CHILTON'S
Foreign Car Repair Manual

German, Swedish, Italian Cars Edition
Volume I

Managing Editor
John Milton

Assistant Managing Editor
John Kelly

Senior Technical Editors
Peter Meyer
John Weise

Technical Editors

John Baxter	Frank Foster	Howard Kenig
Zane Binder	Kerry Freeman	Leo Mealey
Arthur Birney	Jon Jay	Carl Mogerman
Stephen Davis	James Johnson	Svante Mossberg
Joseph DeNuccio		William Wartman

CHILTON BOOK COMPANY

PHILADELPHIA   NEW YORK   LONDON

Copyright © 1971 by Chilton Book Company   All Rights Reserved
Published in Philadelphia by Chilton Book Company and simultaneously in Ontario, Canada, by Thomas Nelson & Sons, Ltd.
ISBN: 0-8019-5632-3   Library of Congress Catalog Card No 73-168562   Manufactured in the United States of America

Complete Service and Repair Procedures for:

BMW (including 2002)

VOLKSWAGEN (including Super Beetle)

MERCEDES-BENZ (including diesel engine service)

AUDI

PORSCHE (including 914)

VOLVO (including 164)

SAAB (including 99)

FIAT

OPEL (including G.T.)

ALFA ROMEO

Acknowledgments

The Chilton Book Company expresses appreciation to the following firms for their assistance: Alfa Romeo, Incorporated, Newark, New Jersey; A Pierburg Auto-U Luftrahrt-Geratebau KG (Zenith carburetors), Neuss/Rhein, Germany; Armolt Corporation (Solex carburetors), Warsaw, Indiana; Bob Yates (SAAB), Langhorne, Pennsylvania; Buick-Opel Division, Fort Washington, Pennsylvania; Daimler-Benz AG, Stuttgart-Unterturkheim, Germany; Fiat Motor Company, Incorporated, New York, New York; Fiat-Roosevelt Motors, Incorporated, Englewood Cliffs, New Jersey; Free Library of Philadelphia, Philadelphia, Pennsylvania; Geon (Weber carburetors), Woodbury, New York; Hoffman Motors Corporation (BMW), New York, New York; Mercedes-Benz of North America, Fort Lee, New Jersey; Moore Motors (Porsche), Philadelphia, Pennsylvania; Porsche-Audi Division, Volkswagen of America, Englewood Cliffs, New Jersey; Robert Bosch Corporation, Long Island City, New York; SAAB-Scania of America, Incorporated, New Haven, Connecticut; S.p.A. Fiat, Torino, Italy; Volkswagen Division, Volkswagen of America, Englewood Cliffs, New Jersey; Volvo Incorporated, Rockleigh, New Jersey; Wilkie Buick (Opel), Philadelphia, Pennsylvania; Wynn's Motors, Incorporated (Volvo), Norristown, Pennsylvania.

NOTE: Although the information in this book is based on factory sources and is as complete as it was possible to make it at time of publication, the possibility exists that later changes were made which could not be included. It must be recognized that such changes are the manufacturer's prerogative, and that the manufacturer cannot be held responsible for them, or the publisher's interpretation of factory information.

ALFA ROMEO SECTION

Index

1625359

Introduction

Alfa Romeo automobiles have been imported into the U.S. since 1956. The company is best known for its two seater sports cars, although sporting sedans, 2+2 models, and even a van have been produced. All models have an aluminum, inline, double overhead camshaft engine.

The early models imported were the 1,300 cc. Giulietta and the larger 2,000 cc. series, both with four-cylinder engines. In 1963, the Giulietta was replaced by the 1,600 cc. Giulia, and the 2,000 cc. series by a 2,600 cc. six-cylinder model. A few 1,300 cc. Giulia models were imported. In 1967, the Giulia Spider was replaced by the Duetto Spider with new styling. No 1968 models were imported, due to a delay in adapting to the U.S. exhaust emission regulations. In 1969, Alfa reappeared on the U.S. market with a 1,750 cc. engine using mechanical fuel injection. The line was limited to only three models: a sedan, a spider, and a 2 + 2, all with the 1,750 cc. engine.

Year and Model Identification

1959 2000 Berlina (sedan)

1959 Giulietta Sprint

1960 Giulietta Spider

1961 Giulietta Sprint

1961 Giulietta Sprint Speciale

1962 Giulietta Sprint

1962 2000 Spider

1963 Giulia Sprint

1963 2600 Spider

1964 Giulia TI

1964 Giulia Sprint GT

1964 Giulia Sprint Speciale

1965 Giulia Spider

1967 Duetto Spider

1967 Giulia Super

1967 1300 Giulia GT Junior

1971 1750 Berlina

1971 1750 GT Veloce

1971 1750 Spider Veloce

Vehicle and Engine Serial Number Identification

Vehicle Number Identification

The vehicle chassis number is stamped on the right side of the engine compartment firewall. In addition, most models have a vehicle data plate which gives the car model and type fastened to the firewall.

Engine Number Identification

The engine number is on the front of the 2,000 cc. cylinder block, just under the cylinder head. On all other engines, the number is on the right side of the cylinder block, toward the front.

Location of typical vehicle chassis number and vehicle identification plate

Location of engine number for all engines except 2,000 cc.

Vehicle Identification

Year	Model	Starting Serial Numbers
1960	Giulietta Series	
	Spider Roadster	1495-05731
	Super Spider Roadster	1495F-05143
	Sprint Coupe	1493-05303
	Sprint Veloce Coupe	1493E-05898
	2000 Series	
	Spider Roadster	10204-00032
1961	Giulietta Series	
	Spider Roadster	1495-08083
	Super Spider Roadster	1495F-07508
	Sprint Coupe	1493-20025
	Sprint Veloce Coupe	1493E-11012
	Sprint Speciale Coupe	10120-00001
	2000 Series	
	Spider Roadster	10204-00105
1962	Giulietta Series	
	Spider Convertible	1495-09308 or AR-167006
	Super Spider Convertible	1495F-10659 or AR-167181
	Sprint Coupe	1493-20750 or AR-158901
	Sprint Veloce Coupe	1493E-23900 or AR-158935
	Sprint Speciale Coupe	10102-00320
	2000 Series	
	Spider Roadster/Convertible	10204-01063
1963	Giulietta Series	
	Spider Convertible	1495-09771 or AR-170180
	Super Spider Convertible	1495F-11039 or AR-171846
	Sprint Coupe	1493-2110S or AR-159014
	Sprint Veloce Coupe	AR-159004
	1600 Giulia Series (Introduced late '62)	
	Sedan	AR-400001
	Sprint Coupe	AR-352001
	Spider Convertible	AR-372001
	2600 Series (Introduced late '62)	
	Convertible	AR-191015
	Coupe	AR-820116
1964	1600 Giulia Series	
	Spider Convertible	AR-372300
	Sprint Coupe	AR-352500
	Sedan	AR-401500
	2600 Series	
	Convertible	AR-191100
	Coupe	AR-820200
1965	1600 Giulia Series	
	TI Sedan	AR-446000
	TI Super Sedan	AR-430000
	Spider Convertible	AR-373959
	Spider Veloce Covertible	AR-379986
	Sprint GT Coupe	AR-353225
	SS Coupe	AR-380000
	TZ Coupe	AR-750000
	2600 Series	
	Berlina Sedan	AR-800074
	Spider Convertible	AR-191320
	Sprint Coupe	AR-820400
1966-71	N.A.	N.A.

General Engine Specifications

Year	Type or Model	Cu. In. Displacement (cc.)	Carburetion	Developed Horsepower @ rpm DIN	Developed Horsepower @ rpm SAE	Developed Torque @ rpm (ft. lbs.)	Bore X Stroke (mm.)	Compression Ratio	Normal Oil Pressure (psi)
1955-1963	Giulietta Berlina	78.6 (1,290)	Solex 32 PBIC	62 @ 6,000	N.A.	N.A.	74 x 75	7.5	N.A.
1957-1965	Giulietta TI	78.6 (1,290)	Solex 35 APAI-G	74 @ 6,200	N.A.	N.A.	74 x 75	8.5	N.A.
1954-1962	Giulietta Sprint, Spider	78.6 (1,290)	Solex 35 APAI-G	80 @ 6,300	N.A.	N.A.	74 x 75	8.5	N.A.
1956-1962	Giulietta Sprint Veloce, Spider Veloce	78.6 (1,290)	Weber 40 DCOE 2 (dual)	90 @ 6,500	N.A.	N.A.	74 x 75	9.1	N.A.
1960-1962	Giulietta SS, SZ	78.6 (1,290)	Weber 40 DCOE 2 (dual)	100 @ 6,500	N.A.	N.A.	74 x 75	9.7	N.A.
1962-1965	Giulia TI	96.0 (1,570)	Solex 32 PAIA 7	92 @ 6,000	104 @ 6,000	N.A.	78 x 82	9.0	50-70
1965-1969	Giulia Super	96.0 (1,570)	Weber 40 DCOE 24 or Solex C 40 PHH 2 (dual)	98 @ 5,500	112 @ 5,500	N.A.	78 x 82	9.0	50-70
1962-1967	Giulia Spider	96.0 (1,570)	Solex 32 PAIA 5	92 @ 6,200	104 @ 6,200	N.A.	78 x 82	9.0	50-70
1964-1967	Giulia Spider Veloce	96.0 (1,570)	Weber 40 DCOE 2 (dual)	112 @ 6,500	129 @ 6,500	N.A.	78 x 82	9.7	50-70
1966-1968	Duetto Spider	96.0 (1,570)	Weber 40 DCOE 27 (dual)	109 @ 6,000	125 @ 6,000	N.A.	78 x 82	9.0	50-70
1962-1964	Giulia Sprint	96.0 (1,570)	Solex 32 PAIA 5	92 @ 6,200	104 @ 6,200	N.A.	78 x 82	9.0	50-70
1963-1967	Giulia Sprint GT, GTC (1965)	96.0 (1,570)	Weber 40 DCOE 27 or Weber 40 DCOE 4 or Solex 40 PHH 2 (dual)	106 @ 6,000	122 @ 6,000	N.A.	78 x 82	9.0	50-70

General Engine Specifications

Year	Type or Model	Cu. In. Displacement (cc.)	Carburetion	Developed Horsepower @ rpm		Developed Torque @ rpm (ft. lbs.)	Bore X Stroke (mm.)	Compression Ratio	Normal Oil Pressure (psi)
				DIN	SAE				
1966-1968	Giulia GT Veloce	96.0 (1,570)	Weber 40 DCOE 27 (dual)	109 @ 6,000	125 @ 6,000	N.A.	78 x 82	9.0	50-70
1965-1968	Giulia Sprint GTA	96.0 (1,570)	Weber 45 DCOE 14 (dual)	115 @ 6,000	133 @ 6,000	N.A.	78 x 82	9.7	50-70
1963-1968	Giulia Sprint Speciale	96.0 (1,570)	Weber 40 DCOE 2 (dual)	112 @ 6,500	129 @ 6,500	N.A.	78 x 82	9.7	50-70
1964-1968	1300 Giulia Sprint	78.6 (1,290)	Solex	80 @ 6,300	N.A.	N.A.	74 x 75	8.5	N.A.
1964-1968	1300 Giulia Berlina	78.6 (1,290)	N.A.	78 @ 6,000	N.A.	N.A.	74 x 75	8.5	N.A.
1965-1968	1300 Giulia GT Junior	78.6 (1,290)	Weber (dual)	103 @ 6,000	N.A.	N.A.	74 x 75	8.5	N.A.
1966-1968	1300 Giulia TI	78.6 (1,290)	Solex	82 @ 6,000	N.A.	N.A.	74 x 75	8.5	N.A.
1969-1971	1750 Berlina, GT Veloce, Spider Veloce	108.4 (1,779)	Mechanical injection	N.A.	132 @ 5,500	137 @ 2,900	80 x 88.5	9.5	50-70
1962-1968	2600 Sedan	158.0 (2,582)	Solex 32 PAIA 4 (dual)	130 @ 5,900	145 @ 5,900	N.A.	83 x 79.6	8.5	50-78
1962-1968	2600 Spider, Sprint	158.0 (2,582)	Solex 44 PHH (triple)	145 @ 5,900	165 @ 5,900	N.A.	83 x 79.6	9.0	50-78

NOTE: Horsepower ratings and compression ratios may vary from year to year.

Tune-Up Specifications

Year	Model	Spark Plugs Make and type	Distributor Gap (in.)	Distributor Point dwell (deg.)	Distributor Point gap (in.)	Basic ignition timing (deg.) [4]	Cranking compression pressure (psi)	Valves Clearance (in.)—Cold In.	Valves Clearance (in.)—Cold Ex.	Intake opens (deg.)	Idle speed (rpm)—minimum
1954-1965	Giulietta Berlina, TI, Sprint, Spider	Lodge HLN Bosch W175 T2	.020-.024	27-33	.014-.016[1] .017-.019[2]	8 BTDC	All cylinders within 10% of each other	.017-.018 .019-.020[3]	.019-.020 .021-.022[3]	22 BTDC 25° 20' BTDC[3]	450
1956-1962	Giulietta Sprint Veloce, Spider Veloce	Lodge RL47 Lodge 2HLN Bosch W225 T2	.015-.018 .022-.026	27-33	.014-.016[1] .017-.019[2]	5 BTDC	As above	.015-.016	.021-.022	34 BTDC	450
1960-1962	Giulietta SS, SZ	Lodge RL47 Bosch W225 T2	.015-.018	27-33	.017-.019[2]	5 BTDC	As above	.011-.012	.019-.020	46 BTDC	N.A.
1962-1967	Giulia TI, TI Super, Spider, Sprint	Lodge 2HLN Bosch W230 T30	.022-.025 .024	N.A.	.014-.016	1-5 BTDC 3-7 BTDC[6]	As above	.019-.020	.020-.022	24° 40' BTDC	500-600
1963-1969	Giulia Super, Sprint GT, CTC, GT Veloce	Lodge 2HL Bosch W230 T30	— .024	N.A.	.014-.016	2-4 BTDC	As above	.019-.020	.021-.022	36° 50' BTDC	600-700
1965-1968	Giulia Sprint GTA	Lodge 2HL Bosch W230 T30	— .024	N.A.	.014-.016	4-6 BTDC	As above	.019-.020	.021-.022	36° 50' BTDC	600-700
1963-1967	Giulia Spider Veloce, SS	Lodge RL47 Bosch W225 T2	.015-.018 .024	N.A.	.014-.016	3.5-6.5 BTDC	As above	.017-.018	.019-.020	29 BTDC	600-700
1966-1968	1600 Duetto Spider	Lodge 2HL Bosch W230 T30	— .024	N.A.	.014-.016	2-4 BTDC	As above	.019-.020	.021-.022	36° 50' BTDC	600-700

Tune-Up Specifications

Year	Model	Spark Plugs Make and type	Gap (in.)	Distributor Point dwell (deg.)	Point gap (in.)	Basic ignition timing (deg.) [4]	Cranking compression pressure (psi)	Valves Clearance (in.)—Cold In.	Ex.	Intake opens (deg.)	Idle speed (rpm) —minimum
1969-1971	1750 Berlina, GT Veloce, Spider Veloce	Lodge HL Bosch WG215 T30	— .024	27-33	.017-.019	1-3 ATDC [5]	As above	.019-.020	.021-.022	36° 50' BTDC	720
1962-1968	2600 Sedan (Berlina)	Lodge 2HLN Bosch W240 T2 Bosch W240 T28	.022-.025 .024 .020	N.A.	.014-.016	5-9 BTDC	As above	.017-.018	.021-.022	33° 20' BTDC	500-600
1962-1968	2600 Spider, Sprint	Lodge 2HLN Bosch W240 T2 Bosch W240 T28	.022-.025 .024 .020	N.A.	.017-.019	5-9 BTDC	As above	.017-.018	.021-.022	20° 30' BTDC	700-750

1 Lucas distributor.
2 Marelli distributor.
3 With camshafts marked between first and second cams by a circle with a cross in the center.
4 The maximum advance should be checked with a stroboscopic timing light at 5,000 rpm. Refer to the Distributor Specifications Chart for maximum advance figures.

5 Injection pump timing marks must be aligned at 70° BTDC of the intake stroke.
6 For TI Super.
NOTE: If any of the figures in the above chart disagree with those given on an engine compartment sticker, the sticker figures should be used.

Firing Order

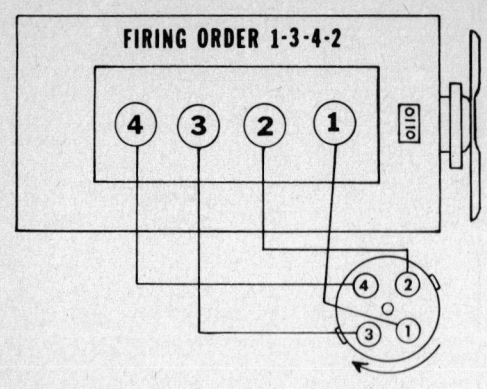

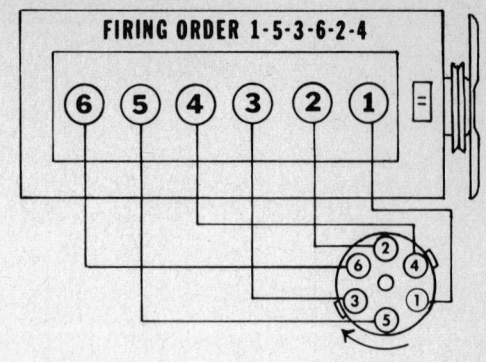

All four cylinder models except 2000; 2000 firing order is 1-2-4-3

2600 six cylinder models

Engine Rebuilding Specifications

Year	Model	Main bearing journals (in.)				Connecting rod bearing journals (in.)		
		Journal diameter	Oil clearance	Shaft end-play	Thrust on No.	Journal diameter	Oil Clearance	Rod side-play
1954-1960	1,290 cc.	Standard 57.074-57.086 1st regrind 56.820-56.832 2nd regrind 56.566-56.578 3rd regrind 56.312-56.324[1]	.001-.002	.003-.010	Center	Standard 44.963-44.975 1st regrind 44.709-44.721 2nd regrind 44.445-44.447 3rd regrind 44.201-44.223[1]	.001-.002	.008-.012
1961-1965	1,290 cc.	Standard 2.3606-2.3611 1st regrind 2.3506-2.3511 2nd regrind 2.3407-2.3411	.001-.002	.003-.010	Center	Standard, 1st regrind as above 2nd regrind 44.455-44.467[1]	.001-.002	.008-.012
1962-1969	1,570 cc.	Standard 2.3606-2.3611 1st regrind	.001-.002	.003-.010	Center	Standard 1.9680-1.9685 1st regrind	.001-.002	.008-.012
1969-1971	1,779 cc.	2.3506-2.3511 2nd regrind 2.3407-2.3411				1.9581-1.9585 2nd regrind 1.9480-1.9485		
1962-1968	2,582 cc.	Standard 2.4795-2.4799 1st regrind 2.4695-2.4699 2nd regrind 2.4595-2.4599	.001-.002	.003-.010	Center	Standard 2.1141-2.1145 1st regrind 2.1041-2.1045 2nd regrind 2.0941-2.0945	.001-.003	.008-.012

1 Given in millimeters

Engine Rebuilding Specifications
Cylinders, Pistons, and Rings

Year	Model	Cylinders (in.)	Pistons (in.)			Rings (in.)	
		Cylinder barrel bore	Piston diameter	Wrist pin diameter and fit	Piston to bore clearance	Side clearance	End-gap
1954-1960	1,290 cc. Giulietta Berlina, TI, Sprint, Spider	Class A (blue) 73.985-73.994 74.185-74.194 74.385-74.394 74.585-74.594 Class B (rose) 73.995-74.004 74.195-74.204 74.395-74.404 74.595-74.604 Class C (green) 74.005-74.014 74.205-74.214 74.405-74.414 74.605-74.614[1]	Mahle Piston Class A (blue) 73.925-73.934[1] 74.125-74.135[4] 74.325-74.335 74.525-74.535 Class B (rose) 73.935-73.944 74.135-74.145 74.335-74.345 74.535-74.545 Class C (green) 73.945-73.954 74.145-74.155 74.345-74.355 74.545-74.555 Borgo Piston Class A (blue) 73.930-73.940 74.130-74.140 74.330-74.340 74.530-74.540 Class B (rose) 73.940-73.950 74.140-74.150 74.340-74.350 74.540-74.550 Class C (green) 73.950-73.960 74.150-74.160 74.350-74.360 74.550-74.560 K.S. Piston Class A (blue) 73.925-73.935 74.135-74.145 Class B (rose) 73.935-73.945 74.335-74.345 Class C (green) 73.945-73.955 74.535-74.545	Black[1] 19.997-20.00 White 19.994-19.997 Fit— Black .0003-.0008 White .0002-.0007	Mahle .002-.003 Borgo .002-.003 K.S. .002-.003	.002-.003	Compression .012-.018 Oil .009-.016
1961-1965	1,290 cc. Giulietta Sprint Veloce, Spider Veloce, SS, SZ	Class A (blue)[1] 73.985-73.994 74.185-74.194 74.385-74.394 74.585-74.594 Class B (rose) 73.995-74.004 74.195-74.204 74.395-74.404 74.595-74.604 Class C (green) 74.005-74.014 74.205-74.214 74.405-74.414 74.605-74.614	Mahle piston[1] Class A (blue)[4] 73.835-73.845 74.035-74.045 74.235-74.245 74.435-74.445 Class B (rose) 73.845-73.855 74.045-74.055 74.245-74.255 74.445-74.455 Class C (green) 73.855-73.865 74.055-74.065 74.255-74.265 74.455-74.465	Black[1] 19.997-20.00 White 19.994 19.997 Fit— Black .0003-.0008 White .0002-.0007	Mahle .006 Borgo .003	.002-.003	Compression .012-.018 Oil .009-.016

Engine Rebuilding Specifications
Cylinders, Pistons, and Rings

Year	Model	Cylinders (in.)	Pistons (in.)			Rings (in.)	
		Cylinder barrel bore	Piston diameter	Wrist pin diameter and fit	Piston to bore clearance	Side clearance	End-gap
1961-1965			Borgo piston Class A (blue) 73.910-73.920 74.110-74.120 74.310-74.320 74.510-74.520 Class B (rose) 73.920-73.930 74.120-74.130 74.320-74.330 74.520-74.530 Class C (green) 73.930-73.940 74.130-74.140 74.330-74.340 74.530-74.540				
1962-1969	1,570 cc.	Class A (blue) 3.0703-3.0706 Class B (pink) 3.0707-3.0710 Class C (green) 3.0711-3.0714	Class A (blue) 3.0677-3.0681 Class B (pink)[6] 3.0681-3.0685 Class C (green) 3.0686-3.0688 Class A (blue)[5][6] 3.0673-3.0677 Class B (pink) 3.0678-3.0681 Class C (green) 3.0682-3.0685	Black .86590- .86602 White .86606- .86614 Fit— Black .0003- .0008 White .0002- .0007	.002- .003 .003[5]	compression .001- .002 chrome compression .002- .003 oil .001- .002	.012- .017
1969-1971	1,779 cc.	Class A (blue) 3.1490-3.1493 Class B (pink) 3.1494-3.1497 Class C (green) 3.1498-3.1501	Class A (blue)[7] 3.1476-3.1479 Class B (pink) 3.1479-3.1483 Class C (green) 3.1483-3.1487	Black .86590- .86602 White .86605- .86614 Fit— Black .0003- .0008 White	.001- .002	Compression .001- .003 Oil .001- .002	Compression .012- .018 Oil .010- .016
1962-1968	2,582 cc. Sedan	Class A (blue) 3.2671-3.2674 Class B (pink) 3.2675-3.2678 Class C (green) 3.2679-3.2682	Class A (blue)[8] 3.2646-3.2649 Class B (pink) 3.2649-3.2653 Class C (green) 3.2653-3.2657	Black .94464- .94476 White .94480- .94488 Fit— .0001- .0003	.002- .003	.001- .002	.012- .017
1962-1968	2,582 cc. Spider, Sprint	Class A (blue) 3.2671-3.2674 Class B (pink) 3.2675-3.2678 Class C (green) 3.2679-3.2682	Class A (blue)[8] 3.2643-3.2647 Class B (pink) 3.2647-3.2651 Class C (red) 3.2651-3.2655	Black .94464- .94476 White .94480- .94488 Fit— .0001- .0003	.002- .003	.001- .002	.012- .017

1 Given in millimeters
4 Measured .434 in. from bottom of piston skirt
5 Spider Veloce, Sprint Speciale, and GTA.

6 measured .472 in. from bottom of piston skirt
7 measured .591 in. from bottom of piston skirt
8 measured .866 in. from bottom of piston skirt

Engine Rebuilding Specifications
Valves

Year	Model	Seat angle (deg.)	Seat (in.) diameter	Valve lift (in.) Intake	Valve lift (in.) Exhaust	Spring pressure (lbs.)	Spring free length (in.)	Stem diameter (in.) Intake	Stem diameter (in.) Exhaust	Stem to guide clearance (in.) Intake	Stem to guide clearance (in.) Exhaust	Valve Guide removable
1954-1965	1,290 cc.	30	N.A.	3.15 [2]	3.15 [2]	Outer 53-55 @ .89 in. Inner — Outer[3] 70-73 @ 1.12 in. Inner 43-45 @ 1.04 in.	Outer 1.70-1.76 Inner 1.55-1.61 Outer 2.00 Inner[3] 1.82	7.976-8.001 or 8.962-8.987[1]	7.950-7.976 or 8.935-8.960[1]	.001-.002	.002-.003	Yes
1962-1969	1,570 cc. (except GTA)	30	Intake 1.6771-1.6784 Exhaust 1.5196-1.5209	N.A.	N.A.	Outer 79-82 @ 1.08 in. Inner 49-51 @ 1.02 in.	Outer Green 2.03 Red 2.08 Inner Green 1.83 Red 1.87	.3528.3538	.3518-.3527	.001-.002	.002-.003	Yes
1965-1969	1,570 cc. GTA	30	Intake 1.7748-1.7754 Exhaust 1.6173-1.6177	N.A.	N.A.	Outer 118-123 @ 1.18 in. Inner 55-57 @ 1.08 in.	Outer 2.03 Inner 1.96	.3329-.3338	.3329-.3338	.001-.002	.001-.002	Yes
1969-1971	1,779 cc.	30	Intake 1.6771-1.6784 Exhaust 1.5196-1.5209	N.A.	N.A.	Outer 79-82 @ 1.08 in. Inner 50-51 @ 1.02 in.	Outer 2.02, 2.08, 2.05 Inner 1.83, 1.88, 1.85	.3532-.3538	.3518-.3527	.001-.003	.002-.003	Yes
1962-1968	2,582 cc.	N.A.	Intake 1.7520-1.7539 Exhaust 1.5945-1.5965	N.A.	N.A.	Outer 98-101 @ 1.18 in. Inner 49-51 @ 1.10 in.	Outer 1.93 Inner 2.03	.3729-.3735	.3912-.3918	.001-.002	.002-.003	Yes

1 Given in millimeters
2 Sprint Veloce, Spider Veloce—3.34
3 1961-1965

Torque Specifications

Year	Model	Cylinder head bolts (ft. lbs.)	Main bearing bolts (ft. lbs.)	Rod bearing bolts (ft. lbs.)	Crankshaft balancer nut (ft. lbs.)	Flywheel to crankshaft bolts (ft. lbs.)	Manifold (ft. lbs.)	
							Intake	Exhaust
1954-1965	1,290 cc.	40-45	22-25	26	N.A.	N.A.	N.A.	N.A.
1962-1969	1,570 cc.	45-46 cold, 48 hot	34-36	36-38	N.A.	30-33	N.A.	N.A.
1969-1971	1,779 cc.	52-54 cold, 55-56 hot	34-36	36-38	N.A.	30-33	Injectors 20-23	N.A.
1962-1968	2,582 cc.	65-69 cold, 67-71 hot	47-50	45-49	92-96	36-40	N.A.	N.A.

NOTE: *Camshaft cap bolts on all models are torqued to 15 ft. lbs. Sparkplugs on all models are torqued to 18-25 ft. lbs.*

Tightening Sequences

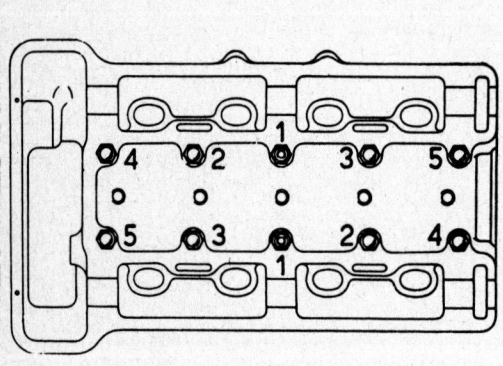
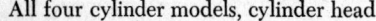

All four cylinder models, cylinder head

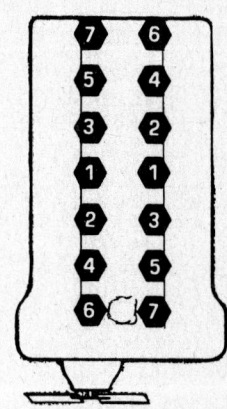

2600 six cylinder models, cylinder head

Electrical Specifications—Battery and Starter

Year	Model	Battery			Starter						Brush spring tension (oz.)
		Capacity (Amp. hrs)	Volts	Grounded terminal	Lock test			No load test			
					Amps.	Volts	Torque (ft. lbs.)	Amps.	Volts	Rpm	
1954-1965	Giulietta Berlina, TI, Sprint, Spider	38	12	Pos.	Lucas 350	8.5	8	50	12	10,000	N.A.
					Marelli 300	7.5	5.4	N.A.	N.A.	N.A.	N.A.
1954-1965	Giulietta Sprint Veloce, Spider Veloce, SS, SZ	38	12	Neg.	Lucas 350	8.5	8	50	12	10,000	N.A.
					Marelli 300	7.5	5.4	N.A.	N.A.	N.A.	N.A.

Electrical Specifications—Battery and Starter

Year	Model	Battery			Starter							Brush spring tension (oz.)
		Capacity (Amp. hrs)	Volts	Grounded terminal	Lock test			No load test				
					Amps.	Volts	Torque (ft. lbs.)	Amps.	Volts	Rpm		
1962-1969	GTA	24	12	Neg.	N.A.	N.A.	N.A.	N.A.	N.A.	N.A.		N.A.
	Giulia TI, Sprint GT, GTC	40	12	Neg.	N.A.	N.A.	N.A.	N.A.	N.A.	N.A.		N.A.
	Giulia Sprint, Spider, SS, SZ	50	12	Neg.	N.A.	N.A.	N.A.	N.A.	N.A.	N.A.		N.A.
	Giulia GT Veloce, Super; 1600 Duetto Spider	60	12	Neg.	N.A.	N.A.	N.A.	N.A.	N.A.	N.A.		N.A.
1969-1971	1750 Berlina, Spider Veloce, GT Veloce	60	12	Neg.	N.A.	N.A.	N.A.	N.A.	N.A.	N.A.		N.A.
1962-1968	2600 Berlina, Spider, Sprint	50	12	Neg.	600	7.0	18.8	40	12.0	9,000		N.A.

Electrical Specifications—Generator and Regulator

Year	Model	Generator				Regulator					
		Part number	Brush spring pressure (oz.)	Field resistance (ohms.)	Maximum output	Part number	Cut-out relay		Maximum current (amps.)	Voltage regulator setting (volts)	
							Volts to close	Reverse current (amps.)			
1954-1965	Giulietta Berlina, TI, Sprint Spider	Lucas C 39 PV 2	20-25	6.2	19 amps	Lucas RB 106 1	12.7-13.3	3.5-5	N.A.	15.6-16.2 @ 68° F, 1.500 gen. rpm	
		Marelli DNA 44 E	N.A.	N.A.	N.A.	Marelli IR 32 B	N.A.	N.A.	N.A.	N.A.	
		Bosch L/J /GEG/160/ 12/2500 R	N.A.	N.A.	160 watts	Bosch RS/ TBC/160/ 12	N.A.	N.A.	N.A.	N.A.	
	Giulietta Sprint Veloce, Spider Veloce, SS, SZ	Marelli DNA 44 E	N.A.	N.A.	N.A.	Marelli IR 32 A	N.A.	N.A.	N.A.	N.A.	
1962-1969	Giulia TI, Sprint, Spider	Bosch LJ/GEG 200/12/ 2700 R 32 mr	N.A.	N.A.	200 watts	Bosch RS/VA 200/ 12 A 2	N.A.	N.A.	N.A.	N.A.	
	Giulia Super	Marelli DN 62 E/P	37	4.7	N.A.	Marelli SD 368 A 300/12	N.A.	N.A.	N.A.	N.A.	
1962-1968	2600 Berlina, Spider, Sprint	Marelli DN 62 C	37	4.7	N.A.	Marelli IR 50 D	11.5-13.0	2.5-7.5	N.A.	138-14.4	

Electrical Specifications—Alternator and Regulator

Year	Model	Alternator			AC Regulator						
		Part number	Field current draw @ 12 V.	Output (amps.)	Part number	Field relay			Regulator		
						Air gap (in.)	Point gap (in.)	Volts to close	Air gap (in.)	Point gap (in.)	Volts @ 125° F
1962-1969	Giulia Spider Veloce, SS, GT, GTC, GTA, Super, GT Veloce; 1600 Duetto Spider	Bosch EG (R) 14 V 25 A 29	N.A.	25	Bosch VA 14 V 25 A	N.A.	N.A.	N.A.	N.A.	N.A.	N.A.
1969-1971	1750 Berlina, GT Veloce, Spider Veloce	Bosch K1 (R, L) 14 V 35 A 20	20-30	35	Bosch AD 1/14 V	N.A.	N.A.	N.A.	N.A.	N.A.	13.8

Distributor Specifications

Year	Model	Distributor	Centrifugal Advance				Vacuum Advance			Maximum advance degrees @ rpm
			Start degrees @ rpm	Intermediate degrees @ rpm	Intermediate degrees @ rpm	End degrees @ rpm	Start degrees @ mm. Hg.	Intermediate degrees @ mm. Hg.	End degrees @ mm. Hg.	
1954-1965	Giulietta Berlina, TI, Sprint, Spider	Lucas DM2	–1—+1 @ 375	.5—2.5 @ 500	8.5—10.5 @ 1,500	16—18 @ 2,375	5—7.5 @ 635	5—7.5 @ 355	2.5—5 @ 304	40-46 @ 5,000
		Marelli S 71 B	–1—+1 @ 400	—	—	18 @ 2,500	0 @ 275	—	6.5 @ 400	40-46 @ 5,000
1960-1962	Giulietta SS, SZ	Marelli S 73 A	–1—+1 @ 400	5 @ 500	11 @ 700	18 @ 2,500	None	None	None	43-49 @ 5,000
1963-1968	Giulia Sprint GT, GTC, Sprint GT Veloce; 1600 Duetto Spider	Bosch JF 4	N.A.	N.A.	N.A.	N.A.	N.A.	N.A.	N.A.	40-43 @ 5,000
1965-1968	Giulia Sprint GTA (dual-plug ignition)	Marelli S 119 A	N.A.	N.A.	N.A.	N.A.	N.A.	N.A.	N.A.	27-31 @ 5,000
1965-1969	Giulia Super	Bosch VJ 4 BR 35mk or Marelli S 103 A	N.A.	N.A.	N.A.	N.A.	N.A.	N.A.	N.A.	43-46 @ 5,000
1962-1967	Giulia, TI, Spider, Sprint	Bosch VJU 4 BR 41mk	N.A.	N.A.	N.A.	N.A.	N.A.	N.A.	N.A.	40-46 @ 5,000
1963-1968	Giulia Spider Veloce, SS	Bosch JF 4	N.A.	N.A.	N.A.	N.A.	N.A.	N.A.	N.A.	43-49 @ 5,000
1963-1967	Giulia TI Super	N.A.	N.A.	N.A.	N.A.	N.A.	N.A.	N.A.	N.A.	43-49 @ 5,300

Distributor Specifications

Year	Model	Distributor	Centrifugal Advance				Vacuum Advance			
			Start degrees @ rpm	Inter-mediate degrees @ rpm	Inter-mediate degrees @ rpm	End degrees @ rpm	Start degrees @ mm. Hg.	Inter-mediate degrees @ mm. Hg.	End degrees @ mm. Hg.	Maximum advance degrees @ rpm
1969-1971	1750 Berlina, GT Veloce, Spider Veloce	Marelli S 103 B	N.A.	N.A.	N.A.	N.A.	N.A.	N.A.	N.A.	31-37 @ 5,000
1962-1968	2600 Berlina	Marelli S 94 A	N.A.	N.A.	N.A.	N.A.	N.A.	N.A.	N.A.	44-47 @ 5,000
1962-1968	2600 Spider, Sprint	Marelli S 93 A (dual-point)	N.A.	N.A.	N.A.	N.A.	N.A.	N.A.	N.A.	44-47 @ 5,000

Capacities and Pressures

Year	Model	Engine crankcase refill after draining (qts.) with filter	with-out filter	Transmission refill after draining (pts.) Manual 4-speed	5-speed	Automatic	Drive axle (pts.)	Fuel tank (gals.)	Cooling system (qts.)	Normal fuel pressure (psi)	Maximum coolant pressure (psi)
1954-1965	Giulietta Berlina, TI	5.6	—	2.8	—	—	2.6	10.5	7.9	N.A.	N.A.
	Giulietta Sprint, Spider	6.0	—	2.8, 3.8 after 1960	—	—	2.6	14.0	7.9	N.A.	N.A.
	Giulietta Sprint Veloce, Spider Veloce	6.0, 6.5 after 1960	—	2.8, 3.8 after 1960	—	—	2.6	21.0, Spider 14.0 after 1960	7.9	N.A.	N.A.
	Giulietta SS, SZ	6.5	—	—	3.8	—	2.6	21.0	7.9	N.A.	N.A.
1962-1969	Giulia GT, GTC, Super, GT Veloce; 1600 Duetto Spider	6.0	—	—	3.8	—	3.0	12.1	7.9	2.8, Super 1.5	N.A.
	Giulia GTA	7.1	—	—	3.8	—	3.0	12.1	7.4	N.A.	N.A.
	Giulia Spider Veloce, SS, TI, Spider, Sprint	6.8	—	—	3.8	—	3.0	14.0, TI 12.1, SS 21.1	7.9	2.8	N.A.
1969-1971	1750 Berlina, GT Veloce, Spider Veloce	7.1	—	—	3.8	—	3.0	12.0	10.0	16-18	N.A.
1962-1968	2600 Berlina, Sprint, Spider	8.3	—	—	3.8	—	4.9	15.8	15.6	N.A.	N.A.

Engine Identification

No. of Cyl.	Cu. In. Displacement (cc.)	Type	Common Designation
4	78.6 (1,290)	Dual overhead camshaft, inline	1,300 cc.
4	96.0 (1,570)	Dual overhead camshaft, inline	1,600 cc.
4	108.4 (1,779)	Dual overhead camshaft, inline	1,750 cc.
4	120.0 (1,979)	Dual overhead camshaft, inline	2,000 cc.
6	158.0 (2,582)	Dual overhead camshaft, inline	2,600 cc.

Brake Specifications

Year	Model	Type		Brake cylinder bore (in.)			Brake drum or disc diameter (in.)	
		Front	Rear	Master cylinder	Wheel cylinder Front	Wheel cylinder Rear	Front	Rear
1954-1965	Giulietta, except SS and SZ	Drum	Drum	1.00	1.00	.875	10.5	10.0
	Giulietta SS and SZ	Drum	Drum	1.00	.875	.875	10.5	10.5
1962-1969	Giulia TI, Spider, Sprint	Drum	Drum	N.A.	N.A.	N.A.	10.5	10.0
	Giulia Spider Veloce, SS	Disc	Drum	N.A.	N.A.	N.A.	N.A.	10.5
	Giulia Sprint GT, GTC, GTA, Super, GT Veloce; 1600 Duetto Spider	Disc	Disc	N.A.	N.A.	GTA only .438	N.A.	N.A.
1969-1971	1750 Berlina, GT Veloce, Spider Veloce	Disc	Disc	N.A.	N.A.	N.A.	10.7	10.5
1962-1968	2600 Berlina, Sprint, Spider	Disc	Drum	N.A.	N.A.	N.A.	N.A.	12.0

Chassis and Wheel Alignment Specifications

Year	Model	Chassis (in.)			Wheel Alignment°					
		Wheel-base	Track Front	Rear	Caster (deg.)	Camber (deg.)	Toe-In (in.)	Kingpin inclination (deg.)	Wheel Inner wheel (deg.)	pivot ratio Outer wheel (deg.)
1954-1965	Giulietta Berlina, TI, Sprint, Sprint Veloce	93.0	50.9	50.0	0°10'- 0°40'[1] 0°30'- 1°[2] 0°-1°[3] 0°20'- 1°20'[4]	0	.118	8°35'	36	28°30'
	Giulietta Spider, Spider Veloce, SS, SZ	88.6	50.9	50.0	0°50'- 1°50'	0	.118	8°35'	36	28°30'
1962-1969	Giulia Sprint GT, GTC, GTA, GT Veloce, Super	92.7, Super 99.0	51.6	50.0	0°30'- 1°30'	0°20'-1°20'	.079-.158	N.A.	N.A.	N.A.
	Giulia Spider, Sprint, Spider Veloce, SS	88.5, Sprint 93.5	50.9	50.0	0°10'- 1°10'	0	.118	N.A.	N.A.	N.A.
	Giulia TI; 1600 Duetto Spider	98.9, Duetto 88.6	51.0, Duetto 51.6	50.0	0°30' 1°30'	0°20'-1°20'	.118	N.A.	N.A.	N.A.
1969-1971	1750 Berlina, GT Veloce, Spider Veloce	101.1	52.1	50.1	1°-2°	—0°10'- +0°50'	.118	N.A.	N.A.	N.A.
1962-1968	2600 Berlina, Sprint, Spider	107.0 101.8 98.5	55.1	54.0	0°10'- 1°10'	.28-.41 in neg., measured at top of wheel rim	.113	N.A.	N.A.	N.A.

1 Berlina up to vehicle No. 148810000
2 Berlina from vehicle No. 148810001
3 TI
4 Sprint and Sprint Veloce

° All wheel alignment figures are for a full passenger and fuel load. The preferred settings are always in the middle of the range given.

Fuses

Model	Circuit	Amperage
2600 Sedan, Spider, Sprint	Right high beam	8
	Left high beam	8
	Right low beam	8
	Left low beam	8
	Rear parking lights, instrument panel lights	8
	Front parking lights, backup lights	8
	Radio, right electric window	8
	Dome light, left electric window	8
	Heater fan, stop lights	8
	Turn signal lights, windshield wiper	8
	Instruments	8
	Ignition	8

Light Bulb Specifications

Year	Usage	Type	Wattage
1954-1965 Giulietta	Headlights	—	45/40
	Stop, turn signal, backup	—	20
	License plate	—	5
	Instruments	—	2.5
	Parking	—	5/20
	Interior	—	3
1962-1969 Giulia Sprint GT, GTC, GTA	Headlights	asymmetric	45/40
	Front parking	globular	5
	Front turn	—	20
	Side turn	tubular	3
	Tail parking/stop	—	5/20
	Tail turn	—	20
	Backup	—	20
	License	globular	5
	Engine compartment, interior	cylindrical	5
	All instrument and warning	tubular	3
	Courtesy (GTA)	cylindrical	5
1962-1969 Giulia Super	Inner headlights	asymmetric	40/45
	Outer headlights	asymmetric	40/45
	Front parking	globular	5
	Front turn	—	20
	Side turn	tubular	3
	Tail parking/stop	—	5/20
	Tail turn	—	20
	Backup	—	20
	License	globular	5
	Lighter lamp	tubular	3
	Engine compartment	globular	5
	Dome, luggage compartment	cylindrical	5
	All warning	tubular	3
1962-1969 Giulia GT Veloce	Headlights	asymmetric	45/40
	Tail parking/stop	—	5/20
	Front turn, tail turn, backup	—	20
	Front parking, license	globular	5
	Side turn	tubular	3
	Engine compartment, dome, map	cylindrical	5
	All instrument and warning	tubular	3
1962-1969 Giulia Spider Veloce, Sprint Speciale	Headlights	—	40/45
	Front parking/turn	—	5/20
	Side turn	—	3
	Tail parking/stop	—	5/20
	Tail turn	—	20
	Backup	—	20
	License	—	5
	Courtesy, engine compartment	—	5
	Lighter lamp, all instrument and warning	—	3
1962-1969 Giulia TI, Spider, Sprint	Headlights	—	45/40
	Front parking	—	5
	Front turn	—	20
	Side turn	—	2.5
	Tail parking/stop	—	5/20
	Tail turn	—	20
	Backup	—	20
	License	—	5
	Inspection light	—	10
	Engine compartment, dome, luggage compartment	—	5
	All instrument and warning	—	3

Light Bulb Specifications

Year	Usage	Type	Wattage
1966- 1969 Duetto Spider	Headlights	asymmetric	45/40
	Tail parking/stop	—	5/20
	Front turn, tail turn, backup	—	20
	Front parking, side turn, license	globular	5
	Engine compartment, courtesy	cylindrical	5
	Lighter lamp, instrument and warning	tubular	3
	Turn signal and high beam warning	tubular	1.2
1969- 1971 1750 Berlina, GT Veloce, Spider Veloce	Headlights, fog lamps	sealed beam	—
	Tail parking/stop	—	5/21
	Front turn and flasher, tail turn and flasher, backup	—	21
	Front parking, license	globular	5
	Engine compartment, courtesy, luggage compartment	cylindrical	5
	Side marker	tubular	4
	Instrument and warning	tubular	3
	Fuel, turn signal, flasher, oil pressure, and brake warning	tubular	1.2
1962- 1968 2600 Berlina, Sprint, Spider	Outer headlights	—	40/45
	Inner headlights	—	45
	Front parking (Sedan, Spider)	—	5
	Front turn (Sedan, Spider)	—	20
	Front parking/turn (Sprint)	—	5/20
	Side turn	—	5
	Tail parking/stop	—	5/20
	Tail turn, backup	—	20
	License, engine compartment, map, dome, luggage compartment	—	5 10
	All instrument and warning	—	2.5

Carburetor Specifications

Model	Carburetor	Choke (primary) diam. (in.)	Main jet	Idling jet	Emulsion air jet	Idling air jet	Starter jet	Accelerator pump jet	Accelerator pump outlet jet	Choke (secondary) diam.	Secondary main jet	Secondary emulsion air jet	Fuel level
Giulietta Berlina 1955-1963	Solex 32 BIC	.83	105	040	160	100	130	—	—	—	—	—	—
	Solex 32 PBIC	.98	130	050	160	100	130	45	—	—	—	—	—
Giulietta TI 1957-1965	Solex 35 APAI-G	.95	130	040	180	100	160	60	—	.95	155	110	—
	Solex 35 APAI-G	.95	125	040	180	100	160	60	—	.95	145	110	—
Giulietta Sprint 1954-1962	Solex 32 PAIAT	.87	115	045	200	100	150	45	—	.91	135	110	—
	Solex 32 PAIAT[1]	.98	135	045	180	100	150	45	—	1.1	180	100	—
	Solex 35 APAI-G	.95	120	040	150	100	160	60	—	.95	150	140	—
Giulietta Spider 1954-1962	Solex 35 APAI-G	.95	120	040	150	100	160	60	—	.95	150	190	—
	Solex 35 APAI-G	.95	115	040	150	100	160	60	—	.95	160	160	—
Giulietta Sprint Veloce, Spider Veloce, SS, SZ 1956-1962	Weber 40 DCO 3	1.1	110[2] 105[3]	050	190	175	—	40	150	—	—	—	4
	Weber 40 DCOE 2	1.1	110	050	200	120	60-F5	35	—	—	—	—	—
Giulia Sprint GT, GTC 1963-1967	Weber 40 DCOE 4	1.2	127	050	220	120	65-F5	35	—	—	—	—	1.12-1.16 in.[5]
	Solex 40 PHH 2	1.2	135	050	135	080	100	35	—	—	—	—	.83 in.[5]
Giulia Sprint GTA 1965-1968	Weber 45 DCOE 14	1.2	135	50-FB	220	120	65-F5	35	—	—	—	—	1.12-1.16 in.[5]
Giulia Super 1965-1969	Weber 40 DCOE 24	1.1	110	050	180	120	65-FS	35	—	—	—	—	1.12-1.16 in.[5]
Giulia TI Super 1963-1965	Weber 45 DCOE 14	1.2	120[2] 115[3]	055	180	120	65	50	—	—	—	—	1.12-1.16 in.[5]
Giulia Sprint GT Veloce 1966-1968	Weber 40 DCOE 27	1.2	120	50-F11	180	120	65-F5	35	—	—	—	—	1.12-1.16 in.[5]

Carburetor Specifications

Model	Carburetor	Choke (primary) diam. (in.)	Main jet	Idling jet	Emulsion air jet	Idling air jet	Starter jet	Accelerator pump jet	Accelerator pump outlet jet	Choke (secondary) diam.	Secondary main jet	Secondary emulsion air jet	Fuel level
Giulia Spider Veloce, SS 1963-1968	Weber 40 DCOE 2	1.2	120[2] 115[3]	055	180	120	65-F5	35	—	—	—	—	1.24-1.26 in.[5]
Giulia TI 1962-1965	Solex 32 PAIA 7	.91	125	045	190	100	120	45	—	.91	130	190	.47 in.[6]
Giulia Spider, Sprint 1962-1967	Solex 32 PAIA 5	.91	125	045	220	100	120	45	—	.91	135	200	.47 in.[6]
1600 Duetto Spider 1966-1969	Weber 40 DCOE 27	.91	120	50-F11	180	120	65-F5	35	—	—	—	—	1.12-1.16 in.[5]
1750 Berlina, GT Veloce, Spider Veloce 1969-1971	Alfa-Spica mechanical fuel injection	—	—	—	—	—	—	—	—	—	—	—	—
2600 Berlina 1962-1968	Solex 32 PAIA 4	.79	105	045	220	100	120	40 or 45	—	.91	110	200	.47-.51[7]
2600 Spider, Sprint 1962-1968	Solex 44 PHH	.95	120	045	160	—	—	50	—	1.3	145	160	1.12-1.18 in.[7]

1 These settings are to be used when 1 mm. (.040 in.) is machined off the cylinder head to increase compression.
2 Winter
3 Summer
4 .95 to .99 in. below level of small bowl covers
5 below float chamber flange
6 above bottom of float chamber
7 distance from level of cover

Wiring Diagrams

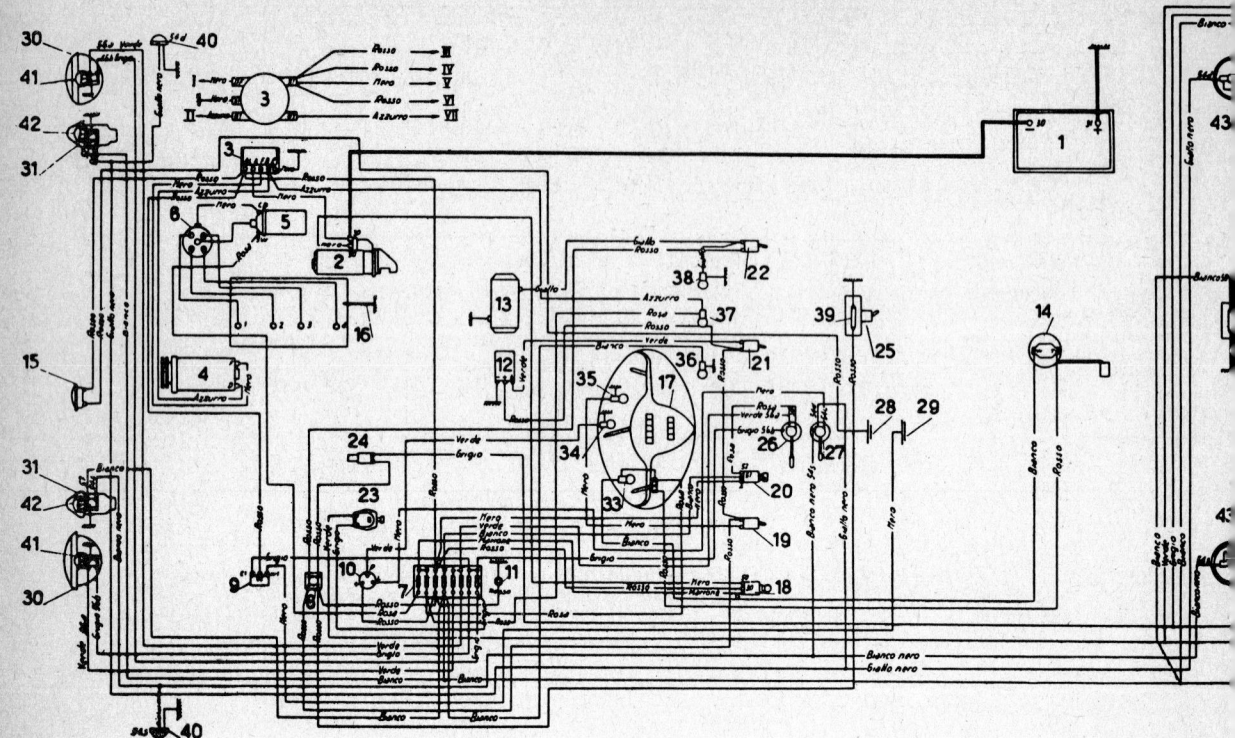

Giulietta Berlina

1. Battery.
2. Starter motor.
3. Regulator.
4. Generator.
5. Ignition coil.
6. Distributor.
7. Fuse box.
8. Terminal board.
9. Electromagnetic switch for turn signals.
10. Turn signal flasher.
11. Socket for inspection lamp.
12. Windshield wiper motor.
13. Heater.
14. Float of fuel level indicator.
15. Electric horn.
16. Ground connection, engine to body.
17. Instrument panel.
18. Ignition switch.

19. Switch for instrument panel lights.
20. Switch for windshield wiper motor
21. Switch for windshield wiper motor.
22. Switch for heater motor.
23. Reserve signal switch.
24. Stop signal switch.
25. Rooflight.
26. Switch for high and low beam.
27. Turn signal switch.
28. Push-button for horn.
29. Push button for blinking headlights.
30. Headlights.
31. Front lamps.
32. Rear lamps.
33. 12 V—2.5 W tell-tale lamp for fuel reserve.
34. 12 V—2.5 W tell-tale lamp for turn signals.

35. 12 V—2.5 W lamps for instrument panel lighting.
36. 12 V—2.5 W tell-tale lamp for high beam lighting.
37. 12 V—2.5 W tell-tale lamp for generator.
38. 12 V—2.5 W tell-tale lamp for heater.
39. 12 V—3 W lamp for roof light.
40. Side blinking lamps.
41. 12 V—45 W—40 W lamps for headlights.
42. 12 V—5 W—20 W lamps for front lamps.
43. 12 V—20 W lamps for rear blinking lights.
44. 12 V—5 W—20 W lamps for rear lamps.
45. 12 V—20 W backup lamps.
46. 12 V—5 W lamp for rear license plate.

Rosso	= Red	Giallo	= Yellow	Bianco	= White
Nero	= Black	Grigio	= Grey	Marrone	= Brown
Azzurro	= Blue	Verde	= Green	Rosa	= Pink
Bianco-nero	= Black and white		Giallo-nero	= Black and yellow	

I. To generator   II. To generator   III. To horn   IV. To fuses   V. To starter motor   VI. To electromagnetic change-over switch   VII. To generator tell-tale lamp

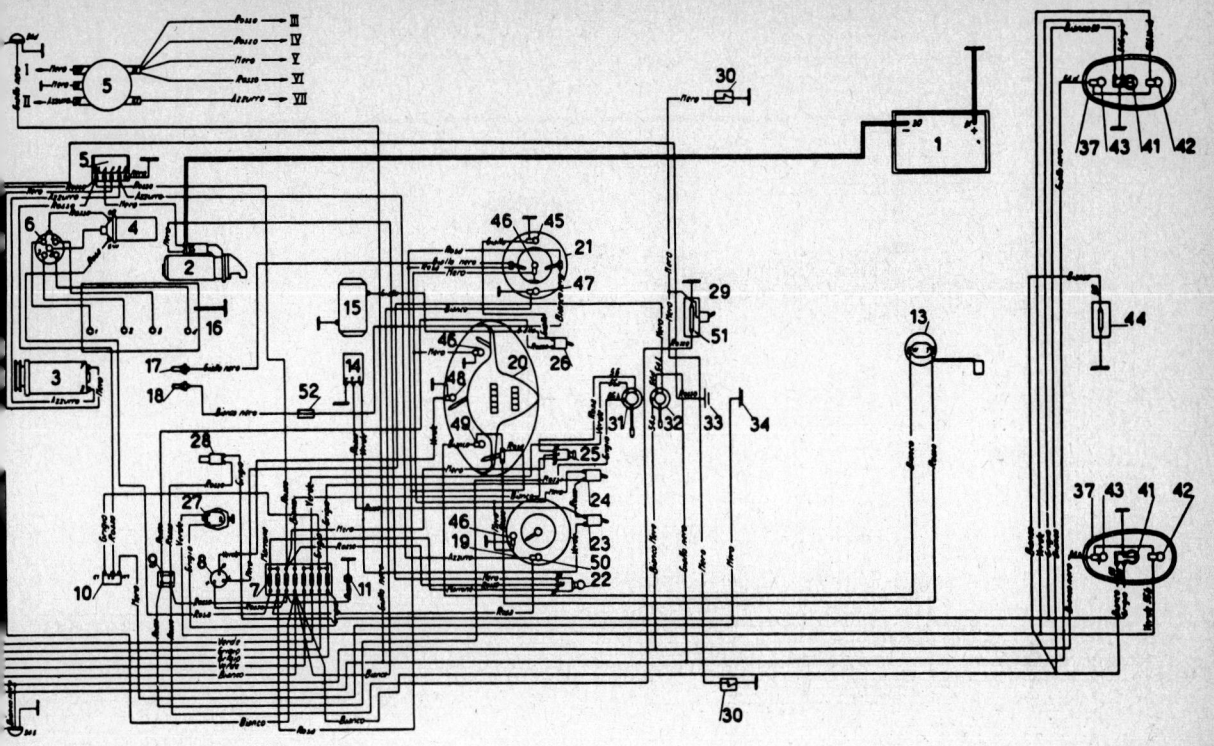

Giulietta TI

1. Battery.
2. Starter motor.
3. Generator.
4. Ignition coil.
5. Regulator.
6. Distributor.
7. Fuse box.
8. Turn signal flasher.
9. Terminal board.
10. Electromagnetic switch for turn signals.
11. Socket for inspection lamp.
12. Horn.
13. Float of fuel level indicator.
14. Windshield wiper motor.
15. Heater.
16. Ground connection, engine to body.
17. Bulb for water temperature.
18. Bulb for oil temperature.
19. Tachometer.
20. Instrument panel.
21. Oil and water temperature.

22. Ignition and starter switch.
23. Switch for windshield wiper motor.
24. Switch for instrument panel lights.
25. Switch for headlamps and parking lights.
26. Switch for heater motor.
27. Backup switch.
28. Stop signal switch.
29. Rooflight.
30. Rooflight switch on doors.
31. Switch for high and low beam.
32. Turn signal switch.
33. Push-button for horn.
34. Push-button for blinking headlights.
35. Headlights.
36. Front lamps.
37. Rear lamps.
38. Side blinking lamps.
39. 12 V—45 W—40 W lamps for headlights.

40. 12 V—5 W—20 W lamps for front lamps.
41. 12 V—5 W—20 W lamps for rear lamps.
42. 12 V—20 W backup lamps.
43. 12 V—20 W lamps for rear blinking lights.
44. 12 V—5 W lamp for rear license plate.
45. 12 V—2.5 W tell-tale lamp for heater.
46. 12 V—2.5 W lamps for instrument panel lighting.
47. 12 V—2.5 W tell-tale lamp for high beam lighting.
48. 12 V—2.5 W tell-tale lamp for turn signals.
49. 12 V—2.5 W tell-tale lamp for fuel reserve.
50. 12 V—2.5 tell-tale lamp for generator.
51. 12 V—3 W lamp for rooflight.
52. Resistance in oil circuit.

Rosso	= Red	Giallo	= Yellow	Bianco	= White
Nero	= Black	Grigio	= Grey	Marrone	= Brown
Azzurro	= Blue	Verde	= Green	Rosa	= Pink
Bianco-nero	= Black and white		Giallo-nero	= Black and yellow	

I. To generator   II. To generator   III. To horn   IV. To fuses   V. To starter motor   VI. To electromagnetic change-over switch   VII. To generator tell-tale lamp

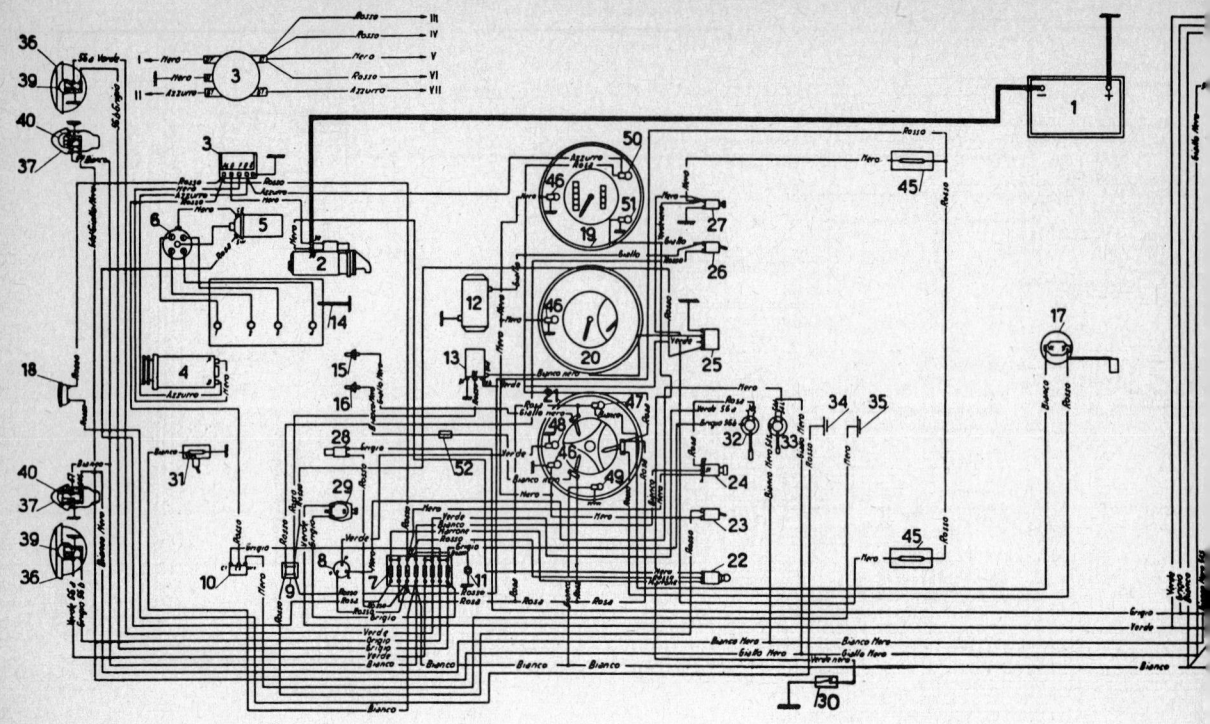

Giulietta Sprint

1. Battery.
2. Starter motor.
3. Regulator.
4. Generator.
5. Ignition coil.
6. Distributor.
7. Fuse box.
8. Turn signal flasher.
9. Terminal board.
10. Electromagnetic switch for turn signals.
11. Socket for inspection lamp.
12. Heater.
13. Windshield wiper motor.
14. Ground connection, engine to body.
15. Bulb for water temperature.
16. Bulb for oil temperature.
17. Float of fuel level indicator.
18. Horn.
19. Speedometer.
20. Tachometer and oil gauge.
21. Oil and water temperature and fuel gauge.

22. Ignition switch.
23. Switch for instrument panel lights.
24. Switch for headlamps and parking lights.
25. Switch for windshield wiper motor.
26. Switch for heater motor.
27. Rooflight switch.
28. Stop signal switch.
29. Backup switch.
30. Rooflight switch on door.
31. Hood light with switch.
32. Switch for high and low beam.
33. Turn signal switch.
34. Push-button for horn.
35. Push-button for blinking headlights.
36. Headlights.
37. Front lamps.
38. Rear lamps.
39. 12 V—45 W—40 W lamps for headlights.

40. 12 V—5 W—20 W lamps for front lamps.
41. 12 V—5 W—20 W lamps for rear lamps.
42. 12 V—20 W lamps for rear blinking lights.
43. 12 V—20 W lamps for backup.
44. 12 V—5 W lamp for rear license plate.
45. 12 V—3 W lamp for rooflight.
46. 12 V—2.5 W lamps for instrument panel lighting.
47. 12 V—2.5 W tell-tale lamp for fuel reserve.
48. 12 V—2.5 W tell-tale lamp for turn signals.
49. 12 V—2.5 W tell-tale lamp for high beam lighting.
50. 12 V—2.5 W tell-tale lamp for generator.
51. 12 V—2.5 W tell-tale lamp for heater.
52. Resistance in oil circuit.

Rosso	= Red	Giallo	= Yellow	Bianco	= White
Nero	= Black	Grigio	= Grey	Marrone	= Brown
Azzurro	= Blue	Verde	= Green	Rosa	= Pink
Bianco-nero	= Black and white		Giallo-nero	= Black and yellow	

I. To generator   II. To generator   III. To horn   IV. To fuses   V. To starter motor   VI. To electromagnetic change-over switch   VII. To generator tell-tale lamp

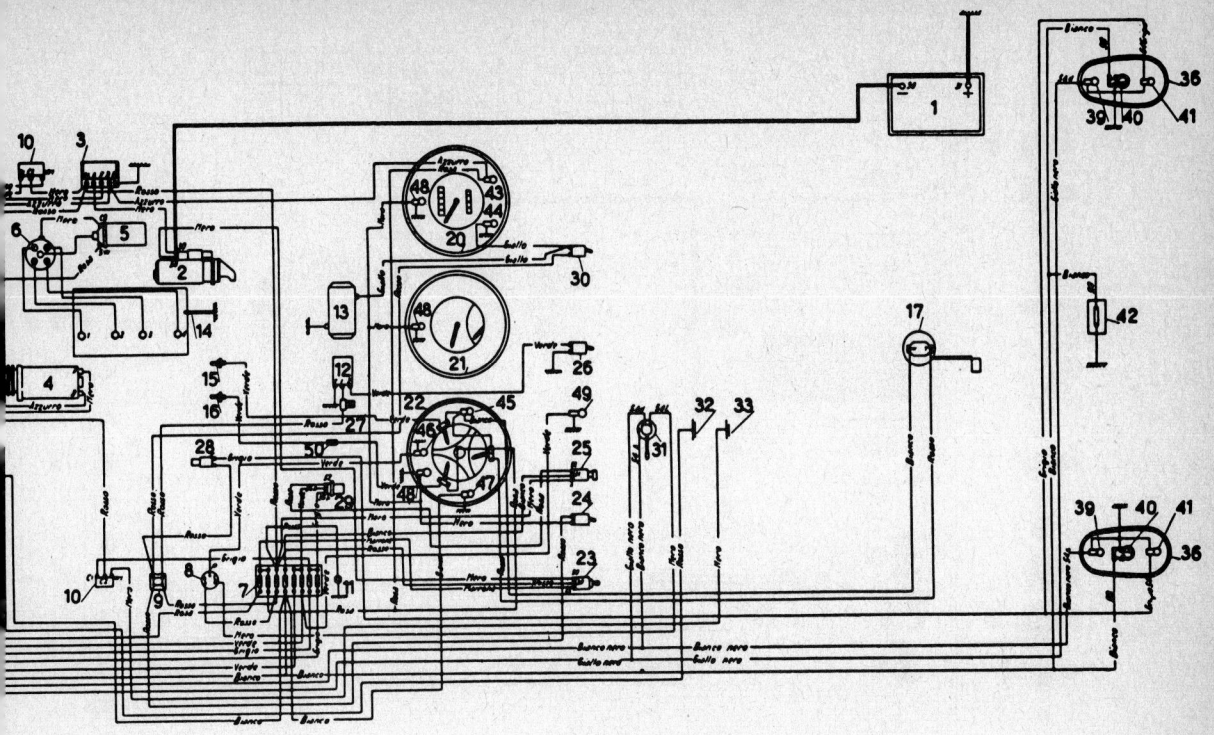

Giulietta Spider

1. Battery.
2. Starter motor.
3. Regulator.
4. Generator.
5. Ignition coil.
6. Distributor.
7. Fuse box.
8. Turn signal flasher.
9. Terminal board.
10. Electromagnetic changeover switch.
11. Socket for inspection lamp.
12. Windshield wiper motor.
13. Heater.
14. Ground connection, engine to body.
15. Bulb for water temperature.
16. Bulb for oil temperature.
17. Float of fuel level indicator.
18. Electric horn.
19. Electric horn.
20. Speedometer.
21. Tachometer and oil gauge.
22. Oil and water temperature and fuel gauge.
23. Ignition switch.
24. Switch for instrument panel lights.
25. Switch for headlamps and parking lights.
26. Switch for windshield wiper motor.
27. Thermal switch.
28. Stop signal switch.
29. Pedal switch for headlamp lights.
30. Switch for heater motor.
31. Turn signal switch.
32. Push-button for horns.
33. Push-button for blinking headlights.
34. Headlights.
35. Front lamps.
36. Rear lamps.
37. 12 V—45 W—40 W lamps for headlights.
38. 12 V—5 W—20 W lamps for front lamps.
39. 12 V—20 W lamps for rear blinking lights.
40. 12 V—5 W—20 W lamps for rear lamps.
41. 12 V—20 W lamps for stop signal.
42. 12 V—5 W lamp for rear license plate.
43. 12 V—2.5 W tell-tale lamp for generator.
44. 12 V—2.5 W tell-tale lamp for heater.
45. 12 V—2.5 W tell-tale lamp for fuel reserve.
46. 12 V—2.5 W tell-tale lamp for turn signals.
47. 12 V—2.5 W tell-tale lamp for high beam.
48. 12 V—2.5 W lamp for instrument panel lighting.
49. 12 V—2.5 W tell-tale lamp for headlamp lighting.
50. Resistance in oil circuit.

Rosso	= Red	Giallo	= Yellow	Bianco	= White
Nero	= Black	Grigio	= Grey	Marrone	= Brown
Azzurro	= Blue	Verde	= Green	Rosa	= Pink
Bianco-nero	= Black and white	Giallo-nero	= Black and yellow		

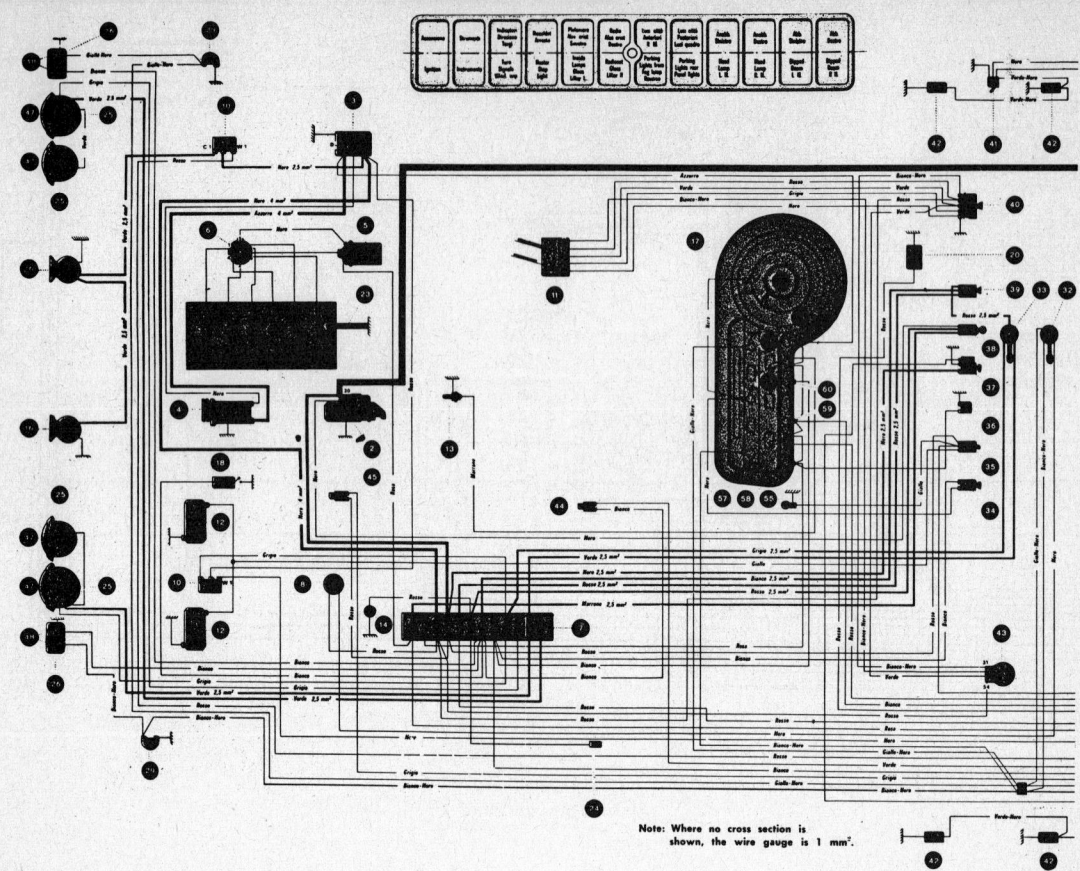

Note: Where no cross section is shown, the wire gauge is 1 mm².

2600 Berlina

1. Battery
2. Starter motor
3. Voltage regulator
4. Generator, D.C.
5. Coil
6. Distributor
7. Fusebox
8. Directional flasher unit
9. Connections
10. Solenoid switch
11. Windshield wiper
12. Blower-heater unit
13. Water temperature gauge bulb
14. Inspection lamp socket
15. Fuel level sender
16. Warning horn
17. Dashboard
18. Engine compartment light
19. Ceiling lamp
20. Map reading lamp
21. Trunk light
22. Fuel pump
23. Engine ground connection
24. Radio set socket
25. Headlamp
26. Front parking light
27. Rear parking light
28. License plate and reverse light
29. Side lamp
30. Signaling knob
31. Warning horn knob
32. Directional light switch
33. Headlamp undipped beam switch

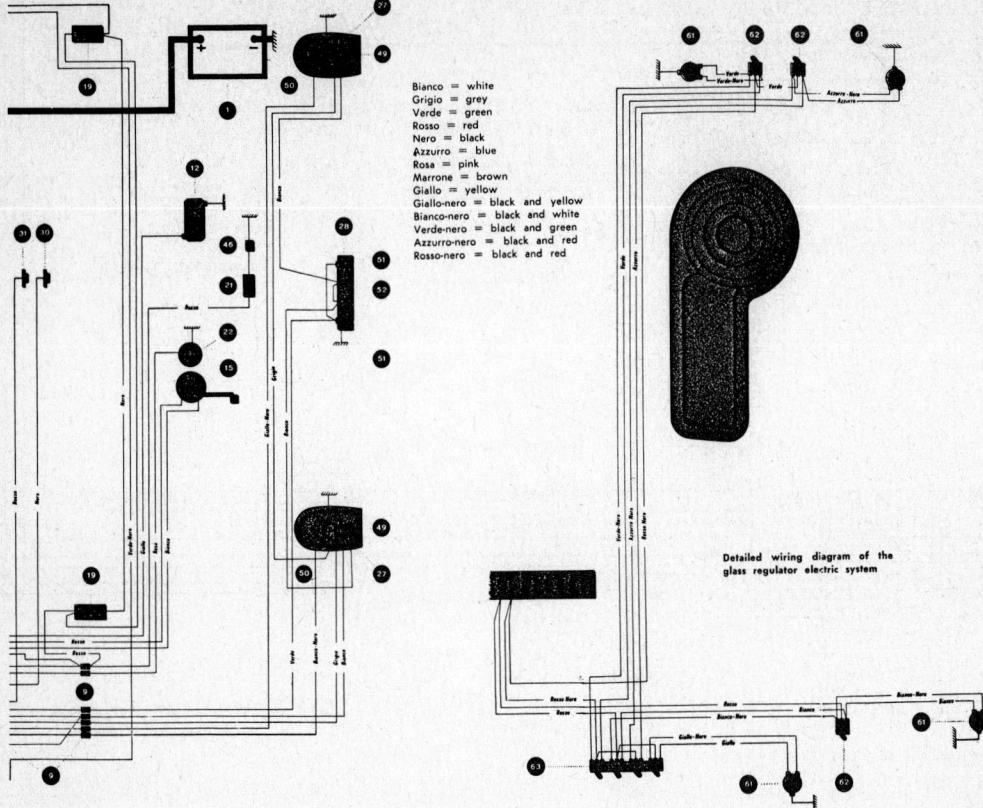

Bianco = white
Grigio = grey
Verde = green
Rosso = red
Nero = black
Azzurro = blue
Rosa = pink
Marrone = brown
Giallo = yellow
Giallo-nero = black and yellow
Bianco-nero = black and white
Verde-nero = black and green
Azzurro-nero = black and red
Rosso-nero = black and red

Detailed wiring diagram of the
glass regulator electric system

2600 Berlina

34. Dashboard light switch
35. Blower-heater unit switch
36. Choke control warning light
    switch
37. Cigarette lighter
38. Ignition switch
39. Headlamp switch
40. Windshield wiper switch
41. Ceiling lamp switch, on door
42. Ceiling lamp switch, pedal
    operated
43. Screen washer switch, pedal
    operated
44. Reverse light switch
45. Stop light switch
46. Trunk light switch

47. Headlamp bulb
48. Front light bulb
49. Rear parking & stop light bulb
50. Rear directional light bulb
51. Reverse lamp bulb
52. License plate light bulb
53. Dashboard light bulb
54. Generator warning light bulb
55. Blower-heater warning light bulb
56. RH directional warning light bulb
57. LH directional warning light bulb
58. Choke control warning light
59. Fuel reserve warning light bulb
60. Parking lamp warning light bulb
61. Glass regulator motor
62. Glass regulator switch
63. Glass regulator switchboard

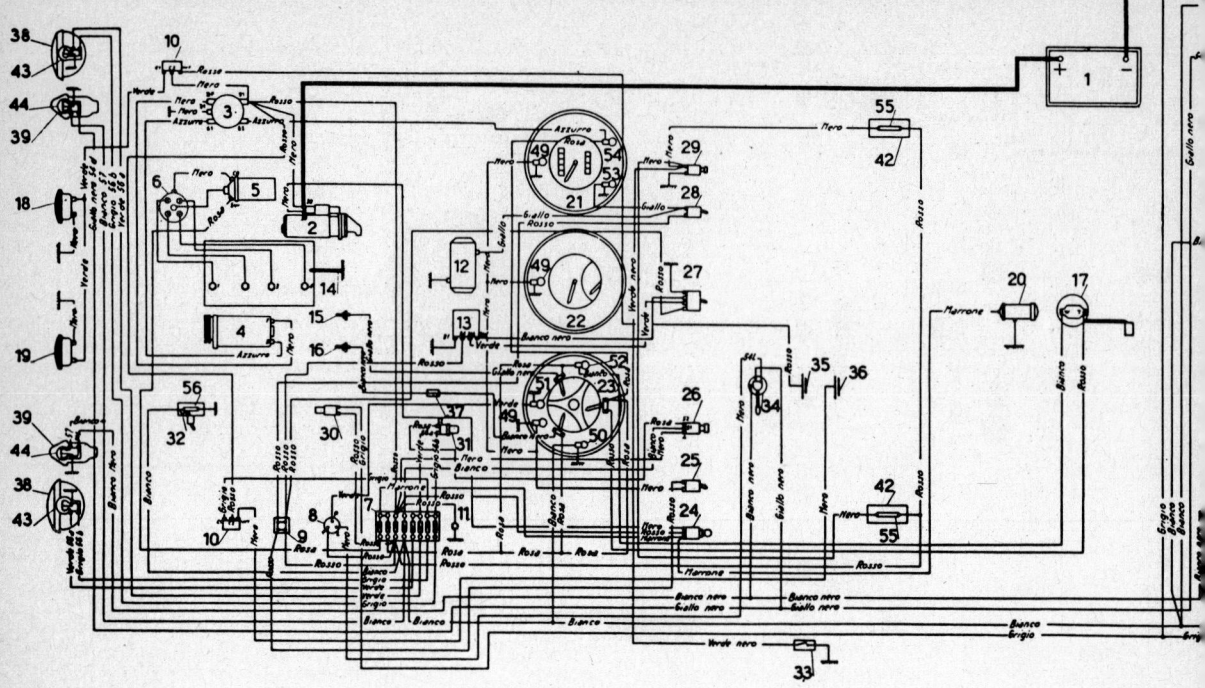

Giulietta Sprint Veloce, Spider Veloce

1. Battery.
2. Starter motor.
3. Regulator.
4. Generator.
5. Ignition coil.
6. Distributor.
7. Fuse box.
8. Turn signal flasher.
9. Terminal board.
10. Electromagnetic changeover switch.
11. Socket for inspection lamp.
12. Heater.
13. Windshield wiper motor.
14. Ground connection, engine to body.
15. Bulb for water temperature.
16. Bulb for oil temperature.
17. Float of fuel level indicator.
18. Horn.
19. Horn.
20. Fuel pump.
21. Speedometer.
22. Tachometer and oil gauge.
23. Oil and water temperature and fuel gauge.

24. Ignition switch.
25. Switch for instrument panel lights.
26. Switch for headlamps and parking lights.
27. Switch for windshield wiper motor.
28. Switch for heater motor.
29. Rooflight switch.
30. Stop signal switch.
31. Pedal switch for headlamp lighting.
32. Hood light with switch.
33. Rooflight switch on door.
34. Turn signal switch.
35. Push-button for horn.
36. Push-button for blinking headlights.
37. Resistance in oil circuit.
38. Headlights.
39. Front lamps.
40. Rear lamps.
41. Rear license lamp.
42. Rooflight.
43. 12 V—45 W—40 W lamps for headlights.

44. 12 V—5 W lamps for front lamps.
45. 12 V—20 W lamps for stop signal.
46. 12 V—5 W lamps for rear lamps.
47. 12 V—20 W lamps for rear blinking lights.
48. 12 V—5 W lamp for rear license plate.
49. 12 V—2.5 W lamps for instrument panel lighting.
50. 12 V—2.5 W tell-tale lamp for high beam.
51. 12 V—2.5 W tell-tale lamp for turn signals.
52. 12 V—2.5 W tell-tale lamp for fuel reserve.
53. 12 V—2.5 W tell-tale lamp for heater.
54. 12 V—2.5 W tell-tale lamp for generator.
55. 12 V—3 W lamp for rooflight. (Sprint Veloce only)
56. 12 V—3 W lamps for hood light.

Rosso	= Red	Giallo	= Yellow	Bianco	= White
Nero	= Black	Grigio	= Grey	Marrone	= Brown
Azzurro	= Blue	Verde	= Green	Rosa	= Pink
Bianco-nero	= Black and white	Giallo-nero	= Black and yellow		

2600 Sprint

Note: Where no cross section is shown, the wire gauge is 1 mm².

2600 Sprint

1. Battery
2. Starter motor
3. Voltage regulator
4. Generator, D.C.
5. Coil
6. Distributor
7. Fusebox
8. Directional flasher unit
9. Engine oil heating resistance
10. Solenoid switch
11. Windshield wiper
12. Blower-heater unit
13. Water temperature gauge bulb
14. Oil temperature gauge bulb
15. Inspection lamp socket
16. Fuel level sender
17. Warning horn
18. Mileage recorder
19. Tachometer and oil pressure indicator
20. Oil & water temperature, fuel level indicators
21. Engine compartment light
22. Ceiling lamp
23. Map reading lamp

24. Trunk light
25. Fuel pump
26. Engine ground connection
27. Radio set socket
28. Headlamp
29. Front parking lamp
30. Rear parking lamp
31. Reserve light
32. License plate light
33. Side lamp
34. Signalling knob
35. Warning horn knob
36. Directional light switch
37. Blower-heater unit switch
38. Choke control push button switch
39. Ceiling lamp switch
40. Ignition switch
41. Headlamp switch
42. Dashboard light switch
43. Cigarette lighter
44. Windshield wiper switch
45. Ceiling lamp switch, on door
46. Screen washer switch, pedal operated
47. Reserve light switch

48. Headlamp undipped beam switch, pedal operated
49. Stop light switch
50. Trunk light push button switch
51. Headlamp bulb
52. Front parking light bulb
53. Rear parking & stop light bulb
54. Rear directional light bulb
55. Reverse light bulb
56. License plate light bulb
57. Dashboard light bulb
58. Generator warning light bulb
59. Blower-heater warning light bulb
60. RH directional warning light bulb
61. LH directional warning light bulb
62. Headlamp warning light bulb
63. Choke control warning light bulb
64. Fuel reserve warning light bulb
65. Parking warning light bulb
66. Glass regulator motor
67. Glass regulator switch
68. Connections

2600 Spider

1. Battery
2. Starter motor
3. Voltage regulator
4. Generator, D.C.
5. Coil
6. Distributor
7. Fusebox
8. Directional flasher unit
9. Engine oil heating resistance
10. Solenoid switch
11. Windshield wiper
12. Blower-heater unit
13. Water temperature gauge bulb
14. Oil temperature gauge bulb
15. Inspection lamp socket
16. Fuel level sender
17. Warning horn
18. Mileage recorder
19. Tachometer
20. Fuel level indicator
21. Water temperature gauge

22. Engine compartment light
23. Map reading lamp
24. Trunk light
25. Fuel pump
26. Engine ground connection
27. Radio set socket
28. Headlamp
29. Front parking lamp
30. Rear parking lamp
31. License plate light
32. Side lamp
33. Signalling knob
34. Warning horn knob
35. Directional light switch
36. Heater switch
37. Choke control switch
38. Ignition switch
39. Headlamp switch
40. Dashboard light switch
41. Windshield wiper switch
42. Screen washer switch, pedal operated

43. Reverse light switch
44. Headlamp undipped beam switch, pedal operated
45. Stop light switch
46. Trunk light switch
47. Headlamp bulb
48. Front parking light bulb
49. Rear parking & stop light bulb
50. Rear directional light bulb
51. Reverse light bulb
52. License plate light bulb
53. Dashboard light bulb
54. Generator warning light bulb
55. Blower-heater warning light bulb
56. Directional warning light bulb
57. Headlamp warning light bulb
58. Choke control warning light bulb
59. Fuel reserve warning light bulb
60. Parking warning light bulb
61. Cigarette lighter
62. Connections

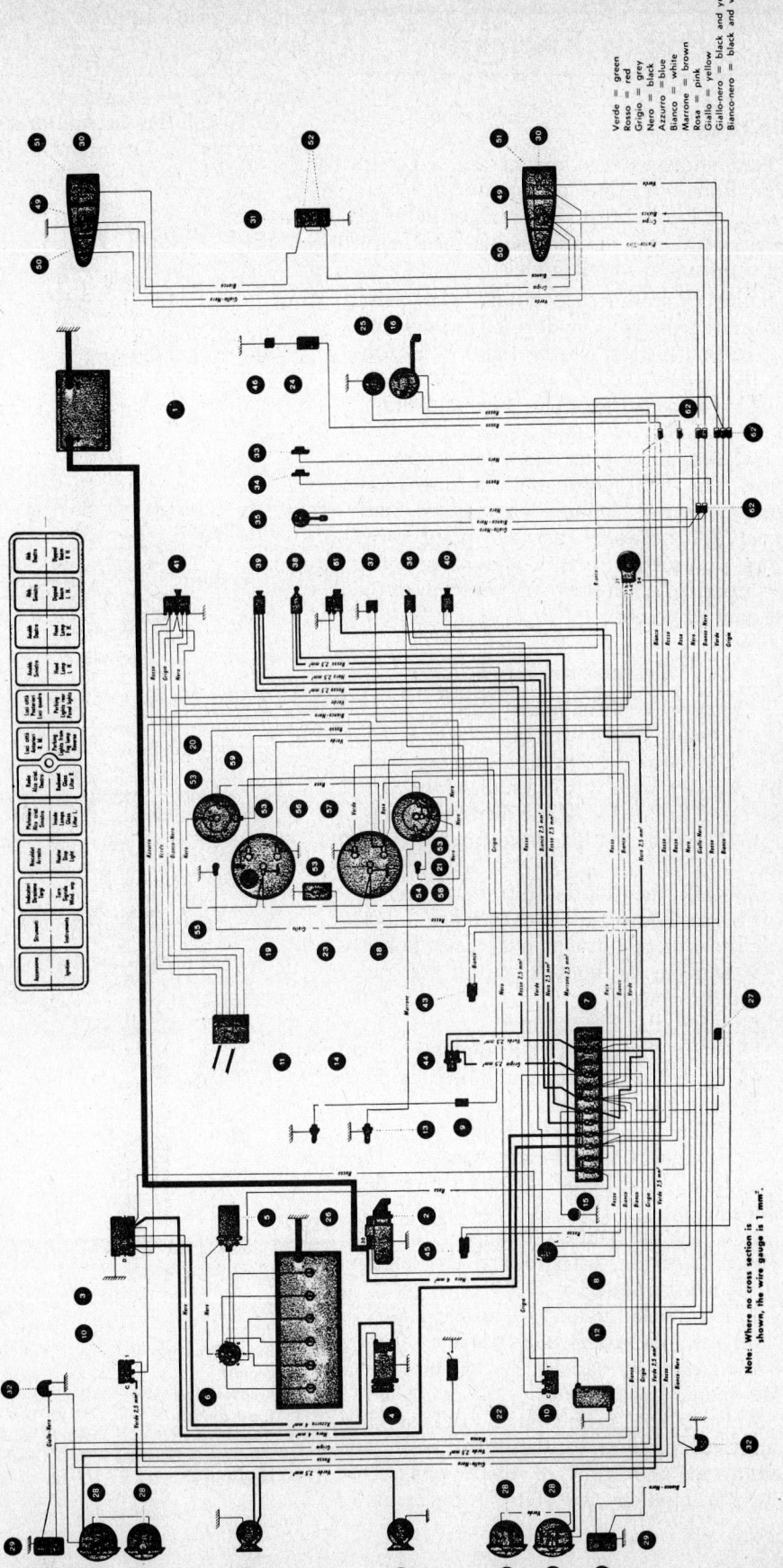

2600 Spider

Verde = green
Rosso = red
Grigio = grey
Nero = black
Azzurro = blue
Bianco = white
Marrone = brown
Rosa = pink
Giallo = yellow
Giallo-nero = black and yellow
Bianco-nero = black and white

Note: Where no cross section is shown, the wire gauge is 1 mm².

Engine Electrical

Distributor

Depending on the model and year, an Alfa Romeo engine may have a Lucas, Bosch, or Marelli distributor. Distributor removal, replacement, and timing procedures are very similar for all models.

Some Marelli distributors, including those used on 1750 models, have two locking screws instead of the more usual one on the contact point plate. Both screws must be loosened for point gap adjustment. Most Marelli and Bosch distributors have an external oiling plug and a felt below the rotor. The dual point Marelli distributor used on some 2600 models has an additional felt between the two point arms. These lubrication points should be oiled very sparingly. Excessive oil could short out the contact points.

DISTRIBUTOR R & R

To remove the distributor:

1. Remove distributor cap.
2. Disconnect distributor primary wire. The primary wire is the small gauge wire connected to the side of the distributor.
3. Disconnect the vacuum advance tube.
4. Mark the relationship between the distributor body and the cylinder block. Note the direction in which the rotor points.
5. Remove the hold-down nut and pull out the distributor.

To replace the distributor:

1. Insert the distributor, matching the marks made before removal and aligning the rotor in its original direction.
2. Replace the hold-down nut.
3. Reconnect the primary wire and the vacuum advance tube. Replace the distributor cap.
4. Check the ignition timing.

To replace the distributor if the engine has been disturbed:

1. Rotate the crankshaft to bring No. 1 cylinder to the compression stroke. Compression pressure can be felt at the spark plug opening while rotating the crankshaft.
2. Bring the static timing mark on the crankshaft pulley into alignment with the pointer on the front of the engine. On Giulietta models, the static timing mark must be centered in the flywheel inspection opening.

3. Turn the rotor toward the location of No. 1 spark plug wire.
4. Install the distributor so that the contact points are just about to begin opening.

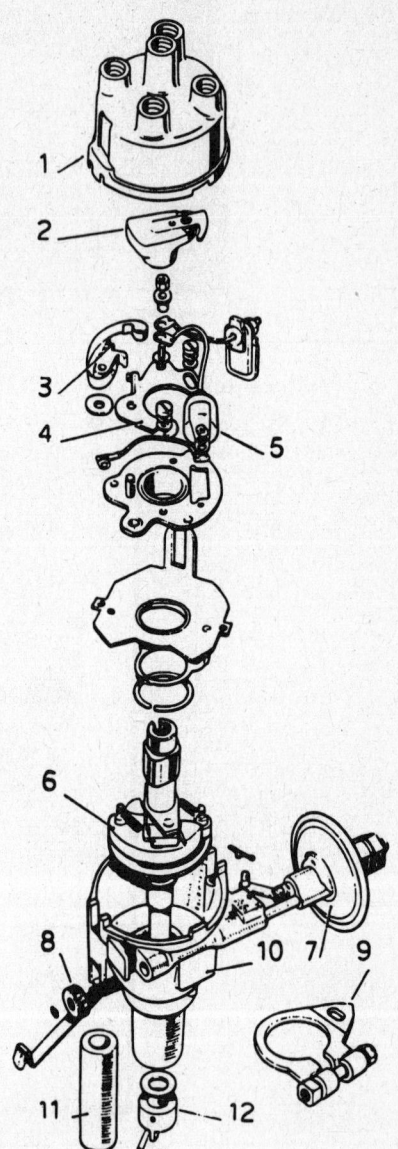

Exploded view of Lucas DM 2 distributor, used on early Giulietta models

1. Cover
2. Rotor
3. Breaker moving contact
4. Breaker plate with fixed contact
5. Condenser
6. Centrifugal advance mechanism
7. Vacuum control unit
8. Knurled knob for minor timing adjustments
9. Clamping plate
10. Distributor body
11. Porous bronze bushing
12. Distributor driving coupling

5. Replace the hold-down nut. Reconnect the primary wire and the vacuum advance tube. Replace the distributor cap.

6. Check the ignition timing.

POINT GAP ADJUSTMENT

Refer to the accompanying illustrations for point gap adjustment.

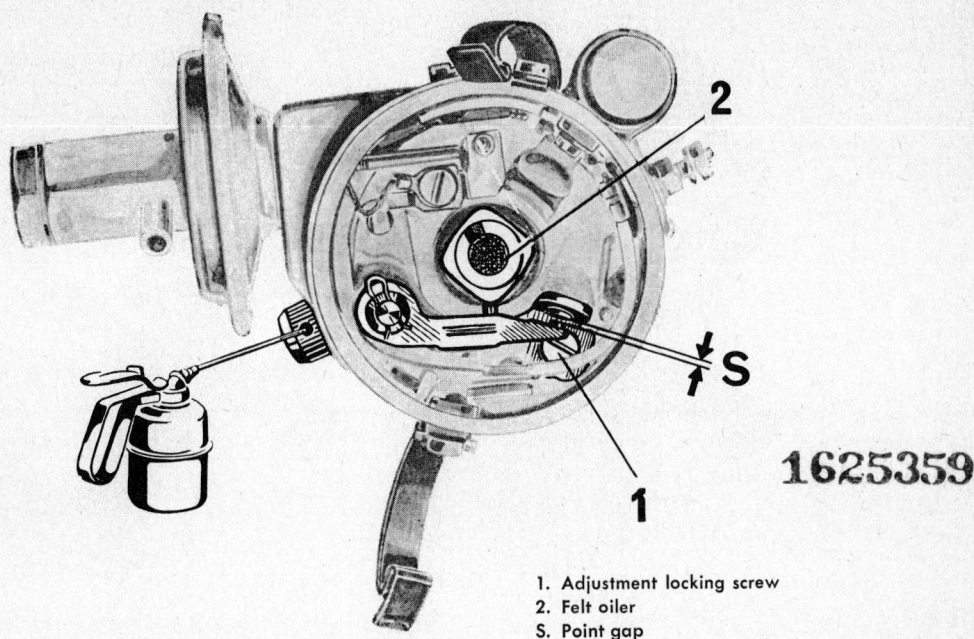

1. Adjustment locking screw
2. Felt oiler
S. Point gap

Typical Bosch distributor

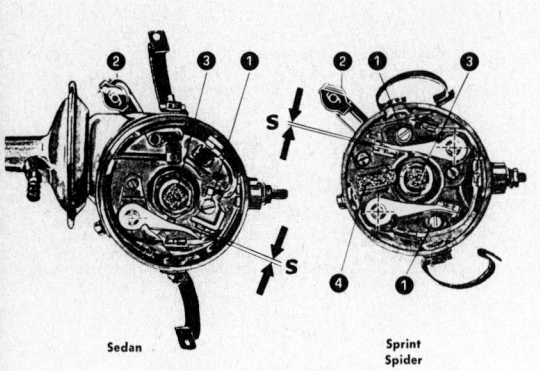

Sedan

Sprint Spider

Marelli distributor used on 2600 models

1. Adjustment locking screw
2. Lubricating plug
3. Lubricating felt
4. Lubricating felt
S. Point gap

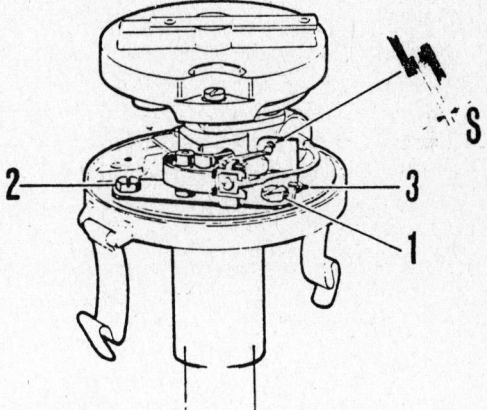

Marelli distributor used on 1750 models

1. Locking screw
2. Locking screw
3. Adjusting screwdriver slot
S. Point gap

IGNITION TIMING

Ignition Timing Marks

On Giulietta engines, the ignition timing marks are on the flywheel, visible through an inspection opening at the left (driver's side) rear of the engine. The marks are AF (static or fixed timing), PMS (top dead center or 0°), and AM (maximum advance).

All other engines have the timing marks on the crankshaft pulley. The marks are F (static or fixed timing), P (top dead center or 0°), and M (maximum advance).

The 1750 engine has an additional mark, I, for setting the injection pump timing at 70° before top dead center of the intake stroke.

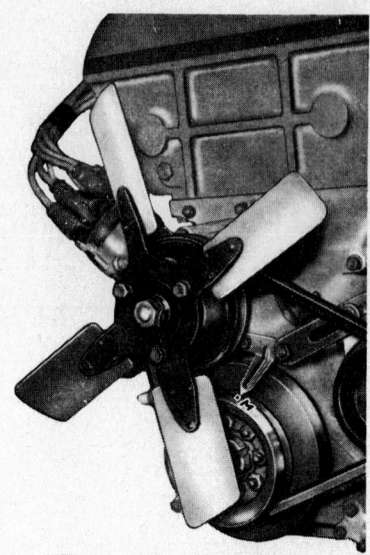

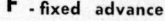

F - fixed advance.   M - maximum advance.

Timing marks on the 2600 engine

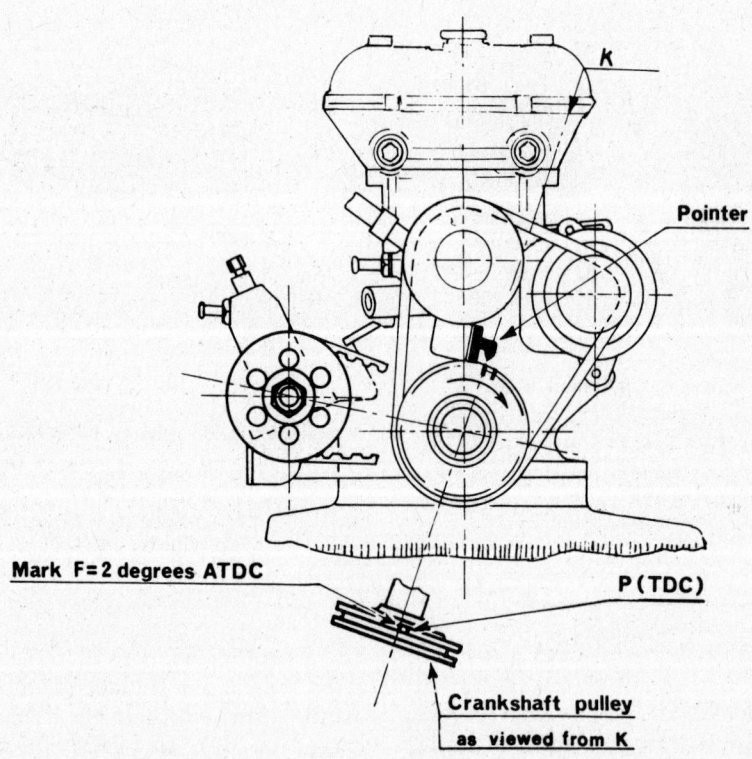

Timing marks on 1750 engine. The maximum advance mark, M, not shown in illustration.

Static Timing

Basic ignition timing can be set statically using a 12 volt test lamp. This method is suitable only for rough initial timing.

Note: basic timing on 1750 engines must be set at operating temperature and idle speed, using a stroboscopic timing light.

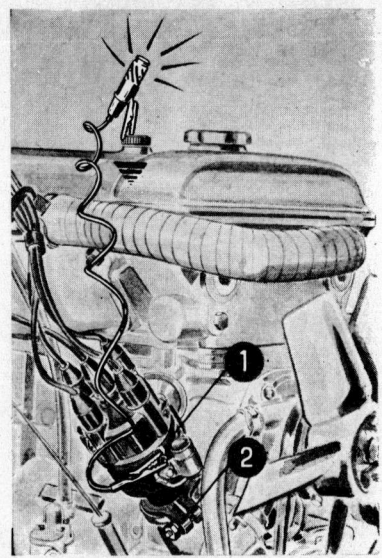

Static timing procedure, used to set initial timing on all models except 1750

1. Distributor primary wire connection
2. Distributor clamp bolt

1. Turn the crankshaft to the compression stroke of No. 1 cylinder.
2. Align the static timing mark with the pointer. Align the mark in the center of the inspection opening on Giulietta models.
3. Remove the distributor cap.
4. Connect the test light between the distributor primary wire connection and a suitable ground. Switch on the ignition.
5. Turn the crankshaft backward about 90°. Then turn the crankshaft slowly in the normal direction of rotation. The light should glow just as the static timing mark reaches alignment with the pointer or the center of the opening. If this is not the case, loosen the distributor clamp screw and advance or retard the timing as necessary. Turn the distributor clockwise (the normal direction of rotor rotation) to retard the timing and counterclockwise to advance it. The Lucas distributor has a knurled knob which can be used for small timing adjustments. Tighten the knob to retard the timing and loosen it to advance the timing.
6. Check the dynamic timing.

Dynamic Timing

To achieve accurate ignition timing at high speeds, the maximum advance must be checked with a stroboscopic timing light. This is normally done at 5,000 rpm. For exceptions, see the Distributor Specifications Table.

1. Disconnect the distributor vacuum advance tube on Giulia and 2600 models. Connect the timing light.
2. Run the engine at the specified speed and direct the light flash onto the timing mark. The maximum advance is correct if the maximum advance mark is aligned with the pointer, or centered in the inspection opening in the case of Giulietta engines.
3. Loosen the distributor clamp and advance or retard the timing as necessary. Tighten the clamp.
4. Reconnect the distributor vacuum advance tube.

Spark Plugs

Alfa Romeo has used three basic types of spark plugs in various models: the normal or exposed electrode plug, the shielded electrode plug, and the surface gap plug. Surface gap plugs need not and can not be adjusted.

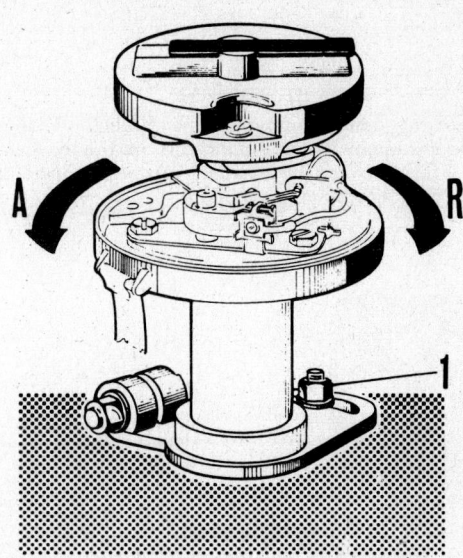

Adjustment of ignition timing

A. Turn distributor body counterclockwise to advance timing
R. Turn distributor body clockwise to retard timing.
1. Distributor hold-down bolt

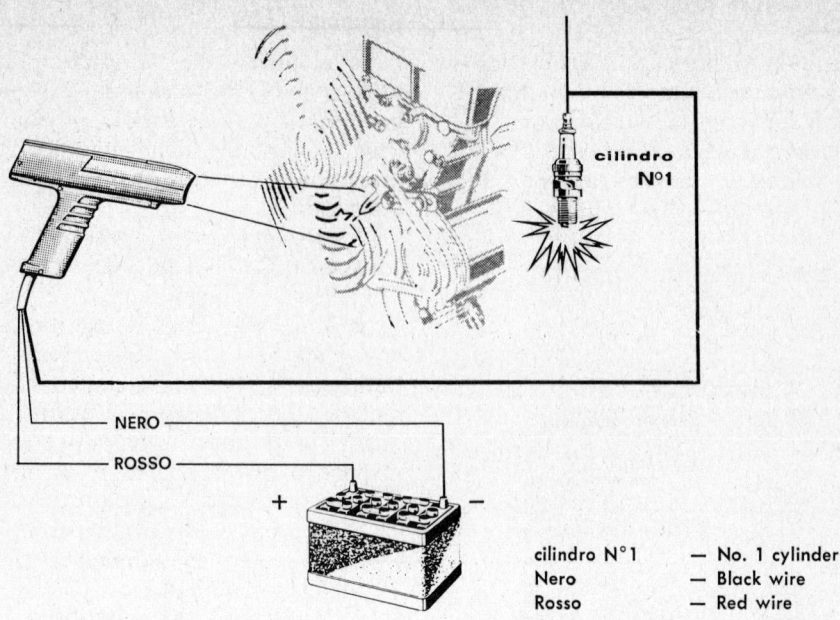

cilindro N°1
Nero
Rosso

cilindro N°1 — No. 1 cylinder
Nero — Black wire
Rosso — Red wire

Checking dynamic timing on all engines except Giulietta

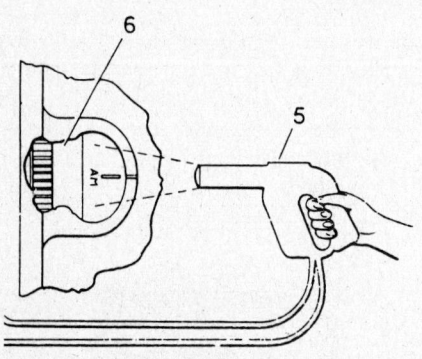

Checking dynamic timing on a Giulietta engine.
The maximum advance mark, AM, on the flywheel,
6, is centered in the flywheel inspection opening.
5 is a stroboscopic timing light.

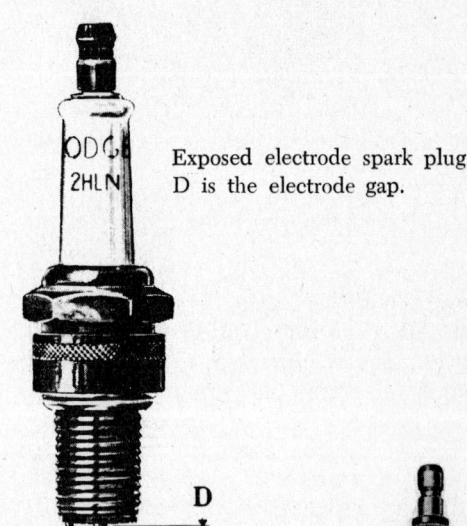

Exposed electrode spark plug.
D is the electrode gap.

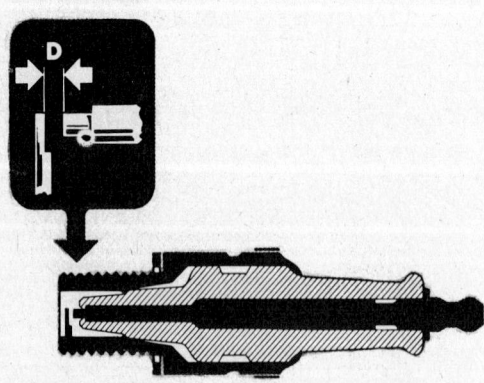

Shielded electrode spark plug. D is the electrode
gap.

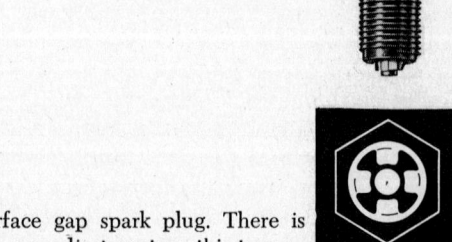

Surface gap spark plug. There is
no gap adjustment on this type.

Generator

A DC generator is used on all Giulietta and 2600 models and on some Giulia models.

BELT TENSION

The belt driving the fan, water pump, and generator must have the correct tension to prevent belt slippage or damage to water pump and generator bearings. There should be about ½″ belt play at the center of the longest span between pulleys on the Giulietta and Giulia, and about ⅜″ on the 2600. Belt tension can be regulated by loosening the nut on the slotted adjusting bracket and tilting the generator toward or away from the engine. In some cases, the bottom pivot bolts on the generator may have to be loosened.

LUCAS GENERATOR AND REGULATOR

A Lucas generator and regulator is used on some Giulietta models. The generator must be lubricated every 6,000 miles. Inject a very few drops of SAE 30 oil into the oil hole at the center rear of the unit. Do not over-oil.

The generator brushes can be removed for inspection through the inspection openings at the rear of the housing. Pull back the brush retaining spring and gently pull

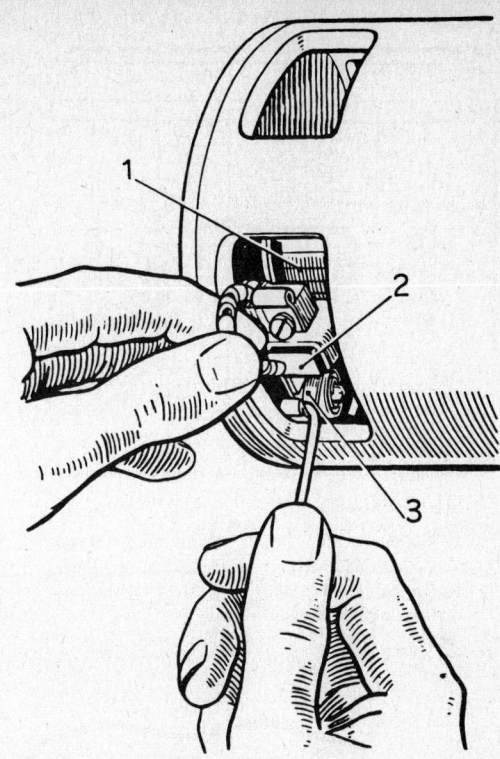

Pull back the brush spring, 3, to remove the brush, 2. 1 is the commutator.

the brush out by its flexible lead. The minimum brush length is .35″ (8.5 mm.). Any brush worn shorter must be replaced.

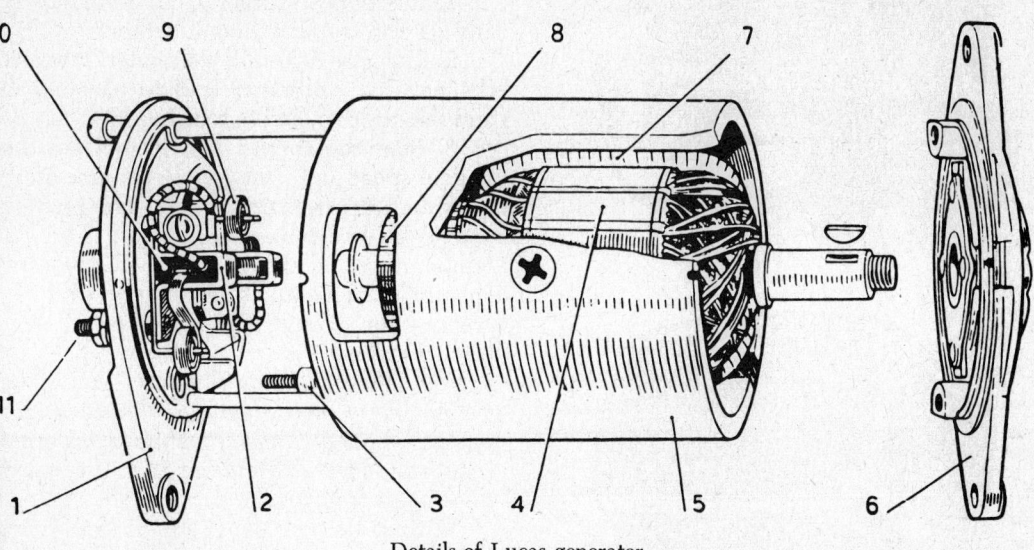

Details of Lucas generator

1. Brush holder endplate
2. Brush holder
3. Terminal (connects to regulator terminal F)
4. Armature
5. Housing
6. Drive side endplate
7. Field coil
8. Commutator
9. Brush retaining spring
10. Brush
11. Terminal (connects to regular terminal D)

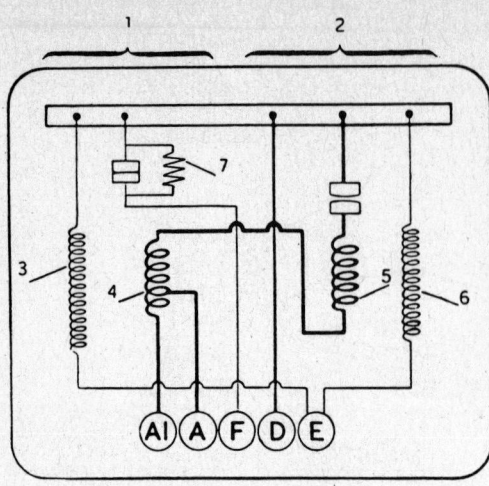

Electrical diagram of the Lucas voltage regulator

1. Regulator unit
2. Cutout unit
3. Regulator shunt coil
4. Regulator series coil
5. Cutout series coil
6. Cutout shunt coil
7. Field resistance

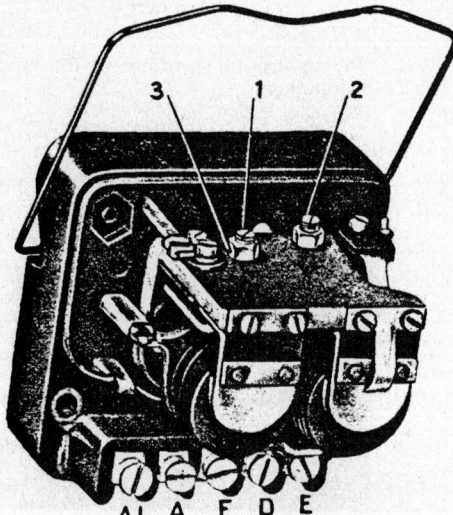

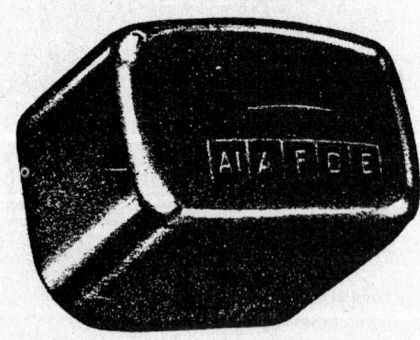

Lucas voltage regulator. 1 is the regulator unit voltage adjusting screw, 2 is the cutout unit voltage adjusting screw, 3 is a locknut.

The Lucas regulator contains a voltage regulator and an undervoltage cutout. The two units are electrically separate.

Lucas Regulator Unit Electrical Adjustment

This adjustment is required to obtain the proper voltage output.

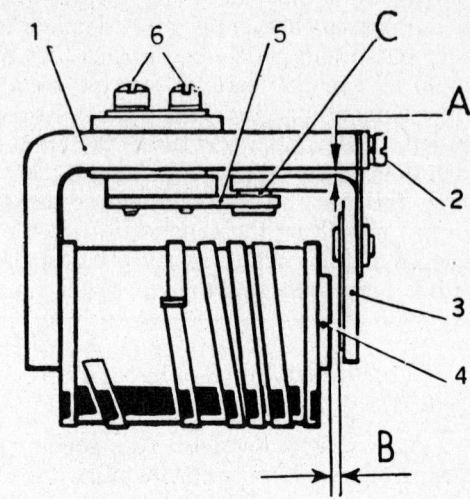

Lucas regulator unit details

1. Regulator bracket
2. Armature retaining screws
3. Armature
4. Core
5. Fixed contact
6. Fixed contact retaining screws

1. Disconnect cables from terminals A and A1 and connect them together.

2. Using a 0-20 volt voltmeter, connect the negative voltmeter lead to terminal D and the positive lead to terminal E.

3. Start the engine. Slowly increase the engine speed until the voltmeter first oscillates and then remains steady. The reading should be 15.6-16.2 volts at 68°F. If the air temperature is above 68°F, the reading should be .3 volts less for every 18°F increase. For every 18°F below 68°F, subtract .3 volts.

Note: When making this test, do not run the engine at more than half throttle or for more than 30 seconds at a time. Inaccurate readings and possible damage will result if this advice is ignored.

4. Stop the engine. If the voltage reading obtained in Step 3 was outside the limits, adjustment is necessary.

5. Remove the regulator cover. With the terminals at the bottom, the regulator unit is on the left. Loosen the locknut and turn the adjusting screw a fraction of a turn.

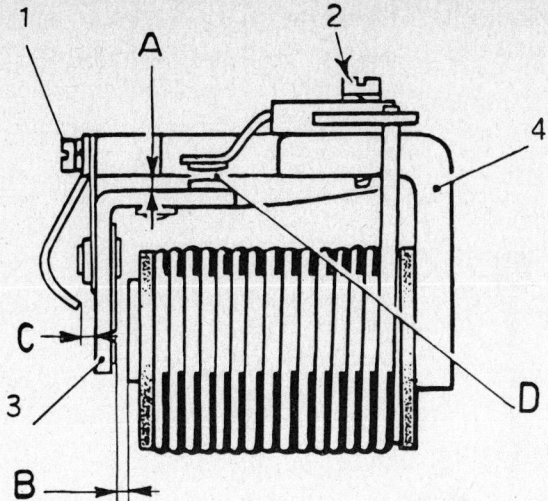

1. Armature retaining screws
2. Fixed contact retaining screws
3. Armature
4. Bracket

Lucas cutout unit details

Turn clockwise to increase the voltage and counterclockwise to reduce it.

6. Repeat Steps 3-5 until the voltage is within limits. Replace cover and reconnect cables.

Lucas Cutout Unit Electrical Adjustment

This adjustment is required in order that the cutout operate at the proper voltage.

1. Remove the regulator cover. The regulator unit is on the right. Connect a 0-20 volt voltmeter across terminals D and E.

2. Start the engine and slowly increase its speed until the cutout contacts close. The voltage at this point should be 12.7-13.3. If the voltage reading is outside these limits, adjustment is required.

3. Loosen the locknut and turn the adjusting screw a fraction of a turn. Turn the screw clockwise to increase the voltage and counterclockwise to reduce it. Tighten the locknut.

4. Check the closing voltage again. Repeat Steps 2-4 until the voltage falls within limits.

Lucas Regulator Unit Mechanical Adjustment

This adjustment is usually required only after cleaning the contacts or otherwise disturbing the regulator unit. The adjustment is as follows:

1. Loosen armature retaining screws (2). Loosen regulator unit adjusting screw.

2. Insert a .020″ (.5 mm.) feeler gauge at A.

3. With the feeler gauge in place, press the armature (3) against the regulator frame (1). Tighten the armature retaining screws (2). Remove the feeler gauge.

4. Check the gap at B. This should be .013-.020″ (.3-.5 mm.). Adjust by bending the fixed contact (5).

5. Press the armature (3) down. The gap at C should be .006-.017″ (.15-.43 mm.).

6. Check the regulator unit electrical adjustment.

Lucas Cutout Unit Mechanical Adjustment

This adjustment is necessary if the cutout unit has been disturbed in any way.

1. Loosen the armature retaining screws (1), the cutout unit adjusting screw, and the fixed contact retaining screws (2).

2. Insert a .014″ (.35 mm.) feeler gauge at A.

3. The gap B must be .012-.015″ (.29-.38 mm.). If it is not, a new armature (3) is needed.

4. Press the armature (3) against the feeler gauge and tighten the armature retaining screws (1).

5. Adjust the gap C to .030-.034″ (.76-.86 mm.) by bending the stop plate.

6. Remove the feeler gauge and tighten the fixed contact retaining screws (2).

7. Insert a .025″ (.63 mm.) feeler gauge at B. Presss the armature against the feeler gauge. Gap D must be .002-.006″ (.05-.15

mm.). Adjust by bending the fixed contact blade.

8. Check the cutout unit electrical adjustment.

Alternator

An AC generator, or alternator, is used on all 1600 Duetto, 1750, and some Giulia models.

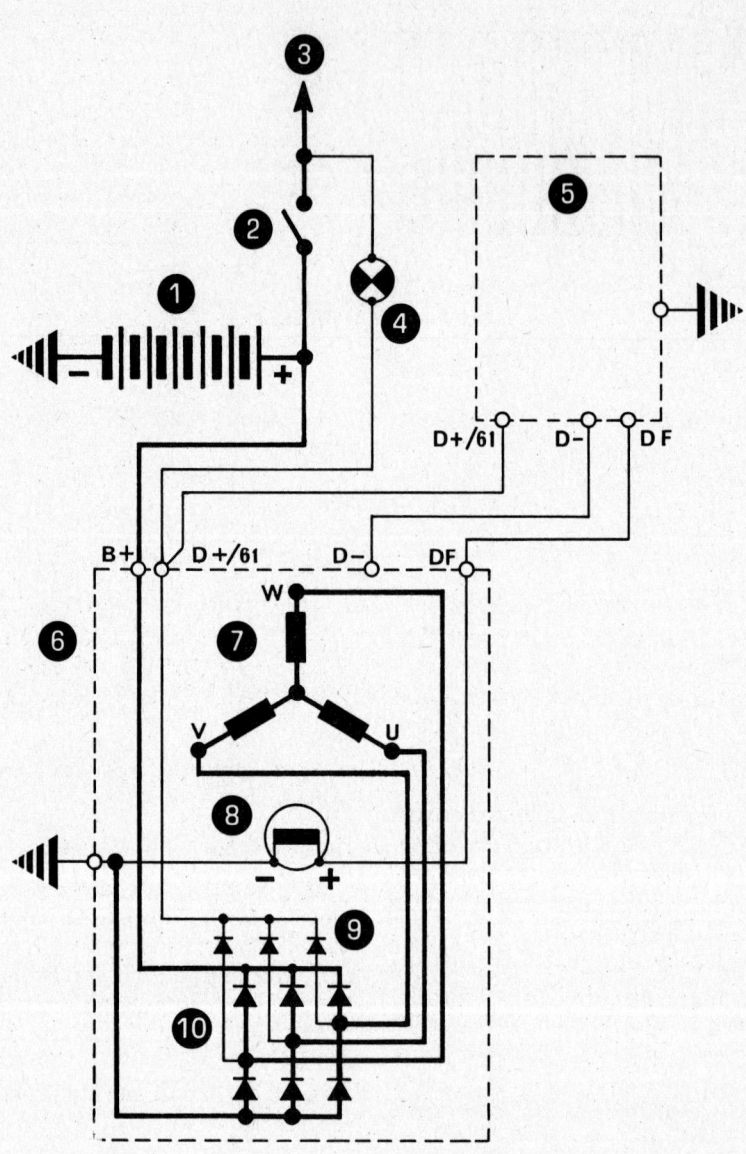

Charging system schematic for vehicles with Bosch alternator and regulator

1. Battery
2. Switch
3. To accessory circuits
4. Warning light
5. Regulator
6. Alternator
7. Stator winding
8. Field winding
9. Field current diode rectifier
10. Output current diode rectifier

D+/61   Field rectifier terminal, connected to regulator terminal D+/61 and to warning light

DF   Field input terminal, connected to regulator terminal DF

B+   Battery terminal

D—   Ground terminal, connected to regulator terminal D—

Belt Tension

The belt driving the fan, water pump, and alternator must have the correct tension to prevent belt slippage or damage to water pump and alternator bearings. There should be about ½″ belt play at the center of the longest span between pulleys. Belt tension is regulated by loosening the nut on slotted adjusting bracket and tilting the alternator toward or away from the engine.

Bosch Alternator and Regulator

The alternator and regulator require no maintenance. The regulator is factory set and a non-adjustable, non-serviceable item.

If charging circuit trouble is suspected, test as follows:

1. Stop engine.
2. Disconnect alternator terminal B+. Connect an ammeter and voltmeter as illustrated.
3. Start the engine. Switch on the headlights. If the readings are 20-30 amps and 12-13 volts, the charging system is satisfactory.
4. Stop engine and reconnect terminal B+.

Battery

All models have a 12 volt battery. The positive terminal is grounded on some Giulietta models. All other models have the more conventional negative ground. See the Battery and Starter Electrical Specifications Chart for details. The battery is located in the trunk of the Giulietta and 2600 and in the engine compartment of the Giulia and 1750.

Fuel System

Electric Fuel Pump

An electric fuel pump is used on all 1750 fuel injected engines, all 2600 engines, and on all other engines using dual sidedraft Weber carburetors. The pump is located beneath the car floor near the fuel tank.

Electric Pump R & R

To remove the fuel pump:

1. Unscrew and plug the inlet and outlet hoses.
2. Disconnect the electrical wiring.
2. Unbolt the pump mounts.
4. Reverse the procedure to install.

Bendix electric fuel pumps have a filter inside the bottom cover. The filter can readily be removed for cleaning, after plugging the inlet line.

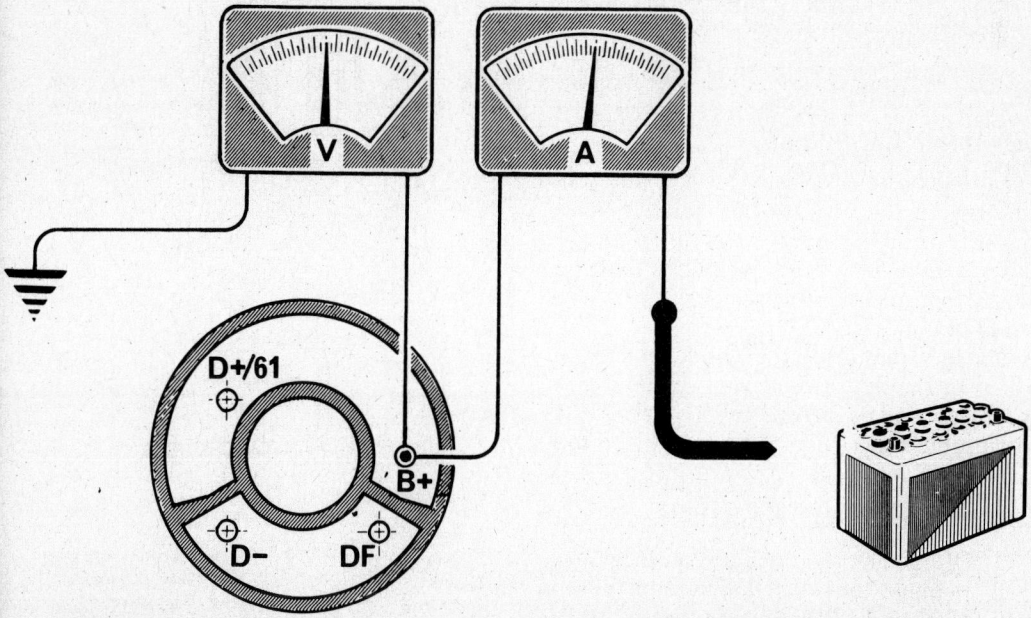

Voltmeter and ammeter connections for charging system test on vehicles with Bosch alternator and regulator

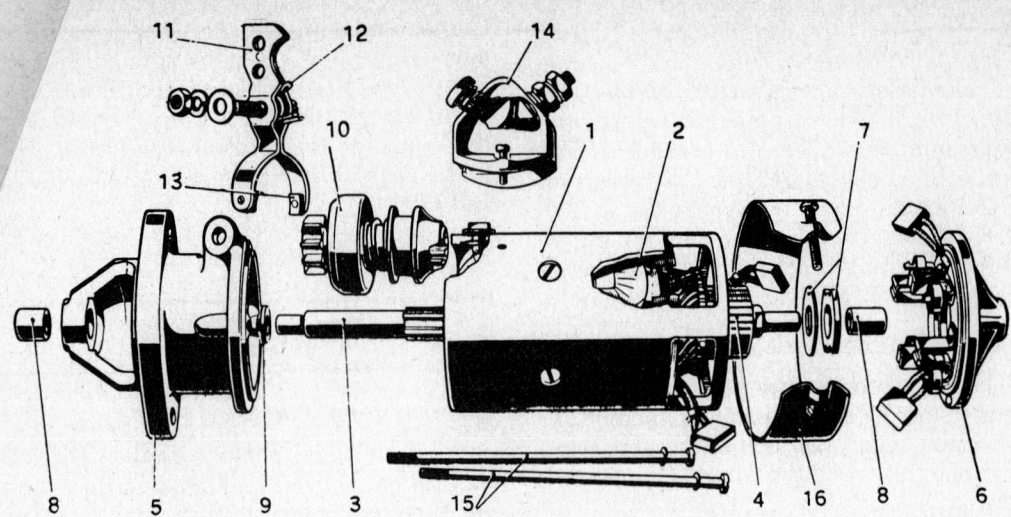

Lucas starter motor used on some Giulietta models

1. Housing	7. Friction discs	12. Return spring
2. Field coil	8. Porous bronze armature shaft	13. Shoes
3. Armature shaft	bushing	14. Switch
4. Commutator	9. Thrust washer	15. Through bolts
5. Drive end bracket	10. Drive assembly	16. Cover
6. Commutator end cover	11. Forked lever	

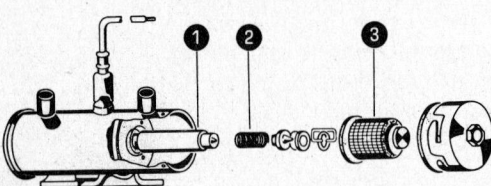

Bendix electric fuel pump. 1 is the pump plunger, 2 is the plunger return spring, and 3 is the fuel filter.

Mechanical Fuel Pump

On the Giulietta engine the fuel pump is mounted on the front of the cylinder head and driven off the exhaust camshaft by a rocker arm. The top of the pump may be readily removed for access to the wire mesh fuel filter.

The fuel pump on the Giulia engine is bolted to the lower right side of the cylinder block and is driven by a pushrod. A replaceable filter is located beneath the top cover of the pump.

GIULIA FUEL PUMP R & R

1. Disconnect the inlet and outlet hoses.
2. Remove the nuts holding the pump to the block and remove the pump.
3. Pull the pushrod from the crankcase.
4. Reverse the procedure to install.

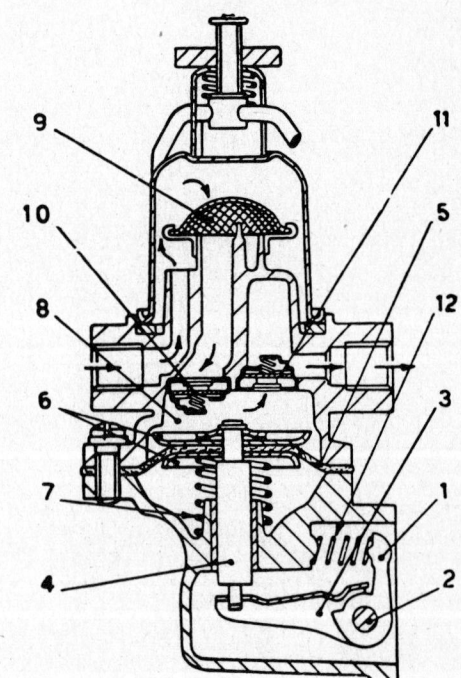

Mechanical fuel pump, Giulietta

1. Rocker arm	
2. Rocker pivot pin	8. Vacuum and pressure chamber
3. Link	
4. Tie rod	9. Fuel filter
5. Diaphragm	10. Suction valve
6. Diaphragm plates	11. Outlet valve
7. Spring	12. Rocker arm spring

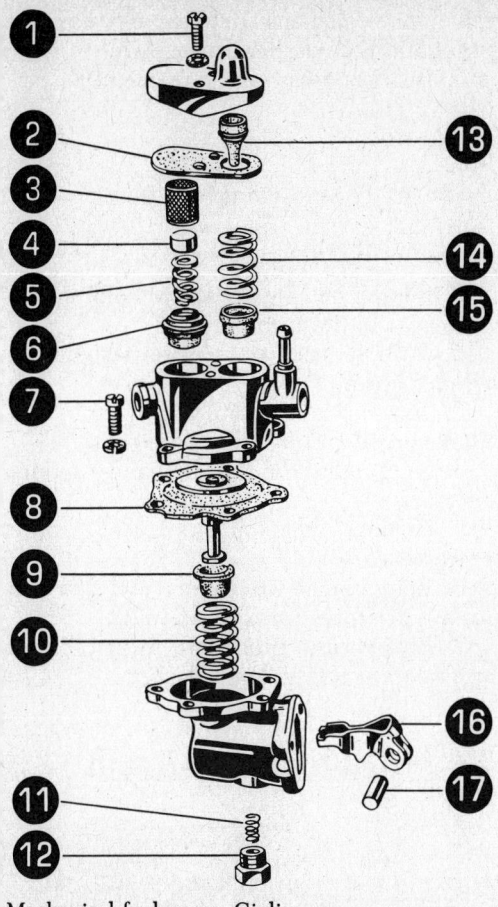

Mechanical fuel pump, Giulia

1. Screws
2. Gasket
3. Fuel filter
4. Spring seat
5. Inlet valve spring
6. Inlet valve
7. Screws
8. Diaphragm assembly
9. Rubber cup
10. Diaphragm return
    spring
11. Rocker arm return
    spring
12. Spring seat
13. Funnel
14. Outlet valve spring
15. Outlet valve
16. Rocker arm
17. Rocker arm pivot pin

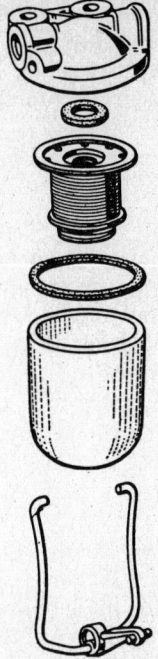

Fuel filter, Giulietta Sprint

Fuel Filters

In addition to the filters located in the fuel pumps, there may be fuel filters in various locations. The Solex downdraft carburetor on the Giulietta Berlina has two screw-in filters. One of these is in unit with the bolt attaching the fuel inlet line; the other is held in by a plug 45° below the fuel inlet. The Giulia TI and the 2600 Berlina have a screw-in filter to one side of the carburetor fuel inlet. The Giulietta Sprint has a filter with a glass sediment bowl in the fuel line near the carburetor. The 1750 fuel injection system has a replaceable in-line filter between the electric pump and

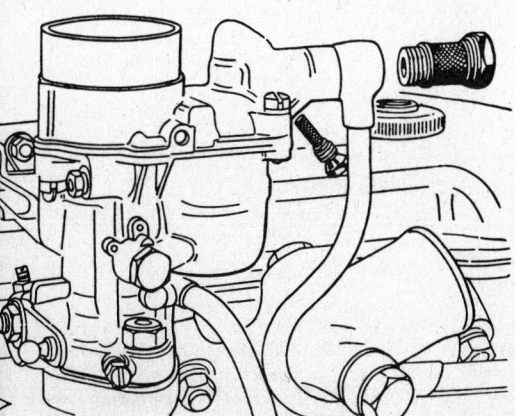

Carburetor fuel filters, Giulietta Berlina

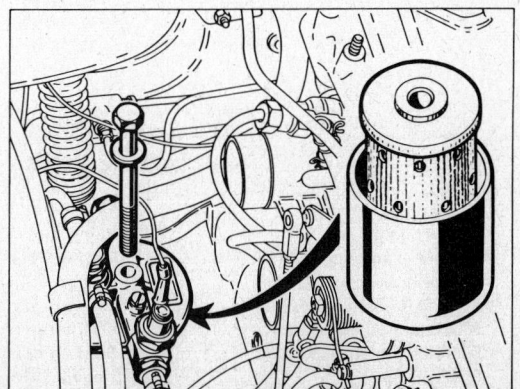

Main fuel system filter, 1750 models

the tank and a main fuel system filter in the fuel line on the right side of the engine. Weber carburetors usually have a filter in the top cover, near the fuel inlet.

Main System Fuel Filter R & R

1750 Fuel Injection System

1. Remove air cleaner assembly by detaching the two upper anchoring straps, loosening the four intake hose clamps, freeing the large and small crankcase ventilation hoses from the oil separator, and disconnecting the four idle hoses from the two equalizers on the cleaner body.

2. Disconnect battery negative terminal. Disconnect starter positive cable if necessary.

3. Thoroughly clean the outside of the filter housing.

4. Loosen the filter bolt and remove the filter and housing. Discard the element.

5. Clean out the filter housing and install a new element. Replace the housing gasket and bolt washer if necessary.

6. Reverse procedure to reassemble.

Carburetor

Solex 32 BIC—Giulietta Berlina

Carburetor R & R

1. Loosen the clamp screw holding the air cleaner to the carburetor.

2. Unbolt the air cleaner from the cylinder head.

3. Disconnect the starting device (choke) cable from the carburetor.

4. Disconnect the fuel line and vacuum tube.

5. Remove the stop from the throttle control lever.

6. Remove the stud nuts and lift the carburetor off the intake manifold.

7. Reverse the procedure to install, using a new mounting flange gasket.

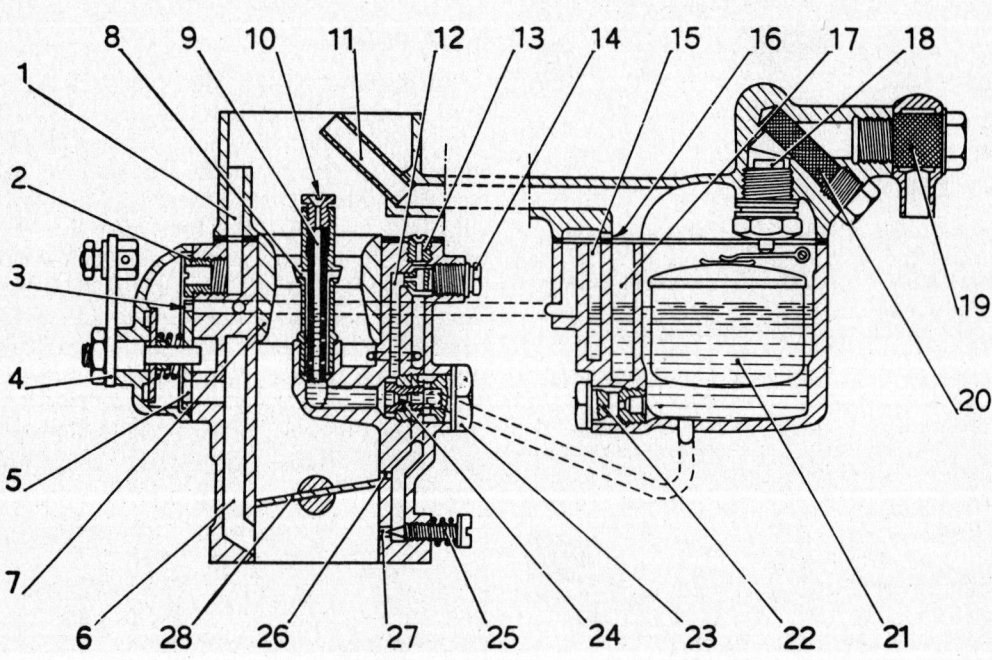

Solex 32 BIC carburetor, used on Giulietta Berlina

1. Starting air intake
2. Starting air jet
3. Hole in rotating disc for fuel
4. Starting control lever
5. Hole in disc for mixture
6. Mixture passage duct
7. Venturi tube (choke)
8. Bleed holes
9. Bleed tube
10. Bleed tube jet
11. Vent tube
12. Idling mixture passage
13. Low speed air plug
14. Low speed jet
15. Starting device well
16. Well air passage
17. Starting device well
18. Needle valve seat
19. Union with fuel intake filter
20. Filter
21. Float
22. Starting jet
23. Main jet holder
24. Main jet
25. Low speed mixture adjustment screw
26. Low speed progression passage
27. Low speed mixture passage
28. Throttle

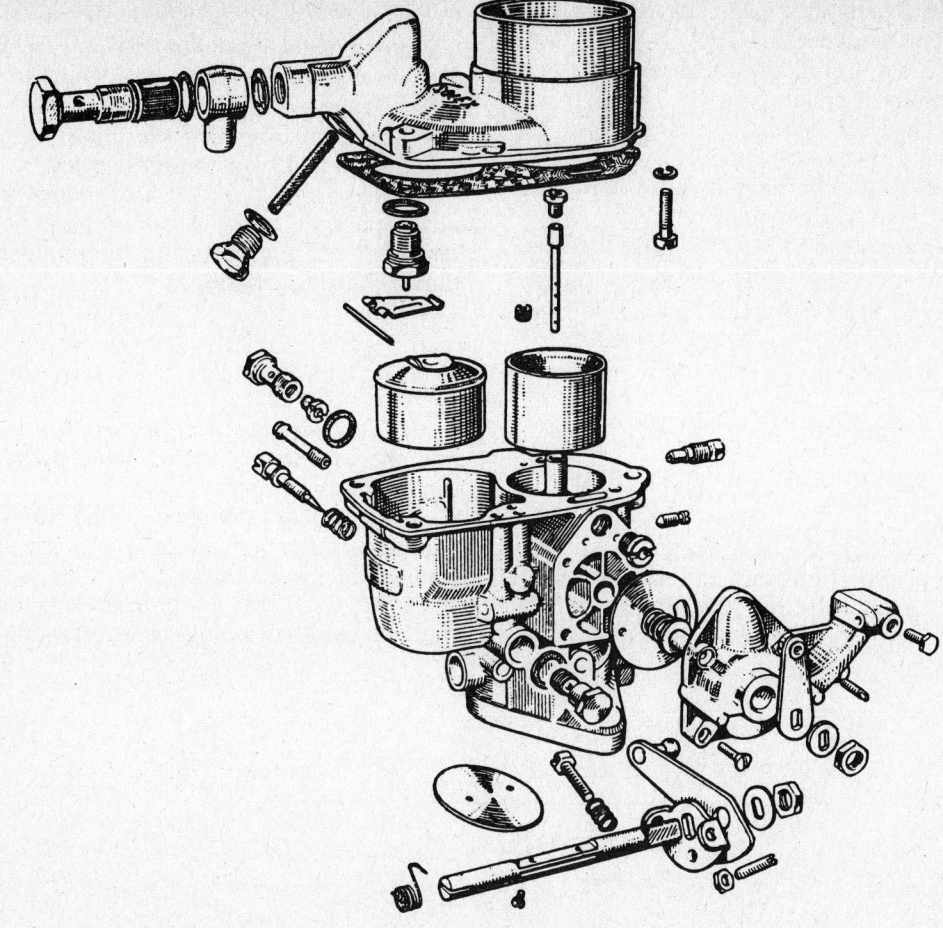

Solex 32 BIC, exploded view

dle Adjustment

Before adjusting the carburetor, first make sure that the ignition system is properly adjusted. Adjust the carburetor with the engine running at normal operating temperature.

1. Increase the engine speed by slightly turning in the throttle minimum opening adjustment screw. When facing the rear (firewall) side of the carburetor, this screw is on the right side of the throttle control lever.

2. Back out the idle mixture screw until the engine speeds up and surges. Turn the screw back in until the engine runs smoothly.

3. Slowly back out the throttle maximum opening adjustment screw, on the left side of the throttle control lever, until the idle speed is about 450 rpm.

4. If the engine begins to race, turn in the idle mixture screw slightly. Do not turn this screw in all the way or the needle will be damaged.

Minor Overhaul and Cleaning

A minor carburetor overhaul can be performed without removing the carburetor from the engine.

1. Remove the air cleaner and wash the element in kerosene.

2. Unscrew the fuel line fitting. Remove the filter and blow it clean with compressed air.

3. Remove the retaining screws and the carburetor cover.

4. Remove the bowl gasket and the float. Clean the float bowl.

5. Remove the jet holders and jets, the idle air and bleed jets, and the bleed tube.

Wash all parts in a safe carburetor solvent and blow them out.

6. Blow out all the carburetor passages with compressed air.

7. Unscrew the needle seat from the cover and clean it carefully.

8. Remove the angled screw and filter from the cover. Blow the filter clean.

9. Remove the screws holding the starting device. Blow through the seat, the tubes, and the cover.

10. Reinstall all the parts, using new gaskets.

SOLEX 35 APAI-G—GIULIETTA TI, SPRINT, SPIDER
SOLEX 32 PAIAT—GIULIETTA SPRINT

Carburetor R & R Idle Adjustment

These procedures are the same as those given previously for the Solex 32 BIC carburetor.

Minor Overhaul and Cleaning

Proceed as for the Solex 32 BIC carburetor, with the addition of these operations:

1. Remove the idle air jet, the left bleed cap and tube, and the pump injector tube. Wash and blow out these parts.

2. Remove the accelerator pump cover, diaphragm, check valve, and jet. Wash and blow out the parts and the pump suction and delivery passages.

SOLEX 32 PAIA 7—GIULIA TI

Carburetor R & R

1. Unscrew the air cleaner wing nut and the carburetor clamp. Remove the air cleaner housing cover.

2. Disconnect the choke cable, the vacuum advance tube, and the fuel hose. Disconnect the throttle linkage.

3. Remove the carburetor mounting stud nuts and remove the carburetor.

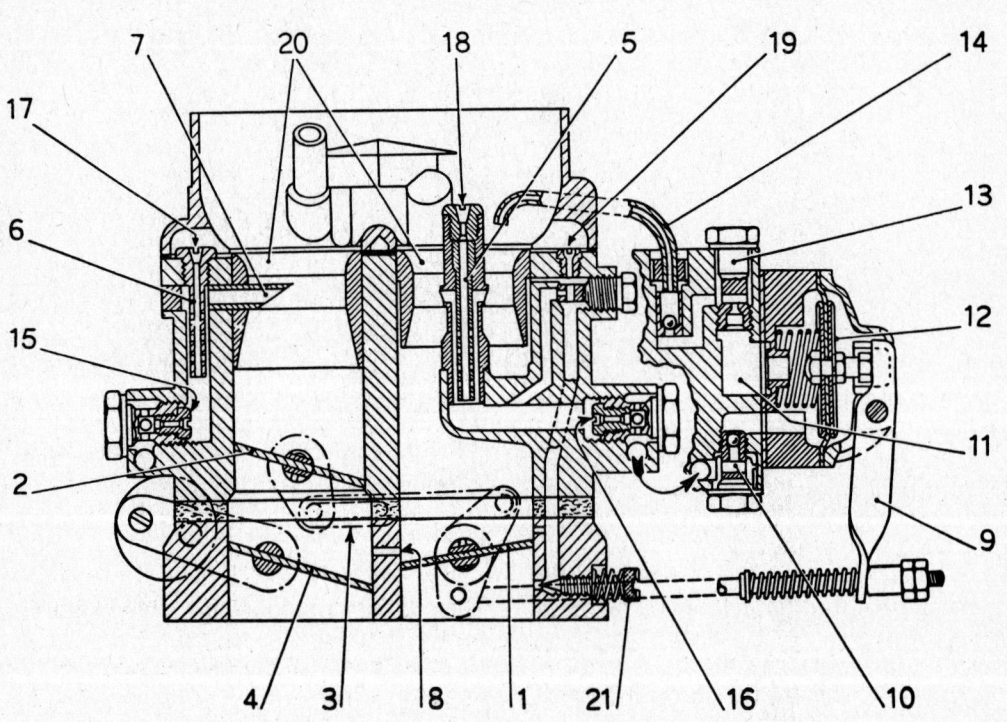

Solex 35 APAI-G carburetor, used on Giulietta TI, Sprint, and Spider

1. Right throttle
2. Left throttle
3. Left throttle control rod
4. Automatic opening throttle
5. Right bleed tube
6. Left bleed tube
7. Left spray tube
8. Drilling between left and right bodies
9. Pump control lever
10. Pump inlet valve
11. Pump pressure chamber
12. Pump diaphragm
13. Pump jet
14. Pump injector tube
15. Left main jet
16. Right main jet
17. Left bleed tube jet
18. Right bleed tube jet
19. Low speed air jet
20. Venturi tubes (choke tubes)
21. Low speed mixture adjustment screw

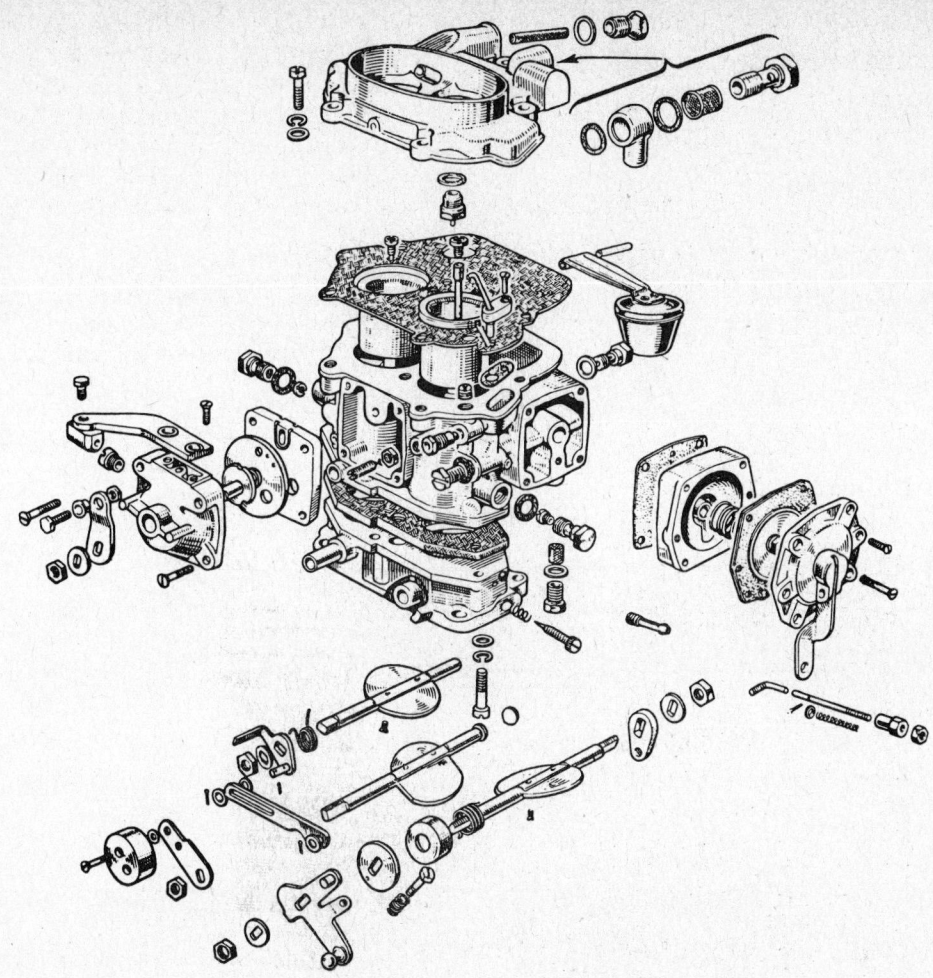

Solex 35 APAI-G, exploded view

4. Reverse the procedure to install, using a new mounting flange gasket.

Idle Adjustment

Before adjusting the carburetor, first make sure the ignition system is set correctly. Adjust the carburetor with the engine running at normal operating temperature.

1. Tighten the 2nd barrel throttle adjusting screw a quarter turn to prevent the 2nd barrel throttle from binding. Tighten the locknut.

2. Slowly run in the 1st barrel throttle idle adjusting screw to speed up the idle.

3. Loosen the idling mixture adjusting screw until the engine begins to surge. Tighten the screw until the engine runs smoothly.

4. Adjust the 1st barrel throttle idle ad-

justing screw until the idle speed is 500-600 rpm.

5. If the engine surges, turn in the idling mixture adjusting screw slightly. Do not run this screw in all the way.

Fuel Level Adjustment

This operation must be performed with the car on a level surface.

1. Idle the engine for one minute, then stop it.

2. Disconnect the fuel line.

3. Remove the carburetor top cover and float.

4. Measure the distance from the fuel level to the float chamber flange. It should be .71-.75" (18-19 mm.). The depth of the fuel should be .47-.51".

5. If the level is not correct, check the needle valve, the thickness of the needle

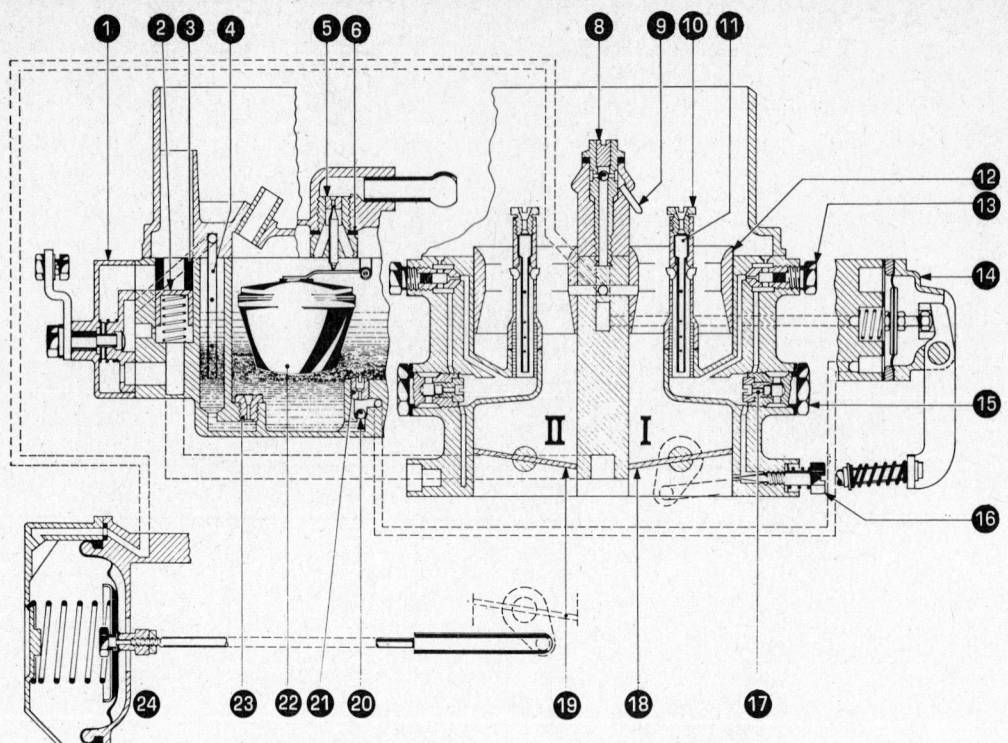

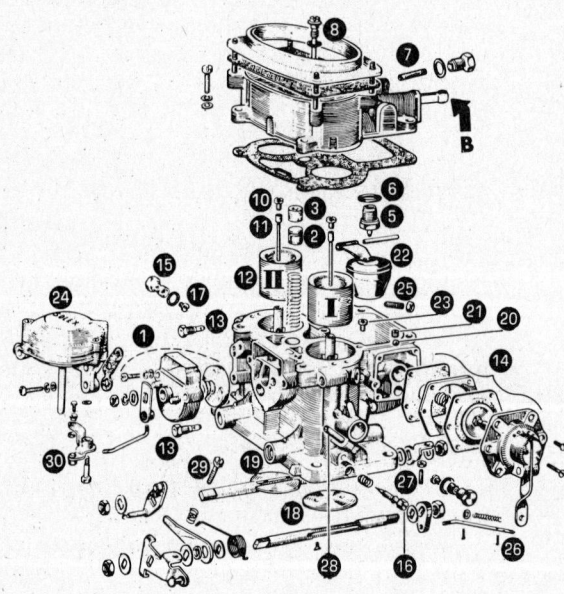

B. Fuel inlet
1. Choke assembly
2. Choke plunger
3. Choke plunger limit stop
4. Choke air metering
5. Needle valve seat
6. Copper gasket for needle valve seat
7. Filter gauze
8. Accelerating pump outlet valve
9. Accelerating pump nozzle
10. Main air metering
11. Mixture tube
12. Venturi
13. Idling jet
14. Accelerating pump
15. Main jet carrier
16. Idling mixture adjusting screw
17. Main jet
18. 1st barrel throttle
19. 2nd barrel throttle
20. Accelerating pump inlet valve
21. Accelerating pump bypass jet
22. Float
23. Choke jet
24. Vacuum capsule
25. Setscrew and locknut for securing venturi
26. Accelerating pump stroke adjuster
27. 2nd barrel throttle adjusting screw
28. Suction port for distributor vacuum advance regulator
29. 1st throttle idle adjusting screw
30. Choke control lever

Solex 32 PAIA 7 carburetor, used on Giulia TI

valve gasket, and the float weight. The gasket is normally .039″ (1 mm.) thick. The float should weigh .25 oz. (7.2 gms.). Adjust the fuel level by adding shims under the needle valve seat.

Solex 32 PAIA 4—2600 Berlina

This carburetor is very similar to the Solex 32 PAIA 7, except that it is used in a dual installation. Idle adjustment procedure is the same; the adjustments must be performed simultaneously on the dual carburetors.

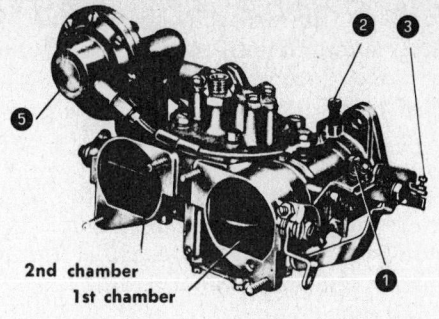

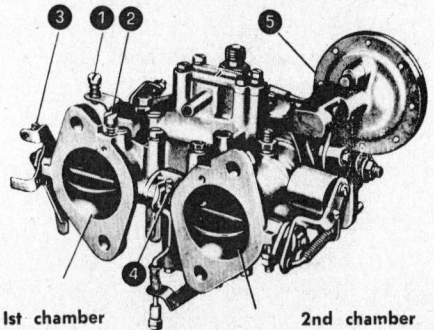

Solex 44 PHH carburetor, used in a triple installation on the 2600 Spider and Sprint

1. 1st chamber throttle adjusting screw
2. 1st chamber idling mixture adjusting screw
3. Choke control lever adjusting screw
4. 2nd chamber throttle adjusting screw
5. Vacuum chamber

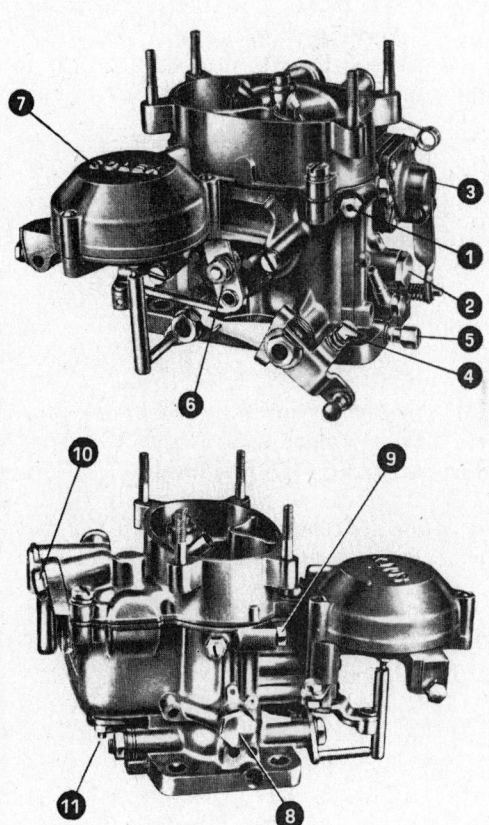

Solex 32 PAIA 4 carburetor, used in a dual installation on the 2600 Berlina

1. Idling jet
2. Main jet No. 1
3. Acceleration pump
4. Adjusting screw for minimum opening of 1st throttle (idle speed)
5. Idle mixture adjusting screw
6. Choke control lever
7. Vacuum chamber
8. Main jet No. 2
9. Idling jet
10. Filter
11. Adjusting screw for minimum opening of 2nd throttle

Solex 44 PHH—2600 Sprint, Spider

Triple Carburetor Adjustments

Before adjusting the carburetors, first make sure that the ignition system is properly adjusted. Adjust the carburetors with the engine at normal operating temperature.

1. Disconnect the links connecting the carburetors to the intermediate control rod.

2. Loosen the 1st chamber throttle adjusting screws.

3. Loosen the 2nd chamber throttle adjusting screws 1-1½ turns.

4. Loosen the choke control lever adjusting screw. Only the rear carburetor has this screw.

5. Adjust the choke control lever adjusting screw so that the gap between the lever and the screw is .012-.016″ (.3-.4 mm.) when the 1st chamber throttle is completely closed. The gap is approximately equal to ¾-1 turn of the screw.

6. Turn the 1st chamber throttle adjusting screws in until they contact the levers. Tighten each screw one more turn.

7. Gently screw the 1st chamber idling mixture adjusting screws in all the way. Back each screw out one turn.

8. Start the engine. Adjust the idling mixture screws until the engine runs smoothly. Adjust the 1st chamber throttle adjusting screws to obtain an idle speed of 700-750 rpm.

9. Check that the 2nd chamber throttles are held closed by the counterweights.

10. Adjust the 2nd chamber throttle adjusting screws to take up any play in the 1st chamber throttles when in the idle position.

11. Connect the intermediate control rod to the carburetors. Adjust the length of the links so that there is ⅛″ (3 mm.) free travel before actuating the carburetors.

12. In wide open throttle position, the throttle should be stopped by the adjusting screw at the throttle pedal to prevent bending of the linkage. When the throttle is released, the throttles should return freely to the idle position.

Solex 40 PHH 2—Giulia Sprint GT, GTC

These carburetors are used in a dual installation, as an alternative to Weber 40 DCOE 4 carburetors. Idling adjustment is the same as for the Weber carburetors.

Fuel Level Adjustment

This operation must be performed with the car on a level surface.

1. Idle the engine for one minute, then stop it.

2. Remove the mixture tube cover and take out one of the main jet carriers. Do not remove the float or float chamber cover.

3. Measure the fuel level through the jet carrier seat. The fuel level should be .83″ (21 mm.) below the cover mating surface.

4. Adjust the fuel level by adding shims under the needle valve seat.

Weber Carburetors

Weber twin-choke sidedraft carburetors are used in dual installations on numerous Alfa Romeo models.

Carburetor R & R

1. Remove hose between air cleaner and air intake box at carburetors.

2. Unscrew the two nuts and remove the air intake box cover.

3. Unbolt and remove the air intake box.

4. Disconnect the choke wire (not used on some models) and the throttle control from the carburetors. Disconnect the fuel lines.

5. Unbolt the carburetors from the intake manifold.

6. Reverse procedure to install.

Carburetor Overhaul and Cleaning

1. Disassemble the carburetors, being careful not to mix the parts of each. Tag the jets to prevent confusion.

2. Wash all parts in a safe solvent and blow out all ducts and passages.

On reassembly:

3. Check that the throttles are perfectly parallel.

4. Check the throttle shaft bearings for play. Check that the acceleration pump is in good working condition.

5. Check that all gasket surfaces are smooth. Replace all gaskets.

Float Level Adjustment—Weber 40 DCO 3

These carburetors are used on the Giulietta Sprint Veloce and Spider Veloce. To check and adjust the fuel level:

1. Remove the small covers in the center of the float bowl covers.

2. Remove the main jet holder.

3. Run the engine.

4. Use a syringe to remove some of the fuel from the bowl. Allow the fuel to reach its level. Stop the engine.

5. Check the level of the fuel. The correct level is .95-.99″ (24-25 mm.) below the small covers.

6. If the level is incorrect, remove the float cover and bend the float tongue to adjust.

Float Level Adjustment—Weber 40 DCOE 4, 40 DCOE 27, 45 DCOE 14

The 40 DCOE 4 is used on the Giulia Sprint GT and the GTC convertible. The 40 DCOE 27 is used on the Giulia Sprint GT Veloce and the 1600 Duetto Spider. The 45 DCOE 14 is used on the Giulia TI Super and Sprint GTA.

Check and adjust the float level as follows:

1. Make sure that the float weight is correct and that it is not damaged or leak-

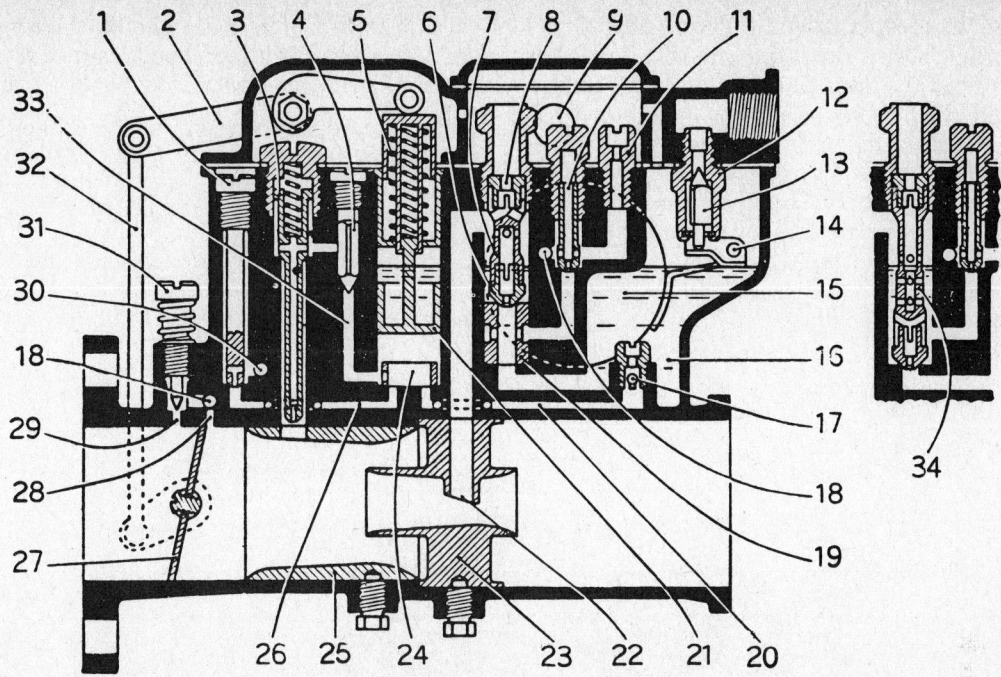

Weber 40 DCO 3 carburetor, used in a dual installation on some Giulietta models

1. Pump drain screw
2. Pump operating lever
3. Pump jet
4. Delivery needle valve
5. Piston return spring
6. Main jet
7. Emulsion bowl
8. Air bleed screw
9. Air intake attachment
10. Idling jet
11. Idle air screw

12. Float needle valve
13. Needle
14. Float fulcrum
15. Float
16. Carburetor bowl
17. Pump suction valve
18. Iding mixture channel
19. Idling communication bushes
20. Pump suction tube
21. Pump piston
22. Jet tube

23. Mixture centering device
24. Piston stop
25. Venturi (choke) tube
26. Pump drain tube
27. Throttle
28. Progression port
29. Idling port
30. Pump drain channel
31. Idle mixture adjusting screw
32. Pump operating rod
33. Pump inlet channel
34. Emulsion bowl

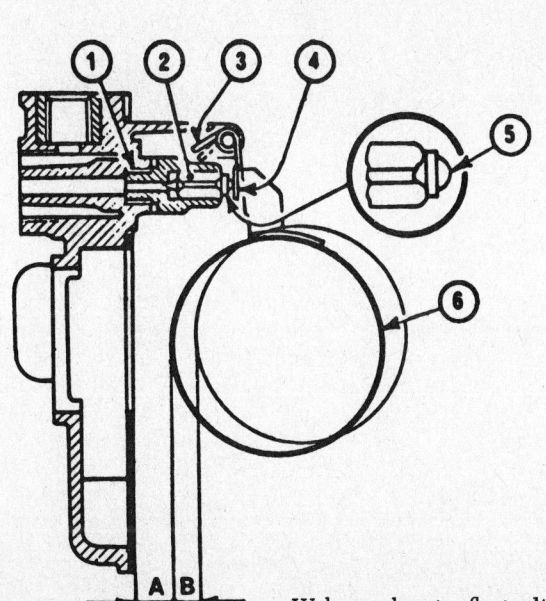

1. Needle valve seat
2. Needle valve
3. Float pivot tail
4. Float tongue
5. Spring-loaded ball
6. Float
A. Measurement of float distance
B. Float travel

Weber carburetor float adjustments

ing. The proper weight is .9 oz. (26 gms.)

2. Check that the needle valve is screwed in firmly and that the spring-loaded ball is not jammed.

3. Hold the carburetor cover in a vertical position so that the float tongue lightly contacts the ball. The floats should be .33" (8.5 mm.) from the cover mating surface with the gasket in place on the cover. This is illustrated as measurement A. Bend the float tongue to adjust.

4. Check that the travel of the float is .26" (6.5 mm.). This is shown as measurement B. Bend the float pivot tail to adjust.

5. The adjustments given above should result in a fuel level 1.12-1.16" (29.0-29.5 mm.) from the upper face of the float chamber. This can be checked as described above for the 40 DCO 3.

6. Install the float and cover. Check that the float moves freely.

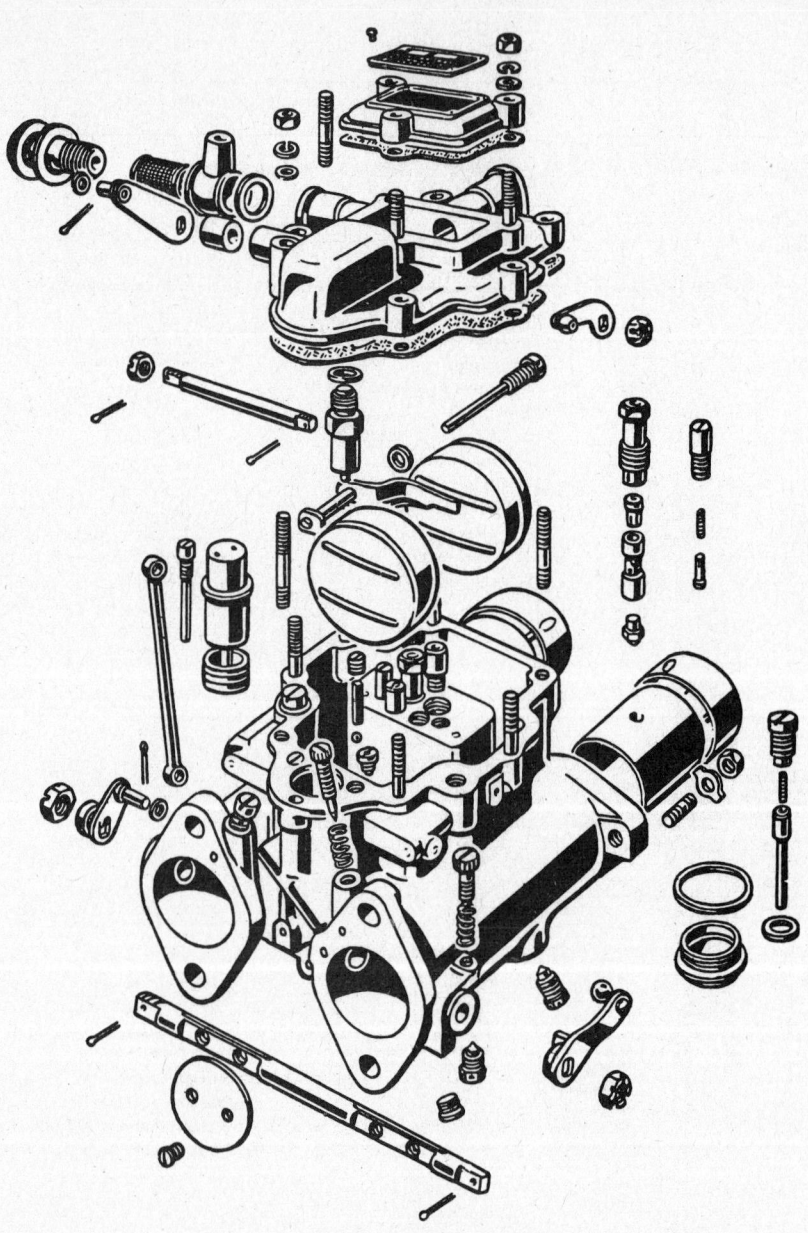

Weber 40 DCO 3, exploded view

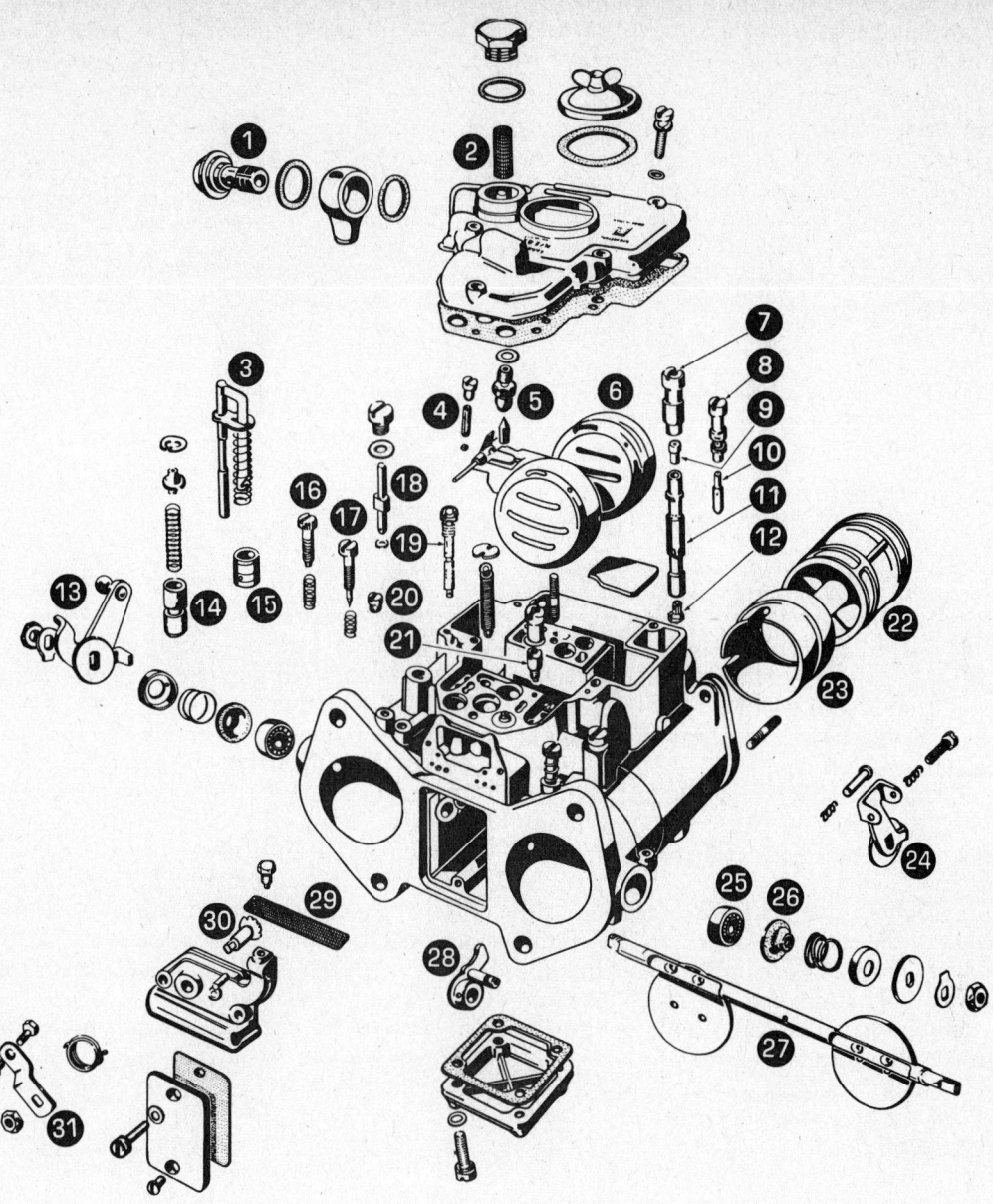

Weber 45 DCOE 14 carburetor, used in a dual installation on Giulia TI Super and Sprint GTA

1. Fuel inlet connector
2. Filter gauze
3. Acceleration pump control rod
4. Acceleration delivery valve
5. Needle valve
6. Float
7. Mixture tube holder
8. Idle jet holder
9. Air restrictor jet
10. Idle jet
11. Mixture tube
12. Main jet
13. Throttle control lever (rear carburetor)
14. Choke valve
15. Acceleration pump plunger
16. Throttle adjusting screw (rear carburetor)
17. Idling mixture adjusting screw
18. Acceleration pump jet
19. Choke jet
20. Steady acceleration port inspection screw
21. Inlet and outlet valve
22. Mixer
23. Venturi (choke tube)
24. Throttle control lever (front carburetor)
25. Ball bearing
26. Dust cover
27. Spindle with throttle valves
28. Acceleration pump control lever
29. Choke air filter gauze
30. Toothed quadrant for choke valve
31. Choke control lever

Float Level Adjustment—
Weber 40 DCOE 2

These carburetors are used on the Giulietta Sprint Veloce, Spider Veloce, Sprint Speciale and Sprint Zagato and also on the Giulia Spider Veloce and Sprint Speciale.

The float level adjusting procedure is the same as for the 40 DCOE 4, 40 DCOE 27, and 45 DCOE 14 with changes to the following steps:

1. The float weight should be .8 oz. (23 gms.).

5. The fuel level should be 1.24-1.26″ (31.0-31.5 mm.) from the upper face of the float chamber.

Idle and Linkage Adjustment—
Weber 40 DCO 3

1. Loosen the clamps securing the control levers to the intermediate shaft on the intake manifold.

2. Set all four idle mixture screws 1½ turns out from the closed position. Never run the screws in tightly. Turn the throttle adjusting screws in ½ turn from the point at which they make contact.

3. Start the engine and adjust the idle mixture and speed. Adjust the throttle adjusting screws on both carburetors in equal increments.

4. Tighten the clamps securing the levers to the intermediate shaft. The throttle discs must all be parallel. Reset the idle speed. Make sure that the two levers on the throttle spindle make contact with the throttle adjusting screws.

5. Make sure that the accelerator linkage allows the carburetors to return to the idling position.

6. Check that wide-open throttle position is reached when the accelerator pedal is floored. An adjustable pedal stop is provided to prevent strain on the linkage.

Idle and Linkage Adjustment—
Weber 40 DCOE 4, 40 DCOE 27,
45 DCOE 14, 40 DCOE 2

1. Check that the electrical system is in good operating condition. Remove and clean the air cleaner element. Check the connections between the carburetors and intake manifolds for tightness.

2. Detach the control linkage (T) from the carburetors.

3. Loosen the idle speed adjusting screw (F) and the throttle synchronizing screw (S) almost completely.

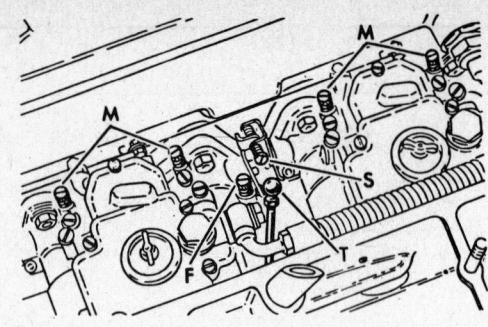

Weber carburetor external adjustments

F. Idle speed adjusting screw
M. Idle mixture adjusting screws
S. Throttle synchronizing screw
T. Control linkage attachment
NOTE: This illustration is not applicable to the 40 DCO 3 carburetors.

4. Operate the throttles to make sure there is no sticking.

5. Make sure the throttles of the rear carburetor are fully closed. Turn in the throttle synchronizing screw (S) until it just makes contact. The throttles of both carburetors should now be parallel.

6. Turn in the idle speed adjusting screw (F) until it makes contact, then tighten it ½-1 turn more. Set all four idle mixture adjusting screws (M) ½-1 turn out from the closed position. Never run these screws in tightly.

7. Start the engine and let it reach normal operating temperature.

8. Run in the idle mixture adjusting screws (M) in small increments until the engine idles smoothly.

9. Run out the idle speed adjusting screw (F) slowly until the idle speed is 600-700 rpm or as given in the Tune-Up Specifications Chart.

10. If the engine starts to race, turn in the idle mixture adjusting screws (M) slightly.

11. Reconnect the throttle linkage (T). Loosen the locknut on the adjustable rod and adjust the rod length so that there is a slight preload against the pedal when in the idling position. Tighten the locknut.

12. Check that wide-open throttle position is reached when the accelerator pedal is floored.

Fuel Injection System

The mechanical fuel injection system has been used since 1969 on the 1750 models. It is a timed, port-injection system.

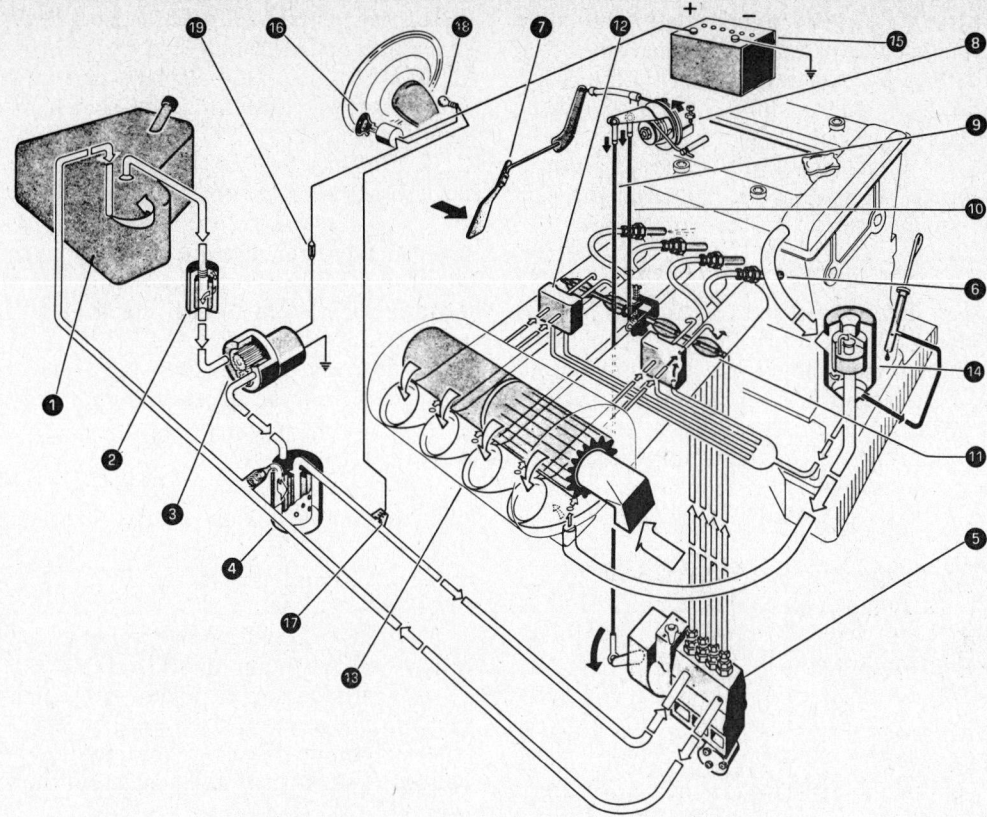

Mechanical fuel injection system, used on 1750 models

FUEL SUPPLY

When the ignition is switched on (16), an electric fuel pump (3) under the rear of the car pumps fuel from the tank (1) through a replaceable in-line filter (2) to the main system filter (4) in the engine compartment. A pressure relief valve in unit with the main system filter keeps pressure at 16-18 psi at this point. If pressure is excessive, some of the fuel pump output is routed back to the tank. A light (18) on the instrument panel gives warning when fuel pressure drops below 7.1 psi. The fuel flows to the injection pump (5) which is driven by a toothed rubber belt from the crankshaft pulley. The pump has four variable displacement plungers actuated by connecting rods driven by a crankshaft turning at half engine speed. Injection pressure is 360-400 psi. The pump is cooled by excess fuel which is then by-passed back to the tank. The pressure within the pump body is maintained by a restrictive orifice at the start of the bypass line. The pump mechanism is lubricated by engine oil. The amount of fuel delivered to the injector nozzles (6) is varied with engine speed and throttle position. In addition, there are devices which compensate for the effects of atmospheric pressure, engine and air temperature, and cold starting. On deceleration, the injection pump delivery is cut off in order to minimize exhaust emissions.

AIR SUPPLY

Engine intake air is filtered through the air cleaner (13) and passes through the throttle valves (11) into the intake ports. The throttle valves are completely closed at idle; idling air must pass from the air cleaner through the equalizers (12) to the intake ports.

Any movement of the accelerator pedal (7) results in the relay crank moving both the pump control rod (9) and the throttle control rod (10).

CRANKCASE VENTILATION

The crankcase ventilation system is not an integral part of the fuel injection system but the systems are interrelated. Crankcase vapors are drawn from the camshaft covers into the oil separator (14). Liquid oil drains back to the sump. When the throttles are fully open, the vapors are drawn into the intake manifold. At lesser throttle openings, the vapors are inducted through the equalizers (12) into the intake ports.

INJECTION SYSTEM SERVICE

Most injection system maintenance and service operations require specialized equipment and knowledge. For this reason, these operations are best left to an authorized repair facility. However, a few simple operations are given here for the convenience of the owner.

Temperature Setting

The temperature setting lever on top of the injection pump control unit is used to adjust the fuel/air ratio for prevailing weather conditions.

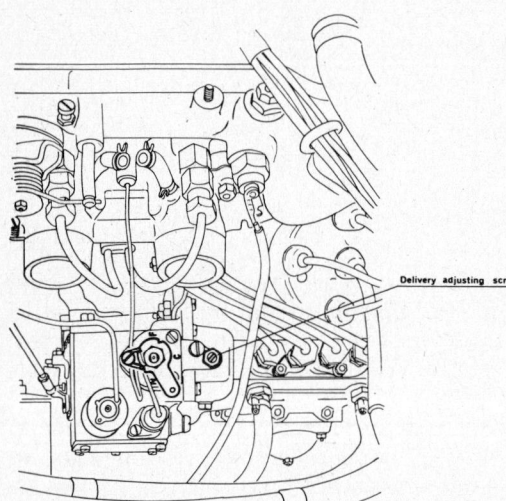

Control unit and injection pump, air cleaner removed. The temperature setting lever is to the left of the delivery adjusting screw, atop the control unit

Setting	Prevailing temperature
N (Normal)	59°F or higher
C (Cold)	32-59°F
F (Freezing)	32°F or lower

Injection Pump R & R

1. Remove air cleaner assembly by detaching the two upper anchoring straps, loosening the four intake hose clamps, freeing the large and small crankcase ventilation hoses from the oil separator, and disconnecting the four idle hoses from the two equalizers on the cleaner body.

2. Disconnect the negative battery terminal and the lead from the cold starting device solenoid.

3. Remove the two screws on the thermostat actuator mounting flange and the two screws clamping the actuator pipe anchoring grommet. Do not remove the thermostat bulb. Remove the actuator from the control unit, being careful not to bend the tube excessively.

4. Disconnect the fuel inlet and by-pass hoses from the injection pump.

5. Disconnect the pump control rod from the control unit.

6. Turn the engine crankshaft to bring No. 1 cylinder to the intake stroke and align the I mark on the crankshaft pulley with the timing pointer on the crankcase front cover.

7. Remove the drive belt cover and take the belt off the pump pulley.

8. Fully loosen the injection tube nuts. Do not remove the tubes from the pump.

9. Unscrew the nuts holding the pipe cluster plate and the injection pump bracket.

10. Loosen the screws attaching the control unit to its bracket at the engine mount.

11. From under the car, remove the four nuts holding the pump support to the engine front cover. Remove the pump and support as a unit.

12. Reverse the procedure to install. Check the pump timing.

Note: An exchange service is available from Alfa Romeo for complete injection pump units. Pumps that have been tampered with have no exchange value.

Injection Pump Timing

1. Turn the engine crankshaft to bring No. 1 cylinder to the intake stroke. The opened valve will be visible through the spark plug hole.

2. Align the I mark on the crankshaft pulley with the timing pointer on the crankcase front cover. This mark corresponds to 70° before top dead center.

3. The mark on the injection pump pulley must be aligned with the reference mark on the pump. The marks may be out of alignment within a tolerance of ±.2" (5 mm.). If the marks are not within tolerance, remove the toothed belt. Line up the marks on the pump and its pulley. Re-

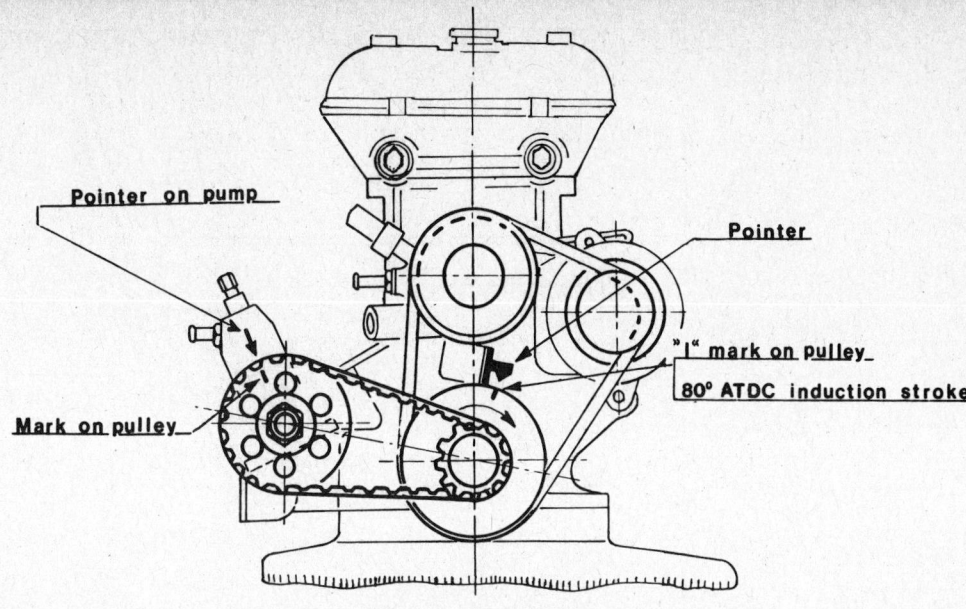

Injection pump timing

place the belt by rotating the pulley in either direction to engage the nearest tooth.

4. Install the protective cover over the belt.

Fuel Cutoff Adjustment

The injection pump cutoff device stops the flow of fuel to the injectors on deceleration. If this device does not completely stop the flow of fuel, the result will be backfiring in the exhaust system. The cutoff device is adjusted by means of a knurled knob at the bottom of the injection pump control unit. The knurled knob can be reached from under the car. To adjust:

1. Turn the knob in.

2. Test by decelerating the engine from about 4,000 rpm in neutral.

3. Repeat Steps 1 and 2 until the engine no longer backfires. If the engine now stalls on deceleration, the knob has been screwed in too far.

Injection Pump Oil Filter Replacement

The injection pump is lubricated by engine oil. The oil filter in the pump support must be replaced:

a. after engine overhaul,

b. when removing the injection pump,

c. after 50,000 miles of service, or

d. if the engine oil has been contaminated, as by water or antifreeze.

To replace the filter:

1. Clean the filter housing cover and the surrounding area thoroughly.

2. Unbolt the cover and remove the element.

3. Clean the filter housing thoroughly with a safe solvent.

4. Insert a new element with the spring facing the cover. Replace the cover gasket if necessary. Install the cover with the retaining nuts loose.

5. Operate the starter for a few seconds until oil oozes past the cover. This is done to bleed air from the pump.

6. Tighten down the cover.

Cooling System

Coolant flow is into the radiator at the top, down through the radiator, through the water pump into the engine block, and out through the cylinder head and thermostat. Cooling system drains are located at the bottom of the radiator and in the side of the engine block. The 2600 Berlina has two additional system drains. These are located on the heater ducts on either side of the engine compartment. On the 2600 Sprint and Spider, there is a drain plug in the heater line below the steering shaft. The 1750 has a drain plug on the heater and air bleed plugs on the water pump and manifold.

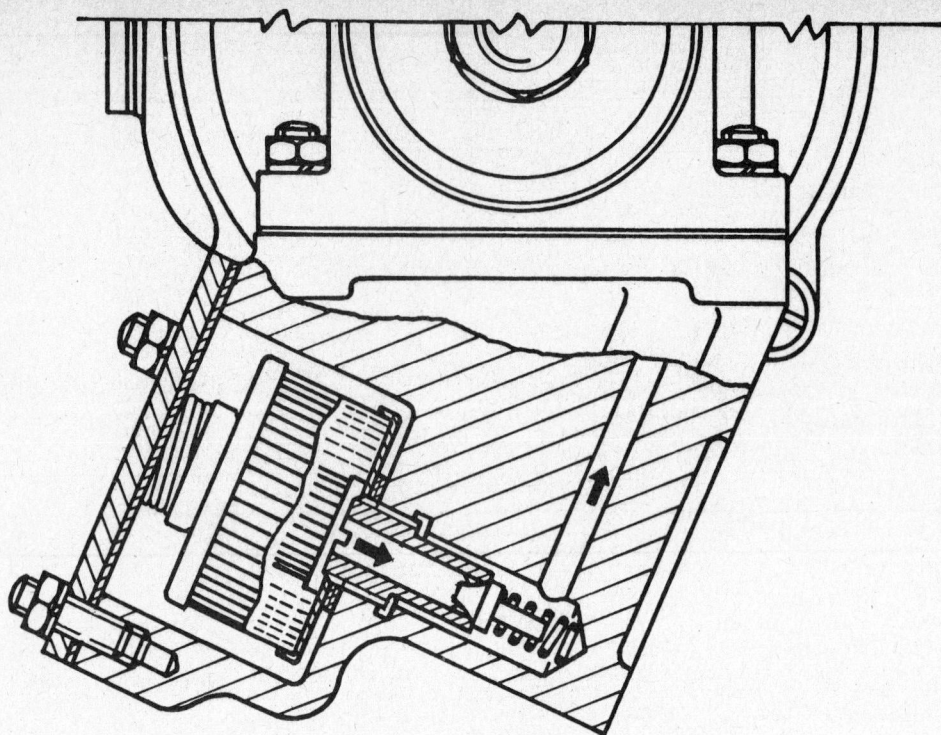

Details of injection pump lubricating oil filter

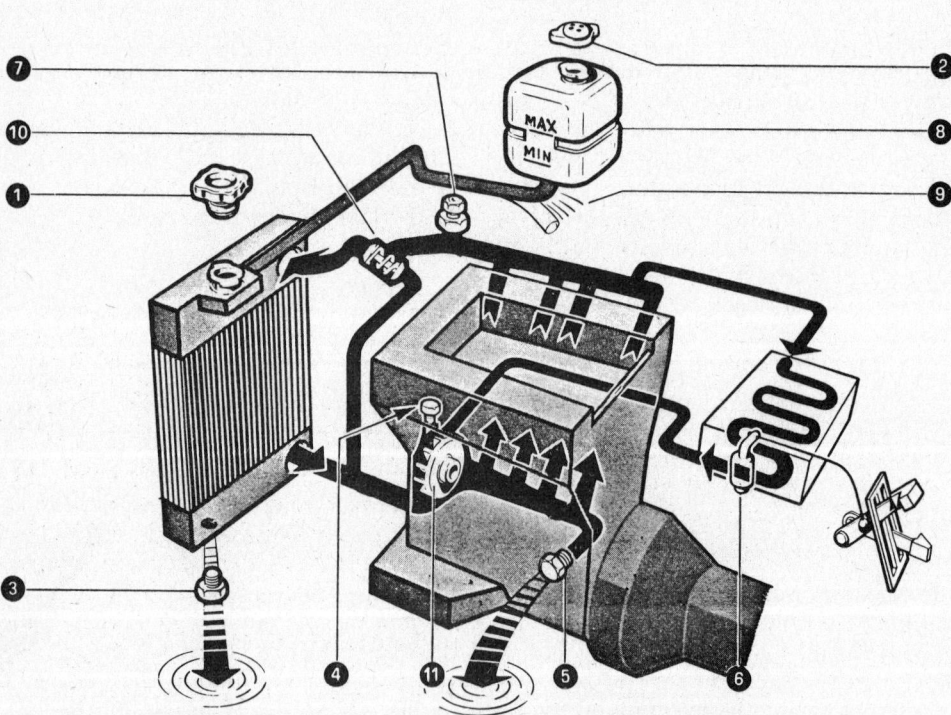

Cooling and heating systems, 1750 models. Note that there are two air bleed screws

1. Radiator filler plug
2. Reservoir filler plug
3. Radiator drain plug
4. Bleed screw on pump
5. Drain plug on crankcase
6. Heater cock

7. Bleed screw on manifold
8. Reservoir
9. Supply line from reservoir to radiator
10. Thermostat
11. Centrifugal pump

Radiator

RADIATOR R&R

Giulietta, Giulia

1. Remove the filler cap and open the drain at the bottom of the radiator. There is another cooling system drain on the side of the engine block.

2. Remove the radiator mounting bolts and rubber pads.

3. Disconnect the upper and lower radiator hoses.

4. Lift out the radiator while tilting it toward the rear of the car.

5. Reverse the procedure to install. Fill the system. Run the engine for a few minutes with the heater on and the radiator cap off, in order to bleed air out of the system.

Water Pump

WATER PUMP R & R

Giulietta

1. Remove radiator.

2. Disconnect heater hose. Disconnect tachometer drive cable.

3. Loosen the generator adjusting bracket and remove the fan belt.

4. Remove the fan nut and lockwasher. Remove the fan and the shaft key.

5. Unbolt and remove the pump.

6. Reverse the procedure to install.

Water pump, Giulietta engines

Giulia

1. Remove radiator.

2. Disconnect tachometer drive cable. Disconnect hose from intake manifold to pump.

3. Loosen the generator or alternator adjusting bracket and remove the fan belt.

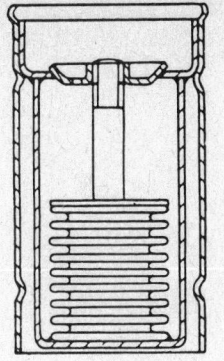

Thermostat, Giulietta engines

4. Unbolt and remove the pump.

5. Reverse the procedure to install.

Thermostat

The cooling system thermostat is in the cylinder head water outlet, except on the Giulietta, which has a capsule thermostat in the upper radiator hose. On most models, the thermostat opens at about 185°F. When reinstalling the thermostat in the 2600 engine, make sure that the small hole in the thermostat faces upward. On the Giulia engine, the spring end of the thermostat must face down.

Installation of thermostat in Giulia engine. The spring end must be down, as shown

Installation of thermostat in 2600 engine. The small hole must be up as shown

---

Engine

Note: Specific repair procedures for the 1750 engine were not available at the time of publication. However, the Giulia engine procedures are generally applicable.

Engine R&R

GIULIETTA

1. Drain coolant. Drain oil. Disconnect battery ground cable.
2. Disconnect:
    a. front and rear crossmembers,
    b. transmission and clutch controls,
    c. oil pressure gauge tube,
    d. starter motor control return spring,
    e. starter electrical cables,
    f. speedometer cable, and
    g. exhaust pipe bracket.
3. Remove the driveshaft center bearing support and unscrew the nut on the rear shaft sliding sleeve.
4. Disconnect the exhaust pipe from the manifold.
5. Unbolt the engine mounting pads from the body.
6. Remove the radiator.
7. Take out the hinge pins and remove the hood.
8. Disconnect the carburetor linkage, heater hoses, generator leads, fuel line, distributor wiring, and tachometer cable.
9. Attach a hook to the engine lifting

bracket and carefully lift the engine/transmission unit out of the car.
10. Reverse the procedure to install.

GIULIA

1. Drain coolant and oil. Disconnect battery ground cable.
2. Detach:
    a. front driveshaft from rear driveshaft at flange.
    b. driveshaft center bearing support,

Components to be disconnected from underneath the car, Giulia

1. Driveshaft flange
2. Driveshaft center bearing support
3. Chassis cross plate
4. Speedometer drive cable
5. Exhaust pipe bracket

Components to be disconnected from underneath the car, Giulia

6. Clutch bottom protection cover
7. Gear selector lever
8. Backup light wiring
9. Clutch lever
10. Exhaust pipe flange
11. Gear engaging lever

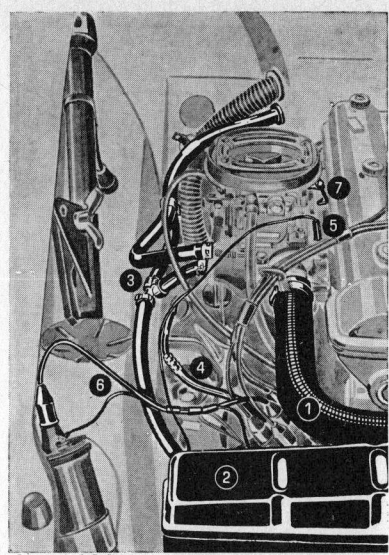

Components to be disconnected in the engine compartment, Giulia

1. Radiator hose
2. Radiator
3. Heater and intake manifold hoses
4. Fuel line
5. Water temperature lead
6. Coil leads
7. Choke cable and throttle linkage

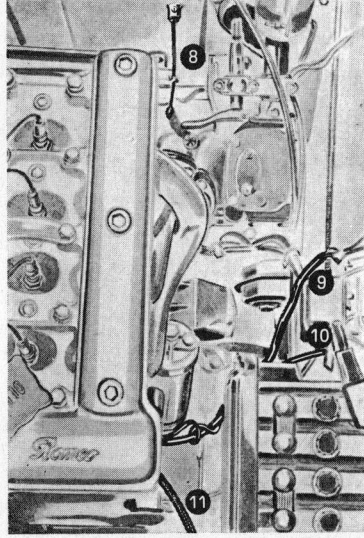

Components to be disconnected in the engine compartment, Giulia

8. Hand throttle
9. Generator or alternator leads
10. Oil pressure gauge connection
11. Engine ground strap

c. chassis cross plate from under front driveshaft,

d. speedometer drive cable,

e. exhaust pipe bracket at transmission,

f. clutch bottom protection cover,

g. gear selector lever,

h. backup light wiring,

i. clutch lever,

j. exhaust pipe at manifold,

k. gear engaging lever, and

l. tachometer cable.

3. Remove:

a. hood support,

b. air cleaner,

c. radiator hoses,

d. radiator,

e. hose from water pump to intake manifold, heater hoses,

f. fuel line,

g. wires for temperature and oil pressure gauges,

h. coil leads,

i. choke cable, hand throttle, and throttle linkage,

j. generator or alternator leads, and

k. engine ground strap and starter leads.

4. Attach hoist to engine and take up the slack.

5. Unbolt transmission supporting crossmember from floor pan and then from transmission.

6. Unbolt engine mounts from chassis. Tilt engine/transmission unit and remove from the car.

7. Reverse procedure to install.

Cylinder Head

CYLINDER HEAD R & R

Giulietta, Giulia, 2600

The cylinder head can be removed without removing the engine from the car. Do not unbolt or remove the head until the engine is thoroughly cold.

1. Drain coolant from radiator and block.

2. Remove exhaust manifold.

3. Remove air cleaner assembly.

4. Disconnect spark plug leads and remove spark plugs.

5. Remove upper radiator hose.

6. Disconnect choke cable and temperature gauge connection.

7. Disconnect fuel line and carburetor linkage. The carburetor(s) and intake manifold will be removed in unit with the head.

8. Disconnect distributor vacuum hose and intake manifold water hoses.

9. Remove camshaft cover from cylinder head.

10. Turn the crankshaft until No. 1 cylinder is at top dead center on the compression stroke, as indicated by the PMS or P mark on the flywheel or crankshaft pulley. The camshaft chain master link should be between the two camshaft sprockets.

11. Loosen the chain tensioner setscrew. There are two screwed-in plugs in the front of the cylinder head, except on the 2600 engine. The chain tensioner setscrew is below the right plug.

The chain tensioner setscrew is at the right side of the cylinder head. The threaded plugs shown are not installed on the 2600 engine

12. Remove the master link.

13. Secure the ends of the chain to prevent them from dropping into the front cover. If the chain is to be removed, attach a 5' length of soft wire to the end of the chain. Pull the chain through its course and leave the wire in place of the chain. The chain can be replaced by pulling it into place with the wire.

Note: If the chain is simply pulled out, the crankcase front cover must be removed to reinstall the chain.

14. Remove cylinder head nuts and two screws securing front cover to head. Re-move head. If it sticks, loosen by tapping with a soft hammer.

To replace head:

15. Reinstall head, using a new gasket. Torque bolts to the figure given in the Torque Specifications Table, using the correct tightening sequence.

16. Check that the top dead center mark on the crankshaft pulley or flywheel is still aligned. Align timing marks on camshaft front journals with marks on journal bearings while No. 1 cylinder cam lobes are facing outward.

When the timing chain is replaced, the camshafts must be aligned as shown. The cam lobes for No. 1 cylinder should face outward

17. Replace chain and master link.

18. Loosen chain tensioner setscrew. Crank engine with starter for a few seconds to allow tensioner to tighten chain. Tighten setscrew.

19. If the camshaft timing marks cannot be aligned after tensioner has been set, loosen the screw holding the sprocket to the camshaft. Remove the locating bolt holding the sprocket to the camshaft flange. Turn the camshaft without moving the chain until the reference marks align. A special pin wrench facilitates this operation. Replace the locating bolt and tighten the screw.

20. Replace the camshaft cover, using a new gasket. Replace all the parts removed in Steps 1-8. Refill the cooling system.

Valve Train

Valve Adjustment

Giulietta, Giulia, 2600

Valve clearance must be checked with the engine cold. Clearance is adjusted by

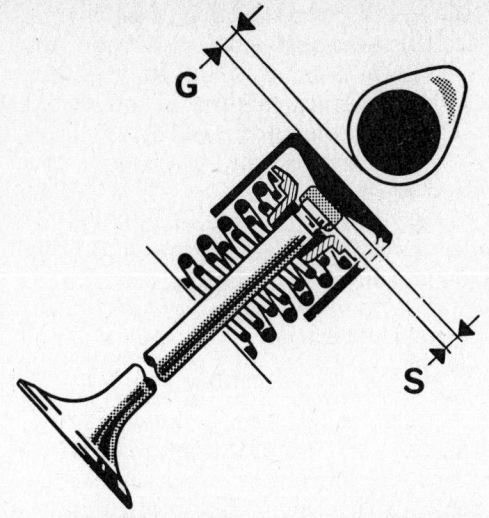

The valve clearance, G, is measured between the valve cup and the base arc of the cam lobe. The thickness, S, of the replaceable valve adjusting pad governs valve clearance

means of replaceable adjusting pads on the valve stems.

1. Remove the camshaft cover.

2. Check the clearance between each valve cup and the base arc of its cam lobe, using feeler gauges. Compare the valve clearance given in the Tune-Up Specifications Chart with the measured clearance. The intake camshaft is on the side of the engine bearing the intake manifold. The exhaust camshaft is on the exhaust manifold side. Note all incorrect clearances.

If the clearances must be adjusted:

3. Turn the crankshaft to align the top dead center mark for No. 1 cylinder.

4. Loosen the chain tensioner as described in Step 11 of Cylinder Head R & R. Detach the master link and remove the chain from the camshaft sprockets. Wire the chain ends up to prevent the chain from falling into the engine.

5. Unbolt the camshaft journal bearings and remove the camshaft(s). Before removing the Giulietta exhaust camshaft, remove the fuel pump rocker arm return spring.

6. Remove the valve cups and adjusting pads on the valves needing adjustment.

7. Using a micrometer, measure the thickness of the valve adjusting pads. Install a new adjusting pad in the proper size to increase or decrease the clearance as necessary. Adjusting pads are available in thicknesses from .05-.10″ (1.3-2.5 mm.)

in increments of .001″ (.025 mm.).

8. Replace valve cups and camshafts. Torque the camshaft bearing caps to 15 ft. lbs.

9. Recheck valve clearances.

10. Proceed with Steps 16-20 under Cylinder Head R & R to replace chain and adjust valve timing.

NOTES ON VALVE TRAIN OVERHAUL

See the Engine Rebuilding Section for general procedures in valve train and cylinder head repair.

Maximum permissible warpage of any cylinder head is .002-.004″. Valve cup to bore clearance should be .001-.002″. Oversize cups are available to correct excessive wear. No more than .004″ camshaft endplay is permissible. Camshaft thrust is taken at the front bearing. Camshaft bearing oil clearance should be less than .004″.

Camshaft and Timing Chains

Two timing chains are used. A short chain links the crankshaft to the idler shaft, directly above the crankshaft. The crankcase front cover must be removed to gain access to this chain. Front cover removal is possible with the engine in place. A longer chain, with a tensioner, links the idler shaft and the two camshafts. Camshaft removal and chain tensioner adjustment is covered under Valve Adjustment.

CRANKCASE FRONT COVER R & R

Giulietta, Giulia, 2600

1. Remove:
   a. radiator,
   b. water pump,
   c. generator or alternator with mounting bracket,
   d. cylinder head,
   e. oil sump (pan),
   f. fuel pump and bracket, and
   g. crankshaft pulley.

2. Unbolt and remove the front cover/oil pump/distributor assembly. It may be necessary to remove the distributor separately.

3. Slide off the sprockets, chain, oil pump drive pinion, and camshaft drive sprocket as a unit. Remove the idler shaft spacer. Check chain and sprockets for stretching or excessive wear.

4. Replace all gaskets and press or drive a new oil seal into the front cover.

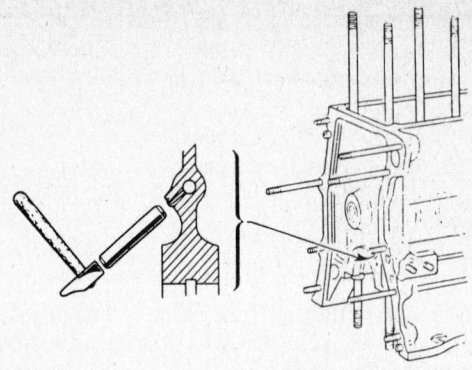

Installation of plug in chain lubricating hole, Giulietta

5. The idler shalt bushings in the crankcase and the front cover may be pulled and pressed out and replaced, if worn excessively. The new bushings must be reamed to fit.

6. On Giulietta engines, check that a plug is installed in the chain lubricating hole in the block. If there is no plug, install one.

To reassemble:

7. Install chain, sprockets, and spacer in unit, being careful to align sprocket timing marks. Use a new spacer if the one removed was worn excessively.

8. Rotate the distributor shaft so that the rotor points to the front. Turn rotor 45° counterclockwise.

9. Loop camshaft chain over idler shaft sprocket. Tie the chain up.

Correct alignment of timing marks on sprockets

10. Install cover assembly with new gasket. On installation, the distributor rotor should turn to point to the front again. It may be necessary to remove and refit the cover to align the rotor correctly.

11. Bolt cover down. Install all items removed in Step 1.

12. Proceed with Steps 16-20 under Cylinder Head R & R to reinstall camshaft chain and adjust valve timing.

Engine Lubrication

OIL FILTER

The 2600 engine uses a throwaway type filter screwed into the right rear side of the cylinder block. The other engines have a replaceable element filter cartridge in a housing on the left side of the engine. On the Giulietta, the housing is secured by a bolt through the bottom. On the Giulia, the housing is secured by a bolt which passes down through the housing bracket.

When draining oil on the 2600, it is recommended that the front of the car be raised slightly.

OIL SUMP R & R

Giulietta

1. Remove the lower front crossmember.

2. Drain oil and replace plug.

3. Remove oil temperature gauge connection.

4. Unbolt and remove sump by sliding toward the rear.

5. Most sumps are held to the crankcase, front and rear, by a spring strap. If these are not installed, it is advisable to scrap the center bolt, front and rear, and install the straps. Use a new gasket on replacement.

Giulia

1. Drain oil and replace plug.

2. Unbolt and remove sump toward front of car.

3. Unbolt sump bottom from sump.

4. On reassembly use new gaskets between sump bottom and sump as well as between sump and crankcase.

OIL PUMP

The gear type oil pump is driven by a pinion on the front of the crankshaft. The pump is located in the engine front cover, and can be removed after removing the oil sump. The distributor is driven from the oil pump driveshaft by an offset key and slot. The General Engine Specifications Chart gives normal oil pressure for highway speeds. Oil pressure at idle may be as low as 7-14 psi (.5-1 kg/cm^2).

Pump R & R

1. Remove oil sump.
2. Turn crankshaft to bring No. 1 cylinder to top dead center of the compression stroke. The PMS or P timing mark should be aligned, and the distributor rotor should point front.
3. On Giulietta only, unbolt suction pipe from center bearing cap and remove pipe.
4. Unbolt the pump from the engine. Remove the distributor.
5. When reinstalling the pump, make sure that the smaller segment of the offset slot and key in the pump driveshaft faces out from the right side of the engine, and that the PMS or P mark is still aligned.

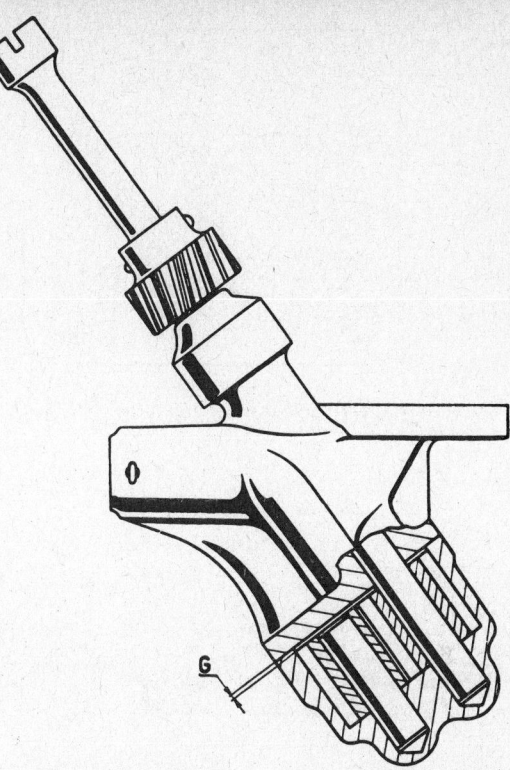

Pump gear end-play is measured at G with a feeler gauge

6. If the pump drive gears will not mesh, remove the pump and rotate the drive pinion one tooth in either direction. Install and bolt down the pump.
7. Install the suction pipe on the Giulietta.
8. When installing the distributor, the rotor must point to the front of the engine, as it did on removal.
9. Replace and refill sump.
10. Check ignition timing.

Pump Inspection—Giulietta, Giulia

1. Pump gear end-play should be .008-.020" (.2-.5 mm.).
2. Pump gear radial clearance between gears and housing should be .001-.002" (.02-.06 mm.).
3. Relief valve spring free length should be 1.9" (48.25 mm.). Under a load of 34.6 lbs. (15.71 kg.), the length should be 1.27" (32.25 mm.).

Pistons and Connecting Rods

The connecting rods are all asymmetrical and must be relocated in their original positions on reassembly. The offsets must be as shown in the illustration.

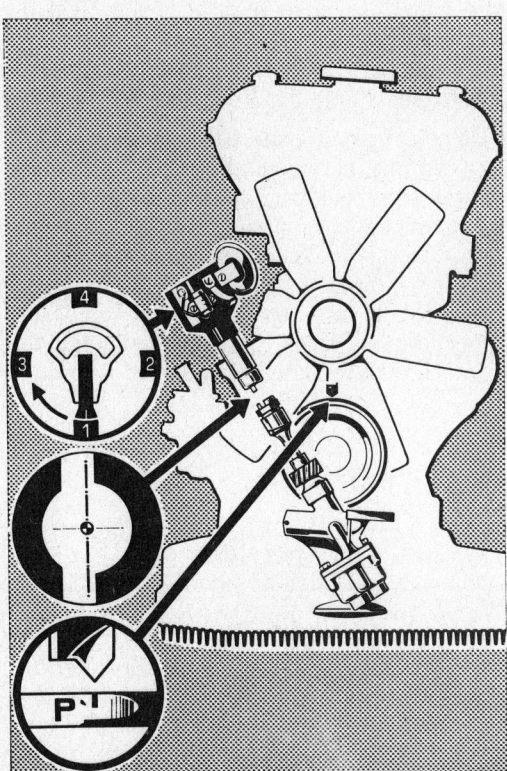

Alignment of units when reinstalling oil pump and ignition distributor. On the Giulietta engine, the P (PMS) mark is on the flywheel. Alignment is the same for the six cylinder 2600 engine

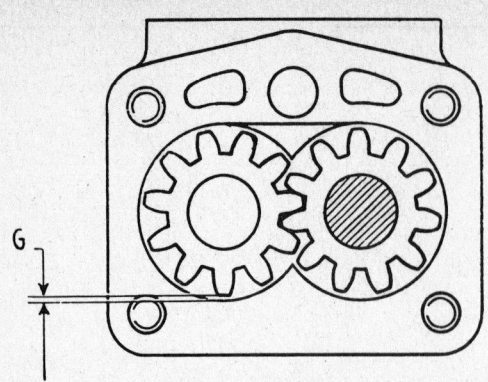

Pump gear radial clearance is measured at G with a feeler gauge

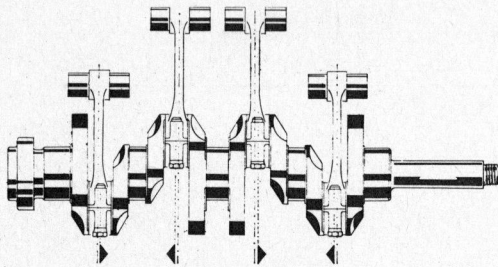

Connecting rods must be installed as shown in the Giulietta and Giulia engines

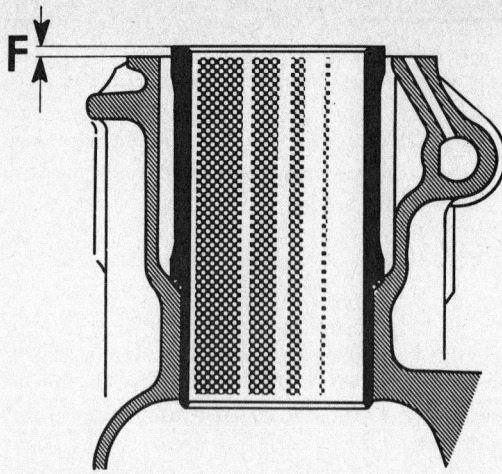

Cylinder liners may project slightly above the block surface

Cylinder Liners

When removing the rod and piston assemblies, fit some sort of a restraining device such as large washers and nuts to the cylinder head mounting studs in order to prevent the liners from being pulled out along with the pistons. The liners can be pulled out by hand after removing the pistons. The liners should be measured for taper and out-of-round by taking two measurements, at right angles to each other, at the points illustrated. When the liners are reinstalled, they may project above the block surface slightly, from .000 to .002".

Flywheel

When replacing the Giulietta flywheel, it is a simple matter to align the PMS mark on the flywheel with the mark on the engine/transmission flange when No. 1 piston is at top dead center.

When replacing the Giulia flywheel, bring No. 1 piston to top dead center. Then align the mark on the flywheel with the centerline of the crankpins, as illustrated.

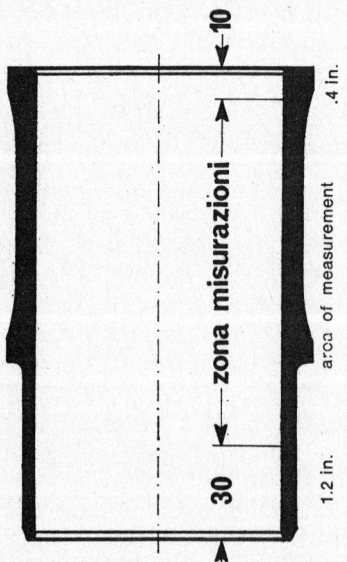

Points at which cylinder liners should be measured to determine wear

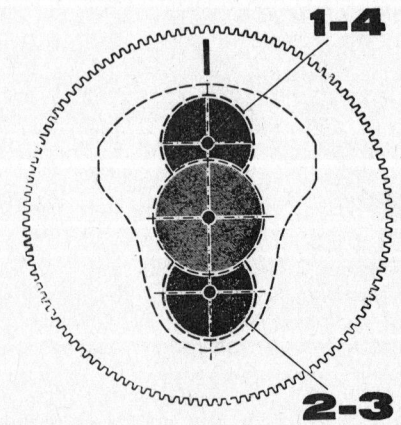

Alignment of the Giulia flywheel on installation

Clutch and Transmission

Clutch and Transmission R&R

If the engine and transmission have been removed from the car in unit as recommended under Engine R & R, it is a very simple matter to separate them. If, however, it is necessary to remove only the clutch or transmission, the following procedures will apply. Note that the transmission must always be removed in order to remove the clutch.

TRANSMISSION R & R

Giulietta

1. Remove clutch actuating rod and bottom clutch cover.
2. Disconnect gearshift actuating rod(s).
3. Disconnect speedometer drive, being careful not to lose washer.
4. Detach engine breather tube from transmission.
5. Unbolt and remove the rubber driveshaft joint.
6. Remove the driveshaft center support and wire up the free end to the body.
7. Remove the exhaust pipe bracket.
8. Support the engine and transmission.
9. On floorshift models, remove the carpet, boot, and shift lever.
10. Unbolt transmission from rear crossmember; remove crossmember.
11. Let the engine/transmission unit down at the rear.
12. Disconnect the flexible gearshift cable from the top of the transmission on early models.
13. Unbolt transmission from engine and remove to the rear.
14. Reverse procedure to reinstall.

Giulia

1. Separate driveshaft sections at the flange.
2. Remove driveshaft center support and chassis cross plate.
3. Disconnect speedometer cable and exhaust pipe bracket.
4. On floorshift models, remove:
   a. carpet and tunnel cover,
   b. boot, and
   c. gearshift lever from swivel.
5. Remove:
   a. clutch bottom cover,
   b. gear selector lever,
   c. backup light wiring,
   d. clutch lever, and
   e. gear engaging lever.
6. Unbolt rear crossmember from floor and transmission; remove crossmember.
7. Unbolt transmission from engine.
8. Remove transmission and driveshaft front section in unit.
9. Unbolt and remove rubber driveshaft joint and driveshaft front section.
10. Reverse procedure to reinstall.

CLUTCH R & R

1. Mark relationship of clutch to flywheel.
2. Unbolt clutch cover evenly and gradually.
3. Remove clutch cover and driven plate. Be careful not to get oil or grease on the facings.
4. Replace the clutch unit on the flywheel, centering the driven plate with a dummy clutch shaft. Tighten the mounting bolts evenly and gradually. Installation can be eased by placing .12″ (3 mm.) thick spacers between the ends of the clutch levers and the clutch cover. These will drop out when the bolts are tightened.

Clutch Linkage

CLUTCH LINKAGE ADJUSTMENT

1750 and 2600 models use hydraulic clutch release linkage with a master cylinder linked to the pedal and a slave cylinder at the clutch arm. Giulietta, Giulia, and 1600 Duetto models use a simple mechanical clutch release linkage.

Mechanical linkage is adjusted at the threaded linkage rod under the car. Hydraulic linkage is adjusted by varying the length of the slave cylinder clutch release rod at the clutch housing. Clutch pedal free-play is the distance the clutch pedal goes down before clutch spring resistance is felt. This can readily be measured with a ruler. Excessive free-play results in the clutch dragging, or not disengaging completely. Insufficient free-play may result in slippage, causing rapid wear of the clutch lining and throwout bearing. On hydraulic systems, free-play between the clutch arm and the slave cylinder may also be checked by moving the clutch arm. There are pro-

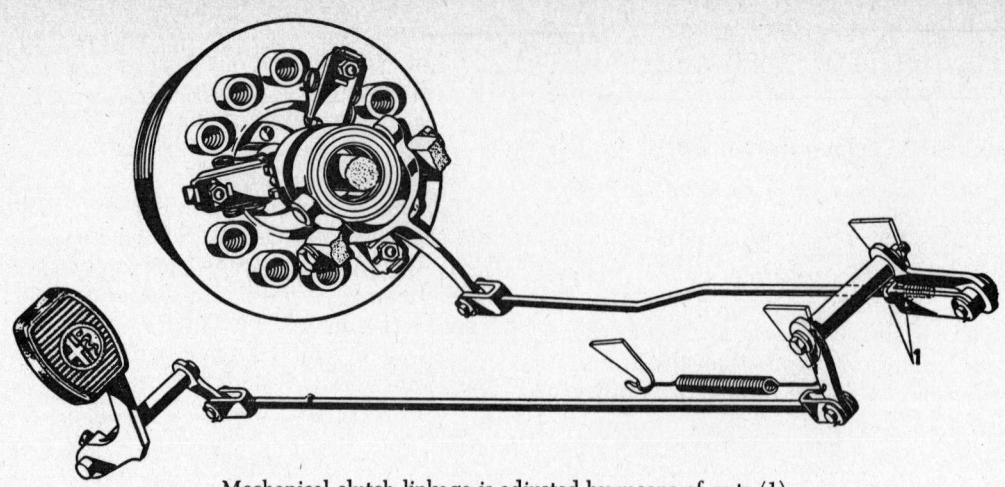

Mechanical clutch linkage is adjusted by means of nuts (1)

visions for bleeding the clutch hydraulic system in the same manner as the brake hydraulic system.

Model	Free-Play at Pedal	Free-Play at Clutch Release Lever
Giulietta, Giulia, 1600 Duetto	.91″	—
1750	.75″	.08-.10″
2600	1.75-2.00″	.12″

Transmission

A four-speed transmission is standard equipment on all Giulietta models except the Sprint Speciale and Sprint Zagato. All other models, to the present, use a five-speed transmission in which fifth gear is an overdrive ratio.

No repair procedures for the four-speed transmission are given here. However, exploded views are presented as an aid in repairing these older models.

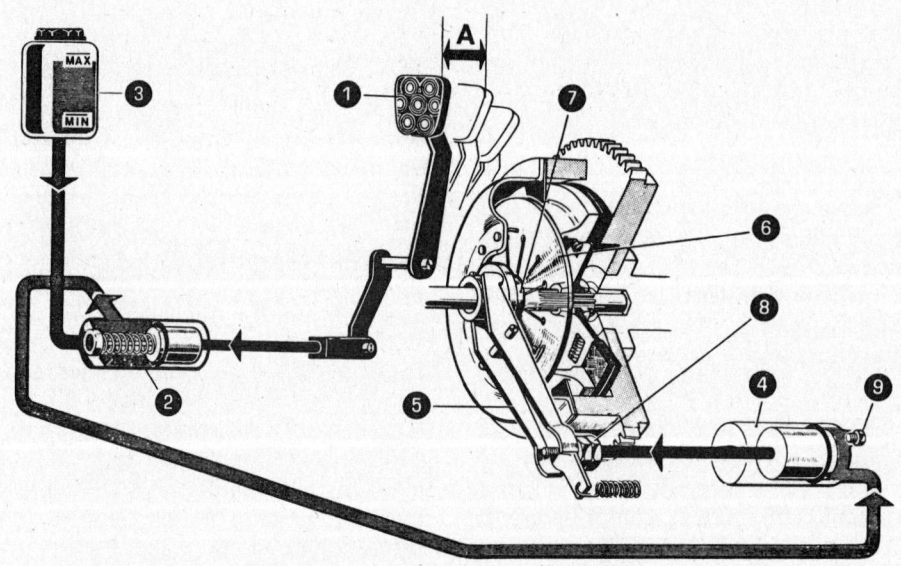

Hydraulic clutch linkage, 1750 models

A. Pedal free travel
1. Pedal
2. Master cylinder
3. Clutch & brake fluid reservoir
4. Slave cylinder
5. Clutch lever
6. Diaphragm spring
7. Throwout bearing
8. Adjusting nuts
9. Air bleed screw

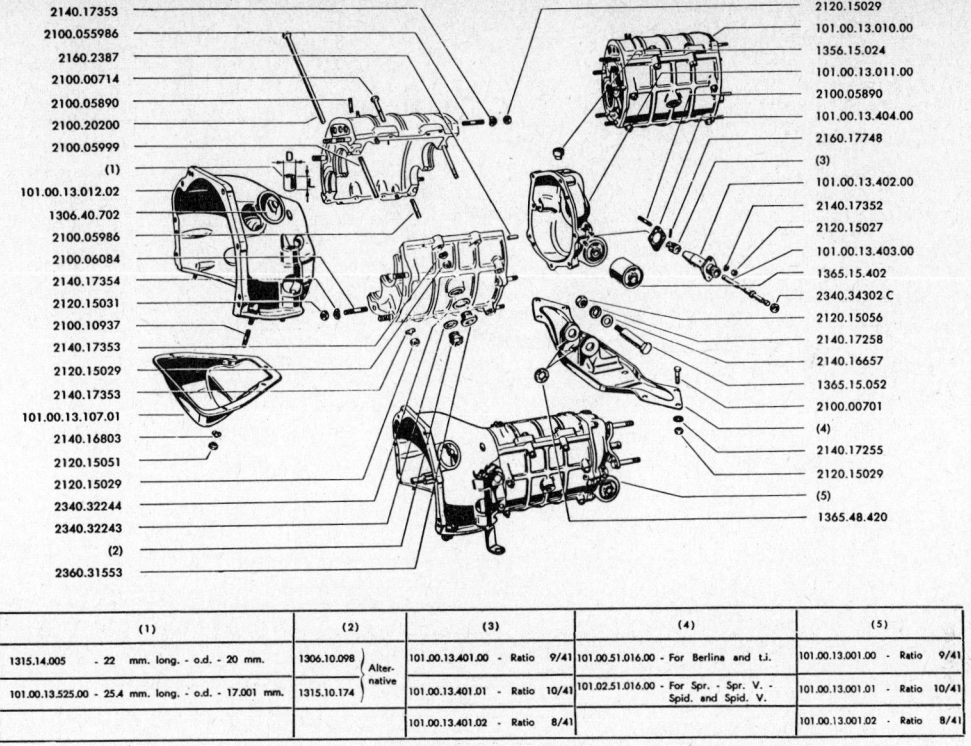

Left labels:
2140.17353
2100.055986
2160.2387
2100.00714
2100.05890
2100.20200
2100.05999
(1)
101.00.13.012.02
1306.40.702
2100.05986
2100.06084
2140.17354
2120.15031
2100.10937
2140.17353
2120.15029
2140.17353
101.00.13.107.01
2140.16803
2120.15051
2120.15029
2340.32244
2340.32243
(2)
2360.31553

Right labels:
2120.15029
101.00.13.010.00
1356.15.024
101.00.13.011.00
2100.05890
101.00.13.404.00
2160.17748
(3)
101.00.13.402.00
2140.17352
2120.15027
101.00.13.403.00
1365.15.402
2340.34302 C
2120.15056
2140.17258
2140.16657
1365.15.052
2100.00701
(4)
2140.17255
2120.15029
(5)
1365.48.420

(1)	(2)	(3)	(4)	(5)
1315.14.005 - 22 mm. long. - o.d. - 20 mm.	1306.10.098 } Alternative	101.00.13.401.00 - Ratio 9/41	101.00.51.016.00 - For Berlina and t.i.	101.00.13.001.00 - Ratio 9/41
101.00.13.525.00 - 25.4 mm. long. - o.d. - 17.001 mm.	1315.10.174 }	101.00.13.401.01 - Ratio 10/41	101.02.51.016.00 - For Spr. - Spr. V. - Spid. and Spid. V.	101.00.13.001.01 - Ratio 10/41
		101.00.13.401.02 - Ratio 8/41		101.00.13.001.02 - Ratio 8/41

Four speed transmission housing and covers, early arrangement shown

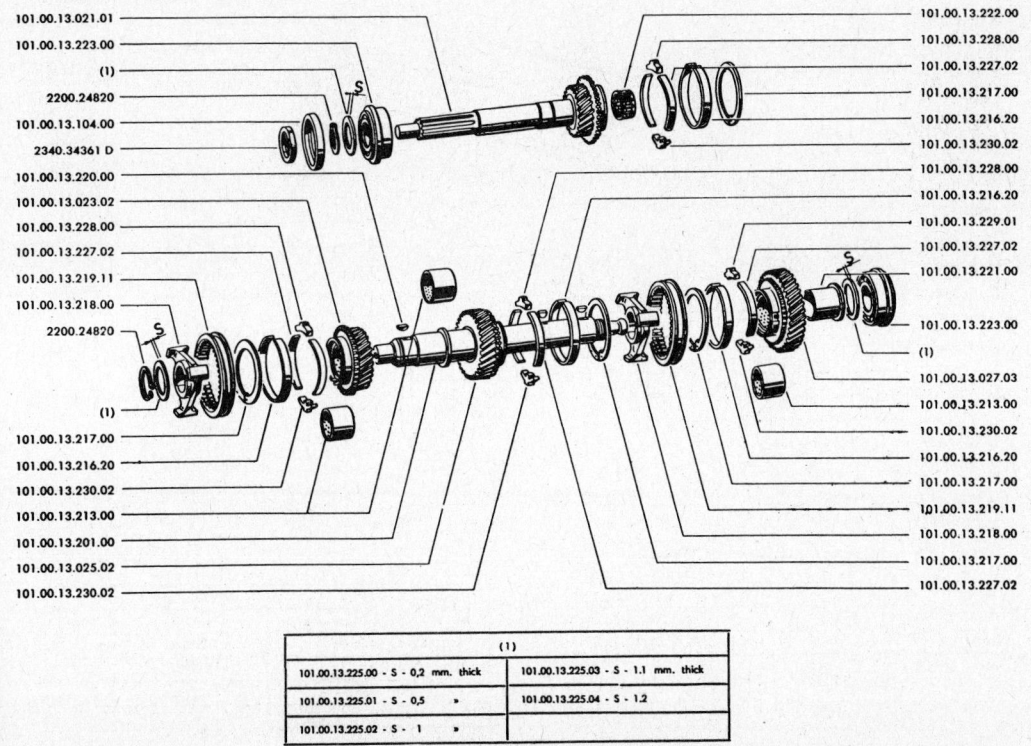

Left labels:
101.00.13.021.01
101.00.13.223.00
(1)
2200.24820
101.00.13.104.00
2340.34361 D
101.00.13.220.00
101.00.13.023.02
101.00.13.228.00
101.00.13.227.02
101.00.13.219.11
101.00.13.218.00
2200.24820
(1)
101.00.13.217.00
101.00.13.216.20
101.00.13.230.02
101.00.13.213.00
101.00.13.201.00
101.00.13.025.02
101.00.13.230.02

Right labels:
101.00.13.222.00
101.00.13.228.00
101.00.13.227.02
101.00.13.217.00
101.00.13.216.20
101.00.13.230.02
101.00.13.228.00
101.00.13.216.20
101.00.13.229.01
101.00.13.227.02
101.00.13.221.00
101.00.13.223.00
(1)
101.00.13.027.03
101.00.13.213.00
101.00.13.230.02
101.00.13.216.20
101.00.13.217.00
101.00.13.219.11
101.00.13.218.00
101.00.13.217.00
101.00.13.227.02

(1)	
101.00.13.225.00 - S - 0,2 mm. thick	101.00.13.225.03 - S - 1.1 mm. thick
101.00.13.225.01 - S - 0,5 »	101.00.13.225.04 - S - 1.2
101.00.13.225.02 - S - 1 »	

Four speed direct drive and main drive shafts

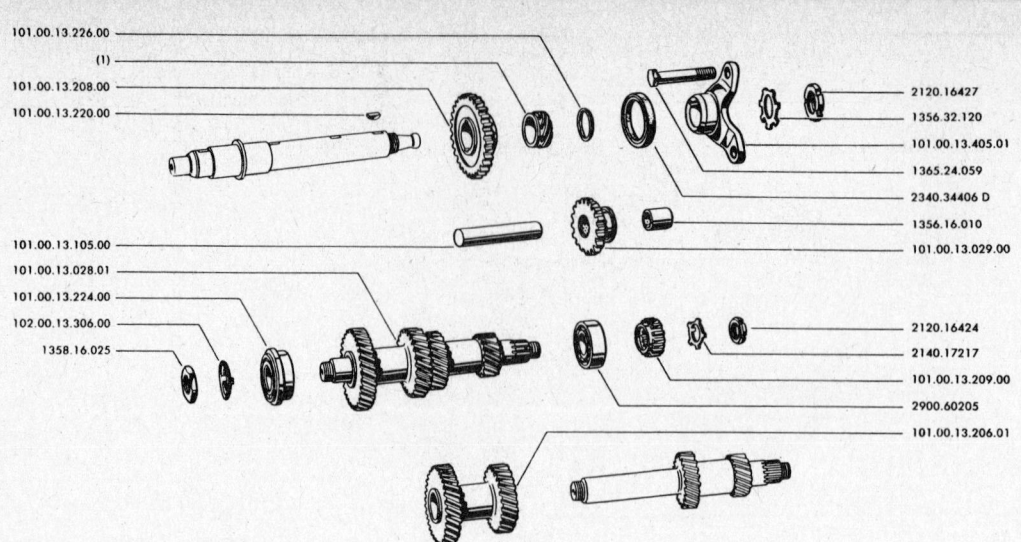

(1)		
101.00.13.400.00	- Ratio	9/41
101.00.13.400.01	- Ratio	10/41
101.00.13.400.02	- Ratio	8/41

Four speed output and reverse shaft assemblies

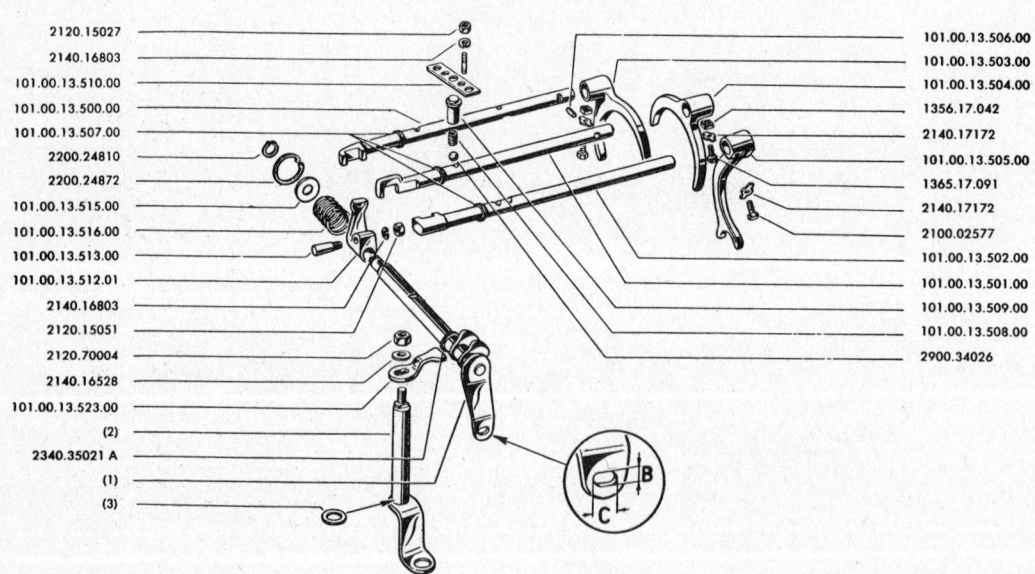

(1)		(2)	(3)			
101.00.13.051.02 - B - 8 mm; C - 11 mm		101.00.13.052.01 dia = 16 mm	101.00.13.529.00 - 0.30 mm thick		101.00.13.529.06 - 0.60 mm thick	
101.00.13.051.04 - B - 16 mm; C - 18 mm		101.00.13.052.02 - dia = 15.875 mm	101.00.13.529.01 - 0.35 »		101.00.13.529.07 - 0.65 »	
			101.00.13.529.02 - 0.40 »		101.00.13.529.08 - 0.70 »	
			101.00.13.529.03 - 0.45 »		101.00.13.529.09 - 0.75 »	
			101.00.13.529.04 - 0.50 »		101.00.13.529.10 - 0.80 »	
			101.00.13.529.05 - 0.55 »			

Four speed internal shifting mechanism

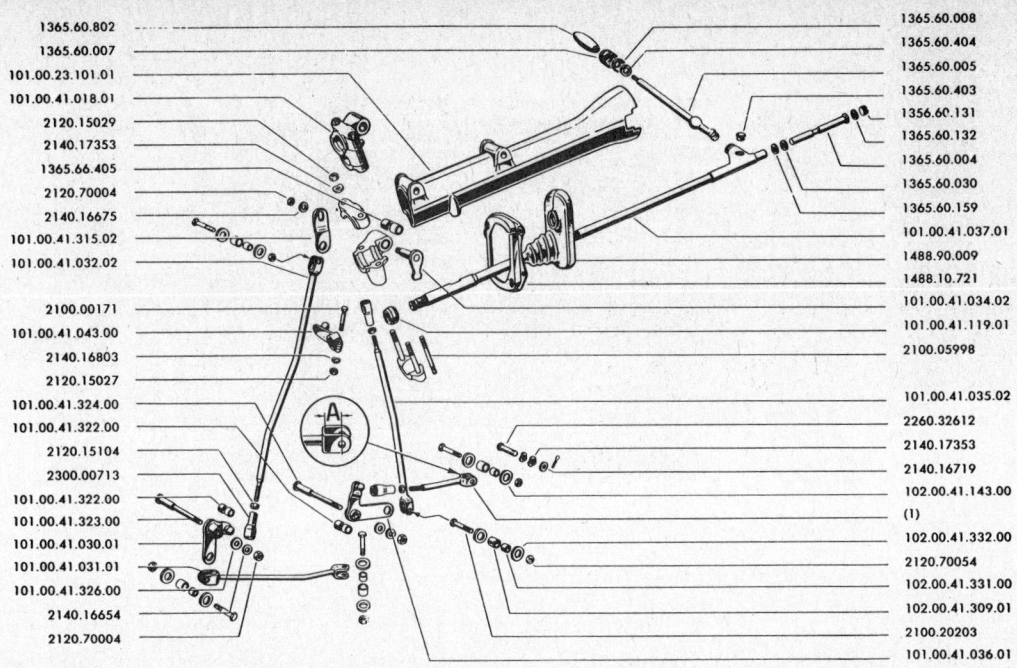

1365.60.802	1365.60.008
1365.60.007	1365.60.404
101.00.23.101.01	1365.60.005
101.00.41.018.01	1365.60.403
2120.15029	1356.60.131
2140.17353	1365.60.132
1365.66.405	1365.60.004
2120.70004	1365.60.030
2140.16675	1365.60.159
101.00.41.315.02	101.00.41.037.01
101.00.41.032.02	1488.90.009
	1488.10.721
2100.00171	101.00.41.034.02
101.00.41.043.00	101.00.41.119.01
2140.16803	2100.05998
2120.15027	
101.00.41.324.00	101.00.41.035.02
101.00.41.322.00	2260.32612
2120.15104	2140.17353
2300.00713	2140.16719
101.00.41.322.00	102.00.41.143.00
101.00.41.323.00	(1)
101.00.41.030.01	102.00.41.332.00
101.00.41.031.01	2120.70054
101.00.41.326.00	102.00.41.331.00
2140.16654	102.00.41.309.01
2120.70004	2100.20203
	101.00.41.036.01

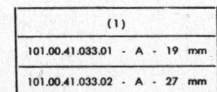

(1)	
101.00.41.033.01	- A - 19 mm
101.00.41.033.02	- A - 27 mm

Four speed column shift linkage

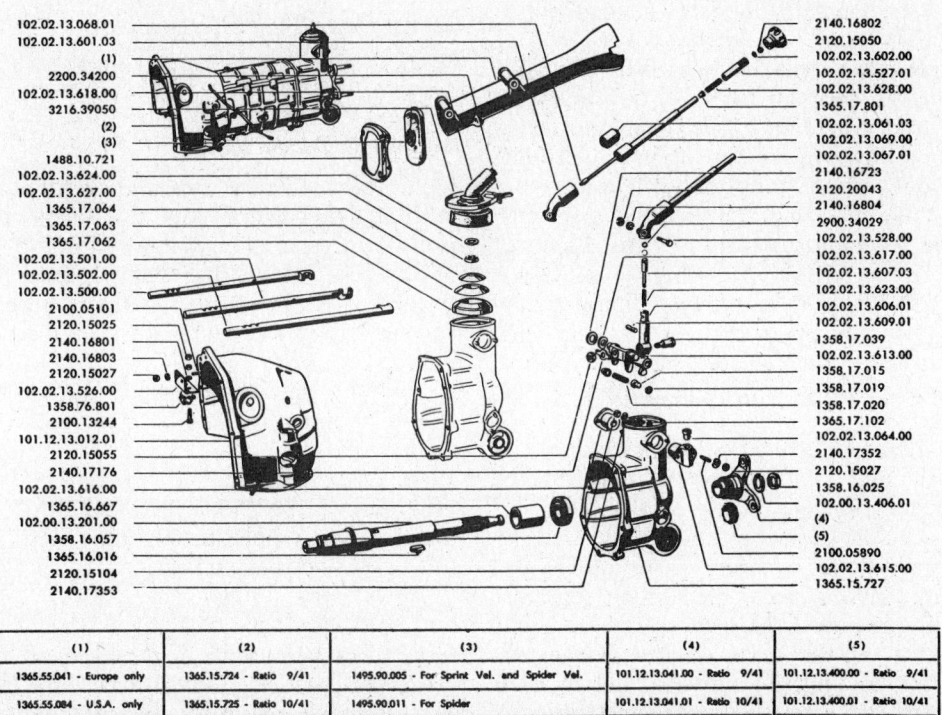

102.02.13.068.01	2140.16802
102.02.13.601.03	2120.15050
(1)	102.02.13.602.00
2200.34200	102.02.13.527.01
102.02.13.618.00	102.02.13.628.00
3216.39050	1365.17.801
(2)	102.02.13.061.03
(3)	102.02.13.069.00
1488.10.721	102.02.13.067.01
102.02.13.624.00	2140.16723
102.02.13.627.00	2120.20043
1365.17.064	2140.16804
1365.17.063	2900.34029
1365.17.062	102.02.13.528.00
102.02.13.501.00	102.02.13.617.00
102.02.13.502.00	102.02.13.607.03
102.02.13.500.00	102.02.13.623.00
2100.05101	102.02.13.606.01
2120.15025	102.02.13.609.01
2140.16801	1358.17.039
2140.16803	102.02.13.613.00
2120.15027	1358.17.015
102.02.13.526.00	1358.17.019
1358.76.801	1358.17.020
2100.13244	1365.17.102
101.12.13.012.01	102.02.13.064.00
2120.15055	2140.17352
2140.17176	2120.15027
102.02.13.616.00	1358.16.025
1365.16.667	102.00.13.406.01
102.00.13.201.00	(4)
1358.16.057	(5)
1365.16.016	2100.05890
2120.15104	102.02.13.615.00
2140.17353	1365.15.727

(1)	(2)	(3)	(4)	(5)
1365.55.041 - Europe only	1365.15.724 - Ratio 9/41	1495.90.005 - For Sprint Vel. and Spider Vel.	101.12.13.041.00 - Ratio 9/41	101.12.13.400.00 - Ratio 9/41
1365.55.084 - U.S.A. only	1365.15.725 - Ratio 10/41	1495.90.011 - For Spider	101.12.13.041.01 - Ratio 10/41	101.12.13.400.01 - Ratio 10/41
	1365.15.726 - Ratio 8/41		101.12.13.041.02 - Ratio 8/41	101.12.13.400.02 - Ratio 8/41

Four speed floorshift arrangement

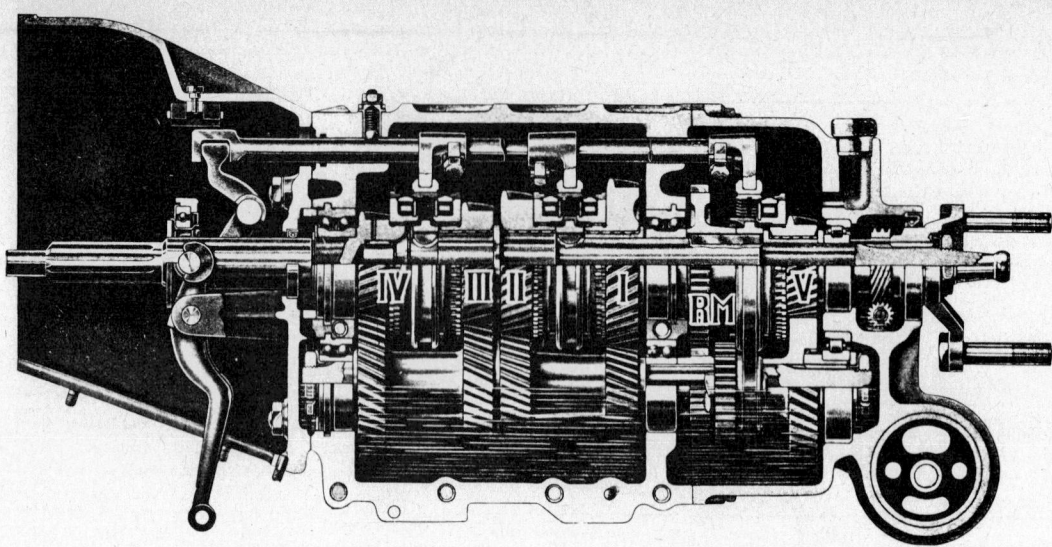

Cutaway view of five-speed transmission. RM is reverse gear

Five-Speed Transmission Overhaul

Disassembly

1. Drain oil. Support transmission on a suitable stand.

2. Block the flexible coupling yoke at the rear of the transmission from turning. Unbolt and remove yoke.

3. On floorshift models, engage third gear. Unbolt and remove rear cover.

4. Remove bolt holding fifth and reverse gear fork at back of transmission. Move rod out to free gear engaging lever at front. Remove backup light switch and throwout bearing from front of housing.

5. Loosen clamp nut holding gear engaging lever on left side of case. Remove lever.

6. At right side, remove small snap-ring from the other end of the gear engaging shaft. Remove the large snap-ring and the reverse gear return spring seat and spring.

7. Remove the gear engaging shaft.

8. Unbolt and remove the clutch housing.

9. Unbolt and separate the case halves. Tap with a soft hammer if necessary. Be careful not to damage the mating surfaces of the case halves. No gasket is used here.

10. Unbolt the plate on the outside of the case holding the shift rod detent ball plungers. Take out the plungers, springs, and balls.

11. Inside the case, loosen the shift fork setscrews, slide out the shift rods, and remove the interlock rollers.

12. If necessary, the outer race of the countershaft rear bearing in the rear cover may be pulled out and pressed back in.

13. Separate the mainshaft from the direct drive shaft. Remove the roller bearing cage.

Direct Drive Shaft Disassembly

1. Remove snap-ring and shim.

2. Press off bearing.

Mainshaft Disassembly

1. Press off rear bearing of fifth gear with its synchronizer hub and sleeve, then press off reverse gear. Remove key.

2. Press off bearing behind first gear. Remove shims, first gear with its bushing, and engaging sleeve for first and second gears.

3. Press off first and second gear synchronizer hub. Remove keys and slide out second gear.

4. Remove snap-ring from the third gear end of the shaft. Press off third and fourth gear synchronizer hub. Slide out third gear and remove keys.

Countershaft Disassembly

1. Clamp the shaft in a soft-jawed vise.

2. Unscrew the nut at the fifth gear end. Remove the roller bearing and the reverse/fifth gear unit.

3. Pull off the intermediate bearing.

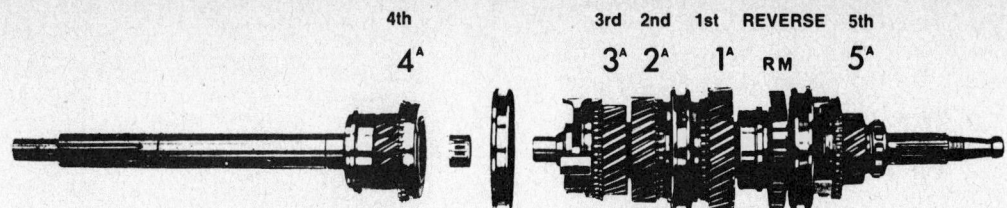

Direct drive shaft at left, mainshaft at right

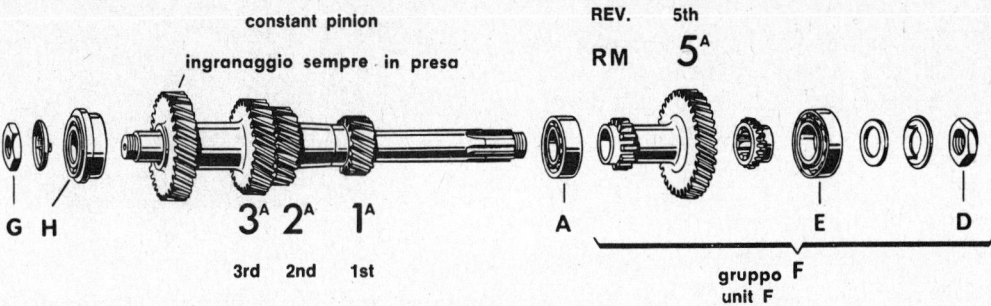

Countershaft

4. Clamp the shaft again and unscrew the front bearing securing nut. Pull off the front bearing.

Synchromesh Unit Repair

1. Remove snap-ring.
2. Check that:
   a. engaging teeth are not worn.
   b. synchronizer sleeves slide freely on their hubs, and
   c. synchronizer rings, stops, and segments are not worn excessively.

3. Reassemble synchronizer units, making sure that all parts are positioned correctly.

Inspection

1. If the mounting pad in the rear cover is to be replaced, pull it out and press the new one in.
2. Check that the mainshaft does not run out more than .002″.
3. Check all bearings for evidence of wear.

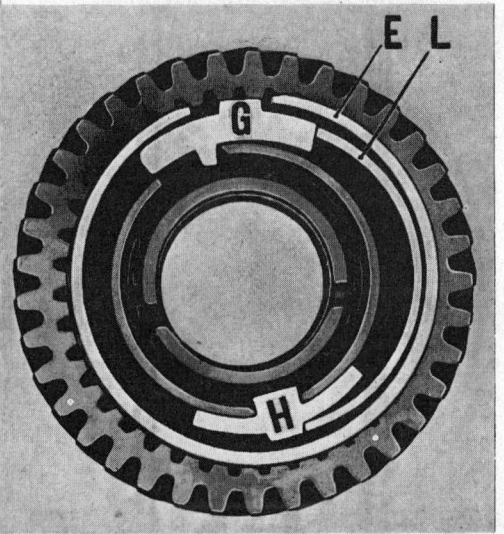

First gear synchromesh unit. Illustration shows strips, L, rings, E, stop, G, and segment, H

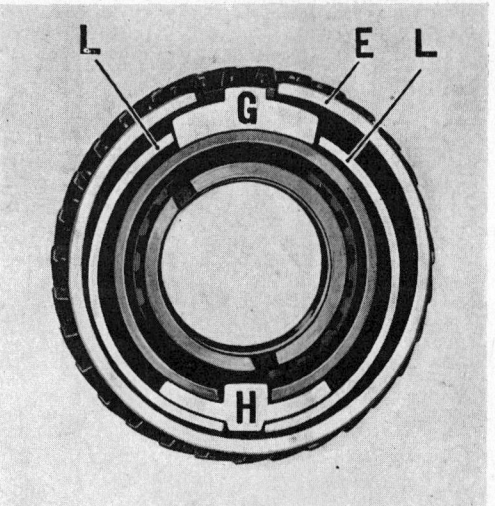

Second and third, fourth and fifth gear synchromesh unit. Illustration shows strips, L, rings, E, stop, G, and segment, H

4. Check shift forks and sleeves for wear. Check clearance between forks and sleeves. Normal clearance is .01-.02″, with a wear limit of .03″.

5. Check that shift interlock mechanism works freely. Any small imperfections in the shift rod notches may be filed away.

6. Check that detent ball spring free length is .6″. Check the balls and notches for good condition.

7. Remove the shaft oil seals from the front and rear covers. Drive in new seals. It is recommended that these seals be replaced whenever the transmission is disassembled.

Reassembly

1. Clamp the mainshaft and assemble in reverse order of Mainshaft Disassembly. Heat synchronizer hubs to 302.°F before installing. With snap-rings installed, there should be no end-play on direct drive shaft and on third and fourth gear hub. Eliminate end-play by use of shims.

With all parts installed and nut torqued to 54-58 ft. lbs., end-play on gears should not exceed .010″ for first gear or .008″ for second and third gears.

2. Assemble the countershaft in reverse order of Countershaft Disassembly. Torque nuts to 58 ft. lbs.

3. Reassemble direct drive shaft in reverse order of Direct Drive Shaft Disassembly.

4. Fit mainshaft and direct drive shafts together. Install flexible coupling yoke onto main shaft and torque nut to 87 ft. lbs. Fit the shafts into the case half and check with calipers that the dimension, A, is 1.65-1.66″. Change the shim between the first gear

Selecting shim to prevent end-play

bushing and the mainshaft bearing inner race to get this measurement.

5. Before installing the shift forks on the shift rods check that, in neutral, the sleeves of third and fourth gears and of first and second gears are equally spaced between the abutments (steps) in the en-

Checking that sleeves are equally spaced between gears

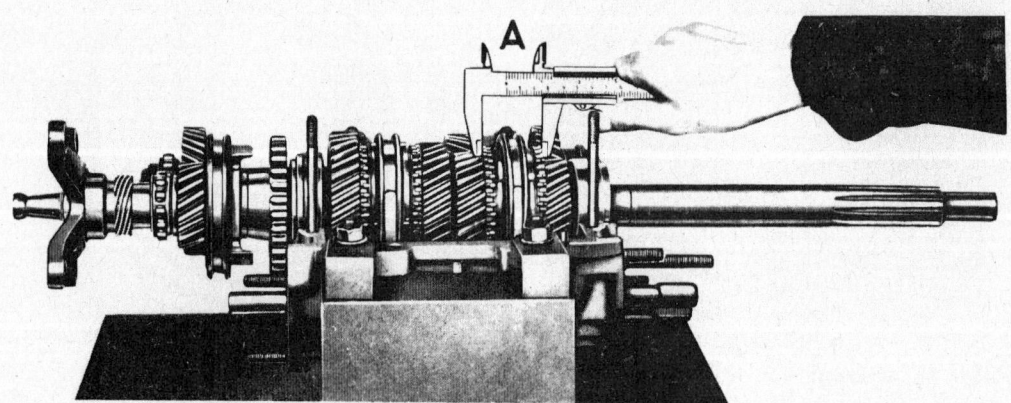

Checking dimension A with mainshaft and direct drive shaft installed

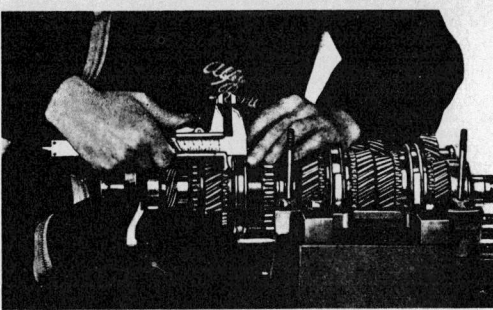

Checking that fifth gear sleeve is the proper distance from the engaging teeth

gaging teeth of the driven gears. Check that the fifth gear sleeve rear edge is .39″ from the abutment in the gear engaging teeth.

6. Before joining the casing halves, set the centering ring into its groove in each half of the case and install the reverse sliding gear onto its spindle.

7. Assemble the case halves. Install the clutch cover, being careful not to damage the seal.

8. On floorshift units, when in neutral position, the inner swivel finger should be engaged with the third and fourth gear shift rod.

Driveshaft and U-Joints

Driveshaft

Most models use a similar two-piece drive shaft. The front, smaller, section is connected to the transmission by a rubber joint and to the rear section by a flange. The front driveshaft section runs in a support bearing. The longer rear section has a universal joint at each end and a sliding spline at the front.

DRIVESHAFT R & R

Giulietta

1. Unbolt rubber joint from transmission coupling.

2. Mark the U-joint flange sections. Unbolt the U-joint from the differential.

3. Unbolt the center bearing and remove the driveshaft assembly.

4. Reverse procedure to install, greasing all fittings. Grease the centering bushing at the extreme front of the shaft. Lubricate the bolts passing through the rubber joint to prevent distortion of the joint.

Guilia, 1600 Duetto, 1750

1. Remove chassis cross plate from under front section.

2. Proceed with Steps 1-4 of the Giulietta procedure, above.

3. Torque bolts at differential flange to 25-29 ft. lbs. Torque rubber joint bolts to 33-40 ft. lbs.

DRIVESHAFT REPAIR

Giulietta

1. Mark flanged joint for reassembly. Separate the sections.

2. Unbolt rubber joint from front section.

3. From front section, remove nut, flange, keys, and center bearing support.

4. Slide forward sleeve off rear section after unscrewing knurled nut holding seal.

5. Take apart U-joints by:
   a. removing snap-rings,
   b. removing grease fitting,
   c. sliding out roller cages, and
   d. removing the spider.

6. Clean all parts in a safe solvent. Check all parts, particularly roller bearings and splines, for wear. Replace the center

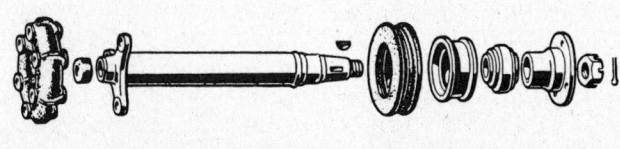

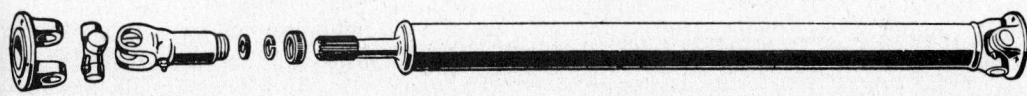

Driveshaft assembly, Giulietta

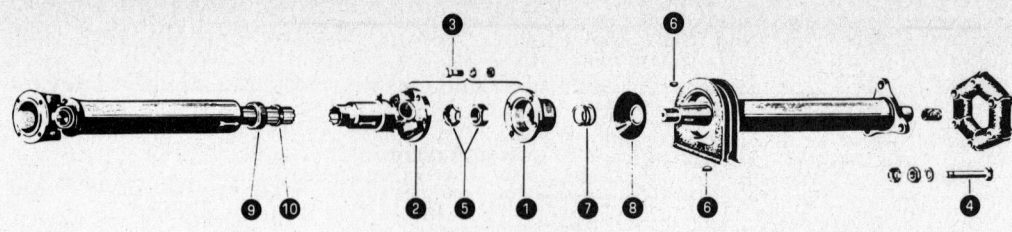

Driveshaft assembly, Giulia

1. Yoke (flanged)
2. Yoke (flanged)
3. Bolt
4. Bolt
5. Nut and lock tab
6. Keys
7. Spring
8. Oil slingers
9. Knurled nut
10. Seal

bearing if worn. Check that spline play is no more than .008″.

7. Reverse procedure to reassemble, aligning marks.

Giulia, 1600 Duetto, 1750

1. Mark flange for reassembly. Separate sections at flange.

2. Unbolt rubber joint from front section. Mark flange half and front shaft section. Remove nut, lock tab, and flange half. Remove shaft keys, spring, and oil slingers.

3. Unscrew knurled nut from rear section. Remove seal and separate splined joint. Pull off bearing and support if it requires replacement. The new bearing should be staked in place to prevent it from sliding out of the support.

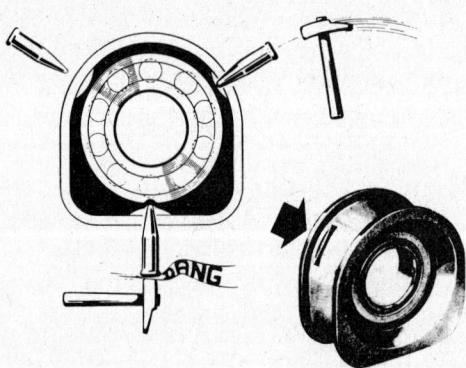

When installing a new driveshaft bearing, stake it in place as shown. The English translation of the word "dang" is "kerboing"

4. Disassemble U-joints as in Step 5 for Giulietta models.

5. Check all parts for wear or damage. Check runout of rear section. It should be no more than .016″ at the center and .004″ behind the splines. Check that spline play is no more than .008″.

6. Reverse procedure to reassemble driveshaft, matching marks made on disassembly.

Drive Axle

The rear axle on all models is the live type, located fore and aft by torque arms, and sideways by a trunnion attached to the frame and to the top of the differential housing. Suspension is by coil springs. Upward movement is restricted by bumper pads and downward movement by limit straps.

Rear Axle Assembly Removal

Removal of the rear axle requires removal of the coil springs, also.

GIULIETTA

1. Remove exhaust system.
2. Disconnect and plug brake tubes.
3. Disconnect handbrake operating rods from cylinders and from rear axle bracket.
4. Disconnect the limit straps. Disconnect shock absorbers at bottom.
5. Loosen wheel lugs.
6. Detach trunnion from top of differential.
7. Jack under the axle tubes to raise the car. Place jackstands under the jack sockets. Remove the wheels.
8. Lower the jack and the rear axle slowly. Remove the rear springs.

Note: Be extremely cautious when installing or removing coil springs. It is advisable to fasten the springs to the torque arms and axle with a heavy chain or cable to prevent their escaping.

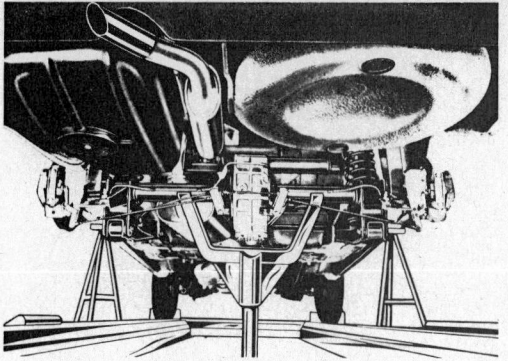

Method of raising and supporting car for rear axle removal

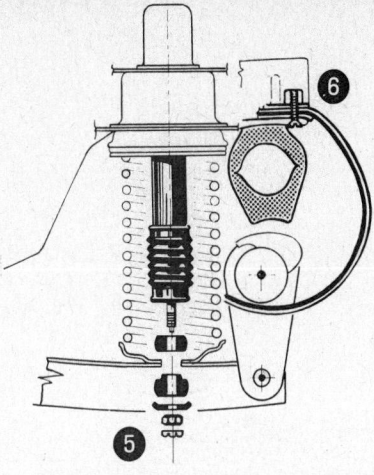

Details of limit straps and bumper pads. 6 is limit strap mounting, 5 is shock absorber lower mounting.

9. Disconnect the torque arms from the body. Disconnect the driveshaft and remove the axle.

GIULIA, 1600 DUETTO, 1750

1. Drain differential.
2. Loosen wheel lugs.
3. Jack under the axle tubes to raise the car. Place jackstands under the jack sockets. Remove wheels.
4. Disconnect and plug brake lines.
5. Unbolt driveshaft from differential.
6. Unbolt trunnion from top of differential.
7. Disconnect handbrake cables from shackles at differential and from levers at brake calipers.
8. Disconnect shock absorbers at bottom. Raise rear axle slightly to unload limit straps. Remove screws holding limit straps and bumper pads.

9. Clamp ends of radius rods to rear axle. A special tool is available for this operation. Remove radius rod pivot bolts at axle. Slowly let down axle ends of radius rods, releasing spring tension.

Note: Be extremely cautious when installing or removing coil springs. It is advisable to fasten the springs to the torque arms and axle with a heavy chain or cable to prevent their escaping.

DISC BRAKES

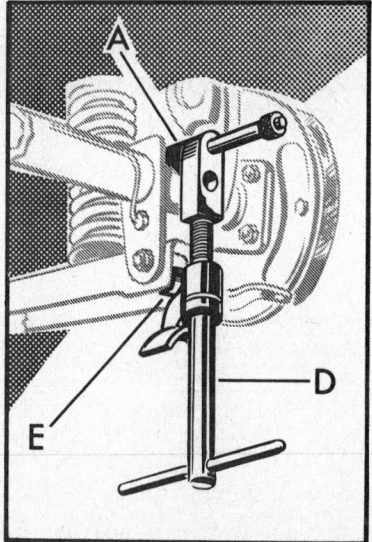

DRUM BRAKES

Special tool used for installing or removing rear coil springs

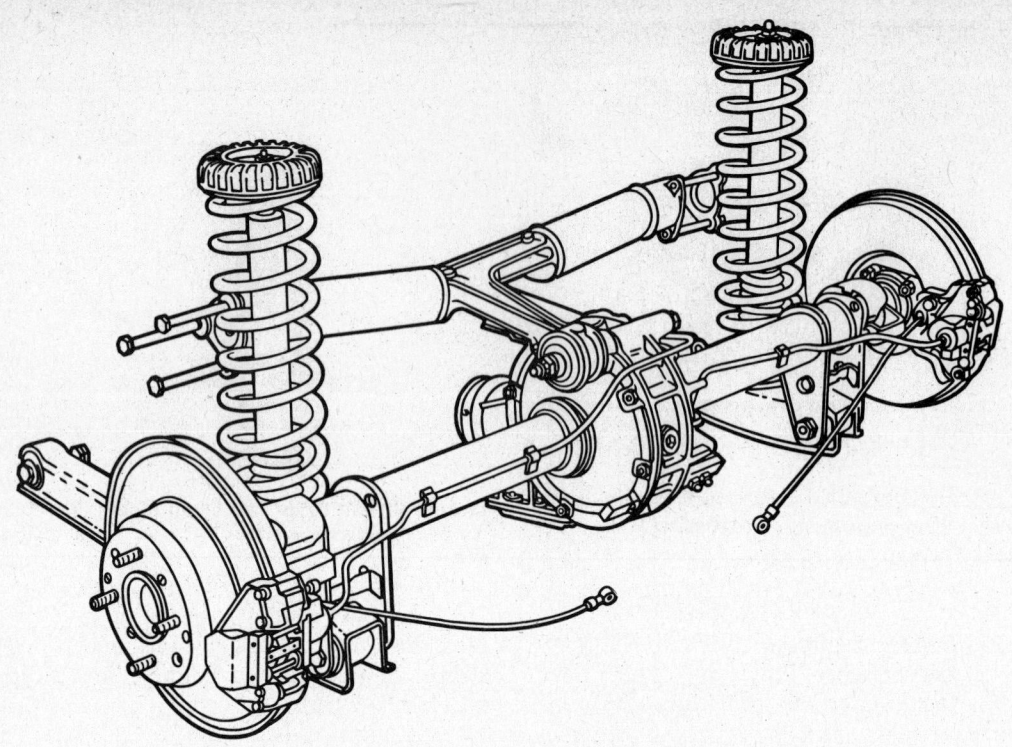

Rear suspension, Giulia, 1600 Duetto, 1750

10. Shift axle to one side to release from the trunnion. Lower and remove rear axle.

Differential Overhaul

Dismantling, adjustment, and reassembly of the differential requires numerous special tools, and measuring devices. For this reason it is not practical to cover these operations here. It is recommended that any differential repairs be entrusted to an authorized service facility.

Front Suspension

Front suspension on all models is independent, utilizing coil springs, A-arms, telescopic shock absorbers, and a cross-chassis stabilizer bar. On the Giulietta, upward movement is limited by pads on the shock absorbers and downward movement by a steel cable between the body and the lower A-arms. The Giulietta shock absorbers are mounted inside the coil springs.

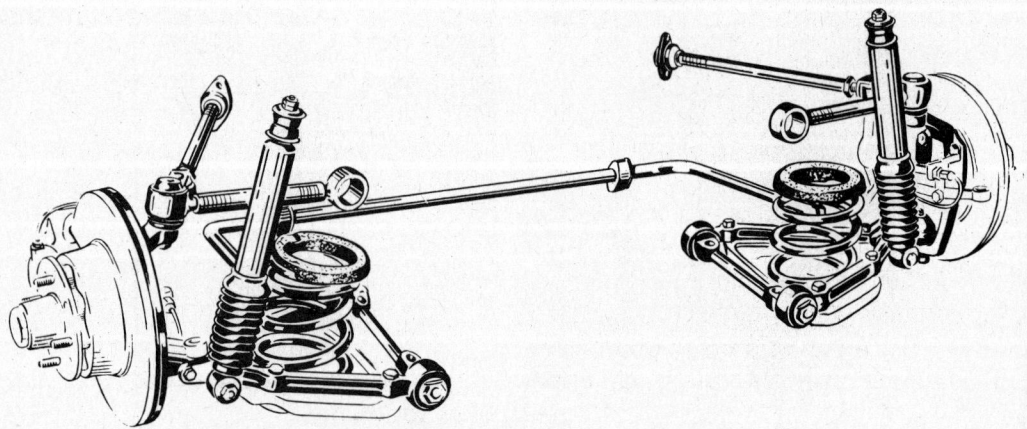

Front suspension. Giulia, 1600 Duetto, 1750

Front Wheel Bearing Adjustment

GIULIA, 1600 DUETTO, 1750

1. Raise wheel.
2. Remove bearing dust cover. Remove cotter pin.
3. Torque castellated nut to 18 ft. lbs. while spinning wheel.
4. Loosen nut ½ turn.
5. Tap lightly on the stub axle end with a soft hammer.
6. Torque the nut to 11 ft. lbs. Back off ¼ turn.
7. Insert the cotter pin. If the holes are not aligned, tighten the nut slightly to align them.
8. Tap stub axle lightly again.
9. After adjustment, end play should be .001-.005″, measured with a dial indicator.
10. Replace dust cover and wheel.
11. If the wheel bearings are to be repacked, use 2.5 ounces of grease for each. Excessive grease will leak out, probably onto the brakes.

Ball Joints

All models, except the 2600, use ball joints in the front suspension. The ball joints are greased on assembly and need no further lubrication. Maximum permissible play of the lower ball joint in its socket is .04″ (1 mm.).

Front End Alignment

CASTER

On the Giulietta, caster is adjusted by moving shims from front to rear, or rear to front, between the body and the upper suspension arm mounting brackets. Caster is adjusted at the upper wishbone strut adjuster on the Giulia, 1600 Duetto, and 1750.

Adjusting caster angle on Giulia, 1600 Duetto, 1750

CAMBER

Camber is not adjustable on Giulia, 1600 Duetto, and 1750 models. On the Giulietta and 2600 it is adjusted by varying the number of shims between the body and the upper suspension arm mounting brackets.

TOE-IN

Toe-in is adjusted at the outer steering arms and the central track rod on all models.

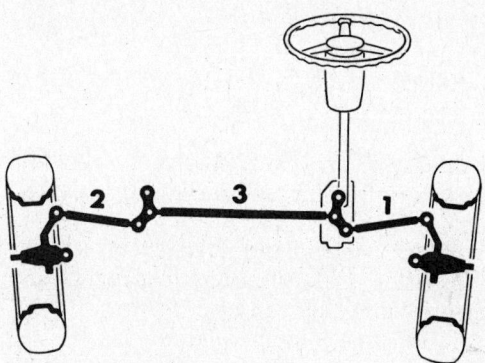

Toe-in is adjusted by equalizing the outer steering arms, 1 and 2, and adjusting the central track rod, 3.

Steering

Steering Wheel R & R

GIULIETTA

1. Disconnect battery ground.
2. Pry off horn button seat ring and button.
3. Unscrew and remove spoke cover.
4. Remove horn/light switches in unit.
5. Unscrew steering wheel nut.
6. Using a puller, remove the steering wheel. Remove the shaft key.
7. Reverse procedure to install.

Steering Column and Box R & R

GIULIETTA

1. Remove steering wheel.
2. Make reference marks on column and bracket.
3. On column shift models, remove shift lever after unscrewing threaded ring holding it to gearshift rod.

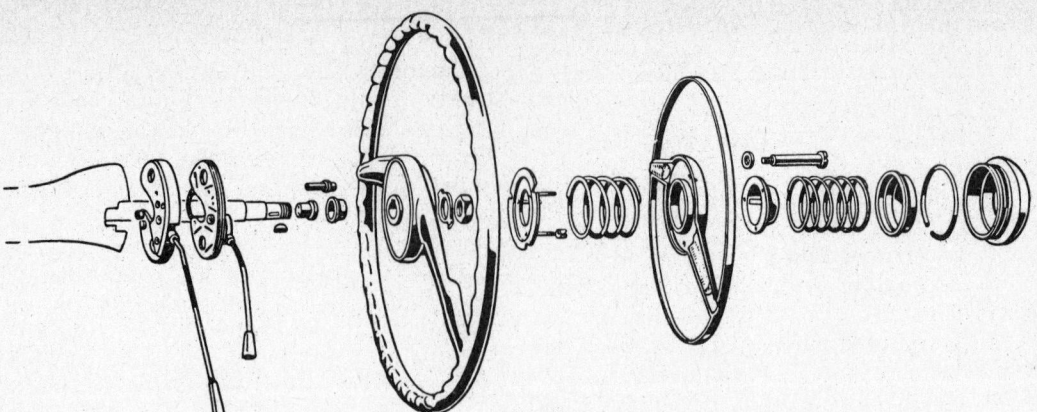

Steering wheel details, Giulietta

4. Loosen column bracket to column clamp screw. Unbolt bracket from instrument panel.

5. Disconnect handbrake lever.

6. After making reference marks, remove column shift rod bearing caps.

7. Remove column bellows.

8. Remove backup light bracket on column shift models after making reference marks.

9. Disconnect both horn wires at bottom of steering box.

10. Unbolt and pull off steering arm from steering box.

11. Unbolt steering box and remove with column.

12. On reinstallation, first hand tighten steering box mounting bolts.
Note: The mounting bolts must be no longer than 2.56″ (65 mm.).

13. Align and bolt down column bracket.

14. Lock down steering box bolts.

15. Reverse Steps 1-10 to complete reinstallation.

Brakes

Giulietta models have hydraulic drum brakes front and rear. The front drums are equipped with light alloy cooling fins. A mechanical handbrake works on the rear wheels only.

Giulia models may have any of an assortment of braking systems. The Giulia TI, Spider, and Sprint have a system very similar to that on the Giulietta, but with three-shoe front drums. The Giulia Sprint Veloce and Sprint Speciale use Girling front disc brakes with drum rear brakes. The 2600 series also uses Girling front discs with finned rear drums. The Giulia Super, GT, GTC, GTA and GT Veloce use Dunlop front discs and drums at the rear. The 1600 Duetto Spider uses the same system. The Giulia GT Veloce may use ATE disc brakes as an alternate installation to the Dunlop units. The Giulia GT and GTC also have a power assist, a Lockheed vacuum booster.

All 1750 models have ATE discs at all four wheels. The system has two vacuum boosters. The 1750 also uses a dual circuit hydraulic system to prevent total loss of braking power in the event of a hydraulic leak. The handbrake actuates a small drum brake located in the center of each rear disc. A modulating valve in the rear hydraulic circuit regulates pressure between front and rear brakes to provide balanced braking action.

Master Cylinder

On all models, brake pedal free-play should be .04-.06″ (1-1.5 mm.).

MASTER CYLINDER R & R

Giulietta

1. Disconnect fluid reservoir from master cylinder. Drain and discard fluid from reservoir.

2. Disconnect stoplight wire.

3. Disconnect rod from clutch pedal.

4. Unbolt brake pedal bracket from body and remove bracket and master cylinder.

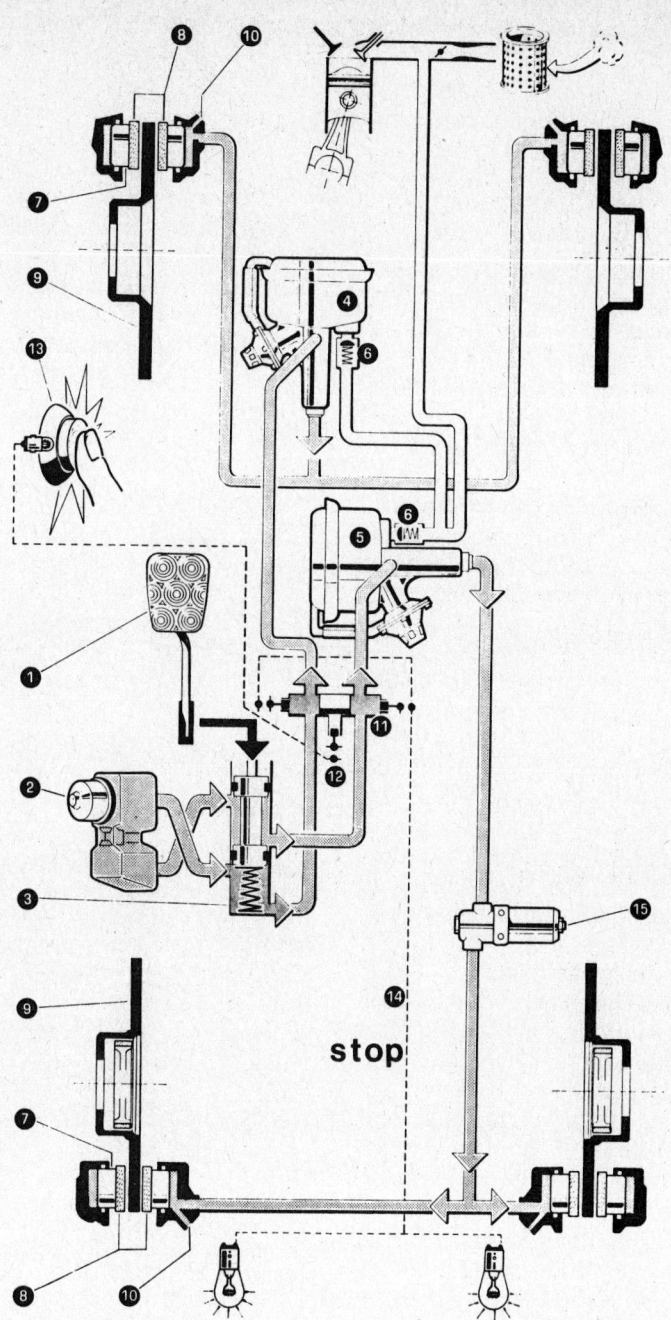

Dual circuit braking system with four-wheel discs, 1750

1. Brake pedal
2. Fluid reservoir
3. Master cylinder
4. Front brake booster
5. Rear brake booster
6. Suction port
7. Plungers
8. Friction Pads
9. Discs
10. Bleed screws
11. Pressure switch cluster
12. Pressure switch for brake warning light
13. Brake warning light
14. Stop light cable
15. Modulating valve

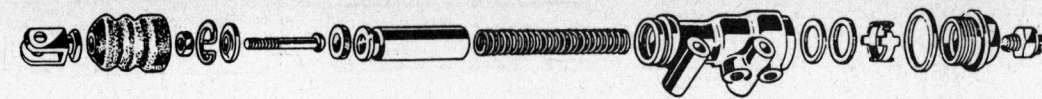

Exploded view of Giulietta master cylinder

MASTER CYLINDER INSPECTION AND REPAIR

1. Check internal surfaces of cylinder body and piston for wear or scoring.
2. Replace any seals either worn or swollen by fluid absorption.
3. Check condition of piston return spring.
4. Check that dust cover bellows is in good condition.
5. On reassembly, be very careful not to damage seals. If actuating rod has been removed, make sure to tighten the lock-nut securing it to the brake pedal link fork.

Hydraulic System Bleeding

Bleeding is required whenever air in the hydraulic fluid causes a spongy feeling pedal and sluggish response. This is often the case after some part of the hydraulic system has been repaired or replaced.

1. Fill the reservoir with the proper fluid. Special fluid is required for disc brakes. Make sure that the fluid level does not go below quarter full during the bleeding operation.
2. Bleed the rear brakes first.
3. Fit a rubber hose over the bleeder screw. Submerge the other end of the hose in clean brake fluid in a clear container. Loosen the bleeder screw.
4. Slowly pump the brake pedal several times until fluid free of bubbles is discharged. An assistant is required to pump the pedal.
5. On the last pumping stroke, hold the pedal down and tighten the bleeder screw.
6. Bleed the front brakes in the same way as the rear brakes. Note that most front drum brakes have two hydraulic cylinders and two bleeder screws. Both cylinders must be bled.
7. Check that the brake pedal is now firm. If not, repeat the bleeding operation.

Drum Brakes

INSTALLING NEW LININGS

1. Remove wheels after supporting car on jackstands.

2. Remove brake drums.
3. Remove brake shoes. Place a heavy rubber band around each cylinder to hold the piston in place. Remove and replace wheel cylinders if necessary.
4. Drill out rivets and rivet on new linings. The rivet heads should be sunk into the lining .08" (2 mm.) or more. The shoe linings must be beveled as illustrated. The rear wheel linings should not be beveled on Giulietta models with two-shoe front brakes.

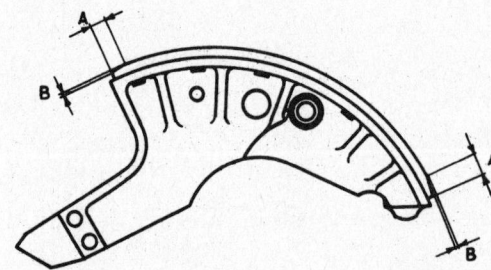

Brake lining beveling required on front shoes. A is .28-.35" (7-9 mm.). B is .02-.04" (.5-1.0 mm.).

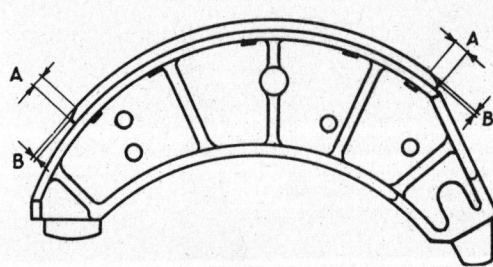

Brake lining beveling required on rear shoes for all models except Giulietta with two-shoe front drums. A is .24-.27" (6-7 mm.). B is .06-.08" (1.5-2.0 mm.).

5. Reinstall shoes. Align shoes using adjusting screws on backing plates.
6. On drums with alloy cooling fins, tap all around the edge of the inner ring (not the braking surface). Any separation of the fins from the drum will be noticed as a change of tone. If necessary, replace drum.
7. If drum is scored, it may be reground. The maximum safe regrind is .040" (1 mm.) off the original diameter.
8. Back off shoe adjusters so that drums

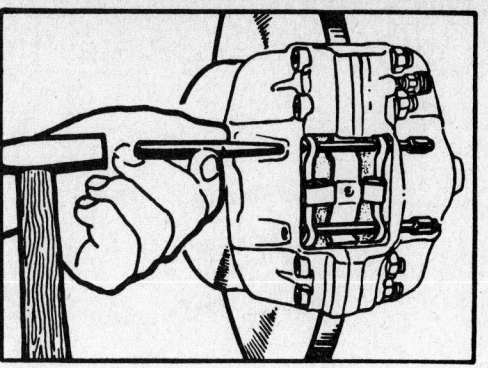

Driving out pad retaining pins, ATE brakes

2600 rear wheel backing plate. 1 is the brake adjuster. 2 is the shoe aligning screw. 3 is the bleed
screw.

Disc Brakes

can be replaced over new linings. Install
drums.

9. Replace wheel. Turn wheel while
tightening one adjusting cam on wheel
backing plate. When a heavy drag is felt,
loosen the cam 1-3 notches until wheel
again rotates freely. Repeat the operation
for the other shoes on the wheel.

*Note: Be sure that the adjuster being
turned is the brake adjusting cam, not the
shoe aligning screw.*

PAD REPLACEMENT

1. Support car and remove wheel.
2. Drive out pad retaining pins.
3. Remove retaining spring.
4. Pull out pads with a hook device.
5. In case one pad is worn more than
the rest, replace whole set of front or rear
pads.
6. Check dust seals and retaining ring.
Replace if worn.
7. Press pistons back to the bottom of
their cylinders. Watch that master cylinder
reservoir does not overflow. If a special tool
for this operation is not available, be extremely careful not to press against the disc
or scratch the piston or cylinder.

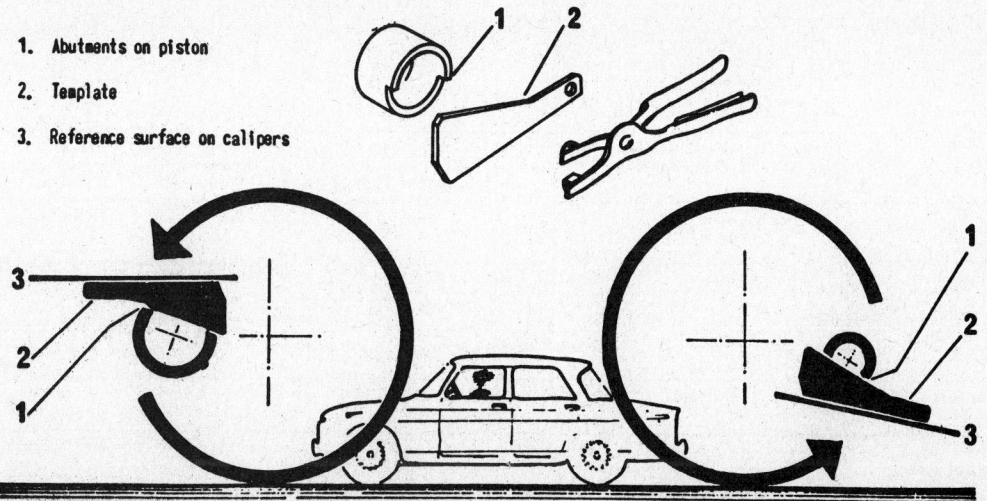

1. Abutments on piston

2. Template

3. Reference surface on calipers

Proper angle for pistons in ATE brakes

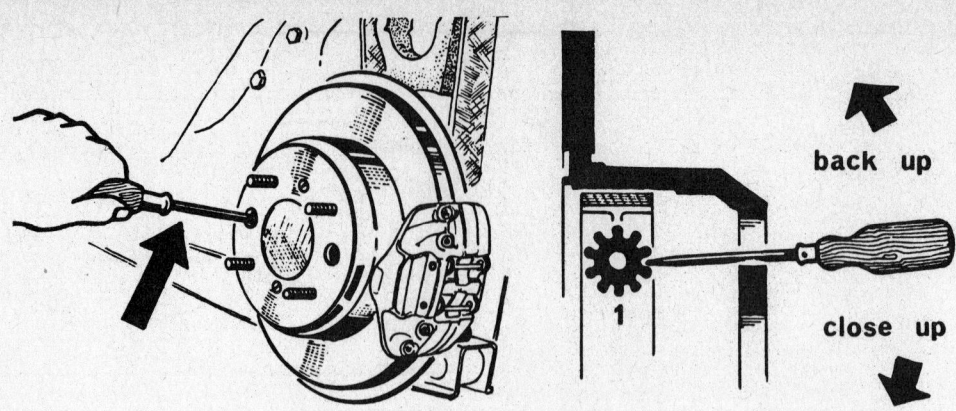

Handbrake adjustment, ATE rear discs

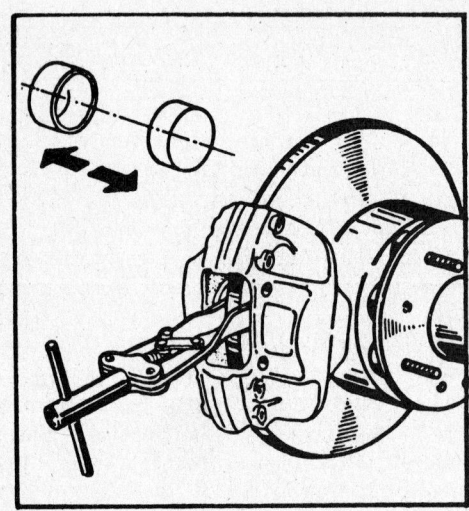

Pushing pistons back into their cylinders with special tool

8. Check that pistons on front and rear wheels are at correct angle as shown.

9. Install new pads, using new retaining pins.

Handbrake

ADJUSTMENT

Models With ATE Rear Discs

1. Raise rear wheels. Remove wheels. Release handbrake.

2. Adjust star wheel until shoe just contacts drum. Back off 2-4 notches.

3. If necessary, slack adjusters in linkage may be taken up.

Models With Drum Rear Brakes

1. Raise rear wheels.

2. Adjust cable linkage slack adjusters so that there is no drag and rear wheels are locked after pulling the lever up halfway.

Disc Brake Repair Specifications

Model	Thickness of New Pad	Minimum Safe Pad Thickness	Maximum Disc Runout	Minimum Disc Thickness After Truing	Caliper Halves Torque	Caliper Mounting Torque
Girling Front	.40-.43″	.12″	.006″	.45″	Inner screws 45-50, Outer screws 25-29 ft. lbs.	72 ft. lbs.
Dunlop Front	.63″	.32″	.006″	.34″	—	—
ATE Front	.59″	.28″	.009″	.45″	—	58 ft. lbs.
ATE Rear	.59″	.28″	.009″	.34″	—	43 ft. lbs.

AUDI SECTION

Index

Introduction

The Audi, produced by Auto Union of Germany and distributed in the United States by Volkswagen of America, has been available in the United States since 1970. Three models, the Super 90, Super 90 station wagon (Variant) and the 100 LS, have been imported using one basic engine. A 1,760 cc. engine is basic, although several modifications are available, producing 100 to 115 horsepower from the slanted four-cylinder, OHV engine. In a departure from tradition, the Audi uses a transaxle behind the forward mounted engine to transmit power to the front drive axle, while a dead axle is used in the rear. Also standard equipment are inboard mounted front disc brakes in conjunction with rear drum brakes and rack and pinion steering. A four-speed transmission is standard but can be replaced with an optional automatic.

Model Identification

1970 Audi sedan Model 100 LS

Vehicle and Engine Serial Number Identification

Vehicle Number Identification

100 LS

Viewing the vehicle in the driving direction, the engine number is stamped on the left side of the engine block, by the clutch housing.

In addition to the engine number, an engine code number is also stamped on the starter end of the cylinder block, just below the cylinder head. This number indicates the cylinder bore of the particular engine.

Model 100 LS engine identification number

Engine code number location

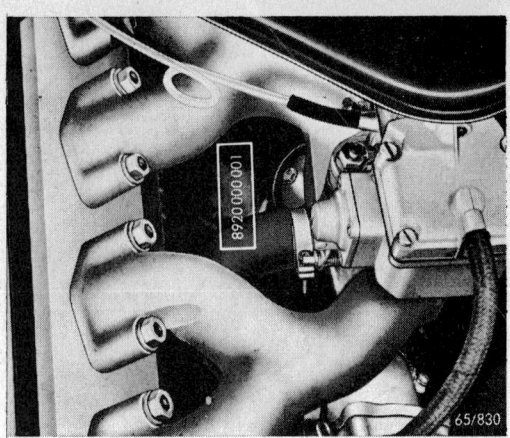

Super 90 engine identification number location
prior to chassis numbers 6842 025 599, etc.

Super 90

Up to chassis numbers 6842 025 559, 6843 018 078 and 6834 000 156 the engine number is stamped on the engine block above the fuel pump. After the above chassis numbers, the engine number is located in the same place as the number on the model 100 LS.

The identical engine code numbers denoting the cylinder bore also appear in the same position on the Super 90.

Engine Code Chart

Piston Size (mm dia.)	Stamped (mm dia.)	Cyl. Bore Size (mm dia.)	Stamped (mm dia.)	Eng. Block Die Stamping
81.465–81.475	81.47	81.505–81.515	81.51	501
81.475–81.485	81.48	81.515–81.525	81.52	502
81.485–81.495	81.49	81.525–81.535	81.53	503
81.715–81.725	81.72	81.755–81.765	81.76	576
81.725–81.735	81.73	81.765–81.775	81.77	577
81.735–81.745	81.74	81.775–81.785	81.78	578
81.965–81.975	81.97	82.005–82.015	82.01	201
81.975–81.985	81.98	82.015–82.025	82.02	202
81.985–81.995	81.99	82.025–82.035	82.03	203
82.465–82.475	82.47	82.505–82.515	82.51	251
82.475–82.485	82.48	82.515–82.525	82.52	252
82.485–42.495	82.49	82.525–82.535	82.53	253

General Engine Specifications

Type	Cu. In. Displacement (ccs.)	Carburetor	Developed Horsepower (DIN or SAE) @ rpm	Developed Torque (ft. lbs.) @ rpm	Bore and Stroke (in.)	Compression Ratio	Normal Oil Pressure (psi)
100 LS	107.5 cu. in (1,760 ccs.)	1–2 bbl. Zenith	115 @ 5,600	119.3 @ 3,200	3.21 x 3.32	10.2:1	14–85
Super 90	107.5 cu. in (1,760 ccs.)	1–2 bbl. Solex	102 @ 5,200	115.7 @ 3,000	3.21 x 3.32	10.6:1	14–85

Tune-Up Specifications

Model	Spark plugs		Distributor		Basic Ignition Timing (deg.)[**]	Cranking Comp. Pressure (p.s.i.)	Valves				
	Make Type [°]	Gap	Point dwell (deg.)	Point gap (in.)			Clearance (in.)		Intake Opens (deg.)	Idle Speed (rpm)	
							Intake (warm)	Exhaust (warm)			
100 LS	N 3	.02–.024	50° ±3°	.016	27° B[1] @ 2,500 rpm	156	.006	.014	8° B	950–1,000	
Super 90	N 3 N 4	.02–.024	50° ±3°	.016	18° B @ 3,000[1] rpm	140–185	.004	.006	6° B	950	

[**] — With vacuum hoses disconnected   1 — 9° BTDC at idle with the vacuum hose connected
[°] — Champion spark plug designation

Firing Order

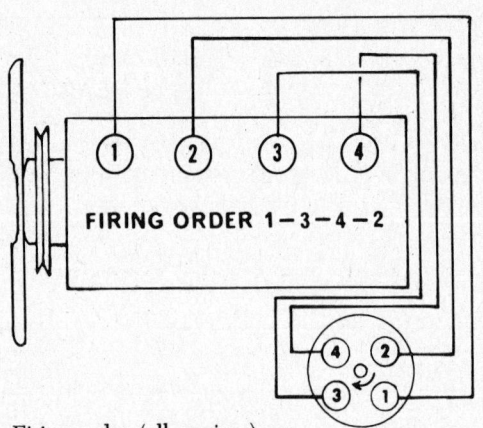

FIRING ORDER 1 – 3 – 4 – 2

Firing order (all engines)

Engine Rebuilding Specifications

Model	Crankshaft								
	Main Bearing Journal (in.)					Connecting Rod Bearing Journals (in.)			
	Journal diameter		Oil Clearance	Shaft End-Play	Thrust On No.	Journal diameter		Oil Clearance	End-Play
	New	Minimum				New	Minimum		
100 LS	2.3622	2.3322	.0015–.0039	.0027–.0074	N.A.	1.8898	1.8598	.0012–.0033	.0043–.0090
Super 90									

Model	Cyl. Block (in.)		Pistons (in.)		Wrist Pin Diameter (Fit)	Rings (in.)		
	Bore		Piston diameter			Side Clearance (max.)	End-Gap (max.)	Piston Clearance
	New	Maximum Oversize	New	Maximum Oversize				
100 LS	3.2085	3.2491	3.2073	3.2479	.9448 (–.00019)	.0059	.039	.0012
Super 90								

Engine Rebuilding Specifications

Model	Valves						
	Seat Angle (Deg.)	Valve Seat Width	Valve lift (in.) Intake	Valve lift (in.) Exhaust	Valve Spring Pressure (lbs.) Intake	Valve Spring Pressure (lbs.) Exhaust	Valve Spring Installed Height (in.)
100 LS	45° 15′	.138″ (max.)	N.A.	N.A.	N.A.	N.A.	N.A.
Super 90							

Model	Valve Stem Diameter (in.)		Stem to Guide Clearance (in.)		Valve Guide Removable
	Intake	Exhaust	Intake	Exhaust	
100 LS	.353	.352	.001	.002	Yes
Super 90	.353	.392	.001	.002	Yes

Distributor Advance Specifications

Model	Distributor Identification	Centrifugal Advance*				Vacuum Advance		
		Start Degrees @ rpm	Intermediate Degrees @ rpm	Intermediate Degrees @ rpm	End Degrees @ rpm	Start Degrees @ in./Hg	Intermediate Degrees @ in./Hg	End Deg's. @ in./Hg
100 LS	Bosch JFUR 4	0° @ 1,300–1,800	10° @ 2,500	18° @ 3,500	22° @ 4,100	0° @ 3.54–5.51	12° @ 9.84	15° @ 15.74
Super 90	Bosch JFUR 4	N.A.	N.A.	N.A.	N.A.	N.A.	N.A.	N.A.

– All degrees are given as crankshaft degrees
All rpm are given as crankshaft rpm

Carburetor Specifications

Model	Carburetor Identification	Venturi		Main Jet		Air Correction Jet		Idle Jet		Idle Air Jet (Bore)	
		Prim. (mm.)	Sec. (mm.)	Prim.	Sec.	Prim.	Sec.	Prim.	Sec.	Prim.	Sec.
00 LS	Solex 32 TDID	24	27	X125 *	X145	160 *	100	g 55 **	50 ***	140	100 ***
uper[2] 90	Solex 32/32 DIDTA[3]	24	27	X120[1]	X140	150	100	g 55	g 80	1.2/ 1.0	Blind/ 1.0

Carburetor Specifications

Model	Carburetor Identi- fication	Injection Rate cc./ stroke	Choke Gap (in.)	Throttle Gap (in.)	Bi-metallic Spring Length (in.)	Float Needle Valve (in.)	Float Needle Valve Seal (in.)	Float Weight (oz.)	Fuel Level (in.)	Float Loca- tion (in.)
100 LS	Solex 32 TDID	1.8 ± .15	.09 ± .006	.063 ± .004	18.5	.079	.079	.26	N.A.	.61–.67
Super[2] 90	Solex 32/32 DIDTA[3]	1.25 ± .15	.09 ± .006	.06 (± .004)	N.A.	.079	.079	N.A.	.63– .71	N.A.

* — Up to engine no. ZZ 016 348: Main jet (Primary)— X 120. Air Correction Jet (Primary)—150
** — with cut-off valve
*** — idle reserve
1 — Use an X115 main jet (primary) in vehicles encountering excessively rich mixture or high fuel consumption.
2 — Additional Specifications:
　Mixture Tube: (Primary) K 20 385 (Secondary) K 20 385
　Atomizer Diameter (mm.): (Primary) 3.2 (secondary) 3.2
　Breather Jet: (Primary) 050 (Secondary) 050
　Injection Tube: (Primary) 60
　Reduction Jet: (Primary) 80

3 — The following departures from the specifications are valid for carburetors from no. 7280 (finned float).
　(A) Idle Fuel Jet: g 50 (replaces g 55)
　(B) Fuel Level: .67"-.74" (instead of .63"-.71")
　(C) Injection Tube: 50 (replaces 60)
　(D) Injection Rate: .9-1.1 cc./stroke (instead of 1.25 cc./stroke)
　(E) A hole (.06" dia.) in the throttle on the bypass bore side

Torque Specifications

Model	Cylinder Head bolts (ft. lbs.)	Main Bearing bolts (ft. lbs.)	Rod Bearing bolts (ft. lbs.)	Crankshaft Balancer bolt (or nut) (ft. lbs.)	Flywheel to Crankshaft bolts (ft. lbs.)	Manifold (ft. lbs.) Intake	Exhaust
100 LS	65**	58*	25–31	130–180	65	17.5	17.5
Super 90	65**	28.9*	25–31	130–180	65	17.3	17.3

* — 100 LS main bearing cap No. 5: 24 ft. lbs.
　Super 90 main bearing cap No. 5: 23 ft. lbs.
** — Torqued according to sequence and in steps (see text)

Torque Sequences

Cylinder head bolts should be torqued, according to the sequence illustrated, and in the following four steps: Step 1, 29 ft. lbs.; Step 2, 43.5 ft. lbs.; Step 3, 58 ft. lbs. and Step 4, 65 ft. lbs.

Super 90 and 100 LS torque sequence

Electrical Specifications

Model	Battery			Starter							Brush spring tension (oz.)
	Capacity (Amp. hours)	Volts	Grounded Terminal	Lock test			No load test				
				Amp.	Volts	Torque	Amps.	Volts	RPM		
100 LS	45	12	Negative	250–300	7	N.A.	N.A.	N.A.	N.A.	N.A.	N.A.
Super 90	45	12	Negative	250–300	7	N.A.	N.A.	N.A.	N.A.	N.A.	N.A.

Model	Alternator					AC Regulator				
	Part Number *	Field Current Draw @ 12V	Output @ Alternator RPM		Brush Spring Tension (oz.)	Part Number *	Regulator			
			X100	X100			Volts to Close	Air Gap (in.)	Point Gap (in.)	Volts at 125°
00 LS	K1 14 V 55A20	N.A.	24 amps @ 22.5	35 amps @ 54.5	10.5–14.0	AD 1 14 V	13.9–14.8	N.A.	.010–.015	N.A.
uper 90										

— Bosch part number

Capacities and Pressures

Model	Engine Crankcase Refill after draining (qts.)		Transmissions Refill after draining			Drive Axle (pts.)	Fuel Tank (gals.)	Cooling System with Heater (qts.)	Normal Fuel Press. (psi) ***	Maximum Coolant Press. (psi)
	With Filter	Without Filter	Manual		Auto. * (gals.)					
			3-Speed (pts.)	4-Speed (pts.)						
00 LS	4.25	N.A.	—	4.2 **	1.6	—	15.3	8	3.55	12.8
uper 90										

* — Figure specified is the total amount. Change amount is .8 gallons.
** — This figure also includes the transaxle.
*** — Measured at the carburetor.

Brake Specifications

Model	Type		Brake Cylinder Bore			Brake Drum or Disc Diameter (in.)	
	Front	Rear	Master Cylinder (in.)	Wheel Cylinder (in.)			
				Front	Rear	Front	Rear
100 LS	Disc	Drum	.817*	—	.6287**	11.02	7.87
Super 90	Disc	Drum					

* — Piston diameter: .807″ (minimum)
   Figure specified is maximum master cylinder bore diameter
** — Figure specified is maximum rear wheel cylinder bore diameter
   Piston diameter: .6197″ (minimum)

Chassis and Wheel Alignment Specifications

Model	Chassis			Wheel Alignment[1]							
	Wheel-base (in.)	Track (in.)		Caster		Camber[°]		Toe-Out (in.)		Wheel Pivot Ratio	
		Front	Rear	Range (deg.)	Pref. Setting (deg.)	Range (deg.)	Pref. Setting (deg.)			Inner Wheel	Caster Wheel
100 LS	105.32	55.9	56.1	—	0° 6' ± 20'	—	0° 11' ± 20'	0 to —.079"		N.A.	N.A.
Super 90	98.03	52.85	52.05	—	0° 10' ± 20'	—	0° 15' ± 20'	0 to —.08"		N.A.	N.A.

° — Rear wheel camber:
    100 LS = 0° 30'
    Super 90 = 1 ± 20' up to chassis nos. 6842 062 322, 6843 051 984 and 6834 007 496
           —30' ± 15' from chassis nos. 6842 062 323, 6843 051 985 and 6834 007 497
1 — Kingpin inclination is dependent upon camber and cannot be adjusted independently

Fuses and Circuit Breakers

Model	Circuit	Amperage		Model	Circuit	Amperage
100 LS	(1) Turn signal, emergency warning light	8			(4) Right overnight light, right tail light, right parking light	8
Super 90	(2) Windshield washer motor and slow action relay, blower motor, horn, temperature gauge, fuel gauge, oil pressure warning light, reverse lights	16			(5) Left high beam	8
					(6) Right high beam, high beam warning light	8
	(3) Windshield wiper motor, brake lights, license plate lights, instrument lights, glove box light, cigarette lighter, clock, interior light	16			(7) Left low beam	8
					(8) Right low beam	8
					(9) Left overnight light, left tail light, left parking light	8

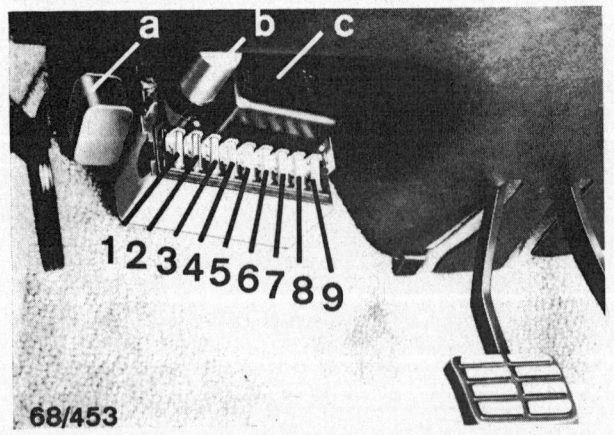

68/453

The fuse box, containing nine fuses, is located in the passenger compartment below the instrument panel. The windshield washer slow action relay (a), the flasher unit (b) and the relay for the high and low beams and the turn signals (c) are also mounted on the fuse box.

Light Bulb Specifications

Model	Usage (Quantity)	Make	Type	Wattage or Candlepower
100 LS	Headlights (2)	N.A.	N.A.	45/40
Super 90	Parking lights (2)			4
	Front turn signals (2)			18
	Rear turn signals (2)			18
	Tail lights (2)			5
	Brake lights (2)			18
	Reverse lights (2)			15
	License plate lights (2)			4
	Interior light (1)			10
	Speedometer			
	Instrument lights (2)			2
	Turn signal warning light (1)			2
	High beam warning light (1)			2
	Combination instrument			
	Instrument light (2)			2
	Oil pressure warning light (1)			2
	Alternator warning light (1)			2
	Fog light (special accessory) (1-2)			35
	Glove box light (1)			2
	Trunk light (1)			3

Wiring Diagrams

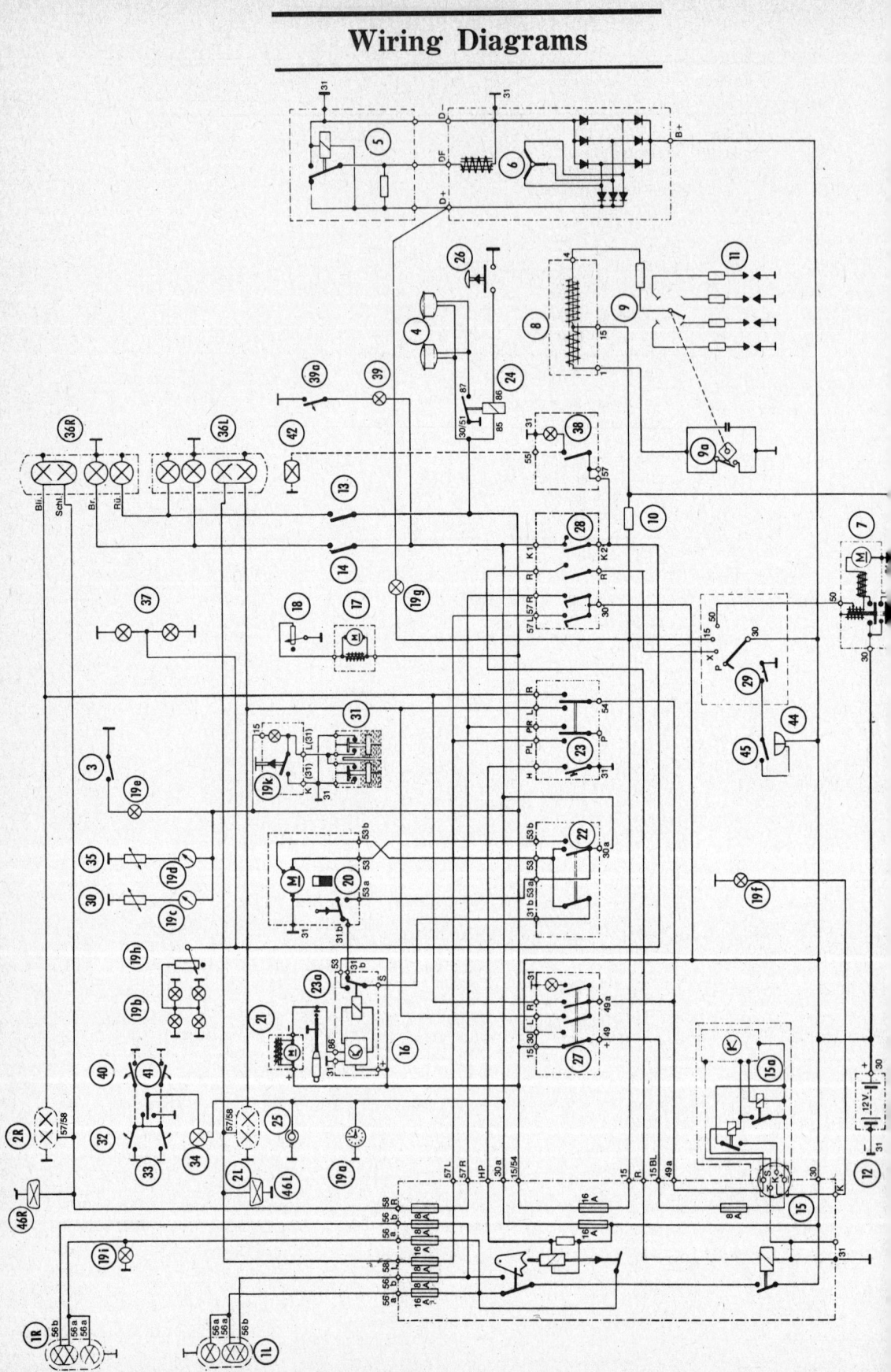

1R Headlight, right
1L Headlight, left
2R Turn signal, right
2L Turn signal, left
3   Oil pressure switch
4   Horn
5   Governor
6   Alternator
7   Starter
8   Ignition coil
9   Distributor
9a Contact breaker
10 Series resistor for position 8
11 Spark plugs
12 Battery
13 Reverse light switch
14 Brake light switch
15 Combination relay
15a Flasher unit
16 Relay, windshield washer
17 Blower motor
18 Series resistor for position 17
19a Clock
19b Instrument illumination
19c Temperature gauge
19d Fuel gauge
19e Oil warning lamp
19f Turn signal warning lamp
19g Battery warning lamp
19h Regulating resistor for position 19b
19i High beam warning lamp
20 Wiper motor
21 Washer motor
22 Wiper switch
23 Turn signal—dip beam switch
23a Washer impulse tracer
24 Multi-connector
25 Cigarette lighter
26 Horn button
27 Emergency warning light switch

28 Light switch
29 Steering-ignition lock
30 Temperature transmitter
32 Door contact switch, front, right
33 Door contact switch, front, left
34 Interior light and switch
35 Fuel tank gauge
36R Tail light, right
36L Tail light, left
37 License plate light
38 Switch, tail fog light
39 Glove compartment light
39a Switch for position 39
40 Door contact switch, rear, right
41 Door contact switch, rear, left
42 Tail fog light (optional extra)

COLOR CODES

ws	white
sw	black
ge	yellow
br	brown
gr	gray
gn	green
rt	red
li	lilac
bl	blue
hlbl	light blue

19k Twin-circuit brake warning lamp
24 Switching relay for position 4
31 Twin-circuit braking system
44 Audible buzzer
45 Door contact switch for position 44
46R ⎫ Side marker lights
46L ⎭

for USA only

Model 100 LS wiring diagram (USA version)

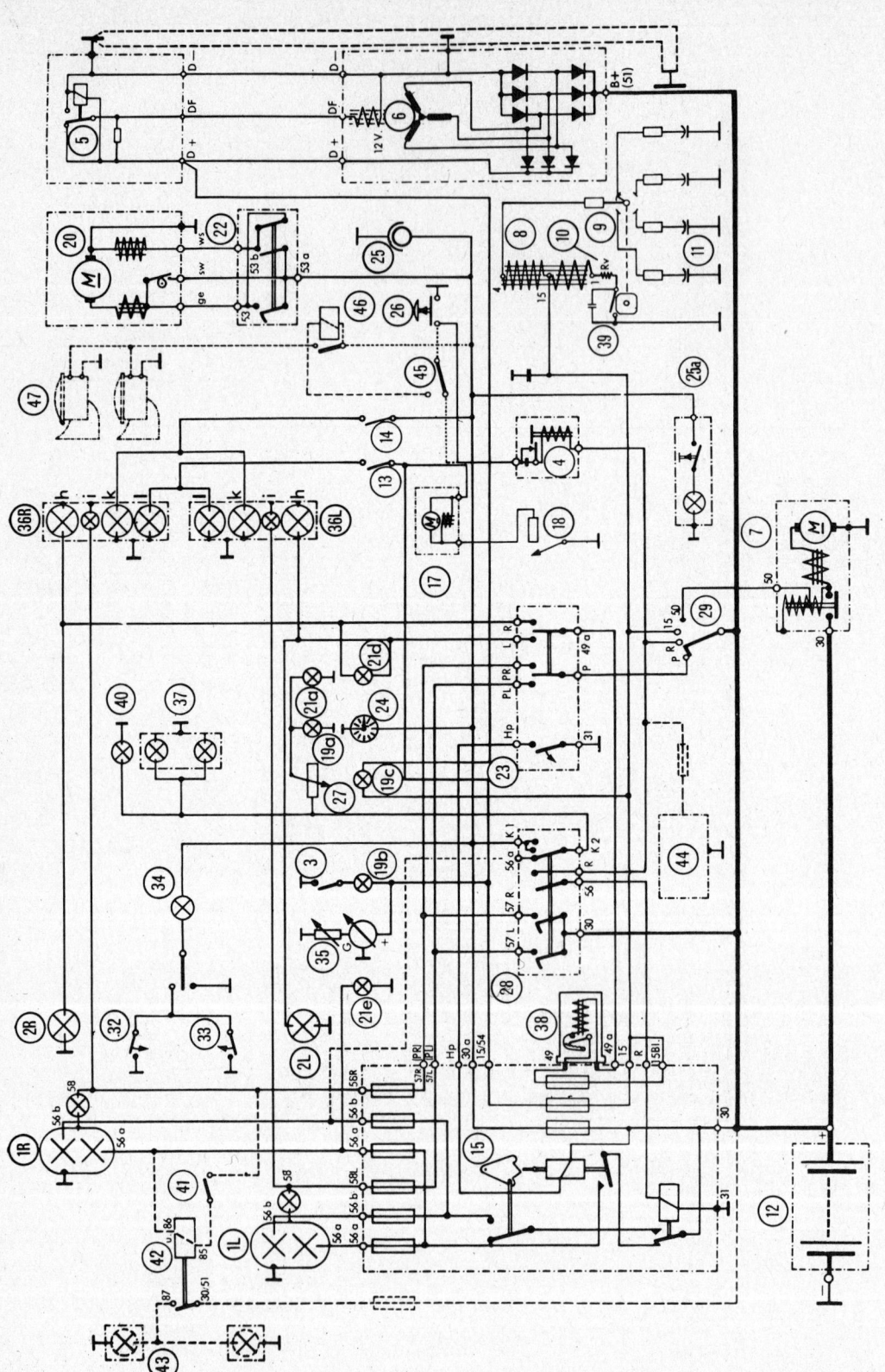

Super 90 wiring diagram (from chassis nos. 6842 040 501 and 6843 030 001).

1R Headlamp, right
1L Headlamp, left
2R Indicator light, right
2L Indicator light, left
3 Oil pressure switch
4 Horn
5 Regulator
6 Alternator
7 Starter
8 Ignition coil
9 Distributor
10 Series resistor, ignition coil
11 Spark plugs
12 Battery 12 volt
13 Reverse light switch
15 Combination relay
16 Connection, left indicator light
17 Fan motor
18 Regulating resistor, fan motor
18a Connector, fan motor
19 Combination instrument
a Instrument illumination
b Oil warning light
c Alternator warning light
20 Windshield wiper motor

21 Speedometer
a Instrument illumination
d Indicator warning light
e High beam warning light
22 Windshield wiper motor switch
23 Indicator—dip beam switch
24 Clock
a Instrument illumination
25 Cigarette lighter
25a Glove compartment light*
26 Horn contact ring
27 Resistor, instrument illumination
28 Light switch
29 Steering—ignition lock
30 Connector, steering—ignition lock
31 Connector, tail light harness
32 Door contact, right
33 Door contact, left
34 Courtesy light
35 Tank fuel gauge
36R Tail light, right
36L Tail light, left
h Indicator light
i Tail light
k Brake light
l Reverse light

37 License plate illumination
38 Indicator unit
39 Contact breaker
40 Trunk light*

OPTIONAL ACCESSORIES

41 Fog lamp switch
42 Relay
43 Fog lamps
44 Radio
45 Horn changeover switch
46 Relay, two-tone horn
47 Two-tone horn
50 Plug connector (Italy)

COLOR CODES

ws white
sw black
ge yellow
br brown
gr grey
gn green
rt red
li lilac
hbl light blue

*Audi Super 90 only

Super 90 wiring diagram (from chassis nos. 6842 040 501 and 6843 030 001).

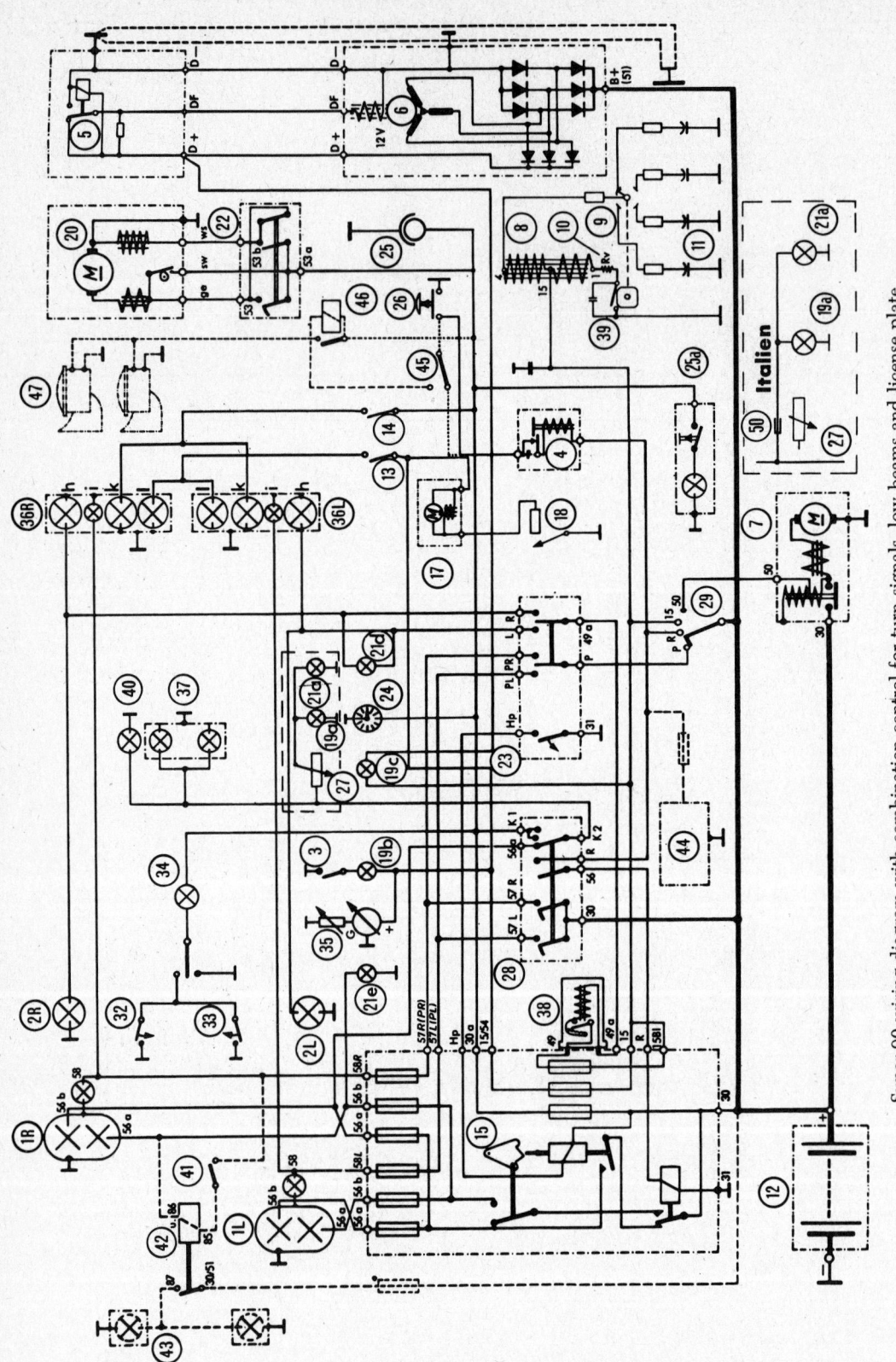

Super 90 wiring diagram with combination control for turn signals, low beams and license plate illumination (from chassis nos. 6842 040 501 and 6843 030 001). Key same as for Super 90 wiring diagram without combination control.

Engine Electrical

Distributor

REMOVAL

Remove the air cleaner. Pry back the retaining clips and remove the distributor cap. Disconnect the green lead at the ignition coil. Detach the vacuum line, being careful not to damage the plastic tube. Loosen the screw at the retaining clamp and pull the distributor from the housing. If the distributor is difficult to remove, the rubber seal is sticking. Carefully pry the distributor loose with a screwdriver.

Contact Breaker

Remove the rotor and dust cap immediately below the rotor. Detach the flat plug and remove the set of contacts. Lubricate the distributor cams with a small amount of molybdenum disulphide grease. Install a new set of breaker points (in reverse order). Lubricate the space between the distributor cam and the contact breaker lever. After installation, set the point gap to specification. Loosen the screw and press the points together. Turn the distributor cam until the breaker lever is at maximum height. Insert a feeler gauge between the points and press them together. Tighten the screw. An exact adjustment can be made with the distributor in the car, using a dwell meter.

INSTALLATION

Distributor installation is the reverse of removal. When installing the distributor, the projections on the shaft, at the bottom of the distributor, must engage the slots in the oil pump driveshaft. Turn the rotor until the two engage. The projections and grooves have been milled off center, making it impossible to install the distributor incorrectly. Lubricate the seal with a small amount of oil.

Ignition Timing

100 LS

A basic timing adjustment can be made in an emergency or after assembly in the following manner. Push the car (in fourth gear) until the ignition timing mark (see illustration) is aligned with the ignition timing mark on the timing cover. This will

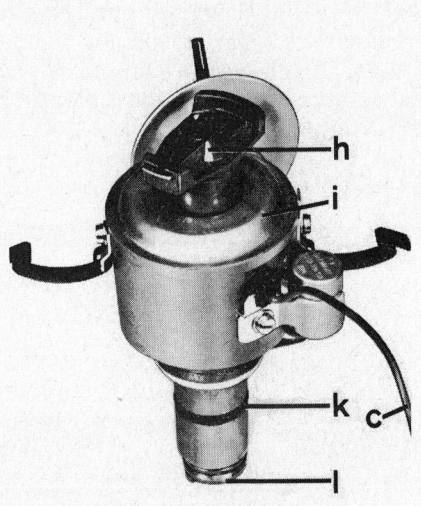

Distributor with cap removed

c   Cable "1" (green)
h   Distributor rotor
i   Dust cap
k   Rubber seal
l   Connection (with 2 projections)

Installed breaker point assembly

c   Cable "1" (green)   n   Bosses
g   Tube, vacuum line   o   Groove
m   Flat plug connection   p   Screw

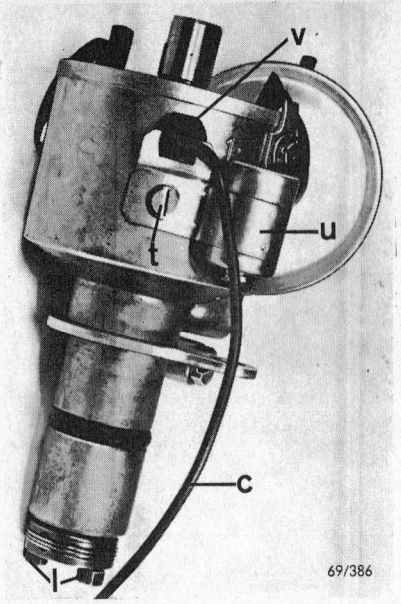

Location of ignition timing mark on 100 LS distributor (M) in relation to the distributor rotor (L).

External view of distributor showing projections which fit slots in the oil pump driveshaft

c   Cable "1" (green)
l   Connections (with 2 projections)
t   Retainer screw for u
u   Condenser
v   Plastic opening

put No. 1 cylinder at TDC. If the distributor rotor is intalled correctly, the rotor will point to the notch on the distributor case, which is the ignition timing setting for No. 1 cylinder. Connect a 12 volt test lamp between the ignition coil terminal on the distributor and ground. With the engine idling in neutral, rotate the distributor clockwise until the lamp stops burning. Turn the distributor counterclockwise until the lamp just lights, and tighten the clamp on the distributor at that point. The ignition is now set at approximately TDC. As soon as possible, check the adjustment with a timing light.

To check the ignition timing with a timing light, connect a timing light to No. 1 cylinder and connect a tachometer. Loosen the distributor clamp screw until it is just possible to turn the distributor by hand. Remove the vacuum hoses. Run the engine to 3,000 rpm and point the timing light at the pulley. Turn the distributor until the 27° BTDC notch on the crankshaft pulley aligns with the mark on the timing cover (see illustration).

Location of 100LS 9° ATDC timing mark used at the idle with vacuum hoses connected.

Location of 100 LS 27° BTDC timing mark (K) on crankshaft pulley and the timing mark (M) on the timing cover

Super 90

The Super 90 can be timed in the same manner as the 100 LS, except that the ignition timing mark on the crankshaft pulley corresponds to 18° BTDC at 3,000 rpm. This mark is the last mark on the pulley.

Alternator

All Audi models in the United States are equipped with alternators. When performing any service to the alternator or alternator system the following precautions should be observed.

A. Leads or cables to any part of the charging circuit should be disconnected only after the engine has been switched off and has stopped running.

B. When working on the electrical system, always disconnect the lead from the negative battery terminal.

C. When performing tests with the engine running, the battery must always be connected.

D. Provisional connections should never be made to the alternator. Always make careful connections.

It is possible to diagnose defects in an alternator system with a test lamp. A test lamp with a minimum of two watts and in good working condition should stop burning when the engine reaches idle speed, or shortly after.

AC Regulator

The AC regulator should be tested by an authorized dealer, using the proper equipment. If a dealer is not readily available, connect an ammeter (40 A range), a voltmeter (20 V range) and an adjustable load resistor for alternators as illustrated. Start the engine and maintain a constant speed of 2,050 rpm (4,000 alternator rpm) and increase the load with the adjustable resistor until the ammeter shows a load of 28-30 A. Read the regulating voltage from the voltmeter, which should match the figure

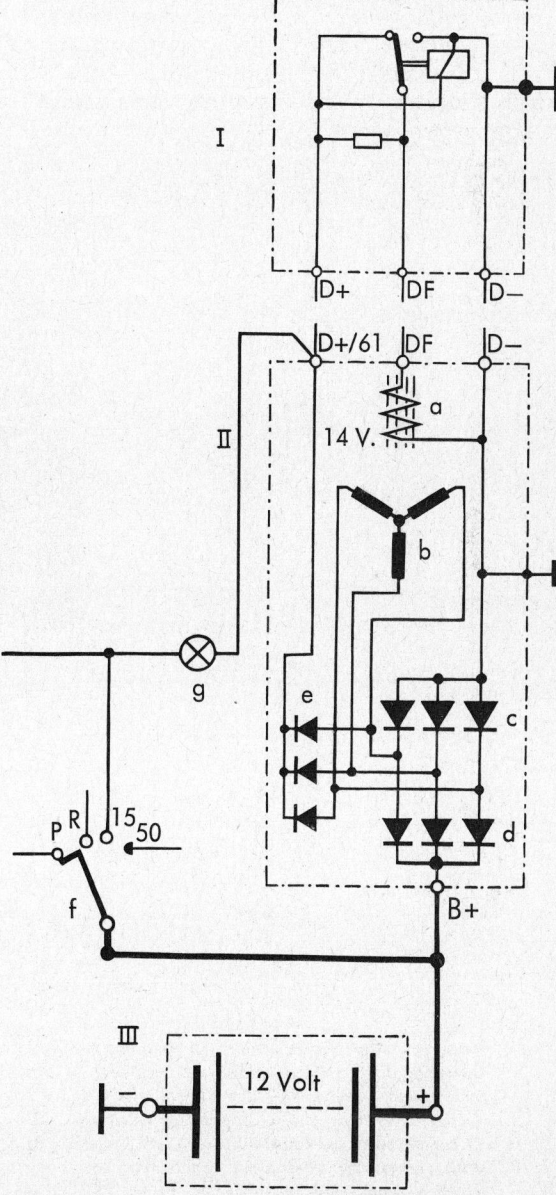

Regulator (two- contact type) (14 volt)
I Alternator (14 volt)
II Battery (12 volt)
a Claw pole rotor with exciter winding
b Stator winding (star connection)
c }
d } Rectifier (silicon diodes)
e Exciter diodes
  Ignition lock*
g Charge warning lamp (2 watt minimum)

* Terminal R on the ignition lock might also be identified with an X.

Alternator connections
D— (ground): Connection to regulator D—
DF (field entrance): Connection to regulator DF
D+/61 (exciter current): Connection to regulator D+ and warning light
B+ (current supply): Connection to battery

Alternator wiring diagram

listed in the specifications. If the readings differ, the test should be repeated with a regulator which is known to be functioning properly. If the regulator is defective, it should be replaced or returned to a dealer for service.

Starter

REMOVAL

Disconnect the battery ground lead. Remove the oil filter. *NOTE: When the oil filter is removed, a certain amount of oil will escape.* Disconnect both leads from the upper terminal of the solenoid. Remove the open cable shoe lead from the lower solenoid terminal. The screw need only be slightly opened to permit removal. Unbolt the starter from the mounting flanges and remove it forward.

INSTALLATION

Installation is the reverse of removal. Be sure that all leads are positioned correctly and are not pinched. If necessary, replace the lower mounting screw in the driving direction. Thoroughly clean the seal and oil filter sealing surface. Lightly lubricate both surfaces and tighten the oil filter to approximately 14-18 ft. lbs. Replace the oil that escaped and run the engine, checking the filter for leaks. *CAUTION: Some starters are equipped with an additional terminal (16) which is under full battery voltage, with a direct connection to the ignition coil. This connection bridges the ignition coil, series resistor creating higher ignition voltage.*

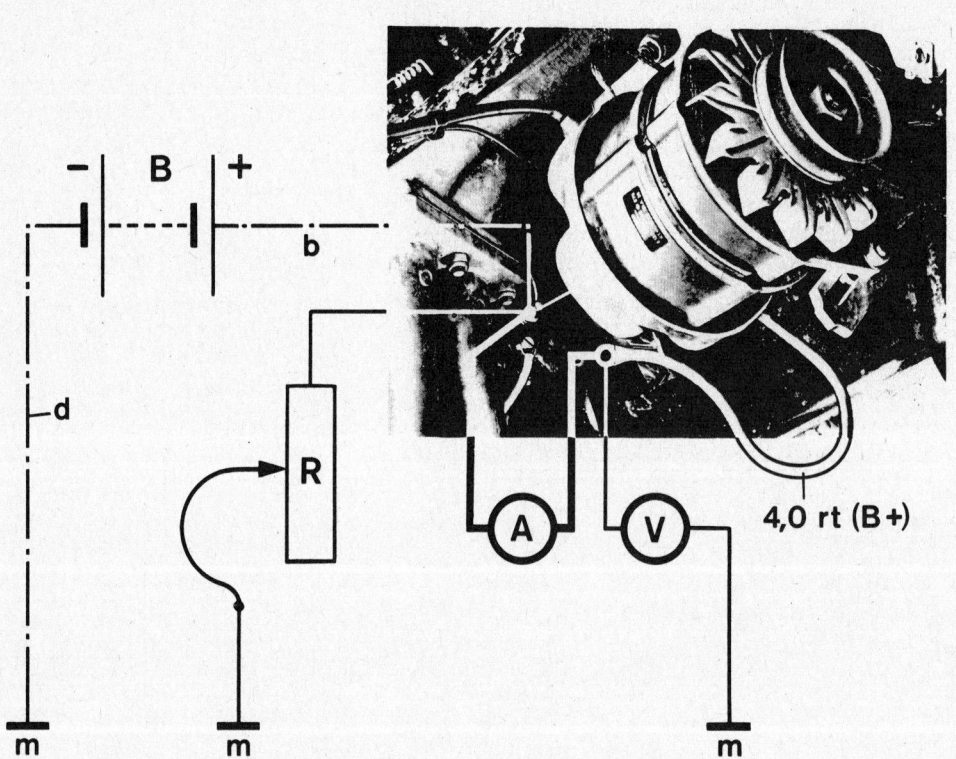

Wiring diagram for testing the regulator

A Ammeter to test loads (range: up to approx. 40 A) connected to the disconnected red lead 4.0 (B +) and starter terminal "30" or a.

V Voltmeter to test voltage (range: up to approx. 20 V) connected to red lead 4.0 (B +) and ground (m).

R Load resistor for alternators (adjustable, loads up to 40 A) connected to starter terminal "30" or a and ground.

B Battery 12 volt (located underneath rear seat).
a Starter terminal "30"
b Lead from terminal a to battery (+)
d Battery ground lead
m Ground
4.0 rt Red cable from alternator terminal B +.

Battery

The battery in the 100 LS is located under the rear seat and is accessible by lifting the front edge of the rear seat. The battery in the Super 90 is located in the engine compartment. Be sure that the terminals are clean and provide an adequate connection. The terminals should be coated (lightly) periodically with petroleum jelly.

Water should be added only to bring the solution level up to the mark, but not above.

Fuel System

Fuel Pump

100 LS

Removal

The fuel pump is located on the left side (driving direction) of the block. Loosen the hose clamps and remove the hoses. Plug both hoses. Remove the two mounting screws and remove the fuel pump.

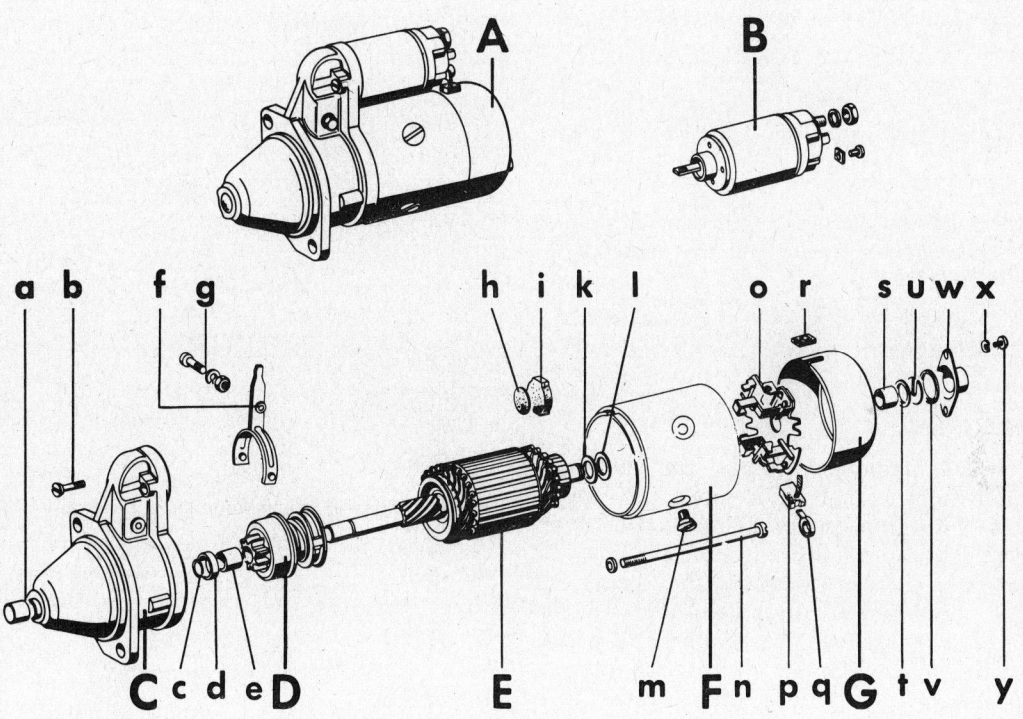

Exploded view of starter (Super 90)

A	Starter	f	Control lever	p	Carbon brush (4 req.)
B	Solenoid switch	g	Cylinder head screw with lock	q	Spring (4 req.)
C	Drive bearing		ring and hex. nut (for control	r	Rubber sleeve, cable
D	Gear ring, complete		lever)	s	Bearing bush (in commutator
E	Armature, complete	h	Plate		bearing)
F	Yoke	i	Rubber seal	t	Shim (as required 0.1, 0.2,
G	Commutator bearing	k	Washer (on armature shaft)		0.3, 0.5, 0.8 mm)
a	Bearing bush and drive bearing	l	Insulator (on armature shaft)	u	Fixing washer
b	Countersunk screw (for Solenoid	m	Countersunk screw (4 req. for	v	Rubber seal ring
	switch)		Pole shoes)	w	End cap
c	Snap-ring	n	Cylinder head screw (2 req.	x	Spring washer (domed)
d	Stop-ring		for washers)	y	Cylinder head screw
e	Bearing bush (2 required for	o	Brush holder plate		
	gear ring)				

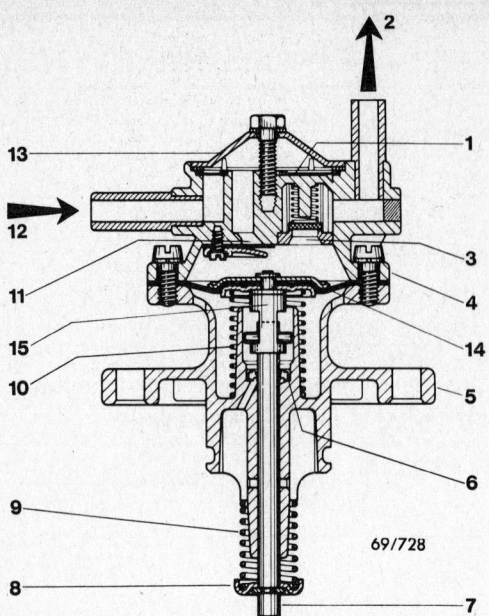

Cross-sectional view of model 100 LS fuel pump

1	Filter screen	9	Spring, pushrod
2	Fuel outlet	10	Spring, diaphragm
3	Outlet valve	11	Inlet valve
4	Pump upper half	12	Fuel intake
5	Pump lower half	13	Cover
6	Oil scraper ring	14	Diaphragm
7	Pushrod	15	Coupling
8	Spring retainer		

Disassembly

Scribe alignment marks on the fuel pump housing halves. Remove the upper half of the fuel pump. Remove the cover from the upper half and clean and inspect the filter screen. Compress the spring on the operating rod (lower half) and remove the circlip. Remove the diaphragm, pushrod and diaphragm spring from the pump lower half. Inspect the mating surfaces and diaphragm.

Assembly

Assembly procedures are the reverse of disassembly, noting the following instructions. The diaphragm must be installed between the housing halves without folds. Depress the pump pushrod when installing the upper pump half. Tighten the pump half retaining screw at 120° intervals. When assembly is complete, check the operation of the pump. Connect a hose (about 24″ long) to the pump suction intake. Place the other end of the hose in a container of gas. Hold the pump approxi-

mately 20″ higher than the gas container and build up pressure by actuating the pushrod at approximately 60 strokes per minute. The pump should begin to produce gas after about 30-40 strokes.

Installation

Installation is the reverse of removal.

SUPER 90

Removal

The fuel pump on the Super 90 model is located on the side of the block, below the carburetor. Remove the fuel supply hose from the carburetor, since access is easier here than at the pump. Remove the intake hose from the pump and the mounting bolts. The rear bolt requires an extension

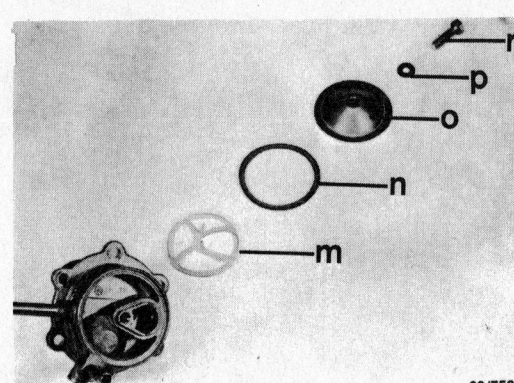

Exploded view of upper pump half (model 100 LS)

m	Filter screen	p	Seal
n	Seal	r	Hex. head screw
o	Cover		

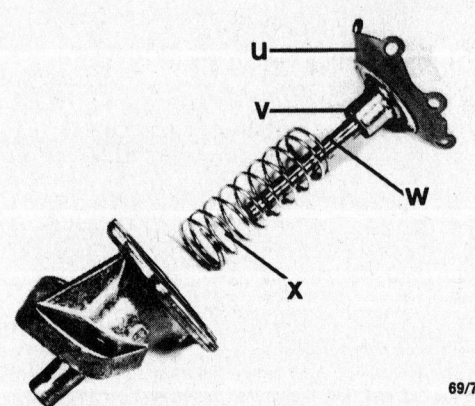

Exploded view of lower pump half (model 100 LS)

u	Diaphragm	w	Pushrod
v	Coupling	x	Diaphragm spring

and joint. Remove the oil dipstick and reach around the radiator to remove the fuel pump from the block. Be sure that no fuel spills into the engine block. Remove the fuel supply hose from the pump.

Disassembly

Clean the outside of the fuel pump and scribe alignment marks. Remove the top plate and filter components (see illustration). Separate the upper half of the pump body from the lower half. Remove the pump lever spring, the shaft circlip and the shaft. Remove the pump lever, then the pump diaphragm. Press back the holder and diaphragm spring and remove the rubber boot from the diaphragm rod.

Assembly

Assemble the pump in the reverse order of disassembly. Inspect the mating surfaces of the housing halves and the diaphragm. The diaphragm should be seated with no folds. This can be accomplished during assembly by depressing the pump lever. Tighten the upper and lower half retaining bolts at 120° intervals. The Super 90 fuel pump can be tested in the same manner as the 100 LS pump.

Installation

Installation is the reverse of removal. Rock the pump to be sure that the lever seats properly on the camshaft.

Fuel Filter

SUPER 90

Maintenance

The fuel pump does not have to be removed to clean the fuel filter. Remove the cap from the pump. Extract the filter screen from below the pump cap, being careful not to lose or damage the sealing ring. Clean the cap, screen and pump upper half. Replace the screen, sealing ring and cap.

Carburetors

REMOVAL

Solex 32/32 TDID (100 LS)

After removing the air cleaner, loosen the clamping spring on the accelerator linkage and disconnect the linkage. Be sure

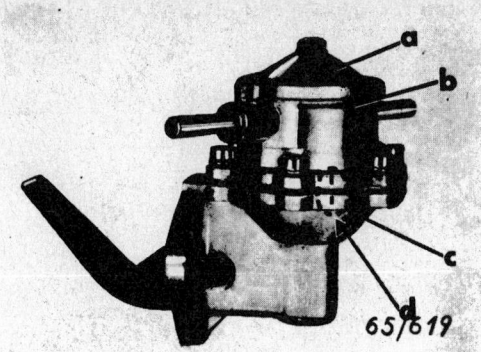

External view of Super 90 fuel pump

    a Cap, upper section
    b Pump upper section
    c Pump lower section
    d Alignment marks

Exploded view of fuel pump upper half components (Super 90)

    a Fuel pump
    b Fuel filter
    c Seal ring
    d Cap
    e Seal ring
    f Hex. head screw

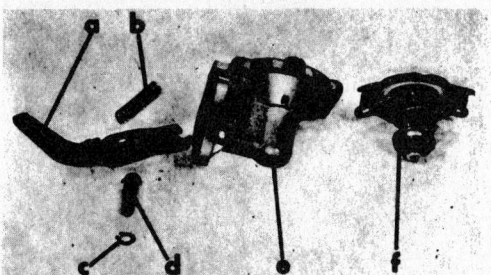

Exploded view of fuel pump lower half components (Super 90)

    a Pump lever
    b Spring
    c Retaining ring
    d Shaft
    e Pump upper section
    f Pump diaphragm, complete

69/1418

Solex 32/32 TDID carburetor components

1	Water connection, automatic choke	8	Carburetor cover
2	Retaining ring	9	Carburetor body
3	Automatic choke	10	Throttle valve
4	Choke lever	11	Atomizer retaining screw (Primary)
5	Choke connecting rod	12	Idle mixture control screw
6	Throttle lever	13	Vacuum connection
7	Idle adjusting screw—sealed with paint	14	Idle air control screw

15	Connecting rod and spring
16	Pump lever
17	Diaphragm pump
18	Idle cut-off valve—idle fuel jet
19	Fillister head cap screws, carburetor cover
20	Fuel connecting tube

Solex 32/32 TDID carburetor components

21	Throttle valve shaft (Primary)	26	Electric connection, thermo starting valve
22	Operating lever	27	Atomizer retaining screw (Secondary)
23	Connecting rod (Secondary)	28	Plug
24	Throttle valve shaft (Secondary)	29	Float chamber
25	Thermo starting valve		

30	Choke
31	Enrichment tube (Primary)
32	Enrichment tube (Secondary)
33	Interior breathing bore

Solex 32/32 TDID carburetor components

15	Connecting rod and spring	34	Stop lever, throttle valve (Secondary)
16	Pump lever	35	Pump lever, throttle valve shaft (Primary)
20	Fuel connecting tube	36	Cover, diaphragm pump

that the plastic washer is not lost. Remove the water hoses. *NOTE: When removing the carburetor from a warm engine, loosen the radiator cap to prevent loss of coolant.* Disconnect the vacuum hose and the lead to the idle cut-off valve. Disconnect the fuel supply hose. Remove the four mounting nuts and remove the carburetor.

Solex 32/32 DIDTA (Model Super 90)

Remove the air cleaner and mark the present setting of the bi-metallic spring. Remove the bi-metallic spring housing together with the clamp ring. There is no need to loosen the water hoses. Remove the clamp spring and disconnect the accelerator linkage. Disconnect the vacuum and fuel hoses and remove the carburetor from the manifold.

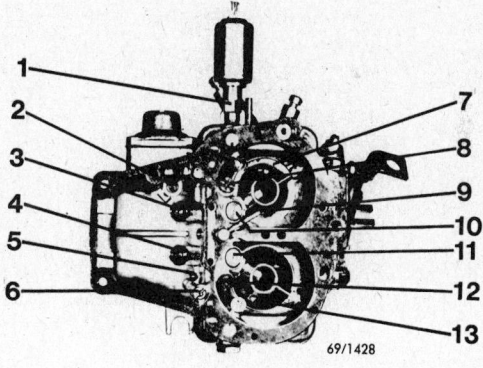

Jet location—Solex 32/32 TDID carburetor

*1	Idle fuel jet with cut-off valve
2	Check valve, diaphragm pump
*3	Main jet (Primary)
*4	Main jet (Secondary)
5	Idle reserve (Secondary)
6	Breathing jet (Secondary)
7	Venturi (Primary)
*8	Air correction jet (Primary)
9	Breathing bore (Primary)
10	Injection tube
11	Breathing bore (Secondary)
*12	Air correction jet (Secondary)
13	Venturi (Secondary)

*Jets to be checked

OVERHAUL

Carburetor repair kits are recommended for each overhaul. Carburetor repair kits are available in three stages and contain all parts and instructions necessary to service the carburetor at each stage. The following summarizes the three basic Solex repair kits.

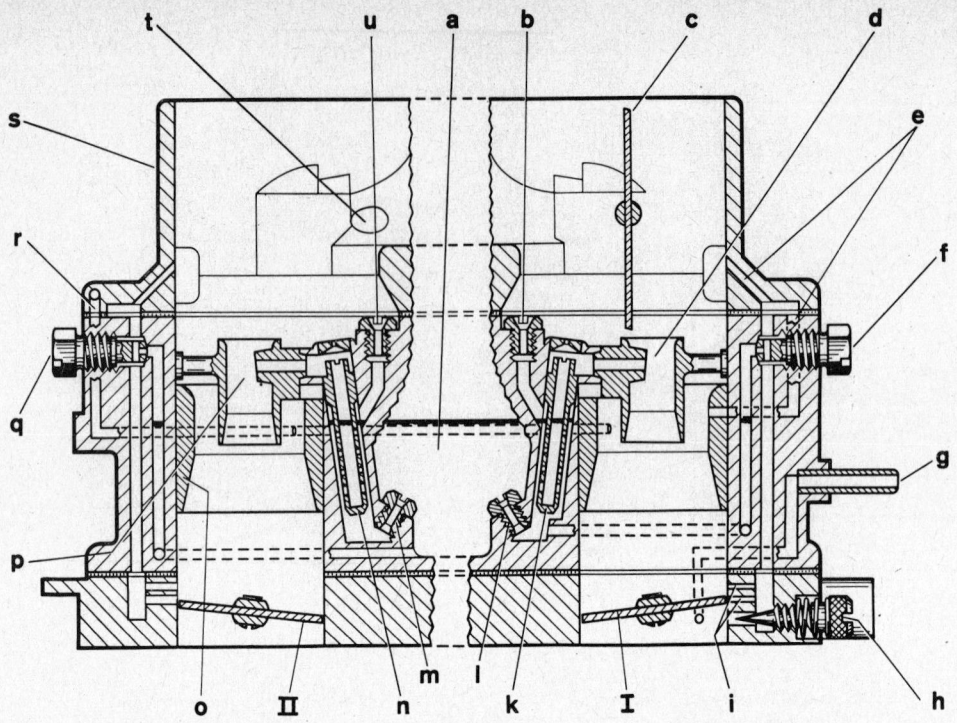

Cross-sectional view of Solex 32/32 DIDTA carburetor

I	Primary Throttle	k	Mixture tube (Primary)
II	Secondary Throttle	l	Main jet (Primary)
a	Float chamber	m	Main jet (Secondary)
b	Air correction jet (Primary)	n	Mixture tube (Secondary)
c	Choke	o	Venturi (Secondary)
d	Outlet arm with atomizer	p	Outlet arm with atomizer (Secondary)
e	Idle air bore	q	Idle jet (Secondary)
f	Idle jet (Primary)	r	Bore, vacuum unit
g	Connection tube, ignition timing	s	Carburetor cover
h	Idle mixture regulating screw	t	Breathing bore
i	Bypass bores	u	Air correction jet (Secondary)

Vit (Vitalization) kit: all gaskets, float needle valve, volume control screw, all diaphragms, spring.

Repair kits: all jets and gaskets, all diaphragms, float needle valve, volume control screw, spring for the pump diaphragm, pump ball valve, main jet carrier, float, complete intermediate rod, intermediate pump lever, complete injector tube, some cover retaining screws and washers.

Gasket kits: all necessary gaskets

When overhauling carburetors, work in a clean dust free area. Disassemble the carburetor carefully, separating similar parts to avoid confusion. Be sure to note all jet sizes. During assembly, seat all screws tightly in their seats and tighten gradually, in rotation. Needle valves should not be tightened into seats, since this will cause uneven jetting. Always use a new flange gasket. Prior to assembly, all parts, except diaphragm and electric choke units, should be cleaned in carburetor cleaner and blown dry with compressed air. Clean all small passages and inspect all points of wear. All jets and valves should be cleaned separately to avoid accidental interchange.

INSTALLATION

Solex 32/32 TDID (100 LS)

Installation is the reverse of removal. Always use a new gasket when replacing the

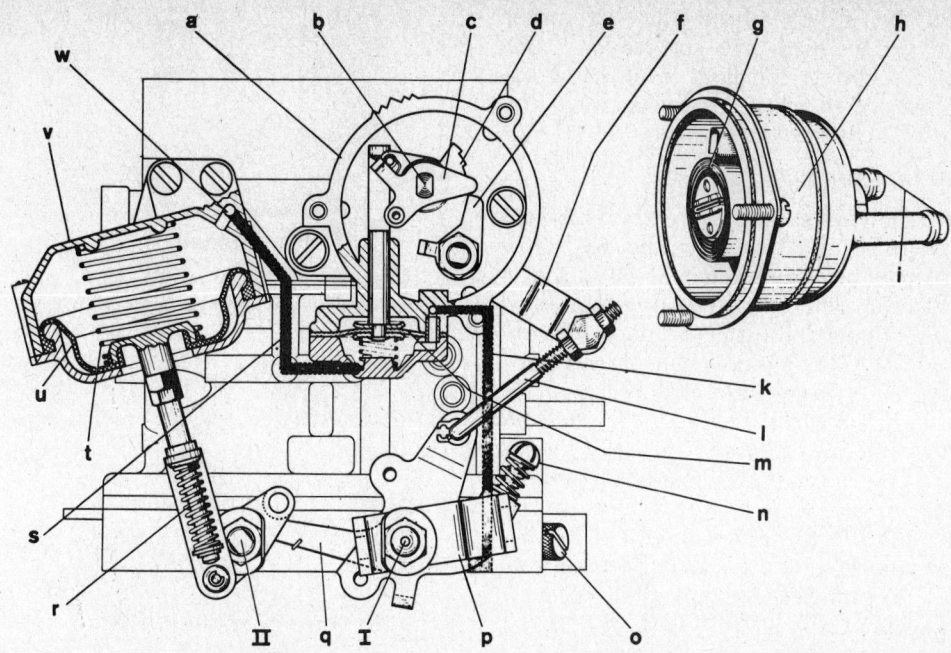

Cross-sectional view of Solex 32/32 DIDTA carburetor

I	Throttle shaft (Primary)	l	Starter rod
II	Throttle shaft (Secondary)	m	Reduction diaphragm
a	Automatic choke housing	n	Idle adjustment screw
b	Choke shaft	o	Idle mixture regulating screw
c	Catch lever	p	Throttle lever
d	Stepped washer	q	Return lever
e	Stop lever	r	Diaphragm rod (Secondary)
f	Starter lever	s	Vacuum spring
g	Bimetallic spring	t	Diaphragm spring
h	Bimetallic spring housing	u	Vacuum diaphragm
i	Warm water connection	v	Vacuum unit
k	Vacuum channel	w	Vacuum bore

carburetor and check the throttle shafts for ease of operation.

Solex 32/32 DIDTA (Super 90)

Installation is the reverse of removal, always using a new flange gasket. Check the throttle shafts for ease of operation.

ADJUSTMENTS—SOLEX 32/32 TDID

Float Level

Remove the air cleaner and disconnect the water hoses. On a warm engine, first remove the radiator cap to prevent loss of coolant. Disconnect the fuel hose. Remove the five screws securing the carburetor cover. Remove the clamping ring from the linkage, but do not loosen the hex nuts. Remove the carburetor cover. The upper edge of the float (arrow in illustration)

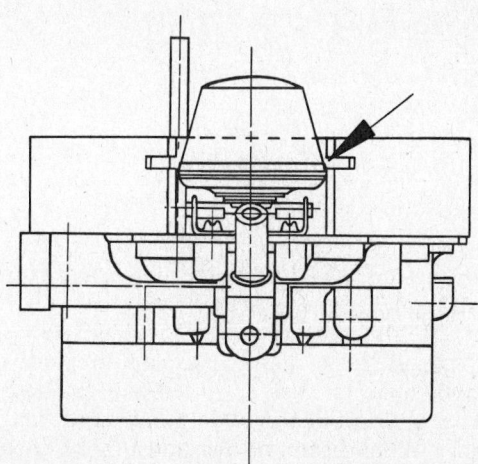

Float level is measured from the upper edge of the float bead (arrow) to carburetor flange surface.

should be .61-.63″ from the carburetor flange surface with the surface at a 45° angle. To correct the float level, bend the metal tab of the float lever. Assemble the carburetor cover to the carburetor.

Pump Injection Rate

Run the engine until the carburetor float chamber is full. Turn the idle set screw completely back and remove the carburetor. Place a container, preferably graduated in cc.'s, underneath the primary venturi. Move the throttle from off to full load position 10 times in an uninterrupted manner. *NOTE: If the carburetor cover is removed to check injection rate, the spring of the injection tube must be depressed to prevent leakage, which will greatly reduce the injection rate.* Measure the amount of fuel injected into the container. The injection rate is the amount of fuel injected divided by 10. Compare this figure with the figure listed in the specifications. There should be no play between the diaphragm and the lever, i.e., the injection process should begin as soon as the throttle lever is moved.

To increase the injection rate, place additional washers between the cotter pin and the pump lever (see illustration). To reduce the injection rate, remove washers from between the lever and the cotter pin, replacing them with thinner washers. An alternative method is to move the cotter pin further towards the outside. If the specified injection rate cannot be obtained, check the diaphragm and replace as necessary. Bend the injection tube to align the injection stream with the increasing throttle gap. *NOTE: If fuel is injected in various directions, and the vehicle runs roughly under acceleration, there is probably some foreign material in front of the jet of the injection tube. If this condition exists, the injection tube should be replaced.*

Automatic Choke

Remove the carburetor. Mark the present housing location (standard: notch a, on illustration, aligned with large tooth b). Remove the housing and bi-metallic spring. Check all the movable parts of the automatic choke for ease of operation. Clean all parts and lubricate sliding surfaces and joints. When installing the housing, be sure that the eyelet of the bi-metallic spring engages the tang above the arm of the follower.

Adjusting injection rate at the pump lever

Exploded view of diaphragm—Solex 32/32 TDID

    c   Mounting screw
    d   Pump cover
    e   Diaphragm
    f   Spring

Standard automatic choke housing location for Solex carburetor

    a   Alignment notch
    b   Large alignment tooth
    c   Mounting screws
    D   Insulator

Choke Gap

With the carburetor removed, mount the carburetor in some holding fixture, so that it is possible to operate the throttle completely. Close the choke tightly. Using a screwdriver, press the diaphragm rod downwards until it rests against the stop. At the same time, hold the choke follower against the stop in a closed position (see illustration). Check the gap between the choke and the housing wall with a drill. The measurement should be as listed in the specifications section. To correct the choke gap, bend the pin (see illustration) upwards or downwards.

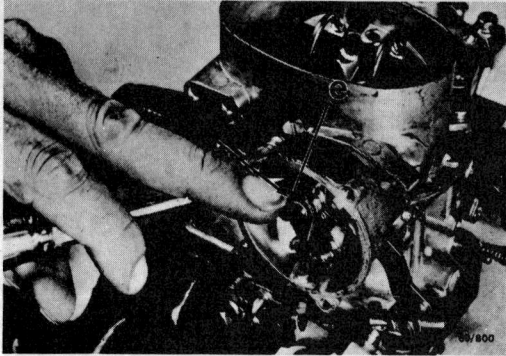

Adjusting the choke gap—Hold the follower (e) against the stop in closed position

Bend the pin (K) to correct the choke gap.

and the housing wall with a drill and compare the measurement with the specifications. Adjust the throttle gap by means of the adjusting nuts on the connecting rod.

Idle Speed

The idle adjustment should be made on an engine which has reached operating temperature (coolant temperature approximately 175°F.) with the air filter installed. The ignition system must have been previously adjusted to specifications. Set the idle speed at 950 rpm by means of the idle adjusting screw (see illustration). The CO content of the exhaust can also be adjusted at this time (see illustration).

Throttle Gap

The throttle gap is set at the factory (2.5° gap) and sealed with paint. This setting should not be disturbed. However, should the throttle gap be disturbed and require adjustment, proceed as follows.

Close the choke gap tightly. The stop lever (see illustration) should rest on the highest step of the stepped washer and hold the throttle open via the connecting rod. Check the gap between the throttle

ADJUSTMENTS—SOLEX 32/32 DIDTA

The same adjustments can be performed on the Solex 32/32 DIDTA as on the Solex 32/32 TDID and in an identical manner. See the Specifications section for differing specifications.

With the choke gap closed tightly, the stop lever (l) rests on the highest step of the stepped washer (m) and holds the throttle open by means of connecting rod (n). The throttle can be corrected by means of adjusting nuts (p).

Adjust the idle speed by means of idle adjusting screw (E). The CO content can be adjusted by means of volume regulating screw (R).

Exhaust System

Super 90 and 100 LS

REMOVAL

Front Exhaust Pipe

Loosen the clip at the primary muffler and remove the flange at the exhaust manifold. Remove the front exhaust pipe.

Primary Muffler and Pipe

Loosen the clamp at the muffler intake. Disconnect the rubber damping loop at the muffler. Remove the primary muffler and pipe.

Tailpipe

Loosen the clamp at the final muffler outlet, disconnect the retaining straps from the tailpipe and remove the tailpipe.

Final Muffler

Disconnect both straps retaining the final muffler and remove the muffler.

When installing the exhaust system, be sure that rubber pad (f) is in position.

INSTALLATION

Install the exhaust system components, reversing the removal procedure. When installing the flange use a new gasket. Tighten the Thermag nuts one after the other, in steps. When installing the tailpipe, be sure that the rubber pad (see illustration) is in position. The pad prevents the tailpipe from contacting the body. Always install the system with new clamps.

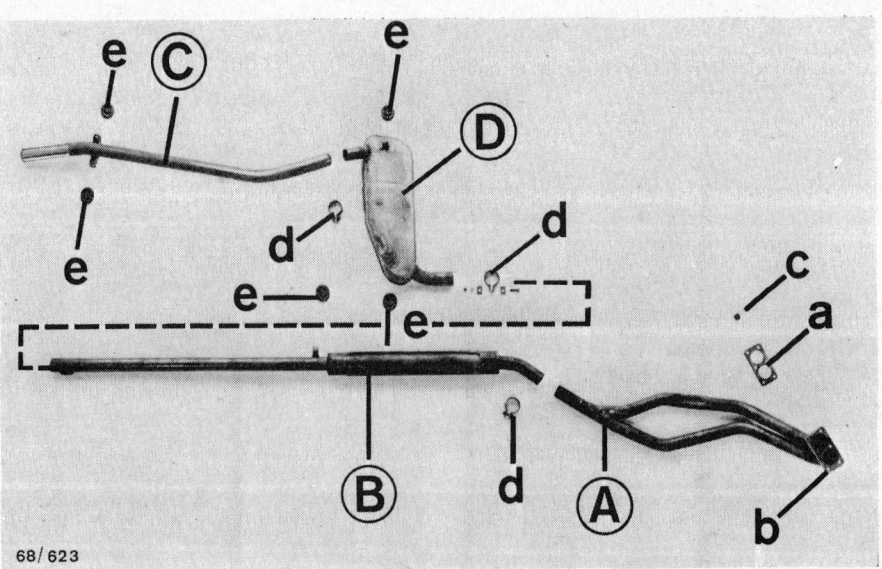

68/623

Exhaust system exploded view

A   Exhaust pipe, front   a   Gasket
B   Primary muffler with pipe   b   Flange
C   Tailpipe   c   Thermag nuts
D   Final muffler   d   Clip with washers, screw, washer and nut
                                    e   Retaining strap

Cooling System

100 LS

RADIATOR

Removal

Allow the engine to cool and carefully remove the radiator cap. Drain the coolant from the engine and radiator. To drain the coolant, place the center heater control lever at the center position (red point). Open the breather plug located on the top radiator hose near the firewall (see illustration). Unscrew the drain plug at the bottom of the radiator. Always use a socket wrench to tighten or remove the plug. Remove the upper coolant hose from the radiator. Detach the mounting strut from the radiator, and swing it forward. Remove the lower coolant hose and unscrew the nut

Remove the water pump pulley with 2 screwdrivers

to release the rubber mounting damper at the rear of the radiator. Do not lose the washer and spring washer. Another rubber damper is located on the right side (as seen in the driving direction) of the radiator and must be removed. Lift out the radiator and cowl. If desired, the cowl can be removed from the radiator by removing the six screws which retain the cowl. When installing the cowl, make sure that the sealing strips are pasted in position (with rubber cement, if necessary).

Installation

Install the radiator and cowl assembly in the reverse of removal. After installing the radiator, be sure that the rubber fan cover rests against the cowl around its complete circumference.

WATER PUMP

Removal

Drain the coolant from the engine. Remove the alternator pulley. Remove the nut from the front of the mounting plate and push the screw towards the rear. Loosen the clamp and pull the lower hose from the water pump. Remove the thermostat (see Thermostat Removal). Unscrew the pulley mounting screws holding the pulley with a screwdriver as illustrated. Remove the pulley using two screwdrivers 180° apart to pry it from the hub. Remove the remaining hose from the pump. Unbolt the mounting plate and remove the mounting plate and water pump.

Disassembly

Audi service procedures do not recommend disassembly of the water pump, due to intricate adjustments and close tolerances.

Open the breather plug (c) to drain the radiator

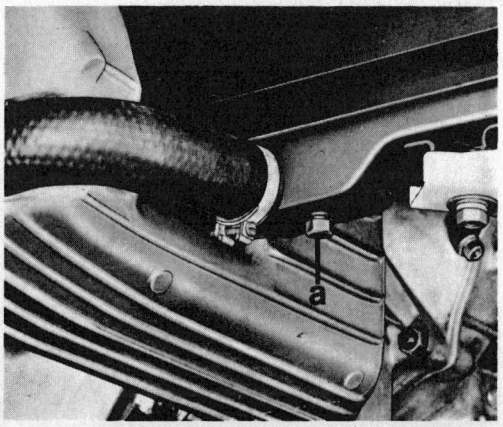

Audi 100 LS drain plug (a) at bottom of radiator

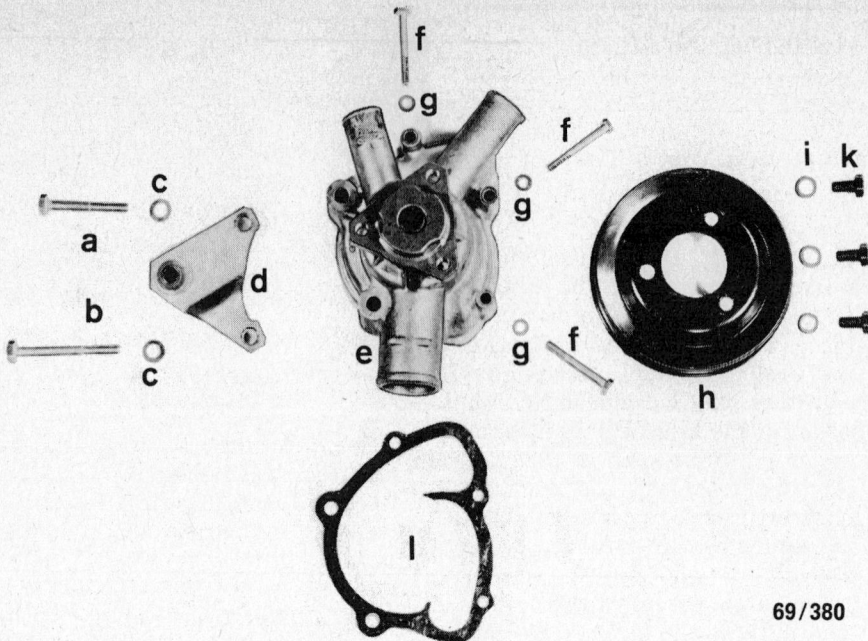

69/380

Exploded view of Audi 100 LS water pump

a	Hex. head screw	e	Water pump	i	Spring washer
b	Hex. head screw	f	Hex. head screw	k	Hex. head screw
c	Spring washer	g	Spring washer	l	Water pump gasket
d	Mounting plate, alternator	h	Pulley		

Installation

To install the water pump, reverse the removal procedures, using new seals and gaskets.

69/379

Installed position of Audi 100 LS thermostat (d)

THERMOSTAT

Removal

Remove the two mounting screws, spring washers, cover and seal. Remove the thermostat. Should it be necessary to replace the complete thermostat, loosen the clamp on the hose leading from the thermostat to the water pump. Remove the retaining screws and remove the thermostat and housing.

Installation

Installation is the reverse of removal. Always use a new gasket and install the thermostat as illustrated.

Super 90

RADIATOR

Removal

Drain the coolant from the radiator and engine. Place the center heater lever at the warm position. Remove the radiator cap and remove the drain plug from the radiator. In addition, remove the drain plug from the engine block. Drain the remaining

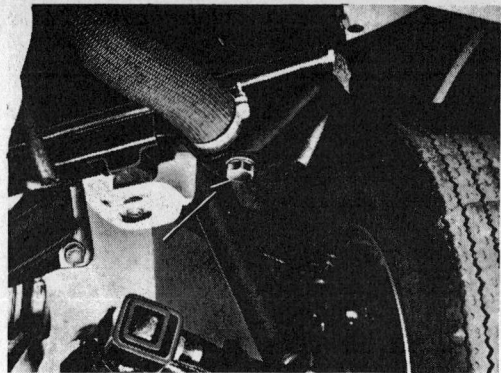

Audi Super 90 drain plug at bottom of radiator (arrow)

coolant from the heater inside the car. Remove the upper and lower hoses from the radiator. Unscrew the mounting nuts (on the right side and behind the radiator) and remove the radiator downwards. If desired, remove the cowl by removing the mounting screws along the side of the radiator.

Installation

To install the radiator, reverse the removal procedures. The gasket between the cowl and radiator must seal the crack completely. Use a rubber cement to paste down the upper and lower gaskets. After installation, be sure that the rubber fan ring is positioned flat around the cowl. It must not be pulled over the front edge of the cowl or it will be damaged by engine vibration.

THERMOSTAT

Removal

Remove the air filter and drain the coolant from the engine. Remove the housing

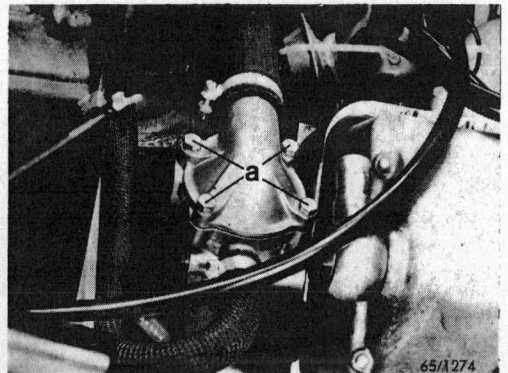

Remove mounting screws (a) and thermostat housing

cover and pull the thermostat from the housing. Check the thermostat by putting it in water and heating the water. The thermostat must open at 174°-181° F. (189° F. for a winter thermostat).

Installation

Installation is the reverse of removal. The thermostat must be installed with the arrow facing the projection of the thermostat housing.

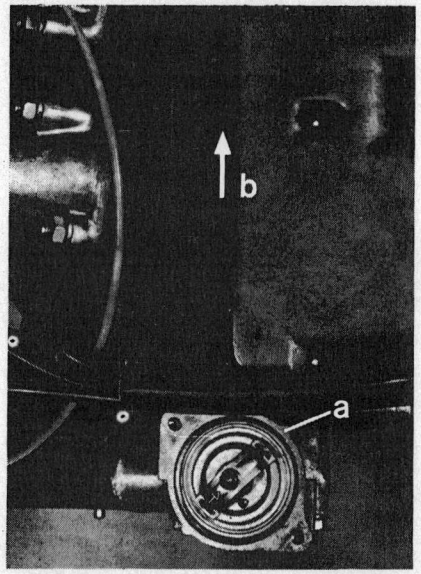

As seen in driving direction (b), align the arrow on the thermostat with the projection (a) on the housing.

WATER PUMP

Removal

From below the car, remove the mounting bolts and detach the V-belt. Drain the coolant and remove the bolt between the two water hoses. Disconnect the water hoses and remove the pump.

Disassembly

Remove the bearing housing. Press the shaft (and bearings) out of the pulley and bearing housing. Press the shaft from the impeller wheel. Be sure that the pump bearings rotate easily. Lift the counter ring from the impeller wheel. Clean all components.

Assembly

Coat the entire surface of the counter ring with glycerine and install it with the

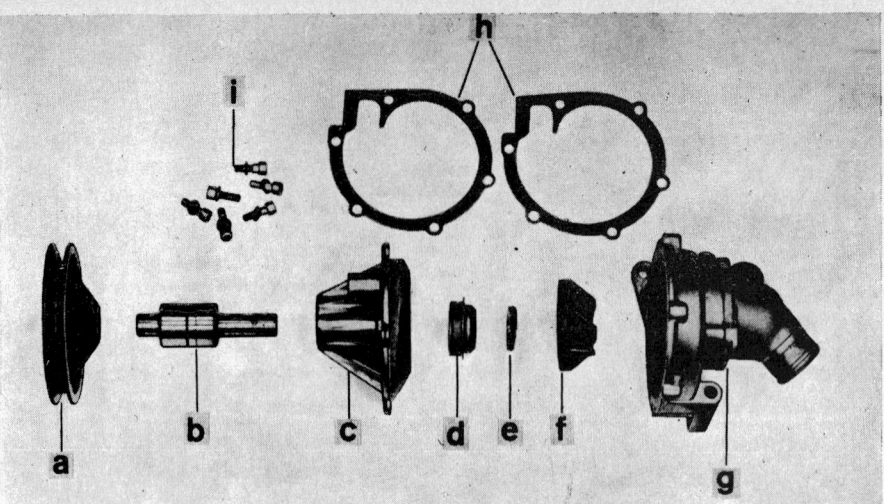

Exploded view of Audi Super 90 water pump

a	Pulley	f	Impeller wheel
b	Water pump bearing with shaft	g	Water pump housing (front and rear sections)
c	Bearing housing	h	Gasket (2 req.)
d	Sliding seal ring	i	Mounting screws
e	Counter ring with rubber ring		

chambered end first. The machined surface must contact the seal ring. Press the counter ring into the impeller wheel by hand, being careful not to damage the rubber ring. Lightly coat the surface of the pump bearing with liquid sealant. Press the bearing into the housing until the bearing is flush with the housing. Press the sliding seal ring into the housing. Press the pulley on the shaft until the pulley hub and shaft are flush. Check the pulley for easy rotation. Place two gaskets between the bearing housing and the water pump housing and tighten the housing. Again be sure that the pulley turns easily.

Installation

Be sure that the sealing surface of the gasket is clean. Install the water pump, reversing the removal operations. Tension the V-belt and tighten the two mounting screws from beneath the car.

Engine

Exhaust Emission Control

The Audi 100 LS and the Super 90 use an identical system to control exhaust emissions. The system is contained in four parts; a triple port intake manifold, an air filter with a flap in the intake to allow self-contained crankcase breathing, a twin box distributor and a heating and cooling circuit to preheat the intake manifold.

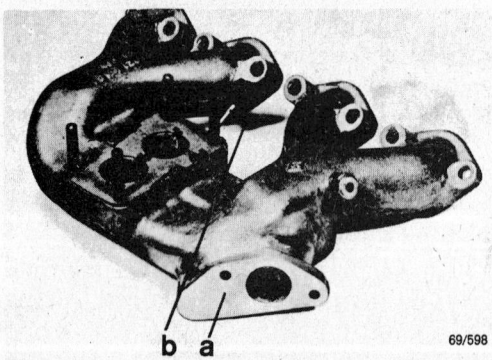

Triple port intake manifold showing thermostat flange (a) and vacuum tube to distributor (b)

The triple port intake manifold is equipped with a separate intake for water, used to preheat the manifold. The preheating and the conduction of the fuel/air ratio from each stage separately, close to the manifold, leads to a more complete combustion and a lower CO content in the exhaust. *NOTE: The primary port of the intake manifold is not circular. Under no circumstances should the gasket be cut to agree with the shape of the gas port.*

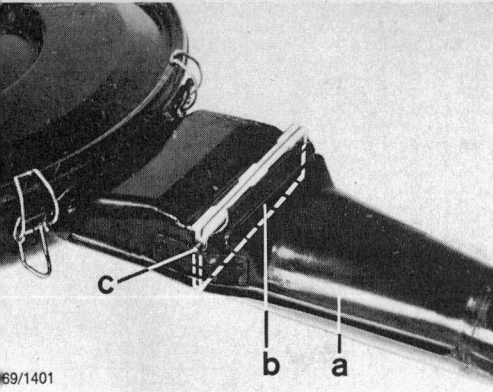

69/1401

Air filter with exhaust emission control equipment

a   Air cleaner inlet
b   Flap, air cleaner inlet
c   Holder and shaft, flap

An oil separator in the cylinder head and a hose between the cylinder head cover and the air filter provide for crankcase breathing. Exhaust gasses and oil vapors are returned to the engine via the air filter and carburetor. A flap (see illustration) in the air filter intake is provided to ensure sufficient vacuum in the air filter and the crankcase. This flap blocks the air intake at idle or low speeds to guarantee suction of vapors from the crankcase and cylinder head. The flap should be checked by hand at its shaft end. The flap must turn easily and should be cleaned and lightly oiled periodically.

The twin box distributor incorporates both centrifugal and vacuum advance mechanisms to assure constant operation of the early ignition control and correct idle speeds. *NOTE: When adjusting the early ignition timing, remove hoses EC and RI (see illustration). When setting the idle speed connect both hoses. These hoses must never be confused.*

The cooling and heating system is designed so that the engine reaches proper operating temperature in a short period of time, ensuring intensive preheating of the intake manifold. The engine should be allowed to run for a short time in winter, before turning the heater on. This will allow the engine to reach operating temperature as quickly as possible.

ADJUSTMENTS

Idle and CO Content

Idle and CO content settings should be made on a warm engine. With the air filter

69/607

Vacuum hoses leading from the distributor

EC   Vacuum connection for early ignition at carburetor
RI   Vacuum connection for retarded ignition at intake manifold

0/88

Basic adjustment screw locations on Solex 32/32 TDID carburetor

1   Intake manifold
2   "Retarded ignition" vacuum connection to intake manifold
3   Idle mixture control screw
4   Idle air control screw
5   "Advanced ignition" vacuum connection to carburetor
6   Idle fuel jet with cut-off valve
7   Idle adjusting screw

installed, remove both vacuum hoses at the distributor. Be sure that the idle cut-off valve and the thermal starting valve are connected and working. Check the ignition timing (see specifications) and adjust if necessary. Replace the vacuum hoses (the

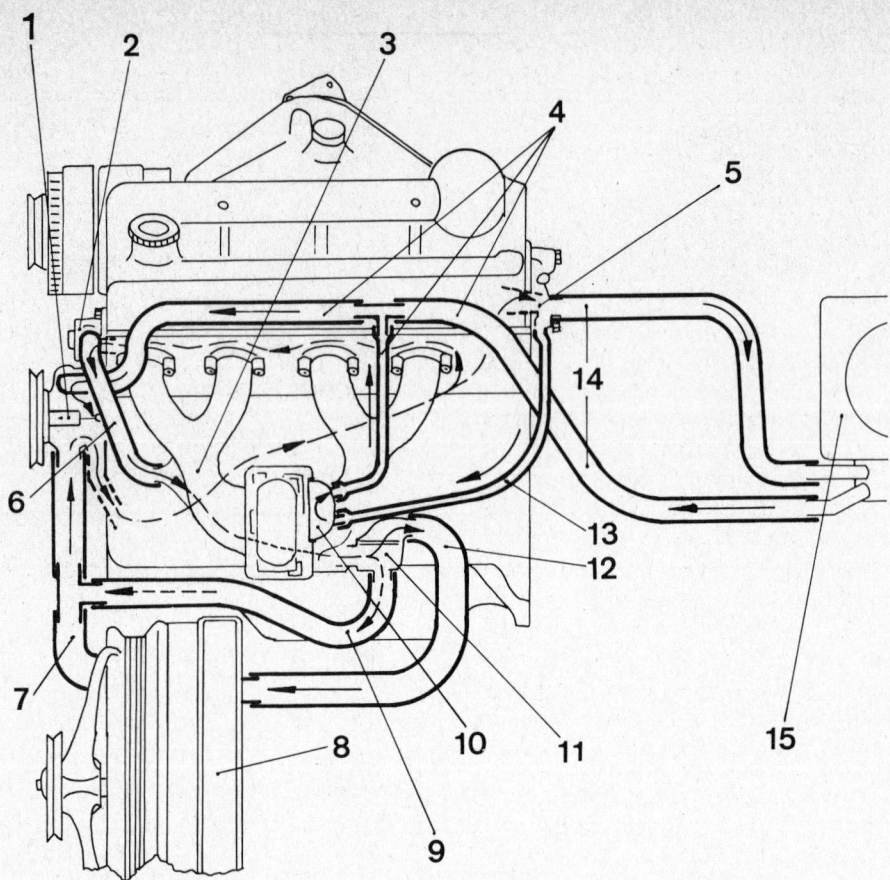

Cooling and heating circuits

1 Water pump	9 Bypass line from intake manifold to water pump
2 Flange, front of cylinder head	10 Preheating, automatic choke
3 Triple port intake manifold	11 Thermostat, intake manifold
4 Return line, heater and automatic choke	12 Radiator circuit
5 Flange, rear of cylinder head	13 Automatic choke circuit
6 Connecting line to intake manifold	14 Heater circuit
7 Radiator circuit from radiator to water pump	15 Heat exchanger, heater
8 Radiator and fan (or electric fan)	

hose from the carburetor connects to the plastic tube and the hose from the intake manifold connects to the metal tube). These hoses should not be confused or an extremely high engine speed will result. Connect a CO analyzer in addition to the tachometer. With the air filter installed, adjust the idle with a long screwdriver. Turn the idle air control screw all the way in, then back it off ½ plus ⅛ turn until the engine idles at approximately 950 rpm. The CO content should be adjusted at the idle mixture screw (1 ± 0.2% by volume). After these adjustments, set the ignition timing at 9° BTDC with both vacuum hoses connected. A final idle setting can be obtained by carefully turning the idle air control

screw. *NOTE: The following may be used to make a final adjustment.*

A. *rpm too high, CO too high—Tighten idle mixture screw*

B. *rpm too high, CO too low—Tighten idle air screw*

C. *rpm too low, CO too high—Loosen idle air screw*

D. *rpm too low, CO too low—Loosen idle mixture and idle air screws*

100 LS

REMOVAL

The transmission and engine must be removed from the car as a unit. Remove the engine hood (only if using a hoist to remove the engine). Unbolt and remove the apron just below the front bumper. Remove the negative connection from the battery. Remove the air filter and carburetor breather hose at the air filter. Drain the coolant and disconnect all hoses between the radiator and engine and the heater and engine. Disconnect the fuel hose at the fuel pump and plug the end of the line. Remove the power brake unit vacuum hose at the intake manifold (if installed). Disconnect the speedometer cable at the transmission, the clutch cable at the mount and the gearshift linkage at the transmission. Disconnect the accelerator linkage at the carburetor, mounting point and connecting rod and remove the throttle shaft. Separate the brake line at the mount and plug the line to prevent loss of fluid. Remove the guard plate from the right engine mount. Disconnect the following electrical wiring from the engine and transmission: ignition leads, idle cut-off valve (if installed), thermostat, four plug pole of regulator, oil pressure switch, starter connections, reverse light switch and ground leads.

Remove the radiator and the fan support together with the fan and stop pad. *NOTE: This operation is only necessary if working with a frame contact hoist or in a pit where the opening in the pit is not large enough to permit lowering the engine with the fan attached. If the opening is large enough, unscrew the stop only.* Remove the front exhaust pipe at the exhaust manifold and at the primary muffler. Unbolt the driveshaft flange at the brake discs. Do not lose the thin insulator from

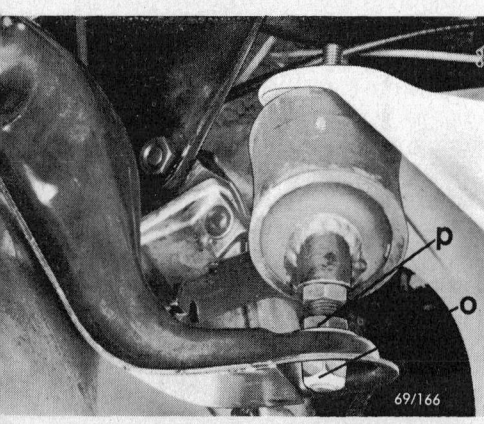

Unscrew the retaining nut (o) from left engine/transmission mount. Do not alter the position of counternut (p).

between the brake disc and the flange. Turn the driveshaft flange slightly in the direction of the wheel and wire it to the upper wishbone. Detach the stabilizer from the lower wishbone, left and right. Position the jack or lifting apparatus and lift the weight from the engine mounts. Remove the bolts retaining the rear cross-member to the body. Remove the retaining nut at the right engine/transmission mount. *Note the position of the washers and sleeve on the right engine/transmission mount.* Remove the retaining nut from the left engine/transmission mount, but do not move the position of the counternut. Remove the engine/transmission unit from the car.

Disassembly

Remove the following external engine attachments: alternator, distributor, carburetor, fuel pump, thermostat, water pump and starter.

Clutch

Remove the transmission from the engine. Mark the location of the clutch with relation to the flywheel (white paint is suitable) since they have been mutually balanced. Hold the flywheel and remove the clutch mounting screws evenly at 120° intervals. Remove the pressure plate and clutch disc.

Exhaust Manifold

Mount the engine on a stand or similar holding fixture. Remove the plate covering the manifold and the eight manifold retaining bolts. Remove the manifold from the cylinder head.

Intake Manifold

Remove the manifold support from beneath the manifold. Unbolt the retaining bolts and remove the manifold.

Cylinder Head

The cylinder head should be removed when the engine has cooled sufficiently to prevent the cylinder head from warping when removed. Remove the rocker arm adjusting nuts and the rocker arms from the studs. Be sure to remove the bearing segments also. Remove the pushrods from their bores, being careful to keep them in the proper order for assembly. Remove the cylinder head bolts in the sequence used for tightening. Remove the cylinder head

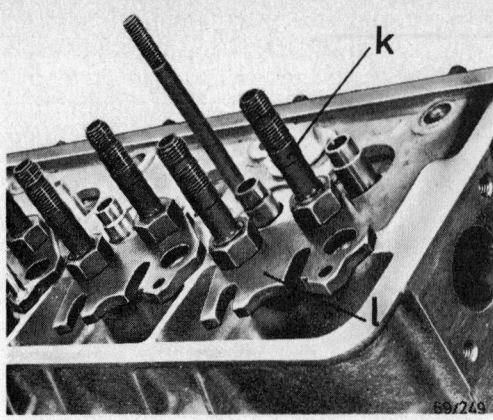

Remove the pushrod guides (l) and the rocker arm studs (k) in emergency cases only.

and place it on a smooth flat surface to avoid scratching the machined finish. Remove the pushrod tappets from their bores in the engine block. The tappets should be identified in some manner, so that they may be installed in the original bore. If further disassembly of the cylinder head is desired, see the Engine Rebuilding section. *NOTE: If the cylinder head is to be disassembled, the rocker arm studs and pushrod guides should not be removed, except in emergency cases. The guides must be aligned in such a manner that the pushrods do not contact the guides.*

Use a Phillips screwdriver to prevent the plunger from springing out of the chain tensioner.

Engine Block and Drive Assembly

Remove the oil pan. Prevent the crankshaft from turning and remove the large retaining nut from the crankshaft pulley. Care should be exercised, since this nut is under a great deal of torque. It may be necessary to tap the pulley lightly with a plastic hammer when removing it. Unbolt and remove the timing chain cover. Bend open the lockplate and remove the hydraulic timing chain tensioner plug. Use a Phillips screwdriver to prevent the plunger from springing out by turning the screwdriver to the left as illustrated. Remove the chain tensioner and unbolt the guide rail. Unbolt the camshaft sprocket and remove the sprocket along with the timing chain.

Scribe alignment marks on the flywheel and crankshaft flange (arrow) before removing flywheel. Prevent the flywheel from turning with some type of counter holder (g).

Scribe alignment marks on the flywheel and crankshaft flange (the two have been balanced together). Hold the flywheel from turning and unbolt the flywheel and remove. Extract the transmission guide bearing from the crankshaft. Remove the oil line from the oil pump and the connection on the opposite side of the block. Remove the oil pump from its mounting. *NOTE: Do not lose the spacer located under the retaining bolt.* Unbolt the connecting rod bearing caps and lay them aside in the proper order. Remove the bearing shells and arrange them in order to assure proper installation in their original position. Push the connecting rods and pistons from the cylinders toward the head side. Arrange these so they will be installed

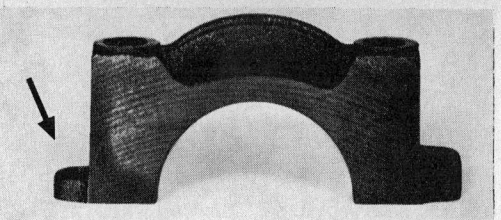

The dowel pin boss of bearing cap no. 4 (oil pump side) is weaker than all other bearing cap bosses.

Do not lose the spacer (l) under the oil pump retaining bolt.

c	Oil pump mounting screw	i	Oil line
d	Oil line mounting screw	l	Spacer
e	Washer	k	Oil pump

in the cylinder from which they were removed. Remove the main bearing caps and bearing shells, arranging these in proper installation order. *NOTE: The dowel pin boss of bearing cap no. 4 (numbered from the front of the engine) is weaker than the dowel pin bosses of all other bearing caps. Extreme care must be taken during assembly to prevent breaking this boss. If this boss is broken the complete engine block must be replaced, since the bearing caps and block are machined together. Bearing caps are not replaceable separately, nor are the corresponding engine blocks. These engine blocks cannot be repaired even at the factory.* Carefully remove the crankshaft from the block. Be sure that no bearing shells stick to the crankshaft, since they could fall and be damaged. Before laying the crankshaft aside, wrap some protective covering around the sealing ring surface to prevent damage. Remove the bearing shells from the block. Remove the oil pressure valve. Unbolt and remove the camshaft guide flange. Pull the camshaft from the engine block. Be careful not to damage the bearing bushings in the block by knocking the camshaft against them.

See the Engine Rebuilding section for any service or replacement to be performed at this point.

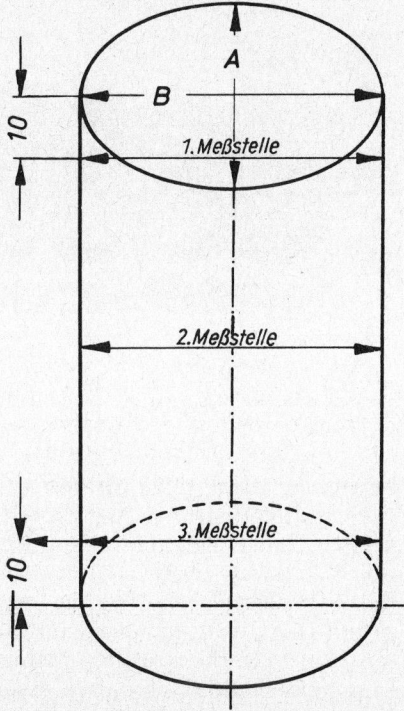

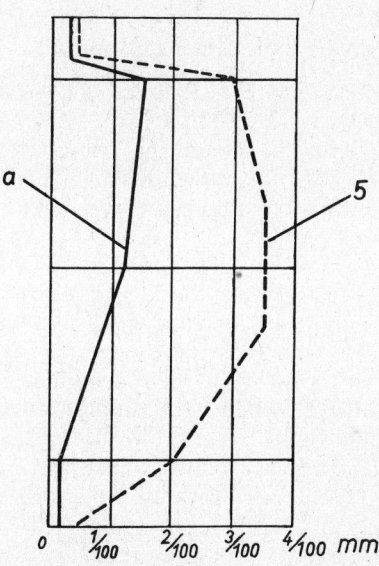

a   normal wear
5   premature wear due to improper lubrication
Meßstelle   check point

Cylinder gauging points and degree of wear chart.

100 LS connecting rod weight class is stamped on the bearing cap (arrow). See chart for weight class identification.

Install the bearing shells in the block.

Connecting Rod Weight Classification 100 LS

Group No.	Weight in Grams
0	815–822
1	823–830
2	831–838
3	839–846
4	847–854
5	855–863
6	–
7	864–871*
8	872–879*
9	880–887*
10	888–895
11	896–903

* Weight class of most connecting rods.

ASSEMBLY

All engine parts should be thoroughly cleaned. Always use new gaskets, seals, locknuts, lockplates and items of similar use. Identical parts of which more than one are installed in an engine (connecting rods, pistons, valves, tappets, pushrods, bearing caps, etc.), are to be installed in their original location when reused. All engines overhauled, or those which have ground cylinders, should be filled with running-in oil and equipped with a run-in oil filter. Consult the chart following Assembly procedures or the Specifications for torque figures.

Install the oil pressure relief valve. Lightly oil the bearing surfaces of the camshaft and carefully guide the camshaft into the block. For a new camshaft, apply molybdenum disulphide to the bearing sur-

faces. Install the camshaft flange. Slide the camshaft sprocket over the pin and tighten the stretch-bolt until the sprocket rests against the flange. Check the camshaft end-play and replace the camshaft flange if the end-play exceeds .004". Install the main and thrust bearing shell halves in the block. Note the end with the projection. Old bearing shells may be replaced in their original positions. If one bearing shell is replaced, however, all must be replaced. Lightly oil the bearing shells and the crankshaft bearing journals and carefully replace the crankshaft in the block. Replace bearing caps and shells and position the bearing caps in order (numbered 1-5),

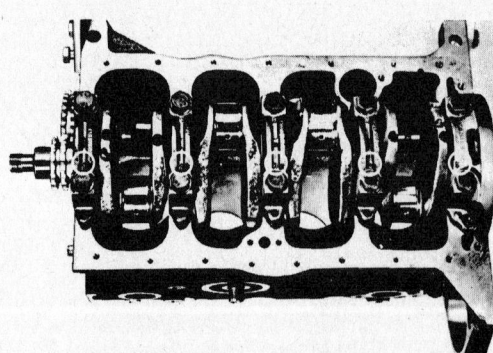

Position the bearing caps in order (numbered 1-5), beginning at the front of the engine.

beginning at the front of the engine. Slide the crankshaft sealing ring onto the crankshaft by hand with the sealing lip towards the crankshaft. Drive the shaft seal up to the stop. Torque the bearing caps. If the piston rings were removed, install the piston rings with the word top facing up. The ring gaps should oppose each other as illustrated. If the wrist pins were removed, they may be installed by heating the piston to

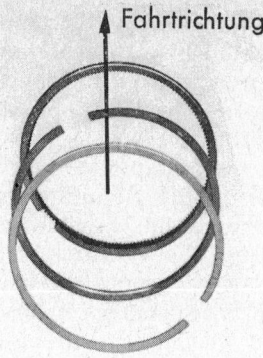

Fahrtrichtung

Piston ring gaps should oppose each other.

approximately 140°F. Lock the wrist pins in place with the wire snaprings. Lightly coat the cylinders with oil. Slide the piston and connecting rod assembly into the proper cylinder from the cylinder head side. Cylinder No. 1 is the front cylinder and the groove in the connecting rod must face towards the camshaft. Install the connecting rod bearing shells and torque the connecting rod bolts. *NOTE: Always use new connecting rod bolts when the engine has been disassembled.* Heat the crankshaft gear to approximately 140°F. Slide the gear on the crankshaft and align with the Woodruff key. Check the end-play (distance between the crankshaft and camshaft gear teeth and the face side of the engine block). Replace the sprockets or gears if the difference between both distances exceeds .02". Secure the guide rail to the block (using a new lockplate). Remove the camshaft sprocket mounting screws (this is necessary to install the timing chain and adjust the valve timing). Turn the camshaft until the punched tooth in the cam-

shaft sprocket aligns with the notch in the guide rail (see illustration). Carefully remove the camshaft sprocket. Do not turn the camshaft while removing the sprocket. Rotate the crankshaft until No. 1 piston is at exactly Top Dead Center. Place the timing chain over the crankshaft gear and insert the camshaft sprocket into the chain so that the camshaft sprocket can be installed with the punched tooth aligned with the notch in the guide rail. *NOTE: During this entire operation, the camshaft or crankshaft may not be turned.* Only timing chains with straight links (see illustration) are to be installed. Never install a chain with indented links. Turn the oil pump until the wide segment of the oil pump driveshaft faces forward (driving direction). Turn the wide segment approximately 15° counterclockwise, and slide the oil pump shaft into the gear teeth of the camshaft. The shaft should rotate slightly. It is important that the No. 1 cylinder be at Top Dead Center and the timing notches aligned when installing the oil pump. Install the spacer

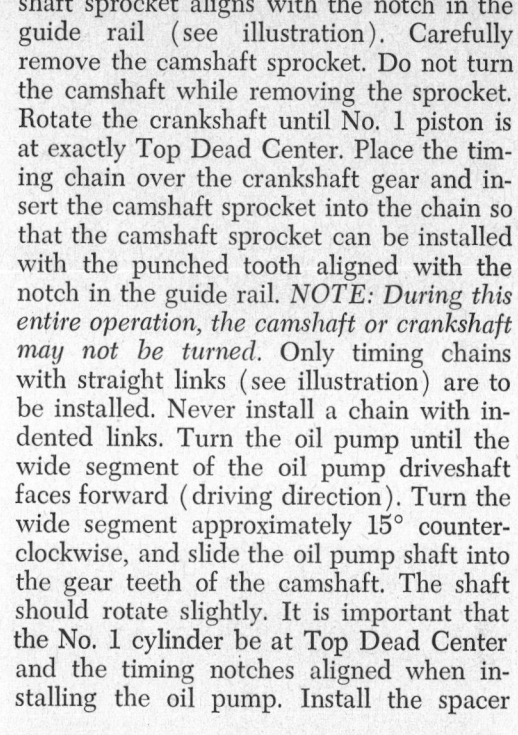

Install the timing chain and camshaft sprocket so that the dot on the camshaft sprocket (arrow) aligns with the notch (arrow) in the guide rail.

Install guide rail (f) and retain with bolts (h) and lockplate (g).

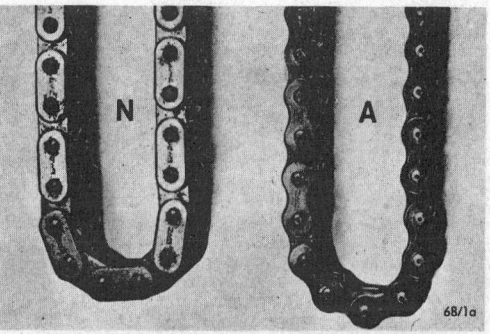

Always install timing chains with straight links (N). Never install chains with indented links (A).

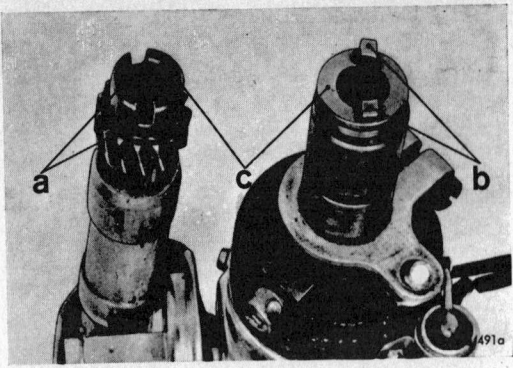

Both slots (a) in the oil pump driveshaft are off-center, as are projections (b) of the distributor driveshaft. Note the wide segment (c) on each shaft.

Turn the oil pump shaft until the wide segment (c) faces forward, as seen in the driving direction. Before installing the pump, turn the shaft approximately 15°, counterclockwise. When the shaft engages the pump it will turn slightly.

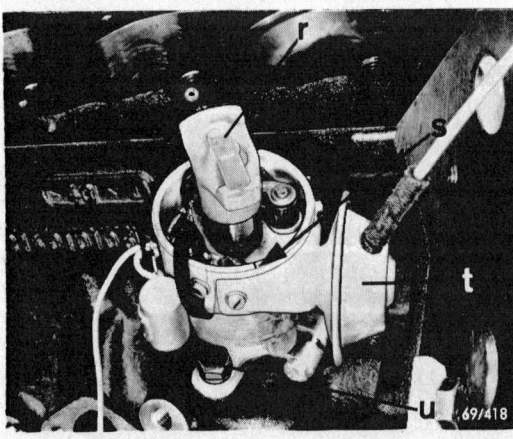

Align the distributor rotor (r) with the notch (s) in the distributor casing. Be sure the vacuum unit (t) is approximately parallel to the engine block, facing the rear. Secure the distributor with bolt (u).

under the mounting bolt and tighten slightly. Install the oil pressure line (there must be no tension on the line). Insert as many seals as necessary and turn the pump slightly to assure a tension free installation. Tighten the oil pump mounting screws and the oil pressure line mounting screws. Align the distributor rotor with the notch in the casing. Insert the distributor so that the vacuum unit is approximately parallel to the engine block and points to the rear of the engine (as seen in driving direction). When installing the distributor, turn the rotor slightly right and left, to allow the distributor shaft projections to engage the oil pump slots. Tighten the distributor mounting bolt. Check the timing. It is correct if:

A. Piston No. 1 is at Top Dead Center
B. The punched tooth of the camshaft sprocket is aligned with the notch in the guide rail
C. The distributor rotor arm is positioned above the notch in the distributor casing.

Lightly oil the valve tappets and place them in their original bores in the engine block. Place a new cylinder head gasket in position and install the cylinder head. Lubricate the cylinder head bolts with graphite before installation. Torque the bolts to specifications. Replace the pushrods in their respective bores and install the rocker arms. The rocker arm mounting screws and adjusting nuts should be coated with molybdenum disulphide. *NOTE: To prevent scoring the cylinder surface after overhauling an engine, the vehicle should not be driven at top speeds for approximately 150 miles.* Install the base plate for the chain tensioner and the tensioner with the plunger. Remove the plug in the end of the assembly and disengage the plunger with an Allen wrench, working through the bore in the chain tensioner. Check to be sure that the plunger moves freely. Turn the wrench in a counterclockwise direction since an automatic adjuster is installed in the plunger. Install the plug with a lock plate and secure. Working from the inside of the timing chain cover, press the pulley shaft seal against the stop in the cover. *NOTE: In case of leaks, this seal can be replaced with the engine in the car, by removing the pulley, prying out the old seal and installing a new seal with the open end facing the engine.* Replace the timing cover gasket and install the timing cover. Place the cork gasket in the front and rear grooves of the oil pan. Installation is made easier by coating the gaskets with high viscosity grease. Place new gaskets on the engine block. Paste the ends of the gaskets to the block with commercial sealing compound. Place the oil pan in position and tighten the screws cross-wise. Use a new seal and torque the oil drain plug to 29 ft. lbs. Install all external engine attachments. *NOTE: When installing the alternator, the upper mounting screw must be installed in the driving direction.* Install the cylinder head cover and fill with oil according to specifications. An engine with ground cylinders should be filled with 6.3 pints of running-in oil. Install the flywheel guide in the crankshaft flange. Heat the flywheel to approximately 176°F. and install it evenly using the alignment marks. *NOTE: A flywheel heated in an oil bath must be cleaned thoroughly in grease solvents.* Allow the flywheel to cool and tighten the stretch-bolts to specification at 180° intervals. Install the transmission needle bearing on the drive pin in such a way as to have the flat side outward with the lettering visible. Complete the remaining engine assembly in reverse order.

When installing the engine, the same distance (X) must exist on both sides between the brake discs and wishbones. Maximum permissible deviation is .08″.

INSTALLATION

Installation procedures are the reverse of removal. The engine and transmission unit must be aligned in such a way that the same distance between brake disc and wishbone exists on each side. The distance between the pulley and front end of the side-member must also be the same on each side. After installation, bleed the brakes.

The same distance (Y) must exist between the pulley and front of the side member, on both sides. Maximum permissible deviation is .08″.

ADJUSTMENTS

Valve Clearance

The valve clearance should be adjusted in the firing order, when the engine has reached operating temperature. See Specifications for proper clearance. To adjust the clearance, turn the self-locking adjustment nuts on each rocker arm. Remove the air filter and rocker cover. The valve clearance of cylinder No. 1 should be adjusted when the valves of No. 1 cylinder overlap those of cylinder No. 4, i.e., when both arms move in opposite directions simultaneously.

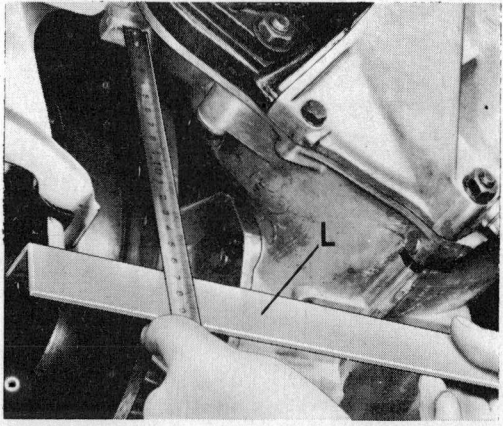

The distance between the castings on the transmission and a rule (L) must not deviate more than .16″.

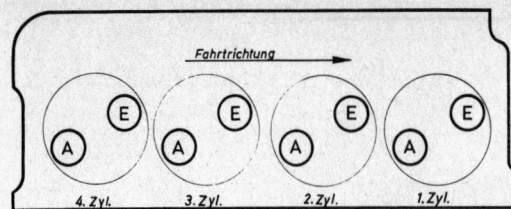

Location of exhaust valves (A) and intake valves
(E) on 100 LS. Arrow indicates forward.

This also applies to:

A. Valve clearance of cylinder No. 3 at
overlap of cylinder No. 2

B. Valve clearance of cylinder No. 4 at
overlap of cylinder No. 1

C. Valve clearance of cylinder No. 2 at
overlap of cylinder No. 3

When making adjustments, tighten the
nut until it is just possible to remove the
feeler gauge. *CAUTION: Do not attempt
to adjust the valve clearance in any other
manner than that described, as the hot oil
under a maximum pressure of 85 psi could
be dangerous.*

100 LS Torque Values

	ft. lbs.
Oil pressure relief valve	18–25
Camshaft flange	18.2
Camshaft sprocket bolts	57–58
Oil pump mounting screws	18–19
Oil pressure line screws	7–8
Distributor mounting bolt	14.5
Rocker arm adjustment nuts (without rocker arm pressure)	
Minimum	10–11
Maximum	32.5
Clutch	23
Oil pan	
(smaller)	6
(larger)	11
Timing cover bolts	7
Engine Mounting Bolts	
Front cross member to stop	18
Engine mount to console	
(left to right)	22
Engine mount to cylinder block	
(left to right)	30
Counternut to engine mount (left)	69
Rear engine mount to transmission	22
Rear cross member to rear engine mount	30
Rear cross member to body	18

Super 90

The removal, disassembly, assembly and
installation instructions for the 100 LS are
also applicable for the Super 90. Torque
values remain the same as do the gauging

points for the cylinders and the connecting
rod weight classification chart. Although
some parts of the 100 LS have been redesigned, such as the fuel pump, and the
carburetors were changed, basically both
models present the same appearance and
require the same service procedures.

Clutch and Transmission

Clutch

100 LS

The Audi 100 LS uses a single plate, dry
disc in conjunction with an F & S MF 215
pressure plate. This clutch pressure plate
cannot be dismantled, so that a new one
must be used for repair.

Removal

Remove the engine from the car and separate the transmission. Mark (with white
paint) the location of the pressure plate.
Remove the pressure plate and clutch.

Paint alignment marks on the pressure plate and
flywheel before removing the pressure plate.

  a Hex head screw
  b Pressure plate
  d Centering drift, clutch

Installation

Always use a dummy shaft to center the
clutch. Slide the clutch disc over the dummy
shaft and slide the shaft into the needle
bearing. Install the pressure plate, aligning
it with the mark made before removal.
Torque the pressure plate mounting screws

Exploded view of Super 90 clutch and pressure
plate assembly

1 Cover plate	6 Pressure plate	11 Adjustment nut
2 Withdrawal ring	7 Disc spring	12 Fillister head screw, lock plate
3 Spring holder	8 Tubular key	13 Serrated washer
4 Spring	9 Swivel-head bolt	14 Clutch disc, complete
5 Lever	10 Ring, adjustment nut	

o 24-27 ft. lbs. Replace the transmission
and install the engine in the car.

SUPER 90

The Super 90 uses a single plate, dry disc
with an F & S KM 200 pressure plate. This
pressure plate may be disassembled for
service. The clutch may be removed and
installed in the same manner as the 100 LS
clutch.

Clutch Pedal Travel

ADJUSTMENT

Super 90 and 100 LS

Turn the adjusting nuts until a travel
(clutch pedal play) of .59" - .78" is obtained. Tighten the lower adjusting nut
(see illustration) *Note: Usually the cause for
the clutch releasing too late is too little
pedal travel. Check the following dimensions:*

A. Total pedal travel 6.1"
B. Clutch play .59"-.78"
C. Remainder .98"-1.18"

Use a wooden block to check the remaining travel. The block should be 1"-1.2"

Clutch pedal adjustment points

a Clutch cable
b Clutch lever
c Upper adjusting nut
d Lower adjusting nut

(the minimum pedal travel allowable).
Place this block of wood beneath the
clutch pedal. Start the engine and push the
clutch pedal all the way down on the block
of wood. Shift into reverse. If the remaining travel is too small (not possible to shift
into reverse) recheck the pedal travel. If

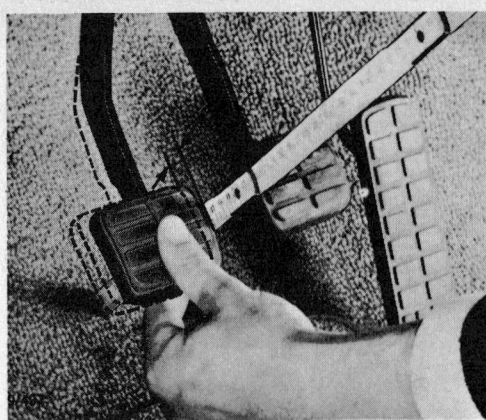

Measuring clutch pedal play

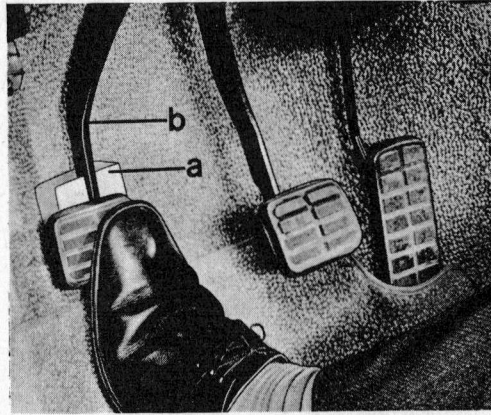

Measuring remaining pedal travel with block of wood

necessary, remove the clutch and replace the clutch disc and pressure plate.

Transmission—Manual

The 100 LS and the Super 90 use the same manual transmission, a four-speed gearbox equipped with Porsche synchronization. The unit also incorporates a built-in differential, because of the front drive axle.

Third and fourth gear wheels are pressed onto the mainshaft and can be replaced in pairs. First, second and reverse gear wheels are integral with the mainshaft. Replacement of first, second or reverse gear involves replacing the mainshaft and the remaining gear wheels. *The mainshaft cannot be separated from first, second or reverse gear wheels.*

REMOVAL

The transmission is removed and installed with the engine. Remove the engine

and unbolt the transmission from the engine (see Engine, Removal).

DISASSEMBLY

The following procedure is suggested for disassembly of the transmission. However, the transmission should only be disassembled to a point which allows replacement of the pertinent parts. Be sure that work is carried out under clean conditions. *NOTE. Gears should always be replaced as matched gears, and separate gears should never be replaced. Only pairs of gears are available as replacement parts.*

Mount the transmission on a stand or holding fixture of some type. Remove the reverse light switch and the bolt beneath the switch. Remove the release bearing by prying out the spring as illustrated. Remove the speedometer bushing.

Shift Rod (In Idle Position)

Remove the two screws and drive the shift rod from the case (with the cover) from the opposite side. Should it be necessary to replace the shaft seal, pry out the seal ring. Install the new seal ring using multi-purpose grease. Drive the new seal into the housing with the sealing lip facing inside. Unscrew the plug and remove the spring, washer and pin. Pull the shift rod out and remove the seal from the cover as necessary.

Stub Axles

Working through ten holes in the flanges (arrow in illustration), remove the four nuts from each side. Press out the stub

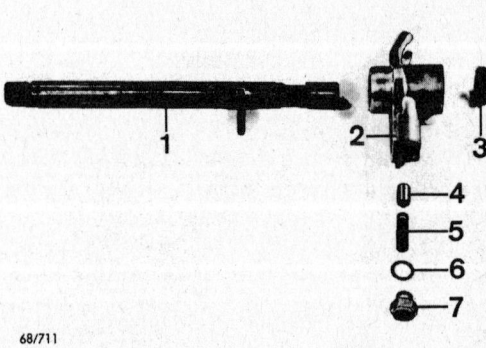

68/711

Exploded view of shift rod.

1	Shift rod	5	Spring
2	Cover, shift rod	6	A 10 x 14 seal
3	Shaft seal	7	Plug
4	Arresting pin		

Cross-sectional view of Audi manual transmission

1	Drive pinion		Shim 0.6 mm
2	Roller bearing		Shim 0.7 mm
3	Spacer		Shim 0.8 mm
4	Sliding gear, 4th speed* Gear, 4th speed*		Shim 0.9 mm
5	Needle bearing two part		Shim 1.0 mm
6	Needle bearing inner race	19	Shim 3.2 mm
7	Operating sleeve		Shim 3.3 mm
8	Guide sleeve		Shim 3.4 mm
9	Sliding gear, 3rd speed* Gear, 3rd speed*		Shim 3.5 mm
10	Needle bearing, two part		Shim 3.6 mm
11	Thrust washer		Shim 3.7 mm
12	Sliding gear, 2nd speed**		Shim 3.8 mm
13	Guide sleeve		Shim 3.9 mm
14	Sliding gear, 1st speed**		Shim 4.0 mm
15	Needle bearing, one part		Shim 4.1 mm
16	Needle bearing, inner race		Shim 4.2 mm
17	Reverse gear**		Shim 4.3 mm
18	Shim 0.2 mm	20	Shim 0.15 mm***
	Shim 0.3 mm	21	Four point bearing
	Shim 0.4 mm	22	Lock plate
	Shim 0.5 mm	23	Hex nut
		24	Shim
		25	Reverse gear ass. (not illustrated)

26	Snap-ring Sp 62
27	Grooved ball bearing 6305 NC 3
28	Circlip A 25 x 1.5 Sd
29	Support disc SS 25 x 35 x 2
30	End cover
31	Shim 50 x 62 x 0.5 mm
	Shim 50 x 62 x 0.3 mm
	Shim 50 x 62 x 0.15 mm
	Shim 50 x 62 x 0.1 mm
32	Gasket, end cover 0.20
	Gasket, end cover 0.25
	Gasket, end cover 0.30
	Gasket, end cover 0.40
33	Transmission cover
34	Transmission case
35	Needle bearing
36	Hex head screw
37	Main shaft****
38	Breather valve
39	Oil slinger
40	Shaft seal 20 x 35 x 10
41	Bushing

* Available in pairs only.

** Available together with main shaft only.

*** If necessary for compensation it is to be installed in bearing end only.

**** Available with 1st, 2nd and reverse gears only.

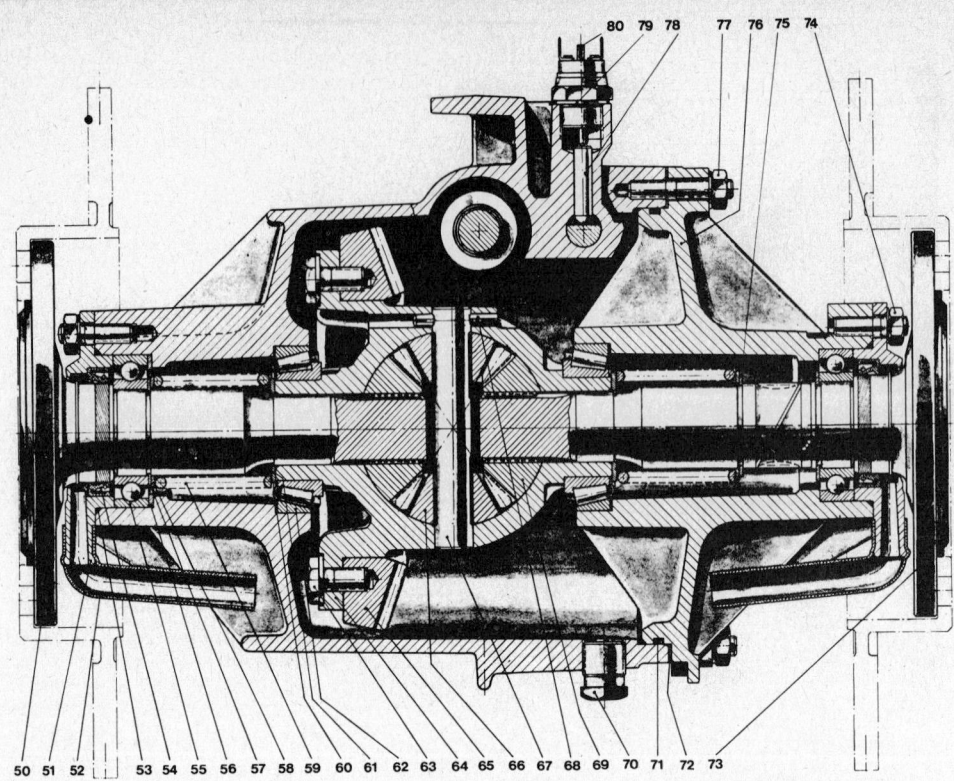

Cross-sectional view of Audi manual transmission through stub axles

50	Stub axle, left		Shim 0.25 mm	70	Magnetic plug M 18 x 1.5
51	Flange		Shim 0.2 mm	71	O-ring
52	Drain hose		Shim 0.15 mm	72	Gasket
53	Cord seal	61	Thrust washer	73	Stub axle, right
54	Shaft seal	62	Taper roller bearing 32008 X	74	Hex nut M 8
55	Grooved ball bearings	63	Hex head screw		with washer B 8 x 15
56	Washer	64	Differential housing	75	Circlip 35 x 1.5
57	Circlip	65	Crown wheel AUDI 100 (37 teeth)	76	Differential flange
58	Washer		Crown wheel AUDI 100 S/LS	77	Hex nut M 8
59	Spring		(35 teeth)		Washer B 8 x 15
60	Shim 1.5 mm	66	Differential bevel gear	78	Pressure pin
	Shim 1.0 mm	67	Shaft	79	Seal A 18 x 22
	Shim 0.8 mm	68	Tubular key 5 x 36	80	Reverse switch
	Shim 0.5 mm	69	Differential pinion		

axles. When dismantling the right stub axle, also remove the circlip. Using a bearing puller, extract the bearing from the flange. If necessary, remove the shaft seal with a drift. This seal is not serviceable; it must be replaced.

End Cover, Differential Flange and Transmission Cover

Unbolt the end cover and note the number and size of shims used for the mainshaft grooved bearing in the end cover. Remove the differential flange retaining nuts and pry off the differential flange. Remove the locating pin and the springs from the case (see illustration). Using a drift, slide in reverse gear (upper selector

Remove the stub axle mounting nuts through the holes in the flange.

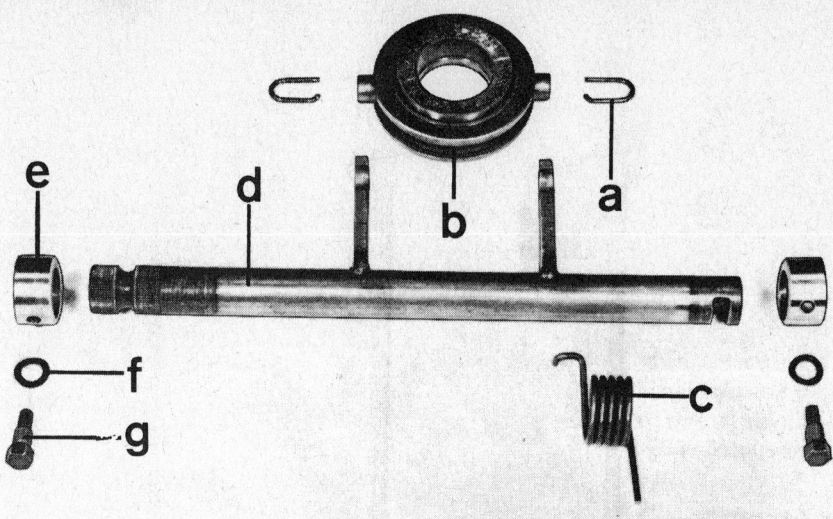

Release shaft components

a   Spring
b   Release bearing
c   Spring
d   Release shaft
e   Bushing
f   B 8 washer
g   Hex head screw

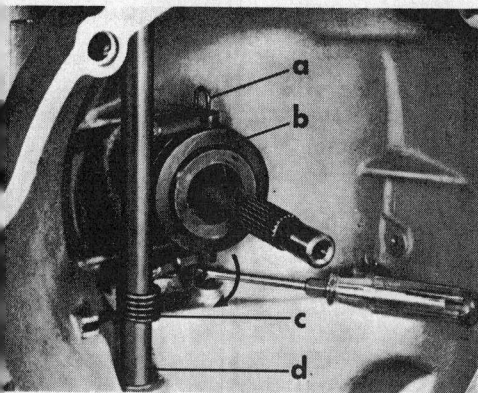

Remove the release bearing by prying out spring

Engage reverse and third gears in order to block drive pinion.

1   Selector rod, reverse
2   Selector rod, 1st/2nd gears
3   Selector rod, 3rd/4th gears
a   M 24 x 1.5 hex nut
b   Lock plate

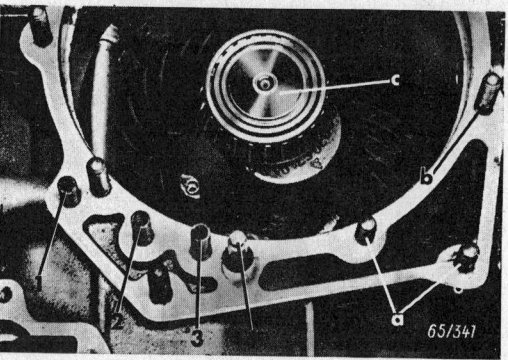

Remove the springs from the side of the transmission case.

1	Spring, reverse	30.0 mm long
2	Spring, 1st/2nd gears	34.7 mm long
3	Spring, 3rd/4th gears	34.7 mm long
4	Location pin, drive pinion roller bearing outer race	
a	M 8 x 15 stud	
b	M 8 x 22 stud (7 required)	
c	Special tool G-11	

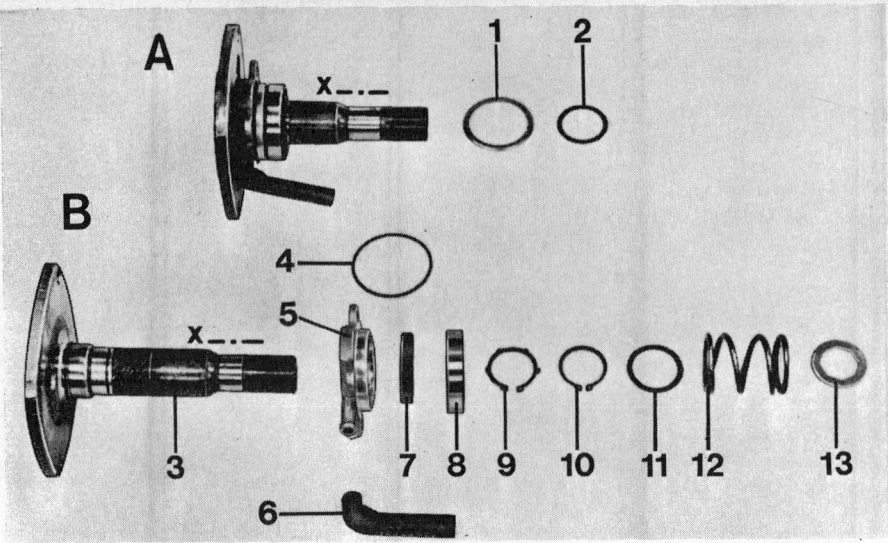

Exploded view of stub axles.

A	Stub axle, left	7	Shaft seal
B	Stub axle, right	8	Grooved ball bearing
1	Washer	9	Circlip
2	Washer	10	Circlip 35 x 1.5
3	Stub axle, right	11	Washer
	(with speedometer drive)	12	Spring
4	Cord seal	13	Thrust Washer
5	Flange	x	Apply Molykote G or LM 348
6	Drain hose		paste to this area when installing

rod) and third gear (lower selector rod) in order to block the drive pinion. Open the lockplate and unscrew the large nut between the selector rods. Unscrew the nine transmission cover retaining nuts, and drive the dowel pin from the case. Drive off the transmission cover with an aluminum drift, using the reinforcements cast in both sides of the transmission cover. Lift the differential out of the transmission case and lay it aside.

Mainshaft

Remove the two circlips from the end of the shaft. Extract the ball bearing. Carefully turn the spindle in a clockwise direction and tap the end of the mainshaft with a plastic hammer. This will also remove the bearing from the cover. *NOTE: Disassembly of the mainshaft requires a press developing approximately 10-12 tons of pressure.* Remove the oil slinger by carefully cutting it open and pulling it off. Do not damage the polished section adjacent to the oil slinger. Remove the circlip, pull off the shim and needle cage. Remove the fourth gear,

needle bearing inner race and third gear using a press.

Drive Pinion

Clamp the transmission cover in a vise equipped with soft jaws. Move the reverse selector rod to the idle position (approximately ½" from the mating surface of the end cover). Place the first and second gear

Remove the circlips (c) and washer (d) from the end of the transmission.

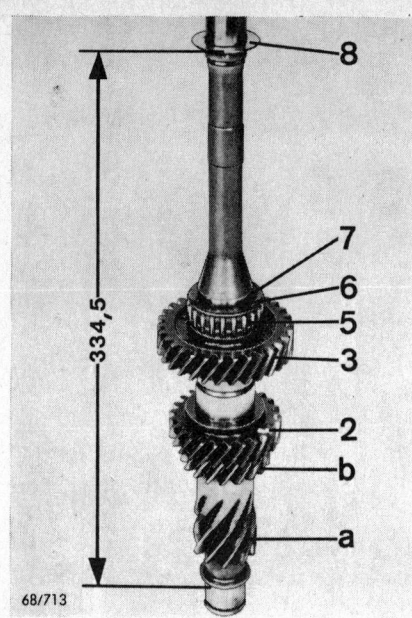

68/713

...ssembled mainshaft, showing distance from ball ...earing collar to oil slinger.

    a   1st and reverse gears
    b   2nd gear
    2   3rd gear
    3   4th gear
    5   Needle (not available separately)
    6   Shim 30 x 40 x 1
    7   Circlip 30 x 1.5
    8   Oil slinger

selector rod in second gear (direction of arrow) and the third and fourth gear selector rod to the idle position. Be very careful of the selector rod and remove the drive pinion. *CAUTION: Due to the complexity of assembling the drive pinion, it should not be disassembled by anyone other than trained service representatives, thoroughly*

65/355

Location of selector rods for removing the drive pinion.

    a   M 16 x 1.5 x 40 hex head screw
    b   Pressure plate
    c   M 8 hex nut
    d   Selector rod, 3rd/4th gears
    e   Selector rod, 1st/2nd gears
    f   Selector rod, reverse

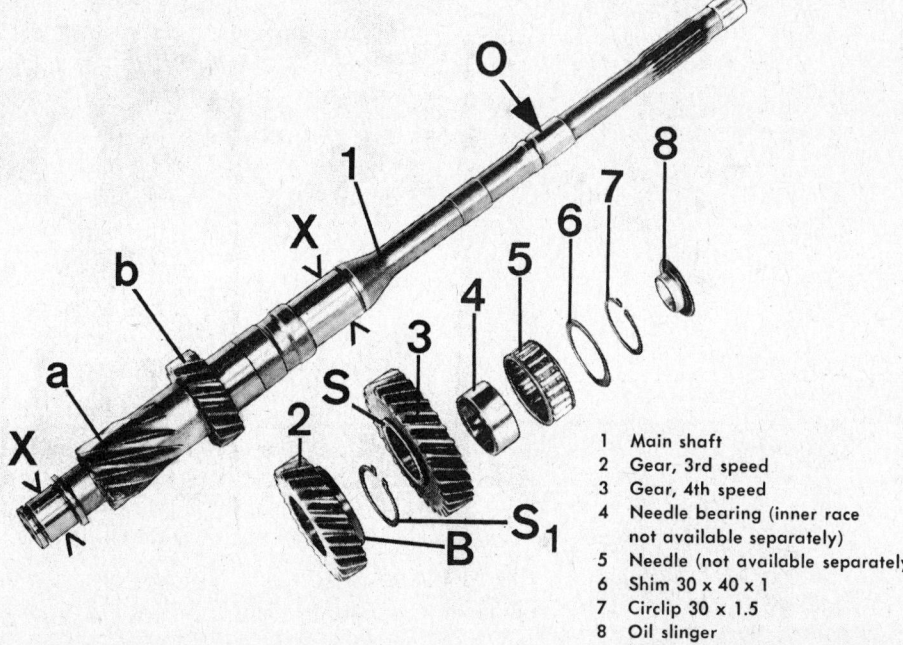

Exploded view of transmission mainshaft.

    1   Main shaft
    2   Gear, 3rd speed
    3   Gear, 4th speed
    4   Needle bearing (inner race
        not available separately)
    5   Needle (not available separately)
    6   Shim 30 x 40 x 1
    7   Circlip 30 x 1.5
    8   Oil slinger
    a   Gear, reverse and 1st speed
    b   Gear, 2nd speed
    S_1 Circlip

familiar with the unit and equipped with special tools. The drive pinion and differential should be laid aside, noting the number and placement of shims and gaskets. Only in this manner can the transmission be assembled in a satisfactory manner. After removing the drive pinion, remove the selector rods and lay aside. Note the arresting pins of the selector rods:

Reverse, first and second gears: .67″

First and second gear and third and fourth gear: .46″

Reverse Gear and Reverse Shift Rail

Remove screw (b) in illustration and the

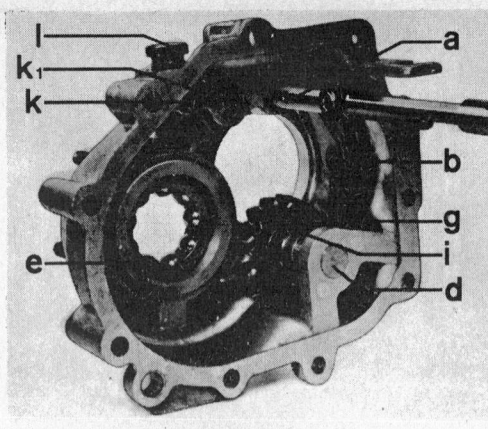

Internal view of transmission cover.

a	Selector rod, reverse
b	M 10 x 1 x 25 hex head, screw
c	B 10 washer
d	Shaft, reverse
e	Four point bearing
f	M 8 x 30 stud
g	Lever, reverse with selector fork
i	Reverse gear with bushing
k	Stop plunger, reverse and 1st/2nd gear
k₁	Stop plunger, 1st/2nd and 3rd/4th speed
l	Filler plug

68/700

Remove hex head screw (b) and washer (c) to remove reverse selector rod (a).

a	Selector rod, reverse
b	M 10 x 1 x 25 hex head screw
c	B 10 washer
d	Shaft, reverse
e	Four point bearing
f	M 8 x 30 stud

washer. Remove the selector rod and the lever. Carefully remove the stop plungers. Press off the four point bearing outer race. Use a pipe with an inside diameter of 70 mm. as a base.

Ring Gear Bearing Outer Race

The transmission case contains two cavities, the stub axle and hub. Use a bearing puller and remove the bearing outer race together with the shims.

Drive Pinion Bearing Outer Race

A groove is milled in the outer race of the roller bearing which engages a pin (see illustration). This pin must be removed before the bearing outer race. Drive the roller bearing outer race from its mounting.

Mainshaft Bearing Outer Race

If not already accomplished, remove the stud which locates the bearing outer race. Use an aluminum or copper drift to drive the outer race, seal and bushing from the clutch housing.

Mainshaft Seal

This seal should always be replaced when repairing the transmission. Simply drive the seal and bushing from the hous-

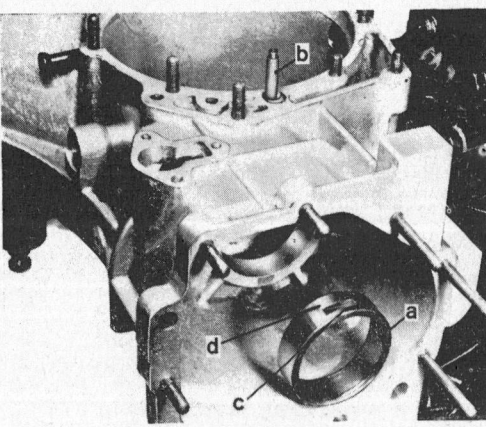

Replacing ring gear taper roller bearing outer race.

a	Roller bearing outer race	c	Narrow end
b	Pin	d	Wide end

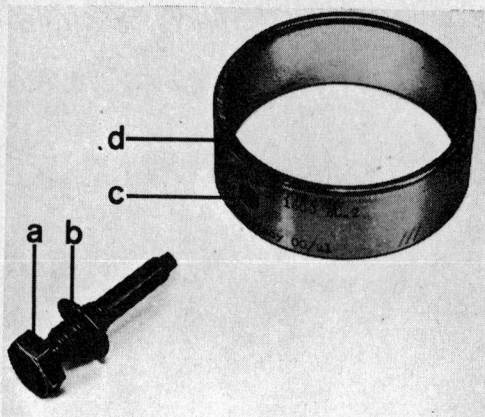

Mainshaft needle bearing outer race and stud.

a Stud
b B 6 washer

c Locating bore
d Needle bearing outer race

Mainshaft seal (20 x 35 x 10).

a 20 x 35 x 10 seal

b Bushing

ng. Install the seal approximately .02″ below the surface of the case.

Left Brake Caliper Studs

Should this operation be necessary, use a bolt extractor or, in emergency cases, two counterlocked flat M 12 hex nuts.

ASSEMBLY

Left Brake Caliper Studs

Before installing new studs, coat the external threads of the studs with a commercial sealant. Install the studs and torque to specification. The upper edge of the stud must be located approximately .02″ below the mating surface for the brake caliper.

Mainshaft Bearing Outer Race

The outer race contains a cavity which the unthreaded part of the stud must engage. It is very important to use extreme care when installing the race. If possible, undercool both parts prior to installation. Drive the outer race into the case in such a way that the cavity in the outer race is in exact alignment with the threaded bore in the case. Should the unthreaded end of the stud not engage the cavity in the race, the race will cant and cause excessive wear and noisy operation. Coat the threads of the stud with sealant and install the stud.

Drive Pinion Bearing Outer Race

Install the bearing outer race with the groove upwards (facing the differential flange opening) so that the pin can engage the groove. Additionally, be sure that the wide end faces the clutch housing. Drive in the outer race until the pin engages the groove (deepest possible penetration). The end of the pin with a groove should face upwards.

Ring Gear Bearing Outer Race

Drive the tapered roller bearing outer race in, up to the stop, without the shims.

Reverse Gear and Reverse Shift Rail

Heat the transmission cover in an oil bath to approximately 176° F. Press a new four point bearing in up to the stop. Slide in the two stop plungers (17 mm. and 11.7 mm.). Install the reverse gear and selector rod in the transmission case in such a manner that the reverse gear faces toward the end cover. Install the selector rods and clamp in position as follows: Screw the hex

Remove the left brake caliper mounting studs.

head screw into the transmission cover until the lever rests against the selector rod and the selector fork is in the groove of reverse gear. The screw should not be screwed into the lever. Turn the screw back until the first thread engages and the lever is pressed against the screw. Torque the screw to specification. This operation will ensure a clearance of approximately .004″ between the selector fork and reverse gear. Check the bearing protrusion as illustrated, with a dial indicator. Check the

Installation of selector rods. Arrow indicates driving direction.

    a   Selector rod, 1st/2nd speed
    b   Selector rod, 3rd/4th speed

Measure bearing protrusion with a dial indicator.

thickness of a new gasket, and choose a gasket in accordance with the following chart:

Bearing Protrusion (mm.)	Gasket Thickness (mm.)
.10–.15	.2 + .05
.16–.18	.25 + .05
.19–.22	.3 + .05
.23–.28	.4 + .05

Install the selector rods (a and b) as illustrated. Place the first and second speed operating sleeve in second and the reverse selector rod in idle.

Drive Pinion

Slide the drive pinion together with the selector rod into the transmission case and at the same time, press the third and fourth

speed operating sleeve in the direction of the arrow (illustration). This will allow the stop plunger to engage the groove of the third and fourth speed selector rods. Install the four point bearing inner race and tighten the nut by hand.

Mainshaft

Heat the third speed gear in an oil bath to approximately 212°F. and press onto the mainshaft. The collar must face the splined end of the shaft. *NOTE: The collar of the fourth speed gear must face the third speed gear.* Heat the needle bearing inner race in an oil bath to approximately 292°F. and press onto the shaft, being careful not to cant the bearing. *NOTE: It is helpful to take hold of the needle bearing with a pipe wrench. Be sure that a piece of pipe (12.6″ long with an inside diameter of 1.2″) is available to drive on the inner race. This operation must be done quickly.* Slide the oil slinger on the shaft until the center of the collar is positioned above the groove on the shaft. Position the oil slinger so that the dimension, as measured from the ball bearing collar to the oil slinger outside surface, is 13.16″ (334.5 mm.). Center punch the oil slinger collar four times, every 90°. Install the mainshaft at an angle in the transmission cover as illustrated. Suspend the mainshaft at a position below the third speed gear. Place the transmission cover in position and carefully press the grooved bearing onto the mainshaft a short distance. Align the transmission cover and continue installing the grooved bearing

Install the mainshaft at an angle.

until it is positioned against the snap-ring in the transmission cover and on the main-shaft.

Differential

Place the differential into the transmission case. Align the drive pinion selector rod in order to mesh reverse and third

...e sure that the selector rod stop plungers are ...ositioned in the bores.

1 Reverse spring, 29.5 mm long
2 1st/2nd speed spring, 34.0 mm long
3 3rd/4th speed spring, 26.0 mm long
4 Locating pin, drive pinion roller bearing outer race

...ear. Apply a thin coat of sealant to the ...ating surfaces of the transmission case ...d cover. Install the transmission cover ...nd shafts in the transmission case. Drive ...e dowel pins in the transmission cover ...d torque the cover retaining nuts to spec-...cation. Work through the opening for ...e shift rod and through the differential ...nge opening and place all selector rods

in idle position. Replace the shims in the differential and drive on the taper roller bearing outer race. *NOTE: Install the thicker shim first so that the thinner shim will not be deformed during later disassembly.* Each time the transmission is repaired, use a new O-ring as a differential flange seal and a new differential flange gasket. Apply a light coat of grease to the O-ring to facilitate assembly. Check to be sure that the selector rod stop plungers are in position (see illustration). Install the springs as illustrated. When installing the locating pin for the roller bearing outer race, be sure that the machined groove in the pin is visible. Install the differential flange in the transmission case and torque the retaining nuts to specification in a crosswise pattern. Apply a light coat of viscous grease to the thrust washer so that it sticks to the circlip.

Stub Axles

Install the left and right stub axles, being careful of the drain hose. Tighten the four stub axle nuts cross-wise according to specification.

End Cover

Place the gasket on the transmission cover and fit the support washer over the mainshaft, followed by the circlip. Use a plastic or rubber hammer and tap the mainshaft downward, in the direction of the transmission case, to ensure that the snap-ring in the grooved bearing rests against the transmission cover. Measure the mainshaft grooved bearing protrusion. When doing so, be sure to use a gasket. Measure the grooved bearing recess in the

Measure the mainshaft grooved bearing protrusion.

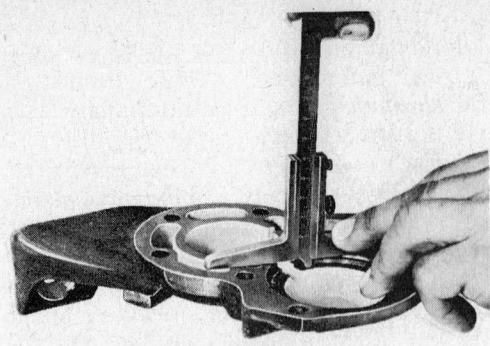

Measure the grooved bearing recess in the end cover.

end cover (from the finished surface to the grooved bearing surface). End cover shims are available in the following sizes: .5, .3, .15 and .1 mm.

Determine the shim thickness as follows: (example)

End cover recess measurement	4.90 mm.
Bearing protrusion measurement	−4.65 mm.
Shim thickness	.25 mm.

i.e., one .15 mm. and one .1 mm. shim.

Apply a light coat of viscous grease and paste the shims(s) in the end cover. Do not forget the shim before tightening the end cover. Coat the mating surfaces with sealant and bolt the end cover to the transmission. Install the reverse light switch and

seal. Coat the sealing surfaces of the transmission case at the shift rod flange with sealant and install the shift rod and cover as illustrated. Turn the transmission and fill with two liters of hypoid transmission oil. Replace the drain plug.

Installation

Installation is the reverse of removal.

Torque Values

Stub Axle°	2.5–3.3 mkp (18.0–23.8 ft. lbs.)
Differential flange°	2.5–3.3 mkp (18.0–23.8 ft. lbs.)
Transmission cover°	2.5–3.3 mkp (18.0–23.8 ft. lbs.)
End cover°	2.5–3.3 mkp (18.0–23.8 ft. lbs.)
Shift rod cover	0.8–1.0 mkp (5.78–7.23 ft. lbs.)
Reverse operating lever	3.0–4.0 mkp (21.7–28.9 ft. lbs.)
Crown wheel— differential housing	70 mkp (50.6 ft. lbs.)
Drive pinion	10.0–11.0 mkp (72.3–79.5 ft. lbs.)
Caliper	4.0–5.0 mkp (28.9–36.1 ft. lbs.)
Oil inlet	3.0–3.5 mkp (21.7–25.3 ft. lbs.)
Oil drain	3.0–3.5 mkp (21.7–25.3 ft. lbs.)
Main shaft needle bearing	0.4–0.6 mkp (2.9–4.3 ft. lbs.)
Speedometer bushing	3.5–4.0 mkp (25.3—28.9 ft. lbs.)
Reverse switch	3.5–4.0 mkp (25.3—28.9 ft. lbs.)
Clutch release shaft	1.0–1.5 mkp (7.23–10.85 ft. lbs.)
Steering lock	0.6–0.9 mkp (4.3–6.5 ft. lbs.)

° The material of M 8 studs and hex nuts has been altered from transmission No. 218 940.
M 8 stud from 8 G to 10 K } In cases of repair only use
M 8 hex nut from 6 G to 8 G } these studs or nuts with new tensile strengths.
In so doing the torque value for M 8 hex nuts has changed from 2.2-3.0 mkp (15.9-21.7 ft. lbs.) to 2.5-3.3 mkp (18.0-23.8 ft. lbs.).

ADJUSTMENTS

Shift Lever

Place the shift rod at idle position and slide on the shift lever. The distance (f) or

Install the shift rod together with the cover.

Distance (f) between center of bolt and shift lever (e) should be 3.3".

stance (g) should be .12" with shift lever in 2nd ar.

e illustration, should be 3.3" (84.0 mm.) the angle should be 23°. The adjustment n be checked by placing the shift rod in cond gear, where the distance between e transmission case and shift lever should , 118" (3 mm.).

tomatic Transmission

The Audi automatic transmission is a hy-ulically operated three-speed unit, shift-automatically within a preselected ve range.

REMOVAL

he automatic transmission can be dis-nected from the engine and removed n the car while the engine is still in the

emove the grill and front apron. The ine must be mounted to the frame in e manner or suspended on a lift or jack

to prevent it from falling from the mounts when the mounts are disconnected. Loosen the brake pipe lines from the brake hoses and plug the ends of the brake hoses. Disconnect the accelerator linkage by pressing the bearing out of the bushing. Disconnect the front exhaust pipe at the exhaust manifold and at the primary muffler. Disconnect and remove the oil filter and starter. Disconnect both driveshafts and suspend them from the upper wishbones. Disconnect the stabilizer at both lower wishbones. Unbolt the holder for the selector cable at the transmission. Remove the selector cable from the lever at the transmission. Remove the selector cable holder. Disconnect the crossmember at the engine mounting and at the support. Place a jack or support under the transmission. Remove the guard and disconnect the left and right engine mountings. Be careful not to alter the position of the left mount, which is fixed by means of counternuts. Insert bolts (⅜" x 8") through each side in place of the engine mounts. Lower the complete power plant until the units rests on the bolts. Disconnect the vacuum hose at the vacuum unit or at the T adaptor. Loosen the torque converter by working through the bore for the starter in the gear ring. Loosen the engine to transmission connections and remove the transmission. Immediately upon removal of the

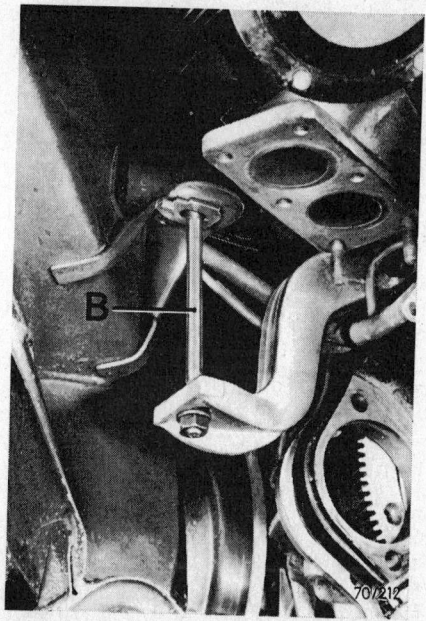

Insert bolts (B) through each engine mount to support the engine.

automatic transmission, secure the torque converter in its original position.

INSTALLATION

To install the transmission, reverse the removal procedure, noting the following instructions. Lift the transmission and bolt it to the engine. Lift both the engine and transmission and install the selector lever holder. When installing the engine mounts, be sure that the projection engages the groove of the mount (see illustration). After installing the engine and transmission

70/215

Loosen the torque converter.

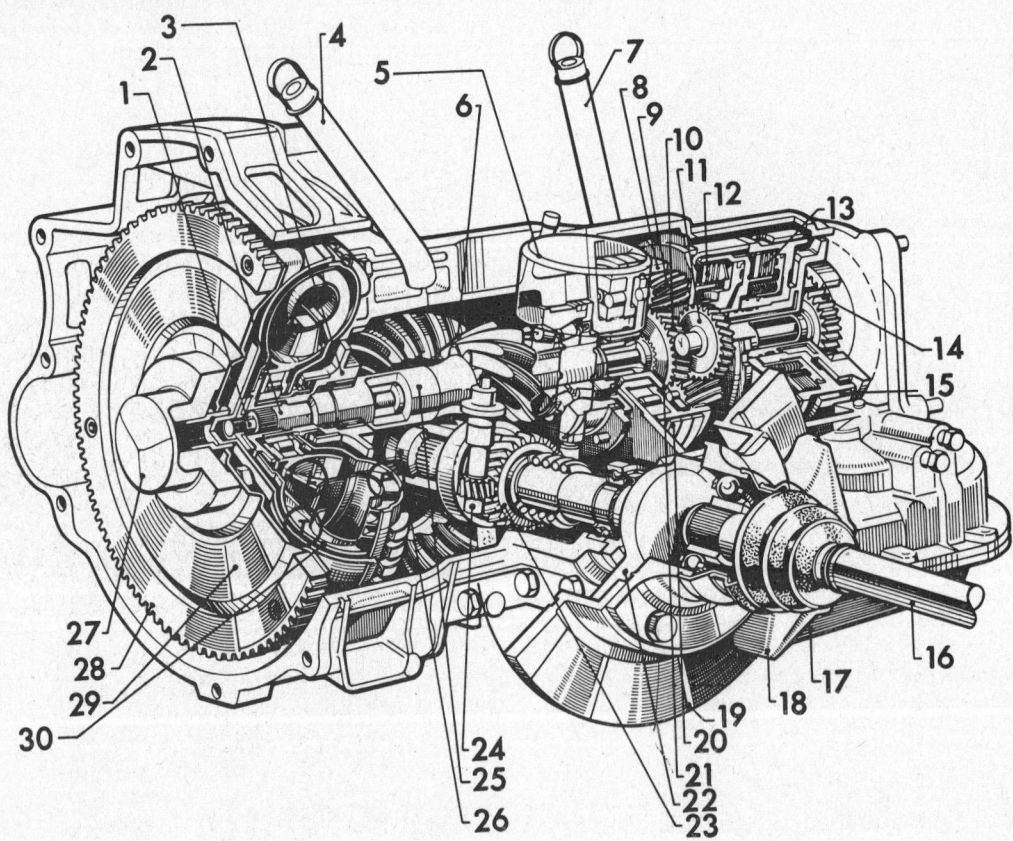

Cut-away view of Audi automatic transmission.

1	Pump shaft	12	Forward clutch	23	Impeller, governor and speedomet drive
2	Turbine shaft	13	Direct and reverse clutch	24	Speedometer pinion shaft
3	Stator support	14	Oil pump	25	Drive pinion shaft
4	Oil filler tube, differential	15	2nd gear brake band	26	Differential
5	Governor	16	Driveshaft	27	Crankshaft, engine
6	Drive pinion	17	Oil pan	28	Gear ring
7	Oil filler tube, planetary gear	18	Brake caliper	29	Drive plate
8	Annulus	19	Brake disc	30	Torque converter
9	Small planetary gear	20	1st gear and reverse brake band	P	Impeller
10	Large sun gear	21	Planetary gear carrier	L	Stator
11	Large planetary pinion	22	Stub axle	T	Turbine

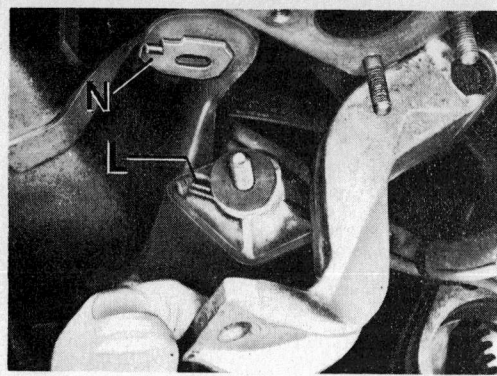

Be sure that the projection (N) engages the groove (L) of the engine mount.

assembly, check the alignment of the unit. Refer to Engine Installation.

ADJUSTMENTS

Selector Lever

Position the selector lever at P. Place the cable through the clamping screw and press the selector lever on the transmission in the direction of the arrow (see illustration) to the stop. Tighten the clamping screw. Start the engine and move the selector lever to D, where the engine speed must decrease before the lever reaches po-

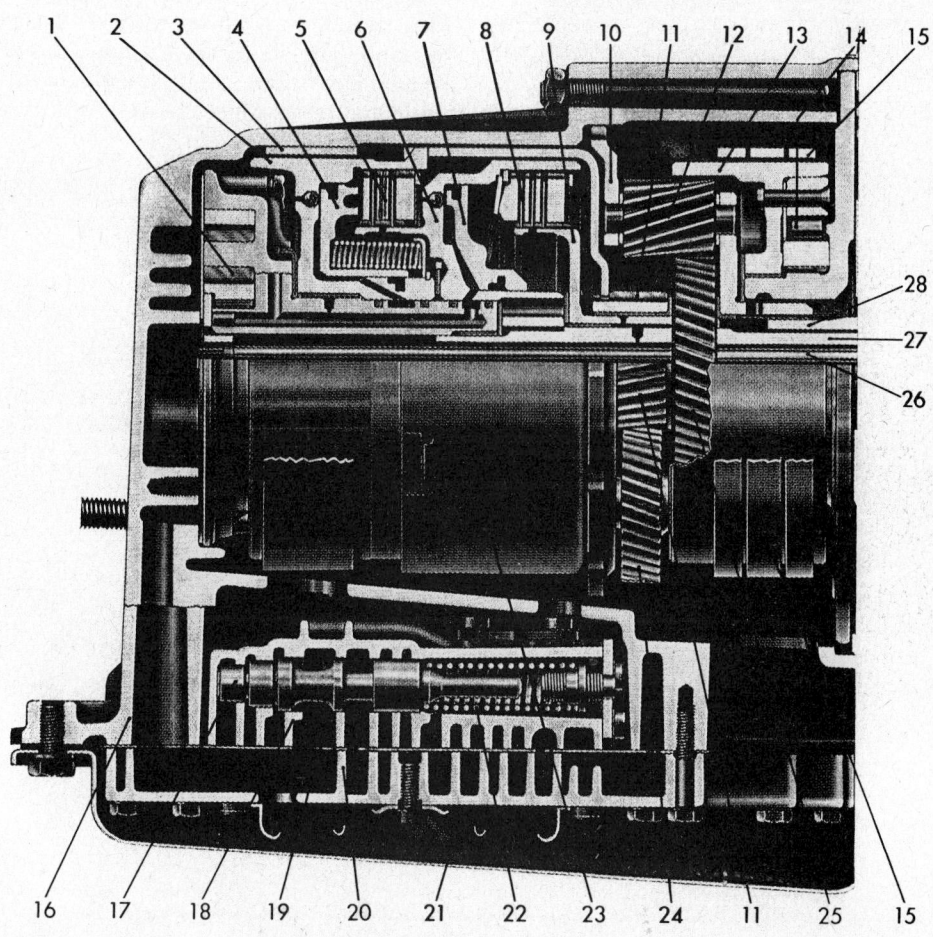

Cross-sectional view of Audi automatic transmission.

1	Oil pump	11	Small sun gear	20	Transfer plate
2	Clutch drum	12	Small planetary pinion	21	Oil strainer
3	2nd gear brake band	13	Annulus	22	Spring, valve
4	Piston, direct and reverse clutch	14	1st gear one-way clutch	23	Drive shell
5	Direct and reverse clutch	15	1st gear and reverse brake band	24	Large planetary pinion
6	Forward clutch drum with ball valve	16	Transmission case	25	Large sun gear
7	Piston, forward clutch	17	Control valve (main)	26	Oil pump shaft
8	Forward clutch	18	Valve body	27	Turbine shaft
9	Forward clutch hub	19	Separator plate	28	Drive pinion shaft
10	Planetary gear carrier				

Selector lever installation.

sition D. Move the selector lever toward R. The engine speed must also fall off before the lever reaches R. If the lever is positioned correctly, the distance from N to D and from N to R must be equal and the engine speed will decrease somewhat. If the distances vary, the selector cable must be adjusted again.

The following check of the selector cable may also be made. Place the lever at N and run the engine at idle. Engage the handbrake and place the lever at R. At this point power transmission and a reduction in engine speed must be noticeable. Increase the idle speed and shift to P. When doing this, the engine speed must increase. Pull the selector lever toward R against the stop. The speed should not drop again. If any conditions are not met, adjust the cable and repeat the check.

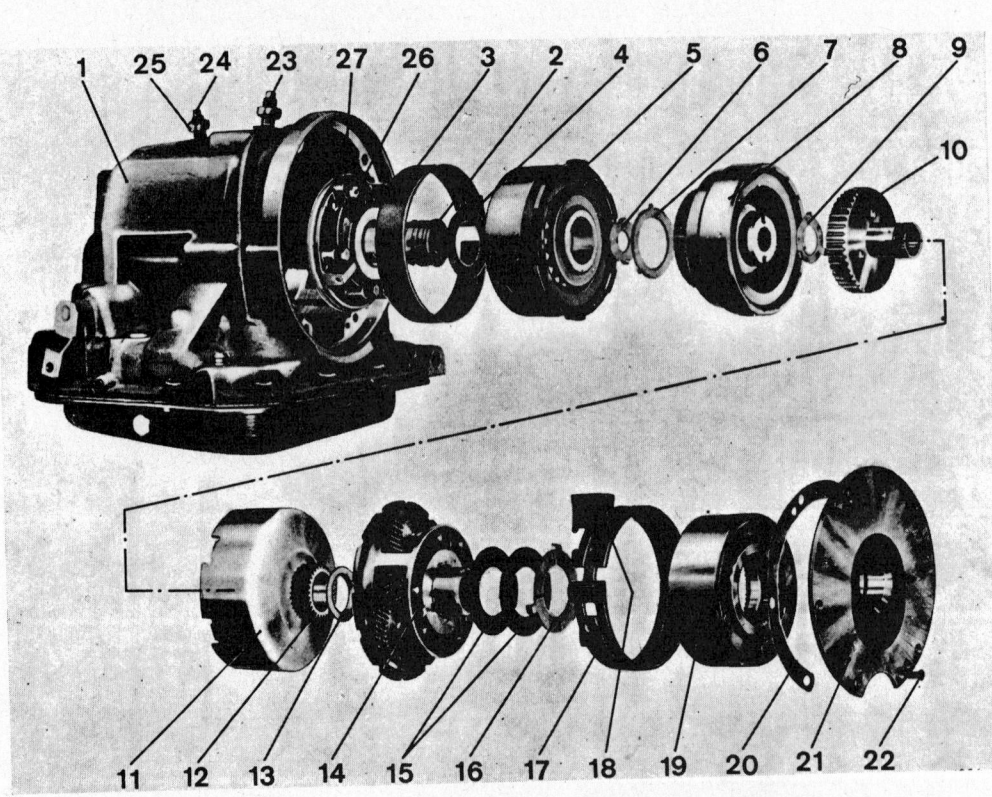

Exploded view of Audi automatic transmission components.

1 Transmission case	11 Drive shell	21 Bearing flange
2 Oil pump	12 Small sun gear	22 Countersunk screw M 6 x 15
3 2nd gear brake band	13 Thrust washer 5	23 Set screw, 1st gear brake band
4 Thrust washer	14 Set of planetary gears	24 Set screw, 2nd gear brake band
5 Direct and reverse clutch	15 Adjusting disc	
6 Thrust washer 2	16 Thrust washer 6	25 Nut, set screw
7 Thrust washer 3	17 1st gear brake band	26 Hex. head screw M 6 x 35
8 Forward clutch	18 Support arm	27 Washer
9 Thrust washer 4	19 Annulus with one-way clutch	
10 Forward clutch hub	20 Gasket, bearing flange	

Vacuum Unit

The vacuum unit must be adjusted after each replacement of the vacuum unit or its seal. This adjustment is also necessary if the gearshift timing is incorrect.

Disconnect the vacuum hose at the vacuum unit and plug the hose with a suitable plug. Remove the screw from the transmission. Connect a pressure gauge (up to 145 psi) to the transmission. Place the selector lever at N and run the engine at 1,000 rpm. Adjust the vacuum unit until the pressure gauge shows a primary gas pressure of 48.4±.28 psi. Remove the pressure gauge and connect the vacuum line to the transmission vacuum unit.

Adjust the vacuum unit by plugging the vacuum line (A), connecting a pressure gauge at (B) and adjusting to specification. 30-106 is a special tool for adjusting vacuum unit.

Drive Axle and Synchronization Joints

The Audi incorporates front wheel drive, using drive axles equipped with Rzeppa (synchronization) joints to absorb lateral movement.

Removal

Remove the driveshaft from the stub axle and detach the driveshaft from the brake disc, noting the insulating washer between the driveshaft and brake disc. Remove the

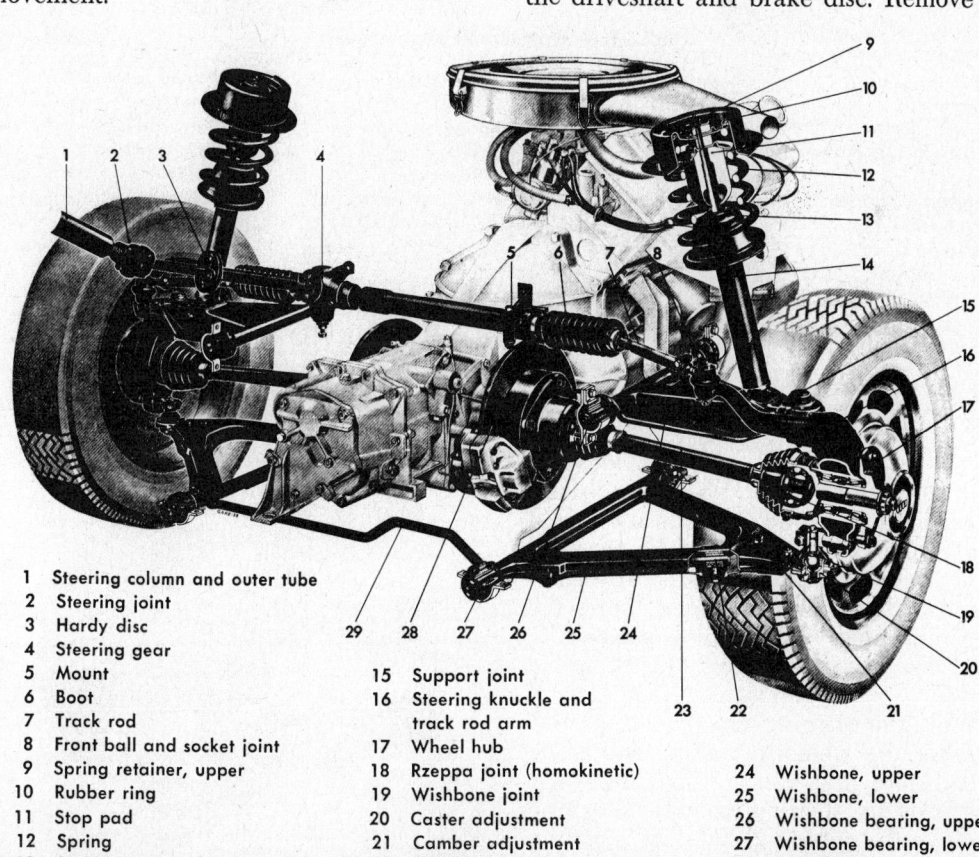

1	Steering column and outer tube
2	Steering joint
3	Hardy disc
4	Steering gear
5	Mount
6	Boot
7	Track rod
8	Front ball and socket joint
9	Spring retainer, upper
10	Rubber ring
11	Stop pad
12	Spring
13	Spring retainer, lower
14	Shock absorber
15	Support joint
16	Steering knuckle and track rod arm
17	Wheel hub
18	Rzeppa joint (homokinetic)
19	Wishbone joint
20	Caster adjustment
21	Camber adjustment
22	Stabilizer bearing
23	Driveshaft
24	Wishbone, upper
25	Wishbone, lower
26	Wishbone bearing, upper
27	Wishbone bearing, lower
28	Brake disc
29	Stabilizer

Audi 100 LS front end components.

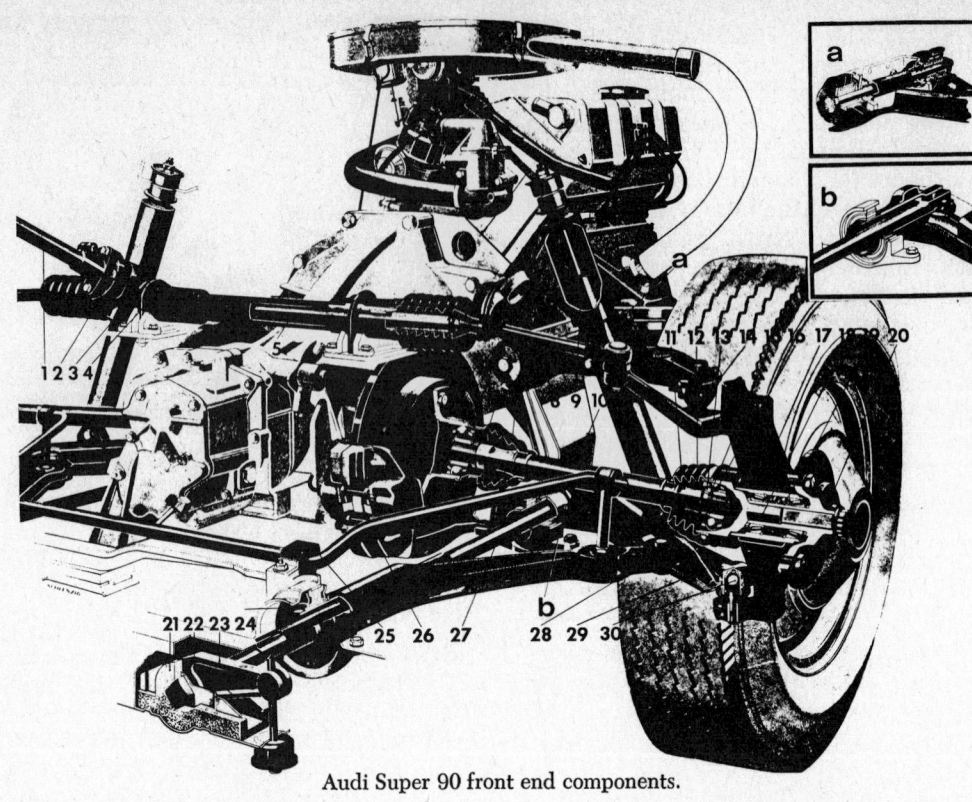

Audi Super 90 front end components.

1	Steering column	9	Shock absorber	17	Steering knuckle	25	Rubber bearing
2	Hardy disc	10	Drive shaft	18	Outer drive joint	26	Stabilizer
3	Steering gear	11	Boot, outer	19	Spacer	27	Front spring
4	Bracket	12	Rzeppa joint, outer	20	Hub	28	Stabilizer strut
5	Rack	13	Springs (2)	21	Pressure piece	29	Wishbone
6	Rzeppa joint, inner	14	Wishbone joint	22	Hex. head screw	30	Support joint assembly
7	Boot, inner	15	Fit ring	23	Adjustment level	a	Wishbone bearing, upper
8	Track rod	16	Snap-ring	24	Strut bearing assembly	b	Stabilizer strut bearing

mounting bolts and cotter pin and remove the castle nuts. Using a universal joint extractor, remove the track rod arm from the track rod arm of the steering knuckle.

DISASSEMBLY

Clamp the steering knuckle in a vise and remove the cotter pin, castle nut and spacer. Cover the threads of the driveshaft to protect them from damage. Using the tools illustrated, or suitable substitutes, press the driveshaft from the steering knuckle.

Clamp the steering knuckle in a vise. Press out the wheel hub and remove the spacer, Nilos ring and ball bearing inner ring. Place the steering knuckle on a tube and drive the outer ball bearing ring from the knuckle. Remove the retaining rings and press out the second ball bearing outer ring.

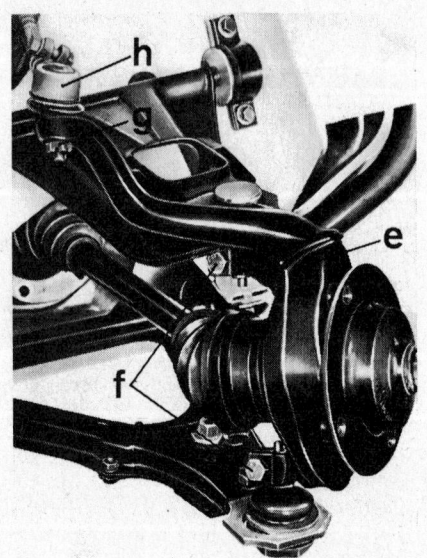

Remove the castle nut (g) from the track rod (h) and the mounting screws (f) from the steering knuckle (e).

Extract the track rod (h) from the track rod arm (e) of the steering knuckle with a universal joint extractor (i).

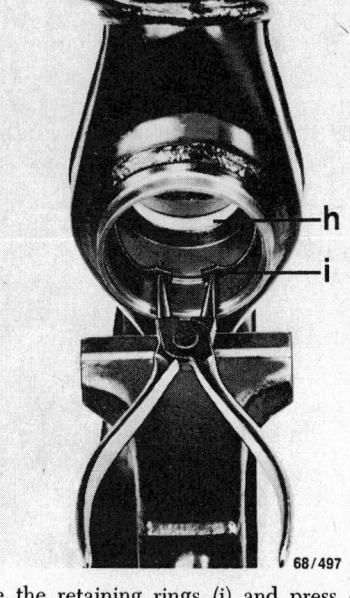

68/497

Remove the retaining rings (i) and press out the outer ring of the ball bearing (h).

ASSEMBLY

Replace the retaining rings. Press in the outer rings using a driver, and fill the space between the rings with approximately 1½ - 2 oz. of Calypsol 5974 LS 5999. Fit the wheel hub into the steering knuckle as follows. Place the spacer and Nilos ring into the wheel hub. Press on the ball bearing inner ring and fit a new spacer bushing. Place the hub into the pre-assembled steering knuckle and press in the second ball bearing inner ring.

Screw the threaded insert onto the driveshaft. Coat the spacer with thick grease

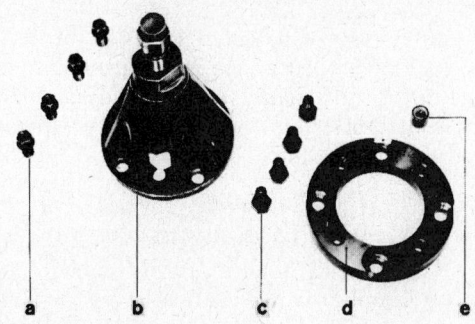

Tool for extracting driveshaft.

a	4 wheel screws	d	Intermediate flange
b	Extractor	e	Pressure cap
c	4 hex. head screws M 14 x 1.5 x 25		

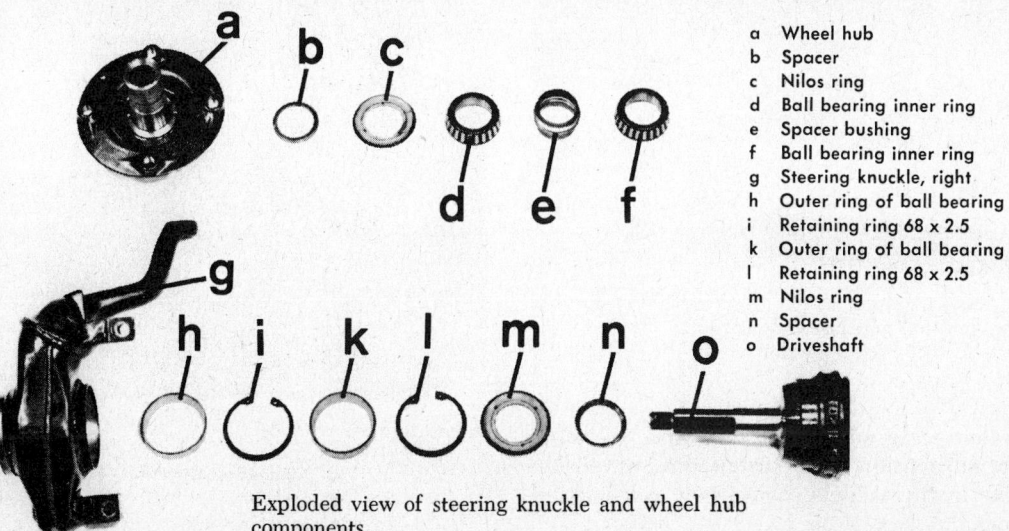

a Wheel hub
b Spacer
c Nilos ring
d Ball bearing inner ring
e Spacer bushing
f Ball bearing inner ring
g Steering knuckle, right
h Outer ring of ball bearing
i Retaining ring 68 x 2.5
k Outer ring of ball bearing
l Retaining ring 68 x 2.5
m Nilos ring
n Spacer
o Driveshaft

Exploded view of steering knuckle and wheel hub components.

and stick the spacer (flat side toward the ball bearing) and the Nilos ring onto the driveshaft. Push the driveshaft into the fitted wheel hub. Replace the spindle, bushing and nut. Fit the driveshaft and be sure that the spacer does not move from its proper position. Further assembly of the unit is the reverse of disassembly.

Installation

Installation is the reverse of removal.

Vehicle Alignment

Appropriate equipment is necessary to perform accurate alignment work. Checking and adjusting should always be carried out in the following sequence. Correct the tire pressure before making any adjustments.

Adjusting caster (100 LS).

a   Camber adjustment   d   Caster adjustment
b   Locknut   e   Screw
c   Screw

GROUND CLEARANCE

100 LS

Ground clearance is the distance (see illustration) from the test surface to the hole in the front bearing shell of the lower wishbone. When the ground clearance falls below the minimum of 8.19″, it must be corrected.

Remove the hydraulic suspension unit. Compress the spring and remove the shock absorber. Insert spacers (1 spacer = .39″)

CASTER

Caster can be adjusted (see illustration) by turning the eccentric nut a after loosening nut b and screw c. After adjustment, try to attain equal values on both wheels and tighten the nuts.

CAMBER

Camber is to be checked (and adjusted) with the wheels in the "straight ahead" position. Camber can be adjusted by turning the eccentric screw e (see illustration). Loosen the nut d and tighten after the adjustment.

Correcting ground height by compressing suspension unit (A) and inserting shim (D). The tool (S) is used to compress the unit.

to correct ground clearance and assemble the suspension unit. Install the suspension unit in the vehicle, using new self-locking nuts.

Adjusting camber (100 LS).

a   Camber adjustment
b   Locknut
c   Lower wishbone

Rear Suspension

The complete rear axle of the Audi is bolted to the body as a unit. The rear axle is attached to two suspension arms. The torsion bars are located in fully sealed tubes in the cross tube. A stabilizer is attached to the rear axle tube. In case of re-pairs, the rear axle may be removed with or without the cross tube.

Rear Axle

REMOVAL (WITHOUT CROSS TUBE)
Depress the brake pedal approximately 1.2″ and retain the pedal in this position.

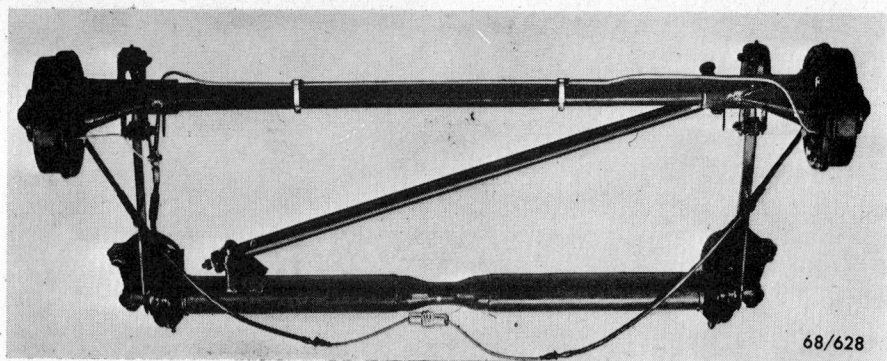

Complete Audi rear axle.

Audi rear axle components.

a	Brake drum and wheel hub	i	Axle tube (stabilizing)	s	Shock absorber
b	Shoe-type brake assembly (brake bracket)	k	Stabilizer	t	Rubber bearing
		l	Cross tube	u	Wheel cylinder
c	Stop pad	m	Torsion bar, rear, left	v	Rear axle, outer (including bearing)
d	Shock absorber	n	Mounting tube	w	Brake drum and wheel hub
e	Suspension arm	o	Torsion bar, rear, right	x	Grease cap
f	Super slip handbrake cable	p	Handbrake adjustment	y	Mounting screw ⎱ Cross tube
g	Brake pipe line	r	Stop pad	z	Mounting screw ⎰ to body
h	Transverse suspension rod				

This will close the compensating bores in the brake master cylinders. Remove both shock absorbers from the rear axle. Jack the vehicle and remove the rear wheels. Loosen the screw on the handbrake cable and remove the grommet in order to slacken the cable. Push out the protecting sleeve from the right and left sides. Remove the rubber boot and pull the handbrake cable out in the direction shown (see illustration). Pull the cable downwards

Remove the brake shoe retaining spring (a).

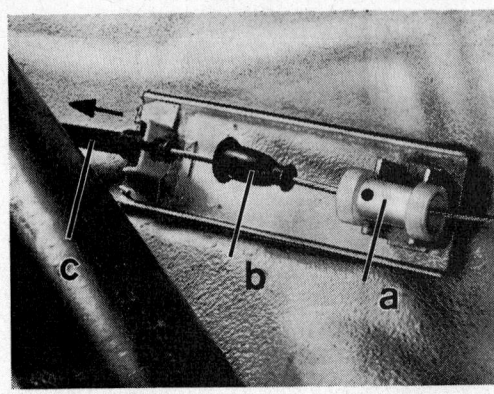

Remove the protective sleeve (a), the rubber boot (b) and pull the cable (c) out in the direction of the arrow.

through the slot in the bracket. Unscrew the brake line from the distributor on the right suspension arm. Remove the brake line and dust cap and plug the distributor. Remove the brake line from the right side brake backing plate and plug the brake line connections. Remove the handbrake cable from the suspension arms by bending open the retaining clamps. Remove the transverse stabilizer bar. Remove the mounting screws from the right and left side suspension arms, just below the axle tube. Lift the rear axle from the suspension arms and place it on suitable stands.

INSTALLATION

Installation is the reverse of removal. Note the angle bracket for the brake line distributor on the right side suspension arm.

Cross Tube With Suspension Arm

REMOVAL

It is not advisable to remove the cross tube or complete rear axle, since a special centering gauge is considered necessary for proper installation of the cross tube.

Wheel Bearings and Rear Stub Axles

REMOVAL

Depress the brake pedal approximately 1.2″ and retain in that position, to close the master cylinder compensating hole. Detach the brake lines from both sides and plug the lines. Pry off the grease cap and remove the cotter pin, castle nut, nut and washer. Remove the wheel and brake drum. Remove the bearing inner ring from the brake drum. Carefully (the spring can fly out) pry out the brake shoe retaining spring. Remove the brake shoes complete with pressure rod and spring, bottom bracket first, then the wheel cylinder. Disconnect the handbrake cable. Unbolt the rear stub axle and brake backing plate. Pry

Remove the retaining screws (a), brake backing plate (b) and stub axles (c).

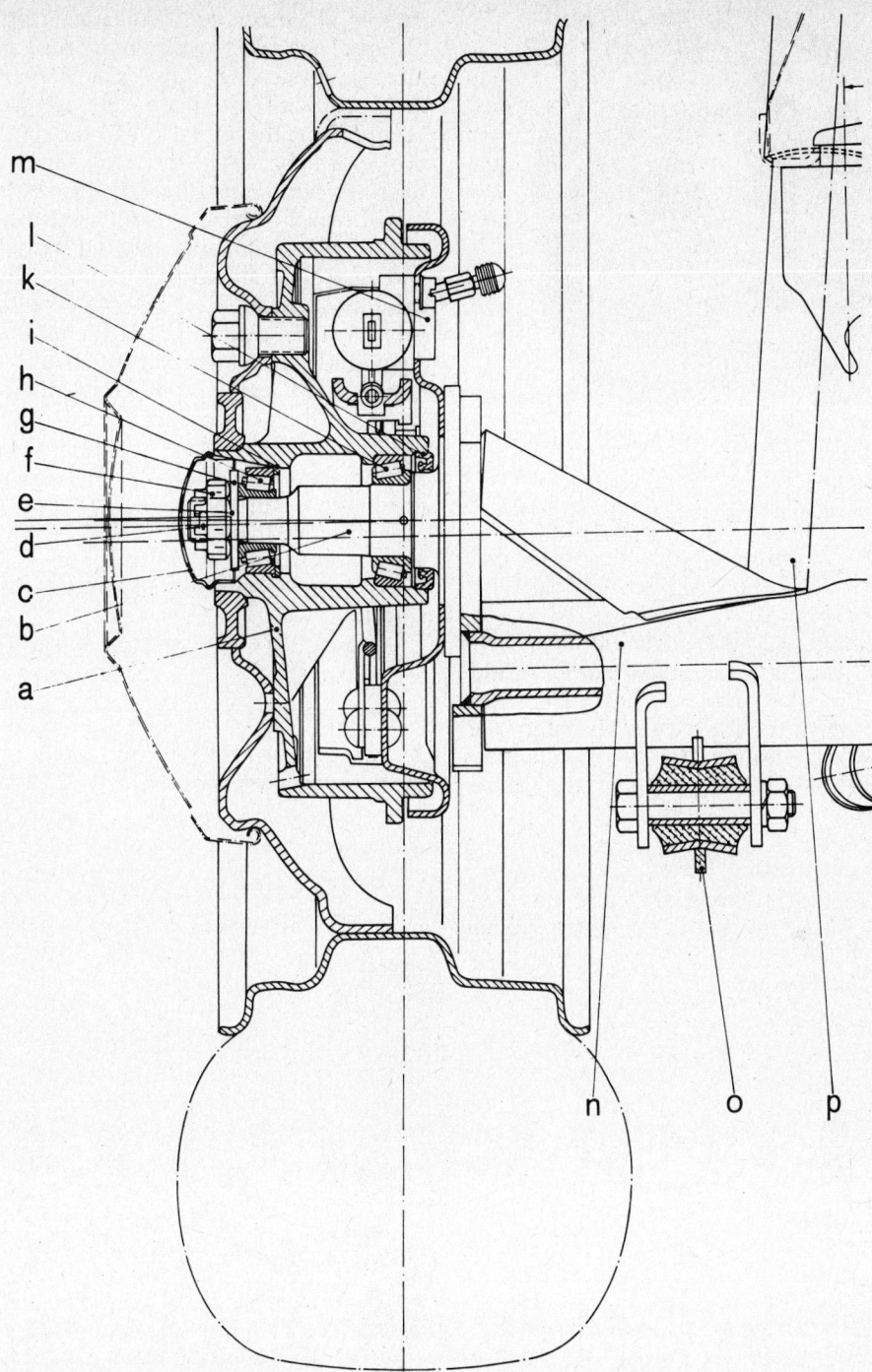

Rear wheel bearing and stub axle assembly.

a   Brake drum, assembled (with centering ring)
b   Rear stub axle
c   Cap
d   Cotter pin 4 x 30 DIN 94
e   Hex. head nut M 16 x 1
f   Castle lock
g   Washer 3.0 mm (0.118 inch)
h   Taper roller bearing LM 11 749/LM 11 710

i   Seeger circlip J 40 x 1.75 V
k   Taper roller bearing L 44 649/L 44 610
l   Shaft seal 38 x 52 x 7
m   Shoe-type brake assembly
n   Rear axle
o   Suspension arm
p   Shock absorber

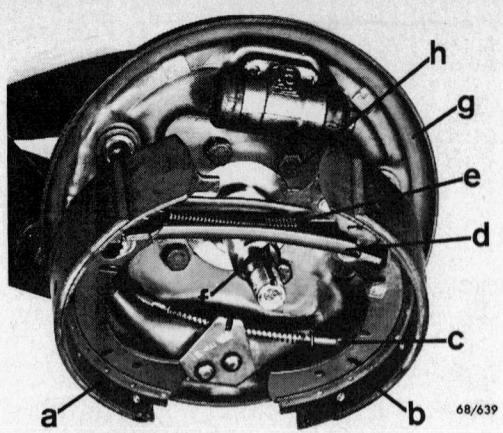

Rear brake shoe assembly

a	Brake shoe	e	Spring
b	Brake shoe with lever	f	Rear stub axle
c	Hand brake cable	g	Brake back plate
d	Pressure rod, left/right	h	Hex. head screw
			M 8 x 20

ring of the inner taper roller bearing with Calypsol wheel bearing grease and push it into the outer ring. Drive a new shaft seal into position (the open side of the seal should face the taper roller bearing). Fill the space between the two taper roller bearings with approximately 10 ozs. of Calypsol wheel bearing grease. Coat the inner ring of the outer roller bearing with grease and install the inner ring. Replace the stub axle and brake backing plate with the groove in the rear stub axle facing upward. Assemble the brake shoes, connect the hand brake cable and insert the brake shoes on the bottom bracket first, then the wheel cylinder at the top. Replace the retaining spring for the brake shoes. Replace the brake drum and wheel, special washer, castle nut and cotter pin. Fill the dust cap with approximately 10 ozs. of Calypsol wheel bearing grease and replace the dust cap.

out the shaft seal (which should always be replaced during rear axle service) and remove the inner ring of the taper roller bearing. Drive the roller bearing outer race from the brake drum. Remove the retaining ring and drive the outer roller bearing from the drum.

INSTALLATION

Replace the retaining ring and drive in the outer ring of the outer taper roller bearing. Press in the outer ring of the inner taper roller bearing. Lightly coat the inner

Steering

The Audi uses a rack and pinion type steering.

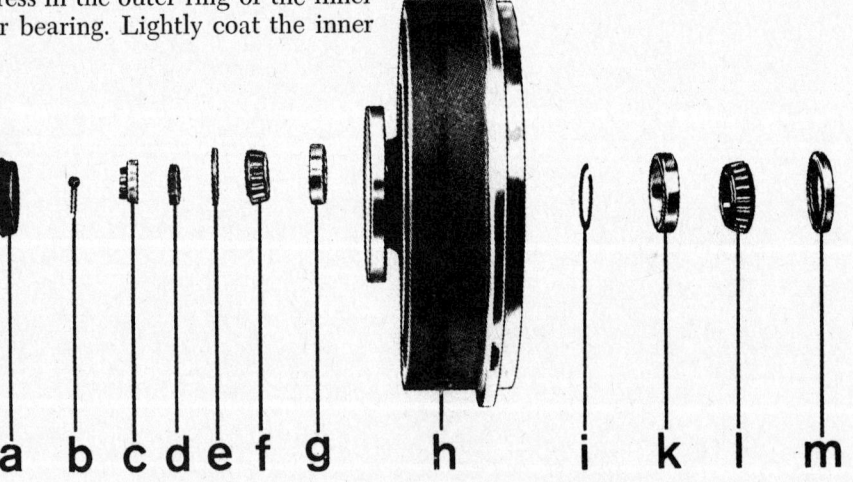

a b c d e f g   h   i k l m

Exploded view of rear brake drum and wheel bearing components.

a	Cap	g	Outer ring—taper roller bearing LM 11749/LM 11 710
b	Cotter pin 4 x 30 DIN 94	h	Brake drum
c	Castle lock	i	Seeger circlip J 40 x 1.75 V
d	Hex. head nut M 16 x 1	k	Outer ring—taper roller bearing L 44 649/L 44 610
e	Washer 3.0 mm (0.118 inch)	l	Inner ring—taper roller bearing L 44 649/L 44 610
f	Inner ring—taper roller bearing LM 11 749/LM 11 710	m	Shaft seal 38 x 52 x 7

Steering Wheel

REMOVAL

Center the steering wheel and pry off the steering wheel pad in an outward direction. Unbolt and remove the steering wheel.

INSTALLATION

Installation is the reverse of removal. Torque the nut to 36 ft. lbs.

100 LS

STEERING COLUMN

Removal

Remove the dashboard panel trim below the dashboard. Remove the steering wheel. Remove the slip ring and pull the ground lead from the slip ring. Remove the three mounting screws (above and below the steering column and at the base of the steering column casing on the right side) and remove the steering column casing. Remove the washers and the column gearshift (if equipped). Remove the steering tube from in front of the clutch and brake

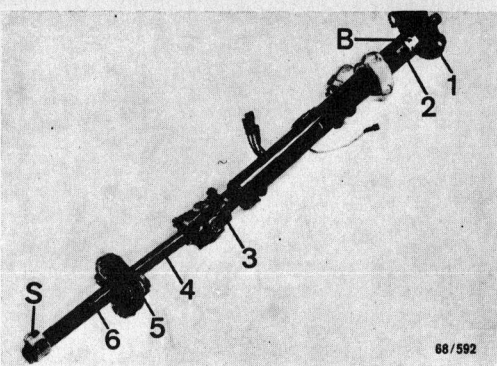

100 LS steering tube and column assembly (assembled).

1	Tube	5	Hardy disc
2	Steering column	6	Tube, welded assy.
3	Steering joint	B	Indicator self-cancelling
4	Intermediate shaft, welded assy.		device
		S	Clip

pedals. Remove the combination switch from the steering tube and disconnect the lead from the terminal of the switch. Disconnect the ignition lock cable at the connections. *NOTE: Be careful to note the colors of the leads to the ignition switch.* Loosen the clamp from the steering column, tube and pinion. Loosen the lower

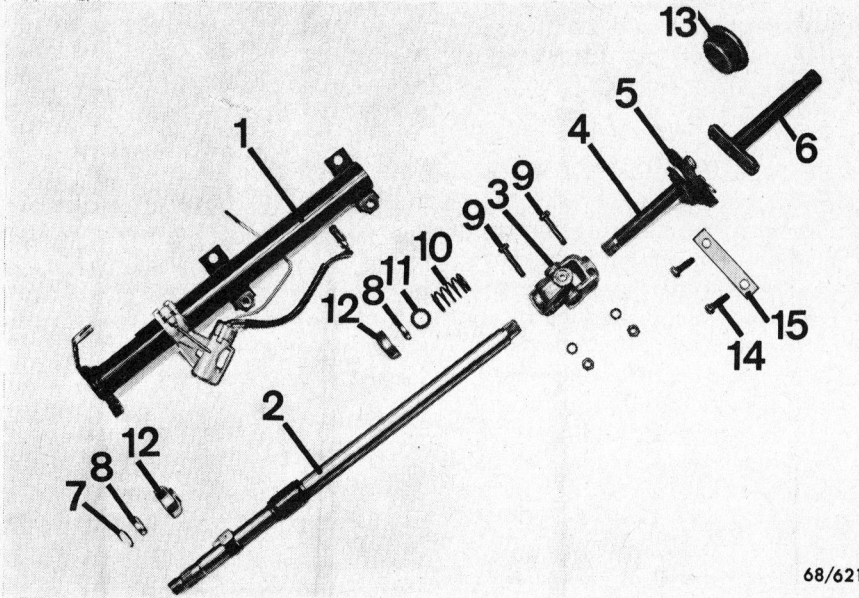

Exploded view of 100 LS steering column and tube.

1	Tube	7	Snap ring	10	Spring
2	Steering column	8	Support ring	11	Washer
3	Steering joint	9	Hex. head screw M 8 x 40	12	Steering column bearing
4	Intermediate shaft, welded assy.		Spring washer B 8	13	Cap
5	Hardy disc		Hex. nut M 8	14	Hex. head screw M 8 x 25
6	Tube, welded assy.			15	Lockplate
	Plug				

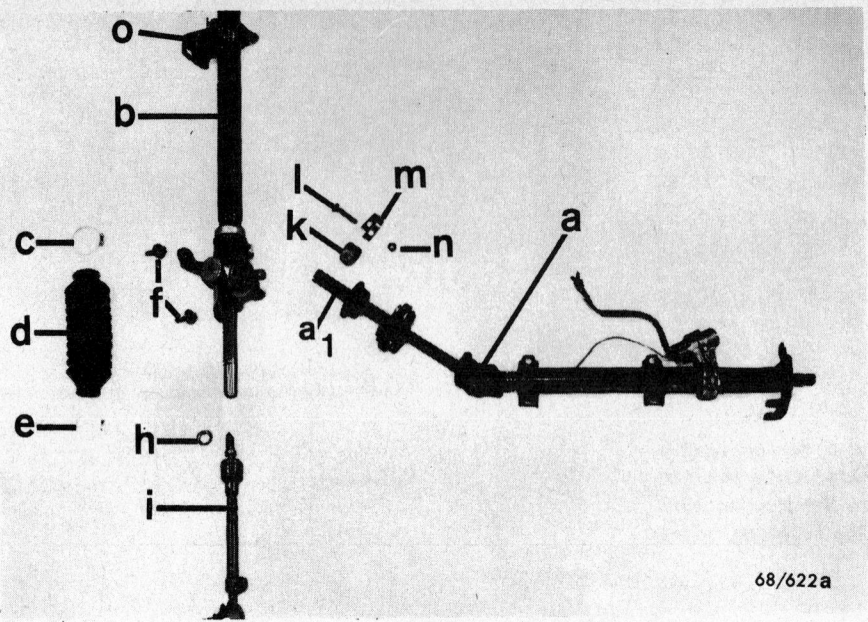

Exploded view of 100 LS steering gear.

a	Steering column	f	Hex. head screw M 8 x 30	m	Lock plate
a₁	Tube		Washer B 8.4	n	Hex. nut M 8
b	Steering gear, LHD		Springer washer B 8	o	Mount
c	Hose clip 45/7 Zy	h	Lockplate		Hex. head screw BM 8 x 70
d	Boot	i	Track rod		Washer A 8.4
e	Hose clip 38/7 Zy	k	Clip		Spring washer B 8
		l	Hex. head screw M 8 x 40		Hex. nut M 8

tube mounting and pull out the steering column.

Disassembly

Remove the tube from the Hardy disc. Pull the steering column out of the tube slightly, and remove the snap ring and support ring. Loosen the connection and remove the steering joint and the spring washer. Remove the steering column bearing by removing the steering column. Remove the intermediate shaft and Hardy disc from the steering joint. Unscrew the Hardy disc from the intermediate shaft. Use a drift to drive the upper steering column bearing from the tube.

Assembly

Assembly is the reverse of disassembly, noting the following points. When installing the steering column bearing, first install the steering column in the tube and drive the bearing into place with an appropriate pipe. Install the steering joint so that the groove is in exact alignment with the threaded hole for the screw. Be sure that the steering column is assembled to the

Hardy disc with the clip upward and the stop for the self-cancelling indicator forward.

Installation

To install the steering column and tube, reverse the removal procedures. Be careful of the color coded wiring and be sure that the washers at the wheel end of the column are installed, thicker washer with the cut-out facing downward.

STEERING GEAR

Removal

Remove the steering gear and pry the track rods out of the steering knuckle. Loosen the mount and steering gear. Slide the steering gear, first to the right, then remove through the engine compartment.

Disassembly

No repair work should be made to the steering gear. If it is defective, replace the unit.

Installation

Installation is the reverse of removal.

Super 90

STEERING COLUMN

Removal

Remove the steering wheel. Remove the blower outlet below the instrument panel. Remove the instrument panel trim. Remove the Bowden cable from its mounting and place the ignition key in the Halt position and remove. Remove the indicator light return switch. Remove the starter switch from the steering ignition lock housing. Remove the spacer, lockrings and washers. Remove the retaining bracket from the steering tube below the dashboard. Slide the hose clamp upward. Turn the ignition key to Garage and pull the steering column outer tube from the end plate. Remove the end plate and the gasket. Bend open the lockplate and remove the steering column tube, being careful of the ground cable. The steering wheel must be turned all the way left to accomplish this.

Installation

Installation is the reverse of removal, noting the following procedures. Before installing the outer tube, fit the hose clamp and end plate on the outer tube. The hose clamp screw should face upward and the end plate should be at an angle of 4° 48′ to the left. Install the end plate in the following manner to prevent leakage. Fit the end plate to the four studs of the firewall. Torque the lower, then the upper nuts to 1.8 ft. lbs. Tighten the hose clamp, steering column outer tube and the end plate connections. Mount the steering casing bracket with the projections engaging the slot in the outer tube. The distance between the upper edge of the steering column and the upper edge of the steering column bearing must be 1.81″. Install the steering column tube mounting parts as illustrated. Center the steering gear and carefully turn the steering wheel until the center position of the rack has been reached. With the rack in the center position, the catch in the indicator return switch must be positioned exactly in the center of the cutout in the steering column outer tube.

STEERING GEAR

Removal

Remove the steering column and tube. Remove the cotter pin and castle nut from the stud of the track rod ball joint. Extract the ball joint, using a ball joint extractor. Remove the supports and brackets used to mount the complete steering gear. Press out the steering gear somewhat and turn

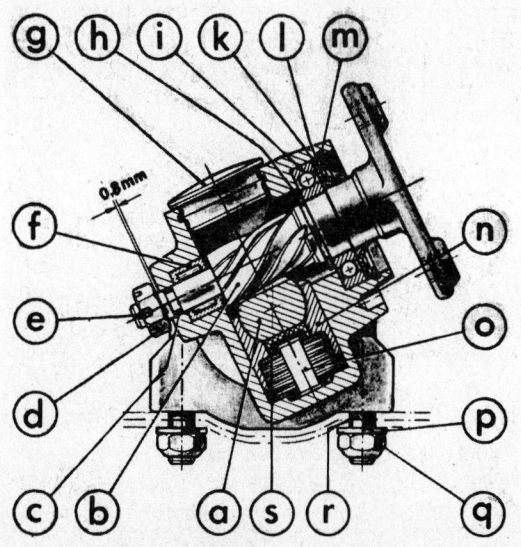

a   Rack
b   Pinion
c   O-Ring
d   Castle nut, 8 x 1
    (Torque 0.5 mkp, 3.6 ft. lbs.)
e   Cotter pin
f   Needle bearing
g   Plug
h   Retaining ring, 20 x 1.2
i   Ball bearing 16004
k   Seal
l   Backing ring
m   Retaining ring, 42 x 1.75
n   Pressure piece
o   Damper, complete
p   Washer
q   Hex. nut, M 8
    (Torque 1.8 mkp, 13 ft. lbs.)
r   Bracket
s   Insert, pressure piece

Cross-sectional view of Super 90 steering gear.

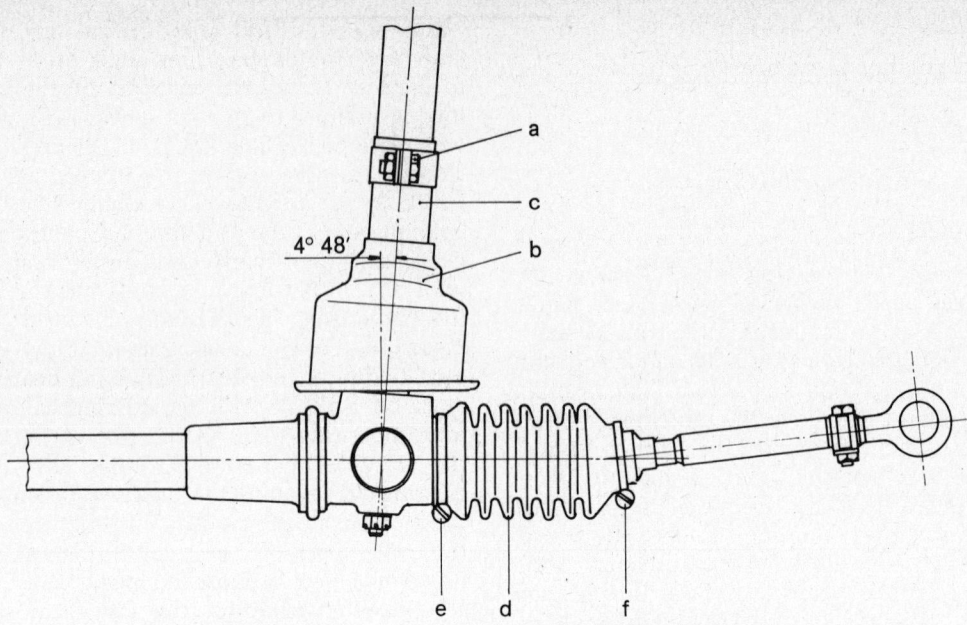

Installation position of Super 90 steering column and tube.

a   Hose clip and connection   d   Boot
b   End plate   e   Fillister head screw/host clip S 52/7
c   Steering column outer tube   f   Fillister head screw/hose clip S 38/7

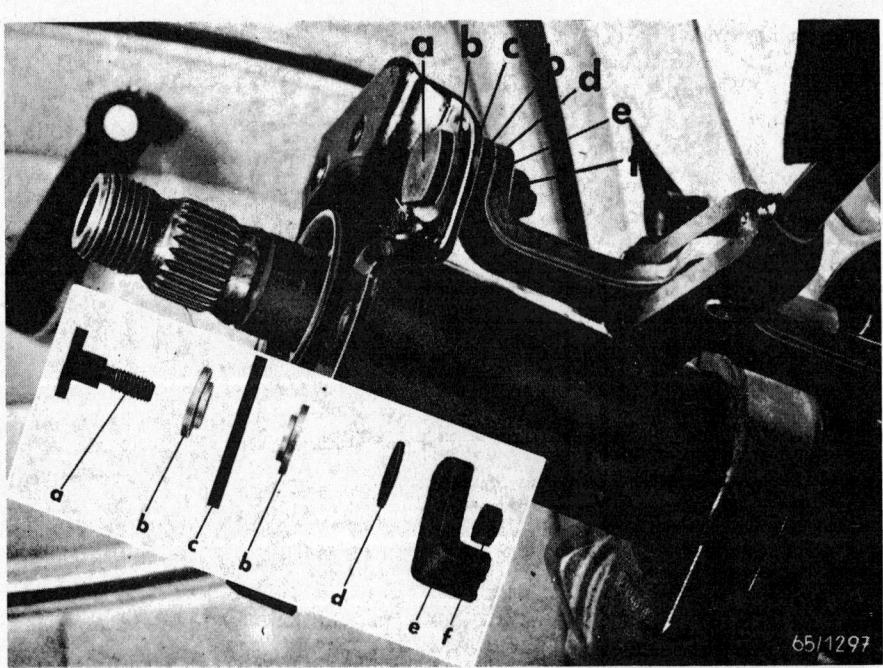

Exploded view of Super 90 steering column tube
mounting components.

a   Shouldered screw   d   Washer B 6.4
b   Plastic washer   e   Head on shift tube
c   Flange—steering column outer tube   f   Hex. nut M 6
b   Plastic washer

the pinion 90° downward in a clockwise direction. Remove the steering gear by pulling it out to the left (as seen in the driving direction).

Installation

Installation is the reverse of removal.

Brakes

The Audi 100 LS and the Super 90 are equipped with hydraulic twin circuit foot brakes, acting on all four wheels. The braking power is transmitted to the wheels through front disc brakes and rear drum brakes. The calipers on the front disc brakes are designed to function as a brake cylinder with one piston each. *NOTE: The housing halves may not be separated, nor the mounting screws loosened, since the passages are cast and sealed at the factory.*

The 100 LS is equipped with a power brake device, which is available on the Super 90 as an option.

NOTE: After any repair has been made to the brake system, it is necessary to pump the brakes several times before the car is driven, to ensure proper contact with the disc brake pads.

Master Cylinder

100 LS

Removal

The 100 LS (with power brakes) uses a tandem master cylinder as described following.

Unscrew the joint nearest the power brake booster on the inside of the master cylinder. Depress and hold the brake pedal about 1½″ down. Release the brake pedal and catch the escaping brake fluid. Remove the brake pipe line nearest the end of the master cylinder. Pull off the cable at the brake light switch. Unscrew the mounting bolts and remove the master cylinder from the power brake booster. Note the round ring between the booster and master cylinder.

Disassembly

Clean the outside of the master cylinder. Remove the brake fluid container, unscrew

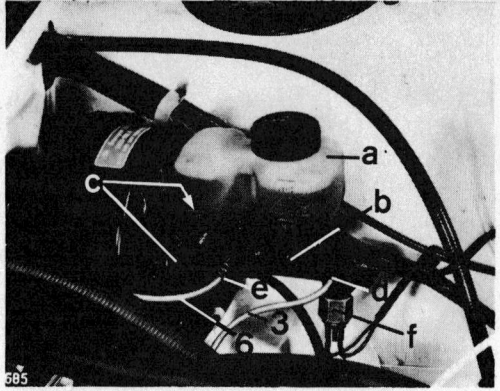

Installed 100 LS brake master cylinder and power brake booster.

a	Brake fluid container
b	Brake master cylinder
c	Mounting nut
f	Brake light switch
3	Brake pipe line to disc brakes
6	Brake pipe line to drum brakes

the brake light switch, remove the circlip and dismantle the unit. It will be necessary to partially unscrew the stop screw to remove the secondary piston.

All parts must be thoroughly cleaned in alcohol only. Dry the parts with compressed air and be sure that the compensating port is not plugged. Visually inspect all components with a magnifying glass. Replace any components that are suspect. Rubber boots and container plugs should always be replaced.

MASTER CYLINDER REPAIR TOLERANCES

Nominal Diameter	*Housing: Min. Diameter*	*Piston: Max. Diameter*
.813″	.817″	.807″

Assembly

Apply a thin coat of ATE brake cylinder paste to the cylinders and boots. Preassemble and install the piston as illustrated. Be sure that the boots are installed correctly and are not damaged. Check the pistons for ease of operation. If the pistons do not return quickly to the stop screw, dismantle the master cylinder and lightly polish the cylinder surface. Further assembly instructions are the reverse of disassembly. Under no circumstances should grease be applied to the pushrod.

Installation

Installation is the reverse of removal. After installing, check the brake fluid level

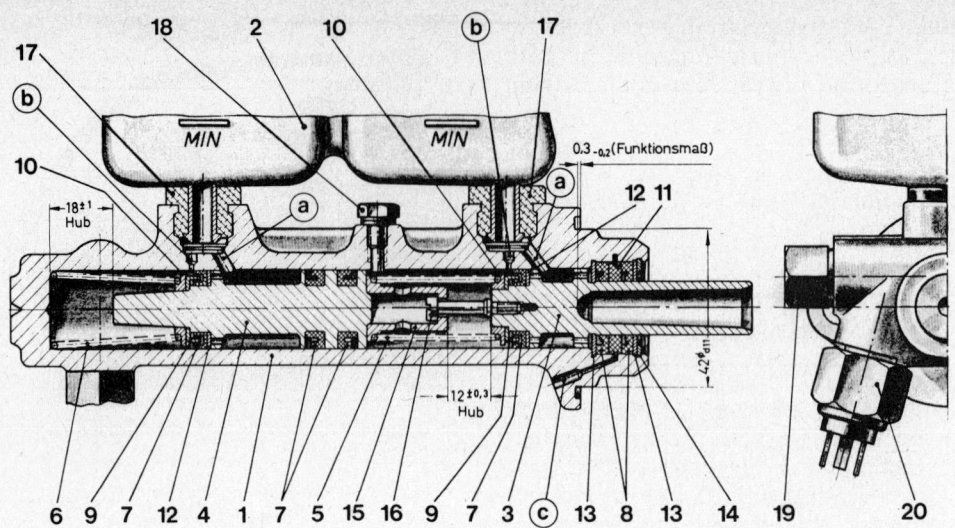

Cross-sectional view of tandem brake master cylinder.

1	Brake master cylinder	9	Support ring	17	Container plug
2	Brake fluid container	10	Spring retainer	18	Stop screw, outer
3	Primary piston	11	Intermediate ring	19	Pressure valve
4	Secondary piston	12	Filler disc	20	Brake light switch
5	Primary spring	13	Stop disc	a	Filling bore
6	Secondary spring	14	Circlip 25 x 1.2	b	Compensating bore
7	Primary boot	15	Stop sleeve	c	Air compensating bore
8	Secondary boot	16	Stop screw, inner		

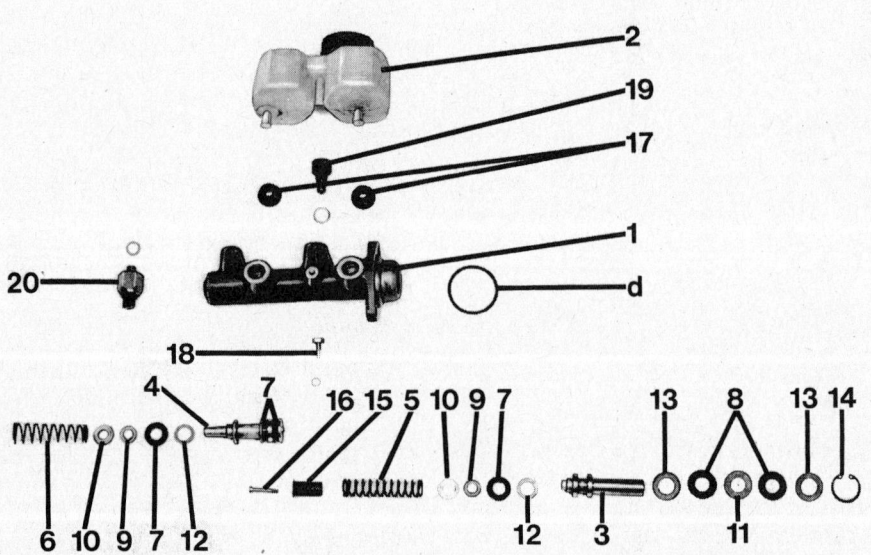

Exploded view of tandem brake master cylinder.

1	Brake master cylinder	9	Support ring	17	Container plug
2	Brake fluid container	10	Spring retainer	18	Stop screw, outer
3	Primary piston	11	Intermediate ring	19	Pressure valve
4	Secondary piston	12	Filler disc	20	Brake light switch
5	Primary spring	13	Stop disc	a	Filling bore
6	Secondary spring	14	Circlip 25 x 1.2	b	Compensating bore
7	Primary boot	15	Stop sleeve	c	Air compensating bore
8	Secondary boot	16	Stop screw, inner		

and bleed the brakes. Be sure to adjust and
test the brakes following any brake service.

SUPER 90

Removal

Remove the instrument panel trim Es pin
(see illustration) after removing the spring

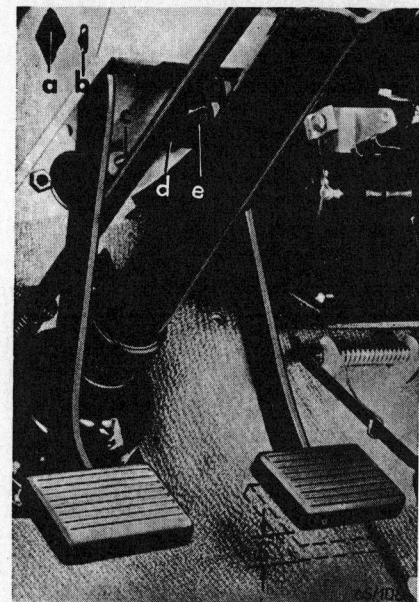

Disconnecting Super 90 brake pedal linkage.

a	Pin (bearing)	d	Counter nut
b	Hex. head screw (top)	e	ES pin
c	Piston rod	S	Play

clip. Pull the flat plug cable connection
from the brake light switch on the master
cylinder. Disconnect the brake line to the
brake discs (on the right of the master cylinder). When doing this, depress the brake
pedal approximately 1½″ and hold in this
position to close the compensating port in
the master cylinder. Release the pedal and
catch the escaping brake fluid. Remove the
master cylinder from the firewall.

Disassembly

Clean the outside of the brake master
cylinder. Remove the snap ring and dismantle the unit. Unscrew the brake fluid
container from the cylinder, being careful
not to lose the sealing ring from beneath
the container. Thoroughly clean all components in alcohol. Dry all components with
compressed air, and visually inspect all

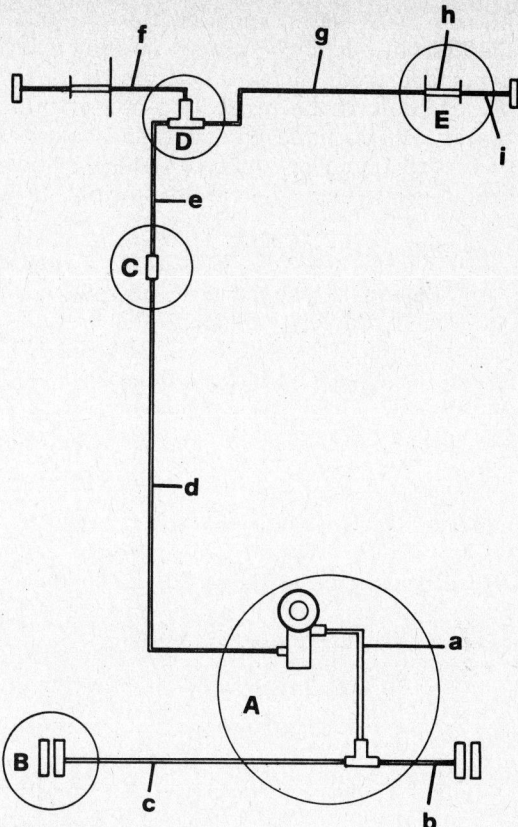

Super 90 and 100 LS brake diagram.

a	Brake hose, 290 mm (11.4 in.)
b	Brake line on gearbox, left
c	Brake line on gearbox, right
d	Brake line, front
e	Brake line, rear
f	Brake line, rear, left
g	Brake line, rear, right
h	Brake hose, rear, 360 mm (14 in.)
i	Brake line on rear axle

Each component of the **AUTO UNION AUDI** brake line
can be replaced separately.

parts for wear, rust or damage. Replace
any parts that are suspected of damage or
wear. Assemble the master cylinder as soon
as possible, following disassembly. Always
replace all rubber components.

MASTER CYLINDER REPAIR TOLERANCES

Nominal Diameter	Housing: Max. Diameter	Piston: Min. Diameter
.750″	.754″	.744″

Assembly

Assembly is the reverse of disassembly.
Apply a thin coat of ATE brake cylinder
paste to the cups and cylinder and assem-

ble the brake master cylinder. Be sure that the filler disc is in the proper position and is not damaged. Check the piston for ease of operation. If the piston does not return quickly, disassemble the unit and lightly polish the cylinder surfaces. At no time should grease be applied to the pushrod.

Installation

Installation is the reverse of removal. Apply a commercial sealant to the firewall and the brake master cylinder. After installation, the following must be done. Fill the master cylinder with brake fluid and bleed the brakes. Actuate the brake pedal several times. Measure the pedal play which should be approximately .2". Measure the clearance between the piston rod and the piston, which should be approximately .04". Check again to be sure that the master cylinder is ¾ full. Test the brakes to be sure they are functioning correctly.

Power Brake Booster (100 LS)

The 100 LS is equipped with a power brake booster which increases pedal pressure transmitted to the master cylinder by approximately 30%. The source of power is the difference in pressure between the engine produced vacuum in the intake manifold and atmospheric pressure. The brake device has been designed to assure the function of the braking system, even if the power brake booster were to fail.

Defective power brake boosters may not be repaired. They must be replaced.

REMOVAL

Remove the brake fluid from the container. Disconnect the brake light switch. Remove the brake lines from the master cylinder and pull the vacuum hose from the booster. Remove the instrument panel trim from below the dash. Remove the pin from the swivel joint of the brake pedal

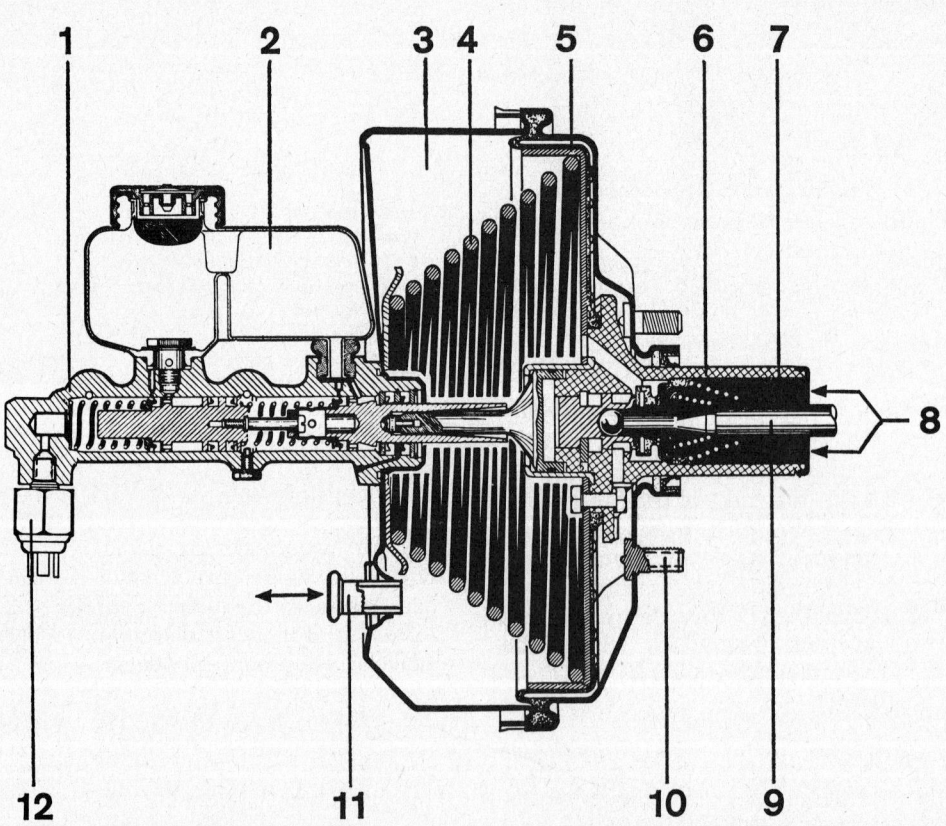

Cross-sectional view of tandem brake master cylinder and power brake booster.

1	Tandem-brake master cylinder	5 Roll diaphragm	9 Pressure rod
2	Brake fluid container	6 Timing housing	10 Mounting bolts, intermediate piece
3	Vacuum cylinder	7 Filter	11 Vacuum-connection
4	Spring	8 Air intake	12 Brake light swtch

linkage. Remove the power brake booster from the firewall. Separate the master cylinder from the booster. Do not lose the seal located between the booster and master cylinder.

INSTALLATION

Installation is the reverse of removal. After installation, check the piston rod clearance and pedal play which should be as follows:

Pedal play	.2″
Piston rod clerance	.04″

Wheel Bearing

Wheel bearing inspection and replacement is covered under Drive Axle and Snychronization Joints.

100 LS Front Brakes

CALIPER AND BRAKE DISC

Removal

The caliper and brake disc can only be removed together. Before removal, be sure that the caliper and disc have been cooled sufficiently.

Depress the brake pedal about 1½″ and hold in this position. Remove the brake pads. Disconnect the brake pipe line at the caliper and plug the opening. Loosen the caliper nuts with a wrench bent at an angle. Unscrew the driveshaft flange and slide it back and upward. Remove the brake disc and caliper, noting the insulating washer between the flange and brake disc.

Disassembly

The housing halves of the calipers may not be separated or loosened. Disassembly of the calipers is not recommended without special tools and training.

Installation

Installation is the reverse of removal. Each caliper should be installed in such a way that the bleeder screw is on top. Bleed and test the brakes.

BRAKE PADS

Replace

Extract the lock clips and remove the retaining pins. While doing this, hold the cross springs in place. Remove the cross

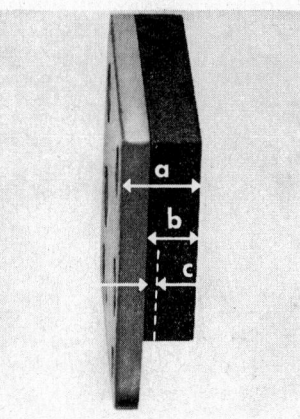

Disc brake pad tolerances.

a	thickness of disc pad with backplate	=	15 mm (0.59 inch)
b	thickness of disc pad—new	=	10 mm (0.394 inch)
c	thickness of disc pad—minimum	=	2 mm (0.078 inch)

69/713

Remove the caliper retaining nuts (100 LS).

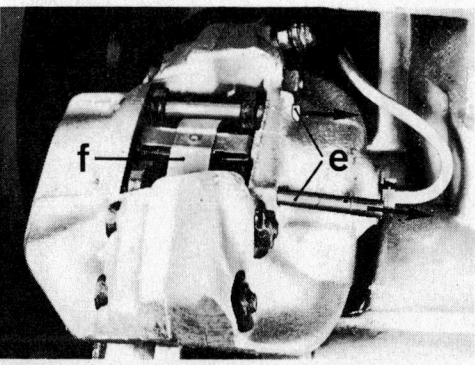

Remove the retaining pins and cross spring from 100 LS disc brake caliper.

springs and pull the brake pads from the calipers.

To install new pads, drain off some of the brake fluid from the master cylinder, since pressing the pistons back to install pads will cause the brake fluid level to rise. Press the pistons completely into the cylinder and check the alignment of the pistons. They should be at an angle of 20° to a gauge as shown; if not they must be rotated. Slide the disc pads into the caliper recess. Replace the retaining spring and install the retaining pins. *NOTE: Never use copper plated lock clips. Always pump the brakes several times to position the pads; otherwise, the brakes will fail.* Test the brakes, but do not apply maximum loads.

New brake pads must be "run-in" and no hard stops should be made with new pads for a distance of approximately 100 miles.

Brake Disc Inspection

The brake disc run-out should be checked with a dial gauge. The maximum

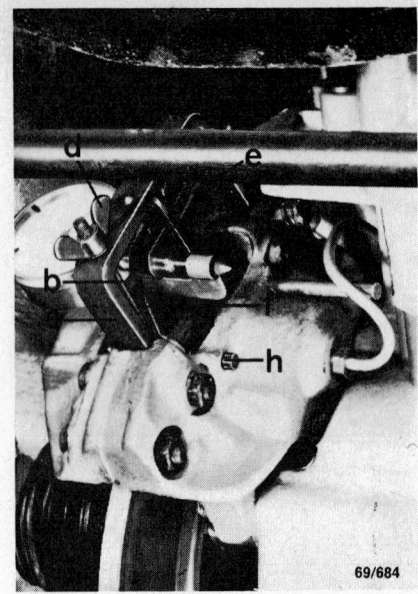

Measuring brake disc run-out.

a	bracket	e	dial gauge holder
b	clamping screw	f	feeler
c	washer	h	retaining pin
d	wing nut		

permissible brake disc run-out is .0047". Brake disc surfaces can be ground a maximum of .0098" per side. The maximum permissible thickness tolerance in any one area of braking surface is .0012". The illustration shows the equipment to measure brake disc run-out.

Super 90 Front Brakes

Brake Pads

Replace

The replacement procedure for brake pads in the Super 90 is identical to that of the 100 LS.

Caliper

Removal

Allow the caliper to cool before removing. To remove the right caliper, first disconnect the battery and remove it. Unscrew the caliper mounting nut. Depress the brake pedal approximately 1½" and hold it, in order to block the compensating port in the master cylinder. Loosen the hex nuts (with the aid of a suitable wrench bent at an angle).

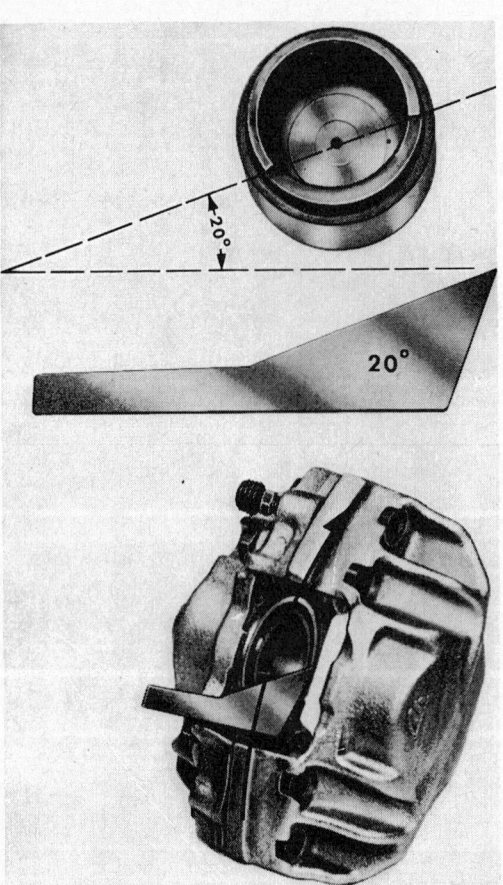

The pistons in the calipers must be aligned using a gauge.

Disassembly

The brake calipers should not be dismantled. See 100 LS Brake Caliper Disassembly.

Installation

Installation is the reverse of removal, noting the following points. The left and right calipers must not be confused, and should always be installed with the bleeder valve upward. Install the calipers without brake pads (these can be installed later). Always use new lockwashers. Refill the master cylinder reservoir and bleed the brakes. Recheck the fluid level and test the brakes (with no load).

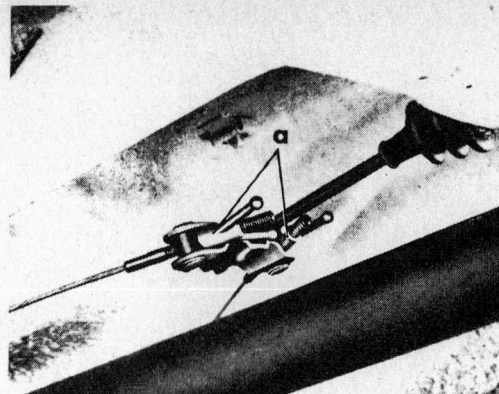

Adjusting a two-piece handbrake cable at the wing nuts (a).

BRAKE DISC

Removal

Jack the vehicle and remove the wheel. Disconnect the steering knuckle from the upper wishbone. Loosen the set screw and drive it out through the bore. Press the wishbone upward until the universal joint pin is clear. Unscrew the driveshaft flange and move it toward the outside. Remove the brake disc downward, being careful not to let the brake disc fall.

Installation

Installation is the reverse of removal.

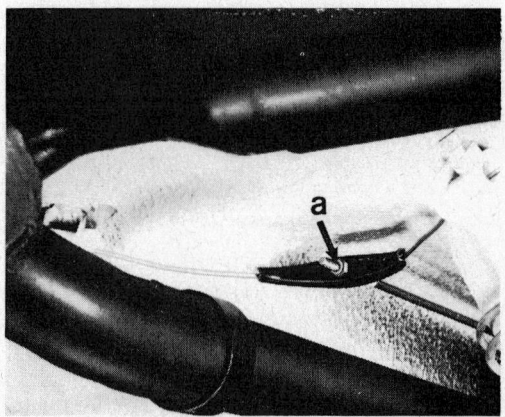

Adjusting a one-piece handbrake cable at the hex nut (a).

Rear Brakes

The rear brakes of the Super 90 and the 100 LS are drum type, hydraulically actuated in service, and used as the parking brake, actuated by a cable. The only service that can be performed is the checking of drums for scoring or out of round condition, replacement of the brake shoes and rebuilding the wheel cylinder.

Parking Brake

ADJUSTMENT

Super 90 and 100 LS

Jack the front of the car. The jack should be placed under the cross tube, never under the slotted axle tube. Be sure the handbrake cable operates easily. Engage the handbrake lever. As it engages the first or second tooth, both wheels must engage simultaneously. When the third or fourth tooth engages the wheels must lock. Using the wing nuts (or the hex nuts in the case of one-piece cables) adjust the cable accordingly. Actuate the brake several times, then loosen the brake and check the wheels for ease of rotation.

Accessories

Heater

100 LS

Removal

Drain the coolant, disconnect the battery, and remove the instrument panel trim from below the dashboard. Remove the breather screw, being careful not to dam-

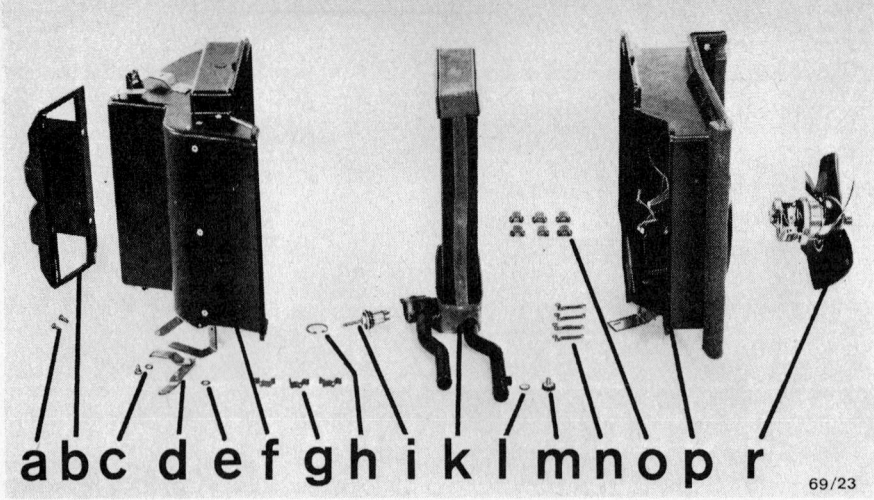

Exploded view of 100 LS heater.

a   Self-tapping screw   g   Spring clip, Bowden cable   m   Breather screw
b   Foot area nozzle   h   Circlip 25 x 1.2   n   Spring, blower motor
c   Hex. head screw   i   Plunger   o   Clip, housing halves
d   Adjusting lever   k   Heater body (heat converter)   p   Housing upper section
e   Nut 5   l   Seal   r   Motor and fan
f   Housing lower section

age the seal. Detach both heater hoses and
the instrument panel trim and the center
shelf. Disconnect the Bowden cables that
control the foot area heater flaps, the windshield flap and the heater valve. Remove
the plug connector from the heater controls
and the lead from terminal 15 of the emergency warning light switch. From the passenger compartment, unbolt the heater and
remove it downward.

Installation

Installation is the reverse of removal.
When installing the Bowden cables, place
the heater levers in the Off position. Place
the leg of the spring clip in the mount and
install the spring clip. The Bowden sleeve
must protrude at least .2″ beyond the
spring clip.

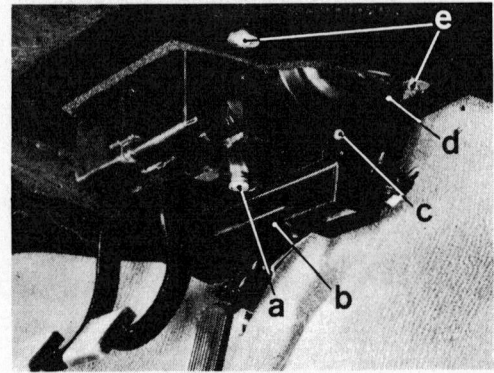

Installed position of Super 90 heater.

a   Drain plug
b   Blower jet
c   Retaining screw for b
d   Retaining screw for b
    (partially replaced by guide pin)
e   Self-tapping screw with washer

SUPER 90

Removal

Drain the coolant, disconnect the battery
and remove the instrument panel trim.
Drain the remaining coolant from the heat
exchanger. Unscrew the blower jet and
remove. Unscrew the Bowden cable (with
mounting for hood lock) and remove the
cable. Disconnect the brown and red flat
plug connections. Remove the right and
left defoster hoses and push them toward
the engine compartment. Remove the Bowden cable from the lever, located just to the
right of the steering column. Disconnect
the cables from the lower and center heater
control levers. Remove the left and right
water drain hoses. Unbolt and remove the
heater.

Installation

Installation is the reverse of removal. Mount the Bowden cables so that they allow the respective control levers a full stroke.

Windshield Wiper Motor

100 LS

Removal

Disconnect the battery negative terminal. Remove the right and left knee protection. From the engine compartment, pull out the rubber grommet to give the wiring harness more play. Pull out the wiper switch and remove the following: WECO connector white lead, yellow lead from ter-

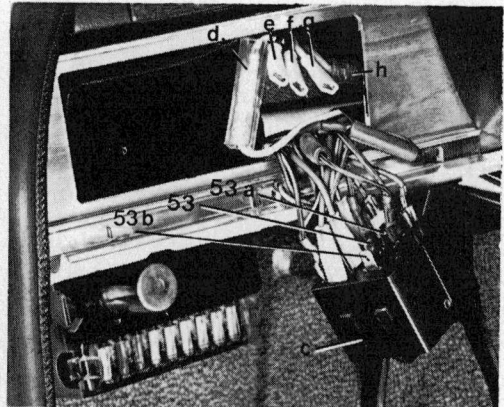

Windshield wiper switch connection (100 LS).

     c   Switch, wipers and warning light
     d   WECO connector, white lead
     e   Yellow lead (terminal 53 b)
     f   Red lead (terminal 53)
     g   Black lead (terminal 53 a)
     h   WECO connector, brown lead

minal 53b, red lead from terminal 53, black lead from terminal 53a and the WECO connector brown lead. Bend open the metal tabs holding the wiring harness and remove the harness which runs below the spray jets, together with the spray jet line. Loosen the nut and pry off the lever for the connecting transmission. Remove the motor and harness.

WINDSHIELD WIPER BASE

Removal

Remove the windshield wiper arms from the studs by prying off the cap and removing the retaining nut. Remove the lower

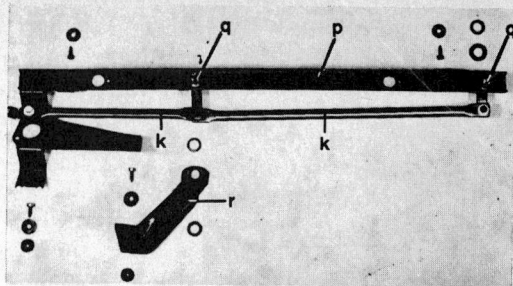

Exploded view of 100 LS windshield wiper base.

     k   Connecting rod   q   Wiper bearing
     p   Wiper base   r   Support

nut, washer and seal from the recess in the body. Remove the mounting screws in the engine compartment and tilt the wiper base to remove.

Installation

Installation of the wiper base and the wiper motor are accomplished by reversing the removal procedures. The lever connected to the wiper motor should be installed at approximately 90° to the driving direction of the vehicle. It should be noticed that wiper arm blades have different angles. The arm with the blade at the greater angle is installed on the driver's side.

Super 90

WINDSHIELD WIPER UNIT

Removal

Remove the wiper arm. The wiper arm is mounted either with a cap nut and domed

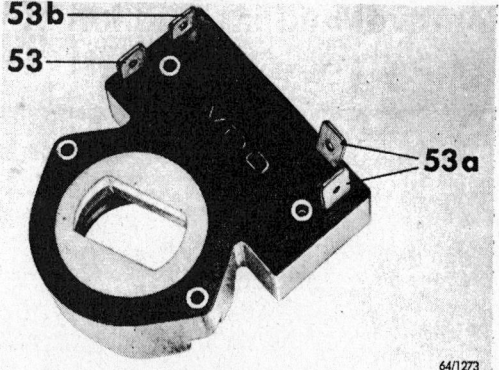

Super 90 wiper switch connections.

     53   Terminal, yellow cable
     53b   Terminal, white cable
     53a   Terminal, black and red/black cables

washer, or, by means of a spring which engages a groove. Pull the windshield washer pump from the dashboard and remove the hoses (long connection to the jets and short connection to the water supply). Remove the ring nut from the dashboard. Remove the switch and pull off the cables. Remove the brown cable from the combination instrument. Drain the coolant and remove the heater. Remove the nut from the wiper arm mounts. Disconnect the hoses from the jets. Tilt the wiper motor and base assembly to remove it.

Installation

Installation is the reverse of removal. Seal the cable hole in the firewall with a plastic sealant if necessary. Operate the wiper motor to be sure that the crank continues running (after the switch is shut off) to its final position (towards the right). Disassemble the crank and mount it properly if this does not occur.

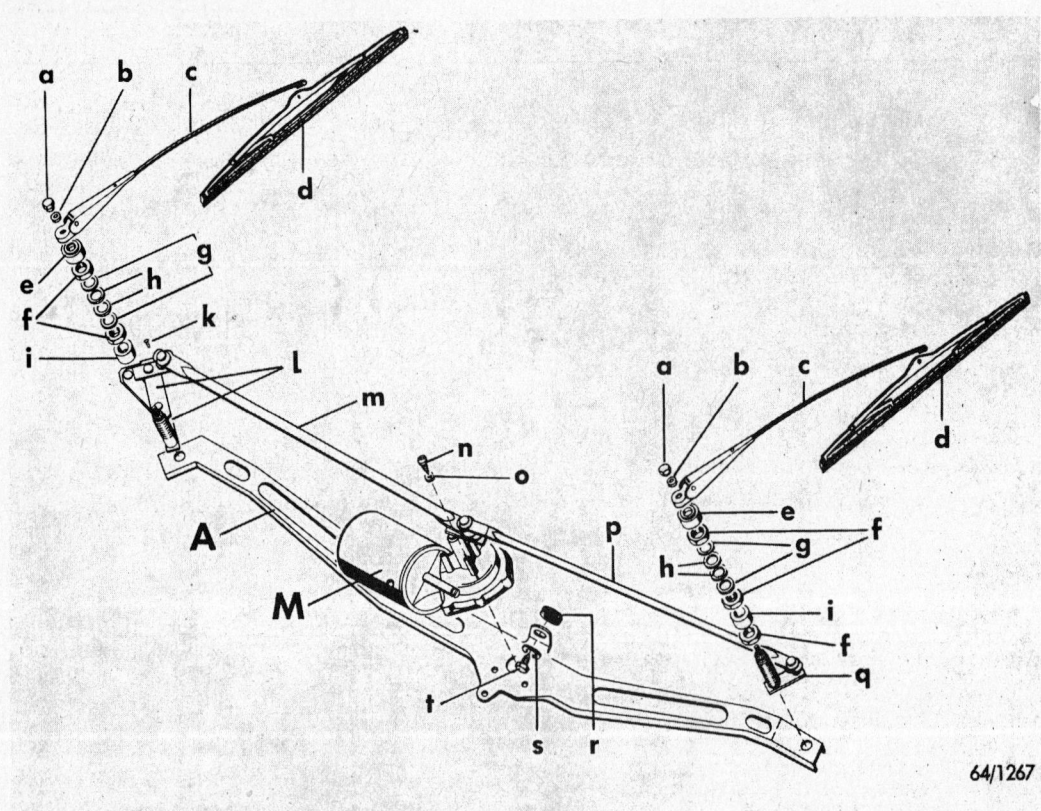

Exploded view of Super 90 wiper base and motor assembly.

A	Windshield wiper base	f	Hex. nut	n	Fillister-head self-tapping screw
M	Wiper motor	g	Washer	o	Lockwasher
a	Cap nut	h	Leather washer	p	Rod (thin)
b	Washer	i	Spacer	q	Wiper bearing
c	Wiper arm	k	Round head rivet 6 x 10	r	Rubber grommet
d	Wiper blade	l	Square joint	s	Washer
e	Seal cap	m	Rod (thick)	t	Hex. head self-tapping screw

BMW SECTION

Index

Model Identification

1600-2

1800

2000

2002

2500

2800

2800 CS

Introduction

The Bavarian Motor Works of Munich, Germany has a 50-year tradition of building engines with from one to twenty-four cylinders. The company was formed as the Bavarian Aircraft Works on March 7th, 1916. BMW engines have set speed and endurance records in the air, on the water, and on the ground. The first production jet aircraft was built by BMW in 1944.

The first motor vehicle to bear the white and blue BMW insignia of the whirling propellor was the BMW motorcycle, introduced in 1923. This machine used a horizontally opposed two cylinder engine and shaft drive, features which are retained in present day BMW motorcycles.

Car production was begun in 1928. The present, highly successful series of BMW automobiles was initiated in 1959, with the BMW 1500.

In 1967, the company introduced the BMW 1600 and 1800 Series, and later the 2002. All have in-line 4-cylinder water cooled engines with displacements upward from 120 cu. in.

In 1969, to satisfy the demand for a larger car that combines the ultimate in passenger comfort with the maneuverability of a sports sedan, BMW introduced the revolutionary 6-cylinder 2500 and 2800. These are full size, elegantly styled cars using fine materials, and are very fast, with amazing acceleration and cruising speeds of 130 miles per hour. General specifications for these cars can be found in this book; however, no repair procedures are available as yet.

In 1969, BMW produced 148,079 vehicles, of which 65,837 were exported.

Vehicle and Engine Serial Number Identification

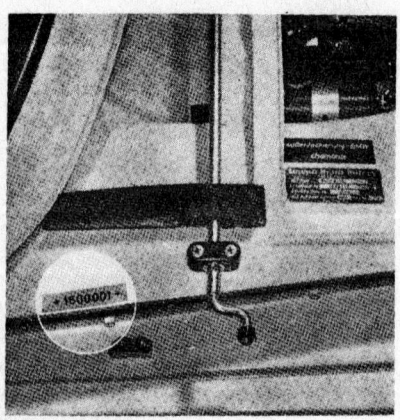

Engine compartment, with Chassis number, left, and Manufacturer's Plate number upper right.

Engine number is located on rear left side of crankcase.

The manufacturer's plate, chassis number and engine number are the means of identifying your car, and must be quoted in all correspondence with the dealer when requesting information or ordering spare parts.

The Manufacturer's Plate is located at the back of the engine compartment on the right. The Chassis Number is also located at the back of the engine compartment next to the lock. The Engine Number is on the rear left hand side of the crankcase.

Firing Order

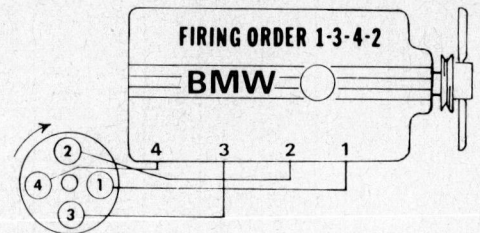

Tightening Sequences

Cylinder head tightening sequence for four cylinder engines.

Cylinder head tightening sequence for BMW 2500, 2800.

General Specifications

Model	Engine			Horsepower (SAE)		Carb. Type	Brakes F/R Disc (DS) Drum (DM)	Elec. Sys. (V.)	Track F/R (In.)	Wheelbase (In.)	Overall Dimensions (Approx. In.)			Wt. (Lbs.)	Tire Size (In.)	Tire Pres. (PSI)*** Std./Rad.	
	No. of Cyl.	Cap. (Cu. In./C.C.)	Comp. Ratio (:1)	BHP	@RPM						Lgth.	Width	Ht.			F	R
1500	4	91/1490	8.8	90	5900	SOLEX 36PDSI	DS/DM	6	52/54	100	177	67	57	2073	6.00-14, 165SR14	24/26	24/26
1600	4	96/1573	8.6	94	5700	SOLEX 36PDSI	DS/DM	6	52/54	100	177	67	57	2073	6.00S-14, 165SR14	24/26	24/26
1600 2 Door	4	96/1573	8.6	96	5800	SOLEX 38PDSI	DS/DM	6**	52/52	99	166	63	55	2070	6.00S-13, 165SR13	24/26	24/26
1600TI	4	96/1573	9.5	118	6200	2 SOLEX 40PHH	DS/DM	12	52/52	99	166	63	55	2070	165SR13	24/26	24/26
1800, 1800A	4	108/1773	8.6	102	5800	SOLEX 38PDSI	DS/DM	6	52/54	100	177	67	57	2073	6.00S-14, 165SR14	24/26	24/26
1800/69	4	108/1766	8.6	102	5800	SOLEX 38PDSI	DS/DM	12	52/54	98	177	67	57	2073	6.00S-14, 165SR14	24/26	24/26
1800TI	4	108/1773	9.5	124	5800	2 SOLEX 40PHH	DS/DM	6	52/54	100	177	67	57	2073	6.00S-14, 165SR14	24/26	24/26
2002, 2000CA	4	121/1990	8.5	113	6000, 5800CA	SOLEX 40PDSIT* or 40PDSI	DS/DM	12	52/52	99,100	166, 178	63, 66	55, 53	2200	165SR13 6.955-14, 175SR (or HR) 14	24/26	24/26
2000, 2000A	4	121/1990	8.5	113	6000	SOLEX 40PDSIT* or 40PDSI	DS/DM	12	52/54	100	177	67	57	2300	175H14, 175SR (or HR) 14	24/26	24/26
2000TI, 2000CS	4	121/1990	9.3	135	5800	2 SOLEX 40PHH	DS/DM	12	52/54	100	177, 178	67, 65	57, 53	2300	6.95H-14, 175SR (or HR) 14	24/26	24/26
2500	6	152/2494	9.0	170	6000	2 ZENITH 35/40INAT	DS/DS	12	57/58	106	185	69	55	2950	DR70X14	27/29	26/28
2800	6	170/2788	9.0	192	6000	2 ZENITH 35/40INAT	DS/DS	12	57/58	106	185	69	57	2950	DR70X14	27/29	26/28
2800CS	6	170/2788	9.0	192	6000	2 ZENITH 35/40INAT	DS/DM	12	57/55	103	183	66	54	2866	DR70X14	27/29	26/28

*With automatic choke.   **Later models have a 12-volt system.   ***For continuous use above 150 KPh (93 mph), add 3 PSI.

Engine Specifications

Model	No. of Cyls.	Displacement Cu. In. (cc) (effective)	Bore In. (mm)	Stroke In. (mm)	Compression Ratio	Torque Ft. Lbs./(KGM)/RPM	Max. Continuous Engine Speed RPM	BHP/RPM SAE
1500	4	91.47 (1499)	3.228(82)	2.795(71)	8.8:1	86.8(12)/3000	5800	90/5900
1600	4	95.99 (1573)	3.307(84)	2.795(71)	8.6:1	91.2(12.6)/3000	5800	94/5700
1600 2 Door	4	95.99 (1573)	3.307(84)	2.795(71)	8.6:1	91.2(12.6)/3000	5800	96/5800
1600TI	4	95.99 (1573)	3.307(84)	2.795(71)	9.5:1	97.3(13.4)/4500	6400	118/6200
1800, 1800A	4	108.2 (1773)	3.307(84)	3.150(80)	8.6:1	105.6(14.6)/3000	5800	102/5800
1800/69	4	107.7 (1766)	3.504(89)	2.795(71)	8.6:1	105.6(14.6)/3000	5800	102/5800
1800TI	4	108.2 (1773)	3.307(84)	3.150(80)	9.5:1	109.2(15.1)/4000	6000	124/5800
2002	4	121.44 (1990)	3.504(89)	3.150(80)	8.5:1	115.7(16)/3000	6000	113/6000
2000, 2000A	4	121.44 (1990)	3.504(89)	3.150(80)	8.5:1	115.7(16)/3000	6000	113/6000
2000TI	4	121.44 (1990)	3.504(89)	3.150(80)	9.3:1	122.9(17)/3600	6000	135/5800
2000CS	4	121.44 (1990)	3.504(89)	3.150(80)	9.3:1	122.9(17)/3600	6000	135/5800
2000CA	4	121.44 (1990)	3.504(89)	3.150(80)	8.5:1	115.7(16)/3000	6000	113/5800
2500	6	152.1 (2494)	3.386(86)	2.82(71.6)	9:1	176(24)/3700	6000	170/6000
2800	6	170.1 (2788)	3.386(85)	3.150(80)	9:1	173.6(24)/3700	6000	192/6000
2800CS	6	170.1 (2788)	3.390(86)	3.150(80)	9:1	173.6(24)/3700	6200	192/6000

Note: Not all these models were imported into the United States.

General Tune-Up Specifications

| Model | Spark Plug Gap In. (mm.) | | | | | | Distributor | | | | | Valves | | | Pressures | |
	Bosch W200 T30	Beru 200/14/3A	Beru 230/14/3A	Champion N9Y	Bosch W215P21 (Platinum Tipped)	Bosch W235P21 (Platinum Tipped)	Point Gap In. (mm)	Dwell Angle°	Point Pressure oz.	Static Timing (Engine Cold)	Dynamic Timing	Clearance (In./mm Cold Engine)[2]	Int. Valve Opens/Closes @.02" (.5mm) Clearance	Int. Valve Opens/Closes @.011" (.28mm) Clearance	Cranking Compression (PSI)	Fuel Pump Pressure (PSI @ 1000 RPM)
1500	.024 +.004 (.6+.1)	.024 +.004 (.6+.1)	.024 +.004 (.6+.1)	.024 +.004 (.6+.1)	.014 (.35)		.016 (.4)	60±1	15.9-19.5	3°BTDC		.0059-.0079 (.15-.20)	4°BTDC 52°ABDC	18°BTDC 66°ABDC		Solex PE 15059 2.99-3.56
1600	.024 +.004 (.6+.1)	.024 +.004 (.6+.1)	.024 +.004 (.6+.1)	.024 +.004 (.6+.1)	.014 (.35)		.016 (.4)	60±1	15.9-19.5	3°BTDC	25°BTDC @1400 ±55 RPM[1]	.0059-.0079 (.15-.20)	4°BTDC 52°ABDC	18°BTDC 66°ABDC	*	Solex PE 15059 2.99-3.56
1600-2 Door	.024 +.004 (.6+.1)	.024 +.004 (.6+.1)	.024 +.004 (.6+.1)	.024 +.004 (.6+.1)	.014 (.35)		.016 (.4)	60±1	15.9-19.5	3°BTDC	25°BTDC @1400 ±55 RPM[1]	.0059-.0079 (.15-.20)	4°BTDC 52°ABDC	18°BTDC 66°ABDC	*	Solex PE 15520 2.99-3.56
1600 TI				.024 +.004 (.6+.1)	.014 (.35)		.016 (.4)	60±1	15.9-19.5	TDC	25°BTDC @2200 ±55 RPM	.0059-.0079 (.15-.20)	4°BTDC 52°ABDC	18°BTDC 66°ABDC	*	Solex PE 15520 2.99-3.56
1800, 1800A	.024 +.004 (.6+.1)			.024 +.004 (.6+.1)		.014 (.35)	.016 (.4)	60±1	15.9-19.5	3°BTDC	25°BTDC @1400 ±55 RPM	.0059-.0079 (.15-.20)	4°BTDC 52°ABDC	18°BTDC 66°ABDC	*	Solex PE 15059 2.99-3.56
1800/69	.024 +.004 (.6+.1)			.024 +.004 (.6+.1)		.014 (.35)	.016 (.4)	60±1	15.9-19.5	3°BTDC	25°BTDC @1400 ±55 RPM	.0059-.0079 (.15-.20)	4°BTDC 52°ABDC	18°BTDC 66°ABDC	*	Solex PE 15581 2.99-3.56
1800TI	.024 +.004 (.6+.1)					.014 (.35)	.016 (.4)	60±1	15.9-19.5	3°BTDC[3]	25°BTDC @2200 ±55 RPM	.0059-.0079 (.15-.20)	4°BTDC 52°ABDC	18°BTDC 66°ABDC	*	Solex PE 15059 2.99-3.56
2002	.024 +.004 (.6+.1)					.014 (.35)	.016 (.4)	60±1	15.9-19.5	3°BTDC	25°BTDC @1400 ±55 RPM	.0059-.0079 (.15-.20)	4°BTDC 52°ABDC	18°BTDC 66°ABDC	*	Solex PE 15517, 15574 2.99-3.56
2000, 2000A	.024 +.004 (.6+.1)					.014 (.35)	.016 (.4)	60±1	15.9-19.5	3°BTDC	25°BTDC @1400 ±55 RPM	.0059-.0079 (.15-.20)	4°BTDC 52°ABDC	18°BTDC 66°ABDC	*	Solex PE 15517, 15574 2.99-3.56
2000 TI						.014 (.35)	.016 (.4)	60±1	15.9-19.5	TDC	25°BTDC @2200 ±55 RPM	.0059-.0079 (.15-.20)	4°BTDC 52°ABDC	18°BTDC 66°ABDC	*	Solex PE 15517, 15574 2.99-3.56
2000 CS	.024 +.004 (.6+.1)					.014 (.35)	.016 (.4)	60±1	15.9-19.5	TDC	25°BTDC @2200 ±55 RPM	.0059-.0079 (.15-.20)	4°BTDC 52°ABDC	18°BTDC 66°ABDC	*	Solex PE 15517, 15574 2.99-3.56
2000 CA	.024 +.004 (.6+.1)					.014 (.35)	.016 (.4)	60±1	15.9-19.5	3°BTDC	25°BTDC @1400 ±55 RPM	.0059-.0079 (.15-.20)	4°BTDC 52°ABDC	18°BTDC 66°ABDC	*	Solex PE 15517, 15574 2.99-3.56

BMW Block, Pistons, and Ring Specifications

Model	Standard Cyl. Bore In. (mm.)	First Rebore In. (mm.)	Second Rebore In. (mm.)	Standard Piston Dia. In. (mm.)	First Oversize Piston Dia. In. (mm.)	Second Oversize Piston Dia. In. (mm.)	Piston Pin Dia. In. (mm.) White	Piston Pin Dia. In. (mm.) Black	Fit in Piston In. (mm.)	Ring End Gap In. (mm.) First and Second Ring	Ring End Gap In. (mm.) Third Ring	Ring Clearance in Groove In. (mm.) First Ring	Ring Clearance in Groove In. (mm.) Second Ring	Ring Clearance in Groove In. (mm.) Third Ring
1500	3.228, .00087 o/s (82, .022 o/s)	3.2383 (82.25)	3.2481 (82.50)	3.2258 (81.935)	3.2356 (82.185)	3.2454 (82.435)	.8662, .00012 u/s (22, .003 u/s)	.8662, .00012 u/s, .00024 u/s (22, .003 u/s, .006 u/s)	.00012–.00032 (.003–.008)	.0118–.0177 (.30–.45)	.0098–.0157 (.25–.40)	.0024–.0034 (.060–.087)	.0014–.0024 (.035–.062)	.00098–.00205 (.025–.052)
1600	3.228, .00087 o/s (82, .022 o/s)	3.2383 (82.25)	3.2481 (82.50)	3.3055 (83.960)	3.3154 (84.210)	3.3252 (84.460)	.8662, .00012 u/s (22, .003 u/s)	.8662, .00012 u/s, .00024 u/s (22, .003 u/s, .006 u/s)	.00012–.00032 (.003–.008)	.0118–.0177 (.30–.45)	.0098–.0157 (.25–.40)	.0024–.0034 (.060–.087)	.0014–.0024 (.035–.062)	.00098–.00205 (.025–.052)
1600-2	3.3071, .00087 o/s (84, .022 o/s)	3.3170 (84.25)	3.3268 (84.50)	3.3055 (83.960)	3.3154 (84.210)	3.3252 (84.460)	.8662, .00012 u/s (22, .003 u/s)	.8662, .00012 u/s, .00024 u/s (22, .003 u/s, .006 u/s)	.00012–.00032 (.003–.008)	.0118–.0177 (.30–.45)	.0098–.0157 (.25–.40)	.0024–.0034 (.060–.087)	.0014–.0024 (.035–.062)	.00098–.00205 (.025–.052)
1600TI	3.3071, .00087 o/s (84, .022 o/s)	3.3170 (84.25)	3.3268 (84.50)	3.3055 (83.960)	3.3154 (84.210)	3.3252 (84.460)	.8662, .00012 u/s (22, .003 u/s)	.8662, .00012 u/s, .00024 u/s (22, .003 u/s, .006 u/s)	.00012–.00032 (.003–.008)	.0118–.0177 (.30–.45)	.0098–.0157 (.25–.40)	.0024–.0034 (.060–.087)	.0014–.0024 (.035–.062)	.00098–.00205 (.025–.052)
1800, 1800A	3.3071, .00087 o/s (84, .022 o/s)	3.3170 (84.25)	3.3268 (84.50)	3.3055 (83.960)	3.3154 (84.210)	3.3252 (84.460)	.8662, .00012 u/s (22, .003 u/s)	.8662, .00012 u/s, .00024 u/s (22, .003 u/s, .006 u/s)	.00012–.00032 (.003–.008)	.0118–.0177 (.30–.45)	.0098–.0157 (.25–.40)	.0024–.0034 (.060–.087)	.0024–.0014 (.035–.062)	.00098–.00205 (.025–.052)
1800/69	3.5039, .00087 o/s (89, .022 o/s)	3.5137 (89.25)	3.5236 (89.50)	3.5024 (88.960)	3.5122 (89.210)	3.5220 (89.460)	.8662, .00012 u/s (22, .003 u/s)	.8662, .00012 u/s, .00024 u/s (22, .003 u/s, .006 u/s)	.00012–.00032 (.003–.008)	.0118–.0177 (.30–.45)	.0098–.0157 (.25–.40)	.0024–.0034 (.060–.087)	.0024–.0014 (.035–.062)	.00098–.00205 (.025–.052)
1800TI	3.3071, .00087 o/s (84, .022 o/s)	3.3170 (84.25)	3.3268 (84.50)	3.3045 (83.935)	3.3144 (84.185)	3.3242 (84.435)	.8662, .00012 u/s (22, .003 u/s)	.8662, .00012 u/s, .00024 u/s (22, .003 u/s, .006 u/s)	.00012–.00032 (.003–.008)	.0118–.0177 (.30–.45)	.0098–.0157 (.25–.40)	.0024–.0034 (.060–.087)	.0014–.0024 (.035–.062)	.00098–.00205 (.025–.052)
2002	3.5039, .00087 o/s (89, .022 o/s)	3.5137 (89.25)	3.5236 (89.50)	3.5024 (88.960)	3.5122 (89.210)	3.5220 (89.460)	.8662, .00012 u/s (22, .003 u/s)	.8662, .00012 u/s, .00024 u/s (22, .003 u/s, .006 u/s)	.00012–.00032 (.003–.008)	.0118–.0177 (.30–.45)	.0098–.0157 (.25–.40)	.0024–.0034 (.060–.087)	.0014–.0024 (.035–.062)	.00098–.00205 (.025–.052)
2000, 2000A, 2000TI, 2000CS, 2000CA.	3.5039, .00087 o/s (89, .022 o/s)	3.5137 (89.25)	3.5236 (89.50)	3.5024 (88.960)	3.5122 (89.210)	3.5220 (89.460)	.8662, .00012 u/s (22, .003 u/s)	.8662, .00012 u/s, .00024 u/s (22, .003 u/s, .006 u/s)	.00012–.00032 (.003–.008)	.0118–.0177 (.30–.45)	.0098–.0157 (.25–.40)	.0024–.0034 (.060–.087)	.0014–.0024 (.035–.062)	.00098–.00205 (.025–.052)

u/s undersize
o/s oversize

Crankshaft, Camshaft, and Connecting Rod Specifications
1500, 1600, 1600-2, 1600TI, 1800, 1800A, 1800/69, 1800TI, 2002, 2000, 2000A, 2000TI, 2000CS, 2000CA

No. of Main Bearings	Crankshaft					Camshaft		Connecting Rods		
	Main Journal Dia. In. (mm.)		Rod Journal Dia. In. (mm.)	Main Bearing Clearance (Radial Play) In. (mm.)	Crankshaft End Play In. (mm.)	Nominal Clearance In. (mm.)	End Play In. (mm.)	Small End Bore In. (mm.)	Big End Bore In. (mm.)	Rod Bearing Radial Play In. (mm.)
	Red	Blue	Standard Size							
	Standard Size									
5	2.165, .00079 U/S .00114 U/S	2.165, .00079 U/S .00114 U/S	1.8898, .00098 U/S .00114 U/S	.0019– .0027	.0024– .0064	.00134– .0064	.00079– .00512	.945, .00083 O/S	2.047, .00039 O/S	.00114– .00287
	(55, .010 U/S, .020 U/S)	(55, .020 U/S, .029 U/S)	(48, .009 U/S, .025 U/S)	(.03– .068)	(.06– .018)	(.034– .075)	(.02– .13)	(24, .021 O/S)	(52, .010 O/S)	(.029– .073)
	First Undersize		First Undersize							
	2.155, .00039 U/S .00079 U/S	2.155, .00079 U/S .00114 U/S	1.8799, .0004 U/S .0010 U/S							
	(54.75, .010 U/S .020 U/S)	(54.75, .020 U/S .029 U/S)	(47.75, .009 U/S .025 U/S)							
	Second Undersize		Second Undersize							
	2.1457, .00039 U/S .00079 U/S	2.1457, .00079 U/S .00114 U/S	1.8701, .0004 U/S .010 U/S							
	(54.50, .010 U/S .020 U/S)	(54.50, .020 U/S .029 U/S)	(47.5, .009 U/S .025 U/S)							

U/S – Undersize   O/S Oversize

Valve Specifications

Model	Running Clearance In. (mm) Int.	Running Clearance In. (mm) Exh.	Overall Length In. (mm) Int.	Overall Length In. (mm) Exh.	Head Dia. In. (mm) Int.	Head Dia. In. (mm) Exh.	Stem Dia. In. (mm) Int.	Stem Dia. In. (mm) Exh.	Guide Inside Dia. In. (mm)	Spring Length Un-Loaded In.
1500,1600, 1600-2, 1600TI, 1800,1800A, 1800/69, 1800TI, 2002,2000, 2000A, 2000TI, 2000CS, 2000CA	.00098- .00216 (.025- .055)	.00157-* .00275 (.040- .070)	4.087± .00079 103.8± .2)	4.106± .00079 (104.3± .2)			.315, .00157 U/S, .0098 U/S (8, .040 U/S, .025 U/S)	.315, .00157 U/S, .00217 U/S (8, .040 U/S, .055 U/S)	.315, .00059 O/S (8, .015 O/S	1.811 (46)
1500,1600					1.535 (39)	1.378 (35)				
1600-2, 1600TI, 1800, 1800A, 1800/69, 1800TI					1.654 (42)	1.378 (35)				
2002,2000, 2000A, 2000TI, CS,CA					1.732 (44)	1.496 (38)				

U/S—undersize O/S—oversize

Torque Specifications

Engine and Gearbox

	KGM	Ft. Lbs.
Cylinder head	6.8–7.2	49.2–52.0
Chain tensioner locking bolt	3–4	21.7–28.9
Main bearing caps	5.8–6.3	42.0–45.6
Connecting rod caps	5.2–5.7	37.6–41.2
Suction pipe attachment to oil pump retainer	0.9–1.1	6.5–8.0
Expansion bolt M12X1-5 (12K)		
with Loctite	9.0–10.0	65.1–72.3
without Loctite	10.0–11.0	72.3–79.6
Flywheel shoulder stud	7.0–7.5	50.6–54.2
Crankshaft pulley	14.0	101.3
Plug on oil pump	5.0	36.2
Water pump pulley	40	28.9
Gearbox mounting		
M 8	2.5	18.1
M 10	4.7	34.0
Gearbox spacer plate	2.0	14.5
Gearbox output flange	15	108.4
Gearbox housing cover	2.5	18.1
Gearbox sealing flange	1.0	7.2
Clutch mounting bolts	1.5–1.9	10.9–13.7
Spark plugs	2.5–3	18.1–21.7
Fuel pump	1.2	8.7
Oil drain plug	6.0	43.4
Oil sump	0.8–1.0	5.8–7.2
Carburetor to manifold (single carb.)	1.0–1.4	7.2–10.1
Hollow bolt for oil supply to camshaft	1.1–1.3	8.0–9.4
Timing case cover top to bottom	0.9	6.5
Distributor flange M 8	2.5	18.1
Distributor flange M 6	1.1	8.0
Cylinder head cover	0.8–1.0	5.9–7.2

Front Axle

	KGM	Ft. Lbs.
Shock absorber leg, center top	8.0	57.8
Shock absorber leg, support	2.5	18
Shock absorber screw ring	12.0+2	86.8+14.5
Shock absorber piston to piston rod	2.5	18
Tie-rod lever to axle	2.5	18
Guide joint to tie-rod lever—minimum	7.0	50.6
Wishbone to front axle (under load)—minimum	15.0	108.5
Front axle to frame	4.7	34.0
Strut to wishbone and axle (under load)—minimum	6.0	43.4
Caliper to axle	9.5	68.7
Steering lever bearing	2.5	18
Steering gear to front axle	4.7	34.0

Torque Specifications

Rear Axle

	KGM	Ft. Lbs.
Drive casing to floor	9	65
Rear axle carrier mounting to floor	12	87
Thrust rod on body floor	2.5	18
Trailing arm on axle beam (under load)	7.5	54
Lower shock absorber mounting (under load)	7.5	54
Final drive attachment	9	65
Large cover on casing	5	36
3-point coupling on pinion—minimum (with Loctite AVV)	15	108
Rubber coupling at gearbox	4.5	33
Ring gear to differential body	8.3	60
Side casing cover	2.5	18
Hexagon bolt on drive flange	9+1	65+7.2
Half-shaft castellated nuts min.	30+5	217+36
Output shaft at driving flange	3	22
Output shaft at half-shaft	3	22
Drive shaft at gearbox	3	22
Rubber bearing at rear axle carrier		
M8	3	22
M10	4.5	32.5
Housing cover (short neck unit)	2.0+0.5	14.5+3.6
Ring gear to differential (short neck unit)	8.5+1	61.5+7.2
Driving flange to half-shaft pinion (short neck unit)	9.0+1	65.1+7.2
Three-arm flange to input bevel pinion—minimum (short neck unit)	15.0	108.5
Output shaft to driving flange (short neck unit)	2.4+0.6	17.4+4.3
Final drive to rear axle carrier (short neck unit)	6.5+1	47.0+7.2
Rubber mounting to body floor (short neck unit)	4.2+0.5	30.4+3.6
Final drive to rubber mounting (short neck unit)	8.1+0.9	58.6+6.5
Drive shaft to final drive (1600–2)	4.5	32.5
Cross-member to final drive (1600–2)	4.5	32.5

Steering

	KGM	Ft. Lbs.
Steering damper to clamp	4.2+0.5	30.4+3.6
Steering damper to retaining strap	4.2+0.5	30.4+3.6
Steering wheel nut	5.5+0.5	39.8+3.6
Joint disc attachment	1.5+0.5	10.8+3.6
Joint flange attachment	2.5	18.0
Steering arm to steering box	14	101.3
Castellated nut on steering guide arm—minimum	8	57.8
Retaining strap to engine mounting	1.9+0.5	13.7+3.6
Clamp to track rod	1.9+0.5	13.7+3.6
Track rod castellated nuts—minimum	3.5	25.3
Steering box to front axle beam	4.7	34.0
Guide lever to front axle beam	2.5	18.0
Track rod clamp bolts	2.5	18.0

Brakes and Wheels

	KGM	Ft. Lbs.
Caliper to kingpin pivot	9.5	68.7
Brake disc to wheel hub	6+0.7	43.4+5.0
Brake hose to caliper	1.3–1.6	8.7–11.6
Pre-pressure valve	1.9	13.7
Wheel nuts	9	65.1
Collar nut on brake line	1.3–1.6	8.7–11.6
Retainer on rear of brake unit (1600–2)	1.9+0.5	13.7+3.6
Retainer on front of brake unit (1600–2)	1.6+0.4	11.6+2.9
Brake unit holder to wheel arch (1600–2)	1.6+0.4	11.6+2.9
Caliper halves	3.4	24.6

Note: See cylinder head tightening sequence.

Electrical Equipment Specifications

Model	Battery		Starter	Generator		Alternator		Regulator			Coil	
	Amp-Hrs.	Volts/Ground	Bosch Type	Bosch Type	Max. Amp. Output	Bosch Type	Max. Amp. Output	Bosch Type	Cut-In V.	Reg. V.	Bosch Type	Mean Watts
1500, 1600, 1600-2	77	6/N	GF(R) 6V	LJ/GEG200/ 6/2400R	50			RS/VA200/ 6A/(1/1)	5.9-6.5	6.3-7.6	TE6B4	12-15
1600-2 (Later Models)	36	12/N	EF(R) 12V			KI/14V/ 35A20	35	AD1/14V			K12V	19
1600TI	44	12/N	EF(R) 12V			KI/14V/ 35A20	35	AD1/14V		13.5-14.2	K12V	19
1800, 1800A	77	6/N	GF(R) 6V	LJ/GEG200/ 6/2400R	50			RS/VA200/ 6A/(1/1)	5.9-6.5	6.3-7.6	TE6B4	12-15
1800/69	77	12/N	EF(R) 12V			KI/14V/ 35A20	35	AD 1/14V		13.5-14.2	TE6B4	12-15
1800TI	66	6/N	GF(R) 6V			KI/7V/ 50A17	50	ADN 1/7V		6.3-7.6	TK6A3	13-16
2002, 2000, 2000A, 2000TI, 2000CS, 2000CA	44	12/N	GF(R) 12V			KI/14V/ 35A20	35	ADN 1/14V		12.6-14.6	K12V	19
2500, 2800	55	12/N	GF(R) 12V			KI/14V/ 35A20	35	ADN1/14V		12.6-14.6	K12V	19

Capacities

Model	Crankcase		Transmission		Rear Axle		Fuel		Cooling Capacity (Pts) (Including Heater)
	Cap. (Pts) (Add .53 for Filter)	Max. Oil Press. (PSI)	Cap. (Pts)	Vis. (SAE)	Cap. (Pts)	Vis. (SAE)	Tank Cap. (Gals)	Pump Press. (PSI @1000 RPM)	
1500	8.6	71-85	2.64	80	1.9	90	14.5	2.99-3.56	14.6
1600	8.6	71-85	2.64	80	1.9	90	14.5	2.99-3.56	14.6
1600-2 Door	8.6	71.85	2.1	80	1.9	90	12.2	2.99-3.56	14.6
1600TI	8.6	71-85	2.1	80	1.9	90	12.2	2.99-3.56	14.6
1800, 1800A	8.6	71-85	2.1*, Note 1	80 ATF TYPE A	1.9 Note 2	90	14.5	2.99-3.56	14.6
1800/69	8.6	71-85	2.1	80	1.9 Note 2	90	14.5	2.99-3.56	14.6
1800TI	8.6	71-85	2.1*	80	1.9	90	14.5	2.99-3.56	14.6
2002	8.6	71-85	2.1	80	1.9	90	12.2	2.99-3.56	14.6
2000, 2000A	8.6	71	2.1, Note 1	80, ATF TYPE A	1.9 Note 2	90	14.5	2.99-3.56	14.6
2000TI	8.6	71	2.1	80	1.9 Note 2	90	14.5	2.99-3.56	14.6
2000CS	8.6	71	2.1	80	1.9 Note 2	90	14.5	2.99-3.56	14.6
2000CA	8.6	71	Note 1	ATF TYPE A	1.9 Note 2	90	14.5	2.99-3.56	14.6
2500	10.6						19.7	–	25.4
2800	10.6						19.7	–	25.4
2800CS, CA	10.6						15.4	–	25.4

Note 1 – ZF automatic transmission capacity is 10 Pts at initial filling and 3.2 Pts. at oil change.
Note 2 – Capacity is 2.74 Pts when the short neck rear axle is used on these models.
*2.64 Pts for long neck gearbox.

Wheel Alignment Specifications

Model	Front Caster	Front Camber*	Front Toe-In* In. (mm.)	Front Toe-Out on 20° Turn*	King Pin Angle	Rear Camber*	Rear Toe-In In. (mm.)
1500, 1600	3°±30'	0° 30'±30'	0–.079 (0–2)	1°±30'	8°±30'	2° negative	.039±.039 (1±1)
1600-2, 1600TI	4°±30'	0° 30'±30'	.059±.059 (1.5±1.5)	1°±30'	8° 30'	2°±20' negative	.039±.039 (1±1)
1800, 1800A	3°±30'	0° 15'±30'[1]	.059±.059 (1.5±1.5)	1°±30'	8° 40'	2° negative	.059±.059 (1.5±1.5)
1800/69	3°±30'	0° 15'±30'	.059±.059 (1.5±1.5)	1°±30'		2° negative	.059±.059 (1.5±1.5)
1800TI	3°±30'	0° 15'±30'	.059±.059 (1.5±1.5)	1°±30'		2° negative	.059±.059 (1.5±1.5)
2002	3°±30'	0° 15'±30'	.059±.059 (1.5±1.5)	1°±30'	8° 40'±30'	2° 20' negative	.059±.059 (1.5±1.5)
2000, 2000A, 2000TI, 2000CS, 2000CA	3°±30'	0° 15'±30'	.059±.059 (1.5±1.5)	1°±30'	8° 40'±30'	2° negative	.059±.059 (1.5±1.5)

*Vehicle loaded: 2x143 lb. (2x65kg) rear seats, 1x143 lb. (1x65kg) front seats, 66 lb. (30kg) in luggage compartment on left side, gas tank full.
[1] 0° 30' up to 1966 model.

Fuses

No.	Fuse (to DIN 72581)	Item
1	8 A	Front parking lights, left and right
2	8 A	License plate lights, right tail light
3	8 A	Instrument lights, left tail light
4	8 A	Interior light, clock, cigar lighter
5	8 A	Stop and turn lights, backup lights
6	16 A	Heater blower, horn, wiper motor, washer unit, fuel and temperature gauges, oil pressure and brake warning lights

Fuse numbers and sizes, and the circuits they control.

Light and Indicator Bulb Wattages

	1500	1600	1600-2	1600 TI	1800, 800A	1800 69	1800 TI	2002	2000, 2000A	2000 TI	2000 CS	2000 CA
Headlights, Low/High	45/40	45/40	45/40	45/40	45/40	45/40	45/40	45/40	45/40	45/40	45/40	45/40
Side and Parking	4	4	4	4	4	4	4	4	4	4	4	4
Front Flashing	18	18	21	21	18	18	18	21	21	21	21	21
Stop	18	18	21	21	18	18	18	21	21	21	21	21
Reverse	15	15	15	15	15	15	15	15	15	15	15	15
Rear Flashing	18	18	21	21	21	21	21	21	21	21	21	21
Tail and Parking	5	5	5	5	5	5	5	5	5	5	5	5
License Plate	5	5	5	5	5	5	5	5	4	4	5	5
Interior	5	5	10	10	10	10	10	10	5	5	5	5
Instrument	2	2	3	3	2	2	2	3			2	2
Battery Charge Indicator	2	2	4	4	2	4	4	4	4	4	4	4
High Beam Indicator	2	2	3	3	2	2	2	3	2	2	2	2
Flashing Indicator	2	2	3	3	2	2	2	3	2	2	2	2
Oil Pressure Indicator	2	2	3	3	2	2	2	3	2	2	2	2
Choke & Fuel Level Indicator	2	2			2	2	2		2	2	2	2
Selector Gate (Automatic Only)					2				2			2
Luggage Compartment											5	5
Engine Compartment											5	5

Wiring Diagrams

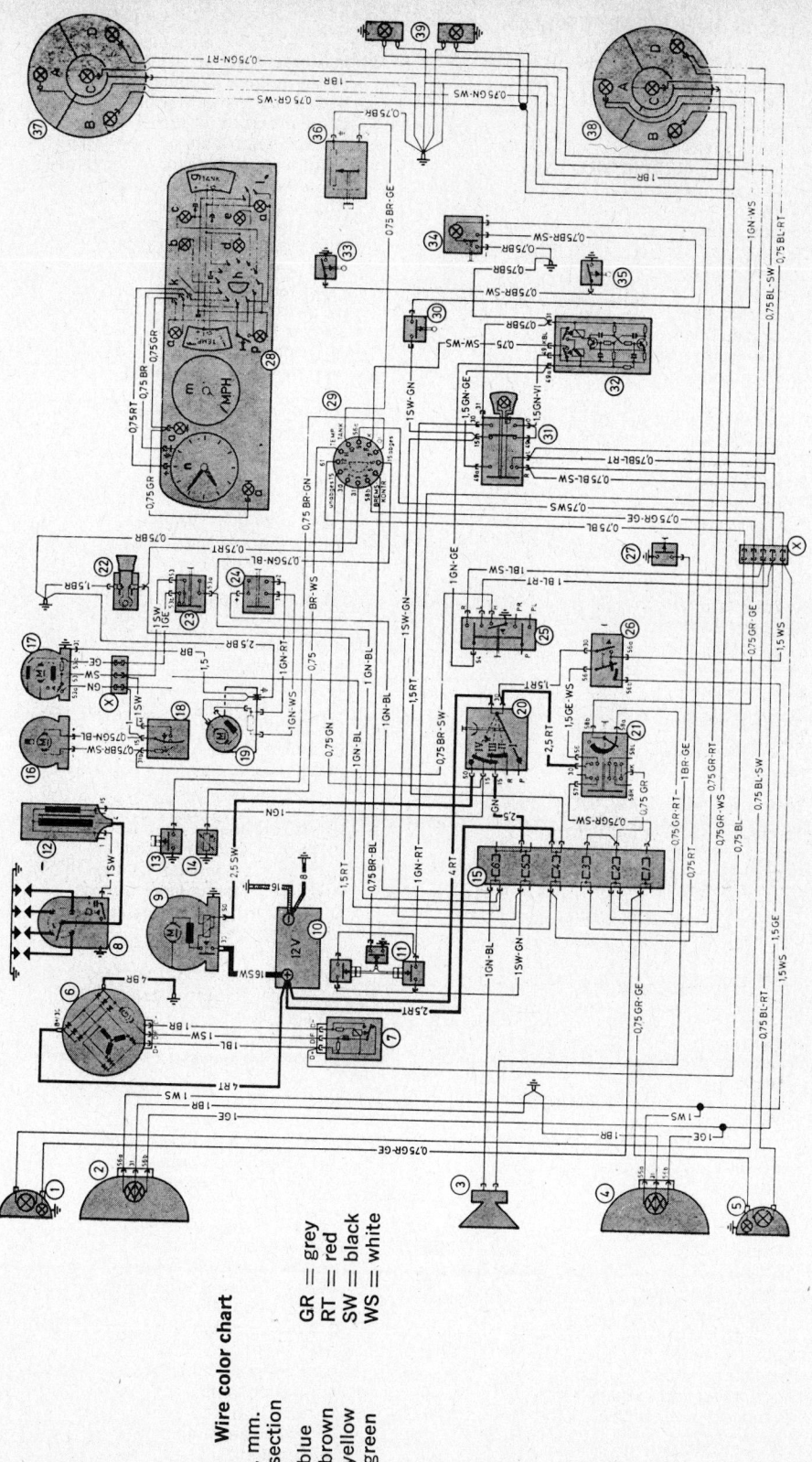

Wiring diagram, BMW 1600-2, US model.

Wire color chart

1.5 sq. mm.
Cross-section

BL = blue   GR = grey
BR = brown   RT = red
GE = yellow   SW = black
GN = green   WS = white

Wiring diagram, BMW 1600-2, US model.

1 Turn signal light (front right)
with parking light
2 Headlight (right)
3 Horn
4 Headlight (left)
5 Turn signal light (front left)
with parking light
6 Alternator
7 Voltage regulator
8 Distributor
9 Starter
10 Battery
11 Stop light switch
12 Ignition coil
13 Oil pressure
14 Water temperature
15 Fuse box
16 Windshield washer pump
17 Windshield wiper motor
18 Washer delay relay
19 Blower motor
20 Ignition switch
   Positions:
   I   Halt (lock)
   II Garage (off)
   III Fahrt (on)
   IV Start (start)
21 Headlight switch
22 Cigar lighter and socket
23 Windshield wiper switch
24 Blower switch
25 Turn signal light and windshield
washer
26 Dimmer switch and headlight flasher
27 Horn button

28 Instrument panel
   a) instrument illumination
   b) battery charge warning light (red)
   c) oil pressure (orange)
   d) high beam warning light (blue)
   e) turn signal indicator light (green)
   f) water temperature gauge
   g) fuel gauge
   h) 12 pole connector
   k) 3 pole connector (clock)
   l) 3 pole connector
   m) speedometer
   n) clock
   p) dual brake system
      and check switch
29 Instrument panel terminals
30 Back-up light
31 Hazard warning signal switch
32 Hazard warning signal relay
33 Courtesy light switch (right)
34 Interior light
35 Courtesy light switch (left)
36 Fuel gauge float contact
37 Rear lamp cluster (right)
   A) Back-up light
   B) Rear light
   C) Turn signal light
   D) Stop light
38 Rear cluster (left)
   A) Back-up light
   B) Rear light
   C) Turn signal light
   D) Stop light
39 License plate lights
X Flat pin connector

Wiring diagram, BMW 2002, US model.

1 Turn signal lamp (front right)
with parking lamp
2 Headlamp (right)
4 Headlamp (left)
5 Turn signal lamp (front left)
with parking lamp
6 Alternator
7 Voltage regulator
8 Distributor
9 Starter
10 Battery
11 Stop lamp switch
12 Ignition coil
13 Oil pressure warning sending unit
14 Water temperature sending unit
15 Fuse box
16 Windshield washer pump
17 Windshield wiper motor
18 Washer delay relay
19 Blower motor
20 Ignition switch
   Positions:
   I   Halt (lock)
   II Garage (off)
   III Fahrt (on)
   IV Start (start)
21 Headlamp switch
22 Cigar lighter and socket
23 Windshield wiper switch
24 Blower switch
25 Turn indicator and windshield
washer switch
26 Dimmer switch and headlamp flasher
27 Horn button
28 Instrument panel
   a) dial illumination

   b) battery charge lamp (red)
   c) Oil pressure lamp (orange)
   d) high beam indicating lamp (blue)
   e) turn indicating lamp (green)
   f) water temperature gauge
   g) fuel gauge
   h) 12-pole connector
   k) 3-pole connector (clock)
   l) 3-pole connector (tachometer)
   m) speedometer
   n) clock
   p) dual brake system warning lamp
      and check switch
29 Instrument panel connecting socket
30 Back-up lamp switch
31 Hazard warning lamp switch
32 Hazard warning lamp relay
33 Courtesy light switch (right)
34 Interior light
35 Courtesy light switch (left)
36 Fuel level sending unit
37 Rear combination lamp, right
   A back-up lamp
   B rear lamp
   C turn signal lamp
   D stop lamp
38 Rear combination lamp, left
   A back-up lamp
   B rear lamp
   C turn signal lamp
   D stop lamp
39 License plate lamps
X Terminal
40 Horn right
41 Horn left
42 Horn relay

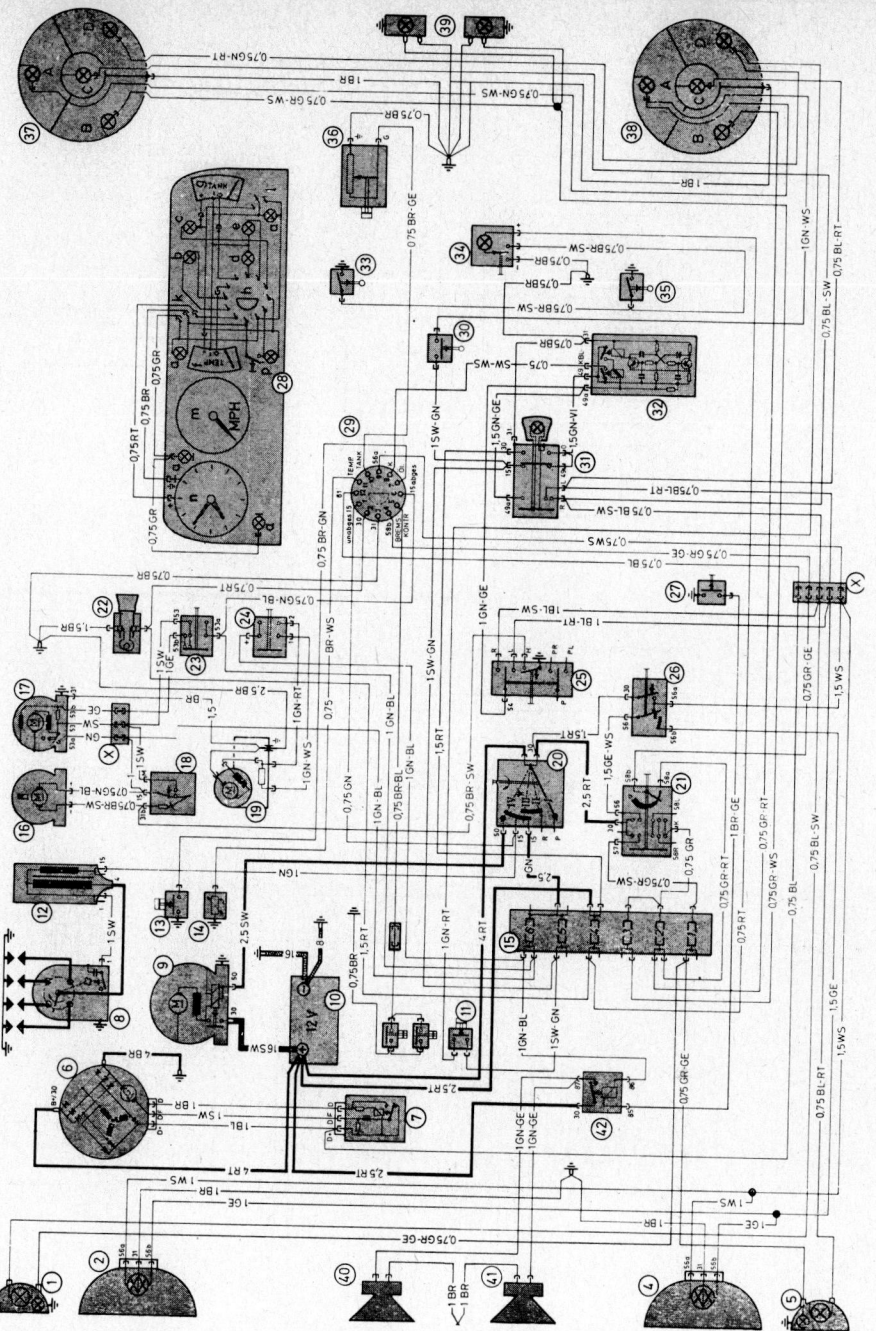

Wiring diagram, BMW 2002, US model.

Wire color chart

1.5 sq. mm.
Cross-section

BL = blue	GR = grey
BR = brown	RT = red
GE = yellow	SW = black
GN = green	WS = white

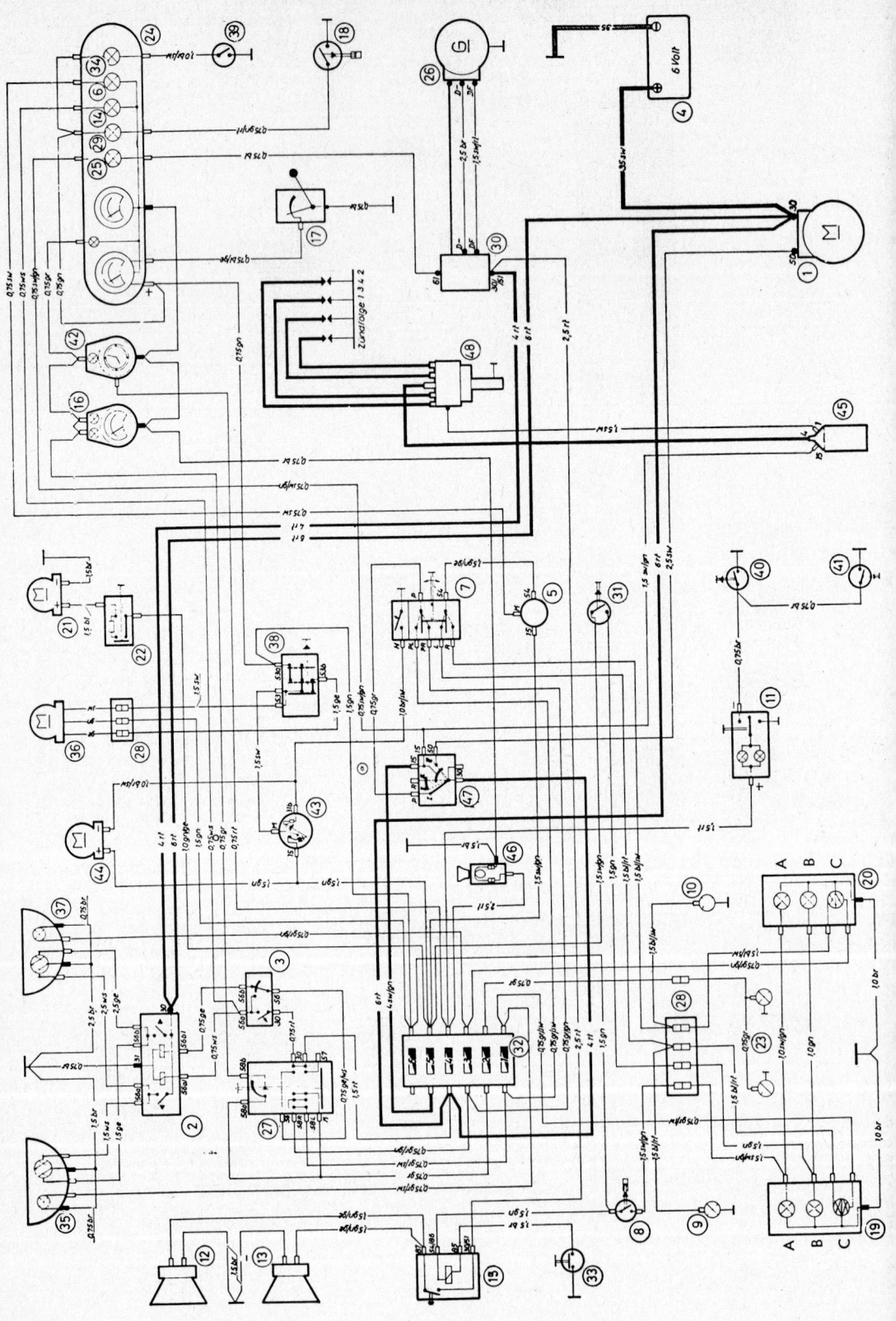

Wiring diagram, BMW 1500, 1600.

1 Starter
2 Dip relay
3 Dip switch
4 Battery
5 Flasher unit
6 Flasher telltale
7 Flasher/parking light switch
  with washer contact
8 Stop light switch
9 Turn indicator front LH
10 Turn indicator front RH
11 Roof light
12 Two-tone horn 1
13 Two-tone horn 2
14 Main beam telltale
15 Horn relay
16 Speedometer
17 Fuel gauge mechanism
18 Oil pressure contact
19 Rear light LH
A Stop light
B Reversing light
C Turn indicator/parking light
  rear
21 Heater blower motor

22 Heater switch
23 Number plate light
24 Combined instrument
25 Battery charge telltale
26 Generator
27 Light switch
28 Cable connector
29 Oil pressure telltale
30 Regulator
31 Reversing light switch
32 Fuse box
33 Horn button
34 Choke telltale
35 Headlight LH
36 Screenwiper motor
37 Headlight RH
38 Screenwiper switch
39 Choke cable contact
40 Door switch LH
41 Door switch RH
42 Clock
43 Delay relay
44 Screenwasher pump
45 Coil
46 Cigar lighter

47 Ignition/starter switch
48 Distributor

Cable coding:
0.75 sq. mm cross-section
Colour:
  BL = blue
  BR = brown
  GE = yellow
  GN = green
  GR = grey
  RT = red
  SW = black
  WS = white

Fuses:
1–2–3–5 = 8 Amp
4–6 = 25 Amp

Ignition / starter switch:
Positions:
  I Halt
  II Garage
  III Fahrt (Drive)
  IV Start

Wiring diagram, BMW 1600-2, 6-volt.

1 Turn indicator RH
2 Headlight RH with parking
  light
3 Foglamp RH
4 Horn
5 Foglamp LH
6 Headlight LH with
  parking light
7 Turn indicator LH
8 Dip relay
9 Generator
0 Regulator/switch unit
1 Distributor
2 Starter
3 Battery (6 Volt)
4 Stop light switch
5 Foglamp relay
6 Foglamp switch
7 Coil
8 Oil pressure contact
9 Water temperature sensor
0 Reversing light switch
1 Fuse box
2 Screenwasher pump
3 Screenwiper motor
4 Delay relay
5 Heater blower motor
6 Ignition/starter switch
7 Light switch
8 Cigar lighter
9 Screenwiper switch
0 Heater switch
1 Flasher unit
2 Turn indicator/parking light/
  screenwasher switch
3 Horn ring

34 Inline fuse for radio
35 Dip switch
36 Instrument panel
37 12-pole plug for "k" on
   instrument panel (view from
   cable side)
38 Radio aerial
39 Radio
40 Door switch RH
41 Interior light
42 Door switch LH
43 Fuel gauge mechanism
44 Rear light RH
45 Number plate light RH
46 Number plate light LH
47 Rear light LH
X Flat pin connector

Cable coding:
1.5 sq. mm cross-section
Colour:
  BL = blue
  BR = brown
  GE = yellow
  GN = green
  GR = grey
  RT = red
  SW = black
  WS = white

Instrument panel:
  a Instrument lighting
  b Clock
  c Speedometer
  d Thermometer
  e Fuel gauge
  f Charge telltale (red)

g Oil pressure telltale
  (orange)
h Main beam telltale (blue)
i Turn indicator telltale
  (green)
k 12-pole plug for Posn. 37
  (seen from connection
  side)
m 3-pole plug for clock cable
n 3-pole plug for revolution
  counter cable
p Revolution counter (special
  equipment, replaces clock)

Special equipment:
Posn. Nos. 3–5–15–16 = Foglamps
       34–38–39 = Radio
       and aerial
       36 p = Revolution
       counter

Fuses:
Nos. 1–2–3–4–5 = 8 Amp.
Nos. 6 = 25 Amp.
Radio = 5 Amp.

Firing order: 1–3–4–2

Ignition / starter switch:
  I Halt
  II Garage
  III Fahrt (Drive)
  IV Start

Rear lights:
  A = Reversing light
  B = Rear light
  C = Turn indicator
  D = Stop light

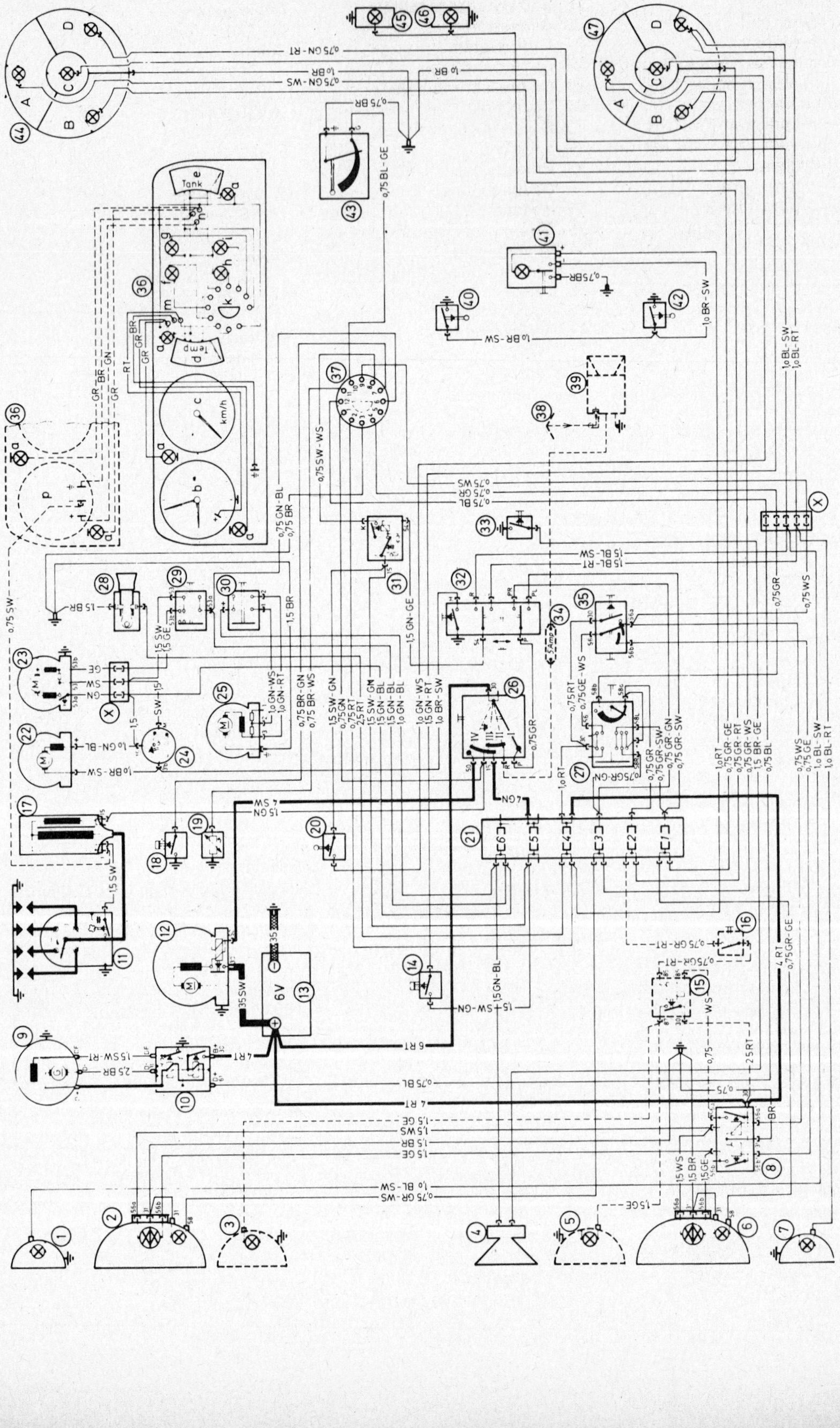

Wiring diagram, BMW 1600-2, 6-volt.

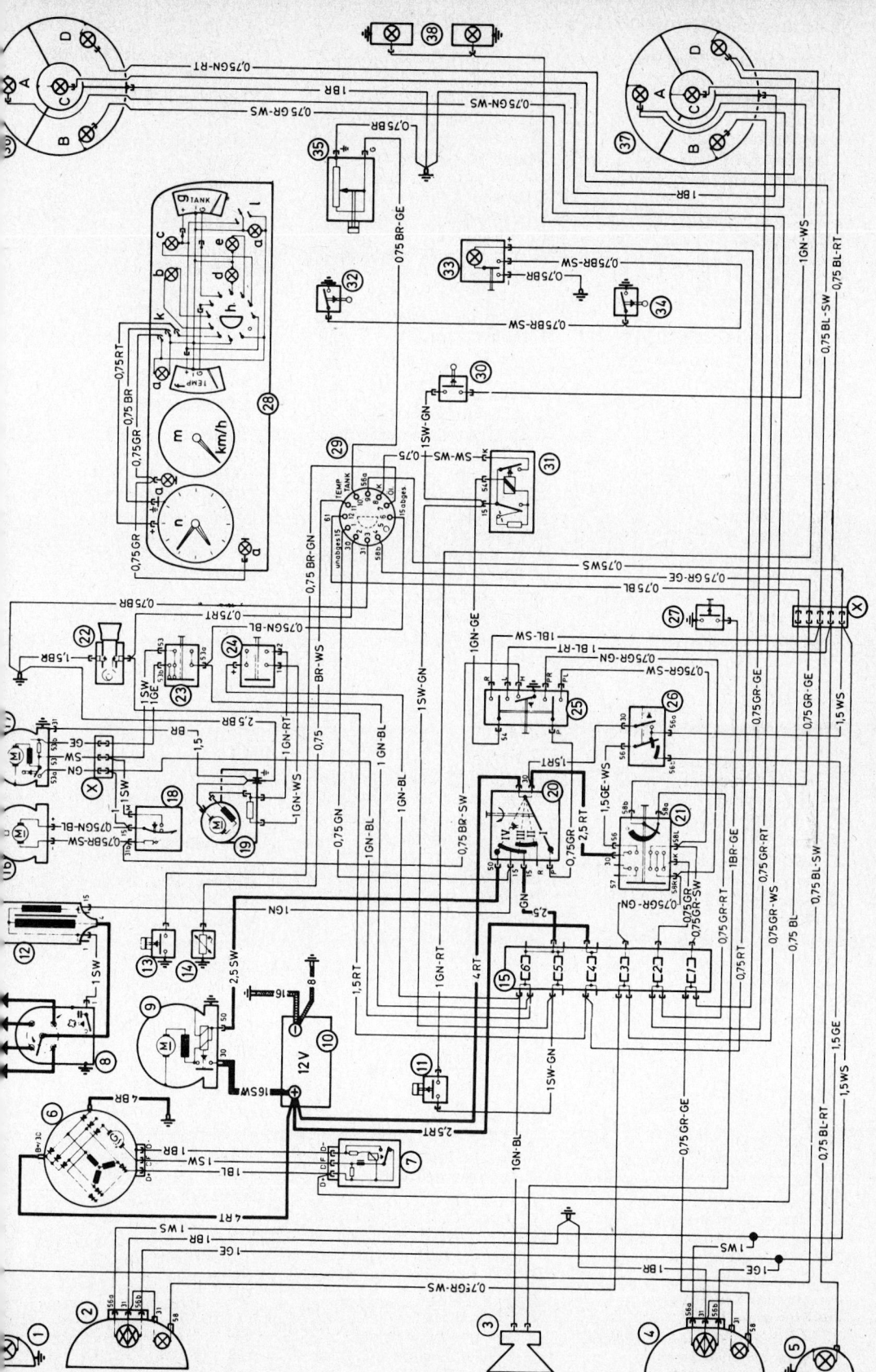

Wiring diagram, BMW 1600-2, 12-volt.

Wiring diagram, BMW 1600-2, 12-volt.

1 Turn indicator front RH
2 Headlight RH with parking light
3 Horn
4 Headlamp LH with parking light
5 Turn indicator front LH
6 Alternator
7 Voltage regulator
8 Distributor
9 Starter
10 Battery
11 Stop light switch
12 Coil
13 Oil pressure contact
14 Remote thermometer contact
15 Fuse box
16 Screenwasher pump
17 Screen wiper motor
18 Delay relay
19 Heater blower
20 Ignition/starter switch
21 Light switch
22 Cigar lighter
23 Screenwiper switch
24 Blower switch
25 Turn indicator/parking light/ screenwasher switch

26 Dip switch/headlight flasher
27 Horn ring
28 Instrument panel
29 12-pole plug for instrument panel (seen from cable side)
30 Reversing light switch
31 Flasher unit
32 Door switch RH
33 Interior light
34 Door switch LH
35 Fuel gauge tank mechanism
36 Rear light RH
37 Rear light LH
38 Number plate light
X Flat pin connector

Instrument panel:
a Instrument lighting
b Charge telltale (red)
c Oil pressure telltale (orange)
d Main beam telltale (blue)
e Turn indicator telltale (green)
f Water temperature gauge
g Fuel gauge
h 12-pole plug
k 3-pole plug for clock

l 3-pole plug for revolution counter
m Speedometer
n Clock

Ignition / starter switch:
I Halt
II Garage
III Fahrt (Drive)
IV Start

Rear lights:
A = Reversing light
B = Rear light
C = Turn indicator
D = Stop light

Firing order: 1–3–4–2

Cable coding:
1.5 sq. mm cross-section

Basic colour:
BL = blue
BR = brown
GE = yellow
GN = green
GR = grey
RT = red
SW = black
VI = violet
WS = white

Wiring diagram, BMW 1600 TI.

1 Turn indicator front RH
2 Headlight RH with parking light
3 Horn RH
4 Horn LH
5 Headlight LH with parking light
6 Turn indicator front LH
7 Alternator
8 Voltage regulator
9 Horn relay
10 Distributor
11 Starter
12 Battery
13 Stop light switch
14 Coil
15 Oil pressure contact
16 Remote thermometer contact
17 Fuse box
18 Screenwasher pump
19 Screen wiper motor
20 Delay relay
21 Heater blower
22 Ignition/starter switch
23 Light switch
24 Cigar lighter
25 Screenwiper switch
26 Blower switch
27 Turn indicator/parking light/ screenwasher switch
28 Dip switch/headlight flasher

29 Horn ring
30 Instrument panel
31 12-pole plug for instrument panel (seen from cable side)
32 Reversing light switch
33 Flasher unit
34 Cable for heated rear window (Special Equipment)
35 Door switch RH
36 Interior light
37 Door switch LH
38 Fuel gauge tank mechanism
39 Rear light RH
40 Rear light LH
41 Number plate light
X Flat pin connector

Instrument panel:
a Instrument lighting
b Charge telltale (red)
c Oil pressure telltale (orange)
d Main beam telltale (blue)
e Turn indicator telltale (green)
f Water temperature gauge
g Fuel gauge
h 12-pole plug
k 3-pole plug for clock
l 3-pole plug for revoluton counter

m Speedometer
n Clock
p Revolution counter

Ignition / starter switch:
I Halt
II Garage
III Fahrt (Drive)
IV Start

Rear lights:
A = Reversing light
B = Rear light
C = Turn indicator
D = Stop light

Firing order: 1–3–4–2

Cable coding:
1.5 sq. mm cross-section

Basic colour:
BL = blue
BR = brown
GE = yellow
GN = green
GR = grey
RT = red
SW = black
VI = violet
WS = white

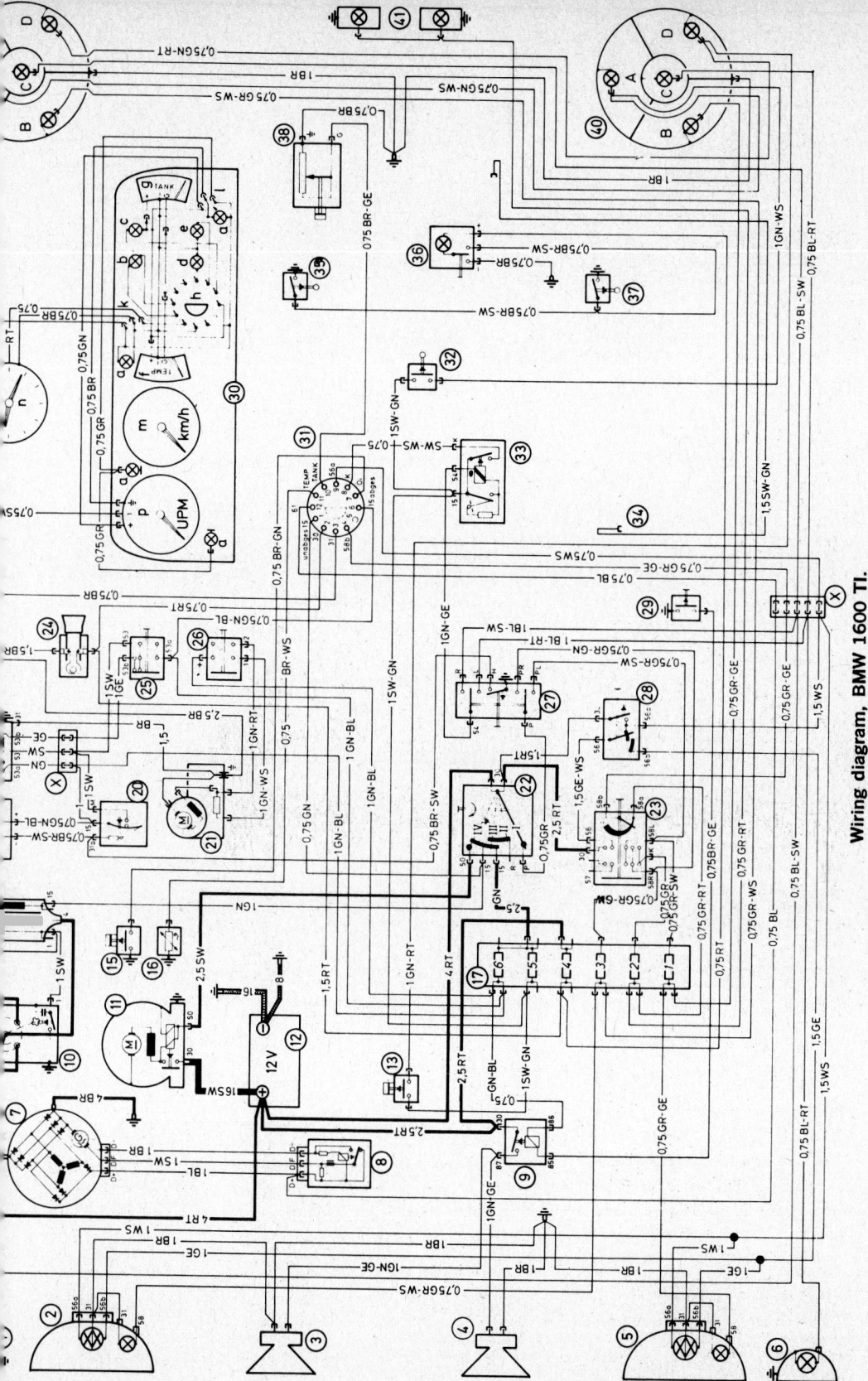

Wiring diagram, BMW 1600 TI.

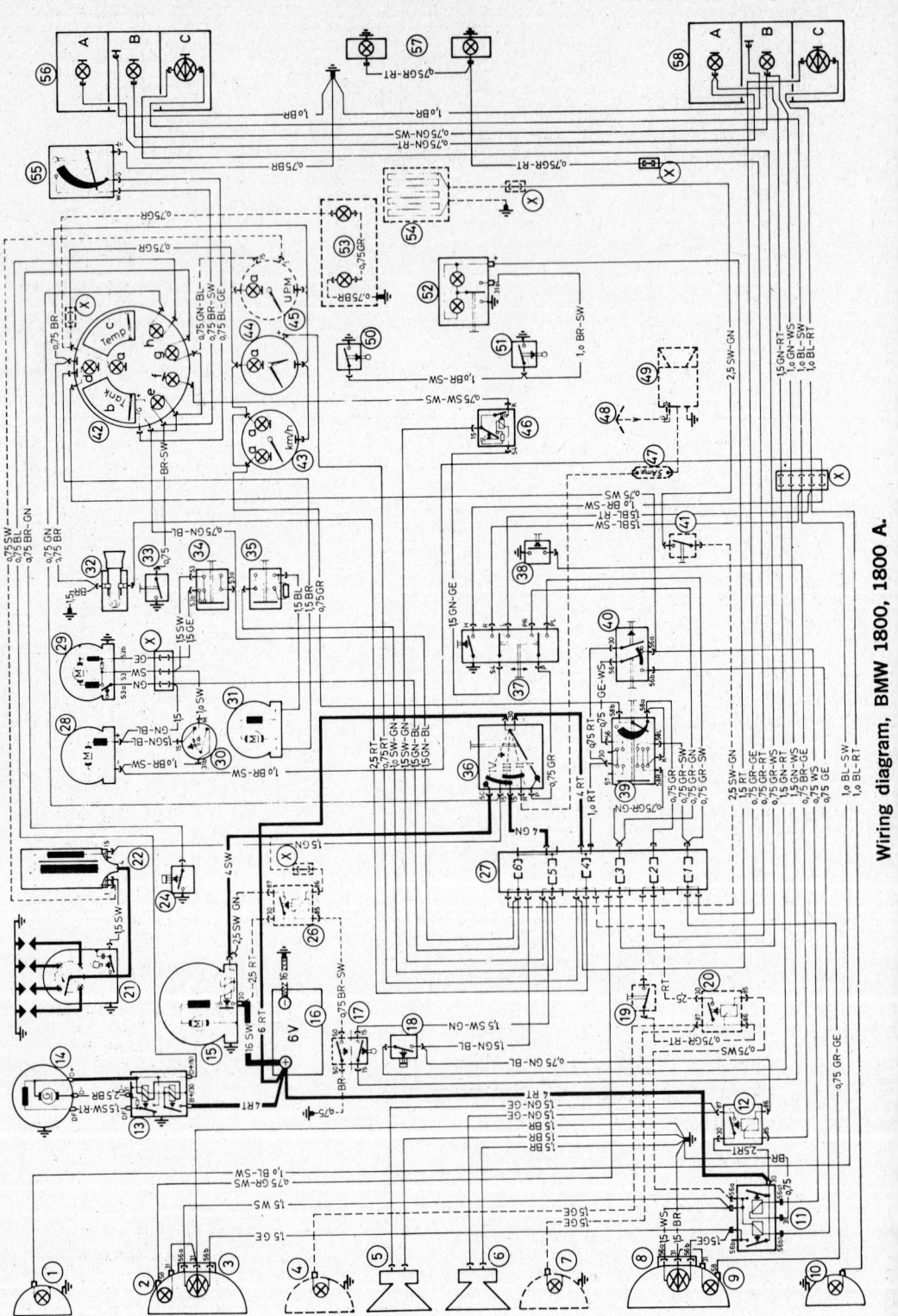

Wiring diagram, BMW 1800, 1800 A.

Wiring diagram, BMW 1800, 1800 A.

1 Turn indicator front RH
2 Parking light RH
3 Headlight RH
4 Foglamp RH
5 Horn RH
6 Horn LH
7 Foglamp LH
8 Headlight LH
9 Parking light LH
10 Turn indicator front LH
11 Dip relay
12 Horn relay
13 Voltage regulator
14 Dynamo
15 Starter
16 Battery
17 Reversing light and starter lock switch
18 Stop light switch
19 Foglamp switch
20 Foglamp relay
21 Distributor
22 Coil
23
24 Oil pressure switch
25
26 Starter relay
27 Fuse box
28 Screenwasher pump
29 Screenwiper motor
30 Delay relay
31 Heater blower motor
32 Cigar lighter
33 Choke cable switch
34 Screenwiper switch
35 Heater switch
36 Ignition/starter switch

37 Turn indicator/parking/light/screenwasher switch
38 Horn ring
39 Light switch
40 Dip switch
41 Switch for heated rear window
42 Combined instrument
43 Speedometer
44 Clock
45 Revolution counter
46 Flasher unit
47 Separate fuse for radio
48 Aerial
49 Radio
50 Door switch RH
51 Door switch LH
52 Interior light
53 Selector lever illumination
54 Heated rear window
55 Fuel gauge mechanism
56 Rear light RH
57 Number plate light
58 Rear light LH
X Flat pin connector

Instruments:
a Instrument lighting
b Fuel gauge
c Thermometer
d Main beam telltale (blue)
e Fuel reserve and choke telltale (white)
f Turn indicator telltale (green)
g Oil pressure telltale (orange)
h Charge telltale (red)

Rear lights:
A = Stop light
B = Reversing light
C = Stop light and turn indicator

Ignition/starter switch:
I Halt
II Garage
III Fahrt (Drive)
IV Start

Special Equipment only:
Item Nos. 4–7–19–20 (foglamps)
41–54 (heated rear window)
47–48–49 (radio and aerial)
45 (Revolution counter in place of clock)

Firing order: 1–3–4–2

For vehicles with automatic gearbox:
Item Nos. 26–53–X (2x): Starter lock switch (17) and all associated cables

Cable coding:
1.5 sq. mm cross-section
Basic colour:
BL = blue
BR = brown
GE = yellow
GN = green
GR = grey
RT = red
SW = black
WS = white

Wiring diagram, BMW 1800 TI, 1800 TISA.

1 Starter
2 Dip relay
3 Dip switch
4 Battery
5 Flasher unit
6 Flasher telltale
7 Flasher/parking light switch with screenwasher contact
8 Stop light switch
9 Turn indicator front LH
10 Turn indicator front RH
11 Interior light
12 Revolution counter
13 Horn
14 Main beam telltale
15 Horn relay
16 Speedometer
17 Fuel gauge tank mechanism
18 Oil pressure contact
19 Rear light unit LH
A Stop light
B Reversing light
C Turn indicator/rear light/parking light
20 Rear light unit RH

A Stop light
B Reversing light
C Turn indicator/rear light/parking light
21 Heater blower motor
22 Heater switch
23 Number plate lamp
24 Combined instrument
25 Charge telltale
26 Dynamo
27 Light switch
28 Cable connector
29 Regulator
30 Reversing light switch
31 Fuse box
32 Horn button
33 Headlight LH
34 Screenwiper motor
35 Headlight RH
36 Screenwiper switch
37 Door switch LH
38 Door switch RH
39 Lock
40 Delay relay
41 Screenwasher pump

42 Coil
43 Cigar lighter
44 Ignition/starter switch
45 Distributor

Cable coding:
0.75 sq. mm cross-section
Basic colour:
BL = blue
BR = brown
GE = yellow
GN = green
GR = grey
RT = red
SW = black
WS = white

Fuses:
1–2–3–5 = 8 Amp
4–6 = 25 Amp

Ignition/starter switch:
Key positions:
I Halt
II Garage
III Fahrt (Drive)
IV Start

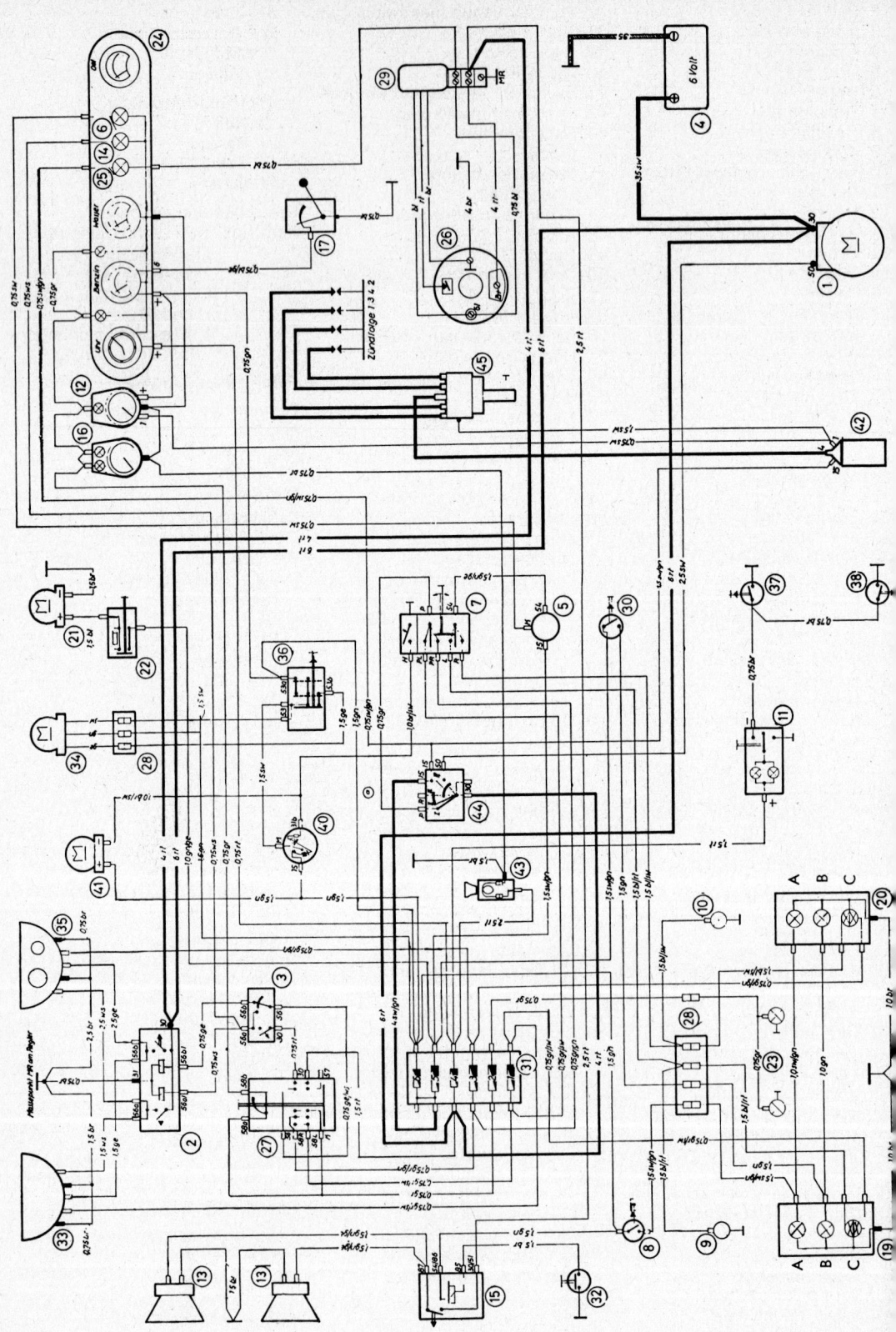

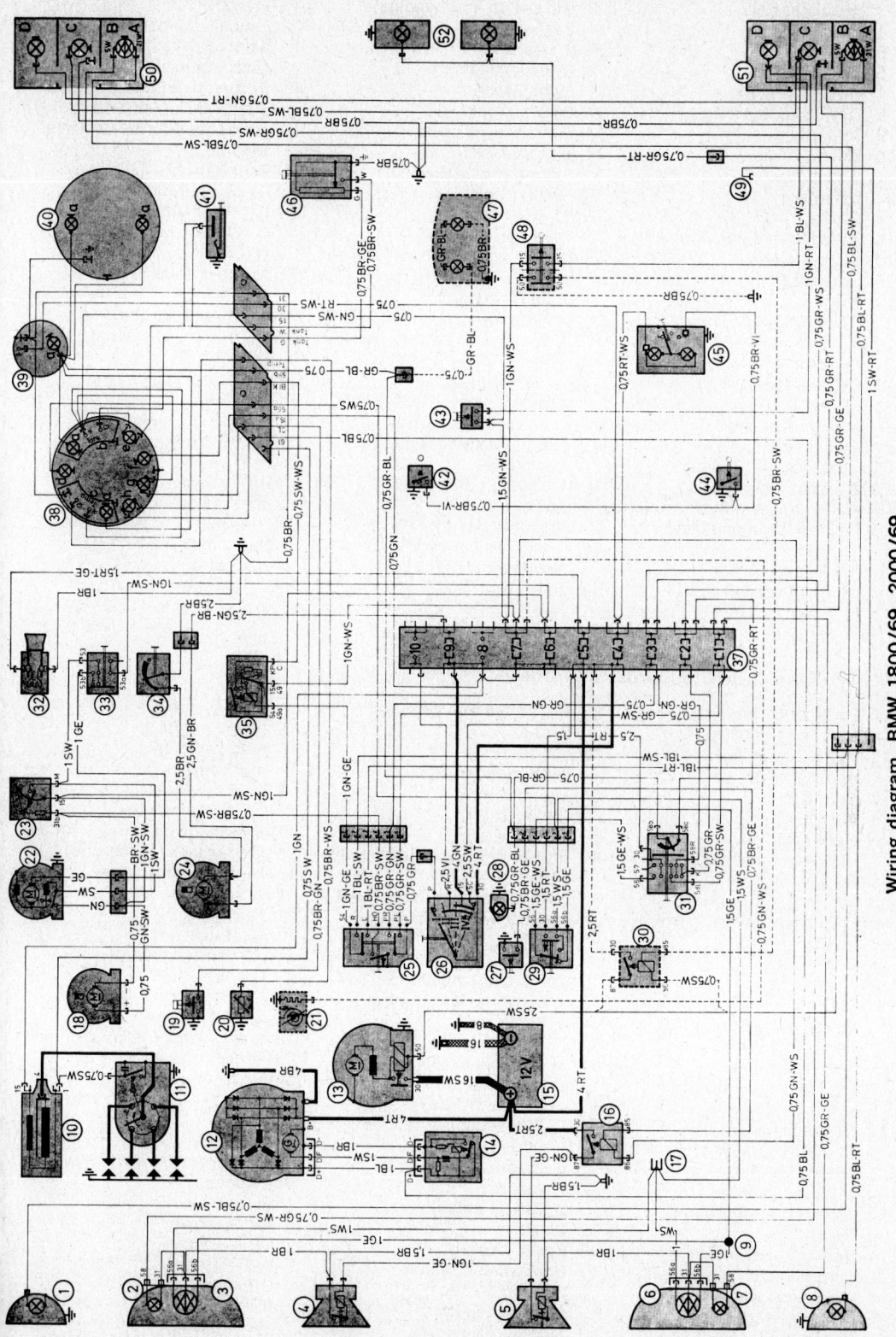

Wiring diagram, BMW 1800/69, 2000/69.

Wiring diagram, BMW 1800/69, 2000/69.

1 Turn indicator front RH
2 Parking light RH
3 Headlight RH
4 Horn RH
5 Horn LH
6 Headlight LH
7 Parking light LH
8 Turn indicator front LH
9 Solder tag
10 Coil
11 Distributor
12 A'ternator
13 Starter
14 Voltage regulator
15 Battery 12 V
16 Horn relay
17 Plug for foglamp relay
18 Screenwasher pump
19 Oil pressure switch
20 Remote thermometer contact
21 Automatic choke
(Automatic only)
22 Screenwiper motor
23 Delay relay
24 Heater blower motor
25 Turn indicator/parking
light/screenwasher switch
26 **Ignition/starter switch:**
   I Halt
   II Garage
   III Fahrt (Drive)
   IV Start

27 Horn ring
28 Switch lighting
29 Dip switch and headlight
flasher
30 Starter relay
(Automatic only)
31 Light switch
32 Cigar lighter
33 Screen wiper switch
34 Blower switch
(continuously variable)
35 Flasher unit
36
37 Fuse box
38 Combined instrument
   a Instrument lighting
   b Fuel gauge
   c Thermometer
   d Main beam telltale (blue)
   e Fuel reserve and choke
   telltale (white)
   f Turn indicator telltale
   (green)
   g Oil pressure telltale
   (orange)
   h Charge telltale (red)
39 Clock
40 Speedometer
41 Choke cable switch
(not Automatic)
42 Door switch RH

43 Stop light switch
44 Door switch LH
45 Interior light
46 Fuel gauge mechanism
47 Selector lever illumination
(Automatic only)
48 Reversing light switch and
starter lock (Automatic only)
49 Connection for heated rear
window
51 Rear light LH
   A = Turn indicator
   B = Tail light
   C = Reversing light
   D = Stop light
52 Number plate light

Firing order: 1–3–4–2
1.5 sq. mm cross-section

Cable coding:
Basic colour:
   BL = blue
   BR = brown
   GE = yellow
   GN = green
   GR = grey
   RT = red
   SW = black
   WS = white
   VI = violet

Wiring diagram, BMW 2000/69, US model.

1 Turn indicator and parking
light front RH
2 High beam headlight (1) RH
3 Headlight (2)
4 Horn RH
5 Horn LH
6 Headlight (2)
7 High beam headlight (1) LH
8 Turn indicator and
parking light front LH
9 High beam relay
10 Coil
11 Distributor
12 A'ternator
13 Starter
14 Voltage regulator
15 Battery 12 V
16 Horn relay
17 Plug for foglamp relay
18 Windshield washer pump
19 Oil pressure contact
20 Remote thermometer contact
21 Automatic choke
(Automatic only)
22 Screenwiper motor
23 Delay relay
24 Heater flower motor
25 Turn indicator/parking light/
windshield washer switch
26 Ignition/starter switch
27 Horn ring
28 Switch lighting

29 Dip switch and headlight
flasher
30 Starter relay
(Automatic only)
31 Light switch
32 Cigar lighter
33 Wiper switch
34 Blower switch (continuously
variable)
35 Hazard warning flasher unit
36 Hazard warning flasher
switch
37 Fuse box
38 Combined instrument:
   a Instrument lighting
   b Fuel gauge
   c Thermometer
   d High beam telltale (blue)
   e Fuel reserve and choke
   telltale (white)
   f Turn indicator telltale
   (green)
   g Oil pressure telltale
   (green)
   h Charge telltale (red)
39 Clock
40 Speedometer
41 Choke cable switch
(not Automatic)
42 Door switch RH
43 Stop light switch

44 Door switch LH
45 Interior light
46 Fuel gauge tank
mechanism
47 Selector lever illumination
(Automatic only)
48 Switch for reversing light and
starter lock (Automatic)
49 Heated rear window
connection
50 Rear light RH
51 Rear light LH
   A = Turn indicator
   B = Rear light
   C = Reversing light
   D = Stop light
52 License plate light
53 Brake fluid level switch
54 Brake fluid level telltale

Firing order: 1–3–4–2

Cable coding:
1.5 sq. mm cross-section
Basic colour:
   BL = blue
   BR = brown
   GE = yellow
   GN = green
   GR = grey
   RT = red
   SW = black
   WS = white

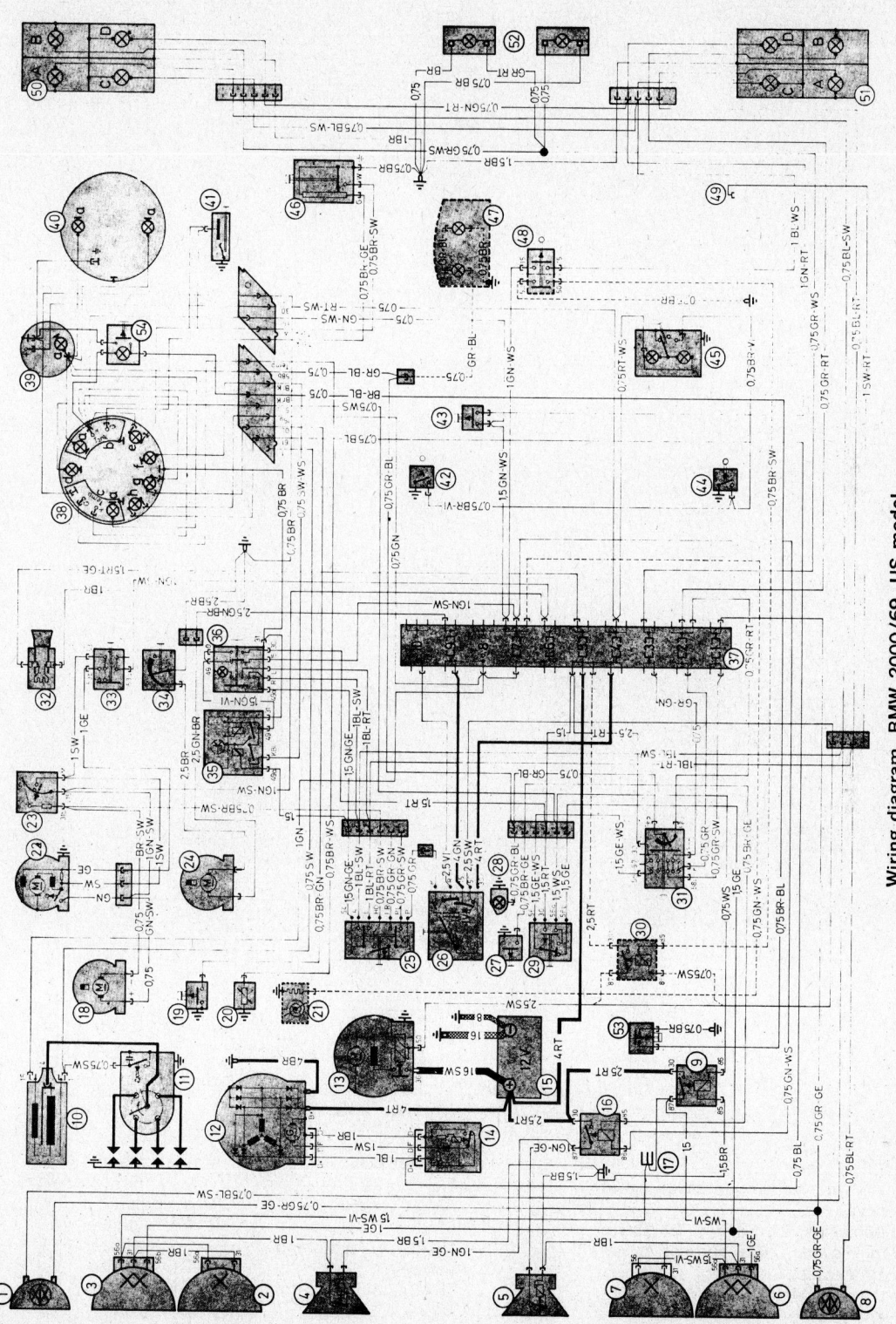

Wiring diagram, BMW 2000/69, US model.

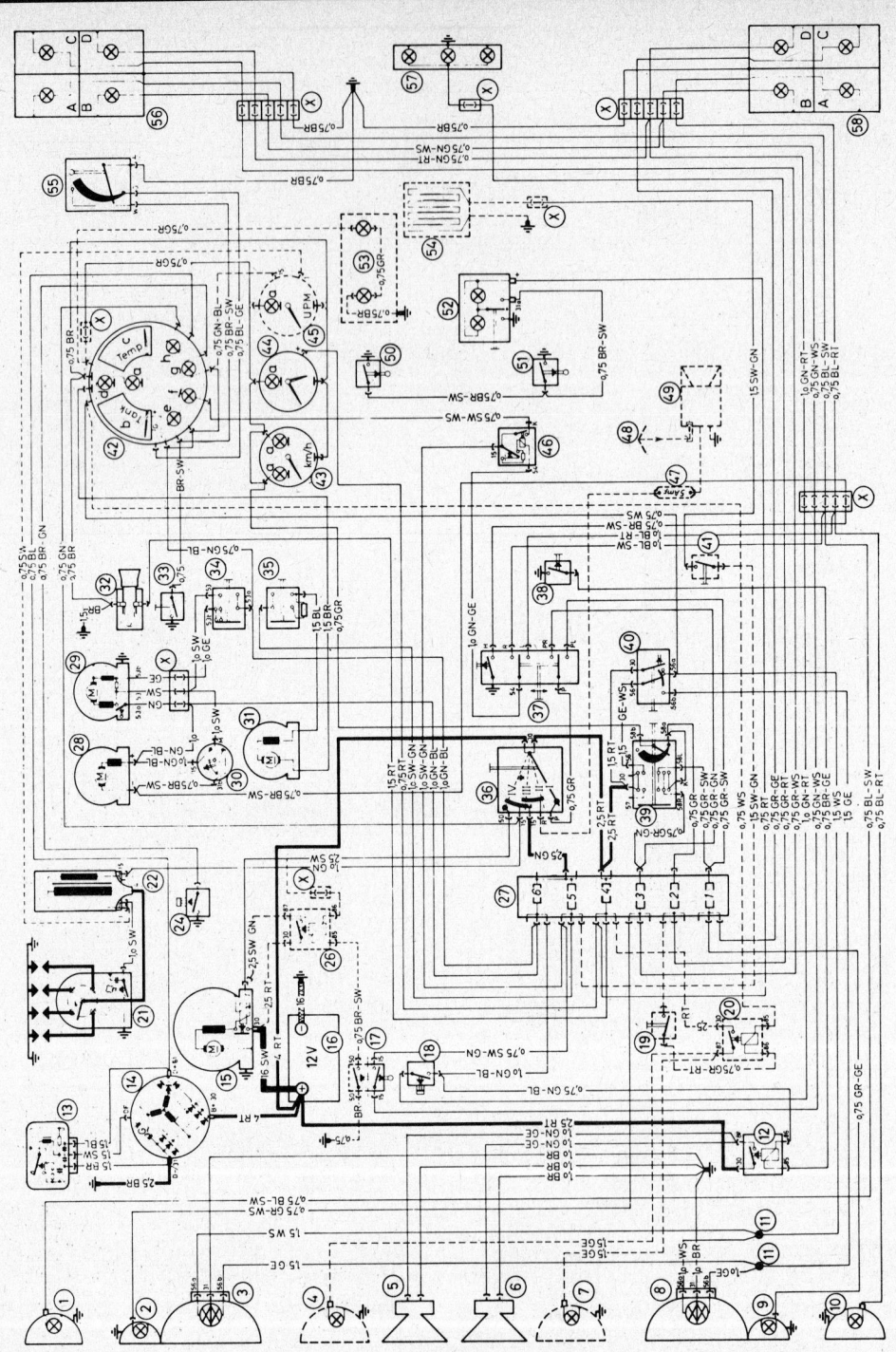

Wiring diagram, BMW 2000, 2000 A, 2000 TI.

Firing order: 1–3–4–2
For vehicles with automatic gearbox:
Item Nos. 27–53–X (2X): Starter lock switch (17) and all associated cables
For TILUX: Revolution counter and heated rear window are standard equipment (clock in combined instrument)

Special Equipment only:
Item Nos. 4–7–19–20 (foglamps)
41–54 (heated rear window)*
47–48–49 (radio and aerial)
45 (Revolution counter in place of clock)*

* Not TILUX

Cable coding:
1.5 sq. mm cross-section
Basic colour:
BL = blue
BR = brown
GE = yellow
GN = green
GR = grey
RT = red
SW = black
WS = white

Wiring diagram, BMW 2000, 2000 A, 2000 TI.

1 Turn indicator front RH
2 Parking light RH
3 Headlight RH
4 Foglamp RH
5 Horn RH
6 Horn LH
7 Foglamp LH
8 Headlight LH
9 Parking light LH
10 Turn indicator front LH
11 Soldered joint
12 Horn relay
13 Voltage regulator
14 Alternator
15 Starter
16 Battery
17 Switch for reversing light and starter lock
18 Stop light switch
19 Foglamp switch
20 Foglamp relay
21 Distributor
22 Coil
23
24 Oil pressure contact
25
26 Starter relay
27 Fuse box
28 Screenwasher pump

29 Screenwiper motor
30 Delay relay
31 Heater blower motor
32 Cigar lighter
33 Choke cable switch
34 Screenwiper switch
35 Heater switch
36 Ignition/starter switch
37 Turn indicator/parking light/screenwasher switch
38 Horn ring
39 Light switch
40 Dip switch
41 Switch for heated rear window
42 Combined instrument
43 Speedometer
44 Clock
45 Revolution counter
46 Flasher unit
47 Separate fuse for radio
48 Aerial
49 Radio
50 Door switch RH
51 Door switch LH
52 Interior light
53 Selector lever illumination
54 Heated rear window
55 Fuel gauge tank mechanism

56 Rear light RH
57 Number plate light
58 Rear light LH
X Flat pin connector

Instruments:
a Instrument lighting
b Fuel gauge
c Thermometer
d Main beam telltale (blue)
e Fuel reserve and choke telltale (white)
f Turn indicator telltale (green)
g Oil pressure telltale (orange)
h Charge telltale (red)

Rear lights:
A = Turn indicator
B = Reversing lights
C = Rear lights
D = Stop lights

Ignition/starter switch:
I Halt
II Garage
III Fahrt (Drive)
IV Start

Wiring diagram, BMW 2000 RE, 2000 A-RE, 2000 TI-RE.

1 Turn indicator front RH
2 Main headlight RH
3 Additional headlight (main beam) RH
4
5 Horn RH
6 Horn LH
7
8 Additional headlight (main beam) LH
9 Main headlight LH
10 Turn indicator front LH
11 Dip relay
12 Horn relay
13 Voltage regulator
14 Alternator
15 Starter
16 Battery
17 Reversing light and starter lock switch
18 Stop light switch
19
20
21 Distributor
22 Coil
23
24 Oil pressure contact
25
26 Starter relay
27 Fuse box
28 Screenwasher pump
29 Screenwiper motor
30 Delay relay
31 Heater blower motor
32 Cigar lighter
33 Choke cable switch
34 Screen wiper switch
35 Heater switch
36 Ignition/starter switch

37 Turn indicator/parking light/screenwasher switch
38 Horn ring
39 Light switch
40 Dip switch
41 Switch for heated rear window
42 Combined instrument
43 Speedometer
44 Clock
45 Revolution counter
46 Flasher unit
47 Separate fuse for radio
48 Aerial
49 Radio
50 Door switch RH
51 Door switch LH
52 Interior light
53 Selector lever illumination
54 Heated rear window
55 Fuel gauge tank mechanism
56 Rear light RH
57 Number plate light
58 Rear light LH
X Flat pin connector

Instruments:
a Instrument lighting
b Fuel gauge
c Thermometer
d Main beam telltale (blue)
e Fuel reserve and choke telltale (white)
f Turn indicator telltale (green)
g Oil pressure telltale (orange)
h Charge telltale (red)

Rear lights:
A = Turn indicator
B = Reversing lights
C = Rear lights
D = Stop lights

Ignition/starter switch:
I Halt
II Garage
III Fahrt (Drive)
IV Start

Firing order: 1–3–4–2

For vehicles with automatic gearbox:
Item Nos. 26–53–X (2X): Starter lock switch (17) with all associated cables

Special Equipment only:
* Standard on 2000 TILUX-RE
Item Nos. 41–54 (heated rear window)*
47–48–49 (radio and aerial)
45 (Revolution counter in place of clock)*

Cable coding:
1.5 sq. mm cross-section
Basic colour:
BL = blue
BR = brown
GE = yellow
GN = green
GR = grey
RT = red
SW = black
WS = white

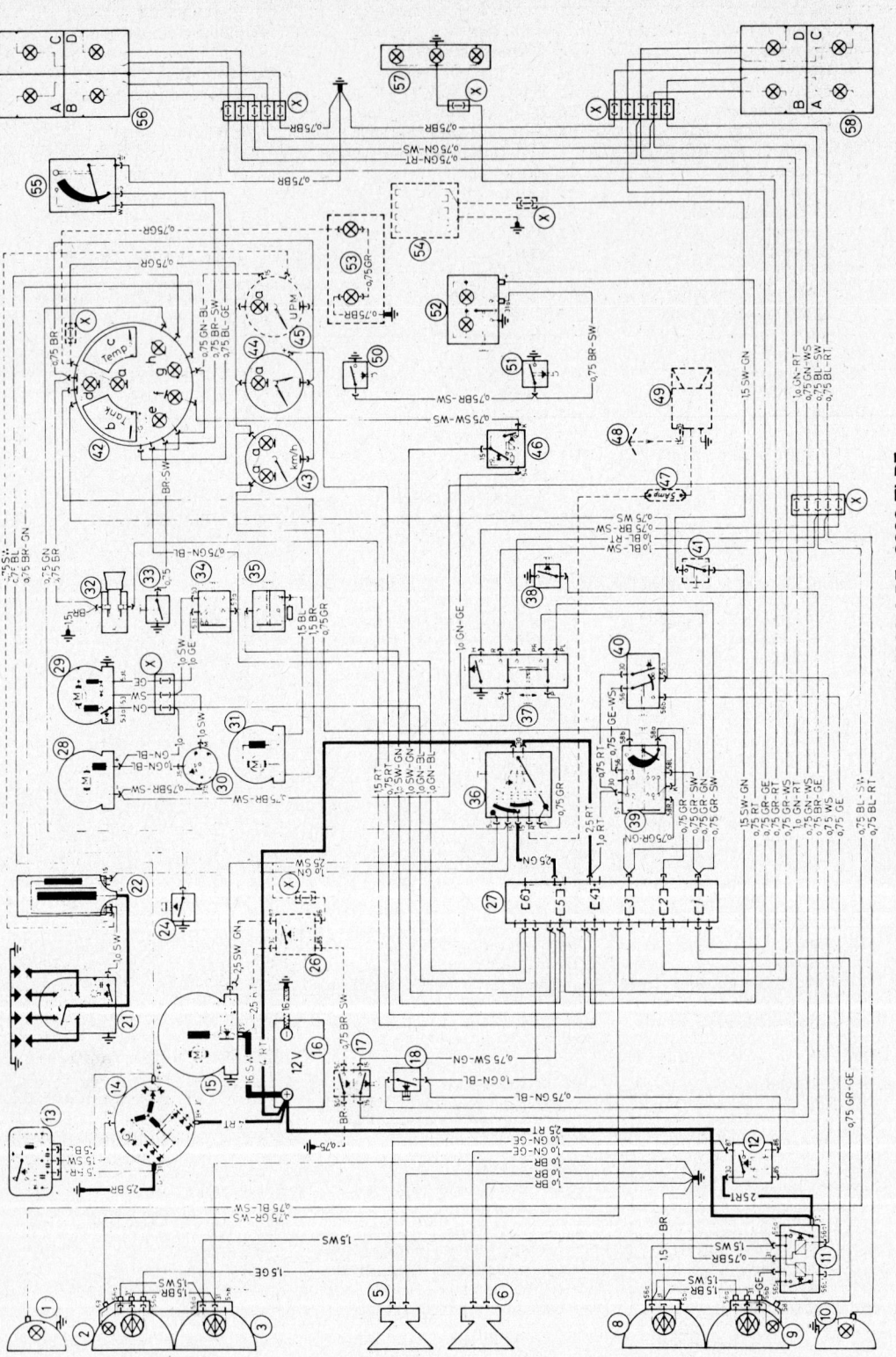

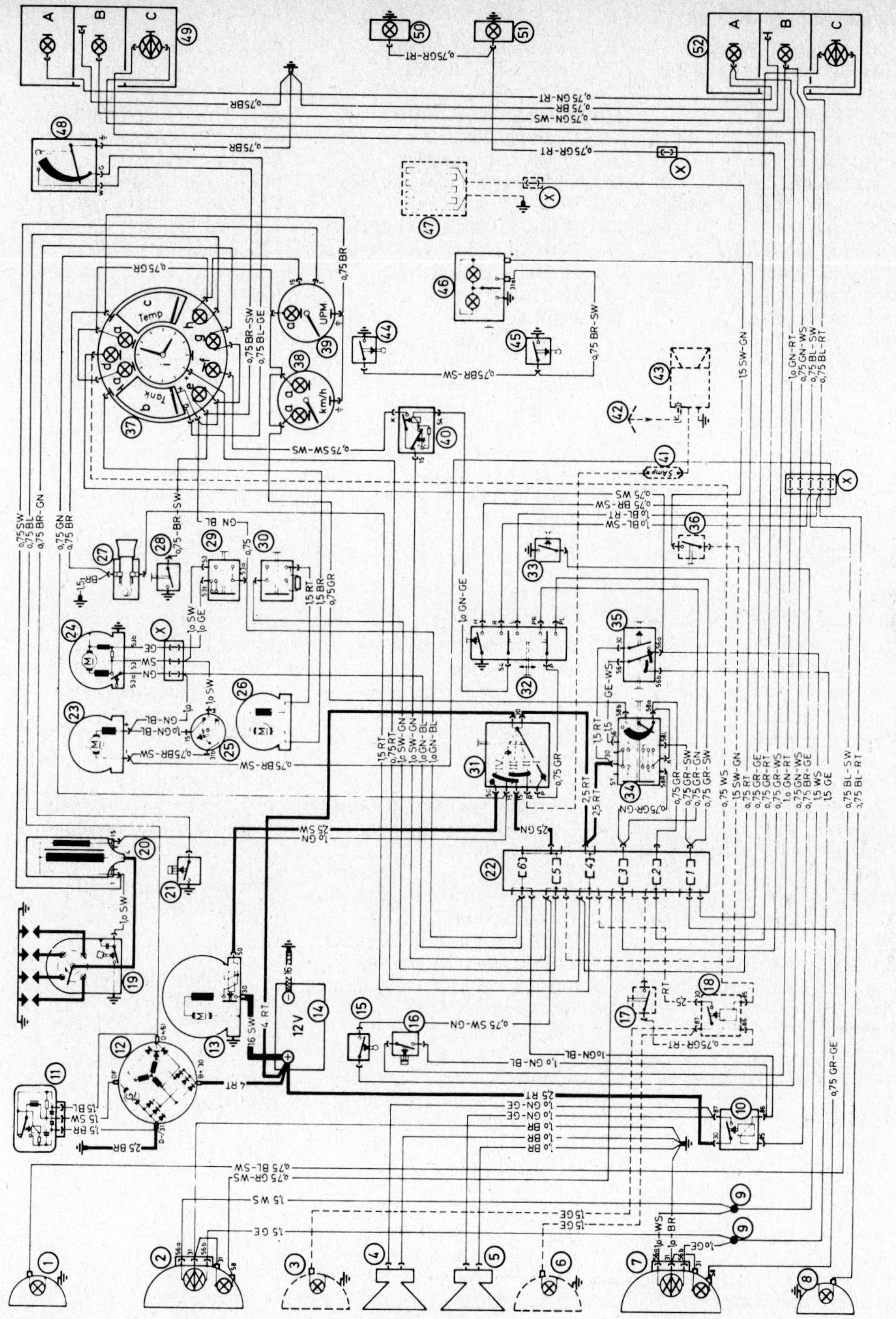

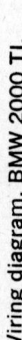

Wiring diagram, BMW 2000 TI.

Rear lights:
A = Stop light
B = Reversing light
C = Rear/parking light and
turn indicator

Ignition/starter switch:
I   Halt
II Garage
III Fahrt (Drive)
IV Start

Firing order: 1–3–4–2

Special Equipment only:
Item Nos. 4–7–19–20 (foglamps)
41–54 (heated rear
window)
47–48–49 (radio and
aerial)

Cable coding:
1.5 sq. mm cross-section

Basic colour:

BL = blue
BR = brown
GE = yellow
GN = green
GR = grey
RT = red
SW = black
WS = white

Wiring diagram, BMW 2000 TI.

1 Turn indicator front RH
2 Headlight RH with parking light
3 Foglamp RH
4 Horn RH
5 Horn LH
6 Foglamp LH
7 Headlight LH with parking light
8 Turn indicator front LH
9 Soldered joint
10 Horn relay
11 Voltage regulator
12 Alternator
13 Starter
14 Battery
15 Reversing light switch
16 Stop light switch
17 Foglamp switch
18 Foglamp relay
19 Distributor
20 Coil
21 Oil pressure contact
22 Fuse box

23 Screenwasher pump
24 Screenwiper motor
25 Delay relay
26 Heater blower motor
27 Cigar lighter
28 Choke cable switch
29 Screen wiper switch
30 Heater switch
31 Ignition/starter switch
32 Turn indicator/parking light/ screenwasher switch
33 Horn ring
34 Light switch
35 Dip switch and headlamp flasher
36 Switch for heated rear window
37 Combined instrument
38 Speedometer
39 Revolution counter
40 Flasher unit
41 Separate fuse for radio
42 Aerial
43 Radio

44 Door switch RH
45 Door switch LH
46 Interior light
47 Heated rear window
48 Fuel gauge tank mechanism
49 Rear light RH
50 Number plate light RH
51 Number plate light LH
52 Rear light LH
X Flat pin connector

Instruments:
a Instrument lighting
b Fuel gauge
c Thermometer
d Main beam telltale (blue)
e Fuel reserve and choke telltale (white)
f Turn indicator telltale (green)
g Oil pressure telltale (orange)
h Charge telltale (red)
i Clock

Wiring diagram, BMW 2000 C, 2000 CA, 2000 CS.

1 Turn indicator front RH
2 Headlight RH
3 Long-range headlight RH
4 Parking light RH
5 Parking light LH
6 Long-range headlight LH
7 Headlight LH
8 Turn indicator front LH
9 Dip relay
10 Dipswitch with headlight flasher
11 Light switch
12 Engine compartment light switch
13 Engine compartment light
14 Horn RH
15 Horn LH
16 Horn relay
17 Horn ring
18 Fuse box
19 Alternator
20 Voltage regulator
21 Coil
22 Distributor
23 Starter
24 Battery
25 Reversing light switch
26 Stop light switch
27 Heated rear window switch
28 Screenwiper motor
29 Screenwiper switch
30 Selector gate light
31 Screenwasher pump
32 Delay relay
33 Heater switch
34 Heater blower motor
35 Cigar lighter
36 Flasher unit
37 Turn indicator/parking light/ screenwasher switch
38 Oil pressure contact

39 Water temperature thermocouple
40 Plug-in connector
41 Electric window lift front RH
42 Terminal board
43 Front window lift switch
44 Terminal board
45 Electrical window lift front LH
46 Electric window lift rear RH
47 Terminal board
48 Rear RH window lift switch
49 Rear LH window lift switch
50 Terminal board
51 Electric window lift rear LH
52 Fuel gauge tank contact
53 Interior light
54 Door switch RH
55 Door switch LH
56 Luggage compartment light switch
57 Luggage compartment light
58 Heated rear window
59 Plug-in connector
60 Turn indicator rear RH
61 Rear light RH
62 Top light RH
63 Reversing light RH
64 Number plate lights
65 Reversing light LH
66 Stop light LH
67 Rear light LH
68 Turn indicator rear LH
69 Choke cable contact
70 Ignition/starter switch
71 Radio
72 Separate fuse
73 Combined instrument
74 Revolution counter
75 Speedometer
76 Clock
77 Rear loudspeaker

Instruments:
a Instrument lighting
b Cooling water thermometer
c Fuel gauge
d Oil pressure telltale
e Choke and fuel reverse telltale
f Battery charge telltale
g Main beam telltale
h Turn indicator telltale

Ignition/starter switch:
Key positions:
  I Lock
  II Garage
  III Fahrt (Drive)
  IV Start

Fuses:
1–2–3–4–5–6 = 8 Amp
7–8 = 25 Amp
Firing order: 1–3–4–2

Cable coding:
0.75 sq. mm cross- section
Colour:
  BL = blue
  BR = brown
  GE = yellow
  GN = green
  GR = grey
  LI = lilac
  RT = red
  SW = black
  WS = white
Items 27–28–59–71–72–77 =
Special equipment
Item 30 only when automatic gearbox fitted
X = When manual gearbox is fitted, conected to instrument lighting; cable for selector gate light is then free.

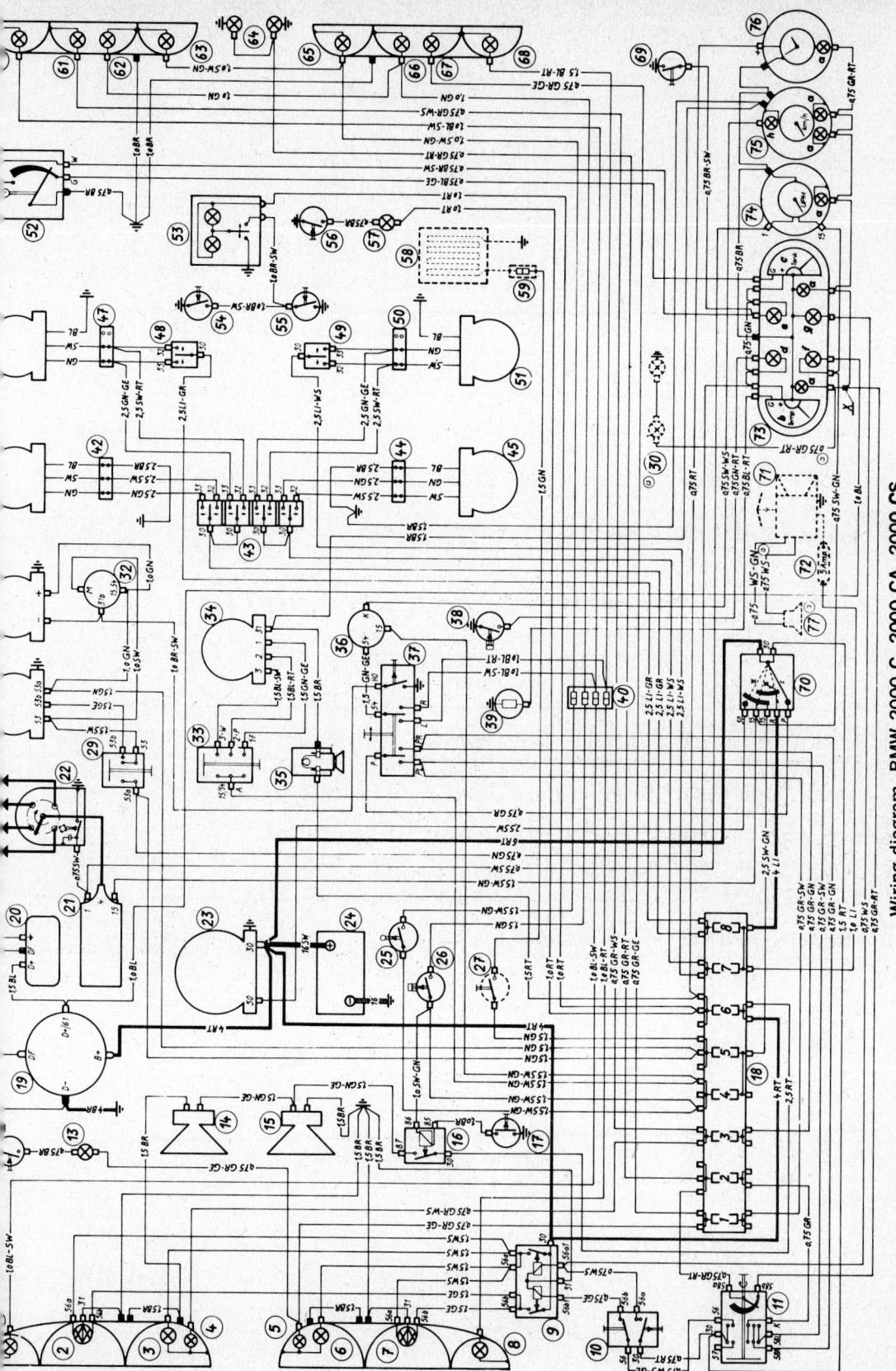

Wiring diagram, BMW 2000 C, 2000 CA, 2000 CS.

Carburetor Specifications

Model	Carburetor Type	Venturi Size	Main Jet Size	Idle (Pilot) Jet Size	Idle Air Port Size	Air Correct. Jet Size	Injection Pump Tube Size	Float Weight Oz./Gr.	Fuel Depth In Chamber In. (mm) Below Joint
1500	Solex 36 PDSI	26	135	47.5	.50	110	.8	1.15/.85	.67-.75 (17-19)
1600	Solex 36 PDSI	26	140	47.5	.50	100	.8	1.15/.85	.67-.75 (17-19)
1600-2	Solex 38 PDSI	26	130	47.5	.50	110	.8	1.15/.85	.67-.75 (17-19)
1600TI	2 Solex 40 PHH	30	0120	50		155	.4	.4/10	***
1800, 1800A	Solex 38 PDSI	30	165, 160**	45,** 47.5	.50	155,** 90	.8	.3/8.5	.67-.75 (17-19)
1800/69	Solex 38 PDSI	30	165, 160**	45,** 47.5	.50	155,** 90	.8	.3/8.5	.67-.75 (17-19)
1800TI	2 Solex 40 PHH	32	0145	57.5		240	.5	.4/10	***
2000, 2000A	Solex 40 PDSIT,* 40 PDSI	30	155	45	.50	130	100	.3/8.5	.67-.75 (17-19)
2002	Solex 40 PDSIT* 40 PDSI	30	155	45	.50	130	100	.3/8.5	.67-.75 (17-19)
2000TI	2 Solex 40 PHH	34	0130	52.5		155	.5	.4/10	***
2000CS	2 Solex 40 PHH	34	0130	52.5		155	.5	.4/10	***
2000CA	Solex 40 PDSIT* 40 PDSI	30	155	45	.50	130	100	.3/8.5	.67-.75 (17-19)

*With automatic choke.　　**With air filter on carburetor.　　***Fuel line marked on exterior of float chamber housing.

Clutch Specifications

Model	Type	Spring Color Coding	Pressure Lbs. Approx.	Minimum Driven Plate Thickness In. (mm)	Clutch Lever Clearance In. (mm)	Pedal Free Travel In. (mm) Approx.
1500	KFS200K single dry plate	green/yellow/green	880±44	.32(8)	.118-.138 (3-3.5)	.8-1.0 (20-25)
1600	KFS200K single dry plate	green/yellow/green	880±44	.32(8)	.118-.138 (3-3.5)	.8-1.0 (20-25)
1600-2	KFS200K single dry plate	green/yellow/green	880±44	.29(7.3)	.118-.138 (3-3.5)	.8-1.0 (20-25)
1600TI	KFS200K single dry plate	blue/white/blue w. yellow stripe	1075±33	.32(8)	.118-.138 (3-3.5)	.8-1.0 (20-25)
1800	KFS200K single dry plate	blue/white/blue w. yellow stripe	1075±33	.32(8)	.118-.138 (3-3.5)	.8-1.0 (20-25)
1800/69	KFS200K single dry plate	blue/white/blue w. yellow stripe	1075±33	.32(8)	.118-.138 (3-3.5)	.8-1.0 (20-25)
1800TI	KFS200K single dry plate	blue/white/blue w. yellow stripe	1075±33	.32(8)	.118-.138 (3-3.5)	.8-1.0 (20-25)
2002	HB225Sph single dry plate	blue/white/blue w. yellow stripe	1075±33	.32(8)	.118-.138 (3-3.5)	.8-1.0 (20-25)
2000	HB225Sph single dry plate	blue/grey/blue	925	.36(9.1)	.158-.177 (4-4.5)	1.4-1.6 (35-40)
2000TI	HB225Sph single dry plate	blue/grey/blue	925	.36(9.1)	.158-.177 (4-4.5)	1.4-1.6 (35-40)
2000CS	HB225Sph single dry plate	blue/grey/blue	925	.36(9.1)	.158-.177 (4-4.5)	1.4-1.6 (35-40)

Gearbox Specifications

Model	Speeds	Synchro-Mesh	Gearbox Ratios:1					Mainshaft End Play In./mm Max.	Counter-shaft End Play In./mm Max.	Pinion Tooth Backlash In./mm	Shaft Runout In./mm Max.
			1st	2nd	3rd	4th	Reverse				
1500, 1600, 1800, 1800TI, 1800/69	4 Fwd, Rev.	1,2,3,4	3.816	2.070	1.330	1.000	4.153	.024/.6	.0079/.2	.00236-.0059/.06-.15	.00079/.02
1600-2, 1600TI, 2002, 2000, 2000TI, 2000CS	4 Fwd, Rev.	1,2,3,4	3.835	2.053	1.345	1.000	4.180	.024/.6	.0079/.2	.00236-.0059/.06-.15	.00079/.02
2500, 2800	4 Fwd, Rev.	1,2,3,4	3.850	2.120	1.375	1.000	4.130	.024/.6	.0079/.2	.00236-.0059/.06-.15	.00079/.02
2800CS	4 Fwd, Rev.	1,2,3,4	3.850	2.080	1.375	1.000	4.130	.024/.6	.0079/.2	.00236-.0059/.06-.15	.00079/.02
1800-A, 2000A, 2000CA, 2002A	3 Fwd, Rev.*		2.56	1.52	1.0	Converter 1-2.2	2.0				

*Automatic ZF3HP-12/B

Equipment Specifications

Type	1500 1600 1600-2 1600T1 1800 1800A 1800/69 1800T1 2002	2000 2000A 2000T1 2000CS 2000CA	All Types	1500 1600	1600-2 1600T1 1800 1800A 1800/69 1800T1 2002 2000T1 2000CS 2000CA
OIL PUMP (Gear type)					
Oil Pressure @					
idling speed, PSI	7.1–21.3	14.2–21.3			
maximum speed, PSI	71–85	71			
Relief valve opening					
pressure, PSI			57–71		
Output, gals/hr.			409		
Gear tooth backlash					
max. in. (mm)			.0028 (.07)		
normal in. (mm)			.0012–.0019 (.03–.05)		
End play				.0028 (.07)	.0035 (.09)
max. in. (mm)				.0019 (.05)	.0019 (.05)
normal in. (mm)					
Free length of pressure					
relief spring, in. (mm)	2.68 (68)	2.70 (68.5)			
OIL PUMP (Rotor Type)					
Outer rotor—housing			.0020–.0079		
clearance, in. (mm)			(.05–.20)		
Rotor—housing, sealing			.0013–.0033		
surface,play, in. (mm)			(.034–.084)		
Inner—outer rotor			.0035–.0106		
clearance, in. (mm)			±.0012 (.09–.27±.03)		
WATER PUMP					
Housing–impeller			.038–.040		
Clearance, in. (mm)			(.8–1.2)		
THERMOSTAT					
Opening temp.			163°–171°F 181° (optional)		
RADIATOR CAP					
Pressure, PSI			12.1–16.3		

Type	1500 1600 1800 1800A 1800T1	1600-2 1600T1	1800/69	2002 2000A 2000T1 2000CS 2000CA	All Types
FUEL PUMP					
Solex PE	15059	15520	15581	15517 and 15574	
Pressure @ 1000 rpm, PSI					2.99–3.56
Output @ specified rpm, GPM	11.9–13.2 @ 5500	11.9–13.2 @ 5500	11.9–13.2 @ 5500	15.8–18.5 @ 5700 1	

1   22.5–26.4 @ 5700–2000TI, 2000CS

Equipment Specifications

Type	1500 1600 1600-2 1600TI 1800 1800/69 1800TI 2002	2000 2000TI 2000CS	All Types	1500 1600 1600TI 1800 1800/69 1800TI 2002	1600-2	2000 2000TI 2000CS
CLUTCH						
Plate I.D. in. (mm)	7.87 (200)	8.50 (216)				
Plate I.D. in. (mm)	5.12 (130)	5.67 (144)				
Bearing:						
Engine side			T450W			
Transmission side			T50S			
Thickness in. (mm)				.41 (10.3)	.37 (9.3)	.37±.0079 (9.3±.2)
Withdrawal arm clearance, in. (mm)	.118–.138 (3–3.5)	.158–.177 (4–4.5)				
Pedal travel, in. (mm)	.8–1.0 (20–25)	1.4–1.6 (35–40)				

Type	All Types	1500, 1600, 1800, 1800A, 1800/69, 1800T1, 2000, 2000A, 2000T1, 2000CS, 2000CA	1600-2, 1600T1, 2002
STEERING			
Min. turning circle (ft.)		34.5	34.1
Steering box ratio	15.5:1		
Overall ratio	17.6:1		
No. of turns lock to lock	3.5		
Max. free play at wheel rim in. (mm)	.79 (20)		

Type	1500 1600 1800T1 With Long Neck Gearbox and Long Neck Final Drive	1600-2 With Universal Gearbox 232 and Long Neck Final Drive	1600 1800 2000 2000T1 2000C 2000CS With Universal Gearbox 232 and Long Neck Final Drive	1800A 2000A 2000CA With Automatic and Long Neck Final Drive	2000 2000C 2000T1 2000CS With Universal Gearbox 232 and Short Neck Final Drive	2000A 2000CA With Automatic and Short Neck Final Drive	2002 With Universal Gearbox 232 and Long Neck Final Drive
DRIVE SHAFT	1-piece	2-piece	2-piece	2-piece	2-piece	2-piece	2-piece
Length in. (mm)	78.3±.06 (1989±1.5)						
Length Front Piece in. (mm)		19.6 (497)	28.9 (735)	23.4 (604)	28.9 (735)	23.4 (604)	20.1 (510)
Length Rear Piece in. (mm)		33.6 (852.5)	30.3 (770)	30.3 (770)	38.8 (985)	38.8 (985)	32.1 (816)
Max. Play in Univ. Joints in. (mm)	.001 (.03) all models						

Equipment Specifications

Type	1500 2002 2000 2000A 2000TI 2000CA	1600 1600–2 1800 1800A 1800/69	1600TI 1800TI 2000CS	1500 2002 2000 2000A 2000TI 2000CA	1500 1600TI 1800TI 2000 2000A 2002 2000TI 2000CS 2000CA
IGNITION ADVANCE DATA*					
Centrifugal, degrees:					
@ 500 rpm	2.5–5.5	0–5	0–4		
@ 750 rpm		9–11	7–9	8.5–10.5	
@ 1000 rpm		11–13	10–12	12–14	
@ 1200 rpm	14–16 (end)		10.5–12.5		
@ 1500 rpm		14–16	13–15		
@ 1900 rpm		16–18 (end)	14–16 (end)		
Max adj: range in distributor (degrees)		16–18			14–16
VACUUM ADVANCE (HG)					
Start: in. (mm)	4.72–5.91 (120–150) **	4.72–5.9 (120–150)			
End: in. (mm)	7.68–8.27 (195–210) **	7.68–8.27 (195–210)			
Adj. range (degrees)	5	5			

* To be measured from distributor shaft on distributor test stand.
** Not applicable to 2000TI.

Rear Axle Specifications

Model	Ratio	No. of Teeth	Basic Pinion/ Ring Gear Adj. Dim. In. (mm) Klingelnberg*	Basic Pinion/ Ring Gear Adj. Dim. In. (mm) Gleason*	Pinion/ Ring Gear Backlash In. (mm)**	Driving Flange To Axle End Play In. (mm)***
1500, 1600	4.375:1	35/8	2.068 (52.52)	2.055 (52.20)	.0028-.0047 (.07-.12)	.039-.059 (.10-.15)
1600TI, 2000TI, 2000CS	3.9:1	39/10	2.068 (52.52)	2.068 (52.52)	.0028-.0047 (.07-.12)	.039-.059 (.10-.15)
1600-2, 1800, 1800A	4.11:1	37/9	2.048 (52.02)	2.065 (52.45)	.0028-.0047 (.07-.12)	.039-.059 (.10-.15)
1600-2, 1800, 1800A, 1800/69, 1800TI, 2000, 2000A	4.10:1	41/10			.0028-.0047 (.07-.12)	.039-.059 (.10-.15)
1800/69, 1800TI	4.11:1	37/9	2.061 (52.34)	2.065 (52.45)	.0028-.0047 (.07-.12)	.039-.059 (.10-.15)
2000, 2000A, 2000CA	4.11:1	37/9	2.068 (52.52)	2.068 (52.52)	.0028-.0047 (.07-.12)	.039-.059 (.10-.15)
2000TI, 2000CS, 2000CA	3.9:1	43/11			.0028-.0047 (.07-.12)	.039-.059 (.10-.15)
2002	3.64:1	40/11			.0028-.0047 (.07-.12)	.039-.059 (.10-.15)

*Distance from face of Pinion to center of differential bearing bore in housing. For pinion heights above 1.2598" (32 mm), the basic adjusting dimension is 2.068" (52.52 mm).
**Short neck: .0031-.0051 (.08-.13)
***Long neck axle

Lubrication Chart

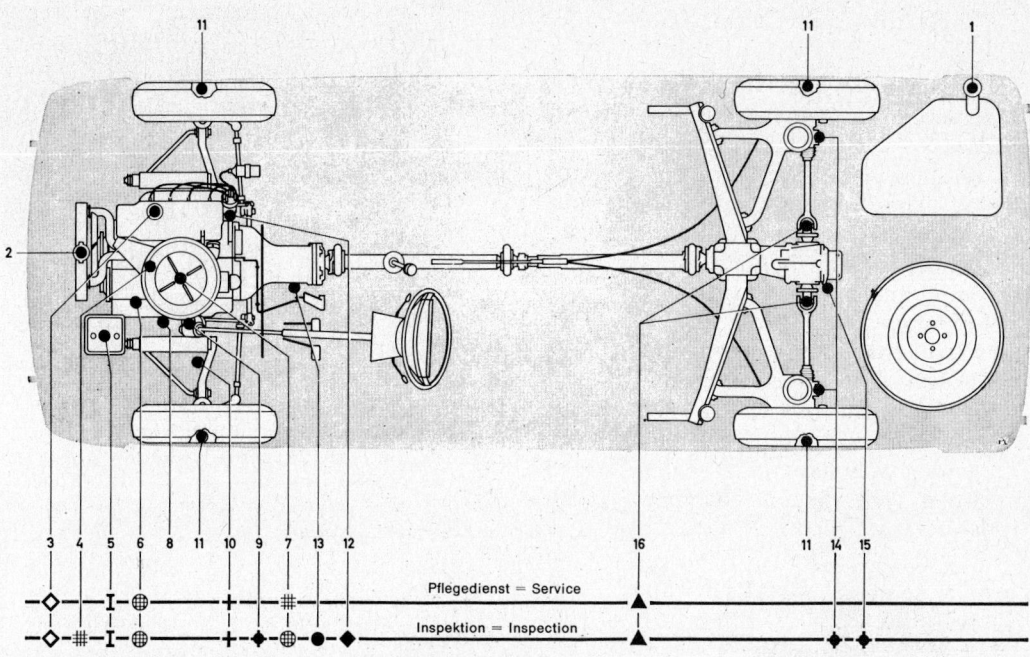

BMW 2002 lubrication chart.

Key to Lubrication Chart

1. Fuel filler		Branded super grade fuel
2. Radiator filler (Coolant outlets are situated at the bottom left of the radiator and the bottom right of the engine block)		Check frost- resistance before and during the cold season.
3. Engine oil filler	◆	Branded HD engine oil
	◇	indicates oil change
4. Fuel pump fine mesh filter	⊞	indicates filter cleaning
5. Battery	I	Distilled water
6. Engine oil filter	⊕	indicates filter renewal
7. induction air filter	⊞	indicates filter cleaning
	⊕	indicates filter renewal
8. Engine oil level dipstick		Check oil level regularly
9. Steering box (permanently filled)	◆	Branded hypoid gear oil SAE 90
10. Hydraulic brake fluid reservoir	+	ATE brake fluid, blue
11. Wheel bearings (examine every 60 000 km/40 000 miles)	▲	Branded multi-purpose grease with drip point 180° C (356° F)
12. Oil nipple for ignition distributor	◆	Branded HD oil, as engine oil
13. Gearbox (change oil every 24 000 km/16 000 miles)	●	Branded gearbox oil, SAE 80 (or, if not available, HD engine oil SAE 30)
14. Half shaft sliding joints (change oil every 24 000 km/16 000 miles) (not used on nomaintenance half-shafts)	◆	Branded hypoid gear oil, SAE 90
15. Final drive	◆	Branded hypoid gear oil, SAE 90
16. Half-shaft universal joint grease nipples (not used on nomainten-ance half-shafts)	▲	Branded multi-purpose grease with drip point 180° C (356° F)

Important instruction to service stations

Strengthened points for single column car lifts with 4 lifting points:

Outer extremity of body under fold directly adjacent to the reinforced points for the car's own jack.

For lifts with 3 lifting points:

At front below the two floor section struts, in line with the front door pillars.

At rear, in the centre of the V-shaped box-section carrier, close to the propeller shaft flange.

Warning: Never jack up directly on to the final drive.

Engine Electrical

Distributor

REMOVAL AND INSTALLATION

To remove the distributor for overhaul or replacement, remove cap and rotate crankshaft to place No. 1 cylinder in firing position with timing marks properly aligned. The distributor rotor should point to the notch on the distributor housing. Disconnect vacuum line and primary ignition wire, and remove fastening bolts and distributor.

Remove distributor (Z) mounting bolts and take out distributor. Remove distributor flange (F). When replacing, coat mating surfaces of distributor and cylinder head (K) with a non-hardening sealer. Install distributor with vacuum chamber (U) on

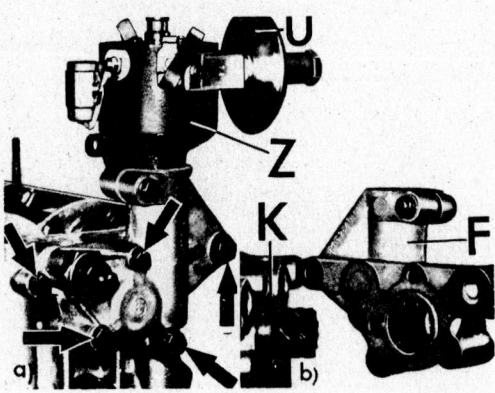

Details of distributor drive.

right when viewed facing forward. Rotor should be just about aligned with mark on distributor housing. Set point gap and dwell angle and adjust ignition timing.

CONTACT POINT ASSEMBLY

When installing points, lightly lubricate distributor cam with high temperature grease. Do not lubricate excessively or lubricant will be thrown onto contact points. Position stationary breaker plate and install lock screw loosely for later adjustment. Install breaker arm on pivot pin. Place spring insulating washer in spring support. Attach breaker arm lead. Install

washer and hairpin clip on pivot pin. Adjust point spacing gap and tighten lockscrew.

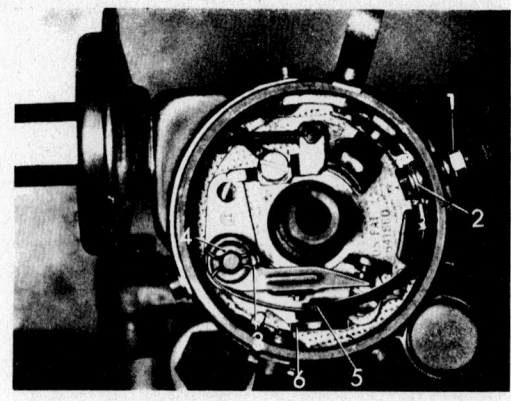

Distributor components: primary wire terminal (1), breaker arm lead (2), clip (3), breaker arm pivot pin (4), breaker arm spring support (5), stationary contact (6). Adjustment screw can be seen beneath contact points.

Point gap can be set by using a feeler gauge; point dwell by using a dwell meter. Accurate measurements with a feeler gauge require careful, precise use of the feeler. The dwell meter, which measures the distance in degrees traveled by the rotating cam while the points are closed, should be first calibrated, switched to the four (or six) cylinder position, and connected between the distributor primary terminal and ground. Remove the distributor cap and rotor. Loosen the breaker set screw approximately ⅛th turn. Observing the dwell meter, reset screw of stationary contact to obtain specified dwell angle of 59-61°. Tighten set screw and recheck dwell. Install rotor and cap, start engine and make a final dwell angle check.

IGNITION TIMING

Timing marks on the crankshaft pulley should be aligned with a pointer on the housing. (Some models have a steel ball in flywheel or inspection opening. Timing is correct when center of steel ball is visible at reference edge). With point gap correctly set and timing marks aligned, distributor housing is rotated counterclockwise slightly until contact points just start to open. The precise instant the points open can be accurately indicated by connecting a (6 or 12 volt) test lamp between the distributor primary terminal and ground. With the ignition switch on, the test lamp will light the moment the contact points open. This method of static timing is only to be used for a rough initial setting.

In using a timing light, connect timing light to No. 1 spark plug. Disconnect all vacuum hoses from the distributor and plug the hoses. Start engine and set idle speed to rpm shown in General Tune-up Specifications Chart. Idle performance must be smooth. Rotate distributor as necessary to align timing marks with timing light pulses. If timing light is not available, timing can be adjusted by marking advance and retard points on the distributor with chalk. With vacuum lines disconnected and engine idling, rotate distributor to point where engine reaches its highest rpm. Mark this point. Next, retard spark by slowly reversing the distributor to the point of lowest rpm. Mark this point. Center distributor between the two marks and tighten it.

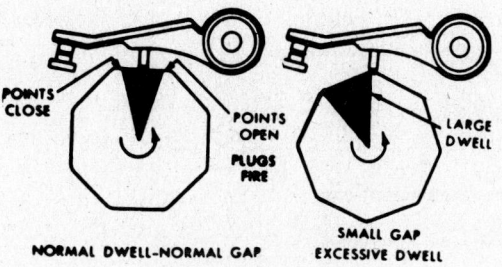

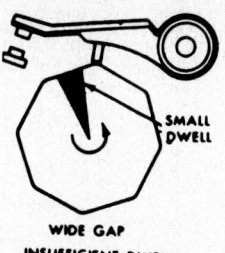

Distributor dwell angle (or cam angle) is determined by contact point gap setting. Dwell is increased by decreasing point gap.

It must be emphasized that the only really accurate way to set ignition timing is by use of a stroboscopic timing light.

Timing is correct when steel ball is centered.

Timing marks on crankshaft pulley:
OT = TDC notch
Z = static timing notch
Z = 2000 rpm timing notch

Ignition Timing of Emission Controlled Engines

Ignition timing of emission controlled engines is checked and if necessary reset as follows with the engine running at normal operating temperature using a timing light and a tachometer.

1. Remove vacuum advance hose from distributor. Set idle speed to exactly 2000 rpm by adjusting idle screw. Direct strobe light at timing mark (steel ball in rim of flywheel) through opening in clutch housing. Some engines have three timing marks on the crankshaft pulley. These are clockwise, OT-top dead center, Z-mark for rough initial static timing, Z-mark for timing at 2000 rpm. There is a corresponding mark on the timing chain cover.

2. If marks do not line up, loosen clamp

on distributor housing and turn until marks are aligned. Re-check engine speed and reset to 2000 rpm if required. Re-tighten distributor housing clamp and re-connect vacuum hose to distributor.

Alternator and Generator

BMW 1500, 1600, 1800, 1800 A, 1800 TI and some 1600-2 models are equipped with 6-volt systems. These use 200 watt DC generators except for the 1800 TI which has a 350 watt alternator. All 12-volt systems employ 450 watt alternators. Starters, generators, alternators, regulators, and coils are all manufactured by Bosch.

Alternator and Regulator

The alternator is a continuous output (even at idle) diode-rectified AC generator. It has three-phase stator (housing) windings assembled on the inside of a laminated core that is the middle section of the housing. Rectifier diodes which change AC to DC are connected to the windings (3 diodes to each phase). If the alternator does not meet output specifications, the alternator and regulator are usually replaced. The alternator requires no lubrica-

tion. The diodes in the alternator are one-way devices, allowing current to flow only from the alternator to the battery; battery current cannot discharge through the alternator. As a result, a current breaker, or cutout relay, is not needed in the regulator. The regulator used with the alternator needs only a voltage regulator which requires no adjustment.

DC Generator and Regulator

The DC generator has a rotating armature with copper windings that intersect lines of magnetic force between magnetic field poles. At the start, the magnetic field is weak because it is only residual. However, as current flows from the armature windings, part of the flow is fed into and excites the magnetic field. Increasing speed intensifies the magnetic field and thereby increases the voltage from the windings. The magnetic field becomes saturated with energy and no further increase in armature speed will add to the output.

Since voltage produced by the generator is in direct proportion to the product of armature speed and exciting current in the magnetic field, a constant voltage output can be maintained by making compensat-

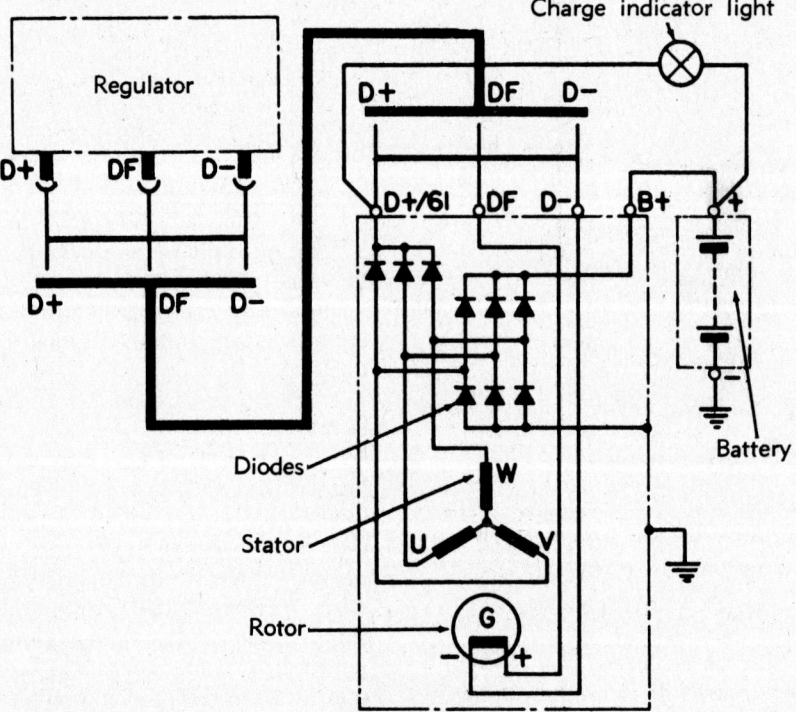

AC charging circuit.

ing adjustments to the exciting current. Armature speed is based on engine rpm and is therefore not independently controllable. The regulator maintains a constant voltage output by interrupting the exciting current.

Testing DC Generator and Regulator

After checking condition and tension of the fan belt, connect a 60-0-60 range ammeter in series with the regulator and battery by disconnecting the red lead from the "B+" regulator terminal and adding an ammeter between the terminal and the red wire. Set engine speed to around 2500 rpm. Output should be at least 20 amperes on a 12-volt DC generator and 50 amperes on a 6-volt unit. A lower output indicates trouble in the generator or regulator. Find the cause by disconnecting the generator field lead (DF) from the regulator and connecting it to the battery side of the ammeter. If output is still low, the generator is faulty.

To test for a faulty regulator, remove the red battery lead from the ammeter and connect a voltmeter positive lead to this terminal. Connect the voltmeter negative lead to ground. Increase engine speed until voltage peaks within 13.5-14.2 range (6.3-7.6 for 6-volt units). If voltage is not in this range, remove cover and adjust spring tension of voltage regulator armature to obtain a middle reading of about 14 volts. If voltage reading fluctuates, clean voltage regulator contacts with fine sandpaper or an ignition file. Do not use emery paper. If voltage continues to fluctuate, or cannot be adjusted to obtain the required reading, the regulator is faulty.

Cutout Relay Adjustment

Connect the positive lead of a voltmeter to the generator armature terminal (D+) at top of regulator. Attach voltmeter negative lead to ground. Connect an ammeter in series with the battery lead and the

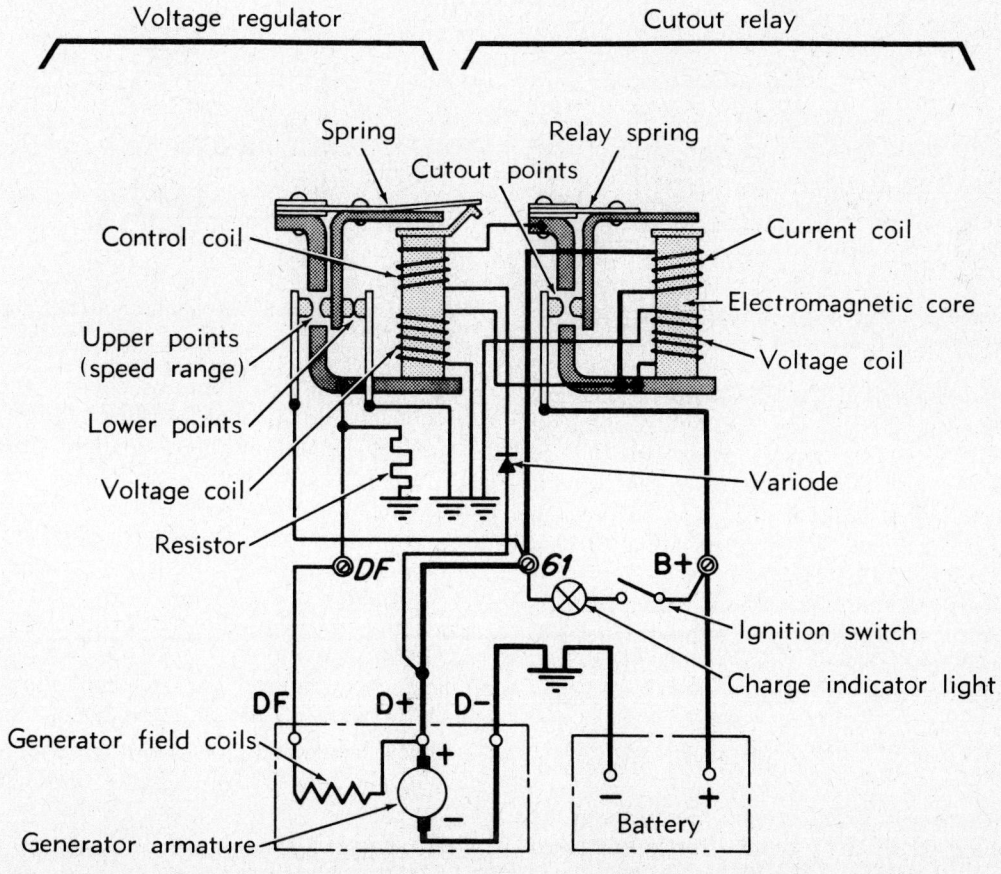

DC charging circuit.

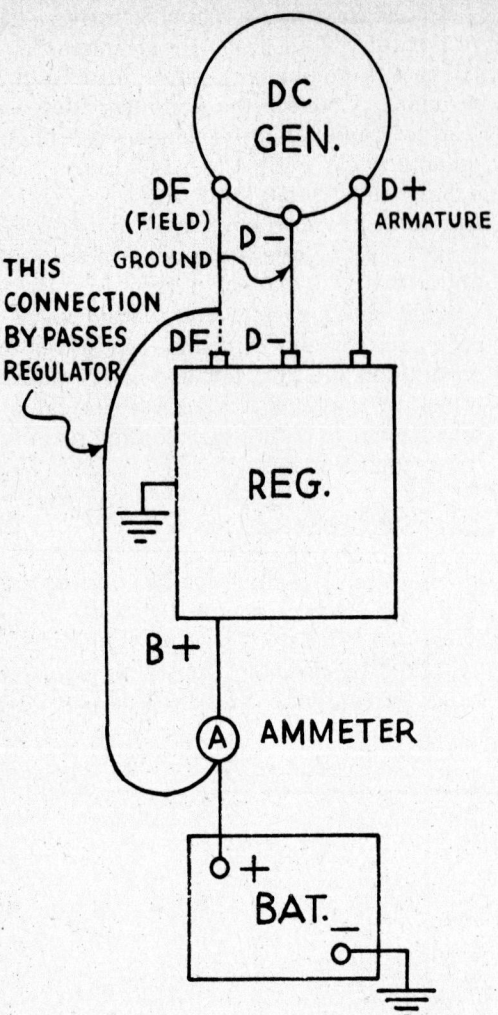

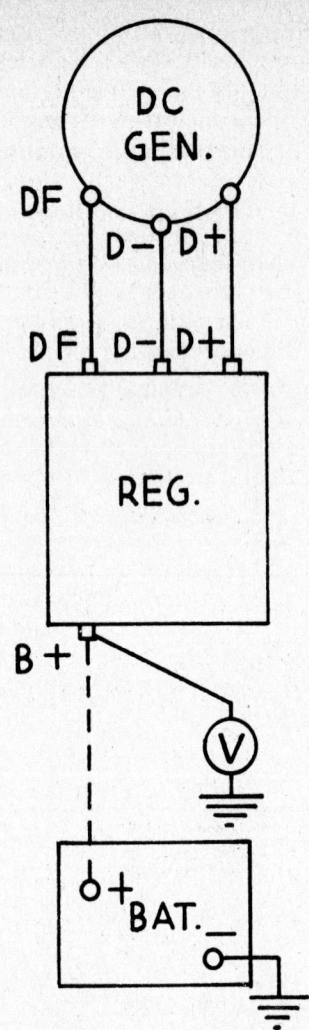

Ammeter connections for testing generator and regulator.

Voltmeter connections for adjusting voltage regulator.

regulator terminal (red lead B+). Increase engine speed and observe voltage increase (until relay points close) and then slightly drop as circuit is completed to the battery. The highest voltmeter reading before the drop is the closing or "cut-in" voltage. This should be 5.9-6.5 volts. If closing voltage is not within limits, adjust by bending the cut-out relay armature spring support. Increase tension to increase voltage — decrease tension to decrease voltage.

DC Generator Overhaul

Remove nut and pulley. Pulley may be pulled off shaft by hand after tapping end of shaft lightly with a plastic covered hammer. Remove lock washer from shaft with

side cutting pliers. Remove cover band, disconnect and lift out brushes. Remove through-bolts and pull housing apart. Take out armature and inspect housing, commutator, and windings for thrown solder.

Check armature for short circuit to ground by use of test prods (commutator bars to shaft) and test lamp. Check around all segments of commutator. Lamp should not light.

Scan commutator bars. Lamp should light by contact between all adjacent bars.

Check field coil for short circuit to ground (housing to DF). Lamp must not light.

Check field coil continuity (D+ to DF). Lamp should light.

Check brush holders in same way for

short circuits to ground, and check brush tension which should be approximately 2 ft. lbs. (.9 kg).

Remove bearing parts from drive end frame. Clean and inspect ball bearings, replace worn parts and pack assemblies with high temperature grease. Wipe generator parts with clean cloth. Grease-cutting compounds might damage armature and coil insulation. Inspect all parts for wear or damage. Soldering must be done with rosin flux: *never use acid flux on electrical connections.* Reassemble using reverse procedure.

Checking for grounded armature of generator.

Checking for armature continuity.

Checking for grounded field of generator.

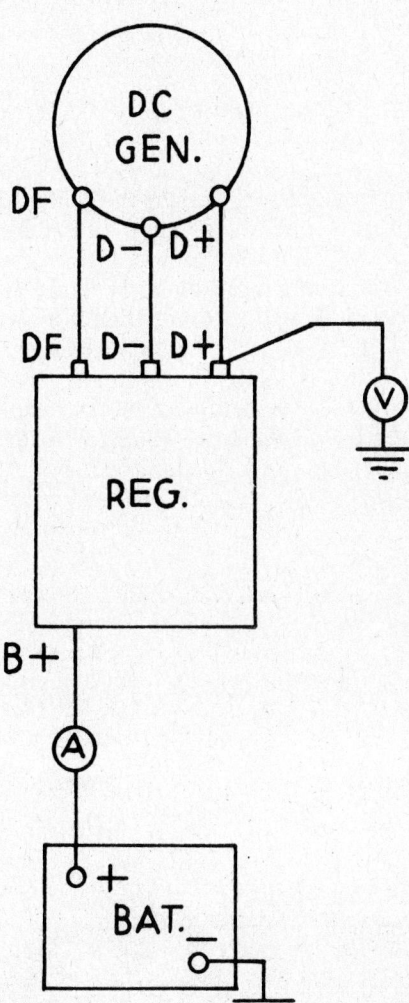

Voltmeter and ammeter connections for adjusting cutout relay.

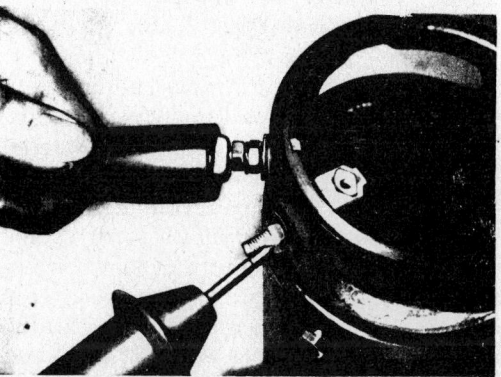

Checking for generator field continuity.

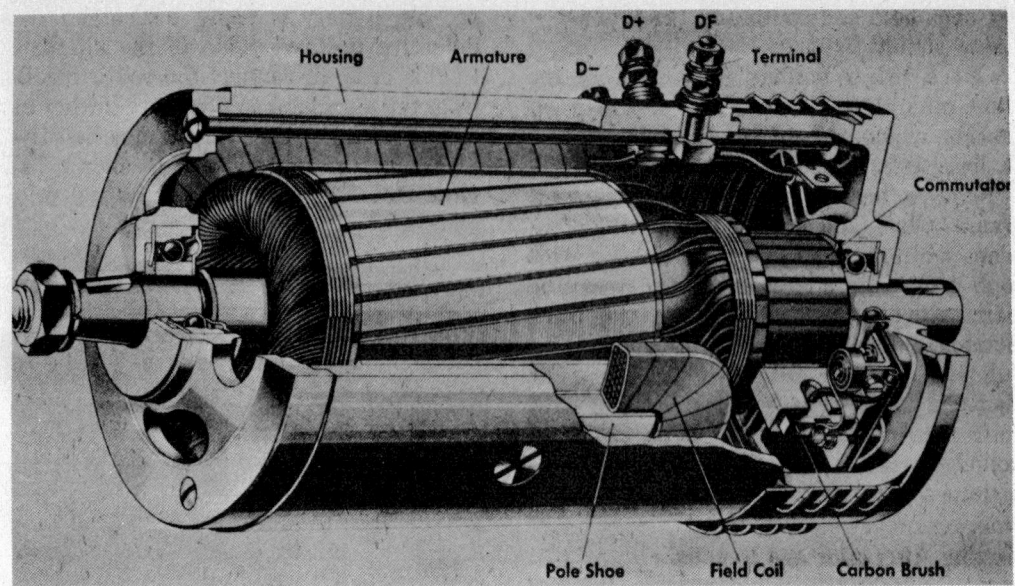

Housing   Armature   D+   DF   Terminal

D−

Commutator

Pole Shoe   Field Coil   Carbon Brush

Cutaway view of Bosch DC generator.

.Testing Alternator and Regulator

WARNING: *the alternator contains diodes which can be damaged by voltage peaks. Therefore, do not disconnect cables between battery, generator and regulator when the engine is running. Also, if battery charger is to be used with the battery in place, disconnect both the positive and negative leads of the battery before connecting the charger to the battery.* The charge warning light serves to excite the field of the alternator. If it does not light with the ignition switch on and engine stopped, it should be checked and replaced if necessary. Also check plug of cable D+ /61 for continuity.

Usually on alternator systems, the warning light will go out while the engine is idling. If it continues to glow brightly, the regulator, generator and cable D+ /61 should be checked for shorts to ground. If the warning lamp glows at half intensity whether the engine is running or stopped, check cable DF and terminal, soldered bridge joints in regulator, carbon brushes, and sliprings, for good conductivity. If warning lamp burns brightly with engine stopped, but glows faintly even when engine is run at moderate to high speeds, the alternator or charge circuit may be faulty. To check this, connect a 4-watt test lamp directly to D+ and B+ on the alternator. If lamp does not glow when engine is run

at moderate speed, then the fault is in the charging circuit. If lamp burns brightly, then goes out, the fault is in the alternator.

If warning lamp glows with the ignition switch off, but goes out when it is switched on, the battery is being discharged by a defective positive diode in the alternator. In this case, disconnect the red cable B+ from the alternator to eliminate further battery discharge. The vehicle may be driven as far as the battery charge allows. The alternator will have to be repaired or replaced.

Further checks for faulty alternator or regulator are made with a voltmeter. Disconnect the red cable (B+) from the alternator. WARNING: *Do not disconnect this cable if the alternator is an SEV type with an electronic regulator.* Connect a voltme-

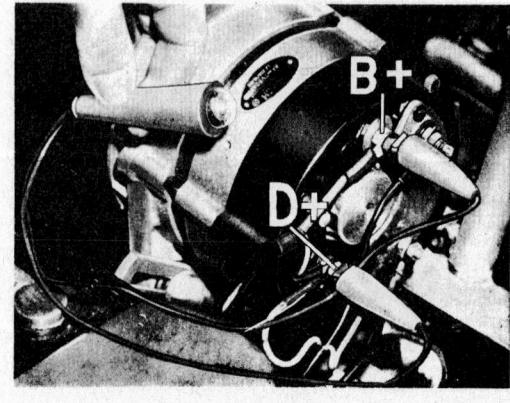

B+

D+

Connections of 4-watt test lamp to alternator.

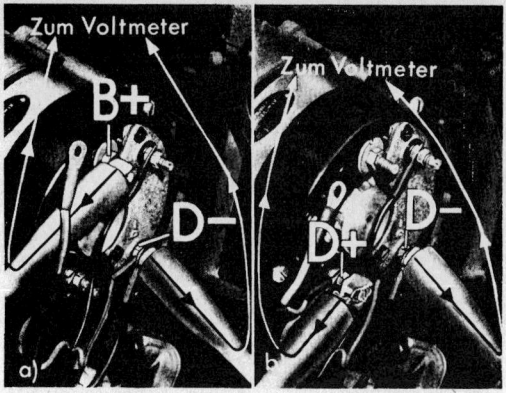

Connections of voltmeter to alternator.

ter to B+ and D-. Accelerate engine. The 6-volt systems should produce a reading of 6.7-7.2 volts, and 12-volt systems a reading of 13.5-14.2 volts. If these values are not obtained, measure the voltage between D+ and D-. If the voltage difference between these two readings (B+ and D-/ D+ and D-) is less than 0.5 volt, the regulator must be replaced. If the voltage is between 1.5 and 4 volts, the alternator is faulty.

Starter

STARTER SERVICING

Disconnect battery ground cable from negative terminal. Remove starter cables and starter. Remove solenoid from motor housing, saving the gasket. Remove support bracket and dust cap. Remove brush holder plate and take out brushes. Remove through-bolts and separate commutator end-frame and field frame assemblies.

Remove bolt, nut and lockwasher from solenoid shift lever fulcrum. Remove armature and drive assembly from shift (yoke) lever. To remove drive assembly from armature, place a cylinder such as a 2″ pipe coupling over the end of the shaft to bear against the pinion stop retainer. Tap the retainer toward the armature to uncover the snap ring. (Models with castle nut, remove cotter pin and left-hand thread castle nut). Remove snap ring from groove in shaft, and slide retainer and pinion drive assembly from shaft. Remove spring.

Carefully inspect all mechanical parts for wear and damage, wash in kerosene, and blow dry with compressed air. Do not submerge armature or roller clutches in solvent. Check condition and tension of brushes. Check field coil and armature commutator with an AC test lamp for short

Starter brush holder plate removed. At reassembly, install washers (1, 2) on armature shaft.

circuits to the shaft and pole pieces. The test lamp should not light.

Check brush holder for shorts, inspect armature commutator for burnt or flat spots. Coat polished metal surfaces, other than the commutator, with engine oil. Lubricate points illustrated. When reassembling starter, lubricate armature shaft with silicone grease. Install assist spring and then the drive assembly with the pinion outward. Slide the pinion stop retainer down over the shaft with the recessed side out. Place a new snap ring on the drive end of the shaft and hold it in place with a block of wood. Tap the block with a hammer to force the snap ring over the end of the shaft, then slide the ring down into the groove in the shaft. Pry stop retainer into position over snap ring.

Lubricate drive housing bushings with silicone grease and set the armature drive assembly with the shift lever in the housing. Lubricate shift lever linkage at solenoid end. Position shift lever and attach bolt, nut and lockwasher. Use care in tightening the pole shoe screws to prevent distortion of parts. Position the field frame over the armature and place washer on commutator end of armature assembly. Install commutator end-frame after lubricating bushing. Install through-bolts and tighten. Connect field leads to motor terminal of solenoid with connecting nut and

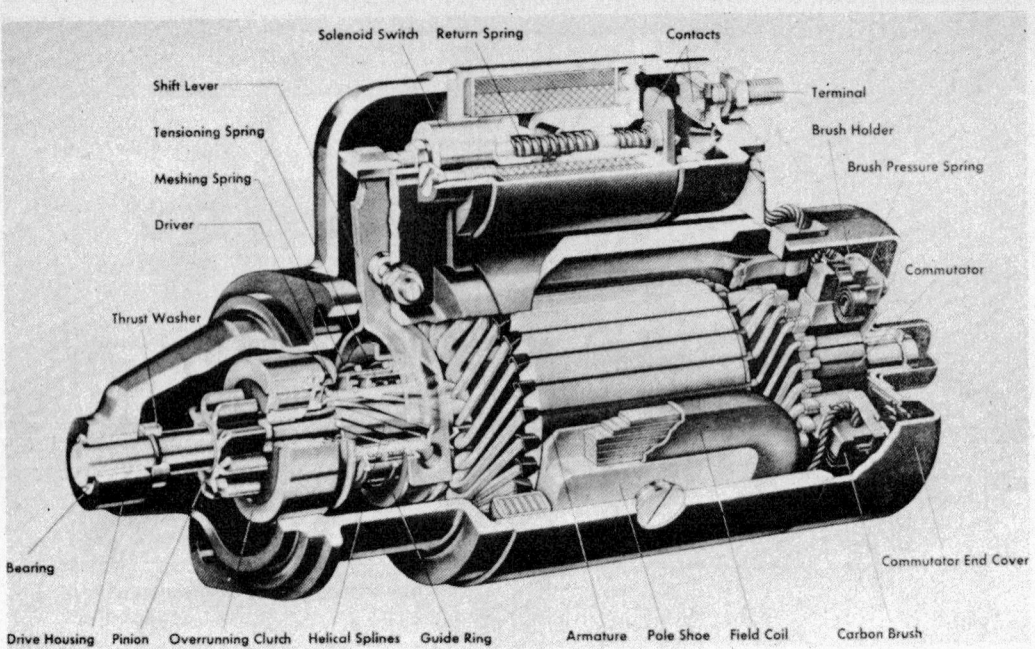

Cutaway view of starter.

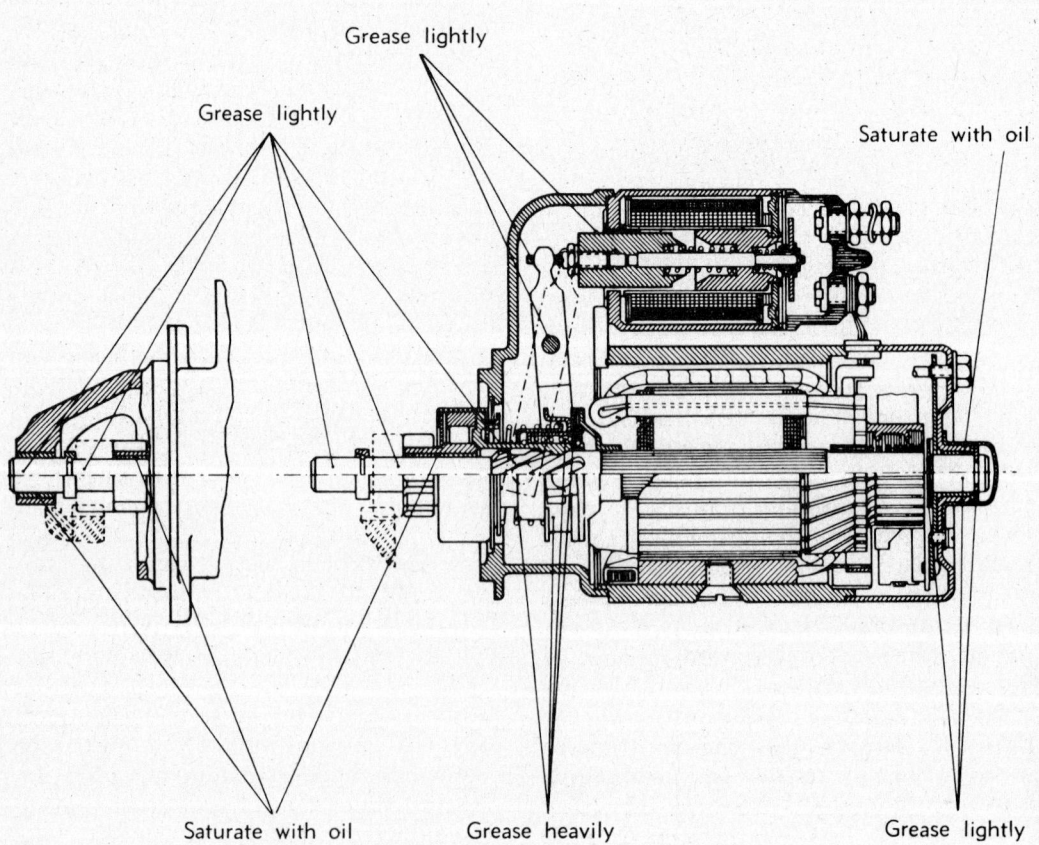

Points to be lubricated when reassembling starter.

washer. Attach solenoid with its gasket to drive housing. Connect the four brushes and install cover band.

Checking starter armature for shorted commutator.

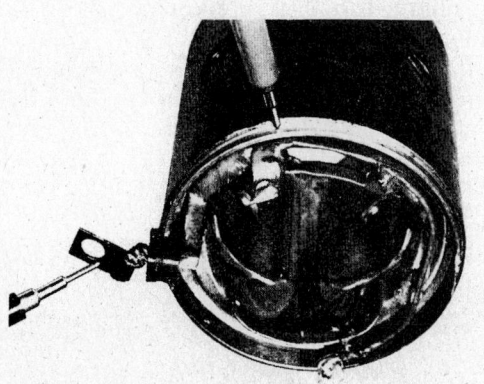

Checking starter for grounded field coil.

Battery

Batteries should be checked periodically for adequate electrolyte level, proper output and good connections. Add nothing but distilled water, and fill when necessary to about 3/16″ above the plates.

Inspect the battery case for cracks and weakness. A leaky battery should be replaced. Check the specific gravity of the battery electrolyte with a hydrometer. Readings from a fully charged battery will depend on the make but will be in the range of 1.260 to 1.310 times as heavy as pure water at 80°F. NOTE: *all cells should produce nearly equal readings.* If one or two cell readings are sharply lower, the cells are defective, and if they continue to be low after charging, the battery must be replaced.

As a battery releases its charge, sulphate ions in the electrolyte become attached to the plates — reducing the density of the fluid. The specific gravity of the electrolyte varies not only with the percentage of acid in the liquid, but also with the temperature. As temperature increases, the electrolyte expands so that specific gravity is reduced. As temperature drops, the electrolyte contracts and specific gravity increases. To correct readings for temperature variation, add .004 to the hydrometer reading for every 10°F that the electrolyte is above 80°F, and subtract .004 for every 10°F that the electrolyte is below 80°F. The drawing shows the total correction to make for any temperature above or below 80°F.

The state of charge of the battery can be determined roughly from the following specific gravity readings:

Hydrometer Readings	Condition
1.260-1.310	Fully charged
1.230-1.250	¾ charged
1.200-1.220	½ charged
1.170-1.190	¼ charged
1.140-1.160	Almost discharged
1.110-1.130	Fully discharged

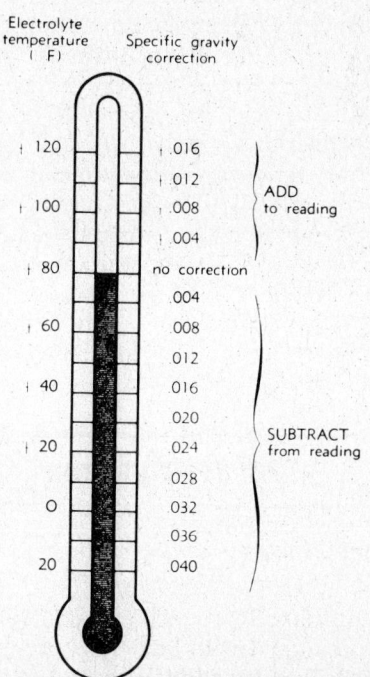

Temperature affects the specific gravity readings of batteries.

Make a light-load voltage test to detect weak cells. First draw off the transient surface charge by operating the starter for three seconds and then turning on the low beam lights. After one minute, test each cell (with lights still on) with the voltmeter. A fully charged battery will have no cell voltage below 1.95 volts and no cell will vary more than .05 volts from the others. A greater variation at full charge indicates a defective cell.

Another battery check requires connecting a charger for three minutes under 40 amperes for a 12-volt battery. Read the battery voltage with the charger still operating. Voltage over 15.5 volts indicates a defective battery. If battery voltage is under this limit and individual cell readings are within 0.1 volt, the battery is usable.

Charging a weak battery is best done by a slow-charge method. If quick charging is attempted, check the cell voltages and the color of the electrolyte a few minutes after charge is started. If cell voltages are not uniform or if electrolyte is discolored with brown sediment, quick charging should be stopped in favor of a slow charge. In either case, do not let electrolyte temperature exceed 120°F.

If high electrical circuit voltage is suspected, the voltage regulator might be cutting in abnormally due to corroded or loose battery connections. The symptoms are hard starting, full ammeter charge and lights flaring brightly. After cleaning, coat battery terminals with petroleum jelly (vaseline) to prevent recurrence of problem.

Overcharging is a common cause of battery failure. A symptom of overcharging is a frequent need for addition of water to the battery. The generating system should be corrected immediately to prevent internal battery damage.

Fuel System

Fuel Pump

BMW 1500, 1600, 1800 and 2000 Series cars are equipped with Solex carburetors, all of which are downdraft except for the sidedraft types used on the 1600 TI, 1800 TI, 2000 TI and 2000 CS. Models 2500, 2800 and 2800 CS use dual Zenith downdraft carburetors. BMW's use Solex mechanical fuel pumps.

FUEL PUMP CLEANING AND ASSEMBLY

Sludge deposited in the fuel chamber or on the filter may be removed after removing the pump cover. Inlet and outlet valves should be inspected and replaced (by replacing the housing) if damaged. Check springs for good condition. Do not stretch springs for greater pressure; if weak or distorted, replace. Wash control mechanism for inlet chamber in fuel oil and lightly lubricate with thin oil. Fuel pump seals, even if only slightly damaged should be replaced. Lightly coat new seals with grease before assembly. If a new diaphragm is to be installed, soak it in kerosene for a few minutes before assembly.

Remove fuel pump. Remove insulating flange and plunger. Disassemble pump by removing screw (1), then screws (6). Remove screws and cover plate (9). Lift lockplate (10) from shaft (11), and tap shaft out

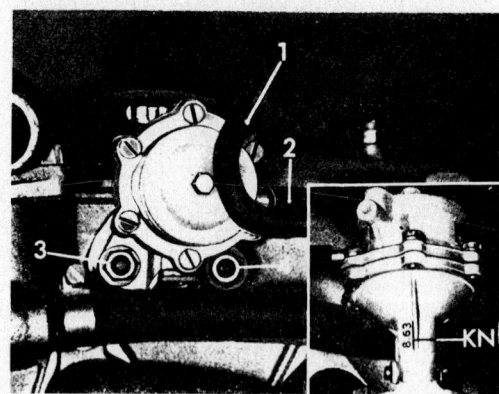

Fuel pump lines (1, 2), mounting bolts (3, 4) and serial number location (KN).

with punch and hammer. Remove rocker arm (13) and its spring (12), and lift up diaphragm (14). Be careful not to change the length of the diaphragm spring which governs pump pressure. The valves in the upper section of the pump are part of the housing and cannot be replaced separately.

Since pump pressure is influenced by plunger length and insulating flange thickness, use replacement parts of the same length and thickness. For vehicles up to chassis No. 917583, combined thickness of

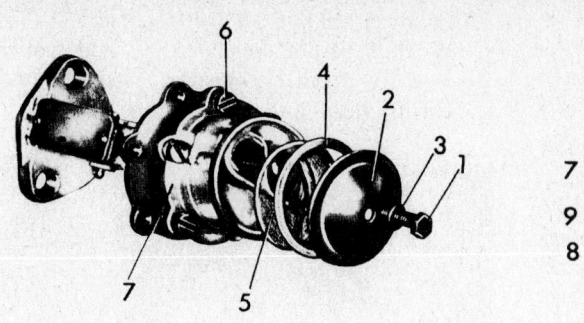 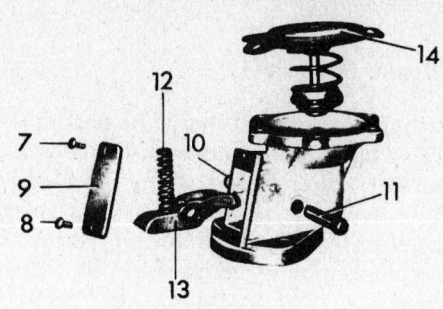

Fuel pump components: assembly screw and washer (1, 3), cap (2), gasket (4), filter (5), upper housing and screws (6, 7), cover plate and screws (8, 9), lockplate (10), shaft (11), rocker arm spring (12), rocker arm (13), diaphragm and spring (14).

flange and gaskets should be .19685" (5 mm); plunger length should be 3.59456" (91.3 mm). For vehicles from chassis No. 917584, thickness of flange and gaskets should be .78742" (20 mm); plunger length should be 4.19299" (106.5 mm). Carefully position diaphragm when reassembling. Pack lower part of pump with grease.

Carburetors

CARBURETOR SERVICING

Carburetor repair kits are recommended for each overhaul. Kits contain a complete set of gaskets and new parts to replace those that generally deteriorate most rapidly. Not substituting *all* of the new

Zenith/Solex carburetor repair kits are of three basic types — repair, Vit, and gasket. The following summarizes the parts in each type:

Vit kits	*Repair kits*	*Gasket kits*
all gaskets	all jets and gaskets	all needed gaskets
float needle valve	all diaphragms	
volume control screw	float needle valve	
all diaphragms	volume control screw	
spring	spring for pump diaphragm	
	pump ball valve	
	main jet carrier	
	float	
	complete intermediate rod	
	intermediate pump lever	
	complete injector tube	
	some cover hold down screws and washers	

parts supplied in the kits can result in poor performance later.

Carburetor Overhaul

Carburetor overhaul should be performed only in a clean, dust-free area. Disassemble carburetor carefully, keeping look-alike parts separated to prevent accidental interchange at assembly. Note all jet sizes. When reassembling, make sure all screws and jets are tight in their seats. Tighten all screws gradually, in rotation. Do not tighten needle valves into seats. Uneven jetting will result. Use a new flange gasket.

Carburetor Cleaning

Wash carburetor parts — except diaphragm and electric choke units — in a carburetor cleaner, rinse in solvent, and blow dry with compressed air. Carburetors have numerous small passages that can be fouled by carbon and gummy deposits. Soak metal parts in carburetor solvent until thoroughly clean. The solvent will weaken or destroy cork, plastic, and leather components. These parts should be wiped with a clean, lint-free cloth. Clean all fuel channels in float bowl and cover. Clean jets and valves separately to avoid accidental interchange. Never use wire or sharp objects to clean jets and passages as this will seriously alter their calibration.

Check throttle valve shafts for wear or scoring that may allow air leakage affecting starting and idling. Inspect float spindle and other moving parts for wear. Replace if worn. Replace float if fuel has leaked into it. Accelerator pump check-valves should pass air one way but not the other. Test for proper seating by blowing and sucking on valve and replace if necessary. Wash valve again to remove breath moisture. Check bowl cover with a straight edge for warped surfaces. Closely inspect valves and seats for wear and damage.

Downdraft Carburetor
Disassembly—1500, 1600,
1600-2, 1800, 1800A, 1800/69,
2000, 2000 A, 2002, 2000 CA

To remove carburetor, disconnect air filter (2) at (1 and 3) and remove filter.

Remove fuel line (6) and vacuum line (7). Disconnect linkage (8), choke cable (17), if installed, from lever (18), and cable sleeve (19) from carburetor. Remove two mounting nuts and carburetor.

Air cleaner removal — all models with single downdraft carburetor.

Disconnecting choke cable — single downdraft carburetor.

Remove carburetor cover (11) with gasket (12). Remove float spindle keeper (13) and lift out float (14) with its shaft. Remove main jet plug (15), washer (18) and main jet (H). Unscrew float needle valve (16) and lift out with its gasket (17). Unscrew air correction jet (19). Unscrew idle mixture adjusting screw (G) and remove with spring. Unscrew idling jet (20). Unscrew enrichment valve (A) and remove with washer. Disconnect pump linkage and remove with washer. Disconnect pump linkage and remove pump cover (21) with linkage. Remove diaphragm (22) and spring (23).

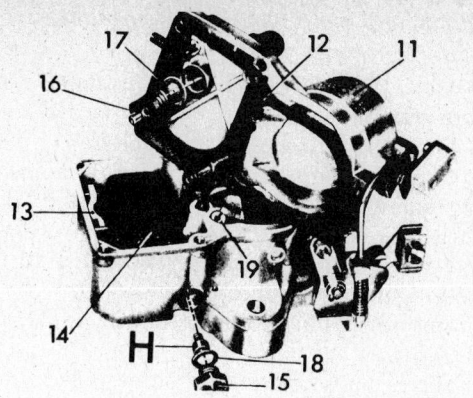
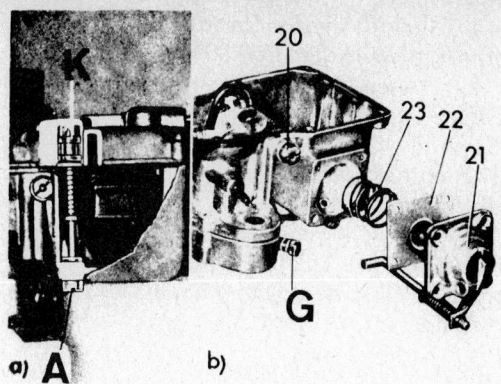

Downdraft carburetor components: cover (11), gasket (12), float spindle keeper (13), float (14), main jet plug (15), float needle valve (16), float needle valve gasket (17), washer (18), main jet (H), air correction jet (19), idling jet (20), pump cover (21), diaphragm (22), spring (23), enrichment valve (A), piston (K), idle mixture adjustment screw (G).

After cleaning and checking components, reassemble carburetor, install on engine, and make the following inspections and adjustments.

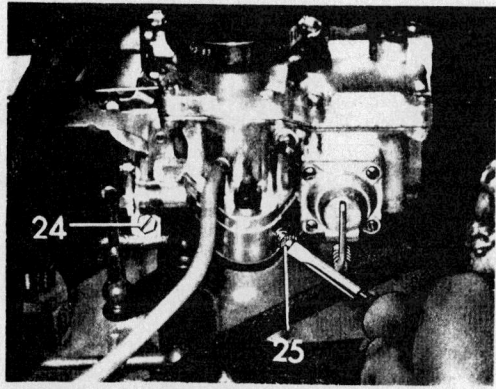

Downdraft carburetor adjustment and fuel level measurement. Idling stop-screw (24), idling mixture adjustment (25), fuel line (26), cover and gasket (27, 28), fuel depth (N).

Warm engine to normal operating temperature. Set idling speed with stop-screw (24). Adjust idling mixture with screw (25) until engine reaches maximum idling speed, then correct idling speed with screw (24). Allow engine to run briefly at idling speed. Shut down engine to check fuel level in carburetor bowl. Remove fuel line (26) and seal off supply line. Remove carburetor cover (27). Fuel level (N) should be .67-.75" (17-19 mm) in depth. Fuel level varies with the thickness of the float needle valve gasket (29). The original thickness of this gasket is .04" (1 mm). If fuel level is not within specifications, replace this gasket. Use a thinner gasket to raise the level and a thicker one to lower the level.

Adjusting Idle for Engines Without Emission Control

Richness of idle speed mixture is determined by the setting of a volume control screw, allowing a very precise adjustment of fuel-air mixture; air intake is through a calibrated orifice located in the body of the carburetor in a recessed space beneath the venturi.

The engine must be warm, and the spark plugs and points in good condition. Gently screw the volume control screw in as far as it will go; then back it out about 2½ turns for a preliminary setting. With the engine idling:

1. Slightly tighten throttle stop screw to adjust idle speed to 700-800, rpm.

2. Loosen volume control screw until engine begins to idle roughly. Then tighten screw slowly until engine idles smoothly. The correct setting gives the fastest possible smooth idle.

3. Slowly loosen throttle stop screw to adjust engine idle to approximately 800 rpm. NOTE: *never completely tighten the volume control screw.*

Adjusting Idle for Engines With Emission Control

Adjust idling of emission controlled engines as follows:

1. Disconnect air hose leading from air pump to exhaust manifold at the pump.

2. Set engine idle speed to 1000 rpm with engine at normal operating temperature.

3. Turn idle mixture adjustment screw (with air hose removed) to obtain 6-8% CO. (If exhaust tester does not give a CO indication, adjust to 75.5% combustion efficiency). Repeat steps 2 and 3 until the specified values have been achieved.

4. Reconnect air hose to pump.

DUAL TWIN-CHOKE CARBURETOR SERVICING—1600 TI, 1800 TI, 2000 TI, 2000 CS

To remove carburetors, disconnect and remove air filter. Remove screws (3 and 4) from support (L). Disconnect choke rod (5) and springs (6). Disconnect fuel lines. Remove mounting nuts and carburetors. Install carburetors in reverse order from above.

Twin carburetor removal. Fuel lines (1, 2), support (L), support screws (3, 4), rod (5), springs (6), Arrows show carburetor mounting screws.

Adjusting Dual Twin-Choke Carburetors

Make the following basic adjustments before starting engine:

Disconnect and remove air filter.

Carefully tighten idling mixture adjusting screws (1-4) until they are fully in, then release one-half turn.

Loosen synchronizing screw (5) until it no longer touches throttle lever (7).

Unscrew idling stop screw (6) as far as it will go.

Screw in synchronizing screw (5) until it just contacts throttle lever (7).

Screw in idling stop screw (6) until it just contacts the throttle plate lever.

Turn idling stop screw (6) in an additional two turns.

All four carburetor throats must be ad-

NOTE: *correct ignition timing and valve adjustment are necessary for proper carburetor tuning.*

Twin carburetor adjustments. Idling mixture adjusting screws (1-4), synchronizing screw (5), idling stop screw (6), throttle lever (7).

justed to pass an equal volume of air. This can be done by using a carburetor synchronizing gauge, or by listening through a short section of water hose to the pitch of the hiss made by the entering air. The gauge is adjusted on the throat of one carburetor for a piston height near the middle of the scale. The unit is then switched to the other carburetor and, if necessary, the carburetor is re-set so that the position of the piston matches that for the first carburetor. The idle stop screws may then be adjusted for equal idling with the help of the synchronizing gauge.

With the engine running at 1200 rpm:

Synchronize carburetor (2) of second cylinder with carburetor (3) of third cylinder by means of adjusting screw (5).

Synchronize carburetor (1) of first cylinder with carburetor (2) of second cylinder by means of adjusting screw (8).

Synchronize carburetor (4) of fourth cylinder with carburetor (3) of third cylinder by means of adjusting screw (9).

Adjust idling mixture screws for maximum engine idling speed.

Set engine idling speed to 800 rpm by means of idling stop screws.

Pump injection volume is adjusted by loosening locknut (15) and turning nut (17) of linkage (16). Screw in to increase volume; screw out to decrease. Correct injection volume is .7-.9 cc.

Choke butterflies are correctly adjusted when clearance at (A) is .008" (.2 mm).

Adjust rod length (B) to 1.614", (41 mm).

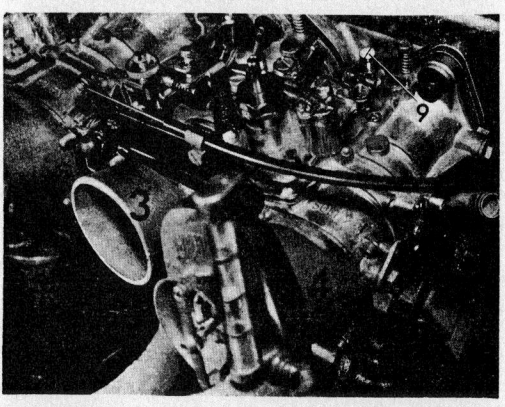

Tuning twin carburetors. Synchronizing adjustments (5, 8, 9), carburetor throats (1-4).

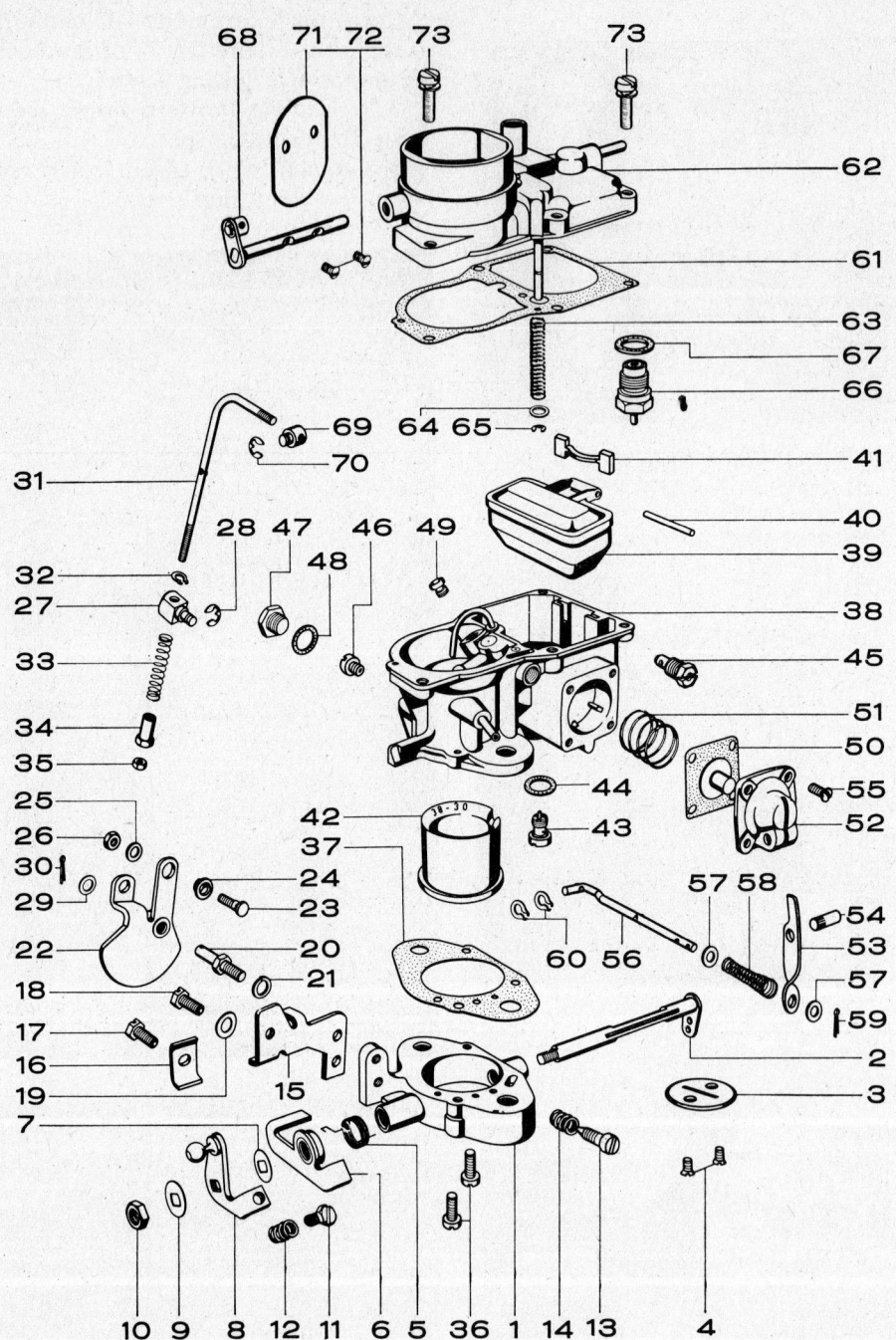

Components of Solex 36 PDSI carburetor used on 1500 and 1600 models.

Components of Solex 36 PDSI carburetor used on 1500 and 1600 models.

— Carburetor compl.
— Throttle body with throttle spindle, throttle butterfly, fixing screws
1 Throttle body
2 Throttle spindle with intermediate lever
3 Throttle butterfly
4 Fixing screw
5 Return spring
6 Intermediate lever compl.
7 Distance washer (between throttle lever and intermediate lever)
8 Throttle lever compl.
9 Tab washer
10 Throttle spindle end nut
11 Slow running adjustment screw (on throttle lever)
12 Slow running adjustment screw spring
13 Volume control screw
14 Volume control screw spring
15 Bowden cable bracket
16 Cable clamp
17 Clamping screw
18 Hexagon screw (for bowden cable bracket)
19 Spring washer (for hexagon screw)
20 Bearing pin
21 Bearing pin spring washer
— Starter lever with clamping screw and roller bracket
22 Starter lever
— Clamping screw compl.
23 Clamping screw
24 Bushing
25 Washer
26 Hexagon nut
27 Grip roller
28 Spring washer
29 Washer
30 Split pin
31 Starter control rod
32 Clamping ring (for starter control rod)
33 Spring (for starter control rod)
34 Shoulder nut (for starter control rod)
35 Hexagon nut (for starter control rod)
36 Throttle body fixing screw
37 Insulating gasket

38 Float chamber with pressed-in emulsion tube and injector tube
39 Float 8.5 gr.
40 Float toggle spindle
41 Holder for float toggle spindle
42 Choke tube
43 Enrichment valve
44 Enrichment valve washer
45 Pilot jet
46 Main jet
47 Main jet screw plug
48 Screw plug washer
49 Air correction jet
50 Diaphragm compl.
51 Diaphragm spring
— Pump cover compl.
52 Pump cover
53 Pump lever
54 Pump lever spindle
55 Fixing screw
— Pump control rod compl.
56 Pump control rod
57 Pump control rod washer
58 Pump control rod spring
59 Pump control rod split pin
60 Pump control rod clip
61 Float chamber cover gasket
62 Float chamber cover compl. with depression actuated piston
— Depression actuated piston compl.
63 Spring (for depression actuated piston)
— Cover plate
64 Washer
65 Spring washer
66 Float needle valve 2 mm with ball
67 Float needle valve washer
68 Strangler spindle compl. (with lever, grip roller)
69 Grip roller
70 Grip roller washer
71 Strangler
72 Strangler fixing screw
73 Assembly screw with spring washer
— Enrichment tube
— Collet

Components of Solex 40 PDSIT carburetor used on 2002, 2000, and 2000 CA models.

— Carburetor compl.
1 Body compl.
2 Enrichment valve compl.
3 Enrichment valve washer
4 Idle jet compl.
5 Main jet
6 Main jet screw plug
7 Screw plug washer
8 Air correction jet
9 Diaphragm compl.
10 Diaphragm spring
11 Pump cover compl.
12 Pump cover fixing screw
13 Choke tube
14 Choke tube fixing screw
15 Hexagon nut
16 Insulating gasket
17 Throttle body compl.
18 Throttle level compl.
19 Toothed washer (on throttle spindle)
20 Throttle spindle end nut
21 Slow running adjustment screw
22 Slow running adjustment screw spring
23 Control rod (between starter and
     throttle lever)
24 Control rod clip
25 Control rod nut
26 Control rod compl. (between intermediate
     lever and pump lever)
27   Control rod
28   Spring
29   Split pin
30   Clip

31   Washer
32   Washer
33 Volume control screw
34 Volume control screw spring
35 Throttle body fixing screw
36 Float compl.
37 Float toggle spindle
38 Float toggle spindle holder
39 Float chamber cover gasket
40 Float chamber cover compl.
41   Spring (for starter diaphragm)
42   Valve cover (for starter diaphragm)
43   Valve cover fixing screw
44   Spindle with abutment lever compl.
45   Strangler lever compl.
46   Strangler lever
47   Clamp roller
48   Clip
49   Hexagon nut
50   Clip
51 Insulating washer
52 Starter cover compl.
53 Starter cover compl.
54   Water connection
55   O-ring
56   Cylindrical screw (with internal hexagon)
57   Washer
58 Retaining ring
59 Fixing screw (for retaining ring)
60 Float needle valve compl.
61 Float needle valve washer
62 Assembly screw

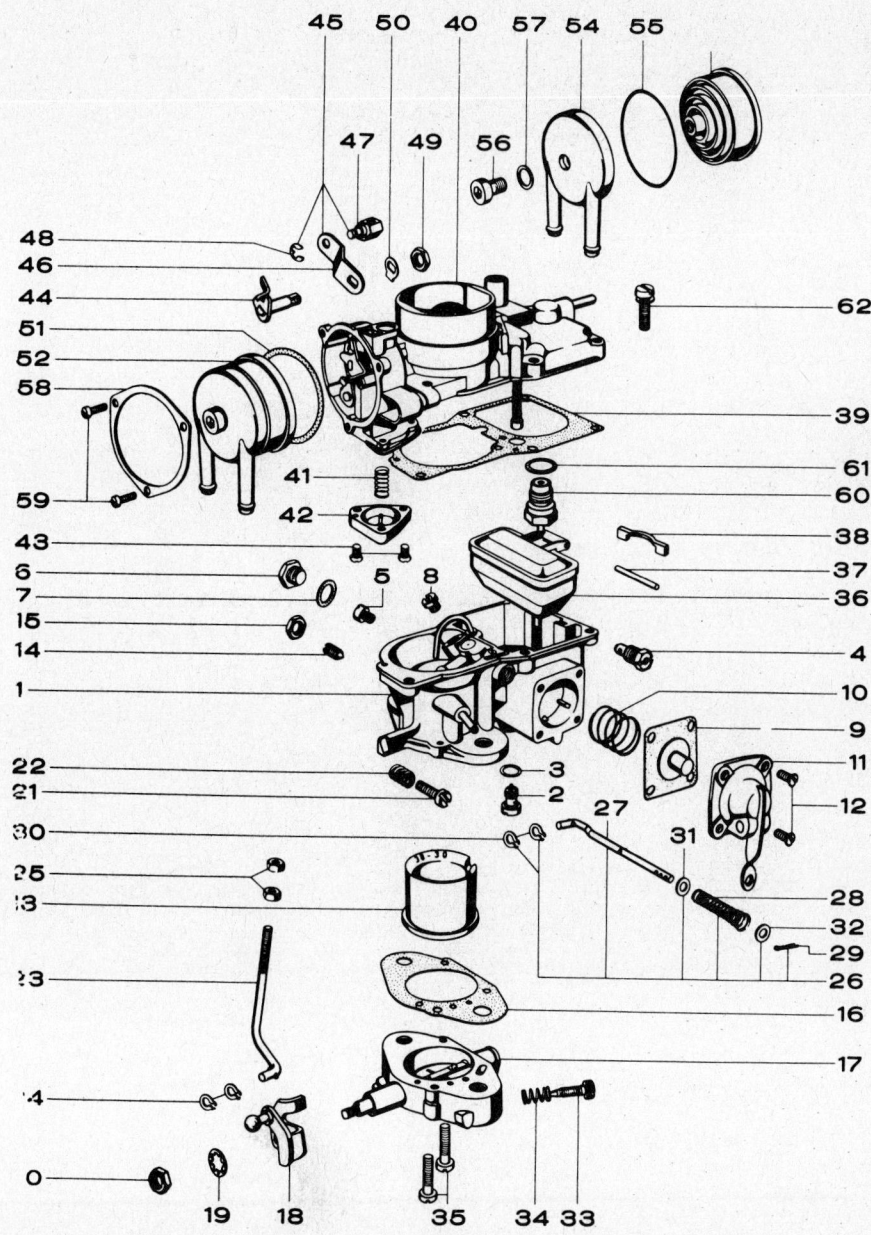

Components of Solex 40 PDSIT carburetor used on 2002, 2000, and 2000 CA models.

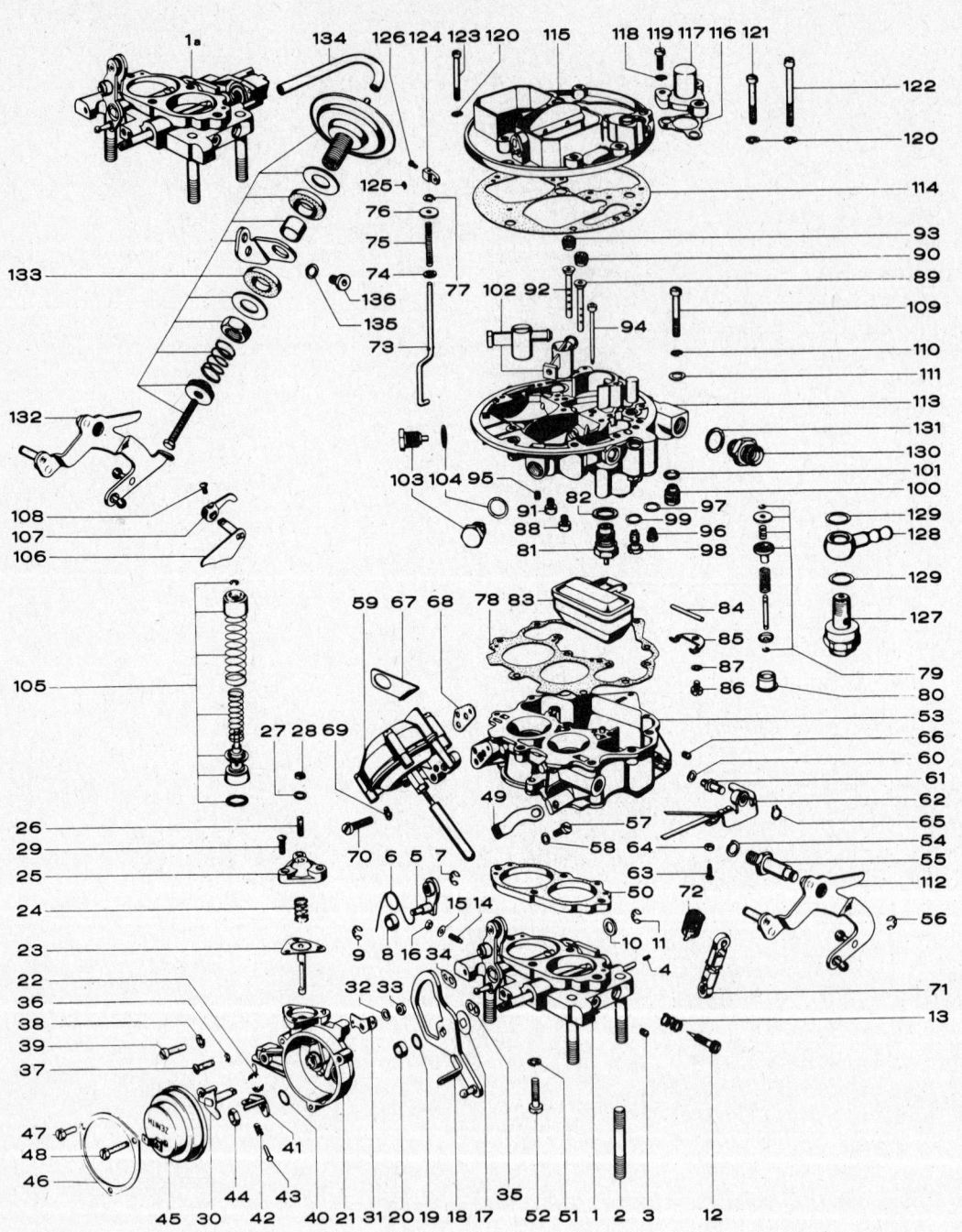

Components of typical Zenith 35/40 INAT downdraft carburetor, used in dual installations on 2500, 2800, 2800 CS.

Components of typical Zenith 35/40 INAT downdraft carburetor, used in dual installations on 2500, 2800, 2800 CS.

1, 1a Throttle valve	46 Stop ring	91 Main jet
2 Pin screw	47 Hex head nut	92 Mixture tube
3 Screw	48 Hex head nut	93 Air correction jet
4 Screw	49 Clamp	94 Idle jet
5 Joint lever	50 Isolation flange	95 Jet
6 Return spring	51 Spring washer	96 Pump suction valve
7 Safety washer	52 Screw	97 Seal ring
8 Roller	53 Float bowl	98 Pump pressure valve
9 Safety washer	54 Spring washer	99 Seal ring
10 Flat washer	55 Bearing bolt	100 Jet
11 Safety washer	56 Safety washer	101 Seal ring
12 Idle mixture screw	57 Cheesehead screw	102 Sprayer
13 Pressure spring	58 Spring washer	103 Pressure screw
14 Adjustment screw	59 Vacuum chamber	104 Seal ring
15 Spring washer	60 Lockwasher	105 Pump piston
16 Hex head nut	61 Bearing bolt	106 Pump lever
17 Flat washer	62 Operating lever	107 Inner pump lever
18 Throttle lever	63 Cheesehead screw	108 Countersunk screw
19 Safety washer	64 Hex head nut	109 Cheesehead screw
20 Spacer	65 Expansion ring	110 Lockwasher
21 Choke body	66 Threaded pin	111 Spring washer
22 Return spring	67 Cable holder	112 Complete operating lever
23 Diaphragm spring	68 Seal ring	113 Platin block
24 Pressure spring	69 Spring washer	114 Carburetor body gasket
25 Valve cover	70 Cheesehead screw	115 Carburetor top
26 Screw	71 Connecting rod	116 Seal ring
27 Seal ring	72 Return spring	117 Cover
28 Hex head nut	73 Connecting rod	118 Lockwasher
29 Countersunk screw	74 Flat washer	119 Cheesehead screw
30 Operating lever	75 Pressure spring	120 Lockwasher
31 Transfer lever	76 Washer	121 Cheesehead screw
32 Spring washer	77 Tension ring	122 Cheesehead screw
33 Hex head nut	78 Seal ring	123 Cheesehead screw
34 Gasket	79 Air valve	124 Joint piece
35 Gasket	80 Bushing	125 Safety washer
36 Star washer	81 Needle valve	126 Cheesehead screw
37 Countersunk screw	82 Seal ring	127 Fuel return valve
38 Spring washer	83 Float	128 Ring hose piece
39 Screw	84 Shaft	129 Seal ring
40 Safety washer	85 Bracket	130 Threaded fitting
41 Stop lever	86 Cheesehead screw	131 Seal ring
42 Pressure spring	87 Spring washer	132 Operating lever
43 Stop screw	88 Main jet	133 Vacuum regulator
44 Hex head nut	89 Mixture tube	134 Rubber hose
45 Choke cover	90 Air correction jet	135 Lockwasher
		136 Cheesehead screw

Components of Weber 45 DCOE 15/16 sidedraft carburetors, used in a dual installation on the 1800 TISA.

1 Jets inspection cover	28 Hexagonal nut	66 Pump plunger
2 Screw securing carburetor cover	29 Gasket for cap	67 Spring for idling adjustment screw
2A Securing screw for well-bottom cover	30 Cap for bottom of bowl	67A Throttle adjusting spring— DCOE 15
	31 Carburetor body	
	34 Lever fixing pin	
3 Gasket for jets inspection cover	35 Pump control lever	68 Idling adjustment screw
	36 Stud bolt	69 Throttle adjusting screw— DCOE 15
4 Normal washer	37 Stud bolt	
4A Normal washer	38 Ball bearing	70 Screw for progression holes inspection
5 Carburetor cover	39 Throttle securing screw	
6 Gasket for carburetor cover	40 Throttle valve	71 Gasket for pump jet
7 Emulsioning tube holder	41 Throttle spindle	72 Pump jet
8 Air corrector jet	42 Starter control securing screw	73 Seal
9 Idling jet-holder	43 Normal washer	74 Screw plug
10 Emulsioning tube	44 Cap securing screw	75 Intake and discharge valve
11 Idling jet	45 Cap for pump opening	76 Starter jet
12 Main jet	46 Gasket for cap	77 Float
13 Plate for carburetor bowl	47 Starter control, including:	78 Fulcrum pin
14 Choke	48 Starter control lever, complete with:	79 Ball for valve
15 Auxiliary venturi		80 Stuffing for ball
16 Dust cover	49 Starter lever	81 Retaining screw for stuffing ball
17 Spring	50 Nut for screw	
18 Spring retaining cover	51 Cable securing screw	82 Gasket for needle valve
19 Shim washer—DCOE 15	52 Lever securing nut	83 Needle valve
19A Shim washer—DCOE 16	53 Lever return spring	84 Gasket for union
20 Air intake horn	54 Sheath securing screw	85 Spherical union
21 Retaining plate	55 Cover for sheath support	86 Gasket for union
22 Auxiliary venturi fixing screw	56 Strainer	87 Screw plug for union
22A Choke fixing screw	57 Starter shaft	88 Strainer
23 Spring washer	58 Spring washer	89 Gasket for filter plug
23A Spring washer	59 Starter valve	90 Filter inspection plug
24 Carburetor anchoring nut	60 Spring for starter valve	91 Plug for protecting strainer
24A Nut for air intake	61 Spring retainer and guide	92 Throttle control lever— DCOE 15, including:
25 Stud bolt	62 Spring washer	
26 Throttle control lever— DCOE 16	63 Spring retaining plate	93 Spring
	64 Pump control rod	94 Throttle adjusting screw
27 Lockwasher	65 Spring for plunger	95 Spring
		96 Throttle control lever

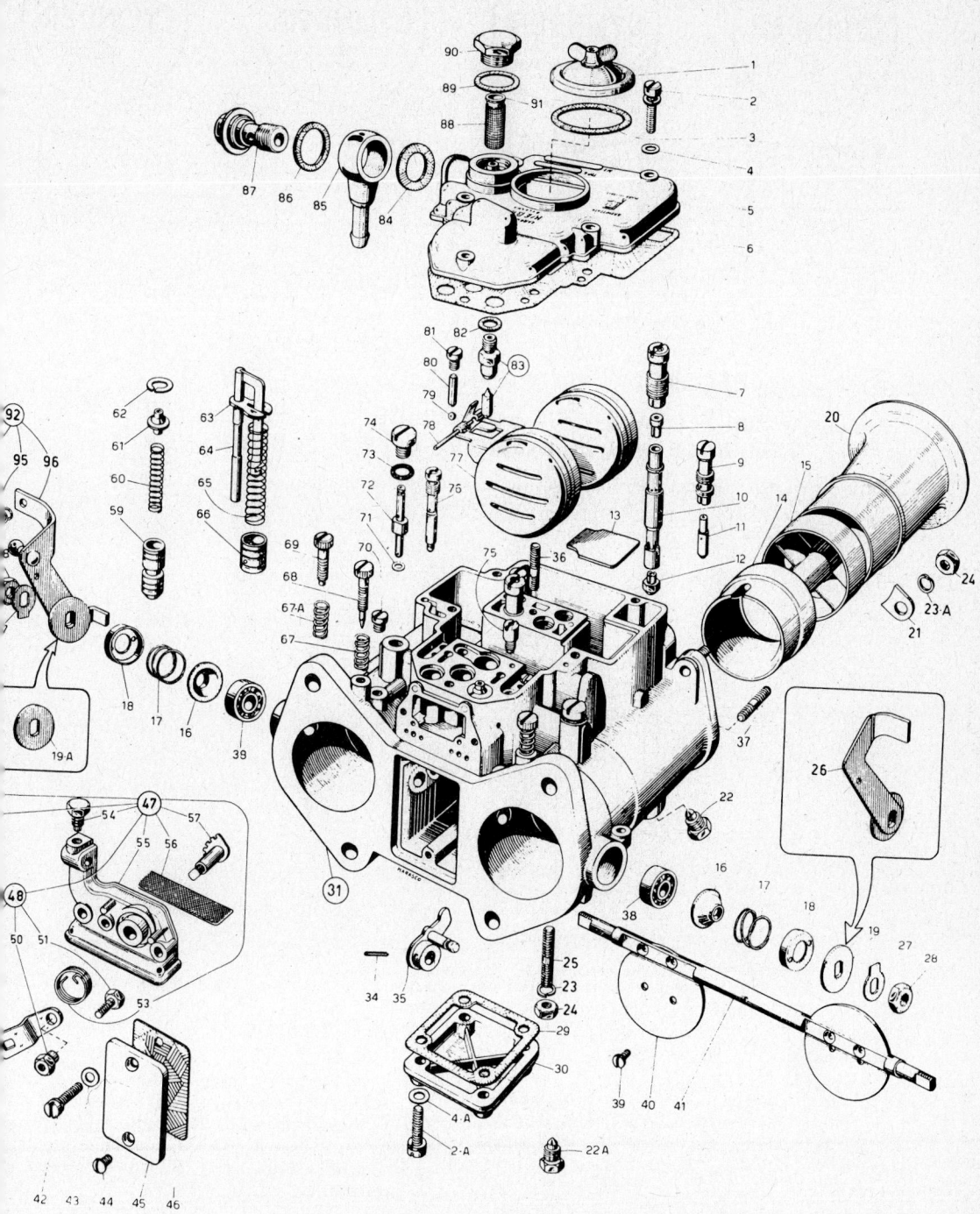

Components of Weber 45 DCOE 15/16 sidedraft carburetors, used in a dual installation on the 1800 TISA.

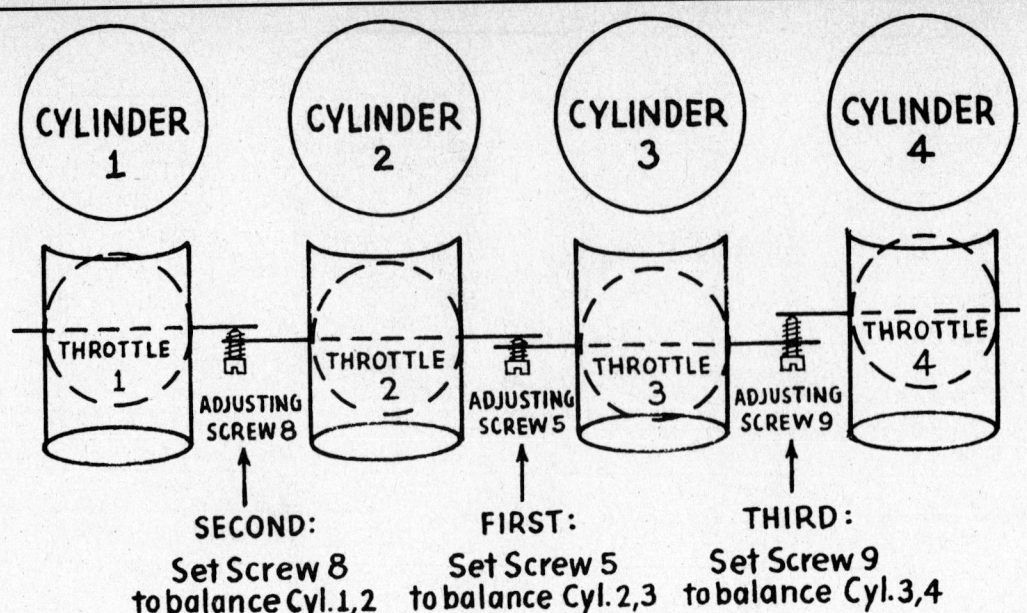

Throttle balancing sequence for dual twin-choke sidedraft carburetors — 1600 TI, 1800 TI, 2000 TI, 2000 CS.

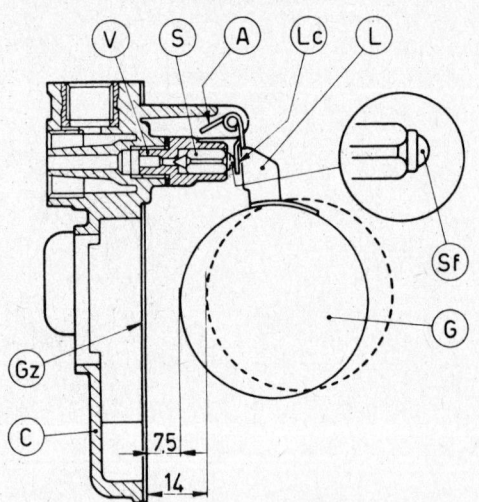

Procedure for adjusting float level on Weber 45 DCOE 15/16 carburetors: Make sure that the weight of the float (G) is correct (26 gr.), that float can pivot freely, and is not pitted.

Make sure that needle valve (V) is tightly screwed in its housing and that pin ball (Sf) of the damping device, incorporated in the needle (S), is not jammed.

Keep the carburetor cover (C) in vertical position as indicated, since the weight of the float (G) could lower the pin ball (Sf) fitted on the needle (S).

With carburetor cover (C) in vertical position and float clip (Lc) in light contact with the pin ball (Sf) of the needle (S), the distance of both half-floats (G) from upper surface of carburetor cover (C), without gasket, must measure 7.5 mm.

After the levelling has been done, check that the stroke of float (G) is 6.5 mm. If necessary adjust the position of the lug (A).

Should the float (G) not be correctly placed, bend the tabs (L) of the float, taking care that the tab (Lc) is perpendicular to the needle axis (S) and that it doesn't have any indentations on the contact surface which might affect the free movement of the needle itself.

Fit the carburetor cover making sure that the float can move without any hindrance or friction.

NOTE — The float level must be checked whenever it is necessary to replace float or needle valve; in the latter case it is advisable to replace the sealing gasket, making sure that the new needle valve is tightly screwed into its housing.

Exhaust System

The BMW exhaust system consists of the exhaust manifold, the exhaust twin-pipe, the exhaust pipe, the muffler, and the tailpipe. The muffler and tailpipe are a unit.

Removal and Installation

Detach the twinpipe from the exhaust manifold and the exhaust pipe. Remove the twinpipe support from the transmission bracket and remove the twinpipe.

NOTE: Support the exhaust pipe from the underpan with a hanger.

Separate the exhaust pipe from the muffler, remove the central support block and remove the exhaust pipe. Remove the tailpipe mount, support the muffler, and remove the muffler mounts. Remove the muffler and tailpipe assembly.

NOTE: To prevent noise, make sure that the exhaust system does not contact the underpan.

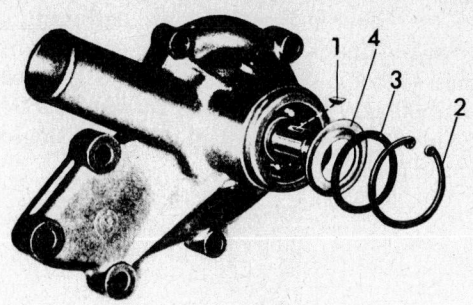

Water pump key (1), snap-ring (2), spacer (3), seal (4).

Use of sleeve (608) to press water pump shaft from impeller (F).

Cooling System

Radiator

REMOVAL AND INSTALLATION

Turn heater control to HOT and allow coolant to drain from radiator and engine block. Remove radiator hoses. Unscrew radiator bolts and lift out radiator. Install in reverse order.

Water Pump

WATER PUMP SERVICING

Remove air filter, radiator, and fan, and pull fan pulley from water pump shaft. Remove mounting screws and water pump. Disassemble by removing flange (on one type), snap-ring, spacer and seal. Remove key from shaft and press shaft with bearing off the impeller. Drive sealing ring (8) out of housing.

When water pump is reassembled, there should be a clearance (A) of .038-.047″ (.8-1.2 mm) between housing and impeller.

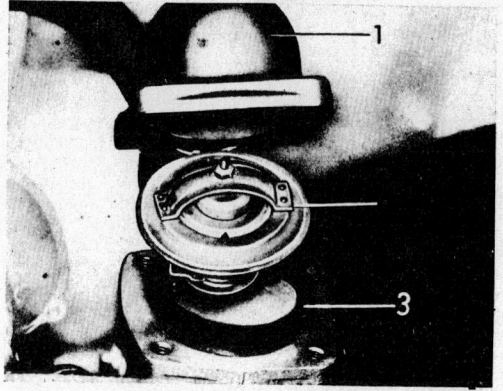

Thermostat components: housing (1), thermostat (2), gasket (3). Opening temperature: 163°-171°F or 181°F.

Engine

The BMW 1500, 1600, 1800 and 2000 Series all have four-cylinder, in-line water cooled engines, with BHP ranging from 90 for the 1500, to 135 for the 2000 TI and 2000 CS cars. The 2500, 2800 and 2800 CS models use two double-barrel Zenith carburetors and six-cylinder, in-line water cooled engines to boost this horsepower to 170 for the 2500 and to 192 for the 2800 and 2800 CS models. All power plants are single overhead camshaft types.

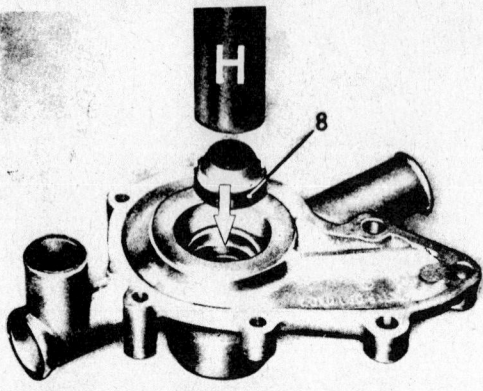

Use of sleeve (H) to drive sealing ring (8) into water pump housing.

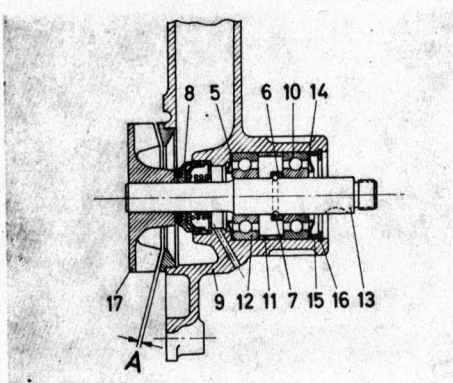

Water pump components: seal (5), lockrings (6, 7), seal ring (8), housing (9), ball bearing (10), spacer (11), ball bearing (12), shaft (13), seal ring (14), spacer (15), circlip (15, 16), impeller (17).
Dimension A = .038"-.047" (.8-1.2 mm).

Exhaust Emission Control

Fresh air flow is directed by a V-belt driven air pump to injector tubes located in each exhaust port immediately behind the exhaust valve. Since exhaust gases at this point are above ignition temperatures, mixture with an excess of oxygen is all that is required to start burning action. This oxidizes the noxious hydrocarbons and changes most of the carbon monoxide to harmless carbon dioxide.

Components of the emission control system such as the air pump, check valve, and gulp valve are maintenance-free. But the air pump V-belt tension should be $\frac{1}{8}$" to $\frac{3}{8}$" slack under thumb pressure and should be adjusted if required. Do not use a pry bar for adjustment. Tighten by hand to avoid pump housing distortion. Inspect hoses, bolts, and nuts of the system for tightness.

ADJUSTMENTS

It is important that all components be kept in precise adjustment for control of exhaust emissions. Properly adjusted dwell angle is essential to ignition timing. Ignition timing and carburetor adjustment procedures for exhaust emission controlled engines are different than for engines without emission control.

If the carburetor cannot be adjusted properly, or backfiring occurs when the throttle is closed, change control valve.

Air pump mounting bolts (1).

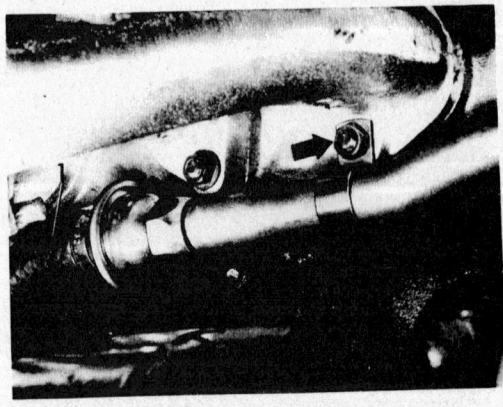

Exhaust gas system check valve hose (1) and pipe manifold clamp (arrow).

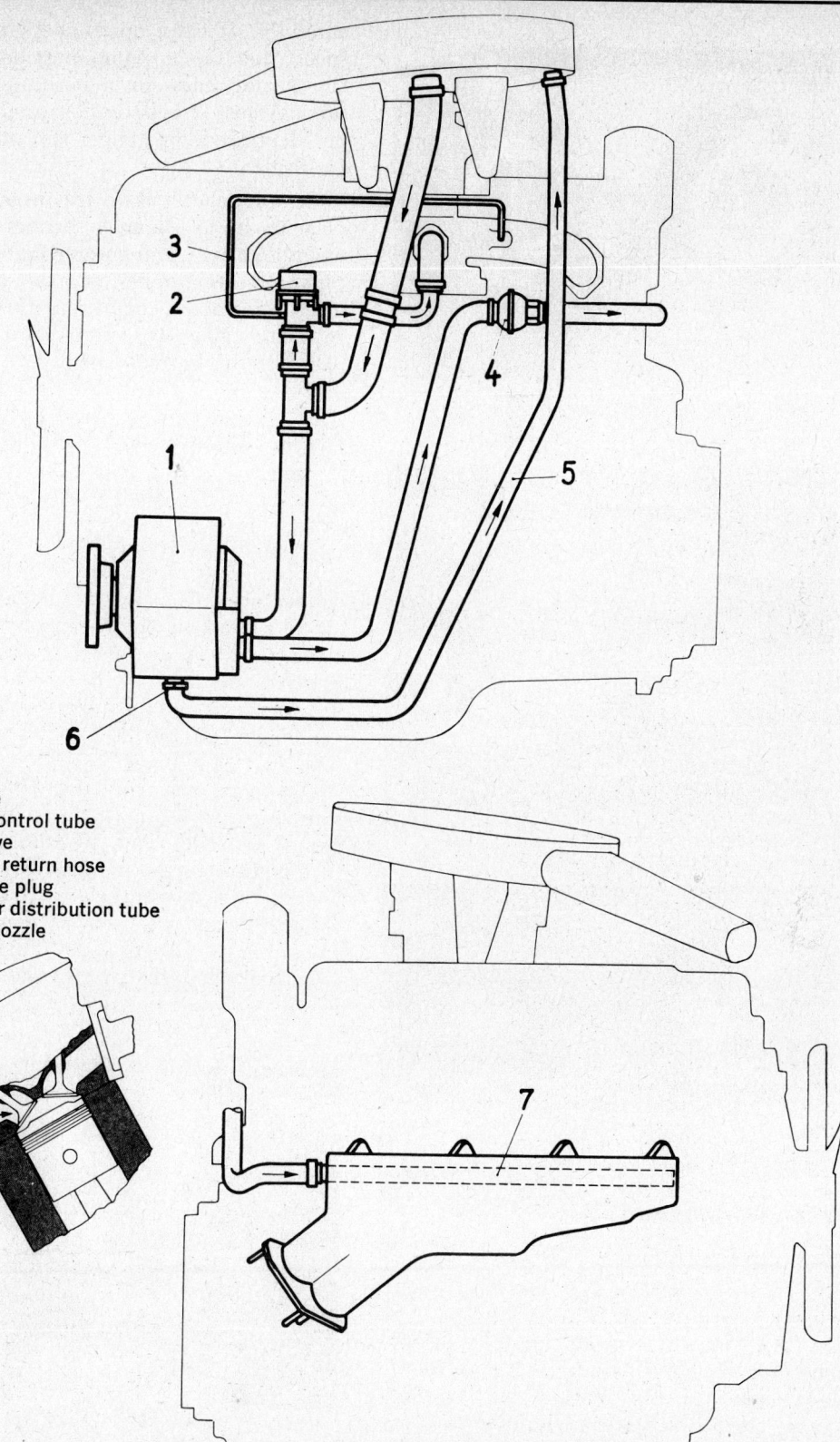

1 Air pump
2 Gulp valve
3 Vacuum control tube
4 Check valve
5 Excess air return hose
6 Relief valve plug
7 Air injector distribution tube
8 Injection nozzle

BMW 2002 emission control system.

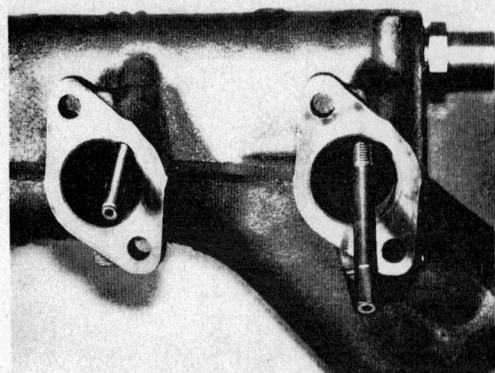

Injection pipes should extend .04" (1 mm) outside manifold flanges.

Pressure regulator unit.

Exhaust emission control system valve.

Check operation of air pump by disconnecting blow-off line, and while accelerating engine, pressing hand lightly on pressure release valve to determine if it is operating. Valve should open at 1700-2000 rpm. If it opens sooner, replace the pressure regulator. Remove regulator with two screwdrivers. Press in new regulator

carefully. If valve opens at higher engine speed, then the air pump must be changed. Check and renew pivot bushings if necessary. Adjust V-belt tension so that it can be depressed by finger pressure .2-.4" (5-10 mm).

Remove check valve for inspection and cleaning by loosening hose from air pump and hose clamp, and unscrewing valve from pipe. Injection pipes may be unscrewed after removing exhaust manifold. When replacing, allow injection pipes to extend .04" (1 mm) beyond flange.

Engine Removal and Installation

REMOVAL

Remove hood by removing hinge bolts after marking their position. Disconnect battery ground cable. Drain radiator and cylinder block by opening drain cocks. Remove radiator cap to speed up draining. Remove air filter with air intake tube, breather tube and air preheater tube.

Remove air preheating regulator (8) with air hose (9).

Disconnect radiator hoses from thermostat and water pump, then remove radiator mounting bolts and radiator. Unscrew temperature sensor (11) from housing (12) and release it from clamps. Disconnect throttle linkage (13), and vacuum line (14) from check valve (15). Pull fuel line (16) from fuel pump (P) and its clamp.

Air filter removal. Filter mounting screws (1, 2), air intake hose clamp (3), heater tube (4), air preheater tube (6).

Preheater regulator removal. Preheater regulator (8), clamp (7), air hose (9), summer-winter lever (10).

Temperature sensor (11), sensor housing (12), throttle linkage (13), vacuum line (14), check valve (15), fuel line (16), fuel pump (P).

Disconnect choke cable (17) from lever (18), and cable sleeve (19) from cable clamp (20) and pull out cable. There is no choke cable on automatic choke models.

Disconnect generator armature wire D+ black/red (22) field wire DF black (23) and brown ground wire (24). Pull plug connector (25) from solenoid switch (26), pull back rubber cover (27) and disconnect starter cable (28). On models with alternator, disconnect red cable at B+ terminal.

Disconnect heater hoses (29 and 30). Disconnect ground band from gearbox flange. Remove socket connection (31) from distributor, and pull connector (32) from oil pressure switch (34).

Disconnect high tension cable from ignition coil and remove distributor cap and rotor.

Remove gearshift lever (D) by first pulling up dust cover (A), rubber housing (B) and dust cover (C), then removing leaf spring and bolt (E) and bolt from shift head (F). On models with pivot ball on shift lever end, pull up rubber boot and packing to remove snap-ring and shift lever.

Jack car and place on stands. Disconnect exhaust pipe from manifold, and disconnect exhaust pipe support. Remove muffler mounting screws. Disconnect drive shaft at the gearbox, and tie up the driven shaft so that it does not fall out of gearbox. Disconnect the reverse light switch and speedometer cable from the gearbox housing.

Remove hydraulic line bracket from clutch housing but do not disconnect line from slave cylinder (40). Disconnect re-

turn spring from clutch arm. Pull back dust cover (38) and remove snap-ring (39) from slave cylinder. Pull slave cylinder forward and take out pushrod. On models with non-hydraulic clutch linkage, remove intermediate shaft.

Attach hoist to engine and take up slack. Remove the right and left hand engine mounting bolts. Support gearbox with a jack. Remove bolt from cap bearing (41) and bolts (42 and 43) from crossmember.

Slowly lower gearbox and lift out engine. Install engine in reverse sequence.

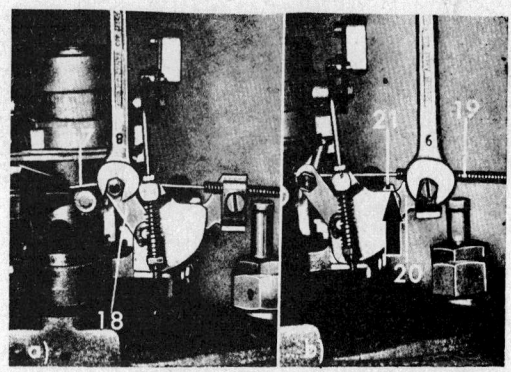

Bowden cable (17), choke lever (18), cable sleeve (19), cable clamp (20). At reassembly, lever (18) must butt against stop (21).

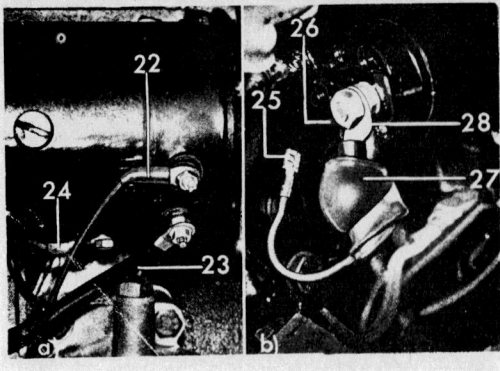

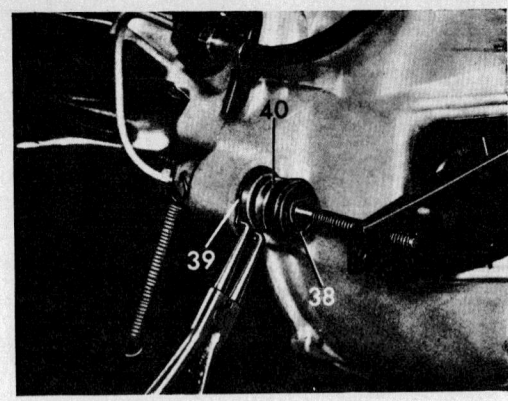

Armature D+, black/red (22), field DF, black (23), ground, brown (24), connector (25), solenoid switch (26), rubber cover (27), cable terminal (28).

Clutch slave cylinder (40), cylinder dust cover (38), and snap-ring (39).

Heater hoses (29, 30), connectors (31, 32), oil pressure switch (34).

Intermediate shaft removal for the 1600-2.

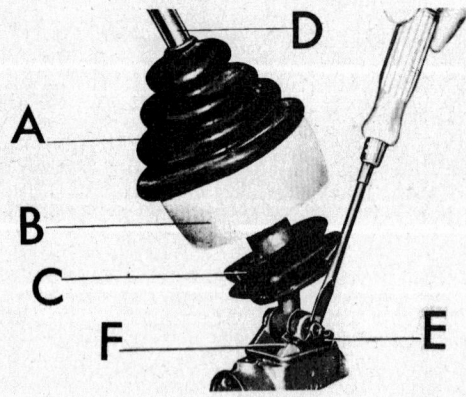

Gearshift lever assembly. Dust covers (A, C), rubber housing (B), lever (D), bolt and leaf spring (E), shift head (F). At reassembly, install bolt (E) in same position.

Cap bearing (41) and crossmember mounting bolts (42, 43).

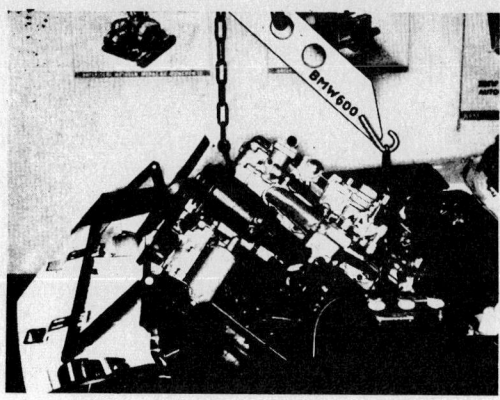
Engine removal and installation.

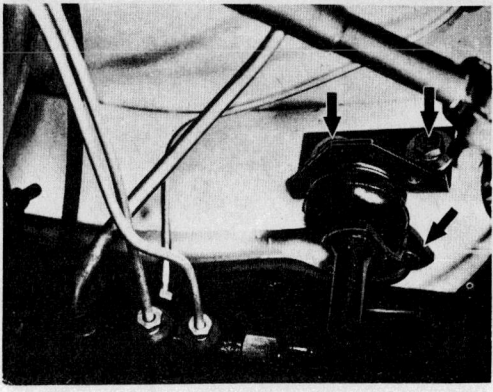
Installation of intermediate shaft.

Installation

When bolting engine of the 1600-2 in place, set right engine support stop as shown in illustration, so that A = .118" (3 mm).

Connect pullrod to intermediate shaft and align shaft bearing support at 90° to the engine before tightening mounting screws.

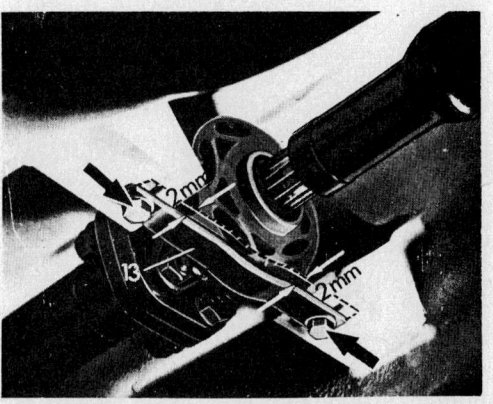
Pre-stress bearing .08" (2 mm) by means of bearing support (13).

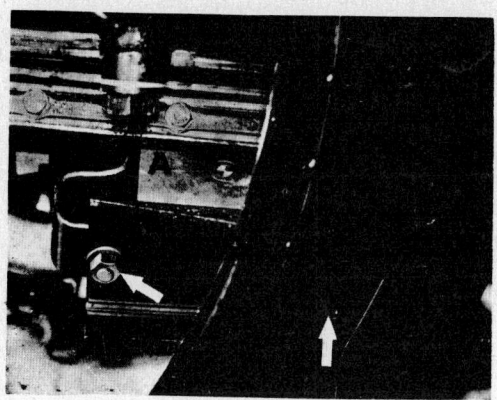
Adjustment of engine mounting stop.

Arrow shows recess in gear shift pin (14) which receives bolt (15).

Tighten drive shaft bolts to 21.8 ft. lbs. torque. Pre-stress center bearing .08" (2 mm).

Install gear shift pin (14) in lever with bolt (15) positioned in centering recess of pin.

Adjust clutch arm play to .1181-.1378" (3-3.5 mm).

When refilling radiator, set heater control lever to "HOT". Run engine until water temperature reaches 176°F. (thermostat opening temperature), turn radiator cap back one notch to release pressure, then check coolant level and retighten cap.

Adjust slave cylinder pushrod for .1181″-.1378″
(3-3.5 mm) correct withdrawal arm clearance.

Cylinder Head

CYLINDER HEAD REMOVAL

Disconnect the following items: radiator
hose from thermostat housing; vacuum hose
from check valve; fuel line from fuel pump;
temperature sensor from thermostat housing; throttle linkage from carburetor; choke
cable from lever and sleeve from clamp;
water hose from intake manifold and heater
hose from cylinder head; and oil dipstick
bracket.

Disconnect wire plug connections on distributor and on oil pressure switch, and
remove distributor cap. Disconnect spark
plug leads and cable from ignition coil.
Detach exhaust pipe from manifold.

Remove nuts and cylinder head cover
with its gasket. Note that when No. 1
cylinder is on TDC, the pointer will be opposite the 2nd notch in the drive pulley.

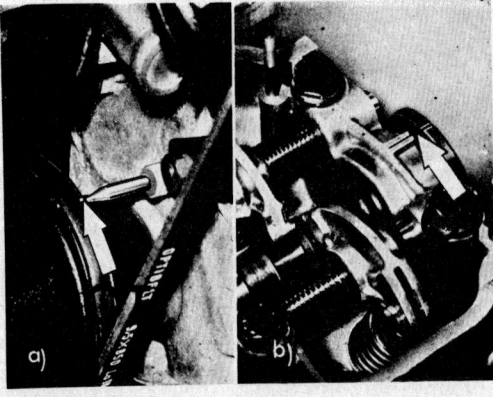

Pointer/drive pulley mark and camshaft/cylinder
head marks coincide at TDC of No. 1 cylinder.

The notch in the camshaft flange must coincide with the notch in the cylinder head.

Detach timing gear cover at top. Loosen
chain tensioner plug (1) and unscrew by
hand. WARNING: *spring is under heavy
pressure. Depress plug when loosening.*

Remove spring (2) and plunger (K).

Bend down lock plate tabs, remove bolts
and camshaft sprocket. Tie up chain with
wire to generator housing. Remove cylinder
head bolts, cylinder head and gasket.

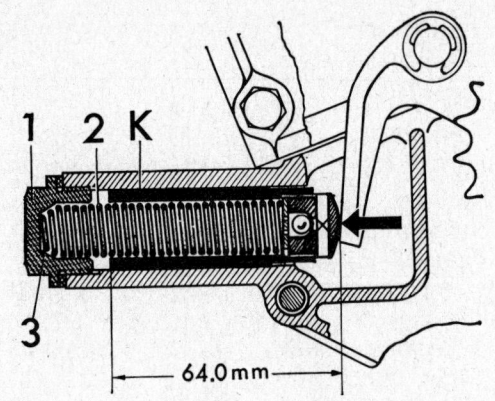

Chain tensioner consists of plug (1), spring (2),
and plunger (K). Spring contacts plug at (3).
Use only plungers of 2.519″ (64 mm) length, or
timing chain will slip.

CYLINDER HEAD INSTALLATION

Tighten cylinder head bolts in sequence
1-10. Tighten in three stages; 21.7 ft. lbs.,
50.5 ft. lbs., and 49.2-52.0 ft. lbs. After test-
running the engine and cooling to 95°F. or
less, give cylinder head bolts a final tightening to 49.2-52.0 ft. lbs. Then check and
adjust valve clearance. CAUTION: *be
sure the gasket water passage holes coincide exactly with those in the block and
the head. The TI cylinder head gasket can
be used on the 1800 cc engine. But under
no circumstances should the cylinder head
gasket of an 1800 cc engine be used on the
TI engine.*

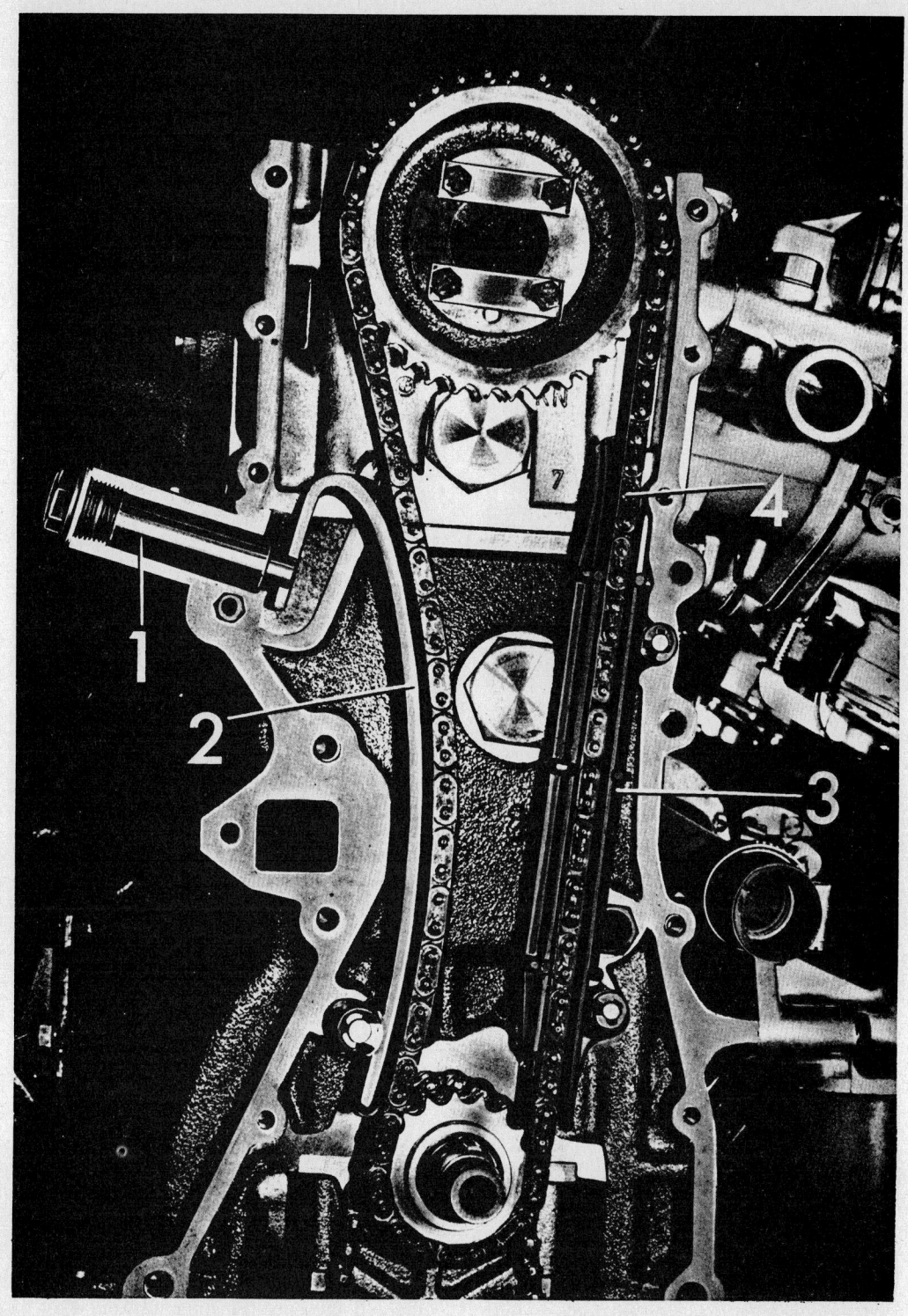

Timing chain tensioning. Plunger of spring tensioner (1), tensioning rail (2), sliding rail (3), chain (4).

Valve Train

CHECKING AND ADJUSTING VALVE CLEARANCE

Check valve clearance with engine cold, pistons on top dead center and in firing order sequence, that is, 1-3-4-2. Proper cold engine clearance for both intake and exhaust valves is:

$$.0059 — .0078'' (.15 — .20 \text{ mm})$$

Two bolts hold guide plate (F) and rocker shafts (K).

ring (2) should cover circlip (4). Notch in camshaft flange should be opposite notch in cylinder head. Guide plate should be thoroughly de-burred, and after assembly, camshaft should revolve easily.

Valve adjustment.

To adjust clearance, loosen locknut and turn eccentric adjuster. Measure clearance with feeler gauge. Hold eccentric in proper position and gently tighten locknut. Recheck clearance.

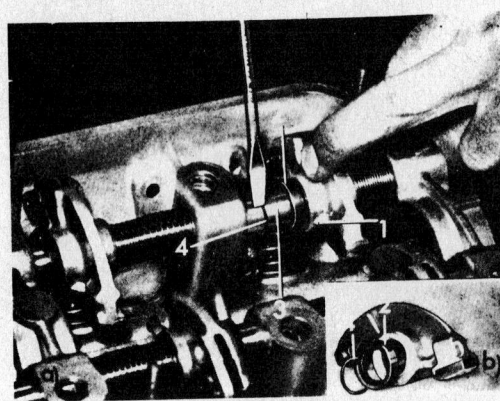

Rocker arms (1), thrust rings (2), rocker shaft (3), circlips (4).

ROCKER ARM REMOVAL AND REPLACEMENT

Remove guide plate bolts and attach rocker arm holder BMW 601 or equivalent device, tightening nuts down evenly. Take out camshaft and guide plate. Remove rocker arm holder.

Push rocker arms (1) and thrust rings (2) far enough to one side on rocker shaft (3) to permit removal of circlips (4). Then drive rocker shafts out the front.

When re-installing, align rocker shafts immediately so that cylinder head bolts can be fitted into their proper recesses. Thrust

VALVE, VALVE GUIDE REMOVAL AND REPLACEMENT

Remove valves with suitable spring compressor. Check spring length. Always replace oil seal rings. A damaged oil seal ring will increase oil consumption. Lay oil seal ring in spring washer. Valve guides can be reamed. To renew valve guides, heat cylinder head to about 356°F. and press guides out into combustion chamber. Press new guides in from rocker shaft side.

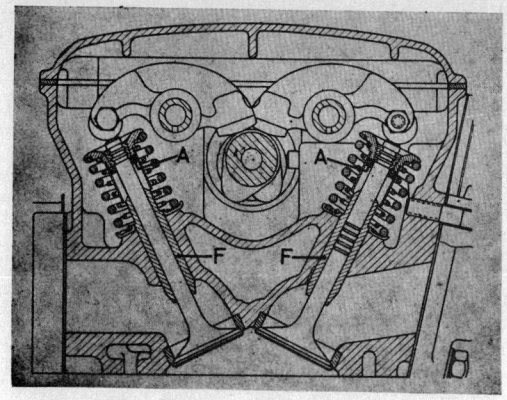

Oil seal rings (A), valve guides (F).

Camshaft and Timing Chain

CAMSHAFT REMOVAL

Rocker Clamp BMW 6025 or an equivalent device facilitates camshaft removal. However, before the clamp frame is fitted into position on BMW 2000 engines, the intake and exhaust valves of No. 2 cylinder

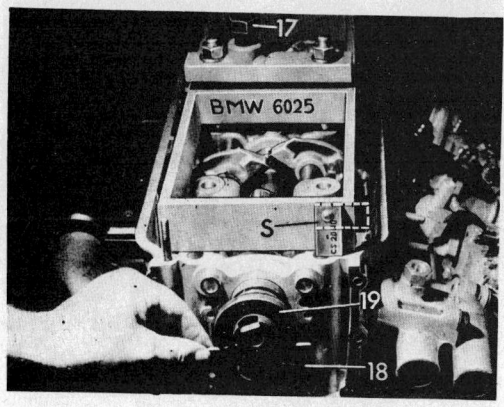

Rocker clamp BMW 6025. Supports (S), tension bolt (17), guide plate (18), camshaft (19).

must be adjusted to maximum valve operating clearance.

Place compression frame in position, lock it and swing down the two supports (S). NOTE: *swing the supports (S) out to side on BMW 1500, 1600, 1800 and 1800 TI engines*. Tighten bolt (17) until camshaft (19) can be withdrawn after removal of guide plate (18).

Installation of new camshaft follows reverse sequence of removal. Before placing cylinder head in position, bring No. 1 cylinder to TDC. The notch on the camshaft flange must be aligned with the mark on the housing. Reset valve operating clearances and ignition timing.

CAMSHAFT INSTALLATION

Install camshaft with notch on flange aligned with mark on housing and with No. 1 cylinder in TDC position. Mount the sprocket with chain fitted onto the camshaft flange. To relieve tension, insert a screwdriver between the tension arm and the timing case cover. Bleed tensioner by filling oil space, pumping piston until oil comes out at plug, then tightening plug. Reset valve clearances and ignition timing.

Cylinder head gaskets.

Insert screwdriver (at arrow) to relieve tension when installing sprocket and chain.

Install cylinder head and timing case covers. Hand tighten bolts (1 and 2). Then tighten bolts 3-8, and finally bolts 1 and 2, to specified torque.

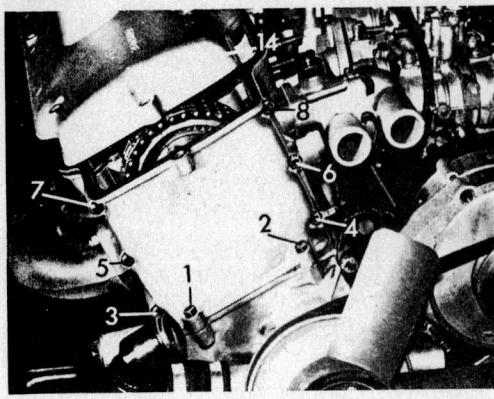

Installing cylinder head and timing case covers. Hand-tighten bolts 1 and 2. Then tighten bolts 3-8, finally bolts 1 and 2.

TIMING CHAIN REMOVAL AND REPLACEMENT

Remove engine, drain oil, remove oil pan and cylinder head cover. Turn crankshaft pulley to set notch opposite pointer, and set notch in camshaft opposite notch in cylinder head. Remove timing gear cover at top. Loosen chain tensioner and remove plunger. WARNING: *tensioner is under heavy spring pressure. Depress plug while removing.*

Remove fan from pulley. WARNING: *do not hold fan blades for leverage; increase fan belt tension by hand and hold onto water pump.* Loosen alternator and remove fan belt. Remove fan pulley with a puller.

Remove alternator and water pump. Remove camshaft sprocket and chain. Lock crankshaft and remove crankshaft pulley nut. Pull off crankshaft pulley. Remove lower timing gear cover and remove chain.

Remove lockring (S) and slide off tensioning wheel (R). Remove sprocket (three bolts) from oil pump housing, and remove housing by pressing gently downward out of the centering sleeves.

With a screwdriver, remove sliding rails

(arrow). Remove key (F) and O-ring (R) from crankshaft.

When reassembling, heat sprocket to temperature of 356-392°F. Note correct position for oil hole (B) under oil pump

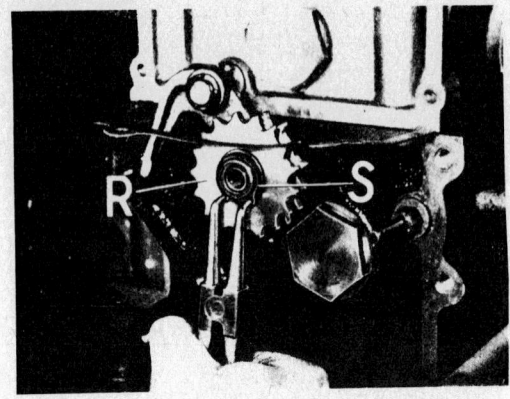

Lockring (S) and timing chain tensioning wheel (R).

Sprocket wheels can be pulled after removing sliding rail (at "a"), key (F) and O-ring (R) at "b."

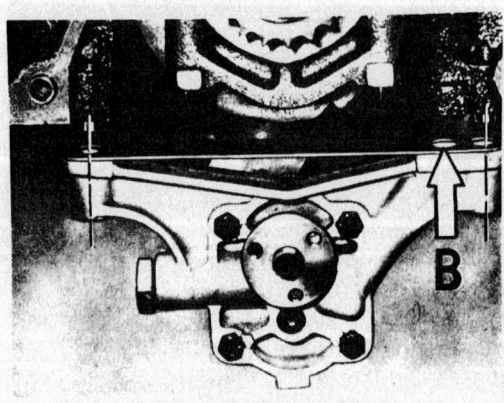

Note position of oil hole (B) in shim.

housing. Install machined faces of sliding rail to face forward toward retainer. Renew O-ring (R).

Chain tension must be set to permit slight depression of the chain (K) with light thumb pressure. Tighten crankshaft pulley to 101.3 ft. lbs. Align notch in camshaft flange with notch in cylinder head. Align pointer with notch in crankshaft pulley. Bend over all lock plates. Renew all copper gaskets and head gasket. Check fan belt for correct tension.

from crankcase and supporting plate. When re-installing pump, adjust chain tension with shims until chain can be just depressed with light finger pressure. Be sure to install shims with oil hole in correct position.

Checking tooth backlash of gear type oil pump.

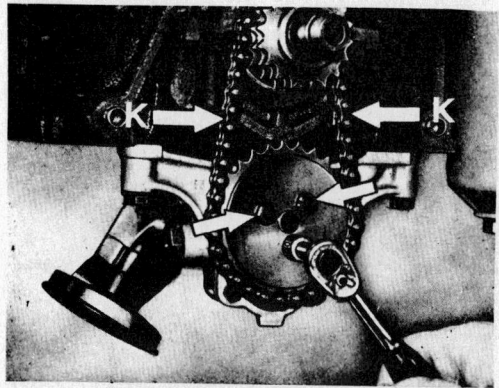

Chain tension should permit slight depression (K) with light finger pressure. Tension is adjusted by shim under oil pump.

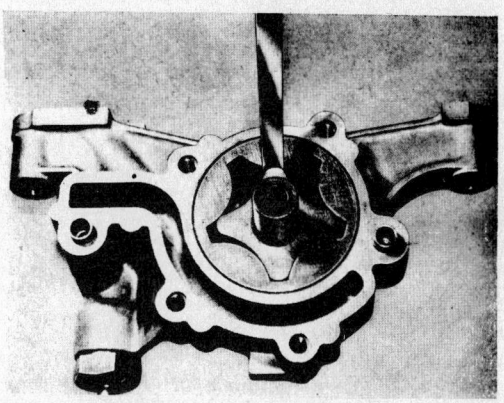

Checking clearance between inner and outer rotors of oil pump.

Engine Lubrication

OIL PUMP SERVICING

Remove oil pan by removing bolts and pulling forward and turning to the left (facing oil pan). Remove drive chain and sprocket. Remove oil pump mounting bolts

Correct position for shim and oil hole (arrow).

Checking play between pump housing and rotor sealing face.

Gear as well as rotor type oil pumps are used on BMW cars. In servicing either, unscrew plug to remove spring and plunger. Spring free length is 2.68″ (68 mm) and should not be changed. Check tooth backlash on the gear type. This should be .001-.002″ (.03-.05 mm) and should not exceed .003″ (.07 mm).

For the rotor type, check clearance between outer rotor and housing. This should be .0020-.0079″ (.05-.20 mm). Clearance between inner and outer rotors should be in the range of .0023-.0118″ (.06-.30 mm). Check play between pump housing and rotor sealing face with a straightedge and feeler gauges. Play should be .0013-.0033″ (.034-.084 mm). If components are not within these specifications they should be replaced.

Measure piston diameter at a point .433″ (11 mm) front skirt edge to find piston clearance.

Piston and Connecting Rods

Servicing Piston and Rod Assemblies

Install rings with "top" marking up as follows: 1. Rectangular ring 2. stepped ring 3. equal chamfer scraper ring. Set ring gaps 180° apart.

Pistons and rods can be serviced without removing engine from car. To remove pistons, remove cylinder head and oil pan, position piston to BDC, remove bearing cap and push piston and connecting rod upward.

Wrist pins can be replaced cold. They are color coded: W on piston crown — wrist pin marked white; S on piston crown — wrist pin marked black. Oil holes in the

connecting rod for wrist pin lubrication should face forward in direction of travel.

Connecting rod bolts are expansion bolts and must be discarded after removal. Do not reuse bolts that have been in service. Rods and bearing caps are marked in pairs for each cylinder and should not be interchanged. Number 4 is at the flywheel end.

Check ring clearance in piston groove and ring end gap with ring inserted in cylinder bore and compare with specifications. Piston clearance in cylinder should be no more than .0016″ (.040 mm) as measured .433″ (11 mm) down from edge of piston skirt. For the 1500 engine, piston clearance should not exceed .00256″ (.065 mm).

Each ring is marked for top and bottom. Install in following grooves in piston:

(top) Rectangular ring
(middle) Stepped ring
(bottom) Equal chamfer scraper ring

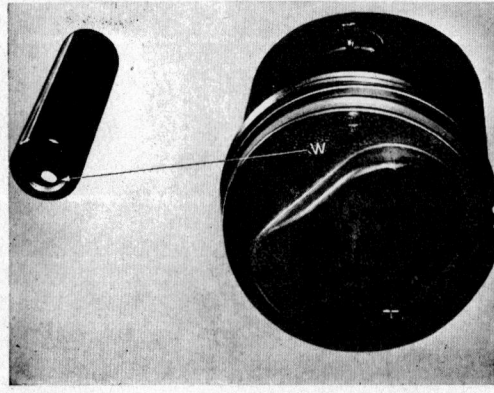

Wrist pins and pistons are color coded. W on piston for white marked wrist pin; S on piston for black marked wrist pin.

Only pistons and rods of the same weight classifications should be used. Weight class of piston is stamped on crown with a + or −. Arrow stamped on the crown points forward in direction of travel. Rod class is coded by means of colors.

Flywheel

FLYWHEEL REMOVAL AND REPLACEMENT

Remove gearbox and clutch assemblies. Maximum permissible out of true at diameter of 7.874″ (200 mm) is .0003″ (.10 mm). Lock flywheel in position. Pry off lock plate and discard plate. Remove bolts and flywheel. At reassembly, use new lock plate and torque bolts to specifications.

CRANKSHAFT REMOVAL AND REPLACEMENT

Remove bottom section of timing cover, drive chain and oil pump. Check crankshaft end play which should not exceed .0024-.0064″ (.06-.18 mm). Remove flywheel. Remove connecting rod and main bearing caps, noting markings. Lift out crankshaft.

Main bearing number 3, the thrust bearing, determines the end play of the crankshaft. Color coding indicates main bearing diameter. The standard diameter crankshaft has a single red or blue dot on the counterweight. Reground crankshafts carry one color stripe (at B) to indicate the 1st undersize main bearing journal, and two

Checking crankshaft end play with a micrometer.

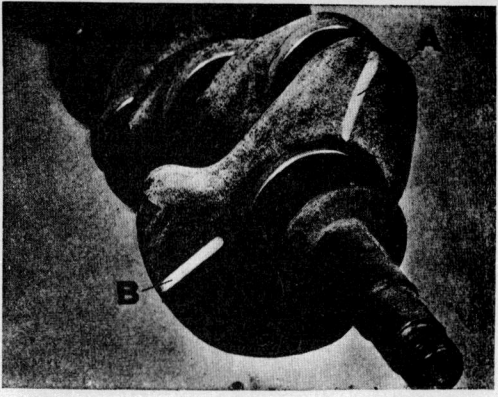

Rod bearing journal diameter marker (A) and main bearing journal diameter marker (B) for reground crankshaft. Single stripe indicates 1st undersize and two stripes indicate 2nd undersize.

stripes to indicate the 2nd undersize. One color stripe (at A) indicates the 1st undersize rod journal, and two stripes, the 2nd undersize. See Crankshaft, Camshaft, and Connecting Rod Specifications chart for sizes.

Check bearing clearance with Plastigage, type PG1. For undersize crankshafts, use corresponding oversize bearing shells. Measure each bearing separately with crankshaft motionless and at TDC. Tighten bearing caps to recommended torque.

Clutch and Transmission

The BMW drive train consists of the gearbox, clutch, drive shaft, differential, and rear axles.

Clutch

A single plate, dry clutch employing conventional coil springs is used on all models. It is hydraulically actuated by a slave cylinder attached to the housing and interconnected by a pushrod to the clutch throwout lever. The hydraulic clutch circuit is entirely independent of the brake circuit. A few models use a mechanically actuated clutch.

CLUTCH ADJUSTMENT

When fully depressed, the clutch pedal should contact the stop. Clearance between pedal plate and hornring must then be 5.7-5.9" (145-150 mm). If clearance is less than 5.3" (135 mm) a piston rod (1) of 4.37" (111 mm) should be used. If clearance is 5.3-5.5" (135-140 mm) a piston rod of 4.29" (109 mm) is used. NOTE: *the maximum clearance of 5.9" (150 mm) should not be exceeded or expansion orifice (3) may damage piston diaphragm (2).*

CLUTCH REMOVAL

To service the clutch it is necessary to remove the transmission. Loosen clutch screws alternately, first on one side then the other. Take off clutch and driven plate. Note that the side of the driven plate with the protruding spring ends and hub faces the gearbox. The clutch plate should be replaced when thickness is .315" (8 mm). When reassembling, center the driven plate and clutch with a suitable shaft, and tighten screws evenly and alternately. Adjust play on throwout lever to figure given in Clutch Specifications Chart.

Centering clutch disc.

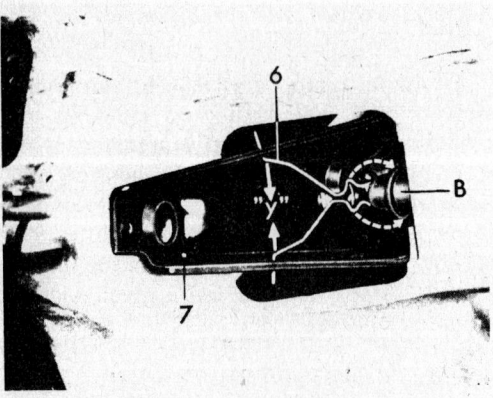

Clutch throwout lever (7), spring (6), collar (B).

Gearbox

BMW's are equipped with two different manual gearboxes beside the automatic type ZF3HP-12 B. The manual types all have 4 forward speeds with Porsche synchronizers. Gear ratios differ slightly.

GEARBOX DISASSEMBLY AND ASSEMBLY—LONG NECK UNIT

Remove engine from its mounting and move far enough forward to allow gearbox to be dropped down at rear. Disconnect and lower steering control lever. Drain gearbox. Partially withdraw shift mechanism from housing after removing lockpin and screwing out the plug, lock bolt and spring. By rotating the mechanism counterclockwise, turn the shift finger until it is clear of the driver. Be careful not to damage seal. NOTE: *the shift mechanism cannot be pulled out completely.* Remove the throwout lever hairpin spring and remove lever.

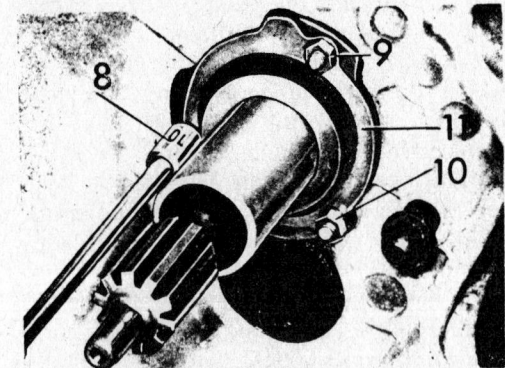

Clutch shaft drive flange (11), nuts (8, 9, 10).

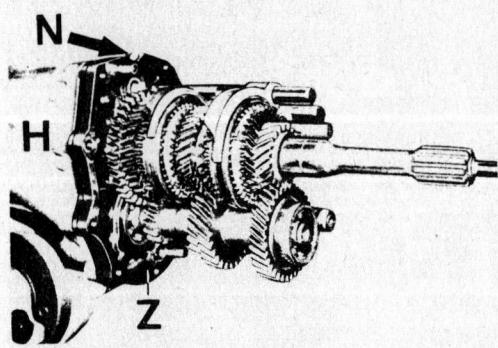

Gearbox disassembly. Housing extension (H), stud (N), spacer (Z).

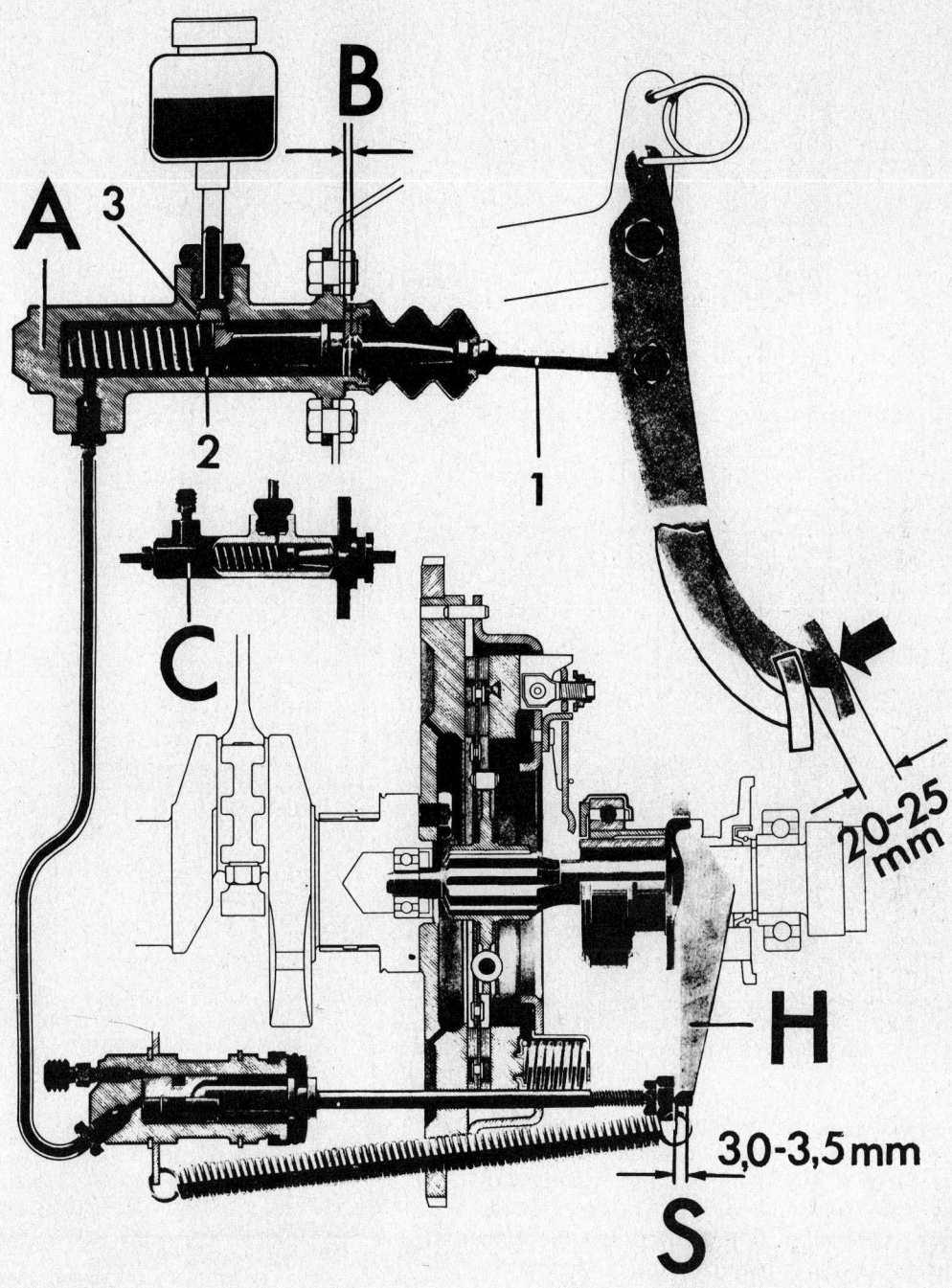

Required pedal free travel and clutch lever clearance (S) for BMW Series 1500, 1600 and 1800. See Clutch Specifications Chart for other models. Piston rod clearance (B) should be .04″ (1 mm). Early master cylinders (C) have a bleed valve. Later types (A) are bled from the slave cylinder.

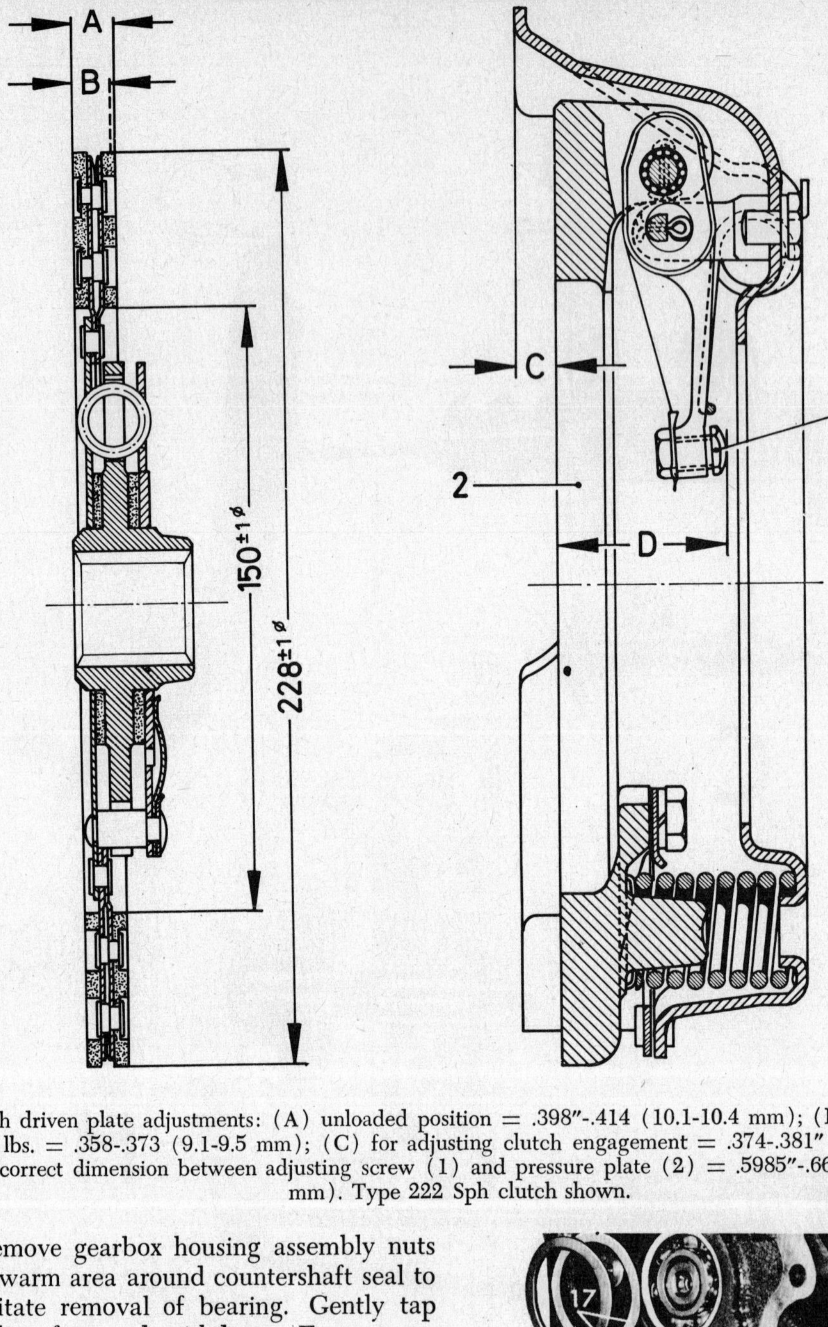

Clutch driven plate adjustments: (A) unloaded position = .398″-.414 (10.1-10.4 mm); (B) loaded with 1058 lbs. = .358-.373 (9.1-9.5 mm); (C) for adjusting clutch engagement = .374-.381″ (9.5-9.7 mm); (D) correct dimension between adjusting screw (1) and pressure plate (2) = .5985″-.6615″ (40.6-42.2 mm). Type 222 Sph clutch shown.

Remove gearbox housing assembly nuts and warm area around countershaft seal to facilitate removal of bearing. Gently tap gearbox free and withdraw. Free spacer (Z) with complete gear train from housing extension by tapping at stud (N) and remove.

Mount gear train together with spacer in a soft jawed vise, remove the countershaft shims (17) and pull bearing. WARNING: *be careful that the countershaft gear does not press the synchronizer out of position.*

Remove clutch shaft (19) and bearing (20) from mainshaft (21).

Removing shims (17) and pulling bearing from countershaft (18).

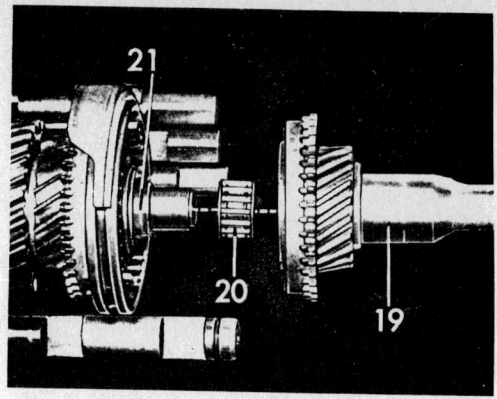

Removing clutch shaft (19) and bearing (20) from mainshaft (21).

Remove shift forks after removing lockpins, then drive shift shafts from spacer.

Mark associated parts to ensure correct reassembly. Recover balls that are released.

Bend down tabs of lockplates and remove screws from mainshaft bearing retainer. *Note position of the special lockplate for correct reassembly. This serves also as a lubricator for the odometer drive.* Drive mainshaft out of spacer.

Clamp mainshaft (36), and remove snapring, thrust washer and guide flange for 3rd and 4th gears. Remove 3rd gear (a) with synchronizer assembly. Remove spacer (b) and bearing (c). Push off spacer ring (d) and thrust washer (e). Lift off 2nd gear (f) with synchronizer assembly, bearing (g), bushing (h) and spacer (i).

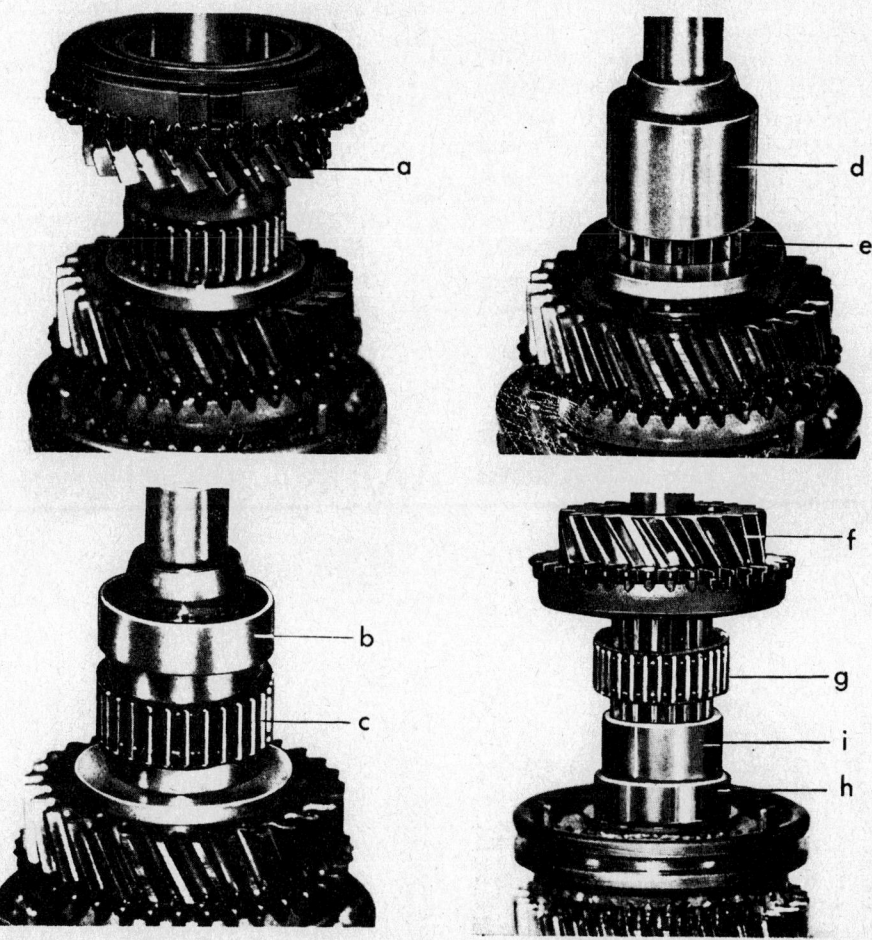

Second and third gear removed. Third gear (a), spacer (b), bearing (c), spacer (d), thrust washer (e), 2nd gear (f), bearing (g), spacer (h), spacer (i).

Spacer (Z) with mainshaft bearing retainer removed. Drive out mainshaft (36) in direction of arrow.

Remove shift sleeve (40), guide flange (41) and 1st gear with synchronizer assembly (42). Take off spacers (43, 44), bearing (45) and reverse gear (46). Remove coupling flange (47) and mark the side (F) facing the reverse gear for correct reassembly. Remove snap-ring (48) and washer (49). Press odometer drive gear

(50) and bearing (51) off mainshaft (52).

Reassemble gearbox in reverse order from above. Assemble mainshaft so that overall dimension measured from hub of reverse gear (60) to smooth surface of guide flange (61) is:

$$5.0394'' \begin{array}{c} +.04'' \\ \text{or} \\ -.08'' \end{array} (128 \begin{array}{c} +.1 \\ \\ -.2 \end{array} \text{mm})$$

Compensate with shims in front of reverse gear.

When assembling shift shafts, and shift forks insert lockpins with their slits facing in the direction of travel of the shafts.

In adjusting gear mesh of mainshaft and countershaft, use shims (91) to adjust play between ball bearing and end seal in intermediate plate to specifications. Install gear train assembly in gearbox housing only in neutral position. Adjust mainshaft end play to specifications by installing a suitable shim on the input end of the mainshaft. Size of shim may be calculated by method shown for Universal 232 gearbox.

Correct length of mainshaft assembly as measured from guide flange (61) to reverse gear (60).

Use of shims (62) in front of reverse gear (60) to obtain correct length of mainshaft assembly.

Adjusting gear mesh: Countershaft (89), bearing (90), shims to take up play (91).

First gear, reverse gear and odometer drive removal. Shift sleeve (40), guide flange (41), 1st gear with synchronizer (42), spacers (43, 44), bearing (45), reverse gear (46), coupling flange (47), position mark (F), snap-ring (48), spring washer (49), odometer drive wheel (50), bearing (51), mainshaft (52).

GEAR BOX DISASSEMBLY— UNIVERSAL 232

Remove engine from its mounting and move far enough forward to allow gearbox to be lowered out of car toward rear. It will be necessary to disconnect and lower parts of the steering linkage also.

Drive out pin and remove shift selector shaft and joint. Mount gearbox on jig, if available and drain oil. Pull bearing from clutch shaft and save shims. Remove gearbox housing cover and warm area around countershaft end-seal to facilitate removal of shaft bearing. Lightly tap to loosen

housing, pull off and remove seal. Remove shift shaft (14) by sliding forward after removing lockpin from side of housing, cutting safety wire and loosening bolt from shift bar.

Place shift shaft (15) in 4th gear position. Remove lockpin (16) and pull shift shaft (15) forward until shift fork (17) can be removed. Catch loose ball bearings. Place shift fork (19) in neutral, push shift shaft (18) to 2nd gear position and drive lockpin out from shift fork (20). Pull shift shaft (18) forward until shift fork (20) can be withdrawn. Catch loose ball bearings. Set shift fork (21) to neutral. Drive

Mainshaft and countershaft assemblies: safety wire (11), lockscrew (12), shift forks (13, 17, 20, 23), shift shafts (14, 15, 18, 24), lockpins (16, 22), shift sleeves (19, 21).

Countershaft bearing retainer (25), ball bearing (26), shift assembly (27), countershaft (28), idler gear (29).

out lockpin (22) from shift fork (23) and pull shift shaft (24) forward until shift fork can be pulled from the reverse gear. Catch loose ball bearings.

Remove bearing retainer (25) and pull bearing (26). Lift out complete shift mechanism (27).

Warm gearbox cover gently, then pull countershaft (28) and idler gear (29) from gearbox housing cover.

Pull clutch shaft (30), shift sleeve (31) and bearing (32). Remove snap-ring (33) and disc. (34). Pull off guide sleeve (35) and 3rd gear (36) with its synchronizer. Pull roller bearing (37). Press mainshaft (38) from speedometer drive gear (39), reverse gear (40), 1st gear (41) with synchronizer, shift sleeve (42), and 2nd gear pinion with synchronizer (43).

GEARBOX ASSEMBLY—UNIVERSAL 232

Inspect synchronizers before reassembly. Front edges of shift sleeve and synchronizer ring must be flush, and shift sleeve teeth should be perfectly sharp. If wear of synchronizer is predominately toward ends of synchronizer ring, ring should be replaced. Wear should be distributed over at least 50% of the periphery. After assembly, it should be easy to turn the synchronizer ring by hand.

The overall dimension of the assembled mainshaft, measured from the ground face of the guide sleeve (35) to the front face of the reverse gear (13) must be 5.429-5.437″ (137.9-138.1 mm). Shims of the proper thickness (Y) to obtain this dimen-

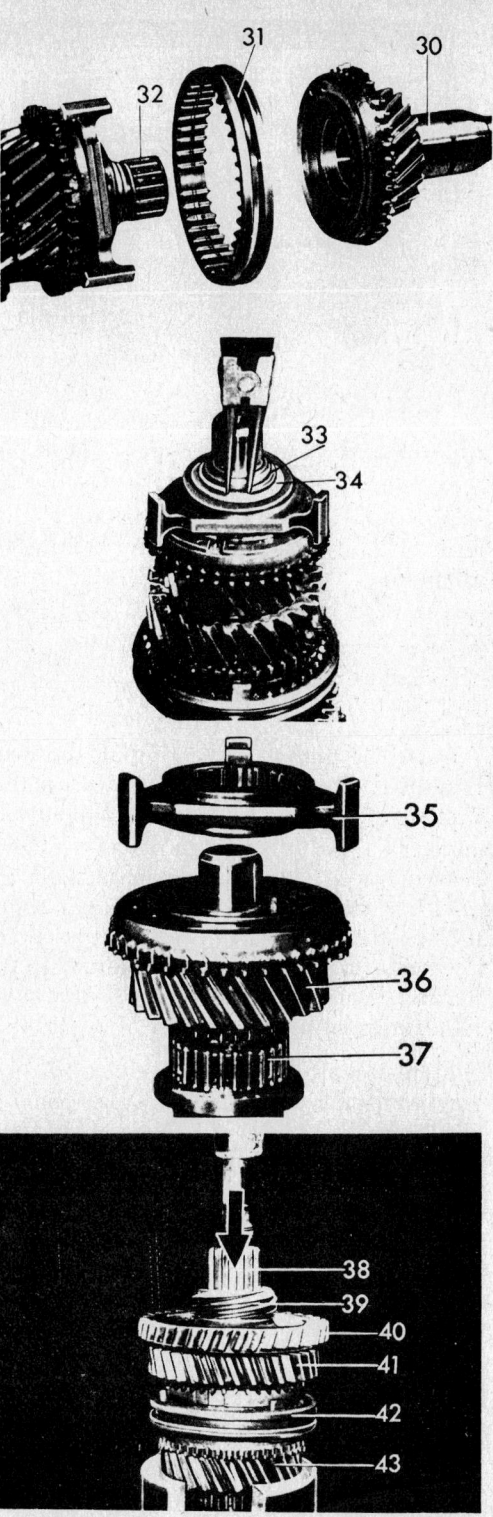

Thickness of shim (X) on mainshaft is determined as described in text.

Clutch shaft disassembly. Clutch shaft (30), shift sleeve (31), bearing (32), disc and snap-ring (34, 33), guide sleeve (35), 3rd gear pinion (36), bearing cage (37), mainshaft (38), speedometer drive (39), reverse gear (40), 1st gear (41), shift sleeve (42), 2nd gear and synchronizer (43).

Mainshaft assembly dimension A. Reverse gear
pinion (13), guide sleeve (35), shim (Y).

sion, if necessary, should be placed at the front of the reverse gear pinion (13). For example:

$$\text{"A" ideal} = 5.433'' \ (138 \text{ mm})$$
$$\text{"A" actual} = 5.394'' \ (137 \text{ mm})$$

"Y" (shim thickness) $= .039''$ (1 mm)

Drive the mainshaft bearing all the way into the gearbox housing. Then measure the distance (C) between the edge of the housing surface (with gasket in place) and the bearing race. This dimension is used to calculate the correct thickness for a shim (X) on the mainshaft. Measure and note thickness (B) of speedometer drive gear. Remove bearing and calculate thickness of (X), for example:

A (mainshaft length) ideal	$= 5.433''$ (138 mm)
add B (thickness of speedo gear):	$.583''$ (14.8 mm)
	$= 6.016''$ (152.8 mm)
subtract C	$1.457''$ (37.0 mm)
D actual (shift sleeve)	$= 4.559''$ (115.8 mm)
D ideal	$= 4.567''$ (116.0 mm)
X (shim thickness)	$= .008''$ (.2 mm)

In fitting the countershaft, the correct thickness for shim (G) is found by first measuring the depth (F) of the housing from its edge to the snap-ring. Then install countershaft into housing cover and measure the height (E) of the shaft with the gasket in position. Find thickness of shim (G) as follows:

	$F =$	$6.496''$ (165.0 mm)
minus	$E:$	$6.480''$ (164.6 mm)
	$=$	$.016''$ (.4 mm)
minus:		$.008''$ (.2 mm) end play
then	$G =$	$.008''$ (.2 mm) (shim thickness)

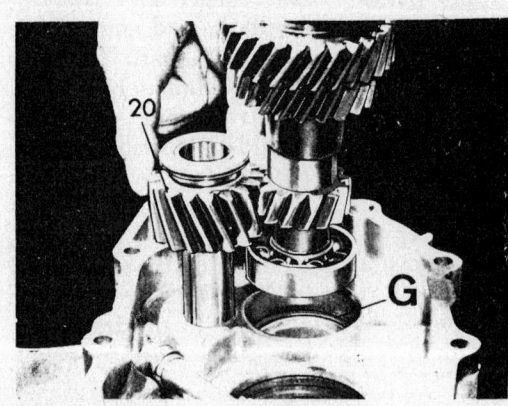

Position of shim (G) in housing cover.

Automatic Transmission

Disassembly and repair of the ZF automatic transmission requires specialized tools and techniques. It is not recommended that this work be attempted by other than an authorized service facility. Only external adjustments are covered in this book.

Throttle Linkage Adjustment

Remove kickdown stop from beneath throttle pedal (10) and adjust to basic

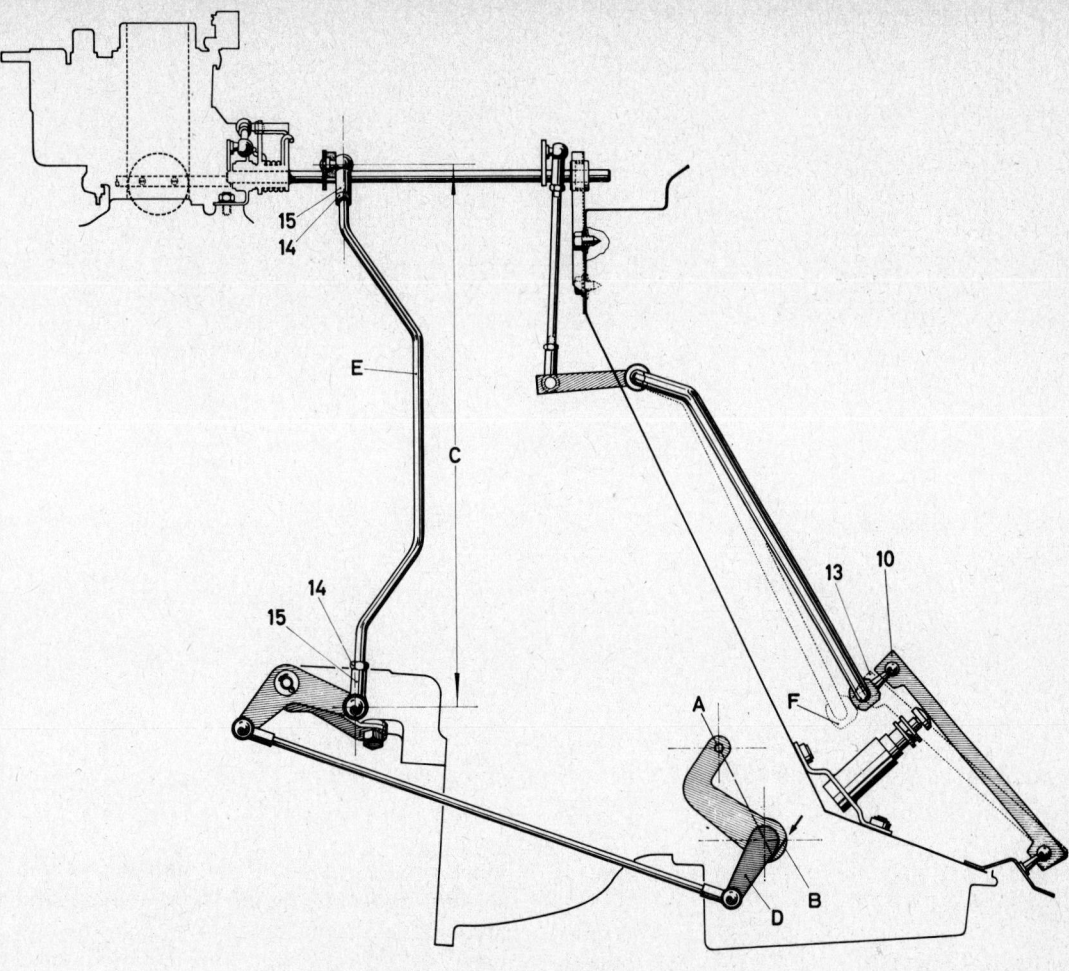

Diagram of throttle linkage and transmission linkage for ZF automatic transmission.

length of 2.618″ (66.5 mm). Replace kickdown stop. When pedal (10) is fully depressed, joint (F) should not be stopped by carpet. If joint (F) hits carpet, readjust kickdown stop to suit. Unhook spring clip and ball swivel at upper end of throttle linkage turnbuckle. Open throttle butterfly fully. If butterfly goes beyond vertical position, bend stop to correct. Press throttle pedal (10) to kickdown contact position and hold throttle butterfly fully open. Adjust turnbuckle to correct length and reinstall ball swivel end and spring clip. Check adjustment by depressing throttle pedal (10) to kickdown position (13). Throttle butterfly should be fully open. If this is not the case, readjust turnbuckle.

TRANSMISSION LINKAGE ADJUSTMENT

Move gear selector lever to position O. Depress throttle pedal (10) to kickdown position (13). Unhook spring clip and ball swivel (15) at top end of turnbuckle (E). NOTE: *any attempt to drive vehicle with transmission linkage disconnected will result in severe damage.* Adjust length (C) of turnbuckle (E) until edge of lever (D) is aligned with index mark (B). Reinstall ball swivel end (15) and spring clip.

Adjust idling speed to approximately 800 rpm. Test drive vehicle, noting speeds at which shifts occur with throttle pedal fully depressed, but not in kickdown position. Any known speedometer error must be

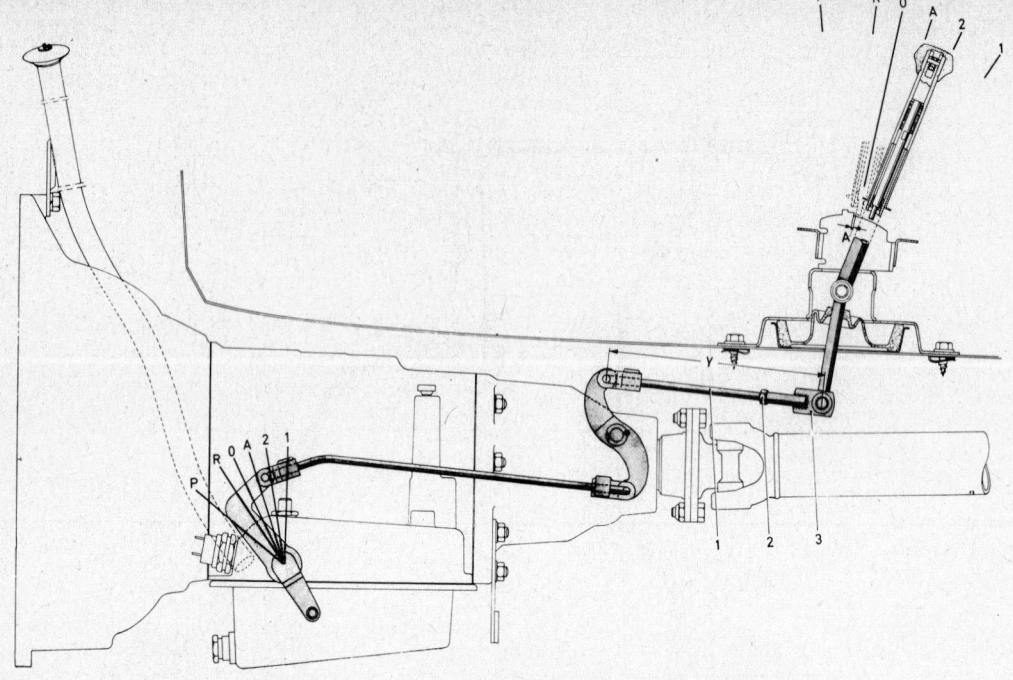

ZF automatic transmission shift linkage, late models.

taken into account. Shift points should be as follows:

	1800 A	2000 A
1st-2nd gear shift	27-31 mph	27-34 mph
2nd-3rd gear shift	53-56 mph	53-59 mph

If shift occurs too early, lengthen turnbuckle (E); if it occurs too late, shorten turnbuckle (E). With throttle pedal in kickdown position (13), the vehicle may be accelerated in each gear up to the maximum permitted engine rpm.

TRANSMISSION SHIFT LINKAGE ADJUSTMENT

There are two types of shift linkage used with the ZF automatic transmission. The first has the shift pattern P-O-A-2-1-R, and a single selector rod. The later unit has the pattern P-R-O-A-2-1 and two selector rods connected by a bellcrank mounted to the transmission extension housing. On the later model, adjustment is made at the rear selector rod.

When adjusting shift linkage, vehicle must not be raised off its wheels. Detach selector rod from hand lever; move hand lever to position O. Move transmission lever to position O, second notch from bottom on early model; third notch from bottom on late model. There should be a clearance (A) of approximately .0394″ (1 mm) between the lever pin and the stop in position O. Adjust length (Y) of selector rod (1) at shackle (3) to obtain this clearance. Reinstall selector rod to hand lever; check for proper shifting into all positions.

Drive Axle, Suspension, and Steering

Final Drive Systems

BMW final drive assemblies differ with the various models. Dimensions of the one and two-piece drive shafts used with the standard long neck, universal, and automatic transmissions and long and short neck final drive units for each of the BMW models are given in the specifications.

REAR AXLE REMOVAL

Push back rubber dust cover from handbrake lever and disconnect handbrake cable. Jack up rear of car, place on stands and remove wheels. Detach muffler and rear part of exhaust system at flange and at its center. Support only one trailing suspension arm with a jack. WARNING: *the shock absorber functions as a restrainer, and should not be removed unless the trailing arm is supported. If the upper shock mount is to be disconnected before jacking the car, the half shaft must be disconnected from the half axle at the same time to prevent damage to the universal joint.*

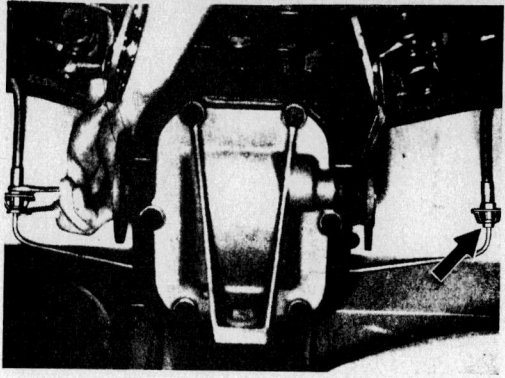

Disconnecting brake lines.

Disconnect half shafts from the differential and loosely wire half shafts to differential. Remove shock absorber from its upper mounting. Lower trailing arm by lowering jack. Remove the coil spring with upper plate and damper rings.

Detach rubber coupling from differential but not from drive shaft.

Disconnect flexible brake line sections from rigid feed lines and plug ends.

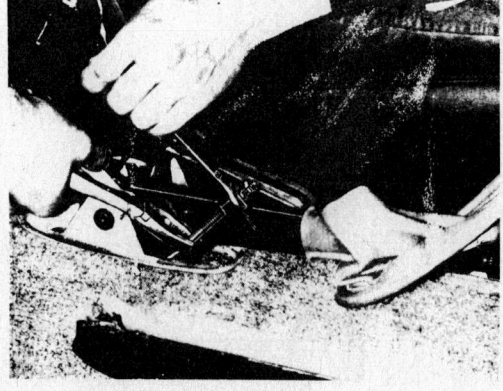

Disconnecting handbrake cable.

Removing rear axle assembly.

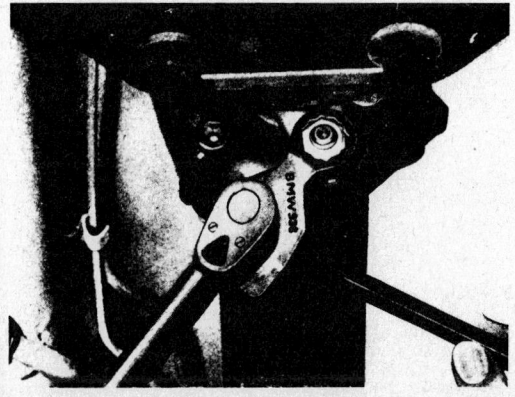

Disconnecting rubber coupling from differential.

Place a jack under differential and detach the rear axle support member from the frame. Remove rear mounting bolt of differential. Lower jack and pull rear axle assembly from under car.

Install rear axle assembly in reverse order from above, tightening bolts to the proper torque specifications. Install coil spring with smooth end up. Bleed brake system.

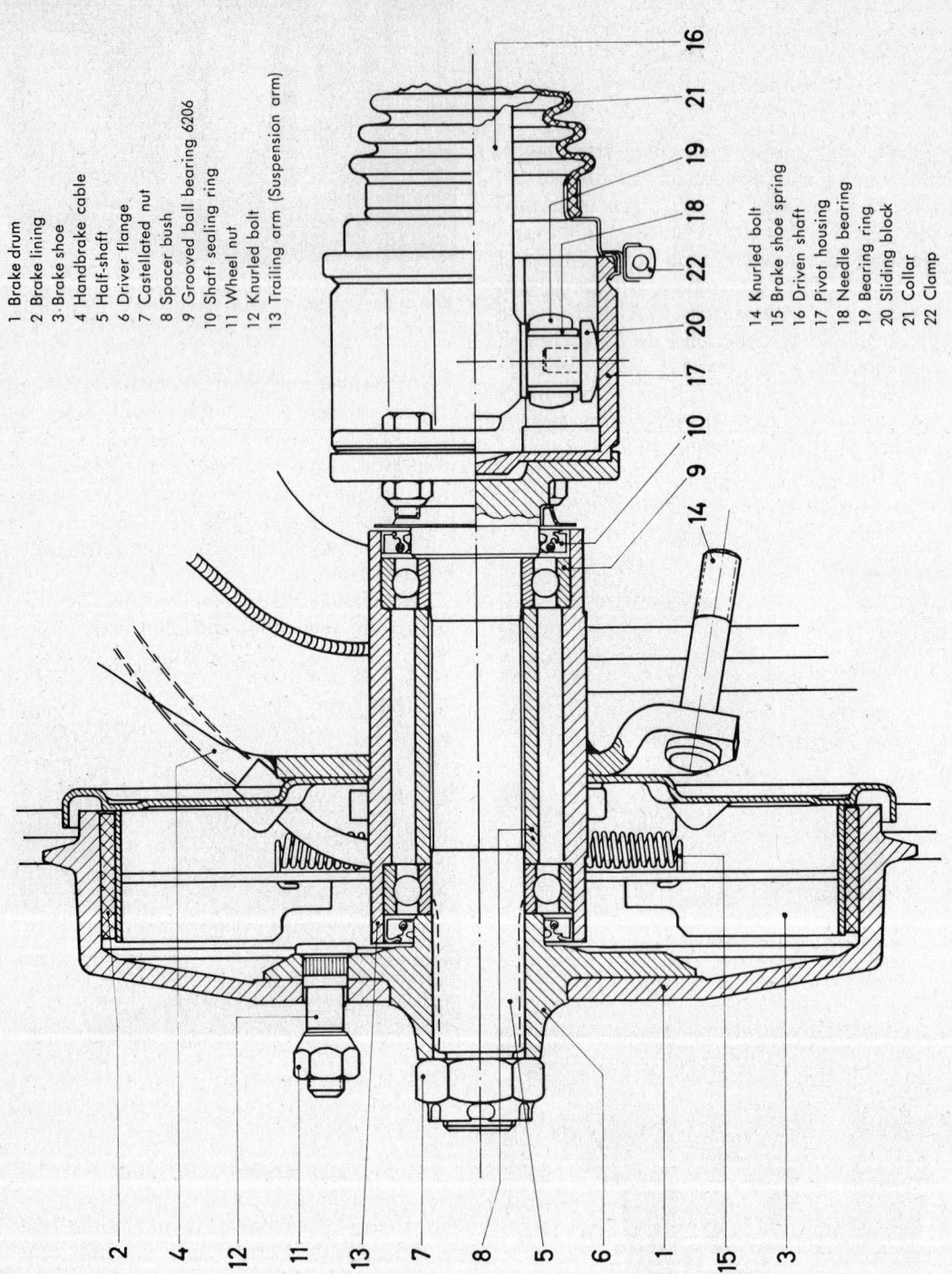

1 Brake drum
2 Brake lining
3 Brake shoe
4 Handbrake cable
5 Half-shaft
6 Driver flange
7 Castellated nut
8 Spacer bush
9 Grooved ball bearing 6206
10 Shaft sealing ring
11 Wheel nut
12 Knurled bolt
13 Trailing arm (Suspension arm)
14 Knurled bolt
15 Brake shoe spring
16 Driven shaft
17 Pivot housing
18 Needle bearing
19 Bearing ring
20 Sliding block
21 Collar
22 Clamp

Rear wheel and axle components.

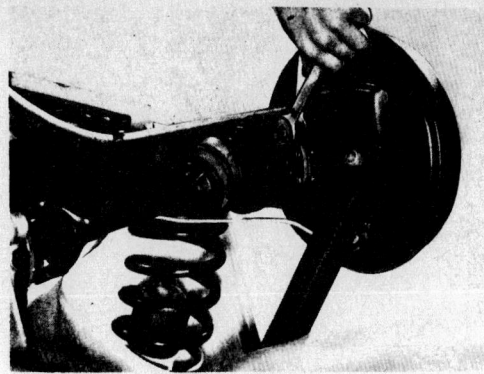

Disconnecting half-shaft from half axle.

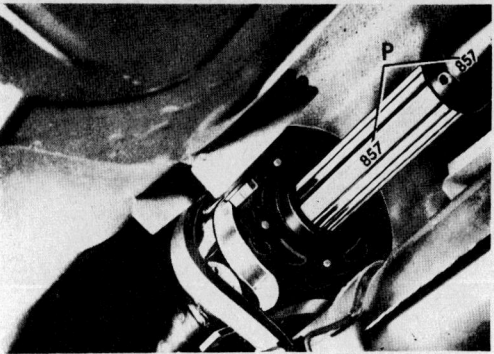

Balanced drive shaft and spline joint pairs are identified by numbers.

TRAILING ARM REMOVAL

To remove trailing suspension arm, disconnect handbrake, support vehicle and remove wheels. Support trailing arm with a jack, remove shock absorber, and disconnect half shaft from half axle. Lower trailing arm with jack, remove coil spring, disconnect brake line and remove trailing arm mounting bolts from frame. Re-install coil spring with smooth end up. Bleed brake system.

DRIVE SHAFT SERVICING

The drive shaft is removed by disconnecting it at both ends after disconnecting and lowering a section of the exhaust system. When installing those with a center bearing, move the bearing forward by about .08" (2 mm). Drive shafts and splined joints are balanced pairs and must not be intermixed.

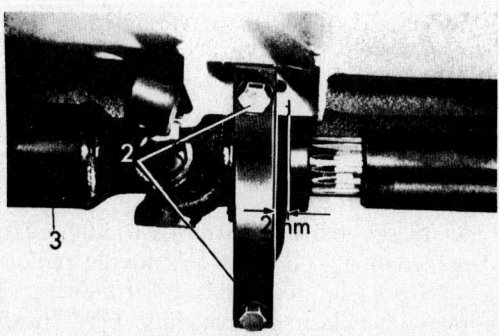

Install center bearing of drive shaft (3), .08" (2 mm) forward, and tighten bolts (2).

REAR AXLE SERVICING

When disconnecting drive shaft from gearbox, tie up universal shaft so it will not slip out. Do not angle the sliding universal joints of the half shafts more than 14°.

Install bearing cap with oil groove down.

In replacing differential bearing, heat the cap to approximately 167° F. Install cap with oil groove at bottom. The ring gear and pinion mesh must then be re-adjusted.

Ring Gear and Pinion Adjustment

These gears are identified by a serial number inscribed on each. Another number appearing on the pinion is the deviation ($\pm$) in hundredths of a millimeter from a basic dimension (D) important to gear adjustment. (See Rear Axle Specifications Chart).

Gear sets use either Klingelnberg (Palloid) or Gleason teeth. The Klingelnberg

Klıngelnberg (Palloid) gear teeth.

Gleason gear teeth.

the pattern in the direction of tooth height, and the backlash changes only slightly.

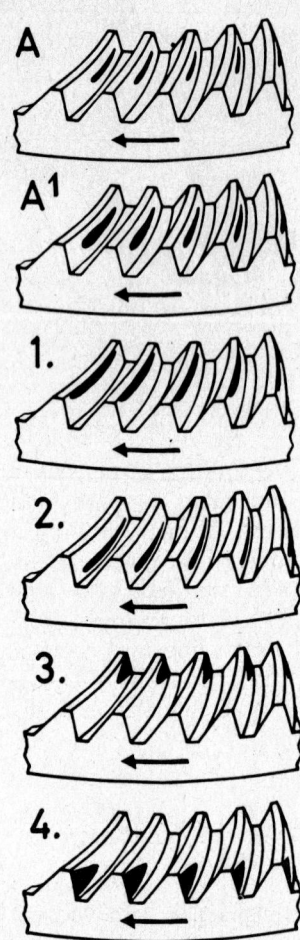

Ring gear/pinion tooth contact patterns produced by Gleason gearing.

inner and outer tooth faces are identical in appearance. With Gleason gears, the outer face is broader than the inside face.

Backlash should correspond to that shown in the table. However, a more decisive test for proper gear adjustment is the tooth contact pattern. This can be altered by changing shims from one side to the other of the bearing cap.

To check tooth adjustment, cover the front and back flanks of the ring gear with blue marking dye. Turn the ring gear at least one revolution in both directions, while maintaining a slight drag on the pinion.

Correct contact pattern made by Gleason teeth under no load is shown in the illustration at (A). When subjected to load, the contact pattern moves somewhat toward the outside as shown at (A1). Displacement of the ring gear primarily changes the backlash, although the pattern is displaced in the axial direction of the teeth. Displacement of the pinion moves

Figures 1, 2, 3 and 4 of the same illustration show the common incorrect patterns which are useful in making corrective adjustments.

1. High, narrow pattern on ring gear (tip contact). Correct by moving pinion toward ring gear, and if necessary, correct backlash by moving ring gear away from pinion.

2. Deep, narrow pattern on ring gear (root contact). Correct by moving pinion away from ring gear axis, and if necessary, correct backlash by moving ring gear toward pinion.

3. Short pattern on smallest end of ring gear tooth (toe contact). Correct by mov-

ing ring gear away from pinion, and if necessary, move pinion closer to ring gear axis.

4. Short pattern on large end of ring gear tooth (heel contact). Correct by moving ring gear toward pinion and, if necessary, move pinion away from ring gear axis.

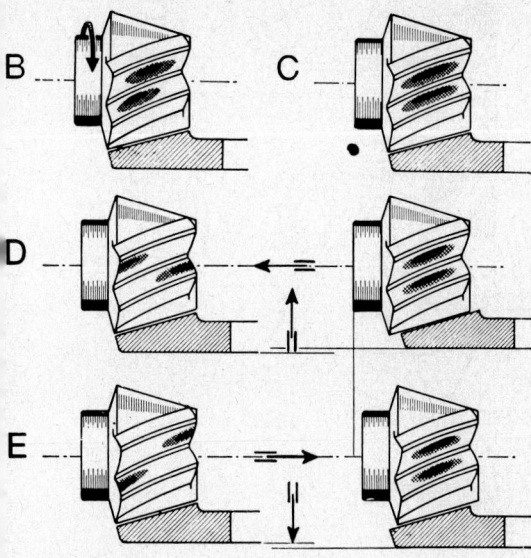

Ring gear/pinion tooth contact patterns produced by Klingelnberg (Palloid) gears.

On Klingelnberg gears, the correct contact pattern should show at about the center point of tooth length and height on both front and back flanks of the pinion.

Figure B shows a correct pattern made with no load.

Figure C shows a correct pattern under load.

Figures D and E show incorrect patterns caused by shimming the pinion in the direction shown by the arrow.

In assembling an overhauled rear drive assembly, the thickness of the shim (X) behind the pinion can be determined using the dimensions obtained as shown by the diagram and given by the Rear Axle Specifications Chart. For example:

1.
$$
\begin{array}{lll}
 & \text{B} & 1.6338'' \ (41.50 \text{ mm}) \\
+ & \text{C} & 1.1024'' \ (28 \text{ mm}) \\
\hline
 & = & 2.7362'' \ (69.50 \text{ mm})
\end{array}
$$

2.
$$
\begin{array}{lll}
 & \text{A} & 4.8031'' \ (122 \text{ mm}) \\
- & (\text{B}+\text{C}) & 2.7362'' \ (69.50 \text{ mm}) \\
\hline
 & = & 2.0669'' \ (52.50 \text{ mm}) \\
 & & \text{D-actual}
\end{array}
$$

3.
$$
\begin{array}{lll}
 \text{(from chart)} & \text{D} & 2.0677'' \ (52.52 \text{ mm}) \\
 & +\text{e} & .0118'' \ (\ .30 \text{ mm}) \\
\hline
 & = & 2.0795'' \ (52.82 \text{ mm}) \\
 & & \text{D-desired} \\
 -\text{D-actual} & & 2.0669'' \ (52.50 \text{ mm}) \\
\hline
 & \text{X}= & -.0126'' \ (-.32 \text{ mm})
\end{array}
$$

In this case, shim thickness must be reduced by .0126'' (.32 mm). If D-actual were greater than D-desired, shim thickness would be increased by .0126'' (.32 mm).

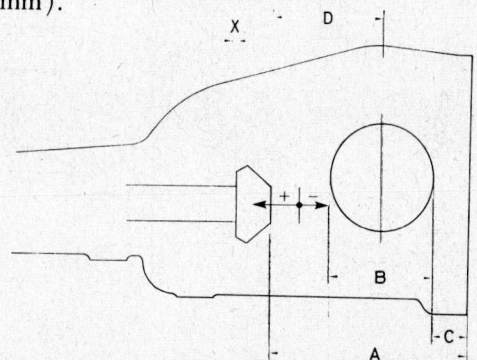

Measurements for determining shim (X) thickness.
A = distance from face of pinion to edge of housing.
B = diameter of bearing cap bore divided by 2.
C = distance from bore to edge of housing.
D = distance from face of pinion to center of bore.
e = deviation (±) from D in hundredths of a mm.
X = shim thickness.

Suspension

Front suspension is the McPherson strut type with lower wishbone, coil springs, and double acting shock absorbers. Rear suspension is fully independent with semi-trailing arms and coil springs. The differential is rubber mounted to the frame. The BMW 2002 also has a rubber mounted front stabilizer bar.

Specifications for wheel alignment are given in the Wheel Alignment Specifications Chart, and are for a normally loaded vehicle. Correct tire pressures, evenly worn tire treads, and wheel bearings without

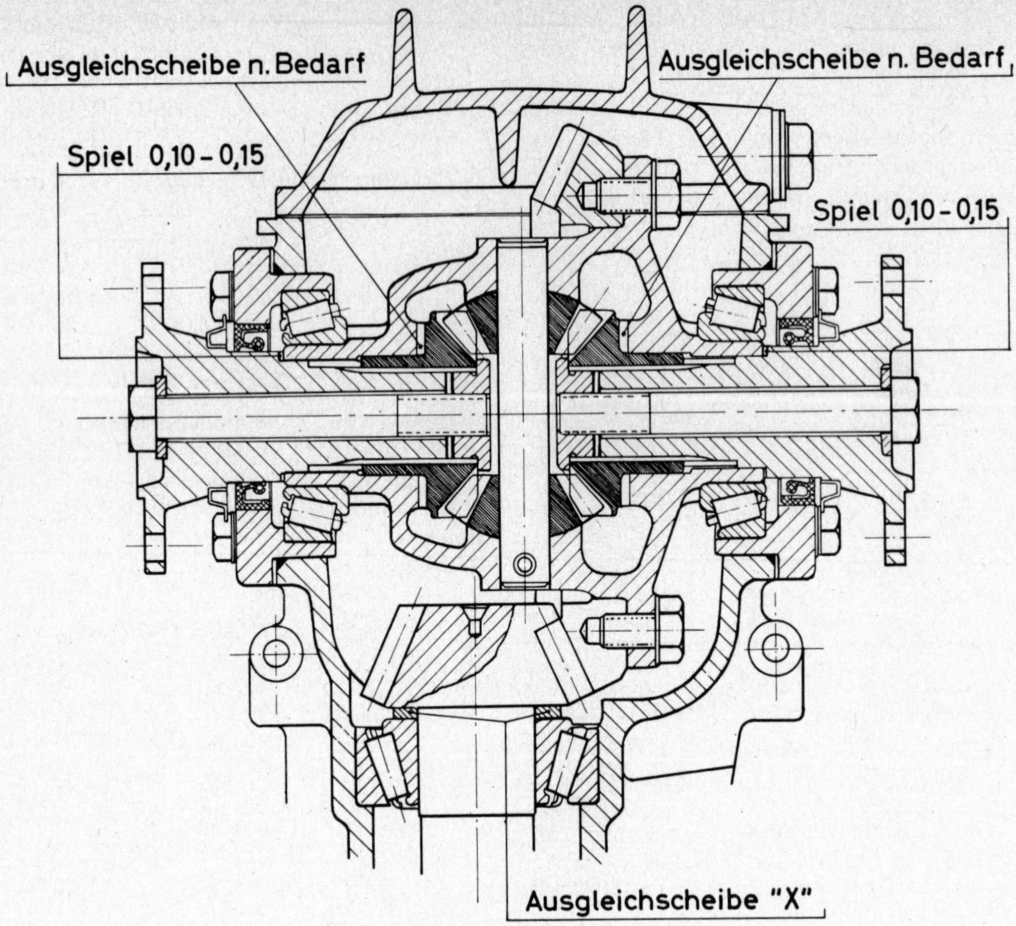

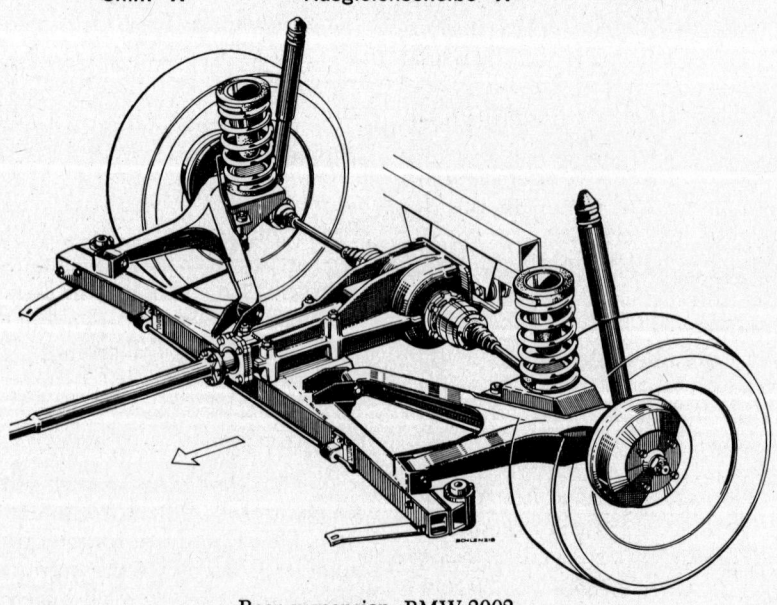

Ausgleichscheibe n. Bedarf

Spiel 0,10 - 0,15

Ausgleichscheibe n. Bedarf

Spiel 0,10 - 0,15

Ausgleichscheibe "X"

Rear axle assembly and adjustment shims.

Shims as required = Ausgleichscheibe n. Bedarf
Clearance   = Spiel 0.10–0.15 mm (0.039–0.059")
Shim "X"   = Ausgleichscheibe "X"

Rear suspension, BMW 2002.

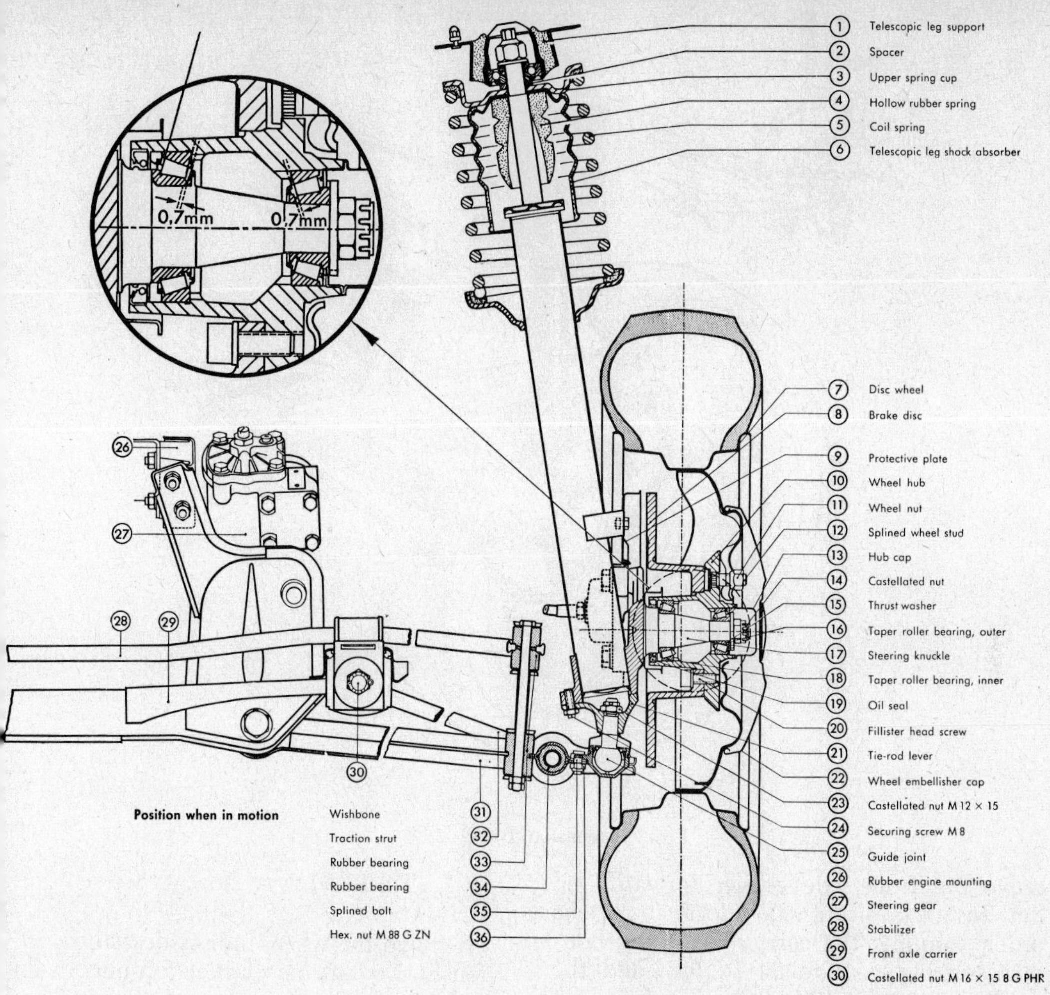

0.7mm 0.7mm

1	Telescopic leg support
2	Spacer
3	Upper spring cup
4	Hollow rubber spring
5	Coil spring
6	Telescopic leg shock absorber
7	Disc wheel
8	Brake disc
9	Protective plate
10	Wheel hub
11	Wheel nut
12	Splined wheel stud
13	Hub cap
14	Castellated nut
15	Thrust washer
16	Taper roller bearing, outer
17	Steering knuckle
18	Taper roller bearing, inner
19	Oil seal
20	Fillister head screw
21	Tie-rod lever
22	Wheel embellisher cap
23	Castellated nut M 12 × 15
24	Securing screw M 8
25	Guide joint
26	Rubber engine mounting
27	Steering gear
28	Stabilizer
29	Front axle carrier
30	Castellated nut M 16 × 15 8 G PHR

Position when in motion

Wishbone	31
Traction strut	32
Rubber bearing	33
Rubber bearing	34
Splined bolt	35
Hex. nut M 88 G ZN	36

Components of BMW front suspension.

excessive play are essential for proper wheel alignment. An optical measuring device must be used to obtain correct wheel alignment.

If there is reason to believe that front and rear wheels do not track, as might be caused by a misaligned rear axle, check and adjust the rear wheel alignment first.

FRONT AXLE CARRIER REPLACEMENT

Jack up the car and place it on jackstands. Remove the wheels. Loosen the nuts from the guide joint. Remove the steering gear from the front axle carrier. Loosen the steering guide lever bearing bracket from the front axle carrier, and tie the bracket and the steering gear to the gearbox.

Front axle carrier mounting screws.

Loosen the left and right engine mounts, and hoist the engine slightly. Support the front axle carrier with a jack and remove the mounting screws. Lower the jack and

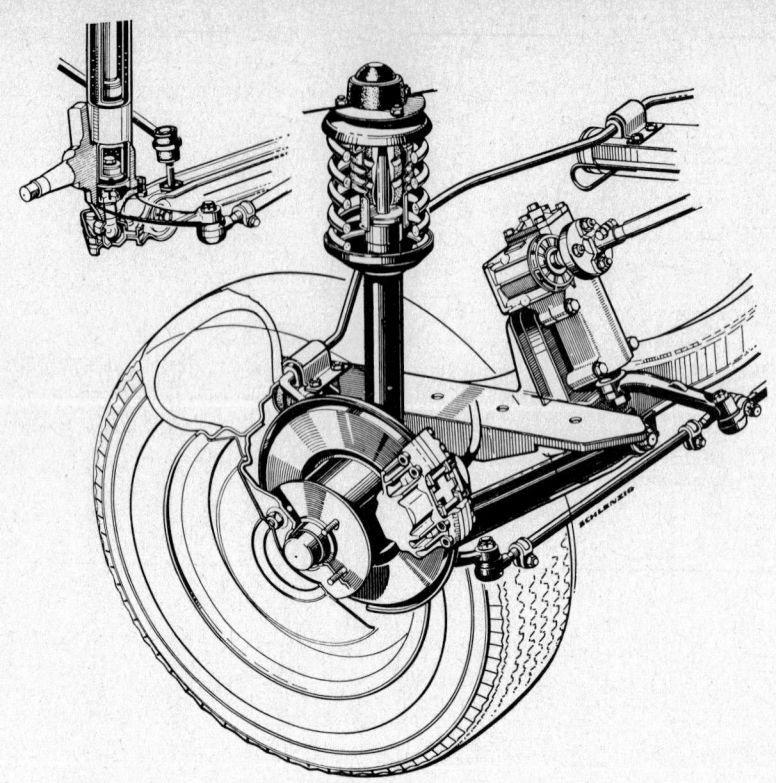

Front suspension, BMW 2002.

move the front axle carrier forward and out. Install the front axle carrier in reverse order, torquing the carrier mounting bolts and steering gear to 34 ft. lbs., and the guide joint nuts to 18 ft. lbs.

WHEEL HUB REMOVAL

Jack the car, support and remove the wheel. Loosen the brake caliper from the shock absorber. Remove the hub cap. Remove the cotter pin and the castle nut. Remove the shoulder disc and pull the wheel hub.

TIE-ROD LEVER REPLACEMENT

Remove the wheel hub as described previously. Loosen the elastic stop-nuts at the guide joint. Remove the safety wire and loosen the tie-rod lever. Remove the cotter pin and castle nut from the ball pivot, and press out the ball pivot. Force the tie-rod lever from the shock absorber. Install in reverse order, tightening tie-rod lever screws to 18 ft. lbs. and installing a new safety wire to hold the cap screws.

Pulling off wheel hub.

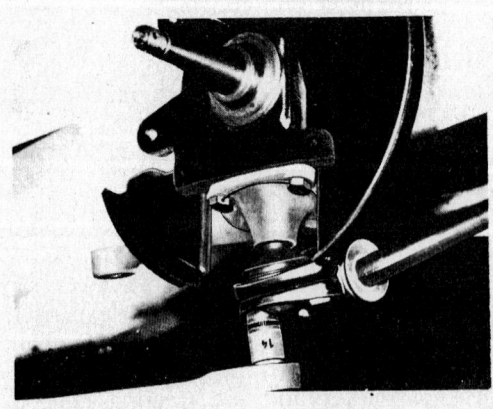

Loosening elastic stop-nuts at guide joint.

Wheel Bearing Renewal

Pull the wheel hub as previously described. Pull out the taper roller bearing with extractor and clean the wheel hub. Press in the outer rings of the bearing. Place the rear taper roller bearing in the hub and press in oil seal. Fill the oil seal with graphite grease. Install the wheel hub and disc on the axle.

Screw on the castle nut and tighten it to 7.2 ft. lbs. Turn the wheel backward and forward a few times to distribute the grease and align the bearings.

Loosen the castle nut one-third turn. Place a screwdriver in the recess of the nose disc. The nose disc must be easily movable to the left and right. Attach a dial indicator to the wheel hub. Just touch the front axle stub with the dial indicator. Adjust the wheel bearing play to between .00079″ (.02 mm) and .00315″ (.08 mm).

Note: Use of a 10-hole castle nut will allow closer adjustment, to between .00079″ (.02 mm) and .00236″ (.06 mm). The play should be adjusted as close to the minimum figure as possible.

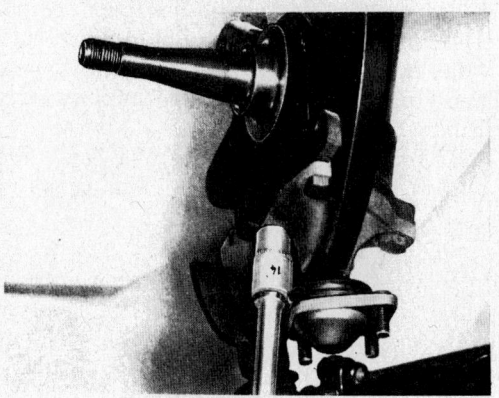

Loosening tie rod lever.

Front End Troubleshooting

When servicing steering and front suspension assemblies, it is advisable to check every front end part because all of the assemblies are so closely interrelated.

First, check the front end for worn or loose-fitting parts. Repair or replace what is faulty. Second, inspect and adjust the steering gear assembly. Third, set the front end alignment. And last, balance the wheels.

To detect front-end troubles quickly, follow these simple procedures:

1. With the front end jacked up, shake both wheels simultaneously to detect any looseness between them. Tie-rod and steering linkage joints sometimes loosen under severe road stresses. Check weaknesses further by shaking and prying against members connected to these joints.

2. Check out wheel suspension joints by having each wheel shaken up and down while the steering knuckle and control arm joints are observed for play.

3. Spin the wheels rapidly to test for deteriorated bearings. Listen for bearing noise and touch bumper to feel vibration that rough bearings create.

4. Rig a piece of chalk so it just clears the wheel rim and rotate the wheel to test for wheel runout. The chalk will mark misaligned, protruding rim areas. Repeat test on inside rim. Wheel should be straightened or replaced if runout exceeds ⅛″.

5. Lower front end to ground and bounce car to check for deteriorated shock absorbers.

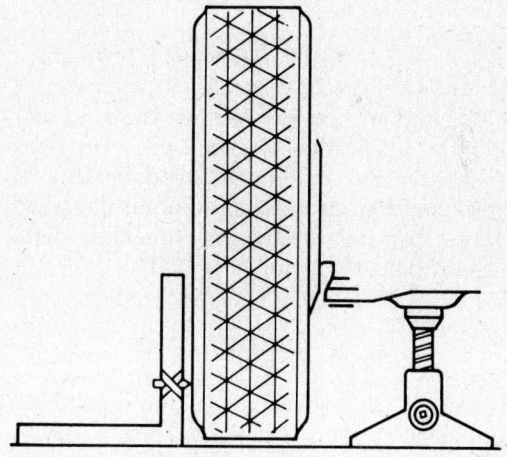

Testing for front wheel runout.

6. Check pre-owned cars for possible front end damage by measuring and comparing the wheelbase on both sides. Measure carefully from common points such as from the rear of the front-wheel rim to the rear of the back-wheel rim. If one side has a shorter or longer wheelbase than is listed in specifications, compare several measurements on both sides between various points until the dislocated part is found.

Diagonal measurements from right front to left rear wheels and from left front to right rear wheels will uncover a distorted chassis (if wheelbase measurements are equal). A twisted chassis will alter tracking and make front end alignment difficult if not impossible.

Vehicle Wandering

Vehicle wandering requires constant steering wheel correction, is annoying and also dangerous. It may be caused by incorrect caster or toe-in, too low tire pressure, excessive or insufficient play in the steering mechanism, worn or stiff steering rod ball joints, stiff control arm system, excessive play in rear end suspension.

Pulling To One Side

Check for uneven tire pressure, weak or uneven front springs, over-tightened wheel bearing, faulty wheel alignment, dragging brake, bent steering rod, or incorrect camber.

Hard Steering

Caused by too-low tire pressure, insufficiently lubricated steering gear or front end, excessive caster, damaged bearing in gear housing or steering column, damaged thrust bearing in steering knuckles, damaged front axle member or body.

Shimmy

Caused by wheels bent, misaligned or unbalanced, worn or warped brake drum, too-low tire pressure, damaged steering rod, loose or worn front wheel bearings.

Front End Alignment

Front end alignment centers on the precise geometric relationship of a number of parts — even when they are changing positions — that provides front wheel stability and control. These geometric angles include steering axis cant, caster, camber, included angle, toe-in, and toe-out (turning

arc). Before any adjustment is made, the condition of the complete front end system should be checked following the procedures given in the previous paragraphs and any defects corrected. Check the air pressure in all the tires. Check that the front tires are worn evenly. If not, replace or rotate them with the rear tires. Front wheel alignment must always be adjusted in this order:

1. Caster
2. Camber
3. Toe-In

Caster

Caster is the cant of the upper ball joint toward the rear of the car (positive). It gives the wheel another type of directional stability by moving the pivot point of the wheel forward of the tire's center. Positioning the pivot point ahead of center causes a drag on the bottom of the wheel (at the center) when it turns, thereby resisting the turn and tending to hold the wheel steady in whatever direction it has been going. The same principle of drag holds a weather vane pointer into the wind. The vane's bulky part seeks the point of minimum resistance behind the pivot.

Too slight a caster angle will cause the wheels to wander or weave at high speed

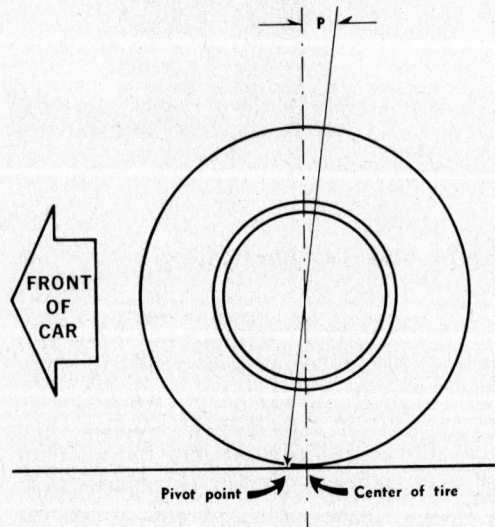

Front wheel caster. P = positive caster. The pivot point ahead of the center line of the tire holds the wheel stable.

and steer erratically when the brakes are applied. Too great a caster angle creates hard steering and shimmy at low speeds. Placing the weight of the car directly over the pivot point allows easiest steering and takes some load off the outside wheel bearings.

Camber

Camber is the angle that the centerline of the wheel makes with the vertical. The top of the wheel cants away from the car so that the center of the tire at the road lies at a point projected along the inclined axis of the upper and lower ball joints (steering axis cant).

Toe-Out

Toe-out (turning arc) is the difference in angle of the two wheels in a turn. As the front end turns, the outside wheel describes a larger circle than does the inside wheel. The turning angle of each is, therefore, not the same and the difference of the two angles is toe-out. If all previously discussed front end angles and measurements are correct and yet toe-out is wrong, one or both of the steering arms are bent.

Toe-In

Usually measured in inches, this is the amount that both wheels are closer together at the front than at the rear. Toe-in is related to wheel camber and compression forces on the steering linkage with forward speed. The greater the camber, the greater is the toe-in, usually. Set toe-in only after checking caster and camber.

Steering Axis Cant

Steering axis cant, or kingpin inclination as termed years ago when kingpins were standard, is the angle (from the vertical) at which the steering knuckle is attached to the upper and lower ball joints. The canted steering knuckle controls wheel directional stability by forcing the wheel to lift the chassis in order to turn from a straight ahead direction. As the steering arm releases its force over the wheel, the wheel returns to its straight ahead position

under the force of the chassis weight. This inclination is not adustable.

Included Angle

This is found by adding the steering axis cant to the positive wheel camber. This total must be equal on both front wheels regardless of what individual differences exist in axis cant and camber between the wheels. If the included angles of the two sides are different, a wheel spindle might be bent, possibly from striking a curb sharply.

Steering

BMW four-cylinder models use ZF-Gemmer worm and roller type steering gear assemblies with a gearbox ratio of 15.5:1 and an overall ratio of 17.58:1. The number of turns lock-to-lock is 3.5 and the wheel turning circle is 31.5 feet. Straight ahead position for the wheels is marked on the worm and steering box. The steering box uses grade SAE 90 hypoid gear oil and has a capacity of .63 pint.

STEERING ASSEMBLY NOTES

When installing the pitman arm, the mark on the steering shaft must line up with the arrow on the pitman arm.

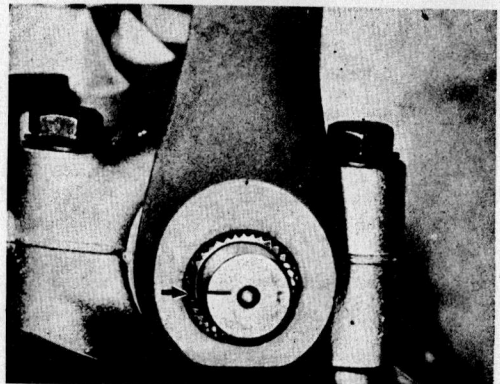

Install pitman arm so that arrow lines up with mark on shaft.

Install the steering shaft in the case so that the mark (B) on the shaft lines up with the mark (C) on the case, and the mark (A) on the shaft points to the middle of the housing seam.

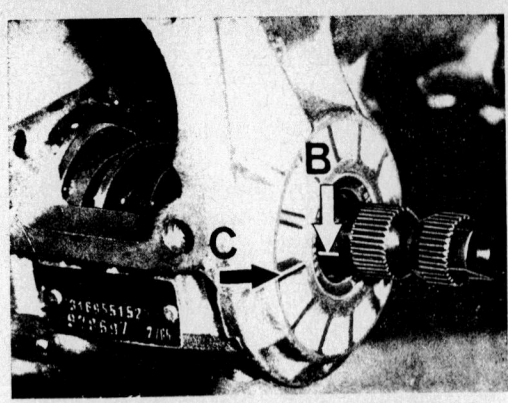

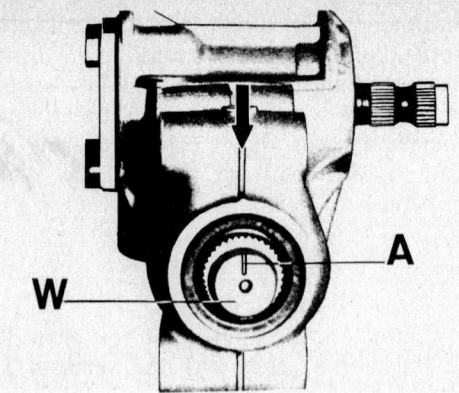

These marks must coincide when installing steering shaft in case.

With the wheels straight ahead, the marking on the worm shaft should be aligned with the marking on the steering gear case.

Markings should line up when wheels are straight.

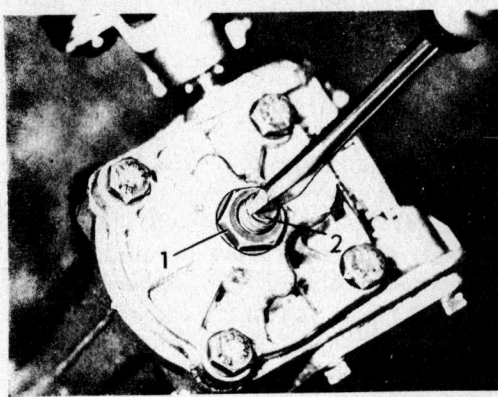

Steering adjustment screw (2) and locknut (1).

Steering Adjustment

This is best made using a friction cocfficient gauge attached to the nut of the steering wheel. The adjustment is correct —without play—with a friction coefficient of .72-1.16 ft. lbs.

Jack up the front of the car with both wheels free. Remove the cover cap from the steering wheel. Turn the steering wheel about one turn to the left. Attach a friction gauge to the wheel, turn the friction gauge to the right beyond the straight-ahead position. Turn the wheel back to the left if another test is required.

Loosen the locknut and turn the adjustment screw while checking the friction coefficient until the proper value is obtained.

Brakes

Disc brakes are on both the front and rear wheels of BMW 2500 and 2800 cars. Other BMW models have disc brakes on the front and drum brakes on the rear. Brakes are power assisted, and the master cylinder has a tandem arrangement whereby each chamber actuates either the front or rear brake cylinders. Failure of either circuit is indicated by a warning light. The twin brake fluid reservoir is located in the engine compartment.

Warning Light Test

Warning of failure of the dual brake system is provided by a 3-watt lamp. Proper functioning of the light system can be tested by turning on the ignition switch and then pressing a small button on the instrument panel. The warning lamp should light when this button is pressed and the ignition switch is on.

Servicing Master Cylinder—2002

Disconnect the brake lines: left front (1), right front (2), and rear (3). Remove the master cylinder.

NOTE: When reassembling, check the rubber ring (4) which, if defective, will prevent vacuum formation. If renewing master cylinder, also check for proper clearance (A) between the pushrod and piston. This should be adjusted to .02″ (.5 mm) with shims (5).

BMW 2002 master cylinder connection ports (1, 2, 3), seal ring (4), shims (5) and proper clearance (A) between pushrod and piston. (A) should be .02″ (.5 mm).

Check all components and replace any that show signs of wear.

Components of BMW 2002 master cylinder: snap-ring (1), stop plate (2), secondary sleeves (3, 5), spacer (4), stop plate (6), piston (7), feeler plate (8), primary sleeve (9), pressure spring (10), bottom valve (11).

Servicing Master Cylinder—1500, 1600

NOTE: The master cylinder has a special bottom valve with a throttle bore (1). If the throttle bore is clogged, the brakes will drag.

Play between piston rod and piston must be .02″ (.5 mm).

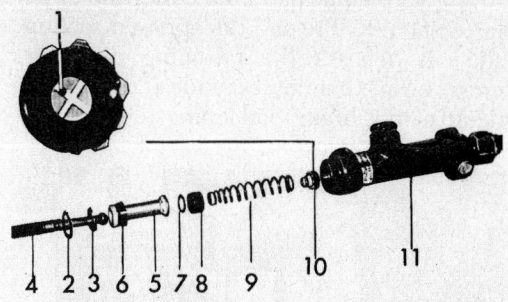

Components of BMW 1500, 1600 master cylinder: snap-ring (2), disc (3), piston rod (4), piston (5, secondary sleeve (6), spacer disc (7), primary sleeve (8), pressure spring (9), bottom valve (10), with throttle bore (1).

Servicing Master Cylinder— 1800, 1800 A, 1800 TI

Check through filling opening with a wire to ensure that compensation bore is not clogged. If bore is clogged, brakes will drag. Play between piston rod and piston must be .02″ (.5 mm).

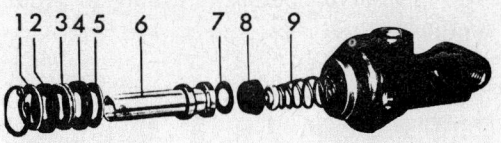

Components of BMW 1800, 1800 A, 1800 TI master cylinder: washer (1), secondary sleeve (2), intermediate ring (3), secondary sleeve (4), stop washer (5), piston (6), spacer disc (7), primary sleeve (8), pressure spring assembly (9).

Servicing Disc Brakes

Disc brakes are self adjusting and therefore require no manual adjustment, but the pad linings should be replaced when they are worn to a thickness of .7″ (2 mm). Brake discs should also be checked for maximum runout which is .0039″ (.10

mm). If the discs should have to be refinished, minimum brake disc thickness is .335" (8.5 mm). To change pads, first remove securing lugs, if so equipped, then drive fastening pins from calipers. Remove cross spring and pull out pads with extractor hook.

When replacing cross springs, place cross spring with embossed area under the upper fastening pin. Preload the opposed section: slide it beneath the fastening pin. The cross spring eliminates undesirable movement of the brake pad linings.

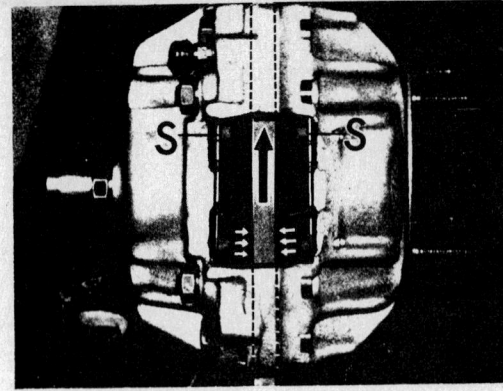

Protective cap (S) installed.

Proper assembly of cross spring.

Return piston to wheel cylinder using piston pressback pliers. Do not use any other tools to avoid damage to wheel cylinder or brake disc. Check brake fluid level in reservoir before returning to avoid overflowing.

For caliper with piston without protective cap, check that 20-degree setting line of piston faces the brake disc inlet. Incorrect adjustment of the piston causes fluttering or squeaking of the disc brake and may prevent correct application of the brake lining to the disc. Installation of the protective cap (S) is recommended where possible. The cap can only be installed on pistons with a shoulder measuring .0315" (.8 mm).

When removing pads that will be used again, mark them to be sure the inside and outside pads will be reassembled in their proper places. Make sure that each pair of wheels (front and rear) have pads of the same type as marked by the manufacturer. NOTE: *bleeding of the hydraulic system after caliper repair is made easier if calipers are filled with fluid before being installed. Remove the bleeder connector and pour in fluid, tilting the caliper.*

Drum Brake Adjustment

To adjust brake shoes, apply brakes forcefully to center the shoes, then with the pedal released, turn the adjustment cams to lock the wheels. Turn cams backward a fraction of a turn until wheel rotates freely, with no noticeable drag, with pedal released. If any brake lines have been disconnected or the pedal operation is spongy, bleed the brake system.

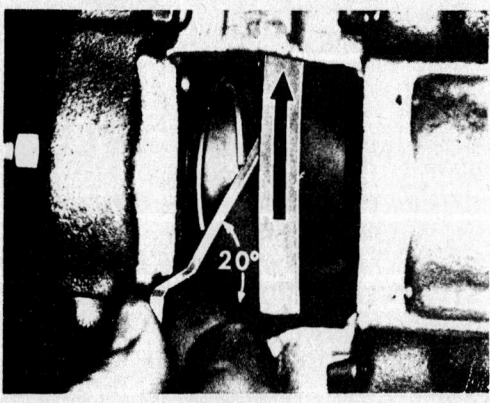

Use of piston gauge to check 20° position of piston.

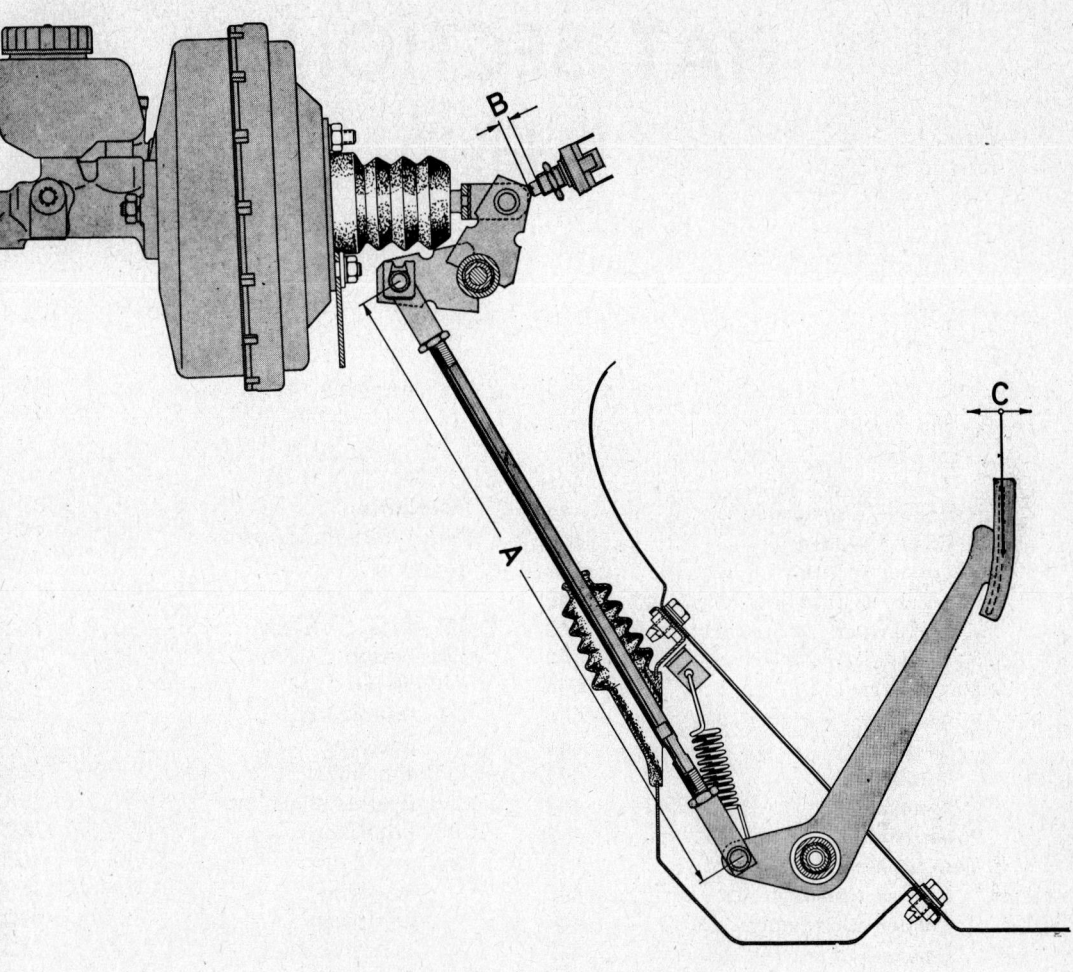

Diagram showing brake pedal, tie rod and stop
light switch adjustments for BMW 1600-2, 2002.
A = 14.52″ (369 mm), B = .24″-.28″ (6-7 mm),
C = ± .19″ (3 mm).

FIAT SECTION

Index

Introduction

Fiat has imported many models into the United States, among them the 124 series, 850 series, 600 series, 1100, 1500 and 1600S series. Almost all series are available in many body styles ranging from roadsters, coupes and cabriolets to station wagons, sedans and Multiplas.

All Fiats are equipped with four-cylinder, inline, water cooled engines. Displacement is as low as 50 cu. in. in the 850 series to 98 cu. in. for the 1971 Sport Coupe and Sport Spyder. Engines are mounted conventionally in most models, except the 850 and 600 series autos.

Fiat 600 Sedan.

Fiat 850 Coupe.

Year and Model Identification

Fiat 124 Sedan.

Fiat 850 Spider.

Fiat 124 Spider.

Fiat 850 Sedan.

Fiat 124 Coupe.

Fiat 1100D Station Wagon.

Fiat 1100R Sedan.

Fiat 1600S Cabriolet.

Fiat 124 Sport Spyder

Fiat 850 Sport Spyder

Fiat 124 Special

Fiat 124 Family Wagon

Vehicle and Engine Identification

An identification plate, mounted on the engine compartment wall, carries the chassis number, serial number and spare parts ordering number. The engine number is found stamped on a pad on the engine block.

Car Model	Serial Number	Type	Displacement cu. in. (cc.)	No. of Cylinders
124 Spyder, Coupe	124AC.000	DOHC	87.7 (1,438)	4
124 Sedan, Station Wagon	124B.040	OHV	73.0 (1,197)	4
124 Special	124B2.040	OHV	87.7 (1,438)	4
124 Sport Coupe	125BC.040	DOHC	98.1 (1,608)	4
124 Sport Spyder	125BC.040	DOHC	98.1 (1,608)	4
600 Sedan	100.000	OHV	38.63 (633)	4
600 Multipla	100.008	OHV	38.63 (633)	4
600D Sedan	100D.000	OHV	46.7 (767)	4
600D Multipla	100D.008	OHV	46.7 (767)	4
850 Sedan	100G3.002	OHV	49.85 (817)	4
850 Coupe	100GC3.040	OHV	49.85 (817)	4
850 Spyder	100GS3.040	OHV	49.85 (817)	4
850 Racer	100GBS.040	OHV	55.1 (903)	4
850 Sports Racer	100GBS.040	OHV	55.1 (903)	4
850 Sport Spyder	100GBS.040	OHV	55.1 (903)	4
850 Sport Coupe	100GBC.040	OHV	55.1 (903)	4
1100/103D Sedan, Station Wagon	103D.000	OHV	66.5 (1,089)	4
1100/103G/103H Sedan	103H.000	OHV	66.5 (1,089)	4
1100D Sedan, Station Wagon	103G.005	OHV	74.5 (1,221)	4
1100R Sedan	103P.000	OHV	66.5 (1,089)	4
1500 Cabriolet	115C.005	OHV	90.37 (1,481)	4
1600S Cabriolet	118B.000	DOHC	95.69 (1,568)	4

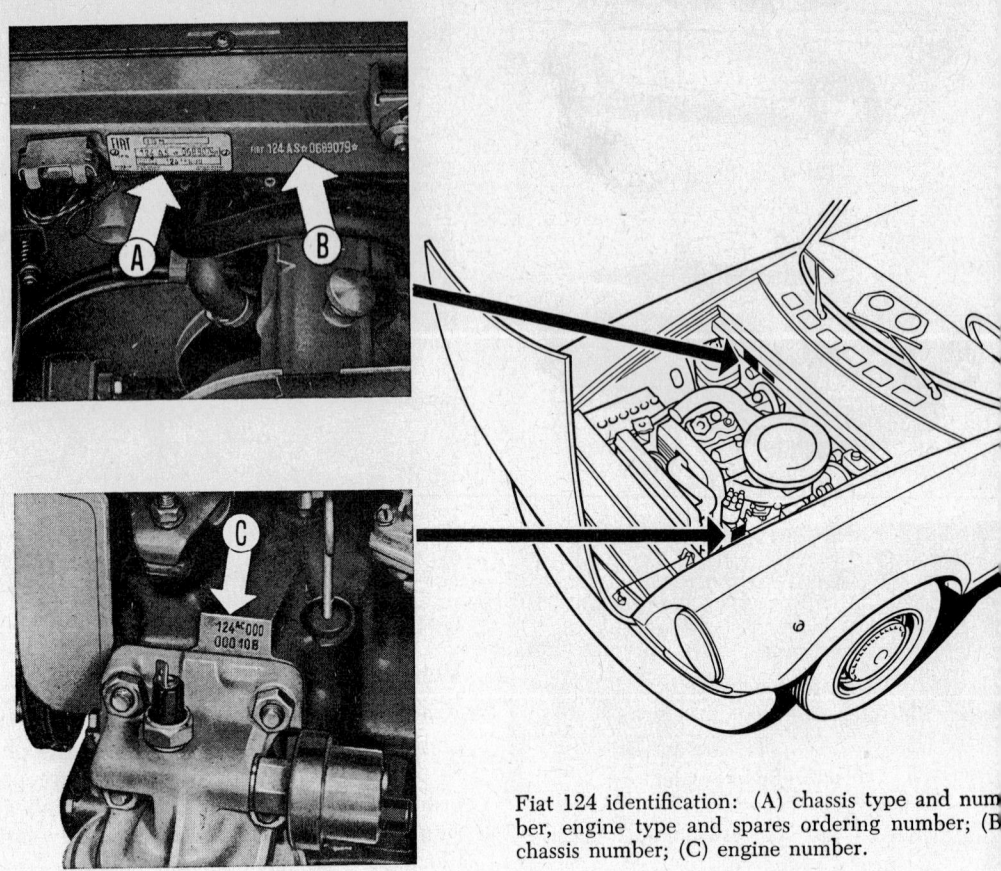

Fiat 124 identification: (A) chassis type and number, engine type and spares ordering number; (B) chassis number; (C) engine number.

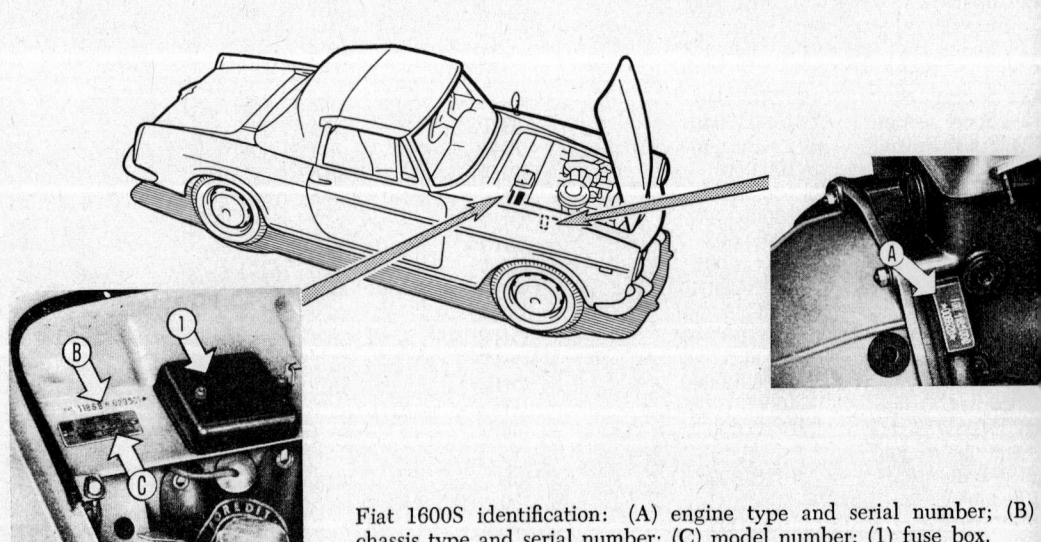

Fiat 1600S identification: (A) engine type and serial number; (B) chassis type and serial number; (C) model number; (1) fuse box.

Fiat 850 identification: (A) model number; (B) chassis type and serial number; (C) engine type and serial number.

General Engine Specifications

Make	No. Cylinders	Displacement (Cu. In./CC.)	Nominal Bore (In./MM.)	Stroke (In./MM.)	Compression Ratio (to 1)	Torque (Ft. lbs./KG.M./RPM)	BHP/RPM (SAE)
124 Spider, Coupe	4	87.7/1438	3.16/80	2.81/71	8.9	82.2/11.4/4000	96/6500
124 Sedan	##4	87.7/1438	3.16/80	2.81/71	N.A.	N.A.	76/5800
	4	73/1197	2.87/73	2.81/71	8.8	64.4/8.9/3400	65/5600
124 Special	4	87.7/1438	3.16/80	2.81/71	8.9	81.0/N.A./3300	76/5400
124 Sport Coupe, Sport Spyder,	4	98.1/1608	3.15/80	3.15/80	8.5	94.3/N.A./4200	104/6000
600	4	38.6/633	2.36/60	2.20/56	7.5	28.9/4.0/3000	28.5/4600
600D	4	46.7/767	2.45/62	2.5/63.5	7.5	40/5.5/2800	32/4800
850 Sedan, Idro-convert	*4	51.4/843	2.56/65	2.5/63.5	8.0③	42.7/5.9/3600④	40/5300④
	**4	49.8/817	2.51/64	2.5/63.5	8.9	44.1/6.1/3600	42/5300
850 Coupe, Spider	**4	49.8/817	2.51/64	2.5/63.5	10.0	45.5/6.3/4000	52/6400
	*4	51.4/843	*2.56/65	*2.5/63.5	①	45.5/6.3/4000	②
850 Sports Racer, Sport Spyder, Sport Coupe	##4	55.1/903	2.56/65	2.68/68.2	9.5	47.7/6.6/4000	58/6500
1100/103D	4	66.3/1089	2.68/68	2.95/75	7.0	52.4/7.2/3200	43/4800
1100/103H	4	66.3/1089	2.68/68	2.95/75	7.8	52.8/7.3/3700	50/5200
1100D/103G	4	74.5/1221	2.83/72	2.95/75	8.1	56.4/7.8/2500	50/5000
1100R	4	66.3/1089	2.68/68	2.95/75	8.1	57.1/8.1/3200	53/5200
1500	4	90.3/1481	3.03/77	3.13/79	9.0	88.9/12.3/3200	83/5400
1600S	#4	95.7/1568	3.15/80	3.07/78	8.6	97.6/13.5/4000	100/6000

① 1966 Coupe—8.8; 1966-67 Spider and 1967 Coupe—9.3.
② 1966-67 Coupe & 1967 Spider—52 @ 6200; 1966 Spider—54 @ 6200.
③ Super version—8.8.
④ Super version—same as 1968-69 standard version.
* 1966-67   ** 1968-69.   # overhead camshafts   ## 1970

Tune-Up Specifications

Model	Spark Plugs Type°	Electrode Gap (In./MM.)	Breaker Point Gap (In./MM.)	Breaker Dwell Angle (Degrees)	Distributor Contact Pressure (Oz./Gr.)	Firing Order	Idle Speed (RPM)°°	Valves Clearance (In./MM.) Int. (Cold) Exh.	Int. Valve Opens (°BTDC)	Electrical System (Volts-Terminal Grounded)
124 Spyder Coupe	N6Y or N9Y	.024/.6	.018/.48	57–63	19.6/550	1-3-4-2	800	.017/.45 .019/.5	26	12N
124 Sedan	N9Y	.024/.6	.018/.48	57–63	19.6/550	1-3-4-2	800	.006/.15 .006/.15	25	12N
124 Special	N9Y	.020–.024	.017–.019	57–63	N.A.	1-3-4-2	800–900	.008 .008	N.A.	12N
124 Sport Coupe, Sport Spyder	N6Y	.020–.024	.015–.017	52–58	N.A.	1-3-4-2	800–900	.018 .020	N.A.	12N
600/D	L7	.024/.6	.018/.48	50	16.8/475	1-3-4-2	800–900	.006/.15 .006/.15	4	12N
850 Sedan	N4	.024/.6	.018/.48	60	17.6/500	1-3-4-2	800–900	.006/.15 .006/.15	16	12N
850 Coupe, Spyder	N3	.020/.5	.018/.48	60	17.6/500	1-3-4-2	800–900	.006/.15 .008/.20	25	12N
850 Racer, Sport Racer, Sport Coupe	N7Y	.020–.024	.015–.017	52–58	N.A.	1-3-4-2	850	.006 .008	N.A.	12N
850 Sport Spyder	N7Y	.020–.024	.015–.017	52–58	N.A.	1-3-4-2	850	.006 .008	N.A.	12N
1100/D	L7	.020/.5	.018/.48	58	19.4/550	1-3-4-2	800–900	.004/.10 .004/.10	16	12N
1100R	Bosch W175T1	.024/.6	.018/.48	58	19.4/550	1-3-4-2	800–900	.004/.10 .004/.10	16	12N
1500	N9Y	.020/.5	.018/.48	60	19.4/550	1-3-4-2	800–900	.008/.20 .010/.25	25	12N
1600S	N9Y	.020/.5	.018/.48	57–63	19.4/550	1-3-4-2	800–900	.012/.30 .014/.35	28	12N

°—Champion, except where noted.
°°—This is only a range, as idle speed will vary with carburetor mixture setting.

Firing Order

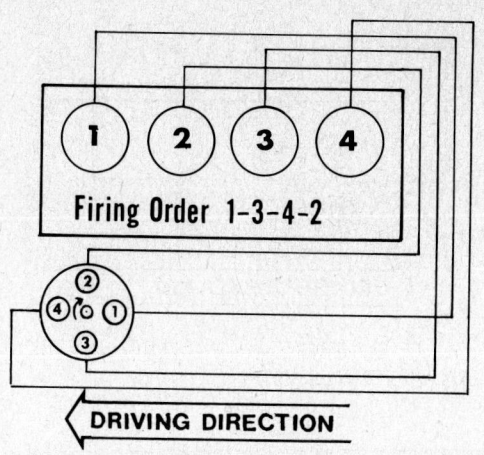

Firing Order—124 Sport Coupe, 124 Sport Spyder

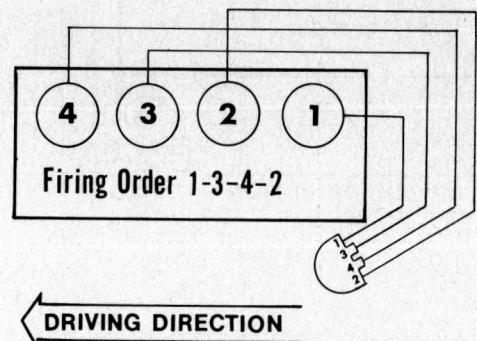

Firing Order—850 Spyder, Sport Spyder

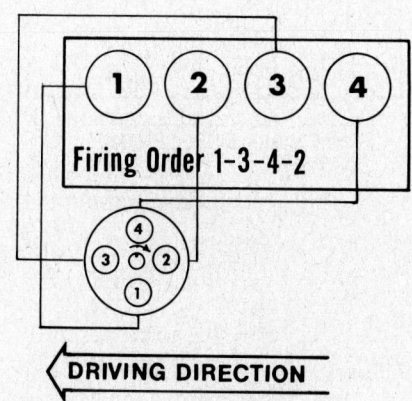

Firing Order—124 Spyder, Coupe

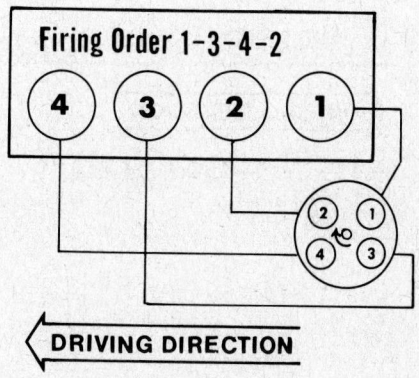

Firing Order—850 Coupe, Sport Coupe, Sedan

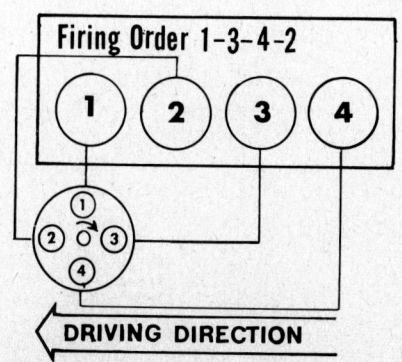

Firing Order—124 Sedan, Station Wagon

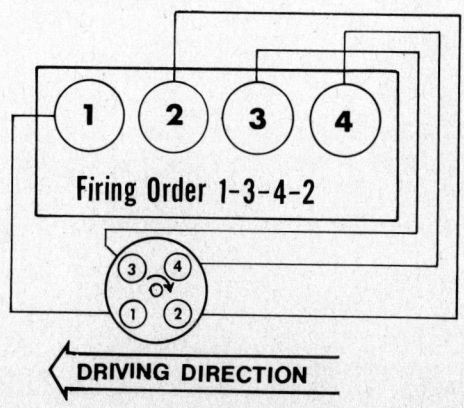

Firing Order—1100/103D, 1100D, Fiat Export, Special Sedan and Family car

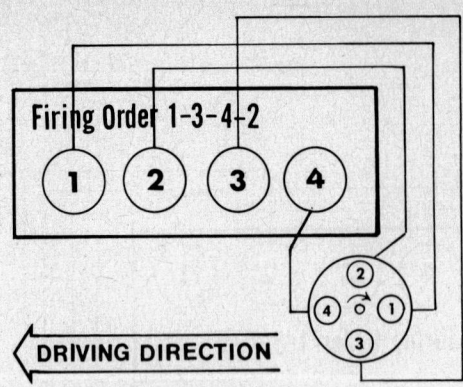

Firing Order—1100R

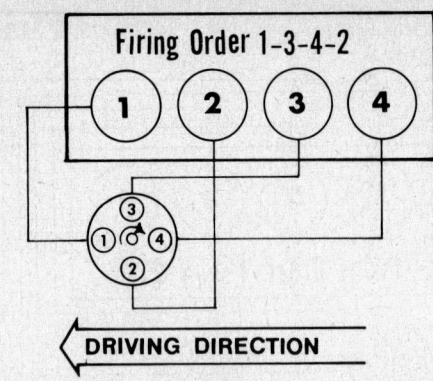

Firing Order—1500 Cabriolet, 124 Sedan (1970), 124 Station Wagon (1970)

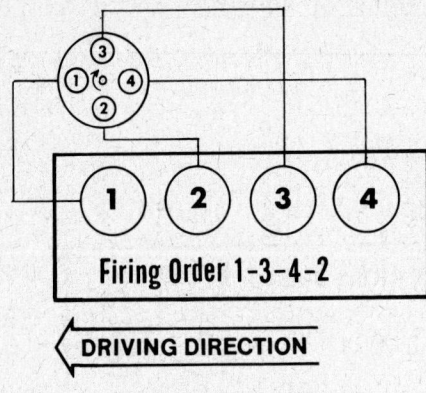

Firing Order—1600S Cabriolet

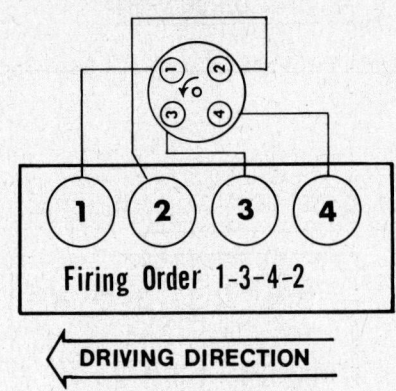

Firing Order—600, 600D

Model	No. Main Bearings	CRANKSHAFT			CAMSHAFT JOURNALS			CONNECTING RODS			Crankshaft End-play (In./MM.)
		Main Journal Diameter (In./MM.)	Rod Journal Diameter (In./MM.)	Main Bearing Clearance (In./MM.)	Diameter Front (In./MM.)	Diameter Middle (In./MM.)	Diameter Rear (In./MM.)	Big End Bore (In./MM.)	Small End Bore (In./MM.)	Rod Bearing Clearance (In./MM.)	
124 Spider Coupe	5	1.9990–1.9998/ 50.77–50.79	1.7910–1.7920/ 45.51–45.53	.00190–.00370/ .050–.095	1.1738–1.1744/ 29.94–29.96	1.7928–1.7934/ 45.73–45.75	1.8085–1.8091/ 46.13–46.15	1.9145–1.9152/ 48.63–48.64	.8637–.8645/ 21.94–21.96	.00102–.00299/ .026–.076	.0024–.0102/ .06–.26
124 Sedan Station Wagon	5	1.9990–1.9998/ 50.77–50.79	1.7910–1.7920/ 45.51–45.53	.00190–.00370/ .050–.095	1.8910–1.8920/ 48.03–48.06	1.7257–1.7266/ 48.83–43.86	1.4517–1.4527/ 36.87–36.90	1.9145–1.9152/ 48.63–48.64	.8637–.8645/ 21.94–21.96	.00102–.00299/ .026–.076	.0021–.0104/ .05–.27
124 Special	5	1.9990–1.9998	1.791–1.792	.0019–.0037	N.A.	N.A.	N.A.	1.9145–1.9152	.8637–.8645	.0010–.00299	.0024–.010
124 Sport Coupe Sport Spyder		N.A.	N.A.	N.A.	N.A.	N.A.	N.A.	N.A.	N.A.	N.A.	N.A.
600	3	1.9996–2.0004/ 50.79–50.81	1.3775–1.3783/ 34.99–35.01	.00059–.00230/ .015–.060	1.4951–1.4961/ 37.97–38.00	1.4951–1.4961/ 37.97–38.00	1.2195–1.2205/ 30.97–31.00	1.5002–1.5007/ 38.11–38.12	.7850–.7863/ 19.94–19.97	.00047–.00225/ .012–.057	.0102–.0138/ .26–.35
600D	3	1.9992–1.9998/ 50.78–50.79	1.5743–1.5751/ 39.99–40.01	.00118–.00276/ .030–.070	1.4951–1.4961/ 37.97–38.00	1.4951–1.4961/ 37.97–38.00	1.2195–1.2205/ 30.97–31.00	1.7188–1.7193/ 43.66–43.67	.8638–.8651/ 21.94–21.97	.00079–.00284/ .020–.067	.0102–.0138/ .26–.35
850 Sedan	3	1.9994–2.0002/ 50.78–50.80	1.5742–1.5750/ 39.98–40.00	.0008–.0024/ .020–.066	1.4951–1.4961/ 37.97–38.00	1.7060–1.7070/ 43.33–43.36	1.2195–1.2205/ 30.97–31.00	1.7188–1.7193/ 43.66–43.67	.7850–.7856/ 19.94–19.95	.00100–.00280/ .026–.071	.0024–.0102/ .06–.36
850 Coupe Spider	3	1.9994–2.0002/ 50.78–50.80	1.5742–1.5750/ 39.98–40.00	.0010–.0028/ .026–.071	1.4951–1.4961/ 37.97–38.00	1.7060–1.7070/ 43.33–43.36	1.2195–1.2205/ 30.97–31.00	1.7188–1.7193/ 43.66–43.67	.7850–.7856/ 19.94–19.95	.00100–.00280/ .026–.071	.0024–.0102/ .06–.26
850 Racer Sport Racer Sport Spyder Sport Coupe	3	1.9994–2.0002	1.5742–1.5750	.0010–.0028	1.4951–1.4961	1.7060–1.7070	1.2195–1.2205	1.7188–1.7193	.7850–.7856	.001–.0028	.0024–.0102
1100/D	3	1.6530–1.6538/ 41.99–42.01	1.5743–15751/ 39.99–40.01	.00078–.00252/ .020–.064	1.4163–1.4173/ 35.97–36.00	1.5344–1.5354/ 38.97–39.00	1.4950–1.4960/ 37.97–38.00	1.7189–1.7194/ 43.66–43.67	.9424–.9433/ 23.94–23.97	.00067–.00252/ .017–.064	.0003–.0102/ .07–.26
1100R	3	1.6530–1.6538/ 41.99–42.01	1.5743–1.5751/ 39.99–40.01	.00078–.00205/ .020–.052	1.4163–1.4173/ 35.97–36.00	1.5344–1.5354/ 38.97–39.00	1.4950–1.4960/ 37.97–38.00	1.7187–1.7193/ 43.66–43.67	.9424–.9433/ 23.94–23.97	.00067–.00270/ .017–.068	.0027–.0102/ .07–.26
1500	3	2.4788–2.4796/ 62.96–62.98	2.0863–2.0871/ 52.99–53.01	.0018–.0035/ .045–.089	1.4163–1.4173/ 35.97–36.00	1.8760–1.8770/ 47.65–47.67	1.8210–1.8220/ 46.25–46.28	2.2330–2.2334/ 56.72–56.73	.9425–.9438/ 23.94–23.97	.0012–.0030/ .031–.076	.0024–.0102/ .06–.26
1600S	5	2.2470–2.2475/ 57.07–57.08	1.8755–1.8763/ 47.64–47.66	.0022–.0032/ .057–.082	1.1016–1.1021/ 27.98–27.99	1.1173–1.1178/ 28.38–28.39	1.1331–1.1336/ 28.78–28.79	2.0210–2.0215/ 51.33–51.34	.8637–.8650/ 21.94–21.97	.0012–.0030/ .031–.076	.0035–.0110/ .09–.28

Engine Rebuilding Specifications (cont'd)

Model	Class A Cyl. Bore (In./MM.)	Class A Piston Dia. (Skirt Top) (In./MM.)	Standard Piston Pin Dia. (In./MM.)	Fit in Piston (In./MM.)	Ring Clearance in Groove (In./MM.) (Maximum)	Ring End-Gap (In./MM.)	Piston Fit in Bore (In./MM.)
124 Spider, Coupe	3.149-151/80-80.05	3.1461-1465/79.91-92	.8649/21.97	.0003/.008	.003/.077 (Top) .002/.057 (2 & 3)	.012/.30 .007/.20	.0031-.0039④ .080-.100④
124 Sedan	2.874-876/73-73.05	2.8724-8728/72.96-97	.8649/21.97	.0003/.008	.003/.077 (Top) .002/.057 (2 & 3)	.007/.20 .007/.20	.0011-.0020/ .030-.050①
124 Special	3.149-3.151	3.1461-3.1465	.8649	.0003	.003 (Top) .002 (2 & 3)	.012 .007	.0031- .0039
124 Sport Coupe Sport Spyder	N.A.	N.A.	N.A.	N.A.	N.A.	N.A.	N.A.
600	2.3622-3626/60-60.01	2.3605-3609/59.95-96	.7085/17.99	.0005/.013	.003/.077 (Top) .002/.057 (2 & 3)	.008/.20 .008/.20	.0013-.0021/ .033-.053①
600D	2.4409-4413/62-62.01	2.4375-4379/61.91-92	.7868/19.99	.0004/.010	.003/.072 (1 & 2) .003/.072 (3rd)	.008/.20 none	.0030-.0037/ .075-.095②
850 Sedan	*2.5197-5216/64-64.05 **2.5591-2.5610/65.00-65.05	*2.5184-5188/63.97-98① **2.5578-2.5582/64.97-64.98	.7862/19.97	.0004/.010	.003/.072 (Top) .002/.052 (2nd) .003/.072 (3rd)	.008/.20 .008/.20 none	.0007-.0015/ .020-.040①
850 Coupe, Spider	*2.5197-5216/64-64.05 **2.5591-2.5610/65.00-65.05	*2.5168-5172/63.93-94② **2.5578-2.5582/64.97-64.98	.7862/19.97	.0004/.010	.003/.072 (Top) .002/.052 (2nd) .003/.072 (3rd)	.008/.20 .008/.20 none	.0023-.0031/ .060-.080②
850 Racer Sport Racer Sport Spyder Sport Coupe	2.5591-2.5610	2.5578-2.5582	.7862	.0004	.003 (Top) .002 (2nd) .003 (3rd)	.008 .008 —	.0023- .0031
1100 103D, 103H	2.6772-6776/68-68.01	2.6734-6738/67.90-91	.8658/21.99	.0003/.008	.002/.05 (1 & 2) .001/.027 (3rd)	.008/.20	.0033-.0041/ .085-.105②
1100/103G	2.8346-8350/72.-72.01	2.8298-8302/71.87-88	.8658/21.99	.0003/.008	.002/.072 (Top) .002/.052 (2 & 3)	.008/.20	.0045-.0053/ .115-.135②
1100R	2.6772-6776/68.-68.01	2.6730-6734/67.89-90	.8658/21.99	.0003/.008	.003/.077 (1 & 2) .003/.072 (3rd)	.018/.30 none	.0038-.0046/ .095-.115②
1500	3.0315-0319/77-77.01	3.0014-0018/76.96-97	.8658/21.99	.0004/.010	.003/.072 (Top) .002/.052 (2nd) .003/.072 (3rd)	.018/.45 .014/.35 none	.0038-.0046/ .095-.115①
1600S	3.1496-1500/80-80.01	3.1157-1161/79.89-90③	.7868/19.99	.0003/.008	.002/.052 (Top) .002/.052 (2nd) .003/.072 (3rd)	.018/.45 .014/.35 .014/.35	.0038-.0046/ .095-.115①

① Measured 1.555" (39.5 mm.) down from top.
② Measured .197" (5 mm.) from skirt top.
③ Measured 1.574" (40 mm.) from bottom ring.
④ Measured 2.057" (52.25 mm.) down from top.
* 817 CC.

Engine Rebuilding Specifications (cont'd)

Model	Valve Clearance (Cold) (In./MM.)		Head Diameter (In./MM.)		Stem Diameter (In./MM.)	Stem Clearance in Guide (In./MM.)	Spring Length Unloaded (In./MM.)		Intake Opens (°BTDC)	Crankshaft Rotation
	Int.	Exh.	Int.	Exh.			Outer	Inner		
Spider, Coupe	.017/.45	.019/.50	1.63/41.4	1.41/36	.3139–.3145 (7.98–7.99)	.0012–.0025 (.032–.065)	2.10/53.9	1.64/41.8	26	CW
Sedan	.006/.15	.006/.15	1.36/34.5	1.22/31	.3143–.3149 (7.98–8.00)	.0008–.0021 (.022–.055)	1.97/50	1.54/39.2	25	CW
Special	.017	.019	1.63	1.41	.3139–.3145	.0012–.0025	2.10	1.64	N.A.	CW
Sport Coupe Sport Spyder	.018	.020	N.A.	N.A.	N.A.	N.A.	N.A.	N.A.	N.A.	N.A.
	.006/.15	.006/.15	.94/24.2	.87/22.2	.2750–.2756 (6.98–7.00)	.0008–.002 (.022–.055)	2.0/51.7	None	4	CW
Sedan	.006/.15	.006/.15	1.06/27	.98/25	.2750–.2756 (6.98–7.00)	.0009–.0022 (.022–.055)	1.71/43.4	None	16	CCW
Coupe Spider	.006/.15	.008/.20	1.14/29	1.02/26	.2750–.2756 (6.98–7.00)	.0012–.0025 (.03–.06)	1.71/43.4	1.47/37.3	25	CCW
Racer Sport Racer Sport Spyder Sport Coupe	.006	.008	1.14	1.02	.2750–.2756	.0012–.0025	1.71	1.47	N.A.	CCW
0/D/R	.004/.10	.004/.10	1.26/32	1.18/30	.3142–.3149 (7.98–8.00)	.0009–.0021 (.022–.055)	1.84/46.9	1.59/40.2	16	CW
0	.008/.20	.010/.25	1.38/35	1.24/31	.3144–.3150 (7.98–8.00)	.0008–.0021 (.022–.055)	1.97/50	1.59/40.2	25	CW
0S	.012/.30	.014/.35	1.59/40.5	1.44/36.5	.3139–.3146 (7.97–7.99)	.0004–.0016 (.010–.040)	1.71/43.4	1.43/36.5	28	CW

Distributor Advance Characteristics

Model	Distributor Identification	Centrifugal Advance°			Vacuum Advance°			Vacuum Retard		
		Start Degrees @ rpm	Intermediate Degrees @ rpm	End Degrees @ rpm	Start Degrees @ in. Hg.	Intermediate Degrees @ in. Hg.	End Degrees @ in. Hg.	Start Degrees @ in. Hg.	Intermediate Degrees @ in. Hg.	End Degrees @ in. Hg.
124 Spider 124 Coupe	Marelli S124A	0 @ 1,000	13 @ 2,500	22–26 @ 4,300	—	—	—	—	—	—
124 Sedan Station Wagon	N.A.	0 @ 1,000	21 @ 2,500	28–32 @ 3,600	—	—	—	—	—	—
124 Special Station Wagon	N.A.	0 @ 1,000	21 @ 2,500	28–32 @ 3,600	—	—	—	—	—	—
124 Sport Coupe Sport Spyder	N.A.	N.A.	N.A.	N.A.	—	—	—	—	—	—
600 Sedan Multipla	N.A.	0 @ 1,600	20 @ 3,200	28–32 @ 4,000	N.A.	N.A.	11 @[1] 11.8	—	—	—
600D Sedan Multipla	N.A.	0 @ 1,600	20 @ 3,200	28–32 @ 4,000	N.A.	N.A.	13 @ 7.87	—	—	—
850 Sedan Coupe Spyder Family	Marelli S110B Marelli S110C	0 @ 1,000	19 @ 3,000	26–30 @ 4,800	N.A.[2]	N.A.[2]	N.A.[2]	—	—	—
850 Racer Sport Racer Sport Spyder Sport Coupe	N.A.	0 @ 900	29 @ 3,000	36–40 @ 4,600	N.A.	N.A.	N.A.	—	—	—
1100, 1100D, 1100R	N.A.	0 @ 800	17 @ 1,500	28–32 @ 2,850	—	—	—	—	—	—
1500 Cabriolet	N.A.	0 @ 800	16 @ 2,500	21 @ 3,900	N.A.	N.A.	15°[3]	—	—	—
1600S	N.A.	N.A.	N.A.	330[4]	—	—	—	—	—	—

1 — 20° from engine number 758493 (Sedan) and engine number 573196 (Multipla)
2 — 10°-16°—Vacuum advance discontinued from engine number 573196
3 — In./Hg, Not Available
4 — Rpm Not Available
° — Crankshaft degrees and crankshaft rpm

Carburetor Specifications

Model	Carburetor Type	Bore (In./MM.) Pri-mary	Second-ary	Venturi (In./MM.) Pri-mary	Second-ary	Main Jet (In./MM.) Pri-mary	Second-ary	Idle Jet (In./MM.) Pri-mary	Second-ary	Main Air Metering Jet (In./MM.) Pri-mary	Second-ary	Idle Air Metering Jet (In./MM.) Pri-mary	Second-ary	Acceler-ator Pump Jet (In./MM.)	Starting Jet (In./MM.) Pri-mary	Second-ary	Float Level (In./MM.) (Distance from cover w/Gasket)
124 Coupe, Spider	Weber 26134DHSA	1.023/26	1.338/34	.905/23	1.062/27	.047/1.20	.054/1.40	.018/.45	.027/.70	.070/1.80	.059/1.50	.063/1.60	.027/.70	.020/.50	.047/1.20	.070/1.80	.2362±.0098 6±.25
124 Sedan Station Wagon	Weber 32DHSA	1.259/32	1.259/32	.905/23	.905/23	.051/1.30	.051/1.30	.018/.45	.030/.80	.070/1.80	.063/1.60	.067/1.75	.027/.70	.016/.40	.063/1.60	–	.2362±.0098 6±.25
124 Special	Weber 32DHSA1	1.259/32	1.259/32	.905/23	.905/23	.051/1.30	.047/1.20	.018/.45	.031/.80	.083/2.10	.063/1.60	.071/1.80	.027/.70	.016/.40	N.A.	N.A.	2.362±.0098 6±.025
124 Sport Coupe Sport Spyder	Weber 26/34 DHSA1	1.023/26	1.338/34	.905/23	1.062/27	.047/1.20	.055/1.40	.018/.45	.027/.70	.071/1.80	.059/1.50	.063/1.60	.027/.70	.020/.50	N.A.	N.A.	2.362±.0098 6±.025
600 Sedan	Weber 26IM	1.024/26	–	.748/19	.177/4.50	.039/1.00①	–	.018/.45	–	.075/1.90	–	–	–	–	.039/1.00	–	.2756/7
	Weber 22IM	.8661/22	–	.6299/16	.177/4.50	.031/.80	–	.018/.45	–	.085/2.15	–	–	–	–	.047/1.20	–	Brass-.2756/7 Nylon-.1969-5
600D Sedan	Weber 28ICP	1.102/28	–	.748/19	–	.039/1.00	–	.0177/.45	–	.075/1.90	–	–	–	.016/.40	Use Butterfly Choke		.2756/7
	Solex C28PIB-2	1.102/28	–	.787/20	–	.042/1.07	–	.0157/.40	–	.063/1.60	–	–	–	.0197/.50	.039/1.00	–	.2756/7
850 Sedan	Weber or Holley 30ICF7	1.181/30	–	.866/22	–	.046/1.17	–	.016/.40	–	.055/1.40	–	–	–	.020/.50	Use Butterfly Choke		.2756/7
	Solex C30PIB4	1.181/30	–	.866/22	–	.043/1.10	–	.016/.40	–	.063/1.60	–	–	–	.020/.50	.039/1.00	–	See Text
850 Coupe Spider	Weber 30DICI②	1.181/30	1.181/30	.827/21	.905/23	.045/1.15	.045/1.15	.018/.45	.020/.50	.073/1.85	.073/1.85	–	–	.016/.40	Use Butterfly Choke		.2362/6
850 Racer Sport Racer Sport Spyder Sport Coupe	Weber 30DICA	1.181/30	1.181/30	.2055	.2055	.045/1.15	.045/1.15	.0157/.40	.0177/.45	.728/1.85	.0669/1.70	.0610/1.55	.0275/.70	.0197/.50	–	–	.2362/6

Carburetor Specifications (cont'd)

Model	Carburetor Type	Bore (In./MM.)		Venturi (In./MM.)		Main Jet (In./MM.)		Idle Jet (In./MM.)		Main Air Metering Jet (In./MM.)		Idle Air Metering Jet (In./MM.)		Accelerator Pump Jet (In./MM.)	Starting Jet (In./MM.)		Float Level (In./MM.) (Distance from cover w/Gasket)
		Primary	Secondary	Primary	Secondary	Primary	Secondary	Primary	Secondary	Primary	Secondary	Primary	Secondary		Primary	Secondary	
1100 Sedan Station Wagon	Weber③ 32IMPE	1.259/32	—	.905/23	—	.049/1.25	—	.018/.45	—	.075/1.90	—	—	—	.0236/.60	.059/1.50	—	.3540/9
	Weber④ 32IMPE4	1.259/32	—	.945/24	—	.047/1.20	—	.018/.45	—	.067/1.70	—	—	—	.0236/.60	.059/1.50	—	.3540/9
	Weber⑤ 36DCD3	1.417/36	1.417/36	.905/23	.905/23	.045/1.15	.045/1.15	.018/.45	—	.078/2.00	.079/2.00	—	—	.0276/.70	.039/1.00	—	.2000/5
	Solex 32PBIC③	1.259/32	—	.945/24	—	.047/1.20	—	.018/.45	—	.075/1.90	—	—	—	.020/.50	.043/1.10	—	.6300/16 (Fuel level)
	Solex 32PBIC④	1.259/32	—	.984/25	—	.045/1.15	—	.018/.45	—	.067/1.70	—	—	—	.016/.40	.049/1.20	—	.6300/16 (Fuel level)
	Solex⑤ C32-35 APATI	1.259/32	1.380/35	.866/22	.905/23	.045/1.15	NA	.018/.45	—	NA	NA	—	—	.020/.50	.040/1.10	—	.2150/5.5
1100R Sedan Station Wagon	Solex 32PHH/5	1.259/32	1.259/32	.866/22	.866/22	.041/1.05	.041/1.05	.016/.40	.016/.40	.071/1.80	.071/1.80	.063/1.60	.063/1.60	.024/.60	.049/1.25		Must use gauge A.95127
1500 Cabriolet	Weber 34DCHD4	1.339/34	1.339/34	.984/25	.984/25	.051/1.30	.055/1.40	.020/.50	.027/.70	.088/2.25	.090/2.30	.075/1.90	—	.027/.70	.059/1.50		.197–.216/5–5.5 (Without gasket)
1600S Cabriolet	Weber 34DCS2/4	1.339/34	1.339/34	.866/22	.866/22	.041/1.05	.041/1.05	.016/.40	.016/.40	.079/2.00	.079/2.00	.031/.80	.031/.80	.016/.40	.031/.80		.256/6.5 (Without gasket)

① After engine #876483—.038"/.97 mm.
② Super feeder—.043"/1.10 mm.
③ 103D engine.
④ 103G engine.
⑤ 103H engine.

Torque Specifications

Model	Cylinder Head bolts (ft. lbs.)	Main Bearing bolts (ft. lbs.)	Rod Bearing bolts (ft. lbs.)	Crankshaft Balancer bolt (or nut) (ft. lbs.)	Flywheel to Crankshaft bolts (ft. lbs.)	Manifold (ft. lbs.)	
						Intake	Exhaust
124 Spyder Coupe Sedan	48.5	59.3	37.6	88.3	58.6	18.1	18.1
124 Special	N.A.	N.A.	N.A.	N.A.	N.A.	N.A.	N.A.
124 Sport Coupe Sport Spyder	N.A.	N.A.	N.A.	N.A.	N.A.	N.A.	N.A.
600 600D	21.7	44.8	16.0	72.3	28.9	N.A.	N.A.
850 Sedan, Idroconvert Coupe, Spyder	(1) 21.7 (2) 36.2	44.8	25.3	72.3	28.9	N.A.	N.A.
850 Racer Sport Racer Sport Spyder Sport Coupe	28.9	44.8	25.3	72.3	28.9	N.A.	N.A.
1100D 1100R	57.8	44.8	25.3	72.3	57.0	N.A.	N.A.
1500	50.6	76.0	47.7	101.3	57.9	N.A.	N.A.
1600S	65.1	76.0	28.9	N.A.	32.5	N.A.	N.A.

Torque Sequences

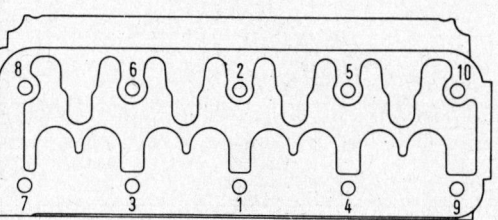

Cylinder head bolt tightening sequence, 124 sedan.

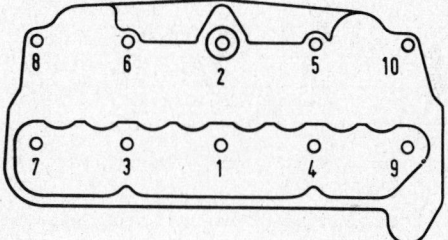

Cylinder head bolt tightening sequence, 600, 850.

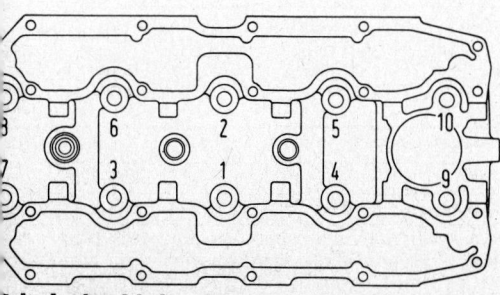

Cylinder head bolt tightening sequence, 124 Coupe and Spider.

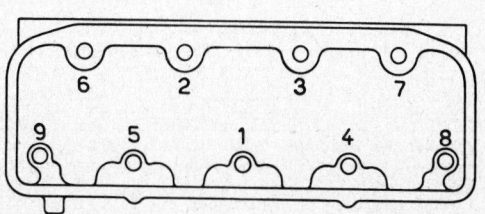

Cylinder head bolt tightening sequence, 1100.

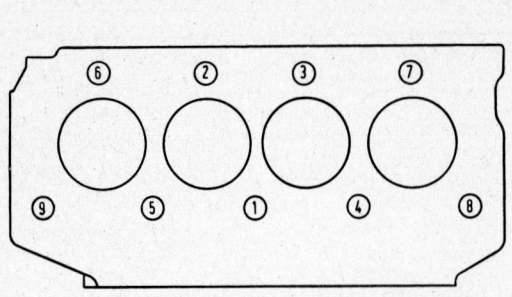

Cylinder head bolt tightening sequence, 1500.

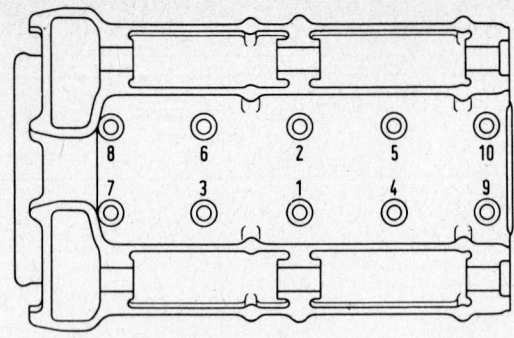

Cylinder head bolt tightening sequence, 1600S.

Electrical Specifications

Model	Battery Cap (Amp.-Hrs.)	Volts/ Ground	Generator Fiat No.	Brush Tension (Oz./KG.)	Alternator Fiat No.	Regulator Fiat No.	Starter Fiat No.	Brush Tension (Oz./KG.)
124 Spider, Coupe	48/60①	12/N	D115/12/28/4E①	25/.7	A12M124/ 12/42M②	GN2/12/28①	E100–1.3–12②	49/1.4
124 Special	48	12/N	N.A.	N.A.	N.A.	N.A.	N.A.	N.A.
124 Sport Coupe Sport Spyder	60	12/N	—	—	A12M124 12/42M	RC1/12B	E100– 1.3/12	N.A.
124 Sedan	48	12/N	D90/12/16/3E	21/.6	—	GN2/12/16	E84–0.8/12	49/1.4
600	32	12/N	D90/12/16/3E③	21/.6	—	GN1/12/16	B76–0.5/12S	40/1.1
600D	36	12/N	D90/12/16/3E	21/.6	—	GN1/12/16	E76–0.5/12S	40/1.1
850, 1100	36/48	12/N	D90/12/16/3CS	21/.6	—	GN2/12/16	E76–0.5/12S	40/1.1
1500, 1600S	48	12/N	D115/12/28/4	25/.7	—	GN2/12/16	E100–1.5/12	40/1.1
850 Racer Sport Racer Sport Spyder Sport Coupe	48	12/N	D90/12/16 3CS	21.6	—	GN2/12/16	E70– 0.5/12	N.A.

① For Spiders with parts serial No. up to 1591914; regulator: Fiat RC1/12B.
② For Spiders with parts serial No. after 1591914.
③ From engine No. 573516.

Electrical Specifications (cont'd)

Fiat Type No.	CUTOUT RELAY Cut-in Volts	Reverse Amps.	Point Gap (In./MM.)	Air Gap Points Closed (In./MM.)	VOLTAGE RELAY Reg. Volts	Air Gap (In./MM.)	CURRENT RELAY Reg. Amps.	Air Gap (In./MM.)	Reg. Resistor (Ohms)	Series Resistor (Ohm
GN2/12/16	12.2–13	< 16	.017/.45	.013/.35	13.9–14.5	.038/.99	15–17	.038/.99	80–90	16–
GN1/12/16	12.4–12.8	< 16	.017/.45	.013/.35	13.9–14.5	.038/.99	15.5–16.5	.038/.99	102–108	—
GN2/12/28	12.4–12.8	< 16	.017/.45	.013/.35	13.9–14.5	.038/.99	26.5–29.5	.038/.99	98.5–111.5	16–
A/4–180/12	12.4–12.8	< 10	.017/.45	.013/.35	14.2–14.8	.038/.99	12.5–13.5	.038/.99	102–108	—
RC1/12B	12.4– 12.8	16	.017	.013	13.9– 14.5	.038 .043	26.5– 29.5	.038– .043	95.5– 111.5	16– 18

Capacities and Pressures

Model	Crankcase Capacity (Pts.)	Oil Pressure (Psi)	Transmission Capacity (Pts.)	SAE Viscosity	Rear Axle Capacity (Pts.)	SAE Viscosity	Fuel Tank Capacity (Gals.)	Cooling Capacity (Pts.)	Tire Pressures (Psi) Front	Rear
124 Spider, Coupe	8	50–71	3.5	90	1.5	90	12	16	23	23
124 Sedan	8	64–86	2.9	90	1.5	90	10*	16	21	25
124 Special	8	N.A.	N.A.	90	1.5	90	10.3	16	N.A.	N.A.
124 Sport Coupe Sport Spyder	N.A.	N.A.	N.A.	90	N.A.	N.A.	11 12	N.A.	N.A.	N.A.
600/D	6.2	36–43	3.2	90	—	—	7	9	14 (Sedan) 24 (Multipla)	23 28
850	7	43–57	4.4	90	—	—	8	16	16	26
850 Racer Sport Racer Sport Coupe Sport Spyder	N.A.	N.A.	4.4	90	—	—	8	N.A.	N.A.	N.A.
1100 Sedan	7	36–43	2.3	90	1.4	90	10	11	21	24
1100 Wagon	7	36–43	2.3	90	1.4	90	8	11	20	28
1100R	7	35.5	2.3	90	1.4	90	9.5	11	21	26
1500	7	57–64	3.4	90	2	90	10	12	23	24
1600S	12.5	85.3	3.4	90	2	90	12	12	24	24

Idroconvert (automatic) transmission capacity: 1.06 gals.
*12 for the Station Wagon.

Brake Specifications

Model	Type Front	Rear	Brake Cylinder Bore Master Cylinder (in.)	Wheel Cylinder (in.) Front	Rear	Brake Drum or Disc Diameter (in.) Front	Rear
124 Spyder, Coupe	Disc	Disc	.75	N.A.	N.A.	8.94	8.94
124 Sedan, Station Wagon	Disc	Disc	.75	1.375	1.375	8.93	8.93
124 Special	Disc	Disc	N.A.	N.A.	N.A.	N.A.	N.A.
124 Sport Coupe Sport Spyder	Disc	Disc	.75	1.875	1.375	8.94	8.94
600 Sedan 600 Multipla	Drum Drum	Drum Drum	.75 1.00	.75 1.125	.75 .75	7.29 8.67	7.29 8.67
600D Sedan 600D Multipla	Drum Drum	Drum Drum	.75 1.00	.875 1.125	.75 .75	7.29 8.67	7.29 8.67
850 Sedan	Drum	Drum	.75	.875	.75	7.29	7.29
850 Coupe 850 Spyder	Disc	Drum	.75	1.772	.75	8.898	7.29
850 Family	Drum	Drum	1.00	1.125	.75	8.672	8.672
850 Racer Sport Racer Sport Spyder	Disc	Drum	.75	1.125	.75	8.898	7.29
850 Sport Coupe	Disc	Drum	N.A.	N.A.	N.A.	N.A.	N.A.
1100, 1100D	Drum	Drum	1.00	1.125	.875	9.85	9.85
1100R Sedan	Disc	Drum	.75	1.875	.75	8.94	9.84
1500 Cabriolet	Disc	Drum	.875	1.344	.75	9.844	9.844
1600S Cabriolet	Disc	Disc	.875	1.50	1.188	10.625	10.625

Wheel Alignment Specifications

Model	Caster	Camber	Toe-In	King Pin Inclination	Capacity Load
124 Spider, Coupe	3.5° −10′ +30′	0.5° ±20′	.118″ ±.039″ (3 ± 1 mm.)	6°	2 persons + 44 lbs (20kg.)
124 Coupe	3.5° −10′ +30′	0.5° ±20′	.07 −.15″ (2–4 mm.)	6°	3 persons + 65 lbs. (30kg.)
124 Sedan	3.5° −10′ +30′	0.5° ±20′	.07 −.15″ (2–4 mm.)	6°	4 persons + 110 lbs. (50kg.)
124 Special	N.A.	N.A.	N.A.	N.A.	N.A.
124 Sport Coupe	3.5° −10′ +30′	0.5° −10′ +30′	.07 −.15″	N.A.	4 persons + 705 lbs.
124 Sport Spyder	3.5° −10′ +30′	0.5° −10′ +30′	.07 −.15″	N.A.	4 persons + 705 lbs.
600	9° ±1°	1° ±15′	0 −.07″ (0–2 mm.)	5.5°	4 persons + 110 lbs. (50kg.)
850	9° ±1°	1° ±15′ (unloaded car)	.23 −.31″ (6–8 mm.) (unloaded car)	4°20′ ±20′	5 persons + 110 lbs. (50kg.)
850 Racer Sport Racer Sport Spyder	9° ±1°	1° ±15′	.07 −.15″	4°20′ ±20′	N.A.
850 Sport Coupe	9° ±1°	1° ±15′	.07 −.15″	4°20′ ±20′	N.A.
1100	2°10′ +10′ −30′	0.5° ±20′	.23 −.36″ (7–9 mm.) (unloaded car)	7°	5 persons + 110 lbs. (50kg.)
1500	2°10′ ±30′	0.5° ±20′	.04 −.12″ (1–3 mm.)	7°	2 persons + 110 lbs. (50kg.)
1600S	1° ±30′	0.5° ±20′	.04 −.12″ (1–3 mm.)	7°	2 persons + 110 lbs. (50kg.)

Fuses and Circuit Breakers

124 SEDAN

Fuse	Amps.	Circuits
1	8	Low oil pressure light, temperature warning light, fuel gauge and reserve warning, wipers, instrument panel, glove compartment light, heater, motor, directionals, stop light
2	16	Interior lights, horns
3	8	LH headlight, low beam
4	8	RH headlight, low beam
5	8	LH headlight, high beam, indicator
6	8	RH headlight, high beam
7	8	LH front parking, indicator, RH rear parking, LH plate light, engine compartment light, luggage compartment light
8	8	RH front parking, LH rear parking, RH plate light

124 SPYDER, COUPE

Fuse	Amps.	Circuits
A	16	Horn, dash, lighter, inspection light
B	8	Engine compartment light, instrument panel, turn signals, stop lights, wipers, ventilation fan
C	8	LH headlight, high beam, high beam indicator light
D	8	RH headlight, high beam
E	8	LH headlight, low beam
F	8	RH headlight, low beam
G	8	LH side light, side light indicator, RH tail light, LH plate light, lighter spotlight, luggage compartment light
H	8	RH front side light, LH tail light, RH plate light
I	8	Oil pressure gauge, low oil pressure light, temperature gauge, fuel gauge and reserve warning light, electric fan clutch, tachometer
L	8	Voltage regulator, alternator field winding

FIAT 299

Fuses and Circuit Breakers (cont'd)

124 SPECIAL

Fuse	Amps	Circuits
N.A.	N.A.	N.A.

124 SPORT SPYDER, 124 SPORT COUPE

Fuse	Amps	Circuits
A	16	Dash lights, horn, interior lights and cigarette lighter
B	8	Engine compartment lights, instrument panel, turn signals and indicators, stop lights, windshield wiper and blower motor
C	8	Left headlight high beam and indicator
D	8	Right high beam
E	8	Left low beam
F	8	Right low beam
G	8	Left side light, side light indicator, right tail light, left license plate light, cigarette lighter spot lamp and trunk light
H	8	Right front side light, left tail light and right license plate light
I	8	Oil pressure gauge and warning light, temperature gauge, fuel gauge and warning light and fan clutch and tachometer
L	8	Voltage regulator and alternator field winding

600

Fuse	Amps	Circuits
1	8	Horn, wipers, rear view mirror
2	8	Directionals, indicator, instrument panel, stop light
3	8	RH headlight, low beam
4	8	LH headlight, low beam
5	8	LH headlight, high beam, RH front parking, LH rear parking, plate light, engine compartment, high beam indicator
6	8	RH headlight, high beam, LH front parking, indicator, RH rear parking

850

Fuse	Amps	Circuits
1	8	Low oil pressure, temperature indicator, fuel gauge and reserve warning, wipers, instrument cluster, electric fan, directionals, stop lights
2	8	Rear view mirror map light, horn
3	8	LH headlight, low beam
4	8	RH headlight, low beam
5	8	LH headlight, high beam, indicator
6	8	RH headlight, high beam
7	8	LH front parking, indicator, RH tail light, LH plate light, engine compartment light
8	8	RH front parking, LH tail light, RH plate light

850 RACER, SPORT RACER, SPORT COUPE, SPORT SPYDER

Fuse	Amps*	Circuits
1	15/54	Oil pressure indicator, temperature indicator, fuel gauge, wiper motor, instrument lights, fan motor, turn signals and indicators and stop lights
2	30	Map light and horn
3	56/b1	Left low beam
4	56/b2	Right side low beam
5	56/a1	Left high beam and high beam indicator
6	56/a2	Right side beam
7	58/1	Left front parking light, parking light indicator, right tail light, left license plate light and engine compartment light
8	58/2	Right front parking light, left tail light and right license plate light

*—All fuses 8 amps.

1100R

Fuse	Amps	Circuits
A	8	Low oil pressure, temperature indicator, fuel gauge and reserve indicator, wipers, instrument panel, electric fan, directional, stop lights
B	8	Courtesy light, horns
C	8	LH headlight, low beam
D	8	RH headlight, low beam
E	8	LH headlight, high beam
F	8	RH headlight, high beam
G	8	LH front parking, indicator, RH rear parking, LH plate light, trunk compartment light
H	8	RH front parking, LH rear parking, RH plate light, engine compartment light

1500, 1600S

Fuse	Amps	Circuits
1	16	Map light, horns, trouble light receptable, lighter, clock
2	8	Fuel gauge and reserve indicator, no-charge indicator, temperature gauge, electric fuel pump, electric fan, temperature indicator and relay switch
3	8	RH headlight, low beam
4	8	LH headlight, low beam
5	8	LH headlight, high beam and indicator
6	8	RH headlight, high beam
7	8	Wiper, heater fan, stop lights, directionals, indicator, instrument panel
8	8	RH parking, LH tail light, RH plate light, engine compartment, lighter spotlight
9	8	LH parking, indicator, RH tail light, LH plate light, trunk light

Light Bulb Specifications

Model	Headlights Low/High	Parking/ Fr. Turn	Side Direc- tionals	Side Markers	Rear Turn	Tail/ Stop	License Plate	Interior	Instrument Panel Lighting	Compart- ments	Indi- cators
124	40/45	20	4	5	20	5/20	5	5	3	3	3
124 Special	40/45	20	4	5	20	5/20	5	5	3	5	3
124 Sport Coupe Sport Spyder	40/45	21	5	4	21	5/21	5	5	3	5	3
600	40/45	5/20	2.5	—	20	5/20	5	3	2.5	5	2.5
850, 1100	40/45	5/20	3	—	20	5/20	5	3	3	5	3
1500, 1600S	40/45	5/20	3	—	20	5/20	5	3	3	5	3
850 Racer Sport Racer Sport Spyder	40/45	5/20	3	—	20	5/20	5	3	3	5	3
850 Sport Coupe	40/45	5/20	3	—	20	5/20	5	3	3	5	3

1. Front direction indicators.
2. Front parking lights.
3. Headlamps (high and low beams).
4. Motorcompressor for electropneumatic horns.
5. Horn control relay switch.
6. Ignition coil.
7. Ignition distributor.
8. Electromagnetic fan switch brush.
9. Electromagnetic fan thermostatic switch.
10. Oil pressure gauge sending unit.
11. Insufficient oil pressure indicator sending unit.
12. Heat gauge thermostatic switch: sends heat gauge pointer to scale end (excessive water temperature) independently of sending unit 17.
13. Alternator.
14. Front side marker lights.
15. Engine compartment lamps.
16. Heat gauge additional resistor.
17. Heat gauge sending unit.
18. Voltage regulator.
19. Battery charge indicator relay.
20. Button switch for electrovalve energizing during fast idle rate adjustments.
21. Electrovalve, exhaust emission control device.
22. Starter motor.
23. Spark plugs.
24. Battery.
25. Switch on clutch pedal for exhaust emission control electropneumatic device.
26. Engine compartment lamps jam switch.
27. Inspection lamp receptacle.
28. Fuses.
29. Stop lights switch.
30. Switch, on the hydraulic circuit, for indicator 55.
31. Windshield washer and wiper foot control.
32. Windshield wiper motor.
33. Windshield wiper intermittent operation cycling switch unit.
34. Flasher, direction indicators.
35. Flasher, indicator 56.
36. Electrofan motor, two-speed.
37. Electrofan motor additional resistor.
38. Outer lighting 3-position switch.
39. Fuel gauge.
40. Fuel reserve indicator.
41. Fuel gauge light.
42. Speedometer light.

43. Parking lights indicator (green).
44. Directional signal arrow tell-tale (green).
45. Headlamp high beam indicator (blue).
46. Insufficient oil pressure indicator (red).
47. Oil pressure gauge light.
48. Oil pressure gauge.
49. Battery charge indicator (red).
50. Engine tachometer.
51. Engine tachometer light.
52. Engine water heat gauge light.
53. Engine water heat gauge.
54. Windshield wiper sweep rate rheostat.
55. Brake system effectiveness and hand brake ON indicator (red).
56. Vehicular hazard warning signal indicator.
57. Panel light rheostatic switch.
58. Jam switches, between doors and pillars, for courtesy lights.
59. Lock switch.
60. Headlamp high/low beam change-over and low beam flashes switch.
61. Direction indicators switch.
62. Windshield wiper control 3-position switch.
63. Electropneumatic horn control button.
64. Electric cigarette lighter (with housing indicator).
65. Vehicular hazard warning signal switch.
66. Electrofan 3-position switch.
67. Courtesy light, with incorporated switch.
68. Rear side marker lights.
69. Switch, on transmission (3rd and 4th gears) for exhaust emission control electropneumatic device.
70. Fuel gauge sending unit.
71. Luggage boot lamp jam switch.
72. Back-up light switch.
73. Switch, on hand brake lever, for indicator 55.
74. Luggage boot lamp.
75. Rear direction indicators.
76. Rear parking and stop lights.
77. Number plate lights.
78. Back-up lamp.

CABLE COLOR CODE

Arancio =	Orange	Giallo =	Yellow	Rosa =	Pink
Azzurro =	Light blue	Grigio =	Grey	Rosso =	Red
Bianco =	White	Marrone =	Brown	Verde =	Green
Blu =	Dark blue	Nero =	Black	Viola =	Violet

124 Sport Spider wiring diagram.

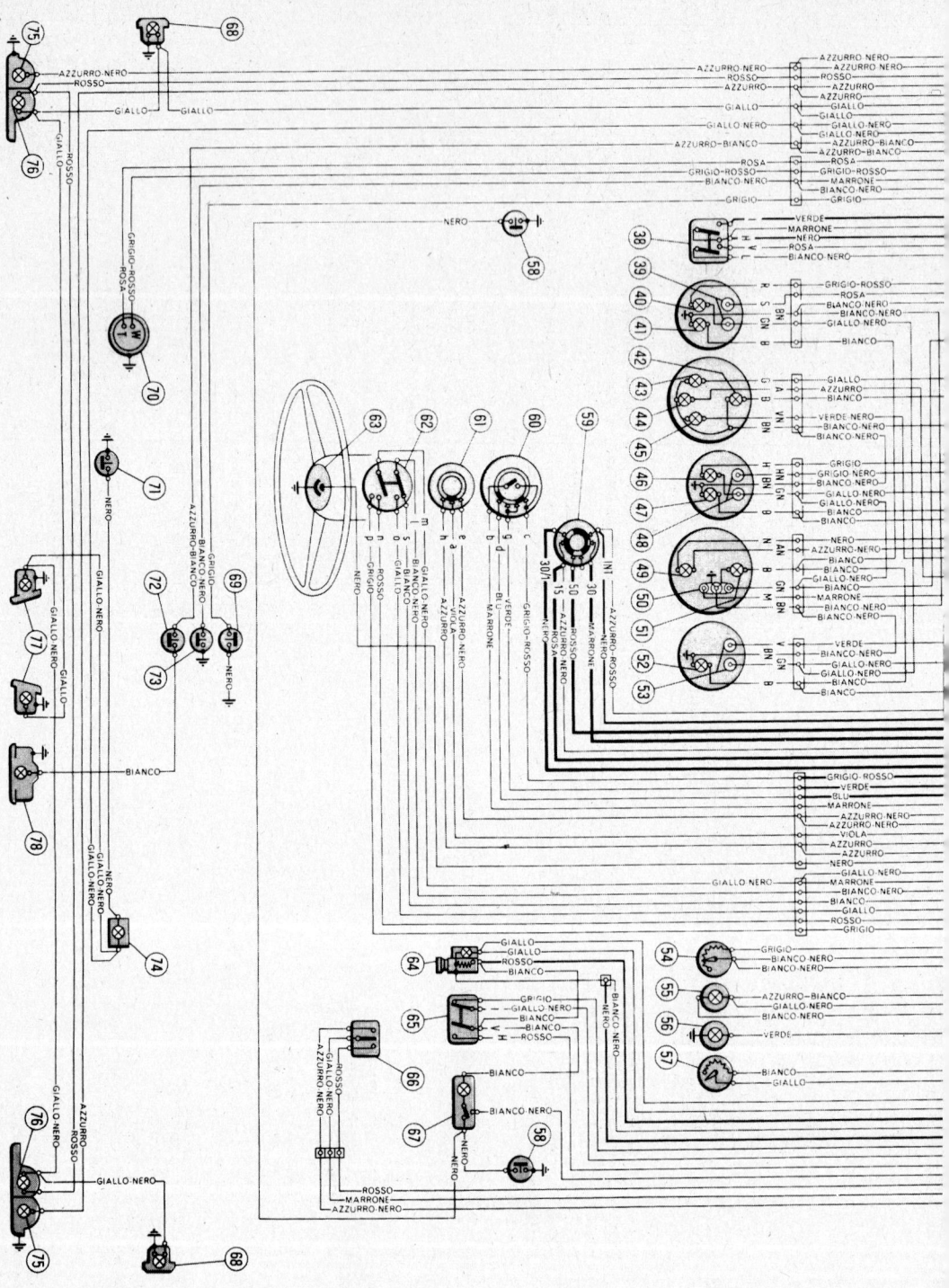

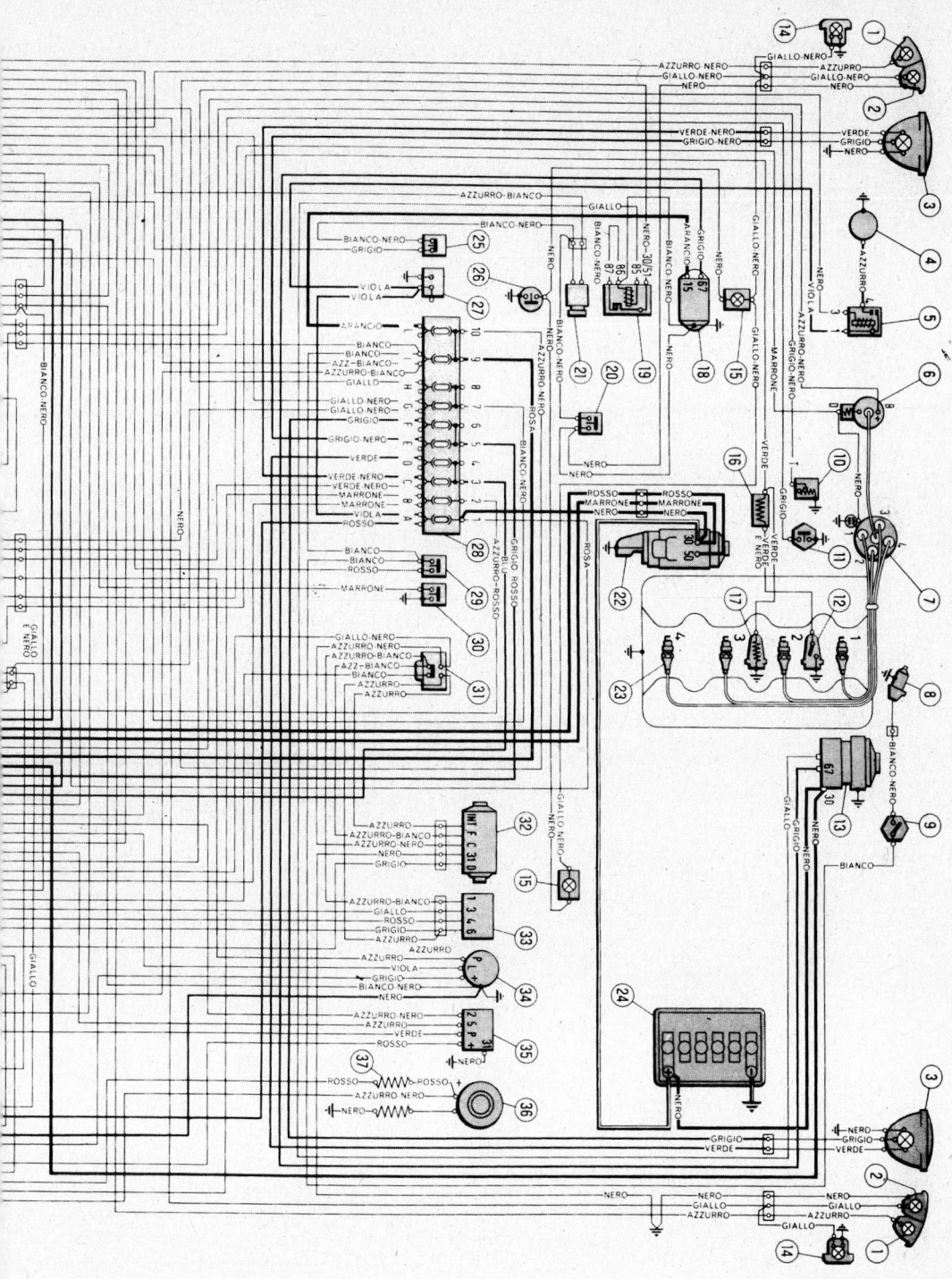

124 Sport Spider wiring diagram.

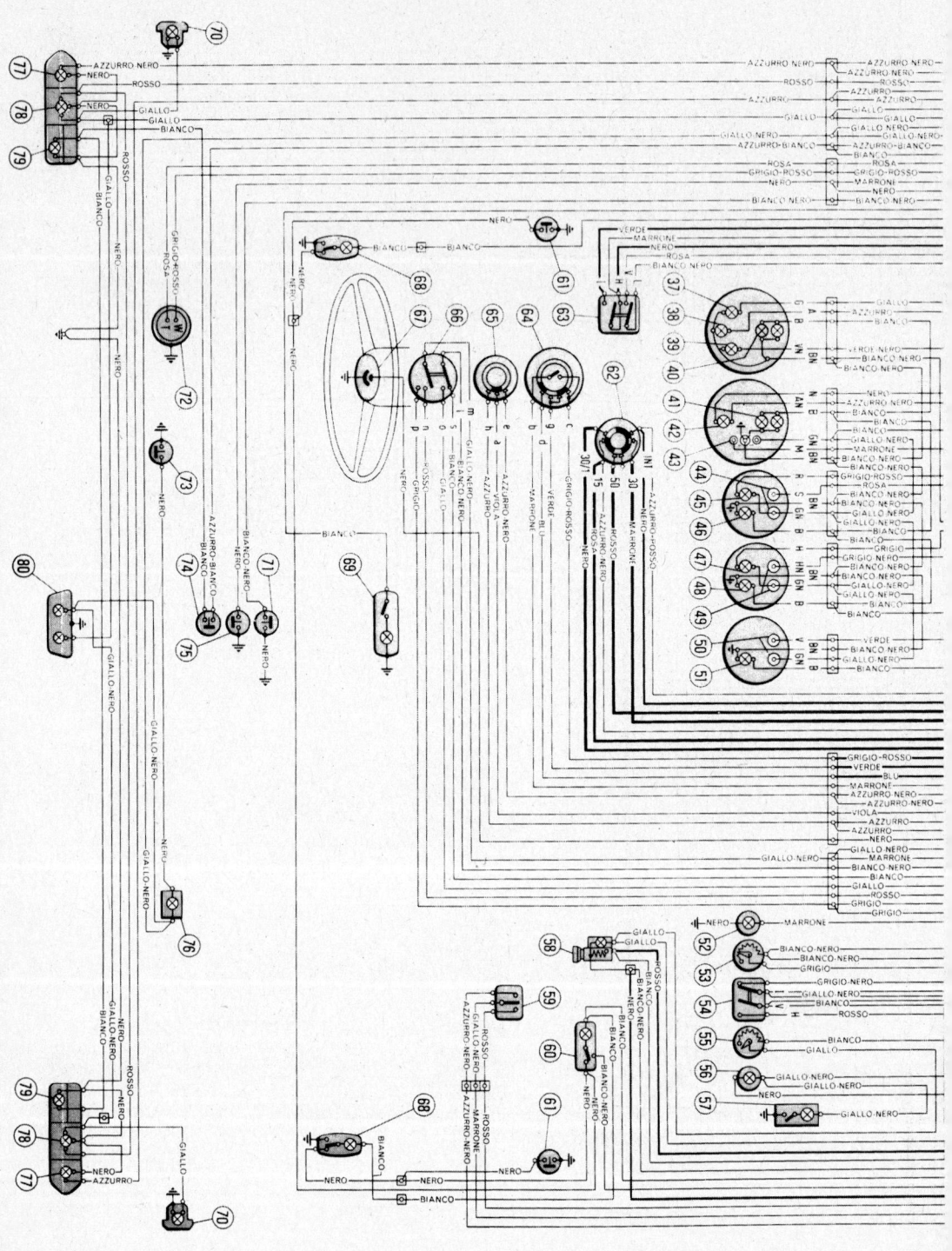

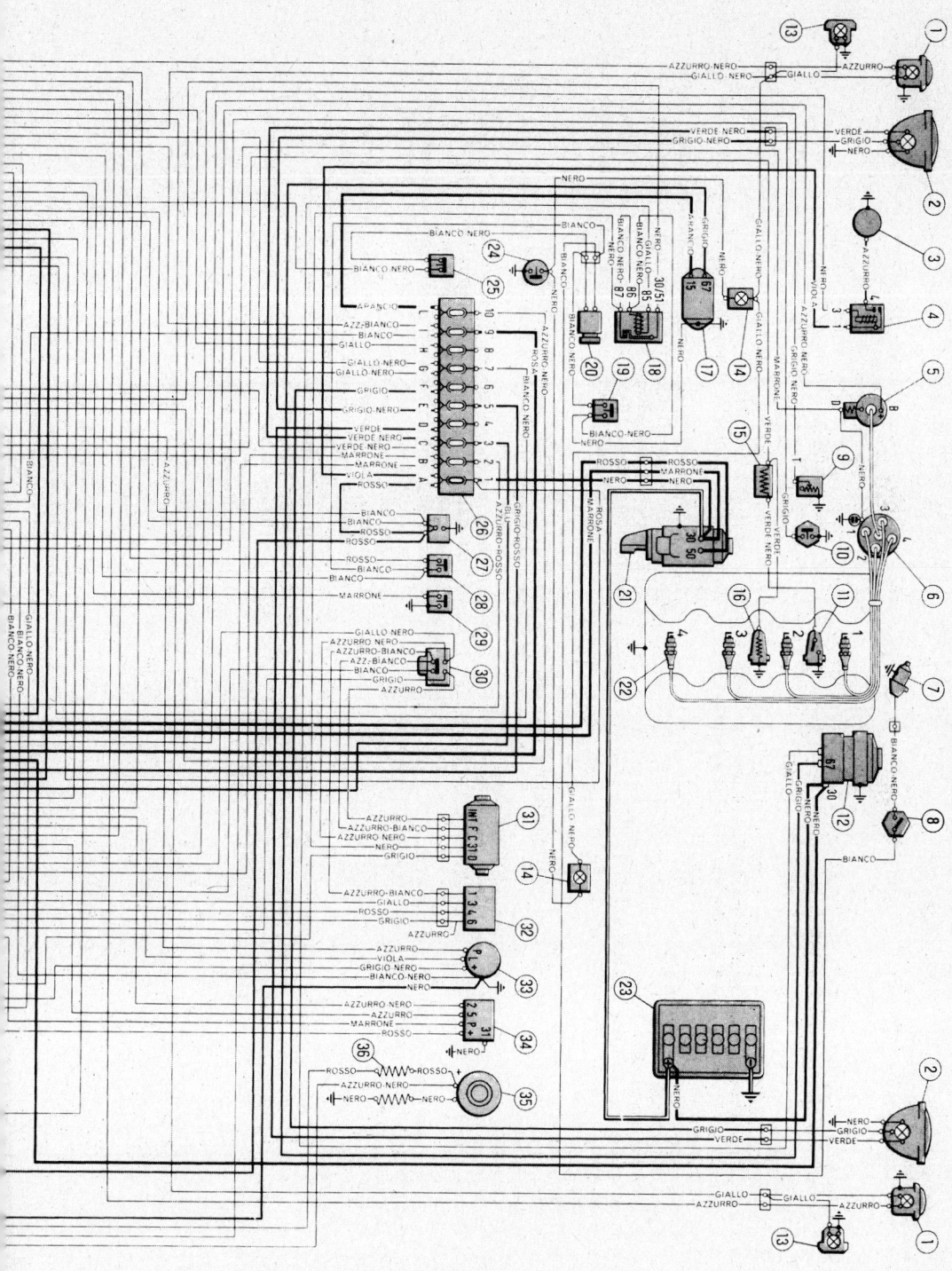

124 Coupe wiring diagram.

1. Front parking and direction indicators.
2. Headlamps (high and low beams).
3. Motorcompressor for electropneumatic horns.
4. Horn control relay switch.
5. Ignition coil.
6. Ignition distributor.
7. Electromagnetic fan switch brush.
8. Electromagnetic fan thermostatic switch.
9. Oil pressure gauge sending unit.
10. Insufficient oil pressure indicator sending unit.
11. Heat gauge thermostatic switch: sends heat gauge pointer to scale end (excessive water temperature) independently of sending unit 16.
12. Alternator.
13. Front side marker lights.
14. Engine compartment lamps.
15. Heat gauge additional resistor.
16. Heat gauge sending unit.
17. Voltage regulator.
18. Battery charge indicator relay.
19. Button switch for electrovalve energizing during fast idle rate adjustments.
20. Electrovalve, exhaust emission control device.
21. Starter motor.
22. Spark plugs.
23. Battery.
24. Engine compartment lamps jam switch.
25. Switch on clutch pedal for exhaust emission control electropneumatic device.
26. Fuses.
27. Inspection lamp receptacle.
28. Stop lights switch.
29. Switch, on the hydraulic circuit, for indicator 56.
30. Windshield washer and wiper foot control.
31. Windshield wiper motor.
32. Windshield wiper intermittent operation cycling switch unit.
33. Flasher, direction indicators.
34. Flasher, indicator 56.
35. Electrofan motor, two-speed.
36. Electrofan motor additional resistor.
37. Parking lights indicator (green).
38. Directional signal arrow tell-tale (green).
39. Headlamp high beam indicator (blue).
40. Speedometer lights.
41. Engine tachometer lights.
42. Battery charge indicator (red).
43. Engine tachometer.

45. Fuel reserve indicator.
46. Fuel gauge light.
47. Insufficient oil pressure indicator (red).
48. Oil pressure gauge light.
49. Oil pressure gauge.
50. Engine water heat gauge.
51. Engine water heat gauge light.
52. Vehicular hazard warning signal indicator.
53. Windshield wiper sweep rate rheostat.
54. Vehicular hazard warning signal switch.
55. Panel light rheostatic switch.
56. Brake system effectiveness and hand brake ON indicator (red).
57. Glove compartment light, with incorporated switch.
58. Electric cigarette lighter (with housing indicator).
59. Electrofan 3-position switch.
60. Courtesy light, front, with incorporated switch.
61. Jam switches, between doors and pillars, for courtesy lights.
62. Lock switch.
63. Outer lighting 3-position switch.
64. Headlamp high/low beam change-over and low beam flashes switch.
65. Direction indicators switch.
66. Windshield wiper control 3-position switch.
67. Electropneumatic horn control button.
68. Courtesy lights, rear, with incorporated switch.
69. Lamp, mirror light, with incorporated switch.
70. Rear side marker lights.
71. Switch, on transmission (3rd and 4th gears) for exhaust emission control electropneumatic device.
72. Fuel gauge sending unit.
73. Luggage compartment lamp jam switch.
74. Back-up light switch.
75. Switch, on hand brake lever, for indicator 56.
76. Luggage compartment lamp.
77. Rear direction indicators.
78. Rear parking and stop lights.
79. Back-up lamps.
80. Number plate lights.

CABLE COLOR CODE

Arancio = **Orange**	Giallo = **Yellow**	Rosa = **Pink**
Azzurro = **Light blue**	Grigio = **Grey**	Rosso = **Red**
Bianco = **White**	Marrone = **Brown**	Verde = **Green**

124 Coupe wiring diagram.

1. Front parking and direction indicator lamps.
2. Headlamps (high and low beams).
3. Horns.
4. Ignition distributor.
5. Spark plugs.
6. Generator.
7. Horn relay switch.
8. Ignition coil.
9. Sending unit, for insufficient oil pressure indicator.
10. Side marker lamps, front (amber).
11. Heat gauge sending unit.
12. Engine compartment lamp, with incorporated switch.
13. Starter.
14. Battery.
15. Electrovalve, exhaust emission control device.
16. Switch, on clutch pedal for exhaust emission control electropneumatic device.
17. Fuses.
18. Switch for indicator 44.
19. Flasher, direction indicators.
20. Stop lights mechanically-operated switch.
21. Windshield wiper motor.
22. Electrofan, two-speed.
23. Vehicular hazard warning signal light flasher.
24. Button switch for electrovalve energizing during fast idle rate adjustments.
25. Generator regulator.
26. Additional resistor for two-speed electrofan motor.
27. Jam switches, between front doors and pillars, for lamps 53.
28. Outer lighting switch.
29. Instrument cluster light switch.
30. Windshield wiper switch.
31. Lock switch.
32. Direction indicators switch.
33. Horn ring.
34. Switch for outer lighting change-over and headlamp flashes.
35. Fuel level gauge.
36. Fuel reserve indicator (red).
37. Insufficient engine oil pressure indicator (red).
38. Generator charge indicator (red).
39. Instrument cluster light.
40. Direction indicators tell-tale (green).
41. Parking lights indicator (green).
42. High beam indicator (blue).
43. Heat gauge.
44. Brake system effectiveness and hand brake ON indicator.
45. Switch for vehicular hazard warning signal lights.
46. Pilot light for vehicular hazard warning signal lights.
47. Electrofan 3-position switch.
48. Glove compartment light, with incorporated jam switch.
49. Switch, on transmission (on 3rd and 4th gear) for exhaust emission control electropneumatic device.
50. Switch, hand brake ON and efficiency check of bulb for indicator 44.
51. Jam switch for back-up lamp.
52. Jam switches, between rear doors and pillars, for lamps 53.
53. Pillar lamps with incorporated switch.
54. Rear side marker lamps (red).
55. Luggage compartment light.
56. Fuel level gauge sending unit.
57. Rear direction indicators.
58. Rear parking and stop lights.
59. Number plate lights.
60. Back up lamp.

NOTE - Mark ▬ means that cable is provided with numbered strip or ferrule.

CABLE COLOR CODE

Azzurro = Blue Grigio = Grey Rosa = Pink
Bianco = White Marrone = Brown Rosso = Red
Giallo = Yellow Nero = Black Verde = Green

124 Sedan and Station Wagon wiring diagram.

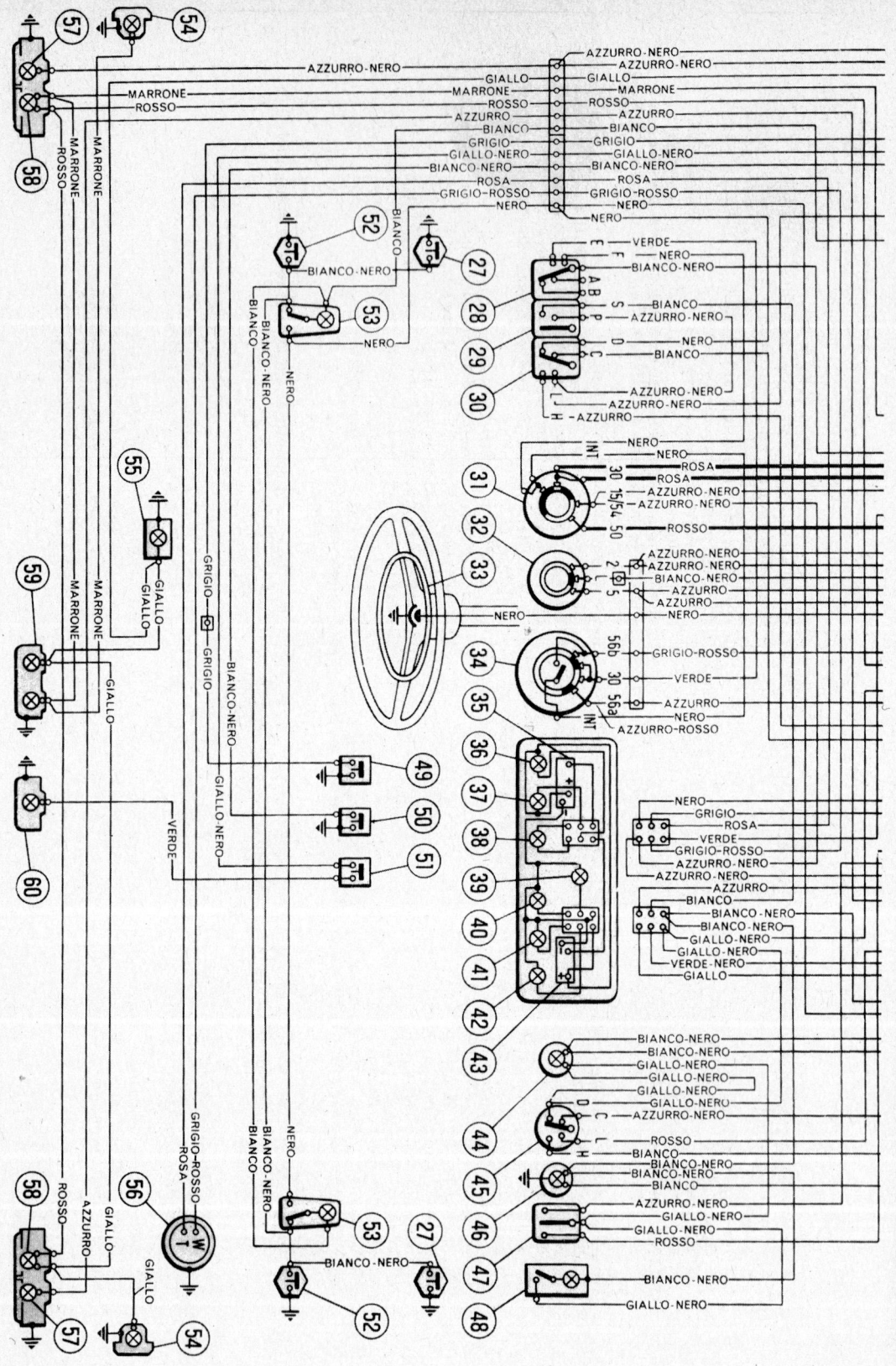

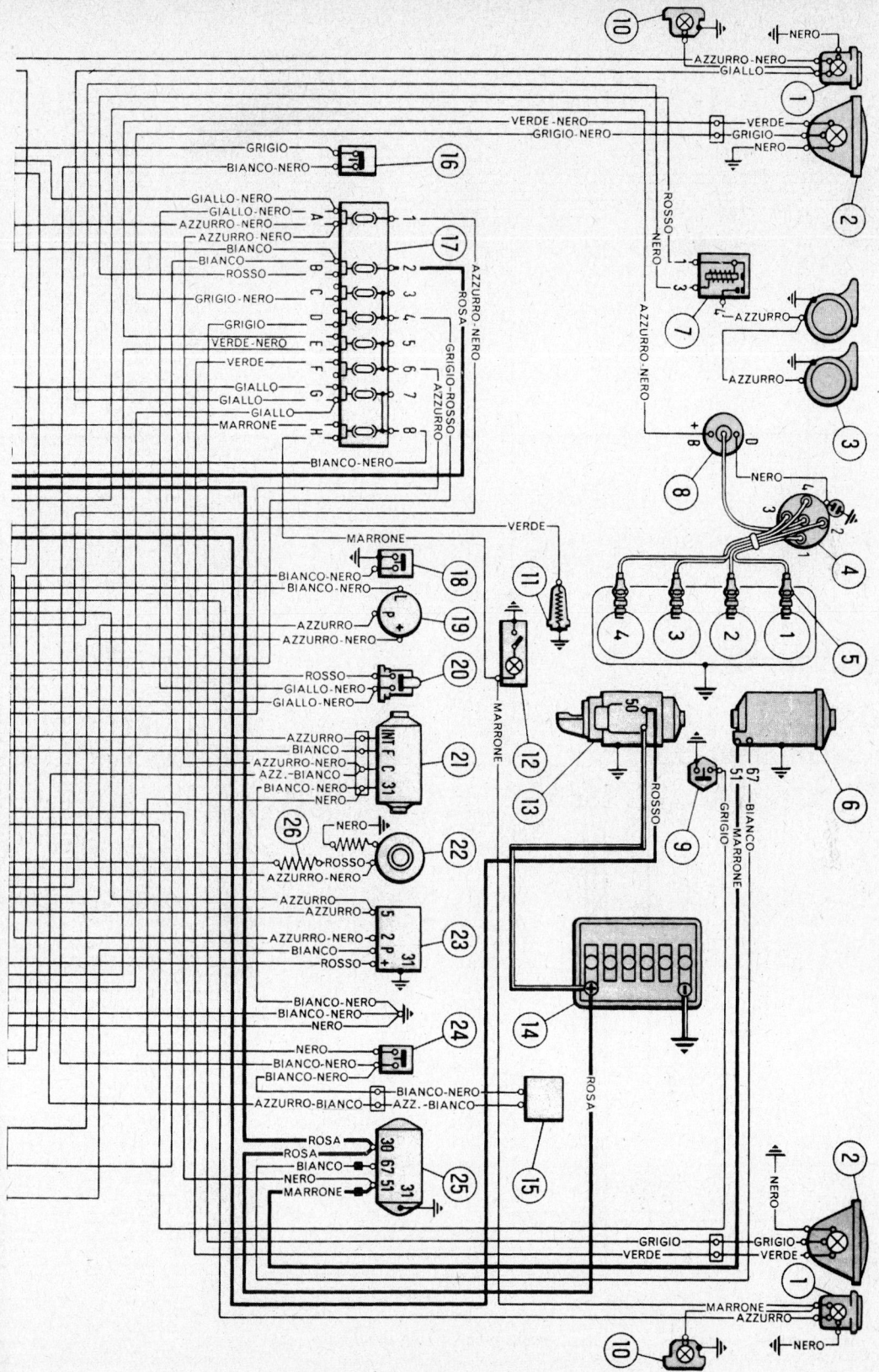

124 Sedan and Station Wagon wiring diagram.

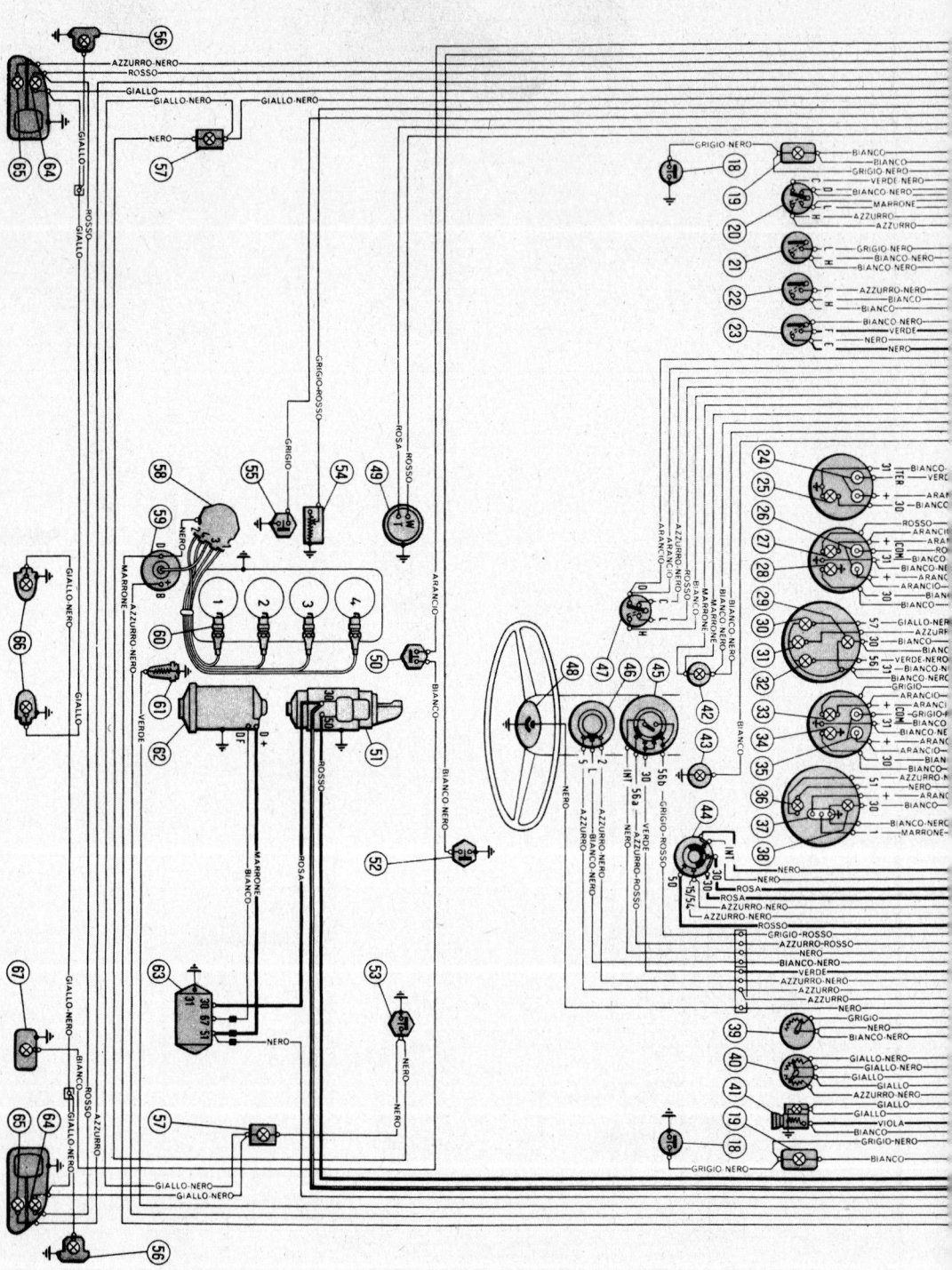

850 Spider wiring diagram.

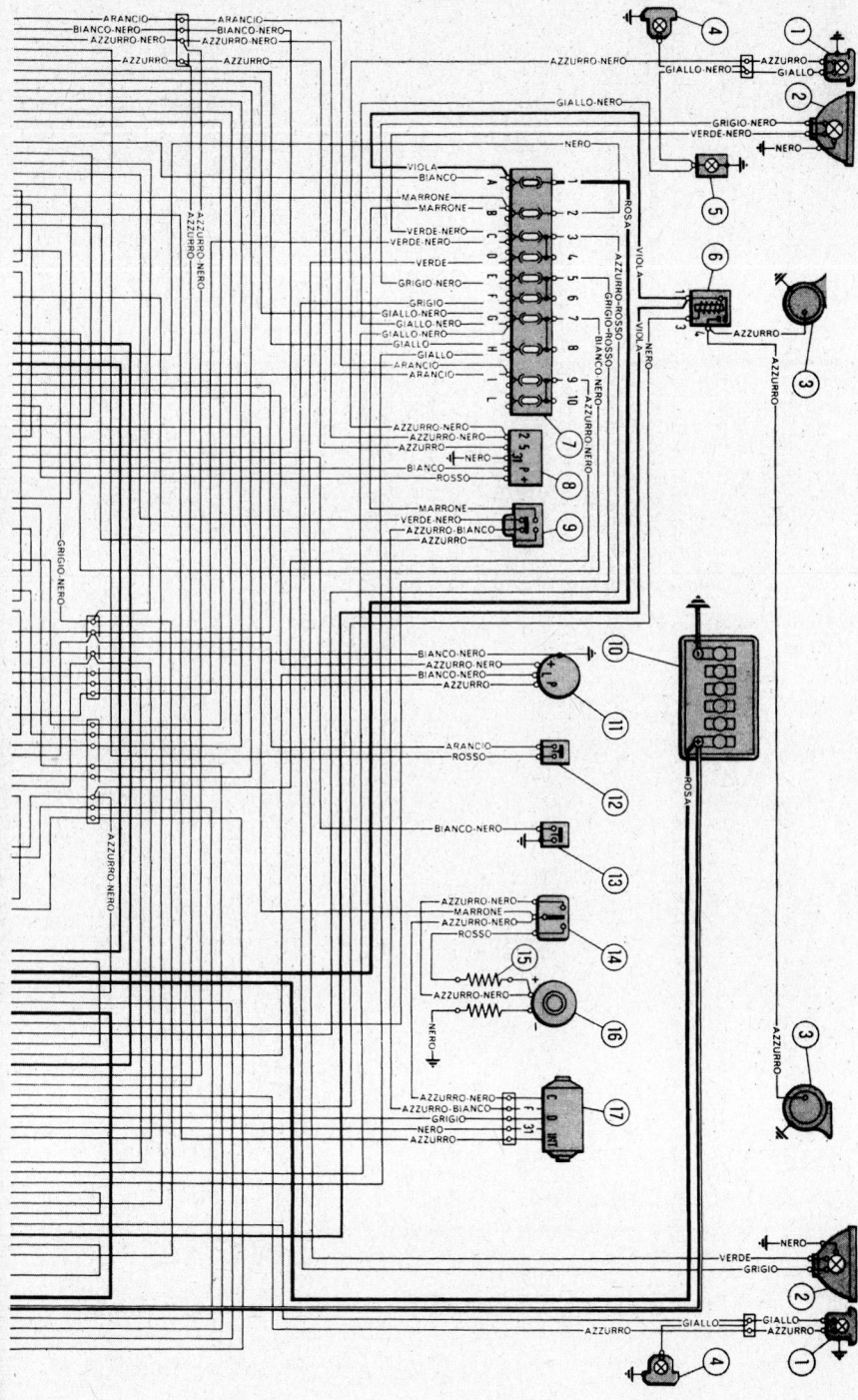

1. Front parking and direction indicators.
2. Headlamps (high and low beams).
3. Horns.
4. Front side marker lights.
5. Front compartment light.
6. Horn relay switch.
7. Fuses.
8. Flasher, vehicular hazard warning signal.
9. Windshield washer and wiper foot control.
10. Battery.
11. Flasher, direction indicators.
12. Stop lights pressure-operated switch.
13. Switch for indicator 42.
14. Switch, 3-position, heating and ventilation fan.
15. Additional resistor, for electrofan motor.
16. Electrofan motor, 2-speed.
17. Windshield wiper motor.
18. Jam switches, between doors and pillars, for courtesy lights.
19. Courtesy lights under facia.
20. Windshield wiper switch.
21. Courtesy lights toggle switch.
22. Instrument cluster light switch.
23. Outer lighting switch.
24. Heat gauge.
25. Heat gauge light.
26. Fuel gauge.
27. Fuel reserve indicator.
28. Fuel gauge light.
29. Speedometer light.
30. Parking lights indicator (green).
31. Direction indicators tell-tale (green).
32. High beam indicator (blue).
33. Insufficient engine oil pressure indicator (red).
34. Oil pressure gauge light.
35. Oil pressure gauge.
36. Generator charge indicator (red).
37. Engine tachometer.
38. Engine tachometer light.
39. Windshield wiper sweep rate adjustment rheostat.

40. Instrument lights and parking light indicator rheostats.
41. Cigarette lighter (w/housing indicator).
42. Indicator, hydraulic service brake effectiveness and hand brake ON.
43. Pilot light, vehicular hazard warning signal ON.
44. Lock switch.
45. Outer lighting change-over and headlamp flashes switch.
46. Direction indicators switch.
47. Switch, vehicular hazard warning signal.
48. Horn button.
49. Fuel gauge sending unit.
50. Jam switch, back up lamp.
51. Starter.
52. Switch, hand brake ON and indicator 42 operation check.
53. Engine compartment lamps jam switch.
54. Sending unit, oil pressure gauge.
55. Sending unit, insufficient oil pressure indicator.
56. Rear side marker lights.
57. Engine compartment lamps.
58. Ignition distributor.
59. Ignition coil.
60. Spark plugs.
61. Sending unit, heat gauge.
62. Generator.
63. Generator regulator.
64. Rear parking and stop lights.
65. Rear direction indicators.
66. Number plate lights.
67. Back up lamp.
NOTE - Mark ▬ means that cable is provided with numbered strip or ferrule.

CABLE COLOR CODE

Arancio = Orange	Giallo = Yellow	Nero = Black	
Azzurro = Blue	Grigio = Grey	Rosa = Pink	
Bianco = White	Marrone = Brown	Rosso = Red	
	Verde = Green	INT	Switch
	Viola = Violet	COM	
		TERM = Heat gauge	

850 Spider wiring diagram.

1. Front parking and direction indicator lamps.
2. Headlamps (high and low beams).
3. Horns.
4. Battery.
5. Horn relay switch.
6. Front side marker lights (amber).
7. Fuses.
8. Flasher, vehicular hazard warning signal.
9. Switch, for indicator 34.
10. Stop lights pressure-operated switch.
11. Flasher, direction indicators.
12. Electrofan, 3-position switch.
13. Electrofan motor, 2-speed.
14. Windshield wiper motor.
15. Additional resistor for electrofan motor.
16. Outer lighting switch.
17. Instrument cluster light switch.
18. Windshield wiper switch.
19. Connectors, electrical, on instrument cluster.
20. Instrument cluster lights.
21. Parking lights indicator (green).
22. High beam indicator (blue).
23. Insufficient engine oil pressure indicator (red).
24. Generator charge indicator (red).
25. Direction indicators arrow tell-tale (green).
26. Fuel reserve indicator (red).
27. Fuel gauge.
28. Heat gauge.
29. Cable for tachometer.
30. Courtesy light, with toggle switch.
31. Lock switch.
32. Switch, vehicular hazard warning signal.
33. Pilot light, vehicular hazard warning signal ON.

34. Indicator, hydraulic service brake effectiveness and hand brake ON.
35. Outer lighting change-over and headlamp flashes switch.
36. Direction indicators switch.
37. Horn button.
38. Jam switches, between doors and pillars, for courtesy light.
39. Fuel gauge sending unit.
40. Jam switch, back up lamp.
41. Spark plugs.
42. Starter with solenoid switch.
43. Switch, hand brake ON and indicator 34 operation check.
44. Rear side marker lights.
45. Sending unit, for insufficient oil pressure indicator.
46. Thermostatic sending unit for heat gauge.
47. Ignition distributor.
48. Ignition coil.
49. Generator.
50. Engine compartment lamp w/incorporated switch.
51. Generator regulator.
52. Rear direction indicators.
53. Rear parking and stop lights.
54. Number plate lights.
55. Back up lamp.

NOTE - Mark ▬ means that cable is provided with numbered strip or ferrule.

CABLE COLOR CODE

Azzurro	= Blue	Rosa	= Pink	Grigio	= Grey
Bianco	= White	Rosso	= Red	Marrone	= Brown
Giallo	= Yellow	Verde	= Green	Nero	= Black
				INT	= Switch

850 Coupe wiring diagram.

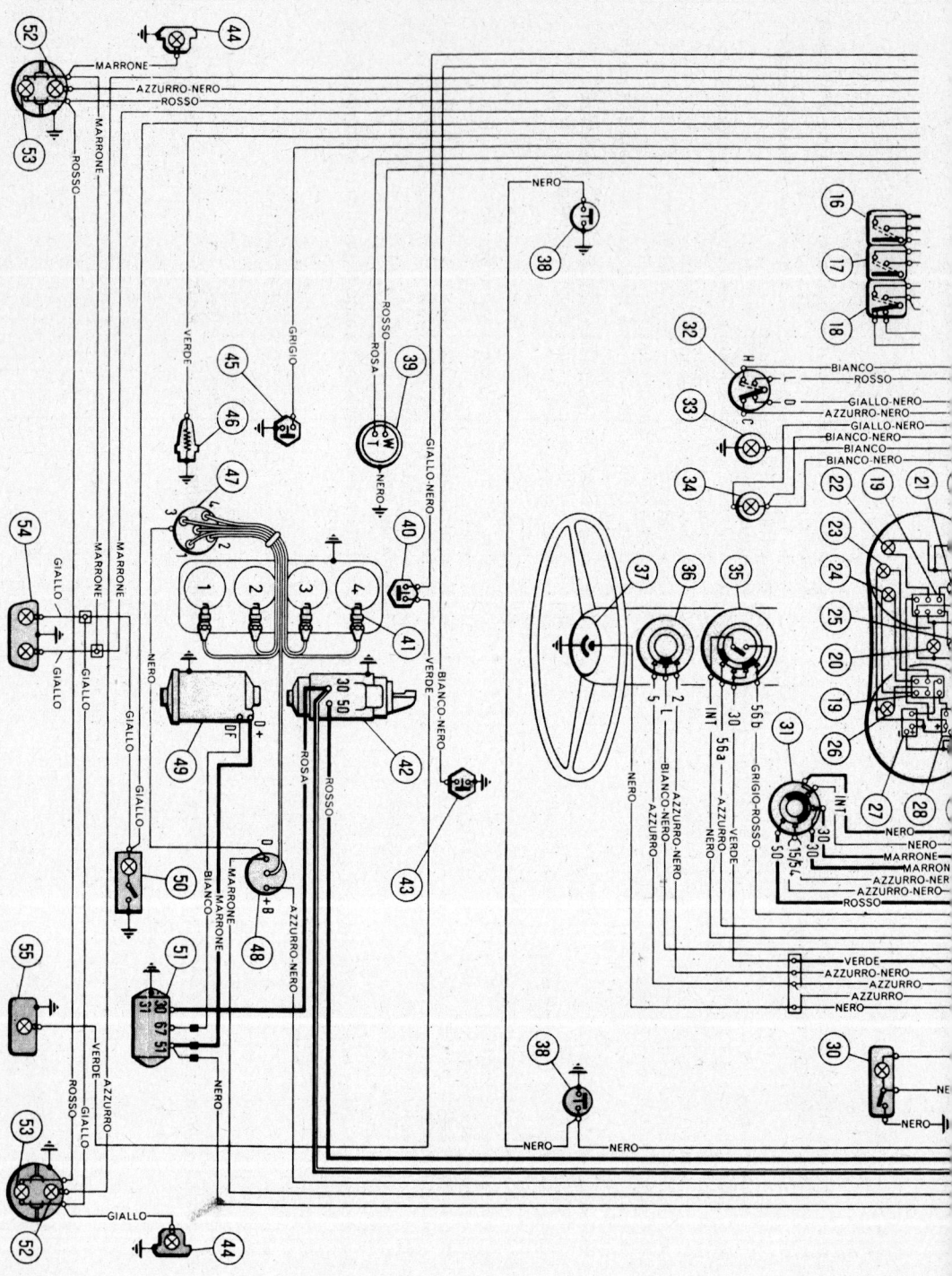

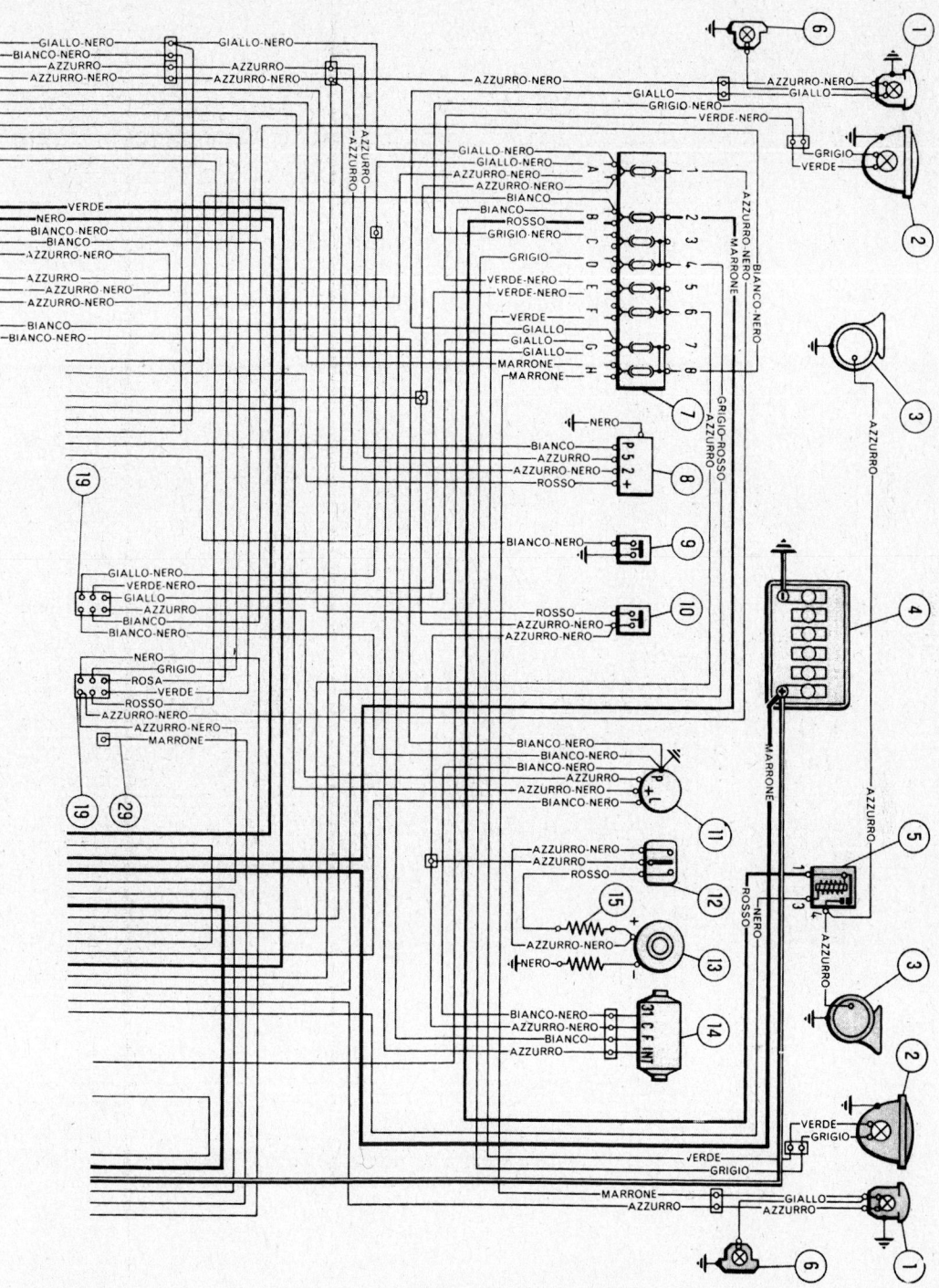

850 Coupe wiring diagram.

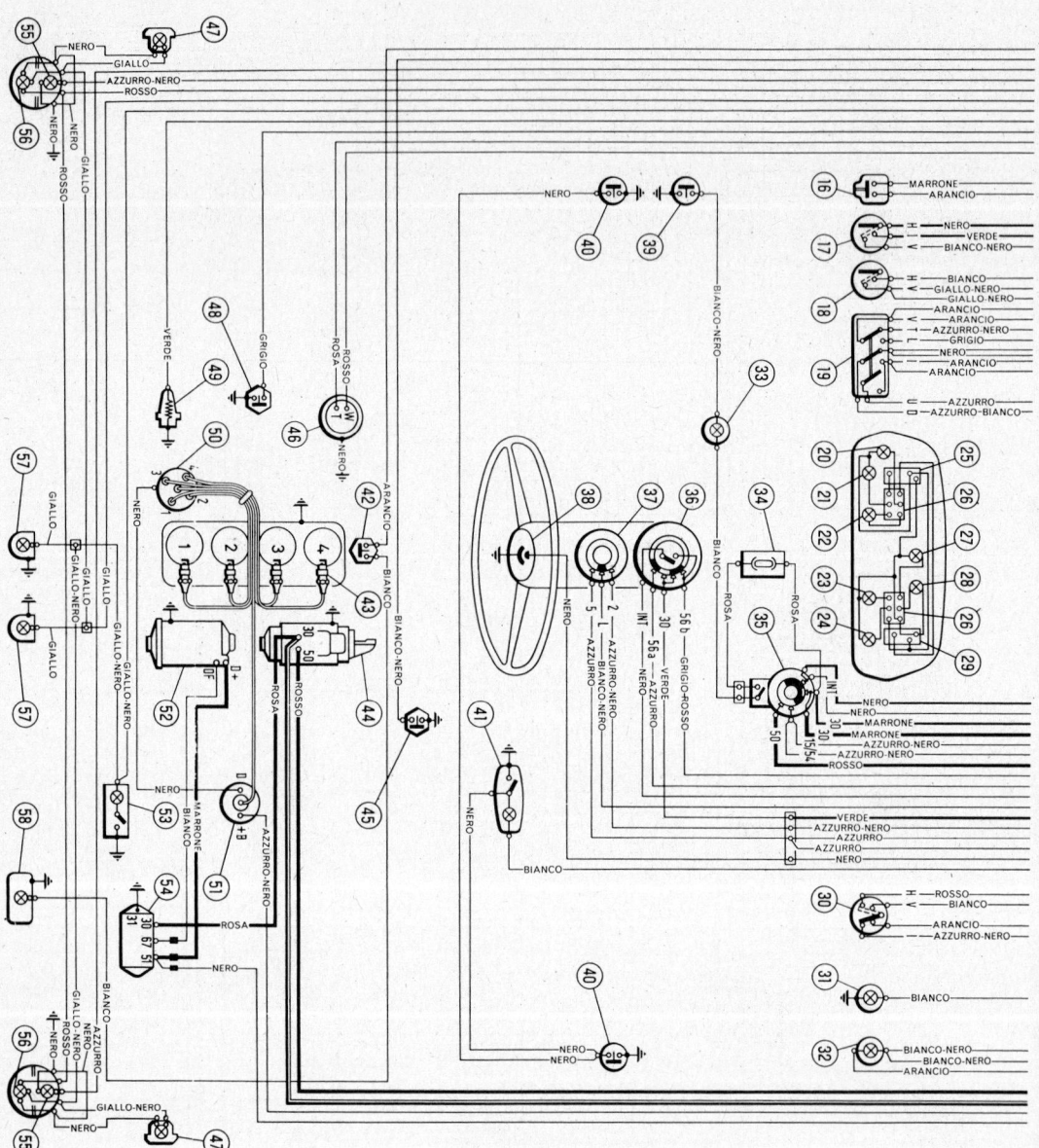

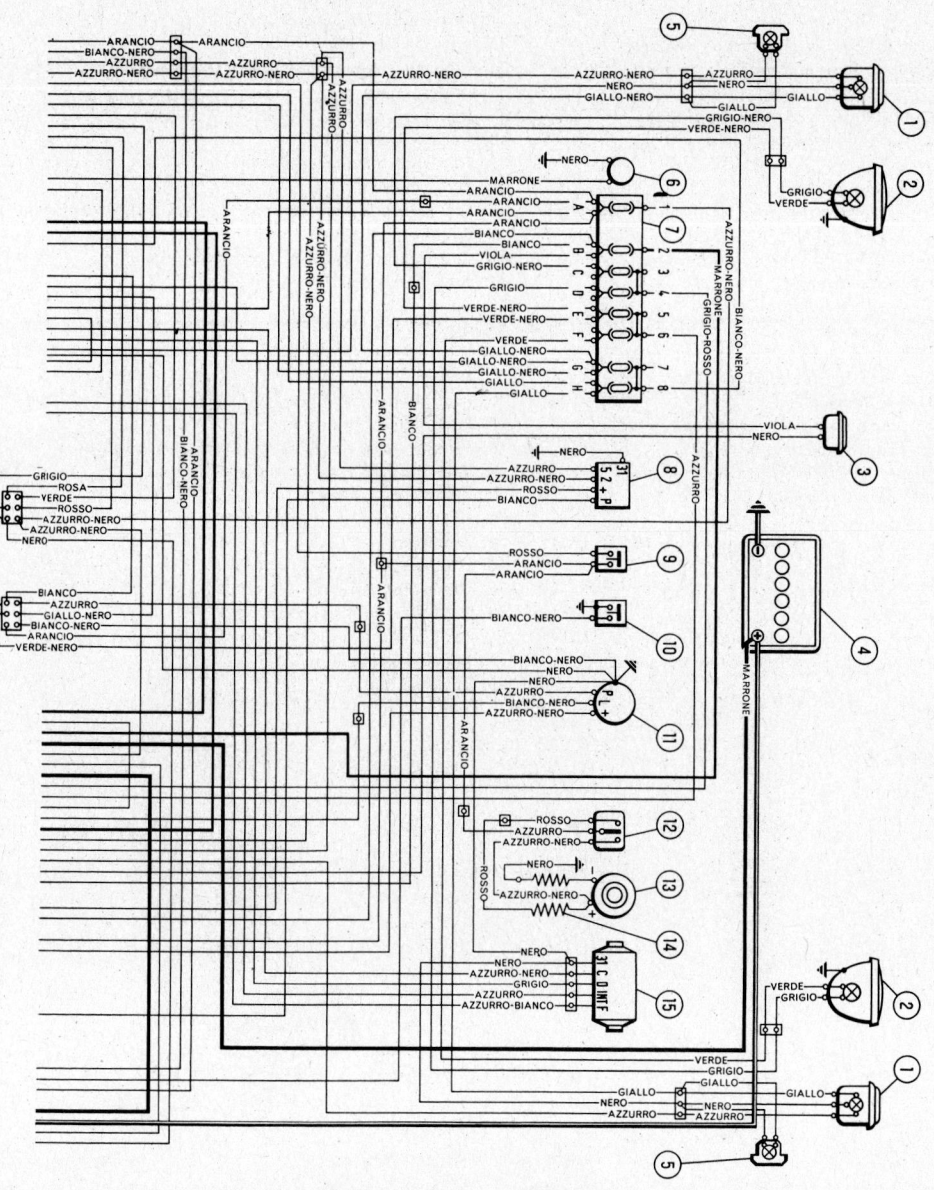

Fiat 850 Sedan wiring diagram

 1. Front parking and direction indicator lamps.
 2. Headlamps (high and low beams).
 3. Horn.
 4. Battery.
 5. Front side marker lamps (amber).
 6. Electric pump, windshield washer.
 7. Fuses.
 8. Flasher, vehicular hazard warning signal.
 9. Stop lights pressure-operated switch.
10. Switch for indicator 32.
11. Flasher, direction indicators.
12. Switch, 3-position, heating and ventilation electrofan.
13. Electrofan motor, 2-speed.
14. Additional resistor, for electrofan motor.
15. Windshield wiper motor.
16. Windshield washer pump button switch.
17. Outer lighting switch.
18. Instrument cluster light switch.
19. Three-position, windshield wiper switch.
20. Fuel reserve indicator (red).
21. Insufficient engine oil pressure indicator (red).
22. Generator charge indicator (red).
23. Parking lights indicator (green).
24. High beam indicator (blue).
25. Fuel gauge.
26. Connectors, electrical, on instrument cluster.
27. Direction indicator tell-tale (green).
28. Instrument cluster light.
29. Heat gauge.
30. Switch, vehicular hazard warning signal.
31. Pilot light, vehicular hazard warning signal ON.

32. Indicator, hydraulic service brake effectiveness and hand brake ON.
33. Remove key indicator.
34. Fuse, indicator 33 protection.
35. Lock switch.
36. High/low beams change-over and headlamp flashes switch.
37. Direction indicators switch.
38. Horn button.
39. Jam switch on steering wheel side door for indicator 33.
40. Jam switches, between doors and pillars, for courtesy light.
41. Courtesy light with incorporated switch.
42. Jam switch, back-up lamp.
43. Spark plugs.
44. Starter.
45. Switch hand brake ON and indicator 32 operation check.
46. Fuel gauge sending unit.
47. Rear side marker lamps (red).
48. Sending unit, insufficient oil pressure indicator.
49. Sending unit, heat gauge.
50. Ignition distributor.
51. Ignition coil.
52. Generator.
53. Engine compartment lamp with incorporated switch.
54. Generator regulator.
55. Rear direction indicators.
56. Rear parking and stop lights.
57. Number plate lights.
58. Back-up lamp.

NOTE: Mark — means that cable is provided with numbered strip or ferrule.

CABLE COLOR CODE

Arancio	Orange
Azzurro	Light blue
Bianco	White
Blu	Dark blue
Giallo	Yellow
Grigio	Grey
Marrone	Brown
Nero	Black
Rosa	Pink
Rosso	Red
Verde	Green
Viola	Violet

Fiat 850 Sedan wiring diagram

1. Front parking lights and direction indicators.
2. Headlamps (high and low beams).
3. Fog lamps.
4. Horns.
5. Battery.
6. Horn relay switch.
7. Front side marker lights.
8. Windshield washer pump.
9. Fuses
10. Fuse, fog lamps.
11. Flasher, vehicular hazard warning signal.
12. Switch for indicator 40.
13. Stop lights pressure operated switch.
14. Flasher, direction indicators.
15. Windshield wiper motor.
16. Battery charge indicator relay.
17. Instrument lights.
18. Electrical connectors for instrument cluster.
19. Direction indicators tell-tale (green).
20. Parking lights indicator (green).
21. Electronic engine tachometer.
22. Fuel reserve indicator (red).
23. Fuel gauge.
24. Heat gauge.
25. Battery charge indicator (red).
26. Insufficient engine oil pressure indicator (red).
27. High beam indicator (blue).
28. Fuse, remove key indicator.
29. Control, pump 8.
30. Outer lighting switch.
31. Instrument cluster light switch.
32. Windshield wiper 3-position switch.
33. Courtesy light with incorporated switch.
34. Lock switch.
35. Jam switches, between doors and pillars, for courtesy lights.
36. Jam switch, on door, for remove key indicator.
37. Electrofan motor.
38. Remove key indicator.
39. Pilot light, vehicular hazard warning signal.
40. Indicator, hydraulic service brake effectiveness and hand brake ON.
41. Switch, vehicular hazard warning signal.
42. Switch, fog lamps.
43. High/Low beams change-over and flashes switch.
44. Direction indicators switch.
45. Horn button.
46. Switch, 3 position, heating and ventilation fan.
47. Switch on clutch pedal for exhaust emission control electropneumatic device.
48. Switch, on transmission (3rd and 4th gears) for exhaust emission control electropneumatic device.
49. Electrovalve, exhaust emission control device.
50. Fuel gauge sending unit.
51. Switch, indicator 40 operation check.
52. Spark plugs.
53. Back-up lamp jam switch.
54. Starter.
55. Insufficient oil pressure indicator sending unit.
56. Press switch for electrovalve energizing during fast idle rate adjustments.
57. Heat gauge sending unit.
58. Ignition distributor.
59. Alternator.
60. Voltage regulator.
61. Fuse, alternator field circuit.
62. Field circuit relay alternator
63. Ignition coil.
64. Engine compartment lamp with incorporated jam switch.
65. Rear side marker lights.
66. Rear direction indicators.
67. Rear parking and stop lights.
68. Number plate lights.
69. Back-up lamps.

CABLE COLOR CODE

Arancio	Orange
Azzurro	Light blue
Bianco	White
Blu	Dark blue
Giallo	Yellow
Grigio	Grey
Marrone	Brown
Nero	Black
Rosa	Pink
Rosso	Red
Verde	Green
Viola	Violet

Fiat 850 Sport Coupe wiring diagram

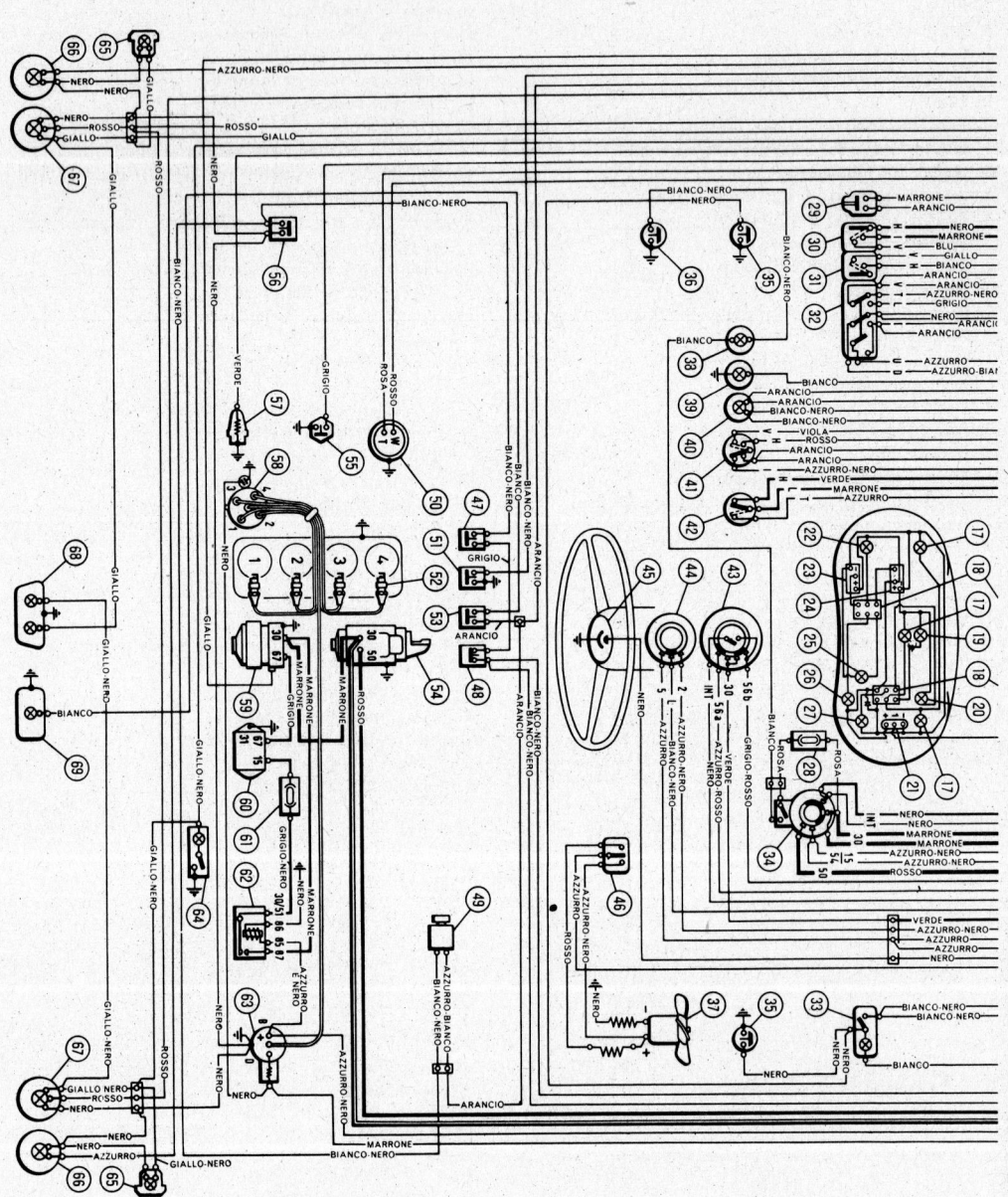

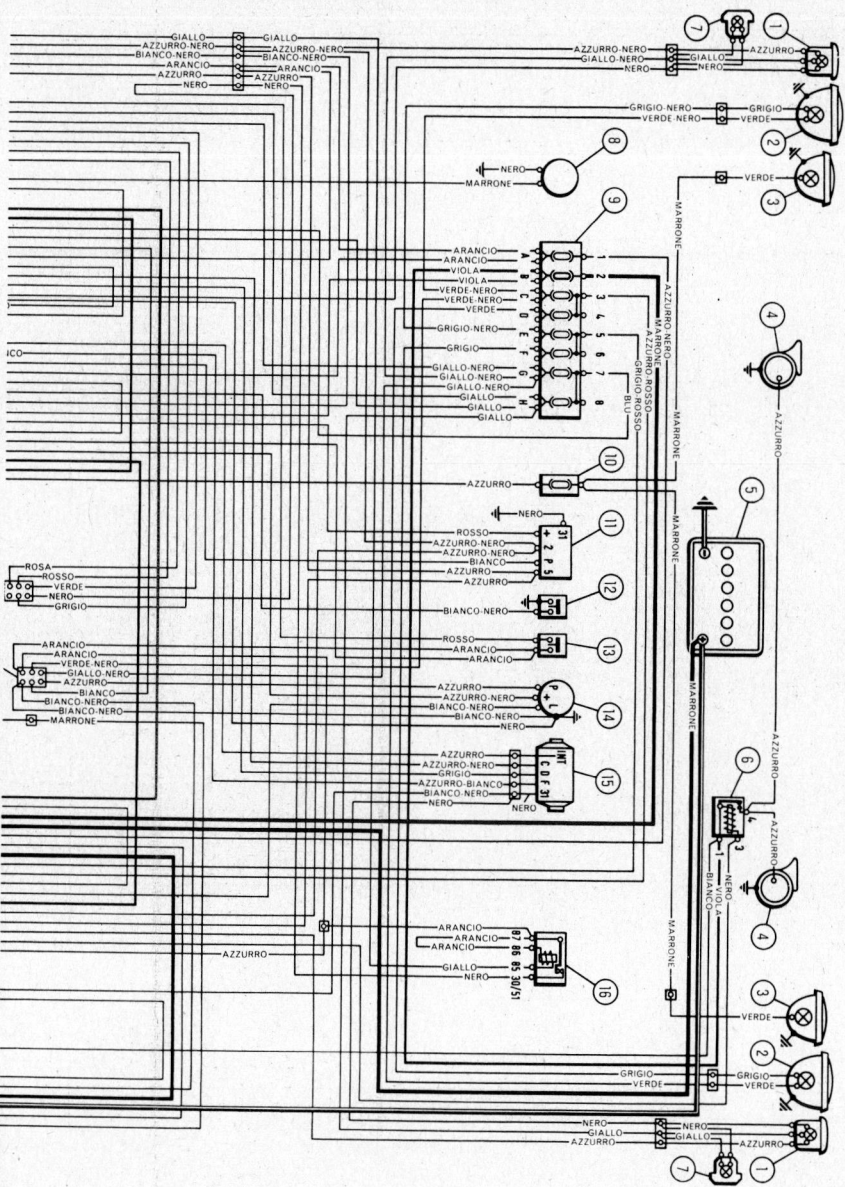

Fiat 850 Sport Coupe wiring diagram

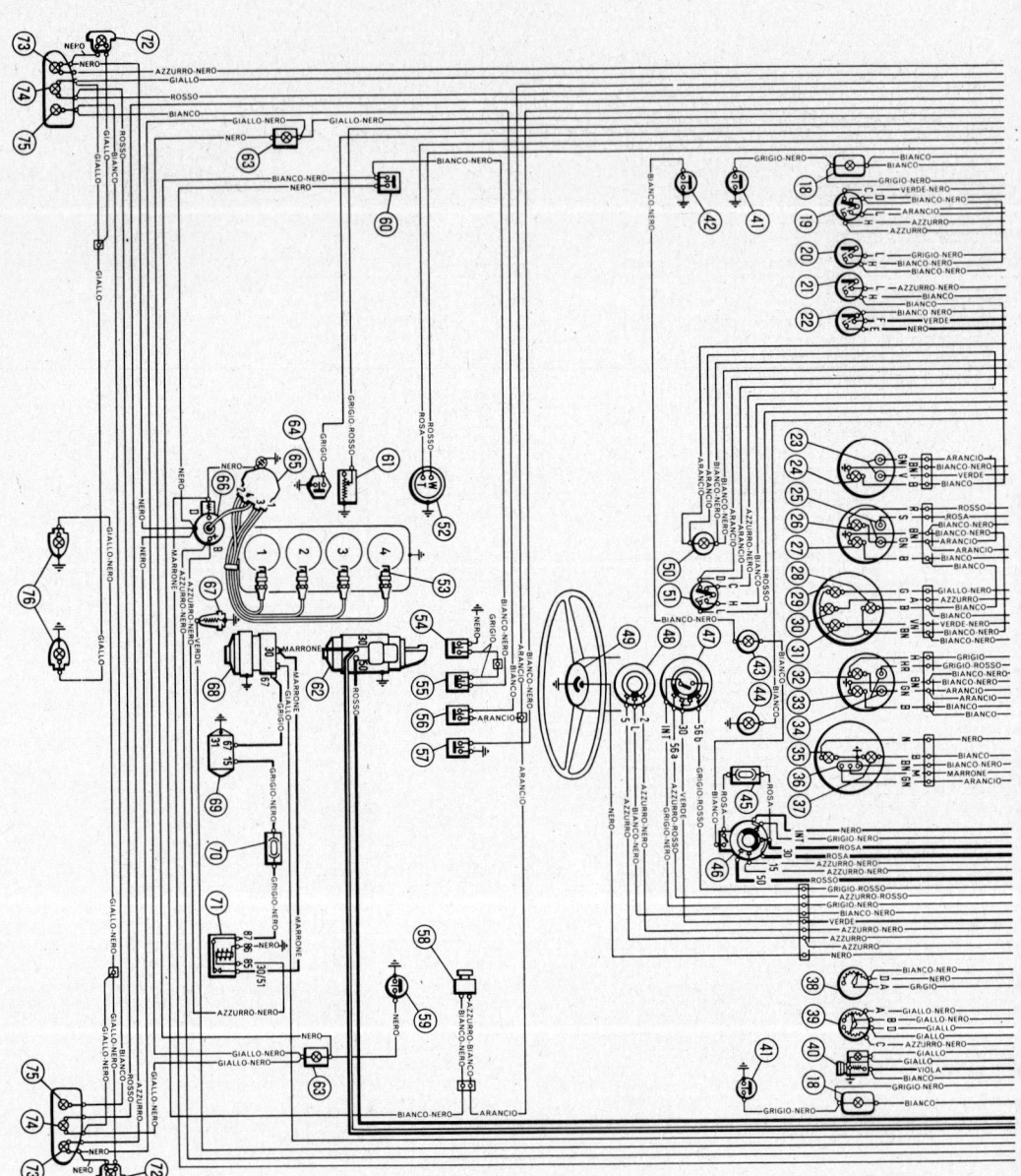

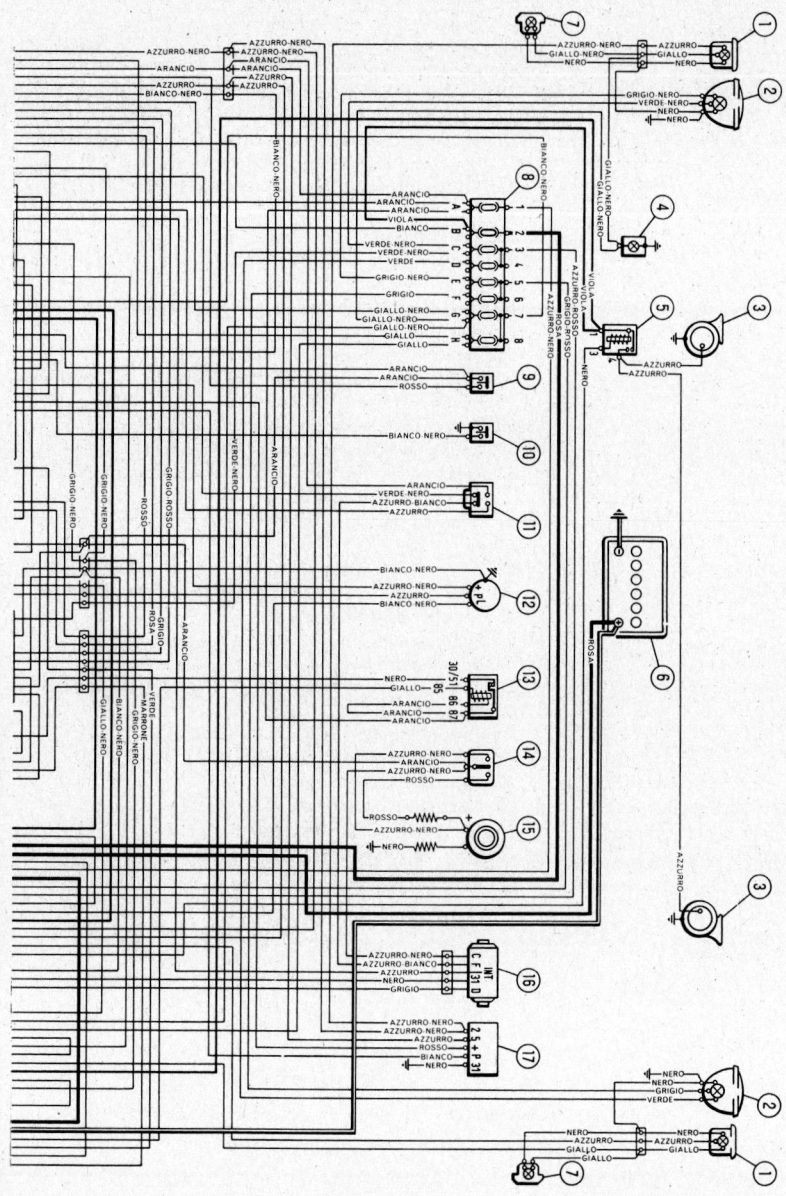

Fiat 850 Sport Spyder wiring diagram

1. Front parking lights and direction indicators.
2. Headlamp (high and low beams).
3. Horns.
4. Front compartment light.
5. Horn relay switch.
6. Battery.
7. Front side marker lights.
8. Fuses.
9. Stop lights pressure-operated switch.
10. Switch for indicator 50.
11. Windshield washer and wiper foot control.
12. Flasher, direction indicators.
13. Battery charge indicator relay.
14. Switch, 3-position, heating and ventilation fan.
15. Electrofan motor, 2-speed.
16. Windshield wiper motor.
17. Flasher, vehicular hazard warning signal.
18. Courtesy lights under instrument board.
19. Windshield wiper switch.
20. Courtesy lights toggle switch.
21. Instrument cluster light switch.
22. Outer lighting switch.
23. Heat gauge.
24. Heat gauge light.
25. Fuel gauge.
26. Fuel reserve indicator.
27. Fuel gauge light.
28. Speedometer light.
29. Parking lights indicator (green).
30. Direction indicators tell-tale (green).
31. High beam indicator (blue).
32. Insufficient engine oil pressure indicator (red).
33. Oil pressure gauge light.
34. Oil pressure gauge.
35. Battery charge indicator (red).
36. Engine tachometer.
37. Engine tachometer light.
38. Windshield wiper sweep rate adjustment rheostat.
39. Instrument lights and parking lights indicator rheostats.
40. Cigarette lighter (w/housing indicator).
41. Jam switches, between doors and pillars, for courtesy lights.
42. Jam switch, on door, for remove key indicator.
43. Remove key indicator.
44. Pilot light, vehicular hazard warning signal.
45. Fuse, remove key indicator.
46. Lock switch.
47. High/Low beams change-over and flashes switch.
48. Direction indicators switch.
49. Horn button.
50. Indicator, hydraulic service brake effectiveness and hand brake ON.
51. Switch, vehicular hazard warning signal.
52. Fuel gauge sending unit.
53. Spark plugs.
54. Switch on transmission (3rd and 4th gears) for exhaust emission control electropneumatic device.
55. Switch on clutch pedal for exhaust emission control electropneumatic device.
56. Jam switch, back-up lamp.
57. Switch, hand brake ON and indicator 50 operation check.
58. Electrovalve, exhaust emission control device.
59. Engine compartment lamps jam switch.
60. Press switch for electrovalve energizing during fast idle rate adjustment.
61. Sending unit, oil pressure gauge.
62. Starter.
63. Engine compartment lamps.
64. Sending unit, insufficient oil pressure indicator.
65. Ignition distributor.
66. Ignition coil.
67. Sending unit, heat gauge.
68. Alternator.
69. Voltage regulator.
70. Fuse, alternator field circuit.
71. Alternator, field circuit relay.
72. Rear side marker lights.
73. Rear direction indicators.
74. Rear parking and stop lights.
75. Back-up lamp.
76. Number plate lights.

CABLE COLOR CODE

Arrancio	Orange
Azzurro	Light blue
Bianco	White
Blu	Dark blue
Giallo	Yellow
Grigio	Grey
Marrone	Brown
Nero	Black
Rosa	Pink
Rosso	Red
Verde	Green
Viola	Violet

Fiat 850 Sport Spyder wiring diagram

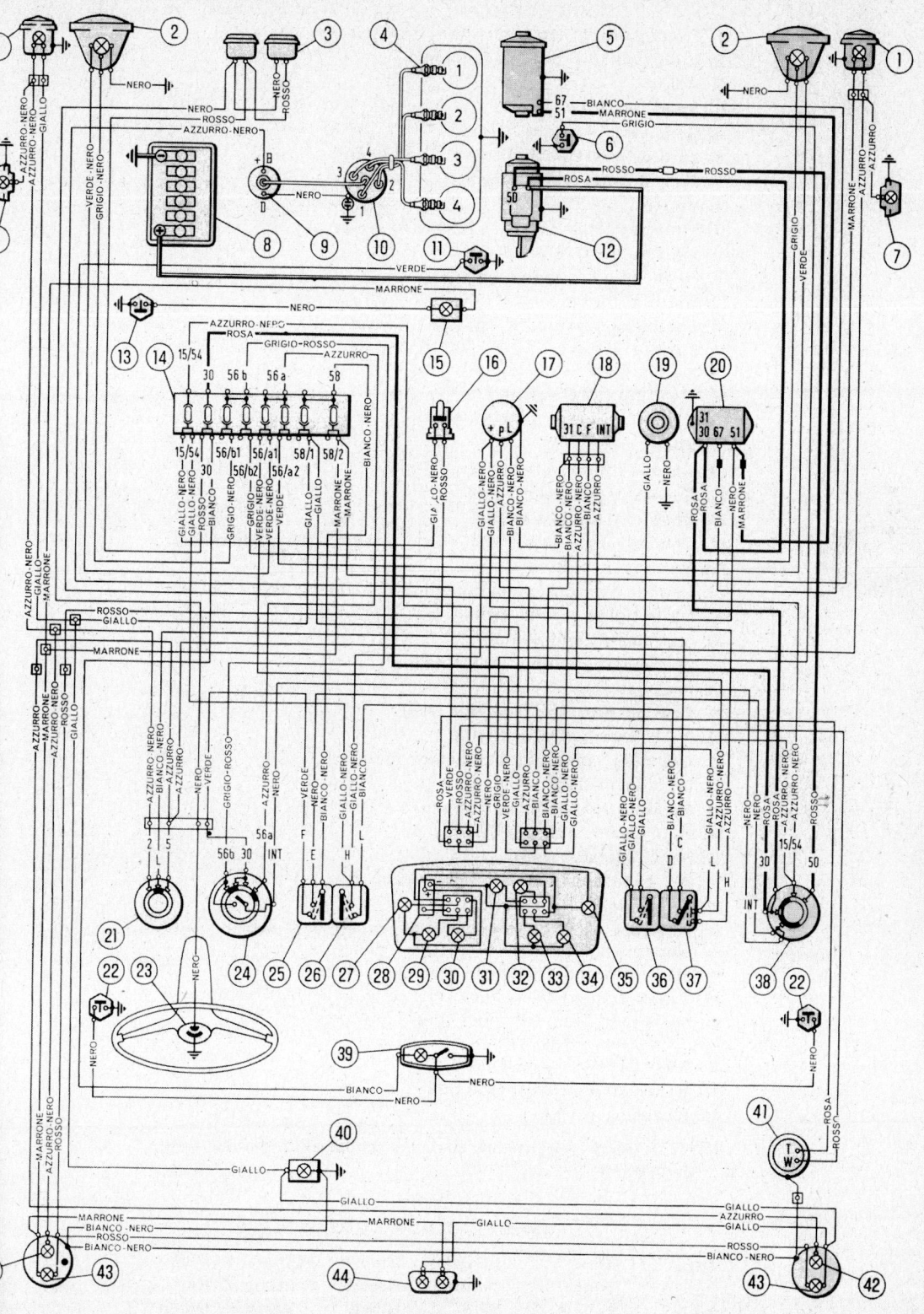

1100R wiring diagram.

1. Front parking and direction signal lights.
2. High and low beam headlamps.
3. Horns.
4. Spark plugs.
5. Generator.
6. Low oil pressure indicator sending unit.
7. Side direction signal lights.
8. Battery.
9. Ignition coil.
10. Ignition distributor.
11. Heat indicator thermal switch.
12. Starting motor.
13. Engine compartment light jam switch.
14. 8-Ampere fuses.
15. Engine compartment light.
16. Stop light jam switch.
17. Direction signal light flasher unit.
18. Wiper motor.
19. Air conditioner electro-fan.
20. Generator regulator.
21. Direction signal switch.
22. Courtesy light jam switches on front quarter door pillars.
23. Horn push button.
24. Change-over switch for outer lighting and low beam flashes.
25. Outer lights master switch.
26. Instrument light switch.
27. Fuel reserve supply indicator (red).
28. Fuel gauge.
29. Low oil pressure indicator (red).
30. No-charge indicator (red).
31. Direction signal light indicator (green).
32. Instrument light.
33. Parking light indicator (green).
34. High beam indicator (blue).
35. Heat indicator (red).
36. Air conditioner electro-fan switch.
37. Windshield wiper switch.
38. Key-type ignition switch, also energizing starting and warning lights circuits.
39. Map light and switch (in rear view mirror).
40. Trunk compartment light (this light is fitted with its own switch on cars with collapsible rear seat back).
41. Fuel gauge tank unit.
42. Rear direction signal lights.
43. Rear parking and stop lights.
44. License plate light.

NOTE - Mark —— means that the cable is provided with numbered strip or ferrule.

CABLE COLOUR CODE

Azzurro = **Blue**	Grigio = **Grey**	Rosa = **Pink**
Bianco = **White**	Marrone = **Brown**	Rosso = **Red**
Giallo = **Yellow**	Nero = **Black**	Verde = **Green**

1100R wiring diagram.

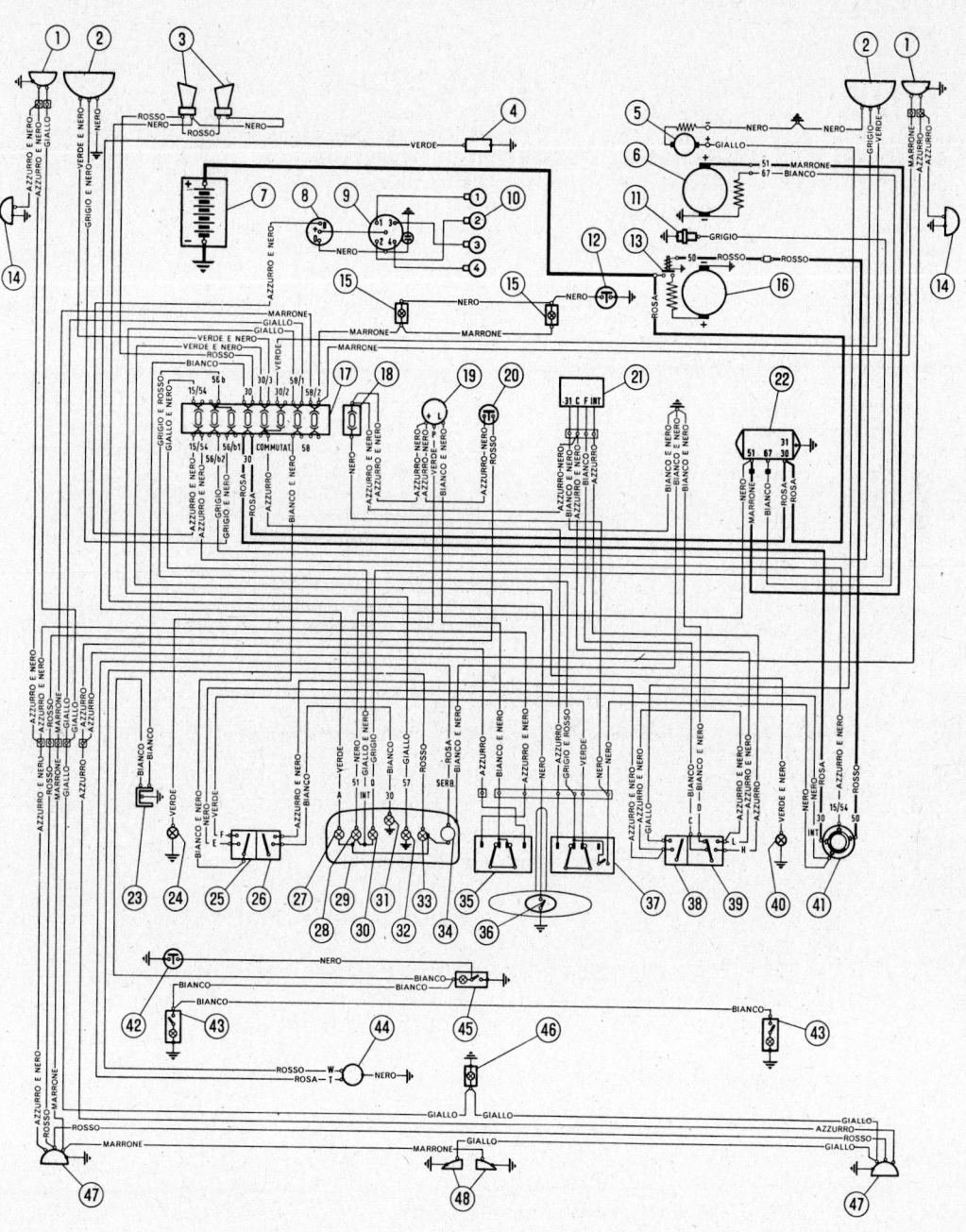

Fiat 1100D wiring diagram

1. Front turn indicator and parking lights.
2. Headlights (high and low beams).
3. Horns.
4. Engine cooling water temperature indicator sending unit.
5. Electrofan, ventilation and heating.
6. Generator.
7. Battery.
8. Ignition coil.
9. Ignition distributor.
10. Spark plugs.
11. Low oil pressure indicator sending unit.
12. Engine compartment lights jam switch.
13. Starter relay switch.
14. Turn indicator side repeaters.
15. Engine compartment lights.
16. Starter.
17. Fuses, 8 Amps.
18. Fuse, 8 Amps.
19. Flasher, turn indicators.
20. Hydraulic, pressure-operated stop lights switch.
21. Windshield wiper motor.
22. Generator regulator.
23. Inspection lamp socket.
24. Turn indicator pilot light (green).
25. Outer lighting switch.
26. Panel light switch.
27. Engine cooling water temperature indicator (red).
28. Generator charge indicator (red).
29. Instrument cluster.
30. Low oil pressure indicator (red).
31. Panel light bulb.
32. Front parking light indicator (green).
33. Low fuel indicator (red).
34. Fuel gauge.
35. Turn indicators switch.
36. Horn button.
37. Front outer lighting selector switch.
38. Electrofan switch.
39. Windshield wiper switch.
40. Headlight high beam indicator (blue).
41. Lock switch.
42. Jam switch, between door and pillar, for bulb incorporated in rear view mirror.
43. Pillar lights, with incorporated switch.
44. Fuel gauge sending unit.
45. Bulb, incorporated in rear view mirror, for courtesy lights.
46. Luggage compartment light.
47. Rear parking, stop and direction indicator lights.
48. License plate light.

NOTE: Mark — means that the cable is provided with numbered strip or ferrule.

CABLE COLOR CODE

Azzurro   Blue

Grigio   Grey

Rosso   Red

Bianco   White

Marrone   Brown

Verde   Green

Giallo   Yellow

Nero   Black   INT-COMMUTAT   Switch   SERB.   Tank.

Fiat 1100D wiring diagram

1. Headlights (high and low beams).
2. Front turn indicator and parking lights.
3. Horn.
4. High water temperature indicator sending unit.
5. Air conditioning unit electrofan.
6. Turn indicator side repeaters.
7. Battery.
8. Ignition coil.
9. Ignition distributor.
10. Spark plugs.
11. Low oil pressure indicator sending unit.
12. Generator.
13. Starter electronmagnetic switch.
14. Starter.
15. Hydraulic, pressure-operated stop lights switch.
16. Engine compartment lights.
17. Engine compartment lights jam switch.
18. Generator regular.
19. Flasher, turn indicators.
20. Windshield wiper motor.
21. Fuel gauge.
22. Windshield wiper three-position switch.
23. Fuses, 8 Amps.
24. Turn indicators pilot light (green).
25. High water temperature indicator (red).
26. Low oil pressure indicator (red).
27. Low fuel indicator (red).
28. Turn indicator switch.
29. Front outer lighting selector switch.
30. Panel light switch.
31. Lock switch.
32. Electrofan switch.
33. Headlight high beam indicator (blue).
34. Inspection lamp receptacle.
35. Outer lighting switch.
36. Front parking lights indicator (green).
37. Generator charge indicator (red).
38. Panel light bulb.
39. Horn button.
40. Jam switch, between door and pillar, for bulb incorporated in rear view mirror.
41. Pillar lights, with incorporated switch.
42. Bulb, incorporated in rear view mirror, for courtesy light.
43. Fuel gauge sending unit.
44. Luggage compartment light.
45. Rear parking, stop and turn indicator lights.
46. License plate light.

NOTE: *Cars with speedometer gauged in miles have a cluster incorporating a heat gauge instead of the temperature indicator. The gauge and its sending unit are not shown in this diagram. Mark — means that the cable is provided with numbered strip or ferrule.*

CABLE COLOR CODE

Azzurro Blue

Grigio Grey

Rosso Red

Bianco White

Marrone Brown

Verde Green

Giallo Yellow

Nero Black   INT-COMMUTAT Switch   SERB. Tank.

Fiat Export, Special Sedan and Family car wiring diagram

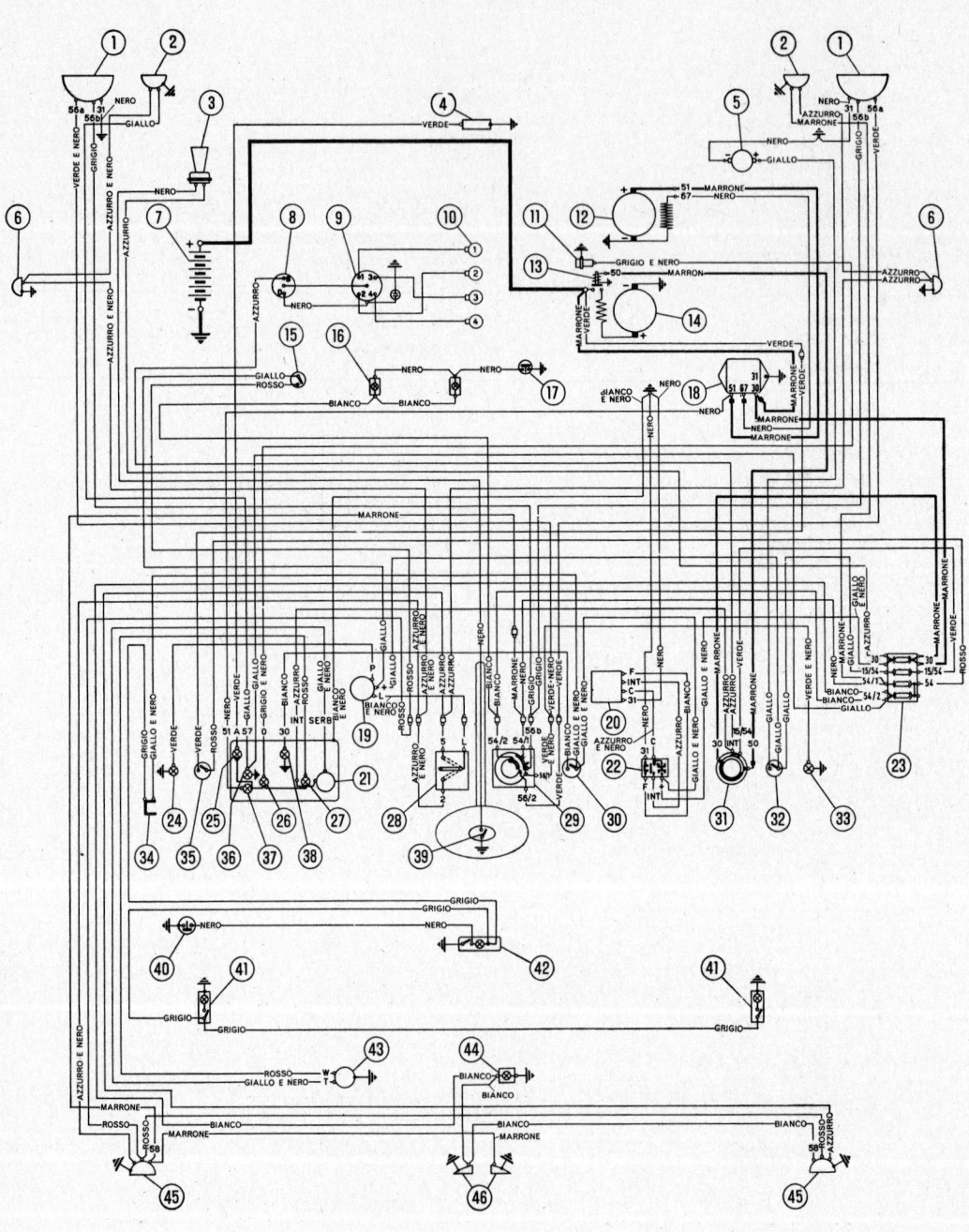

Fiat Export, Special Sedan and Family car wiring diagram

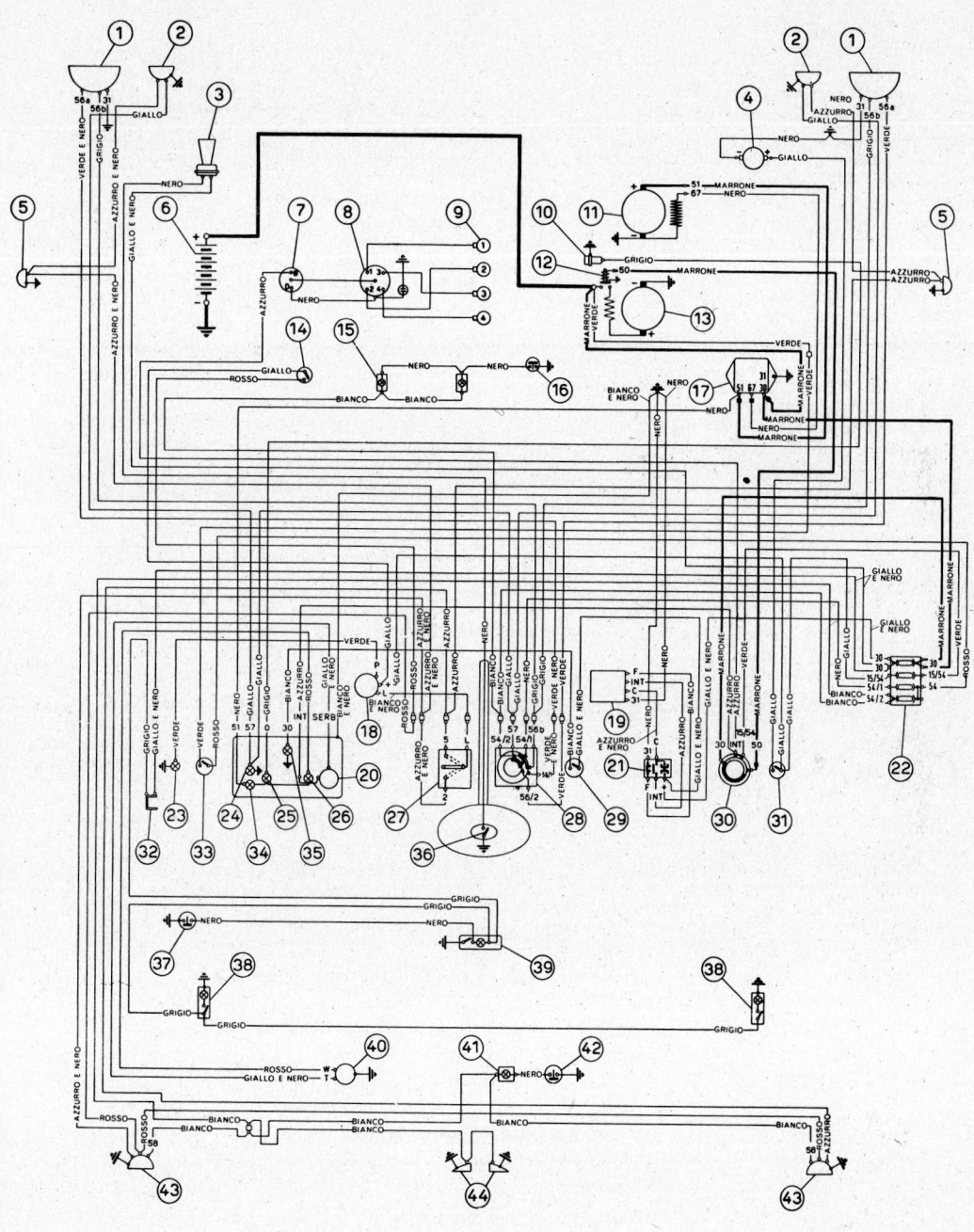

Fiat 1100/103D wiring diagram

1. Headlights (high and low beams).
2. Front turn indicator and parking lights.
3. Horn.
4. Air conditioning unit electrofan.
5. Side turn indicator repeaters.
6. Battery.
7. Ignition coil.
8. Ignition distributor.
9. Spark plugs.
10. Low oil pressure indicator sending unit.
11. Generator.
12. Starter relay switch.
13. Starter.
14. Hydraulic, pressure-operated stop light switch.
15. Engine compartment lights.
16. Engine compartment light jam switch.
17. Generator regulator.
18. Flasher, turn indicators.
19. Windshield wiper.
20. Fuel gauge.
21. Windshield wiper three-position switch.
22. 8-A fuses.
23. Turn indicators pilot light (red).
24. Front parking lights indicator (green).
25. Low oil pressure indicator (red).
26. Low fuel indicator (red).
27. Turn indicators switch.
28. Front outer lighting selector switch.
29. Panel light switch.
30. Lock switch.
31. Electrofan switch.
32. Inspection lamp receptacle.
33. Outer lighting switch.
34. Generator charge indicator (red).
35. Panel light bulb.
36. Horn control pushbutton.
37. Jam switch, between door and pillar, for courtesy light in rear view mirror.
38. Inner lights, with incorporated switch.
39. Bulb, incorporated in rear view mirror, for courtesy light.
40. Fuel gauge sending unit.
41. Luggage compartment light.
42. Jam switch, luggage compartment light.
43. Rear parking, stop and turn indicator lights.
44. License plate lights.

NOTE: *Mark — means that the cable is provided with numbered strip or ferrule.*

CABLE COLOR CODE

Azzurro　Blue

Grigio　Grey

Rosso　Red

Bianco　White

Marrone　Brown

Verde　Green

Giallo　Yellow

Nero　Black　　　INT-COMMUTAT　Switch　　SERB.　Tank.

Fiat 1100/103D wiring diagram

1. Front direction signal and parking lamps.
2. Headlamps (high and low beams).
3. Horns.
4. Electromagnetic fan thermal switch.
5. Low oil pressure indicator sending unit.
6. Electromagnetic fan switch brush.
7. Temperature gauge sending unit.
8. Generator.
9. Direction signal side repeaters.
10. Engine compartment lights.
11. Horn control relay switch.
12. Ignition coil.
13. Ignition distributor.
14. Heat indicator sending unit.
15. Generator regulator.
16. Flasher unit, direction indicators.
17. Stop light jam switch.
18. Temperature gauge resistor.
19. Temperature gauge silicon diode.
20. Heater electrofan.
21. Spark plugs.
22. Map light under dashboard.
23. Starting motor.
24. Windshield wiper motor.
25. Fuses.
26. Engine compartment light jam switch.
27. Outer lighting master switch.
28. Jam switches on doors for courtesy light.
29. Direction signal pilot light (green).
30. Front parking light indicator (green).

31. Heat gauge indicator (red).
32. Direction signal switch.
33. Horn button.
34. Outer lighting change-over switch and headlamp flasher.
35. Fuel and temperature gauge light.
36. No-charge indicator (red).
37. Fuel gauge and reserve supply indicator.
38. Low oil pressure indicator (red).
39. Temperature gauge.
40. Electric clock light.
41. Electric clock.
42. Speedometer light.
43. Headlamp high beam indicator (blue).
44. Lock switch for ignition, warning lights and starting (controls also the anti-theft device).
45. Windshield wiper switch.
46. Instrument lights switch.
47. Electrofan switch.
48. Map light switch.
49. Trouble light receptacle.
50. Cigar lighter (w/spot light).
51. Battery.
52. Fuel gauge sending unit.
53. Deck light.
54. Deck light jam switch.
55. Rear direction signal lights.
56. Tail and stop lights.
57. License plate lights.

NOTE: *Mark — means that the cable is provided with numbered strip or ferrule.*

TERM   Temperature gauge -- INT   Switch

CABLE COLOR CODE

Azzurro	Blue
Bianco	White
Giallo	Yellow
Grigio	Grey
Marrone	Brown
Nero	Black
Rosa	Pink
Rosso	Red
Verde	Green

Fiat 1500 Cabriolet wiring diagram

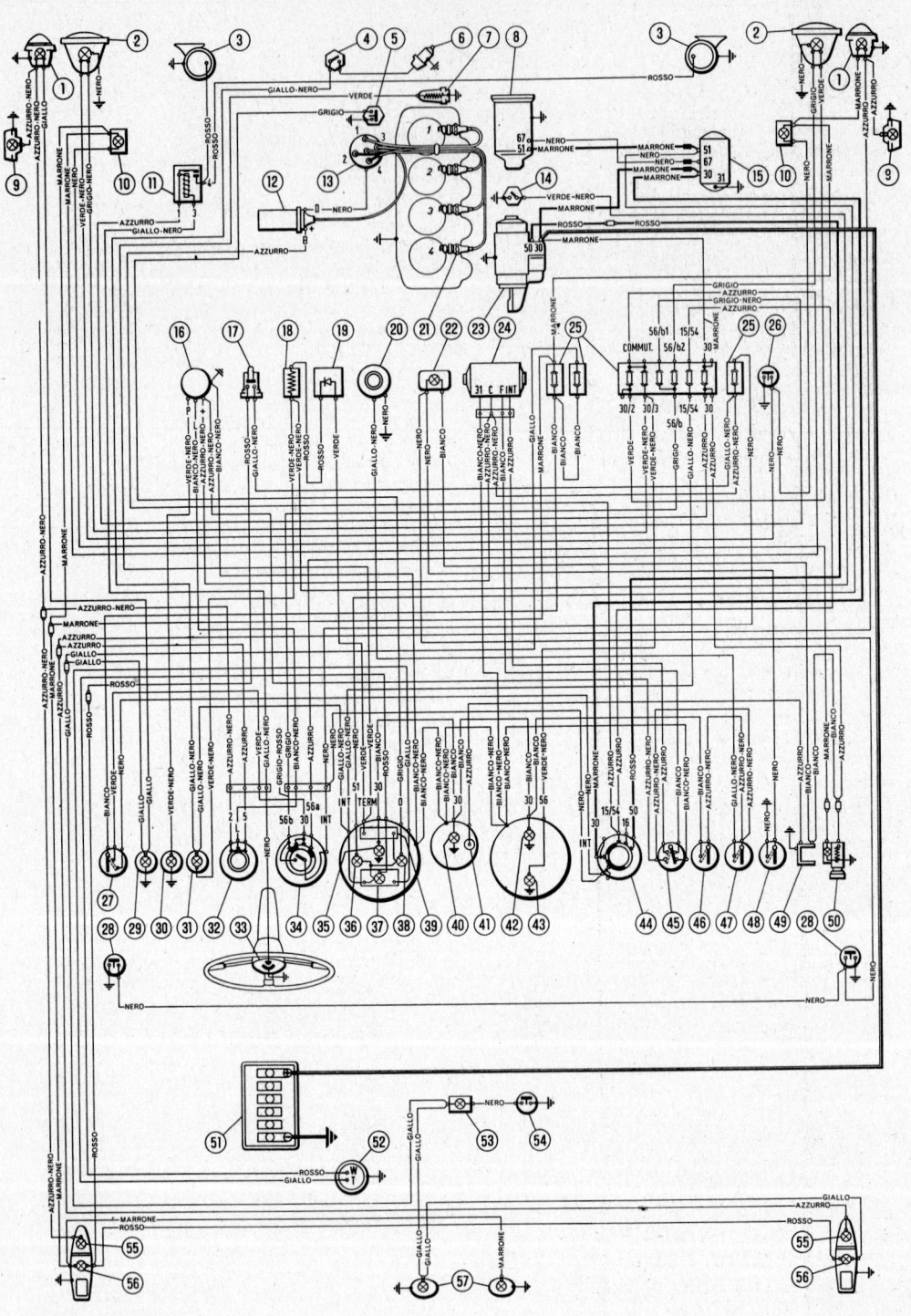

Fiat 1500 Cabriolet wiring diagram

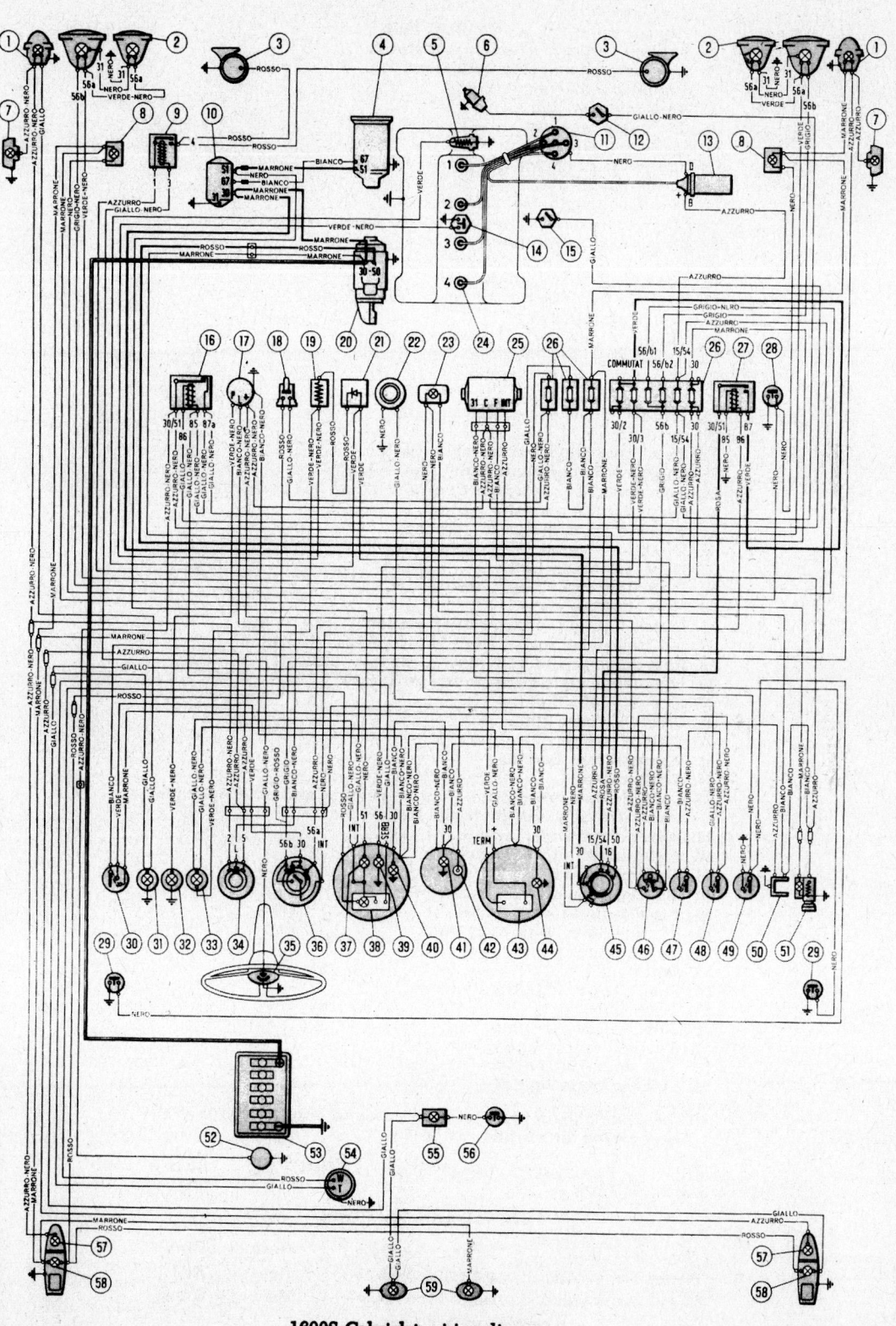

1600S Cabriolet wiring diagram.

1. Front direction signal and parking lamps.
2. Dual headlamps (high and low beam).
3. Horns.
4. Generator.
5. Temperature gauge sending unit.
6. Cooling radiator electromagnetic fan.
7. Direction signal side repeaters.
8. Engine compartment lights.
9. Horn relay switch.
10. Generator regulator.
11. Ignition distributor.
12. Thermal switch for fan 6.
13. Ignition coil.
14. Thermal switch for indicator 33.
15. Low oil pressure sending unit for relay switch 16.
16. Relay switch for pump 52.
17. Flasher unit, direction signal light.
18. Stop light jam switch.
19. Resistor for electric temperature gauge.
20. Starting motor.
21. Silicon diode for temperature gauge.
22. Ventilation and heating electrofan.
23. Map light under dashboard.
24. Spark plugs.
25. Windshield wiper motor.
26. Fuse box.
27. Headlamp high beam relay switch.
28. Engine compartment light jam switch.
29. Jam switches, between door and pillar, for courtesy light.
30. Outer lighting master switch.
31. Parking light indicator (green).
32. Direction signal pilot light (green).
33. Heat indicator (red).
34. Direction signal light switch.
35. Horn button.
36. Outer lighting change-over switch.
37. No-charge indicator (red).
38. Fuel gauge with red reserve supply indicator.
39. Headlamp high beam indicator (blue).
40. Speedometer light.
41. Electric clock light.
42. Electric clock.
43. Temperature gauge.
44. Tachometer.
45. Lock switch for ignition, warning lights and starting (controls also the anti-theft device).
46. Windshield wiper switch.
47. Instrument lights switch.
48. Electrofan switch.
49. Map light switch.
50. Trouble light receptacle.
51. Cigar lighter, with spot light.
52. Electric fuel pump.
53. Battery.
54. Fuel gauge sending unit.
55. Deck light.
56. Jam switch for lamp 55.
57. Rear direction signal lights.
58. Tail and stop lights.
59. License plate lights.

NOTE - Mark ▬ means that the cable is provided with numbered strip or ferrule.

TERM. = Temperature gauge — INT-COMMUTAT. = Switch
SERB. = Tank

CABLE COLOR CODE

Azzurro = Blue	Grigio = Grey	Rosa = Pink
Bianco = White	Marrone = Brown	Rosso = Red
Giallo = Yellow	Nero = Black	Verde = Green

1600S Cabriolet wiring diagram.

1. Front parking and direction indicator lamps.
2. Headlamps (high and low beam).
3. Horn.
4. Fuel gauge sending unit.
5. Battery.
6. Stop lamp pedal-operated switch.
7. Side direction lights.
8. Direction indicator switch.
9. High beam indicator.
10. Parking light indicator.
11. High water temperature indicator.
12. Winking device (flasher unit).
13. Generator charge indicator.
14. Low engine oil pressure indicator.
15. Instrument cluster light.
16. Fuel gauge, with reserve supply indicator.
17. Outer lighting switch.
18. Instrument cluster light switch.
19. Ignition lock switch.
20. Direction indicator pilot light.
21. Windshield wiper motor.
22. Windshield wiper switch.
23. 8-A fuses.
24. Horn button.
25. Outer lighting change-over switch.
26. Jam switch, between door and pillar, for rear view mirror light.
27. Lamp incorporated in rear view mirror, for car interior illumination, with toggle switch.
28. Starter switch.
29. Starter.
30. Sending unit, for low oil pressure indicator.
31. Engine compartment light, with automatic switch.
32. Ignition distributor.
33. Generator.
34. Thermostatic sending unit for excessive water temperature indicator.
35. Spark plugs.
36. Ignition coil.
37. Generator regulator.
38. Rear parking, stop and direction indicator lamps.
39. Number plate lamp.

NOTE: Mark — means that cable is provided with numbered strip and ferrule.

CABLE COLOR CODE

Azzurro	Blue
Bianco	White
Giallo	Yellow
Grigio	Grey
Marrone	Brown
Nero	Black
Rosa	Pink
Rosso	Red
Verde	Green
Azzurro e Nero	Black and Blue
Bianco e Nero	Black and White
Giallo e Nero	Black and Yellow
Verde e Nero	Black and Green
Grigio e Nero	Black and Grey
Commutat.	Switch
Serb.	Tank
INT.—Inter.	Switch

Fiat 600, 600D wiring diagram

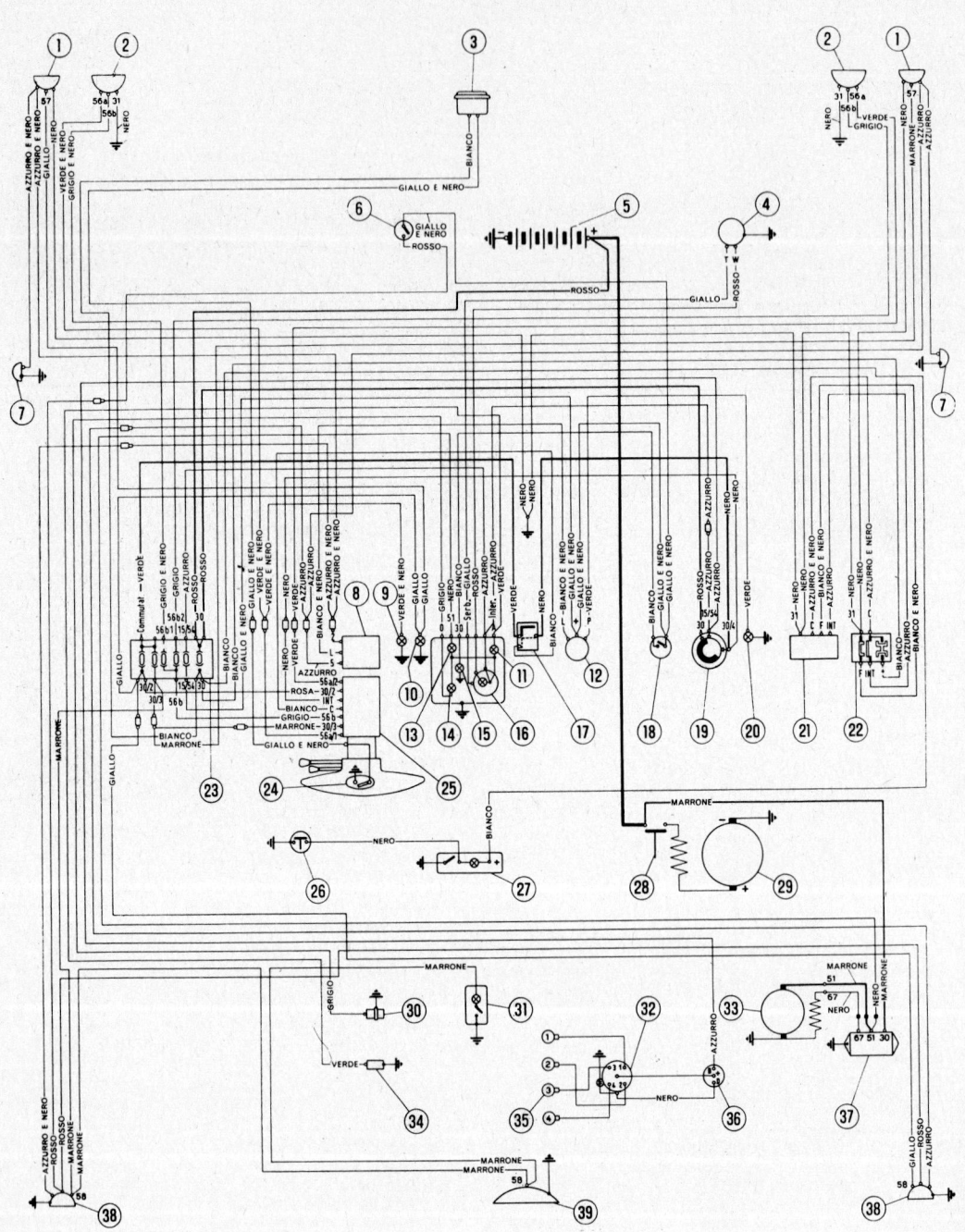

Fiat 600, 600D wiring diagram

Engine Electrical

Distributor

All Fiat distributors are similar, both in appearance and operation. Fiat 850 series, 600, 600D and 1500 Cabriolet models are equipped with distributors using vacuum and centrifugal advance mechanisms. All other Fiat models are fitted with distributors employing only centrifugal advance.

REMOVAL

Removal procedures are similar for all Fiat distributors. Remove the high tension leads from the distributor. Remove the low tension leads and disconnect the vacuum advance (if equipped). Loosen the clamp bolt at the base of the distributor mounting and carefully remove the distributor from the engine.

DISASSEMBLY

Since all Fiat distributors are basically alike, a typical disassembly procedure is given. Remove the distributor cap (124 distributor caps are held in place by two screws instead of clips). On 850 distributors, remove the centrifugal advance springs and the centrifugal advance weights. On other units, remove the condenser and rotor. Disconnect and remove the breaker points assembly. Remove the breaker carrier plate. Remove the distributor drive gear and the distributor driveshaft, complete with weights and cams.

ASSEMBLY

Assembly is the reverse of disassembly.

INSTALLATION

If the auxilliary shaft or camshaft has been removed, the following procedure is suggested for installation of the distributor.

Rotate the crankshaft to bring No. 1 cylinder to Top Dead Center of the compres-

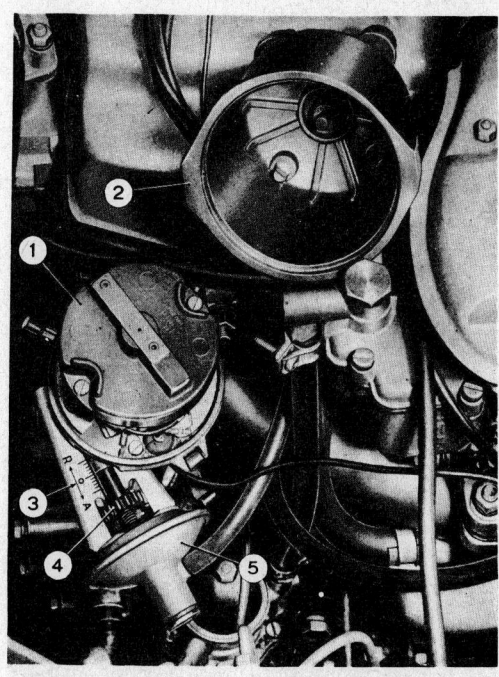

Distributor components, Fiat 1500: (1) rotor; (2) distributor cap; (3) octane selector; (4) octane selector adjustment; (5) vacuum advance.

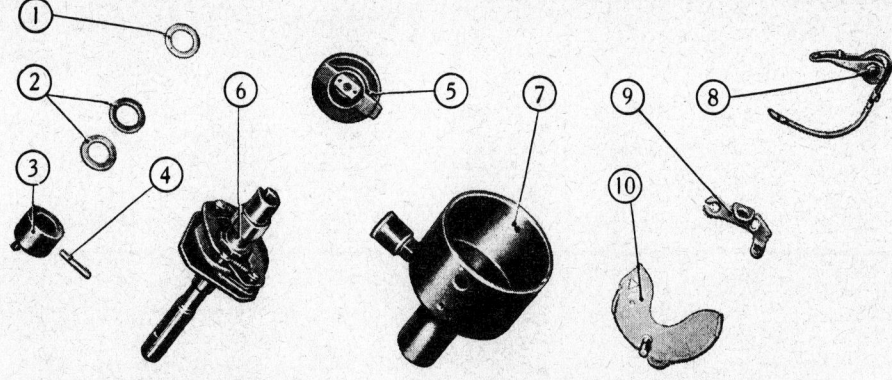

1. Washer between weight carrier plate and body.
2. Washer between body and coupling.
3. Coupling.
4. Pin, coupling.
5. Rotor.

6. Shaft, complete with weights and cams.
7. Body.
8. Breaker arm.
9. Stationary contact bracket.
10. Breaker carrier plate.

Exploded view of typical Fiat distributor

sion stroke (both valves closed). Turn the crankshaft until the timing marks are aligned. Position the distributor rotor opposite No. 1 contact in the cap. At this point, the contact breaker points are about to open. Fit the distributor in its housing and tighten the clamp bolt. Replace the distributor cap and connect the spark plug wires in the firing order. Check the ignition timing with a timing light and check the point dwell with a dwell meter.

Timing Marks

The timing marks for various engines are as follows:

1500—mark on the centrifugal oil filter ½" ahead of the mark on the timing gear cover;

1600—mark on the centrifugal oil filter indexed with the mark on crankcase;

Timing marks for the Fiat 124: (1) Mark for 10° advance; (2) mark for 5° advance; (3) mark for 0° advance; (4) reference mark on fan belt pulley.

1100—mark on the timing gear cover aligned with the mark on the pulley;

850—mark on the centrifugal oil filter ½" ahead of mark on the timing gear cover. NOTE: *850 engine rotates counterclockwise.*

600—mark on the pulley .35" ahead of mark on the timing gear cover;

600D—mark on the pulley ½" ahead of mark on the timing gear cover;

124—mark on the pulley aligned with the first (shortest) mark on distributor drive housing.

Fiat 1500 timing marks

Fiat 1100 and 600 timing marks

Fiat 850 timing marks

Distributor Octane Selector

FIAT 1500

This is a manual adjustment which varies the static advance of the distributor ±5° to provide the most efficient timing for the octane rating of the fuel. When low octane fuel is used, the adjustment can be rotated to retard (R) the timing by 5°. Conversely, with high octane fuel, the timing can be advanced (A) 5°. The normal advance setting for middle octane ratings is at "0" marking on the shaft.

Generator

DC generators are two-pole, shunt-wound types with three-unit regulators for control of generator voltage, current, and cutout. Before making regulator tests and adjustments it is necessary to temperature-stabilize the unit. This can be done by operating the unit at 15-16 volts, with the cover on, until operating temperature is reached.

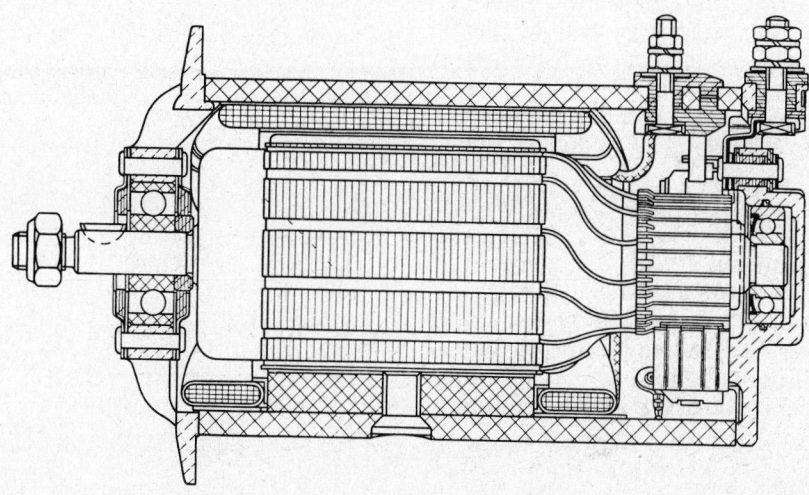

Fiat generator D90/12/16/3E

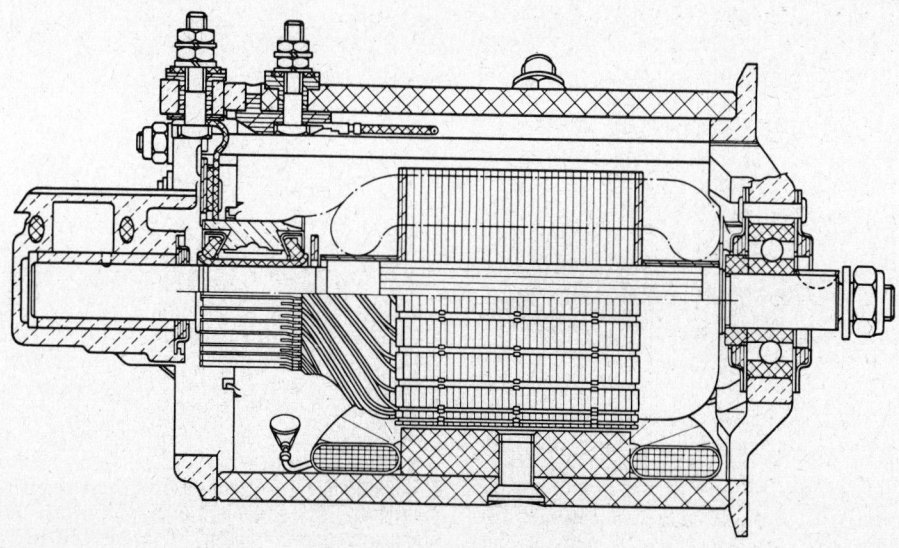

Fiat generator D115/12/28/4E

Voltage Regulators

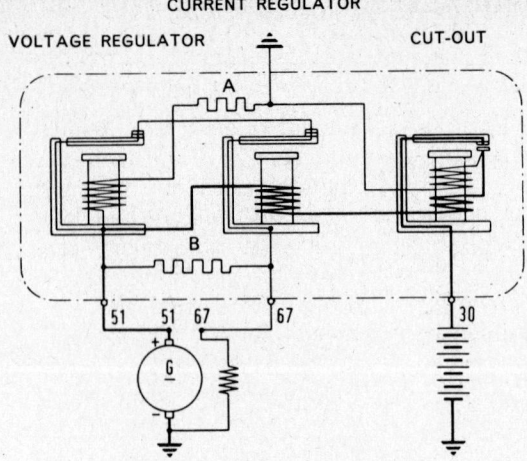

Cut-Out

Measure the air gap for the cut out relay between the clapper and the edge of the core nearest the contacts. Make the cut in adjustment with the unit at 60-95° F. Adjust by bending the spring tension arm until the points close at the proper specification.

Check the reverse current by connecting a two way ammeter in series with the battery lead to the regulator. Run the generator to 4,500 rpm and gradually reduce speed, noting the reverse current at the point when the contacts open. See Specifications for the proper amperage. The range between cut in and cutout action can be adjusted by enlarging or reducing the air gap.

Diagram showing generator, battery and GN2/-12/16 regulator connections. Series resistor at (A); regulating resistor at (B).

Voltage Regulator

With the regulator at 122° F., increase generator speed to 4,500 rpm. Set the generator to ½ its rated output. If necessary, set the regulator by bending the spring tension arm until the voltage reads according to specifications. Increasing spring tension will raise the voltage.

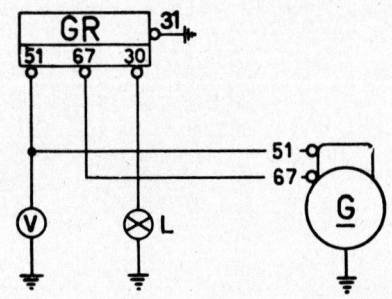

Current Regulator

With the regulator connected and stabilized at a temperature of 122° F., run the generator to 4,500 rpm. Adjust the rheostat until the voltmeter reads 13 volts. At this

Adjustment of regulator cutout relay closing (cut-in) voltage. DC voltmeter with a 20-volt range (V), and three-watt 12 volt lamp (L) are connected as shown.

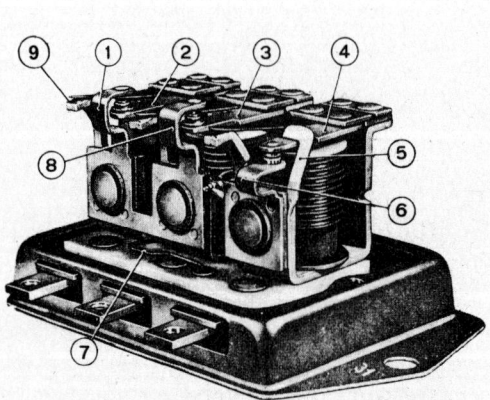

Fiat GN2/12/16 regulator components: (1) fixed contact arm; (2) voltage relay armature; (3) current relay armature; (4) cutout relay armature; (5) air gap adjustment arm; (6) cutout relay fixed contact arm; (6) (7) lead to series resistor; (8) current relay fixed contact arm; (9) relay spring tension arm.

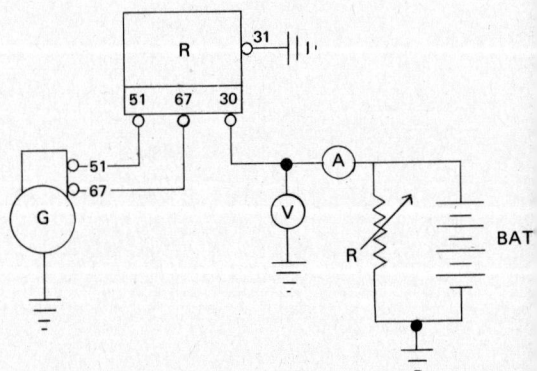

Connections for voltage and current regulator adjustment. V = 20-volt range voltmeter; A = 20-ampere range ammeter; R = 25 ampere 3-ohm rheostat.

point the ammeter should read the generator's rated output. Adjust the current to the correct value by bending the spring tension arm. Increasing the tension will increase the current.

Alternators

Fiat 124 Sport Coupe and late Spyder and 124 models are equipped with a 770 watt alternator, replacing the 400 watt generator. The alternator is a self rectifying, three phase current generator, using silicon diodes in a bridge circuit. The RC1/12B voltage regulator is a dual vibrating contact type, requiring no adjustment.

Certain precautions should be observed when working on this, or any other, AC charging system.

1. Never switch battery polarity.
2. When installing a battery, always connect the grounded terminal first.
3. Never disconnect the battery while the engine is running.
4. If the molded connector is discon-

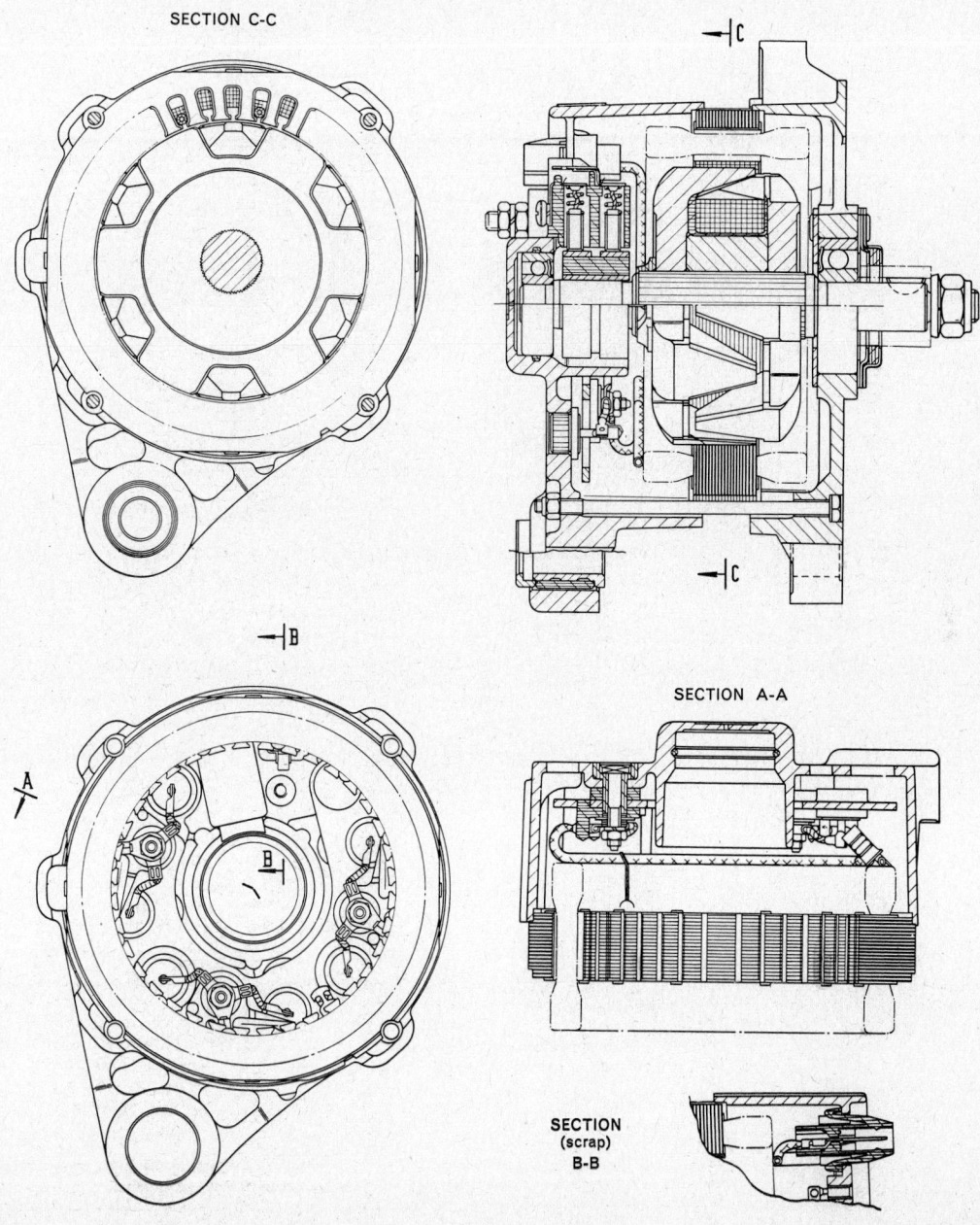

SECTION C-C

SECTION A-A

SECTION (scrap) B-B

Fiat alternator A12M-124/12/42

nected from the alternator, do not ground the hot wire.

5. Never run the alternator with the main output cable disconnected.
6. Never electric weld around the vehicle, without disconnecting the alternator.
7. Never apply any voltage, other than battery voltage, when testing.
8. Never apply more than 12 volts to "jump" a battery, for starting purposes.

Starter

REMOVAL

Front Engine Models

Jack the car and place jackstands beneath the frame. Disconnect the battery positive terminal to prevent accidental shorting. Remove the exhaust manifold and muffler to provide clearance. Disconnect the wires from the starter, tagging each

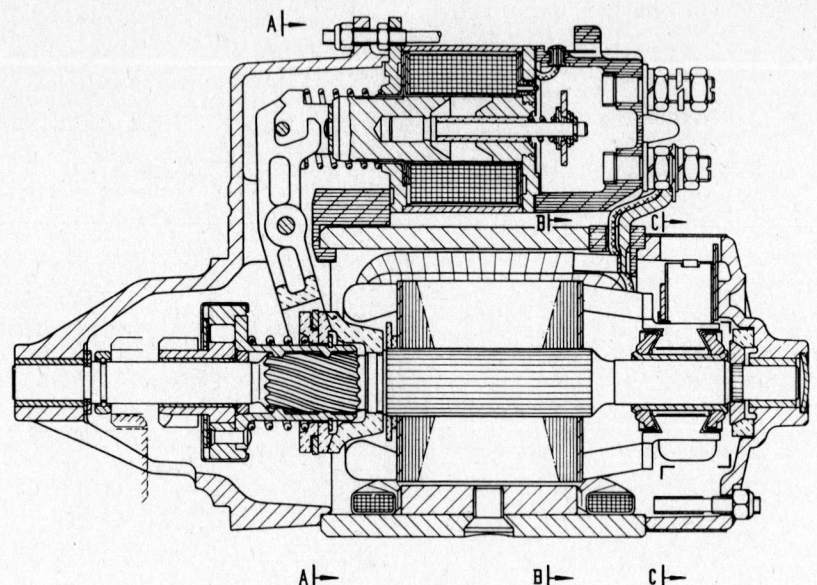

Longitudinal section of complete motor.

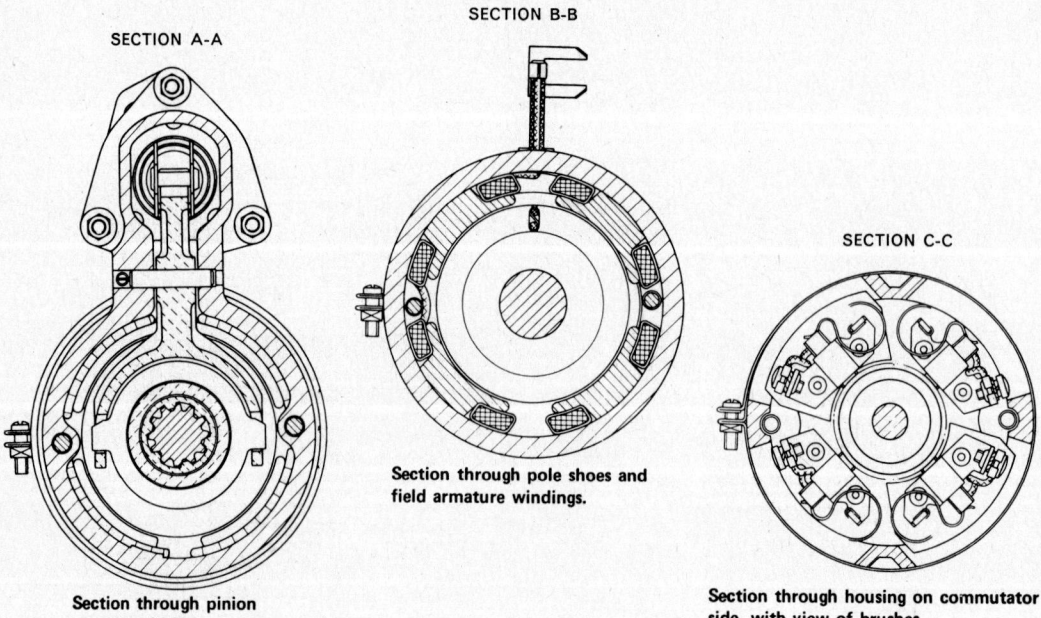

SECTION A-A

Section through pinion engaging device.

SECTION B-B

Section through pole shoes and field armature windings.

SECTION C-C

Section through housing on commutator side, with view of brushes.

Fiat starter E100-1.3/12.

wire to facilitate later identification. Remove the mounting bolts and pull the starter from the housing.

Rear Engine Models

Raise the car at the rear and set it on two stands at the control arms. Disconnect the battery plus cable to prevent shorting. Disconnect and remove the lower linings of the compartment. If necessary, remove the exhaust manifold and muffler. Disconnect the wires from the starter motor and tag each wire to facilitate later identification. Remove the mounting bolts and the starter.

Disassembly

The starter can be broken down into the following subassemblies: solenoid, commutator end head, frame, armature, drive and pinion end head.

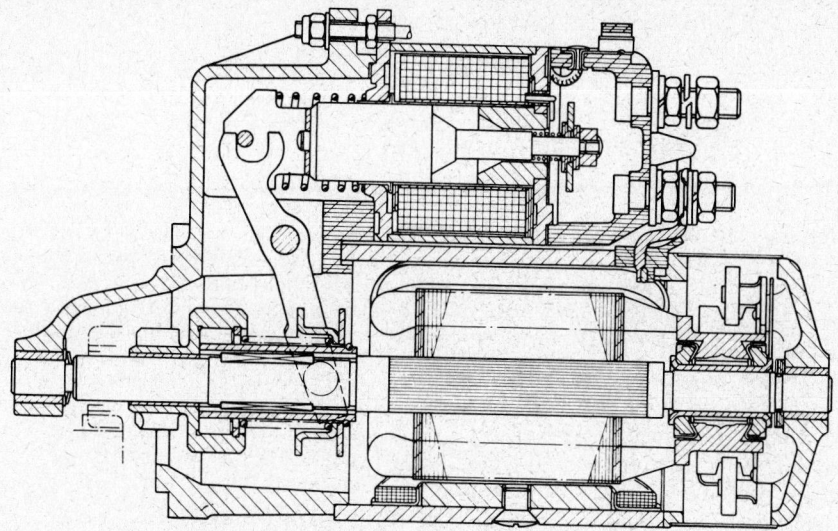

Longitudinal section view of starting motor assembly.

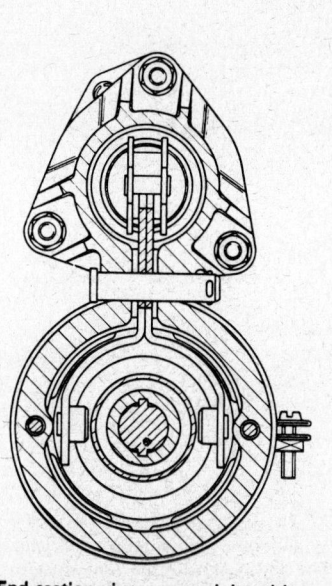

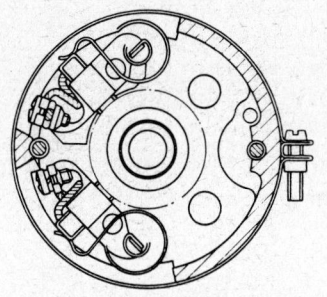

End section view across commutator end head with view of brushes.

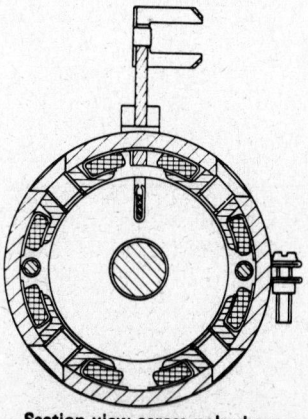

End section view across pinion drive.

Section view across pole shoes and field winding.

Fiat starter E76-0.5/12.

To disassemble, disconnect the starter motor lead from the solenoid and remove solenoid. Remove brush cover and disconnect brush holder. Lift brushes slightly and retain them in their holders by arranging springs against their sides. Unscrew two self-locking nuts and take off brush holder bracket, saving the fiber and steel thrust washers. Slide frame off pinion end. Remove cotter pin from linkage pivot and remove pivot. The armature can then be taken out, along with the drive and fork lever.

Assembly

Assembly is the reverse of removal.

Installation

Installation for all models is the reverse of removal.

Battery

All Fiat batteries are 12 volt units, grounded from the negative side. The only maintenance associated with the battery is to keep it filled with clean (preferably, distilled) water. The terminals should also be kept lightly coated with petroleum jelly to prevent corrosion.

Fuel System

Fuel Pump

All Fiats use mechanical type fuel pumps, operated from the camshaft or auxiliary shaft, except the model 1600S, which uses an electric type.

REMOVAL

Mechanical

Remove and plug the fuel lines leading to the fuel pump. Remove the mounting nuts and carefully remove the fuel pump from the block (or crankcase). If the pump is equipped with a pushrod, remove the pushrod, gasket and insulator from the mounting.

Electric

The electric fuel pump is mounted underneath the car floor, outside the battery housing. Disconnect the electric connection from the pump. Remove and plug the fuel intake and outlet lines. Remove the mount-

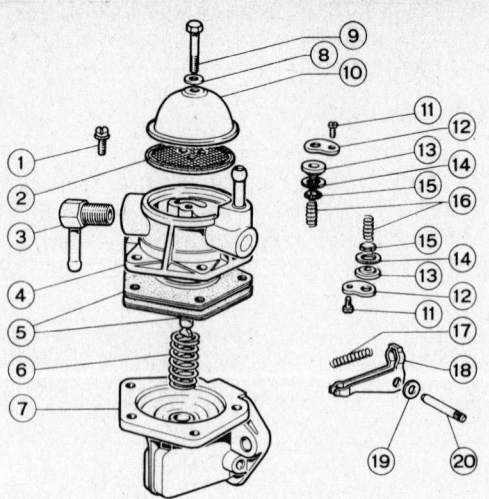

Fuel pump, 850. (1) pump bodies interlocking screws; (2) filter gauze; (3) connector; (4) upper body; (5) diaphragms; (6) spring; (7) lower body; (8) plain washer; (9) cover mounting screw; (10) pump cover; (11) valve housing locking screws; (12) valve housings; (13) valve plugs; (14) plug seals; (15) suction and delivery valves; (16) valve springs; (17) operating lever reaction spring; (18) yoke lever; (19) thrust washer; (20) yoke lever pin.

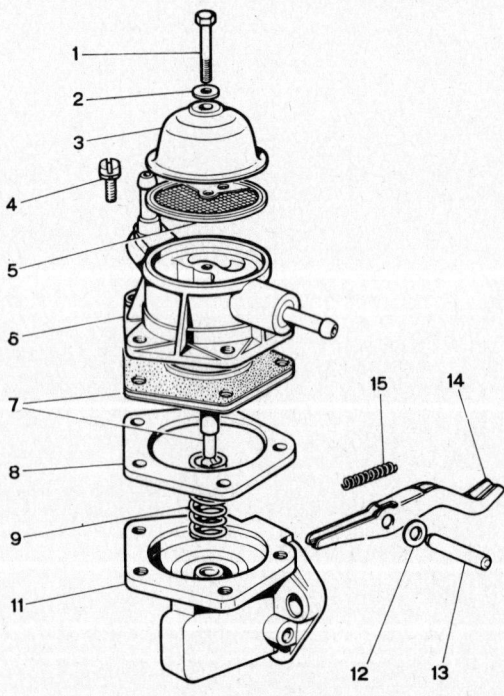

Fuel pump, 124. (1) cover fixing screw; (2) lockwasher; (3) cover; (4) screw fixing upper to lower body; (5) filter; (6) upper body; (7) diaphragm; (8) spacer; (9) spring; (11) lower body; (12) flat washer; (13) pivot pin; (14) operating lever; (15) spring.

ing bolts and remove the pump from the mounting bracket.

SERVICE

Mechanical

Sludge deposited in the fuel chamber or on the filter may be removed with the pump cover off. Intake and outlet valves should be inspected and replaced if damaged. Check springs for good condition.

Control mechanism for the intake chamber diaphragm should be washed in kerosene and lightly lubricated with thin oil. Lightly coat new fuel pump seals with grease before assembly. If a new diaphragm is to be installed, soak it in kerosene for a few minutes before assembly.

Electric

With the ignition switch off and the pump de-energized, the plunger (6) is held in its resting position by the spring(7). In this position, contacts (5) are held closed by the action of a swinging permanent magnet attracted by the plunger. When ignition switch is turned on, a coil is energized through the closed contacts, pulling the plunger down, compressing the spring and releasing the permanent magnet at the top. The contacts then open, de-energizing the coil and allowing the plunger to return to the top by spring action to repeat the cycle.

During the plunger upstroke, the intake

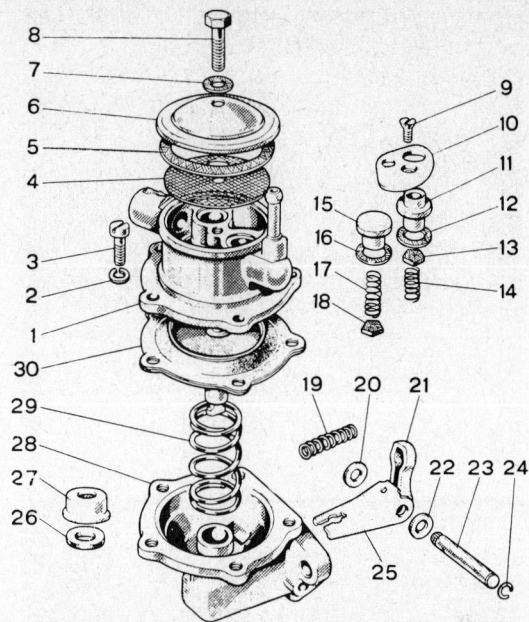

Fuel pump, 600. (1) upper body; (2) lockwasher; (3) screw; (4) filter; (5) seal; (6) cover; (7) gasket; (8) screw; (9) screw; (10) plate; (11) plug; (12) gasket; (13) inlet valve; (14) spring; (15) plug; (16) gasket; (17) spring; (18) outlet valve; (19) spring; (20) washer; (21) control rocker; (22) washer; (23) pin; (24) snap ring; (25) lever; (26) felt; (27) cup; (28) pump lower body; (29) spring; (30) diaphragm.

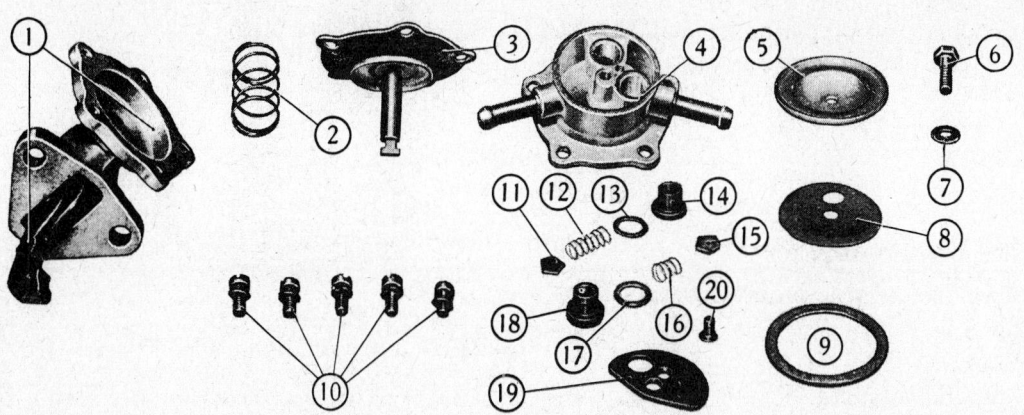

Fuel pump, 1100. (1) pump lower body and rocker arm; (2) diaphragm spring; (3) diaphragm; (4) pump upper body; (5) upper body cover; (6) cover screw; (7) screw gasket; (8) filter screen; (9) cover gasket; (10) upper-to-lower body screws; (11) outlet valve; (12) valve spring; (13) gasket; (14) outlet valve plug; (15) inlet valve; (16) valve spring; (17) gasket; (18) inlet valve plug; (19) valve plug retaining plate; (20) plate retaining screw.

1. Pump assembly.   4. Fuel inlet connection.
2. Fuel delivery connection.   5. Bottom cover nut.
3. Electric connection.

Location of 1600S electric fuel pump

valve (13) is opened and fuel is sucked
into the chamber (8). During the down-
stroke, fuel passes into the chamber above
the plunger through the lift valve (12).
Fuel is filtered by plastic strainer (4), and
magnetic particles are trapped by magnet
(23). The strainer and magnetic trap
are accessible by removing the pump bottom.

INSTALLATION

Mechanical—Except 850

Installation is the reverse of removal.

850

Before replacing the fuel pump, adjust
the projection of the pump pushrod. Fit
the insulating spacer to its seat with a gasket. Slide in the pushrod. The projection
of the pushrod should be .0394"–.0591". If
the projection is not within specified limits,
adjust the projection by replacing the gas-

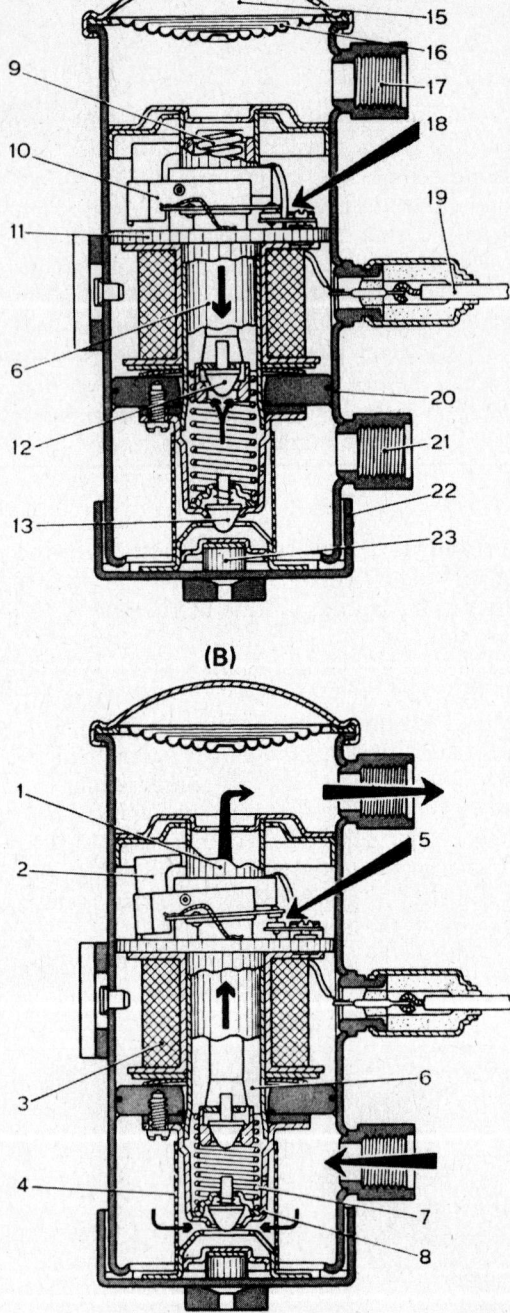

Electric fuel pump of the 1600S Cabriolet. Operation is described in the text. (1) tube; (2) magnet; (3) coil; (4) strainer; (5) contacts (open); (6)
plunger; (7) plunger spring; (8) valve carrier casing; (9) damper spring; (10) breaker arm; (11)
breaker base; (12) fuel lift valve; (13) fuel inlet
valve; (14) cover; (15) air chamber; (16) diaphragm; (17) delivery connection; (18) contacts
(closed); (19) current lead; (20) pump body; (21)
inlet connection; (22) cover; (23) magnet.

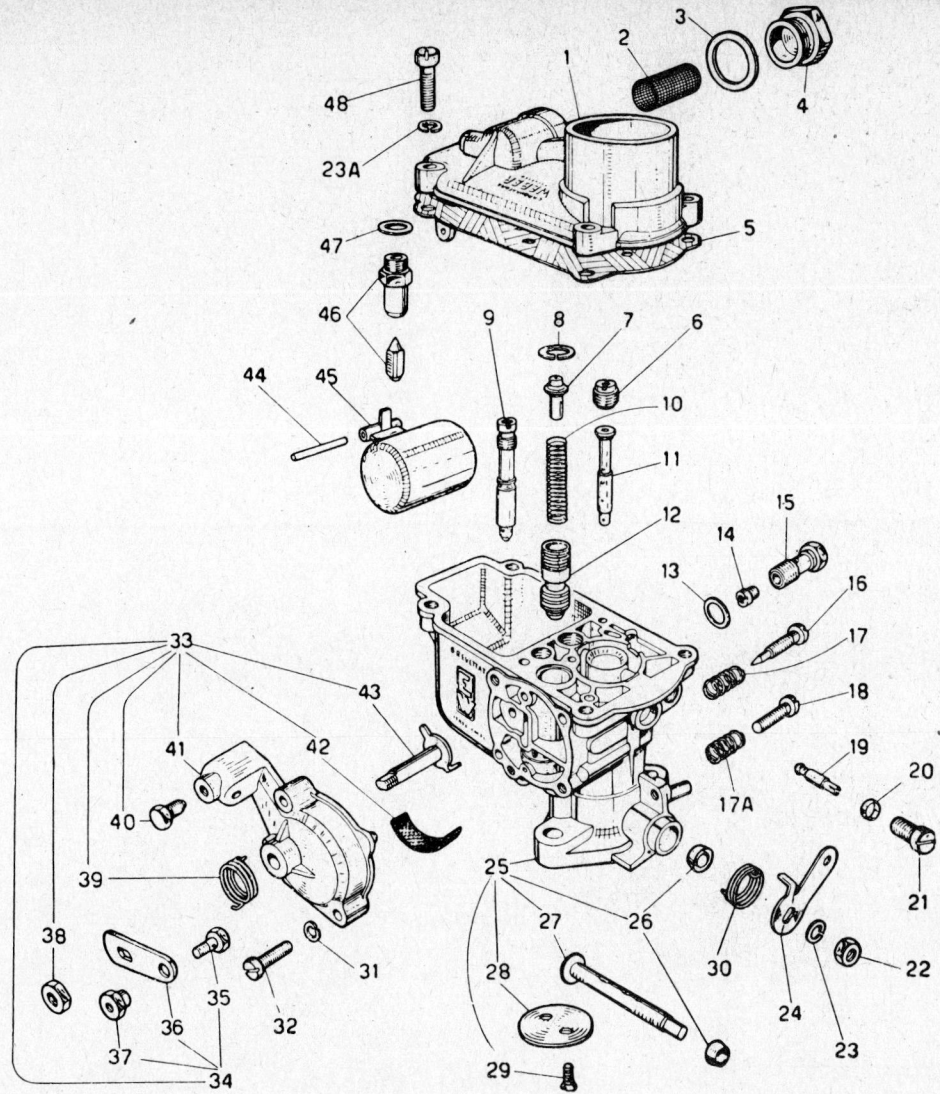

1	Carburetor cover	18	Idle speed adjustment screw	33	Cover with sheath support
2	Filter gauze	19	Idle jet		including:
3	Gasket for filter inspection plug	20	Grommet for idle jet holder	34	Starter lever complete with:
4	Filter inspection plug	21	Idle jet holder	35	—Cable fixing screw
5	Gasket for carburetor cover	22	Throttle control lever nut	36	—Starter control lever
6	Air corrector jet, emulsion tube	23	Spring washer for lever nut	37	—Nut for cable fixing screw
7	Spring guide and retainer	23A	Spring washer, carburetor cover	38	—Starter control lever fixing nut
8	Spring retaining washer		fixing screw	39	—Starter control lever return
9	Starter jet	24	Throttle control lever		spring
10	Starter valve spring	25	Carburetor body	40	—Sheath fixing screw
11	Emulsion tube		including:	41	—Cover with sheath support
12	Starter valve	26	—Spindle grommet	42	—Starter, air filter gauze
13	Main jet gasket	27	—Throttle spindle	43	—Starter valve control shaft
14	Main jet	28	—Throttle valve	44	Float fulcrum pin
15	Main jet holder	29	—Throttle fixing screw	45	Float (brass)
16	Idle mixture adjustment screw	30	Throttle control lever return spring	45	Float (nylon)
17	Spring, idle mixture adjustment	31	Spring washer for screw, sheath	46	Needle valve
	screw		support cover	47	Gasket for needle valve
17A	Spring, idle mixture adjustment	32	Fixing screw, sheath support cover	48	Carburetor cover fixing screw
	screw				

(*) Calibrated parts

Exploded view—Weber 22IM carburetor

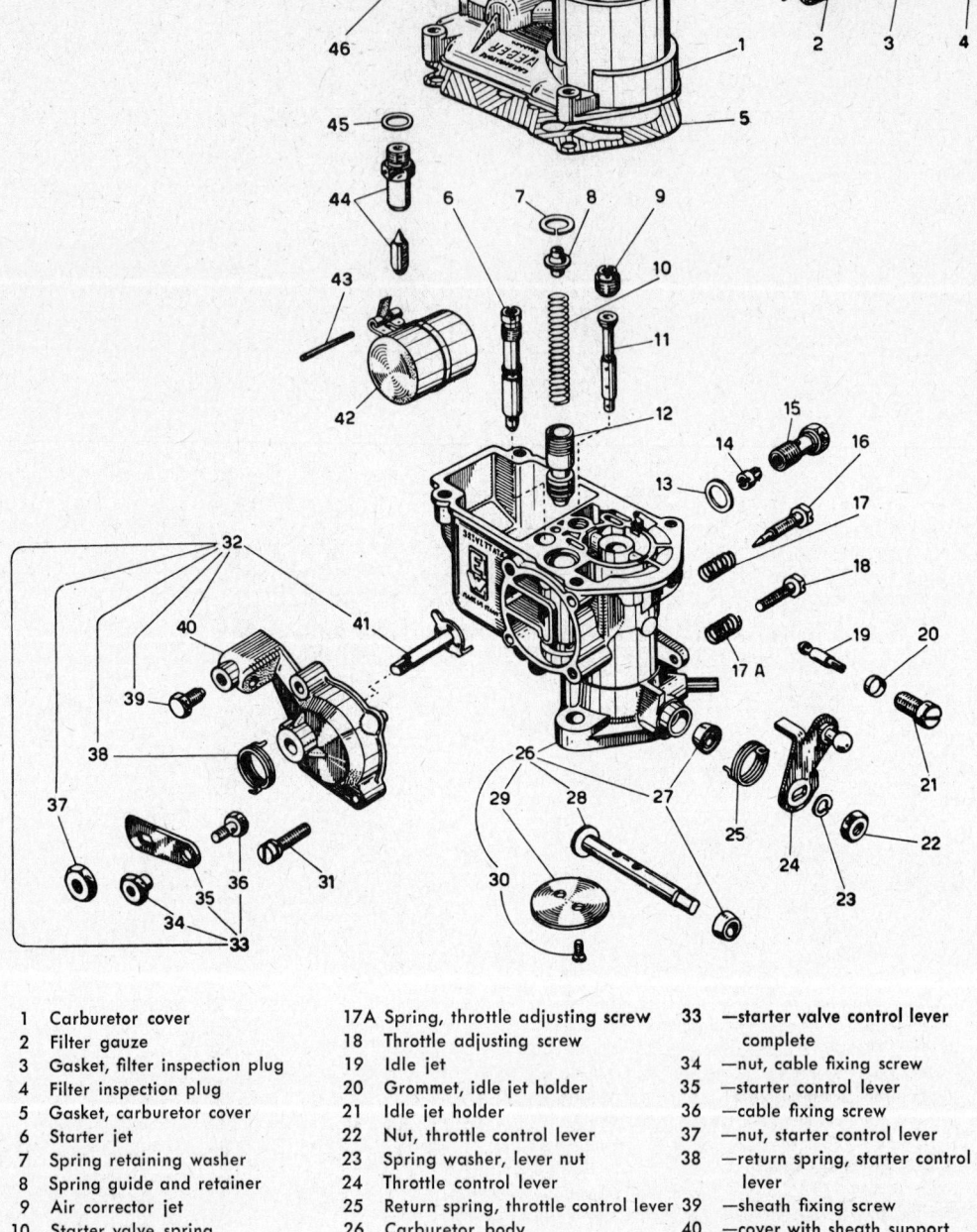

1	Carburetor cover	17A	Spring, throttle adjusting screw	33	—starter valve control lever
2	Filter gauze	18	Throttle adjusting screw		complete
3	Gasket, filter inspection plug	19	Idle jet	34	—nut, cable fixing screw
4	Filter inspection plug	20	Grommet, idle jet holder	35	—starter control lever
5	Gasket, carburetor cover	21	Idle jet holder	36	—cable fixing screw
6	Starter jet	22	Nut, throttle control lever	37	—nut, starter control lever
7	Spring retaining washer	23	Spring washer, lever nut	38	—return spring, starter control
8	Spring guide and retainer	24	Throttle control lever		lever
9	Air corrector jet	25	Return spring, throttle control lever	39	—sheath fixing screw
10	Starter valve spring	26	Carburetor body	40	—cover with sheath support
11	Emulsion tube		including:	41	—starter valve control shaft
12	Starter valve	27	—spindle grommet	42	Float
13	Gasket, main jet holder	28	—throttle valve spindle	43	Float fulcrum pin
14	Main jet	29	—throttle valve	44	Needle valve
15	Main jet holder	30	—throttle valve fixing screw	45	Gasket, needle valve
16	Idle adjustment screw	31	Sheath support fixing screw	46	Carburetor cover fixing screw
17	Spring, idle adjustment screw	32	Cover with sheath support		
			including:		

(*) Calibrated parts.

Exploded view—Weber 26IM1 carburetor

ket with another. Service gaskets are available in the following thicknesses:

A = .0106″-.0130″
B = .0276″-.0315″
C = .0472″-.0512″

Further installation is the reverse of removal.

Electric

The electric fuel pump must be mounted vertically, with the pump cover uppermost. Prior to mounting the pump, sand the mounting bracket and the pump mounting surface, in order to be sure of a good ground. The pump is provided with a welded bracket for mounting. Connect all lines and check for leaks.

Carburetors

Over the years, Fiats have been equipped with either Weber or Solex carburetors, in either one- or two-barrel models. Only one, the 1600S, has a multiple carburetion system. For the carburetor usage on each engine, consult the specifications.

WEBER 22IM AND 26IM

These carburetors are single-throat, downdraft types, with progressive action starting devices.

Adjustments

Idle speed adjustment is made by means of the throttle stop screw and the idle mixture screw. Adjust, with engine warm, by first setting throttle stop screw to minimum opening that allows steady operation. Then turn mixture screw in or

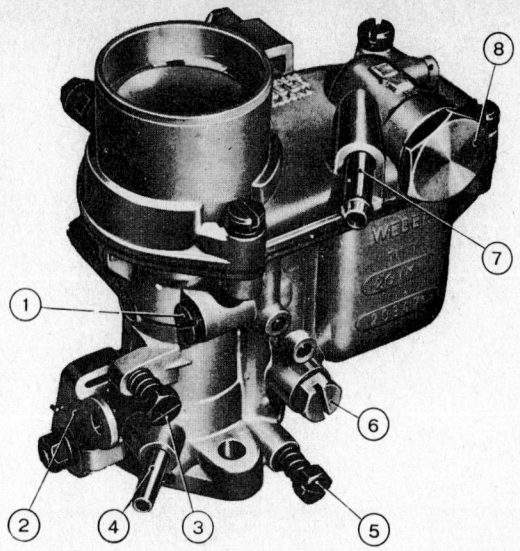

Weber 26IM carburetor. Idle jet holder (1); throttle lever (2); idle speed adjustment (3); vacuum advance line (4); idle mixture adjustment (5); main jet holder (6); fuel inlet (7); strainer (8).

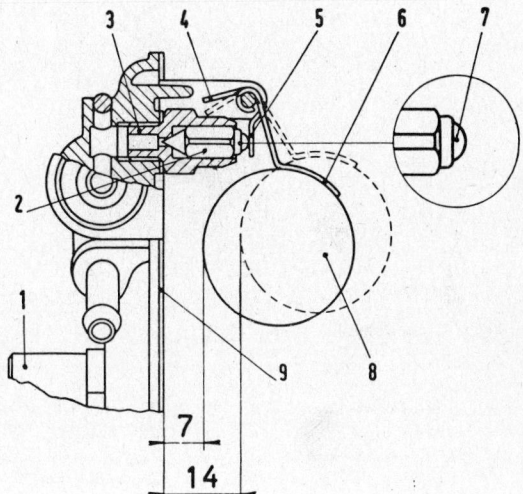

Float adjustment for Weber 26IM carburetor. (1) carburetor cover; (2) needle; (3) needle valve; (4) lug; (5-6) arms; (7) needle ball; (8) float; (9) cover gasket.

out to achieve fast, smooth idle. Readjust throttle stop screw for proper idle speed.

Float level adjustment is checked with the carburetor cover held vertically. When adjustment is correct, float arm (5) just touches ball (7) of needle (2) when float is .28″ (7 mm.) away from cover gasket (9). Float travel is .28″ (7 mm.). These dimensions are .20″ (5 mm.) and .28″ (7 mm.), respectively, for the Weber

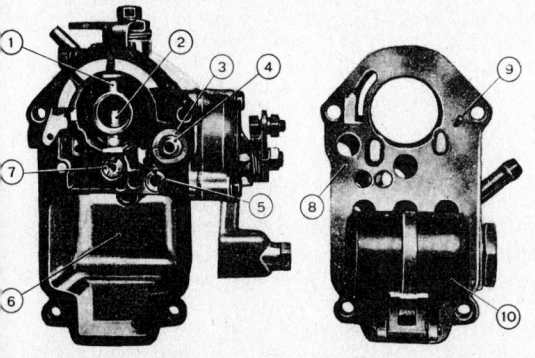

Weber 26IM carburetor. (1) secondary venturi; (2) nozzle tube; (3) choke valve spring lock ring; (4) spring retainer and guide; (5) choke jet; (6) fuel bowl; (7) emulsion well with air bleed jet; (8) gasket and carburetor cover; (9) cover locating dowel; (10) float.

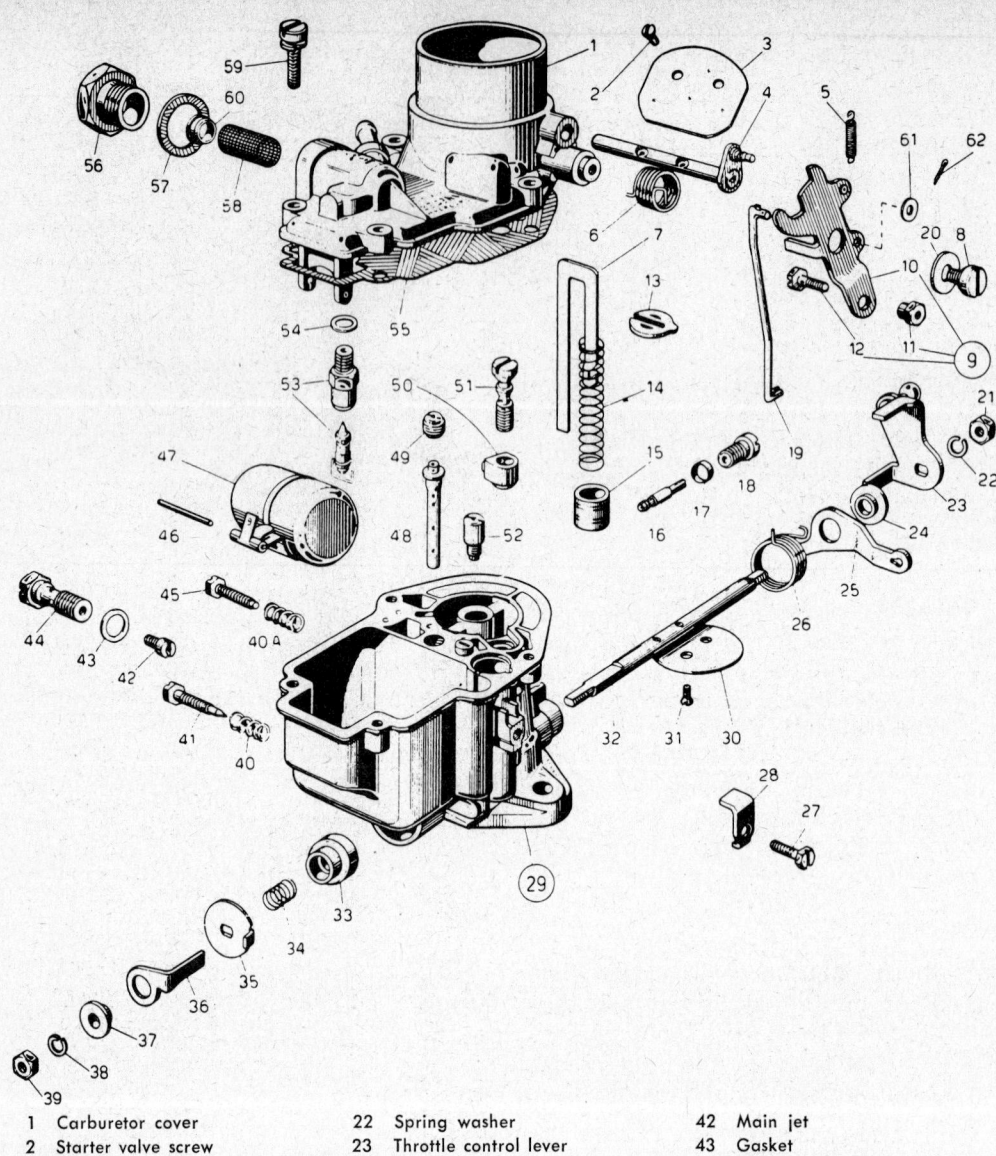

1	Carburetor cover	22	Spring washer	42	Main jet
2	Starter valve screw	23	Throttle control lever	43	Gasket
3	Starter valve	24	Bushing	44	Main jet holder
4	Starter valve shaft	25	Lever for fast idling	45	Throttle adjustment screw
5	Lever spring	26	Main shaft return spring	46	Float fulcrum pin
6	Starter shaft return spring	27	Plate fixing screw	47	Float
7	Pump control rod	28	Sheath retaining plate	48	Emulsion tube
8	Starter lever fulcrum screw	29	Carburetor body	49	Air corrector jet
9	Starter control lever, complete	30	Throttle	50	Pump jet
10	—Lever	31	Throttle fixing screw	51	Pump delivery valve
11	—Nut for screw	32	Main shaft	52	Pump intake valve
12	—Cable fixing screw	33	Diaphragm	53	Needle valve
13	Spring retaining plate	34	Diaphragm holding spring	54	Gasket
14	Spring, pump plunger	35	Shim, pump control	55	Cover gasket
15	Pump plunger	36	Loose lever	56	Filter plug
16	Idle jet	37	Bush	57	Gasket
17	Seal	38	Spring washer	58	Filter gauze
18	Idle jet holder	39	Nut for shaft	59	Cover fixing screws
19	Rod	40	Spring, idle adjustment screw	60	Filter protector
20	Washer	40A	Spring, throttle adjustment screw	61	Washer
21	Lever fixing nut	41	Idle adjustment screw	62	Cotter pin

(*) Calibrated parts.

Exploded view—Weber 28ICP carburetor

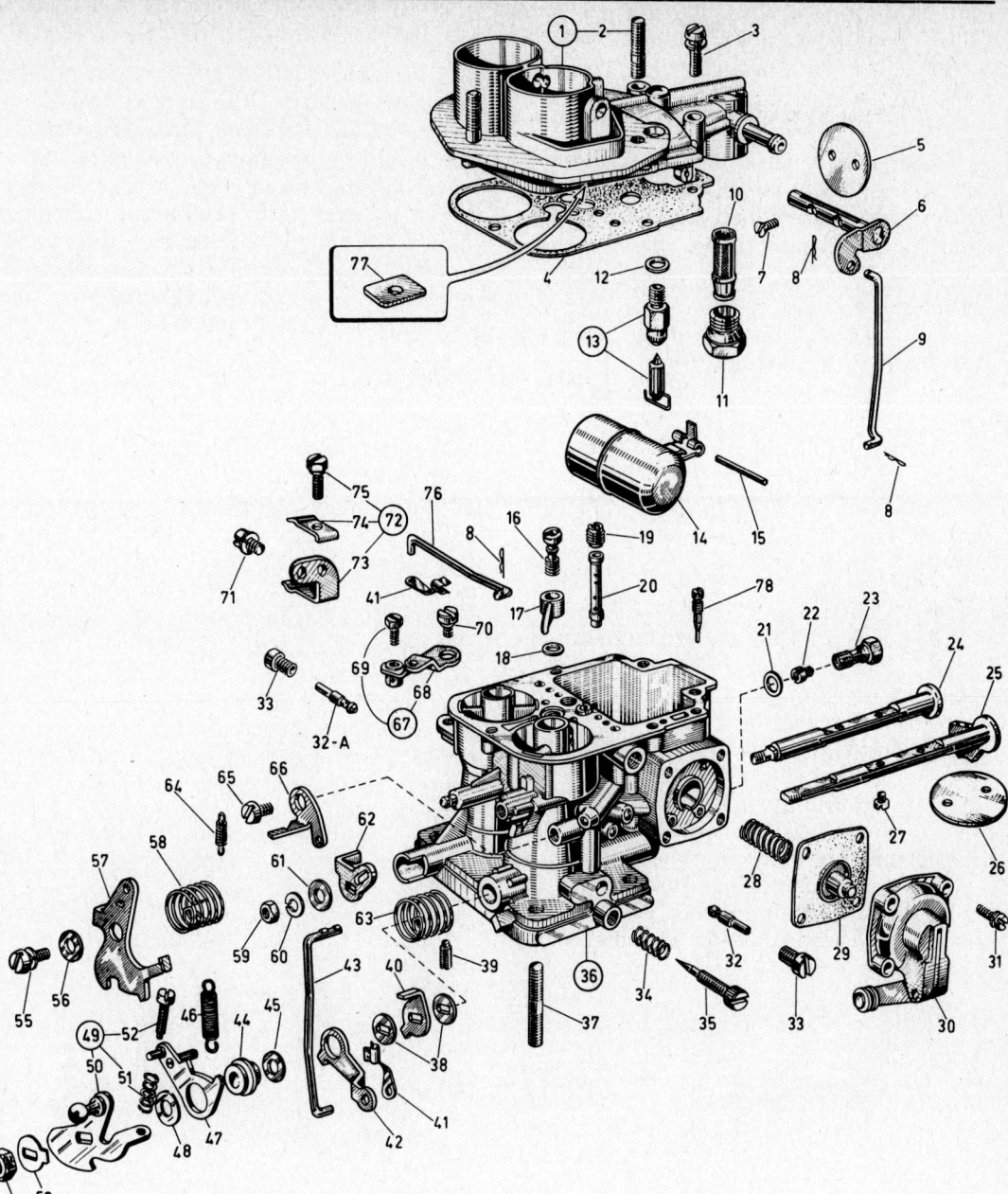

Exploded view—Weber #30DC1 carburetor

22IM. Bend float arms to correct float position.

WEBER 28ICP AND 30ICF

Weber 28ICP and 30ICF carburetors are similar single-throat, downdraft types with manual starting and lean mixture controls, plus accelerator pump.

Adjustments

Float level adjustment is identical to the Weber 26IM carburetor.

WEBER 30DIC

This is a dual-throat carburetor, with manual choke and a super-feeder device as part of the secondary throat. An accelerator pump is provided for smooth running.

Adjustments

Idle is adjusted on a warm, running engine. Adjust the throttle stop screw to a point where the engine runs steadily. Adjust the volume control screw to a point that allows highest steady engine speed at selected degree of throttle restriction. Adjust the throttle opening to the best idle speed, controlling the mixture rate with the volume control screw.

Follow the instructions for float adjustment, detailed under Weber 22IM adjustment. Float level is 6 mm. and float stroke is 14 mm.

WEBER 34DCHD4

The Weber 34DCHD4 is a downdraft, doublethroat carb. The primary throttle is controlled by the accelerator. The secondary throttle is vacuum controlled, and begins opening when vacuum in the first throat is sufficient to actuate a diaphragm. As the secondary throttle opens, vacuum in the secondary throat assists throttle opening as required. A mechanical linkage closes the secondary throttle.

Adjustments

Idle speed adjustments are made with the engine warm. Adjust only the throttle stop screw and the volume control screw of the primary throat. Turn throttle stop screw until engine idles smoothly, then adjust volume control screw for mixture which gives highest engine speed. Finally, reduce engine speed with throttle stop screw to prescribed idle speed.

With the float hanging in a vertical position, adjust the distance from the float to the carburetor cover, obtaining a distance of 5-5.5 mm. The float tang should lightly contact the needle valve. Bend the float arm to adjust this measurement. Float stroke should be adjusted to 13 mm. in the above manner.

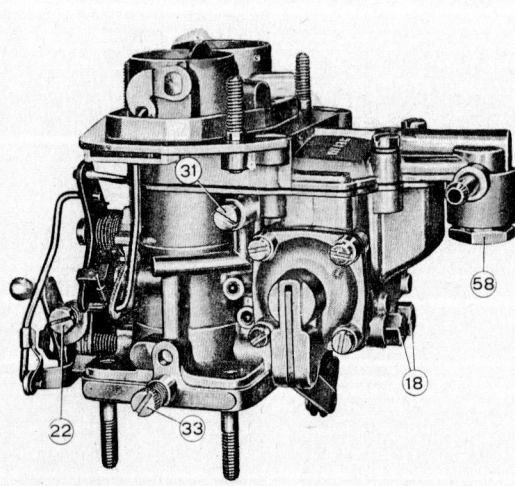

Weber 30DICI carburetor adjustments, controls and jet locations. (18) main jets; (22) throttle stop screw; (31) idle jet; (33) volume control screw; (58) strainer inspection plug.

Weber 34DCHD4 carburetor adjustments, controls and jet locations. (1) idling jet; (2) vacuum advance line connector; (3) main jet; (4) volume control screw; (5) throttle stop screw; (6) primary throat throttle control lever; (7) primary throat throttle spindle.

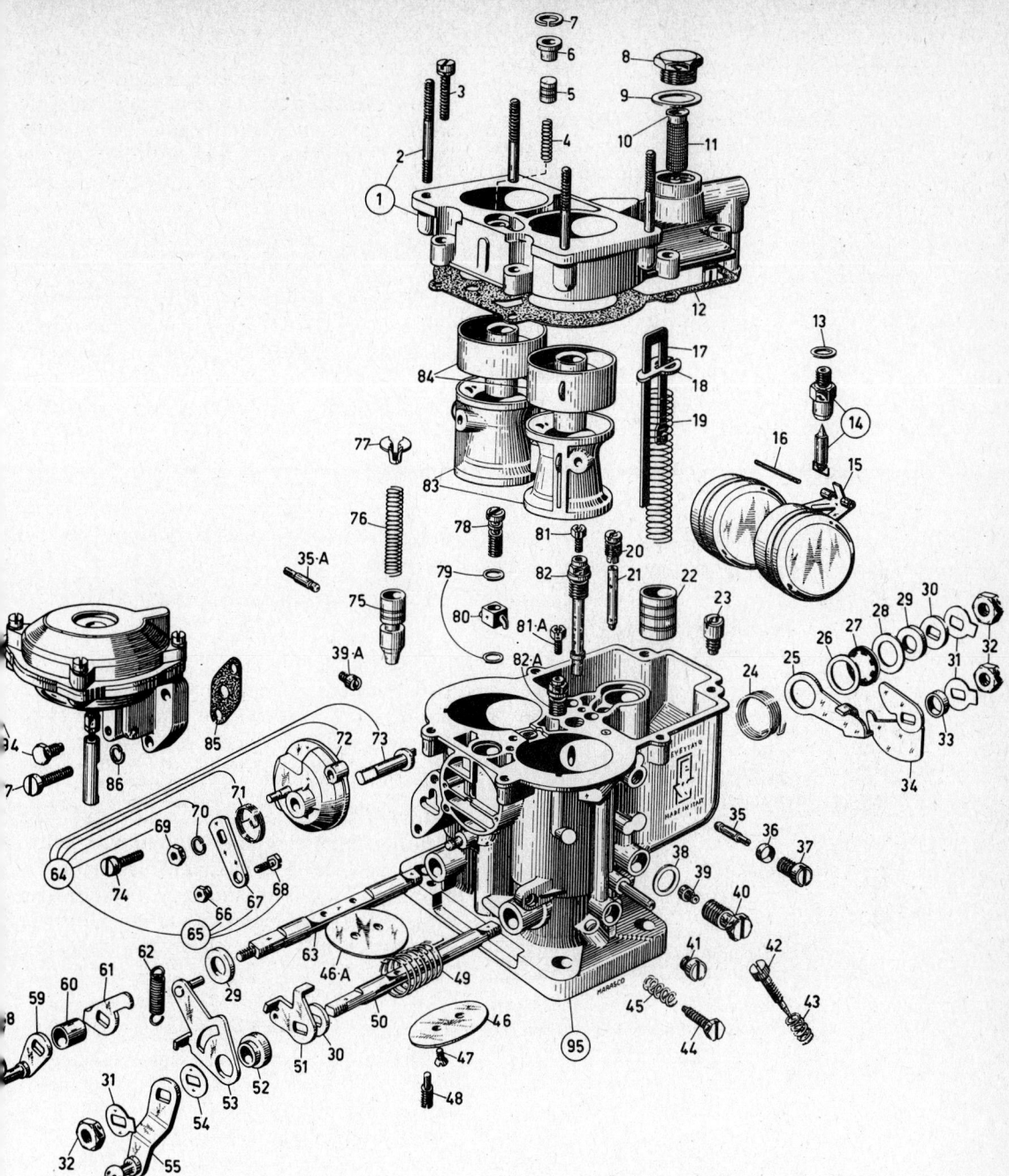

Exploded view—Weber 34DCHD4 carburetor

Weber 34DCS

Weber 34DCS2 (front) and 34DCS4 (rear) carburetors are double-barrel types with synchronous throttles, choke and accelerator pump. The throttles are operated by gears, but open in opposite directions.

Adjustments

Adjustments for these carburetors are the same as for the Weber 34DCHD4.

Solex 30PIB

The Solex 30PIB is a single-throat, downdraft carb with a manual choke and a diaphragm type power accelerator pump.

Adjustments

Float level adjustment is made by first removing float, then placing it on gauge A.95126, making sure arms contact both

Adjustments and controls for Weber 34DCS carburetors. (1) idle mixture adjusting screw; (2) throttle adjusting screw; (3) choke control lever link; (4) throttles control lever rod.

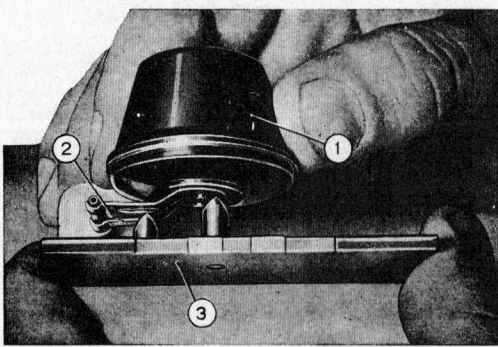

Solex 30PIB float adjustment. (1) float; (2) float arm; (3) gauge A.95126.

dowels. The float should be level. If not, correct float level by bending float arm, then fit gauge needle seat as shown in diagram. Needle should allow gauge to slide freely. Set dowel at needle to prevent gauge from sliding. The position of the needle is changed, if necessary, by use of shims.

Solex C32PHH

This is a dual-throat, sidedraft carburetor, each throat feeding two cylinders. An opening between the throats provides reciprocal fuel mixture balance, and each throat has its own idling and main fuel system.

Adjustments

Idle speed is adjusted by means of the throttle stop screw and the volume control screw.

Solex 32PBIC and Weber 32IMPE

These Solex and Weber carbs are interchangeable single-barrel, downdraft types with a throat diameter of 1.26″ (32 mm.) and are equipped with a progressive starting device and an accelerator pump.

Adjustments

Idle adjustments are made with the throttle stop screw and idle mixture screw. Solex fuel level adjustment is made by changing the gasket under the needle valve seat, using a thinner gasket to raise the level and a thicker one to lower it.

Solex C32-35 APATI and Weber 36DCD3

These carburetors are interchangeable double-barrel downdraft types, having a throat diameter of 1.417″ (36 mm.). They are equipped with a progressive action starting device and accelerating pump.

Adjustments

Float position is adjusted by bending the float arm until the float clears the cover (without gasket) by .2″ (5 mm.).

Weber 30DICA

This carburetor is a dual-throat, downdraft unit using a differential throttle opening. It is fitted with a pneumatic device which stops the throttle from completely closing during fast idle.

Current Setting		32PHH/6 CR182	32PHH/9 CR185
Choke tube	K	23	22
Main jet	Gg	115	105
Correction jet	a	190	180
Pilot jet	g	45	40
Needle valve	P	1.6	1.6
Float	F	gr. 9	gr. 9
Fuel jet	Gst	125	125
Injector tube		cal. 40	cal. 60

Solex C32PHH-6 and PHH-9 components and specifications. The PHH-6 settings are for the Fiat 124 and the PHH-9 settings are for the 1100R.

1. Body
2. Throttle butterfly 10° (124)
— Throttle butterfly 8° (1100R)
3. Throttle spindle
4. Throttle screw
8. Idle adjustment screw
9. Screw spring
10. Throttle lever assembly
13. Lock washer
15. Volume control screw
23. Starter valve
36. Throttle lever nut
39. Starter valve spring
41. Cable screw
45. Starter cover
48. Cable support
50. Support screw
62. Float assembly
64. Float spindle washer (only 1100R)
65. Float chamber gasket
70. Main jet
74. Pilot jet
75. Starter jet
80. Air cap screw
84. Emulsion air cap assembly

93. Central diffuser screw
98. Nut for screw
99. Emulsion tube assembly (124)
101. Choke tube
102. Choke tube screw
103. Float chamber cover assembly
110. Float spindle
112. Filter screen
114. Filter plug washer
115. Needle valve washer (124)
116. Needle valve
126. Float chamber assembly screw
127. Lock washer
154. Ball
158. Pump actuating lever
160. Pump control rod
166. Pump assembly screw
167. Pump gasket
175. Washer
192. Yoke
196. Throttle spring
209. Roller bracket
210. Circlip
218. Filter plug

258. Lock washer
264. Lock washer
336. Pump rod adjustment nut
337. Lock nut
342. Pump rod spring
343. Control rod retaining washer
354. Bushing
358. Starter return spring
371. Diaphragm
374. Diaphragm pump body
376. Diaphragm spring
377A. Pump cover
378. Pump cover screw
386. Throttle return spring
387. Return spring stop pin
389. Nut washer
394. Circlip
472. Stud
573. Pump channel anti-siphon
574. Grub with sealing ring
582. Pivot
583. Blow by disc
599. Sealing ring
602. Plug washer
617. Threaded plug
621. Central diffuser

1. Body
2. Throttle butterfly 8°
3. Throttle spindle
4. Throttle butterfly screw
8. Adjustment screw
9. Screw spring
10. Throttle lever
13. Throttle spindle washer
15. Volume control screw
23. Starter valve
31. Starter lever
32. Starter cable screw
33. Control lever bushing
34. Starter cable screw nut
36. Starter spindle and throttle spindle nut
43. Starter air jet (Ga)
45. Starter cover
46. Starter cover screw
50. Cable sheath locking screw
53. Starter spindle washer
62. Float (F)
65. Float chamber gasket
70. Main jet (Gg)
71. Main jet carrier
72. Main jet carrier washer
73. Correction jet (a)
74. Pilot jet (g)
75. Starter fuel jet (Gs)
76. Gp, Gs and pump inlet valve washer
84. Idling air bleed (u)
86. Emulsion tube (s)
101. Choke tube (K)
102. Choke tube fixing screw
103. Float chamber cover
109. Float toggle
110. Float toggle spindle
115. Needle valve washer
116. Needle valve
126. Float chamber screw
127. Washer
136. Flange washer
158. Pump actuating lever
160. Pump control rod
166. Pump assembly screw
167. Pump body gasket
196. Throttle spindle return spring
217. Filter screen
218. Filter plug
338. Pump injector high assembly
339. Pump injector support screw
340. Pump injector support gasket
342. Pump rod spring
343. Control rod washer
344. Control rod split washer

349. Pump valve
350. Pump jet (Gp)
353. Pump filter screen
354. Sealing washer
356. Washer
371. Pump membrane
375. Pump body
376. Pump membrane spring
377A. Pump cover
378. Pump cover screw
389. Stop washer
449. Flange stud (short)
449. Flange stud (long)
548. Intermediate lever screw

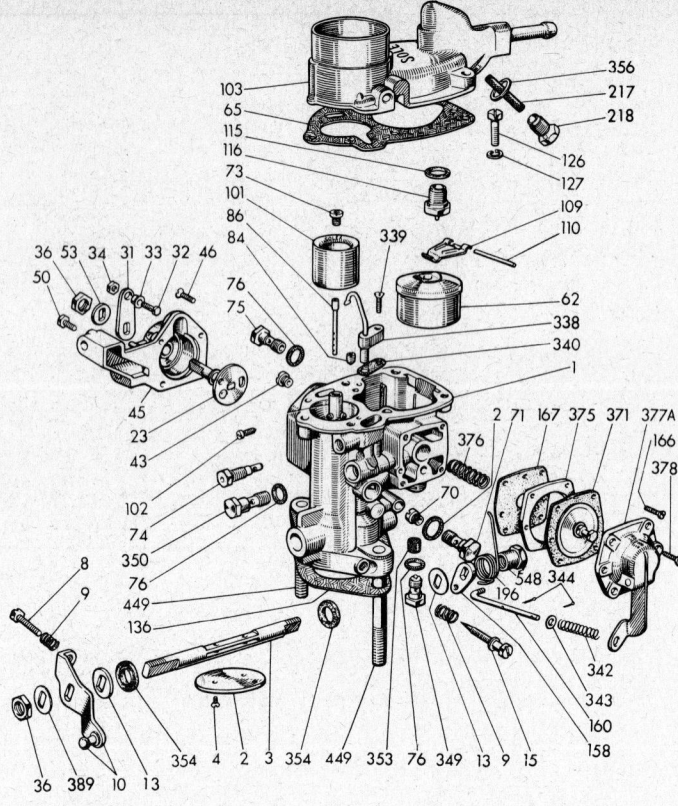

Solex C32PBIC components and specifications, Fiat 1100.

Carburetor Setting			
	103 D.037*	103 D	103 D. Premier
Choke tube K =	24	24	20.5
Main jet Gg =	120	120	102
Correction jet a =	205	185	200
Pilot jet g =	45	45	40
Idling air bleed u =	100	100	100
Emulsion tube s =	17 T	17 T	17 T
Needle valve P =	1.5	1.5	1.5
Float F =	12.5	12.5	12.5
Accelerating pump =			
Pump jet Gp =	50	50	40
Starter =			
Air jet Ga =	4	4	3.5
Fuel jet Gs =	110	110	125

*With special air filter

1   Throttle chamber
2a   Throttle butterfly, 8°
2b   Throttle butterfly, 17°
2c   Automatic throttle, 17°
3a   Right-hand throttle
        spindle
3b   Left-hand throttle
        spindle
3c   Automatic throttle
        spindle assembly
4   Throttle screw
8   Adjustment screw
9   Screw spring
10a RH throttle lever
        assembly
10c LH throttle lever
        assembly
13   Washer
15   Volume control screw
16   Float chamber gasket
17   Float chamber screw
23   Starter valve
31   Starter lever
32   Starter cable screw
33   Control lever bushing
34   Starter cable nut
36   Lever nut
36a Starter lever nut
45   Starter cover
46   Starter screw
48   Cable sheath support
50   Cable sheath locking
        screw
61   Float chamber
62   Float (F)
63   Float spindle
65   Float chamber gasket
70   Main jet (Gg)
71   Main jet carrier
72   Main jet washer
73   Correction jet (a)
74   Pilot jet (g)
75   Starter jet (Gs)
76   Gs, H, Gp gasket
84   Pilot jet air bleed
86a Emulsion tube
        (RH carburetor)
86b Emulsion tube
        (LH carburetor)
98   Choke tube screw nut
101a RH choke tube
        (first carburetor) (K)
101b LH choke tube (second
        carburetor) (K)
102 Choke tube screw
103 Float chamber cover
115 Needle valve washer
116 Needle valve assembly
        (P)
126 Float chamber screw
127 Lock washer
128 Cable sheath support
        screw
158 Pump actuating lever
160 Pump rod
166 Pump assembly screw
167 Pump body gasket
175 Washer

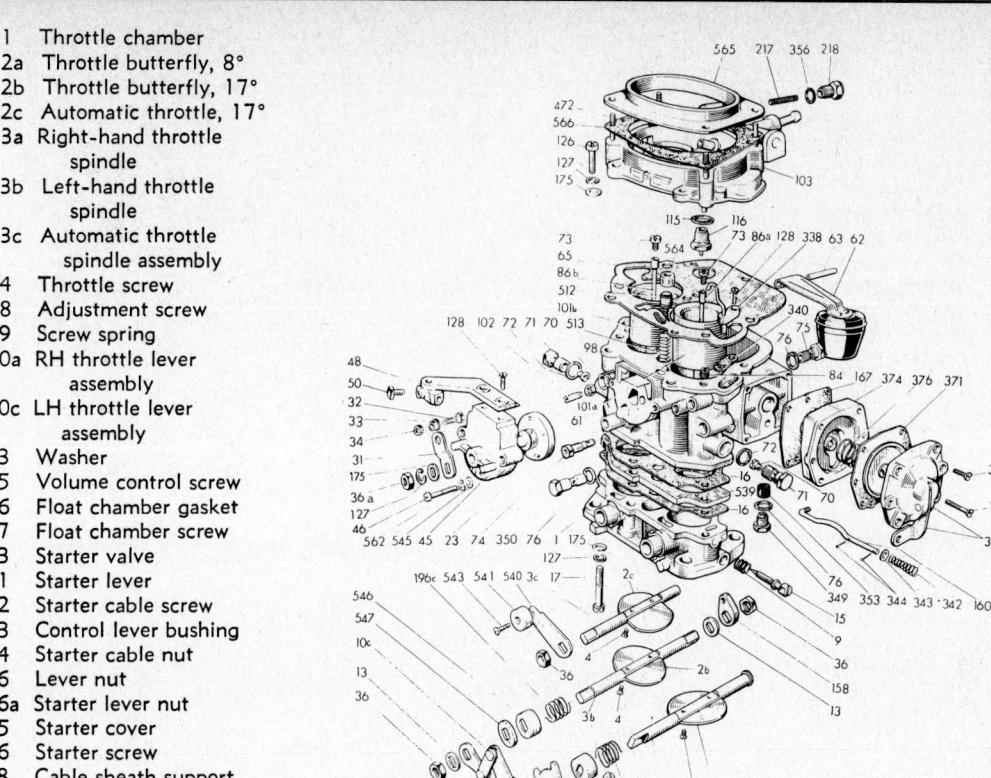

Solex C32-35 APATI-2 components and specifications, Fiat 1100.

196a RH throttle return spring
196c LH throttle return spring
217 Filter screen
218 Filter plug
338 Pump injector assembly
        (high)
340 Pump injector gasket
342 Pump rod spring
343 Control rod washer
344 Control rod split pin
349 Pump inlet valve
        assembly (H)
350 Pump jet (Gp)
353 Pump filter screen
356 Filter plug washer
371 Membrane assembly
374 Pump body assembly
376 Pump membrane spring
377A Pump cover assembly
378 Pump cover screw
472 Cover stud
512 Starter piston
513 Spring for starter piston
539 Heat insulator
540 Counterweight lever
541 Counterweight
543 Counterweight screw
545 Screw washer
546 Spring cup

547 Thrust washer
562 Washer (for fixing
        screw)
563 Throttle spindle bushing
564 Boot for starter piston
565 Flange for air intake
566 Gasket for item 565

Carburetor Setting		
	I	II
Choke tube	22	23
Main jet	112	115
Correction jet	200	160
Pilot jet	40	60
Idling air bleed	120	—
Emulsion tube	0	C. 20705
Needle valve	1.5	—
Float	8 gr.	—
Pump jet	60	—
Fuel jet	105.	

1 Carburetor cover
2 Carburetor cover screw
3 Lock washer, starter plunger seat
4 Seat, starter plunger
5 Starter plunger
6 Spring, starter plunger
7 Filter plug
8 Gasket, filter plug
9 Filter gauze
10 Gasket, carburetor cover
11 Float fulcrum pin
12 Gasket, needle valve
13 Plunger shaft
14 Plunger spring retaining plate
15 Pump plunger spring
16 Needle valve complete
17 Float
18 Starter air corrector jet
19 Starter jet
20 Pump plunger
21 Intake valve with exhaust orifice
22 Idle jet
23 Seal, idle jet holder
24 Idle jet holder
25 Gasket, main jet holder
26 Main jet primary duct
26A Main jet secondary duct
27 Main jet holder

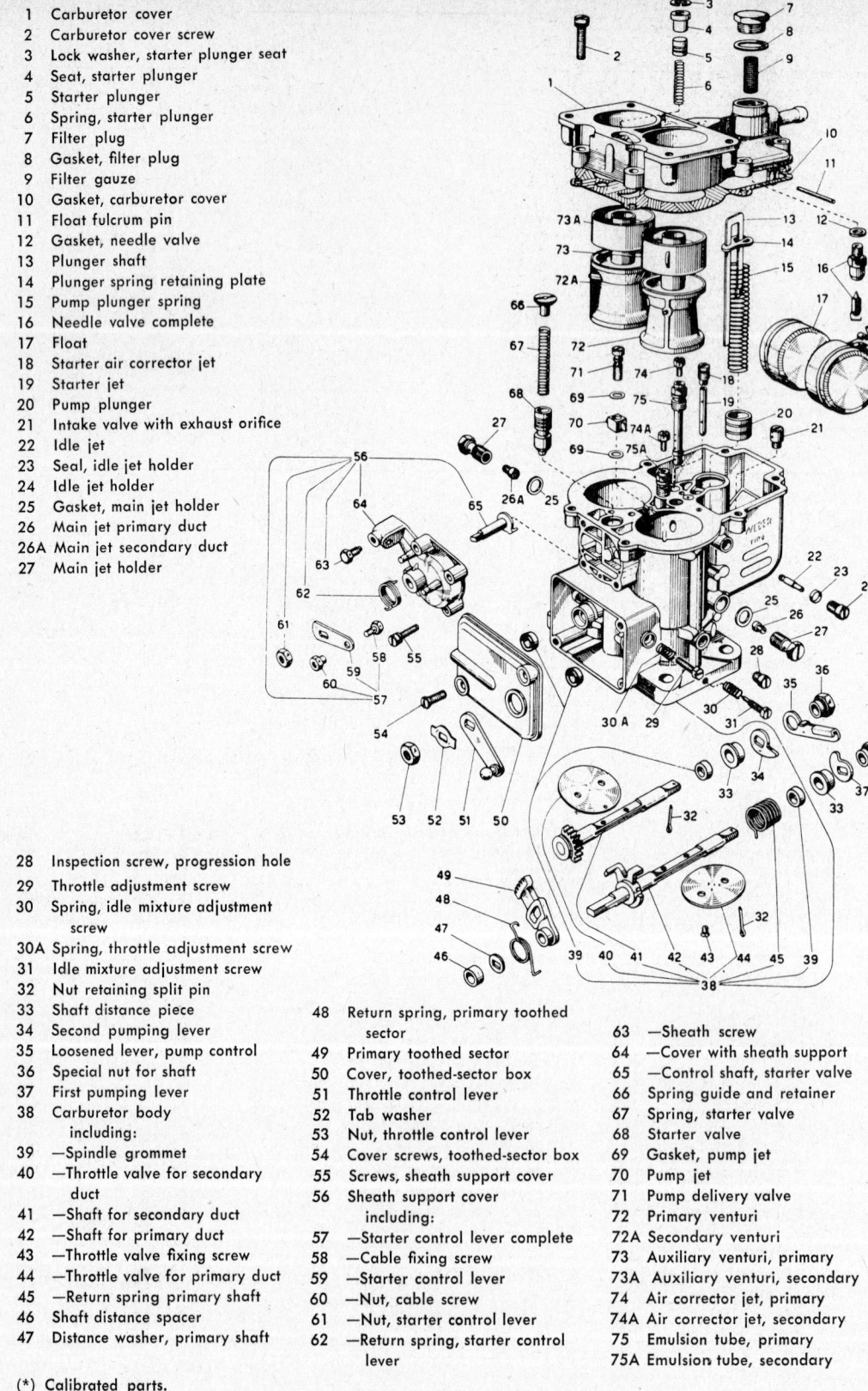

28 Inspection screw, progression hole
29 Throttle adjustment screw
30 Spring, idle mixture adjustment
    screw
30A Spring, throttle adjustment screw
31 Idle mixture adjustment screw
32 Nut retaining split pin
33 Shaft distance piece
34 Second pumping lever
35 Loosened lever, pump control
36 Special nut for shaft
37 First pumping lever
38 Carburetor body
    including:
39 —Spindle grommet
40 —Throttle valve for secondary
    duct
41 —Shaft for secondary duct
42 —Shaft for primary duct
43 —Throttle valve fixing screw
44 —Throttle valve for primary duct
45 —Return spring primary shaft
46 Shaft distance spacer
47 Distance washer, primary shaft

48 Return spring, primary toothed
    sector
49 Primary toothed sector
50 Cover, toothed-sector box
51 Throttle control lever
52 Tab washer
53 Nut, throttle control lever
54 Cover screws, toothed-sector box
55 Screws, sheath support cover
56 Sheath support cover
    including:
57 —Starter control lever complete
58 —Cable fixing screw
59 —Starter control lever
60 —Nut, cable screw
61 —Nut, starter control lever
62 —Return spring, starter control
    lever

63 —Sheath screw
64 —Cover with sheath support
65 —Control shaft, starter valve
66 Spring guide and retainer
67 Spring, starter valve
68 Starter valve
69 Gasket, pump jet
70 Pump jet
71 Pump delivery valve
72 Primary venturi
72A Secondary venturi
73 Auxiliary venturi, primary
73A Auxiliary venturi, secondary
74 Air corrector jet, primary
74A Air corrector jet, secondary
75 Emulsion tube, primary
75A Emulsion tube, secondary

(*) Calibrated parts.

Exploded view—Weber 36DCD 3 carburetor

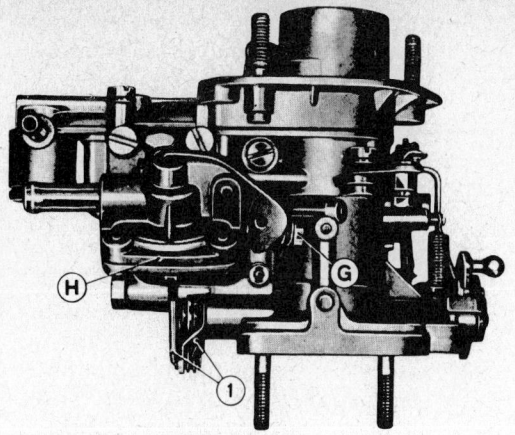

1. Linkage
   G. Fast idle setting screw
   H. Fast idle vacuum control device

Weber 30DICA carburetor

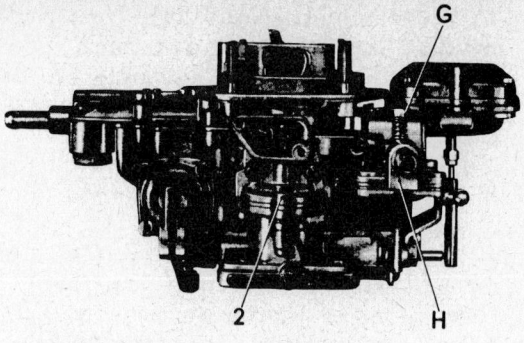

2. Vacuum device
   H. Vacuum operated device for fast idle speed control
   G. Adjustment screw for fast idle speed

Weber DHSA1 carburetor

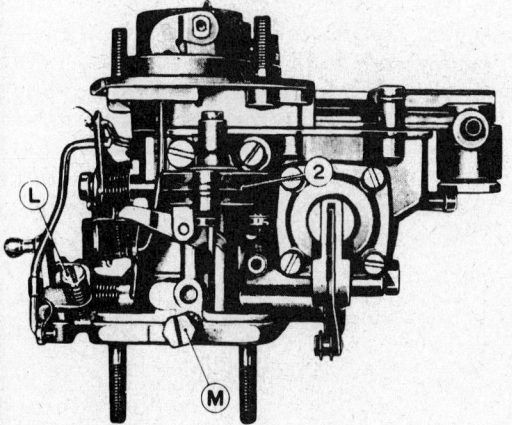

2. Vacuum device
   L. Idle setting screw
   M. Mixture adjusting screw.

Weber 30DICA carburetor

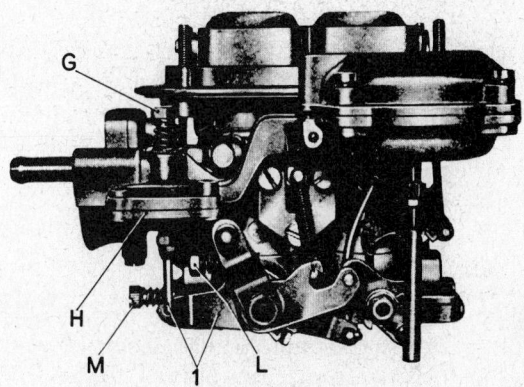

1. Linkage
   G. Adjustment screw for fast idle speed
   H. Vacuum operated device for fast idle speed control
   L. Idle running setting screw
   M. Idle mixture metering screw

Weber DHSA1 carbureor

Adjustments

Idle adjustment procedures are the same as for the Weber 22IM or Weber 30DIC.

Float level adjustment of Weber carburetors is a procedure basically similar for all models. Follow instructions for float level adjustment, given under Weber 22IM adjustment. Consult the specifications for the proper dimensions.

WEBER 32DHSA 1 AND 26/34 DHSA 1

This carburetor is a dual-throat unit, using a differential throttle opening and vacuum control of the secondary throttle. It also incorporates a pneumatic device, which prevents the throttle from completely closing during fast idle.

Adjustments

See the adjustment procedures under Weber 22IM for float level and idle adjustment. Consult the specifications for proper dimensions.

SERVICE

Carburetor repair kits are recommended for each overhaul. Kits contain a complete set of gaskets and new parts to replace those that generally deteriorate most rapidly. All of the new parts supplied in the kits should be used for maximum performance.

Carburetor overhaul should be performed only in a clean, dust-free work area. Disassemble and assemble carburetor carefully, referring to exploded view drawings. Keep look-alike parts separated to prevent accidental interchange at assembly and note all jet sizes. When reassembling, make sure all screws and jets are tight in their seats. Tighten all screws gradually and take care not to tighten needle valves too tightly. Always use a new carburetor flange gasket.

Wash carburetor parts, except diaphragm, in carburetor cleaner, rinse in solvent, and blow dry with compressed air. Carburetors have numerous small passages that can be fouled by carbon and gummy deposits. Soak metal parts in carburetor solvent until thoroughly clean. The solvent will weaken or destroy cork, plastic and leather components and these parts should be wiped with a clean, lint-free cloth only. Clean all fuel passages in the float bowl and cover and clean jets and valves separately to avoid accidental interchange. Never use wire or sharp objects to clean jets and passages, as this can seriously alter their calibration.

Check the throttle valve shafts for play that can cause air leakage, then inspect float spindle and other moving parts for wear. Replace float if gasoline has leaked into it. Accelerator pump check valves should pass air one way but not the other. Test for proper valve seating, by blowing and sucking on valve, and replace if necessary. Check the bowl cover with a straightedge for warped surfaces and inspect valves and seats closely for wear.

Exhaust System

Removal of the exhaust system from front-engined Fiats presents no special difficulties or problems. It is a conventional exhaust system consisting of tailpipe, muffler, exhaust pipe and exhaust manifold.

The muffler and headers are removed as a unit from Fiats equipped with rear mounted engines. On the Fiat 850 the lower splash shield must be removed. The single header (or four headers, in the 850 Spyder and Coupe) are unbolted from the engine. Finally, unbolt the two mounting nuts just above the muffler.

Replace the muffler and header assembly, by reversing the removal procedure.

Cooling System

124 Sedan

Cooling is by forced water circulation using a centrifugal pump. The cooling system consists of a water pump mounted on the crankcase, radiator in front of the engine, auxiliary tank, thermostat, fan and water temperature gauge sending unit.

RADIATOR

Removal

Open the petcock at the bottom of the radiator and drain the coolant from radiator and cylinder block. Remove the hose connecting radiator and thermostat cover. Remove the hose connecting radiator and water pump. Remove the pipe connecting the radiator to the auxiliary tank. Unbolt and remove the radiator.

Installation

Installation is the reverse of removal.

WATER PUMP

Removal

If necessary, remove the radiator from the vehicle. Unbolt and remove the fan from the water pump flange. Remove the hose connecting water pump and radiator. Remove the water pump from the mounting.

Installation

Installation is the reverse of removal.

THERMOSTAT

Removal

Drain off part of the water in the radiator (to a level below the outlet in the cylinder head). Remove the hose connecting the radiator to the thermostat cover. Remove the cover and withdraw the thermostat.

Inspection

Immerse the thermostat in water and

heat the water. When the temperature reaches 185-192° F., the thermostat valve should begin to open. The valve should be completely open when the water temperature reaches 212° F. If the thermostat does not meet specifications, it is defective and must be replaced.

Installation

Installation is the reverse of removal.

BY-PASS THERMOSTAT

On later models, a by-pass thermostat is installed. This type of thermostat is connected to the water pump, cylinder head and radiator by three hoses. It enables a large volume of water to be circulated, ensuring a more uniform heat distribution inside the engine.

124 Sport

The cooling system used on 124 Sport models operates in basically the same manner as that on 124 Sedan models. The fan, on 124 Sport models, is fitted with an electro-magnetic clutch, enabling the fan to operate only when the temperature of the water, by the dash indicator, is above 192°

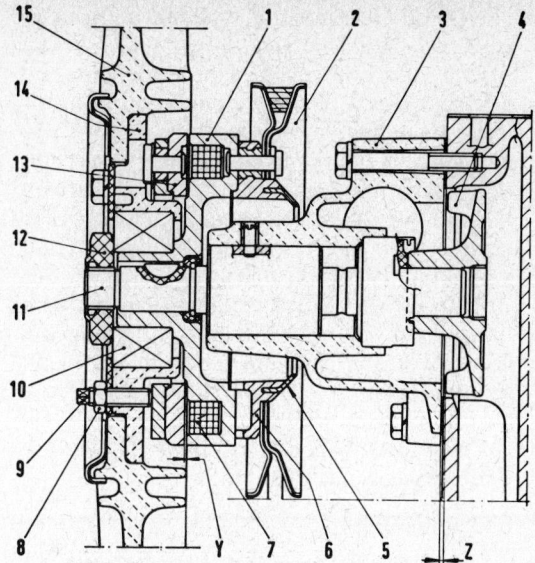

1. Pulley hub and body of electro-magnet
2. Pulley
3. Pump body
4. Pump rotor
5. Contact ring
6. Contact ring hub
7. Magnet coil
8. Locknut
9. Magnet air-gap adjusting screw
10. Fan bearing
11. Water pump spindle
12. Nut
13. Armature of electro-magnet
14. Fan hub
15. Fan

Y 0.25-0. 35mm (0.0098" to 0.0137")   Z 1 mm (0.0394")

Cross-section of water pump and electro-magnetic fan clutch

F. Removal and service procedures for the 124 Sport models are identical to 124 Sedan models.

ELECTRO-MAGNETIC FAN CLUTCH

Inspection

Check that the air gap between the body and armature of the electromagnet is .0098"-.0137". If the air gap does not meet specifications, adjust as follows.

Unscrew the locknuts of the three adjusting screws. Make the adjustment by means of the screws, checking the adjustment each time with a feeler gauge, opposite the screw which has been adjusted. When the adjustment is complete, lock the nuts on the screws.

1. Fan hub locknut
2. Water pump spindle
3. Electro-magnet air-gap adjusting screws and locknuts
4. Screws fixing fan to hub
5. Fan

Fan and electro-magnetic clutch installed on engine

NOTE: *Occasionally, the fan will fail to run, even after the leads to the thermostatic switch are connected. The fault may be due to a break in the magnetic winding or lead. As a temporary measure, the fan can be made to run continuously in the following manner. Unscrew the three locknuts on the air gap adjusting screws. Tighten the screws until the armature adheres to the magnet body. Tighten the three nuts.*

A defective thermostatic switch can also be temporarily repaired, by connecting the two thermostatic switch leads to the same terminal, causing the fan to run continuously. As soon as possible, replace the thermostatic switch or change pulley, complete with magnet and brush ring.

600 and 600D

Sedans of this type are cooled by forced water circulation through a centrifugal pump. An upright pipe radiator, located next to the engine, is cooled by a fan. The radiator is equipped with a thermostat to control air flow, via a lever to the butterfly valve.

The Multipla uses the same system, except for a thermostat in the pipe between the cylinder head and radiator, replacing the butterfly valve.

WATER PUMP

Removal

Remove the right front, lower apron. Drain the radiator through the petcock under the radiator. Loosen the drive belt from the pulley. Remove the pump intake hose and disconnect the engine ground cable. Remove the water pump, complete with fan and air conveyor.

Installation

Installation is the reverse of removal.

THERMOSTAT

Removal (Sedan)

Remove the radiator and loosen the ringnut securing it to the radiator. Remove the thermostat.

Testing (Sedan)

Immerse the thermostat in water and heat the water. The thermostat should open at 167-176° F. and be completely open at 221° F.

Installation (Sedan)

Installation is the reverse of removal.

Removal (Multipla)

The thermostat is located in the water outlet pipe in front of the cylinder head. Unscrew the thermostat with a wrench and remove it.

Testing (Multipla)

Immerse the thermostat in water and heat the water. The thermostat should begin to open at 161-170° F. and be completely open at 185° F.

Installation (Multipla)

Installation is the reverse of removal.

850

The cooling system used on 850 model Fiats consists of a radiator, fan, water pump, thermostat and connecting hoses.

RADIATOR

Removal

Remove the engine right-side apron and drain the coolant from the radiator. Disconnect the coolant intake and outlet hoses from the radiator. Disconnect the lockring securing the air conveyor to the radiator. Disconnect the engine ground cable and the pipe from the radiator to the expansion tank. Remove the radiator mounting screws and lift out the radiator.

Installation

Installation is the reverse of removal.

WATER PUMP

Removal

Remove the engine right-side apron. Drain the coolant from the radiator. Remove the drive belt from the pulley and disconnect the hoses at the cylinder head and radiator. Remove the lockring holding the air conveyor to the radiator. Remove the securing bolts and remove the water pump and air conveyor assembly.

Installation

Installation is the reverse of removal.

THERMOSTAT

Removal

The thermostat is situated at the front

end of the cylinder head. Drain the coolant from the engine and radiator. Remove the hose from the thermostat housing and withdraw the thermostat.

Installation

Installation is the reverse of removal.

WATER PUMP DRIVE BELT

Adjust Tension

Correct belt tension is approximately ½". To adjust the tension, loosen the generator mounting bolts. Correct the tension of the belt, setting the position of the generator support. Remove the pulley locknuts. Remove the pulley half and shift one or more shims outside. Fit the pulley half and secure. NOTE: *This procedure is only valid to stretch the water pump drive belt.*

1500 and 1600S

These Fiat models use a cooling system similar to that used on Fiat 124 models. The equipment and service are similar, including the electro-magnetic fan clutch.

1. Adjustable generator support
2. Support fixing nuts
3. Generator pulley
4. Water pump and fan drive pulley
5. Pulley-to-hub mounting nuts
6. Spacer rings, belt tension adjustment

Adjusting water pump, fan and generator drive belt tension

Engine

Exhaust Emission Control

FIAT 124 AND 850 (1970-ON)

Air pollution control is provided by the Fiat FD1 system, which consists of a specially calibrated carburetor, a new water-heated intake manifold, modified centrifugal spark advance and a fast idling device to limit intake vacuum during deceleration. The second barrel of the carburetor is equipped with a vacuum diaphragm unit (H) and linkage (1), which prevents the throttle from closing completely during deceleration when the fast idling device goes into operation. Another vacuum device (2), in parallel with the fast idle unit, matches engine mixture requirements during warm-up.

Fast idle operation is provided by three switches and a solenoid. One switch (A) on the side of the transmission is open when the car is standing, but closed when third and fourth gears are engaged. A second switch installed near the clutch pedal closes when the pedal is released. When both these switches are closed the solenoid valve (1) is energized, which opens the vacuum line that actuates the fast idle diaphragm unit (H) on the carburetor. The third switch (2) is a pushbutton switch to energize the solenoid when the car is standing still. Adjustment of the fast idle speed then can be made by turning a screw (G).

Carburetor adjustment is made by first adjusting the set screw (L) for 800 rpm idle speed. If an analyzer is available, adjust mixture screw (M) for an output of 3% carbon monoxide. Press pushbutton (2), then set fast idle speed to 1500 rpm by adjusting screw (G). Before pressing pushbutton (2) to release the solenoid, rev up engine with accelerator and recheck fast idle speed. Readjust screw (G), if necessary, and press pushbutton (2) to OFF position.

GAS VAPOR RECIRCULATION

124 and 850

The Fiat 124 and 850 Sport models are additionally equipped with a system to re-

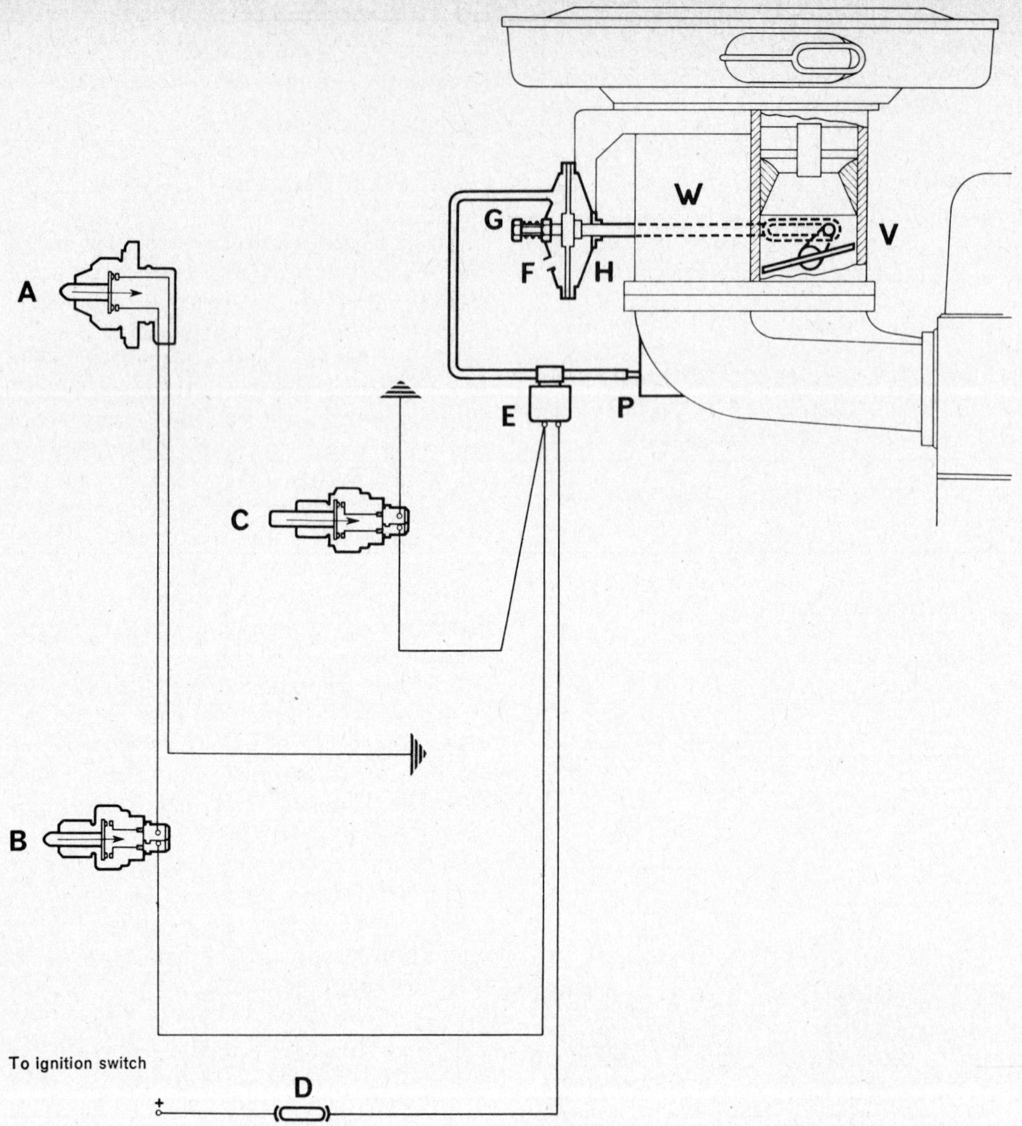

A

G

W

F   H   V

E   P

C

B

To ignition switch

D

+

Fiat 124 FD1 system for exhaust emission control. (A) switch on gearbox (closed when third
and fourth gear engaged); (B) switch on clutch pedal (closed with clutch pedal released);
(C) switch for fast idle speed control; (D) fuse; (E) solenoid valve; (F) compensating orifice;
(G) throttle adjustment for fast idle; (H) fast idle speed control; (P) vacuum connection on intake manifold; (V) throttle; (W) carburetor.

Fast idle control switch (A) mounted on transmission.

Solenoid valve (1) and pushbutton test switch (2)
of FD1 exhaust emission system.

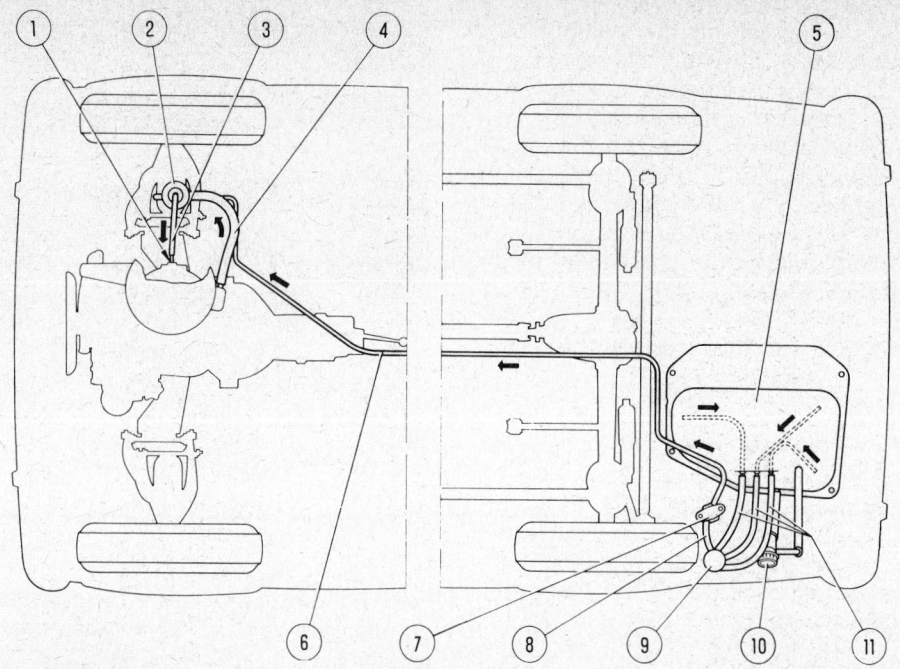

1. Calibrated orifice
2. Activated carbon filter
3. Line to engine intake manifold
4. Hot air purge tube
5. Fuel tank (limited filling type
6. Vapor vent line
7. Three-way control valve
8. Vapor outlet
9. Vapor-liquid separator
10. Sealed filler cap
11. Vapor intake

Fuel vapor recirculation system (124 Station Wagon)

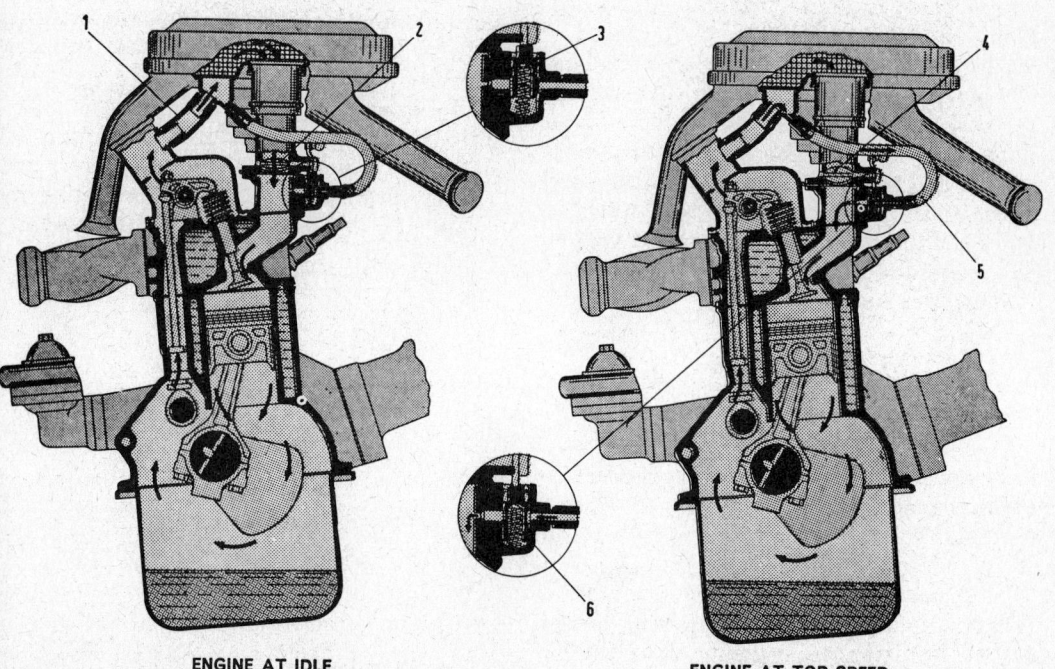

ENGINE AT IDLE   **ENGINE AT TOP SPEED**

Operation of the Fiat 850 exhaust emission system. With engine at idle speed vapors are sucked back through (1) to air cleaner and carburetor. Breather valve (3) and throttle (2) are closed. At top speed, part of vapors are sucked through (1). As valve (4) opens, breather valve (6) opens too, and most vapors are drawn through line (5) into intake manifold for combustion.

circulate gas vapors from the fuel tank. The system consists of a hermetically sealed gas tank cap, vapor separator, a three way valve and activated carbon filter.

The carbon filter is placed in the engine compartment to absorb fuel vapors coming from the tank. When the engine is running, a blast of hot air regenerates the activated carbon and conveys the gas vapors in the intake manifold to the filter.

850 Exhaust Emission System
(Prior to 1970)

With the engine at idle speed, vapors are sucked through to the air cleaner and carburetor. The breather and throttle are now closed. At top speed part of the vapors are sucked through to the air cleaner. As the valve opens, the breather valve opens also, and most vapors are drawn into the intake manifold for combustion.

Removing 124 transmission.

Engine Mechanical

The Fiat 124, 600, 850, 1100, 1500 and 1600S models all have four-cylinder, inline, water-cooled engines. The 600 and 850 engines are rear mounted.

The engine used in the 124 Spider and Coupe sport cars differs from that used in the 124 sedan and station wagon. Major differences are a larger bore in the sports models and their double overhead camshaft valve train, as opposed to the overhead valve design used in the sedan and wagon. There are also slight differences in carburetion, lubrication and cooling.

All Fiat 124 Models

Removal

Removal of 124 sedan and sports car engines is facilitated by removing the radiator and the transmission. Proceed as follows:

Jack the car and place on stands. Drain radiator, auxiliary tank, block and heater system by first moving heater lever to far right, then opening radiator drain cock and removing plug on right-hand side of block. Speed up draining by removing radiator and auxiliary tank caps.

Disconnect battery leads. Then disconnect ignition coil, generator, starter, low oil pressure and water temperature indicator wires.

Disconnect accelerator rod, sliding it out of lever ball joint end toward dash. Remove air filter. Detach choke cable from carburetor. Disconnect line from fuel pump and detach exhaust pipe from manifold. Disconnect radiator and heater hoses.

Remove the upper two screws that hold the radiator to the body, then remove the radiator by sliding it off the lower support bracket.

Working from inside car, remove gearshift lever by pressing down upper part of sleeve (5) and, with a screwdriver, releasing spring ring (4) from its seating in lower part of lever (5). Upper part of

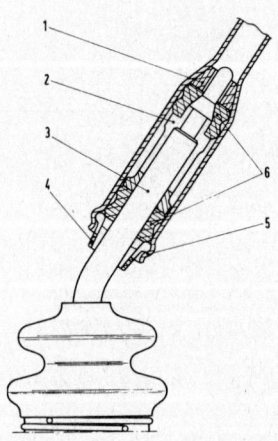

Fiat 124 gearshift lever assembly: (1) shoulder; (2) spacer; (3) lever; (4) spring; (5) sleeve; (6) rubber bushings.

A clamp (tool A70025) holds universal (4) together while removing drive shaft spider screws (1) and transmission spider screws.

124 Sedan, Special, Station Wagon (OHV)

Disassembly

To facilitate disassembly, mount the engine on some type of engine stand.

Drain the oil from the engine and remove the dipstick. Dismantle the clutch assembly, by removing the six bolts and washers securing it to the flywheel. If the air filter was not removed earlier, remove it by disconnecting the two crankcase ventilation pipes and removing the four screws. Disconnect the fuel pump to carburetor fuel line. Remove the fuel pump from the mounting studs. Remove the distributor bracket from the stud and the distributor from the engine. Remove the oil and water temperature sending units. Remove the generator, bracket, fan and drive belt. Disconnect the accelerator rod from the carburetor throttle lever. Remove the valve cover from the cylinder head. Remove the heater delivery and return water pipes, which are connected to the cylinder head and water pump outlet. Remove the thermostat cover and gasket and withdraw the thermostat. Remove the water outlet from the cylinder head. Remove the carburetor, complete with shields, spacers and gaskets. Remove the intake and exhaust manifolds. Unscrew the oil filter and remove the gasket. Remove the water pump and fan assembly from the crankcase. Loosen the four

lever can then be slipped from the lower part (3). In assembly, it will be necessary to insert shoulder ring (1), rubber bushing (6), spacer (2), rubber bushing (6) and spring ring (4) into the upper part of sleeve (5), then press upper lever down over lower lever to seat spring ring.

Remove transmission cover, then, from under car, disconnect driveshaft spider and transmission mainshaft from universal.

Note: This is facilitated by placing the band, Tool A.70025, on the coupling itself. Disconnect speedometer cable from transmission and disconnect flexible cable from clutch fork. Remove flywheel cover, electrical ground cable and exhaust pipe bracket clip. Remove heat shield from exhaust manifold and three bolts that hold starter to front of transmission.

Position a hydraulic jack under transmission for support. Remove four bolts which mount transmission to crankcase, then remove crossmember that holds transmission to car floor.

Supporting transmission jack, move it toward rear of car so as to withdraw clutch shaft from the pilot bushing and clutch hub. Lower jack and pull transmission from under car. Remove starter from engine compartment.

Using a chain hoist, pass the rear sling under the crankcase and the front sling under the thermostat housing. Support engine with hoist, remove front mounts and lift engine clear.

Remove air filter by disconnecting two crankcase ventilation pipes and removing four screws.

self-locking nuts and remove the rocker shaft assembly from the cylinder head. Withdraw the pushrods from their bores, keeping them in the proper order for assembly. Loosen the ten bolts and remove the cylinder head. Withdraw the tappets from their guides, keeping them in the proper order. Unlock the tap washer under the nut which secures the fan drive pulley. Using a flywheel holder, remove the nut from the pulley. Remove the pulley from the crankshaft. Remove the oil pan from the cylinder block. Loosen the bolts, and withdraw the front timing gear cover. Unlock the tab washer and remove the bolt securing the timing gear (larger) to the camshaft. Remove the camshaft sprocket and timing chain. Use a gear puller to remove the crankshaft sprocket from the crankshaft. Do not forget to remove the key from the slot in the crankshaft. Remove the flywheel from the crankshaft. Using a puller, withdraw the ball race carrying the transmission direct drive shaft from its seat in the crankshaft. Withdraw the driven gear of the oil pump and distributor drive from the end of its spindle. Remove the oil pump assembly, complete with suction pipe and gasket. Remove the connecting rod caps and bearing shells, keeping them in the proper order for assembly. Carefully, push the connecting rods, complete with pistons, rings and bearings, from the upper end of the block. Remove the rear cover plate of the crankcase. Unbolt the five main bearing caps and remove these, keeping them in correct order. Carefully, lift the crankshaft from the block and lay it down where it will not be damaged. Remove the bearing shells and the thrust half bearings from the rear main bearing. Remove the camshaft end plate and carefully remove the camshaft.

Assembly

Lubricate the camshaft bearings and journals. Insert the camshaft and fit the retainer plate over the front end of the shaft. Carefully, lubricate the main bearing half shells and seat them in the block. Lubricate the crankshaft journals and seat the crankshaft in the block. Install the thrust half-rings in the rear main bearing seat. Fit the main bearing caps and half-bearings, tightening the caps to specification. Replace the ball race of the transmission direct drive shaft. Install the rear crankcase cover plate and tighten the six

bolts. Turn the crankshaft to bring the crankpins of Nos. 1 and 4 cylinders to their highest point (with the engine upside down). Fit the flywheel, aligning the reference mark on the flywheel with the crankpins. Torque the retaining bolts to specification. Lubricate the pistons and fit the piston, ring and connecting rod assembly to their respective cylinders. The piston must be fitted to the correct cylinder. The number stamped on the connecting rod and cap indicates the cylinder number. When the assembly is complete, the number on the cap must be on the side away from the camshaft. Refit the oil pump to the cylinder block. Connect the connecting rods and torque to specification. Replace the driven gear of the oil pump and the distributor drive on its spindle. Oil the camshaft journals and insert the camshaft into the block, being careful not to damage the bearings. Replace the camshaft gear on the camshaft and torque the bolt to specifications. Replace the key and gear on the crankshaft along with the timing chain. Be sure that the marks on the two gears align. Insert the tappets into their proper bores in the cylinder block. Place the cylinder head gasket on the block and fit the cylinder head, complete with valves and springs. Insert the ten cylinder head bolts and torque according to specifications, in no less than two stages. Insert the pushrods into their proper housings. Replace the rocker assembly over the studs on the cylinder head. Torque the nuts to specification. Check the valve timing as follows. Fit a degree wheel or sector scale and bring No. 1 cylinder to the beginning of intake stroke. Bring the mark on the flywheel (TDC of Nos. 1 and 4 cylinders) in line with zero on the degree wheel or sector scale. At this point, the marks on the timing gears should be aligned. Adjust the final clearance of the valves and rockers. Replace the timing gear cover. Install the fan drive pulley over the front end of the crankshaft with its tab washer and nut. Torque to specification. Replace the fuel pump, inserting a gasket and spacer between the pump and the block. Fit the oil filter bracket and oil filter. Replace the intake and exhaust manifolds on the cylinder head. Install the water pump to the front of the cylinder block with gaskets. Replace the thermostat. Fit the water return pipe from the heater to the water pump and exhaust manifold. Replace the water temperature sending

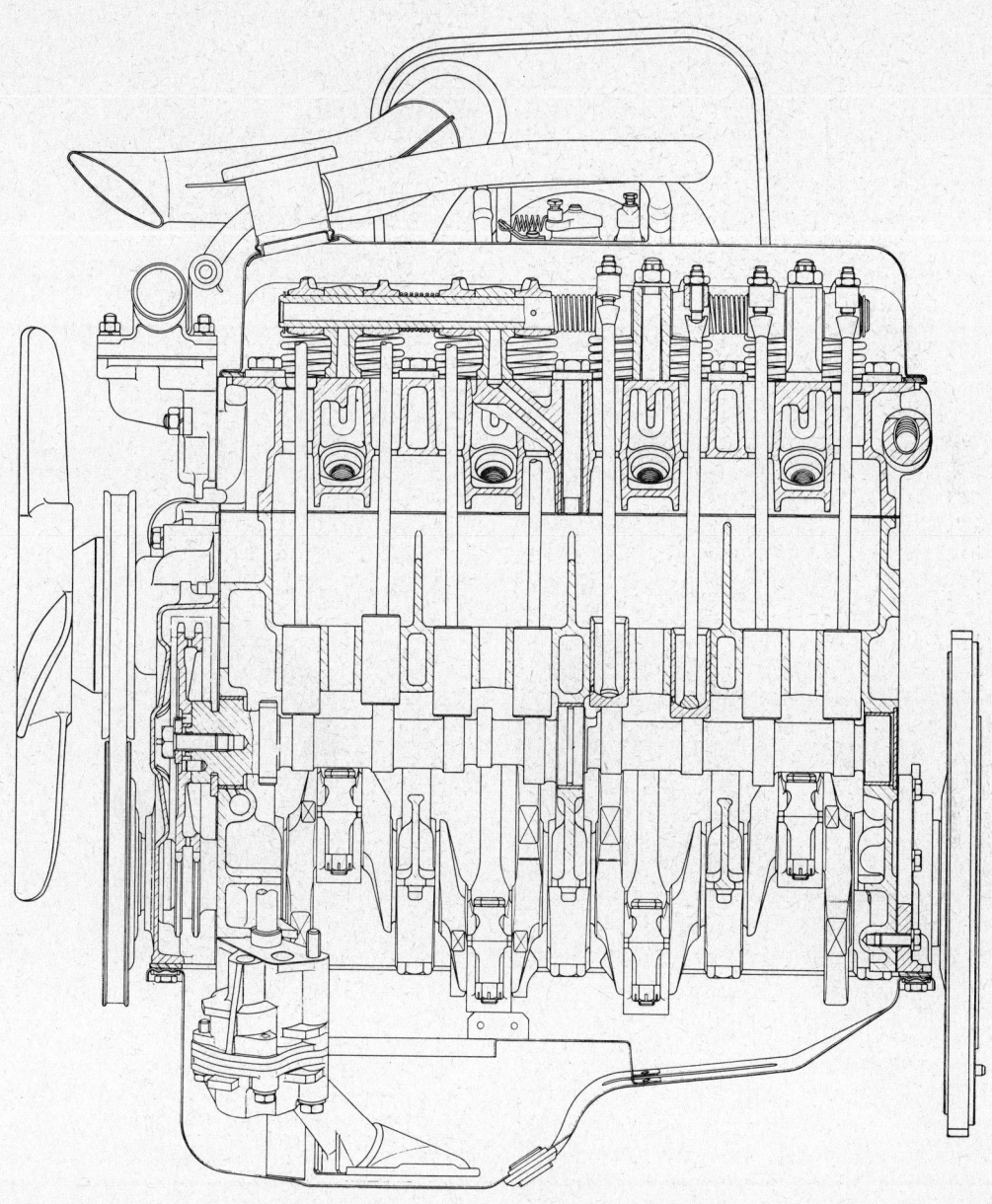

Cross-section of Fiat 124 sedan engine (OHV) through the valve mechanism

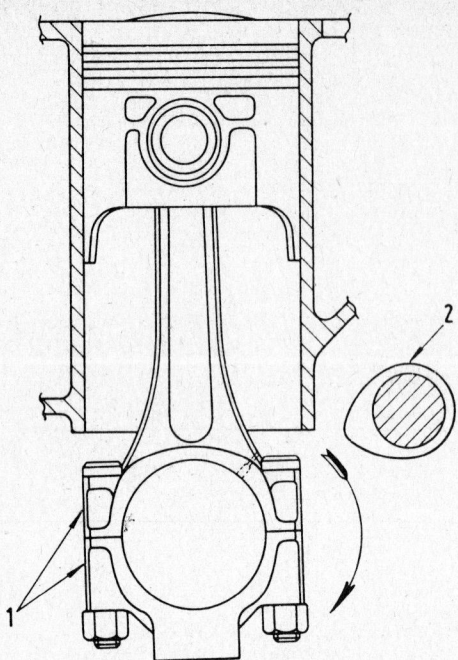

Timing marks aligned on 124 camshaft drive sprockets.

Install rod-piston assembly with cylinder number identification (1) away from camshaft (2). Arrow shows engine rotation from front.

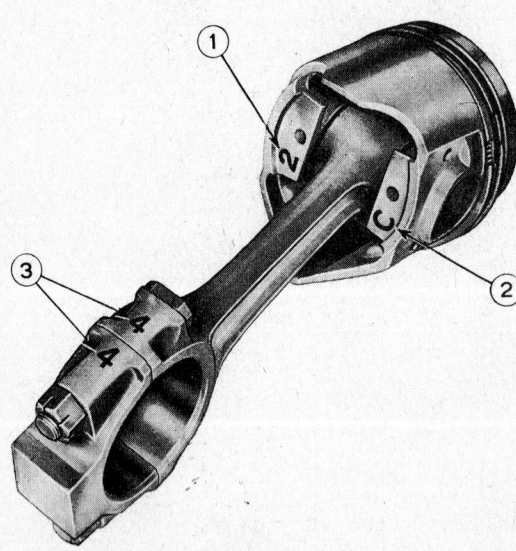

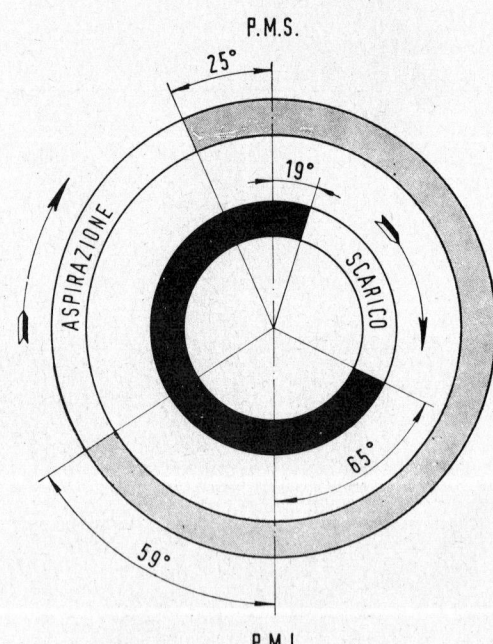

Valve timing diagram for 124 sedan, with a tappet clearance of .0147" (.375 mm.) Outer ring is intake valve, and inner ring is exhaust valve.

Piston and rod assemblies are marked (1) for class of bore, (2) piston class, and (3) piston cylinder number. Metal may be removed from areas (1) and (2) to equalize piston weights.

unit in the cylinder head. Fit the oil pressure sending unit to the oil filter bracket. Replace the cooling system drain plug in the crankcase. Replace the spacer, gasket, carburetor and heat shield over the intake manifold studs, in that order. Connect the fuel line to the fuel pump and carburetor.

Replace the distributor and time the ignition. To do this, bring No. 1 cylinder to the end of compression stroke (both valves closed) and fit the degree wheel. Turn the flywheel until the reference mark on the flywheel shows 10° B.T.D.C. Mesh the oil pump and distributor drive pinion with the camshaft. Turn the distributor drive spindle so that the rotor is facing No. 1 cylinder contact. The breaker points should be just beginning to open. Without moving the distributor spindle, insert the distributor into the housing and insert the spindle in the toothed end of the driving gear. Clamp the distributor in place, and replace the distributor cap. Fit the fan pulley and fan on the hub of the water pump spindle. Replace the lower generator supports, generator and upper generator support. Fit the belt over the three pulleys (drive pulley, fan pulley and generator pulley). Adjust the belt tension and clamp the generator to the upper bracket. Fit the gasket and rocker cover to the cylinder head and replace the spark plugs. Connect the accelerator control rod to the lever on the cylinder head cover. Replace the clutch assembly on the flywheel. Replace the oil pan on the block. Fill the engine with oil and replace the dipstick.

124 SPYDER, COUPE, SPORT SPYDER, SPORT COUPE (DOHC)

Disassembly

These Fiat models use a double overhead camshaft engine. This engine is identical to the overhead valve model, except for the two cylinder heads (and two camshafts), timing belt instead of timing chain, an idler sprocket for the timing belt and an auxiliary shaft to drive the distributor and oil pump.

Follow the disassembly procedure suggested for the 124 overhead valve engine, noting the above differences.

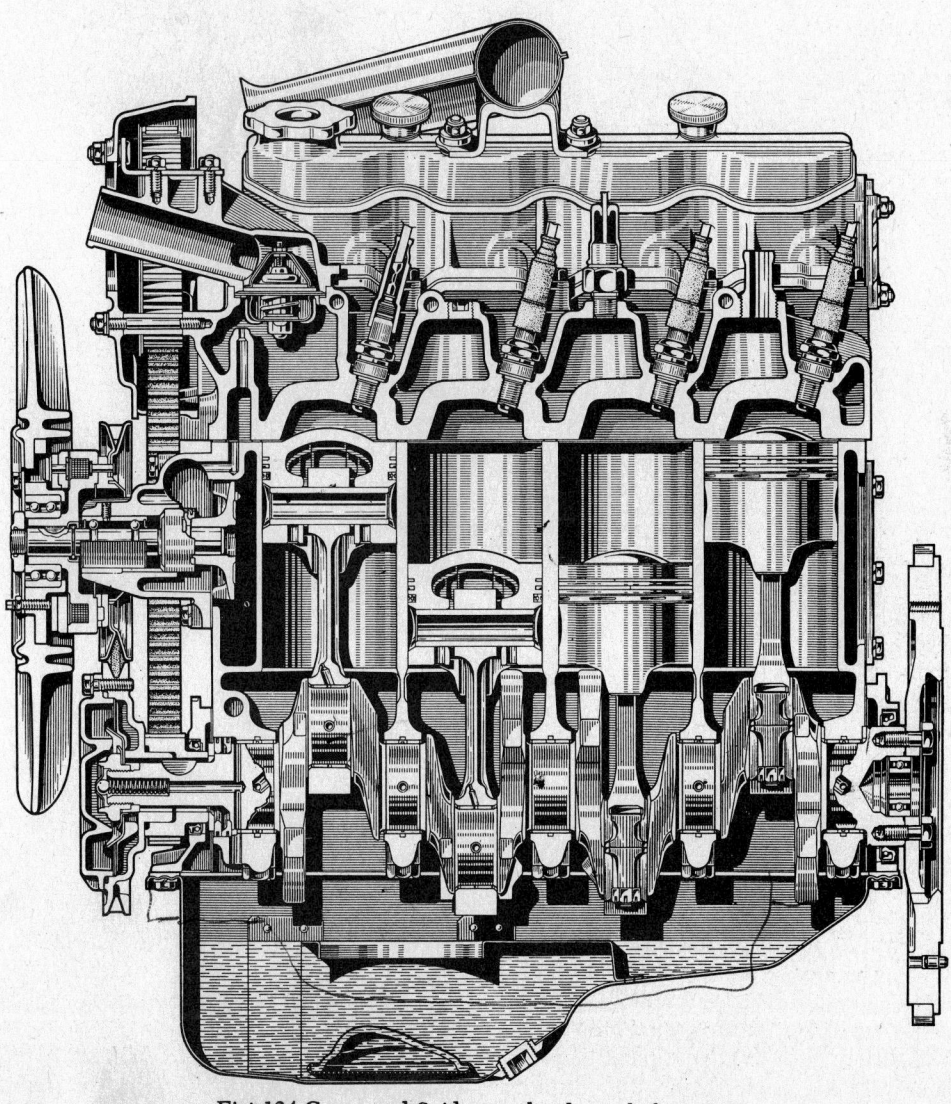

Fiat 124 Coupe and Spider overhead camshaft engine.

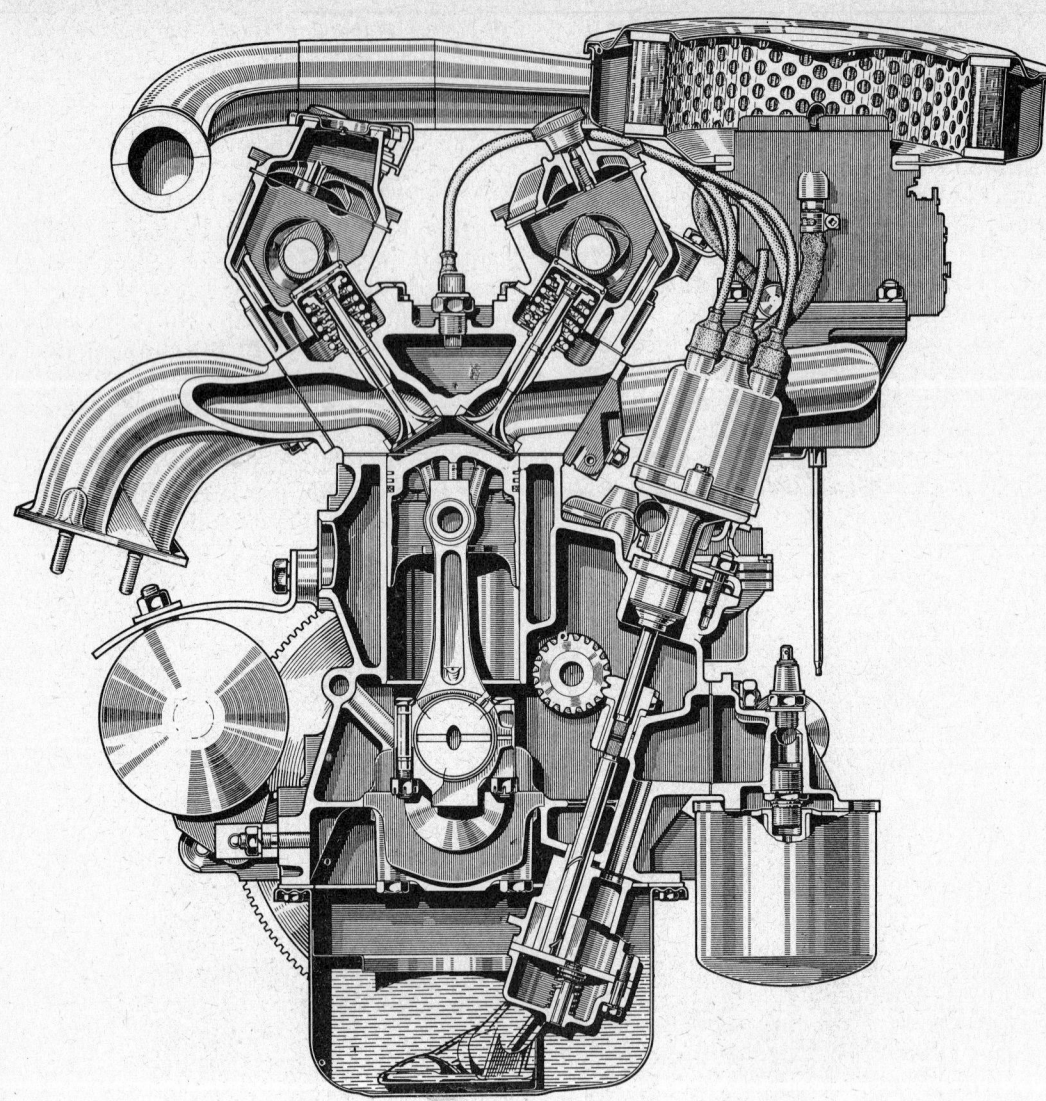

Fiat 124 Coupe and Spider overhead camshaft engine.

Assembly

Assemble the engine following the procedure outlined for the 124 overhead valve engine. The following departures should be noted.

To install the cylinder heads and time valves, crank pistons Nos. 1 and 4 to TDC. Screw two dummy studs into the crankcase to index the cylinder heads. Align the cylinder head gasket and carefully position the cylinder head on the crankcase, piloting it over the dummy studs.

NOTE: *Care should be taken when replacing the cylinder heads, since the valves protrude from the head face. These can be knocked against the block and bent.*

Start some of the head screws, manually, and remove the pilot studs. Torque the cylinder head bolts in the proper sequence, to specification. Position the camshafts, so that the reference mark on each gear is aligned with the fixed pointer at the front of the cylinder head.

NOTE: *Once the head has been fitted, avoid turning the camshafts until the timing belt is installed.*

Fit the timing belt, being careful not to disturb the alignment of the camshafts and fixed pointer. Fix a spring balance to the upper right arm of the timing belt idler. Adjust the belt tension by applying a force of 60 lbs. in a direction bisecting the angle formed by the timing belt as it passes around the idler. Tighten the nuts to clamp the idler. Check the belt tension at two or three points, turning the crankshaft ½ turn in the direction of rotation only.

NOTE: *The timing belt must be changed every 25,000 miles. Under no circumstances, may the timing belt be used more than 37,000 miles.*

To change the timing belt without removing the radiator or engine, follow the procedure outlined.

Drain part of the water in the cooling system and remove the upper radiator hose. Remove the upper section of the air duct. Check the ignition timing and remove the timing cover. Check the valve timing and hold the camshaft gears and engage a low gear while applying the handbrake. Remove the lower protection plate from the engine. Loosen the generator mounting nut and tensioner bolt. Remove the generator drive belt and slacken the timing belt idler locknuts. Remove the timing belt and fit a new belt over the camshaft gears and idler. Fix a spring scale and apply a force of 60 lbs. in a direction bisecting the angle formed by the timing belt as it passes around the idler. Clamp the idler with the locknuts and check the tension at two or three places, turning the crankshaft ½ turn in the direction of rotation only.

Valve adjustment is necessary only if the clearance is .004″ less than the figure listed in the specifications. This applies only to overhead camshaft engines. Tappet clearance is measured between the camshaft lobe and the tappet, directly beneath it. It is not necessary to remove the camshaft to adjust clearance.

Install timing belt (3) with camshaft gears at top (exhaust left and intake right) locked by tool (4) and positioned with reference marks opposite pointers on (1). Idler pulley (8), locked by screws (7 and 9), exerts tension on belt. Auxiliary drive gear is held in place by (6).

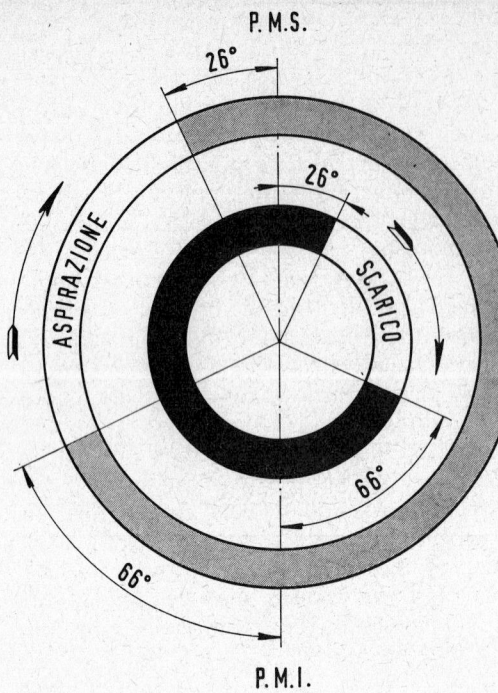

P.M.S.
26°
26°
ASPIRAZIONE
SCARICO
66°
66°
P.M.I.

Aspirazione Inlet   Scarico Exhaust
P.M.S. T.D.C.   P.M.I. B.D.C.

Fiat 124 Sport Spyder and Sport Coupe valve timing diagram for theoretical tappet clearance of
.019".

Check the valve clearance by removing
the rocker cover. Remove the covers from
over the camshafts. Rotate the crankshaft
until the cam lobe, which controls the tappet to be checked, is perpendicular to the
tappet. In this position, the valve in ques-

tion is closed. Use a feeler gauge to measure the clearance between the cap plate
and the cam lobe.

To adjust the tappet clearance, rotate
the camshaft until the valve is fully open.
Hold the tappet down and rotate the camshaft to allow the extraction of the tappet
by means of a jet of compressed air
through the notch in the tappet. Insert the
new cap plate of correct thickness, determined by the feeler gauge measurement.
Cap plates are available in 30 different
thicknesses in graduations of .0019". The
thickness is marked on the face of the plate,
but it is good practice to measure the cap
plate to be sure that the thickness is as
marked.

INSTALLATION

Installation is the reverse of removal.

600, 850

REMOVAL

Jack car from the rear and place on
stands. Disconnect the positive terminal
of the battery and the fuel line at the tank.
Tilt back of rear seat forward and remove
screws and floor covering. Remove starter
and two upper bolts that hold the transmission to the engine.

Remove apron under engine, then unbolt flywheel housing from transmission.
Disconnect the exhaust pipe at the manifold and the muffler at the oil sump. Drain

A. Use tool (1) to adjust clearance between cap
plate (4) of tappet (5) and cam (3). Arrow shows
notch for removing cap plate.

B. Rotate camshaft in direction of arrow until cam
meets stop (A) to free cap plate from cam.

the cooling system and disconnect the water hoses at the radiator. Disconnect the fuel line at the fuel pump. Disconnect oil pressure and water temperature indicators. Remove the air cleaner and disconnect the carburetor choke and accelerator linkage. Disconnect ignition coil and generator.

Attach a chain hoist to the engine and lightly take up the slack. Remove the two bottom bolts that hold the engine to the transmission, then remove the rear central engine support nut, washer and rubber bushing. Remove the two nuts, one on each side, that hold the bumper to the brackets and the four nuts and two screws that hold the lower body panel. Lift engine from car.

Removing engine from 850, using special adapter A60534 (3) and hydraulic jack (4).

DISASSEMBLY

Disassembly of Fiat 600 and 850 engines is almost identical to that for the Fiat 124 overhead valve engine. All three engines

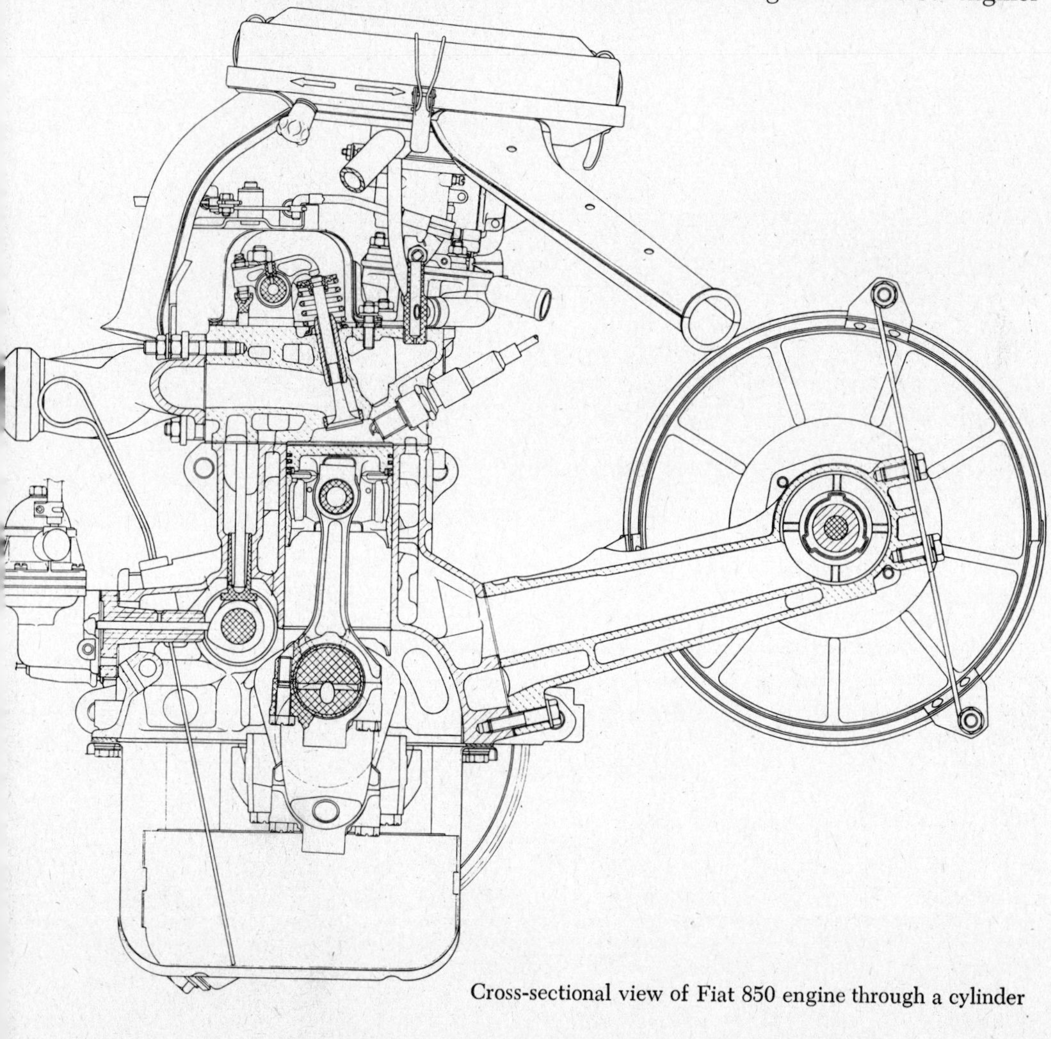

Cross-sectional view of Fiat 850 engine through a cylinder

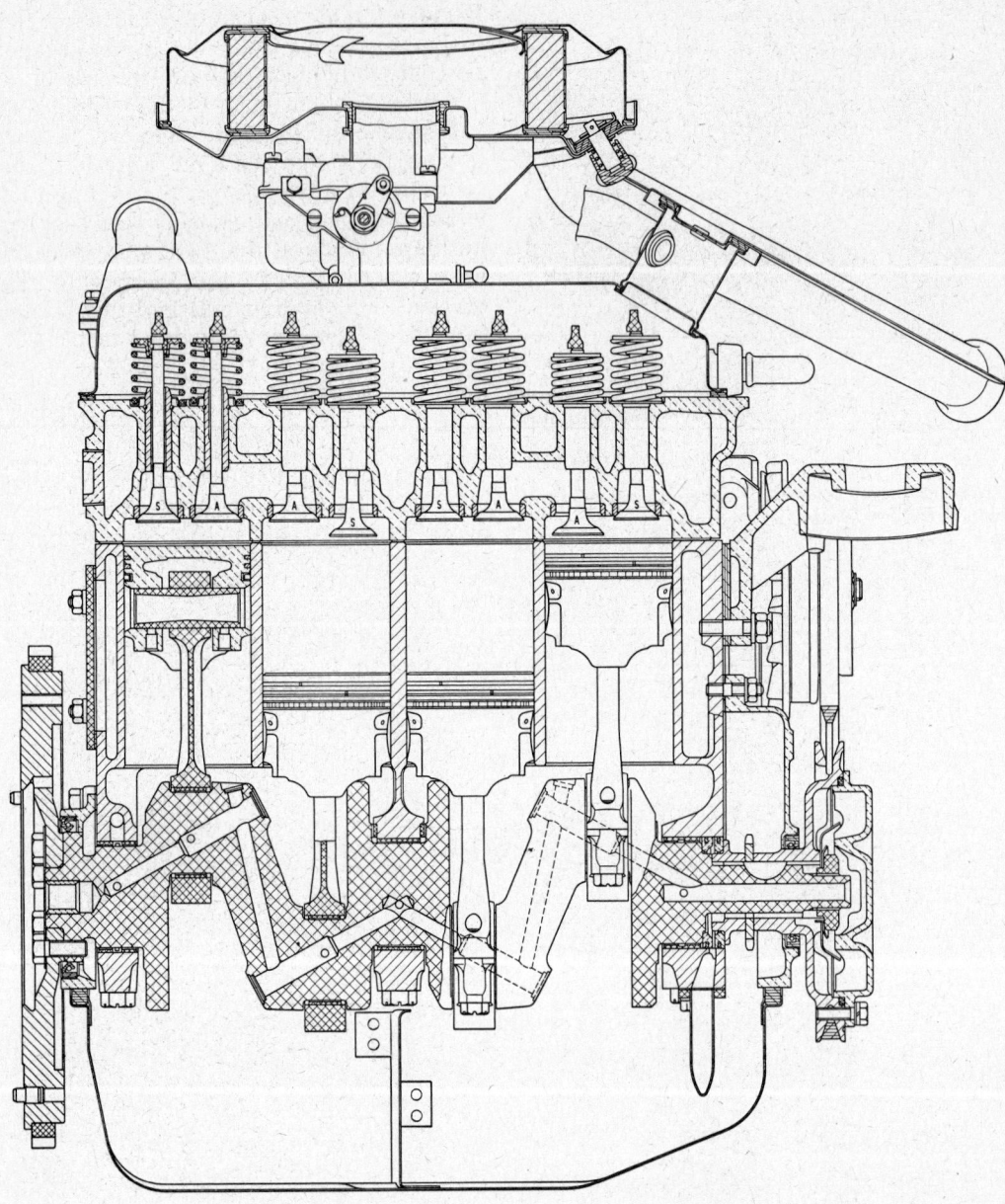

Cross-sectional view of Fiat 850 engine across the cylinders

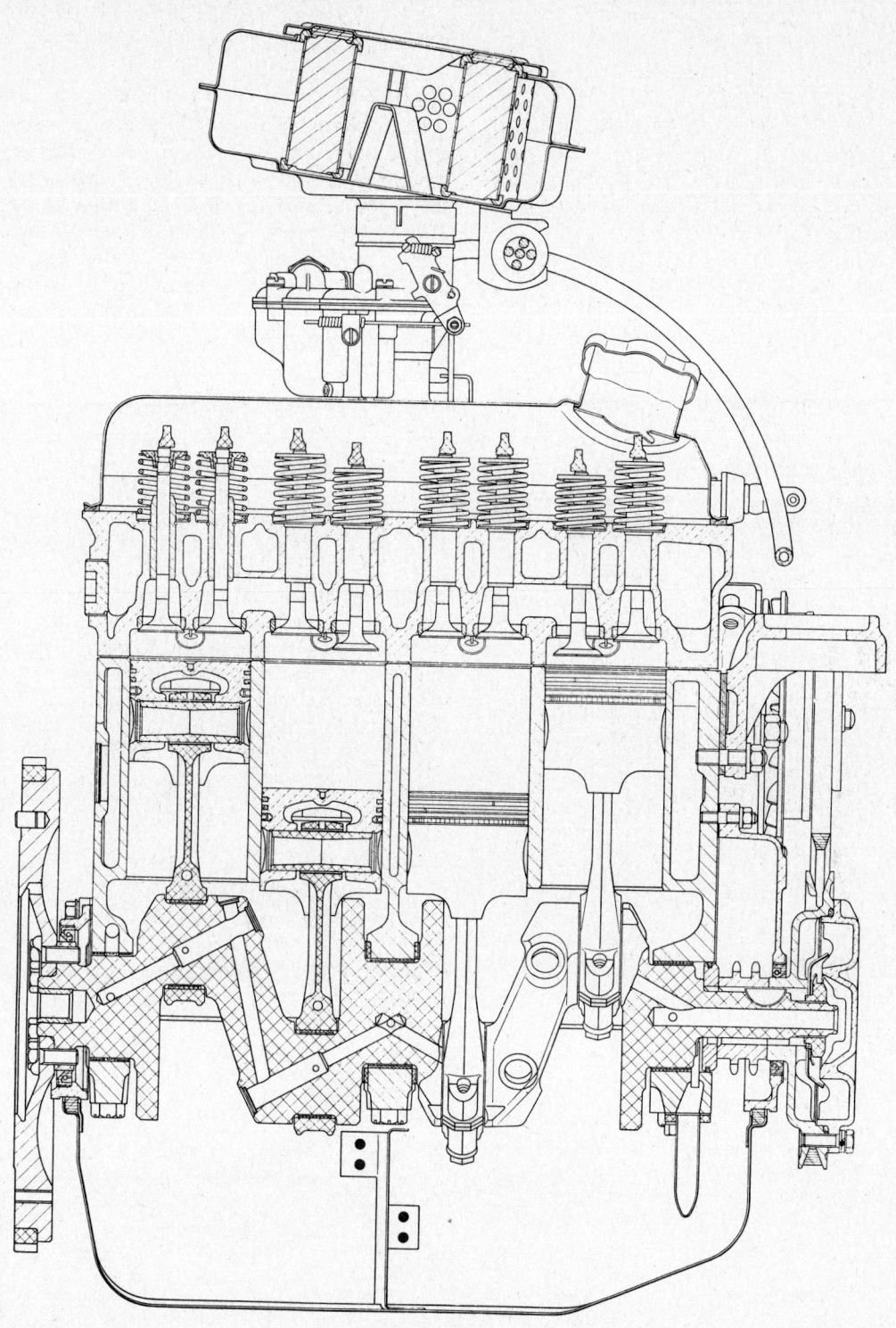

Fiat 600D engine.

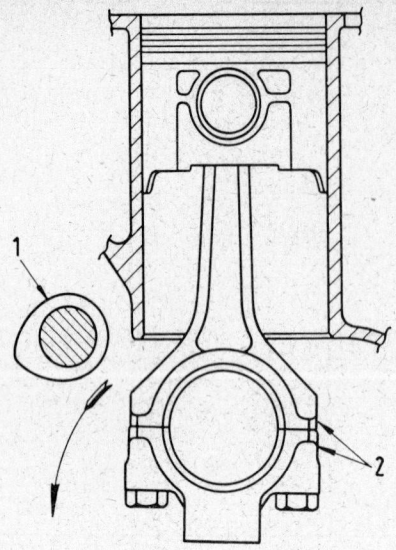

1. Camshaft
2. Location of connecting rod identification number
   Arrow shows engine direction of rotation.

Fiat 850 piston installation

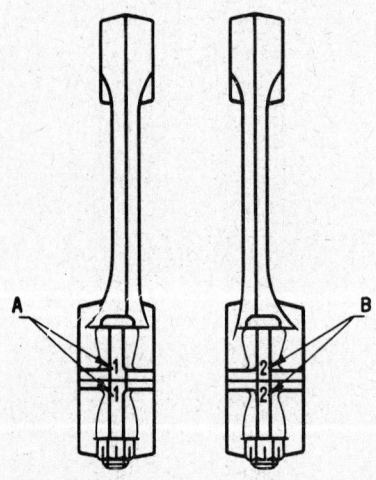

Letter A indicates the side where numbers must be stamped for connecting rods of cylinder No. 1 and 3 — B, the side where numbers must be stamped for connecting rods of cylinder No. 2 and 4.

Fiat 600 connecting rods

are inline, four-cylinder, overhead valve engines, differing only in internal specifications. Basically disassembly of all three engines is identical, excepting external attachments.

ASSEMBLY

Follow the procedure outlined for the Fiat 124 overhead valve engine.

VALVE TIMING—850

Crankshafts of the 850 Spider, Coupe and Sedan engines rotate counterclockwise. To check valve timing, temporarily set tappet clearance of cylinder No. 1 at .0148″ (.375 mm.). Turn flywheel until mark (showing TDC of No. 1 and No. 4 cylinders) is opposite zero on a sector scale (A.95694). In this position, the marks on the timing sprockets should be aligned.

VALVE TIMING—600

Install a degree wheel or sector scale, and rotate the flywheel to bring the timing mark to 4° (10° up to engine number 466800) which is the beginning of the intake stroke of No. 1 cylinder. Temporarily adjust No. 1 cylinder valve clearance to .0177″ (.0082″ up to engine number 466800). Turn the camshaft until No. 1 cylinder intake valve begins to open. Check the timing marks on crankshaft and camshaft sprockets. They should be aligned. Adjust the final valve clearance to .0059″ (.0039″ up to engine number 466800).

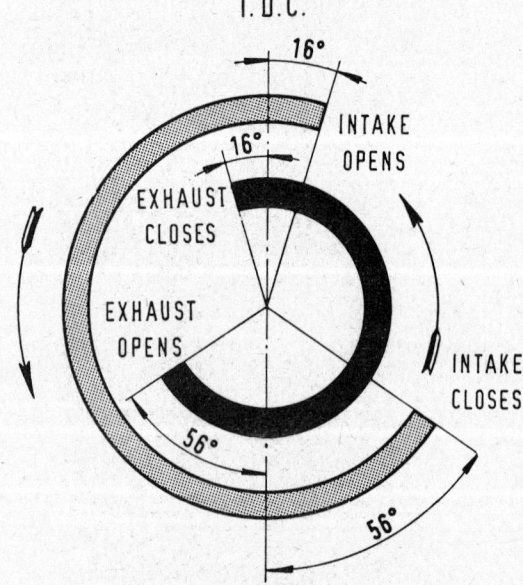

Valve timing diagram for the 850 sedan at increased tappet clearance of .0148″ (.375 mm.). Note counterclockwise rotation of crankshaft.

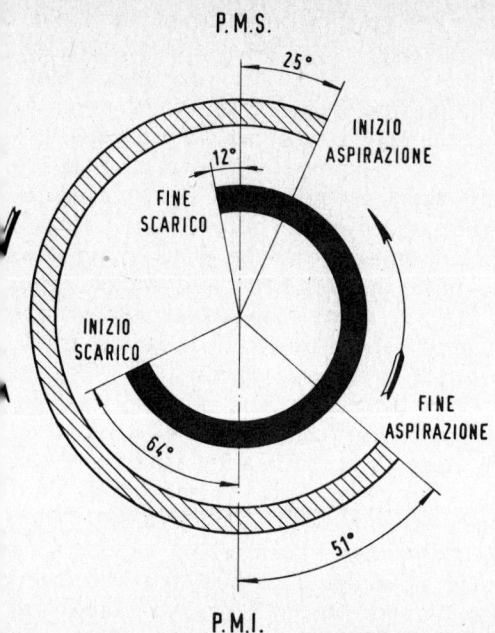

P.M.S.

25°

INIZIO
ASPIRAZIONE

12°

FINE
SCARICO

INIZIO
SCARICO

64°

FINE
ASPIRAZIONE

51°

P.M.I.

Valve timing diagram for the 850 Spider and
Coupe at increased tappet clearance of .0148"
(.375 mm.). Crankshaft rotates counterclockwise.
Outer circle shows opening and closing of intake
valve, and inner circle, exhaust valve opening and
closing.

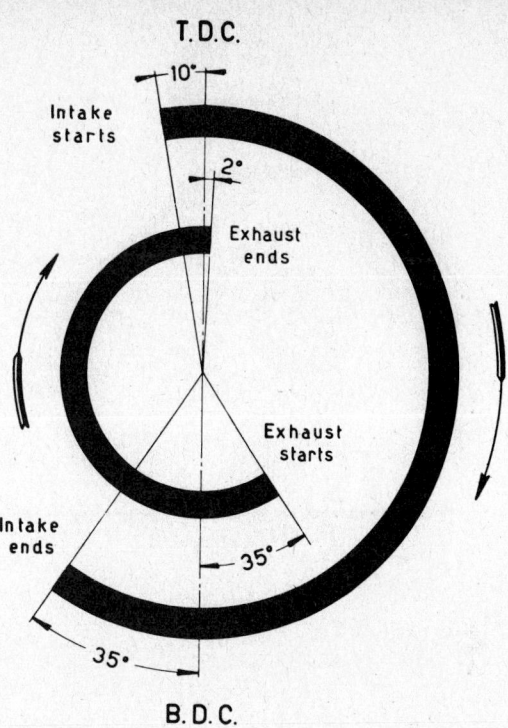

T.D.C.

10°

Intake
starts

2°

Exhaust
ends

Exhaust
starts

Intake
ends

35°

35°

B.D.C.

Fiat 600 valve timing diagram with theoretical
valve lash of .0082" (up to engine number 466800)

Fiat 850 valve timing marks—Chain stretchers
should always be turned outward as shown

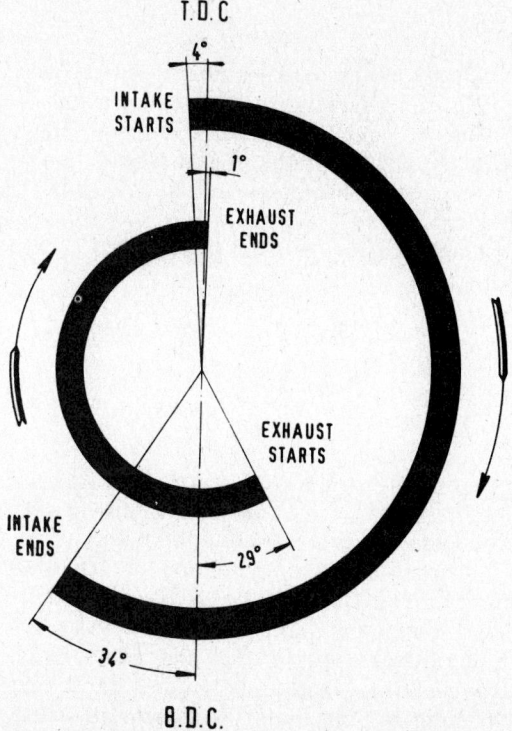

T.D.C

4°

INTAKE
STARTS

1°

EXHAUST
ENDS

EXHAUST
STARTS

INTAKE
ENDS

29°

34°

B.D.C.

Valve timing diagram for tappet clearance of
.0177" (.45 mm.), 600.

Fiat 600 timing marks

INSTALLATION

Use reverse procedure to install engine, taking utmost care when inserting clutch shaft into splined hub of clutch disc.

1100, 1100D and 1100R

REMOVAL

These engines can be removed from the vehicle by following the procedure suggested for removal of the 124 engine. However, in this case, the engine hood should be removed, the air cleaner should be removed before the engine is removed and the transmission need not be removed.

DISASSEMBLY

To disassemble these engines, follow the procedure outlined for the 124 overhead valve engine.

ASSEMBLY

Assembly is the same procedure as that used for 124 overhead valve engines. The following differences should be noted.

Pistons, like the cylinders, are divided into three classes (A, B, C) based on their skirt diameters, and must always be installed into cylinders of the same class. Pistons are also grouped in sets according to their weight, with a maximum tolerance among pistons of the same set of ±.07 oz. (±2 gr.). Only pistons of the

same set may be installed in an engine. Weight and class letter are stamped on piston tops. Piston skirt wear always must be added to cylinder (or liner) wear to find the actual clearance between the two parts. If clearance is in excess of .0078″ (.20 mm.), cylinders (or liners) need reboring and oversize pistons must be used.

New rings should be checked for side clearance in the grooves and for end gap. If gap is more than recommended, try another set of rings. If it is too small, widen it by filing or grinding.

Connecting rods and pistons must be assembled so that the number stamped on the connecting rod bearing saddle and cap faces the slotted side of the piston skirt. Rods have an .078″ (2 mm.) offset. When installing them, be sure the offset side is adjacent to the main bearing. The cylinder number stamped on the connecting rod must face the side opposite the camshaft. When installing new rods, stamp rods 1 and 3 with their numbers on one side, and rods 2 and 4 with their numbers on the opposite side.

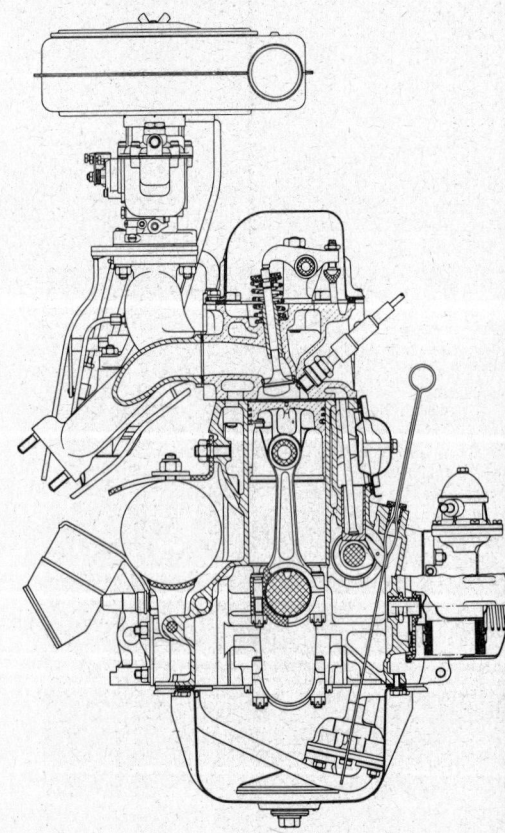

Cross-sectional view of Fiat 1100 engine through a cylinder

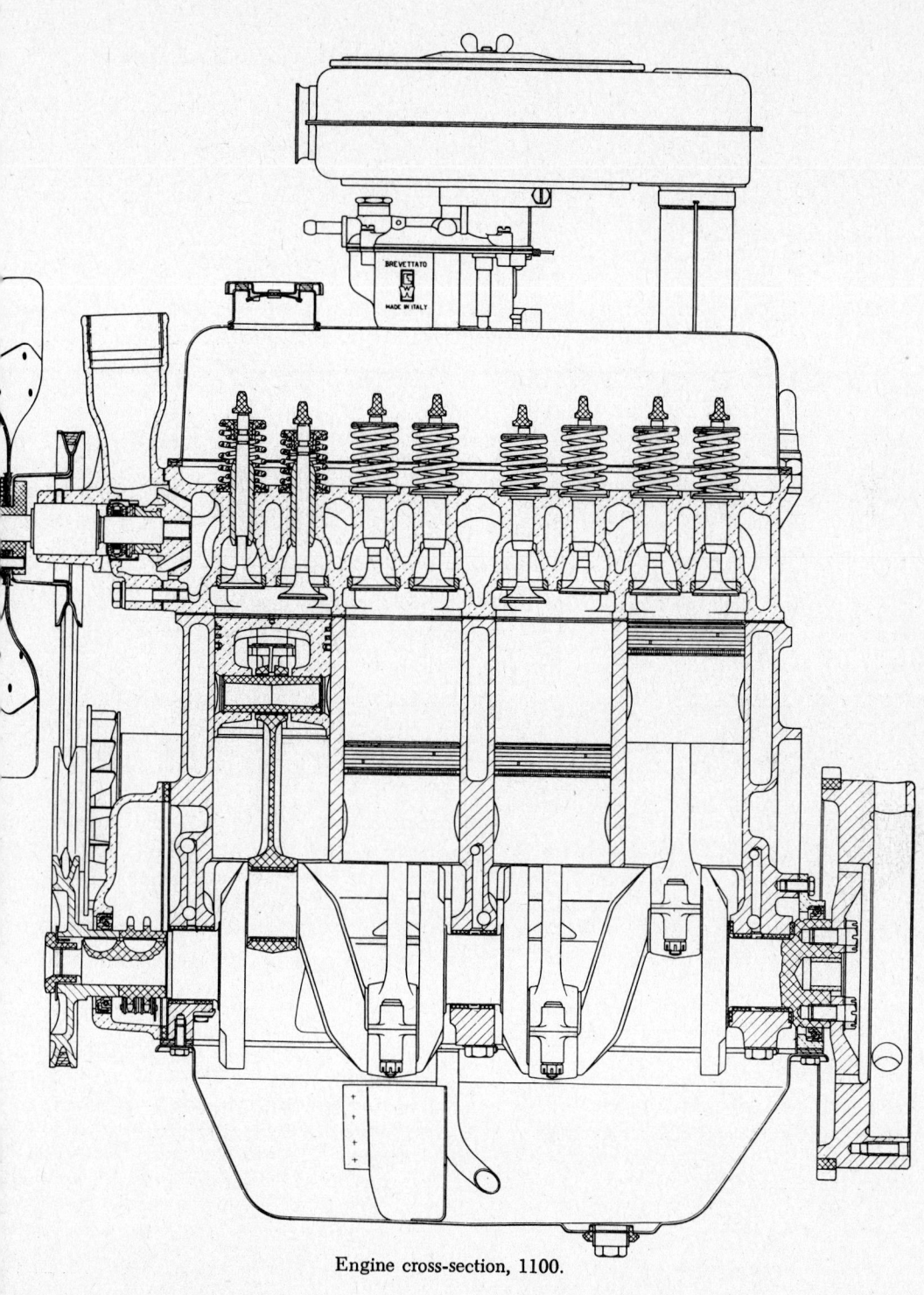

Engine cross-section, 1100.

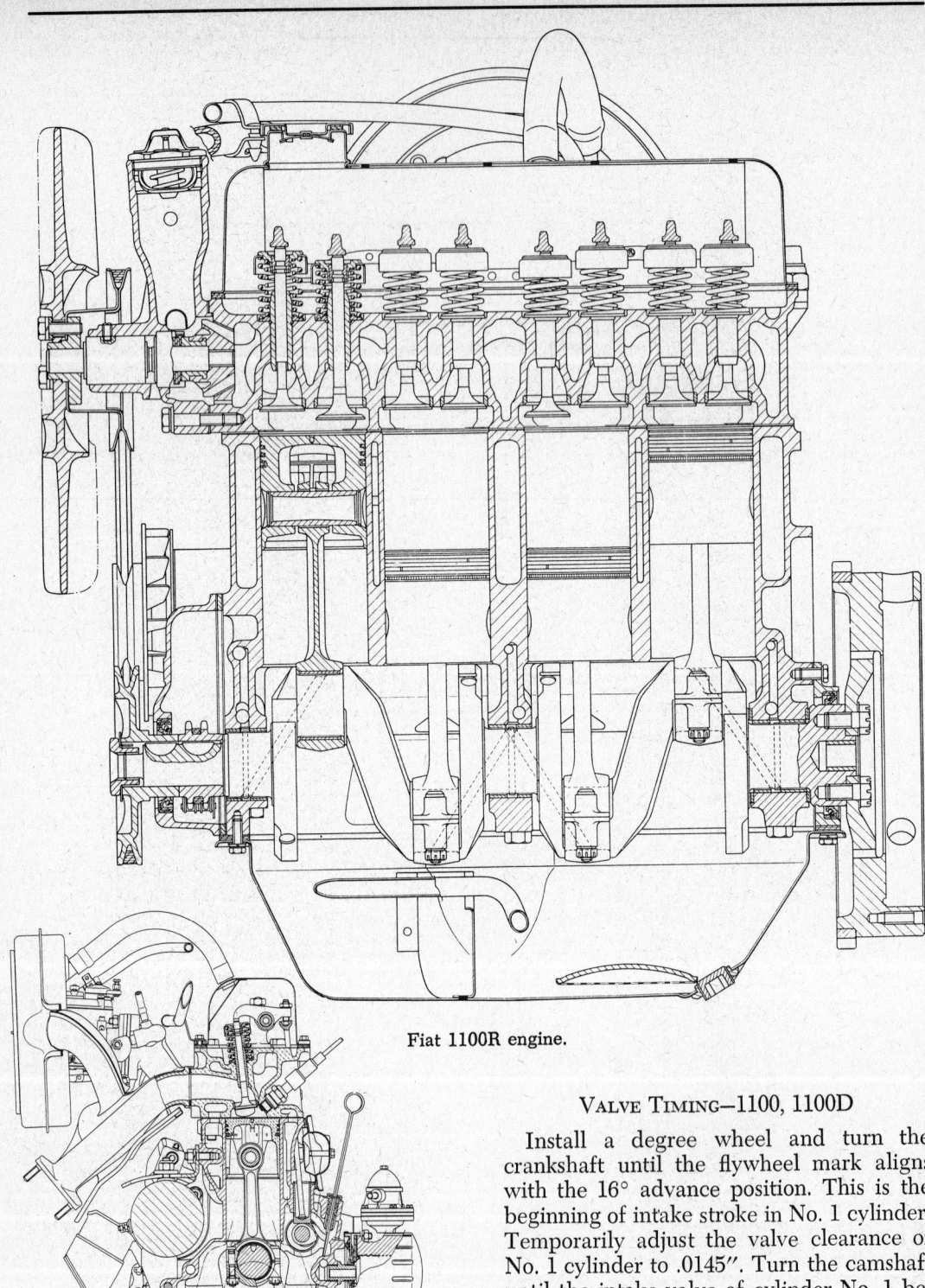

Fiat 1100R engine.

Cross-sectional view of Fiat 1100R engine through a cylinder

Valve Timing—1100, 1100D

Install a degree wheel and turn the crankshaft until the flywheel mark aligns with the 16° advance position. This is the beginning of intake stroke in No. 1 cylinder. Temporarily adjust the valve clearance of No. 1 cylinder to .0145″. Turn the camshaft until the intake valve of cylinder No. 1 begins to open. At this point the timing marks on the camshaft and crankshaft should be aligned.

Valve Timing—1100R

To be sure that the valves on 1100R engines are timed properly, insert the driven

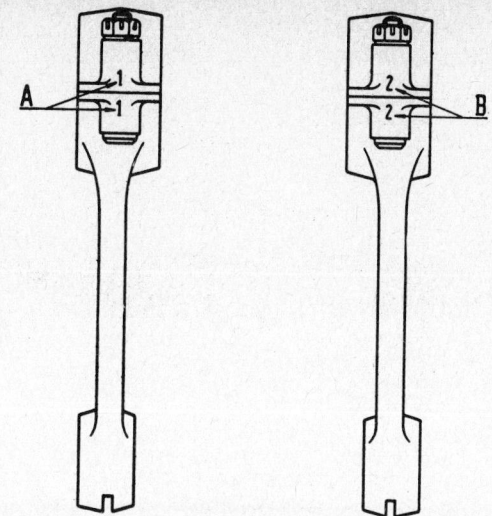

Connecting rod identification, Fiat 1100. Cylinder numbers for rods 1 and 3 are stamped on side "A", rods 2 and 4 are stamped on side "B". Sides are identified by rod offset between bearing and wrist pin.

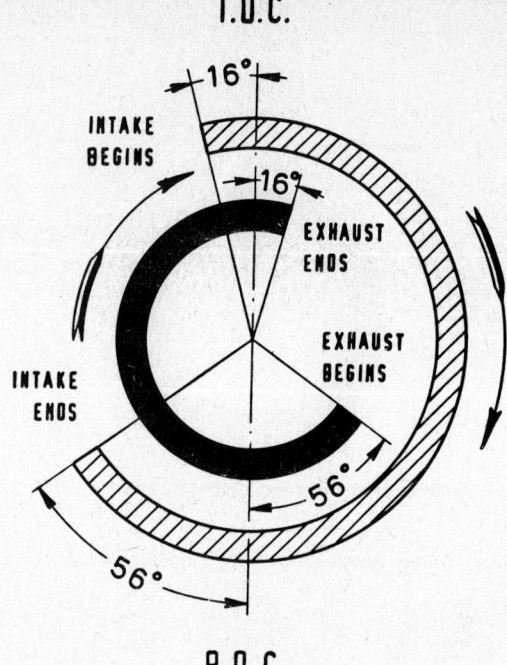

Fiat 1100 and 1100D valve timing diagram with theoretical valve lash of .0145"

STEPPED OILSCRAPER RING   COMPRESSION RING

RADIAL-SLOT OILSCRAPER RING   EXPANSION SLOT

REFERENCE NUMBERS

Fiat 1100 piston and connecting rod assembly— Reference numbers must face opposite the camshaft when installed

sprocket on the front end of the crankshaft. Install the driven sprocket on the camshaft and rotate the camshaft until the valve timing marks are aligned. Without removing the camshaft, take out the driven sprocket and mesh the timing chain with the sprockets. Install the driven sprocket so that the timing marks are aligned. Fit the plain washer and lockplate.

Fiat 1100 and 1100D valve timing marks

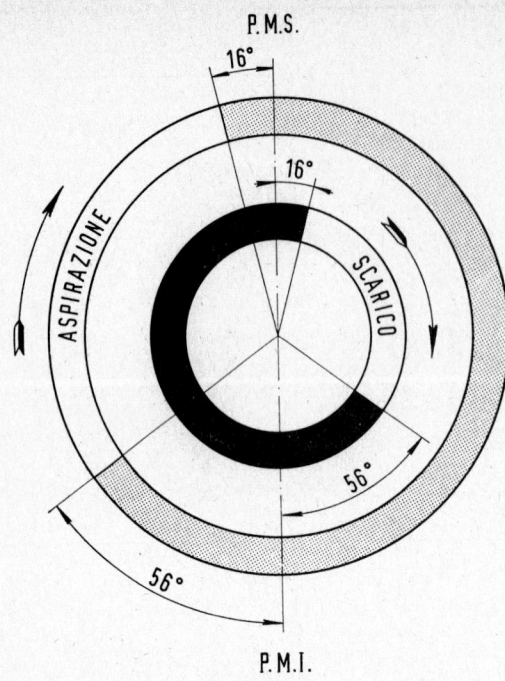

P.M.S.

16°

16°

ASPIRAZIONE   SCARICO

56°

56°

P.M.I.

P.M.I.   B.D.C.
Aspirazione   INTAKE
P.M.S.   T.D.C.
Scarico   EXHAUST

Fiat 1100R valve timing diagram with valve lash of .0146"

Valve Lash—1100, 1100D, 1100R

Adjust at the overlap in the firing order, using the following information.

Intake Stroke Begins (Cylinder No.)	Adjust Valves (Cylinder No.)
1	4
3	2
4	1
2	3

Installation

Installation is the reverse of removal.

1500 Cabriolet

Removal

Follow removal procedures for Fiat 124.

Disassembly

Disassembly procedures are the same as for the 124 overhead valve engine.

Assembly

Follow the assembly procedures for the overhead valve 124 engine. Note the following procedures.

Pistons of the 1500 engine (115C.005) are domed-type with a cavity on one side of the dome to allow for intake valve opening. Assemble the connecting rod to the piston so that the number stamped on the rod face is on the opposite side of this cavity. Install the assembly into the cylinder with the rod assembly number facing away from the camshaft.

Fiat 1100R timing marks

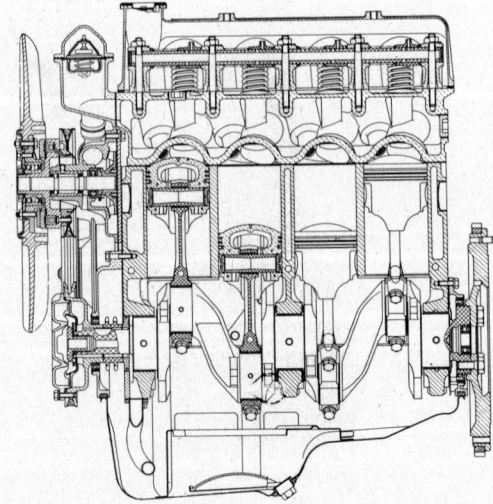

Cross-section of Fiat 1500 engine through the cylinders

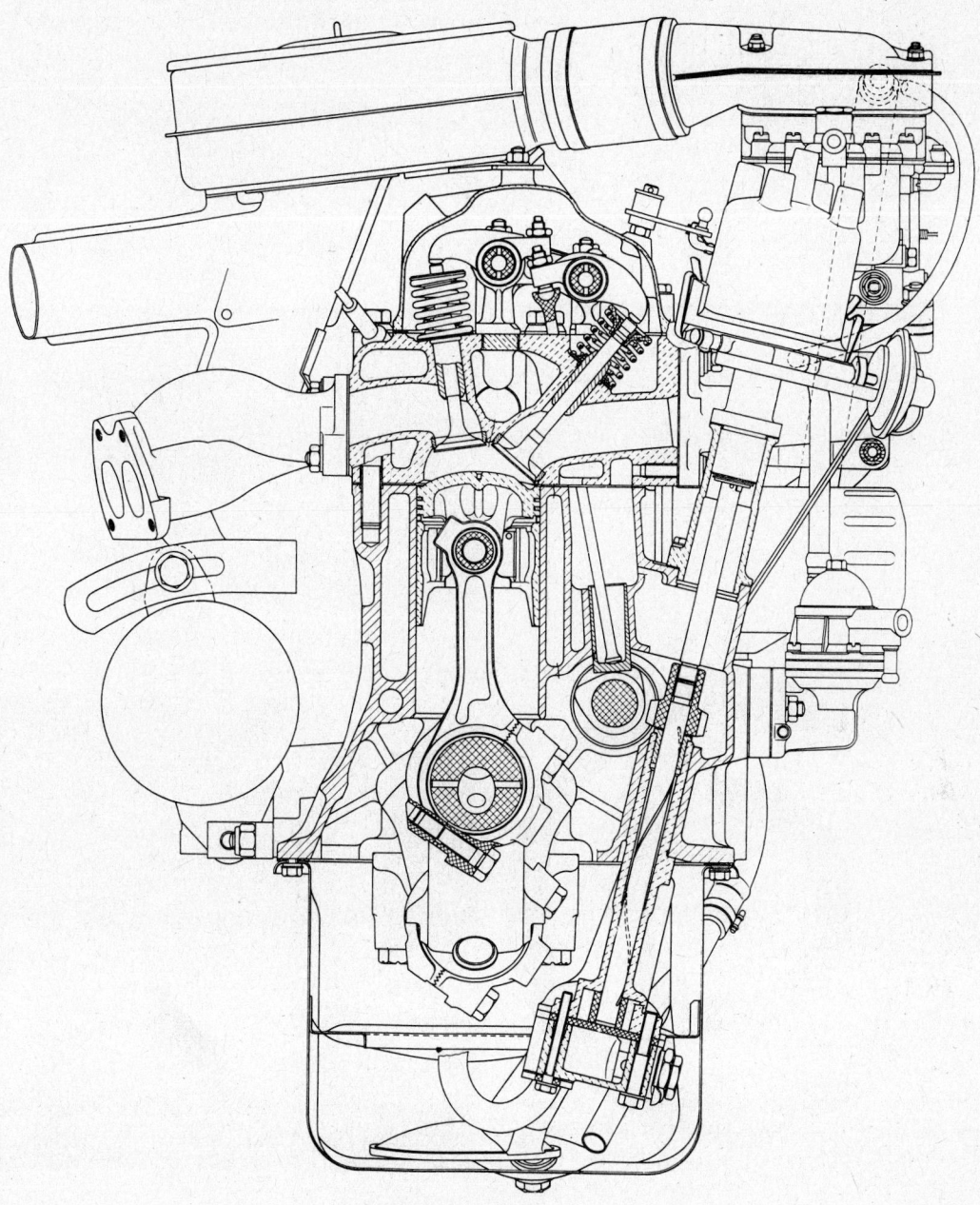

Engine cross-section, 1500.

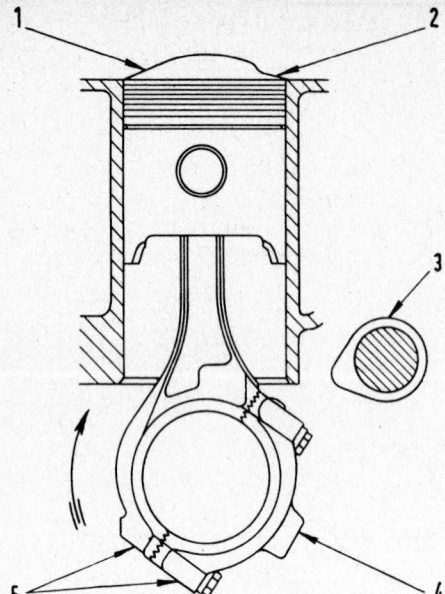

Proper connecting rod/piston position, Fiat 1500. Piston bore size and wrist pin group number (1); piston cavity (2); camshaft position (3); wrist pin bushing size number (4); piston assembly number (5).

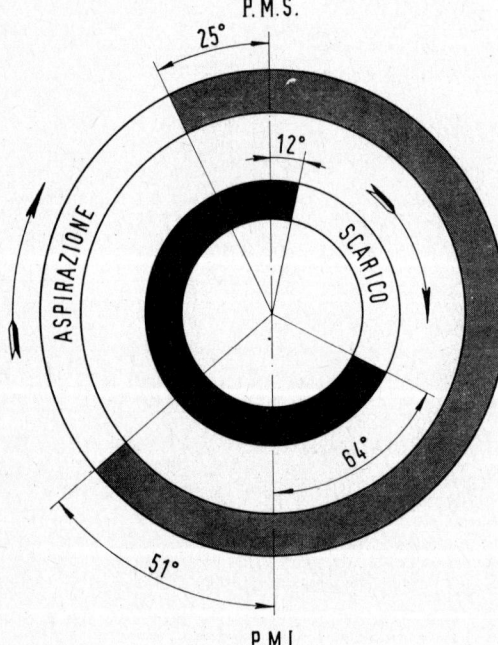

P.M.S.

25°

12°

ASPIRAZIONE

SCARICO

64°

51°

P.M.I.

ASPIRAZIONE   INTAKE
P.M.I.   B.D.C.
SCARICO   EXHAUST
P.M.S.   T.D.C.

Fiat 1500 valve timing diagram with valve lash of .0177″

VALVE TIMING

Use the procedure detailed for timing the 1100R valves.

VALVE LASH

Valve lash adjustment is exactly the same procedure used for the Fiat 1100R engine.

Fiat 1500 valve timing marks

1. Feeler gauge
2. Heat indicator sending unit
3. Exhaust valve rocker arm
4. Tappet clearance adjusting screw and nut
5. Pushrod
6. Intake valve rocker arm
7. Cup
8. Rocker shaft support

Adjusting Fiat 1500 valve lash

1600S Cabriolet

REMOVAL

Follow the removal procedure for 124 engines.

DISASSEMBLY

This engine is very similar to the 124 overhead camshaft engine. The 1600S engine uses three timing chains and two ad-justable chain tensioners. Otherwise, the operation and disassembly procedures for this engine are similar to the 124 overhead camshaft engine.

ASSEMBLY

Follow the 124 overhead camshaft engine assembly procedures, which are similar to the 1600S assembly procedures. Note the following procedures.

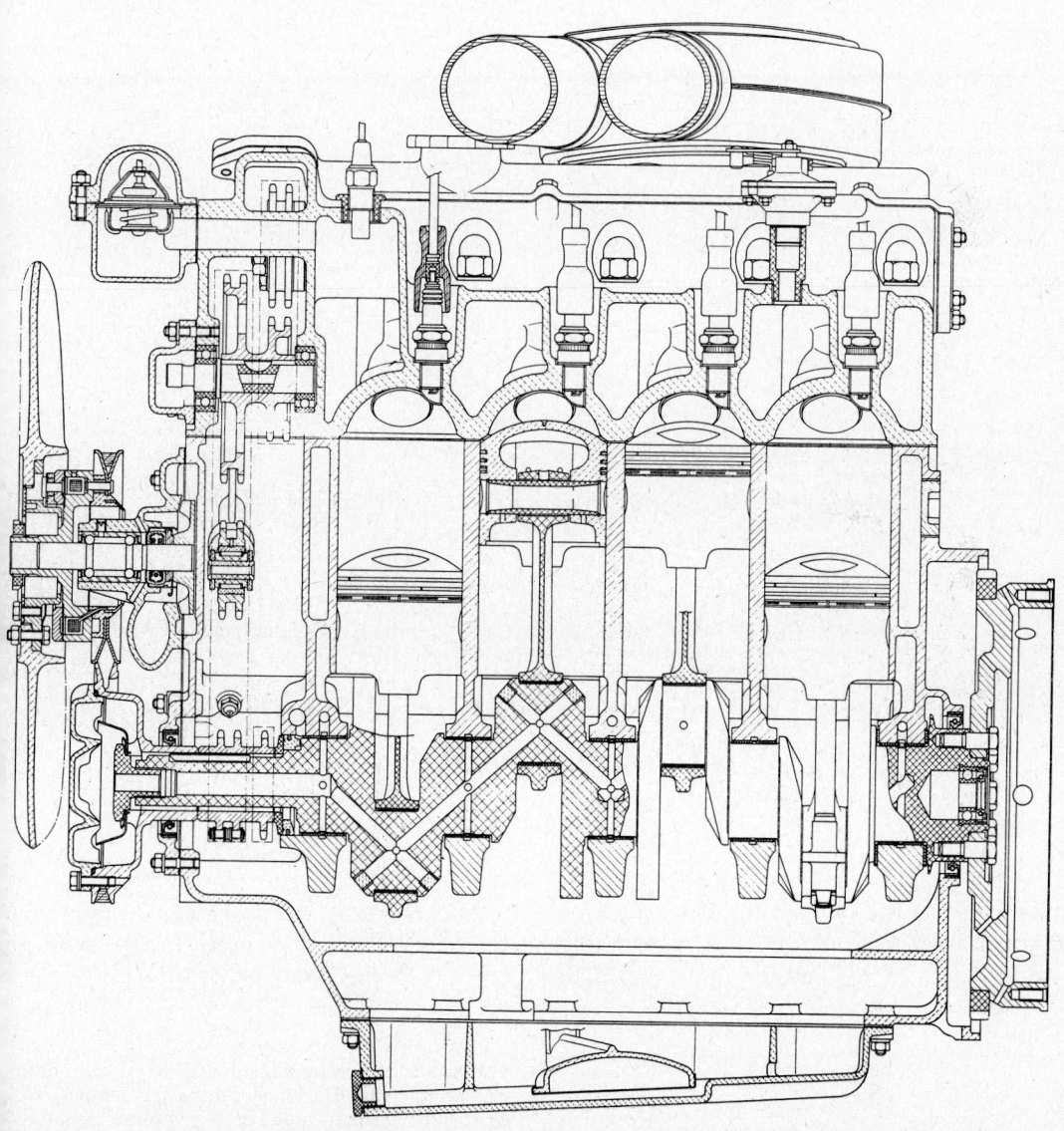

Engine cross-section, 1600S.

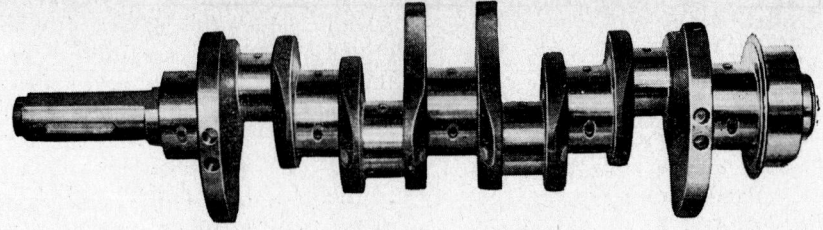

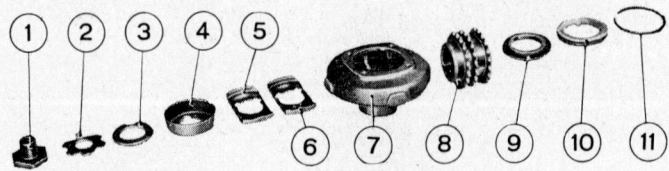

1. Centrifugal oil filter
   mounting screw
2. Lockplate
3. Washer
4. Oil slinger
5. Baffle plates
6. Baffle plates

7. Filter thrower
8. Timing gear drive
   sprocket
9. Thrust ring
10. Oil seal disc
11. Oil seal ring

Fiat 1600S crankshaft components

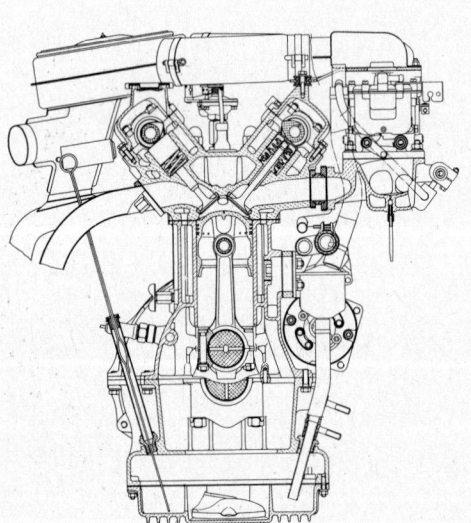

Cross-section of Fiat 1600S engine through a
cylinder

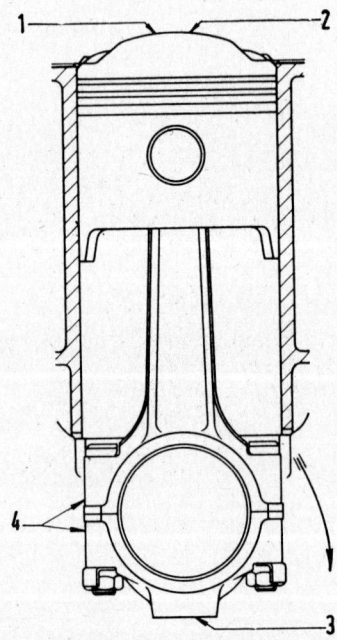

Connecting rod assembly of 1600S model. Bore
size group letter (1); wrist pin group number (2);
wrist pin bushing number (3); piston assembly
number (4).

OIL PUMP

Oil pump and distributor are chain-driven from the crankshaft. Driveshaft end-play is determined by a thrust washer in the pump housing and can be adjusted by substituting oversize washers, which are available in increments of .0039" (.10 mm.) from .0669" (1.7 mm.) to .1181" (3 mm.). Select a thrust washer having a thickness equal to the gap between the face of the shaft and a straightedge held across the crankcase. Insert washer and install pump with paper gasket. End-play will then be determined by thickness of gasket.

TAPPET CLEARANCE

Tappet clearance adjustment in the 1600S engine (118B.000) is made by first removing the camshafts, then changing valve endcaps. Endcaps are supplied in thicknesses ranging from .08" (2 mm.) to .126" (3.2 mm.) in increments of .002" (.05 mm.). Before removing camshafts, check clearance between tappets and cam lobes to determine which valves need adjustment. Turn flywheel until reference mark lines up with mark on crankcase and removable link of camshaft drive chain is accessible. Take out the removable link

and tie the two ends of the chain outside the housing to keep the chain from falling into the case. *Without changing position of crankshaft, which would also change the timing,* remove camshaft by first loosening center bearing screws, then front and rear screws. Loosen screws evenly to avoid distorting camshaft with unequal valve spring pressure. Exhaust valve camshaft is marked "S", intake valve camshaft is marked "A".

VALVE TIMING

Valve timing check is made by turning the flywheel until its reference mark lines up with the mark on the crankcase. In this position, marks on the camshafts should line up with marks on camshaft bearings. Using a sector scale, turn flywheel and check valve angles at opening and closing of intake and exhaust strokes. Adjustment can be made, if required, by relocating the holes in the flanges of the camshafts relative to the sprocket holes. Moving the mounting position one hole, right or left,

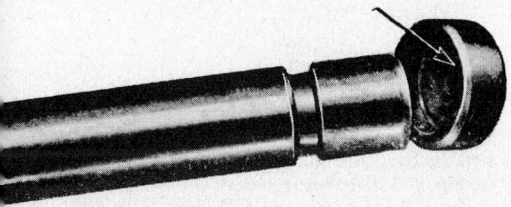

Fiat 1600S upper timing chain link retainer (arrow shows correct position)

Valve stem and cap for adjusting tappet clearance

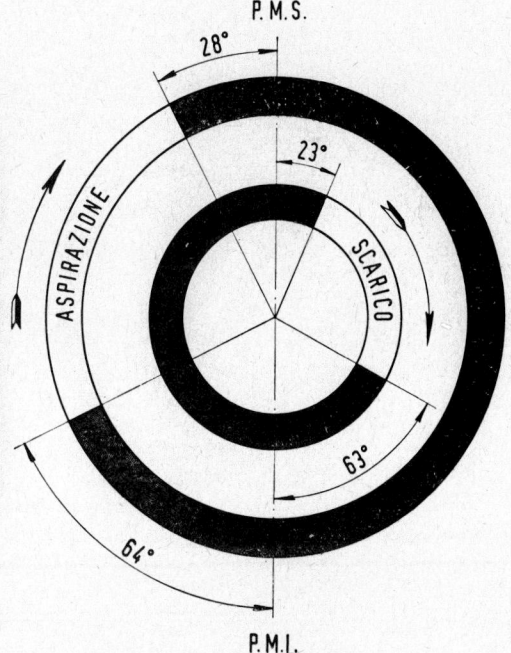

ASPIRAZIONE   INTAKE
P.M.S.   T.D.C.

SCARICO   EXHAUST
P.M.I.   B.D.C.

Fiat 1600S valve timing diagram with tappet clearance of .0138" (exhaust) and .0118" (intake)

Timing marks on flywheel and crankcase, 1600S.

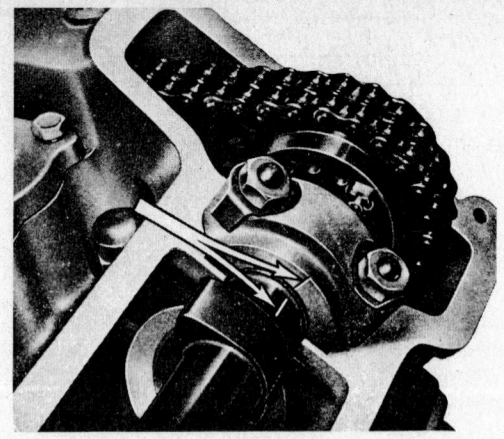

Timing marks on camshaft and bearing, 1600S.

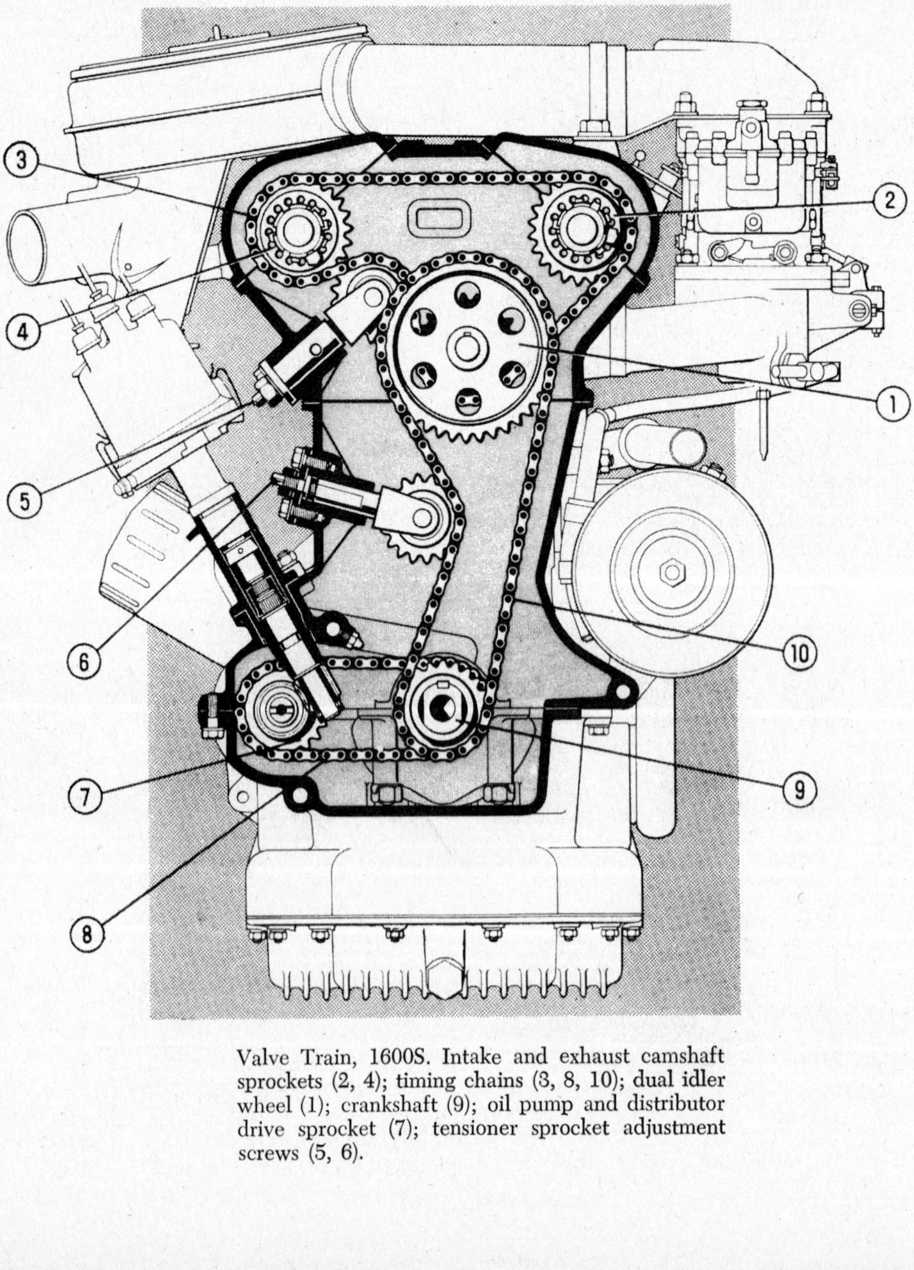

Valve Train, 1600S. Intake and exhaust camshaft
sprockets (2, 4); timing chains (3, 8, 10); dual idler
wheel (1); crankshaft (9); oil pump and distributor
drive sprocket (7); tensioner sprocket adjustment
screws (5, 6).

results in an angular displacement of 1°42′51″. Remove the locknut and the sprocket-to-camshaft locating screw. Relocate the camshaft to obtain correct timing, install locating screw and tighten locknut.

TIMING CHAIN TENSIONER

Timing chain tension adjustment is made by turning the tensioner sprocket screw counterclockwise to increase, and clockwise to reduce, tension. Do not overtighten. Chain tension is correct when it sags .039–.079″ (1–2 mm.) under hand pressure.

Timing chain is adjusted on model 1600S by turning screws (3) after loosening locknuts (1, 2).

Oil Filters

Fiat 124, 850, 1500 and 1600S cars have two oil filters. One is the conventional cartridge; the other is a centrifugal type mounted on the front end of the crankshaft. A pulley on the front of this filter drives the belt for the fan, water pump and generator.

Oil is forced into the filter through one of two openings in the crankshaft, and returns to the crankcase through a ball check valve and the other opening in the shaft.

Tighten the nut holding the hub to the shaft to 72.3 ft.lbs. (10 kg.m.) for 124 and 850 models, and 101.3 ft.lbs. (14 kg.m.) for 1500 and 1600S models.

Clutch and Transmission

The drive train for Fiat models, except the 600 and 850, consists of the clutch, gearbox, drive shaft, hypoid and rear axle. The 600 and 850 have rear-mounted engines and utilize a clutch and transaxle (gearbox, differential and axle) assembly to transmit power to the rear wheels.

Clutch

A single-plate, dry clutch is used on all models. Pressure plates are of two types, those having conventional coil springs and those having a single diaphragm spring.

All are mechanically operated except the 1600S Cabriolet, which has a hydraulic servo. This system consists of a pedal-actuated master cylinder and a slave cylinder which has an adjustable pushrod connected directly to the clutch throw-out lever. The hydraulic clutch circuit is entirely independent of the brake circuit, although it utilizes brake fluid. Capacity of the system is .36 pints.

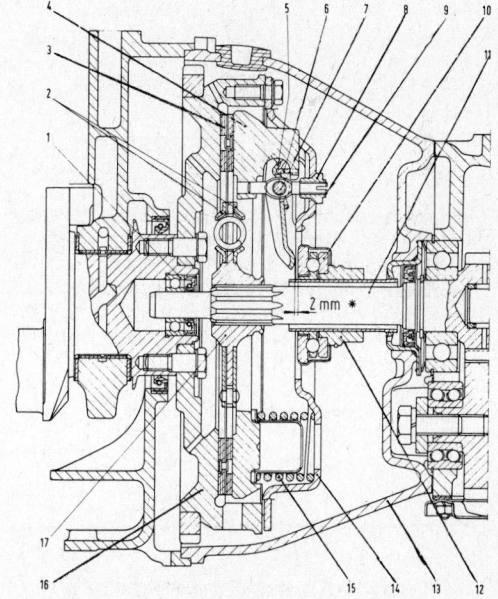

Coil spring clutch assembly of the 1600S Cabriolet. (1) front ball bearing, clutch shaft; (2) driven plate flanges; (3) driven plate linings; (4) pressure plate; (5) release levers; (6) fulcrums; (7) release lever pin; (8) eyebolt nut; (9) eyebolt; (10) throwout bearing; (11) clutch shaft; (12) throwout sleeve; (13) bell housing; (14) clutch cover; (15) pressure springs; (16) flywheel; (17) driven plate hub.

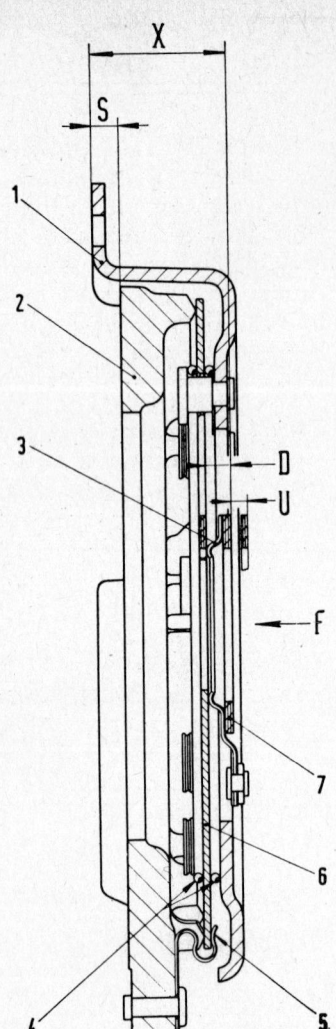

Clutch plate assembly and specifications for the 124 Coupe and Spider. (1) clutch plate; (2) thrust ring; (3) withdrawal flange; (4) spring spacers; (5) spring retainer; (5) (6) diaphragm spring; (7) friction ring; (S) thickness of ring gauge = .32" (8.2 mm.); (X) distance to be maintained = 1.57-1.68" (40-43 mm.); (D) withdrawal stroke - .31" (8 mm.); (U) maximum wear limit - .19" (5 mm.); (F) load to move withdrawal flange - 728 lbs. (330 kg.).

PEDAL TRAVEL ADJUSTMENT

Should pedal free travel be less than specified because of clutch plate facing wear, adjustment should be made (see dimensions in table), otherwise the clutch will slip. Prior to making adjustments, check all cable and rod grommets and bushings for possible wear.

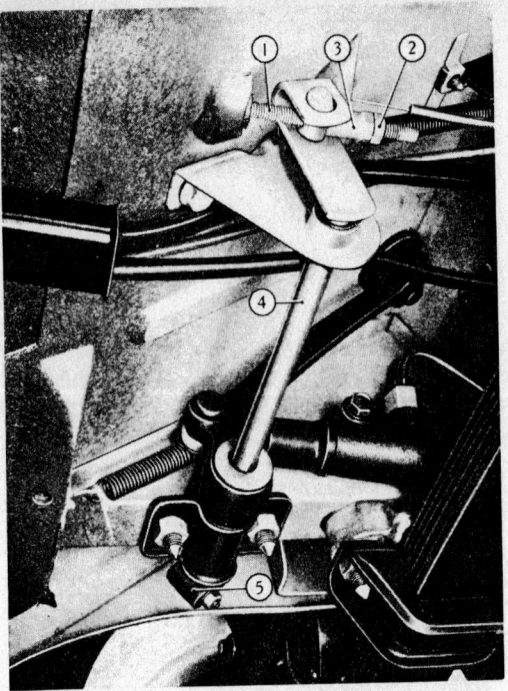

To adjust free-play on 600, loosen locknut (2) on cable (1) and turn (3) either in, (to reduce), or out, (to increase). Shaft (4) is actuated by pedal (5).

REMOVAL

The clutch is removed with the transmission. Jack the car and remove the transmission. It is important that the clutch shaft never be allowed to rest on the withdrawal flange, since the support plates of the flange will be bent. Mark the position of the clutch in relation to the flywheel to facilitate assembly. Remove the bolts securing the clutch cover to the flywheel. The bolts should be removed evenly to prevent distortion of the clutch.

INSTALLATION

Check the condition of the pilot bushing which is pressed into the crankshaft. If necessary, replace this bushing. Installation of the clutch is the reverse of removal. Use an old mainshaft or wooden dummy shaft to center the clutch disc.

Transmission

124 (4-SPEED)

The transmission is of the conventional type, four forward gears and one reverse. All gears are fully synchronized. The transmission is in three parts, front bell housing, main transmission case and rear cover.

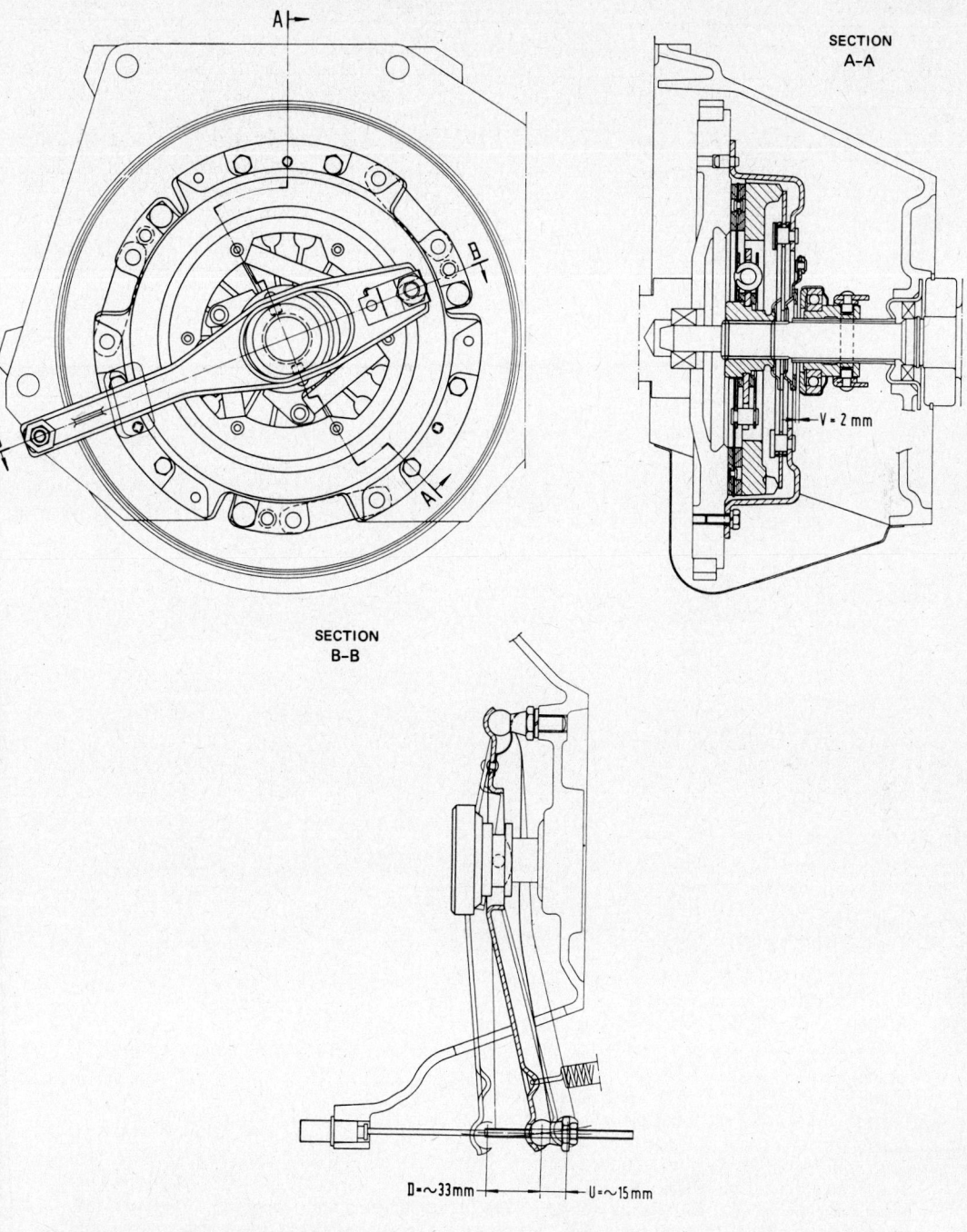

**SECTION
A-A**

V = 2 mm

**SECTION
B-B**

D=~33mm   U=~15 mm

Diaphragm spring clutch assembly of 124 viewed from throwout fork side. (V) in A-A=free travel of throwout sleeve; (D) in B-B = travel of throwout lever; (U) in B-B = maximum movement of lever due to wear.

Clutch Specifications

Model	Type	Plate Actuator	Plate Dia. (In./MM.)	Pedal Free-Travel (In./MM.)
124 (All Models) Spider, Coupe	Dry, Single Plate	Diaphragm Spring	7.87/200	.98/25①
124 Sedan	Dry, Single Plate	Diaphragm Spring	7.16/182	.98/25①
600/D	Dry, Single Plate	6 coil springs	6.10/155	.78/20
850 (All Models)	Dry, Single Plate	Diaphragm Spring	6.2/160	.9–1/23–25①
1100	Dry, Single Plate	6 coil springs	7.25/184	.6–.8/15–20
1100R	Dry, Single Plate	6 coil springs	7.25/184	.78/20
1500	Dry, Single Plate	6 coil springs	7.87/200	.71–.87/18–22
1600S	Dry, Single Plate°	6 coil springs	8.5/216	.71–.87/18–22

° Hydraulic operation.
① Release flange Travel = .31″/8 MM.

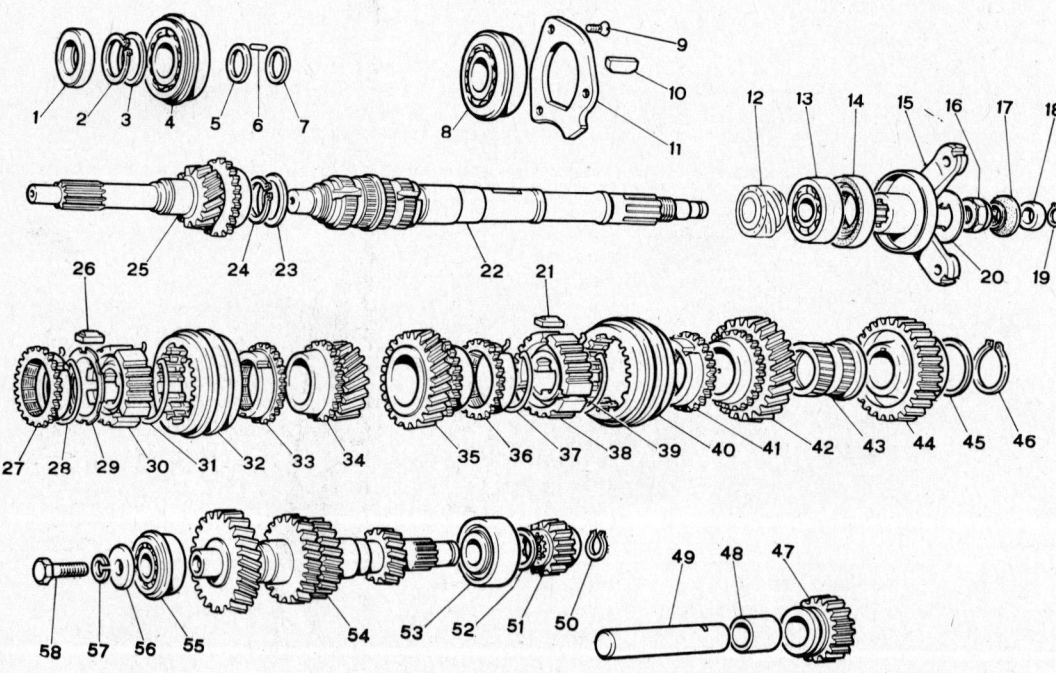

Transmission components. 124 Sedan. (1) inner cover seal; (2) bearing retaining ring; (3) spring washer; (4) direct drive shaft ball bearing; (5) and (7) thrust rings of needle roller bearing between direct drive and mainshaft; (6) needle roller; (8) mainshaft intermediate ball bearing; (9) bearing retaining plate fixing screw; (10) key; (11) mainshaft intermediate ball bearing retaining plate; (12) speedometer drive gear (13) mainshaft rear ball bearing; (14) rear cover oil seal; (15) flexible coupling spider; (16) spider fixing nut; (17) sealing ring; (18) flexible coupling centering ring; (19) snap-ring; (20) lockwasher; (21) and (26) sliding sleeves dogs; (22) mainshaft; (23) spring washer; (24) mainshaft assembly retaining snap-ring; (25) direct drive and fourth gear shaft; (27, 33, 36 and 41) synchronizing rings; (28, 31, 37 and 39) dog retaining rings; (29) spring washer; (30) third-fourth gear sliding sleeve hub; (32) and (40) sliding sleeves; (34) third speed driven gear; (35) second speed driven gear; (38) first-second gear sliding sleeve hub; (42) first speed driven gear; (43) first gear bush; (44) reverse driven gear; (45) spring washer; (46) reverse driven gear retaining snap-ring; (47) reverse idler gear; (48) reverse idler gear bush; (49) reverse idler gear spindle; (50) snap-ring; (51) reverse driving gear; (52) spring washer; (53) layshaft rear roller bearing; (54) layshaft with first, second and third gears; (55) layshaft font double-row ball bearing; (56) flat washer; (57) spring washer; (58) layshaft front ball bearing fixing bolt.

Cross-section of 124 Sedan clutch and transmission.

Removal

Working from inside the car, remove the gear lever and cover plate. Underneath the car, remove the flexible coupling from the spider on the mainshaft. Remove the speedometer drive from the support on the transmission. Disconnect the clutch withdrawal fork return spring. Remove the locknut and unscrew the adjusting rod from the flexible cable. Remove the flywheel cover from the bell housing. Remove the bolt securing the exhaust pipe bracket to the transmission. Detach the exhaust piping. Remove the starter motor heat shield and starter motor. Support the transmission, and remove the four bolts securing the transmission to the engine. Move the transmission carefully away from the engine and lower it to the ground.

Disassembly

Remove the drain plug and drain the oil from the transmission. Remove the oil filler plug. Place the transmission upside down and remove the lower cover and gasket. Remove the clutch withdrawal fork and slide the thrust bearing and control sleeve from the central support. Remove the bell housing and gasket. At the same time remove the center cover of the direct drive shaft with the oil seal and spring washer. It may be necessary to remove the seal on the bench. Remove the bolts securing 3rd

1. Detent ball spring, reverse gear selector rod
2. Detent ball spring for 3rd and 4th gears
3. Detent ball spring, 1st and 2nd gears

Removing the detent balls and springs from the central case (124 4-speed)

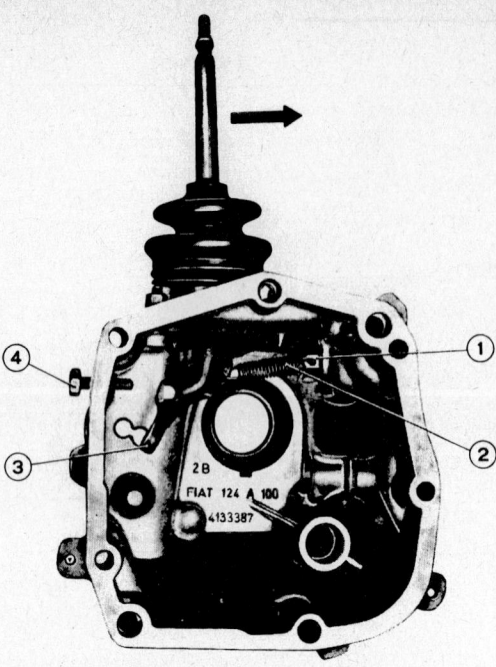

1. Anchor screw for gear lever return spring
2. Gear lever return spring
3. Gear lever
4. Gear lever sidetravel stopscrew
   The arrow shows the direction in which the lever must be moved to disengage it from the selector rods, so that the rear cover can be removed.

Inside view of rear transmission case (124 4-speed)

and 4th gear selector forks. NOTE: *When the bolts have been removed the fork can be moved along the bar and the two gears can be engaged simultaneously.* Slide the rubber dust cover from the end of the mainshaft. Remove the snap-ring and flexible coupling ring. Lock the mainshaft by proceeding according to the note above, and remove the spider from the mainshaft. Remove the speedometer drive support and gasket from the rear transmission cover. Remove the selector rod detent ball spring cover plate from the main casing. Remove the springs from the recesses, followed by the detent balls. NOTE: *The reverse gear selector rod ball spring is not of the same compression as the other two springs. Keep this one separate from the other two.* Remove the rear cover complete with gear lever, by proceeding as follows. Remove the stop screw which limits the side movement of the lever. Remove the nuts retaining the cover to the main body. Move the gear lever to the left to disengage it from the selector rods and remove the rear cover.

Remove the gear lever from the rear cover. Slide the rear ball bearing and speedometer drive gear from the mainshaft. Slide the reverse gear selector rod, complete with fork, from its seat in the main case and, at the same time, remove reverse gear from its spindle. Remove the snap-ring retaining reverse driving gear and remove the gear from the end of the layshaft. Remove the snap-ring retaining the driven gear from the reverse gear train. Remove the spring washers, driven gear of the reverse gear train, and remove the Woodruff key from its seat. NOTE: *Before removing the retaining clip of the reverse gear driven train, the spring washer must be compressed.* Engage two gears to prevent the shafts from turning and remove the retaining bolt and front ball bearing from the layshaft. Tilt the layshaft and remove it from the main case. Remove the 3rd and 4th gear selector rods from the case and remove the bolt and spring washer holding the 1st and 2nd gear selector forks to the rod. Remove the rod, followed by the 1st-2nd and 3rd-4th gear forks. The three safety rollers will be released as the selector rods are removed. Remove the plate which retains the mainshaft intermediate ball bearing. Withdraw the bearing from its housing. NOTE: *When separating the direct drive shaft from the mainshaft, the 23 needle roller bearings will be free to spin or fall inside the case. It is advisable to remove these and check the exact number immediately.* Withdraw the reverse gear spindle from the main case. Remove the direct drive and 4th gear shaft from the mainshaft, complete with ball bearing and 4th gear synchronizing ring. Tilt the mainshaft and remove it from the case, complete with gears, hubs, sliding sleeves and synchronizing rings. Remove the following parts from the mainshaft: 1st gear and bushing, 1st gear synchronizing ring, 1st and 2nd gear hub and sliding sleeve, 2nd gear synchronizing ring and 2nd gear. Remove the snap-ring from its seat in the front end of the mainshaft and remove the following parts: spring washer, 3rd-4th gear hub, sliding sleeve, synchronizing ring, and 3rd gear. Remove the snap-ring from the direct drive and 4th gear shaft and remove the spring washer and ball bearing.

Assembly

Assemble the following parts on the mainshaft, in the order given: 3rd gear and synchronizing ring, 3rd-4th gear sliding sleeve (with three dogs and two springs) and spring washer. Insert the snap-ring in the groove, securing the parts listed above to the front of the mainshaft. Slide the 2nd gear and synchronizing ring, 1st-2nd gear sliding sleeve and hub (with three dogs and two springs) and 1st speed synchronizing ring and gear with bushing onto the rear end of the shaft. NOTE: *The synchronizing ring dog springs must be fitted so that the ends of the springs are not attached to the same dog.* Tilt the mainshaft and insert it into the transmission case. Working from the rear end of the mainshaft, use a driver and insert the intermediate ball bearing. Install the reverse idler gear shaft, then fit the shaft and bearing retaining plate. Secure the plate to the main case and stake the nuts in place. Fit the ball bearing and spring washer to the direct drive shaft and insert the spring retaining clip of the bearing in the groove. Fit the inner thrust ring in the recess of the direct drive shaft. Coat the 23 needle rollers with heavy grease and insert these, followed by the outer thrust ring. Insert the direct drive shaft in the main case and slide it onto the end of the mainshaft, seating the 4th gear synchronizing ring and toothed spring washer between them. Fit the 1st and 2nd gear selector fork to the sliding sleeve and slide the corresponding selector rod into the fork from outside. Replace the locating roller of this bar to its seat and secure the fork to the rod. Install the 3rd-4th gear selector fork and rod in the same manner. Do not lock the fork to the rod at this point, since it will be necessary to use this fork to lock the transmission at a later time. Insert the layshaft with 1st, 2nd, 3rd and direct drive gears, into the main case. Replace the front ball bearing and rear ball bearing of the layshaft. Lock the shafts by engaging two gears at the same time. Use the flat washer, spring washer and bolt to secure the front bearing to the layshaft. Fit the key to the mainshaft and install the reverse driving gear and spring washer. Retain these with a snap-ring. Fit the spring washer and reverse driving gear to the end of the layshaft and secure them with a snap-ring. Insert the reverse selector rod locating roller in its seating, and fit the selector fork to the rod. Retain this with a bolt and spring washer. Install the selector rod in its guide and at the same time, fit the reverse idler gear to its spindle. Install the speedometer drive gear and rear ball bearing on the mainshaft. Fit the gear shifting assembly to the rear transmission cover, as follows. Drive a new oil seal with inner spring into place. Fit the gear shifting lever to the cover. Attach the gear lever return spring to the lever and replace the screw in the cover. Mount the lever assembly on the rear cover and fit the rear cover to the main transmission case. Be sure to fit a gasket between the two cases. Replace the speedometer drive support with a gasket under it. It is held in place by a nut on a

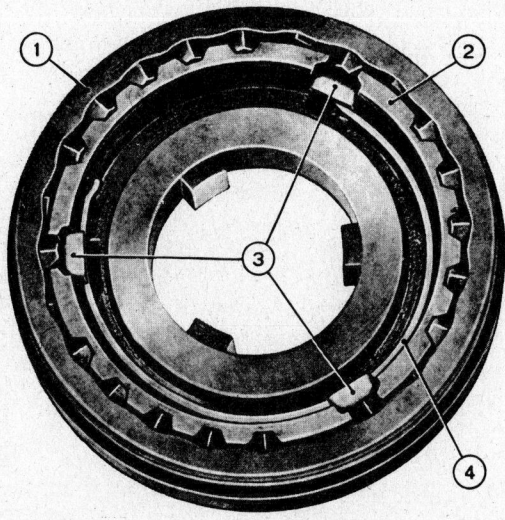

1. Sliding sleeve
2. Hub
3. Dogs
4. Dog retaining spring

Sliding sleeve type synchronizer

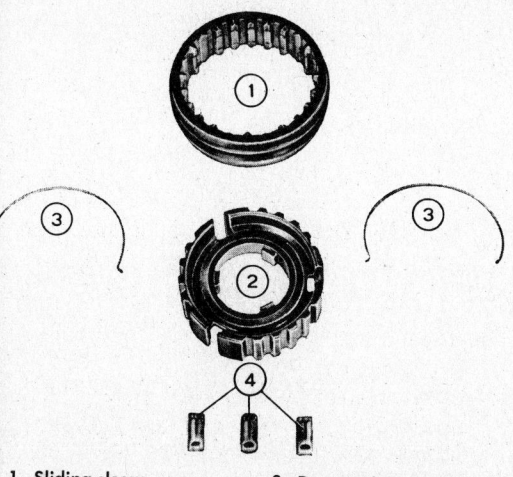

1. Sliding sleeve
2. Hub
3. Dog retaining spring
4. Dogs

Exploded view of sliding sleeve type synchronizer

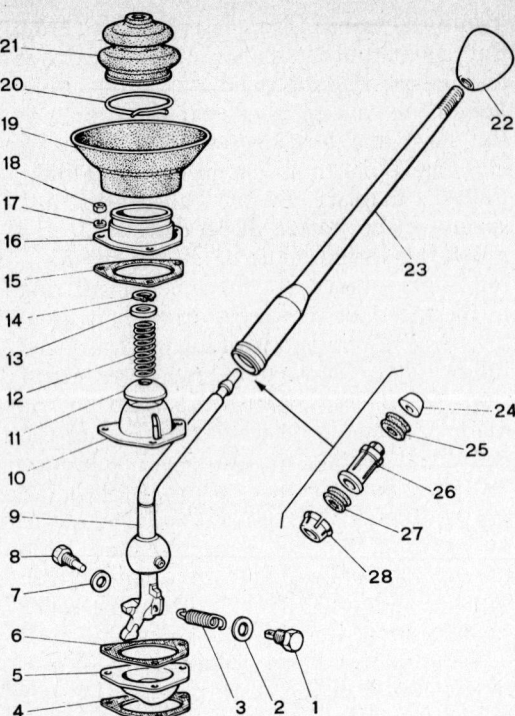

1. Gear lever return spring anchor screw
2. Flat washer
3. Lever return spring
4. Gasket
5. Socket plate
6. Gasket
7. Flat washer
8. Gear lever stop screw
9. Lower part of gear lever with ball
10. Upper socket plate
11. Dome washer
12. Spring
13. Cup washer
14. Retaining snap-ring
15. Gasket
16. Flange
17. Spring washer
18. Nut
19. Grommet
20. Spring clip
21. Rubber boot
22. Knob
23. Upper part of gear lever
24. Shoulder block
25. Rubber bushings
26. Spacer
27. Rubber bushings
28. Spring-ring

Exploded view of 124 sedan gearshift assembly

stud in the cover. Install the flexible spider and flat washer on the tail of the mainshaft. Lock the gears and tighten the nut, bending up the tab washer. Install the dust cover on the mainshaft and drive the cou-

pling centering ring into place and insert the snap-ring in the groove. Drive an oilseal into the cover of the direct drive shaft and attach this cover to the front of the transmission body. Insert a sealing ring between them. Install the spring washer of the cover and fit the bell housing to the main case, with a gasket. Fit the 3rd and 4th gear selector fork to the selector rod and secure with a bolt and washer. Replace the three selector rod detent balls and springs in their proper bores. Note that the reverse spring is different from the other two. Fit the lower cover and gasket to the main case. Install the oil drain plug. Fit the clutch release sleeve and thrust bearing to the cover of the cover of the direct drive shaft and install the fork lever. Turn the transmission right side up, and fill with 2.75 pints of Fiat W 90/M oil. The oil must come to the brim of the filler hole. Replace the filler plug.

Installation

Install the transmission in reverse order to removal. Be sure to center the clutch with an old mainshaft or wooden dummy shaft.

Specifications

Gear backlash	.0039"
Clearance between	
1st gear and bushing	.0019"-.0039"
2nd and 3rd gears and seats	.0019"-.0039"
Clearance between reverse gear and bushing	.0019"-.0039"
Clearance between flanks of sleeve splines and hub splines	.0027"-.0063"
Radial bearing clearance	.0019" (max.)
Axial bearing clearance	.0196" (max.)
Shaft runout	.00098" (max.)

124 (5-Speed)

This transmission, previously optional on 124 Spyder and Coupe models, has now become standard. Basically, it is the same unit as the 4-speed, with the addition of a fifth gear or overdrive. The transmission is in three parts. The front body is bolted to the crankcase and houses the clutch and withdrawal sleeve, with a thrust bearing. The center body is bolted to the front body and contains the 1st, 2nd, 3rd and 4th

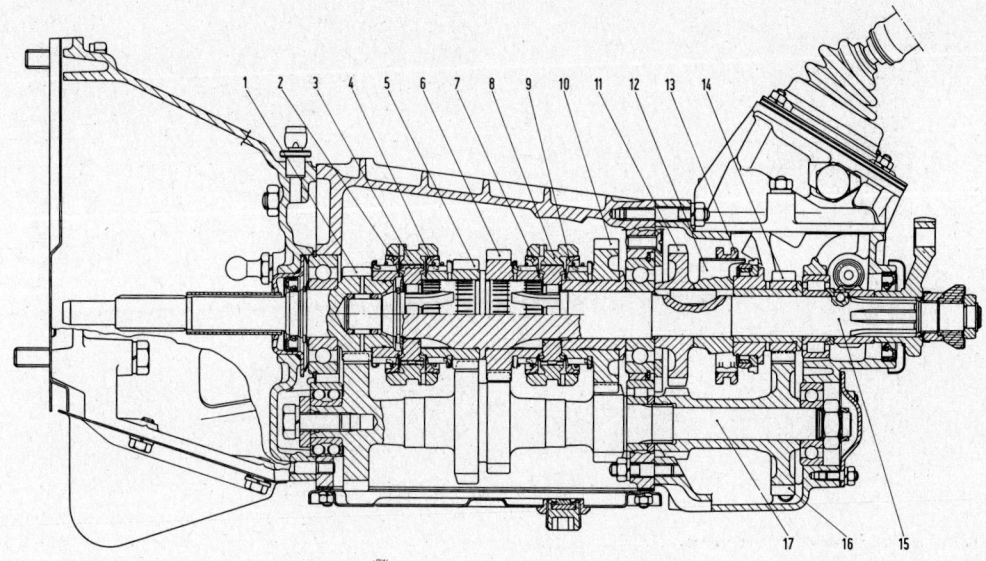

1. Constant mesh 4th gear pinion and main drive
2. Synchronizing ring
3. Sliding sleeve, 3rd and 4th gear
4. Synchronizing ring
5. 3rd gear pinion
6. 2nd gear pinion
7. Synchronizing ring
8. Sliding sleeve, 1st and 2nd gears
9. Synchronizing ring
10. 1st gear pinion
11. Reserve gear pinion
12. Hub
13. Sliding sleeve, 5th gear
14. Pinion and synchronizer complete, 5th gear
15. Mainshaft
16. Gear assembly for 5th and reverse gears
17. Countershaft
18. Reverse shaft

19. Reverse sliding pinion
20. 5th and reverse selector bar
21. 3rd and 4th gear selector bar
22. 1st and 2nd gear selector bar
23. 5th and reverse selector fork
24. Gear lever ball
25. Reverse spring
26. Gear lever ball socket
27. Ball socket retaining plate
28. Gear lever guide plate
29. 5th gear and reverse guard plate
30. Gear lever guide plate
31. Resistance-spring spindle, 1st, 2nd 5th and reverse
32. 3rd and 4th gear selector fork
33. 1st and 2nd gear selector fork
34. Sleeve hub, 3rd and 4th gears
   A. Stop dog
   B. Safety stop for reverse

Cross-sectional view of 124 5-speed transmission

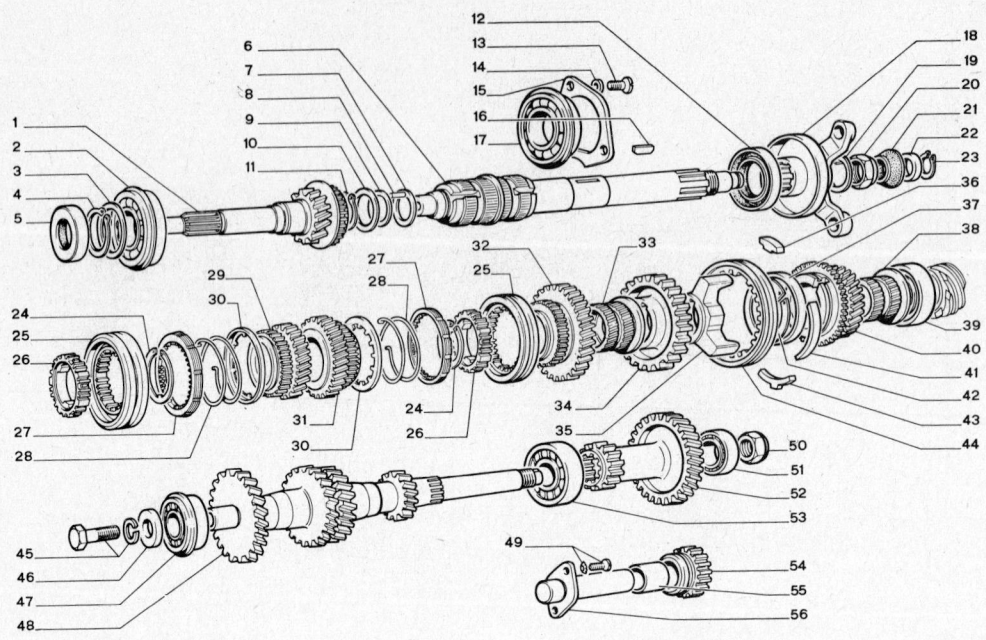

1. Constant mesh and fourth gear shaft
2. Front ball bearing
3. Spring washer
4. Snap-ring
5. Gasket
6. Mainshaft
7. Thrust washer
8. Needle rollers
9. Thrust washer
10. Spring washer
11. Snap-ring
12. Gasket
13. Plate fixing screws
14. Toothed washer
15. Bearing retainer plate
16. Woodruff key
17. Intermediate ball bearing
18. Joint sleeve
19. Lockwasher
20. Nut

21. Seal ring
22. Positioning ring
23. Snap-ring
24. Snap-ring
25. Sliding sleves, 1st, 2nd, 3rd, and 4th gears
26. Sliding sleeve hubs
27. Synchronizing ring
28. Springs
29. 3rd speed gear
30. Cup
31. 2nd speed gear
32. 1st speed gear
33. 1st speed gear bushing
34. Reverse gear
35. Sliding sleeve hub, 5th speed gear
36. Stop plate
37. 5th speed gear synchronizing ring
38. 5th speed gear bushing
39. Rear roller bearing
40. 5th speed gear

41. Spring
42. Snap-ring
43. Thrust plate
44. 5th gear sliding sleeve
45. Screws and spring washer, locking bearing
46. Plain washer
47. Front ball bearing, countershaft
48. Countershaft and gears for 1st, 2nd, 3rd and constant mesh
49. Screws and toothed washer fixing reverse gear shaft
50. Nut
51. Rear ball bearing
52. Reverse and 5th speed gears
53. Intermediate roller bearing
54. Reverse gear
55. Reverse gear bushing
56. Reverse gear shaft

Exploded view of 124 5-speed components

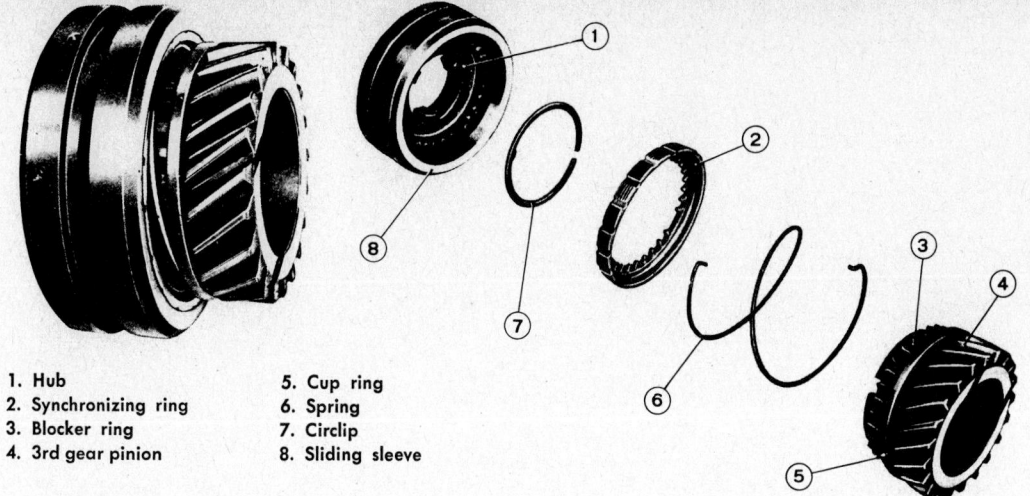

1. Hub
2. Synchronizing ring
3. Blocker ring
4. 3rd gear pinion
5. Cup ring
6. Spring
7. Circlip
8. Sliding sleeve

Exploded view of sliding sleeve type synchronizer used on 5-speed transmission (1st, 2nd, 3rd and 4th gears)

gears. The rear cover is bolted to the center body and carries 5th and reverse gears, along with the selector bars. It also contains the mainshaft roller bearing and countershaft ball bearing. The upper part of the rear cover holds the gearshift lever, which is slightly different from the 4-speed unit. NOTE: *Starting with chassis number 0005752, a new gearshift mechanism is used in production.*

All forward gears are sychronized. The 1st, 2nd, 3rd and 4th gears use a blocker type synchronizer with a sliding sleeve. The 5th gear is synchronized by a spring-ring type synchronizer.

Overhaul

Disassembly and assembly are basically the same procedures as those outlined for the 124 (4-speed). Specifications remain identical to those for the 4-speed unit.

When assembling a synchronizer, be sure that the returned ends of the spring are inserted in the slots in the blocker ring, without distorting the normal diameter of the spring. This should be done before the circlip is fitted.

1100, 1100D AND 1100R

The 1100 Fiats use a 4-speed transmission composed of three units. The bell housing is attached to the engine crankcase and houses the clutch and throwout bearing. A center body, bolted to the bell housing carries the following parts: main transmission gears; direct drive shaft; mainshaft and

bearings; 3rd and 4th gears and synchronizer rings; 3rd and 4th speed sliding sleeve; 1st and reverse sliding gear; layshaft with constant mesh; 1st and 3rd speed gears; layshaft front and rear bearings; reverse shaft and gear; 1st, 3rd, 4th and reverse selector rods and forks and the gear shifting dog shaft. The transmission extension, or rear case, contains the rear part of the mainshaft, which carries the 2nd speed gear, synchronizer ring, sliding sleeve and fork and speedometer drive gear. The parking brake drum is also mounted on the mainshaft end, outside the transmission extension.

Removal

Remove the driveshaft bracket. Detach the front exhaust pipe support bracket from the rear transmission case. Loosen the nuts and swing the bracket outwards. Disconnect the driveshaft from the front joint. Remove the transmission rear crossmember. Disconnect the clutch release control lever tie rod, gear selection control rod from the relay lever, gearshift dog shaft and the parking brake control rod. Detach the speedometer drive connection and remove the flexible cable from the clip. Remove the exhaust piping and starter. Remove the clutch release fork lever return spring and remove the flywheel cover plate. Disconnect the ground strap and disconnect the upper nuts securing the transmission to the engine. Support the transmission and withdraw the unit straight back. Lower the

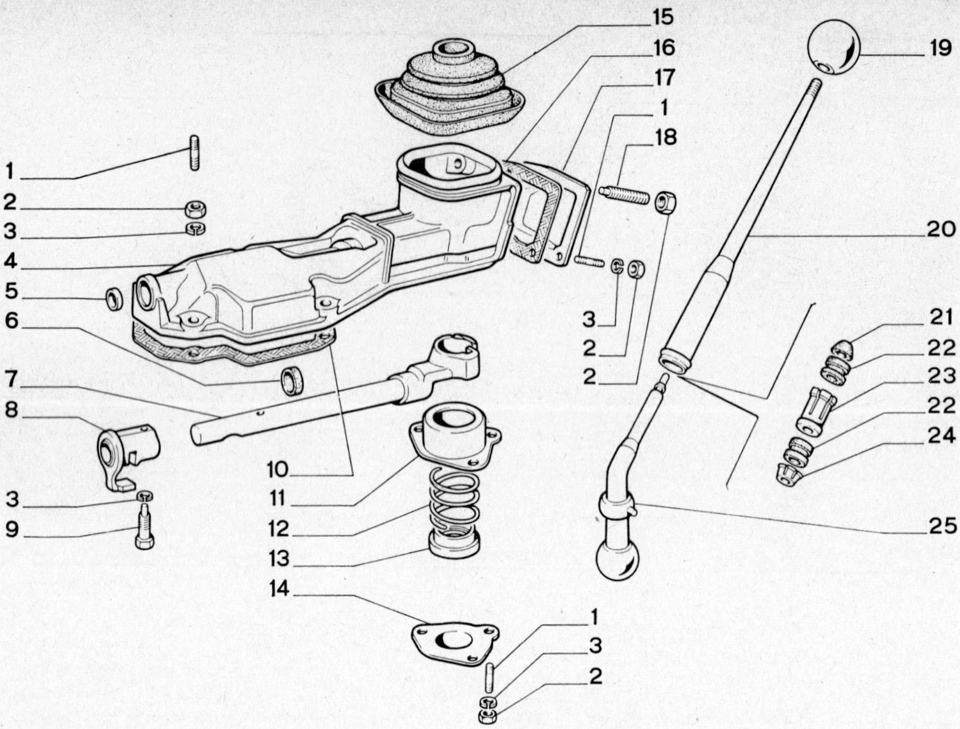

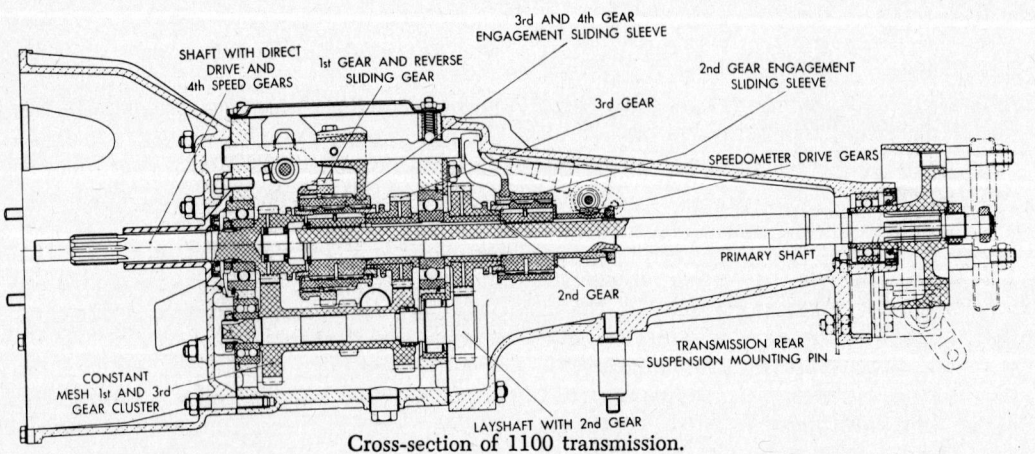

1. Studs
2. Nuts
3. Spring washers
4. Support
5. Plug
6. Gasket
7. Gear selector and actuating bar
8. Dog
9. Screw
10. Gasket
11. Cover, spring retaining
12. Reverse stiffening spring
13. Upper ball socket, pivot lever

14. Lower ball socket, pivot lever
15. Boot
16. Gasket
17. Cover
18. Pin
19. Grip
20. Lever jacket
21. Pad
22. Resilient bushings
23. Spacer
24. Snap-ring, lever jacket
25. Pivot lever, gearshift

Exploded view of 124 5-speed gearshift mechanism

Cross-section of 1100 transmission.

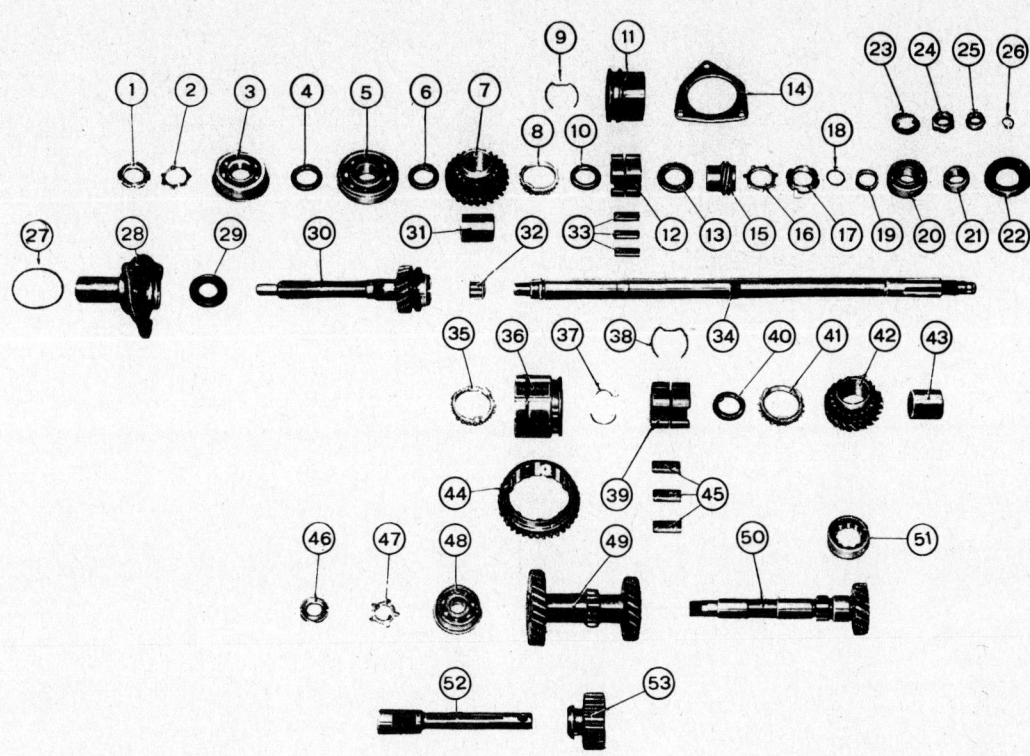

1. Constant mesh shaft nut
2. Tab washer
3. Direct drive shaft bearing
4. 3rd gear ring
5. Intermediate bearing
6. 2nd gear ring
7. 2nd gear
8. Synchronizing ring
9. Shifting plate spring
10. 2nd gear rear ring
11. 2nd gear sliding sleeve
12. Hub
13. Shifting plate thrust ring
14. Plate
15. Speedometer driving gear
16. Tabwasher
17. Nut
18. Snap-ring
19. Retainer ring

20. Rear bearing
21. Spacer
22. Rear seal
23. Plate
24. Parking brake drum locking nut
25. Flexible joint centering ring
26. Snap-ring
27. Front cover gasket
28. Front cover
29. Seal
30. Constant mesh and 4th gear shaft
31. 2nd gear bushing
32. Front roller bearing
33. Shifting plates for synchronizer gear
34. Main shaft
35. 4th gear synchronizer ring
36. 3rd and 4th gear sliding sleeve
37. Stop semi-rings

38. Shifting plate spring
39. Sliding sleeve hub
40. 3rd speed gear front ring
41. 3rd gear synchronizer ring
42. 3rd gear
43. 3rd gear bushing
44. 1st and reverse gear
45. Synchronizer ring shifting plates
46. Nut
47. Tabwasher
48. Ball bearing
49. Gear cluster on layshaft for constant mesh, 1st and 3rd gear
50. Layshaft with 2nd gear
51. Rear roller bearing
52. Reverse shaft
53. Reverse gear

NOTE: *Starting from engine No. 470163 rings 10 and 40 have been incorporated in hub.*

Exploded view of 1100 4-speed transmission

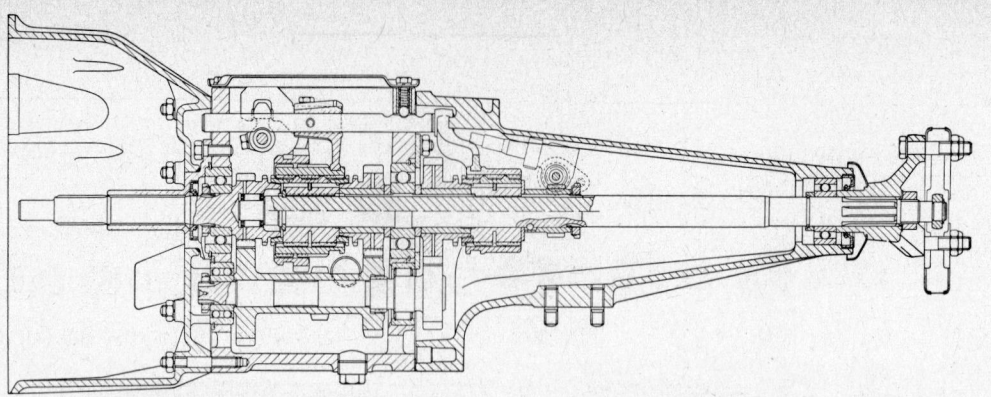

Cross-section of 1100R 4-speed transmission

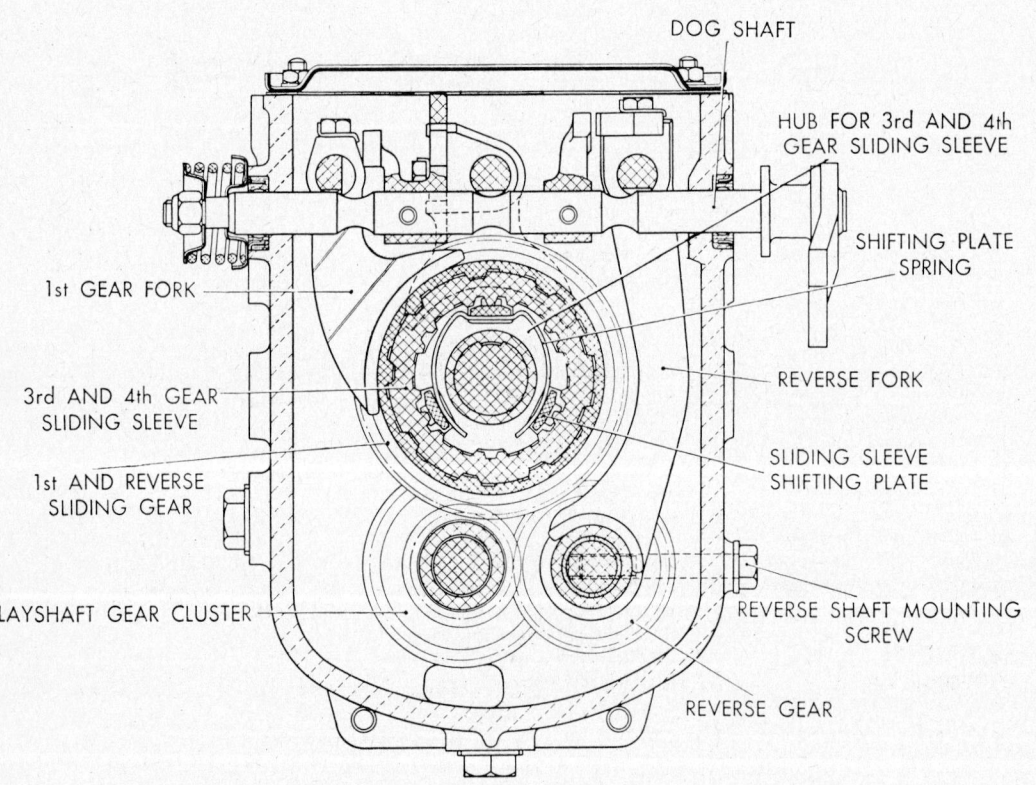

Cross-section of 1100R 4-speed transmission through the gear shifting dog shaft

transmission to the ground. The front end of the engine may have to be lifted with a hoist to permit withdrawal of the transmission.

Overhaul

Most Fiat manual transmissions employ the same basic operating principles and similar moving parts. Refer to the illustrations and disassembly and assembly procedures already given.

Installation

Installation is the reverse of removal.

Specifications

Gear backlash	.004″
Gear bore to gear bushing clearance (2nd and 3rd)	.002″-.004″
Reverse shaft to gear bushing clearance	.0013″-.0031″
Ball bearing radial clearance	.002″ (max.)
Ball bearing axial clearance	.02″ (max.)
Shaft runout	.0008″ (max.)
Oil	
Type	Fiat W 90
Quantity	1.5 qts.
	1.16 qts. (1100R)

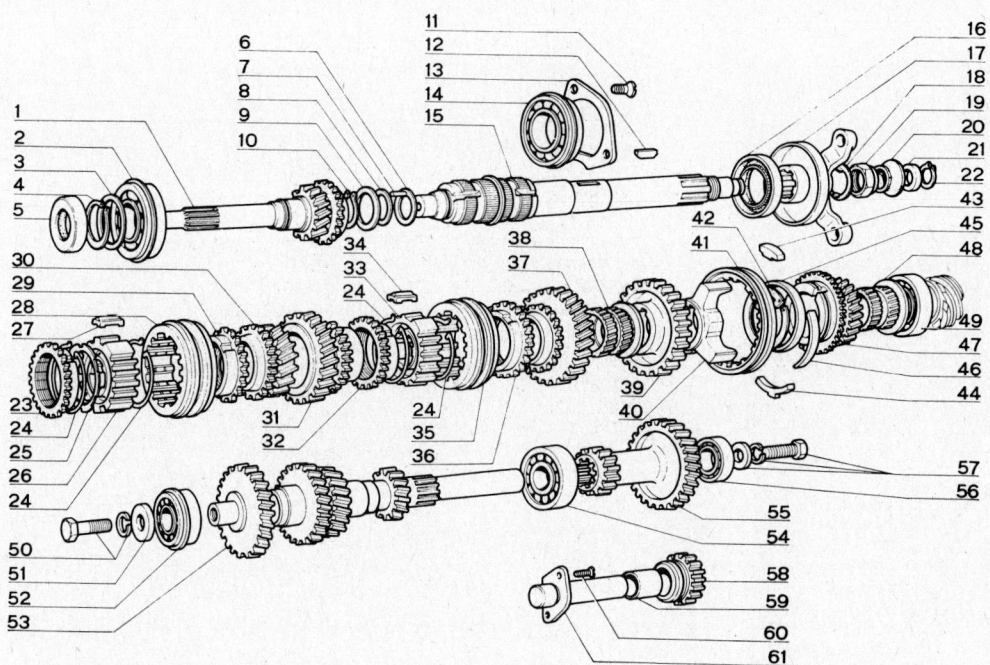

Transmission components, 1500, 1600S. (1) clutch shaft; (2) front ball bearing; (3) lock washer; (4) snap-ring; (5) seal; (6) thrust ring; (7) needle rollers; (8) thrust ring; (9) lock washer; (10) snap-ring; (11) plate screws; (12) Woodruff key; (13) bearing plate; (14) intermediate ball bearing; (15) mainshaft; (16) seal; (17) flexible joint yoke sleeve; (18) lock washer; (19) nut; (20) seal ring; (21) flexible joint dowel ring; (22) snap-ring; (23, 29, 32, 36) third and fourth, first and second synchromesh rings; (24) shifting plate springs; (25) lockwasher; (26) third and fourth slip sleeve hub; (27, 34) shifting plates; (28) third and fourth slip sleeve; (30) third speed gear; (31) second speed gear; (33) first and second slip sleeve hub; (35) first and second slip sleeve; (37) first speed gear; (38) first speed gear bushing; (39) reverse gear; (40) overdrive slip sleeve hub; (41) overdrive slip sleeve; (42) snap-ring; (43) stop plate; (44) thrust plate; (45) overdrive synchromesh ring; (46) spring; (47) overdrive gear; (48) overdrive gear bushing; (49) rear roller bearing; (50) bearing lock screw and washer; (51) washer; (52) countershaft front ball bearing; (53) countershaft with first, second, third and constant mesh gears; (54) center ball bearing; (55) reverse and overdrive gear; (56) rear ball bearing; (57) bearing lock screw, spring washer and plain washer(*); (58) reverse gear; (59) reverse gear bushing; (60) reverse gear shaft screws; (61) reverse gear shaft.
(*) the countershaft rear ball bearing locking design shown in figure has been adopted up to 1500 Cabriolet Chassis No. 043092 Parts serial No. 1425734, and 1600S Cabriolet Chassis No. 042439 Parts serial No. 1427679.

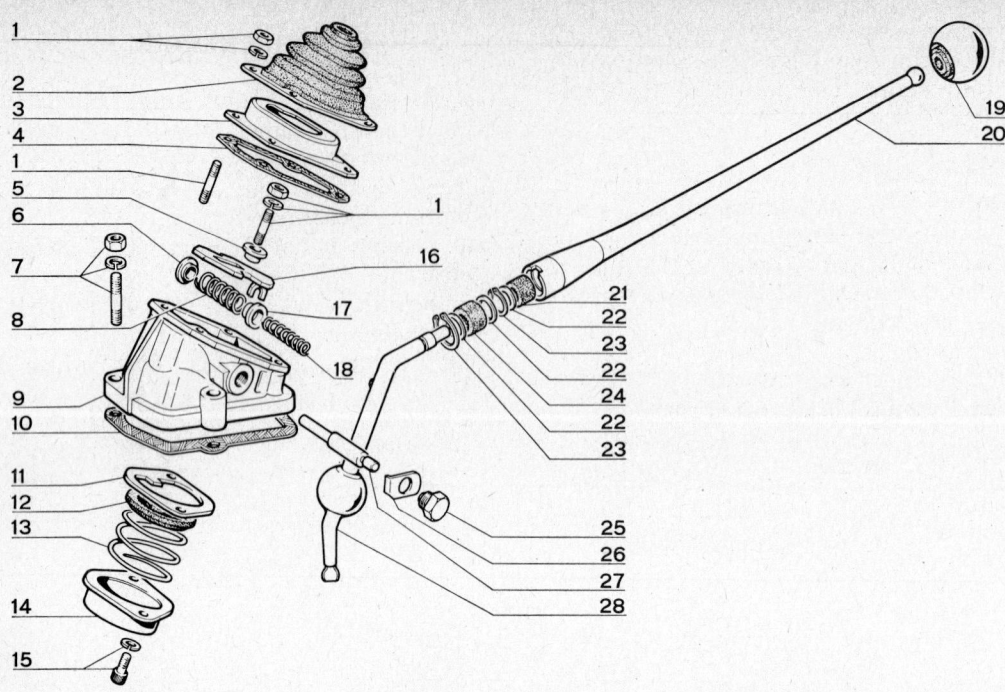

1. Nuts, lockwashers and studs
2. Boot
3. Overdrive and reverse control safety plate
4. Gaskets
5. Spacer
6. Cup
7. Nuts, lockwashers and studs
8. Overdrive and reverse stiffening spring
9. Housing
10. Gasket
11. Fulcrum pin and lever positioning plate
12. Fulcrum pin ball socket
13. Reverse stiffening spring
14. Spring cover
15. Screw and lockwashers
16. Fulcrum pin guide plate
17. Cup
18. First and second stiffening spring
19. Grip
20. Gearshift lever
21. Upper rubber bushing
22. Plain washers
23. Bushing snap-rings
24. Lower rubber bushing
25. Plug
26. Lockplate
27. Spring spindle
28. Lever fulcrum pin

Exploded view of 1500 and 1600S gearshift mechanism

1500 AND 1600S CABRIOLET

Basically, this is a very similar unit to the transmission currently in use on Fiat 124 models. It is a 5-speed unit, with the 5th speed functioning as overdrive. It also is built in three parts, described under the Fiat 124 (5-speed) transmission. Consult the procedures under Fiat 124 (4-speed) for assembly and disassembly.

Specifications

Gear backlash	.0039″
Ball bearing radial clearance	.002″ (max.)
Ball bearing axial clearance	.02″ (max.)
Shaft runout	.001″ (max.)
Oil	
Type	Fiat W 90M
Quantity	1.7 qts.

850 TRANSAXLE

The transmission and differential are incorporated into a single case. The transmission uses four forward gears, all synchronized, the 4th gear being an overdrive. Synchronizing rings are of the sliding type.

Transmission is controlled manually through a gearshift lever on the floor.

Removal

Disconnect cable from positive terminal of battery. Remove engine compartment lid, upper headlining, generator and starter. Jack car up at the rear and place on stands. Disconnect shock absorbers from lower mountings. Remove axle shaft universal joints. Disconnect clutch and speedometer cables and gearshift rod.

Support transaxle unit with a jack and remove unit mounting screws from engine. Remove flywheel cover and screws that

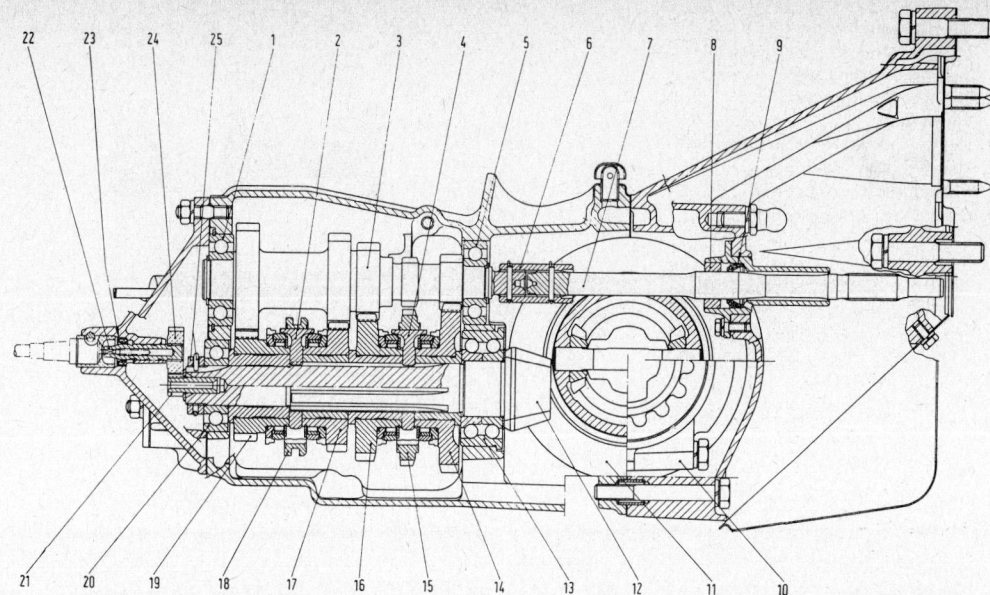

Transaxle assembly of the 850 Series. (1) front ball bearing of countershaft; (2) third and fourth slip sleeve hub; (3) countershaft with drive gears; (4) first and second slip sleeve hub; (5) rear ball bearing of countershaft; (6) countershaft-to-input shaft sleeve; (7) input shaft; (8) input shaft bushing; (9) oil seal; (10) differential carrier cap; (11) ring gear; (12) drive pinion-output shaft; (13) drive pinion rear ball bearing; (14) first driven gear; (15) first and second slip sleeve and reverse gear; (16) second driven gear; (17) third driven gear; (18) third and fourth slip sleeve; (19) fourth driven gear; (20) output shaft-drive pinion front ball bearing; (21) speedometer drive gear; (22) speedometer driven shaft; (23) oil seal; (24) speedometer driven gear; (25) output shaft-drive pinion nut and retainer.

hold transaxle support bracket to body. Adjust position of jack to permit disengagement of clutch shaft from plate, then lift out transaxle.

Disassembly

Remove the left side mounting bracket and tie the axle shafts up, to prevent them from falling or being damaged. Place the transaxle on a work stand or large smooth bench and drain the oil. Carefully, dismantle the transmission and differential unit. For ease of assembly, it will be wise to mark the position of the differential carrier caps and bearing adjusters.
NOTE: *The transmission components can be removed from the gearbox without removing the differential unit, unless the layshaft and drive pinion are removed. If there is no evidence of malfunction in the differential, do not disturb it.*

Remove the support with the speedometer drive pinion. Disassemble the front housing and extract the gear selector lever and gasket. Lock the layshaft and drive pinion and remove the cotter pin and nut.

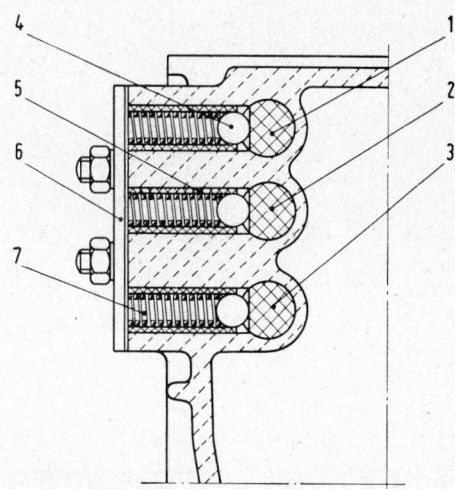

1. Reverse selector rod
2. 3rd and 4th speed selector rod
3. 1st and 2nd speed selector rod
4. Selector rod positioning balls
5. Ball and spring guide bushings
6. Cover
7. Detent ball spring

Location of transaxle detent balls

1. 4th speed driving gear
2. 1st speed and reverse driving gear
3. 3rd speed driving gear
4. 2nd speed driving gear
5. Clutch shaft
6. Sleeve, clutch shaft to primary shaft
7. Sleeve locking snap-rings
8. Primary shaft rear bearing
9. Gear cluster driving gear
10. Primary shaft

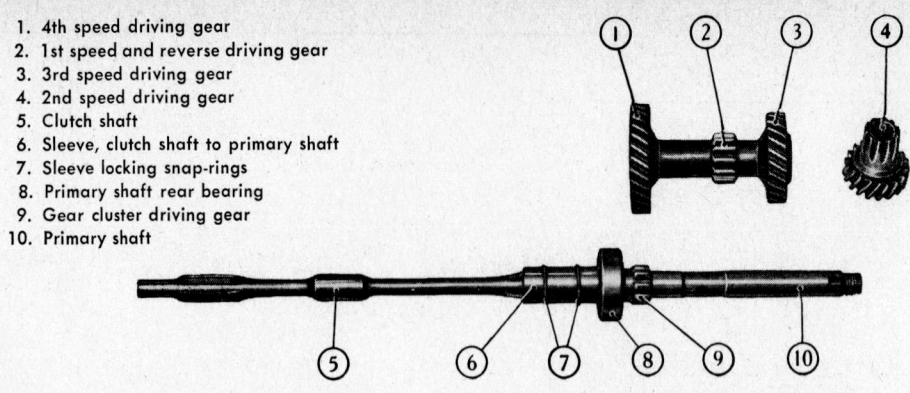

Exploded view of clutch and primary shafts

Remove the speedometer drive gear from the layshaft, followed by the retainer cover, springs and detent balls. Remove the second gear sliding sleeve with fork and selector rod and the hub (with springs). Slide out the reverse control upper rod and fork, red locking ball, intermediate rod and safety roller and 3rd and 4th gear selector forks. Remove the synchronizer ring, 2nd speed driven gear and bushing. Unscrew the primary shaft nut and remove the wash-er. Remove the 2nd speed drive gear, ball bearing and reverse shaft retaining plate and slide out the reverse shaft with gear. Remove the front housing to center body mounting plate and from the plate, remove the primary shaft front bearing and layshaft front bearing. Remove from the layshaft: 3rd speed driven gear and bushing; synchronizer; 3rd and 4th speed sliding sleeve and hub; first and reverse driven gear; fourth speed synchronizer and driven gear

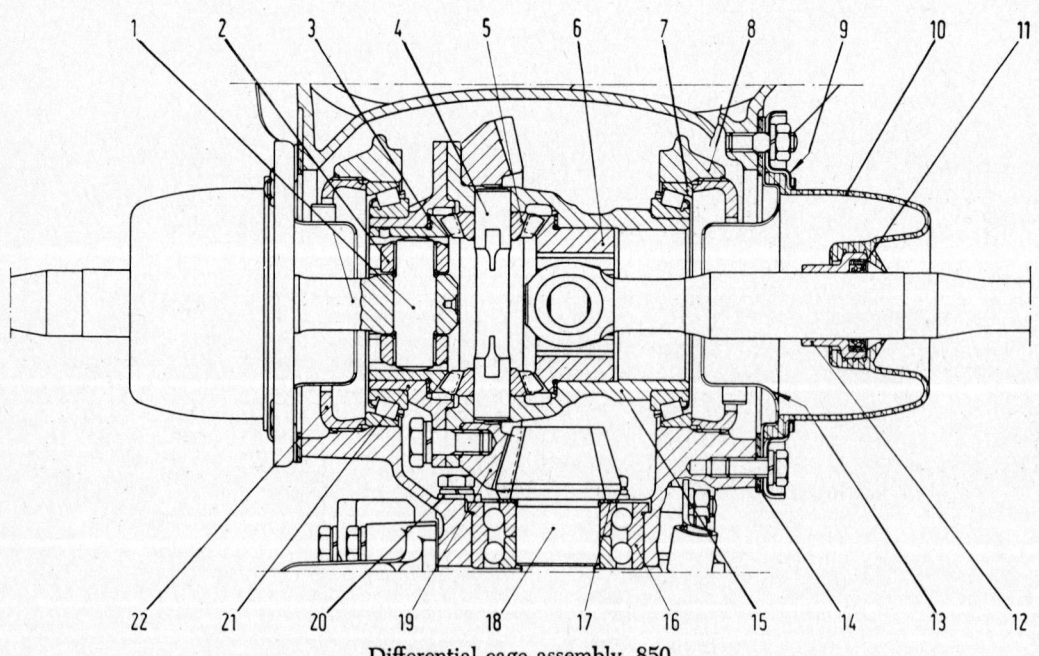

Differential cage assembly, 850.

(1) axle shaft; (2) axle shaft slip joint; (3) side gear thrust ring; (4) pinion gear shaft; (5) pinion gear; (6) side gear; (7) differential cage roller bearing; (8) differential cage carrier cap; (9) oil boot cover; (10) oil boot; (11) oil seal; (12) oil seal retainer; (13) oil boot baffle; (14) baffle gasket; (15) differential cage half; (16) drive pinion rear ball bearing; (17) drive pinion shim; (18) drive pinion; (19) ring gear; (20) bearing retainer plate; (21) differential cage half; (22) roller bearing adjuster.

with bushing. Through the front end, remove the primary shaft containing the 1st, 3rd, 4th and reverse drive gears, rear bearing and clutch shaft. Remove the clutch release control assembly from the rear housing. The seal ring and intermediate support bushing will remain in the gearbox rear housing.

Inspection

Thoroughly clean all parts and inspect them for cracks, burrs, wear and runout. Any parts not meeting specifications should be replaced. Carefully file away all burrs with a dead file.

850 DIFFERENTIAL

Disassembly

After disassembling the gearbox, remove the side gear lateral sleeves, bearing adjuster lockplate, bearing adjuster and bearing housing with seals from both ends of the differential. Pull out the roller bear-

ing outer ring. Remove the rear body of the central case and remove the differential case. Extract the bevel pinion and bearing after removing the retaining plate. Disassemble the bevel pinion bearing with an arbor press. Pull the roller bearing and inner rings from the differential case. Loosen the screws joining the two differential halves and the ring gear. Remove the idle pinion carrier shaft, idle pinions and side gears and thrust washers.

Assembly

A shim of suitable thickness must be installed between pinion and rear ball bearing to set the pinion depth, thereby obtaining the correct backlash between ring gear and pinion. Shims are supplied in the following thicknesses: .108″, .110″, .112″, .114″, .116″, .118″, .120″, .122″, .124″, .126″, .128″, .130″, .132″ and .134″. Ideally, the determination of shim thickness is made with a suitably machined dummy pinion and dial indicator. In the

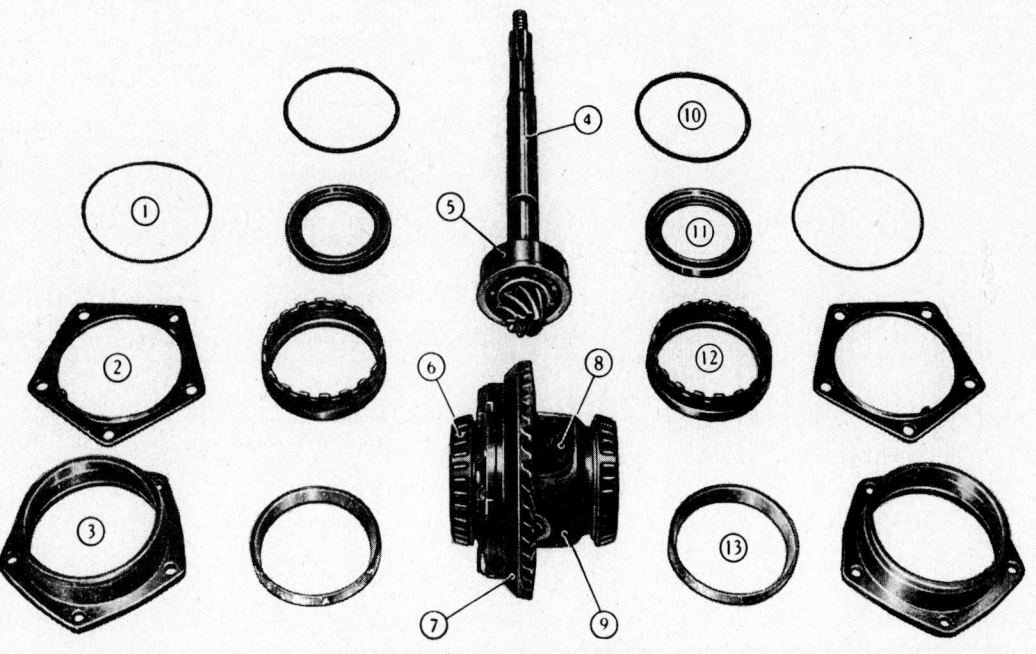

1. Gasket for plate
2. Plate securing adjuster 12
3. Roller bearing housing
4. Bevel drive pinion
5. Rear ball bearing for bevel drive pinion
6. Roller bearing inner ring
7. Final drive ring gear
8. Side gear
9. Differential case
10. Bearing housing seal ring
11. Oil seal
12. Roller bearing adjuster
13. Bearing outer ring

Exploded view of typical differential and final drive components absence of a dummy pinion, the following method may be used.

If the original ring gear and drive pinion are being replaced, install the same shim as was removed. This should give an adequate setting of pinion depth. If either a new ring gear or drive pinion are being replaced (they should be replaced in matched sets), compare the number stamped on the drive pinion and ring gear being replaced with that stamped on the original ring gear and drive pinion. By comparing these numbers and the original shim from the pinion, an approximate shim thickness can be determined.

Gather a number of shims of varying thicknesses. Fit the side gears with the thrust rings, idle pinions and idle carrier shaft. Insert the ring gear in the left case half and mate the case halves. The side gears must be adjusted, through the thrust rings, to obtain the proper rotational torque. Check the rotational torque by locking one of the side gears. The torque required to turn the other side gear may not be greater than 3.6 ft. lbs. Shims to adjust this value are available in the fol-

lowing sizes: .0394″, .0512″ and .0591″. Install the two roller bearing inner rings. Install this complete assembly in the gearbox-differential case. Install the two bearing housings with seals and roller bearing outer rings. Also install the two oil seals, bearing adjusters and seals. The bearing lockplates should be installed after setting.

Mount a dial indicator and set it at zero. With the adjuster rings slightly in touch with the bearings, tighten one adjuster ring and measure the amount of divarication at the case. Slacken the opposite adjuster ring; the dial indicator must return to zero. Tighten the second adjuster ring again, until a divarication of .008″-.010″ is obtained. Rotate the ring gear through several revolutions to ensure final seating of the bearings. The bearings are now preloaded. Mount and zero the dial indicator again and set the backlash to .004″-.006″, by rotating the bearing adjusters. To prevent any alteration of bearing preload, rotate one adjuster ring the same amount as the other, but in an opposite direction.

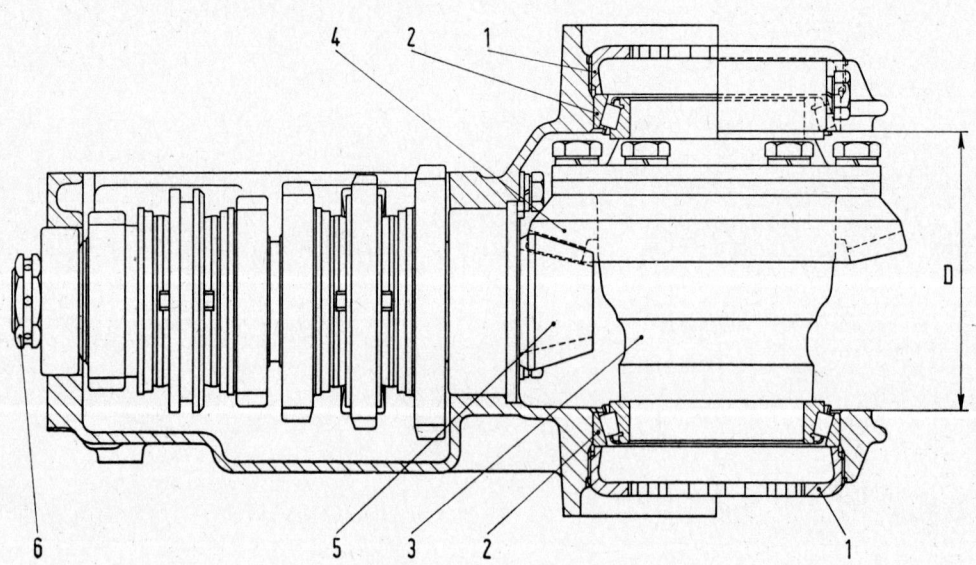

1. Bearing adjuster
2. Roller bearings
3. Differential cage
4. Ring gear
5. Drive pinion
6. Drive pinion nut
D   Distance between differential carrier caps; tighten bearing adjusters until D increases by .008″-.010″ (0.20 to 0.25 mm). (850 Fiat)

Diagram for checking differential cage bearing preload

PULL SIDE

COAST SIDE

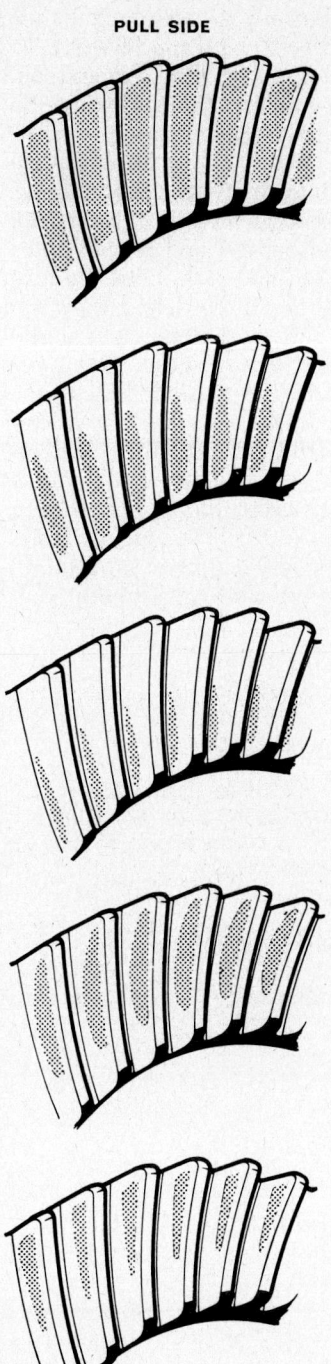

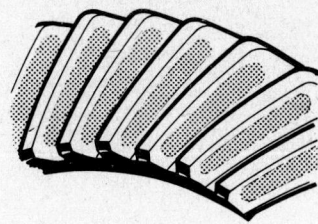

Correct tooth contact.

Contact pattern should be evenly spread over ring gear teeth, on both pull and coast sides.

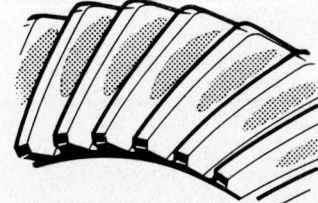

Incorrect contact.

Pull side: heavy contact at tooth toe, toward the center.

Coast side: heavy contact at tooth heel, toward the center.

Move pinion away from ring gear by reducing thrust washer thickness.

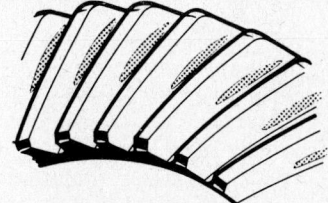

Incorrect contact.

Pull side: heavy contact on toe, at tooth flank bottom.

Coast side: heavy contact on heel, at tooth flank bottom.

Move pinion away from ring gear by reducing thrust washer thickness.

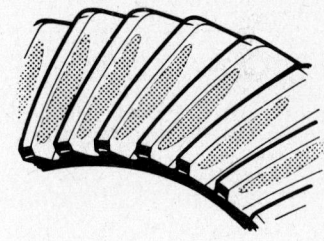

Incorrect contact.

Pull side: heavy contact at tooth heel and toward the center.

Coast side: heavy contact at tooth toe and toward the center.

Move the pinion toward ring gear by increasing thrust washer thickness.

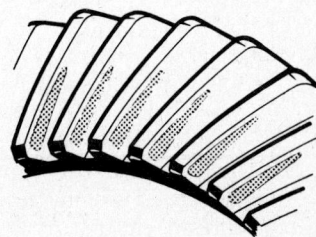

Incorrect contact.

Pull side: heavy contact on heel, at tooth face.

Coast side: heavy contact on toe, at tooth face.

Move the pinion toward ring gear by increasing thrust washer thickness.

Ring gear tooth contact patterns and adjustments.

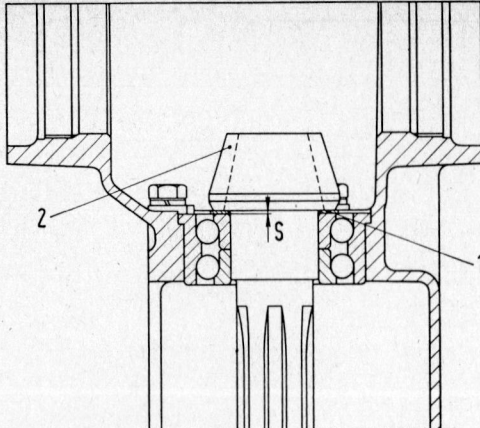

1. Drive pinion shim
2. Drive pinion
S. Shim thickness

Diagram for fitting drive pinion shim

Finally, the gears should be coated with red lead and a check of the gear tooth contact pattern made. Work the differential under load. A contact pattern will be left on the teeth. Consult the illustrations to determine if the pinion should be moved away from the ring gear or toward the ring gear. The pinion depth can be controlled by the shim. Replace the shim with another, depending upon the results of the gear tooth contact pattern. The differential must be disassembled to do this and the bearings must be preloaded again during assembly.

850 Transmission

Assembly

Through the casing front end, install the primary shaft with 1st, 3rd, 4th and reverse speeds drive gear assembly, complete with rear bearing and clutch shaft. Fit the layshaft with the following parts: 4th speed gear and bushing, 3rd and 4th speed gear synchronizer assembly, hub and 3rd and 4th speed siding sleeve (to which the 1st speed driven gear must be keyed), 3rd speed synchronizer ring and driven gear with bushing. Install the mounting plate for the center housing to front body. Install the primary shaft front bearing and the layshaft front bearing. Fit the reverse shaft with gear and bushing and install the retaining plate. Key the 2nd speed driving gear in position and secure with

nut and washer. Tighten this nut to a torque of 43.4 ft. lbs. (early type) and 73.0 ft. lbs. (later gearboxes). Fit the 2nd speed driven gear, bushing, synchronizing ring and sliding sleeve hub to the layshaft. Install the sliding sleeve with 1st and 2nd speed selector rod and fork. Position the three synchronizer inner springs. Insert the selector rod safety roller. Slide the following parts into position: 3rd and 4th speed intermediate selector rod and fork; safety roller and ball set and reverse speed upper selector rod and fork. Lock the forks on rods. Install the three detent balls and springs and secure with the cover. Install the speedometer driven gear. Screw the nut into place on the layshaft and torque to 40 ft. lbs. Fit the speed selector lever and gasket to the front housing. Fit the front housing to the central body and at the same time insert the speed selector lever on the selector lever dogs. Install the speedometer drive pinion support. Install the cotter pin and nut on the shaft.

Installation

Installation is the reverse of removal.

600, 600D

Removal, disassembly, assembly and installation procedures for the 850 transaxle also apply to the transaxle used on the Fiat 600 and 600D.

Specifications (850)

Ball bearing radial clearance	.002″ (max.)
Ball bearing axial clearance	.02″ (max.)
Shaft runout	.0008″ (max.)
Differential cage bearings	
Preload (divarication measured at carrier caps wth dial indicator)	.008″-.010″
Final drive backlash	.004″-.006″
Oil	
Type	Fiat W 90M
Quantity	4.44 pts.

Idroconvert

The Idroconvert transmission (automatic) is available as an option on 850 Fiats and some 124 Fiats. Basically the unit is a torque converter coupled to a 4-speed transmission, controlled by a gear lever with an integral knob switch.

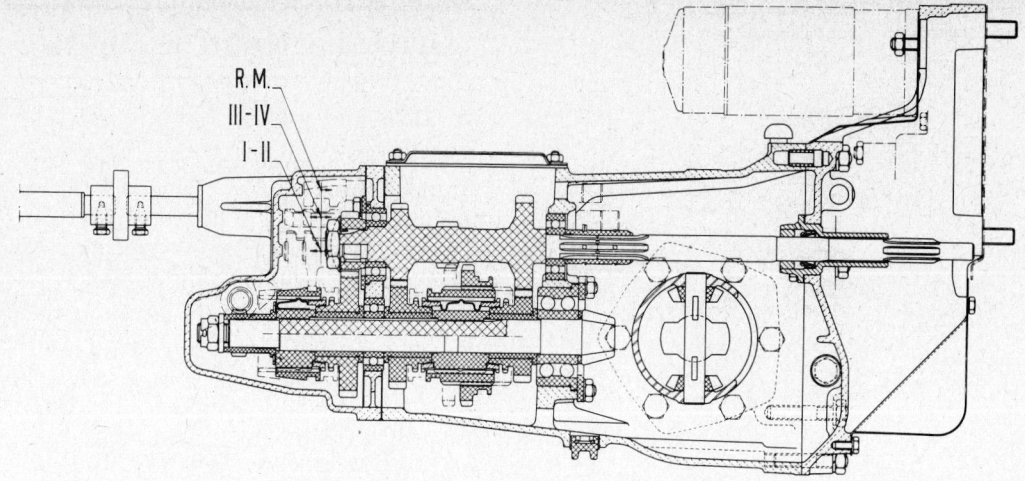

R.M.
III-IV
I-II

Cross-sectional view of Fiat 600 transaxle

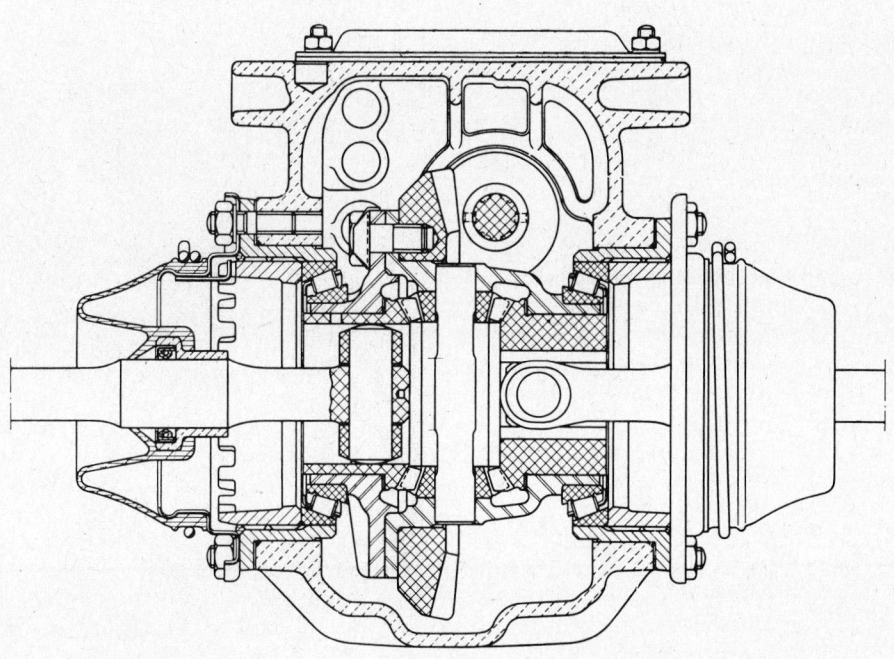

Cross-sectional view of Fiat 600 differential through the ring gear and axle shaft joints

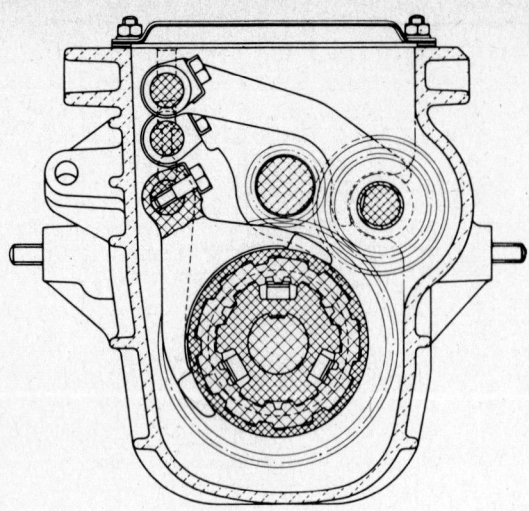

Cross-sectional view of 600 transaxle through 3rd and 4th gear engagement sleeves

REMOVAL

Removal and installation of this unit are the same as those for the manual transmission.

Adjustment

The only necessary adjustment is idle speed. Warm the engine and apply the handbrake. Engage 4th gear. If the engine tends to stall, increase the idle slightly to correct the condition.

Shift Linkage

1100R

The linkage connecting gearshift and transmission consists of two adjustable rods, which are connected to the operating lever on the transmission case.

Adjustment

Loosen the locknuts and vary the length of the control rods by screwing them in or out to obtain suitable shifting.

600, 600D

Adjustment

Remove the cover from alongside the gearshift lever. Loosen the lever support retaining screws. Push the support forward if 1st or 3rd gear engagement is improper. Move the support rearward if 4th and reverse need adjustment. Tighten the mounting screws and replace the components.

Driveshaft and U-Joints

124, 1500 and 1600S

These Fiat driveshafts are in two parts, a tubular front piece connected to the transmission through a flexible spider coupling and a solid rear piece, connected to the front piece by a universal joint and to the rear axle by a splined sleeve.

REMOVAL

Driveshaft

Proceed as follows to remove the entire driveshaft assembly from the car. Remove the sleeve of the front shaft from the coupling. Detach the retaining clip to the brake hose from the cover of the rear shaft and disconnect the hose from the rear brake pipe. Release the brake pipe from the clips. Remove the bolts securing the rear shaft cover to the differential housing. Disconnect the hand-brake return spring from the central support. Unscrew the four nuts securing the central pillow block to the underside of the vehicle. Slide the driveshafts toward the front of the car.

1. Bolts fixing sliding sleeve on driveshaft to the flexible joint
2. Nuts and bolts fixing transmission sleeve to flexible joint
3. Tool A. 70025
4. Flexible joint

Spider joint connecting driveshaft to transmission

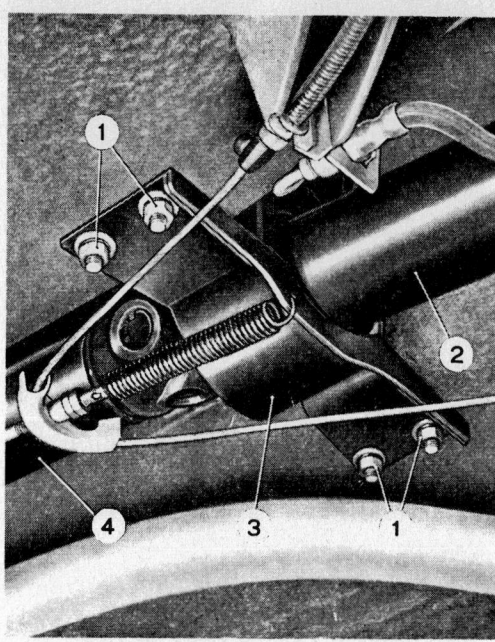

1. Bolts fixing pillow block to body
2. Tubular cover of rear shaft
3. Pillow block housing
4. Front shaft

Driveshaft central pillow block

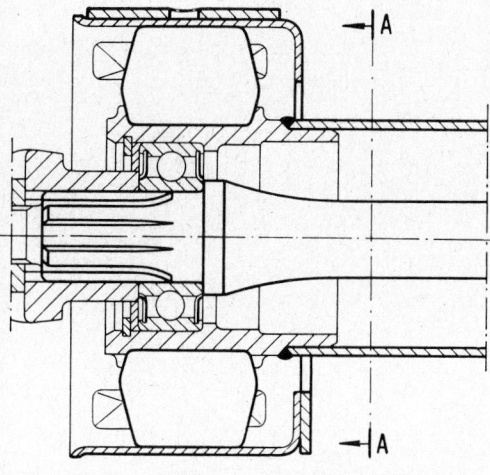

Cross-sectional view of central pillow block and driveshaft

DISASSEMBLY

Driveshafts

Remove the spider of the universal joint. Remove the universal joint fork and the snap-ring holding the bearing dust cover. Slide the rear shaft, complete with

bearing out of the tubular cover. Extract the bearing from the end of the shaft. When the cover has been removed the sliding sleeve can be removed from the front shaft.

ASSEMBLY

Assembly is the reverse of disassembly.

INSTALLATION

Installation is the reverse of removal, noting the following points. Be sure that the marks on the front shaft and corresponding spider are aligned. This will ensure that the shaft balance carried out at the factory is maintained. Before tightening the nuts fixing the central pillow block, check the clearances at the pillow block. Gap D should be wider than gap S by .039″ with the car unloaded. Gap S should be wider than gap D by .112″-.157″ with the car loaded.

1100, 1100D and 1100R

These cars have basically the same driveshaft as the 124 series, although some 1100 series Fiats were equipped with a single piece driveshaft. Service operations and removal and installation procedures remain similar for both types.

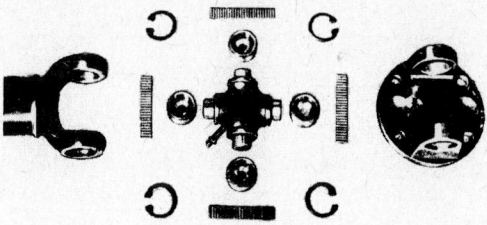

Exploded view of typical Fiat universal joints

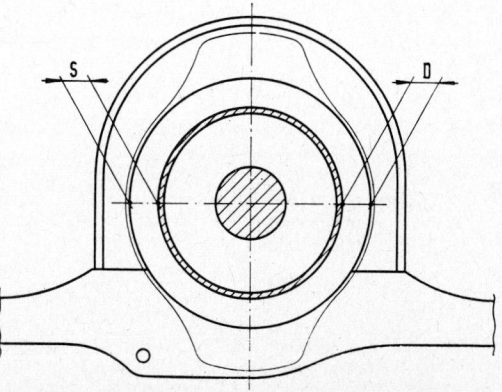

Cross-sectional view of driveshaft and central pillow block showing loaded and unloaded gaps

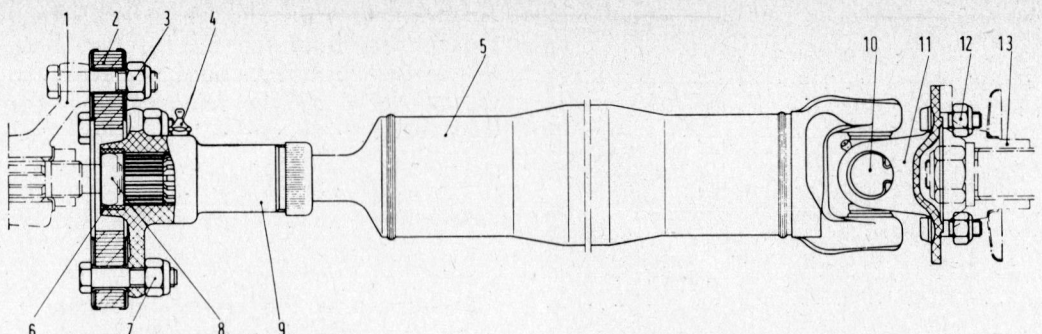

1. Slip yoke on transmission mainshaft
2. Flexible joint
3. Flexible joint-to-slip yoke self-locking nut
4. Slip yoke lubricated
5. Shaft
6. Flexible joint centering bushing
7. Flexible joint-to-shaft nut

8. Mainshaft ring for flexible joint bushing
9. Slip yoke
10. Universal joint spider
11. Universal joint yoke flange
12. Driveshaft-to-pinion end flange nut
13. Drive pinion end flange

Fiat 1100 one-piece driveshaft

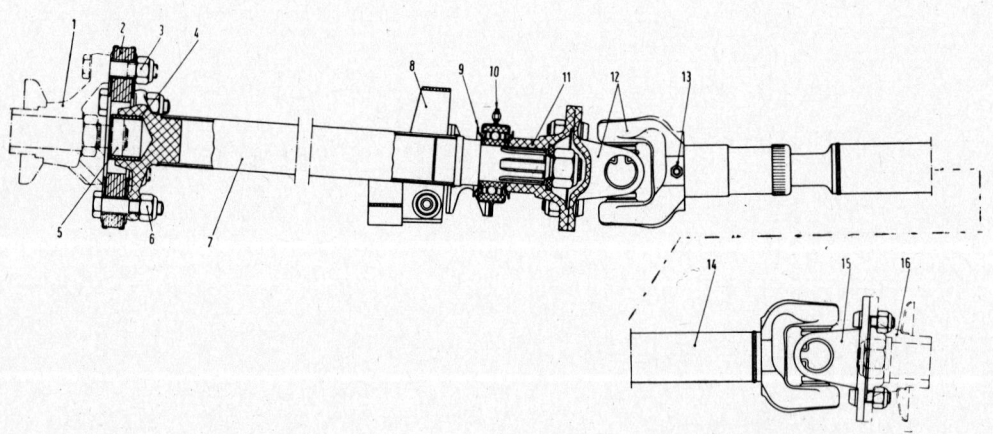

1. Slip yoke on transmission mainshaft
2. Flexible joint
3. Flexible joint-to-slip yoke self-locking nut
4. Flexible joint centering bushing
5. Mainshaft ring for flexible joint bushing
6. Flexible joint-to-front driveshaft nut
7. Front propeller shaft
8. Center bearing bracket

9. Center bearing dust shield
10. Driveshaft center bearing housing
11. Front driveshaft-to-rear driveshaft sleeve flange
12. Front universal joint
13. Slip yoke lubricator
14. Rear driveshaft
15. Universal joint yoke flange
16. Drive pinion end flange

Fiat 1100 two-piece driveshaft

850 and 600

These cars are rear engined vehicles and are equipped with a transaxle, having no need for a driveshaft of conventional design.

Drive Axle and Suspension

The rear axle is of the semi-floating, hypoid design with the wheels mounted directly on the axle shafts. The axle shafts have integral wheel hubs supported inside by the side gears and outside by the flanges of the axle housing.

124

REAR AXLE

Removal

Jack the car and remove the wheels from the axle shaft hubs. Plug the brake line reservoir outlet with a wooden plug. Remove the brake hose from the pipe. Remove the driveshaft. Disconnect the handbrake cable from both brake calipers. Remove the two trailing arms of the stabilizer bar from the brackets on the axle housing. Remove the brake regulator control rod. Support the axle housing with a hydraulic jack. Remove the upper shock absorber mounting nuts. Remove the trailing arms from the axle housing. Remove the crossrod. Lower the axle assembly to the ground.

Installation

Fit the springs and isolating rings to the seats on the axle housing. Fit the rubber bushings to the upper stems of the shock absorbers. Connect the trailing arms and cross-rod to the axle housing with the nuts finger tight. Extend the shock absorbers and lift the axle with the jack, allowing the upper stems of the shock absorbers to enter the holes in the body. Secure the ends of the shock absorbers from inside the luggage compartment. Connect the brake regulator tie rod to the mounting on the axle housing. Connect the stabilizer tie-rods to the axle housing, but do not tighten. Fit the driveshaft. Connect the brake hoses to the piping and check the brake fluid level. Bleed the brake system. Fill the axle and loosely fit the wheels. Lower the car and with the car loaded, tighten all rear suspension nuts.

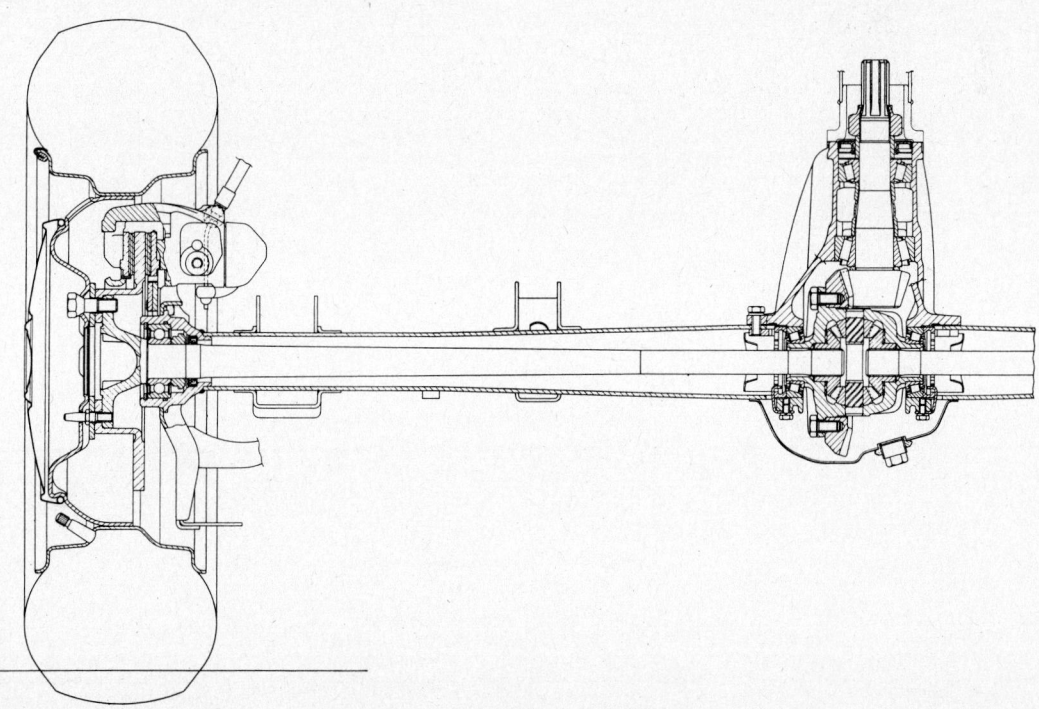

Rear axle assembly, 124 Coupe and Spider.

AXLE SHAFTS

Removal

Jack the rear of the car and remove the wheels. Remove the caliper support bracket assembly without disconnecting the brake fluid lines. Remove the snap-ring which retains the bearing dust cover.

The values of dimensions a, b, c, d, e, f and g are given in the table

Dimensions to be checked	Pre-modification* in.	mm	Post-modification* in.	mm
a	.63	16	.82	21
b	2.42	61.5	2.53	64.5
c	.078	2	.102	2.6
d	1.22	31	1.35	34.5
e	2.44	62	2.55	65
f	.393	10	.314	8
g	.866	22	1.082	27.5

*Modification of rear axle dimensions with vehicles carrying spare parts number 069548 and above.

Using a slide hammer, remove the axle shaft, complete with snap-ring, dust cover, bearing and bearing retaining collar. Extract the shaft oil seal and O ring. NOTE: *Always use a hydraulic press to remove the axle shaft bearing retaining collar.*

Installation

Fit the oil seal and O ring to the housing. Insert the complete axle shaft and fit the snap-ring to the housing. Fit the brake disc to the axle shaft hub with two centering screws. Fit the caliper support bracket and caliper assembly to the axle. Fit the wheel and lower the car to the ground.

DIFFERENTIAL

Removal

To remove only the differential, use the following procedure.

Unscrew the drain plug in the lower part of the axle housing and drain the gear oil. Jack the rear of the car and remove the rear wheels. Withdraw the axle shafts, far enough to disengage them from the side gears. Unbolt and remove the differential from the housing.

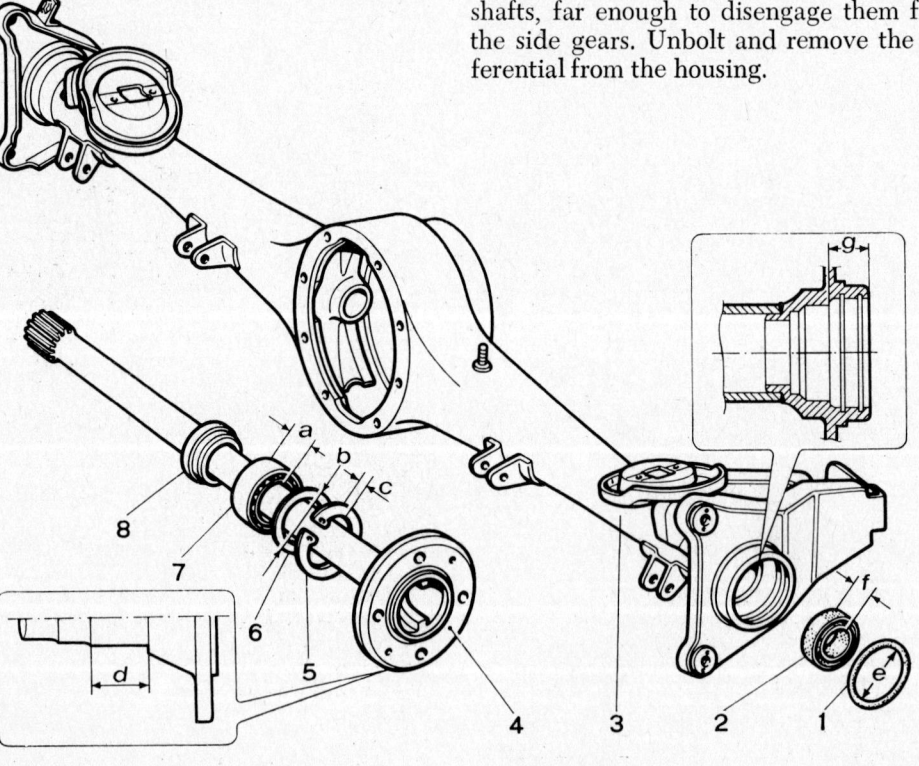

1. O ring
2. Oil seal
3. Axle housing
4. Axle shaft
5. Snap-ring
6. Dust shield
7. Ball bearing
8. Bearing retaining collar

Exploded view of 124 rear axle and axle shaft assembly

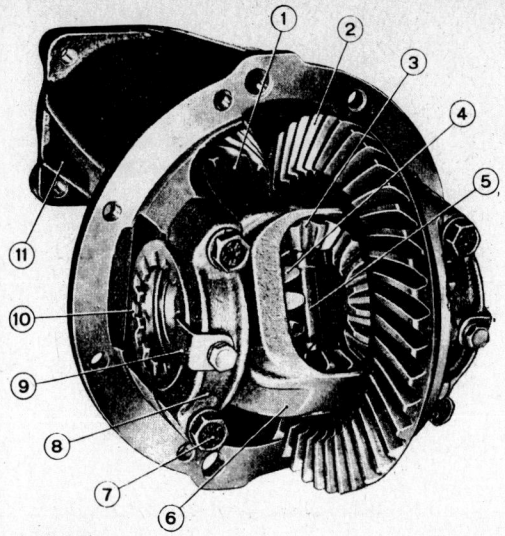

1. Pinion
2. Ring gear
3. Pinion gear
4. Side gear
5. Pinion gear shaft
6. Differential case
7. Differential case bearing cap screw
8. Differential case bearing cap
9. Ring lockplate
10. Bearing retaining ring
11. Differential housing

Typical Fiat differential

Disassembly

Remove the bolts and lockplates from the bearing caps. The lockplates hold the bearing adjusters in place. Matchmark the caps and bosses and remove the bearing cap bolts. Remove the caps, retaining rings and roller bearing outer races. Withdraw the differential case from the carrier, complete with gears, ring gear and inner bearing races. Turn the carrier upside down and by holding the pinion, unscrew the pinion nut. Withdraw the pinion, complete with thrust ring, rear roller bearing inner race and collapsible spacer. Remove the oil seal, oil slinger and inner race from the front bearing. Remove the outer race of the rear roller bearing with a drift. Slide the collapsible spacer from the pinion and pull the inner race of the rear roller bearing and thrust washer from the pinion. Remove the inner races of the bearings in which the differential case runs. Remove the ring gear and, using a drift, remove the pinion gears shaft. Rotate the side gears and remove these and their thrust washers from the case.

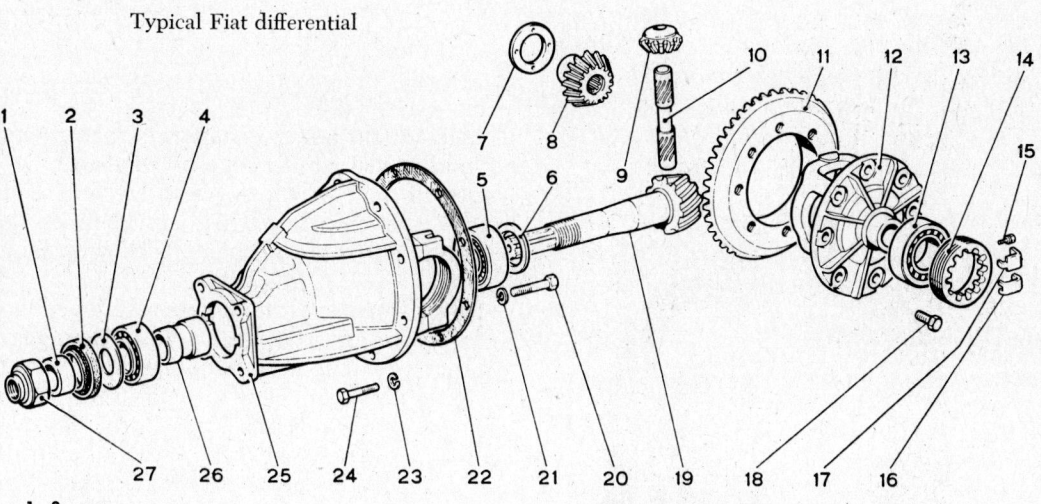

1. Spacer
2. Oil seal
3. Oil slinger
4. Front roller bearing
5. Rear roller bearing
6. Pinion shaft rear roller bearing thrust washer
7. Side gear thrust ring
8. Side gear
9. Pinion gear
10. Pinion gear shaft
11. Ring gear
12. Differential case
13. Differential case roller bearing
14. Bearing adjuster ring
15. Locking plate clip bolt
16. Locking plate
17. Locking plate
18. Bolts fixing ring gear to differential case
19. Bevel pinion
20. Carrier cap bolts
21. Spring washer
22. Gasket
23. Spring washer
24. Differential carrier to axle housing bolt
25. Differential carrier
26. Collapsible spacer
27. Bevel pinion nut

Exploded view of typical Fiat differential assembly

Inspection

Check all gears for damage or wear. Very slight wear damage can be corrected with very fine abrasive paper. Inspect the side gear thrust washers. If the thrust washers are only slightly defective polish them. Be sure that the case and carrier are not cracked.

Assembly

Assemble the side gears and thrust washers in the case. Insert the pinion gears through the opening in the case and engage them with the side gears. Align the holes in the pinion gears with the holes in the case and insert the pinion gears shaft. Check the axial play in each side gear. The play should be from 0-.039″. If the side gear play is excessive, replace the thrust washers with thicker ones, to bring the axial play within specifications. Service thrust washers are supplied in the following sizes: .076″, .078″, .080″ and .082″. If the thrust washers were changed, measure the clearance again. If new thrust washers fail to bring the clearance within specifications, the side gears are excessively worn and must be replaced. Fit the ring gear to the case and torque the bolts to 72.0 ft. lbs. Fit the inner races of the roller bearings with a driver of proper size.

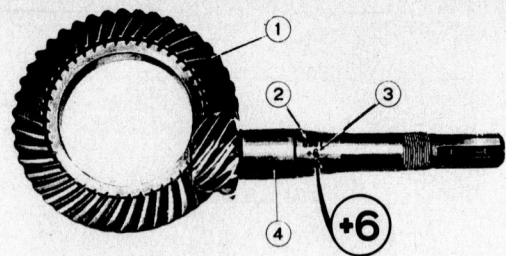

1. Ring gear
2. Serial production and matching number
3. Centesimal value of difference between actual and nominal distance
4. Bevel pinion

Ring gear and pinion markings

At this point assembly of the pinion requires a trial and error method to determine the thickness of the pinion thrust washer, which controls pinion and ring gear mesh, compensating for differences in machining between pinion and carrier. Assemble several thrust washers of varying thicknesses and several collapsible spacers. Pinion bearing thrust washers are in the following thicknesses: .100″, .102″, .104″, .106″, .108″, .110″, .112″, .114″, .116″, .118″, .120″, .122″, .124″, .1259″, .1279″, .1299″ and .1311″.

If the pinion, ring gear, pinion bearings and differential carrier are not changed, the same collapsible spacer and pinion thrust washer may be re-used. However, if any of those parts are installed new, the thrust washer and collapsible spacer will have to be replaced with new parts.

By comparing the number stamped on the pinion and ring gear (old or new gear sets), a reasonable determination of thrust washer thickness can be made. The number, stamped on the pinion, and preceded by a (+) or (−) sign, is the difference, in hundredths of a millimeter, between the actual fitting clearance and the nominal fitting clearance. Select a thrust washer thought to be of nearly proper size (or as close to the proper size as possible). Assemble the pinion and bearings and insert the pinion assembly in the carrier. Fit the front roller bearing inner race, the oil seal, oil slinger and spacer on the front of the carrier.

The pinion bearings are preloaded in the following manner. Clamp the pinion and torque the pinion nut to 108.5-166.4 ft. lbs., constantly checking the rotational

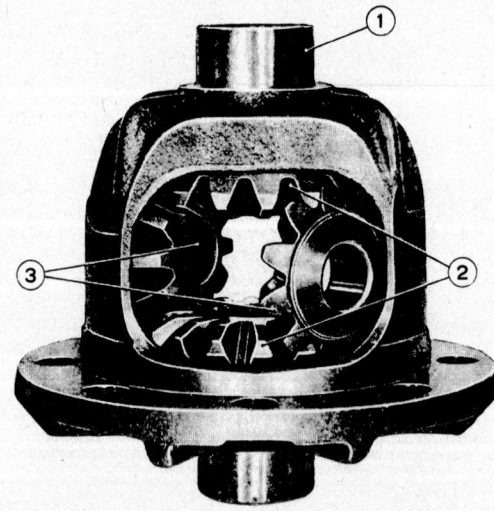

1. Differential case
2. Side gears
3. Pinion gears
Arrange the pinion gears as shown in the figure and push them into place by rolling them on the side gear.

Assemble the side gears in the differential case

torque. The rotational torque of the pinion must be between 1.2-1.5 ft. lbs. *NOTE: If the tightening of rotational torque is exceeded, the collapsible spacer will have to be replaced. If the proper rotational torque cannot be obtained, the spacer will have to be removed and replaced with another.*

Fit the differential case into the carrier, complete with bearing outer races. Fit the two bearing retaining and adjusting rings and bring them into light contact with the bearings. Fit the bearing caps and torque the bolts to 36.0 ft. lbs. Temporarily adjust the ring gear and pinion backlash to .0031"-.0047". Alternately, tighten the two bearing adjusting rings the same number of turns, until the differential case bearing cap divergence measures .0063"-.0078". The ring gear backlash must remain as set.

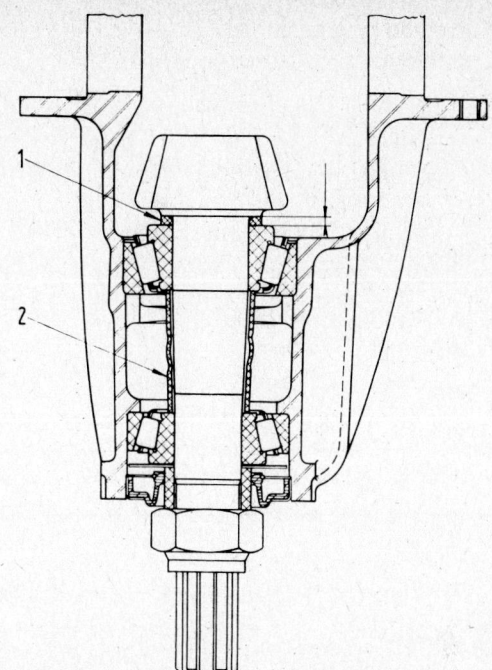

1. Rear bearing thrust ring
2. Collapsible spacer between roller bearings

Diagram for fitting pinion

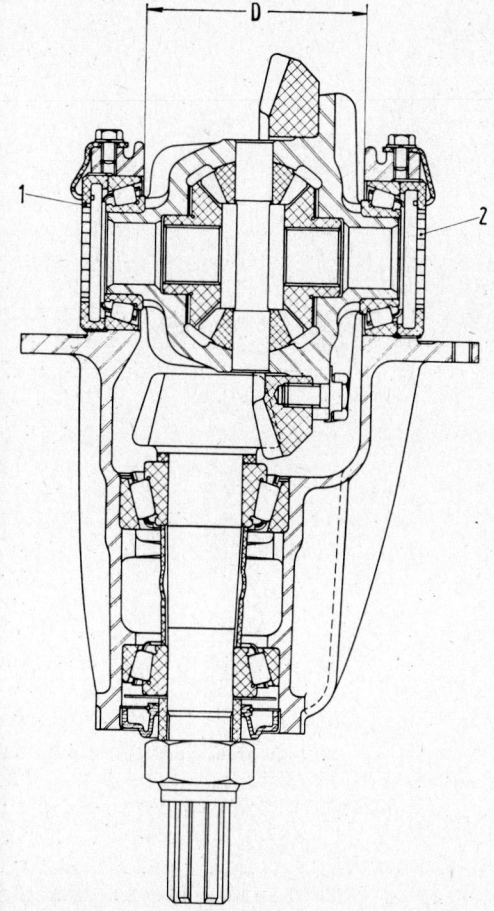

D. Distance between differential case bearing caps: tighten adjusting rings 1 and 2 to increase dimension D.

Diagram for checking the differential case bearing preload

Using a dial gauge, adjust the ring gear backlash to .0032"-.0047". It is important that if one adjuster ring is turned, the other be turned an equal amount, ensuring that the preload is not altered.

Coat the ring gear with red lead and check the tooth contact pattern, as illustrated under the 850 transaxle. Depending on the results of this test, the pinion thrust washer may have to be replaced with another of different thickness, either thicker or thinner, depending on the direction in which the pinion must be moved. Bear in mind that if this operation is necessary, the entire process will have to be repeated.

Installation

Installation is the reverse of removal.

Specifications

Pinion nut torque	108.5-166.3 ft. lbs.
Pinion turning torque	1.2-1.5 ft. lbs.
Bearing preload	
Differential cap spread	.0063"-.0090" (increase)*
Side gear axial clearance	0-.0039"

Pinion and ring gear
  backlash   .0031″-.0047″**
Oil
  Type   Fiat W 90/M
  Quantity   1 pt. 26 oz.
  *—124 Sport Spyder, Sport Coupe .0063″-
  .0078″
  **—124 Sport Spyder, Sport Coupe .0039″-
  .0059″

1100, 1100D and 1100R

REAR AXLE

This rear axle and differential are of
the same design as the 124 rear axle, except that the 1100 series Fiats have rear
drum brakes, and utilize leaf springs.

Removal

Jack the rear of the car and remove the
rear wheels and the rubber bumpers on
the underframe. Plug the brake reservoir
outlet and disconnect the hose from the
three-way connection on the axle housing.
Detach the stabilizer bar from the axle
housing. Disconnect the driveshaft from
the pinion flange. Remove the spring U-
bolts and detach the shock absorbers from
the lower attachment plate. Support the
rear axle with a hydraulic jack and remove the assembly from the car. The leaf
springs need not be removed.

Installation

Installation is the reverse of removal.

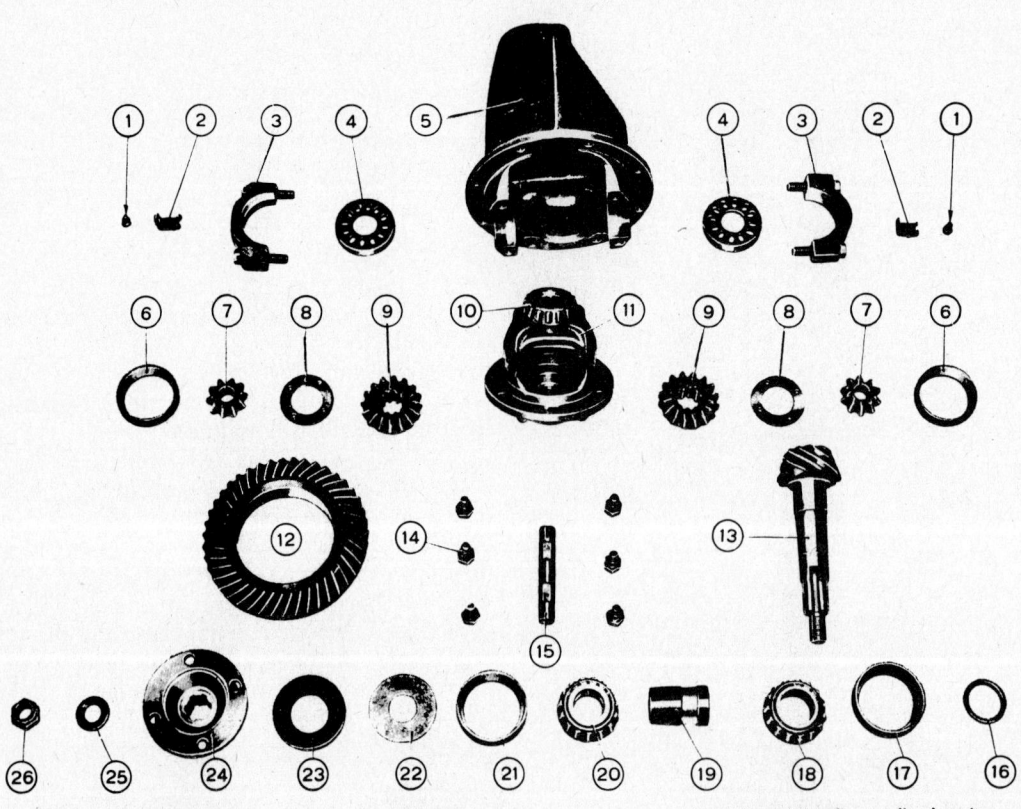

1. Adjustable lockplate screws	11. Differential case	20. Drive pinion front roller bearing
2. Side roller bearings adjuster	12. Ring gear	inner ring
lockplate	13. Drive pinion	21. Roller bearing outer ring
3. Differential bearing caps	14. Ring gear-to-differential case	22. Oil slinger
4. Side roller bearing adjusters	screws	23. Oil seal
5. Differential carrier	15. Pinion gear shaft	24. Drive pinion end flange
6. Roller bearing outer rings	16. Drive pinion rear bearing thrust	25. Pinion flange lock washer and
7. Pinion gears	washer	self-locking nut
8. Side gear thrust washers	17. Roller bearing outer ring	26. Pinion flange lock washer and
9. Side gears	18. Roller bearing inner ring	self-locking nut
10. Roller bearing inner ring	19. Collapsible spacer	

Exploded view of 1100 differential components

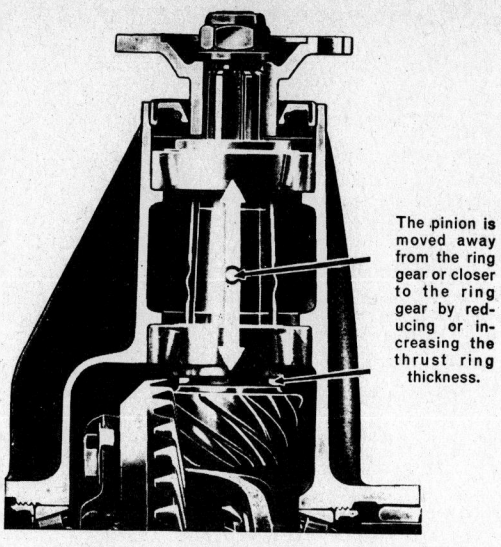

The pinion is moved away from the ring gear or closer to the ring gear by reducing or increasing the thrust ring thickness.

Pinion depth adjustment (applicable to all front-engine, rear axle Fiats)

Be sure to unplug the brake line reservoir and to bleed the brake system. Lower shock absorber nuts are torqued to 63 ft. lbs.

AXLE SHAFTS

Removal

Axle shaft removal is similar to 124 axle shaft removal after removing the wheels, brake drum and brake backing plate.

Installation

Installation is the reverse of removal.

DIFFERENTIAL

Removal

Differential service is identical to the service operations on the 124 Fiat rear axle.

Specifications

Ring gear to pinion backlash	.0028″-.0047″
Side gear backlash	.004″
Pinion nut torque	58-116 ft. lbs.
Pinion rotational torque	1-1.3 ft. lbs.
Bearing preload differential cap spread	.008″-.010″
Side gear thrust washers	.079″ and .081″
Pinion bearing thrust washers *	in .002″ increments, from .106″-.132″

Oil Type	Fiat W 90
Quantity	.67 qt.

*—1100R pinion bearing thrust washers are supplied as follows: .1004″, .1024″, .1043″, .1063″, .1083″, .1102″, .1122″, .1142″, .1161″, .1181″, .1201″, .1240″, .1260″, .1280″, 1299″

1500 and 1600S

Rear axle, axle shaft and differential service procedures for 124 and 1100 Fiats are applicable to the 1500 and 1600S Fiats.

Specifications

Pinion nut torque	58-116 ft. lbs.
Pinion rotational torque	1.08-1.16 ft. lbs.
Bearing preload Differential cap divergence	.0051″ (approx.)
Side gear turning toque (loose differential case and other side gear locked)	21.7-36.2 ft. lbs.
Ring gear and pinion backlash	.0031″-.0047″
Oil Type	Fiat W 90/M
Quantity	.95 qt.

850

REAR SUSPENSION

Removal

Jack the car at the rear and set it on stands. Remove a wheel and disconnect a shock absorber at the rear. Tie the axle shaft off from the wheel shaft joint. Disconnect the handbrake control cable from the brake shoe actuating lever. Plug the brake fluid reservoir outlet and detach the brake hose from the brake line. Disconnect the sway bar at the control arm and the transmission mounting bracket. Back out the screws mounting the control arm to the body, at the front and the rear, noting the number of shims. Using a hydraulic jack, lower the rear suspension. Repeat this procedure to lower the other arm.

Disassembly

Disassemble the control arm. This operation should not present any particular

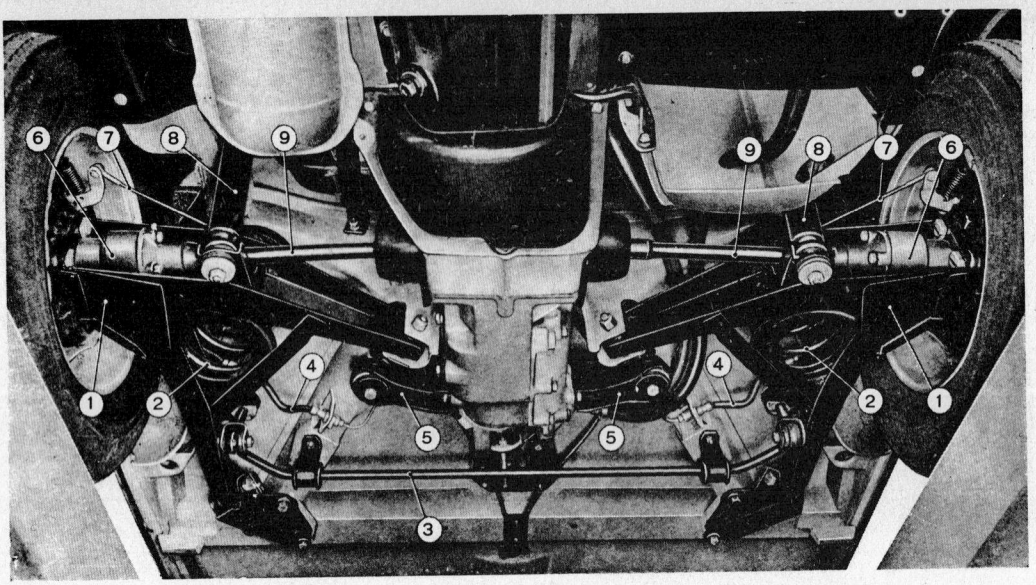

1. Control arms
2. Coil springs
3. Sway bar

4. Hydraulic brake lines
5. Transmission mounting brackets
6. Flexible joints

7. Handbrake control cable
8. Shock absorbers
9. Axle shafts

850 rear suspension in place on vehicle

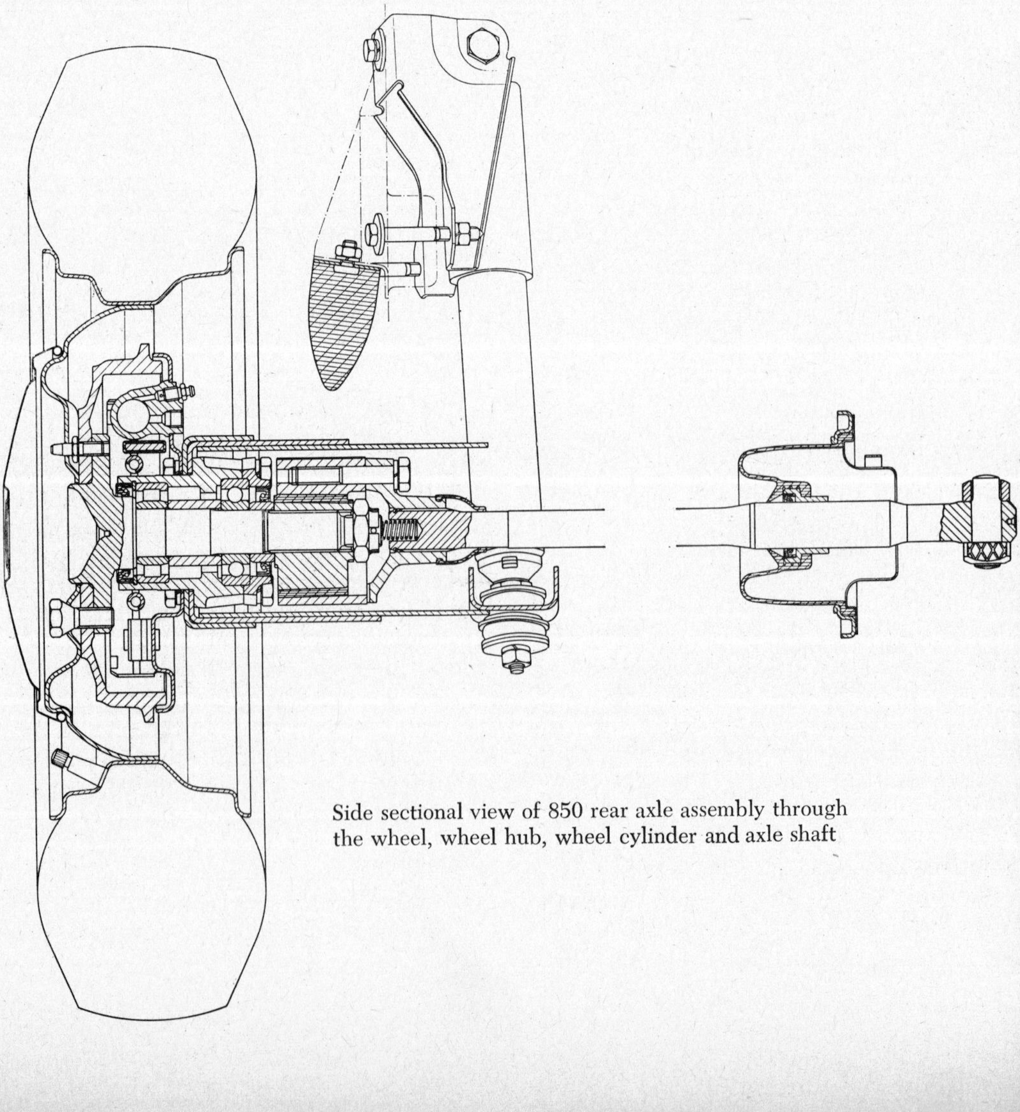

Side sectional view of 850 rear axle assembly through the wheel, wheel hub, wheel cylinder and axle shaft

difficulty, but the following points should be noted.

After the wheel hub has been removed, remove the ball bearing retainer plate. Withdraw the ball bearing with a slide hammer. Remove the roller bearing cup with a driver. *NOTE: Whenever the roller bearing has been removed, it must be re-*

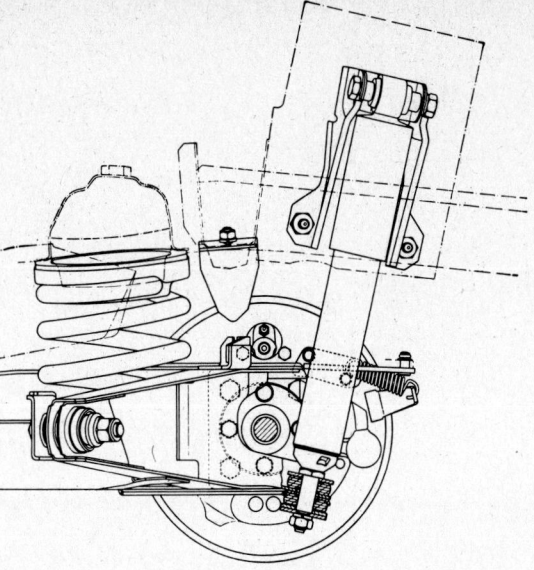

Sectional view of rear suspension across the sway bar mounting

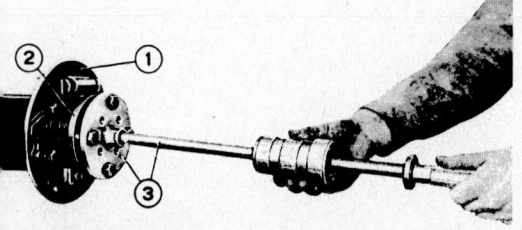

1. Brake backing plate
2. Wheel hub
3. Slide hammer for rear wheel hubs

Removing 850 rear wheel hub

placed with a new one. A driver should be used for removal of control arm bushings. Check the ball and roller bearings for wear. Sliding surfaces of the wheel shaft must show no signs of binding. Always use new spring type oil seals which have been removed.

Assembly

To assemble the control arm, reverse the disassembly procedure. Liberally lubricate the bearing cups and bushings with Fiat MR 3 grease and install, using a driver.

COIL SPRINGS

Check to be sure that coil springs are in good condition and show no cracks. Examine the rubber seats and replace these if they are damaged. Coil springs are graded with two colors: yellow paint spot

and green paint spot. Coil springs on any one car must show same paint color identification.

Installation

Raise the suspension and set it at the mounting points. Temporarily tighten the front mounting screws. Slide the rear end of the control arm into the body bracket. Install the coil spring with rubber seats.

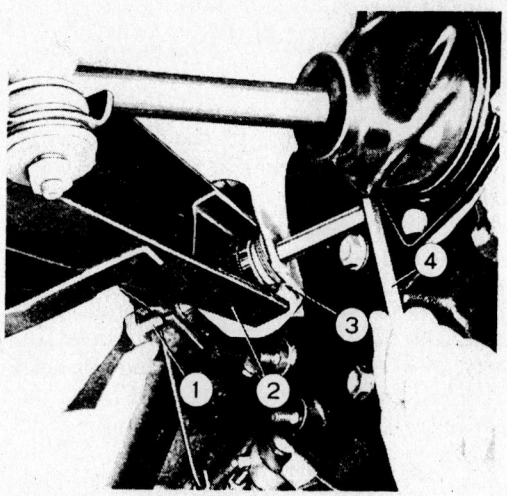

1. Control arm rear lockpin
2. Control arm
3. Shims
4. Tool—A. 74143

Fastening 850 rear control arm to body

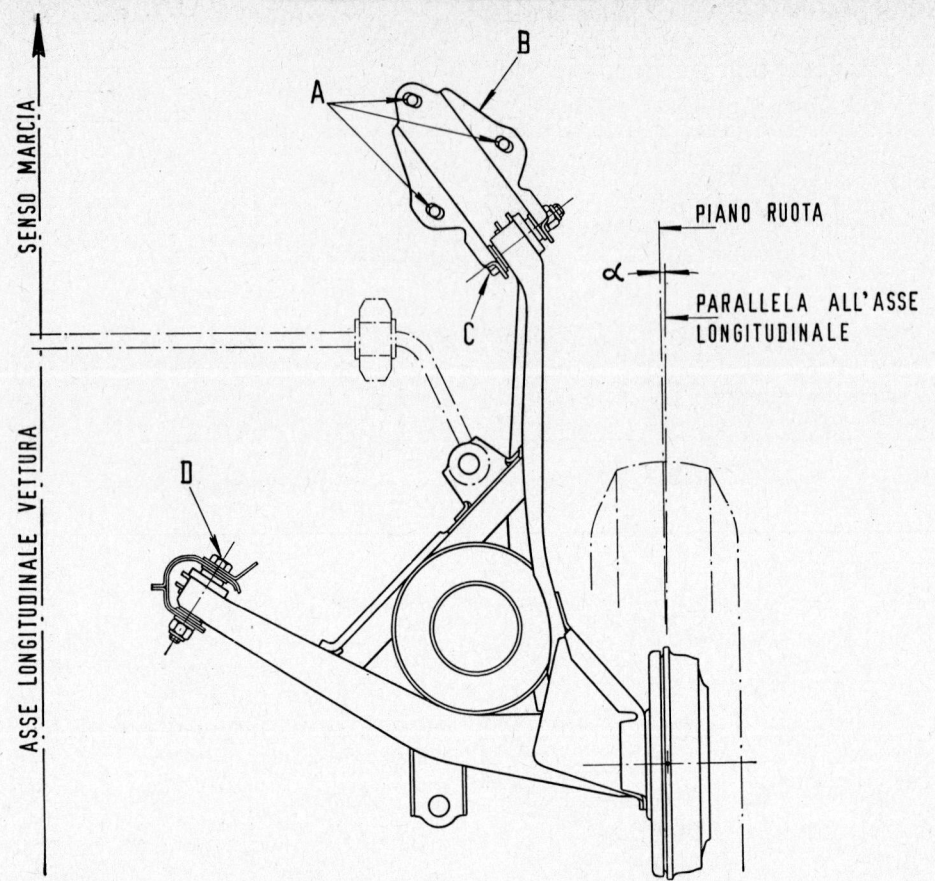

A. Screws, front bracket to underbody (recommended torque 28.9 to 36.2 ft. lbs.—4 to 5 kgm.). Tighten these screws after adjusting toe-in with wheel in vertical position—B. Front bracket of control arm—C-D. Screws and nuts, control arm to underbody. These nuts should be drawn up with 65.1 ft. lbs. (9 kgm) of torque with care under full load— α Toe-in angle, with wheel in vertical position: 0° 12′ ± 6′.
Senso marcia—Director of drive. Asse longitudinale vettura—car centerline. Piano ruota—Wheel plane. Parallela al'asse longitudinale—Parallel to car centerline.

Diagram for setting 850 rear end geometry

Secure the axle shaft to the flexible joint and the shock absorber to the control arm. Insert the shims in the same amount and position as removed, between the "estend-block" and the mounting bracket. Tie up the brake line and handbrake control cable. Remove the plug from the brake fluid reservoir to restore fluid circulation. Install the transmission mounting bracket and sway bar. Fit the wheels and bleed the brakes.

FLEXIBLE JOINT

Replace

Jack the rear of the car and remove the wheel. Remove the axle shaft to flexible joint sleeve screws. Slide the sleeve back on the axle shaft and remove the inner spring. Remove the cotter pin and screw the nut out four complete turns. Attach a slide hammer to the wheel hub and pull the wheel hub part way out. Turn the nut all the way out and replace the flexible joint with a new one. By working the mounting nut, reset the wheel hub to its original position. Torque the nut to 101 ft. lbs. and thread the cotter pin. If the cooter pin does not align with a hole, advance the nut further. Complete the assembly by reversing the disassembly procedures.

600 and 600D

The 600 series rear suspension is basically similar to the 850 rear suspension.

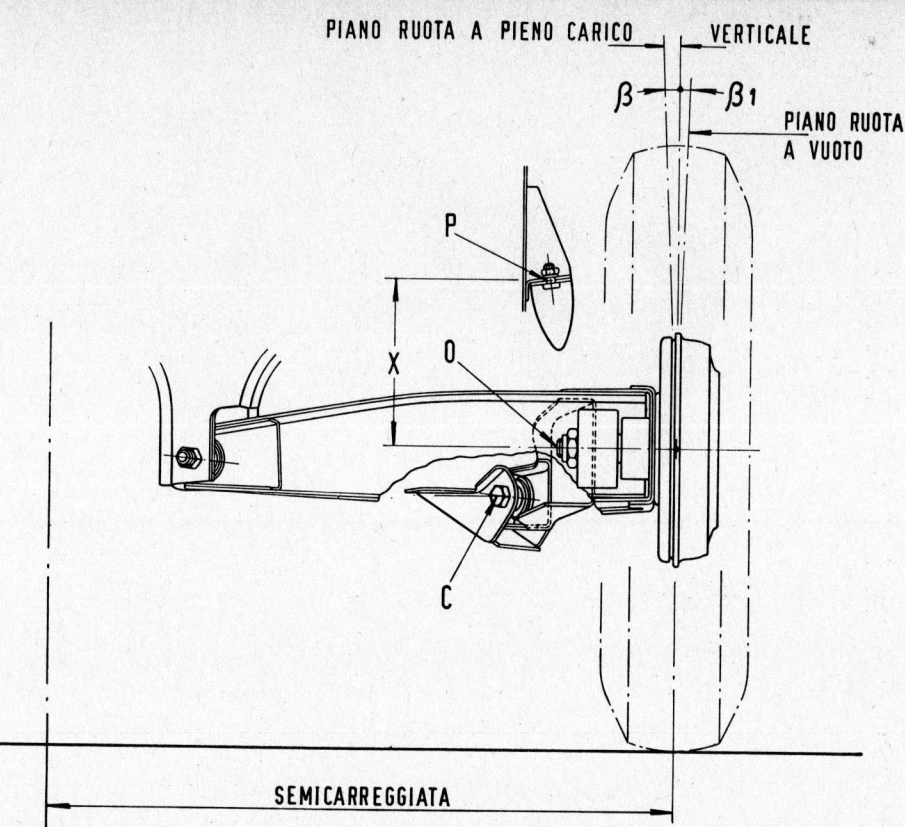

PIANO RUOTA A PIENO CARICO — VERTICALE

β — β1

PIANO RUOTA A VUOTO

P

O

X

C

SEMICARREGGIATA

C. Screw and nut, control arm to front bracket
O. Wheel center
P. Rubber buffer screw hole center

X. Distance (some 6.102″—155 mm) of wheel center from P; in this position the wheel shold be at right angle to floor

β —2° 15 to 2° 40.
β1—1° 15′ to 1° 30′.
Piano ruota a pieno carico—Wheel plane, full load

Verticale—Vertical
Piano ruta a vuoto—Wheel plane, no load
Semicarreggiata—Thread half

Diagram for checking rear suspension and rear end geometry

REAR SUSPENSION

Removal

Removal procedures are basically similar to the 850. The floor lining behind the rear seat must be removed to unbolt the shock absorber mounting nuts.

Disassembly

Disassembly and assembly are similar to the 850.

Installation

Installation is the reverse of removal. The wheel bearings must be preloaded, a procedure unique to the 600 series Fiats. The bearing housing should be torqued to 43.4 ft. lbs., checking the bearing ro-

tational torque, at the same time. Rotational torque should be approximately .36 ft. lbs. If the rotational torque exceeds this figure, a new flexible joint should be installed.

Front Suspension

The Fiat 124 and 600D have coil springs at front and rear, while models 600 and 850 have transverse leaf springs at the front and coil springs at the rear. The Fiat 1100, 1500 and 1600S models have coil springs at the front and longitudinal leaf springs in the rear.

124

The front suspension is of the wishbone type, with coil springs, hydraulic shock ab-

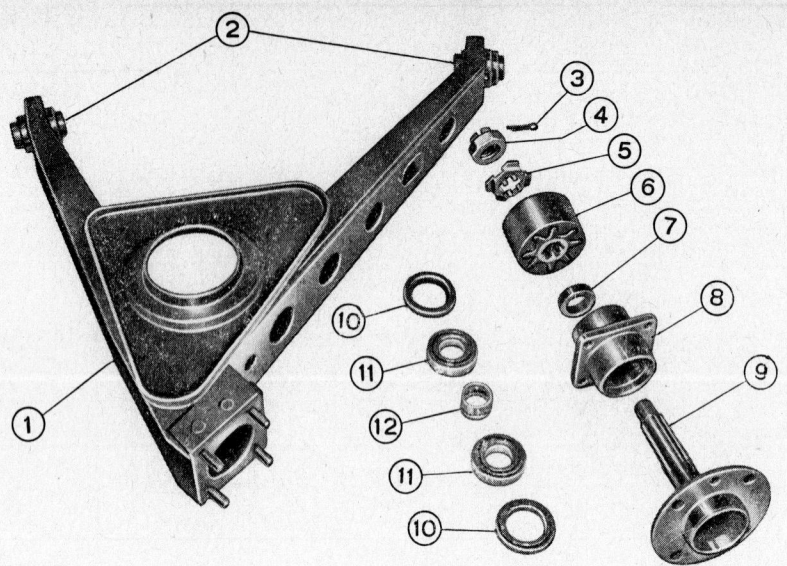

1. Swinging arm
2. Estendblock, arm mounting on body floor
3. Cotter pin
4. Wheel shaft mounting nut
5. Lockplate
6. Flexible joint

7. Spacer, bearing housing-to-joint
8. Bearing housing
9. Wheel shaft
10. Bearing housing oil seals
11. Roller bearings
12. Resilient spacer

Fiat 600 control arm and wheel shaft components

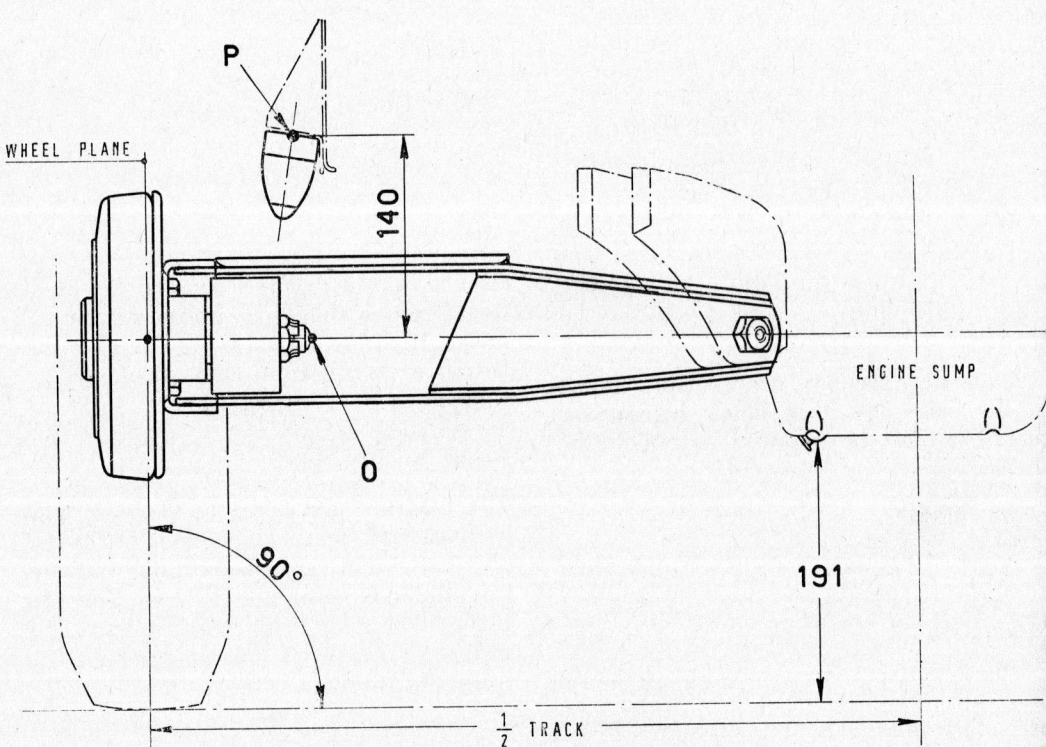

Diagram for checking and adjusting Fiat 600 toe-in

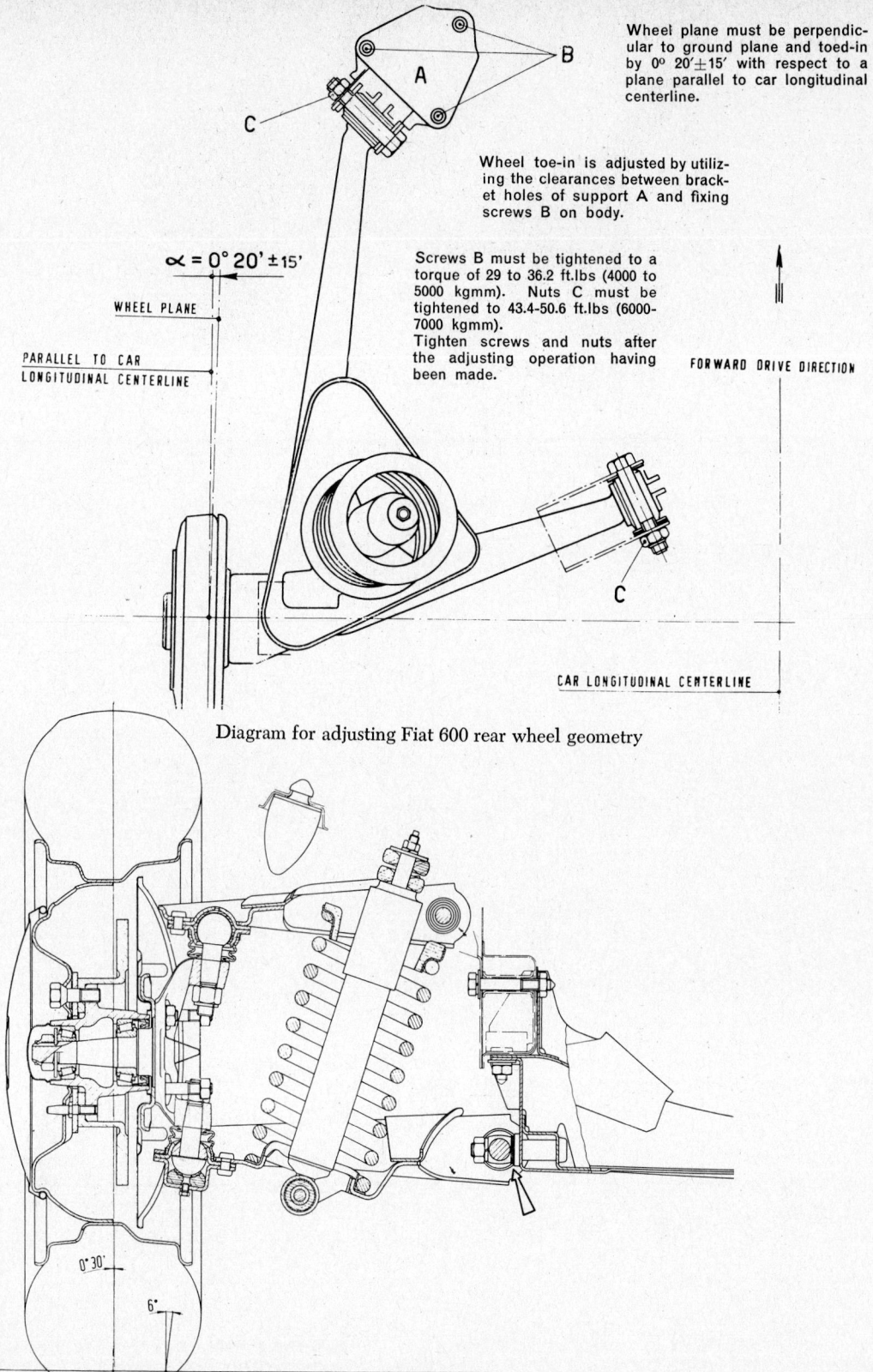

Wheel plane must be perpendicular to ground plane and toed-in
by 0° 20′±15′ with respect to a
plane parallel to car longitudinal
centerline.

Wheel toe-in is adjusted by utilizing the clearances between bracket holes of support A and fixing
screws B on body.

Screws B must be tightened to a
torque of 29 to 36.2 ft.lbs (4000 to
5000 kgmm). Nuts C must be
tightened to 43.4-50.6 ft.lbs (6000-
7000 kgmm).
Tighten screws and nuts after
the adjusting operation having
been made.

FORWARD DRIVE DIRECTION

$\alpha = 0° 20′ ±15′$

WHEEL PLANE

PARALLEL TO CAR
LONGITUDINAL CENTERLINE

CAR LONGITUDINAL CENTERLINE

Diagram for adjusting Fiat 600 rear wheel geometry

0° 30′

6°

Left front suspension of 124 showing kingpin setting and camber angle for loaded
car. Arrow points to shims for camber adjustment.

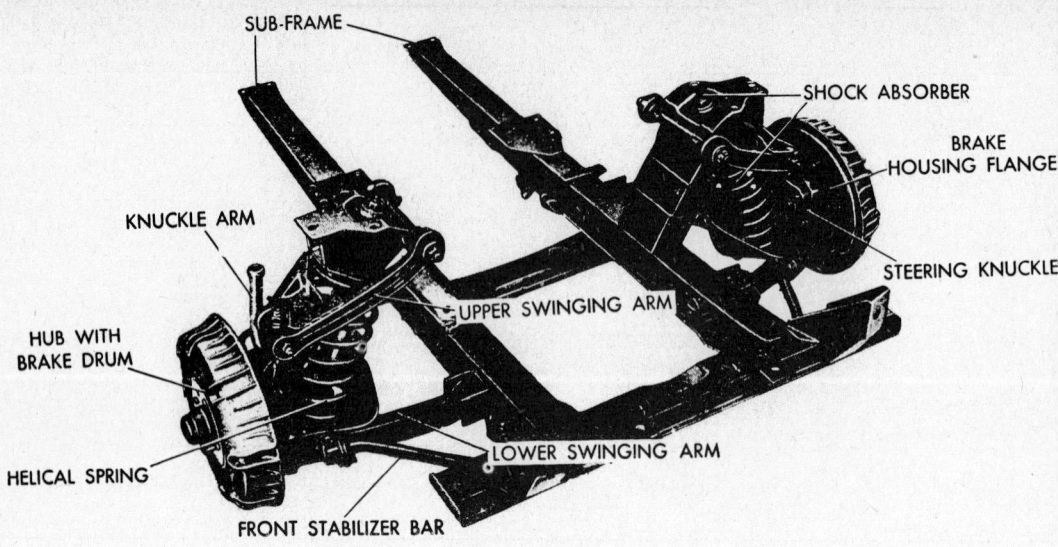

Fiat 1100 front suspension and subframe assembly

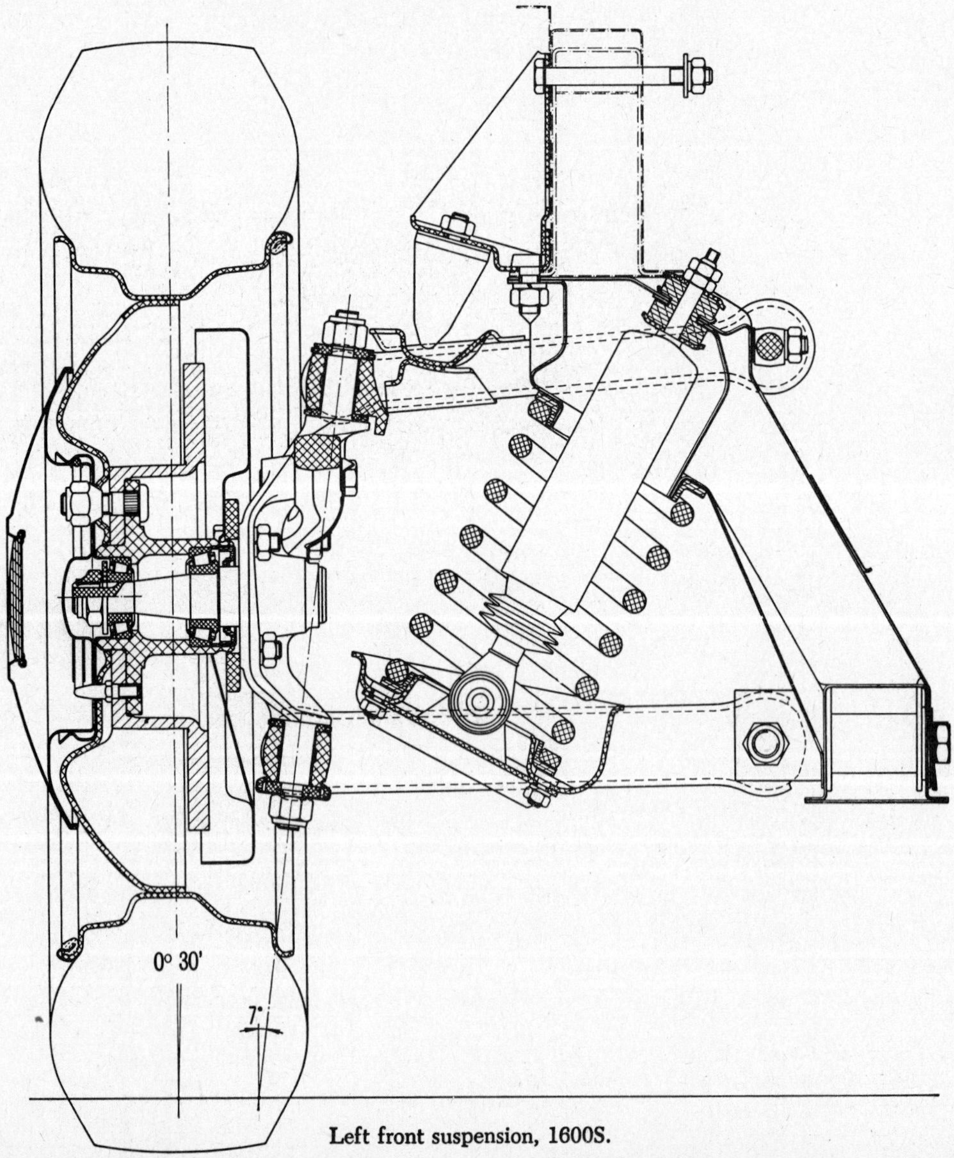

$0° 30'$

$7°$

Left front suspension, 1600S.

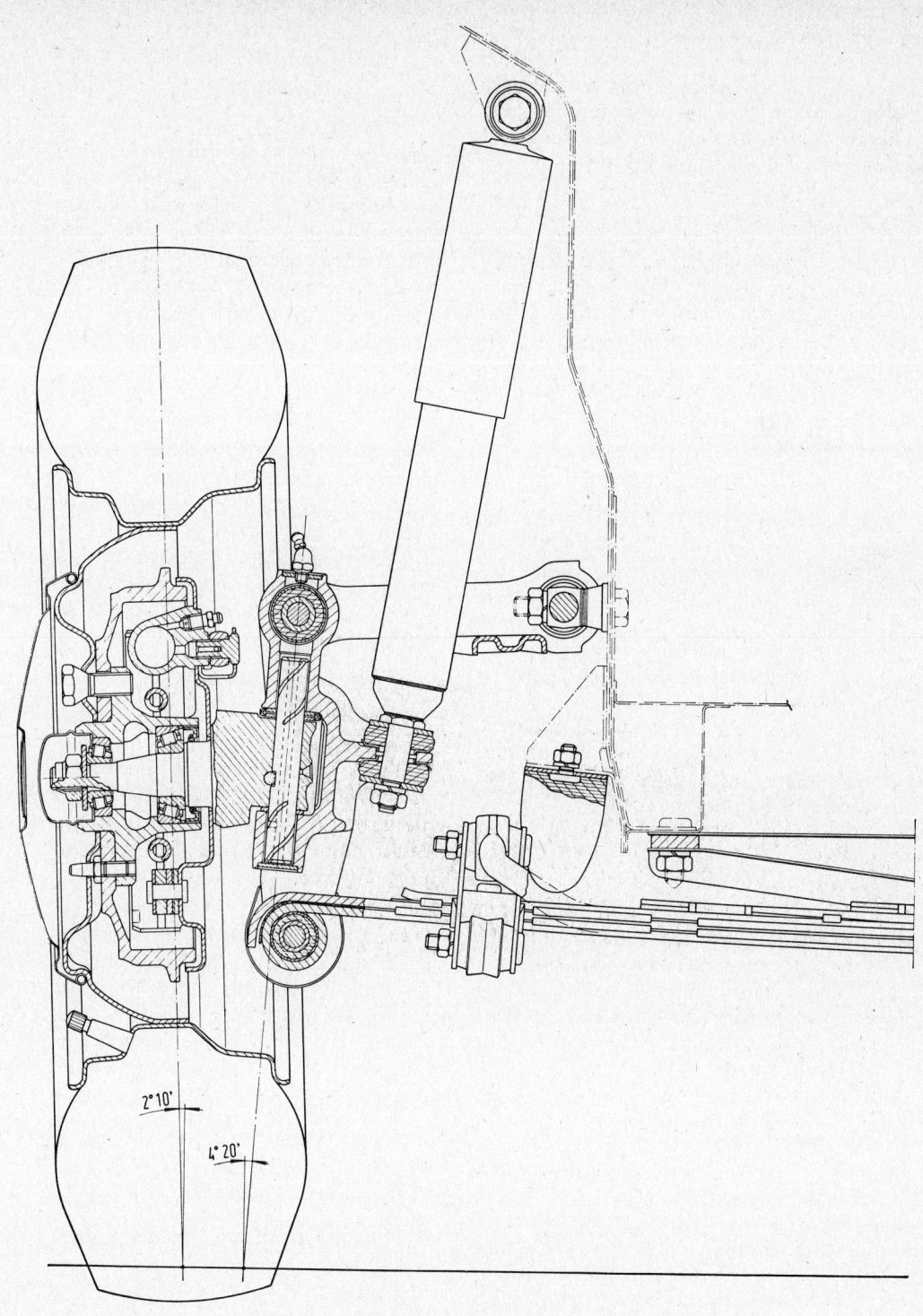

Left front suspension, 850.

sorbers and stabilizer bar. Upper and lower control arms are connected to the knuckles through ball joints, lubricated for life. The two ball joints are hosed in the control arm and riveted in position. Two lower control arms are connected to the lower crossmember of the frame.

Ball Joint Inspection

Check that the ball joints are perfectly seated in their sockets and that the arms are not loose in them. The whole arm must be changed if the joints are not secure in the arm or if they show signs of wear. The ball joint seals must also be in place, to prevent the entry of water or other matter.

1100, 1100D AND 1100R

Basically, the 1100 series Fiats use the suspension used on the 124. The 1100 has a subframe which mounts the entire suspension. To remove the front suspension, the entire subframe pictured must be removed. If this operation is performed, be sure to support the engine from a lift or hoist.

Upper and lower control arms are connected to the subframe by rubber bushings and to the steering knuckle pillars, by spiders and self-tapping bushings.

1500 AND 1600S

An independent wheel front suspension is used, with hydraulic shock absorbers (1500) and pneumatic shock absorbers (1600S). A sway bar is attached to the lower control arms and coil springs on the lower control arm and boxed plate of pillar at top.

850 AND 600

The suspensions used on these Fiats are basically alike in design and operation. Independent front wheel suspension consists of a transverse leaf spring secured to the body and king pins. The leaf spring also acts as a stabilizer. Telescopic, hydraulic shock absorbers are anchored to the body and to the steering knuckle pillar.

The 600 Multipla uses a different front suspension, consisting of independent wheels and control arms connected to the wheels, counteracted by coil springs. Shock absorbers and a tranverse stabilizer bar are also mounted.

Front Wheel Alignment

124, 1100, 1500, 1600S AND 600D

Camber

Camber angle adjustment is made by changing the number of shims under the two bolts that hold the lower control arm (upper arm on the 1100, 1500, 1600S) to the frame crossmember. Camber is increased by removing shims and reduced by adding shims. Add or remove the same number for each bolt, otherwise caster will be affected.

Caster

Caster angle is increased by moving these shims from the front bolt to the rear and decreased by moving them from the rear bolt to the front.

Toe-in adjustment is made by first loosening the clamp bolts, then turning the sleeves to lengthen or shorten the left- and right-hand tie-rods.

600 AND 850

Camber and caster angle and adjustment are made by means of shims installed under the two bolts that hold the control arm to the frame. Camber angle is increased by adding the same number of shims under each bolt; decreased by removing the same number of shims from under each bolt.

Caster is increased by moving shims from the rear bolt to the front bolt and reduced by moving shims from the front bolt to the rear bolt.

Toe-in is adjusted by turning sleeves to lengthen or shorten the left-and right-hand tie-rods.

Steering

Fiat 124, 600D, 1100, 1500 and 1600S models utilize worm and roller type steering assemblies with a ratio of 16.4 to 1. The wheel turning circle is 28 feet for the 600D and approximately 34.5 feet for the 124, 1100, 1500 and 1600S. The 600 and 850 models employ worm and sector systems with a ratio of 13 to 1 and 'wheel turning circle of 28.5 feet for the 600 and 31.5 feet for the 850.

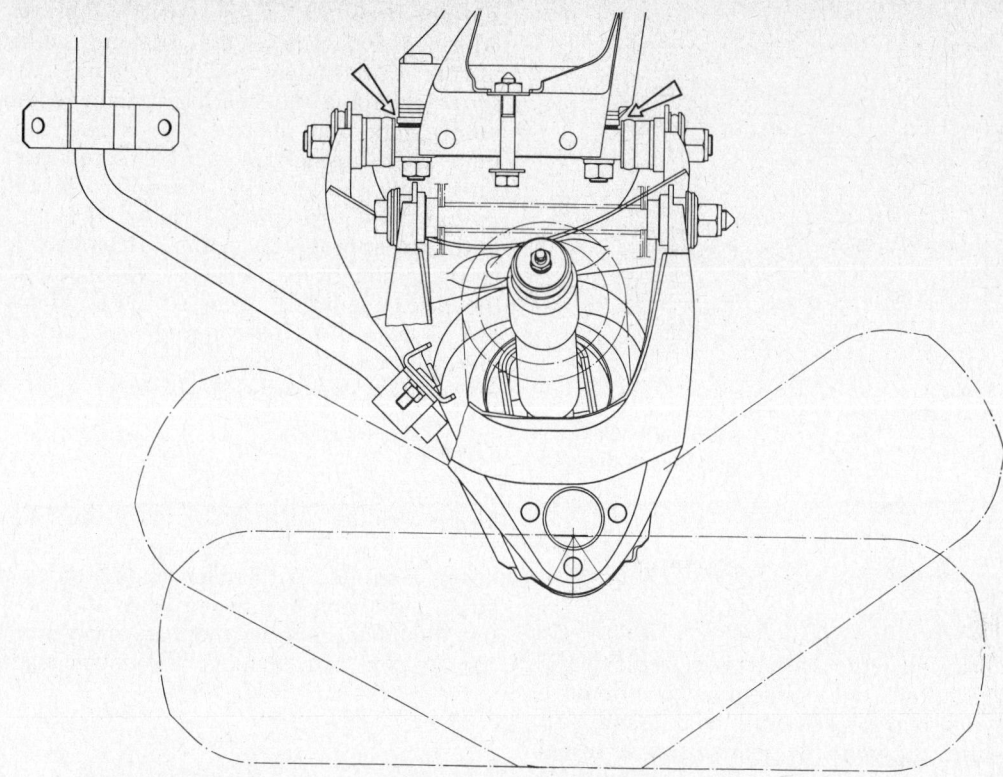

Left front suspension showing shims (at arrows) for adjusting caster and camber, 124.

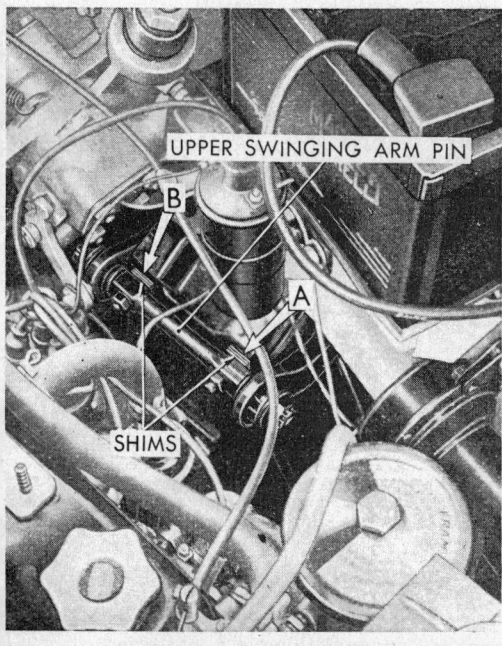

Adjustment points for 1100 front wheel caster and camber—Shims are mounted at points A and B

Camber on 600 and 850 is increased by adding shims (at arrows) to the wishbone mounting bolts (A and B). Caster is increased by moving shims from rear bolt to front bolt.

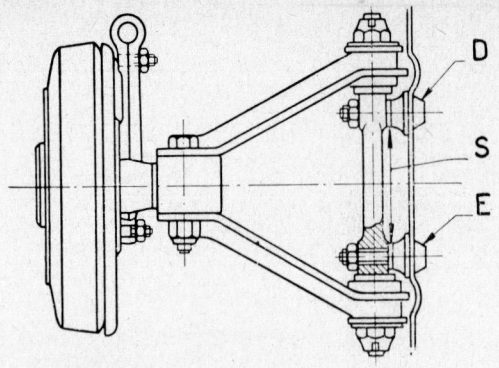

S—Shims.
D and E—Points where shims must be installed.

Fiat 600 front wheel camber adjustment diagram

Steering Gear
124 SEDAN, COUPE AND SPYDER

Removal

Disconnect the battery and remove the horn button and emblem cover. Remove the steering wheel retaining nut and pull the steering from the shaft, using a wheel puller. Remove the turn signal switch half covers and unscrew the retaining collar of the turn signal switch. This is located on the bracket fixing the steering column to the body. Disconnect the steering column bracket from the ignition switch (threaded ring) and remove the retaining collar of the turn signal switch. Remove the screw clamping the steering column to the worm shaft and remove the steering column from inside the car. Unscrew the nuts fixing the left-hand steering arm and intermediate arm pins. Remove the pins with an appropriate puller. Remove the steering box from the body by removing the three mounting screws. *NOTE: Shims can be placed on the steering box bolts to ensure proper alignment. Note the number and placement of such shims.*

Disassembly

Drain the oil from the steering box. Using a puller, remove the drop arm from the roller shaft. Remove the roller shaft cover, complete with roller shaft adjusting screw, adjusting disc, lockwasher and locknut. Remove the roller shaft assembly from the steering box. Remove the worm shaft

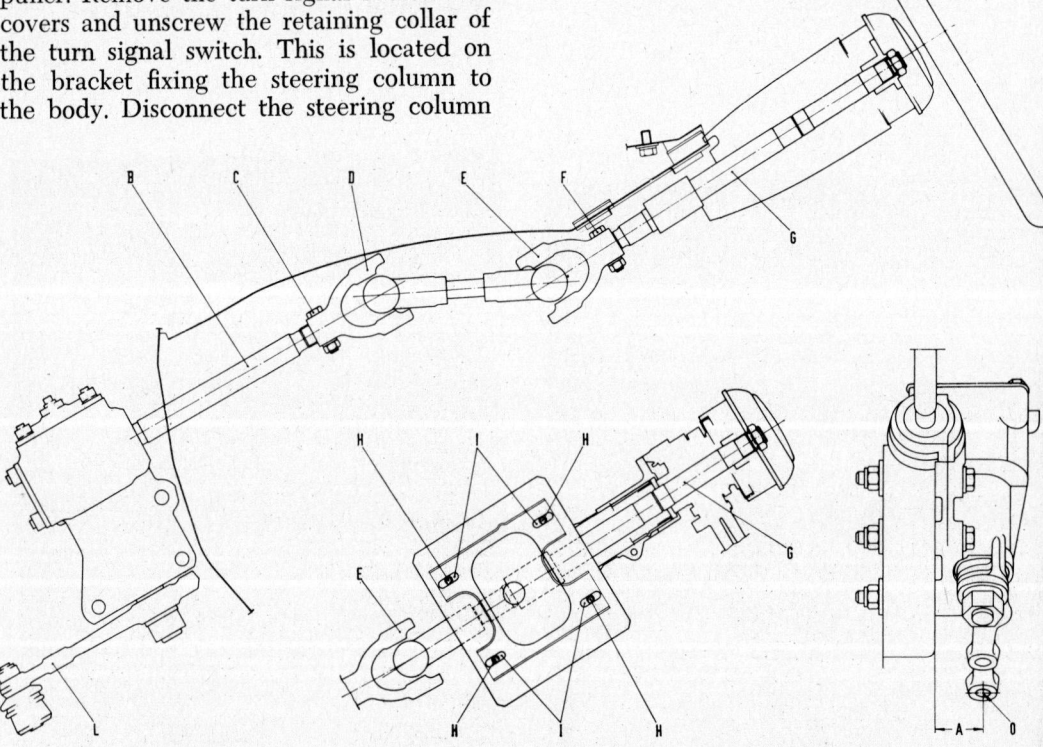

Steering components, Fiat 124 Coupe and Spider. (B) lower steering column; (C) lower universal joint fork bolt; (D and E) universal joint forks; (F) upper steering column universal joint fork bolt; (G) upper steering column; (H) steering column guide bracket fixing screws; (I) slots; (L) steering arm; (O) center of steering arm eye. A = 42.5 mm. (1.67″) approx. This dimension must be respected when fitting steering assembly to car.

thrust cover and the front bearing adjusting shims. Turn the worm shaft to withdraw the front roller bearing. Use a puller and remove the outer race of the rear roller bearing. Remove the worm and shaft from the steering box along with the inner race of the inner roller bearing.

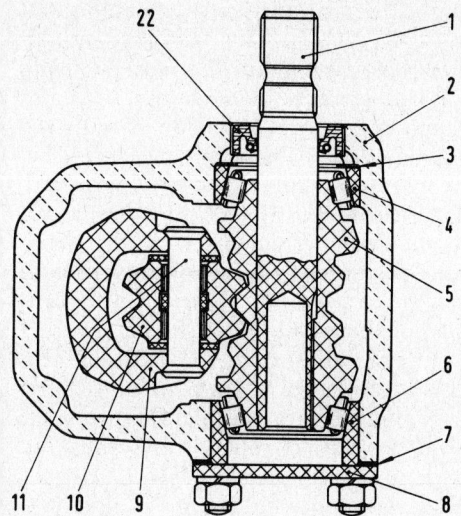

Section through steering box assembly on C/L of worm shaft.

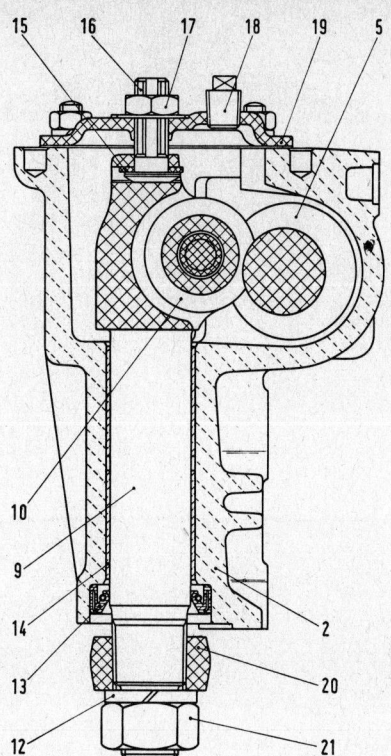

Section through steering box assembly on C/L of roller shaft.

1. Steering shaft
2. Steering box
3. Worm upper bearing shim
4. Upper roller bearing
5. Worm
6. Lower roller bearing
7. Worm lower bearing shim
8. Worm thrust cover
9. Roller shaft
10. Roller
11. Roller pin

12. Spring washer under drop arm nut
13. Roller shaft oil seal
14. Roller shaft bush
15. Roller shaft adjusting disc
16. Roller shaft adjusting screw
17. Locknut
18. Plug
19. Steering box cover
20. Drop arm
21. Drop arm nut
22. Steering shaft oil seal

Withdraw the outer race of the worm shaft rear roller bearing, which will release the shims under the race. *NOTE: Shims are supplied for service to the worm shaft front and rear roller bearings, in thicknesses from .0039"-.0059".* Remove the roller shaft oil seal. If the roller shaft bushings are worn, extract these.

Assembly

Check the clearance between bushings and roller shaft. This should be .00031"-.00201" (.0039" max.). After pressing the bushes into the steering box, they should be reamed to correct diameter (1.1298"-1.1306").

Drive in the roller shaft bushes. Fit the shims and outer race of the roller shaft rear bearing into the box, using a drift. The same number and placement of shims, found at the time of disassembly, must be used. Fit the inner races of the two roller bearings to the worm and install the worm in the box. Drive the outer race of the front roller bearing into the box and fit the thrust cover. Place shims between the thrust cover and the box as required. Check the rotational torque of the worm shaft, which must be .09-.47 ft. lb. If the torque is lower than the specification, reduce the shims; if higher, increase the shims. Fit the roller shaft oil seal. Fit the

1. Adjusting screw locknut
2. Roller shaft adjusting screw
3. Roller shaft
4. Adjusting screw plate
5. Steering box cover studs
6. Lockwasher

Fit the steering box cover with roller shaft adjusting screw.

1. Lockwasher
2. Adjusting screw
3. Drop arm

Adjusting worm and roller clearance

roller shaft cover with adjusting plate, lockwasher and locknut. Temporarily fit the drop arm to the roller shaft. With steering box on the bench, the drop arm should be free to rotate through 30° 40′ ±1° 40′ on either side of the central position. Move the arm in both directions, and check that, through at least 30° in either direction, the clearance between roller and worm is nil. *NOTE: The clearance adjustment between arm and roller must be made with drop arm in mid-position.* If any clearance is present, eliminate it with the adjusting screw. When the clearance between worm and roller has been adjusted, check the turning torque of the worm shaft, which should now be .64-1.22 ft. lbs., from the mid position of the drop arm, through a travel of at least 30° right or left. Turning torque should be ≦ 50 ft. lbs. beyond the angle of 30°, up to the limit of arm travel. During worm and roller adjustment, if the correct mesh does not exist between worm and roller, shims must be inserted to give correct contact. Repeat the adjustment of the worm bearing and the worm and roller. Finally, key the drop arm to the roller shaft, and torque the retaining nut to 173.5 ft. lbs. Fill the steering box with a .23 qt. of Fiat W 90 oil and fit the plug tightly.

Installation

Insert the steering column through the opening in the dashbord. Fit the end of the worm shaft of the steering box to the steering column. *NOTE: If the car is fitted with an anti-theft key switch, fit the steering shaft, so that the keyway is on the left.* Fit the steering box to the body and do not tighten the nuts. Be sure to replace the shims in the proper position. Lock the end of the steering shaft over the splined worm shaft. Replace the supporting bracket to the steering column and connect it to the instrument panel, without tightening the nuts. Connect the lefthand intermediate and side rod pins to the drop arm and secure them with self-locking nuts. Fit the steering wheel temporarily, and turn the wheel several times to steady and settle the assembly. Tighten the steering box mounting nuts. Fit the turn signal switch to the bracket and steering column. Attach the steering column bracket to the instrument panel. Be sure the front wheels are positioned straight ahead, and fit the steering wheel, with spokes horizontal. Stake the nut in place. Connect the turn signal switch and the ignition switch. Fit the two half collars to the turn signal switch and replace the horn button and emblem.

124 SPECIAL, SPORT COUPE AND SPORT SPYDER

Removal, disassembly, assembly and installation procedures are basically alike to the 124 Sedan. During installation, check that no play exists between the bracket and column on the side opposite the bearing on the steering wheel side. Also be sure the universal joints do not bind the steering linkage.

1100

Removal

Disconnect the battery, remove the horn button and disconnect the horn. Remove the steering wheel with a wheel puller. Disconnect the turn signal assembly and remove the switch unit and gearshift lever. Remove the steering column to dashboard mounting bracket. Remove the complete gearshift lever and steering column support. Disconnect the link rod at the pitman arm. Remove the steering column hole cover pad from the dashboard. Detach the gearshift control rod levers and pull out the gearshift main control rod. Be sure to unlock the rod return spring. Remove the three screws securing the steering housing. From the engine compartment, pull the steering column down and out.

Disassembly

Disassembly procedures for the 124 steering gear are valid for the 1100 steering gear.

Installation

Installation is the reverse of removal.

1500 AND 1600S

Removal, Installation and service procedures for these steering gears are basically alike to those procedures for 124 and 1100 Fiats.

850

Removal

Pry off the horn button by inserting a

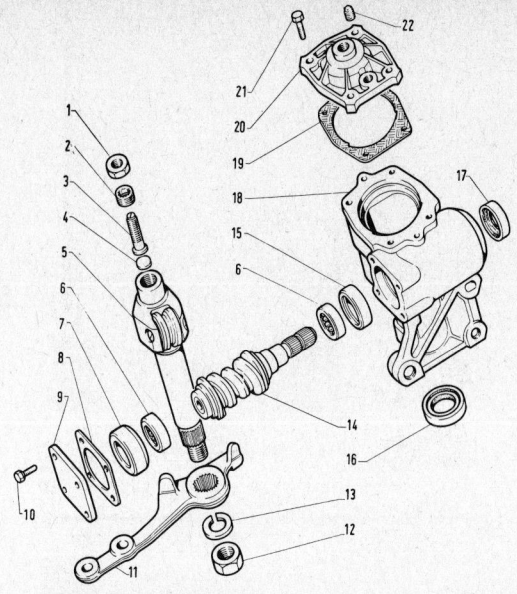

1. Adjusting screw nut
2. Screw ring
3. Adjusjusting screw
4. Plug
5. Roller shaft
6. Ball bearings
7. Bearing retainer
8. Shims
9. Worm screw thrust cover
10. Cover screws
11. Pitman arm
12. Nut, pitman arm to roller shaft
13. Washer
14. Worm screw
15. Bearing retainer
16. Roller shaft seal
17. Steering column seal
18. Steering gear housing
19. Gasket
20. Steering housing upper cover
21. Upper cover screws
22. Oil filler plug

Exploded view of newer type 124 steering gear

screwdriver between the button and wheel hub. Disconnect the horn and remove the steering wheel, using a wheel puller. Working from the luggage compartment, loosen the steering column to worm screw. Jack the front of the car and support it on stands. Disconnect the steering rods from the pitman arm. Remove the mounting nuts and the steering gear.

Disassembly

Drain the oil from the steering gear. Using a puller, remove the pitman arm. Remove the worm sector and shaft assembly. Remove the bearing lock and adjusting nut. Slide the worm free, complete

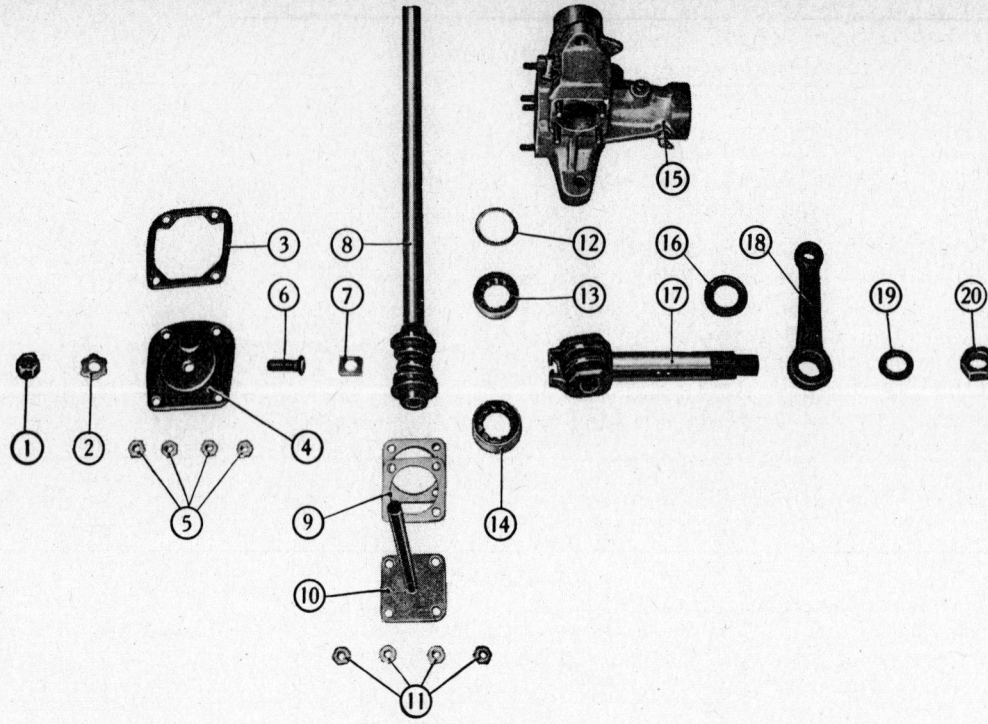

1. Adjusting screw nut
2. Lockplate
3. Cover gasket
4. Side cover
5. Cover stud nuts
6. Roller shaft adjusting screw
7. Adjusting screw plate
8. Worm and shaft
9. Worm front bearing shim
10. Thrust cover
11. Thrust cover-to-box studs
    mounting nuts
12. Rear bearing shims
13. Rear roller bearing
14. Front roller bearing
15. Steering housing
16. Seal, roller shaft
17. Roller shaft
18. Pitman arm
19. Pitman arm nut lockwasher
20. Pitman arm-to-roller shaft nut.

Exploded view of Fiat 1100 steering gear

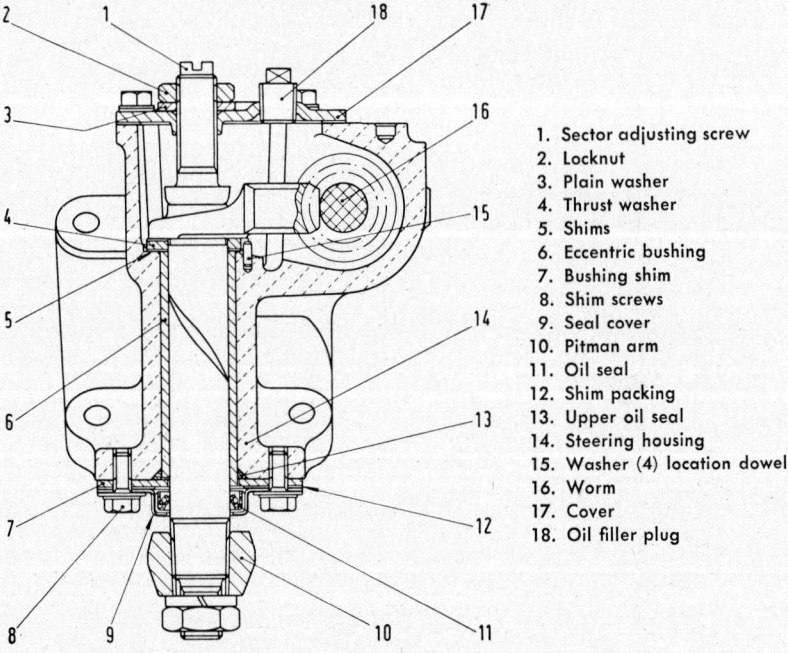

1. Sector adjusting screw
2. Locknut
3. Plain washer
4. Thrust washer
5. Shims
6. Eccentric bushing
7. Bushing shim
8. Shim screws
9. Seal cover
10. Pitman arm
11. Oil seal
12. Shim packing
13. Upper oil seal
14. Steering housing
15. Washer (4) location dowel
16. Worm
17. Cover
18. Oil filler plug

Sectional view of 850 steering gear

1. Oil filler plug
2. Sector adjusting screw

Adjusting worm and sector gear lash (Fiat 850)

with roller bearing cones. Tap out the roller bearing cups and oil seals with a driver.

Assembly

Check the clearance between bushing and sector shaft. The clearance of new parts should be 0-.0016″. Wear limit is .004″. *NOTE: Steering worm and sector are assembled with a touch fit at tooth flank. Adjustment is by turning the eccentric bushing on the worm sector.*

Assembly is the reverse of disassembly, noting the following points. New bushings should always be reamed to obtain specified clearance. Thoroughly wash all components and lubricate them.

Adjustment

This procedure is valid for adjustment after overhaul or as a routine procedure. Disconnect the pitman arm. Back out the

1. Nut
2. Toothed washer
3. Plain washer
4. Screw
5. Support
6. Steering wheel
7. Shaft
8. Screw
9. Toothed washer
10. Screw
11. Lockplate
12. Plain washer
13. Cover
14. Gasket
15. Pin
16. Plain washer
17. Self-locking nut
18. Nut
19. Worm
20. Plain washer
21. Adjusting screw
22. Thrust washer
23. Shim
24. Worm sector and shaft
25. Cotter pin
26. Lower sleeve

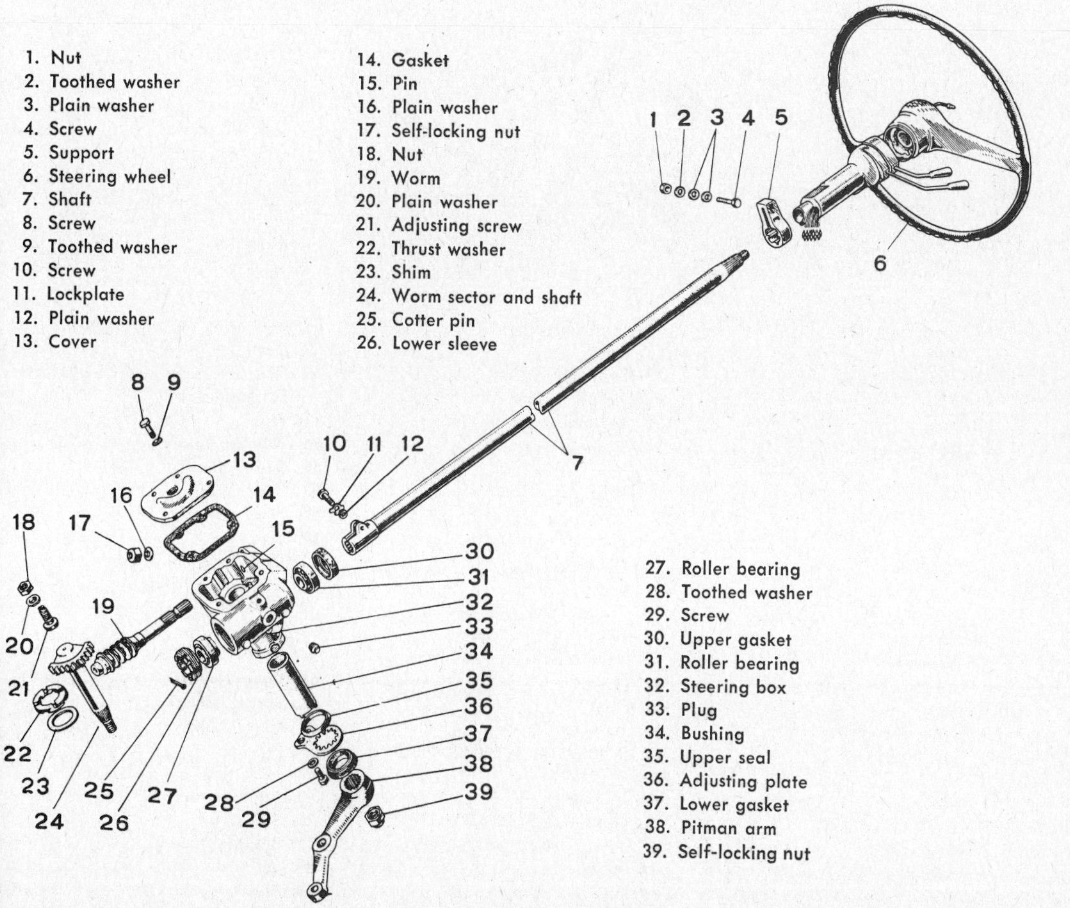

27. Roller bearing
28. Toothed washer
29. Screw
30. Upper gasket
31. Roller bearing
32. Steering box
33. Plug
34. Bushing
35. Upper seal
36. Adjusting plate
37. Lower gasket
38. Pitman arm
39. Self-locking nut

Exploded view of 600 Sedan steering gear components

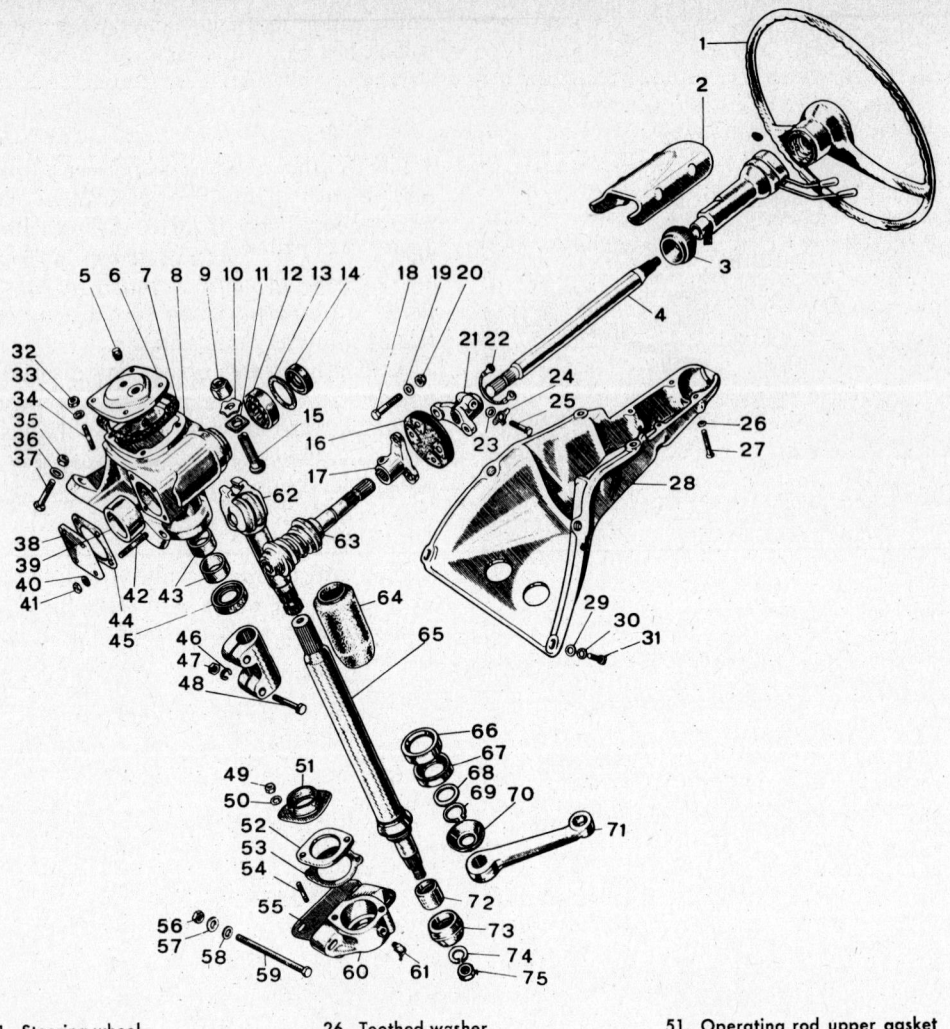

1. Steering wheel
2. Cover
3. Rubber bushing
4. Shaft
5. Plug
6. Upper cover
7. Gasket
8. Box
9. Nut
10. Lockplate
11. Lockplate
12. Rear roller bearing
13. Shim
14. Gasket
15. Adjusing screw
16. Flexible joint plate
17. Sleeve
18. Screw
19. Plain washer
20. Self-locking nut
21. Sleeve
22. Horn ground cable
23. Plain washer
24. Lockplate
25. Locking screw

26. Toothed washer
27. Screw
28. Support
29. Plain washer
30. Toothed washer
31. Screw
32. Nut
33. Toothed washer
34. Stud
35. Self-locking nut
36. Plain washer
37. Screw
38. Front cover
39. Front roller bearing
40. Toothed washer
41. Nut
42. Stud
43. Bushing
44. Shim (thickness .0039''-.0059'';
    0.10-0.15 mm)
45. Gasket
46. Spring washer
47. Nut
48. Screw
49. Nut
50. Toothed washer

51. Operating rod upper gasket
52. Cover
53. Shim (thickness .0039''-.0059'';
    0.10-0.15 mm)
54. Stud
55. Adjusting plate
56. Self-locking nut
57. Plain washer
58. Plain washer
59. Screw
60. Operating rod support
61. Lubrication fitting
62. Roller shaft assembly
63. Worm shaft
64. Boot
65. Operating rod
66. Socket halves
67. Socket halves
68. Washer
69. Snap-ring
70. Lower gasket
71. Pitman arm
72. Bushing
73. Joint
74. Spring washer
75. Nut

Exploded view of 600 Multipla steering gear components

screw which retains the shim. Turn the eccentric bushing, through the shim, to move the sector toward the worm. Bushing rotation should allow subsequent insertion of retaining screws in the shim. Should the shim screws already be in the last hole, move the shim one serration on, then secure. If too much play exists at the worm bearings, turn the lower adjuster nut, locking it in place after adjustment. Use a cotter pin to lock the nut. The sector and worm teeth should mesh perfectly. Add or remove shims to move the sector as required. These shims, under the thrust washer are available in .0039" thickness. Replace any seal which is damaged.

600 (SEDAN)

Removal

Remove the horn button, disconnect the horn and remove the steering wheel. Inside the car, remove the steering shaft to worm screw mounting nut. Jack the front of the car and disconnect the steering arms at the pitman arm. Remove the battery to gain access to the upper steering box mounting nut. Disengage the worm from the steering column and remove the steering box.

Assembly

Assembly and disassembly procedures for the 600 steering gear are the same as for the 850 steering gear.

600 MULTIPLA

The 600 Multipla steering gear is of the worm screw and roller type.

124 Sport Series (1971) and 850 Sport Series (1971)

These models are equipped with a collapsible steering column, consisting of three sections, coupled by two universal joints. *NOTE: When installing this steering column on a car, it is necessary to twist the heads off the stretchbolts.*

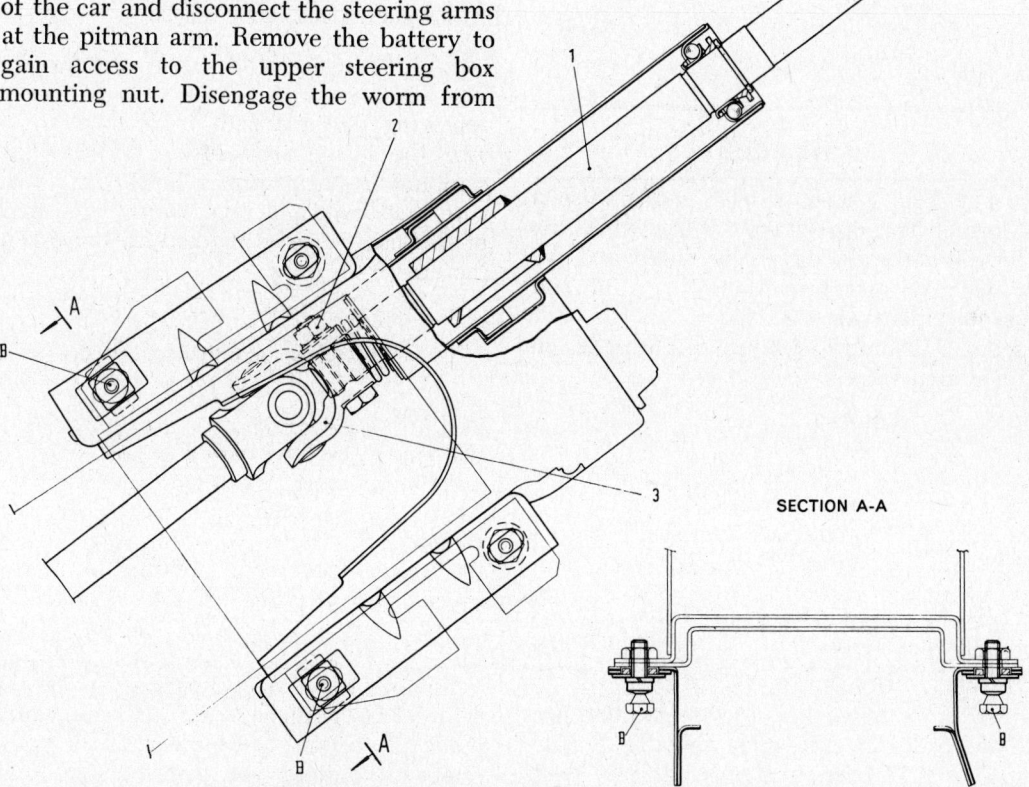

SECTION A-A

1. Steering column upper section
2. Screw, fork to steering column upper section
3. Fork
B. Screws, steering column support to body (to be tightened until screw heads are twisted off).

Schematic view of 124 Sport series (1970-71) collapsible steering column

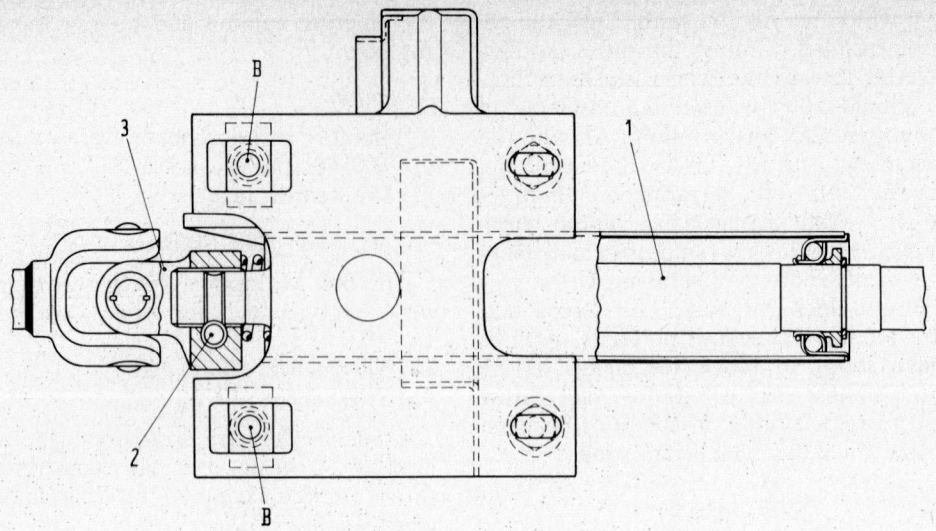

B

3

1

2

B

1. Steering column upper section
2. Attaching screw, yoke to steering column upper section
3. Yoke
B. Attaching screws steering column support to body (upon installation tighten screws until screw heads are twisted off).

Schematic view of 850 Sports series (1970-71) collapsible steering column

Brakes

The Fiat 124 and 1600S models use a fourth wheel disc brake system, while the 850 Spider and Coupe, the 1100R and the 1500 have disc brakes on the front and drum brakes on the rear. The 600, 850 sedan, 1100 and 1100D use drum brakes on on all four wheels.

124 and 1600S

All four disc brakes are self-adjusting and rear brakes are equipped with a regulator, operated by a torsion bar for proper rear wheel trim during braking.

A vacuum servo (power brake) system acts on all four wheels to lessen the required pedal pressure. Maximum runout for brake discs is .006″ (.15 mm.). To correct for excessive runout, machine the disc. Thickness, however, must be at least .374″ (9.5 mm.). Discs showing damage, deep scoring, or wear exceeding .019″ (.5 mm.) on either face must be changed.

Friction pads can be inspected for wear from outside the caliper. If damaged, or worn to .06″ (1.5 mm.) (.12″, or 3 mm. for the 1600S), replacement is necessary. When removing reusable pads mark them to be sure the inside and outside pads are assembled in their proper positions. Make sure that front and rear wheels have pads of the same type as marked by the manufacturer.

MASTER CYLINDER

Removal

Remove the reservoir cover and plug the fluid outlet port. Disconnect the pipe between the reservoir and master clyinder. Remove the three way connection from the master cylinder. Unbolt the master cylinder from the firewall.

Disassembly

Remove the boot from its groove in the cylinder body. Remove the snap-ring which holds the piston. From the cylinder body, remove the following parts: piston, sealing ring, valve ring carrier, valve ring and piston return spring.

Assembly

Inspect the bore of the cylinder and hone any deep irregularities. The honing must

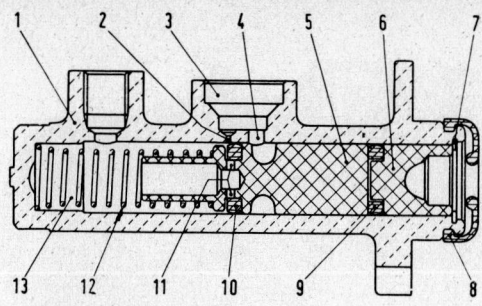

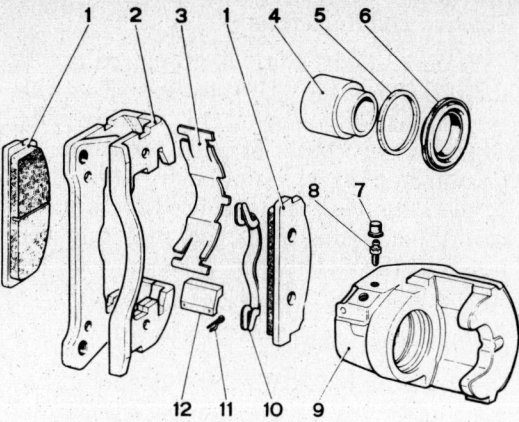

1. Cylinder body
2. Compensating port
3. Seating for union of line from reservoir
4. Feed port
5. Floating valve carrier
6. Piston
7. Snap-ring
8. Rubber boot
9. Sealing ring
10. Floating valve ring
11. Port to allow fluid to pass to compress floating valve sealing ring
12. Piston return spring
13. Pressure chamber

Cross-section of 124 master cylinder

1. Friction pad
2. Caliper bracket
3. Flat radial spring to secure caliper
4. Piston
5. Seal
6. Piston protecting cap
7. Bleed connection protecting cap
8. Bleed connection
9. Caliper body
10. Spring
11. Cotter pin
12. Caliper locking block

Exploded view of 124 front brake caliper and bracket

be slight, otherwise, the bore will be increased, in which case, the cylinder body will have to be replaced. Clean all parts thoroughly in brake fluid.

Assemble the parts, reversing the disassembly order.

Installation

Installation is the reverse of removal. Do not forget to bleed the brake system.

FRONT BRAKES

Caliper Removal

Jack the car and remove the wheels. Plug the outlet port of the brake fluid reservoir. Disconnect the brake hose from the caliper by unscrewing the junction. Remove the cotter pins, which hold the locking blocks in place and remove the locking blocks. Remove the caliper flat springs, friction pads and springs. Without removing the brake disc from the car, check the brake disc runout. If there are any deep score marks on the disc, be sure these do not exceed .019″. Past this dimension, discs must be replaced.

Caliper Disassembly

Remove the dust boot. Direct a jet of air into the fluid inlet coupling to remove the piston from the caliper cylinder. Remove the seal. *NOTE: When pistons are*

1. Brake disc
2. Friction pad locking spring
3. Caliper support bracket
4. Friction pad

Removing disc brake pads on Fiat 124

removed piston seals must always be changed. Wash all parts in hot water and dry with compressed air.

Friction Pad Replacement

Friction pads must be replaced when their thickness is .059″ or less. The caliper must be removed to change pads. There are two types of pads, identified by an orange or black paint stripe. Only pads of the same class may be used on any one car. When fitting pads, be sure that the inner distance between pads is not less than .413″.

Caliper Assembly

Fit the piston seal to the caliper cylinder. Insert the piston and push it to the far end of the cylinder. Fit the dust boot, making sure that the lip enters the under-cut in the caliper body.

Caliper Installation

Fit the spring and friction pads to the caliper bracket. Install the flat spring and

1. Caliper body
2. Bleed connection
3. Gaiter
4. Handbrake cam lever
5. Handbrake cable anchorage
6. Piston protection boot
7. Piston
A. Reference mark
B. Slot engaging friction pad rib

Fiat 124 rear brake caliper

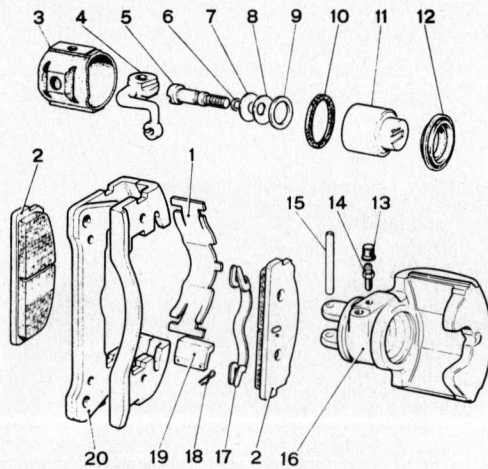

1. Flat radial spring securing caliper
2. Friction pad
3. Boot over handbrake lever end
4. Handbrake cam lever
5. Self-adjusting pin
6. Pin sealing ring
7. Disc spring
8. Disc spring
9. Disc spring thrust washer
10. Piston seal
11. Piston complete with self-adjusting device
12. Piston protection cap
13. Cap for bleed connection
14. Bleed connection
15. Handbrake cam lever pivot pin
16. Caliper body
17. Spring
18. Cotter pin
19. Caliper locking block
20. Caliper bracket

Exploded view of 124 rear brake caliper and bracket

caliper to the caliper bracket. Insert the locking blocks to retain the caliper. Replace the cotter pins. Connect the brake hose to the caliper and tighten the connection. Unplug the brake fluid reservoir and fill the reservoir. Bleed the brakes.

REAR BRAKES

Caliper Removal

Rear caliper removal is the same as front caliper removal.

Caliper Disassembly

Remove the dust boot and unscrew the piston from the handbrake plunger. To do this use a screwdriver in the slot in the head of the piston. Remove the seal and the handbrake gaiter. Remove the pivot pin on which the cam lever turns and remove the lever along with the plunger seal, disc spring and spring thrust washer. *NOTE: When the pistons are removed from the caliper, the piston seals must always be changed.*

Caliper Assembly

Fit the self-adjusting plunger with seal, spring and thrust washer. Install the handbrake cam lever and fit the pivot pin in the fork of the caliper body. Fit the handbrake lever gaiter. Replace the rubber piston seal in the caliper body. Screw in the piston until it is properly seated and the mark cut in the piston is opposite the bleed connection.

Friction Pad Replacement

This operation is identical to pad replacement of front brakes.

Caliper Installation

Follow the procedure for front brake caliper installation. Connect the handbrake cable to the cam lever.

Power Brake Booster (124)

Fiat 124's are fitted with a power brake booster operating on all four wheels. It utilizes depression in intake manifold vacuum to increase the normal brake pedal pressure exerted by the driver.

Rear Brake Pressure Regulator

Installation

Before connecting it into the brake line, attach brake regulator to its bracket with two screws (A and B), but do not tighten them until a later adjustment is made. Attach torsion bar (D) to body with bracket (E). Locate end of torsion bar (D') at a distance (X) of 5.78″ (5.0″ for the station wagon) from the underside of the body, then lift boot (C) and rotate the regulator on screw (A) until the opposite end of the bar (D') lightly contacts piston (F) projecting from the regulator. Holding the regulator in this position, tighten screws A and B, coat the area of the bar that contacts the piston and pin (I) with grease, and place boot (C) in position.

Attach link (G) to end (D') of torsion bar and to the lug on the axle housing. Complete assembly by connecting brake

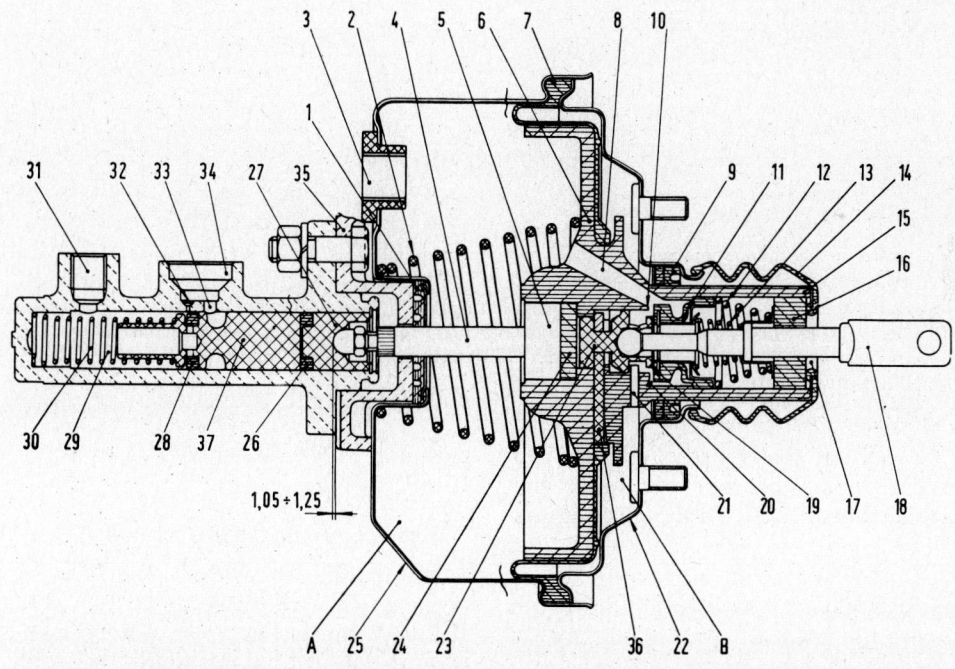

Components of power brake system, 124. (1) front seal; (2) piston return spring; (3) vacuum line union; (4) piston rod; (5) working piston; (6) actuating piston; (7) diaphragm; (8) vacuum duct; (9) rear seal; (10) vacuum port; (11) valve; (12) piston-valve return spring; (13) retaining valve return spring; (14) guide tube rubber boot; (15) actuating piston guide tube; (16) filter element; (17) servo unit air intake; (18) valve control rod; (19) atmospheric pressure passage; (20) vacuum hole; (21) vacuum and air passage; (22) rear body; (23) piston-valve; (24) reaction disc; (25) front body; (26) seal ring; (27) hydraulic piston; (28) floating ring-valve; (29) master cylinder; (30) hydraulic piston return spring; (31) union for connection to 3-way brake distributor; (32) compensating hole; (33) master cylinder inlet port; (34) union for line from reservoir to master cylinder; (35) mounting flange; (36) piston retaining plate; (37) floating ring-valve carrier; (A) front chamber; (B) rear chamber.

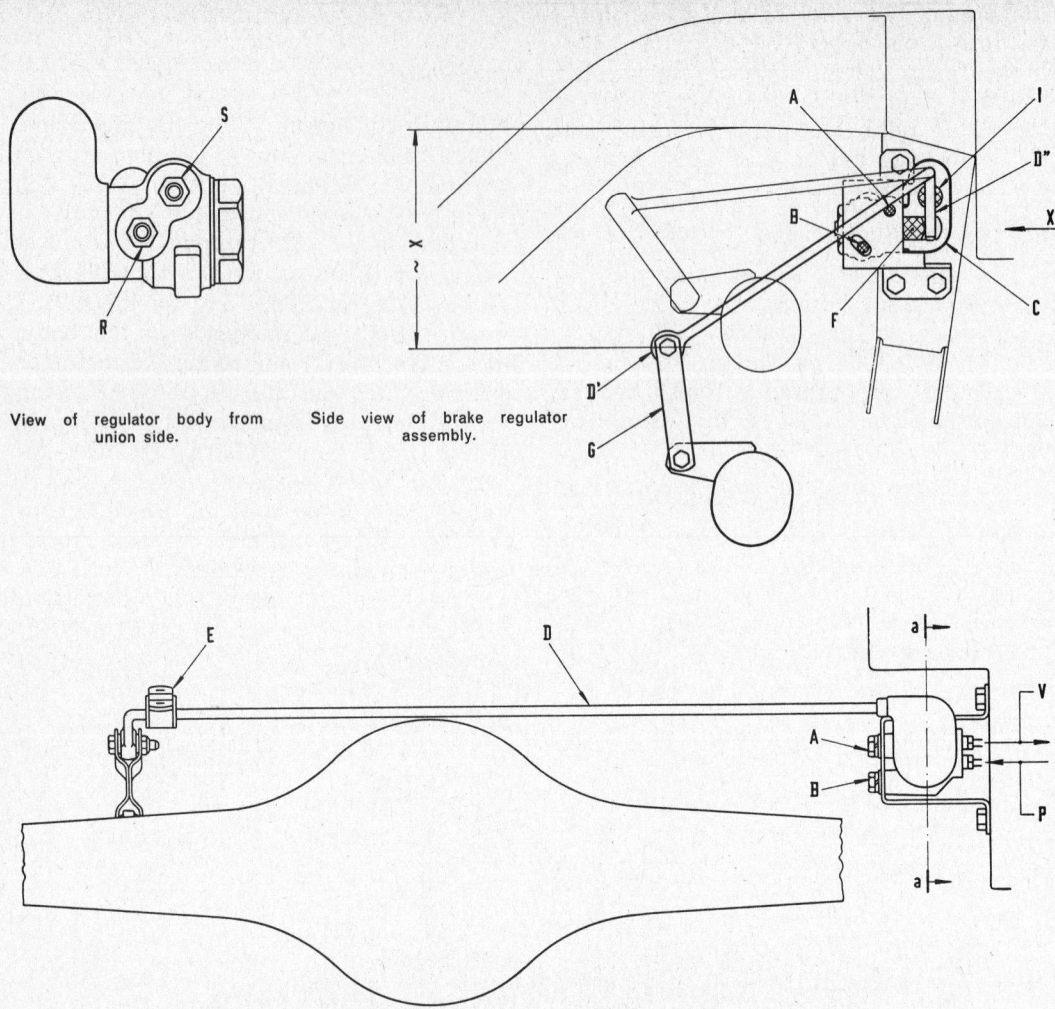

View of regulator body from
union side.

Side view of brake regulator
assembly.

Assembly and adjustment of rear brake regulator, 124. (A and B) regulator mounting screws;
(C) boot; (D, D', D'') torsion bar; (E) torsion bar body mounting; (F) piston; (G) link to bracket
on axle; (I) pin; (P) line to master cylinder; (R) union for line from master cylinder; (S) union
for line to rear brakes; (V) line to rear brakes.

line (P) from the master cylinder to lower union (R) of regulator, and line (V) which feeds the rear calipers to upper union (S).

FRICTION PAD REPLACEMENT (1600S)

These friction pads can be replaced without removing the calipers. Jack the car and remove the wheel. Replace the lining pads if worn below .1181". Remove the fasteners and slide off the retaining pins. Remove the plates which carry the lining pads. Push the pistons into the cylinder bores. Insert the plates with a new set of lining pads and install the retaining pins, cotter pins and fasteners. Reset the pistons before driving, by pumping the brake pedal until solid resistance is felt.

HANDBRAKE ADJUSTMENT

Using the lever, disengage the handbrake cable. Pull the lever up two notches. Unscrew the locknut on the tensioner and turn the adjusting nut until the cable is stretched. Tighten the locknut. The cable is correctly tensioned when the car is held by a movement of the lever through three notches.

850 Spyder and Coupe, Sport Spyder and Sport Coupe, 1100R and 1500

These cars employ disc brakes at the front and drum brakes at the rear. The

1. Shield
2. Disc
3. Wheel hub
4. Caliper
5. Plates with lining pads
6. Pad spring retainers
7. Brake fluid line to caliper inboard half
8. Bridge pipe, inboard-to-outboard caliper half

1600S left front wheel disc brake assembly

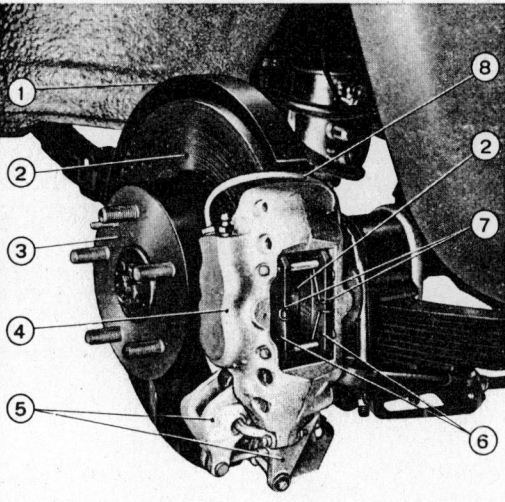

1. Shield
2. Disc
3. Wheel hub
4. Caliper
5. Manual brake mechanism
6. Plate with lining pads
7. Pad spring retainers
8. Bridge pipe, inboard-to-outboard caplier half

1600S left rear wheel disc brake assembly

disc brakes require no adjustment, but the friction pads should be replaced when they are worn to a thickness of .08" (2 mm.) for the 850 and 1100R, and .12" (3 mm.) for the 1500.

MASTER CYLINDER

The master cylinder removal and disassembly does not present any difficulties. Basically, the procedures outlined for the 124 Fiat are applicable.

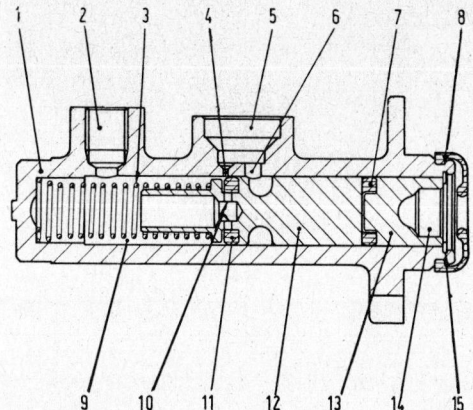

1. Body
2. Brake delivery line T-fitting seat
3. Piston return spring
4. Transfer port
5. Reservoir hollow screw seat
6. Master cylinder fluid intake port
7. Seal ring
8. Rubber boot
9. Fluid compression chamber
10. Floating valve ring fluid passage ports
11. Foating and sealing valve ring
12. Valve ring carrier
13. Piston
14. Pushrod seat
15. Snap-ring

Cross-sectional view of 1600S master cylinder

1. Brake caliper
2. Lining pads
3. Fluid hose
4. Caliper mounting bracket
5. Brake disc
6. Caliper U-bolts

Replacing 1100R brake pads

Disc brake assembly, 1500. (1) shield; (2) fluid line connecting caliper halves; (3) friction lining pad and plate assemblies; (4) fasteners; (5) inboard caliper half; (6) brake disc; (7) outboard caliper half; (8) wheel hub; (9) bleeder screw.

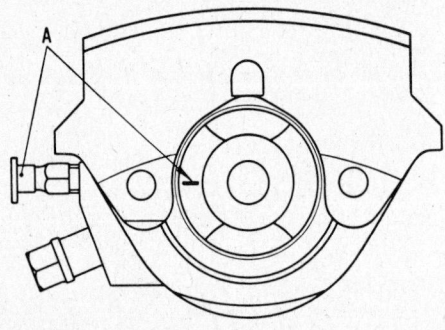

850 disc brake caliper diagram—Mark (A) is to be aligned toward the bleeder screw

FRONT BRAKES

Pad Replacement

Remove the caliper from the mounting brackets. Remove the retaining plates and slide off the pins. Tip the clamps to remove the caliper from the bracket. Replace the pads and push the piston to the bottom of the cylinder. Make sure that the mark on the piston faces the bleeder screw. Replace the caliper.

Brake Calipers

The only service which can be performed to brake calipers is the renewal of seals and pistons. To remove pistons from front calipers, remove the nut and depress the pin at the end. Replace calipers and bleed brakes.

REAR BRAKES

Drum Inspection

Jack the car and remove the rear wheels. Remove the brake drums. Check for scoring or out-of-round.

600, 1100/D and 850 Sedan

The shoes of these drum brakes are self-centering and no manual adjustments are needed to center the shoes with respect to the drum.

To adjust brakes, apply full pedal to center the shoes, then, with the pedal depressed, turn the adjustment cams to full stop. While keeping pedal down, turn cams backward a fraction of a turn at a time until wheel rotates freely with pedal released. If any brake lines have been disconnected, or the pedal operation is spongy, bleed the brake system.

MASTER CYLINDER

Disassembly

Remove the master cylinder from the car. Remove the rubber boot from its retaining flange and take out the rod. Remove the boot retaining flange, two gaskets and the plunger stop plate. Remove the following from the master cylinder body: plunger, valve, valve ring carrier, valve ring and return spring.

Assembly

Assembly is the reverse of disassembly.

WHEEL CYLINDERS

Disassembly

Jack the car and remove the wheels and brake drums. Unfasten and remove the rubber boots. The plungers, valve rings and cups on the ends of the reaction spring will be pushed out by the expansion of the spring.

Assembly

Assembly is the reverse of disassembly. Valve rings should be renewed and all parts lubricated before assembly.

BRAKE DRUMS

Inspect drums for scoring or an out-of-

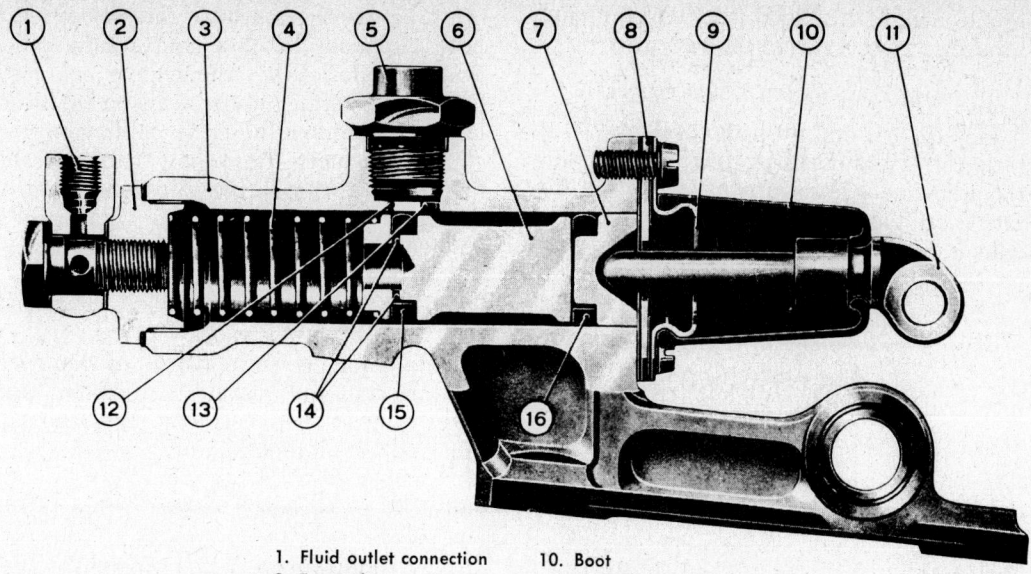

1. Fluid outlet connection
2. Front plug
3. Body
4. Plunger return spring
5. Fluid intake connection
6. Valve carrier
7. Plunger
8. Stop plate
9. Boot retaining flange
10. Boot
11. Pushrod
12. Compensating hole
13. Fluid intake hole
14. Valve ring compression holes
15. Valve ring
16. Valve ring

Cutaway view of 1100 master cylinder

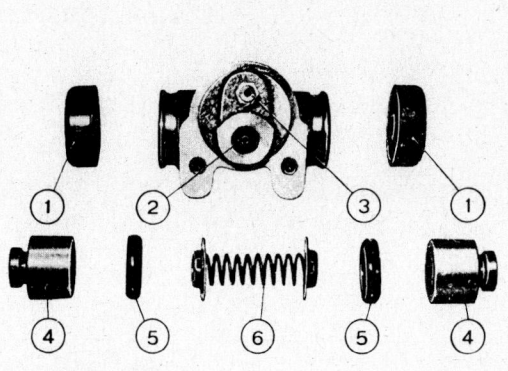

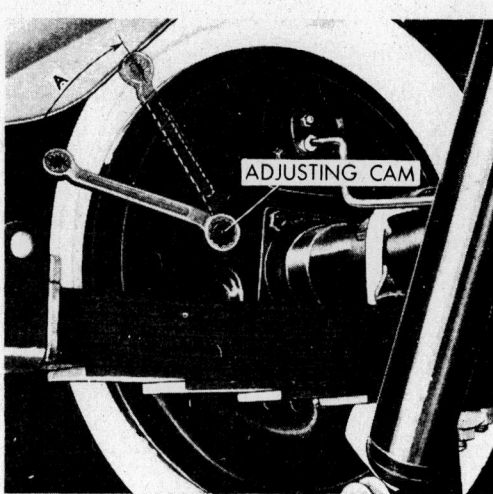

A—Adjusting cam nut angle. It must be: 20° for used linings and 25° for new linings.

Brake shoe clearance adjustment

1. Rubber boots
2. Fluid intake connection
3. Bleeder screw
4. Plunger
5. Valve rings
6. Plunger spring and cups

Exploded view of wheel cylinder components

round condition. Bleed the brake system following any service to the system.

SHOE CLEARANCE ADJUSTMENT

Jack the car and push the brake pedal to lock the shoes against the drum. Rotate the adjustment nuts outward (to stop). Rotate them back about 20° and be sure the wheels turn freely.

Accessories

124

WINDSHIELD WIPER MOTOR

Removal

The windshield wiper motor is removed from the engine compartment side in the following manner.

Unscrew the left-hand spacer nut and remove the left-hand wiper blade and arm. Remove the retaining nuts from the bracket and pull the motor back slightly. Remove the clip connecting the right half-link to the motor and remove the motor.

Installation

Installation is the reverse of removal.

HEATER

Removal

Drain the engine cooling system and the heater radiator. The lower heater lever must be moved to the right. Loosen the hose clips on the flow and return pipes to the heater. From the engine compartment, remove the rubber seals on the heater pipes. Remove the valve cable from the clip. Disconnect the yellow cable to the fan. Release the spring clips and remove the fan housing. Lower the radiator and remove the air intake shutter control cable. Remove the heater from the car.

Installation

Installation is the reverse of removal. Be sure that the gasket between fan and body is positioned correctly. Run the engine and top off the radiator.

850

WINDSHIELD WIPER MOTOR

Removal

Remove the instrument cluster. Remove the lockrings of the control switches and ornamental plate. Remove the instrument panel lining which is fastened with tight clips. The wiper assembly can be removed through the opening in the instrument panel.

Installation

Installation is the reverse of removal.

MERCEDES-BENZ SECTION

Index

453

190, 190Dc Sedans

220b, 220Sb, 220SEb Sedans

220SEb/C Convt. (coupe similar)

300SL, 300SEL Sedans (to 1965)

230SL, 250SL Sports Cars

300SEb, 300SEL Sedans (1966 up)

200, 200D Sedans

230/8 Sedans

220D/8, 220/8 Sedans

250/8 Sedan

280SL/8 Sports Car

250/8 Coupe

300SEL/8 6.3 Sedan

280S/8, 280SE/8, 280SEL/8, 300SE/8, 300SEL/8 Sedans

250SE Convt. (coupe similar)

300SE Coupe (convt. similar)

230S Sedan

230 Sedan

Introduction

All models imported into the United States from about 1964 are covered, with the exception of the type 600. It is recognized that few if any 600 owners are interested in doing their own work and that the Mercedes-Benz dealer can provide the best service for this model. In general, however, the engine and transmission used in the 300 SEL/8 6.3 is identical to that used in the 600, with minor modifications for this application.

Identification

Type plate

 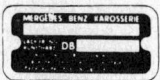 

Chassis number   Body and paint   Engine number

Identification plates.

Since the Mercedes-Benz design is in continuous development and evolution, the newest developments are put into production as soon as they become available. Therefore, while it is true that arbitrary cut-off chassis numbers are chosen each

year to designate the onset of the "new" model year, it does not necessarily mean that a 1968 car is radically different from a 1969 model. Especially, it does not mean that an "old" 1968 is now obsolete.

All this is great for the owner, but it presents a problem when ordering parts. The solution is found in the comprehensive Daimler-Benz identification plates, found in various places, but usually under the hood and on the door posts. Consulting the illustration pertaining to your model (220, 230 S, etc.), find the locations of the chassis number plate, type plate and engine plate. With these numbers, plus the engine and other subsystem serial numbers, one is armed with all the information he needs to identify his car.

When ordering parts, it is necessary to give the complete chassis number, plus the numbers of the concerned area. For example, when ordering pistons or a distributor cap you must give the engine number as well as chassis number. If you are ordering front suspension components, give the front axle number. Identification of the various subsystems is covered in their respective chapters, excepting engine identification.

The model/engine identification chart gives a picture of the model/engine/chassis combinations that have been imported to the United States since about 1964. Some models were in production much earlier and are included because of popularity.

All models that are now out of production, as well as current models, are shown in the next chart, along with their starting and ending chassis numbers. This is especially useful where the same designation has been carried over to a different vehicle.

1. Type plate
2. Chassis number plate
3. Body and paint number plate
4. Engine number plate

Identification plate location—sedans.

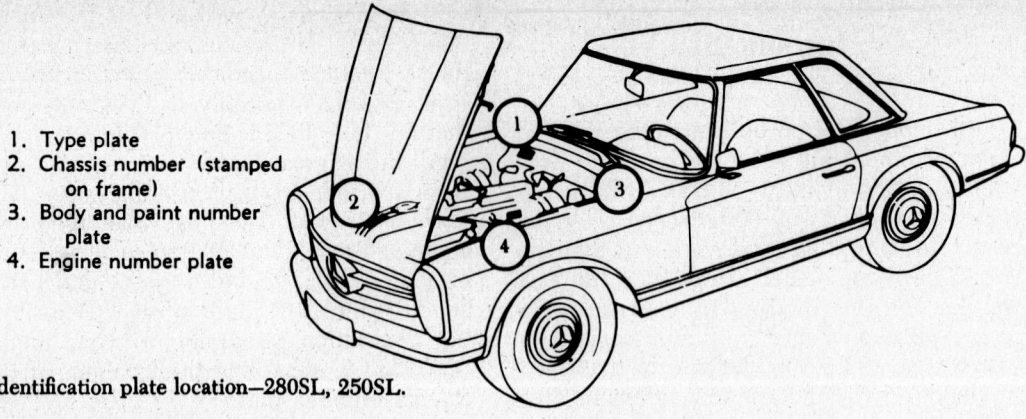

1. Type plate
2. Chassis number (stamped on frame)
3. Body and paint number plate
4. Engine number plate

Identification plate location—280SL, 250SL.

1. Type plate
2. Chassis number
3. Body and paint number plate
4. Engine number plate

Identification plate location—230SL.

An example of this is the 230. While the 230 is now out of production and the 230/8 has taken its place, the two have the same designation on the trunk lid. (The "/8" does not appear.) The chassis number immediately indicates whether you have a "new" 230, although the more modern styling should be a clue.

It should be noted that the center number (10 or 12) in the chassis number indicates the type transmission. A "10" indicates that the car is equipped with a manual transmission, while a "12" indicates an automatic. These numbers, of course, will vary with individual transmission options for individual cars.

On Mercedes-Benz models imported recently into the United States the certification plate has been relocated from the left windshield pillar to the center door pillar.

This change was effected with the following chassis end numbers:

Model	Chassis Type	Chassis End No.
220 D/8	115 110	076 285
220/8	115 010	034 047
230/8	114 015	033 510
250/8	114 010	030 983
280 S/8	108 016	031 250
280 SE/8	108 018	031 833
280 SE/8 Cp./Conv.	111 024/025	003 144
280 SEL/8	108 019	032 041
280 SL/8	113 044	010 704
300 SEL/8	109 016	002 047
300 SEL/8 6.3	109 018	002 390

Model/Engine Identification

Model	Chassis	Engine Model	Engine Type
190c	110.010	M121B.V.	121.924
200	110.010	M121B.XI	121.940
190Dc	110.110	OM621.III	621.912
200D	110.110	OM621.VIII	621.918
230	110.011	M180.VI	180.945
		M180.X①	180.949①
220b	111.010	M180.IV	180.940
220Sb	111.012	M180.V	180.941
230S	111.010	M180.VIII	180.947
250S	108.012	M108.I	108.920
220SEb	111.014	M127.III	127.982
250SE	108.014	M129.I	129.980
230SL	113.042	M127.II	127.981
250SL	113.043	M129.III	129.982
220SEb/C	111.021(coupe)	M127.V	127.984
220SEb/C	111.023(convt.)	M127.V	127.984
250SE/C	111.021(coupe)	M129.I	129.980
250SE/C	111.023(convt.)	M129.I	129.980
300SE	112.014(sedan)	M189.III(1st version)	189.984(1st version)
300SE	112.015(long wb)	M189.V(2nd version)	189.986(2nd version)
300SE②	112.021(coupe)	M189.IV(1st version)	189.985(1st version)
300SE②	112.023(convt.)	M189.VI(2nd version)	189.987(2nd version)
300SEb	108.015	M189.VIII	189.989
300SEL	109.015	M189.VII	189.988
300SE③	112.021(coupe)	M189.VI	189.987
300SE③	112.023(convt.)	M189.VI	189.987
220D/8	115.110	OM615	615.912
220/8	115.010	M115	115.920
230/8⑤	114.015	M180	180.954
250/8⑥	114.010	M114	114.920
280S/8	108.016	M130	130.920
280SE/8	108.018(sedan)	M130	130.980
280SE/8④	108.019(long wb)	M130	130.980
280SE/8	111.024(coupe)	M130	130.980
280SE/8	111.025(convt.)	M130	130.980
280SL/8	113.044	M130	130.983
300SEL/8 2.8	109.016	M130	130.981
300SEL/8 6.3	109.018	M100	100.981

①   *INAT carburetors from chassis No. 017649.*
②   *To August, 1965.*
③   *From August, 1965.*
④   *Also known as 280SEL/8*
⑤   *Not imported after August, 1969.*
⑥   *Not imported after 1968.*
wb   *wheelbase*
convt.   *convertible*

Out of Production Models

Model	Starting Serial No.	Ending Serial No.
190c	110.010—10—000001	110.010—10—130557
200	110.010—10—130558	110.010—10—200761
190Dc	110.110—10—000001	110.110—10—225647
200D	110.110—10—225648	110.110—10—387263
230	110.011—10—000001	110.011—10—040258
220b	111.010—10—000001	111.010—10—069692
220Sb	111.012—10—000001	111.012—10—161126
230S	111.010—10—069693	111.010—10—110798
250S	108.012—10—000001	④
220SEb	111.014—10—000001	111.014—10—082687
250SE	108.014—10—000001	108.014—10—055181
230SL	113.042—10—000001	113.042—10—019832
250SL	113.043—10—000001	113.043—10—005196
220SEb/C (coupe)	111.021—10—000001	111.021—10—082990
220SEb/C (convt.)	111.023—10—000001	111.023—10—082990
250SE/C (coupe)	111.021—10—082991	111.021—10—089205
250SE/C (convt.)	111.023—10—082991	111.023—10—089205
300SE (sedan)	112.014—10—000001	112.014—10—005137
300SE (long wb)	112.015—10—000001	112.015—10—005137
300SE (coupe)①	112.021—10—000001	112.021—10—005137
300SE (convt.)①	112.023—10—000001	112.023—10—005137
300SEb	108.015—10—000001	108.015—10—002737
300SEL	109.015—10—000001	109.015—10—002369
300SE (coupe)②	112.021—10—005138	112.021—10—009875
300SE (convt.)②	112.023—10—005138	112.023—10—009875

Current Models

Model	Starting Serial No.	Ending Serial No.
220D/8	115.110—10—000001	
220/8	115.010—10—000001	
230/8	114.015—10—000001	⑤
250/8	114.010—10—000001	
280S/8	108.016—10—000001	
280SE/8 (sedan)	108.018—10—000001	
280SE/8 (long wb)③	108.019—10—000001	
280SE/8 (coupe)	111.024—10—000001	
280SE/8 (convt.)	111.025—10—000001	
280SL/8	113.044—10—000001	
300SEL/8	109.016—10—000001	
300SEL/8 6.3	109.018—12—000001	

①	*To August, 1965.*
②	*From August, 1965.*
③	*Also known as 280SEL/8.*
④	*Still in production, but not imported after 1968.*
⑤	*Not imported as of August, 1969.*
wb	*wheelbase*
convt.	*convertible*

General Engine Specifications

Engine Model	Engine Type	Bore and Stroke (mm.)	Displace. (cc.)	Compress. Ratio	Firing Order	Number Cylinders	Horsepower @ rpm (SAE)	Torque @ rpm (ft. lbs.)	Max. rpm	Number Main Bearings
M121B.V	121.924	85.00x83.60	1,897	8.7:1	1-3-4-2	4	90 @ 5,200	113 @ 2,700	6,000	3
M121B.XI	121.940	87.00x83.60	1,988	9.0:1	1-3-4-2	4	105 @ 5,200	113 @ 3,600	6,000	5
M180.VI	180.945	82.00x72.80	2,306	9.0:1	1-5-3-6-2-4	6	118 @ 5,400	137 @ 3,800	6,000	4
M180.X ①	180.949	82.00x72.80	2,306	9.0:1	1-5-3-6-2-4	6	135 @ 5,600	145 @ 4,200	6,000	4
M180.IV	180.940	80.00x72.80	2,195	8.7:1	1-5-3-6-2-4	6	105 @ 5,000	133 @ 3,300	6,000	4
M180.V	180.941	80.00x72.80	2,195	8.7:1	1-5-3-6-2-4	6	124 @ 5,200	139 @ 3,700	6,000	4
M180.VIII	180.947	82.00x72.80	2,306	9.0:1	1-5-3-6-2-4	6	135 @ 5,600	145 @ 4,200	6,000	4
M108.I	108.920	82.00x78.80	2,496	9.0:1	1-5-3-6-2-4	6	146 @ 5,600	157 @ 4,200	6,300	7
M127.III	127.982	80.00x72.80	2,195	8.7:1	1-5-3-6-2-4	6	134 @ 5,000	152 @ 4,100	6,000	4
M129.I	129.980	82.00x78.80	2,496	9.5:1	1-5-3-6-2-4	6	170 @ 5,600	174 @ 4,500	6,300	7
② M129.I	129.980	82.00x78.80	2,496	9.5:1	1-5-3-6-2-4	6	170 @ 5,600	174 @ 4,500	6,300	7
M127.II	127.981	82.00x72.80	2,306	9.5:1	1-5-3-6-2-4	6	170 @ 5,600	159 @ 4,500	6,500	4
M129.III	129.982	82.00x78.80	2,496	9.5:1	1-5-3-6-2-4	6	170 @ 5,600	174 @ 4,500	6,500	7
C ② M127.V	127.984	80.00x72.80	2,195	8.7:1	1-5-3-6-2-4	6	134 @ 5,000	152 @ 4,100	6,000	4
M189.III ③	189.984	85.00x88.00	2,996	8.7:1	1-5-3-6-2-4	6	185 @ 5,200	204 @ 4,000	6,000	7
M189.V ③	189.986	85.00x88.00	2,996	8.8:1	1-5-3-6-2-4	6	195 @ 5,500	203 @ 4,100	6,000	7
M189.IV ③	189.985	85.00x88.00	2,996	8.7:1	1-5-3-6-2-4	6	185 @ 5,200	204 @ 4,000	6,000	7
⑥ M189.VI ⑤	189.987	85.00x88.00	2,996	8.8:1	1-5-3-6-2-4	6	195 @ 5,500	203 @ 4,100	6,000	7
M189.VIII	189.989	85.00x88.00	2,996	8.8:1	1-5-3-6-2-4	6	195 @ 5,500	203 @ 4,100	6,000	7
M189.VII	189.988	85.00x88.00	2,996	8.8:1	1-5-3-6-2-4	6	195 @ 5,500	203 @ 4,100	6,000	7
M115	115.920	87.00x92.40	2,197	9.0:1	1-3-4-2	4	116 @ 5,200	142 @ 3,000	6,000	5
M180	180.954	81.75x72.80	2,292	9.0:1	1-5-3-6-2-4	6	135 @ 5,600	145 @ 3,800	6,300	4
M114	114.920	82.00x78.80	2,496	9.0:1	1-5-3-6-2-4	6	146 @ 5,600	161 @ 3,800	6,300	7
M130	130.920	86.50x78.80	2,778	9.0:1	1-5-3-6-2-4	6	157 @ 5,400	181 @ 3,800	6,500	7
⑩ M130	130.980	86.50x78.80	2,778	9.5:1	1-5-3-6-2-4	6	180 @ 5,750	193 @ 4,500	6,500	7
M130	130.983	86.50x78.80	2,778	9.5:1	1-5-3-6-2-4	6	180 @ 5,750	193 @ 4,500	6,500	7
M130	130.981	86.50x78.80	2,778	9.5:1	1-5-3-6-2-4	6	180 @ 5,750	193 @ 4,500	6,500	7
6.3 M100	100.981	103.00x95.00	6,332	9.0:1	1-5-4-8-6-3-7-2	8	300 @ 4,100	434 @ 3,000	5,250	5

carburetors from chassis No. 110,011-10-017649.
e and convertible.
ersion.
wheelbase.
d version.

⑥ Coupe to August, 1965.
⑦ Convertible to August, 1965.
⑧ From August, 1965. (Same engine as previous second version 300SE convertible)
⑨ Not imported as of August, 1969.
⑩ Sedan, coupe, convertible and long wheelbase (280SEL/8).

NOTE: 250C (coupe) uses 280S/8 carbureted engine.

General Diesel Engine Specifications

Model	Engine Model	Engine Type	Bore & Stroke (mm.)	Displace. (cc.)	Compress. Ratio	Firing Order	No. of Cyl.	H.P. @ rpm (SAE)	Torque & rpm (ft. lbs.)	Number Main Bear.
190Dc	OM621.III	621.912	87 x 83.6	1,988	21:1	1-3-4-2	4	60 @ 4,200	87 @ 2,400	3
200D	OM621.VIII	621.918	87 x 83.6	1,988	21:1	1-3-4-2	4	60 @ 4,200	87 @ 2,400	5
220D/8	OM615	615.912	87 x 92.4	2,197	21:1	1-3-4-2	4	65 @ 4,200	96 @ 2,400	5

Tune-up Specifications

Model	Engine Type	Spark Plugs ▲	Plug Gap (in.)	Point Gap (in.)	Point Dwell (deg.)	Valve Clearance (in.) Intake	Valve Clearance (in.) Exhaust	Valve Timing (deg.) Intake Opens *	Ignition Timing (deg.) **	Idle Speed Manual Transmission N	Idle Speed Automatic Transmission N	Idle Speed Automatic Transmission D	Cranking Compression Pressure (psi) Normal Range
190c	121.924	L87Y	.020	.016-.020	48-52	.003	.006	10 B	48	800-850	850-950	600 ⑨	139-154
200	121.940	N6Y	.023	.016-.020	48-52	.003	.007	11 B	43	800-850	850-950	600 ⑨	147-162
230	180.945 180.949 ①	N6Y	.023	.016-.020	37-41	.003	.007	11 B	37	750-800	800-850	550 ⑨	147-162
220b	180.940	N6Y	.023	.012-.016	37-41	.003	.006	10 B	35	750-800	800-850	550 ⑨	147-162
220Sb	180.941	N6Y	.023	.012-.016	37-41	.003	.006	10 B	35	750-800	800-850	550 ⑨	147-162
230S	180.947	N6Y	.023	.012-.016	37-41	.003	.007	11 B	37	750-800	800-850	550 ⑨	147-162
250S	108.920	N6Y	.023	.012-.016	37-41	.003	.007	11 B	37	750-800	800-850	550 ⑨	147-162
220SEb	127.982	N6Y	.023	.012-.016	37-41	.003	.006	10 B	28	750-800	750-800	600 ⑨	147-162
250SE	129.980	N6Y	.020	.012-.016	37-41	.003	.007	11 B	30	750-800	750-800	750 ⑨	162-177
250SE/c ②	129.980	N6Y	.020	.012-.016	37-41	.003	.007	11 B	30	750-800	750-800	750 ⑨	162-177
230SL	127.981	N6Y	.020	.012-.016	37-41	.003	.007	10 B	30	750-800	750-800	600 ⑨	162-177
250SL	129.982	N6Y	.020	.012-.016	37-41	.003	.007	11 B	30	750-800	750-800	750 ⑨	162-177
220SEb/c ②	127.984	N6Y	.023	.012-.016	37-41	.003	.006	10 B	28	750-800	750-800	600 ⑨	147-162
300SE	189.984	N6Y	.020	.014-.018	47-51	.004	.010	7 B	28	650-700	680-720	600 ⑨	147-162
300SE ④	189.986 ⑤	N6Y	.020	.014-.018	47-51	.004	.008	18 B	28	650-700	680-720	600 ⑨	147-162
300SE ⑩	189.986 ③	N6Y	.020	.014-.018	47-51	.004	.008	18 B	28	650-700	680-720	600 ⑨	147-162
300SE ⑥ 300SE ⑦ ②	189.987 ⑤	N6Y	.020	.014-.018	47-51	.004	.008	18 B	28	650-700	680-720	600 ⑨	147-162
300SEb	189.989	N6Y	.020	.014-.018	47-51	.004	.010	18 B	28	650-700	680-720	600 ⑨	147-162
300SEL	189.988	N6Y	.020	.014-.018	47-51	.004	.010	18 B	28	650-700	680-720	600 ⑨	147-162
220/8	115.920	N6Y	.023	.016-.020	48-52	.003	.007	11 B	43	850-950	850-950	650-700	147-162
230/8	180.954	N6Y	.023	.012-.016	37-41	.003	.007	11 B	37	800-900	800-900	650-700	147-162
250/8	114.920	N6Y	.023	.012-.016	37-41	.003	.007	11 B	37	800-900	800-900	650-700	147-162
280S/8	130.920	N6Y	.023	.012-.016	37-41	.003	.007	11 B	37	800-900	800-900	650-700	147-162
280SE/8 ⑧	130.980	N6Y	.020	.012-.016	37-41	.003	.007	11 B	30	700-800	700	700	162-177
280SL/8	130.983	N6Y	.020	.012-.016	37-41	.003	.007	11 B	30	700-800	700	700	162-177
300SEL/8	130.981	N6Y	.020	.012-.016	37-41	.003	.007	11 B	30	700-800	700	700	162-177
300SEL/8 6.3	100.981	UN12Y	.020	.012-.016	34-38	.004	.010	4B-2A	26 ⑪	550	550	600	147-162

NOTE: On 1970-1971 models with transistor ignition, only a transistorized dwell meter c...

① INAT carburetors.
② Coupe and convertible.
③ First version.
④ Long wheelbase.
⑤ Second version.
⑥ Convt. to Aug., 1965.
⑦ From Aug., 1965; same engine as previous second version 300 SE convt.
⑧ Sedan, coupe, convertible and long wheelbase 280 SEL/8.

⑨ In gear with power steering in lock position.
⑩ Coupe to Aug., 1965.
⑪ At 3,000 rpm.
▲ For normal driving.
* Preload test value of .016". See Chapter 2 for procedure and additional timing values.
** At 4,500 rpm, vacuum line disconnected and plugged. See *Distributor Specifications* Chart.

A After top dead center.
B Before top dead center.
NOTE: On dual-point distributors, check each separately by inserting insulator between each contact set in turn. Dwell values gi... are total both sets.
NOTE: To counteract wearing of fiber contac... block, adjust dwell to lower end of range (wider gap).

CAUTION

General adoption of anti-pollution laws has changed the design of almost all car engine production to effectively reduce crankcase emission and terminal exhaust products. It has been necessary to adopt stricter tune-up rules, especially timing and idle speed procedures. Both of these values are peculiar to the engine and to its application, rather than to the engine alone. With this in mind, car manufacturers supply idle speed data for the engine and application involved. The information is clearly displayed in the engine compartment of each vehicle.

Diesel Tune-up Specifications

Model	Valve clearance ① ② Intake (in.)	Valve clearance ① ② Exhaust (in.)	Intake valve opens (deg.) ⑤	Injection pump setting (deg.)	Injection nozzle pressure (psi) New	Injection nozzle pressure (psi) Used	Idle speed (rpm) ③	Cranking compression pressure (psi)
190Dc	.004④	.016	12.5B	26B	1564–1706	1422–1706	700–800	284–327
200D	.004④	.016	12.5B	26B	1564–1706	1422–1706	700–800	284–327
220D/8	.004④	.016	12.5B	24B	1564–1706	1422–1706	700–800	284–327

B = Before Top Dead Center
① With cold engine.
② With warm engine — intake .008, exhaust .018
③ Manual transmission in neutral, automatic transmission in drive range.
④ In cold weather (below 5°F.), increase to .006 cold.
⑤ See Text for more complete specifications.

Tune-up Values for U.S. Versions with Exhaust Emission Controls*

Model	Point Gap (In.)	Dwell Angle (Deg.)	Dwell Angle (%)	Ignition Timing at Idle Speed	Basic Timing at 4,500 rpm	Ignition Timing at 1,500 rpm	Ignition Timing at 3,000 rpm	Compression Pressure (psi)	Spark Plug Type
200	.016—.020	50 ±2	55 ±3	TDC ±2° B ④	43° B	24—31° B ⑤	31—37° B ⑤	142—156 120 min.	Bosch W215T28 Beru D215/14/3
230, 230S	.012—.016	38 +3 −1	63 +5 −2	TDC ⑤	37° B	19—28° B ⑤	29—35° B ⑤	142—156 120 min.	Bosch W215T28 Beru D215/14/3
250S	.012—.016	38 +3 −2	63 +5 −2	TDC ⑤	37° B	19—28° B ⑤	29—35° B ⑤	142—156 120 min.	Bosch W215T28 Beru D215/14/3
250SE, 250SL	.012—.016	38 +3 −1	63 +5 −2	2A ±2° ④	30° B	12—19° B ⑤	30° B ⑤	156—170 127 min.	Bosch WG235T28 Beru D235/14/3S
220/8	.016—.020	50 ±2		3A +3° ④ −2	43° B			142—156 120 min.	Bosch W200T27 Beru ED200/14/3
230/8	.012—.016	38 +3 −1		TDC ④ ⑤	37° B	19—28° B ④ ⑤	29—35° B ⓒ ⑤	142—156 120 min.	Bosch W200T27 Beru ED200/14/3
250/8	.012—.016	38 +3 −1		TDC ④ ⑤	37° B	19—28°B ④ ⑤	29—35° B ④ ⑤	142—156 120 min.	Bosch W200T27 Beru ED200/14/3
280S/8	.012—.016	38 +3 −2		TDC ⑤	37° B	19—28° B ⑤	29—35° B ⑤	142—156 120 min.	Bosch W200T27 Beru ED200/14/3
280SE/8	.012—.016	38 +3 −1		2A ±2° ④	30° B	12—19° B ⑤	30° B ⑤	156—170 127 min.	Bosch WG215T28 Beru D215/14/3S
280SL/8	.012—.016	38 +3 −1		2A ±2° ④	30° B	12—19° B ⑤	30° B ⑤	156—170 127 min.	Bosch WG215T28 Beru D215/14/3S
300SEL/8	.012—.016	38 +3 −1		2A ±2° ④	30° B	12—19° B ⑤	30° B ⑤	156—170 127 min.	Bosch WG215T28 Beru D215/14/3S
300SEL/8 6.3	.012—.016	36 ±2	60 ±3	2A ±2° ⑤	26° B	13—21° B ⑤	26° B ⑤	156—170 127 min.	W215P21 D215/14/3P

*This chart covers U.S. versions exclusively. If the car is of European origin, for that market, specifications may differ slightly.

① P or N unless otherwise noted.
② Manual or automatic — no accessories operating other than alternator.
③ Adjusted if a 1.0 mm. (.039") ring placed under float needle.
④ With vacuum.
⑤ Without vacuum.

⑥ In 2, 3, 4 or R range only.
A. After top dead center.
B. Before top dead center.
F. Front.
R. Rear

Model	Carburetor Type	CARBURETION Main Jet (No.)	Air Correction Jet (No.)	Idle Fuel Jet (No.)	Idle Air Jet (mm.)	Injection Tube (mm.)	Injection Rate (cc./stroke)	Fuel Level (mm.)	Idle Speed ② in N (rpm)	EXHAUST GAS VALUES (% CO/% SUN) Idle Manual Trans.	Idle Auto Trans. ①
200	Solex 38 PDSI	137.5	80	62.5	1.6	0.5	0.7—1.0	③	850—900	2.0—2.5/82—83	2.0—2.5/82—83
230, 230S	35/40 INAT Zenith	115F 120R	100F 130R	45	1.3		0.7—1.0	21—23	800—850	0.5—1.0/85—86	0.5—1.0/85—86
250S	35/40 INAT Zenith	115F 125R	100F 120R	45	1.3		0.7—1.0	21—23	800—850	0.5—1.0/85—86	0.5—1.0/85—86
250SE, 250SL	Fuel Inj.								700—750	2.5—3.5/80—82	2.5—3.5/80—82
220/8	Solex PDSI 36—40	137.5	80	62.5	1.6	0.5	0.7—1.0	③	850—950	2.0—2.5/82—83	2.0—2.5/82—83 ⑥
230/8	35/40 INAT Zenith	115F 120R	100F 130R	45	1.3		0.7—1.0	21—23	800—900	1.5—3.0/81—84	1.5—3.0/81—84
250/8	35/40 INAT Zenith	115F 125R	100F 120R	45	1.3		0.7—1.0	21—23	800—900	0.5—1.0/85—86	0.5—1.0/85—86
280S/8	35/40 INAT Zenith	115F 125R	90F 110R	45	1.3		0.7—1.0	21—23	800—900	0.5—1.0/85—86	0.5—1.0/85—86
280SE/8	Fuel Inj.								700—800	3.0—4.5/79—81	3.0—4.5/79—81
280SL/8	Fuel Inj.								700—800	3.0—4.5/79—81	3.0—4.5/79—81
300SEL/8	Fuel Inj.								700—800	3.0—4.5/79—81	3.0—4.5/79—81
300SEL/8 6.3	Fuel Inj.								550—600		2.0—3.0/81—83 ⑥

Exhaust Gas Values (Under Load)

Fuel Injected Engines

Model	230SL, 250SE, 250SL, 300SE, 300SEb, 300SEL (with six-cylinder inj. pump)			250SEb, 300SE (with two-cylinder inj. pump)	280SE/8, 280SL/8, 300SEL/8	
Adjustment	Vacuum (mm.Hg./in.Hg.)	Exhaust gas values (% CO/ % SUN)		Exhaust gas values (% SUN)	Vacuum (mm.Hg./in.Hg.)	Exhaust gas values (%CO/ % SUN)
Full load @ 3,000 rpm (third gear) ①		2.0–3.0/81–83		78–80		1.5–2.5/ 82–84
Partial load @ 1,500 rpm (third gear) ②	300/11.8	1.0–2.0/81–85 (230SL— 83–86 SUN)		83–86	300/11.8	0.1–0.5/ not readable
Partial load @ 2,500 rpm (third gear) ③	300/11.8	0.5–1.0/84–87		84–87	300/11.8	0.1–0.5/ not readable
Idle speed (neutral) ④	300–400/11.8–15.7 (six-cyl. pump) 420–480/16.4–18.8 (two-cyl. pump)	2.5–3.5/80–82		79–81	300–400/ 11.8–15.7	3.0–4.5/ 79–81

①   *Adjusted at control rod end.*
②   *Adjusted at black screws.*
③   *Both vacuum and exhaust gas values must be obtained. On two-cylinder injection pump, adjust at white screws.*
            On six-cylinder injection pump, white screws cannot be moved with pump installed; remove pump first.
④   *Check again in Drive range if equipped with automatic transmission.*

Exhaust Gas Values (No Load)

Carbureted Engines

Model	Exhaust gas values (%CO/ % SUN)			
	Idle speed	1,500 rpm	3,000 rpm	4,500 rpm
190c, 200, 220b, 220Sb, 230, 230S, 250S	3.5–4.5/79–81	1.0–4.0/80–85	0.2–0.3/82–87	.05–1.5/84–89

Firing Order

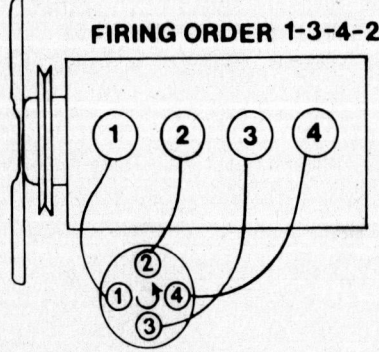

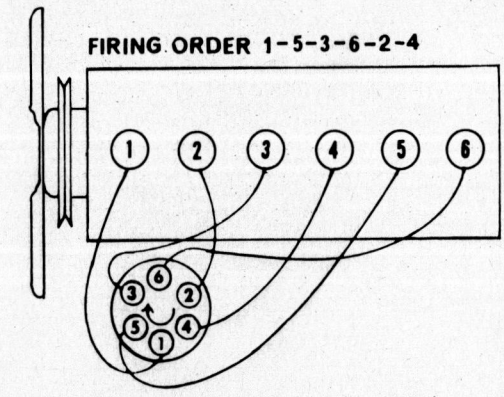

Carburetor Specifications

Model	Carb. Type	Air Horn Ø (mm.)	Main Jet	Air Correct. Jet	Mixing Tube	Emuls. Chamber Vent	Idle Fuel Jet	Idle Air Jet Bore	Enrich. Valve	Accelerator Pump	Inject. Amt. (cc./stroke)	Pump Jet	Inject. Tube	Choke Fuel Jet	Choke Air Bore (mm.)	Float Needle (mm.)	Float Wt. (gm.)	Fuel Level (mm.)	Bypass Bores (mm.)
190c	S 34PICB	28	0145	170	49		50	1.5		No. 72 neutral	1.0–1.2	80	high .5 graded	230⑦	6.5⑤	2.0	5.7	17–19	1.2
200	S 38PDSI	28	137.5	80	N.R.	0.5	62.5④	1.6		neutral	0.7–1.0⑤		high .5 graded		8.5	2.0	8.5	⑥	1.5/1.3
220b	S 34PICB	24	0120	200	44		50	1.0		No. 72 neutral	0.9–1.2	50	high .5 graded	180	4.0	1.5	5.7	17–19	1.25
230	S 38PDSI	26	135	180	N.R.	0.5	50	1.6	90⑦	neutral	1.0–1.3⑤		high .4 graded*			2.0	8.5	⑥	1.5/1.3
220Sb ①①	Front	23	0115⑧	200	44		50	1.4⑨	60⑧	No. 831 neutral	1.3–1.7	80	high .5 graded	90 ⑩	2.0 ⑩	2.0	7.3	19–21	1.2/1.8
	Rear	27	135	190							1.3–1.7								
220Sb ②	Front	23	112.5	100	4S		45	1.5			0.8–1.2		.5 graded			2.0	8.5		18–20
	Rear	27	120	150	4N											2.0	8.5		18–20
230, 230S	Front	24	115	100⑫	4S		45	1.3			0.7–1.0		.5 graded			2.0	8.5		21–23
	Rear	28	120	130	4N											2.0	8.5		21–23
250S	Front	24	120	110	4S		45	1.3			0.7–1.0		.5 graded			2.0	8.5		21–23
	Rear	28	120	120	4N											2.0	8.5		21–23

1 Solex 34PAITA carburetors.
2 Zenith 35/40 INAT carburetors.
3 Up to chassis No. 10–105281 or 12–107377—choke air bore 4.0 and jet 180.
4 Up to chassis No. 161599—idle fuel jet 55, idle air bore 1.0 and bypass bores 1.3/1.0.
5 Automatic transmission front carburetor—0.6–0.9 cc./stroke.
6 Float level O.K. if 1.0 mm. (0.039") seal ring installed under float needle.
7 Up to chassis No. 006122—100.
8 Some models with carburetor No. 4 413 610 had 0112.5 main jet and No. 50 enrichment jet (front carburetor).
9 Up to engine No. 10–068125, 11–004644 and 12–000390—1.5 with bypass bores 1.15/1.15.
10 Up to engine No. 10–031160 and 11–003114— 100 with 3.0 mm. choke air bore.
11 Pump diaphragm bolt length — 18.7–18.9 mm., plate diameter 32 mm. (22 mm. on carburetor No. 4 509 149).
12 Up to chassis No. 019242 (230) and 094927 (230S) — 90.
* Front carburetor, automatic transmission — .5 graded.

NOTE: Carburetor repair kits are of three basic types—repair, Vit, and gasket. The following summarizes the parts in each type:

Vit kits
all gaskets
float needle valve
volume control screw
all diaphragms
spring

Repair kits
all jets and gaskets
all diaphragms
float needle value
volume control screw
spring for pump diaphragm
pump ball value
main jet carrier
float
complete intermediate rod
intermediate pump lever
complete injector tube
some cover hold-down screws
and washers

Gasket kits
all needed gaskets

Crankshaft Specifications

Model	Stand. Main Bearing Journal Diam. (mm.)	Stand. Connect. Rod Bearing Journal Diam. (mm.)	Journal out-of-round Tolerance (mm.)	Maximum Journal Taper (mm./in.)	Journal Fillet Radii (mm./in.)	Flywheel Flange Runout (mm./in.)	Maximum Unbalance (cm. g.)	Main Bearing Oil Clearance (mm./in.)	Crankshaft End-Play (mm./in.)
190c	69.955–69.965	51.955–51.965	.005–.01	.01/.0004	2.5–3.0/.097–.117	.010/.0004	15	.045–.060/.0017–.0023	.100–.175/.004–.007
200	69.955–69.965	51.955–51.965	.005–.01	.01/.0004	2.5–3.0/.097–.117	.010/.0004	15	.045–.060/.0017–.0023	.100–.175/.004–.007
190Dc	69.955–69.965	51.955–51.965	.005–.01	.01/.0004	2.5–3.0/.097–.117	.010/.0004	15	.045–.060/.0017–.0023	.100–.175/.004–.007
200D	69.955–69.965	51.955–51.965	.005–.01	.01/.0004	2.5–3.0/.097–.117	.010/.0004	15	.045–.065/.0017–.0025	.100–.175/.004–.007
230	59.955–59.965	47.955–47.965	.005–.01	.01/.0004	2.5–3.0/.097–.117	.012/.0005	15	.045–.060/.0017–.0023	.100–.175/.004–.007
220b	59.955–59.965	47.955–47.965	.005–.01	.01/.0004	2.5–3.0/.097–.117	.012/.0005	15	.045–.060/.0017–.0023	.100–.175/.004–.007
220Sb	59.955–59.965	47.955–47.965	.005–.01	.01/.0004	2.5–3.0/.097–.117	.012/.0005	15	.045–.060/.0017–.0023	.100–.175/.004–.007
230S	59.955–59.965	47.955–47.965	.005–.01	.01/.0004	2.5–3.0/.097–.117	.012/.0005	15	.045–.060/.0017–.0023	.100–.175/.004–.007
250S	59.955–59.965	47.055–47.965	.005–.01	.01/.0004	2.5–3.0/.097–.117	.012/.0005	15	.045–.060/.0017–.0023	.100–.175/.004–.007
220SEb	59.955–59.965	47.055–47.965	.005–.01	.01/.0004	2.5–3.0/.097–.117	.012/.0005	15	.045–.060/.0017–.0023	.100–.175/.004–.007
250SE	59.955–59.965	47.055–47.965	.005–.01	.01/.0004	2.5–3.0/.097–.117	.012/.0005	15	.045–.060/.0017–.0023	.100–.175/.004–.007
230SL	59.955–59.965	47.055–47.965	.005–.01	.01/.0004	2.5–3.0/.097–.117	.012/.0005	15	.045–.060/.0017–.0023	.100–.175/.004–.007
250SL	59.955–59.965	47.055–47.065	.005–.01	.01/.0004	2.5–3.0/.097–.117	.012/.0005	15	.045–.060/.0017–.0023	.100–.175/.004–.007
250SE/C	59.955–59.965	47.055–47.065	.005–.01	.01/.0004	2.5–3.0/.097–.117	.012/.0005	15	.045–.060/.0017–.0023	.100–.175/.004–.007
300SE	59.950–59.970	51.950–51.970	.005–.01	.01/.0004	2.5–3.0/.097–.117	.015/.0006	20	.030–.055/.0012–.0023	.100–.240/.004–.010
300SEb	59.950–59.970	51.950–51.970	.005–.01	.01/.0004	2.5–3.0/.097–.117	.015/.0006	20	.030–.055/.0012–.0023	.100–.240/.004–.010
300SEL	59.950–59.970	51.050–51.970	.005–.01	.01/.0004	2.5–3.0/.097–.117	.015/.0006	20	.030–.055/.0012–.0023	.100–.240/.004–.010
300SE/C	59.950–59.970	51.050–51.970	.005–.01	.01/.0004	2.5–3.0/.097–.117	.015/.0006	20	.030–.055/.0012–.0023	.100–.240/.004–.010
220D/8	69.955–60.965	51.950–51.970	.005–.01	.01/.0004	2.5–3.0/.097–.117	.010/.0004	15	.030–.055/.0012–.0023	.100–.240/.004–.010
220/8	69.955–69.965	51.955–51.965	.005–.01	.01/.0004	2.5–3.0/.097–.117	.010/.0004	15	.045–.065/.0017–.0025	.100–.175/.004–.007
230/8	59.955–59.965	51.955–51.965	.005–.01	.01/.0004	2.5–3.0/.097–.117	.012/.0005	15	.045–.065/.0017–.0025	.100–.175/.004–.007
250/8	59.955–59.965	47.955–47.965	.005–.01	.01/.0004	2.5–3.0/.097–.117	.012/.0005	15	.045–.065/.0017–.0025	.100–.175/.004–.007
280S/8	59.955–59.965	47.955–47.965	.005–.01	.01/.0004	2.5–3.0/.097–.117	.012/.0005	15	.045–.065/.0017–.0025	.100–.175/.004–.007
280SE/8	59.955–59.965	47.955–47.965	.005–.01	.01/.0004	2.5–3.0/.097–.117	.012/.0005	15	.045–.065/.0017–.0025	.100–.175/.004–.007
280SEL/8	59.955–59.965	47.955–47.965	.005–.01	.01/.0004	2.5–3.0/.097–.117	.012/.0005	15	.045–.065/.0017–.0025	.100–.175/.004–.007
280SL/8	59.955–59.965	47.955–47.965	.005–.01	.01/.0004	2.5–3.0/.097–.117	.012/.0005	15	.045–.065/.0017–.0025	.100–.175/.004–.007
300SEL/8 2.8	59.955–59.965	47.955–47.965	.005–.01	.01/.0004	2.5–3.0/.097–.117	.012/.0005	15	.045–.065/.0017–.0025	.100–.175/.004–.007
300SEL/8 6.3	69.955–69.965	54.940–54.960	.005–.01	.01/.0004	2.5–3.0/.097–.117	.015/.0006	40	.045–.065/.0017–.0025	.100–.240/.004–.010

Cylinder Head Specifications

Model	Height of New Head (mm.)	Maximum Material Removal (mm./in.)	Maximum Longitudinal Eccentricity (mm./in.)	Maximum Lateral Eccentricity (mm./in.)	Total Compress. Space with Head Installed (cc.)	Compress. Ratio (:1)	Combust. Chamber Volume with Valves and Plugs (cc.)
190c	84.8—85.0	1.0/.039	0.1/.0039	0/0	60.8—64.1	8.7	51.1—52.1
200	84.8—85.0	1.0/.039	0.1/.0039	0	61.4—64.6	9.0	49.5—50.5
190Dc	84.8—85.0	0.8/.031	0.1/.0039	0	23.5—25.5③②	21.0	
200D	84.8—85.0	0.8/.031	0.1/.0039	0	23.5—25.5③②	21.0	
230	84.8—85.0	0.8/.031	0.1/.0039	0	④	④	④
220b	84.8—85.0	0.8/.031	0.1/.0039	0	①	①	①
220Sb	84.8—85.0	0.8/.031	0.1/.0039	0	①	①	①
230S	84.8—85.0	0.8/.031	0.1/.0039	0	④	④	④
250S	84.8—85.0	0.8/.031	0.1/.0039	0	④	④	④
220SEb	84.8—85.0	0.8/.031	0.1/.0039	0	①	①	①
250SE	84.8—85.0	0.8/.031	0.1/.0039	0	48.0—50.7	9.5	40.7—41.7
230SL	84.8—85.0	0.8/.031	0.1/.0039	0	45.3—48.0	9.5	37.5—38.5
250SL	84.8—85.0	0.8/.031	0.1/.0039	0	not available	9.5	not available
250SE/C	84.8—85.0	0.8/.031	0.1/.0039	0	48.0—50.7	9.5	40.7—41.7
300SE	See illus. A & B	0.8/.031	0.08/.0031	0	62.0—65.0 ②	8.8	
300SEb		0.8/.031	0.08/.0031	0	62.0—65.0	8.8	
300SEL		0.8/.031	0.08/.0031	0	62.0—65.0	8.8	
300SE/C		0.8/.031	0.08/.0031	0	62.0—65.0	8.8	
220D/8	84.8—85.0	0.8/.031	0.1/.0039	0	27.0—28.0③②	21.0	
220/8	84.8—85.0	1.0/.039	0.1/.0039	0	67.8—71.1	9.0	57.6—58.6
230/8	84.8—85.0	0.8/.031	0.1/.0039	0	47.0—49.7	9.0	37.6—38.6
250/8	84.8—85.0	0.8/.031	0.1/.0039	0	51.0—53.7	9.0	42.4—43.4
280S/8	84.8—85.0	0.8/.031	0.1/.0039	0	not available	9.0	not available
280SE/8	84.8—85.0	0.8/.031	0.1/.0039	0	not available	9.5	not available
280SEL/8	84.8—85.0	0.8/.031	0.1/.0039	0	not available	9.5	not available
280SL/8	84.8—85.0	0.8/.031	0.1/.0039	0	not available	9.5	not available
300SEL/8 2.8	84.8—85.0	0.8/.031	0.1/.0039	0	not available	9.5	not available
300SEL/8 6.3	See illus. D	0.5/.020	0.08/.0031	0	98.0—102.0	9.0	86.7—88.7

① As of engine numbers:

180 940—10—044 200   127 982—10—031 774
180 940—12—000 517   127 982—12—004 498
180 941—10—091 448   127 984—10—006 556
180 941—12—003 491   127 984—12—001 611

Combustion Chamber	Compress. Ratio (:1)	Total Compress. Space (cc.)	Compress. Space in Head (cc.)
No. 1 cylinder	8.7	49.5-53.1	39.0-40.0
No. 2 cylinder	8.5	48.2-50.8	37.7-38.7
No. 3-6 cylinders	8.3	46.9-49.5	36.4-37.4

② Total compression space with cylinder head installed is determined by piston shape.

③ Prechamber end to cylinder head surface distance 'c' must be readjusted to 0.2145—0.2301" if head is milled by installing a thicker gasket at (13) (illustration C).

Model		230, 230S, 250S	230, 230S	250S	230, 230S	250S
④ Combustion Chamber	Compress. Ratio (:1)	Total Compress. Space (cc.)			Compress. Space in Head (cc.)	
No. 1 cylinder	8.6	49.3-52.6	53.4-57.0		40.1-41.1	44.3-45.3
No. 2 cylinder	8.8	48.0-51.2	52.0-55.5		38.8-39.8	42.9-43.9
No. 3-6 cylinders	9.0	47.0-49.2	51.0-53.7		37.6-38.6	41.6-42.6

Valve Specifications

Model	Minimum Valve Head Edge Thickness (mm./in.)		Valve Seat Width (mm.)		Valve Seat Angle (deg.)	Valve Stem Diameter (mm.)	
	intake	exhaust	intake	exhaust		intake	exhaust
190c	1.0/.039	1.5/.058	1.25—2.00	1.25—2.00	45+15'	8.970	9.950
200	1.0/.039	1.5/.058	1.25—2.00	1.25—2.00	45+15'	8.970	9.950
190Dc	1.0/.039	1.5/.058	1.25—2.00	1.25—2.00	45+15'	8.920	9.920
200D	1.0/.039	1.5/.058	1.25—2.00	1.25—2.00	45+15'	8.920	9.920
230	1.0/.039	1.5/.058	1.25—2.00	1.25—2.00	45+15'	8.970	9.950
220b	1.0/.039	1.5/.058	1.25—2.00	1.25—2.00	45+15'	8.970	9.950
220Sb	1.0/.039	1.5/.058	1.25—2.00	1.25—2.00	45+15'	8.970	9.950
230S	1.0/.039	1.5/.058	1.25—2.00	1.25—2.00	45+15'	8.970	10.950
250S	1.0/.039	1.5/.058	1.25—2.00	1.25—2.00	45+15'	8.970	10.950
220SEb	1.0/.039	1.5/.058	1.25—2.00	1.25—2.00	45+15'	8.970	9.950
250SE	1.0/.039	1.5/.058	1.25—2.00	1.25—2.00	45+15'	8.970	10.950
230SL	1.0/.039	1.5/.058	1.25—2.00	1.25—2.00	45+15'	8.970	9.950
250SL	1.0/.039	1.5/.058	1.25—2.00	1.25—2.00	45+15'	8.970	10.950
250SE/C	1.0/.039	1.5/.058	1.25—2.00	1.25—2.00	45+15'	8.970	10.950
300SE	1.0/.039	1.8/.070	1.50—2.00	1.50—2.00	45+15'	8.970	11.950
300SEb	1.0/.039	1.8/.070	1.50—2.00	1.50—2.00	45+15'	8.970	11.950
300SEL	1.0/.039	1.8/.070	1.50—2.00	1.50—2.00	45+15'	8.970	11.950
300SE/C	1.0/.039	1.8/.070	1.50—2.00	1.50—2.00	45+15'	8.970	11.950
220D/8	1.5/.058	1.5/.058	1.30—1.60	2.60—2.90	30+15'	9.920	9.940
220/8	1.0/.039	1.5/.058	1.25—2.00	1.25—2.00	45+15'	8.970	10.940
230/8	1.0/.039	1.5/.058	1.25—2.00	1.25—2.00	45+15'	8.970	10.940
250/8	1.0/.039	1.5/.058	1.25—2.00	1.25—2.00	45+15'	8.970	10.940
280S/8	1.0/.039	1.5/.058	1.25—2.00	1.25—2.00	45+15'	8.970	10.940
280SE/8	1.0/.039	1.5/.058	1.25—2.00	1.25—2.00	45+15'	8.970	10.940
280SEL/8	1.0/.039	1.5/.058	1.25—2.00	1.25—2.00	45+15'	8.970	10.940
280SL/8	1.0/.039	1.5/.058	1.25—2.00	1.25—2.00	45+15'	8.970	10.940
300SEL/8 2.8	1.0/.039	1.5/.058	1.25—2.00	1.25—2.00	45+15'	8.970	10.940
300SEL/8 6.3	1.0/.039	1.5/.058	1.25—2.00	1.25—2.00	45+15'	8.970	11.940

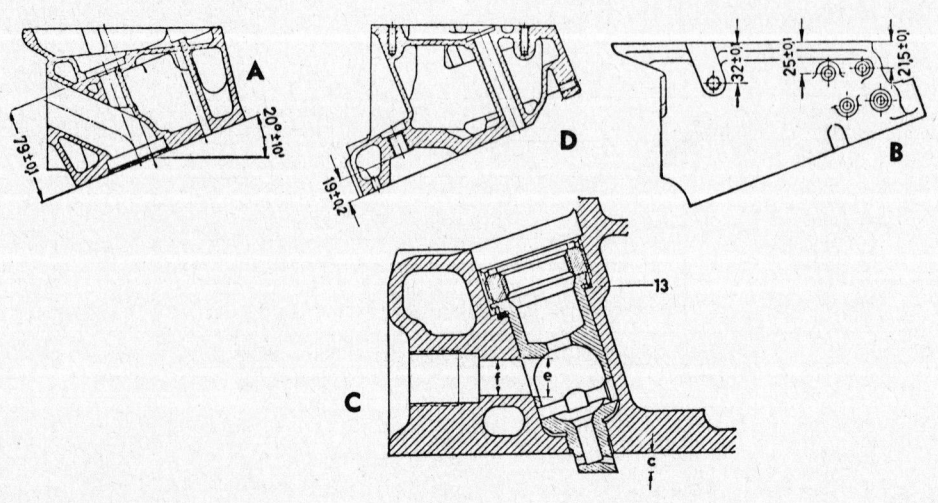

Piston Specifications

Model	Standard Bore Diameter (mm.)	Piston Sidewall Clearance (mm./in.)	Piston Pin Diameter (mm.)	Piston Pin Running Fit (mm.)	Max. Weight Deviation in Engine Pistons (g.)	Rods (g.)	Piston Ring End Gap (mm.) ⑤	Piston Ring Groove Clear. (mm.)
190c	85.000—85.022	.03—.04/.0012—.0015	25.994—26.000	.012—.023	4.0	5.0	①	.055—.077③
200	87.000—87.022	.03—.04/.0012—.0015	26.000—25.995	.012—.023	4.0	5.0	②	.060—.092③
190Dc	87.000—87.022	.07/.0027	26.000—25.995	.012—.023	4.0	5.0	①	.080—.112③
200D	87.000—87.022	.07/.0027	26.000—25.995	.012—.023	4.0	5.0	①	.080—.112③
230	82.000—82.022	.03—.04/.0012—.0015	25.000—24.995	.012—.023	4.0	5.0	②	.060—.092③
220b	80.000—80.019	.03—.04/.0012—.0015	23.994—24.000	not avail.	4.0	5.0	①	.080—.112
220Sb	80.000—80.019	.03—.04/.0012—.0015	23.994—24.000	not avail.	4.0	5.0	①	.080—.112
230S	82.000—82.022	.03—.04/.0012—.0015	23.994—24.000	not avail.	4.0	5.0	②	.060—.092
250S	82.000—82.022	.03—.04/.0012—.0015	25.000—24.995	not avail.	4.0	5.0	②	.060—.092
220SEb	80.000—80.019	.03—.04/.0012—.0015	23.994—24.000	not avail.	4.0	5.0	①	.080—.112
250SE	82.000—82.022	.03—.04/.0012—.0015	25.000—24.995	not avail.	4.0	5.0	②	.060—.092
230SL	82.000—82.022	.03—.04/.0012—.0015	23.994—24.000	not avail.	4.0	5.0	①	.060—.092
250SL	82.000—82.022	.03—.04/.0012—.0015	25.000—24.995	not avail.	4.0	5.0	not avail.	not avail.
250SE/C	82.000—82.022	.03—.04/.0012—.0015	25.000—24.995	not avail.	4.0	5.0	②	.060—.092
300SE	85.000—85.022	.03—.04/.0012—.0015	25.994—26.000	.007—.018	4.0	5.0	①	.060—.092
300SEb	85.000—85.022	.03—.04/.0012—.0015	26.000—25.995	.007—.018	4.0	5.0	①	.060—.092
300SEL	85.000—85.022	.03—.04/.0012—.0015	26.000—25.995	.007—.018	4.0	5.0	①	.060—.092
300SE/C	85.000—85.022	.03—.04/.0012—.0015	26.000—25.995	.007—.018	4.0	5.0	①	.060—.092
220D/8	87.000—87.022	.02—.03/.0008—.0012	26.000—25.995	.012—.023	4.0	5.0	not avail.	not avail.
220/8	87.000—87.022	.02—.03/.0008—.0012	25.000—24.995	.012—.023	4.0	5.0	not avail.	not avail.
230/8	④	.02—.03/.0008—.0012	25.000—24.995	.012—.023	4.0	5.0	not avail.	not avail.
250/8	82.000—82.022	.02—.03/.0008—.0012	25.000—24.995	.012—.023	4.0	5.0	not avail.	not avail.
280S/8	86.500—86.522	.02—.03/.0008—.0012	25.000—24.995	.012—.023	4.0	5.0	not avail.	not avail.
280SE/8	86.500—86.522	.02—.03/.0008—.0012	25.000—24.995	.012—.023	4.0	5.0	not avail.	not avail.
280SEL/8	86.500—86.522	.02—.03/.0008—.0012	25.000—24.995	.012—.023	4.0	5.0	not avail.	not avail.
280SL/8	86.500—86.522	.02—.03/.0008—.0012	25.000—24.995	.012—.023	4.0	5.0	not avail.	not avail.
300SEL/8 2.8	86.500—86.522	.02—.03/.0008—.0012	25.000—24.995	.012—.023	4.0	5.0	not avail.	not avail.
300SEL/8 6.3	103.000—103.022	.02—.03/.0008—.0012	26.000—25.995	.007—.018	4.0	8.0	①	.06—.092

① Top — .55—.70/.022—.028
II — .45—.60/.018—.023
III — .30—.45/.012—.016
IV — .30—.45/.012—.016

② 3 Ring Pistons (No Ring No. IV), otherwise same as footnote #1.

③ I See Space
II & III & IV .040 — .072
IV Type 300 SEL/8 6.3 — .05—.082

④ Engine No. 180.945
180.949   82.000—82.022
180.954   81.750—81.772

⑤ If Rings are coated with Molybdenum, the end gap is 0.15—0.2 mm. less than the indicated figures

Connecting Rod Specifications

Model	Connecting Rod Big End Internal Diam. (mm.)	Connecting Rod Small End Internal Diam. (mm.)	Connecting Rod Bore Out-of-Round Max. (mm./in.)	Connecting Rod Length (mm.)	Connecting Rod Bearing Clearance (mm./in.)	Connecting Rod Side-Play (mm./in.)
190c	55.600—55.619	29.000—29.021	.01/.0004	148.95—149.05	.045—.060/.0018—.0023	.110—.260/.004—.010
200	55.600—55.619	29.000—29.021	.01/.0004	148.95—149.05	.045—.060/.0018—.0023	.110—.260/.004—.010
190Dc	55.600—55.619	29.000—29.021	.01/.0004	148.95—149.05	.045—.060/.0018—.0023	.110—.260/.004—.010
200D	55.600—55.619	29.000—29.021	.01/.0004	148.95—149.05	.045—.060/.0018—.0023	.110—.260/.004—.010
230	51.600—51.619	28.000—28.021	.01/.0004	124.95—125.05	.045—.060/.0018—.0023	.110—.260/.004—.010
220b	54.000—54.019	27.000—27.021	.01/.0004	134.95—135.05	.045—.060/.0018—.0023	.110—.260/.004—.010
220Sb	54.000—54.019	27.000—27.021	.01/.0004	134.95—135.05	.045—.060/.0018—.0023	.110—.260/.004—.010
230S	51.600—51.619	28.000—28.021	.01/.0004	124.95—125.05	.045—.060/.0018—.0023	.110—.260/.004—.010
250S	51.600—51.619	28.000—28.021	.01/.0004	124.95—125.05	.045—.060/.0018—.0023	.110—.260/.004—.010
220SEb	54.000—54.019	27.000—27.021	.01/.0004	134.95—135.05	.045—.060/.0018—.0023	.110—.260/.004—.010
250SE	51.600—51.619	28.000—28.021	.01/.0004	124.95—125.05	.045—.060/.0018—.0023	.110—.260/.004—.010
230SL	51.600—51.619	27.000—27.019	.01/.0004	124.95—125.05	.045—.060/.0018—.0023	.110—.260/.004—.010
250SL	51.600—51.619	28.000—28.021	.01/.0004	124.95—125.05	not avail.	not avail.
250SE/C	51.600—51.619	28.000—28.021	.01/.0004	124.95—125.05	not avail.	not avail.
300SE	55.600—55.619	29.000—29.021	.01/.0004	163.95—164.05	not avail.	not avail.
300SEb	55.600—55.619	29.000—29.021	.01/.0004	163.95—164.05	.050—.070/.0020—.0028	.110—.260/.004—.010
300SEL	35.600—55.619	29.000—29.021	.01/.0004	163.95—164.05	.050—.070/.0020—.0028	.110—.260/.004—.010
300SE/C	55.600—55.619	29.000—29.021	.01/.0004	163.95—164.05	.050—.070/.0020—.0028	.110—.260/.004—.010
220D/8	55.600—55.619	29.000—29.021	.01/.0004	148.95—149.05	not avail.	not avail.
220/8	55.600—55.619	29.000—29.021	.01/.0004	148.95—149.05	not avail.	not avail.
230/8	51.600—51.619	28.000—28.021	.01/.0004	124.95—125.05	not avail.	not avail.
250/8	51.600—51.619	28.000—28.021	.01/.0004	124.95—125.05	not avail.	not avail.
280S/8	51.600—51.619	28.000—28.021	.01/.0004	124.95—125.05	not avail.	not avail.
280SE/8	51.600—51.619	28.000—28.021	.01/.0004	124.95—125.05	not avail.	not avail.
280SEL/8	51.600—51.619	28.000—28.021	.01/.0004	124.95—125.05	not avail.	not avail.
280SL/8	51.600—51.619	28.000—28.021	.01/.0004	124.95—125.05	not avail.	not avail.
300SEL/8 2.8	51.600—51.619	28.000—28.021	.01/.0004	124.95—125.05	not avail.	not avail.
300SEL/8 6.3	58.050—58.150	29.000—29.021	.01/.0004	165.95—166.05	.045—.065/.0018—.0026	.22—.35/.0088—.0140

Torque Specifications
(Ft.lbs.)

Model	Cylinder head bolts		Rocker arm mounting bolts	Rocker block bolts	Connecting rod cap bolts	Main Bearing cap bolts	Flywheel bolts		Oil pan bolts	Spark or glow plugs
	Cold ①	Hot ②					Man.	Auto.		
190c	58	65	72		27	65	40+3.5	33+3.5	5.8	21—26
200	58	65	72		27	65	40+3.5	33+3.5	5.8	21—26
190Dc	65	65		27	27	65	40+3.5	33+3.5	5.8	36
200D	65	65		27	27	65	40+3.5	33+3.5	5.8	36
230	58	65	72		44	58	47+3.5	47+3.5	5.8	21—26
220b	58	65	72		27	65	40+3.5	33+3.5	5.8	21—26
220Sb	58	65	72		27	65	40+3.5	33+3.5	5.8	21—26
230S	58	65	72		44	58	47+3.5	47+3.5	5.8	21—26
250S	58	65	72		43	58	69+3.5	69+3.5	5.8	21—26
220SEb	58	65	72		27	58	47+3.5	47+3.5	5.8	21—26
250SE	58	65	72		43	58	69+3.5	69+3.5	5.8	21—26
230SL	58	65	72		27	58	69+3.5	47+3.5	5.8	21—26
250SL	58	65	72		43	58	69+3.5	69+3.5	5.8	21—26
220SEb/C	58	65	72		27	58	47+3.5	47+3.5	5.8	21—26
250SE/C	58	65	72		43	58	69+3.5	69+3.5	5.8	21—26
300SE	72	80		27	27	36±1.4	32+1.4	32+1.4	5.8	21—26
300SEb	72	80		27	27	36±1.4	32+1.4	32+1.4	5.8	21—26
300SEL	72	80		27	27	36±1.4	32+1.4	32+1.4	5.8	21—26
220D/8	65	65		27	40	65	21+7③	21+7③	8	36
220/8	58	65	58		40	65	21+7③	21+7③	8	22
230/8	58	65	58		45-2.1	58	21+7③	21+7③	8	22
250/8	58	65	58		45-2.1	58	21+7③	21+7③	8	22
280S/8	72	80			45	65	21+7③	21+7③	8	22
280SE/8	72	80			45	65	21+7③	21+7③	8	22
280SL/8	72	80			45	65	21+7③	21+7③	8	22
300SEL/8	72	80			45	65	21+7③	21+7③	8	22

NOTE: Lubricate all bolts with engine oil before insertion; do not use Molykote.

① *36 ft.lbs. for M 10 bolts.*
② *43 ft.lbs. for M 10 bolts.*
③ *Plus tightening angle —* 220/8, 220D/8: 60° + 10°.
           230/8, 250/8,
           280S/8, 280SE/8,
           280SL/8, 300SEL/8: 90° + 10°.

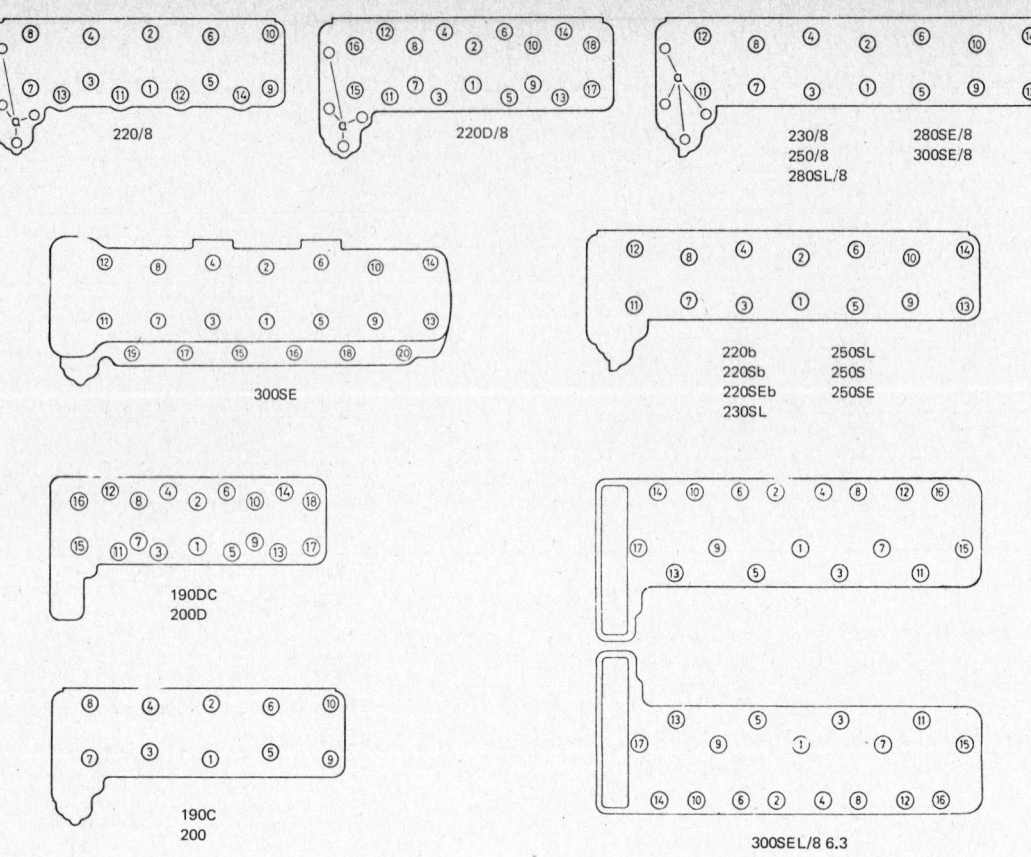

Cylinder head torque sequence.

Battery Specifications

Model	Battery Capacity (Ah @ 20 hrs.)	Model	Battery Capacity (Ah @ 20 hrs.)	Model	Battery Capacity (Ah @ 20 hrs.)
190c	52⑤	250SE	55	220D/8	88
200	44	230SL	55⑦	220/8	44
190Dc	66	250SL	55	230/8	44
200D	66	220SEb/C①	55⑦	250/8	44
230	44	250SE/C①	55	280S/8	55
220b	52⑤⑥	300SE③	66	280SE/8③①	55
220Sb	52⑤⑥	300SE①②	66	280SL/8	55
230S	44	300SEb	66	300SEL/8	66
250S	44	300SEL	66	300SEL/8 6.3	66
220SEb	55⑦	300SE①④	66		

① Coupe and convertible.
② To August, 1965.
③ Long wheelbase.
④ From August, 1965.
⑤ Second version; first version—56.
⑥ From March, 1965—44.
⑦ Second version; first version—60.

Acid level—5mm. above separator or level mark.

Specific gravity—Full charge .... 1.280 (1.230 tropics)
                   Half charge .... 1.210 (1.160 tropics)
                   Discharged .... 1.140 (1.090 tropics)

Charging current— Initial 5%
                   Standard 10%
                   Quick 75%

Maximum acid temperature during charging—40°C. (104°F.)
Freezing temperature—Full charge .... —68°C. (—40 tropics)
                      Half charge .... —40°C. (—13 tropics)
                      Discharged .... —12°C. (—13 tropics or
                                                            —6 for phase II models)

Model	Type Starter (Bosch)	Short Circuit Test Amps.	volts	Load Test Amps.	volts	Speed (rpm)	Idling Test Amps.	volts	Speed (rpm)	Solenoid Yoke Length (mm.)	Generator Type Used
190c	EF(R)12V0, 8PS 0 001 208 003	250–285	6	165–200	9	1,100–1,450	35–45	12	6,400–7,900	19±1	LJ/GG 240/12/2400/AR8, LJ/GK 300/12/1450 AR2, LJ/GEG 160/12/2500 R8, G 114 V 30 A 25 or K 114 V 38 A 15
200	EF(R)12V0, 8PS 0 001 208 025	250–285	6	165–200	9	1,100–1,450	35–45	12	6,400–7,900	19±1	K 114 V 35 A 20
190Dc	JD(R)12VI, 8PS 0 001 354 064	670–750	6	310–350	9	1,250–1,450	60–80	11.5	6,000–7,100	49±.2	same as 190c
200D	JD(R)12VI, 8PS 0 001 354 064	670–750	6	310–350	9	1,250–1,450	60–80	11.5	6,000–7,100	49±.2	K 114 V 35 A 20
230	EF(R)12V0, 8PS 0 001 208 003	250–285	6	165–200	9	1,100–1,400	35–45	12	6,400–7,900	19±1	K 114 V 35 A 20
220b	EED 0.8/12 R 45	340–400	8.5	180	10	1,100–1,400	30–50	11.5	5,000–7,500	32.4±1	same as 190c
220Sb	EF(R)12V0, 8PS 0 001 208 003	250–285	6	165–200	9	1,100–1,450	35–45	12	6,400–7,900	19±1	same as 190c
230S	EF(R)12V0, 8PS 0 001 208 003	250–285	6	165–200	9	1,100–1,450	35–45	12	6,400–7,900	19±1	K 114 V 35 A 20
250S	EF(R)12V0, 8PS 0 001 208 026	250–285	6	165–200	9	1,100–1,450	35–45	12	6,400–7,900	19±1	K 114 V 35 A 20
220SEb	EF(R)12V0, 8PS 0 001 208 003	250–285	6	165–200	9	1,100–1,450	35–45	12	6,400–7,900	19±1	same as 190c
250SE	EF(R)12V0, 8PS 0 001 208 026	250–285	6	165–200	9	1,100–1,450	35–45	12	6,400–7,900	19±1	K 114 V 35 A 20
230SL	EF(R)12V0, 8PS 0 001 208 009	250–285	6	165–200	9	1,100–1,450	35–45	12	6,400–7,900	19±1	K 114 V 35 A 20
250SL	EF(R)12V0, 8PS 0 001 208 026	250–285	6	165–200	9	1,100–1,450	35–45	12	6,400–7,900	19±1	K 114 V 35 A 20
300SE, 300SEb, 300SEL	GE(R)12VI, 3PS 000 1 307 019	500–550	7	270–310	9	1,200–1,400	40–60	11.5	6,500–8,000	32.2±1	LJ/GK 300/12/1450/AR53 K 114 V 38 A 15
220D/8	2.5/12	1,000–1,200	6	650–750	9	1,000–1,200	80–95	12	7,500–8,500	19±1	K 114 V 35 A 20
220/8	EF 0.8/12 or 1.4/12 250–285	250–285	6	165–200	9	1,100–1,450	35–45	12	6,400–7,900	19±1	K 114 V 35 A 20
230/8	EF 0.8/12 or 1.4/12 250–285	250–285	6	165–200	9	1,100–1,450	35–45	12	6,400–7,900	19±1	K 114 V 35 A 20
250/8, 280S/8, 280SL/8, 300SEL/8	EF 0.8/12 or 1.4/12 250–285	250–285	6	165–200	9	1,100–1,450	35–45	12	6,400–7,900	19±1	K 114 V 35 A 20
300SEL/ 8 6.3	EJB 12V/1.8	—	—	—	—	—	—	—	—	—	K 114 V 55 A 20

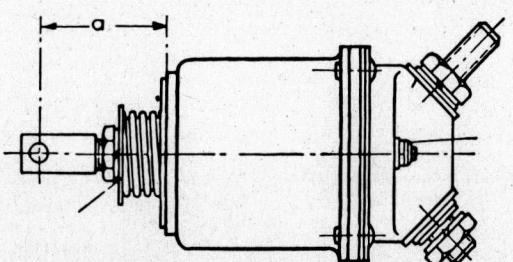

Solenoid yoke length with linkage drawn in..

Generator and Regulator Specifications

Generator Specifications   Regulator Specifications

Generator Type	Setting Load (Watts/Amps)	Rated Voltage Speed (rpm)	Test Speed (rpm) cold	Test Speed (rpm) warm	Resistance of Exciter Coil	Associated Regulator Bosch RS/...	Cut-In Voltage (volts)	Return Current (Amps.)	Regulating Voltage (without load)	Load at Double Rated Speed (Starting of reg. Amps.) cold	warm
LJ/GEG 160/12/2500R8	160/30	1,900	2,500	2,600	4.8 +0.5 ohms	UA 160/12/15	12.7–13.4	2.5–6.6	13.8–14.6	19.5–22.5	17.5–20.5
LJ/GG 240/12/2400R8	240/30	1,700	2,300	2,500	4.8 +0.5 ohms	UA 240/12/38	12.7–13.4	5.0–9.0	13.8–14.6	30.0–34.0	27.0–31.0
LJ/GG 240/12/2400AR8						UAA 240/12/43	12.5–13.2	5.0–11.5	13.5–14.5	29.0–33.0	27.5–32.0
G 114 V 30 A 25 0 101 302 023	–/30	1,700	2,300	2,500	4.8 +0.5 ohms	0 190 309 002 UAA 240/12/43	12.5–13.2	5.0–11.5	13.5–14.5	29.0–33.0	27.5–32.0
LJ/GK 300/12/1450AR53	300/38	1,150	1,500	1,500	5.2 +0.5 ohms	UA 300/12/43	12.5–13.2	5.0–11.5	13.5–14.5	37.0–41.0	35.5–40.0
K 114 V 38 A 15 0 101 402 076	–/38	1,100	1,450	1,500	5.2 +0.5 ohms	UAA 300/12/43 0 190 309 010	12.5–13.2	5.0–11.5	13.5–14.5	37.0–41.0	35.5–40.0
LJ/GK 300/12/1450AR2	300/38	1,100	1,450	1,500	5.2 +0.5 ohms	UA 300/12/43	12.5–13.2	5.0–11.5	13.5–14.5	37.0–41.0	35.5–40.0
K 114 V 38 A 15 0 101 402 071	–/38	1,100	1,450	1,500	5.2 +0.5 ohms	UA 300/12/43 0 190 300 079	12.5–13.2	5.0–11.5	13.5–14.5	37.0–41.0	35.5–40.0
K 114 V 35 A 20 0 120 400 504 ④	490/35	2,000			4.0 +0.4 ohms ③	AD 1/14/1 ADN 1/14 V ①	N.A.		13.5–14.2 13.9–14.8②		28.0–30.0

① Suppressed version.
② With load.
③ Between slip rings.
④ Do not test without regulator—see text.

Capacities

Model	Fuel Tank (gals.) **	Crankcase (qts.) Max. **	Min. **	Radiator (qts.) **	Rear Axle (pts.) **	Oil Filter (pts.) **	Transmission (pts.) Man. **	Auto. **	Power Steering (pts.) **	Manual Steering (pts.) ***
190c	13 3/4	4 1/4	2 1/2	10 1/2	5 1/4	1	3	7 1/2①	3	5/8
200	17 1/4	4 1/4	2 1/2	10 1/2	5 1/4	1	3	7 1/2①	3	5/8
190Dc	13 3/4	4 1/4	2 1/2	10 1/2	5 1/4	2	3	7 1/2①	3	5/8
200D	17 1/4	4 1/4	2 1/2	10 1/2	5 1/4	2	3	7 1/2①	3	5/8
230	17 1/4	5 3/4	3 3/4	14 3/4	5 1/4	1	3	7 1/2①	3	5/8
220b	17 1/4	5 3/4	3 3/4	12	5 1/4	1	3	8③	3	5/8
220Sb	17 1/4	5 3/4	3 3/4	12	5 1/4	1	3	8③	3	5/8
230S	17 1/4	5 3/4	3 3/4	12	5 1/4	1	3	8③	3	5/8
250S	21 1/2	5 3/4④	3 3/4	11	5 1/4	1	3	8③	3	5/8
220SEb	17 1/4	5 3/4	3 3/4	12	5 1/4	1	3	8③	3	5/8
250SE	21 1/2	5 3/4④	3 3/4	11	5 1/4	1	3	8③	3	5/8
230SL	17 1/4	5 3/4	3 3/4	11 1/2	5 1/4	1	3	8③	3	5/8
250SL	21 1/2	5 3/4④	3 3/4	13 1/2	5 1/4	1	3	8③	3	5/8
220SEb/C	17 1/4	5 3/4	3 3/4	12	5 1/4	1	3	8③	3	5/8
250SE/C	21 1/2	5 3/4④	3 3/4	11	5 1/4	1	3	8③	3	5/8
300SE	21 1/2	6 1/4	4 1/4	17 3/4	5 1/4	1	3	10⑥	3 1/4	
300SE*	21 1/2	6 1/4	4 1/4	17 3/4	5 1/4	1	3	10⑥	3 1/4	
300SEb	21 1/2	6 1/4	4 1/4	17 3/4	5 1/4	1	3	10⑥	3 1/4	
300SEL	21 1/2	6 1/4	4 1/4	17 3/4	5 1/4	1	3	10⑥	3 1/4	
220D/8	17 1/4	4 1/4⑧	2 1/2	11 1/4	2 1/2	2	3	9 3/4④⑤	3	5/8
220/8	17 1/4	4 1/4	2 1/2	11	2 1/2	1	3 1/2	8 3/4②	3	5/8
230/8	17 1/4	5 3/4④	3 3/4	11	2 1/2	1	3 1/2	9 3/4④⑤	3	5/8
250/8	17 1/4	5 3/4④	3 3/4	10 1/2	2 1/2	1	3 1/2	9 3/4④⑤	3	5/8
280S/8	21 1/2	5 3/4④	3 3/4	11	5 1/4	1	3	8③	3	5/8
280SE/8	21 1/2	5 3/4④	3 3/4	11 1/4	5 1/4	1	3	8③	3	5/8
280SL/8	21 1/2	5 3/4④	3 3/4	13 1/4	5 1/4	1	3	8③	3	5/8
300SEL/8	21 1/2	5 3/4④	3 3/4	11	5 1/4	1	3	8③	3	5/8
300SEL/8 6.3	27 3/4	6 3/4	5 1/4	19	5 1/4	2		16 1/2⑦	3 1/4	

*	Coupe and convertible, first and second versions.
**	All figures rounded off to nearest quarter.
***	Rounded off to the nearest eighth.
①	Initial filling — 9 1/2 pts.
②	Initial filling — 11 3/4 pts.
③	Initial filling — 10 pts.
④	With oil cooler — 6 1/4 qts.
⑤	Initial filling — 11 1/2 pts.
⑥	Initial filling — 12 pts.
⑦	Initial filling — 18 1/2 pts.
⑧	Oil cooler added after chassis No. 052 894; add 1 pt. extra.

Maintenance Intervals
(All Figures in Thousands of Miles)

Model	Automatic Trans. Fluid		Engine Oil		Oil Filter	Oil Bath Air Filter	Inj. Pump Oil	Chassis	Heat Riser Valve
	Check & Refill	Change ⑨	Check & Refill	Change	Change	Change	Check	Lube	Lube (Kerosene)
190c	3.0	12.0	3.0	6.0	6.0			3.0 ⑩	3.0
200	3.0	12.0	3.0	6.0	6.0			3.0 ⑩	3.0
190Dc	1.9	11.4		1.9	5.7	1.9	11.4	1.9 ⑪	5.7
200D	3.0	12.0		3.0	3.0	3.0	12.0	3.0 ⑩	6.0
230	3.0	12.0	3.0	6.0	6.0			3.0 ⑩	6.0
220b	1.9	11.4	1.9	5.7	5.7			1.9 ⑪	5.7
220Sb	1.9	11.4	1.9	5.7	5.7			1.9 ⑪	5.7
230S	3.0	12.0	3.0	6.0	6.0			3.0 ⑩	6.0
250S	3.0	12.0	3.0	6.0	6.0			3.0 ⑩	6.0
220SEb	1.9	11.4	1.9	5.7	5.7		5.7	1.9 ⑪	
250SE	3.0	12.0	3.0	6.0	6.0		12.0	3.0 ⑩	
230SL ⑭	1.9	11.4	1.9	5.7	5.7		5.7 ⑮	1.9 ⑪	
250SL	3.0	12.0	3.0	6.0	6.0		12.0	3.0 ⑩	
220SEb/C①	1.9	11.4	1.9	5.7	5.7		5.7	1.9 ⑪	
250SE/C②	3.0	12.0	3.0	6.0	6.0		12.0	3.0 ⑩	
250SE/C③	3.0	12.0	3.0	6.0	6.0		12.0	3.0 ⑩	
300SE④	1.9	11.4	1.9	5.7	5.7		5.7	1.9 ⑪	
300SE⑤	1.9	11.4	1.9	5.7	5.7		5.7	1.9 ⑪	
300SE⑥	1.9	11.4	1.9	5.7	5.7		5.7	1.9 ⑪	
300SEb	3.0	12.0	3.0	6.0	6.0		12.0	3.0 ⑩	
300SEL	3.0	12.0	3.0	6.0	6.0		12.0	3.0 ⑩	
300SE⑦	3.0	12.0	3.0	6.0	6.0		12.0	3.0 ⑩	
300SE⑧	3.0	12.0	3.0	6.0	6.0		12.0	3.0 ⑩	
220D/8	3.0	12.0		3.0	3.0	3.0	12.0	3.0 ⑩	6.0
220/8	3.0	30.0	3.0	6.0	6.0			3.0 ⑩	3.0
230/8	3.0	12.0	3.0	6.0	6.0			3.0 ⑩	3.0
250/8	3.0	12.0	3.0	6.0	6.0			3.0 ⑩	3.0
280S/8	3.0	12.0	3.0	6.0	6.0			3.0 ⑩	3.0
280SE/8	3.0	12.0	3.0	6.0	6.0		12.0	3.0 ⑩	
280SEL/8	3.0	12.0	3.0	6.0	6.0		12.0	3.0 ⑩	
280SE/8 ①	3.0	12.0	3.0	6.0	6.0		12.0	3.0 ⑩	
280SL/8	3.0	12.0	3.0	6.0	6.0		12.0	3.0 ⑩	
300SEL/8	3.0	12.0	3.0	6.0	6.0		12.0	3.0 ⑩	
300SEL/8 6.3	3.0	12.0	3.0	6.0	6.0		12.0	3.0 ⑩	

①   Coupe and convertible
②   Coupe
③   Convertible
④   Long wheelbase
⑤   Coupe to August, 1965
⑥   Convertible to August, 1965
⑦   Coupe from August, 1965
⑧   Convertible from August, 1965
⑨   Transmission oil filter every 30,000 miles
⑩   Every 1,500 miles or every month under adverse conditions, at least every two months regardless

Maintenance Intervals
(All Figures in Thousands of Miles)

Model	Manual Trans. Oil — Change	Power Steering Fluid — Refill	Manual Steering Oil — Refill	Rear Axle Oil — Change	Level Control Fluid — Refill	Brake Fluid — Refill	Clutch Fluid — Refill	Wheel Bearings — Repack	Parking Brake Rails — Lube	Door [12] Hinges [17] — Lube
190c	12.0	3.0	12.0	12.0		3.0	3.0	12.0	6.0	12.0
200	12.0	3.0	12.0	12.0		3.0	3.0	12.0	6.0	12.0
190Dc	11.4	1.9	11.4	11.4		1.9	1.9	11.4	5.7	11.4
200D	12.0	3.0	12.0	12.0		3.0	3.0	12.0	6.0	12.0
230	12.0	3.0	12.0	12.0		3.0	3.0	12.0	6.0	12.0
220b	11.4	1.9	11.4	11.4		1.9	1.9	11.4	5.7	11.4
220Sb	11.4	1.9	11.4	11.4		1.9	1.9	11.4	5.7	11.4
230S	12.0	3.0	12.0	12.0		3.0	3.0	12.0	6.0	12.0
250S	12.0	3.0	12.0	12.0		3.0	3.0	12.0	6.0	12.0
220SEb	11.4	1.9	11.4	11.4		1.9	1.9	11.4	5.7	11.4
250SE	12.0	3.0	12.0	12.0		3.0	3.0	12.0	6.0	12.0
230SL [14]	11.4	1.9	11.4	11.4		1.9	1.9	11.4	5.7	11.4
250SL	12.0	3.0	12.0	12.0		3.0	3.0	12.0	6.0	12.0
220SEb/C [1]	11.4	1.9	11.4	11.4		1.9	1.9	11.4	5.7	11.4
250SE/C [2]	12.0	3.0	12.0	12.0		3.0	3.0	12.0	6.0	12.0
250SE/C [3]	12.0	3.0	12.0	12.0		3.0	3.0	12.0	6.0	12.0
300SE [4]	11.4	1.9		11.4	1.9 [13]	1.9	1.9	11.4	5.7	11.4
300SE [5]	11.4	1.9		11.4	1.9 [13]	1.9	1.9	11.4	5.7	11.4
300SE [6]	11.4	1.9		11.4	1.9 [13]	1.9	1.9	11.4	5.7	11.4
300SEb	12.0	3.0		12.0		3.0		12.0	6.0	12.0
300SEL	12.0	3.0		12.0	3.0 [13]	3.0		12.0	6.0	12.0
300SE [7]	12.0	3.0		12.0	3.0 [13]	3.0		12.0	6.0	12.0
300SE [8]	12.0	3.0		12.0	3.0 [13]	3.0		12.0	6.0	12.0
220D/8	12.0	3.0	12.0	12.0	3.0	3.0	3.0	12.0	6.0	12.0
220/8	12.0	3.0	12.0	12.0	3.0	3.0	3.0	12.0	6.0	12.0
230/8	12.0	3.0	12.0	12.0	3.0	3.0	3.0	12.0	6.0	12.0
250/8	12.0	3.0	12.0	12.0	3.0	3.0	3.0	12.0	6.0	12.0
280S/8	12.0	3.0	12.0	12.0	3.0	3.0	3.0	12.0	6.0	12.0
280SE/8	12.0	3.0	12.0	12.0	3.0	3.0	3.0	12.0	6.0	12.0
280SEL/8	12.0	3.0	12.0	12.0	3.0	3.0	3.0	12.0	6.0	12.0
280SE/8 [1]	12.0	3.0	12.0	12.0	3.0	3.0	3.0	12.0	6.0	12.0
280SL/8	12.0	3.0	12.0	12.0	3.0	3.0	3.0	12.0	6.0	12.0
300SEL/8	12.0	3.0		12.0	3.0	3.0	3.0	12.0	6.0	12.0
300SEL/8 6.3		3.0		12.0	3.0 [13]	3.0		12.0 [16]	6.0	12.0

[1] Every 1,000 miles under adverse conditions

[2] At same mileage, oil miscellaneous hinges, joints, linkages, distributor felt

[3] Antifreeze unit for air suspension below 41° F. Fill to top of corrugation with ethyl alcohol

[4] To August, 1965. From August, 1965 same as 230S except injection pump interval

[5] From August, 1965—12,000 miles

[6] Also every spring and fall

[7] At same mileage, grease water pump and wedge in contact breaker if applicable

Distributor Specifications

Model	Bosch Distributor Number	Basic Timing Test Light ±1°	Basic Timing Strobe Light (starter speed) *	800 rpm w/o & w vacuum	Dynamic Timing (No Load) 1,500 rpm w/o vacuum	Dynamic Timing (No Load) 3,000 rpm w/o vacuum	Dynamic Timing (No Load) 4,500 rpm w/o vacuum	Range of Vacuum Advance	Start of Vacuum Advance at No-Load rpm
190c	VJUR4BR27T	2°B	3°B	8-13°B	22-27°	28-32°	37-41°	11 ±3°	1,000-1,200
200	IFUR4 0231 115 052 ⑧	5°A	6°B	9-15°B	23-29°	29-35°	43°	11 ±3°	1,000-1,200
	0231 115 060 ⑦			TDC ±2°	24-31°	31-37°	43°		
230, 230S, 250S	IFUR6 0231 116 038	1°B	3°B	5-15°B	20-27°	25-31°	37°	10 ±3°	1,400-1,600
	IFUR6 0231 116 048	1°B	3°B	5-15°B	20-27°	25-31°	37°	10 ±3°	1,800-2,000
	IFUR6 0231 116 052 ⑦			TDC ②	19-28°	29-35°	37°		
220b, 220Sb	VJUR6BR47T 0231 116 038	2°A	TDC	4-11°	18-23°	23-27°	33°	11 ±2°	1,400-1,600 1,800-2,000 ①
220SEb, 220SEb/C	VJUR6BR45T	2°A	TDC	TDC	11-15°	26°	26°	14 ±3°	800-1,000
	VJUR6BR49T	2°A	TDC	0-3°B	11-15°	26°	26°	14 ±3°	800-1,000
	VJUR6BR61T	4°B	6°B	4-7°B	15-19°	26°	26°	14 ±3°	800-1,000
250SE, 250SL, 250SE/C	IFUR6 0231 11 6047	3°B	5°B ②		13-20°	30°	30°		
	IFUR6 0231 11 6051 ⑦	6°B	8°B ②	2°A ±2°	12-19°	30°	30°		
230SL	VJUR6BR49	2°B	4°B	4-7°B	15-19°	30°	30°	14 ±3°	800-1,000
				8°B	10-12°	30°	30°	14 ±3°	800-1,000
300SE	ZV/PBUR6RI	1°B	3°B	8-15°B	21-26°	26°	26°	11 ±2°	800-1,000
300SE ③④	ZV/PBUR6RIT 0231 141 001	3°B	4°B	8-15°B	21-26°	26°	26°	11 ±3°	800-1,000
300SE ⑤	PFUR6 0231 141 002	3°B	4°B	8-18°B	21-28°	28°	28°	11 ±3°	800-1,000
300SEb, 300SEL	PFUR6 0231 141 004 ⑥	TDC	1°B	2°B	14-24°	28°	28°	8 ±3°	800-1,000
220/8	JFUR4 0231 115 065			2°A +3/-2° ⑨			43°		
	JFUR4 0231 115 060 ⑦	5°B		TDC ±2°	25-32°	31-37°	43°		
230/8 250/8	JFUR6 0231 116 052 ⑦	TDC		TDC	19-28°	29-35°	37°	10 ±3°	1,800-2,000
280S/8	JFUR6 0231 116 052 ⑦	TDC		TDC	19-28°	29-35°	37°	10 ±3°	1,800-2,000
280SE/8, 280SL/8	JFUR6 0231 116 051 ⑦			2°A±2° ⑨	12-19°	30°	30°	10 ±3°	
300SEL/8	JFUR6 0231 116 051 ⑦			2°A±2° ⑨	12-19°	30°	30°	10 ±3°	
300SEL/8 6.3	TFUR8 0231 119 004 ⑦			2°A±2°	13-21°	26°	26°	10 ±3°	600-620

* With spark plugs installed.
① 250S, 230S, 230 with 180.949 engine.
② Without vacuum advance.
③ Long wheelbase.
④ Coupe to August, 1965.
⑤ Coupe and convertible from August, 1965.
⑥ Manual transmission only.
⑦ Exhaust emission control only.
⑧ Without exhaust emission control.
⑨ With vacuum advance only.

NOTE: *The timing light check at cranking speed is only for finding approximate ignition timing values. To help eliminate errors, check cylinders No. 1 and No. 4 on four-cylinder engines, No. 1 and No. 6 on six-cylinder engines; the values should vary not more than 1.5°.*

Distributor Advance Curves

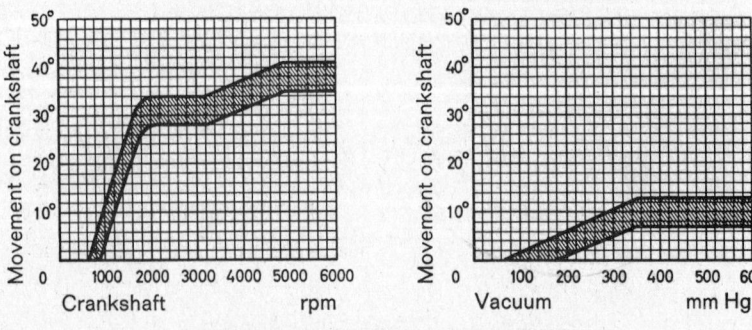

JFUR 6 0231 116 052 for 230/8, 250/8.

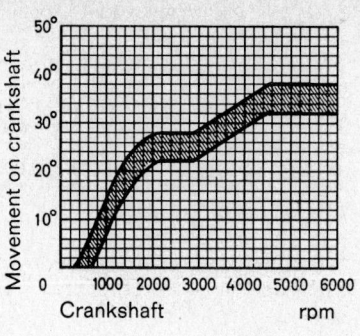

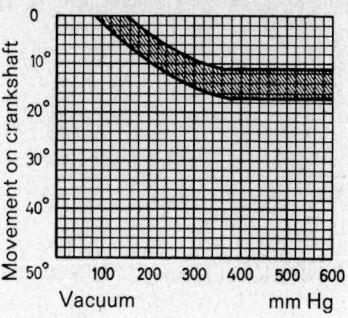

JFUR 4 0231 115 060 for 220/8.

Automatic governor control movement

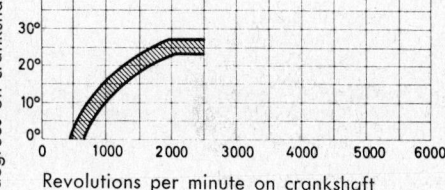

Automatic vacuum control movement

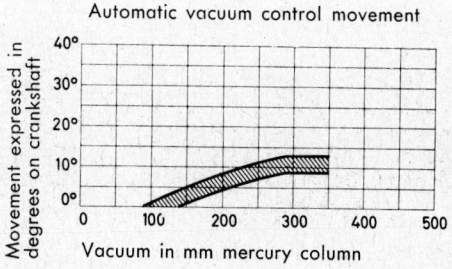

ZVI/PBUR 6 R1 for 300SE.

Automatic governor control movement

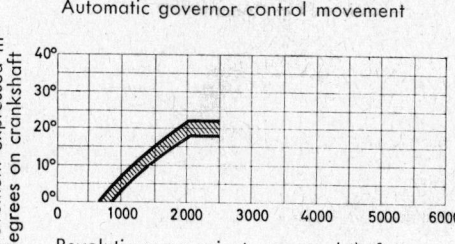

Automatic vacuum control movement

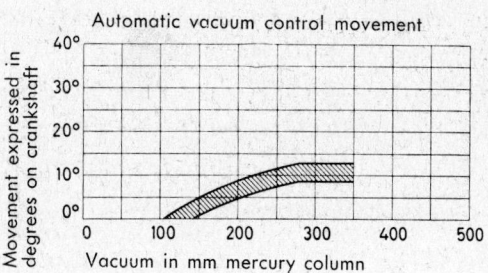

VJUR BR 61 T for 220SEb (third version).

Automatic governor control movement

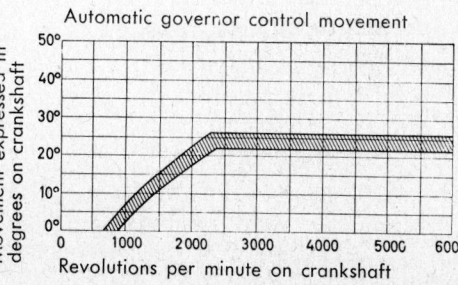

Automatic vacuum control movement

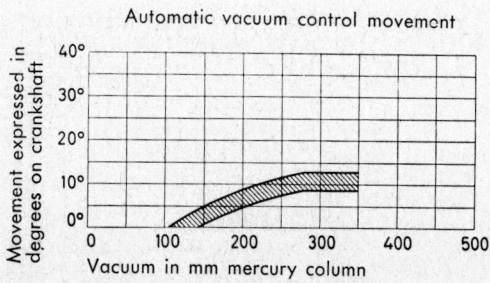

VJUR 6 BR 49 T for 220SEb (second version).

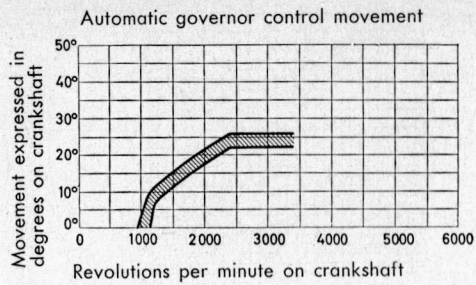

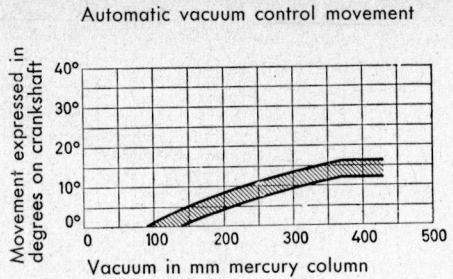

VJUR 6 BR 45 T for 220SEb (first version).

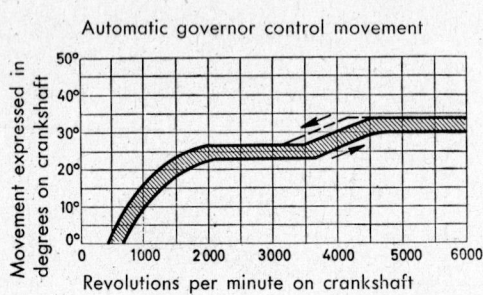

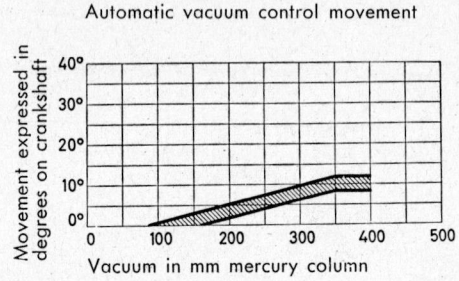

VJUR 6 BR 47 T for 220 b, 220Sb.

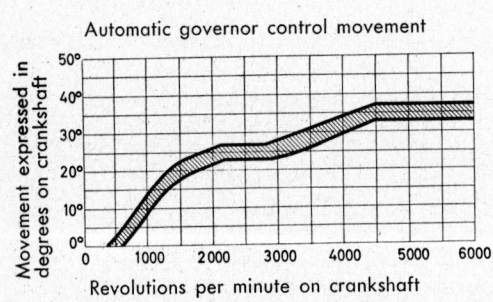

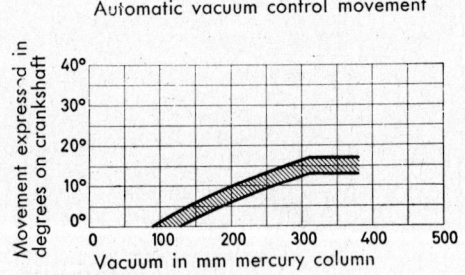

VJUR 4 BR 27 T for 190c.

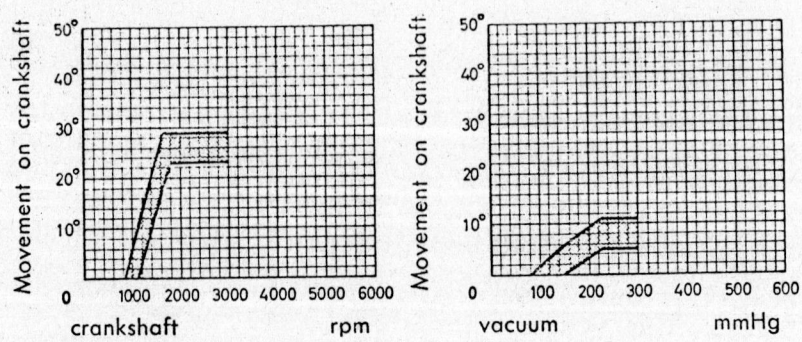

PFUR 6 (R) 0231 141 004 for 300SEb, 300SEL (second version) all manual transmission.

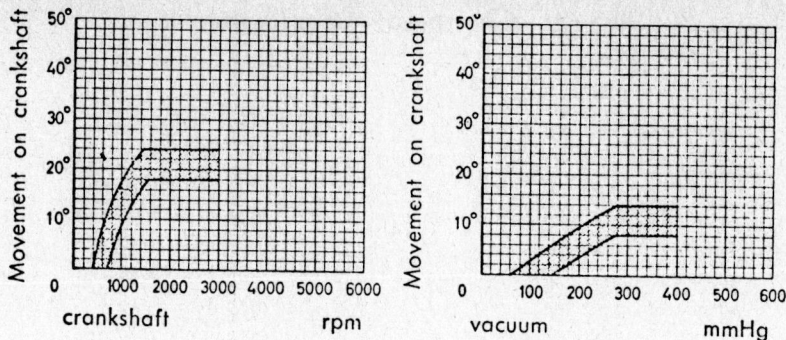

ZV/PBUR 6 R 1 T 0231 141 001 for 300SE (185 H.P.).
PFUR 6 (R) 0231 141 002 for 300SEb, 300SEL (first version), 300 SE
(195 H.P.)

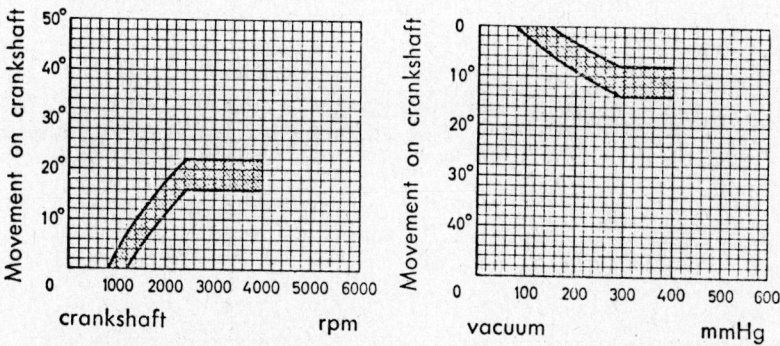

JFUR 6 (R) 0231 116 051 for 230SL (fourth version), 250SE (second
version), 250SL.

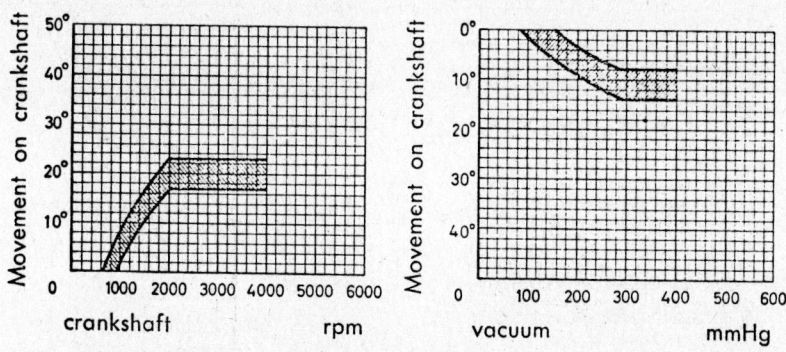

JFUR 6 (R) 0231 116 047 for 230SL (third version), 250SE (first version).

Wheel Alignment Specifications

Model	Front Camber		Front Caster		Front Toe-in (in.)	King Pin Inclination	Rear Toe-in (in.)
	Curb ▲	Test ★	Manual	Power			
190c	+0°30' ± 10'	0°20' −20'	3°30' ± 15'	4° ± 15'	.080 ± .040	5°30' ± 10'	± .080
200	+0°30' ± 10'	0°20' −20'	3°30' ± 15'	4° ± 15'	.080 ± .040	5°30' ± 10'	± .080
190Dc	+0°30' ± 10'	0°20' −20'	3°30' ± 15'	4° ± 15'	.080 ± .040	5°30' ± 10'	± .080
200D	+0°30' ± 10'	0°20' −20'	3°30' ± 15'	4° ± 15'	.080 ± .040	5°30' ± 10'	± .080
230	+0°30' ± 10'	0°20' −20'	3°30' ± 15'	4° ± 15'	.080 ± .040	5°30' ± 10'	± .080
220b	+0°30' ± 10'	0°20' −20'	2°45' ± 15'	4° ± 15'	.080 ± .040	5°30' ± 10'	± .080
220Sb	+0°30' ± 10'	0°20' −20'	2°45' ± 15'	4° ± 15'	.080 ± .040	5°30' ± 10'	± .080
230S	+0°30' ± 10'	0°20' −20'	3°30' ± 15'	4° ± 15'	.080 ± .040	5°30' ± 10'	± .080
250S	+0°30' ± 10'	0°20' −20'	3°30' ± 15'	4° ± 15'	.080 ± .040	5°30' ± 10'	± .080
220SEb	+0°30' ± 10'	0°20' −20'	2°45' ± 15'	4° ± 15'	.080 ± .040	5°30' ± 10'	± .080
220SEb/C	+0°30' ± 10'	0°20' −20'	3°30' ± 15'	4° ± 15'	.080 ± .040	5°30' ± 10'	± .080
250SE	+0°30' ± 10'	0°20' −20'	3°30' ± 15'	4° ± 15'	.080 ± .040	5°30' ± 10'	± .080
230SL	+0°10' + 20'	0° + 20'	3°30' ± 15'	4° ± 15'	.080 ± .040	5°30' ± 10'	± .080
250SL	+0°10' + 20'	0° + 20'	3°30' ± 15'	4 ± 15'	.080 ± .040	5°30' ± 10'	± .080
300SE, SEL	+0°20' − 20'			4° ± 15'	.080 ± .040	5°30' ± 10'	± .080
300SEb	+0°30' ± 10'	0°20' −20'	3°30 15'	4° ± 15'	.080 ± .040	5°30 ± 10'	± .080
220D/8	0° ± 10'	0° ± 10'	2°30' ± 20'	3°30' ± 20'	.200 ± .040	6° ± 10'	.040 +.080 −.040
220/8	0° ± 10'	0° ± 10'	2°30' ± 20'	3°30' ± 20'	.200 ± .040	6° ± 10'	.040 +.080 −.040
230/8	0° ± 10'	0° ± 10'	2°30' ± 20'	3°30' ± 20'	.200 ± .040	6° ± 10'	.040 +.080 −.040
250/8	0° ± 10'	0° ± 10'	2°30' ± 20'	3°30' ± 20'	.200 ± .040	6° ± 10'	.040 +.080 −.040
280S/8	0° ± 10'	0° ± 10'	2°30' ± 20'	3°30' ± 20'	.200 ± .040	6° ± 10'	.040 +.080 −.040
280SE/8	0° ± 10'	0° ± 10'	2°30' ± 20'	3°30' ± 20'	.200 ± .040	6° ± 10'	.040 +.080 −.040
280SL/8	0° ± 10'	0° ± 10'	2°30' ± 20'	3°30' ± 20'	.200 ± .040	6° ± 10'	.040 +.080 −.040
300SEL/8	0° ± 10'	0° ± 10'	2°30' ± 20'	3°30' ± 20'	.200 ± .040	6° ± 10'	.040 +.080 −.040
300SEL/8 6.3	0°20' −20'	+0°20' −20'		6° ± 15'	.080 ± .040	5°30'± 10'	± .080

▲   *Check in this attitude.*
★   *Adjust in this attitude, with proper test load.*
①   *Station wagon — +2° ± 30'.*
②   *Station wagon — +1° ± 30'.*
③   *Coupe and Convertible — +0°30' ± 1°.*
④   *Station wagon — +0°30' ± 1°.*
⑤   *Operate level valve connecting rods at left and right front and center*
     rear (by hand) until specified level reached.
⑥   *With air suspension — −0°45' ± 15' curb, -0°45' ± 1° test.*

TEST LOADS: Sedan, Coupe, Convertible — 286 lbs. front seat, 143 lbs. rear seat
                Sports cars — 330 lbs. front seat, 88 lbs. in trunk
                Station Wagon — same as sedan

Wheel Alignment Specifications *(Continued)*

	Rear Wheel Camber							
	Without Level Control				With Level Control			
	Standard Suspension		H.D. Suspension		Standard Suspension		H.D. Suspension	
Model	Curb ▲	Test ★	Curb ▲	Test ★	Curb ▲	Test ★	Curb ▲	Test ★
190c	+1°30' ± 30'	−0°45' ± 30'	+2°15' ± 30' ①	+0°30' ± 30' ②	+0°30' ± 1°	−0°45' ± 30'	+1° ± 1° ④	+0°30' ± 1° ④
200	+1°30' ± 30'	−0°45' ± 30'	+2°15' ± 30'	+0°30' ± 30'	+0°30' ± 1°	−0°45' ± 30'	+1° ± 1° ④	+0°30' ± 1° ④
190Dc	+1°30' ± 30'	−0°45' ± 30'	+2°15' ± 30' ①	+0°30' ± 30' ②	+0°30' ± 1°	−0°45' ± 30'	+1° ± 1° ④	+0°30' ± 1° ④
200D	+1°30' ± 30'	−0°45' ± 30'	+2°15' ± 30'	+0°30' ± 30'	+0°30' ± 1°	−0°45' ± 30'	+1° ± 1° ④	+0°30' ± 1° ④
230	+1°30' ± 30'	−0°45' ± 30'	+2°15' ± 30'	+0°30' ± 30'	+0°30' ± 1°	−0°45' ± 30'	+1° ± 1°	+0°30' ± 1°
220b	+1°30' ± 30'	−0°45' ± 30'	+2°15' ± 30'	+0°30' ± 30'	+0°30' ± 1°	−0°45' ± 30'	+1° ± 1°	+0°30' ± 1°
220Sb	+1°30' ± 30'	−0°45' ± 30'	+2°15' ± 30'	+0°30' ± 30'	0° ± 1°	−0°45' ± 30'	+0°45' ± 1°	+0°30' ± 1°
230S					0° ± 1°	−0°45' ± 30'	+0°45' ± 1° ④	+0°30' ± 1° ④
250S					0° ± 1°	−0°45' ± 30'	+0°45' ± 1°	+0°30' ± 1°
220SEb	+1°30' ± 30'	−0°45' ± 30'	+2°15' ± 30'	+0°30' ± 30'	0° ± 1°	−0°45' ± 30'	+0°45' ± 1°	+0°30' ± 1°
220SEb/C	+1°30' ± 30'	−1°15' ± 30'	+1°30' ± 30'	+0°30' ± 30'	0° ± 1°	−0°45' ± 30'	+0°30' ± 1°	+0°30' ± 1°
250SE					0° ± 1°	−0°45' ± 30'	+0°45' ± 1° ③	+0°30' ± 1°
230SL	+1°45' ± 30'	−1°45' ± 30'	+1°30' ± 30'	+1°30' ± 30'				
250SL	+1 30' ± 30'	−1 45' ± 30'	+1 30' ± 30'	+1 30' ± 30'				
300SE, SEL					⑤ ⑥	⑤ ⑥		
300SEb					0° ± 1°	−0°45'	+0°45'	+0°30' ± 1°
220D/8	−0°45' ± 20'	−0°45' ± 20'	−0°5' ± 20'	−0°5' ± 20'	−1°15' ± 20'	−1°15' ± 20'	−0°5' ± 20'	−0°5' ± 20'
220/8	−0°45' ± 20'	−0°45' ± 20'	−0°5' ± 20'	−0°5' ± 20'	−1°15' ± 20'	−1°15' ± 20'	−0°5' ± 20'	−0°5' ± 20'
230/8	−0°45' ± 20'	−0°45' ± 20'	−0°5' ± 20'	−0°5' ± 20'	−1°15' ± 20'	−1°15' ± 20'	−0°5' ± 20'	−0°5' ± 20'
250/8	−0°45' ± 20'	−0°45' ± 20'	−0°5' ± 20'	−0°5' ± 20'	−1°15' ± 20'	−1°15' ± 20'	−0°5' ± 20'	−0°5' ± 20'
280S/8	−0°45' ± 20'	−0°45' ± 20'	−0°5' ± 20'	−0°5' ± 20'	−1°15' ± 20'	−1°15' ± 20'	−0°5' ± 20'	−0°5' ± 20'
280SE/8	−0°45' ± 20'	−0°45' ± 20'	−0°5' ± 20'	−0°5' ± 20'	−1°15' ± 20'	−1°15' ± 20'	−0°5' ± 20'	−0°5' ± 20'
280SL/8	−0°45' ± 20'	−0°45' ± 20'	−0°5' ± 20'	−0°5' ± 20'	−1°15' ± 20'	−1°15' ± 20'	−0°5' ± 20'	−0°5' ± 20'
300SEL/8	−0°45' ± 20'	−0°45' ± 20'	−0°5' ± 20'	−0°5' ± 20'	−1°15' ± 20'	−1°15' ± 20'	−0°5' ± 20'	−0°5' ± 20'
300SEL/8 6.3					−0°45' ± 15'	−0°45' ± 1°		

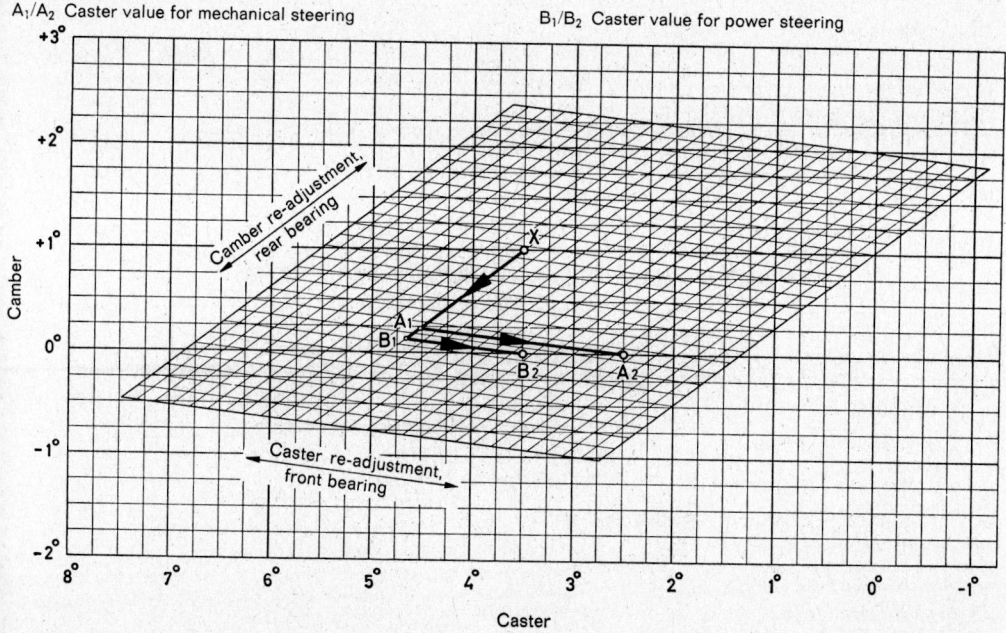

A₁/A₂ Caster value for mechanical steering   B₁/B₂ Caster value for power steering

The relationship of caster to camber for phase II models.

Clutch Pressure Plate Specifications

Clutch Pressure Plate—Coil Spring Type

Specification		190c 190Dc 200 200D	220b 220Sb 220SEb Sedan	220 SEb/C	230 230S 230SL 250S 250SE	300SE 300SEb 300SEL
Control dimension "e" between cover plate and release levers with new driven plate installed	(mm.)	17.5±0.2		7.0±0.2		18±0.2
Resulting adjusting dimension of worn-out driven plate	(mm.)	24.5		14		11
Adjusting dimension "d" for clutch assembly	(mm.)	41.4		36.8		42.5
Travel "i" of release levers because of permissible wear of driven plate	(mm.)			7		
Throwout travel "h" of release levers	(mm.max.)			10		10.6
Free-play "g" between throwout bearing and release levers (clutch free-play)	(mm.)			2		
Maximum permissible difference between the release levers ①	(mm.)			0.3		
Thickness "c" of pressure plate	(mm.)	15		16.5		14.5
Regrind dimension of the pressure plate ②	(mm.max.)			1		
Maximum permissible unbalance of the pressure plate	(cmg.)	20		15		
Contact pressure	(pounds)	1045		1185±55		1360
Clutch springs	Number			9		
	Color code	colorless and gold		yellow and gold		light blue and gold
	External diameter (mm.)	29		28.6		27.4
	Wire gauge	4		4.1		4.2
	Free length (mm.)	50		55.1		58.5
	Length under load (mm.)	32.4		37.2		39.5
	Load (kg.)	53+6		61.5±2.5		69±3.5

①   *Press down the release levers several times before measuring.*

②   *If the reduction in thickness exceeds .020", shims corresponding in thickness to the total amount of material removed should be placed between the clutch springs and the cups to restore the total spring pressure.*

Clutch Pressure Plate—Diaphragm Spring Type

Specification		220D/8 220/8	230/8 250/8
Contact pressure	(pounds)	1080—1235	1185—1320
Max. permissible unbalance	(cmg.)	15	20
Throwout travel "e" at thrust ring	(mm.)		9
Travel "f" of thrust ring due to permissible wear of driven plate	(mm.)		8
Control dimension "d" for new driven plate	(mm.)	48	47.9
for driven plate with max. wear	(mm.)	56	55.9

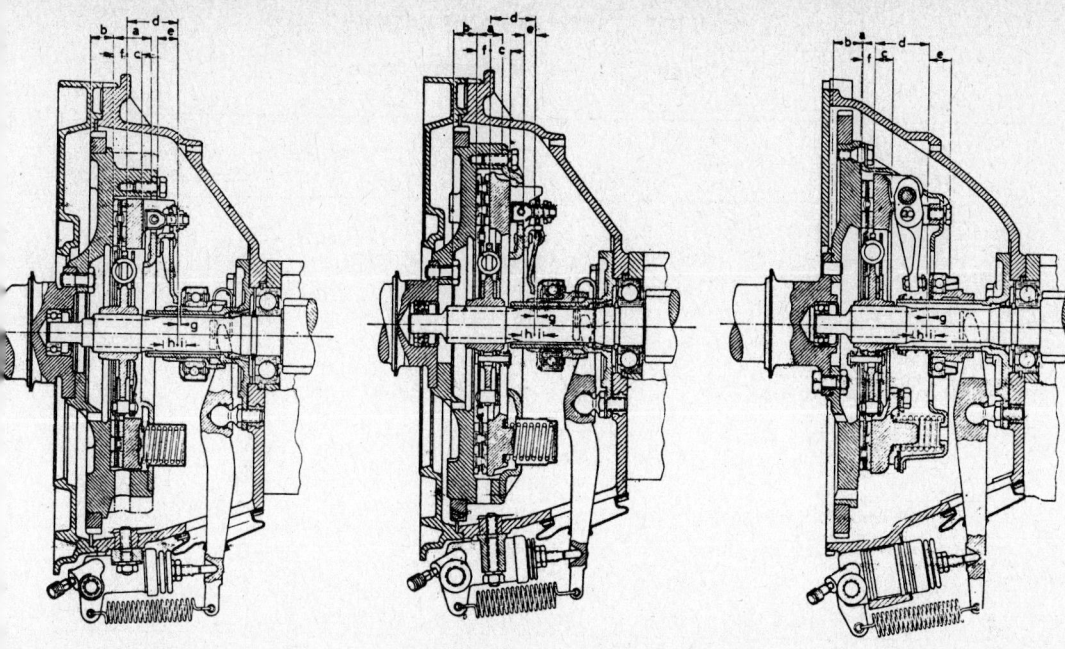

Clutch used on 190c, 190Dc, 200 and 200D models.

Clutch used on 220b, 220Sb, 220-SEb, 230SL, 230, 230S, 250S, and 250SE models.

Clutch used on 300SE and 300-SEL with manual transmission and on 300SEb.

a = Clearance between clutch face and clutch clamping face on the flywheel
b = Clearance between clutch face and flywheel attaching flange
c = Thickness of clutch pressure plate
d = Adjusting dimension for clutch assembly
e = Control dimension between cover plate and release levers for new driven plate

f = Thickness of new driven plate compressed
g = Free-play between throw-out bearing and release levers (clutch free-play)
h = Throwout travel
i = Travel of release levers because of driven plate wear

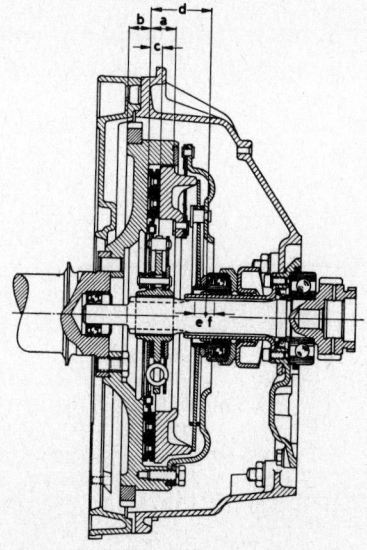

a. Indicates the distance between the clutch face and the contact face at the flywheel;
b. Indicates the distance between the clutch face and the flywheel attaching flange;
c. Indicates the thickness of the new driven plate in compressed condition (clutch contact pressure);
d. Indicates a control dimension between the clutch face at the flywheel and the external thrust ring face at the clutch with new driven plate.
e. Indicates the throwout travel
f. Indicates the thrust ring travel due to permissible wear of the driven plate.

Diaphragm spring clutch used on phase II models.

Clutch Plate Specifications

Clutch Plate—Coil Spring Type

Specification			190c 190Dc 200, 200D	220b 220Sb 220SEb	230, 230S 230SL 250S, 250SE	300SE 300SEb 300SEL
Thickness of the driven plate "f"						
	released	(mm.)	10.3+0.3		10.3+0.4	10.6+0.4
	compressed	(mm.)	9.1+0.3		+0.4 9.1-0.1	+0.4 9.3-0.1
Thickness of facing		(mm.)	3.5		3.8	3.5
Permissible wear of facing thickness on either side		(mm.)		1		
Permissible unbalance		(cmg.)		5		
Permissible runout		(mm.)		0.5		
Permissible radial play on driveshaft		(mm.)		0.04±0.01		
Torsion damper — Free motion torque, traction side		(mkg.)	17.3		20	30
Torsion damper — Stop angle		(deg.)	8°30'		5°	4°
Torsion damper — Friction torque		(mkg.)	0.6—0.9		1.4—1.7	0.9—1.2

Clutch Plate—Diaphragm Spring Type

Specification			220D/8 220/8	230/8 250/8
Thickness of driven plate "c"				
	released	(mm.)	10.3	
	compressed	(mm.)	8.9	
Thickness of lining		(mm.)	3.8	
Permissible wear on lining thickness (per side)		(mm.)	1	
Permissible unbalance		(cmg.)	5	
Permissible runout		(mm.)	0.5	
Permissible radial play on driveshaft		(mm.)	0.04 ±0.01	
Torsion damper — Free motion torque traction side		(mkg.)	17	20
Torsion damper — Stop angle		(deg.)	8°30'	5°
Torsion damper — Friction torque		(mkg.)	0.6—0.9	1.4—1.7

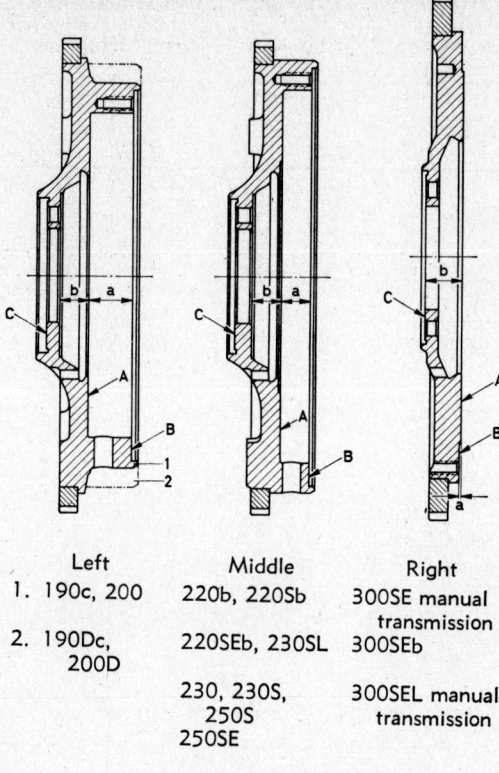

Left	Middle	Right
1. 190c, 200	220b, 220Sb	300SE manual transmission
2. 190Dc, 200D	220SEb, 230SL	300SEb
	230, 230S, 250S 250SE	300SEL manual transmission

Flywheel tolerances.

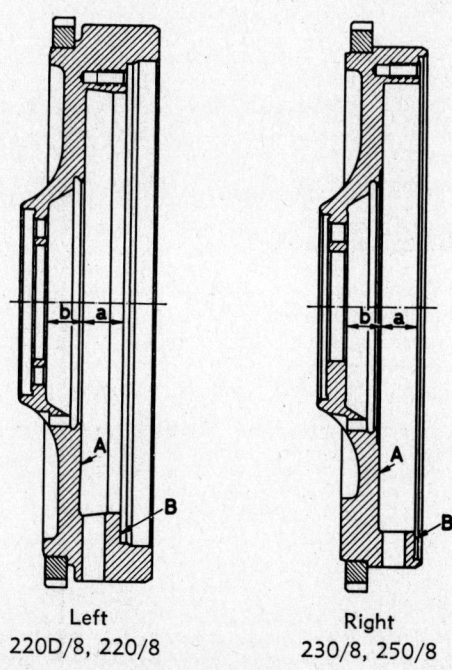

Left	Right
220D/8, 220/8	230/8, 250/8

Flywheel tolerances.

Throwout Bearing Specifications

Throwout Bearing—Coil Spring Clutches

Specification		190c to 230SL	300SE
Internal diameter of the throwout bearing	(mm.)	39.988 / 40.000	49.988 / 50.000
External diameter of the throwout bearing	(mm.)	40.006 / 39.995	50.006 / 49.995
Oversize (+) or play (−) of the throwout bearing on the throwout unit	(mm.)	−0.005	+0.018
Internal diameter of the throwout unit	(mm.)	35.600 / 35.639	40.100 / 40.139
External diameter of the transmission case front cover	(mm.)	35.500 / 35.438	40.000 / 39.938
Clearance between throwout unit and neck at transmission case front cover	(mm.)	0.1—0.2	

Throwout Bearing—Diaphragm Spring Clutches

Specification		220D/8—250/8
Internal diameter of throwout bearing	(mm.)	41.6
External diameter of throwout bearing	(mm.)	68.000 / 67.987
Internal diameter of bearing seat within throwout unit	(mm.)	67.970 / 68.000
Seat tolerance between throwout bearing external dia. and throwout unit internal dia. Force fit (+); play (−)	(mm.)	+0.030 to −0.013
Internal diameter of throwout unit	(mm.)	34.050 / 34.112
External diameter of guide tube at transmission case front cover	(mm.)	34.000 / 33.938
Play between throwout unit and guide tube at transmission case front cover	(mm.)	0.050—0.174

Hydrak Automatic Hydraulic Clutch Specifications

Drive Plate for Clutch

Specification		220b 220Sb	220SE 220SEb
Clearance "a" between the clutch face and the clamping face for the pressure plate ①	(mm.)	1.5+0.1	19.4±0.1
Thickness "b" of drive plate			
new	(mm.)	14.5	31.0
when repaired	(mm.)	13.5	30.0
Permissible runout of mounted drive plate	(mm.)	0.05	

①   If the clutch face "A" is being reconditioned, the drive plate at the clutch clamping face "B" for the pressure plate should be machined so that the dimension "a" is maintained.

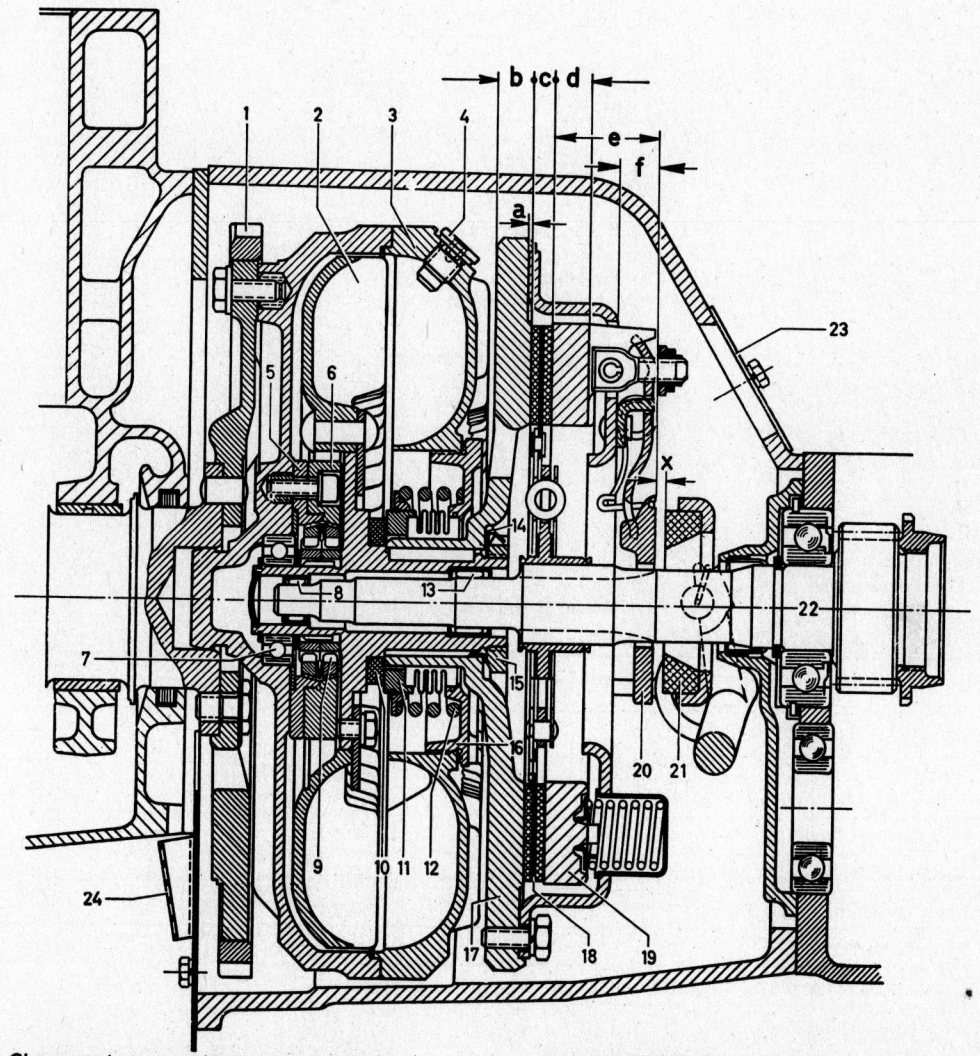

a = Clearance between clutch face and clutch clamping face for the clutch pressure plate
b = Thickness of drive plate
c = Thickness of driven plate
d = Thickness of pressure plate

e = Adjusting dimension of release levers between clutch face and contact ring
f = Adjusting dimension between cover plate and contact ring
x = Clutch free-play

Hydrak clutch.

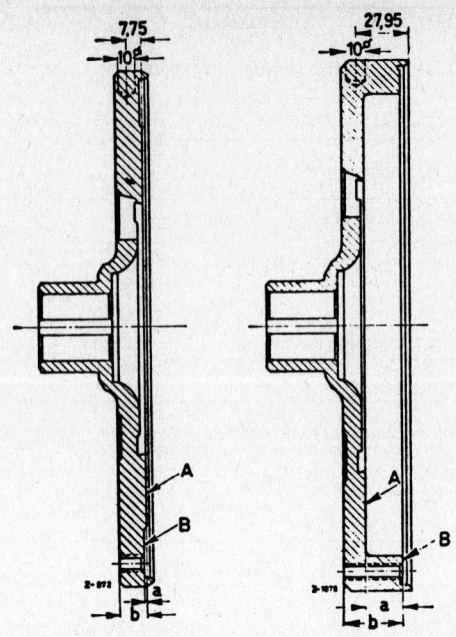

Left—220b, 220Sb   Right—220SE, 220SEb
A = Clutch face
B = Clutch clamping face for pressure plate
a = Clearance between clutch face and clutch
      clamping face
b = Thickness of drive plate

Hydrak drive plates.

Clutch Driven Plate

Specification		220b 220Sb	220SE 220SEb
Thickness of the driven plate "c"			
released	(mm.)	8.8+0.3	9.8+0.3
compressed	(mm.)	7.8+0.3	9.1+0.3
Thickness of facing	(mm.)	3.5	4.2
Permissible wear of facing thickness on either side	(mm.)	1	
Permissible unbalance	(cmg.)	5	
Permissible runout	(mm.)	0.5	
Permissible radial play on the drive shaft	(mm.)	0.04±0.01	
Torsion damping			
Free motion torque, traction side	(mkg.)	17.5	20
Stop angle	(degrees)	3°15′	5°
Friction torque	(mkg.)	0.4—0.8	0.9—1.3

Clutch Pressure Plate

Specification			220b 220Sb		220SE 220SEb	
Adjusting dimension "f" for new driven plate with clutch installed ①	(mm.)		15.5			
Resulting adjusting dimension of worn-out driven plate	(mm.)		23.5			
Thickness "d" of the pressure plate ②	(mm.)		15		16.5	
Regrind dimension of pressure plate	(mm.)		1			
Permissible unbalance of pressure plate	(cmg.)		15			
Thrust pressure	(pounds)		1055		1155	
Clutch springs	Number		3	6	3	6
	Color code		white with gold line	yellow with gold line	brown with gold line	yellow with gold line
	External diameter	(mm.)	25.6	25.75	29.0	28.6
	Wire gauge	(mm.)	3.6	3.75	3.8	4.1
	Free length	(mm.)	44	45	58.7	55.5
	Length under load	(mm.)	29.2		37.2	
	Load	(kg.)	45+4	56+4	46±3	61.5±2.5

① *Press down the release levers several times before measuring. It is important that the distance from the cover plate should be identical for all three release levers and that the difference should not exceed .012".*

② *If the reduction in thickness exceeds .020", shims corresponding in thickness to the total amount of material removed should be placed between the clutch springs and the cups and/or the pressure plate to restore the total spring pressure. The selection and the color designation of the springs can be seen from the table. The tolerance of pressure springs of the same color designation within a clutch should be as small as possible.*

Fuses

Fuse No.	Amps.	Lead	Consumer Units	Remarks
1	8	30	Roof light, reading light, clearance lights, electric clock, flash approach signal	Permanently live circuit
2	25	54	Windshield wipers, windshield washer, 1st and 2nd horn, cigar lighter	
3	8	54	Free for optional equipment or automatic transmission	Can be switched off by ignition starter switch in steering lock
4	8	54	Flash signal system, choke control or automatic choke control, fuel level mechanism and reserve gauge on pre-phase II carbureted models, stop light and reverse light on pre-phase II carbureted models, fuel pump on injected models	
5	8	54	Reversing light, fuel gauge, fuel reserve gauge, pilot light for parking and service brakes, defroster blower on pre-phase II carbureted models, idle increase and flash signal system on pre-phase II injected models	
6	8 (carb.) 25 (injec.)	54 54	Stop light, heater blower, upper beam flasher on all pre-phase II models, auto. starter, electromagnetic solenoid, and blower on injected pre-phase II models.	
7	8	58	Right tail light, right parking light, right license plate light[1]), instrument lighting, trunk compartment lighting	Can be switched off by light switch
8	8	58	Left tail light, left parking light, left license plate light[1]), fog lights, license plate light	
9	8	56a	Right upper beam, upper beam pilot light	Can be switched off by dimmer switch
10	8	56a	Left upper beam	
11	8	56b	Right lower beam	
12	8	56b	Left lower beam	

1) On Models 230 and 250.
The ignition is not fuse-protected.
There is a separate fuse for the radio, which can be switched on in the ignition lock position 1 (garage) and 2 (driving).
The radio is switched off in the 0 position.

Light Bulbs
All Models—1960-70

Usage	Wattage
Main headlights	45/40
Fog lights	35
Parking lights	4
Reverse lights	15
Tail lights	5
Brake lights	15
Flashers	18
License plate	10
Instrument and pilot	2
Clearance	3[1]
Interior	10

1 On 190c and 190Dc, 2 watts

Wiring Diagrams

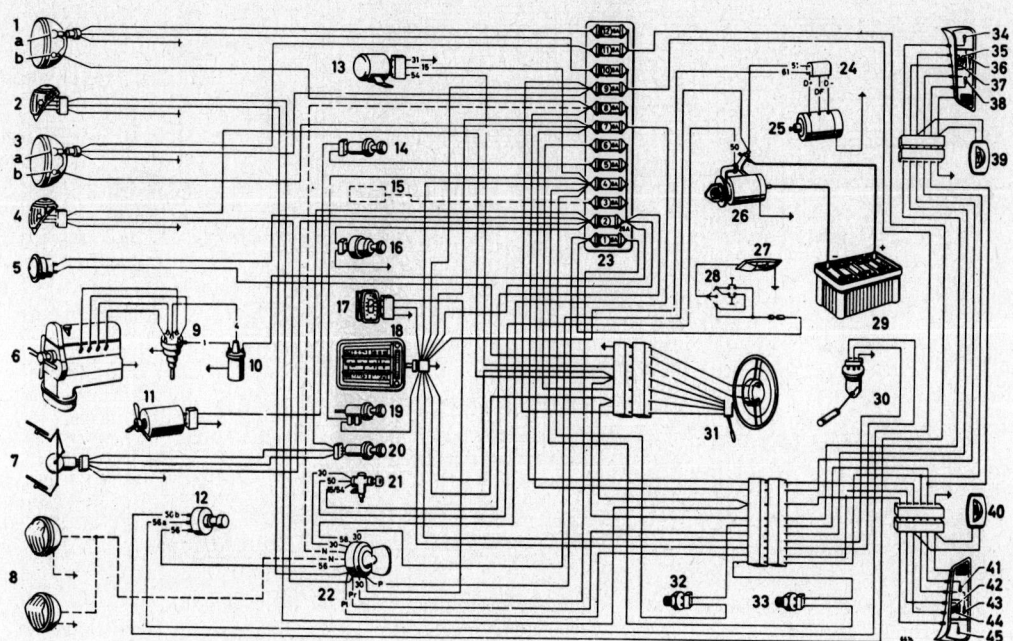

1a.	Headlight left, upper beam and lower beam	12.	Foot dimmer switch
1b.	Headlight left, parking light	13.	Flash signal mechanism
		14.	Heater blower switch
2.	Clearance and flash signal lights left	15.	Free for optional extra
		16.	Cigar lighter
3a.	Headlight right, upper beam and lower beam	17.	Clock
		18.	Instrument cluster
3b.	Headlight right, parking light	19.	Choke control
		20.	Windshield wiper switch
4.	Clearance and flash signal lights right	21.	Ignition starter switch
		22.	Light switch with additional positions for clearance light and pull switch for fog lights
5.	Horn		
6.	Engine		
7.	Windshield wiper	23.	Fuses
8.	Fog light (optional extra)	24.	Regulator
9.	Distributor	25.	Generator
10.	Ignition coil	26.	Starter
11.	Heater blower motor	27.	Reading light
		28.	Door contact switch

29.	Battery
30.	Fuel level indicator
31.	Flash signal switch with upper beam flash signal switch
32.	Stop light switch
33.	Reversing light switch
34.	Flash signal right
35.	Clearance light right
36.	Reversing light right
37.	Tail light right
38.	Stop light right
39.	License plate light right
40.	License plate light left
41.	Stop light left
42.	Tail light left
43.	Reversing light left
44.	Clearance light left
45.	Flash signal left

Wiring diagram—190c.

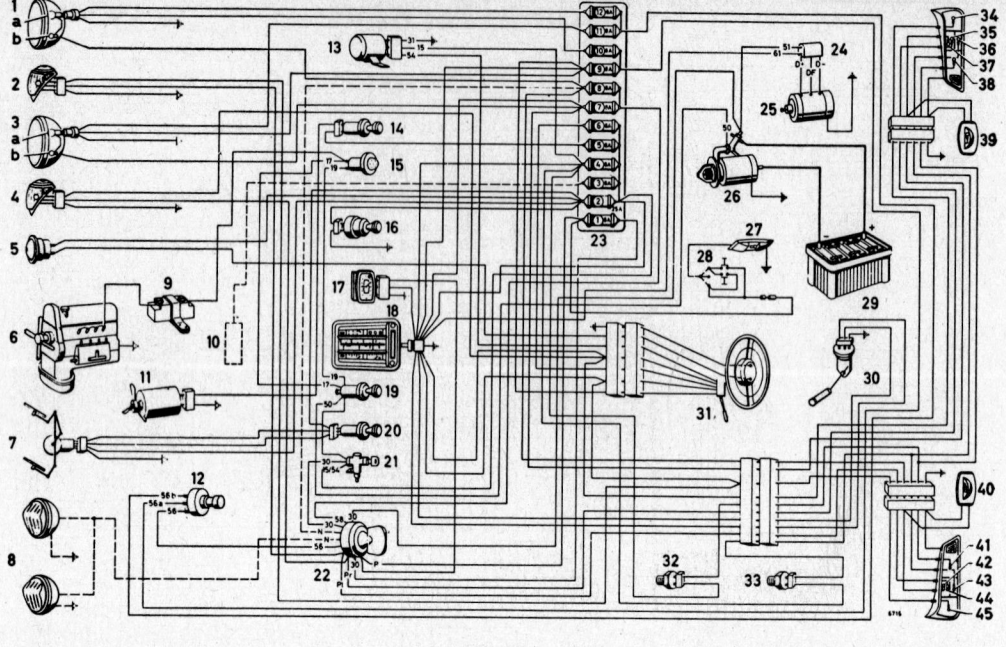

1a. Headlight left, upper beam and lower beam
1b. Headlight left, parking light
2. Clearance and flash signal lights left
3a. Headlight right, upper beam and lower beam
3b. Headlight right, parking light
4. Clearance and flash signal lights right
5. Horn
6. Engine
7. Windshield wiper
8. Fog light (optional extra)
9. Glow plug resistance
10. Free for optional extra
11. Heater blower motor

12. Foot dimmer switch
13. Flash signal mechanism
14. Heater blower switch
15. Glow plug indicator resistor
16. Cigar lighter
17. Clock
18. Instrument cluster
19. Glow plug starter switch
20. Windshield wiper switch
21. Steering lock
22. Light switch with additional positions for clearance light and pull switch for fog lights
23. Fuses
24. Regulator
25. Generator
26. Starter
27. Reading light
28. Door contact switch

29. Battery
30. Fuel level indicator
31. Flash signal switch with upper beam flash signal switch
32. Stop light switch
33. Reversing light switch
34. Flash signal right
35. Clearance light right
36. Reversing light right
37. Tail light right
38. Stop light right
39. License plate light right
40. License plate light left
41. Stop light left
42. Tail light left
43. Reversing light left
44. Clearance light left
45. Flash signal left

Wiring diagram—190Dc.

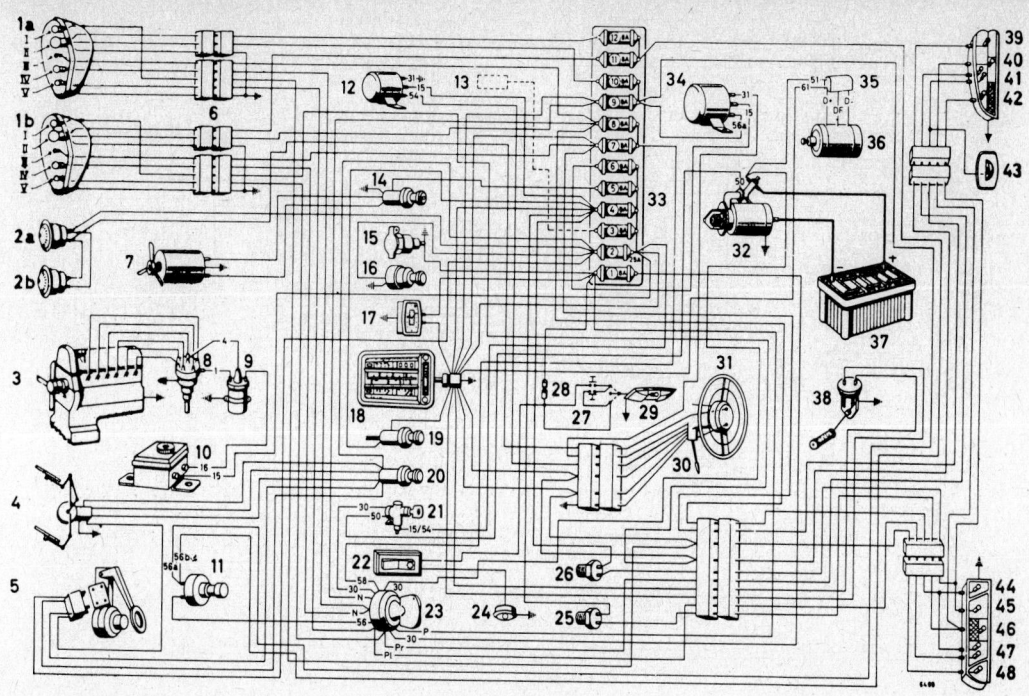

1a.	Lighting unit left	10.	Series resistance	29.	Reading light
	I. Flash signal light	11.	Foot dimmer switch	30.	Flash signal switch and
	II. Upper beam and lower	12.	Flash signal mechanism		upper beam signal
	beam	13.	Automatic clutch		switch
	III. Parking light		(optional)	31.	Steering wheel with horn
	IV. Fog light	14.	Heater blower switch		ring
	V. Clearance light	15.	Socket	32.	Starter
1b.	Lighting unit right	16.	Cigar lighter	33.	Fuses
	I. Flash signal light	17.	Clock	34.	Upper beam flash
	II. Upper beam and lower	18.	Instrument cluster		mechanism
	beam	19.	Choke control	35.	Regulator
	III. Parking light	20.	Windshield wiper switch	36.	Generator
	IV. Fog light	21.	Ignition starter switch	37.	Battery
	V. Clearance light	22.	Roof light switch	38.	Fuel level indicator
2a.	Horn right		(220 Sb)	39.	Flash signal right
2b.	Horn left	23.	Rotary light switch with	40.	Reversing light right
3.	Engine		positions for clearance	41.	Clearance light and tail
4.	Windshield wiper, two-		light left and right and		light right
	stage		pull switch for fog lights	42.	Stop light right
5.	Foot pump with switch for	24.	Roof light	43.	License plate light right
	windshield washer	25.	Reversing light switch	44.	License plate light left
6.	Plug connections	26.	Stop light switch	45.	Stop light left
7.	Heater blower motor	27.	Door contact switch	46.	Reversing light left
8.	Distributor	28.	Plug connections	47.	Tail and clearance light left
9.	Ignition coil			48.	Flash signal left

Wiring diagram—220b, 220Sb (first version).

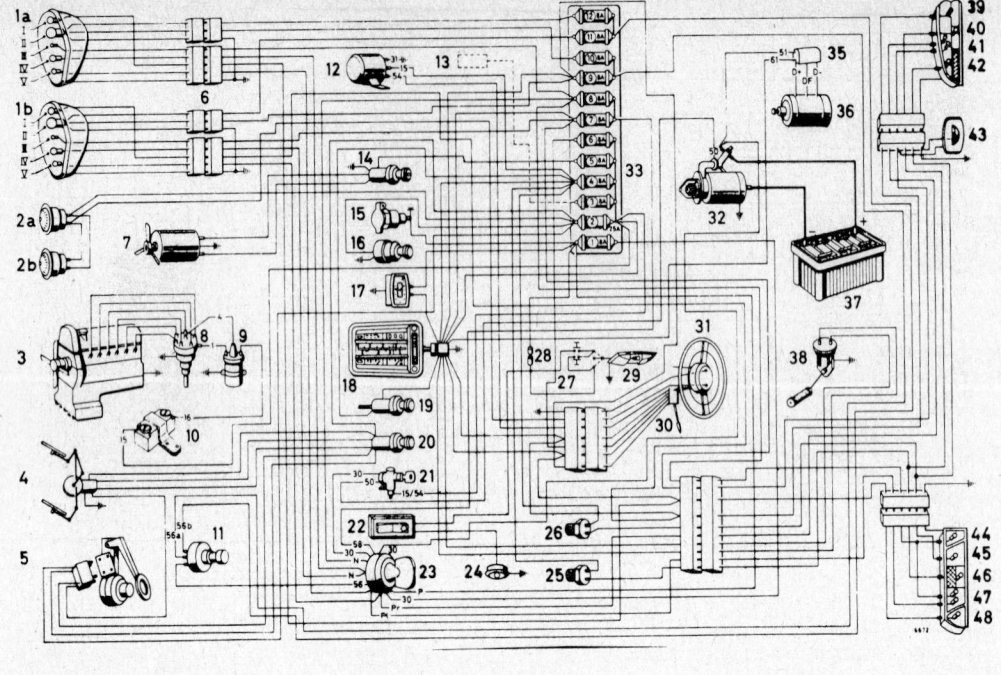

1a.	Lighting unit left	8.	Distributor	28.	Plug connection
I.	Flash signal light	9.	Ignition coil	29.	Reading light
II.	Upper beam and lower	10.	Series resistance	30.	Flash signal switch and
	beam	11.	Foot dimmer switch		upper beam flash signal
III.	Parking light	12.	Flash signal mechanism		switch
IV.	Fog light	13.	Free for optional extra	31.	Steering wheel with horn
V.	Clearance light	14.	Heater blower switch		ring
1b.	Lighting unit right	15.	Socket	32.	Starter 12 volts
I.	Flash signal light	16.	Cigar lighter	33.	Fuses
II.	Upper beam and lower	17.	Clock	35.	Regulator
	beam	18.	Instrument cluster	36.	Generator 12 volts
III.	Parking light	19.	Choke control	37.	Battery 12 volts
IV.	Fog light	20.	Windshield wiper switch	38.	Fuel level indicator
V.	Clearance light	21.	Steering lock	39.	Flash signal right
2a.	Horn right	22.	Roof light switch	40.	Reversing light right
2b.	Horn left		(only Model 220 S)	41.	Clearance light and tail
3.	Engine	23.	Light switch with additional		light right
4.	Windshield wiper		positions for clearance	42.	Stop light right
	(two-stage in 220 S)		light and pull switch for	43.	License plate light right
5.	Foot pump for windshield		fog lights	44.	License plate light left
	washer with switch for	24.	Roof light (only Model	45.	Stop light left
	windshield wiper		220 S)	46.	Reversing light left
6.	Plug connections	25.	Reversing light switch	47.	Tail and clearance light left
7.	Heater blower motor	26.	Stop light switch	48.	Flash signal left
		27.	Door contact switch		

Arrangement Model 220 S   Model 220

Wiring diagram—220b, 220Sb (second version).

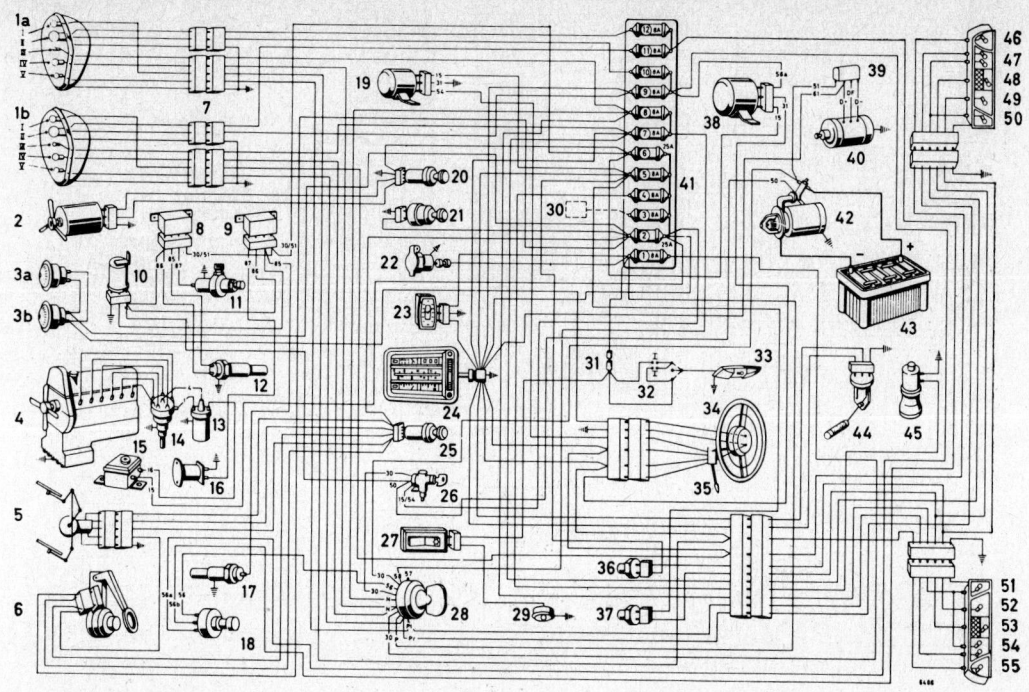

1a. Lighting unit left	11. Electro-magnetic starting	34. Steering wheel with horn
I. Flash signal light	valve	ring
II. Upper beam and lower	12. Thermo time switch	35. Flash signal switch and
beam	13. Ignition coil	upper beam flash signal
III. Parking light	14. Distributor	switch
IV. Fog light	15. Series resistance for	36. Stop light switch
V. Clearance light	ignition coil	37. Reversing light switch
1b. Lighting unit right	16. Magnet for mixture control	38. Beam flash signal
I. Flash signal light	17. Thermo switch	39. Regulator (Lima)
II. Upper beam and lower	18. Foot dimmer switch	40. Generator
beam	19. Flash signal mechanism	41. Fuses
III. Parking light	20. Switch for heater blower	42. Starter
IV. Fog light	motor	43. Battery
V. Clearance light	21. Cigar lighter	44. Fuel level indicator
2. Heater blower motor	22. Socket	45. Electric fuel feed pump
3a. Horn right	23. Electric clock	46. Flash signal right
3b. Horn left	24. Instrument cluster	47. Tail light and clearance
4. Spark plugs (engine)	25. Windshield wiper switch	light right
5. Windshield wiper	26. Steering lock	48. Reversing light right
6. Foot pump and switch for	27. Roof light switch	49. Stop light right
windshield washer	28. Rotary light switch	50. License plate light right
7. Plug connection	29. Roof light	51. Licnse plate light left
8. Relay for electromagnetic	30. Free for optional extra	52. Stop light left
starting valve	31. Plug connection	53. Reversing light left
9. Relay for automatic starter	32. Door contact switch left	54. Tail light and clearance
aid	and right	light left
10. Time switch	33. Reading light	55. Flash signal left

Wiring diagram—220b, 220Sb (first version).

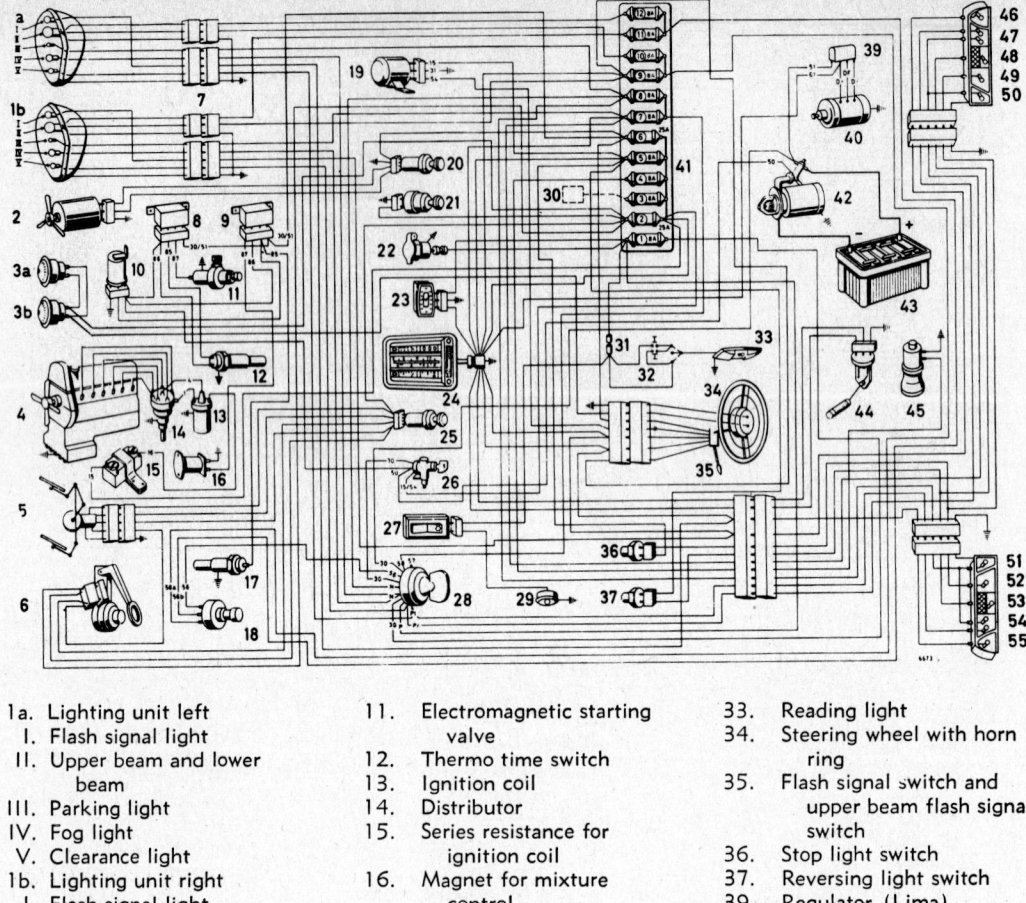

1a.	Lighting unit left
I.	Flash signal light
II.	Upper beam and lower beam
III.	Parking light
IV.	Fog light
V.	Clearance light
1b.	Lighting unit right
I.	Flash signal light
II.	Upper beam and lower beam
III.	Parking light
IV.	Fog light
V.	Clearance light
2.	Heater blower motor
3a.	Horn right
3b.	Horn left
4.	Spark plugs (engine)
5.	Windshield wiper, two-stage
6.	Foot pump and switch for windshield washer
7.	Plug connection
8.	Relay for electromagnetic starting valve
9.	Relay for automatic starter aid
10.	Time switch (delay switch)
11.	Electromagnetic starting valve
12.	Thermo time switch
13.	Ignition coil
14.	Distributor
15.	Series resistance for ignition coil
16.	Magnet for mixture control
17.	Thermo switch
18.	Foot dimmer switch
19.	Flash signal mechanism
20.	Switch for heater blower motor
21.	Cigar lighter
22.	Socket
23.	Electric clock
24.	Instrument cluster
25.	Windshield wiper switch
26.	Steering lock
27.	Roof light switch
28.	Rotary light switch
29.	Roof light
30.	Free for optional extra
31.	Plug connection
32.	Door contact switch left and right
33.	Reading light
34.	Steering wheel with horn ring
35.	Flash signal switch and upper beam flash signal switch
36.	Stop light switch
37.	Reversing light switch
39.	Regulator (Lima)
40.	Generator
41.	Fuses
42.	Starter
43.	Battery
44.	Fuel level indicator
45.	Electric fuel feed pump
46.	Flash signal right
47.	Tail light and clearance light right
48.	Reversing light right
49.	Stop light right
50.	License plate light right
51.	License plate light left
52.	Stop light left
53.	Reversing light left
54.	Tail light and clearance light left
55.	Flash signal left

Wiring diagram—220SEb sedan (second version).

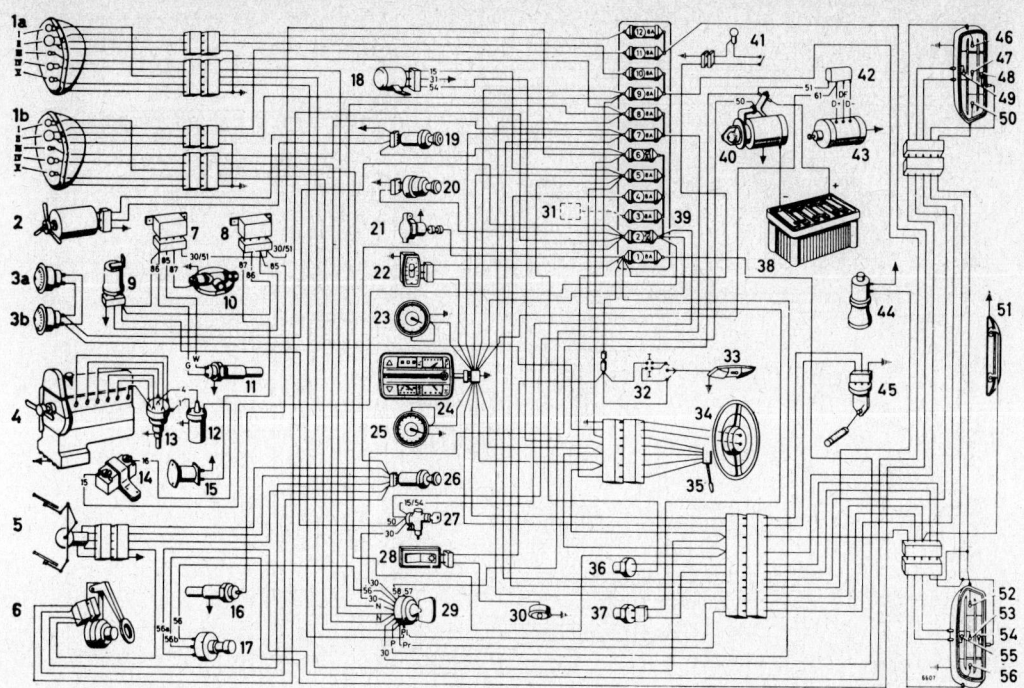

1a. Lighting unit left	10. Electromagnetic starting	31. Optional extra
I. Flash signal light	valve	32. Door contact switch left
II. Upper beam and lower	11. Thermo time switch	and right
beam	(for para 10)	33. Reading light
III. Parking light	12. Ignition coil	34. Steering wheel with horn
IV. Fog light	13. Distributor	ring
V. Clearance light	14. Series resistance for	35. Flash signal switch and
1b. Lighting unit right	ignition coil	upper beam flash signal
I. Flash signal light	15. Solenoid switch for	switch
II. Upper beam and lower	mixture control	36. Reversing light switch
beam	16. Thermo switch	38. Battery
III. Parking light	(for para 15)	39. Fuses
IV. Fog light	17. Foot dimmer switch	40. Starter
V. Clearance light	18. Flash signal mechanism	41. Glove compartment light
2. Heater blower motor	19. Blower switch with pilot	42. Regulator (generator)
3a. Horn right	light	43. Generator
3b. Horn left	20. Cigar lighter	44. Electric fuel feed pump
4. Spark plugs (engine)	21. Socket	45. Fuel level indicator
5. Windshield wiper, two-	22. Electric clock	46. Flash signal right
stage	23. Speedometer	47. Tail light right
6. Foot pump for windshield	24. Instrument cluster	48. Reversing light right
washer with switch for	25. Revolution counter	49. Clearance light right
windshield wiper	26. Windshield wiper switch	50. Stop light right
7. Relay for electromagnetic	27. Steering lock	51. License plate light
starting valve	28. Roof light switch	52. Stop light left
8. Relay for automatic starter	29. Rotary light switch	53. Tail light left
aid	30. Roof light	54. Reversing light left
9. Time switch for automatic		55. Clearance light left
starter aid		56. Flash signal left

Wiring diagram—220SEb Coupe.

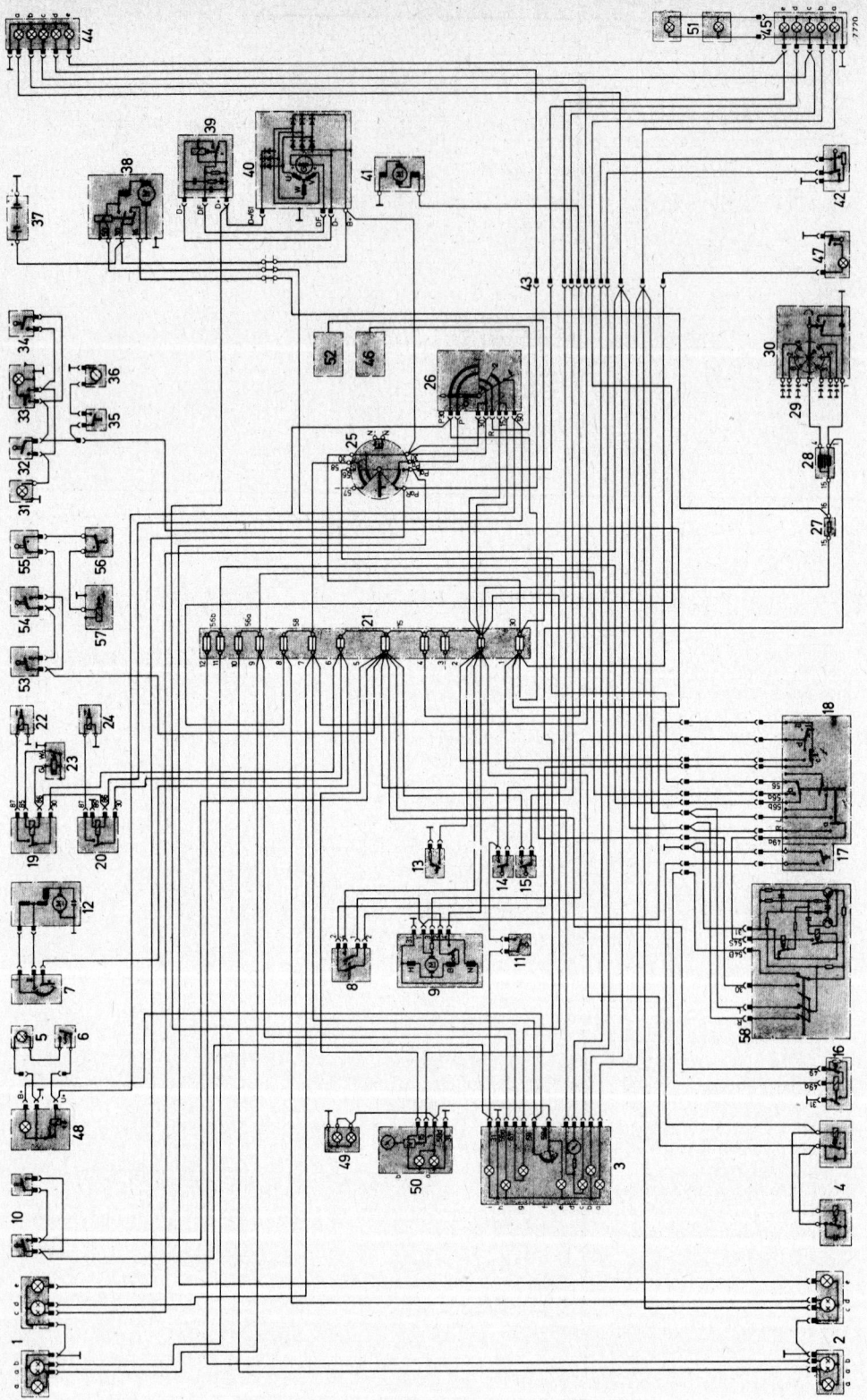

Wiring diagram—280SE/8 Coupe and Convt.

Wiring diagram—280SE/8 Coupe and Convt.

1. Light assembly (right side)
2. Light assembly (left side)
   a. High beam
   b. Low beam
   c. Turn signal light
   d. Parking light
   e. Side light
3. Instrument cluster
   a. Turn signal light indicator, left
   b. Turn signal light indicator, right
   c. Low fuel level warning light
   d. Fuel gauge
   e. Instrument illumination
   f. Instrument illumination rheostat
   g. Generator (alternator) charge warning light
   h. High beam indicator
   i. Parking brake and brake fluid level warning light
4. Horn system
5. Glove compartment light
6. Switch for glove compartment light
7. Heater blower switch
8. Windshield washer foot pump
9. Wiper motor
10. Brake fluid level warning light control element
11. Parking brake warning light control element

12. Heater blower motor
13. Cigar lighter
14. Stop light switch
15. Back-up light switch
16. Sending unit for turn signal light
17. Horn ring
18. Combination switch
    a. Turn signal light switch
    b. Headlight dimmer switch
    c. Windshield wiper switch
    d. Windshield wiper speed control switch
19. Relay for starter valve
20. Relay for mixture control
21. Fuses
22. Magneto for starter valve
23. Thermo time switch
24. Magneto for mixture control
25. Headlight switch
26. Ignition starter switch
27. Series resistance
28. Ignition coil
29. Spark plugs
30. Distributor
31. Entrance light
32. Courtesy light switch, left door
33. Reading light
34. Courtesy light switch, right door
35. Switch for dome light, rear
36. Dome light, rear

37. Battery
38. Starter
39. Voltage regulator
40. Alternator
41. Fuel feed pump
42. Fuel gauge sending unit
43. Rear light unit wiring harness connecting plug
44. Rear light unit (right side)
45. Rear light unit (left side)
    a. Turn signal light
    b. Tail light
    c. Back-up light
    d. Side light
    e. Stop light
46. Spare wire for extras (radio)
47. Trunk light
48. Electric clock
49. Speedometer light
50. Tachometer
    a. Tachometer light
    b. Electric indicating system
51. License plate light
52. Automatic antenna (optional)
53. Switch, 3rd gear ⎫
54. Switch, 4th gear ⎬ for exhaust emission control system
55. Switch, clutch pedal
56. Switch, accelerator pedal shaft ⎭
57. Magneto
58. Hazard warning light transmitter

Wiring diagram——280SE/8 sedan.

1. Light assembly (right side)
2. Light assembly (left side)
   a. High beam
   b. Low beam
   c. Turn signal light
   d. Parking light
   e. Side light
3. Instrument cluster
   a. Turn signal light indicator, left
   b. Turn signal indicator, right
   c. Low fuel level warning light
   d. Fuel gauge
   e. Electric clock
   f. Instrument illumination rheostat
   g. Instrument illumination
   h. Generator (alternator) charge warning light
   i. High beam indicator
   k. Parking brake and brake fluid level warning light
4. Dual horn system
5. Glove compartment light
6. Switch for glove compartment light
7. Heater blower switch
8. Windshield washer foot pump
9. Wiper motor
10. Brake fluid level warning light control element

11. Parking brake warning light control element
12. Heater blower motor
13. Cigar lighter
14. Stop light switch
15. Back up light switch
16. Sending unit for turn signal light
17. Horn ring
18. Combination switch
    a. Turn signal light switch
    b. Headlight dimmer switch
    c. Windshield wiper switch
    d. Windshield wiper speed control switch
19. Relay for starter valve
20. Relay for mixture control
21. Fuses
22. Magneto for starter valve
23. Thermo time switch
24. Magneto for mixture control
25. Headlight switch
26. Ignition starter switch
27. Series resistance
28. Ignition coil
29. Spark plugs
30. Distributor
31. Entrance light
32. Courtesy light switch, left front door
33. Reading light
34. Courtesy light switch, right front door
35. Switch for dome light

36. Dome light, rear
37. Battery
38. Starter
39. Voltage regulator
40. Alternator
41. Fuel feed pump
42. Fuel gauge sending unit
43. Rear light unit wiring harness connecting plug
44. Rear light unit (right side)
45. Rear light unit (left side)
    a. Turn signal light
    b. Tail light
    c. Back up light
    d. Side light
    e. Stop light
46. Spare wire for extras (radio)
47. Trunk light
48. License plate light
49. Door contact, rear, right
50. Door contact, rear, left
51. Switch, accelerator pedal shaft ⎫
52. Switch, clutch pedal
53. Solenoid, injection pump ⎬ for exhaust emission control system
54. Switch, gear-shift position (in 3rd and 4th gear closed) ⎭
55. Hazard warning light transmitter

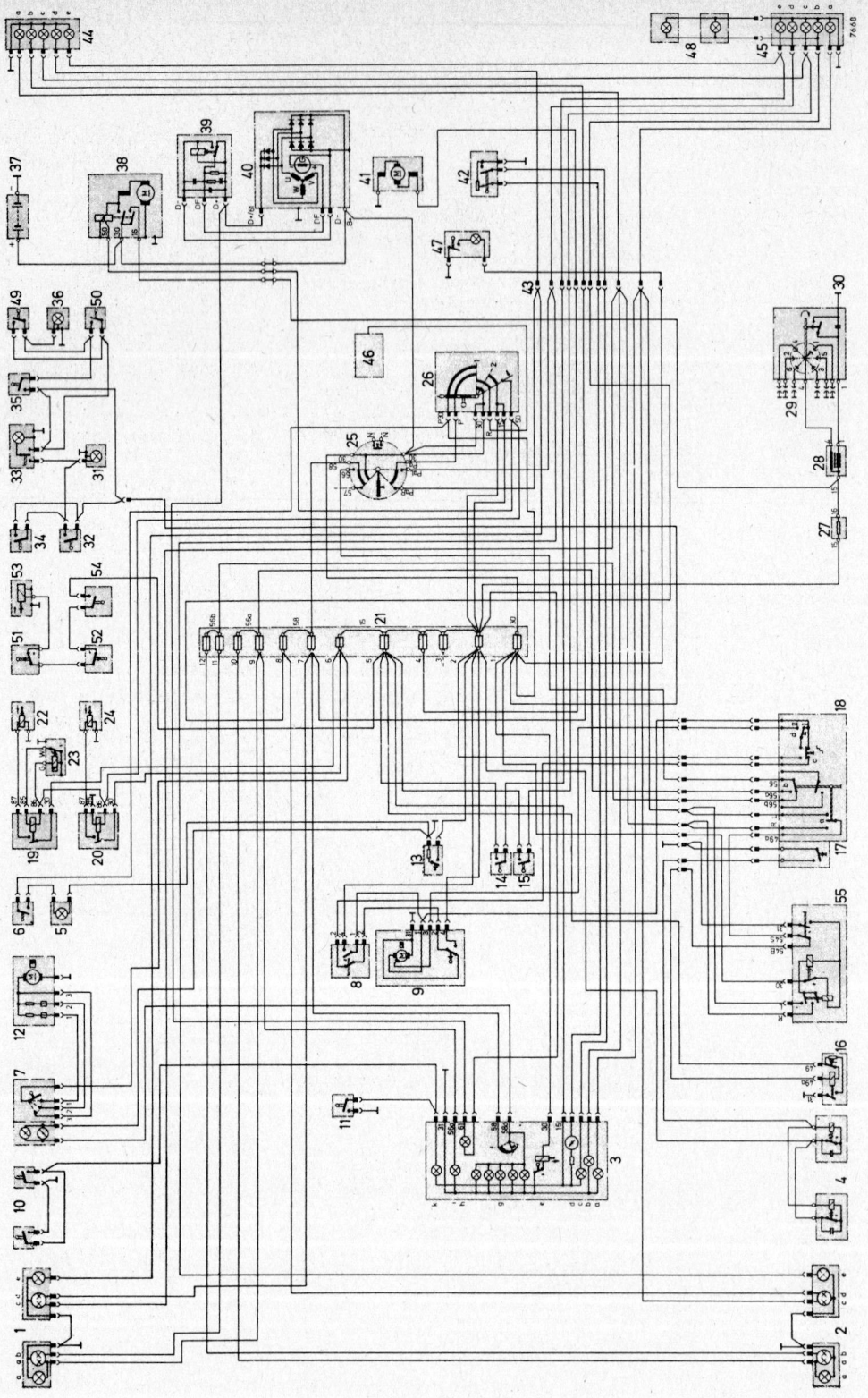

Wiring diagram—280SE/8 sedan.

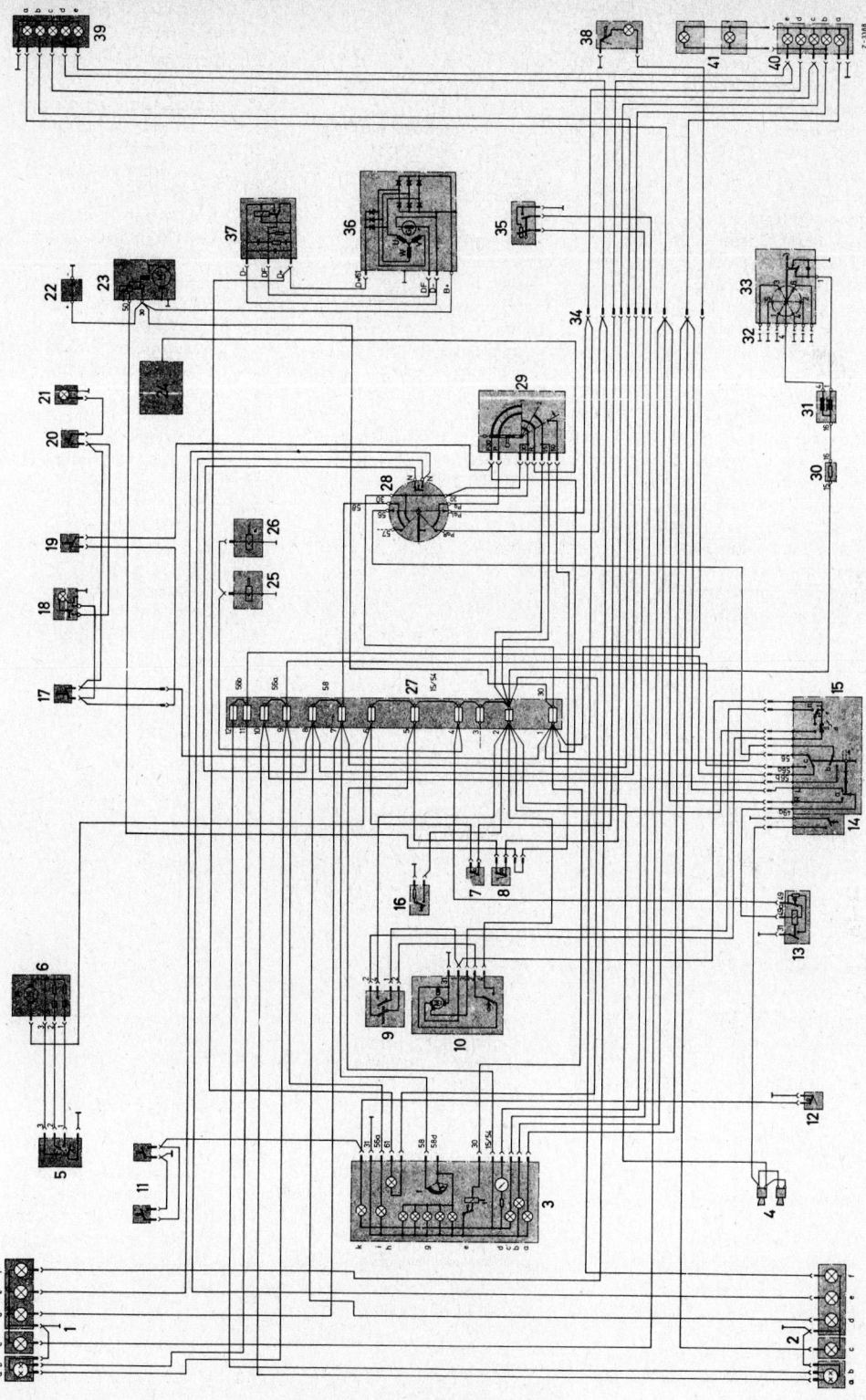

Wiring diagram—230/8, 250/8.

Wiring diagram—230/8, 250/8.

Opposite

1. Right lighting unit
2. Left lighting unit
  a. Upper beam
  b. Lower beam
  c. Flash signal
  d. Parking light
  e. Fog light
  f. Clearance light
3. Instrument cluster
  a. Left signal indicator
  b. Right signal indicator
  c. Fuel reserve warning light
  d. Fuel level indicator
  e. Electric clock
  f. Control resistance for
    instrument lighting
  g. Instrument lighting
  h. Charging light
  i. Upper beam control
  k. Brake control
4. Two-tone horn mechanism
5. Blower switch (air intake)
6. Blower motor (air intake)
7. Stop light switch
8. Reversing light switch
9. Foot pump windshield
  washer
10. Wiper motor
11. Control switch for brake
    fluid
12. Control switch for parking
    brake
13. Flash signal mechanism
14. Horn ring
15. Combination switch
  a. Flash signal switch
  b. Flash approach signal
    switch
  c. Hand dimmer
  d. Windshield wiper switch
  e. Wiper speed switch
16. Cigar lighter
17. Front left door contact
18. Reading light
19. Front right door contact
20. Roof-light switch (on
    Model 250 only)
21. Rear roof light (on Model
    250 only)
22. Battery
23. Starter
24. Lead for optional extra
    (radio)
25. Automatic start mechanism
    on rear carburetor
26. Automatic start mechanism
    on front carburetor
27. Fuses
28. Rotary light switch
29. Ignition starter switch
30. Series resistance
31. Ignition coil
32. Spark plugs
33. Distributor
34. Sleeve union for tail light
    wiring harness
35. Fuel level indicator
36. Generator
37. Voltage regulator
38. Trunk compartment light
39. Right tail light
40. Left tail light
  a. Flash signal
  b. Tail light
  c. Reversing light
  d. Clearance light
  e. Stop light
41. License plate light

Wiring diagram—220D/8.

1. Right lighting unit
2. Left lighting unit
  a. Upper beam
  b. Lower beam
  c. Flash signal
  d. Parking light
  e. Fog light
  f. Clearance light
3. Instrument cluster
  a. Left signal indicator
  b. Right signal indicator
  c. Fuel reserve warning light
  d. Fuel level indicator
  e. Electric clock
  f. Control resistance for
    instrument lighting
  g. Instrument lighting
  h. Charging light
  i. Upper beam control
  k. Brake control
4. Two-tone horn system
5. Blower switch (air intake)
6. Blower motor (air intake)
7. Stop light switch
8. Reversing light switch
9. Foot pump windshield
  washer
10. Wiper motor
11. Control switch for brake
    fluid
12. Control switch for parking
    brake
13. Flash signal mechanism
14. Horn ring
15. Combination switch
  a. Flash signal switch
  b. Flash approach signal
    switch
  c. Hand dimmer
  d. Windshield wiper switch
  e. Wiper speed switch
16. Cigar lighter
17. Front left door contact
18. Reading light
19. Front right door contact
20. Fuses
21. Lead for optional extra
    (radio)
22. Battery
23. Starter
24. Rotary light switch
25. Steering lock
26. Glow starter switch
27. Glow plug resistance contro
28. Glow plugs
29. Sleeve union for tail light
    wiring harness
30. Fuel level indicator
31. Generator
32. Voltage regulator
33. Trunk compartment light
34. Right tail light
35. Left tail light
  a. Flash signal
  b. Tail light
  c. Reversing light
  d. Clearance light
  e. Stop light
36. License plate light

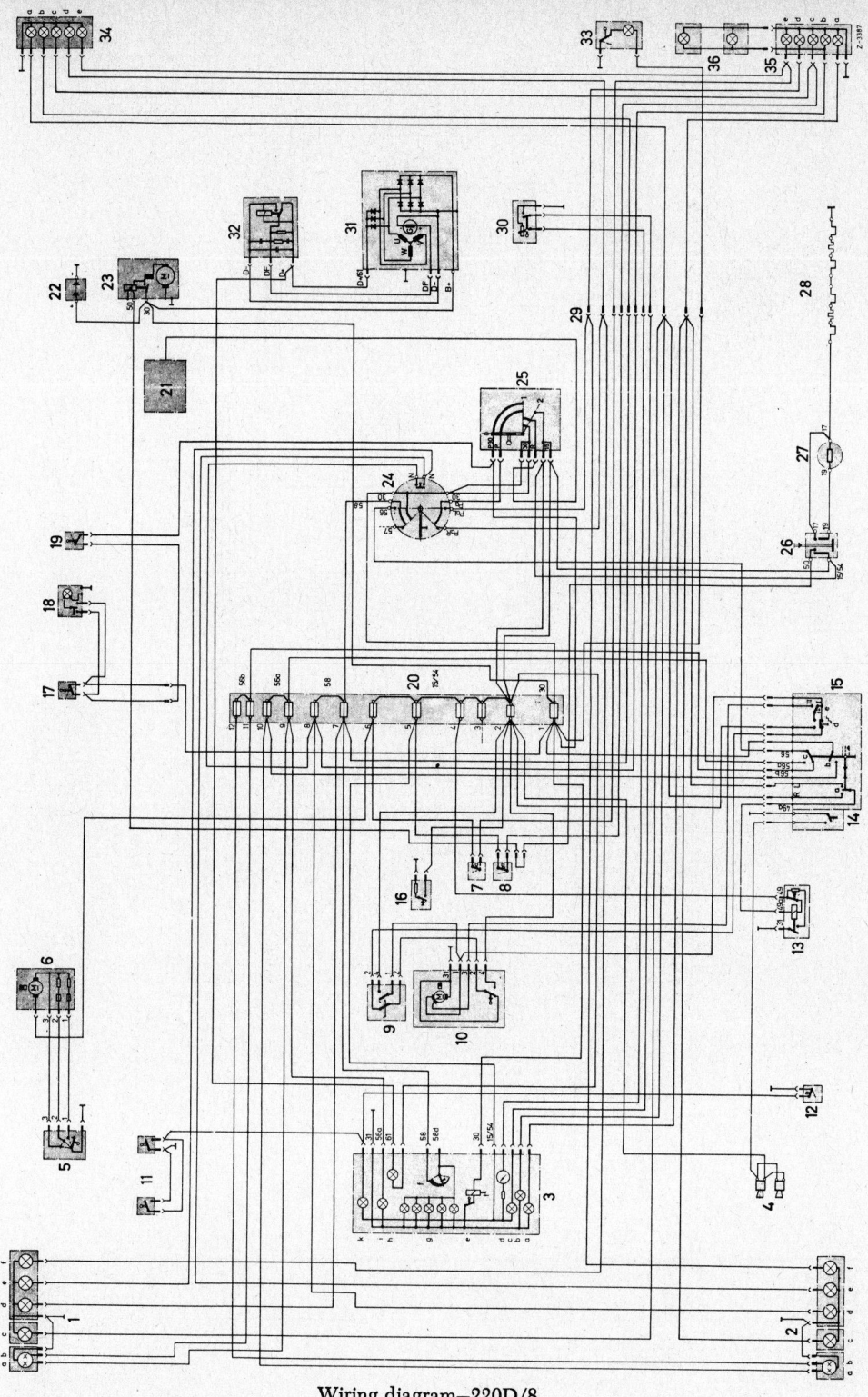

Wiring diagram—220D/8.

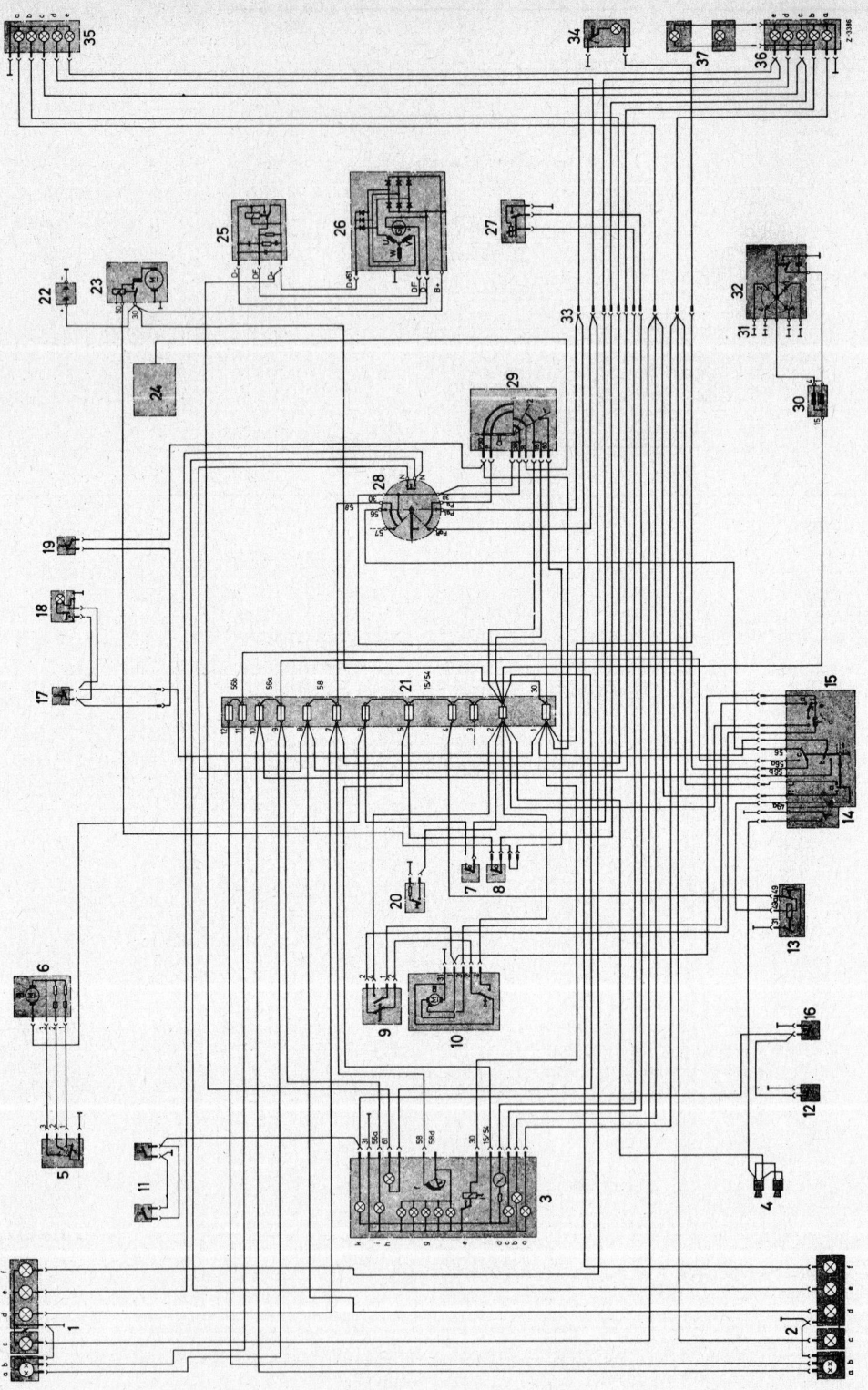

Wiring diagram—220/8.

Wiring diagram—220/8.

1. Right lighting unit
2. Left lighting unit
   a. Upper beam
   b. Lower beam
   c. Flash signal
   d. Parking light
   e. Fog light
   f. Clearance light
3. Instrument cluster
   a. Left signal indicator
   b. Right signal indicator
   c. Fuel reserve warning light
   d. Fuel level indicator
   e. Electric clock
   f. Control resistance for instrument lighting
   g. Instrument lighting
   h. Charging light
   i. Upper beam indicator
   k. Brake control
      Choke control indicator
4. Two-tone horn system
5. Blower switch (air intake)
6. Blower motor (air intake)

7. Stop light switch
8. Reversing light switch
9. Foot pump (windshield washer)
10. Wiper motor
11. Control switch for brake fluid
12. Control switch for parking brake
13. Flash signal mechanism
14. Horn ring
15. Combination switch
    a. Flash signal switch
    b. Flash approach signal switch
    c. Hand dimmer
    d. Windshield wiper switch
    e. Wiper speed switch
16. Choke cable control switch
17. Front left door contact
18. Reading light
19. Front right door contact
20. Cigar lighter

21. Fuses
22. Battery
23. Starter
24. Lead for optional extra (radio)
25. Voltage regulator
26. Generator
27. Fuel level indicator
28. Rotary light switch
29. Ignition starter switch
30. Ignition coil
31. Spark plugs
32. Distributor
33. Sleeve union for tail light wiring harness
34. Trunk compartment light
35. Right tail light
36. Left tail light
    a. Flash signal
    b. Tail light
    c. Reversing light
    d. Clearance light
    e. Stop light
37. License plate light

Engine Electrical

Distributor

REMOVAL AND INSTALLATION

Remove the distributor cap, primary wire, vacuum line, and clamp bolt. Mark the position of the distributor body with relation to the block, and the position of the rotor with relation to the distributor body, then pull the distributor from the engine. *NOTE: Do not rotate engine with distributor out, otherwise initial ignition timing will have to be determined.*

BREAKER POINT REPLACEMENT

To replace the contact points, remove the distributor cap, rotor and plate. Remove the distributor contact holder (3) by removing screw (4) and prying the cable from the connecting terminal (1), or by removing the connecting terminal screw (depending on design). To reinstall, reverse removal procedure, remembering to check that the distributor cam is properly lubricated with a tiny amount of grease.

To adjust points initially, set block at the highest spot on the cam and set gap to approximate center of range by inserting a screwdriver into the adjusting slot of the contact holder (3) between the two bosses (2). In some cases, the points are adjusted by turning an eccentric cam with a small screwdriver. While it is possible to set the gap using a feeler gauge, it is much more accurate to use the dwellmeter.

A. Contact breaker pair (contact closed)
1. Connecting terminal from low-voltage cable 1 to ignition coil and to cable from breaker arm
2. Bosses on contact breaker plate
3. Contact holder with adjusting slot
4. Fixing screw for contact holder
5. Vacuum box with diaphragm
6. Notch on distributor housing rim of distributor for cylinder 1
7. Pull rod for vacuum control

Distributor components—single contact set.

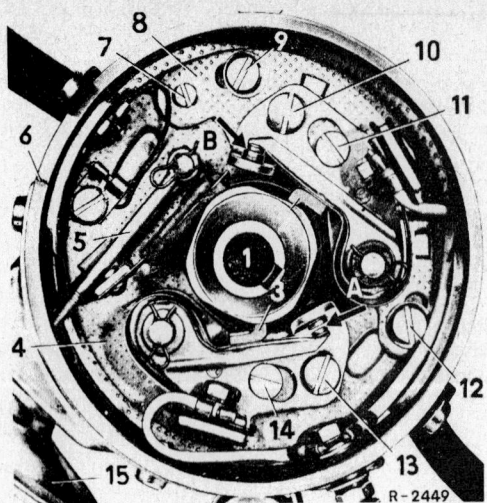

A. Contact breaker point set
    (points open)
P. Contact breaker point set
    (points closed)
1. Distributor shaft with 4 cams
2, 3. Slide for movable breaker arm
4. Base plate with contact
    breaker point set A
5. Pull rod for vacuum advance
6. Mark for cylinder 1
7. Adjusting cam-head bolt (for
    correcting ignition interval
    between both contact breaker
    point sets)
8. Intermediate plate (adjustable on base
    plate) with contact breaker point
    set B
9, 12. Fastening screw of intermediate plate
    (with contact breaker point set B)
10, 13. Fastening screw of contact breaker point
    set
11, 14. Adjusting cam-head screw for contact
    breaker point gap and/or dwell angle
    adjustment
15. Vacuum box with diaphragm

Distributor components—double contact sets.

The 300 SEL 6.3 engine has a dual-point distributor, similar to models used on previous 300 series engines. To check dwell with this distributor, each point set must be blocked off, in turn, using a fiber plate or other insulator. Dwell angle, in this case, is checked at starter cranking speed, ignition switch on and center coil wire removed.

To check total dwell, replace the distributor cap, start the engine and run at 4,000 rpm. The dwell angle may drop not more than 3° from previous check, and must be over 32° in any case. If angle is less than 32°, replace the points.

To replace the points, remove the distributor plate and rotor, then remove contact sets A and B (see illustration). This can be accomplished by removing the cotter pins from the bearing posts and removing screws (10 and 13). Remove the screw from the cable terminal, then remove the points.

To install, reverse the above procedure, making sure that the points are parallel to each other when closed. The lubrication felt should be moistened with a drop of oil at this time.

To adjust the point gap, loosen screw (13) for set A and screw (10) for set B. Then, turn eccentric screws (11 and 14) to obtain an approximate .012–.016″ gap. Tighten screws (10 and 13) and check dwell. If it is out of specification, adjust each set identically, in small increments, until proper value for both sets is obtained.

DISTRIBUTOR MODIFICATIONS

Due to the general increase in the use of rock salt on winter roads, the ignition system is more subject to corrosion and cross-firing of spark plug wires and to surface discharge across the distributor cap. In addition to standard commercial ignition sprays, it is advisable when conducting a tune-up to change the ignition system components to update and protect the system.

Since October, 1967 all cars have been equipped with a new-type distributor cap, which is made of polyester and pre-sprayed on the inside for moisture protection. When the new cap is employed, it is also possible to use a new-type rotor, also made of polyester with polycarbonate radio suppression built-in.

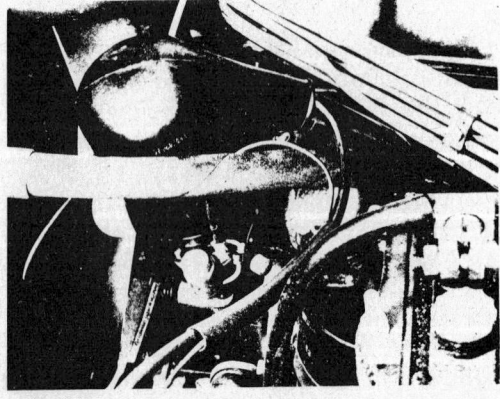

Rubber distributor cover protects against moisture, salt and dirt.

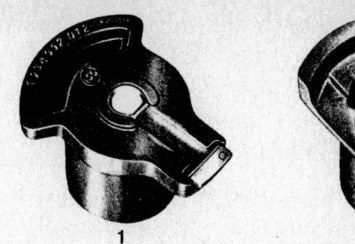

1. Old type (part No. 000 158 15 31)
2. New type (part No. 000 158 20 31)

Distributor rotors.

The new caps have the same parts numbers as the old-type caps, but they can be easily recognized by their shiny inner coating. The following parts numbers are applicable:

190c, 200 ....000 158 18 02
220b, 250 SE 000 158 16 02
300 SE, 300 SEL 000 158 17 02

The new-type rotor, part No. 000 158 20 31 (for 200–250 SE models), is to be used with all four- and six-cylinder models having a CAST-IRON distributor housing, a conical rotor seat and a 0.513″ diameter rotor driveshaft.

Rotor 000 158 21 31 is to be used ONLY with a new-type distributor having an ALUMINUM housing, cylindrical rotor seat and a 0.562″ diameter rotor driveshaft.

By using force, the rotor, 000 158 20 31, can be pushed onto the rotor driveshaft of the aluminum distributor, but the rotor will not make good contact with the carbon center button of the cap. The other rotor, 000 158 21 31, can be slipped onto the older cast-iron distributor, but it will wobble and damage the cap. Do not interchange these rotors.

In addition to these parts, a protective cover for the distributor, part No. 000 158 06 85, has been made available for all four- and six-cylinder distributors. If the cover is not presently installed, a longer high-tension wire (25.19″) is needed. This can be ordered, along with the cover, under part No. 130 150 09 18.

When installing this cover on fuel-injected engines, make sure that the spark plug wires go underneath the fuel injection tubes.

Also, on the 300 SEL/8, a modification of the hose between the air suspension pump and the antifreeze container is necessay. The end connected to the rear fitting of the antifreeze container must be removed and connected to the front fitting. The plug removed from the front fitting can be used to block the fitting just vacated, and the hose shortened to 9⅝″ for clearance.

Ignition Timing

Setting the ignition timing varies somewhat for different models, but in general, there are two ways of doing it. One is by use of a "timing" light or stroboscope; the other is more simple and involves using a small 12-volt light bulb with two leads soldered to its terminals. It must be noted that the latter method is not to be considered a substitute for a strobe light, and is generally only useful for finding approximate timing values after the distributor has been removed.

To set the timing using a strobe light, first make sure that the contact gap (or dwell) is correct—timing is influenced by this value. Then, connect the timing light leads to the battery posts, observing correct polarity, and the third lead into No. 1 spark plug wire at some point. A good way to do this is to slip a small nail into the appropriate distributor cap tower, then connect the lead to the nail.

Run the engine at the speed specified in the *Tune-up Specifications* while shining the light on the timing index area. Timing

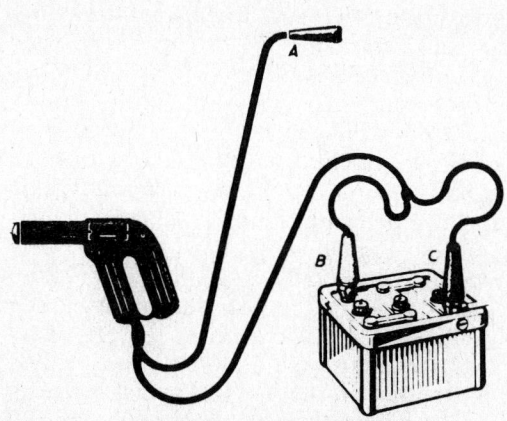

A. To No. 1 cylinder
B. To battery positive terminal
C. To battery negative terminal

Timing light hook up.

must be replaced if the advance curve is incorrect. (Distributor No. 0231115064.)

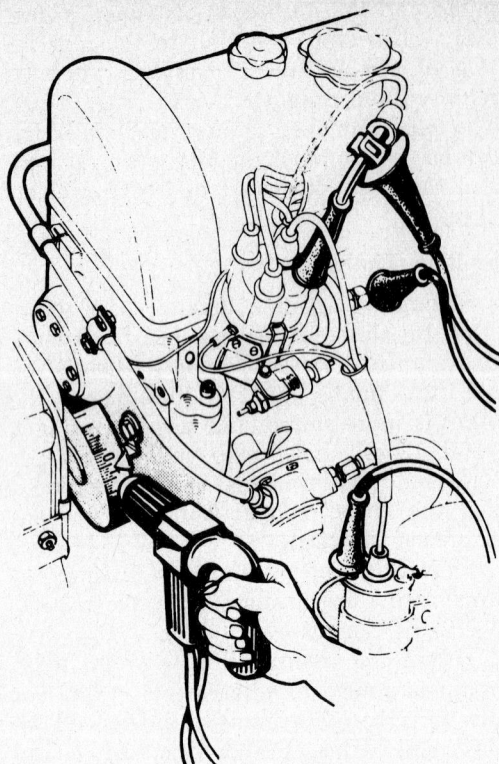

Checking timing using a strobe light.

is normally checked at 4,500 rpm (3,000 rpm for 6.3) with the vacuum line disconnected and plugged. *CAUTION: Make sure cables are out of the fan.*

Timing is adjusted by loosening the distributor clamp bolt and rotating the distributor. To advance timing, rotate the distributor opposite the normal direction of rotation; to retard timing, rotate in the normal direction.

The *Distributor Specifications* table gives timing values for various engine speeds, with and without the vacuum line connected. This enables one to measure the full range of the automatic advance unit. Hook up the timing light and a tachometer and run the engine at various speeds (with vacuum connected) and plot the values against rpm. The total advance curves can be found in graphic form in the Specifications. To adjust the advance curve, adjust the stop nut on the pull rod which connects the vacuum advance diaphragm to the breaker plate. Screwing the nut in advances the spark and decreases the range and vice versa.

On the 220/8, however, the vacuum unit cannot be adjusted properly and, therefore,

SETTING TIMING IF ENGINE HAS BEEN DISTURBED

To set the basic timing after the distributor has been removed, connect a small 12-volt test lamp between ground and the coil distributor terminal. Remove No. 1 spark plug and the coil high-tension lead. Slowly bump the engine over, holding a finger loosely in the spark plug hole. When the rotor of the distributor comes around to the mark on the housing, and the finger is forced out of the spark plug hole by compression pressure, the proper conditions for setting timing are established.

With the key on and a wrench on the crankshaft sprocket (never use the camshaft sprocket) nut, turn the engine over slowly in the direction of normal rotation until the light bulb just lights. Note the position of the timing marks with relation to the pointer. The values should correspond with those for static timing given in the *Distributor Specifications* chart. If an adjustment is to be made, always rotate the engine through a complete engine cycle to come up on No. 1 again, in order to take up slack in the distributor drive.

The values obtained in this check are usually 1–2° later than those obtained by using a strobe light at starter speed. "Later" means that the light bulb might light at perhaps 2° BTDC, whereas the strobe would indicate 3½° BTDC for the same setting.

Checking the timing at starter speed, using the strobe light, is identical to that check made at 4,500 rpm, excepting that all spark plug wires except No. 1 are grounded to prevent accidental starting.

To set the ignition timing on the 300 SEL/8 6.3 V8 engine, disconnect the vacuum line from the distributor and plug it. With the strobe light connected to No. 1 spark plug wire, run the engine at 3,000 rpm and observe timing mark (26° BTDC). If necessary, loosen distributor clamp and rotate distributor to obtain correct value. To advance timing, turn against direction of rotation; to retard timing, turn in same direction as rotation.

It is necessary then, because of the dual-point design, to check the timing at No. 5 cylinder. The values obtained should be the same for both cylinders No. 1 and No. 5. If not, reset intermediate plate (8) and/or contact sets A and B (see illustration) with respect to each other by loosening screws (9 and 12), then turning bolt (7) to reset intermediate plate (8). The dwell angle might have to be reset at this time as well.

This distributor is best set up on an ignition test stand at the dealer, as the points have to be perfectly synchronized for perfect operation.

Generator and Regulator

The generator is actually a DC shunt-wound electric motor operating in a manner opposite to that of a normal motor. Instead of current being supplied to the unit and mechanical power being "generated", mechanical power is supplied to the unit via a V-belt driven by the engine, and the resultant generated current used to recharge the battery and power the various electrical subsystems of the vehicle. Engine speed varies, however, and thus so does generator speed (and current output). In order to keep the current constant for a fixed load, a regulator is utilized. In effect, this acts as an electrical "switch" to cut off current at a predetermined value, thus preventing system damage from "too much" current. *NOTE: This is why turning on the headlights on long, high-speed runs does nothing to prevent overcharging.*

IN-CAR GENERATOR TESTING—MODELS WITH THREE-ELEMENT REGULATOR

Hold the positive lead of a voltmeter to terminal #51 at the regulator and connect the negative lead to ground. The rated battery voltage should be indicated (12 volts). Turn on the ignition switch and check that the charging light goes on. Disconnect the blue wire from terminal D+ (#61) at the regulator; the charging light should now go out. If the light stays on, the blue wire is grounded somewhere along its length.

To test the regulator, connect a voltmeter between terminal D+ (#61) and the D— terminal at the regulator. Start the engine and disconnect the red wire from terminal B+ (#51) at the regulator and tape its end. Increase the engine speed and watch the voltmeter; when the needle no longer rises the regulating voltage has been achieved. No voltage indicates a mal-

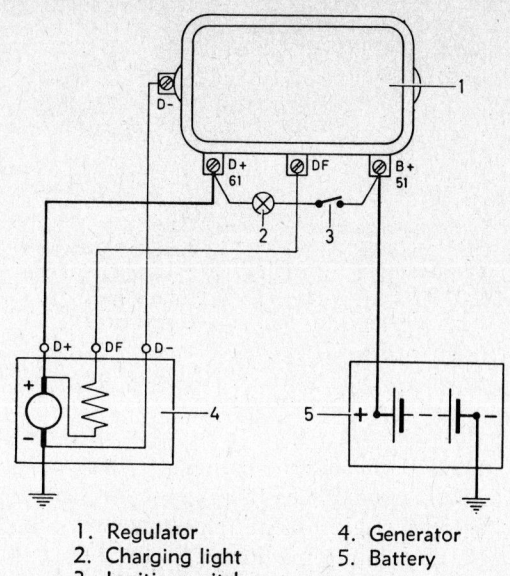

1. Regulator
2. Charging light
3. Ignition switch
4. Generator
5. Battery

Generating circuit.

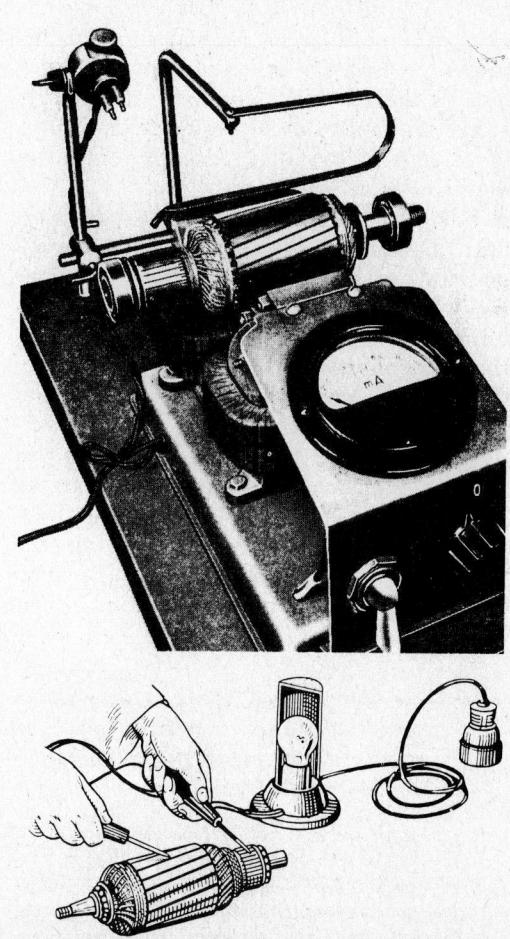

Armature testing. Top—using armature growler; Bottom—using 40-watt bulb. Dampness sometimes causes slight illumination.

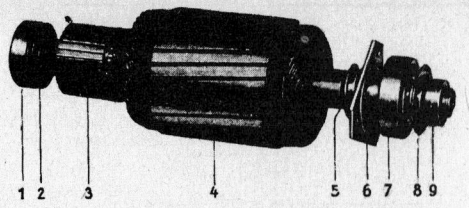

1. Annular grooved bearing
2. Splash disc
3. Collector
4. Armature
5. Splash disc
6. Cover disc
7. Annular grooved bearing
8. Splash disc
9. Spacer ring

Generator armature.

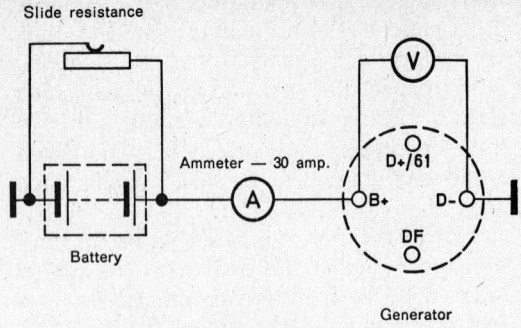

Alternator test.

adjusted or malfunctioning regulator. In this case, sometimes polarizing the generator solves the problem. Disconnect the fan belt and connect a jumper wire between terminal DF and regulator terminal D—. Connect a jumper between regulator terminals B+ (#51) and D+ (#61). The generator should now spin (working like an electric motor) in its normal direction of rotation. Repeat the regulating voltage test. If the voltage is too low (see table), either the generator or regulator is faulty; if voltage is too high, usually only the regulator is at fault.

Test the regulator current regulation next. Disconnect the battery ground cable and the red wire from regulator terminal B+ (#51). Connect an ammeter between terminal #51 and the wire just removed, then reconnect the battery ground cable. Turn on all accessories and start the engine. Speed up the engine and check the ammeter reading; it now should indicate the regulating current. No current indicates a defective regulator, which must be replaced as a unit. Allow the engine to slow to idle speed. The ammeter should now indicate a slight *discharge* (reverse current).

IN-CAR GENERATOR TESTING—MODELS WITH THREE-PHASE GENERATOR (ALTERNATOR) AND SINGLE-ELEMENT REGULATOR

CAUTION: On this model, never disconnect the generator leads or battery cables with the engine running, as induced peak voltage will destroy the sensitive diode rectifiers. Never short terminals to ground for the same reason (polarization).

Always observe battery polarity when jump-starting and never use a battery charger as a "hot shot". Charge batteries with cables disconnected.

To test regulation, connect a voltmeter between the generator B+ terminal and ground, after disconnecting battery ground cable. Disconnect the red wire at the B+ generator terminal and connect an ammeter (30–0–30) between the terminal and the wire just disconnected. Reconnect the battery ground cable and start the engine;

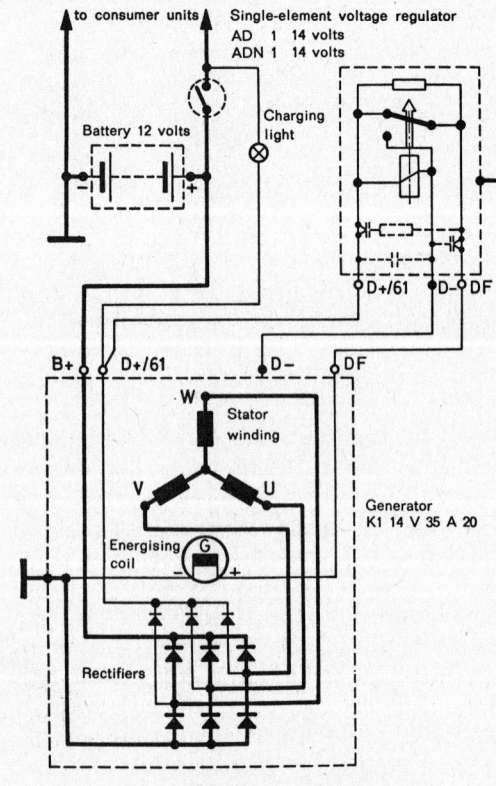

Alternator circuit.

Generator Diagnosis

Condition	Probable Cause	Correction
Battery not charging or not charging enough	1. Brushes not touching commutator, sticking, worn, broken or oil-fouled. 2. Commutator oily. 3. Commutator worn. 4. Faulty connections. 5. Defective battery. 6. Generator windings shorted. 7. Defective voltage regulator. 8. Fanbelt too loose; pulleys worn.	1. Clean or replace brushes. 2. Clean commutator. 3. Machine commutator and undercut segments. 4. Tighten connections or replace wires. 5. Check battery and/or replace. 6. Test generator and repair. 7. Replace regulator. 8. Tighten fanbelt; replace pulleys.
Ammeter light does not light with engine off and ignition on	1. Ammeter light bulb burnt out. 2. Battery discharged. 3. Defective battery. 4. Loose connections. 5. Defective voltage regulator.	1. Install new bulb. 2. Charge battery. 3. Test and/or replace battery. 4. Tighten connections. 5. Replace regulator.
Ammeter light does not go out at high engine speed	1. Wire at terminal No. 61 shorted. 2. Defective voltage regulator. 3. Defective generator.	1. Replace wire or fix short. 2. Replace regulator. 3. Test and/or repair generator.
Ammeter light flickers	1. Loose fanbelt. 2. Pulleys worn. 3. Generator brushes sticking.	1. Tighten fanbelt. 2. Replace pulleys. 3. Check brushes and replace if necessary.

turn on all electrical accessories (headlights on high beam, radio, air conditioner, etc.). Run the engine at 2,200 rpm and check the meter readings, comparing them to the specifications table.

If the voltage falls outside the specified limits, connect the voltmeter between the generator D+ and D— terminals and repeat the test. If the difference in the two voltmeter readings is greater than 0.5 volt, the alternator is at fault; if less than 0.5 volt, the regulator. *NOTE: Remember, loose connections can result in false readings.*

GENERATOR REMOVAL AND INSTALLATION

Disconnect the battery ground cable and the wires at the generator. Tag the wires for easy assembly. Loosen the generator bracket pivot bolts, then loosen the swing bracket bolt and move the generator inward to remove the V-belt. Remove all bolts and remove generator. Installation is the reverse of removal. *NOTE: Fanbelt tension should be such that thumb pressure on the longest belt section results in .25"– .50" belt deflection.*

Starter

All Mercedes-Benz passenger cars are equipped with 12-volt Bosch electric starters of various rated outputs. The starter motor is actually nothing but a simple series-wound electric motor of high torque output, fitted with a drive pinion and a device to mesh the pinion with the flywheel ring gear. The carrier, which is connected to the pinion through the overrunning clutch, runs in splines machined in the armature shaft. When the armature rotates, these splines force the pinion into mesh. When the engine starts, the overrunning (one-way) clutch releases the pinion and the unit disengages. The starter is actuated and the pinion engaged by an electric solenoid mounted on top of the starter motor.

REMOVAL

Disconnect the ground cable at the battery, then disconnect wires at the solenoid. *NOTE: Tag wires for ease in installation.*

On early models, unbolt the starter from the bellhousing and remove the ground cable, then remove starter from beneath the car. On phase II cars, unbolt nuts (5) and

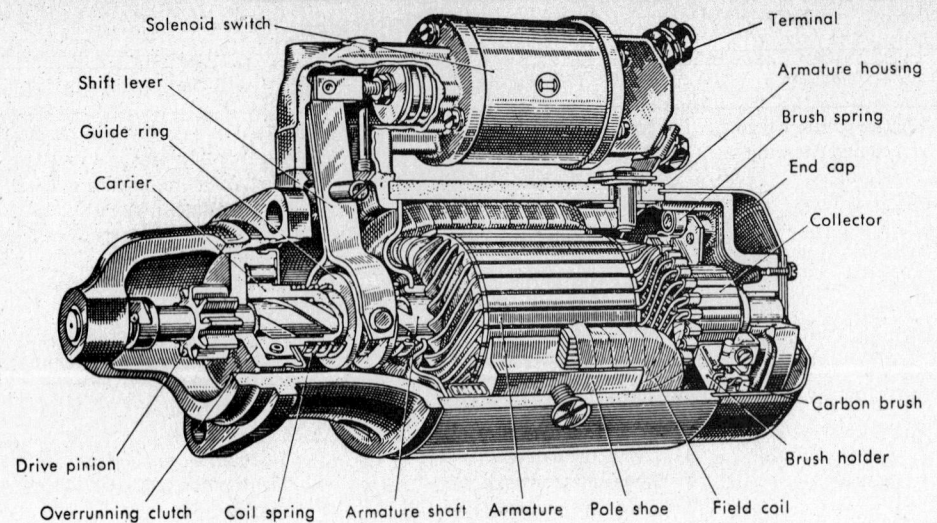

Starter motor.

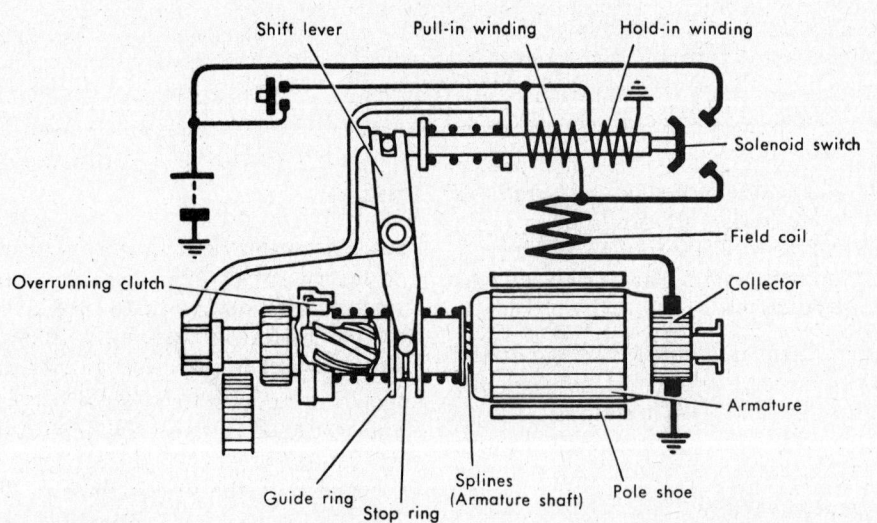

Starter motor in schematic form.

(7), as well as screws (4). Remove bracket (8), then unbolt starter from bracket (9).

DISASSEMBLY AND ASSEMBLY

Remove the end cap (4) and lift out the brushes. Disconnect the cable that runs between the field coil and the solenoid (at the solenoid end). Unscrew the nut in front of commutator bearing and remove washers. Unscrew the nuts from the armature housing bolts and remove drive bearing end frame and armature. *NOTE: Lay armature brake components on bench, in order, for easy assembly.*

Remove the bolts that hold the solenoid, then remove solenoid. Disassemble shift lever mechanism, knocking the pin out with a drift. Then remove shift lever and armature from drive bearing end frame. Inspect the overrunning clutch; it should turn clockwise only (seen from drive pinion end), then check the pinion gear itself for chipped or broken teeth. Remove the armature shaft snap-ring and inspect the bearings. New bearings must be pressed into the housing ends. The brushes must be washed in carbon tet to remove all grease and replaced if worn badly. New brushes can be lightly sanded with emery

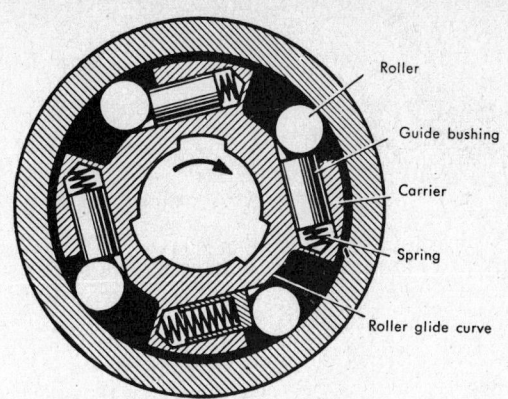

Overrunning clutch.

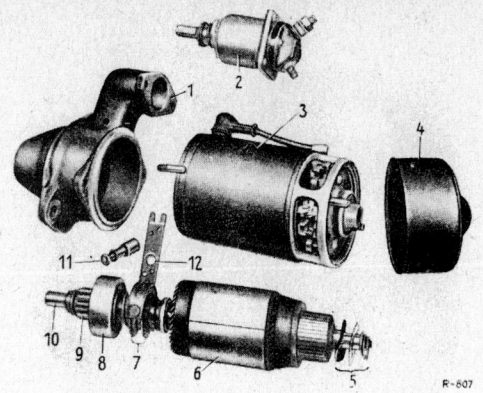

1. Drive bearing
2. Solenoid switch
3. Armature housing
4. End cap
5. Parts of armature brake
6. Armature
7. Guide ring
8. Overrunning clutch
9. Pinion
10. Armature shaft
11. Pivot pin
12. Shift lever

Starter disassembled.

Starter removal—Phase II cars.

1. Terminal 30
2. Terminal 50
3. Solenoid
4. Hex head screw SW 13
5. Hex nut SW 17
6. Exhaust manifold
7. Hex nut SW 17
8. Holding bracket
9. Holding bracket

1. Ground strap
2. Hexagon screws
3. Solenoid switch
4. Connecting bolt
5. Starter
6. Connecting cable
7. Hexagon nut
8. Hexagon screws

Starter motor installed.

cloth so that they slide freely in their holders. If brushes are replaced, it is a good idea to replace the brush springs as well.

Clean the commutator with carbon tet and check for burned areas. The commutator can be turned down on a lathe to make it perfectly round. The segments then must be undercut to a depth of .024″–.032″ using a suitably ground hacksaw blade. *NOTE: Do not sand armature with emery paper, because metallic particles in paper may short out segments.*

Check solenoid yoke length "a" and adjust, if necessary, by loosening locknut and screwing shaft in or out. Assembly is the reverse of disassembly.

ARMATURE TESTING—STARTER DISASSEMBLED

Lay the disassembled armature in the jaws of an armature growler and turn on the current. Slowly rotate the armature while holding a 6″ length of hacksaw blade against the metal segments. If the blade is magnetically attracted to any part of the armature (buzzes), the armature must be replaced.

Use the test prods to test pairs of commutator segments. If the light goes on it indicates a short circuit in the commutator.

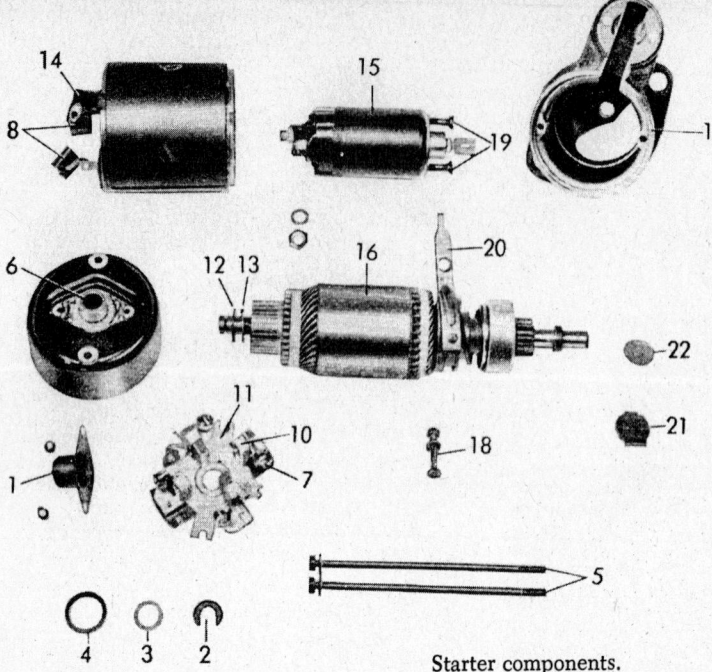

1. Protective cover
2. Locking plate
3. Compensating washer
4. Seal
5. Armature housing screws
6. Collector
7. Brush springs
8. + Carbon brushes
10. Guides
11. Brush holder
12. Thrust washer
13. Compensating washer
14. Connection exciter coil
15. Solenoid switch
16. Armature
17. Driving end shield
18. Bolt with nut
19. Fixing screws
20. Shift fork
21. Rubber seal
22. Steel washer

Starter components.

Starter Diagnosis

Condition	Probable Cause	Correction
Starter does not crank or cranks sluggishly	1. Battery discharged. 2. Battery defective. 3. Battery terminals loose or corroded; defective cables. 4. Starter terminals or brushes shorted to ground. 5. Carbon brushes in starter not contacting commutator, oily or broken. 6. Defective solenoid switch. 7. Excessive voltage drop in cables, damaged cables, loose connections.	1. Charge battery. 2. Test and/or replace battery. 3. Tighten, clean and grease terminals. 4. Fix short. 5. Check brushes, clean and/or replace; check for free movement in holders. 6. Replace solenoid. 7. Check leads and connections.
Starter turns but does not engage	1. Pinion binding. 2. Teeth on pinion or ring gear damaged.	1. Disassemble and clean pinion. 2. Remove burrs, replace ring gear or pinion.
Starter turns but stalls when pinion is engaged	1. Battery discharged. 2. Brush spring tension inadequate. 3. Solenoid defective. 4. Excessive voltage drop in cables.	1. Charge battery. 2. Check and/or replace brushes/springs. 3. Replace solenoid. 4. Check leads and terminals.
Starter turns after ignition switch released	1. Ignition switch faulty. 2. Solenoid sticking.	1. Replace switch. 2. Replace solenoid or free up.
Pinion does not engage, starter spins freely	1. Pinion or ring gear damaged or dirty. 2. Solenoid spring weak or broken.	1. Clean gears or replace. 2. Replace spring.
Pinion engages but starter breaks free and spins	1. Overrunning clutch slipping.	1. Replace pinion and clutch.

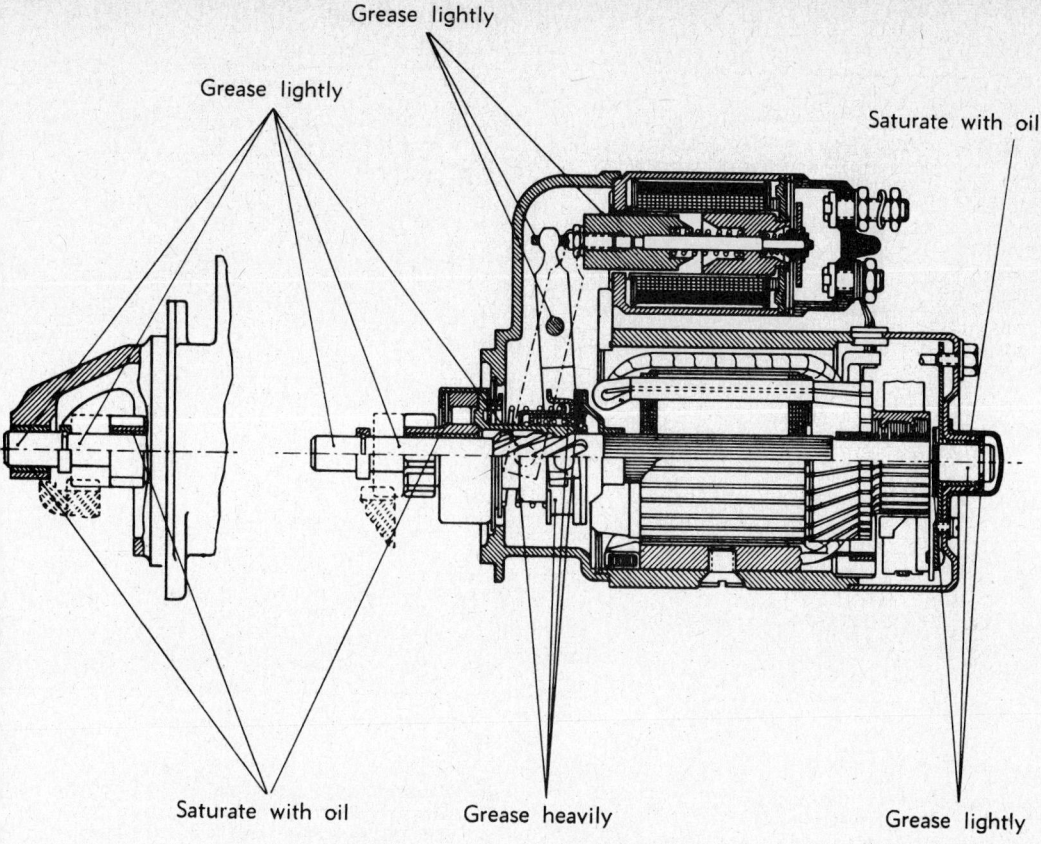

Grease lightly

Grease lightly

Saturate with oil

Saturate with oil

Grease heavily

Grease lightly

Lubrication points on Bosch starter.

FIELD COIL TESTING— STARTER DISASSEMBLED

Connect the prods from the armature growler between ground and the lead that normally goes to the solenoid (or use an ohmmeter). If the light goes on, or the ohmmeter indicates continuity. the field coil is grounded and must be replaced.

Fuel System

Fuel Pump

Fuel pumps used on Mercedes-Benz models are of two general types—electric (for all injected engines) and diaphragm (for all carbureted engines). Testing for pressure and volume, and vacuum, will tell whether the pump needs to be replaced. Diaphragm-type fuel pumps are serviced as units only, no parts being available for repairs. Electric pumps can be repaired if necessary.

To check fuel pump pressure, disconnect the feed line from the pump to the carburetors and insert a T-fitting, with appropriate fittings or short sections of neoprene hose, into the line. Attach a 0–10 psi pressure gauge to the T and crank the engine. To check fuel volume, disconnect the T-fitting and hold the open end of the fuel discharge line to the mouth of a graduated container.

Delivery pressure of the Bosch electric fuel pump used on fuel injected models is measured between the fuel filter and damper unit; it should not be less than 5.9 psi with a minimum terminal voltage of 10 volts @ 3.1–3.5 Amperes. As with mechanical pumps, check the filter for stoppage before assuming the pump is faulty. *NOTE: It is not necessary, or desirable, for the engine to be running; turn on the ignition and pump should work.*

Measure delivery volume at a point behind the return line damper nut. *NOTE: Use new fuel filter element. Volume should*

Fuel Pump Specifications

Model	Pump Type	Delivery Pressure psi @ Starter Speed	Delivery Pressure psi @ Idle Speed	Measuring Point	Discharge Pressure psi @ 3,000 rpm	Discharge Pressure psi @ Idle Speed	Discharge Pressure psi @ 3,000 rpm	Vacuum [1] mm. Hg. Idle Speed	Vacuum mm. Hg. Starter Speed
190c 200, 230 220b 220Sb 230S 250S	DVG diaphragm [7]	1.77-2.35	2.21-2.94	Behind pump outlet					230-320
220/8 230/8 250/8	APG diaphragm	1.77-2.35	2.21-2.94	Behind pump outlet					230-320
190Dc 200D 220D/8	Bosch FP/K22M2/8		1.20-2.20	Between inj. pump & main filter	32.0	29.0	37.0	2.9-5.9	
220SEb 300SE [2]	Bosch FP/ESB5RC25/ 12AI	8.8-13.2 [3]		Behind fine filter		17.6 [3][4]			
230SL 250SE 250SL 300SE 300SEb 300SEL [5]	Bosch FP/ESB5RC25/ 12AI	13.2-16.1 [3]		Behind fine filter		19.1 [3][6]			

[1] Measured in front of pump inlet.
[2] With two-cylinder injection pump.
[3] With engine not running and a minimum of 11 volts at terminals.

[4] Measured behind damper unit in fuel return line.
[5] With six-cylinder injection pump.
[6] Behind fuel overflow valve on injection pump.
[7] Pump tappet clearance — .016-.020".

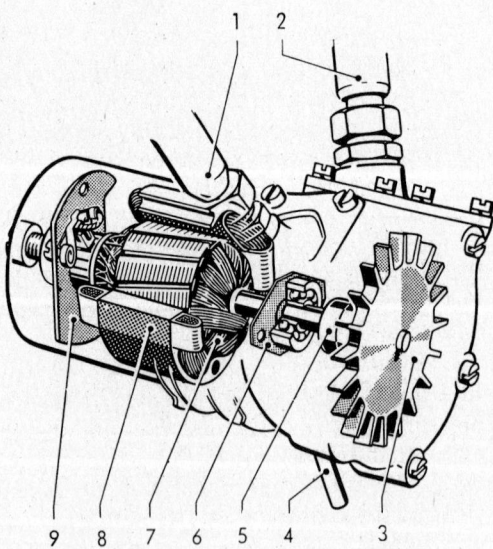

1. Connection, delivery side, with check valve
2. Connection, suction side
3. Vane
4. Leak-off pipe
5. Slide ring seal
6. Mounting plate
7. Armature
8. Laminated pole
9. Brush holder plate

Bosch electric fuel pump internal parts.

1. Threaded union with check valve (delivery side)
2. Screw plug
3. Terminal 30
4. Terminal 31
5. Threaded union (suction side)
6. Pump cover

Bosch electric fuel pump.

be 3.5 qts. per minute with 10 volts @ 3.1–3.5 Amperes at pump terminals.

Check the pump-to-motor seal for leakage by disconnecting the bypass pipe (4). With pump warm (after shutting off engine) there should be no rapid dripping.

The pump itself can be cleaned of dirt by removing the pump cover (6), after match-marking the cover and case. *NOTE: Maximum impeller play on key is ±18°.*

Carburetor

IDLE AND LINKAGE ADJUSTMENT—190c

The 190c is equipped with one Solex 34 PICB carburetor. To adjust, first check the throttle butterfly shaft for ease of movement. Detach pushrod (9) from lever (11) and disconnect return spring (1). Turn out the idle screw (8) until the butterfly is completely closed, then turn the screw in until the butterfly is almost ready to open. From this position, turn screw in exactly one turn. Open the butterfly all the way and make sure the limit screw (12) contacts the full load stop on the housing, then reconnect the pushrod (9) and return spring (1). Press the accelerator pedal to the floor and make sure the butterfly opens fully.

To adjust idle speed, screw in the idle mixture screw (7) until it seats, then back it out exactly two turns. *NOTE: Do not overtighten—which would damage the needle seat.*

Start the engine and allow it to warm up, connect a tachometer between the distributor-to-coil *primary* wire and ground, and adjust idle speed to 750–800 rpm. Adjust the *mixture* screw until the highest, smoothest idle speed is attained, then re-adjust screw (8) to get 750–800 rpm idle speed again.

1. Clamp screw	8. Idle adjustment
2. Clamp screw	screw
3. Control lever	9. Pushrod
4. Rod	10. Return spring
5. Rod	11. Throttle valve lever
6. Control lever	12. Aperture limiting
7. Idle mixture ad-	screw
justment screw	13. Choke control

Type 190c carburetor.

During idling or low speed operation, the engine needs little fuel and, as a consequence, the danger of vapor lock under high temperature conditions is increased. To compensate for this, a fuel return valve is incorporated into the carburetor. This valve is operated by the spring-loaded accelerator pump arm to allow excess fuel to run back through the valve and return

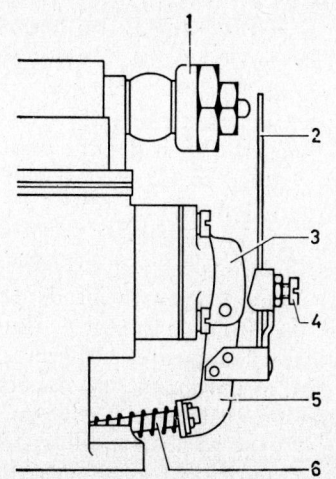

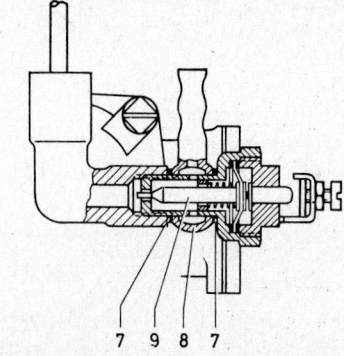

1. Return valve	5. Pump arm
2. Spring-loaded the	6. Connecting rod
pump arm head	7. Fiber gasket
3. Accelerator pump	8. Ring connector
4. Adjusting screw	9. Valve pin

Scavenging device on 190c.

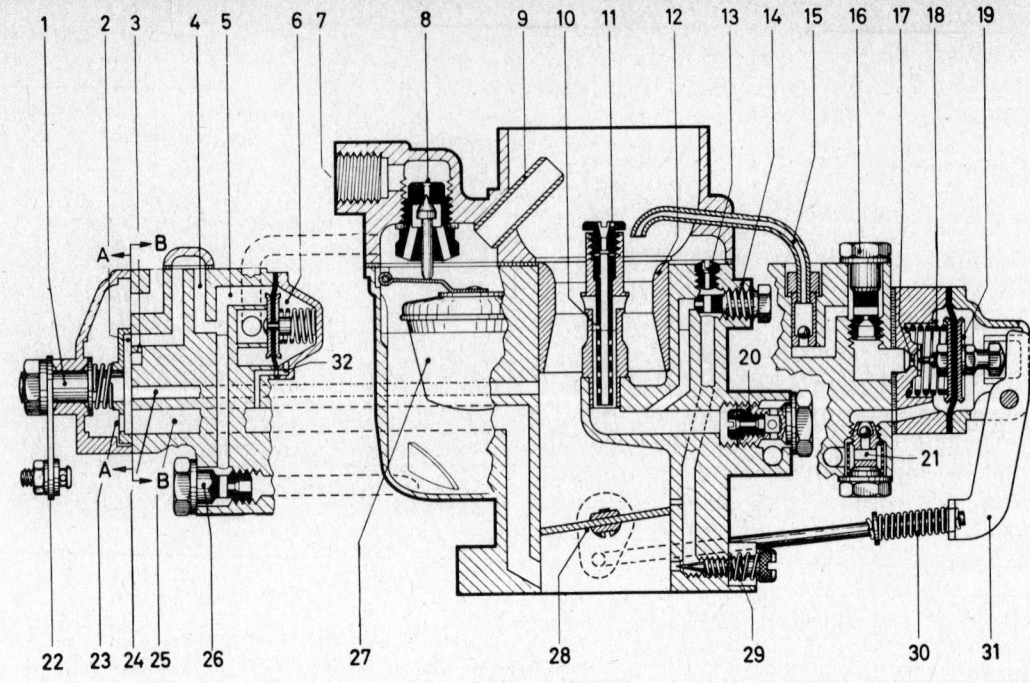

1. Starter rotary slide valve
2. Graded intake bore in starter flange for fuel canal (4)
3. Graded intake bore in starter flange for fuel slot
4. Fuel canal to starter system
5. Air canal from starter air valve to fuel canal (4)
6. Starter air valve
7. Fuel-line connection in carburetor cover
8. Float needle valve
9. Vent tube for float chamber
10. Mixing tube holder with mixing tube
11. Air correction jet
12. Air horn
13. Idle air jet
14. Idle fuel jet
15. Injection tube
16. Pump jet
17. Bore
18. Diaphragm spring
19. Pump diaphragm
20. Main jet plug with main jet
21. Ball valve
22. Starter lever
23. Starter air bore in starter rotary slide valve
24. Additional air canal
25. Starter mixture canal
26. Starter fuel jet
27. Float
28. Throttle valve
29. Idle mixture adjustment screw
30. Connecting rod with compression spring
31. Pump arm
32. Vacuum canal for starter air valve

Solex 34PICB carburetor.

line to the fuel tank, thus cooling the fuel and preventing vapor lock.

To adjust the valve, push the accelerator linkage until the accelerator pump lever (5) is fully against its stop, then turn adjusting screw (4) until return valve (1) is completely closed.

IDLE AND LINKAGE ADJUSTMENT—
220b AND 220Sb

Early models of the 220 b series used two Solex 34 PICB carburetors with "straight" linkage, while later models used progressive linkage. The 220 Sb used two Solex 34 PAITA carburetors with both "straight" and progressive linkage, while later models used two Zenith 35/40 INAT carburetors with progressive linkage.

To adjust the linkage on both 220 b and 220 Sb models using Solex carburetors, first detach pushrods (2) and (6) (or (3) and (5) for progressive linkage) and check their length. Pushrod (2) should be 3.34" long (center to center of ball sockets); pushrod (5) should be 3.86" long; pushrods (6) and (3) should be 7.41" long. Pack the ball sockets with chassis grease and reinstall, then detach pushrods (8), or (1), from the front and rear carburetors and check the linkage and carburetor butterflies for ease of movement; oil if necessary.

Operate pushrod (8) to open the butterfly and make sure the limit screw (12) contacts the full load stop with the butterfly fully open (220 b).

On 220 Sb models, the limit stop on the

1. Double lever
2. Pushrod
3. Eccentric screw
4a. Ball socket, left-hand thread
4b. Ball socket, right-hand thread
5a. Hexagon nut, left-hand thread
5b. Hexagon nut, right-hand thread
6. Pushrod

7. Relay lever
8. Spring-loaded pushrod
9. Throttle valve lever
10. Return spring
11. Idle adjustment screw
12. Aperture limiting screw
13. Coil spring for choke control
14. Choke control
15. Clamping screw for choke control
16. Connecting rod

17. Fuel line
18. Idle fuel jet
19. Pump jet
20. Idle mixture adjustment screw
21. Main jet
22. Union for tester
23. Screw plug
24. Vacuum line distributor
25. Pump arm
26. Accelerating pump

Type 220b with Solex 34PICB carburetors.

second carburetor must contact the housing with the butterflies of *both* carburetors fully open. Unscrew the idle screw (11) on both carburetors until the butterflies are completely closed, then turn them in until the butterflies are just ready to open. From this point, turn the screws in one turn.

On cars having "straight" linkage, adjust eccentric screw (3) so that the slot is at right angles to the front relay lever, with the eccentric pointing upward. On cars having progressive linkage, install a screw (4), similar to the one shown, having a ⅝"

diameter head. Pull back on the bellcrank until it contacts the eccentric screw (3) or the homemade screw (4) and make sure that the butterfly lever is resting against the idle adjustment screw. Adjust the pushrods so that, in this position, it is possible to snap them over their ball sockets without forcing. Remove screw (4) and depress the accelerator pedal to the floor to make sure the butterflies open fully.

In the case of the 220 Sb having INAT carburetors, disconnect pushrods (9) and (13) and check linkage for ease of movement, then check that bellcrank (7) con-

1. Double lever
2. Pushrod
3. Eccentric screw
4a. Ball socket, left-hand thread
4b. Ball socket, right-hand thread
5a. Hexagon nut, left-hand thread
5b. Hexagon nut, right-hand thread
6. Pushrod
7. Relay lever
8. Spring-loaded pushrod
9. Throttle valve lever

10. Return spring
11. Idle adjustment screw
12. Return spring
13. Clamp
14. Relay lever
15. Connecting rod (to starter lever)
16. Connecting rod
17. Fuel pressure line
18. Idle fuel jet
19. Pump jet
20. Idle mixture adjustment screw
21. Main jet of stage 1
22. Union for tester
23. Screw plug

24. Vacuum line, distributor
25. Pump arm
26. Accelerating pump
27. Adjustment screw and lock nut
28. Spring-loaded pump arm head
29. Fuel return valve
30. Fuel return line
31. Coil spring for choke control
32. Rubber bushing
33. Adjusting nut
34. Choke control
35. Clamping screw for choke control

Type 220Sb with Solex 34PAITA carburetors.

tacts the housing with the butterfly fully open. Adjust idle screws (4), after unloading chokes, by unscrewing until the butterflies are fully closed, then turning in until the butterflies are just ready to open and continuing exactly one turn more after that point.

The connecting rods (1) then must be adjusted to 1.58″ in length and the pushrod (9) adjusted so that, with the butterfly levers resting against idle stop screws, it can be pushed onto its ball sockets without forcing.

Idle speed adjustment is the same for both the 220 b and 220 Sb. First screw in the idle mixture screws (20) or (6) until bottomed, then back out 1½ turns on 220 b and two turns on 220 Sb. Start the engine and allow it to warm up, then, on engines having progressive linkage, disconnect pushrods (5) or (13). On engines having "straight" linkage, turn the eccentric screw (13) to gain enough clearance between the screw and bellcrank (7) for idle adjustment.

Connect a tachometer between the coil-to-distributor primary wire and ground, then evenly adjust idle speed screws (11) or (4) on *both* carburetors to attain 750–800 rpm idle speed. Now adjust the idle

1. Spring-loaded
     pushrod
2. Relay lever
3. Pushrod
4. Adjustment screw
     or fillister
     head screw
     M 8 DIN 85
5. Pushrod
6. Adjusting ring
7. Relay lever
8. Roller
9. Quadrant lever
10. Cylinder cover
11. Threaded bolt
12. Bearing bracket

Type 220Sb with Solex 34PAITA carburetors and progressive linkage.

1. Connecting rod
2. Throttle valve lever
3. Quadrant lever
4. Idle adjustment screw
5. Pump arm
6. Idle mixture adjustment
     screw
7. Reversing lever
8. Float chamber vent valve
9. Pushrod
10. Adjustment screw
11. Lever
12. Fuel return valve
13. Pushrod
14. Relay lever
15. Adjusting ring
16. Roller
17. Quadrant lever

Type 220Sb with Zenith 35/40 INAT carburetors.

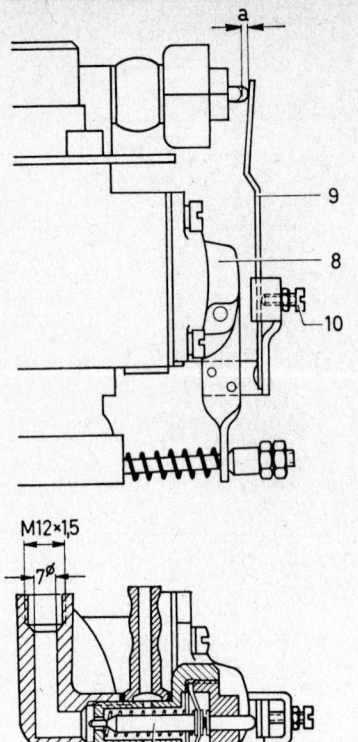

3. Valve pin
4. Fiber gasket
5. Ring connector
8. Accelerating pump
9. Spring-loaded pump arm head
10. Adjusting screw
a. = 0.4—0.6 mm. (.016-.024")

Scavenging device on 220b and 220Sb.

mixture screws, evenly, to attain the smoothest, fastest idle speed possible, then readjust idle speed screws evenly to get 750–800 rpm engine speed.

On 220 Sb models having INAT carburetors, check the float chamber vent. With the butterfly in idle position, the lever (7) should lift the valve pin (8) .060"–.080"; adjust by carefully bending lever (7). On engines having progressive linkage, attach pushrods (5) or (13) and adjust the knurled nuts (6) or (15) so that the roller (8) or (16) rests against the limit stop without tension. On engines having "straight" linkage, adjust eccentric screw (3) to give .008" clearance between it and the bellcrank (7). Make sure the chokes operate in synchronization.

The 34 PAITA carburetors have a fuel return valve incorporated into the accelerator pump system in the same manner as on 190 c models. To adjust this valve, depress the spring-loaded pushrod at the butterfly lever of the front carburetor and back out the idle speed screw until the throttle butterfly is completely closed. Now, screw in adjusting screw (10) on the accelerator pump arm until the return valve is completely closed, then back out the adjusting screw to the point where the return valve pin has covered a distance ("a") of .016"–.024"; lock the adjusting screw. Improper adjustment of the return valve often results in a lack of fuel at high speeds.

Idle and Linkage Adjustment 200, 230, 230S and 250S with Solex 36/40 PDSI Carburetors

These models use two Solex 36/40 PDSI-2 carburetors. Since the advent of the closed crankcase breather system in 1965, it is sometimes difficult to attain smooth idle speed. (The engine sucks in unburnt crankcase vapor, which impairs combustion efficiency at low speeds.) Before adjusting carburetors, adjust the ignition timing and check the spark plugs. Start the engine and allow it to come to operating temperature, then remove the air cleaner.

To adjust carburetors, disconnect pushrods (1) and (15) and turn in the idle mixture screws (8) until they seat (don't overtighten). Turn the screws out ¾ turn for 200 and 230 models, 1¼ turns for 230 S and 250 S. Check that, as accelerator pedal is depressed, both throttle butterflies open fully and together. Re-adjust pushrod length to achieve this.

Connect a tachometer between engine ground and the distributor-to-coil primary wire and adjust idle speed screws (6) evenly to obtain specified idle speed (see Chapter 2). Now, adjust idle mixture screws (8) evenly to attain the smoothest, fastest idle speed possible, then re-adjust idle speed screws evenly to specified idle speed again. *NOTE: On 230 S and 250 S models, idle speed is adjusted by turning the knurled screws on the plastic connecting rods.*

Recheck throttle butterfly synchronization and check length of pushrod (1); it should be equal in length to the distance

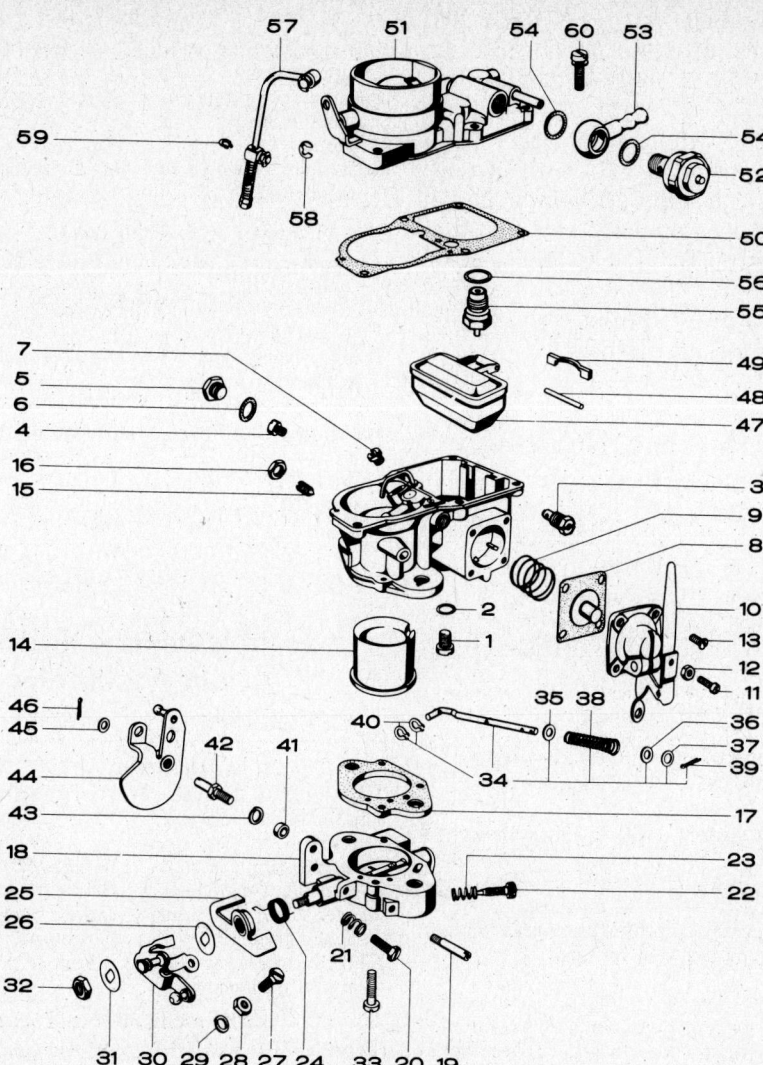

1. Cheesehead screw	21. Pressure spring	41. Washer
2. Seal ring	22. Idle volume control screw	42. Bearing bolt
3. Idle jet	23. Pressure screw	43. Lockwasher
4. Main jet	24. Return spring	44. Choke lever
5. Plug screw	25. Operating lever	45. Washer
6. Seal ring	26. Spacer washer	46. Cotter pin
7. Air correction jet	27. Choke adjustment screw	47. Complete float
8. Diaphragm	28. Hex head nut	48. Float pin
9. Diaphragm spring	29. Lockwasher	49. Hold-down
10. Pump cover	30. Throttle lever	50. Seal ring
11. Cheesehead screw	31. Safety washer	51. Carburetor top
12. Hex head nut	32. Hex head nut	52. Fuel return valve
13. Countersunk screw	33. Cheesehead screw	53. Ring hose piece
14. Venturi	34. Pump connecting rod	54. Seal ring
15. Venturi lockscrew	35. Flat washer	55. Needle valve
16. Hex head nut	36. Flat washer	56. Seal ring
17. Isolation gasket	37. Flat washer	57. Choke connecting rod
18. Complete throttle valve	38. Pressure spring	58. Safety washer
19. Connection tube	39. Cotter pin	59. Expansion ring
20. Idle adjustment screw	40. Expansion ring	60. Cheesehead screw

Solex 36/40 PDSI carburetor (U. S. version).

between bearing bolts (3) on 200 and 230 models. *NOTE: It must be possible to connect all pushrods without binding or forcing.*

Adjust pushrod (15) so that roller (18) contacts the limit stop at (17) without tension, then check that the accelerator pedal is fully against its stop with both throttle butterflies fully open. If not, adjust linkage at firewall.

Reconnect all pushrods and recheck idle speed, then install air cleaner.

Troubleshooting Guide— Solex Carburetors

PROBLEM	SOLUTION
Hard cold start	
Choke valves do not move easily.	Free up choke valves.
Choke valves not closing properly.	Adjust starter cable.
Throttle valve opening angles too small.	Check throttle valve angle.
Rough running of engine during warm-up	
Starter valve vacuum diaphragm defective.	Replace diaphragm.
Vacuum bore for starter valve clogged.	Check performance of starter valve; blow out bore with compressed air.
Compression springs at starter connecting rod not adjusted correctly.	Adjust compression springs.
Throttle valve opening angle out of synchronization.	Adjust and synchronize throttle valve opening angle.
Rough idle	
Idle fuel jet or idle air bore clogged.	Clean jet and bore.
Idle canal and by-pass bores clogged.	Clean bores and canal.
Float leaks.	Replace float.
Float adjustment wrong.	Adjust float.
Damaged idle mixture adjustment screw or damaged seat in chamber.	Replace idle mixture adjustment screw and/or throttle valve assembly.
Injection tube dripping after fuel injection.	Check relief bores for clogging and clean relief bores.
Gaskets leaking at carburetors, at suction tube, or at vacuum connections.	Find leaks by pressure test and stop them.
Idle speed too high	
Throttle valve jammed.	Free up valve.
Ball heads on control linkage sticking.	Replace ball heads.
Dashpot too far out.	Adjust dashpot.

Poor acceleration	
Injection tube clogged.	Clean injection tube.
Pump diaphragm faulty.	Replace diaphragm.
Injection amount wrong; injection angle wrong.	Adjust injection amount and direction.
Baffle plate incorrectly installed.	Install baffle plate properly.
Engine stalls when engaging gear.	
Dashpot maladjusted.	Adjust dashpot.
High fuel consumption	
Float needle valve leaking; wrong float adjustment.	Replace float needle valve and gasket.
Loose idle or main jet.	Tighten jets.
Injection amount too large.	Adjust injection amount.
Wrong type of jets installed.	Install proper jets.

Troubleshooting Guide— Zenith Carburetors

PROBLEM	SOLUTION
Hard cold start	
Choke valves sticking.	Free up valves.
Choke valves do not close.	Free up valves.
Bi-metal spring in starter cover defective.	Replace bi-metal spring.
Starter cover has insufficient preload.	Increase starter cover preload.
Throttle valve opening angle insufficient.	Adjust cold start idle increase.
Engine stalls after cold start	
Starting mixture too rich or too lean.	Adjust pilot throttle gap.
Starter valve vacuum diaphragm defective.	Replace vacuum diaphragm.
Rough idle	
Choke valves do not open.	Replace fuse.
Fuse for automatic choke blown.	Replace heater coil.
Heater coil in starter cover burnt.	Replace heater coil.
Choke valves jam.	Free up choke valves.
Idle fuel jet or idle air bore clogged.	Clean jet or bore.
Idle canal and/or by-pass bores clogged.	Clean idle canal and/or bypass bores.
Floats leak.	Replace floats.
Float adjustment wrong.	Adjust float.
Damaged idle mixture adjustment screw or damaged seat in chamber.	Replace idle mixture adjustment screw and/or throttle valve component.
Gaskets leaking at carburetors, at intake manifold, or at vacuum connections.	Use new gaskets.

Idle speed too high

Throttle valve jammed. — Free up valve.
Ball heads at control linkage sticking. — Replace ball heads.
Vacuum control too far out. — Adjust vacuum control.
Float chamber vent valves do not move easily. — Replace vent valves.

Poor acceleration

No injection or injection amount too small. — Clean injection tube.
Injection tube clogged. — Slide sleeve back over and make sleeve smoother.
Accelerating pump sleeve has too little preload. — Clean intake valve.
Injection amount too large. — Adjust injection amount.
Injection angle wrong — Bend injection tube to proper angle.

Hard hot starting

Float chamber vent valve does not open far enough. — Adjust vent valve.
Vent valve blocked. — Clean vent valve.

High fuel consumption

Float needle valve leaking. — Replace float needle valve and gasket.
Float adjustment wrong. — Adjust float.
Injection amount too large. — Adjust injection amount.
Wrong type of jets installed. — Install proper jets.
Choke valves do not open all the way. — Check choke valves for ease of movement. Check performance of heater coil in starter cover.

CARBURETOR MODIFICATIONS—200

To obtain the best performance possible without stalling, some modifications to the model 200 carburetor were made in production. Cars not having these modifications can be improved in the following manner:

On automatic transmission models, carefully bend the injection tube of the front carburetor toward the venturi wall, as illustrated. This helps to eliminate flat spots. In serious cases of hesitation when starting out from rest, modify the rear carburetor in the same manner.

On all cars, the lower bypass bore (3) can be enlarged to 1.5 mm. (from 1.3 mm.); the upper bypass bore (2) enlarged to 1.3 mm. (from 1.0 mm.); the idle bore (1) enlarged to 1.6 mm. (from 1.0 mm.); the idle fuel jet (7) changed from 55 to

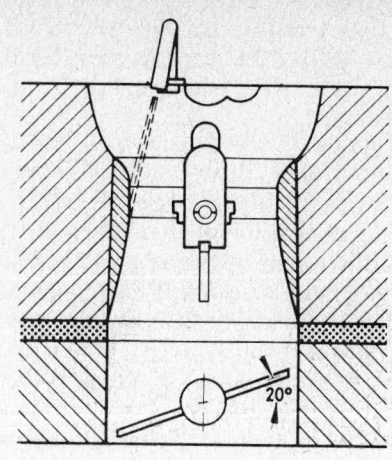

Bending injection tube—type 200 front carburetor.

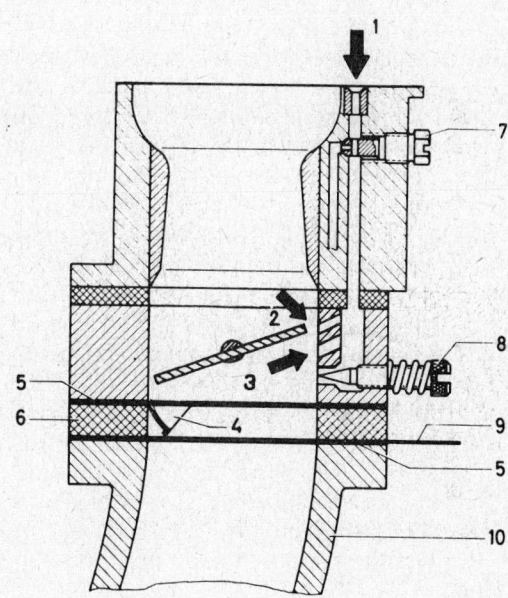

1. Idle air bore
2. Bypass bore
3. Bypass bore
4. Deflector plate
5. Gasket (seal)
6. Gasket (seal)
7. Idle fuel jet (nozzle)
8. Mixture adjustment screw
9. Screening plate
10. Suction tube

Carburetor modifications to type 200.

62.5 and a fuel deflector plate (4) installed. *NOTE: The carburetors must be removed and disassembled.*

Use a No. 52 drill for enlarging bore (1), a No. 53 drill for bore (3) and a No. 55 drill for bore (2). *CAUTION: Use a hand drill only; turn drill very slowly and determine proper drill angle before starting.*

Idle and Linkage Adjustment—230, 230S, 250S with Zenith INAT Carburetors

The basic set-up is similar to the one pictured for 220 Sb models having Zenith carburetors. First check the spark plugs and ignition timing, then start the engine and allow it to warm up. Remove the air cleaner and disconnect the pushrod and bellcrank linkage from front carburetor, then connect rubber hose (⅜″ inside diameter) between camshaft cover and intake manifold bypass connector. Connect a tachometer between engine ground and the distributor-to-coil primary wire and adjust carburetor idle speed screws evenly to obtain 800–850 rpm. Adjust mixture screws evenly, after seating fully (without overtightening) to get the smoothest, fastest possible idle speed, then readjust idle speed screws evenly to 800–850 rpm. Connect the pushrods, making sure they seat properly with no tension or binding and reconnect bellcrank linkage to front carburetor. There should be .004″–.008″ clearance between the bellcrank and roller.

If car is equipped with automatic transmission, place selector lever in "D" and adjust spring (7) by turning nut (8) to obtain an idle speed of 650–700 rpm. Then, shift transmission into neutral and check that actuating lever (10) contacts the idle stop screw (1). If the lever rests against the hex screw (9), turn the screw clockwise and shift the selector lever to "D" position. Readjust the spring (7) to obtain 650–700 rpm.

If car is equipped with manual transmission, emission control system and air conditioning, adjust spring (7) to obtain a clearance of .004″ between the hex screw (9) and actuating lever (10).

With the above adjustments completed, disconnect tachometer and breather hose and reinstall air cleaner. *NOTE: Remember to reconnect hose to intake manifold.*

Choke, Pre-Throttle and Fast Idle Adjustment—230, 230S, 250S with Zenith INAT Carburetors

Check that the choke butterflies operate smoothly, then check the alignment of the index marks on the choke housing. The choke springs are preloaded .196″ normally, although in cases of stalling during warm-up a preload of .118″ may be required.

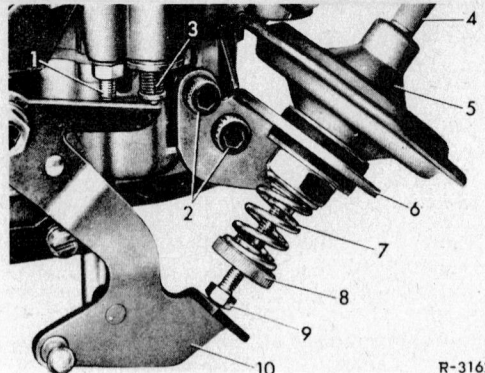

1. Idle stop screw
2. Allen head screw
3. Vent valve
4. Vacuum hose
5. Idle compensator
6. Bracket
7. Compression spring
8. Knurled nut
9. Hex head screw
10. Actuating lever

Dashpot adjustment—230, 230S, 250S with INAT carburetors.

1. Marking for cars up to 3,000 miles
2. Choke housing marking
3. Choke housing cover marking
4. Choke housing cover

Choke adjustment—230, 230S, 250S with INAT carburetors.

1. Choke housing cover
2. Choke housing
4. Throttle lever
5. Connecting rod

Adjusting pre-throttle gap—230, 230S, 250S with INAT carburetors.

1. Control lever
2. Control lever (hot start)
3. Adjusting screw
4. Step cam
5. Diaphragm control rod
6. Return spring

Adjusting pre-throttle gap—230, 230S, 250S with INAT carburetors.

1. Choke valve
2. Measuring pin (pre-throttle gap)
3. Connecting rod
4. Starter valve
5. Set screw

Adjusting pre-throttle gap—230, 230S, 250S with INAT carburetors.

To adjust the pre-throttle gap, first warm up the engine, then lift the accelerator linkage slightly and place a screwdriver between the choke housing and throttle lever. Lift connecting rod (5) to the stop position of diaphragm rod and release linkage. The clearance at this point between the throttle butterfly and carburetor throat should be .079″–.083″. Clearance is measured by inserting the shank of a No. 47 or No. 45 drill. If necessary, adjust setscrew (5) on the starter valve. Repeat procedure for the other carburetor.

To adjust fast idle, first warm up engine, then, with engine not running, lift accelerator linkage and insert a screwdriver between the choke housing and throttle lever. Lift the connecting rod (5) and release accelerator linkage. This should place the adjusting screw on the highest point of the cam.

Start engine, after connecting a tachometer, and check engine speed; it should be 2,400–2,600 rpm. Repeat procedure for the other carburetor. *NOTE: Turning adjusting screw clockwise increases engine speed and vice-versa. If engine is cold, fast idle speed should be 1,800 rpm.*

CARBURETOR ACCELERATOR LEVER MODIFICATIONS—230, 230S, 250S WITH INAT CARBURETORS

If the engine stalls or hesitates during acceleration, a modified accelerator cam lever can be installed and the accelerator pump fuel delivery volume increased. First remove the air cleaner, then the car-

1. Choke housing cover
2. Choke housing
3. Adjusting screw

230, 230S, 250S choke housing showing adjusting screw.

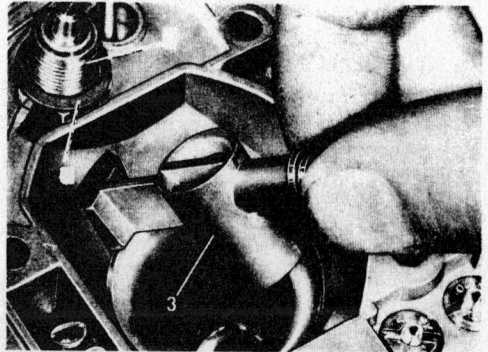

Removing atomizers—230, 230S, 250S with INAT carburetors.

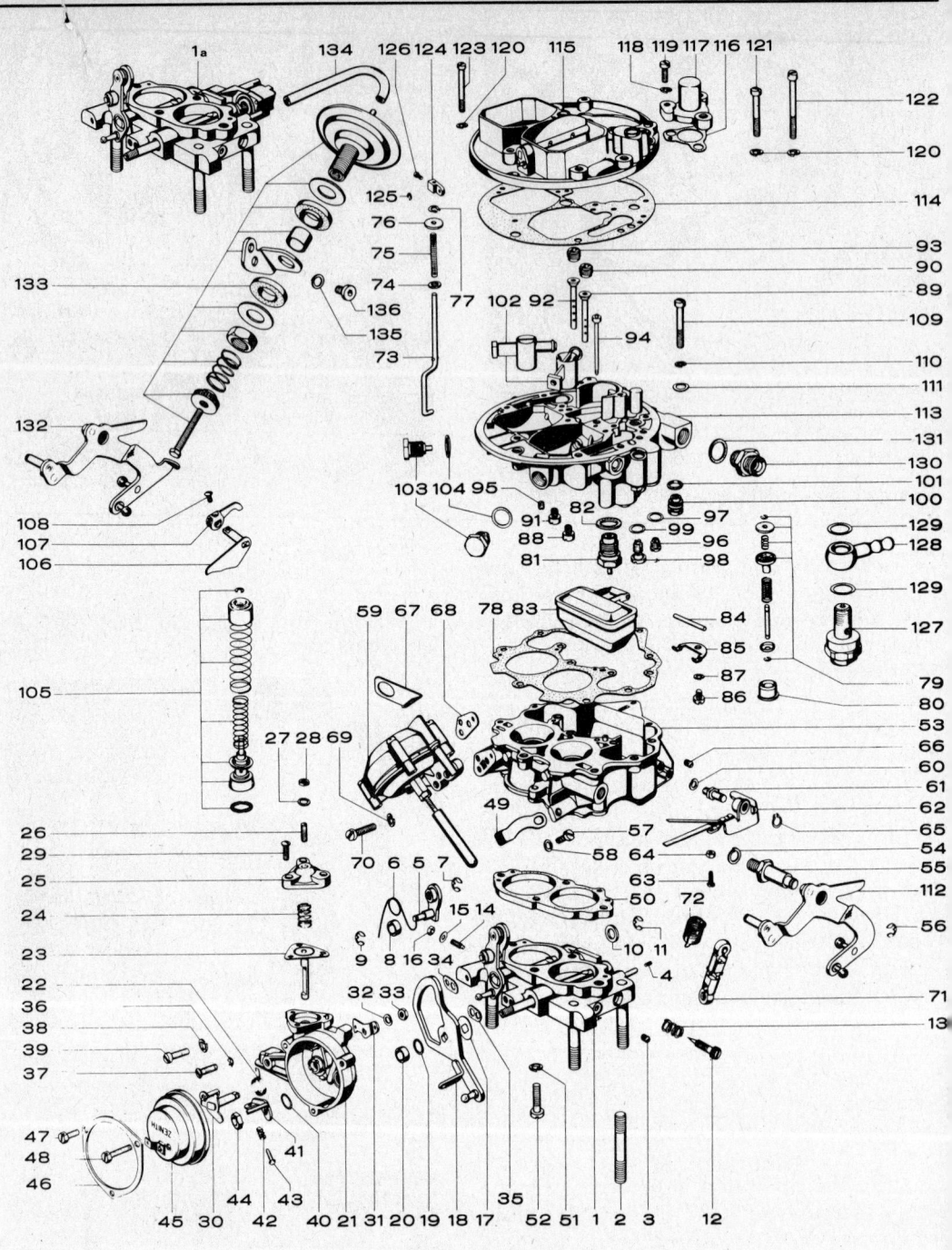

Zenith 35/40 INAT carburetor.

Zenith 35/40 INAT carburetor.

2. Pin screw
3. Screw
5. Joint lever
6. Return spring
7. Safety washer
8. Roller
9. Safety washer
10. Flat washer
11. Safety washer
12. Idle mixture screw
13. Pressure spring
14. Adjustment screw
15. Spring washer
16. Hex head nut
17. Flat washer
18. Throttle lever
19. Safety washer
20. Spacer
21. Choke body
22. Return spring
23. Diaphragm spring
24. Pressure spring
25. Valve cover
26. Screw
27. Seal ring
28. Hex head nut
29. Countersunk screw
30. Operating lever
31. Transfer lever

32. Spring washer
33. Hex head nut
34. Gasket
35. Gasket
36. Star washer
37. Countersunk screw
38. Spring washer
39. Screw
40. Safety washer
41. Stop lever
42. Pressure spring
43. Stop screw
44. Hex head nut
45. Choke cover
46. Stop ring
47. Hex head nut
48. Hex head nut
49. Clamp
50. Isolation flange
51. Spring washer
52. Screw
53. Float bowl
54. Spring washer
55. Bearing bolt
56. Safety washer
57. Cheesehead screw
58. Spring washer
59. Vacuum chamber
60. Seal ring

69. Spring washer
70. Cheesehead screw
71. Connecting rod
72. Return spring
73. Connecting rod
74. Flat washer
75. Pressure spring
76. Washer
77. Tension ring
78. Seal ring
79. Air valve
80. Bushing
81. Needle valve
82. Seal ring
83. Float
84. Shaft
85. Bracket
86. Cheesehead screw
87. Spring washer
88. Main jet
89. Mixture tube
90. Air correction jet
91. Main jet
92. Mixture tube
93. Air correction jet
94. Idle jet
95. Jet
96. Pump suction valve
97. Seal ring

98. Pump pressure valve
99. Seal ring
100. Jet
101. Seal ring
102. Sprayer
103. Pressure screw
104. Seal ring
105. Pump piston
106. Pump lever
107. Inner pump lever
108. Countersunk screw
109. Cheesehead screw
110. Lockwasher
111. Spring washer
114. Carburetor body gasket
115. Carburetor top
116. Seal ring
117. Cover
118. Lockwasher
119. Cheesehead screw
120. Lockwasher
121. Cheesehead screw
122. Cheesehead screw
123. Cheesehead screw
124. Joint piece
125. Safety washer
126. Cheesehead screw

Additional parts for carburetor 000.120-13 DB 16

1. Throttle valve
60. Lockwasher
61. Bearing bolt
62. Operating lever

63. Cheesehead screw
64. Hex head nut
65. Expansion ring
112. Complete operat-

ing lever
113. Complete platin block
127. Fuel return valve

128. Ring hose piece
129. Seal ring
130. Threaded fitting
131. Seal ring

Additional parts for carburetor 000.120-14 DB 17

1. Throttle valve
4. Screw
66. Threaded pin
67. Cable holder

112. Complete operat- ing lever
113. Platin block

Additional parts for carburetor 000.120-23 DB 27

1. Throttle valve
67. Cable holder
113. Platin block
132. Operating lever

133. Vacuum regulator
134. Rubber hose
135. Lockwasher
136. Cheesehead screw

Additional parts for carburetor 000.120-15 DB 18

1a. Throttle valve
60. Lockwasher
61. Bearing bolt
62. Operating lever

63. Cheesehead screw
64. Hex head nut
65. Expansion ring
67. Cable holder

112. Complete operat- ing lever
113. Platin block
127. Fuel return valve

128. Ring hose piece
129. Seal ring
130. Threaded fitting
131. Seal ring

buretor tops and pre-atomizers (3). Remove the hold-down screw from each inner pump lever and push outer pump levers and shafts out.

Remove accelerator pump plungers and inspect the leather washers; replace if necessary. Clean the pump cylinders with alcohol, then reinstall pump plungers and check the pump injection action. *NOTE: Depressing the pump lever slowly should result in 0.7–1.0 cc. fuel injection per stroke. If less than this, bend inner pump lever to increase pump plunger stroke.*

Check that the fuel discharge tube directs the fuel spray to a point .39"–.59" below the upper edge of the intermediate plate block. Carefully, bend the tube, without crushing it, to adjust.

Reassemble carburetors, using the modified cam lever (as illustrated), then adjust carburetor synchronization and idle speed as described previously.

IDLE SPEED AND LINKAGE
ADJUSTMENT—220/8

The 220/8 uses two 36/40 PDSI Solex

1. Fastening screw
2. Fastening screw
3. Plunger assembly
4. Cam lever
5. Outer pump lever

Bending lever—230, 230S, 250S with INAT carburetors.

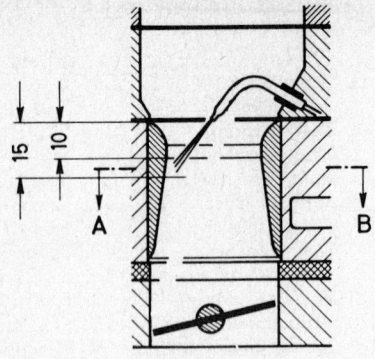

Section A-B

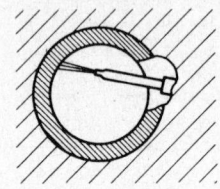

Fuel discharge tube modifications.

carburetors in a set-up quite similar to that used on early 230 models.

First warm up engine, then detach pushrods (15) and (4). Adjust pushrod (1) so that its length equals the distance between the lever pivot pins (3). Adjust idle speed by turning screws (6) evenly, then adjust idle mixture screws(8) evenly for the fastest, smoothest idle. Readjust idle speed screws to obtain specified idle speed, then place pushrod (4) in such a position that the bellcrank (2) is .040″ from the limit tab on the intake manifold. Install push-

rod (4), after adjusting it to a length where it goes onto its ball sockets without binding or tension.

Adjust pushrod (15) by turning the knurled nut (14) so that the roller rests in its slot without tension (on cars with manual transmission) or so that the lever (5) is against the idle stop (on cars with automatic transmission).

1. Push rod
2. Angle relay lever
3. Pivot pin
4. Pushrod
5. Throttle lever
6. Idle adjustment screw
7. Starter adjustment screw
8. Idle fuel adjustment screw
9. Starter link rod
10. Fuel return valve
11. Flat spring
12. Adjustment screw of fuel return valve
13. Angle relay lever stop
14. Adjusting ring
15. Pushrod
16. Angle relay lever
17. Quadrant lever
18. Roller

Carburetor adjustment—type 220/8.

Vacuum Control Valve
Adjustment—220/8

Automatic Transmission Models

Loosen bolt (6) to give .040″ clearance between it and the bellcrank (7). *NOTE: In "D" range.*

Automatic Transmission Models with No Accessories or Air Conditioned Models, Any Transmission

Place selector lever in "D" or, if equipped with manual transmission, turn on air conditioner. Adjust bolt (6) to obtain specified idle speed, then adjust nut (4) to rest against stop (5).

Models with Two or More Accessories

Place car in "D" or, if equipped with manual transmission, turn on one accessory (air conditioning, full lock on power steering, etc.). Adjust bolt (6) to obtain specified idle speed, then adjust nut (4) to give .080″ clearance between it and stop (5).

Accelerator Pump Adjustment—220/8

Check the accelerator pump in the same manner as with Zenith INAT carburetors. On the front carburetor used in automatic transmission applications, the fuel spray

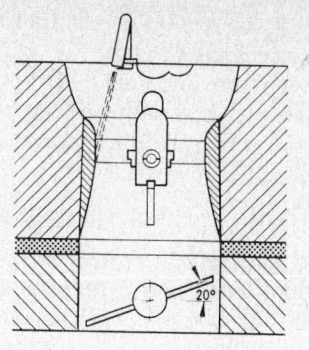
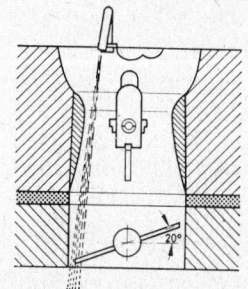
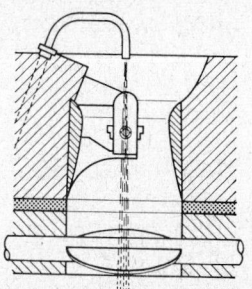

Fuel spray adjustment—220/8.

must hit the side of the venturi, not shoot directly into the carburetor throat. On both carburetors used in manual transmission applications, and on the rear carburetor in automatic transmission applications, the fuel spray must be parallel to the venturi axis and go through the gap between the venturi and throttle butterfly when the butterfly is opened 20°.

1. Vacuum hose
2. Closing damper
3. Bracket
4. Polystop nut
5. Stop
6. Hexagon bolt
7. Angle relay lever
8. Pushrod
9. Starter adjustment screw
10. Idle adjustment screw
11. Mixture adjustment screw

Dashpot adjustment—220/8.

1. Fuel return valve
2. Flat spring
3. Adjusting screw
4. Shim
5. Pump lever
6. Connecting rod

Accelerator pump adjustment—220/8.

The amount (volume) of fuel delivered by the accelerator pump is adjusted by adding or removing shims (4) between the pump lever (5) and the cotter pin on the pump rod (6). Adding shims increases volume, and vice-versa.

CUT-OFF VALVE INSTALLATION—220/8

If the engine "overruns" after shutting off the ignition, electric fuel cut-off valves can be installed in place of the existing idle jets. Replace both idle jets with the new cut-off valves, connect the valves together and route the wire to the fuse box. Loosen the fuse box mounting and connect wire to Terminal No. 3 (output side), then re-install fuse box. *NOTE: Needed are two cut-off valves, part No. 000 072 00 17; one wiring harness, part No. 110 540 28 09.*

CHOKE ADJUSTMENT—220/8

Adjust idle speed and check throttle linkage for ease of movement. Detach pushrod (19) at rear carburetor and clamp choke cable (18) so that its end is in alignment with clamp (11). Push choke lever (7) forward against stop (10), then press choke control in until there is .040″ clearance between it and dashboard. Tighten choke cable at lever (7) by tightening screw (8).

Turn the shoulder nut (8) on the choke link (1) so that distance "a" equals 1.12″

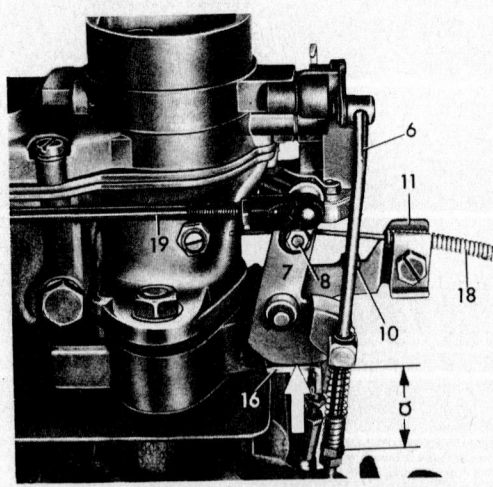

6. Starter link rod
7. Starter lever
8. Clamping screw
10. Stop
11. Bowden cable clamp
16. Follower link lever
18. Starter cable coil
19. Connecting rod

Choke adjustment—220/8.

at the rear carburetor. Set lever (7) as illustrated (arrow) by adjusting connecting link (19).

IDLE SPEED AND LINKAGE ADJUSTMENT— 230/8, 250/8 with INAT CARBURETORS

Warm up engine, remove air cleaner and detach control rods (11) and (16). Adjust idle speed screws (1) evenly to obtain specified idle speed, then turn mixture screws (7) in until they seat (do not over-tighten) and adjust outwards evenly to obtain the fastest, smoothest idle speed. Recheck idle speed and adjust screws (1) if necessary.

On cars having manual transmission, adjust length of control rod (16) so that the roller rests against the end of the slot without tension. On cars having automatic transmission, hold throttle butterfly lever (8) against the idle stop and adjust control rod (16) so that it can be easily hooked up without binding.

DASHPOT ADJUSTMENT—230/8, 250/8 WITH INAT CARBURETORS

If car is equipped with automatic transmission, place selector lever in a drive range and, with engine not running, back out hex bolt (9) until vent valve (3) is raised .020″–.040″. Then start engine and adjust compression spring (7) by turning nut (8) to obtain specified idle speed. *NOTE: With parking brake locked.*

Place selector lever in "N" and check that the lever (10) is against the idle stop. If the lever touches hex bolt (9), back out the bolt and readjust spring (7) with car in "D".

If car is equipped with manual transmission, start engine, make sure all accessories are turned off, and adjust nut (8) to give .004″ clearance between hex bolt (9) and the actuating lever (10).

AUTOMATIC CHOKE ADJUSTMENT— 230/8, 250/8 WITH INAT CARBURETORS

Check that the choke butterflies operate without binding, then check the choke housing cover; the marks must line up. *NOTE: The spring is preloaded .20″.*

Turn on the ignition switch and make sure the throttle butterflies open after a few minutes (engine cold). To adjust the pilot throttle gap with the engine running, lift accelerator linkage and insert a screw-

1. Idle adjustment screw	8. Actuating lever	14. Fuel return valve
2. Throttle valve lever	9. Hexagon bolt	15. Hexagon nut
3. Test union	10. Adjustment nut	16. Control rod
4. Pump lever	11. Connecting rod	17. Lever
5. Idle stop screw	12. Adjustment screw	18. Lever
6. Float chamber vent valve	13. Return valve lever	19. Adjustment screw
7. Idle mixture adjustment screw		

Carburetor adjustment—types 230/8, 250/8, 280S/8.

driver between the choke housing (2) and the throttle lever (4). Press the relay lever (5) upwards until it touches the stop on the diaphragm rod, then release linkage. Measure the clearance between the choke butterfly and the carburetor bore; it should be .096″. If necessary, adjust by turning screw (5) on the starter valve.

Start the engine and allow it to warm up. Shut off the engine, raise the accelerator linkage and insert a screwdriver between the starter housing (2) and the throttle lever (4) of one carburetor. Press the relay lever upward and release linkage. This should cause the adjustment screw (3) inside the choke housing to come to rest on the top notch of the cam (4).

Hook up a tachometer and start the engine; adjust screw (3) to obtain proper fast idle. Adjust the other carburetor in the same manner.

Fuel Injection

Mercedes-Benz passenger cars use intermittent intake pipe fuel injection units with mechanical two- or six-element pumps. An electric fuel pump draws fuel from the supply tank and forces it through a filter into the suction chamber of the injection pump. Excess fuel flows back to the fuel tank via fuel return lines. The injection pump plungers force the fuel through the pressure valves into the fuel distribution lines and injection valves. The injection valves spray atomized fuel into the intake ports in the cylinder head, where it is mixed with air from the air venturi. The fuel-air mixture then enters the combustion chambers, where it is ignited by a conventional electric ignition system.

The injection pump and its attendant control linkage can only be accurately tested and adjusted using special test apparatus and tools not readily available. For this reason it is recommended that all work on the fuel injection system be carried out by an authorized Mercedes-Benz dealer.

Many troubles in starting can be traced to the cold start electrical system incorporated. A study of the wiring diagrams, and use of an ohmmeter or other continuity

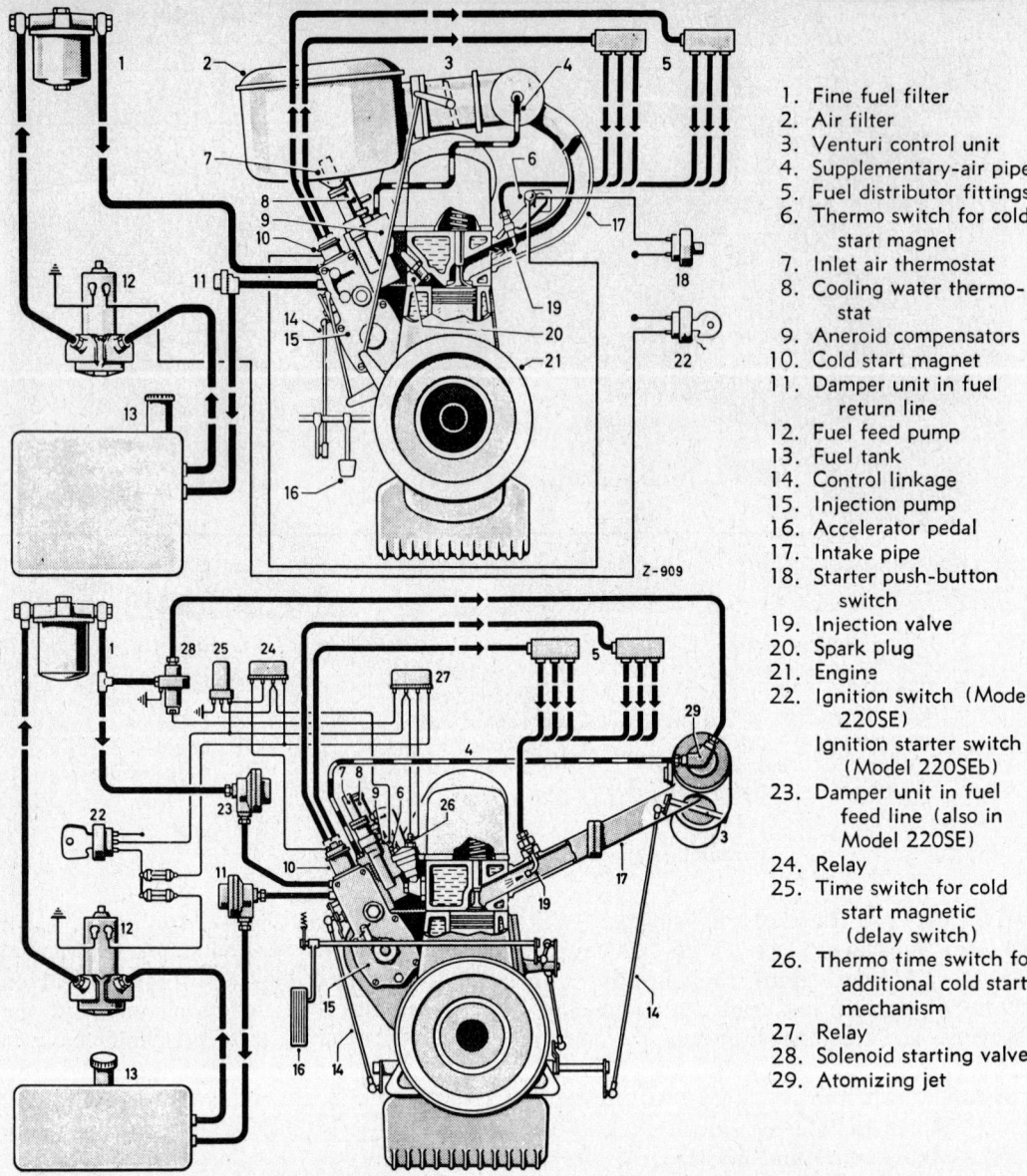

1. Fine fuel filter
2. Air filter
3. Venturi control unit
4. Supplementary-air pipe
5. Fuel distributor fittings
6. Thermo switch for cold start magnet
7. Inlet air thermostat
8. Cooling water thermostat
9. Aneroid compensators
10. Cold start magnet
11. Damper unit in fuel return line
12. Fuel feed pump
13. Fuel tank
14. Control linkage
15. Injection pump
16. Accelerator pedal
17. Intake pipe
18. Starter push-button switch
19. Injection valve
20. Spark plug
21. Engine
22. Ignition switch (Model 220SE)
    Ignition starter switch (Model 220SEb)
23. Damper unit in fuel feed line (also in Model 220SE)
24. Relay
25. Time switch for cold start magnetic (delay switch)
26. Thermo time switch for additional cold start mechanism
27. Relay
28. Solenoid starting valve
29. Atomizing jet

Top—injection system used on 220SE with ZEA pump.

Bottom—Injection system used on 220SEb with ZEA pump.

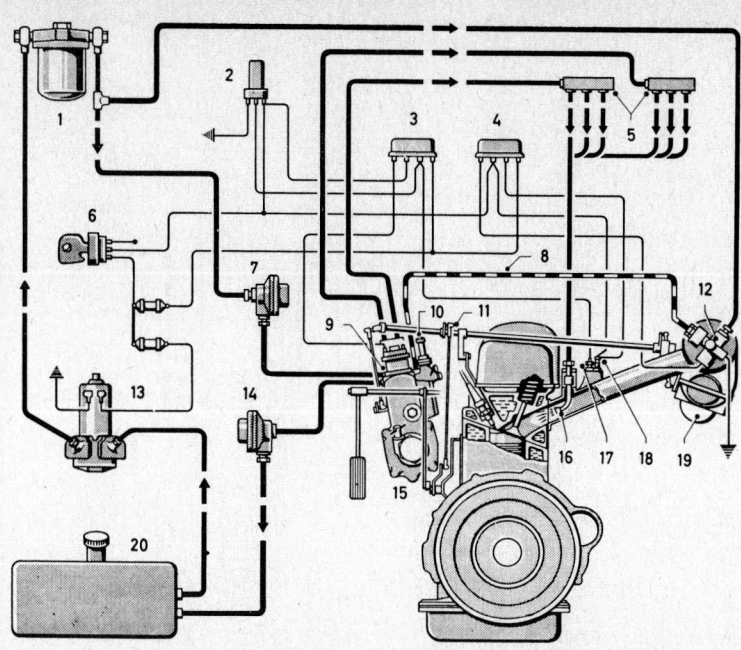

1. Fine fuel filter
2. Time switch
3. Relay
4. Relay
5. Fuel distributor fittings
6. Ignition starter switch
7. Damper unit (feed line)
8. Supplementary air pipe
9. Cold start magnet
10. Cooling water thermo-
    stat
11. Control linkage
12. Solenoid starting valve
    with atomizing jet
13. Fuel feed pump
14. Damper unit (return
    line)
15. Injection pump
16. Injection valve
17. Thermo switch in cool-
    ing water circulation
    system
18. Thermo time switch in
    cooling water circu-
    lation system
19. Venturi control unit
20. Fuel tank

Injection system used on 300SE with ZEA pump.

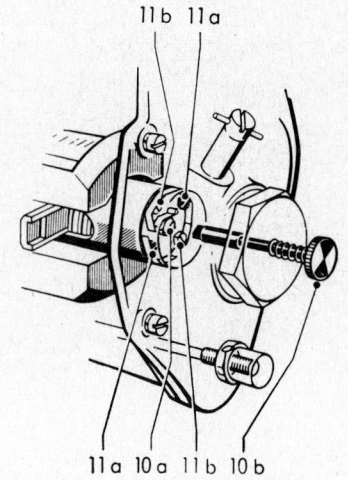

10a. Adjustment screw (black) for idle up to
     approx. 1,000 rpm
10b. Spring-loaded idle control knob
11a. Adjustment screw (black) for partial load or
     medium engine speed range from approx.
     700 to approx. 4,000 rpm
11b. Adjustment screw (white) for partial load or
     upper engine speed range from approx.
     2,000 rpm

ZEA pump adjustment screws.

tester, will often help isolate problem components.

Idle speed can be adjusted by turning the idle screw on the air venturi and the spring-loaded idle control knob on the injection pump to obtain smooth operation. *NOTE: The knob must be pushed in against spring pressure. Turning counterclockwise leans the mixture and vice-versa. Do not exceed three notches in either direction.*

It must be emphasized, however, that adjustments of this nature are extremely critical in light of emission control regulations, and that the use of a CO meter is necessary to obtain best operation.

Other simple service procedures include checking the linkage for ease of movement and the injection control rod for binding. Detach the pushrod at the adjustment lever and push the lever to the full load stop position. Allow the lever to return slowly until it rests against the idle stop, making sure there is no binding in the system.

To check the fuel control rod, start the engine and allow it to warm up. If, after operating the adjusting lever, the idle speed can be *considerably* increased by backing out the idle air screw on the air

1. Inlet air thermostat
   (no longer installed
   on the ZEB Injec-
   tion pump)
2. Cold start magnet
3. Pin
4. Guide pin for cam
   lever
5. Reversing lever
6. Starting delivery lever
7. Fuel control rod head
8. Relay lever
9. Eccentric bushing
10a. Idle adjustment screw
   (black) up to
   appr. 1,000 rpm
10b. Spring-loaded idle
   control knob
11a. Adjustment screw
   (black) for partial
   load or medium
   speed range of
   appr. 700 to appr.
   4,000 rpm
11b. Adjustment screw
   (white) for partial
   load or top speed
   range as from appr.
   2,000 rpm
12. Dipstick
13. Governor sleeve stop
   screw
14. Joint
15. Governor springs
16. Flyweights
17. Supporting lever
18. Governor sleeve
19. Sliding piece
20. Plug with lubricating
   plate
21. Camshaft
22. Fixing screw for roller
   tappet
23. Roller tappet
24. Plunger spring
25. Control sleeve
26. Mobile toothed
   quadrant

27. Fixing screw for pump
   element
28. Fuel return pipe
29. Pump element
30. Pipe union
31. Clamping jaws
32. Pressure pipe
33. Fuel feed pipe

34. Fuel control rod
35. Drive lug
36. Cam plate
37. Cam lever
38. Air filter
39. Cooling water thermo-
   stat

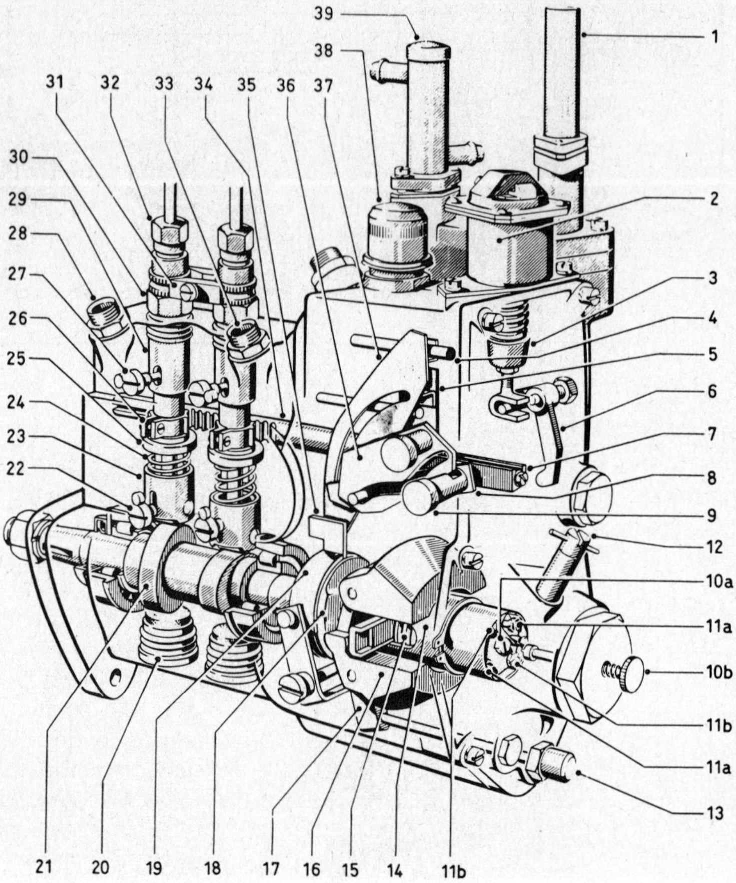

ZEA injection pump.

S = Starting position of fuel
      control rod
V = Full load position
L = Idle position
2. Cold start magnet
3. Pin
4. Guide from cam lever
5. Reversing lever
6. Starting delivery lever
7. Fuel control rod head
8. Relay lever
9. Eccentric axle
10a. Idle adjustment screw
      (black) for up to appr.
      1,000 engine rpm
11a. Adjusting screw (black)
      for partial load or
      medium speed range of
      appr. 700 to appr.
      4,000 engine rpm
11b. Adjusting screw (white)
      for partial load or top
      speed range as from
      appr. 2,000 engine rpm
13. Governor sleeve stop screw
14. Joint
15. Governor springs
16. Flyweights
17. Supporting lever
18. Governor sleeve
19. Sliding piece
34. Fuel control rod
35. Drive lug
36. Camshaft

37. Cam lever	66. Control lever
63. Venturi control unit	67. Adjustment lever
64. Throttle valve	68. Pushrod
65. Throttle valve lever	69. Axle
	70. Pullrod

ZEA injection pump control linkage.

1. Damper unit (return
   line)
2. Cooling water hose
3. Rubber hose for sup-
   lementary air line
4. Injection pipes
5. Cooling water
   thermostat
6. Cooling water hose
7. Pushrod
8. Cold start magnet
9. Full-load stop
10. Adjustment lever
11. Damper unit (feed
   line)
12. Idle stop
13. Fuel hose (feed line)
14. Fuel line connection
   cold start valve
15. Fuel line (return line)
16. Hexagon nut
17. Oil line
18. Oil container for
   power steering
19. Thermo time switch
20. Thermo time switch

Two-cylinder injection pump—220SEb illustrated.

Gasoline Injection Pumps

Model	Transmission version	Engine type	Bosch designation DB Part No.	Remarks
220SE	Mech. transmission	127.980	EP/ZEA 2 KL 75 R 1 000 074 28 01	Cam plate and cam lever have positive connection. Idle adjustment screw not adjustable from outside. One adjustment screw for total partial load range. (Replaced by R 3 pump)
			EP/ZEA 2 KL 75 R 2 127 070 00 99	Cam plate and cam lever have non-positive connection. Idle adjustment screw adjustable from outside by means of spring-loaded idle control knob. Two adjustment screws for lower and upper partial load range. (Replaced by R 3 pump)
			EP/ZEA 2 KL 75 R 3 127 070 00 01	Differs from R 2 injection pump in insulating flanges fitted between thermostats and corrector assembly. Cut-off temperature for supplementary air and mixture enrichment during warm-up period by means of cooling water thermostat is between 65-68° C (on R 1 and R 2 injection pumps appr. 60° C). Inlet air thermostat with spring cup which limits adjustment by inlet air thermostat to 30 to 35° C.
220SE Convertible and Coupe		127.983	EP/ZEA 2 KL 75 R 3 Z 127 070 02 01	Differs from R 3 injection pump in modified partial-load and full-load adjustment.
220SEb	Mech. transmission		EP/ZEA 2 KL 75 R 4 003 074 38 01	Differs from R 3 Z injection pump only in modified adjustment lever. Replaced by R 6 pump.
			EP/ZEA 2 KL 75 R 6[1] 003 074 68 01	Differs from R 4 injection pump in the adjustment lever which is suitable for top and bottom control linkage.
			EP/ZEB 2 KL 75 R 11 127 070 05 01	Two-cylinder injection pump with mechanical control. (Replaced by R 14 pump)
		127.982 127.984	EP/ZEB 2 KL 75 R 14 127 070 16 01	Differs from R 11 injection pump in modified pressure valves.
			EP/ZEA 2 KL 75 R 7 004 074 06 01	Differs from R 6 injection pump in better governing or warming-up air and steeper end of idle governing (increased idling speed).
	Automatic transmission		EP/ZEB 2 KL 75 R 13 127 070 08 01	Differs from R 11 injection pump in steeper idle adjustment curve. (Replaced by R 16 pump)
			EP/ZEB 2 KL 75 R 16 127 070 17 01	Differs from R 13 injection pump in modified pressure valves.
230SL	Mech. and automatic transmission	127.981	PES 6 KL 70/120 R 11 127 070 07 01	Six-cylinder injection pump with mechanical control via three-dimensional cam.

Model	Transmission version	Engine type	Bosch designation DB Part No.	Remarks
250SE 250SL	Mech. and automatic transmission	129.980 129.981 129.982	PES 6 KL 70 A 120 R 18 129 070 03 01	Differs from R 11 injection pump in longer pump housing, modified three-dimensional cam. (Replaced by R 18z pump)
			PES 6 KL 70 A 120 R 18z 129 070 06 01	Differs from R 18 injection pump in ball pressure valves, no oil check valve and slightly richer adjustment.
			PES 6 KL 70 A 120 R 18y 129 070 08 01	USA version (exhaust gas purification). Differs from R 18z in stop magnet, modified three-dimensional cam and guide tube for full-load adjustment screw.
300SE 300SE (long)	Automatic transmission		EP/ZEB 2 KL 75 R 12 003 074 99 01	Two-cylinder injection pump with mechanical control. (Replaced by R 15 pump)
			EP/ZEB 2 KL 75 R 15 189 070 00 01	Differs from R 12 injection pump in modified pressure valves.
	Mech. transmission	189.984 189.985	EP/ZEB 2 KL 75 R 17 189 070 01 01	Differs from R 12 injection pump by flatter idle adjustment curve. (Replaced by R 18 pump)
			EP/ZEB 2 KL 75 R 18 189 070 02 01	Differs from R 17 injection pump in modified pressure valves.
	Mech. and automatic transmission	189.986 189.987	PES 6 KL 70 A 120 R 12 189 070 03 01	Six-cylinder injection pump with mechanical control via three-dimensional cam.
			PES 6 KL 70 A 120 R 12 189 070 03 01	Up to engine no. 189.987-10-000 480 or 189.987-12-000 871
			PES 6 KL 70 A 120 R 19 189 070 05 01	As from engine no. 189.987-10-000 481 or 189.987-12-000 872.
300SEb 300SEL	Mech. and automatic transmission	189.989 189.988	PES 6 KL 70 A 120 R 19 189 070 05 01	Differs from R 12 injection pump in longer housing, modified return-line union, start mechanism (cable harness) modified. (Replaced by R 19 pump. Part No. 189 070 07 01)
			PES 6 KL 70 A 120 R 19 189 070 07 01	Differs from R 19 injection pump, Part No. 189 070 05 01, in being without oil check valve and with ball pressure valves.

1 On Model 220 SEb, the ZEA injection pump can be replaced by the ZEB injection pump in the case of engines with overhead control linkage.

venturi, the fuel control rod is probably binding and the injection pump must be replaced.

Injection Pump Removal

Remove the battery and drain off some of the engine coolant. Referring to the illustration, disconnect coolant hoses (2) and (6), the air line (3), the oil line (17), and the fuel lines that go to the pump.

Detach the control rod (7) and disconnect the wire from the cold start magnet.

Unscrew nuts (16) and, on six-cylinder pumps (as opposed to two-cylinder pumps) unscrew the rear pump bracket. Remove the pump to the rear and remove coupling sleeve. *NOTE: If the drive lug on the injection pump camshaft must be replaced, use a puller. The drive lug must be held with soft-jawed pliers while removing the cam hold-down nut and two bolts may have to be removed to make room for the puller, depending on the type puller used.*

1. Control lever
2. Cooling water hose
3. Supplementary air line
4. Injection pipes
5. Cooling water thermostat
6. Cooling water hose
7. Control rod
8. Cold start magnet
9. Full-load stop
10. Adjustment lever
11. Air cleaner
12. Idle stop
13. Fuel line (feed line)
14. Aneroid compensator
15. Fuel line (return line)
16. Hexagon screw
17. Oil line
18. Spring-loaded idle control knob
19. Housing for the thermostat switches
20. Hexagon screw

Six-cylinder injection pump—230SL illustrated.

Injection Pump Installation

Models 220SEb and 300SE with Two-Cylinder Pump

Set the crankshaft and injection pump in the installation position; No 1 cylinder at TDC (ignition) mark on pump camshaft lined up with mark on flange of pump.

Push the coupling sleeve onto the drive lug and install the pump. Connect all lines, attach the control rod and check the adjustment of the control linkage, then install battery, top up coolant and check injection pump oil level.

Models 230SL, 250SE, 250SL, 300SE, 300SEb, and 300SEL with Six-Cylinder Pump

Set crankshaft and injection pump in the installation position; No. 6 cylinder to 20° ATDC on intake stroke for 230SL, 250SE, 250SL and No. 6 cylinder to 60° ATDC for 300SE, 300SEb and 300SEL, with mark on pump camshaft lined up with mark on flange of pump.

Push the coupling sleeve onto the drive lug and install the pump. Connect all lines, attach the control rod and check the adjustment of the control linkage, then install

battery, top up coolant and check injection pump oil level. *NOTE: Injection pump element #1 is connected to No. 6 cylinder, etc.*

Exhaust System

Pre-Phase II Models

Removal

Disconnect the exhaust pipe at the exhaust manifold, then unscrew the bracket from mounting plate on the rear transmission cover. If rubber rings (10) are installed detach and remove them.

NOTE: On cars equipped with air suspension, detach the connecting rod for the level adjustment valve from the torsion bar lever on the rear axle. Loosen the lower clamp (5) and pull the torsion bar (2) down out of the way.

Disconnect the rubber rings (1) from the main muffler (4) and, on cars with dual exhausts, unscrew the nuts (1) that hold the main muffler. Remove the exhaust system assembly as a unit on 230SL, in two pieces for all others, making sure to note

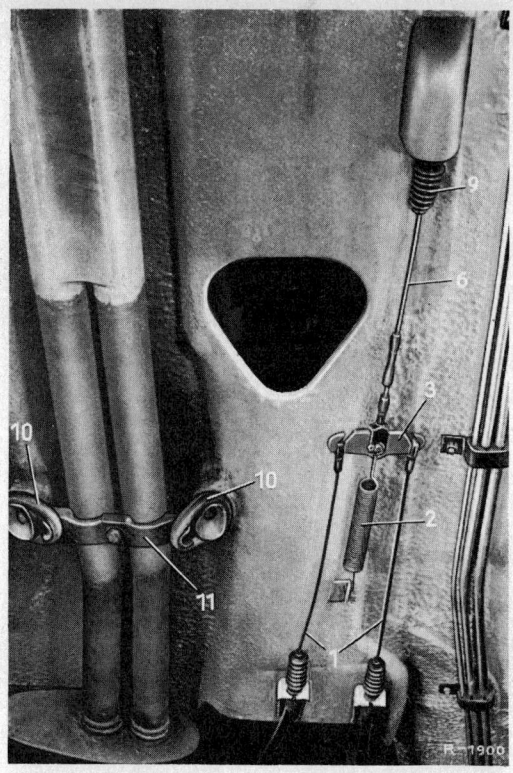

Disconnecting exhaust system—pre-Phase II models.

1. Rear brake cable
2. Return spring
3. Equalizer
6. Front brake cable
9. Rubber grommet
10. Rubber ring
11. Lower bracket

Disconnecting air suspension connecting rod—pre-Phase II models.

1. Rear axle tube
2. Torsion bar
3. Chassis base panel bracket
4. Rubber mounting
5. Clamp
6. Bracket
7. Retainer
8. Fixing strap
9. Bearing bracket
10. Connecting link

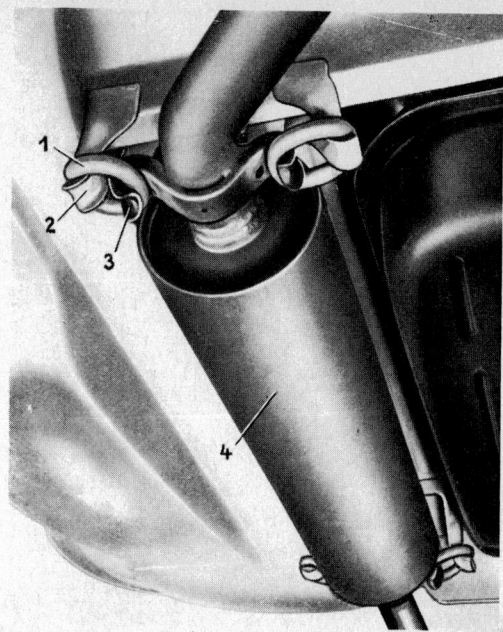

Disconnecting main muffler—pre-Phase II models.

1. Rubber ring
2. Chassis base panel bracket
3. Main muffler bracket
4. Main muffler

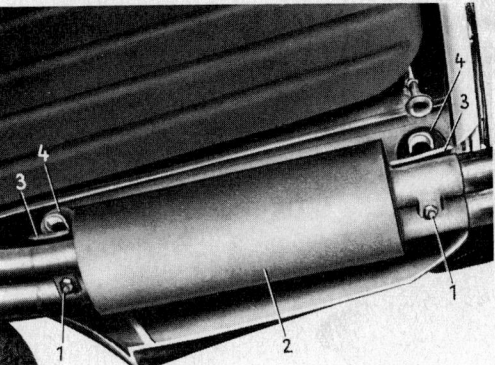

Insulating plate positioning—pre-Phase II models.

1. Hexagon nut
2. Main muffler
3. Insulating plate
4. Rubber ring

position of any insulating plates that go between the rubber rings and exhaust pipes.

INSTALLATION

Connect the exhaust pipe loosely to the manifold, then attach rubber rings to the main muffler and, on cars having dual exhausts, fit the insulating plates and nuts.

Place new seal rings (gaskets) on the front pipe and tighten the self-locking nuts that hold it to the manifold flange. Screw the exhaust pipe bracket to the transmission so that no tension exists on the exhaust system, then attach the rubber rings, if used, to the chassis floor. *NOTE: On cars equipped with air suspension, fold the torsion bar up in place and reconnect it. Attach the connecting rod to the torsion bar lever.*

Phase II Models

REMOVAL

Disconnect the front exhaust pipe at the exhaust manifold, then loosen the pipe clamps (8) at the connection or, for four-cylinder 220/8, disconnect the flange that connects the two pipe sections.

Disconnect and remove the clamp (6) between the transmission support bracket (4) and the exhaust pipe, then disconnect the rubber rings that attach the main muffler to the chassis floor pan. Separate and remove mufflers and pipes.

INSTALLATION

To install, reverse removal procedure. Some assembly tips follow:

1. On 220/8, the self-locking nuts at the pipe connecting flange between the front and rear pipes must be tightened so that

Pipe connecting flange—220/8.

1. Hexagon bolt   4. Self-locking nut
2. Washer   5. Front exhaust pipe
3. Pressure spring   6. Center exhaust pipe

Manifold flange connection—220D/8.

1. Hexagon bolt   3. Pressure spring
2. Washer   4. Self-locking nut

tension springs are 36 mm. (1.4″) long as measured at "b".

2. On 220D/8, the self-locking nuts at the pipe-to-manifold flange must be tightened so that tension springs are 31 mm. (1.2″) long as measured at "a".

Cooling System

Radiator

REMOVAL AND INSTALLATION

To remove the radiator, drain the coolant and the oil cooler (if so equipped). Then, remove the fan shroud and loosen the

Disconnecting exhaust system—Phase II models.

1. Front exhaust pipe   5. Tension bracket
2. Rear exhaust pipe   6. Clamp
3. Pre-silencer   7. Self-locking nuts
4. Transmission-mounted   8. Pipe clamp
   support bracket

Radiator mount and thermostat location.

upper and lower hose clamps. Remove the hoses at the radiator, being careful not to crush the outlets. If the hoses are deteriorated it is best to cut them away with a sharp knife.

Unscrew the connections of the engine oil cooler and transmission oil cooler (automatic). Detach the hold-down bolts and the rubber pads on each side of the radiator and pull the radiator upward.

On the 230 SL, the bleeder hose from the radiator top tank must be removed, as well as the battery and hood.

When reinstalling, always measure the distance B1 and B2 (as illustrated). If the distances "a" (thickness of rubber pads) added to B2 do not equal B1, shims must be added, otherwise the radiator will be overstressed and the solder joints will tend to crack. ("Horseshoe" shims are available at most auto parts jobbers.)

Always make sure that the fan clears the shrouding all around *before* starting the engine, and that there is sufficient clearance between all hoses and the fanbelts.

Water Pump

Two basic types of water pumps have been used in Mercedes-Benz models—an oil lubricated model used on 190c, 190Dc, 200, 220D, 220b, 220Sb, 220SEb, 230, 230S, 230SL and some 300SE models. This pump was replaced in production by a maintenance-free unit on the 250S, 250SE, 250SL, 300SE, 300SEb and 300SEL models as well as on the Phase II cars. Dimensions and illustrations of both types follow.

Thermostat

The thermostat used is as illustrated. With the Mercedes-type cooling system, removing the thermostat does not aid in cooling. Coolant flows straight back into the engine through the bypass hose and results in an overheated engine.

Engine

Exhaust Emission Controls

In order to meet Federal standards for hydrocarbon emission for 1968 import,

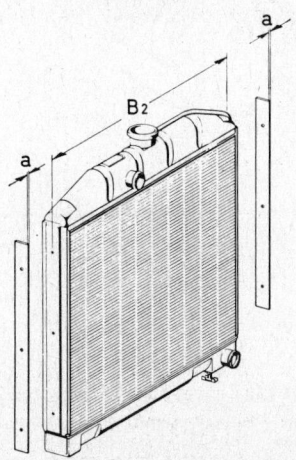
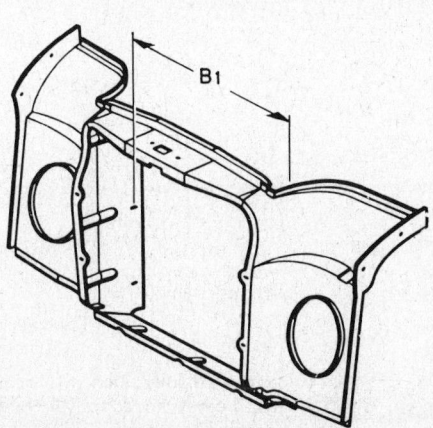

Measurements needed to determine spacer thickness.

Model	Water pump without water pump housing and pulley Part No.	Distance "a" and "b" in illustrations	Illustration
190c, 190Dc, 200, 200D, 220b, 220Sb, 220SEb, 230, 230S, 230SL	121 200 06 20	a = 22.8—23.2 b = 88.8—89.0	#1
250S, 250SE, 250SL	121 200 08 20	a = 22.8—23.2 b = 60.35—62.25	#2
300SE	189 200 04 20	a = 35.6—36.0	#1 #2
300SEb, 300SEL	189 200 07 20	a = 35.7—35.9	#2

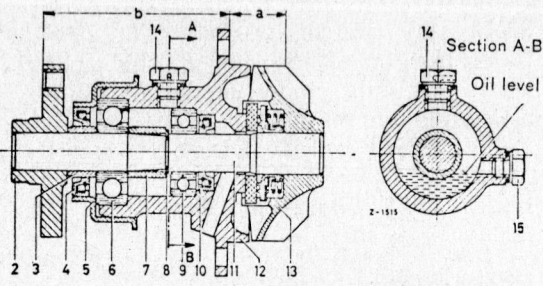

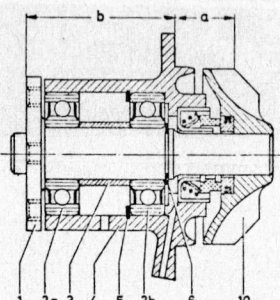

Oil lubricated pump used on models listed in chart as #1.

2. Hub
3. Spacer ring
4. Sealing ring
5. Sealing ring retainer
6. Annular grooved bearing
7. Spacer sleeve
8. Snap-ring
9. Annular grooved bearing
10. Sealing ring
11. Water pump shaft
12. Bearing housing
13. Impeller
14. Filler screw with breather bore
15. Oil level checking screw

Sealed pump used on models listed in chart as #2.

1. Hub with water pump shaft
2a. Front ball bearing
2b. Rear ball bearing
3. Spacer sleeve
4. Bearing housing
5. Snap-ring
6. Snap-ring
10. Impeller

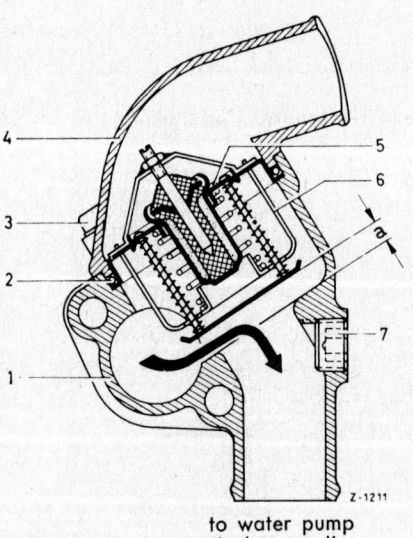

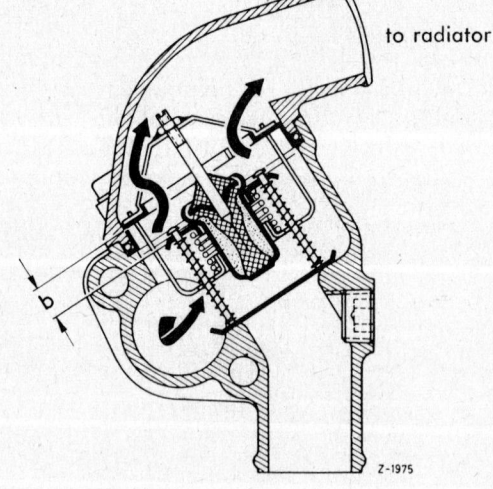

to radiator

to water pump via by-pass line

Thermostat action.

Main valve closed — Bypass valve fully open
Stroke "a" = 6—6.5 mm. from 0 to appr. 74—78°C.
1. Cooling water thermostat
2. Sealing ring
3. Hexagon socket screw
4. Cover

Main valve open — Bypass valve closed
Stroke "b" = 8—9 mm. at appr. 91—94° C.
5. Corrugation
6. Cooling water thermostat element
7. Plug

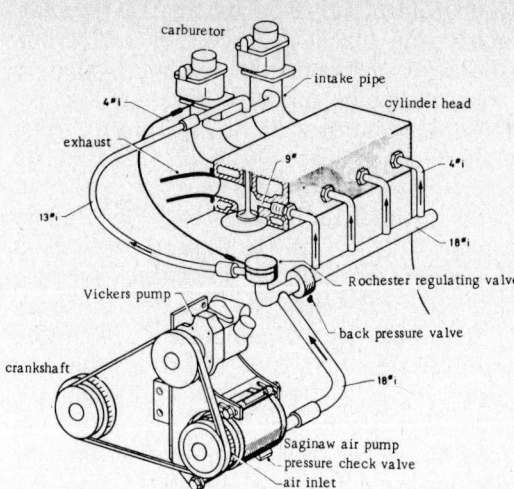

Manifold Air Oxydation System—230, 230S, 250S.

some modifications were necessary on models imported to the United States. The type 200 carburetor and distributor were modified so that vacuum control works only during idling and deceleration, when the throttle is contacting the idle stop, to retard the ignition spark. The carburetor was modified so that, even with the ignition timing maladjusted, the mixture cannot become too rich.

The 230, 230 S and 250 S presented a more difficult emission problem. As a result, in addition to carburetor and distributor modifications, similar to those used on the 200, a port burning (afterburner) system was incorporated. This system, known as the "Manifold Air-Oxydation System", should be familiar to American mechanics, for it utilizes many U.S.-made components. A V-belt driven air pump forces clean air, under slight pressure, to the exhaust ports. This air combines with the hot exhaust gases and "afterburning", or more complete combustion, takes place.

The distributor was modified by increasing the advance range of the centrifugal advance mechanism and incorporating a device to retard the ignition spark at idle and under deceleration. The carburetors were essentially unchanged, although some models were rejetted and on all models manufacturing tolerance limits tightened up.

The illustration shows the afterburner system in schematic form. The Saginaw rotary vane air pump, driven at 0.94 en-

gine speed, draws fresh air, through a centrifugal air filter, into a chamber. This chamber is vented to the atmosphere by a pressure check valve, which protects the pump by allowing excess pressure to escape. The air is compressed by the rotary vanes and is forced through a pipe and one-way (back pressure) valve into the air distribution manifold, thence into each exhaust port.

The back pressure valve allows the air from the pump to flow only one way, thus acting as a pump protective device in the event that exhaust pressure exceeds pump output (as it would if the V-belt broke).

In addition, an air regulating valve (Rochester) is incorporated into the system. During deceleration, a vacuum forms in the intake manifold. This vacuum evaporates the fuel drops adhering to the inside of the manifold and enriches the mixture. The air regulating valve supplies air from the pump to the intake manifold to compensate for this. A control mechanism for the air regulating valve, similar to a standard vacuum advance unit, meters air with relation to the intake manifold vacuum.

Fuel injected models required little modification. The three-dimensional cam on the injection pump was changed slightly and the full-load adjustment capability increased. In addition, an electric solenoid switch was incorporated to stop fuel delivery under deceleration.

The air venturi throttle butterfly setting was closed down to 4° from the previous 7°.

Exhaust Emission Control System Modifications—230/8

The 230/8 is equipped with two emission control systems, one using a Saginaw air pump and injection tubes and another that superseded the Saginaw type after chassis number 018 018 (January, 1969).

The new system complies with Federal standards through engine modifications rather than use of an air pump system. During deceleration, the rear carburetor vacuum control unit (dashpot) is governed to hold the throttle butterfly open above 1,800 rpm engine speed. This is accomplished through use of a relay and solenoid valve connected to a vacuum hose that runs between the intake manifold and the vac-

1. Idle stop screw
2. Vent valve
3. Vacuum hose to valve
4. Vacuum hose connecting valve
5. Compression ring
6. Knurled nut
7. Hex head adjustment screw
8. Actuating lever
   and vacuum control unit

Dashpot adjustment—230/8 with emission control.

1. Mounting bracket
2. Electrical speed relay
3. Solenoid valve
50 mm. = 2"

Solenoid valve—230/8 with emission control.

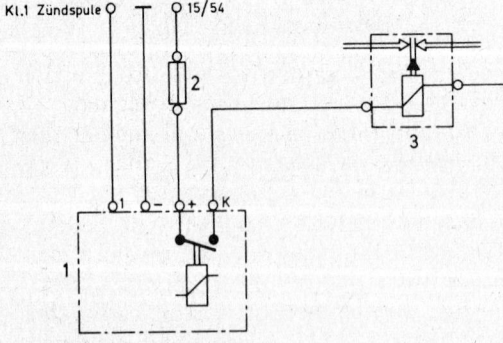

1. Speed relay switch
2. Fuse #5
3. Solenoid valve
K1. 1 Zündspule = Terminal 1 - ignition coil

Fuel cut-off valve—230/8 with emission control.

uum control valve on the rear carburetor. At engine speeds in excess of 1,800 rpm, the relay activates the solenoid valve to shut off intake manifold vacuum and expose the control valve diaphragm to atmospheric pressure. Without vacuum, a spring pushes adjustment screw (7) outward to hold the throttle butterfly slightly open. *NOTE: The idle speed adjustment procedure described previously for the 230/8 is still valid.*

To adjust the vacuum control valve properly, turn the hex screw (7) to lift the vent valve (2) .020"–.040" (engine not running). Start the engine and make sure all power accessories are shut off. Adjust spring (5) by turning nut (6) to give .004" clearance between screw (7) and lever (8). When the engine is warmed up, remove vacuum hose (4) and check engine speed; it should not exceed 1,750 rpm. Adjust by turning screw (7).

To test the relay, first connect a tachometer, then pull off the connector at the solenoid valve and hook a 12-volt test light to the connector. Start the engine and gradually increase speed; test light should go on at 2,000 $^{+50}_{-30}$ rpm and should go off when speed drops below 1,750–1,800 rpm.

TROUBLESHOOTING FUEL SHUT-OFF VALVE—INJECTED ENGINES

Manual Transmission

Connect a 12-volt test light between the solenoid and ground, then switch on the ignition. The light should go on in first and fourth gears without touching the accelerator pedal.

Now, to check the switches on the transmission cover or column jacket, move shift lever to neutral, first, second and reverse positions *without* touching the clutch or accelerator pedals; the test light should go out.

To check the switch on the clutch pedal, place lever in third *or* fourth gear and depress clutch pedal *without* touching the accelerator pedal; the test light should go out.

To check the micro-switch on the throttle linkage, engage third *or* fourth gear and depress the accelerator pedal *without* touching the clutch pedal; the test light should go out in this position as well.

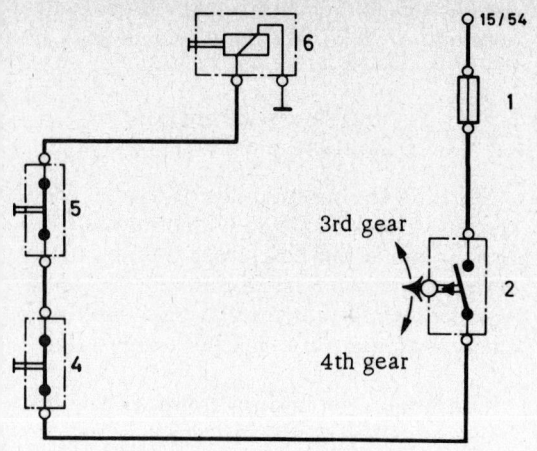

1. Fuse
2. Operating contact switch on jacket tube, third and fourth gear
4. Contact switch on clutch pedal
5. Micro-switch on control shaft
6. Stop solenoid on injection pump

Stop solenoid—columnshift manual transmission.

Automatic Transmission

Connect a tachometer between ground and the coil-to-distributor primary wire, then connect a 12-volt test light between the stop solenoid and ground. Place the instruments inside the passenger compartment, then start the engine and test drive the car on a level road. To check the micro-switch on the throttle linkage, accelerate in lever position "4" until the transmission shifts into fourth gear, then let off the accelerator pedal and watch the test light and tachometer. The test light must remain lit until the speed drops to 1,150 rpm.

To check the oil pressure switch on the transmission, place the lever in "3" and accelerate in third gear to 1,600 rpm. At this point, shift the lever into "2" and let off the accelerator pedal; the light should go out.

To check the "tachometer" sending unit, switch on the ignition and disconnect the plug and hook the 12-volt lamp between terminal No. 1 (black wire) and ground. Start the engine and check the lamp; at 1,400 rpm it must go on. *NOTE: To adjust the micro-switch on the throttle linkage, remove the plug on the dual-circuit relay and connect the 12-volt light between terminals No. 87a and No. 86. Shift lever into "2",*

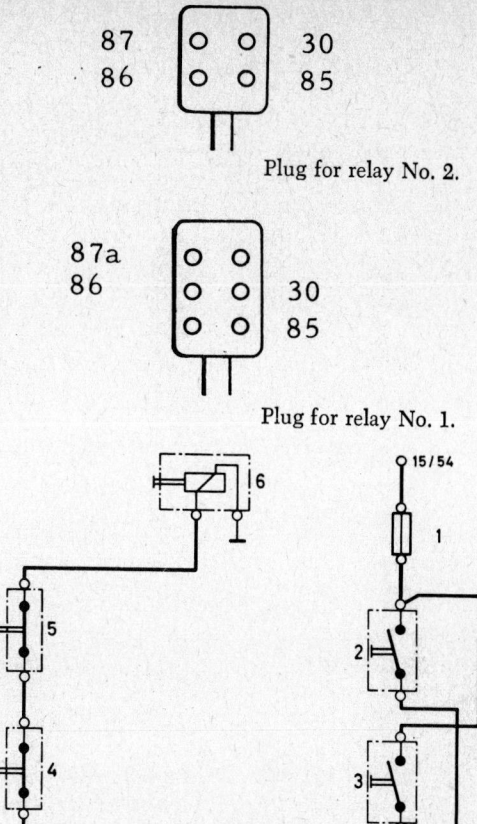

Plug for relay No. 2.

Plug for relay No. 1.

1. Fuse
2. Operating contact switch on gearbox cover (3rd gear)
3. Operating contact switch on gearbox cover (4th gear)
4. Contact switch on clutch pedal
5. Micro-switch on control shaft
6. Stop solenoid on injection pump

Stop solenoid—floorshift manual transmission.

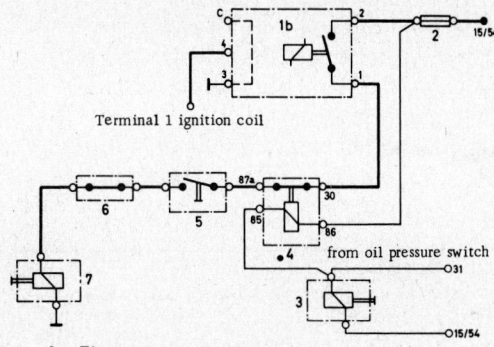

Terminal 1 ignition coil

from oil pressure switch

1. Electronic tachometer
2. Fuse
3. Solenoid for idle speed compensator
4. Dual circuit relay
5. Starter locking and back-up light switch
6. Micro-switch on control shaft
7. Stop solenoid in injection pump

Stop solenoid—automatic transmission.

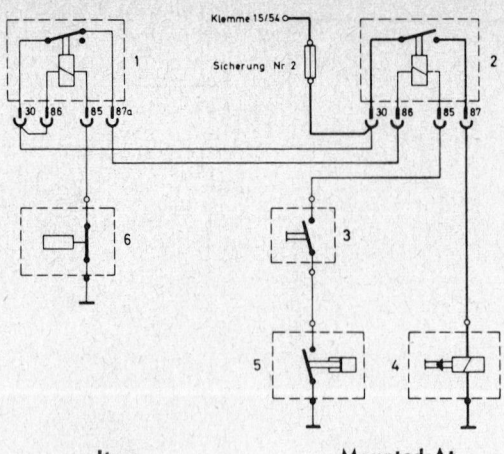

Item	Mounted At
1. Alternating Relay no. 1	left of radiator
2. Operating Relay no. 2	left of radiator
3. Micro-switch	firewall
4. Stop solenoid switch	injection pump
5. Oil pressure switch	transmission
6. Temperature switch	engine block

Klemme = Terminal
Sicherung = Fuse

Stop solenoid—after August, 1969.

"3", "4" or "R" and adjust micro-switch adjusting screw so that, when actuating linkage, light goes out before throttle butterfly moves.

The introduction of a new automatic transmission in mid-1969 necessitated a modification of the stop solenoid circuit. On models 280 SE/8, 280 SEC/8 and 300 SEL/8, the oil pressure switch on the transmission controls the solenoid. The switch does not operate at coolant temperature below +62° F.

To test the "62° F." switch. remove the plug from relay No. 1 and connect a 12-volt test light between terminals No. 30 and No. 85. The test light should go on below 62° F. temperature.

To test the micro-switch on the throttle linkage, connect the oil pressure switch terminal to ground, then remove the four-prong plug from relay No. 2 and connect the test light between the brown-white wire (No. 85) and the red-black wire (No. 30). Turn on the ignition switch and depress the accelerator pedal; the light should go out. Reconnect the terminal to the oil pressure switch.

To test the oil pressure switch, remove the plug from relay No. 2 and connect the test light between terminals No. 30 and No. 85. Test drive the car on a level road.

Accelerate to 25 mph, then release the accelerator pedal; the light should stay lit while decelerating above 15 mph.

TROUBLESHOOTING THE PORT INJECTION SYSTEM

Start the engine and allow it to idle. The pressure check valve should be noise-free. Now, remove the hose from the air pump outlet fitting and make sure air is being expelled. Hold the outlet fitting closed and check that the pressure check valve operates.

Disconnect the hose in front of the back pressure valve. With the engine idling, no exhaust should escape from the valve. Now, remove the hose in front of the Rochester valve. With the engine idling, the valve should not suck in air (a small amount is, however, permissible if idling is unaffected). Speed the engine up and allow it to come back to idle speed. During deceleration the valve should open for about one second to suck in air.

TIGHTENING AIR PUMP V-BELT— 230/8, 250/8

Remove the battery, then loosen the three bolts that hold the pump. Tighten the belt by turning the toothed tensioning bolt counterclockwise, then tightening the clamping nut. Tighten the air pump bolts and install the battery.

AIR PUMP REMOVAL AND INSTALLATION

Remove the battery, drain coolant, disconnect water and oil cooler lines and re-

Air pump hold-down bolts.

1. Air pump bracket	3. Clamping nut for tensioning bolt
2. Fixing bolts	4. Spacer washers

Air pump tensioning bolt.

1. Air pump
2. High pressure pump for power steering

3. Tensioning bolt
4. Fixing screws for V-belt pulley

1. Steering relay arm
2. Tie-rods
3. Steering shock absorber

Lowering transmission.

Front limit stop used with four-cylinder engines.

move the radiator. Loosen and remove air pump hose, then remove the three hold-down bolts and the three pulley screws. Remove belt and pulley and slide pump forward to remove.

To install, place pump in position and screw in hold-down bolts loosely, making sure spacer washers are properly positioned. Place pulley and belt on pump and tighten the pulley screws. *NOTE: Never use screws that are longer than ½", otherwise they will scrape and ruin the front bearing seal.* Tighten the V-belt, tighten the three hold-down bolts and check that the relief valve muffler is positioned with its three holes pointing down. Install radiator, air pump hose, coolant and water and oil lines. Install battery and check oil and water levels.

Engine R & R

First, remove the hood, then drain the cooling system and disconnect the battery. While not strictly necessary, it is better to remove the battery completely to prevent breakage by the engine as it is lifted out.

Remove the fan shroud, radiator and disconnect all heater hoses and oil cooler lines.

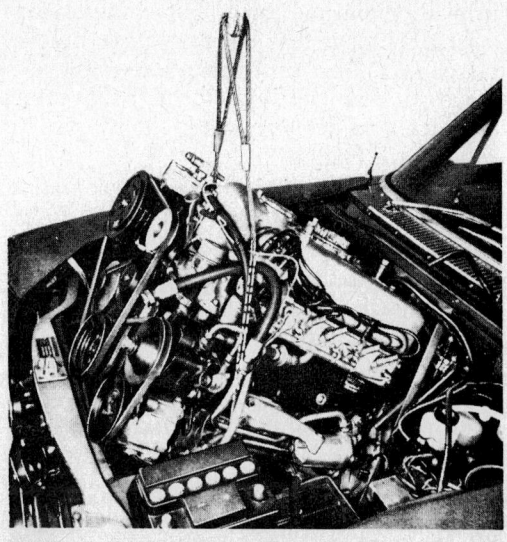

Removing engine.

Remove air cleaner and all fuel, vacuum and oil hoses (e.g., power steering and power brakes). Plug all openings to keep out dirt.

CAUTION: Air conditioner lines should not be indiscriminately disconnected without taking proper precautions. It is best to swing the compressor out of the way while still connected to its hoses. Never do any welding around the compressor—heat may cause an explosion. Also, the refrigerant, while inert at normal room temperature, breaks down under high temperature into hydrogen fluoride and phosgene (among other products), which are highly poisonous.

Remove the viscous coupling and fan and, on applicable engines, disconnect the carburetor choke cable. On diesel engines, disconnect the idle control and starting cables. On all engines, disconnect accelerator linkage. On 6.3 V8, remove generator. On six-cylinder engines with three-groove crankshaft pulley, remove the heater pipe on the firewall. Disconnect all ground straps and electrical connections. It is a good idea to tag each wire for easy reassembly.

Detach the gearshift linkage and the exhaust pipes from the manifolds. Loosen the steering relay arm and pull it down out of the way, along with the center steering rod and hydraulic steering damper. The hydraulic engine shock absorber should be removed. Remove hydraulic line from clutch housing and the oil line connectors from automatic transmission (see illustration). Unbolt clutch slave cylinder from bellhousing, after removing return spring. Remove the exhaust pipe bracket attached to the transmission and place a wood-padded jack under the bellhousing, or place a cable sling under the oil pan, to support the engine.

Mark the position of the rear engine support and unbolt the two outer bolts, then remove the top bolt at the transmission and pull the support out. Disconnect speedometer cable and the front driveshaft U-joint. Push the driveshaft back and wire it out of the way.

Unbolt the engine mounts on both sides, and, on four-cylinder engines, the front limit stop. Unbolt the power steering fluid reservoir and swing it out of the way; then, using a chain hoist and cable as illustrated, lift the engine and transmission upward and outward. An angle of about 45° will allow the car to be pushed backwards while the engine is coming up.

Reverse the procedure to install, making sure to bleed the hydraulic clutch, power steering, power brakes and fuel system.

CYLINDER HEAD
REMOVAL

In order to perform a valve job or to inspect cylinder bores for wear, the head must be removed. While this may seem fairly straightforward, some precautions must be observed to ensure that valve timing is not disturbed.

Drain the radiator and remove all hoses and wires. Remove the camshaft cover and associated throttle linkage, then press out the spring clamp (2) from the notch in the rocker arm (3). Push the clamp outward over the ball cap of the rocker, then depress the valve, using a tool similar to the one illustrated, or a large screwdriver, and lift the rocker arm out of the ball pin head (1).

Remove the rocker arm supports and the camshaft sprocket nut. On diesels, the rockers and their supports must be removed together. Using a suitable puller, remove the camshaft sprocket, after having first marked the chain, sprocket and cam for ease in assembly. Remove the sprocket and chain and wire it out of the way. *CAUTION: Make sure the chain is securely wired so that it will not slide down into the engine.*

Unbolt the manifolds and exhaust header pipe and push them out of the way, then loosen the cylinder head hold-down bolts in the reverse order of that shown in torque diagrams for each model. It is good practice to loosen each bolt a little at a time, working around the head, until all are free. This prevents unequal stresses in the metal.

Reach into the engine compartment and gradually work the head loose from each end by rocking it. Never, under any circumstances, use a screwdriver between the head and block to pry, as the head will be scarred badly and may be ruined.

Valve Train
VALVE SEAL INSTALLATION—
HEAD INSTALLED

In cases of excessive oil consumption traced to faulty valve stem seals, the seals can be replaced with the head installed.

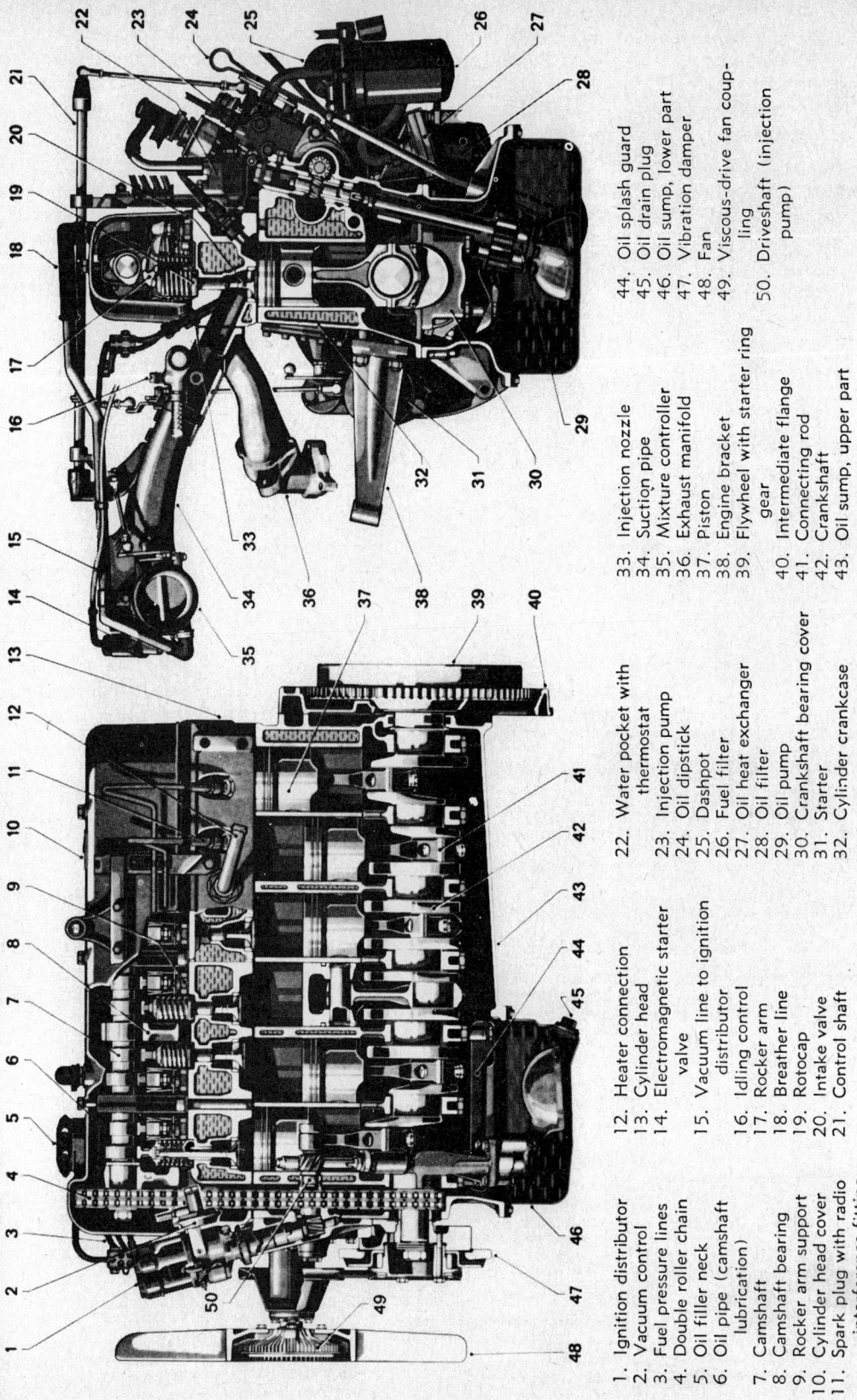

1. Ignition distributor
2. Vacuum control
3. Fuel pressure lines
4. Double roller chain
5. Oil filler neck
6. Oil pipe (camshaft lubrication)
7. Camshaft
8. Camshaft bearing
9. Rocker arm support
10. Cylinder head cover
11. Spark plug with radio interference fitting
12. Heater connection
13. Cylinder head
14. Electromagnetic starter valve
15. Vacuum line to ignition distributor
16. Idling control
17. Rocker arm
18. Breather line
19. Rotocap
20. Intake valve
21. Control shaft
22. Water pocket with thermostat
23. Injection pump
24. Oil dipstick
25. Dashpot
26. Fuel filter
27. Oil heat exchanger
28. Oil filter
29. Oil pump
30. Crankshaft bearing cover
31. Starter
32. Cylinder crankcase
33. Injection nozzle
34. Suction pipe
35. Mixture controller
36. Exhaust manifold
37. Piston
38. Engine bracket
39. Flywheel with starter ring gear
40. Intermediate flange
41. Connecting rod
42. Crankshaft
43. Oil sump, upper part
44. Oil splash guard
45. Oil drain plug
46. Oil sump, lower part
47. Vibration damper
48. Fan
49. Viscous-drive fan coupling
50. Driveshaft (injection pump)

Longitudinal and cross-section—250SE engine (M 129).

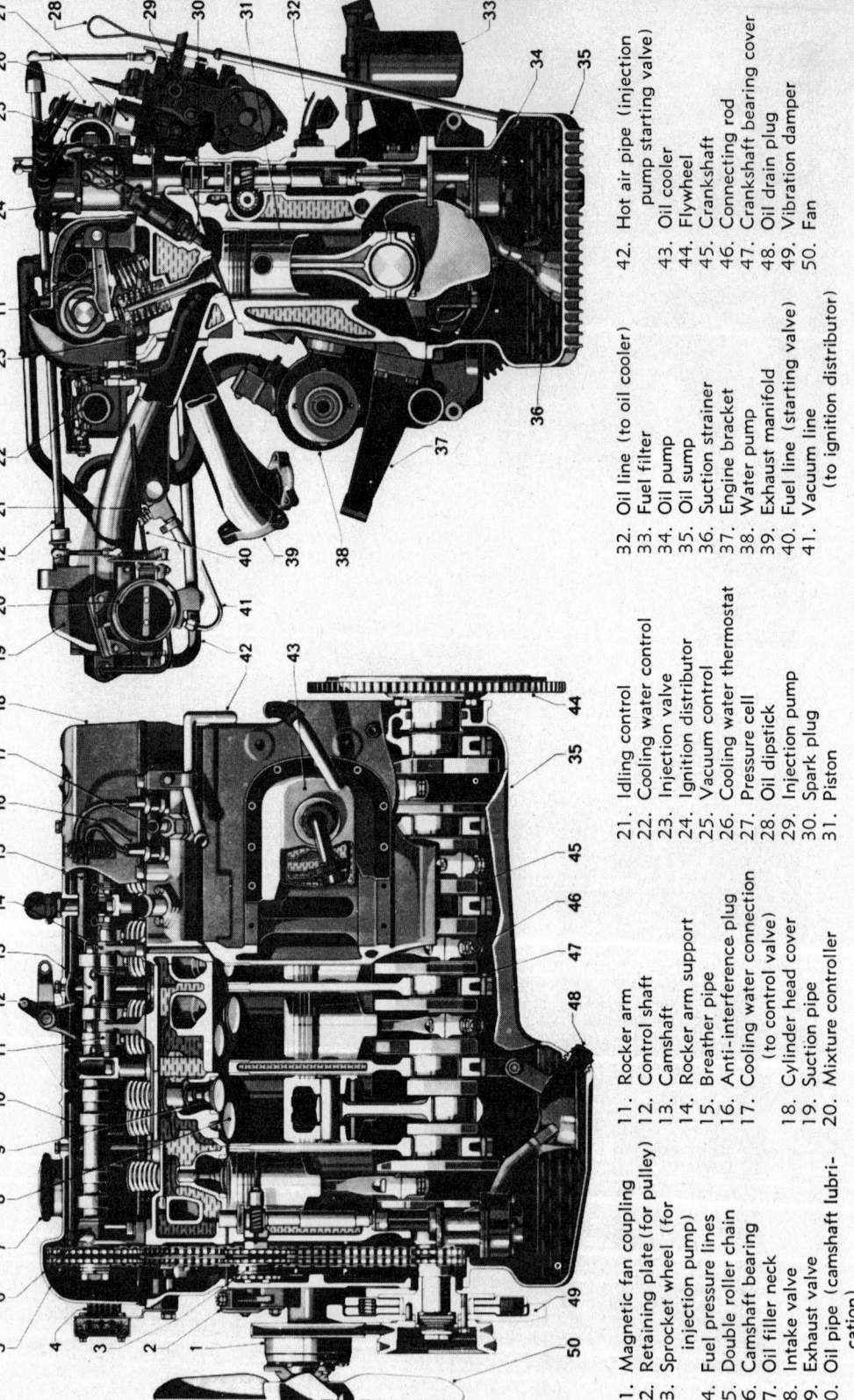

1. Magnetic fan coupling
2. Retaining plate (for pulley)
3. Sprocket wheel (for injection pump)
4. Fuel pressure lines
5. Double roller chain
6. Camshaft bearing
7. Oil filler neck
8. Intake valve
9. Exhaust valve
10. Oil pipe (camshaft lubrication)
11. Rocker arm
12. Control shaft
13. Camshaft
14. Rocker arm support
15. Breather pipe
16. Anti-interference plug
17. Cooling water connection (to control valve)
18. Cylinder head cover
19. Suction pipe
20. Mixture controller
21. Idling control
22. Cooling water control
23. Injection valve
24. Ignition distributor
25. Vacuum control
26. Cooling water thermostat
27. Pressure cell
28. Oil dipstick
29. Injection pump
30. Spark plug
31. Piston
32. Oil line (to oil cooler)
33. Fuel filter
34. Oil pump
35. Oil sump
36. Suction strainer
37. Engine bracket
38. Water pump
39. Exhaust manifold
40. Fuel line (starting valve)
41. Vacuum line (to ignition distributor)
42. Hot air pipe (injection pump starting valve)
43. Oil cooler
44. Flywheel
45. Crankshaft
46. Connecting rod
47. Crankshaft bearing cover
48. Oil drain plug
49. Vibration damper
50. Fan

Longitudinal and cross-section—300SE engine (M 189).

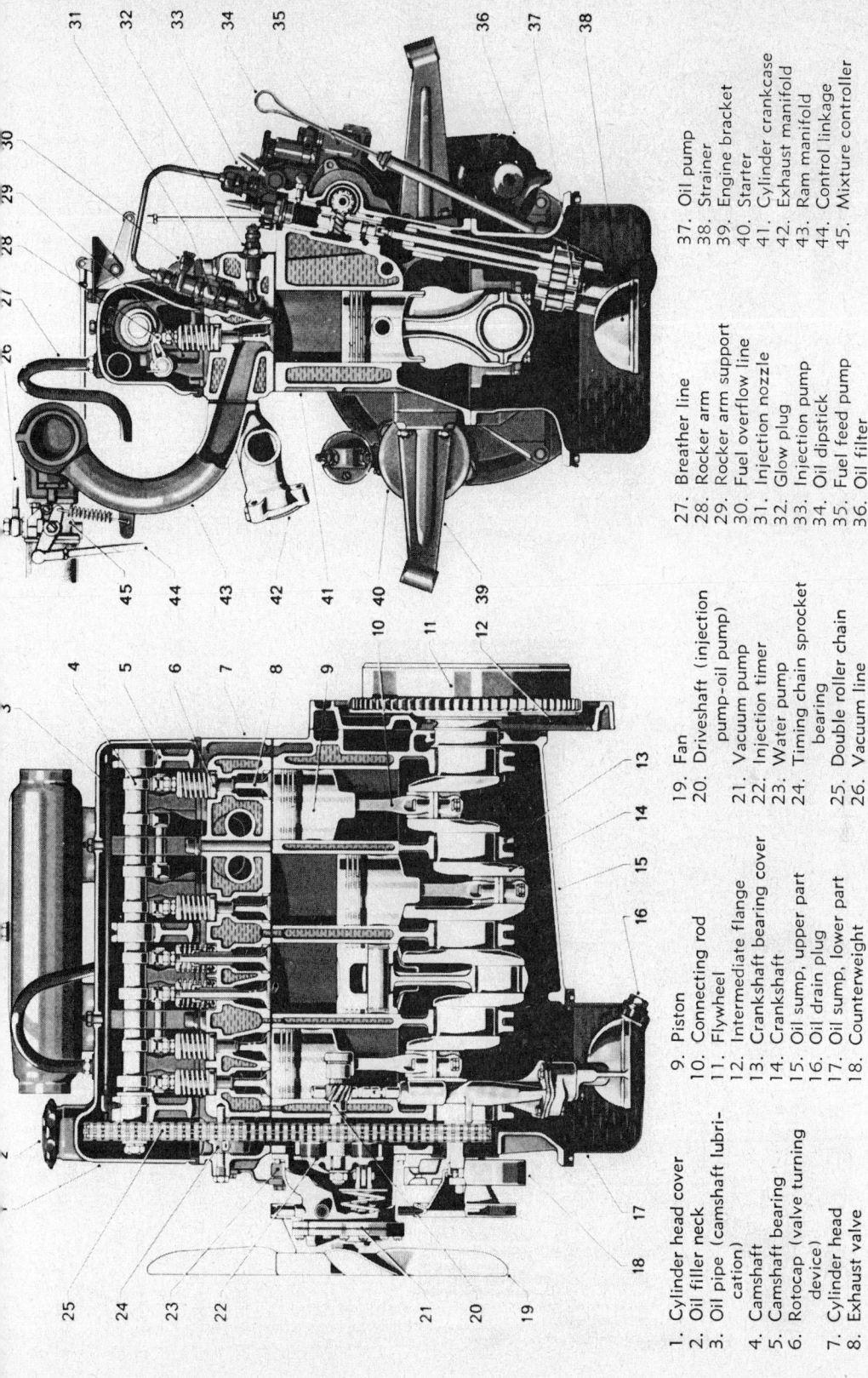

1. Cylinder head cover
2. Oil filler neck
3. Oil pipe (camshaft lubrication)
4. Camshaft
5. Camshaft bearing
6. Rotocap (valve turning device)
7. Cylinder head
8. Exhaust valve
9. Piston
10. Connecting rod
11. Flywheel
12. Intermediate flange
13. Crankshaft bearing cover
14. Crankshaft
15. Oil sump, upper part
16. Oil drain plug
17. Oil sump, lower part
18. Counterweight
19. Fan
20. Driveshaft (injection pump-oil pump)
21. Vacuum pump
22. Injection timer
23. Water pump
24. Timing chain sprocket bearing
25. Double roller chain
26. Vacuum line
27. Breather line
28. Rocker arm
29. Rocker arm support
30. Fuel overflow line
31. Injection nozzle
32. Glow plug
33. Injection pump
34. Oil dipstick
35. Fuel feed pump
36. Oil filter
37. Oil pump
38. Strainer
39. Engine bracket
40. Starter
41. Cylinder crankcase
42. Exhaust manifold
43. Ram manifold
44. Control linkage
45. Mixture controller

Longitudinal and cross-section—200D engine (OM 621).

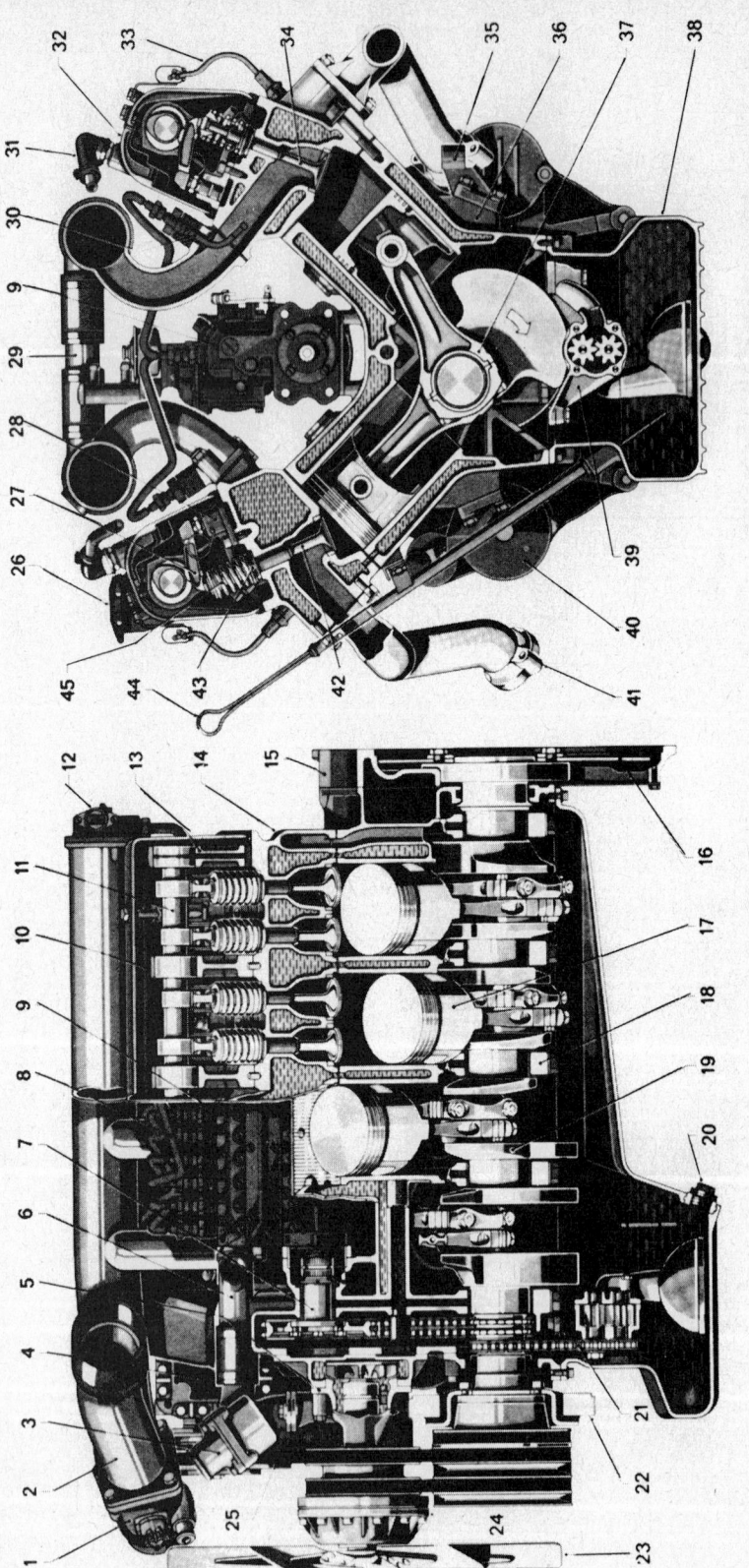

1. Venturi control unit
2. Intake pipe
3. Cooling water thermostat
4. Compressor for air-conditioning system
5. Water pump
6. Cooling water line
7. Driveshaft (injection pump)
8. Fuel delivery lines
9. Injection pump
10. Oil pipe (camshaft lubrication)
11. Camshaft
12. Electromagnet. Starting valve
13. Camshaft bearing
14. Cylinder head
15. Intermediate flange
16. Follower disc
17. Piston
18. Crankshaft bearing cover
19. Crankshaft
20. Oil drain plug
21. Roller chain (oil pump drive)
22. Vibration damper
23. Fan
24. Hydraulic fan coupling
25. Hydraulic pump
26. Oil filler neck
27. Rocker arm
28. Rocker arm support
29. Expansion line
30. Injection valve
31. Breather pipe
32. Cylinder head cover
33. Ignition cable with anti-interference plug
34. Intake valve
35. Engine support
36. Cylinder crankcase
37. Connecting rod
38. Oil sump
39. Oil pump
40. Starter motor
41. Exhaust manifold
42. Outlet valve
43. Rotocap (valve turning device)
44. Oil dipstick
45. Valve spring

Longitudinal and cross-section—300SEL/8 6.3 engine (M 100).

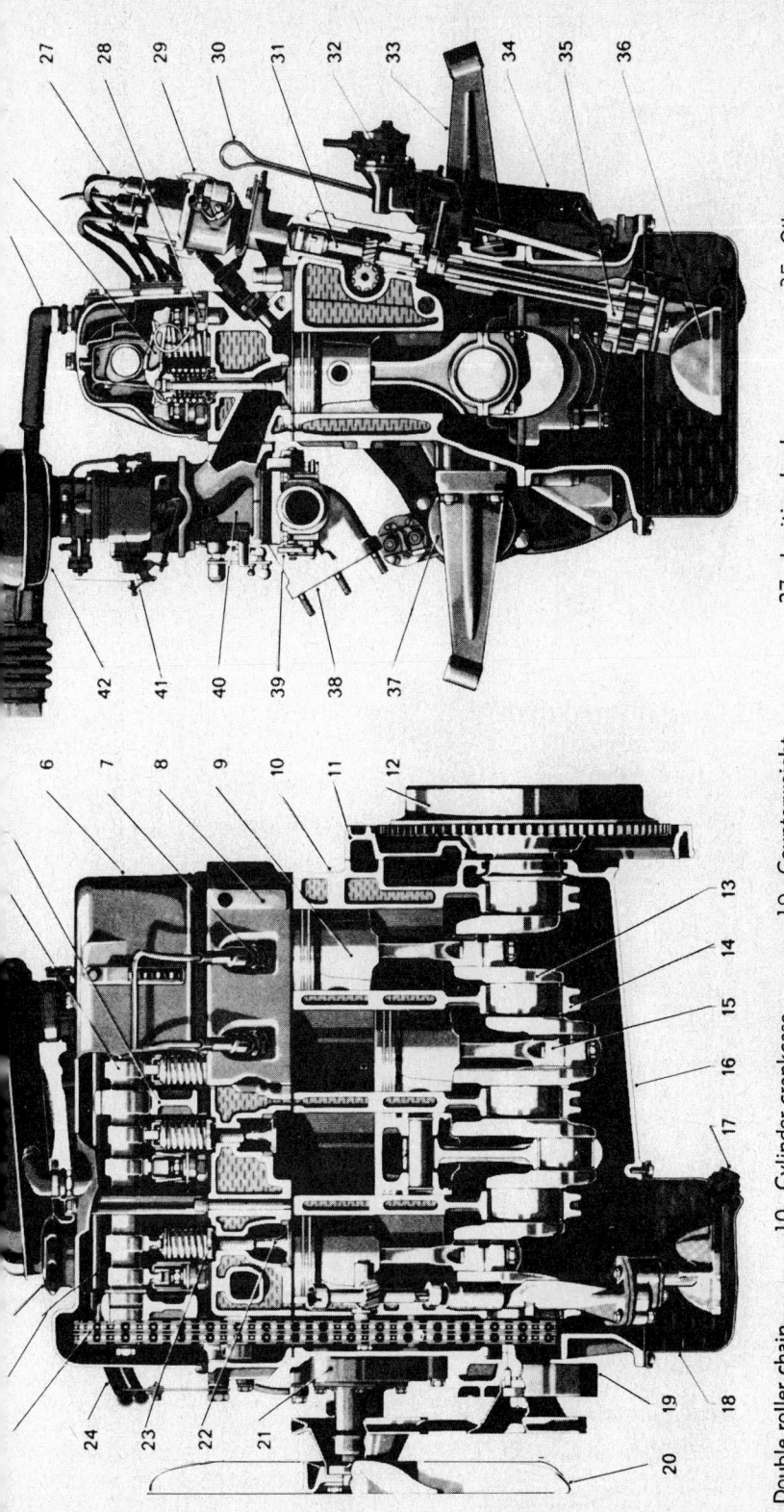

Longitudinal and cross-section—200 engine (M 121).

1. Double roller chain
2. Oil pipe (camshaft lubrication)
3. Oil filler neck
4. Camshaft
5. Camshaft bearing
6. Cylinder head cover
7. Spark plug
8. Cylinder head
9. Piston
10. Cylinder crankcase
11. Intermediate flange
12. Flywheel
13. Crankshaft
14. Crankshaft bearing cover
15. Connecting rod
16. Oil sump, upper part
17. Oil drain plug
18. Oil sump, lower part
19. Counterweight
20. Fan
21. Water pump
22. Intake valve
23. Rotocap (valve turning device)
24. Fuel line
25. Breather line
26. Rocker arm
27. Ignition leads
28. Rocker arm support
29. Ignition distributor
30. Oil dipstick
31. Driveshaft (oil pump-ignition distributor)
32. Fuel pump
33. Engine bracket
34. Oil filter
35. Oil pump
36. Strainer
37. Starter
38. Exhaust manifold
39. Thermo spiral (heater flap)
40. Suction pipe
41. Carburetor
42. Scoop (twin-carburetor system)

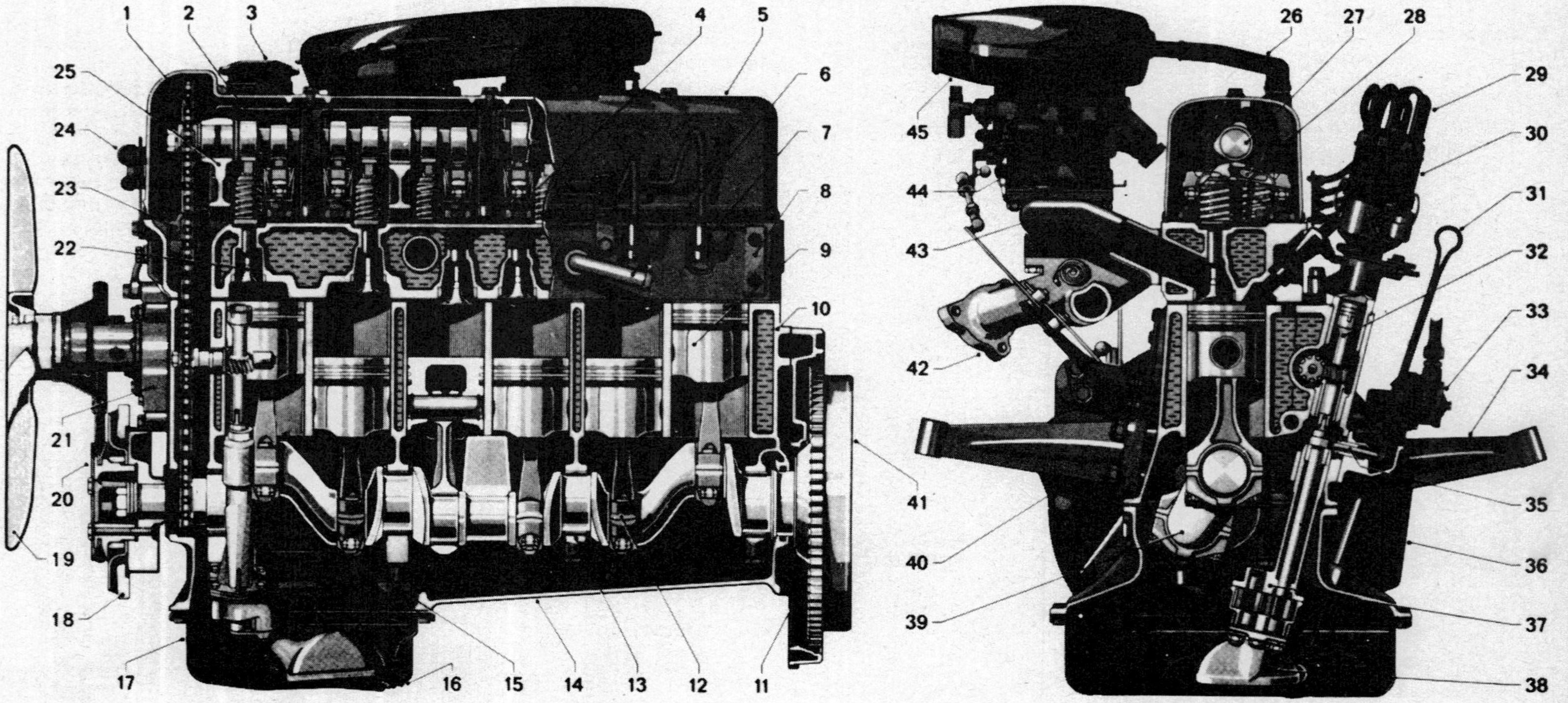

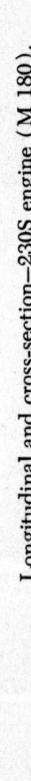

Longitudinal and cross-section—230S engine (M 180).

1. Single roller-chain
2. Oil pipe (camshaft lubrication)
3. Oil filler neck
4. Rocker arm support
5. Cylinder head cover
6. Heater connection
7. Spark plug with anti-interference plug
8. Cylinder head
9. Piston
10. Cylinder crankcase
11. Intermediate flange
12. Connecting rod
13. Crankshaft bearing cover
14. Oil sump, upper part
15. Oil splash guard
16. Oil drain plug
17. Oil sump, lower part
18. Vibration damper
19. Fan
20. Pulley
21. Water pump
22. Exhaust valve
23. Timing chain sprocket bearing
24. Fuel lines
25. Camshaft bearing
26. Breather pipe
27. Camshaft
28. Rocker arm
29. Ignition cables
30. Ignition distributor
31. Oil dipstick
32. Driveshaft (oil pump ignition distributor)
33. Fuel pump
34. Engine support
35. Plunger (fuel pump)
36. Oil filter
37. Oil pump
38. Suction strainer
39. Crankshaft
40. Starter motor
41. Flywheel with toothed ring
42. Exhaust manifold
43. Intake pipe
44. Compound carburetor
45. Scoop (double carburetor system)

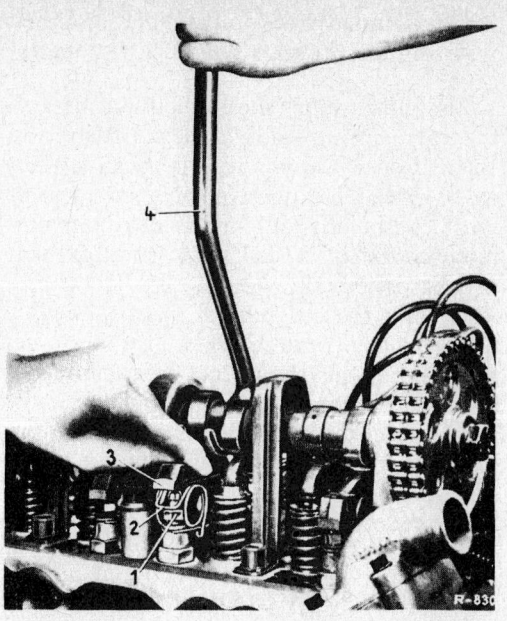

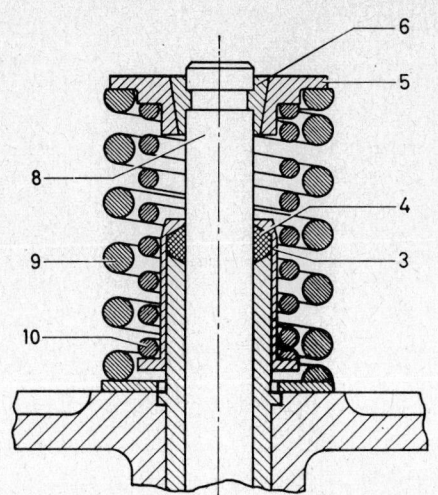

1. Ball pin head
2. Spring clamp
3. Rocker arm

4. Tool for removal
   (112 589 08 -
   61 00)

Removing valve train.

1. Snap-ring	5. Valve spring
2. Valve spring	retainer
washer	6. Valve retainer
3. Sealing ring	7. Pressure piece
retainer	8. Intake valve
4. Silicone valve seal	9. Outer valve spring
	10. Inner valve spring

Intake valve—300SE.

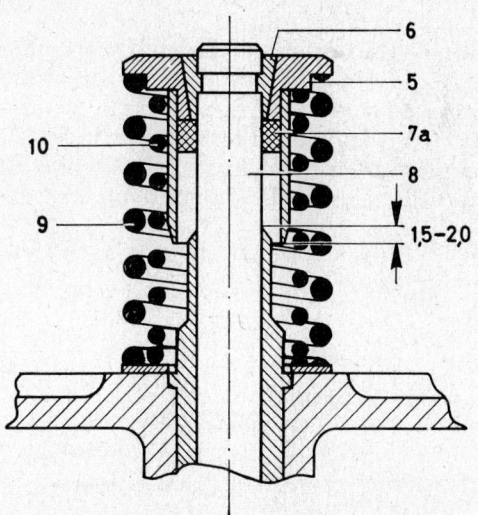

1. Valve retainer   2. Magnet

Removing valve spring with cylinder head installed.

1. Snap-ring	6. Valve keeper
2. Thrust collar	7. Pressure piece
3. Sealing ring	8. Exhaust valve
retainer	9. Outer valve spring
4. Valve seal	10. Inner valve spring
5. Valve spring	
retainer	

Exhaust valve—300SE.

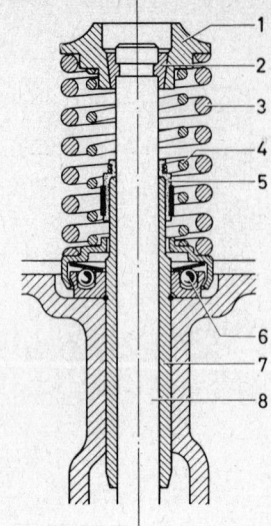

1. Valve spring   5. Teflon valve seal
   retainer   6. Rotocap
2. Valve keeper   7. Valve guide
3. Outer valve spring 8. Valve
4. Inner valve spring

Intake and exhaust valve—230SL.

Remove the camshaft cover and any obstructing linkage, then turn the engine over by hand to bring the pistons of the affected cylinders up to TDC.

Break the center out of an old spark plug and braze an air fitting onto it. Screw the fitting into the spark plug hole of the affected cylinder and maintain at least 180 psi pressure in the cylinder. This will hold the valve closed. It is important that the piston be exactly at top dead center, otherwise the air pressure will turn the engine over.

The illustration shows how to depress the valve spring using a special Mercedes-Benz tool. Automotive jobbers usually stock similar inexpensive tools, and one of these can be adapted, or one can be manufactured out of ¼" flat stock, suitably bent and hardened, and some heavy washers.

Striking the valve stem sharply with a hammer sometimes loosens stubborn retainers, but this should not be done unless absolutely necessary. The diagrams show some typical valve seal configurations; but it is best to examine the seals you are working on and compare with new ones, because different versions were used in production.

VALVE CLEARANCE

Valve (tappet) clearance should be checked with the engine cold. On the 190c, 220b, 220 Sb and 220 Seb, clearance is measured between the sliding surface of the rocker arm and the cam base circle of the camshaft. The newer 220/8, 230/8 and 250/8 series engines also have clearance measured in this manner.

On the 300 SE series, however, clearance is measured between the valve stem end and the adjusting screw or ball socket.

To measure clearance, remove spark plug wires and high-tension wire. Detach the air vent line at the valve cover and remove the cover screws and cover. Some models have a plastic vacuum line routed

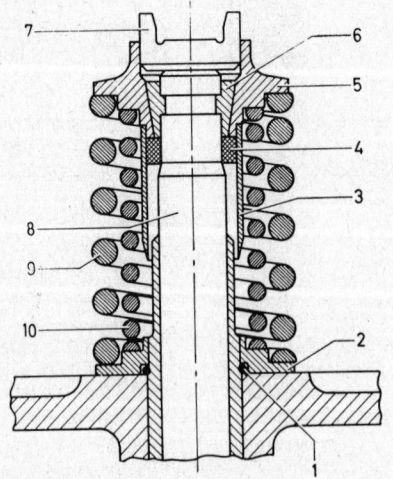

Exhaust valve—220b, 220Sb, 220SEb. Intake and exhaust valve—190c.

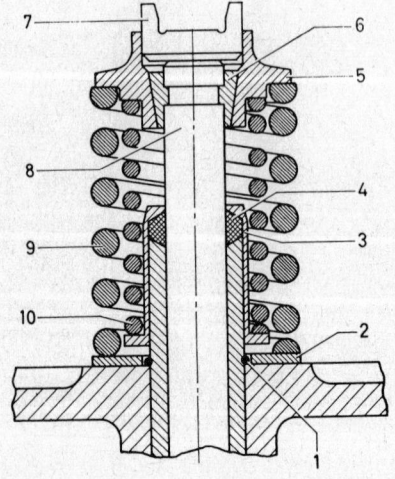

Intake valve—220b, 220Sb, 220SEb.

1. Adjusting screw and ball cup
   for exhaust valve
2. Rocker arm (exhaust)
3. Valve spring retainer and
   sealing ring retainer for
   exhaust valve
4. Sealing ring (exhaust)
5. Cylinder head
6. Valve guide (exhaust)
7. Exhaust valve
8. Valve seat ring (exhaust)
9. Valve seat ring (intake)
10. Intake valve
11. Valve guide (intake)
12. Washer
13. Sealing ring retainer (intake)
14. Sealing ring (intake)
15. Inner valve spring
16. Outer valve spring
17. Valve spring retainer (intake)
18. Valve cone halves
19. Rocker arm (intake)
20. Adjusting screw (intake)
a = Distance between jointing sur-
    face cylinder head and intake
    valve spring retainer
b = Distance between joining sur-
    face cylinder head and exhaust
    valve spring retainer

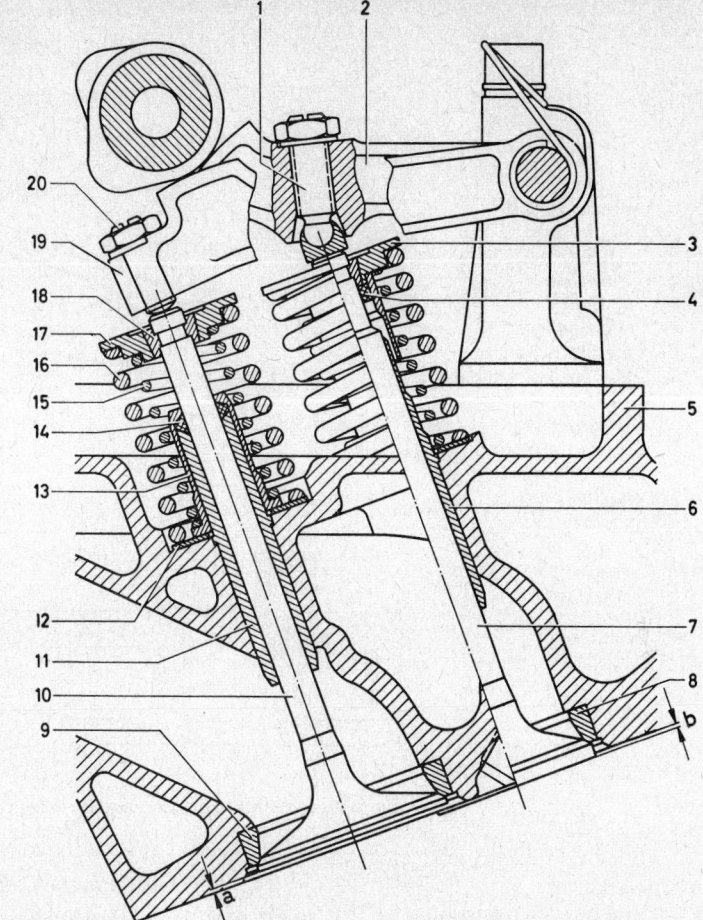

Valve arrangement—300SE.

close to the cover. This line cannot be kinked or bent, therefore it is best to remove it entirely by disconnecting each end and lifting it out of the way. Also, on some models, such as the 220 SEb and 300 SE, the air control shaft running over the valve cover must be removed, as well as the air cleaner.

Check the cylinder head bolts for correct torque and, if necessary, tighten to specifications.

Rotate the camshaft by turning the crankshaft pulley bolt with a 22 mm. wrench until the lobe of the cam is not pressed against the rocker arm, but is on the opposite side of, and at right angles to, the sliding surface of the rocker arm (see illustration). Some models, such as the 300 SE, have holes in the vibration damper plate to assist in crankshaft rotation. In this case, a screwdriver may be used, carefully, to turn the pulley.

Insert the proper feeler gauge between the sliding surface of the rocker arm and the cam base circle, or, in the case of the 300 SE, between the valve stem and the adjusting screw. Adjust until the feeler can just be pulled through with a little tension.

Adjustment is accomplished by turning the ball pin (3) at the hex collar. To increase clearance, screw the ball pin head inward; to decrease, screw outward. This adjustment ideally should be performed using a special adapter and a torque wrench. The illustration shows what this adapter looks like and how it is used. The shape of the tool is dictated by the need for accurate torque readings since, using it, the wrench can be directly lined up with the ball pin head.

In any case, the torque of the ball pin head in its base should be 10–11 ft.-lbs. (14.4–25 ft.-lbs for phase II models). If the torque is too little, the ball pin head

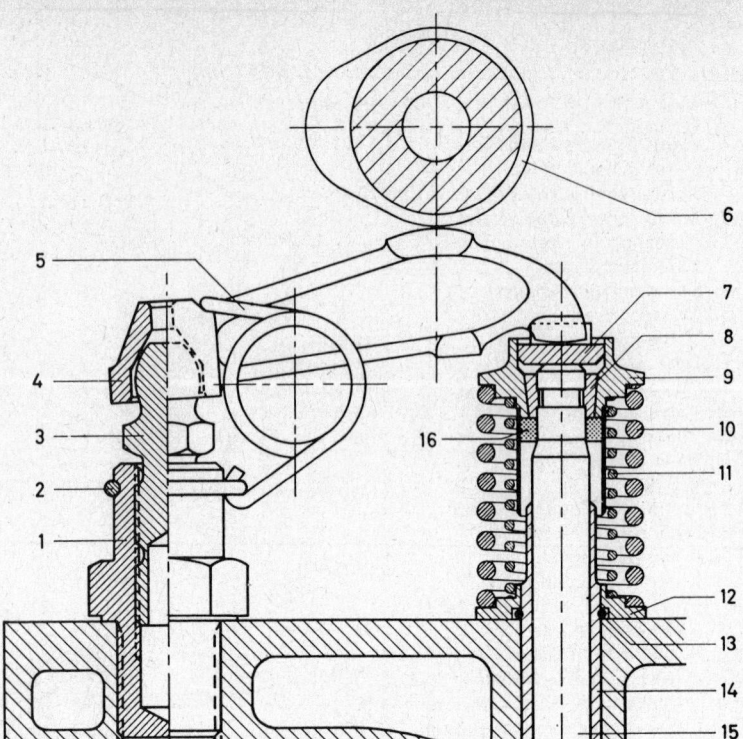

1. Ball pin base
2. Annular spring
3. Ball pin head
4. Rocker arm
5. Spring clamp
6. Camshaft
7. Pressure piece
8. Valve cone half
9. Valve spring retainer
   and sealing ring
   retainer
10. Outer valve spring
11. Inner valve spring
12. Pressure piece
13. Snap-ring
14. Valve guide
15. Valve
16. Sealing ring

Valve arrangement—gasoline engines except 300SE.

will tend to vibrate and clearance will not remain as set.

If the tappet clearance is too small and the ball pin head cannot be screwed in far enough to remedy it, a thinner pressure piece can be installed in the spring retainer (9). Standard thickness is 0.177" (4.5 mm.), but pieces are available in

0.137" (3.5 mm.) and 0.0985" (2.5 mm.) thicknesses as well.

To replace the pressure piece, the rocker arm must be removed. On the 300 SE, the clearance is adjusted by unscrewing the

Adjusting valve clearance.

Torque wrench adapter for adjusting ball pin.

locknut on the rocker arm and turning the adjusting screw in or out.

During extremely cold weather (—13° F.), the intake valve clearance may be opened up to aid cold starting. When the weather warms up, however, the clearance must be reset to normal values.

Model		Winter	Summer
300 SEL/8	6.3	.006″	.004″
220/8		.005″	.003″
230/8		.005″	.003″
250/8		.005″	.003″
250 S		.005″	.003″
280 S/8		.005″	.003″
280 SE/8		.005″	.003″
280 SL/8		.005″	.003″
300 SEL/8		.005″	.003″

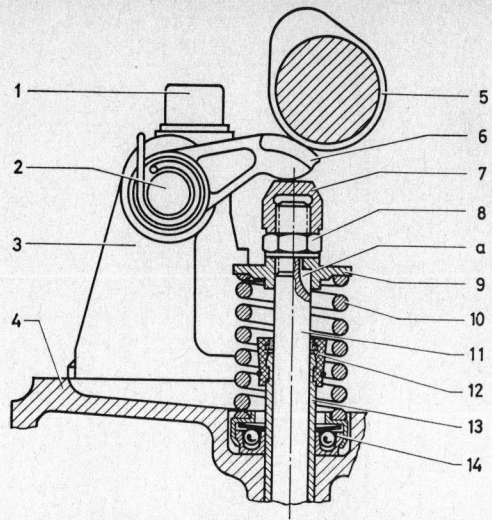

Diesel Engines

Valve adjustment for diesel engines is basically the same as that given for gasoline engines. On the diesel, however, the feeler gauge must be inserted between the rocker arm (6) and the cap nut (7), as in the illustration.

Remove the camshaft cover and turn the engine, using a wrench on the crankshaft pulley nut (22 mm.), until the TDC mark and the pointer line up.

This job can be accomplished easily if someone helps. First, a wrench must be placed on the valve spring retainer hex nut as illustrated (17). The hex nut (8) then must be loosened with another open end wrench, (bent to fit) (14), while the cap nut (7) is held with another wrench (16). The illustration shows this set up clearly.

Turn the cap nut (7) to adjust, then tighten the locknut (8) and recheck. Go on to the other cylinders, turning the crankshaft to TDC position for each adjustment.

Camshaft and Timing Chain

VALVE TIMING

Checking valve timing is too inaccurate at the standard tappet clearance, therefore timing values are given for an assumed tappet clearance of 0.4 mm. (0.016″).

To check timing, remove the rocker cover and spark plugs. Cut the degree wheel from the back endpaper of this book and glue it to a piece of stiff cardboard, bakelite or aluminum. A pointer must be made out of a bent section of ³⁄₁₆″ brazing rod or coathanger wire, and attached to

a. Groove in valve shaft
1. Extending screw
2. Rocker arm shaft
3. Rocker arm block
4. Cylinder head
5. Camshaft
6. Rocker arm
7. Cap nut
8. Hexagon nut
9. Valve spring retainer and sealing ring retainer
10. Valve spring
11. Valve shaft
12. Valve sealing ring
13. Valve guide
14. Valve rotator

Valve arrangement on diesel engines (220D/8 shown).

6. Rocker arm
7. Cap nut
8. Hexagon nut
9. Valve spring retainer with sealing ring retainer
14. Special wrench (621 589 01 01 00)
15. Feeler gauge
16. Special wrench (621 589 01 01 00)
17. Special wrench (621 589 00 03 00)

Adjusting valves on diesel engine.

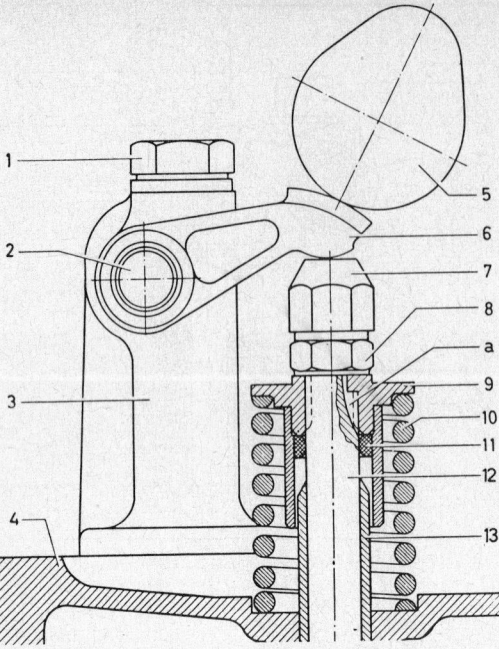

a. Groove in valve
    stem
1. Necked-down bolt
2. Rocker arm shaft
3. Rocker arm
    bracket
4. Cylinder head
5. Camshaft
6. Rocker arm

7. Cap nut
8. Hex nut
9. Valve spring re-
    tainer with seal
    ring holder
10. Valve spring
11. Rubber seal ring
12. Valve stem
13. Valve guide

On 190Dc and 200D, align camshaft with rocker
arm as shown for valve adjustment.

the engine as illustrated. *NOTE: If the degree wheel is attached to the camshaft as shown, values read from it must be doubled.*

With a 22 mm. wrench on the crankshaft pulley, turn the engine, in the direction of rotation, until the TDC mark on the vibration damper registers with the pointer (see inset) and the distributor rotor points to the No. 1 cylinder mark on the housing. Turn the loosened degree wheel until the pointer lines up with the 0° (OT) mark, then tighten it in this position. Continue turning the crankshaft in the direction of rotation until the camshaft lobe of the associated valve is vertical (e.g., points away from the rocker arm surface). To take up tappet clearance, insert a feeler gauge thick enough to raise the valve slightly from its seat between the rocker arm cone and the pressure piece (see illustration).

The next step involves the use of a dial indicator. Attach the indicator to the cylinder head so that the feeler (3) rests against the valve spring retainer of No. 1 cylinder intake valve. Preload the indicator at least 0.008″, then set to zero, making sure the feeler (3) is exactly perpendicular on the valve spring retainer. It may be necessary to bleed down the chain tensioner at this time to facilitate readings.

Turn the crankshaft in the normal direction of rotation, again using a wrench on the crankshaft pulley, until the indicator reads 0.016″ less than zero reading.

1. Pointer for graduation
    on crankshaft
2. TDC mark or graduation
    on degree wheel of
    crankshaft
3. Degree wheel from end-
    paper
4. Pointer on camshaft
5. Dial micrometer with
    feeler and holder
6. Bracket for camshaft
    cover
7. Distributor rotor arm
8. Mark on distributor
    housing for 1st cyl-
    inder

Adjusting valve timing.

1. Feeler gauge
2. Valve spring retainer
3. Dial indicator prod
4. Dial indicator holder
5. Dial indicator

Adjusting valve timing.

Note the reading of the degree wheel at this time, remembering to double reading if wheel is mounted to camshaft sprocket. Again turn the crankshaft until the valve is closing and the indicator again reads 0.016″ less than zero reading. Make sure, at this time, that preload has remained constant, then note the reading of the degree wheel. The difference between the two degree wheel readings is the timing angle (number of degrees the valve is open) for that valve.

The other valves may be checked in the same manner. comparing them against other and the opening values given in the *Tune-up Specifications*. It must be remembered that turning the crankshaft contrary to the normal direction of rotation results in inaccurate readings. If valve timing is not to specification, the easiest way of bringing it in line is to install an offset Woodruff key in the camshaft sprocket. This is far simpler than replacing the entire timing chain, and it is the factory-recommended way of changing valve timing provided the timing chain is not stretched too far or worn out. Offset keys are available in the following sizes:

Offset	Part No.	For a correction at crankshaft of
2° (.7 mm.)	621 991 04 67	4°
3°20′ (.9 mm.)	621 991 02 67	6½°
4° (1.1 mm.)	621 991 01 67	8°
5° (1.3 mm.)	621 991 00 67	10°

Valve Timing Figures

Model	camshaft code number[1]	Intake valve opens BTDC	Intake valve closes ATDC	Exhaust valve opens BTDC	Exhaust valve closes ATDC	Mini. dist. betw. intake valve and piston with crankshaft adjusted to 5° after intersection TDC
190c	42 [3] 46 [4] 49 [5]	10°	46°	44°	12°	.0351″
190Dc 200D	02 [3] 12 [4] 13 [5] 17 [6]	12.5°	41.5°	45°	9°	.0394″ [7]
200	50 [6]	11°	53°	47°	21°	
220b 220Sb 220SEb	61 [2] 70 [3] 79 [4] 82 [5]	10°	46°	44°	12°	
230 230S	86	11°	53°	47°	21°	
230SL	76 [4] 84 [5]	10°	58°	51°	23°	.0351″
250S 250SE 250SL	86	11°	53°	47°	21°	
300SE [8]	39 [2] 42 [3]	7°	47°	49.5°	11.5°	
300SE [9] 300SEb 300SEL	46	18°	58°	53°	15°	
220/8	61	11°	47°*	48°**	16°	.0351″
220D/8	18	12.5°	41.5°*	45°**	9°	.0507″ [7]
230/8 250/8	0835	11°	47°*	48°**	16°	.0351″
280S/8 280SE/8 280SE/C/8	0835	11°	47°*	48°**	16°	.0351″
280SE/8 300SEL/8	0935	12°	56°*	53°**	21°	.0351″
300SEL/8 6.3 #	left-16 right-17 same	L-5° R-7° 2.5°	L-50°* R-48°* 52.5°*	L-40°** R-42°** 37.5°**	L-15.5° R-13.5° 18°	.0351″

[1] The code number on individual camshafts is stamped on the end face.
[2] Hollow shaft.
[3] Solid shaft for external lubrication with grooved bearings.
[4] Solid shaft for external lubrication without grooved bearings (except No. 1).
[5] Solid shaft for external lubrication without grooved bearings.
[6] Cams
[7] On models 200D and 220D/8, the minimum distance (.058″) between the exhaust valve and piston head at 5° before TDC must also be measured.
[8] With engine types 189.984 and 189.985.
[9] With engine types 189.986 and 189.987.
* ABDC
** BBDC
\# Top line—with new chain; bottom line—after 12,000 miles, both sides.

The Woodruff key must be installed with the offset toward the "right", in the normal direction of rotation, to effect advanced valve opening; toward the "left" to retard.

Advancing the intake valve opening too much can result in piston and/or valve damage. (The valve will hit the piston.) To check the clearance between the valve head and the piston, the crankshaft must be positioned at 5° ATDC (on intake stroke). The procedure is essentially the same as for measuring valve timing.

As before, the dial indicator is set to zero after being preloaded, then the valve is depressed until it touches the top of the piston. As the normal valve head-to-piston clearance is approximately .035″, you can see that the dial indicator must be preloaded at least .042″ so there will be enough movement for the feeler.

If the clearance is much less than .035″, the cylinder head must be removed and checked for carbon deposits. If none exist, the valve seat must be cut deeper into the head. Always set the ignition timing after installing an offset key.

Diesel Engines

After valve timing is checked, measure the distance between the exhaust valve and the piston at 5° BTDC as well as the intake valve to piston clearance at 5° ATDC. (All measurements taken at top of exhaust stroke.) The clearance must be at least .050″, intake and exhaust.

TIMING CHAIN REPLACEMENT

This operation can be done with everything in place. Remove only the camshaft cover, spark plugs, chain tensioner and the rocker arm blocks.

With a high-speed grinder, grind off two chain rivets and remove one link. Connect the end of the new chain to one end of the old using a removable link (similar to ones used on motorcycle chains). Now, simply pull the old chain out from the other end while feeding in the new chain. *NOTE: Go in normal direction of rotation.* Make sure the new chain turns the camshaft as it goes around. Unhook the old chain and connect the new one together with the removable link, inserting the link from front to rear with the closed end facing direction of rotation (see illustration).

Install and bleed the chain tensioner, then install rocker arm blocks and adjust valve clearance. Check the valve timing and correct, if necessary, using an offset Woodruff key, or by removing the camshaft sprocket and resetting the chain the necessary number of teeth. Reinstall spark plugs and camshaft cover.

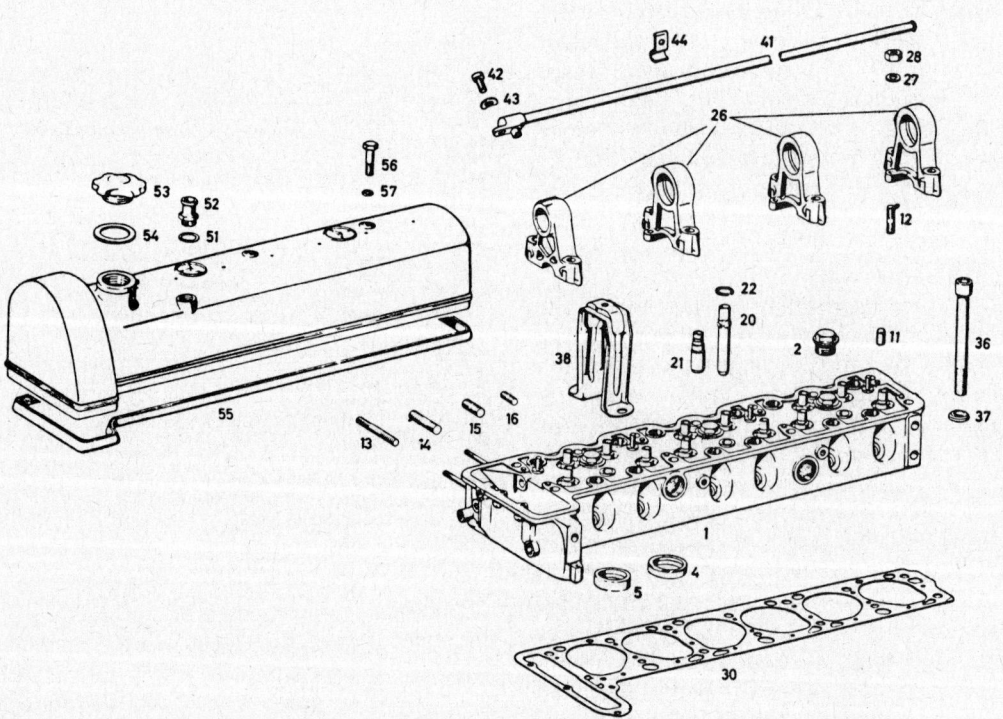

Six-cylinder head and associated parts—250SL, 280SL illustrated.

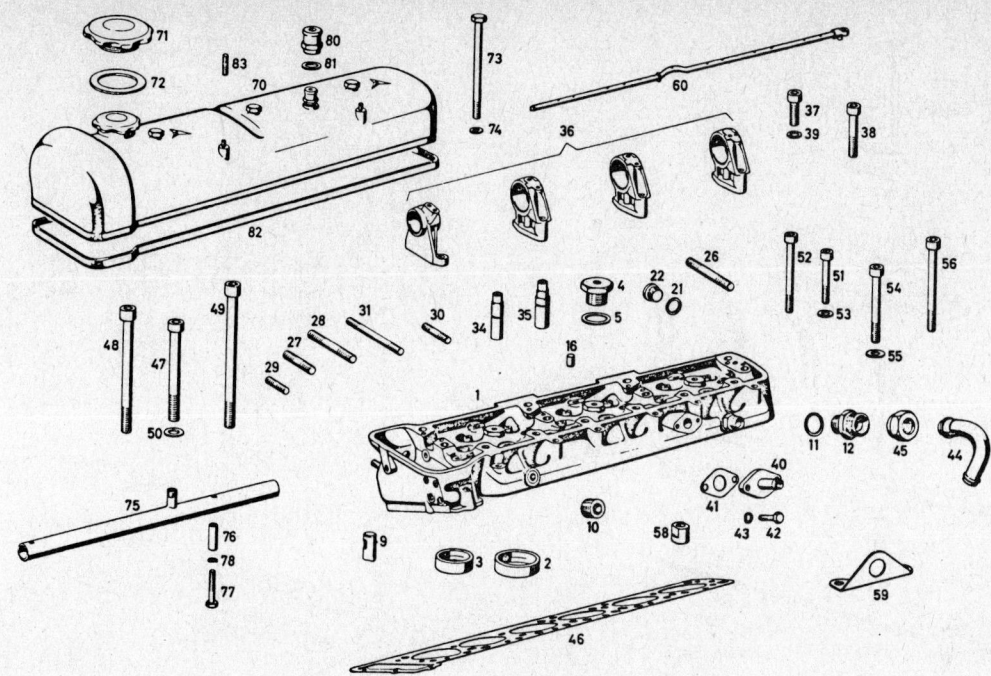

Cylinder head and associated parts—300SE.

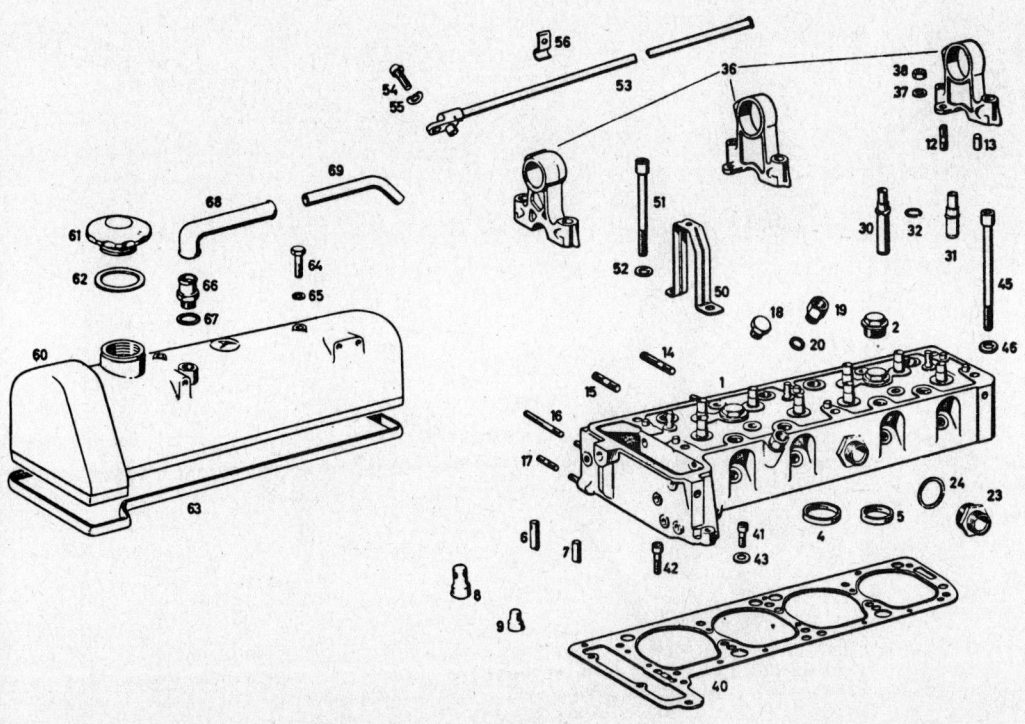

Four-cylinder head and associated parts.

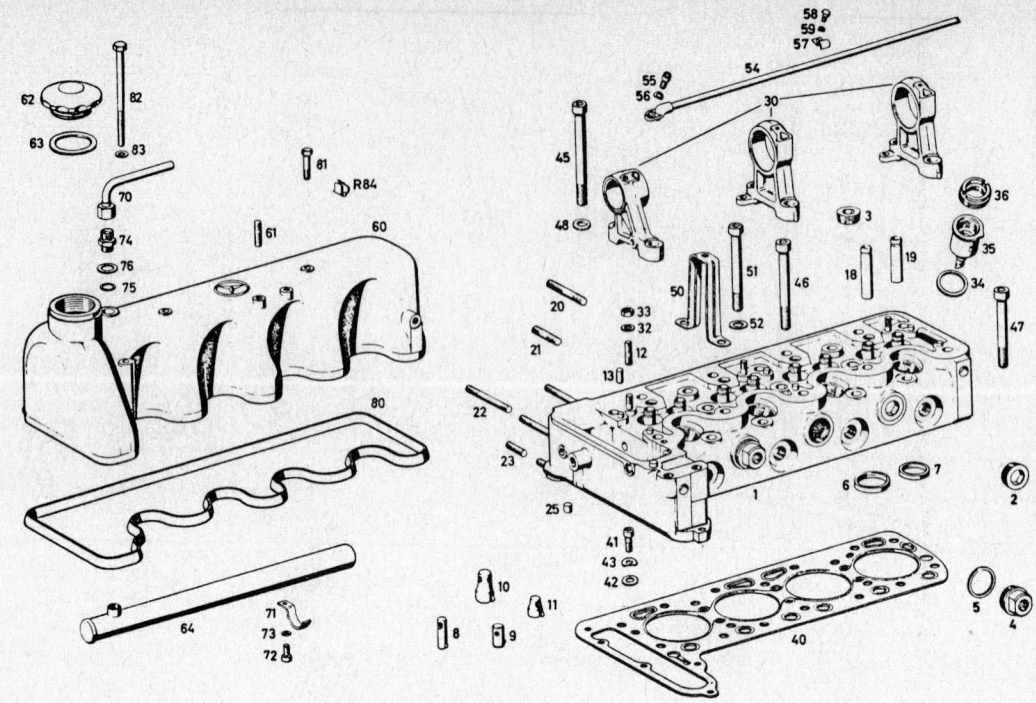

Diesel cylinder head and associated parts.

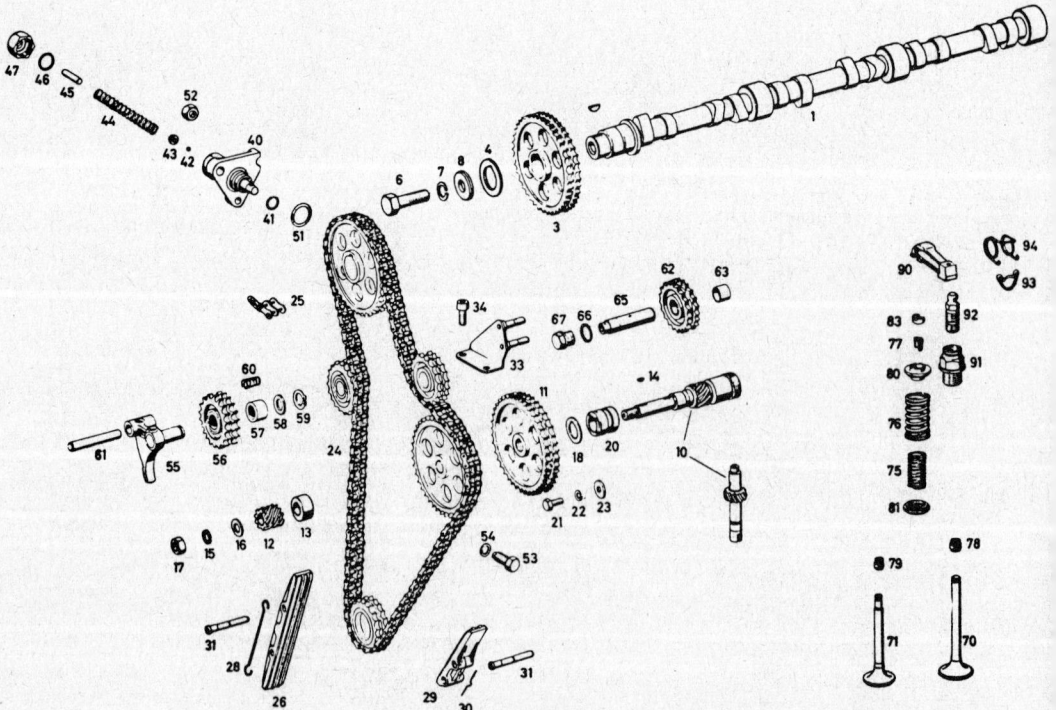

Six-cylinder valve train—250SL, 280SL illustrated.

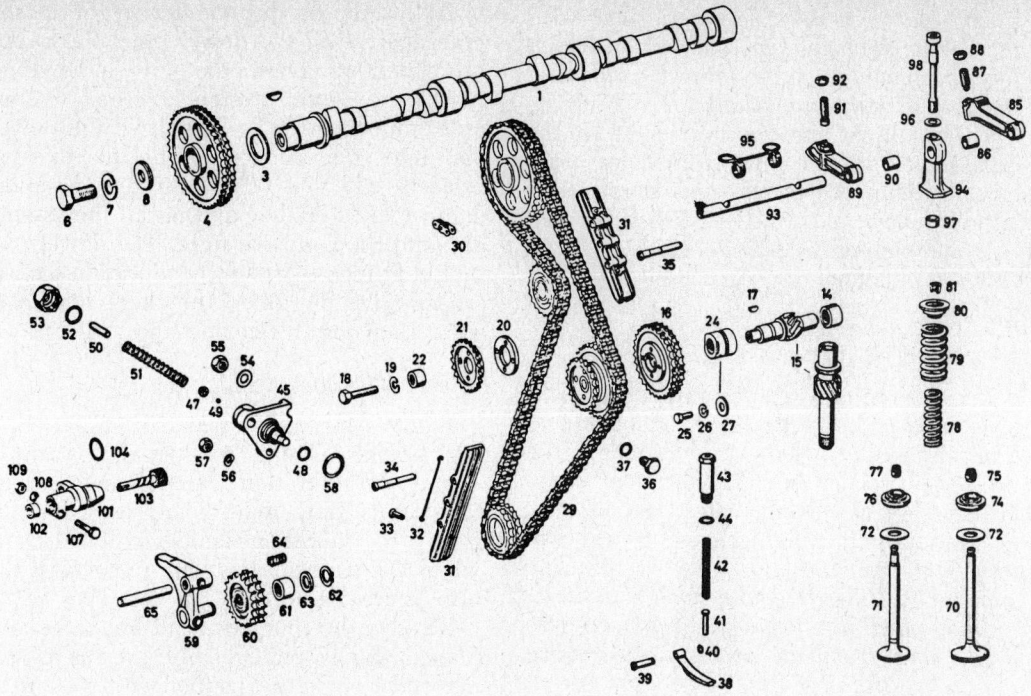

Valve train—300SE.

1. Spring clip   2. Link

Timing chain link.

VIBRATION DAMPER REMOVAL
AND INSTALLATION

190c, 190Dc, 200, 200D

Remove the radiator, then remove the fan belt. Loosen the large center stretch bolt that holds the pulley, then remove the bolt, washer, pulley and counterweight from the crankshaft. It will be necessary to use a puller to get the pulley off the end of the crank. *NOTE: If counterweight is damaged so much that it must be replaced with*

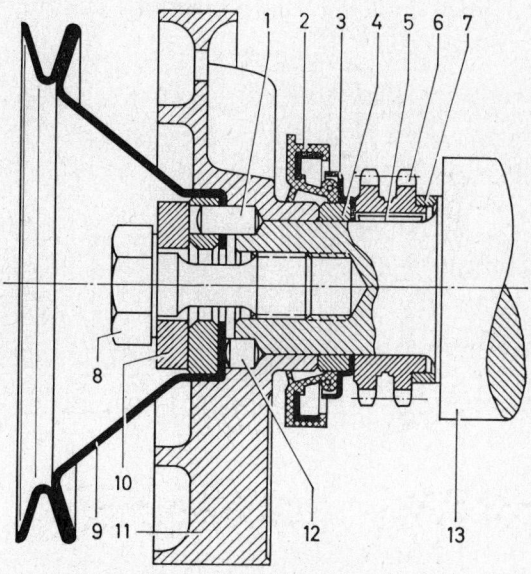

Vibration damper and counterweight—4 cylinder engines.

1. Cylindrical pin 8h 8X16 DIN 7
2. Oil seal
3. Oil thrower
4. Spacer ring
5. Woodruff key
6. Crankshaft sprocket
7. Compensating ring
8. Stretch bolt
9. V-pulley
10. Washer
11. Counterweight
12. Cylindrical pin 8H 8X8 DIN 7
13. Crankshaft

a new unit, it will be necessary to remove the engine from the car. The reason is that the new counterweight must be balanced together with the crankshaft.

To install, fit the counterweight to the crankshaft with the dowel pin holes properly lined up. Drive the pins home, then install pulley and washer. Install stretch bolt and tighten to 129 ft. lbs. Install fan belt and radiator.

All 6-Cylinder Engines
Except 300SE, 300SEb, 300SEL

Remove the radiator and fan belt. Loosen and remove the three hex-head bolts that hold the pulley. Remove the pulley, the pressed-on spacer and the vibration damper. Remove the center stretch bolt that holds the counterweight, then pull the counterweight from the end of the crank using a puller. *NOTE: If counterweight is damaged so much that it must be replaced with a new unit, it will be necessary to remove the engine from the car. The reason is that the new counterweight must be balanced together with the crankshaft. The vibration damper, on the other hand, is balanced independently and can be replaced with the engine installed.*

To install, fit the counterweight to the crankshaft with the dowel pin holes properly lined up. Drive the pins home, then install the center stretch bolt and washer and tighten to 129 ft. lbs. Drive the dowel pin into the counterweight so that it projects .118″ (—.008″). Fit the vibration damper to the pulley and install the assembly onto the counterweight. The dowel pin should fit in the bore in the vibration damper. Install and tighten the three hex-head bolts, then install fan belt and radiator.

300SE, 300SEb, 300SEL

Remove the radiator and the fan mounting bracket. Using two small C-clamps, clamp the vibration damper together at two points 180° apart. The reason for this is that the vibration damper will fall apart when the hex-head bolts are removed if the clamps are not in place.

Remove the four hex-head bolts, the lock plate and the pulley. Unscrew the center nut and remove it together with the thrust washer and vibration damper. The hub can be removed from the crank, if necessary, using a jaw-type puller.

Clamping 300 series vibration damper together.

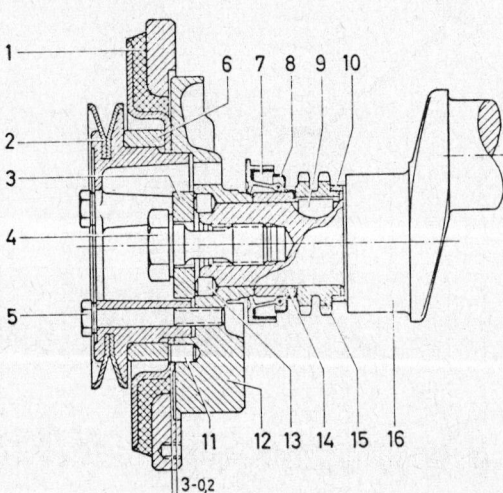

Vibration damper and counterweight—6 cylinder except 300 series.

1. Vibration damper
2. V-pulley
3. Washer
4. Stretch bolt
5. Hex bolt
6. Spacer ring
7. Oil seal
8. Oil thrower
9. Woodruff key
10. Compensating ring
11. Dowel pin 8h
    8X12 DIN 7
12. Counterweight
13. Dowel pin 8X8
    N 37 b
14. Spacer ring
15. Crankshaft sprocket
16. Crankshaft

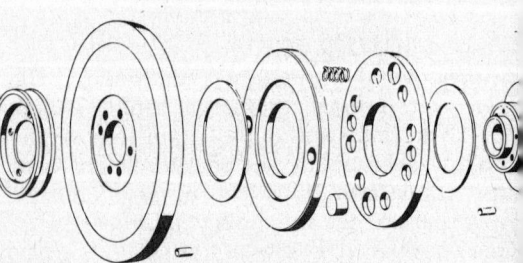

Vibration damper assembly sequence—300 series.

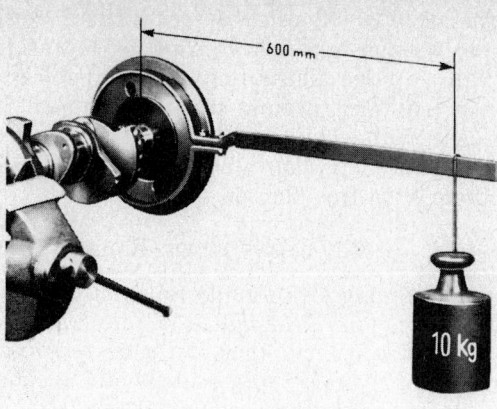

Checking vibration damper frictional rotating
torque—300 Series.

Release the two C-clamps and carefully disassemble the vibration damper. Clean the mating surfaces of the damper, and the two bakelite discs, with #80 sandpaper. Clean with greaseless solvent and reassemble, using *new* rubber shear blocks. Apply the two C-clamps and tighten them evenly. Install the rear disc (dry) onto the crank hub and install the vibration damper, making sure dowel pin holes are properly lined up. Install the center bolt and tighten to 144 ft. lbs., making sure the lock plate holes are lined up with the corresponding holes in the damper. Remove the C-clamps, then install the pulley and the four-hex-

head bolts and lockwashers. Tighten bolts to 18 ft. lbs.

After mounting the damper, check the friction torque required to rotate it. The torque should be 4.5-7 mkp. (32-52 ft. lbs.), as measured around the outer circumference of the damper. To do this, attach a 22 lb. weight to a lever arm about 24″ long and see if the damper rotates.

Install the fan mounting bracket and radiator.

FRONT SEAL INSTALLATION

Most leaky front seals can be replaced with the engine in the car. An exception is the silicone rubber seal used in 230, 230 S, 230 SL, 250 S, 250 SE and 250 SL models. This seal, (part No. 108 031 00 81) white-yellow in color, should be replaced only with the engine disassembled, because the sealing surface would be scraped off as the seal was installed into the housing. A new seal, however, was developed so that replacement is possible with the engine in place; it can be used on these older engines as well.

This new seal, part No. 108 031 01 81, is black in color and can be used on all 2.2, 2.3 and 2.5 liter engines. The following table indicates how the various versions of oil seal may be used when repairs are being carried out.

Part No.	Material (color)	Model	Repair	Observations
180 031 06 81	Perbunan (blue)	220b 220Sb 220SEb 220SEb/C	With engine disassembled and with engine installed	Only with oil thrower and spacer sleeve Part No. 180 031 04 51 (16.25 mm.)
108 031 00 81	silicone (white/yellow)	230 230S 230SL 250S 250SE 250SE/C 250SL	Only when engine is disassembled	Without oil thrower, but with wider spacer sleeve, Part No. 108 031 01 51 (16.9—17 mm.)
108 031 01 81	polyacryl (black)	220b/Sb/SEb 220SEb/C 230 230S 230SL 250S 250SE 250SE/C 250SL	When engine is installed	With oil thrower and spacer sleeve, Part No. 180 031 04 51 (16.25 mm.), or without oil thrower but with wider spacer sleeve Part No. 108 031 01 51 (16.9—17 mm.)

The oil seals obtainable as spare parts for all four-cylinder engines and engines for Models 300SE, 300SEb and 300SEL may be used for disassembled and installed engines, with or without oil thrower.

TIMING CHAIN TENSIONER

To accurately check the chain tensioner requires special test equipment. However, if the tensioner is bad enough to cause chain rattle, it will suffice to remove it, clamp it down, fill it with oil and bleed it, then push down slowly. If the tensioner is good, it will require quite high pressure to compress, and will compress only very slowly.

To remove the tensioner, first take off the camshaft cover and drain the radiator to a level below the thermostat housing. Remove the housing and the idler pulley bracket. The tensioner now can be easily removed. Check the tensioner and, if necessary, replace it. Parts are available separately, but the pressure pin (9) and housing (4) *must* be replaced together for proper operation.

To bleed the tensioner after installation, fill the oil case in the cylinder head with engine oil and, using a screwdriver, push the tension sprocket bearing as far as it will go (see illustration). Slowly release the tensioner, making sure the oil case is filled with oil at all times. Repeat the procedure until no air bubbles issue and there is no free-play on the tensioner.

TIMING CHAIN GUIDE RAILS

The timing chain guide rails must be removed before cleaning an engine block in the hot tank, and they must be removed from the cylinder head before milling. The rails are held in place by pivot bolts and pressed-in pins or by pressed-in pins alone, depending on location. The pressed-in pins normally are removed using a special tool; however, a simple workable tool can be made in the shop using a spacer sleeve having an inside diameter greater than the outside diameter of the pin and either an M6 metric bolt or a ¼-20 USS bolt. If a

Bleeding chain tensioner.

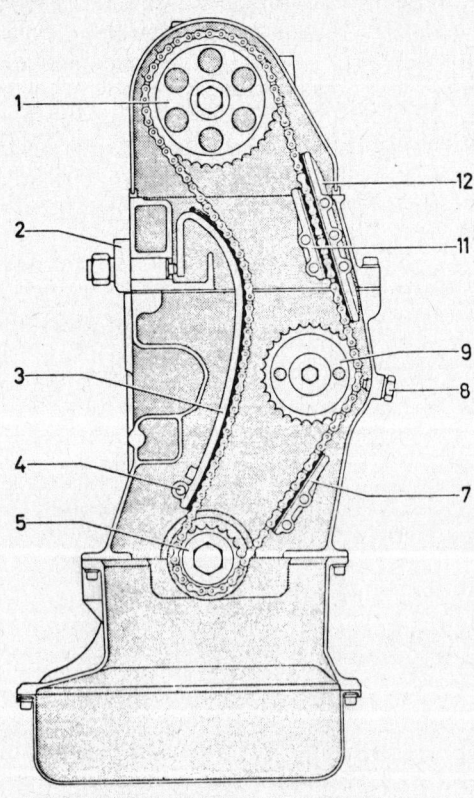

Typical gasoline engine timing chain rail arrangement for phase II cars.

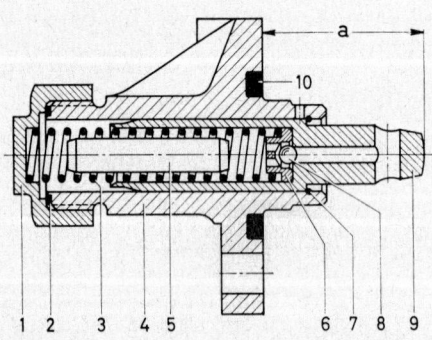

Chain tensioner.

1. Cap nut	6. Ball retainer
2. Sealing ring	7. Snap-ring
3. Pressure spring	8. Ball
4. Housing	9. Pressure pin
5. Pin	10. O-ring

1. Camshaft sprocket	8. Locking screw
2. Chain tightener	9. Intermediate gear
3. Tensioning rail	driving oil pump
4. Pivot pin	and distributor
5. Camshaft sprocket	11. Chain guide, inside
7. Chain guide	12. Chain guide, outside

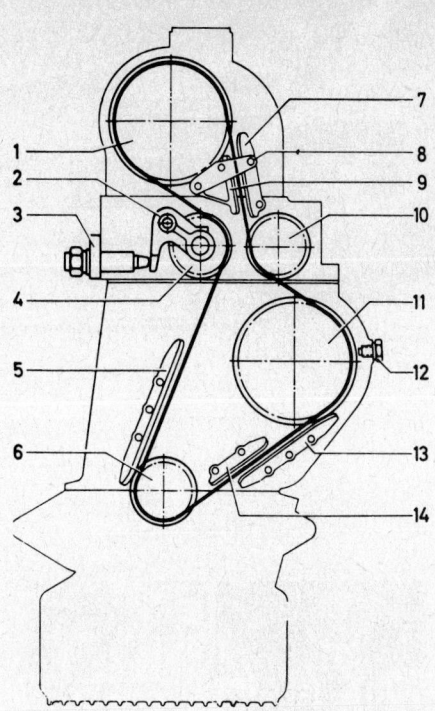

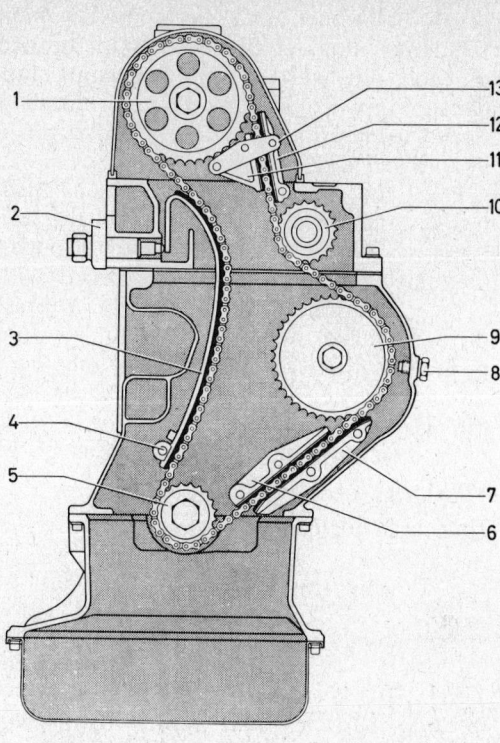

1. Camshaft sprocket
2. Idler sprocket support with idler sprocket
3. Chain tightener
4. Idler sprocket
5. Guide rail, outer
6. Crankshaft sprocket
7. Guide rail, outer

8. Holder for guide rail, inner
9. Guide rail, inner
10. Guide sprocket
11. Intermediate sprocket
12. Locking screw
13. Guide rail, outer
14. Guide rail, inner

Timing chain configuration—190Dc, 200D.

1. Camshaft sprocket
2. Chain tensioner
3. Tensioning rail
4. Pivot pin for tensioning rail
5. Crankshaft sprocket
6. Inner chain guide
7. Outer chain guide
8. Safety screw

9. Idling gear (drive for injection timer, injection pump and oil pump)
10. Diverter sprocket
11. Inner sliding rail
12. Outer sliding rail
13. Inner sliding rail retainer

Timing chain configuration—220D/8.

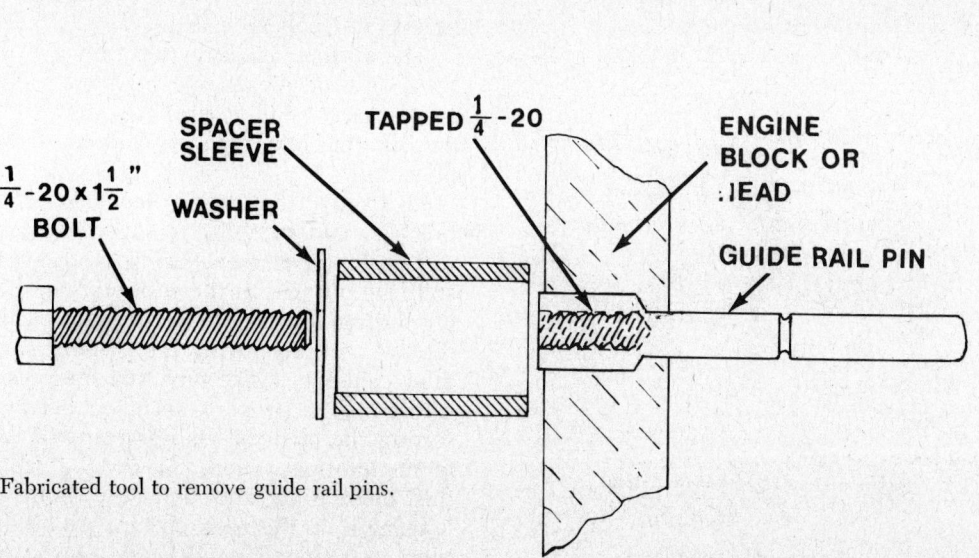

Fabricated tool to remove guide rail pins.

metric bolt is not available (must be about 1½″ long), tap out the threads in the end of each pin with a ¼-20 bottoming tap. Clean chips from threads and obtain a sleeve, as described previously, and a washer and ¼-20 x 1½″ USS bolt.

Place the components in order, as illustrated, and tighten the bolt in the pin threads. The pin will gradually pull out of the block far enough to be removed with pliers. When installing pins, use a brass drift to make sure the threads are not peened over. NOTE: *Some guide rails have a lock wire which fits in a groove in each pin. This wire must be held out of the way with a screwdriver while tightening the "puller" bolt.*

Engine Lubrication

OIL CHANGE AND FILTER

The engine oil is changed by removing the drain plug in the oil pan (see illustration). It is best to drain the oil while hot, because particles and contaminants will then be in suspension and drained out with the oil.

If the car has an oil cooler, the oil must be drained by removing the drain plug at the bottom of the cooler (see illustration). It is recommended that the oil filter be removed before draining the oil cooler in order to provide a pressure release in the oil system, ensuring complete draining. The copper and copper-asbestos gaskets on the oil pan and oil cooler plugs may be reused if they are not scored badly, but it is advisable to renew them after a few oil changes to prevent seepage.

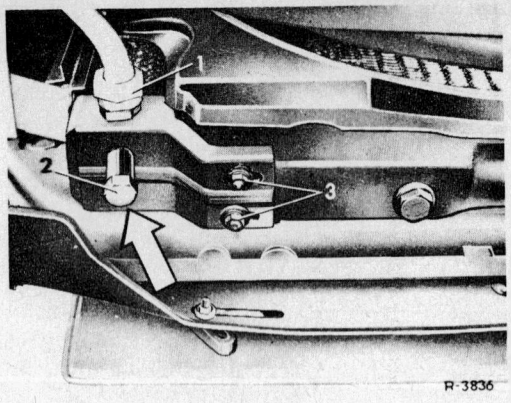

1. Pipe joint
2. Oil drain plug
3. Hold-down nuts

Oil cooler.

Oil filter.

Tightening torque for the oil pan drain plug is approximately 36 ft.lbs., for the oil cooler drain plug 14 ft.lbs. and for the lower oil filter bolt 29 ft.lbs.

The oil filter is located on the lower left-hand side of the engine on most models. It is either a full-flow or a combined full and partial-flow type, depending on application.

To remove the filter element, loosen the bolt (2) and carefully remove the housing (1) and filter element, being careful not to spill the oil. Clean the inside of the housing with a kerosene-soaked, lint-free rag to remove any sediment, then insert a new filter element. Make sure that the pressure spring (7) is properly installed before inserting the element—its absence will result in no filtering action. As can be seen in this illustration, the bolt that holds the housing is, in this case, on top. An oil drain plug is provided on the side of the filter

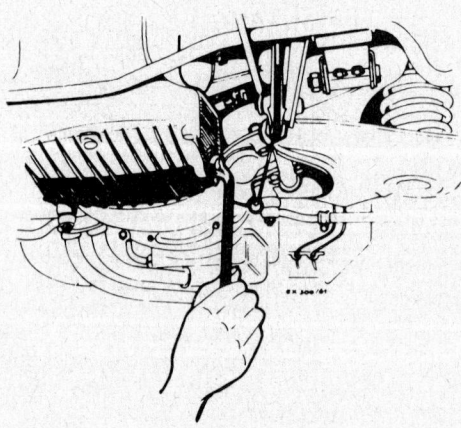

Engine oil drain plug.

Seal filter element at "a" and blow through with compressed air.

housing to allow pre-draining the housing before removal.

OIL PUMP

All Mercedes-Benz automobiles use a gear-type oil pump, the specifications for each model being given below. To remove the pump, first remove the oil pan. Check gear backlash and clearance between pump housing and gears, plus all other dimensions shown in the chart. If pump is not to specifications, it must be replaced.

Flywheel

The flywheel and crankshaft are balanced together as a unit, therefore disassembly must be preceded by matchmarking these components for correct assembly positioning.

Stretch bolts are used to hold some newer flywheels in place. These are easily identified by their "hourglass" shape (see illustrations). These bolts are deformed, or stretched, when tightened, and their usefulness must be determined by measuring their diameter at the stretch point.

Stretch bolts must be torqued to the prescribed "preload" initial reading, then the wrench turned through a certain number of degrees rotation. This method ensures that the bolts will not loosen in service.

After pretightening, do not slack up on the wrench, but immediately turn the required number of degrees. While not strictly accurate, the number of degrees can be estimated.

1. Bolt
2. Upper section
3. Filter element (full flow)
4. Rubber seal ring
5. Filter element (partial flow)
6. Lower section
7. Spring and retainer
8. Oil drain screw
a. Bypass bore

Oil filter cutaway.

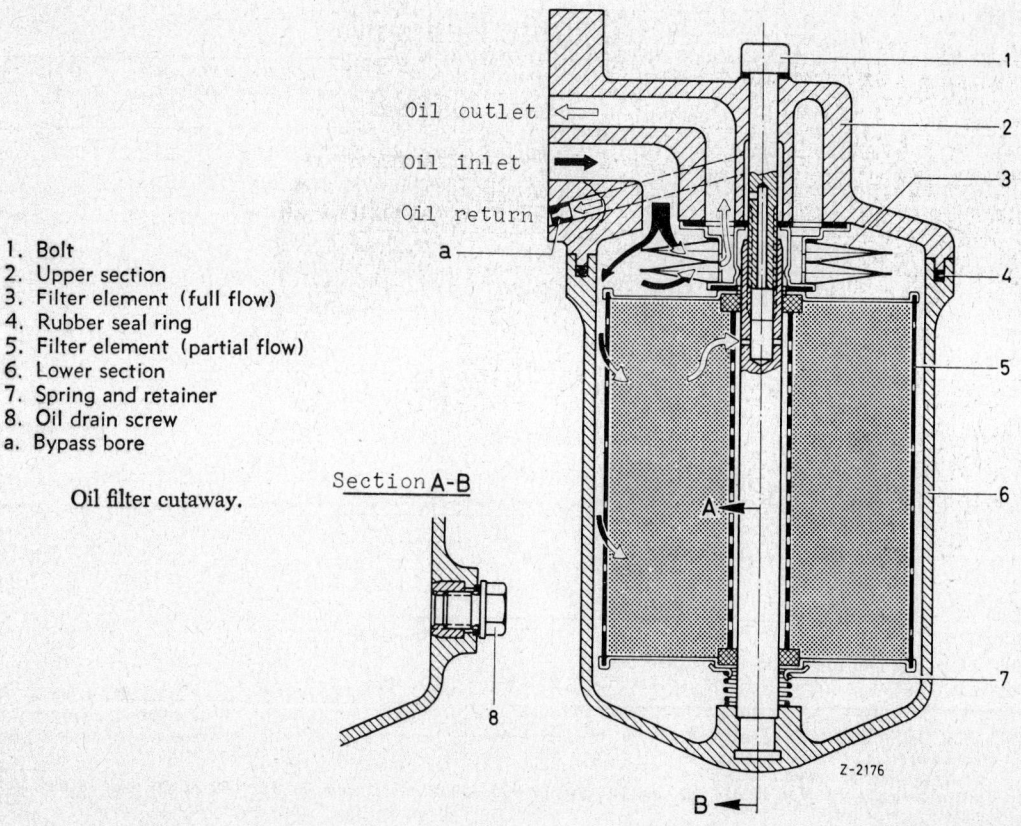

Oil Pump Specifications

Model	190c 190Dc 200 200D	220b 220Sb 220SEb 230SL	230 230S 250S 250SE 250SL	300SE 300SEb 300SEL
Internal diameter of bearing bushing in housing base and top (mm.)			12.000 / 12.018	
Driveshaft diameter (mm.)			11.984 / 11.973	
Gear spindle diameter (mm.)			11.973 / 11.964	
Radial play of driveshaft (mm.)			0.016—0.045	
Radial play of gear spindle (mm.)			0.027—0.054	
Diameter of oil pump gears (mm.)			36.450 / 36.411	
Diameter of bore in housing base and top (mm.)			36.500 / 36.525	
Play between oil pump gears and pump housing (mm.) — Radial play			0.025—0.057	
Play between oil pump gears and pump housing (mm.) — End-play	0.046—0.082	0.050—0.092	0.040—0.082	
Backlash (mm.)			0.05—0.10	
Minimum play between pump housing and helical gear, cam or follower (mm.)		0.2[1]		1.5

1 *Does not apply to Models 190Dc, 200D, 220SEb, 230, 250SE, and 250SL*

Oil Pump Delivery

Model	Part No.	Gear height (mm.)	Pump speed (rpm)	Delivery (kg/min.)	Vacuum suction side (mm. Hg.)	Pressure delivery (atm.[2])	Oil temp. (° C)
190c	121 180 15 01	16	2500	19.5—24.5			
190Dc 200[3]	621 180 05 01 121 180 21 01		345—350	2.33—3.43			
200	121 180 23 01		2500	27—33.7			
200D	621 180 09 01		345—350	3.07—4.72			
220b 220Sb	180 180 09 01	22	2500	26.5—33	400	5[1]	100 at n = 2500
220SEb	127 180 02 01						
230 230S	108 180 00 01		345—350	3.0—4.62			100—106 at n = 345-350
230SL	129 180 00 01						
250S	108 180 01 01	28	2500	33.6—42			
250SE 250SL	129 180 01 01		345—350	3.83—5.88			
300SE 300SEb 300SEL	189 180 02 01	30	2500	36.0—45.0			
			345—350	4.1—6.3			

Type of oil: for all models engine oil SAE 10
1 *Pressure in front of pump = 0 kg/cm²*
2 *Counter pressure = 2.0—2.1 kg/cm²*
3 *Up to engine nos. 121 940 10 025 718 and 121 940 12 003 493 oil pump, Part No. 121 180 21 01, with 16 mm. gear height was installed.*

Springs for Oil Relief Valves

Model	Part No. of spring	Outer diameter (mm.)	Wire gauge (mm.)	Free length (mm.)	Loaded length pre-tension (mm.) (kg.)		Loaded length final tension (mm.) (kg.)		Opening pressure of the oil relief valve (atm.)
In the Crankcase (Pressure maintenance valve)									
190c to 300SEL	127 993 02 01	8.7—9	1.3	43.6	39	2.0	30.5	5.25 to 5.95	5.5—6.5
In the Oil Filter									
190c to 300SEL	181 993 06 01	12.25	1.25	49	32	2.26	24	3—3.6	2.2—2.5

Special Diesel Engine Service

When overhauling an older OM621 series engine, many components from the OM615 engine can be used to help increase reliability. The injection timer from the OM615 often helps reduce diesel knock, and also increases chain and slide rail life.

The newer camshaft has wider lobes and rocker arms and can be used if the complete rocker assembly is installed. Always check valve timing after effecting such a change.

It is also possible to use the stronger OM615 valve springs. This is especially

Standard Transmission   **Automatic Transmission**

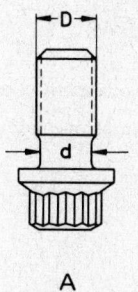 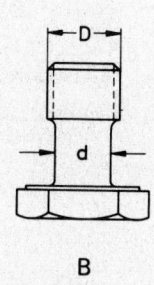 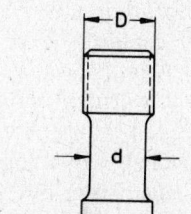

A   B   C

	A	B			C
Part No.	615 032 05 71	621 032 00 71	108 032 01 71	108 990 03 19	108 990 04 19
Thread Diameter	M 10 x 1	M 10 x 1	M 12 x 1	M 10 x 1	M 12 x 1
Diameter "d" of Stretch Bolt When New (mm.)	.33"-.01" (8.5-0.2)	.31"-.01" (8.0-0.2)	.36"-.01" (9.2-0.2)	.31"-.01" (7.7-0.2)	.36"-.01" (9.2-0.2)
Minimum Diameter	.31" (8.1 mm.)	.30" (7.6 mm.)	.34" (8.8 mm.)	.29" (7.3 mm.)	.34" (8.8 mm.)
Installed in Engines of Models:	220/8 220D/8	230/8	250/8 280S/8 280SE/8 280SE/8 Cp/Cv. 300SEL/8 280SL/8	220/8 220D/8 230/8	250/8 280S/8 280SE/8 280SE/8 Cp/Cv. 300SEL/8 280SEL/8

Stretch bolts used on Mercedes-Benz flywheels.

Flywheel matchmarks (arrows) and angle of rotation tightening—four-cylinder illustrated.

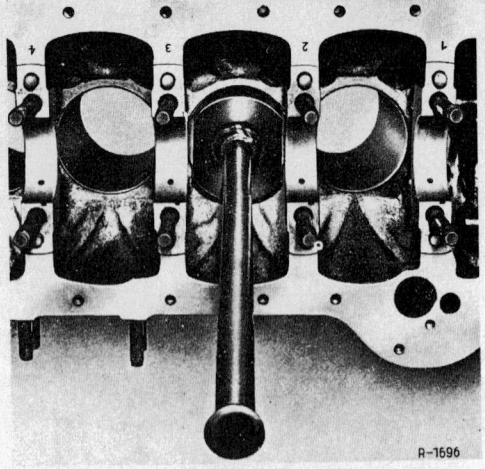

Driving out cylinder liner—300SE.

desirable in older engines that have had several valve jobs; the valves seat deeper in the head and reduce spring tension.

Cylinder Liner Removal and Replacement

Some aluminum block engines, the 300 SE for example, have thin grey iron liners installed into the bores. When these liners become worn or damaged, they must be replaced, because boring is not feasible.

Obviously, this job is not one for the home mechanic, but it is included for the sake of machine shops and garages not familiar with the Mercedes-Benz.

If only one cylinder is to be relined, anchor the remaining liners using small retainers similar to those illustrated.

Completely strip the block and degrease it using Gunk or kerosene. Heat the block evenly for 30–45 minutes at a temperature of 575–640° F. in an oven.

After removal from the oven, drive the liners out from the bottom using a suitable drift. If the liner will not move, it can be split, or bored, but care must be taken not to damage the block.

After the block has cooled to room temperature, carefully clean the bores in the block and measure their diameter. Measure the O.D. of the new cylinder liners and compare with specifications.

Ideally, the block should be pressure checked before installing new liners. Oil galleries should withstand 90 psi, water jackets 30 psi, without leaking.

Heat the block again and insert the liners from the top, being careful of align-

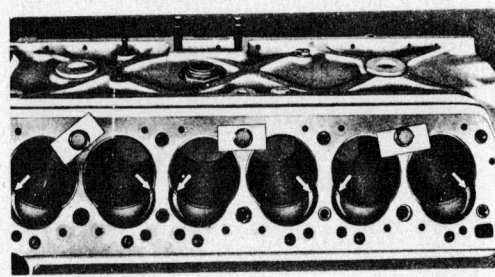

Retaining plates to hold liners if only one liner is to be replaced.

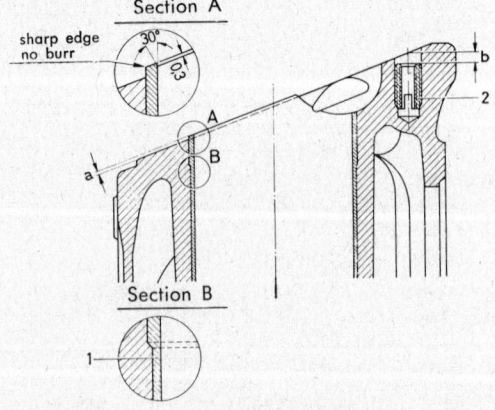

1. Liner   2. Threaded bushing

Machining 300SE liners.

ment. After cooling, the projecting liners must be milled square with relation to the block (see illustration). The liners must then be honed to final finish tolerances and the valve recesses re-machined.

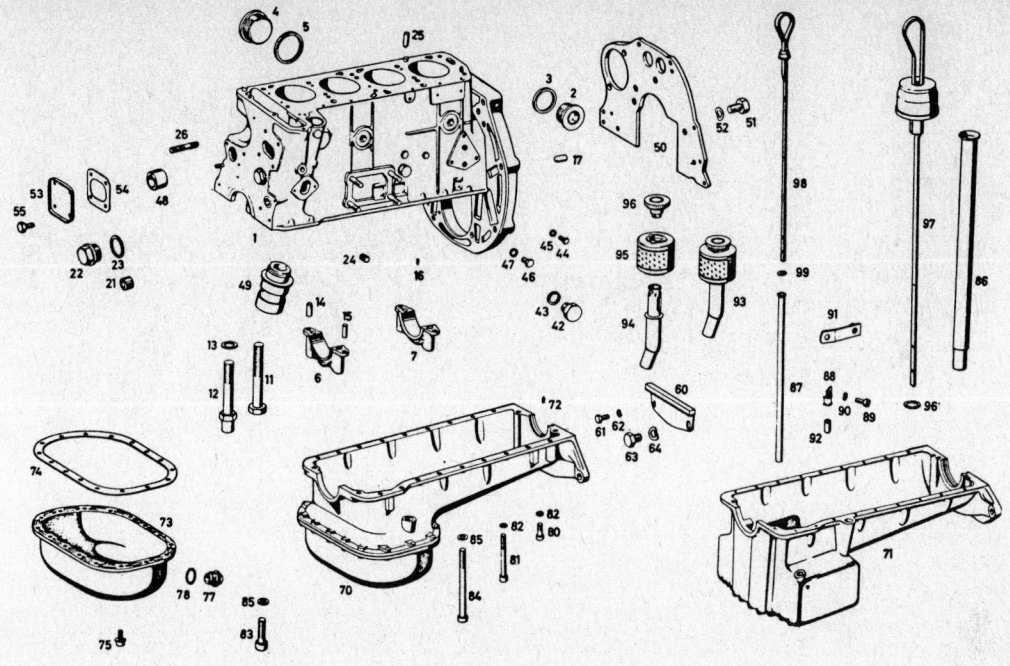

Four-cylinder engine block and associated parts.

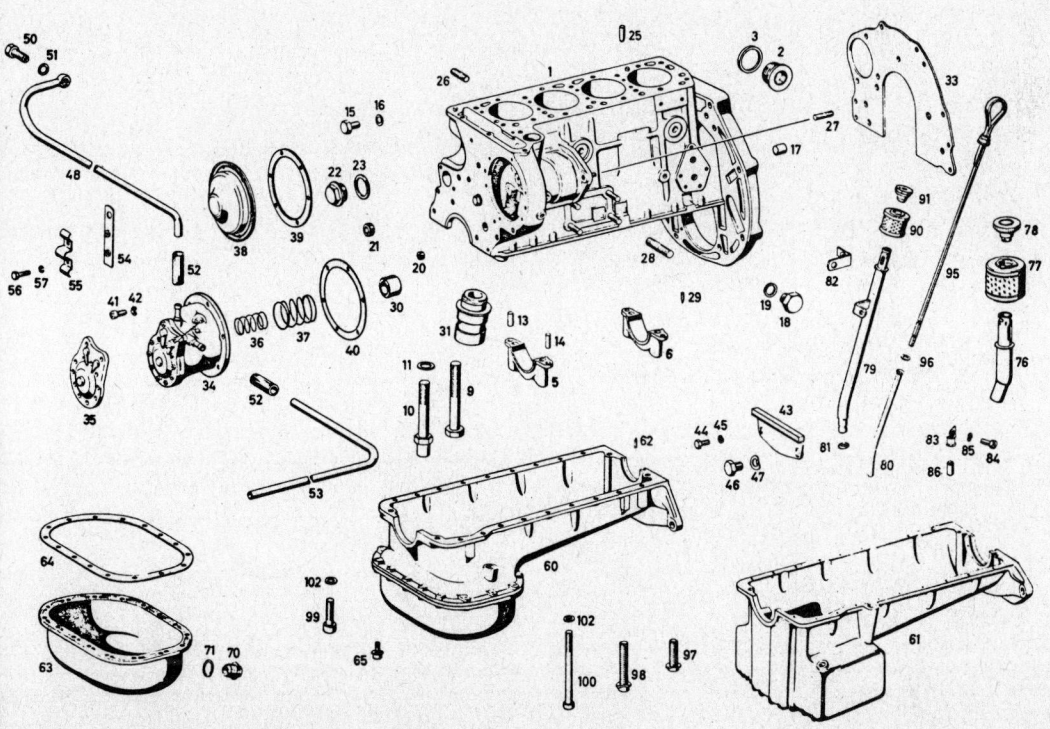

Diesel engine block and associated parts.

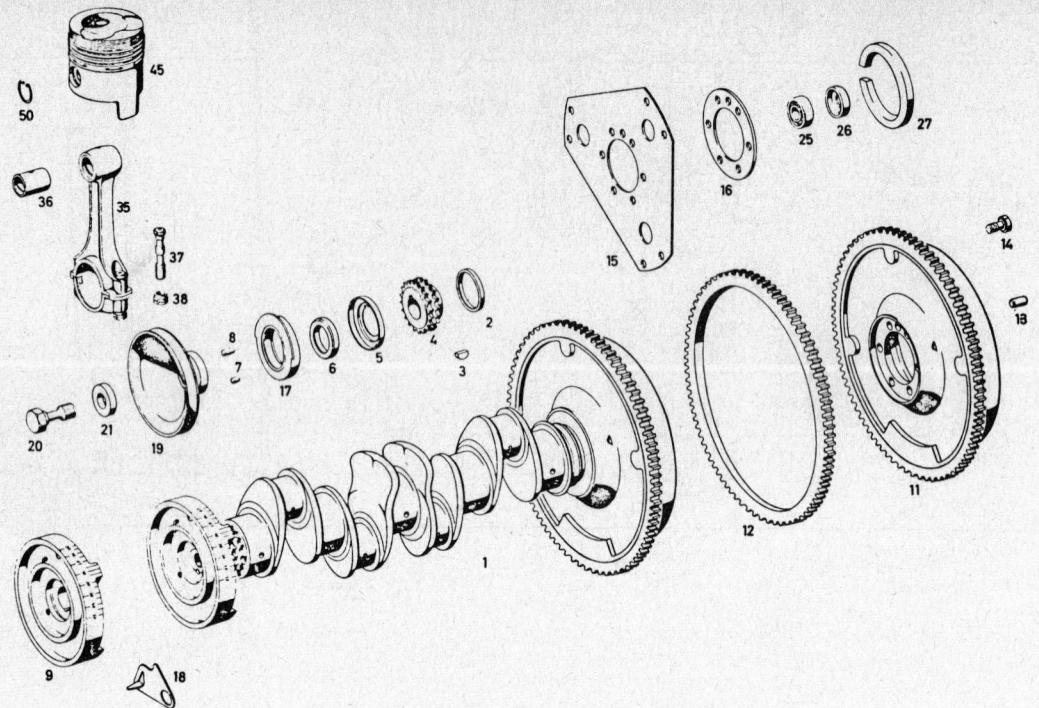

Diesel crankshaft and associated parts.

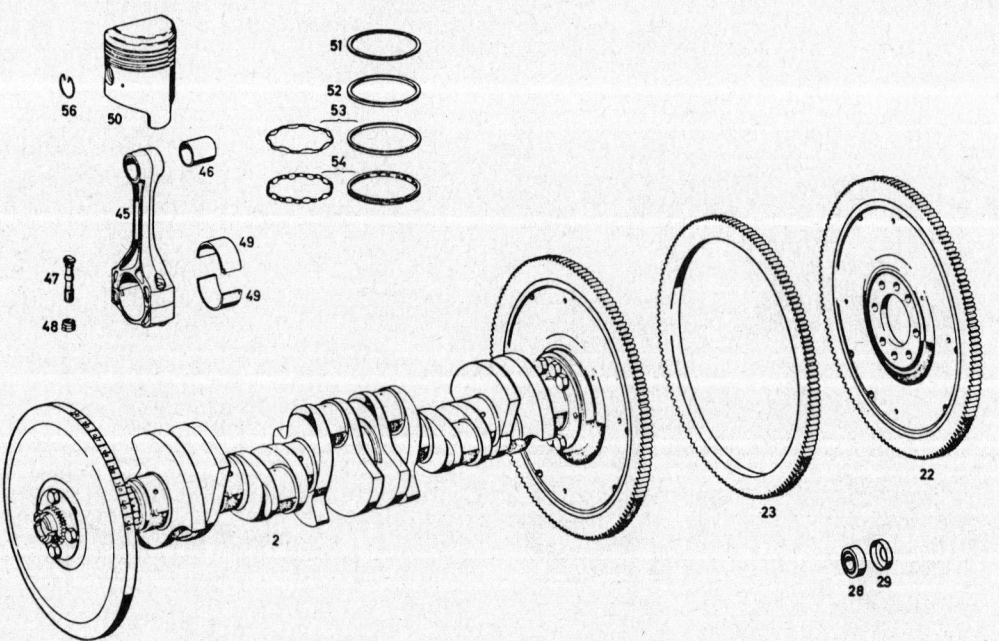

Type 300SE crankshaft and associated parts.

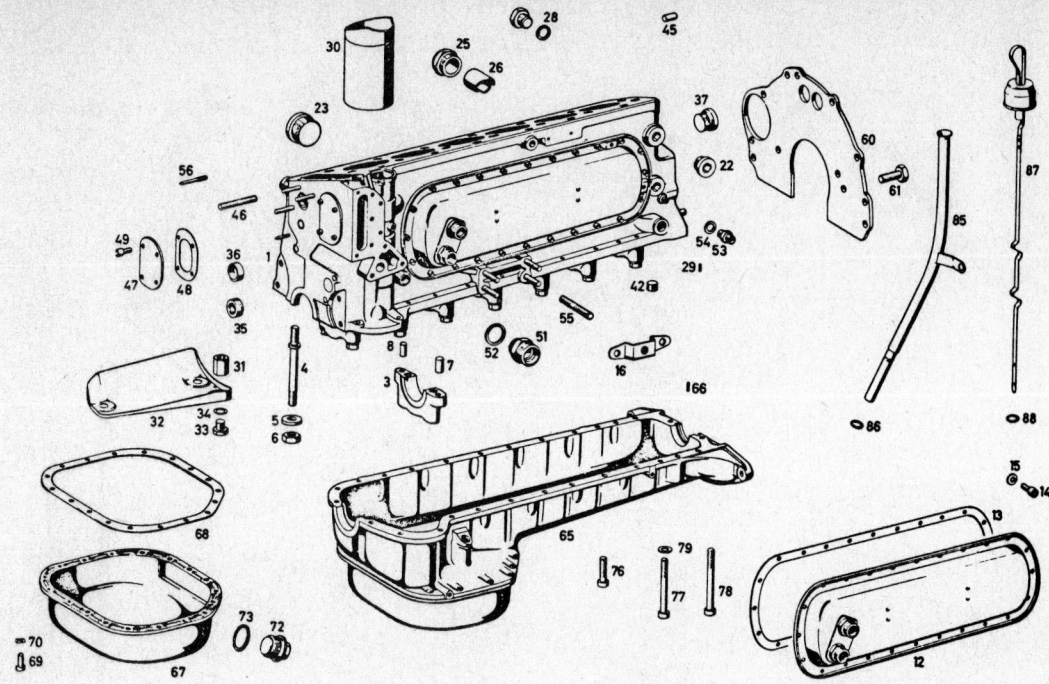

Type 300SE engine block and associated parts.

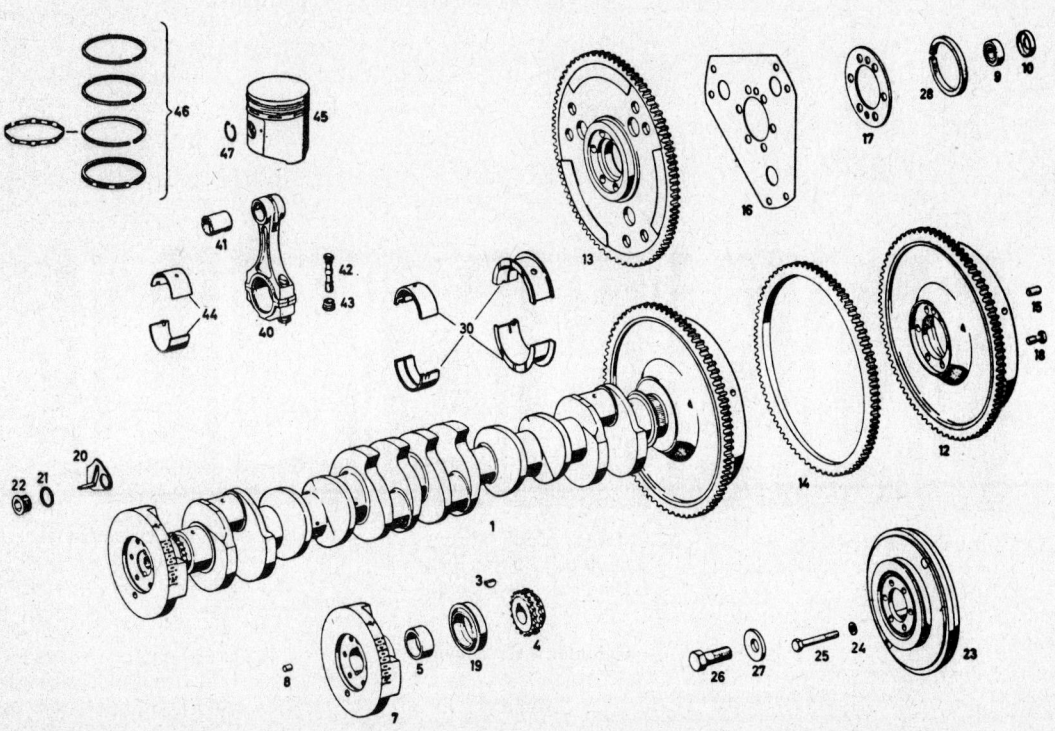

Six-cylinder crankshaft and associated parts—250, 280 illustrated.

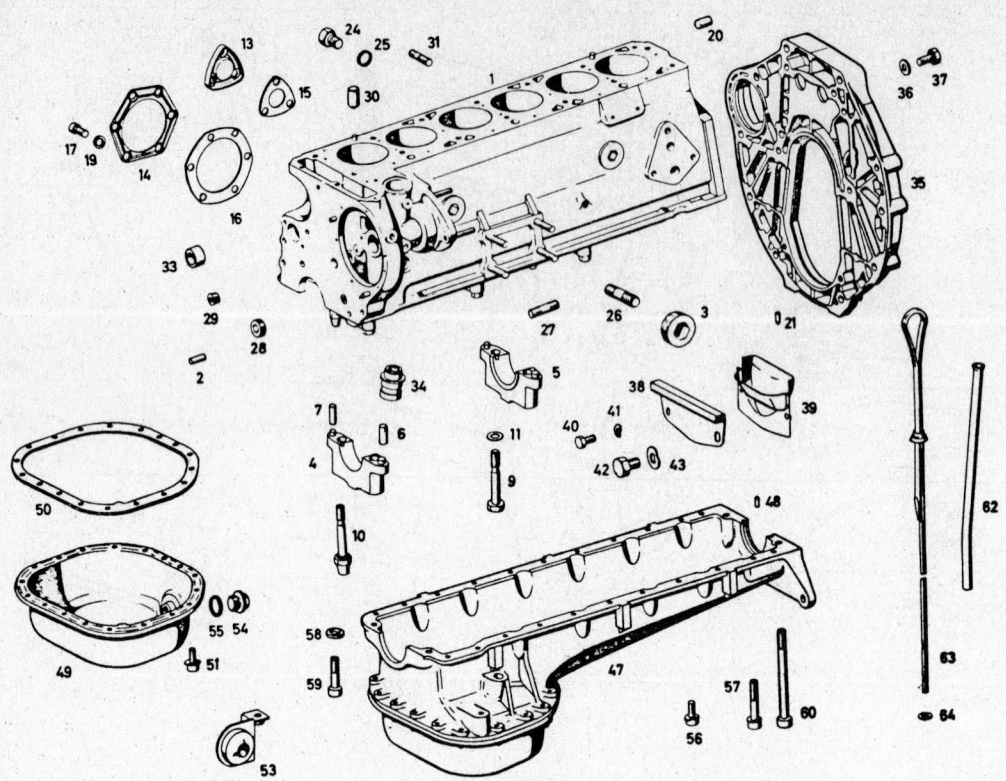

Six-cylinder engine block and associated parts—250, 280 illustrated.

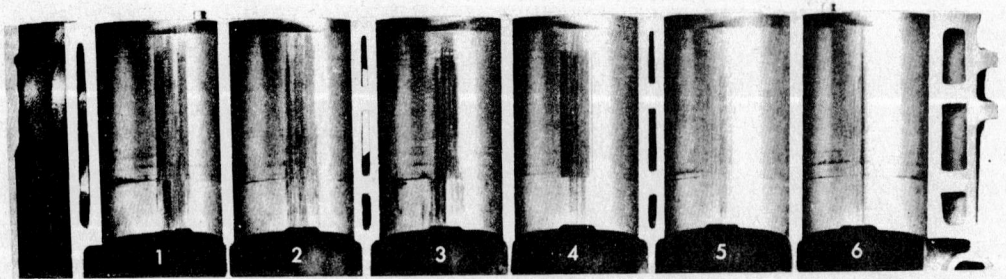

1, 2, 3 Piston skirt seizure re-   4. Piston skirt and oil ring   5, 6 Score marks caused by a
     sulted in this pattern. Engine   seizure caused this damage.   split piston skirt. Damage is
     must be rebored   Engine must be rebored   not serious enough to warrant
                                                                                    reboring

Cylinder wall damage.

7. Ring seized longitudinally,
   causing a score mark
   1 3/16" wide, on the land
   side of the piston groove.
   The honing pattern is destroyed and the cylinder
   must be rebored

8. Result of oil ring seizure.
   Engine must be rebored

9. Oil ring seizure here was not
   serious enough to warrant
   reboring. The honing
   marks are still visible

Cylinder wall damage.

Manual Transmission

Removal and Replacement

To remove, first jack up the car at all four corners and place on axle stands. Remove the negative battery cable and unhook all shift rods. With column-mounted gearshift lever, remove rods (2) and (1) at the relay arm from under the hood. On floorshift models, unhook the rods (1) and (2) at the transmission side cover by prying upwards on the clips from the open end with a screwdriver. On models having a top cover shift mechanism, the floor tunnel must be removed to reach the shift rods. On older models having the clutch slave cylinder held to the clutch housing with two bolts, remove the cylinder completely and swing it out of the way. On newer models it is sufficient to remove the hose at point "A" (see illustration) and plug it to prevent fluid loss.

Remove the speedometer cable and the exhaust pipe bracket and wire them out of the way. Now, on pre-1965 models, disconnect the driveshaft by unbolting the center bearing support and the front U-joint plate at the transmission, then sliding the shaft back and out of the way. On later models, a double nut configuration is used. Holding one nut with a wrench, loosen the other, then unbolt the shaft from the transmission tailshaft. Remove the center bearing support on these models as well.

NOTE: It is a good idea to scribe marks on the center bearing support bracket for ease in assembly.

Mark the position of the rear crossmember and slightly jack up the engine with a block of wood between the jack and the oil pan. This serves to take the weight off the crossmember bolts during removal and prevents stripped threads. Unscrew all crossmember bolts that hold it to the body and transmission and remove the crossmember. Unbolt the bellhousing and starter bolts and pull the transmission straight backward, while rotating clockwise 90° to clear obstructions. Make absolutely sure the mainshaft is out of the clutch before lowering the transmission, otherwise the clutch hub will be damaged.

Installation is the reverse of removal except that the rear U-joint must be split on some models and the driveshaft pushed further back for clearance. Always coat the mainshaft splines and pilot bushing surfaces with Vaseline or Molykote grease before installing. Don't forget the ground cables under the nuts, and take care that all bolts are tightened evenly and the 300 SE dowel pins properly lined up. The center bearing support must not be cocked or it will soon disintegrate under torque loads, so tighten its mounting bolts finger tight until everything else is torqued, then tighten them. The driveshaft double clamp nuts get torqued to about 140 ft.-lbs. Bracing the hold-down wrench on the body pan

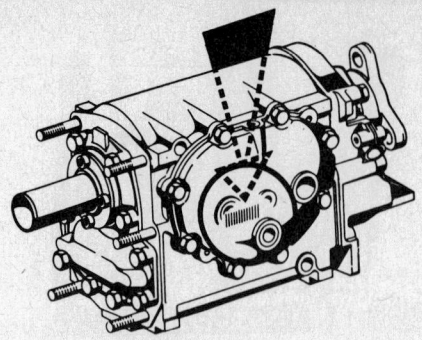

Transmission identification numbers—side cover.

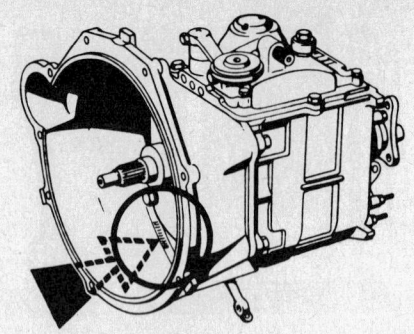

Transmission identification numbers—top cover.

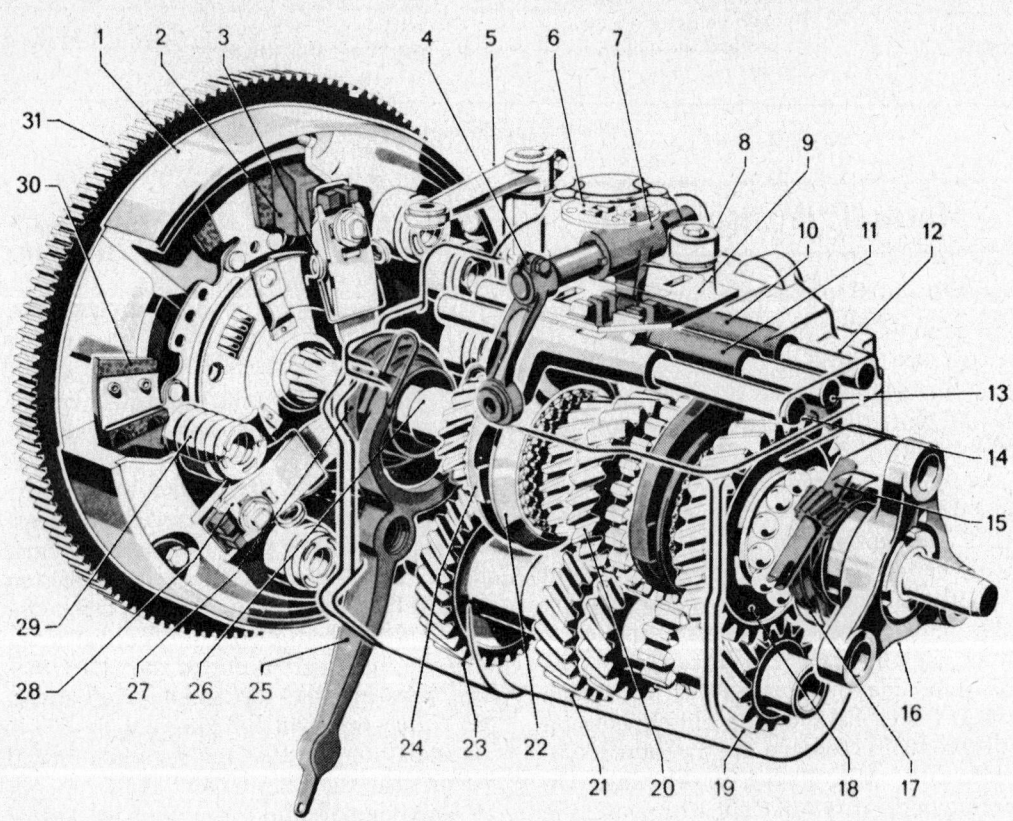

1. Flywheel
2. Clutch pressure plate
3. Spring
4. Lever (for shifter shaft)
5. Selector lever
6. Gate plate
7. Shifter dog
8. Vent
9. Guide plate
10. Shifter head (reverse gear)
11. Shifter fork (1st and 2nd gear)
12. Shifter rod (reverse gear)

13. Shifter rod (1st and 2nd gear)
14. Shifter rod (3rd and 4th gear)
15. Speedometer drive
16. Three-armed flange
17. Helical gear
18. Helical gear (1st gear)
19. Countershaft
20. Helical gear (2nd gear)
21. Countershaft gear (3rd gear)
22. Sliding sleeve (3rd and 4th gear)

23. Countershaft gear (4th gear)
24. Shifter fork (3rd and 4th gear)
25. Release fork
26. Drive shaft
27. Release body (with release bearing)
28. Lever
29. Clutch spring
30. Clutch lining
31. Starter ring gear

Transmission internal parts—top cover model illustrated.

1. Selector rod
2. Shift rod
3. Cover
4. Relay lever
5. Fixing clip
6. Selector lever
7. Flexible speedometer drive
8. Spring-loaded ball connector

Columnshift levers.

1. Shift rod for 1st and 2nd gear
2. Shift rod for 3rd and 4th gear
3. Shift rod for reverse gear
4. Shift lever for reverse gear
5. Flexible speedometer driveshaft
7. Pressure hose for clutch actuation
8. Pressure line for clutch actuation
13. Clamping screws for exhaust pipe support
A. Pressure hose fitting to pressure line

Transmission and clutch linkage must be disconnected.

5. Flexible speedometer drive shaft
6. Clamp screw
7. Pressure hose for clutch mechanism
8. Pressure line for clutch actuating mechanism
9. Propeller shaft bolt
10. Fixing screw for fastening crossmember to chassis base panel
11. Fixing screw for fastening crossmember with rubber mounting to transmission
12. Fixing nuts (covered) for exhaust pipe strut
13. Bolts for exhaust pipe clamping bracket
14. Clamping bracket
A. Pressure hose fitting to pressure line

Crossmember must be unbolted before removing transmission.

1. Pushrod
2. Hexagon nut
3. Pressure pin
4. Hexagon screw
5. Extraction cylinder
6. Bleed screw
7. Rubber cover cap
8. Line
9. Hose
10. Return spring
11. Throwout fork
12. Cuff

Clutch slave cylinder.

is not recommended without some insulation to distribute the load.

Use a 24″ section of pipe on the wrench handle, but don't put full weight on it or the nut might be distorted. CAUTION:

On all Allen-head bolts, use the proper size key with a short extension. Use of too small American keys may round the bolt heads to such a degree that removal without drilling is impossible. Unfortunately,

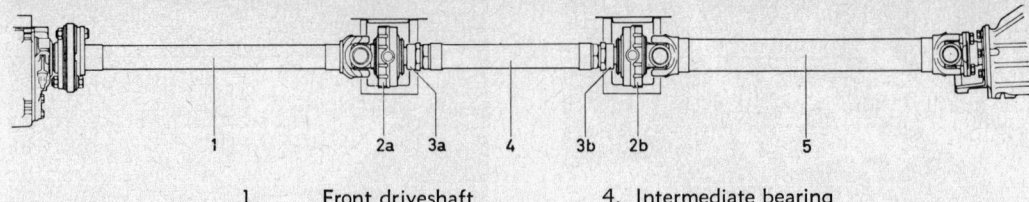

1.   Front driveshaft
2a., 2b. Intermediate bearing
3a., 3b. Clamp nut

4. Intermediate bearing
5. Rear driveshaft

Three-piece driveshaft.

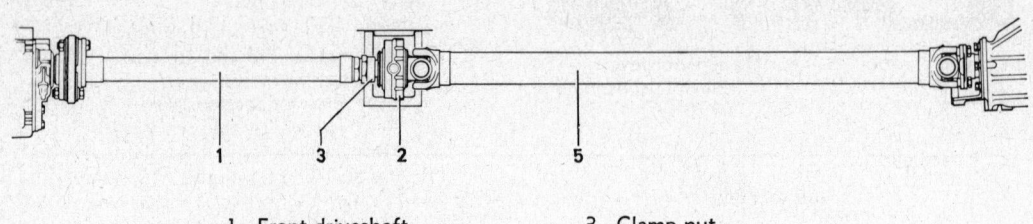

1. Front driveshaft
2. Intermediate bearing

3. Clamp nut
5. Rear driveshaft

Two-piece driveshaft.

Double clamp nuts on driveshaft.

Lowering transmission.

Allen bolts are extremely hard, and almost impossible to drill out with any success if they are in an awkward position. Grinding an oversize American key to fit is O.K. if the grinding is done slowly so as not to destroy the temper of the steel from frictional heating.

Separating Transmission and Bellhousing

The reason for removing both the transmision and bellhousing together is immedi-

1. Shift rod for 1st and 2nd gear
2. Shift rod for 3rd and 4th gear
4. Shift rod for reverse gear

Side cover shift linkage rods.

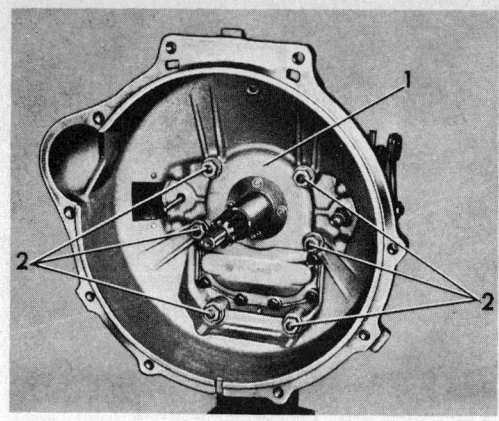

Bolts (2) that secure bellhousing (1) to transmission.

Throwout bearing (1) and fork (2).

Removing throwout fork (2) from ball pin (3).

ally equipped with an automatic transmission quite sensitive to misalignment, therefore the bellhousing was aligned at the factory and stamped with the car engine number for identification. Since the manual transmission-equipped cars used the same bellhousing, it is necessary to use the old bellhousing with any replacement transmission, or it is necessary to realign the new housing.

To remove the housing, pull off the throwout bearing, then the throwout fork. The non-anchored end of the fork must be pulled outward, then to the left to disengage the ball socket pivot. (Directions "A" and "B" in illustrations.) Unscrew the bolts that hold the transmission to the housing, then tap the housing lightly with a fiber hammer to separate it from the transmission nose piece. The housing is easily distorted, so never use a steel hammer.

Transmission Inspection

"Locked-up" transmissions or shifting problems may be caused by defective parts in the shifting mechanism of the transmission itself. After making sure that the shift rods are all in proper adjustment, check the first and second gear shift yoke needle bearings and the shift detent mechanism.

Drain the transmission oil and remove the clamp bolt and reverse shift lever at

ately obvious when the unit is out: the transmission hold-down bolts can be reached only from the inside. Bolt configurations vary slightly with the different models, but, in general, removal procedure is identical. The exception is the 300 SE with manual transmission. This model was usu-

1. Transmission cover
2. Shift lever for 1st and 2nd gear
3. Shift lever for 3rd and 4th gear
4a. Shift lever finger for reverse gear
8. Fixing bolt for detent cage
9. Locking plate
10. Transmission vent
12. Clamp screws

Side shift cover.

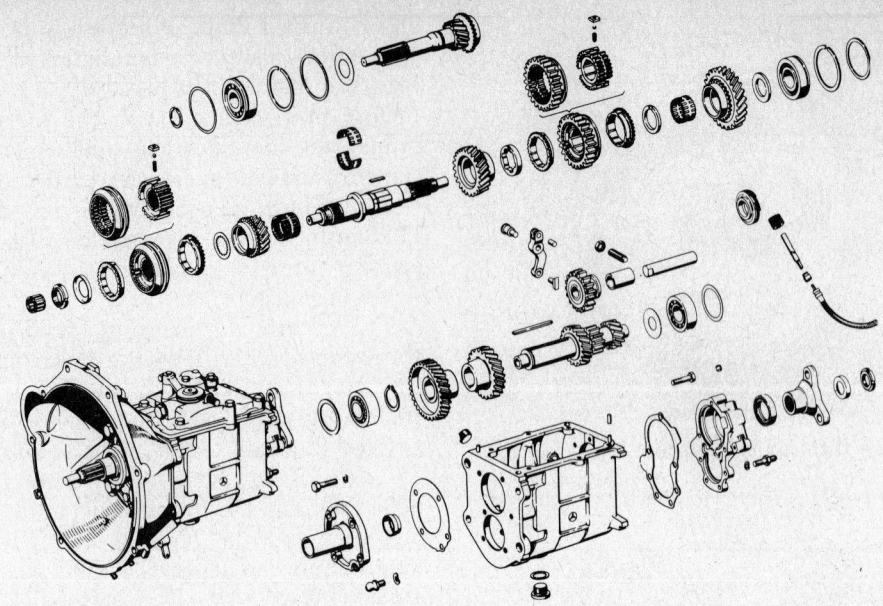

Internal transmission parts—220SEb, 190c, 190Dc, 200, 200D, 230, 300SE, 250S, 250SE, 280S, 280SE, 300SEb, 230SL, 250SL, 280SL.

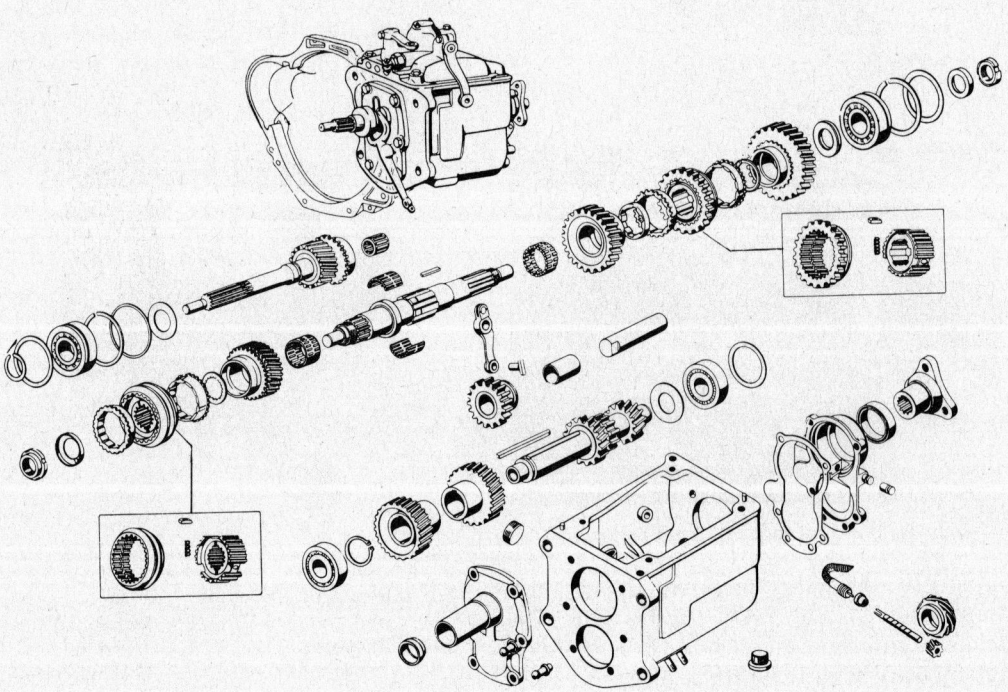

Internal transmission parts—top cover.

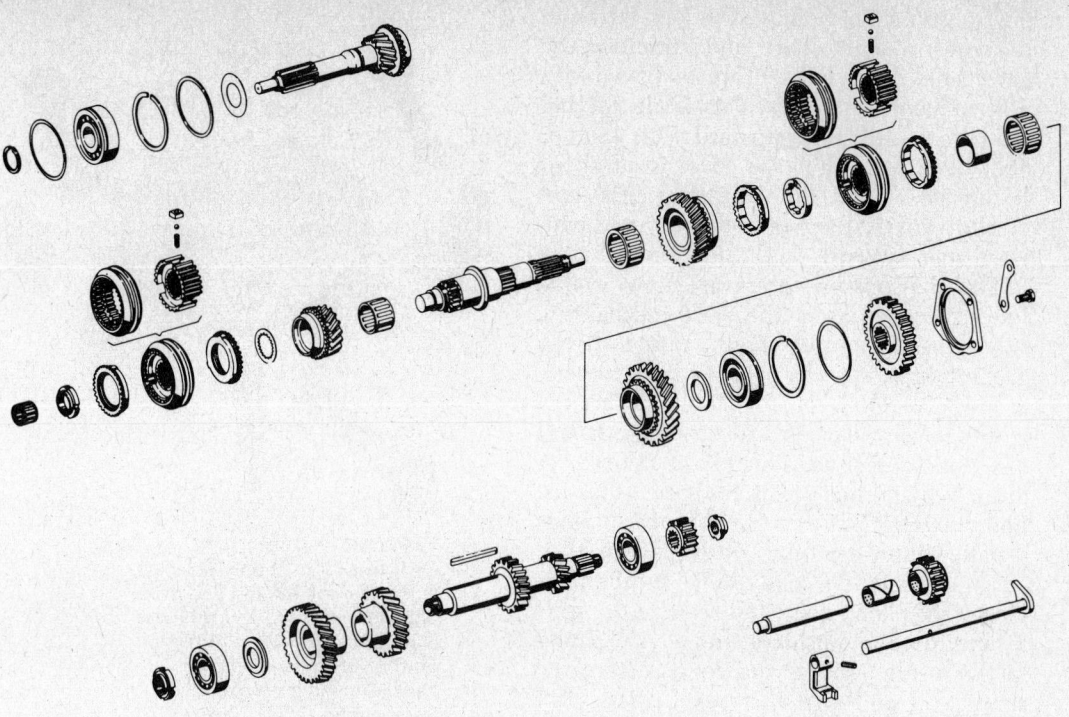

Internal transmission parts—side cover used on phase II models.

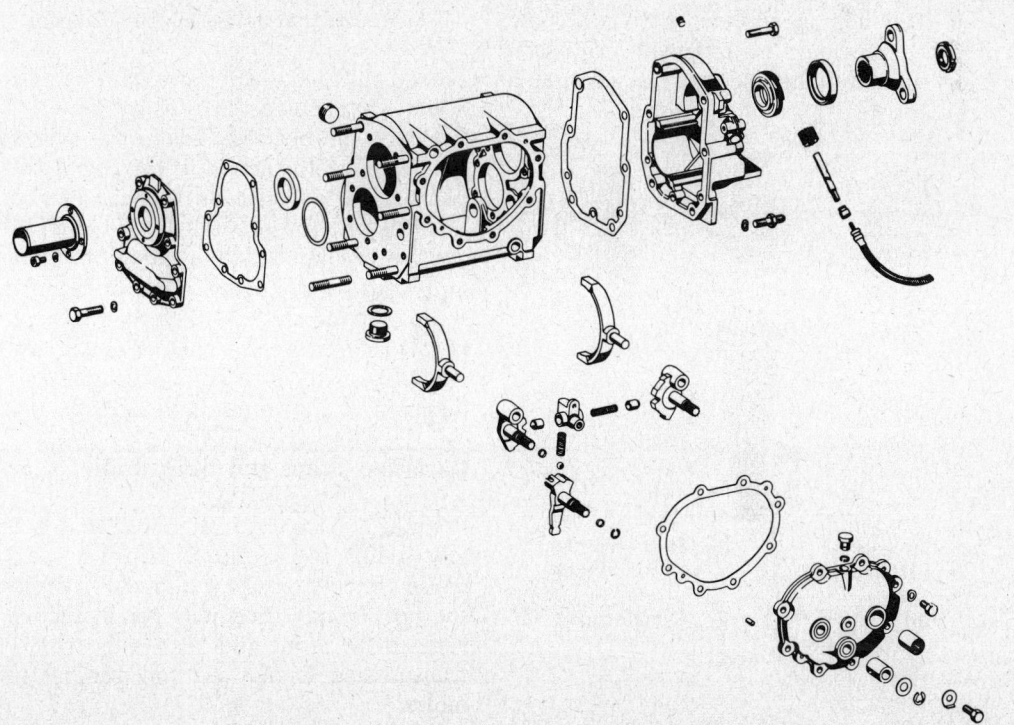

Transmission case—side cover used on phase II models.

the transmission. Remove the lock tab from the reverse shift shaft and unscrew the cover hold-down bolts. Tap the cover with a fiber hammer to loosen it, while driving the reverse shift shaft upward with another fiber hammer. When the cover is off about ¾", reach in and slide the shift forks out of shift yokes, then pull the cover downward and upward.

The transmission gears are now visible for inspection, as is the shift mechanism. When inspecting gear teeth, rotate all the gears to make sure no part has been missed. A chipped tooth is as bad as a broken tooth, for it weakens the entire gear and can lead to transmission failure. Work the gears by hand and check the synchronizers. Badly burred or worn synchronizing rings usually cause "grinding" during shifting.

To disassemble the shift mechanism, loosen the clamp bolts and remove the shift levers from the outside of the cover. Going to the inside, remove the circlips from the shafts and pull out shift yokes (2a) (3a) and the reverse detent lever (4a). Using a screwdriver, bend back the lock tab on bolt (8) and unbolt the detent cage (7) and locating pin. The detent balls should not be scarred and should move in and out easily, although under spring tension. If they are immovable even under pressure, or if they flop in and out with ease, the detent cage should be replaced. The shift yokes then must be checked for wear, as a

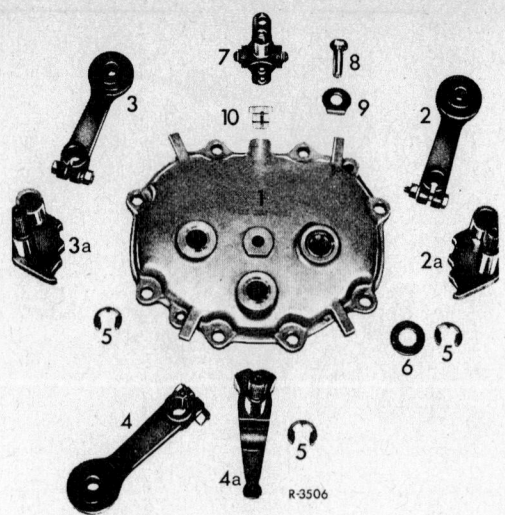

1. Transmission cover
2. Shift lever for 1st and 2nd gear
2a. Shift yoke for 1st and 2nd gear
3. Shift lever for 3rd and 4th gear
3a. Shift yoke for 3rd and 4th gear
4. Shift lever for reverse gear
4a. Shift lever finger for reverse gear
5. Shaft circlip
6. Washer (only for 1st and 2nd gear)
7. Detent cage
8. Fixing screw
9. Locking plate
10. Transmission vent
Note: A taller vent is available to prevent water leaking into transmission.)

Side cover shift linkage and internal parts.

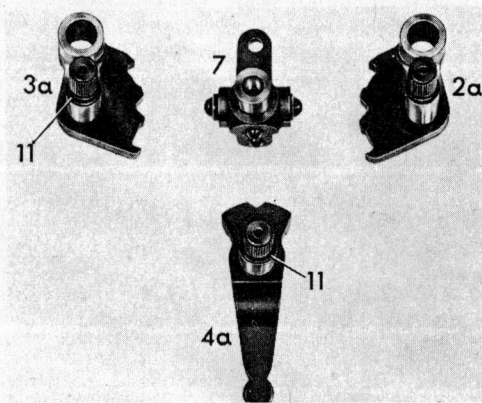

2a. Shift yoke for 1st and 2nd gear
3a. Shift yoke for 3rd and 4th gear
4a. Shift lever finger for reverse gear
7. Detent cage
11. O-ring

Shifter components—side cover (showing detent ball and cage).

burred shift yoke will more than likely ruin a new detent cage in a short time.

Check the bearings where the shift rods pass through the cover. If the caged needle bearings are scored or broken, new ones must be pressed into place. Use of an arbor press is recommended, although some ingenuity and a large bench vise can be utilized in an emergency. Don't forget to replace the O-rings, because they will almost always leak after once being disturbed. Adjustment of the levers is described later.

Replacing Front and Rear Seals

Fluid leaking from the front seal is usually visible in the clutch housing and can cause clutch slippage if allowed to progress too far. In any case, it is good practice to replace the front and rear seals while the transmission is out, just on general principles.

After the clutch housing is removed, un-

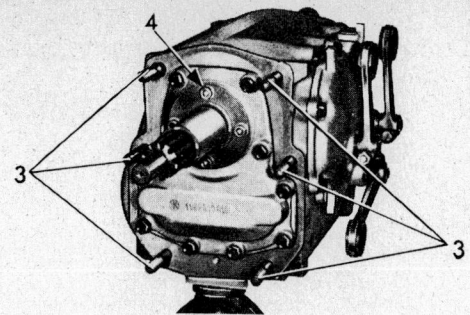

Transmission front cover installed.

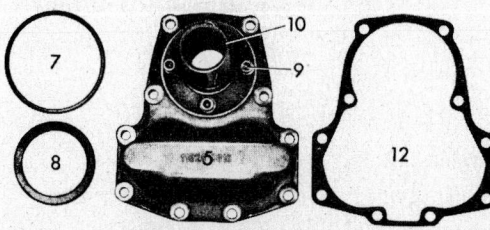

5. Transmission front cover
7. Spacer washer for driveshaft
8. Spacer washer for countershaft
9. Fixing bolts
10. Mounting tube
12. Paper gasket

Transmission front cover removed.

Transmission front cover (5), showing seal (11) and installation tool (10).

7. Spacer washer for driveshaft
8. Spacer washer for countershaft

Front transmission bearings.

screw the front cover bolts and remove the cover. The thrust washers must be replaced in exactly the same position, so note their order when removing.

Unbolt the nose piece from the front cover, then press the old seal out. It is recommended that an arbor press with a 1¾″ adapter be used, but a slide hammer with a screw attachment can be used for this job. It is important, however, that the new seal is *pressed* into the cover, not hammered. The thrust washers can be held in place with wheel bearing grease during installation of the cover. *NOTE: Use non-hardening Permatex on the cover and bolt threads to prevent leaks.*

To remove the rear seal, insert a bar through the rear flange and remove the lock tab and nut. Remove the flange, then remove the cover bolts and cover. The gear train can now be inspected for wear and the seal replaced. *CAUTION: When installing, the reverse shaft must be properly aligned with the keyed portion of the cover or breakage of the cover will result.*

1. Transmission case rear cover
8. Fitting sleeve
9. Seal
10. Paper gasket

Transmission rear cover and gasket.

Rear transmission cover (1) must be aligned with keyed portion of reverse shaft (11) and sleeve (8).

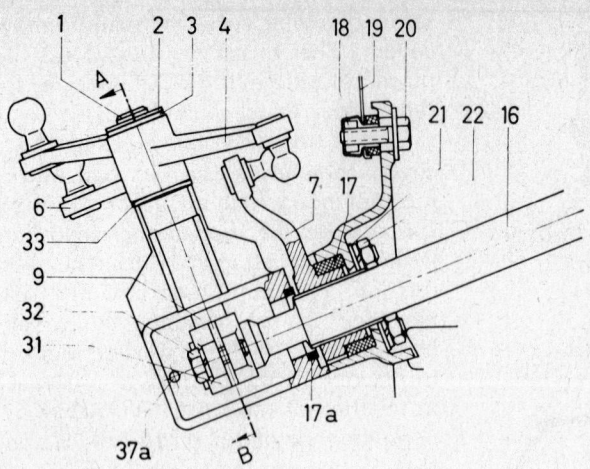

1. Relay lever shaft
2. Snap-ring
3. Washer
4. Relay lever
6. Selector lever
7. Lever on shift tube
9. Selector shaft
16. Shift tube
17. Vulkollan bushing
17a. Spacer ring
18. Cage nut
19. Front panel
20. Hexagon screw with washer
21. Washer
22. Hexagon nut with lockwasher
31. Selector lever on shift tube
32. Hexagon screw (clamp screw)
33. Spring washer
37a. Water outlet bore

Second version columnshift linkage.

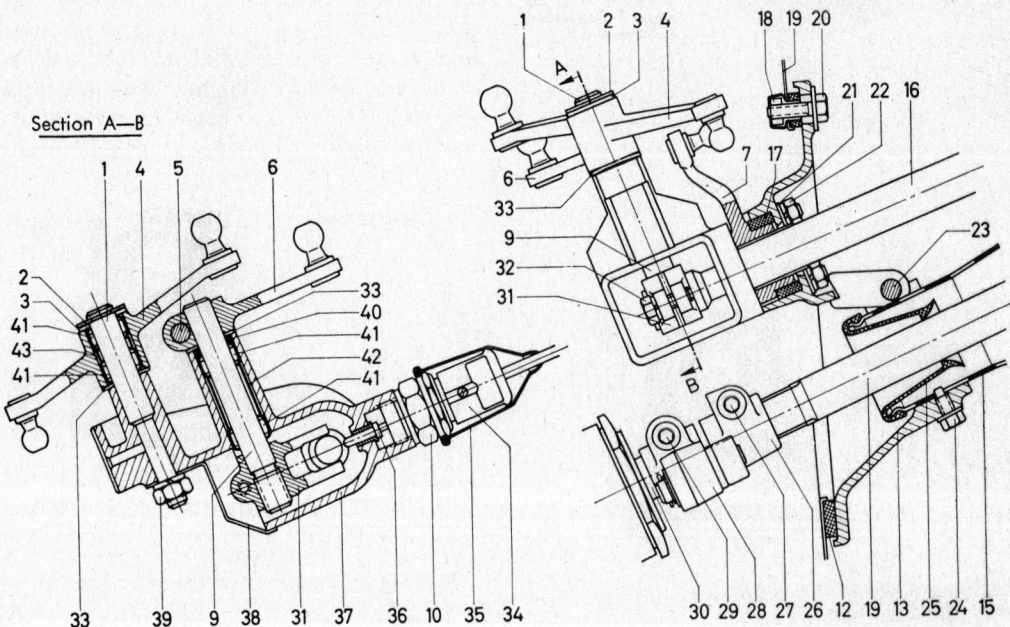

First version columnshift linkage.

1. Relay lever shaft
2. Snap-ring
3. Washer
4. Relay lever
5. Hexagon screw (clamp screw)
6. Selector lever
7. Lever on shift tube
9. Selector shaft
10. Reversing light switch
12. Rubber gasket
13. Cover plate
15. Steering column jacket
16. Shift tube
17. Vulkollan bushing

18. Cage nut
19. Steering tube
20. Hexagon screw with washer
21. Washer
22. Hexagon nut with lockwasher
23. Hexagon screw (clamp screw)
24. Stud screw with lockwasher
25. Rubber sleeve
26. Upper flange
27. Hexagon socket screw
28. Lower flange (clamp screw)
29. Hexagon socket screw (clamp screw)

30. Steering worm
31. Selector lever on shift tube
32. Hexagon screw
33. Spring washer
34. Plug connection
35. Protective cap
36. Pressure pin
37. Bearing assembly
38. Cover
39. Hexagon nut with lock-washer
40. Sealing ring
41. Needle bearing
42. Spacer sleeve
43. Spacer sleeve

Linkage Adjustments—Columnshift

Proper adjustment of the columnshift linkage is dependent on both the position of the levers at the transmission and the length of the shift rods.

TOP COVER TRANSMISSION

Check that the levers are not binding anywhere in their travel, then place the shift lever in neutral and loosen the clamp bolt (5) at the selector lever (6). Then pull the selector lever forward in the direction of travel and pull the relay lever (4) forward by the lower leg. This should engage fourth gear.

Remove the rubber cover on the shift lever at the steering column and have a helper pull the shift lever upward until about .080″ separates the shift tube collar and the recess in the steering tube jacket. Tighten the clamp bolts (5) on the selector lever, preloading the spring washer (33) while doing so.

Now, try shifting through all the gears, using the clutch of course. When engaging reverse, a resistance should be felt. If not, the reverse gear interlock on the top cover probably is weak and a new spring should be installed. When the shift lever is in second or fourth gear, it should vary only

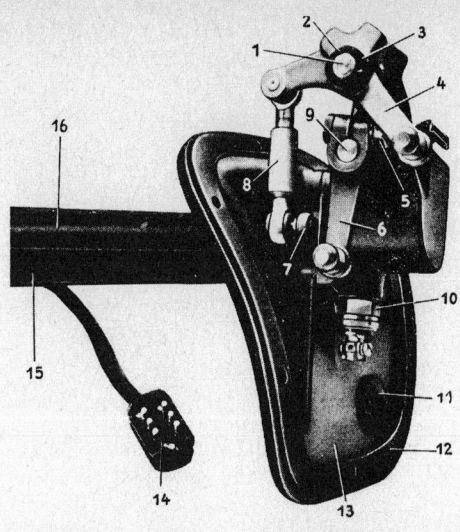

1. Shaft
2. Snap-ring
3. Spring washer
4. Relay lever
5. Hexagon nut
6. Selector lever
7. Lever on shift tube
8. Spring-loaded ball connector
9. Selector shaft
10. Backup light switch
11. Rubber grommet
12. Rubber gasket
13. Cover plate
14. Plug connection
15. Steering column jacket
16. Shift tube

Columnshift lower bearing assembly.

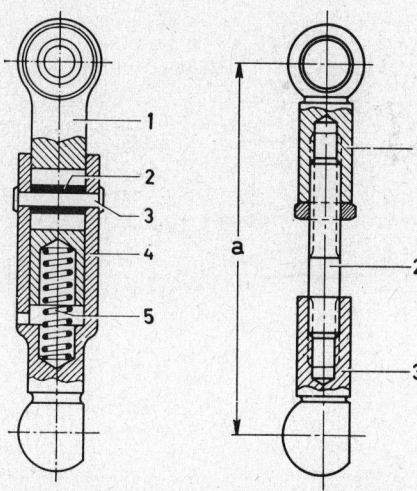

Left	Right
1. Spring-loaded ball connector	1. Ball connector
2. Polyamide bushing	2. Stud bolt
3. Cylindrical pin	3. Ball connector
4. Spring-loaded ball connector (outer part)	a = Adjusting dimension
5. Pressure spring	

Spring-loaded ball connector and new-type connecting rod which replaces it.

1. Shift tube
2. Hexagon nuts for attaching the bearing assembly of the steering wheel shift system
3. Cover plate
4. Cable for reversing light switch
5. Steering column jacket
6. Tightening strap for steering column jacket

Columnshift lower bearing assembly.

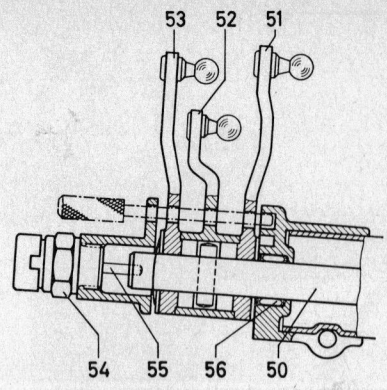

51. Reverse lever
52. 1st and 2nd gear lever
53. 3rd and 4th gear lever

Columnshift levers—phase II models (side cover).

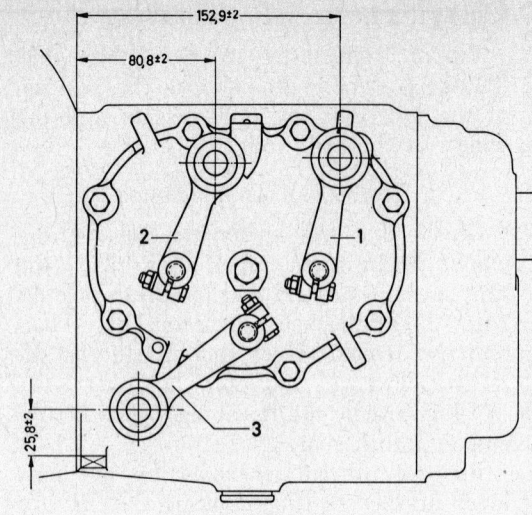

1. 1st and 2nd gear lever
2. 3rd and 4th gear lever
3. Reverse lever

Side cover columnshift transmission levers—phase II models.

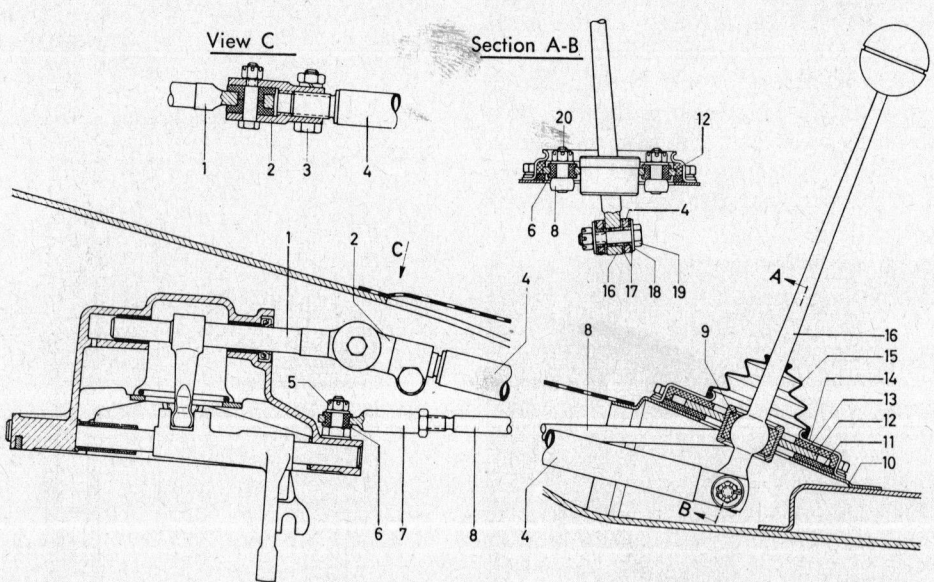

View C   Section A-B

1. Shifting shaft	12. Shift lever bearing
2. Yoke end	12a. Shift lever bearing, new version
3. Hexagon screw	13. Upper bearing cover
4. Shift tube	14. Cover plate 1st version, sheet metal
5. Castle nut	14a. Cover plate 2nd version, vulcollan
6. Bushing	15. Cuff
7. End piece	16. Shift lever
8. Pushrod	17. Bushing
9. Ball socket (vulcollan)	18. Washer
9a. Split ball socket	19. Hexagon screw
9b. Internal circlip	20. Castle nut
9c. Corrugated washer	
10. Transmission tunnel	
11. Lower bearing cover	

2nd Version

Floorshift lever—top cover transmission.

about ⅝″ from the horizontal. Small corrections to this can be made by shortening or lengthening the shift rod.

If shifting is hard, the shift tube (16) may be touching the steering column passage or, in first version units. the lever (7) may be binding in its bearing. To correct the latter condition, loosen the steering column strap (6) (see illustration) and the firewall cover plate and correct any misalignment.

If the selector lever (31) binds in the shift tube (16), it must be removed and checked for straightness. The selector lever dogs may be bent apart or ground down to fit. Grease all the ball sockets and check that the lower bearing assembly at the bottom of the steering column hasn't pulled off its studs.

The spring-loaded ball connector in the bearing assembly often wears and causes hard shifting. Replace it with the newer type connecting rod and adjust length to 67 mm. (2⅝″).

SIDE COVER TRANSMISSION

Check the positioning of the shift levers at the transmission (see illustration) and correct by loosening clamp bolts. The diagram shows the levers in neutral.

Next, go to the lower steering column and lock the three levers by inserting a .2156″ rod (a No. 3 drill will do) through the levers and the hole in the bearing block.

With the shift levers at the lower steering column locked and the levers at the transmission adjusted, try hooking the shift rods into their respective levers. If they are too long or short, adjust their length by loosening the locknuts and turning the ball socket ends. Remove the locking rod and try shifting through the gears. Very slight further adjustments may clear up any binding.

Linkage Adjustments—Floorshift

TOP COVER TRANSMISSION

To adjust, move the shift shaft (1) against the reverse gear stop and engage second gear by actuating the shaft. Then move the shift lever (16) into the first or second gear shifting plane and insert the shift tube (4) into the yoke serrations at least ⅝″ and tighten the clamp bolt. Try

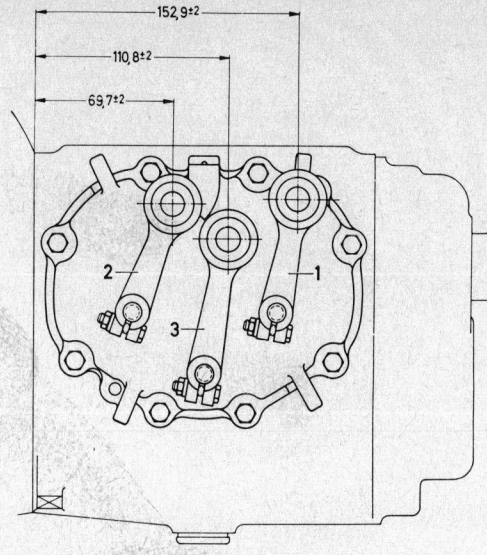

1. 1st and 2nd gear lever
2. 3rd and 4th gear lever
3. Reverse lever

Floorshift transmission levers—phase II (side cover).

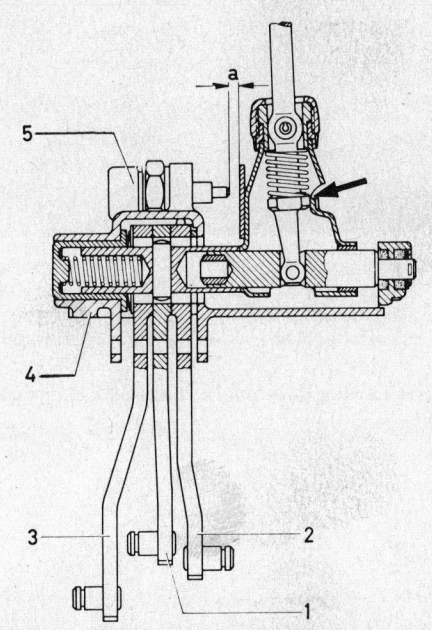

1. Shift lever for 1st and 2nd gear
2. Shift lever for 3rd and 4th gear
3. Shift lever for reverse gear
4. Bearing block
5. Backup light switch
6. Adjusting dimension for reversing light switch, 4±1 mm. – gearshift lever in shifting plane 1st or 2nd gear

Floorshift lever—phase II (side cover).

Diaphragm spring clutch pressure plate.

Clutch hold-down device—300SE models.

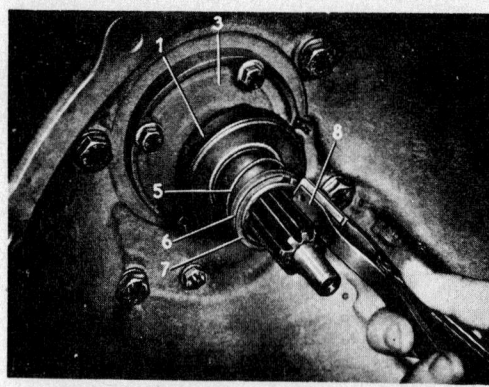

1. Throwout unit with bearing	5. Return spring
	6. Spring retainer
3. Transmission case front cover	7. Snap-ring
	8. Snap-ring pliers

Removing throwout bearing—300SE models.

1. Throwout unit and bearing	3. Transmission case front cover
2. Spring clip	4. Throwout fork

Removing throwout bearing.

shifting through all the gears. If the shift lever hits the bearing (12), adjust both pushrods (8) an *equal* amount.

SIDE COVER TRANSMISSION

The adjustment procedure is the same as that for side cover column shift transmissions, with the exception of the lever positioning at the transmission. The three shift levers and bearing block (where the locking rod is inserted) are found underneath the floor tunnel, which must be removed.

CAUTION: On all types of transmissions, never hammer or force a new shift knob on with the shift lever installed, as the plastic bushing connected to the lever will be destroyed and cause hard shifting.

Clutch

Removal and Installation

To remove the clutch, first remove the transmission and bellhousing. On 300 SE models, place hold-down clamps, or equivalent, as illustrated. Now, loosen the clutch pressure plate hold-down bolts evenly, 1–1½ turns at a time, until tension is relieved. Never remove one bolt at a time, as damage to the pressure plate is possible. Examine the flywheel surface for blue heat marks, scoring or cracks. If the flywheel is to be machined, always machine an equal amount from surfaces "A" and "B" in order to maintain distance "a".

To reinstall, coat splines with high temperature grease and place clutch disc against flywheel, centering it with a clutch

Clutch pilot shaft (1) is necessary for proper alignment during installation.

pilot shaft. A wooden shaft, available at automotive jobbers, is satisfactory, but an old transmission mainshaft works best. Tighten the pressure plate hold-down bolts evenly 1–1½ turns at a time until tight, then remove pilot shaft.

CAUTION: Most clutch plates have the flywheel side marked as such, (Kupplungsseite). Do not assume that the pressure springs always face the transmission, since some do not (e.g., 300 SE, 230, 230 S, 230 SL, 250 S and 250 SE).

Diagnosis

The most common problems with both the coil and diaphragm spring type clutches concern "sticking" or "squealing".

If the clutch pedal itself is not hitting anything, the problem may be in the clutch master cylinder or the hydraulic slave cylinder. Disassemble these units and check

their cylinder walls. Binding is evidenced by shiny, worn spots, and the application of a special grease (available at the dealer) will usually stop the problem. Score marks, however, require cylinder replacement.

To bleed the hydraulic clutch, remove the caps from both the brake and clutch reservoirs and connect a section of hose to a bleed screw on one of the front brake calipers (or drums). Open the bleed screw and pump the brakes in order to fill the hose with fluid. When this is accomplished, connect the hose to the bleed screw on the clutch slave cylinder, open that bleed screw, top up the reservoirs and pump the brakes slowly. As the pedal is pumped, air bubbles should escape from the system, but it is extremely important that the brake fluid reservoir never run dry. If it does, the brakes must be bled as well.

When no more air bubbles come out of the clutch fluid reservoir, close the clutch bleed screw, then the brake bleed screw. Test both pedals for proper operation. If the clutch pedal feels spongy or low, repeat the procedure until all air is evacuated. Remember to top up both brake and clutch reservoirs with a recommended fluid.

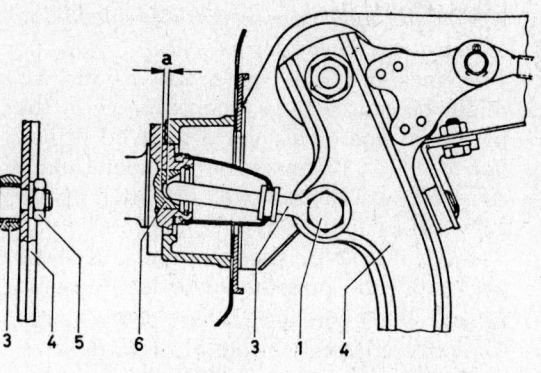

1. Adjusting screw
2. Bushing in piston rod
a = clearance between piston and piston rod
3. Piston rod
4. Clutch pedal
5. Hexagon nut
6. Piston

To adjust clearance between piston pushrod and supply cylinder (outside), loosen hex nut (5), then turn adjusting bolt to give clearance "a" of .008–.020". The clearance cannot be measured, it must be judged by touch. Make sure the mark on the adjusting bolt points toward the pedal pivot pin.

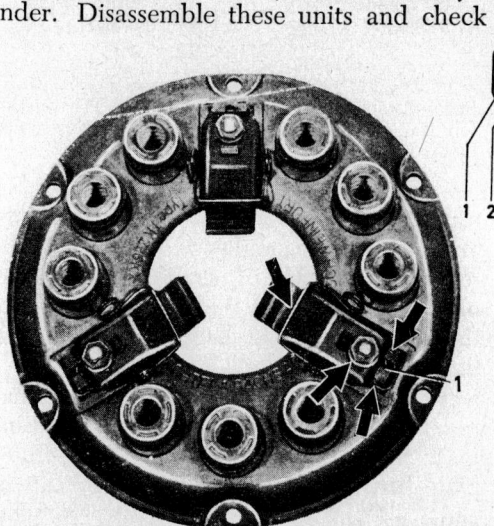

Lubrication points on coil spring clutch pressure plate.

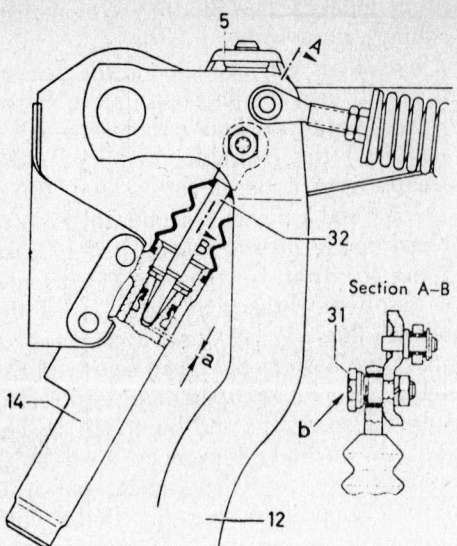

1. Pushrod   8. Line from supply
2. Hexagon nut   cylinder
3. Pressure pin   9. Pressure hose
4. Hexagon screw   10. Return spring
5. Extraction cylinder   11. Throwout fork
6. Bleed screw   12. Cuff
7. Protective cap

First version clutch slave cylinder. The pushrod length can be adjusted by removing the spring and loosening the locknut.

5. Rubber stop for   nut and lock-
   clutch pedal   washer
12. Clutch pedal   32. Piston rod
14. Supply cylinder   a = Clearance between
31. Adjusting screw   piston and pis-
    with hexagon   ton rod
                         b = Line marking

Inside clutch supply cylinder. Clearance is adjusted in the same way as for outside cylinder, except that the mark on the adjusting bolt must point toward the rear.

1. Pushrod   8. Line from supply
4. Stud screw   cylinder
5. Extraction cylinder   9. Pressure hose
6. Bleed screw   10. Return spring
7. Protective cap   11. Throwout fork
                                  12. Cuff

Second version clutch slave cylinder. The pushrod length can be adjusted in the same way as for the first version cylinder.

NOTE: It may be necessary to bleed the clutch master cylinder as well.

A sticking pedal on a 250 S—300 SE might be caused by a blocked valve in the hydraulic line. This valve may be drilled out to 0.118″ (3 mm.), but all metal chips must be carefully removed or clutch operation will be impaired.

Squealing and sticking may also be caused by the pressure plate lugs binding against the openings in the cover plate. The arrowed points in the illustration show the lubrication points. Use Molykote paste on these areas, as well as on the throwout bearing surface and transmission nose piece. If lubrication does not stop the noise, filling the affected parts is O.K. if too much material is not removed.

The normal adjustment of the pedal over-center spring is 2.64″ (67 mm.). Increasing this to 2.83″ (72 mm.) also helps alleviate sticking. The reason for clutch slippage is usually pretty easy to spot—oil on the clutch plate. This can be either transmission oil from a leaking front transmission seal, or engine oil from a leaking rear main bearing oil seal. Never just replace the disc; find the leak and fix it or the new clutch will be ruined in a short time.

A clutch worn down near the rivets must be replaced or flywheel and/or pressure plate damage is certain. Check the clutch plate linings for looseness. If they can be slid back and forth on the rivets, the plate must be discarded no matter how little wear is in evidence.

Driven Plate

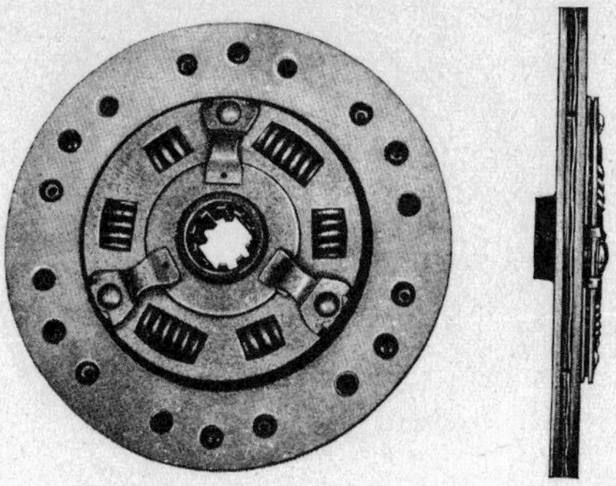

Pressure Plate

Models 190 c,
190 Dc, 200
and 200 D

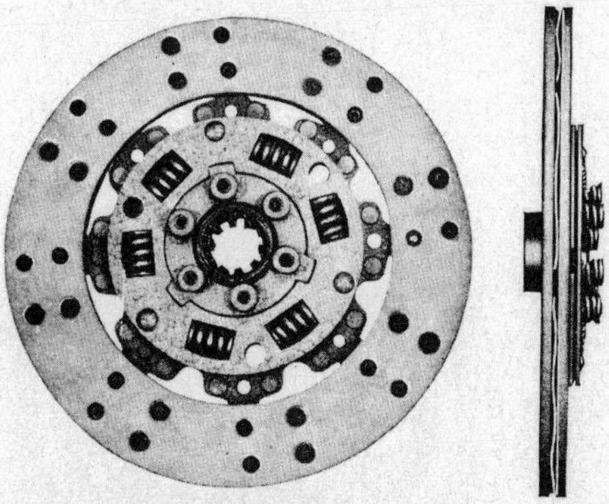

Models 220 b,
220 Sb
and 220 SEb

with single
spring-loaded
facing

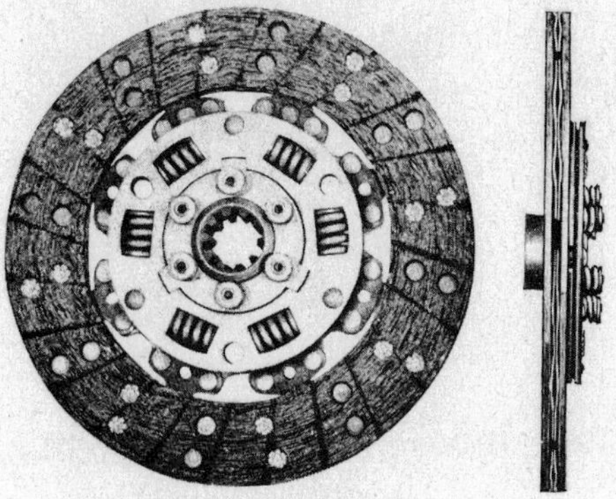

Models 220 b,
220 Sb, 220 SEb
and 230 SL

with double
spring-loaded
facing

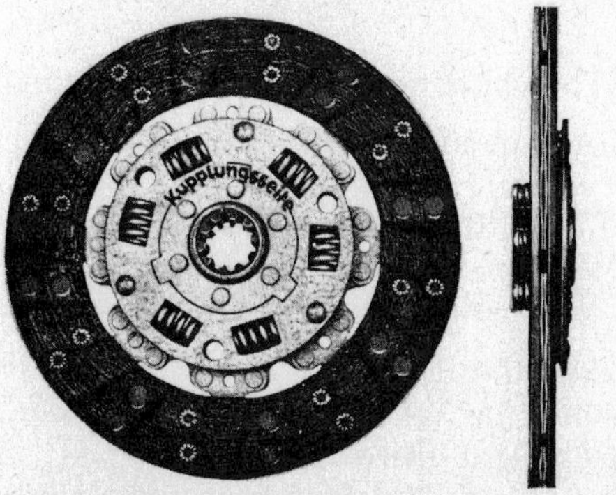

Models 230,
230 S, 250 S,
250 SE and
230 SL

with double
spring-loaded
facing

1 Sheet-metal ring for better engine speed adaptability

Clutch types used in various models.

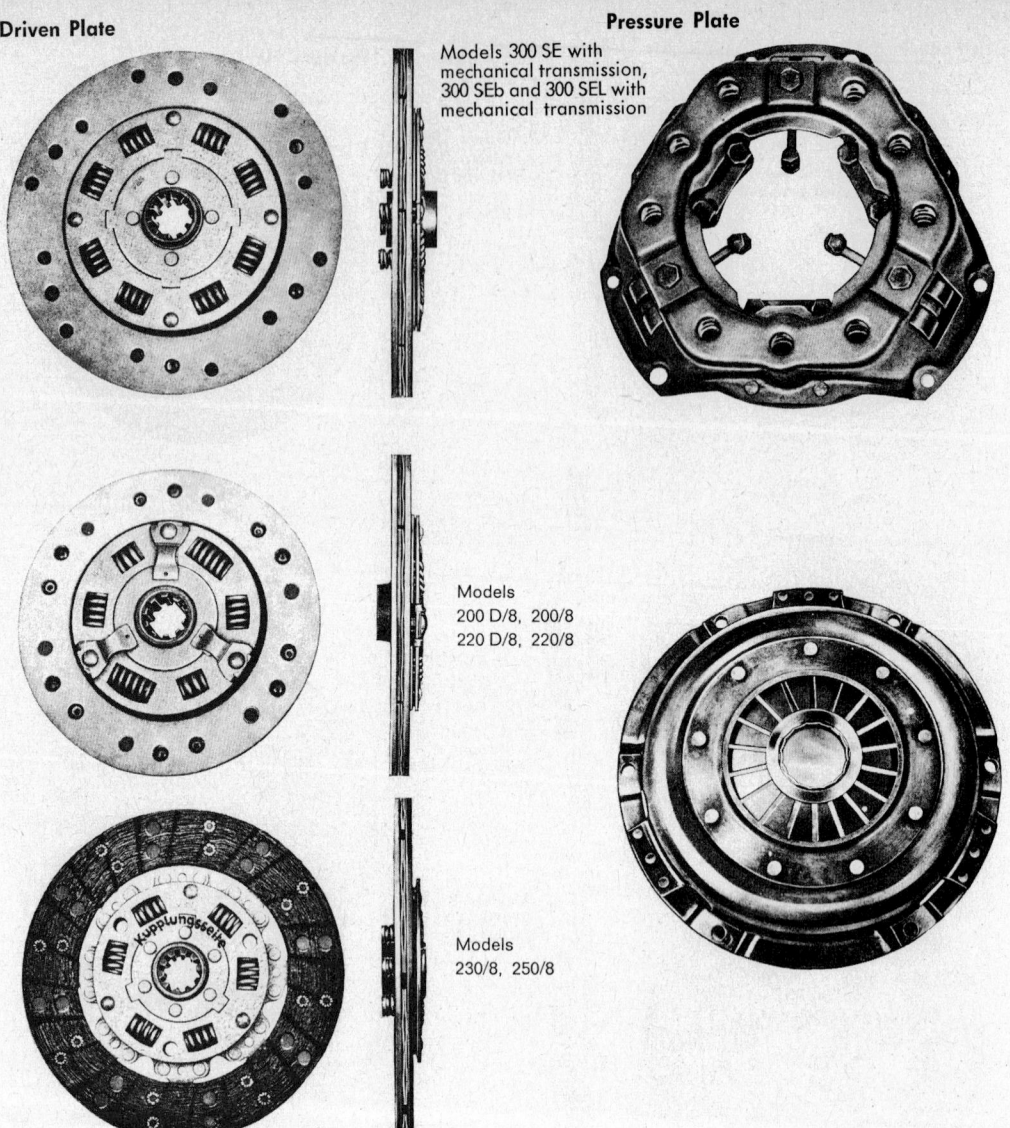

Driven Plate

Pressure Plate

Models 300 SE with mechanical transmission, 300 SEb and 300 SEL with mechanical transmission

Models 200 D/8, 200/8 220 D/8, 220/8

Models 230/8, 250/8

Clutch types used in various models.

Hydraulic Automatic (Hydrak) Clutch

Operation

This type of clutch is an interim step between a straight mechanical set-up and an automatic transmission. It is similar in operation to some Chrysler Corporation units of the early fifties and the Volkswagen automatic stickshift.

The clutch consists of four main groups:

1. A hydraulic coupling (i.e. torque converter).
2. A conventional clutch.
3. A servo assembly for operating clutch.
4. A servo control unit.

Actually, the car is driven in the same manner as a standard transmission car except that there is no clutch pedal and the car may be left in gear while idling.

When the shift lever is touched, an electrical circuit is actuated that operates

Hydrak Hydraulic Automatic Clutch Diagnosis

Condition	Probable Cause	Correction
Slow acceleration, engine races during shifting	1. Insufficient oil in torque converter. 2. Driven plate of clutch oily.	1. Check stall speed and refill. 2. Replace driven clutch plate.
Clutch slips too long after shifting	1. Coasting—adjusting screw on reducing valve screwed in too far. 2. With accelerator pedal depressed—adjusting screw on rear axle switch screwed in too far. 3. With accelerator pedal partly depressed—spring-loaded diaphragm incorrectly adjusted.	1. Adjust control element. 2. Adjust rear axle switch. 3. Replace control element.
Coasting downshift too harsh	1. Adjusting screw on reducing valve unscrewed too far.	1. Adjust control element.
Shifting harsh during acceleration	1. Rear axle switch adjusting screw unscrewed too far. 2. Defective rear axle switch. 3. Limit switch in servo jammed "off".	1. Adjust rear axle switch. 2. Replace rear axle switch. 3. Free up or replace switch.
Intermittent harsh shifting (down-shift)	1. Reducing valve plugged or dirt at valve head.	1. Remove and clean valve.
Clutch slips under acceleration or on hills	1. Driven plate of clutch oily. 2. Servo pull rod incorrectly adjusted.	1. Replace driven clutch plate. 2. Adjust pull rod.
Driven clutch plate continues spinning at idle speed	1. Driven plate hub jammed in splines. 2. Broken or warped linings on clutch plate. 3. Defective needle bearing in Hydrak unit.	1. Free up and install new driven plate if necessary. 2. Replace clutch driven plate. 3. Replace Hydrak unit.
Clutch does not disengage during shifting	1. Servo pull rod incorrectly adjusted. 2. Lines leaking; supply cylinder leaking. 3. Bellows in servo defective. 4. Needle bearing in Hydrak unit broken. 5. Broken electrical circuit. 6. Shift lever switch contacts burned or corroded. 7. Control valve electromagnet defective.	1. Adjust pull rod. 2. Repair leak. 3. Replace servo assembly. 4. Replace Hydrak unit. 5. Trace circuit and repair break. 6. Clean contact points in switch. 7. Replace electromagnet.
Clutch does not engage after shift.	1. Contact of shift lever switch sticking.	1. Clean contact points in switch and adjust switch.

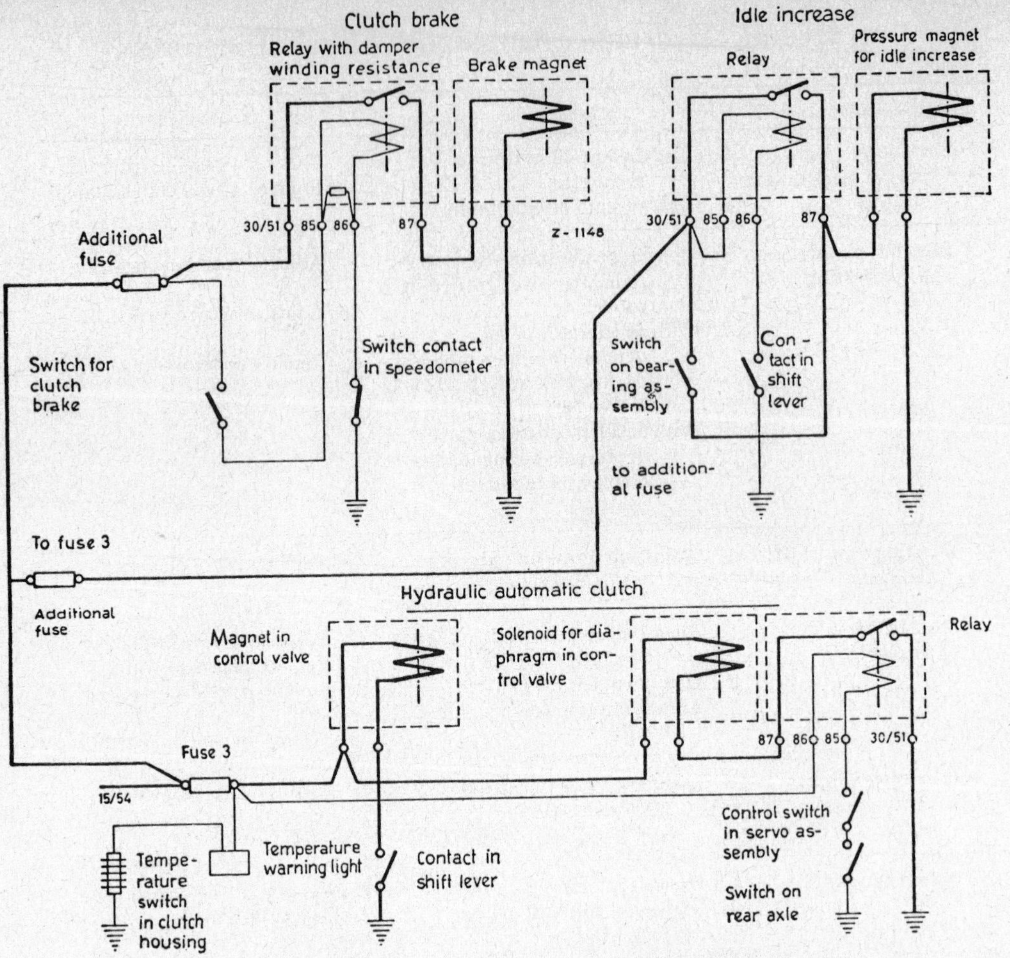

Clutch brake

Relay with damper winding resistance   Brake magnet

Idle increase

Relay   Pressure magnet for idle increase

30/51   85   86   87   Z-1148   30/51   85   86   87

Additional fuse

Switch for clutch brake

Switch contact in speedometer

Switch on bearing assembly

Contact in shift lever

to additional fuse

To fuse 3

Additional fuse

Hydraulic automatic clutch

Magnet in control valve

Solenoid for diaphragm in control valve

Relay

87   86   85   30/51

Fuse 3

15/54

Temperature switch in clutch housing

Temperature warning light

Contact in shift lever

Control switch in servo assembly

Switch on rear axle

Electrical circuits—220SE Hydrak clutch.

the clutch servo through a control valve. All this valve does is open one side of the servo diaphragm to manifold vacuum, leaving the other side exposed to normal 14.7 psi atmospheric pressure. The resultant movement of the diaphragm is transmitted mechanically to a normal clutch throwout arm to release the clutch. To overcome one of the hazards of this type system, a free-wheeling device automatically locks the engine and differential together during coasting, thus allowing the driver to use engine compression for slowing down, as well as allowing the car to be pushstarted.

The torque converter consists of two units, the primary unit, which is bolted to the crankshaft, and the secondary unit, to which the clutch and transmission is attached. The power loss through the coupling is negligible for all practical purposes, being around 2%.

1. Screw plug
2. Hydraulic coupling
3. Mechanical clutch

KFX 12 Hydrak clutch unit.

1. Cover plate with temperature switch
2. Cover plate
3. Clutch brake

Underside of Hydrak clutch husing.

1. Cover plate
2. Cover plate for cooling air inlet
3. Clutch brake
4. Cable connection at clutch brake
5. Clutch housing
6. Jointing flange
7. Cover plate for cooling air outlet

Underside of Hydrak clutch installed in 220SE.

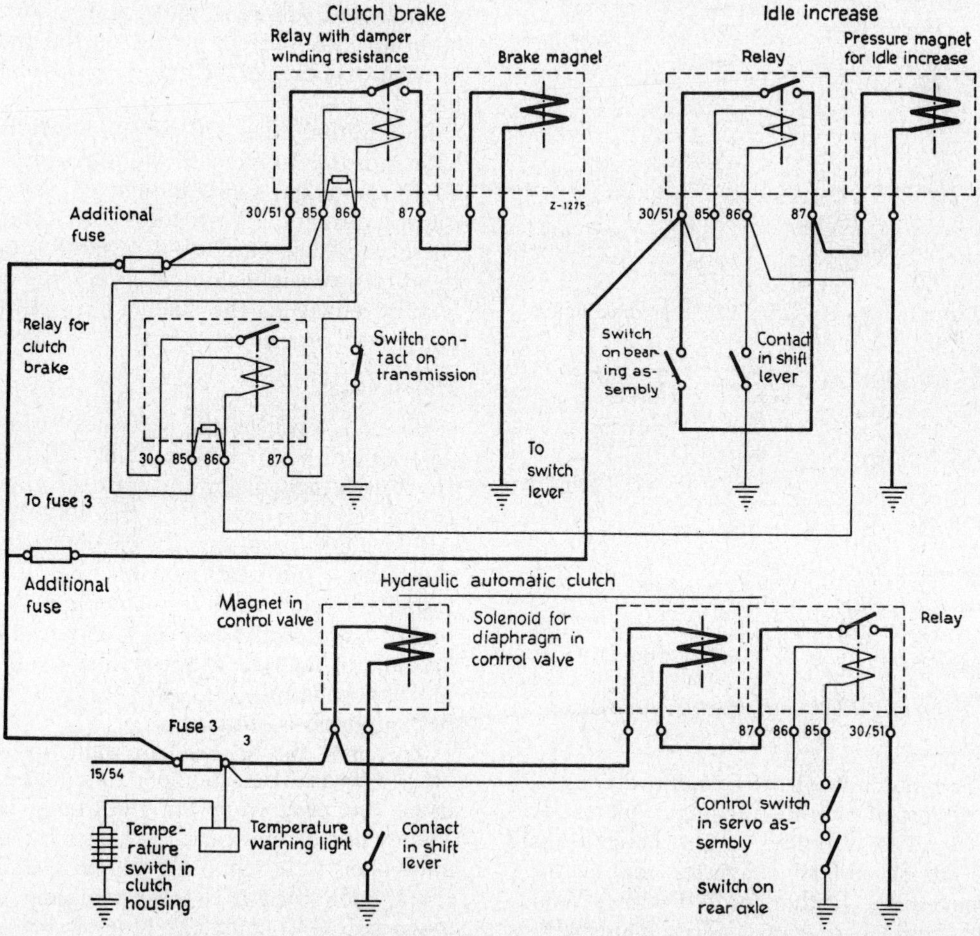

Electrical circuits—220SEb Hydrak clutch.

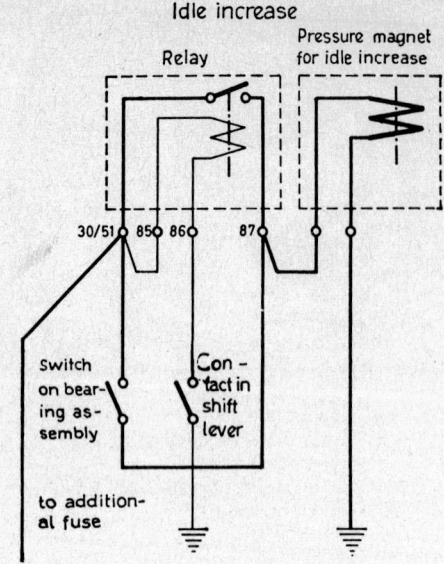

Idle speed circuit.

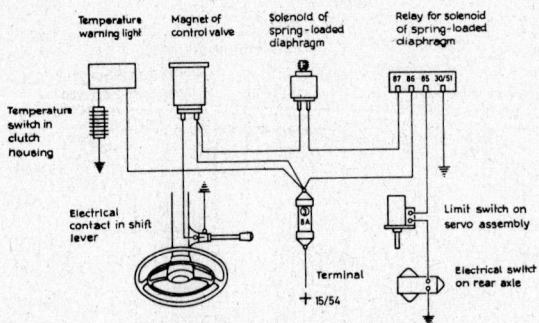

Electrical circuits—220b, 220Sb Hydrak clutch.

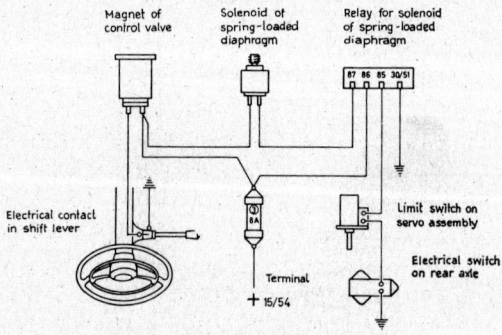

Electrical circuits—219, 220S, Hydrak clutch.

The clutch itself consists of a drive plate, a driven plate and a contact plate. The drive plate is bolted to the flanged shaft of the secondary converter unit with a grooved nut, further located with a Woodruff key. The transmission mainshaft is centered in two needle-type pilot bearings in the shaft of the secondary converter unit.

The clutch housing has a temperature controlled flap that allows cooling air to circulate when the coupling oil temperature reaches about 180° C. (356° F.).

The servo assembly is pretty straight-forward; a limit switch on the servo breaks the circuit to the control element solenoid when the clutch is engaged. In addition, the control element is influenced by a switch on the rear axle via a relay.

The 220 SE and SEb, the last models to have the Hydrak clutch, had a larger clutch plate to handle the additional power of their fuel-injected engines. In order to eliminate rough engagement on starting, with attendant chattering, an electric brake located on the clutch housing serves to stop the disc as soon as the gearshift lever is touched. To make sure the clutch brake is never actuated except when stopped or creeping slowly, an additional switch in the speedometer breaks the circuit to the unit at speeds above 5 mph. The 220 SEb has a somewhat different setup, and above 5 mph an eddy current switch on the transmission case breaks the circuit to the clutch brake.

In addition, the 220 SE and 220 SEb have a device to increase the idle speed by 40–60 rpm when a gear is engaged. Touching the gearshift lever causes a solenoid to energize which, through a pushrod, opens the throttle a slight amount. When the gear is fully engaged, the solenoid deactivates and speed returns to normal.

Maintenance

The oil level in the converter can be determined by making a stall speed test. Hook up a tachometer and start the engine. If the oil level is correct, the stall speed will be 1,600–1,800 rpm for carbureted versions and 1,750–1,950 rpm for 220 SE and 220 SEb models. The test is made with the brakes on, fourth gear engaged and the accelerator floored. If the stall speed is too high, there is too little oil in the converter or the clutch is slipping.

To check the oil level or refill the unit, lift the carpet from the floor tunnel and remove the plug from the right-hand side. The engine should be turned over by hand until one of the coupling plugs is visible. It's a good idea to let the coupling cool down before opening the plug, as pressure build-up may force a stream of hot oil out the hole. Always replace the gaskets and torque to no more than 21 ft.-lbs. The filling capacity is 1.5 liters ATF Type A.

The cooling air cover plates should be cleaned every 5,000 miles at least, because a blocked plate will cause the converter to overheat badly.

Adjustments

CLUTCH FREE-PLAY

Measured at the pull rod, the free-play should be .39"–.47" for the 220 S, .23"–.31" for the 220 b, 220 Sb, 220 SE, and 220 SEb. On the 220 SE, only the long pull rod may be adjusted.

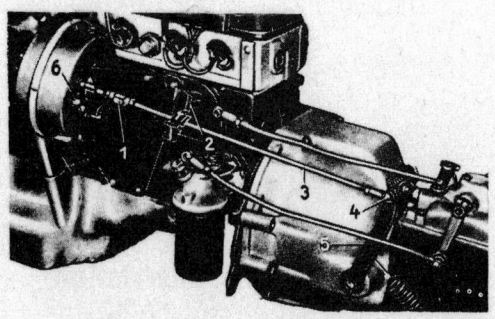

1. Turnbuckle
2. Adjusting clamps
   (180 589 12 23)
   for adjusting the
   free-play
3. Pull rod
4. Connector head
5. Throwout lever
6. Limit switch

Hydrak linkage as installed on 219 and 220S.

1. Relay
2. Threaded ring
3. Screw plug
4. Adjusting screw
   and locknut
5. Hose to servo
   assembly
6. Hose to vacuum
   supply reservoir
7. Screw plug
8. Servo assembly
9. Control element
10. Vacuum tube from
   intake manifold

Control element installation–220SE.

CONTROL ELEMENT

The control element can be adjusted to regulate the "harshness" of the shift by turning screw (2). Screwing inward makes shifting smoother and screwing outward roughens the shift. If shifting is irregular in spite of adjustment, there could be dirt in the reducing valve (18).

To disassemble, unscrew the threaded lock ring and carefully remove the spring (6), damper sleeve (4), damper weight (5) and the valve head.

ELECTRICAL SWITCH AT REAR AXLE

Remove the cover plate from inside the trunk. With the car level, the handbrake released and the shift lever in neutral, hook a test light between the positive battery terminal and the "+" terminal of the switch.

Adjust the spring-loaded screw until the light just comes on. Backing the screw out causes harsher shifts, and vice-versa.

Switches with longer transmission arms ("B" in illustration) require a further screw adjustment of ½–¾ turn inward after the light comes on.

SHIFT LEVER SWITCH

Connect a test light between the positive battery terminal and the black wire at the control element solenoid. Loosen the locknut and screw the cover cap in until the two contacts touch and the light comes on. Back the cap off to give .008"–.012" (.2–.3 mm.) clearance.

CLUTCH BRAKE

Using a protractor and a piece of heavy cardboad, make a gauge and pointer similar to the one illustrated. Press the gauge onto the relay lever, then unscrew the grease fitting and attach the pointer.

Push either the short or long pushrod forward until the throwout bearing contacts the clutch. Zero the gauge and pointer and detach the long pull rod. Connect a test light between the clutch brake switch and ground, then move the relay lever (2) forward until the pointer is opposite the 11° mark on the gauge (that is, the pointer moves through 11° of arc). At this point, the test light should come on. If not, adjust the switch bracket—forward if the brake engages early, rearward if it engages late.

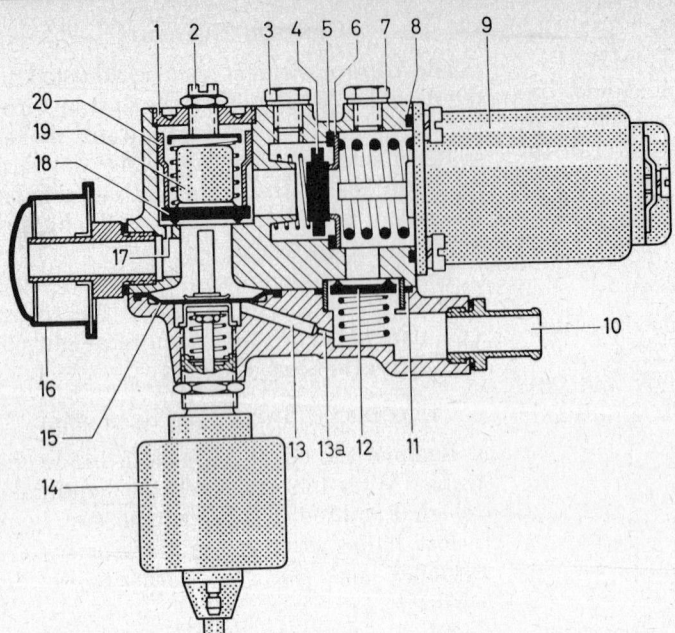

1. Threaded ring
2. Adjusting screw with lock-nut
3. Screw plug
4. Control valve
5. Rubber washer
6. Valve head
7. Screw plug
8. Rubber washer
9. Electromagnet for control valve
10. Vacuum union for intake manifold
11. Rubber washer
12. Check valve
13. Vacuum canal
13a. Throttle in vacuum canal
14. Solenoid for spring-loaded diaphragm
15. Spring-loaded diaphragm
16. Air cleaner
17. Jet in reducing valve
18. Reducing valve
19. Damper weight
20. Damper sleeve

Control element.

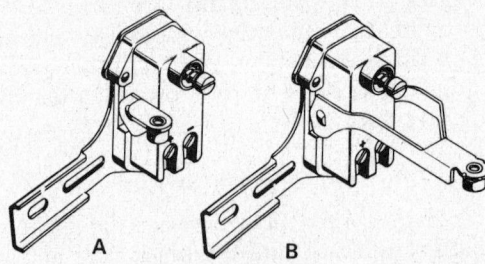

Rear axle switches.

Automatic Transmission

Due to the complexity of this automatic transmission, and the special tools needed for any practical service, it is recommended that any work other than simple adjustment of the shift linkage be done by an authorized Mercedes-Benz dealer.

Even such a job as removal and replacement requires a special jack, and hydraulic

1. Bearing for relay lever
2. Relay lever
3. Pinion rim grease fitting
4. Graduated disc
5. Turnbuckle
6. Long pull rod
7. Spring for the switch of the clutch brake
8. Pointer
9. Short pull rod

Adjusting linkage.

1. Bearing for relay lever
2. Long pull rod
3. Turnbuckle
4. Relay lever
5. Spring for clutch brake switch
6. Short pull rod
7. Bracket for servo assembly
8. Servo assembly

Linkage as installed on 220SE.

pressure testing and troubleshooting require instruments not easily obtainable.

Shift Linkage Adjustment—Columnshift

With the full weight of the car on its suspension, remove shift rod (7) and set the range selector lever (at transmission) and gearshift lever in neutral. The shift rod (7) should be exactly the right length so that it fits on the ball sockets at inter-

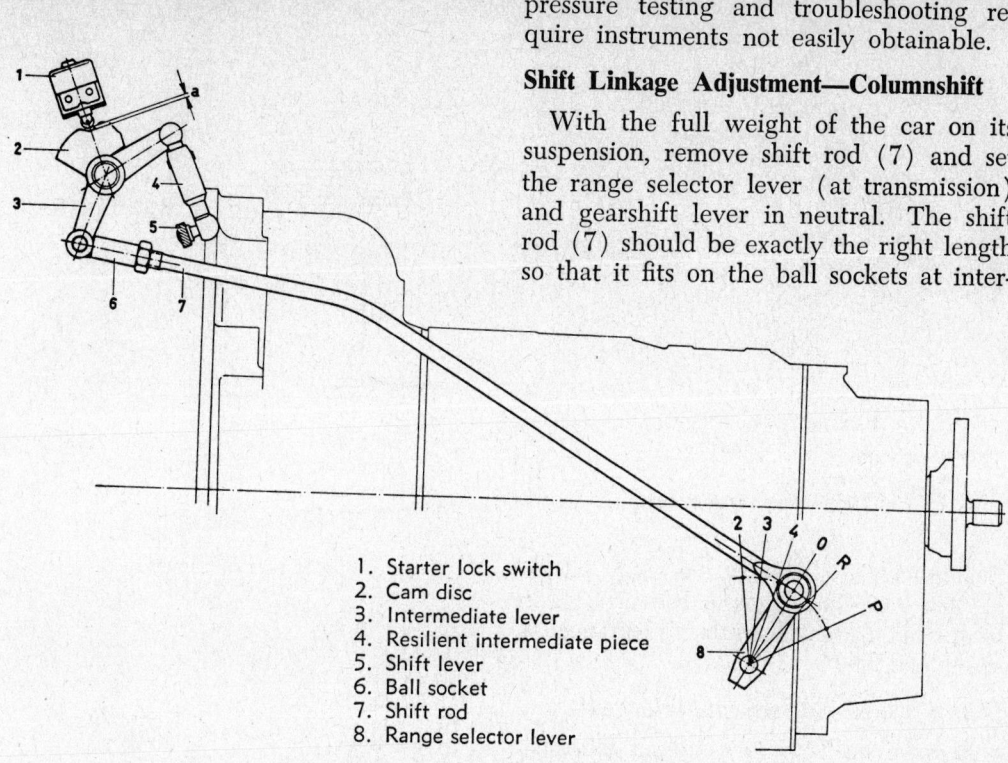

1. Starter lock switch
2. Cam disc
3. Intermediate lever
4. Resilient intermediate piece
5. Shift lever
6. Ball socket
7. Shift rod
8. Range selector lever

Automatic transmission columnshift linkage.

1. Selector lever
2. Selector lever bottom section
3. Adjusting lug
4. Shift rod
5. Additional lever
6. Range selector lever
7. Cable pulls
8. Adjusting stop
9. Starter lock and back up light switch

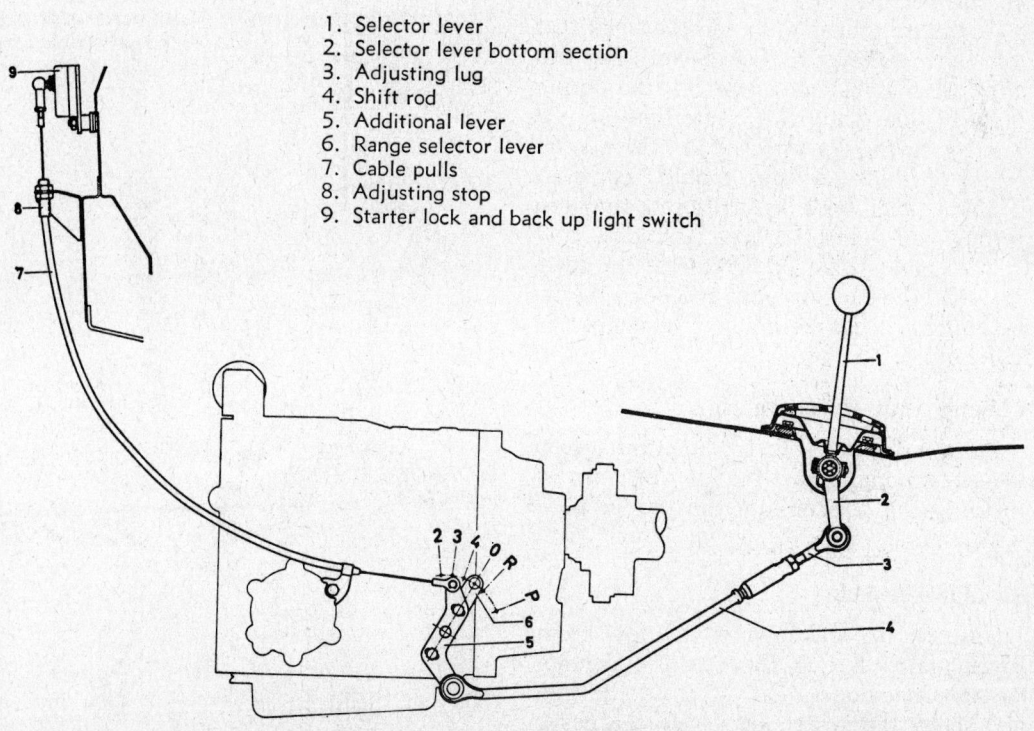

Automatic transmission floorshift linkage.

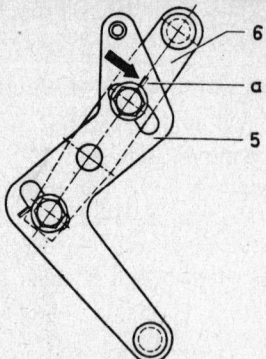

5. Additional lever
6. Range selector lever
▲ Adjusting mark

Additional lever arrangement.

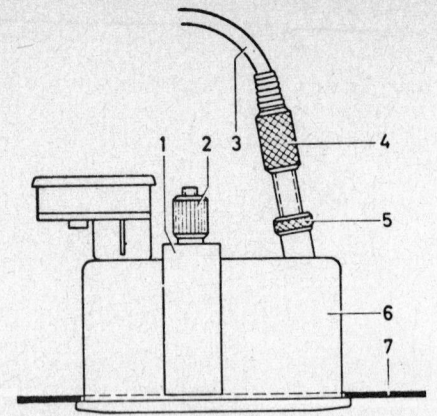

1. Clamp   5. Locknut
2. Clamp nut   6. Housing
3. Bowden cable   7. Instrument panel
4. Knurled nut

Adjusting selector lever pointer.

mediate lever (3) and lever (8) without any tension. On models with neutral safety switch set up as illustrated, clearance "a" should be .040".

Shift Linkage Adjustment—Floorshift

Remove shift rod (4) and set the range selector lever (6) and the gearshift lever (1) in neutral. There should be about .040" play between the lever and the sleeve neutral detent.

At the transmission, loosen the bolts that told the extra lever to the selector lever and align the adjusting mark on the upper oblong hole with the centerline of the selector lever. On the 230 SL, the center-lines of both levers should coincide. Tighten bolts, hook up shift rod, and test through all gearshift lever positions.

The cable attached to the extra lever operated the back-up light and neutral safe-ty switch. It can be adjusted at point (8) if required.

Column Shift Range Indicator

Place the gearshift lever in neutral, loosen locknut (5) and adjust the knurled nut (4) to bring the pointer into the proper posi-tion.

Kickdown Switch

Unscrew the kickdown switch (4) from cover plate (2) on the steering column jacket. Check operation of throttle linkage and screw the switch back into the cover plate until the throttle valve lever is 3/16" from the full-load stop screw (2) when the

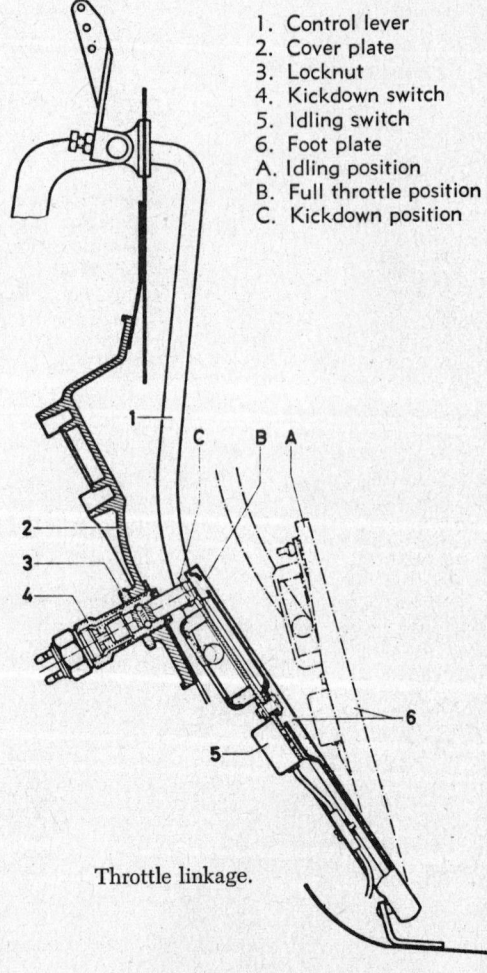

1. Control lever
2. Cover plate
3. Locknut
4. Kickdown switch
5. Idling switch
6. Foot plate
A. Idling position
B. Full throttle position
C. Kickdown position

Throttle linkage.

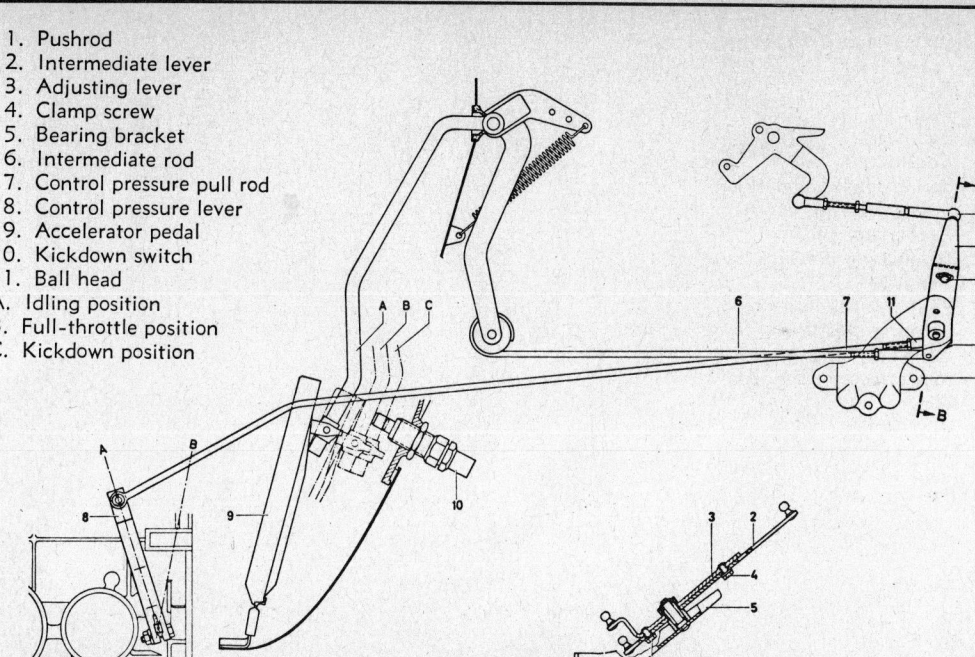

1. Pushrod
2. Intermediate lever
3. Adjusting lever
4. Clamp screw
5. Bearing bracket
6. Intermediate rod
7. Control pressure pull rod
8. Control pressure lever
9. Accelerator pedal
10. Kickdown switch
11. Ball head
A. Idling position
B. Full-throttle position
C. Kickdown position

Throttle rod (control pressure) linkage.

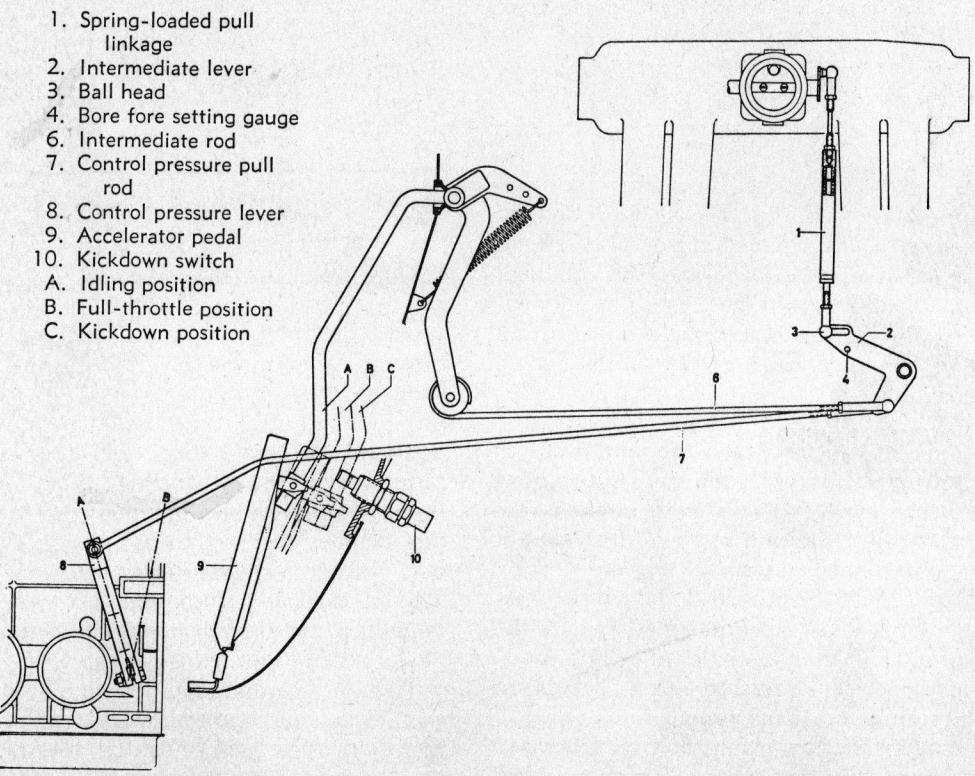

1. Spring-loaded pull linkage
2. Intermediate lever
3. Ball head
4. Bore fore setting gauge
6. Intermediate rod
7. Control pressure pull rod
8. Control pressure lever
9. Accelerator pedal
10. Kickdown switch
A. Idling position
B. Full-throttle position
C. Kickdown position

220D/8 control pressure linkage. A special gauge is required to adjust this linkage properly.

1. Spring-loaded connecting rod
2. Angle lever
3. Pushrod
4. Ball head
5. Control rod
6. Spring-loaded stop (kick-down change-down)
7. Accelerator pedal
8. Modulating pressure trans-mitter
9. Test connection for modu-lating pressure
10. Basic adjustment screw

Positions of accelerator pedal
A. Idling
B. Full throttle
C. Kickdown
a. Kickdown travel
b. Non-extended length of connecting rod

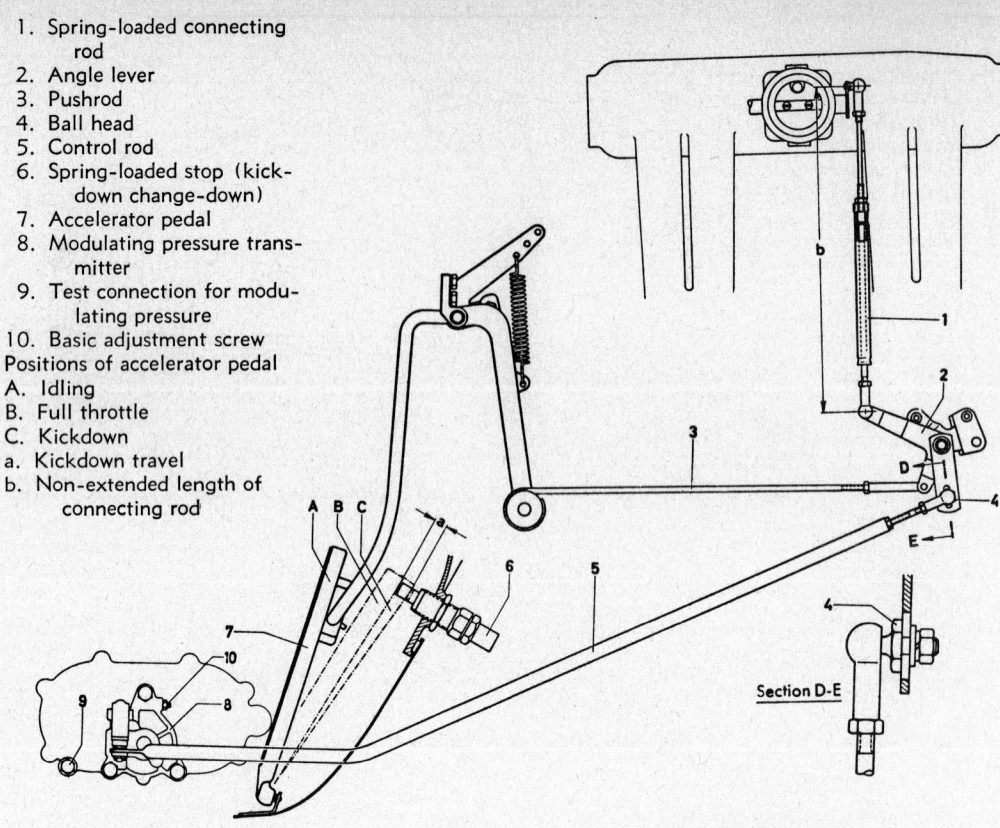

190Dc and 200D control pressure linkage. It is difficult to adjust this linkage without special gauges.

gas pedal rests against the switch (position "B"). When the pedal is depressed to position "C", there should be ³⁄₆₄″ between the throttle valve lever and the full load stop on the venturi housing. On fuel injected models, the injection pump adjusting lever should rest against the full load stop.

Control Pressure Linkage

On the 220/8, detach the pull rod (7) from the socket (11) and push the control pressure lever (8) so that it contacts the stop. Adjust the pull rod length so that it may be connected without tension.

On the 230/8 and 250/8, detach the linkage at the rear carburetor and detach the pull rod (7) from the ball head (11), pressing the control pressure lever (8) against the stop at the same time.

Loosen the two clamp bolts at lever (4) and turn adjusting lever (3) until the ball socket can be hooked up without forcing it.

Front Wheel Camber and Caster

On older models, camber is adjusted by turning an eccentric bolt on the steering knuckle. Newer phase II models have a provision for adjusting both camber and caster at the same time. This is accomplished by turning two eccentric pins on the lower control arm mountings—the front pin changes caster, the rear changes camber. *NOTE: Vehicles must be fully loaded. This is especially important on phase II models, as the rubber mountings may twist in the control arm if load is too light.*

To adjust camber on older models, loosen the hex bolt (2) and remove it and the lock plate (3). The camber can be adjusted by turning the eccentric thus exposed. In some cases, camber cannot be adjusted using the

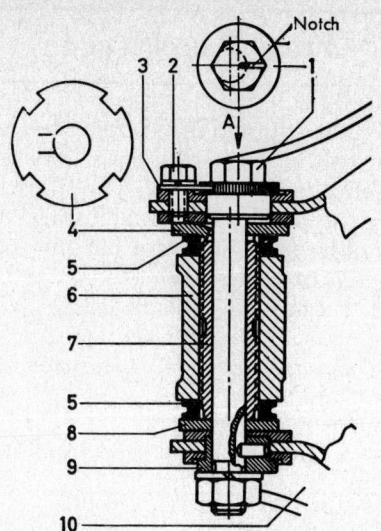

1. Eccentric bolt for camber adjustment
2. Hexagon screw with lockwasher
3. Locking plate
4. Adjusting washer
    for caster adjustment
5. Rubber sealing ring
6. King pin
7. Threaded bolt
8. Eccentric bushing with drive pin
10. Upper control arm

Camber and caster adjustment.

1. Front axle sub-frame
3. Lower control arm
7. Suspension joint
27. Torsion bar connecting linkage
29. Torsion rubber mounting
30. Eccentric bolt

Lower control arm, showing eccentric adjusters.

eccentric alone. Install or remove shims (3) between pivot pin (6) and upper control arm (2) and front axle support (7). If a shim is removed from between the front axle support and the pivot pin, it must be reinstalled between the locking plate and the hex bolt.

On phase II models, caster and camber are interrelated. When caster is increased, the camber is changed in a positive direction; when caster is decreased, the reverse is true. When camber is adjusted in the positive direction, caster is changed negatively.

Changing camber by 0°15′ results in 0°20′ caster change; changing caster by 1° results in a 0°7′ camber change. The diagram illustrates this relationship between caster and camber. For example, x = measured caster of 3°30′, measured camber of +1°. Set correction camber to +0°14′ (A1) and/or +0°8′ (B1), then adjust caster (A2) and/or (B2).

Adjustment of front wheel caster on older models is accomplished by swiveling the front axle support on the eccentric bolts at the flat springs on the longitudinal front axle support. Differences in caster between the left and right sides can be minimized by turning the threaded bolt (7) on top of the steering knuckle.

First, loosen the four bolts that hold the rear motor mount. This relieves any tension on the mount during adjustment. Loosen the hex bolts (10) and (13) on the right and left of the flat spring, then loosen the locknut (15) for eccentric bolt (14). Remove the support strut which goes to the front axle support, then matchmark the flat spring and the chassis. Adjust the eccentric evenly on both sides. If left- and right-side

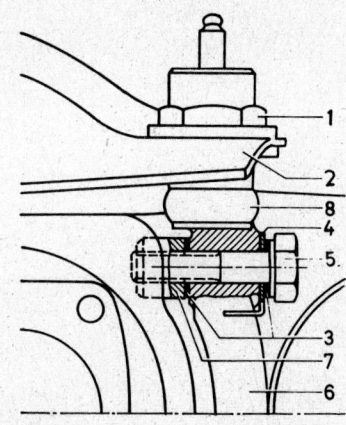

1. Threaded bushing
2. Upper control arm
3. Shim
4. Lock plate
5. Bolt
6. Pivot pin
7. Front axle support
8. Rubber seal

Upper control arm bushings.

20. Tie-rod   24. Steering relay
20a. Clamp   lever
21. Center tie-rod

Tie-rod adjustment.

Front Wheel Toe-In

Toe-in is adjusted by changing the length of the two tie-rods with the wheels in the straight ahead position. The illustration shows one tie-rod and its adjusting points. Some older models have a hex nut locking arrangement rather than the newer clamp (20a), but adjustment is the same. *NOTE: Install new tie-rods so that the left-hand thread points toward left-hand side of car.*

Front End Service

Steering Knuckle/Ball Joint Replacement

caster differs, loosen the hex nut of the eccentric bolt and turn the threaded bolt. *CAUTION: Never alter caster by turning the upper control arm pivot pin.*

To check the steering knuckles or ball joints, jack up the car, placing the jack directly under the front spring plate. This unloads the front suspension to allow the

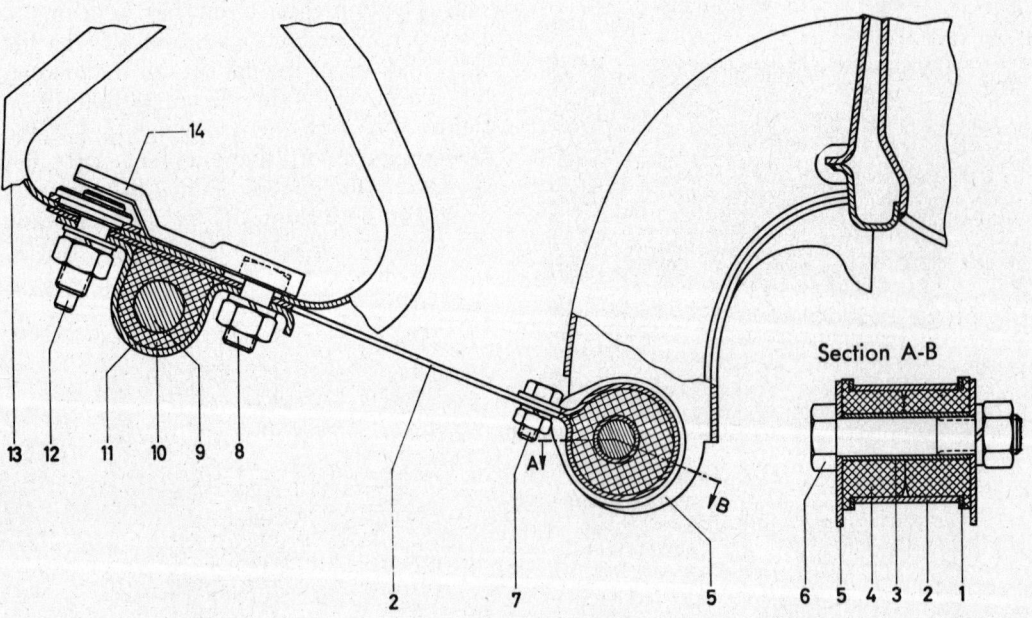

Section A-B

1. Spacer ring
2. Flat spring
3. Spacer tube
4. Rubber mounting
5. Bearing bracket at front axle support
6. Hexagon screw with nut and lockwasher

7. Hexagon screw (clamping screw) with nut and lockwasher
8. Square screw with nut and lockwasher
9. Torsion bar
10. Rubber mounting for torsion bar

11. Bracket for rubber mounting
12. Eccentric with nut, lockwasher, and washer
13. Bearing bracket on chassis base panel
14. Cage for square screw and eccentric

Longitudinal support (flat spring) on second version front axle.

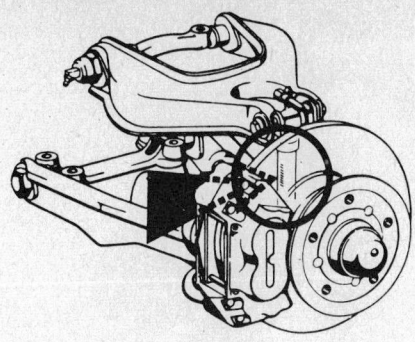

Front suspension identification number location.

cars with disc brakes, remove the brake caliper and unscrew the brake hose and line from the steering knuckle.

Disconnect the tie-rod from the knuckle arm and, on older models, remove the shock absorber.

Referring to the two illustrations, on models having king pins, place a support rod (1) in position (or place a screw jack under the lower control arm), then loosen

3. Lower control arm	14. Bracket
4. Upper control arm	18. Caliper
5. Steering knuckle	20. Tie-rod
6. Guide joint	24. Steering relay lever
7. Suspension joint	27. Torsion bar connecting linkage
10. Front spring	
11. Front shock-absorber	32. Cover plate
12. Torsion bar	33. Bracket for brake hose
13. Rubber mounting for torsion bar	

Ball joint suspension.

1. Supporting fixture
2. Eccentric bolt of upper steering knuckle mounting
3. Threaded pin of lower mounting

Steering knuckle removal.

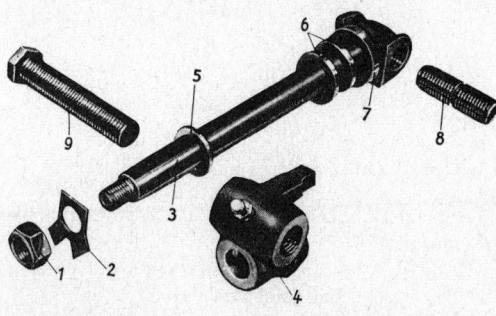

1. Hexagon nut	6. Thrust washer
2. Locking plate	7. Dust cover
3. King pin	8. Threaded pin top
4. Steering knuckle support	9. Threaded pin bottom
5. Shim	

Steering knuckle components.

maximum play to be observed. On older models having king pins, the maximum allowable play between the king pin and bearing bushing is 0.016"; the king pin end-play is the same. Late model ball joints need be replaced only if dried out with plainly visible wear and/or play.

To replace steering knuckles on cars equipped with drum brakes, first remove the brake drum, then disconnect the brake hose where it hooks to the steel line. On

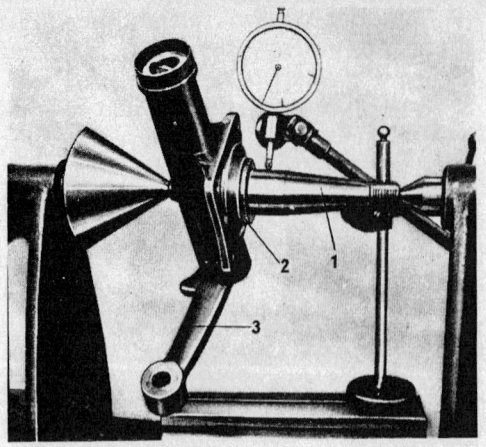

1. Wheel spindle
2. Contact surface for seal
3. Steering arm

Checking spindle runout.

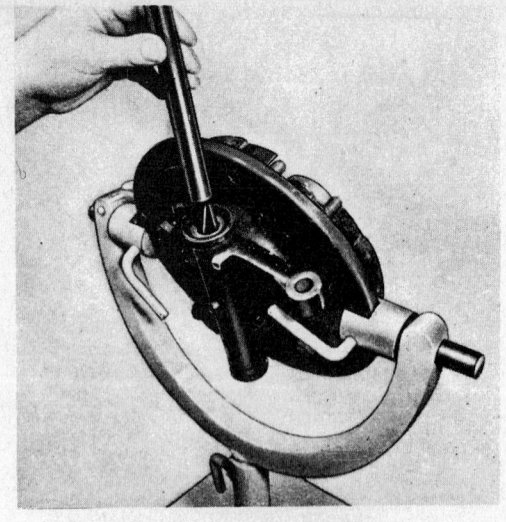

Reaming king pin bushings.

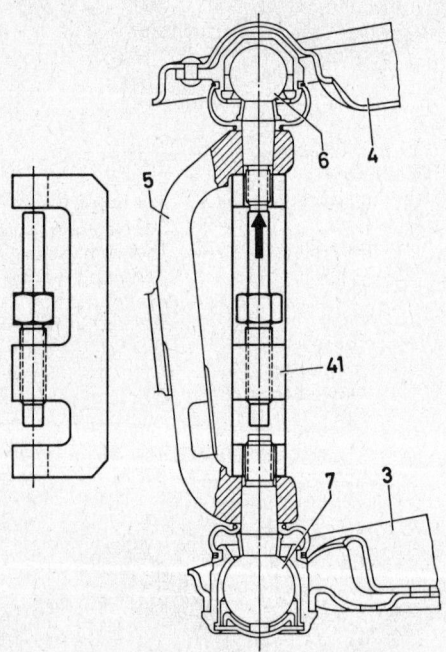

3. Lower control arm
4. Upper control arm
5. Steering knuckle
6. Guide joint
7. Suspension joint
41. Puller (115 589 02 33 00)

Ball joint removal.

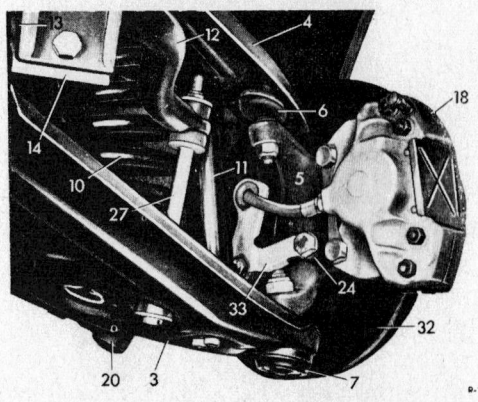

3. Lower control arm	13. Rubber mounting
4. Upper control arm	14. Bracket
5. Steering knuckle	18. Brake caliper
6. Ball joint	20. Tie-rod
7. Suspension joint	24. Steering relay lever
10. Front spring	27. Torsion bar con-
11. Front shock-	necting linkage
absorber	32. Cover plate
12. Torsion bar	33. Bracket

Front suspension components (ball joint).

bolt (2) and remove. Remove the cotter pin and castle nut (3) from the lower control arm and unscrew the threaded pin, then remove the entire knuckle assembly. On models having ball joints, remove the nuts at the ball joints (7) and (6), then press the ball joints from the knuckle from the inside. The upper joint can be removed without special tools by striking the knuckle support with a hammer at point (5) (see illustration). Then, after the upper joint is disconnected, strike the knuckle support at the corresponding lower ball joint in the same manner.

To disassemble, remove front brake shoes and wheel cylinders (if so equipped), then the front wheel hub. *NOTE: It may be necessary to remove the disc brake dust cover as well.*

Unscrew the threaded pin from the upper knuckle support and the hex nut (1) from the king pin. Strike the king pin sharply with a hammer to unseat the lower knuckle support (4), then remove the lower support and shim washer.

Check the spindle for runout (wobble) by suspending it in the jaws of a lathe and checking with a dial indicator, then check the knuckle arm for distortion and the knuckle support for internal wear and cracks. The king pin bushings can be driven out using a drift. New bushings are *pressed* in, then reamed to size.

Control Arm Replacement

On models having threaded control arm supports, first remove the steering knuckle, then unscrew the threaded bushings (4) and the pivot pin (2). Remove the rubber seals (3) and the control arm.

On models having hex bolt supports, support the control arm with a jack, then disconnect the sway bar (27) and shock absorber. Remove the front coil spring, then disconnect the brake hose from the steel line, plug the line to prevent fluid loss

1. Threaded bushing
1a. Groove
2. Code number on control arm
3. Pivot pin

Threaded pivot pin bushing.

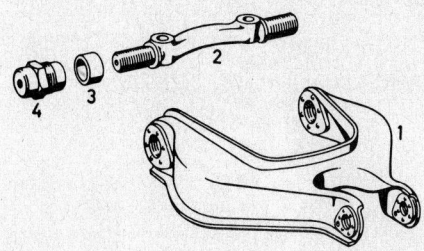

1. Upper control arm	3. Rubber sealing ring
2. Pivot pin	4. Threaded bushing

Upper control arm and shaft.

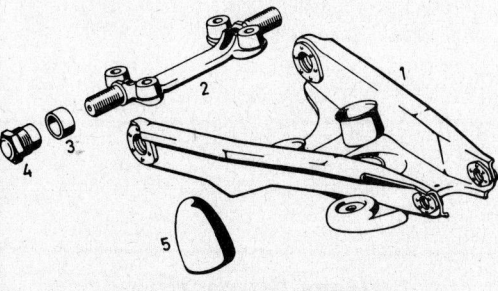

1. Lower control arm	4. Threaded bushing
2. Pivot pin	5. Additional rubber
3. Rubber sealing ring	buffer

Lower control arm and shaft.

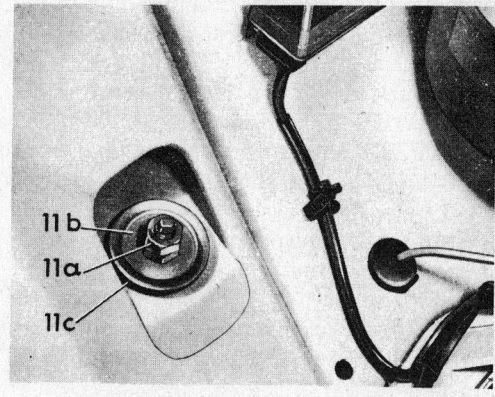

11a. Hexagon nuts
11b. Cup
11c. Rubber ring

Shock absorber upper mounting.

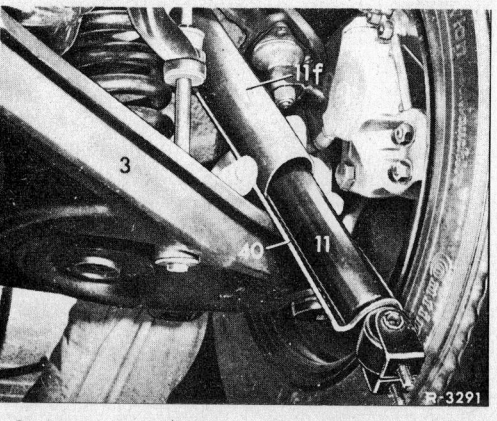

3. Lower control arm	11f. Protective sleeve
11. Shock-absorber	40. Stirrup

Shock absorber removal.

and unscrew the hex bolts. *NOTE: The bolts are installed from the inside—the nut always goes on the outside of the control arm.*

To install, reverse removal procedure. On models having threaded bushings, make sure the bushing rotates freely on the pivot pin.

Front Shock Absorber Replacement

Shock absorbers are normally replaced only if excessively leaking (oil visible on outside cover) or if internally worn to a point where the car no longer rides smoothly and rebounds after hitting a bump. A good general test of shock absorber condition is made by bouncing the front of the car by standing on the bumper. If the car rebounds more than two or three times after jumping off the bumper, it can be assumed that the shock absorbers need replacement.

To replace, jack up the car and support the lower control arm with a jack stand. Remove the upper and lower mounting bolts, compress the shock absorber and remove. On some early models it may be necessary to remove the battery and air cleaner to gain access to the upper bolts. *NOTE: The steel stirrups must be removed and changed over to the new shock absorbers. Use new rubber bushings throughout.*

Front Spring Replacement

Jack up the front of the car and remove the front wheels. On cars having drum brakes, remove the brake drum. Remove the front shock absorber and disconnect the sway bar. On cars having pivot pins and threaded bushings, unscrew the two outer bolts that attach the pivot pin to the frame. Place a jack under the inner control arm, then remove the two inner bolts and gradually lower the jack and arm. When the spring tension is relieved, remove spring and its rubber bumpers.

On cars having eccentric adjusters, first punchmark the position of the adjusters, then loosen the hex bolts. Support the lower control arm with a jack, then knock out the eccentric pins and gradually lower the arm until spring tension is relieved. The spring can now be removed. *NOTE: Check caster and camber after installing new spring.*

3. Lower control arm	12. Torsion bar
4. Upper control arm	29. Rubber mounting
6. Guide joint	44. Jack cradle
7. Suspension joint	47. Angled intermediate brace
10. Front spring	
11. Front shock-absorber	

Removing front coil spring—phase II models.

1. Front spring	4. Pivot pin for lower control arm
2. Lower control arm	
3. Jack cradle	

Removing front coil spring—early models.

Rear Suspension

Rear Shock Absorber Replacement

Jack up the car and support the axle tube

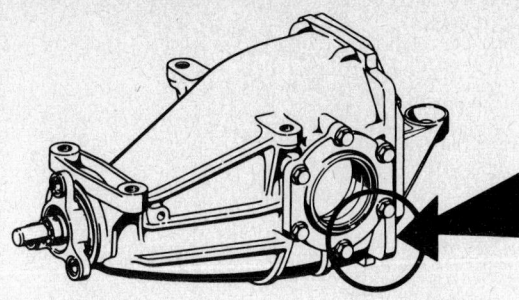

Differential identification number location.

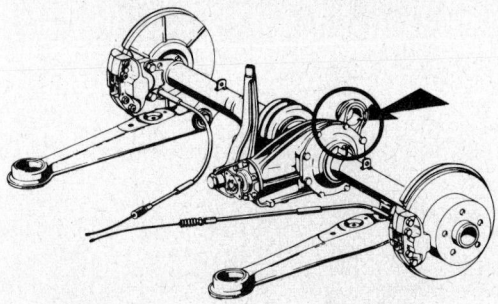

Differential identification number location.

or the lower control arm. From inside the trunk, remove the rubber cap, locknut and hex nut. Then, from underneath the car, remove the lower mounting nut (or bolt), lockwasher and associated components. The shock absorber can now be removed.

NOTE: Use new rubber bushings throughout.

On cars with automatic level control, open the bleed screw (11a) in the line to the rear suspension units and drain about a pint of hydraulic fluid into a clean jar. Remove the back seat and the two cover plates. Seal off hydraulic line (B2) on the suspension unit and plug the banjo fitting with a bolt and nut, then unscrew nuts (5a) and remove washer and rubber gasket. Unbolt the lower bolts on the trailing arm (19) and remove the suspension unit.

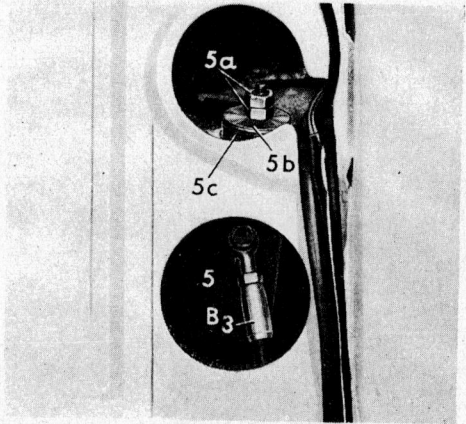

5. Suspension unit
5a. Hexagon nuts
5b. Washer
5c. Upper rubber ring
B3. Hydraulic fluid line from spring accumulator to suspension unit

Level control removal (shock absorber unit).

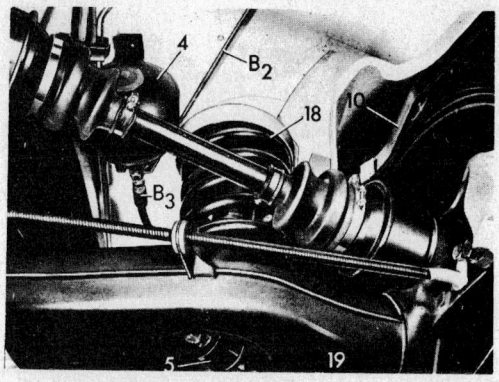

4. Spring accumulator
5. Suspension unit
10. Torsion bar
18. Rear spring
19. Oblique control arm
B2. Hydraulic fluid line from level control to spring accumulator
B3. Hydraulic fluid line from spring accumulator to suspension unit

Level control and rear suspension—phase II models.

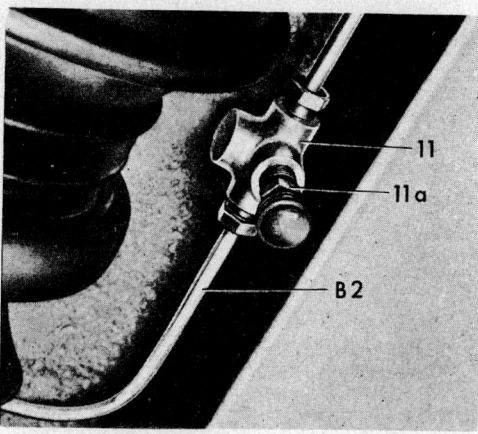

11. Coupling
11a. Bleed screw
B2. Hydraulic fluid line from level control to spring accumulator

Level control system fitting and bleed screw.

NOTE: Use new gaskets throughout. Use only special fluid for level system.

Rear Spring Replacement

Jack up the car, place on stands and remove the rear wheel, then support the control arm on a jack. Install two spring compressors similar to those illustrated and jack up the control arm to compress the

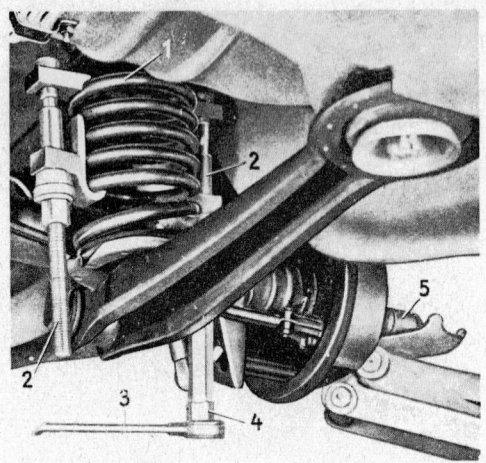

1. Rear spring
2. Spring tensioner
   (111 589 04 31)
3. Ratchet ½" square
4. Hexagon special
   socket (24 mm.)
5. Flange

Rear coil spring removal.

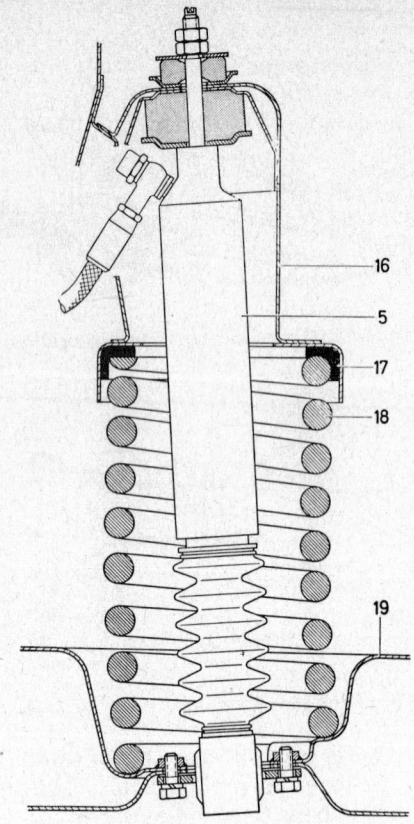

5. Suspension unit
16. Dome on chassis
    base panel
17. Rubber mounting
18. Rear spring
19. Oblique control
    arm

Level control shock absorber.

1. Upper spring plate on chassis base panel
2. Upper rubber mounting
3. Rear spring
4. Lower rubber mounting
5. Lower spring plate
6. Torque arm
7. Support for lower shock-absorber suspension
8. Lower shock absorber suspsenion
9. Rear shock absorber

Rear coil spring and trailing arm.

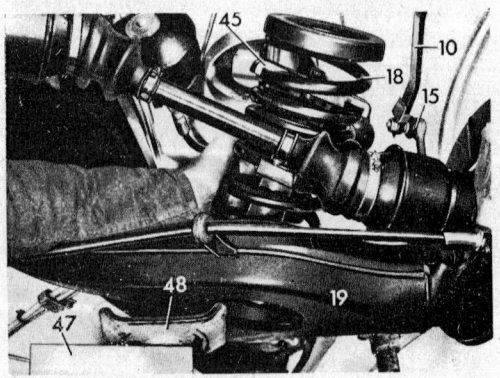

10. Torsion bar
15. Connecting rod
17. Rubber mounting
18. Rear spring
19. Oblique control
    arm
45. Spring tensioner
    (115 589 00
    31 00)
47. Angled intermedi-
    ate brace
48. Jack cradle

Removing rear coil spring—phase II models.

spring. Tighten the spring compressors, then lower the jack and control arm gradually until the spring and rubber mounting pads can be removed. *NOTE: Fasten the rubber mounting plate to the spring, using masking tape for easy installation.*

NOTE: On phase II models, the shock absorber must be removed.

Compensating Spring Replacement

STEEL COIL-TYPE

Jack up the car from the rear and support

1. Compensating spring
2. Cuff
3. Hose clamp or snap-ring
5. Bearing ring
10. Eye on rear axle housing

Steel coil compensating spring removal.

on jack stands. Compress the spring as illustrated until tension on the right axle tube bracket is relieved, then unbolt the bracket and remove the spring. *NOTE: On 230 SL and 250 SL, it may be necessary to detach the lower shock absorber bolts to allow the axle tubes to swing downward far enough for spring removal.*

HYDROPNEUMATIC-TYPE

Jack up the car from the rear and support on jack stands. Unscrew the Allen bolts that hold the ball joint bracket, then unscrew nut (7) and remove spring and washer. The left shock absorber lower mounting must be removed and the control

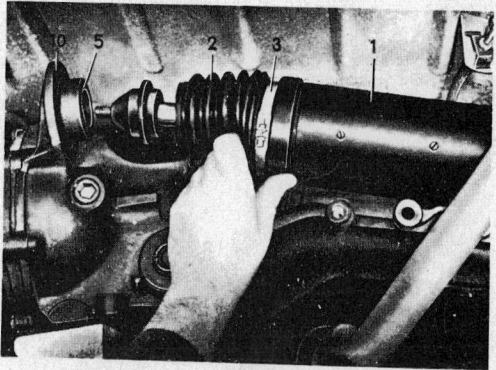

Hydropneumatic compensating spring removal.

1. Compensating spring
2. Cuff
3. Hose clamp or snap-ring
4. Hose clamp
5. Bearing ring
6. Washer
7. Hexagon nut (polystop)
8. Hexagon socket screw

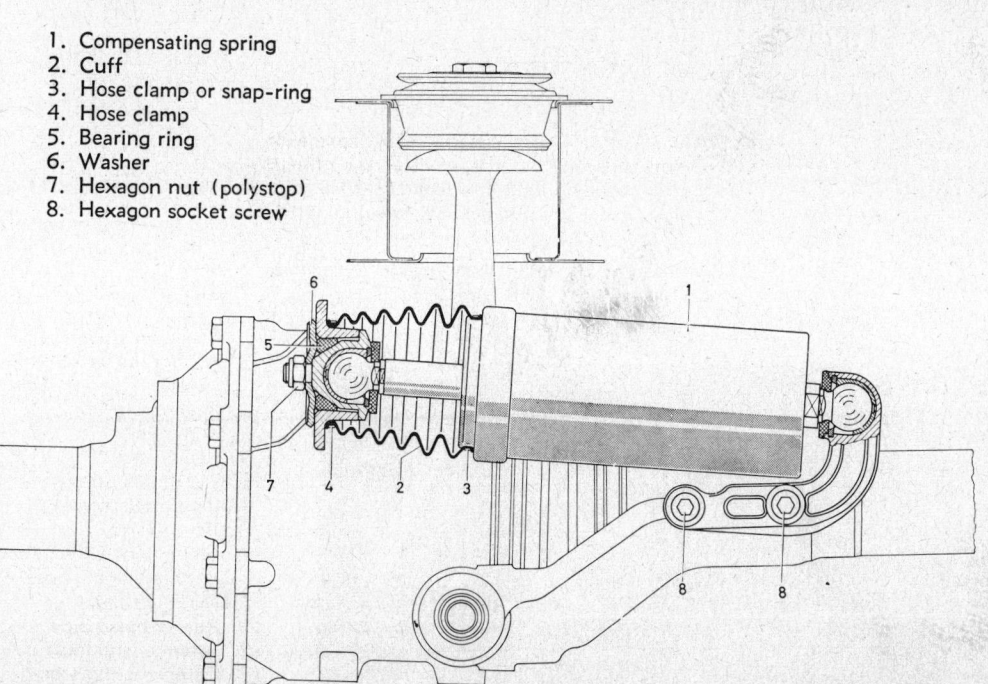

Hydropneumatic compensating spring.

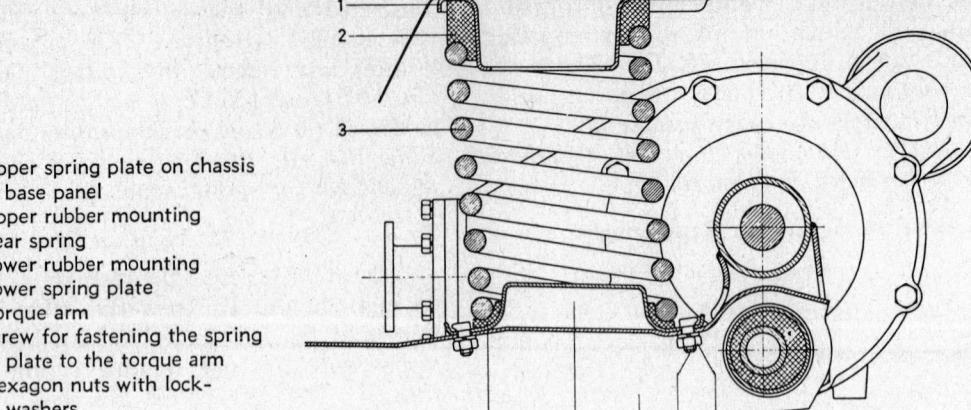

1. Upper spring plate on chassis
   base panel
2. Upper rubber mounting
3. Rear spring
4. Lower rubber mounting
5. Lower spring plate
6. Torque arm
7. Screw for fastening the spring
   plate to the torque arm
8. Hexagon nuts with lockwashers

Rear wheel camber adjustment—older models.

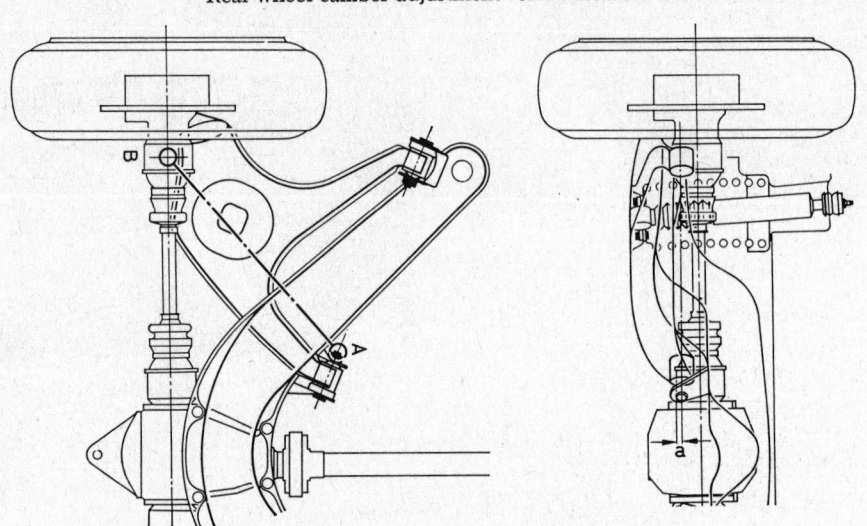

a = oblique control arm position (difference in
height between the axis of the rear oblique
control arm mounting (A) and the lower edge
of the cup for the outer homokinetic joint (B).

Rear wheel camber adjustment—phase II models.

1. Rear shock absorber
2. Rubber buffer for axle
   tube
3. Rear spring
4. Brake line
5. Brake hose
6. Distributor fitting
7. Rear brake cable
8. Torque arm
9. Brake line (connection
   to left brake hose)
10. Main muffler
11. Rear exhaust pipe
12. Intermediate muffler
13. Compensating srping

Rear suspension—cars with enclosed axle shafts.

arm supported with a jack to allow the axle tube to drop low enough for installation.

Rear Wheel Camber

Rear wheel camber is adjusted by turning the lower spring plate (5) or by installing upper rubber mounting pads (2) of different thicknesses. On phase II models, rear wheel camber is adjusted by changing the actual position of the trailing rear control arms, each specific arm position corresponding to a specific camber value.

On early models, remove the rear coil spring, then unbolt the lower spring plate and adjust, or use thicker or thinner upper spring pads.

Differential

Differential Removal

MODELS HAVING ENCLOSED AXLE SHAFTS

Jack up the rear of the car and remove the rear wheels. If equipped with drum brakes, remove the drums; if equipped with air suspension, remove the sway bar. Remove the rear exhaust pipe and the two mufflers, then loosen the parking brake adjuster wingnut and disconnect the brake

1. Hexagon nut and locknut
2. Cup
3. Rubber buffer
4. Retainer on chassis base panel
5. Cross strut
6. Hexagon nut (locknut)
7. Rear link
8. Hexagon screw and spring washer
9. Front link
10. Hexagon screw and spring washer
11. Hexagon screw for connecting pin of the rear axle suspension
12. Support for rear axle suspension
13. Hexagon screws (clamping screws)

Rear torque link removal—190c, 190Dc, 220b, 220Sb, 220SEb, 300SE models.

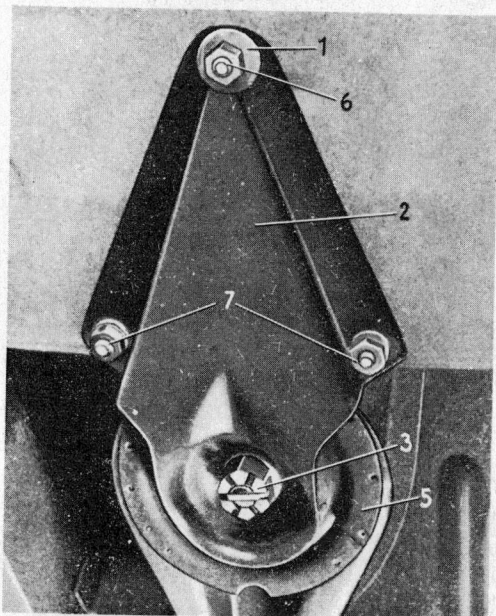

1. Washer
2. Mounting plate
3. Shouldered castle nut
5. Torque arm
6. Welded-in hexagon screw with nut and lockwasher
7. Hexagon screws with nuts, lockwashers and washers

Trailing arm mounting plate.

1. Cheese head screws
2. Locking plates
3. Hexagon nuts
4. Oil drain plug

Rear universal joint removal.

cables. Disconnect the rear universal joint
and push the driveshaft forward, then remove the compensating spring. Remove
the rear coil springs, as described previously, and, on cars with air suspension, disconnect the spring piston from the torque
arm. *NOTE: Do not remove from bellows.*

If car is equipped with drum brakes, disconnect the brake lines from the wheel cylinders and brake hoses, then remove lines
and retainers from axle tubes. If equipped
with disc brakes, disconnect hoses from
lines at the calipers.

Remove the front link (9) from the cross
strut by loosening bolts (8) and (10); push
the strut out of the way. Remove the trailing arm brackets (2) from the chassis.
*NOTE: Tape any shims found beneath the
plate to the appropriate trailing arm.*

If equipped with air suspension, disconnect brake support chassis mount by removing rear seat and unscrewing the castle
nut thus exposed. Pull the bolt out from
beneath the car. Jack up the axle tubes
slightly to unload the shock absorbers, then
disconnect the lower shock mounts. Raise
the axle tubes to a horizontal position.

Place a 24″ section of 2 x 4 (wood) over
the top of the differential housing, the long
axis lined up with the axle tubes, then,
using short sections of chain or rope, fasten
the axle tubes to the ends of the 2 x 4 so
that the axle tubes remain in a horizontal
position and do not sag at their ends. This
is to prevent damage to the inner sliding
joint of the axle shafts.

From inside the trunk, unbolt the differential housing from the chassis, then
gradually lower the entire rear differential
housing and axle tube assembly to the floor.

Models Having Exposed Axle Shafts

Jack up the rear of the car as high as
possible; support rear axle subframe on jack
stands (both sides). Drain oil from differential housing, remove hubcaps and the
two bolts (one per side) that hold the axle
to the axle flange. The rear axle splined
shaft then must be pressed from the axle
flange. (The illustration shows this being
done using the proper tool.) Place a jack
under the differential housing and jack up
the housing slightly. then unscrew the Allen
bolt (43). *NOTE: This bolt is tightened
to 87–115 ft.-lbs.*

From inside the trunk, remove the four

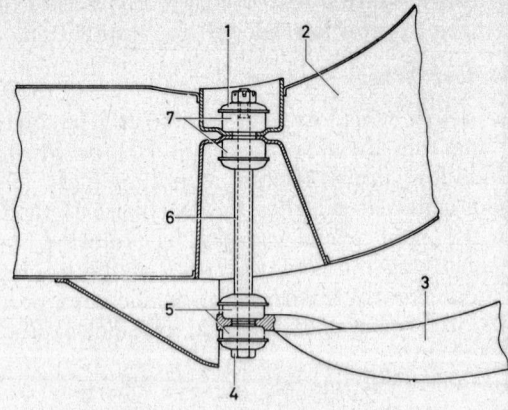

1. Cup
2. Side member
3. Lever for brake support
4. Hexagon screw
5. Lower rubber buffer
6. Spacer tube
7. Upper rubber buffer

Hold-down bolt through chassis base.

Loosening axle bolt.

42. Rear rubber mounting
43. Hexagon socket bolt
45. Breather
46. Screw plug for filling
47. Screw plug for draining

Differential mounting bolts.

Loosening driveshaft clamp nuts.

Lowering differential.

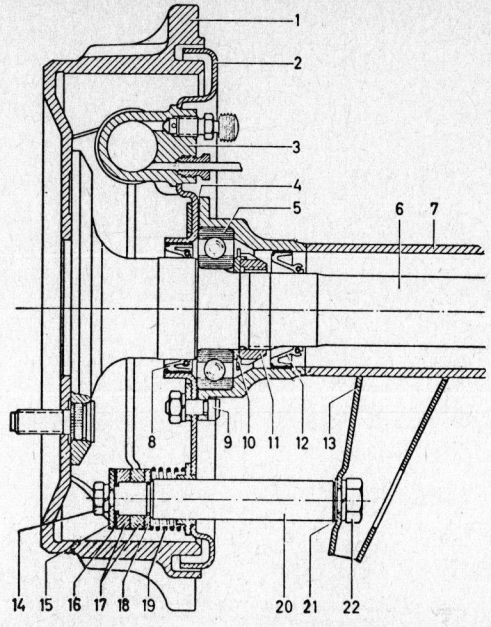

1. Brake drum
2. Brake anchor plate
3. Wheel cylinder
4. Seal
5. Annular grooved bearing
6. Rear axle shaft
7. Axle tube
8. Outer seal
9. Fitted screw
10. Locking plate
11. Grooved nut
12. Inner seal
13. Bracket
14. Hexagon screw with lockwasher
15. Washer
16. Brass washer
17. Brake shoe
18. Washer
19. Pressure spring
20. Anchor pin
21. Washer
22. Hexagon screw with lockwasher

Axle shaft—drum brakes.

plugs and unbolt the differential housing from the subframe (17 mm. socket). Now, loosen the driveshaft center bearing support bracket, push back the rubber dust cover and loosen the locknut. Disconnect the rear universal joint from the flange and push the driveshaft forward out of the way, then lower the entire rear differential housing assembly and axle shafts to the floor.

Axle Shaft Removal

MODELS HAVING ENCLOSED AXLE SHAFTS
(190c, 190 Dc, 200, 200 D,
220b, 220 Sb, 220 SEb,
230, 230 S, 230 SL, 300 SE Sedan,
300 SE/c UP TO AUGUST, 1965)

Jack up the rear of the car, remove the wheel and, if equipped with drum brakes, remove the brake drum and shoes. Disconnect brake line from wheel cylinder and remove the backing plate anchor bolt from the rear.

If the car is equipped with disc brakes,

remove the brake caliper, the brake disc and the hold-down plate. Remove the backing plate/grease retainer bolts, then, using a puller as illustrated or a slide hammer, pull out the axle shaft. *NOTE: Axle bearings must be removed with a special puller or an arbor press ONLY—never hammer on the bearings.*

Removing axle shaft.

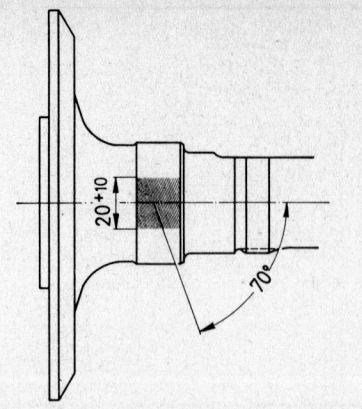

Left rear axle shaft with right-hand thread pattern.

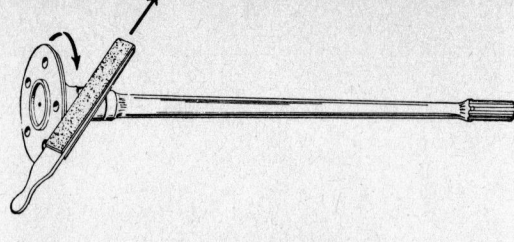

Right rear axle shaft with left-hand thread pattern. Flange of rear axle shaft pointing to headstock.

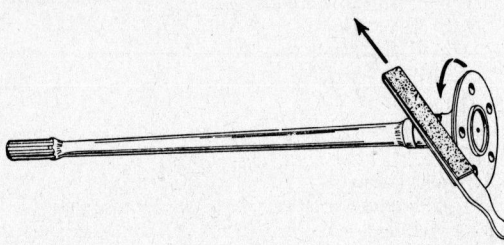

Left rear axle shaft with right-hand thread pattern. Flange of rear axle shaft pointing to tailstock.

If the outer axle seal surface no longer has discernible oil return grooves, recut the grooves using a flat piece of wood (paint stirrer) and 180 grit emery paper. The left axle shaft gets a right-hand pattern; the right axle shaft a left-hand pattern (see illustrations). *NOTE: When inserting axle shaft into sliding joint, anchor joint by removing 10 mm. plug on axle tube and rotating sliding joint so that depression in joint lines up with hole; insert suitable punch.*

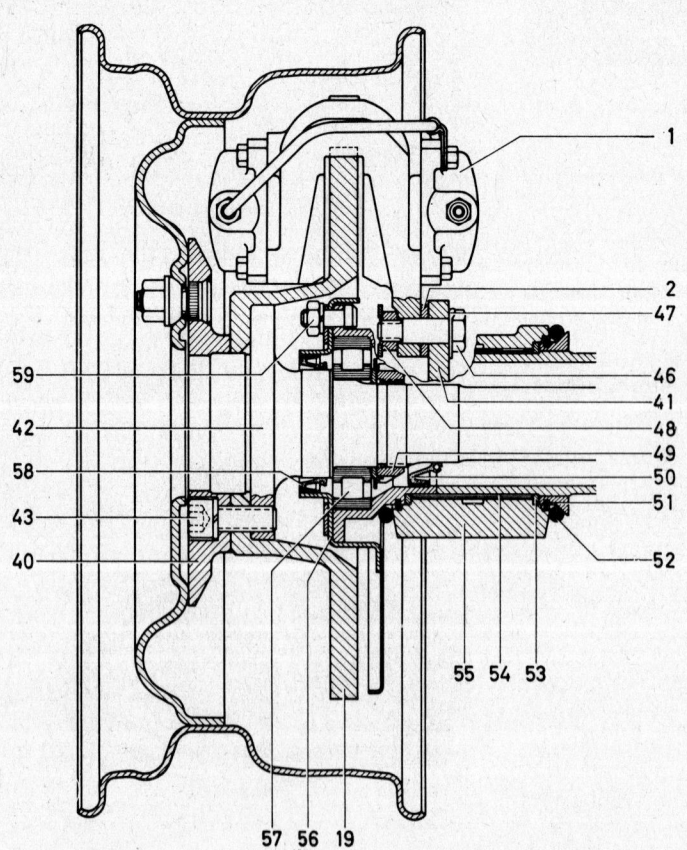

1. Brake caliper
2. Shim
19. Brake disc
40. Wheel fixing disc
41. Fixing eye on the bearing housing
42. Rear axle shaft
43. Hexagon socket screw
46. Hexagon fitting screw
47. Locking plate
48. Bracket
49. Grooved nut with lock
50. Seal
51. Sealing ring
52. Rubber ring
53. Split shim
54. Bearing shell
55. Bearing housing
56. Sealing ring retainer
57. Barrel roller bearing
58. Seal
59. Fitting bolt with hexagon nut and lockwasher

Axle shaft—disc brakes.

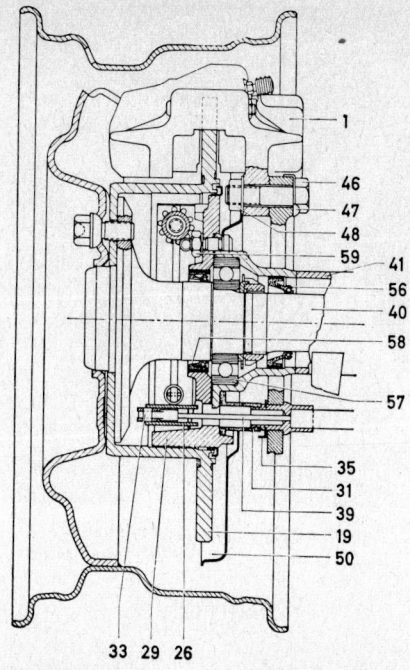

1. Brake caliper
19. Brake disc
26. Expansion lock
29. Back plate
31. Rubber sleeve
33. Pin for brake cable
35. KL lock for brake cable
39. Brake cable
40. Rear axle shaft
41. Axle tube
46. Hexagon fitting bolt
47. Locking plate
48. Bracket with weld-on nut
50. Cover plate
56. Seal
57. Grooved ball bearing
58. Seal
59. Fitting bolt with hexagon nut and lockwasher

Axle shaft arrangement.

Differential mounting bolt (43) and rear mount (42).

9. Rear axle housing
27. Side gear
30. Differential housing
33. Lock ring

Lock ring for axle shaft—phase II models.

Models Having Enclosed Axle Shafts
(250 S, 250 SE, 300 SEb, 300 SE/c from August, 1965, 300 SEL)

Jack up the rear of the car and remove the wheel, brake caliper and disc, then remove the parking brake shoes. Unbolt the backing plate and dust cover and pull the axle from the housing using a puller or slide hammer (see previous section). *NOTE: The grooved nut is threaded to the shaft; bearings must be removed and replaced using an arbor press. Use punch, as previously described, to anchor sliding joint during axle installation.*

Models Having Exposed Axle Shafts
(Phase II Models)

Jack up the rear of the car and remove the wheel and center axle hold-down bolt (in hub). Drain differential oil and place

Removing axle shaft and spacer ring (11).

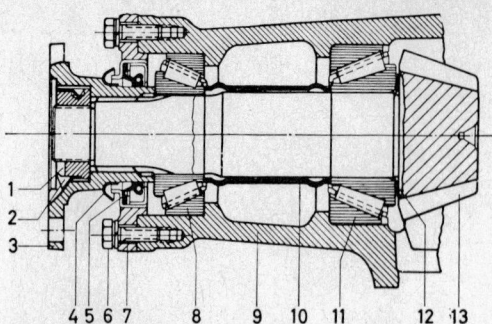

1. Grooved nut
2. Locking plate
3. Joint flange
4. Protective washer
5. Seal
6. Hexagon screw
7. Cover
8. Front annular taper roller bearing
9. Rear axle housing
10. Spacer sleeve
11. Rear annular taper roller bearing
12. Compensating washer
13. Drive pinion

Pinion seal configuration.

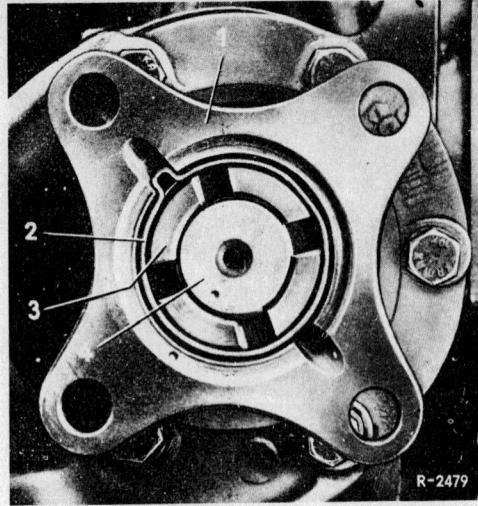

1. Joint flange
2. Locking plate
3. Grooved nut
4. Drive pinion

Grooved pinion nut.

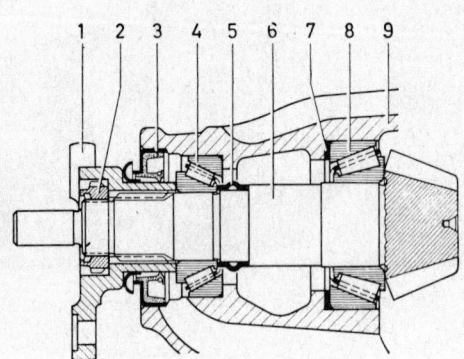

1. Joint flange
2. Self-locking grooved nut
3. Sealing ring
4. Front taper roller bearing
5. Spacer sleeve
6. Drive pinion
7. Shim
8. Rear taper roller bearing
9. Rear axle housing

Pinion seal configuration—phase II models.

Pinion seal removal (3).

"L" for right and left units. Always use new lock rings.

CAUTION: Check end-play of lock ring in groove. If necessary, install thicker lock ring to eliminate all end-play, while still allowing lock ring to rotate.

Pinion Seal Replacement

Drain the differential oil, jack up rear of car and remove wheels and brake drums. Support the axle tubes or lower arms on jack stands so that axles are in a horizontal position, then disconnect the driveshaft rear universal joint. Punchmark the flange and housing, then remove the grooved nut. Using a puller, remove the flange. NOTE: If flange is scored, it must be replaced.

Pull or pry the seal from the housing and

a jack under the differential housing. Unbolt rubber mount (42) from the chassis and the differential housing, then remove the differential housing cover to expose the ring and pinion gears. Press the shaft from the axle flange, as described previously. Using a screwdriver, remove the axle lock ring inside the differential case (see illustration) and pull the axle from the housing. NOTE: Axle shafts are stamped "R" and

install new seal (press into place). Reinstall components and carefully tighten the grooved nut until the torque required to turn the differential assembly at the pinion shaft is 26–30 cm.-kg. (22–26 in.-lbs.) for models having enclosed axle shafts and 15–20 cm.-kg. (13–17 in.-lbs.) for models having exposed axle shafts. This corresponds to about 108–144 ft.-lbs. on the grooved pinion nut. If the turning torque is excessive, a new collapsible spacer sleeve must be installed. Never back off on the grooved nut to achieve desirable pinion turning torque, as the bearings will be improperly preloaded and eventually destroyed.

Ring and Pinion Gear Replacement and Adjustment

(190c, 190 Dc, 200, 200 D, 220b,
220 Sb, 220 SEb, 230,
230 S, 230 SL, 300 SE Sedan, 300 SE/c
UP TO AUGUST, 1965)

With the rear differential housing removed, first remove the right-hand axle and tube, then loosen the hold-down bolt and

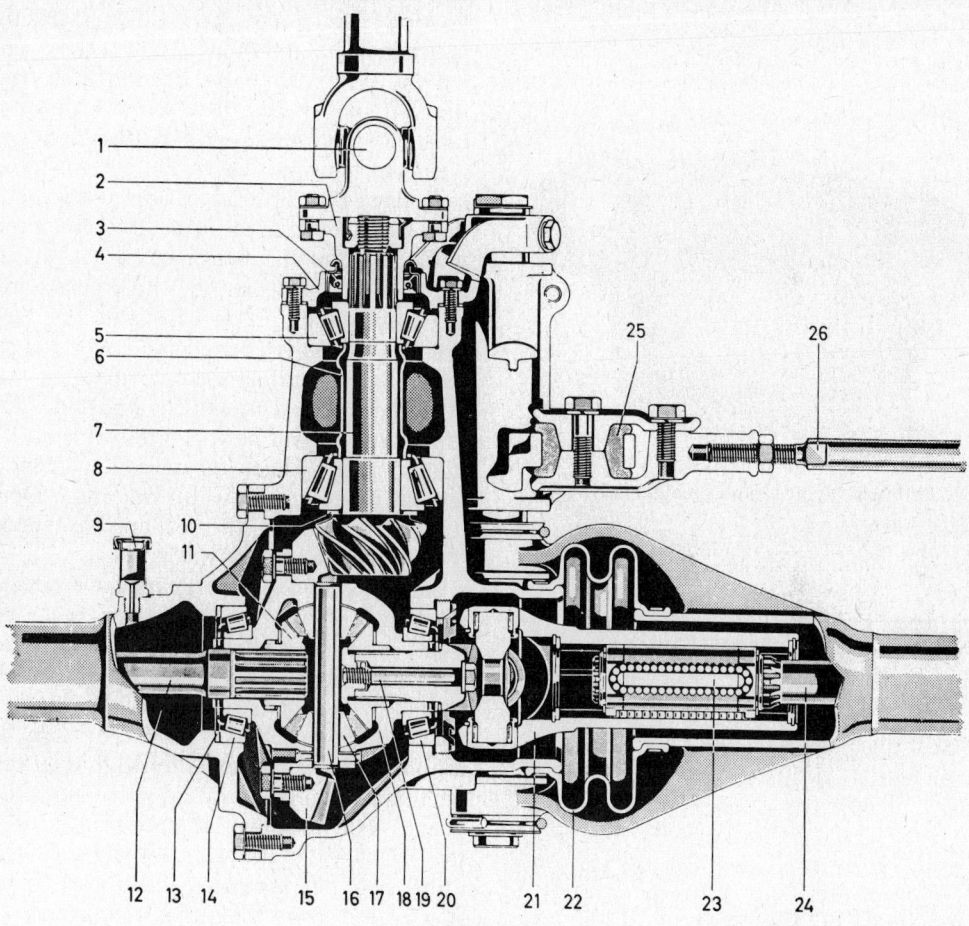

1. Driveshaft	10. Compensating washer	20. Annular taper roller bearing for differential
2. Joint flange	11. Left differential side gear	21. Outer yoke with universal joint
3. Seal	12. Left rear axle shaft	
4. Cover	13. Compensating washer	22. Rubber sleeve
5. Front annular taper roller bearing	14. Annular taper roller bearing for differential	23. Sliding sleeve with cylindrical rollers
6. Spacer sleeve	15. Ring gear	24. Right rear axle shaft
7. Drive pinion	16. Differential pinion shaft	25. Rubber mounting
8. Rear annular taper roller bearing	17. Differential pinion gear	26. Cross strut for rear axle suspension
9. Bleed screw	18. Differential housing	
	19. Clamp screw with lock-washer	

Typical differential construction—models having enclosed axle shafts.

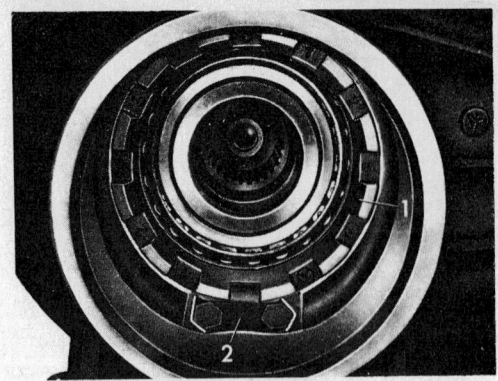

Threaded ring (1) and lock tabs (2).

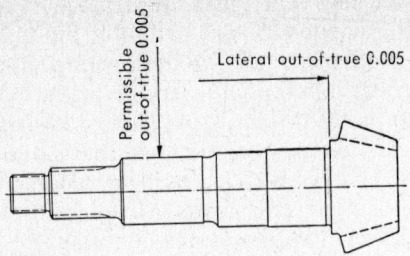

R-1093

Left axle tube (1) and breather (2).

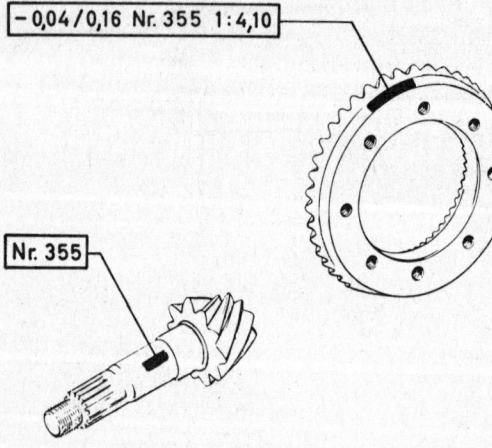

— 0,04/0,16 Nr. 355 1:4,10

Nr. 355

— 0.04 Deviation "a" from basic adjustment
       "D nom." in the direction minus 0.04
       mm.
  0.16 Backlash
No. 355 Gear set (ring gear and pinion) No. 355
1:4.10 Gear ratio drive pinion to ring gear

Ring and pinion markings.

pull out the slip joint. Remove the right-
and left-hand axle shafts and unbolt the
bearing flange and axle tubes from the
housing. The differential now can be removed. Press the outer bearing race from
the left axle tube, then remove the lock
tabs (2) and unscrew the threaded ring
from the housing. Drive the outer bearing
race from the right-hand side of the housing, then remove the grooved pinion nut
while holding the flange steady in a vise.
The pinion shaft can now be pressed into
the empty differential case and removed.
Remove the pinion flange and cover and the
inner pinion bearing; the outer bearing race
must be pressed from the housing. The
inner bearing can now be pressed from the
pinion shaft. Check the pinion for runout
and the bearing seats for scoring. Don't
forget to remove the collapsible spacer
sleeve from the pinion shaft.

The ring and pinion gears have several
markings etched on their surfaces: the
serial number, the pinion depth tolerance
deviation (in mm.), the gear ratio and the
backlash clearance (in mm.). Backlash is
constant, being $.0062'' \pm .0008''$, while the
individual gear markings indicate tolerance
deviation from the norm for those *particular*
gears. For instance, if the ring gear is
marked with a minus (—) sign (and a
dimension), it indicates the pinion deviation is away from the ring gear; a plus (+)
sign indicates the reverse. The proper
pinion depth can be computed for any
combination of ring and pinion gears, and
the thickness of the compensating washer
determined, from these markings. Since
special tools are required for computation
of the proper washer thickness, a "red
lead" test will be described later.

The factory procedure involves measuring distance "B", the distance between the
front end of a "perfect" dummy pinion
shaft of known thickness ("C" nom.) and

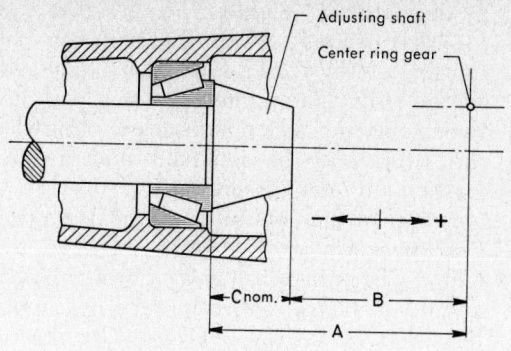

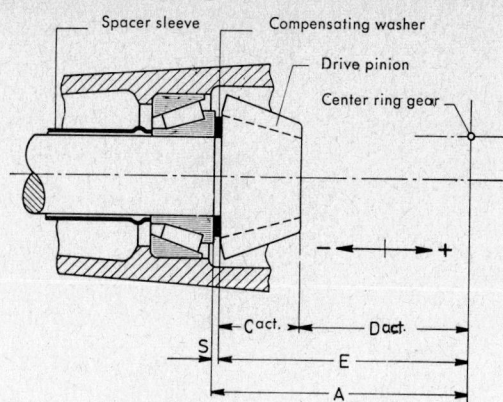

C nom. = Nominal height of adjusting shaft

B = Distance between front end of adjusting shaft and center ring gear

A = Distance between inner race of rear taper roller bearing and center ring gear

C act. = Actual height of drive pinion

D act. = Actual distance between front face of drive pinion and center ring gear (adjusting dimension)

E = Distance between compensating washer and center ring gear

A = Distance between inner race of rear taper roller bearing and center ring gear

S = Thickness of compensating washer

the center of the ring gear to determine distance "A" (see illustrations). Then the actual distance ("D" act.) is computed by adding to (or subtracting from, as the case may be) the "perfect" distance between the front of the pinion gear as installed, the dimension "a" etched on the gear to be used. (Dimension "a" is the amount of deviation from the "perfect" pinion thickness.) From the illustration, it can be seen that "S", the thickness of the compensating washer needed to bring the pinion and ring gears into perfect mesh, is determined by subtracting distance "E" from the previously determined distance "A". Distance "E" is found by adding the actual thickness of the pinion gear to be used (measured with a micrometer) to the distance "D act.", also previously computed. This enables the washer thickness to be accurately determined before the components are assembled, thus saving much time and trouble over the trial and error "red lead" method.

$$S = (B + 34.50) - [(58.00 \pm a) + C \text{ act.}]$$

S = thickness of compensating washer

B = distance between front of dummy "perfect" pinion and center of ring gear

± a = manufacturing tolerance deviation etched on gear

C act. = actual thickness of pinion to be used

NOTE: C nom. = 34.50 (mm.)

D nom. = 58.00 (mm.)

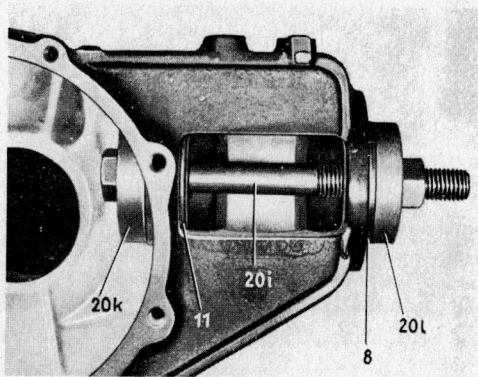

8. Front bearing outer race
11. Rear bearing outer race
20. Fixture (111 589 12 61 00)) or homemade
20i. Hexagon screw
20k. Installing washer
20l. Installing washer

Installing outer pinion bearing races.

To assemble, first install the outer bearing races (front and rear) of the pinion shaft into the housing, using a tool similar to the one illustrated. Push the compensating washer "S" onto the pinion shaft and press on the inner bearing race. *NOTE: If "red lead" method of determining washer thickness is to be used, pick a washer on the basis of markings on old gears and old washer thickness. If ring and pinion gears are to be reused, a new washer of the same thickness as the one used before should be installed.*

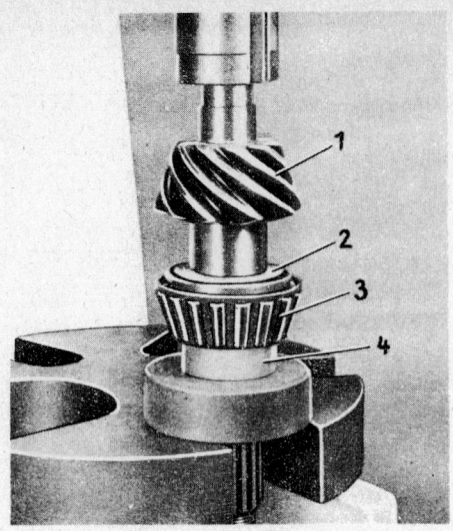

1. Drive pinion
2. Compensating washer
3. Rear annular taper roller bearing
4. Pressure sleeve with support

Pressing on inner bearing race.

Install the pinion into the differential housing, slide on a new collapsible spacer sleeve and press on the inner bearing race, after coating it with hypoid lubricant. Press a new pinion seal into place in the housing cover and install the cover. Press the driveshaft universal joint flange onto the drive pinion splines, after coating splines with Molykote. *NOTE: Observe matchmarks made during disassembly.*

Install the grooved nut and lock plate and tighten the nut until a torque of 16–18 cm.-kg. (14–15 in.-lbs.) for new bearings, or 5–10 cm.-kg. (4–9 in.-lbs) for old bearings, is needed to turn the drive pinion in its bearings. Tap the housing gently with a fiber hammer to seat the bearings. *CAUTION: Remember, as the grooved nut is tightened, the collapsible sleeve is deformed to provide proper bearing preload. As a consequence, the sleeve must be REPLACED if torque on the grooved nut is exceeded. Never loosen the grooved nut to obtain desired pinion rotating torque.*

Insert the compensating washer into the left axle tube flange and press in the outer race of the roller bearing. Screw in the threaded ring about three turns and press the outer bearing race into the differential housing until it rests against the ring. Install the differential into the housing and

attach the bearing flange and left axle tube to the housing. Tighten the threaded ring to approximately 25 ft.-lbs. and tap the housing gently with a fiber hammer to seat the bearing. There must be some play between the ring and pinion gears, otherwise the ring must be removed and a new washer (thinner) inserted.

Set up a dial indicator to measure ring gear backlash at the outer edge of the teeth. Check backlash at four or five points around the gear circumference—it should be .0062" ± .0008". *NOTE: Clamp the drive pinion so that only ring gear backlash is measured.*

If backlash is excessive, a thicker compensating washer must be installed between the bearing flange and the outer bearing race (in differential, *not* on pinion) and vice-versa. A .040" washer results in approximately .003"–.004" change in backlash.

Red Lead Tooth Pattern Test

In order to determine whether the ring and pinion gears are in perfect mesh a "red lead" test must be made. This is espe-

Correct Meshing

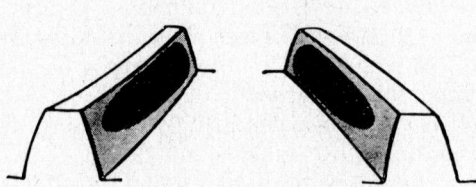

Contact at Dedendum (incorrect)

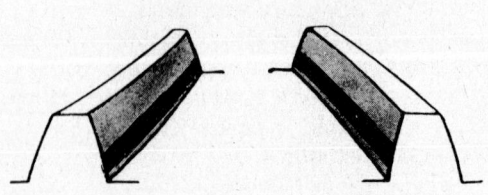

Contact at Addendum (incorrect)

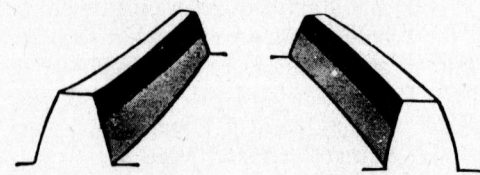

cially necessary if pinion depth compensating washer "S" was arbitrarily selected without computation. Coat the teeth of the ring and pinion gears with red lead, mechanic's blue dye or lipstick. Rotate the pinion shaft while holding a piece of soft wood against the ring gear (the wood acts as a brake). Compare the tooth pattern obtained with the illustrations. The ideal ring gear "wear" pattern is usually not exactly as shown; it is only necessary that the outer portions of the gear teeth are not touched. If the outer (upper) portions of the teeth are covered, a thicker compensating washer "S" is indicated for the drive pinion. At the same time, a thinner washer is needed in the left axle tube flange to correct backlash. If the inner gear teeth surfaces are covered, a thinner compensating washer "S" and a thicker left axle tube washer are necessary. This will, of course, require complete disassembly of the unit and a new collapsible spacer on the drive pinion. It is for this reason that it is best to have the proper equipment available for computation of compensating washer "S" thickness before assembly, as this trial and error method is most time consuming.

After the proper pinion depth and backlash has been achieved, adjust the initial tension on the differential bearings by tightening or backing out the threaded ring. At the same time, check the torque required to rotate the pinion shaft (and complete gear train). *NOTE: The torque required to turn the pinion shaft before installation of ring gear is known; it should increase by 7–8 cm.-kg. (6–7 in.-lbs.) after installation.*

Continue assembly in reverse order of disassembly.

Ring and Pinion Gear Replacement and Adjustment (250S, 250SE, 300SEb, 300SE/c from August, 1965, 300SEL)

Disassembly is basically the same as in the previous section, although some small design differences are apparent. For instance, the compensating washer "S" on the drive pinion is installed between the outer bearing race of the rear bearing and the front face of the bearing seat (see illustrations).

Computation of washer thickness is the same as in the previous section, with the following exceptions:

C nom. = 67.00 (mm.)
D nom. = 66.00 (mm.)

4. Dished washer	16. Locking pin
5. Differential pinion	17. Differential pinion
14. Thrust washer	shaft
15. Differential side gear	21. Bearing ring

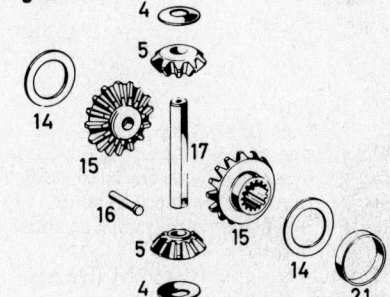

Spider gears and associated parts.

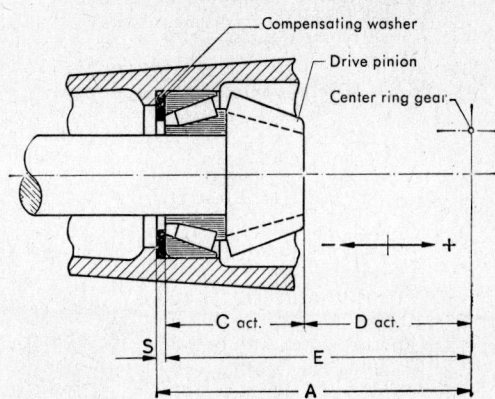

C act. = Actual height of drive pinion plus height of taper roller bearing

D act. = Actual distance between front face of drive pinion and center ring gear (adjusting dimension)

E = Distance between compensating washer and center ring gear

A = Distance between front face of bearing mounting for the rear taper roller bearing and center ring gear

S = Thickness of compensating washer

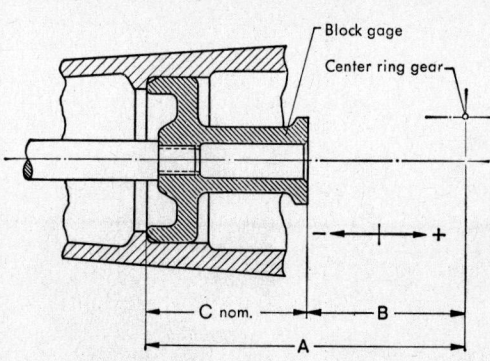

C nom. = Height of block gage

B = Distance between front face block gage and center ring gear

A = Distance between front face of bearing mounting for the rear taper roller bearing and center ring gear

Standard Differential

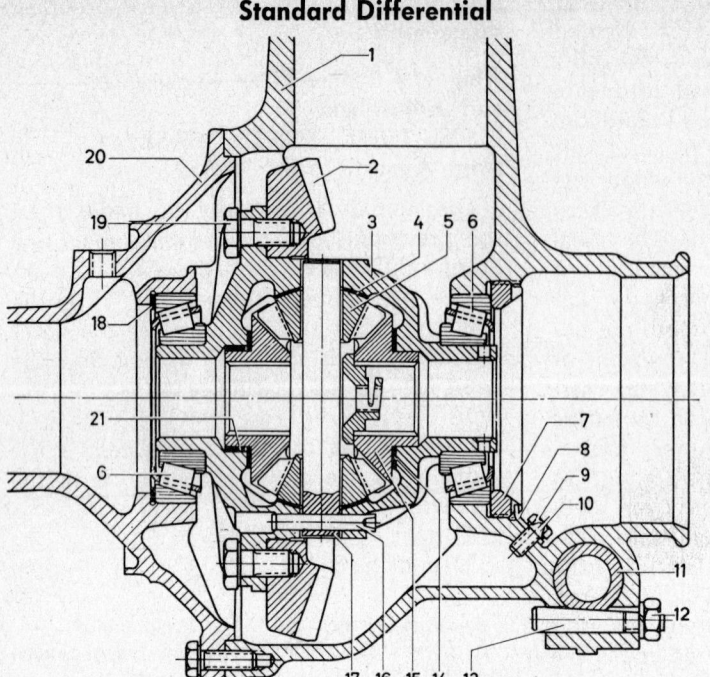

1. Rear axle housing
2. Ring gear
3. Differential gear housing
4. Dished washer
5. Differential pinion
6. Taper roller bearing
7. Threaded ring
8. Lock
9. Hexagon screw
10. Locking plate
11. Connecting pin
12. Hexagon nut with lock-washer
13. Conical screw wedge
14. Thrust washer
15. Differential side gear
16. Locking pin
17. Differential pinion shaft
18. Compensating washer
19. Hexagon screw
20. Bearing flange with left axle tube
21. Bearing ring

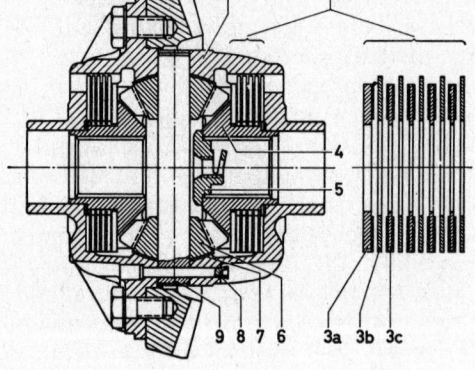

1. Ring gear
2. Differential housing
3. Friction clutch
3a. Friction clutch with one-side sinter coating
3b. Friction clutch without coating
3c. Friction clutch with both-side sinter coating
4. Differential side gear
5. Nut for right differential side gear
6. Differential pinion
7. Dished washer
8. Locking pin
9. Differential pinion shaft

Positive traction differential clutch parts.

3a. Friction clutch with one-side sinter coating
3b. Friction clutch without coating
3c. Friction clutch with both-side sinter coating
4. Differential side gear
5. Nut for right differential side gear
6. Differential pinion
7. Dished washer
8. Locking pin
9. Differential pinion shaft

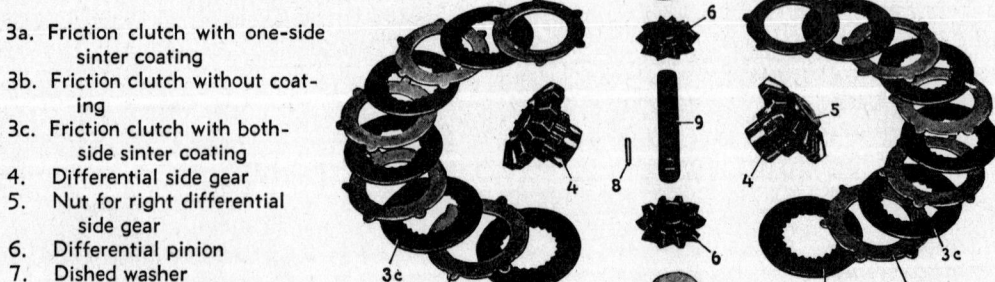

Positive traction differential parts.

Steering

Steering Wheel Removal and Installation

WHEELS WITHOUT SHOCK ABSORBER IN COLUMN (UP TO 1967)

Pry the center trademark plate from the end of the column. Loosen the hex-head nut that holds the wheel to the steering tube and remove the wheel from the serrations. The wheel should come off by hand without the use of a puller. *NOTE: Matchmark wheel and steering tube before removal.*

Before installing, check the positions of retainer (11) for contact ring (12), and check that the tension spring (30) is in place. Place the wheel on the end of the steering tube with the matchmarks lined up. Install the hex-head nut and lockwasher and tighten the nut to 57 ft. lbs.

WHEELS WITH SHOCK ABSORBER IN COLUMN (AFTER 1967)

The shock absorber is simply a collapsible spacer installed between the wheel and the steering tube. This is not the entire collapsible steering column as is found in most recent American cars—simply a spacer. If it is necessary to work on the steering column jacket, steering tube or shift tube, the wheel must be removed complete with the shock absorber. The wheel can, however, be removed from the shock absorber to do work on the horn contact switch.

Remove the trademark plate by prying, then remove the five hex-head nuts from the steering tube studs. Remove the steering wheel. If it is necessary, remove the center hex-head nut from the end of the shaft and remove the shock absorber along with the wheel. When installing, tighten the hex-head nut that holds the shock absorber to 36 ft. lbs. The five hex-head nuts that hold the wheel to the shock absorber are tightened to 8-10 ft. lbs.

Removing center hex-head nut—wheels without shock absorber.

11. Retainer for contact ring
12. Horn contact ring
13. Steering column jacket
16. Rubber cover for turn signal switch
17. Turn signal switch
19. Steering tube
30. Spring

Steering wheel and horn components—wheels without shock absorber.

1. Hex-head nut
2. Steering wheel
3. Horn ring

Nuts (1) that hold wheel to steering column shock absorber.

1. Hexagon nut with
   spring washer
2. Steering wheel
3. Horn ring
4. Hexagon nut with
   spring washer
5. Steering tube
6. Steering column
   shock-absorber
7. Slip ring with cable
12. Contact ring
13. Annular grooved
    bearing
16. Mounting plate
19. Needle bearing
20. Vulkollan ring
23. Guide pin
24. Spring seat pin
25. Pressure spring
26. Shift tube
27. Shift lever
28. Ball socket
29. Cap
30. Rubber cover
31. Combined switch
32. Rubber cover

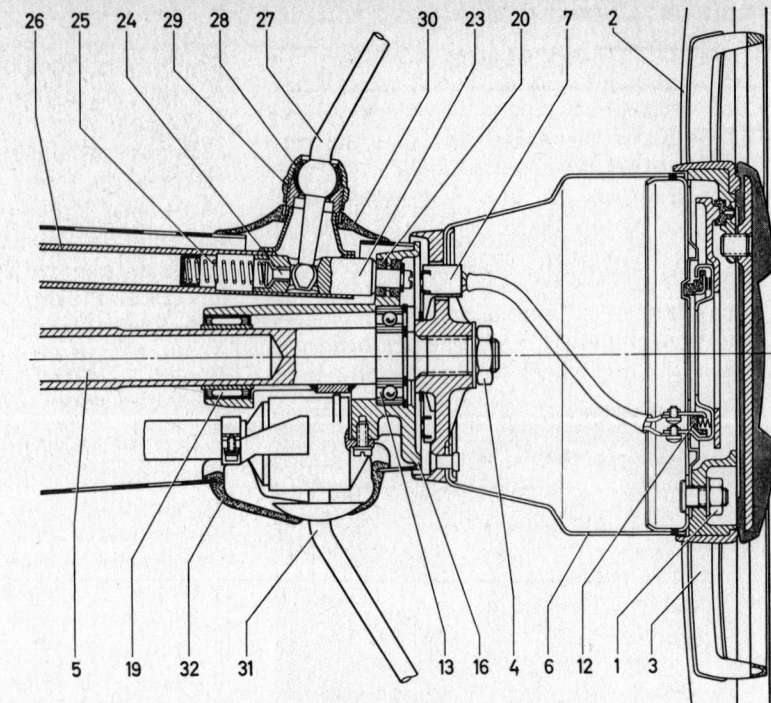

Layout of steering wheel with shock absorber.

Manual Steering Gear Removal and Installation

PRE-PHASE II MODELS

Remove the clamp bolt (8) from the lower steering coupling. Detach the center tie-rod from the steering arm, then unscrew the bolts (5) that hold the gear box to the frame. Detach the steering box shaft from the coupling and remove the gear box from underneath the car. The pitman arm can be removed from the gear box with a puller.

1. Cover plate
2. Steering column jacket
3. Rubber gasket boot
4. Lower flange of steering coupling
5. Hexagon screws for fastening the steering
   assembly to the chassis base panel
6. Upper flange of steering coupling
7. Steering tube
8. Hexagon socket screw (lower clamping screw)
9. Hexagon socket screw (upper clamping screw)

10. Screw plug in steering housing cover
11. Adjusting screw for pressure assembly of
    steering shaft
12. Hexagon nut (locknut for adjusting screw)
13. Steering gear arm
14. Tie-rod
15. Castle nut with cotter pin
16. Ball joint for center tie-rod
17. Ball joint for tie-rod
18. Center tie-rod

To install, attach the pitman arm (observing matchmarks) to the gear box, then remove the oil fill plug and fill the box with the required lubricant. Place the steering box in its centered position (this can be found by observing the steering worm shaft

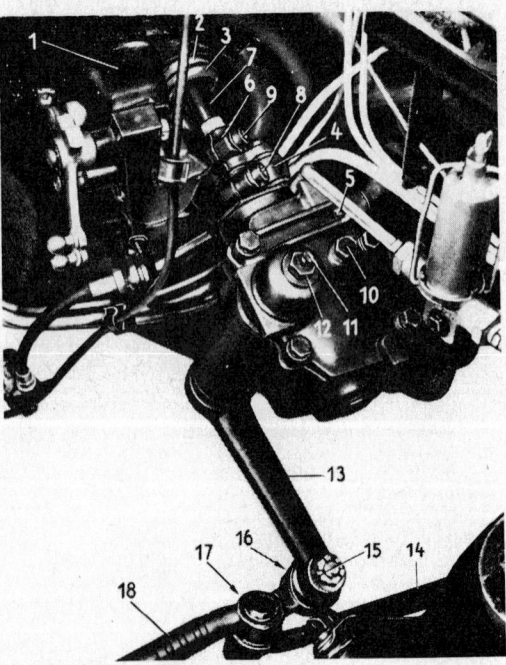

Manual steering gear assembly—pre-phase II models.

while looking down through the bore in the housing cover). Center the steering wheel (the cancelling cam for the turn signal should be opposite the center of the turn signal switch) and install the gear box from beneath the car. Insert the steering shaft of the box into the lower coupling. Install the three chassis-to-gear box bolts and tighten. Tighten the lower clamp bolt, after making sure steering wheel and gear box are both in centered positions. Reattach the center tie-rod to the pitman arm.

PHASE II MODELS

Remove the socket screw from the upper flange of the steering coupling. Detach the tie-rod and center tie-rod from the pitman arm. Remove the pitman arm from the gear box using a puller. The pitman arm can be removed from the gear box with the two tie-rods still attached if desired. In any case, however, the pitman arm must be removed from the gear box before the box will come out of the car. Detach the steering shock absorber from the bracket on the chassis, then remove the three hex-head bolts that secure the gear box to the frame side member. Press the steering worm shaft off the coupling and remove the gear box from underneath the car.

5. Steering tube
8. Steering column jacket
8a. Assembly hole in steering column jacket
33. Rubber boot

34. Cover plate
35. Hexagon screw with washer
41. Rubber grommet
42. Fixing screw
50. Assembly pin

Inserting assembly pin to center telescopic steering tube.

20. Tie-rod
20a. Clamp on tie-rod
21. Center tie-rod
21a. Plastic ring
22. Steering gear arm

25. Steering shock-absorber
27. Steering
35. Fixture 100 589 04 33 00 (tie-rod end puller)

Removing pitman arm—phase II models

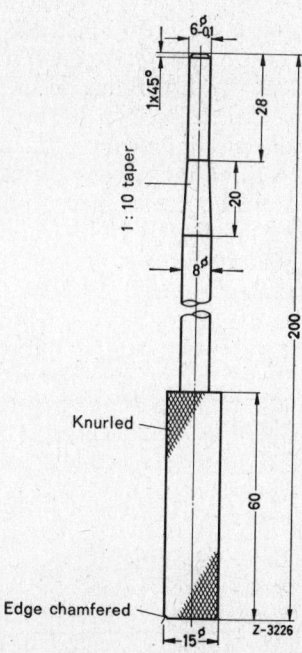

Dimensions for the garage-made assembly pin.

To install, reverse removal procedure, making sure to center the gear box and steering wheel as with previous models (previous procedure).

CAUTION: The telescopic steering tube must be fixed in position with an assembly pin inserted through hole (8a) as illustrated, otherwise the tube will be shifted out of position when the steering box is ininstalled.

Power Steering Gear
Removal and Installation

Suck the oil from the power steering reservoir using a syringe. Detach the high-pressure hose and oil return hose from the steering assembly. Cap both lines to prevent entry of dirt, then remove the clamp screw from the lower part of the coupling flange. On phase II cars, remove rubber plug (41) from cover plate (34) and remove U-joint socket screw. Detach the tie-rod and center tie-rod from the pitman arm, using pullers or a tie-rod splitter. Remove the hex-head bolts that hold the gear box to the chassis, then press the worm shaft stub from the steering coupling and remove the gear box from underneath the car.

To install, first install pitman arm (if has been removed) aligning matchmarks. Tighten pitman arm nut to 110 ft. lbs and install cotter pin. Remove the screw plug from the steering box. Turn the worm shaft until the center of the power piston is directly below the bore in the housing. On pre-phase II cars, check the dimension "a" in the illustration—the dimension can be changed by changing the position of the pitman arm on its shaft. Center the steering wheel, and shaft. This can be determined on pre-phase II cars by removing the rubber cover from the turn signal switch and observing whether the cancelling cam for the turn signals is opposite the center of the switch.

Press the worm shaft stub into the steering shaft coupling, making sure not to damage the serrations. *NOTE: On phase II cars, install assembly pin as for manual steering.* Install and tighten the hex-head screws that

hold the gear box to the chassis, then install and tighten the coupling clamp screw. Install plug in gear box, using a new gasket, attach tie-rods to pitman arm and check that the steering knuckle arms rest against their stops at full left and right lock.

Check toe-in and correct if necessary. Remove the dust covers from the fluid lines, then reconnect the high- and low-pressure lines. Fill the reservoir and connect a hose between the bleed screw on the steering and the reservoir. Open the bleed screw and, with engine running, bleed the system and top up.

Brakes

The brake systems used on Mercedes-Benz automobiles are of three basic types: drums front and rear, discs front and drums rear, and discs front and rear. The drum brakes are manually adjusted or automatically adjusted, while the disc brakes are all automatically adjusted.

Disc brakes have certain advantages over drum types. They are not as sensitive to heat build-up, thus they don't "fade" as quickly. Also, dirt and water do not affect brake action, because such contaminants are thrown off by centrifugal force or scraped off by the pads.

Most models imported into this country have one of the disc brake arrangements, the more recent models having the four-wheel discs exclusively.

The drum brake system is of conventional construction, utilizing two hydraulic wheel cylinders operating leading and trailing brake shoes.

The front disc/rear drum system has a master hydraulic cylinder with a special check valve and a power brake unit to supply the increased hydraulic pressure needed to actuate this design. There is also a pressure valve that maintains a residual pressure of 7.4–11.8 psi in the rear brake hydraulic system.

When the brake pedal is depressed, the master cylinder piston is forced forward, displacing hydraulic fluid. Since the volume of the system is constant, this displacement results in increased pressure, which is exerted on the front caliper pistons and/or wheel cylinders, thus forcing the

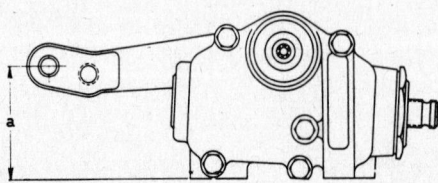

Brake System Diagnosis

Condition	Probable Cause	Correction
Brake pedal soft or "spongy"	1. Air in hydraulic system. 2. Brake fluid low. 3. Brake fluid boiling. 4. Leaking master cylinder. 5. Worn friction pads or linings. 6. Leaking wheel or pressure cylinder. 7. Damaged check valve.	1. Bleed hydraulic system. 2. Top up fluid; bleed system. 3. Let system cool down; bleed if necessary. 4. Check and replace master cylinder seals or master cylinder. 5. Replace pads or linings. 6. Replace units or damaged seals. 7. Replace check valve.
Brakes heat up or fail to release	1. Clogged compensating port in master cylinder. 2. Pushrod/piston clearance too small (single circuit). 3. Sticking wheel or pressure cylinder piston. 4. Rubber seals swollen by use of incorrect brake fluid. 5. Parking brake cables sticking. 6. Drum-brake self-adjusters binding. 7. Brake shoe return springs weak. 8. Rear drum-brake (aluminum shoes) pushrod clearance too small. 9. Check valve sticking, allowing residual pressure in system. 10. T-50 power brakes—vacuum piston or check ball in slave cylinder sticking. 11. T-51 power brakes—brake pushrod and master cylinder piston bind.	1. Clean port with stiff wire. 2. Adjust brake pedal free-play. 3. Repair wheel or pressure cylinder. 4. Clean and rebuild entire system. 5. Readjust parking brake; lube cable. 6. Check for wear; lining/shoe clearance. 7. Replace return springs. 8. Adjust pushrod clearance. 9. Replace check valve. 10. Replace damaged components. 11. Replace power brake unit.
Brakes do not stop car fast enough (normal pedal travel, hard pedal)	1. Brake linings or friction pads oily or greasy. 2. Brake linings or friction pads heat glazed. 3. Friction pads worn. 4. Brake discs or drums worn or dusty.	1. Replace linings or pads; replace rear grease seals or front hub seals. 2. Replace linings or friction pads. 3. Replace friction pads. 4. Replace or clean discs or drums.
Brakes do not stop car fast enough (long pedal travel and hard pedal)	1. Vacuum hose or connections leaking. 2. Damaged seal between master cylinder and vacuum unit. 3. Damaged master cylinder seals. 4. Damaged or leaking control valve. 5. Low engine vacuum. 6. Check valve sticking. 7. T-50 power brakes—leaking check valve in slave cylinder. 8. T-50 power brakes—vacuum piston sticking. 9. Diesel only—defective vacuum pump.	1. Tighten or replace hose. 2. Replace seal. 3. Replace seals or master cylinder. 4. Replace power brake unit. 5. Check manifolds and valves for leaks. 6. Replace vacuum line and check valve. 7. Replace power brake unit. 8. Replace power brake unit. 9. Repair vacuum pump.

Brake System Diagnosis *(Continued)*

Condition	Probable Cause	Correction
Brakes rattle or chatter	1. Rear shock absorbers worn. 2. Rear suspension/spring broken. 3. Excessive wheel wobble/bent rim/tires out of round.	1. Replace shock absorbers. 2. Repair faulty components. 3. Replace rims/tires.
	Disc Brakes 1a. Excessive disc runout. 2a. Friction pads wearing unevenly. 3a. Brake discs uneven thickness. 4a. Brake discs grease-coated, rusty.	1a. Correct runout. 2a. Replace pads; break in carefully. 3a. Install new disc so that difference does not exceed 0.0012". 4a. Clean brake discs.
	Drum Brakes 1b. Brake drums out of round. 2b. Brake drum wall thickness unequal. 3b. Unequally worn brake linings.	1b. Replace or machine drums; must be less than 0.0008" variation. 2b. Replace brake drums if variation exceeds 0.040". 3b. Replace brake linings
Brakes dragging on one side (drum brakes)	1. Brake linings worn unevenly. 2. Brake shoes on one side too large in diameter. 3. Brake drums out of round or scored. 4. Internal diameter of drums unequal. 5. Brake linings oily or greasy. 6. One shoe sticking on anchor pin. 7. Wheel cylinder sticking. 8. Brakes unequally adjusted. 9. Dust in brake drums. 10. Heat glazed linings.	1. Replace linings. 2. Replace shoes. 3. Replace or machine. 4. Equalize diameter by grinding. 5. Replace linings; replace grease seals or front hub seals. 6. Clean and lubricate pin. 7. Recondition or replace wheel cylinder. 8. Adjust brakes or check self-adjuster operation. 9. Blow out dust with compressed air. 10. Replace or sand linings.
Brakes dragging on one side (disc brakes)	1. Friction pads oily or greasy. 2. Friction pad on one side worn. 3. Brake caliper not parallel to disc. 4. One friction pad heat glazed. 5. Clearance in one caliper insufficient.	1. Replace pads and seals. 2. Replace pads, both sides. 3. Adjust caliper using shims. 4. Replace all pads. 5. Dunlop—check clearance, replace pressure cylinder if necessary. Girling/Teves—check pistons for ease of movement.
Brakes squealing	**Disc Brakes** 1. Friction pad loose on piston guide (Dunlop). 2. Piston cocked in caliper (Teves). 3. Friction pad has insufficient play in caliper gap. **Drum Brakes** 1a. Faulty shoe-to-anchor contact. 2a. Too much clearance between brake shoe eye and anchor pin. 3a. Unequally worn or glazed linings. 4a. Dust in brake drums.	1. Reseat pad. 2. Check piston position. 3. Grease rear and side pad surfaces with Molykote. 1a. Straighten contact plates. 2a. Adjust clearance. 3a. Replace brake linings. 4a. Blow out dust and sand linings.

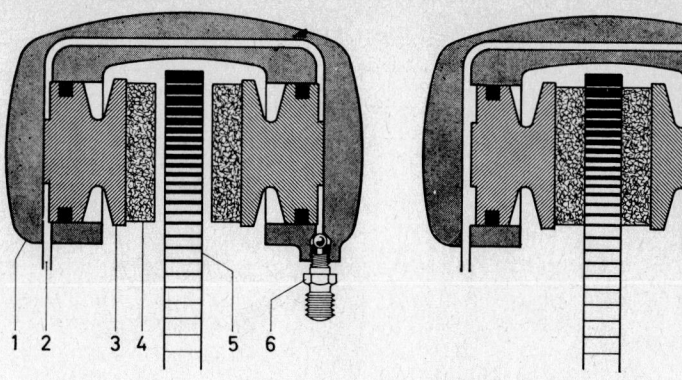

Girling disc brake. Left—Non-applied position. Right—Applied position.

friction pads or brake shoes against the disc or drums.

Pressure is in direct proportion to the effort applied to the brake pedal, although disc/drum systems utilize a proportioning valve to maintain a front/rear pressure ratio, thereby reducing the possibility of premature rear wheel lock-up.

When the pedal is released, hydraulic pressure drops and the brake return springs (on drum brakes) and wobbling action of the disc (on disc brakes) return the shoes/pads to their proper positions and force the displaced fluid back into the master cylinder.

Brake Types

GIRLING DISC BRAKES

There are three versions of this brake system. On the first and second versions, the steering knuckle bracket is riveted to the knuckle and the caliper is aligned with the disc by shims. The third version has a combination bracket and knuckle and no shims are used to locate the calipers.

The first and second versions can be distinguished from the third version by the external hydraulic line that connects the inner and outer pistons. The third version has an internal passage connecting the pistons.

DUNLOP DISC BRAKES

This type brake is used at both front and rear wheels. The caliper is attached to the steering knuckle bracket (or to rear axle housing) and fits around the rotating brake disc. Pistons on each side of the disc keep tension constant and prevent any distortion.

1. Front wheel hub	9. Brake caliper
2. Brake disc	10. Stirrup
4. Connecting line with pipe clip	11. Brake line
6. Friction pad with fitting plate	18. Bleed screw

Dunlop front disc brake.

As with the other disc systems, the Dunlop brake is self-adjusting and maintains a good pedal regardless of pad wear.

There is an automatic adjustment mechanim within the caliper pistons but it cannot be disassembled, nor does it require any maintenance.

The rear wheel discs require a separate mechanism to provide parking brake action. As with drum brakes, a separate handbrake is used to mechanically activate the brake linings or, in this case, friction pads.

The illustrations show how the system works. When the lever (32) is activated by the handbrake, lining carriers (18) and (19) are pivoted on the caliper assembly (1) and the pads are pressed against the

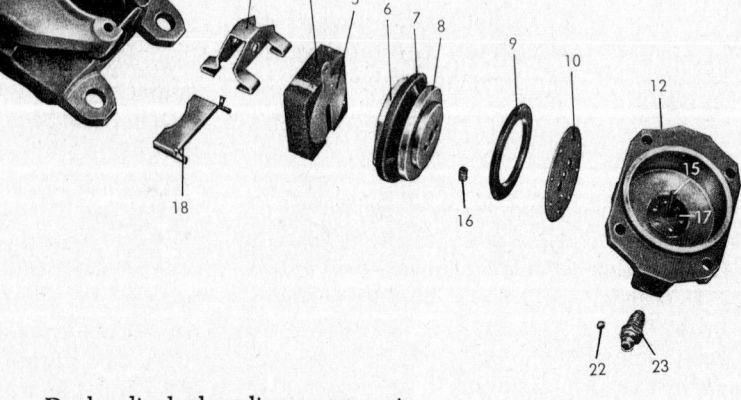

1. Brake caliper
12. Connecting line
13. Pipe clip
18. Outer lining carrier
19. Inner lining carrier
32. Tension lever
35. Cover plate
36. Adjustment screw

Rear parking brake mechanism—Dunlop.

1. Brake caliper
2. Stirrup
3. Hexagon screw with hexagon nut and serrated lockwasher
4. Friction pad with fitting plate (foot brake)
12. Pressure cylinder
19. Brake disc
20. Connecting line with pipe clip
24. Locking plate
25. Swing bolt
26. Leg spring
27a. Outer lining carrier
27b. Inner lining carrier
29. Friction pad with fitting plate (handbrake)
31. Adjustment screw
34. Tension lever
38. Brake line
40. Wheel fixing disc
41. Brake support lever
42. Rear axle shaft

Dunlop rear disc brake.

disc. The pads are also automatically adjusted in this application.

When the clearance of the pads becomes greater than .008", the pin (27a) advances into the next notch of adjusting nut (26). When the handbrake is released, the adjustment is completed.

TEVES DISC BRAKES

The operation and construction of this type system is similar to the third version Girling disc brakes. At the front, the caliper is attached to the steering knuckle/caliper bracket without use of aligning

1. Brake caliper
2. Stirrup
4. Friction pad
5. Fitting plate
6. Lining pressure plate
7. Dust cap
8. Piston
9. Piston seal
10. Piston plate
12. Pressure cylinder
15. Return pin
16. Friction spring
17. Spring plate
18. Retaining plate
22. Ball
23. Bleed screw

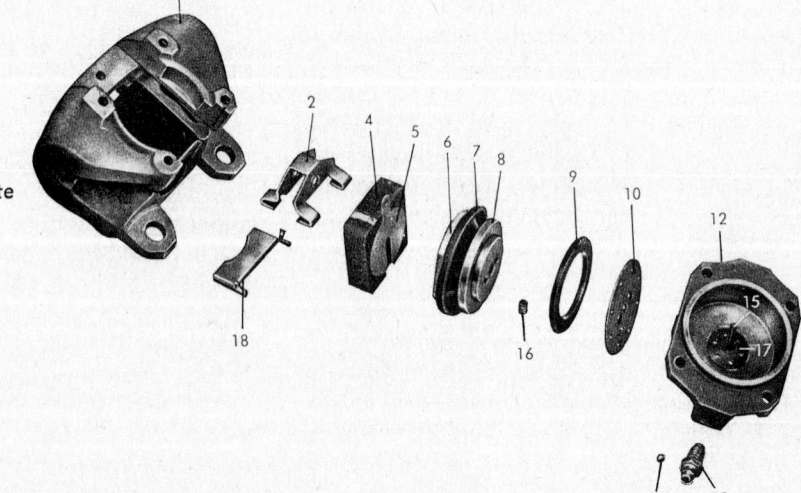

Dunlop disc brake caliper components.

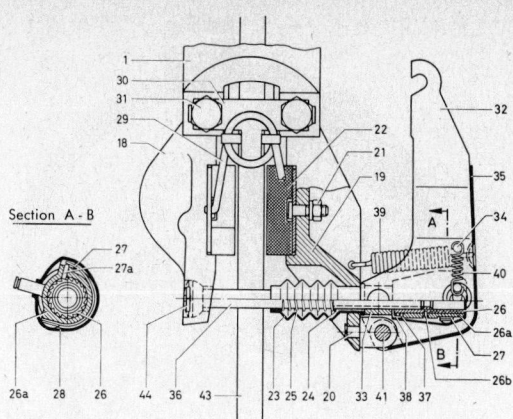

Section A - B

1. Brake caliper
18. Outer lining carrier
19. Inner lining carrier
20. Bearing bracket
21. Cheesehead screw
    with hexagon
    nut and crimped
    washer
22. Friction pad with
    mounting plate
23. Rubber grommet
24. Plastic bushing
25. Pressure spring
26. Adjusting nut
26a. Adjusting sleeve
26b. Snap-ring
27. Flat spring
27a. Pin

28. Rubber cap
29. Leg spring
30. Locking plate
31. Swing bolt
32. Tension lever
33. Driving block
34. Pin on tension
    lever
35. Cover plate
36. Adjustment screw
37. Retaining spring
38. Cup
39. Return spring
40. Return spring
41. Collar bolt
43. Brake disc
44. Cotter pin

Rear brake caliper and parking brake mechanism—
Dunlop.

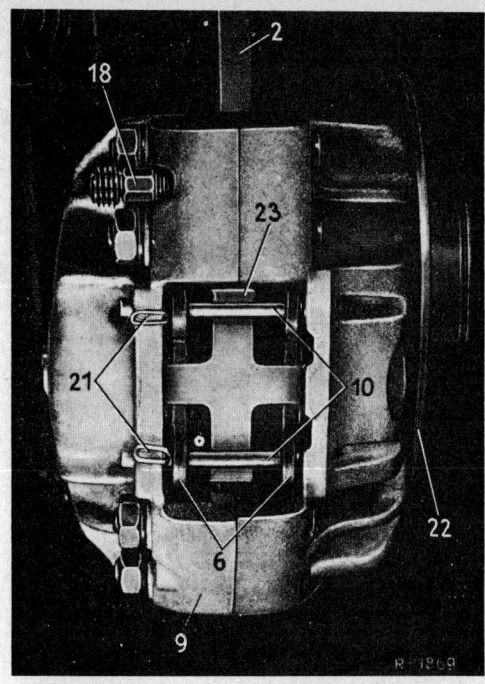

2. Brake disc
6. Friction pad
9. Brake caliper
10. Lock pin

18. Bleed screw
21. Locking clip
22. Front wheel hub
23. Cross leaf spring

Teves disc brake.

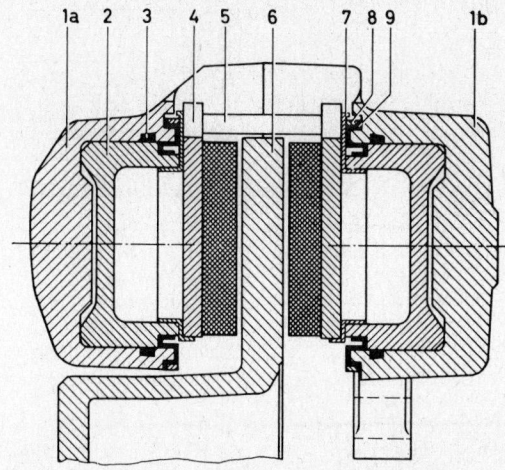

1a. Outer brake caliper
    half
1b. Inner brake caliper
    half
2. Piston
3. Piston seal
4. Friction pad

5. Lock pin
6. Brake disc
7. Heat screening
   plate
8. Clamp ring
9. Dust cap

Friction pad and caliper piston location—Teves.

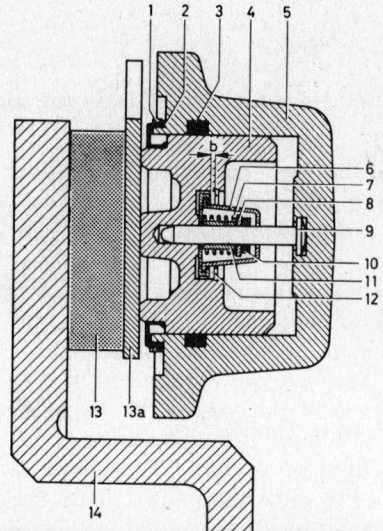

1. Clamp ring
2. Dust cap
3. Piston seal
4. Piston
5. Pressure cylinder
   of brake cali-
   per
6. Stop cap
7. Pressure spring
8. Spacer washer

9. Guide pin
10. Clamp rings
11. Spacer sleeve
12. Lock ring
13. Friction pad
13a. Base plate
14. Brake disc
b. Clearance be-
   tween stop cap
   and lock ring

Caliper piston and associated parts—Teves.

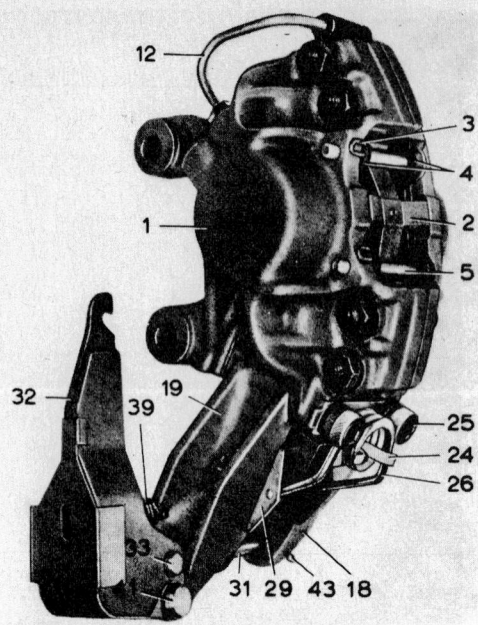

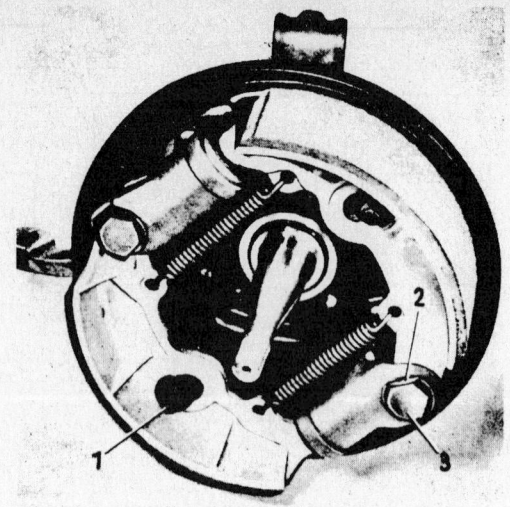

1. Hexagon screw
2. Locking plate
3. Anchor pin

Typical drum brake.

1. Brake caliper	25. Swing bolt
2. Cross leaf spring	26. Leg spring
3. Locking clip	29. Friction pad (park-
4. Friction pad (serv-	ing brake)
ice brake)	31. Adjustment screw
5. Lock pin	32. Tension lever
12. Connecting line	33. Crosshead
18. Outer lining carrier	39. Return spring
19. Inner lining carrier	41. Collar bolt
24. Retaining plate for	43. Cotter pin
leg spring	

Rear brake caliper and parking brake mechanism—
Teves.

shims. The two halves of the caliper are
bolted together permanently. *NOTE: These
bolts should never be removed for any
reason.*

The rear calipers are equipped with an
automatic adjusting mechanism and, in
addition, a disc-wobble compensator. This
last feature is required because of the large
movement of the axle shafts, especially on
turns. Without the compensator, the pistons would be required to move a longer
distance to press the pads against the disc,
thus increasing brake pedal travel.

Lining Replacement

Front Lining Replacement—
Drum Brakes with Mechanical
Adjustment

Jack up the car and remove the brake
drum. Using brake spring pliers, or a
screwdriver, remove the two return springs.
If pliers are used, always place a piece of

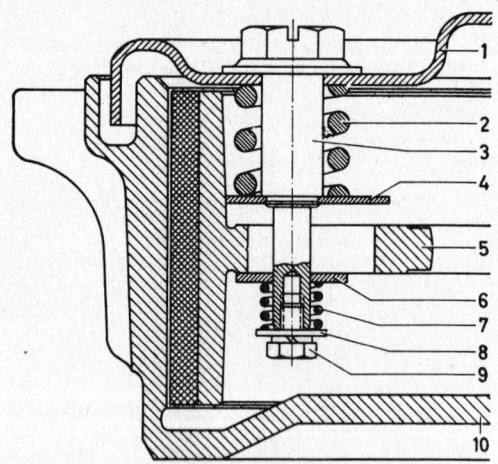

1. Brake anchor plate	6. Washer
2. Pressure spring	7. Pressure spring
3. Adjustment bolt	8. Washer
4. Eccentric plate	9. Hexagon screw
5. Brake shoe	10. Brake drum

Guide pin and components—mechanical adjusters.

rubber tile, or equivalent, on the lining for
protection.

Remove the hold-down bolts, washers
and coil springs, then unscrew the stop
bolts from the rear of the wheel cylinder.
Bend the lock tabs back and unscrew the
anchor pins from the wheel cylinder.
NOTE: One version has the anchor pin

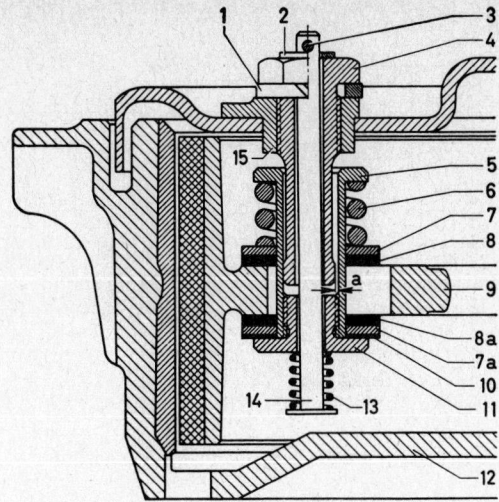

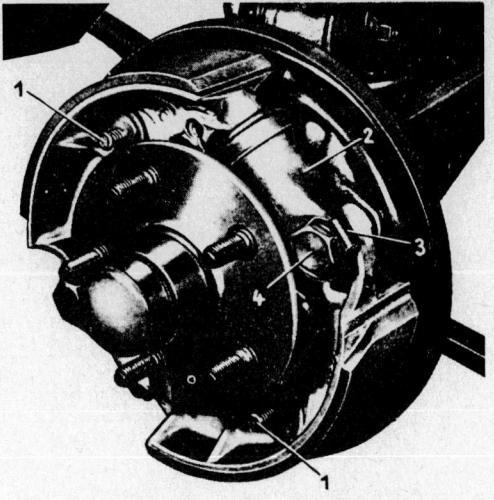

1. Guide pin   3. Locking plate
2. Brake wheel cylinder   4. Anchor pin

Lining installed. Note chamfered lining edges.

1. Lockwasher	8 and 8a. Friction
2. Washer	washers
3. Cotter pin	9. Brake shoe
4. Bolt	10. Washer
5. Adjusting sleeve	11. Tensioning screw
6. Pressure spring	12. Brake drum
7. and 7a. Thrust	13. Pressure spring
washers	14. Guide pin
	a. clearance

Guide pin and components—self-adjusters.

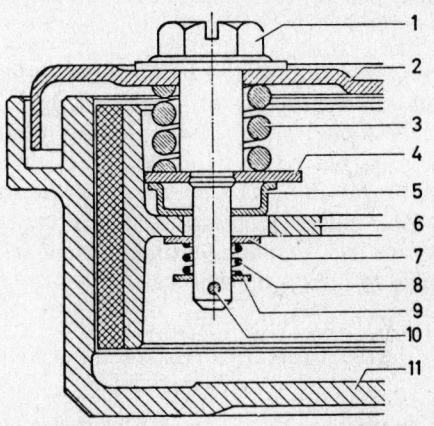

1. Adjustment bolt	7. Washer
2. Brake anchor plate	8. Pressure spring
3. Pressure spring	9. Washer
4. Eccentric plate	10. Cotter pin
5. Cup washer	11. Brake drum
6. Brake shoe	

Guide pin and components used on 2″ wide shoes —rear mechanical.

screwed directly into the wheel cylinder, therefore the rear bolt does not need loosening.

Remove the brake shoes and blow the backing plates off with compressed air. The edges of new brake shoes should be chamfered before installation to allow faster lining break-in without dust build-up.

Install the new brake shoes and all other components. Then adjust the brakes as outlined later in this chapter.

Front Lining Replacement—
Drum Brakes with Self-Adjusters

Jack up the car and remove brake drum and return springs. Remove the cotter pins (3) on guide pin (14) from behind the backing plate, then remove the washer, guide pin and spring (13).

Loosen the bolts (4) from behind the backing plate and remove along with lockwashers. Then remove the stop bolts (2) and lockwashers. *NOTE: Some versions do not require removal of the stop bolts.*

Bend the lock tabs (6) away from the anchor pins and remove the pins, then brake shoes. Remove the retaining pins from the wheel cylinder, blow the backing plate off with compressed air and install the new shoes, first chamfering the edges of the lining. *CAUTION: The automatic self-adjusters must be checked before installing the brake drums. Using a large*

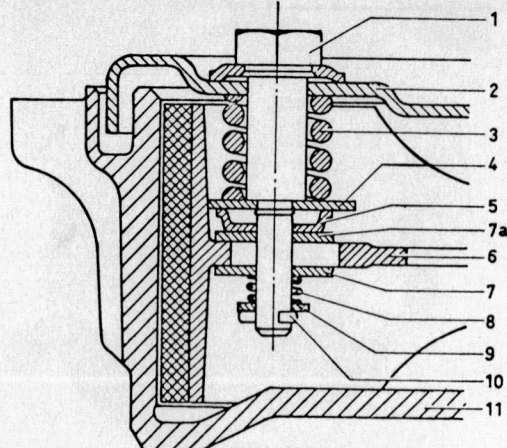

1. Adjustment bolt   7. Washer
2. Brake anchor plate   7a. Washer
3. Pressure spring   8. Pressure spring
4. Eccentric plate   9. Washer
5. Cup washer   10. Cotter pin
6. Brake shoe   11. Brake drum

Guide pin and components used on 2.6″ wide shoes—rear mechanical.

screwdriver, work the brake shoes outward and inward as far as they will go. The brake shoes must remain in any position they are placed, even when gently tapped. Before installing the drums, force the shoes to their innermost position and, before driving the car, pump the brake pedal a few times to adjust the brakes.

Rear Lining Replacement— Drum Brakes with Mechanical Adjustment

There were three versions used—two with cast-iron shoes 2″ and 2.6″ lining width and one with cast aluminum shoes having 2.6″ linings.

To replace lining on models with cast-iron shoes, jack up car and remove brake drum and return spring. Remove the cotter pin, washer, spring and rear washer. Remove the hex bolt from the anchor pin and remove all washers. The brake shoes and parking brake cable now can be removed, as well as the spring. Clean the backing plate with compressed air and install new shoes, first chamfering the lining edges. Coat the anchor pins with a light coat of grease, then reinstall all components. Adjust the brakes as outlined later in this chapter. *NOTE: The washer arrangements on the 2″ and 2.6″ brakes differ—see illustrations.*

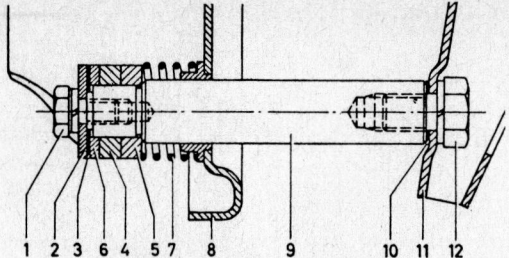

1. Hexagon screw   7. Pressure spring
2. Washer   8. Brake anchor plate
3. Brass washer   9. Anchor pin
4. Outer brake shoe   10. Shim
5. Inner brake shoe   11. Bracket
6. Washer   12. Hexagon screw

Anchor pin and components—rear mechanical.

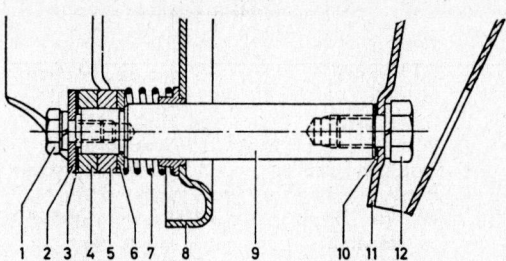

1. Hexagon screw   7. Pressure spring
2. Washer   8. Brake anchor plate
3. Brass washer   9. Anchor pin
4. Outer brake shoe   10. Shim
5. Inner brake shoe   11. Bracket
6. Washer   12. Hexagon screw

Anchor pin and components—rear mechanical.

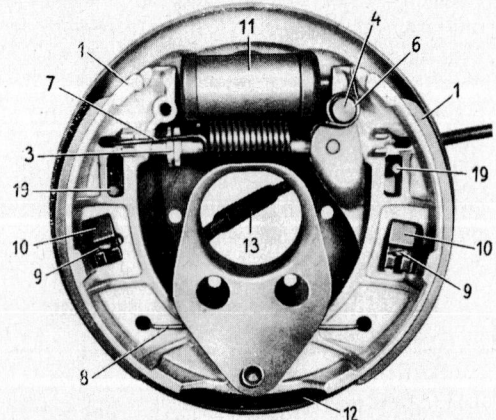

1. Brake shoes   9. Retaining pin
3. Pushrod   10. Flat spring
4. Collar bolt   11. Wheel cylinder
6. Brake lever spring   12. Brake anchor plate
7. Upper return spring   13. Brake cable
8. Lower return   14. Eccentric plate
      spring

Aluminum 2.6″ wide shoes.

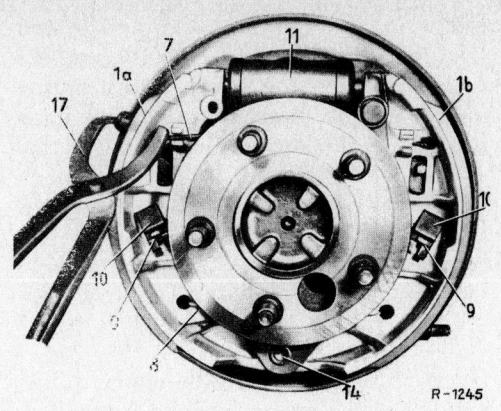

1a. Front brake shoe	10. Flat spring
1b. Rear brake shoe	11. Wheel cylinder
7. Upper return spring	14. Brake shoe anchor pin
8. Lower return spring	17. Brake spring pliers
9. Retaining pin	

1b. Rear brake shoe
2. Brake lever
16. Pry bar 1½″ wide

Removing rear brake shoe

Shoe removal. Note pad under pliers to protect linings.

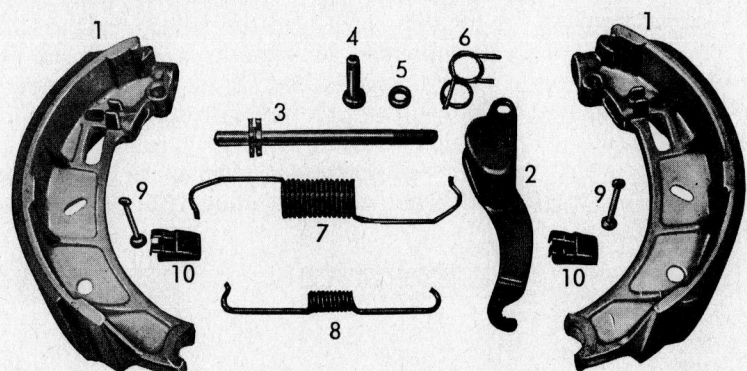

1. Brake shoes
2. Brake lever
3. Pushrod
4. Collar bolt
5. Sleeve
6. Return spring
7. Upper return spring
8. Lower return spring
9. Retaining pin
10. Flat spring

Brake components.

The aluminum brake shoes require a slightly different replacement procedure. After removing the brake drum, detach the upper and lower return springs, then, using a screw driver, press off the two shoe retaining clips and remove the associated pins.

Rotate the two eccentrics (19) until the shoes are out to the end of their travel, then insert a suitable piece of flat steel between the brake cable lever and the rear shoe and remove the shoe. Now remove the front shoe and disconnect the rear shoe from the brake lever. Unscrew the pushrod from the brake lever and remove the upper return spring from the pushrod.

To install new shoes, first coat the pushrod threads with a good graphite grease or Molykote, then hook the return spring to the pushrod, with the long end toward the thread. Screw the pushrod into the brake lever and attach the lever, pushrod and *both* return springs to the rear brake shoe. Place a punch through one retaining hole to lock the return spring in position, insert the flat steel pry bar between the brake shoe and lever, attach, the brake cable and install the shoe to the backing plate. Install the front shoe, after coating the anchor pins and pivot points with grease, then turn the two eccentrics to adjust the brakes inward. Insert the re-

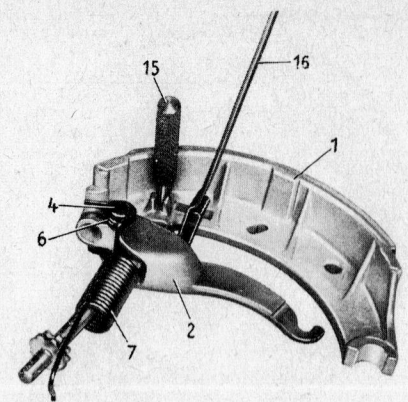

1. Brake shoes
2. Brake lever
4. Collar bolt
6. Brake lever spring
7. Upper return spring
15. Retaining pin
16. Spreader

Retaining pin (punch) placement.

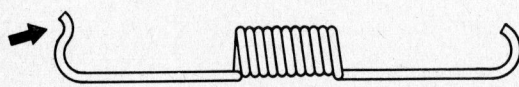

Spring used with rear drums having self-adjusters.

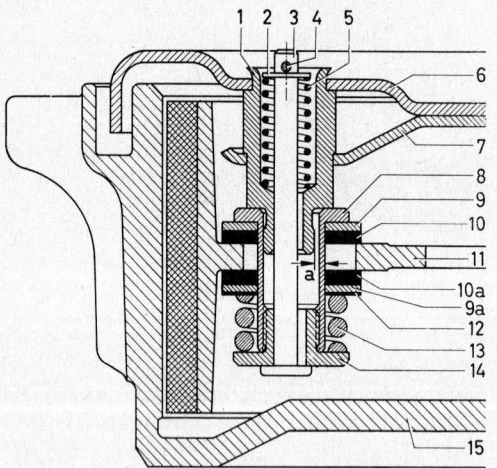

1. Bolt
2. Washer
3. Guide pin
4. Cotter pin
5. Pressure spring
6. Brake anchor plate
7. Bow
8. Adjusting sleeve
9. and 9a. Thrust washer
10. and 10a. Friction washer
11. Brake shoe
12. Washer
13. Pressure spring
14. Tensioning screw
15. Brake drum
a. Clearance

Guide pin and components. Pin can be reversed for ease in installation, with cotter pin end facing forward—self-adjusters.

taining pins through the backing plate and shoes and snap the clips onto the ends of the pins. Attach the upper return spring and remove the punch from the retaining hole. Attach the lower return spring so that the end with the kink in its hook is attached to the front brake shoe. Install the brake drums and adjust the brakes as outlined later.

REAR LINING REPLACEMENT— DRUM BRAKES WITH SELF-ADJUSTERS

Jack up the car, remove the brake drums, then detach the brake shoe and brake lever return springs. Remove the cotter pins from the automatic adjusters, then the washers, pins and springs. Remove the brake shoes and detach the handbrake cable, then remove the washer and spring from the anchor pin. Remove the spring-loaded pins from one wheel cylinder, then remove the activating pin (2) from the guide pin (5) and check the springs (3) for tension. Clean the backing plate with compressed air, chamfer the edges of the new lining, and install. It will be necessary to compress the pressure spring during installation using a small C-clamp. *NOTE: The left- and right-hand return springs are different—see illustration. Check the auto-*

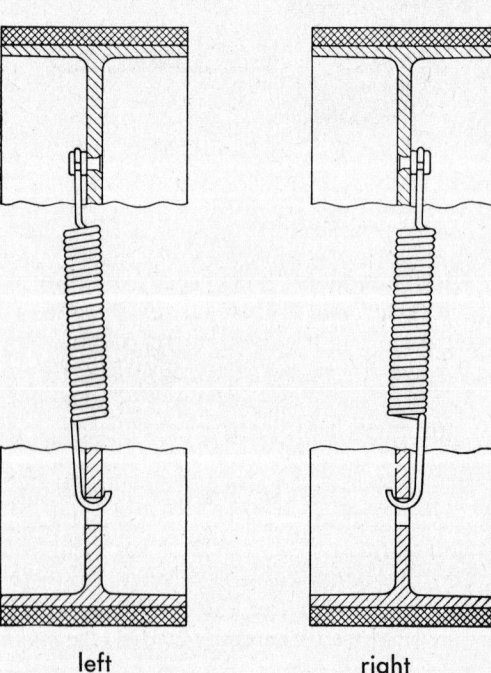

left   right

Return springs—self-adjusters.

1. Front wheel hub
2. Brake disc
3. Brake caliper
4. Connecting line
5. Bleed screw
6. Friction pad
7. Spring clip

Girling disc brakes.

1. Friction pad
2. Brake caliper
3. Brake disc

Pad removal—Girling.

matic adjusters as outlined in Front Lining Replacement—Drum Brakes With Self-Adjusters, then adjust the handbrake as outlined later.

PAD REPLACEMENT—GIRLING DISC BRAKES

The construction of this type brake allows complete pad inspection without disassembly. Check the pads and replace only if worn to .080″ or less, or if the disc and pads are oil-coated.

To remove, pull the spring clips (7) out of the retaining pins and remove the pins. Using a wire hook, bent from ³⁄₁₆″ welding rod, pull the pads from the calipers. Blow off the brake assembly with compressed air and push the pistons back out of the way. *NOTE: This sometimes forces fluid from the master cylinder reservoir.*

Before pushing the pistons back, remove the inner heat shield, if present, to prevent damage. These shields, by the way, can be replaced with anti-squeak plates, available at authorized dealers, if brake squealing is a problem.

Making sure the dust caps are properly seated by pressing them back with a screwdriver, install new pads, then insert retaining pins and clips. Pump the brake pedal a few times to seat the pads, then

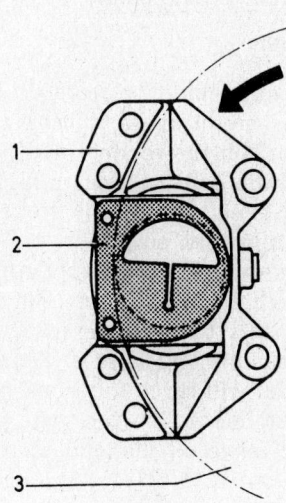

1. Calipers
2. Anti-squeal plate
3. Brake disc

Girling anti-squeal plate installation.

check the master cylinder reservoir and fill if necessary.

As with all new brakes, disc brake pads should be carefully broken in or they will become heat glazed and useless. In other words, *no hard stops* for several hundred miles.

1. Front wheel hub
2. Brake disc
4. Connecting line
6. Friction pad
9. Brake caliper
10. Stirrup
11. Brake line
18. Bleed screw

Dunlop disc brake configuration. Stirrup (10) must be removed before pads can be replaced.

1. Brake caliper
4. Friction pad
12. Pressure cylinder
19. Brake disc
47. Hook

Pad removal using hook (47)—Dunlop.

PAD REPLACEMENT—DUNLOP DISC BRAKES

A. Foot Brake

Dunlop pads should be replaced if worn to ¼″ or less in thickness, or if oil covered. To check, unbolt the retainer (10) and remove it and the bolt. If worn, remove pads with a hook, then blow off the brake assembly with compressed air.

Before installiing new pads, push the pistons back into their bores. The illustration shows this being done using special piston pliers, but, if care is exercised, a piece of steel will serve the same purpose.

Check the guide for the pad pressure plate and remove all dirt and score marks with emery paper. *NOTE: Pushing pistons back may displace brake fluid from master cylinder reservoir.*

Install pad onto piston guide bolt, making sure it is properly engaged. Attach the pad retainer and bolt and pump the brake pedal to seat the pads. Do not abuse the brakes for several hundred miles; otherwise, the pads will become heat glazed.

B. Parking Brake

The parking brake (handbrake) pads must be replaced if worn to .18″ or less, or if oil covered.

To remove, pull the cotter pin on the outer lining carrier (27a) and back out the adjustment screw (31) a few turns. Detach

1. Brake caliper
4. Connecting line

Holding caliper pistons in retracted position using special tool (48a)—Dunlop.

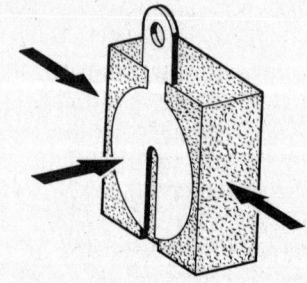

Dunlop friction pad lubrication points. Even one drop of grease on pad friction surface will result in erratic brake action.

1. Brake caliper
2. Stirrup
3. Hexagon screw with hexagon nut and serrated lockwasher
4. Friction pad with fitting plate (service brake)
12. Pressure cylinder
19. Brake disc
20. Connecting line with pipe clip
24. Locking plate
25. Swing bolt
26. Leg spring
27a. Outer lining carrier
27b. Inner lining carrier
29. Friction pad with fitting plate (handbrake)
31. Adjustment screw
34. Tension lever
38. Brake line
40. Wheel fixing disc
41. Brake support lever
42. Rear axle shaft

Rear brake caliper and disc arrangement—Dunlop.

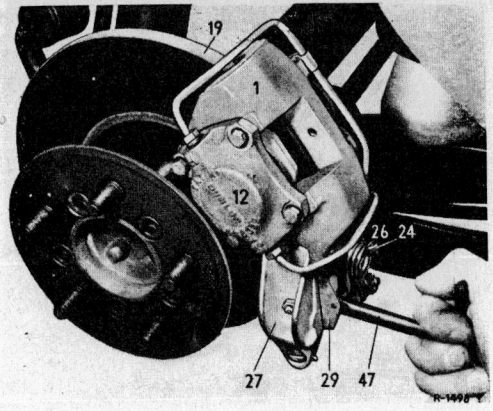

1. Brake caliper
12. Pressure cylinder
19. Brake disc
24. Locking plate
26. Leg spring
27. Lining carrier
29. Friction pad
47. Removal hook

Removing rear friction pads—Dunlop.

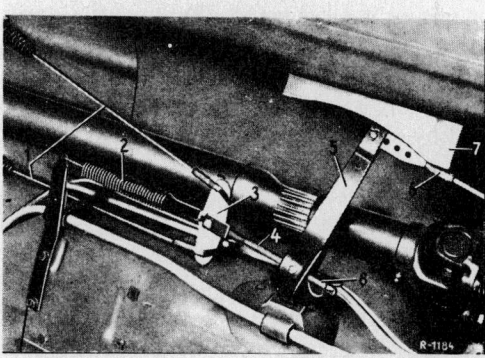

1. Rear brake cables
2. Return spring
3. Equalizer
4. Tensioning screw
5. Relay lever
6. Center brake cable
7. Relay lever guide
8. Wingnut for handbrake adjustment

Parking brake cables must be slackened—Dunlop.

the hairpin spring (26) and loosen the nut that holds the pads to the lining carriers. Pull the pad from the carrier using a hook, then clean the pad guide on the lining carrier with emery paper.

Loosen the parking brake cables by backing out the wingnut at the relay lever, then install the new friction pads. Install the hairpin spring and adjust the pads by turning screw (31) until a clearance of .020" exists between the pads and disc. Lock the adjusting screw with a cotter pin, then seat the pads by pulling the handbrake on a few times. Adjust the handbrake cables as outlined later.

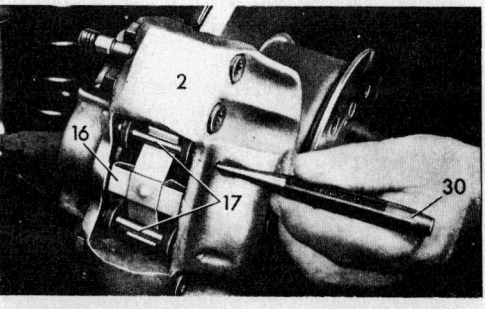

2. Brake caliper
16. Cross-leaf spring
17. Retaining pin
30. Drift

Driving out retaining pin—Teves.

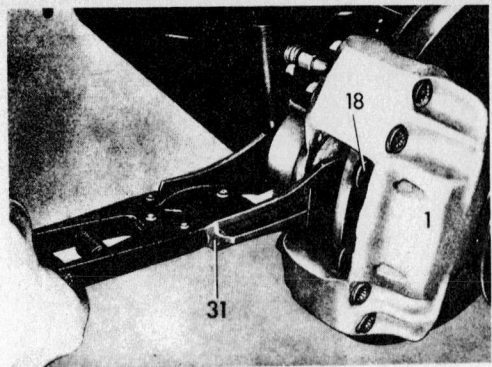

1. Brake caliper
18. Friction pad

Holding pistons in retracted position using special pliers (31)—Teves.

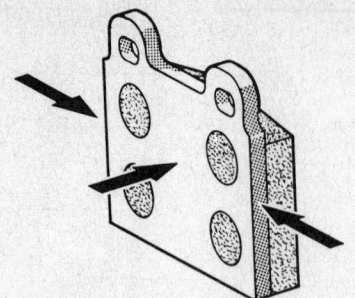

Friction pad lubrication points—Teves.

PAD REPLACEMENT—TEVES
DISC BRAKES

Pads must be replaced if worn to .080″ or less, or if oil covered. Remove the cover plate (front only) and drive the retaining pins out of the caliper, using a drift. Remove the "cross" spring, then remove one pad by pulling out on both tabs with bent pieces of welding rod. Blow off the brake assembly with compressed air and clean the pad guide in the caliper. Check the dust covers for cracks. If cracks exist, the caliper must be disassembled and the cover replaced.

Press one piston back into its bore, using special pliers or a flat piece of steel bent to fit. *NOTE: Fluid may be displaced from the master cylinder reservoir.*

Install one friction pad, then push the other piston back and install the other pad. *NOTE: One pad must always remain in caliper, because pushing one piston back would bring the other forward too far.*

Install the "cross" spring and retaining pins, then seat the pads by pumping the brake pedal a few times.

Hard stopping for the first few hundred miles could ruin the new pads by causing heat glazing.

LINING REPLACEMENT—TEVES
DRUM PARKING BRAKE

To replace rear parking brake lining, first remove the brake caliper and disc (as described later in this chapter), then detach the lower return spring (31), using brake spring pliers. Turn the axle flange

15. Rear axle shaft flange	31. Lower return spring
20. Brake shoes	39. Brake spring pilers
24. Compression spring	

Removing parking brake linings—Teves.

13. Support web	20. Brake shoes
15. Rear axle shaft flange	24. Compression spring

Removing retaining springs using special tool (40) —Teves.

11. Cover plate	20. Brake shoes
13. Support web	22. Adjustment device
15. Rear axle shaft flange	29. Upper return spring

Lifting parking brake shoes over axle flange—Teves.

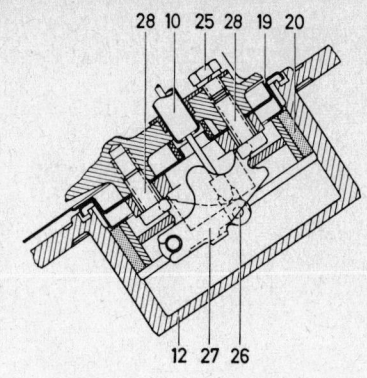

10. Brake cable	26. Pin
12. Brake disc	27. Expansion lock
19. Cover plate	28. Hexagon socket screw
20. Brake shoes	

Cross-section of parking brake assembly—Teves.

so that a threaded bolt hole aligns with a retainer spring (24). Depress the spring as illustrated, then turn 90° and remove. Remove the other spring in the same manner, then pull the brake shoes apart at the lower end and remove upward. Detach the upper return spring and star wheel adjuster, then press out pin (26) from the expansion lock (27) and remove lock from brake cable.

Coat all moving surfaces with Molykote paste, then attach the expansion lock to the brake cable and press the lock into the backing plate. Adjust the star wheel to its innermost position, after lubricating threads, and install it and the upper return spring onto the new shoes. Slip the shoes over the axle and hook them to the expansion lock, then hook up the retainer spring and lower return spring. The long-hooked end is attached last. Install brake disc, caliper and adjust parking brake.

Disc Brake Caliper Replacement

To remove the caliper, first remove the brake line (11) from the caliper (9). *NOTE: Plug the line to prevent fluid loss.* The lines are arranged as follows:

Girling (1st version)—line is attached to inner position bore by a hollow bolt. The brake hose connector points upward and

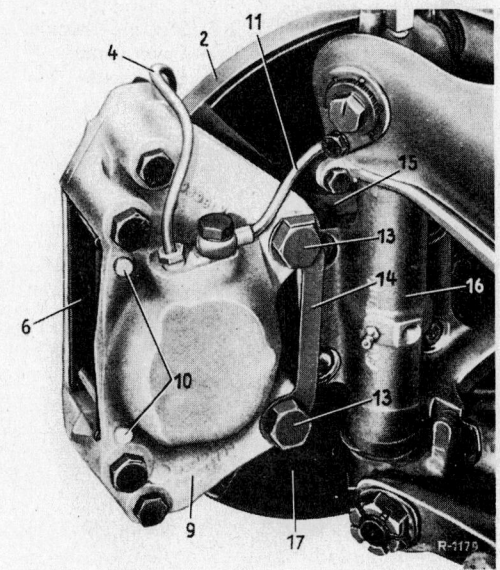

2. Brake disc	13. Hexagon fitting screw
4. Connecting line	14. Locking plate
6. Friction pad	15. Steering knuckle bracket
9. Brake caliper	16. Steering knuckle
10. Locking pin	17. Cover plate
11. Brake line with connector	

Girling disc brake (first version).

the bleed screw is in the outer caliper half.

Girling (2nd version)—line is attached to outer piston bore. Hose connector is connected behind steering knuckle and bleed screw is on inner cylinder.

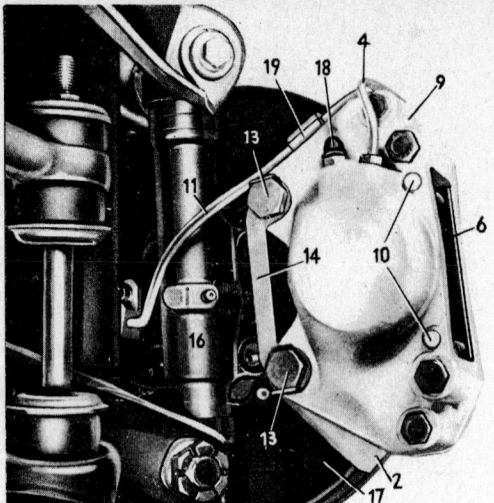

2. Brake disc
4. Connecting line
6. Friction pad
9. Brake caliper
10. Locking pin
11. Brake line with
    connector

13. Hexagon fitting
    screw
14. Locking plate
16. Steering knuckle
17. Cover plate
18. Bleed screw
19. Rubber lug

Girling disc brake (second version).

2. Brake disc
6. Friction pad
9. Brake caliper
10. Locking pin
11. Brake line with
    connector
13. Hexagon fitting
    screw

14. Locking plate
16. Steering knuckle
17. Cover plate
18. Bleed screw with
    rubber cap
20. Heat screening
    plate

Girling disc brake (third version).

Girling (3rd version)—line is connected to inner piston bore and there is no external connecting line.
Teves—same as 3rd version Girling.

1. Feeler gauge
2. Brake disc
3. Brake caliper
M = Measuring point

Measuring caliper to disc clearance on Girling brakes.

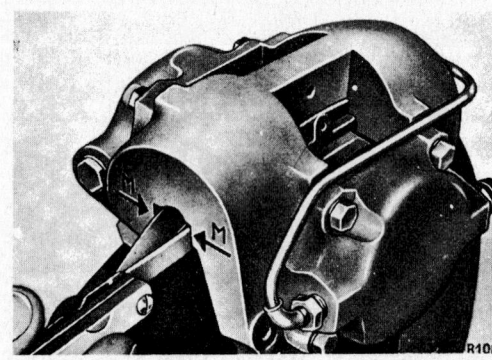

Measuring caliper to disc clearance on Dunlop brakes. M = Measuring point.

Dunlop—the brake line is attached to the outer piston bore.
NOTE: The caliper need not be removed unless the disc or hub must come off.
Next, bend back the lock tabs (14) and remove the hold-down bolts (13). The caliper can be removed at this time. Any shims should be taped together and their positions noted.
To install, reverse the removal procedure, paying special attention to shim placement. Always use a new lock tab—bending weakens the metal.
It is extremely important that the brake disc be exactly parallel to the caliper. Using a feeler gauge, measure the clearance

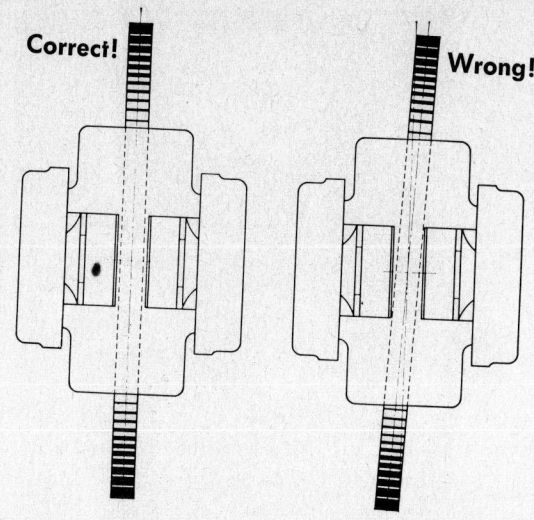

Correct!   Wrong!

If the caliper and disc are misaligned uneven friction pad wear will result.

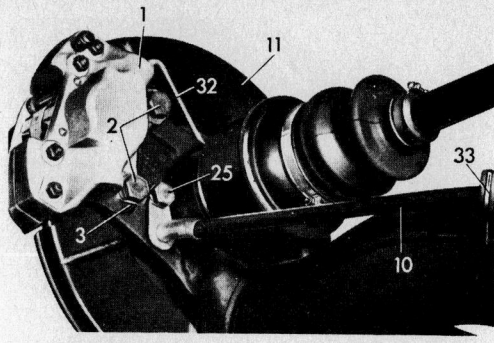

1. Brake caliper
2. Hexagon screw
3. Locking plate
10. Brake cable
11. Cover plate

25. Hexagon screw
32. Brake line
33. Bracket for brake cable with rubber grommet

Teves rear brake caliper used on phase II models.

at the top and bottom of the caliper (between disc and caliper) and on both sides of the disc (see illustrations). If the clearance varies beyond specifications, position the brake caliper by adding or subtracting shims as required.

Tighten all bolts to proper torque specifications, then install the lock tabs. Connect the brake line, using new copper gaskets, then bleed the system as outlined later in this chapter.

Before test driving the car, turn the steering wheel to the extreme left and right positions and make sure that the brake lines do not rub anywhere. Pump the brake pedal to seat the pads and check for "sponginess". If the pedal is spongy, bleed the brakes again.

Brake Disc Removal

FRONT

Removal for the various types is similar. First, remove the brake caliper, then the front hub. Fasten the hub in a vise or holding fixture (be careful not to distort the housing), matchmark the disc and hub, then unbolt the brake disc.

Inspect the disc for burning (blue color), cracks and scoring. The disc becomes scored slightly in normal service; therefore,

1. Brake caliper
2. Stirrup
3. Hexagon screw with hexagon nut and serrated washer
4. Friction pad with mounting plate (service brake)
12. Pressure cylinder
19. Brake disc
20. Connecting line with pipe clip
24. Locking plate
25. Swing bolt

26. Leg spring
27a. Outer lining carrier
27b. Inner lining carrier
29. Friction pad with mounting plate (handbrake)
31. Adjustment screw
34. Tension lever
38. Brake line
40. Wheel fixing disc
41. Brake support lever
42. Rear axle shaft

Dunlop rear brake caliper used on 300SE models.

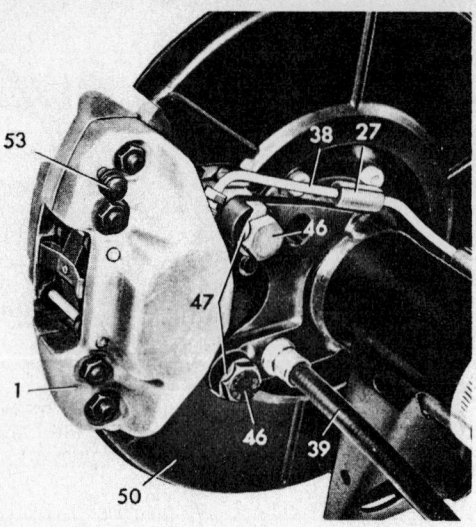

1. Brake caliper   47. Locking plate
27. Rubber ring   50. Cover plate
38. Brake line   53. Bleed screw with
39. Brake cable   rubber cap
46. Hexagon fitting
    screw

Rear brake caliper as used on 250S, 250SE and 300SEb models.

1. Brake disc   4. Hexagon bolt
2. Dial gauge   5. Distance sleeve
3. Dial gauge holder   6. Cover plate

Checking runout of brake disc using a dial indicator.

Brake disc, showing unacceptable level of damage.

1. Brake caliper   16. Cross-leaf spring
12. Brake disc   17. Retaining pin
14. Fitting pin   18. Friction pad
15. Rear axle shaft
    flange

Teves rear disc replacement.

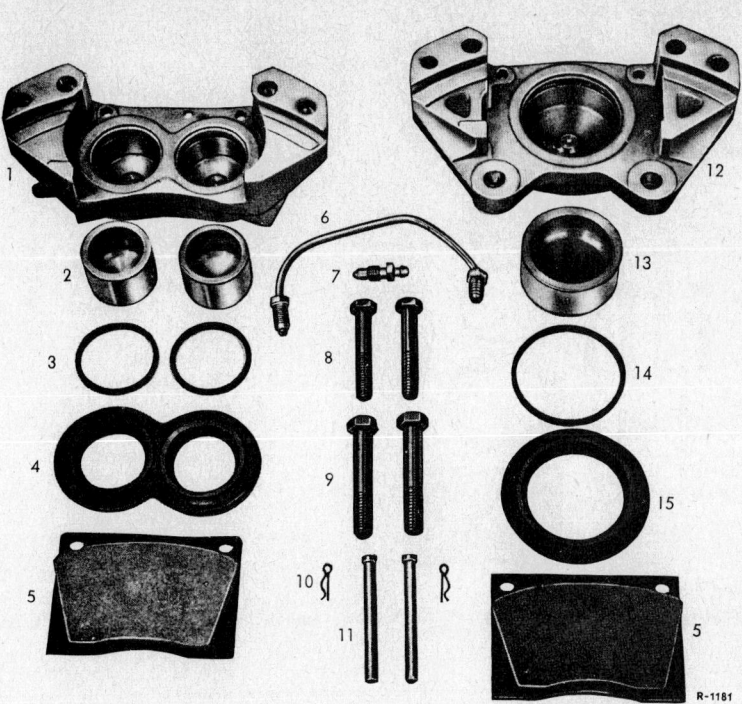

1. Outer caliper half
2. Piston
3. Piston seal
4. Dust cap
5. Friction pad
6. Connecting line
7. Bleed screw
8. Hexagon screw
9. Hexagon screw
10. Spring clip
11. Retaining pin
12. Inner caliper half
13. Piston
14. Piston seal
15. Dust cap

Girling caliper components (first and second versions).

replace it only if the depth of individual scores exceeds .020".

To ensure proper alignment, clean the hub and disc with emery paper to remove all rust and/or burrs, then bolt the disc to the hub. It is a wise precaution to use new lockwashers under the bolts. Install the hub and disc, then check the disc for run-out (wobble), using a dial indicator as illustrated. If runout is excessive, it sometimes helps to remove the disc and reseat it on the hub. Install the caliper assembly and bleed the brakes.

REAR

Remove the brake caliper and unbolt disc from rear axle flange. *NOTE: The parking brake must be released.*

Discs that will not come off can be gently tapped with a fiber hammer. Before installing, coat the axle flange with Moly-kote grease, then install disc and caliper and check runout. Bleed the brakes before moving the car.

Piston Seal Replacement— Girling Disc Brakes

CAUTION: Although exploded views show caliper halves disassembled, the two halves should NEVER be unbolted.

Remove brake caliper and friction pads, as previously described. On versions having an external connecting line, insert a wood block about ¾" thick into the caliper gap and force the piston out using compressed air (7–8 psi). Remove the wood and the piston. On versions having an internal connecting passage, clamp the inner piston and force the two outer pistons out using compressed air. Remove the clamp, block the outer caliper passage, and blow out the inner piston.

Remove the dust boots and remove the piston seals. Check the cylinder bores for wear or corrosion. If the bores are scored, do *not* hone them—replace the entire caliper assembly.

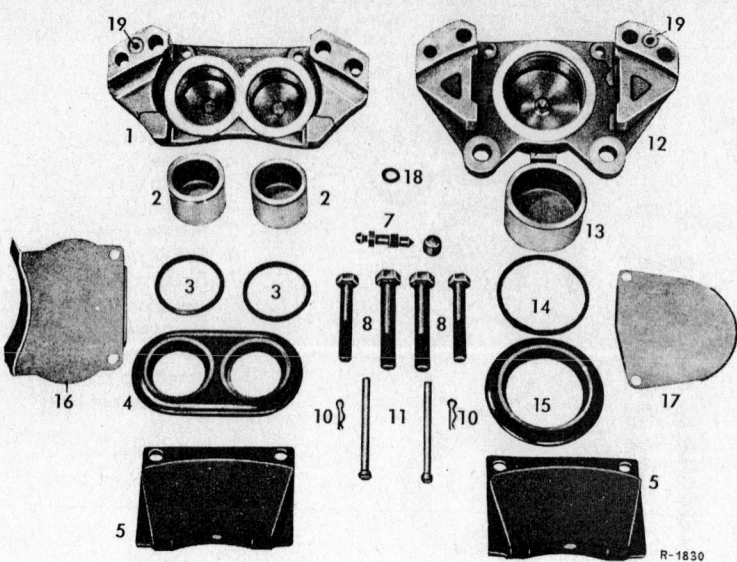

1.	Outer caliper half
2.	Piston
3.	Piston seal
4.	Dust cap
5.	Friction pad
7.	Bleed screw
8.	Hexagon screw
10.	Spring clip
11.	Retaining pin
12.	Inner caliper half
13.	Piston
14.	Piston seal
15.	Dust cap
16.	Heat screening plate
17.	Heat screening plate
18.	Rubber sealing ring
19.	Connecting passage in caliper halves

Girling caliper components (third version).

Before installing new seals, clean all passages with brake fluid and compressed air. Install the seals, dust caps and pistons, coating everything with brake fluid before assembly. Install the connecting line (if present) and brake caliper, then bleed the brakes.

Piston Seal Replacement— Teves Disc Brakes

CAUTION: Do not unbolt the two caliper halves for any reason. NOTE: Remove the brake caliper for easier service.

Remove the friction pads, brake line and dust cap, then pry the clamp ring from the housing. Using a rubber-backed piece of flat steel, hold one piston in place while blowing the other one out with compressed air (7–8 psi). *NOTE: If a piston is stuck, clamp the other piston in place and pump the brake pedal. The hydraulic pressure will force the piston out. This is a messy operation, so protect exterior paint from splashing brake fluid.*

Remove the piston seals from the cylinder bores and examine the bores. Scored bores necessitate replacement of the entire caliper, since the inner surface is chrome plated and cannot be honed. Clean the

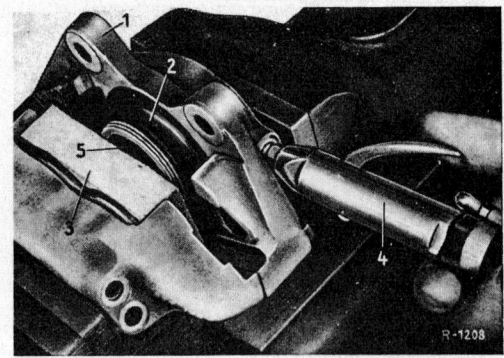

1. Brake caliper	4. Compressed air
2. Dust cap	5. Piston
3. Piece of wood	

Removing caliper piston—Girling.

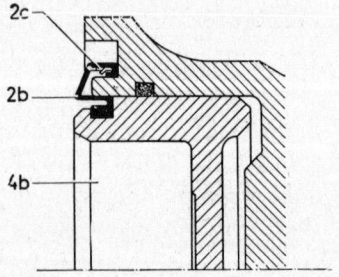

2b. Dust cap	4b. Piston
2c. Closed clamp ring	

Piston seal and dust cover—Teves.

bores with crocus cloth only, never emery paper.

Install the new seals, coating them with brake fluid beforehand, then install the piston so that the projection points downward. *NOTE: If the projection is in any other position, the brakes may squeal badly.*

Install the dust cap, clamp ring and heat shield. The recess in the heat shield must fit the piston projection, but be above the shield level by about .004". *NOTE: The heat shields differ for inner and outer pistons.*

Install the friction pads and the caliper assembly, then bleed brakes. *IMPORTANT: The rear brake pistons must be installed with the piston projection facing upward.*

| 1. Brake caliper | 23. Holding fixture |
| 2. Piston | |

Holding fixture in place—Teves.

Wheel Cylinder Service—Drum Brakes

Any time the brakes are inspected, the wheel cylinders should also be inspected. Wheel cylinder malfunctions usually fall into two general categories—leakage and sticking or binding.

The best leakage check is simply to peel back the rubber dust cover. If fluid seeps out, or if the cover is wet on the inside, the wheel cylinders should be rebuilt. It is best to rebuild all wheel cylinders at once, for if one is leaking, the rest are sure to follow. Use new seals throughout.

FRONT WHEELS

To disassemble, unscrew the bleed screw and remove actuating pin (8), metal boot (6) and rubber dust cover (7). Remove the piston (5), cap (4), cap expander (3) and stop spring (2) from the housing.

Clean the cylinder bore with alcohol or brake fluid, then examine the bore. Scored or rusted wheel cylinders are normally replaced. Honing destroys the surface and, with the single-end design of these cylinders, is difficult to do properly. Assembly is the reverse of disassembly. *NOTE: Coat all parts with brake fluid.*

REAR WHEELS

To replace wheel cylinders, remove the brake shoes, disconnect brake lines and un-

Double-end wheel cylinder installed.

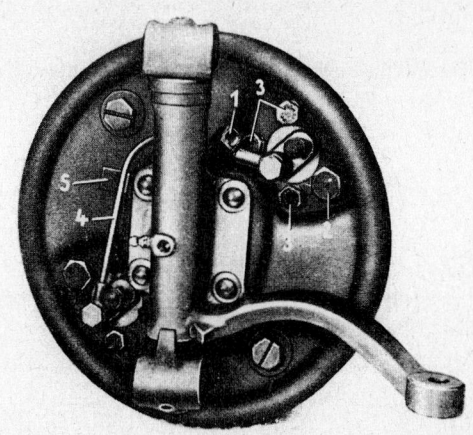

1. Square socket at the brake line	3. Hexagon screw
2. Stop screw or hexagon screw	4. Brake line
	5. Rubber pad

Rear of backing plate.

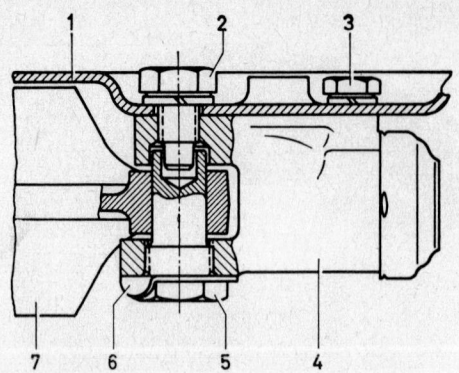

1. Brake anchor plate   5. Anchor pin
2. Stop screw   6. Locking plate
3. Hexagon screw   7. Brake shoe
4. Brake wheel cylinder

First version wheel cylinder mounting—front.

1. Pressure bolt   6. Pressure spring
2. Rubber cap   7. Wheel brake
3. Piston   cylinder
4. Blind hole cup

Wheel cylinder components—rear.

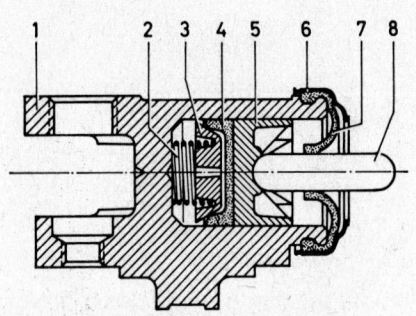

1. Brake wheel cylinder   5. Piston
    housing   6. Metal boot
2. Spring   7. Rubber boot
3. Piston cup expander   8. Actuating pin
4. Cup

Wheel cylinder internal parts—front.

1. Piston   4. Rubber boot
2. Bolt   5. Guide pin
3. Cup spring

Wheel cylinder with spring-loaded pin—rear.

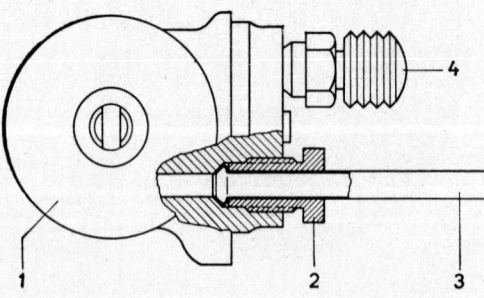

1. Wheel cylinder   3. Brake line
    housing   4. Bleed screw
2. Cap screw

Wheel cylinder external parts—front.

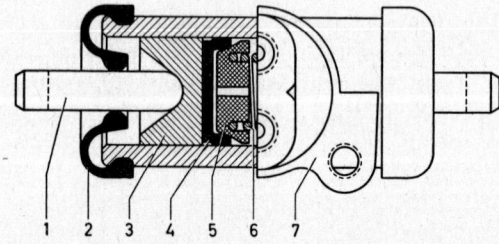

1. Actuating pin   5. Piston cup expander
2. Rubber boot   6. Spring
3. Piston   7. Wheel cylinder
4. Cup

Wheel cylinder with rigid pin—rear.

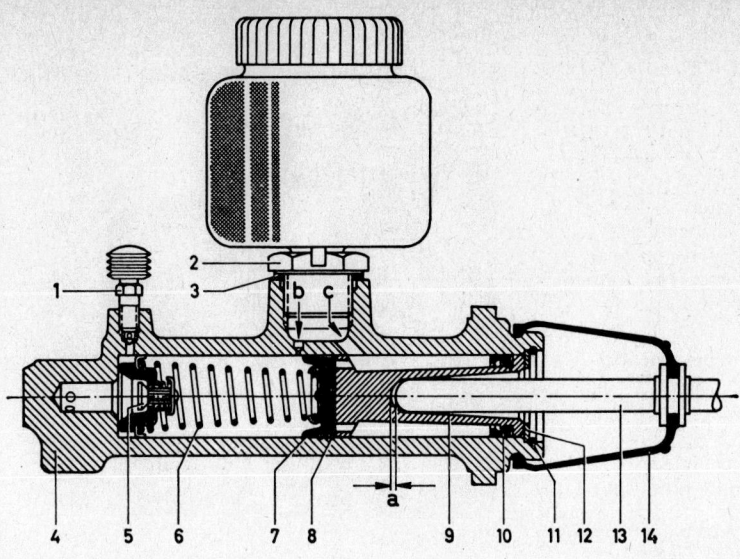

1. Bleed screw
2. Tubular screw
3. Sealing ring
4. Housing
5. Check valve
6. Pressure spring
7. Primary cup
8. Piston cup washer
9. Piston
10. Secondary cup
11. Piston stop ring
12. Piston stop washer
13. Piston pushrod
14. Boot
a = Clearance between piston and pushrod
b = Compensating ports
c = Connecting ports

Single circuit master cylinder.

bolt cylinder from the rear. Bleed brakes after installing new cylinders.

Inspection and disassembly is essentially the same and, while it is *possible* to hone wheel cylinder bores, it is recommended that the entire cylinder be replaced. Coat all parts with brake fluid before assembly.

Single Master Cylinder Service

The function of the master cylinder is to convert the mechanical action of the foot pedal into hydraulic pressure, which acts on the wheel cylinders (caliper pistons) to actuate the brake shoes (pads) and stop the car. The basic design of all master cylinders is the same, whether single or dual type. Operation is very similar to that of the wheel cylinder in reverse. A pushrod moves a piston against spring pressure, displacing hydraulic fluid in a closed system. Since the volume is constant, pressure rises. This pressure serves to operate the wheel cylinders of drum brakes or caliper pistons of disc brakes.

The master cylinder should be checked if fluid loss is experienced, or if the fluid constantly becomes aerated.

To remove, first drain the master cylinder

1. Screw cap (master cylinder)
2. Screw cap (supply cylinder)
3. Bleed screw (supply cylinder)
4. Bleed screw (master cylinder)
5. Brake line
6. Brake line
7. Brake line
8. Brake line
9. Brake line
10. Line from supply cylinder to extraction cylinder
11. Stop light switch
12. Plug connection
13. Flash signal mechanism
14. Plug connection
15. Upper beam flash mechanism
16. Plug connection

Master cylinder installed.

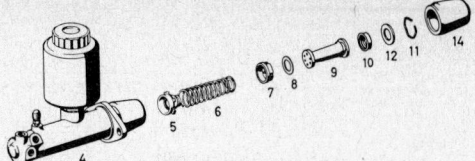

4. Master cylinder   9. Piston
5. Check valve   10. Secondary cup
6. Pressure spring   11. Piston stop ring
7. Primary cup   12. Piston stop washer
8. Piston cup washer   14. Boot

Single circuit master cylinder components.

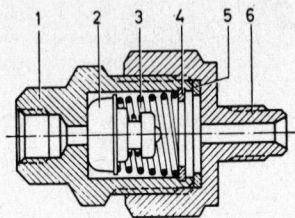

1. Housing   4. Piston stop ring
2. Check valve   5. Sealing ring
3. Pressure spring   6. Threaded union

Check valve.

1. Screw cap   cylinder to ex-
   (master cylinder)   traction cylinder
2. Screw cap   11. Stop light switch
   (supply cylinder)   12. Plug connection
3. Bleed screw   13. Primary pressure
   (master cylinder)   valve
4. Bleed screw   14. Relay
   (supply cylinder)   15. Relay
5. Brake line   16. Assembly plate
6. Brake line   17. Relay
7. Brake line   18. Relay
8. Brake line   19. Inspection lamp
9. Brake line   socket
10. Line from supply

Master cylinder installation—front disc/rear drum system.

by opening the bleed screw, then disconnect all brake levers and the stop light switch. On cars with front disc/rear drum systems, first disconnect the brake line at the primary pressure valve, then unscrew the valve from the master cylinder.

To install, reverse removal procedure, making sure that stop light switch and primary pressure valve threads seal tightly. The master cylinder pushrod clearance must be maintained by adjusting the pedal freeplay—see section on brake adjustment in this chapter.

To bleed the master cylinder, pump the pedal and maintain pressure while having the bleed screw cracked open. When the pedal goes to the floor, hold it there and tighten the bleed screw (to prevent sucking air into hydraulic system). Continue this procedure until no more air bubbles issue from the bleed screw opening, then top up the fluid level and bleed the brakes at the wheels.

Disassembly is simple, just remove the dust boot and the snap-ring, then pull out

all internal parts. While it is possible to hone rusted or corroded bores, it is not recommended, because this destroys the surface and a lasting repair is not usually achieved. If the cylinder bore is good, replace the rubber sealing caps with new components, clean all passages and parts with brake fluid and reassemble the master cylinder. It is a good idea to replace the check valve at this time, as well as the pressure spring.

Dual Master Cylinder Service

The dual master cylinder operates in the same manner as the single piston model. It, however, has a safety feature which the single unit lacks—if a leak develops in one brake circuit (rear wheels, for example),

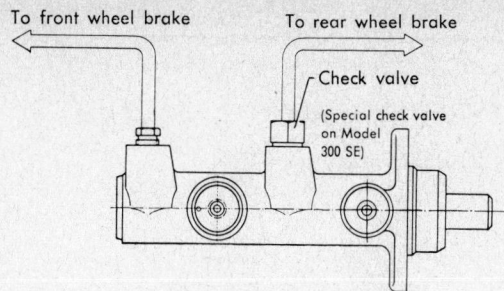

Tandem master cylinder.

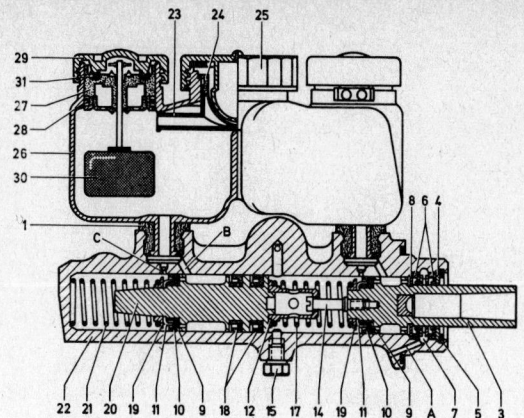

the other circuit will still operate.

Failure of one system is immediately obvious—the pedal travel increases appreciably and a warning light is activated. This warning light is operated by a simple switch attached to a float in the reservoir/s. When the fluid falls below a certain level, the switch activates the circuit. *CAUTION: This design was not intended to allow driving the car for any distance with, in effect, a two-wheel brake system. If one brake circuit fails, braking action is correspondingly lower. Front circuit failure is the more serious, however, since the front brakes contribute up to 75% of the braking force required to stop the car. Repair any leaks immediately!*

1. Plug
3. Piston (pushrod circuit)
4. Piston stop washer
5. Piston stop ring
6. Vacuum seal
7. Spacer ring
8. Support ring
9. Piston cup washer
10. Primary cup
11. Thrust ring
12. Spring retainer
14. Connecting screw
15. Stop screw
17. Pressure spring
18. Ring cup
19. Spring retainer
20. Piston (intermediate piston)
21. Pressure spring
22. Housing
23. Splash guard
24. Strainer
25. Screw cap
26. Reservoir
27. Contact insert
28. O-ring
29. Cover cap
30. Float
31. Sealing ring
A. Leak port
B. Connecting port
C. Compensating port

Tandem master cylinder internal parts.

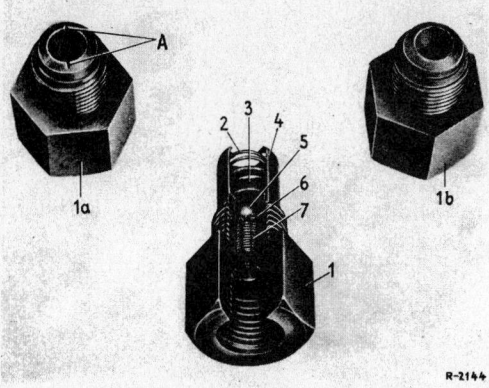

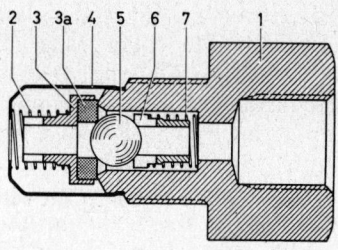

Left

1. Connector with check valve
1a. Connector for special check valve
1b. Connector for check valve
2. Pressure spring
3. Spring retainer
4. Metal sleeve
5. Ball
6. Spring sleeve
7. Pressure spring
A. Notches in the connector for the special check valve

Right

1. Connector
2. Pressure spring
3. Spring retainer
3a. Rubber ring
4. Metal sleeve
5. Ball
6. Spring sleeve
7. Pressure spring

Check valves used in first version Tandem master cylinders.

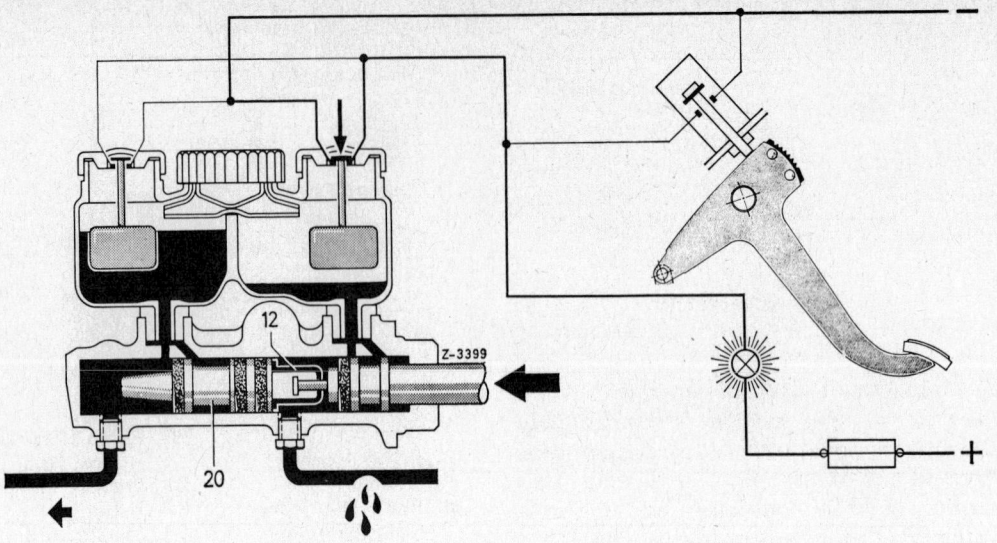

Tandem master cylinder warning light circuit indicates a leak in any one circuit.

To remove the master cylinder, first open a bleed screw at one front, and one rear, wheel. Pump the pedal to empty the reservoir completely, then disconnect the switch connectors using a small screwdriver. Disconnect the two brake lines and plug the ends with bleed screw caps or equivalent. Unbolt the master cylinder from the power brake unit and remove.

To disassemble, pull the reservoir out of the top of the cylinder, then remove screw cap (25), strainer (24) and splash shield (23). Unscrew the cover caps (29) and take out inserts (27) and O-rings (28). Push the piston inward slightly and remove the stop screw (15). Remove the piston stop ring (5) in the same manner, then pull out the piston and other components. The spring must be unscrewed from the piston.

Assembly precautions are similar to that of single master cylinder. *NOTE: Do not hone the cylinder bore. If slight rust marks do not come out with crocus cloth, replace the master cylinder.*

CAUTION: Always use a new O-ring between the master cylinder and power brake unit.

1. Tandem master cylinder	6. Power brake
2. Reservoir	7. Reservoir for supply cylinder
3. Plug connection	8. Vacuum line
4. Screw cap	9. Brake line to right front wheel brake
5. Cover cap	

Tandem master cylinder installation.

attached brackets and cables, then detach the pushrod from the brake pedal and unbolt the brake unit from the firewall. Installation is the reverse of removal; make sure to use a new O-ring seal between the master cylinder and power brake unit.

Power Brake Unit Replacement

Remove the master cylinder and the vacuum line at the brake unit. Remove all

Bleeding Brakes

Always bleed the brakes after performing any service, or if the pedal seems

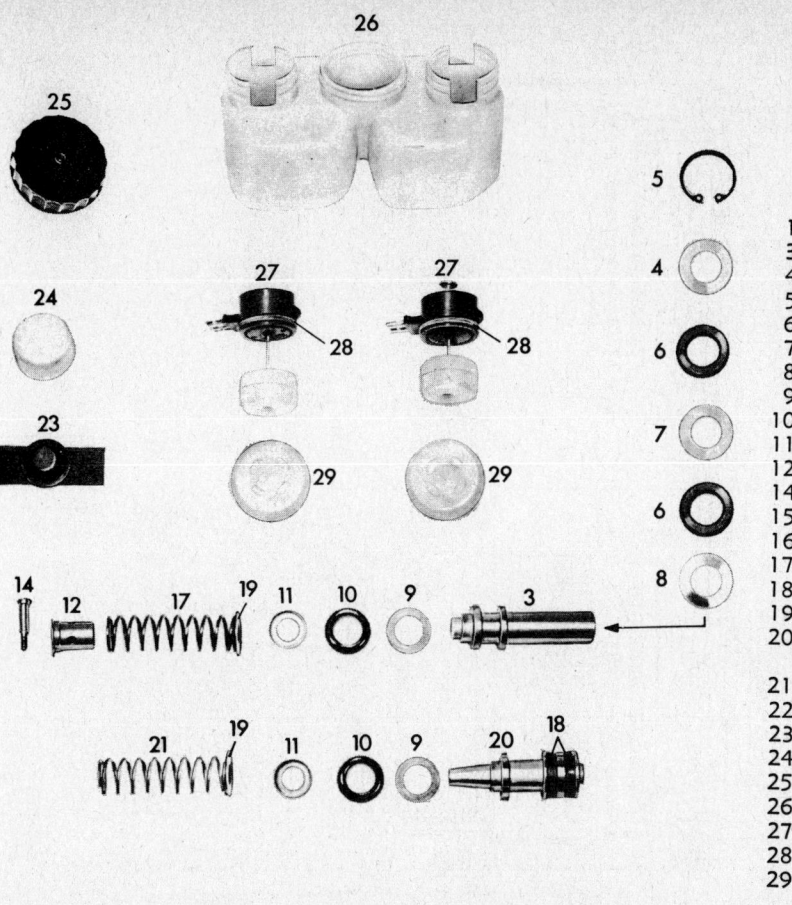

1. Plug
3. Piston (pushrod circuit)
4. Piston stop
5. Piston stop ring
6. Vacuum sealing ring
7. Spacer ring
8. Support ring
9. Piston cup washer
10. Primary cup
11. Thrust ring
12. Spring retainer
14. Connecting screw
15. Stop screw
16. Sealing ring (copper)
17. Pressure spring
18. Ring cup
19. Spring retainer
20. Piston (intermediate piston)
21. Pressure spring
22. Housing
23. Splash guard
24. Strainer
25. Screw cap
26. Reservoir
27. Contact insert
28. O-ring
29. Cover cap

Exploded view of tandem master cylinder.

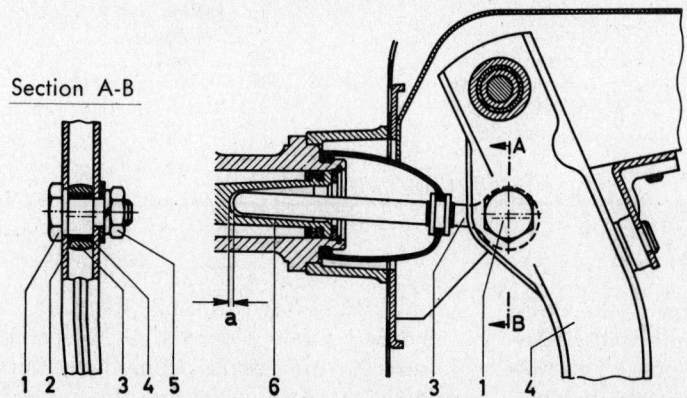

Section A-B

1. Adjusting screw
2. Polyamide bushing
3. Pushrod
4. Brake pedal
5. Hexagon nut
6. Piston
a. = Clearance between pushrod and piston

Adjustment of brake pedal free-play on models with single circuit master cylinder.

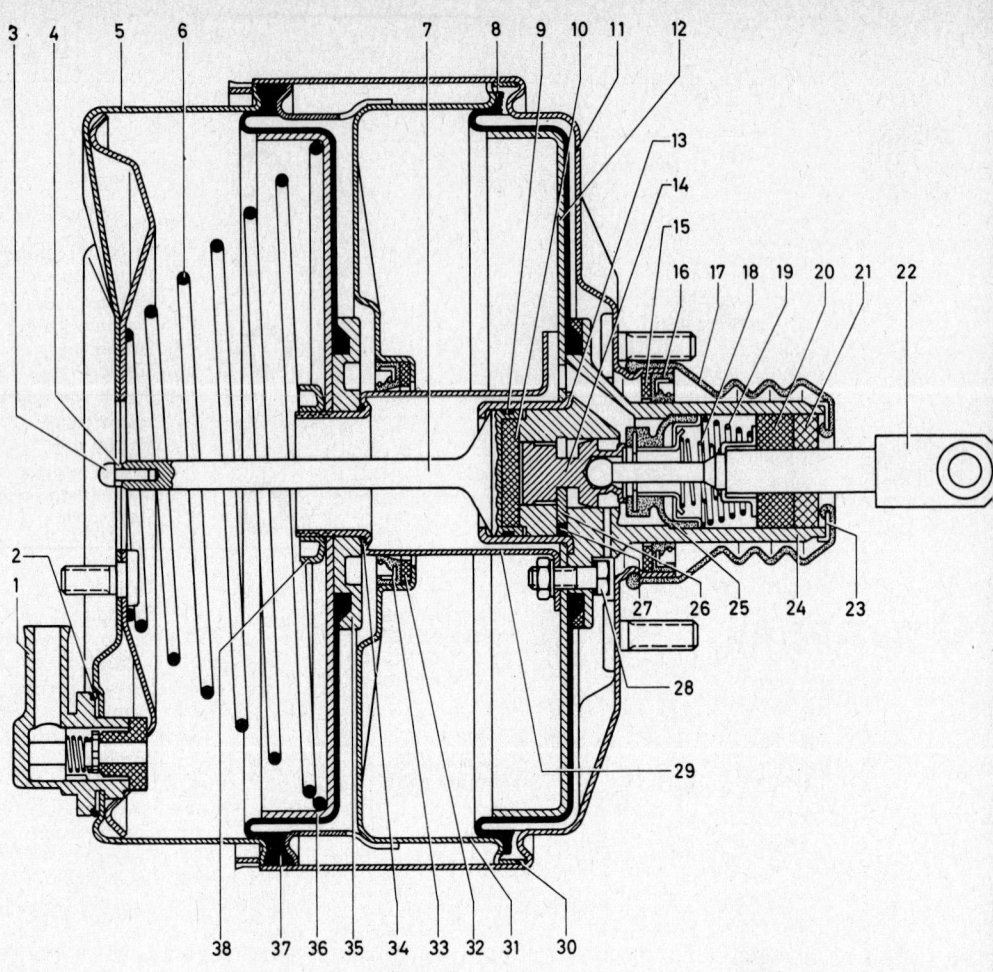

1. Check valve	14. Valve plunger	27. Seal
2. O-ring	15. Guide ring	28. Hexagon screw with washer
3. Pressure button	16. Sealing ring	and hexagon nut
4. Compensating washer	17. Boot	29. Spacer tube
5. Front vacuum cylinder	18. Poppet return spring	30. Ring
6. Pressure spring (piston	19. Valve rod return spring	31. Center vacuum cylinder
return spring)	20. Air cleaner	32. Guide ring
7. Pushrod	21. Muffler	33. Sealing ring
8. Roller-type diaphragm	22. Valve operating rod	34. O-ring
10. Reaction disc	23. Muffler bracket	35. Support
11. Rear vacuum cylinder	24. Control housing	36. Diaphragm retainer
12. Diaphragm retainer	25. Poppet assembly	37. Roller-type diaphragm
13. Guide bushing	26. Stop disc	38. Sheet-metal nut

T 51/200 power brake unit.

spongy ("soft"). The location of the bleed screws can be seen by consulting the illustrations throughout this chapter. The procedure is simple, first have an assistant pump the brakes and hold the pedal. Then, starting at the point farthest from the master cylinder, slightly open the bleed screw. When the pedal hits the floor, close the bleed screw before allowing pedal to return (to prevent air from being sucked into the system). Continue this procedure until no more air bubbles exit from bleed screw hole, then go to the next wheel. To prevent fluid splashing on car (it eats

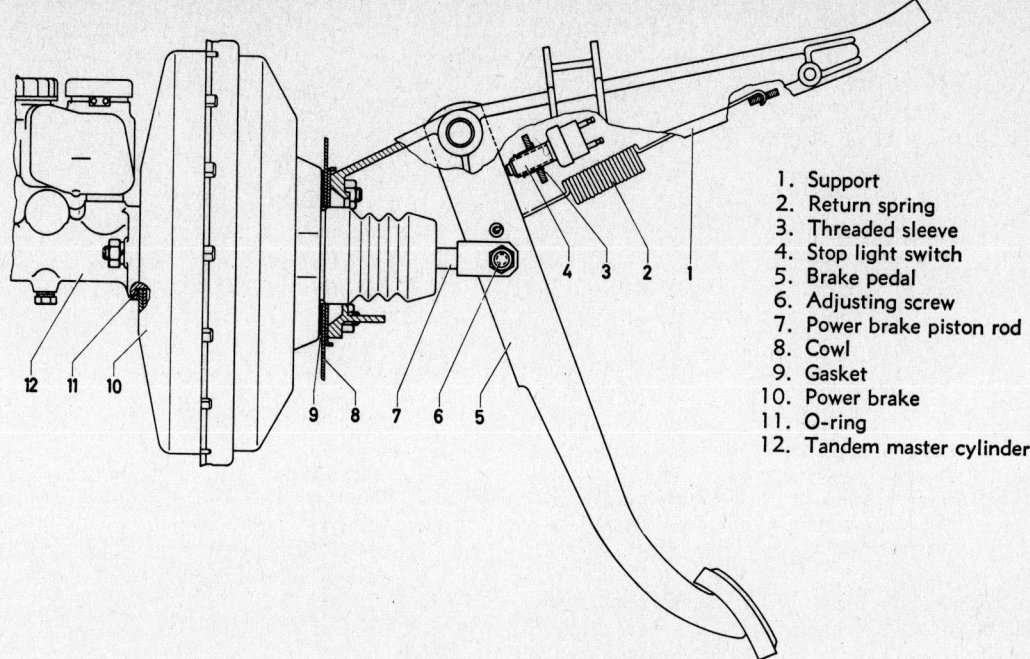

1. Support
2. Return spring
3. Threaded sleeve
4. Stop light switch
5. Brake pedal
6. Adjusting screw
7. Power brake piston rod
8. Cowl
9. Gasket
10. Power brake
11. O-ring
12. Tandem master cylinder

Power brake unit used on phase II models.

paint), place one end of a section of hose on the bleed screw and the other in an open jar of brake fluid. This fluid is filled with microscopic air bubbles after bleeding

Section A-B

2. Piston rod of power brake
3a. Adjusting screw with hexagon nut and lockwasher
4. Pivot pin with hexagon nut and lockwasher
12. Clutch pedal
13. Brake pedal
14. Supply cylinder
17. Pedal support
21. Bushings in the pedals
25. Bushings in the brake pedal
26. Hexagon screw with hexagon nut and lockwasher

Adjustment of brake pedal free-play on models with tandem master cylinder (all except 230SL).

process is completed, therefore it should be discarded.

SEQUENCE OF BLEEDING OPERATIONS

A. *Single master cylinder, drum brakes or four-wheel discs.* First bleed the master cylinder, then the power brake (if installed). Start bleeding at right rear wheel and work toward master cylinder.

B. *Single master cylinder, discs front/ drums rear.* First bleed the master cylinder, then the power brake unit. Bleed the brake caliper farthest from master cylinder (depending on model), then the other brake caliper. Bleed the drum brakes last, again starting with the brake farthest from master cylinder.

C. *Dual master cylinder.* Bleed only the circuit that has been opened. If both circuits have been opened, first bleed the circuit connected to the pushrod bore, then the other circuit.

Brake Adjustment

DRUM BRAKES

To adjust the brakes, turn the cam bolts until definite drag is felt, then back off the

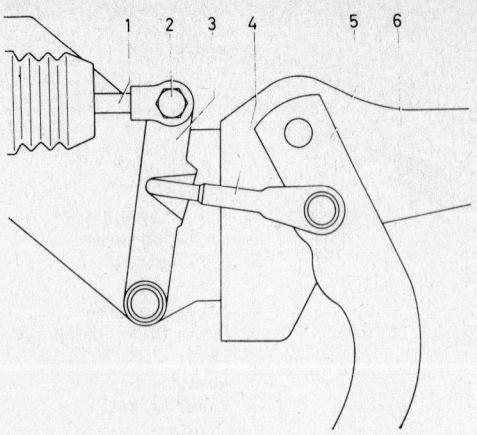

1. Piston rod of power   3. Relay lever
   brake   4. Pushrod
2. Adjusting screw   5. Brake pedal
   with hexagon nut   6. Pedal support
   and lockwasher

Adjustment of brake pedal free-play on type 230SL.

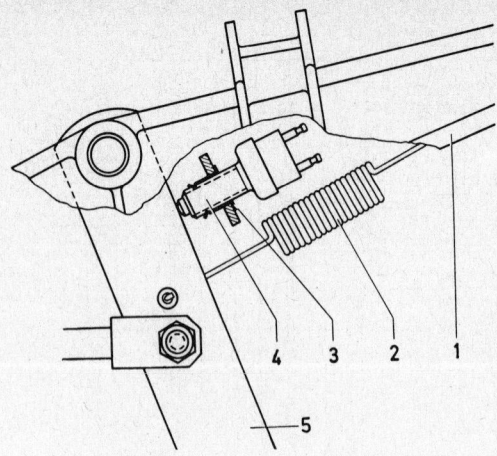

1. Pedal support   4. Switch
2. Return spring   5. Pedal
3. Threaded sleeve

Adjustment of stop light switch.

bolts until the wheel turns freely again.

Single Circuit Brake Pedal Free-Play

Check the brake pedal free-play—it should be .16″–.20″. If adjustment is necessary, loosen hex nut (5) on the pedal and turn the adjustment bolt (1). (The .16″–.20″ free-play should equal .20″–.28″ pushrod/master cylinder clearance.)

NOTE: Some cases of locked brakes are caused by insufficient pushrod/master cylinder clearance. If the master cylinder piston cannot return fully, the compensating port in the master cylinder is not uncovered and residual hydraulic pressure holds the brake shoes against the drums.

NOTE: Disc brakes require no adjustment.

Dual-Circuit Brake Pedal Free-Play

The brake pedal travel should be 6.08″ on all models. To adjust on all models except 230 SL, turn adjusting bolt (3a) until the notch on the bolt head points rearwards. This gives maximum travel, and adjustment is made from this point. *NOTE: If pedal hits brass threads of stop light switch, use shims under switch so that switch button protrudes 0.16″.*

On the 230 SL, remove the plastic ring from the bolt head and remove the stop light switch. Turn adjusting bolt (2) on the relay lever until the notch on the bolt head faces rearward. Adjust the stop light switch so that the button protrudes 0.16″ and the brake lights operate with a pedal depression of 0.8″. Now, pump the brake pedal a few times and jack up the front of the car. Spin one wheel and open the bleed screw of the brake caliper on that wheel. If this results in a freer-spinning wheel, the stop light switch must be further adjusted, because it is holding the brake pedal forward and allowing residual pressure to stay in the system.

PARKING BRAKE ADJUSTMENT

On cars equipped with cast-iron brake shoes (rear), tighten wingnut (1) on brake lever (3) or the wingnut (8) on relay lever (5) until the brake holds when the handle is pulled out 2.4″–2.6″. If the rear wheels do not spin free with the handbrake all the way in, readjust until they do spin.

On cars equipped with aluminum rear brake shoes, the distance is 2.4″.

If adjustment is not possible by this method, adjust the rear wheel brakes, then back out the cable wingnut at the relay lever and allow the cables to hang loosely. Adjust pushrod (3) by turning adjustment wheel (2) to give .040″ clearance at "b". It is advisable to remove the brake drum

1. Wingnut
2. Front brake cable
3. Brake lever
4. Support rod
5. Cotter pin
6. Pivot pin
7. Center brake cable

Parking brake linkage—first version.

1. Front brake cable
2. Hexagon screw with locking plate
3. Pull rod for supporting the handbrake lever mounting
4. Handbrake lever
5. Center brake cable
6. Cotter pin

Parking brake linkage—second version.

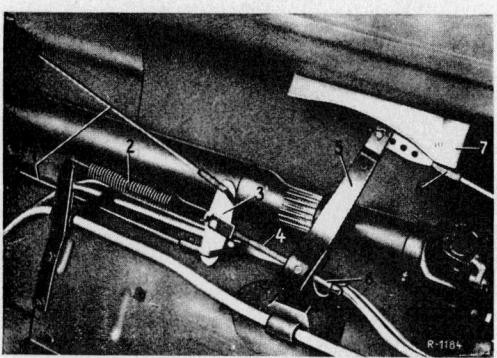

1. Rear brake cables
2. Return spring
3. Equalizer
4. Tensioning screw
5. Relay lever
6. Center brake cable
7. Guide for relay lever
8. Wingnut for adjusting the handbrake

Parking brake linkage—second version.

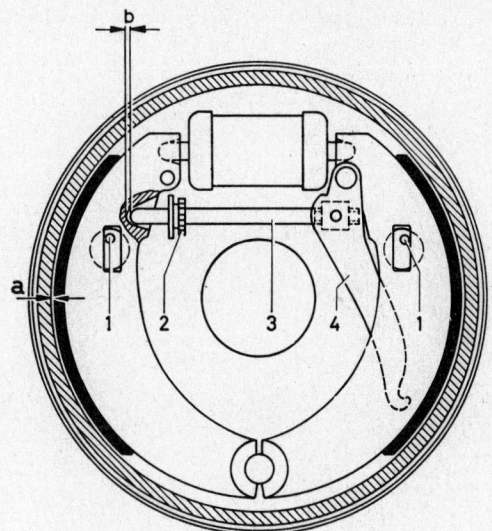

1. Eccentric
2. Adjusting star wheel
3. Pushrod
4. Brake lever

Parking brake pushrod adjustment—drum brakes with aluminum shoes.

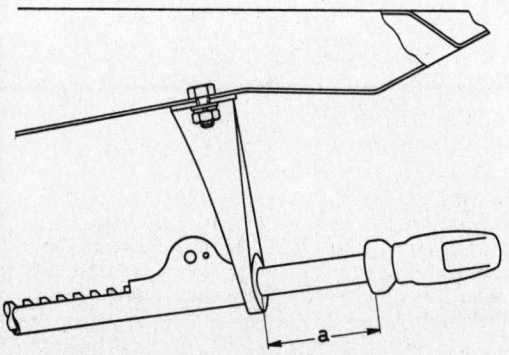

Handbrake travel—drum brakes (see text).

for this job. The brakes, if correctly adjusted, should not touch the pushrod, and there should be .010"–.012" clearance between the linings and drums.

The relay lever should be adjusted to give 0.8"–1.6" at "a".

Lever Handbrake—SL Models

Adjust the drilled adjustment wheel (10) by inserting a drill rod into the holes. The

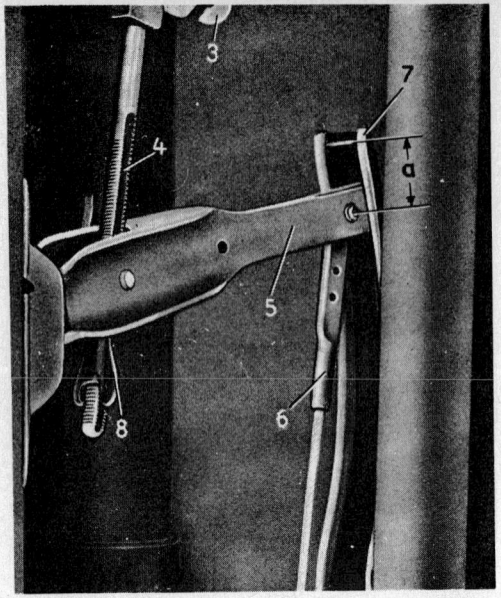

3. Equalizer
4. Tensioning screw
5. Relay lever
6. Center brake cable
7. Guide for relay lever
8. Wingnut

Relay lever adjustment.

lever should have to come up only three notches in order to hold the car on a slight grade.

Teves Drum-Type Parking Brake

If the floor pedal can be depressed more than two notches before actuating the brakes, adjust by jacking up the rear of the car, then removing one lug bolt and adjusting the star wheel with a screwdriver. Move the screwdriver upward on left (driver's) side, downward on right (passenger's) side to tighten the shoes. When the wheel is locked, back off about 2–4 "clicks". With this type system, the adjusting bolt on the cable relay lever only serves to equalize cable length; therefore, do not attempt to adjust brakes by turning this bolt.

PARKING BRAKE WARNING LIGHT—
220/8 TO 250/8

The red parking brake warning light should go out when the brake is released. If the master cylinder reservoirs are full,

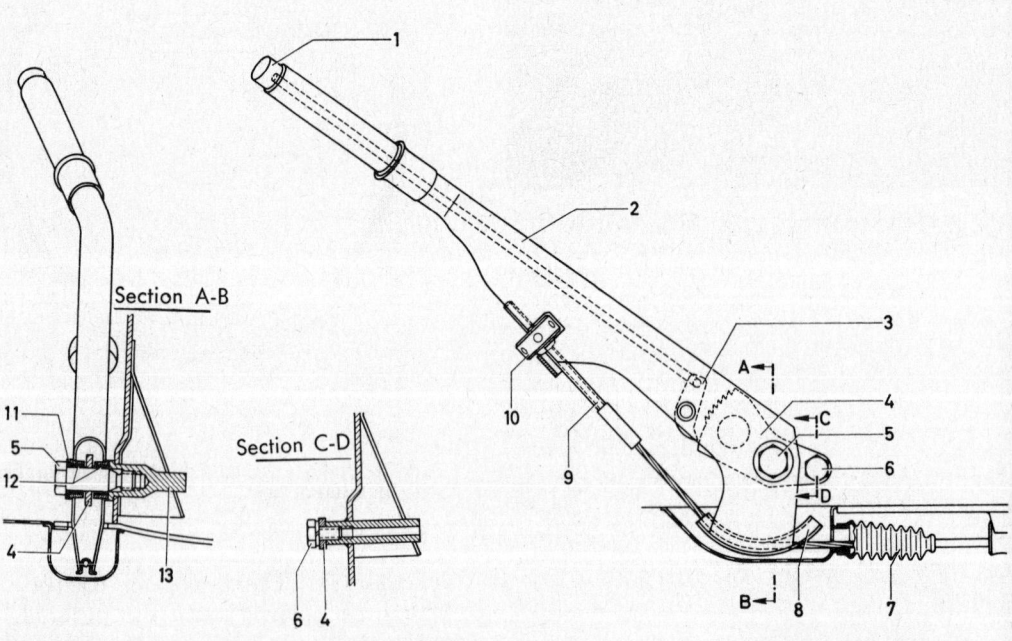

Section A-B
Section C-D

1. Push button
2. Handbrake lever
3. Pawl
4. Toothed segment
5. Pivot pin
6. Hexagon screw with
   lockwasher
7. Rubber sleeve
8. Brake cable guide
9. Front brake cable
10. Circular four-hole nut
11. Washer
12. Bearing bushing
13. Threaded member for
    fastening brake lever to
    chassis base panel

Handbrake lever adjustment—SL models.

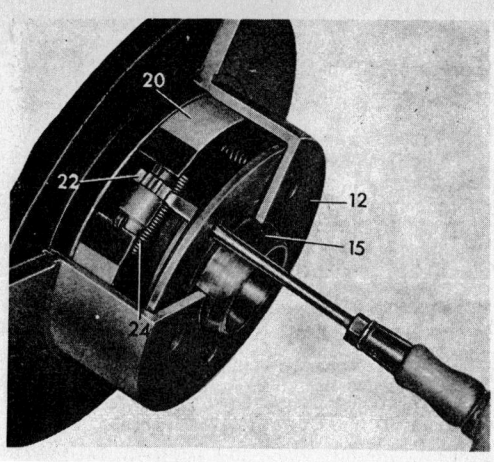

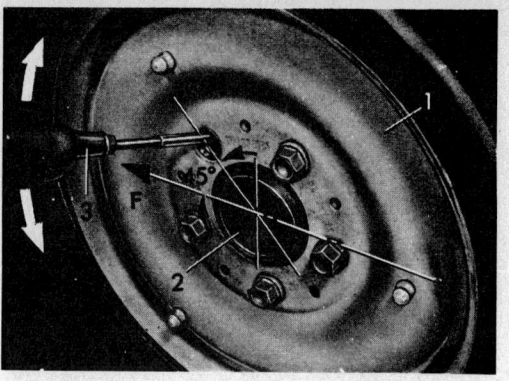

1. Disc wheel
2. Rear axle shaft

3. Screwdriver
F = Direction of travel

Parking brake shoe adjustment—wheel installed—
Teves.

12. Brake disc
15. Rear axle shaft
    flange
20. Brake shoes

22. Adjustment device
24. Upper return
    spring

Adjusting parking brake shoes—wheel removed—
Teves.

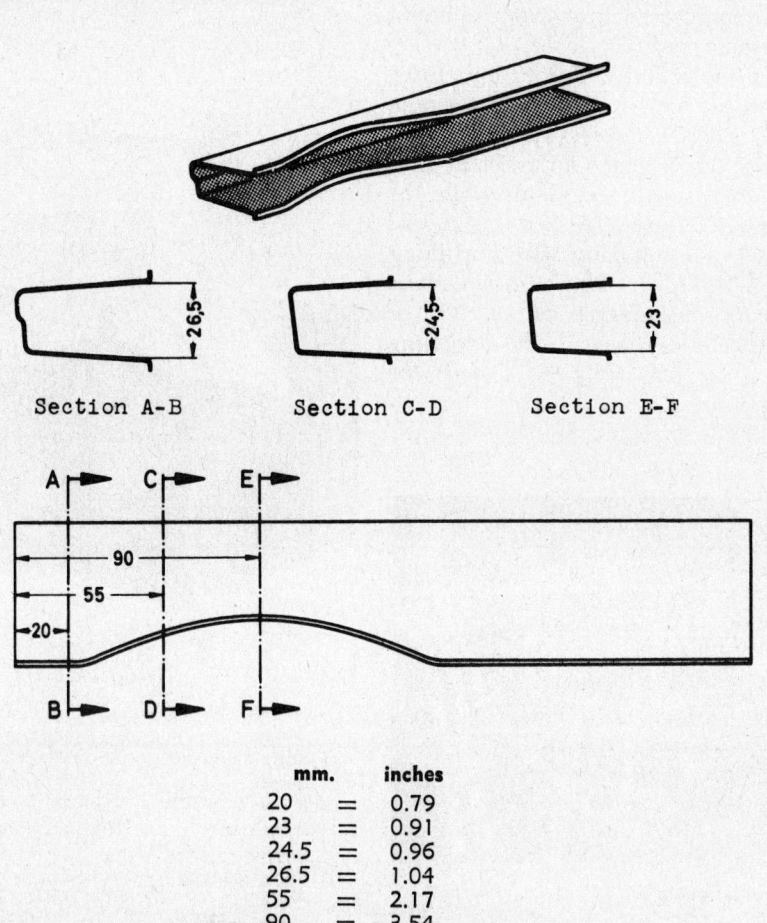

Section A-B   Section C-D   Section E-F

mm.		inches
20	=	0.79
23	=	0.91
24.5	=	0.96
26.5	=	1.04
55	=	2.17
90	=	3.54

From section E-F, the groove
width runs into the existing
width.

Parking brake modifications necessary if warning light doesn't go out—220/8 to 250/8.

and the light still does not go out, check the intermediate relay lever and its guide rail for binding. Working from underneath the car, clean the guide rail thoroughly, then remove the cotter pin and bend the rail to conform with the measurements illustrated. Grease the guide rail and re-assemble.

If the light still does not go out, bend the switch contact carrier slightly to the left, making sure that the switch itself is not acting as a stop for the pedal linkage.

Brake Pressure Regulator

The brake pressure regulator serves to "split" the hydraulic pressure in the brake system in proportion to the braking requirement at the front and rear wheels. This prevents premature lock-up with attendant loss of braking control.

To check the unit for proper operation, jack up the car and, with normal vacuum in the brake booster, depress the pedal with about 65 lbs. force. Have an assistant hold a hand on the pressure regulator while the pedal is slowly released. A distinct "knock" will be felt in the regulator if it is working properly. *CAUTION: The unit cannot be serviced with any degree of success, or safety. Always replace malfunctioning regulators, not forgetting to bleed the brakes after doing so.*

1. Brake force regulator
2. Bracket
3. Brake line from tandem brake master cylinder
4. Brake hose to left rear wheel brake
5. Bracket at frame floor

Brake pressure regulator.

Heater

Removal of Heater Core and Blower Assembly

SEDANS UP TO 1966

Remove the connecting duct for the rear seat heating system. Unsnap the two large clips on the heater box (from under the dash). Remove the lockwasher on the air flap lever, then detach the two cables from the air flap lever. Disconnect the outer cable clamps that hold the control cables to the lever assembly. Detach the short link from the motor crank of the windshield wiper motor, then remove the right defroster nozzle.

Unsnap the large clips that hold the left defroster nozzle. Disconnect the control ca-

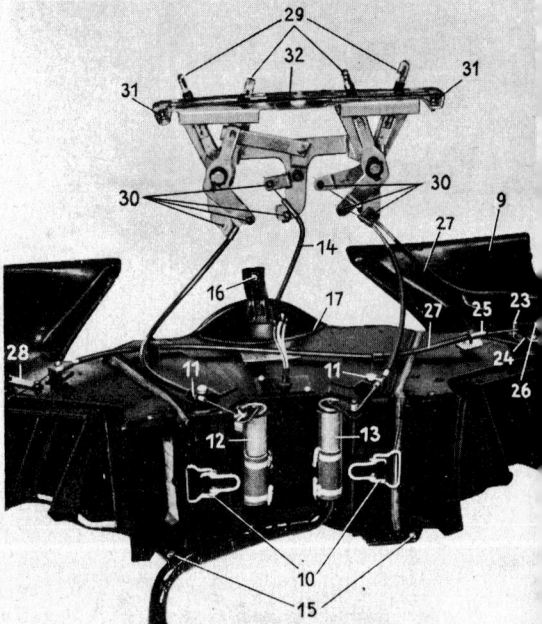

8. Left defroster nozzle	15. Fixing screw
9. Right defroster nozzle	16. Fixing screw
10. Cover	17. Heater box
11. Wire cable for regulating valve	23. Lock washer
12. Left regulating valve	24. Air flap lever
13. Right regulating valve	25. Wire cable
14. Wire cable for fresh-air flap	26. Wire cable
	27. Outer cable sheath
	28. Air flap lever
	29. Control lever
	30. Fixing screw
	31. Fixing nut
	32. Escutcheon

Heater system seen from under dashboard.

bles at the valves (11, 12, 13 in illustration). Detach the cable (14) for the fresh air flap. Unscrew the two hold-down screws (15) from the firewall and the screw (16) from the water tank bracket. The left defroster nozzle is not removed, simply pushed around to get the required clearance. Drain the coolant from the radiator and block, then disconnect the heater motor wires at the junction block. Disconnect the water hoses that go to the return pipe (from under the hood—on firewall), then disconnect the water hose from the connection on the firewall under the master cylinder. Remove the rubber grommets from the firewall where the heater pipes go through, then remove the entire heater box (containing both core and blower) from under the dash.

MODELS 250S, 250SE, 300SEb, 300SEL

Drain the coolant from the radiator and block, then detach the battery ground cable. Disconnect the feed and return pipes of the heater core at the firewall (from under the hood). Remove the steering wheel, then remove the connecting duct for the rear seat heater. Remove the right defroster

nozzle as follows: remove the right cover panel below the instrument panel, then remove glove box, upper instrument panel padding and clips that hold the right nozzle. Pull off connecting hose (5) from nozzle (7), disconnect right defroster nozzle from center defroster nozzle and remove right nozzle. Now, remove center defroster nozzle as follows: remove speaker grill and the self-tapping screw in the speaker recess. Pull the center nozzle from the left nozzle and remove center nozzle.

Remove the model designation panel from the dashboard, then remove radio. Remove ashtray and ashtray housing. Disconnect blower wires at junction block. Disconnect all heater cables, then remove the three heater box hold-down screws. Remove the two screws that hold the clips (8) at the left defroster nozzle. Disconnect the speedometer cable at the transmission and at the speedometer, then pull it up and out of the left defroster nozzle.

Lift the left defroster nozzle, fold the rubber ring (13) and slide the nozzle with aperture (14) over the steering lock. Remove the heater box, complete with blower,

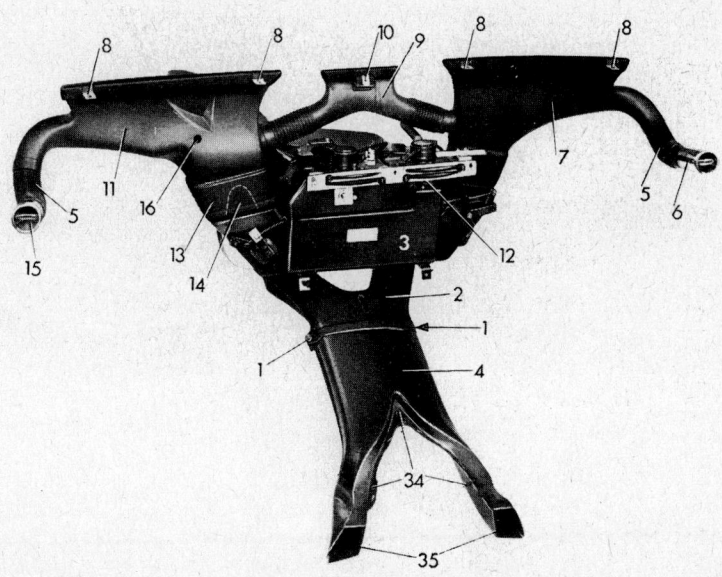

1. Screw on connecting duct	7. Right defroster nozzle	14. Aperture
2. Connecting duct	8. Clips	15. Left annular nozzle
3. Heater box	9. Center defroster nozzle	16. Hole for speedometer cable
4. Heating duct for rear compartment heating	10. Self-tapping screw	34. Oval head tapping screw
5. Connecting hose	11. Left defroster nozzle	35. Seal
6. Right annular nozzle	12. Cable plug	
	13. Rubber ring	

Heater system seen from under dashboard—250S, 250SE, 300SEb, 300SEL.

to the lower right. *NOTE: When installing, first install the left-hand heater box screw due to clearance problems.*

PHASE II CARS (220/8 to 250/8)

Drain coolant from radiator and block, then disconnect the three hoses where they go through the firewall. Remove the rear seat heater duct, then remove right defroster nozzle as follows: remove right cover underneath instrument panel, then remove glove box. Detach the connecting hose from the right annular nozzle (3) and remove the two nuts (4) that hold the right defroster nozzle (5). Remove right nut (11) and center nut (12) from instrument panel. Slightly lift the instrument panel, then remove right duct and nozzle down and to the right.

Remove the left cover underneath the instrument panel, then remove the two nuts from the heater box slotted brackets. Back out the screw on the supporting bracket at the transmission tunnel, then reach through the glove box opening and remove the rubber boot from the center air duct. Disconnect the center air flap linkage, then remove left nut (11) on instrument panel. Disconnect cable connections at right side of heater box, then slightly raise instrument panel and remove heater box, with core. Remove three blower screws and pull out blower, disconnecting plug when visible.

Windshield Wipers

Motor Removal and Installation

PRE-PHASE II SEDANS

Remove the right cover under the instrument panel. Detach the short link (1) from

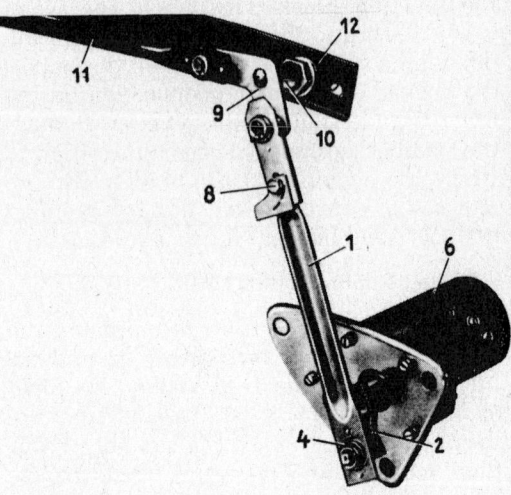

1. Link	9. Tandem lever
2. Motor crank	10. Adjusting gauge
4. Washer	11. Long link
6. Wiper motor	12. Holding plate
8. Locking screw	13. Wiper shaft

Wiper motor and connections—pre-phase II models.

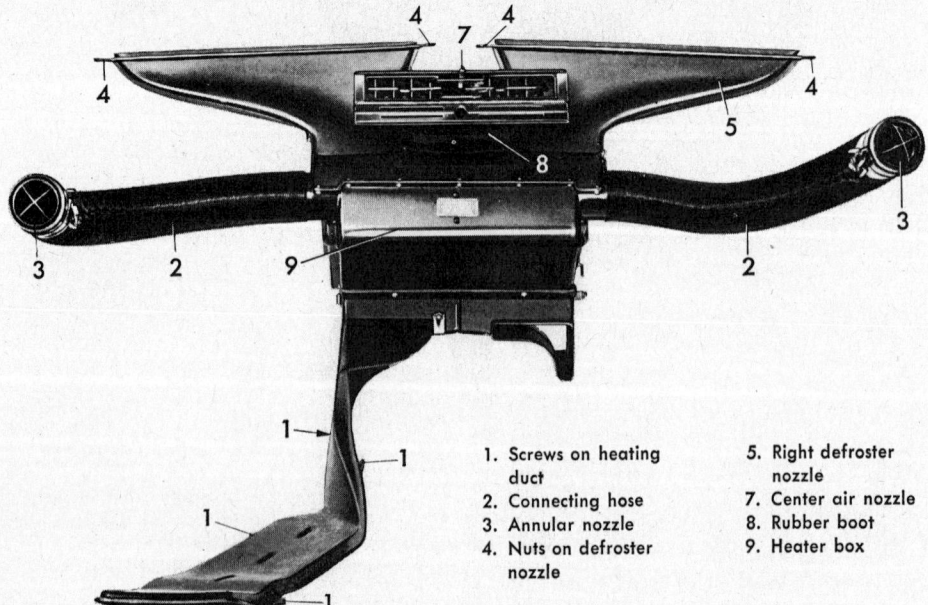

1. Screws on heating duct	5. Right defroster nozzle
2. Connecting hose	7. Center air nozzle
3. Annular nozzle	8. Rubber boot
4. Nuts on defroster nozzle	9. Heater box

Heater system seen from under dashboard—phase II models.

the motor crank (2) by removing the snap-ring and washer (4). From under the hood, pull out the six-pin plug and remove the three hold-down screws. Remove the motor.

To install, hold the motor in position and install the three screws through the firewall. Insert the six-pin plug and put the motor in "park" position by switching it on and off again quickly. Attach the short link (1) to the motor crank (2), together with washer (4) and snap-ring. Install the right cover under the instrument panel.

PHASE II SEDANS

Remove the cover plate under the left side of the dashboard. Detach the ball joint from the link rod (2), then remove the three hold-down nuts from the studs. From under the hood, disconnect the cable plugs and remove the motor. Installation is the reverse of removal.

1. Setscrew
2. Link rod
3. Threaded pin
4. Sealing washers
5. Ball joint on motor

Wiper motor and connections—phase II models.

Diesel Engine Troubleshooting and Tune-up

The diesel and gasoline engines used by Mercedes-Benz differ essentially in only one way—how the fuel is ignited. Both types are four-stroke cycle engines, that is, their operating cycles consist of (1) an intake stroke, whereby air (or air-fuel mixture) is pulled into the combustion chamber, (2) a compression stroke, during which the air (or air-fuel mixture) is compressed and heated, (3) a power stroke, caused by the burning (ignition) of the injected fuel and air mixture, and (4) an exhaust stroke, which literally pushes the burnt and unburnt gases out of the engine.

A diesel engine does not have an ignition system as such, although there are glow plugs for starting. To ignite its fuel-air mixture, the diesel depends on the heating effect of compression pressure. If the pressure is high enough, through high compression ratios and combustion chamber design,

FOUR STROKE DIESEL CYCLE

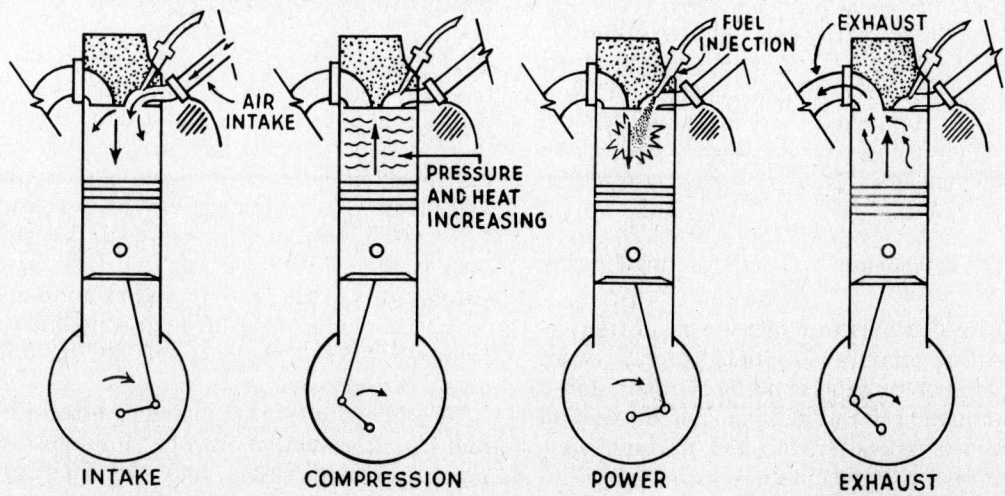

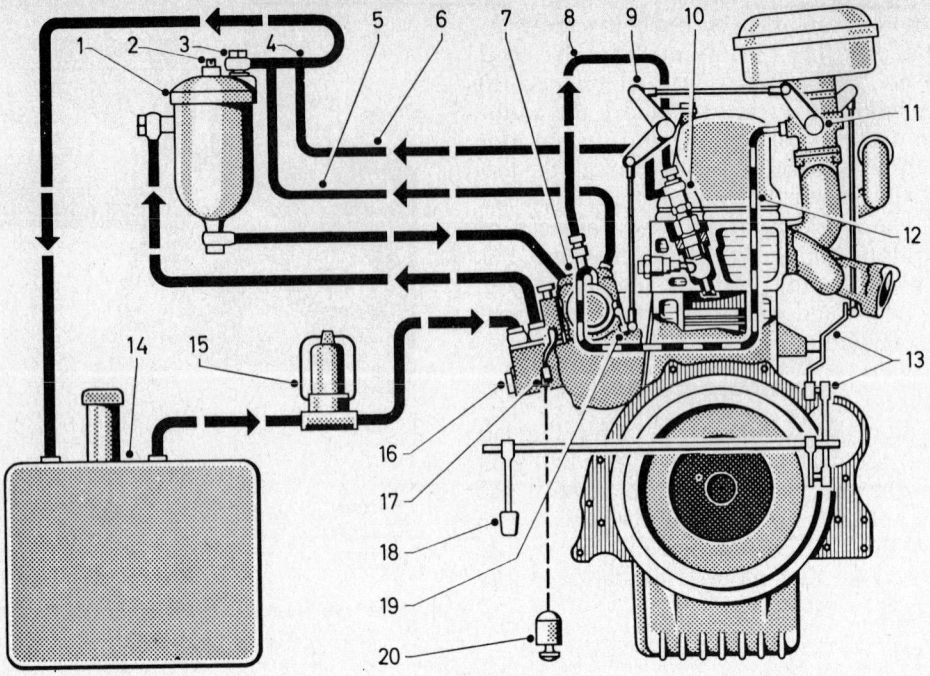

1. Main fuel filter
2. Vent screw
3. Hollow screw with throttle screw
4. Fuel return line
5. Overflow line
6. Injection nozzle leakage line
7. Injection pump

8. Pressure line from injection pump to injection nozzle
9. Angular lever for auxiliary mechanical control
10. Injection nozzle
11. Venturi control unit
12. Vacuum line with throttle screw
13. Linkage and lever for accelerator pedal control
14. Fuel tank
15. Fuel prefilter

16. Fuel feed pump with hand pump
17. Adjusting lever
18. Accelerator pedal
19. Lever for auxiliary mechanical control
20. Heater plug starting switch with starting and stopping cable

Diesel operation in schematic form.

the fuel-air mixture will ignite of its own accord.

The diesel, having no ignition system, is simplified to an extent, although the timed fuel injection required may offset this to a degree. Advantages lie in increased fuel economy using lower grades of fuel, along with long life due to rugged construction.

Troubleshooting a Non-Starting Engine

Any discussion of diesel engine troubleshooting must involve fuel injection, since most poor running conditions stem from a malfunction in this system. The illustration shows a typical engine and its fuel injection system in schematic form.

The fuel feed jump, driven by the injection pump, acts the same as the fuel pump of any gasoline engine, pumping fuel from the tank to the engine. The fuel passes through two fuel filters, the transparent prefilter and the larger main filter. From there it goes into the suction chamber of the injection pump, in which a constant fuel pressure is maintained by the overflow valve. At a *minimum* pressure of 11.8 psi surplus fuel flows back into the fuel tank via this valve. The fuel pump has a pumping capacity much greater than is necessary in order to keep the chamber always full of bubble-free fuel.

The injection pump plungers force the fuel from the suction chamber through the pump pressure valves into the injection

Diesel Engine Troubleshooting Chart

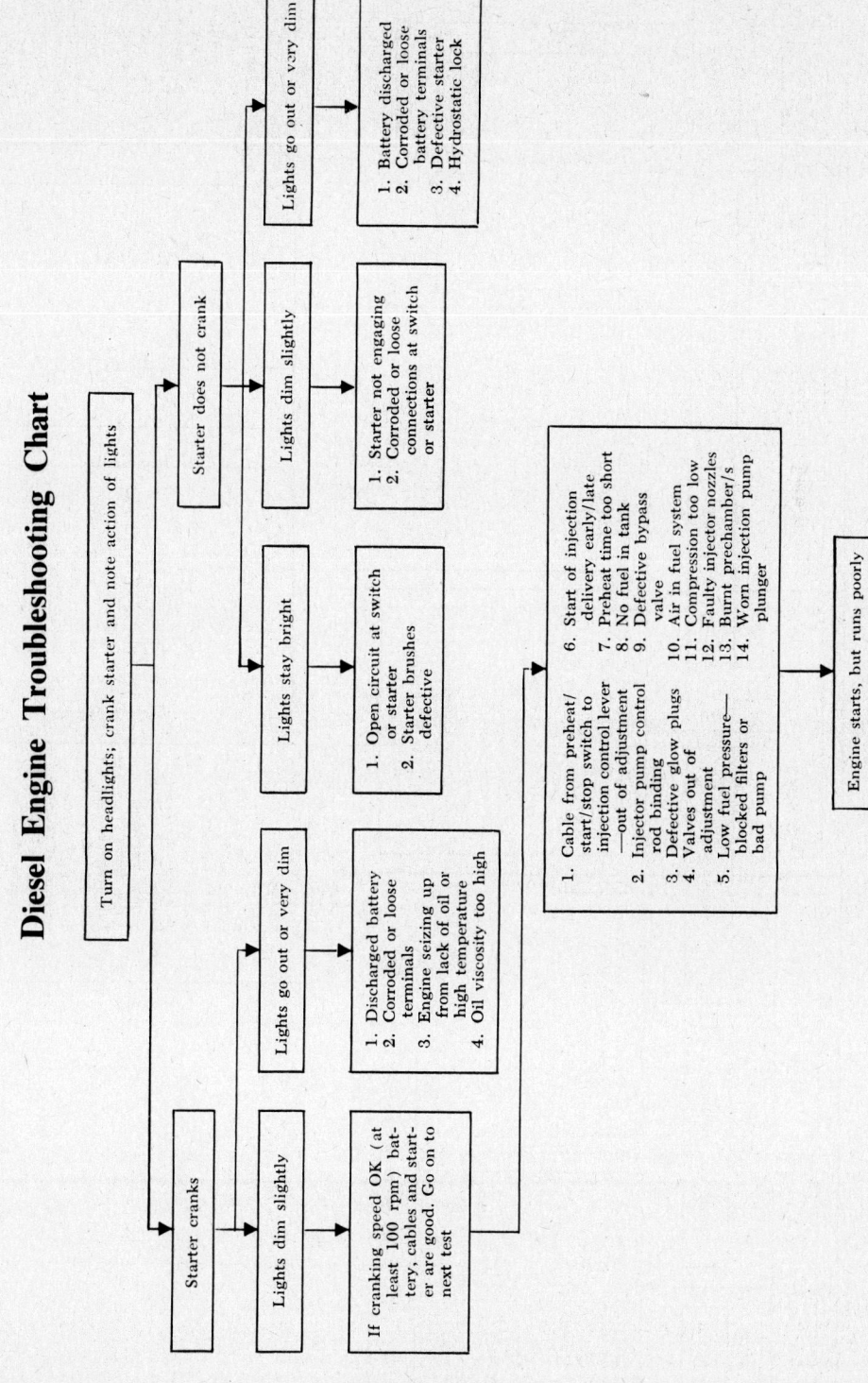

Turn on headlights; crank starter and note action of lights

Starter cranks

Lights dim slightly

If cranking speed OK (at least 100 rpm) battery, cables and starter are good. Go on to next test

Lights go out or very dim

1. Discharged battery
2. Corroded or loose terminals
3. Engine seizing up from lack of oil or high temperature
4. Oil viscosity too high

Starter does not crank

Lights stay bright

1. Open circuit at switch or starter
2. Starter brushes defective

Lights dim slightly

1. Starter not engaging
2. Corroded or loose connections at switch or starter

Lights go out or very dim

1. Battery discharged
2. Corroded or loose battery terminals
3. Defective starter
4. Hydrostatic lock

Engine starts, but runs poorly

1. Cable from preheat/ start/stop switch to injection control lever —out of adjustment
2. Injector pump control rod binding
3. Defective glow plugs
4. Valves out of adjustment
5. Low fuel pressure— blocked filters or bad pump
6. Start of injection delivery early/late
7. Preheat time too short
8. No fuel in tank
9. Defective bypass valve
10. Air in fuel system
11. Compression too low
12. Faulty injector nozzles
13. Burnt prechamber/s
14. Worn injection pump plunger

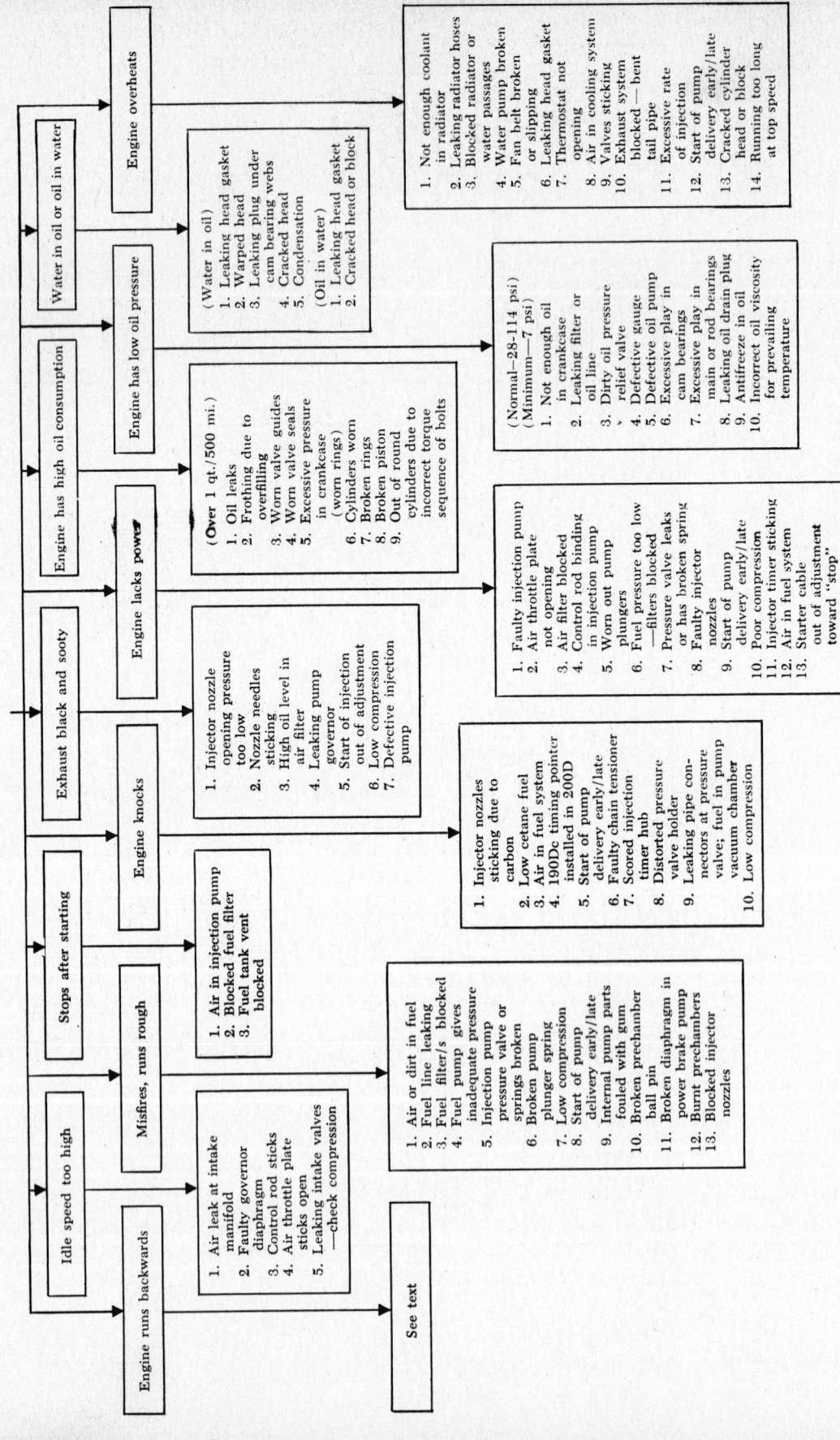

Engine overheats
1. Not enough coolant in radiator
2. Leaking radiator hoses
3. Blocked radiator or water passages
4. Water pump broken
5. Fan belt broken or slipping
6. Leaking head gasket
7. Thermostat not opening
8. Air in cooling system
9. Valves sticking
10. Exhaust system blocked — bent tail pipe
11. Excessive rate of injection
12. Start of pump delivery early/late
13. Cracked cylinder head or block
14. Running too long at top speed

Water in oil or oil in water

(Water in oil)
1. Leaking head gasket
2. Warped head
3. Leaking plug under cam bearing webs
4. Cracked head
5. Condensation

(Oil in water)
1. Leaking head gasket
2. Cracked head or block

Engine has high oil consumption

(**Over** 1 qt./500 mi.)
1. Oil leaks
2. Frothing due to overfilling
3. Worn valve guides
4. Worn valve seals
5. Excessive pressure in crankcase (worn rings)
6. Cylinders worn
7. Broken rings
8. Broken piston
9. Out of round cylinders due to incorrect torque sequence of bolts

Engine has low oil pressure

(Normal—28-114 psi)
(Minimum—7 psi)
1. Not enough oil in crankcase
2. Leaking filter or oil line
3. Dirty oil pressure relief valve
4. Defective gauge
5. Defective oil pump
6. Excessive play in cam bearings
7. Excessive play in main or rod bearings
8. Leaking oil drain plug
9. Antifreeze in oil
10. Incorrect oil viscosity for prevailing temperature

Engine lacks power
1. Faulty injection pump
2. Air throttle plate not opening
3. Air filter blocked
4. Control rod binding in injection pump
5. Worn out pump plungers
6. Fuel pressure too low —filters blocked
7. Pressure valve leaks or has broken spring
8. Faulty injector nozzles
9. Start of pump delivery early/late
10. Poor compression
11. Injector timer sticking
12. Air in fuel system
13. Starter cable out of adjustment toward "stop"

Exhaust black and sooty
1. Injector nozzle opening pressure too low
2. Nozzle needles sticking
3. High oil level in air filter
4. Leaking pump governor
5. Start of injection out of adjustment
6. Low compression
7. Defective injection pump

Engine knocks
1. Injector nozzles sticking due to carbon
2. Low cetane fuel
3. Air in fuel system
4. 190Dc timing pointer installed in 200D
5. Start of pump delivery early/late
6. Fuel chain tensioner
7. Scored injection timer hub
8. Distorted pressure valve holder
9. Leaking pipe connectors at pressure valve; fuel in pump vacuum chamber
10. Low compression

Stops after starting
1. Air in injection pump
2. Blocked fuel filter
3. Fuel tank vent blocked

Misfires, runs rough
1. Air or dirt in fuel
2. Fuel line leaking
3. Fuel filter/s blocked
4. Fuel pump gives inadequate pressure
5. Injection pump pressure valve or springs broken
6. Broken pump plunger spring
7. Low compression
8. Start of pump delivery early/late
9. Internal pump parts fouled with gum
10. Broken prechamber ball pin
11. Broken diaphragm in power brake pump
12. Burnt prechambers
13. Blocked injector nozzles

Idle speed too high
1. Air leak at intake manifold
2. Faulty governor diaphragm
3. Control rod sticks
4. Air throttle plate sticks open
5. Leaking intake valves —check compression

Engine runs backwards

See text

lines—thence to the injection nozzles, at a spray pressure of 1564–1706 psi. The spray must pass through the prechamber before reaching the main combustion chamber. Surplus fuel at the injectors is passed through leakage lines into the fuel tank.

The fuel volume is influenced by the accelerator pedal position, engine load and speed, and controlled by the pneumatic governor on the rear of the injection pump.

If the engine will not start, as usually happens in cold weather with a poorly maintained car, try turning the idle speed adjuster knob all the way counterclockwise, pre-glow for a full minute, push the clutch all the way in and the accelerator pedal halfway down. Then, try to start the engine. If the engine does not start after 10–15 seconds, pre-glow again and repeat the procedure. If the engine fires a few times but just won't catch, hold the starter on for a longer period.

This assumes, of course, that the starter motor turns the engine over at all. The most common cause of the starter not working, or working sluggishly, is a low battery, sometimes in combination with "summer" oil. The diesel, having such a high compression ratio (21:1) is difficult to turn over with high viscosity oil working against it.

If, after checking the battery, starter, cables, and oil, the engine still will not start, a check of one, or all, of the following areas is in order:

1. Cable from pre-glow/start-stop switch to injection control lever.
2. Injection pump control rod.
3. Compression pressure (including valve adjustment).
4. Glow plugs.
5. Fuel pressure.
6. Start of injection pump delivery.

CABLE

To adjust the cable, first disconnect the ground cable from the negative battery post. Push the control knob all the way in to the "stop" position. In this position, the adjusting lever on the injection pump will

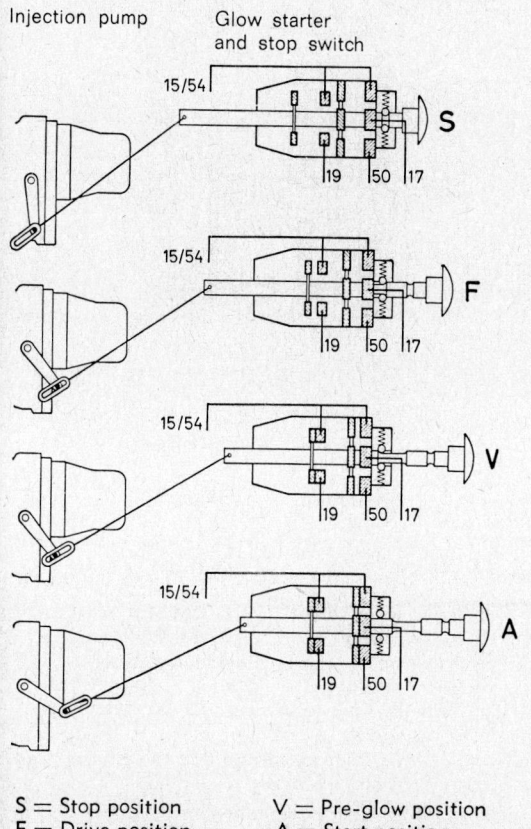

S = Stop position   V = Pre-glow position
F = Drive position   A = Start position

Starting cable positions.

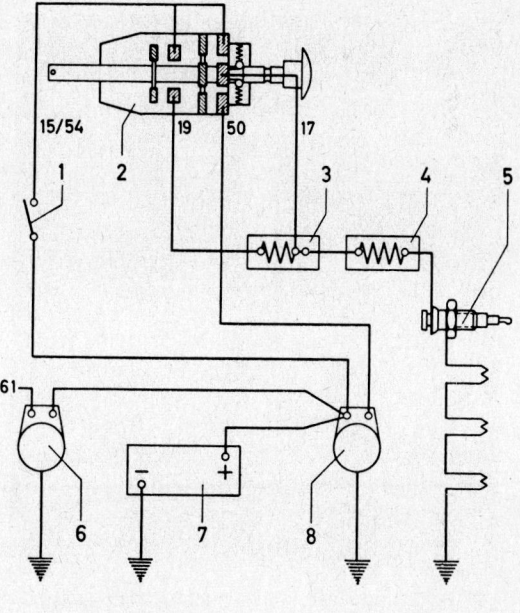

1. Main switch   5. Glow plug
2. Push pull switch   6. Generator
3. Glow plug control   7. Battery
4. Resistor   8. Starter

Diesel starting system.

be pushed completely forward. Next, pull the knob to the "start" position. In this position, the pin of the adjusting lever should rest against the end of the eye (2).

Now, release the knob. The adjusting lever should return to the "driving" position. In both this and the pre-glow position, the adjusting lever pin must clear the eye end by at least .080″. If not, adjust the cable by loosening the bolt and moving the coil spring outer housing (4) with relation to the angle bracket (3). Also, make sure the adjusting lever (1) is firmly attached to the pump shaft by tightening the clamp screw. Check the cable and adjusting lever for free movement and check that the lever is pulled all the way back when the knob is pulled to the starting position. Reconnect the battery cable and try to start the engine. *NOTE: If both the start and stop positions cannot be adjusted properly, it is best to sacrifice a little starting delivery to gain a full stop position on the lever.*

CONTROL ROD

The control rod runs through the center of the injection pump, one end sticking out of the end housing, covered with a protective cap. If this rod is sticking in the stop position, no fuel is delivered to the injectors and the engine will not start. Remove the end cap and check the rod for binding.

COMPRESSION

The only difference in testing is that the glow plugs instead of the spark plugs are removed for the test. Individual cylinder pressures should not vary more than 45 psi.

Don't forget, valve clearances set too close will result in poor compression readings for the diesel, too.

Some engines have a valve rotator (6) installed. If this rotator fails, compression will be low. Usually, the replacement of the rotator will bring compression back up to par.

GLOW PLUGS

The glow plugs provide a means for ignition during starting and perform the same

1. Adjusting lever (starting and stopping cable lever)
2. Eye with rubber molding of starting and stopping cable
3. Angle bracket
4. Coil spring

Starting cable adjustment.

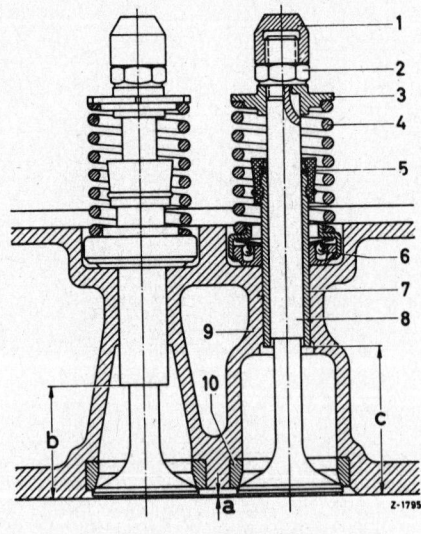

Intake   Exhaust

1. Cap nut
2. Hexagon nut
3. Valve spring disk
4. Valve spring
5. Valve seal
6. Valve rotator
7. Valve guide— exhaust
8. Exhaust valve
9. Cylinder head
10. Valve seat— exhaust

a = Distance from separating line of cylinder head to valve disk
b = Distance from separating line of cylinder head to front face of intake valve guide
c = Distance from separating line of cylinder head to front face of exhaust valve guide

Diesel valve set-up, showing rotator.

Testing glow plugs.

function as normal spark plugs, although they do so in a different manner.

The light on the dashboard indicating when the glow plugs are hot enough to fire can also serve as a troubleshooting aid. If the light does not glow, it usually indicates a faulty plug.

Test the plugs by having an assistant hold the starting knob in the preheat position while shorting the plugs to ground, in turn, with a screwdriver. Each plug should produce a spark if working properly. While bridging the connections, the light should light. If, after disconnecting the ground lead (10) of the preheating system, the light still stays lit, a short circuit in the system is indicated. This is usually caused by a carboned up plug electrode or by a lead touching the cylinder head. Check the leads first. If they seem O.K., pull the knob to the preheat position and disconnect one plug power lead at a time, starting from the ground end, until the light goes out, indicating the faulty plug.

Glow plugs can be cleaned, but it is better to replace them if they are badly carboned. To remove the plugs, loosen the cable (10), if this has not been done already, by removing the knurled nut (11). Unscrew the other nuts and remove the insulators (9) and the bus bars (8). Using a 21 mm. socket, unscrew and remove the glow plugs.

1. Union nut for mounting the injection line
2. Hex. nut for mounting the fitting
3. Fitting
4. Connection head of leak oil line
5. Hollow screw
6. Nozzle holder
7. Glow plug
8. Bus bar
9. Connection insulator
10. Connection cable or ground cable resp. (on both outer glow plugs)
11. Knurled nut

Diesel starting and injection components.

a. Groove in cylinder head
b. Lug securing prechamber
c. Distance between prechamber (5) and cylinder head
d. Max. permissible measure of a retracted ball pin with respect to the outer dia. of the prechamber (.020")
1. Nozzle holder
2. Threaded ring
3. Seal ring between prechamber and cylinder head
4. Seal ring between prechamber and nozzle holder (nozzle plate)
5. Prechamber (ball pin version)
6. Ball pin in the prechamber
7. Glow plug

Glow plug and prechamber.

Before installing new plugs, clean the ducts and prechamber bores with a stiff bristle brush or a small scraper. The ball pin in the prechamber is easy to break, so don't go much deeper than 2″ into the plug hole. Crank the engine a few times to blow out any carbon particles loosened by the scraping, then insert the plugs. Do not exceed 35 ft.-lbs. torque.

It might be a good idea to recheck these new plugs to ensure that all connections are tight and not grounded and that the plugs are not faulty.

FUEL PRESSURE

The fuel pump is mounted on the side of the fuel injection pump, and can be easily identified by the hand priming pump. Its job, like that of the gasoline engine fuel pump, is to deliver a constant fuel volume, at adequate pressure, to the injection pump. With the diesel engine it is extremely important that the fuel is air-free, without bubbles. A fuel bypass valve is located in the injection pump to maintain constant fuel pressure for the engine load. This valve opens at a pressure of 14.7–22 psi, sending excess fuel back into the supply system.

As with most things mechanical, accurate testing is possible only with the proper instruments. A general check of fuel pressure can be made, however, if one assumes that the bypass valve is functioning properly. Disconnect the return line at the fitting and hold the line over an open coffee can. Start the engine and watch the line. If fuel comes out, it can be assumed that the fuel pressure is sufficient, as a pressure of at least 14.7 psi is required to open a good bypass valve.

It is also good practice to check the discharge line from the fuel filter, as a blocked filter will deliver no fuel. Check the tank before assuming the worst about a fuel pump—gauges have been known to be wrong. It may be a good idea to disconnect the input line from the fuel tank and blow back through it with low-pressure compressed air. A line free of debris will allow the air to bubble in the tank. *CAUTION: High pressure air will blow out the fuel tank filter.*

Defective fuel pumps should be replaced, as it is not really feasible to rebuild them without the proper tools. To check the pump, unscrew the hand pump and remove the suction valve. Unscrew the plug

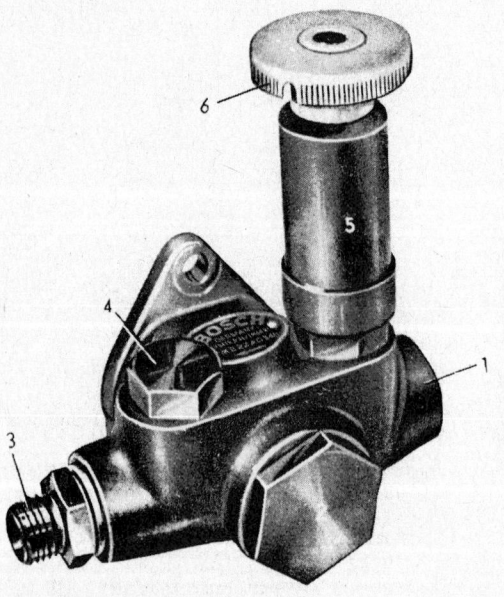

1. Connector at suction end	5. Hand pump and cap lug to
2. Screw plug to plunger	suction valve
3. Connector at discharge end	6. Handle of hand feed pump
4. Screw plug to pressure valve	7. Roller tappet guide

8. Guard ring
9. Guide pin and/or guide
   plate on roller tappet
10. Roller tappet

Diesel fuel pump.

(4) covering the pressure valve and remove the valve. Worn valve seats can be reground sometimes, but it is better to replace them. To check the plunger, remove the plug (2) and pull the plunger and spring. If it is badly scored or worn the pump must be replaced. If the pump is only clogged with gum, it is possible to clean it with lacquer thinner or carbon tet, but a new rubber O-ring should be used on the hand pump during reassembly.

START OF INJECTION PUMP DELIVERY

As the piston comes up on compression stroke, there is a delay, caused by the fuel having to come from the pump to the injector nozzle, which must be compensated for. For example, if injection takes place too early, temperatures may not yet be high enough for ignition (piston has not come up far enough to compress the air). To compensate for this lag, the injection pump begins to deliver fuel to the nozzle 26° before top dead center is reached for 190 Dc and 200 D and 24° BTDC for 220 D/8.

To check the start of delivery, remove the negative battery cable and set the piston of No. 1 cylinder at top dead center by lining up the TDC mark on the crankshaft pulley with the pointer. If TDC is achieved, both intake and exhaust valves of No. 1 cylinder will be closed (springs not compressed).

This can be checked by removing the camshaft cover and observing the relationship of the rockers to the valve stems. Now, using a wrench on the crankshaft pulley nut (never use the camshaft pulley nut, as the timing chain rails will be damaged), turn the engine over 1¾ turns, in the normal direction of rotation.

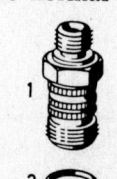

1. Pipe union
2. Rubber sealing ring
3. Coil spring
4. Sealing ring
5. Pressure valve plate with pressure valve

Pressure valve components.

1. Adjustment lever of injection pump	4. Tachometer drive
2. Hand-operated fuel pump	5. Overflow pipe
	6. Bleed screw
3. Jaws for locking two pipe unions	7. Fuel container
	8. Fuel return lines

Measuring start of pump delivery.

Unscrew the injection line at the pipe union of the first pump cylinder (see illustration). Remove pipe union (1), rubber O-ring (2), spring (3) and the pressure valve. Replace the union and screw on an overflow pipe (5) (see illustration).

Detach the starting cable from the lever at the injection pump and make sure that the lever is in the full delivery position. If this is not done the test may be inaccurate.

Either connect an auxiliary fuel container to the injection pump or fill the main fuel filter by operating the hand pump (2) and cracking the bleed screw (6) to ensure that the fuel is air-free.

With the wrench on the crankshaft pulley, turn the engine over slowly in the normal direction of rotation until the fuel stream from the overflow pipe stops dripping. *NOTE: Another drop may follow 10–15 seconds later, but this is normal.*

At this point, the pump piston covers

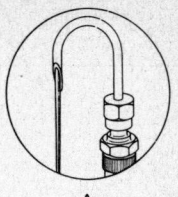 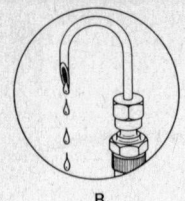 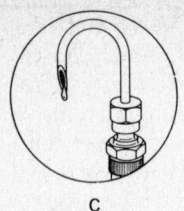

A. Solid fuel stream
B. Fuel begins to drip
C. One drop follows 10-15
    seconds later

Overflow pipe during test.

the intake core in the pump cylinder and the start of delivery point has been reached. The crankshaft pointer should read 26° BTDC or 24° BTDC, depending on model.

Repeat the test by continuing to turn the crankshaft in the direction of rotation—two turns. At the end of the second revolution the fuel should cease dripping again at the proper point.

To adjust the start of delivery, loosen the bolts of the front flange and rotate the pump toward the engine to begin delivery earlier, or away from the engine to delay delivery. It may be necessary to disconnect the injector tubes so that the pump will be free enough to rotate.

Remove all test equipment and reassemble, using a new seal (4) in the pressure valve assembly. The pressure valve assembly pipe union must be tightened to exactly 25 ft.-lbs. with the threads coated with Vaseline. Bleed the fuel system by opening bleed screw (6) and pumping the hand pump to evacuate any air. Reattach the starting cable and adjust as mentioned previously.

Troubleshooting a Poorly Running Engine/Tune-up

A careful study of the troubleshooting chart will reveal most of the symptoms of poor running associated with diesel engines of this type, along with their probable causes. You will also note that many items are found in more than one column, because the breakdown or malfunctioning of one component part could cause any number of problems, depending on whether other components are involved in this breakdown. For instance, a blocked fuel filter could cause the engine to stop immediately after starting, cause it to misfire or run badly, or even not start at all. In

such cases of multiple listings, test or repair procedures given for one will be valid for all, unless specifically stated otherwise.

In order to eliminate repetition, the most common testing and repair procedures follow in no particular order or sequence. Simply consult the troubleshooting chart and find the associated test.

ENGINE RUNS BACKWARD

Under the right conditions the diesel engine can run backward (although poorly)

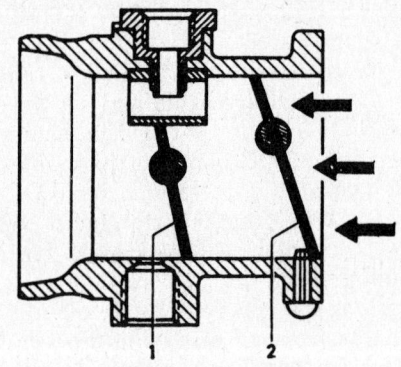

1. Throttle valve
2. Check throttle valve

Air check valve to prevent engine from running backwards. Arrows show the valve closed, as it would be if engine attempted to run backwards.

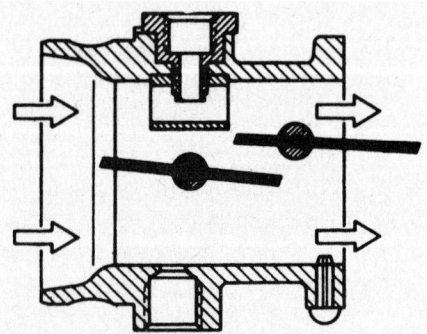

Air check valve as it operates normally.

accompanied by smoke issuing from the air cleaner. This is not a common condition, but one that can be damaging to the engine.

For example, if reverse gear is accidentally engaged while coasting forward, or if the engine stalls under load and restarts itself, the engine can run backward. To stop it, engage a gear and let out the clutch suddenly, or block the exhaust pipe with a rag. This can also happen if an attempt is made to start the engine without preheating. If the switch is moved from the start to the preheat position, the beginning of preheat may coincide with engine revolutions, causing extremely early ignition. If this happens, the air filter will quickly catch fire and the engine can seize up due to lack of oil, so quick action is necessary.

Since 1962, diesel engines have had a check throttle valve installed to prevent this situation, so a check of that valve will usually isolate the problem. Lubricate the valve every 5,000 miles with engine oil to prevent recurrence.

Engine Stops After Starting

Can be caused by blocked fuel tank, fuel filter, or an air-locked injection pump. Remove tank filler cap and try starting the engine. Remove fuel line to injection pump and crank engine. Check fuel volume. Bleed fuel system.

Idle Speed Too High

Air leaks at the intake manifold can be located by squirting some soapy water at any suspected joints with the engine running. Solution will be sucked in or bubble if a leak exists.

The injection pump governor diaphragm cannot be checked accurately unless the pump is placed on a test stand. It is possible, however, to determine roughly whether or not the governor is operating. First, with the engine idling, squirt a soapy water solution over the intake manifold, vacuum line, governor housing and air venturi housing joints to check for leakage.

Remove the starting cable from the control lever of the injection pump and remove the sleeve (3) over the control rod. Unscrew vacuum line at (1) and actuate the control lever (2), making sure the control rod goes to its full stop position, while holding thumb over fitting (1).

1. Vacuum union
2. Control lever
3. Protector sleeve over control rod

Checking vacuum chamber.

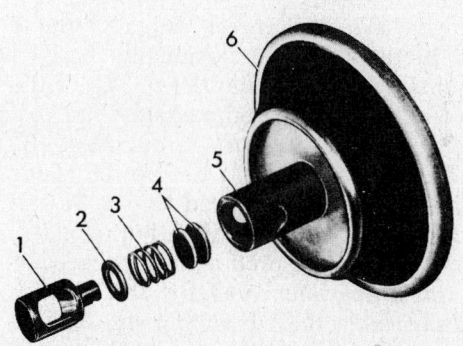

1. Compensator pin
2. Shim for compensator spring
3. Compensator spring
4. Shims for compensator spring
5. Sleeve
6. Diaphragm

Vacuum diaphragm components.

1. Prod of dial indicator
2. Sleeve of diaphragm
3. Piece of tubing
4. Pin, 6 mm. in diameter
5. Compensator pin

Assembling and checking diaphragm assembly.

Release control lever and observe control rod. If diaphragm of the pump governor is functioning, the control rod will move slightly, but will be restrained by vacuum produced in the housing. Removing the thumb should allow the control rod to move. If this test indicates the diaphragm to be faulty, remove the four bolts and take out the diaphragm for inspection.

It is possible, although not the best procedure, to replace the diaphragm with the injection pump in place, but care must be taken in assembly. For example, it is easy to lose the compensator mechanism components (1, 4 and 5 in illustration). It is also necessary to use a dial indicator to measure the maximum compensator travel (see illustrations).

To measure this travel, obtain a pin 6 mm. in diameter (approximately 0.235″) and insert it through the sleeve (2) of the old diaphragm and compensator pin (5). Placing the assembly on a large socket (3) is necessary for stability. Set up the gauge as illustrated, with the prod tip on the end of the compensator pin, slightly preloaded. Press down on the prod and measure existing travel (maximum travel is .043″–.105″).

Disassemble the old diaphragm and insert the shims into the new one. Now measure maximum travel of the diaphragm. The difference in readings should not exceed .0024″. Shims are available to make corrections.

Uneven Running, Metallic Noise, Blue Smoke

The usual cause of this condition is a broken ball pin in the prechamber, a jammed injection nozzle or a leaky vacuum pump system.

With the car stationary, rev the engine a few times and note the exhaust. If intermittent clouds of black smoke are emitted, it indicates one or more of the injection nozzles is faulty. To determine which nozzle is malfunctioning, allow the engine to idle. Loosen the cap nuts (7) of each injection tube, one at a time, about ½ turn, then retighten. If there is no change in the rough idle, it indicates a faulty nozzle. A good nozzle will be indicated by a further roughening of the idle when the cap nut is unscrewed.

To remove the nozzle, take off the cap nut (7) and unscrew the nut (6) that holds the banjo fitting (5 and 3). Remove bolt

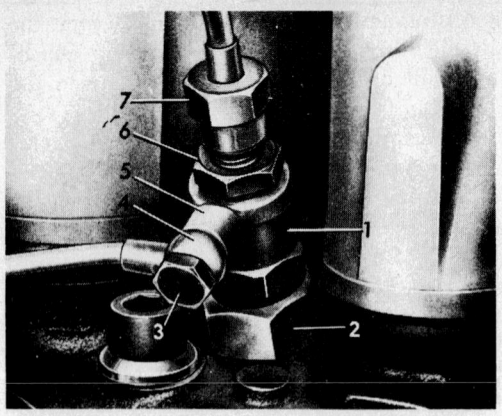

1. Nozzle holder
2. Cap nut of nozzle holder assembly
3. Hollow bolt
4. Union head of leak-off oil pipe
5. Through-way jointing piece
6. Hexagon nut anchoring the through-way jointing piece
7. Cap nut anchoring the injection pipe

Injection nozzle.

(3) and the overflow line. Then, unscrew the nozzle assembly and seal (6).

Examine the prechamber for carbon deposits and clean it if necessary. To disassemble the nozzle holder, remove the **cap nut (5)** (see illustration) with a 27 mm. box wrench, then pull out the nozzle **assembly (2)** and jet needle (1). Remove the nozzle element (3), thrust pin (4) and spring (6) from the nozzle holder. It is very easy to crush or distort the nozzle holder, therefore do *not* clamp it in a vise to disassemble. Individual nozzle components are run-in together and never should be interchanged.

Nozzle testing requires special equipment capable of producing accurately measured pressure while allowing observation of the spray pattern. Since this equipment is not readily available, and jury-rigged setups do not produce good results, it is recommended that the dealer do any nozzle testing.

In any case, malfunctioning nozzles are usually only carboned up and, if care is exercised, they can be hand-cleaned.

Brush any carbon away using a brass-bristle brush or a piece of kerosene-soaked wood. Never use a steel scraper, because any burrs will ruin the injector. Using a sharpened brass rod, scrape any deposits from the grooves and orifices, then soak in solvent and blow out with compressed air.

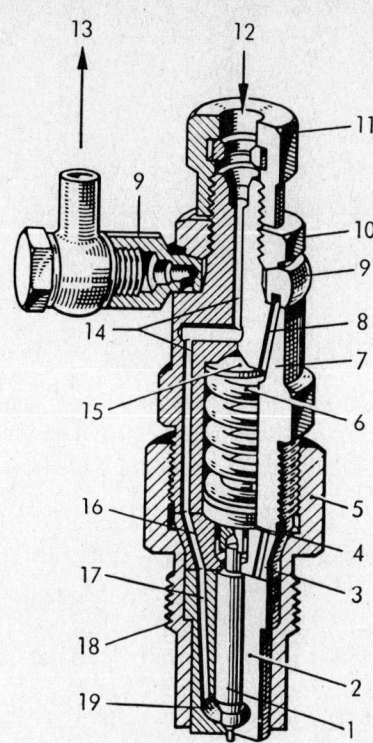

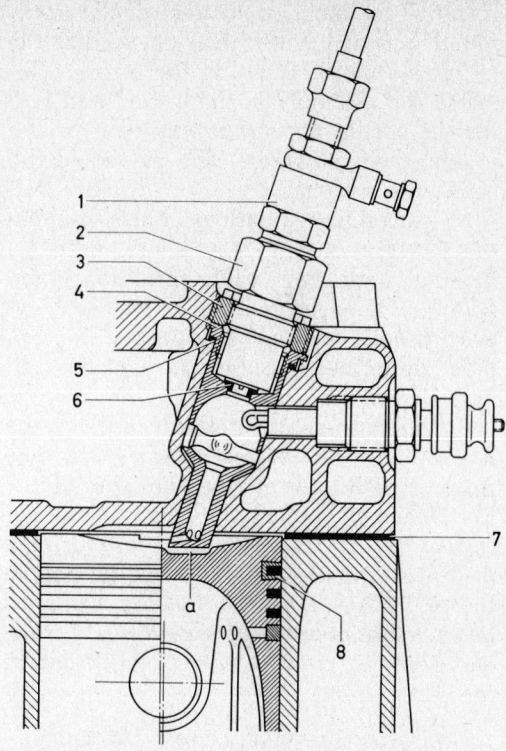

1. Jet needle
2. Nozzle assembly
3. Nozzle element
4. Thrust pin
5. Cap nut for fixing injection nozzle
6. Compression spring
7. Nozzle holder
8. Drain hole in the nozzle holder
9. Through-way jointing piece with annular canal for leak-off oil union
10. Hexagon nut for fixing the through-way jointing piece
11. Cap nut for fixing the injection pipe
12. Fuel feed
13. Leak-off oil drain back to fuel tank
14. Pressure canal in the nozzle holder
15. Special washers belonging to compression spring (machined steel disks)
16. Annular groove and feed bores in nozzle element
17. Annular groove and pressure canal in nozzle assembly
18. Mounting thread
19. Pressure chamber in nozzle assembly

Nozzle holder/injection assembly.

1. Nozzle holder
2. Cap nut of nozzle holder
3. Threaded ring
4. Prechamber
5. Sealing ring
6. Seal
7. Cylinder head gasket
8. Piston ring liner
a. Piston base recess

Nozzle holder installed.

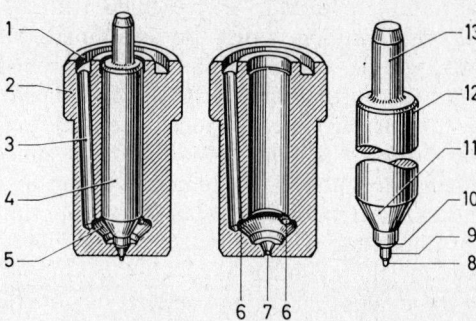

1. Annular groove
2. Nozzle assembly
3. Intake bore
4. Jet needle
5. Pressure chamber
6. Mouth of intake bore in pressure chamber
7. Mouth of nozzle
8. Injection pin
9. Throttle pin
10. Needle seating surface
11. Thrust shoulder
12. Needle shaft
13. Thrust shank

Injector nozzle.

Examine for burrs or scratches and out-of-round injection holes, then check that the jet needle moves freely in the nozzle. Immerse the assembly in diesel fuel and pull the jet needle about one-third out of the nozzle, then release it. The jet should fall of its own weight.

In emergency situations, burrs keeping the jet from sliding may be removed by lapping with fine valve grinding compound. Damaged seating surfaces, however, usually will not be restored by lapping; therefore, it is best to replace such damaged units.

Assemble the unit carefully, checking the illustrations for correct parts assembly. Any dirt will prevent free operation of the jet. When tightening the cap nut, do not exceed 50 ft.-lbs.—excessive torque may distort the nozzle and cause the jet needle to bind. *CAUTION: Always use new seals when reassembling and installing injectors, and never try to stop leaks by overtightening connections.*

UNEVEN RUNNING, DRONING NOISE, VERY HEAVY BLUE SMOKE

This condition is usually caused by a cracked diaphragm in the power brake vacuum pump. Engine oil is sucked through the crack into the vacuum hose, then into the intake manifold. The result can be burned prechambers if not corrected in time, as well as general carbon build-up in the combustion chamber. Remove the hose from the vacuum pump to the intake manifold. If it is filled with oil, the prechambers must be examined for damage. If the prechamber is scorched badly or burnt away, it must be replaced. Unfortunately, special tools are required for this job. In light of the difficulty sometimes encountered in removal even *with* the special tools, it is almost certain that any substitute will not work, and may even damage the cylinder head. Leave this job to the dealer and confine activity to general scraping and cleaning of the chamber. This usually will be sufficient if the condition was caught in time. To alleviate the cause of the problem, the vacuum pump diaphragm must be replaced.

To check the diaphragm, detach the vacuum hose between the pump and the power brake and, using a T-fitting connector similar to the one illustrated, hook a vacuum gauge into the line. With the en-

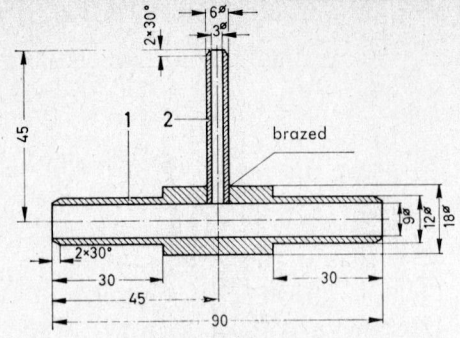

T-fitting for vacuum test.

gine running at 2,000 rpm, the gauge should show a little over 21 in. Hg. (vacuum) after about 10 seconds.

ENGINE KNOCKS

"Knocking" of the engine falls into four general categories:

1. Knocking during idling.
2. Knocking under partial load at low speed.
3. Knocking under partial load at high speed.
4. Hard knocking, engine shaking on mounts.

Unless the noise has some mechanical cause, bad connecting rod bearings for instance, diesel knock can be considered harmless to everything but the driver's ears.

Knocking During Idling

This is a normal condition with diesel engines and nothing really can be done about it. Injection nozzle replacement, although often done, is not a guarantee that the noise will stop. In fact, the new clean nozzles will often make the noise more pronounced.

Knocking at Partial Load at Low Speed

This usually occurs with a cold engine, and becomes less as the engine heats up. The most common cause of this is use of diesel fuel with too low a cetane rating (equivalent to "octane" for gasoline). Try mixing about a quart of engine oil with each tank of fuel or change fuel brands.

Oftimes air in the fuel system will cause this problem as well. Check all fuel lines and hoses, from the tank all the way up. The fuel filter and hand pump can also

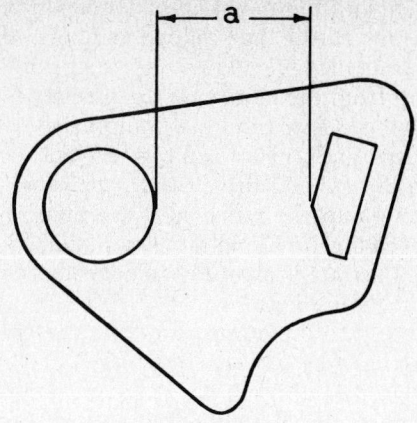

Timing pointer.

develop leaks. Bleed the fuel system, as described previously, and check the fuel pump vacuum (idle speed=6-12 in. Hg.) and pressure (open pressure of relief valve at idle=11-21 psi).

Although highly unlikely at this late date, some 200 D engines may have had timing pointers installed from the 190 Dc engine. This will retard the ignition by 3° or so. Check the pointer with the illustration and table.

Type	Pointer Part Number	Measurement
190 Dc	121 032 01 15	a = 1″ (25.0 mm.)
200 D	121 032 02 15	a = 1¹⁄₁₆″ (27.0 mm.)

Check the start of fuel delivery, as previously outlined, and check the fuel filters.

Injection lines of a different diameter may be exchanged for older types to eliminate knocking. The new lines are ¹⁄₁₆″ (1.5 mm.) in diameter (inside).

Knocking at Partial Load At Higher Speeds

This type of knocking usually happens in third gear traveling at 30–45 mph. It can be distinguished by the fact that it gets louder as the engine heats up.

This is often caused by a faulty timing chain tensioner. When the chain loses tension it vibrates, causing a rattle. In addition, the injection timer hub can be scored to such a degree that injection timing is retarded.

The injection timer can be removed and checked in the following manner:

1. Remove radiator (on 220 D/8).
2. Detach vacuum and pressure hoses from vacuum pump. Remove vacuum pump.
3. Remove cover screws and cover. Remove hex nut and washer from shaft.
4. Remove camshaft cover.
5. Remove hex screw and holder along with inner guide rail (on 190 Dc and 200 D.)
6. Remove the camshaft sprocket bolt.
7. Turn the crankshaft, using a wrench on the pulley nut, in the direction of rotation until the TDC mark for 220 D/8 models and the 45° BTDC mark on 190 Dc and 200 D models coincides with pointer.
8. Matchmark the position of the chain with the injection timer. (Use paint dots.)
9. Matchmark position of chain on camshaft sprocket.
10. Remove chain tensioner.
11. On 220 D/8, remove screw (13) and the inner and outer sliding rails (11 and 12). (See illustrations in engine section.)
12. Pull the camshaft sprocket, making sure the thrust washers are not lost.
13. Unscrew locking screw and pull the upper guide rail pivot pin.
14. Using a strip of sheet metal or cardboard between the chain and the gear teeth, remove chain from the intermediate sprocket.
15. Pry off the injection timer, being careful not to turn over the engine or camshaft.

Inspect the timer. If scored badly or broken internally, replace it, remembering to transfer matchmarks from old timer. When reassembling, follow removal procedure in reverse, being careful to line up the matchmarks. A bent piece of brazing rod will hold the guide rail in place while inserting the pivot pin. Don't forget to bleed the chain tensioner.

Hard Knocking and Shaking Of Engine

The main cause of this is a sticking injector nozzle. These can be tested as described earlier in this chapter, as well as the pressure valve holders, another cause of the problem.

Leaks between the pipe connectors and pressure valve holders can cause fuel to leak into the governor vacuum chamber. Replacement of the seals will stop the problem, but the fuel must be drained from the vacuum chamber. Unscrew the oil level plug and loosen the governor housing bolts. Drain the fuel by pulling the housing away.

INJECTION PUMP

In many cases of poor running, the injection pump itself is at fault. Fuel that is extremely gritty will cause wear of the pump plungers, and plunger springs can break in service. Accurate testing of the pump must be carried out on a test stand. Aside from testing the governor vacuum and control rod, little else other than visual inspection for broken or worn parts can be accomplished without this apparatus.

To remove the pump for service, unscrew all injection lines, the vacuum line and fuel lines. Plug the lines, then detach the connecting rod for the auxiliary mechanical control and the starting cable at the adjusting lever. Turn the crankshaft, in the normal direction of rotation, to line up the 45° BTDC mark with the pointer (No. 1 piston on compression stroke).

Matchmark the pump and flange. Unscrew the nut at the bell-shaped support, then the front flange hold-down nuts. Pull the pump from the crankcase, then remove the coupling sleeve from the pump drive collar or driveshaft. New pumps do not come with the splined drive collar, therefore the old one must be removed if the pump is to be exchanged. Using a puller similar to the one illustrated, carefully remove the collar and Woodruff key.

To install the pump, note that the crankshaft has not moved from the 45° BTDC position, then insert the Woodruff key into its groove in the driveshaft, making sure the shaft is dirt free. Install the drive collar and hex nut, using a tape-wrapped pair of pliers to hold the collar while tightening the nut. It is extremely important that the splines are not damaged in any way during this operation. Try sliding the coupling sleeve onto the drive collar. If it slides on easily, it can be pressed onto the driveshaft (see illustration). Remove the oil overflow pipe plug at the rear of the injec-

Section A–B

1.	Segment plate of the injection timing device	11.	Bearing bushing, front	27.	Stud bolt
2.	Intermediate sprocket	12.	Bearing bushing, rear	28.	Gasket
3.	Bushing	13.	Coupling sleeve	30.	Injection pump
4.	Washer	14.	Snap-ring	31.	Hex nut with washer
5.	Lockwasher	15.	Hex nut	32.	Washer
6.	Hex nut	16.	Lockwasher	33.	Screw plug
7.	Woodruff key	17.	Follower	34.	Rubber ring
8.	Segment flange of inj. timing device	18.	Cover	35.	Hex hd. screw
9.	Centrifugal weight roller of the inj. timing device	19.	Lockwasher	36.	Pressure piece
		20.	Fill. hd. screw	37.	Bearing bushing
10.	Intermediate gear shaft (driveshaft for injection pump and for helical gear 39 or for oil pump)	21.	Gasket	38.	Bearing body
		22.	Lockwasher	39.	Helical gear (drive for oil pump and revolution counter)
		23.	Hex hd. screw		
		24.	Butting ring (steel washer)		
		24a.	Grooved pin	40.	Bearing bushing
		25.	Cylinder crankcase		

Injection timer and tachometer drive.

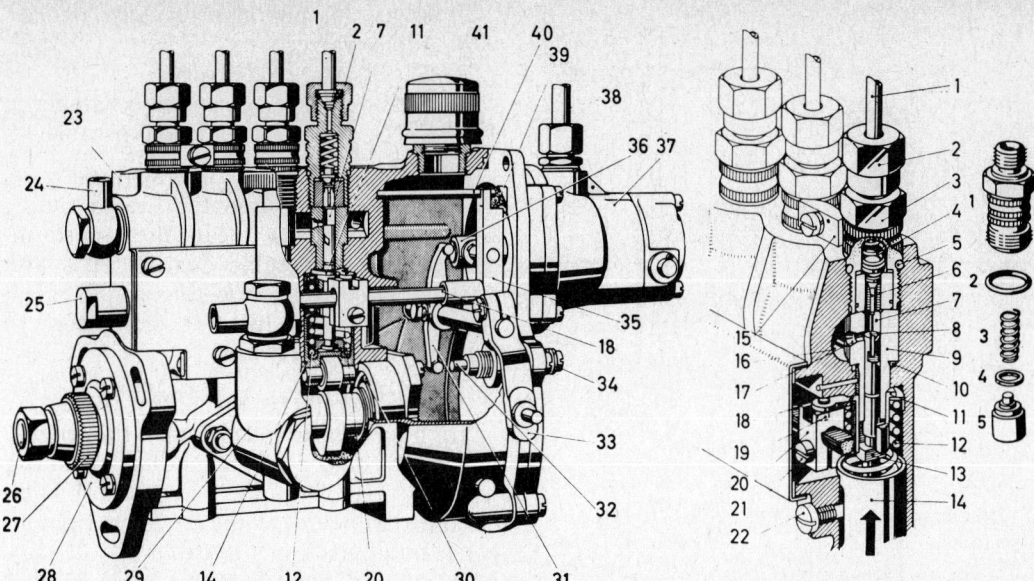

1. Pressure pipe (injection pipe)
2. Cap nut
3. Pipe union
4. Valve spring
5. Seal between pipe union and injection pump housing
6. Pressure valve with pressure valve holder
7. Pressure chamber
8. Plunger ⎫ = forming pump
9. Cylinder ⎭ element
10. Seal
11. Governor sleeve with steering arm
12. Tappet spring
13. Plunger vane
14. Roller tappet
15. Clamping jaws (to grip the pipe unions)
16. Suction chamber
17. Control bore (feed and return bore)
18. Control rod
19. Pin on control sleeve rotating lever
20. Adjustable clamping piece with guide groove
21. Clamp screw
22. Tappet guide screw
23. Injection pump housing
24. Fuel feed union
25. Control rod guide bearing and start-metering stop
26. Camshaft (drive side)
27. Link stud
28. Bearing base-plate with gasket and centering
adjustment
29. Fuel feed pump
30. Journal bearing
31. Rocker arm
32. Stop pin for full load stop
33. Setting lever
34. Setting lever stop, also adjustment screw with full load stop
35. Guide lever
36. Diaphragm pin with pressure pin and compensator spring
37. Diaphragm assembly
38. Vacuum line
39. Diaphragm
40. Guide pin
41. Air cleaner and oil filler bore

Diesel fuel injection pump.

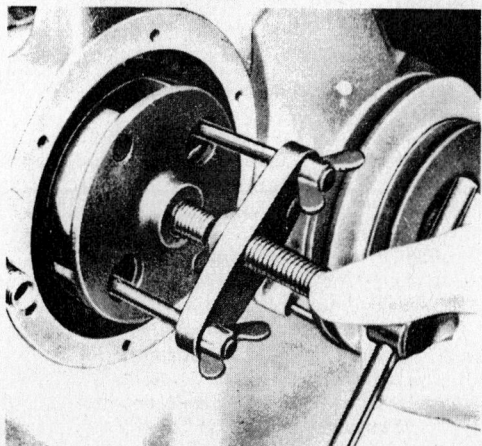

Removing injection timer.

Matchmarks on drive collar.

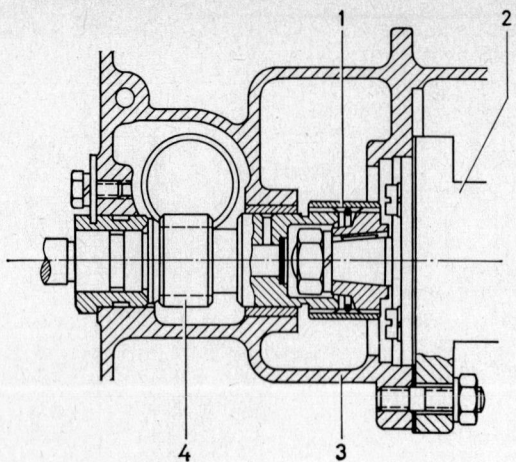

1. Coupling sleeve
2. Injection pump
3. Crankcase
4. Idling gear shaft
(driveshaft for
injection pump
and oil pump)

Injection pump drive.

tion pump and adjust start of delivery position by aligning marks as illustrated. Apply light finger pressure to the follower in a direction opposite normal direction of rotation (left). This pressure should cause the drive collar to jump two teeth. Grease the paper gaskets with Vaseline and install them to side of crankcase, then install pump, finger-tightening the bolts in the slotted holes. Turn the crankshaft in direction of rotation to 26° BTDC (or 24° BTDC for 220 D/8) and check the start of delivery, as outlined previously.

Diesel Engine Tune-up

Some of the tune-up procedures have been covered in the troubleshooting section. For those who are not having any problems and wish to tune their engines as part of normal maintenance procedure, these tune-up jobs are listed below. (Starred items have been covered previously.)

1. Adjust idle speed.
*2. Check pneumatic governor for leakage.
3. Adjust idle control cable.
4. Adjust additional mechanical control (Stupser).
5. Adjust no-load maximum speed (governor).
6. Adjust full-load maximum speed (governor).

7. Adjust for minimum exhaust smoke.
8. Adjust valves.
*9. Check start of delivery.
*10. Check glow plugs and prechamber.
*11. Check and adjust start/stop cable.

While not a regular tune-up procedure, checking and adjustment of valve timing should be done, as it can affect performance to a considerable degree. It is also good practice to check this if the chain tensioner has been removed or replaced to rectify a noise condition.

IDLE SPEED ADJUSTMENT

To adjust idle speed, start the engine and allow it to come to normal operating temperature. Turn the idle control knob on the dashboard to the extreme right to get enough slack in the cable (4). It may be necessary to readjust the cable bracket to get the required free-play.

Since there is no electric ignition system, a mechanical tachometer take-off drive is provided, as shown in the illustration. (If such a tachometer is not available, adjust

1. Vent line of crankcase ventilation system
2. Connecting rod (approximate length 310 mm.) to control valve lever (Venturi control unit)
3. Angle relay lever
4. Idle adjustment cable
5. Vacuum line between injection pump governor and Venturi control unit
6. Connecting rod (approximate length 205 mm.) to additional mechanical control lever (butt bolt)
7. Lever of additional mechanical control (butt bolt)

Diesel control linkage.

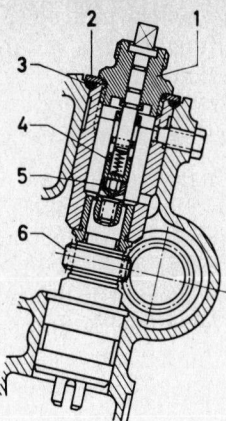

1. Revolution counter drive or adapter
2. Cover plate
3. Rubber ring
4. Follower or connecting piece between adapter and helical gear
5. Cylindrical screw with hexagon socket
6. Helical gear (driving oil pump and revolution counter)

Tachometer drive and oil pump drive.

1. Full-load stop screw
2. Front control valve
3. Connecting rod from front control valve lever to angle lever for injection pump butt bolt operation
4. Idle stop screw
5. Vacuum line to injection pump
6. Check valve lever with stop for automatic opening and rubber damping (in this position the check valve is open)
7. Follower on rear control valve lever for automatic opening of check valve
8. Rear control valve lever
9. Connecting rod (approx. 250 mm. long) to reversing lever, pushrod, control shaft, pedal lever, foot-plate
10. Power brake line to vacuum pump

Air venturi and associated linkage.

the idle speed by ear to about 700–800 rpm, manual transmission in neutral and automatic in drive, with the parking brake on fully and the wheels chocked. The ammeter light will go out when sufficient speed is reached.

To adjust the idle speed, turn the idle screw on the air intake in or out. If the vacuum line(5) is leaking, the idle speed will not drop when the screw is turned, so make sure both the line connections and the pneumatic governor are good before proceeding. Drain any fuel that might have leaked into the governor housing by unscrewing the oil level plug and loosening the governor housing bolts.

IDLE CONTROL CABLE

Turn the idle control knob on the dashboard to the extreme right and adjust the cable to provide .004″–.008″ clearance between the adjusting ring and the relay lever. The cable must be checked for binding as well, and lubricated if necessary.

ADDITIONAL MECHANICAL CONTROL

This control mechanism helps to eliminate idle speed variations, i.e., "hunting".

With the idle speed properly adjusted, detach the connecting rods [(2) (6) and (9) in illustration] and measure their length, center to center between ball sockets.

Connecting rod No. 2–310 mm. (12.1″)
Connecting rod No. 6–205 mm. (8.1″)
Connecting rod No. 9–250 mm. (9.8″)

With the rods adjusted, detach connecting rod No. 6 from the relay lever (3) and push it down until it rests against the idle stop. In this position, clearance between the ball socket and head should be .04″. If it requires more than .04″ lift to reattach the connecting rod, unscrew the ball socket.

MAXIMUM SPEED ADJUSTMENT NO-LOAD CONDITIONS

This adjustment must be made using a tachometer. The purpose of this adjustment is to limit the maximum engine revolutions so that the engine will never exceed its design speed in service. First, warm up the engine and press the accelerator to the floor. The full-load stop at the air venturi should be contacted by the linkage and the engine speed should not exceed 5,000 rpm.

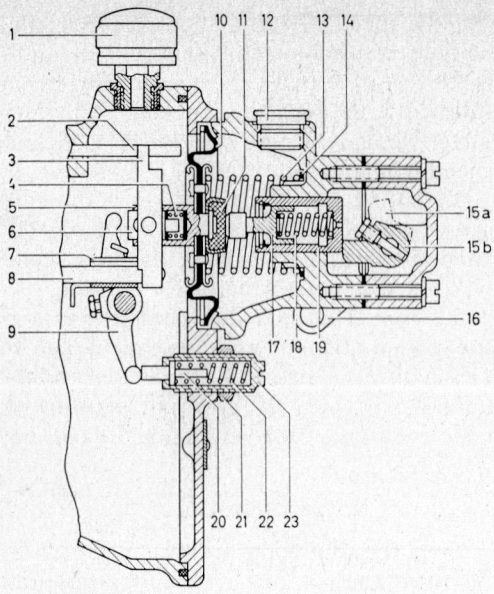

1. Air cleaner
2. Guide rod
3. Guide lever
4. Compensator
   spring
5. Diaphragm sleeve
6. Compensator pin
7. Start-metering
   stop
8. Control rod
9. Double-link rocker
10. Diaphragm
11. Rubber buffer
12. Vacuum union to
    vacuum chamber
13. Control spring
14. Backing ring
15a. Switch cam, full-

load position
15b. Switch cam, idle
     position
16. Lever for automatic
    auxiliary gov-
    ernor system
17. Stop stud (butt
    bolt)
18. Auxiliary spring
19. Butt bolt housing
    or spring hous-
    ing, sliding
20. Stop stud for full-
    load stop
21. Setting nut
22. Spring
23. Full-load stop
    screw

Vacuum system in idle position.

The speed can be adjusted by turning the full-load stop screw (1). If the throttle plate is already all the way open and the speed is not up to par, the injection pump control spring tension may be increased by shimming (see illustration). A .004″ shim will usually increase the engine speed by about 120–150 rpm, depending on the original tension of the spring.

CAUTION: At first glance this appears to be an easy way to increase the engine speed range, thus the power output. Unfortunately, the power output decreases sharply above 5,000 rpm, and the reliability

of the engine suffers as well, to the point of almost certain bearing failure or crankshaft destruction.

MAXIMUM SPEED AT FULL-LOAD

If all aspects of engine and chassis performance have been checked and/or adjusted to produce optimum power and the car will not reach its maximum speed, the full-load stop screw can be adjusted further, or the injection pump control spring tension can be increased slightly. However, under no circumstances should the engine speed under no-load conditions be allowed to go over 5,000 rpm. If no-load engine speed is O.K., check the speedometer for accuracy, using a stopwatch and a turnpike measured mile.

Model	Max. speed in second gear (mph)	Max. speed in third gear (mph)	Top speed (mph*)
190 Dc	34	54	77
200 D	34	54	80
220 D/8	35	57	83

*Depends on transmission power drain.
NOTE: The best full-load engine speed is 4,350 rpm.

EXHAUST SMOKE EMISSION

If the emission of black exhaust smoke seems excessive, test in the following manner: make all engine checks and adjustments and, with the engine fully tuned, road test the car on a slight grade. Accelerate in third gear from about 15 mph to the third-gear shift point mark on the speedometer. Have a passenger watch the exhaust smoke while doing this. If the smoke remains black and can be seen extending three or four feet behind, the maximum fuel delivery rate is too high. Adjust by screwing in the full-load stop screw on the *injection pump governor* about ¼ turn (see illustration). Repeat the road test and adjust in small increments until the smoke disappears. *CAUTION: Do not exceed ½ turn total.*

If the smoke level is still objectionable, the full-load stop screw on the *air venturi* can be adjusted to reduce maximum speed slightly, or the injection pump start of delivery can be retarded 2°.

OPEL SECTION
Index

695

Introduction

Opel A.G., owned by General Motors since 1929, began importing and selling the Opel Rekord through the Buick Motor Division dealer network in 1958. In 1964, the Opel line was expanded to include the Kadett Models, a sedan, a coupe and a station wagon. Since then the Opel has become more Americanized, adding such options as a fully automatic 3-speed transmission in 1969. A sport version of the Kadett, the Rallye, with improved performance and special trim, was introduced in 1967, followed by the Opel GT, a two seat sports coupe based on the Kadett Rallye running gear, in 1969.

Year and Model Identification

1964-65 Kadett Sedan

1966-67 Kadett Coupe

1966-70 Kadett Station Wagon

1967-70 Kadett Coupe

1967-70 Rallye Coupe

1969-70 GT

Vehicle and Engine Serial Number

Vehicle Identification Number

KADETT

Opel Kadett vehicle-identification numbers run consecutively from the first Kadett produced in 1964. The first two digits of the serial number (reading from the left) indicate the model. The other numbers indicate production sequence. The identification plate is located in the engine compartment either on the right fender wall or on the left side of the fire wall.

GT

The GT is numbered in an identical manner to the Kadett. Identification plates are located on the right side of the cowl

Model Identification Plate located in Engine compartment.

and on the left side of the instrument panel at the base of the windshield.

Engine Serial Number

KADETT AND GT

The engine number, stamped on the engine housing just above the crankcase dipstick, is prefixed with numbers and letters to indicate engine displacement and power. Reading from the left, the first two digits represent engine identification. Engines with an "S" designation are designed to run on premium gas.

Vehicle Identification

Year Model Number & Name	Starting Chassis Serial Numbers
1964 31, 2 dr sedan 32, Sport Coupe 34, Kadett Caravan	– 0 223 661
1965 (from 8-24-64 2-Door Sedan Sport Coupe Kadett Caravan New Coil (from Dec.)	– 0 399 251 31 0 407 849 32 0 416 103 34 0 409 311 0 489 948
1966 2-Door Sedan Sport Coupe Kadett Caravan 4-Door Sedan 4-Door Deluxe (L) 2-Door Deluxe (L) Caravan Deluxe (L)	31 0 654 963 (Last Unit 32 0 654 980 Imported) 34 0 654 965 to 957 592 36 0 654 966 to 957 470 37 0 655 506 to 957 600 38 0 656 052 to 957 598 39 0 655 583
1967 (from late August, 1966) 2-Door Sedan Sport Coupe Rallye (from 11-5-66) Caravan Deluxe (L)	31 0 957 604 to 1 223 566 32 0 957 603 to 1 228 102 32 1 041 613 39 0 957 662 to 1 231 606

Year Model Number & Name	Starting Chassis Serial Numbers
1968 31, 2-dr sedan 39, Deluxe (L) station wagon 92, Rallye Coupe 99, 2-dr Sport Coupe Deluxe "LS"	311243154 391242823 921280093 991286203
September 2-Door Coupe Caravan "L"	311249264 321239547 (67-1/2) 391249269 1.1US 000 448 1.5S 0 001 167 1.9S 0 144 099
October	391278809 921278980 (GM Rallye) 1.1US 001 878 1.5S 0 004 542 1.9S 0 151 061
November	311309932 991309933 (LS Sport Coupe) 1.1US 003 699 1.5S 0 008 508 1.9S 0 158 470
December	311343043 991343042 (LS Sport Coupe) 1.1US 005 544 1.5S 0 016 685 1.9S 0 164 067

Vehicle Identification

Year Model Number & Name	Starting Chassis Serial Numbers
1969 January	311368692
	921368693
	(Deluxe Sport Coupe, Model 95)
	1.1US 008 094
	1.5S 0 020 934
	1.9S 0 169 809
February	311398391
	911398387
	1.1US 013 373
	1.5S 0 028 808
	1.9S 0 176 833
March	391424148
	911424150
	1.1US 015 455
	1.5S 0 033 142
	1.9S 0 182 374
May	919 088 213[1]
June	919 091 048[1]
July	9 100 153[1]
August	9 104 923[1]
	311 550 095[2]
September	9 113 662[1]
	391 576 367[2]
	931 559 041 GT[2]
October	9 123 841[1]
	311 601 896[2]
	941 602 249 GT[2]
November	9 134 890[1]
	911 630 295[2]
	941 630 311 GT[2]
December	919 144 965[1]
	911 656 931[2]
	941 656 936 GT[2]
1970 January	9 154 026[1]
	311 681 493[2]
	941 681 527 GT[2]
February	919 164 634[1]
	921 714 442[2]
	941 714 445 GT[2]
March	319 174 208[1]
	911 743 235[2]
	941 743 245 GT[2]
April	319 184 280[1]
	391 777 151[2]
	941 777 158 GT[2]
May	319 196 158[1]
	311 807 907[2]
	931 807 911 GT[2]
June	319 206 992[1]
	391 838 651[2]
	941 838 648 GT[2]

Year Model Number & Name	Starting Chassis Serial Numbers
July	9 218 812[1]
	1 867 336[2]
	941 867 347 GT[2]
31	Built at Antwerp, Belgium
39	319 226 095
91	399 226 072
92/95	919 226 160
93(93/94)	929 226 061
	Built at Bochum, Germany
	311 892 279
	391 891 974
	911 898 881
	921 892 066
August	9 227 783[1]
	1 888 684[2]
	941 888 798[3]
September	9 233 208[1]
	1 912 265[2]
	941 912 266[3]
October	399 246 274[1]
	1 948 000[2]
	941 948 005[3]
November	399 259 947[1]
	1 983 547[2]
	941 983 580[3]
December	9 271 593[1]
	312 018 193[2]
	942 018 199[3]
1971 January	399 283 899[1]
	2 048 746[2]
	942 048 756[3]
February	929 295 513[1]
	2 082 517[2]
	942 082 518[3]
March	929 295 513[4]
	312 113 439[2]
	942 113 440[3]
April	9 308 895[1]
	312 147 476[2]
	942 147 481[3]
May	9 325 062[1]
	2 182 510[2]
	942 182 518[3]
June	9 339 598[1]
	312 210 650[2]
	942 210 670[3]
July	9 357 845[1]
	312 245 306[2]
	Not Produced[3]

First Model 30 built on May 13, 1970
  Antwerp, Belgium: Chassis Number 319 329 970
First Model 30
  Bochum, Germany: Chassis Number 312 186 123
1 Antwerp, Belgium
2 Bochum, Germany
3 GT (Bochum)
4 Strike at Antwerp, Belgium

General Engine Specifications

Year	Model	Displacement cu. in (cc)	Developed Horsepower (SAE) @ RPM	Developed Torque (ft.lbs.) @ RPM	Bore and Stroke	Compression Ratio	Carburetor
1964-1965	1.0	60.2(987)	46 @ 5200	54 @ 3100	2.84 x 2.40	7.8:1	1-1 Bbl w/ manual choke
	1.0S	60.2(987)	54 @ 5500	56 @ 3800	2.84 x 2.40	8.8:1	1-1 Bbl w/ manual choke
1966-1967	1.1	65.8(1077)	54 @ 5600	59 @ 3000	2.95 x 2.40	7.8:1	1-Solex 1 Bbl w/ manual choke
	1.1S	65.8(1077)	60 @ 5600	63 @ 3200	2.95 x 2.40	8.8:1	1-Solex 1 Bbl w/ manual choke
	1.1SR	65.8(1077)	67 @ 6000	62 @ 5000	2.95 x 2.40	9.2:1	1-Solex 1 Bbl w/ manual choke
	1.1R	65.8(1077)	60 @ 6000	58 @ 3400	2.95 x 2.40	8.2:1	1-Solex 1 Bbl w/ manual choke
1968	1.1	65.8(1077)	55 @ 5600	59 @ 2850	2.95 x 2.40	8.2:1	1-Solex 1 Bbl w/ manual choke
	1.5L	91.0(1491)	80 @ 5100	87 @ 3400	3.25 x 2.75	9.0:1	1-Solex 2 Bbl w/ manual choke
	1.9L	115.8	102 @ 5200	115 @ 3100	3.66 x 2.75	9.0:1	1-Solex 2 Bbl w/ automatic choke
1969	1.1US (AIR)*	65.8(1077)	55 @ 5600	59 @ 2850	2.95 x 2.40	8.2:1	1-Solex 1 Bbl w/ manual choke
	1.1R (OECS)**	65.8(1077)	55 @ 5600	59 @ 2850	2.95 x 2.40	8.2:1	2-Solex 1 Bbl w/ manual choke
	1.1SR (OECS)**	65.8(1077)	55 @ 5600	59 @ 2850	2.95 x 2.40	9.2:1	2-Solex 1 Bbl w/ manual choke
	1.9L	115.8	102 @ 5200	115 @ 3100	3.66 x 2.75	9.0:1	1-Solex 2 Bbl w/ automatic choke
1970	1.1R (OECS) **	65.8(1077)	63 @ 6000	58 @ 4000	2.95 x 2.40	8.2:1	2-Solex 1 Bbl w/ manual choke
	1.1SR (OECS)	65.8(1077)	67 @ 6000	62 @ 5000	2.95 x 2.40	9.2:1	2-Solex 1 Bbl w/ manual choke
	1.9S	115.8	102 @ 5400	115 @ 3300	3.66 x 2.75	9.0:1	1-Solex 2 Bbl w/ automatic choke

* -- Air Injector Reactor System used on 1.1 liter engines imported to United States during 1969.
** -- Opel Emission Control System used on all 1.1 liter engines as noted above.

Tune-up Specifications

Year	Model	Spark Plugs Make/Type	Spark Plugs Gap in.(mm)	Spark Plugs Thread (mm)	Distributor Point Dwell Angle (degs.)	Distributor Point Gap in.(mm)	Basic Ignition Timing (degs.)	Cranking Compression Pressure (psi)	Valves Clearance in.(mm) Intake Hot	Intake Cold	Exhaust Hot	Exhaust Cold	Intake Valve Opens (degs. BTDC)	Idle Speed (RPM)
1964-1965	10 10S	AC44F	.035 (0.88)	14	50-55	.014-.016 (0.35-0.40)	TDC	140+7.5	.008 (0.20)		.008 (0.20)	—		600-800 750-800
1966-1967	11 11S 11SR	AC44F	.028-.031 (0.70-0.78)	14	48-55	.016-.020 (0.40-0.51)	TDC	140+7.5	.006 (0.15)	.008 (0.20)	.010 (0.25)	.012 (0.30)	36	600-800 800-900 950-1000
1968	1.1	AC43FS	.030 (0.76)	14	48-52	.018 (0.45)	TDC	140+7.5	.006 (0.15)		.010 (0.25)	—	44	850-900
1968	15S	AC44XLO	.030 (0.76)	14	48-52	.018 (0.45)	TDC	140+7.5	.012 (0.30)		.012 (0.30)	—	34	750-800
1968	19S	AC43FS	.030 (0.76)	14	48-52	.018 (0.45)	TDC	140+7.5	.012 (0.30)		.012 (0.30)	—	44	750-800
1969	1.1R	AC43FS	.028-.031 (0.70-0.78)	14	47-53	.016 (0.40)	TDC	140+7.5	.006 (0.15)		.010 (0.25)	—	44	925-975
	1.1SR								.012 (0.30)		.012 (0.30)	—	46	925-975
	1.9S												44	850-900
1970	1.1R 1.1SR	AC43FS	.028-.031 (0.70-0.78)	14	47-53	.016 (0.40)	TDC	140+7.5	.006 (0.15)		.010 (0.25)	—	46	925-975
	1.9								.012 (0.30)		.012 (0.30)	—	44	850-900

Firing Order

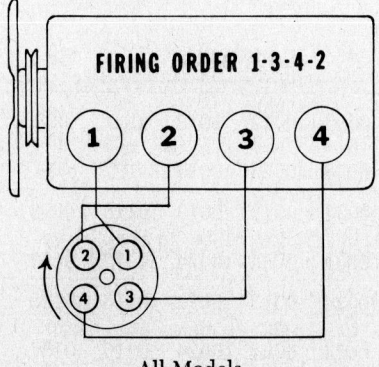

FIRING ORDER 1-3-4-2

1 2 3 4

All Models

Engine Rebuilding Specifications

All measurements in inches and (millimeters)

ENGINE	CRANKSHAFT							CONNECTING ROD		
	Main-bearing Journal Diameter	Crankshaft End Play	Journal-to-bearing Clearance	Thrust Bearing Effective Length	Journal and Crankpin — Maximum Out-of-round	Maximum Taper	Connect-ing-rod Journal Diameter	Connect-ing rod Bearing Length	Journal-to-bearing Clearance	Rod-to-journal Side Clearance
1.1 and 1.0	2.1260 (54.00)	.004 to .008 (.10–.20)	.0004 to .0022 (.010–.056)	1.1438 (29.052)	.0002 (.0051)	.0004 (.010)	1.7711 (44.986)	.9087 (23.081)	.0006 to .0025 (.0152–.0635)	.004 to .010 (.102–.254)
1.5 and 1.9	2.2829 to 2.2835	.0017 to .0061	.0009 to .0025	1.0807 to 1.0831	.0002	.0004	2.0461 to 2.0467	0.9843 to 0.9873	.0006 to .0023	.0043 to .0095

ENGINE	CAMSHAFT						OIL PUMP
	Number of Bearings	Diameter of Bearing Journal inches			Journal-to-bearing Clearance inches	Camshaft End Play inches	Clearance between Gears inches	Gear-to-housing Clearance (gears protrude) inches
		#1	#2	#3				
1.1 and 1.0	3	1.613	1.594	1.574	.001 to .003	.007 to .013	.004 to .008	.002 to .004
1.5 and 1.9	3	--	—	—	.001 to .003	.004 to .040	.004 to .008	Maximum .004

EN-GINE	CYLINDER BORE		PISTON IN BORE	PISTON RINGS						PISTON PINS		
	Maximum Out-of-Round inches	Maximum Taper inches	Clearance inches	Ring Clearance in Groove inches			Gap in Ring (With ring in bore) inches		Diameter inches	Offset in Piston	Fit in Piston inches	Fit in Connecting Rod
				Top	Center	Bottom	Compression	Oil				
1.0 1.1	.003	.005	.0004 to .0008	.0024 to .0034	.0013 to .0025	.0013 to .0025	.010 to .016	.008 to .014	.079	Toward distributor	.00024 to .00047	Press
1.5	.0005	.0005	.0012	.0024 to .0034	.0013 to .0024	.0013 to .0024	.0118 to .0177	.0098 to .0157				Press
1.9	.0005	.0005	.0012	.0024 to .0034	.0013 to .0024	.0013 to .0024	.0118 to .0216	.0098 to .0157				Press

Engine Rebuilding Specifications

Pistons

Index Number for Cylinder Bore	Cylinder Bore Dia. mm	Production Piston Dia. in mm (Marking on Top of Piston)	Service Replacement Piston Dia. in mm (Marking on Top of Piston)
5	71.95	71.93	71.93
6	71.96	71.94	71.95
7	71.97	71.95	71.95
8	71.98	71.96	71.97
9	71.99	71.97	71.97
00	72.00	71.98	71.99
01	72.01	71.99	71.99
02	72.02	72.00	72.01
03	72.03	72.01	72.01
04	72.04	72.02	72.03
05	72.05	72.03	72.03
06	72.06	72.04	72.05
07	72.07	72.05	72.05
08	72.08	72.06	72.07
09	72.09	72.07	72.07
10	72.10	72.08	

Standard Production Sizes (left margin)

Index Number for Cylinder Bore	Cylinder Bore Dia. mm	Pistons Not Avail. For Service Replacement
5 mm Oversize 72.45	72.45	72.43
72.46	72.46	72.45
72.47	72.47	72.45
72.48	72.48	72.46
1 mm Oversize 72.95	72.95	72.93
72.96	72.96	72.95
72.97	72.97	72.95
72.98	72.98	72.96

ENGINE	VALVE	TAPPET CLEARANCE ADJUSTMENT—HOT inches and (millimeters)	VALVE SPRING PRESSURE (lbs @ inches) Spring Compressed	Spring Open
1.5 and 1.9	Intake	.012″ (0.30 mm)	72.75 @ 1.63″	125.66 @ 1.32″
	Exhaust	.012″ (0.30 mm)	68.34 @ 1.38″	131.61 @ 1.06″

ENGINE	VALVE	TAPPET CLEARANCE ADJUSTMENT—HOT inches and (millimeters)	VALVE SPRING PRESSURE (lbs @ inches) Spring Compressed	Spring Open
1.1	Intake	.006″ (0.15 mm)	34 @ 1.34″	91 @ 1.04″
	Exhaust	.010″ (0.25 mm)		
1.0	Intake	.008″ (0.2 mm)	34 @ 1.43″	92 @ 1.04″
	Exhaust	.008″ (0.2 mm)		

ENGINE	VALVE HEAD Diameter inches and (millimeters) Intake	Exhaust	VALVE FACE ANGLE	VALVE SEAT ANGLE	OVERCUT OF VALVE SEAT
1.0	1.220 (30.99)	1.063 (27.00)	44°	45°	25°
1.1	1.259 (31.98)	1.063 (27.00)	44°	45°	25°
1.5	1.496	1.259	44°	45°	30°
1.9	1.574	1.338	44°	45°	30°

Engine Rebuilding Specifications

EN-GINE	VALVE CLEARANCE IN GUIDE inches and (millimeters)		VALVE—SIZE RANGES inches	Oversize Mark	VALVE STEM DIAMETER inches and (millimeters)		VALVE GUIDE BORE inches and (millimeters)
	Intake	Exhaust			Intake	Exhaust	
1.1 and 1.0	.0006 to .0018 (.015–.045)	.0014 to .0026 (.035–.066)	Standard	—	.2756 to .2760 (7.000–7.010)	.2748 to .2752 (6.980–6.990)	.2766 to .2774 (7.025–7.045)
			.0030 oversize	1	.2785 to .2789 (7.075–7.085)	.2778 to .2781 (7.055–7.065)	.2795 to .2803 (7.100–7.120)
			.0059 oversize	2	.2815 to .2819 (7.150–7.160)	.2807 to .2811 (7.130–7.140)	.2825 to .2833 (7.175–7.195)
			Service oversize .0098	A	.2854 to .2858 (7.250–7.260)	.2846 to .2850 (7.230–7.240)	.2864 to .2872 (7.275–7.295)
1.5 and 1.9	.001 to .0025	.002 to .0035	Standard	—	.3538 to .3543	.3524 to .3528	.3553 to .3562
			.0030 oversize	1	.3567 to .3572	.3553 to .3559	.3582 to .3592
			.0059 oversize	2	.3597 to 3602	.3583 to .3588	.3615 to .3622
			Service oversize .0118	A	.3656 to .3661	.3642 to .3647	.3671 to .3681

Models and Years They Were Imported

Model Description	1964	1965	1966	1967	1968	1969	1970
30 2-door Sedan (Economy)	–	–	–	–	–	–	x
31 2-door Sedan (Standard)	x	x	x	x	x	x	x
32 Sport Coupe	x	x	x	x	–	–	–
34 Caravan 1000 (Wagon)	x	x	–	–	–	–	–
36 4-door Sedan (Standard)	–	–	x	–	–	–	–
37 4-door Deluxe ("L") Sedan	–	–	x	–	–	–	–
38 2-door Deluxe ("L") Sedan	–	–	x	–	–	–	–
39 Caravan "L" Deluxe Wagon	–	–	x	x	x	x	x
91 2-door Sport Sedan	–	–	–	–	x	x	x
92 GM Rallye Coupe	–	–	–	x	x	x	
93 Opel GT	–	–	–	–	–	x	x
95 Deluxe Sport Coupe	–	–	–	–	x	x	x
99 Deluxe "LS" Sport Coupe	–	–	–	–	x	x	x

Engine Identification

No. of Cyl.	Displacement Cu. In. (cc)	Type	Starting Engine Serial Nos. (Code)
4	60.2 (987)	1.0	372 326
4	60.2 (987)	1.0S	058 862
4	65.8 (1077)	1.1 (1.1)	2 214 216 698
4	65.8 (1077)	1.1S (also 1.1S & 1.1R	0 000 077 1 095 102 270
4	65.8 (1077)	1.1SR	3 513
4	91.0 (1491)	1.5S (1968 only)	0 000 100
4	115.8 (1898)	1.9S	

Torque Specifications

Year	Model	Cylinder Head Bolts (ft. lbs.)	Main Bearing Bolts (ft. lbs.)	Rod Bearing Bolts (ft. lbs.)	Crankshaft Balancer Bolts (or nut) (ft. lbs.)	Flywheel to Crankshaft Bolts (ft. lbs.)	Manifold Bolts (ft. lbs.)	
							Intake	Exhaust
1964-1965	1.0 1.0S	35	45	20	30	25		
1966	1.0 1.1	35	45	20	30	25		
1966-1967	1.0 1.1	35	45	20	30	25		
1968	1.1	35	45	20	30	25		
	1.5 1.9	72 cold 58 warm	72	36	54	43	33	33
1969	1.1	35	45	20	30	25		
	1.9	72 cold 58 warm	72	36	54	43	33	33
1970	1.1	35	45	20	30	25		
	1.9	72 cold 58 warm	72	36	54	43	33	33

Note: unless otherwise noted
10mm bolt (15mm head)—30 ft. lbs.
8mm bolt (13mm head)—15 ft. lbs.
6mm bolt (10mm head)—60 in. lbs.

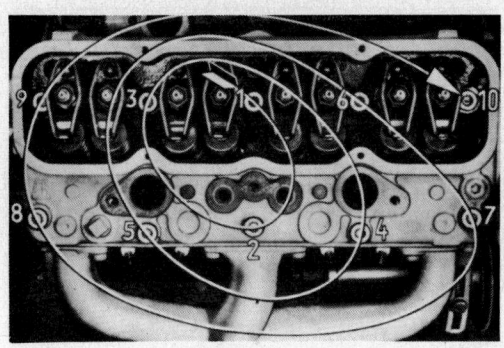

Cylinder head—OHV engines

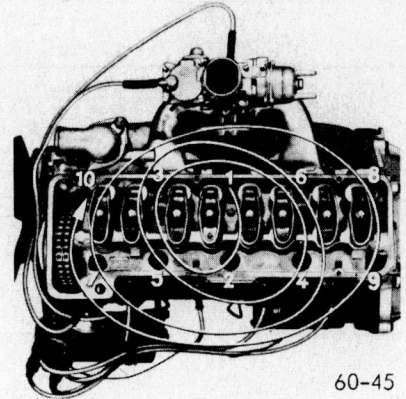

60-45

Cylinder head—CIH engines

60-42

Combination manifold—CIH engines

Electrical Specifications

| Year | Model | Battery | | | Starter | | | | | | Brush Spring |
| | | Cap. (Amp-Hours) | Volts | Grounded Terminal | Lock Test | | | No Load Test | | | Tension (oz.) |
					Amps	Volts	Torque	Amps	Volts	RPM	
1964-1965	1.0 1.0 S	66-77	6	Negative	370-470	3.2-3.8	–	50-70	5.5	8,000-9.500	28-32
1966-1967	1.1	44	12	Negative	270-310	7.5-8.5	–	25-45	11.5	8,000-9,500	28-32
	1.9	44	12	Negative	270-310	7.5-8.5	–	25-45	11.5	8,000-9,500	28-32
1968	1.1	44	12	Negative	270-310	7.5-8.5	–	25-45	11.5	8,000-9,500	28-32
	1.5 & 1.9	44	12	Negative	280-320	6 min	–	35-45	12	6,400-7,900	40-46
1969	1.1	44	12	Negative	270-310	7.5-8.5	–	25-45	11.5	8,000-9,500	28-32
	1.9	44	12	Negative	280-320	6 min	–	35-45	12	6,400-7,900	40-46
1970	1.1	44	12	Negative	270-310	7.5-8.5	–	25-45	11.5	8,000-9,500	28-32
	1.9	44	12	Negative	280-320	6 min	–	35-45	12	6,400-7,900	40-46

| Year | Model | Generator | | | | | Regulator | | |
		Part Number	Brush Spring Press. (oz)	Field Resistance (ohms)	Max Output (Amps)	Part Number	Cut-out Relay Closing Volts	Maximun Current (Amps)	Voltage Regulator Setting* xx RPM
1964-1965	1.0	LJ/GEG 200/6/	15-21	–	30	RS/VA 200/6 A1	6.0-6.5	–	7.0-7.4 @ 1500 RPM
	1.0S	2600 FR 33							
1966-1967	1.1, 1.1S, & 1.1SR	EG14V25 A27	15-21	–	30	VA14V 25A	12.3-13.2	–	13.6-14.5 @ 1500 RPM
1968	1.1	EG (R) 14 V25A27	15-21	3.5-4	25	VA14V 25A	12.3-13.2	–	13.6-14.5 @ 2500 RPM
	1.5 & 1.9S	EG(R) 14 V25A25	15-21	3.5-4	25	VA14V 25A	12.3-13.2	–	13.6-14.5 @ 2500 RPM
1969	1.1	EG (R) 14 V25A27	15-21	3.5-4	25	VA14V 25A	12.3-13.2	–	13.6-14.5 @ 2500 RPM
	1.9	EG (R) 14 25A27	15-21	3.5-4	25	VA14V 25A	12.3-13.2	–	13.6-14.5 @ 2500 RPM
1970	1.1	EG (R) 14 25A27	15-21	3.5-4	25	VA14V 25A	12.3-13.2	–	13.6-14.5 @2500 RPM

Electrical Specifications

Year	Model	Alternator (AC Generator)					Field Relay			AC Regulator		
		Part Number	Field Current Draw @ 12V	Output* Generator RPM							Regulator	
				Volts	Amps @ 2500 RPM		Air Gap (ins.)	Point Gap (ins.)	Closing Voltage	Air Gap (ins.)	Point Gap (ins.)	Volts @ 2000 Engine RPM
1966-1967		K114V 35A20	–	14	30 min		–	–	–	–	–	13.5-14.5
1968	1.1, 1.5S & 1.9S	K114V 35A20	–	14	30 min		–	–	–	–	–	13.5-14.5
1969	1.1 & 1.9	K114V 35A20	–	14	30 min		–	–	–	–	–	13.5-14.5
1970	1.1 & 1.9	K114V 28A20	–	14	30 min		–	–	–	–	–	13.5-14.5

Distributor Advance Characteristics

Year	Model	Distributor Ident.	Centrifugal Advance			Vacuum Advance		
			Start Degrees @ RPM	Intermediate Degrees @ RPM	End Degrees @ RPM	Start in./Hg.	Intermediate Degrees @ in./Hg.	End Degrees @ in./Hg.
1964-1965	1.0 1.0S	VJU4BR43	8-18.5 @ 1,000	24-31 @ 2,000	29-36 @ 3,000	2-6	–	@ 5.5-9
1966-1967	1.1 & 1.9	1FU4(R)	3.5-15.5 @ 1,000	25-30 @ 2,000	30-35 @ 3,000	2-4	–	13-18 @ 6.5-7.5
1968	1.1	VJU4(R)	@ 900-1200	24-31 @ 1700	39-46 @ 4200	1-3	–	10-16 @ 5
	1.5 & 1.9	JFU4	@ 800-1100	17-23 @ 1500	31-37 @ 3200	3-6	–	18-24 @ 13
1969	1.1	VJU4(R)	@ 900-1200	24-31 @ 1700	39-46 @ 4200	1-3	–	10-16 @ 5
	1.9	JFU4	@ 800-1100	17-23 @ 1500	31-37 @ 3200	3-6	–	18-24 @ 13
1970	1.1	VJU4(R)	@ 900-1200	24-31 @ 1700	39-46 @ 4200	1-3	–	10-16 @ 5
	1.9	JFU4	@ 800-1100	17-23 @ 1500	31-37 @ 3200	1-3	–	18-24 @ 13

Carburetor Specifications

Engine	Carburetor Make	Opel No.	Venturi Diameter (K) (mm)		Main Jet (Gg)		Air Bleed (correction) Jet (a)		Idle Jet (g)		Float Bowl (mm.)		Accel Jet (mm.)
			Prim	Sec	Prim	Sec	Prim	Sec	Prim	Sec	Needle Valve	Float Level (F)	
1.0	Carter	2865352	21	–	36	–	75	–	60	–		12	50
1.0S	Carter	2877419	21	–	75	–	200	–	60	–		12 (15/32")	50
1.1	Solex E15303	2 891 001	28	–	x130	–	150	–	45	–	1.5	7.3	50
1.1S	Solex E15307	2 891 002	28	–	x130	–	150	–	50	–	1.5	7.3	50
1.1	Solex E15486	2 891 018	26	–	x117.5	–	100	–	50	–	1.5	7.3	50
1.1S	Solex E15487	2 891 019	28	–	x130	–	110	–	50	–	1.5	7.3	55
1.1SR	Solex	Rallye Front 2 891 643 Rear 2 891 644			x117.5	–	110	–	55	–			
1.1 (1968)	Solex 35 PDSI	2891 512A	26	–	x132.5	–	700	–	47.5	–	1.5	2 ①	
1.5S (1968)	Solex 32 SDID	2891 513A	22	24	x110	x975	120	100	52.5	75	2	2 ①	
1.9S (1968)	Solex 32 DIDTA-4	2891 514A	24	28	x117.5	x155	120	80	50	75	2	2 ①	
1.1 (1969)	Solex 30 PDSI	2891 512B	26	–	x132.5	–	70	–	45	–	1.5	1 ①	
1.1SR (1969)	Solex 35 PDSI-2		26	–	x115	–	110	–	50	–	1.5	1 ①	
1.9 (1969)	Solex 32 DIDTA-4	2891 749A	24	28	x117.5	x155	120	80	g50	g75	2	2 ①	
1.1R (1970)	Solex 30 PDSI	2891 820A	24	–	x107.5	–	130	–	45	–	1.5	1 ①	
1.1SR (1970)	Solex 35 PDSI-2	3441 005A	26	–	x115	–	110	–	50	–	1.5	1 ①	
1.9S (1970)	Solex 35 DIDTA-4 GT-32TDID-2	2891 749A	24	28	x117.5	x155	120	80	g50	g75	2	2 ①	

① Indicates thickness of the seal ring under needle valve rather than distance from fuel level to float bowl flange.
Note: Carburetor tune-up specifications are in Chapter 2.

Capacities and Pressures

Year & Model	Crankcase (qts.) Refill after Drain		Transmission (pts.) Refill after Drain			Rear Drive Axle (pts.)	Fuel Tank (U.S. Gals.)	Fuel Pump Press. (psi)	Cooling System		
	With Filter	Without Filter	3-speed	Manual 4-speed	Auto				Cap. (qts.) With Heater	Max Press. (psi)	Thermostat Opens @ (°F)
1964-1965 1.0	3	2.6	–	1.3	–	1	8.7	2-2 ¾	5.5	8.5	180
1966-1967 1.1	3	2.6	–	1.4	–	1 ¼	10.6	3.1-3.7	5 w/o htr 5.5 w htr	7.8-9.2	189
1968 1.1L	3	2.75	–	1.4	–	1.5	10.6	3.1-3.7	5.0	10.4-12.2	180
1.5L	3 ¼	3	–	2.5	–	2.5	10.6	2.0 Min	6	10.2-12.2	190
1.9L	3 ¼	3	–	2.5	–	2.5	10.6	2.0 Min	6	10.2-12.2	190
1969 1.1L 1.1R 1.1SR	3	2.5	–	1.4	13	1.5	10.6 (13.2- Opel GT)	2.0 Min	5.5 5 w/o htr	8.5	180
1.9S	3 ¼	3	–	2.5	13	2.5	10.6 (13.2- Opel GT)	2.0 Min	6	10.2-12.2	190
1970 1.1R 1.1SR	3	2.5	–	1.4	10.5	1.5	10.6 (13.2- Opel GT)	3.1-3.7 @ 195ORPM	5.5 5.0 w/o htr	10.4-12.4	189
1.9S	3 ¼	3	–	2.5	10.5	2.5	10.6 (13.2- Opel GT)	3.1-3.7 @ 195ORPM	6	13.2-15.2	189

Brake Specifications

Year & Model	Type Front	Rear	Brake Cylinder Bores Master Cyl. (ins.)	Wheel Cyl. (ins.) Front	Rear	Brake Drum/Disc Diameter (ins.) Front	Rear	Brake Disc Thickness Min (ins.)	Brake Pad & Lining Min Thickness (ins.) Before Replacement
1964-1965 31	Drum	Drum	0.750-0.752	0.875-0.878	0.625-0.628	7.880-7.910	7.880-7.910	–	–
32									
34									
1966-1967 31	Drum	Drum	0.750-0.752	15/16	5/8	7.880-7.910	7.880-7.910	–	–
32									
37	Fixed Caliper Disc	Drum	0.750-0.752	–	5/8	9.370	7.880-7.910	0.425-0.433	0.280
38								0.390-0.433 (1967)	0.280
39									
1968 31	Drum	Drum	0.750-0.752	15/16	5/8	7.880-7.910	7.880-7.910	–	–
39									
91	Fixed Caliper Disc		0.810-	–	5/8	9.370	7.880-7.910	0.394 Min 0.430 New	0.280
92									
99									
1969 31	Drum	Drum	13/16	15/16	5/8	7.870-7.910 (1.1)	7.870-7.910 (1.1)	–	–
39									
91	Drum	Drum	13/16	15/16	5/8	9.060-9.090 (1.9)	9.060-9.090 (1.9)	–	–
92									
93	Fixed Caliper Disc		0.810	*	5/8	9.370	–	0.394 Min-0.433 New	0.280
95									
1970 31	Drum	Drum	13/16	15/16	5/8	7.870-7.900 (1.1)	7.870-7.900 (1.1)	–	–
39									
91						9.060-9.090 (1.9)	9.060-9.090 (1.9)		
92									
93	Fixed Caliper Disc		0.810	**	5/8	9.370	–	0.394 min-0.433 new	0.280
95									

* Caliper cylinder bores for front wheels are: 1.770 inches for 1.1 engined models; and 1,890 inches for 1.9 engined models.

** Caliper cylinder bores for front wheels are: 1.730 inches for 1.1 engined models; and 1.770 inches for 1.9 engined models.

Chassis and Wheel Alignment Specifications

Year & Model	Wheel base	Chassis Track (in.) Front	Rear	Wheel Alignment Caster Range (Degrees)	Pref. Setting (Degrees)	Camber Range (Degrees)	Pref. Setting (Degrees)	Toe-in (in.)	King-pin Inclination (Degrees)	Wheel Pivot Ratio Inner Wheel	Outer Wheel
1964-1965											
31	91.5	47.2	47.4	0-+2		½ - 2		1/32 min-			
32		47.6	47.8					3/16 max			
34		47.2	47.4								
1966-1967											
31	95.1	49.2	50.4	+1- -2	1½*	+½ - -1	¾	1/32 min-			
32	95.1	49.2	50.4					1/8 max			
37 †	95.1	49.2	50.4								
38 †	95.1	49.2	50.4								
39	95.1	49.2	50.4								
1968											
31	95.1	49.2	50.4	+1- -2	1½*	+½ - -1	¾	1/32 min			
32	95.1	49.2	50.4					1/8 max			
37	95.1	49.2	50.4								
38	95.1	49.2	50.4								
39	95.1	49.2	50.4								
1969											
31	95.1	59.2	50.2	+1- -2	1½*	+½ - -1 (Kadett)	¾ (Kadett)	1/32 min-		20	18½
39	95.1	49.2	50.2					1/8 max			
91	95.1	49.2	50.2			+½ - - 1 (GT)	½ (GT)				
92	95.1	49.2	50.2								
93	95.7	49.4	50.6								
95	95.1	49.2	50.2								
1970											
31	95.1	49.2	50.2	1-3 (Kadett)	2	+½ - 1 ½ 1 (Kadett)		1/32 min-		20	18½
39	95.1	49.2	50.2	2-4 (GT)	3	+½ - 1 ½ (GT) 1		1/8 max			
91	95.1	49.2	50.2								
92	95.1	49.2	50.2								
93	95.7	49.4	50.6								
95	95.1	49.2	50.2								

* Left and right wheel angles must be within one degree of each other.
† Opel Kadett Deluxe (2 dr. and 4 dr. models) cars made in 1966 only.

Fuses and Circuit Breakers

Circuit & Location	Amp.

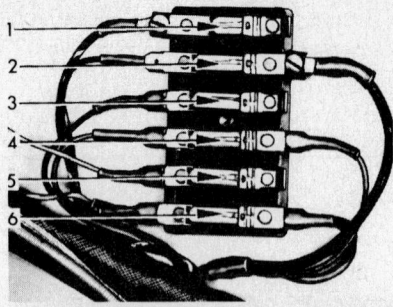

1964-1965
(Behind left wheelhouse panel)

1 Horn, windshield wiper	25
2 Direction signal lamps, stop lights	8
3 Heater motor	8
4 Interior lamp	8
5 Left tail lamp	8
6 Right tail lamp, license plate lamp, instrument lights	8

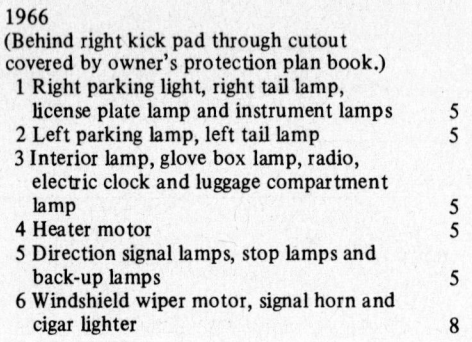

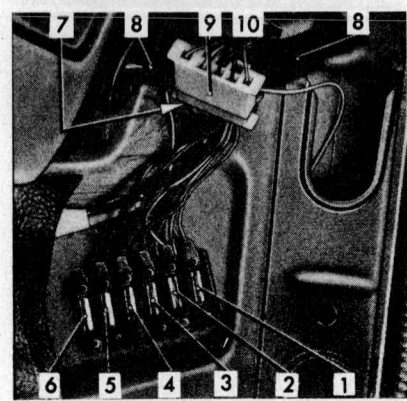

1966
(Behind right kick pad through cutout covered by owner's protection plan book.)

1 Right parking light, right tail lamp, license plate lamp and instrument lamps	5
2 Left parking lamp, left tail lamp	5
3 Interior lamp, glove box lamp, radio, electric clock and luggage compartment lamp	5
4 Heater motor	5
5 Direction signal lamps, stop lamps and back-up lamps	5
6 Windshield wiper motor, signal horn and cigar lighter	8

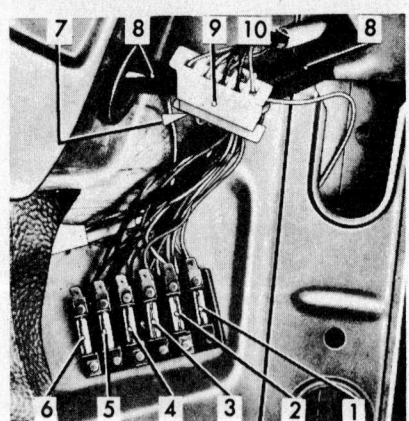

1966-1967
(Behind right kick pad through cutout)

1 Right parking lamp, right tail lamp, license plate lamps and instrument lamps	5
2 Left parking lamp and left tail lamp	5
3 Dome lamp, glove box lamp, radio, electric clock and hazard warning flasher	5
4 Heater motor and cigar lighter	8
5 Direction signal lamps, stop lamps and back-up lamps	5
6 Windshield wiper motor and horn	8

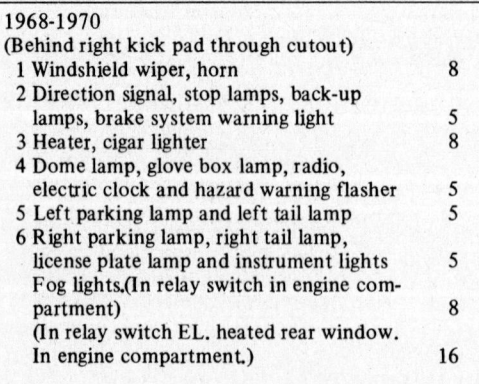

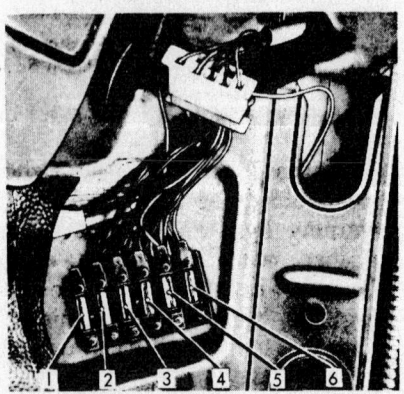

1968-1970
(Behind right kick pad through cutout)

1 Windshield wiper, horn	8
2 Direction signal, stop lamps, back-up lamps, brake system warning light	5
3 Heater, cigar lighter	8
4 Dome lamp, glove box lamp, radio, electric clock and hazard warning flasher	5
5 Left parking lamp and left tail lamp	5
6 Right parking lamp, right tail lamp, license plate lamp and instrument lights	5
Fog lights.(In relay switch in engine compartment)	8
(In relay switch EL. heated rear window. In engine compartment.)	16

Light Bulb Specifications

Year & Usage	Type (Buick Opel Part No.)	Wattage
1964-1965		
Headlamp	5956006	6V - 6006
Parking lamp	N-15610	6V - 3W
Stop lamp	N-48080	6V - 18W
Direction signal lamp	N-48080	6V - 18W
Tail lamp	N-15600	6V - 5W
License plate lamp	N-15610	6V - 3W
Instrument lights	N-44780	6V - 3W
Interior lamp	12 24 626	6V - 5W
Oil pressure indicator lamp	N-31620	6V - .6W
Direction signal indicator lamp	N-31620	6V - .6W
Headlight high beam indicator lamp	N-31620	6V - .6W
Charging indicator bulb	N-31620	6V - .6W
1966-1967		
Headlamp	5956007	12V -45/40W
Parking lamp	N-21 840	12V - 4W
Direction signal lamp, front	N-51 230	12V -18W
Direction signal lamp, rear	N-51 230	12V -18W
Electric clock	N-31 600	12V -2W
Instrument lamp	N-59 140	12V -3W
Direction signal indicator lamp	N-59 140	12V -3W
Headlamp high beam indicator lamp	N-59 140	12V -3W
Charging indicator lamp lamp	N-59 140	12V -3W
Oil pressure indicator lamp	N-59 140	12V -3W
Interior lamp	12 24 627	12V -5W
Stop lamp	N-51 230	12V -18W
Tail lamp	N-15 630	12V -5W
License plate lamp	N-21 840	12V -3W
Back-up lamp	N-58 220	12V -15W
1968-1970		
Headlamp	5956007	12V -45/40W
Parking lamp	N-21 840	12V -4W
Direction signal lamp, front and rear	N-51 230	12V -18W
Electric clock lamp	N-31 600	12V -2W
Instrument lamp	N-59 140	12V -3W
Direction signal indicator lamp	N-59 140	12V -3W
Headlamp high beam indicator lamp	N-59 140	12V -3W
Charging indicator lamp	N-59 140	12V -3W
Oil pressure indicator lamp	N-59 140	12V-3W
Dome lamp	12 24 627	12C -5W
Stop lamp	N-51 230	12V -18W
Tail lamp	N-15 630	12V -5W
License plate lamp	N-21 840	12V -3W
Back-up lamp	N-58 220	12V -15W
Glove box lamp	N-21 840	12V -3W
Tachometer lamp	N-51 250	12V -3W
Fog light	Z-723	12 -35W
Ammeter lamp	N-31 600	12V -2W
Oil pressure gauge lamp	N-31 600	12V -2W
Hazard warning flasher indicator lamp	N-62 440	12V -1.2W

Wiring Diagrams

1966 and 1967 Kadetts (except Rallye)

1. Headlight
2. Front direction signal lamp
3. Parking lamp
4. Horn
5. Regulator
6. Generator
7. Temperature sending unit
8. Spark plugs
9. Distributor
10. Coil
11. Oil pressure switch
12. Starter
13. Battery
14. Heater blower motor
15. Stop light switch
16. Wiper motor
17. Interior lamp switch
18. Lights and windshield wiper switch
19. Heater blower motor switch
20. Instrument light
21. High beam lamp
22. Direction signal indicator light
23. Temperature gauge
24. Oil pressure light
25. Generator light
26. Fuel gauge
27. Clock
28. Clock light
29. Cigar lighter
30. Fuse box
31. Direction signal flasher
32. Printed circuit
33. Combination switch for turn signal, dimmer switch, horn and passing signal
34. Hazard warning switch
35. Steering—ignition lock
36. Back-up lamp switch
37. Dome light
38. Fuel gauge—tank unit
39. Luggage compartment light
40. Rear turn signal light
41. Stop light
42. Tail light
43. Back-up light
44. License plate light

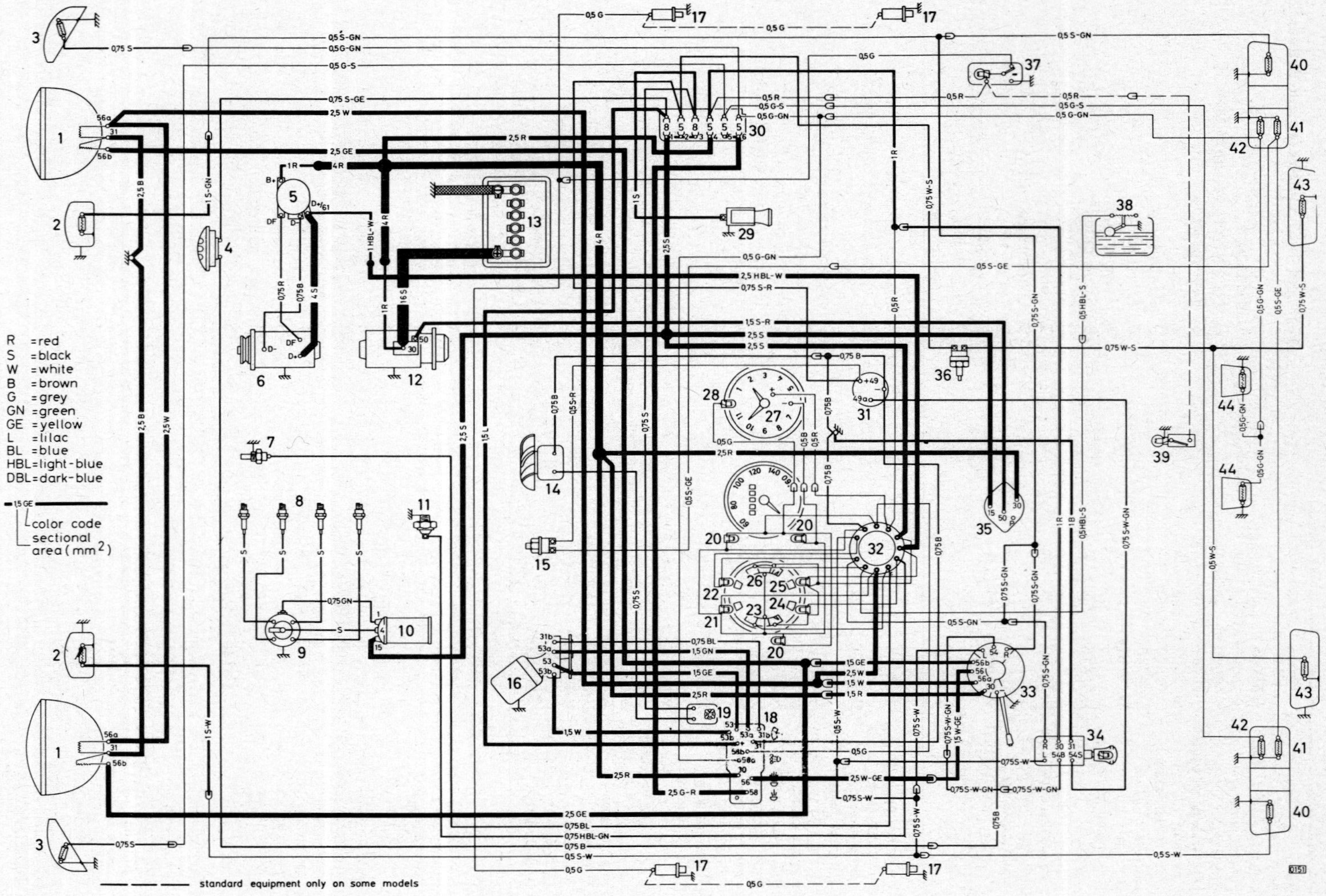

Wiring Diagram for 1966 and 1967 Kadetts (except Rallye)

R = red
S = black
W = white
B = brown
G = grey
GN = green
GE = yellow
L = lilac
BL = blue
HBL = light-blue
DBL = dark-blue

color code
sectional area (mm 2)

standard equipment only on some models

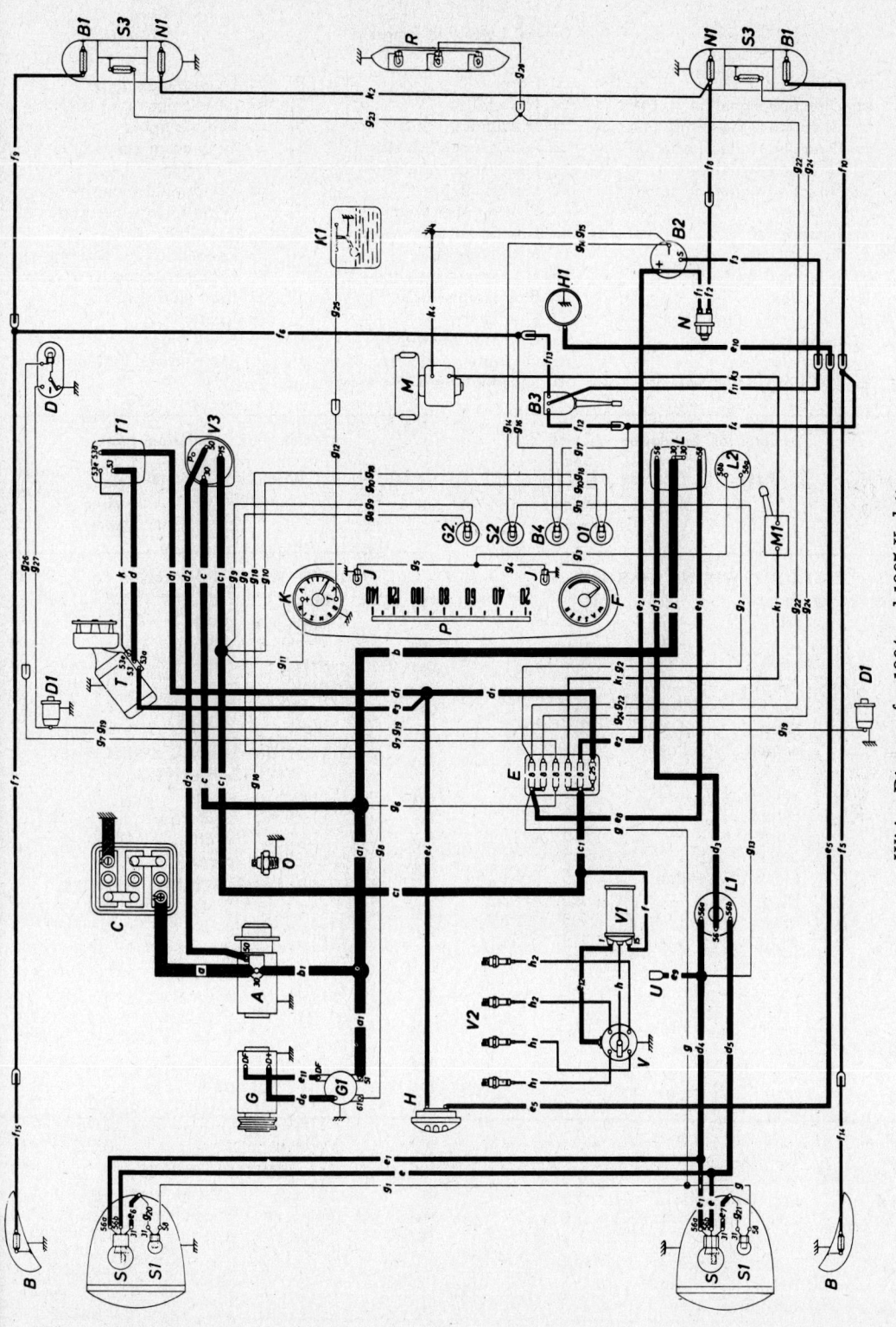

Wiring Diagram for 1964 and 1965 Kadetts

1964 and 1965 Kadetts

Capital Letters in Diagram

A	=	Starter	H	=	Horn	R	=	License plate lamp
B	=	Direction signal lamp, front	H_1	=	Horn button	S	=	Headlamps
B_1	=	Direction signal lamp, rear	J	=	Instrument lights	S_1	=	Parking lights
B_2	=	Direction signal flasher unit	K	=	Fuel gauge dash unit	S_2	=	High beam indicator lamp
B_3	=	Direction signal switch	K_1	=	Fuel gauge tank unit	S_3	=	Tail lamp
B_4	=	Direction signal indicator lamp	L	=	Light switch	T	=	Windshield wiper motor
C	=	Battery	L_1	=	Foot dimmer switch	T_1	=	Windshield wiper motor switch
D	=	Interior lamp	L_2	=	Instrument light switch			
D_1	=	Interior lamp switch	M	=	Heater motor	U	=	Connection for passing signal or fog lamp relay
E	=	Fuse box	M_1	=	Heater motor switch			
F	=	Temperature indicator	N	=	Stop lamp switch	V	=	Ignition distributor
G	=	Generator	N_1	=	Stop lamp	V_1	=	Ignition coil
G_1	=	Regulator	O	=	Oil pressure switch	V_2	=	Spark plugs
G_2	=	Charging indicator lamp	O_1	=	Oil pressure indicator lamp	V_3	=	Steering and ignition lock
			P	=	Speedometer with odometer			

Code	Color of Insulation		Cross Sectional Area (mm^2)	Code	Color of Insulation		Cross Sectional Area (mm^2)	Length (inches)
	Base	Tracers			Base	Tracers		
FRONT WIRING HARNESS				**REAR WIRING HARNESS**				
a_1	red	—	10	f_8	black	red	1	
b, b_1	red	—	6	f_9	black	green	1	
c	red	—	4	f_{10}	black	white	1	
c_1	black	—	4	g_{22}, g_{23}	grey	red	0.5	
d	yellow	—	2.5	g_{24}	grey	black	0.5	
d_1	black	yellow	2.5	g_{25}	light blue	black	0.5	
d_2	black	red	2.5	k_3	black	red	0.75	
d_3	white	yellow	2.5	**DIRECTION SIGNAL SWITCH WIRING HARNESS**				
d_4	white	—	2.5					
d_5	yellow	—	2.5	e_{10}	brown	—	1.5	
e	yellow	—	1.5	f_{11}	black	white/green	1	
e_1	white	—	1.5	f_{12}	black	white	1	
e_2	black	red	1.5	f_{13}	black	green	1	
e_3, e_4	black	yellow	1.5	**INTERIOR LAMP WIRING HARNESS**				
e_5, e_6, e_7	brown	—	1.5					
e_8	grey	red	1.5	g_{26}	red	—	0.5	
e_9	white	—	1.5	g_{27}	grey	—	0.5	
f	black	—	1	**SINGLE WIRES**				
f_1, f_2	black	red	1	a	black	—	25	36
f_3	black	white/green	1	d_6	black	special wire	2.5	
f_4, f_5	black	white	1	e_{11}	red	—	1.5	9.3
f_6, f_7	black	green	1	e_{12}	green	red	1.5	9.4
g, g_1	grey	—	0.5	f_{14}	black	white	1	9.1
g_2	grey	green	0.5	f_{15}	black	green	1	9.1
g_3, g_4, g_5	grey	—	0.5	g_{28}	grey	red	0.5	19.7
g_6, g_7	red	—	0.5	k_3	black	—	0.75	29.5
g_8	light blue	white	0.5	k_4	brown	—	0.75	18.5
g_9, g_{10}, g_{11}	black	—	0.5	**IGNITION WIRES**				
g_{12}	light blue	black	0.5	h	blue	special wire	—	7.1
g_{13}	white	—	0.5	h_1	blue	special wire	—	24
g_{14}, g_{15}	brown	—	0.5	h_2	blue	special wire	—	19.7
g_{16}	black	green	0.5					
g_{17}	black	white	0.5					
g_{18}	light blue	green	0.5					
g_{19}	grey	—	0.5					
$g_{20}, 21$	brown	—	0.5					
k	blue	—	0.75					
k_1	black	—	0.75					

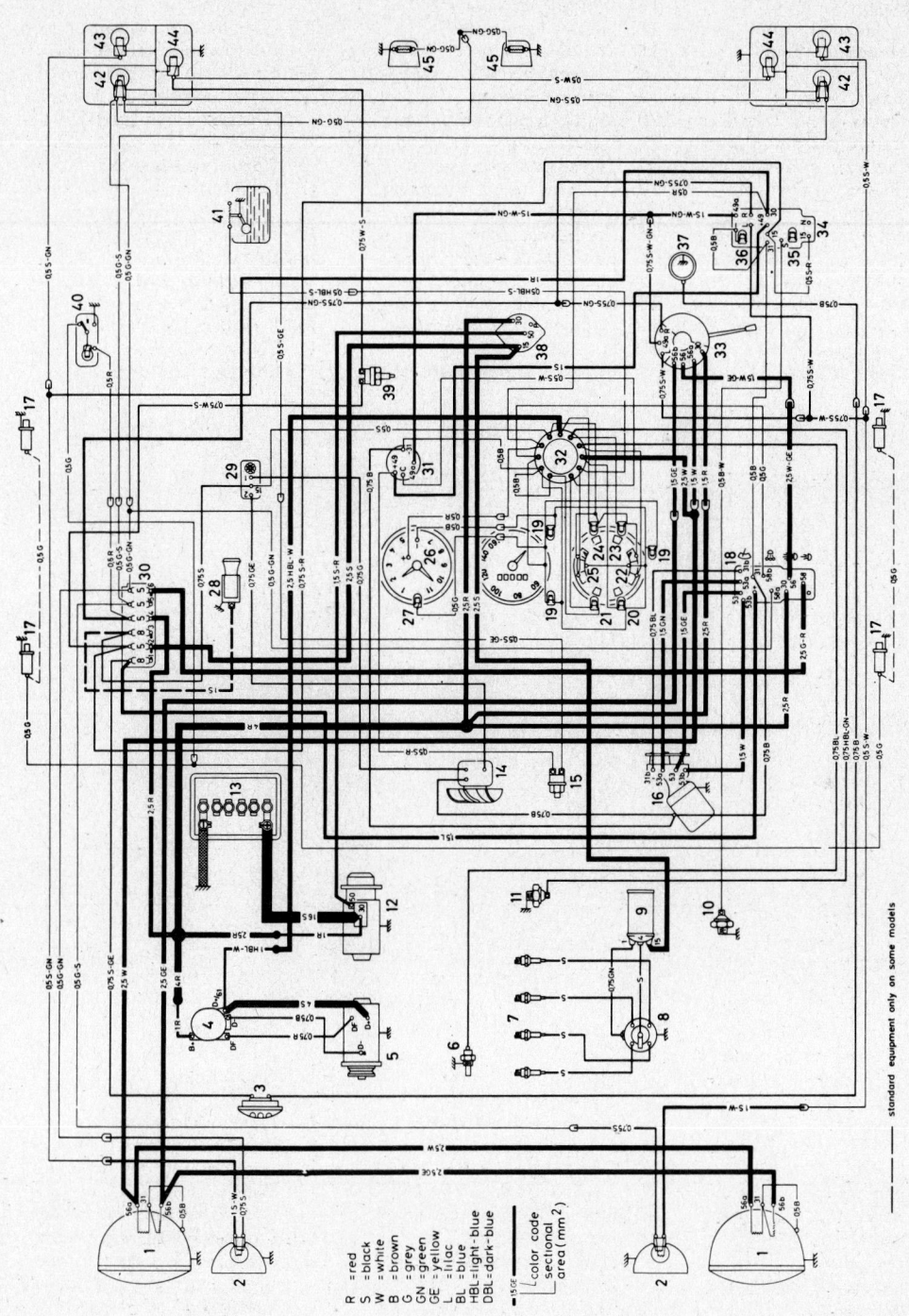

Wiring diagram for 1968 Kadett.

R = red
S = black
W = white
B = brown
G = grey
GN = green
GE = yellow
L = lilac
BL = blue
HBL = light - blue
DBL = dark - blue

color code
sectional
area(mm²)

standard equipment only on some models

Wiring diagram for 1968 Kadett.

1. Headlight
2. Front direction signal lamp and parking lamp
3. Horn
4. Regulator
5. Generator
6. Temperature sending unit
7. Spark plugs
8. Distributor
9. Ignition coil
10. Switch, brake warning light control
11. Oil pressure switch
12. Starter
13. Battery
14. Heater blower motor
15. Stop light switch
16. Windshield wiper motor
17. Interior lamp switch
18. Combined lights and windshield wiper switch
19. Instrument lamp
20. High beam indicator lamp
21. Direction signal indicator lamp
22. Temperature gauge
23. Oil pressure indicator lamp
24. Generator light
25. Fuel gauge dash unit
26. Electric clock
27. Electric clock light
28. Cigar lighter
29. Heater blower switch
30. Fuse box
31. Direction signal flasher unit
32. Printed circuit
33. Combination switch for turn signal and dimmer switch
34. Combined fog light, brake warning light and hazard warning light switch
35. Brake warning switch light
36. Hazard warning switch light
37. Horn button
38. Ignition and starter switch
39. Back-up lamp switch
40. Dome light
41. Fuel gauge-tank unit
42. Tail and stop lamp
43. Direction signal lamp
44. Back-up lamp
45. License plate lamp

Wiring diagram for 1968 Rallye.

1. Headlight
2. Front direction signal lamp and parking lamp
3. Fog light
4. Fog light relay
5. Horn
6. AC regulator
7. AC generator
8. DC generator
9. Connector
10. DC regulator
11. Temperature sending unit
12. Spark plugs
13. Oil pressure switch
14. Ignition coil
15. Distributor
16. Switch, brake warning light control
17. Windshield wiper motor
18. Starter
19. Battery
20. Fuse box
21. Heater blower motor
22. Stop light switch
23. Electric windshield wiper switch (foot pump)
24. Combined lights and windshield wiper switch
25. Interior lamp switch
26. Instrument light
27. High beam indicator lamp
28. Direction signal indicator lamp
29. Fuel gauge dash unit
30. Generator light
31. Oil pressure indicator lamp
32. Temperature gauge
33. Printed circuit
34. Tachometer
35. Direction signal flasher unit
36. Heater blower switch
37. Cigar lighter
38. Oil pressure gauge
39. Electric clock
40. Ammeter
41. Ignition and starter switch
42. Combination switch for turn signal and dimmer switch
43. Horn button
44. Hazard warning switch light
45. Brake warning switch light
46. Combined fog light, brake warning light and hazard warning light switch
47. Back-up lamp switch
48. Dome light
49. Fuel gauge-tank unit
50. Tail and stop lamp
51. Direction signal lamp
52. Back-up lamp
53. License plate lamp

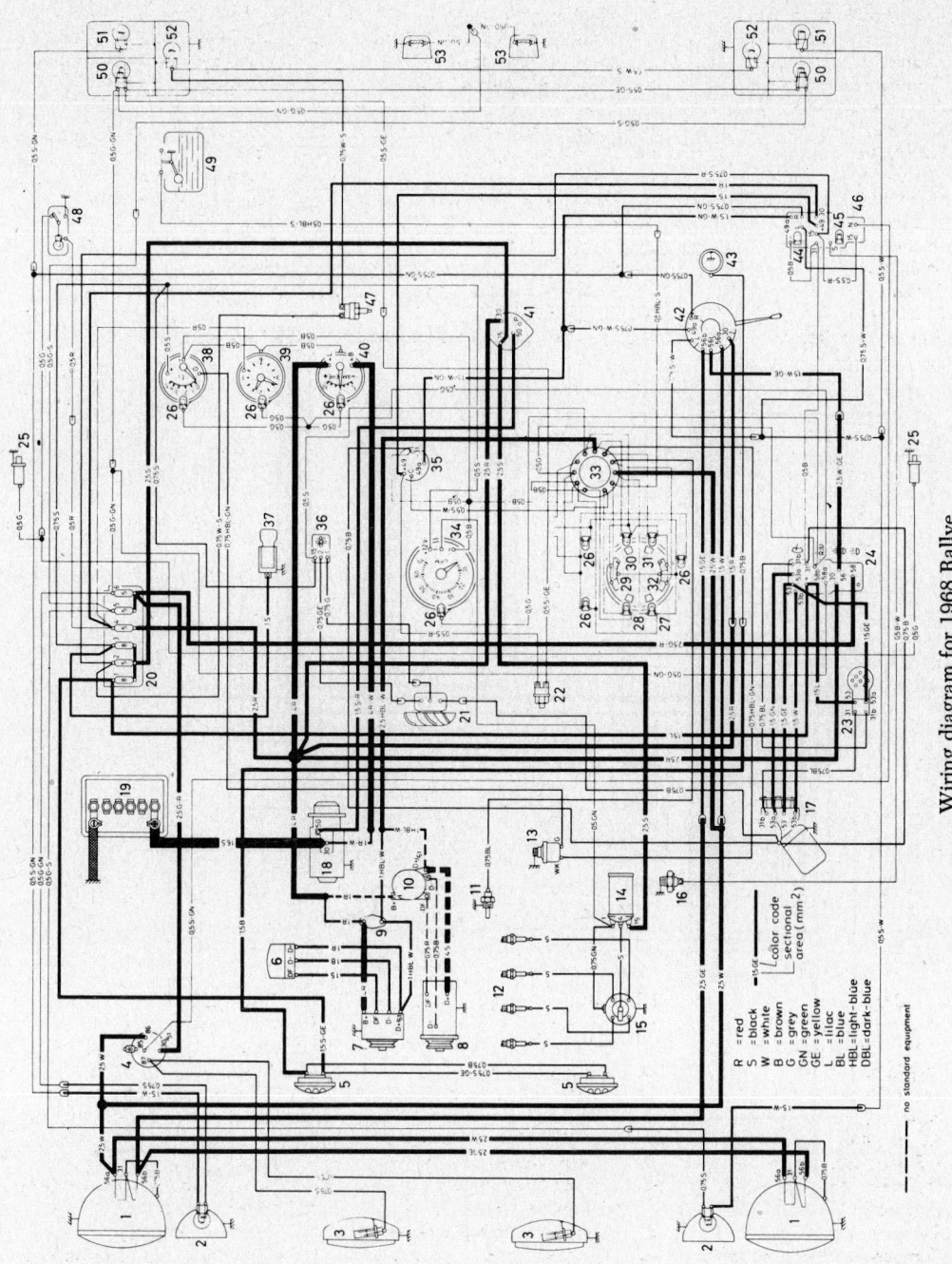

Wiring diagram for 1968 Rallye.

R = red
S = black
W = white
B = brown
G = grey
GN = green
GE = yellow
L = lilac
BL = blue
HBL = light-blue
DBL = dark-blue

15 GE ← color code
sectional
area (mm²)

------- = no standard equipment

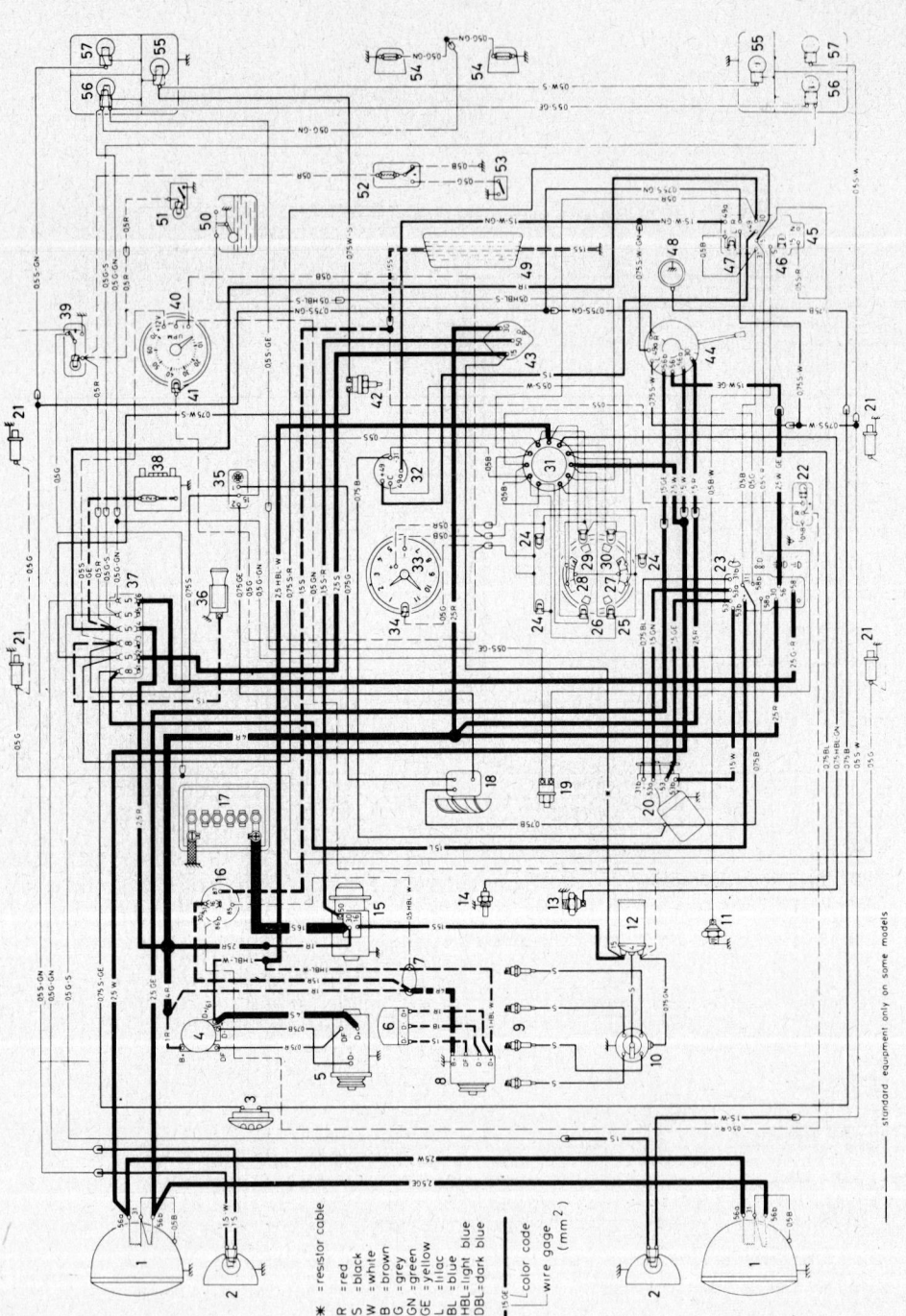

Wiring diagram for 1969 Kadett.

*— standard equipment only on some models

✱ = resistor cable

color code
R = red
S = black
W = white
B = brown
G = grey
GN = green
GE = yellow
L = lilac
BL = blue
DBL = dark blue
HBL = light blue

wire gage (mm²)

Wiring diagram for 1969 Kadett.

1. Headlight
2. Front direction signal lamp and parking lamp
3. Horn
4. Regulator
5. Generator
6. Alternator
7. Connector
8. Alternator—regulator
9. Spark plugs
10. Distributor
11. Low brake indicator switch
12. Coil
13. Oil pressure switch
14. Temperature sending unit
15. Starter
16. Relay, electrically heated back window
17. Battery
18. Heater blower motor
19. Stop light switch
20. Windshield wiper motor
21. Door jamb switch
22. Switch, electrically heated back window
23. Combined lights and windshield wiper switch
24. Instrument lamp
25. High beam indicator lamp
26. Direction signal indicator lamp
27. Temperature gauge
28. Fuel gauge dash unit
29. Generator light
30. Oil pressure indicator lamp
31. Printed circuit
32. Direction signal flasher unit
33. Clock
34. Electric clock light
35. Heater blower switch
36. Cigarette lighter
37. Fuse box
38. Radio
39. Dome light
40. Tachometer
41. Tachometer light
42. Back-up lamp switch
43. Ignition and starter switch
44. Combination switch for turn signal and dimmer switch
45. Fog light switch and hazard warning light switch
46. Low brake indicator light
47. Hazard warning flasher
48. Horn button
49. Electrically heated back window
50. Fuel gauge——tank unit
51. Trunk light
52. Luggage compartment light
53. Luggage compartment light switch
54. License plate lamp
55. Back-up lamp
56. Tail and stop lamp
57. Direction signal lamp

Wiring diagram for 1969 Rallye.

1. Headlight
2. Front direction signal lamp and parking lamp
3. Fog light
4. Fog light relay
5. Horn
6. AC regulator
7. AC generator
8. DC generator
9. Connector
10. DC regulator
11. Temperature sending unit
12. Spark plugs
13. Oil pressure switch
14. Ignition coil
15. Distributor
16. Switch, brake warning light control
17. Windshield wiper motor
18. Starter
19. Battery
20. Fuse box
21. Heater blower motor
22. Stop light switch
23. Electric windshield wiper switch (foot pump)
24. Combined lights and windshield wiper switch
25. Interior lamp switch
26. Instrument light
27. High beam indicator lamp
28. Direction signal indicator lamp
29. Fuel gauge dash unit
30. Generator light
31. Oil pressure indicator lamp
32. Temperature gauge
33. Printed circuit
34. Tachometer
35. Direction signal flasher unit
36. Heater blower switch
37. Cigar lighter
38. Oil pressure gauge
39. Electric clock
40. Ammeter
41. Ignition and starter switch
42. Combination switch for turn signal and dimmer switch
43. Horn button
44. Hazard warning switch light
45. Brake warning switch light
46. Combined fog light, brake warning light and hazard warning light switch
47. Back-up lamp switch
48. Dome light
49. Fuel gauge-tank unit
50. Tail and stop lamp
51. Direction signal lamp
52. Back-up lamp
53. License plate lamp

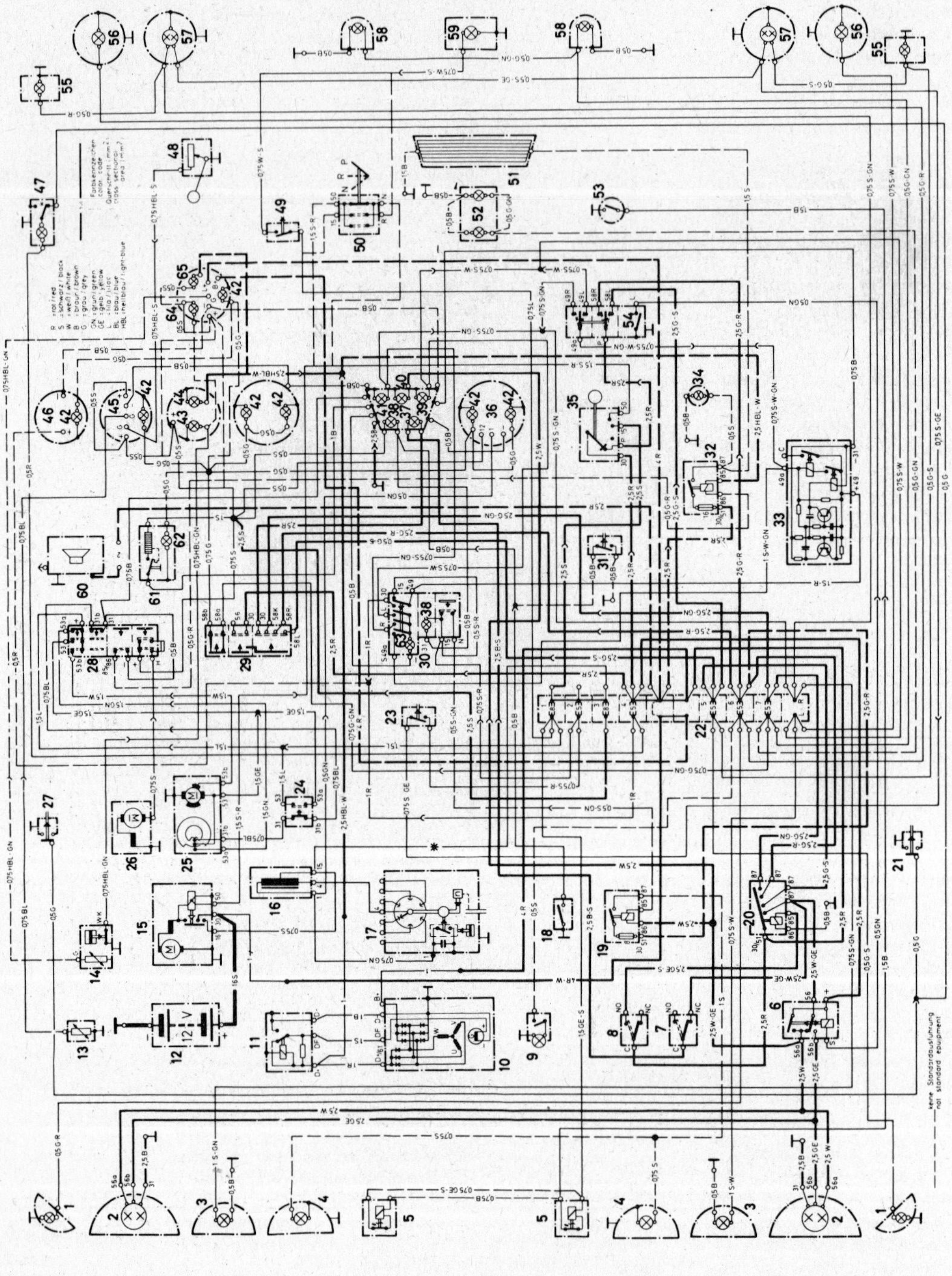

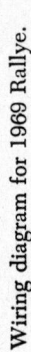

Wiring diagram for 1969 Rallye.

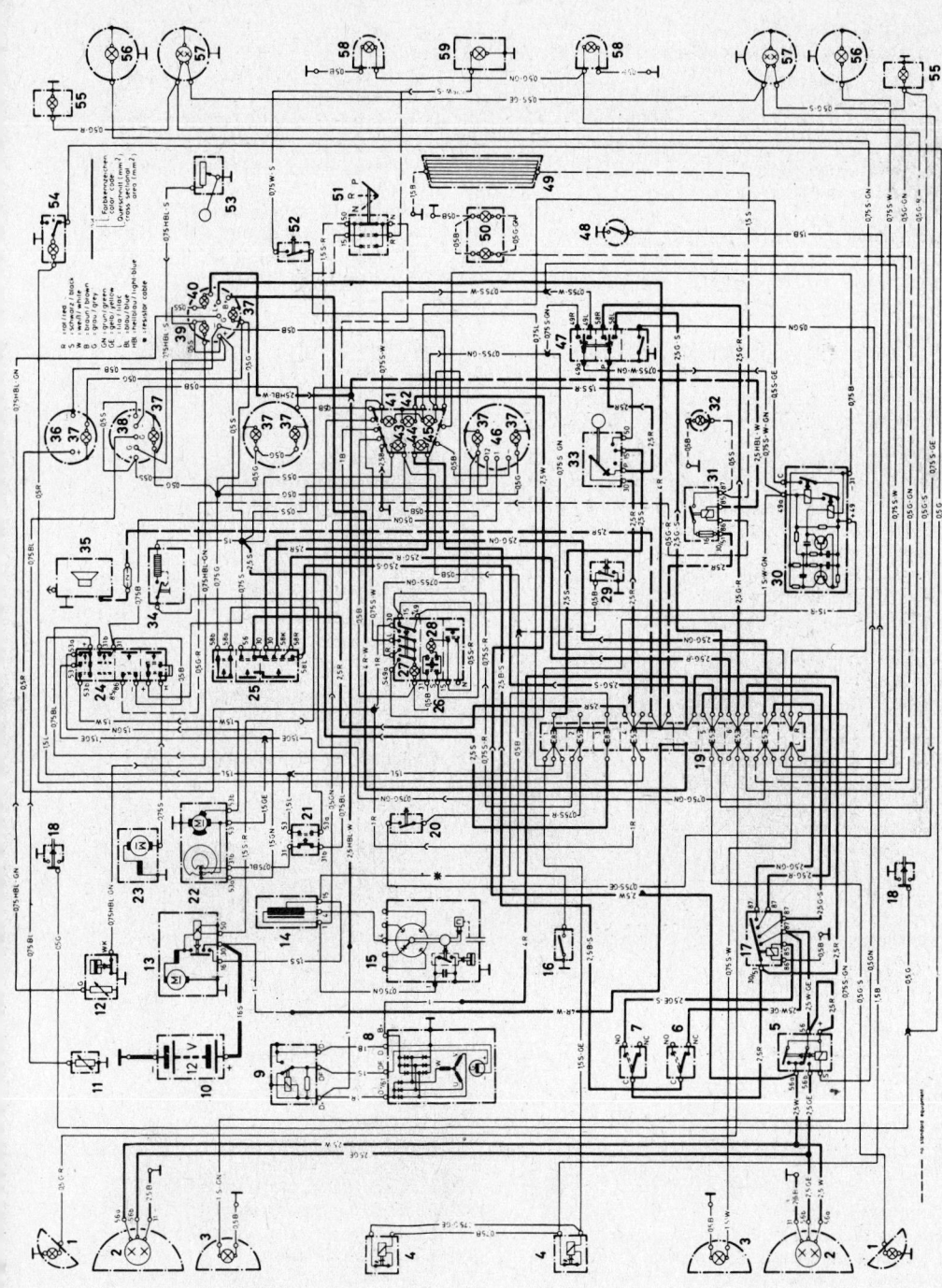

Wiring diagram for 1969 GT.

Wiring diagram for 1969 GT.

1. Side marker and parking light
2. Headlamp high and low beams
3. Direction signal lamp
4. Horn
5. Dimmer relay
6. Headlamp indicator lamp switch
7. Headlamp relay switch
8. A.C. generator
9. Regulator
10. Battery
11. Temperature sender
12. Oil pressure sender
13. Starter
14. Ignition coil
15. Distributor
16. Brake warning light control switch
17. Headlamp relay
18. Interior lamp switch
19. Fuse box
20. Stop light switch
21. Wiper switch and pump assy.
22. Windshield wiper motor
23. Blower
24. Windshield wiper, heatable back window and blower switch
25. Parking light and instrument light switch
26. Hazard warning flasher, brake system warning light switch
27. Hazard warning flasher indicator lamp
28. Brake system warning light
29. Parking brake indicator lamp switch
30. Flasher unit
31. Heatable back window relay
32. Heatable back window indicator light
33. Ignition and starter switch
34. Cigar lighter
35. Radio
36. Electric clock
37. Instrument light
38. Temperature indicator and fuel gauge dash unit
39. Oil pressure gauge with oil pressure indicator lamp
40. Ammeter with charging indicator light
41. Direction signal indicator lamp, right
42. Headlamp high beam indicator lamp
43. Parking brake indicator lamp
44. Headlamp high beam indicator lamp
45. Direction signal indicator lamp, left
46. Tachometer
47. Signal switch
48. Horn contact
49. Heatable back window
50. Selector lever indicator lamp
51. Selector lever switch
52. Back-up lamp switch
53. Fuel gauge tank unit
54. Interior lamp
55. Side marking light
56. Direction signal lamp
57. Stop and tail lamp
58. License plate lamp
59. Back-up lamp

Wiring diagram for 1970 Kadett.

1. Headlamp, high and low beams
2. Direction signal and parking lamp
3. Horn
4. Regulator
5. Generator
6. A.C. regulator
7. Connector
8. A.C. generator
9. Spark plug
10. Distributor
11. Brake control switch
12. Ignition coil
13. Oil pressure switch
14. Temperature sending unit
15. Starter
16. Relay
17. Battery
18. Blower motor
19. Stop lamp switch
20. Windshield wiper motor
21. Door jamb switch
22. Electrically heated back window switch
23. Light and windshield wiper switch
24. Instrument lamps
25. Headlamp high beam indicator lamp
26. Direction signal indicator lamp
27. Temperature indicator
28. Fuel gauge dash unit
29. Charging indicator lamp
30. Oil pressure indicator lamp
31. Multiple plug
32. Direction signal flasher unit
33. Electric clock
34. Electric clock lamp
35. Blower switch
36. Cigar lighter
37. Fuse box
38. Radio
39. Interior lamp
40. Tachometer
41. Tachometer lamp
42. Back-up lamp switch
43. Ignition and starter switch
44. Signal switch
45. Fog lamp and hazard warning flasher switch
46. Brake control lamp
47. Hazard warning flasher indicator lamp
48. Horn button
49. Electrically heated back window
50. Fuel gauge tank unit
51. Luggage compartment lamp
52. Load compartment lamp
53. Load compartment lamp switch
54. License plate lamp
55. Back-up lamp
56. Direction signal lamp
57. Tail lamp
58. Side marker light
59. Solenoid valve
60. Tachometer relay
61. Warning buzzer
62. Warning buzzer switch

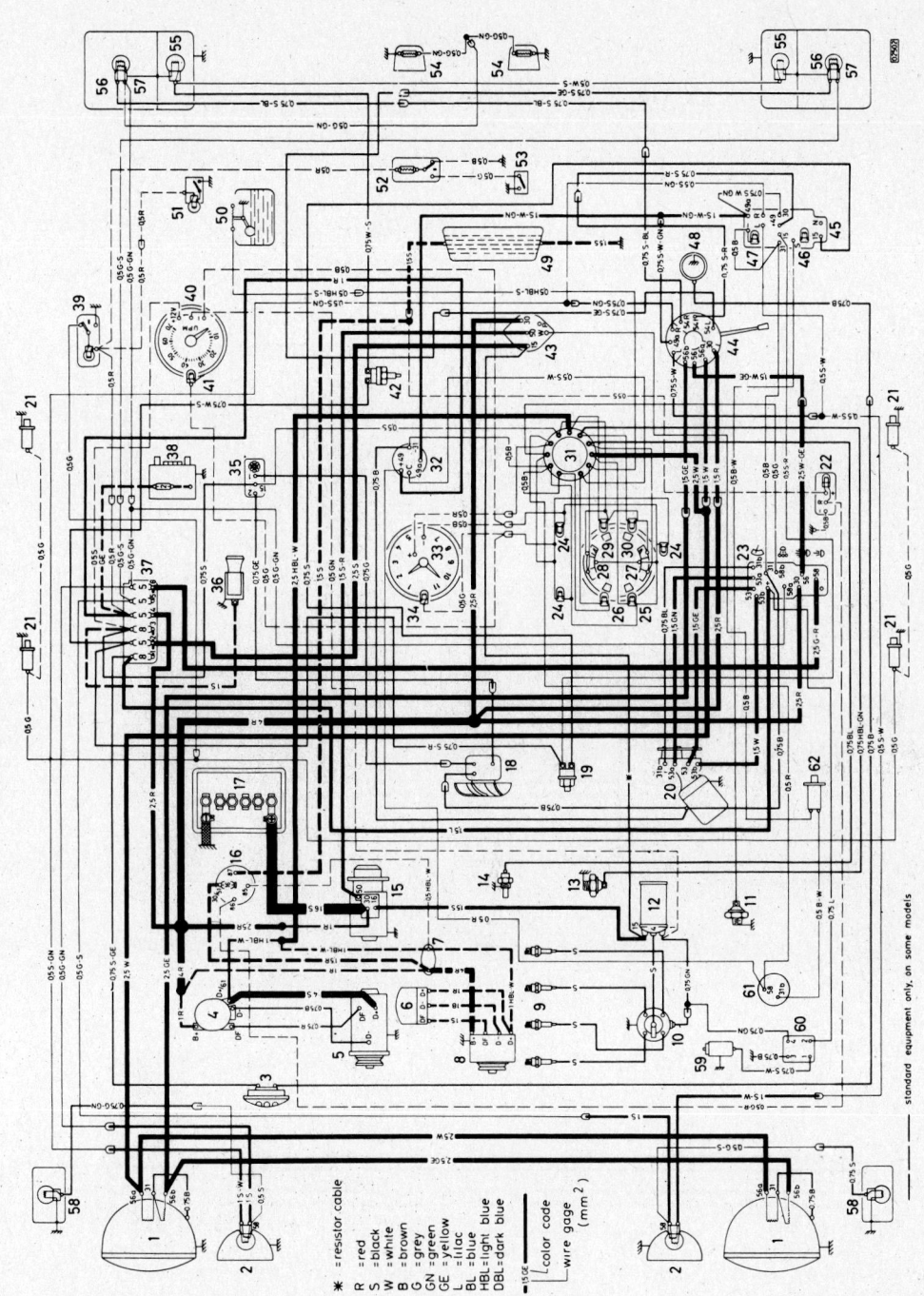

Wiring diagram for 1970 Kadett.

* = resistor cable

	color code
R = red	
S = black	
W = white	
B = brown	
G = grey	
GN = green	
GE = yellow	
L = lilac	
BL = blue	
HBL = light blue	
DBL = dark blue	

wire gage (mm²)

standard equipment only, on some models

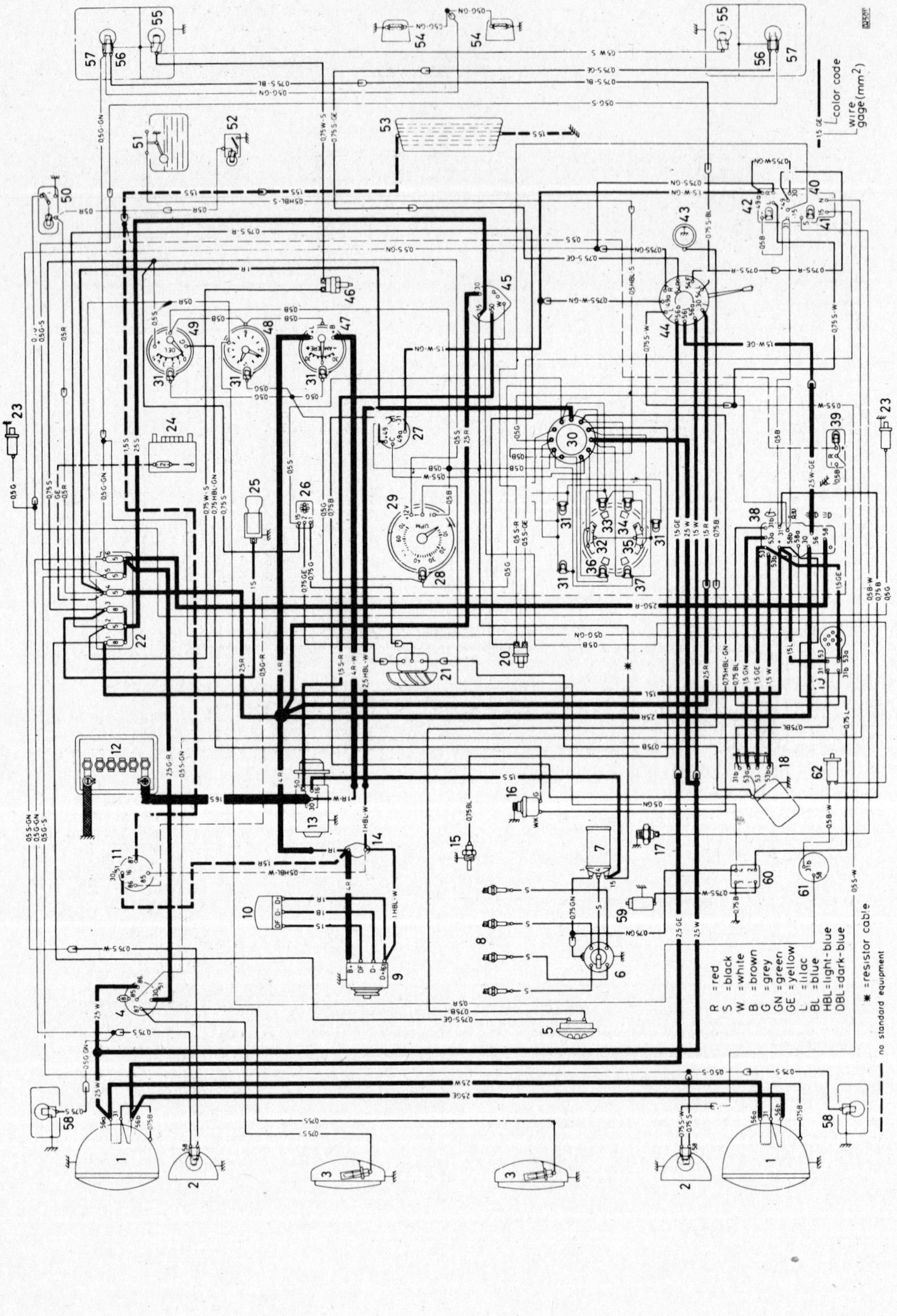

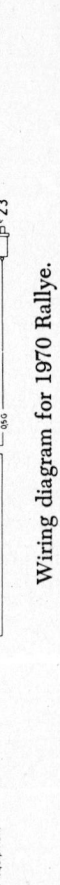

Wiring diagram for 1970 Rallye.

R	= red
S	= black
W	= white
B	= brown
G	= grey
GN	= green
GE	= yellow
L	= lilac
BL	= blue
HBL	= light-blue
DBL	= dark-blue

* = no standard equipment

= resistor cable

Color code
wire
gage (mm²)

Wiring diagram for 1970 Rallye.

1. Headlamp
2. Direction signal lamp and parking lamp
3. Fog lamp
4. Fog lamp relay
5. Horn
6. Distributor
7. Ignition coil
8. Spark plugs
9. A.C. Generator
10. Regulator
11. Electrically heated back window relay
12. Battery
13. Starter
14. Terminal
15. Temperature sending unit
16. Oil pressure switch
17. Brake warning light switch
18. Windshield wiper motor
19. Wiper switch and pump assembly
20. Stop lamp switch
21. Blower motor
22. Fuse box
23. Interior lamp switch
24. Radio
25. Cigar lighter
26. Blower motor switch
27. Direction signal flasher unit
28. Tachometer lamp
29. Tachometer
30. Multiple plug
31. Instrument lamps
32. Fuel gauge dash unit

33. Charging indicator lamp
34. Oil pressure indicator lamp
35. Temperature indicator
36. Direction signal indicator lamp
37. Headlamp high beam indicator lamp
38. Windshield wiper instrument light and light switch
39. Electrically heated back window with warning light
40. Fog lamp switch
41. Brake warning light
42. Hazard warning light switch
43. Horn button
44. Signal switch
45. Ignition and starter switch
46. Back-up lamp switch
47. Ammeter
48. Electric clock
49. Oil pressure gauge
50. Interior lamp
51. Fuel gauge tank unit
52. Luggage compartment lamp
53. Electrically heated back window
54. License plate lamp
55. Back-up lamp
56. Direction signal lamp
57. Tail lamp
58. Side marker light
59. Solenoid valve
60. Solenoid valve relay
61. Warning buzzer
62. Warning buzzer switch

Wiring diagram for 1970 GT with manual transmission.

1. Side marker and parking light
2. Headlamp high and low beams
3. Direction signal lamp
4. Horn
5. Dimmer relay
6. Headlamp indicator lamp switch
7. Headlamp relay switch
8. A.C. generator
9. Regulator
10. Battery
11. Temperature
12. Oil pressure sender
13. Starter
14. Ignition coil
15. Distributor
16. Brake warning light control switch
17. Headlamp relay
18. Interior lamp switch
19. Fuse box
20. Stop light switch
21. Wiper switch and pump assembly
22. Windshield wiper motor
23. Blower

24. Windshield wiper, heatable back window and blower switch
25. Parking light and instrument light switch
26. Hazard warning flasher, brake system warning light switch
27. Hazard warning flasher indicator lamp
28. Brake system warning light
29. Clutch warning switch
30. Flasher unit
31. Heatable back window relay
32. Heatable back window indicator light
33. Ignition and starter switch
34. Cigar lighter
35. Radio
36. Electric clock
37. Instrument lights
38. Temperature indicator and fuel gauge dash unit
39. Oil pressure gauge with oil pressure indicator lamp
40. Ammeter with charging indicator light
41. Direction signal indicator lamp, right

42. Headlamp high beam indicator lamp
43. Parking brake and clutch indicator lamp
44. Headlamp high beam indicator lamp
45. Direction signal indicator lamp, left
46. Tachometer
47. Signal switch
48. Horn contact
49. Heatable back window
50. Selector lever indicator
51. Selector lever switch
52. Back-up lamp switch
53. Fuel gauge tank unit
54. Interior lamp
55. Side marking light
56. Direction signal lamp
57. Stop and tail lamp
58. License plate lamp
59. Back-up lamp
60. Warning buzzer
61. Warning buzzer switch
62. Revolution relay
63. Solenoid valve
64. Headlamp relay switch

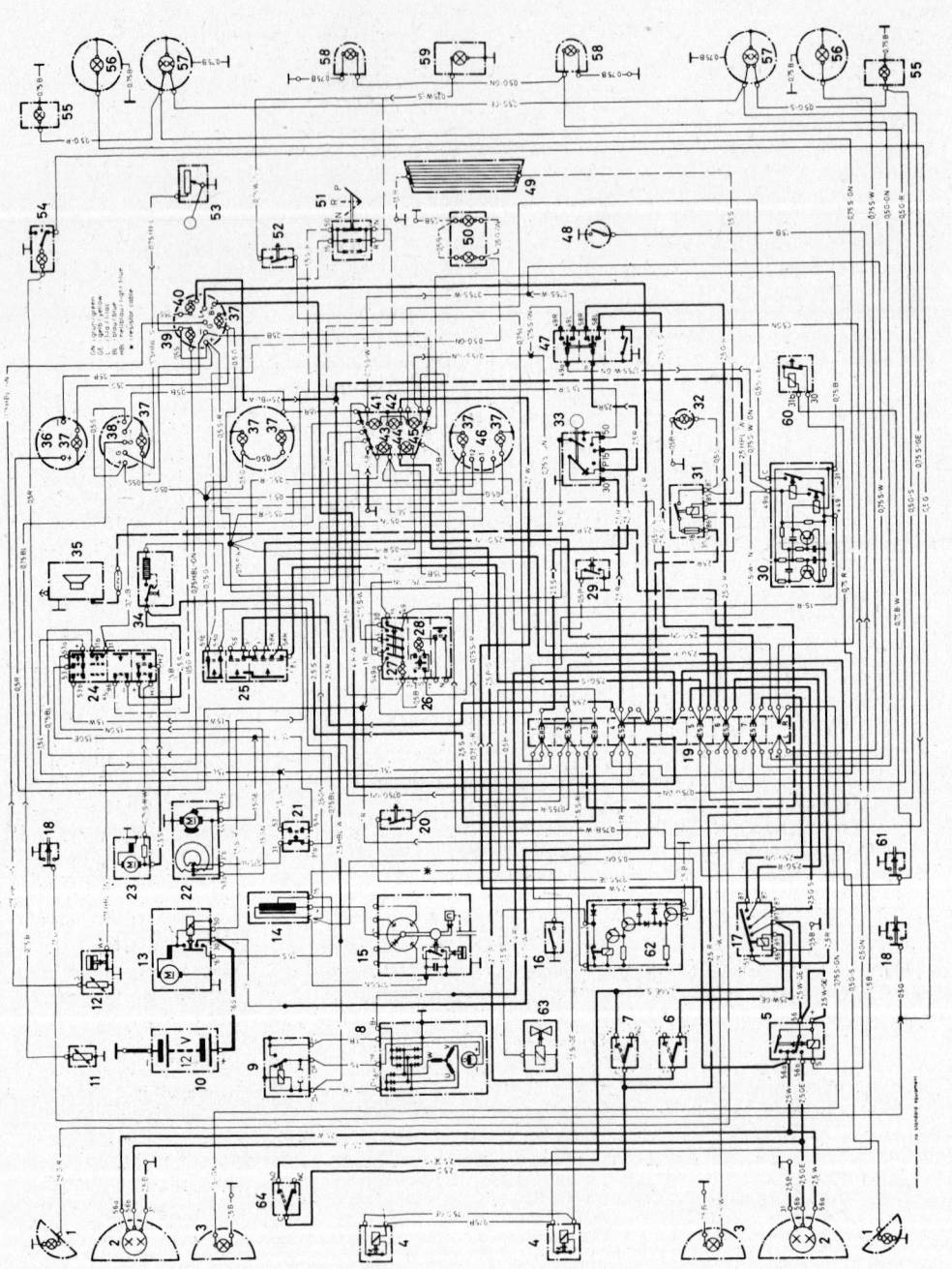

Wiring diagram for 1970 GT with manual transmission.

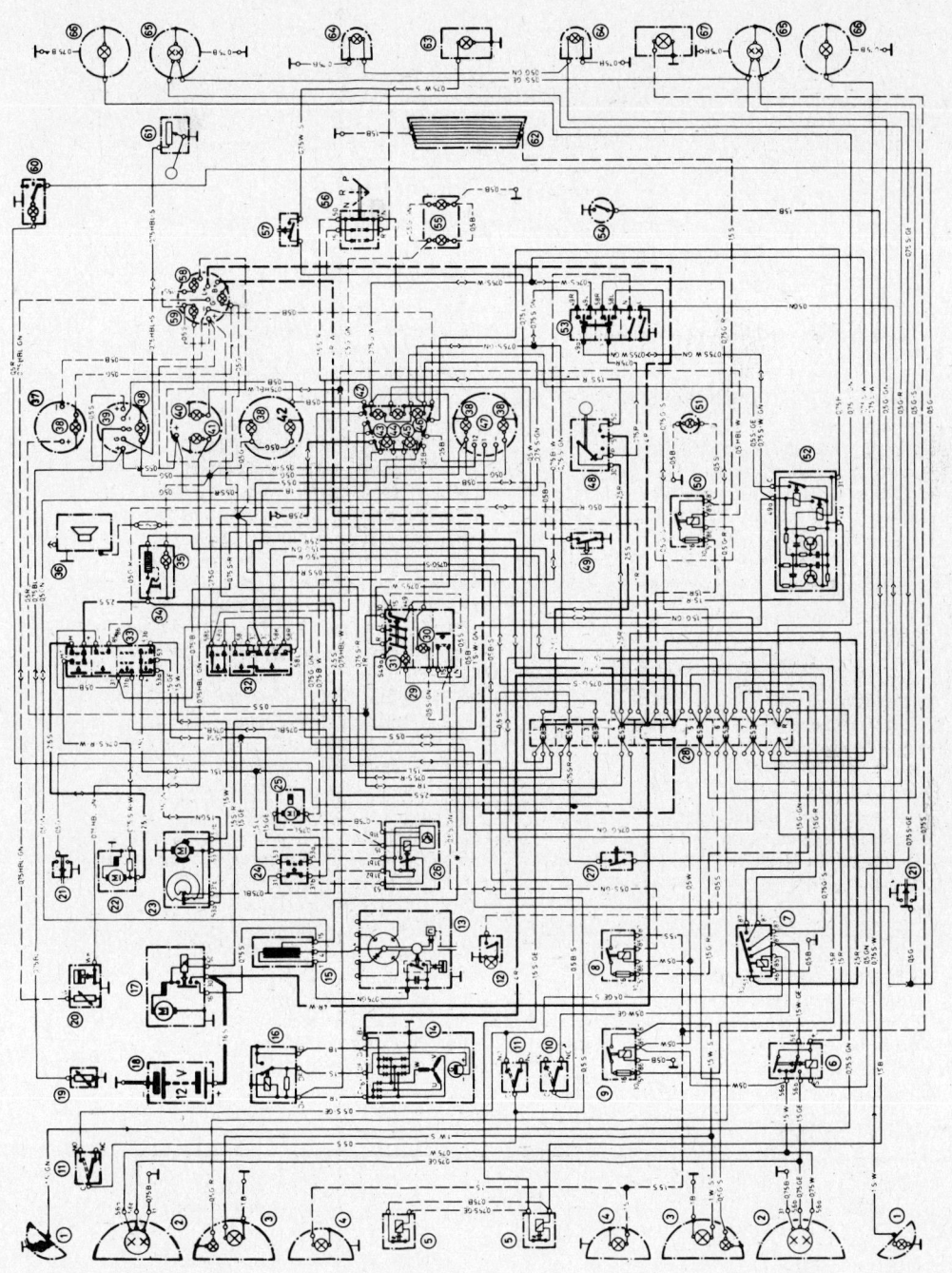

Wiring diagram for 1970 GT with automatic transmission.

Wiring diagram for 1970 GT with automatic transmission.

1. Direction signal lamp
2. Headlamp high and low beams
3. Long range headlamp with parking light
4. Fog lamp +)
5. Horn
6. Dimmer relay
7. Headlamp relay
8. Fog lamp and fog tail lamp relay +)
9. Long range headlamp relay
10. Headlamp indicator lamp switch
11. Headlamp and long range headlamp switch
12. Engine compartment lamp +)
13. Distributor
14. A.C. Generator
15. Ignition coil
16. Regulator
17. Starter
18. Battery
19. Temperature sender
20. Oil pressure sender
21. Interior lamp switch
22. Blower
23. Windshield wiper motor
24. Wiper switch and pump assy.
25. Windshield washer pump +)
26. Retarding relay +)
27. Stop light switch
28. Fuse box
29. Hazard warning flasher, fog lamp and fog tail lamp switch +)
30. Fog tail lamp indicator lamp +)
31. Hazard warning flasher indicator lamp
32. Parking light and instrument light switch
33. Windshield wiper, heatable back window +) and blower switch
34. Cigar lighter

+) Special Equipment

35. Cigar lighter lamp +)
36. Radio +)
37. Electric clock +)
38. Instrument lamp
39. Temperature indicator and fuel gauge dash unit
40. Charging indicator lamp
41. Oil pressure indicator lamp
42. Direction signal indicator lamp, right
43. Parking brake indicator lamp +)
44. Headlamp high beam indicator lamp
45. Headlamp indicator lamp
46. Direction signal indicator lamp, left
47. Tachometer
48. Ignition and starter switch
49. Parking brake indicator lamp switch +)
50. Heatable back window relay +)
51. Heatable back window indicator lamp +)
52. Flasher unit
53. Signal and windshield washer switch
54. Horn contact
55. Selector lever lamp +)
56. Selector lever switch +)
57. Back-up lamp switch
58. Ammeter with charging indicator lamp +)
59. Oil pressure indicator with oil pressure indicator lamp +)
60. Interior lamp
61. Fuel gauge tank unit
62. Heatable back window +)
63. Back-up lamp
64. License plate lamp
65. Tail and stop lamp
66. Direction signal lamp
67. Fog tail lamp +)

Engine Electrical

Distributor

REMOVAL AND INSTALLATION

Kadett and GT

To overhaul distributor, remove distributor cap, place No. 1 cylinder in the firing position (timing marks aligned), disconnect vacuum line and primary ignition wire, and remove bolt, clamp and distributor.

Replace paper gasket on distributor housing if necessary.

Install distributor with vacuum advance unit pointing rearward and parallel with engine. Turn rotor to align mark on tip with breaker point hold-down screw so that shaft seats itself. If distributor was set in wrong, rotor will be 180° out of place. Set distributor into position and hand tighten bolt. The mark on the rotor should be nearly aligned with mark on distributor housing. Align marks on rotor tip and housing, set breaker point gap or dwell angle, and adjust ignition timing.

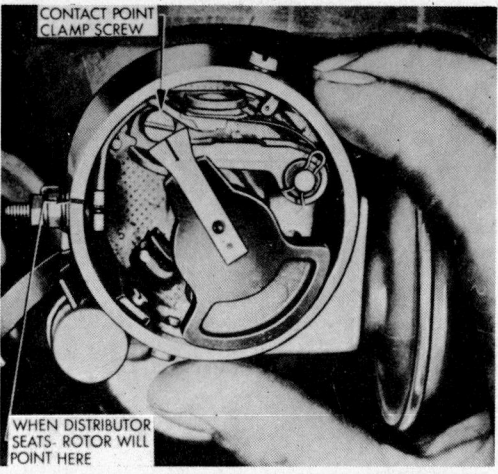

CONTACT POINT CLAMP SCREW

WHEN DISTRIBUTOR SEATS- ROTOR WILL POINT HERE

Distributor and rotor positioned for installation

BREAKER POINTS

Kadett and GT

When installing points, lightly lubricate distributor cam with high temperature grease. CAUTION: *Excessive lubricant will throw off into contact points.* Position support on breaker plate and install lock screw loosely for later adjustment. Install breaker arm on pivot pin. Position spring insulating washer correctly in spring support. Plug-in breaker arm wire. Adjust gap to specifications. Tighten.

Point gap can be set by using a feeler gauge or a dwell meter. Accurate measurements with a feeler gauge require careful, precise usage of the feelers.

A dwell meter should be calibrated first, switched to the four-cylinder position, and connected between the distributor primary terminal and ground. Remove the distributor cap and rotor. Loosen the breaker set screw approximately ⅛ turn. Observing the dwell meter, reset screw of stationary contact to obtain specified dwell angle. Tighten set screw and recheck dwell. Install rotor and cap, start engine, and make a final dwell angle check.

IGNITION TIMING

Kadett and GT

Timing marks for overhead-valve engines are located on the crankshaft pulley and timing chain cover. The 15S and 19S engines have timing marks in the form of a steel ball embedded in the flywheel and a pointer in a window on the right side of the flywheel housing. Timing is correct when the timing marks are aligned at the moment No. 1 cylinder reaches top dead center (TDC).

Basic timing is set by rotating distributor housing counterclockwise slightly until contact points just start to open. Timing marks must line up at this point. Install distributor cap, and connect spark plugs.

Adjust ignition timing after setting point gap. A fast and easy way to adjust timing is with a stroboscope.

Connect strobe light to No. 1 spark plug. Disconnect all vacuum hoses from distributor and plug the hoses. Start engine and reduce idle speed below 500 rpm for 1.1 liter engine and 700 rpm for 1.5 and 1.9 liter engines. Idle performance must be smooth. Slowing the idle is essential to keep the centrifugal advance in distributor from engaging. Rotate distributor as necessary to align timing marks with strobe pulses.

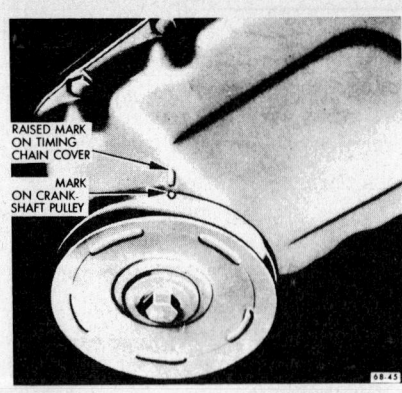

Ignition timing marks—1.1 liter engine.

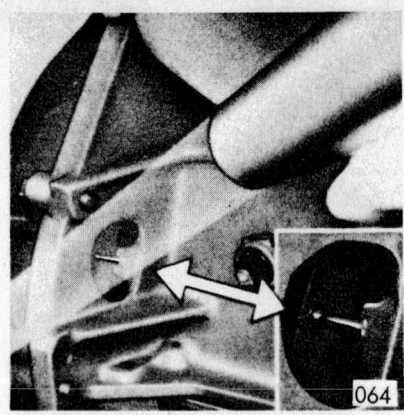

Ignition timing marks—CIH engines.

AC Generator and Regulator

An AC generator and regulator are installed on the Rallye as standard equipment, and on all models using heavy duty electrical options (i.e., fog lights, heated rear window) since 1967. All 1971 Opels are equipped with an AC generator and regulator.

ALTERNATOR

The AC Generator—alternator—has a rotor carrying the field windings mounted in ball bearings at both ends. Lubrication is maintained by sealed-in grease.

The alternator is a continuous output (even at idle) diode-rectified generator. It has three-phase stator (housing) windings assembled on the inside of a laminated core that is the middle section of the housing. Rectifier diodes are connected to the windings (3 diodes to each phase) which change AC voltage into direct current. If the generator does not meet output specifications, it is usually replaced as a unit.

AC REGULATOR

The diodes in the alternator only allow current to flow from the generator to the battery. Battery current cannot discharge through the generator. As a result a current breaker is not needed in the regulator. The AC regulator needs just the voltage regulator unit.

NOTE: *The following precautions should be observed when servicing a vehicle equipped with an alternator:*

1. Never operate the alternator on an open circuit (battery disconnected).

2. When installing a battery, connect the ground terminal (negative) before connecting the positive.

3. When arc welding anywhere on the vehicle, disconnect the alternator.

DC Generator and Regulator

The DC generator has its armature supported by a ball bearing at the drive end and a sintered bronze bushing behind the commutator. Lubricate the bushing by removing the plastic plug from the end support.

DC GENERATOR

The DC generator has a rotating armature with copper windings that intersect lines of magnetic force between magnetic field poles. At the start the magnetic field is weak because it is only residual. However, as current flows from the armature windings, part of the flow is fed into and excites the magnetic field. Increasing speed intensifies the magnetic field and thereby increases the voltage from the windings. The magnetic field becomes saturated with energy and no further increase in armature speed will add to the output.

DC REGULATOR

Since voltage produced by the generator is in direct ratio to the product of armature speed and exciting current in the magnetic field, a constant voltage output can be easily maintained by making compensating adjustments to the exciting current. Armature speed is based on engine rpm and is therefore not independently controllable. The regulator maintains a constant voltage output by interrupting the exciting current.

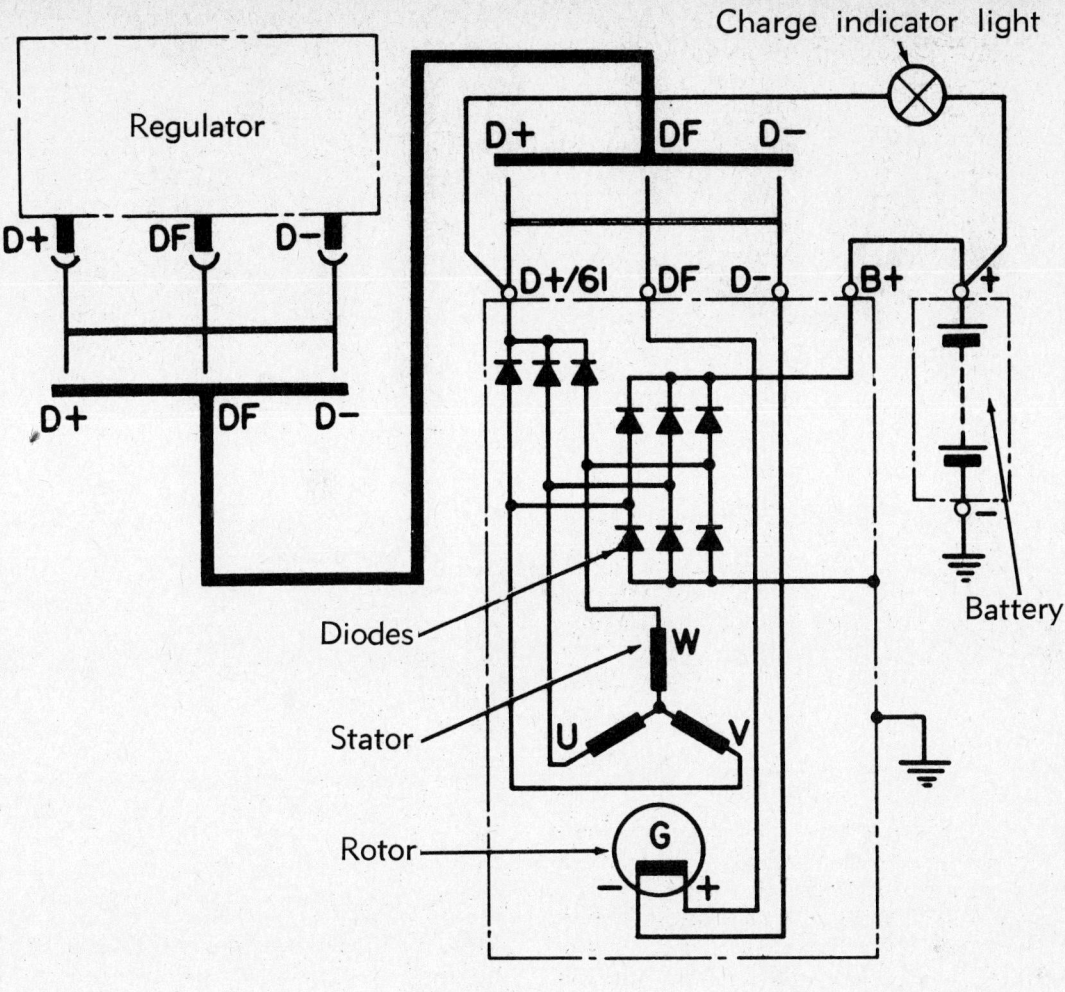

AC Charging Circuit

The Bosch regulator used on the Kadett (coded "V" type) has a semi-conductor component, a variode, having a variable resistance under different voltage loads, ranging from high resistance at low voltages to extremely low resistance at high voltage levels. Diagram shows the variode lead running parallel to the main current lead. (Main lead runs from D+ via the cutout current winding to the cutout contact; variode lead runs from main lead to the control winding on the regulator core.) The variode lead picks up the voltage drop that resistance causes in the main current lead. The resistance of the main current lead determines the activation of the variode and should not be altered or replaced separately.

TESTING AND ADJUSTING
GENERATOR AND REGULATOR

After checking condition and tension of fan belt, turn off all accessories, set engine speed up to around 2500 rpm, and attach ammeter in series with regulator and battery by disconnecting red lead from "B+" regulator terminal and adding ammeter between terminal and red wire. Output must be 20 amperes minimum on a 12-volt DC generator, 30 amperes on an AC generator, and 50 amperes on a 6-volt DC unit (at 2000 rpm). A lower output indicates malfunction in the generator or regulator. Identify the cause by disconnecting the generator field lead from the regulator (three-way connector in AC unit) hooking it through the ammeter and by-passing the

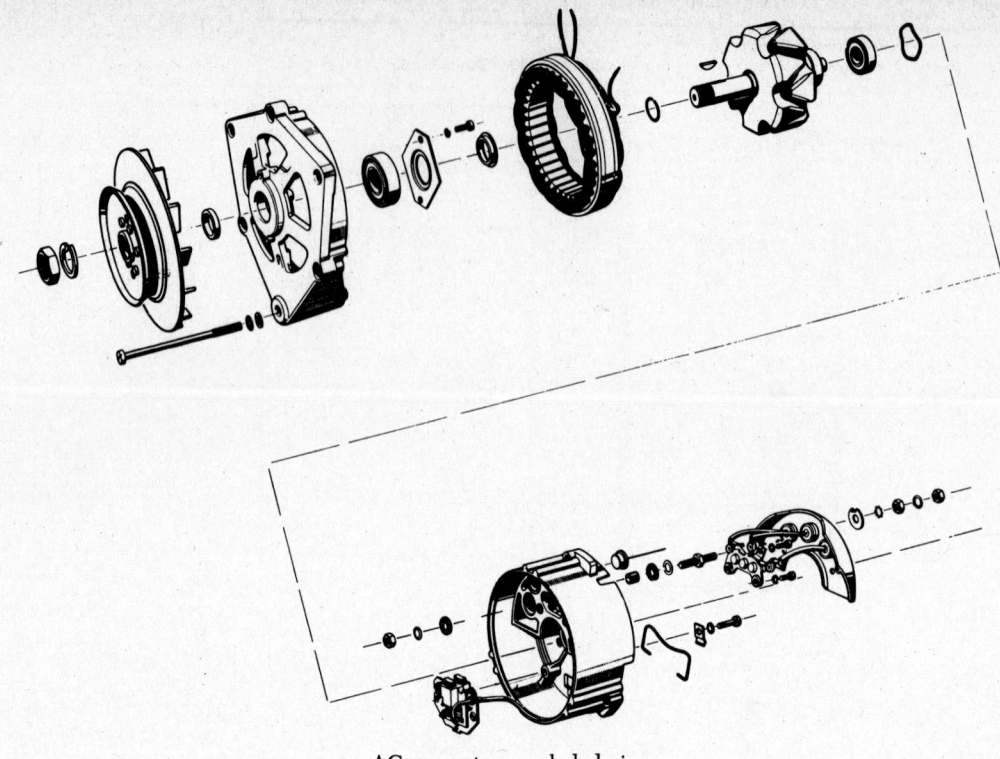

AC generator—exploded view

regulator. If output is still low, generator is faulty.

Remove red battery lead from regulator "B+" terminal and connect voltmeter positive lead to this terminal. Run voltmeter negative lead to ground. Increase engine speed until voltage peaks within 13.5-14.5 range. Six-volt regulator limits voltage to 7.0-7.5 volts.

If voltage reading is not in range, remove regulator cover and adjust voltage regulator armature spring tension to obtain a middle reading of 14.0 volts. If reading fluctuates, voltage contacts are dirty. Reseal AC voltage regulator cover carefully, using tape.

Adjusting Cutout Relay Closing Voltage — DC Regulator

Connect voltmeter positive lead to regulator "61" (lower rear) terminal. Attach negative lead to ground. Connect ammeter in series with "B+" (upper rear) terminal and disconnected red wire to battery. Increase engine speed and observe voltage increase (until cutout relay points close)

and then drop slightly as circuit is completed to battery. The highest voltmeter reading before the drop is the closing voltage. Closing voltage: 12.3-13.2 volts; 5.9 to 6.5 volts. If closing voltage is not within limits, adjust closing voltage by bending cutout relay spring support. Increase spring tension to increase closing voltage—decrease spring tension to decrease closing voltage.

IMPORTANT: *The wire leading from regulator to generator is permanently attached to the regulator.* The resistance of this wire is closely tuned with the variode and coils. Its length must not be changed. Should wire damage occur, replace the regulator and wire as a unit.

GENERATOR REMOVAL AND INSTALLATION

NOTE: *Always disconnect the battery terminals prior to removal of the generator.*

DC Generator

Code for identification and remove the three leads from the generator. Remove the adjusting bolt, loosen the lower mounting

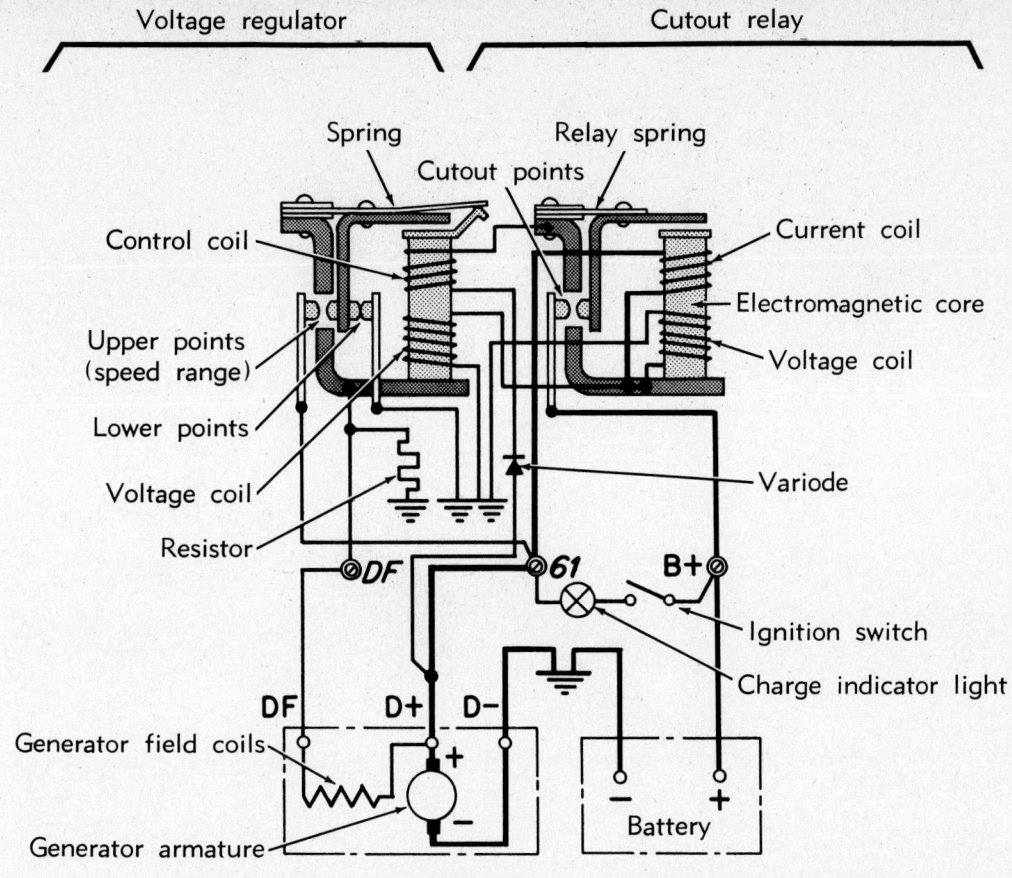

DC Charging Circuit

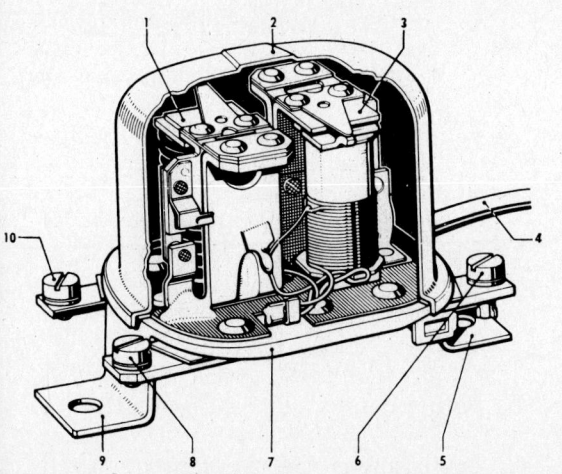

1. Cutout relay with current and voltage coils
2. Cover
3. Voltage regulator with voltage and control coils
4. Wire connection (D+ terminal)
5. Mounting bracket
6. Terminal "DF"
7. Base plate
8. Terminal B+
9. Mounting bracket
10. Terminal "61"

Bosch Regulator for DC Generator

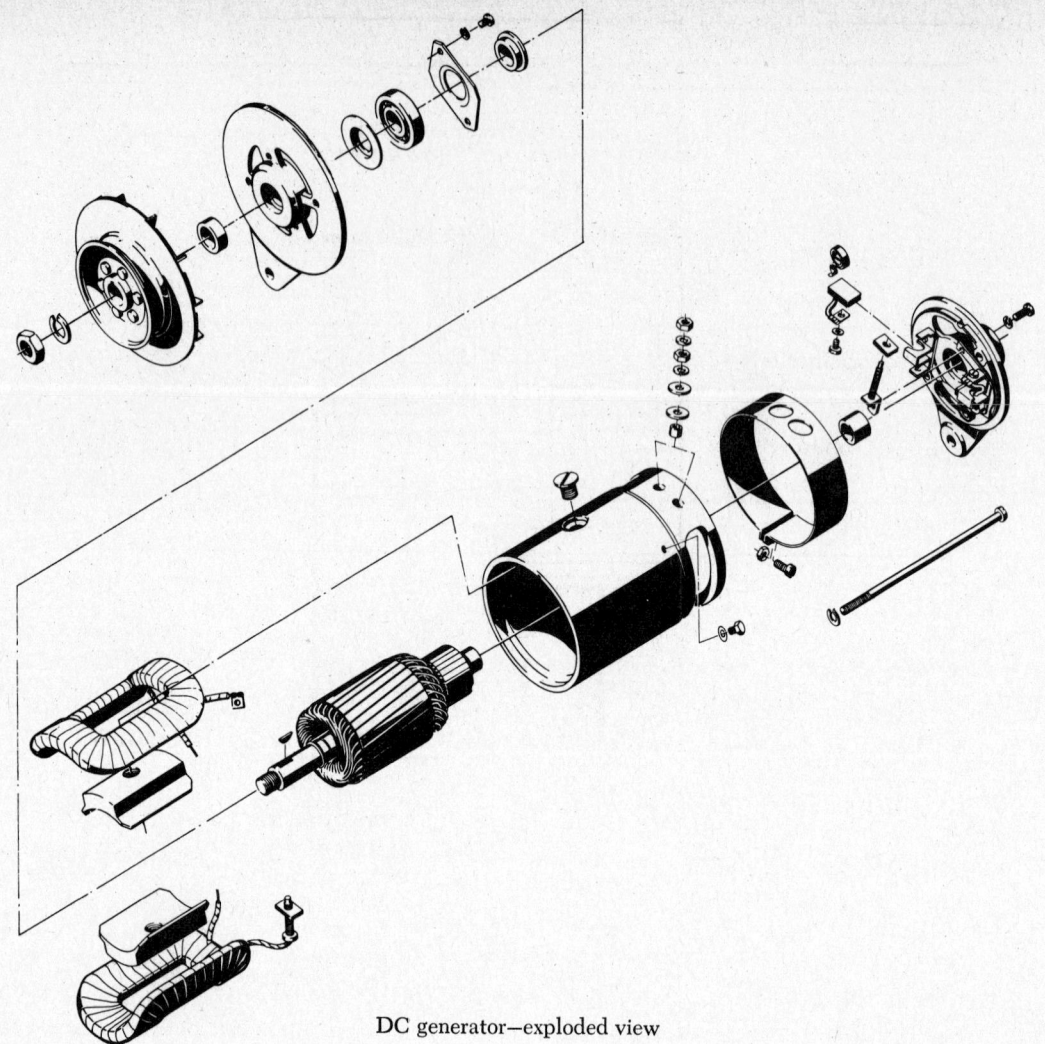

DC generator—exploded view

bolts and remove the fan belt. Swing the generator downward, and remove the two mounting bolts and the generator. When installing, the generator must be polarized, by momentarily attaching a jumper wire from the D+ terminal to the D− terminal of the regulator.

AC Generator

Disconnect the battery lead and the wiring connector from the alternator. Remove the upper adjusting bolt, loosen the lower mounting bolt, and remove the fan belt. Swing the alternator downward, and remove the through-bolt and alternator.

CAUTION: *Do not attempt to polarize the regulator of an AC charging system. To do so will cause serious damage to the charging system.*

Installation is the reverse of removal.

Battery

KADETT AND GT

Kadetts have used 12-volt batteries from 1966. Earlier models were equipped with 6-volt, 66 amp-hour Varta or Mareg batteries. However the 77 amp-hour Delco is a frequent replacement. The Kadett 12-volt electrical system requires that the battery produce at least 9 volts while starter is cranking the engine. The 6-volt system can tolerate a minimum of 4.5 volts output under the cranking load.

Batteries should be checked periodically for proper output and good connections. A weak power supply lowers the efficiency of the engine as well as placing a greater drag on the generator circuit.

Inspect the battery case for cracks and

weakness. Check the density (specific gravity) of the battery electrolyte with a hydrometer. Readings from a fully charged battery will depend on the make but will fall in the range of 1.260 to 1.310 times as heavy as pure water at 80°F. NOTE: *All cells should produce nearly equal readings.* If one or two cell readings are sharply lower, they are defective.

The amount of charge remaining in a battery can be roughly determined from the specific gravity ranges shown in the chart below.

Hydrometer Readings	Condition
1.260-1.310	Fully charged
1.230-1.250	¾ charged
1.200-1.220	½ charged
1.170-1.190	¼ charged
1.140-1.160	Almost discharged
1.110-1.130	Fully discharged

Perform a light-load voltage test to detect weak cells. First draw off the transient (surface) charge by operating the starter for three seconds and then turning on the low beam lights. After one minute, test each cell (with lights still on) with a voltmeter. A fully charged battery will have no cell voltage below 1.95 volts and no cell should vary more than .05 volts from the others. A greater variation at full charge indicates a defective cell.

CAUTION: *When jump starting, ensure that cable polarity is correct, and that the jumper cables are disconnected as soon as the vehicle starts, to avoid damaging the charging system.*

Starter

The starter is a brush-type, series-wound motor equipped with an over-running clutch and operated by a solenoid. The field frame carries the pole shoes and the field coils. The armature has a spline which carries the over-running clutch and pinion assembly. The armature shaft is supported in two bushings which are permanently packed with lubricant.

As the starter is energized, the shift lever moves against the spring and by means of the guide ring sends the pinion into mesh with the flywheel. After the pinion meshes, the solenoid contact disc closes the circuit and the engine is cranked. When the en-

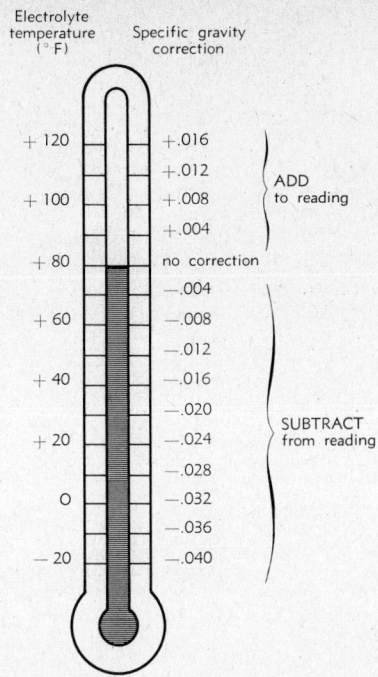

Effect of temperature on the specific gravity of battery electrolyte

gine starts, the increased speed of the flywheel causes the pinion to over-run the clutch and armature. The pinion continues in full mesh until the starter current is interrupted. Then the shift lever spring returns the pinion to its neutral position.

Disconnect ground strap from battery before starting any work on electrical parts of installed starter.

Removal and Installation

OHV Engines

To remove the starter while the engine is in the chassis, it is necessary to remove the air cleaner and disconnect the choke control cable. Hoist front of car and support it. Disconnect right engine mount (starter side), and tail pipe at rear of car. Loosen one bolt and remove the other bolt from left engine mount. Raise engine on starter side and remove bracket to gain access to starter. Disconnect starter wiring and remove starter.

Installation of starter is in reverse sequence of steps for removal. When reinstalling bolts attaching the engine-mount bracket to the crankcase, use appropriate non-hardening permatex to prevent leaks.

Starter installation—OHV engines

Starter installation—CIH engines.

Removing starter stud—CIH engines.

CIH Engines

To remove the starter of the CIH engines, disconnect the starter wiring. Remove the starter support bracket, the two starter bolts, nuts and lockwashers. Drive out the stud for clearance and remove the starter. To install the starter, reverse the removal procedure; finger tighten all bolts first, then tighten bolts at the engine before the others.

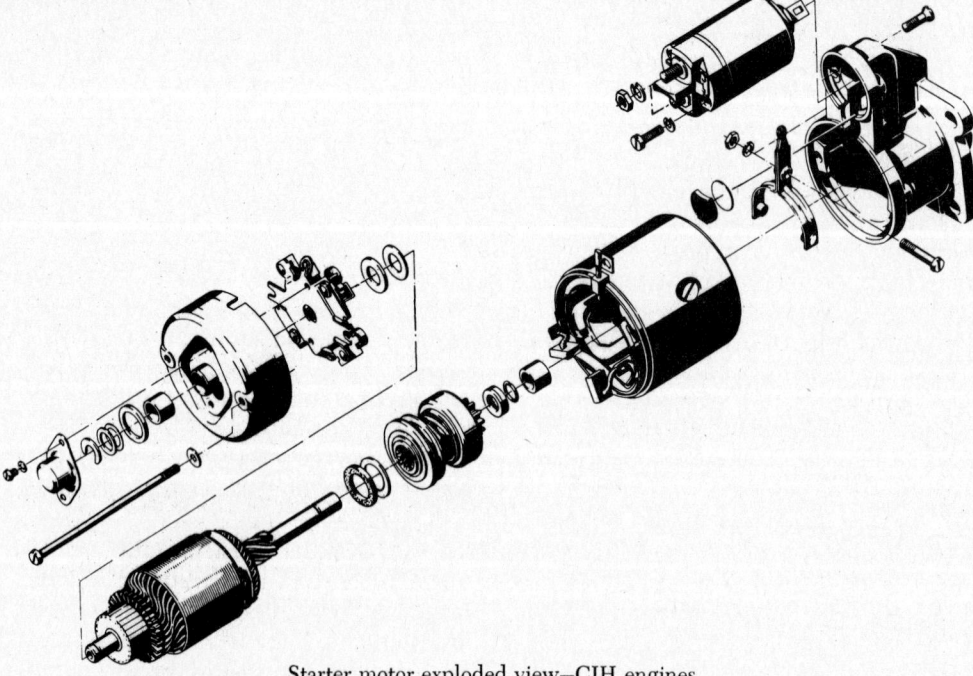

Starter motor exploded view—CIH engines

Fuel System

Fuel Pump

Fuel pressure is determined by diaphragm spring tension in the fuel pump. A weak spring causes low fuel pressure. Extreme spring tension creates fuel pressures that are too high. Pressure for normal engines at carburetor height is a minimum of 2 psi.

Quantity of fuel delivered to the carburetors is determined by the length of stroke of the pump diaphragm which varies with pump linkage wear and distance the pump is from its cam lobe. Stroke is adjusted by changing the thickness of the flange gaskets between pump and engine housings.

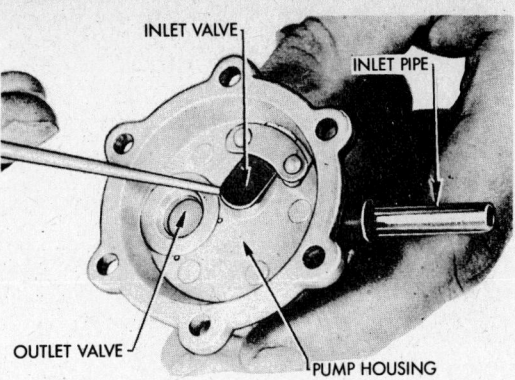

Upper housing of fuel pump has valves that cannot be replaced separately.

SERVICE

OHV Engines

Carefully remove fuel lines to prevent rupturing them, plug the ends, and remove pump from engine housing. NOTE: *The fuel pump is lower than the tank. The tank line will feed gas if not plugged.* Scratch a mark across the diaphragm flanges to simplify later reassembly. This avoids accidental changing of the lead-in angle of the fuel lines which might occur if the top section is put back on facing a different direction.

Remove screws from the diaphragm flanges and separate the two sections of the pump. Remove spring from fuel pump rocker arm. Remove retainer clips from rocker arm pin and punch out pin. Remove rocker arm and lift pump diaphragm out of housing. NOTE: *Diaphragm cannot be disengaged unless rocker arm is removed.*

Disassemble the top section by removing hex retaining screw, cover, filter screen and gasket. Inlet and outlet check valves cannot be removed. If a valve is damaged, upper housing must be replaced.

Work rubber oil seal off diaphragm rod and slide off seal retainer and diaphragm spring. Wash parts in solvent and dry with air. Replace weak or worn diaphragm, spring and linkage. Replace upper section having valves, if necessary. Replacement-part kits are available.

Metal parts coated with white oxide

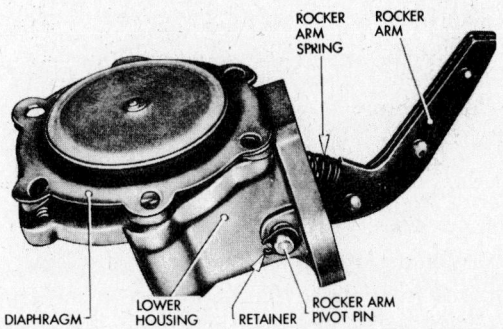

Lower housing of fuel pump is disassembled by punching out pivot pin. Remove rocker arm spring first.

CIH Engines

A pushrod type fuel pump, driven by the distributor shaft, is used. Since no replacement parts are available for this pump, service is limited to cleaning the fuel have been water damaged and should be replaced to prevent fouling of carburetor jets.

Reassembly of the fuel pump is the reverse of disassembly.

Cleaning fuel pump fuel strainer

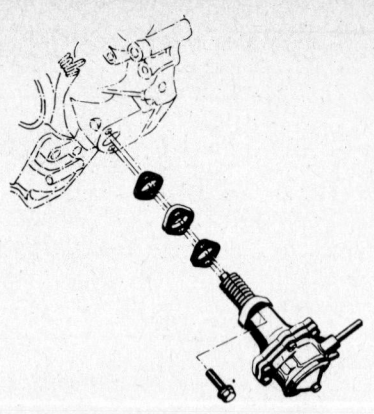

Fuel pump installation—CIH engines

strainer (under the pump cover), or replacement of the entire pump should leaks or pressure loss occur.

Carburetor

REMOVAL AND INSTALLATION

1 X 1 bbl.

Remove the fuel line and all vacuum hoses from the carburetor. Disconnect the choke cable and the throttle control rod, unbolt the two mounting nuts, and remove the carburetor. When installing, ensure that the rubber O-ring is installed and properly seated in the manifold, and that the choke plate is fully open when the control is pushed in completely.

2 X 1 bbl.

Remove the fuel lines and all vacuum hoses from the carburetors. Disconnect the choke cable from the choke control rod, and remove the cable bracket and cable from the carburetor. Disconnect the throttle control rod, unbolt the mounting nuts, and remove the carburetors. When installing, ensure that the rubber O-rings are properly seated in the manifold, the choke plate is fully open when the control is pushed in completely, and that the carburetors are synchronized (see below).

1 X 2 bbl.

Remove the fuel line and all vacuum hoses from the carburetor, and the water lines from the choke housing (automatic choke). Disconnect the choke cable (where applicable) and the throttle control rod, unbolt the four mounting nuts,

and remove the carburetor. Prior to installation of the carburetor, adjust the automatic choke (by rotating the choke housing) so that it is nearly closed at room temperature.

Installation is the reverse of removal.

ADJUSTMENTS

Before adjusting carburetor idle speed, check for binding of the throttle linkage:
1. Lubricate all pivot points with 1-2 drops of engine oil while moving throttle controls.
2. Lubricate accelerator pump rods.
3. Disconnect all ball joints, fill cups with high temperature grease, reconnect.
4. Move linkage back and forth to check for proper functioning.

Of utmost importance in tuning is the reminder that carburetors can only be adjusted satisfactorily when the engine is in good mechanical condition and timing is perfect.

Synchronization of Twin Carburetors

Prior to adjusting the carburetors, the engine must be at operating temperature. Loosen the screw on the coupling between the carburetors, leaving clearance between the screw and the shaft pick-up.
NOTE: *On cars equipped with Opel Emission Control System, shut off the center unit by pulling the hose from the front carburetor to the center unit and plugging the carburetor nipple and the intake manifold vacuum port.*

Back out the throttle idle adjust screw and close the idle mixture screw on the front carburetor, so that the engine runs on the rear carburetor only. Start the engine, and adjust the rear carburetor so that the engine runs as smoothly as possible at 700 rpm. Reverse the procedure and adjust the front carburetor in a similar manner.
NOTE: *Record the number of turns as the idle mixture screw is closed on the rear carburetor.*

Back out the idle mixture screw on the rear carburetor the number of turns recorded, and adjust the idle, using the rear throttle screw, to 1,000 rpm.

Idle Speed Adjustment — OHV Engines Through 1967

Perform the following steps to adjust the idle speed of the Carter and Solex carburetors used on 1.0 and 1.1 liter engines.

1. If carburetor was disassembled, set the basic mixture adjustment by screwing the idle-mixture jet(s) closed until the screw gently touches its seat. Reopen the screw on Carter ¾ turn; Solex, 1½ turns.

2. Set the idle speed to highest rpm within specifications by adjusting the throttle stop screw.

Carburetor	Standard engine	"S" engine
Carter, 1.0-liter	600-800 rpm	750-800 rpm
Solex, 1.1-liter	600-800 rpm	800-900 rpm

3. Adjust idle-mixture screw(s) until the highest possible rpm is achieved.

4. Turn the throttle stop screw again, lowering rpm to normal engine idle.

5. Readjust the idle-mixture screw(s) until the engine runs perfectly. The engine should not die by quick-shutting of the throttle or quick release of the clutch pedal in neutral.

6. Adjust throttle control linkage (if possible) so that it slips on without changing carburetor adjustment.

Idle Speed Adjustments — 1968 Engines

The carburetors used on 1968 engines have an adjustable idle air-bypass system, with an air passage entrance above the throttle valve, a passage exit below the throttle valve, and an air (speed) adjusting screw in between. Idle speed adjustment is made only with the by-pass air adjusting screw, not by changing the throttle stop-screw position. However, if the stop screw setting has been disturbed accidentally, adjust it first with air cleaner installed and choke valve open. Follow the throttle stop-screw adjustment procedures below.

1. With engine idling, fully close idle air-adjustment screw (uppermost screw).

2. Adjust idle-mixture screw to achieve the highest possible idle speed. Idle speed should now be 650-700 rpm.

3. If idle is not 650-700 rpm, adjust *throttle stop screw* as required to obtain this speed. The throttle valve is now properly reset.

Continue with the air and mixture adjustments (taking care not to disturb the throttle stop screw) until engine idles perfectly.

1. With air cleaner installed and choke

valve open, adjust idle speed with air adjusting screw (uppermost screw) to 850-900 rpm (750-800 rpm, CIH engines).

2. Adjust idle mixture needle (located in lower throttle body) until the highest possible rpm is achieved.

3. If idle speed is now over 900 rpm (800, CIH engines). readjust idle air screw to 850-900 rpm (750-800, CIH).

4. Whenever idle speed is changed, always make a careful mixture needle adjustment last.

Idle Speed Adjustments— 1969-70 OHV Engines

The twin carburetor system has factory-balanced carburetors, therefore individual throttle stop screws and idle mixture needles never should be disturbed. If the adjustments are disturbed accidentally, a basic adjustment, as follows, must be performed to balance the carburetors.

1. Connect a tachometer, start the engine and run until operating temperature is reached.

2. Adjust idle speed, using idle speed screw in center unit between carburetors, to 975 rpm.

3. Adjust idle mixture screw located at left of front carburetor to obtain highest rpm. If idle speed exceeds 1,000 rpm, reduce speed using center unit idle speed screw, then readjust idle mixture screw for highest rpm.

4. Reduce speed 50 rpm by slightly leaning idle mixture screw for best performance.

On manual transmission cars, it may be necessary to adjust the deceleration mixture to obtain correct dashpot action. Connect a jumper wire between the battery positive post, and the solenoid valve terminal. This will hold the solenoid valve open so that the intake vacuum can open the diaphragm valve. Move carburetor linkage to give engine speed of at least 3,000 rpm, then release. The engine should idle at 1,000-1,900 rpm. If it does not, turn in deceleration speed screw to decrease speed and check again.

To check operation of the computer, connect a test light between the solenoid valve and ground, then increase engine speed. Test light should come on between 2,100 and 2,500 rpm. If light does not come on, the computer must be replaced.

Carburetor adjusting screws on 1.1 OECS engine.

1. Throttle stop screw
2. Idle mixture needle
3. Center unit air speed screw
4. Center unit mixture needle

5. Deceleration mixture screw
A. Carburetor linkage coupling screw
B. Choke stop screw

Idle Speed Adjustments —
1969-70 1.9 Engines

The throttle valve has been properly positioned by the manufacturer and should not require adjustment, but should it be necessary to adjust it, use the following procedure.

Fully close the idle air adjusting screw until seated. Adjust idle mixture needle and throttle stop screw at 650-700 rpm to obtain the best possible mixture.

NOTE: *Now that the throttle stop screw has been set, do not move it. All further adjustments are made with the idle air and mixture screws.*

If it was not necessary to adjust the throttle stop, proceed by raising the idle speed to 850 rpm with the idle air (speed) adjusting screw and the idle mixture needle. Adjust idle mixture needle to midpoint of highest rpm range. If idle speed is too high, reset idle air speed adjusting screw to obtain 850 rpm.

NOTE: *Always adjust idle mixture after changing idle speed.*

The fast idle speed is adjusted by turning the nuts on the throttle connecting rod. Shortening the rod decreases, and lengthening increases engine speed. The fast idle should be 2,700 ±200 rpm, with the throttle lever resting on the highest step of the fast idle cam.

OVERHAUL PROCEDURES

Carburetor part-replacement kits are recommended for each overhaul. Kits contain a complete set of gaskets and new parts to replace those that generally deteriorate most rapidly. Not substituting *all* of the new parts supplied in the kits usually results in poor performance later.

Wash carburetor parts—except for diaphragm—in a carburetor cleaner, rinse in solvent, and blow dry with compressed air. Remember, breath carries moisture which induces oxidation. Clean diaphragm only in solvent to prevent deterioration. Clean jets and valves separately to avoid interchanging them during reassembly.

Check throttle shaft, float spindle(s), and other moving parts for wear. Replace if worn. Replace float if gasoline has leaked into it. The accelerator pump check valve ("no-return" ball valve) should pass air one way but not the other. Test for proper valve seating by blowing and sucking on valve and replace if necessary. Wash it again to remove breath moisture. Clean all fuel channels in the float bowl and the cover thoroughly but carefully. Blow out these channels in both directions so that ball valves and seats are clean and action is free.

Replace the accelerator pump diaphragm because it loses properties when exposed to air. Replace the carburetor flange gasket.

In all cases, take care not to tighten needle valves into seats. Uneven jetting will result.

Carter Carburetor—1.0 Liter Engine

Disconnect choke cable and throttle-choke connecting rod at throttle end, unscrew air horn attaching bolts, and lift off air horn and choke assembly.

Remove fuel inlet filter cover and screen. Unhook metering rod spring, turn metering rod ¼ turn and lift out of housing. NOTE: *Small washer on metering rod acts as dust cover.*

Remove link to accelerator plunger rod and take off accelerator lever-to-throttle connecting rod at throttle end.

Loosen float bowl cover screws. Lift and rotate bowl cover. Slide off accelerator pump lever. Remove float cover assembly, remove float, needle, seat and gasket. Remove accelerator pump rod.

Pull out accelerator pump plunger. Remove idle jet tube, idle well plug and idle well jet. Remove main metering jet. Remove accelerator pump passage plug and accelerator pump discharge jet.

Remove accelerator pump check valve plug, strainer, inlet check valve and outlet check valve. Remove passage-plug and

nozzle-jet from main metering nozzle. Remove throttle body and plastic spacer from float bowl. Remove idle mixture adjustment screw.

Assemble the carburetor as follows:

Bolt throttle body and plastic spacer to main carburetor body. Place choke wire clamp under bolt near idle mixture adjustment.

Install all jets, check valves and end plugs with gaskets. NOTE: *Idle well jet must be installed before low speed jet tube.*

Install float needle, seat, and float on float bowl cover. Leave gasket off for the moment.

Check float by placing 12 mm (.47″) float gauge under float. It must pass under entire float. If adjustment of float is necessary, reset by bending small tang that contacts float needle. Be careful to bend only tang and *not* arm or float body.

Inspect accelerator pump plunger, replace worn parts and install it in float bowl. Install float bowl cover gasket; slide accelerator pump lever over pivot on cover. Install accelerator pump rod and float bowl cover.

Use metering-rod gauge in place of metering rod (horizontal surface of gauge cut-out should just contact lower side of rod pivot with throttle closed tightly) and bend accelerator pump rod at lower angle, if necessary, to gain proper adjustment. See drawing. Remove gauge, place washer

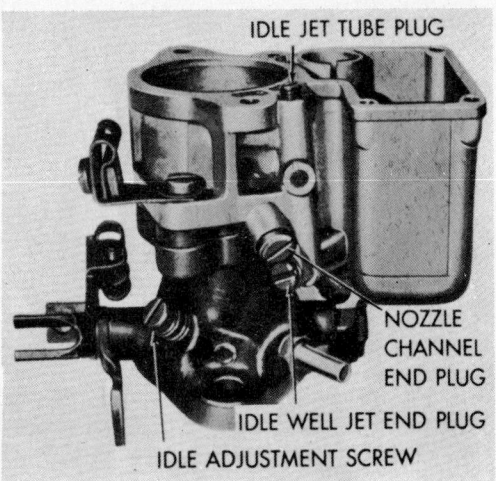

Carter Carburetor on 1964 and 1965 Kadetts

on metering rod and install rod. Secure with spring and complete connections.

Attach the choke to the fast-idle cam operating rod (angle down) and install air horn (float bowl cover) on carburetor body. No gasket is used between air horn and carburetor body.

Install inlet filter screen and cover. Be certain gasket is positioned under attaching bolt.

Check choke valve assembly for free operation and screw-in idle adjustment until it gently touches seat. Then back off ¾ turn for basic starting adjustment.

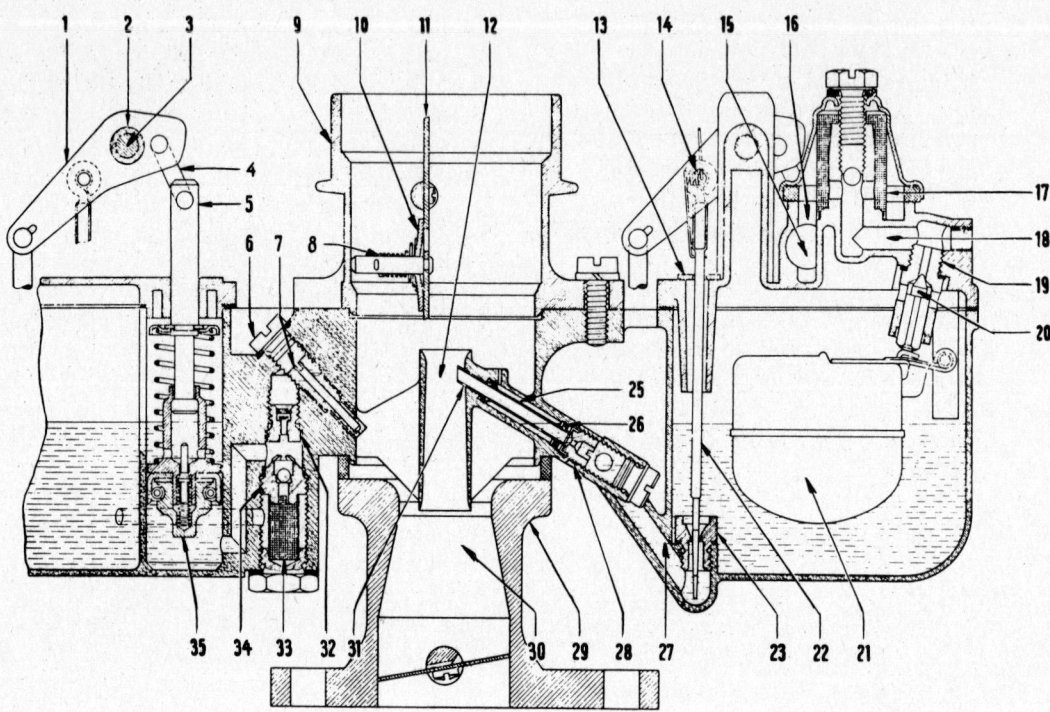

Cross-section of the Carter Carburetor

1. Accelerator pump lever
2. Bushing for accelerator pump lever
3. Pin for accelerator pump lever
4. Accelerator pump link
5. Accelerator pump plunger
6. Accelerator pump passage plug
7. Accelerator pump discharge jet
8. Choke valve spring
9. Air horn
10. Choke valve
11. Choke
12. Primary venturi
13. Metering rod dust washer
14. Metering rod retaining spring
15. Fuel inlet
16. Sediment bowl
17. Fuel inlet filter
18. Fuel passage
19. Float seat
20. Float needle
21. Float
22. Metering rod
23. Main metering jet
25. Nozzle channel
26. Nozzle
27. Nozzle jet passage
28. Nozzle jet
29. Carburetor throttle body
30. Main venturi
31. Bleed hole in nozzle
32. Accelerator pump outlet check valve
33. Strainer
34. Accelerator pump inlet check valve
35. Accelerator pump plunger with relief valve and plunger seat

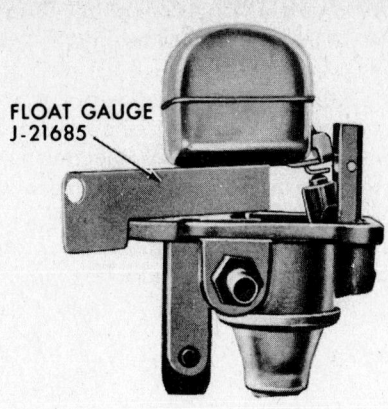

Float Adjustment of Carter Carburetor

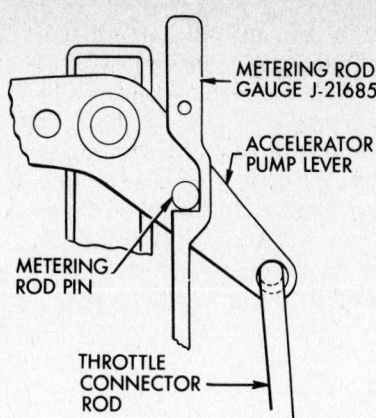

Metering rod Adjustment on Carter Carburetor

Solex Carburetor – 1.1 Liter Engine

Referring to illustration, remove the float chamber cover screws. Place cover on clean paper.

Disconnect the accelerator pump lever from its pump control rod and then unscrew the four corner screws to remove pump assembly.

Remove the idle mixture (volume) adjustment screw from throat below throttle butterfly. Remove throttle body from main housing by loosening screws underneath. Unscrew idle jet from housing.

Using next illustration, remove air correction jet (high speed air bleed) from throat. From the float chamber, lift out the float spring, the spindle (pin), and the float. Loosen venturi (choke tube) fastening screw and remove venturi. Take out main metering jet. Remove power circuit plug, if applicable.

From the float bowl cover (air horn), remove the float needle valve and washer, and the plug from accelerator-jet passage or the check-valve carrier, whichever applies. Pump nozzle is not removable on older Solex carburetors.

Assemble the carburetor as follows:

Referring to illustrations and using new gasketing and other soft parts where needed, place the washer, spring and pump-cover arm over the pump control rod and secure them with the cotter pin or locking nut provided. Adjust length to obtain injection quantity specifications.

If accelerator pump was taken apart, reassemble by placing spring in pump body lower section, and diaphragm assembly in pump cover, and by fastening both groups together with short center pump-cover screws. Hold pump arm steady while tightening screws to keep diaphragm from distorting. In assembling the carburetor, tighten all screws gradually (one and then another) as though using torque procedures.

Screw in plugs, jets and carriers. and idle adjusting screw(s). Screw in idle adjustment until it gently touches seat and then back off 2 turns for basic starting adjustment.

Screw in a *new* needle valve and seal ring with thickness of .040″. Other thicknesses will give an incorrect float level. Install float assembly with spring ends pressing against pivot pin (spindle). Put on float-chamber cover, using new gasket.

Check the radial play of the throttle plate (butterfly) shaft. Too much play allows air leakage and affects starting and idling. Replace throttle body if necessary.

Solex Carburetor – 1968 1.5 Liter Engine

Remove the carburetor cover and the float valve from the cover. Remove the enrichment system cover. Remove the injection tube, with the ball valve and spring, from the float chamber. Remove the float with the spindle and leaf spring. Remove the idle jets and the high speed jets. Remove the metering jets and the accelerator pump inlet ball valve, then the enrichment jet.

Remove the retainer ring from the pump connecting rod, then remove the accelerator pump. Remove the idle mixture adjusting screw and idle air adjusting screw from the throttle valve body.

Assemble the carburetor as follows:

Screw in the jets. *CAUTION: Never mix parts from the primary and secondary barrels.* With stop screw, adjust throttle valve of secondary barrel so that a gap of 0.002″ exists (this prevents jamming in the bore).

Screw in float needle valve, together with copper seal ring. Insert injection tube so that the bent end points into the center of the primary barrel. Install new gasket and carburetor cover. Arrange washers on vent valve, one on each side of the lever, and insert cotter pin. Fuel injection may be adjusted by adding or removing washers. Adding washers increases injection and removing them decreases injection. The lower vent valve spring should be compressed

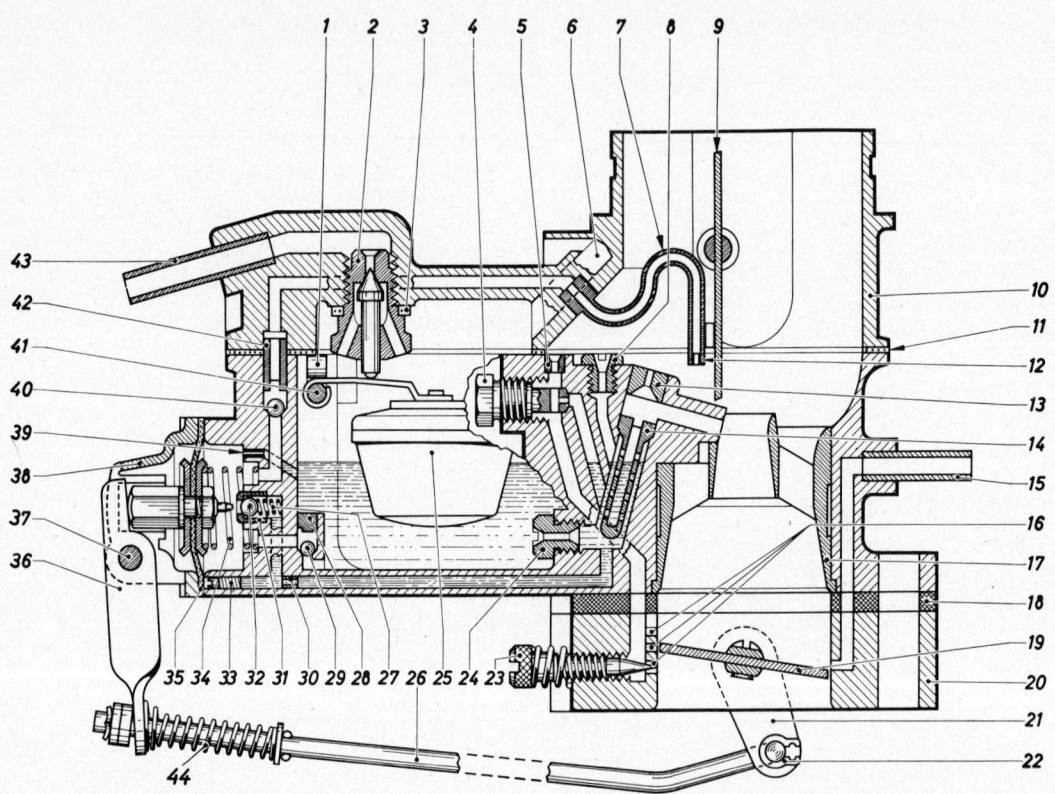

Cross-section of the Solex 35-PDSI Carburetor, used on early 1966 Kadetts

1. Leaf spring	16. Idle port and off-idle ports	31. Power by-pass valve seat
2. Float needle valve	17. Venturi	32. Power by-pass valve
3. Copper seal ring	18. Insulating flange gasket	33. Channel plug (power by-pass)
4. Idle jet	19. Throttle valve	34. Diaphragm return spring
5. Idle air bleed	20. Throttle body	35. Diaphragm
6. Bowl vent	21. Throttle lever	36. Pump lever
7. Accelerator pump nozzle	22. Clip	37. Pump lever shaft
9. High-speed bleeder	23. Idle mixture screw	38. Pump cover
9. Choke	24. Main jet	39. Fuel reduction jet to float
10. Air horn	25. Float	chamber
11. Air horn gasket	26. Pump rod	40. Fuel outlet ball valve
12. Pump nozzle jet	27. Thrust spring	41. Float arm pivot
13. Main nozzle bleeder	28. Fuel inlet ball stop	42. Ball valve sleeve
14. Main well tube	29. Pump inlet ball valve	43. Fuel inlet
15. Vacuum line fitting	30. Power by-pass restriction	44. Duration spring

¼" with the throttle valve completely closed.

Solex Carburetor — 1.9 Liter Engine

The carburetor used on the 1.9 liter engine is an automatic choke version of the carburetor used on the 1.5 liter engine. Disassemble the carburetor as follows:

Pry clamp ring from lower end of throttle lever to choke link. Pry off vacuum case connecting lever. Remove vent valve rod cotter pin, clamp ring, washers and thrust spring. Unscrew carburetor cover and remove float needle valve and seal ring. Remove vacuum diaphragm cover from choke housing and enrichment cover from carburetor cover. Unscrew retaining ring from automatic choke body and take off cover. Unscrew vacuum diaphragm case from carburetor cover and remove reduction jet.

Proceed to disassemble the carburetor in the same manner as the manual choke (1.5 liter) version.

If the brass bushings in the vacuum case are worn, the vacuum case must be replaced. While the carburetor is disassembled, the hot idle compensator may be checked by heating it in water until it opens. Opening temperature should be 194°F.

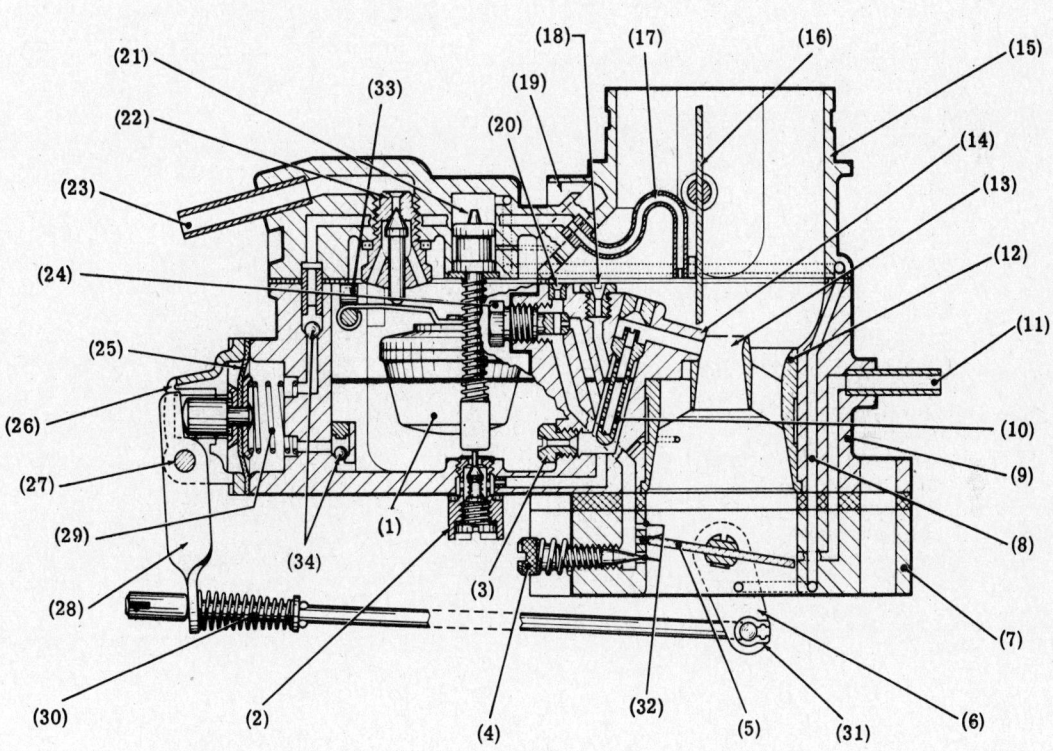

Cross-section of the Solex 35-PDSI-2 Carburetor, used on late 1966 and later Kadetts

 1. Float
 2. Power valve
 3. Main metering jet
 4. Idle mixture screw
 5. Throttle valve
 6. Throttle lever
 7. Throttle body
 8. Vacuum passage to power valve
 9. Float bowl
10. Main well tube
11. Vacuum fitting
12. Main venturi
13. Boost venturi
14. Main nozzle
15. Air horn
16. Choke
17. Accelerator pump nozzle
18. High speed bleeder
19. Bowl vent
20. Idle air bleed
21. Vacuum piston
22. Float needle valve
23. Fuel inlet
24. Idle jet
25. Pump diaphragm
26. Pump cover
27. Pump lever shaft
28. Diaphragm return spring
29. Pump lever
30. Duration spring
31. Clip
32. Idle and off-idle ports
33. Leaf spring
34. Check ball

Assemble the carburetor as follows:

Install vacuum diaphragm case assembly. Install gasket between automatic choke cover and automatic choke body. Install automatic choke cover so that the catch of the bi-metal spring is positioned on the bent end of the intermediate lever. Align and tighten the automatic choke cover. The valve should be nearly closed at room temperature.

A	Automatic choke cover (water temp)
B	Choke adjustment screws
C	Cover of choke control mechanism
D	Float chamber vent tube
E	Enrichment diaphragm chamber
F	Fuel inlet
G	Float cover screws
H	Idle jet
I	Accelerator pump screws
J	Vacuum pipe for distributor advance
K	Idle air (speed) adjusting screw
L	Accelerator pump adjustment
M	Connection for A.I.R.
N	Idle mixture (volume) adjustment
O	Throttle stop screw
P	Throttle lever
Q	Choke-throttle connecting rod
R	Venturi set screw
S	Secondary throttle control rod
T	Hot water hose connections
U	Enrichment air jet
V	Check valve carrier for accelerator pump
W	Injection nozzle for accelerator pump
X	Main nozzle bleed (emulsion tube underneath)
Y	Primary venturi (choke tube)
AA	Air channel of progression circuit for secondary venturi
BB	Control arm for outside ventilation channel to float bowl
CC	High speed air bleed (main air jet)
DD	Primary main metering jet (secondary main metering jet not visible)
EE	Fuel inlet to check valve
FF	Enrichment fuel inlet
GG	Control rod for the inside-outside ventilator for the float bowl
HH	Enrichment tube
II	Secondary-throttle diaphragm chamber
JJ	Vacuum-choke diaphragm chamber
KK	Choke valve
LL	Vacuum passage to enrichment chamber
MM	Needle valve carrier
NN	Float bowl ventilation passage

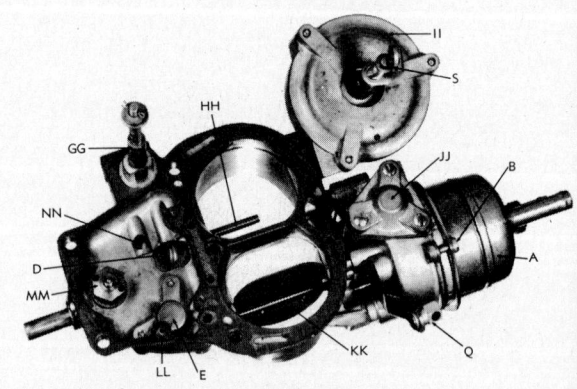

Solex 2-barrel carburetor, used on the 1.5 and 1.9 liter engines (automatic choke version)

Throttle and Choke Linkage

ADJUSTMENTS

A throttle linkage comprised of rods and ball studs is used. Adjustments are made using a threaded rod located adjacent to the floorboard in the engine compartment. The throttle should be adjusted so that it operates freely, and permits the throttle plate(s) of the carburetor(s) to close fully.

The choke cable is adjusted so that the choke plate will be fully open when the control is pushed in completely.

Exhaust System

Exhaust Pipe, Muffler and Tailpipe

REMOVAL AND INSTALLATION

Single Muffler System

To remove the exhaust pipe, unbolt the pipe from the manifold, loosen the exhaust pipe to muffler clamp, and pull the pipe from the muffler. To remove the muffler and tailpipe assembly, remove the muffler strap, the tailpipe support, and the O-rings. Prior to installation, check the condition of the O-rings, and replace if cracked or hardened.

Installation is the reverse of removal. NOTE: *Following the installation of the exhaust system, ensure that no part contacts the underside of the vehicle, to prevent excessive vibration and noise.*

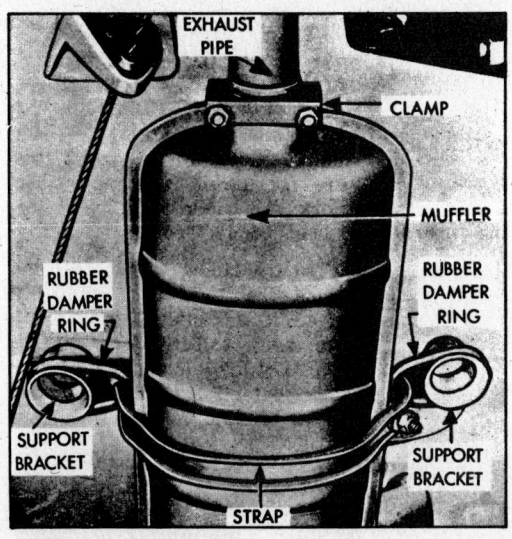

Muffler support assembly

Dual Muffler System

The dual muffler system is serviced in the same manner as the single muffler system. Each muffler may be removed separately. When removing only the rear muffler, the front muffler and exhaust pipe should be supported.

NOTE: *On Rallye models, the rear muffler and the dual tailpipes are a permanent assembly, and are serviced as a unit.*

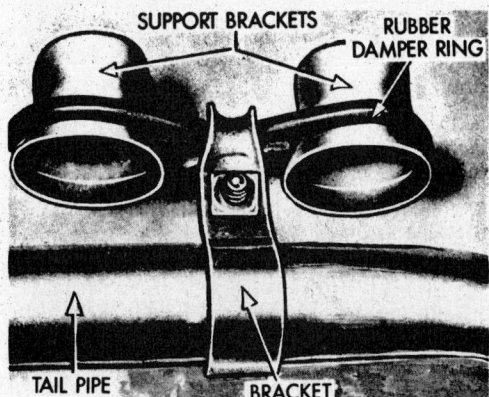

Tailpipe support assembly

Cooling System

Radiator

REMOVAL AND INSTALLATION

Remove the upper and lower hoses from the radiator and drain the coolant. Unbolt the lower attaching nut and slide the radiator upward and out of the vehicle.

Installation is the reverse of removal.

Water Pump

REMOVAL AND INSTALLATION

OHV Engines

Remove the lower radiator hose in order to drain coolant. Loosen the generator mounting bolts and remove the fan belt. Remove the fan mounting bolts and the fan, and all hoses from the water pump. Remove the water pump mounting bolts and remove the pump.

Install in the reverse order of removal.

CIH Engines

Remove all radiator hoses, drain the coolant, and remove the radiator and shroud. Loosen the generator mounting bolts and remove the fan belt. Unbolt and remove the fan. Remove the pulleys from the water pump shaft and the crankshaft. Disconnect all hoses from the water pump, remove the mounting bolts, and remove the water pump and gasket.

Install in the reverse order of removal.

SERVICE

All Engines

All Opel water pumps are of the non-serviceable type, and must be replaced if roughness or excessive play is evident in the bearing.

Thermostat

CAUTION: *The thermostat must be installed in the proper position, to permit the cooling system to function properly.*

Thermostat Usages

Year	Opening Temperature (degrees F.)	
	OHV Engines	CIH Engines
1964	180	—
1965	180	—
1966	180	—
1967	180	—
1968	180	190
1969	180	190
1970	189	189

Engine

Exhaust Emission Control

1968-69

The exhaust emission control system on the 1968-69 Opel limits the amount of unburned hydrocarbons and carbon monoxide discharged into the atmosphere and is separated from the PCV system. The air pump injects clean filtered air into each exhaust port immediately after the exhaust valve. This air allows the hot exhaust gases to burn any unburned fuel and carbon monoxide before it reaches the atmosphere. On sudden closing of the throttle, some of the air is fed into the intake manifold through the control valve to further reduce the pollutants. The entire system is designed to be relatively maintenance free, and internal parts of the pump are not available separately—if the pump is defective it must be replaced.

To see if the pump is operating, remove the hose at the check valve while the engine is idling and check for air discharge. If there is no air delivery, the pump is defective and should be replaced, and the check valve must be inspected as a possible source of trouble.

The check valve should be examined occasionally, and always checked when the pump is replaced, for defective operation. If the valve leaks, hot exhaust gases may damage the pump. Check the hose from the pump to the check valve—if it is hot while the engine is running, or brittle, remove the air cleaner and the hose. If the black rubber on the valve is burned at all, replace the valve and check the pump for damage.

If backfiring occurs when the throttle is closed at high speeds, or while shifting, the control valve is malfunctioning and must be replaced.

NOTE: *When cleaning the engine compartment, mask off the centrifugal fan filter located behind the pulley assembly.*

The design of the 1969 1.9 liter engine ignition system includes two vacuum control units, one advance and one retard. The advance unit is supplied with vacuum from the primary barrel of the carburetor just above the throttle valve. This port supplies no vacuum during idling or closed throttle deceleration, but supplies full vacuum when the throttle valve is opened enough to uncover this port.

The retard unit is supplied with intake manifold vacuum at all times. During idling and deceleration, when there is vacuum to the advance unit, the retard unit will cause the timing to be retarded 4-9°. During partial throttle operation, there is vacuum to the advance unit and the retard unit has no effect on timing.

1970

The 1970 exhaust emission control system is designed to reduce unburned hydrocarbons and carbon monoxide through the use of: (1) leaned out carburetion, (2) heated air, (3) mixture control on engine deceleration, and, (4) tuned spark timing. This system does away with the air pump and related equipment as used on earlier cars.

The exhaust manifold provides heated air for a stable intake temperature and accurate mixture by means of a "stove" mounted on the exhaust manifold. This heated air is drawn through the heated air pipe into the snorkel of the air cleaner. The temperature control air cleaner has a sensor that is designed to mix the heated air with colder outside air so the carburetor inlet air temperature averages about 115 ±20°F. This is done with the sensor, two doors in the air cleaner, and a vacuum motor. The motor operates the doors so that as one opens the other closes, mixing heated and cold air to keep temperature constant. The doors are spring loaded, so that when there is no vacuum from the engine the cold air door is open. When the engine is running, the amount of vacuum delivered to the motor is regulated by the sensor and the amount of vacuum available from the engine. Thus when underhood temperature rises above 135°F., the sensor allows no vacuum to the motor and the door for the heated air closes completely, admitting only cold air. When accelerating hard, manifold vacuum drops and the motor gets no vacuum regardless of the temperature, so again the cold air door is open. When decelerating, the manifold vacuum is high and, if the underhood temperature is less than 135°F., the cold air door closes and only heated air is admitted. The hot air door opens fully at 9″ of vacuum and the cold air door opens fully below 5″ of vacuum.

1.1 engines now use two carburetors, and a leaner idle is achieved because of more accurate air metering and better distribution. An additional air-fuel mixture valve is attached to the balance tube on the intake manifold. This allows an additional fuel-air mixture to be drawn into the intake manifold when decelerating, keeping combustion efficiency high and reducing the harmful emissions. This valve draws in the additional fuel-air mixture from the front carburetor on deceleration at engine speeds above 1,800 rpm to prevent backfiring.

The deceleration control mechanism of the mixture valve unit consists of an electromagnetic valve, a diaphragm valve and a deceleration mixture screw. The electromagnetic valve operates in relation to engine speed. Above 1,800 rpm, the valve is held open and below 1,800 rpm the valve is closed. The diaphragm valve is operated by intake manifold vacuum, and can operate only above 1,800 rpm, when the electromagnetic valve is open. Therefore, at speeds over 1,800 rpm, when there is high engine vacuum (e.g., during deceleration), additional fuel-air mixture is supplied to the intake manifold to limit emission of pollutants.

The ignition timing of the 1.1 liter engine incorporates a combined advance-retard unit. At engine idle, high engine vacuum acts to retard the timing, as does the vacuum developed during deceleration, to a maximum of 10° ATDC. During acceleration, and other periods of low engine vacuum, the familiar advance mechanism takes over to advance the timing as usual.

The 1970 1.9 liter engine ignition system has the two units combined into one—a double acting, diaphragm unit. It operates exactly as the two units do for the 1969 engine, and is similar to the unit on the 1.1 liter engine.

Engine Assembly

REMOVAL AND INSTALLATION

Kadett

Mark hood mounting location and remove engine hood. Remove radiator bolts and hoses and slide radiator upward and out of engine compartment.

Remove shift lever by placing shift in neutral, raising cover, and unscrewing lock cap. Push lock cap down and turn counterclockwise.

The Sport Coupe and Rallye use a snapring to retain the shift lever. Remove the ring using snap-ring pliers and lift out the shift lever.

Detach fuel line and throttle rod (from both carburetor and rear support). Disconnect battery cables, control cables and wires for carburetor, heater, starter, generator and distributor. Unfasten heater hoses and exhaust pipe from its manifold.

Raise car and support front and rear

with frame stands. Detach clutch cable from yoke and remove cable from transmission mount. CAUTION: *Do not twist cable.* Remove flywheel cover plate. Disconnect back-up light switch, speedometer cable, parking brake cable assembly and oil filter housing.

To remove 1964-65 Kadett engine and transmission, support universal-joint bracket with floor jack so it can be lowered, and attach lift equipment to engine from above. Mark position of U-joint bracket to underbody and remove four bracket-underbody bolts and lower driveshaft to its limit of travel. CAUTION: *Be careful of brake and gasoline lines when lowering driveshaft.* Slightly moving front driveshaft side to side, remove upper and then lower driveshaft to transmission bolts.

To remove 1966-70 Kadett engine and transmission, support transmission with floor jack so it can be lowered, and attach lift equipment to engine from above. Loosen transmission mount bolts. Mark mates of driveshaft U-joint and flange. Remove U-joint bolts, work the driveshaft slightly forward, lower rear end of shaft and slide it out toward rear.

When removing engine and transmission as unit on all models, unscrew rear engine-mount bolts (behind transmission). NOTE: *Although front engine rubber mounts are same size, the mounting bracket on starter side of engine is larger.* Lift out unit through engine compartment.

When removing engine without transmission, loosen bell - housing - to - engine bolts. Support transmission on floor jack and remove transmission mounting bolts; lower transmission to align it with the engine. Remove two lower bell housing bolts (attaching to crankcase) and, to prevent warping clutch disc, install guide pins (J-21722). Remove right side of front engine-mounting bolts for movement to work transmission and engine apart. Remove upper bell-housing bolts, and slide transmission back off guide pins and clutch spline while rotating transmission slightly if necessary. Remove front-mount bolts from other side of engine and lift out engine.

GT

The removal of the 1.1 liter engine from the GT is similar to removal from the Kadett, except that the engine must be supported by a hoist after removing all the usual items. With the engine supported, unbolt the transmission crossmember from the transmission and the frame, and the engine crossmember from the engine and frame. Pull the engine as far forward as possible and carefully lift the engine and transmission from the car.

Installation and removal of the 1.9 liter engine from the GT is possible only from the bottom of the car. The engine rests on a separate crossmember, not on the front suspension crossmember.

Disconnect all electrical and water connections to the engine. It is not necessary to remove the radiator. Remove all vacuum connections. Be sure to remove the T-fitting from the intake manifold before engine removal. Remove the choke cable, heater control cable, throttle linkage, heater hose and gearshift lever. Raise the vehicle at both front and rear and support on stands. Disconnect the speedometer cable from the transmission, the clutch cable, driveshaft, exhaust pipe at manifold, and engine ground strap. Lift the engine so the forward mounts are somewhat relieved of strain, then unbolt the transmission crossmember from the transmisssion and frame. Carefully lower the engine and transmission.

To install the engine, reverse the above procedure. Note that extreme care must be used when installing, until the crossmembers are properly secured to support the engine.

Remove sport shift lever by extracting snap rings under boot.

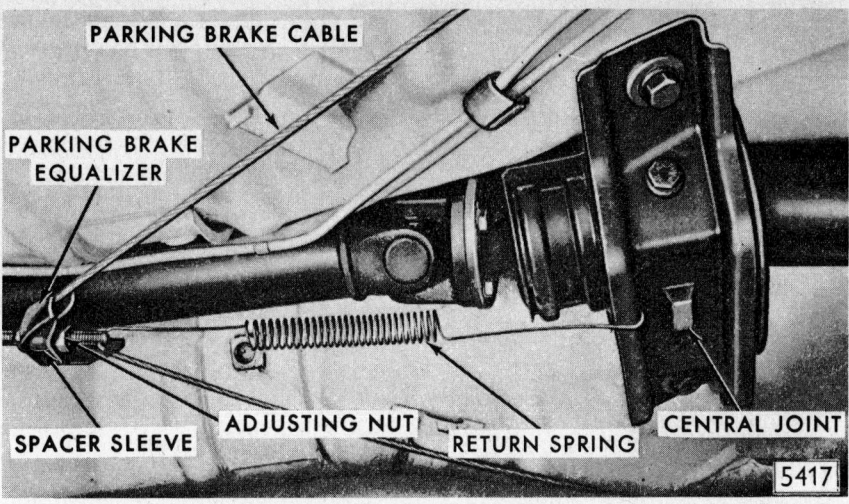

Mark mates of driveshaft joint flanges before removing bolts. Parking brake can be disassembled at the equalizer.

Manifolds

Intake Manifold

OHV Engines

OHV engine intake manifolds are held in place by three star-type bolts. The center bolt is accessible only after removing the carburetor.

Install manifold with new gasket and tighten star bolts beginning with center bolt. Install reinforcing bracket bolt. Place new O-ring into carburetor flange groove, position carburetor, and install spark plug wire support clamp under carburetor hold-down nut. Screw on and tighten carburetor hold-down nuts.

Exhaust Manifold

OHV Engines

Prior to removal of the exhaust manifold, the hose must be removed from the check valve on vehicles equipped with the A.I.R. emission control system. Following this, and on vehicles not equipped with this system, the manifold may be unbolted and removed. The injection nozzles may be removed from the manifold by removing the distributor tube pipe fittings, and lightly tapping the nozzles until they slide out.

Install in the reverse order of removal.

Center intake manifold bolt is located in manifold below carburetor.

Combination Manifold

CIH Engines

To remove the combination manifold, proceed as follows: Disconnect the throttle linkage at the carburetor, remove the fuel, vacuum and water hoses, unbolt the A.I.R. control valve, and remove the PCV valve from the rocker cover. The manifold and carburetor may now be removed as a unit.

When installing the manifold, tighten the two inner nuts until snug. Then continue to tighten in the specified sequence, tightening to 33 ft. lbs.

Cylinder Head

Removal and Installation

CAUTION: *Remove the cylinder head when it is cold, and in the reverse of the tightening sequence, to prevent warpage.*

OHV Engines

Remove the cylinder head as follows: Remove the distributor cap and spark plug wires, drain the radiator, remove the fan belt, and remove the intake and exhaust manifolds. Remove the rocker cover, the rocker nuts and ball seats, and the rocker arms and pushrods. On models equipped with A.I.R., the pump, pump hose, pump belt and control valve must also be removed. Remove the cylinder head using a star wrench.

Installation is the reverse of removal. When installing, coat both sides of the head gasket with graphite grease, and install with the side marked "oben" facing up.

CIH Engines

To remove the 1.5 and 1.9 liter CIH cylinder head, remove the distributor cap and spark plug wires, drain radiator, and remove the fan belt. If the cylinder head is being removed for gasket change only, there is no reason to remove the manifold assembly, otherwise remove the manifolds. Remove the rocker arm cover, rotate the camshaft so the recess in the shaft allows removal of all bolts. Use a 12mm. serrated drive to remove the 12 bolts. Remove the three bolts attaching plate to front of cylinder head, plastic screw from end of camshaft, and the three bolts attaching the camshaft sprocket to the camshaft. Slide the sprocket off the camshaft and remove the cylinder head.

To install the 1.5 and 1.9 liter CIH engines cylinder head, reverse the removal procedure, making sure to install the coolant passage gasket in the timing case. Tighten the cylinder head bolts to 72 ft. lbs. Slide the camshaft sprocket, with chain, onto camshaft and guide pin and fasten with bolts. Install plastic adjusting screw and close front access hole. Check cam-

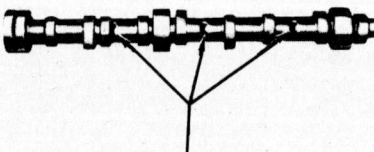

RECESSES VERTICAL FOR REMOVAL OF LEFT ROW OF CYLINDER HEAD BOLTS

Recesses in camshaft—CIH engines.

shaft end clearance between the cover and the plastic screw—if it exceeds 0.004-0.008", readjust cover with a suitable drift.

Valve Train

VALVE ADJUSTMENT

Adjust valves cold. Set each piston to TDC compression stroke and adjust intake valve to .008" lash and exhaust valve to .012" lash on pushrod engines.

Adjust valve clearance with engine *at operating temperature* (hot) and at slow idle to:

Pushrod intake valve	.006"
Pushrod exhaust valve	.010"
CIH intake and exhaust valves	.012"

It is best to adjust valve clearances immediately after road test.

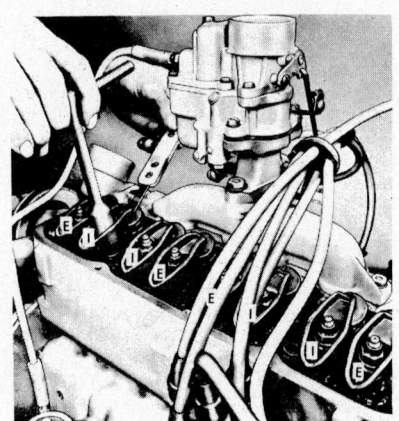

Adjusting Valve Clearance

SERVICE

To service the valve train, remove the cylinder head and support it at its ends with blocks of wood on a clean surface. NOTE: *Do not rest CIH cylinder head directly on its gasket surface with the valves and camshaft installed.* Remove the rocker nuts, rocker balls, and rocker arms.

Using valve spring compressor (J-8062) remove keys (keepers), caps and springs. When using scrapers or wire brushes for removing carbon, avoid scratching valve seats and valve faces. Cut a chisel from hardwood for chipping carbon from the cylinder chamber. The wood is less likely to score the metal surfaces.

Inspect valve guides. Worn or pitted

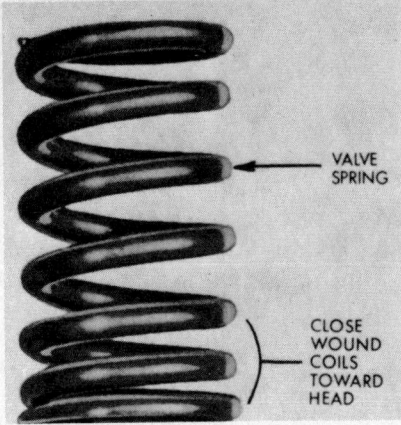

Install valve springs with closely wound coils toward the cylinder head.

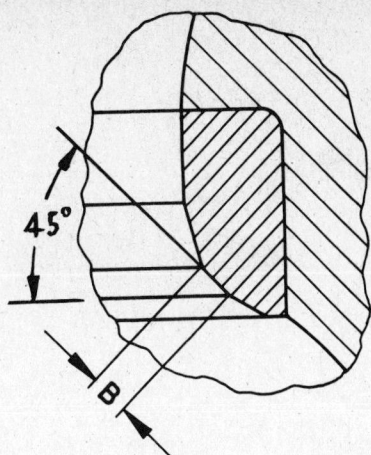

Valve Seat Surfaces

guides can be reamed to accept oversize valves. Valves are marked near stem. (NOTE: Always check valve stem diameter since oversize valves, on occasion, are used in production.)

Grind valve seats to 45° angle. Seat width should be:

Valve	Seat width
Intake	.050" to .060"
Exhaust	.065" to .075"

Resurface valves to 44°—inlet and exhaust.

NOTE: *CIH engines utilize aluminum coated intake valve faces. These valves must not be resurfaced or lapped with grinding compound.*

Correct the valve seat width using a 25° (OHV engines) or 30° (CIH engines) cutting tool. The top of the valve seat on OHV engines should be at least .040" (intake) or .060" (exhaust) above the clean combustion chamber.

Lube with engine oil and install valves, valve springs (with closely wound coils toward cylinder head), caps and cap retainers.

Camshaft and Timing Chain

TIMING COVER REMOVAL AND INSTALLATION

OHV Engines

Having removed fan belt, unscrew crankshaft pulley bolt and work pulley off by hand. If pulley sticks, tap against rear of pulley with rubber hammer. Remove timing chain cover and oil slinger (deflector).

Install in the reverse order of removal.

CIH Engines

Remove the engine mounting nuts, raise the engine, and support the engine on blocks of wood (see illustration). Unbolt and remove the radiator and shroud assembly. Dismount the generator and remove the generator mounting brackets. Remove the A.I.R. pump drive belt, pump and bracket. Remove the fuel pump, the distributor, and the timing chain tensioner assembly. Unbolt and remove the crankshaft pulley and remove the water pump. Drain and lower the oil pan, remove the timing cover bolts (NOTE: *the bolt in the water pump housing must be removed before the timing cover can be removed*), and remove the timing cover.

Install in the reverse order of removal.

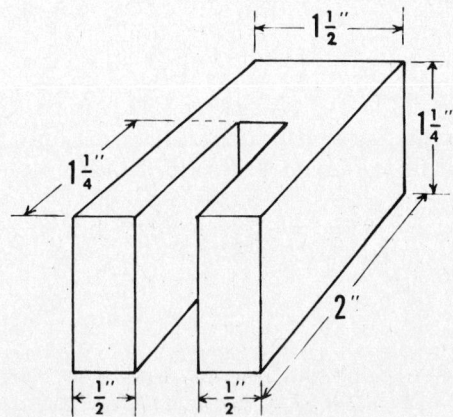

Block of wood used to raise engine

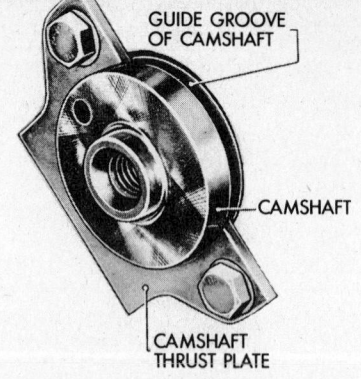

Punch out outer-seal retainer and cork seal but do not remove inner-seal retainer.

Camshaft thrust plate mounts in guide groove with closed side facing crankshaft.

Oil Seal Replacement

OHV Engines

If replacing crankshaft oil seal in timing chain cover, support chain cover securely on bench and punch out *outer*-seal retainer and cork seal from cover. (CAUTION: Do not remove *inner*-seal retainer.)

Install new seal through front of cover. Drive flush with cover carefully, to avoid distortion to cover.

CIH Engines

To replace the timing cover oil seal with the cover installed, remove all V-belts, unbolt and remove the crankshaft pulley, and pry out the oil seal using a screwdriver. Lubricate the new seal, and press it into the timing cover. Reinstall the crankshaft pulley, and torque the bolt to 72 ft. lbs.

Camshaft Removal and Installation

OHV Engines

The engine must be out of car and inverted to remove camshaft and bearings. After taking off rocker assemblies and timing chain, remove distributor, invert engine, and take off camshaft thrust plate, camshaft and engine front plate. If lifters are to be removed, oil pan must be off.

Liberally prelube the camshaft with STP and insert it into the crankcase. Place a new paper gasket on engine front plate and install it on the crankcase.

Install camshaft in crankcase and camshaft thrust plate into guide groove in

front camshaft journal so that closed side of plate is facing crankshaft. Torque bolt to 60 in.-lb.

CIH Engines

Remove the cylinder head, loosen the self-locking retaining nuts and swing the rocker arms off the lifters. Remove the lifters and place in a suitable holding fixture so that they can be replaced in their original positions. Remove the covers from access holes on the back and left of the head. Support the camshaft so it will not damage the bearing surfaces, and remove from the front of the head. The 1.9 liter engine camshafts are identified by the bead or red spot between the second and third exhaust cams on the camshaft.

To install, reverse removal procedure,

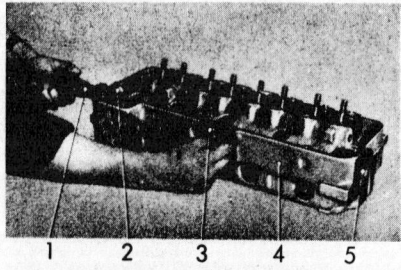

Camshaft removal—CIH engines.

1. Camshaft
2. Front access hole
3. Lateral access hole
4. Cylinder head
5. Rear access hole

lubricating the camshaft liberally with STP and taking care not to damage the bearing surfaces.

TIMING CHAIN TENSIONER REMOVAL AND INSTALLATION

OHV Engines

Prior to removal of the timing chain tensioner, the timing cover must be removed.

Timing-chain tensioner is spring loaded. To remove, hold tensioner by its slipper and body so parts won't fly, and unbolt assembly.

Timing chain tensioner should be checked for wear (defective parts are not available separately) before reassembly. Install compression spring and adjusting piston into plunger sleeve with guide pin fitted into helical slot of adjusting piston.

With ⅛″ Allen wrench, turn adjusting piston clockwise into plunger sleeve until guide pin emerges on top of helical slot thereby blocking piston (for installation). Oil the sliding parts, slip plunger sleeve into tensioner body, and bolt body with nut and lockwasher to engine housing.

Remove end plug and lock plate from timing chain tensioner. Through end-plug hole insert ⅛″ Allen wrench and release piston. The tensioner now exerts proper tension and no further manual adjustment is required. Install tensioner end plug using ⁷⁄₁₆″ wrench together with new lock plate and secure plug by bending up tab.

CIH Engines

The timing chain tensioner is removed and installed by threading the assembly in and out of the left side of the timing cover. The tensioner is adjusted automatically depending on engine oil pressure, therefore no manual adjustment is provided.

TIMING CHAIN REMOVAL AND INSTALLATION

OHV Engines

Prior to the removal of the timing chain, the timing cover and the timing chain tensioner must be removed.

Position sprockets into chain links (noting that sprocket punch marks and painted edge of chain face *outward*) and assemble on shafts. If new chain is required, chain and sprockets must be replaced as a set.

If timing chain is to be reused, mark the forward side with paint so it can be installed correctly. The painted edge must face outward so chain will turn in the same direction as before.

Remove camshaft sprocket retaining bolt and special washer. Crankshaft is keyed; camshaft has lock pin. Pull off camshaft and crankshaft sprocket together with timing chain.

When installing timing chain on pushrod engines, place crankshaft sprocket (19 teeth) and camshaft sprocket (38 teeth) on their shafts with punch marks facing outward. Turn both shafts so that sprocket punch marks face each other directly. Proper alignment of sprockets assures perfect valve timing.

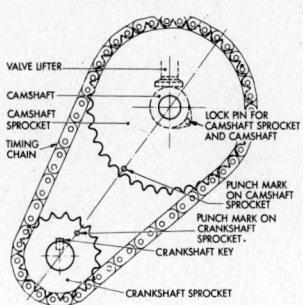

Timing chain installation—OHV engines

CIH Engines

In order to remove the timing chain, all ancillaries, the cylinder head, the crankshaft pulley, and the timing case cover must be removed. If the chain is to be reused, mark it for identification, so that it may be installed in the original position. Unbolt the pulley from the camshaft, and slide the pulleys and the chain from the camshaft and crankshaft.

Reinstall timing chain by reversing the

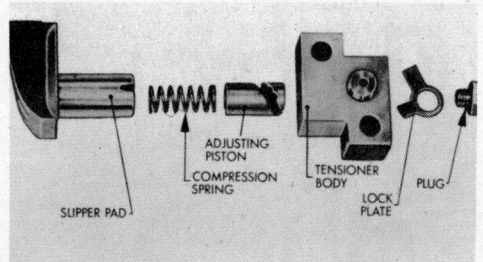

Chain tensioner—OHV engines

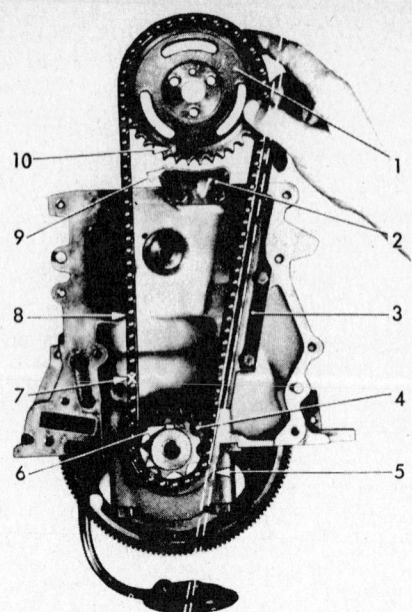

Timing chain installation—CIH engines

1. Camshaft sprocket
2. Camshaft sprocket support
3. Long damper block
4. Crankshaft sprocket
5. Chain and damper block parallel
6. Crankshaft key
7. Paint mark on front of timing chain
8. Timing chain
9. Mark on camshaft sprocket support
10. Mark on camshaft sprocket

removal procedure, noting the following procedures. Clean and check all parts for wear and replace as necessary. The sprockets are replaced in sets only, although the chain may be replaced without having to use new sprockets.

Turn the crankshaft so the key for the sprocket is on top and vertical. Assemble the chain and camshaft sprocket, then place the chain on the crankshaft sprocket. Make sure the front of the chain, marked with paint, is facing forward, and that it moves in the original direction if using the original chain.

Make sure that the camshaft sprocket mark aligns with the mark on the support, and that the chain is parallel with the damper block. At this time, the No. 1 and No. 4 pistons will be at TDC, and the timing mark on the flywheel and cylinder block will coincide. Recheck after sprocket has been fixed to camshaft—the valves for the No. 1 cylinder must be closed at this time.

Engine Lubrication

SYSTEM TYPE

OHV Engines

The gear-type oil pump draws oil through a fine mesh screen into pump housing and then forces it through the full-flow type oil filter into the main oil gallery. From this area oil is fed to all crankshaft and camshaft bearings. Oil thrown off the crankshaft lubricates the cylinder walls. The rest of the oil is fed to the cylinder head oil gallery where it lubricates the valve mechanism.

A by-pass valve in the oil filter mount prevents the oil supply from being blocked by a clogged filter element.

CIH Engines

The gear type pump draws oil, through a fine mesh screen and a passage in the block, into the pump housing, cast integral with the timing cover. Oil is then pumped through a full flow filter and into the main gallery, which lubricates the crankshaft, the connecting rods, and the cylinder walls through a spurt hole on the connecting rod, and into a branch which lubricates the valve train.

A bypass and a relief valve are provided to prevent oil blockage in the filter and excessive oil pressure.

OIL PAN REMOVAL AND INSTALLATION

Kadett

In order to remove the oil pan from the Kadett, the front suspension must be removed as an assembly (see Suspension Section). Support the engine slightly to remove weight from the engine mounts. Disconnect the clutch cable at the pivot arm. Remove the crossmember to frame and body bolts and the engine mount bolts, and remove the crossmember. The oil pan bolts and oil pan may now be removed.

Install oil pan gasket by placing gasket end-tabs in slots in front and rear main bearing caps. Install small gasket strips in grooves in front and rear main bearing caps. Torque oil pan bolts to 5 ft-lbs. NOTE: *Flat washers are used on oil pan attaching bolts adjacent to rear main bearing.*

GT

To remove the oil pan from the 1.1 liter GT engine, with the engine in the chassis, support the engine with a suitable sling, and lift slightly to remove weight from the mount. Disconnect the clutch cable at the pivot arm. Remove the crossmember to engine and crossmember to frame bolts, then the crossmember itself. Remove the oil pan.

To remove the oil pan from the 1.9 liter GT engine, with the engine in the chassis, support the engine with Opel tool J-23375 or equivalent. Install the tool by removing upper engine mount nut and installing the fixture, then replacing and tightening the nut. The engine is now supported by the frame. The front suspension need not be removed. Remove the front engine support crossmember, then the oil pan.

Installation is the reverse of removal.

Oil Pump Service

OHV Engines

With oil pan off, remove two pump-mount star bolts (J-21736 wrench), oil pump, gasket, oil pump cover and screen assembly. Slide out pump gears. Remove pressure-relief-valve plug, gasket, relief valve, spring and check ball. See exploded view.

Wash all parts thoroughly and inspect relief valve for wear or scoring. Check relief-valve spring to see that it is not worn or collapsed. Thoroughly clean pickup screen.

Install oil pump gears in housing. Using feeler gauge check gear lash between gears. Clearance must be .004"-.008". Place straight edge over gears. Since gears extend above housing, gap between housing and straight edge should be .002"-.004".

Reassemble pump parts and (using new gasket) install pump cover and screen assembly on oil pump body.

Check oil pump for smooth operation, fill housing with engine oil and install pump (with new gasket) on crankcase. Torque bolts to 15 ft.-lbs.

CIH engines

The oil pump is cast integrally with the timing cover, adjacent to the oil filter. The pump gears may be removed by removing the six pump cover mounting bolts. Otherwise, pump service is the same as OHV engine pump service. NOTE: *The oil pan must be removed to gain access to the screen assembly.*

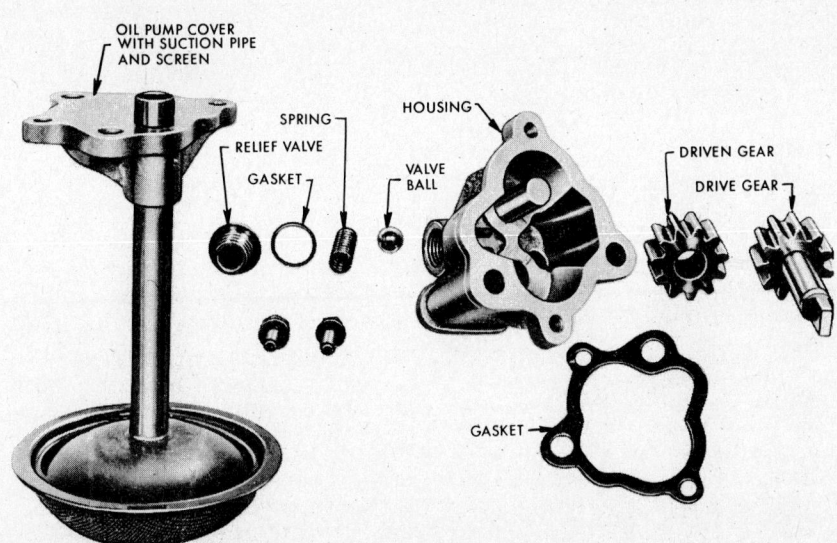

Exploded view of oil pump—OHV engines

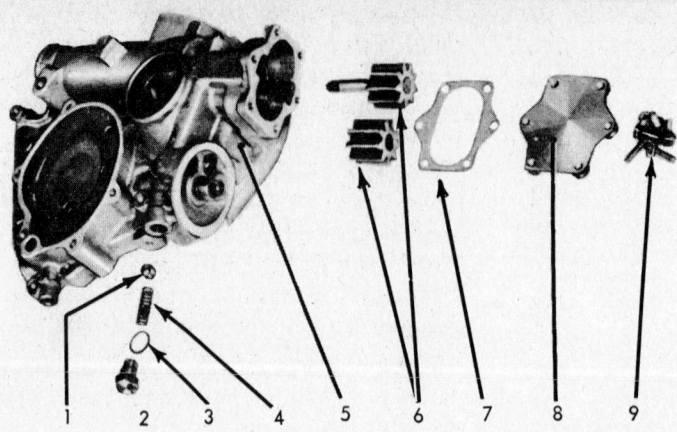

1. By-pass valve ball
2. Plug, by-pass valve
3. Gasket
4. Spring
5. Timing case
6. Oil pump gears
7. Cover gasket
8. Cover
9. Cover attaching screws

Exploded view of oil pump—CIH engines

Pistons and Connecting Rods

POSITIONING

The pistons and connecting rods are installed as shown below.

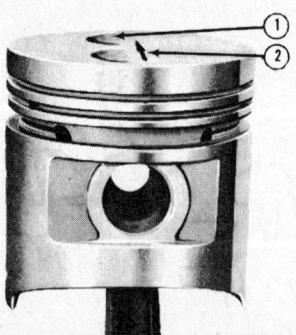

1. NOTCH IN PISTON HEAD FOR VALVES
2. RUBBER STAMPED ARROW POINTING TOWARD THE FRONT
3. NOTCH IN CONNECTING ROD CAP POINTING TOWARD THE REAR

OHV engines

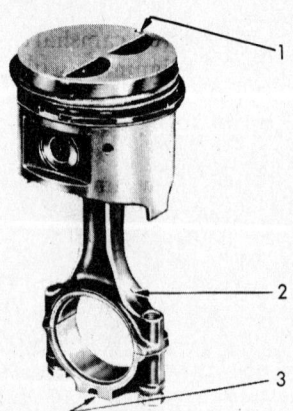

1. NOTCH IN PISTON HEAD POINTING TOWARD THE FRONT
2. OIL HOLE IN CONNECTING ROD POINTING TOWARD THE RIGHT (MANIFOLD SIDE)
3. NOTCH IN CONNECTING ROD CAP POINTING TOWARD THE REAR

CIH engines

PISTON RINGS

The piston rings are installed on all engines as shown below.

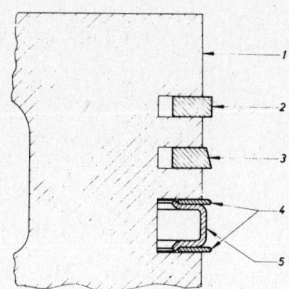

1. PISTON
2. NO. 1 COMPRESSION RING – INSTALLED WITH EITHER SIDE UP.
3. NO. 2 COMPRESSION RING – INSTALLED WITH "TOP" MARKING TOWARDS THE TOP.
4. UPPER AND LOWER STEEL BAND RING – INSTALLED WITH EITHER SIDE UP.
5. INTERMEDIATED RING – INSTALLED WITH EITHER SIDE UP.

Arrangement of piston rings

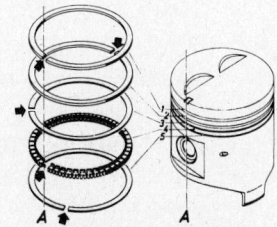

1. NO. 1 COMPRESSION – GAP IN FRONT
2. NO. 2 COMPRESSION – GAP IN REAR
3. UPPER STEEL BAND – 1 - 2 IN. TOWARDS THE LEFT OF INTERMEDIATE RING GAP.
4. INTERMEDIATE RING – GAP IN FRONT
5. LOWER STEEL BAND – 1 - 2 IN. TOWARDS THE RIGHT OF INTERMEDIATE RING GAP.
"A" VERTICAL LINE FOR PISTON AND RINGS, FRONT

Location of ring gaps.

Clutch and Transmission

Clutch Linkage Adjustment

OHV ENGINES

Clutch pedal free play (pedal lash) must be adjusted occasionally to compensate for normal wear of the clutch facings. As the driven plate (clutch disc) wears thinner, pedal free play decreases.
Clutch pedal free play should measure ¾" to 1" (20-25 mm) from the released-pedal rest point to start of clutch disengagement (see diagram).

Adjust free play at clutch housing by loosening clutch cable lock nut at release fork and screw ball-stud nut along cable shaft until proper play is reached. Hold hexagon end of cable, to permit loosening of locknut and turning of ball stud.

CIH ENGINES

Clutch pedal free play should be adjusted to between ¾ and 1¼", by turning the ball stud located on the right side of the clutch housing. Cable length is not adjustable. Turning the ball stud clockwise decreases, and counterclockwise increases pedal travel.

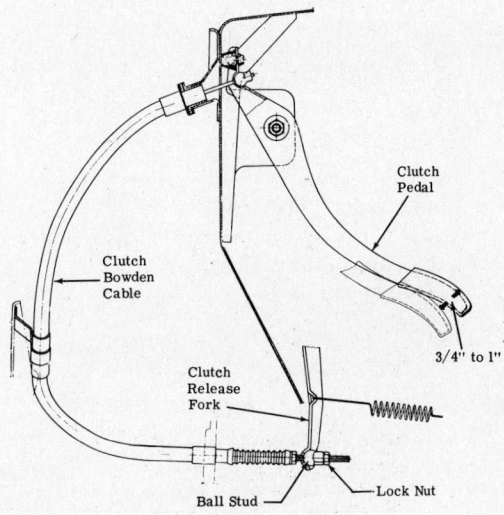

Clutch free play adjustment—OHV engines

Shift Linkage Adjustment

MANUAL TRANSMISSIONS

The shift linkage is attached directly to the transmisssion and no linkage adjustment is possible.

AUTOMATIC TRANSMISSION

Remove the lock clip holding the control rod to the selector lever. Remove the control rod from the selector lever and place both the selector lever and the transmission shift lever in the drive position. Adjust the control rod by turning, until it slides freely over the pin on the selector lever, and install the lock clip.

Transmission Kick-down Valve

Opel models equipped with an automatic transmission use a kick-down valve, to facilitate automatic downshifting, controlled by the accelerator. This linkage is adjusted as follows:

With the accelerator linkage in full throttle position, the detent ball must be resting firmly against the lever. To adjust the cable, loosen and tighten upper and lower adjusting nuts as necessary.

To check the adjustment, grasp the linkage and pull the detent cable through the detent. If about ⅜" of travel is obtained between slide linkage and stops on linkage rod, and a noticeable resistance is felt due to the detent valve's being pulled open, correct adjustment has been made.

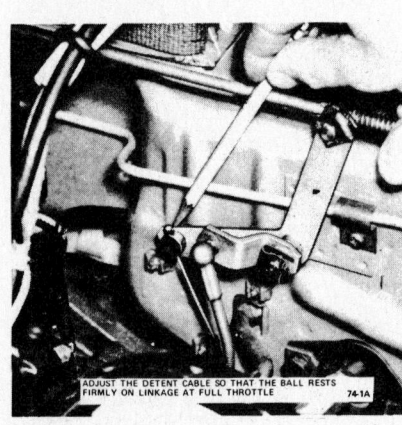

Transmission kick-down adjustment

Clutch Removal and Installation
OHV ENGINES

Remove the transmission from the vehicle (see procedure below). Check for assembly alignment marks on the clutch cover flange and flywheel. If no marks are present, punch or scribe marks for installation purposes. Loosen the four clutch cover retaining bolts one turn at a time, and remove the pressure plate and driven disc.

Hold the clutch disc and pressure plate against the flywheel, and insert a clutch pilot tool. Align the mating marks on the flywheel and clutch cover (if using the original pressure plate) and tighten the four retaining bolts evenly and gradually to 15 ft. lbs. Install the transmission (see below).

CIH ENGINES

Remove the transmission from the vehicle (see procedure below). Unbolt the exhaust pipe from the exhaust manifold. Disconnect the clutch return spring and cable from the clutch fork, and unbolt the starter from the flywheel housing. Remove the clutch support to bellhousing bolts, back out the clutch support to cylinder block bolts, and swing support downward. Remove the bellhousing lower cover and the bellhousing. If the pressure plate assembly is to be reused, ensure that alignment marks are present on the flywheel and the clutch cover flange. Loosen the clutch cover retaining bolts one turn at a time until spring pressure is released, and remove the pressure plate and driven disc.

Installation is the reverse of removal. When installing the clutch onto the flywheel, use a pilot tool, to ensure proper alignment of the driven disc, and torque the cover bolts gradually to avoid distortion.

Manual Transmission

REMOVAL AND INSTALLATION

All Models

Remove the air cleaner and throttle rod from the engine. Remove the standard shift lever by pulling up the boot, pushing the lock cap down and turning it counterclockwise. The sport shift lever is removed by removing the boot, and removing the snapring that retains the lever. Disconnect the clutch cable from the clutch fork, the speedometer cable from the speedometer drive housing, and the wires from the back-up lamp switch. Unhook the parking brake cable return spring, and remove the cable adjusting nut, equalizer, and spacer. Mark the relative positions of the driveshaft U-joint flange and the drive pinion extension shaft flange at the central joint, support the vehicle at its rear jack brackets, loosen the bolt locks and remove the flange bolts. Work the driveshaft slightly forward, swing the end of the shaft down, and remove the shaft and thrust spring. NOTE: *Plug the end of the transmission to prevent fluid loss.*

Remove the lower bolt on each side of the crankcase, and install guide pins to prevent clutch disc warpage when removing the transmission. Support the engine from below, and unbolt the right engine mount. Remove one rear transmission mounting bolt, loosen the other, and raise the front of the engine to provide clearance for removal of the transmission. Remove the remaining transmission to crankcase bolts, and the rear mounting bolt, and slide the transmission back and out of the vehicle.

Installation is the reverse of removal.

Automatic Transmission

REMOVAL AND INSTALLATION

NOTE: *When removing or installing the automatic transmission, ensure that the front of the transmission is always above the rear of the transmission, to prevent the converter from falling out.*

Kadett

From the top of the transmission, before the car is raised, disconnect the battery. Remove 2 upper housing bolts, remove the filler tube and converter housing bolt. On the 1.9 liter engine, remove the two upper starter bolts.

Raise the car and remove the flywheel cover pan. Disconnect the exhaust system at exhaust manifold and remove the driveshaft. Drain the oil pan, loosen the transmission support, place a jack under the transmission, and remove the support. Lower the transmission enough to remove the speedometer cable and modulator vacuum line. Remove the detent cable and linkage at selector lever or transmission. Mark the flywheel and converter for assembly and remove flywheel-to-converter bolts. Remove the converter housing-to-engine bolts. Pry the transmission from the engine. Disconnect the cooler lines. Move the transmission back and install a clamping tool to hold converter. Lower transmission to bench.

Installation is the reverse of removal. When installing, ensure that the marks on the flywheel and the converter align properly.

GT

To remove the transmission from the GT, disconnect the battery and pull the throttle control rod off the ball pin. Raise the car. Remove the heat shield from the right side and the exhaust pipe. Remove the driveshaft and detach rear engine support from

the transmission crossmember. Support the transmission with a jack.

Unscrew the transmission crossmember from side members. Lower transmission as far as possible then drain the oil. Detach selector rod from ball pin at the outer transmission selector lever. Remove the cooler lines and pull vacuum line from modulator. Detach detent cable from accelerator pedal and unscrew detent cable from transmission. Remove speedometer cable, then unscrew engine support brackets from torque converter housing. Slacken only the front attaching bolt. Remove the torque converter housing cover plate and mark flex plate and converter for assembly.

Unscrew the three torque converter-to-flex plate attaching bolts. Pry the transmission loose from the engine. Move transmission back and insert a clamping tool to hold converter, then lower transmission to bench.

Installation is the reverse of removal. When installing, rotate the converter, to ensure that the marks on the flex plate and the converter align properly.

Manual Transmission

OVERHAUL

OHV Engines

Remove transmission case cover (6 bolts) that supports shift housing and discard the gasket. Invert transmission to drain oil. Using suitable pliers, remove reverse gear stop spring from transmission case cover.

To remove speedometer driven gear, pry cover out of upper right side of rear bearing retainer (speedometer drive housing). Using small punch, push speedometer driven gear out through upper opening and discard speedometer gear shaft seal.

Shift shafts, forks and detents are removed through top of case. Take the six retaining snap rings from shift shafts (located front and rear of shift forks and shift head). Pull the three detent (lock-ball) retaining plugs out, and remove the springs and balls.

(NOTE: For the following steps, be certain the shift shafts are in neutral position. This assures that the interlock pins at the rear of the shafts will not interfere with shaft removal.)

1. Remove lower attaching bolt of rear-

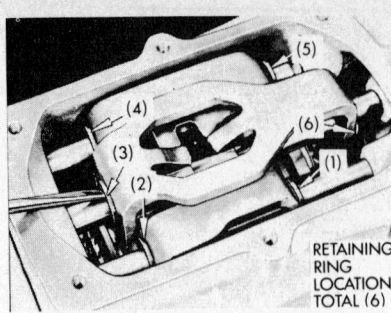

Removing Snap-rings from Shafts

Shift head is center assembly; forks are on shafts to either side of head.

bearing retainer and rotate bearing retainer until rear of 1st and 2nd speed (middle) shift shaft is exposed. Use brass drift to drive shaft and end plug forward out of case.

(CAUTION: During shaft removal or replacement, be certain that the spring washer on each shaft does not fall into retaining ring groove and block shaft movement, damaging shaft or washer.)

2. Rotate rear-bearing retainer until a hole lines up with 3rd and 4th speed shifter shaft and drive the shaft out toward the front. Remove spring washers and shaft end plugs.

3. Rotate rear bearing retainer until a hole lines up with the reverse-gear shifter shaft and drive the shaft out towards the front.

4. Lift out shift forks, shift head and reverse lever.

If removing and disassembling mainshaft assembly with rear-bearing retainer, mark with paint the relative position of 3rd- and 4th-speed clutch sleeve and 1st-and-2nd-speed sliding gear as well as corresponding synchronizer rings and clutch hubs. Marks are made to assure the same tooth or spline contact on reassembly.

Turn rear-bearing retainer so that hole for countergear shaft is accessible. Drive countergear shaft out of transmission case

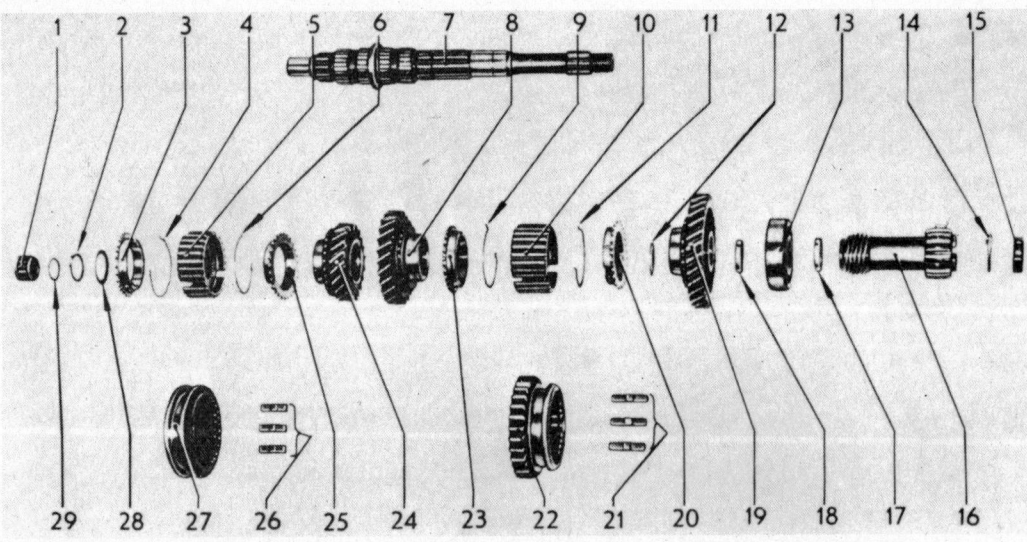

Mainshaft and component parts—Transmission used with OHV engines.

1. Needle bearing assembly
2. Snap ring
3. 4th-speed synchronizer ring
4. Clutch key spring
5. 3rd-and-4th-speed clutch hub
6. Clutch key spring
7. Mainshaft
8. 2nd-speed gear
9. Clutch key spring
10. 1st-and-2nd-speed clutch hub
11. Clutch key spring
12. Snap ring
13. Ball bearing
14. Lock plate
15. Nut
16. Mainshaft sleeve
17. Spacer between ball bearing and sleeve
18. Spacer between bearing and 1st-speed gear
19. 1st-speed gear
20. 1st-speed synchronizer ring
21. Keys for 1st-and-2nd-speed sliding gear
22. 1st-and-2nd-speed sliding gear
23. 2nd-speed synchronizer ring
24. 3rd-speed gear
25. 3rd-speed synchronizer ring
26. Keys for 3rd-and-4th-speed clutch sleeve
27. 3rd-and-4th-speed clutch sleeve
28. Spring washer
29. Thrust ring

toward the rear. Use caution with lock ball on shaft. Pull mainshaft assembly and rear-bearing retainer out of transmission case together. Slide 3rd-and-4th speed clutch sleeve off clutch hub and remove keys and front clutch key spring.

Clamp mainshaft assembly into a vise having soft jaws and remove mainshaft nut and lockplate. Press from mainshaft, the mainshaft ball bearing, the rear-bearing retainer, two spacers, the mainshaft sleeve, and 1st-speed gear. Slide 1st-and-2nd-

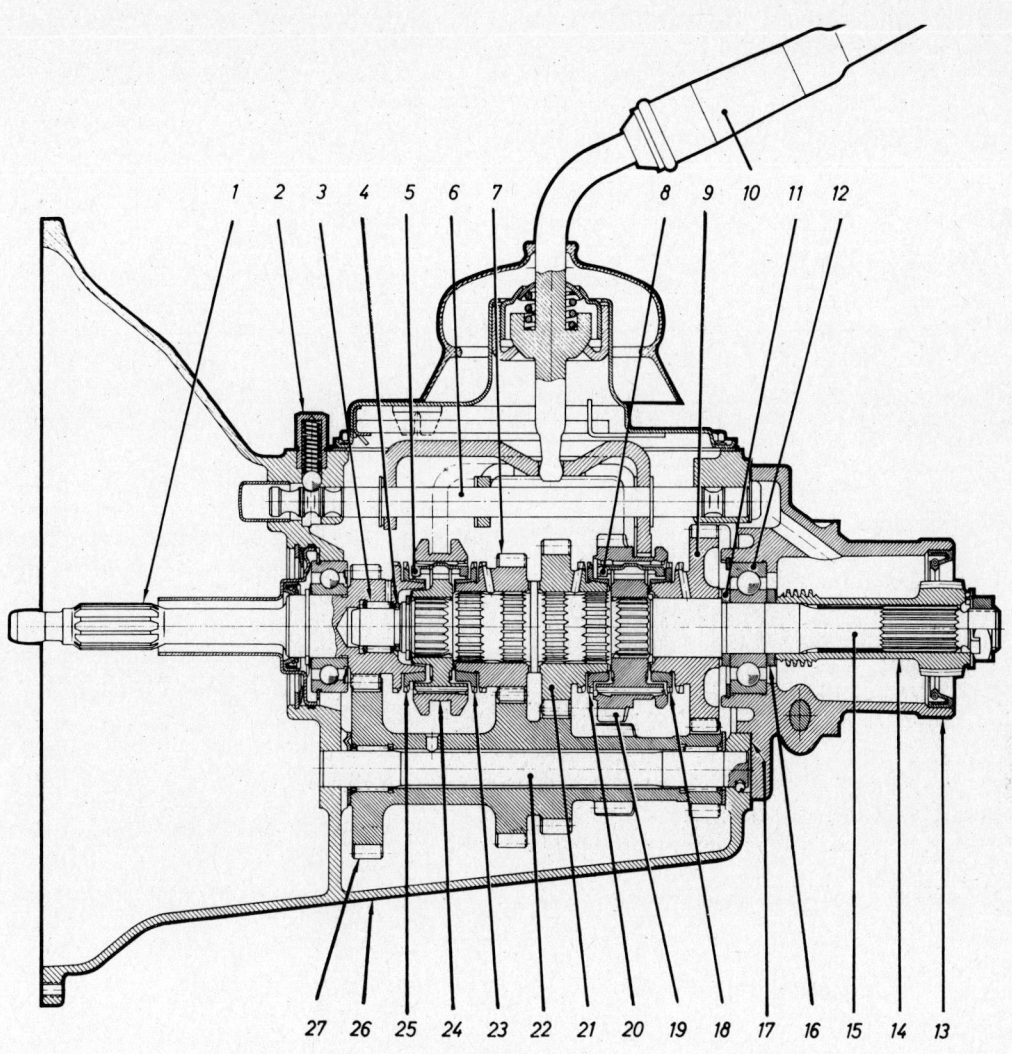

Sectional view of transmission used with OHV engines

1. Clutch gear
2. Lock ball and spring plug
3. Needle bearing assy.
4. Thrust ring
5. Key for 3rd-and-4th-speed clutch sleeve (3)
6. 1st-and-2nd-speed shifter shaft
7. 3rd-speed gear
8. Key for 1st-and-2nd-speed clutch sleeve (3)
9. 1st-speed gear

10. Gearshift lever
11. Spacer between 1st-speed gear and ball bearing
12. Ball bearing
13. Speedometer drive housing (bearing retainer)
14. Mainshaft sleeve
15. Mainshaft
16. Spacer between ball bearing and mainshaft sleeve
17. Gasket between speedometer drive housing and transmission case

18. 1st-speed synchronizer ring
19. 1st-and-2nd-speed sliding gear
20. 2nd-speed synchronizer ring
21. 2nd-speed gear
22. Countergear shaft
23. 3rd-speed synchronizer ring
24. 3rd-and-4th-speed clutch sleeve
25. 4th-speed synchronizer ring
26. Transmission case
27. Countergear

speed sliding gear off clutch hub and remove keys and rear clutch key spring.

NOTE: *Keep synchronizer rings with their respective gears—perhaps by wiring them together. Always discard used synchronizer keys and key springs.*

Take snap-ring out of rear-bearing retainer and with a hammer handle carefully push out ball bearing. Pull oil seal ring out of rear-bearing retainer.

Remove snap-ring behind 1st and 2nd-speed clutch hub from mainshaft. Place next-to-largest slot in press plate under 2nd-speed gear (between 2nd and 3rd gears) and press gear, 1st-2nd clutch hub and 2nd-speed synchronizer ring off rear of shaft. Remove front clutch-key spring.

Remove snap-ring from front of mainshaft, insert mainshaft in press plate and press 3rd-speed gear, 3rd-4th clutch hub and 3rd-speed synchronizer ring off front of mainshaft. Remove rear clutch-key spring from clutch hub.

Inspection of mainshaft assembly. Examine shaft, bearing, gears, hubs, and synchronizer rings for excessive wear, chipping, nicks or scoring. Wash ball bearing in solvent, blow dry, and check for roughness or other wear. Use new synchronizer key springs when reassembling. Oil all parts with SAE 90 transmission lubricant.

To remove main drive gear and bearing assembly, disengage yoke spring, yoke (from ball stud) and release bearing. Remove snap ring and dished washer that retains release-bearing sleeve and main drive gear. Release-bearing sleeve (thrust-bearing guide) and seal assembly can be slid off front of pilot shaft. Grasp pilot (spline) shaft and with slight rocking motion, withdraw main drive gear and bearing assembly from front of transmission case. Remove and discard O-ring between clutch-gear bearing and case.

To disassemble main drive gear and bearing assembly, remove caged-needle bearing and thrust ring from gear end of shaft (this bearing may have come out with mainshaft assembly). Remove ball-bearing retaining snap ring and dished washer over spline shaft.

Using press plate and adapter press bearing forward off main-drive-gear shaft. When using press, do not allow shaft to tip or bend. Examine all parts and races for abnormal wear or damage. Try spline for sliding fit into clutch disc hub. Examine

release bearing sleeve and inner seal for damage. Remove seal by carefully driving out with punch from rear. Using seal driver for installation, drive seal in until it bottoms in sleeve.

Removal of countergear and reverse sliding gear. Lift countergear assembly from bottom of transmission case and remove through rear of case. Remove thrust washers. Use long (12″) brass drift through pilot gear opening to drive reverse sliding gear shaft out toward rear of transmission case. Remove gear from case. Do not lose ball imbedded in shaft.

Wash gears, bearings and shafts in solvent and blow dry. Check all parts thoroughly for abnormal wear, nicks or scoring. Reverse sliding gear should rotate freely on shaft without excessive side play (clearance). However, bushings are not serviced separately. If abnormal wear exists, replace gear and bushings. If wear is unusually severe, shaft may also require replacement.

NOTE: *If replacement of caged needle bearings is required, 26 individual needles are to be installed for service replacement instead of two caged bearing assemblies. Place new thrust washers on front and rear of countergear assembly (1966-up only).*

Clean transmission case thoroughly prior to reassembly and oil each part as it is reinstalled in housing.

Put reverse sliding gear in housing with the long bearing hub facing the rear. Install shaft making sure ball is seated in its groove. Using plastic mallet, drive shaft until end is flush with the case. Coat countergear thrust washers with petroleum jelly and position in the case with dimples in slots provided. Start *countergear shaft* through rear of transmission case. Leave it flush with rear thrust washer. Hold front thrust washer in place with screwdriver. Coat ends of the *countergear assembly* with petroleum jelly and insert new thrust washers. Using countergear needle-bearing loader (J-22414), install bearing needles into each end of assembly.

Mainshaft Assembly With Rear-Bearing Retainer. The clutch hubs and sliding sleeves are factory mated and should be returned to their original position. However, the keys and springs may be replaced individually if worn or broken.

From front of the mainshaft install 3rd-speed gear on mainshaft. Assemble so gear turns freely on mainshaft. Place 3rd-speed synchronizer ring over 3rd-speed cone. Install rear clutch-key spring in 3rd-4th clutch hub so that hooked spring end rests in a hub slot.

Using press plate (J-21684), press 3rd-4th clutch hub onto mainshaft so that the original tooth-alignment is restored. Secure clutch hub with snap ring.

Slide 2nd-speed gear from the rear onto mainshaft. Gear must turn freely. Place 2nd-speed synchronizer ring on 2nd-speed gear cone.

(NOTE: Install caged needle bearings in countergear assembly if bearing replacement is not required.)

With loading tool (J-22414) in place, position countergear assembly in bottom of case, large end forward, taking care not to disturb thrust washers and loose needles. Do not tap countergear *shaft* through its assembly until after installation of main drive gear and mainshaft.

Place spring washer over reverse shift lever pin and install lever.

To assemble main drive gear and bearing assembly, raise transmission case on end (bell housing up). Lubricate and position new main-drive-gear bearing "O" ring in groove. Install main-drive-gear assembly (using installer J-21708). Rap tool lightly with plastic mallet until locating snap ring is against case. Lubricate seal in release bearing sleeve and install sleeve over spline shaft until flange touches bearing. Place dished washer on sleeve flange, dished-out side down, and install snap ring. It may be necessary to tap snap ring down with punch to start it into groove. To assure good snap ring engagement, grip ends of snap ring with expanding (external) snap-ring pliers and force ring back in groove.

Place transmission case, bell housing down, over hole in bench to protect main-drive-gear shaft.

Install both clutch key springs in 1st-2nd clutch hub so that hooks of both springs rest in the same hub slot as 3rd-4th hub springs are positioned opposite each other. Press 1st-2nd clutch hub onto mainshaft so that original teeth mate. Install 1st-2nd keys (longer style) and 1st-2nd sliding gear (forked groove to rear) on clutch hub with splines in line with paint markings.

Secure 1st-2nd clutch hub on mainshaft with snap ring. Slide 1st-speed synchroni-

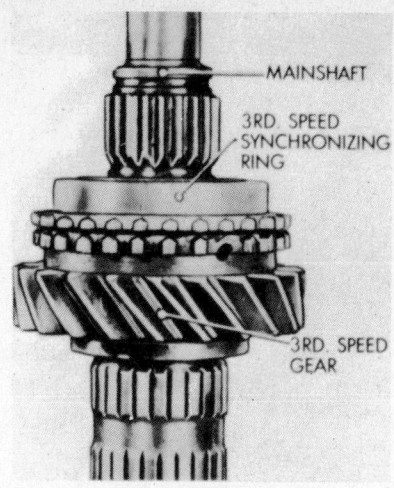

Assembling Gears on Mainshaft

Clutch Key Spring Positions

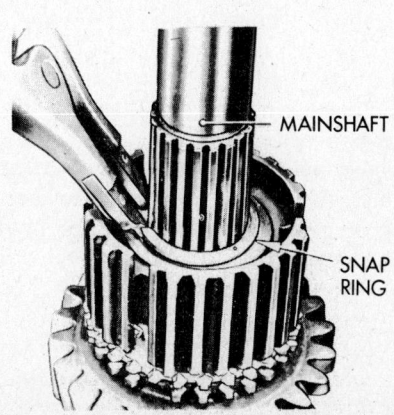

Installing Snap Ring That Holds 3rd-4th Clutch Hub

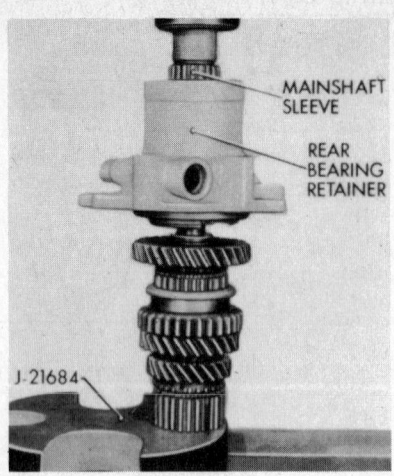

MAINSHAFT
SLEEVE

REAR
BEARING
RETAINER

J-21684

Installing Rear Bearing Retainer and Sleeve on Mainshaft

zer ring (line up paint markings), 1st-speed gear and spacer onto mainshaft. Oil seal-ring lips and drive seal ring into rear-bearing retainer to its stop (using installer J-21740).

Press rear bearing into bearing retainer near outer race and install snap ring. If bearing has been replaced, a new snap ring must be selected according to width of bearing outer-race. (NOTE: Replacement bearing boxes marked "A" use a silver snap ring. Boxes marked "B" use a blue snap ring. Boxes marked "C" use a black snap ring.)

Slide mainshaft assembly through rear bearing retainer, place spacer and main-shaft sleeve onto mainshaft and (with press plate J-21684) press all parts onto main-shaft. Position front 3rd-4th clutch key spring. Install the 3 keys (short design) and 3rd-4th sleeve over hub along with synchronizing ring—noting paint marks.

Install thrust ring and needle-bearing as-sembly on mainshaft. Install 4th-speed synchronizer ring on clutch gear. Place a new rear-bearing retainer gasket on retain-er. Place mainshaft assembly into trans-mission case. Line up paint markings on 4th-speed synchronizer ring and 3rd-4th clutch sleeve.

Line up countergear assembly and its thrust washers with shaft holes in front and rear of case. Coat inner surface of front shaft hole in case with sealer, rotate rear-bearing retainer and gasket out of way and install countergear shaft. Make certain lo-cating ball is in place and enters groove in

case. Tap shaft in until rear of shaft is flush with case. Position rear-bearing retainer, coat lower attaching bolt with an appro-priate sealer, and tighten bolt to a torque of 25 ft.-lb.

Secure transmission firmly in vise, loosely install nut and lockplate on mainshaft, place drive-pinion-flange wrench (J-22399) on mainshaft sleeve. Counterhold mainshaft sleeve and torque nut to 18 ft.-lb. Secure nut with lockplate.

NOTE: On installed transmissions, with drive shaft removed, drive-pinion-flange wrench can be used to counterhold main-shaft sleeve while checking torque of main-shaft nut.

Installing Shifter Shafts. Lubricate and install interlock pins (passage in rear top of case). Coat retaining plugs with sealer and drive in until plugs bottom. Pins must be located between shift shafts.

Place mainshaft gear train in neutral and loosely position shift forks and shifter head in case. From front of transmission, insert short shifter shaft into hole on right side. Place shaft through reverse idler fork, in-stall spring washer (dished-out side toward the front) and feed shaft through shifter head. Next insert 1st-2nd shifter shaft into center hole, install spring washer (dished-out side toward front) and feed shaft through shifter fork and shifter head. In-sert 3rd-4th shifter shaft into left hole, feed through shifter fork and install spring wash-er (dished-out side toward the rear).

Install six new snap rings into shifter shaft grooves. The spring washers are lo-cated between the shifter forks or shifter head and the snap rings. Apply sealer to shaft caps (plugs) and place in front end of case. Tap in until plugs bottom on shoulder in shaft hole.

Lubricate and install detent balls and springs. Then apply sealer carefully to retainer plugs and drive them into case until they bottom.

When installing speedometer drive gear, apply sealer to gear cap and tap it into place.

To assemble and install transmission case cover, place reverse-speed stop spring into transmission cover, grease cover gasket, place shift forks and head in neutral, and position gasket and cover plate. Use sealer on all threads. Torque cap screws to 7 ft.-lbs.

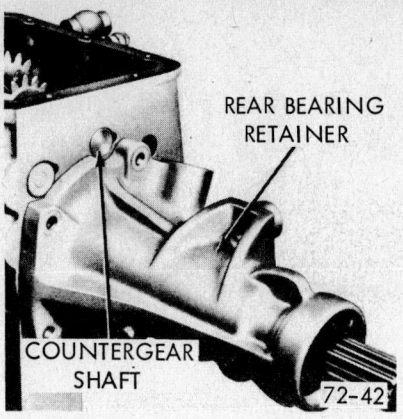

Countergear shaft removal.

CIH Engines

Remove the cotter pins that secure the shift control rod and remove the control rod. Remove the pin that secures the selector lever to the intermediate shaft. Take the two bolts from the rear bearing retainer and remove the selector lever, locknut and selector ring.

Remove the case cover and drain the oil. Turn the rear bearing retainer until the countergear shaft is exposed. From the front, drive out the shaft and remove from the case. NOTE: *To remove the pins, use a ⅛″ pin punch.*

Position of lock pins for shifter forks and selector dogs.

Drive out reverse intermediate lever pivot and remove the lever. Turn the selector shaft so the lock pins are in a vertical position. Drive pins out of 3rd and 4th speed intermediate lever, then 1st and 2nd speed intermediate lever.

With a screwdriver, pry out selector shaft

seal rings on case. Pull out both lock ball plugs with a slide hammer. Remove thrust springs and balls.

With transmission in first gear, drive lock pins out of shifter dogs and selector dogs. From the rear of the transmission, drive out both shifter shafts with a brass drift. Drive the reverse shifter shaft from the rear of the case. The shifter fork will remain in the case.

Turn the rear bearing retainer until reverse idler gear shaft is exposed. Push out shaft from front, remove shaft, idler gear, and shifter fork.

Removing reverse idler gear shaft.

Pull transmission case extension, with mainshaft assembly, out of case. Remove snap-ring from rear bearing retainer groove and remove mainshaft from rear bearing retainer. Remove the loose parts, such as keys, clutch sleeve, and synchronizer ring.

Remove snap-ring in front of clutch hub, and behind speedometer drive gear. Remove the drive gear lock ball from the mainshaft, then remove all loose parts from the shaft.

Supporting 2nd speed gear, press out large clutch hub and needle bearing inner sleeve. Supporting the 3rd speed gear, press off the small clutch hub.

Examine the shafts, gears, bearings and hubs for excessive wear, nicks, scoring and chipping. Replace worn bearings, synchronizer rings, keys, and clutch key springs.

IMPORTANT: *The clutch hubs and sliding discs are a selected assembly and should be kept together as originally assembled.*

From the front, install the 3rd and 4th speed gear onto the mainshaft (the gear must turn freely on the shaft). Install 3rd speed synchronizer ring onto the third

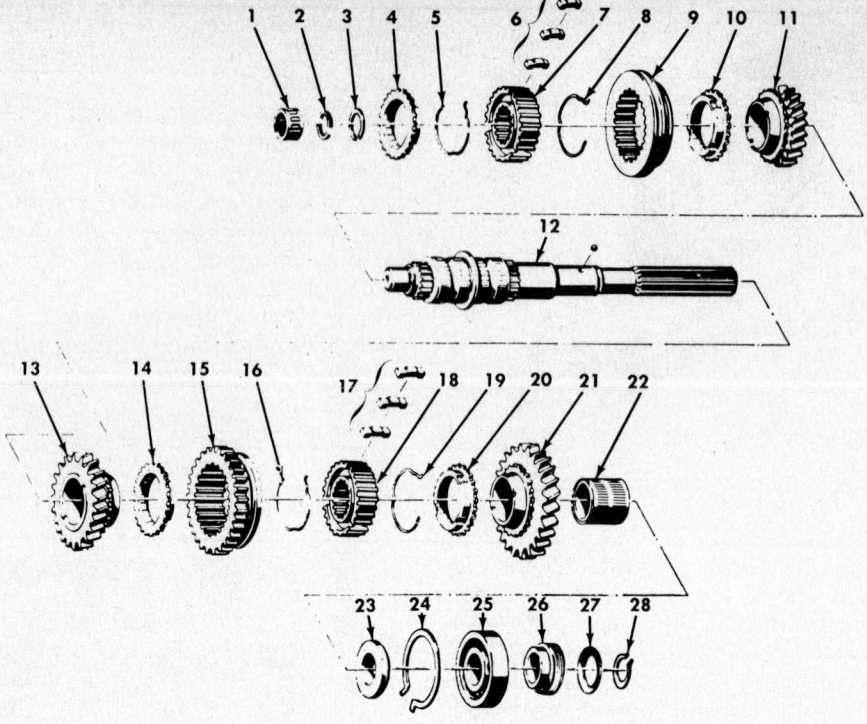

Exploded mainshaft assembly.

1. Needle bearing assembly—mainshaft in main drive gear
2. Thrust ring
3. Snap-ring
4. 4th speed synchronizer ring
5. Clutch key spring
6. Keys for 3rd and 4th speed clutch sleeve
7. 3rd and 4th speed clutch hub
8. Clutch key spring
9. 3rd and 4th speed clutch sleeve
10. 3rd speed synchronizer ring
11. 3rd speed gear
12. Mainshaft
13. 2nd speed gear
14. 2nd speed synchronizer ring
15. Clutch sleeve
16. Clutch key spring
17. Keys for 1st and 2nd speed clutch sleeve
18. 1st and 2nd speed clutch hub
19. Clutch key spring
20. 1st speed synchronizer ring
21. 1st speed gear
22. 1st speed gear needle bearing
23. Spacer plate
24. Transmission case extension snap-ring
25. Ball bearing
26. Speedometer drive gear
27. Dished washer
28. Snap-ring

speed cone. Install rear clutch key into 3rd and 4th speed clutch hub so that the hooked spring end rests in one of the slots.

Press 3rd and 4th speed clutch hub onto mainshaft so that the original tooth contact is obtained; secure it with a snap-ring. From the rear, place the 2nd speed gear onto the mainshaft. Place the 2nd speed synchronizer ring on the 2nd speed gear cone.

Install both clutch key springs into 1st and 2nd speed clutch hub so the hooks of both springs rest in the same hub slot and the ends of the springs are opposite each other. Press the 1st and 2nd speed clutch hub onto the mainshaft so the original tooth contact is obtained.

Press needle bearing onto mainshaft. Install 1st and 2nd speed keys and sliding gear

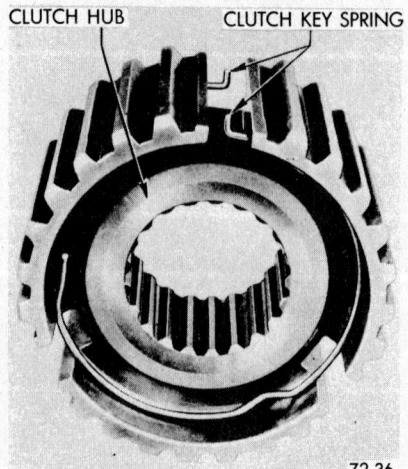

Installation of clutch key springs.

Spacer ring and needle bearing installation on mainshaft.

(with forked groove to the rear) onto the clutch hub.

Slide needle bearing, synchronizer ring, 1st speed gear, space plate (chamfer to the rear) and transmission case extension snap-ring onto mainshaft. Press on rear bearing. Slide speedometer drive gear and dished washer onto mainshaft and secure with snap-ring.

Place mainshaft assembly into rear bearing retainer up to its stop and secure with snap-ring. Position 3rd and 4th speed clutch key spring in position. Install keys and 3rd and 4th speed sleeve over hub, along with synchronizer ring. NOTE: *Arrows on keys point towards shifter fork groove.*

Install new gasket onto rear bearing retainer and slide mainshaft assembly into case. From the side, slide spacer ring and needle bearing onto mainshaft. Install clutch gear onto transmission case up to snap-ring stop.

Turn the transmission case extension until the bore for the reverse idler gear shaft is exposed. Place lock ball into shaft and, from rear of case, install shaft. At the same time, install the reverse idler gear and reverse shifter fork. The shifter fork groove of the idler gear and the shoulder of the shifter fork go toward the front.

Insert the 1st and 2nd speed shift shafts at the front of the case, with the notches down, pushing through the L-shaped shifter dog first. Push the 1st and 2nd speed selector shaft through the shifter forks, positioning the shoulder toward the front of the case. Drive the lock pins in place, allowing them to protrude 1/16-5/64".

Insert the 3rd and 4th speed shift shaft from the front of the case, with the notches down, pushing it through the 3rd and 4th speed shifter fork. Install the lock pin, allowing 1/16-5/64" to protrude.

Install the reverse shift shaft from the rear of the case, with notches up, pushing it through the reverse shifter fork; install the lock pin.

Insert the selector shaft in the case, push through the 1st and 2nd speed intermediate lever, then the 3rd and 4th speed intermediate lever, then insert lock pins.

Engage reverse speed intermediate lever and 3rd and 4th speed intermediate lever, install pivot pin. End-play on reverse speed intermediate lever should be 0.004-0.012". Insert both lock balls and thrust springs into bores in transmission case and drive in plugs.

Coat the thrust washers with bearing

Position of "L" shaped dog.

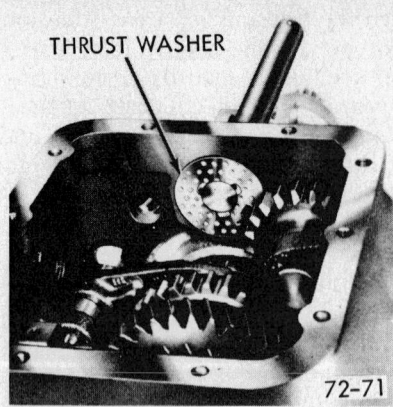

THRUST WASHER

72-71

Countergear thrust washer installation.

grease and stick to transmission case. Turn the transmission case to expose counter-gear shaft. Place lock ball into the shaft from the rear so the thrust washer is held in place. Hold the opposite thrust washer in place with a short drift.

Insert the countergear into the transmission case. Insert the shaft into the counter-gear and drive it into the case, paying attention to the lock ball.

Align the rear bearing retainer and torque bolts to the transmission case. Install lock ball and thrust spring into top transmission bore. Install case cover gasket, cover and bolts.

Driveshaft

The 1964-65 Kadett driveshaft is comprised of a torque tube, which serves as a rear engine mount, and a differential pinion extension, that are joined by a U-joint at a central bracket.

1966 and later models added a rear engine mount crossmember, located at the rear of the transmission, eliminating the need for the torque tube. The central bracket and the pinion extension tube are retained, a short driveshaft being used to connect the transmission to the extension tube at the central bracket. Models equipped with OHV engines use only one U-joint immediately in front of the central bracket, while models with CIH engines use one at each end of the short driveshaft.

Removal and Installation

1964-65

The 1964-65 driveshaft is removed after the central joint bracket has been detached. Support central joint with a jack, then remove the hex-head support-bracket bolts. Let the driveshaft hang free by lowering the jack. Swing the central-joint-support bracket downward and place a support stand under the bellhousing. Where the pinion flange and driveshaft meet, make a mark. Then remove the four attaching bolts, and slide shaft slightly forward into support tube.

The driveshaft may now be removed with or without the torque tube. To remove the shaft and torque tube, remove the four torque tube mounting bolts at the rear of the transmission and the two central support bracket mounting bolts, and slide the tube and shaft rearward. The shaft may be removed alone by sliding rearward out of the torque tube.

Installation is the reverse of removal. When installing the torque tube ensure that the engine mounts are not in a stressed position (engine too far forward or rearward). A pry slot is provided in the tube support bracket to move the engine in either direction.

1966-70 OHV Engines

Raise the rear of the vehicle and disconnect the parking brake equalizer from the rod. Remove one rear engine mount bolt and loosen the other. Mark the mating parts of the driveshaft and pinion extension, and remove the mounting bolts. Slide the shaft slightly forward, and remove the shaft and thrust spring. Install a plug to avoid fluid loss from the transmission.

Install in the reverse order of removal. Insert the small end of the thrust spring into the transmission, and torque the flange bolts to 18 ft. lbs.

1968-70 CIH Engines

Removal and installation is similar to the OHV engine models, except that the rear engine mount need not be loosened. When installing, torque rear U-joint U-bolts to 11 ft. lbs.

Drive Axle

General

Rear suspension on Kadetts from 1964 through 1967 is designed with leaf springs. The axle assembly is attached to the springs with support brackets. The attachment point of the axle to each rear spring is forward of center to reduce driving and coasting stresses on the springs. A plastic pad is placed between the leaves of each rear spring to prevent friction and squeaking. The rear springs have a progressive action, becoming stiffer with increased load.

Rear suspension for 1968 and later models was completely redesigned with coil springs, a track bar, and a roll stabilizer.

Rear wheel rates were reduced, as a result of the design change, from 102 psi to 95 psi.

The coil springs are mounted on the axle. Two (lower) control arms connect the axle to the body. The differential torque-tube mount at the central joint is (in effect) an upper control arm. Using the torque tube as a control arm allows for a lower underbody and additional cushion depth in the rear passenger seat. Because this suspension design directs greater stress to the axle tube, metal thickness of the tube is increased.

Spring Removal and Installation

1964-65

Raise car and support it with stands. Remove wheel. Loosen slightly the rear axle housing outer and inner nuts. Remove U-bolts, lower rubber pad, and the brake cable grommet from its bracket. Supporting spring with jack, extract front eye bolt. Then remove rear shackles. Bushing is one piece rubber and steel. Note order of bushing lengths for reassembly.

Reassemble rear spring in reverse sequence tightening shackle and eye bolts to 11 ft.-lbs., U-bolts and housing attachment nuts to 18 ft.-lbs.

1966-70

Raise the vehicle and support it at its rear jack brackets. Disconnect the shock absorbers and (if equipped with stabilizer)

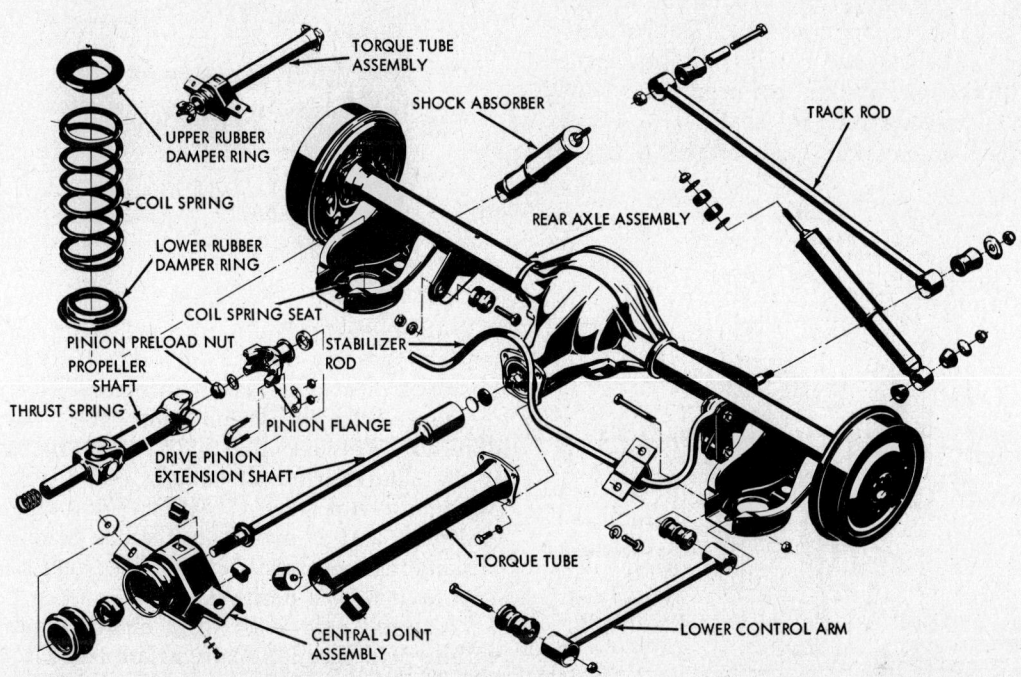

Rear suspension, driveshaft, and central joint—CIH engines

stabilizer and shackles from the rear axle brackets. Lower the rear axle as far as possible and remove the springs. NOTE: *When lowering rear axle do not stress brake hose.*

Install the springs, checking to ensure that they are properly seated in the damper rings and seats. Jack up the rear axle at the differential housing, compressing the springs in their seats. Attach the shock absorbers to the rear axle, torquing the nuts to 15 ft. lbs. Attach stabilizer, and torque bolts to 25 ft. lbs.

OUTER BEARING AND SEAL RECONDITIONING

OHV Engines

With wheel assembly and brake drum off, use access holes in axle shaft flange to remove four nuts holding brake backing plate to axle housing.

Install axle pulling tools (J-2619 and J-8805) on axle shaft flange, attach puller with wheel lug nuts, and pull axle shaft.

NOTE: The rear axle oil seal is positioned in the axle shaft ball bearing and can be replaced only together with ball bearing. The ball bearing outer race is provided with a rubber ring which seals the ball bearing against the rear axle housing. This prevents oil from leaking out and dirt and moisture from entering. The ball bearing is packed and should not be cleaned with solvent. The oil seal need not be oiled on installation of axle shaft.

Saw or chisel through retaining ring as

shown. Install slotted plate (J-21721) into ram and yoke. Press off bearing and water deflector.

A rear axle that is damaged or worn beyond the following tolerances should be replaced. Maximum radial runout of axle shaft at ball bearing seat is .002". Permissible axial runout of axle shaft flange near larger diameter (4.92") is .004".

Install new deflector on axle shaft if available. Use original deflector again only if in good condition. To install new water deflector on axle shaft. use installer ring (J-21721) in a ram and yoke. Press on deflector until installer stops snugly against shaft shoulder.

Press on bearing (using installer ring J-21721-2) so that oil seal in bearing faces shaft splines. NOTE: New bearing is needed if oil seal is worn.

Press on bearing retainer so that shoulder faces bearing. (CAUTION:The recess in the installer ring must face the slotted plate to avoid damage to the retaining ring surface.)

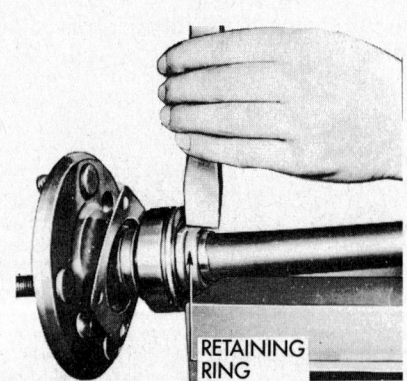

Removing Retaining Ring

With a depth gauge, measure depth of rear-axle-bearing seat in axle housing (backing plate and gaskets in place). Next measure width of bearing outer race. The difference between the two measurements is the shim thickness needed (end play). Maximum end play is .002". To reduce end play, add as many .004" shims behind bearing as necessary. A slight crush fit (up to .006") is desirable.

To install axle shaft, coat shaft splines with hypoid gear lubricant, insert axle shaft into housing, and (using mallet) drive it into housing completely. Torque nuts to 20 ft.-lbs.

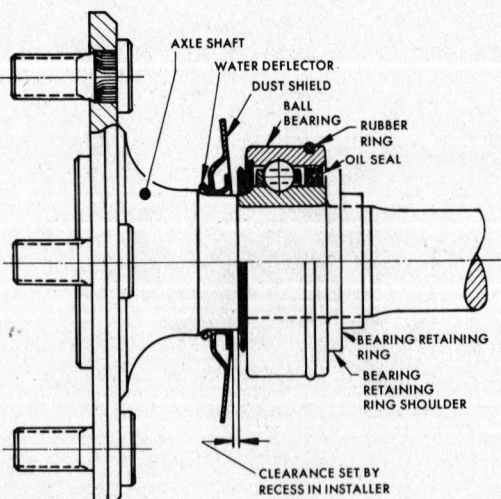

Rear axle outer bearing and oil seal—OHV engines

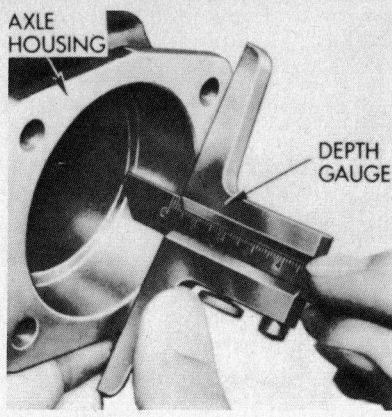

Rear Axle Bearing Seat Depth

CIH Engines

With wheel assembly and brake drum off, remove the differential cover and allow oil to drain. Use access holes in axle shaft flange to remove four nuts that hold the brake locking plate to the axle housing.

Remove axle shaft retaining ring from inner end of axle shaft. Position a screwdriver behind the inner end of the axle shaft to remove axle shaft. If axle sticks, install axle shaft pulling tools to facilitate removal.

To install a new oil seal or bearing, pull off old bearing with remover, slide hammer and adapter. Drive in new seal and bearing.

An axle that is damaged or worn beyond tolerance should be replaced. Maximum radial runout of axle shaft is 0.002″, maximum axial runout of axle shaft flange is 0.004″.

Position new paper gasket and the bolts on backing plate and install axle shaft. (Be sure not to damage oil seal when installing axle shaft.)

Install new retaining ring on inner end of axle shaft. Install new cover gasket and cover and tighten bolts to 18 ft. lbs. Fill differential with 2½ pints of SAE 80 or 80-90 rear axle lubricant. Install axle shaft retainer nuts and tighten them to 20 ft. lbs.

Axle Removal and Installation

1964-65

Prior to removal of the axle, the drive pinion extension flange must be separated from the U-joint by bending back the lock plate and removing the four flange attaching bolts.

On all leaf-spring models remove four bolts securing axle to spring support. Lift axle assembly up and move to the left so that right wheel brake assembly will clear right spring. Lower right end of axle and remove assembly from vehicle.

To reinstall axle assembly, raise left end of axle assembly up and over left spring so that right end of assembly will clear right spring. Raise right end and move complete assembly to the right so that brackets on axle housing are aligned with spring seat support. Screw on bolts finger tight. Align and connect driveshaft to pinion flange. Torque bolts to 18 ft.-lbs. Support torque tube with a floor jack and raise until central-joint-support bracket aligns with threaded holes in floor panel. Install finger-tight two bracket-to-floor attaching bolts.

Raise car, and remove support stands and place them under rear springs at U-bolts. Next torque bracket-to-floor bolts to 30 ft.-lbs. Torque spring bolts to 18 ft.-lbs. Connect shock absorbers at axle brackets and torque to 15 ft.-lbs.

Continue installation in reverse sequence to removal. Bleed brakes and fill differential with hypoid gear lubricant.

1966-70

Raise the rear of the vehicle and support with jack stands at the jack brackets. Remove both rear wheels and one rear brake drum. Disconnect the parking brake rod from the equalizer, and the cable from the actuating lever on the side with the drum removed. Separate the cable from the lower control arm brackets and hang the free end over the exhaust pipe.

Unbolt the shock absorbers, the track rod, and (if so equipped) the stabilizer shackles, from the rear axle brackets. Mark the mating parts of the driveshaft to pinion extension flange, separate the flange, and tie the driveshaft out of the way. Disconnect and cap the brake hoses at the differential, lower the axle enough to remove load from the springs, and remove the springs.

Unbolt the central joint bracket from the under pan and the lower control arms from the axle brackets, and roll the axle out from under the vehicle.

Install in the reverse order of removal. When installing the central joint to the underpan, place a load of aproximately

350 lbs. in the trunk, support the vehicle by the differential housing (raise off of the jack stands), and torque the bolts to 33 ft. lbs. Following installation of the axle, the brake system must be bled.

DIFFERENTIAL RECONDITIONING

The 1964-65 pinion extension shaft is removed as follows:

With driveshaft disconnected and central joint disassembled, remove pinion shaft nut and pinion flange.

Unscrew bolts attaching torque tube to differential flange and (using hammer and piece of wood) tap torque tube loose. Pry off tube using screwdrivers. (CAUTION: Pry off tube evenly to avoid distortion of pinion shaft.) Drive out torque tube bearing and protective cap using brass drift.

The 1966-70 pinion extension shaft is removed as follows:

With driveshaft disconnected and central joint disassembled, remove bolts attaching rear torque tube to axle housing, break the flange seal with a block of wood as shown, and withdraw pinion-shaft extension and torque tube from axle housing. Remove self-locking nut on pinion-shaft (immobilize flange with a wrench which can be clamped in a vise). Pull off pinion flange with puller, taking care to protect threads.

Remove pinion-shaft extension from torque tube using soft mallet against shaft at central-joint end. Remove ball bearing from its cushion. Reinstall with flange facing toward front of car. Pack area in front of bearing with water-resistant grease. Unscrew the two bolts and pull central joint support from torque tube, exposing support cushions. Replace cushions if necessary. Torque new ones to 29 ft.-lbs. Put central-joint support in place on one cushion and then pry the support over the other with a screwdriver. Bolt together and torque to 15 ft.-lbs.

Inserting pinion-shaft extension into torque tube from the rear, tap into place with soft-face mallet. Position pinion flange, tap into place far enough to start pinion nut (use soft-face mallet), install new nut on flange, secure flange and torque nut to 73 ft.-lbs.

Install torque tube and central-joint assembly on rear axle housing using a new gasket.

Prior to draining differential, remove brake pipe assembly, including pipes attaching wheel cylinder, junction block at differential housing, and hose bracket on torque tube.

Loosen differential bolts and drain lubricant by breaking loose cover at bottom. Remove cover. Next check pinion depth, ring gear-to-pinion backlash, and side bearing preload. If adjustments meet specifications, it is not necessary to disassemble pinion and differential.

Mark side-bearing caps and housing with punch for proper reinstallation. Remove attaching bolts and caps. Using suitable wood levers (such as hammer handles), pry out differential assembly. Do not drop or interchange bearing races. Remove both differential side bearings with bearing puller (J-2241-2 and adapter J-21683). Do not interchange bearings or shims.

Remove bolts attaching ring gear to differential case. Evenly tap ring gear off case with brass drift and hammer. Drive out pinion-shaft lock pin with a small punch. Remove pinion gears, side gears, and shims.

Using a suitable sharp-pointed tool, pry pinion oil seal from its seat. (To prevent damage to the flange, lay a large screwdriver against the flange as a base for prying.)

Place wrench on preload adjusting nut and continue disassembly by following paragraphs below that apply.

1964-65 models require installing pinion flange to help hold pinion shaft steady. Turn wrench counterclockwise to remove preload nut. Tap out pinion shaft, its inner bearing and tension ring carefully with plastic hammer. Remove oil deflector and outer bearing from rear axle housing.

1966-67 models have pinion with splined sleeve. Grip sleeve to hold pinion from turning while removing pinion nut. Remove thrust cap. Tap pinion from housing with soft-face hammer.

Tap out pinion bearing races, noting shims behind inner bearing outer race. Press off pinion inner bearing.

Clean all mating surfaces free of foreign matter or burrs. Press on pinion bearings and races, lubricating bearings amply. After checking pinion depth, complete installation in reverse of disassembly. At the point where no further end play is detectable

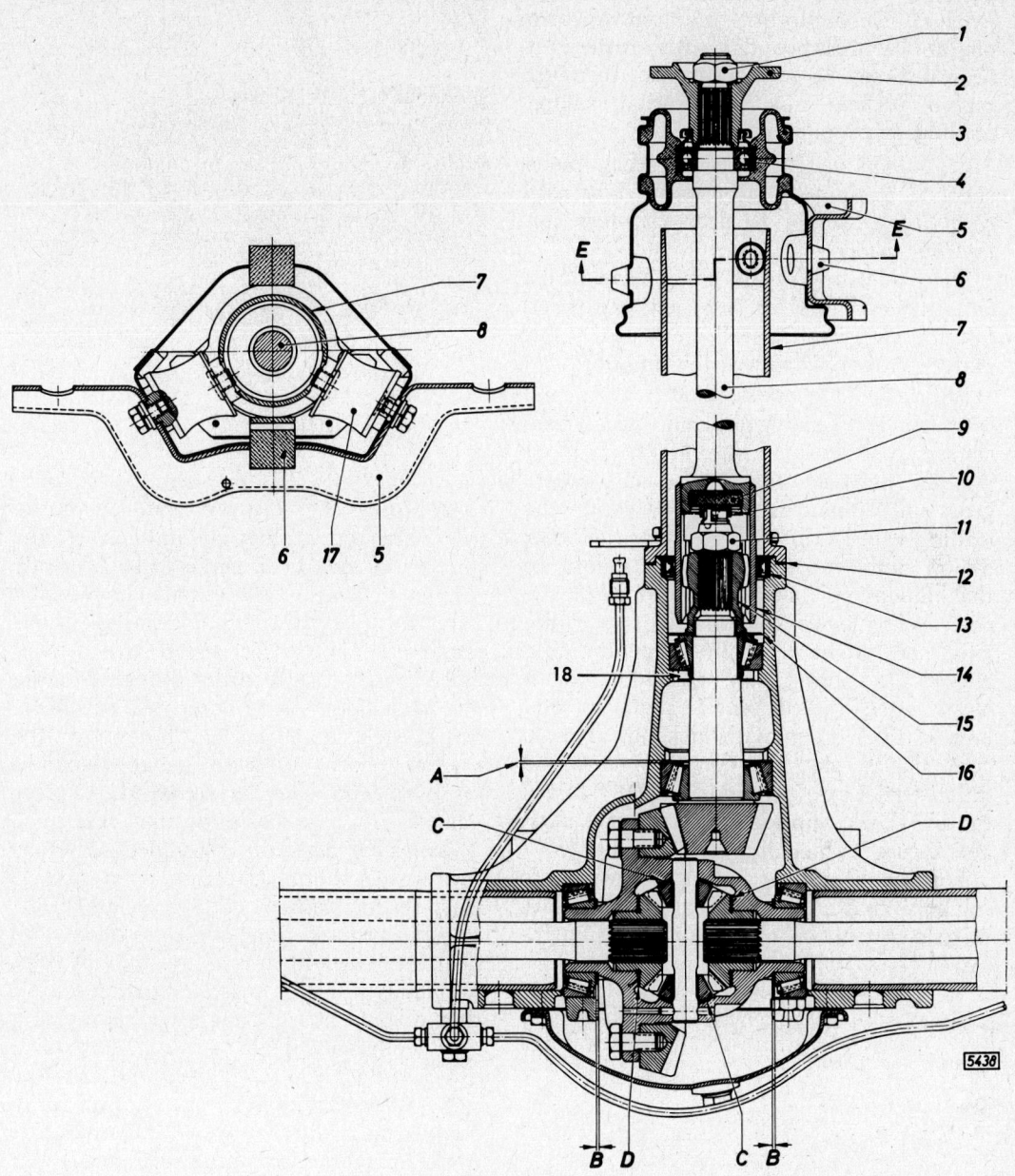

Pinion and Differential, since 1966.

1. Self-locking nut
2. Drive-pinion-shaft extension flange
3. Rubber cushion
4. Ball bearing with sheet metal casing
5. Central joint support
6. Rubber cushion on central joint support
7. Torque tube
8. Drive pinion extension
9. Hard rubber disc
10. Thrust cap
11. Hex. nut
12. Paper gasket
13. Oil seal
14. Slip joint
15. Splined sleeve
16. Oil deflector
17. Rubber cushion
18. Collapsible spacer
A = Shims for drive-pinion height adjustment
B = Shims for ring gear and pinion backlash adjustment
C = Spherical washer
D = Shim for differential side gears

when tightening the pinion preload adjusting nut, preload specifications are nearly reached. Check torque required to turn pinion (in inch-pounds) after turning it several times to seat bearings. Readjust pinion preload nut as required, taking readings while pinion is turning.

CAUTION: After preload has been checked, *final tightening must be done very carefully so as not to over-compress collapsible spacer.*

Stake adjusting nut to slots, drive thrust cap onto end of shaft (use new cap if old fits loosely), and install new seal after soaking in hypoid lube a few minutes.

Lubricate side gears, pinion gears and washers. Install side gears and thrust washers into case. Position one pinion (without washer) between side gears and rotate gears until pinion is directly opposite the loading opening in the case. Place another pinion between side gears and align so that pinion-axle holes line up with holes in case. When holes are aligned, rotate pinions back toward loading opening just enough to permit sliding pinion thrust washers in. Install pinion shaft so that hole in shaft aligns with lock pin holes in case. If clearance between side gears and differential case exceeds .006", install thicker shims. Slip lock pin in pinion shaft and secure by peening case.

Position ring gear on differential case (plate) so that holes in gear align with holes in case. Attach bolts and torque to 30 ft.-lbs.

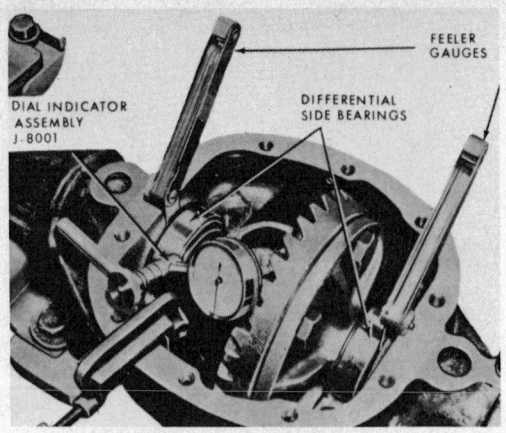

Adjusting Differential Tolerances

To adjust side-bearing preload and to set proper ring gear-to-pinion backlash, the differential side bearings must be precisely shimmed. Place differential side-bearing outer races on bearings and install differential case in carrier. Insert two sets of feeler gauges between the differential case and each side-bearing outer race as shown. Work each gauge to the bottom of the pedestal bore. Increase gauge thickness until all end play is removed. Replace gauges with shims of same thickness.

Ring gear backlash (clearance) is set by readjusting differential case from side to side. Set backlash by adding feelers at one side bearing and removing from other until gear tooth clearance is an average of .005", within .004"-.008" range. A dial indicator that mounts at right angles with the ring gear teeth is available.

When end play is removed and backlash is correct, select shims to thickness of feeler gauges. In addition add .002" to each side to obtain side bearing preload. Remove side bearings (using puller J-2241-2 and adapter J-21683), fit shims behind respective bearings and reseat the bearings. Place outer races on side bearings and set differential case into its carrier. Using a plastic hammer, tap case in until seated at bottom of bores. Tighten bearing-cap bolts to 30 ft.-lbs. Rotate case several times to seat bearings.

Check backlash and side bearing preload using an inch-pound torque wrench connected at right angles to the assembly as shown. Preload should be 10-20 in.-lbs.

Bolt Tightening Sequence on Ring Gear

Differential Specifications

Pinion Bearing Preload

1.0 AND 1.1 LITER ENGINES

	(average)	(range)
New bearings	8 in.-lbs.	5-11 in.-lbs.
Original bearings	4 in.-lbs.	3-5 in.-lbs.

1.5 AND 1.9 LITER ENGINES

	(average)	(range)
New bearings	9 in. lbs.	7–12 in. lbs.
Original bearings	6 in. lbs.	5–7 in. lbs.

Pinion depth setting (from pinion marking) +.002″ to —.001″

Shims for setting pinion depth

Notches in shim	Shim thickness (inch)
One side flattened	.0016-.0024
0	.0094-.0102
1	.0104-.0112
2	.0114-.0122
3	.0124-.0132
4	.0134-.0142
5	.0144-.0152

Clearance from differential side gears to case max. 0.006″

Shims for setting clearance

Notches in shim	Shim thickness (inch)
0	0.019–0.020
1	0.023–0.024
2	0.027–0.028
3	0.031–0.032

Maximum runout, axle shaft bearing-seat	0.002″
Maximum lateral runout, rear axle shaft-flange (at largest flange diameter)	0.004″
Maximum lateral runout, ring gear	0.003″
Lash, ring gear to drive pinion	0.004–0.008″
Differential side bearing preload	New bearings: 20–30 ft. lbs.
	Old bearings: 10–20 ft. lbs.

Shims for setting preload

Notches in shim	Shim thickness (inch)
0	0.0056–0.0062
1	0.0066–0.0072
2	0.0076–0.0082
3	0.0085–0.0092
4	0.0094–0.0102
5	0.0104–0.0112
6	0.0193–0.0201
7	0.0386–0.0398

Front Suspension

General

All Opel models use independent front wheel suspension attached to a cross member and a transverse steel-band spring. Road shock is dampened by direct shock absorbers. The entire suspension can be removed as a unit. No maintenance lubrication is needed.

Kadett front suspension for 1966-67 models differs from that of earlier models, with larger cross member, longer two-leaf spring, tapered seats for ball joints, and rubber bumper to eliminate spring and cross member interference.

The 1968 suspension was modified from the 1967 design by a change to a softer spring. As a result, wheel rates dropped from 99 pounds per square inch to 80 psi and ride softness improved. Other changes were made to handle the additional weight of two optional engines but are adopted on all models for simplified part servicing. The modifications include the following:

. . . Shaft for lower control arm is redesigned with larger offset to accommodate three-leaf spring.

. . . Lower ball-joint and stud are larger.

. . . Tapered roller bearings replace ball bearings.

. . . Steering knuckle spindles and wheel hubs are changed to hold tapered bearings. (Drum-brake steering knuckles and front hubs for ball bearings on models prior to 1968 are not interchangeable to disc-brake knuckles and hubs).

. . . Rubber is vulcanized to inner sleeve of lower control arm for greater durability. Hardness of rubber is reduced for softer ride.

The front end for the 15S and 19S engines uses a three-leaf transverse spring to properly suspend the greater weight. A rubber bushing is vulcanized to the spring inner sleeve. The three-leaf assembly is not interchangeable with the standard suspension.

REMOVAL AND INSTALLATION AS A UNIT

Kadett

Block and brake wheels, jack up front end (place block of wood between jack

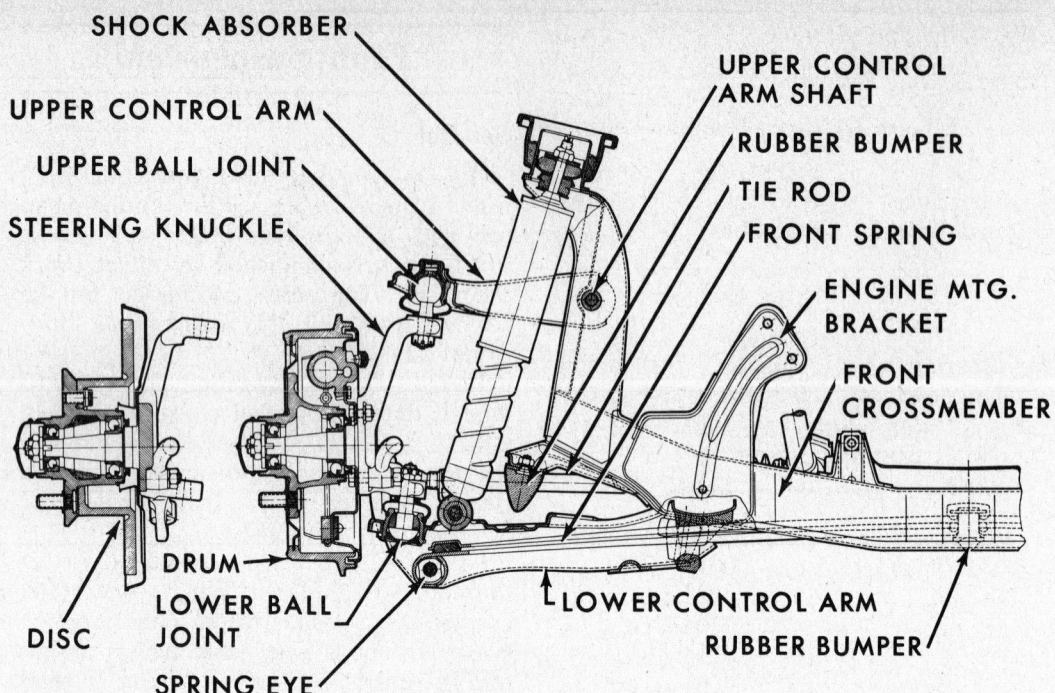

SHOCK ABSORBER

UPPER CONTROL ARM

UPPER BALL JOINT

STEERING KNUCKLE

UPPER CONTROL ARM SHAFT

RUBBER BUMPER

TIE ROD

FRONT SPRING

ENGINE MTG. BRACKET

FRONT CROSSMEMBER

DRUM

LOWER BALL JOINT

DISC

SPRING EYE

LOWER CONTROL ARM

RUBBER BUMPER

Opel Front Suspension

and cross member to prevent damage), and support car with stands at rear of front frame rails.

Support power plant at rear of transmission with a stand; remove clamping bolt and nut from steering mast flange, and take out stop bolt from mast guide below steering wheel. Gently lift steering column from mast flange until it stops against direction signal mechanism. Prop wood spacer between housing and steering wheel hub.

Disconnect brake hoses, front engine support bolts, rubber mounts, clutch cable at engine mount, shock-absorber plastic cover, and upper shock-absorber attaching nuts.

Remove cross-member attaching nuts and lower the cross member. Watch that engine mounting bracket does not interfere with starter cables.

Installation is easier if rubber dampening block is lubricated to reduce friction of mounting brackets. Slide engine mounting bracket over rubber block, attach cross member to front frame rail with new nuts, and torque to 30 ft-lbs. Bolt down engine and complete installation in reverse sequence to disassembly. Make sure direction signal switch is in central (not engaged) position when lowering steering

column into mast. Tighten steering-mast clamp bolt to 25 ft-lbs. Adjust front end alignment.

GT

For the GT, proceed as outlined above, but note the following steps: loosen the steering mast at the lower universal joint and take out the clamp bolt. Loosen the clamp at the upper universal joint and lift the steering mast upward until it is free of the lower universal joint. It is also necessary to remove the air cleaner. Before removing the engine mount nuts, unscrew the radiator from the support on the crossmember.

Installation is the reverse of removal. When installing the steering mast, center the steering wheel and front wheels. Tighten the lower universal joint clamp bolt to 22 ft. lbs. and then the upper bolt to 14 ft. lbs.

BALL JOINT REMOVAL AND INSTALLATION

Upper

Remove upper ball joint if there is excessive play in the ball stud. With wheel off, unscrew castle nut from upper ball joint stud. Discard cotter pin. Press ball stud from steering knuckle (puller J-21687) and remove two bolts attaching ball joint to upper control arm. Replace ball joint if dust cap is damaged.

Install upper ball joint with the off-center holes in flange showing towards the steering knuckle spindle. Tighten control-arm nuts to 18 ft.-lbs. and castle nut to 29 ft.-lbs.

Lower

Maximum axial play of Kadett lower ball joints is .080 inches. Greater play or worn parts require replacement of joint. New lower ball joints have axial play of .020 inches or less.

When removing lower ball joint, back off castle nut only two turns. Strike the ball stud to break it loose. Do not remove nut. Compress transverse spring (compressor J-21689) 3⅛" from lower spring leaf. Disconnect shock absorber to lower control-arm attachment, compress it and swing it aside. Then remove castle nut from ball-joint stud.

NOTE: prior to the removal of the lower ball joint from the control arm, note the position of the locating notch, shown in illustration, in the rim of the ball-joint housing. Scribe or mark the control arm to facilitate realignment of the replacement ball joint.

Pry off dust-cap retainer and dust cap carefully and press ball stud out of lower control arm.

When reinstalling lower ball joint, the notch in the ball joint bottom plate (identifying the direction of the elongated slot) must point towards the brake drum backing plate. Alignment must be within 2° of lower control-arm centerline. Improper positioning of the ball joint will cause binding and fracture. Do not press ball joint

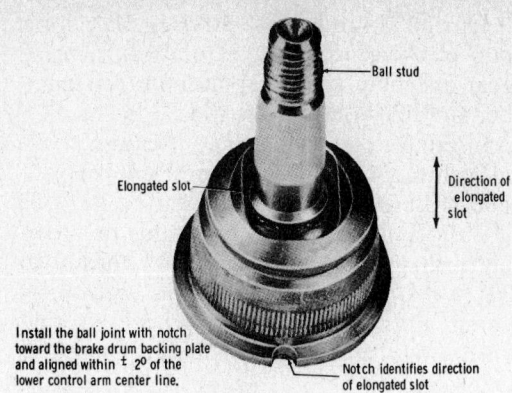

Install the ball joint with notch toward the brake drum backing plate and aligned within ± 2° of the lower control arm center line.

Lower ball joint installation

onto bottom plate, but only onto joint housing.

Install dust cap on lower ball joint and fill with chassis lubricant (GM-742). Attach dust cap retainer. Press ball joint into steering knuckle (using J-9519-3 and J-21690). Install castle nut and torque to 45 ft.-lbs. Use new cotter pin.

Steering

Steering Gear and Wheel

STEERING WHEEL REMOVAL AND INSTALLATION

Disconnect the ground strap from the battery, pry out the horn cap, and disconnect the horn wires. Bend the lockplate tabs down, and remove the steering wheel nut and washer. Mark the relative position of the steering wheel and shaft, install a conventional steering wheel puller, and remove the steering wheel.

Prior to installation, lightly lubricate the sliding parts of the turn signal mechanism with lubriplate. Ensure that the match marks align, and install in the reverse order of removal.

STEERING GEAR REMOVAL AND INSTALLATION

Remove flexible-coupling bolt above gear box (see exploded view) and the stop bolt located below steering wheel in steering mast jacket. Lift out steering column from mast about three inches and position it with block of wood.

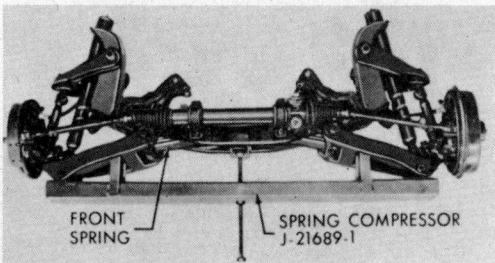

FRONT SPRING   SPRING COMPRESSOR J-21689-1

Transverse spring is compressed for removing lower ball joint.

Detach tie rod ends, pressing ball studs out of steering arms. Unfasten steering gear assembly from suspension cross member and lift it off with tie rods.

Install the steering gear as follows:

Position steering gear on front suspension cross member and tighten bolts to 25 ft.-lbs. Position tie-rod ball studs on steering arm; install castle nuts and torque to 30 ft.-lbs. Lock into position with new cotter pins. Set steering wheel so that flat, lower portion of steering mast is parallel to ring-coupling bolt hole.

Position the mast in the flexible coupling and set clearance between steering-wheel hub and directional signal housing between 3/32" and 1/8". Tighten flexible coupling to 23 ft.-lbs. Reinstall stop bolt in steering mast jacket. Turn steering wheel ½ turn both right and left. If any resistance is noticeable, remove the steering mast and find the cause. NOTE: *do not over-tighten stop bolt in plastic bushing.*

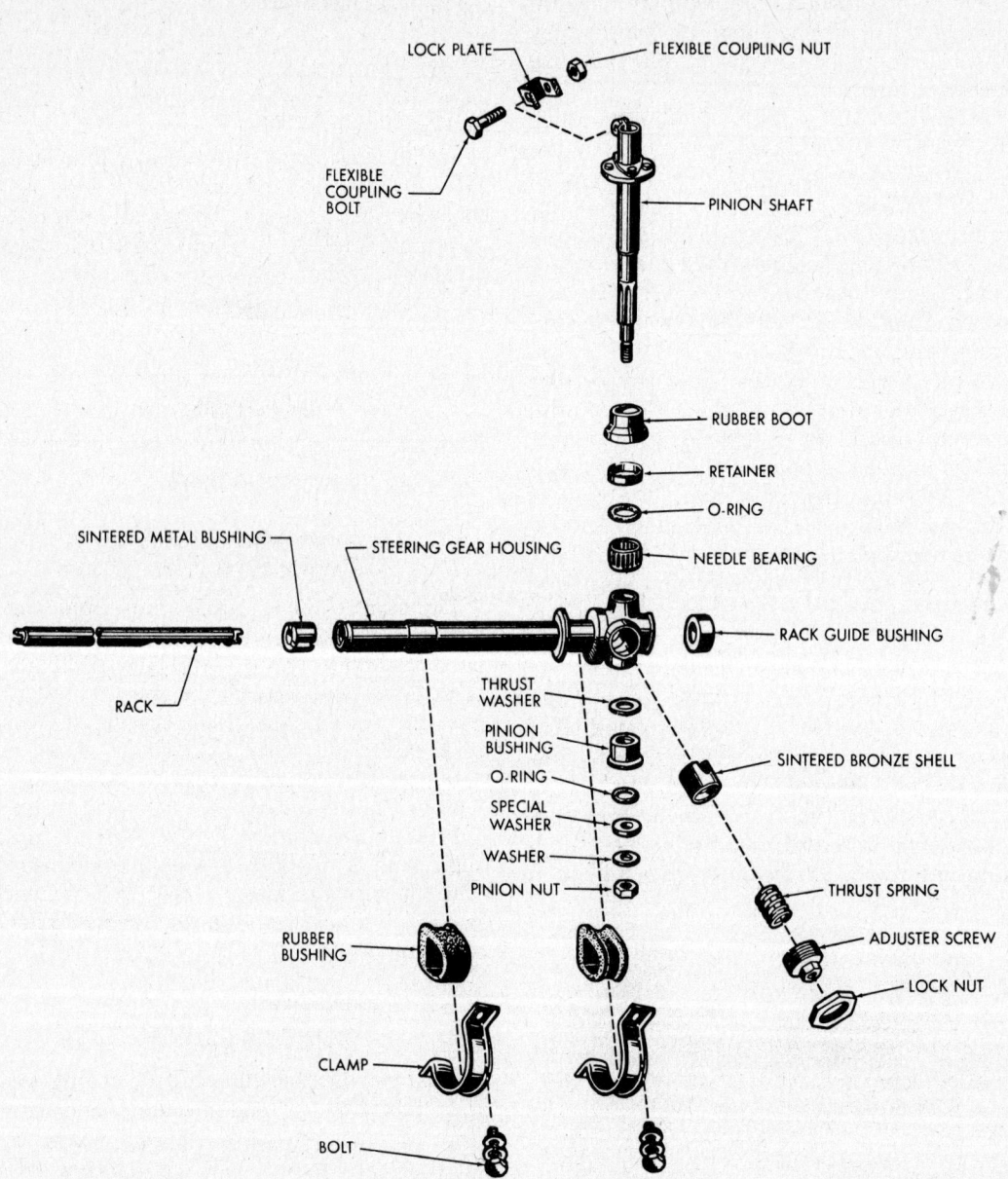

Steering Gear Assembly in Exploded View

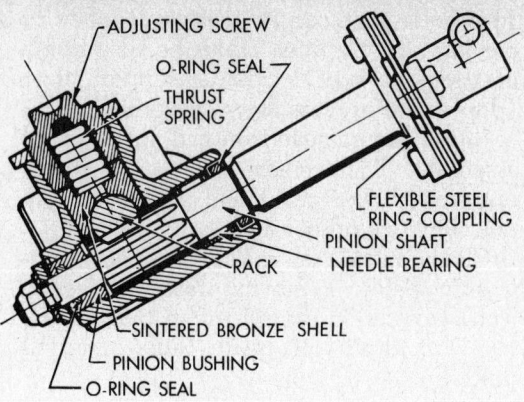

ADJUSTING SCREW
O-RING SEAL
THRUST
SPRING
FLEXIBLE STEEL
RING COUPLING
PINION SHAFT
RACK
NEEDLE BEARING
SINTERED BRONZE SHELL
PINION BUSHING
O-RING SEAL

Steering gear assembly adjusting screw determines rack-to-pinion clearance.

Steering Gear Reconditioning

To disassemble steering gear, clamp housing in soft-jaw vise and slip clamps and bellows off housing to expose ball joint screws. Unscrew tie rod ball studs from racks, holding rack secure with open end wrench. Remove adjusting screw from gear housing and take out thrust spring and sintered bronze shell.

Grip gear assembly so pinion shaft is held by vise and take off pinion nut and washers. Discard pinion nut. Pull pinion shaft and rack from housing. Remove O-rings from retainer and pinion bushing. Take out thrust washer.

When restoring gear assembly, use new O-rings in retainer and pinion bushing. Coat all moving parts, and fill long end of housing with 1¾ oz of lubricant.

Insert long toothless end of rack into short end of housing until rack protrudes from both ends equally (approx. 2⅞″).

Inspect the three air passages in the sintered metal bushing. They must be clean and dry. Blocked vents allow vacuum to build—sucking bellows into and jamming rack teeth.

Set pinion shaft into housing so that its spline meshes with twelfth tooth of the rack (use sleeve J-21712). Position pinion shaft so that flexible coupling is on top—perpendicular to rack. Tighten new pinion nut over washers to only 10 ft.-lbs. to avoid binding.

Set sintered bushing in position, fill adjustment hole with lubricant, and restore thrust spring and screw assembly.

Assemble remaining parts and install unit on car before making a final back lash adjustment.

Steering Gear Adjustment

Set steering gear to high point by positioning front wheels straight ahead with center steering wheel spoke pointing directly downward. Flexible-coupling bolt hole will thereby be positioned parallel to the rack.

Thread adjusting screw into steering gear housing until resistance is felt. (The screw pushes the sintered bronze shell against the rack). Back off adjusting screw ¹⁄₁₂ of a turn (a quarter turn = ³⁄₁₂) and check for free movement of rack, left and right. If not free, delicately back off screw further until rack does move freely. Hold adjuster screw in position and tighten lock nut to 65 ft.-lbs.

Fill area under pinion shaft rubber boot with steering gear lubricant and slide boot into position.

Brakes

Master Cylinder

The drum-type brake system requires a minimum "static" pressure of 4¼ psi on the brake fluid at all times to hold the wheel cylinder cups firmly against the cylinder walls, preventing loss of fluid or entrance of air. Disc brakes, on the other hand, require that all pressure be released to disengage brake pistons.

Kadetts for 1966 with front disc brakes used a master cylinder with the disc-brake circuit entering the master cylinder ahead of the static pressure check valve.

Dual master cylinders, having two brake circuits working independently of each other for front and rear brakes, were introduced on the 1967 Kadetts. One type of dual cylinder was used for the all-drum system requiring a static fluid pressure. A second type provided a pressure-free circuit for the front disc brakes.

Single Master Cylinder Overhaul

Disconnect and tape brake lines entering master brake cylinder. Remove the

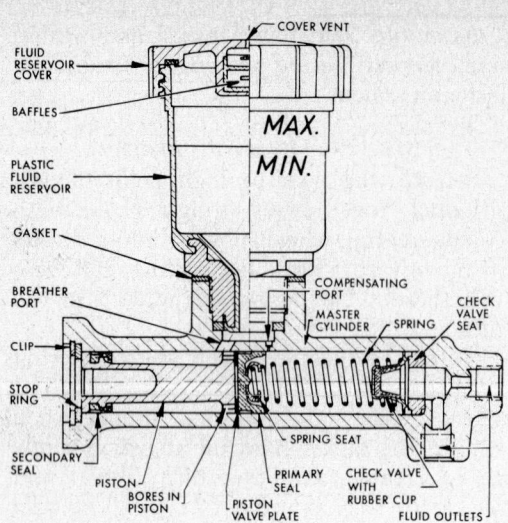

Single Brake Master Cylinder

two bolts that secure master cylinder to cowl wall. Depress brake pedal slightly and remove master cylinder support plate (depression in plate faces master cylinder).

Inside car, remove trim pad above pedal assembly. Then remove actuating pushrod nut from brake pedal and slide assembly out. Remove rubber dust cap.

Clean outside of master cylinder thoroughly before removing reservoir cover. Turn cylinder over and pump pushrod by hand to drain all brake fluid. Discard fluid.

Remove snap ring and stop ring from end of master cylinder. Remove piston with its components. Remove brake fluid reservoir, washer, and gasket. NOTE. *left hand threads on reservoir.*

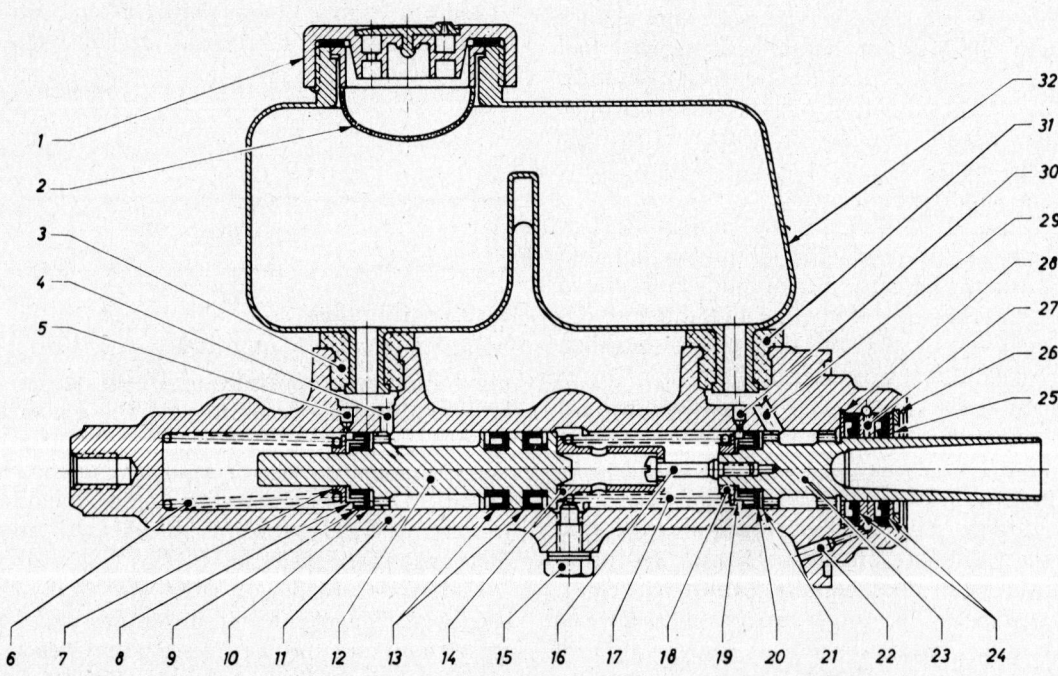

Dual Brake Master Cylinder

1. Cover with seal ring
2. Screen
3. Sealing plug
4. Feed port
5. Compensating port
6. Piston spring
7. Piston spring collar
8. Support ring
9. Primary seal
10. Plate
11. Dual brake master cylinder housing
12. Intermediate piston (for front brake circuit)
13. Secondary seal
14. Stop sleeve
15. Stop screw with seal ring
16. Stop screw
17. Piston spring
18. Piston spring collar
19. Support ring
20. Primary seal
21. Plate
22. Drain port
23. Piston (rear brake circuit)
24. Secondary seals
25. Stop plate
26. Circlip
27. Intermediate ring
28. Stop plate
29. Feed port
30. Compensating port
31. Sealing plug
32. Twin brake fluid container

Inspect master cylinder bore and clean with brake fluid and brush. Check by-pass and compensating ports for restrictions.

Reassemble single master cylinder by first installing reservoir, gasket and washer on cylinder. NOTE. *left hand threads.*

Dip all parts in brake fluid and install valve seat washer, check valve, spring and attached spring seat, primary cap, thin steel washer, and piston with secondary cup. Push piston into bore; then install stop washer and lock ring. Check for free operation. Test proper seating of lock ring with a hard pull on rod.

Dual Master Cylinder Overhaul

Disconnect and tape brake lines entering master cylinder. Remove master cylinder from support bracket and brake booster. Pour out brake fluid and lift out fluid container (reservoir) and its sealing plugs.

Screw static pressure valve out of housing. Push piston into cylinder to point where a rod ¹⁄₁₀-inch thick will slip into the feed port to hold piston in this position. Remove stop screw at bottom and circlip at booster end of housing and take out both pistons together with springs.

Unscrew stop screw from rear-brake-circuit piston. Remove remaining parts.

Clean master cylinder parts with brake fluid and dry with compressed air. Clear compensating and feed ports. Polish cylinder bore and pistons.

Maximum piston diameter	.82 inch
Minimum piston diameter	.81 inch

Replace rubber seals and static pressure valve. Coat parts with brake fluid for reassembly. Assemble intermediate piston and insert it into cylinder bore with thrust spring and spring seat. The smaller diameter of the tapered thrust spring must face piston. With a drift push piston into housing and insert rod into feed port. Install stop screw with new seal ring.

Insert preassembled piston for rear brake circuit into cylinder bore and install circlip into groove in housing. Check piston for free movement. If required, place washers under the head of the stop screw. Push piston partly into housing and remove rod from feed port.

Screw in new static pressure valves. Coat new sealing plugs thinly with brake fluid and insert them into housing. Push twin brake fluid container into sealing plugs.

Brake Booster

The brake booster available on 1967 and later Kadetts reduces required foot pressure for braking approximately 25%. The booster is mechanically controlled by the foot pedal and conveys this pressure along with an engine vacuum assistance to the dual master cylinder. A vacuum control valve prevents air from flowing back into booster when engine is not running. The valve must be replaced when defective.

Checking Brake Booster Operation

The operation of the brake booster can be checked easily.

1. With engine off, use up all vacuum by depressing brake pedal several times.

2. Hold pedal down and start engine. As vacuum builds, the pedal will move farther (held under same foot pressure) as power is developed by booster.

Disc Brakes

Pad Inspection and Reconditioning

Disc brake friction pads can be checked for wear without disassembling the caliper if a gauge is available that measures the distance from the inside of one friction pad backing plate to the other when the brake is engaged. Both brake friction pads must be replaced if either pad is worn down to a thickness of .08″ or less.

If no gauge is available, tap dowel pins from brake caliper towards center of car after pin retainer has been removed. Mark friction pads for later reassembly and pull pads from caliper. Oily, cracked, or defaced pads need replacement. Pads themselves must measure at all times greater than .08 inch thick. Remove high spots on friction pads with cut stone file before reinstalling.

If installing new friction pads, force both caliper pistons into their caliper bores completely with a clamp. NOTE: *Open bleeder valve on caliper to prevent brake reservoir overflow.*

Replace friction pad retaining spring.

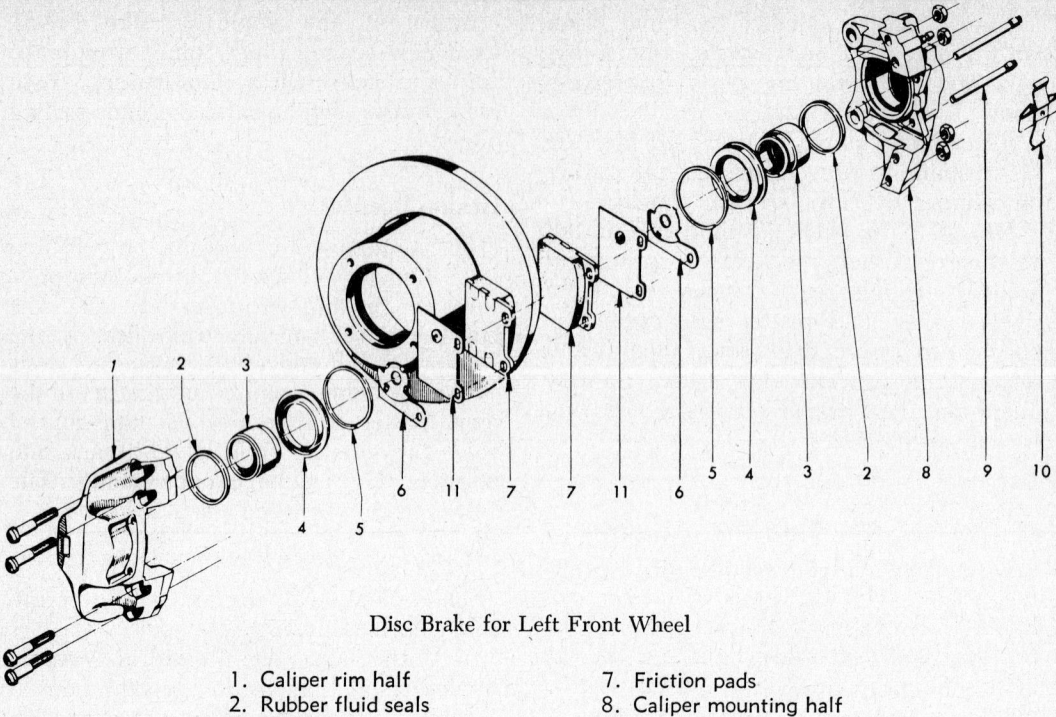

Disc Brake for Left Front Wheel

1. Caliper rim half
2. Rubber fluid seals
3. Hollow pistons
4. Rubber seals
5. Clamp rings
6. Retainer plates
7. Friction pads
8. Caliper mounting half
9. Dowel pins for friction pads
10. Cross-shaped retaining spring
11. Pad backing plate

Press brake pedal several times to seat pads. Bleed and add brake fluid. Avoid forceful braking for 125 miles to break in pads.

CALIPER RECONDITIONING

Remove caliper from wheel backing plate. Loosen brake line at union, unfasten caliper and brake hose bracket and remove brake pipe (plugging hose at union).

Caliper halves are not disassembled for repair work. From opening for friction pads, lift retainer plates from each piston. Next pry clamp rings from rubber seals and remove seals. Keep twin parts from the two halves separated.

Check caliper piston seals and clamp rings for deterioration or damage. Clean ring recesses with *denatured* alcohol.

A special clamp (J-22429) is recommended for forcing pistons from caliper halves.

New rubber seals are recommended for reinstallation with cleaned clamp rings. Make sure that seals are securely seated on their collars and clamp rings are correctly positioned on the seals. Push retainer plates into pistons with handle of screwdriver. Attach brake pipe and caliper to front end, making sure that mating surfaces of caliper and steering knuckle are clean and smooth. Tighten caliper attaching bolts to 50 ft.-lbs.

DISC INSPECTION

The discs should be inspected visually for scratches, nicks, or scoring. The discs may be checked for lateral runout using a dial indicator, mounted perpendicular to the disc, ½″ from its circumference. Disc parallelism is checked with a micrometer.

Minimum thickness of brake disc	.390 inch
Maximum unevenness	.002 inch
Maximum lateral runout	.001 inch

If runout or parallelism exceed the above specifications, the disc should be machined or replaced. NOTE: *In no case should the disc be machined beyond the minimum thickness.* If it is impossible to true disc without exceeding this figure, the disc should be replaced. The disc is removed by unbolting the caliper and suspending it on a piece of heavy wire (NOTE: do not stress the brake hose), and removing the wheel hub. Support the wheel backing plate in a vise, and unbolt the disc hat from the hub using a star wrench. The disc may now be pulled from the hub. CAUTION: *Do not drive the hub out of the disc.*

The disc is installed in the reverse order of removal. When installing the disc on the hub, ensure that the mating surfaces are free of dirt, and torque the star bolts to 36 ft. lbs. Before installing the disc on the car, repack the wheel bearings.

Drum Brakes

WHEEL CYLINDER INSPECTION AND OVERHAUL

Carefully pull lower edges of wheel cylinder boots away from cylinders and note if interior is wet—an indication of brake fluid seepage past the piston cup. If so, cylinder overhaul is required.

Clean dirt from all surrounding surfaces and then disconnect and seal off brake line (tape is often satisfactory for sealing). Remove cylinder from backing plate.

Dismantle boots, pistons, cups and spring from cylinder. Remove bleeder valve. Discard boots and cups; clean other parts with fresh brake fluid. Use no fluid containing even a trace of mineral oil.

Light scratches and corrosion can be polished from pistons and bore with fine emery cloth or steel wool. Dip all parts in brake fluid and reassemble. After in-

stallation, adjust brakes and road test for performance.

BRAKE DRUM INSPECTION

The drums should be checked for cracks, scoring and concentricity. Slight scores may be polished out using emery cloth. Eccentricity or serious scores should be removed by turning the drum providing the maximum diameter is not exceeded.

Maximum eccentricity of drum: .004 inch

NOTE: Eccentricity is measured by measuring and comparing the diameter of the inner and outer edge of the machined surface in two places 90° apart.

Standard drum inner diameter 7.880 inches

Maximum diameter after turning 7.910 inches

To regain center contact with brake shoes, grind linings to .02 inch under drum diameter.

Before reinstalling brake drum, inspect all brake pipe and hose connections for fluid leakage. Tighten these connections and apply heavy pressure to brake pedal to recheck seal. Inspect rear wheel backing plate for leaks from wheel bearing oil seals. Replace seals if needed. Check all backing plate bolts for tightness. Clean away all dirt from assemblies and repack wheel bearings.

If rear wheel backing plate was removed, use new gaskets lightly coated with grease. Torque plate to 21 ft.-lbs. Seal the outside of the backing plate near the brake shoe hold-down springs with body sealing compound.

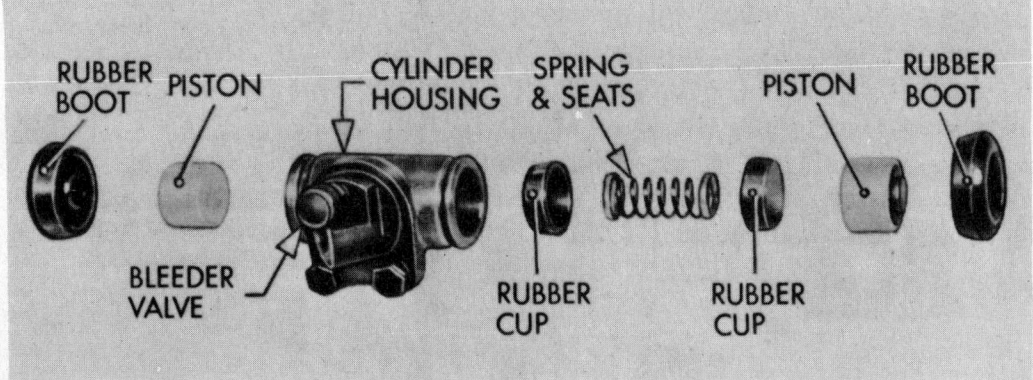

Brake Cylinder for Front Wheel (drum).

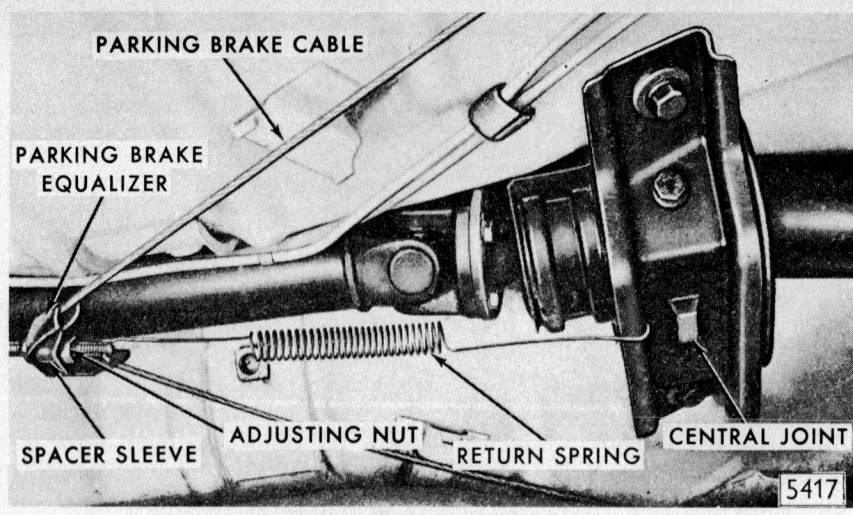

PARKING BRAKE CABLE

PARKING BRAKE
EQUALIZER

SPACER SLEEVE

ADJUSTING NUT

RETURN SPRING

CENTRAL JOINT

5417

Parking brake cable adjustment

ADJUSTMENT

The drum brakes are adjusted using two eccentrics mounted on the backing plate. Turning the eccentrics in the direction of the arrows stamped on the backing plate increases shoe-to-drum contact. When adjusting the front shoes, turn the eccentrics, while turning the wheel forward, until the wheel locks. Then back off the eccentric until the wheel is just free to turn.

Adjust the rear shoe in a similar manner, turning the wheel rearward rather than forward.

Parking Brake

ADJUSTMENT

Lift the rear of the vehicle, and support with jack stands. Release the parking brake lever and loosen the nut in front of the equalizer. Pull the brake lever up three notches (clicks), and tighten the nut behind the equalizer until the rear brakes begin to bind. Tighten the nut in front of the equalizer, and lubricate the cable in the area of the equalizer to ensure proper operation.

Heater

Core Removal and Installation

KADETT

Drain the coolant by removing the lower radiator hose. Disconnect the heater hoses at the heater, remove the housing retaining screws, and remove the core.

Install in the reverse order of removal.

Blower Removal and Installation

KADETT

Disconnect the wire leading to the blower and the air distributor door control cable. Remove the hoses from the air distributor, and remove the air distributor. Remove the screws mounting the blower to the housing, and remove the blower.

Install in the reverse order of removal.

Heater Assembly Removal and Installation

GT

Drain the coolant by removing the lower radiator hose, and remove the hoses from the heater in the engine compartment. Disconnect the hood lock control cable from the lock bar. Remove the console by removing two screws under the ash tray, two screws retaining the headlamp lever handle, and prying the console up to release four retaining snaps. Lower the steering column, and separate the two plug connectors from it.

Remove the two plugs from the sides of the instrument panel, adjacent to the heater control, and remove the screws through the openings. Detach the speedometer cable from the speedometer, and remove the flasher unit, located adjacent to the hood

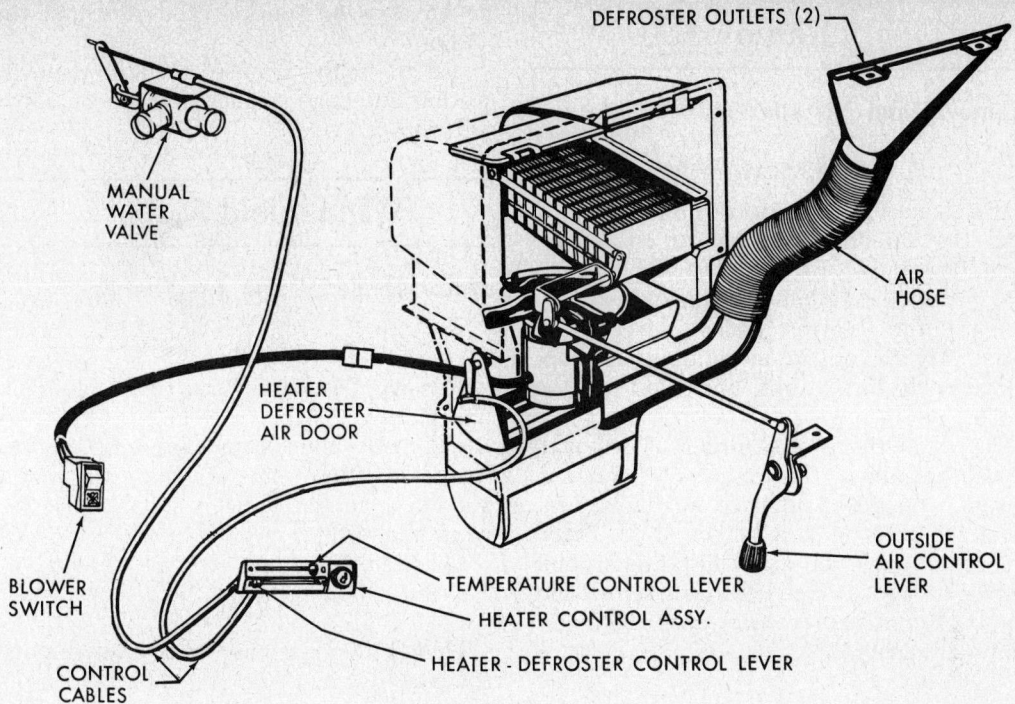

DEFROSTER OUTLETS (2)

MANUAL
WATER
VALVE

AIR
HOSE

HEATER
DEFROSTER
AIR DOOR

BLOWER
SWITCH

TEMPERATURE CONTROL LEVER

HEATER CONTROL ASSY.

CONTROL
CABLES

HEATER - DEFROSTER CONTROL LEVER

OUTSIDE
AIR CONTROL
LEVER

Heater assembly—Kadett

release. Disconnect five plug connectors from the left underside of the instrument panel. Remove two retaining screws from the radio bracket, and one nut from the left side of the instrument panel, and pull the panel out from the top. If so equipped, mark for identification and remove the wires from the ammeter.

Unbolt the heater control panel, and the heater support bracket, located at the upper right corner of the radio bracket.

Remove all screws from the dash panel padding, and remove it from the dash. Disconnect all duct hoses, remove one bolt from the top and two nuts from the bottom of the case, and remove the heater assembly.

Install in the reverse order of removal, checking all connections such as hoses to ensure that they are airtight. Correct any leaks with body sealer.

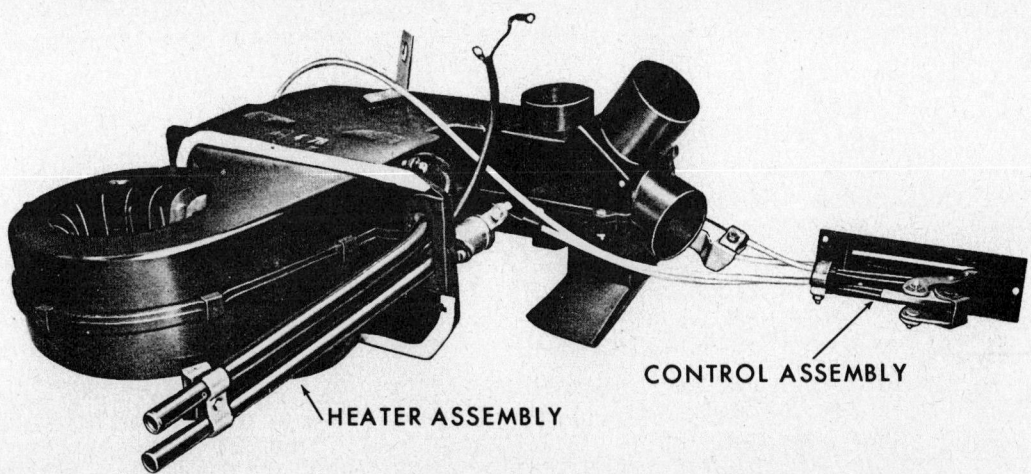

CONTROL ASSEMBLY

HEATER ASSEMBLY

Heater assembly—GT

Radio

Removal and Installation

KADETT

Disconnect the battery ground cable, and the antenna and speaker connectors from the radio. Remove the knobs from the radio, and unbolt the mounting nuts. Remove the receiver bracket lower screw from the receiver, loosen the upper bolt approximately three turns, and slide out the radio.

Install in the reverse order of removal. When installing the radio, the antenna trimmer should be adjusted as follows: extend the antenna to a height of 31″, tune the radio to a barely audible station around 1400 KC, and turn the trimmer screw (on the bottom of the receiver) until maximum volume is achieved.

RALLYE

The procedure is identical to the Kadett, except that the glove box and the right defroster duct must be removed, and the radio installed and removed through the glove box opening.

GT

In order to remove the radio from the GT, the dash and instrument panel must be removed (see Heater Removal). After this is complete, remove the radio knobs and the mounting nuts, disconnect the antenna and the speaker, and slide out the radio.

Install in the reverse order of removal, noting antenna trimmer adjustment above (Kadett).

Windshield Wipers

Motor Removal and Installation

KADETT

Remove the crank arm nut and crank arm from the wiper motor drive shaft, located above the clutch and brake pedals. Unbolt the three nuts attaching the motor and drive to the firewall and remove the wiper motor.

Install in the reverse order of removal.

GT

Unbolt the retaining nuts, and remove the wiper arms. Remove the three bolts retaining the wiper posts to the deflector panels, and allow the posts to drop out of the panels. Unscrew the left and center deflector panels, and remove the left panel, including the motor and linkage.

Remove the crank arm nut from the wiper drive, and separate the linkage from the motor. Unbolt the three retaining nuts, and remove the motor from the deflector panel.

Install in the reverse order of removal. When installing the wiper arms, ensure that they are in the proper position at rest.

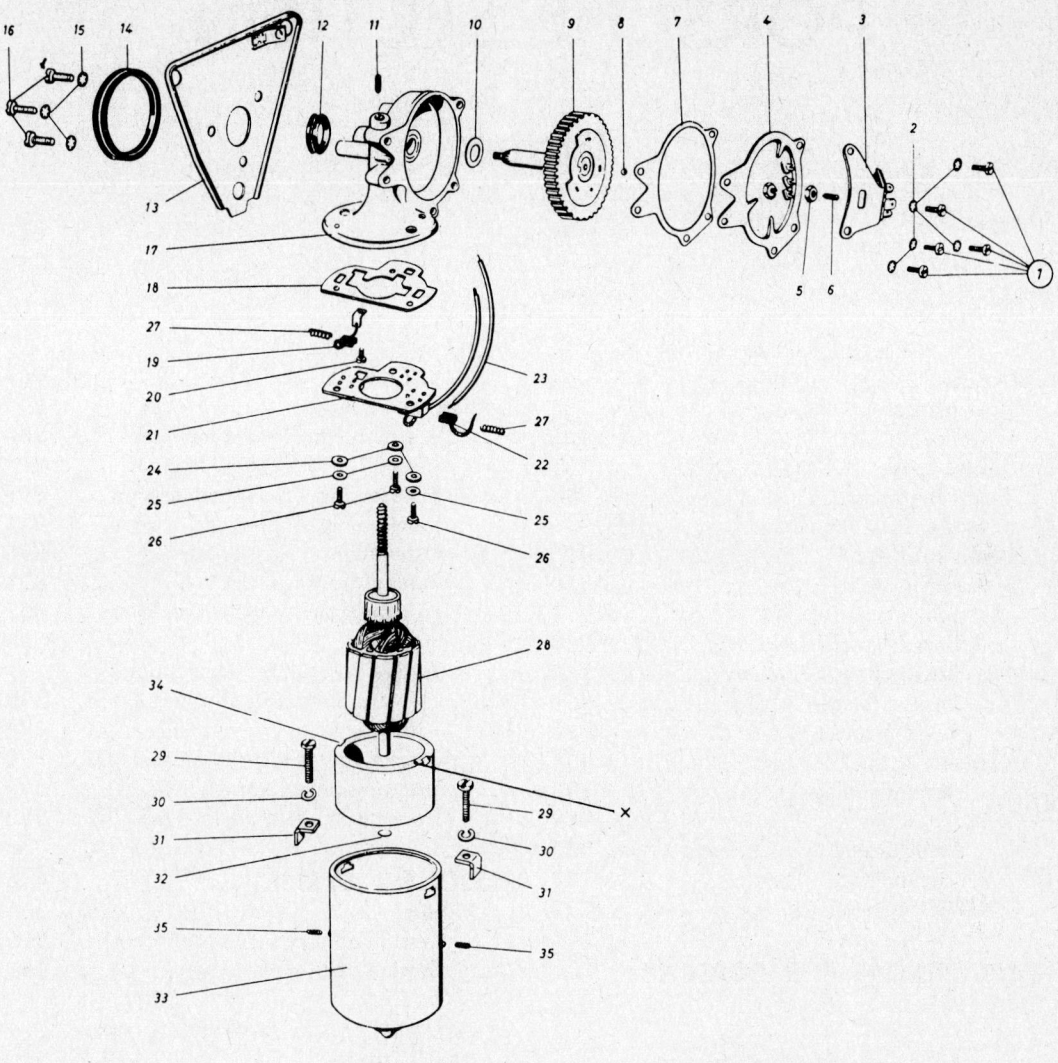

Windshield Wiper Motor—NOTE: *The magnet must be installed with the paint dot facing the drive end.*

1. Attaching screws
2. Toothed washers
3. Contact plate
4. Transmission cover
5. Hex. nut
6. Threaded end-play pin
7. Gasket
8. Ball
9. Driven gear
10. Washer
11. Threaded end-play pin
12. Sleeve
13. Mounting plate
14. Gasket
15. Toothed washers
16. Attaching screws
17. Transmission housing
18. Insert
19. Negative brush
20. Attaching screw
21. Retaining plate
22. Positive brush
23. Wire
24. Rubber bushings
25. Washers
26. Attaching screws
27. Thrust spring
28. Armature
29. Attaching screws
30. Lockwasher
31. Angle brackets
32. Cone
33. Motor housing
34. Magnet ring
35. Magnet threaded pin locators
X   North pole paint marking on this side

PORSCHE SECTION

Index

Year and Model
Identification

1959 Model 356A

1960 Model 356B Roadster

1961 Model 356B Hardtop

1962 Model 356B Cabriolet

1963 Model 356B Coupe

1964 Model 356C Coupe

1965 Model 911 Coupe

1966 Model 911S Coupe

1967 Model 912 2+2 Coupe

1967 Type 911S 2+2 Coupe

1968 Model 911L 2+2 Coupe

1968 Targa Convertible

1969 Model 911E Coupe

1970 Model 914—Four cylinder

Introduction

Porsche was introduced late in 1949, beginning with the 356 model. The body was unitized to a box-construction frame, powered by a modified VW engine, the 1100. The 1300 engine was introduced in 1951, quickly followed by the 1500 in October, 1951. A convertible was introduced in 1952, followed by the 1300S engine in 1954.

In 1955, the 356A Porsche was introduced, followed in 1956 by the 1600 and 1600S engines. The 356B series, from 1960, used the Super-90 engine until 1963, when the 356C and SC, powered by modified S-90 engines, became the Porsche standard. The 912 Porsche, introduced in 1965, was powered by a modified 1600SC engine, but shared the same body style as the six-cylinder 911, first displayed in 1963, in Germany. The 911S was introduced in 1967, and the 911L in 1968. The latest model Porsche, the 914, has been available since 1969, with a four or six-cylinder engine.

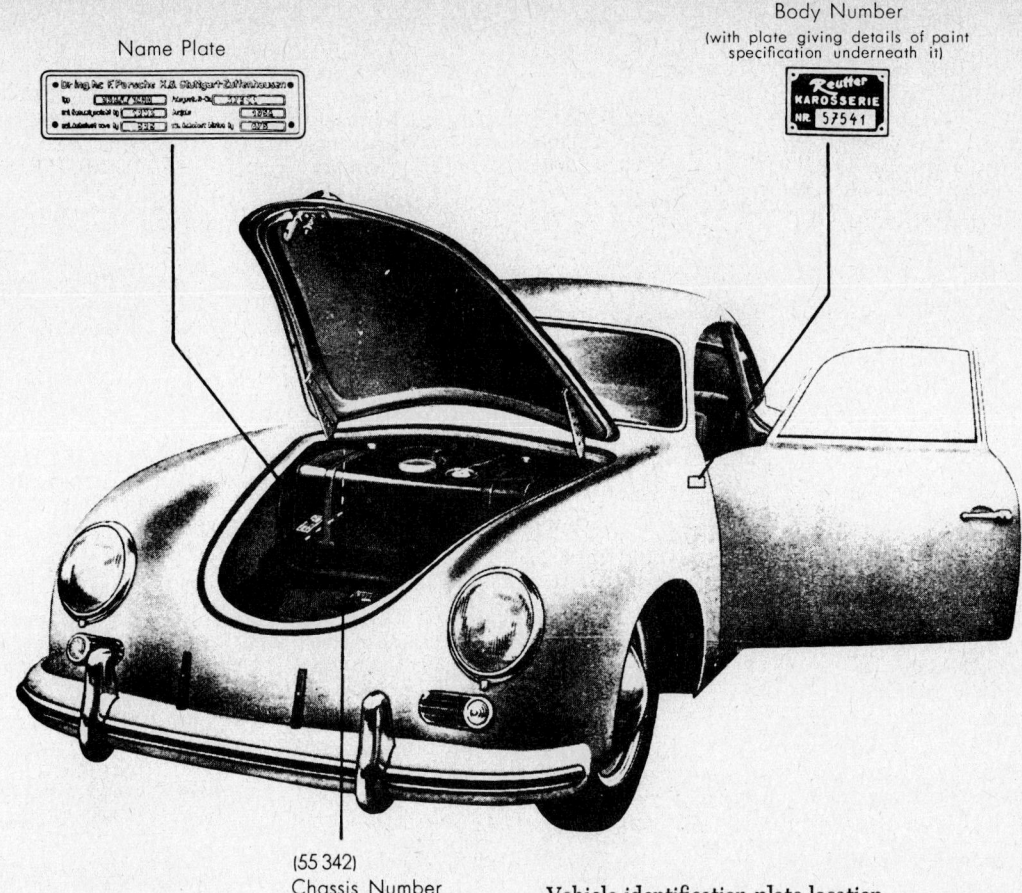

Name Plate

Body Number
(with plate giving details of paint
specification underneath it)

(55 342)
Chassis Number

Vehicle identification plate location

Model Identification

Vehicle and Engine Serial Number Identification

Vehicle Number

Porsche vehicle identification numbers run consecutively for each body shell. The chassis number plate is located in the front luggage compartment on the left side.

Porsche Starting Serial Numbers

1950	1100 series	5001-5410
1951	1100 series	5411-5600
		5132-5162
	1300 series	10001-10170
		10350-10432
	1500 series	10531-11125

1952	1100 series	10433-10469
	1300 series	11126-12084
	1500 series	
	Cabriolet	12301-12387
	Coupe	50001-50098
	1500S series	15001-15116

1953	1100, 1300, 1500, 1500S series	
	Coupe	50099-51645
	Cabriolet	60001-60394

1954	1100, 1300, 1300S (until May), 1300A (June to Nov.), 1500 (until Nov.), 1500S (until Nov.), 1300S, 1500, 1500S (preceding three from Nov.)	
	Coupe	51646-53008
	Cabriolet	60395-60722
	Speedster	80001-80200

1955	1300 series 1300S series 1500 series 1500S series	until Oct.
	Coupe	53009-55000
	Cabriolet	60723-61000
	Speedster	80201-81900

1300 series   }
1300S series   } from Oct.*
1600 series   }
1600S series   }

Coupe	55001-55390
Cabriolet	61001-61069
Speedster	81901-82000

* — Began 356A after October, 1955.
   Classified as a 1956 model

1956   1300, 1300S, 1600, 1600S series

Coupe	55391-58311
Cabriolet	61070-61499
Speedster	82001-82050

1957   1300, 1300S (until Sept.)

Coupe	58312-59090
Cabriolet	61500-61700
Speedster	82851-83691

1600, 1600S (from March)

Coupe	100001-101692
Cabriolet	61701-61892

1600, 1600S (from Sept.)

Coupe	101693-102504
Cabriolet	150001-150149
Speedster	83792-84366

1958   1600 series, 1600S series

Coupe	102505-106174
Cabriolet	150150-151531
Speedster	84367-84922
Convertible	85501-85886

1959   1600, 1600S series
      (until Sept.)

Coupe	106175-108917
Cabriolet	151532-152475
Speedster	85887-86830

1600, 1600S series (from Sept.)*

Coupe	108918-110237
Cabriolet	152476-152943
Roadster	86831-87391

* — Began 356B after September, 1959 (classified 1960 model)

1960   1600, 1600S, 1600 S-90 series

Coupe	110238-114650
Cabriolet	152944-154560
Roadster	87392-88920

1961   1600   }
       1600S   } until Sept.
       1600 S-90   }

Coupe	114651-117476
Karmann/Hardtop	200001-201048
Cabriolet	154561-155569
Roadster	88921-89483

1600   }
1600S   } from Sept.*
1600 S-90   }

Coupe	117601-118950
Karmann/Hardtop	201601-202200
Cabriolet	155601-156200
Roadster	89601-89800

* — Classified as 1962 model

1962   1600   }
       1600S   } until July
       1600 S-90   }

Coupe	118951-121099
Karmann/Hardtop	202201-202299
Karmann/Coupe	210001-210899
Cabriolet	156201-156999

1600   }
1600S   } from July*
1600 S-90   }

Coupe	121100-123042
Karmann/Coupe	210900-212171
Cabriolet	157000-157768

* — Classified 1963 model abroad

1963   1600   }
       1600S   } until July
       1600 S-90   }

Coupe	124239-132304
Karmann/Coupe	212172-214400
Cabriolet	157769-158700

1600C   } from July*
1600SC   }

Coupe	126001-128104
Karmann/Coupe	215001-216738
Cabriolet	159001-159832

* — Began 365C in July, 1963

1964   1600C, 1600SC series

Coupe	128105-131927
Karmann/Coupe	216739-221482
Cabriolet	159833-161577

1965   1600C, 1600SC series

Coupe	138928-
Karmann/Coupe	221483-
Cabriolet	161578-

911 series (Coupe)	300001-300235

911 series (from Jan. to June)

Coupe	300236-303290

912 series (July to Dec.)*

Coupe	350001-351970
Karmann/Coupe	450001-454470

* — Classified as 1966 model

1966   911 series

Coupe	303391-305100

912 series

Coupe	351971-353000
Karmann/Coupe	454470-485100

911 series*

Coupe	305101-307350

911S series*

Coupe	305101S-307360S

912 series

Coupe	354001-354970
Karmann/Coupe	458101-461140

* — Classified as 1967 models

1967   911 series

Coupe	307351-308522
Convertible	500001-500718

911S series

Coupe	307361S-308523S
Convertible	500001S-500718S

912 series
Coupe	354971-355601
Karmann/Coupe	464141-463204
Convertible	550001-550544

911 (USA) * w/emission control
Coupe	11830001-
Karmann/Coupe	11835001-
Convertible	11880001-

911 L series*
Coupe	11810001-
Convertible	11860001-

911 T series*
Coupe	11820001-
Karmann/Coupe	11825001-
Convertible	11870001-

911S series*
Coupe	11800001-
Convertible	11850001-

911 L (USA)* w/emission control
Coupe	11805001-
Convertible	11855001-

912 (USA)* w/emission control and 912 series
Coupe	12820001-
Karmann/Coupe	12800001-
Convertible	12870001-

* — Classified as 1968 models

Engine Number

The engine number is stamped below the generator mount on 356 and 912 models. The engine number is to the right of the blower on the crankcase of 911 models.

PORSCHE ENGINE SERIAL NUMBERS

Year Mfg.	Vehicle and Engine Model Designation	Engine Ser. Nos.
1950	356/1100	0101-0411
1951	356/1100	0412-0999
		10001-10137
	356/1300	1001-1099
		20001-20821
	from Oct. 356/1500	30001-30737
1952	356/1100	10138-10151
	356/1300	20822-21297
	till Sept. 356/1500	30738-30750
	from Sept. 356/1500	30751-31025
	from Oct. 356/1500S	40001-40117
1953	356/1100	10152-10161
	356/1300	21298-21636
	356/1500	31026-32569
	356/1500S	40118-40685
	from Nov. 356/1300S	50001-50017
1954	356/1100	10162-10199
	356/1300	21637-21780
	till May 356/1300S	50018-50099
	June to Nov. 356/1300A	21781-21999
	till Nov. 356/1500	32570-33899
	till Nov. 356/1500S	40686-40999
	from Nov. { 356/1300	22001-22021
	356/1300S	50101-
	356/1500	33901-34119
	356/1500S	41001-41048

Year Mfg.	Vehicle and Engine Model Designation	Engine Ser. Nos.
1955		
till Oct. {	356/1300	22022-22245
	356/1300S	-50127
	356/1500	34120-35790
	356/1500S	41049-41999
from Oct. {	356A/1300	22246-22273
	356A/1300S	50128-50135
	356A/1600	60001-60608
	356A/1600S	80001-80110
1956	356A/1300	22274-22471
	356A/1300S	50136-50155
	356A/1600	60609-63926
	356A/1600S	80111-80756
1957 till Sept.	356A/1300	22472-22999
	356A/1300S	50156-50999
	356A/1600	63927-66999
	356A/1600S	80757-81199
from Sept. {	356A/1600	67001-68216
	356A/1600S	81201-81521
1958	356A/1600	68217-72468
	356A/1600S	81522-83145
1959 till Sept. {	356A/1600	72469-79999
	356A/1600S	83146-84770
from Sept. {	356B/1600	600101-601500
	356B/1600S	84771-85550
1960	356B/1600	601501-604700
	356B/1600S	85551-88320
	356B/1600S-90	800101-802000
1961 till Sept. {	356B/1600	604701-606799
	356B/1600S	88321-89999
		085001-085670
	356B/1600S-90	802001-803999
from Sept. {	356B/1600	606801-607750
	356B/1600S	700001-701200
	356B/1600S-90	804001-804630
1962 till July {	356B/1600	607751-608900
	356B/1600S	701201-702800
	356B/1600S-90	804631-805600
from July {	356B/1600	608901-610000
	356B/1600S	702801-705050
	356B/1600S-90	805601-806600
1963	356B/1600	610001-611000
		0600501-0600600
		611001-611200
till July {	356B/1600S	705051-706000
		0700501-0701200
		706001-707200
	356B/1600S-90	806601-807000
		0800501-0801000
		807001-807400

Year Mfg.	Vehicle and Engine Model Designation	Engine Ser. Nos.	Year Mfg.	Vehicle and Engine Model Designation	Engine Ser. Nos.
from July {	356C/1600C	710001-711870 730001-731102	1967	911	909001-911000
	356C/1600SC	810001-811001 820001-820522		911	911001-911190
1964	356C/1600C	711871-716804		911S	960001 961144
	356C/1600SC	731103-733027 811002-813562 820523-821701		912	750001-753430 836001-836610
1965	356C/1600C	716805	1967 1967	911	911191-912050
	356C/1600SC	733028 813563 821702		911S	961141 962178
from Sept. 64	1965 911	900001-900360		912	753431-756195 836611-837070
1965	1965 911	900361 903550	1968	911USA	3280001-
	from Jan. to June 912	740001-744210		911USA	3380001-
	1966 from July to Dec.	830001-832090		911L	3080001-
1966	1966 911	903551-907000		911L	3180001-
	911	907001-909000		911T	2080001-
	912	744211-750001 832091-836000		911T	2180001-
				911S	4080001-
				911S	4180001-
				911L USA	3280001-
				911L USA	3380001-
				912	1080001- 1085001-
				912USA	1280001-

General Engine Specifications

Model	Type—cylinders— valve & cam arrangement— camshaft drive	Displacement— cubic inches (cubic centim.)	Bore—Stroke— inches (millimeters)	Compression Ratio (to 1)	Max. Brake Horsepower— SAE hp/rpm (DIN hp/rpm)	Maximum Torque SAE ft-lb/rpm (DIN mkg/rpm)	Power Output SAE hp/cu in. (DIN hp/liter)	Maximum Speed—mph	Potential Fuel Consumption— Miles/gallon
914/6	Horiz-6- OHC-chain	121.4 (1991 cc)	3.15–2.598 (80–66 mm)	8.6	125 @ 5800 (110 DIN)	131 @ 4200 (16 mkg)	.9/cu. in.	123	21.3
914	Horiz-4- OHV-push- rods-gears	102.5 (1679 cc)	3.543– 2.598 (90–66 mm)	8.2	85 @ 5000 (80 DIN)	99.45 @ 3500 (97.65 mkg)	1.2/cu. in.	109	25.5
911 and 911L	Horiz-6- OHC-chain	121.5 (1991 cc)	3.15–2.60 (80–66 mm)	9.0	148@6100 (130 DIN)	129@4200 (17.8 mkg)	1.22/cu in. (65/liter)	130	24 (96 oct.)
911S	Horiz-6- OHC-chain	121.5 (1991 cc)	3.15–2.60 (80–66 mm)	9.8	180@6600 (160 DIN)	132@5200 (18.2 mkg)	1.49/cu in. (80/liter)	140	23 (96 oct.)
912	Horiz-4- OHV-push- rods-gears	96.5 (1582 cc)	3.25–2.91 (82.5– 74.0 mm)	9.3	102@5800 (90 DIN)	90@3500 (12.4 mkg)	1.06/cu in. (57/liter)	115	27 (96 oct.)

General Engine Specifications

Model	Type—cylinders—valve & cam arrangement—camshaft drive	Displacement—cubic inches (cubic centim.)	Bore—Stroke—inches (millimeters)	Compression Ratio (to 1)	Max. Brake Horsepower—SAE hp/rpm (DIN hp/rpm)	Maximum Torque SAE ft-lb/rpm (DIN mkg/rpm)	Power Output SAE hp/cu in. (DIN hp/liter)	Maximum Speed—mph	Potential Fuel Consumption—Miles/gallon
356SC	Horiz-4-OHV-push-rods-gears	96.5 (1582 cc)	3.25–2.91 (82.5–74.0 mm)	9.5	107@5800 (95 DIN)	91@4000 (12.6 mkg)	1.11/cu in. (60/liter)	115	27
356C	Horiz-4-OHV-push-rods-gears	96.5 (1582 cc)	3.25–2.91 (82.5–74.0 mm)	8.5	88@5200 (75 DIN)	90½@3600 (12.5 mkg)	0.91/cu in. (47.5/liter)	109	28
1600 S-90	Horiz-4-OHV-push-rods-gears	96.5 (1582 cc)	3.25–2.91 (82.5–74.0 mm)	9.0	102@5500 (90 DIN)	89@4300 (12.3 mkg)	1.06/cu in. (57/liter)	112	27 (92 oct.)
1600S	Horiz-4-OHV-push-rods-gears	96.5 (1582 cc)	3.25–2.91 (82.5–74.0 mm)	8.5	88@5000 (75 DIN)	86@3700 (11.9 mkg)	0.91/cu in. (47.5/liter)	109	29 (88 oct.)
1600	Horiz-4-OHV-push-rods-gears	96.5 (1582 cc)	3.25–2.91 (82.5–74.0 mm)	7.5	70@4500 (60 DIN)	81@2800 (11.2 mkg)	0.73/cu in. (38/liter)	100	31 (86 oct.)
1500S	Horiz-4-OHV-push-rods-gears	90.8 (1488 cc.)	3.15–2.91 (80–74 mm)	8.2	82 @ 5400 (70 DIN)	79.5 @ 3600 (11.0 mkg)	1.04/cu. in.	105	30
1500	Horiz-4-OHV-push-rods-gears	90.8 (1488 cc)	3.15–2.91 (80–74 mm)	7.1	64 @ 4800 (55 DIN)	78 @ 2800 (10.8 mkg)	1.17/cu. in.	96	32
1300S	Horiz-4-OHV-push-rods-gears	78.75 (1290 cc)	2.93–2.91 (74.5–74 mm)	8.2	70@5500 (60 DIN)	65@3600 (9.0 mkg)	0.89/cu. in. (46.5 liter)	99	30 (86 oct.)
1300 (356B and 1300A)	Horiz-4-OHV-push-rods-gears	78.75 (1290 cc)	2.93–2.91 (74.5–74 mm)	6.5	51@4200 (44 DIN)	59½@2800 (8.25 mkg)	0.65/cu. in. (34/liter)	90	30 (86 oct.)
1300 (356)	Horiz-4-OHV-push-rods-gears	78.46 (1286 cc)	3.15–2.52 (80–64 mm)	6.5	51@4200 (44 DIN)	59½@2800 (8.25 mkg)	0.65/cu. in. (34/liter)	90	35 (88 oct.)
1100	Horiz-4-OHV-push-rods-gears	66.27 (1086 cc)	2.9–2.52 (73.5–64 mm)	7.0	47@4200 (40 DIN)	51.8@2800 (7.15 mkg)	0.71/cu. in. (37/liter)	87	39 (88 oct.)

Firing Order

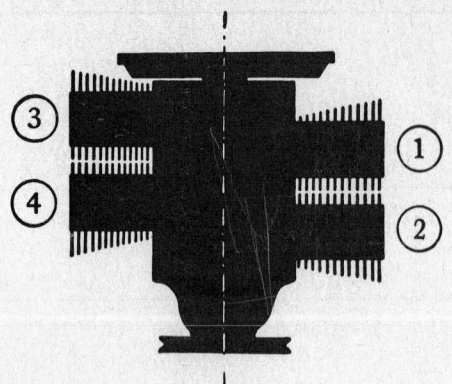

Firing order of 4-cyl. engines, 1-4-3-2. (Front of engine is at top of picture.)

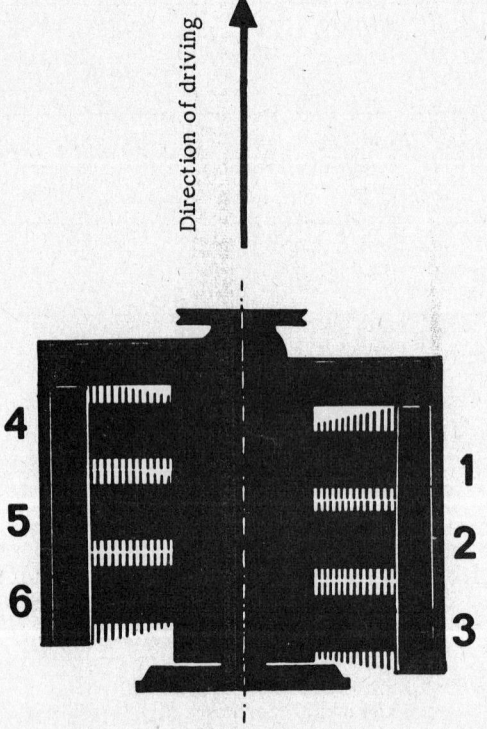

Direction of driving

FIRING ORDER   1 - 6 - 2 - 4 - 3 - 5

Firing order of 2,000, 2,000S and 914/6 engines

Carburetors for Porsche Engines

356 ENGINES
32 PBI Solex
  1100–369 (1950–1954)
  1300–506 (1951–1955)
  1300S–589 (1954)
  1500–546 (1952–1954)
  1500–527 60 hp (1952)

40 PBIC (PICB) Solex
  1300S–589 (1953)
  1500S–528 (1952–1954)
  1500–527 60 hp (1952)

356A ENGINES
32 PBI Solex
  1300–506/2 (1954–1957)

32 PBIC Solex
  1300S–589/2 (1955–1957)
  1600–616/1 (1955–1957)

40 PICB Solex
  1300S–589/2 (1955–1957)
  1600S–616/2 (1955–1957)

40 OCM 2 Weber
  1600 GS

PII Solex
  1500 GS (1955)
  1500 RS (1955)

LATE 356A AND 356B ENGINES
32 NDIX Zenith
  1600–616/1 (1958 & 1960)
  1600–616/2 (1958 & 1960)
  1600S–616/12 (from 700 001)
  1600C–616/15

356C AND 912 ENGINES
40 PII-4 Solex
  1600S–90 616/7
  1600SC–616/16
  912

911, 911S, 911L ENGINES
40 PI Solex
  2000–901/1

40 IDA 3C–3C1 Weber
  2000–901/01 (from #907 001)

40 IDA (S) Weber
  2000S (before 960 502)

40 IDA 3C–3C1 Weber
  2000S (#960 502)

40 IDAP 3C/40 IDAP 3C1 Weber
  901/14
  901/17
  (engines equipped with EECS)

914, 914/6 ENGINES
40 IDT P1 3C1 Weber
40 IDT P1 3C Weber

SPECIAL ENGINES
40 DCM 1 Weber
  1500 RS–550

46 IDM 1 Weber
  1500 RSK

46 IDA 3C–3C1 Weber
  Carrera 6

48 IDA–IDA 1 and 46 IDA2–IDA3 Weber
  904 GT and 8/C–V engines

Distributor Advance Characteristics

Model	Distributor Identification	Centrifugal Advance				Vacuum Advance		Vacuum Retard	
		Start Degrees @ rpm	Intermediate Degrees @ rpm	Intermediate Degrees @ rpm	End Degrees @ rpm	Start @ ins./Hg	End Deg's @ ins./Hg	Start @ ins./Hg	End Degrees @ ins./Hg
914/6	Marelli S 112 EX	0° @ 1,000	15-19° @ 2,000	24-28° @ 4,000	35° @ 6,000	*	*	*	*
914	Bosch 022 905 205 B	0° @ 1,000-1,200	14-17° @ 1,500	14-17° @ 2,100	22-25° @ 2,900	3.93-5.12	12-15° @ 7.48	2.36-3.93	8-10° @ 5.91
914	Bosch 022 905 205 A	0° @ 1,000-1,200	9-12° @ 1,500	15-18° @ 2,200	22-25° @ 2,900	3.93-5.12	12-15° @ 7.48	2.36-3.93	8-10° @ 5.91
911	Bosch JFR 6	N.A.	N.A.	N.A.	N.A.	N.A.	N.A.	N.A.	N.A.
912	Bosch 0231-129 022	5°-14° @ 1,000	21°-26° @ 2,000	29°-34° @ 3,000	30°-35° @ 3,100	*	*	*	*
356C and 356B	Bosch VJR 4 BR18 (MK)	0° @ 600-900	10° @ 1,000-1,200	20° @ 1,600-2,200	33° @ 2,900-5,300	*	*		
356A	Bosch VE 4 BRS 383	0° @ 540-700	10° @ 1,040-1,400	20° @ 1,800-2,280	30° @ 2,700-3,000	*	*	*	*
356	Bosch VE 4 BRS 383	0° @ 540-700	10° @ 1,040-1,400	20° @ 1,800-2,280	30° @ 2,700-3,000	*	*	*	*

* — Distributors not equipped with vacuum advance or retard

Carburetor Specifications

Engine Type	914/6	911-2000 (to 907000)	912	1600 SC and 1600 S-90	1600 C	1600 S (from 1958) (616/2)	1600 (from 1958) (616/1)	1600 S (thru 1957) (616/2)
Carburetor	Weber 40 IDT P1 3C1 Weber 40 IDT P1 3C	40 PI	Solex 40 PII-4	Solex 40-PII-4	Zenith 32 NDIX (dependent idling)	Zenith 32 NDIX (dependent idling)	Zenith 32 NDIX (dependent idling)	Solex 40 PICB (independent idling)
Venturi or Choke Tube (K)	27	30	32	32	28	28	24	29
Main Jet (Gg) (at 1300' altitude average)*	105	125	0120	0115	0130	0130	0115	0130
Air Correction Jet (a)	170	180	180	180	210	220	230	200
Idling Jet (g)	45	55	57.5	57.5	55	50	50	45
Idling Air Bleed (u)	145	1.0	1.8	1.8	140	140	120	2.0
Acceleration Pump Type		0.5 mm	72	72				82
Acceleration Pump Jet (Gp)	50	50	50	50	40	40	50	70
Pump Injection Quantity (warm to cold seasons) from 2 strokes, each nozzle	0.5 cc./stroke	0.40 cc to 0.65 cc	0.45 cc to 0.62 cc	0.45 cc to 0.65 cc	0.25 cc to 0.35 cc	0.2 cc to 0.3 cc	0.2 cc to 0.3 cc	0.55 cc to 0.75 cc (per stroke)
Injection nozzle (i)		0.8 mm	high-type with 0.4 restrictor	high-type with 0.4 restrictor	0.8 short	0.8 short	0.8 short	high 0.8
Float Needle Valve (spring-loaded)	1.75	2.0	175	175	125	125	125	2.0
Fuel Pump Pressure (psi)								
Weight of Float		7 grams	7.4 grams	7.4 grams	5.2 g per float	5.2 g per float	5.2 g per float	23 with fins
Float Level	12.5-13.0 mm. from upper edge of carburetor housing without seal	(fuel level) 15 to 20 mm below intake duct	to inspection port	to inspection port	18.5 ± 1.0 mm (.728″ ± .04″)	18.5 ± 1.0 mm (.728″ ± .04″)	18.5 ± 1.0 mm (.728″ ± .04″)	
Main Jet Carrier			6.0	60				
Emulsion (Mixture) Tube Number (s)	F1	8	25	25	1S	1S	1S	22
Transition (Intermediate) Ports	1.7/1.4/1.0	1.7/1.4/1.0	1.7/1.4/1.0	1.7/1.4/1.0	1.4/1.4	1.4/1.4	1.4/1.4	1.2/1.0/0.8
Stabilizing Bore								
Starter Air Bleed (Ga)				—	—	—	—	—
Starter Fuel Jet (Gs)				—	—	—	—	—

* Decrease size 3% for each additional 1650' altitude. (e.g. jet size 0120 = 1300'; jet size 0115 = 4600')

Carburetor Specifications

Engine Type	356 B 1600 S-90 1960	356A 1500 GS-GT 1958	Carrera 4 Spyder		1600 (thru 1957) (616/1)	1300 S (589/2)	1300 S (589/2)	1300 S 1954	(589) 1953
Carburetor	Solex 40 PII-4	Solex 40 PII-4	Solex 40 PII	Solex 40 PII	Solex 32 PBIC (independent idling)	Solex 40 PICB (independent idling)	Solex 32 PBIC (independent idling)	Solex 32 PBI	Solex 40 PBIC
Venturi or Choke Tube (K)	32	34	34	34	26	26	24	24	26
Main Jet (Cg) (at 1300' altitude average)*	0115	0110	0120	0102.5/0105	0112.5	0105	0105	160	105
Air Correction Jet (a)	180	180	260	140	200	150	200	160	150
Idling Jet (g)	60	50	50	45	50	50	50	50/55	50
Idling Air Bleed (u)		1.5	2.0	2.0	1.5	2.0	1.5	1.0	2.0
Acceleration Pump Type	180	82	82	82	72	83	72	72	83
Acceleration Pump Jet (Gp)	50	50	60	85	60	50	60	80	50
Pump Injection Quantity (warm to cold seasons) from 2 strokes, each nozzle	.45 cc (per stroke)	.45 cc (per stroke)			0.5 cc to 0.7 cc (per stroke)	0.7 cc to 0.9 cc (per stroke)	0.5 cc to 0.7 cc (per stroke)	0.5 cc to 0.7 cc (per stroke)	0.7 cc to 0.9 cc (per stroke)
Injection nozzle (i)	high 0.4	high 0.4			high 0.8	high	low	high 1.2	low
Float Needle Valve (spring-loaded)	175 suspended	2.0	2.0	2.0	1.5	2.0	1.5	2.0	2.0
Fuel Pump Pressure (psi)	1.9–2.6 psi	2.3–2.8 psi							
Weight of Float	7.4 grams	10 grams	10 grams	10 grams	5.7 grams	21 grams	5.7 grams	12.5 grams	21 grams
Float Level								16 ± 1.5 mm	16 ± 1.5 mm
Main Jet Carrier									
Emulsion (Mixture) Tube Number (s)	25	21	33		33	28 (open end)	33	0	28
Transition (Intermediate) Ports	1.7/1.4/1.0	1.5/1.2/1.0	1.0/1.0		1.0/1.0	1.2/1.0/0.8	1.0/0.8	1.2/1.5	0.8/1.0/1.2
Stabilizing Bore								yes	no
Starter Air Bleed (Ga)							—	3.5	—
Starter Fuel Jet (Gs)							—	120	—

* Decrease size 3% for each additional 1650' altitude. (e.g. jet size 0120 = 1300'; jet size 0115 = 4600')

Carburetor Specifications

	1300 (506/2) 1954–1957	1500 S (528) 1952	1500 S (528) 1953	1500 S (528) 1954	1500 60 hp (527) (1952)	1500 60 hp (527) (1952)	1500 (546) (1952–54)	1300 (1951–54) (506)	1100 (1950–54) (369)
Engine Type									
Carburetor	Solex 32 PBI (dependent idling)	Solex 40 PBIC (dependent idling)	Solex 40 PBIC (independent idling)	Solex 40 PBIC (PICB) (independent idling)	Solex 32 PBI	Solex 40 PBIC (dependent idling)	Solex 32 PBI	Solex 32 PBI	Solex 32 PBI
Venturi or Choke Tube (K)	23	26 (29-sport)	26 (29-sport)	26 (29-sport)	26	26 (29-sport)	24	24	23
Main Jet (Cg) (at 1300' altitude average)*	0125	117.5 (135-sport)	107.5 (117.5-sport)	85 (97.5 or 102.5 sport)	115	115 (130-sport)	120	115	110
Air Correction Jet (a)	220	160	160	160	180	160	260	240	230
Idling Jet (g)	50	55	50	55	55	55	55	60	60
Idling Air Bleed (u)	1.0	2.2	1.0	2.0	1.0	1.0	1.0	1.0	1.0
Acceleration Pump Type	72	82	82	83	72	82	72	73	73
Acceleration Pump Jet (Gp)	60	60	85 (110-sport)	80 (90-sport)	55	60	55	55	50
Pump Injection Quantity (warm to cold seasons) from 2 strokes, each nozzle	0.5 cc to 0.7 cc (per stroke)	0.7 cc to 0.9 cc (per stroke)	0.7 cc to 0.9 cc (per stroke)	0.7 cc to 0.9 cc (per stroke)	0.5 to 0.7 cc (per stroke)	0.7 to 0.9 cc (per stroke)	0.5 to 0.7 cc (per stroke)	0.5 to 0.7 cc (per stroke)	0.5 to 0.7 cc (per stroke)
Injection nozzle (i)	high 0.8	high 0.8	high 1.2	low	high	high 0.8	high 0.8	high 0.8	high 0.8
Float Needle Valve (spring-loaded)	1.5	2.0	2.0	2.0	2.0	2.0	2.0	1.5	1.5
Fuel Pump Pressure (psi)									
Weight of Float	12.5 grams	21	21	21	12.5 grams	21 grams	12.5 = metal 5.7 = plastic	12.5 grams	12.5 grams
Float Level	16 ± 15 mm	16 ± 15 mm		20 (+1 mm)	20 (+1 mm)	20 (+1 mm)	16 ± 1.5 mm	16 ± 1.5 mm	16 ± 1.5 mm
Main Jet Carrier									
Emulsion (Mixture) Tube Number (s)	33	23	28	28	23	23	28	23	23
Transition (Intermediate) Ports	1.2/1.2	1.3/1.5	1.3/1.5	0.8/1.0/1.2	1.2/1.2	1.3/1.5	1.2/1.2	1.2/1.2	1.2/1.2
Stabilizing Bore	yes	no	yes 1.8	no	yes 1.5	yes 1.8	yes	yes	yes
Starter Air Bleed (Ga)	3.5	—	—	3.5	3.5	—	3.5	3.5	3.5
Starter Fuel Jet (Gs)	120	—	—	120	120	—	120	120	120

* Decrease size 3% for each additional 1650' altitude. (e.g. jet size 0120 = 1300'; jet size 0115 = 4600')

Carburetor Specifications

	901/14 and 901/17	2000S (from #960 502)	2000S (to #960 502)	2000 (from #907 001)	1500 RS (550)	Carrera 6
Engine Type						
Carburetor	Weber 40-IDAP 3C 40 IDAP 3C1	Weber 40 IDS 3C 40 IDS 3C1	Weber 40 IDA (S)	Weber 40 IDA 3C 40 IDA 3C1	Weber 40 DCM 1	Weber 46 IDA 3C-3C1
Venturi	30	32	32	30	34	42
Pre-Atomizer (aux. venturi)	4.5	4.5	4.5	4.5	3.5	4.5
Main Jet	125	125	135	125	Rear 1.15 Front 1.20	1.70
Air Correction Jet	180	185	170	180	1.75	1.45
Idle Jet	52	55	55	55	45 X 45	0.70
Idle Air Bleed	110	110	110	110	(holder) 1.20	
Acceleration Pump Jet	50	50	50	50	0.55	0.50
Emulsion Tube	F 26	F 3	F 26	F 26	F 4	F 24
Float Weight	25.5 grams				67 grams	25.5 grams
Float Level (top of float to top edge of housing, no gasket)	12.5–13.0 mm (.492″–.512″)	12.5–13.0 mm (.492″–.512″)	12.5–13.0 mm (.492″–.512″)	12.5–13.0 mm (.492″–.512″)	10.5 to 11.5	12.5 to 13
Fuel Level (from top edge of housing with fuel pressure 3.6 psi)	20.75 ± 1 mm	20.5–21.0 mm (.807″–.827″)	20.5–21.0 mm (.807″–.827″)	20.5–21.0 mm (.807″–.827″)		
Float Needle Valve	1.75	1.75	1.75	1.75	3.0	1.75
Enrichment Jet	70					
Pump Jet	closed					
Pump Cam	adjustable					
Pump Inlet Valve	closed					
Injection Quantity (per stroke)	0.5 ± 0.1 cc	0.8 ± 0.2 cc	0.8 ± 0.2 cc	0.8 ± 0.2 cc		
Float Chamber Vent (diameter)	6.0 mm	4.5 mm	4.5 mm	6.0 mm		
Mixture Outlet	5 mm					
Idle Mixture Outlet	1.0 mm					
Bypass Orifices	0.8/1.1/ 1.35 mm					

Engine Rebuilding Specifications

Model	Crankshaft (ins.) — Main Bearing Journals° Jour. Diameter New▲	Jour. Diameter Min.	Oil Clearance	Shaft[4] End-Play	Connecting Rod Bear. Jour. — Jour. Diameter New	Jour. Diameter Min.▲	Oil Clearance	End-Play	Thrust on No.	Cylinder Bore New	Cylinder Bore Max.	Pistons (ins.) — Mahle Piston Diameter New	Mahle Piston Diameter Max.	Schmidt[5] Piston Diameter New	Schmidt[5] Piston Diameter Max.	Wrist Pin Diameter (Fit) Mahle	Wrist Pin Diameter (Fit) Schmidt
914/6	2.2429-2.2437	N.A.	.0004-.0028	.0043-.0077	2.2429-2.2437	N.A.	.0011-.0034	.0078-.0157	1	3.1496	3.1701-3.1705	3.1484	3.1685	3.1480	3.1685	.86614 / 0 to -.00016	.86614 / 0 to -.00016
914	2.3610-2.3618	2.3296-2.3304	N.A.	.0028-.0051	2.1646-2.1654	N.A.	N.A.	.004-.016	1	3.543	3.583-3.5834	3.5417	3.5815	—	—	.94472-.94582	—
911	2.2429-2.2437	N.A.	.0004-.0028	.0043-.0077	2.2429-2.2437	N.A.	.0011-.0034	.0078-.0157	1	3.1496-3.1500	3.1696-3.1700	3.1470-3.1474	3.1671-3.1675	—	—	(Press)	
912	2.1654[6]	N.A.	.001-.003[8]	.005-.007	2.0866	N.A.	.0016-.0036	.0039-.0118	1	3.2479	3.2679-3.2682	3.2301-3.2311	3.2311	—	—	.8660-.8661[7]	(Press)
356C (1600SC)	2.1641-2.1649	N.A.	.001-.003[1]	.005-.007	2.0866	N.A.	.0016-.0036	.0039-.0118	1	3.2479	N.A.	3.2460 ±.0002	3.2661 ±.0002	—	—	(Press)	
356C (1600C)	2.1641-2.1649	N.A.	.001-.003[1]	.005-.007	2.0866	N.A.	.0016-.0036	.0039-.0118	1	3.2479	N.A.	3.2460 ±.0002	3.2661 ±.0002	—	—	(Press)	
356B (1600 cast iron)	1.9685	N.A.	.001-.003	.005-.007	2.0866	N.A.	.0016-.0036	.0039-.0118	1	3.2479	3.2657	3.2479	3.2657	—	—	(Press)	
356B (1600S light alloy)	1.9685	N.A.	.001-.003	.005-.007	2.0866	N.A.	.0016-.0036	.0039-.0118	1	3.2479	3.2657	3.2479	3.2657	3.2456	3.2659[2]	(Press)	(Press)
356A (1600 1600S)	1.9687	N.A.	.0018-.0039	.005-.007	2.0866	N.A.	.0016-.0036	.0039-.0118	1	3.2479	3.2657	3.247	3.2657	—	—	(Press)	
356A (1300 1300S)	1.9687	N.A.	.0018-.0039	.0055-.0067	2.0866	N.A.	.0016-.0036	.0039-.0118	1	2.9329	N.A.	2.933	N.A.	—	—	(Press)	
356 (1300S 1500S)	1.9687	³	.0018-.0039	.004-.0055[9]	³	³	.002	N.A.	1	2.9329 / 3.1496	N.A.	2.9275-2.9277 / 3.1440-3.1442	2.9283-2.9285 / 3.1448-3.1450	—	—	(Press)	
356 (1300 1500)	1.9687	N.A.	.0018-.0039	.004-.0055	2.0937	N.A.	.002	N.A.	1	3.1496	N.A.	3.1560	N.A.	—	—	(Press)	
356 (1100)	1.9687	N.A.	.0018-.0039	.004-.0055	1.9687	N.A.	.002	N.A.	1	2.8936	2.9133	2.890	2.911	—	—	.78716-.78724	(Press)

Model	Side Clearance				End-Gap			
	Ring 1	Ring 2	Ring 3	Ring 4	Ring 1	Ring 2	Ring 3	Ring 4
914/6	.0032-.0043	.0020-.0032	.0012-.0024	—	.0118-.0177	.0118-.0177	.0098-.0157	—
914	.0024-.0035	.0016-.0028	.0008-.0020	—	.0138-.0217	.0118-.0217	.0098-.0157	—
911	.0029-.0042	.0023-.0028	.0010-.0020	—	.0118-.0177	.0118-.0177	.0098-.0157	—
912	.0030-.0042	.0018-.0028	.0010-.0020	—	.012-.018	.012-.018	.012-.018	—
356C-(1600SC)	.0030-.0042	.0018-.0028	.0018-.0028	.0010-.0022	.004-.018	.004-.018	.004-.018	.004-.018
356C (1600C)	.0030-.0042	.0024-.0031	.0014-.0024	.0010-.0022	.010-.020	.010-.020	.010-.020	.010-.020
356B (1600 cast iron)	.0030-.0042	.0024-.0031	.0014-.0024	—	.010-.020	.010-.020	.010-.020	—
356B (1600S-light alloy)	.0018-.0028	.0010-.0020	.0010-.0020	—	.004-.018	.004-.018	.004-.018	—
356A (1600 1600S)	.0014-.0019	.0014-.0019	.0006-.0012	—	.004-.0118	.004-.0118	.004-.0118	—
356A (1300 1300S)	.0014-.0019	.0014-.0019	.0006-.0012	—	.004-.0118	.004-.0118	.004-.0118	—
356- (1300S 1500S)	.0014-.0019	.0014-.0019	.0006-.0012	—	.004-.012	.004-.012	.004-.012	—
356- (1300 1500)	.0014-.0019	.0014-.0019	.0006-.0012	—	.004-.012	.004-.012	.004-.012	—
356- (1100)	.0014-.0019	.0014-.0019	.0006-.0012	—	.012-.018	.012-.018	.012-.018	—

1 Crankshaft Journal Clearance:
Bearing 1 - .0011"-.0031"
Bearing 2, 3 - .0014"-.0035"
Bearing 4 - .0016"-.0041"

2 Pistons made by Mahle and Nural.

3 Uses roller bearing crankshaft.

* — First main bearing journal diameter given is for 1-7 bearings (six cylinder engines) and 1-3 bearings (four cylinder engines). The second journal size is for the last bearing. The bearing nearest the distributor drive gear (No. 1) is at the other end.

4 Crankshaft end-play measured at the thrust bearing.

5 Schmidt piston ring side clearance:
Ring 1 (Top)   .0028" – .0039"
Ring 2   .0016" – .0028"
Oil Ring   .0008" – .0020"

6 Specification given is for No. 2 and 3 main bearing. No. 1 main bearing journal is 1.9865".

7 Piston pin specification is for pin color coded white.

8 912 and 356 B oil clearance:
No. 2 and 3 bearing: .0018"-.0039"
No. 4 bearing: .0016"-.0041"

9 Type 356 No. 4 bearing
Oil clearance: .0016"-.0044"

▲ Crankshaft main bearing journals may be ground .030" undersize. Before any attempts are made to regrind bearing journals of any kind consult an authorized Porsche dealer. Connecting rod bearing journals may also be reground. Consult an authorized Porsche dealer for exact specifications.

Engine Rebuilding Specifications (con't)

Model	Valve Seat Angle	Minimum Valve Face Contact (ins.)		Valve Lift (ins.)		Valve Spring Pressure (lbs.)		Valves				Valve Guide Removable
								Valve Spring Installed Height (ins.)		Stem Diameter (ins.)		Stem-to-Guide Clearance (ins.)	
		Intake	Exhaust	Intake	Exhaust	Intake	Exhaust	Intake	Exhaust	Intake	Exhaust	Intake	Exhaust	
914/6	45°	.0453	.0571	N.A.	N.A.	N.A.	N.A.	1.42 ±.01	1.42 ±.01	.3531 –.0005	.3524 –.0005	N.A.	N.A.	Yes
914	30° °°°	.0709	.0787	N.A.	N.A.	159.8-184.1	159.8-184.1	1.18	1.18	.3126-.3130	.3508-.3512	.0177	.0177	Yes
911	45°	.0453	.0571	.453 [1]	.413 [1]	176.4	165.3	1.417 ±.012	1.417 ±.012	.3527 –.0004	.3526 –.0004	.0011-.0022	.0019-.0030	Yes
912	45°	.044	.055	N.A.	N.A.	79.3 ±3.32	79.3 ±3.32	1.61	1.57	.3929-.3933	.3921-.3925	.0014-.0024	.0022-.0031	Yes
356C-1600SC	45°	N.A.	N.A.	.425	.362	N.A.	N.A.	1.61	1.575	.3929-.3933	.3921-.3925	N.A.	N.A.	Yes
356C-1600C 356B-1600 (cast iron)	45°	N.A.	N.A.	.394	.339	N.A.	N.A.	1.67	1.63	N.A.	N.A.	N.A.	N.A.	Yes
356B-1600S (light alloy)	45°	.043	.055	.425	.362	N.A.	N.A.	1.675 [2]	1.635 [2]	.3929-.3932	.3920-.3924	.0014-.0024	.0022-.0032	Yes
356A-1300 1600	45°	.043	.055	.325	.325	83.3	83.3	1.25	1.25	.3929-.3933	.3921-.3925	.00138-.00236	.00216-.00315	Yes
-1300S -1600S				.378	.364									
356-1100	45°	.043	.055	.325	.325	83	83	1.234	1.234	.313-.314	.3127-.3131	.00137-.00236	.00216-.00315	Yes
356-1300 -1500	45°	.043	.055	.325	.325	83	83	1.234	1.234	.31318-.31362	.31279-.31318	.00137-.00236	.00275-.00374	Yes
356-1300S -1500S	45°	.043	.055	.378	.364	83	83	1.234	1.234	.31318-.31362	.31279-.31318	.00137-.00236	.00275-.00374	Yes

°°° – Seat angle of 914 engine is 30° (Intake) and 45° (Exhaust)

1 Valve Lift Type 2,000 T Engine: Intake – .382"
Exhaust – .350"

2 Replaced in mid-year—Intake – 1.614"
Exhaust – 1.575"

Tune-up Specifications

Model	Spark Plugs Make Type°	Gap	Distributor Point dwell	Point gap	Basic Ignition Timing (deg.)	°° Dynamic Ignition Timing (deg. @ rpm)	Cranking Comp. Pressure (p.s.i.)	Valves Clearance (in) Intake (Cold)	Exhaust (Cold)	Intake Opens (deg.)	Idle Speed (rpm)
914/6	W230-T30	.024"	40°±3°	.016"	N.A.	35° BTDC @ 6,000 rpm	140-150	.0039"	.0039"	15° B	900-950
914	W175-T21	.028"	44°-50°	.016"	5° B	27° BTDC @ 3,500 rpm	128-156	.0039"	.0039"	12° B	900-950
911 911L	W250-P21	.014"	38°±3°	.016"	5° B	35° BTDC @ 6,000 rpm (load)	128-156	.004"	.004"	29° B	1200-1400
911S	W265-P21	.014"	38°±3°	.016"	5° B	31° BTDC @ 6,000 rpm (load)	128-156	.004"	.004"	29° B	850-950
912	W225-T1	.020"-.024"	47°-53°	.016"	3° B	N.A.	°°°	.004"	.006"	17° B	1000
1600SC 1600S-90	W225-T1	.020"-.024"	47°-53°	.016"	3° B	N.A.	°°°	See Valve Clearance Chart		17° B	1000
1600C 1600S 1600	W225-T1	.020"-.024"	47°-53°	.016"	5° B	N.A.	°°°	See Valve Clearance Chart		10° B	750-850
1300S 1600S (356A)	W240-T1	.028"	50°	.016"	5° B	N.A.	°°°	See Valve Clearance Chart		15° B	750-850
1300 1600 (356A)	W225-T1	.028"	47°-53°	.016"	5° B	N.A.	°°°	See Valve Clearance Chart		5° B	750-850
356 Engines	W225-T1	.028"	47°-53°	.016"-.020"	5° B	N.A.	°°°	See Valve Clearance Chart		2½° B	750-850

° — All spark plug references are to Bosch spark plugs.
B }
BTDC — Before Top Dead Center

°° — With vacuum hoses disconnected
°°° — No compression figures listed—all cylinders within 10 p.s.i. of each other

Valve Clearances (Cold)

Vertical notes for the 3-Piece Crankcase columns:
- [A] Valve Clearance for engines beginning with Engine No. P-84771 (356B) with light-alloy rocker arm bracket and light-alloy pushrods.
- [B] From engine No. 700001 (616/12) with light-alloy rocker arm brackets and two-metal pushrods.
- [C] From engine No. 820641 or 811-362 (6-6/16) resp. with "Biral"-cylinders and two metal pushrods.

Engine		2-Piece Crankcase With Steel Pushrods (in.)	With Light-Alloy Pushrods (in.)	3-Piece Crankcase (in.) [A]	(in.) [B]	(in.) [C]
1100	Intake	.008				
	Exhaust	.006				
1300	Intake	.004	.008	.004		
	Exhaust	.004	.006	.006		
1300A	Intake		.008			
	Exhaust		.006			
1300S	Intake		.008	.004		
	Exhaust		.006	.010		
1500	Intake	.004	.008	.004		
	Exhaust	.004	.006	.006		
1500S	Intake	.006	.008	.004		
	Exhaust	.004	.006	.006		
1600	Intake			.004		
	Exhaust			.006		
1600S	Intake			.004	.006	.004
	Exhaust			.006	.004	.006
1600S-90	Intake			.006		
	Exhaust			.004		
1600C	Intake			.004		
	Exhaust			.006		
1600SC	Intake			.006		.004
	Exhaust			.004		.006

Cylinder and Piston Sizes

356 Engines

1300 AND 1300S SERIES

Type 1300

piston diameter 3⁵/₃₂″ (80 mm.)
special characterstics:
nose type (formerly also flat)
2 compression rings
1 oil ring above piston boss

For cylinder bore 2.933″ dia (74.5 mm)

Group	Dia. of cylinder (in.)	Dia. of piston (in.)
A	2.928347—2.928543	2.927559—2.927755
B	2.928543—2.928740	2.927755—2.927953
C	2.928740—2.928937	2.927953—2.928149
D	2.928936—2.929134	2.928149—2.928347
E	2.929134—2.929330	2.928347—2.928543

Type 1300S

piston diameter 3.925″ (74.5 mm.)
special characteristics:
flat piston with recess for exhaust valve; exceptionally
broad bevel.
2 compression rings over piston pin boss
1 oil ring below piston pin boss

1500 AND 1500S SERIES

For cylinder bore 3.15″ dia (80 mm)

Group	Dia. of cylinder (in.)	Dia. of piston (in.)
A	3.144882—3.145078	3.144094—3.144290
B	3.145078—3.145275	3.144290—3.144488
C	3.145275—3.145471	3.144488—3.144684
D	3.145471—3.145669	3.144684—3.144882
E	3.145669—3.145865	3.144882—3.145078

Type 1500

piston diameter 3⁵/₃₂″ (80 mm.)
special characteristics:
flat piston with recess for exhaust valve; narrow bevel
between crown of piston and top land
distance from crown to boss (a) 4³/₆₄″ (17 mm.)

Type 1500S

piston diameter 3⁵/₃₂″ (80 mm.)
special characteristics:
flat piston with recess for exhaust valve; broad bevel on
rim of crown
distance piston crown to piston pin boss (a) 0.77″

Clearance between piston and cylinder

1300	= 0.0006″
1300 Super	= 0.0006″
1500	= 0.001″
1500 Super	= 0.001″

1100 Series

Color	Dia. of cylinder	Dia. of fitted piston
Standard size	blue 2.89330" —2.89366"	2.890945"
Basic size 2.8937	rose 2.89370" —2.89405"	2.89134"
Over size	blue 2.912992"—2.913346"	2.91063"
Basic size 2.9134	rose 2.91338" —2.91374"	2.91102"

Clearance between cylinder and piston:
0.008"

The 1100 series engine takes pistons of identical color designation only, while other 356 series engines use pistons belonging to the same letter group.

Type 1100

piston diameter $2^{29}/_{32}$" (74 mm.)
special characteristics:
domed crown with recess for exhaust valve
2 compression rings
1 oil ring above the piston pin boss

356A Engines

1300 and 1300S Series

Nominal cylinder bore = 74.5 mm
(2.933 in)

Group	Cylinder bore (mm.)	Piston dia. (mm.)	Group	Cylinder bore (mm.)	Piston dia. (mm.)
A	74.460—74.465	74.440—74.445	F	74.485—74.490	74.465—74.470
B	74.465—74.470	74.445—74.450	G	74.490—74.495	74.470—74.475
C	74.470—74.475	74.450—74.455	H	74.495—74.500	74.475—74.480
D	74.475—74.480	74.455—74.460	I	74.500—74.505	74.480—74.485
E	74.480—74.485	74.460—74.465	K	74.505—74.510	74.485—74.490

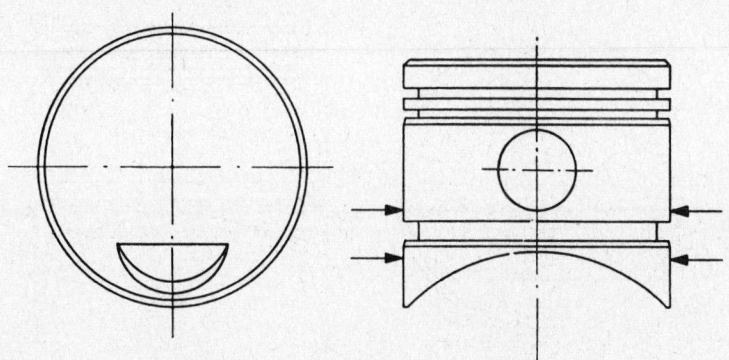

Type 1300

Type 1300
Piston diameter 74.5 mm. (2.933 in.)
Characteristic features:
Flat crown with recess for exhaust valve. Narrow

bevel between piston crown and top land
2 compression rings above piston pin boss
1 oil scraper ring below piston pin boss
Check diameter at points shown by arrows.

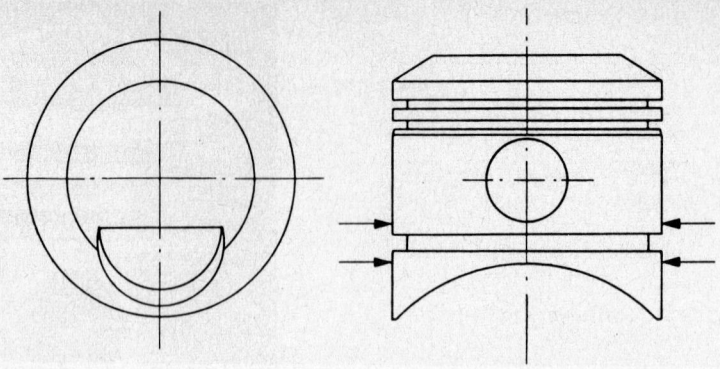

Type 1300S

Type 1300 S
Piston diameter 74.5 mm. (2.933 in.)
Characteristic features:
Flat crown with recess for exhaust valve. Exceptionally broad bevel between piston crown and top land

2 compression rings above piston pin boss
1 oil scraper ring below piston pin boss
Check diameter at points shown by arrows.

1600 and 1600S Series

Nominal cylinder bore = 82.5 mm (3.248 in)

Group	Cylinder bore (mm.)	Piston dia. (mm.)
A	82.460—82.465	82.440—82.445
B	82.465—82.470	82.445—82.450
C	82.470—82.475	82.450—82.455
D	82.475—82.480	82.455—82.460
E	82.480—82.485	82.460—82.465
F	82.485—82.490	82.465—82.470
G	82.490—82.495	82.470—82.475
H	82.495—82.500	82.475—82.480
I	82.500—82.505	82.480—82.485
K	82.505—82.510	82.485—82.490

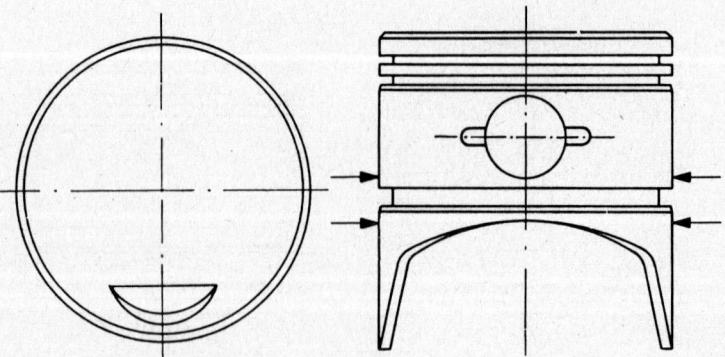

Type 1600

Type 1600
Piston diameter 82.5 mm. (3.248 in.)
Characteristic features:
Flat crown with recess for exhaust valve. Narrow bevel between piston crown and top land
2 compression rings above piston pin boss
1 oil scraper ring below piston pin boss
Check diameter at points shown by arrows.

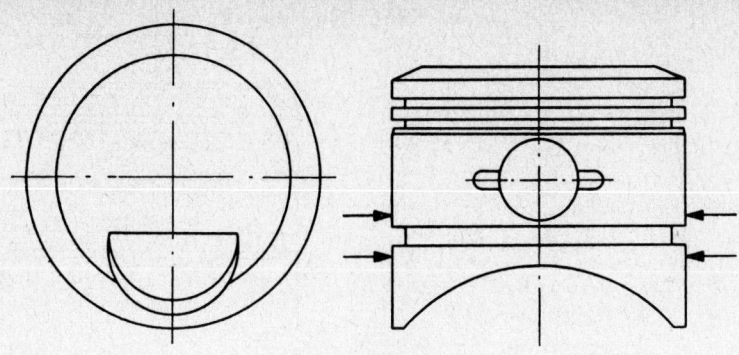

Type 1600S

Type 1600 S
Piston diameter 82.5 mm. (3.248 in.)
Special characteristics:
Flat crown with recess for exhaust valve. Excep-

tionally broad bevel between piston crown and
top land
2 compression rings above piston pin boss
1 oil scraper ring below piston pin boss

Clearance between cylinder and piston

Type 1300 ⎫	
Type 1300S ⎬ 0.015—0.025 mm	
Type 1600 ⎪ (0.0006 to 0.001 in)	
Type 1600S ⎭	

A number and a letter will be found on the top fin of each cylinder and the crown of each piston. Matched pistons and cylinders are marked with the same serial number and letter, the letter indicating the size group.

356B Engines

1600S Series (Light Alloy)

Group	Cylinder dia. (mm.)	Piston dia. (mm.)
A	82.460—82.465	82.440—82.445
B	82.465—82.470	82.445—82.450

Group	Cylinder dia. (mm.)	Piston dia. (mm.)
C	82.470—82.475	82.450—82.455
D	82.475—82.480	82.455—82.460
E	82.480—82.485	82.460—82.465
F	82.485—82.490	82.465—82.470
G	82.490—82.495	82.470—82.475
H	82.495—82.500	82.475—82.480
I	82.500—82.505	82.480—82.485
K	82.505—82.510	82.485—82.490

Matched cylinder and piston pairs are stamped with the same group identification letter. The pistons are marked on the crown and the cylinders on the base. Only cylinders and pistons of the same size group may be paired.

Type 1600S

1600 S Engine
Piston diameter 82.5 mm.
Characteristic features:
Wide bevel around edge of piston crown.

2 compression rings above piston pin boss
1 oil scraper ring under piston pin boss
Dimensions given for point D_1.
Dimension A = 30 mm. ($1^3/_{16}$ in.)

356C Engines

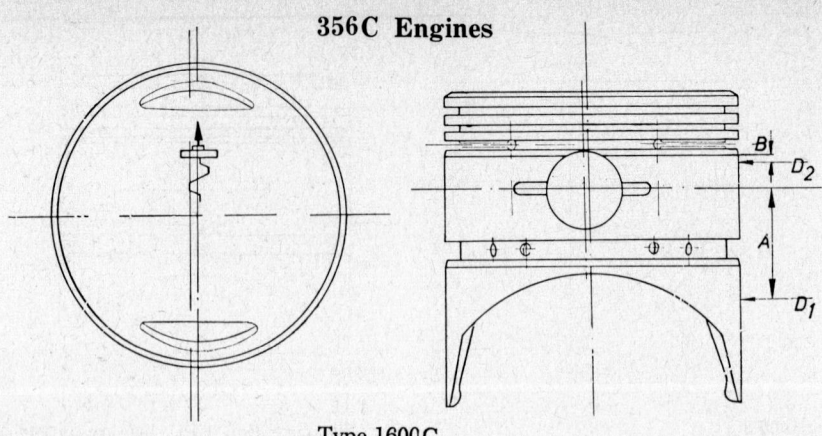

Type 1600C

Piston diameter 82.5 mm.
Characteristic features:
Narrow bevel around edge of piston crown.
3 compression rings above the piston pin boss.

1 oil scraper ring below piston pin boss
Dimensions given for points D_1 and D_2.
Dimension A = 30 mm. ($1^3/_{16}$ in.)
Dimension B = 2 mm. ($^5/_{64}$ in.)

Group	Cylinder Dia. (mm.)	Piston Dia. (mm.)
A	82.460—82.465	82.430—82.435
B	82.465—82.470	82.435—82.440
C	82.470—82.475	82.440—82.445
D	82.475—82.480	82.445—82.450
E	82.480—82.485	82.450—82.455
F	82.485—82.490	82.455—82.460
G	82.490—82.495	82.460—82.465
H	82.495—82.500	82.465—82.470
I	82.500—82.505	82.470—82.475
K	82.505—82.510	82.475—82.480

Piston cylinder clearance, new, should be from 0.025 to 0.035 mm (.00098 to .00138 in.).

912 Engine

STANDARD SIZE (mm.)

Group	Cylinder Diameter	Piston Diameter
—1	82.485—82.494	82.47
0	82.495—82.504	82.48
+1	82.505—82.514	82.49

1ST OVERSIZE

Group	Cylinder Diameter	Piston Diameter
—1 KD 1	82.985—82.994	82.97
0 KD 1	82.995—83.004	82.98
+1 KD 1	83.005—83.014	82.99

Wear limit is a clearance of 0.2 mm (.008″) between piston and cylinder. Exact piston to cylinder clearance can be determined only by measuring each component separately.

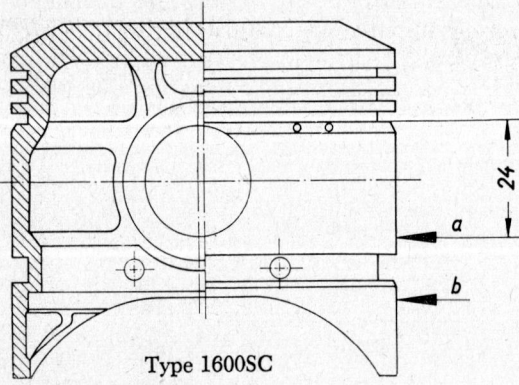

Type 1600SC

Nominal piston diameter 82.5 mm.
Characteristic features:
Broad bevel around high piston crown.
Three compression rings above the piston pin
one oil control ring below the piston pin.
Nominal diameter measuring point at arrows and "b".

Matching cylinder and piston pairs are marked with the same letter. The cylinders are marked at the base while the pistons are marked on the face.

Only cylinders and pistons of the same size group are to be matched.

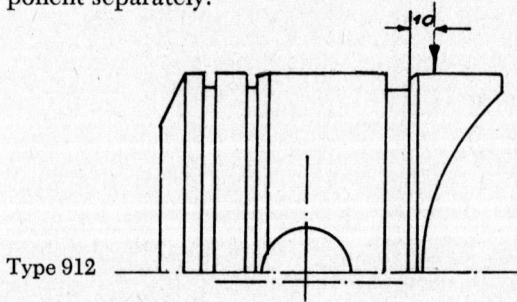

Type 912

Characteristic feature:
Conspicuously broad bevel around the piston top perimeter.
Two compression rings above the piston pin, one oil scraper below the piston pin.
Nominal diameter measuring point shown by arrow.

Type 911

911 Engine

Cylinder marking	Cylinder diameter mm. (in.)	Piston marking	Piston diameter mm. (in.)	Clearance between cylinder and piston mm. (in.)
Normal		Normal		
—1	79.990 —80.000 (3.1492— 3.1496")	—1	79.925 —79.935 (3.1466— 3.1470")	0.055
0	80.000 —80.010 (3.1496— 3.1500")	0	79.935 —79.945 (3.1470— 3.1474")	to 0.075 (.0022
+1	80.010 —80.020 (3.1500— 3.1504")	+1	79.945 —79.955 (3.1474— 3.1478")	to .0029")
Oversize				
—1 KD 1	80.490 —80.500 (3.1689— 3.1692")	—1 KD 1	80.425 —80.435 (3.1663— 3.1667")	0.055
0 KD 1	80.500 —80.510 (3.1692— 3.1696")	0 KD 1	80.435 —80.445 (3.1667— 3.1671")	to 0.075 (.0022
+1 KD 1	80.510 —80.520 (3.1696— 3.1700")	+1 KD 1	80.445 —80.455 (3.1671— 3.1675")	to .0029")

914/6 Engine

Size Class	Dim. Group	Cylinder dia. mm (in.)	Mahle Piston dia. D1 mm (in.)	Schmidt Piston dia. D1 mm (in.)
Normal size 80.0 mm dia. (3.15")	0	80.00—80.01 (3.1496—3.1500)	79.97 (3.14843)	79.96 (3.14804)
	1	80.01—80.02 (3.1500—3.1504)	79.98±0.005 (3.14882±.00020)	79.97+0.006 (3.14843+.00024)
	2	80.02—80.03 (3.1504—3.1508)	79.99 (3.14921)	79.98–0.007 (3.14882–.00028)
Oversize 1 80.5 mm dia. (3.17")	0 KD 1	80.05—10.51 (3.1693—3.1697)	80.46 (3.1677)	80.46 (3.1677)
	1 KD 1	80.51—80.52 (3.1697—3.1701)	80.47 (3.1681)	80.47 (3.1681)
	2 KD 1	80.52—80.53 (3.1701—3.1705)	80.48 (3.1685)	80.48 (3.1685)

	Installation clearance	Wear limit
(Mahle)	(.0010—.0018")	(.0094")
(Schmidt)	(.0014—.0022")	(.0098")

914 Engine

Size class	Color	Cylinder dia. mm. (in.)	Piston dia. mm. (in.)
Standard size 90.0 mm dia. (3.54″)	Blue	89.990—89.999 (3.54292—3.54327″)	89.95 (3.54134″)
	Pink	90.000—90.009 (3.54331—3.54366″)	89.96 (3.54173″)
	Green	90.010—90.020 (3.54370—3.54409″)	89.97 (3.54212″)
1st Oversize 90.5 mm dia. (3.56″)	Blue	90.490—90.499 (3.56260—3.56295″)	90.45 (3.56103″)
	Pink	90.500—90.509 (3.56299—3.56334″)	90.46 (3.56142″)
	Green	90.510—90.520 (3.56338—3.56377″)	90.47 (3.56181″)
2nd Oversize 91.0 mm dia. (3.58″)	Blue	90.990—90.999 (3.58229—3.58264″)	90.95 (3.58071″)
	Pink	91.000—91.009 (3.58268—3.58303″)	90.96 (3.58110″)
	Green	91.010—91.020 (3.58307—3.58346″)	90.97 (3.58149″)

Installation clearance in mm. (in.)
0.04—0.06 (.0016—.0024)

Torque Specifications

Model	Cylinder Head bolts (ft. lbs.)	Main Bearing bolts (ft. lbs.)	Rod Bearing bolts (ft. lbs.)	Crankshaft Pulley bolt (or nut) (ft. lbs.) [1]	Flywheel to Crankshaft bolts (ft. lbs.)	Manifold (ft. lbs.) Intake	Exhaust
914/6	21.7-23.9	25.3	36.2	57.9	108.5	*	*
914	23.1	23.9	23.9	43.4	79.6		
911	23.9	25.3	36.2	57.9	108.5		
912	21.7	28.9	32.5	N.A.	253-268		
356C-1600 S-90	21.8	29.0	32.0	72.0	326-363		
356B-1600	22.0	29.0	32.6	72.0	254-268		
356A-1300 1600	22.0	22.0	25-29	72.0 [2]	250-267		
356-1100 1300 1500	22.0	22.0	36.0	N.A.	250-260		

1 No crankshaft balancer — specification given is for crankshaft pulley
* No specification given — tighten uniformly and carefully
2 1600 Engine only

Tightening Sequences

Cylinder head—Models 356, 356A, 356B, 356C

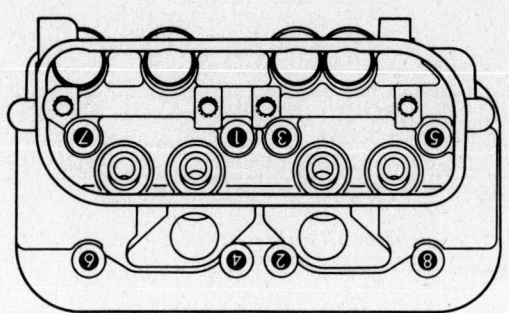

Cylinder head—Model 914 (four cylinder)

Electrical Specifications

Model	Battery			Starter							Brush spring tension (oz.)
	Capacity (Amp. hours)	Volts	Grounded Terminal	Lock test			No load test				
				Amp.	Volts	Torque (ft. lbs.)	Amps.	Volts	RPM[1]		
914/6*	N.A.	12	Neg.	160-200	9	1100-1400 rpm	35-50	12	6400-7900		N.A.
914**	N.A.	12	Neg.	170-205	9	900-1300 rpm	35-45	12	7400-9100		N.A.
911	45	12	Neg.	160-200	9.0	1100-1400 rpm	33-50	11.5	6400-7900		42.3 +4.5 —1.8
912	45	12	Neg.	160-200	9.0	1100-1400 rpm	33-50	11.5	6400-7900		42.3 +4.5 —1.8
356C	84	6	Neg.	340-400	8.5		30-50	11.5	5000-7500		28-32
356B 356A	84	6	Neg.	450-520	3.5	6.5-6.9	60-80	5.5	5300-7300		28-32
356	84	6	Neg.	420-480	3.5	6.5-6.9	60-80	5.5	5500-7500		28-32

* — Starter type 033 911 023A
** — Starter type   311 911 023B
1 — All rpm figures are generator rpm

Electrical Specifications

Model	Generator				Regulator				
	Part Number °°	Brush Spring Pressure (oz.)	Field Resistance (ohms)	Output (Amps) °°°	Part Number °°	Cut-out Relay		Maximum Current (amps)	Voltage Regulator Setting (in.)[3]
						Volts to Close	Reverse Current (amps)		
912	EG (L) 14V 25A 20	15.8-21.1	3.5	N.A.	RS/VA 200/12 A5	12.4-13.1	2-7.5	N.A.	N.A.
356C	LJ/GEG/ 200/6/ 2600 L19	16-21	1.0-1.1	36	RS/UA 200/6/23	6.3-6.7	4-9	47-51[2]	.010-.016
356B	LJ/GEG/ 200/6/ 2600 L19	16-21	1.0-1.1	36	RS/UA 200/6/23	6.3-6.7	4-9	47-51[2]	.010-.016
356A	LJ/GE 160/6/ 2500 L2	16-21	1.2-1.32	26	RS/UA 160/6/24	6.3-6.7	4.5-8.5	37-41[1]	.010-.016
356-1500S	LJ/GE 160/6/ 2500 L2	16-21	1.2-1.32	26	RS/UA 160/6/15	6.3-6.7	4.5-8.5	37-41[1]	.010-.016
356-1500	130/6/ 2600 AL 16	16-21	1.2-1.32	21	RS/UA 160/6/13	6.3-6.7	4.5-8.5	37-41[1]	.010-.016
356-1300S	130/6/ 2600 AL 16	16-21	1.2-1.32	21	RS/UA 160/6/13	5.5-6.5	2.0-5.5	37-41[1]	.010-.016
356-1300 1100	130/6/ 2600 AL 15	16-21	1.2-1.32	21	RS/G 130/ 6/1°	5.5-6.5	2.0-5.5	37-41[1]	.010-.016

° — Regulator identification number for Model 1300 — RS/G/130/6/11
°° — All part numbers refer to Bosch equipment
°°° — Generator output is rated at 2500 generator rpm. This is roughly equivalent to engine idling speed, since the generator is driven at 1.8 times engine speed.
1 — Maximum current (cold) is 40-44 amps. Figure specified is (warm).
2 — Maximum current (cold) is 50-54 amps. Figure specified is (warm).
3 — Figure specified for voltage regulator setting is contact gap.

Model	Alternator				AC Regulator						
	Part Number °	Field Current Draw @ 12V	Output @ Alternator RPM		Part Number °	Field Relay			Regulator		
			amps.	amps.		Air Gap (in.)	Point Gap (in.)	Volts to Close	Air Gap (in.)	Point Gap (in.)	Volts at 125°
914/6	K 1	N.A.	N.A.	N.A.	ADN	N.A.	N.A.	N.A.	N.A.	N.A.	N.A.
914	K 1	N.A.	N.A.	N.A.	ADN	N.A.	N.A.	N.A.	N.A.	N.A.	N.A.
911	K 1 (RL) 14 V 35 A 20	N.A.	28-30	3,000	AD1/14V	N.A.	N.A.	N.A.	N.A.	N.A.	N.A.

° — All part numbers refer to Bosch equipment.

Capacities and Pressures Specifications

Model	Engine Crankcase (with 1 filter) quarts	Transmission & Differential		Fuel Tank (with reserve) gallons	Brake Reservoir ounces	Steering Gear ounces	Windshield Washer quarts
		Tunnel pints	Split pints				
914/6	9.6	N.A.	—	16.4	¾ full	N.A.	N.A.
914	3.7*	N.A.	—	16.4	¾ full	N.A.	N.A.
911	9.5	5¼	—	16.4	7	—	2.1
912	5.3	5¼	—	16.4	7	—	2.1
356C	5.3	7.4	—	13.2	8½	8½	—
356B	5.3	7.4	—	13¾	8½	8½	—
356A	5.3	7.4	5¼	13¾	8½	4¼	—
356	5.3	—	5¼	13¾	8½	4¼	—
356 (early)	3.7	—	5¼	13¾	8½	4¼	—

* without oil filter change — 3.2 qts.

Brake Specifications

Model	Type		Brake Cylinder Bore			Brake Drum or Disc Diameter (ins.)		Maximum Drum Machining Tolerance
	Front	Rear	Master Cylinder (ins.)	Wheel Cylinder (ins.) Front	Rear	Front	Rear	
914/6	Disc	Disc	.75	1.9*	1.5*	11.122 —.012	11.260 —.008	.709" **
914	Disc	Disc	.6874	1.7*	1.3*	11.063 —.008	11.102 —.008	.394" **
911	Disc	Disc	.75	1.890[1]	1.378[1]	11.102	11.220	.02" ***
912	Disc	Disc	.75	1.890[1]	1.378[1]	11.102	11.220	.02" ***
356C	Disc (ATE)	Disc (ATE)	.75	1.890	1.378	10.81	11.22	N.A.
356B (early)	Disc (Porsche)	Disc (Porsche)	N.A.	1.299	.984	N.A.	N.A.	N.A.
356B	Drum	Drum	.75	.75	.75	11.024-11.062	11.024-11.062	11.1023"
356A	Drum	Drum	.75	.75	.75	11.024-11.062	11.024-11.062	11.10"
356	Drum	Drum	.75	.75	.75	11.0236-11.0630	11.0236-11.0630	11.1023"

* — Caliper piston diameter
** — Minimum disc thickness after refinishing — The disc thickness must be refinished symmetrically, i.e., uniformly from both sides.
*** — Disc machining tolerance from base metal
1 — Cylinder diameter

Chassis and Wheel Alignment Specifications

Model	Chassis					Wheel Alignment						
	Wheel-base (ins.)	Track (ins.)		Caster		Camber (Deg.)		Toe-In		King-pin Inclination (deg.)	Wheel Pivot Ratio	
		Front	Rear	Range (deg.)	Pref. Setting (deg.)	Front	Rear	Front (in.)	Rear		Inner Wheel	Outer Wheel
914/6	96.5	53.3	N.A.	±30′	6°±30′	0° ±30′	N.A.	N.A.	——	N.A.	N.A.	N.A.
914	96.5	52.7	N.A.	±30′	6°±30′	0° ±30′	N.A.	N.A.	——	N.A.	N.A.	N.A.
911 L	87.05	53.8	52.8	±30′	6° 45′ ±45′	0° ±20′	—1° 6′	+40′ total left + right	0°	N.A.	N.A.	N.A.
911 S	87.05	53.27	52.18	±30′	6° 45′ ±45′	0° ±20′	—1° 6′	+40′ total left + right	0°	N.A.	N.A.	N.A.
911	87.05	53.8	52.6	±30′	6° 45′ ±45′	0° ±20′	—1° 6′	+40′ total left + right	0°	N.A.	N.A.	N.A.
912	87.05	53.8	52.6	±30′	6° 45′ ±45′	0° ±20′	—1° 6′	+40′ total left + right	0°	N.A.	N.A.	N.A.
911 (thru 1965)	87.05	52.64	51.85	±45′	6° 45′ ±45′	0° ±20′	—1° 6′	+40′ total left + right	0°	N.A.	N.A.	N.A.
356 C	82.68	51.42	50.08	±30′	5°±30′	0° 40′ ±30′	+10′ to +1° 30′	.0394 .118	.00″- .059″	4° 30′	N.A.	N.A.
356 B	82.7	51.4	50.1	±30′	5°±30′	0° 40′ ±30′	+10′ to +1° 30′	.0394 .118	.00″- .059″	4° 30′	N.A.	N.A.
356 A	82.7	51.4	50.1	±30′	5°±30′	0° 40′ ±30′	+30′ to +2°	.04-.12	0″±10′	4° 30′	N.A.	N.A.
356	82.7	50.8	49.2	±30′	2½-3	¾±¼	1-3	¼-⅜	0″±1/16″	4° 30′	N.A.	N.A.

Fuses and Circuit Breakers

Model	Circuit	Amperage
356 356A	Stop light, fuel gauge, blinker unit	8
	Trouble light, cigarette lighter	25
	Horn	25
	Interior light, windshield wiper	8
	Left fog light	8
	Right fog light	8
	Left tail light, left parking light, license plate light	8
	Right tail light, right parking light, license plate light	8
	Left low beam and back-up light	8
	Right low beam and back-up light	8
	Left high beam indicator light	8
	Right high beam	8
356B 356C	Combined stop and flashing light	8
	Cigarette lighter, plug socket, windshield wiper	25
	Supplemental heating	—
	Inside lamp	8
	Right fog light	8
	Left fog lamp	8
	Right side light, right tail light, license plate light	8
	Left side light, left tail light, license plate light	8
	Right low beam	8
	Left low beam, back-up light	8
	Right high beam	8
	Left high beam, pilot light	8
911	Stop light, blinkers, back-up lights	15
	Interior light, cigarette lighter, clock	15
	Auxiliary heater	40
	Windshield wipers and washer	40
	Fog lamps	15
	Trunk light, license plate light	15
	Right parking light	15
	Left parking light	15
	Right low beam	15
	Left low beam	15
	Right high beam, high beam indicator light	15
	Left high beam	15
912	Stop light, blinkers, back-up lights	15
	Interior light, cigarette lighter, clock	15
	Auxiliary heater	15
	Windshield wipers and washer	40
	Fog lamps	15
	Trunk light, license plate light	15
	Right parking light	15
	Left parking light	15
	Right low beam	15
	Left low beam	15
	Right high beam, high beam indicator light	15
	Left high beam	15

Light Bulb Specifications

Model	Usage	Wattage
356A	High beam	35/35
	Parking blinker light	15/5
	Interior light	5
	Speedometer light	.6
	Tachometer light	.6
	Combination oil temperature and fuel gauge light	1.2
	Stop blinker light	15
	Tail light	5
	License plate light	10
	Back-up light	25
356B 356C	Sealed beam headlight	45/40
	Front parking light (in turn signal)	4
	Front turn signal	15
	Turn signal, brake light	15
	Tail light	5
	License plate light	5
	Back-up light	25
	Interior light	15
	Tachometer light	.6
	Speedometer light	.6
	High beam indicator light	.6
	Turn signal indicator light	1.2
	Combination instrument light	1.2
	Generator indicator light	1.2
	Oil pressure light	1.2
911 912	Headlights	45/40
	Foglamps	35
	Back-up light	25
	Stop lights	18/5
	Turn signals	18
	Interior lights	10
	Trunk light	5
	Parking lights, license plate light	4
	Instrument lights, control lights	2

Wiring Diagrams

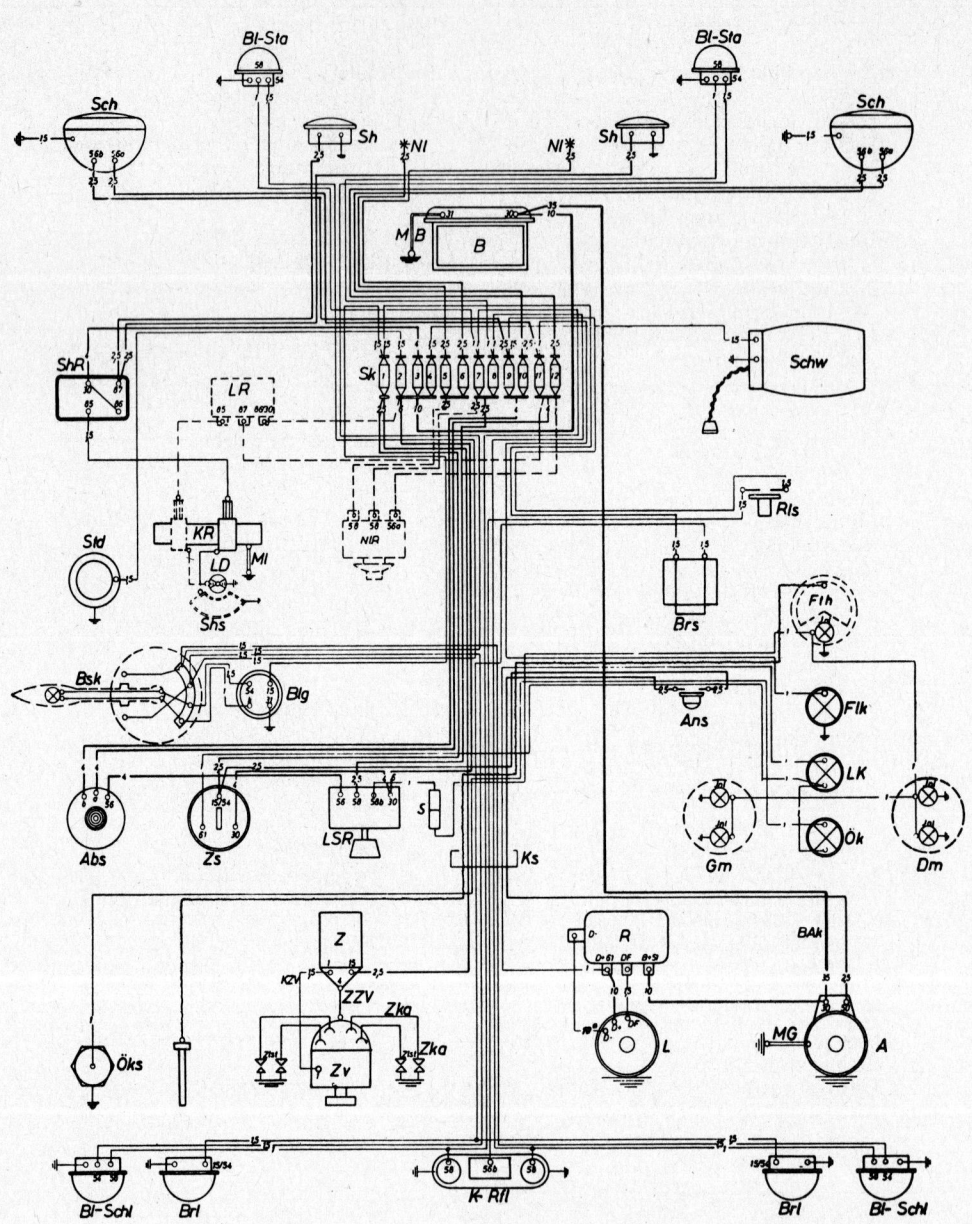

Wiring diagram—Model 356 (Speedster)

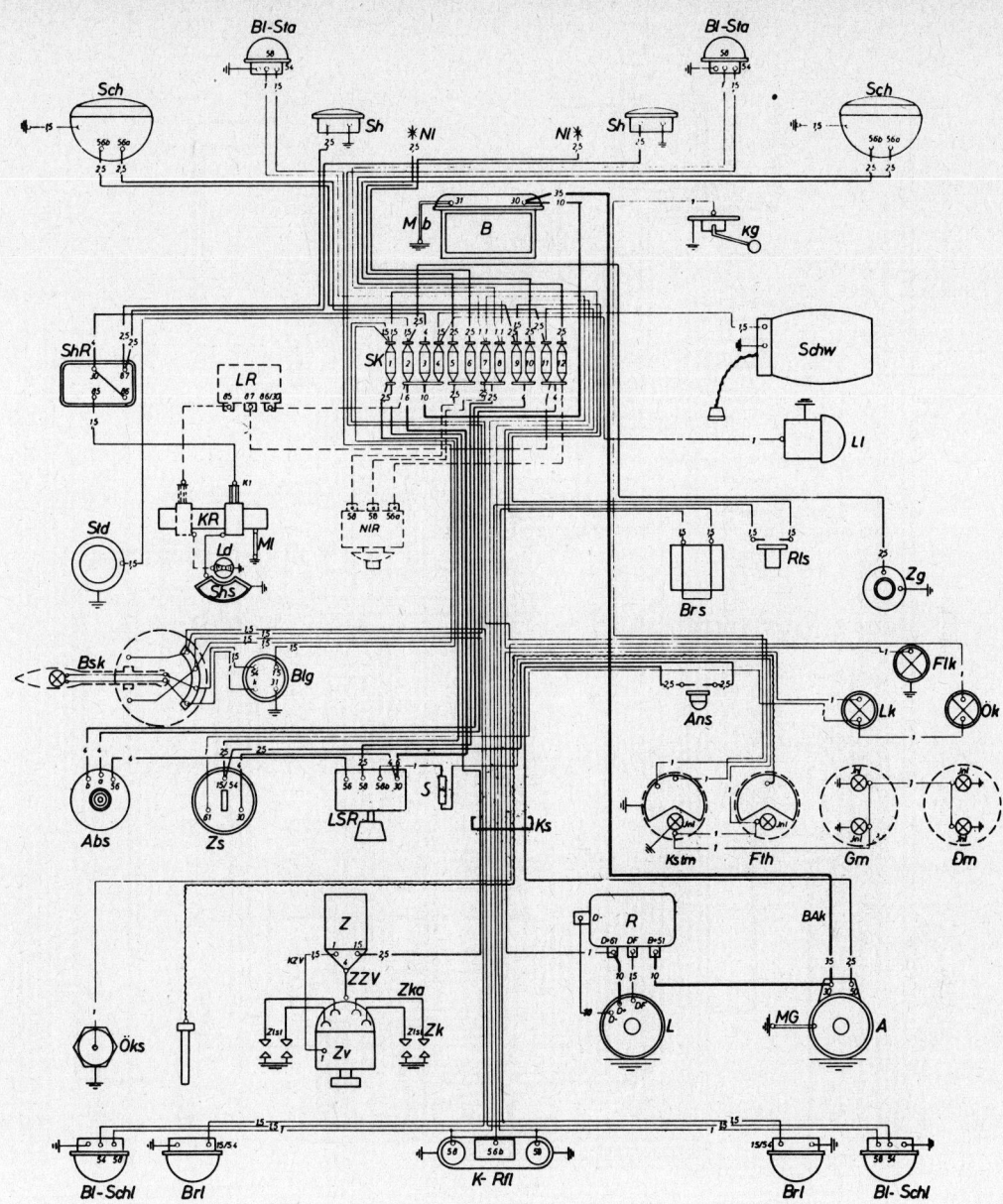

Wiring diagram—Model 356

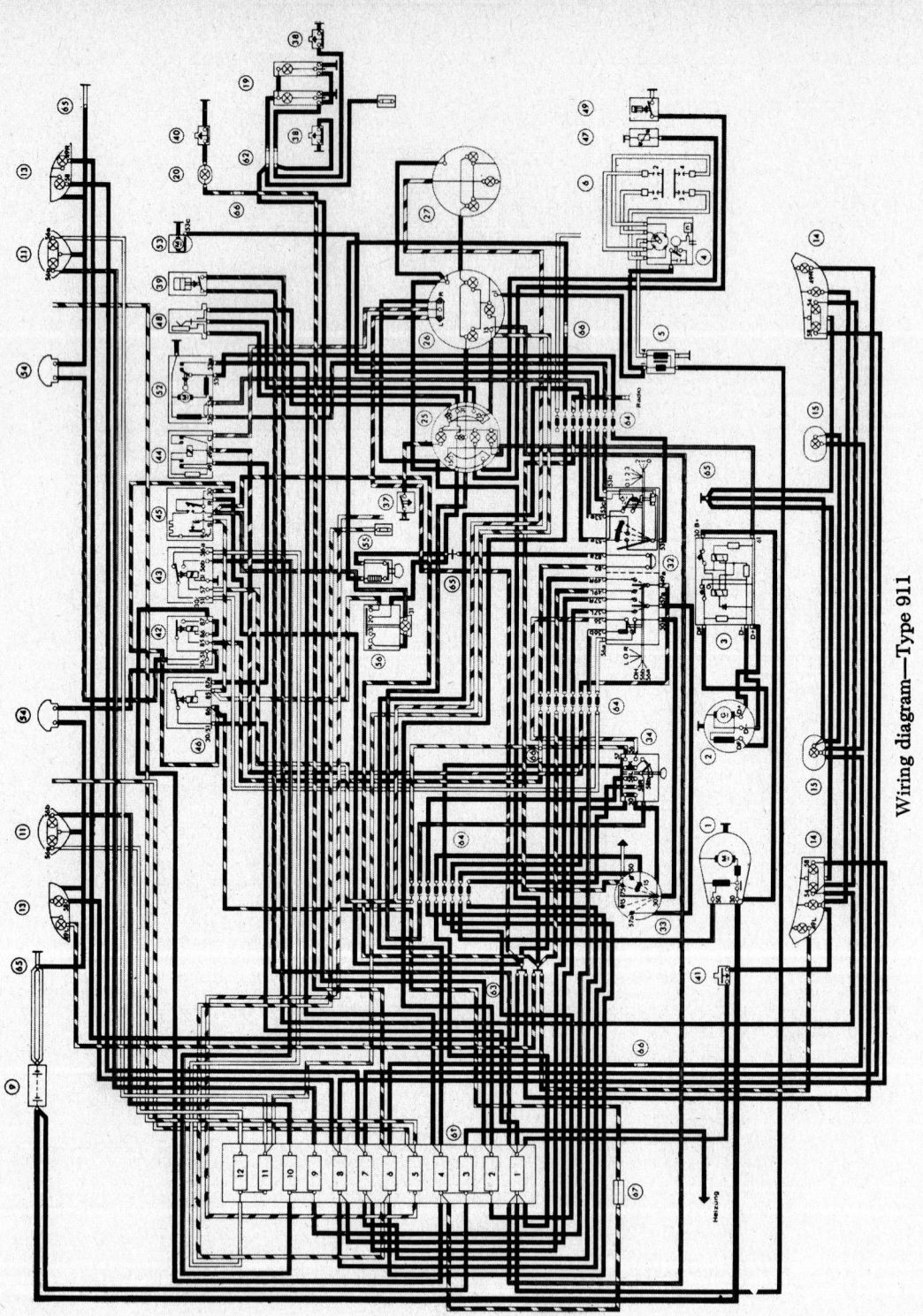

Wiring diagram—Type 911

1. Starter motor
2. Alternator
3. Control box
4. Ignition distributor
5. Ignition coil
6. Spark plugs
7. Fuel pump
8. Resistor
9. Battery
11. Headlamps
12. Fog lamps
13. Blink/parking lights
14. Tail/stop/blink/back-up lights
15. License plate light
19. Interior light
20. Trunk light
24. Small combination instrument
25. Large combination instrument
26. Transistorized tachometer
27. Speedometer
28. Clock
32. Blink/dimmer/signal/wiper/ washer switch with signal knob on steering wheel
33. Starter/ignition switch
34. Light switch
36. Fog lamp switch with control light

37. Handbrake control light switch
38. Door post contact switch
39. Brake light switch
40. Trunk light switch
41. Back-up light switch
42. Signal horn relay
43. Relay for light signal
44. Blink light unit
45. Control light unit
46. Control light relay
47. Oil temperature transmitter
48. Fuel tank unit
49. Oil pressure transmitter
50. Oil level transmitter
51. Resistor relay
52. Windshield wiper motor
53. Windshield washer pump
54. Signal horn
55. Cigarette lighter
56. Control light switch
57. Control light fuse
61. Fuse box

Ground leads or cables:
a) battery—body
b) transmission—chassis
c) steering column control switch —body

d) fuel spout—body
e) windshield wipers—body
f) instruments—body
g) heater—body

Fuses
1. Stop light, blinkers, back-up lights
2. Interior light, cigarette lighter, clock
3. Auxiliary heater
4. Windshield wipers and washer
5. Fog lamps
6. License plate light, trunk light
7. Parking light, RH
8. Parking light, LH
9. Low beam, RH
10. Low beam, LH
11. High beam, RH, high beam control light
12. High beam, LH

IMPORTANT
Disconnecting of battery with running engine results in immediate destruction of alternator.

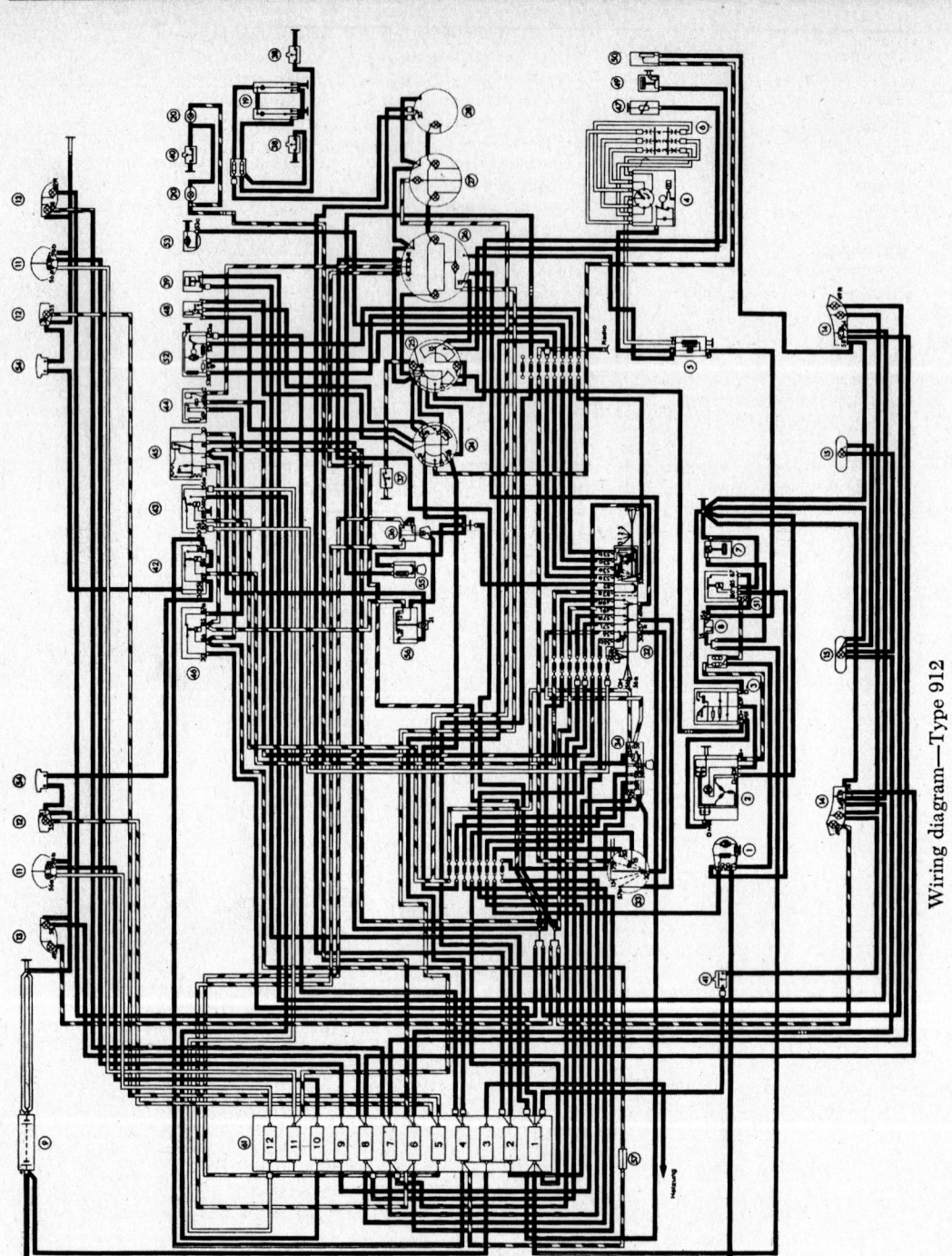

Wiring diagram—Type 912

1. Starter
2. Generator
3. Regulator
4. Distributor
5. Ignition coil
6. Spark plugs
9. Battery
11. Headlight
13. Parking and turn signal light
14. Tail, stop, turn signal and back-up light
15. License plate light
19. Interior light
20. Luggage compartment light
25. Large combination instrument
26. Transistorized tachometer
27. Speedometer
32. Combined switch for turn signal, low beam, head-light signal, wiper, washer and horn button
33. Ignition switch
34. Main light switch
37. Hand brake indicator light switch
38. Door contact switch
39. Stop light switch

40. Luggage compartment light switch
41. Back-up light switch
42. Horn relay
43. By-pass relay for high beam signal
44. Turn signal flasher
45. Warning signal flasher
46. Warning signal relay
47. Oil temperature sending unit
48. Fuel tank sending unit
49. Oil pressure sending unit
52. Wiper motor
53. Washer pump
54. Horn
55. Cigarette lighter
56. Warning signal switch
61. Fuse box
62. Two-pole plug connector
63. Cable distribution block
64. Eight-way disconnect
65. Ground
66. Signal-pole plug connector
67. Warning signal fuse with holder

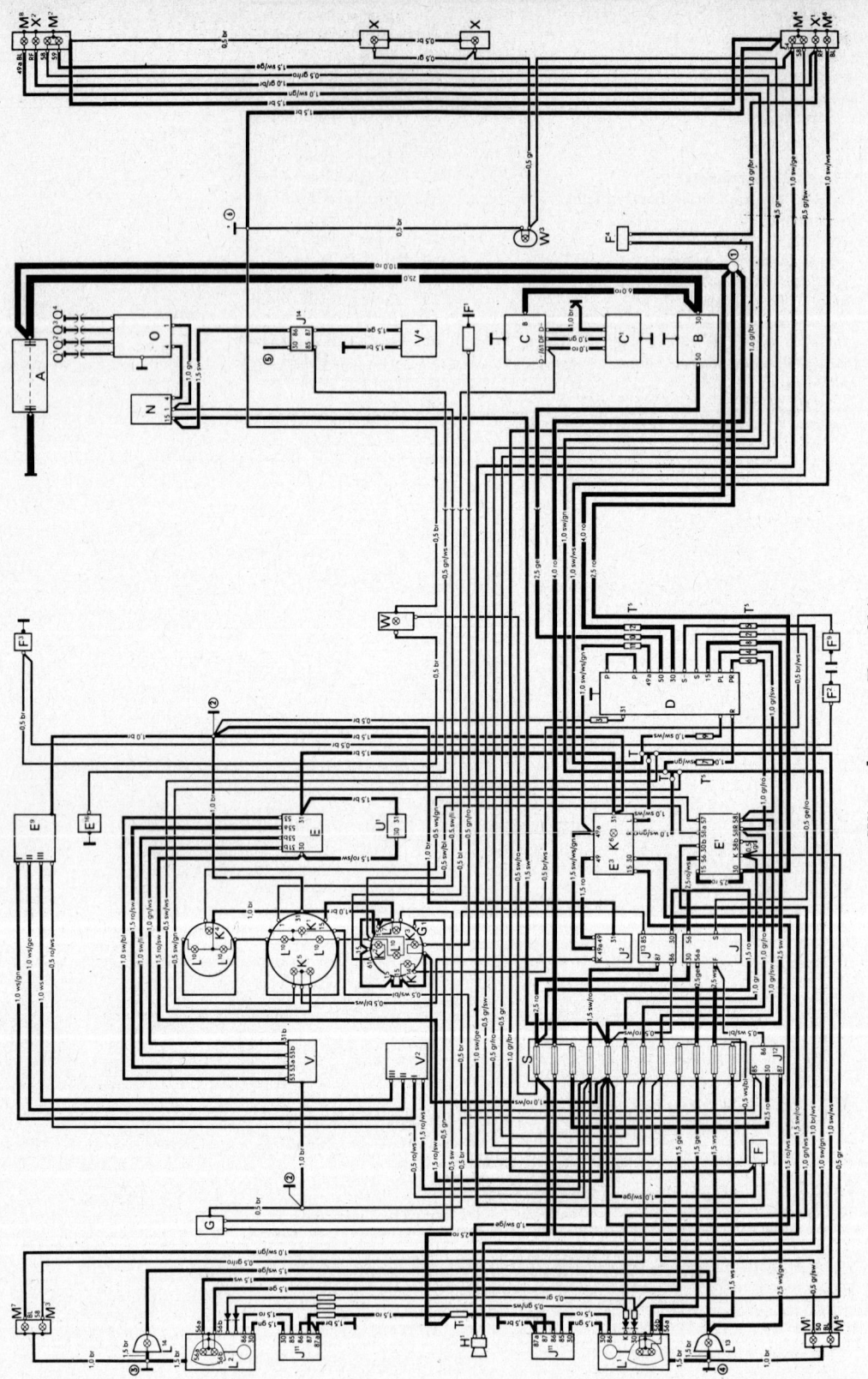

Wiring diagram—Type 914

A	Battery	L 14	Lamp for high beam right
B	Starter	M 1	Lamp for parking light left
C	Generator	M 2	Lamp for tail and brake light right
C 1	Regulator switch	M 3	Lamp for parking light right
D	Ignition starter and blinker switch	M 4	Lamp for tail and brake light left
E	Windshield wiper switch	M 5	Lamp for blinker light front left
E 1	Light switch	M 6	Lamp for blinker light rear left
E 3	Warning light switch	M 7	Lamp for blinker light front right
E 9	Fan motor switch	M 8	Lamp for blinker light rear right
E 16	Hot air blower switch	N	Ignition coil
F	Brake light switch	O	Ignition distributor
F 1	Oil pressure switch	Q 1	Spark plug for cylinder 1
F 2	Door contact switch left	Q 2	Spark plug for cylinder 2
F 3	Door contact switch right	Q 3	Spark plug for cylinder 3
F 4	Backup light switch	Q 4	Spark plug for cylinder 4
F 9	Hand brake indicator light switch	S	Fusebox
G	Fuel gauge transmitter	T	Line connector
G 1	Fuel gauge indicator	T 1	Line connector, single
H 1	Horn	T 5	Plug connection
J	Hand dimmer and headlight flasher relay	U 1	Cigar lighter
J 2	Warning blinker relay	V	Windshield wiper motor
J 11	Retractable headlamp motor relay	V 2	Fan motor front
J 12	High beam relay	V 4	Hot air blower
J 13	Fan motor relay front	W	Interior light
J 14	Warm air blower relay	W 3	Trunk light
K 1	High beam indicator light	X	Number plate light
K 2	Alternator indicator light	X 1	Backup light left
K 3	Oil pressure indicator light	X 2	Backup light right
K 4	Parking lamp indicator light	1	Positive connection—fuse holder
K 5	Blinker indicator light	2	Frame connection point—fuse holder
K 6	Warning blinker system indicator light	3	Frame connection point—retractable headlamp right
K 14	Hand brake indicator light	4	Frame connection point—retractable headlamp left
L 1	Retractable headlamp with motor left	5	Relay plate in engine compartment fuse 30
L 2	Retractable headlamp wih motor right	6	Frame connection point—relay plate
L 7	Lamp for fuel gauge (reserve)		
L 10	Instrument lights		
L 13	Lamp for high beam left		

Engine Electrical

Distributor

REMOVAL

After removing the distributor cap, inspect it for carbon paths which accumulate in areas of high voltage leakage. Discard the cap if any are present. Otherwise, clean the inside of the cap and check for cracks. Remove corrosion from the copper contacts and inspect the condition of the center carbon brush. The brush should extend from the cap, be clean and without cracks. If any contacts are deeply scored, replace the cap.

Inspect the distributor rotor for burns and, if necessary, replace it. With the rotor arm off, lubricate the distributor cam with non-corrosive, high-temperature grease.

NOTE: Do not allow grease or dirt to contaminate breaker points.

Carefully examine the contact-breaker assembly in the distributor for the following poor-performance conditions:

1. Points are blackened, pitted, or worn excessively. (Points in extended service normally become dull gray without losing efficiency).

2. Movable contact-point arm has lost spring action.

3. Fiber rubbing block on breaker arm is badly worn or loose.

4. Coil primary wire (attached to the breaker assembly with the condenser) is twisted, frayed or short-circuited on the distributor plate.

5. Condenser lead connection is loose or damaged.

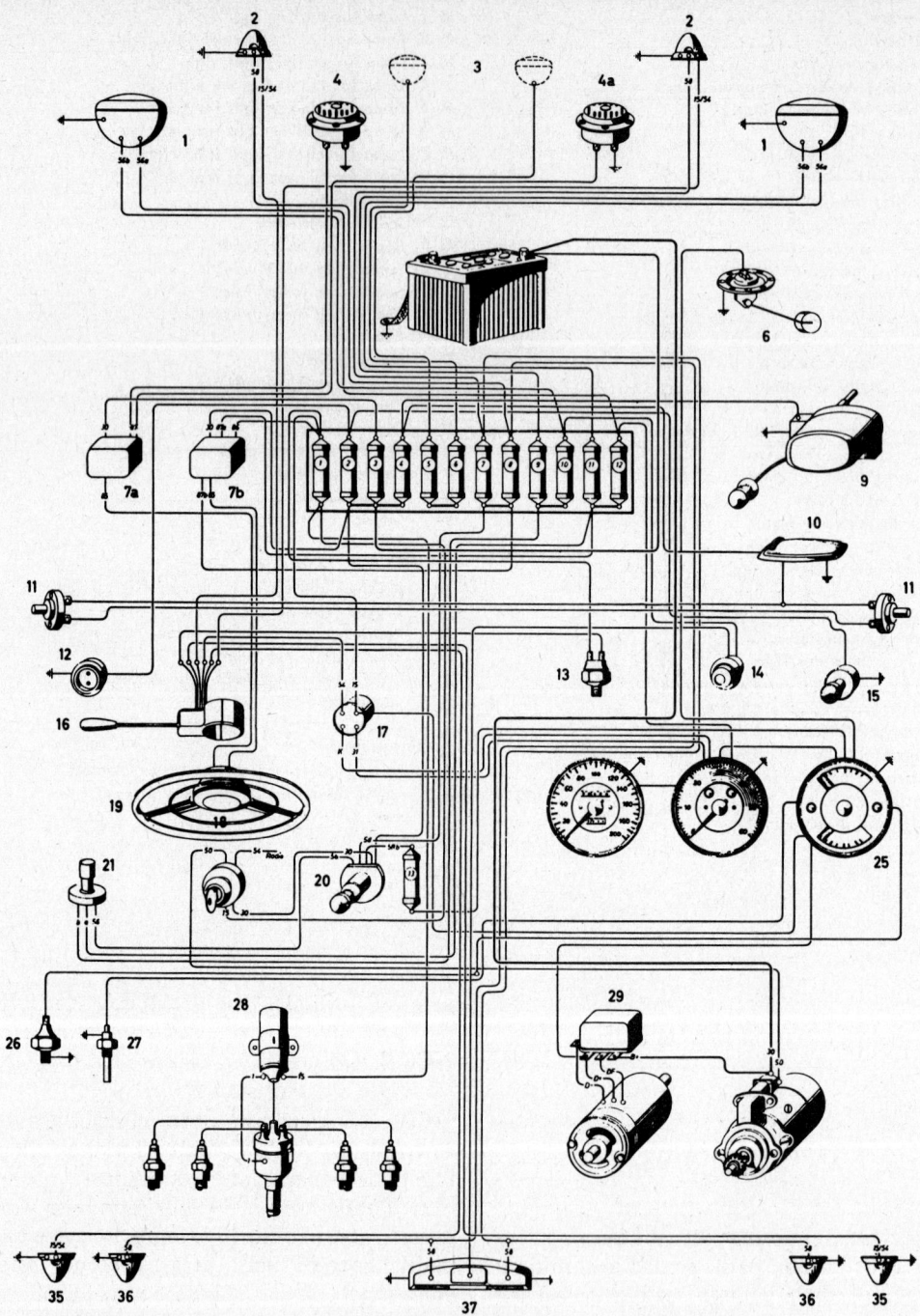

356A wiring diagram (electrical circuit for 356 and early 356B models is similar).

1 Headlight	10 Interior light*	20 Light switch
2 Turn signal, parking light	11 Door contact switch*	21 Dimmer switch
3 Fog light (optional)	12 Dash socket	25 Oil temp. and fuel gauge
4 Horn (high pitch)	13 Stop light switch	26 Oil pressure grounding switch
4a Horn (low pitch)	14 Back-up light switch	27 Oil temp. sending unit
6 Sending unit (fuel gauge)	15 Cigarette lighter*	28 Ignition coil
7 Horn relay	16 Turn signal switch	29 Voltage regulator
7b Relay for light signal*	17 Blinker unit	35 Turn signal, stop light
9 Windshield wiper motor	18 Light signal button*	36 Tail light
* not on Speedster	19 Horn ring	37 License plate light

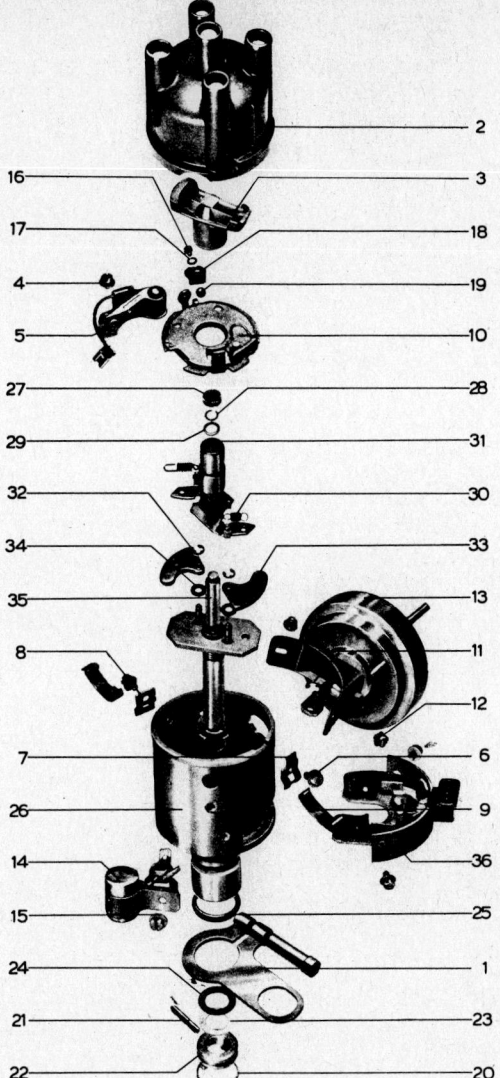

1. Holder for ignition distributor
2. Ignition distributor head
3. Distributor rotor
4. Fastening screw for contact breaker
5. Contact breaker
6. Cheesehead screw
7. Fastening plate with lug for holding spring
8. Fastening plate for holding spring
9. Holding spring
10. Contact breaker plate
11. Circlip for pull rod attachment
12. Cheesehead screw
13. Vacuum box
14. Condenser
15. Cheesehead screw
16. Cheesehead Screw
17. Spring ring
18. Holding spring for ball
19. Ball
20. Circlip for drive gear
21. Pin for drive gear
22. Drive gear
23. Compensating washer 0.1 mm.
24. Fiber washer
25. Rubber sealing ring
26. Distributor housing
27. Felt washer
28. Circlip
29. Thrust ring
30. Return spring
31. Distributor cam
32. Circlip
33. Flyweight
34. Washer
35. Distributor shaft
36. Releasing contacts

Exploded view of Type 914 Ignition distributor

6. Ground wire (pigtail) between the breaker assembly plate and the distributor housing is frayed or loose.

If any of the distributor components is faulty, replace it and then find the cause so that the new part can give good service. Contact points that are slightly burned can be cleaned with a thin cut-stone or point file.

To overhaul distributor, remove distributor cap, place No. 1 cylinder in the firing position (timing marks aligned), disconnect vacuum line and primary ignition wire, and remove retaining screw clamp and distributor.

Replace paper gasket on distributor housing if necessary.

BREAKER POINTS AND IGNITION TIMING

When installing points, lightly lubricate distributor cam with high temperature grease. CAUTION: *Excessive lubricant will throw off into contact points.* Position support on breaker plate and install lock screw loosely for later adjustment. Install breaker arm on pivot pin, lightly lubricating pin with high temperature grease. Position spring insulating washer in spring support. Connect breaker arm wire.

Adjusting point gap. The breaker points must be correctly set before adjusting ignition timing because every 0.1 mm (.004″) gap difference alters the ignition timing by almost 3° of crankshaft angle.

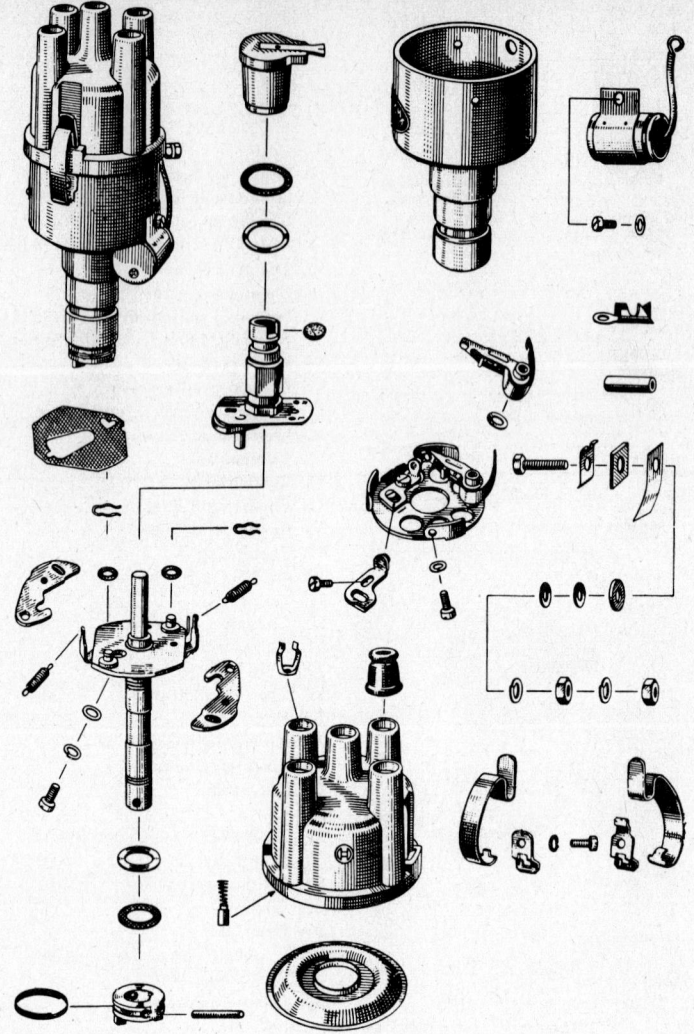

Distributor VJ 4 BR.

Point gap can be set by using a feeler gauge or a dwell meter. Accurate measurement with a gauge requires careful, precise use of the feelers. With the distributor cap and rotor off, turn the crankshaft until a cam lobe on the distributor shaft has fully opened the contact points. Loosen the breaker set screw and turn the eccentric adjusting screw until the correct gap is obtained. Tighten clamping screw and check the gap on all cam lobes. Make sure gauge being used is clean.

A dwell meter should be calibrated, switched to the four-cylinder position, and connected between the distributor primary terminal and ground. Mark the crankshaft pulley at the correct angle. Remove the distributor cap and rotor. Loosen the breaker set screw approximately ⅛ turn. Observing the dwell meter, reset screw of stationary contact to obtain specified dwell angle. Tighten set screw and recheck dwell. Install rotor and cap, start engine, and make a final dwell angle check.

Basic timing is set by rotating distributor housing slightly until contact points for cylinder #1 just start to open. Measure off and mark the correct timing point on the crankshaft pulley and align this point with the joint or stamped mark on the crankcase. Loosen distributor clamping screw. Connect one lead of a 6-volt or 12-volt test lamp

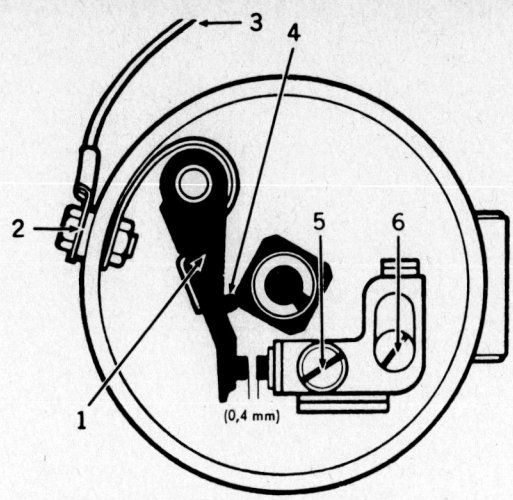

Contact-breaker assembly in distributor.

1 Contact arm
2 Terminal for coil wire and condenser wire
3 Primary wire from coil
4 Fiber rubbing block
5 Set screw
6 Eccentric screw

to the primary post (terminal 1) on the distributor and the other test lead to ground. Switch on ignition and rotate the distributor clockwise until the breaker points close. Then return the distributor counterclockwise very slowly until the test lamp lights. Carefully tighten distributor clamp, install distributor cap and connect spark plug wires.

Adjust ignition timing after setting point gap. A fast and easy way to adjust timing is with a stroboscope. A second method does not require the strobe light.

Connect strobe light to No. 1 spark plug. Disconnect all vacuum hoses from distributor and plug the hoses. Start engine and reduce idle speed to below 500 rpm. Idle performance must be smooth. Slowing the idle is essential to keep the centrifugal advance in the distributor from engaging. Rotate distributor as necessary to align timing marks with strobe pulses.

The 911 and 914/6 engines have distributors with timing ranges that fluctuate. For this reason they are set in the fully advanced position which is at an engine speed of 6,000 rpm. At this point the distributors are advanced to 35° before top dead center. Measure across the top edge of the crankshaft pulley *to the right* 35.4 mm (1.394″) and mark this point, which is 35° BTDC.

1. Set gap of breaker points (0.4 mm).
2. Set ignition.
3. Mark crankshaft pulley.
4. Connect strobe light.
5. Warm up engine.
6. Loosen distributor clamp so distributor can be rotated by hand.
7. Set engine at constant speed of 6000 rpm and light up pulley with strobe light.
8. Turn distributor until timing mark lines up with crankcase joint.

If strobe light is not available, timing can be adjusted by measuring the advance and retard points with chalk or other marker. Disconnect vacuum hoses from distributor and plug the hoses. Start engine and reduce idle speed to below 500 rpm. When idle performance is smooth, slowly advance the distributor to point where engine reaches its highest rpm. Mark this point. Next retard the spark by slowly reversing the distributor to the point of highest rpm. Mark this point. Center the distributor between the two marks and tighten it.

INSTALLATION

Install distributor with rotor pointing to #1 cylinder notch and with crankshaft set at Top Dead Center for that cylinder. Make sure the spacer spring is properly seated in the distributor drive head. Adjust rotor back and forth slightly until shaft seats itself. If distributor was set in wrong, rotor will be 180° out of place. Set distributor into position and hand tighten clamp. The mark on the rotor should be nearly aligned with mark on distributor housing. Align marks on rotor tip and housing, set breaker point gap or dwell angle, and adjust ignition timing.

The centrifugal advance mechanism can be simply checked by removing the distributor cap and turning the rotor clockwise until it stops. When the rotor is released it should return to original position by itself. If it does not return freely, the mechanism springs are faulty or the bearing surfaces are gummed. A "pinging" noise in the engine can be caused by a defective advance mechanism. The exact operation of the advance unit can be tested with an ignition test set.

DC Generator

The DC generator has its armature supported at each end of the shaft by ball bearings which are lubricated with heat resistant grease and require no attention under normal conditions. If bearings are lubricated during an overhaul of the generator, never use chassis grease.

Two carbon brushes are held by spring pressure against the commutator. These brushes should be inspected every 6,000 miles and replaced if worn badly to prevent damage to the commutator. A steel band around one end of the generator housing covers the brushes and commutator.

The commutator consists of copper sections which are insulated from each other and from the armature shaft. The sections receive electrical current from an armature coil (winding) and pass the current to the brushes. Occasionally, the insulation between the commutator sections must be trimmed back below the commutator surface.

DC Regulator

Since generator voltage is determined by 1) the speed of the armature and 2) the exciting current in the magnetic field, a constant voltage output can be maintained theoretically by controlling the exciting current or the armature speed. However, armature speed is based on engine rpm and is therefore not independently controllable. So the regulator maintains a constant voltage output by interrupting the exciting current.

The indicator lamp on the dash panel,

1. Elbow connector
2. Screw for hose clip
3. Thread connection for hose clip
4. Hose clip
5. Rubber sleeve
6. Wiring alternator
7. Suction cover for alternator
8. Nut
9. Spring washer
10. Rubber sleeve for suction cover
11. Nut for B+ connection
12. Washer
13. Washer
14. Serrated washer
15. Contact washer
16. 3-pole plug housing
17. Seal for suction cover
18. Positive diode carrier
19. Positive diodes
20. Screw
21. Connecting screw for stator winding
22. Exciting diode carrier
23. Exciting diodes
24. Seal
25. Negative diodes
26. Positive diode carrier fastening bolts
27. Brush holder fastening screws
28. Washer
29. Spring ring
30. Alternator housing
31. Carbon brush
32. Pressure spring for carbon brush
33. Brush holder plate
34. Stator
35. Spring washer
36. Ball bearing, slip ring
37. Claw pole rotor
38. Bearing plate
39. Ball bearing bearing plate
40. Screw
42. Ball bearing, drive end
42. Intermediate ring
43. Pulley
44. Housing screw
45. Washer
46. Washer
47. Nut

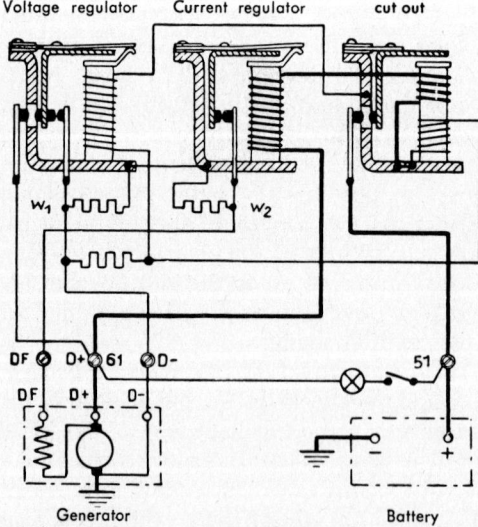

DC charging circuit including the regulator-cutout (across top) and the generator (at bottom).

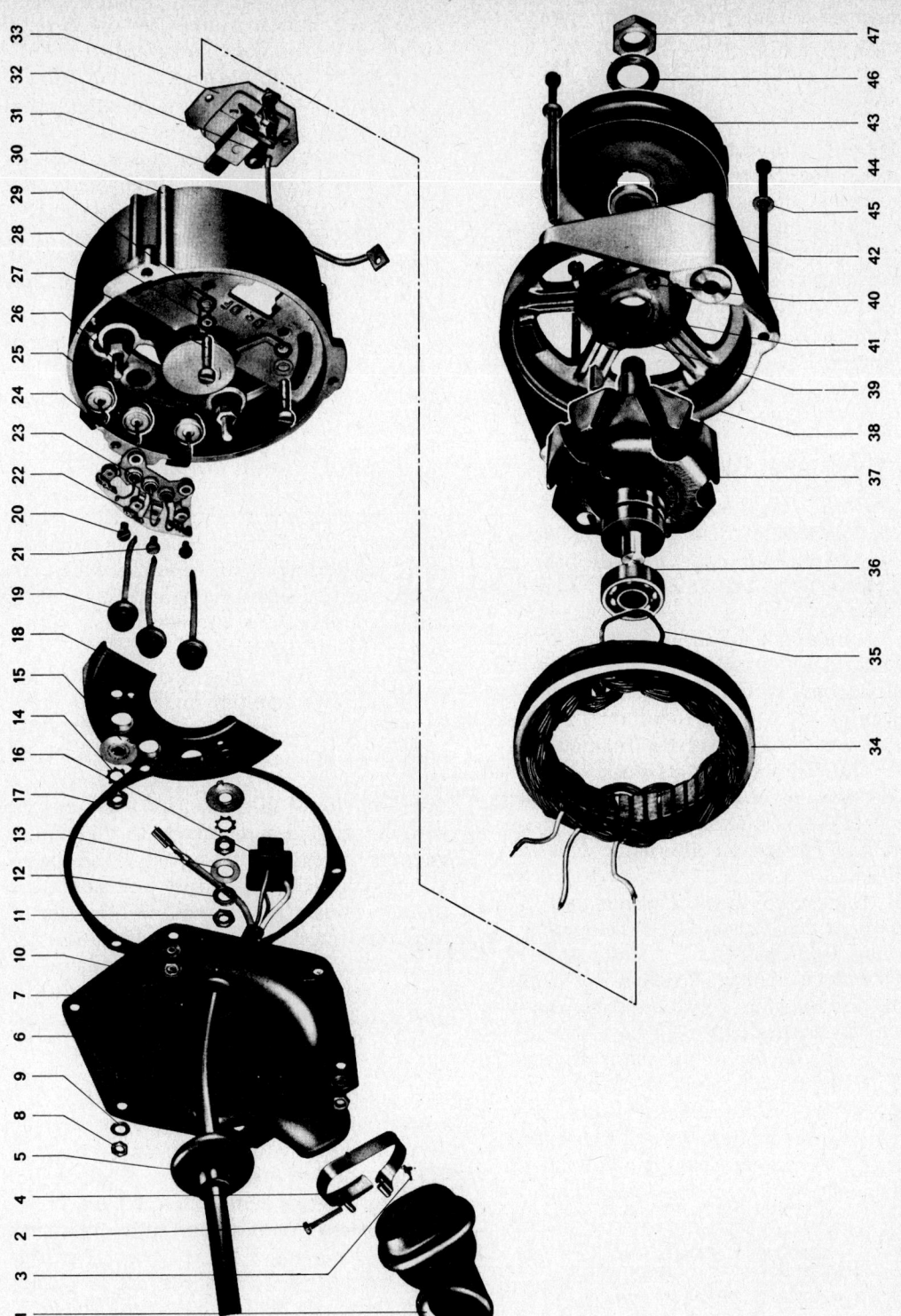

Alternator used on Type 914

connected through the ignition switch to terminals 51 and 61 of the regulator, lights up (with ignition on) whenever the generator voltage is less than the battery voltage.

If the output of the generator is less than the electrical charge of the battery, the battery would discharge through the generator. The regulator serves the second function of cutting off the generator to prevent the discharge.

When replacing a regulator, first check that the field coils of the generator are not grounded. Polarize DC generator to prevent damaging the regulator and to ensure proper charging.

AC Generator (Alternator)

The AC Generator—alternator—has the field windings carried in a rotor that is mounted at both ends in ball bearings. Lubrication is maintained by sealed-in grease.

The capability of the alternator to produce substantial current at idle speed presents a potential danger when testing. One precaution is to use a rheostat in the field circuit when bypassing the regulator in a test. The rheostat permits positive control of the amount of current allowed through the field circuit and also prevents high current from ruining the alternator while testing.

Warning: Keep battery ground cable disconnected while changing wires on alternator and regulator.

To prevent damage to electrical components and to assure reliable test results, observe the suggestions below.

1. Check tension of alternator drive belt.
2. Disconnect battery cables, clean them and test condition and charge of battery. Battery must be more than half charged.
3. Be absolutely sure of polarity before connecting battery in the test circuit. Reversed polarity will ruin the alternator diodes.
4. Disconnect both battery cables when making a battery charger hook-up. Never use a battery charger to start engine. Be sure of polarity hook-up when using a booster battery for starting.
5. Never ground the alternator output or the battery terminal.
6. Never ground the field circuit between alternator and regulator.

7. Never run any alternator on an open circuit with the field energized.
8. Never try to polarize an alternator.
9. Do not test alternator by attempting to run it like a motor.
10. The regulator cover must be in place when making test readings because the regulator parts are temperature sensitive.
11. The ignition switch must be off when removing or installing the regulator cover.
12. Use only insulated tools to make adjustments to the regulator.
13. When adjusting engine idle speed, put an electrical load on the engine by turning on the lights, heater, and other accessories.

Starter

The starter is a brush-type, series-wound motor operated by a solenoid. The armature shaft, supported in two bushings which are permanently packed with lubricant, has a spline which carries an overrunning clutch and a pinion assembly.

When the starter is switched on, the solenoid throws the pinion gear into mesh with the flywheel by means of the actuating lever and guide ring. When the solenoid (while moving the lever) reaches a contact disc, the circuit to the starter is completed and the engine is cranked. If the pinion gear cannot engage the flywheel, the spring absorbs the solenoid thrust and holds the pinion against the flywheel until the starter turns and meshes the teeth. The overrunning clutch breaks the connection between engine and starter as soon as the speed of the flywheel exceeds that of the starter pinion. The pinion continues in full mesh until the starter spring returns it to a neutral position. A brake is mounted at the commutator end of the starter to stop the armature quickly for another start if needed.

Disconnect ground strap from battery before working on any electrical parts of installed starter. With ground strap off, starter can be removed if the battery, regulator and ignition switch cables are detached from terminals 30 and 50 on the solenoid. Remove starter by unscrewing flange bolts.

OVERHAUL

Checking starter brushes and commutator. Remove starter end cap to inspect brushes for wear and free movement in

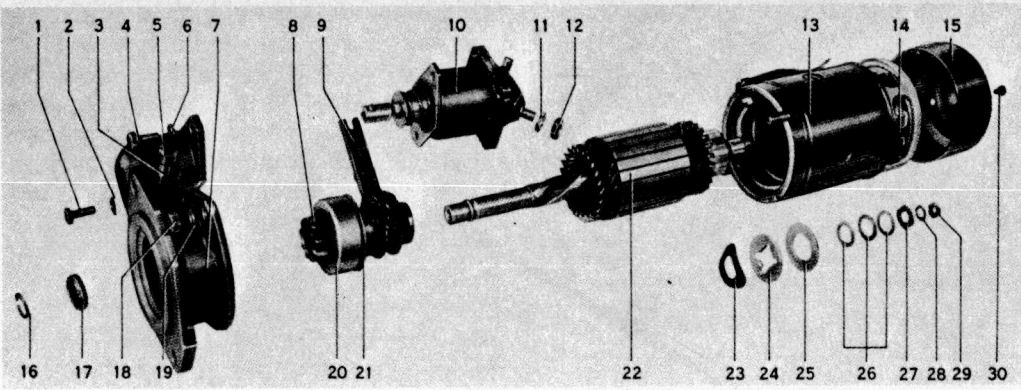

Parts of Bosch starter.

1 Starter flange bolt	12 Nut for terminal	22 Armature
2 Lock washer	13 Armature housing	23 Spring washer of armature
3 Pivot pin for lever	14 Brush for commutator	brake
4 Solenoid flange bolt	15 Starter end cap	24 Holding washer
5 Pivot pin screw head	16 Lock ring for armature shaft	25 Thrust washer
6 Lock washer	17 Pinion stop collar	26 Shims
7 Drive housing	18 Lock securing armature	27 Drive washer
8 Drive pinion gear	housing	28 Lock washer
9 Pinion actuating lever	19 Lock washer	29 Nut
10 Solenoid	20 Overrunning clutch assembly	30 End-cap screw
11 Lock washer	21 Thrust washer	

their guides. Replace brushes which are excessively worn, oil saturated or have loose connectors. Install brushes with the flexible connectors positioned so they will not hinder brush movement. Use a complete set even if only one brush is needed. Test tension of brush springs, replacing weak ones.

Clean the commutator with a lint-free cloth wrapped around a piece of wood and dampened in solvent or carbon tetrachloride. If commutator won't come clean or shows burned spots or scrapes, the starter should be disassembled.

Overhauling starter. Remove starter and cap and lift brushes from commutator. Clamp armature shaft at the drive pinion in a vise (with soft jaws) and remove the nut at the commutator end of the starter. Remove nuts on hook studs that hold motor housing and slide housing off. Note arrangement of plates, washers and shims of the armature brake.

Place armature in a vise with the pinion gear facing up to remove the drive assembly from the armature. Place a hollow drift or ½" pipe coupling if handy over the end of the shaft to bear against the pinion stop collar. Tap the collar toward the armature to uncover the lock ring. Remove the lock ring from the groove in the shaft and discard it, then slide the collar (not reusable)

from the shaft. Polish burrs from the shaft and then withdraw armature from housing.

Wipe starter parts with clean solvent-dampened cloth. Carefully inspect all parts for wear or damage. Wash non-electrical parts in gasoline, carbon tetrachloride, or trichlorethylene and dry immediately with compressed air. Do not submerge drive assembly or armature in cleaning solvent. The drive assembly has lubricant packed in the overrunning clutch. The bushing of the commutator bearing is only cleaned as far as it is accessible. The drive pinion should be cleaned in solvent only if it is oily and will not mesh at low temperatures.

Often the armature does not show evidence of damage. However, open circuits in the armature sometimes cause burned spots between adjacent commutator segments due to the brush deposits which bridge the insulation between segments. Inspect commutator and soldered connections. Check the windings and commutator for short circuits to the shaft or core with an AC test lamp. The lamp should not light when one probe touches the core and the other touches the commutator or the windings. Dampness can cause slight illumination.

The commutator segments are separated by mica plates. If the commutator is out of

Check starter armature for damage with 40-v AC test lamp. Dampness sometimes causes slight illumination.

round by more than .05 mm (.002″) and scored or burned it should be turned on a lathe to obtain a true surface. Do not remove more metal than is necessary. The mica must be undercut 0.3 to 0.5 mm (.012″ to .020″). A thin hacksaw blade is a good tool if carefully used. Slightly chamfer (a slight bevel) sides of commutator segments and remove all burrs from the undercut slots to provide a smooth running surface for the brushes. Metal chips remaining between the segments will cause short circuits.

Check for shorts in the brush holder plate and in the exciter windings. Inspect windings for burns. Any soldering must be done with rosin flux.

Field coils can be tested (when installed in housing) with an AC test light. Test for a grounded circuit in the coils by touching one probe to the coil connection and the other to the housing. Lamp should not light. Test each field coil individually for open circuits with a 6-volt test lamp in series with the battery.

Coat polished metal surfaces, other than the commutator, lightly with silicone grease. Bearing points, armature brake, helical spline, actuating lever, and pinion should be greased with special-purpose, high temperature grease. If replacing the bushing in the commutator bearing, the new bushing (oilite) must be placed in a hot oil bath for one half hour prior to assembly.

Install a new pinion stop collar and lock ring, securing collar on the lock ring with a punch.

Assemble starter in reverse sequence to disassembly, checking that armature end play is within range 0.1 to 0.3 mm (.002 to .012″).

Use sealing compound for (see illustration) 1) holes for slotted screws in end cap,

2) rubber seal between housing and end cap, 3) holes in housing for hook studs, 4) joint faces between armature housing and drive housing, 5) joint faces between starter and transmission, 6) joint faces between solenoid and drive housing.

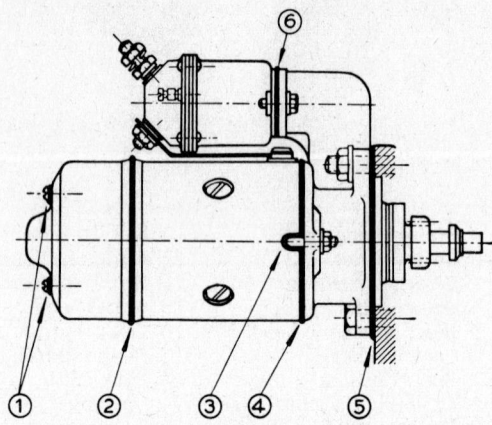

Use compound to seal areas shown on starter. Points are described in text.

Hold cable ends from twisting while terminal nuts are tightened; do not use excessive force.

Solenoid

Checking solenoid. Remove connector strap from solenoid switch and remove flange bolts holding solenoid. Pull out starter pinion to free solenoid shaft from actuating lever and lift solenoid off the lever.

Total armature travel of the solenoid should be 10 ± 0.2 mm ($.394 \pm .008″$). Of

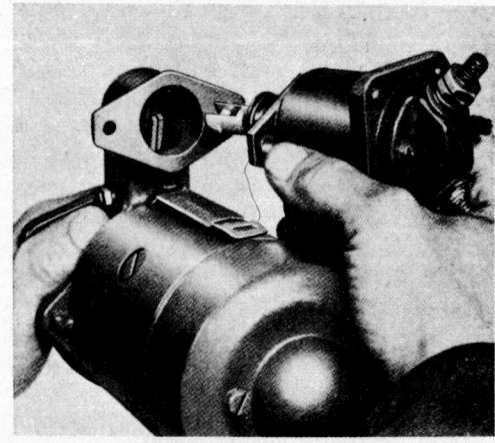

To remove solenoid, lift solenoid shaft (with pin) off the forked lever in the housing.

this, 3 mm (.118″) is contact reserve. To check travel, connect a 6-volt lamp between the main terminals and push in the armature. Measure the travel remaining after the test lamp lights. When installed in the starter, the solenoid switch must pull the armature in when 4 volts are applied between terminal 30 and ground. If it does not, check for proper seating of starter brushes.

If installing a new solenoid switch, adjust the plunger so that the centerline of the pivot in the yoke is 32.4 ± 0.1 mm (1.275 ± .004″) from the solenoid flange.

Battery

The 12-volt electrical system is standard on 914, 912 and 911 models. Battery output averages 45 amperes per hour. Earlier models are equipped with 6-volt, 84 amp-hour batteries. The 12-volt system requires that the battery produce at least 9 volts while the starter is cranking the engine. The 6-volt system can tolerate a minimum of 4.5 volts output under the cranking load.

Batteries should be checked periodically for proper output and good connections. A weak power supply lowers the efficiency of the engine as well as placing a greater drag on the generator.

Inspect the battery case for cracks and weakness. Check the density (specific gravity) of the battery electrolyte with a hydrometer. Readings from a fully charged battery will depend on the make but will fall in the range of 1.260 to 1.310 times as heavy as pure water at 80°F. NOTE: *All cells should produce nearly equal readings.* If one or two cell readings are sharply lower, those cells are defective. The average test voltage of each cell is 2 volts. It increases to about 2.5 to 2.7 volts while the battery is being charged and decreases to between 2.1 and 2.0 volts soon after the charging current has been cut off. The battery is discharged when the cell voltage has dropped to approx. 1.8 volts under no-load test condition.

As a battery releases its charge, sulphate ions in the electrolyte become attached to the battery plates—reducing the density of the fluid. The specific gravity of the electrolyte varies not only with the percentage of acid in the liquid, but also with temperature. As temperature increases, the elec-

trolyte expands so that specific gravity is reduced in this second way. As temperature drops, the electrolyte contracts and gravity increases. To correct readings for temperature variation, add .004 to the hydrometer reading for every 10°F. that the electrolyte is above 80°F. and subtract .004 for every 10° that the electrolyte is below 80°. The drawing shows the total correction to make for any temperature above or below 80°F.

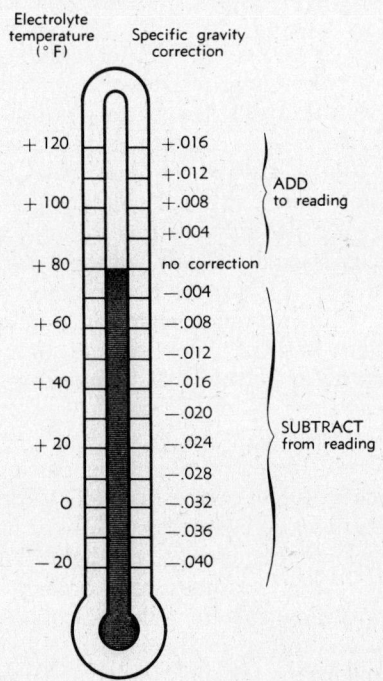

Temperature affects the specific gravity readings of batteries.

The amount of charge remaining in a battery can be roughly determined from the specific gravity ranges shown in the chart.

Perform a light-load voltage test to detect weak cells. First draw off the transient (surface) charge by operating the starter for three seconds and then turning on the low beam lights. After one minute, test each cell (with lights still on) with a voltmeter. A fully charged battery will have no cell voltage below 1.95 volts and no cell should vary more than .05 volts from the others. A greater variation at full charge indicates a defective cell.

Hydrometer Readings	Condition
1.260–1.310	Fully charged
1.230–1.250	¾ charged
1.200–1.220	½ charged
1.170–1.190	¼ charged
1.140–1.160	Almost discharged
1.110–1.130	Fully discharged

Another battery check involves connecting a charger for three minutes under 40 amperes for a 12-volt battery (75 amps for 6-v). Read the battery voltage with the charger still operating. Voltage over 15.5 v for 12-volt battery (7.75 for 6-v) indicates a defective battery. If battery voltage is under this limit and individual cell readings are within 0.1 volts, the battery is usable.

Charging a weak battery is best done by a slow-charge method. If quick charging is attempted, check the cell voltages and the color of the electrolyte a few minutes after charge is started. If cell voltages are not uniform or if electrolyte is discolored with brown sediment, quick charging should be stopped in favor of a slow charge. In either case, do not let electrolyte temperature exceed 120°F.

If high voltage in the circuit is suspected, the voltage regulator might be cutting in abnormally due to corroded or loose battery connections. The symptoms are hard starting, a full ammeter charge, and lights flaring brightly. After cleaning, coat battery terminals with petroleum jelly (vaseline) to prevent recurrence of problem.

Overcharging the battery is a common cause of battery failure. A symptom of overcharging is a frequent need for more water in the battery. The generating system should be corrected immediately to prevent internal battery damage.

Caution: fire or sparks near a charging battery will cause the battery gasses to explode.

Fuel System

Fuel Filters

Every Porsche has a fuel filter screen located in the fuel pump. These can be quickly opened and cleaned. When assembling filter, check fit of gasket.

All 356 models have an additional fuel filter attached to the fuel cock at the tank. The filter is accessible beneath the dash panel. To clean the filter at the fuel cock, close the cock, unscrew the wing nut, remove and rinse the filter in clean gasoline.

A sediment screen is located in the fuel tank above the fuel cock. To clean the tank and sediment screen, close the fuel cock and disconnect the fuel hose from it. Remove the cotter pin at the fuel cock operating rod and pull the rod back slightly. Remove the flexible vent hose (bleeder hose) and the gas gauge from the tank. Detach and remove tank from the luggage compartment. Empty tank, remove fuel cock, and flush both with gasoline and dry with compressed air.

Fuel Pump

TYPE 914

Removal

Pinch the fuel hoses to prevent spillage and remove the cable plug. Cut the hose clamps and pull off, catching the fuel. Lift the fuel pressure hose to prevent draining of the fuel loop line. Unscrew the retaining nuts and remove the pump.

Installation

Fit the hoses to the pump. The pressure hose must be fitted with a hose clamp. Mount the pump on its supports and remove the clamps pinching the fuel lines. Replace the cable plug, ensuring that the protective cap is installed correctly.

TYPE 914/6

Removal

The fuel pump employed on the 914/6 is an electric type, similar to the type used on some previous models. Remove the right-hand hot air hose and detach the cable plug. Loosen the nuts securing the anti-vibration mount. Remove the clip from the pressure line. Disconnect the fuel hoses (suction line "S" and return line "R") which are attached by hose clips. Catch any fuel which may flow from the line.

Installation

Check plug connection for corrosion and be sure to connect the plug correctly. With-

Electric fuel pump—Type 914/6

out distorting the anti-vibration mounts, connect the hoses to the pump. Be sure to seat the protective cap correctly as a protection against corrosion.

356 SERIES, 911, 912

The rod-operated mechanical fuel pumps used on most pushrod engines are powered at camshaft speed by a cam that is part of the distributor drive gear. Two common types, an "L" shaped unit and a newer, horizontal (straight-line) pump, are simply constructed and easily checked for malfunction.

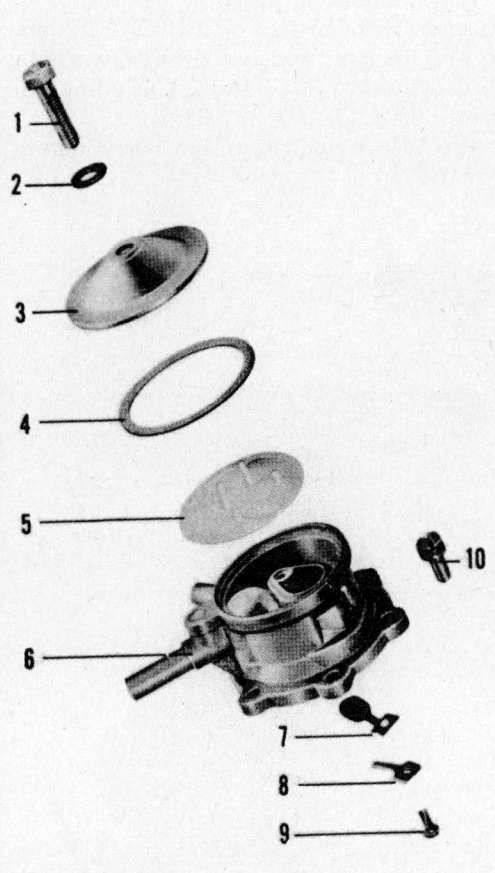

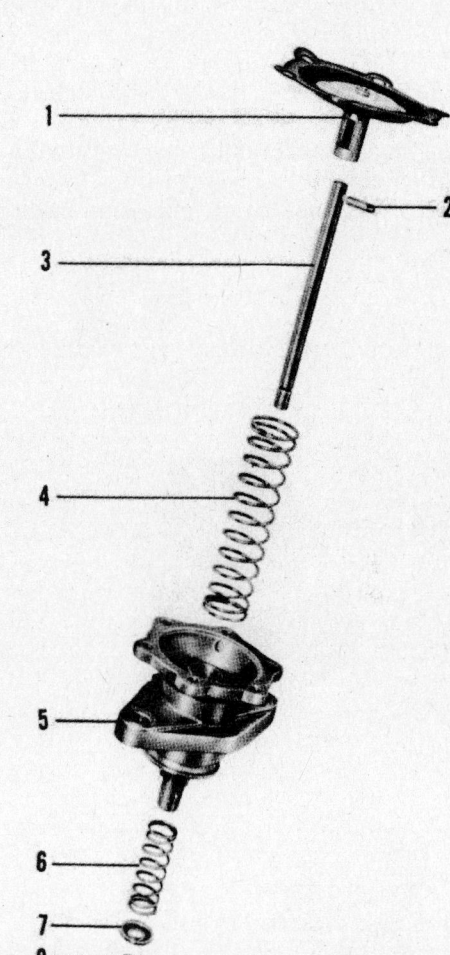

Straight-line fuel pump.

Left side
5 Fuel strainer
6 Valve housing
7 Leaf spring valve
8 Valve limiter
9 Self threading screw

Right side
1 Diaphragm
3 Plunger
4 Diaphragm spring
5 Diaphragm housing
6 Plunger spring
7 Spring seat
8 Lock ring

A third type, a dual fuel pump, was used with Solex 40 PI (overflow circuit) carburetors on the early 911 and 911S models before the Weber carburetion system was adopted.

A Bendix electric fuel pump is used on the 911, 911S and several racing engines including the Carrera. The pump is sealed and contains helium gas to keep contact erosion at a minimum. The electric pump has a removable filter within a hex-locking cover on the bottom. The cover also has a magnetic trap.

Fuel pressure is determined by the degree of compression of the diaphragm spring in the fuel pump. A weak spring causes low fuel pressure; extreme spring tension creates pressures that are too high. Excessive pump pressure causes carburetor flooding and, in almost all cases, leads to dilution of oil around the cylinder rings. Insufficient pump pressure causes lean combustion mix-

ture and, thus, a rough running engine with misfiring at high rpm and meager power output.

Over the years, as engine displacements increased and carburetion designs improved, fuel pump pressure requirements have risen. Generally, fuel pumps on 356 models maintain pressures within the range of 1.3 to 1.9 psi (.09–.13 atm) at engine speeds from 1000 to 3000 rpm. The fuel pump delivers at least 167 cc/minute.

The 356A models have pump pressures in a range from 1.8 to 2.4 psi.

The 356B models pump gasoline at a rate between 1.9 and 2.7 psi (.13–.18 atm) and deliver 300 cc/minute at 4500 rpm.

The straight-line (horizontal) fuel pump on later 356B models, on all 356C models, and on the 912, works at a pressure within 2.9 to 3.5 psi (.20–.24 atm). This pump delivers 500 cc/minute at 4500 rpm.

The 911 engines require a much higher

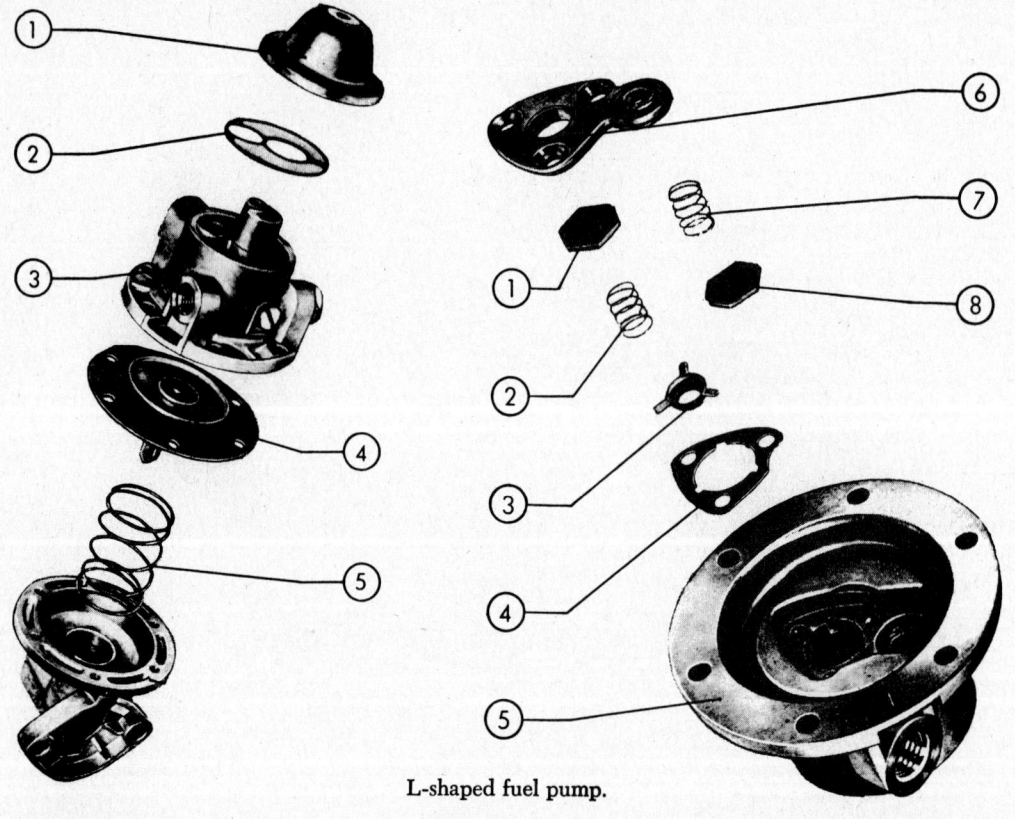

L-shaped fuel pump.

Left side	Right side	
1 Fuel pump cover	1 Exhaust valve plate	6 Valve retainer plate
2 Fuel strainer	2 Exhaust valve spring	7 Intake valve spring
3 Valve housing	3 Seat for exhaust valve spring	8 Intake valve plate
4 Diaphragm	4 Gasket for retainer plate	
5 Diaphragm spring	5 Valve housing	

pressure, between 4.1 and 4.9 psi (.28–.33 atm), and a greater volume, 900 cc/minute, because they are larger in displacement.

The fuel pump used on the type 914 operates at a pressure of 28 psi, while the fuel pump on the type 914/6 operates at 4½ psi.

Removal

Remove fuel lines carefully to prevent rupturing them, plug the ends of the pipes, and remove pump from engine housing. *Note:* the tank line will feed gas by gravity if not plugged. Scratch a mark across the diaphragm flanges to simplify later reassembly. This prevents accidental changing of the lead-in angle of the fuel lines which might occur if the top section is put back on facing a different direction.

Reconditioning Mechanical Pumps

Remove screws from the diaphragm flanges and separate the two sections of the pump. Press down on diaphragm to release rocker arm link. Remove retainer clips from rocker arm pin and punch out pin. Take out link, rocker arm and rocker arm spring.

Disassemble the top section by removing hex retaining screw, cover and pulsator. Carefully remove valve covers so that parts don't fly out.

Wash parts in solvent and dry with air. Replace worn valves, valve seats, diaphragm, linkage and spring. Replacement-part kits containing these parts are available.

Metal parts coated with white oxide have been water damaged and should be replaced to prevent fouling of carburetor jets.

Reassembly of the fuel pump is the reverse of disassembly. Assemble the rocker arm and link and hold them together with thin rod or metal inserted through pivot pin holes. Install diaphragm spring and diaphragm. Then turn over pump so rocker link drops toward diaphragm connection. Press diaphragm in and hook it onto link. Insert rocker pivot pin and secure it.

Press in rocker arm linkage enough to make diaphragm stay flat between the flanges while turning in flange screws until screw heads touch lock washers. At this point, push rocker linkage in as far as possible to stretch diaphragm and tighten down flange screws. Premature diaphragm wear

is avoided by pre-stretching the diaphragm in this way.

Carburetors

Through the years Porsches have been equipped with Solex, Zenith and Weber carburetors. Similar in design, all three have several conventional circuits in common—float, starting, idle, progression, main feed, acceleration, and enrichment.

ALTITUDE CORRECTION

Thinner air at high altitudes, 3600–4500 feet (1200–1500 m), causes the fuel-air mixture to be richer. Solex among others has available an altitude corrector that is fitted in place of the main jet carrier. It progressively reduces the flow of fuel into the main jet as atmospheric pressure decreases in higher altitudes.

In substantially different altitudes, the main jet size must be different. To compensate for higher altitudes, the main jet is approximately 6% smaller for every 3,000 feet.

SOLEX PBI AND PBIC

Referring to the exploded view drawing remove screws holding the float chamber cover. Place cover on clean paper and screw out needle valve. Remove the four screws fastening the cover of the disc-valve starter, take off the assembly, and then remove starter fuel jet located to left of cover. Remove starter air jet.

When removing all assemblies, keep "twin" components separated to prevent accidental interchanges when reassembling carburetors. Note all jet sizes.

Remove air correction jet (high speed air bleed) from emulsion (main vent) assembly in throat, extract the emulsion tube from inside, and take out the emulsion tube holder. Remove the accelerator pump *injector* screw and the injection assembly. The 32 PBIC has high and low injectors.

From the float chamber, lift out (except with the 40 PBIC, which unscrews) the float toggle (float arm), its spindle (pin), and the float. The 40 PBIC has a float-holding screw located on side of float chamber accessible from outside.

Disconnect the accelerator pump lever from its pump control rod and then unscrew the four corner fixing screws to remove pump assembly. Remove the pump inlet valve, strainer, and washer from under the

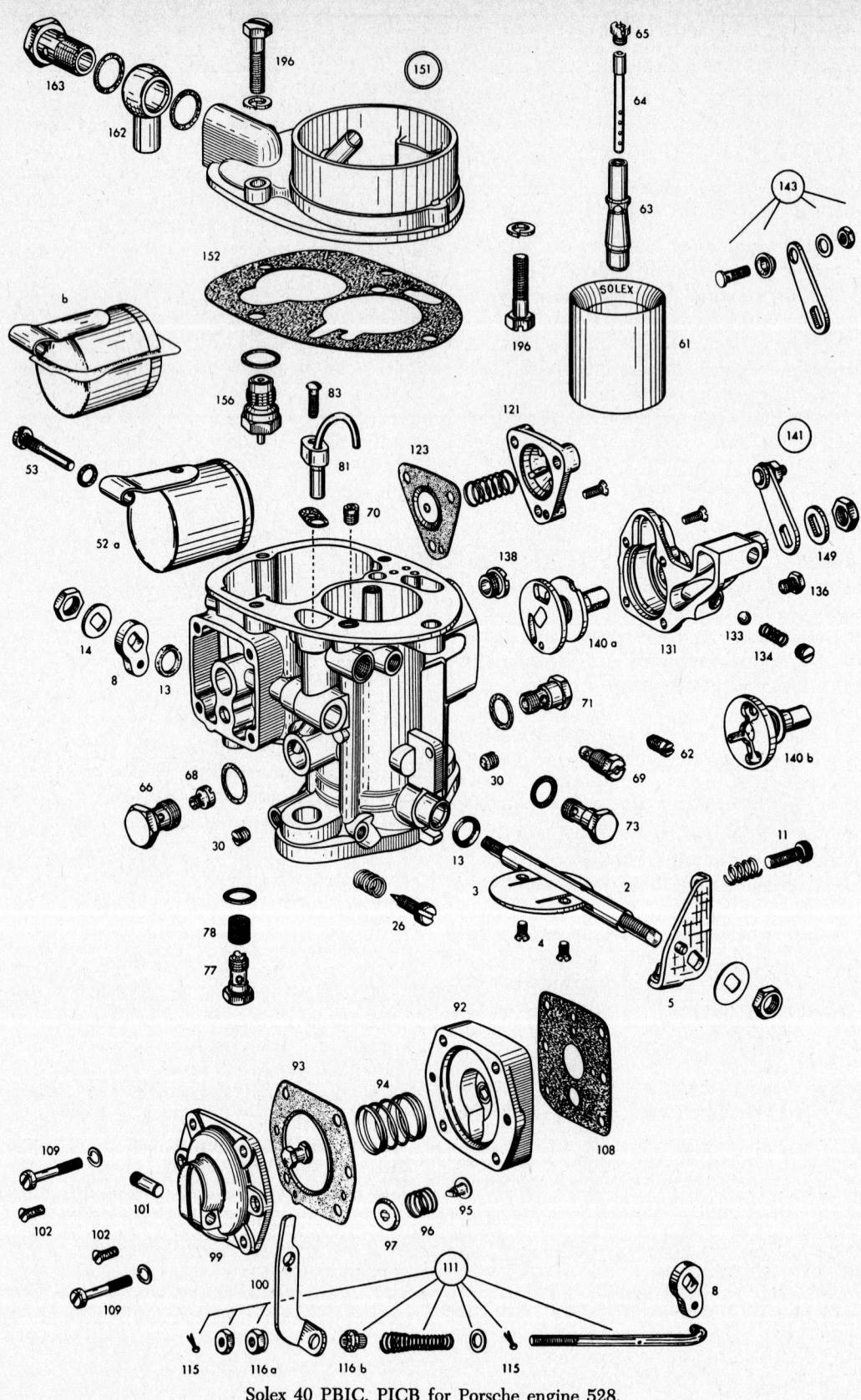

Solex 40 PBIC, PICB for Porsche engine 528.

accelerator housing. Unscrew the accelerator pump jet from housing that extends to side of accelerator pump. Take out the main (metering) jet carrier and jet from the carburetor housing.

Remove the idle volume control screw (idle mixture adjustment) from throat below throttle butterfly. Remove idle (pilot) jet and idle (pilot) air bleed. The venturi (choke tube) is removable by loosening a set screw.

SOLEX PII AND PII-4

When removing and cleaning assemblies, keep "twin" components separated to prevent accidental interchanges when reassembling carburetor.

Referring to exploded view diagram, remove the float chamber cover screws. Take off cover and remove two screws and springs securing float pivot. (See exploded views, parts 68, 69, except for 40 PII). Place cover on clean paper and unscrew float needle valve and washer. Remove both air correction jets (high speed air bleed) near float chamber and emulsion (main vent) tubes—40 PII emulsion tubes are threaded.

Unscrew each pump injector fixing screw and extract the injection assemblies.

From the float chamber, lift out securing plate, pivot and arm for adjustment of fuel level—not on 40 PII. Take out float and its spindle (pin).

Disconnect the accelerator pump lever from its pump control rod and then un-

screw the four corner fixing screws to remove pump assembly. Remove the pump inlet valve, its strainer and washer from under the accelerator housing (see exploded views, part numbers 42, 43, 44). Unscrew both accelerator pump jets from housings that extend to sides of accelerator pump. Don't lose small ball check ("no-return") valve. Take out both main (metering) jet carriers, jets and washers—see exploded views, parts 27, 28, 29—from the carb housing below the accelerator pump.

Remove both idle volume control screws (idle mixture adjustments) located next to bottom carburetor flanges. Remove idle fuel jets (pilot) and idle air bleeds. Unscrew enriching jet (located next to idle air bleeds in 40 PII-4 for Super 90 models).

Enriching tubes are located in the float cover assembly. Venturi (choke tube) is removable by releasing the set screw.

PJJ CARBURETORS

Some Solex carburetors on Porsches were factory stamped PJJ. These are PII carburetors.

SOLEX 40 PI-1

The Solex 40 PI-1 carburetor differs from conventional designs by having a single carrier assembly holding all jets suspended in a pocket of the carburetor body but accessible from the top without removing the carburetor cover. Each carburetor uses an overflow fuel-level system that is fed from

2 Butterfly spindle	70 Pilot air bleed (idle)	116a Pump lever adjustment nut
3 Butterfly	71 Starter fuel jet	116b Pump lever bushing
4 Screws for butterfly	73 Pump jet	121 Vacuum starting device
5 Throttle stop plate	77 Ball check-valve seat	123 Diaphragm for valve
8 Transfer lever	78 Ball valve filter	131 Manual starting device
11 Idle speed screw	81 Low injector	133 Ball valve
13 Dust ring	83 Injector fixing screws	134 Spring for ball valve
14 Throttle shaft washer	92 Accelerator pump housing	136 Attaching screw
26 Volume control screw (idle mixture)	93 Diaphragm	138 Air jet
	94 Diaphragm spring	140a Starting device rotating plate
30 Threaded plug	95 Valve	
52 Float 21 gr.	96 Valve spring	140b Starting device rotating plate 3–5
53 Float holding screw	97 Spring retainer	
61 Venturi	99 Pump cover	141 Starting device control lever
62 Venturi fixing screw	100 Pump lever	143 Control lever assembly
63 Emulsion tube holder	101 Spindle for lever	149 Spindle washer
64 Emulsion tube (No. 28)	102 Pump cover screws	151 Float chamber cover
65 Air correction jet	108 Pump gasket	152 Cover gasket
66 Main jet holder	109 Filister-head cover screws	156 Needle valve 2 mm
68 Main jet	111 Connecting rod assembly	162 Banjo fitting
69 Pilot jet (idle)	115 Cotter pins	163 Banjo bolt
		196 Fixing screw

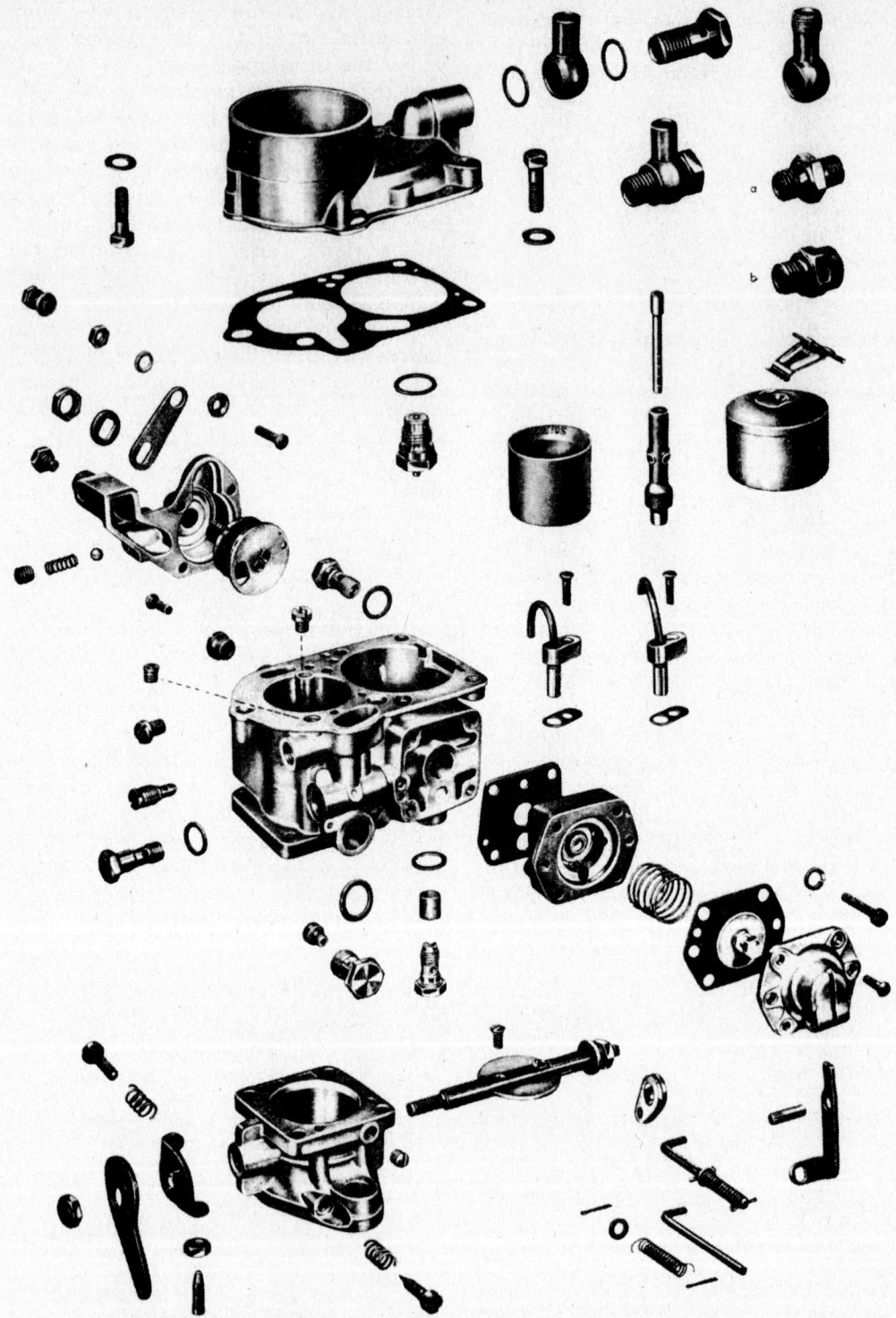

Solex 32 PBIC for Porsche engines 616/1 and 589/2. (See 40 PBIC for part names.)

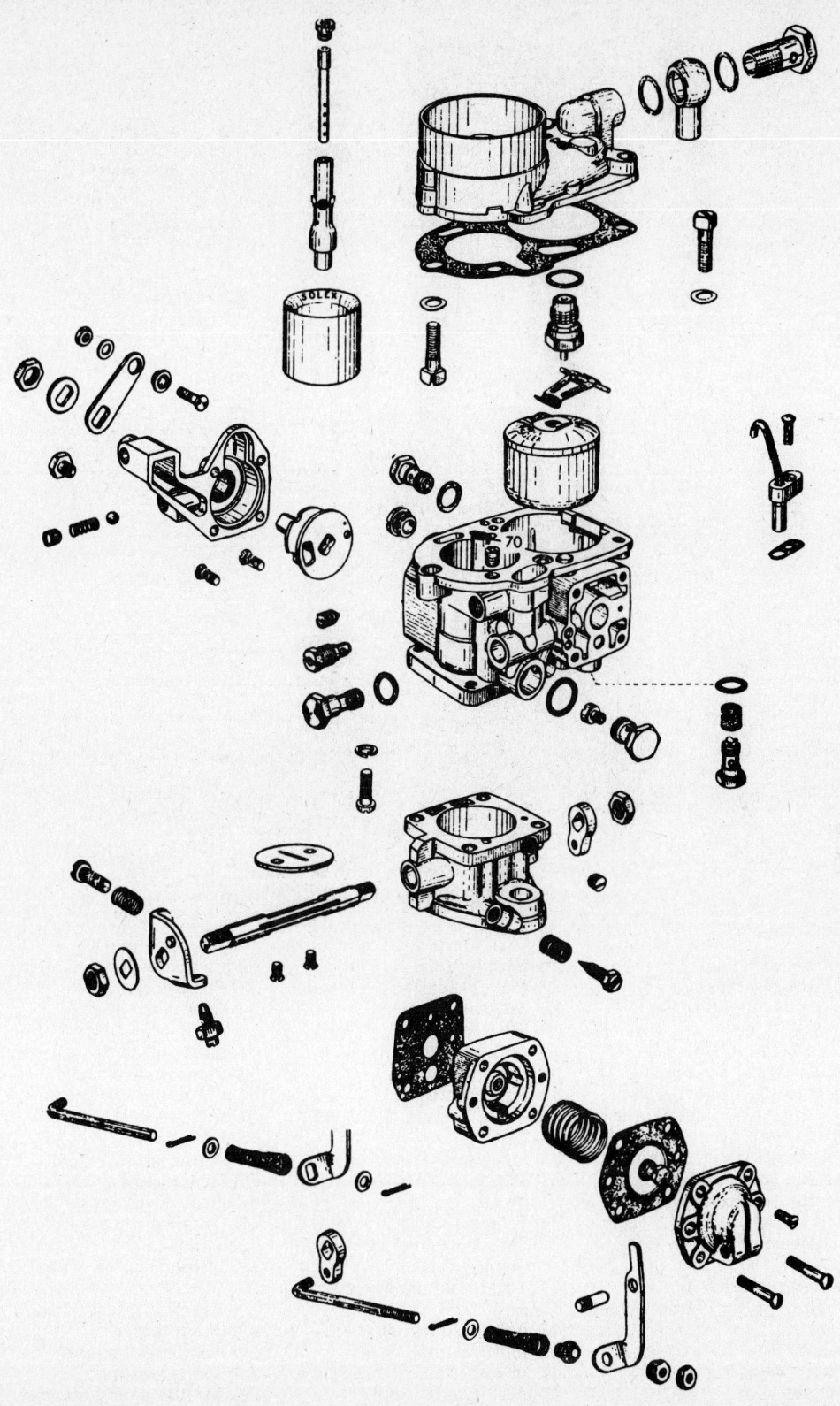

Solex 32 PBI for Porsche engines 369, 506, 589, 546, 527. (See 40 PBIC for part names.)

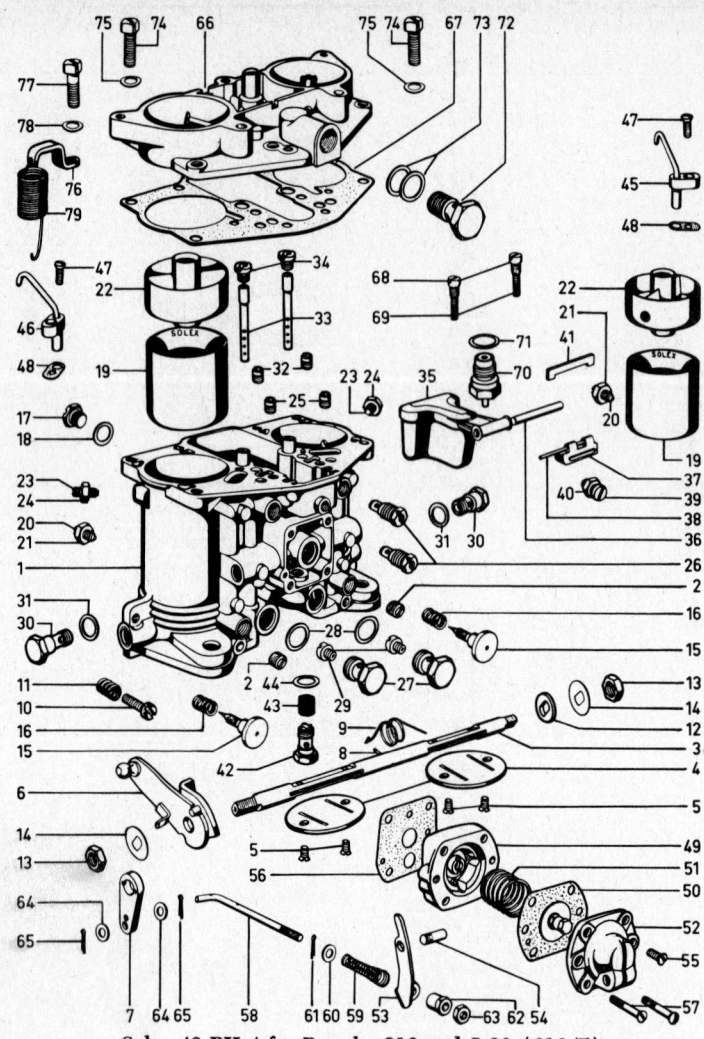

Solex 40 PII-4 for Porsche 912 and S-90 (616/7).

3 Throttle spindle	26 Pilot jet (idle fuel jet)	52 Pump cover
4 Throttle butterfly	27 Main jet carrier	53 Pump rocker
5 Throttle butterfly screw	28 Jet-carrier washer	54 Rocker spindle
6 Throttle lever	29 Main jet	56 Pump cover gasket
7 Pump actuating lever	30 Acceleration pump jet	57 Lower pump fixing screws
8 Return-spring stop pin	32 Enrichment jet	58 Pump control rod
9 Throttle shaft return spring	33 Emulsion tube	61 Cotter pin
10 Slow running adjustment screw (idle speed)	34 Air correction jet	62 Pump adjustment nut
11 Adjustment-screw spring	35 Float	63 Lock nut
12 Throttle shaft washer	36 Float spindle	65 Cotter pin
13 Throttle shaft end nut	37 Toggle for fuel level adjustment	66 Float chamber cover
14 Stop washer	38 Toggle spindle	67 Float cover gasket
15 Volume control screw (idle mixture)	39 Set screw (fuel level adjustment)	68 Distance screw for float toggle spindle
16 Control-screw spring	41 Toggle-spindle locking plate	69 Distance screw spring
17 Screw plug (for checking fuel level)	42 Ball check valve	70 Float needle valve 1.75 mm with spring-loaded ball
19 Venturi (K)	43 Ball valve screen	72 Banjo bolt
20 Venturi fixing screw	45 Injector tube	74 Float cover screws
22 Diffuser	47 Injector tube fixing screw	75 Spring washers
23 Diffuser fixing screw	49 Acceleration pump	76 Throttle spring support
25 Pilot air bleed (idle air jet)	50 Diaphragm	77 Assembly screw on support
	51 Diaphragm spring	79 Throttle lever spring

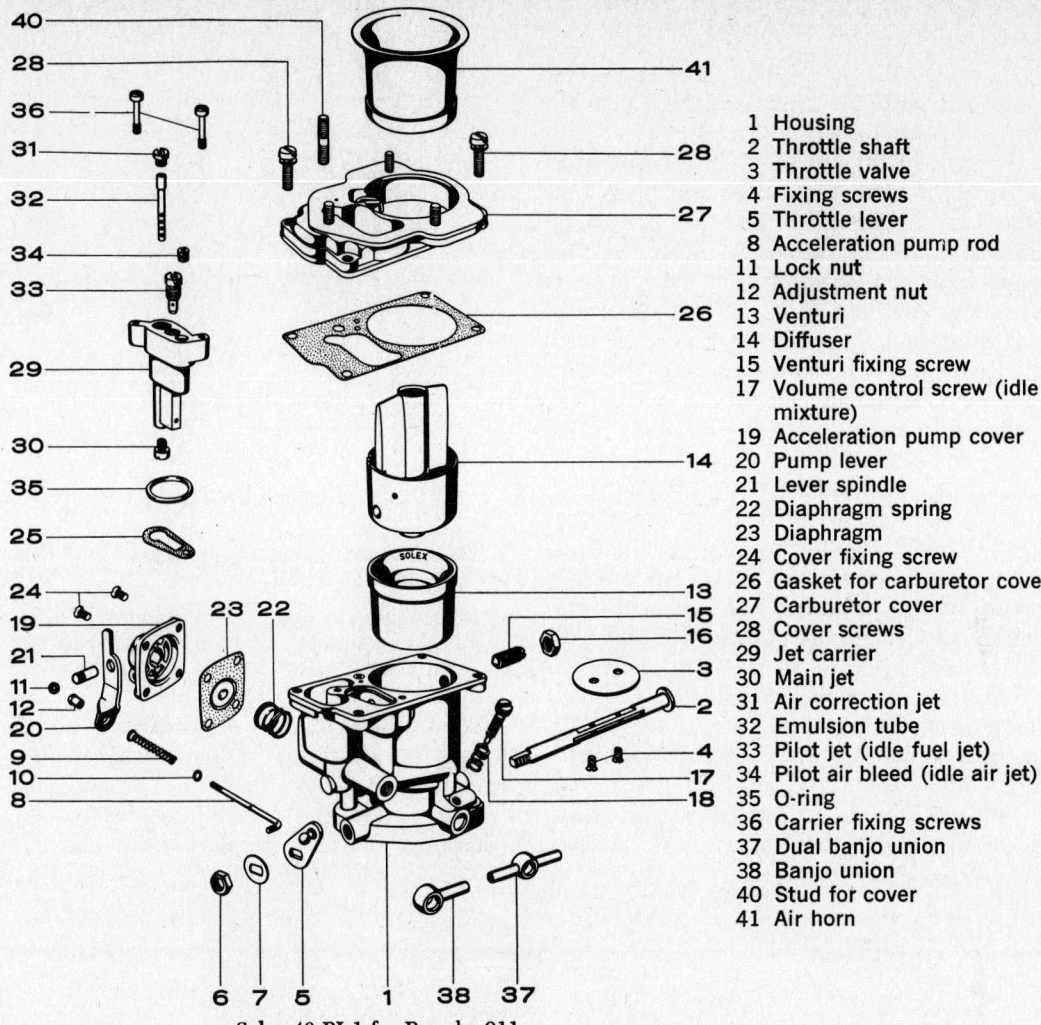

Solex 40 PI-1 for Porsche 911.

1 Housing
2 Throttle shaft
3 Throttle valve
4 Fixing screws
5 Throttle lever
8 Acceleration pump rod
11 Lock nut
12 Adjustment nut
13 Venturi
14 Diffuser
15 Venturi fixing screw
17 Volume control screw (idle mixture)
19 Acceleration pump cover
20 Pump lever
21 Lever spindle
22 Diaphragm spring
23 Diaphragm
24 Cover fixing screw
26 Gasket for carburetor cover
27 Carburetor cover
28 Cover screws
29 Jet carrier
30 Main jet
31 Air correction jet
32 Emulsion tube
33 Pilot jet (idle fuel jet)
34 Pilot air bleed (idle air jet)
35 O-ring
36 Carrier fixing screws
37 Dual banjo union
38 Banjo union
40 Stud for cover
41 Air horn

a separate float chamber common to all the carbs. Accelerator pump disassembly is similar to procedures outlined above for other Solex carburetors.

When removing assemblies, note jet sizes so that mistakes of interchanging jets are avoided in reassembly of carburetor.

Assembly

Referring to exploded view diagrams, and using new gasketing and other soft parts where needed, place the washer, spring and pump-cover arm over the pump control rod and secure them with cotter pin, horseshoe lock, or locking nut provided.

If accelerator pump was taken apart, reassemble by placing spring in pump body lower section, and diaphragm assembly in pump cover and by fastening both groups together with short center pump-cover screws. Hold pump arm steady while tightening screws to keep diaphragm from distorting. In assembling carburetor parts, tighten all screws gradually (one and then another) as though using torque procedures.

Replace emulsion tubes (with open ends up), jets and carriers, pump check valve(s) and idle adjusting screw(s). Install starter unit (if applicable). In many cases the starter jet has the same thread size as the correction jets. *Check stamped jet sizes against specifications.* Screw in idle adjustment until it gently touches seat and then back off 1½ turns for the basic setting.

Use a *new* needle valve and seat. Install float assembly and put on float-chamber cover with new gasket.

Zenith 32 NDIX

Later 1600 and 1600S models were equipped with the Zenith 32 NDIX dual-throat carburetor.

Throttle linkage to the Zenith carburetor is different from that used on Solex, but otherwise, disassembly of the Zenith is similar to that of the Solex. After the top cover has been taken off, the fixing screw, air correction jets, emulsion tube holders and emulsion tubes can be removed from the center cluster. Both idling air jets can also be unscrewed. Note jet sizes so that mistakes in re-assembly are avoided.

Remove retaining screw for jet cover plate on side and remove the two main and two idling jets. Both idling mixture screws are located beside the jet housing. The starter fuel jet and accelerator pump jets are located on the opposite side. Beneath the pump cylinder are the pump valve and ball check valve.

When removing assemblies, keep "twin" components separated to prevent accidental interchanges when reassembling carburetor.

When reassembling the Zenith, use new gasketing and other soft parts where

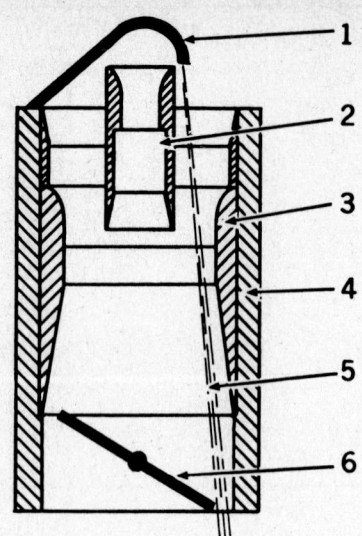

Position of acceleration pump nozzle is critical. Keep it aimed as shown.

1 Acceleration nozzle
2 Auxiliary Venturi
3 Main Venturi
4 Carburetor body
5 Injected fuel
6 Throttle valve

needed. Check plunger of accelerator pump for perfect condition. Replace floats if they leak. Check all jets for correct size. Install venturi with the restriction facing up (stamped size can be read from above).

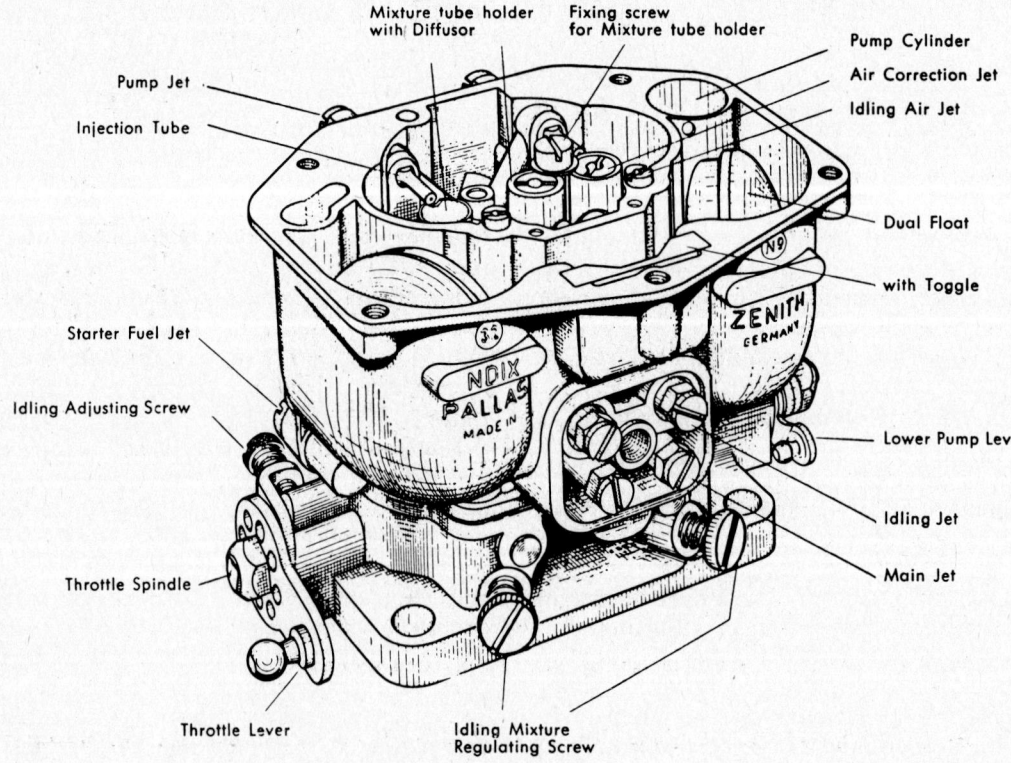

Zenith NDIX (cover removed).

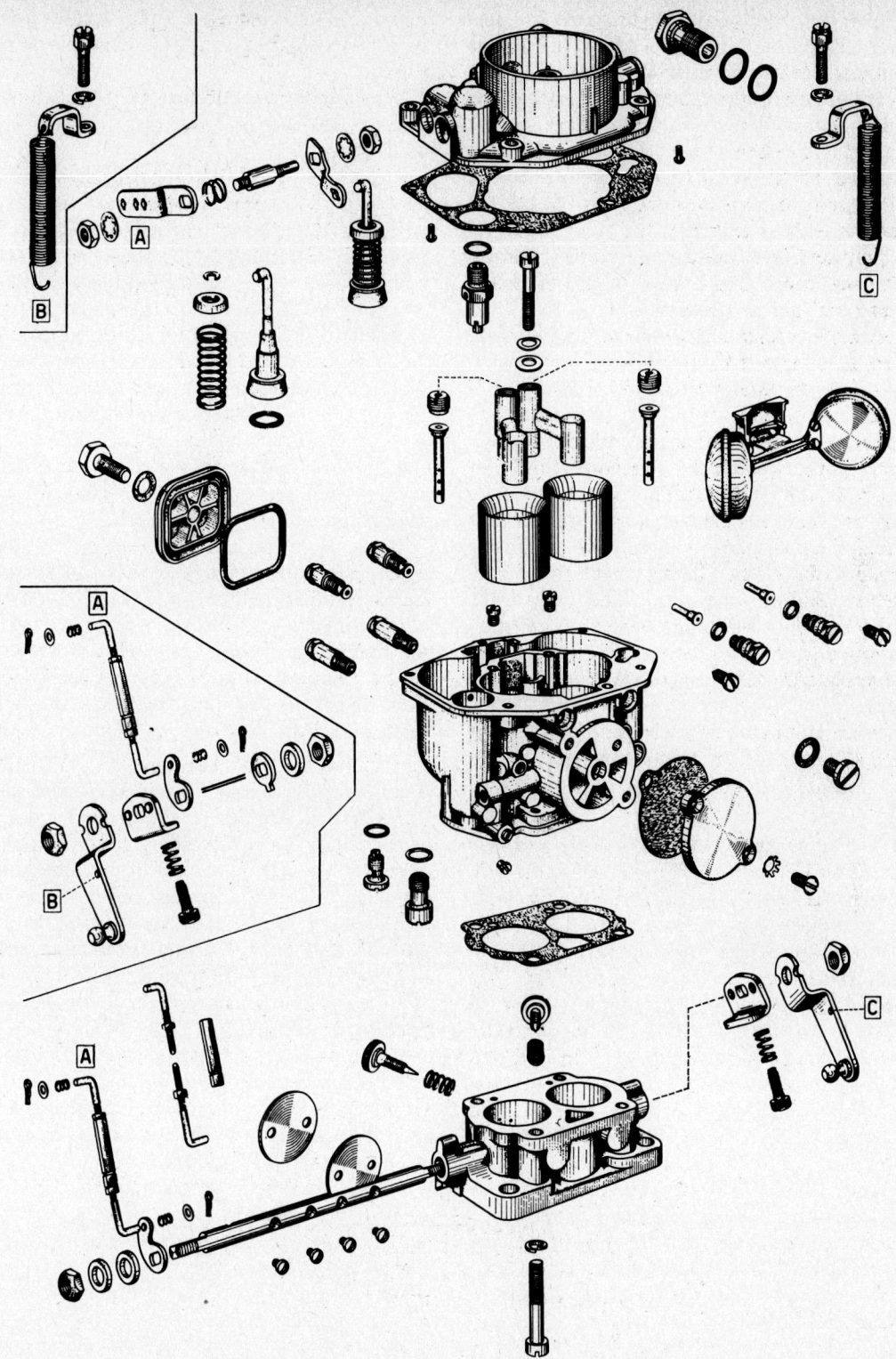

Zenith 32 NDIX for Porsche engines 616/1 and 616/2.

Do not overtighten venturi fixing screw. Check clearance of throttle valve shaft. Ex- cessive clearance allows extra air to enter which causes poor starting and idling.

Check tip of idle adjustment screw for perfect condition. Replace screw if tip is burred, bent or broken off.

Install emulsion tubes (with open ends up), jets and carrier assemblies, pump valve, ball check valve, and idle adjusting screws. (NOTE: in some cases, different jets have the same thread sizes. Check jet sizes against specifications.)

Screw in idle adjustment until it gently touches seat and then back off 1½ times for basic starting adjustment.

Place float assembly on a level surface and check if both floats and brackets touch. If necessary straighten floats carefully. Insert float assembly into chamber and check for either float touching. Bend float brackets as required. Install float assembly and put on float chamber cover.

Use a *new* needle valve and seat so that the jetting surface of the valve is perfectly smooth and clean. Check needle valve gasket for perfect condition. The thread for the valve must be intact. Check sealing surfaces of carburetor cover. The carburetor cover gasket is held by two rivets. When replacing the gasket, the rivets can be removed with a sturdy knife. The new gasket must be secured by two rivets.

Weber Carburetors

The Porsche 356A, 1600 G.S. and the Carrera G.T. were equipped originally with Weber 40 DCM 2 carburetors having floats on two sides, dual throats and all jets clustered in the center to counteract for movement stresses.

The Porsche 1500RSK has a Weber 46 IDM 1 carburetor with a single, centrally located float and jets that feed through two independent carburetor throats into separate intake manifold flanges. Central float location is another design for good carburetion under movement forces.

Both the 40 DCM 2 and 46 IDM 1 are disassembled easily from top to bottom if circuit components are removed in groups. Keep "twin" components separated to prevent accidental interchanges when reassembling carburetor.

The Porsche 904 G.T. has Weber 48 IDA carburetors. The Porsche 911 (from engine #907001) and the 911S use Weber 40 IDA and 40 IDA(S) or IDS carburetors, respectively. Each cylinder has its own carburetor; three carburetors on each cylinder bank are grouped into an assembly with two float chambers and one accelerating pump.

The Weber carburetors on the Porsche 911 and 911S are removed and disassembled as follows:

Detach carburetor preheating hose from air cleaner assembly. Unsnap fasteners and withdraw air cleaner cartridge. Detach oil breather hose from oil filler stack. Withdraw condensation water hose from bottom of air cleaner housing. Unsnap fasteners of air cleaner ducts at carburetors and remove air cleaner assembly. Detach fuel hoses. Detach carburetor control links from throttle levers. Unscrew carburetor retaining nuts from intake ducts. Withdraw carburetor assembly, taking care that spring washers do not fall into the intake ducts. Close off intake ducts with paper or cloth.

Remove air cleaner lower assembly and carburetor top. Remove filter body retaining screws and filter body. Remove plug screw and float needle valve. Remove main jet carrier and main jet, air adjustment screw, stopper screw, idle metering jet, venturi set screws, and throttle valve adjusting screw. Unscrew air correction jet and shake out the emulsion tube. If the emulsion tube is stuck it can be pulled out easily with a slightly tapered punch gently pushed into the tube to gain hold. Remove check valve and pump nozzle. Loosen preatomizer by light tapping and remove it. Withdraw venturis. Remove float pivot pin and lift out float. Unscrew retaining nuts of the accelerator pump and remove cover. Remove diaphragms, pump lower assembly, springs, and valve.

Clean carburetor parts, channels and ports with gasoline or solvent and dry with compressed air (breath containing moisture induces oxidation). *Do not use wire or needles to scrape out jets.*

Check looseness of throttle shafts. Excessive play permits extra air to enter the intake throats. The throttle valve when closed, must be air tight.

Check pump diaphragms for good condition, replace if necessary. Check tips of idle adjustment screws and air adjustment screws for possible damage or defects. After installing the venturis, safety-wire the set screws.

Check jet sizes with specifications at installation. The contour of the main jet bore

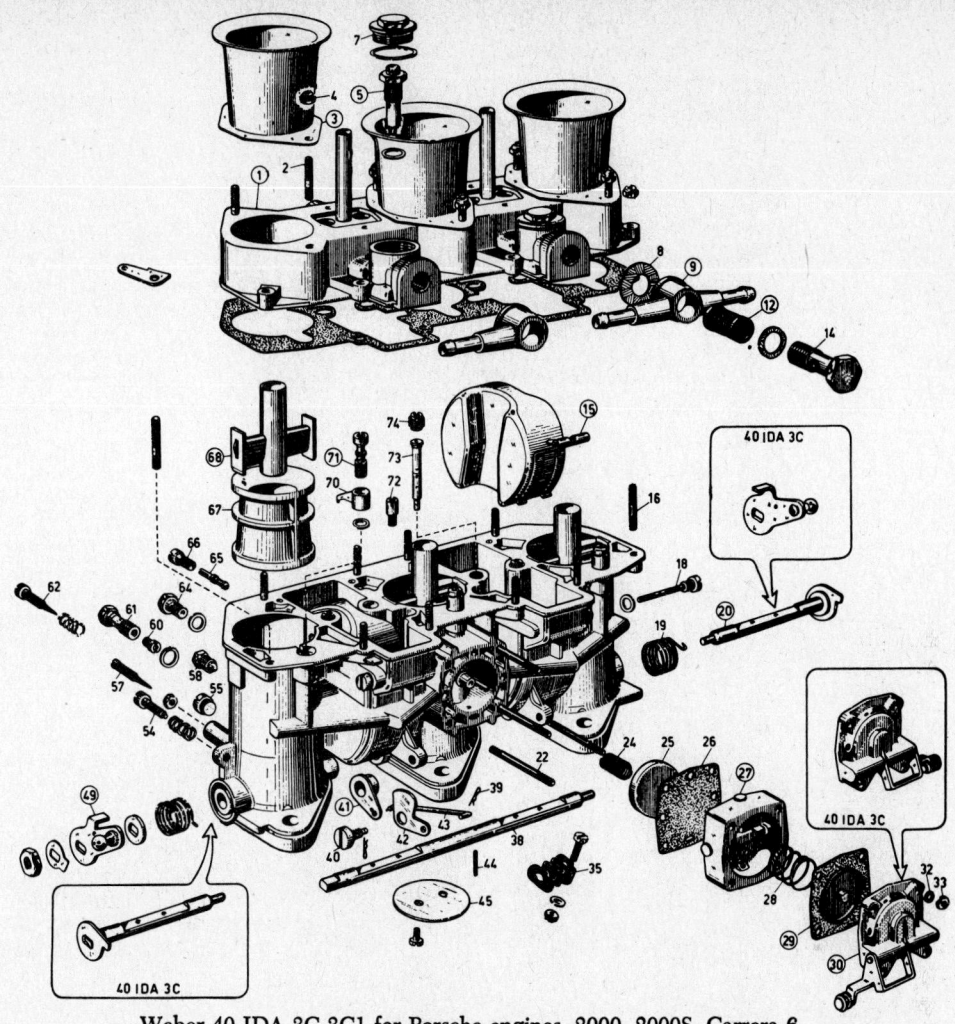

Weber 40 IDA 3C-3C1 for Porsche engines, 2000, 2000S, Carrera 6.

1 Carburetor cover	27 Pump body	55 Progression hole inspection
2 Air horn studs	28 Diaphragm spring	plug
3 Air horn	29 Pump diaphragm	57 Air adjusting screw
4 Fastening nut	30 Pump cover—40 IDA 3C1	58 Choke fixing screw
5 Needle valve	32 Lock washer	60 Main jet
7 Plug over needle valve	33 Stud nut	61 Main jet holder
8 Fuel inlet gasket	35 Elastic joint	62 Idle mixture adjusting screw
9 Filter body of fuel inlet	38 Throttle spindle	63 Gasket
12 Fuel screen	39 Cotter pins	64 Plug
14 Inlet end cap	40 Fulcrum screw for accelera-	65 Idling jet
15 Fuel floats	tion pump	66 Idling jet holder
16 Carburetor cover studs	41 Pump lever	67 Choke tube (venturi)
18 Fulcrum screw for float	42 Pump cam	68 Auxiliary venturi
19 Throttle valve spring	43 Control rod	70 Acceleration pump jet
20 Throttle shaft for 40 IDA 3C1	44 Spring pin	71 Delivery valve
22 Accelerator-pump fixing studs	45 Throttle valve	72 Intake valve
24 Valve spring	49 Control lever—40 IDA 3C1	73 Emulsion tube
25 Pump valve	54 Throttle adjusting screw (idle	74 Air corrector jet
26 Diaphragm	speed)	

is machined with consideration given to the direction of flow. The identifying number is stamped into the side of the jet. The idle air bleed is drilled into the carburetor body and cannot be changed.

Install the carburetors, using new gaskets at intake ducts. The sealing surfaces must be completely clean. Adjust control linkage with the throttle valves fully closed.

Disassembly of the Weber 40 IDT P1

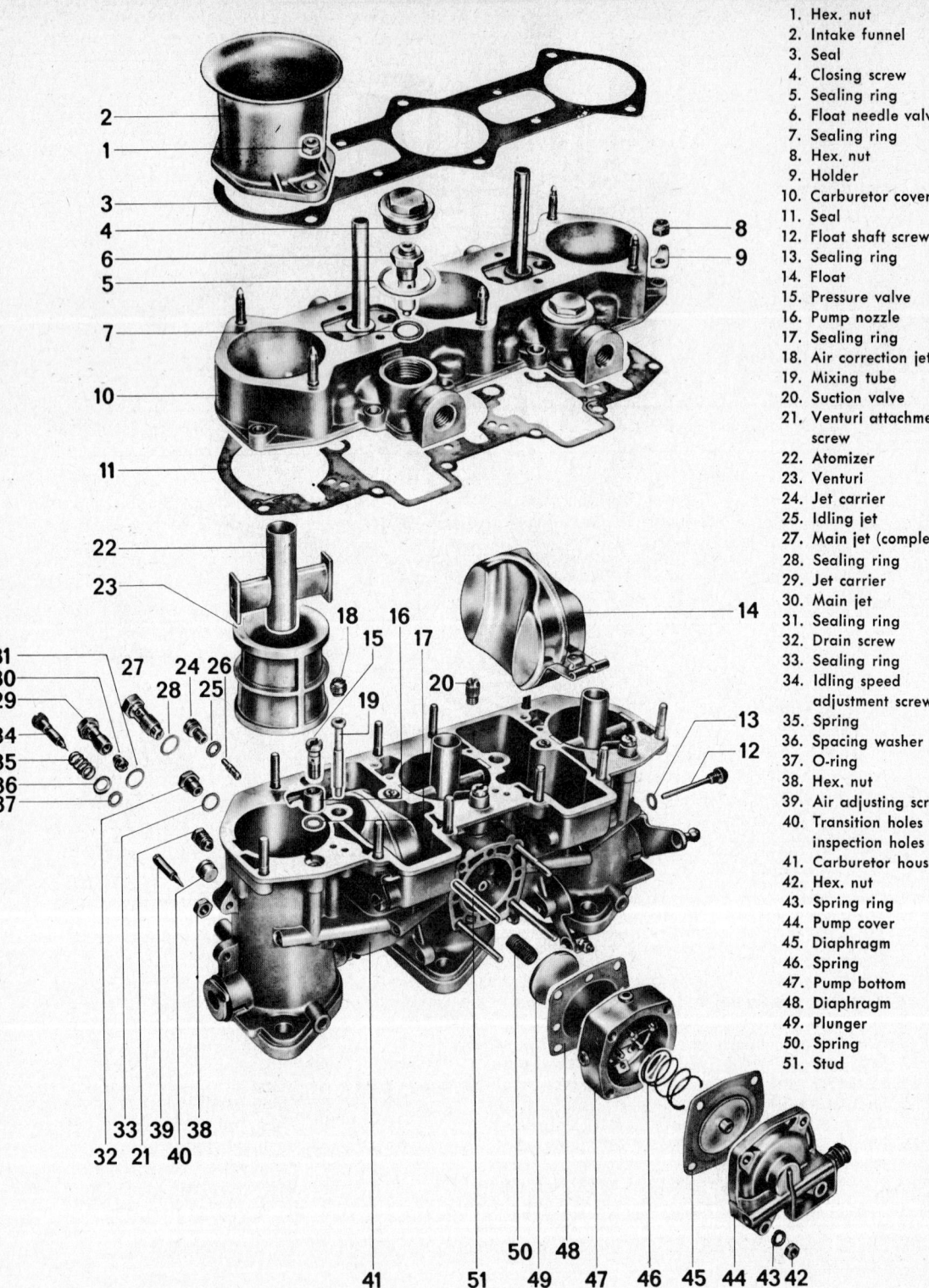

1. Hex. nut
2. Intake funnel
3. Seal
4. Closing screw
5. Sealing ring
6. Float needle valve
7. Sealing ring
8. Hex. nut
9. Holder
10. Carburetor cover
11. Seal
12. Float shaft screw
13. Sealing ring
14. Float
15. Pressure valve
16. Pump nozzle
17. Sealing ring
18. Air correction jet
19. Mixing tube
20. Suction valve
21. Venturi attachment screw
22. Atomizer
23. Venturi
24. Jet carrier
25. Idling jet
27. Main jet (complete)
28. Sealing ring
29. Jet carrier
30. Main jet
31. Sealing ring
32. Drain screw
33. Sealing ring
34. Idling speed adjustment screw
35. Spring
36. Spacing washer
37. O-ring
38. Hex. nut
39. Air adjusting screw
40. Transition holes inspection holes
41. Carburetor housing
42. Hex. nut
43. Spring ring
44. Pump cover
45. Diaphragm
46. Spring
47. Pump bottom
48. Diaphragm
49. Plunger
50. Spring
51. Stud

Weber carburetor 40 IDT P1 3C1/3C for Porsche 914/6

3C1/3C carburetor is approximately the same as previous model Weber carburetors used on the Porsche. NOTE: When re-moving the carburetor from the intake manifold, be sure that no corrugated washers drop into the intake ducts.

ADJUSTMENTS

With clean carburetors installed and proper fuel pump pressure feeding the float chamber, several basic tune-up adjustments can be made to the carburetors.

Float level

With the engine idling, the fuel pump delivering gas at the specified pressure, and the car sitting perfectly level, the needle valves on the carburetors should be partially closed and near the height indicated in specifications. Shut off the engine. The needle valve should close completely. It is only necessary to turn on the ignition to fill the fuel bowl if the engine has an electric fuel pump.

Float level is adjusted by installing a thicker or thinner gasket under the needle valve. Thin gaskets raise the fuel level. Thick gaskets lower it. Further adjustment is possible by bending the float arm. The proper level is most easily determined with a gauge that fits into the main jet carrier or into the special plug holes provided on some carburetors. If the gauge glass is not marked, measure the distance from the fuel level to the flange of the fuel bowl.

If a gauge is not available, there are other ways of accurately determining fuel level. A spare main jet carrier can be drilled out on the end and fitted with flexible, transparent tubing. Extend the tube upright and measure the distance from the fuel level to the fuel bowl flange.

Another method of measuring fuel level is to shut off the fuel supply (after the needle valve has closed) and remove the float cover. Measure the distance from the float bowl flange to the fuel level. *Note:* the highest point of the surface of the fuel (the meniscus) is around the edges of the bowl and float. Measure only to these edges. When the gauge touches the meniscus, the fuel surface will visibly jump up to the bottom edge of the gauge. Measure at this position.

Float Level
Specifications
Flange to Fuel
Surface

Carburetor	(h) Distance
32 PBI	16 ± 1.5 mm
32 PBIC	19 ± 1.0 mm
40 PICB	$20.5 \pm .05$ mm

The 40 PII-4 float level is easily corrected with the engine idling by turning the adjustment screw while spotting the fuel level at the screw threads of the float leveling port. Turn adjusting screw in to lower the float level; turn it out to raise the level. Turning the screw in pushes the float down, which in turn, forces some gas out through the inspection port. Allow the engine to use up the excess fuel before making another adjustment.

The fuel level in Weber carburetors can be set before the carburetor is installed on the engine. With float moving freely and the needle valve tightened into position insert friction spring between a half-float and the bowl. Raise the float above the bowl flange to height specifications listed. Measure the depth of the needle valve (in closed position) from its base (with gasket) to its tip that touches the float arm. Bend the tab on the float arm until this measurement matches the needle valve measurement. Inexpensive gauges are available (shown in the illustration) for accurate measurements.

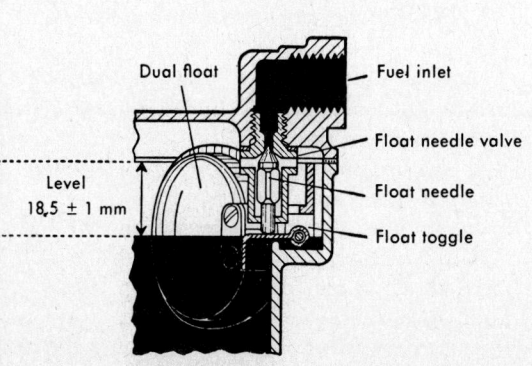

Dual float — Fuel inlet

— Float needle valve

Level 18.5 ± 1 mm — Float needle

— Float toggle

Float system
Float level in Zenith NDIX.

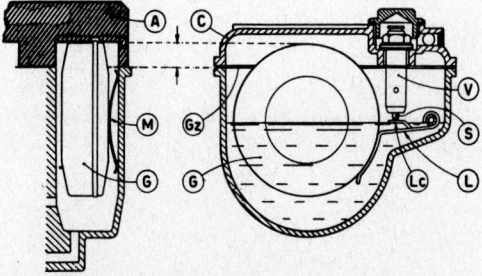

Float level adjustment on Weber carburetors.

A	Gauge	L	Float arm
C	Float bowl cover	Lc	Float arm tab
Gz	Gasket	V	Needle valve
G	Float	S	Needle tip

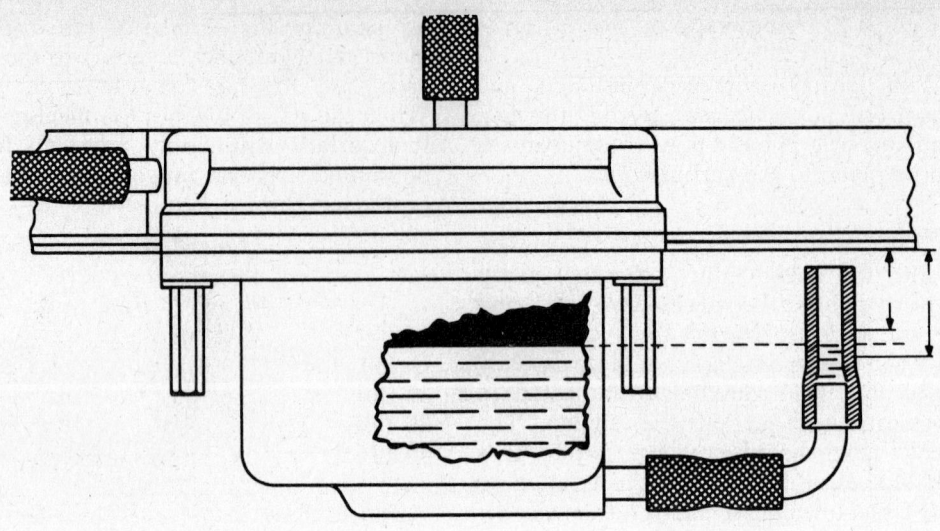

Transparent hose can be used to see fuel level in float chamber on 911. Set level between 15 mm to 20 mm.

Accelerator Pump

The amount of fuel discharged by the accelerator pump is adjusted (except on Weber) by changing the location of the accelerator pump arm on the pump connecting rod. Harness a small vial with a thin wire and place it in the carburetor throat to catch all of the gas discharged from the ejector nozzle. When the float bowl is full, operate the pump rod (or throttle rod) a few times and then measure the quantity in the vial. Divide this amount by the number of strokes taken to get the average volume ejected with each stroke. Check this amount (average ejection with one stroke) with the specifications.

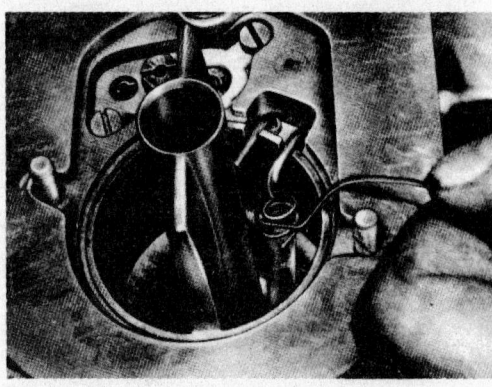

Vial catches fuel ejected by acceleration pump.

The pump jet size determines the *duration* of each ejection, *not* the quantity injected. The accelerator pump rod sets the *quantity* that is injected. Injection quantity on the Weber 40 IDA is not adjustable.

Throttle Linkage

Check adjustment of the throttle linkage before adjusting synchronization and idling of the carburetors. All throttle valves must open and close in unison and have free travel from idle to full power.

1. Lubricate all moving joints with 1–2 drops of engine oil while moving throttle controls. Do not lubricate the plastic-coated parts because dust and grit will cling to them, causing the smooth surface to eventually wear away.

2. Lubricate accelerator pump rods and linkage.

3. Disconnect all ball joints and sockets, partly fill cups with high temperature grease, and reconnect.

4. Move linkage back and forth to check for free movement.

To remove throttle linkage from the 911 and 912, detach throttle rod at ball joint on cross-shaft at air blower housing. Remove floor mat to gain access to opening in floorboard. Remove hex bolts retaining gearshift lever base and take out lever with base. Remove handbrake lever with base. Remove attaching clamps of throttle rod through openings for shift and brake levers. Detach throttle rod from ball joint on rear cross-shaft (beneath transmission). Pulling rearward, slip out throttle linkage.

To remove throttle linkage from all 356 models. Unhook ball joint on accelerator pedal and unfasten pedal. Remove left section of floor board for access to the pedal pivot lever (bell crank). Loosen ball socket of long accelerator rod from pivot lever.

Fuel Injection

Type 914

The fuel pump sucks fuel from the tank to the ring line via the filter. A pressure regulator at the end of the ring line restricts fuel pressure to 28.4 psi. Electro-magnetic injection valves are connected to the ring line by distributors. The pressure regulator returns excess fuel to the tank via a second line. The overflow line from the fuel pump also enters this line. The fuel pump is provided with a pressure relief valve which responds when the pressure rises

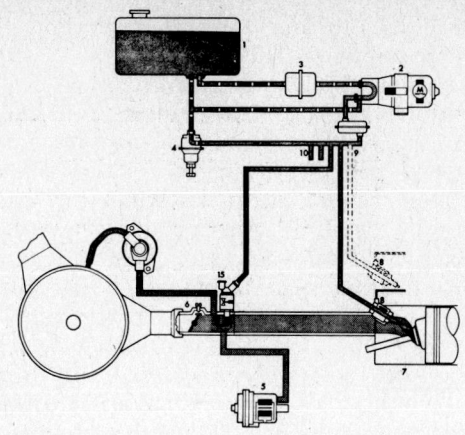

Basic fuel circuit diagram of Type 914 electronic fuel injection

1. Fuel tank	6. Throttle valve
2. Pump	7. Cylinder
3. Filter	8. Injection valve
4. Pressure regulator	9/10. Fuel distributor
5. Pressure feeler	15. Cold starting valve

considerably above the rated value, for example, through a fault of the pressure regulator. Pressure in the ring line is maintained when the pump is cut out by a

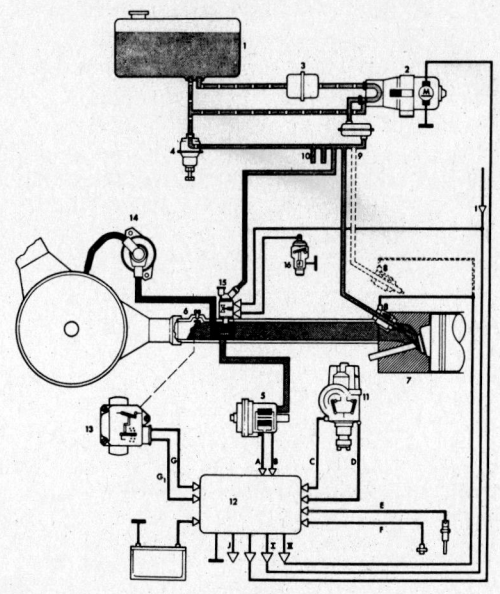

Basic circuit diagram of Bosch Electronic Fuel Injection used on Porsche Type 914

1. Fuel tank
2. Fuel pump
3. Fuel filter
4. Pressure regulator
5. Pressure feeler
6. Intake air distributor
7. Cylinder head
8. Injection valves
9. Fuel distributor
10. Fuel distributor
11. Ignition distributor with releasing contacts (ZV-contact I, ZV-control II)
12. Control unit
13. Throttle valve switch with acceleration enrichment
14. Supplementary air valve
15. Cold starting nozzle
16. Thermal switch for cold starting device
A + B —from pressure feeler
    (signal load condition)
C + D —from ignition distributor contacts
    (signals speed and release)
E + F —from temperature feelers
    (signal warming up)
G   —from throttle valve switch (switching off fuel delivery under overrunning cond.)
G 1 —(Acceleration enrichment)
H   —from pressure switch
    (signal full load enrichment)
     —from starter, terminal 50 solenoid switch
    (signal start enrichment)
    Bridging of full load safety device
I   —to injection valves cylinder 1 and 4
II   —to injection valves cylinder 2 and 3

check valve in the pressure connection of the fuel pump. The injection valves are opened electrically, in two groups, by the control unit. When the valves open, fuel is injected as a result of fuel pressure. The ejection duct in the injection valve is accurately calibrated. In addition, the fuel pressure is kept constant, so that the quantity of injected fuel depends only upon the time span during which the valve is open. The injection time is "computed" by the control unit. The information which the electronic system processes in the control unit arrives from individual information transmitters on the engine as follows:

The moment of injection is determined by the ignition distributor contacts in accordance with the position of the camshaft.

The injection time, or quantity of fuel injected, are determined by two factors, engine speed and load condition of the engine. Engine speed is fed into the control unit by the releasing contacts of the ignition distributor. The load imposed on the engine is sensed by the pressure condition in the intake distributor. This pressure is converted into an electrical value, transmitted to the control unit, by a pressure feeler, which is connected to the intake distributor by a hose line.

Electronic fuel injection ignition distributor release contacts

The control unit processes this information into a new signal. The new signal opens the valves for a longer or shorter period of time. Thus, the control unit, correlating load and engine speed, transmits an electronic signal to the valves to inject more or less fuel, thereby supplying basic fuel requirements.

In addition to basic fuel requirements, an accurately measured fuel quantity must be injected when starting at low temperatures, when warming up the engine and under full load (warming-up enrichment).

Warming-up enrichment depends upon engine temperature, which is electrically measured by two sensors in the intake dis-

Block circuit diagram of electronic fuel injection control unit

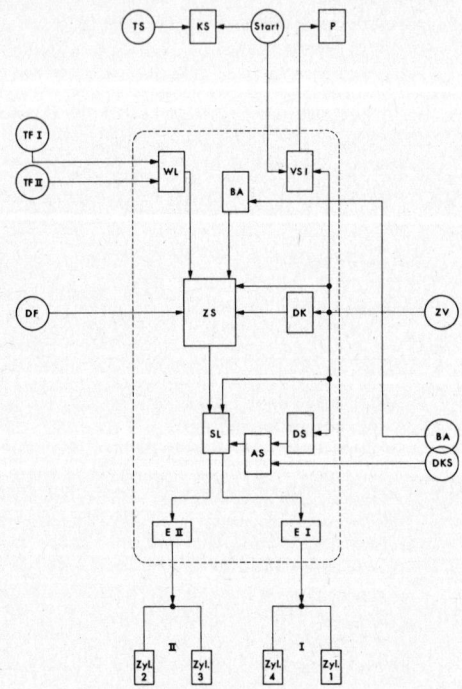

Zv	—Ignition distributor contacts
BA	—Acceleration enrichment
DKS	—Throttle valve switch
TF I	—Temperature feeler I
TF II	—Temperature feeler II
DF	—Pressure feeler
Zyl 1	
Zyl 4	—Injection valves for cylinders 1-4
KS	—Cold starting valve
TH	—Thermo switch
P	—Fuel pump
St	—Start signal
VSi	—Overflow safety device
BA	—Acceleration enrichment
WL	—Warming up enrichment
Zs	—Time switch
DK	—Engine speed correction
DS	—Engine speed switch
AS	—Shutoff function
SL	—Switching logic
E I, E II	—End stages for valve groups I and II

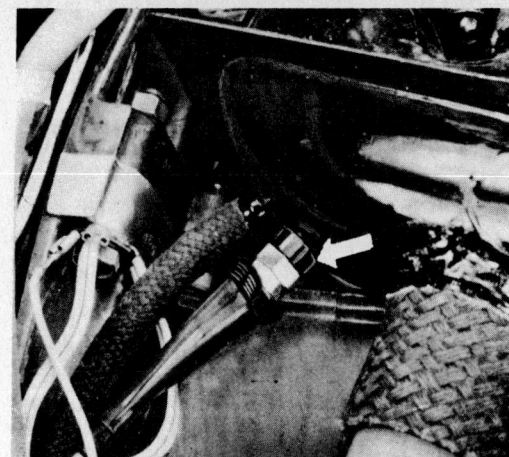

Electronic fuel injection temperature feeler in the intake air distributor

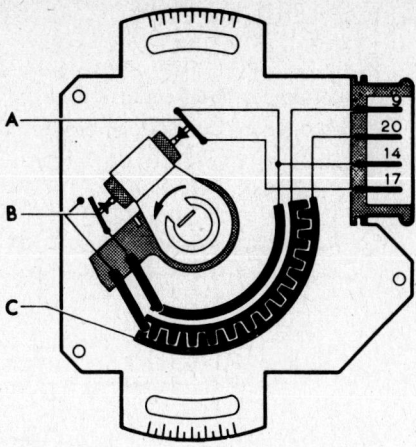

Electronic fuel injection pressure feeler

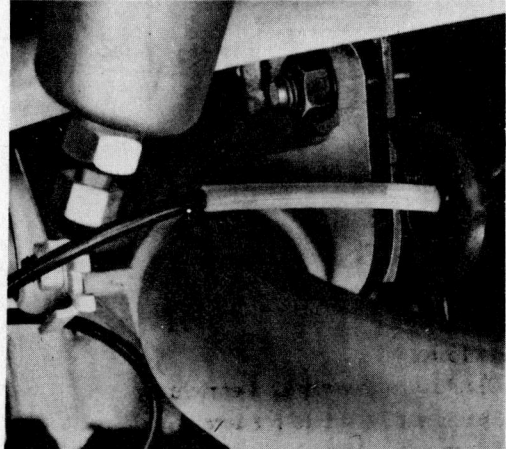

Temperature feeler in the cylinder head

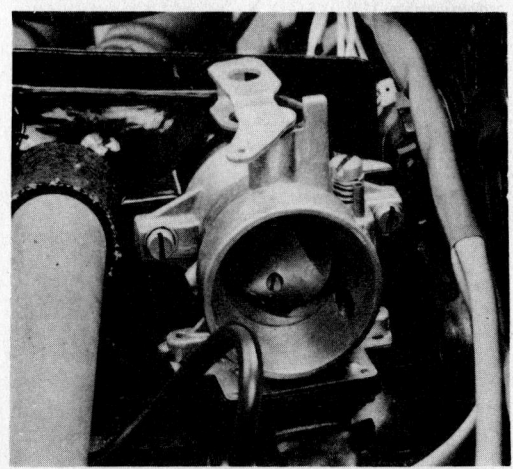

Electronic fuel injection throttle valve switch

tributor and the cylinder head. These signals are also processed by the control unit in the proper ratio with regard to basic fuel requirements, and transmitted electrically to the injection valves.

During overrunning conditions, using the engine to brake going downhill, no fuel should be injected. Under this condition, the engine speed increases and the throttle valves are closed. During overrunning conditions, when the engine speed is above 1,800 rpm the throttle valve switch will switch off fuel delivery. When the engine reaches 1,250 rpm during overrunning conditions, fuel delivery is again switched on, and transition into idling is ensured.

To keep the structural requirements of the control unit small, two valves each are connected in parallel. Valve group I = cylinders 1 and 4. Valve group II = cylinders 2 and 3. The valves in any one group inject simultaneously. The valves of cylinders 1 and 3 will inject each time past the open intake valves during the intake stroke. The injection valves of cylinders 2 and 4 are already injecting against the closed intake valves during the exhaust stroke and, in effect, are storing fuel.

While driving, air volume is controlled by a throttle valve installed in front of the intake air distributor. At idling speed the throttle valve is completely closed. Idling air requirements are supplied via the idling air duct in the throttle valve connection. The idling speed is adjusted by changing the cross-section of the idling air duct by means of an adjusting screw on the throttle valve connection.

Engines which are not fully warmed re-

Special Notes:

1 - Do not use force when inserting plugs into plug guides.
2 - Watch out for good condition of plug and plug lug (no corrosion).
3 - Watch out for good seat of protective rubber cap.

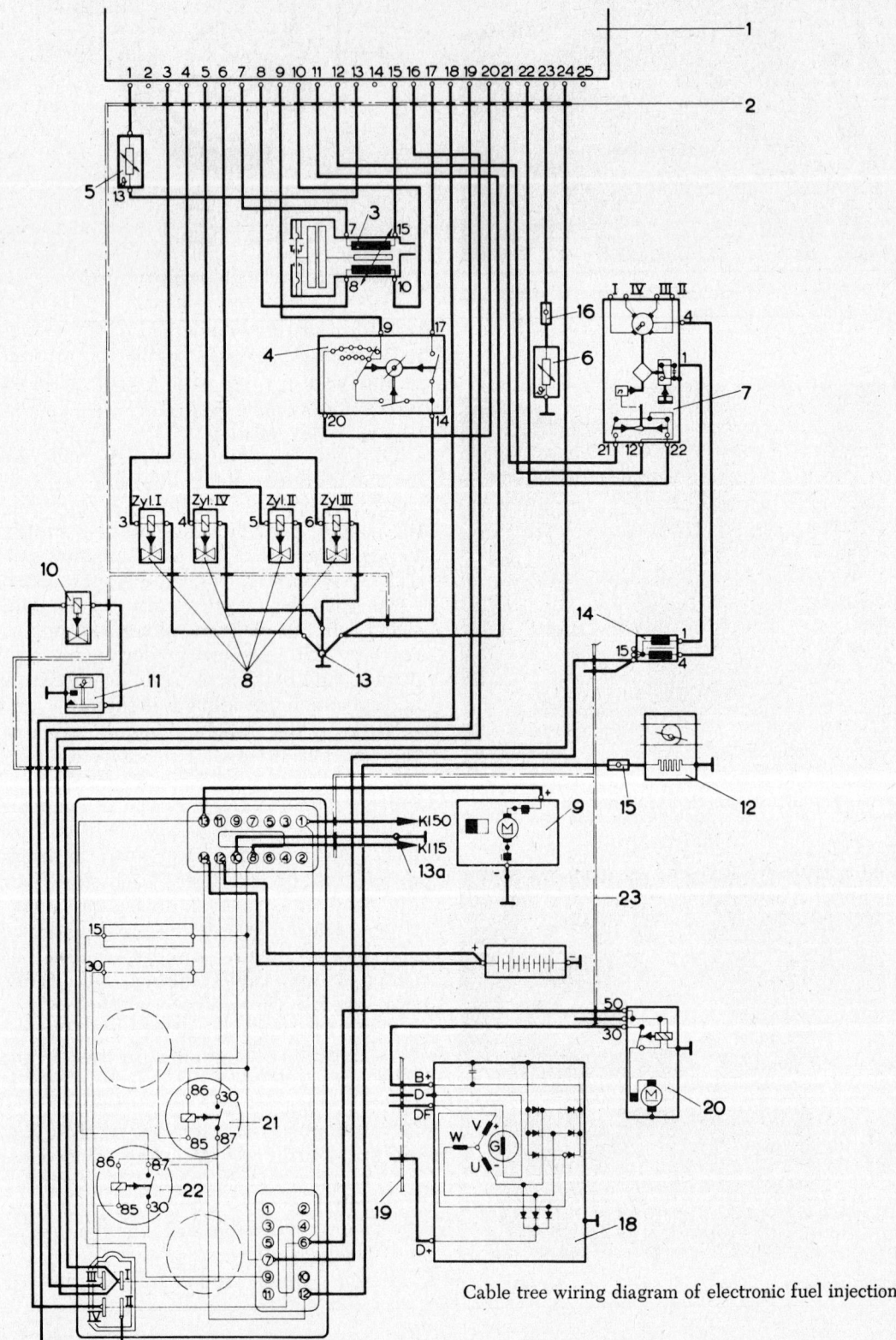

Cable tree wiring diagram of electronic fuel injection

1. Control unit
2. Electronic cable line
3. Pressure feeler
4. Throttle valve switch acceleration enrichment
5. Temperature feeler I (intake distributor)
6. Temperature feeler II (cylinder head)
7. Ignition distributor with impulse release
8. Injection valve
9. Fuel pump
10. Fuel valve
11. Thermo switch for fuel enrichment
12. Supplementary air valve
13. Ground connection (on engine housing)
14. Ignition coil
15 ⎫
16 ⎭ Line connectors
17. Regulator for alternator
18. Alternator
19. Cable line alternator
20. Starter (starter motor)
21. Voltage supply relay
22. Pump relay
23. Lines not included in main cable line

quire additional air. This is controlled by the supplementary air valve or rotary valve. It will change the effective cross-section of the air duct, depending on the temperature of the engine compartment and the temperature of an electric heater installed in the supplementary air valve. The rotary valve is turned by a bi-metallic spring which reacts to the temperature

Exploded view of injection valves and intake pipes used on electronic fuel injection

components. The electric heater of the supplementary air valve is connected to terminal 87 of the pump relay.

During cold starts (below 41° F.) additional fuel is injected directly into the air intake distributor to keep the mixture preparation at maximum efficiency. To accomplish this, a cold start device is installed in the air intake distributor. A cold starting valve is installed in the ring line and is electrically connected through a thermal switch and terminal 50 of the starter.

Warning: *No service or adjustment of this system should be attempted unless thoroughly familiar with the entire system.*

INJECTION VALVES

Removal

Loosen the retaining nuts of both valves on one side. Check the valves for proper operation and leaks.

Installation

Place the internal valve bearing into the proper hole of the intake pipe. Place the valve holder on the valve, followed by the external valve bearings. Be sure that the valve plugs connect correctly (grey protective caps at front, black at the rear). Front and rear, as used here, apply to direction of car travel.

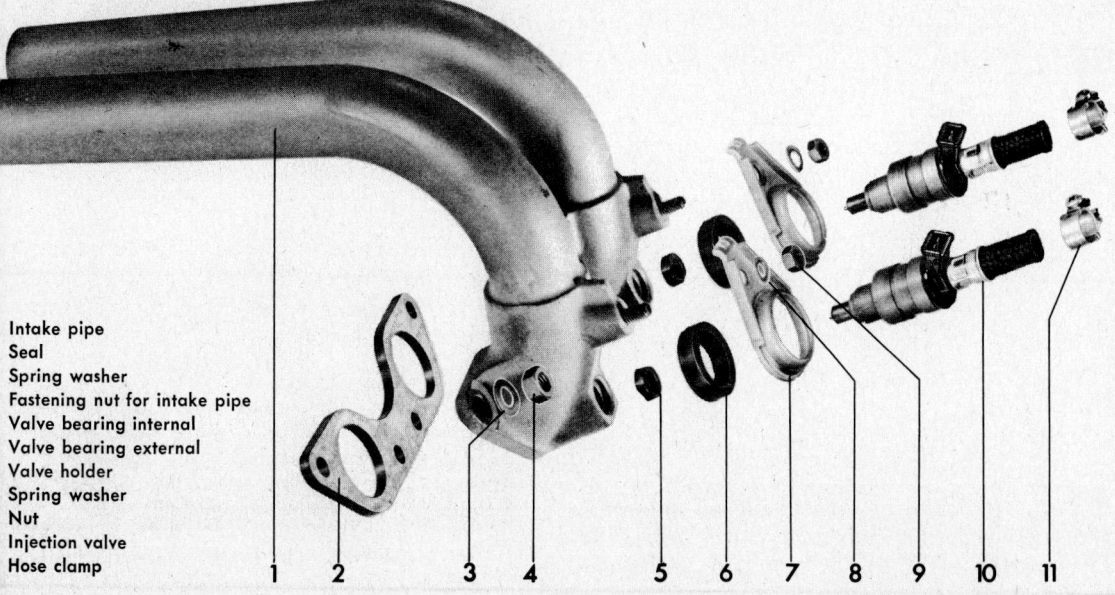

Intake pipe
Seal
Spring washer
Fastening nut for intake pipe
Valve bearing internal
Valve bearing external
Valve holder
Spring washer
Nut
Injection valve
Hose clamp

1   2   3   4   5   6   7   8   9   10   11

INTAKE PIPES

Removal

Intake pipes on both sides can be separately removed and installed. Remove the
injection valves and unscrew the four nuts.
Loosen the fuel valve line fastening plates
on the front intake pipe. Remove the intake pipe, making sure that no parts fall
into the cylinder head.

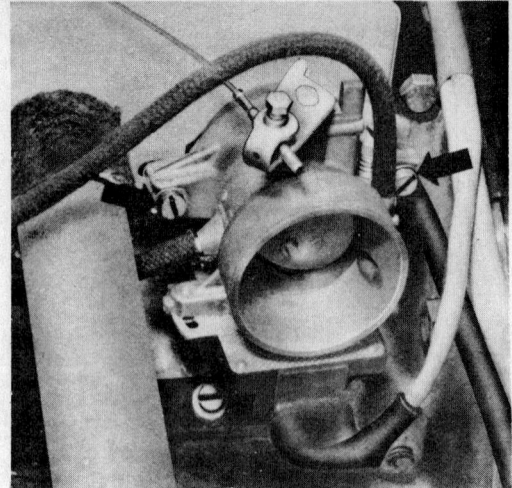

Intake connection on electronic fuel injection

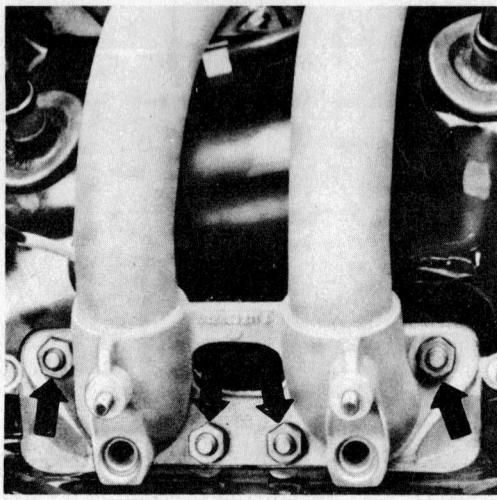

Removal of intake pipes

Installation

Installation is the reverse of removal.
Before installing, check the seal between
the intake pipe and cylinder head for damage.

THROTTLE VALVE SWITCH

Removal

Remove the air filter. Disconnect the
throttle valve return spring. Remove the
intake connection, but do not remove the
Bowden cable for throttle valve or the
connecting hoses for the ignition distributor. Remove the throttle valve switch.

ADJUSTMENTS

Pressure Regulator

A pressure gauge of tested accuracy
must be used to test the pressure regulator.
The pressure gauge can be connected into
the fuel line on either side of the engine,
between the injection valves. On some
models a T fitting is provided. Other mod-

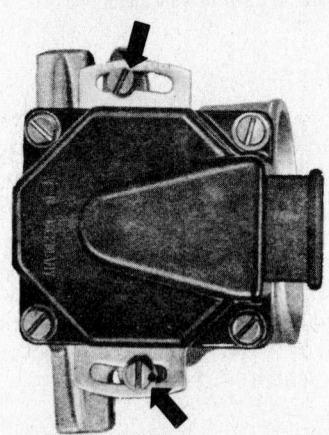

Throttle valve switch on electronic fuel injection

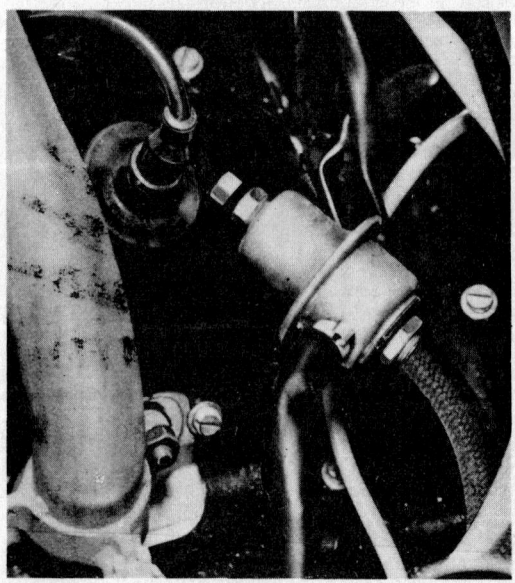

Pressure regulator adjustment—electronic fuel injection

els require the use of a special Bosch tester made for the system, or, a T fitting can be made from suitable diameter hose and clamps. After the pressure gauge is connected, switch on the ignition. Disconnect the cable running between the ignition distributor and the ignition coil. Operate the starter and read the pressure on the pressure gauge, which should be 28.4 psi. If this specification is not attained, adjust the pressure regulator by means of the adjusting screw. Turning the adjusting screw clockwise (see illustration) will decrease the pressure, while turning the screw in the opposite direction, counterclockwise, will increase the pressure.

Idling Speed

Remove the air filter and connect a tachometer. Start the engine and set the idle speed at 900 rpm. Turning the adjustment screw (see illustration) clock-

Throttle valve switch connections—electronic fuel injection

Idling speed adjustment—electronic fuel injection

wise, in the direction of (a) increases idle speed. Turning the screw in the direction of (b), or counterclockwise, decreases the idle speed.

Throttle Valve Switch

The switch contact on the throttle valve switch should open when the throttle valve is turned 2° from its closed position. Connect an ohmmeter to connections 14 and 17 (see illustration). Close the throttle valve and carefully turn the throttle valve switch until the ohmmeter registers 0. Then turn the throttle valve switch by one more division mark, or 2°, to the right, or counterclockwise (see illustration).

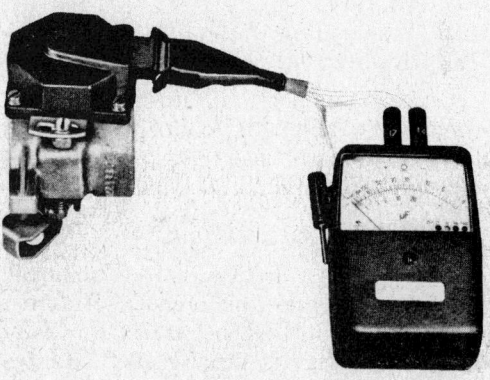

Throttle switch adjustment—electronic fuel injection

TYPE 911E

The fuel injection in the 911E is mechanical and especially sensitive to adjustments and service. *This system should not be tampered with by anyone except trained Porsche service representatives.*

Exhaust System

Muffler

REMOVAL

If the engine is mounted in the car, remove the rear cover plate and tail pipes. Loosen the exhaust pipe clamps. Remove the exhaust pipe flange nuts and the support straps, if equipped. Remove the muffler by tapping with a rubber mallet and pulling the muffler straight back.

INSTALLATION

Installation is the reverse of removal, observing the following precautions. Before installing, carefully inspect the exhaust pipes and muffler for leaks. Straighten bent or dented pipes. Especially check the welded joint between the muffler and lower pipes for cracks or leaks, which could allow escaping exhaust gasses to enter the passenger compartment. Always install new gaskets. Check the fit of pipe joints to front exhaust pipes. Align these joints before installing the muffler. With the engine installed in the car, the exhaust pipes and muffler must not touch the body.

Junction Box

REMOVAL (ENGINE REMOVED FROM CAR)

Unscrew the bolt on the junction box. Remove the bolts on the exhaust flange and loosen the exhaust pipe clamp. Remove the junction box and exhaust pipe.

INSTALLATION

Installation is the reverse of removal, observing the following points. Check the junction box and exhaust pipes for damage. Clean exhaust pipe gasket surfaces and install new gaskets.

Cooling System

All Porsche engines are air cooled by means of an engine covering which conducts cooling air to various sections of the engine. In the event that any portion of the cooling system is dismantled, assembly should be carried out with extreme care to prevent the possibility of air leaks which will severely affect cooling.

Most Porsche cooling fans are V-belt driven. The belts are subject to considerable stress. As a safeguard to adequate cooling, V-belt tension and condition are of utmost importance. V-belts should remain free of grease and oil. Most solvents, except for gasoline, will remove grease or oil from V-belts, followed by rinsing in water. Extensive V-belt exposure to grease or oil will warrant replacement.

V-belt

TENSION ADJUSTMENT (EXCEPT 914)

Loosen the nut at the pulley of the generator and remove the outer half of the pulley. Pulley spacers should be mounted

V-belt pulley spacers for tension adjustment (except 914)

according to needs. The tension is correct when the V-belt can be depressed ¾"-⅝" under thumb pressure. Removal of spacers between pulley halves will increase tension, while adding spacers will decrease tension. If only one spacer remains between pulley halves, the V-belt should be replaced. Mount the outer pulley half followed by the unused spacers. This will assure a constant availability of spacers. Replace and tighten the special nut. Carelessly tightened pulleys will wear quickly at the hub.

TENSION ADJUSTMENT (914)

Remove the cover for the cover plate. Loosen the socket screw and adjust the V-

V-belt tension adjustment—914 only

belt tension by moving the alternator left or right. Tighten the screw when the adjustment is complete.

Engine

Removal

All 356/A/B/C engines are removed from the car without the transmission. The 911 and 912 engines are removed with the transmission, only the axles remain in place. The 914 and 914/6 are also removed with the transmission.

TYPE 356 A/B/C

Disconnect negative cable from battery to front compartment. Shut off fuel valve at tank.

(Models since 356B—disconnect heater air hose and T-joint or connecting duct from blower housing).

Remove air cleaners and rear cover-plate on engine. Remove throttle linkage at ball joint. Detach choke cable if choke is manual. Slip off hose to intake of fuel pump and detach fastening clip. (356C—remove fuel pump shield).

Disconnect wires from generator, blower housing, and ignition coil. Detach leads to oil-pressure and oil-temperature sensors. Oil-temperature unit is below by-pass oil filter. (912—remove tachometer connection from the ignition coil).

Raise rear of car and place on stands. Remove heater control cables, linkage and ducts from engine. (Since 356B—control cables are accessible in engine compartment).

Remove hose to fuel pump. Detach tachometer drive. (Since 356B—loosen tailpipe clamps and remove pipe extensions from muffler).

Remove the two engine lower-mount nuts from studs. Support engine with suitable jack. Securing two engine upper-mount bolts, unscrew the nuts. Pull engine from gear box until mainshaft clears the clutch plate. Then lower engine from the car.

TYPE 912 AND 911

Preliminary removal procedures vary for Type 912 and 911. For Type 912, follow the steps outlined under Type 356, up to

and including removal of the heater and control cables, which are accessible in the engine compartment.

Preliminary removal steps for the 911 engine are as follows:

Disconnect battery. Detach hot air duct from air cleaner and remove air cleaner. Detach oil tank vent hose.

Detach wires from the electric fuel pump. Separate multiple connector on cable between alternator and voltage regulator. Detach cable fasteners from body. Disconnect ignition coil leads to engine. Detach fuel hose from connector at float chambers. Unscrew throttle linkage from bell housing. Remove oil breather hose from oil filler. Detach cable from oil pressure sensor.

Raise rear of car at least three feet and place on stands. Drain engine oil and detach oil hoses from oil tank.

At this point, final removal steps are identical for Type 912 and 911.

Scratch connecting flanges (for matching purposes) and detach cables from engine starter. Detach clutch cable from clutch control lever.

Detach ground strap. Disconnect backup light cable. Disconnect throttle linkage from forward cross shaft (at transmission).

Remove tunnel cover in rear of passenger compartment. Expose shiftrod joint by sliding rubber boot toward front of car. Remove safety wire and unscrew bolt. Separate joint.

Place jack under balance point of engine-transmission and apply slight tension on jack. Unbolt engine and transmission mounts from body and lower engine on jack with care. Pull unit out to the rear. Unbolt transmission from engine.

TYPE 914 AND 914/6

Essentially, removal procedures for the Type 914 and 914/6 are alike. However, in place of disconnecting the fuel injection system from the four-cylinder engine, the fuel lines to the carburetors must be detached from the six-cylinder engine.

Scribe alignment marks on the engine compartment lid and hinges and remove the lid. Disconnect the battery. Remove the air filter and heater hoses. Remove the cables from the fuel injection components and place these out of the way. In the case of the four-cylinder engine, disconnect the line from the fuel pump to the car-

Fuel injection components for engine—removal

1. Voltage supply relay 4-pole
2. Two injection valves left 2-pole
3. One throttle valve switch 4-pole
4. Temperature feeler 1-pole
5. Mass connections 3-pole
6. Cold starting valve 2-pole

7. Thermal switch 1-pole
8. Ignition distributor release contact 3-pole
9. Temperature feeler 1-pole
10. Two injection valves right 2-pole
11. Pressure feeler 4-pole

buretor. Disconnect the throttle valve cable (both engines) and push it through the engine cover plate. Unbend the metal plate and separate the fuel hoses at the connecting points near the pressure feeler. Be sure to plug the ends of the hoses coming from the tank. Loosen the nut retaining the starter. Raise the vehicle and remove the exhaust muffler molding. Remove the lower components for warm air flow. Detach the protective covering and unscrew the shift rod holder. Remove the protective covering and unscrew the bolt with the ball (see illustration) and re-

move the rear shift rod. Remove the heater flap box, hoses and cables. Loosen the adjusting nut and hex nut for guide roller, bend the holding plate and pull the clutch cable forward. Loosen the speedometer driveshaft and detach. Remove the starter and the ground strap on the luggage floor pan. Loosen the universal shafts on the transmission and suspend from wire hooks from the body. Unscrew the four nuts on the transmission supports (see illustration) and also the left and right nuts on the engine mounts. Carefully lower the engine/transmission assembly from the car.

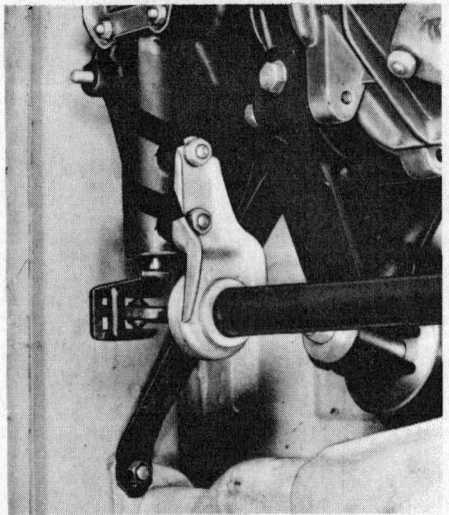

Remove the rear shift rod

Remove the transmission supports and engine mounts

Installation

Type 356 A/B/C, 912, 911

Install engines in reverse sequence to the removal procedures, noting the precautions listed below:

1. Before attaching engine to transmission, check transmission input shaft for run-out. 2. Check clutch throwout bearing. 3. Fill flywheel bushing in gland nut (hollow bolt) with graphite grease. 4. Check and coat with graphite grease the transmission shaft splines and pilot journal, starter shaft bushing, and gear teeth of starter drive pinion and flywheel gear. 5. Thoroughly clean the mating surface of engine and transmission joining flanges. 6. Care must be exercised when guiding the transmission for attachment to the engine since damage may occur to the flywheel bushing, throwout bearing, or transmission input shaft. To align the clutch plate splines with those on the input shaft, slightly turn the crankshaft pulley, with transmission in gear, until alignment is achieved. 7. Mate engine to transmission by aligning lower-mount studs or bolts first. Screw on nuts hand tight to the point where the flanges are snug. Tighten down top nuts and then bottom nuts, torquing equally. 8. Adjust clutch free-play, carburetor linkage, (choke cable), accelerator linkage and heater cables.

Type 914, 914/6

The installation procedure is the reverse of the removal process. During installation, note the following points.

On vehicles equipped with a manual transmission, check the clutch throwout bearing for wear before attaching the transmission. Only wipe off the throwout bearing, do not wash in any solvent. Coat the throwout bearing guide bushing, input shaft, and bushing for starter shaft lightly with molybdenum disulphide paste. When positioning the engine/transmission unit, be sure that the fuel lines near the injection valves are not pinched and that the hand brake cables are above the engine mounts. Tighten the engine mount screws to 21.7 ft. lbs. and the transmission support nuts to 14.5 ft. lbs. Tighten the universal shaft attachment screws to 32.5 ft. lbs. Always use new lockwashers. Adjust the free play of the clutch. Properly seat the engine com- partment seal. Adjust the throttle valve cable and carefully connect the cable and protective rubber caps.

Disassembly—Four-Cylinder Engines

Place engine on stand and drain oil. Remove front, rear and side engine shrouds. Remove muffler, exhaust pipes and heat exchangers. Both supports for engine rear shield must be off. Loosen exhaust pipe clamps behind heat exchangers and the straps supporting the muffler. Break away stuck pipe connections by tapping joints lightly with rubber mallet.

Detach coil wires at distributor and remove distributor cap. Disconnect leads from spark plugs. Remove air cleaners, throttle linkage, fuel lines, carburetors (cover intake openings) and fuel pump with its insulating flange. Disconnect oil lines to filter. After the actuating plunger of the fuel pump is out and hex nut holding distributor base plate is removed, lift out distributor and withdraw distributor pinion shaft by pushing up and turning to the left through orifice of fuel pump flange. Cautiously pick up thrust washer from base of pinion shaft so it won't fall into crankcase. Take spring from pinion shaft.

Remove V-belt and oil filler. Unscrew retaining bolts on blower housing. Unfasten generator from support and detach wiring. Disconnect hot air duct from blower housing. Lift off blower housing (the generator and blower can be removed without removing entire housing). Detach oil cooler. Remove cylinder shrouds (and lower air ducts if export heater is standard equipment). Remove generator carrier and then seal off opening to eliminate foreign matter.

Remove rocker covers, rocker arms, and rocker arm carriers. Pull out pushrods and mark them for reassembly. Remove intake manifolds, cylinder heads (allen-wrench nuts), pushrod tubes and air deflector baffles. Remove cylinders and pistons, marking each for reassembly. Remove crankshaft pulley with woodruff key. Detach exhaust muffler brackets.

Two-piece crankcase. Remove oil pump cover and take out gears. Extract oil pump housing from crankcase.

Three-piece crankcase. Remove oil pump cover and take out gears. Remove timing gear cover and counter-pressure oil line with rubber plugs. Remove oil seal, deflector, bearing No. 4 and bypass valve located in timing gear cover. *Note for removing bearing:* After deforming oil seal at recess slot in seat (strike seal through recess slot with punch and hammer), pry out seal with screwdriver, withdraw oil deflector, remove bearing set screw, and take out bearing No. 4. Remove any burrs from oil-seal seat, heat timing cover to 140°F and punch out bearing.

All engines. Remove clutch and flywheel. Evenly loosen clutch retaining bolts, slackening each by one or two turns at a time in a cross sequence until spring pressure is relieved to avoid distortion of spring housing. Slip off clutch assembly and disc. Loosen flywheel gland nut and remove flywheel and soft iron gasket. If oil seal is removed, clean seat for oil seal and hone down sharp edges from outer surface perimeter, making sure to clean away any metal filings.

Remove oil drain plug, bypass and pressure relief valves, oil strainer and magnetic element.

Disassemble crankcase by removing crankcase retaining nuts and two retaining nuts for camshaft bearing at flywheel end. Break the crankcase halves free with rubber mallet. *Prying halves apart will damage mating surfaces.* Unbolt crankshaft and camshaft. Remove camshaft end plug. Withdraw valve lifters. Remove bearing inserts and crankshaft oil seal at bearing No. 1. Mark bearing inserts.

Rocker Carriers and Cylinder Heads

Reworked cylinder heads should be checked for altered combustion chamber displacement. Deviation from uniform displacement of all cylinders must be within ± 1 cc. Displacement values should be stamped on the heads.

Four-cylinder Engines

Rocker carriers and cylinder heads are accessible after lower air duct, side shield, cylinder shrouds, intake duct, carburetors and rocker covers are removed.

Remove the hex nuts from the rocker arm shafts and lift out the shafts with the rocker arms, springs, washers and spacers. Remove the retaining bolts from the rocker carrier and lift off the carrier. The pushrods should be marked if removed.

The cylinder head retaining nuts are the allen-wrench type and are located above and below the valve stems. Carefully re-

move washers under allen nuts before moving cylinder head. Cylinders are numbered from the flywheel on the right side as 1 and 2 (right when facing front of car), and on the left side, as 3 and 4.

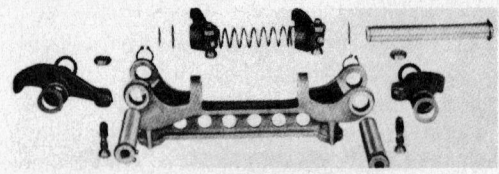

Rocker arm assembly for 1600.

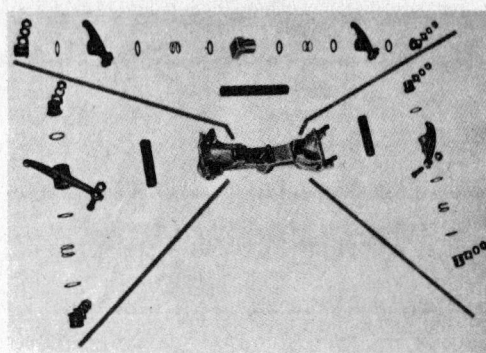

Rocker arm assembly for 1600S.

Installation of cylinder head must be made carefully to ensure proper seating. Head will warp when tightened if it is not properly seated on cylinders.

Proper sealing against oil leaks is another precaution to take. Insert pushrod tubes, after they have been stretched slightly at the bellows, between the crankcase and the head with the weld seams facing up. Check for precise O-ring seating at each end of the tubes (gaskets have trapezoid shape). Lubricate O-rings used under cylinder head nuts (use no sealing compound). Position air deflector baffles after noting if cutout is rounded for the cap nut or squared for the hex nut. Coat cylinder head nuts with graphite paste and tighten lightly (7 ft-lbs.) in sequence shown. Next, torque nuts to 22 ft-lbs. (3 mkg) in proper sequence.

6	2	4	8
7	3	1	5

Squirt oil into hollow pushrods until it reaches other end and then insert pushrod in tube and seat its end in the valve lifter.

When installing carrier and rockers, inspect retaining bolts, coat threads and base of bolt heads with graphited oil, use new spring washers, and tighten. Torque carrier

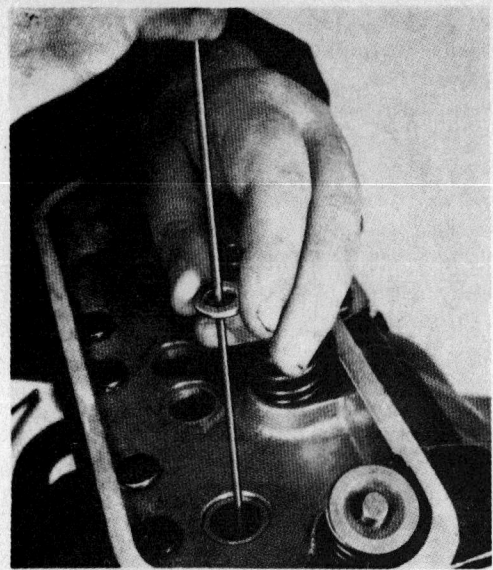
Place one washer under each cylinder head nut.

bolts to 36 ft-lbs. (5 mkg); rocker shaft nuts to 18 ft-lbs. (2.5 mkg).

Valves, Guides and Seats

To remove valves from individual heads, place each head on valve compressing tool and compress springs. Take out valve keepers (cotters), slowly release tool and remove spring seats. Lift out valve springs, sealing caps (except 911 engine after May, 1965), washers and adjustment spacers.

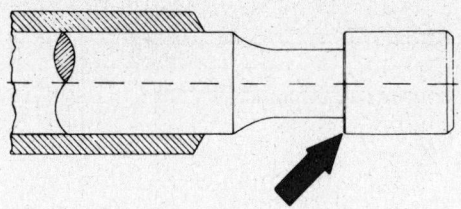
Remove burrs from valve stem ends to avoid gouging valve guides.

Before removing valve from cylinder head, hone down burrs from keeper seats on the valve stem to prevent damage to valve guide.

Valves. Clean valves of carbon deposits and inspect for wear and pitting. Grind off only enough metal to clean face. Do not exceed dimensions listed.

Valve stems with ridges or other excessive wear need replacement because they cannot be ground or straightened. Valves with

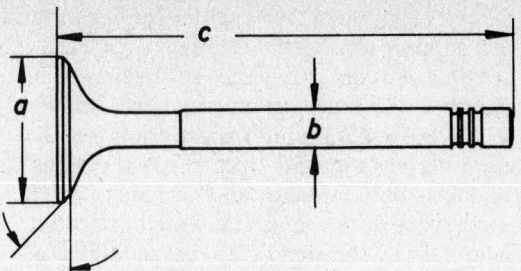
Critical valve measurements.

warped stems, traces of seizure, or damaged keeper seats must be replaced.

Seating valves (lapping) is easily done with a suction cup or other valve-turning device and fine-texture grinding compound. Grinding compound is soluble in water, not in grease or oil. Wash and flush all surfaces thoroughly with water, dry and lubricate with oil promptly.

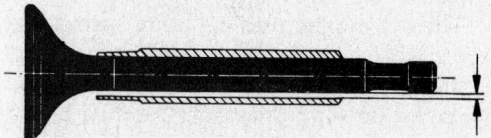
Clearance between the valve and its guide.

Valve guides. Check valve guides for firm contact with cylinder head. The bore of each valve should be measured from both ends with a plug gauge of 10 mm diameter. Clearance between guide and valve stem is listed in specifications.

Replacing valve guides with standard workshop equipment is not recommended because the cylinder head can easily be damaged. Replacing valve guides requires heating cylinder head to 355°F and punching out guides toward combustion chamber or drilling out guides. Oversized guides are needed for replacement and must be machined down to bore size of guide seat. Overlap for intake and exhaust guides is .041 to .06 mm. Guides must be pressed into cylinder head from rocker arm side. Tallow is needed for lubrication. Fitted guides are reamed to specifications.

Install sealing caps when valves are returned to the guides. Pull each cap over guide so base of cap rests against guide.

Beginning May, 1965, the 911 engines use a support washer for valve springs with a center bore diameter of 17 mm rather than 14 mm. Valve stem seals need not be removed on these newer engines for access to the support washers.

Valve springs. All valve springs used in same engine must be of equal free length so valves function uniformly. Spring tension can vary only 5% from specifications. Though both intake and exhaust valve springs are of the same free length, effective length (and tension) can be modified at installation by adding spacers under the springs. Keep steel washer between spacers and spring to prevent damage and wear to spacers.

The 356 and 356A models and the 911 have engines with an outer and an inner spring for each valve. The early 356B used a single 47 mm spring at each valve but this was later replaced with a 49 mm spring. All valve springs of the 1600 S-90 engine have an additional 1.5 mm steel washer under the 49 mm spring to increase spring pressure still more.

The 912 engine uses a 47 mm spring that gives greater tension than the 49 mm spring. Install valve springs so that closely wound coils rest on support washers. Adjust length (not necessary for inner spring) by adding or removing spacers.

and should be lightly reworked with cutter. When refacing seat, maintain specified *seat width* on 45° bevel. The outside bevel (15° on all 356 models, 25° on the 912, and 30° on the 911) can be reworked only if the plane of the surface does not extend into cylinder head metal. If milled surface of this bevel meets the head, have valve seat replaced. Always mill 45° bevel first to obtain correct seat width.

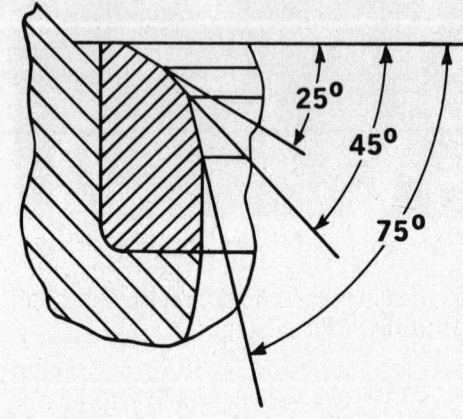

Valve seat angles are measured from a horizontal plane. (See text for correct angles for different engines.)

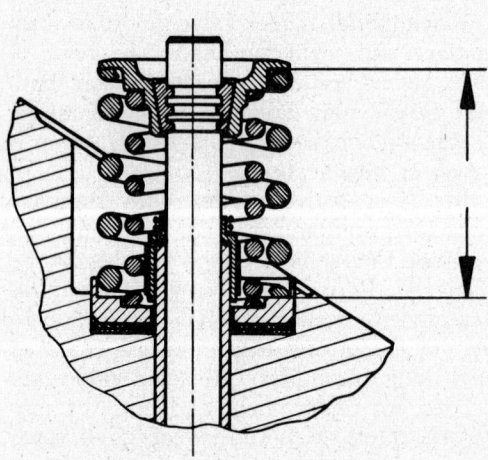

Valve spring length is measured from the resting points of the spring at each end.

In cases where dual springs are used, if either outer or inner spring does not meet tension specifications, *both* springs (inner and outer) must be replaced together.

Valve seats. Valve seating can be checked with valves installed by pouring gasoline into valve ports. If gasoline leaks through, the valve does not seat on entire surface

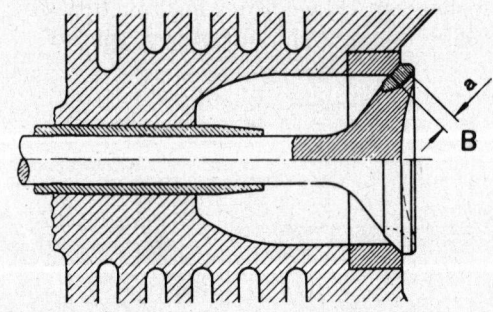

Valve seat width.

Valve seats on the 911 can be refaced only to the extent that dimension A of spring (see illustration) remains within range of 45.85 to 47.05 mm.

Replacing a valve seat requires special tools not usually available. The seat insert must be ground from the head until loosened. Then the seat is driven out. A new valve seat insert must be machined to match bore size. Overlap required for intake seat is 0.15 to 0.19 mm, exhaust seat is 0.10 to

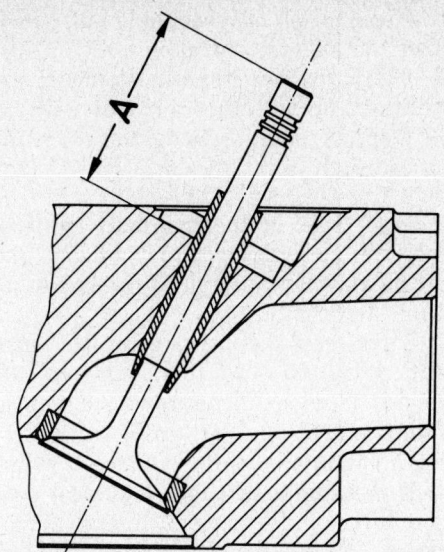

Dimension "A" is critical on 911 engines (see text).

Valve clearance adjustment on pushrod engines.

0.15 mm (except for 911 which is 0.16 to 0.20 mm). The cylinder head is heated to 395°F and the new seat insert is driven into bore. The cylinder head must cool slowly. Reheat cylinder head to 395° for two hours and again allow to cool slowly.

VALVE CLEARANCE AND TIMING

Valve clearance. Valve clearance is best adjusted with engine cold at temperature near 68°F. Insufficient clearance causes burnt, pitted and warped valves and seats. It alters valve timing and causes the engine to run noisily and unevenly. Equally detrimental, excessive clearance intensifies wear in valve components and upsets valve timing. Also, the engine will not perform smoothly or quietly.

Adjust valve clearance in cylinder sequence, 1–2–3–4, on four-cylinder engines, and in firing order, 1–6–2–4–3–5 on the 911 while rotating crankshaft counterclockwise. Start by setting No. 1 piston on top dead center (TDC) of compression stroke (move pulley clockwise). Both valves are closed and the TDC (or OT or Z1) mark on the crankshaft pulley is aligned with the mark on the crankcase. The distributor rotor faces a notch in the distributor housing (distributor cap is off). Loosen locknut on adjusting screw and set clearance by turning the screw while checking clearance with feeler gauge. Hold adjusting screw when tightening locknut. Recheck clearance.

On 911, next turn pulley 120° to check clearance in valves of #6 cylinder. TDC of #2 cylinder is 120° farther on pulley.

Valve timing. Timing points of valves are checked after valve clearance has been temporarily set at 1.00 mm in cold engine. After checking timing, reset clearance to normal specifications.

Valves that have been refaced (ground on machine) or lapped (ground in seats) must be seated first. Therefore, set reworked valves to additional clearance of 0.15 mm over specifications and run engine for half hour. After test run, set valve clearance to 1.00 mm (cold) and check timing. Last, return valve clearance to specifications.

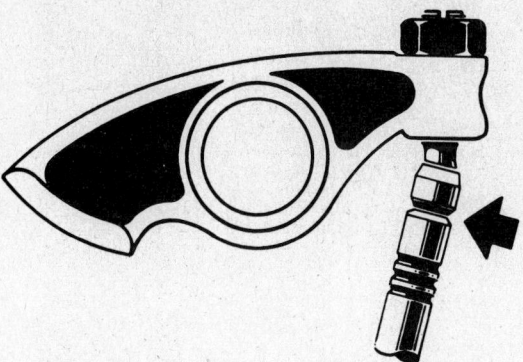

Adjust valve clearance on 911 below rocker on valve side.

Valve timing adjustment for 911. Turn crankshaft until the mark Z1 on the crankshaft pulley lines up exactly with the crankcase joint. Taking care that the valves and pistons do not collide with each other, turn both camshafts (tool P 202) to bring the punch marks, stamped on the face of the camshafts, exactly above the shaft vertical center (see arrow in illustration). Back off a little if the slightest resistance is felt during the turn. Then turn the free shaft to bring the valves and pistons into proper harmony before continuing with the first shaft.

With the crankshaft timing marks aligned and the camshaft punch marks exactly on the top, the engine is timed at firing point in cylinder 1 with overlapping in cylinder 4. Find which hole in the camshaft sprocket lines up with a corresponding hole in the sprocket flange and insert aligning dowel pin.

Slip on washer and tighten retaining nut to 72.3 ft-lbs. (10 mkg).

Adjust cylinder 1 intake valve clearance to 0.10 mm (.004″) and attach dial gauge. The gauge sensor must be positioned exactly on the edge of the valve spring retaining collar. Adjust the gauge to a preload of 10 mm (.39″) to provide for sensor travel when the cam lobe depresses the valve. Depress the chain tensioner with a screwdriver to tighten the chain (on the side to be measured) and turn crankshaft one complete turn until the timing marks are aligned again. The dial gauge should read between 4.2 and 4.6 mm (.165″–.181″). A preferred range is 4.25 to 4.45 mm.

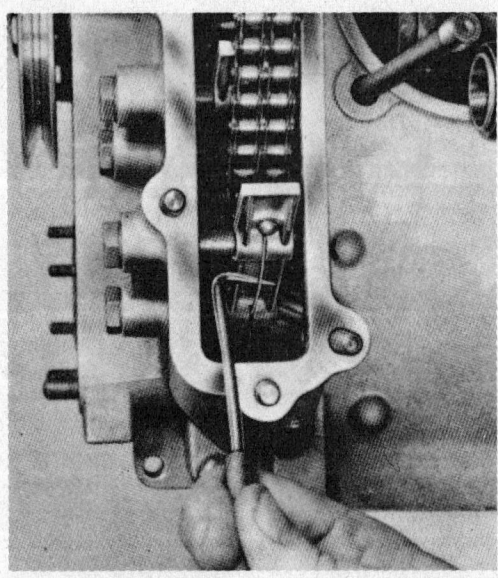

To detach timing chain guide, the spring must be lifted from its groove.

If the gauge shows a lower or higher reading, the camshaft has to be readjusted as follows:

1. Remove sprocket retaining nut, spring washer and aligning dowel pin.

2. Check that the crankshaft pulley mark is still lined up with the crankcase joint.

3. Depress tensioner to tighten chain and turn camshaft until the dial gauge indicates 4.4 to 4.45 mm (.173″-.175″).

4. Find hole in the camshaft sprocket which lines up with the sprocket flange and insert the dowel pin. Replace spring washer and nut and tighten.

5. Turn crankshaft two complete turns to the right and read dial gauge. If the specified value is still not obtained, repeat the steps above.

When valves overlap in cylinder 1, cylinder 4 is at firing point (TDC). Repeat procedure for cylinder 4 valve timing adustment.

CYLINDERS AND PISTONS

With cylinder heads off, the pushrods should be withdrawn and marked according to position. Also remove the pushrod tubes to protect them. Take off air deflector plates between the cylinders and remove and mark the cylinders according to position.

Inspect cylinder walls for scoring, roughness, or ridges from excessive wear. With an accurate cylinder gauge or bore micrometer, check for cylinder taper and out-of-round at top, middle and bottom of bore, both parallel and at right angles to the centerline of the engine.

Out-of-round on cylinder bore must not exceed 0.02 mm.

Though cylinders and pistons are best replaced in sets, the cylinder (if in good condition) might be honed for smallest possible oversize piston and rings, if necessary. Obtain piston first and then rework cylinder bore to match the size. If boring cylinders, obliterate old size numbers and stamp on new sizes.

Measure cylinders at a point approximately ¾ inch below top edge and 1 inch above lower edge of bore.

All cylinders are coded at the base to indicate the bore diameter size group. Pistons are marked identically on their tops. Replace cylinders and pistons (in sets) which are worn close to maximum clearance.

Cylinder-piston sets for engines of older Porsches are grouped according to size and then stamped with the letter of that group, A through K. Sizes range in 10 groups from .04 mm undersize to .01 mm oversize.

Cylinder-piston sets for newer engines are designated as standard (with −1, 0, +1, and +2 groups), or as oversize (−1KD, 0KD, and +1KD groups). Pistons are available in a second oversize (−1KD2, 0KD2, +1KD2 groups), ranging from 83.47 mm to 83.49 mm. Cylinder-piston sets installed in one engine may not differ in size by more than four groups.

The cylinders are available in height groups (distance between flanges at crankcase and head) and are marked accordingly with a triangle enclosing the number 5, 6, 7 or 8. Only cylinders of the same height groups can be installed in the same bank.

Pistons. Mark pistons to ensure reassembly in original position and location. Remove piston pin circlips, making sure they don't fall into crankcase. Heat pistons to approximately 175°F (with electric piston heater), knock out piston pins with drift and remove pistons.

Use a ring expander to remove piston rings, expanding rings as little as possible to avoid breaking or bending them.

Measure piston diameter (dial gauge is recommended) at a point approximately 10 mm below the bottom ring at right angles to the piston pin. Double check this by measuring the diameter between the last compression ring and the oil scraper, above or below the piston pin.

Replace pistons that show traces of scoring or wear. Cylinders that are in good condition need not be replaced if a new piston of the same size group is available.

Cut a chisel from hardwood for chipping carbon from the cylinder chamber and piston. The wood is less likely to score the metal surfaces. Remove carbon deposits from piston crown and the ring grooves. Signs of uneven contact or carbon deposits on one side of the piston may indicate poor connecting rod alignment. Traces of deposits or discoloration on piston side at a right angle to the piston axis might be caused by a bent connecting rod.

To install the pistons correctly on the connecting rods, attach the piston to the connecting rod with the arrow on the piston crown facing the flywheel. If piston is not marked, determine the direction by noting the machined pockets in the crown for valve clearance. Position these pockets under the valves.

Pistons for engines up to #900727 on the 911 model are slightly higher in the valve pocket area. If the cylinder head or piston is replaced in these engines, check that the minimum distance between the piston valve pocket and the valve face is not less than 0.8 mm (.0314″). Place several strips of a plastic gauging compound in the valve pockets. Fit and tighten cylinder head and rocker carrier. With camshaft installed, adjust timing and rotate engine several times. Remove cylinder head and measure the plastic compound for proper clearance. Grind valve seats if necessary to obtain clearance needed.

Piston pins. Since 1957, piston pins are off center in the pistons (with the exception of the 911) to minimize piston slap. The angle that the connecting rod pushes the piston into the cylinder is opposite that angle at which the rod is pushed out (because the connecting rod must go around the crankshaft). The piston is pressed toward each wall in turn. If the piston pin (wrist pin) is off center, the connecting rod slides the piston against the opposite wall before the combustion forcefully slams it against that side (piston slap). All of this movement occurs within the clearance limits of the piston to the cylinder.

The piston pin is held in the piston by a press fit (interference fit). If a piston pin can be pushed into the cold piston by hand, the pin is too small. Yet, a pin that is too large will cause the piston to scrape the cylinder walls as engine temperature rises. A color code marking inside the piston on the piston pin boss indicates the proper size of the pin for that piston.

Piston pin clearance in the connecting rod bushing is ideally .02 to .036 mm. If the clearance approaches the wear limit of .050 mm (.002″), fit a new piston pin to a new connecting rod bushing.

Install piston pins when they are cold and the pistons are heated to 175°F. If a piston heater is not available, the piston can be heated by dipping it in hot oil. Insert piston pin circlip on end of pin that will face toward the flywheel. Oil the cold pin, and slide the pin into the piston with slight pressure *in one continuous move* until the cir-

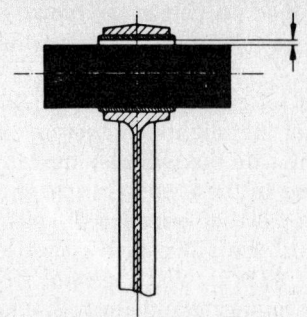

Piston pin clearance in connecting rod (max. .05 mm).

clip touches. Install other retainer. The gap of the circlips should face the top of the piston or the crankshaft.

Piston rings. Remove rings from piston with ring expander to prevent deforming ring. Check piston rings for proper condition, ring gap and ring groove clearance. The size of the gap in the ring can be measured with a feeler gauge. Place the ring in the cylinder and push it down somewhat with a piston so that it sits in the bore evenly. The optimum gap size is listed below. The side play of the ring in its piston evenly. The side play of the ring in its piston groove, called ring side clearance, must be within the limits listed.

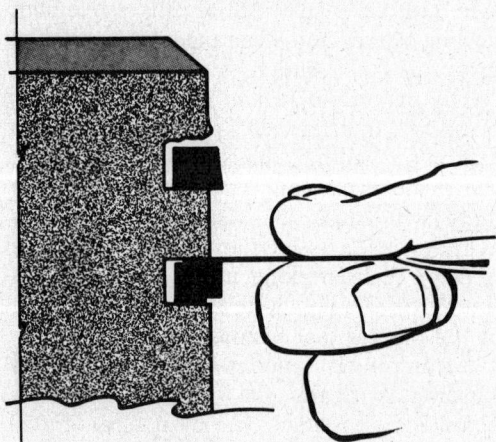

Measuring side clearance of rings.

Install piston rings with their top side (marked) facing the piston crown. Use an expander to prevent damage to the piston or ring. Stagger piston ring gaps so that they are approximately 120° apart if there are three rings (120° = ⅓ total distance around), and 90° apart if there are four rings (¼ the total circumference).

CAMSHAFT, CRANKSHAFT AND CONNECTING RODS

The camshaft, crankshaft and connecting rods are accessible for service after the crankcase halves have been opened. See section *Disassembling Porsche Engines* for procedures on dismantling crankcase.

Camshaft on pushrod engines. With crankcase separated, take out the camshaft and inspect its condition. The cam lobes must not be excessively worn or have ripples; the gear must have good tooth contact; the bearings must be smooth; and the shaft must be straight. Lubricate camshaft with graphite oil.

When the camshaft is installed, the gear tooth with the inscribed circle is placed between the two crankshaft gear teeth that have punch marks. Check gear side clearance (backlash) for every tooth, measuring while rocking gears back and forth. Install camshaft end plug.

Camshafts are available with five gear sizes. Each gear is stamped with a size code that shows in hundredths of a millimeter how much the pitch circle radius differs from standard size. The numbers −2, −1, 0, +1, +2 respectively equal −.02 mm, −.01 mm, standard size, +.01 mm, and +.02 mm oversize.

Camshaft removal for the 911 is described in the section ROCKER CARRIERS AND CYLINDER HEADS.

Crankshaft. With pistons out, the crankcase disassembled, and the camshaft withdrawn, the crankshaft with the connecting rods can be removed. Mark all bearing inserts for later installation (mark insert of bearing 1 at the crankcase joint to aid in locating dowel pin seat). Place crankshaft in bench mount and remove connecting rods.

The crankshaft drive pinion for the timing gear and the drive gear for the distributor are locked onto the crankshaft by a woodruff key. Using lock ring pliers (VW 161a), remove gear lock ring from crankshaft. Remove the distributor drive gear, spacer and camshaft drive gear from crankshaft using a puller and block. Polish out minor scoring in the seating surface with fine grit polishing cloth saturated with engine oil. Inspect gears for wear and tooth contact.

To install the distributor and camshaft

drive gears, insert woodruff key for each gear, heat each gear to 175°F and press them onto crankshaft using special guide tube (VW 427). Fit camshaft gear with beveled edge facing flywheel. Install gear lock ring on crankshaft and check gears for firm seating when they have cooled.

Check crankshaft for whip, cracks and wear. Burrs on bearing surfaces can be honed smooth with a fine oil stone or grit cloth. Clear oil galleries with compressed air, and flush with oil. If crankpin journals are scored or ridged, the crankshaft must be replaced or reground and refitted for undersized bearings. Use an outside micrometer to check for out-of-round, not to exceed 0.03 mm (.0012″).

The plain bearing crankshaft can be sent to the factory for regrinding. Undersize bearings are available in three size groups for standard and oversize main bearing bores.

End play of the crankshaft is measured at the crankshaft pulley when the engine is installed in chassis, and at the flywheel when the engine is disassembled. In both cases use a dial gauge for precision. When measuring end play at the crankshaft pulley, attach gauge holder to a stud in the timing gear cover; when measuring at the flywheel, attach the holder to the engine mounting flange. Optimum end play is 0.14 to 0.17 mm (.0055″ to .0067″) with a wear limit of 0.22 mm (.0087″).

If measuring end play with the crankshaft out, position bearing 1 on its crankshaft journal and install spacer. Spacers are available in thicknesses from 0.8 to 1.05 mm (.0315 to .0413″) and are marked alphabetically from A through F.

Attach flywheel to the crankshaft and torque the gland nut to 253–271 ft-lbs. (35–37.5 mkg). Measure end play with feeler gauge.

With the crankshaft mounted in the crankcase, end play is calculated as follows:

1. Place gauge base on the end of the crankshaft and measure distance from crankshaft end to the thrust flank of bearing 1 while crankshaft is pushed to flywheel.

2. Place gauge base on the flywheel hub and measure depth of seat (flywheel hub takes up the thrust, hub seat rests on crankshaft end).

3. From the difference in readings, and adding the thickness of the soft iron gasket, the thickness of the required spacer can be determined. Thickness of soft iron gaskets ranges between 0.10 to 0.14 mm (.004–.006″) but only one gasket can be used.

Example:

Crankshaft-end to Bearing 1 thrust flank	4.015 mm
Crankshaft seat depth in flywheel hub	−3.025 mm
	0.990 mm
Soft iron gasket thickness	+0.100 mm
	1.090 mm
Required end play	−0.140 mm
Spacer Thickness =	0.950 mm

Connecting rods. Porsche connecting rod bearings are insert halves assembled in rod and cap, except in 1300S and early 1600S engines which have roller bearings. If work is needed on the connecting rods with roller bearings, the crankshaft and rods should be returned to the factory.

Mark the insert-type connecting rods and caps for correct reassembly. Unbolt connecting rods from the crankshaft and inspect bearings and journals. If connecting rod bearings are chipped, scored or excessively worn, they should be replaced. New bearings are available in standard and undersizes. Lightly bevel the butting edges of the bearing inserts to prevent gouging of the journal when bearing cap is tightened. Polish edges of oil passages in crankshaft journals and bearings so they are smooth.

Check the weight of each connecting rod. Weight difference should not exceed 0.2 oz. Check connecting rod alignment and straightness.

Check the piston pin bushing. The pin should enter the bushing with light finger pressure. New bushings are press fitted to the rod and must be drilled out (not reamed) to accept the piston pin.

Check dowel pin in bearing 1 for firm seating. Install bearing halves, placing insert of bearing 1 on crankshaft journal so the off-centered dowel pin bore is closest to the flywheel side. Set crankshaft in position.

Thoroughly clean and oil all parts before assembling them. Match punch marks for correct reassembly and then torque connecting rod retaining nuts to 32.5 ft-lbs. (4.5 mkg). Visually check for tight fit of the cap with the rod. Minor stresses which might result from tightening the rod on the crankshaft can be relieved by light hammer taps. The tightened connecting rods should move freely under their own weight.

Side clearance between the connecting rods and the crankshaft should be between 0.15 to 0.20 mm (.006 to .008″).

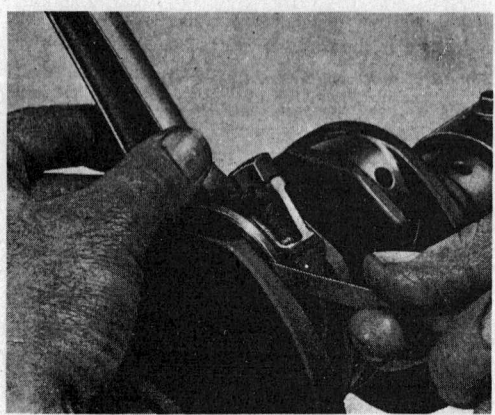

Measuring side clearance (range 0.1 to 0.3 mm) between connecting rods and crankshaft.

Disassembly—911 Engine

Follow the disassembly procedure for any Porsche engines up to rocker carriers and cylinder heads. Further disassembly of the 911 engine is as follows:

Removal of cylinder heads on the 911 involves removing the overhead camshafts. All three cylinder heads on each bank can be removed as a unit complete with camshaft and rockers or each cylinder head can be removed individually. For access to the cylinder heads and valves the camshaft housing must be disassembled and removed.

Rockers. Scribe mark on rockers for later installation. Remove 5 mm allen retaining screws in rocker shafts, holding cone-nut that is released on other end of shaft. Push out shafts and lift away rockers. *Position camshaft so that cam lobe does not press against the rocker being removed.*

Camshaft. Remove timing chain cover at each camshaft. Unbolt chain tensioner and intermediate wheel, using tools P 202 and P 203. Withdraw dowel pin from camshaft wheel with tool P 212. Remove sliding wedges and withdraw wheel and flange. Take key from camshaft, unscrew three sealing ring screws, and remove sealing ring

together with O-ring and gasket. Withdraw camshaft toward rear. Note that both camshafts turn in the same direction and there-

Camshaft seals in chain housing of 911.

1 Paper gasket	5 Spacer
2 O-ring	6 Camshaft sprocket
3 Sealing flange	flange
4 Thrust plate	

fore require that the cam lobes be positioned differently.

Cam housing. Unscrew hex nuts and the three allen screws to lift off camshaft housing. Each housing fits either cylinder bank.

Cylinder head. Loosen cylinder head securing nuts (using tool P 119) and remove the cylinder head. Cylinders are numbered from the crankshaft pulley on the left bank as 1, 2 and 3 (left when facing front of car), and on the right bank as 4, 5 and 6.

The upper and lower sealing surfaces of the cylinder head (between head and camshaft and between head and cylinder) should not be machined. Permitted distortion at the cylinder seating surface must not exceed 0.15 mm (.0059″). Examine the mating surfaces to ensure that they are in good condition.

When installing cylinder heads, use new cylinder head gaskets with perforations set toward cylinder. Carefully position each head, insert washers and tighten hex nuts lightly.

The camshaft housing is sealed to the cylinder heads only with sealing compound. Assemble camshaft housing and oil return pipes on the cylinder heads, but only hand-tighten.

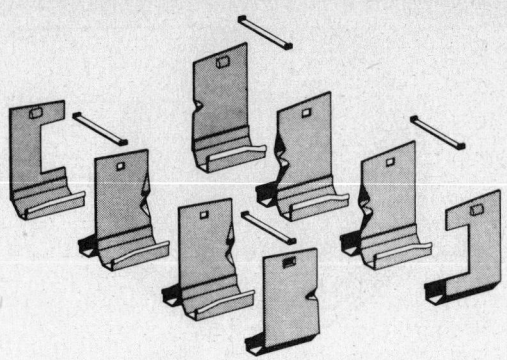

Installed positions of air deflector plates for 6-cyl. engines.

The Porsche factory workshop manual suggests that at this point in reassembly, the cylinder head be torqued down first and then the camshaft housing. Some mechanics prefer to torque the camshaft housing first for more accurate tensioning. Either way, the camshaft must be checked frequently for free turning. If tightening one side binds the crankshaft, tightening the opposite side must free it again. If not, the housing must be loosened and tightening steps must be made in a different sequence.

Tighten cylinder head to 21.6–23.8 ft-lbs. (3.0 to 3.3 mkg). Tighten camshaft housing to 15.9–18.1 ft-lbs. (2.2 to 2.5 mkg).

Warning: Pistons for engines up to No. 900727 are slightly higher in the valve pocket area. If it becomes necessary to replace the cylinder head of an engine having these pistons, the minimum distance between the piston valve pocket and the valve head must be determined during assembly, and must be not less than 0.8 mm (.0314").

From this point, further disassembly of the 911 engine is the same as the four-cylinder procedure.

Type 914

DISASSEMBLY

Mount the engine on a stand. Drain the engine oil and remove the muffler and heat exchanger. Remove the rear engine cover plate. Remove the intake distributor and intake pipe with the injection valves (on fuel injection engines). Remove the ignition distributor and the front engine cover plate. Remove the cooling blower impeller. Remove the cooling blower housing with the alternator attached. Remove the engine mount. Remove the front and rear cylinder jackets with the warm air guides. Remove the oil cooler, oil filter and oil pump. Remove the rocker arm shafts with the protective tubes, pushrods and tappets. Remove the cylinder heads, cylinders and pistons. Remove the clutch and flywheel. Disassemble the crankcase, being careful not to score any of the mating surfaces by trying to pry the halves apart. Remove the camshaft and crankshaft with the connecting rods.

ASSEMBLY

Assembly is the reverse of disassembly, noting the following procedures. Check the riveting of the camshaft gear and the camshaft. Check the camshaft for out-of-true using V-blocks. The maximum allowable wear is .0016". Check the end play of the guide bearing which should be .0016-.0051". The oil holes in the crankshaft bearing journals and bearings should have no sharp edges. Carefully remove any metallic foreign substances. Install the crankshaft and connecting rods. Install the camshaft and gear so that the tooth marked with a 0 is located between the two teeth of the crankshaft gear which are identified with a punch mark (see illustration). Coat the mating surfaces of

Type 914 valve timing marks

the housing halves with a thin coat of sealing compound. Be sure that no sealing compound enters the oil ducts. Assemble the crankcase halves and lightly tighten the screw for the oil intake pipe. Screw on the sealing nuts with the sealing ring on the outside and tighten to the specified torque. Rotate the crankshaft to ensure free rotation. Grease the needle bearing in the flywheel with a small amount of multi-purpose grease. Moisten the left ring with engine oil, wiping off any excess. Install the flywheel and adjust the axial play of the crankshaft. Measure the axial play by installing the flywheel with two spacing washers but without the sealing rings. Using a dial gauge, measure the play by rotating the flywheel. The thickness of the third spacer can be computed by subtracting .0039″ from the measured result. Remove the flywheel and install the sealing ring, felt ring and three spacers. Three spacers must always be installed for the required thickness. Spacers are available in the following sizes: .0094″, .0118″, .0126″, .0134″, .0142″ and .0150″. Each spacer is marked for proper identification. The axial play of the crankshaft, measured with the engine assembled and the flywheel screwed on, should be .0028-.0051″. On vehicles equipped with a Sportomatic transmission, the flywheel is replaced with a carrier plate retained to the crankshaft with five screws. The felt ring and needle bearing have also been eliminated. Clean the contact surface of the clutch disc and flywheel. Check the splining of the input shaft and coat lightly with molybdenum disulphide powder, applied with a brush. The clutch disc should slide easily. Check the throwout bearing. Do not wash in any solvent but wipe it clean. Replace bearings which are contaminated or noisy. Grease the guide bushing lightly with molybdenum disulphide paste. Center the clutch disc and clutch on the flywheel using an input shaft. When a new clutch is installed, the balancing marks should be 180° apart. A white paint stripe on the outside edge of the flywheel indicates the heavy end, and a white paint stripe indicates the heavy end of the clutch. Tighten the bolts to 14.5 ft. lbs. Clean all pistons and check for wear. Check the marking of the pistons according to the following designations:

A—The letter next to the arrow is the index of the spare parts number.

B—The punched in arrow indicates that the piston must be installed with the arrow facing the flywheel.

C—The color dot (blue, pink or green) indicates the paired size of the piston.

D—A statement of weight class (+ or —) is punched in or printed.

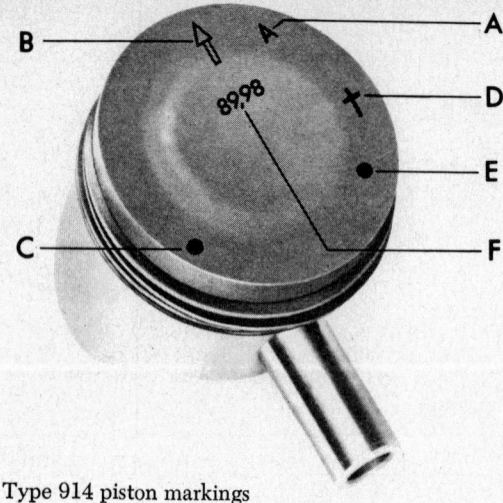

Type 914 piston markings

E—The weight class is indicated by a color dot (brown = —weight and grey = +weight).

F—Number indicates the piston size in mm.

Fit the compression and oil scraper rings. The designation Top should face up. Insert the locking rings of pistons 1 and 2 on the side facing the flywheel. The locking rings of pistons 3 and 4 should be fitted on the impeller side. Fit the piston pin. The piston pin may slide in easily by hand, which is normal. Should the pin not fit easily, heat the piston to approximately 176° F. and slide in the piston pin without bottoming the pin on the locking ring. Seat the second locking ring. Lubricate the piston and piston pin. Compress the piston rings. Lubricate the cylinder bore and fit the cylinder bore. The sealing ring must also be fitted. The studs of the crankcase may not touch the cooling fins of the cylinder. Check the cylinder head for cracks and the spark plug threads for damage. Replace the sealing ring and the cylinder head. Pre-tighten the cylinder head nuts slightly and finally tighten according to sequence. Replace the baffle plate. Insert the tappets with engine oil. Slide the protective tubes with new sealing rings up to the stop, taking care not to damage the sealing rings. Slide the bearing pieces on the rocker arm shafts so that the slots face downward and the broken edges outward when settling on the studs. The clip securing the protective tubes should enter the slots of the bearing pieces and rest against the bottom

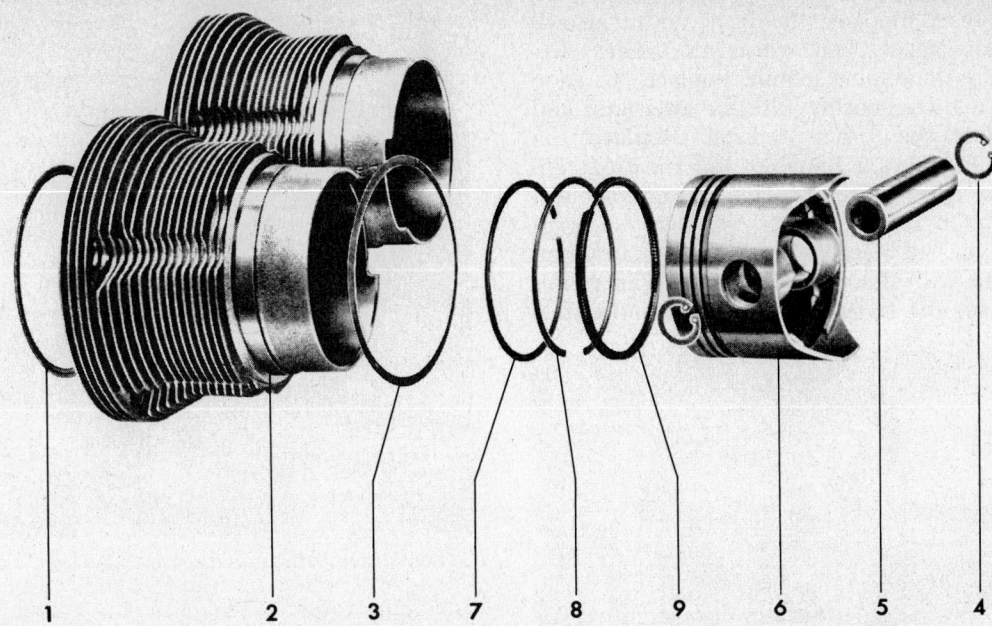

Type 914 exploded view of cylinders and pistons

1. Gasket
2. Cylinder
3. Gasket
4. Snap-ring
5. Wrist pin
6. Piston
7. Upper compression ring
8. Lower compression ring
9. Oil control ring

edges of the protective tubes. Lubricate the gear wheel and driveshaft and insert into the oil pump housing. Install the oil pump cover with the lubricated rubber sealing ring. Check the gear wheels for proper running. Install the oil pump with new seal into the crankcase. The journal of the driveshaft should be in alignment with the slot in the camshaft gear. Center the oil pump by two crankshaft revolutions and tighten the nuts. Clean the sealing sur-

face on the flange for the oil filter. Lubricate the rubber seal slightly and screw the filter in until the filter is seated. Tighten the oil filter. Replace the oil cooler after checking for leaks and tightening all weld-

Installation of Type 914 rocker arm shafts and bearing pieces

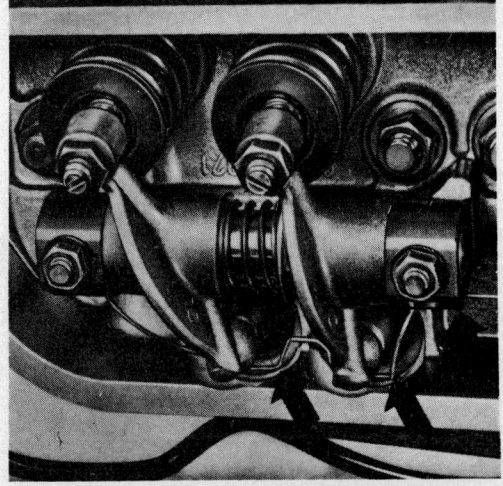

Protective tube securing clips—Type 914

ed seats. Replace the front and rear cylinder jackets and warm air guides. Replace the engine mount. Replace the cooling blower housing with the alternator and adjust the V-belt tension. Replace the cooling blower impeller and the front engine cover plate. Replace the ignition distributor. Bring cylinder No. 1 to the firing point. The black notch should be in alignment with the reference mark. The center off-set slot in the head of the ignition dis-

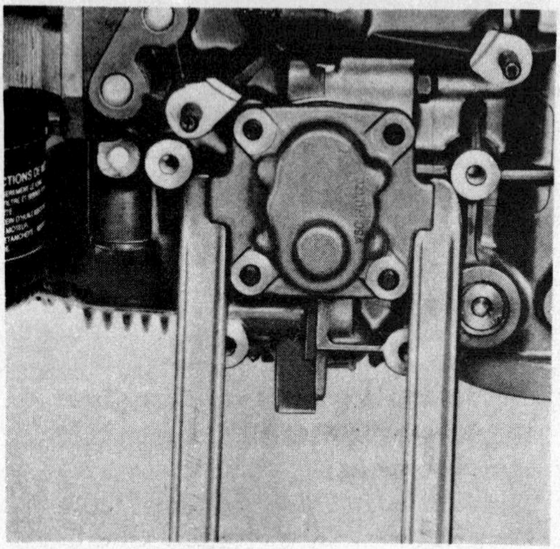

Oil pump installed—Type 914

tributor driveshaft should be at an angle of approximately 12° in relation to the longitudinal axis of the engine. Turn the

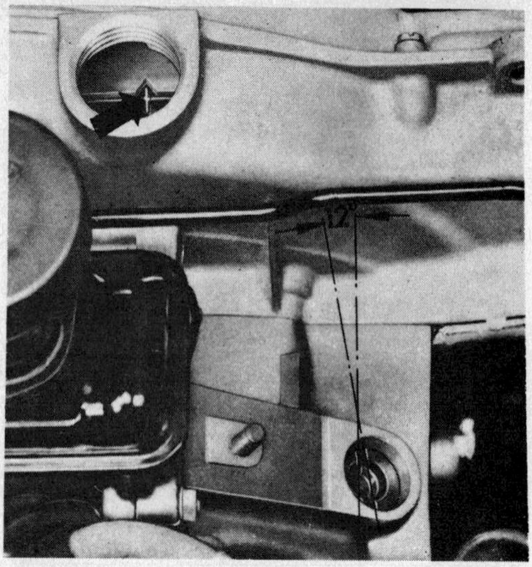

Distributor installation reference marks—Type 914

distributor rotor to the mark for cylinder 1 on the distributor housing. Insert the ignition distributor. Replace the oil filler neck with the oil vent. Replace the intake distributor with the intake pipes and injection valves. Mount the rear engine cover plate. Replace the exhaust muffler and heat exchanger. Fill the engine with oil and replace the engine in the car. Adjust the ignition timing.

Exploded view of double oil pump used on Type 914 equipped with Sportomatic transmission

1. Sealing nut M 8
2. Closing screw
3. Spring
4. Piston
5. Cover
6. Seal for intermediate plate and cover
7. Gear wheel outside top
8. Gear wheel outside bottom
9. Sealing ring for intermediate plate
10. Intermediate plate
11. Plate spring
12. Shaft bottom with gear wheel inside
13. Shaft toy with gear wheel inside
14. Housing for double oil pump
15. Seal for oil pump housing

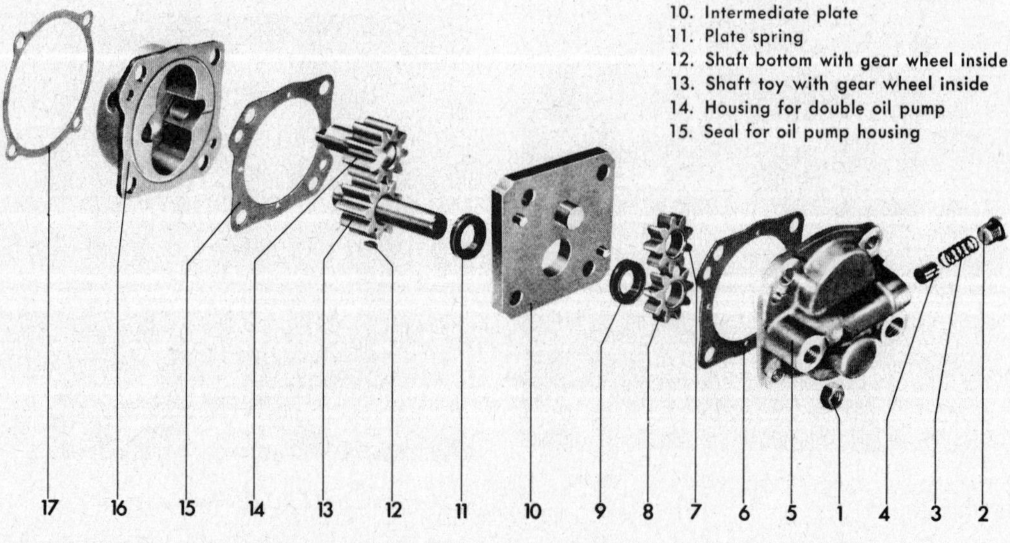

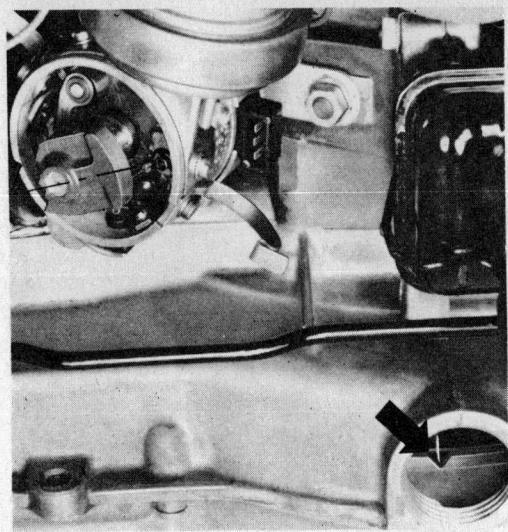

Distributor rotor alignment mark—Type 914

2,000 engine, although the engine used in the Type 914/6 differs slightly in compression ratio, torque values and some specifications. The following torque values are for use with the engine found in the Type 914/6.

Screw bolts crankcase half: 15.9 - 18.1 ft lbs.

Screw bolts crankcase half (Bearing points): 25.3 ft. lbs.

Connecting rod bolts: 36.2 ft. lbs.

Cylinder head bolts: 21.7 - 23.9 ft. lbs.

Camshaft housing on cylinder heads: 15.9 ft. lbs.

Nut on camshaft: 72.3 ft. lbs.

Rocker arm shafts: 13.0 ft. lbs.

Flywheel attachment: 108.5 ft. lbs.

Crankshaft V-belt pulley: 57.9 ft. lbs.

Alternator V-belt pulley: 28.9 ft. lbs.

VALVES

Procedures for removing, servicing and adjusting valves in the Porsche 914 engine are identical to the procedures described for all four-cylinder engines.

Type 914/6

All service procedures for the engine in the Type 914/6 are identical to those for the Type 911. Both cars use the Type

Lubrication

If any malfunction is encountered in the engine lubrication system, and especially if the oil cooler leaks, check the operation of the pressure relief valve.

FOUR-CYLINDER ENGINES

The oil pump (10) draws oil through a strainer (5) in the sump, and forces it through a bypass valve (7) to the main oil circuit.

The 356 and early 356A engines with a

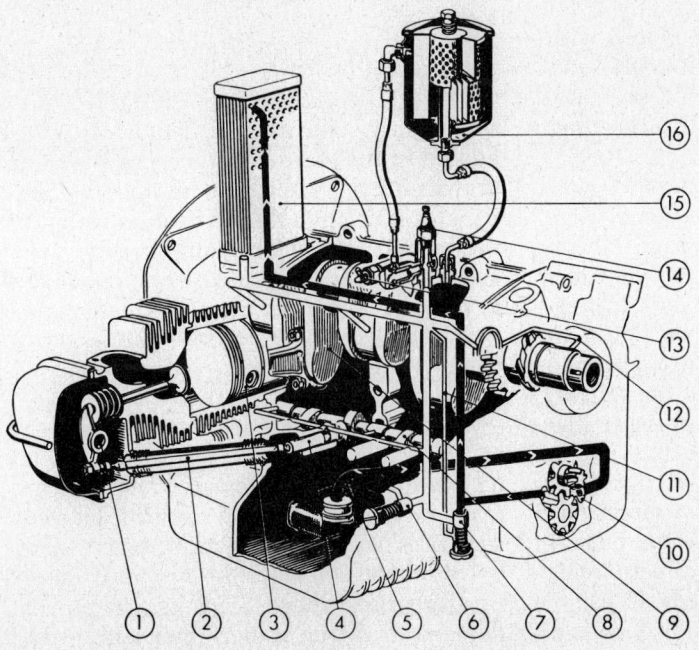

1 Rocker shaft bearing
2 Pushrod
3 Piston pin located above oil ring (356C)
4 Tappet
5 Oil line from sump strainer
6 Pressure relief valve
7 Oil cooler by-pass valve
8 Camshaft
9 Crankshaft
10 Oil pump
11 Counter-pressure line to by-pass valve
12 #4 bearing lubrication line
13 Oil pressure sensor
14 Oil temperature sensor
15 Oil cooler
16 By-pass oil filter

Oil system of 4-cyl. engines at operating temperature.

two-piece crankcase have a single valve for both oil-cooler bypass and oil-pressure relief functions. As the valve plunger is forced down, it first opens a bypass circuit leading directly to lubrication points, and at higher oil pressure, a pressure-relief passage to the sump.

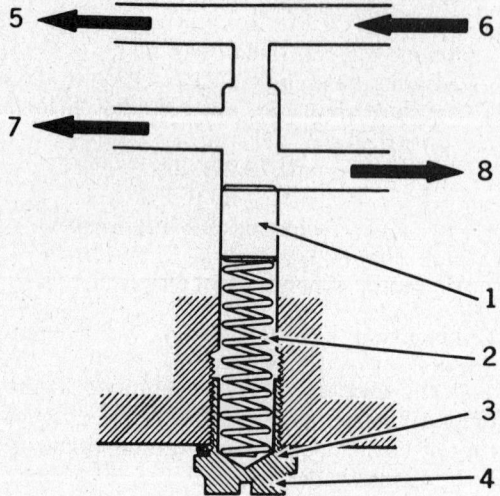

Combination pressure-release and cooler-bypass valve used on 356 and early 356A engines.

1 Piston	6 From oil pump
2 Spring (compressed)	7 Directly to lubrica-
3 Seal	tion points
4 Screw plug	8 To the sump
5 Through oil cooler to	
lubrication points	

Later 356A models were introduced with one valve for bypassing the oil cooler and another for releasing excessive oil pressure. This design was adopted for all succeeding models, including the 912.

When the engine is not running, the spring-loaded plunger in the bypass valve holds the main oil circuit passage closed. As soon as the oil pump begins to function, the plunger is depressed by oil pressure (minimum, 19 psi) and oil flows directly to all lubrication points, bypassing the oil cooler (15). As oil fills the circuit, some flows through a counter-pressure line (11) to a cavity below the bypass valve plunger. The oil pushes the plunger upward, closes the passage of the direct circuit, and forces all oil through the cooler. The bypass valve reopens the direct circuit only if pumping pressure exceeds 44 psi.

Some 356A engines are designed with a thermostat which opens at approximately

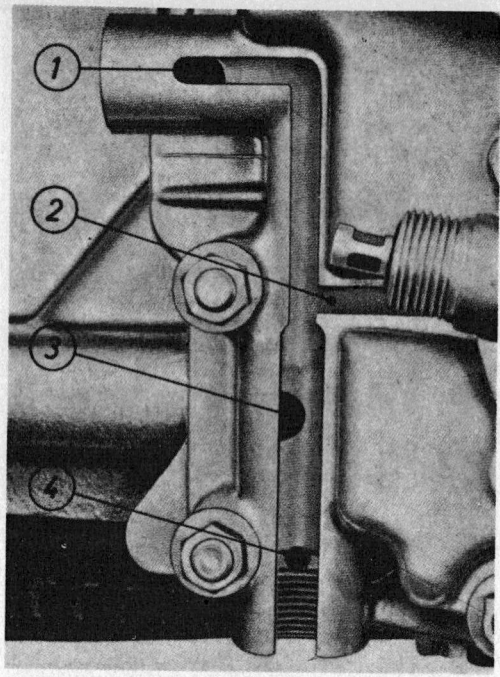

Oil cooler bypass valve.

1 To oil cooler
2 From oil sump
3 Directly to lubrication points by bypassing the oil cooler
4 From back-pressure line

176°F and sends oil through the oil cooler. 356A engines without thermostats have the opening in the timing case sealed off by a blind flange.

TYPE 911

The 911 engine (Type 2000) has dry-sump lubrication using a double oil pump housed in the crankcase. One pump section draws oil from a separate oil tank and distributes it through the lubrication circuit of the engine. The other pump section scavenges oil from the crankcase and delivers it through a bypass filter to the separate tank. The scavenger pump is the larger of the two because it pumps oil containing air bubbles.

A thermostat redirects the oil around the oil cooler directly to the bearings when oil temperature drops below 176°. A pressure relief valve bleeds the oil circuit if oil pressure rises above 88 psi ($\pm$11 psi). A safety valve releases oil from the system if the oil pressure rises above 113.7 psi, to prevent damage to the oil cooler, filter and hoses.

Valves in the filter base and filter body

Location of oil pressure units on 6-cyl. engines.

1 Pressure relief valve
2 Safety valve

bypass the filter if oil pressure exceeds 28.4 psi.

TYPE 914/6

The oil system of the Type 914/6 engine is identical to the Type 911.

OIL STRAINER

The oil strainer at the bottom of the engine (easily removed for cleaning) screens oil in two ways. Submerged in oil, the pump tube sucks the oil through a fine strainer and under a magnet, trapping both metallic and other foreign matter.

When assembling oil strainer, clean gasket remnants from strainer and cover flanges, check that the suction tube fits into screen and magnet snugly, use new gaskets on both sides of strainer flange, and do not overtighten cover, especially if thick gaskets are used.

The 356C engine has the oil strainer in the crankcase sump equipped with a centrifugal valve to prevent air from entering lubrication system during severe cornering.

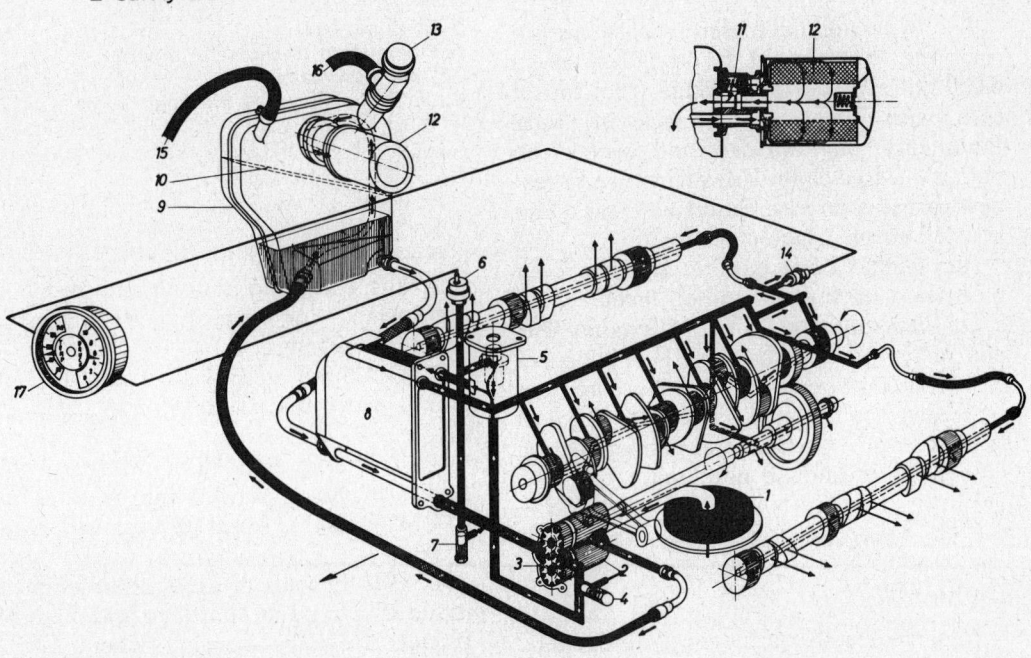

Dry sump oil system—911.

1 Strainer	7 Pressure relief valve	13 Oil fill pipe
2 Scavenger pump	8 Oil cooler	14 Temperature sensor
3 Pressure pump	9 Oil tank	15 Vent for crankcase
4 Safety valve	10 Screen to prevent foaming	16 Vent to carburetor intake
5 Cooler bypass thermostat	11 Pypass valve	17 Temperature-pressure gauge
6 Pressure sensor	12 Full-flow filter with safety valves	

Two valves, attached to a common sliding stem, open alternately to either side. In a curve, the sliding stem is forced centrifugally to the outside as is the oil in the sump. The inside valve closes and prevents air from entering suction pipe.

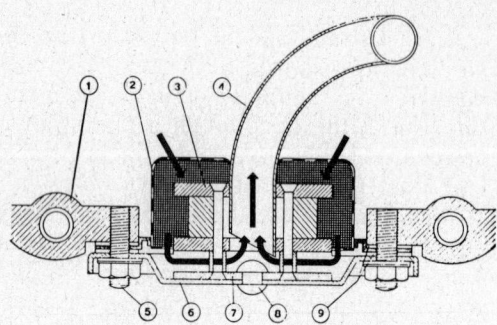

Oil flow through strainer in sump.

1 Crankcase	6 Oil strainer cover
2 Oil strainer	7 Disc
3 Magnetic filter	8 Rivet
4 Oil suction tube	9 Gasket
5 Stud	

CARTRIDGE OIL FILTER

The bypass oil filter used in Porsches is a cartridge that should be replaced every 6,000 miles. Remove cartridge from top of case with slight counterclockwise turn. Pump dirty oil from case and wipe clean with a lint-free cloth. Use slight turn to seat new cartridge in case. Insert new gasket on housing cover. Tighten securely.

Run engine a few minutes and check for oil leaks. Check crankcase oil level.

Oil filter replacement for 911 engine. One end of the oil filter on the 911 engine has female threads ¾″ x 16 UNF-2A. The filter is screwed off counterclockwise. Inspect sealing surface on base and rubber seal on filter before installing new unit.

OIL PUMP AND TACHOMETER DRIVE

Disassembly

Remove engine rear cover plate (generator end) and cover plate between lower sections of air ducts. Pull off crankshaft belt pulley and detach shield under pulley. Unbolt oil pump cover having tachometer drive attached. Slip out gears of pump. The oil pump housing can be extracted with a puller (tool VW 201).

Oil pump and tachometer drive.

1 Gasket
2 Oil pump gear with tachometer drive pinion
3 Oil pump gear
4 Thrust washer
5 Oil pump cover
6 Pinion shaft (tachometer drive)
7 Light alloy washer
8 Thrust bearing plug for pinion shaft

Note the following:

1. Inspect pump housing and gear bearing surfaces for wear. Excessive wear reduces oil pressure.

2. Optimum gear lash (clearance between gears) is 0.03 to 0.08 mm (.001–.003 in).

3. Tolerable end play of gears, with gasket in place, is .035 mm to 0.10 mm (.0014″–.0039″). Limit of wear is 0.20 mm (.008″).

4. Play in shaft of driven gear might be reduced by tapping shaft end with hammer. If not, exchange housing when shaft is loose.

5. Check pump cover with straight edge for warp, excessive wear and scoring. Cover can be honed flat.

6. Place pump cover partially over gears (without gasket) to check clearance between gears and housing. Measured with

feeler gauge, gap must not exceed 0.1 mm (.0039″).

7. Use new gasket of proper thickness but do not use any sealer. Gasket thickness for 356 and 356A = 0.08 mm (.003″); 356 B, C, and 912 = 0.20 mm (.008″) or 0.16 mm compressed.

8. Clean crankcase seat for pump housing before installation.

9. Replace tachometer drive with its pinion-shaft gasket.

From numbers P-67001 and P-81201 in Types 1600 and 1600S engines, the oil pump housing is cast in the timing case and, therefore, not extractable. Otherwise, all oil pumps are alike. *Note: Timing case with cast oil-pump housing is not interchangeable with other types owing to a modified lubrication circuit.*

The 911 oil pump can be removed only when the crankcase sections of the engine have been separated.

Loosen bolts securing oil pump and withdraw pump together with intermediate shaft and connecting shaft. Detach pump from shafts. Clean with solvent and dry with compressed air, checking proper function by rotating driveshaft at steady speed. Examine seals at inlet and outlet. If pump is damaged or inoperative, it must be replaced.

Installing oil pump, connect shafts to the

drive chains, ensure proper fitting of the seals, and tighten down unit.

OIL COOLER

The oil cooler can be quickly removed with a 10 mm box wrench after the blower housing has been taken off. Discard inlet and outlet ring gaskets on mounting flange. (Exception: cooler for 911 is accessible after upper, front (toward flywheel) and right hand cover plates are removed. Unscrew upper and lower nuts on base of cooler. Leave lower pipe attached to cooler, but remove hose leading to it. Hold hex flange on pipe to prevent cracking pipe from cooler).

A suspect cooler is best tested under air pressure of 85 psi (up to 147 psi for 912). Always check the pressure relief valve if cooler has been leaking. Use new gaskets at installation. After installing cooler, test again with air pressure.

Note for 356A: type 1600 from engine number P-67001 and type 1600S from P-81201 have wider oil bores to the oil cooler (9.75 mm) than do older engines. If necessary, replace original soft-soldered oil coolers with new brazed coolers, but do not interchange sizes. Small oil bores (7.75 mm dia.)—replace cooler with #616-07-012-1 (green paint dot). Large oil bores (9.97 mm dia.)—replace cooler with #616-07-017.

Model	914		914/6		911		912, 356B, 356A	
Oil Pressure	Normal	Min.	Normal	Min.	Normal	Min.	Normal	Min.
Idling, warm								7.3 psi
Pressure at 2500 rpm, warm	42 psi	28 psi	81-103 psi @		81-103 psi @		44 psi	29 psi
Oil Pressure Switch Opens	2-6.4 psi		5000 rpm		5000 rpm		4¼ to 8⅜ psi	

Emission Control (USA)

Exhaust emissions from gasoline engines depend heavily upon fuel/air ratio, but are also affected by the firing point, temperature and proper tuning of an engine. To reduce toxic fumes, the ignition distributor and carburetor are properly adjusted in relation to each other. A pneumatically actuated throttle valve adjuster with an electromagnetic valve is controlled by a speed switch, preventing an increase

of hydrocarbons by opening the throttle valves in dependence of intake pipe vacuum.

THROTTLE VALVE ADJUSTER

The throttle valve adjuster slightly opens the throttle valves under over-running conditions to prevent the intake pipe vacuum from increasing to the same level as with the throttle valves closed. As a result the

Vacuum reduction for throttle valve adjuster

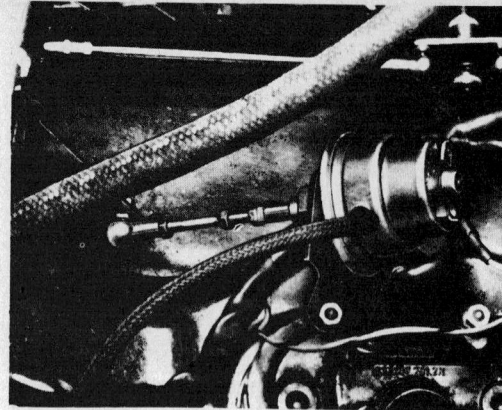

Throttle valve adjuster

engine is provided with an ignitable fuel/air ratio under over-running conditions, and no major portion of the fuel will enter the exhaust system unburned. Backfiring is also substantially eliminated.

SPEED SWITCH

At speeds above 1,600 rpm the speed switch, which receives pulses from the contact breaker, sets the electromagnetic changeover valve to its through position, allowing the intake pipe vacuum to influence the diaphragm. Upon deceleration, the increasing vacuum will pull the actuating rod of the throttle valve adjuster, which, in turn, will slightly turn the carburetor linkage in the direction of full throttle. The throttle valves will be unable to close completely and the path of the supplementary mixture to the intake pipes is not obstructed. The magnetic valve closes below $1,500 \pm 50$ rpm and the vacuum end

Speed switch for exhaust emission control system

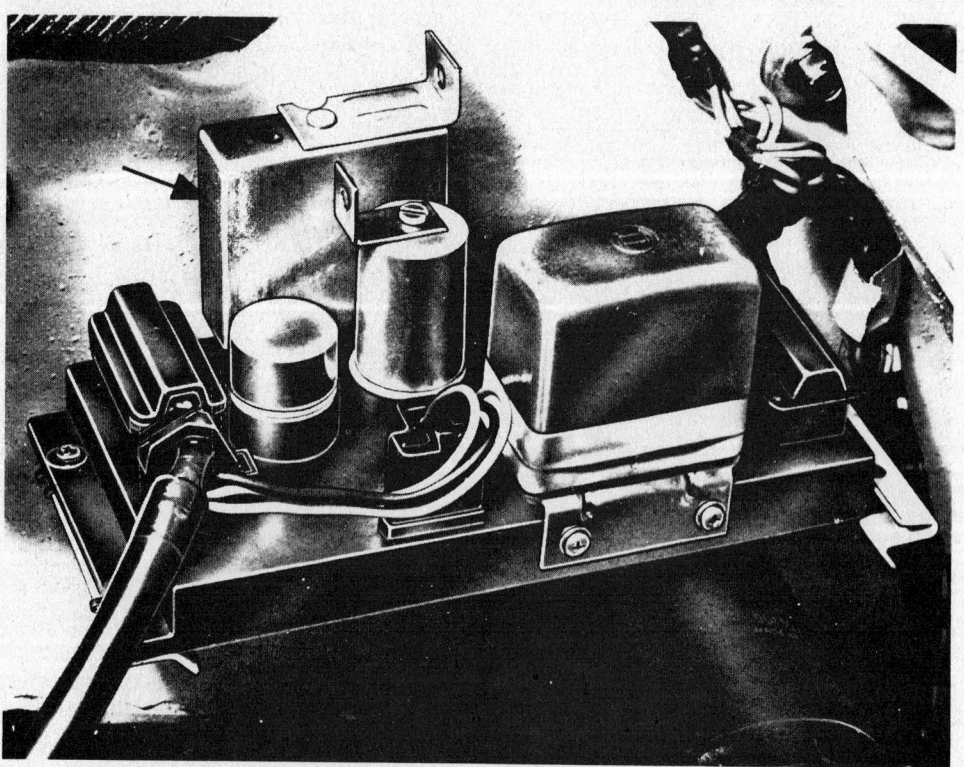

of the diaphragm is vented allowing the throttle valves to close in idling position.

ADJUSTMENTS—TYPE 914 and 914/6

Firing Point and Idling Speed

Adjust the firing point and idling to specification. Adjust the point gap to .016″ or the closing angle to 40° ± 3°. Adjust the ignition at idling speed (900-950 rpm) to 4° ATDC. Run the engine until warm (minimum 140° F.) and check that the firing point at 6,000 rpm is 35° BTDC. If the firing point at 6,000 rpm is not as specified, set the firing point at idle speed back to 2° ATDC. Synchronize the carburetors. If an exhaust gas analyzer is available, adjust the idle mixture control screws, at idle, until the CO content according to the exhaust gas analyzer is 4.5 ± .5%.

Throttle Valve

Pull the cable from the insulated connection on the adjuster. Connect this cable

Actuating the changeover valve on the throttle adjuster

to the positive side of the battery, to actuate the changeover valve. Run the engine and turn the actuating rod of the adjuster so that after accelerating once (approximately 3,000-4,000 rpm) slow deceleration will produce a speed of 1,250-1,300 rpm. Use an external tachometer, not the vehicle tachometer. Replace the cable on the speed switch and accelerate to 3,000-4,000 rpm again. Upon deceleration, idling speed should be 900-950 rpm.

Speed Switch

Connect a test lamp to the poles of the adjuster. The lamp should light at a speed of 2,000-3,000 rpm. The lamp should go out at 1,500 ± 50 rpm (cut-out speed). If the above does not occur, replace the speed switch.

Test lamp connected to the throttle adjuster to check the speed switch

Clutch and Transmission

Clutch

The Porsche drive train consists of a dry single-plate clutch, a transmission-differential, and ball-jointed half axles.

REMOVAL

With transmission and engine out of the chassis and separated, remove the retaining bolts on the clutch cover by loosening them alternately and evenly, one turn at a time to avoid distortion. Remove the pressure plate and clutch disc.

Inspect clutch parts for wear and damage. Check friction surfaces of flywheel and pressure plate for scoring, ends of release fingers for wear, and clutch facings for wear or oil saturation. A flywheel that is scored or discolored can be polished or lightly machined. Inspect clutch disc for distortion. Lateral runout should not exceed 0.6 mm (.023″) at the outer diameter. The thickness of the disc from one facing to the other (when not pressed together) should be 10.1 to 9.7 mm (0.397″ to 0.382″). Test-out the disc hub on the shaft drive splines for easy slip fit, without side play.

Check the release bearing for wear, binding, or roughness. *NOTE: Do not clean disc or release bearing in solvent.* Inspect surface on drive spline and check bushing in flywheel gland nut. The drive shaft bushing in the flywheel is pressed in from the crankshaft side.

Check ends of diaphragm spring (except on early Porsches) for marks from the thrust bearing. Running marks of less than 0.3 mm (.011″) in depth are not harmful.

Check bearing surface of the pressure plate for cracks, burns and wear. Pressure plates with inward deflections of up to 0.3 mm are usable. Use a straight edge to determine unevenness. Check for cracks on the pressure plate and cover at the spring connections. Check rivet attachments for tightness. The diaphragm spring is mounted in the cover between two wire rings with a rivet connection. Clutches with visible wear on the rivet head or wire ring are not usable. Premature clutch slippage is often caused by drag in the area where the diaphragm pivots on the housing. Coat the diaphragm spring between the wire rings with a light coat of molybdenum-sulphide grease (MoS_2) before fitting the clutch.

The clutch release fork is fastened to the pivot shaft by two roll pins inserted into each other at each end of the bearing fork. Remove the clutch pivot shaft by driving out the roll pins in the fork. The slits in the new roll pins must be placed opposite to each other but only facing directly up or directly down. Also inspect the bushings that hold the pivot shaft in the clutch housing. The bushings can be driven out with a drift.

When assembling clutch, partly fill the flywheel bushing with special graphite grease or MoS_2 grease. Fit clutch disc with a drift or a cut-off clutch sliding shaft so that it is exactly centered in the flywheel. Position clutch on flywheel with dowel pins. Fit the clutch and tighten bolts evenly (only one or two turns at a time) to prevent distortion of the cover. Torque to 25.3 ft-lbs. (3.5 mkg).

After gearbox is fitted to engine, pull the clutch release lever toward the axle. There must be a distance of at least 20 mm (¾″) between the release lever and the gearbox housing.

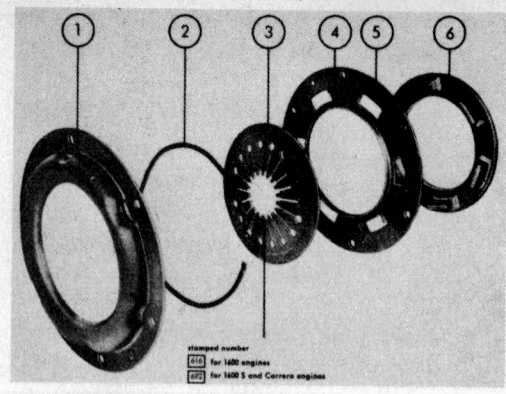

Diaphragm clutch assembly.

1 Cover	4 Tensioners
2 Lock ring	5 Counter plate
3 Disc spring	6 Pressure plate

The mainshaft seal in the clutch housing can be replaced without removing or disassembling the transmission. Remove the clutch release bearing and its guide. Pry out the oil seal with a screwdriver, taking care not to damage the seat in the housing. Apply sealing compound to the outside of the new oil seal so that no compound touches the sealing lip. Lubricate the mainshaft and the sealing lip. With special tool, press new seal into position. If transmission is disassembled, removal of the old seal is simplified by driving it out from the inside.

To remove the clutch control cable, detach the floor mats, raise the tunnel cover from the front, and disconnect the cable from the shackle. Pull out clutch cable to the rear; detach cable from clutch housing; check condition of cable cover and bellows; and smear cable with grease before sliding it into the cover from the rear.

Adjustments

Pedal Free Play

Clutch pedal free play should measure from ¾ to 1 inch (20–25 mm) from the resting position of the clutch pedal to the point where disengagement begins. The adjustment is possible at both the pedal base and at the clutch housing. At the pedal, the floor mat and transmission cover must be removed for access to the clutch cable. At the clutch housing, the clutch cable is accessible on early Porsches only after the left

Clutch pedal free play can be measured at the clutch housing.

rear wheel is removed. On either end of the cable, loosen the lock nut and screw the adjusting nut along the shaft until proper play is achieved. Hold cable with pliers if necessary. Depress the foot pedal a few times and recheck the free play. Tighten the lock nut and grease the threaded rod.

Pedal Travel

Clutch pedal travel (the distance from point of clutch engagement to the floor) must be adjusted to eliminate gear clash

Clutch pedal travel is adjusted at base of pedal to eliminate clash when engaging reverse gear.

whenever the clutch is serviced. With engine idling and the transmission at operating temperature, depress the clutch pedal and check ease of shifting into reverse gear. Engagement will be noticeable but clash-free if adjustment is correct. Gear clash is eliminated by moving the pedal stop (the strip of flat metal at the base of the pedal) up or down as required.

Transmission

The manual transmissions in Porsches have been modified over the years as power output has increased. The earliest Porsches had a transmission almost identical to the VW type, a split-case, non-synchronized assembly. In 1953, a "519" gearbox with ring-

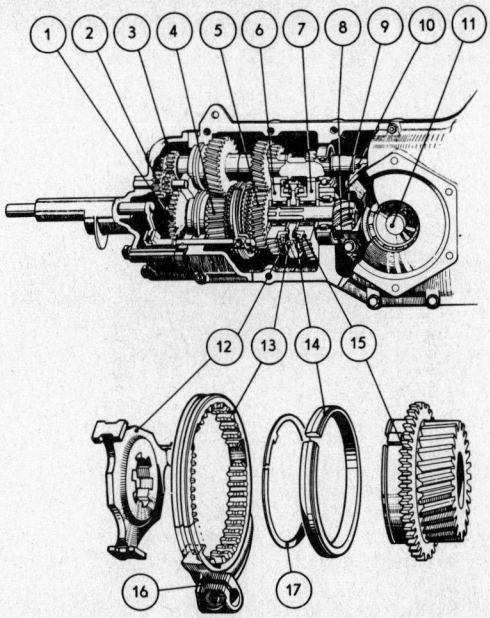

Cutaway of "519" split-case synchronized transmission (1952–55).

1 Gear 2 for reverse gear
2 Gear 3 for reverse gear
3 Transmission housing end cover
4 Gear 2 for 4th gear
5 Gear 2 for 3rd gear
6 Gear 2 for 2nd gear
7 Gear 2 for 1st gear
8 Housing for differential with crown gear
9 Bevel pinion
10 Main shaft
11 Rear axle shaft
12 Three-pronged shift guide
13 Operating sleeve
14 Synchronizing ring
15 Gear 2 and synchronizing clutch shoulder
16 Selector fork
17 Safety ring

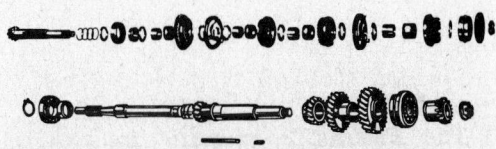

Shafts of "519" split-case transmission. Top: pinion shaft. Bottom: main shaft.

type synchronization on all forward speeds became the standard.

A one-piece tunnel-housing was introduced as "type 644" late in 1955. The tunnel design allowed service operations without a

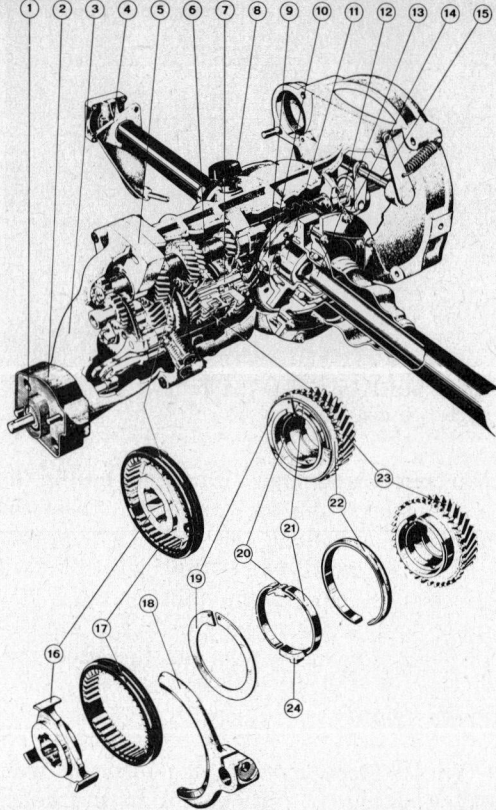

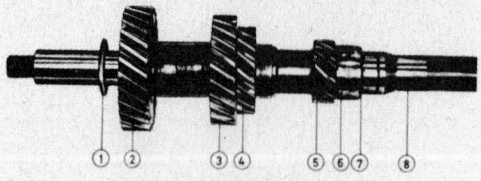

Shafts of "644" tunnel-housing transmission.

Main shaft (top)
  1 Spacer
  2 Driving gear for IV speed
  3 Driving gear for III speed
  4 Driving gear for II speed
  5 Driving gear for I speed
  6 Inner race of roller bearing
  7 Retaining ring
  8 Drive shaft
Pinion shaft (bottom)
  9 Spacer
 10 Bearing washer
 11 Shift collar for III, IV gear
 12 Shift collar for I, II gear
 13 Roller bearing, inner race with rollers and cage
 14 Bevel pinion and shaft

complete teardown. The "644" transmission was developed into "type 716" (in 1959) that featured a more efficient synchromesh mechanism with progressive servo action.

The "741" gearbox again modified the synchro gears along with shift shaft and mounting changes.

A five-speed manual transmission was available as an option with the introduction of the Type 912. This transmission later became standard on the higher performance models.

The Porsche Sportomatic transmission system has three main units: the hydraulic torque converter, an automatic shifting

"741" transmission with lock-type synchronization (356B). (*Single mount,* thru transmission #35000; *double mount,* from transmission #35001). A self-servo lock synchronization and a single-mount transmission support are modifications of the "741" from the "644." The single support with a lower gear shift rod provides extra rear seat clearance. A double-mount casing with low-shift rod was introduced with transmission #35001.

  1 Oil seal
  2 Front transmission mounting
  3 Gearbox cover
  4 Axle tube end flange with shock absorber extension
  5 Intermediate plate
  6 Main shaft
  7 Pinion shaft and pinion
  8 Breather
  9 Differential pinion
 10 Ring gear
 11 Differential side gear
 12 Clutch release bearing guide
 13 Rear axle shaft
 14 Clutch release bearing
 15 Clutch release pivot shaft
 16 Spider
 17 Sliding sleeve
 18 Selector fork
 19 Lock ring
 20 Brake band stop
 21 Brake band
 22 Synchronizing ring
 23 Third gear on pinion shaft with synchronizing element
 24 Slider

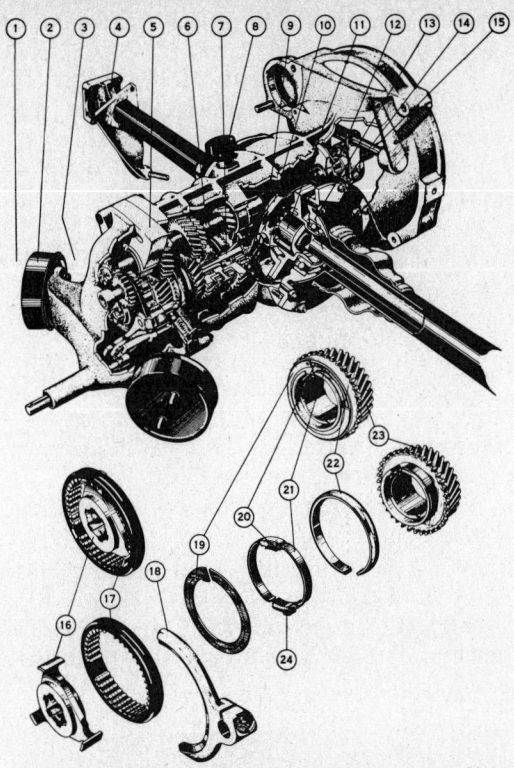

"741" transmission modifications (since transmission #50001). Service operations are not changed. See single-mount "741" illustration for part names of synchromesh assembly.

clutch and the Porsche four-speed gearbox with a parking lock device added.

The hydraulic torque converter, of the "Trilock" design with a pump wheel, turbine and stator, operates on regular engine oil supplied from the engine's oil reservoir by a special oil pump.

The pump wheel, connected directly to the engine's crankshaft, establishes a rotational flow of oil and forces it through the turbine, causing the turbine to rotate. The rotational energy (or torque) of the turbine is the force that drives the rear wheels. The

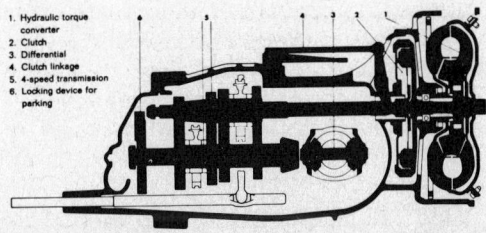

1. Hydraulic torque converter
2. Clutch
3. Differential
4. Clutch linkage
5. 4-speed transmission
6. Locking device for parking

Porsche sportomatic transmission includes a torque converter, an electric clutch, and the standard 4-speed transmission.

stator receives the oil flow from the turbine and redirects it in a way to augment the flow from the pump wheel—thus providing an increase of torque that improves the efficiency of the turbine. When the engine is accelerated, the turbine and the stator gradually approach a 1:1 ratio with the pump wheel. When the three parts of the converter are synchronized in the higher rpm range, they function as a hydraulic clutch with slippage of only 3.5%.

The shifting clutch is a single plate dry clutch which is automatically and very quickly disengaged when the gear selector is moved. This action is produced by a sole-noid-controlled vacuum cylinder. A micro-switch on the gear-selector lever activates the solenoid and a second switch on the lever keeps the clutch disengaged during idling. The coupling speed is controlled by engine rpm.

REMOVAL

Transmission removal steps are similar for all Type 356 Porsches. The engine must be removed before the transmission and differential unit can be removed. Type 912, 911, 914 and 914/6 Porsche engines are removed with the engine and transmission as a single unit. For all transmission removal procedures except Type 356, follow the steps detailed in the Engine section. Removal and installation of Type 356 transmissions follows.

To remove transmission from the chassis (all 356 models), detach the battery ground lead; break loose the rear axle nuts; jack up the car; and take off the wheels. Next remove the engine. Remove axle nuts and pull off brake drums.

Remove brake shoes and springs. Disconnect brake line from wheel cylinder and plug it. Detach clamp holding brake hose on axle tube. Loosen bracket for hand brake cable and remove cable unless backing plate will be used again, in which case the cables need not be removed and the backing plate can be temporarily suspended from the chassis. Remove bolts from rear wheel bearing cap (transmission oil will run out), remove brake backing plate, and put bearing cap and spacer back on temporarily.

Remove the floor tunnel cover that is forward of the back seat. Push the rubber shift rod boot forward. Loosen locking bolt

Adjust or remove shift linkage in tunnel ahead of rear seat.

on clamp and work the shift rod forward out of the clamp.

Lift radius arms with special tool and remove shock absorbers. Remove mounting bolts from axle tube suspension flange. The front bolt is an adjustable stop and should not be disturbed. Remove angle bracket and rubber buffer. Remove nuts from front transmission mount. Disconnect the ground strap, throttle linkage, torque rod, starter cable, and the plug for the back-up light switch. Remove shackle from clutch lever by removing pin. If the rear bracket for the cable is not slotted, the shackle must be unscrewed so that the cable can be pulled through the bracket.

Remove both cover plates from transmission mount bolts and remove the bolts, lowering axles and transmission. Do not place transmission on its flange.

INSTALLATION

Installation of the transmission is the reverse of removal, observing the following points. To prevent damage to the axle boots, do not turn them in their sockets. Connect starter and generator cables to solenoid. The torque rod should be adjusted so there is no tension between the transmission and mount. Check rod again after road test. Adjust gear shift linkage by placing shaft lever in second gear position, engaging second gear in the gearbox, and connecting shift rod to shaft without tension. Tighten clamp in tunnel and test shifting. The clutch cable housing should be bowed gently between the chassis and the bracket on the transmission. Adjust clutch pedal free play after

engine is installed. Bleed and adjust brakes.

Tighten rear axle nuts to 400 ft.-lbs. (55 mkg) and insert cotter key. Tighten rear wheel nuts to 95 ft.-lbs. (13 mkg). Fill transmission and adjust camber and toe-in of rear wheels after road test.

DISASSEMBLY

Four-Speed Manual

Porsche transmissions are machined so that all cast parts are interchangeable. However, disassembly requires adjustment of tolerances with special tools.

Drain transmission oil and remove the starter, the transmission rear mount (near clutch), the axle tubes, and the transmission front housing with the selector rod. Remove the reverse idler II from the reverse gear shift fork and attach the mainshaft holder.

Remove reverse idler II from reverse gear shift fork.

Engage 4th gear. Remove cotter key from pinion shaft castle nut. Loosen nut on pinion shaft and pull off reverse gear III and key from main shaft. Next remove reverse gear I and key. Remove intermediate plate with main and pinion shafts from transmission housing. For reassembly note thickness of gaskets used. The two dowel pins should remain in the intermediate plate. Hold plate in soft-jaw vise, and remove three plugs covering selector rod locks.

One ball and spring fits into each of the shift lock bores of the first, second and reverse gears. A ball, spring and spacer tube fit into the shift lock bore of the 3rd and

1 Reverse gear I (on main shaft)
2 Reverse gear II (held by selector fork)
3 Selector rod for reverse gear
4 Reverse gear III (mounted on pinion shaft)
5 Selector rod, 1st and 2nd gear
6 Plug for selector rod lock, reverse gear
7 Plug for selector rod lock, 1st and 2nd gear
8 Selector rod 3rd and 4th gear
9 Tapped holes to extract gear
10 Plug for selector rod lock, 3rd and 4th gear

Four-speed transmission intermediate plate

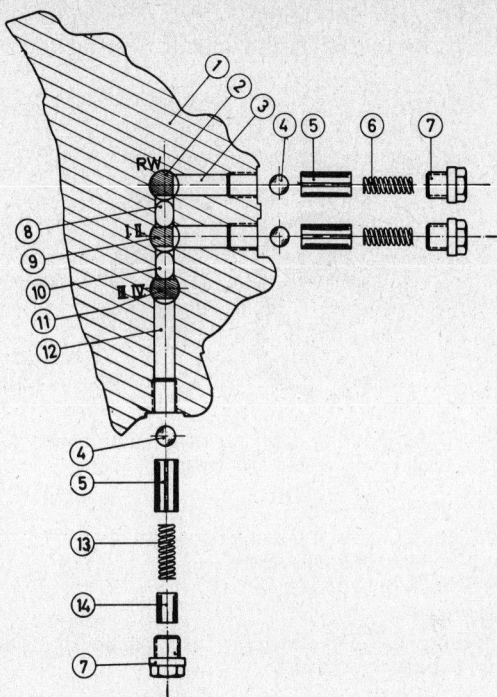

Arrangement of Selector Interlocks.

1 Intermediate plate
2 Shift rod for reverse gear
3 Bore for reverse gear interlock (seat for part 5)
4 Locking ball
5 Guide bushing
6 Reverse gear lock spring (free length 25.7 mm, 1.012 in.)
7 Retaining plug
8 Interlock pin
9 Shift rod for 1st and 2nd gear
10 Interlock pin
11 Shift rod for 3rd and 4th gear
12 Bore for 3rd and 4th gear interlock
13 Lock spring for 3rd and 4th gear (free length 23.2 mm, .913 in.)
14 Spacer plug

4th gears. Remove bolts holding shift forks and pull shift rods out of intermediate plate. Interlock pins are located in the connecting passage between the shift rods for reverse and 1st and 2nd gear and between the shift rods for 1st and 2nd gear and 3rd and 4th gear.

Remove pinion and main shaft simultaneously from intermediate plate. The dowel pins must be pushed to one side so that the plate will lie flat on the press. If ball bearings or seats appear damaged, the intermediate plate must be dismantled. Installing a new plate requires adjustment of the ring and pinion and preload on the double roller bearing.

Remove rear axle drive assembly.

Remove both lock rings from the bearing race of the main shaft and the lock ring inside the gearbox from the bearing race of the pinion shaft. Remove main shaft bearing from transmission housing. Remove bearing race from pinion shaft. Heating the housing to 220°F makes removing the races easier. Remove oil deflector plate from differential housing and, if necessary remove main shaft oil seal.

Assembly

Four-Speed Manual

Clean transmission housing and inspect for wear, external damage, or cracks. In case of severe damage (e.g. ring or pinion fracture) check if the bearing seats have also been damaged. Inspect wear of starter bushing. Inspect clutch pivot shaft bushings for wear. Check roller bearings of main and pinion shafts for wear or damage. Check main shaft for runout. Install outer lock ring of pinion shaft bearing. Install rear lock ring for mainshaft bearing using special pliers. Heat transmission housing to 220°F and install bearing races.

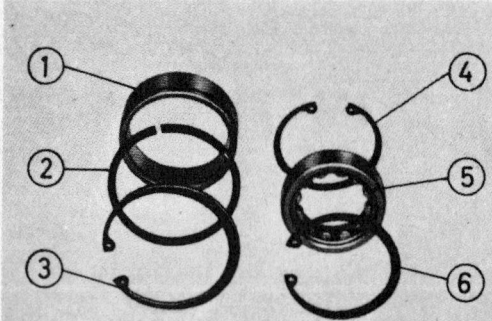

1 Roller bearing outer race for pinion shaft
2 Lock ring (installed on bearing race)
3 Lock ring
4 Lock ring
5 Roller bearing outer race with cage and
   rollers for main shaft
6 Lock ring

Bearing assembly for main and pinion shaft of four-speed transmission

1 Main shaft
2 Intermediate plate
3 Pinion gear
4 Selector fork 1st and 2nd gear
5 Selector fork 3rd and 4th gear
6 Shift rod with fork for reverse gear
7 Shift rod for 1st and 2nd gear
8 Shift rod for 3rd and 4th gear

Assembled intermediate plate

Main shaft: Outer race with cage and rollers.

Pinion shaft: Outer race with mounted lock ring.

Install lock rings on both bearings. Install oil deflector plate and secure with copper lock washer. Install main-shaft seal. Insert main and pinion shafts in special tool P 55 and adjust height with adjusting screw until the faces of the fourth gears of both shafts are flush.

Press main and pinion shafts into intermediate plate simultaneously (tool P 55). There should be at least 0.2 mm (.079″) clearance between the upper faces of the 4th gears of both shafts and the surface of the intermediate plate. Hold intermediate plate with main and pinion shafts in a soft-jaw vise. Install shift rods and selector forks in the following order:

1) Reverse gear selector rod.
2) First interlock pin.
3) 1st and 2nd gear selector rod and fork.

4) Second interlock pin.
5) 3rd and 4th gear selector rod and fork.

If the bushings for the selector rod locks have been removed or if a new intermediate plate is used, the bushings must be installed in the three bores using special tools. Inspect springs of gear shift locks. Replace damaged springs. The correct free length for reverse gear is 25.7 mm (1.012″), minimum 25.2 mm (.992″). Free length for forward gear springs is 23.2 mm (.915″), minimum 22.7 mm (.895″). Install a locking ball and spring in each of the three gear lock bores using the correct spring for reverse gear. Install spacer plug in the 3rd and 4th gear lock bore. Screw in the retaining plugs. Install intermediate plate in gearbox with main and pinion shafts. The dowel pins must fit tight in the intermediate plate. Secure intermediate plate to transmission housing. Engage 1st gear using a screwdriver. Install reverse gear I on main shaft and tighten castle nut to 18 ft-lb. (2.5 mkg).

Assembled pinion shaft.

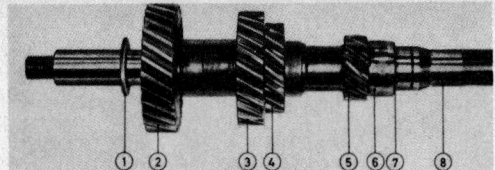

Parts of main shaft.

1 Spacer
2 4th gear
3 3rd gear
4 2nd gear

5 1st gear
6 Inner race of roller bearing
7 Lock ring
8 Main shaft

Install reverse gear III on pinion shaft and tighten castle nut to 145 ft-lbs. (20 mkg). Loosen castle nut and re-tighten to 70 ft-lbs. (10 mkg). With selector forks free on shafts, check locking of selector rods. As soon as a gear is engaged, the other rods

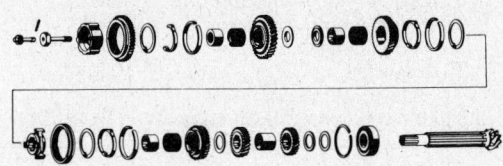

Pinion shaft for 911.

Input shaft for 911.

must be locked in position. In cases where the intermediate plate, the transmission housing or pinion have been exchanged, the ring and pinion adjustment must be made. Remove intermediate plate with main and pinion shafts from transmission housing and secure in vise.

Install reverse gear II in selector fork. Insert shaft for reverse idler through reverse idler into intermediate plate. This will provide a proper guide for the reverse gear selector rod and assure the proper position for adjusting selector forks for forward speeds. Install selector rod guide. The selector forks should be adjusted so that the sliding sleeve in a neutral position is exactly centered between the synchronizing rings. This adjustment must be exact to

Check that the selector rod heads are parallel to each other.

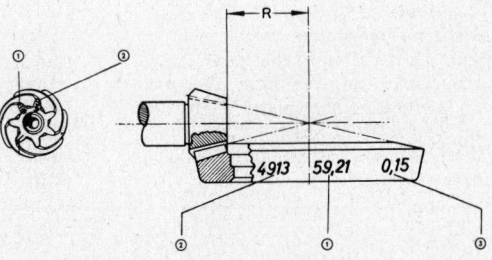

Adjusting ring and pinion gears.

1 Setting dimension "R" for ring and pinion gears
2 Matching set number
3 Backlash for the ring pinion gears at setting "R"
"R" Distance between ring gear centerline and face of pinion

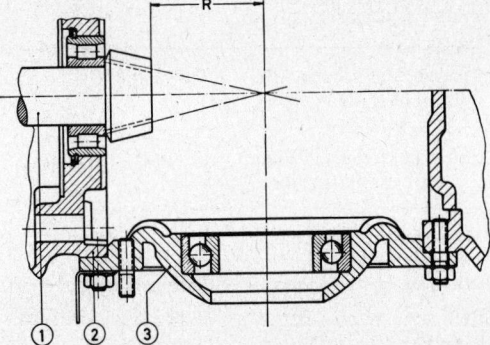

Shims for 1st gear on pinion shaft. R = distance between centerline of differential and face of pinion. Basic size for 7:31 ratio is 59.80 mm. Real setting is marked on gears. Make up the difference in sizes with shims placed between inner race of roller bearing and the thrust washer for the 1st gear.

1 Pinion and shaft
2 Transmission housing
3 Differential cover plate, left side

insure proper gear synchronization. After completion of fork adjustment, tighten clamping bolts to 18 ft-lb. (2.5 mkg). Check that the selector rod heads are parallel to each other. After the proper shims for ring and pinion clearance have been determined, install intermediate plate in transmission housing. Secure pinion and drive shaft castle nuts with cotter keys.

Torque Values for Transmission 741

	Foot-Pounds Torque
Castle nut on main shaft	18.0
Castle nut on pinion shaft	72.5
Bolts for differential ring gear	43.5
Bolts for bearing retaining plate on intermediate plate	14.5
Bolts on selector forks	18.0
M 8 bolts on transmission housing	14.5
Rear axle nuts	400

Transmission Tolerances— Type 741

	Range mm Normal	Wear Limit mm
Selector fork side clearance in sliding sleeve 1st and 2nd gear 3rd and 4th gear	0.10–0.30	0.5
Clearance of reverse idler II on idler shaft	0.032–0.068	0.25
Runout of main shaft on pilot bearing surface	0.1 max.	0.2
Main shaft clearance in in pilot bushing	0.082–0.168	0.2
Runout of main shaft between bearings	0.03 max.	0.04
Rear axle shaft play in spline	0.03–0.10	0.15
Rear axle clearance between fulcrum plates	0.05–0.15	0.25
Runout of axle shaft	0.00–0.02	0.03

Torque Values for Transmission 901

Location	Foot-Pounds Torque
M 8 Hexagon nuts on transmission housing	18.08
M 6 Hexagon nuts on guide tube	7.23
M 6 Socket head screw for withdrawal fork	7.23
M 8 Hexagon bolt with pin (angular drive)	18.08
M 12 drain plug on intermediate plate	18.08
M 24 oil filter plug	14.46–18.08
M 24 magnetic oil drain plug	14.46–18.08
Hexagon bolt for clamping plate of intermediate plate	18.08
M 24 Hexagon nut on first motion shaft	72.33–86.79
M 12 Crown nut on first motion shaft	43.39–47.01
M 14 Crown nut on first motion shaft (reinforced type)	65.09–79.56
M 12 Expansion screw on drive shaft	79.56–86.79
M 8 Hexagon bolt of selector forks	18.08
M 12 Hexagon bolts for securing crown wheel	68.71–72.33
M 10 expansion screw for joint flange of differential	32.54–36.16
M 8 ball pin for withdrawal fork	15.18–16.63

Torque Values for 914 Manual Transmission and Sportomatic

	ft. lbs.
Hex. nuts on transmission housing	18.0
Hex. screw with trunnion (angle drive)	10.8
Closing screw on intermediate plate	21.7
Closing screw oil inlet	18.0
Magnetic plug oil drain	18.0
Hex. screws for intermediate plate clamping plate	18.0
Hex. nut on input shaft	80
Crown nut on input shaft	72
Expanding screw of pinion shaft	87
Hex. screws of shift forks	18.0
Hex. screws for ring gear attachment	72
Expanding screws for universal flange of differential	25.3—18.9
Hex. nuts on converter housing and servo motor	18.0
Hex. nuts on converter housing and starter	32.5
Closing screw on front gearbox cover for parking lock	34.0
Double hex. socket screws for clutch pressure plate	10.8
Double hex. socket screws for freewheel support	10.8
Double hex. screw for converter-drive plate	17.4—18.8
Bridging switch	25.3—28.9
Backup light switch	25.3—28.9
Hollow screw of angle drive in guide bushing	15.9—17.4

Transmission Tolerances

	TYPE 901 Normal Range	Wear Limit	TYPE 741 Normal Range	Wear Limit
Backlash between gears—all speeds	0.06 to 0.12 (0.0023″–0.0047″)	0.22 (0.0086″)	.06 to 0.20	0.30
Side clearance of gears on pinion shaft with drive shaft				
1st speed	0.3 to 0.4 (0.011″–0.015″)	0.5 (0.019″)	0.25 to 0.35	0.4
2nd speed	0.2 to 0.3 (0.007″–0.011″)	0.4 (0.015″)	0.2 to 0.3	0.4
3rd speed end play	0.2 to 0.3 (0.007″–0.011″)	0.4 (0.015″)	0.2 to 0.3	0.4
4th speed	0.2 to 0.3 (0.007″–0.011″)	0.4 (0.015″)	0.2 to 0.3	0.4
Selector shaft play in the guides	0.095 to 0.156 (0.0037″–0.0061″)	0.4 (0.015″)	0.095 to .0061	0.4
Runout of selector shafts		0.10 (0.0039″)		0.10

DISASSEMBLY

Five-Speed Manual

Mount the transmission on a stand and drain the oil. Remove the starter and the caps from the universal joint mounting flanges. Shift the transmission into 5th gear by turning the inner shiftrod clockwise to its stop. Pull the shift rod out and block the input shaft. Remove the universal joint mounting flanges. Remove the side cover retaining nuts and remove the differential unit. Remove the transmission support from the front cover and remove the front cover. Use caution when performing the latter operation as the reverse gear components can fall out. Remove the retaining screw from the selector fork (1st and reverse gear) and remove the gear and selector fork. Remove the bolt from the pinion shaft (transmission engaged in 5th gear and pinion shaft blocked). Remove the roll pin from the castle nut with a punch. Remove the castle nut and 1st gear from the input shaft. Shift into neutral and remove the nuts from the inner shift rod guide fork. Withdraw the guide fork. Remove the inner shift rod through the rear access hole. Insert a screwdriver into the guide fork opening and shift into 5th gear. Remove the intermediate plate with the gear clusters. CAUTION: *The gear clusters can be inserted or removed only when the transmission is in 5th gear.* Mount the intermediate plate and gear clusters in a vise equipped with soft jaws. Remove the 1st and reverse gear spider wheel. Remove gear II of 1st speed and the needle bearing cage. Withdraw the selector shaft and detent ball from the 1st and reverse gear shaft. Remove the 2nd and 3rd gear selector fork, selector shaft, and detent. Remove the 4th and 5th gear selector fork, selector shaft and detent. The selector forks for 2nd and third, and 4th and 5th gears should be marked to prevent confusion during assembly. Remove the detent ball spring and detent. Drive the aligning dowels in the intermediate plate flush with the plate and remove the throttle linkage. Using a press, remove the input and pinion shafts together from the intermediate plate. Care should be used to ensure that the bearing balls do not fall from the double-row offset ball bearing. Disassemble the intermediate plate. Remove the bearing brace plate. Heat the intermediate plate to approximately 248° F. and press out the four point ball bear-

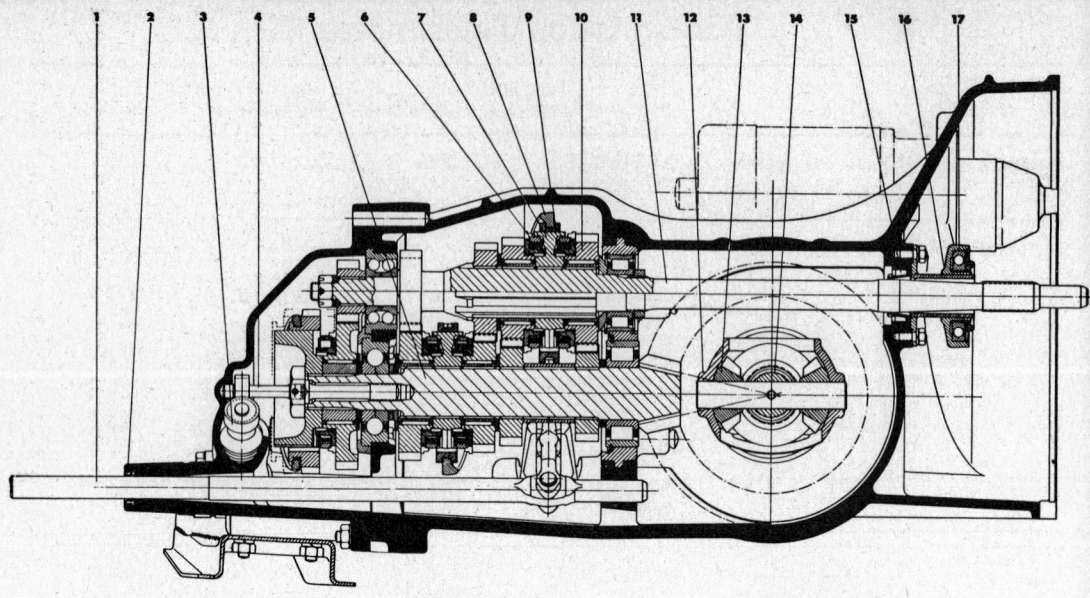

1. Shift rod	7. Spider	12. Differential carrier
2. Oil seal	8. Shift fork	13. Bevel spider gear
3. Tachometer drive	9. Sliding sleeve	14. Side gear shaft
4. Gear shaft	10. Gear 1, 5th speed	15. Oil seal
5. Pinion shaft	11. Input shaft	16, 17. Clutch throwout bearing
6. Synchronizing ring		

Cross-section view of Porsche five-speed transmission and differential

ing and the double-row ball bearing. Drive the dowel pins from the plate and, if necessary, remove the detent bushings individually. From the case center web, remove the spring retainers of the input shaft bearing and the front retainer of the pinion shaft. Heat the housing to approximately 248° F. and tap both bearing races from the case using a plastic hammer. Remove the input shaft oil seal.

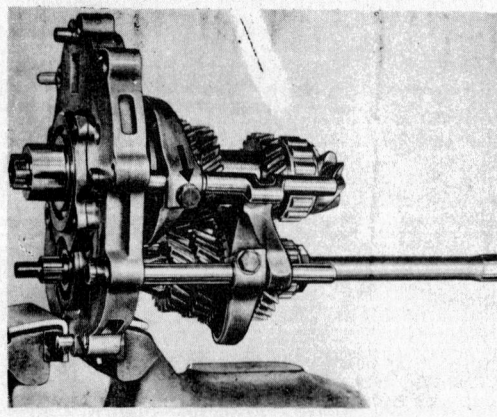

Remove retaining screw for 2nd and 3rd gear

ASSEMBLY

Five-Speed Manual

Assembly is the reverse of disassembly, noting the following points. Clean the housing and check for external wear, damage or cracks. Check the roller bearings of the input shaft and pinion shaft. Check the input shaft for run-out. Install the proper spring retainer into the outer bearing race of the pinion shaft roller bearing. Replace rear spring retainer of the input shaft roller bearing into the bore. Heat the transmission housing and install the outer race of the input shaft roller bearing and the spring retainer. Install the outer race of the pinion shaft roller bearing with the spring retainer mounted on the race. Install the front spring retainer. Install the input shaft oil seal. Assemble the intermediate plate. Clean all parts and check for wear. Heat the intermediate plate and install the four point ball bearing and the double-row ball bearing, These should seat well on the intermediate plate. Grease and insert any loose balls from the bearings. Position the bearing brace plate. Insert the retaining bolts

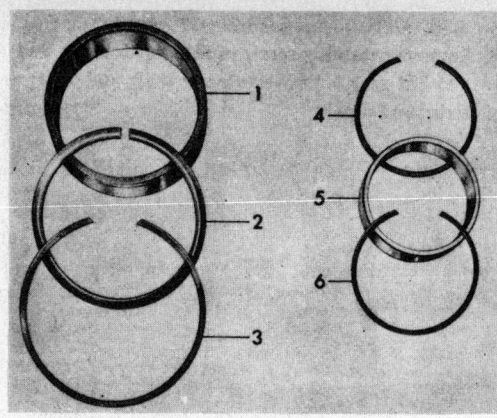

1. Pinion shaft roller bearing outer race
2. Spring retainer (mounted onto outer race)
3. Spring retainer
4. Spring retainer
5 Outer race of pinion shaft roller bearing
6. Spring retainer

Proper positioning of pinion shaft spring retainers

and lock plates. Torque to 18 ft. lbs. Install the detent bushings, making sure that no bushings protrude from the selector shaft bores. Assemble, in reverse order of disassembly, the pinion shaft and input shaft. Insert the intermediate plate (with 5th gear engaged) and lightly tighten in a cross sequence at the four housing studs. Install gear I of 1st speed on the input shaft and tighten the nut to 43-47 ft. lbs. Secure the castellated nut with a pin. Re-

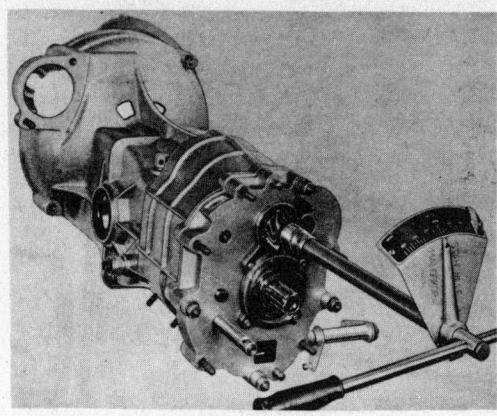

Install gear I of 1st speed on the input shaft

place the thrust washer on the pinion shaft with the small collar facing the bearing. Guide the needle bearing race into place. Install the needle bearing and gear II of 1st speed. Install the spider wheel of 1st and reverse gear. Oil the pressure seat of the pinion shaft bolt (which has an extension for tachometer take-off). Torque to 80-86 ft. lbs. with the input shaft blocked. Place the intermediate plate into a vise with soft jaw liners. Install the selector

shafts and forks in the reverse order of removal, noting the following procedures. Place the selector fork of 4th and 5th gear onto the sliding sleeve and push the 4th and 5th gear selector shaft through until it enters the bore in the intermediate plate. Secure the shift arm to the selector shaft with a roll pin and slightly tighten the fork retaining screw (with the spring wash-

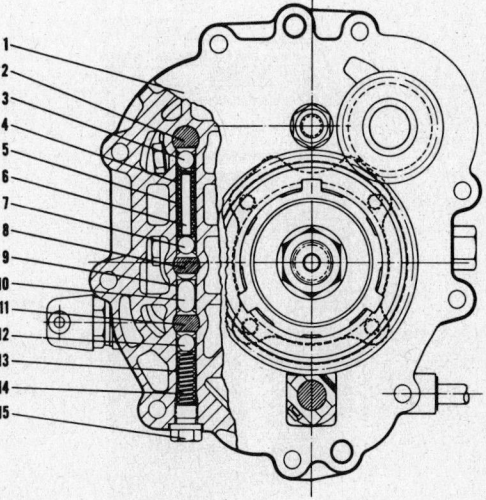

Arrangement of detent components

1. Intermediate plate
2. Selector shaft of 4th and 5th speed
3. Ball
4. Detent bushing
5. Detent spring of 2nd thru 5th speed
6. Detent pin
7. Ball
8. Selector shaft of 2nd and 3rd speed
9. Detent bushing
10. Detent pin
11. Selector shaft of 1st and reverse speed
12. Ball
13. Detent bushing
14. Detent spring (reverse speed)
15. Cap screw

er). Into the detent bore which connects the selector shaft bores, place the ball, detent pin and long spring for detents 2 through 5. Repeat the operation for the selector fork of 2nd and 3rd gear with the selector shaft of 4th and 5th gear in neutral and the detent ball of 2nd and 3rd gear pushed down. Move 2nd and 3rd gear selector shaft into neutral and insert the detent. Install the selector shaft of 1st and reverse gear, followed by the detent ball and the short spring. Torque the cap screw to 18 ft. lbs. Slide the selector fork and sliding gear of 1st and reverse gear together onto the spider wheel and selector shaft. Slightly tighten the retaining screw and washer. Check the springs of the detent. Adjust the selector fork of 1st and reverse gear. Press the assembled reverse twin gear (with bearings and shaft) against the intermediate plate to be sure that 1 mm. of clearance exists between reverse gear and the sliding gear with the transmission in neutral. Eliminate the free-

Side clearance between 1st and reverse gear selector shaft and 2nd and 3rd gear selector shaft

Side clearance between 4th and 5th gear selector shaft and 2nd and 3rd gear selector shaft

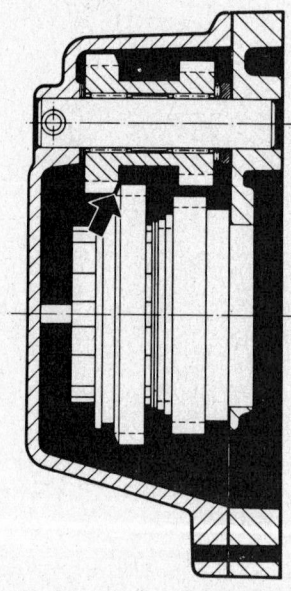

1 mm. clearance between reverse gear and sliding gear with transmission in neutral

play that may exist between the selector fork and the sliding gear by pushing the sliding gear in the direction of the car's travel to ensure that during operation the sliding gear will not strike the reverse gear. Tighten the selector fork retaining screw to 18 ft. lbs. Make sure that the selector shaft actuating tabs have a clearance of .079"-.118" in relation to 2nd and 3rd gear. Adjust the selector forks of 2nd and 3rd gears, and 4th and 5th gears. The sliding sleeve must be adjusted to a position in the exact center of both synchronizing rings when the transmission is in neu-

tral. Torque all selector fork retaining screws to 18 ft. lbs. with a clearance as listed above. Assemble the inner shift rod, making sure that the tapered bore in the rod points in the same direction as the inner shift rod. Press the retaining pin in and hold with a cotter pin. The inner shift rod must be installed at the same time as the gear cluster asssembly. It is best to insert the shift rod into the housing first. Install the intermediate plate with gear clusters and gaskets, which have been determined at the time of pinion and ring gear adjustment (see Four-Speed Transmission Assembly). Shift into neutral and guide the inner shift rod into position at the selector shaft tabs and into the rear guide bore. Install the guide fork of the inner shift rod, using a new gasket. Be certain that the inner shift rod enters the guide fork. Assemble the front case cover and install. Heat the cover to approximately 248° F. and install the reverse gear shaft making sure that the oil passage in shaft points down. Drive in the retaining pin. Heat the bronze thrust washer (248° F.) and install on the reverse gear shaft until it seats firmly against the cover. Install the bearing cages and spacer bushings. Install the reverse gear, thrust needle bearing and thrust washer. Insert the tachometer elbow drive into the cover, making sure that the set screw lines up with that in the cover. Install the set screw and washer and torque to 18 ft. lbs. Replace a new paper gasket on the intermediate plate and install the front housing. To bring the helical reverse gear past the sliding gear of reverse and 1st, pull the reverse gear and its needle bearing with the thrust washer as far to the end of the shaft as possible. NOTE: *The machined recess in the thrust washer must align with the outer collar of the pinion shaft ball bearing.* Torque the cover retaining nuts to 18 ft. lbs. Install the transmission support.

Gearshift

SPORTOMATIC

Removal

The gearshift is accessible after the tunnel cover mat has been removed. Sliding out the front seats may be easiest way to get to the floor mats. Disconnect heater cables from heater flaps. Mark position of shift lever bracket to avoid extra adjustments when installing. Remove allen screws holding the bracket and lift the assembly over to one side. Remove lock ring from threads of the heater control and turn out the knob completely. In the rear tunnel opening, slide rubber boot forward on shift rod, loosen the clamp and pull the shift rod out of the connection toward the front. Remove shaft from shift lever opening.

Exploded view of Sportomatic converter housing

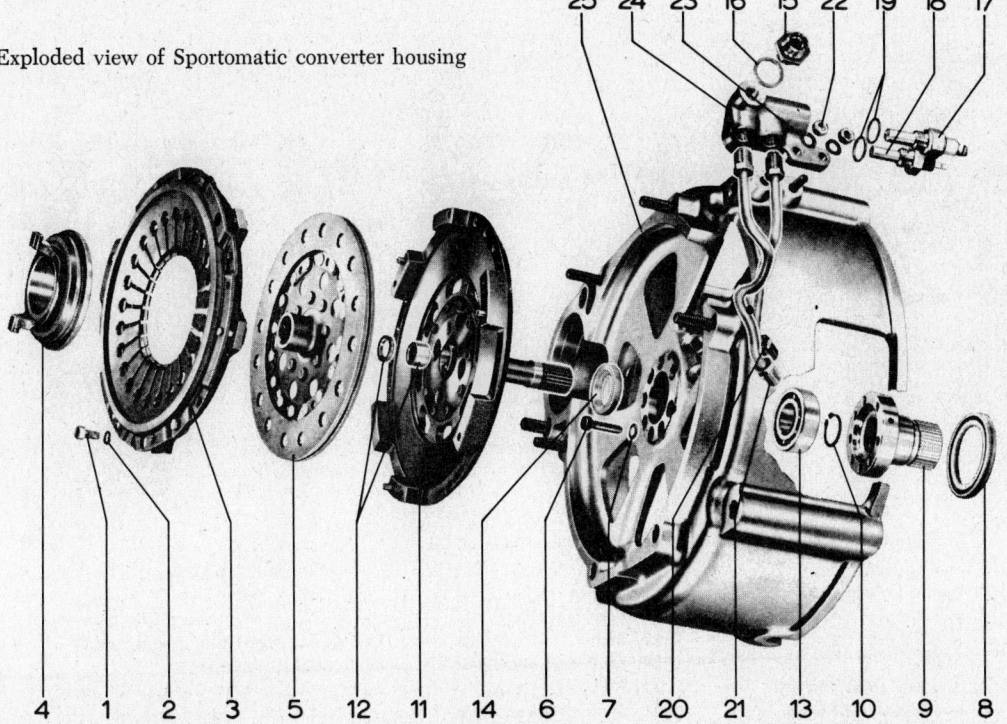

1. Internal screw
2. Spring ring
3. Plate spring clutch with pressure plate
4. Throwout bearing
5. Clutch plate
6. Internal screw
7. Sealing Washer
8. Sealing ring
9. Freewheeling unit
10. Locking ring
11. Carrier plate
12. Sealing ring and needle bearing
13. Grooved ball bearing
14. Sealing ring
15. Double connection
16. Sealing ring
17. Tele-thermometer transmitter
18. Temperature switch
19. Sealing ring
20. Pressure pipe
21. Return flow pipe
22. Nut
23. Spring plate
24. Switch housing
25. Converter housing

1. Torque converter
2. Nut
3. Spring washer
4. Nut
5. Spring washer
6. Converter housing
7. Cotter pin
8. Washer
9. Bolt
10. Nut
11. Spring washer
12. Servo motor
13. Transmission

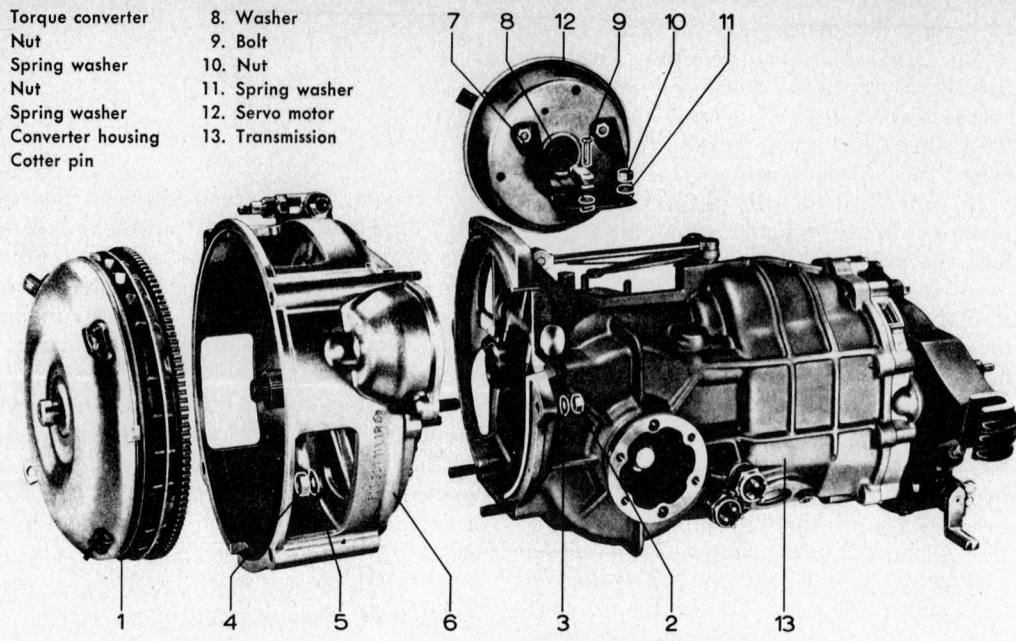

Sportomatic servo motor, converter housing and transmission

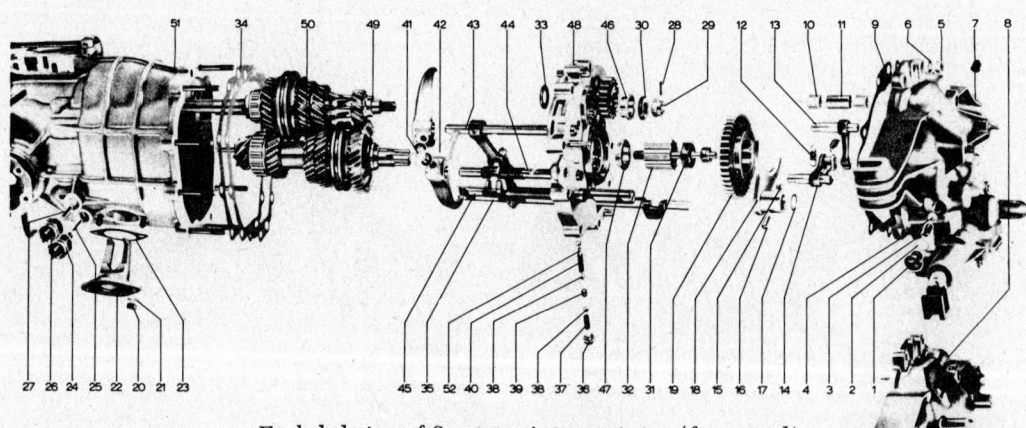

Exploded view of Sportomatic transmission (four speed)

1. Closing screw	19. Gear wheel reverse gear	37. Spring
2. Sealing ring	20. Nut	38. Ball 9 mm. dia.
3. Spring for parking lock	21. Spring ring	39. Locking piece
4. Ball 9 mm.	22. Fork piece	40. Spring with pin for gear lock
5. Self-locking screw	23. Seal	41. Screw with spring washer
6. Washer	24. Bridging switch	42. Shift forks
7. Gearbox cover 914	25. Plunger	43. Shift rod 3rd and 4th gear
8. Gearbox cover 914/6	26. Switch backup lights	44. Shift rod 1st and 2nd gear
9. Seal	27. Plunger	45. Shift rod for parking lock and
10. Needle bearing	28. Clamping sleeve	reverse gear
11. Spacer bushing	29. Castle nut	46. Bearing inner race
12. Draw spring	30. Washer	47. Bearing inner race
13. Pawl for parking lock	31. Expanding screw	48. Intermediate plate
14. Lever for parking lock	32. Spline shaft sleeve	49. Driving shaft
15. Ball 7 mm.	33. Axial needle bearing	50. Driven shaft
16. Bolt	34. Seal	51. Transmission housing
17. Locking ring	35. Shift rod	52. Pin, gear lock
18. Shift fork for reverse gear	36. Closing screw	

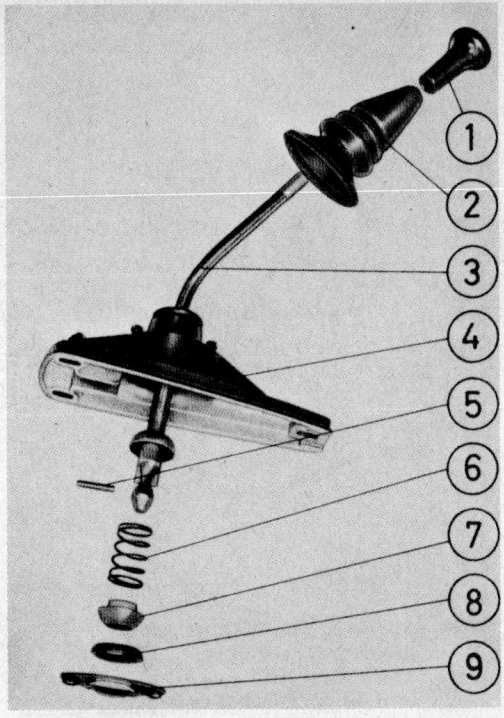

1 Gear shift knob   6 Spring
2 Rubber boot   7 Ball
3 Gear shift lever   8 Socket
4 Gear shift bracket   9 Retaining plate
5 Roll pin

Type 356 gearshift

Type 356 gearshift—lower assembly

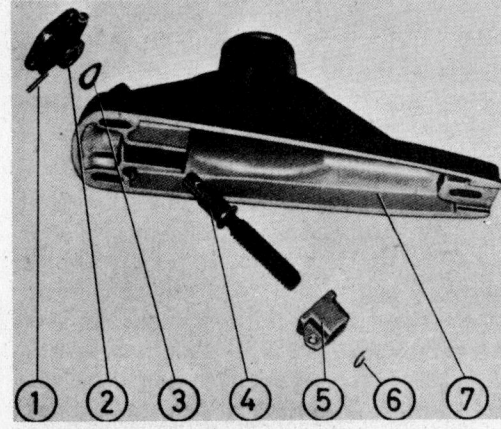

1 Roll pin
2 Heater control knob
3 Spring washer
4 Spindle for heater control
5 Heater cable anchor
6 Lock ring
7 Gear shift bracket

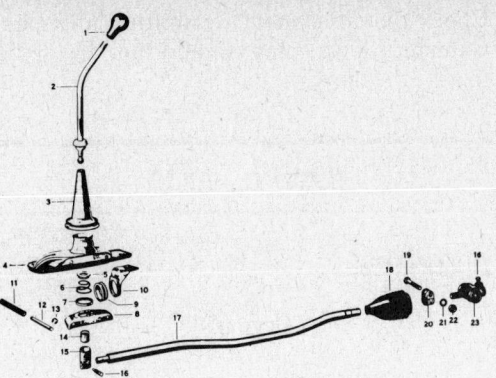

Gearshift Assembly for 911–912.

1	Gearshift knob	12	Guide pin
2	Gearshift lever	13	Retainer
3	Dust boot	14	Ball socket
4	Gearshift base	15	Shift rod joint
5	Spring seat	16	Tapered screw
6	Gearshift spring	17	Shift rod
7	Spring seat	18	Dust boot
8	Gearshift stop plate	19	Hex bolt
9	Guide bushing	20	Clamp
10	Guide bracket	21	Serrated washer
11	Stop plate thrust spring	22	Hex nut
		23	Shift rod coupling

Type 911-912 gearshift assembly—Type 914 and 914/6 gearshift assembly is identical from the shift lever to the springs. Below the springs the parts differ.

INSTALLATION

When installing the shift assembly, thread the heater cable anchor with its eye toward the front of the car. Lubricate all moving parts. Center the shift and guide and install shift housing with position marks aligned. If adjustment is necessary, place shift lever and transmission in second gear and adjust rod at clamp (forward of rear seat) so there is no tension.

Shift Linkage

ADJUSTMENT

Type 911 and 912

Remove the cover from the rear of the center tunnel. Loosen the bolt in the shift rod clamp. Place the transmission in neutral and move the shift lever of the transmission selector shaft completely forward. Move the gearshift lever completely forward to stop. Insert a serrated washer under the bolt and torque to 18 ft. lbs.

Check the adjustment by shifting all gears. Gearshift lever play should be the same in all directions.

Drive Axle

Differential

TYPE 356

Disassembly

With the brake backing plates off and the axle tubes removed, the differential can be lifted through the left side opening of the transmission.

Hold the differential in a vise to remove bolts from ring gear. Remove differential carrier cover and rear axle with gear and

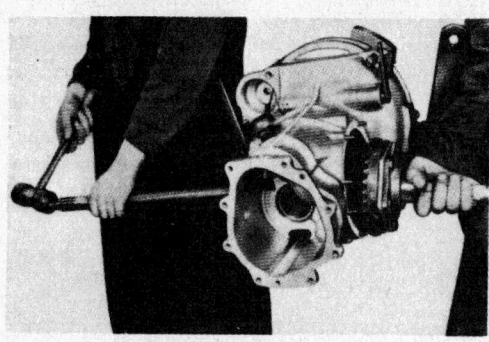

Remove entire differential with axles from the left opening of transmission housing.

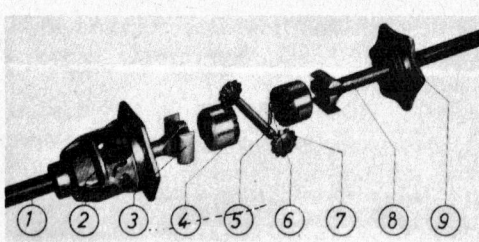

1 Half-axle, right
2 Differential carrier
3 Fulcrum plate
4 Differential side gear
5 Differential pinion shaft
6 Pin
7 Differential pinion gear
8 Half-axle, left
9 Cover

Exploded view of Type 356 differential assembly

side gears. Check rear axles and differential gears for wear and damage. (The side gear has 17 teeth; the pinion gear, 11). Inspect rear axle alignment. Small deviations may be corrected using press. Permissible run-out measured on ball bearing seat is 0.03 mm (.0012"). Inspect ring gear for wear and damage. If necessary, replace together with the pinion.

The differential gears are exchanged in pairs. The rear axle shafts and differential gears (divided into 3 size groups) must have the same color markings. The assembly tolerance of the rear axle (measured on the large diameter of the flat end) is 0.03 to 0.10 mm (.0012" to .0039"). Excessive clearance causes rear axle noises.

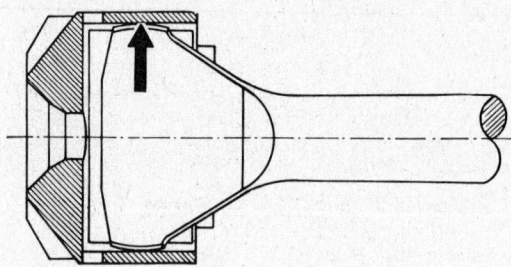

Excessive clearance causes rear axle noises.

Assembly

Lubricate and assemble cleaned parts, checking rear axle clearance, fulcrum plates

Type 356 differential measurements

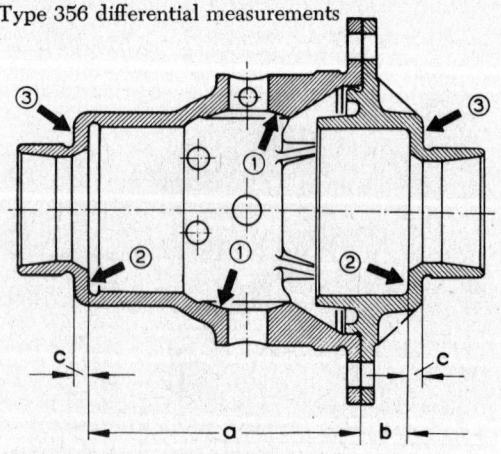

1 Bearing surface for differential pinion
2 Bearing surface for side gear
3 Surface for spacer ring
a Depth of differential carrier 109 mm (4.290 in.)
b Depth of differential carrier cover 19 mm (.750 in.)
c Minimum wall thickness 4.0 mm (.157 in.)

and rear axle gear. Use over-size fulcrum plates to eliminate excessive play. Permissible clearance is 0.05 mm (.002″). Secure differential pinion shaft by peening locking pin. Clean surfaces on differential carrier and ring gear before installing. Install bolts with locking plates or safety wire.

Differential Side Gear & Axle Shaft Identification (Type 356)

Paint Mark	Side Gear Inner Diameter	Axle Shaft Outer Diameter
Blue	2.3609″- 2.3622″	2.3583″- 2.3597″
Pink	2.3630″- 2.3638″	2.3601″- 2.3609″
Green	2.3642″- 2.3649″	2.3613″- 2.3622″

Rear axle shafts and differential side gears are paired and fall into the above three groups. The marking on the side gear in the form of a dot, is painted in the recess of the gear. The axle shaft marking in the form of a circle, is painted about six inches from the flat end of the shaft.

Type 912, 911, 914 and 914/6

Disassembly

The differential can be removed without removing the engine and transmission assembly. However, to make adjustments or to replace parts, the engine and transmission assembly should be removed.

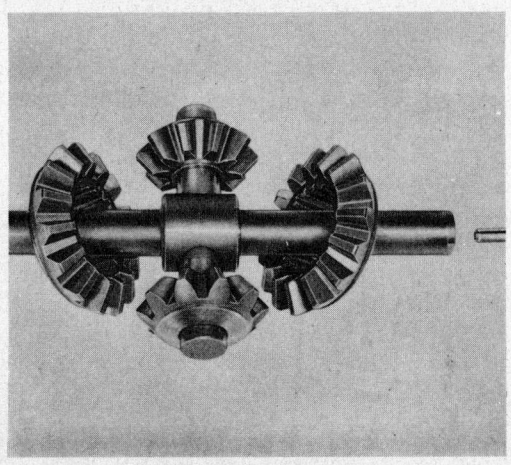

Internal view of differential

Detach both rear axle half-shafts at the differential flanges. Detach the clutch cable and rear throttle linkage. Remove the differential side bearings. Note the thickness of the spacer for correct assembly. Remove the pin retaining the shaft. Using a driver, remove the spider gear and the side gear shaft. Turn the spider gears to the side and pull through the opening in the differential carrier. Remove the ring gear. Remove the differential side gears through the larger opening in the differential carrier.

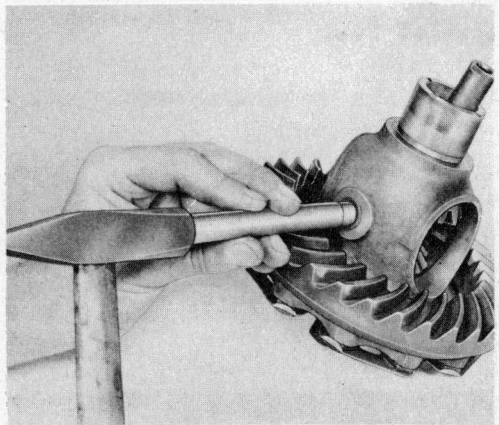

Remove the spider gear shaft

Assembly

Coat the sides of the side and spider gears inside the differential carrier with molybdenum disulphide paste and insert the gears through the side openings of the differential carrier. Position these with the aid of the axle flanges. Slide the spider gears through the side opening and position them so that the shaft will pass through. Rotate the spider gears until their bores align with those in the carrier. Insert the side gear shaft and drive the spider gear shaft in, orienting the roll pin bore towards the axles. Drive the roll pin into place. Prior to this assembly, remove the axle flanges. Place the ring gear on the carrier and torque the bolts to 69-72 ft. lbs. Insert the bolt locking plates in the grooves of the bolts and bend the plates down over one of the bolt sides. Determine the thickness of the spacers to be used. Install the side bearings. Install the outer races of the side bearings by heating the transmission housing or cover to approximately 248° F. Adjust the ring gear. Be sure that the side

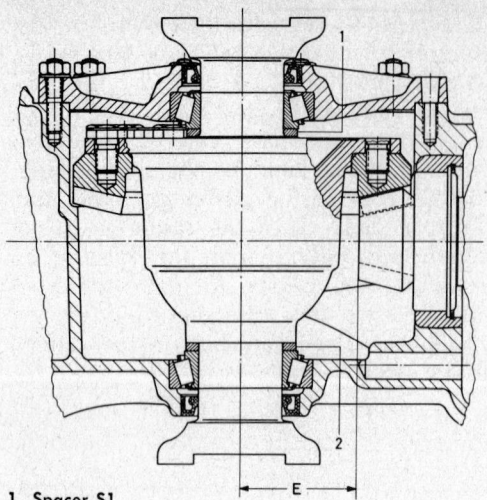

1. Spacer S1
2. Spacer S-2
E. Adjustment value

Cross-sectional view of differential adjustment spacers

bearing outer races are well seated in the transmission housing or cover. Install, on the ring gear side of the differential carrier, a spacer (S1, see illustration) .138" thick. On the other side, place a spacer (S2, see illustration) .118" thick. Place these spacers under the side bearings and install the side bearings. Insert the differential with side bearings into the transmission housing. Install the transmission housing cover (without oil seal) onto the housing along with a gasket .0079" thick. Slightly tighten the cover with two nuts (180° apart) to 18 ft. lbs. and check the gap between the cover and the gasket with

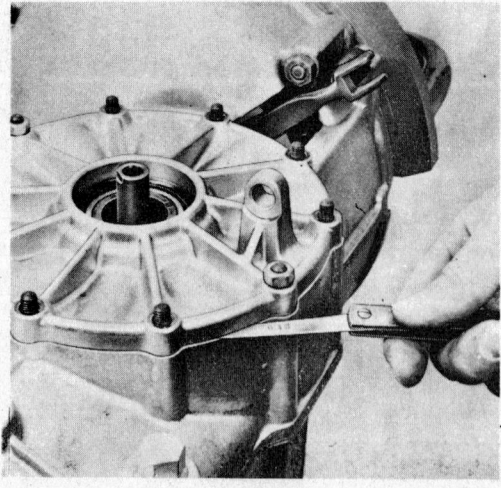

Check the gap between cover and gasket with feeler gauge.

a feeler gauge. This should be approximately .006". Select a ring gear side spacer to provide a preload clearance of .006".

EXAMPLE

Clearance determined by feeler gauge: .016"

Minus desired preload clearance: .006"

The installed .138" thick spacer (S1) to be replaced by one .010" thinner i.e., .128".

Tighten the housing cover using a .0079" gasket. Insert the axle flange with a thrust washer and tighten the bolt slightly. Measure the drag of the installed differential (the pinion shaft must not be engaged and the axle flange oil seal must not be present). The differential drag should be between 15.6 and 20.8 in. lbs. This measurement will indicate that the side bearing is properly preloaded. If not, replace the spacer with one of proper thickness. Withdraw the differential, remove both side bearings and measure the total thickness of all spacers with a micrometer. Measure each spacer at four different points. This figure indicates the spacer thickness of ring gear adjustment. In preparation for further ring and pinion adjustment, spacer S1 should be .0393" thinner than ½ of spacer total, and spacer S2 should be .0393" thicker than ½ of spacer total.

EXAMPLE

$$\text{Total thickness of spacer S1 + S2} \quad .246''$$

$$\text{Thickness of spacer S1} \left(\frac{.246''}{2}\right) \begin{array}{r} .123'' \\ - .039'' \\ \hline .084'' \end{array}$$

$$\text{Thickness of spacer S2} \left(\frac{.246''}{2}\right) \begin{array}{r} .123'' \\ + .039'' \\ \hline .162'' \end{array}$$

Spacers are available in increments of .004" from .08" to .020". Due to a .010" washer, adjustments to the nearest .002" are possible. The calculated thickness of spacers should be rounded off to match the actual (available) spacer thickness, as long as rounding-off does not alter the value of total spacer thickness (S1 + S2). Permissible variation in spacer thickness should not exceed .0007". Be sure to remove any burrs from the spacers before measuring. Adjust the pinion shaft depth. This has been roughly adjusted through determination and placement of proper spacers.

Assemble the pinion shaft and ring gear and make a gear tooth contact pattern (see illustration). Depending upon the results obtained from this test, the pinion will have to be moved closer to, or farther from, the ring gear. For this purpose paper gaskets are available from Porsche dealers in sizes of .004″, .006″, and .008″.

Proper tooth contact—The left side is the drive side and the right side is the coast side.

Heavy heel contact is shown on the left (drive side) and on the right (coast side). Move the ring gear closer to the pinion.

Heavy toe contact is illustrated. The drive side is on the left, while the coast side is on the right. Move the ring gear away from the pinion.

Heavy heel contact is shown on the left (drive side) and heavy toe contact is shown on the right (coast side). Move the pinion away from the ring gear.

Heavy toe contact is shown on the left (drive side) while heavy heel contact is shown on the right (coast side). Move the pinion toward the ring gear.

Gaskets may be installed in thickness ranging from .004″ - .020″. If this is insufficient for obtaining proper gear tooth contact pattern, it will be necessary to disassemble the pinion shaft and change the adjustment shims accordingly. Adjust the ring gear backlash. Insert the preassembled intermediate plate with gears, selector shafts and paper gaskets (determined at the time of pinion adjustment)into the transmission housing. Place spacer bushings on four opposing studs on the housing and tighten. The pinion shaft stretchbolt must be torqued to 79-86 ft. lbs. before making any measurements. Install the differential unit, side bearings and spacers (S1 and S2) into the transmission housing. Install the side cover with a .008″ paper gasket. When tightening the side cover retaining nuts, continuously check to ensure that the ring and pinion gear do not bind or jam. Torque all side cover nuts to 18 ft. lbs. Block the pinion shaft at the stretchbolt and insert the axle flange into the differential. Mount a dial gauge on the assembly and measure the amount of gear backlash. Repeat the measurement at every 90° of gear rotation. The values must not differ by more than .002″ at each point of measurement. The exact amount of gear backlash is etched on the ring gear (ring and pinion gears may only be installed in matched sets which are mated at the factory). Gear backlash should be between .0047″ and .007″. To adjust the amount of ring gear backlash, spacers (S1 and S2) can be replaced. If the amount of backlash is to be adjusted, care must be taken to be sure that the total spacer thickness is not changed. Check the axle flange oil seals and replace if defective. Replace the engine and transmission assembly if these were removed or attach both rear axle half-shafts at the differential flanges and connect the throttle linkage and clutch cable.

ZF MULTIPLE DISC SELF LOCKING DIFFERENTIAL (OPTIONAL)

Conventional differentials transmit torque to the wheel which is easiest to turn. This path of least resistance is eliminated to a great degree by the self locking differential. The torque transmitted to the differential does not transfer directly to the spider gears, but over the two side gear rings which cannot rotate but slide

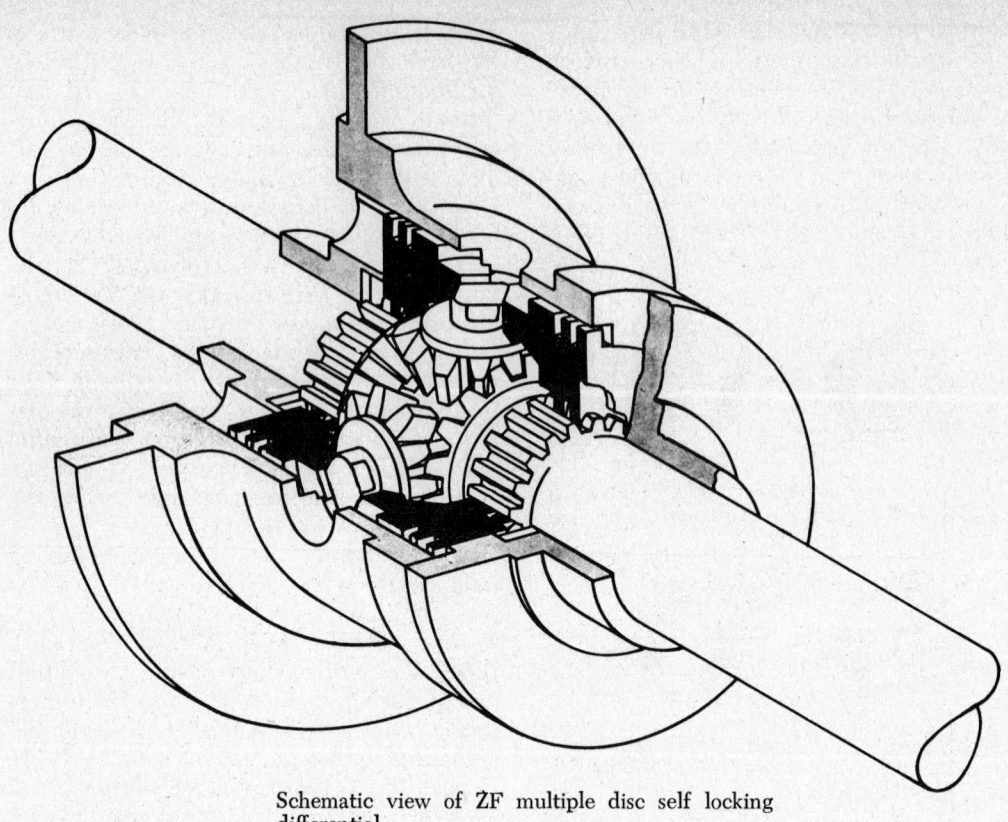

Schematic view of ZF multiple disc self locking
differential

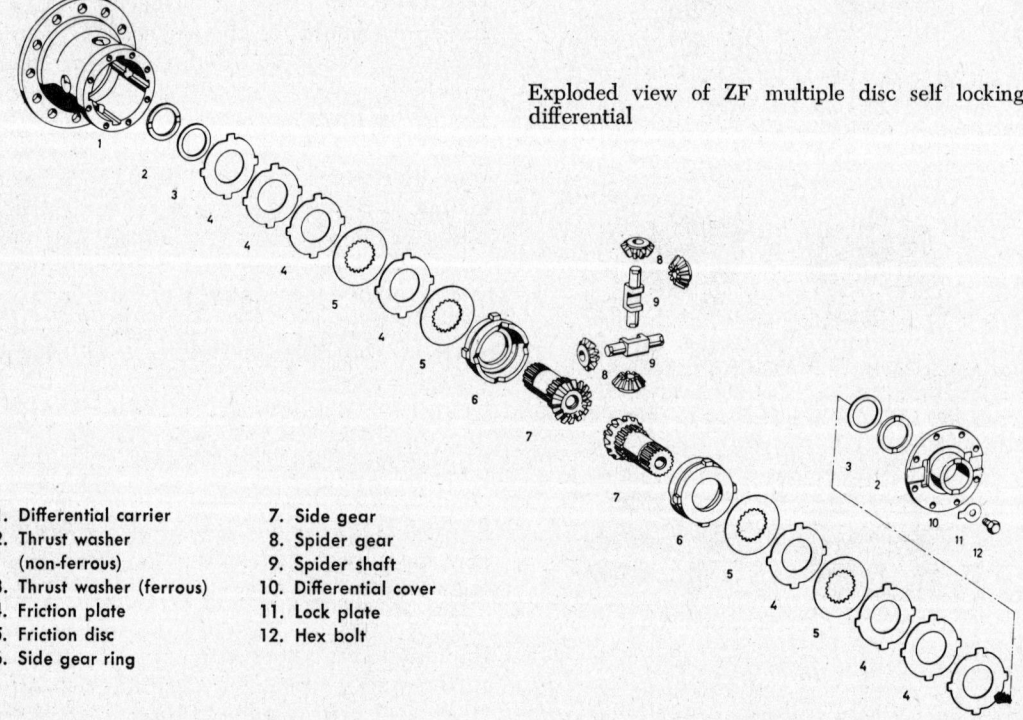

Exploded view of ZF multiple disc self locking
differential

1. Differential carrier
2. Thrust washer
   (non-ferrous)
3. Thrust washer (ferrous)
4. Friction plate
5. Friction disc
6. Side gear ring

7. Side gear
8. Spider gear
9. Spider shaft
10. Differential cover
11. Lock plate
12. Hex bolt

axially in the differential carrier. The force resulting from the transfer of torque forces the side gears apart exerting pressure on the preloaded friction discs. The axle shafts become locked to the differential unit preventing the possibility of the torque taking the path of least resistance. The ZF differential offers the dual advantage of a constant locking effect in the differential and a torque governed locking effect which is always proportionate to engine torque.

Lubrication

The only lubricant approved for this differential (ZF-optional) is Shell Transmission Oil S 1747A. This oil is known as indicated in the following countries:

United States: Shell HDR Gear Oil 90 E.P.
Canada: Shell HDR Gear Oil 90
Australia: Shell SCL Gear Oil 90

Disassembly

Remove the differential from the car following the procedure outlined in the standard differential section. Unlock the safety plate tabs and remove the bolts and cover. Remove the thrust washers, friction plates and discs, side gear ring and side gear. Withdraw the spider gears and spider shafts from the differential carrier.

Remove spider gears and shafts from differential carrier

Remove friction plates and discs, thrust washers, side gear ring and side gear.

Remove the second side gear, side gear ring, multiple disc retarder and thrust washers from the differential carrier. Note the sequential location of the retarder discs and plates. The original arrangement must not be disturbed. The ZF self locking differential is preset at the factory for an effectiveness of 50%. This value has been

Remove the second side gear, side gear ring, multiple disc retarders and thrust washers from the differential carrier.

carefully determined and increasing the preset effectiveness is not recommended. With the differential disassembled, check the differential carrier thrust surfaces for wear or grooving. Check the friction plate locating grooves for wear. Check the thrust surface of the differential cover. Check the side gear thrust surfaces, which should not be obviously worn or grooved. The side gear rings must move freely in the differential carrier.

Assembly

Coat all contact surfaces of the friction discs with MOLYKOTEPASTE "G" prior to assembly. Also coat the contact surfaces of the friction plates, side gear rings and spider shafts. The entire retarder assembly must be checked for an installation length of 3.213″ - 3.240″ under a pressure of 220 lbs. (See illustration, distance "a".) The tolerance between minimum and maximum includes the maximum permissible wear of all parts. Determine the length of the assembly with the differential out of the carrier and placed in a press. If the value cannot be reached, it will be necessary to determine which parts are worn and replace them. The wear may occur at the friction plates or discs, the side gear rings or the slanted ramps of the spider shafts. Place the differential carrier on a bench with the large opening up. The non-ferrous thrust washer fits into the differential carrier with the machined recess down. Insert the ferrous thrust washer on top of the nonferrous thrust washer. Place the friction discs and plates into the carrier in the same sequence as removed. A friction plate is placed at the differential carrier as well as the cover. In differentials equipped with preloaded friction disc and plate assemblies, be sure that the undulated friction discs are placed next to the differential carrier and the differential cover. The plate undulation should be arranged so that a free space exists between the differential carrier or differential cover and the mating friction plate (see illustration). Special attention should be

given to the proper positioning of the friction discs and plates. The self locking effectiveness could have been inadvertently changed. Place one side gear ring onto the friction discs and plates. Insert one side gear so that the splines engage the teeth of the friction disc. Place two spider gears on each spider shaft. Place the spider shafts across each other and insert their seats into the differential carrier. Place the second side gear on the four spider gears

Place the second side gear onto the four spider gears, followed by the second side gear ring.

Plate undulation arrangement

Undulated friction plate

Oil groove

Differential carrier or cover , respectively

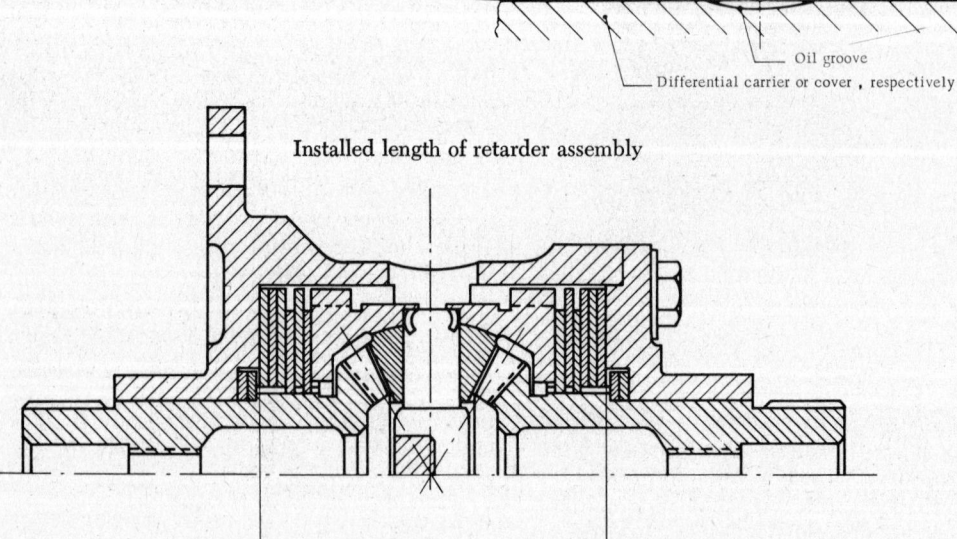

Installed length of retarder assembly

a

and place the second side gear ring on top. Insert the second set of friction discs and plates. Particular attention should be given to the oil groove, as in the installation

Replace the second set of friction discs and plates.

of the first set. Place the ferrous thrust washer, followed by the non-ferrous thrust washer, with the machined groove facing up, onto the side gear. Place the differential cover on the differential carrier, and torque the bolts to 18 ft. lbs. The assembled differential must turn freely without binding under a torque of 7.2-10.8 ft. lbs. Moderate noises may occur, when going through sharp curves under power, but these are inherent in the design of the unit and will not damage the differential. NOTE: *The ZF multiple disc self locking differential may be installed with Nadella half shafts only.*

Axle Tubes

TYPE 356, 912 AND 911

Removal

Remove the brake drums and the brake backing plates. Loosen the nuts on the bearing cover of the axle tubes and remove the axle tube with the bearing cover and the gasket. Drive the dowel pin from the bearing flange. Press the bearing flange from the axle tube. Remove the boot and bearing cover from the axle tube.

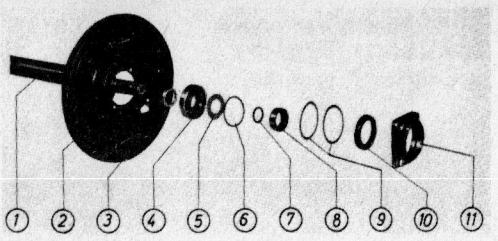

Rear wheel bearings and axle tube.

1 Axle tube
2 Brake backing plate
3 Spacer ring, inner
4 Ball bearing
5 Washer
6 Seal
7 Seal
8 Spacer ring, outer
9 Shims
10 Oil seal
11 Bearing cover

Exploded view of rear axle tube

Installation

Axle tube installation is the reverse of removal. Inspect the rear axle tube boot and replace if worn. Clean the mating surfaces of the bearing flange and coat the bearing flange and axle tube with a light coat of grease. Press the flange on the tube. Install new axle flange gaskets (.004"-.012") as required. After installation, the axle tube must move freely with no noticeable play. To remove play, add or subtract gaskets. If this will not remove play, it may be necessary to replace the axle tube.

Half Shafts

REMOVAL

Raise the car and remove both rear wheels. Remove the cotter pin from the castellated nut and remove the nut. Remove the Allen bolts from the half shaft flange, knock the half shaft from its seat and remove.

INSTALLATION

Place a new gasket ring on the half shaft stub, lightly oil the splines and insert the stub in the wheel hub. Torque the Allen bolts in the half shaft flange as follows:
Nadella half shaft: 34 ft. lbs.
Lobro half shaft: 31 ft. lbs.
The flange surface of the half shaft must be free of grease at the time of installation. Tighten the half shaft castellated nut to a torque of 217-253 ft. lbs. and secure with a new cotter pin.

Universal Shaft

Type 914 and 914/6

Removal

   Unlock the castellated nut of the universal shaft and remove the nut. Remove the heat exchanger. Loosen the universal shaft screws from the universal flange and remove the universal shaft. Be sure the flange surfaces are not damaged.

1. Hex. nut	17. Spring washer
2. Spring ring	18. Holding plate
3. Bearing Bolt	19. Protective cover
4. Washer	20. Hex. bolt
5. Spring strut	21. Lock washer
6. Hex. bolt	22. Shim plate
7. Spring washer	23. Shim
8. Caliper	24. Self-locking hex. nut
9. Hex. bolt	25. Hex. bolt
10. Brake disk	26. Spring ring
11. Cotter pin	27. Bearing cap
12. Castle nut	28. Radial taper ball
13. Washer	bearing
14. Universal shaft	29. Self-locking hex. nut
15. Wheel hub	30. Control arm bearing
16. Hex. bolt	31. Rear axle control arm

Exploded view of Type 914 rear hub assembly

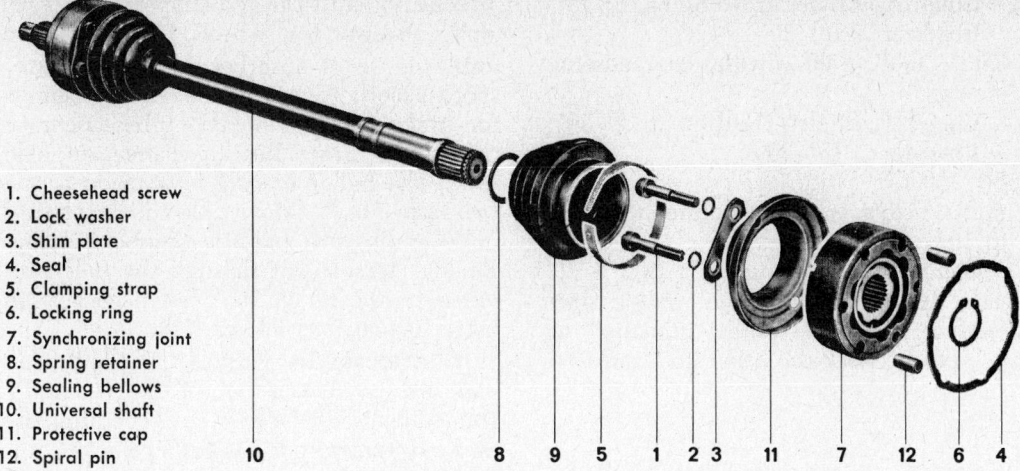

1. Cheesehead screw
2. Lock washer
3. Shim plate
4. Seal
5. Clamping strap
6. Locking ring
7. Synchronizing joint
8. Spring retainer
9. Sealing bellows
10. Universal shaft
11. Protective cap
12. Spiral pin

10   8   9   5   1   2 3   11   7   12   6   4

Exploded view of Type 914 universal shaft

Installation

Use a new seal for the flange and be sure that the flange surfaces are absolutely free of burrs and grease. Use new lockwashers and tighten the universal shaft screws on the flange to a torque of 31 ft. lbs. Be sure that the lockwashers rest with their hollow end against the shim plate. Torque the castellated nut to 217-253 ft. lbs.

of the radius arm. Draw in a line that runs across the arm perpendicular to the top edge (90° on protractor). With the chassis level drop a plumb line from the top of the radius arm at the drawn-in line and measure the angle that the plumb line makes with the drawn line.

356B 1600, 1600S (without compensating spring)

Suspension

Rear Wheel

The rear wheels are independently suspended. The splined ends of the torsion bars fit into a splined socket which is welded to the central chassis tube. The rubber-mounted trailing radius arms are connected to the splined outer ends of the torsion bars. The axle tube flanges are bolted to the trailing ends of the radius arms. Suspension is adjusted by engaging the desired splines of the torsion bar. Suspension dampening is controlled by double acting adjustable shock-absorbers.

Correct adjustment of the torsion bar may be obtained by measuring the angle of the radius arm with respect to the horizontal position of the automobile. The radius arm must be unloaded. Place the flat edge of a protractor against the top edge

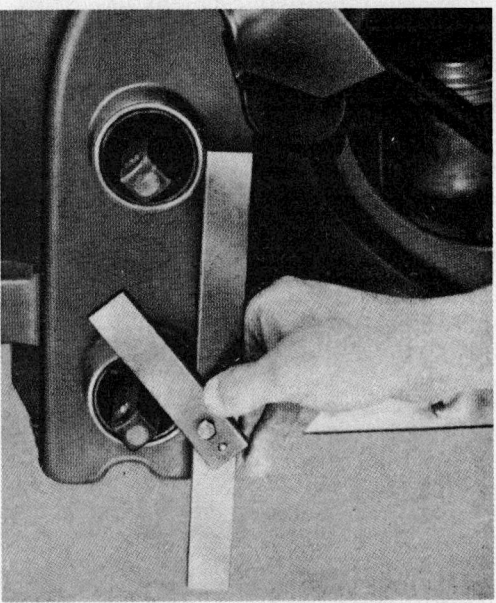

Check torsion bar adjustment. The angle is 40°.

Coupe, Cabriolet/Hardtop = 16° 13′
Roadster = 14° 30′
356B 1600 S-90 (with compensating spring)

Coupe, Cabriolet/Hardtop = 15° 30′
Roadster = 13° 30′
356B 1600GS (with compensating spring that was not original equipment) = 12° to 13°

Camber: −0.5° to 1.5°

The adjustment of both radius arms should be identical. When adjusting one side, always check the other and correct if

necessary. Hoist car and support it on level dolly. Remove rear wheels. Lift radius arm until the shock-absorber is free. Remove shock-absorbers and release holding clamps for brake hoses from axle tubes. Remove three bolts from bearing flange on axle tube. The buffer bracket is fastened to the two upper bolts. Move axle tube rearward out of radius arm and inner rubber bearing. Remove torsion bar through the hole provided in the body. It is not necessary to mark torsion bars left or right.

If the torsion bar is fractured, the broken end can be driven out of the internally splined central tube by a steel rod after the opposite torsion bar has been removed. Inspect torsion bars for damaged splines and condition of paint, especially for traces of rust. Grease the splines of the torsion bar. Install torsion bar so that its splines engage the socket in the frame. Position radius arm on outer end of torsion bar.

Measure angle between unloaded radius arm and horizontal (as described with plumb line). A noticeable variation between the actual angle of the radius arm and the specified angle can be corrected by changing the position of the radius arm, the torsion bar, or both. The different number of splines on either end of the torsion bar permit diverse adjustment. When the inner end of the torsion bar is advanced one spline it turns 9°. When the radius arm is moved one spline it gives a change of 8° 10′. As a result the minimum adjustment of the radius arm is 0° 50′. The adjustment of the right and left radius arms may vary up to ±30′. The greater angle should be on the driver side.

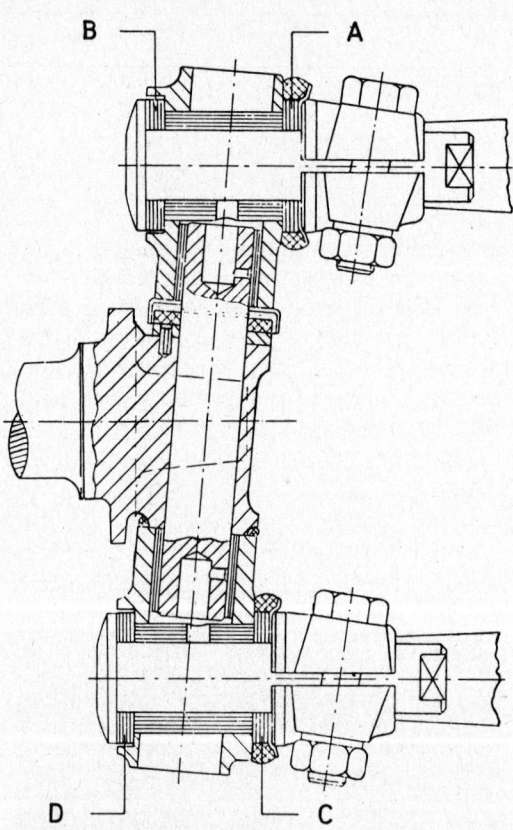

Shims on suspension arm.

Offset (toward inside) of top		Upper suspension shims		Lower suspension shims	
inches	(mm)	inner (A)	outer (B)	inner (C)	outer (D)
.200	(5)	3	7	7	3
.217	(5.5)	4	6	7	3
.236	(6)	4	6	6	4
.246	(6.5)	5	5	6	4
.276	(7)	5	5	5	5
.295	(7.5)	6	4	5	5
.315	(8)	6	4	4	6
.335	(8.5)	7	3	4	6
.354	(9)	7	3	3	7

Front Wheel

TYPE 356, 912 AND 911

There are two major front suspension systems on Porsches, both with torsion bars. The 912 and 911, which share the same body shell, have each front wheel independently suspended on a shock-absorber strut that is mounted at the top to the wheel well and at the bottom to a transverse control arm attached through a torsion bar to a crossmember. The torsion bar is adjustable and the shock absorber has a progressively-acting rubber buffer. **Cornering** qualities are enhanced by a transverse stabilizer that connects with both wheel struts. The front axle has no lubrication points but the front wheel bearings must be repacked with new grease when repairs are made.

All 356 models have a front axle consisting of two rigid tubes, welded to the frame, each of which carries a torsion bar that is anchored in the center. Suspension arms attached to the torsion bars support the stub axle of each wheel. The front axle tubes, suspension arms and steering knuckle approximately form a parallelogram. A stabilizing bar connects both wheels.

The front axle should be lubricated at regular intervals of 6000 miles under normal conditions but more often than one every two months in adverse environments. Perfect lubrication of the front axle is with the chassis raised off its wheels. Grease should be applied to the nipples until excess grease begins to emerge at the edges of the joints. The front wheel bearings are best cleaned and repacked with grease once a year.

After servicing steering or front suspension it is advisable to check every front end part because all of the assemblies are so closely interrelated. First, check the front end for worn or loose-fitting parts. Repair or replace what is faulty. Second, inspect and adjust the steering gear assembly. Third, set the front end alignment. And lastly, balance the wheels.

To find front-end troubles quickly, follow these simple checks.

1. With the front end jacked up, rock or shake both wheels simultaneously to detect any looseness between them. Tie-rod and steering linkage joints sometimes loosen under severe road stresses. Check for weakness in the joints by shaking and prying against members connected at these joints.

2. Check-out wheel suspension joints by having each wheel shaken up and down while the steering knuckle and control arm joints are observed for play.

3. Spin the wheels rapidly to test for deteriorated bearings. Listen for bearing noise and touch the bumper to feel vibration that rough bearings create.

4. Rig a piece of chalk (as shown) so it just clears the wheel rim and then rotate the wheel to test for wheel runout. The chalk will strike misaligned, protruding rim areas. Repeat test on inside of rim. Wheel

should be straightened if runout exceeds ⅛ inch.

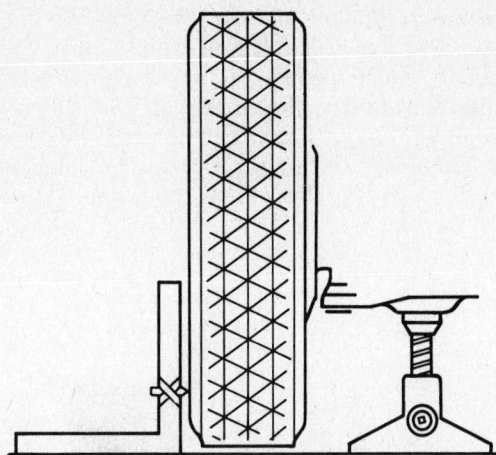

The chalk will mark areas of wheel runout.

5. Lower front end to ground and rebound fenders to check for deteriorated shock absorbers.

6. Check pre-owned cars for possible front end damage by measuring and comparing the wheelbase on both sides. Measure carefully from common points such as from the rear of the front wheel rim to the rear of the back wheel rim. If one side has a shorter or longer wheelbase than is listed in Porsche specifications, compare several measurements on both sides between various points until the dislocated part is found.

Diagonal measurements from right front to left rear wheels and from left front to right rear wheels will uncover a distorted chassis (even if wheelbase measurements are equal). A twisted chassis will alter tracking and make front end alignment difficult if not impossible.

FRONT END ALIGNMENT

Front end alignment centers on the precise geometric relationship of a number of parts—even when they are changing positions—so that there is always wheel stability and control. The geometric angles include steering axis inclination, caster, camber, included angle, toe-in, and toe-out (turning arc).

Steering axis inclination, or kingpin slant as termed when kingpins were standard, is the angle (from the vertical) of the steering knuckle or shock-absorber strut (in 911 and 912). The slant of the steering knuckle controls wheel direction stability by forcing the wheel to lift the chassis in order to turn from a straight ahead direction. As the steering wheel is released from a turn, the front wheels return to the straight ahead position under the force of the chassis weight. The inclination is not adjustable.

Camber is the angle that the wheel makes with vertical. The top of the wheel slants

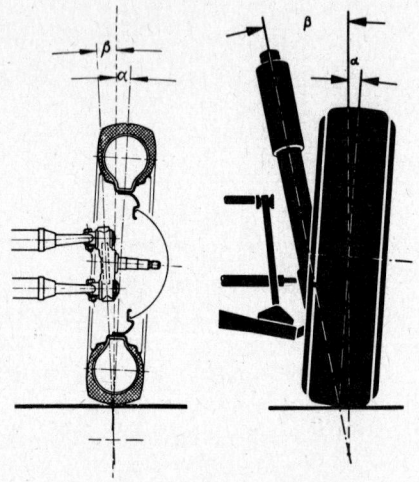

Camber and inclination angle of front wheels. Left side: Angle a = camber ($0°40'\pm30'$). Angle β = inclination ($4°30'$). Rear wheel camber = $+45'\pm$ 35'.

out from the car (positive) so that the center of the tire meets the road at a point projected along the steering axis inclination. Placing the weight of the car directly over this pivot point allows easiest steering and takes some load off the outside wheel bearing.

Rear wheel camber affects the steering performance of the car. Early Porsches in some cases have an oversteering response. This characteristic can be lessened by adjusting the radius arms so that the rear wheels have a zero or a slight negative camber. Remember that significant negative camber increases wear on tires and reduces suspension travel.

On 912–911 suspensions, rear wheel camber is adjusted by the inside eccentric nut located ahead of the fixed control arm.

Included angle is found by adding the steering axis inclination to the wheel camber. This total must be equal on both front

wheels regardless of individual differences in axis cant or camber between the wheels. If the included angles of the two sides are different, a wheel spindle might be bent, possibly from striking a curb sharply.

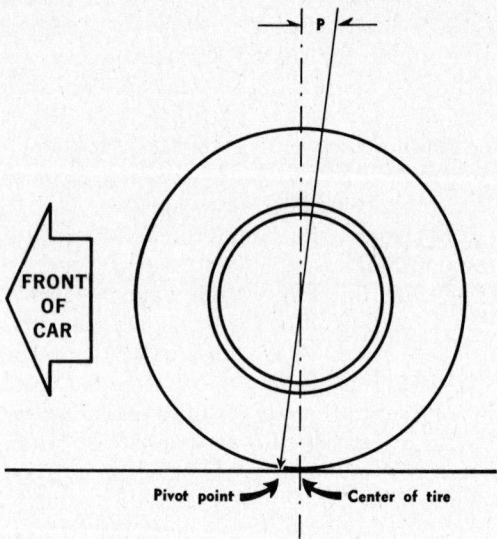

Positive caster. The pivot point ahead of the center-line of the tire holds the wheel stable.

Positive caster is the slant of the top of the steering knuckle (or shock-absorber strut) toward the rear of the car. Caster gives the wheel another type of directional stability by moving the pivot point of the wheel forward of the tire's center. Positioning the pivot point ahead of center causes a drag on the bottom of the wheel (at the center) when it turns, thereby resisting the turn and tending to hold the wheel steady in whatever direction it is going. The same principle of drag holds a weather vane pointer into the wind. The vane's bulky part seeks the point of minimum resistance behind the pivot.

Too slight a caster angle will cause the wheels to wander or weave at high speed and steer erratically when the brakes are applied. Too great a caster angle creates hard steering and shimmy at low speeds.

Caster and camber values in all models might exceed the specification limits if the body is tilted or if torsion bars are not properly adjusted. If torsion bars are set and caster or camber is still not correct, there is damage to some part of the front end.

Caster and camber cannot be adjusted on

911 models up to chassis serial number 302 694, and on numbers 302 736 and 302 805. Measurements not meeting specifications indicate damage or wear to the suspension strut or other parts.

Caster and camber adjustments can be made on other 911 and 912 suspensions. Pull back enough trunk carpeting for access to the three retaining screws of the strut position adjustment. Scrape off and clean the pressure plates and the movable dish ring with a tar solvent. Mark position of the single-hole and two-hole plates and loosen retaining screws.

Reset dish ring together with suspension strut end toward side of car to obtain the desired camber adjustment; resetting the dish ring by 1 mm equals a 6 minute change in suspension strut angle. Reset dish ring and suspension strut toward front or back of car for caster adjustment. Reseal surfaces around the pressure plates and dish ring with non-hardening sealer.

Toe-in, usually measured in inches, is the amount that both wheels are closer together

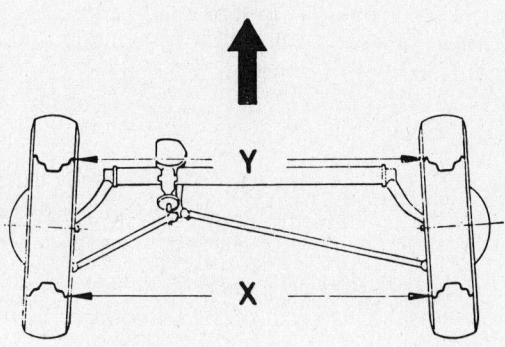

Toe-in of front wheels: x-y = 2±1 mm (.0788″± .0394″). Rear wheel toe-in: .00±.059″, 0.0±1.5 mm (0°±10′).

relation to the dash. Mark this spoke with chalk, tape or a piece of string. Turn wheel to opposite lock, and note position of lower spoke to dash. The points on the dash should be in the same relative position (on opposite sides of the wheel) if steering wheel is perfectly placed on its shaft. Set the steering wheel to its midpoint (wheels straight ahead) and adjust the left and right tie rods. One turn of the tie rod changes toe-in approximately one-third inch. Make adjustments on 912–911 suspension with wheels pressed together at the front under a force of 33 lbs. Note that the car must be at curb weight with a full gas tank and a spare wheel on board.

Rear wheel toe-in can be corrected by adjusting position of the axle tube. Minimum toe-in increases driving stability and ensures minimum tire wear. If one rear wheel has toe-in while the other has toe-out, the rear axle is not parallel to the front axle. On 912–911 suspensions, tracking is adjusted by the eccentric nut located forward of the camber adjustment. It is possible that if the tracking adjustment required a considerable change at the eccentric, the position of the camber eccentric nut might be in the extreme right or left end of the oblong cavity in the radius arm. In such a case the eccentric nut should be turned around 180° (a half turn) to prevent binding.

Turning angle differential. The difference angle, sometimes called toe-out, is the difference between the arcs that the two wheels make in a turn. As the front end turns, the outside wheel describes a larger circle than does the inside wheel. The turning angle of the inside wheel (right wheel

at the front than at the rear. Toe-in is related to wheel camber and compression forces on the steering linkage with forward speed. The greater the camber, the greater is the toe-in, usually. Set toe-in only after checking caster and camber.

Toe-in must be adjusted with the steering gear at its midpoint since otherwise the wheel turning angle would not be the same on both sides. Turn steering wheel to lock, holding wheel against stop and note the position of the lower spoke of the wheel in

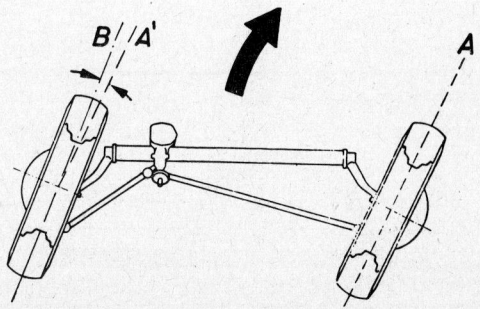

Difference of turning angles when wheel on **inside** of curve is set at 20°, the outside wheel is less **by** (3°10′±20′).

in a right turn) is greater than the outside wheel in the front end trapezoid arrangement of all 356 models. The difference of the two angles is often called toe-out. However the parallel tracking layout of the 912–911 suspension is designed so that there is no significant angular difference between the wheels in a turn. Angular differential (opposite of toe-out in this system) results from the toe-in value of the front wheels and the mechanical clearance in the steering parts.

In either the trapezoid or the parallel-tracking suspension, move wheels to extreme left and right and determine difference angle for each turn. Both angles should be equal if there is no damage to any front end parts. If the front end is otherwise aligned and the difference angles are not equal, the trouble is in the steering mechanism. The 356 Porsche (not 356A or after) can have the difference angles corrected by moving the steering gear along the axle tube toward the greater angle. Subtract the smaller angle from the large one. Divide this result in half (remember that $1° = 60'$). Correct this angle to the distance the steering box must be moved. $10' = 1.2$ mm; $30' = 3.5$ mm. The 356A and newer models have a dowel pin that holds the position of the steering box—adjustment is not possible.

Chassis height adjustment is critical for complete front end and rear suspension alignment. Check height measurements only after car is at curb weight with a full gas tank and a spare tire. Check tire pressure; measure height from a level floor; mark dead center of wheel on hub caps of front wheel. Set the suspension at proper attitude by depressing front of car several times (push down on the bumper at center) and allowing the body to rebound by itself. Measure the vertical distance between the front wheel center and the floor. Make second measurement from center of torsion bar to floor.

The difference between wheel center and torsion bar center should be 108 mm (4¼″) on the 911 and 912. On these cars the torsion bar is adjustable at the adjustment screw. Difference in height between right and left sides must not be more than 5 mm. See the next section, *Wheel and Suspension Disassembly*, for details on other models.

Rear end height is measured (in principle) in the same way as for the front end, however, the torsion bar is set in a rubber mount which gives somewhat under the weight of the body. Therefore, measure from the floor to the bottom of the bushing. Then measure from the bottom of the bushing mount to the top and divide it in half. Add this distance to the first measurement from the floor to get the theoretical center of the torsion bar. The difference between the wheel center and the torsion bar center is 12 mm ± 5 mm, but the right side should not vary from the left more than 8 mm. Chassis height is adjustable by moving the radius arm on the torsion bar splines.

DISASSEMBLY-TYPE 911 AND 912

Raise car and remove both wheels. Unscrew brake cover shrouds. Disconnect hydraulic line from brake caliper, using a prop to hold brake pedal slightly down so that fluid from reservoir will not drain into lines. Detach caliper line and brake hose from supporting bracket, and pull both out with the retaining spring. Remove caliper mounting bolts and take off entire caliper assembly.

Remove grease cap from wheel hub, unscrew the wheel nut and withdraw the bearing washer. Slide off the wheel hub, brake disc and bearing. Remove the brake carrier (mount for caliper).

Unlock and remove the castle nut on the ball stud, the castle nuts on the transverse control arm, and the hex nut at the top of the shock-absorber strut (in luggage compartment). The strut is now free.

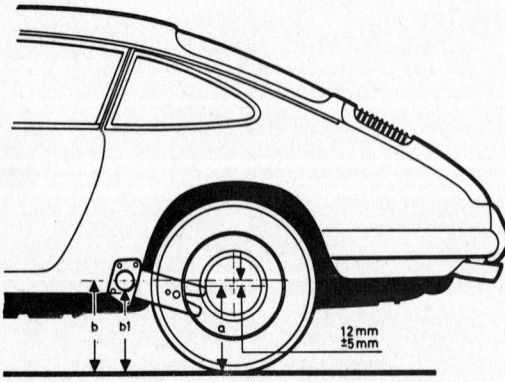

Rear axle height adjustment. 12±5 mm (0.47°± 0.2″).

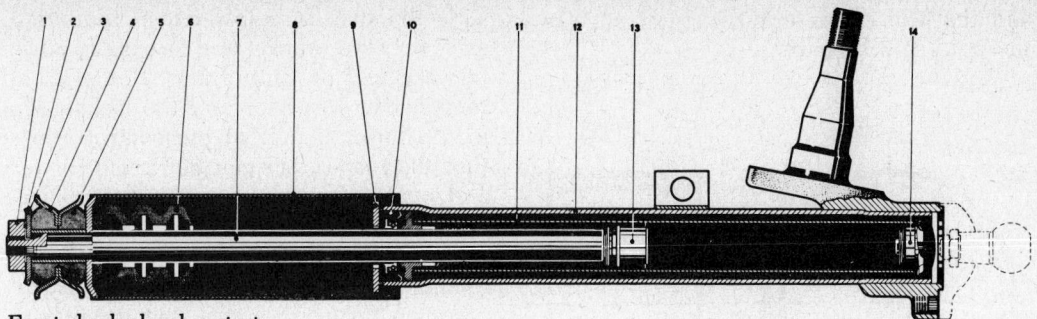

Front shock-absorber strut.

1 Hex nut	6 Rubber buffer	11 Cylinder
2 Safety plate	7 Piston rod	12 Strut tube
3 Washer	8 Shielding tube	13 Piston
4 Bracket (on vehicle)	9 Stop disc	14 Bottom valve
5 Rubber bushing	10 Oil seal	

Shock-absorber Strut

To dismantle shock-absorber strut, secure it in a soft-jaw vise with the spindle up. Remove upper shielding tube and extract rubber buffer. Unlock and remove the hex nuts holding the steering lever and ball joint. The ball joint can be pressed from its seat with a puller. The spacing ring (on the wheel spindle) for the inside bearing can be driven off with a drift punch.

Check spindle and shock-absorber strut for straightness and alignment with special tools. Both must be replaced as a unit. Check the steering control lever with tool P 284 for the seat deviation of the tie rod joint, for the height alignment of the steering lever, and for the condition of the ball stud. Check condition of the rubber dust cover and replace if necessary.

The shock-absorber strut is assembled and installed in reverse order to disassembly. Heat the bearing distance ring to 300°F. and push it into place. Fill rubber boot of each new ball joint with multipurpose grease, making sure that the tapered end of the stud is not greased and torquing castle nut to 32½ ft-lbs. If cotter pin opening appears above the top of the castle nut, place a spacer under the nut. Tighten steering lever hex bolts to 34 ft-lbs. Install rubber dry. Tighten hex nut on the strut to 58 ft-lbs. Install castle nuts in transverse control arm to 54 ft-lbs., using washers and cotter keys. Screw tight the castle nut on the ball stud of the tie rod to 32½ ft-lbs. Tighten brake carrier bolts to 34 ft-lbs.

The damping action of the shock absorbers is adjustable. The 912 models are fitted with shock absorbers that are adjusted to the softest setting; the 911 vehicles have the shock absorbers set one turn harder (to the right).

With the wheels removed, unlock the hex nut at top of strut and remove nut while supporting the transverse control arm with a jack. Press plunger rod and shielding tube fully down and turn plunger rod to left, without forcing it, until the adjusting lug engages the mating recess in the bottom valve. Mark the shielding tube and the shock-absorber body at the point where the lug engages. Turn the shielding tube farther to the left to determine if an adjustment was previously made to harder setting and, if so, by how much. Starting from the original position, turn the tube one-half or more turns to the right until the desired damping action has been reached. Pull plunger rod up again to disengage the adjusting components. Maximum adjustment range is 2¼ turns. Make certain that the left and right shock-absorber struts are adjusted to an equal degree. The degree of damping action can easily be felt by pumping the plunger rod.

Wheel Bearings

Remove the wheel hub, with brake disc and bearings. Using a shop press, press out the wheel bearings. If necessary to remove the brake disc from the wheel hub, mark the brake disc position on the wheel hub first. With wheel hub heated to 300°F., press out the inner tapered roller bearing and the seal. Press out the outer race of the outer roller bearing.

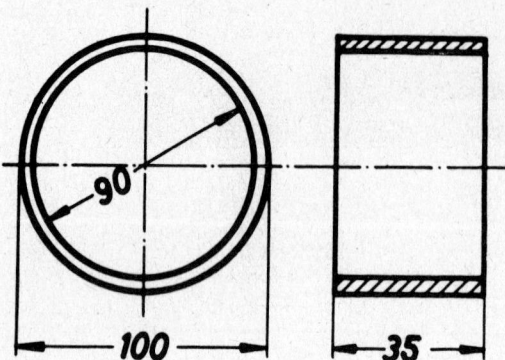

Homemade spacer for pressing out the outer race of the outer roller bearing (dimensions in mm).

Thoroughly clean both tapered bearings and check for wear or damage. Heat wheel hub to 300° and press in the outer race of the inner roller bearing. Insert the inner race in the inner roller bearing and press oil seal in until it is flush with the wheel hub housing. Press in the outer race of the outer roller bearing. Place brake disc on the wheel hub with marks aligned and install bolts from inside to outside so that bolt heads rest against the brake disc. Use new spring washers under the nuts. Torque disc bolts to 16½ ft-lbs.

Fill wheel hub with 1½ oz. of multipurpose lithium grease, coat the bearings with grease, and install them. Settle the wheel bearings in their seats by lightly tightening the clamping nut while turning the hub. Loosen nut slightly and work screwdriver against bearing and washer with light pressure. Tighten clamping nut to 18 ft-lbs. Lightly coat the nut and washer with grease and install grease cap without filling it with grease.

Install brake caliper and spring washers (tightening to 50½ ft-lbs.), brake line and hose, and brake cover shroud. Bleed brake system and adjust wheel alignment.

Transverse Control Arm and
Torsion Bar

To remove the transverse control arm, take off the undershield. Turn the torsion bar adjusting screw out. Unlock and remove castle nuts from control arm below the shock-absorber strut. Pull out the bolts and slide the strut assembly out of the control arm. Remove bracket and bearing cap from forward end of control arm. Remove both torsion bar dust caps and the locking ring in the forward part of the control arm so that the torsion bar can be driven forward and out of the arm. Loosen the bolt that retains the control arm in the body crossmember. Push the arm toward the front of the car while turning it about its axis. The piece on the control arm that fits into the crossmember is called a "flanbloc." It is not possible to press the flanbloc off the arm without damaging the arm. The two must be replaced together.

Drive the torsion bar adjusting lever out of the crossmember by striking it with a punch inserted through the opening for the control arm. Take care not to damage the torsion bar splines.

Check the control arm with a special tool. Visually check the rubber bushing and flanbloc for wear. Check torsion bar for damaged splines and rust.

When installing the control arm, position it in the crossmember so that the end that attaches to the strut slants down 10 degrees from the crossmember. This adjustment

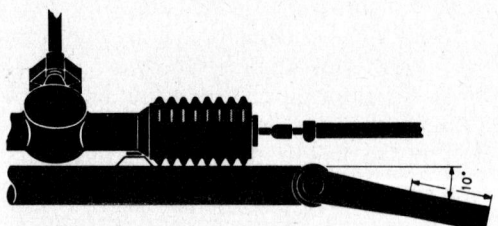

Position the control arm end at 10° angle to crossmember.

must be exact to prevent twisting damage to the flanbloc and to avoid uneven springing. Lightly coat the torsion bar and mounting splines with grease. Install the bar through the front of the control arm, lock it in place and put on the cap. Torsion bars are marked right or left on their ends. Place the bearing cap so that the proper edge faces the control arm bushing. Insert the rubber bushing on the control arm so that the narrow collar comes to rest against the thrust washer of the arm. Prior to assembly, coat the rubber bushing with glycerine paste and make sure that the bushing is not pinched along the sides between the cap and bracket when tightening. Lightly tighten the forward bracket boot first. Torque to 34 ft-lbs. Tighten the castle nuts on the arm under the strut to 54 ft-lbs., using washers and cotter keys.

Install the torsion bar adjusting lever onto the splined torsion bar in the crossmember when the control arm has been pushed down until the stop is struck in the shock-absorber strut (use tire iron or other lever). Position adjusting lever with adjusting screw turned out and leaving as little clearance at the adjustment point as possible. The lever should have a coat of grease before installation. Slightly tighten the adjusting screw and install lock ring and dust cover. Adjust height of front end and check wheel alignment.

Front End Crossmember

The front end crossmember can be checked for alignment (after it is removed from the chassis) by using two perfectly straight tubes of 54 mm outside diameter and 350 mm long. When tubes are fastened in crossmember, they cannot be out of parallel more than 2.0 mm (between a and b and between a flat surface and the edge of a tube).

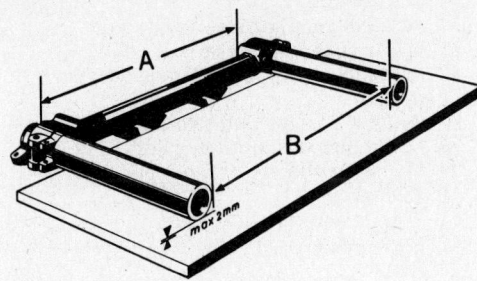

Checking alignment of front-end crossmember with straight tubes on flat surface. (A=B±2 mm; neither tube can be more than 2 mm off flat surface).

Stabilizer Assembly

Loosen clamping bolts to stabilizer lever and slip lever from square end of stabilizer. Loosen the stabilizer support by removing the support retaining bolts and squirting a little rust solvent or penetrating oil onto the support and rubber bushing. Pry both parts loose with 2 large screwdrivers. Remove support retaining bolts on the other side and pull out stabilizer together with bushing and support. Using a shop press, remove the stabilizer from the support and the rubber bushing (use penetrating oil).

Visually check rubber grommets in the stabilizer shackle for wear and coat the stabilizer and rubber bush with gylcerine paste or similar rubber lubricant. Lightly tighten both supports, center the stabilizer, and torque hex bolts to 18 ft-lbs. Position each stabilizer lever onto the square end of the stabilizer so that the square end protrudes approximately 1 mm beyond the lever. Tighten shackle retaining bolts to 18 ft-lbs.

DISASSEMBLY-TYPE 356

Raise car and remove both wheels. Pull out the speedometer shaft cotter pin on the left front wheel. Take off grease caps on axles, unscrew the wheel nuts (both axles have right hand threads) and withdraw the bearing washers. Pull off brake drums. If an inner bearing does not come off freely, use a puller. Unbolt the brake backing plate. Though it is not necessary to disconnect the brake hose, care must be taken not to twist or bend it.

Remove tie rod at ball joint with special tool. Remove hex bolts that clamp the upper and lower suspension arms to the steering knuckle (kingpin). Tap off knuckle from suspension arms.

Shock-absorber

Remove the shock-absorber and inspect its bushings for wear. The shock-absorber is

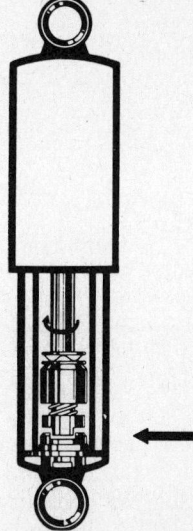

Shock absorber adjustment. Compress shock absorber completely and turn plunger rod counterclockwise without applying force, until the lug of the adjusting cam engages the recess of the bottom valve.

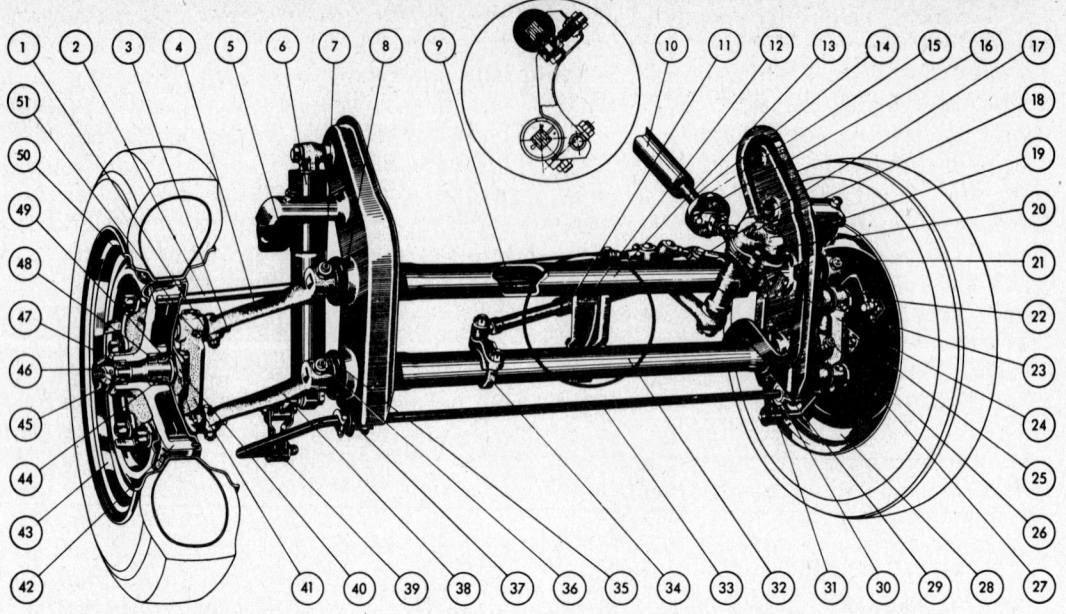

Cutaway view of front suspension on all 356 models. Close-up circle shows torsion bar adjustment screws.

 1 Hex. head clamping screw
 2 Tie rod, right
 3 Suspension arm link pin
 4 Upper suspension arm, right
 5 Rubber stop, right
 6 Shock absorber
 7 Retaining screw for upper suspension arm, right
 8 Upper suspension arm seal, right
 9 Torsion bar
10 Tubular jacket
11 Steering damper
12 Carrier plate (stop)
13 Upper axle tube
14 Drag link tube
15 Ground strap
16 Joint disc
17 Tie rod, left
18 Steering gear adjusting screw
19 Rubber stop, left
20 Steering gear
21 Retaining screw for upper suspension arm, left
22 Connection for brake line
23 Parking brake bell crank
24 Suspension arm link, left (steering knuckle)
25 Stub axle
26 Brake anchor plate, left

27 Retaining screw for lower suspension arm, left
28 Rim
29 Retaining clip for parking brake lever shaft
30 Anti-roll bar bearing
31 Mounting shackle for anti-roll bar, left
32 Lower axle tube
33 Anti-roll bar
34 Retaining clip for steering damper
35 Lower suspension arm seal, right
36 Retaining screw for lower suspension arm, right
37 Bearing cap for anti-roll bar, right
38 Lower suspension arm, right
39 Mounting shackle anti-roll bar, right
40 Stub axle
41 Suspension arm link, right
42 Brake drum
43 Rim
44 Spacer
45 Hub cap
46 Clamping nut
47 Front wheel bearing, outer
48 Front wheel bearing, inner
49 Front wheel bearing, seal
50 Grease nipple
51 Brake anchor plate, right

adjustable to a greater firmness (from the factory set soft position) by pressing down the upper housing completely and turning plunger counterclockwise without applying force until the lug of the adjusting cam on the bottom of the plunger engages the recess of the bottom valve. Then turn ½ or more revolutions in a clockwise direction to make dampening more firm to a maximum of two complete revolutions (from maximum softness). Pull upper section back enough to disengage the adjustment valve. Spread and compress both front shock-absorbers to feel if adjustments are identical.

Non-adjustable shock-absorbers require

no maintenance. A slight loss of fluid does not necessitate replacement of the shock absorber since small losses are replenished from an internal oil reservoir. Working the shock-absorber by hand can indicate whether a shock-absorber is working but does not give an indication of its effectiveness. Check bushings and rubber mounts for wear.

Torsion Bars

Remove suspension arms at torsion bars on one side. Loosen the retaining screws and lock nuts of the torsion bars in the center of the axle tubes. Pull out the suspension arm of the opposite side together with the torsion bar. Check bars for cracks and broken weld areas. Check suspension arms, plastic bushings and needle bearings for wear. The bushings are removable with special tools.

Coat torsion bars with grease and install in position, bringing the countersink in the center of the torsion bar in line with the hole for the retaining screw. Tighten screw and check position of torsion bars. Make a gauge to measure the torsion bar angle with two straight strips of metal. The angle must be 40° as shown. Correct the torsion bar adjustment by turning the threaded set pin (above retaining screw). One full turn corrects the torsion bar by 2° 50′ (close to 3°).

The front axle tubes are checked for alignment with special gauge, VW 256a.

Stabilizer Assembly

The stabilizer assembly is unbolted at the ends of the axle tubes and at the shackles to the lower suspension arms. Check all parts for damage.

Suspension Arm/Steering Knuckle Adjustment

Rock each front wheel by hand to check clearance between the suspension arm and the steering knuckle. Excessive play should be adjusted out. First loosen the hex nuts holding the suspension arm to the knuckle. Tighten the mounting studs (suspension arm link pins) fully into steering knuckle and back off slightly (max. ⅛ turn) so there is free movement between the suspension arms and the knuckle. If adjustment is not possible, the shims are worn excessively. ·Finally tighten. the clamping bolts of the suspension arms, and check the toe-in adjustment of the wheels.

Steering Knuckle and Stub Axle

The bushings of the steering knuckle can be pressed out; the bores of the bushings are checked by gauge VW 259. Hole in bushing must line up with grease nipple. Check clearance of king pin in its bushings. If pressing in new king pin bushings, insert bushings from inside of steering knuckle. Line up the groove in the upper bushing with that in knuckle or file in a groove if there is none. Heat stub axle in oil bath to 176° and press in king pin. Steering knuckle must swivel freely when moved by hand.

TYPE 914 AND 914/6

The front suspension used on the Type 914 and 914/6 is identical to that used on the Type 912 Porsche.

Steering

Three types of steering boxes have been used on the Porsche. Up to 1958, a worm-and-nut type was used, having a half-moon shaped nut that travels up and down a steering shaft worm (cam). The worm-and-nut type was replaced with a Ross single-peg design manufactured by ZF in Germany. The roller-mounted peg rides along the worm. The ZF gearbox is interchangeable with the worm-and-nut type. A rack-and-pinion steering design was adopted for the 912–911 body shell.

Porsche Type 914 and 914/6 also use an identical rack and pinion unit, shared by the Type 912 and 911.

Adjustments

WORM AND NUT TYPE

The worm-and-nut type steering gear is adjusted for worm-shaft end play and for steering nut clearance while the wheels are off the ground. Loosen the lock nut and set screw for the sector shaft on top of box. Loosen adjusting sleeve clamp bolt and tighten adjusting sleeve clockwise until the worm-shaft end play is taken up. *Do not overtighten.* Tighten the clamping bolt.

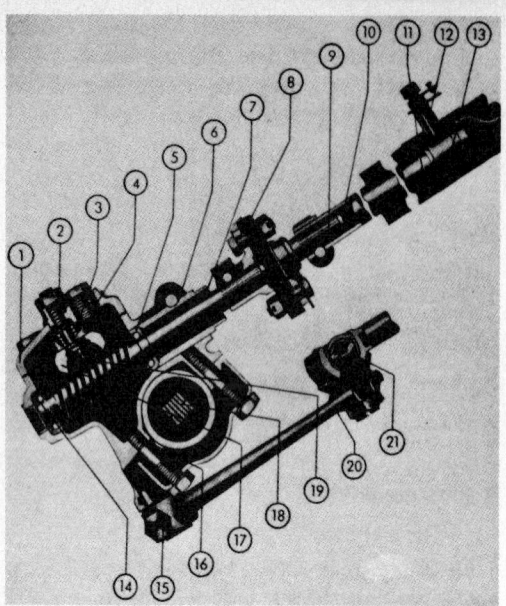

Worm-and-nut steering gear.

1	Steering box cover	12	Carbon brush
2	Set screw	13	Commutator ring
3	Pressure spring	14	Lower thrust
4	Filler plug		bearing
5	Upper thrust bearing	15	Retaining nut
6	Adjusting sleeve		for pitman arm
7	Oil seal	16	Steering worm
8	Coupling disc	17	Sector shaft
9	Splined sleeve for	18	Torsion bar
	steering column	19	Steering nut
	(double-arm flange)	20	Pitman arm
10	Steering column	21	Tie rod joint
11	Steering column tube		

Check steering action for easy movement. Position the sector shaft arm at right angle to the steering worm (wheels straight ahead). Tighten sector-shaft adjusting screw as far as it will go and back off ⅛ turn. Tighten lock nut. If hard steering persists, check tension of spring below adjusting screw. Steering movement should be smooth from lock to lock and without any binding or excessive play. In roadtest, wheels should naturally return to straight ahead position.

ZF Type Single Peg

Unlike the worm-and-nut steering gear, the ZF single-peg gear is designed so that only in the center of its range, with front wheel deflections between ±2°, there is no play. If the wheels are turned more than 3° in either direction there must be play in the steering mechanism. This de-

sign makes it possible to adjust the steering gear accurately and to adjust for wear without any danger of the peg binding at some point along its travel. When checking the play in the steering, the front wheels must be placed directly in the straight ahead position. The central position of the steering gear is indicated by a line on the spindle of the steering worm and a notch on the steering box. It is possible to bring these two marks into alignment at points other than the pressure point, so turn the steering wheel to full lock (in either direction), back it off just about one full revolution and then align the marks.

Accurate adjustment of the pressure point (center) is critical. Sometimes an adjustment made on a bench is too tight, causing binding when placed under a load. There should be almost no play in the mid-position, with greater play at each end. Disconnect tie rods and steering damper from drop arm. Unscrew lock nut on steering gear and tighten adjusting screw (right hand thread) until a slight resistance is felt when turning the steering wheel through its central position. Tighten lock nut and fasten tie rod and steering damper.

The pressure point should not be noticeable when car is being driven. Under no circumstances should one try to eliminate steering shocks by increasing the pressure point. (If measuring device is available, set the pressure point to 4.34–6.08 inch-pounds). In general, it is advisable to have the pressure point a little free than too tight. Maximum play of the steering wheel in the central position should be 0.4 inch (10 mm).

Rack and Pinion Type

The rack-and-pinion steering boxes have adjustment steps that vary according to the type of steering-rack pressure block.

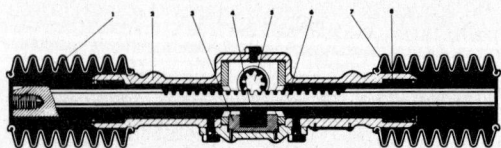

Rack and pinion steering gear.

1	Thread for tie rod joint	5	Steering pinion
2	Housing	6	Steering rack
3	Adjusting nut	7	Rubber boot
4	Pressure block	8	Bushing

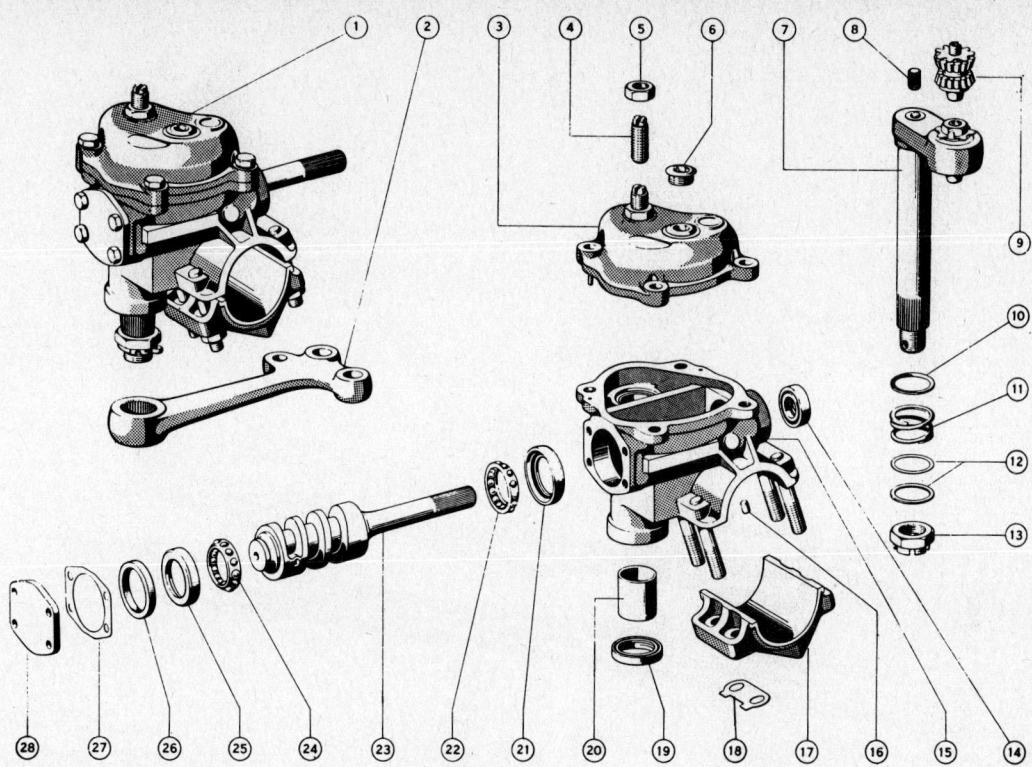

ZF-type steering gear.

1 Steering box, complete	10 Thrust washer	19 Seal
2 Steering drop arm	11 Compression spring	20 Bearing bushing
3 Steering box cover	12 Thrust washers	21 Ball race, top
4 Adjusting screw	13 Castle nut	22 Ball cage
5 Lock nut for adjusting screw	14 Radial oil seal	23 Steering worm
6 Oil filler plug	15 Steering box	24 Ball cage
7 Rocker shaft	16 Dowel pin	25 Ball race, bottom
8 Thrust pin	17 Clamp	26 Spacer
9 Steering peg roller bearing	18 Lock plate	27 Adjusting washer
		28 End plate

Steering gear *with dust boot seat* has a steel pressure block with a plastic contact surface. Remove the base plate and use it as a wrench to tighten the adjusting nut to seating contact. Back off the nut by three teeth. Check the steering drag at the steering wheel nut with a torque wrench. The maximum drag with the tie rods and steering damper disconnected should be 8.6 in.-lbs. (10 cmkg). Minimum drag should not be less than 3½ in.-lbs. (4 cmkg). When installing the base plate, the four pins in the plate must easily fit into teeth of the adjusting nut. Move the nut a little if necessary.

Steering gear *without dust boot seat* has

Adjusting drag of rack-and-pinion steering gear. Pins in cover fit between teeth of the steering-drag adjustment nut.

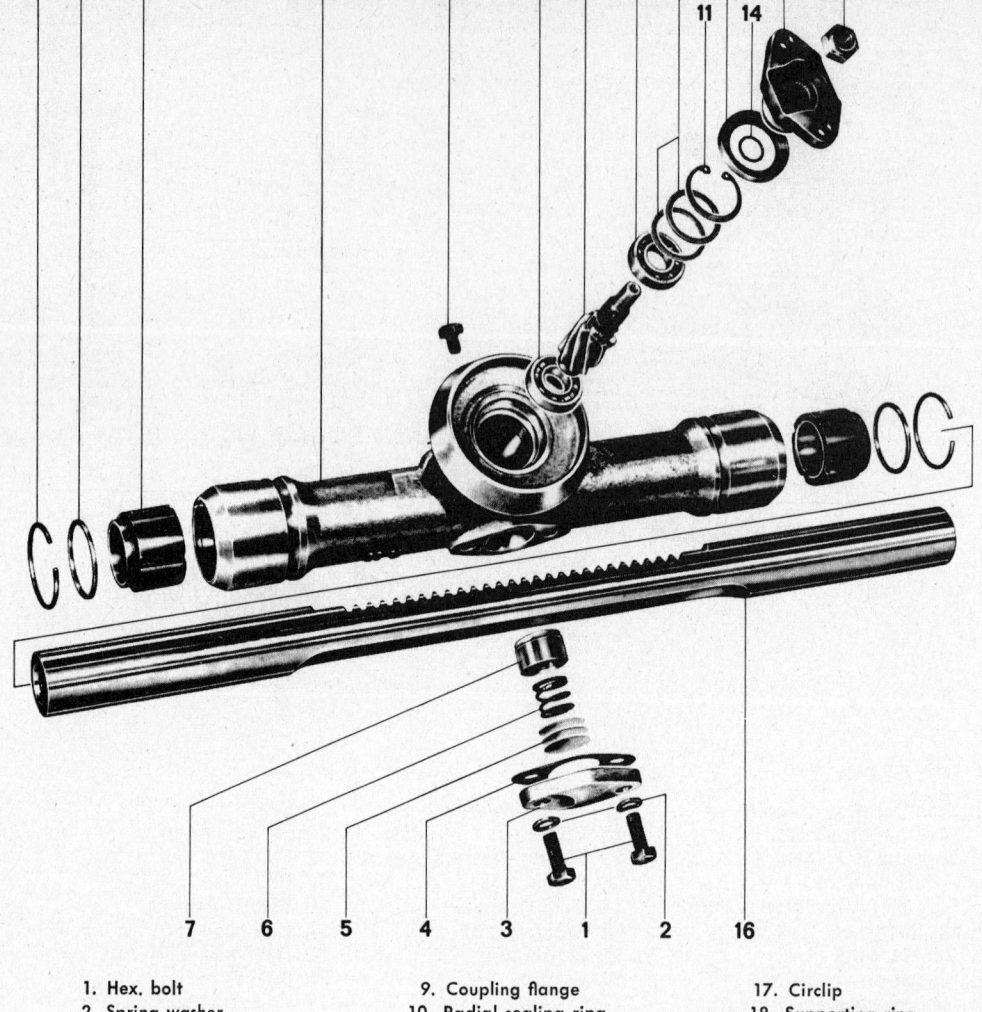

1. Hex. bolt	9. Coupling flange	17. Circlip
2. Spring washer	10. Radial sealing ring	18. Supporting ring
3. Housing cover	11. Locking ring	19. Bearing bushing
4. Seal	12. Compensating washer	20. Grooved ball bearing
5. Adjusting washer	13. Drive pinion	21. Hex. bolt
6. Compression spring	14. Round cord ring	(filler screw M 8x8)
7. Thrust piece	15. Grooved ball bearing	22. Steering gear housing
8. Self-locking hex. bolt	16. Rack	

Exploded view of Type 914 and 914/6 rack and pinion steering

a plastic pressure block. Remove base plate and tighten adjusting nut to a maximum drag of 8.7 in.-lbs. (10 cmkg).

Disassembly

To remove the worm-and-nut and the ZF-type steering boxes, jack up front of car and remove left front wheel. Remove steering box cover in trunk. Disconnect battery. Loosen steering damper at drop arm (Pitman arm). Press out tie rod ends from drop arm. Turn steering towards right or turn drop arm completely counterclockwise. Loosen steering column from steering coupling and remove clamp on steering gear after unlocking and removing hex nuts. Remove steering gear from front axle and pull out towards front. After installation, adjust toe-in. Disassembly of the steering gear is not recommended; the units are sealed at the factory.

However, if necessary to disassemble steering gear, detach steering coupling, pull off the drop arm with puller, and take off the top of the steering box. Lift out the sector shaft (rocker shaft).

On ZF-type only, remove end plate; take out shims and spacer ring; and tap out steering worm downward. Do not mix up bearing cage and race—all parts must be refitted to original position. Remove oil seal. Clean all parts and check worm and peg for wear. A new worm requires new taper bearing and enough shims to ensure that worm turns freely but has no play; a new peg requires a new locking plate. Fit new seals and insert worm with upper bearing, which should be packed with grease, through the lower opening. Pack the lower bearing with grease and fit in place. Then fit outer race.

On worm-and-nut type only with sector shaft out, take off steering nut and remove hex bolt of adjusting sleeve. Remove steering worm, adjusting sleeve, gasket, and upper thrust bearing. Press cap and lower thrust bearing inward from outside. Clean all parts and check for wear. After installing worm, press in upper thrust bearing with VW special tools. When installing the adjusting sleeve, provide the steering worm with a protecting sleeve to prevent damage of the seal lip by the splines. Do not turn sector shaft when inserting it into steering box. Thrust pin and spring tolerances are critical to steering adjustment and wear of parts.

Load on assembled spring
0.8″ (20.3 mm) = 132 to 165 lbs. (60–75 kg)
Thrust pin = .79″ (20.1 mm)
Pin shaft length = .78″ (19.9 mm)
Fill steering box with ½ pint SAE 90 hypoid gear oil.

To remove rack-and-pinion steering unit from the chassis, remove carpeting from trunk on steering side, detach heating duct of auxiliary heater from the steering post and lay duct to the side. Open steering gear access door and remove intermediate shaft cover. It might help to pry up one of the two prongs in the spring clip with a small screwdriver. Detach the heater fuel pump and lay it to the side. Undo lower hex bolt of the universal joint, loosen castle nut, and pull universal joint off the steering shaft. Remove allen bolts holding steering shaft. Slip off dust boot and unbolt the steering coupling.

From under car, remove undershield; detach ball joint from tie rod; unscrew steering housing bolts; remove crossmember brace on the right side; and withdraw to the right the steering assembly. Unlock and remove bolt from tie rod yoke and remove tie rod.

Check tie rods for damage and the ball joints for serviceable condition: when moving the ball stud, slight friction must be felt. If the ball stud can be moved freely and axial play is detectable, the ball joint should be replaced. Coat the yoke bolt with grease, install, and torque to 34 ft-lbs. (4.7 mkg). Install crossmember brace without binding. Torque hex nuts to 47 ft-lbs. (6.5 mkg) and hex bolts to 34 ft-lbs. (4.7 mkg). Using new lockwashers, install and torque steering box bolts to 34 ft-lbs.

Torque ball joint castle nuts to 32.5 ft-lbs. securing with cotter key. Install steering coupling retaining bolts, using new safety washers.

Brakes

Porsches from the Type 356C have been equipped with disc brakes. The brakes are ATE type (Dunlop licensed).

The 912 and 911 Porsches are equipped with ATE-type (Dunlop licensed) disc brakes. The disc brakes have calipers which house two hydraulic cylinders and friction pads per wheel. Earlier Porsches use drum brakes with two single-thrust brake cylinders in each front wheel (two leading shoes) and the conventional two-direction cylinder (one leading shoe, one trailing) in each rear wheel.

Since 1950, the brake system has been considerably developed. The very first Porsches were fitted with VW brakes, but late in 1950 the two-leading-shoes design (Duplex) was adopted. Contact pressure of the brake shoe against the drum is greater in the Duplex system because the action of *both* shoes is augmented by wheel rotation. By 1953 the drums were larger (280 mm from 240 mm) and made of light alloy with cooling fins. More recently the 356 B introduced a cross-finned drum.

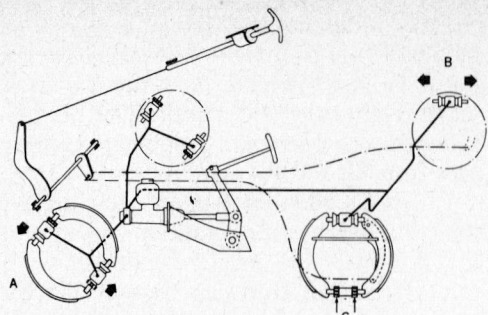

Direction of brake lining travel in drum brakes.

A Duplex design (both front wheels)
B Simplex design (both rear wheels)
C Brake adjustment nuts

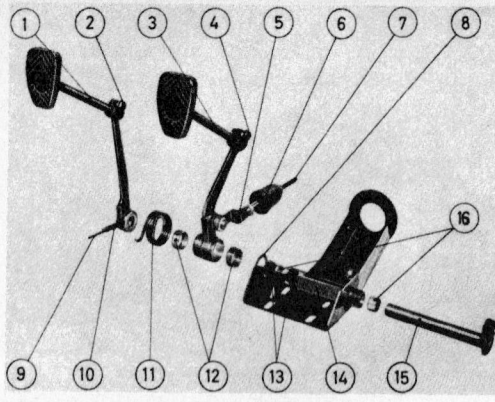

Pedal assembly on 356 models.

1 Clutch pedal	8 Washer
2 Clamp screw	9 Roll pin
3 Brake pedal	10 Heavy roll pin
4 Clamp screw	11 Return spring
5 Connecting link	12 Bushings
6 Rubber boot	13 Rubber buffer pads
(inverted after	14 Pedal bracket
installing)	15 Clutch pedal shaft
7 Push rod	16 Pedal shaft bushings

Drum Brakes

ADJUSTMENTS

Drum brakes are checked by applying the brake pedal. If it travels to within two inches of the floor mat and has a hard feel, the brake shoes require adjustment or relining. A spongy feel indicates the need for bleeding.

The four-wheel disc brakes are not adjustable but should be checked frequently for proper fluid level and inspected every 6000 miles for friction pad wear.

Brake Pedal Height

Brake pedal height is not adjustable on either drum or disc systems because the master cylinder pushrod connects directly to the brake pedal. If pedal binding occurs, take the assembly apart at the pedal pivot and clean it.

Brake Shoes

Adjust brake shoes by turning adjustment eccentrics on wheel backing plate. All have a right-hand thread requiring adjustments as listed.

Right rear wheel:
      FRONT nut, turn downward
      REAR nut, turn upward
Left rear wheel:
      FRONT nut, turn upward
      REAR nut, turn downward
Right front wheel:
      UPPER nut, turn upward
      LOWER nut, turn downward

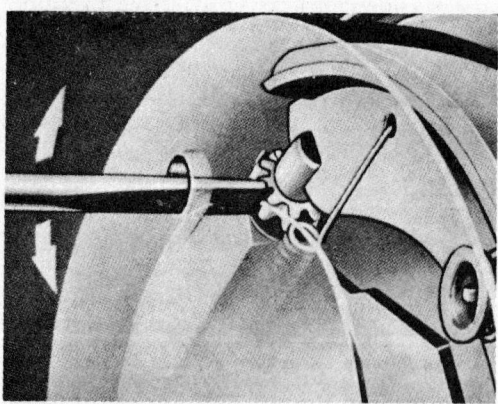

All brake adjustment nuts have right-hand thread.

Left front wheel:
      UPPER nut, turn downward
      LOWER nut, turn upward

Completely depress the brake pedal several times to allow the brake shoes to centralize in the brake drums. Rotate brake drum forward until the adjusting hole in the drum is in line with one of the adjusting nuts. Insert a screwdriver through the hole and turn the adjusting nut, using screwdriver as a lever, until the brake lining contacts the brake drum tightly. Back off adjusting nut by 7 or 8 notches to allow the brake drum to rotate freely.

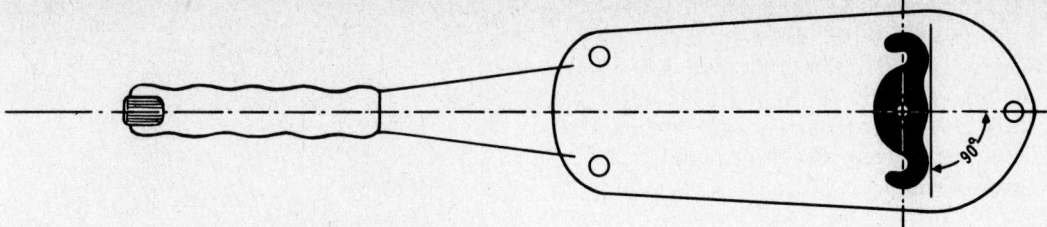

Looking down on 911-912 hand brake. Cable equalizer (seen through holes) must be straight as shown.

Parking Brake

Adjust parking brake with lever pulled up about three inches. Test for cable free movement and equal tightening action at both brakes. If braking action is equal, adjustment of the center cable is enough. Secure cable with lever at the three-inch position and with rear brakes just beginning to engage drum. Lubricate cable. Set parking brake only after foot brakes have been adjusted.

The parking brake for *cars with disc brakes* is an adjustable drum brake design that fits inside the rear wheel brake disc. To adjust parking brake, remove rear wheels, release handbrake and push the disc

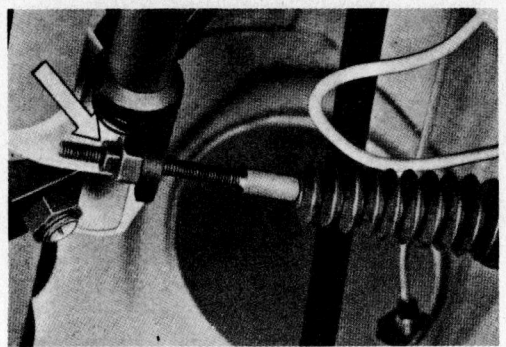

Parking brake adjustment.

friction pads to sides so that discs rotate freely. Loosen handbrake cables. Insert screwdriver into adjustment opening in drum of rear disc and turn adjustment nut until disc begins to drag slightly. Repeat procedure on opposite wheel. Then remove slack from cables. Pull tunnel cover and handbrake lever boot up at the rear and check the position of the cable equalizer by looking through the two inspection holes in handbrake bracket. The equalizer must

be straight when handbrake is pulled up. Reset (if necessary) and tighten the cable conduit adjusting nuts.

Next back off adjusting sprocket in each wheel by approx. 4–5 teeth so brake discs turn freely. Check for clearance at the handbrake lever. The handbrake should be tight when pulled up four clicks.

Brake Bleeding

Bleed the brake system to remove air from the brake cylinders. Air, being compressible, cushions fluid movement from the brake pedal to the wheel cylinders, reducing brake effectiveness and making the pedal spongy. Bleeding operation should begin at farthest point from master cylinder. Bleed the left and then the right rear wheels before front ones. On drum brakes, next bleed right front upper cylinder and then right front lower one. Bleed left front upper cylinder before left front lower cylinder, which is last.

After filling reservoir to "MAX" level, clean dirt from each bleeder valve, remove cap, and fit valve with hose to drain fluid into jar that has some fluid in it. Hose prevents fluid from seeping to lining. Fluid in jar prevents air from being accidentally sucked back into the line.

Open valve almost ¾ turn, depress brake pedal, close valve and allow pedal to return slowly. Repeat steps until no more bubbles enter jar. Keep pedal depressed until bleeder valve is closed. Replacement fluid is drawn from the reservoir so keep fluid level high in the reservoir to prevent air from entering the lines through the master cylinder. Throw out the fluid that was discharged during bleeding operation because all of the bubbles will not settle out. *Caution: brake fluid will destroy paint.*

Disc brakes are bled in the same way, starting with the bleeder valves of the rear wheels. Bleed outer and then inner valve of left rear wheel. Next bleed outer and then inner valve of right rear wheel. Then bleed right front wheel and finally, the left front wheel.

Brake System Flushing

Complete flushing of brake system is suggested whenever new brake system parts are installed. Fluid with any trace of mineral oil should not be used to flush system.

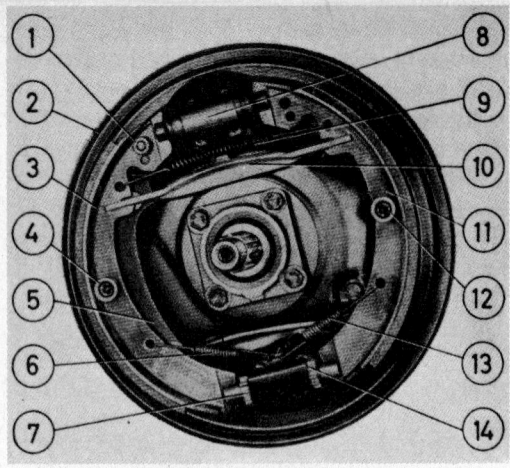

Drum brake—right rear.

1 Pivot bolt for parking brake actuating lever
2 Brake back plate
3 Secondary brake shoe
4 Pressure spring with collar
5 Parking brake cable
6 Return spring
7 Adjusting nut
8 Brake cylinder
9 Return spring
10 Pressure rod
11 Primary brake shoe
12 Pressure spring with collar
13 Return spring
14 Adjusting nut

BRAKE SHOES

Replacement

Remove drum assembly for access to brake shoes. Remove return springs, spring retainers, dowel pins and springs on shoes. Place clamps on brake cylinder plungers. Brake shoes are specially bonded—replace shoes and linings as unit. If brakes are replaced on one side, do same for other side so that braking effectiveness is equal. Keep hands cleans while handling new linings.

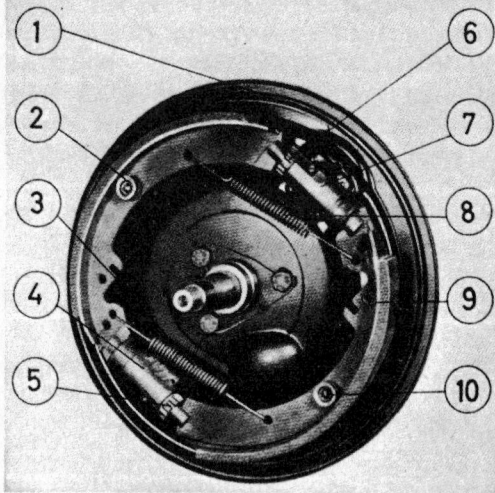

Drum brake—right front.

1 Brake back plate
2 Pressure spring with collar
3 Return spring
4 Lower brake cylinder
5 Lower adjusting nut
6 Upper adjusting nut
7 Upper brake cylinder
8 Return spring
9 Brake shoe with lining
10 Pressure spring with collar

WHEEL CYLINDERS

Overhaul

Carefully pull lower edges of wheel cylinder boots away from cylinders and note if interior is wet—an indication of brake fluid seepage past the piston cup. If so, cylinder overhaul is required.

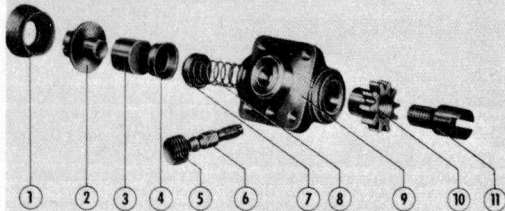

Front wheel brake cylinder—drum brakes.

1 Boot
2 Plunger
3 Piston
4 Rubber cup
5 Dust cap
6 Bleeder valve
7 Spring seat
8 Stop spring
9 Wheel brake cylinder housing
10 Adjusting nut
11 Adjusting screw

Clean dirt from all surrounding surfaces and then loosen connecting line and unscrew wheel brake cylinder. Tape is often satisfactory for sealing off brake line. Remove brake hose if bottom cylinder is being removed.

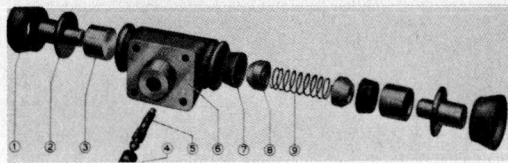

Rear wheel brake cylinder—drum brakes.

1 Boot	6 Wheel brake cyl. housing
2 Plunger	7 Rubber cup
3 Piston	8 Spring seat
4 Dust cap	9 Stop spring
5 Bleeder valve	

Dismantle boots, plungers, pistons, cups, spring seats and spring from cylinder. Unscrew bleeder valve. Replace boots and cups if possible; clean other parts with fresh brake fluid. Use no fluid containing even a trace of mineral oil.

Light scratches and corrosion can be polished from pistons and bore with fine emery cloth or steel wool. Dip all parts in brake fluid (use brake cylinder paste if available) and reassemble.

Install the wheel brake cylinders with the piston side showing in direction of forward rotation. The shoe must be placed with the notch in the web facing the piston. Check oil seal and bearings for condition. Clean brake drum hub and bearing and repack with grease. Adjust, bleed and road test the brakes for performance.

Brake Drums

Reconditioning

Thoroughly clean and inspect brake drums for cracks, scoring and out-of-round. Polish out slight scores with emery cloth. Shallow grooves can be removed by boring if oversized linings are obtainable. Out-of-round drums cause excessive wear on other brake parts as well as on tires. Drums can only be worn down or machined to 2.0 mm beyond their original size. Maximum tolerable runout is .004 inch (0.1 mm). Measure for run-out by checking along open and closed edges of machined surface and at right angles. Inside diameter variations of brake drums on opposite sides must be less than .008″ (0.2 mm) for equal braking.

To regain center contact with brake shoes, grind linings to .020 inches under drum *diameter*.

When reinstalling brake drum, inspect all brake pipe and hose connections for fluid leaks. Tighten these connections and apply heavy pressure to brake pedal to check seal. Inspect wheel bearing oil seals. Check all backing plate bolts for tightness. Clean away all dirt from assemblies and repack wheel bearings.

Master Cylinder

The master cylinder has a by-pass port in the cylinder wall which compensates for fluid expansion or contraction by allowing excess fluid to flow into or out of the reservoir. Fouling of this port can cause dragging of the shoes (brake lights will stay on). The piston pushrod must be adjusted at the brake pedal for .04″ free play, or the main piston cup will not clear the bypass port.

A double-action check valve controls the fluid pressure balance between the master cylinder and the brake lines. The check valve is pressure loaded by a spring.

Open front hood, fold back rubber mat and unscrew cover to steering gear. Jack up front of car. Disconnect cable on stop light switch. Unscrew brake lines from master cylinder and plug ends. Remove floor board on pedal side. Pull protective cap from master cylinder rod and remove master cylinder.

Empty and remove fluid reservoir. Unscrew stop light switch. Remove spring for stop plate. Take out stop plate and piston (with secondary piston cup). Remove washer, main piston cup, return spring with spring retainer, check valve and valve seat.

Clean all parts only with brake fluid. Gasoline, benzol, glycerine and other petroleum base products destroy rubber parts. The cleaned and dry piston must move with suction in both directions in the cylinder. Replace the two piston cups whenever rebuilding a master cylinder. Apply a thin film of brake cylinder paste on piston, cylinder wall and rubber parts. Firmly seat the lock ring. Align the mark at the bottom of

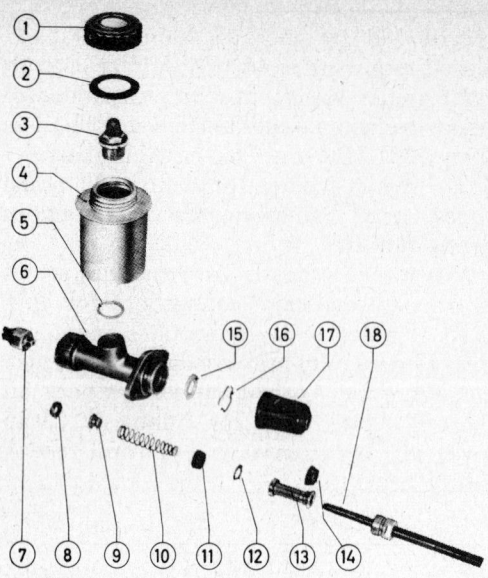

Master cylinder—drum brakes.

1 Cover
2 Gasket
3 Threaded nipple and strainer
4 Fluid reservoir
5 Gasket
6 Master cylinder housing
7 Stop light switch
8 Valve seat
9 Check valve
10 Pressure spring
11 Main piston cup
12 Washer
13 Piston
14 Secondary piston cup
15 Piston stop plate
16 Locking ring
17 Boot
18 Brake push rod

Disc Brakes

A disc-type system consists of a brake disc which rotates with the wheel and a caliper having a hydraulic cylinder and piston on each side of the disc. The caliper presses friction pads against each side of the disc to stop the car.

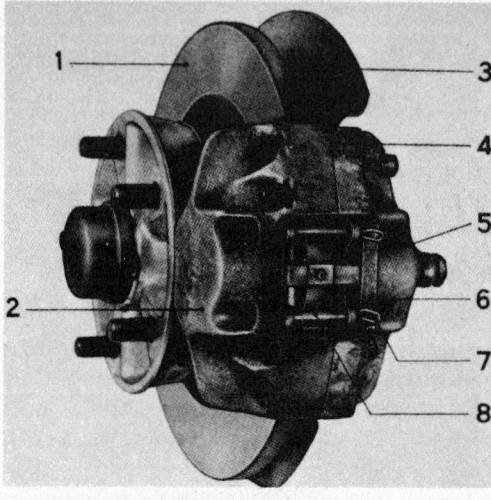

Disc brake assembly.

1 Brake disc
2 Outside caliper half
3 Disc shroud
4 Inside caliper half
5 Inside friction pad
6 Cross-spring
7 Pin retainer
8 Dowel pin holding friction pads

the reservoir with the stop-light switch and the center line of the master cylinder housing. Check that the ventilation hole in the reservoir cover is free.

Install in reverse order to removal. Seal flange on master cylinder with compound. Adjust clearance between brake pushrod and piston in master cylinder, after loosening the locknut on the brake pushrod. Clearance approximately .04″. Adjust and bleed brakes.

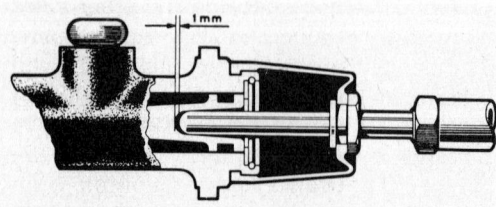

Cross-section at brake pedal adjustment in master cylinder (.04″).

The caliper which is mounted to the wheel suspension is in halves called the mounting (inside) half and the rim (outside) half. The friction pads are positioned by dowel pins which run through both caliper halves.

Friction Pads

Friction pads can be checked for wear without disassembling the caliper if an inexpensive gauge is used to measure the distance from the inside of one friction pad backing plate to the other while the brake is engaged. Clearance between the friction pad plates and the cross-spring in the center must be greater than 2 mm (.08″) on each side. See illustration. Both brake friction pads must be replaced if either pad is worn down so that braking remains equal.

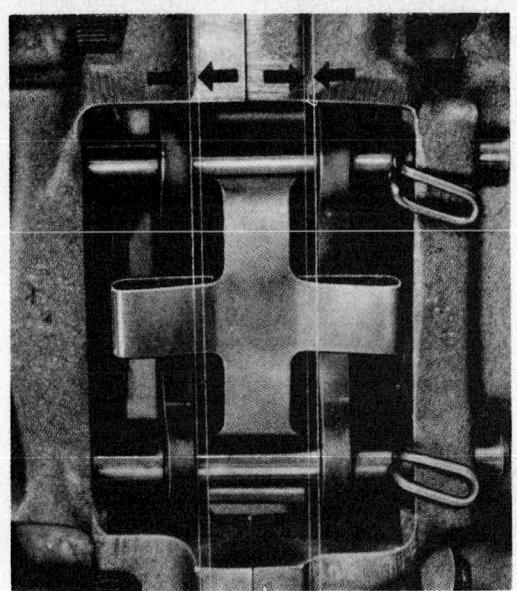

Measuring friction pad thickness.

If no gauge is available, pull out the retainers and tap dowel pins from brake caliper toward other side of car while depressing the cross-spring. Mark friction pads for later reassembly and pull pads from caliper. Oily, cracked, or defaced pads need replacement. Pads themselves must measure at all times greater than .08″ thick. Remove high spots on friction pads with cut stone file before reinstalling.

If installing new friction pads, force both caliper pistons completely into their caliper bores with a clamp or piece of smooth hardwood. *NOTE: open bleed valve on caliper to prevent brake reservoir overflow.* Clean area with alcohol. Clean brake disc with fine emery cloth and smooth off ridges at outside and inside of disc.

Replace friction pad cross-spring and retaining pins. Press brake pedal several times to seat pads. Bleed calipers and add brake fluid to reservoir. Avoid forceful braking for 125 miles to break in new pads.

CALIPERS

Remove caliper from wheel backing plate to inspect all other brake assembly parts. Detach brake line at union, plugging hose at union, and unfasten caliper with shield.

Caliper halves are *not* disassembled for repair work unless their joint leaks brake fluid. NOTE: *Do not disassemble Type 914 or 914/6 rear calipers, as this may destroy the automatic adjusting device.* From opening for friction pads, lift retainer plates from each piston. Next pry clamp rings from rubber seals and remove seals with plastic pin to prevent damage to the groove. Keep twin parts from the two halves separated.

Remove brake piston seal with a plastic pin to prevent damage to the groove.

Check caliper piston seals and clamp rings for deterioration or damage. Clean ring recesses with denatured alcohol. New rubber seals are recommended for installation with cleaned clamp rings. Make sure that seals are securely seated on their collars and clamp rings are correctly positioned on the seals. Push retained plates into pistons with handle of screwdriver.

To force pistons from caliper halves, loosen bleeder valve and carefully blow hydraulic fluid out of caliper at pressure of about 14 psi. Place caliper in a vise and depress one piston into caliper. Clamp it in. Put a thin piece of hardwood in front of that piston and force the other piston out with air pressure. Start with pressure of 29 psi and raise it if necessary. *Keep fingers out of caliper slot.* Clean parts with alcohol. Repair kits with replacement parts are available.

Insert clean piston into cylinder. Position cut-back part of piston ridge under the alignment tool when flat edge of tool is flush with top of caliper as shown.

Attach brake pipe and caliper to front end, making sure that mating surfaces of

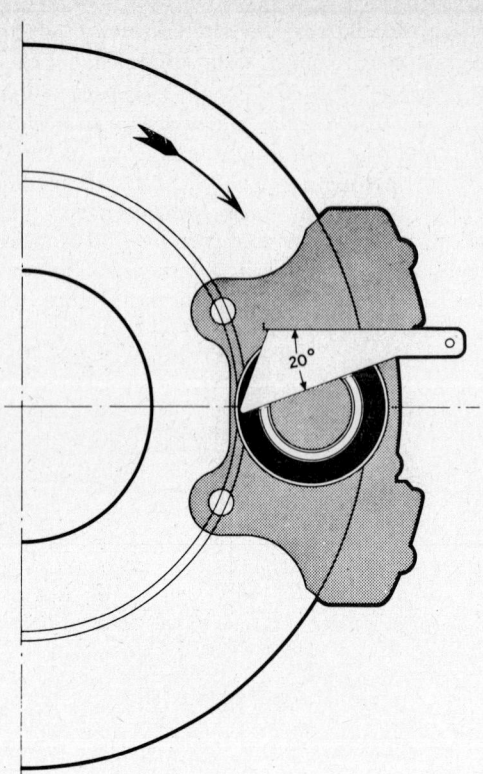

Positioning brake piston in caliper.

The master cylinder for disc brakes is a simple design that requires minimum maintenance. When cleaning assembly, use alcohol only. Check parts for wear, making sure that no dirt has clogged the ports. All parts are accessible after removing lock ring with small screwdriver.

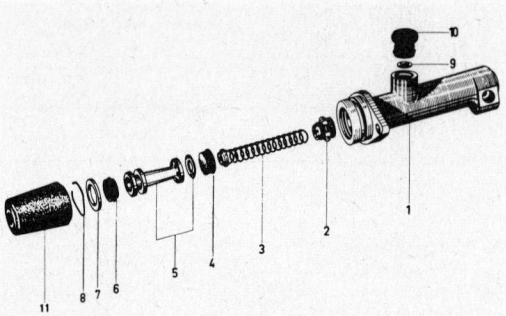

Master cylinder—disc brakes.

1 Housing
2 Special check valve
3 Spring
4 Primary piston cup
5 Piston with washer
6 Secondary piston cup
7 Piston stop plate
8 Lock ring
9 Washer
10 Rubber grommet
11 Rubber boot

caliper and steering knuckle are clean and smooth. Tighten caliper attaching bolts to 45 ft. lbs.

DISC RUNOUT

Check brake disc for lateral runout which should not exceed .008″ (0.2 mm) when measured half an inch from its circumference edge. If runout is greater, remove disc (by taking off wheel hub), secure it carefully in a vise, mark position and remove star head bolts. Remove disc evenly with puller. Check mating surfaces and shoulder for dirt, burrs or high spots. Torque new bolts to 73 ft-lbs. (10 mkg) in a cross pattern. Repack wheel bearings.

To remove master cylinder from chassis, unsnap accelerator pedal, unfasten floormat, and remove floor board. Withdraw rubber boot from cylinder and drain brake fluid reservoir. Remove undershield covering steering gear. Detach hydraulic lines and stop-light switch from master cylinder. Remove hose connecting reservoir with cylinder and dismount master cylinder from body.

When installing master cylinder, seal the flange to the body with compound. Provide clearance of 1.0 mm (.04″) between piston rod and piston in cylinder. Check vent passage in reservoir. Fill system with fresh brake fluid and bleed it. Check brake lights. Install undershield.

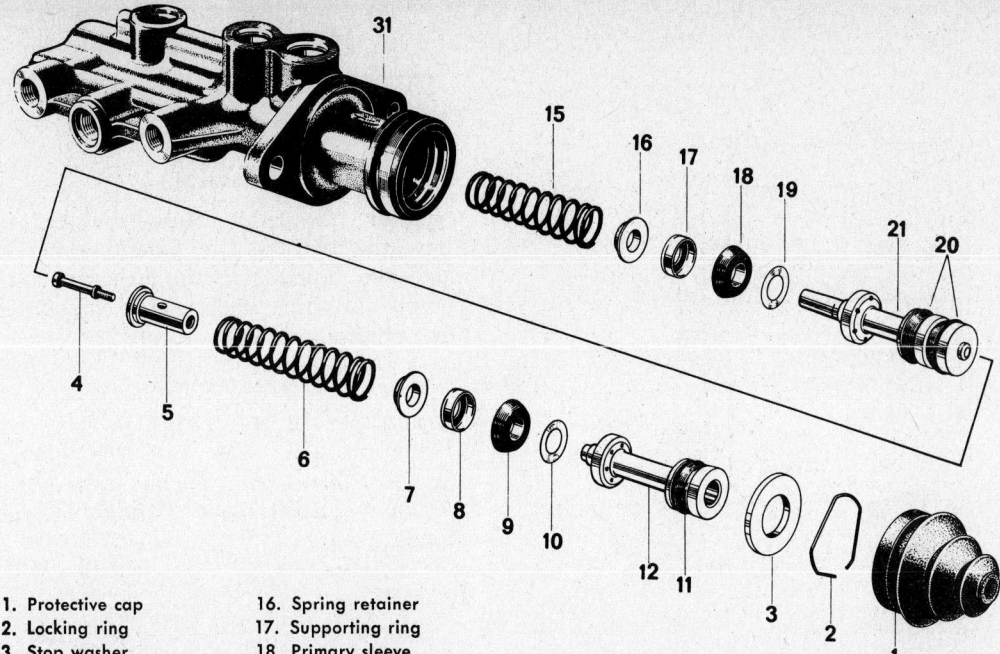

1. Protective cap
2. Locking ring
3. Stop washer
4. Stop screw for stroke restriction
5. Stop sleeve
6. Compression spring for pressure piston
7. Spring retainer
8. Supporting ring
9. Primary sleeve
10. Filling disk
11. Grooved sleeve piston
12. Pressure piston
13. Stop screw
14. Sealing ring
15. Compression spring for intermediate piston
16. Spring retainer
17. Supporting ring
18. Primary sleeve
19. Filling disk
20. Separating sleeve
21. Intermediate piston
22. Brake warning switch
23. Round cord ring
24. Screw
25. Round cord ring
26. Compression spring
27. Piston
28. Sleeve
29. Tank plug
30. Washer
31. Tandem master brake cylinder housing

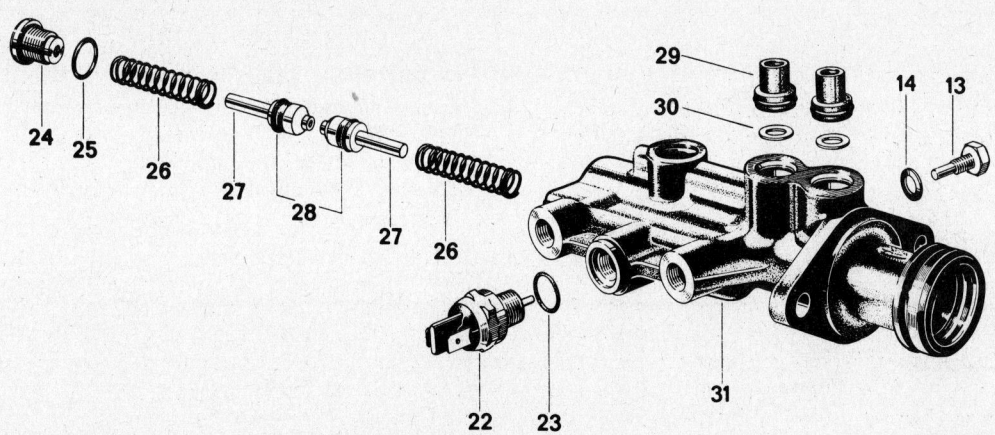

Exploded view of Type 914 and 914/6 tandem master cylinder

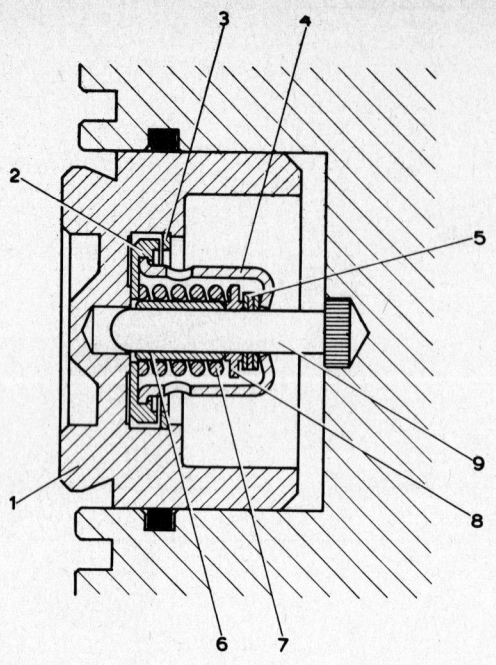

1. Piston
2. Stop washer
3. Lock washer
4. Spring housing
5. Friction disk
6. Spacing sleeve
7. Compression spring
8. Spacing washer
9. Friction pin

Type 914 and 914/6 adjusting and lateral wobble compensating device to keep the lifting clearance in the brake system constant under larger piston strokes.

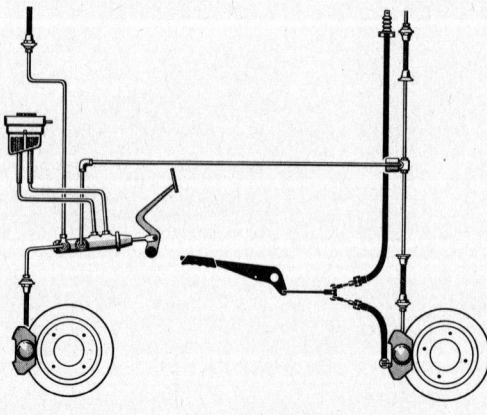

Schematic diagram of Type 914 and 914/6 hydraulic brake system

Heating System

Type 356

REMOVAL

Remove the engine from the car. Unscrew the bolt on the junction box. Remove the bolts from the exhaust flange. Loosen the pipe clamp and remove the junction box and exhaust pipe.

INSTALLATION

Install the heater in the reverse order of removal. Be sure that the junction box and exhaust pipe do not leak. Always use new gaskets and straighten bent flanges.

Type 912

REMOVAL

Remove the engine from the car. Remove the rear engine shield and detach the clamps from the holders. Remove the exhaust muffler. Remove the nuts from the front and rear flanges. Remove the securing claws from the exhaust pipe ends. Remove the retaining bracket and sheetmetal cover from the heat exchanger. Remove the shroud from the front and rear lower ducts. The heat exchanger can be removed after removing the front or rear flange from the cylinder head.

INSTALLATION

Installation is the reverse of removal. Note the inspection detailed for Type 356.

Type 911

REMOVAL

Detach and remove the connecting hose from the heat exchanger to the valve chamber. Remove the heater hose from the heat exchanger. Remove the heat exchanger.

INSTALLATION

Installation is the reverse of removal, noting the inspections detailed under Type 356.

Type 914 and 914/6

Installation and removal procedures are similar to the above for this type vehicle.

Windshield Wipers

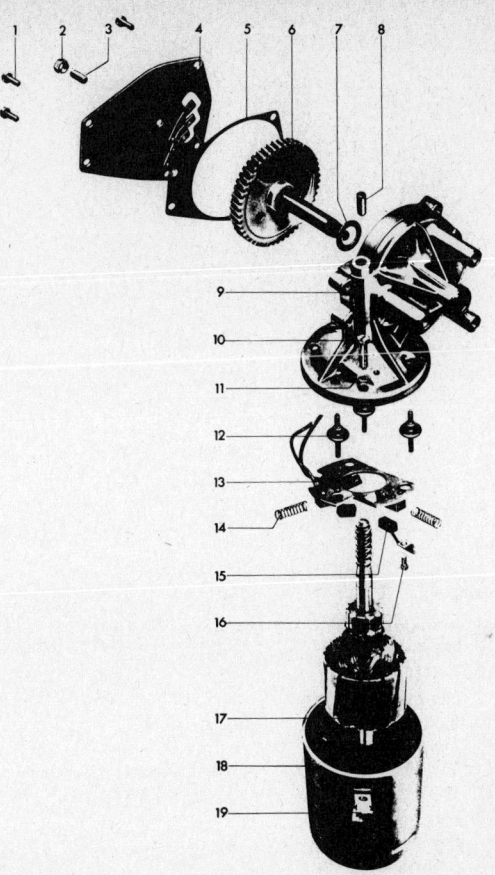

Type 356

REMOVAL

Detach the wiper linkage from both wiper arms. Remove the clamping screw from the drive lever. Detach the cables and connections. Remove both fixing screws. Detach the wiper motor.

INSTALLATION

Grease all the joints and proceed in the reverse of removal.

Type 914 and 914/6

REMOVAL

Disconnect the battery ground cable. Remove the wiper arms. Remove the bearing cap, hollow washer and rubber seal. Remove the container. Remove the fresh air blower housing. Loosen the nut from the anti-vibration bearing under the instrument panel. Remove the windshield wiper frame with the motor. Disconnect the lines.

INSTALLATION

Connect the wires according to the wiring diagram. Replace the windshield wiper frame with the motor. Be sure that the anti-vibration bearing is in place. Replace the nut on the bearing to avoid distortion. Replace the windshield wiper arms and connect the battery. Check the system for proper function. Replace the fresh air blower housing.

Exploded view of Type 914 windshield wiper motor

1. Screw
2. Hex. nut
3. Adjusting screw
4. Cover with contacts
5. Seal
6. Worm gear with drive shaft
7. Thrust washer
8. Adjusting screw
9. Bearing of gear unit
10. Hex. screw
11. Spring ring
12. Rubber bearing
13. Brush holder plate
14. Spring
15. Ground carbon
16. Screw
17. Armature
18. Pole housing with permanent magnet
19. Holding bracket

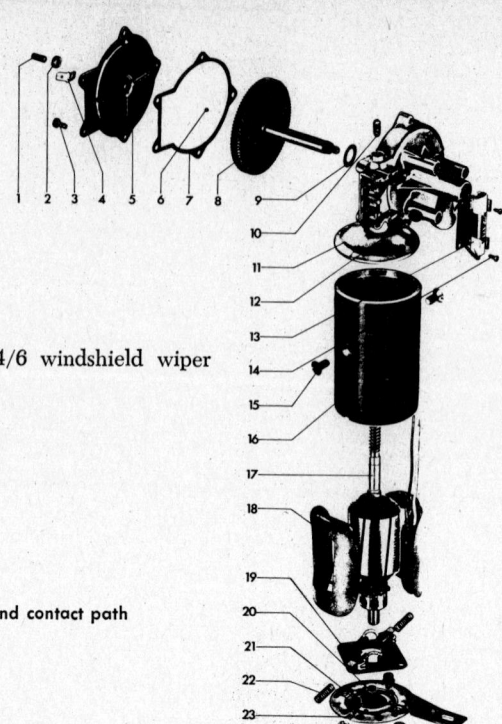

Exploded view of Type 914/6 windshield wiper motor

1. Adjusting screw
2. Counter nut
3. Screw
4. Ground plug
5. Cover
6. Ball
7. Seal
8. Worm gear with drive shaft and contact path
9. Thrust washer
10. Adjusting screw
11. Bearing of gear unit
12. Rubber sleeve
13. Preresistance
14. Oval head sheet screw for preresistance
15. Screw for pole shoes
16. Pole housing
    Pole shoes
17. Armature
18. Field winding
19. Brush holder plate
20. Thrust washer
21. Rubber bearing
22. Spring for carbon brush
23. Bearing plate
24. Spring ring
25. Oval head screw

SAAB SECTION

Index

Year and Model Identification

Introduction

The SAAB, a product of the Swedish aircraft firm SAAB Aktiebolag, was first introduced in 1949 to meet the demand for economical, dependable automobiles in the immediate post-war period. Designated the Model 92, the original design proved so sound that it has lasted to this day in the form of the Model 96, and its station wagon version the Model 95. The Sonett, SAAB's sport car, shares many components with the Monte Carlo 850 and V4 models and is covered in this book along with those models.

1956 93

1958 93B

1958 GT 750

1959 93F

1964 96

1959 95

1965 Monte Carlo 850

1960 96

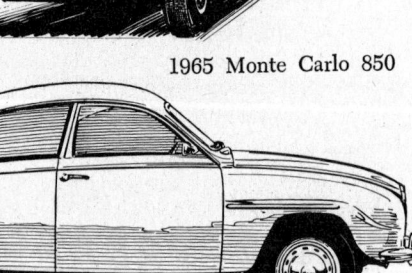

1965 96

1963 95

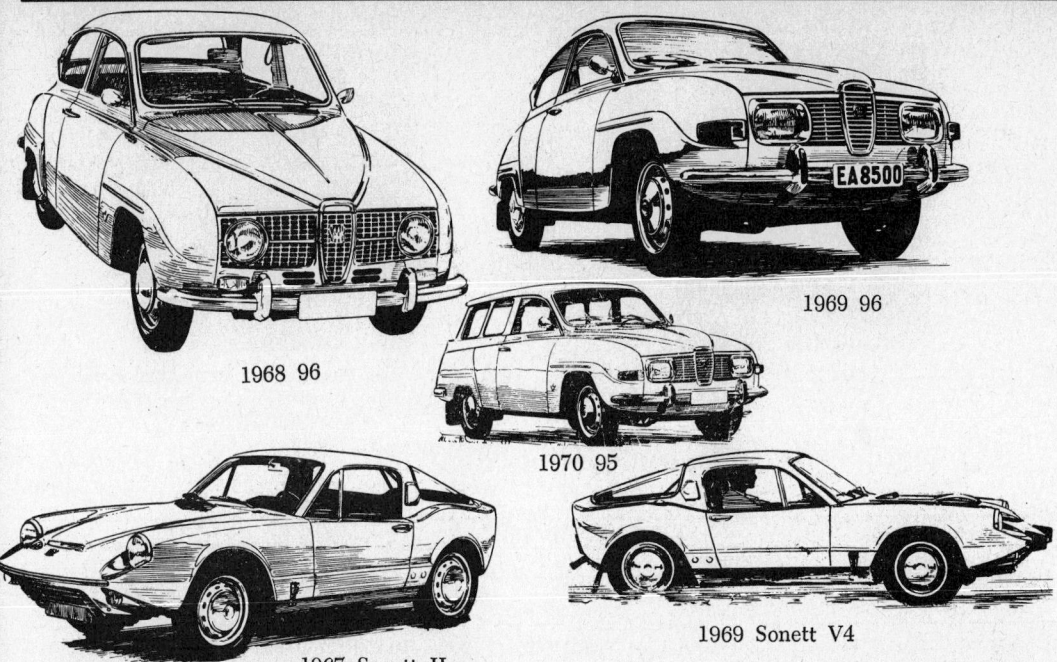

1968 96

1969 96

1970 95

1967 Sonett II

1969 Sonett V4

Vehicle and Engine Serial Number Identification

Vehicle number identification

The chassis number is found stamped on a plate attached to the firewall under the hood, as well as on the left-hand side of the support member underneath the front edge of the back seat. On 1969–70 models, however, the number is embossed on a tab visible through the driver's side windshield. The chart shows the cut-off chassis numbers for the different models.

Location of Chassis number on models up to 1969

Location of Chassis number on 1969-70 models

Engine number identification

The engine serial number is located on the right side of two-stroke engines. On models through 1965, the number is directly below the thermostat housing along the juncture of the cylinder head and block. On 1966 and later models, the number is above the starter, along the juncture of the block and crankcase. On the V4 engine, the number is on the block, directly ahead of the left valve cover.

Location of engine serial number—two-stroke to 1965

Location of engine serial number—two-stroke from 1966

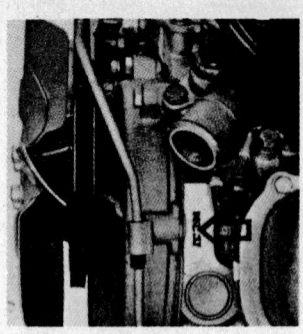

Location of engine serial number—four-stroke V4

Vehicle Identification

| Model | Model Year | | | | | |
	1960	1961	1962	1963	1964	1965
GT–750	100,001–112,500	112,501–139,600	139,601–150,000			
95	1–1,700	1,701–3,684	3,685–6,623	6,624–10,800	10,801–N.A.	23,101–28,701
96 (incl. Sport)	100,101–112,500	112,501–139,600	139,601–168,000	168,001–201,400	201,401–N.A.	310,001–349,693

| Model | Model Year | | | | |
	1966	1967	1968	1969	1970
GT–750					
95	30,001–37,300	42,001–50,197	52,001–62,059	65,001–74,986	80,001–
96 (incl. Sport)	370,001–400,750	420,001–458,526	470,001–507,018	520,001–552,859	560,001–

General Engine Specifications

Model	Year	Type	Cu. In. Displacement	Developed Horsepower @ rpm (DIN)	Developed Torque (DIN) @ rpm (ft. lbs)	Bore and Stroke (in.)	Compression Ratio
GT 750	1958-1960	3 cyl., two-stroke	46 (748 cc.)	45 @ 4,800	61 @ 3,500	2.60 X 2.87	9.8:1
95 and 96	1960-1964	3 cyl., two-stroke	51.9 (841 cc.)	38 @ 4,250	59 @ 3,000	2.76 X 2.87	7.3:1
95 and 96	1965	3 cyl., two-stroke	51.9 (841 cc.)	40 @ 4,250	60 @ 3,000	2.76 X 2.87	8.1:1
Sport Monte Carlo 850	1965-1966	3 cyl., two-stroke	51.9 (841 cc.)	55 @ 5,000	68 @ 3,800	2.76 X 2.87	9.0:1
95 and 96	1966-1967	3 cyl., two-stroke	51.9 (841 cc.)	42 @ 4,250	62 @ 3,100	2.76 X 2.87	8.5:1
Sonett II	1967	3 cyl., two-stroke	51.9 (841 cc.)	60 @ 5,200	69.4 @ 4,000	2.76 X 2.87	9.0:1
95 and 96	1967-1970	V4, four-stroke	91.4 (1498 cc.)	65 @ 4,700	85 @ 2,500	3.54 X 2.32	9.0:1
Sonett II and III	1968-1970	V4, four-stroke	91.4 (1498 cc.)	65 @ 4,700	85 @ 2,500	3.54 X 2.32	9.0:1
95 and 96, Sonett III	1971	V4, four-stroke	103.6 (1698 cc.)	65 @ 4,700	85 @ 2,500	3.54 X 2.63	8.0:1

Tune-Up Specifications

Year	Model	Engine	Spark Plugs (Bosch) Type[1]	Gap (in.)	Distributor Dwell (deg.)	Gap (in.)	Basic Ignition Timing (deg.)	Cranking Compression Pressure (psi)	Valves Clearance (in.) Warm In.	Ex.	Intake Opens (deg.)	Idle Speed
1958- 1960	GT 750	3 cyl., 750 cc.	M240TI	.028[2] .033[3]	80-84	.012- .016	2 BTDC	138 ± 7				N.A.
1960- 1964	95 and 96	3 cyl., 850 cc.	M225TI	.028[2] .032[3]	77-83	.012- .016	10 BTDC[4] 7 BTDC[5]	112 ± 7				N.A.
1965	95 and 96	3 cyl., 850 cc.	M240TI	.032	80-84	.012- .016	7 BTDC	121 ± 7: cyl. 1,3 114 ± 7: cyl. 2				600- 750
1965 1966 1967	Sport Monte Carlo 850 Sonett II	3 cyl., 850 cc.	MGV260 T31S	.022- .024 .028- .047 (max)[6]	75-82	.014- .018	10 BTDC	128 ± 7				600- 750
1966- 1967	95 and 96	3 cyl., 850 cc.	M240TI	.032	75-82	.014- .018	10 BTDC	121 ± 7: cyl. 1,3 114 ± 7: cyl. 2				600- 750
1967- 1970	95 and 96	V4, 1,500 cc.	W225T35[7] W200T30[8]	.024- .028	50 ± 2	.016	6 BTDC @ 500 rpm[9]	N.A.	.014	.016	21 BTDC	800- 900
1968- 1969	Sonett II	V4, 1,500 cc.	W225T35[7] W200T30[8]	.024- .028	50 ± 2	.016	10 BTDC @ 1,000 rpm[9]	N.A.	.016	.016	21 BTDC	900
1971	95 and 96	V4, 1,700 cc.	W145T30	.025	50 ± 2	.016	3 BTDC @ 800 rpm[9]	N.A.	.014	.016	N.A.	800- 900

1 For normal driving; see text for chart of recommended plugs for other uses.
2 With normal ignition cables.
3 With resistance ignition cables.
4 With VJ3 BR8T distributor.
5 With VJU3 BR1T and VJU3 BR2T distributors.
6 Sport with capacitative discharge ignition system.
7 Black or silver painted engine.
8 Blue painted engine.
9 Vacuum hose disconnected.

NOTE: If these specifications differ from those on the engine compartment sticker, use the sticker figures.

Firing Order

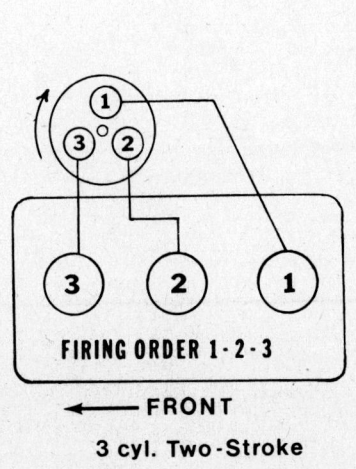

FIRING ORDER 1-2-3

← FRONT

3 cyl. Two-Stroke

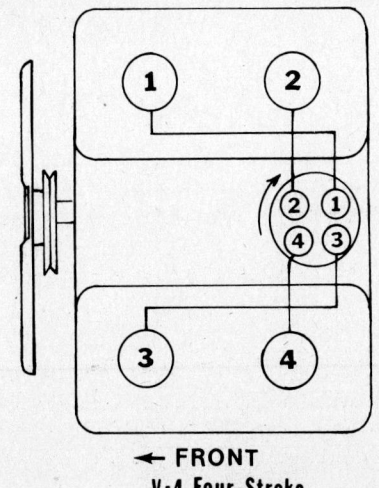

← FRONT
V-4 Four-Stroke
FIRING ORDER 1-3-4-2

Engine Rebuilding Specifications
Crankshaft

Year	Model	Main Bearing Journals				Connecting Rod Bearing Journals			Side-play at piston pin (in.)
		Journal diameter (mm.)	Oil clearance (in.)	Shaft end-play (in.)	Thrust on No.	Journal Diameter (mm.)	Oil clearance (in.)	Side-play (in.)	
	GT 750 to chassis No. 118.980, early 850[1]			.002			.0006-.0008	.003-.005	.158
to 1965	Late GT 750, late 850[2]			.002			.0006-.0008	.081-.084	.004-.016
1965-1967	All two-stroke[2]			.002			.0004-.0006	.081-.091	.004-.016
1967-70	1,500 cc. V4	57.000-56.990 (red) 56.990-56.980 (blue)[3]	.0005-.002 (Std.) .0006-.002 (U/S)	.0005-.002 (Std.) .0006-.002 (U/S)	Center Bearing	53.99-53.89 (blue) 54.00-53.99 (red)[4]	.0006-.002 (Std.) .0006-.003 (U/S)	N.A.	[5]

1 Rods guided by crankshaft.
2 Rods guided by piston.
3 Undersizes available: .05, .25, .50, .75, 1.00 mm.
4 Undersizes available: .25, .50, .75, 1.00 mm.
5 Piston and connecting rod are not to be separated.
   They are available only as an assembly.
U/S: undersize.

Engine Rebuilding Specifications
Valves

Model	Seat angle (deg.)	Seat width (in.)	Valve lift (in.)		Valve spring pressure (lbs.) @ length (in.)	Valve spring free length (in.)	Stem diameter (mm.)		Stem to guide clearance (in.)		Valve guide removable
			In.	Ex.			In.	Ex.	In.	Ex.	
1,500 cc. V4	45	.059-.070	.38	.38	39-47 @ 1.59[1]	1.78[2]	8.043-8.025 Standard 8.243-8.225 8.443-8.425 8.643-8.625 8.843-8.825 Oversize	8.017-7.999 Standard 8.217-8.199 8.417-8.399 8.617-8.599 8.817-8.799 Oversize	.001-.002	.002-.004	No

1 Monte Carlo, Sonnett: 59-66 @ 1.59.
2 Monte Carlo, Sonnett: 185.

Engine Rebuilding Specifications
Block, Pistons, Rings

Model	Block — Bore (mm.) Std.	Block — Bore (mm.) Oversize	Pistons — Piston diameter (mm.) Std.	Pistons — Piston diameter (mm.) Oversize	Wrist pin diameter (in.) and fit	Piston clearance (in.)	Rings — Side clearance (in.)	Rings — End-gap (in.)
GT 750	65.994-66.001 Class A / 66.001-66.008 AB / 66.008-66.015 B / 66.043-66.053 C	66.508-66.515 Class 0.5 A / 66.515-66.522 0.5 B / 67.008-67.015 1.0 A / 67.015-67.022 1.0 B	65.907-65.914 Class A / 65.914-65.921 AB / 65.921-65.928 B / 65.926-65.963 C	66.421-66.428 Class 0.5 A / 66.428-66.435 0.5 B / 66.921-66.928 1.0 A / 66.928-66.935 1.0 B	.702[1]	.003-.004 max. .007	.003-.005 Upper / .002-.004 Center / .002-.004 Lower	.010-.020
850, 1960-1964	69.987-69.994 Class A / 69.994-70.001 AB / 70.001-70.008 B / 70.036-70.046 C	70.501-70.508 Class 0.5 A / 70.508-70.515 0.5 B / 71.001-71.008 1.0 A / 71.008-71.015 1.0 B	69.930-69.937 Class A / 69.937-69.944 AB / 69.944-69.951 B / 69.979-69.986 C	70.444-70.451 Class 0.5 A / 70.451-70.458 0.5 B / 70.944-70.951 1.0 A / 70.951-70.958 1.0 B	.702[1]	.002-.003 max. .006	.003-.005 Upper / .003-.005 Center / .002-.004 Lower	.010-.020
95 and 96 Two-stroke, 1965-1967	69.987-69.994 Class A / 69.994-70.001 AB / 70.001-70.008 B / 70.036-70.046 C	70.501-70.508 Class 0.5 A / 70.508-70.515 0.5 B / 71.001-71.008 1.0 A / 71.008-71.015 1.0 B	69.927-69.939 Class A / 69.934-69.946 AB / 69.941-69.953 B / 69.976-69.988 C	70.444-70.451 Class 0.5 A / 70.451-70.458 0.5 B / 70.944-70.951 1.0 A / 70.951-70.958 1.0 B	.75[1]	.002-.003 max. .006	.003-.005 Upper / .003-.005 Center / .002-.003 Lower	.010-.020
Sport, Monte Carlo 850, and Sonett II Two-stroke, 1965-1967	69.987-69.994 Class A / 69.994-70.001 AB / 70.001-70.008 B / 70.036-70.046 C	70.501-70.508 Class 0.5 A / 70.508-70.515 0.5 B / 71.001-71.008 1.0 A / 71.008-71.015 1.0 B	69.895-69.902 Class A / 69.902-69.909 AB / 69.909-69.916 B / 69.944-69.951 C	70.409-70.416 Class 0.5 A / 70.416-70.423 0.5 B / 70.909-70.916 1.0 A / 70.916-70.923 1.0 B	.75[1]	.003-.004 max. .006	.004 Upper / .003-.004 Center / .002-.004 Lower	.010-.020

Engine Rebuilding Specifications
Block, Pistons, Rings

Model	Block (mm.) Bore		Pistons Piston diameter (mm.)		Wrist pin diameter (in.) and fit	Piston clearance (in.)	Rings Side clearance (in.)	End-gap (in.)
	Std.	Oversize	Std.	Oversize				
1,500 cc. V4, 1967-1970	90.030-90.040	90.530-90.540 91.030-91.040	89.978-90.002	90.478-90.502 90.978-91.002	Piston and rod supplied as assembly.	.001-.002	.002-.003 Upper .002-.003 Center .001-.008 Lower	.010-.020 Upper .010-.020 Center .015-.055 Lower

1 Should fit with light thumb pressure. Pin should be easily rotatable with two fingers.

Torque Specifications
V4 Engine (ft./lbs.)

Spark plugs	Main bearing	Connecting rod	Crank-shaft gear	Flywheel	Cam-shaft thrust plate	Cam-shaft gear	Cylinder head	Intake manifold bolts	Intake manifold nuts	Intermediate plate to block	Timing cover	Water pump to timing cover	Balance shaft pulley	Oil pump to block	Oil pan	Ther-mostat housing	Valve cover	Rocker shaft	Oil filter
22-29	72	25	36	50	15	36	40, then 50, then 68	2.9-5.8, then 16-21[1]	2.2-3.6, then 11-13[2]	15	15	7	36	11	4	15	4	32	1/2 turn after contacting block

1 Figures given apply thru chassis No. 95/66.249 and 96/524.379. For later models: 2.9-5.8, then 15-18. For Sonett: 4, then 11, then 15, then 18.

2 Figures given apply thru chassis No. 95/66.249 and 96/524.379. For later models: 2.9-5.8, then 15-18.

Torque Specifications
Two-Cycle Engine (ft./lbs.)

Model	Spark plugs	Cylinder head	Crankcase halves	Flywheel bolts	Crankshaft pulley
750 cc.	32[1]	[2] Bolts marked 80 — 47 ft. lbs. 100 — 58 ft. lbs.	5/16" — 18 3/8" — 29	22	36
850 cc.	32[1]	36[2]	5/16" — 18 3/8" — 29	22	36

1 Bosch MGV260T31S: 14.
2 See text for correct method of tightening bolts.

Torque Specifications
Transmission (ft./lbs.)

Transmission case end cover	Differential bearings	Ring gear bolts	Pinion shaft nut	Primary shaft nut	Counter-shaft nut
18	29	18	initially 87, then 44	36	60

Torque Specifications
Suspension and Wheels (ft./lbs.)

Castle nut, front wheel hub	Castle nut, rear wheel hub	Tie-rod end	Wheel bolts
122-144	65-72	25-36	58-72

Tightening Sequences

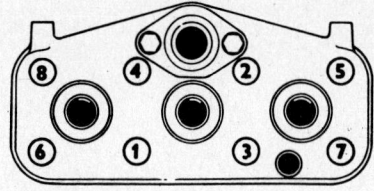

Cylinder head bolt tightening sequence—750 cc. engines

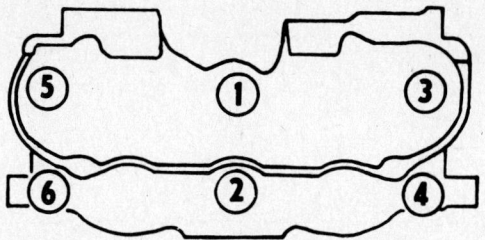

Cylinder head bolt tightening sequence—V4

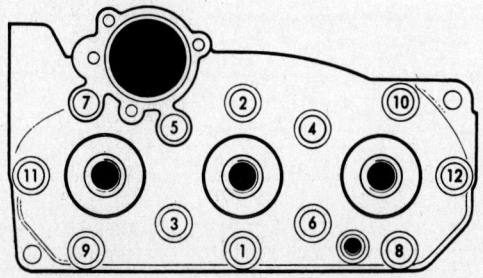

Cylinder head bolt tightening sequence—850 cc. engines

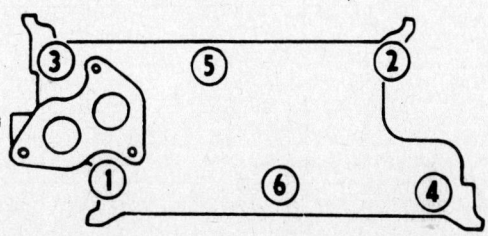

Intake manifold tightening sequence—V4

Electrical Specifications
Battery and Starter

Year	Model	Battery			Starter
		Capacity (Amp. hours)	Volts	Grounded terminal	Brush spring tension (oz.)
1960-64	2-cycle	34	12	Neg.	16-25
1965-1966	2-cycle	34	12	Neg.	19-25
1967	2-cycle	44	12	Neg.	19-25
1967-1970	V4	44	12	Neg.	41-46
1971	V4	60	12	Neg.	N.A.

Electrical Specifications
Generator and Regulator

Year	Model	Generator			Regulator				
		Bosch part number	Brush spring pressure (oz.)	Maximum output (Amps.)	Bosch part number	Cut-in voltage	Reverse current relay (Amps.)	Maximum output (watts)	Voltage setting @idle
1960-1963	All	LJ/GEG 160/12/2500+W30 R4	16-21	20	RS/TBA 160/12/1	12.1-13.1	3-9	240	14.3-15.3
1963-1964	All	LJ/GEG 160/12/2500+W30 R4	16-21	20	RS/VA 200/12/A2	12.3-13.3	2-7.5	300[1]	13.8-14.8
1965-1966	95, 96, Sport[2]	EG(R) 14V 25A 31	16-21	25	VA 14V 25A or RS/VA 200/12/A2	12.4-13.1	2-7.5	300[1]	13.5-14.5

1 Warm.
2 Sport: 1965 only.

Electrical Specifications
Alternator and AC Regulator

Year	Model	Alternator			AC Regulator				
		Bosch part number	Brush spring pressure (oz.)	Maximum output (Amps.)	Bosch part number	Cut-in voltage	Reverse current relay (Amps.)	Maximum current (watts)	Voltage setting
1966	Monte Carlo 850	K1 ↔ 14V 35A 20	10.5-14	35	AD 1 14V	N.A.	N.A.	N.A.	N.A.
1967	95, 96 2-stroke	K1 ↔ 14V 35A 20	10.5-14	35	AD 1 14V	N.A.	N.A.	N.A.	N.A.
1967	Sonett 2-stroke	K1 ↔ 14V 35A 20	10.5-14	35	ADN 1 14V	12.4-13.1	2-7.5	300, warm	13.5-14.5
1967-1970	All V4	K1 ↔ 14V 35A 20	10.5-14	35	AD 1 14V	N.A.	N.A.	N.A.	N.A

Distributor Specifications

Distributor Model (Bosch Designation Plus Factory Parts No.)	Used on SAAB Models	Point Gap (in.)	Distributor Dwell Angle (deg.)	Contact Pressure (oz.)	Direction of Rotation	Condenser Type	Dynamic Timing (deg.)	Basic Timing (deg.) ▲	Ignition Coil Designation
VJ3BR7T	GT-750	.012–.016	80–84	38–42	CW	LMKO Z30Z	22B†•	2B•	ZS/KZ 2/12 A or TK 12 A 10
VJ3BR8T	95 (up to 4836) / 96 (up to 148268)	.012–.016	77–83	14–19	CW	LMKO 1Z30Z	20B†	10B	ZS/KZ 1/12A, TK 12 A 4 or K–12
VJ3BR9T	GT-850 (up to Sport 96 1965)	.012–.016	80–84	39–42	CW	LMKO 1Z30	20B†	10B	ZS/KZW 1/12 (1/6), E3LC–134 or TKW 12 (1/6)
VJ3BR10T / VJ3BR11T	GT–850 (up to Sport 96 1965)	.012–.016	77–83	14–19	CW	LMKO 1Z30	20B†	10B	KW12V
VJU3BR1T	95 (from 4837) / 96 (from 148269)	.012–.016	77–83	14–19	CW	LMKO 1Z42Z	17B†◉	7B	K–12
VJU3BR2T / JFU3 (R) 0 231 144 002	95 (from 10801) / 96 (from 201401)	.012–.016	77–83 (VJU3) / 80–84 (JFU3)	14–19	CW	LMKO 1Z42	17B†◉	7B	K–12
JF3 (R) 0 231 120 023	Sport 96 (up to 1965) / Sonett 2-stroke	.014–.018	75–82	14–19	CW	LMKO 1Z30	20B†	10B	KW12V
JFU3 0 231 144 004	GT–850 (from 1966)	.014–.018	75–82	18–22	CW	LMKO 1Z42	20B†◉	10B	KW12V
JFUR4 0 231 146 044 / JFUR4 0 231 146 024	95 (1967-68) / 96 (1967-68)	.016	50±2	14–19	CW	1 237 330 091	6B†◉	6B	K–12
JFUR4 0 231 146 033 / JFUR4 0 231 146 073	95 (1967-68) / 96 (1967-68) Sonett V4	.016	50±2	14–19	CW	1 237 330 091 / 1 237 330 113••	6B†◉ / 10B††	6B	K–12
JFUR4 0 231 146 084	95 (1969-70) / 96 (1969-70)	.016	50±2	14–19	CW	1 237 330 091	6B†◉	6B	K–12

▲ With test light, engine not running.
† At 3,000 rpm.
‡ At 500 rpm.
◉ With vacuum line disconnected and plugged.
• If equipped with dual carburetor and open exhaust −20° (22 mm. below upper mark) and TDC (upper mark).
•• Sonett V4
†† At 1,000 rpm (Sonett V4).

Distributor Advance Specifications

Distributor Type or Designation	Range (deg.)	Begins (rpm)	Centrifugal Advance (degrees @ dist. rpm)				Vacuum Advance		
			5° (rpm)	10° (rpm)	15° (rpm)	Stops (rpm)	Range (deg.)	Begins (in. Hg.)	Stops (in. Hg.)
VJ3 BR7 T	18–22	400–800	700–1,000	900–1,250	1,150–1,500	1,500–2,000	---	---	---
VJ3 BR8 T	17–21	900–1,300	1,200–1,600	1,400–4,700	4,600–5,300	5,300–6,000	---	---	---
VJU3 BR1 T	17–21	900–1,300	1,200–1,600	1,400–4,700	4,600–5,300	5,300–6,000	8.5–11.5	4.73–5.51°	5.51–6.30
VJU3 BR2 T	17–21	900–1,300	1,200–1,600	1,400–4,700	4,600–5,300	5,300–6,000	8.5–11.5	4.73–5.51°	5.51–6.30
JFU3 0 231 144 002	20	900–1,300	1,100–1,500	3,800–4,300	4,400–4,900	5,000–5,500	10	4.73–5.51°	5.51–6.30
JFU3 0 231 144 003	15	900–1,300	1,100–1,500	3,800–4,300	4,200–4,700	4,500–5,000	15	2.36–3.15	4.73–5.51
JF3 (R) 0 231 120 023	10	800–1,200	1,100–1,500	---	---	1,400–1,800 (@ 10°)	---	---	---
JFU3 0 231 144 004	10	800–1,200	1,100–1,500	---	---	1,400–1,800 (@ 10°)	15	2.36–3.15	4.73–5.51
0 231 146 044	12–14	375–425	450–500	1,025–1,400	---	1,800	7.7–9.0	6.69–8.67	16.9–18.1
0 231 146 024	.12–14	375–425	450–500	1,025–1,400	---	1,800	7.7–9.0	6.69–8.67	16.9–18.1
0 231 146 033	12.5–14.5	300–400	450–500	950–1,250	---	1,650	7.7–9.0	6.69–8.67	16.9–18.1
0 231 146 073	12.5–14.5	300–400	450–500	950–1,250	---	1,650	7.7–9.0	6.69–8.67	16.9–18.1
0 231 146 084	11.5–13.5	500–615	790–910	1,300–1,800	---	2,400	6.5–8.5	3.54–5.51	9.68

° Should return to zero before 3.94 in. Hg. (100 mm. Hg.) is reached.

Brake Specifications

Year	Model 1	Type		Brake cylinder bore			Brake drum or disc. diameter (in.)	
		Front	Rear	Master cylinder (in.)	Wheel cylinder (in.)		Front	Rear
					Front	Rear		
1960-1964	Type I	Drum	Drum	.875	.875	.750	9	8
1960-1964	Type II	Drum	Drum	.750	.8[2]	.750	9	8
1960-1964	Type III	Drum	Drum	.750	.8[2]	.750	9	8
1965-1966	95, 96	Drum	Drum	.750	.8	.750	9	8
1965-1966	Sport, Monte Carlo 850	Disc	Drum	.750	2	.750	10.75	8
1967-1968	95, 96 Monte Carlo	Disc	Drum	.750	2	.625[3]	10.50	8
1969-1970	95, 96	Disc	Drum	.813	2	.625[3]	10.50	8
1967-1969	Sonett	Disc	Drum	.750	2	.625	10.50	8

2 95, 96: .750.
3 95, 1967-1969: .750.

Capacities and Pressures

	Model	Engine Crank-case refill after draining (qts.)		Transmission refill after draining (pts.)	Fuel tank (gals.)	Cooling system with heater (qts.)	Normal fuel pressure (psi)	Maximum coolant pressure (psi)
		With filter	Without filter					
1960-1964	95			4	11.5	8.1	N.A.	3.5-4.5
1960-1964	96, GT 750			4	10.5	8.1	N.A.	3.5-4.5
1965-1967	95			3	11.5	6.9	2.1-3.5	3.4-4.3
1965-1967	96			3	10.5	6.9	2.1-3.5	3.4-4.3
1965-1966	Sport, Monte Carlo 850			3	10.5	6.9	2.1-4.3	3.4-4.3
1967	Sonett 2-stroke			3	15.8	6.9	N.A.	3.4-4.3
1967-1970	95 V4	3.3	3.0	3	11.5	7.9[1]	3.4-4.3	2.2-4.3
1967-1970	96, Monte Carlo V4	3.3	3.0	3	10.5	7.9[1]	3.4-4.3	2.2-4.3
1968-1970	Sonett V4	3.3	3.0	3.6	15.8	7.6	3.4-4.3	2.2-4.3
1971	95 V4	3.5		3	11.1	7.5	3.4-4.3	2.2-4.3
1971	96 V4	3.5		3	10.0	7.5	3.4-4.3	2.2-4.3

1 1969-1970: 7.5.

Brake System Application

System	Model	Serial No.
Type I	95	Up to 3130
	96	Up to 134999
	GT-750	Up to 134999
Type II	95	3131 to 10800
	96	135000 to 201400
	GT-750	135000 to 201400
Type III	95	From 10801
	96	From 201401
	96 Sport (GT-850)	From 201401
	Sonett	All

Chassis and Wheel Alignment Specifications

Year	Model	Chassis			Wheel alignment					
		Wheel-base (in.)	Track (in.)		Caster	Camber	Toe-in.	Kingpin Inclination (deg.)	Wheel pivot ratio (deg.)	
			Front	Rear	Range (deg.)	Range (deg.)	(in.)		Inner wheel	Outer wheel
1960-1971	All sedan and wagon	98	48	48	1.5-2.5	.5-1.0	.04-.12	6-8	21-24	20
1967	Sonett	85	48	48	1.5-2.5	—.25-+.25	0-.08	6-8	21-24	20
1968-1969	Sonett	85	50.5	50.5	1.5-2.5	—.25-+.25	0-.08	6-8	21-24	20

Light Bulb Specifications

Year and model	Usage	Wattage	Candlepower
1960-64, All	Headlights	50/40	
	Turn signal/parking	25/7	32/4
	Turn signal/stop	25	32
	Tail	5	
	License plate	5	
	Courtesy	5	
	All warning and instrument	2	
	Backup	25	
	Trunk	4	
1965-1967, All two-stroke sedan and wagon	Headlights	50/40	
	Parking/flasher, front	25/5	32/4
	Stop/flasher, rear	25	32
	Tail	5	
	License plate	5	
	Dome	5	
	Driving and fog	45	
	All warning and instrument	2	
	Backup	32	
	Trunk	4	
1967-68, All V4 sedan and wagon	Headlights	50/40	
	Parking/turn signal, front	21/5	
	Stop/turn signal, rear	21	
	Tail	5	
	License plate	5	
	Backup	21/5	
	Dome	5	
	Driving and fog	45	
	All warning and instrument	2	
	Clock	4	
	Tachometer	2	
	Trunk	4	
1969-71, All V4 sedan and wagon	Headlights	50/40	
	Parking/turn signal, front	5/21	
	Turn signal, rear	21	
	Tail	5	
	Stop	21	
	License plate	5	
	All warning and instrument	2[2]	
	Dome	5	
	Trunk	4	
	Backup	21	
	Side position	4	
	Tachometer	2	

Light Bulb Specifications

Year and model	Usage	Wattage	Candlepower
1967-1969, Sonett	Parking, front	6	
	Flasher, front	25	
	Stop/flasher, rear	25	
	Tail	5	
	License plate	5	
	Map reading	5	
	All warning and instrument	2	
	Backup	32[1]	
	Clock	4	

1 1968-69: 25.
2 1971:1.2.
NOTE: All fuses are 8 ampere.

Carburetor Specifications

Year	Model	Type	Main jet	Main jet holder	Choke tube (mm.)	Emulsion jet	Emulsion tube	Idle fuel jet	Idle air jet	Starting air jet	Starting fuel jet	Accelerator pump jet	Needle valve	Float weight (oz.)	Float level (in.)	Compensating jet	Low speed fuel jet	Bypass fuel jet	Bypass air jet
1960	GT 750	Solex 40 AI or 40 BI	150		28	250	1	45	100	3.5	190		2.0	.75	[1]				
1960-1964	850 cc.	Solex 40 AI or 40 BI	135		28	250	1	45	100	3.5	190		2.0	.75	[1]				
1965	850 cc.	Solex 40 BI	140		28	250	1	40	100	3.5	190		1.5	.75	[1]				
1960	GT 750	Solex 44 PII	150		32	300	19	50	140				2.5	.35	[1]				
1960	GT 750	Zenith 34 VNN	107		30	200		50	140				2.0	.22-.24	[1]	110			
1965-1967	850 cc.	Zenith 34 VNN	105		30	200		45	50				1.5	.22-.24	[1]	105			
Thru 1964	Monte Carlo	Solex 34 BIC	115		28		21	55-60	120	3.5	160			.20	[1]	120			
1965	Sport	Solex 34W	120	A	28	200	21	35		3.5	170		1.5	.20	[1]				
1966-1967	Monte Carlo 850	Solex 34 W2(Y)	135 [2]	A	28	220	21	35		3.5	170		1.2	.20	[1]		55		
1966-1967	Monte Carlo 850	Solex 34 W2(Z)	120	A	28	200	21	35		3.5	170		1.2	.20	[1]		55		
1967	Sonett	Solex 40 DHW	130 [3]		33	240		45	100				2.0	.26	[1]			65	100
1967-1968	Sedan and Wagon	Solex 28-32 PDSIT-7	125		25.5	110		50	1.5			50	1.5	.26	[1]				

Carburetor Specifications

Year	Model	Type	Main jet	Main jet holder	Choke tube (mm.)	Emulsion jet	Emulsion tube	Idle fuel jet	Idle air jet	Starting air jet	Starting fuel jet	Accelerator pump jet	Needle valve	Float weight (oz.)	Float level (in.)	Compensating jet	Low speed fuel jet	Bypass fuel jet	Bypass air jet
1967-1968	Sedan and Wagon	Solex 32 PDSIT-4	127.5		25.5	95 or 100		50 or 42.5	1.5			50	1.5	.26	[1]				
1968-1969	Sonett	Solex 32 PDSIT-4	122.5		25.5	100		50	1.5			50	1.5	.26	[1]				
1969-1970	95 and 96	FoMoCo C8GH-9510-G	140										2.0		[1]				
1969	95 and 96, USA models	FoMoCo C8GH-9510-H	135										2.0		[1]				
1970	95 and 96, USA models	FoMoCo 70TW-9510-AA	135										2.0		[1]				
1971	95 and 96, USA models	Autolite 71TW-LA																	

1 See text.
2 Outer carburetors: 120.
3 Outer carburetors: 122.5.

Wiring Diagrams

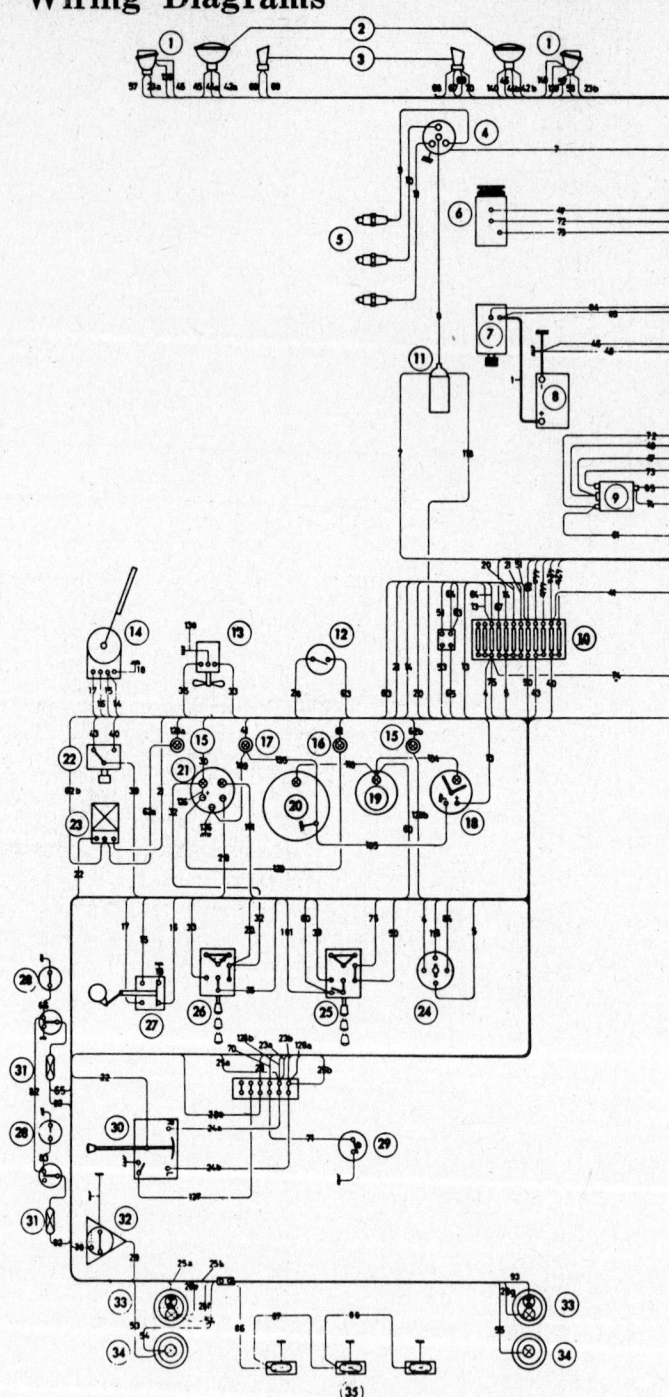

1. Turn signals and side lights
2. Headlights
3. Horn
4. Distributor
5. Spark plugs
6. Generator
7. Starter
8. Battery
9. Relay
10. Fuse box
11. Ignition coil
12. Stop light switch
13. Heater fan motor
14. Wiper motor
15. Turn indicator repeater light
16. Charge indicator light
17. High beam indicator lamp
18. Electric clock
19. Coolant thermometer
20. Speedometer and odometer
21. Fuel gauge
22. Dimmer switch
23. Flasher unit
24. Ignition and starter switch
25. Headlight switch and instrument illumination rheostat
26. Heater fan switch
27. Windshield wiper switch
28. Courtesy light switch
29. Horn button
30. Turn indicator switch
31. Courtesy light with switch
32. Fuel tank gage
33. Stop lights and turn indicators
34. Tail lights
35. License plate light

Wiring diagram—SAAB 95 (station wagon) 1965

Black: 1, 7, 18, 19, 45, 46, 47, 49, 71, 105, 109, 135, 136, 139, 140.

Red: 5, 8, 9, 10, 11, 21, 28, 28e, 28f, 28g, 32, 39, 61, 63, 65, 67, 68 72, 92, 126, 129.

Green: 16, 22, 50, 51, 53, 54, 55, 57, 58, 60, 86, 87, 88, 101, 104, 110.

Gray: 4, 25b, 29, 35, 44a, 62a, 62b, 64, 69, 70, 74, 75, 85, 93.

White: 20, 23b, 24b, 40, 42b, 66, 82, 83, 118, 128a.

Yellow: 17, 23a, 24a, 33, 43, 44b, 73, 84, 128b.

Brown: 14, 15, 30, 137.

Blue: 13, 25a, 41, 42a.

1. Turn signal indicators and side lights
2. Headlights
3. Horn
4. Distributor
5. Spark plugs
6. Generator
7. Starter
8. Battery
9. Voltage regulator
10. Fuse box
11. Ignition coil
12. Series resistance
13. Stop light switch
14. Heater fan motor
15. Wiper motor
16. Direction indicator repeater light
17. Charge indicator light
18. High beam indicator light
19. Electric clock
20. Coolant thermometer
21. Speedometer and odometer
22. Fuel gauge
23. Dimmer switch
24. Flasher
25. Ignition and starter switch
26. Headlight switch and instrument
26. Headlight switch and instrument illumination rheostat
27. Warning flasher switch with control lamp
28. Heater fan switch
29. Windshield wiper switch
30. Courtesy light switch
31. Horn button
32. Direction indicator switch
33. Courtesy light with switch
34 Fuel tank gauge
35. Stop light and turn indicators
36. Tail lights
37. License plate light

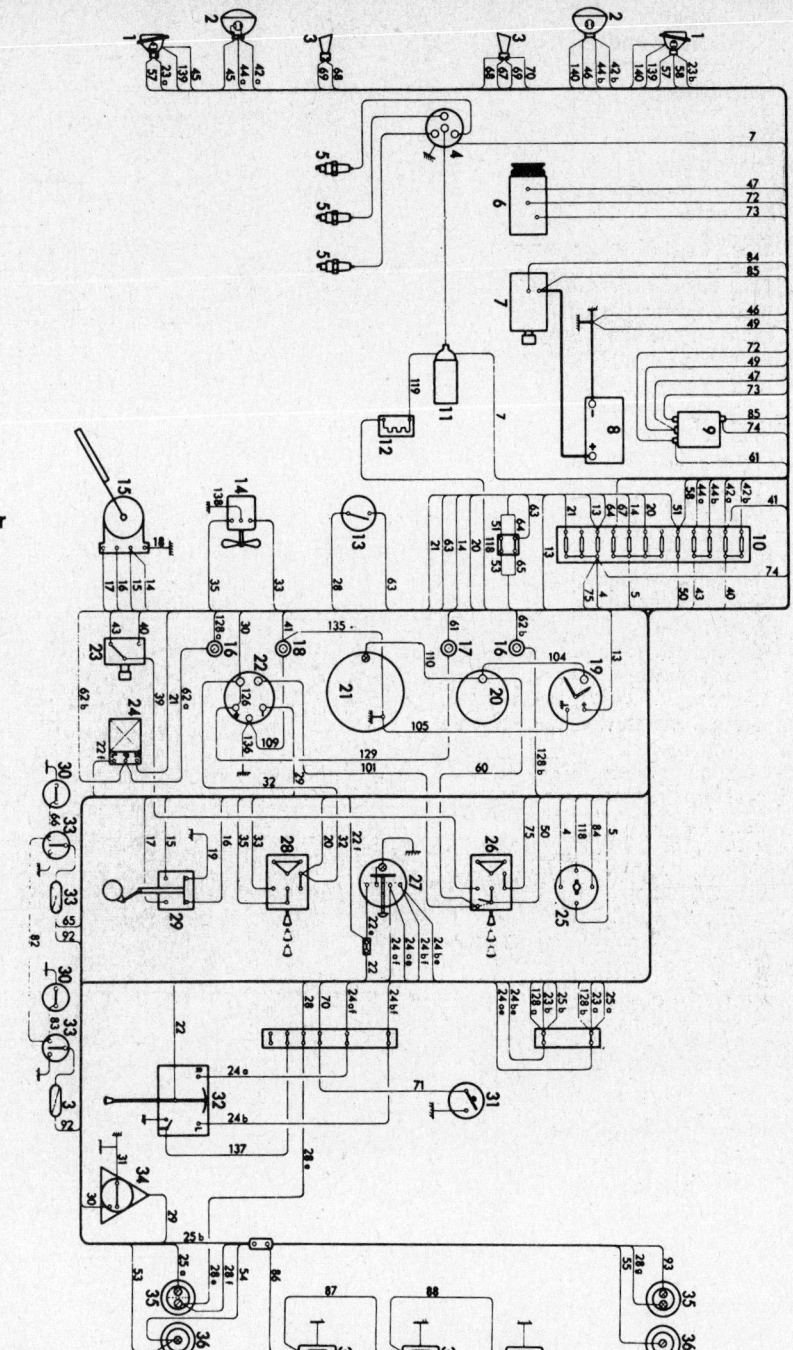

Wiring diagram—SAAB 95 (station wagon) 1966 USA version

Black: 7, 18, 19, 45, 46, 47, 49, 71, 105, 109, 135, 136, 138, 139, 140.

Red: 5, 21, 28, 28e, 28f, 28g, 32, 39, 61, 63, 65, 67, 68, 72, 92, 126, 129.

Green: 16, 22, 22e, 22f, 50, 51, 53, 54, 55, 57, 58, 60, 86, 87, 88, 101, 104, 110, 119.

Grey: 4, 25b, 29, 35, 44a, 62a, 62b, 64, 69, 70, 74, 75, 85, 93.

White: 20, 23b, 24b, 24be, 24bf, 40, 42b, 66, 82, 83, 118, 128a.

Yellow: 17, 23a, 24a, 24ae, 24af, 33, 43, 44b, 73, 84, 128b.

Brown: 14, 15, 30, 137.

Blue: 13, 25a, 41, 42a.

1. Turn signal indicators and side lights
2. Headlights
3. Horn
4. Distributor
5. Spark plugs
6. Voltage regulator
7. Alternator
8. Starter
9. Battery
10. Fuse box
11. Ignition coil
12. Stop light switch
13. Heater fan motor
14. Wiper motor
15. Direction indicator repeater light
16. Charge indicator light
17. High beam indicator light
18. Electric clock
19. Temperature gauge
20. Speedometer with odometer
21. Fuel gauge
22. Dimmer switch
23. Flasher
24. Ignition and starter switch
25. Headlight switch and instrument illumination rheostat
26. Warning flasher switch with control lamp
27. Heater fan switch
28. Windshield wiper switch
29. Courtesy light switch
30. Courtesy light with switch
31. Horn button
32. Direction indicator switch
33. Fuel tank gauge
34. Stop lights and direction indicators
35. Tail lights
36. License plate light

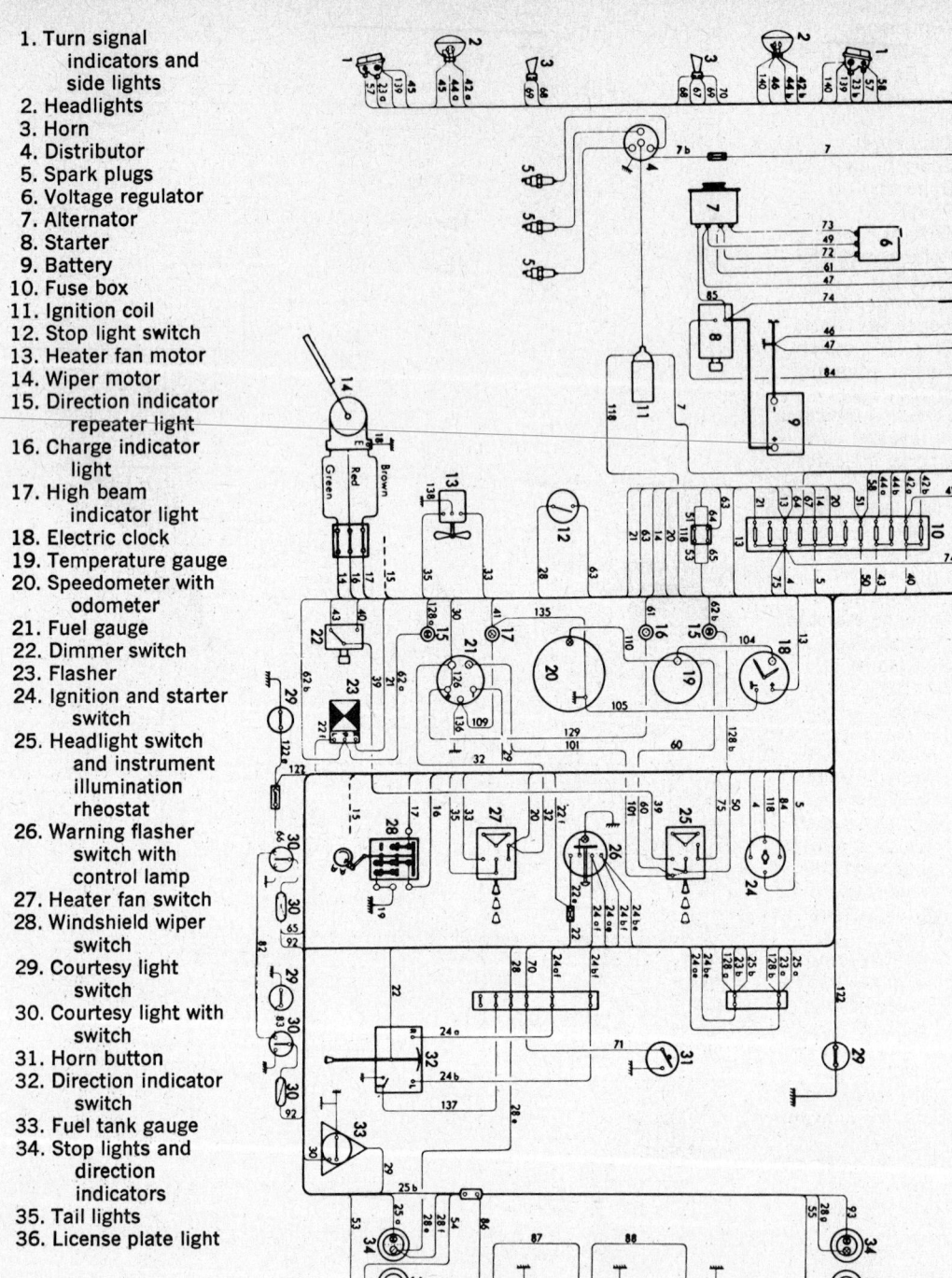

Wiring diagram—SAAB 95 (station wagon) 1967 USA version

Black: 7, 7b, 18, 19, 45, 46, 47, 49, 71, 105, 109, 135, 136, 138, 139, 140.

Red: 5, 21, 28, 28e, 28f, 28g, 32, 39, 61, 63, 65, 67, 68, 72, 92, 126, 129.

Green: 16, 22, 22e, 22f, 50, 51, 53, 54, 55, 57, 58, 60, 86, 87, 88, 101, 104, 110.

Grey: 4, 25b, 29, 35, 44a, 62a, 62b, 64, 69, 70, 74, 75, 85, 93.

White: 20, 23b, 24b, 24be, 24bf, 40, 42b, 66, 82, 83, 118, 122, 122e, 128a.

Yellow: 17, 23a, 24a, 24ae, 24af, 33, 43, 44b, 73, 84, 128b.

Brown: 14, 15, 30, 137.

Blue: 13, 25a, 41, 42a.

1. Turn signal
    indicators and
    side lights
2. Headlights
3. Horn
4. Distributor
5. Spark plugs
6. Generator
7. Starter
8. Battery
9. Relay
10. Fuse box
11. Ignition coil
12. Stop light switch
13. Heater fan motor
14. Wiper motor
15. Direction indicator
    repeater light
16. Charge indicator
    light
17. High beam indicator
    light
18. Electric clock
19. Coolant
    thermometer
20. Speedometer and
    odometer
21. Fuel gauge
22. Dimmer switch
23. Flasher
24. Ignition and starter
    switch
25. Headlight switch
    and instrument
    illumination
    rheostat
26. Heater fan switch
27. Windshield wiper
    switch
28. Courtesy light
    switch
29. Horn button
30. Direction indicator
    switch
31. Courtesy light with
    switch
32. Fuel tank gauge
33. Stop lights, turn
    indicators and
    tail lights
34. License plate light
35. Trunk light

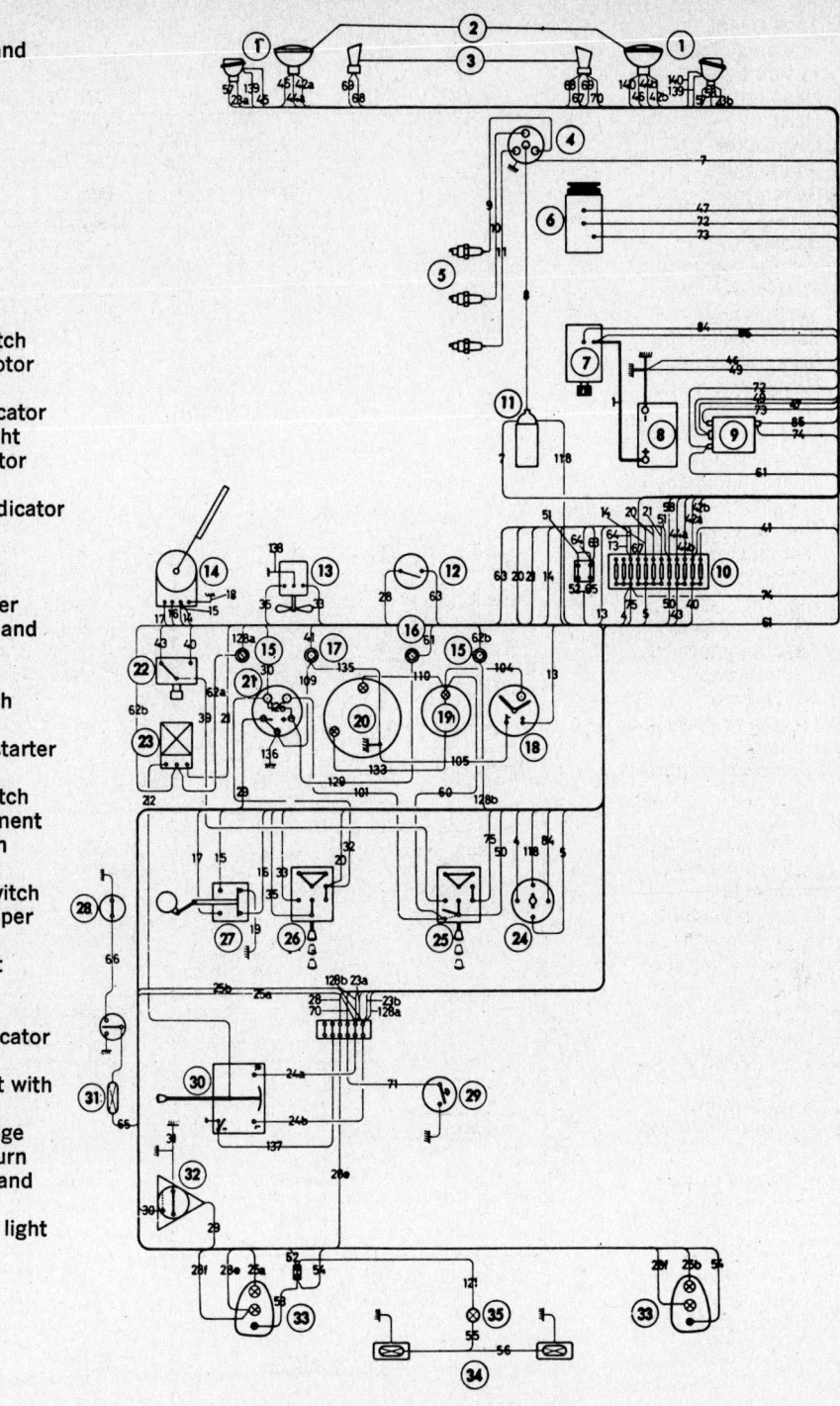

Wiring diagram—SAAB 96 1965

Black: 1, 7, 18, 19, 45, 46, 47, 49, 71, 105,
    109, 135, 136, 139, 140.
Red: 5, 8, 9, 10, 11, 21, 28, 28e, 28f, 32, 39,
    61, 63, 65, 67, 68, 72, 126, 129.
Green: 16, 22, 50, 51, 52, 53, 54, 55, 56, 57,
    58, 60, 69, 70, 85, 101, 104, 110, 121, 133.

Grey: 4, 25b, 29, 35, 44a, 62a, 62b, 64, 74, 75.
White: 20, 23b, 24b, 40, 42b, 66, 118, 128a.
Yellow: 17 23a, 24a, 33, 43, 44b, 73, 84, 128b.
Brown: 14, 15, 30, 137.
Blue: 13, 25a, 41, 42a.

1. Turn signal indicators and side lights
2. Headlights
3. Horn
4. Distributor
5. Spark plugs
6. Generator
7. Starter
8. Battery
9. Voltage regulator
10. Fuse box
11. Ignition coil
12. Series resistance
13. Stop light switch
14. Heater fan motor
15. Wiper motor
16. Direction indicator repeater light
17. Charge indicator light
18. High beam indicator light
19. Electric clock
20. Coolant thermometer
21. Speedometer and odometer
22. Fuel gauge
23. Dimmer switch
24. Flasher
25. Ignition and starter switch
26. Headlight switch and instrument illumination rheostat
27. Warning flasher switch with control lamp
28. Heater fan switch
29. Windshield wiper switch
30. Courtesy light switch
31. Horn button
32. Direction indicator switch
33. Courtesy light with switch
34. Fuel tank gauge
35. Stop lights, turn indicators and tail lights
36. License plate light
37. Trunk light

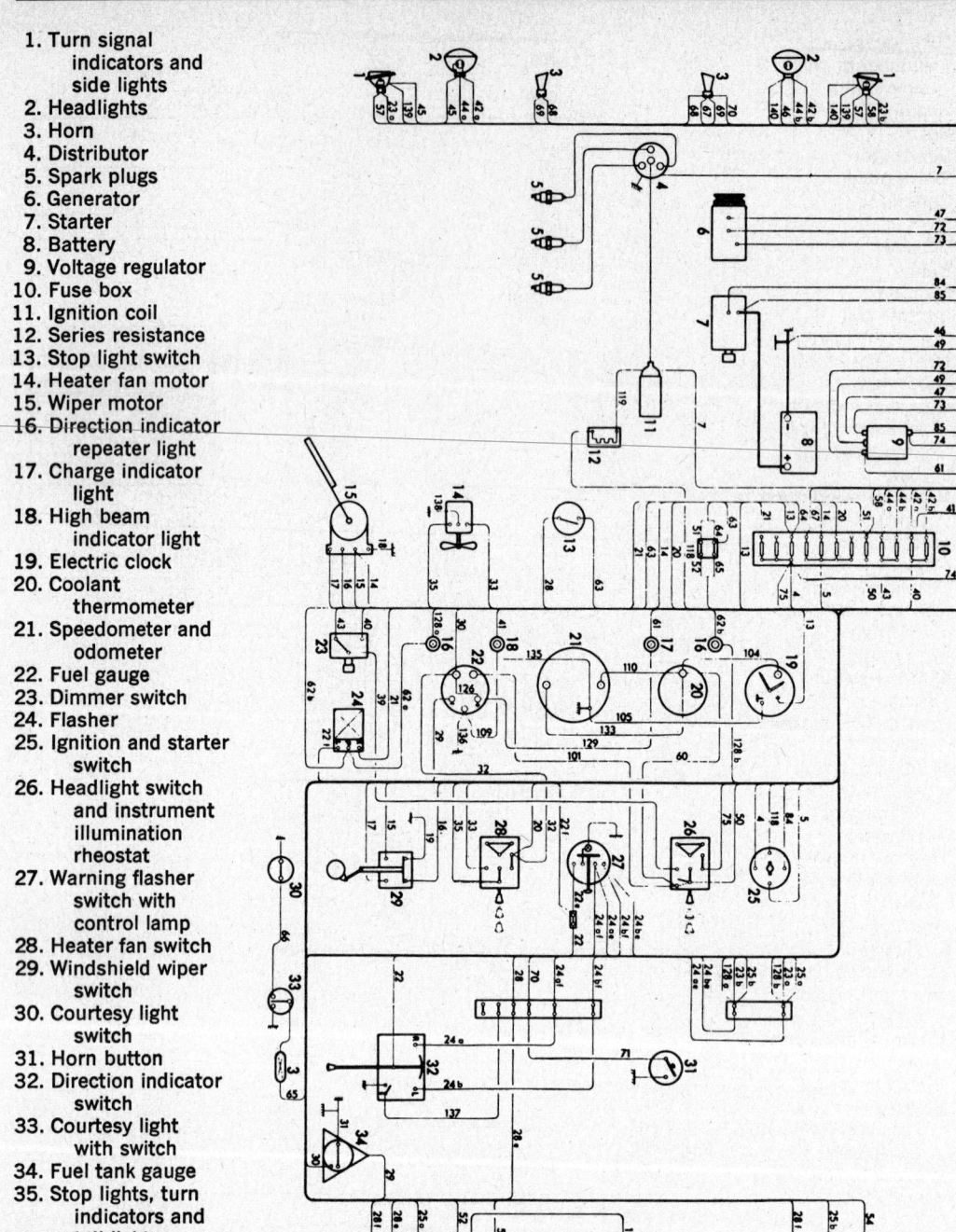

Wiring diagram—SAAB 96 1966 USA version

Black: 7, 18, 19, 45, 46, 47, 49, 71, 105, 109, 135, 136, 138, 139, 140.

Red: 5, 21, 28, 28e, 28f, 32, 39, 61, 63, 65, 67, 68, 72, 126, 129.

Green: 16, 22, 22e, 22f, 50, 51, 52, 53, 54, 55, 56, 57, 58, 60, 101, 104, 110, 121, 133.

Grey: 4, 25b, 29, 35, 44a, 62a, 62b, 64, 69, 70, 74, 75, 85.

White: 20, 23b, 24b, 24be, 24bf, 40, 42b, 66, 118, 128a.

Yellow: 17, 23a, 24a, 24ae, 24af, 33, 43, 44b, 73, 84, 128b.

Brown: 14, 15, 30, 137.

Blue: 13, 25a, 41, 42a.

1. Turn signal indi-
      cators and side
      lights
2. Headlights
3. Horn
4. Distributor
5. Spark plugs
6. Voltage regulator
7. Alternator
8. Starter
9. Battery
10. Fuse box
11. Ignition coil
12. Back-up light switch
13. Stop light switch
14. Heater fan motor
15. Wiper motor
16. Direction indicator
      repeater light
17. Charge indicator
      light
18. High beam indicator
      light
19. Electric clock
20. Temperature gauge
21. Speedometer with
      odometer
22. Fuel gauge
23. Dimmer switch
24. Flasher
25. Ignition and starter
      switch
26. Headlight switch
      and instrument
      illumination
      rheostat
27. Warning flasher
      switch with
      control lamp
28. Heater fan switch
29. Windshield wiper
      switch
30. Courtesy light
      switch
31. Courtesy light with
      switch
32. Horn button
33. Direction indicator
      switch
34. Fuel tank gauge
35. Back-up lights
36. Stop lights, direc-
      tion indicators
      and tail lights
37. License plate light
38. Trunk light

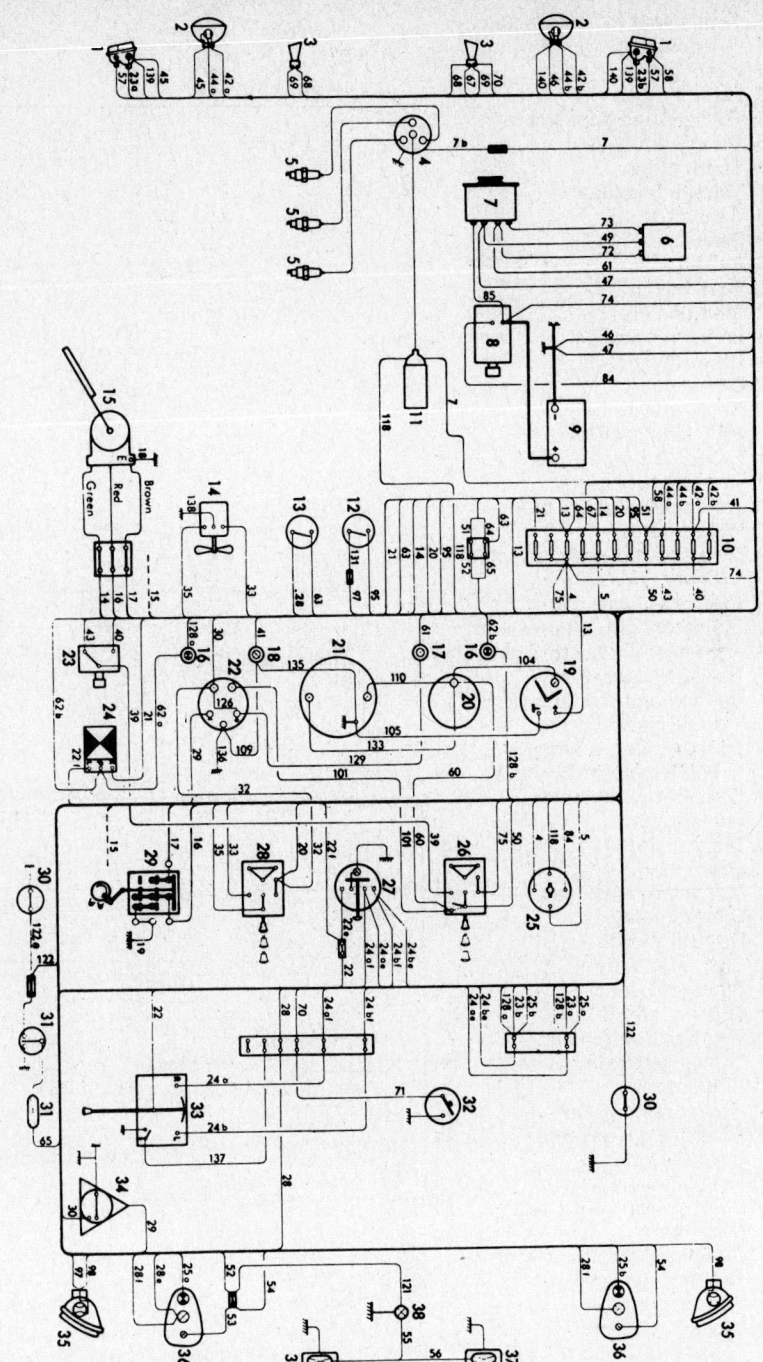

Wiring diagram—SAAB 96 1967 USA version

Black: 7, 7b, 18, 19, 45, 46, 47, 49, 71, 105,
    109, 135, 136, 138, 139, 140.

Red: 5, 21, 28, 28e, 28f, 32, 39, 61, 63, 65, 67,
    68, 72, 126, 129.

Green: 16, 22, 22e, 22f, 50, 51, 52, 53, 54,
    55, 56, 57, 58, 60, 101, 104, 110, 121, 133.

Grey: 4, 25b, 29, 35, 44a, 62a, 64, 69, 70, 74,
    75, 85.

White: 20, 23b, 24b, 24be, 24bf, 40, 42b, 66,
    95, 97, 98, 118, 122, 122e, 128a, 131.

Yellow: 17, 23a, 24a, 24ae, 24af, 33, 43, 44b,
    73, 84, 128b.

Brown: 14, 15, 30, 137.

Blue: 13, 25a, 41, 42a.

1. Turn signal indicators and
   side lights
2. Headlights
3. Horn
4. Foglight and spotlight
5. Distributor
6. Spark plugs
7. Voltage regulator
8. Generator
9. Starter
10. Battery
11. Fuse box
12. Ignition coil
13. Series resistance
14. Oil warning relay
15. Oil gauge
16. Back-up light switch
17. Stop lamp switch
18. Heater fan motor
19. Temperature meter
20. Windshield-washer pump
21. Wiper motor
22. Direction indicator repeater
    light
23. Charge indicator light
24. Indicator light, oil pressure
25. High beam indicator light
26. Indicator light, fuel
27. Ignition and starter switch
28. Electric clock
29. Speedometer, odometer
    and tripmeter
30. Coolant thermometer
31. Fuel gauge
32. Tachometer
33. Flasher
34. Maneuvre relay, light
35. Dimmer relay
36. Dimmer switch
37. Cigarette lighter
38. Spotlight switch
39. Foglight switch
40. Headlight switch and
    instrument illumination
    rheostat
41. Heater fan switch
42. Windshield wiper and
    washer switch
43. Courtesy light switch
44. Courtesy light with switch
45. Horn button
46. Direction indicator switch
47. Fuel tank gauge
48. Back-up lights
49. Stop lights, direction
    indicators and tail lights
50. License plate light
51. Trunk light

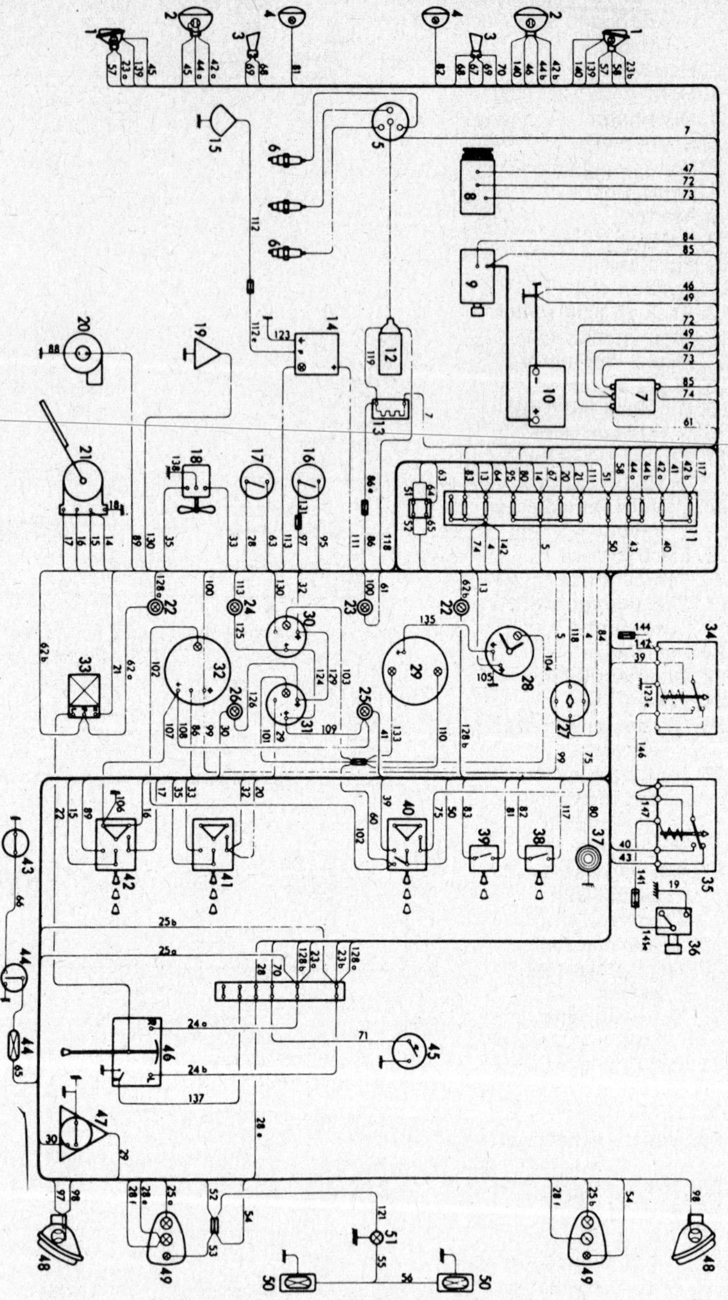

Wiring diagram—SAAB Monte Carlo 850 1965
USA version

Black: 7, 18, 19, 45, 46, 47, 49, 71, 80, 88,
  105, 106, 107, 108, 109, 123, 123e, 124,
  125, 135, 138, 139, 140.

Red: 5, 21, 28, 28e, 28f, 32, 39, 61, 63, 65, 67,
  68, 72, 83, 86, 86e, 111, 126, 129.

Green: 16, 22, 50, 51, 52, 53, 54, 55, 56, 57,
  58, 60, 82, 101, 102, 103, 104, 110, 119,
  121, 133, 146, 147.

Grey: 4, 25b, 29, 35, 44a, 62a, 62b, 64, 69, 70,
  74, 75, 85, 89, 113, 117, 142, 144.

White: 20, 23b, 24b, 40, 42b, 66, 95, 97, 98,
  118, 128a, 131.

Yellow: 17, 23a, 24a, 33, 43, 44b, 73, 81, 84,
  99, 100, 112, 112e, 128b, 130.

Brown: 14, 15, 30, 137, 141, 141e.

Blue: 3, 25a, 41, 42a.

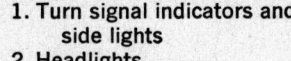

1. Turn signal indicators and
   side lights
2. Headlights
3. Horn
4. Foglight and spotlight
5. Distributor
6. Spark plugs
7. Voltage regulator
8. Generator
9. Starter
10. Battery
11. Fuse box
12. Ignition coil
13. Series resistance
14. Oil warning relay
15. Oil gauge
16. Back-up light switch
17. Stop lamp switch
18. Heater fan motor
19. Temperature meter
20. Windshield-washer pump
21. Wiper motor
22. Direction indicator repeater
    light
23. Charge indicator light
24. Indicator light, oil pressure
25. High beam indicator light
26. Indicator light, fuel
27. Ignition and starter switch
28. Electric clock
29. Speedometer, odometer
    and trip meter
30. Coolant thermometer
31. Fuel gauge
32. Tachometer
33. Flasher
34. Maneuvre relay, light
35. Dimmer relay
36. Dimmer switch
37. Cigarette lighter
38. Spotlight switch
39. Foglight switch
40. Headlight switch and instru-
    ment illumination
    rheostat
41. Warning flasher switch
42. Heater fan switch
43. Windshield wiper and
    washer switch
44. Courtesy light switch
45. Courtesy light with switch
46. Horn button
47. Direction indicator switch
48. Fuel tank gauge
49. Back-up lights
50. Stop lights, direction indi-
    cators and tail lights
51. License plate light
52. Trunk light

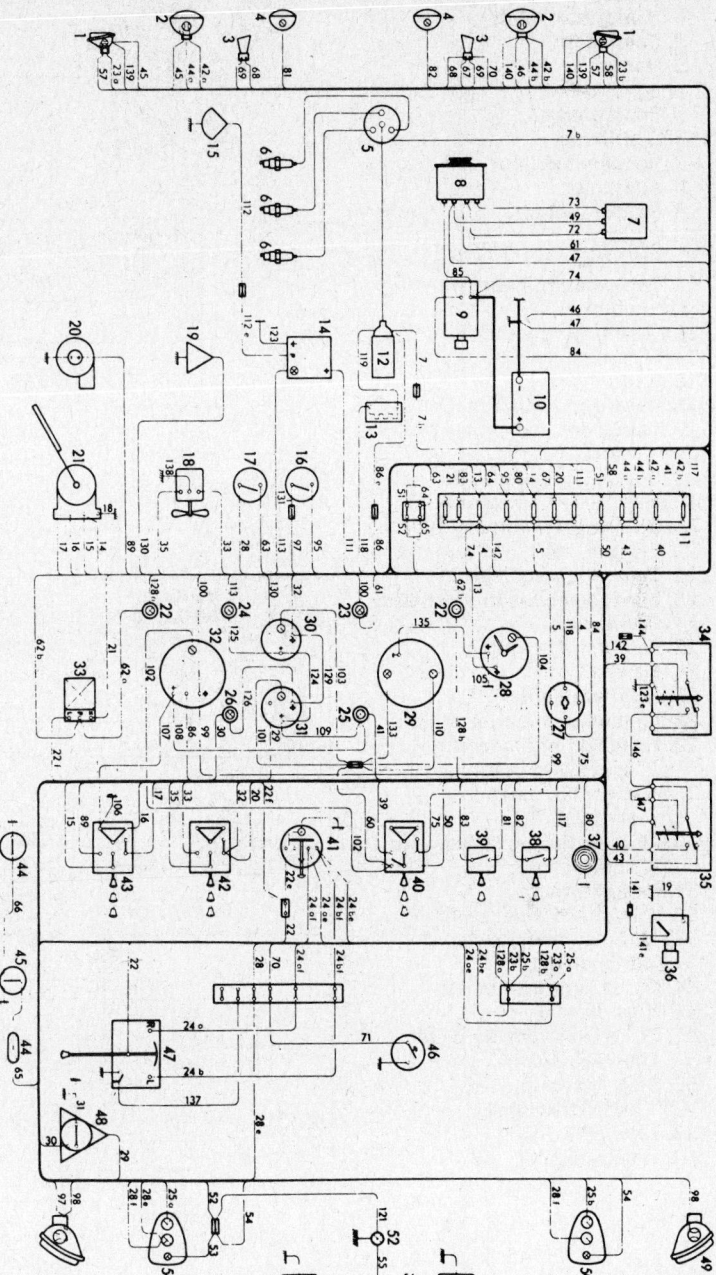

Wiring diagram—SAAB Monte Carlo 850 1966 USA version

Black: 7, 7b 18, 19, 31, 45, 46, 47, 49, 71, 80,
88, 105, 106, 107, 108, 109, 123, 123e, 124,
125, 135, 138, 139, 140.

Red: 5, 21, 28, 28e, 28f, 32, 39, 61, 63, 65, 67,
68, 72, 83, 86, 86e, 111, 126, 129.

Green: 16, 22, 22e, 22f, 50, 51, 52, 53, 54, 55,
56, 57, 58, 60, 82, 101, 102, 103, 104, 110,
119, 121, 133, 146, 147.

Grey: 4, 25b, 29, 35, 44a, 62a, 62b, 64, 69, 70,
74, 75, 85, 89, 113, 117, 142 144.

White: 20, 23b, 24b, 24be, 24bf, 40, 42b, 66,
95, 97, 98, 118, 128a, 131.

Yellow: 17, 23a, 24a, 24ae, 24af, 33, 43, 44b,
73, 81, 84, 99, 100, 112, 112e, 128b, 130.

Brown: 14, 15, 30, 137, 141, 141e.

Blue: 3, 25a, 41, 42a.

1. Parking and turn signal
   indicator lights
2. Headlights
3. Horns
4. Ignition coil
5. Spark plugs
6. Distributor
7. Voltage regulator
8. Alternator
9. Starter motor
10. Battery
11. Fuse box
12. Temperature gauge sending
    unit
13. Oil pressure switch
14. Stop light switch
15. Heater motor
16. Windshield wiper motor
17. Turn signal indicator
    warning lights
18. Charge indicator light
19. High beam indicator light
20. Oil pressure warning light
21. Electric clock
22. Temperature gauge
23. Speedometer with odometer
24. Fuel gauge
25. Foot dimmer switch
26. Flasher
27. Cigarette lighter
28. Ignition and starter switch
29. Headlight and parking
    light switch with instru-
    ment illumination
    rheostat
30. Warning flasher switch with
    control light
31. Heater switch
32. Windshield wiper switch
33. Automatic door switch for
    dome light
34. Dome light with switch
35. Horn ring
36. Direction indicator switch
37. Fuel tank sending unit
38. Stop light and direction
    indicator light
39. Tail lights
40. License lights

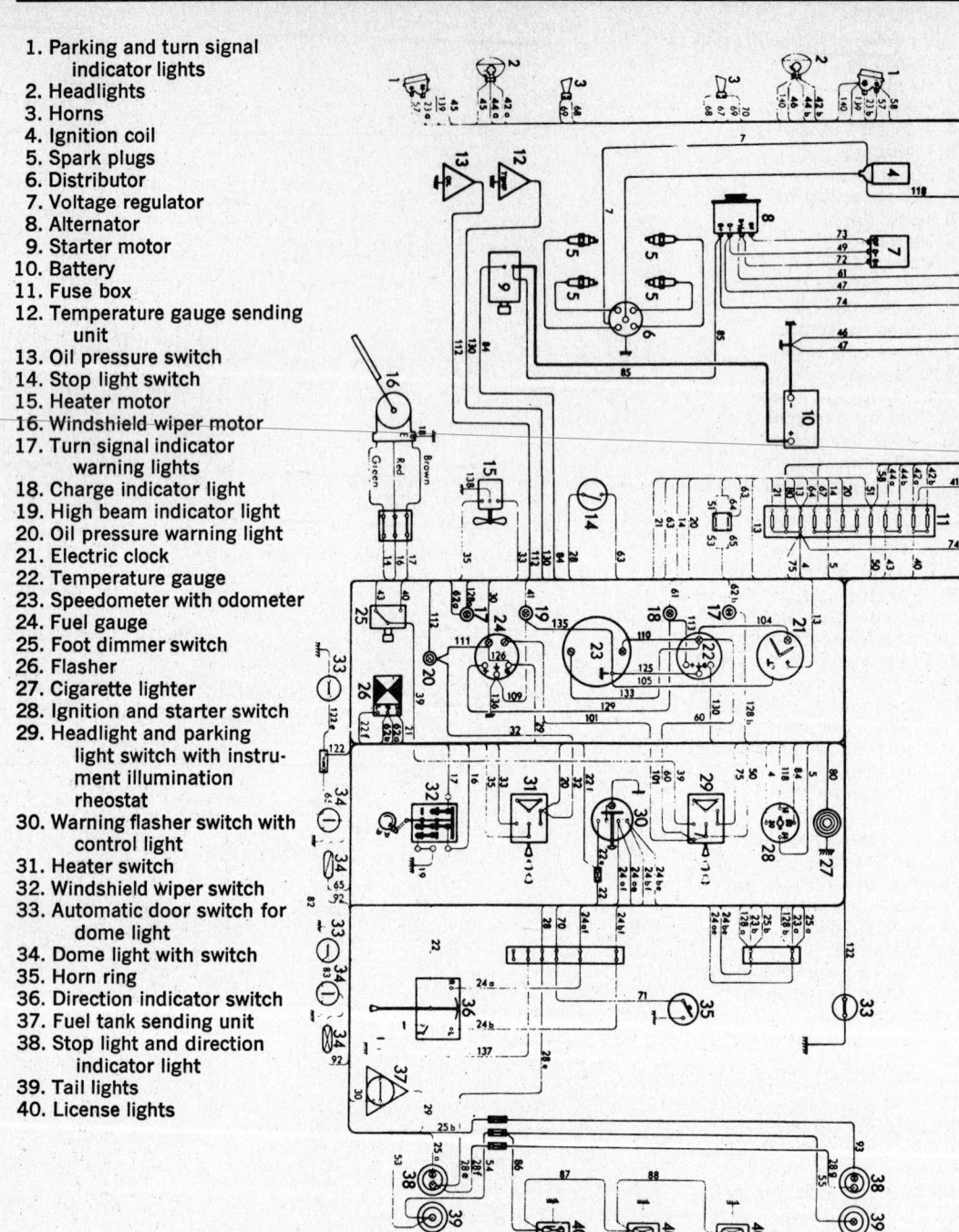

Wiring diagram—SAAB 95 (station wagon) 1967 USA version

Black: 7, 18, 19, 45, 46, 47, 49, 71, 80, 105,
109, 125, 135, 136, 138, 139, 140.

Red: 5, 21, 28, 28e, 28f, 28g, 32, 39, 61, 63,
65, 67, 68, 72, 92, 111, 113, 126, 129.

Green: 16, 22, 22e, 22f, 50, 51, 53, 54, 55,
57, 58, 60, 86, 87, 88, 101, 104, 110, 133.

Grey: 4, 25b, 29, 35, 44a, 62a, 62b, 64, 69, 70,
74, 75, 85, 93.

White: 20, 23b, 24b, 24be, 24bf, 40, 42b, 66,
82, 83, 118, 122, 122e, 128a.

Yellow: 17, 23a, 24a, 24ae, 24af, 33, 43, 44b,
73, 84, 128b.

Brown: 14, 30, 130, 137.

Blue: 13, 25a, 41, 42a, 112.

1. Turn signals and side lights
2. Headlights
3. Horn
4. Ignition coil
5. Spark plugs
6. Distributor
7. Voltage regulator
8. Alternator
9. Starter
10. Battery
11. Fuse box
12. Temperature gauge sending unit
13. Oil pressure switch
14. Back-up light switch
15. Stop light switch
16. Brake warning contact
17. Heater fan motor
18. Windshield washer pump
19. Wiper motor
20. Charge indicator light
21. Direction indicator repeater light
22. Brake warning light
23. High beam indicator light
24. Oil pressure warning light
25. Temperature gauge
26. Speedometer with odometer
27. Fuel gauge
28. Dimmer switch
29. Flasher
30. Ignition and starter switch
31. Headlight switch
32. Instrument illumination rheostat
33. Heater fan switch
34. Warning flasher switch
35. Courtesy light switch
36. Courtesy light with switch
37. Switch for windshield wiper, washer and signal horn
38. Direction indicator switch with headlight flasher
39. Fuel tank gauge
40. Stop lights and direction indicators
41. Tail lights
42. Back-up lights
43. License plate light

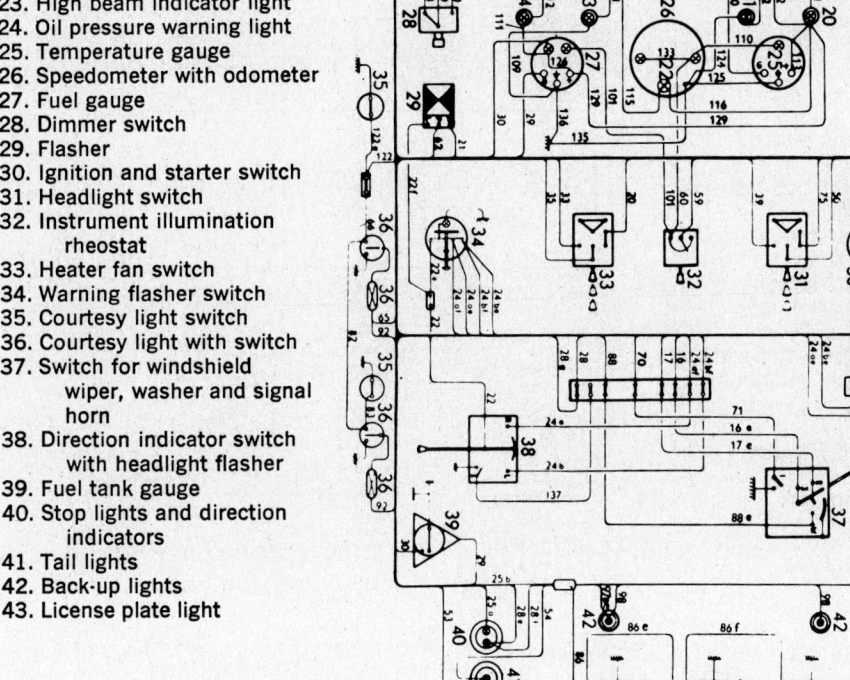

Wiring diagram—SAAB 95 (station wagon) 1968 USA version

Black: 7, 45, 46, 47, 49, 69, 70, 88, 88e, 109, 124, 125, 135, 136, 138, 139, 140.

Red: 5, 21, 28, 28e, 28f, 28g, 32, 39, 61, 63, 65, 67, 68, 72, 72e, 92, 111, 113, 116, 126, 129.

Green: 22, 22e, 22f, 50, 51, 53, 54, 55, 57, 58, 59, 60, 86, 86e, 86f, 101, 110.

Grey: 4, 16, 16e, 25b, 29, 35, 44a, 62, 64, 74, 75, 85, 93.

White: 20, 23b, 24b, 24be, 24bf, 40, 40c, 42b, 66, 82, 83, 95, 97, 97ae, 98, 118, 112, 122e, 131.

Yellow: 23a, 24a, 24ae, 24af, 33, 43, 44b, 73, 84, 115.

Brown: 14, 15, 30, 89, 130, 137.

Blue: 17, 17e, 25a, 41, 42a, 112.

1. Parking light and turn signals
2. Headlights
3. Horn
4. Ignition coil
5. Spark plugs
6. Distributor
7. Voltage regulator
8. Alternator
9. Starter
10. Battery
11. Fuse box
12. Temperature transmitter
13. Oil pressure switch
14. Back-up light switch
15. Stop light switch
16. Brake warning contact
17. Heater fan motor
18. Windshield washer pump
19. Windshield wiper motor
20. Charge indicator light
21. Direction indicator repeater light
22. Brake warning light
23. High beam indicator light
24. Oil pressure warning light
25. Electric clock (Extra equipment)
26. Temperature gauge
27. Speedometer and odometer
28. Fuel gauge
29. Flasher unit
30. Dimmer relay
31. Ignition and starter switch
32. Headlight switch
33. Instrument illumination rheostat
34. Heater fan switch
35. Warning flasher switch
36. Courtesy light switch
37. Courtesy light with switch
38. Switch for windshield wiper,
       washer and signal horn
39. Direction indicator switch with
       headlight flasher and dimmer
       switch
40. Fuel transmitter
41. Back-up light and direction
       indicators
42. Tail light and stop light
43. License plate light

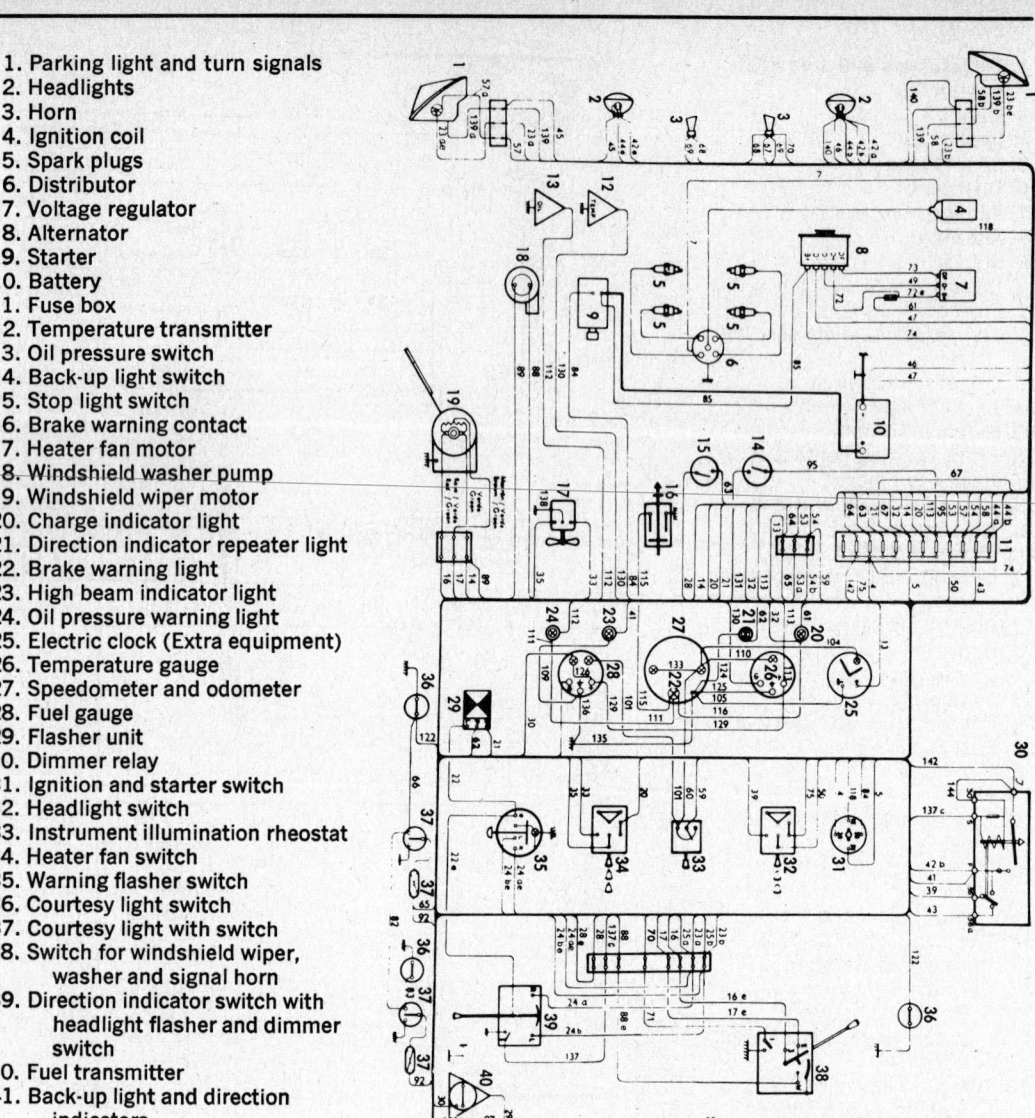

Wiring diagram—SAAB 95 (station wagon) 1969 USA version

4 grey	24a yellow	42b white	58 green	73 yellow	101 green	131 white
5 red	24ae yellow	43 yellow	58b green	74 grey	104 green	133 green
7 black	24b white	44a grey	59 green	75 grey	105 black	135 black
13 blue	24be white	44b yellow	60 green	82 white	109 black	136 black
14 brown	25a blue	45 black	61 red	83 white	110 green	137 brown
16 grey	25b grey	46 black	62 grey	84 yellow	111 red	137c brown
16e grey	28 red	47 black	63 red	85 grey	112 blue	138 black
17 blue	28e red	49 black	64 grey	86 green	113 white	139 black
17e blue	28f red	50 green	65 red	86e green	115 yellow	139a black
20 white	29 grey	53 blue	66 white	86f green	116 red	139b black
21 red	30 brown	53a blue	67 red	88 black	118 white	140 black
22 green	32 red	53e green	68 red	88e black	122 white	142 grey
22e green	33 yellow	54 green	69 black	89 brown	124 black	144 grey
23a vellow	35 grey	54b green	70 black	92 red	125 black	

1. Parking and turn signal
   lights
2. Headlights
3. Horns
4. Ignition coil
5. Spark plugs
6. Distributor
7. Voltage regulator
8. Alternator
9. Starter motor
10. Battery
11. Fuse box
12. Temperature gauge,
    sending unit
13. Oil pressure switch
14. Back-up light switch
15. Stop light switch
16. Heater motor
17. Windshield wiper motor
18. Direction indicator warning
    lights
19. Charge indicator light
20. High beam indicator light
21. Oil pressure warning light
22. Electric clock
23. Temperature gauge
24. Speedometer with
    odometer
25. Fuel gauge
26. Foot dimmer switch
27. Flasher
28. Cigarette lighter
29. Ignition and starter switch
30. Headlight and parking light
    switch with instrument
    illumination rheostat
31. Warning flasher switch with
    control light
32. Heater switch
33. Windshield wiper switch
34. Automatic door switch for
    dome light
35. Dome light with switch
36. Horn ring
37. Direction indicator switch
38. Fuel tank sending unit
39. Back-up lights
40. Stop lights, direction
    indicator and tail lights
41. License lights
42. Trunk light

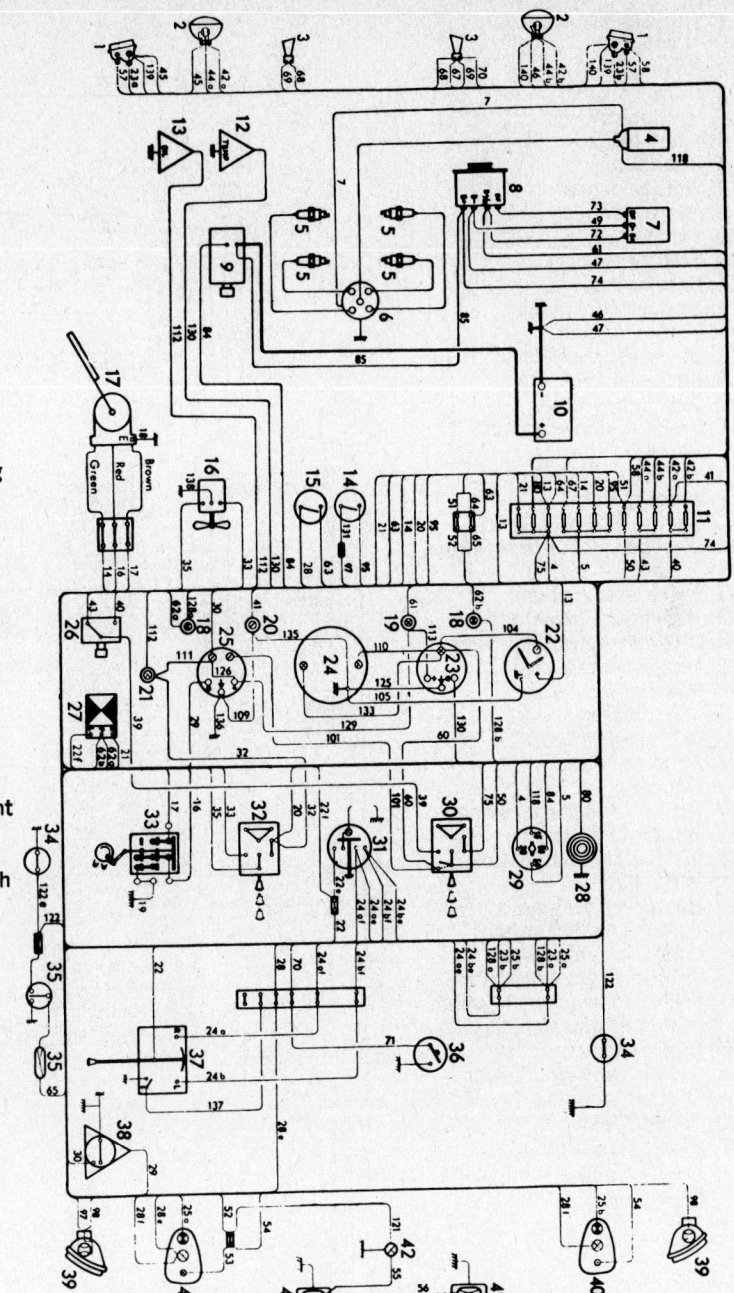

Wiring diagram—SAAB 96 1967 USA version

Black: 7, 18, 19, 45, 46, 47, 49, 71, 80, 105,
109, 125, 135, 136, 138, 139, 140.

Red: 5, 21, 28, 28e, 28f, 32, 39, 61, 63, 65, 67,
68, 72, 111, 113, 126, 129.

Green: 16, 22, 22e, 22f, 50, 51, 52, 53, 54, 55,
56, 57, 58, 60, 101, 104, 110, 121, 133.

Grey: 4, 25b, 29, 35, 44a, 62a, 62b, 64, 69, 70,
74, 75, 85.

White: 20, 23b, 24b, 24be, 24bf, 40, 42b, 66, 95,
97, 98, 118, 122, 122e, 128a, 131.

Yellow: 17, 23a, 24a, 24ae, 24af, 33, 43, 44b,
73, 84, 128b.

Brown: 14, 30, 130, 137.

Blue: 13, 25a, 41, 42a, 112.

1. Turn signals and side lights
2. Headlights
3. Horn
4. Ignition coil
5. Spark plugs
6. Distributor
7. Voltage regulator
8. Alternator
9. Starter
10. Battery
11. Fuse box
12. Temperature gauge, sending unit
13. Oil pressure switch
14. Back-up light switch
15. Stop light switch
16. Brake warning contact
17. Heater fan motor
18. Windshield washer pump
19. Wiper motor
20. Charge indicator light
21. Direction indicator repeater light
22. Brake warning light
23. High beam indicator light
24. Oil pressure warning light
25. Temperature gauge
26. Speedometer with odometer
27. Fuel gauge
28. Dimmer switch
29. Flasher
30. Ignition and starter switch
31. Headlight switch
32. Instrument illumination rheostat
33. Heater fan switch
34. Warning flasher switch
35. Courtesy light switch
36. Courtesy light with switch
37. Switch for windshield wiper, washer and signal horn
38. Direction indicator switch with headlight flasher
39. Fuel tank gauge
40. Back-up light
41. Stop lights, direction indicators and tail lights
42. License plate light
43. Trunk light

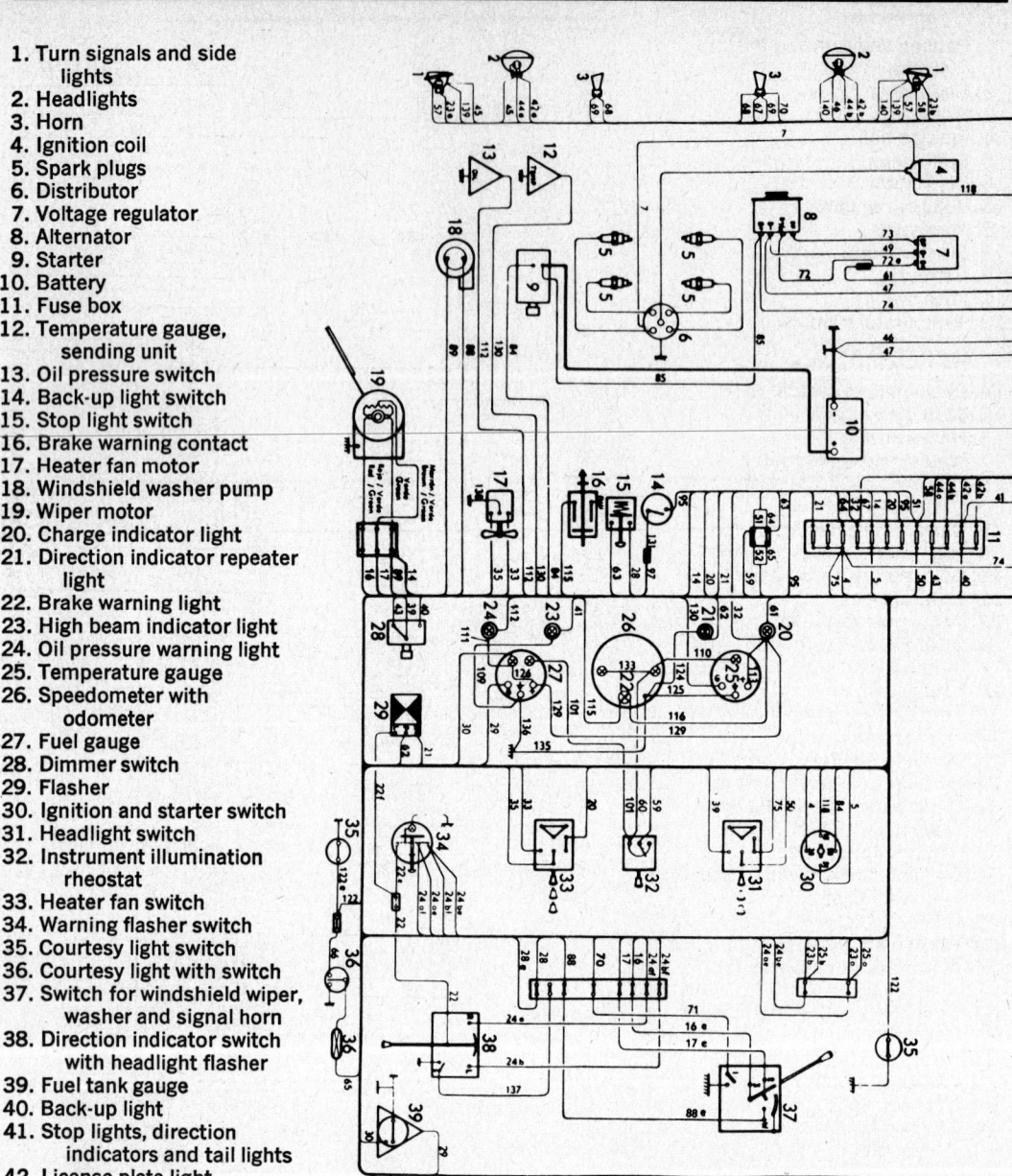

Wiring diagram—SAAB 96 1968 USA version

Black: 7, 45, 46, 47, 69, 70, 71, 88, 88e, 109, 124, 125, 135, 136, 138, 139, 140.

Red: 5, 21, 28, 28e, 28f, 32, 39, 61, 63, 65, 67, 68, 72, 72e, 111, 113, 116, 126, 129.

Green: 22, 22e, 22f, 50, 51, 52, 53, 54, 55, 56, 57, 58, 59, 60, 101, 110, 121, 133.

Grey: 4, 16, 16e, 25b, 29, 35, 44a, 62, 64, 74, 75, 85.

White: 20, 23b, 24b, 24be, 24bf, 40, 42b, 66, 95, 97, 98, 118, 122, 122e, 131.

Yellow: 23a, 24a, 24ae, 24af, 33, 43, 44b, 73, 84, 115.

Brown: 14, 30, 89, 130, 137.

Blue: 17, 17e, 25a, 41, 42a, 112.

1. Parking light and direction
   indicators
2. Headlights
3. Horn
4. Ignition coil
5. Spark plugs
6. Distributor
7. Voltage regulator
8. Alternator
9. Starter
10. Battery
11. Fuse box
12. Temperature transmitter
13. Oil pressure switch
14. Stop light switch
15. Back-up light switch
16. Brake warning contact
17. Heater fan motor
18. Windshield washer pump
19. Windshield wiper motor
20. Charge indicator light
21. Direction indicator repeater light
22. Brake warning light
23. High beam indicator light
24. Oil pressure warning light
25. Electric clock (Extra equipment)
26. Temperature gauge
27. Speedometer with odometer
28. Fuel gauge
29. Flasher unit
30. Dimmer relay
31. Ignition and starter switch
32. Headlight switch
33. Instrument illumination rheostat
34. Heater fan switch
35. Warning flasher switch
36. Courtesy light switch
37. Courtesy light with switch
38. Switch for windshield wiper
    washer and signal horn
39. Direction indicator switch with
    headlight flasher and dimmer
    switch
40. Fuel transmitter
41. Back-up lights
42. Stop lights, direction indicators
    and tail light
43. License plate light
44. Trunk light

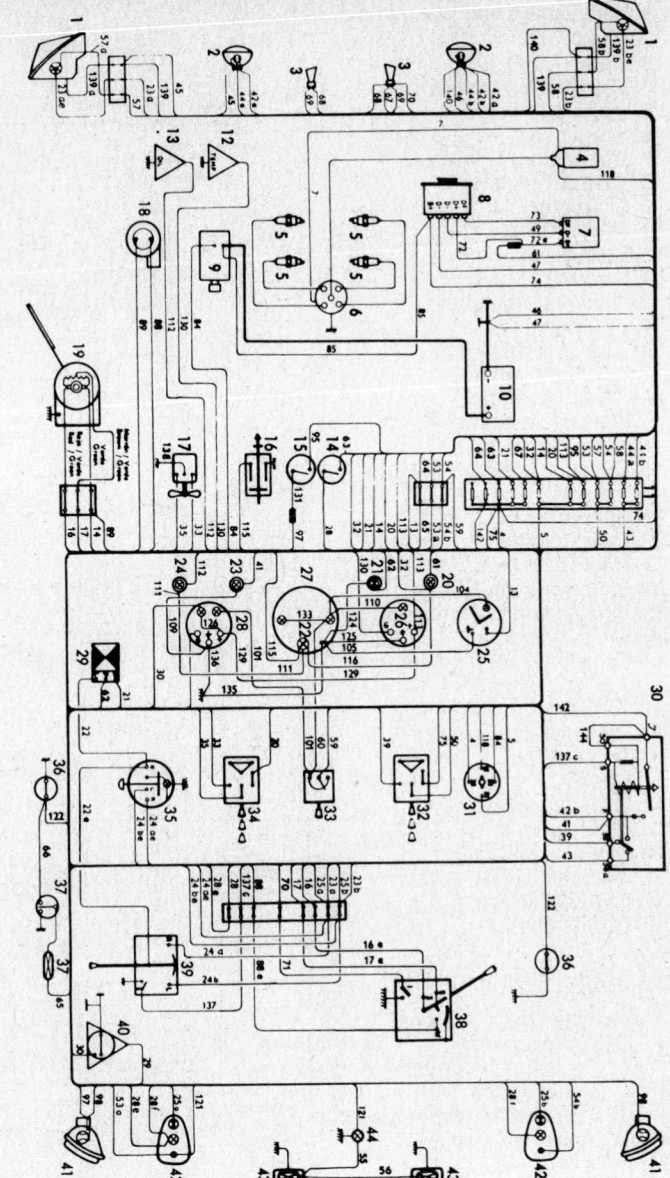

Wiring diagram—SAAB 96 1969 USA version

4 grey	24ae yellow	44a grey	60 green	85 grey	121 green	142 grey
5 red	24b white	44b yellow	61 red	88 black	122 white	144 grey
7 black	24be white	45 black	62 grey	88e black	124 black	
13 blue	25a blue	46 black	63 red	89 brown	125 black	
14 brown	25b grey	47 black	64 grey	95 white	126 white	
16 grey	28 red	49 black	65 red	97 white	129 white	
16e grey	28e red	50 green	66 white	98 white	130 brown	
17 blue	28f red	53 blue	67 red	101 green	131 white	
17e blue	29 grey	53a blue	68 red	104 green	133 green	
20 white	30 brown	54 green	69 black	105 black	135 black	
21 red	32 red	54b green	70 black	109 black	136 black	
22 green	33 yellow	55 green	71 black	110 green	137 brown	
22e green	35 grey	56 green	72 red	111 red	137c brown	
23a yellow	39 red	57 red	72e red	112 blue	138 black	
23ae yellow	41 blue	57a blue	73 yellow	113 white	139 black	
23b white	42a blue	58 green	74 grey	115 yellow	139a black	
23be white	42b white	58b green	75 grey	116 red	139b black	
24a yellow	43 yellow	59 green	84 yellow	118 white	140 black	

1. Turn signals and side lights
2. Headlights
3. Horn
4. Foglight and spotlight
5. Ignition coil
6. Spark plugs
7. Distributor
8. Voltage regulator
9. Alternator
10. Starter
11. Battery
12. Fuse box
13. Temperature meter
14. Oil gauge
15. Back-up light switch
16. Stop light switch
17. Heater fan motor
18. Windshield-washer pump
19. Wiper motor
20. Direction indicator repeater lights
21. Charge indicator light
22. Indicator light, oil pressure
23. High beam indicator light
24. Indicator light, fuel
25. Ignition and starter switch
26. Electric clock
27. Speedometer, odometer and trip meter
28. Temperature gauge
29. Fuel gauge
30. Tachometer
31. Flasher
32. Maneuvre relay, light
33. Dimming relay
34. Dimming switch
35. Cigarette lighter
36. Spotlight switch
37. Fog light switch
38. Headlight switch and instrument illumination rheostat
39. Warning flasher switch
40. Heater fan switch
41. Windshield wiper and washer switch
42. Courtesy light switch
43. Courtesy light with switch
44. Horn button
45. Direction indicator switch
46. Fuel tank gauge
47. Back-up lights
48. Stop lights, direction indicators and tail lights
49. License plate lights
50. Trunk light

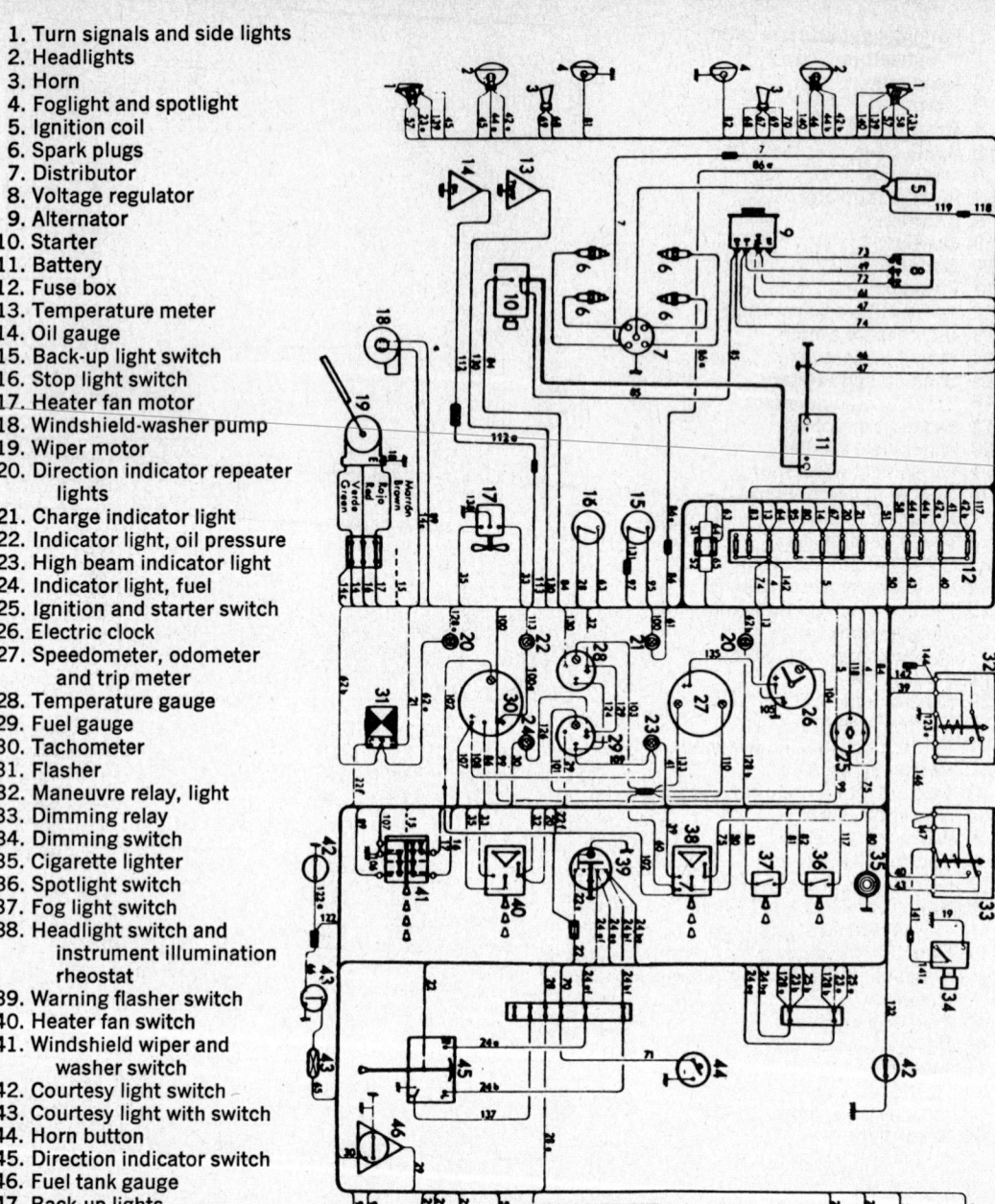

Wiring diagram—SAAB Monte Carlo 1967 USA version

Back: 7, 7b, 18, 19, 45, 46, 47, 49, 71, 80, 105, 106, 107, 108, 109, 123e, 124, 135, 138, 139, 140.

Red: 5, 21, 28, 28e, 28f, 32, 39, 61, 63, 65, 67, 68, 72, 83, 86, 86e, 126, 129.

Green: 16, 22, 22e, 22f, 50, 51, 52, 53, 54, 55, 56, 57, 58, 60, 82, 101, 102, 103, 104, 110, 119, 121, 133, 146, 147.

Grey: 4, 25b, 29, 35, 44a, 62a, 62b, 64, 69, 70, 74, 75, 85, 89, 113, 117, 142, 144.

White: 20, 23b, 24b, 24be, 24bf, 40, 42b, 66, 95, 97, 98, 118, 122, 122e, 128a, 131.

Yellow: 17, 23a, 24a, 24ae, 24af, 33, 43, 44b, 62b, 73, 81, 84, 99, 100, 100e, 112, 112e, 128b, 130.

Brown: 14, 14c, 15, 30, 137, 141, 141e.

Blue: 13, 25a, 41, 42a.

1. Turn signals and side lights
2. Headlights
3. Horn
4. Ignition coil
5. Spark plgs
6. Distributor
7. Voltage regulator
8. Alternator
9. Starter
10. Battery
11. Fuse box
12. Temperature gauge, sending unit
13. Oil pressure switch
14. Back-up light switch
15. Stop light switch
16. Brake warning contact
17. Heater fan motor
18. Windshield-washer pump
19. Wiper motor
20. Direction indicator repeater light
21. Brake warning light
22. Charge indicator light
23. Indicator light, oil pressure
24. High beam indicator light
25. Indicator light, fuel
26. Ignition and starter switch
27. Electric clock
28. Speedometer, odometer and trip meter
29. Temperature gauge
30. Fuel gauge
31. Tachometer
32. Dimmer switch
33. Flasher
34. Cigarette lighter
35. Switches for extra equipment
36. Headlight switch
37. Instrument illumination rheostat
38. Heater fan switch
39. Warning flasher switch
40. Courtesy light switch
41. Courtesy light with switch
42. Switch for windshield wiper, washer and signal horn
43. Direction indicator switch with headlight flasher and dimmer switch
44. Fuel tank gauge
45. Back-up lights
46. Stop lights, direction indicators and tail lights
47. License plate light
48. Trunk light

Wiring diagram—SAAB DeLuxe 1968 USA version

Black: 7, 23a, 45, 46, 47, 49, 71, 80, 88, 88e, 105, 107, 108, 109, 124, 135, 138, 139, 140.

Red: 5, 21, 28, 28e, 28f, 32, 39, 61, 63, 65, 67, 68, 72, 72e, 86, 86e, 111, 113, 116, 126, 129.

Green: 22, 22e, 22f, 50, 51, 52, 53, 54, 55, 56, 57, 58, 59, 101, 102, 103, 104, 110, 121, 133.

Grey: 4, 16, 16e, 25b, 29, 35, 44a, 62a, 62b, 64, 69, 70, 74, 75, 85.

White: 20, 23b, 24b, 24be, 24bf, 40, 42b, 66, 95, 97, 98, 99, 118, 122, 122e, 128a, 131.

Yellow: 24a, 24ae, 24af, 33, 43, 44b, 73, 84, 115, 128b.

Brown: 14, 30, 89, 130, 137, 137c.

Blue: 13, 17, 17e, 25a, 41, 42a, 112.

1. Parking light and direction indicators
2. Headlights
3. Horn
4. Ignition coil
5. Spark plugs
6. Distributor
7. Voltage regulator
8. Alternator
9. Starter
10. Battery
11. Fuse box
12. Temperature transmitter
13. Oil pressure switch
14. Back-up light switch
15. Stop light switch
16. Brake warning contact
17. Heater fan motor
18. Windshield washer pump
19. Windshield wiper motor
20. Direction indicator repeater light
21. Brake warning light
22. Charge indicator light
23. Oil pressure warning light
24. High beam indicator light
25. Indicator light, fuel
26. Ignition and starter switch
27. Electric clock
28. Speedometer, odometer and trip meter
29. Temperature gauge
30. Fuel gauge
31. Tachometer
32. Flasher unit
33. Dimmer relay
34. Cigarette lighter
35. Switches for extra equipment
36. Headlight switch
37. Instrument illumination rheostat
38. Heater fan switch
39. Warning flasher switch
40. Courtesy light switch
41. Courtesy light with switch
42. Switch for windshield wiper, washer and signal horn
43. Direction indicator switch with headlight flasher and dimmer switch
44. Fuel transmitter
45. Back-up lights
46. Stop lights, direction indicators and tail lights
47. License plate light
48. Trunk light

Wiring diagram—SAAB DeLuxe 1969 USA version

4 grey	23b white	32 red	53 blue	68 red	98 white	124 black
5 red	23be white	33 yellow	53a blue	69 black	99 white	126 white
7 black	24a yellow	35 grey	54 green	70 black	101 green	128a white
13 blue	24ae yellow	39 grey	54b green	71 black	102 green	128b yellow
14 brown	24af yellow	41 blue	55 green	72 red	103 green	129 white
16 grey	24b white	42a blue	56 green	72e red	104 green	130 brown
16e grey	24be white	42b white	57 blue	73 yellow	105 black	131 white
17 blue	24bf white	43 yellow	57a blue	74 grey	107 black	133 green
17e blue	25a blue	44a grey	58 green	75 grey	108 black	135 black
20 white	25b grey	44b yellow	58b green	80 black	109 black	137 brown
21 red	28 red	45 black	59 green	84 yellow	110 green	137c brown
22 green	28e red	46 black	61 red	85 grey	111 red	138 black
22e green	28f red	47 black	62a grey	86 red	112 blue	139 black
23a yellow	29 grey	49 black	62b grey	86e red	113 white	139a black
23ae yellow	30 brown	50 green	63 red	88 black	115 yellow	139b black
			64 grey	88e black	116 red	140 black
			65 red	89 brown	118 white	142 grey
			66 white	95 white	121 green	144 grey
			67 red	97 white	122 white	

1. Parking light and direction
   indicators
2. Headlights
3. Horn
4. Ignition coil
5. Spark plugs
6. Distributor
7. Voltage regulator
8. Alternator
9. Starter
10. Battery
11. Fuse box
12. Temperature transmitter
13. Oil pressure switch
14. Back-up light switch
15. Stop light switch
16. Brake warning contact
17. Heater fan motor
18. Windshield washer pump
19. Windshield wiper motor
20. Cigarette lighter
21. Contact for warning buzzer
22. Buzzer
23. Clock
24. Speedometer and odometer
25. High beam indicator light
26. Direction indicator repeater light
27. Brake warning light
28. Temperature and fuel gauges
29. Indicator light, fuel amount
30. Oil pressure warning light
31. Charge indicator light
32. Flasher unit
33. Dimmer relay
34. Ignition and starter switch
35. Hazard warning flasher switch
36. Instrument illumination rheostat
37. Headlight switch
38. Heater fan switch
39. Dome lamp switch
40. Dome lamp with switch
41. Switch for windshield wiper, and
    washer
42. Signal horn contact
43. Direction indicator switch with
    headlight flasher and dimmer
    switch
44. Fuel transmitter
45. Back-up light and direction
    indicators
46. Tail light and stop light
47. License plate light

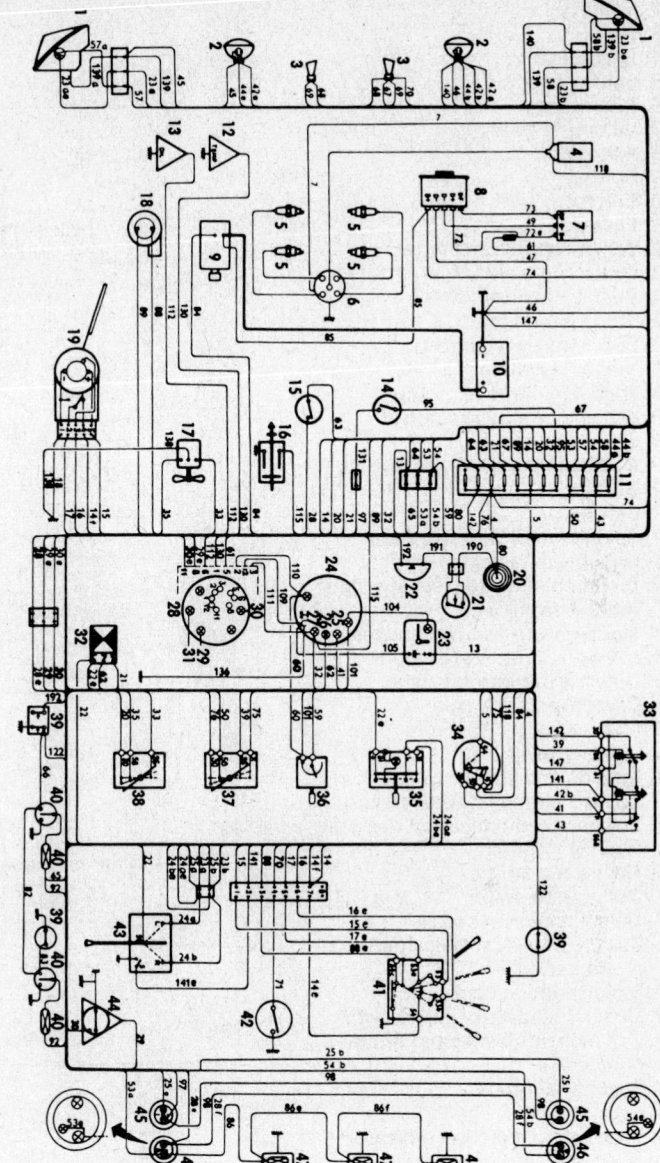

Wiring diagram—SAAB 95 (station wagon) 1970 USA version

4 grey	22e green	30e brown	53a blue	67 red	86e green	118 white
5 red	23a yellow	32 red	53e green	68 red	86f green	122 white
7 green	23ae yellow	33 yellow	54 green	69 black	88 black	130 brown
13 blue	23b white	35 grey	54b green	70 black	88e black	131 white
14 brown	23be white	39 yellow	54e green	71 black	89 brown	136 black
14e brown	24a yellow	41 blue	57 blue	72 red	92 red	138 black
14f brown	24ae yellow	42a blue	57a blue	72e red	95 white	139 black
15 red	24b white	42b white	58 green	73 yellow	97 white	139a black
15e red	24be white	43 yellow	58b green	74 grey	98 white	139b black
16 grey	25a blue	44a grey	59 green	75 red	101 green	140 green
16e grey	25b grey	44b yellow	60 green	76 grey	104 green	141 brown
17 blue	28 red	45 black	61 red	80 black	105 black	141e brown
17e blue	28e red	46 black	62 grey	82 white	109 black	142 grey
18 black	28f red	47 black	63 red	83 white	110 green	147 black
20 white	29 grey	49 black	64 grey	84 yellow	111 red	190 yellow
21 red	29e green	50 green	65 red	85 grey	112 blue	191 grey
22 green	30 brown	53 blue	66 white	86 green	115 yellow	192 black

1. Parking light and direction indicator
2. Headlights
3. Horn
4. Ignition coil
5. Spark plugs
6. Distributor
7. Voltage regulator
8. Alternator
9. Starter
10. Battery
11. Fuse box
12. Temperature transmitter
13. Oil pressure switch
14. Back-up light switch
15. Stop light switch
16. Brake warning contact
17. Heater fan motor
18. Windshield washer pump
19. Windshield wiper motor
20. Cigarette lighter
21. Contact for warning buzzer
22. Buzzer
23. Clock
24. Speedometer with odometer
25. High beam indicator light
26. Direction indicator repeater light
27. Brake warning light
28. Temperature and fuel gauges
29. Indicator light, fuel amount
30. Oil pressure warning light
31. Charge indicator light
32. Flasher unit
33. Dimmer relay
34. Ignition and starter switch
35. Hazard warning flasher switch
36. Instrument illumination rheostat
37. Headlight switch
38. Heater fan switch
39. Dome lamp switch
40. Dome lamp with switch
41. Switch for windshield wiper, and
      washer
42. Signal horn contact
43. Direction indicator switch with
      headlight flasher and dimmer
      switch
44. Fuel transmitter
45. Back up light
46. Stop lights, direction indicators
      and tail light
47. License plate light
48. Trunk light

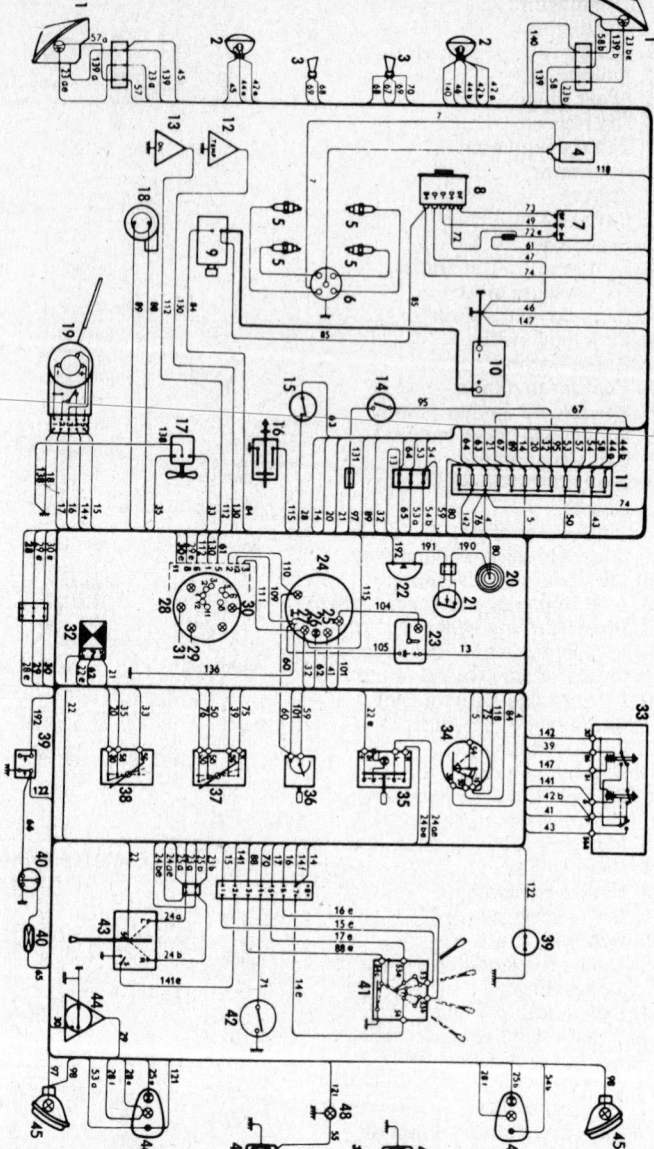

Wiring diagram—SAAB 96 1970 USA version

4 grey	22e green	30e brown	53a blue	67 red	95 white	138 black
5 red	23a yellow	32 red	54 green	68 red	97 white	139 black
7 green	23ae yellow	33 yellow	54b green	69 black	98 white	139a black
13 blue	23b white	35 grey	55 green	70 black	101 green	139b black
14 brown	23be white	39 yellow	56 black	71 black	104 green	140 black
14e brown	24a yellow	41 blue	57 blue	72 red	105 black	141 brown
14f brown	24ae blue	42a blue	57a blue	72e red	109 black	141e brown
15 red	24b white	42b white	58 green	73 yellow	110 green	142 grey
15e red	24be white	43 yellow	58b green	74 grey	111 red	147 black
16 grey	25a blue	44a grey	59 green	75 red	112 blue	190 yellow
16e grey	25b grey	44b yellow	60 green	76 grey	115 yellow	191 grey
17 blue	28 red	45 black	61 red	80 black	118 white	192 black
17e blue	28e red	46 black	62 grey	84 yellow	121 green	
18 black	28f red	47 black	63 red	85 grey	122 white	
20 white	29 grey	49 black	64 grey	88 black	130 brown	
21 red	29e green	50 green	65 red	88e black	131 white	
22 green	30 brown	53 blue	66 white	89 brown	136 black	

1. Turn signals and side lights
2. Headlights
3. Horn
4. Foglight and spotlight
5. Distributor
6. Spark plugs
7. Voltage regulator
8. Generator
9. Starter
10. Battery
11. Fuel pumps
12. Fuse box
13. Ignition coil
14. Series resistance
15. Oil warning relay
16. Oil gauge
17. Cooling fan
18. Thermostat contact
19. Temperature transmitter
20. Back-up light switch
21. Stop lamp switch
22. Heater fan motor
23. Wiper motor
24. Windshield-washer pump
25. Charge indicator light
26. Indicator light oil pressure
27. Indicator light fuel
28. Direction indicator repeater
    light
29. High beam indicator light
30. Ignition and starter switch
31. Tachometer
32. Coolant thermometer
33. Fuel gauge
34. Speedometer, odometer and
    trip meter
35. Electric clock
36. Cigarette lighter
37. Flasher
38. Maneuver relay, headlight
    flasher
39. Maneuver relay, light
40. Dimmer relay
41. Dimmer switch
42. Spotlight switch
43. Fog light switch
44. Headlight switch and in-
    strument illumination
    rheostat
45. Windshield wiper and
    washer switch
46. Map reading light with
    switch
47. Map reading light switch
48. Fuel tank gauge
49. Heater fan switch
50. Cooling fan switch
51. Warning flasher switch
52. Direction indicator switch
    with headlight flasher
53. Horn button
54. Stop lights and direction
    indicator lights
55. Tail lights
56. Back-up lights
57. License plate light

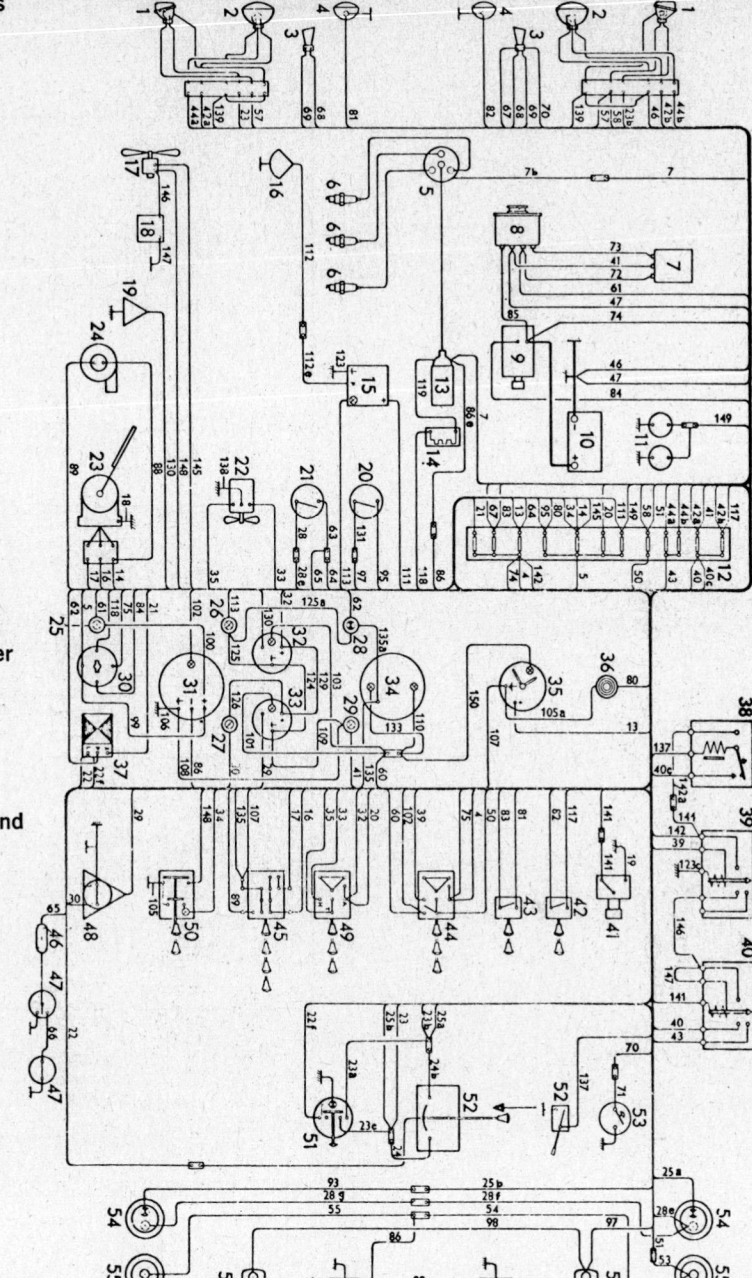

Wiring diagram—SAAB with two-stroke engine (Sonett II)

Black: 1, 7, 7b, 18, 19, 41, 46, 47, 71, 80, 105, 105a, 106, 107, 108, 109, 123, 123c, 124, 125, 125a, 135, 135a, 138, 138, 147

Red: 5, 21, 28, 28e, 28f, 28g, 32, 34, 39, 61, 63, 65, 67, 68, 72, 83, 86, 86e, 111, 126, 129

White: 20, 23a, 23b, 24b, 40, 40c, 42b, 95, 97, 98, 118, 131

Green: 16, 22, 22f, 50, 51, 53, 54, 55, 57, 58, 60, 82, 86, 88, 101, 102, 103, 110, 119, 133, 145, 146, 147, 148, 150

Yellow: 17, 23, 23c, 24a, 33, 43, 44b, 62, 66, 73, 81, 84, 99, 100, 112, 112e, 130

Blue: 13, 25a, 41, 42a, 64, 149

Grey: 4, 25b, 29, 35, 44a, 69, 70, 74, 75, 85, 89, 93, 113, 117, 142, 142a, 144

Brown: 14, 30, 88, 137c, 141

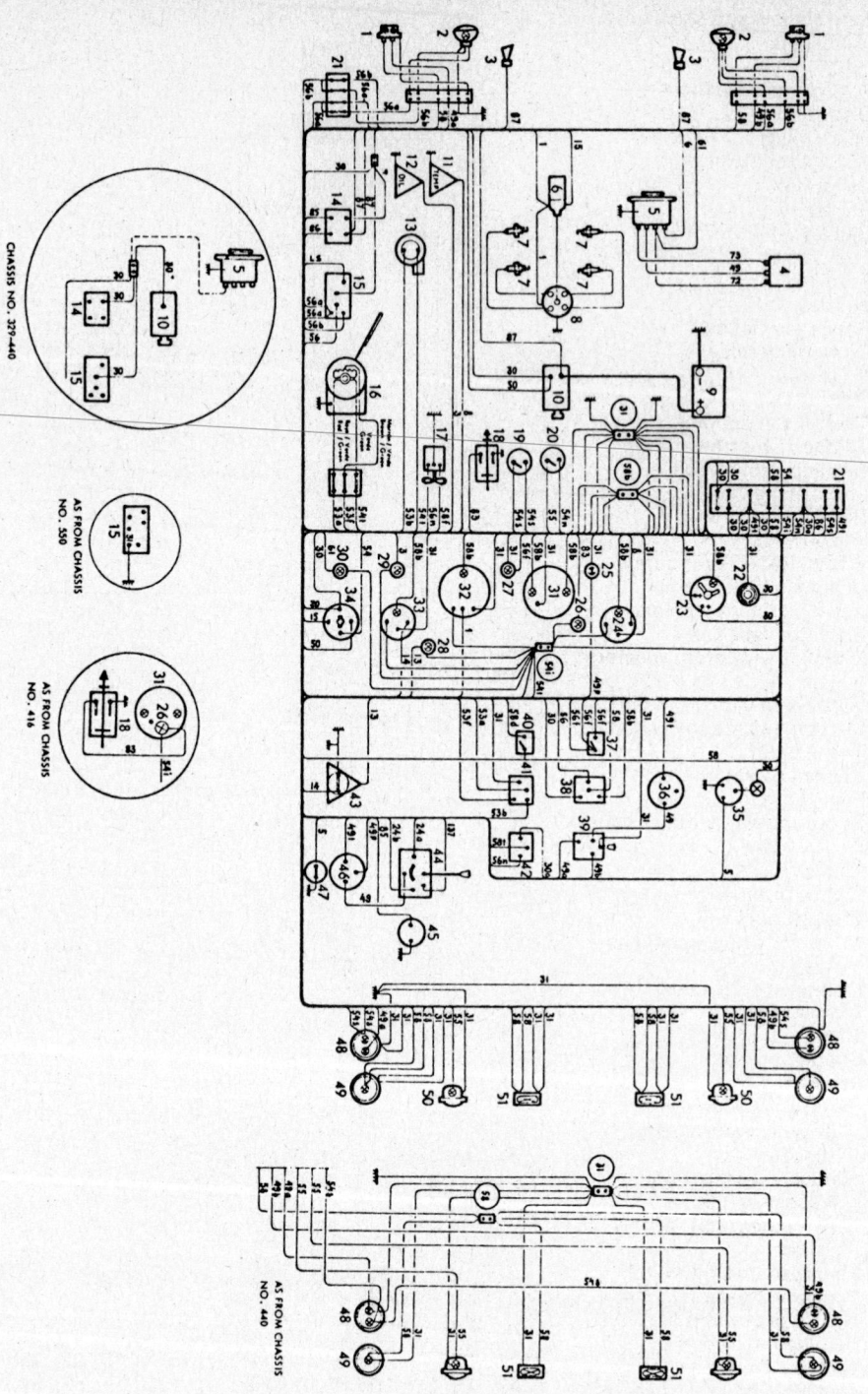

Wiring diagram—SAAB Sonett with V4 engine (Sonett II)

Black: 31, 85, LS.

Red: 1, 6, 15, 30, 30a, 49t, 50, 54, 54i, 54n, 54r, 54s, 54t, 61, 72, 86, 87.

White: 24b, 49b, 55, 56a.

Green: 49, 53a, 58, 58b, 58d.

Yellow: 8, 24a, 49p, 53f, 54h, 56b, 73.

Blue: 49b, 56a, 56f.

Grey: 14, 49a, 53b, 56, 58t.

Brown: 3, 5, 13, 83, 137.

Wiring diagram—SAAB Sonett with V4 engine (Sonett II)

1. Turn signals and side lights
2. Headlights
3. Horn
4. Voltage regulator
5. Alternator
6. Ignition coil
7. Spark plugs
8. Distributor
9. Battery
10. Starter
11. Temperature transmitter
12. Oil pressure switch
13. Windshield-washer pump
14. Relay, signal
15. Maneuver relay, light
16. Wiper motor
17. Heater fan motor
18. Brake warning contact
19. Stop lamp switch
20. Back-up light switch

21. Fuse box
22. Cigarette lighter
23. Electric clock
24. Temperature gauge
25. Direction indicator repeater light
26. Brake warning light
27. High beam indicator light
28. Indicator light fuel
29. Indicator light oil pressure
30. Charge indicator light
31. Speedometer, odometer and trip meter
32. Tachometer
33. Fuel gauge
34. Ignition and starter switch
35. Map reading light with switch
36. Warning flasher relay
37. Spotlight switch

38. Headlight switch and instrument illumination rheostat
39. Warning flasher switch
40. Fog light switch
41. Windshield wiper and washer switch
42. Heater fan switch
43. Fuel tank gauge
44. Direction indicator switch with headlight flasher and dimmer switch
45. Horn button
46. Flasher relay
47. Map reading light switch
48. Stop lights and direction indicator lights
49. Tail lights
50. Back-up lights
51. License plate light

1. Parking and turn signal lights
2. Headlights
3. Horns
4. Distributor
5. Spark plugs
6. Generator
7. Fuel pump
8. Starter motor
9. Battery
10. Voltage regulator
11. Fuse box
12. Ignition coil
13. Heater fan motor
14. Windshield wiper motor
   a. SWF
   b. Bosch
15. Stop-light switch
16. Instruments cluster
17. Dip switch
18. Door switch for roof light
19. Road-light switch
20. Heater fan switch
21. Instrument-lighting switch
22. Turn indicator repeater light
23. Ignition and starting switch
24. Windshield-wiper switch
25. Cigar lighter
26. Turn indicator switch
27. Horn button
28. Fuel-gauge sender unit
29. Roof light and switch
30. Rear roof light
31. Stop lights and turn indicator lights
32. Parking lights
33. License light
34. Door switch for roof light

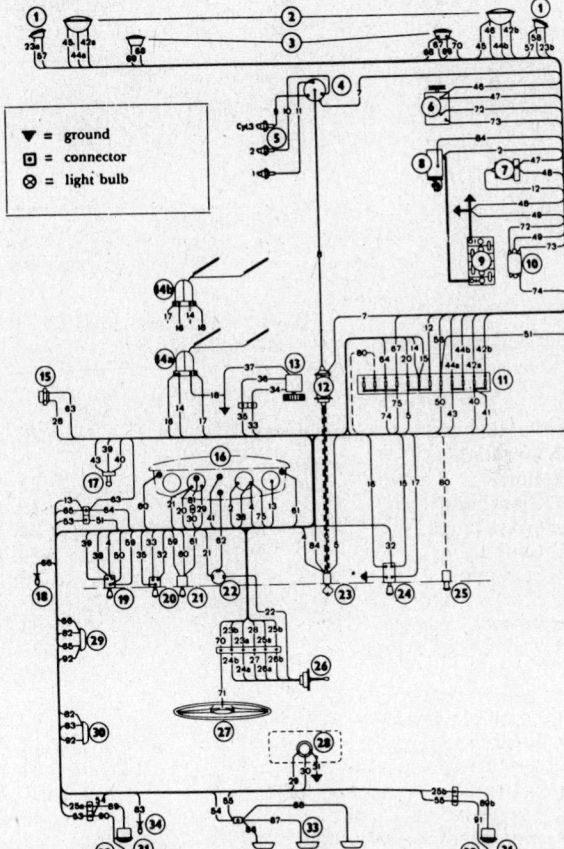

Wiring diagram—SAAB 95 (station wagon) up to chassis No. 10,800

Grey: 4, 12, 13, 25b, 26b, 29, 35, 36, 38, 44a, 62, 64, 69, 70, 74, 75, 76.

White: 23b, 24b, 40, 41, 42b.

Yellow: 17, 25a, 26a, 30, 43, 44b, 66, 73, 81, 82, 83, 84, 89a, 89b.

Blue: 42a.

Black: 1, 7, 18, 19, 23a, 24a, 32, 37, 45, 46, 47, 48, 49, 71, 77, 78, 79, 80.

Red: 2, 5, 8, 9, 10, 11, 14, 15, 20, 21, 27, 28, 33, 34, 39, 63, 65 67, 72, 92.

Green: 16, 22, 50, 5, 52, 53, 54, 55, 56, 57, 58, 59, 60, 61, 86, 87, 88, 90, 91.

NOTE: Saab 95 cars up to chassis No. 1700 have the same wiring as the Saab 93 from chassis No. 49801, except for leads to rear lights.

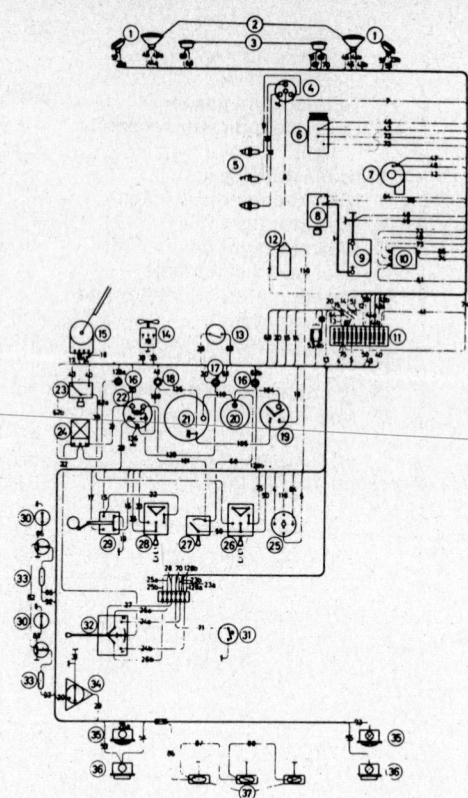

Wiring diagram—SAAB 95 (station wagon) from
chassis No. 10,801

1. Parking and turn signal lights
2. Headlights
3. Horns
4. Distributor
5. Spark plugs
6. Generator
7. Fuel pump
8. Starter motor
9. Battery
10. Voltage regulator
11. Fuse box
12. Ignition coil
13. Stop-light switch
14. Heater fan motor
15. Windshield-wiper motor
16. Turn-indicator repeater light
17. Charge indicator light
18. High beam indicator light
19. Electric clock

20. Coolant thermometer (lighting)
21. Speedometer and odometer
22. Fuel gauge
23. Dip switch
24. Turn indicator flasher
25. Ignition and starter switch
26. Headlight switch
27. Instrument-lighting rheostat
28. Heater fan switch
29. Windshield-wiper switch
30. Door switches for courtesy light
31. Horn button
32. Turn indicator switch
33. Courtesy lights with switch
34. Fuel gauge sender unit
35. Stop lights, and turn indicator lights
36. Tail lights
37. License lights

Black: 1, 7, 18, 19, 23a, 24a, 45, 46, 47, 48, 49,
71, 105, 109, 135, 136.

Red: 5, 8, 9, 10, 11, 14, 20, 21, 27, 28, 32, 39,
61, 63, 65, 67, 68, 72, 92, 126, 129.

Green: 16, 22, 50, 51, 53, 54, 55, 58, 59, 60,
86, 87, 88, 101, 104, 110.

Grey: 4, 12, 25b, 26b, 29, 35, 44a, 62a, 62b, 64,
69, 70, 74, 75, 85, 93.

White: 23b, 24b, 40, 42b, 66, 82, 83, 118, 128a.

Yellow: 17, 26a, 33, 43, 44b, 73, 84, 128b.

Brown: 15, 30.

Blue: 13, 25a, 41, 42a.

1. Parking and turn signal lights
2. Headlights
3. Horns
4. Distributor
5. Spark plugs
6. Generator
7. Fuel pump
8. Starter motor
9. Battery
10. Voltage regulator
11. Fuse box
12. Ignition coil
13. Heater fan motor
14. Windshield-wiper motor
    a. SWF
    b. Bosch
15. Stop-light switch
16. Instrument cluster
17. Dimmer switch
18. Door switches for courtesy light
19. Headlight switch
20. Heater fan switch
21. Instrument-lighting switch
22. Turn indicator flasher
23. Windshield-wiper switch
24. Ignition and starter switch
25. Trunk light
26. Turn indicator switch
27. Wheel with horn button
28. Fuel-gauge sender unit
29. Courtesy light with switch
30. Stop and turn indicator lights
31. License lights

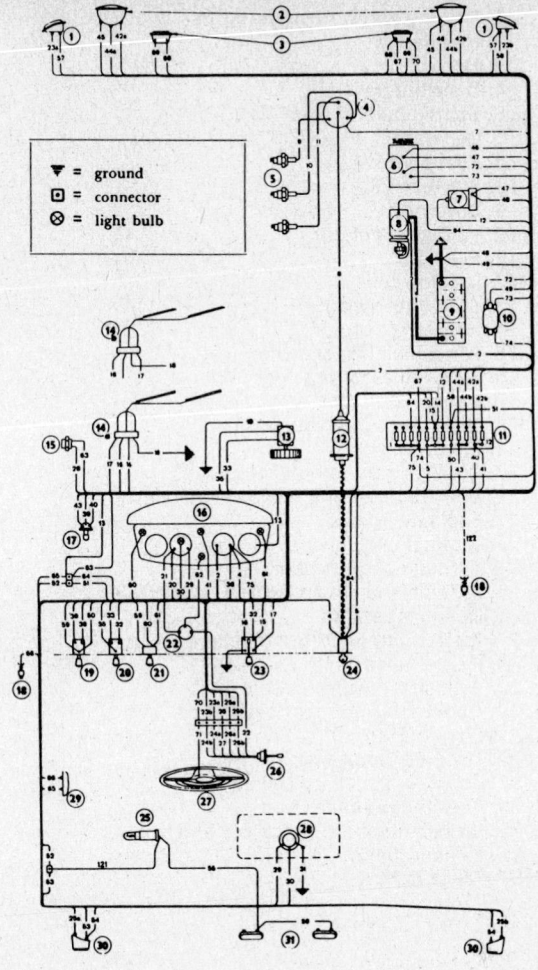

▽ = ground
▢ = connector
⊗ = light bulb

S 267

Wiring diagram—SAAB 96 up to chassis No. 201,400

Black: 1, 7, 18, 19, 23a, 24a, 32, 37, 45, 46, 47, 48, 49, 71, 77, 78, 79.

Red: 2, 5, 8, 9, 10, 11, 14, 15, 20, 21, 27, 28, 33, 39, 63, 65, 67, 68, 72.

Green: 16, 22, 50, 51, 52, 53, 54, 55, 56, 57, 58, 59, 60, 61, 121.

Grey: 4, 12, 25b, 26b, 29, 35, 38, 44a, 62, 64, 69, 70, 74, 75, 76.

White: 23b, 24b, 40, 41, 42b.

Yellow: 17, 25a, 26a, 30, 43, 44b, 66, 73, 81, 84, 122.

Blue: 42a.

1. Parking and turn signal lights
2. Headlights
3. Horns
4. Distributor
5. Spark plugs
6. Generator
7. Fuel pump
8. Starter motor
9. Battery
10. Voltage regulator
11. Fuse box
12. Ignition coil
13. Stop-light switch
14. Heater fan motor
15. Windshield-wiper motor
16. Turn-indicator repeater light
17. Charge indicator light
18. High beam indicator light
19. Electric clock
20. Coolant thermometer (lighting)
21. Speedometer and mileage recorder
22. Fuel gauge
23. Dimmer switch
24. Turn indicator flasher
25. Ignition and starter switch
26. Headlight switch
27. Instrument-lighting rheostat
28. Heater fan switch
29. Windshield-wiper switch
30. Door switch for courtesy light
31. Horn button
32. Turn indicator switch
33. Courtesy light with switch
34. Fuel gauge sender unit
35. Stop lights, turn indicators and tail lights
36. License lights
37. Trunk light

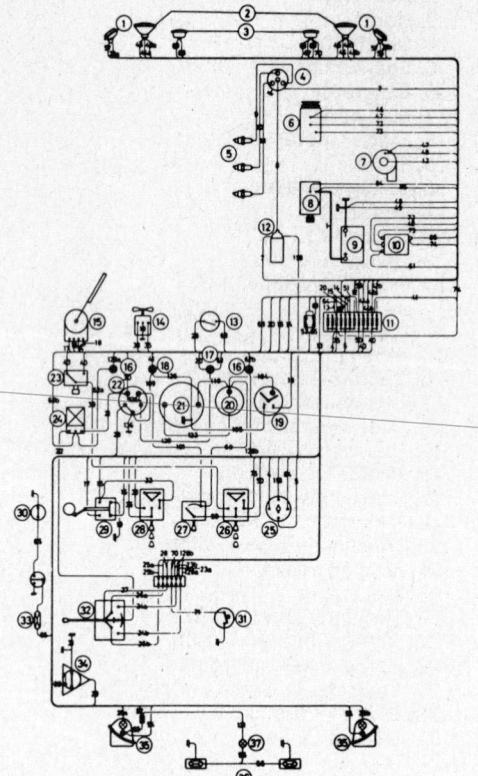

Wiring diagram—SAAB 96 from chassis No. 201,401

Black: 1, 7, 18, 19, 23a, 24a, 45, 46, 47, 48, 49, 71, 105, 109, 135, 136.

Red: 5, 8, 9, 10, 11, 14, 20, 21, 27, 28, 32, 39, 61, 63, 65, 67, 68, 72, 126, 129.

Green: 16, 22, 50, 51, 52, 53, 54, 55, 56, 57, 58, 59, 60, 101, 104, 110, 121, 133.

Grey: 4, 12, 25b, 26b, 29, 35, 44a, 62a, 62b, 64, 69, 70, 74, 75, 85.

White: 23b, 24b, 40, 42 b, 66, 118, 128a.

Yellow: 17, 26a, 33, 43, 44b, 73, 84, 128b.

Brown: 15, 30.

Blue: 13, 25a, 41, 42a.

1. Parking and turn signal lights
2. Headlights
3. Horns
4. Extra lights
5. Distributor
6. Spark plugs
7. Generator
8. Fuel pump
9. Starter motor
10. Battery
11. Voltage regulator
12. Fuse box
13. Resistance
14. Ignition coil
15. Heater fan motor
16. Windshield-wiper motor
17. Windshield-washer pump
18. Stop-light switch
19. Dimmer switch
20. Instruments
21. Halda Speed Pilot
22. Door switch
23. Light switch
24. Heater fan switch
25. Flasher unit
26. Windshield wiper switch
27. Ignition and starter switch
28. Cigar lighter
29. Back-up light switch with ind. light
30. Switch for optional lights
31. Instrument illumination switch
32. Extra switch
33. Turn indicator switch
34. Horn button
35. Courtesy light with switch
36. Fuel gauge, sender unit
37. Tail, stop and turn indicator signal lights
38. Back-up lights
39. License plate lights

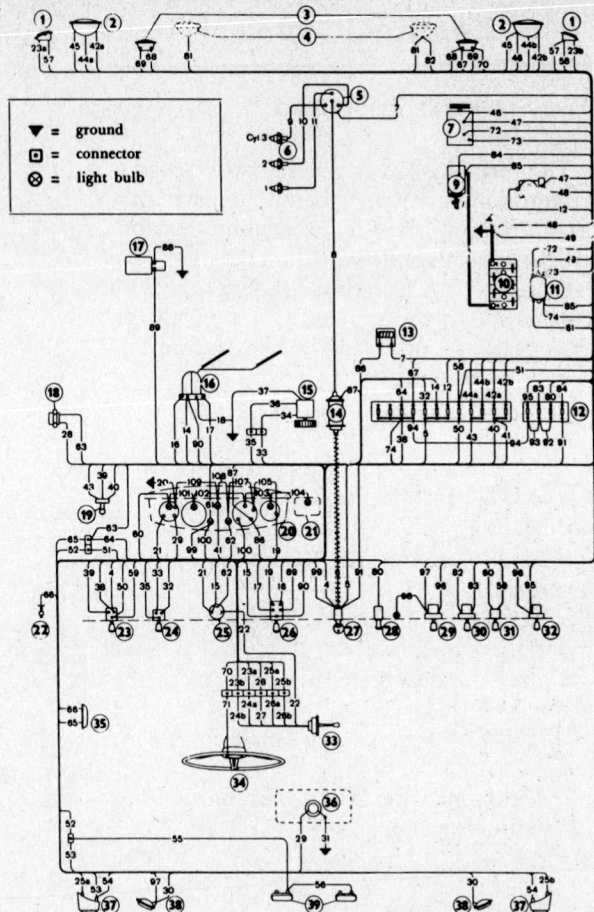

Wiring diagram—SAAB GT-750

Black: 1, 7, 18, 19, 20, 23a, 24a, 32, 37, 45, 46, 47, 48, 49, 71, 80, 88, 89, 91, 105, 107, 108, 109.

Red: 5, 8, 9, 10, 11, 14, 15, 21, 27, 28, 33, 34, 39, 61, 63, 65, 67, 68, 72, 86, 90.

Yellow: 17, 25a, 26a, 43, 44b, 66, 73, 84, 99, 100.

Green: 16, 22, 50, 51, 52, 53, 54, 55, 56, 57, 58, 59, 60, 81, 82, 83, 101, 102, 103, 104.

Blue: 12a, 62.

Grey: 4, 12, 25b, 26b, 29, 35, 36, 38, 44a, 64, 69, 70, 74, 85, 87, 92, 93, 94.

White: 23b, 24b, 30, 40, 41, 42b, 95, 96, 97, 98.

Engine Electrical

Two-Stroke Distributor

The principal differences between distributors involve the vacuum advance governors. One, JFU3 (R), a vacuum distributor, is connected to a vacuum take-off on the carburetor. When setting the ignition with a stroboscope, the vacuum governor always must be disconnected by removing the line from the distributor.

REMOVAL

1. Disconnect the battery ground cable and the distributor primary lead.
2. Remove the distributor cover and, if applicable, remove the line at the vacuum chamber.
3. Loosen the locking bolt on the retainer under the distributor.
4. Pull the distributor up and out of the engine. NOTE: *With VJU3BR1T and VJU3BR2T, the generator bracket must be moved.*
5. Disconnect the spark plug wires from the distributor cap.

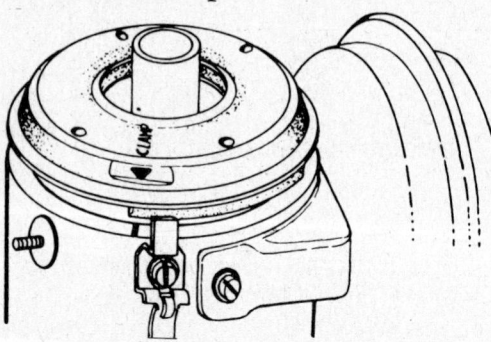

Condensation trap

INSTALLATION

1. Remove the spark plugs and turn the crankshaft so that the mark on the pulley faces the centermost mark on the engine block.
2. a. *Distributors 0 231 144 002/JFU 3, VJU3BR1T, and VJU3BR2T:* Install the distributor into the engine so that the vacuum chamber faces the rear with a clearance of about 0.4–0.6″ between it and the engine block. At the same time, the marks on the rotor and distributor housing should coincide.

b. *Distributor JF 3 (R), VJ3BR7T, and VJ3BR8T:* Install the distributor into the engine so that the oil cup points forward and slightly to the right. At the same time, the marks on the rotor and distributor housing should coincide.

c. *Distributors 0 231 144 003/JFU3 and 0 231 144 004/JFU3.*

Install the distributor into the engine so that the vacuum chamber faces forward and slightly to the right. At the same time, the marks on the rotor and distributor housing should coincide.

3. Reconnect the distributor primary wire and the battery ground cable.
4. Install the distributor cap. The spark plug wire for the No. 2 cylinder must be installed into the tower opposite the distributor rotor when the mark on the pulley faces the centermost mark on the engine block. The two remaining spark plug wires are installed clockwise. The one for the No. 3 cylinder first and for No. 1 cylinder afterwards.
5. Adjust the timing and, if applicable, reconnect the hose to the vacuum chamber. The vacuum hose must be installed so that its highest point is higher than the float chamber.

DISTRIBUTORS 0 231 120 023/JF3 (R), VJ3BR7T, AND VJ3BR8T DISASSEMBLY

1. Remove the rotor 4, which is fastened to the cam by means of the stop screw 7.
2. Lift off the condensation shield.
3. Loosen the nut 31 for the condenser wire.
4. Remove clip 9 and lift breaker arm 12.
5. Remove screw 33, together with contact washer 34, insulating washer and insulating strip 35. Retrieve the insulating washers 32.
6. Loosen the screw and remove contact plate 11.
7. Loosen and remove the three screws 39 which hold breaker plate 13. Two of these screws also hold the retaining springs 37.
8. Remove the retaining springs and lift up breaker plate 13.
9. File off and drive out the riveted slotted pin 23 which holds the distributor pinion 47 to the shaft 22.

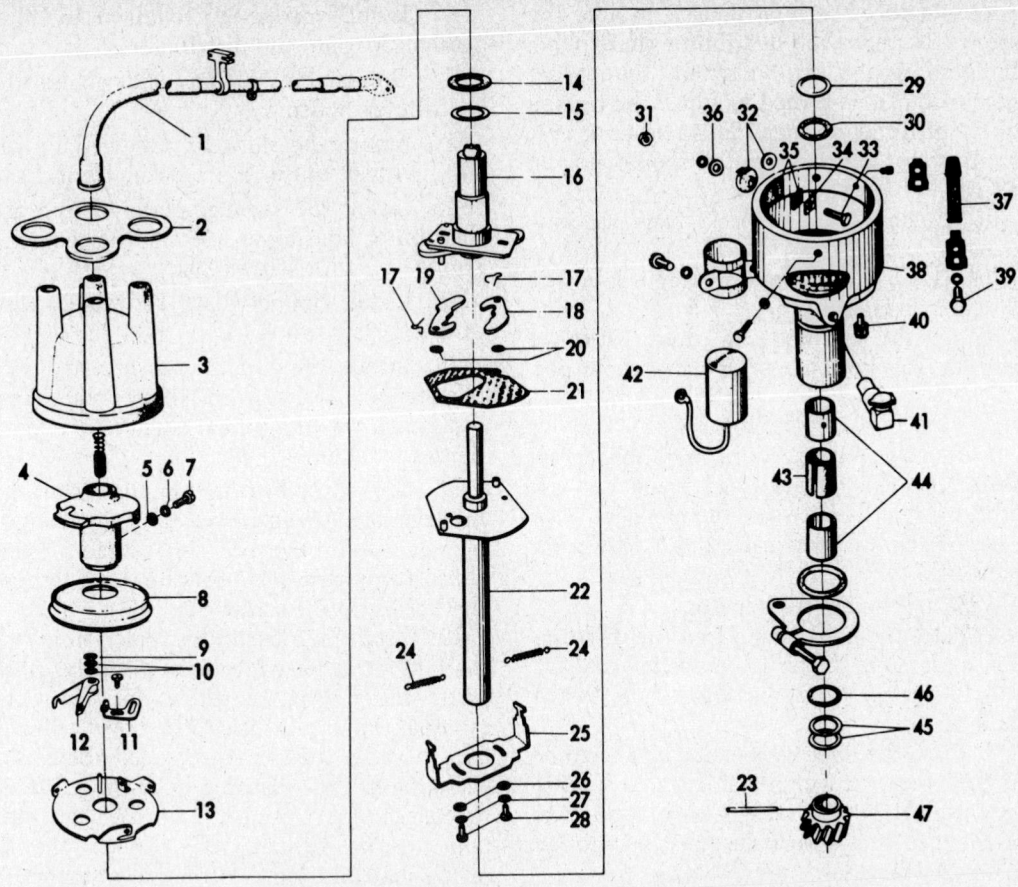

Distributor 0 231 120 023/JF3 (R) (VJ3 BR11T)

1. Ventilation hose	17. Damping spring	33. Contact screw
2. Retainer, ventilation hose	18. Fly weight	34. Contact washer
3. Distributor cap	19. Fly weight	35. Insulating washer
4. Distributor arm (rotor)	20. Fiber washer	36. Washer
5. Washer	21. Fiber plate	37. Retaining spring
6. Spring washer	22. Distributor shaft	38. Distributor housing
7. Screw, distributor arm	23. Slotted pin	39. Screw for retaining spring
8. Condensation shield	24. Spring	40. Bleed nipple
9. Clip	25. Clamp	41. Lubricator
10. Shim	26. Washer	42. Capacitor
11. Contact plate	27. Spring washer	43. Felt bushing
12. Breaker arm	28. Screw	44. Bushing
13. Contact breaker plate	29. Shim	45. Shim
14. Fiber washer	30. Fiber washer	46. Fiber washer
15. Shim	31. Nut for contact screw	47. Distributor pinion
16. Breaker arm	32. Insulating washer	

10. Lift out the distributor shaft, together with the vacuum advance governor. Collect washers 29 and 30, as well as any shims 45.

11. Unhook the two springs 24 from spring holder 25 and lift off breaker cam 16. Collect the spacers 15 and the fiber washer 14.

12. Unhook the springs from the breaker cam. If necessary, bend the spring holders carefully.

13. Remove the damping springs 17 and lift off the governor weights 18 and 19. Remove the fiber washers 20 from beneath the weights.

14. Remove the fiber plate 21. Note the screws 28 under the distributor shaft plate. If these screws are loosened, the spring holder 25 can be turned to adjust the tension of the governor springs. This tension is correctly set at the factory and should not be altered.

15. Remove condenser 42 from the distributor housing.

16. Remove the rubber ring from the distributor housing.

17. If the bushings in the distributor housing are worn, press or drive them out.

ASSEMBLY

1. If new bushings are installed, press them into the housing and place the felt lubricating pad between them.

2. Attach the condenser to the distributor housing.

3. Install a new rubber ring.

4. Place the fiber plate 21 on the distributor shaft steel plate; align it so that its oblong cut-out faces the round hole in the steel plate.

5. Place the fiber washers 20 on the stubs of the governor weights and smear a little grease on the stubs. Any grease applied to bearings or sliding surfaces must be applied in small quantities.

6. Put the governor weights 18 and 19 on the stubs. The weights must be positioned with the slide projections facing downwards towards the fiber plate.

7. Secure the weights with the damping springs 17.

8. Hook the governor springs 24 onto the holders on the breaker cam 16 and bend the holders down to prevent the springs from loosening during assembly.

9. Grease the distributor shaft, then install the breaker cam onto it. The pins on the bottom of the breaker cam must fit into the grooves in the governor weights. Make sure the longer pin is fitted into the corresponding hole in the distributor shaft plate. Note that the pins of the breaker cam must be inserted properly in order to stretch the damping springs.

10. Hook the governor springs onto the spring holders on clamp 25.

11. Check that the ignition advance mechanism functions properly by turning the breaker cam clockwise.

12. Install spacer 29, followed by fiber washer 30, onto the distributor shaft.

13. Grease the shaft and slide it into the distributor housing.

14. Mount the shim 15, followed by the fiber washer 14, on the breaker cam.

15. Install the breaker plate 13 into the distributor housing and secure the retaining springs 37 with screws 39.

16. Install contact plate 11; loosely turn down the screw.

17. Install screw 33 for the primary wire connection, along with the contact and insulating washers, then connect the condenser.

18. Grease the bearing pin and install the breaker arm. Adjust axial play and height in relation to the breaker contact, using shims 10. Secure using the clip 9 and tighten the nut 31 on the screw 33.

19. Install the distributor pinion onto the shaft, after having adjusted the axial play of the latter using the shims 45. The permissible axial play is 0.004–0.008″. Note that the fiber washer 46 is placed above the shim, against the distributor housing. When driving in and riveting the slotted shaft pin, take care not to damage the shaft, pinion, or the shaft bearing. The height of the rivet bead must not exceed 0.02″.

20. Adjust the point gap to 0.014–0.018″. Tighten the screw for the contact plate. If the gap is adjusted using a dwellmeter tester, the dwell angle should be 75–82°.

21. Install the condensation shield over the breaker mechanism so the arrow points toward the mark on the distributor housing.

22. Screw on the rotor.

DISASSEMBLY AND ASSEMBLY OF DISTRIBUTORS 0 231 144 002/JFU3 (VJU3BR2T), 0 231 144 003/JFU3, AND VJU3BR1T

Follow the same general procedure as outlined for 0 231 120 023/JF3 (R). Use the part identification and location number from the corresponding illustrations. See the chart for setting clearances and dwell.

Ignition Timing

The firing order is 1–2–3. No. 1 cylinder is the rear cylinder. Ignition setting is done with No. 2 cylinder at TDC.

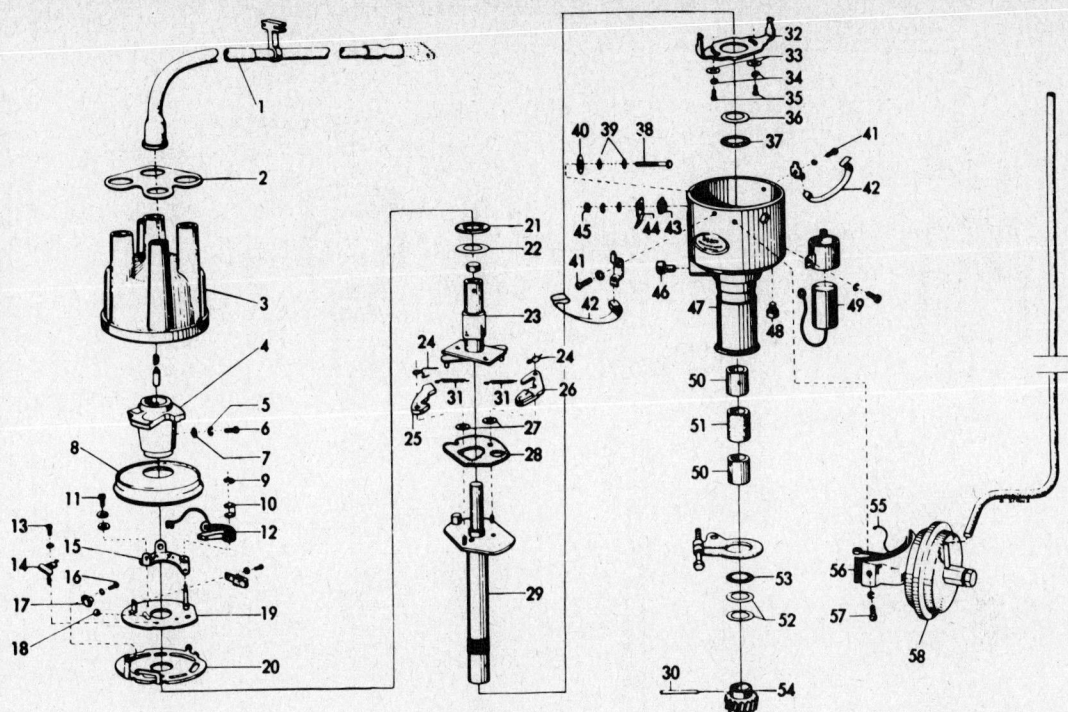

Distributor 0 231 144 002/JFU3 (VJU3 BR2T)

1. Ventilation hose
2. Retainer, ventilation hose
3. Distributor cap
4. Distributor arm (rotor)
5. Spring washer
6. Screw, distributor arm
7. Washer
8. Condensation trap
9. Clip
10. Shim
11. Screw for contact plate
12. Breaker arm
13. Screw for pivot
14. Pivot
15. Contact-breaker plate
16. Screw for ball retainer
17. Ball retainer
18. Ball
19. Self-adjusting breaker plate

20. Stationary breaker plate
21. Fiber washer
22. Shim
23. Breaker cam
24. Locking spring
25. Fly weight
26. Fly weight
27. Fiber washer
28. Fiber plate
29. Distributor shaft
30. Pin
31. Regulator spring
32. Clamp
33. Washer
34. Spring washer
35. Screw for clamp
36. Shim
37. Fiber washer
38. Contact screw
39. Contact washer

40. Fiber washer
41. Screw, retaining spring
42. Retaining spring
43. Insulating washer
44. Connection
45. Nut, contact screw
46. Lubricator
47. Distributor housing
48. Bleeder nipple
49. Capacitor
50. Bushing
51. Felt bushing
52. Shim
53. Fiber washer
54. Distributor pinion
55. Earthing connection,
    vacuum chamber
56. Sealing strip
57. Screw, vacuum chamber
58. Vacuum chamber

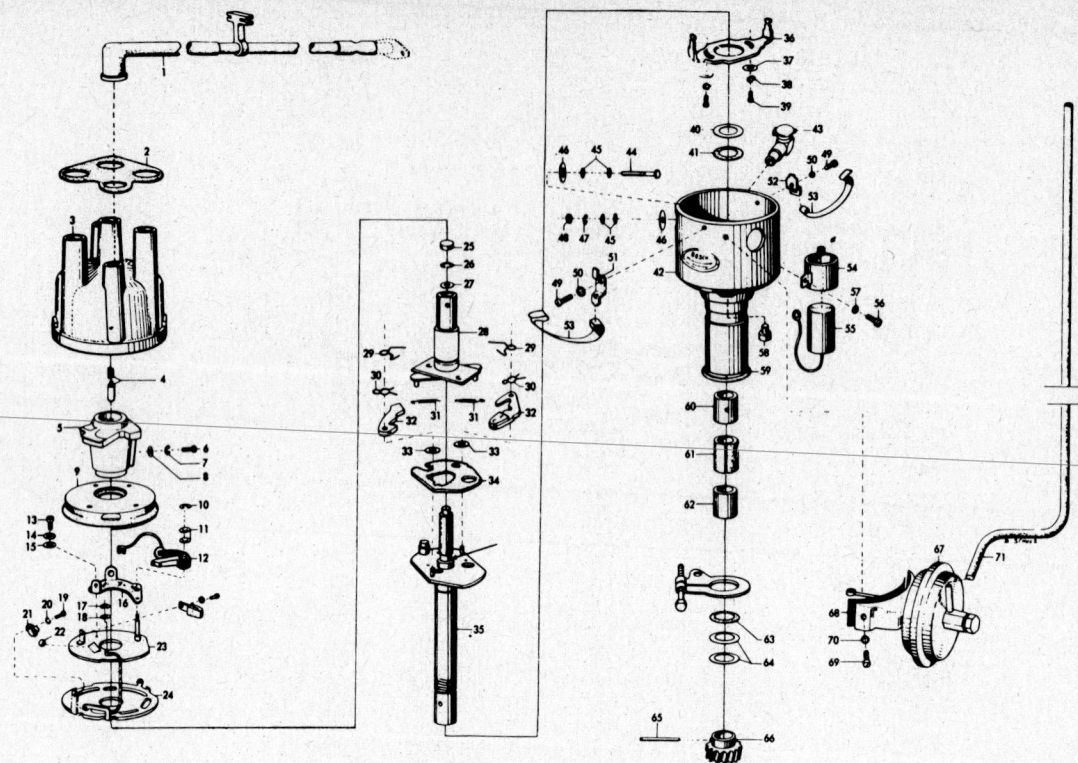

Distributor 0 231 144 003/JFU3, 0 231 144 004/JFU3

1. Ventilation hose
2. Retainer, ventilation hose
3. Distributor cap
4. Center carbon brush with spring
5. Rotor
6. Screw for rotor
7. Spring washer
8. Flat washer
9. Condensation shield
10. Clip
11. Shim
12. Breaker arm
13. Screw for contact plate
14. Spring washer
15. Flat washer
16. Contact-breaker plate
17. Clip
18. Flat washer
19. Screw for ball holder
20. Spring washer
21. Ball holder
22. Ball
23. Self-adjusting (moving) breaker plate
24. Stationary breaker plate

25. Lubricating felt
26. Retaining washer
27. Washer
28. Breaker cam
29. Damping spring (Monte Carlo 850)
30. Locking spring (Saab 95/96)
31. Governor spring
32. Governor weight
33. Fiber washer
34. Fiber plate
35. Distributor shaft
36. Clamp
37. Flat washer
38. Spring washer
39. Screw for clamp
40. Spacer
41. Fiber washer
42. Distributor housing
43. Lubricator
44. Contact screw
45. Contact washer
46. Insulating washer
47. Spring washer
48. Nut for contact screw

49. Screw for retaining-spring holder
50. Spring washer
51. Retaining-spring holder with lug
52. Retaining-spring holder without lug
53. Retaining spring
54. Capacitor clip
55. Capacitor
56. Screw for capacitor clip
57. Spring washer
58. Bleed nipple
59. Rubber ring
60. Upper bushing
61. Felt bushing
62. Lower bushing
63. Fiber washer
64. Shim
65. Serrated pin
66. Distributor pinion
67. Vacuum chamber
68. Sealing strip
69. Screw for vacuum chamber
70. Spring washer
71. Vacuum hose

The ignition timing should be checked and adjusted using a strobe timing light at an engine speed of 3,000 rpm. This is more reliable than setting static timing using a test lamp.

At the front end of the engine there are four marks: one mark on the pulley and three on the engine block. These marks are used as follows:

a. When the mark on the pulley coincides with the upper mark on the engine block, No. 2 piston should be at TDC. This upper mark is used to determine if the pulley mark is in the correct position, and when remarking the pulley after installing a new crankshaft or pulley.

b. When the mark on the pulley coincides with the middle mark on the engine block, it shows the basic ignition setting for No. 2 cylinder. It is used when adjusting the static ignition timing on a stationary engine using a test lamp and when installing the distributor.

c. When the mark on the pulley coincides with the lower mark on the engine block, it shows the ignition position for No. 2 cylinder at an engine speed of approximately 3,000 rpm. This mark is utilized for ignition setting using a strobe timing light. Note that the engine revolutions must be within the limits shown after the first step on the

timing curve. If the engine is equipped with a vacuum advance distributor, always remove the hose to the vacuum chamber before setting ignition timing.

Degrees on the Crankshaft	Distance on Pulley from Upper Mark
1°	0.04″
7°	0.30″
10°	0.43″
15°	0.65″
17°	0.74″
20°	0.87″

NOTE: *Mark is TDC for No. 2 cyl. Pulley dia. = 4.961″.*

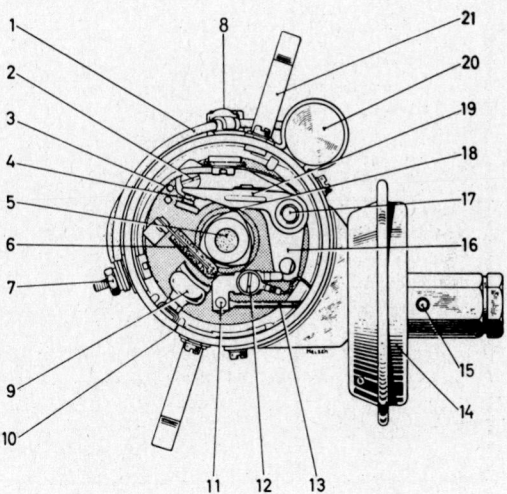

Checking length of vacuum chamber control arm. To adjust length, hold nut (1) and loosen locknut (2), then screw the arm in or out until correct length is obtained.

A=1.68 ± 0.008″ }
B=0.137 ± 0.0059″ } Up to 1965

A=1.68 ± 0.008″ }
B±0.197 = 0.0059″ } From 1966

Breaker points and components—distributor JFU 3

1. Condenser cable
2. Locking screw
3. Adjusting lug for breaker points
4. Breaker points
5. Lubricating felt pads
6. Lubricating felt pads
7. Connection for low tension cable
8. Lubricator
9. Bearing
10. Ignition setting mark
11. Pivot (SAAB 95/96 1965 model)
12. Pivot screw (SAAB 95/96, 1965 model)
13. Control arm
14. Vacuum chamber
15. Vacuum-hose connection
16. Contact plate with stationary breaker point
17. Stub for breaker arm
18. Fiber lug
19. Breaker arm
20. Condenser
21. Retaining spring

Bosch designation	0 231 144 002/JFU3 (VJU3 BR2T)	0 231 120 023/JF3 (R) (VJ3 BR11T)	0 231 144 003/JFU3	0 231 144 004/JFU3
Model	Saab 95/96, model 1965	Saab Sport model 1965	Saab 95/96 as from model 1966	Saab Monte Carlo 850 as from model 1966
Ignition timing	Centrifugal and vacuum regulation	Centrifugal regulation	Centrifugal and vacuum regulation	Centrifugal and vacuum regulation
Breaker gap	0,012-0,016 in. (0,3-0,4 mm)	0,014-0,018 in. (0,35-0,45 mm)	0,014-0,018 in. (0,35-0,45 mm)	0,014-0,018 in. (0,35-0,45 mm)
Dwell angle	80-84°	75-82°	75-82°	75-82°
Basic setting of ignition with the aid of a test lamp with engine standing still, and when fitting a distributor				
Ignition position in degrees on pulley B.T.D.C.	7°	10°	10°	10°
Stroboscope setting of ignition at approx. 3000 r/m				
Ignition position in degrees on pulley B.T.D.C.	17° Set the ignition, with the vacuum hose disconnected	20°	15° Set the ignition, with the vacuum hose disconnected	20° Set the ignition, with the vacuum hose disconnected
Checking the mark on pulley. The piston in cyl. 2 shall be at T.D.C. The mark on the pulley shall now coincide with the upper mark on the engine block.				

Ignition timing settings

Dynamic Timing Using Strobe Light

1. Check the breaker points and arm and adjust to the correct gap. When installing the rotor, always use a new spring washer to prevent the screw from working loose. Inspect all wires, cap, spark plugs and connections and be certain everything is in good condition.

2. Turn the crankshaft in the normal direction of rotation until the mark on the pulley coincides with the middle mark on the engine block.

3. Turn the distributor so that the mark on the rotor is opposite the mark on the edge of the distributor housing and the vacuum chamber points rearwards on the SAAB 95 and 96 (1965) and that the distributor housing lubricator points forward and a little to the right on the SAAB Sport (1965). From 1966, the distributor must be turned so that the vacuum chamber points forward and a little to the right.

4. Connect the strobe light to the spark plug wire or cap tower of No. 2 cylinder and start the engine. Gradually increase the

Distributor Bosch designation	VJ3 BR7T	VJ3 BR8T	1. VJU3 BR1T 2. VJU3 BR2T
Model	Saab GT 750	Saab 95 up to chassis No. 4836 Saab 96 up to chassis No. 148268	1. Saab 95 from chassis No. 4837 2. Saab 95 from chassis No. 10801 1. Saab 96 from chassis No. 148269 2. Saab 96 from chassis No. 201401
Ignition advance	centrifugal reg.	centrifugal reg	centrifugal and vacuum reg.
Breaker gap	0.3—0.4 mm	0.3—0.4 mm	0.3—0.4 mm
Dwell angle	80°—84°	77°—83°	77°—83°
Basic setting of ignition with aid of test lamp stationary engine Ignition position in degrees on crankshaft B.T.D.C.	S 203 2° (see note*)	S 204 10°	S 205 7°
Stroboscope setting at 3.000 r.p.m. approx Ignition position in degrees on crankshaft B.T.D.C.	S 206 22° (see note**)	S 206 20°	S 207 17° NB with disconnected vacuum hose
Check that the mark on the pulley tallies The 2nd cylinder shall be at T.D.C.	S 208	S 208	S 209

The following applies for GT 750 if equipped with double carburetors and special exhaust system:
* Basic setting = 0° (upper setting mark)
**Stroboscope setting = 20° (22 mm below the upper setting mark)

Ignition timing settings

engine speed. A noticeable change in the ignition setting will be observed somewhere between 1,000 and 2,000 rpm; a further increase in engine speed should result in no change. Adjust the timing within this rpm range by loosening the locking bolt and turning the distributor housing; in the normal direction of rotation to retard, against to advance. When the mark on the pulley coincides with the lower mark on the engine block, secure the distributor by tightening the locking bolt.

Static Timing Using Test Light

If a strobe light is not available, the ignition timing can be adjusted using a small 12-volt test light between the chassis ground and the primary wire on the distributor.

1. Remove the distributor cap, rotor, and condensation trap. Examine the points and adjust the gap.

2. Reinstall the condensation trap and rotor.

3. Turn the crankshaft until the mark on

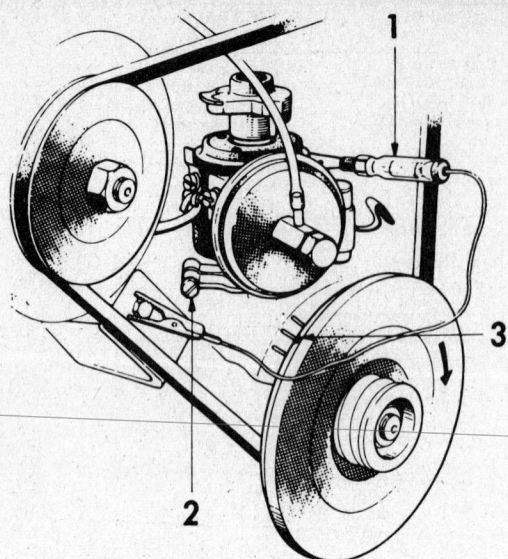

Setting ignition timing using the test light method

1. Test light
2. Lock screw
3. Timing marks

Spark plugs should be chosen according to the type of driving done. While "cold" plugs may be good for racing and high-speed, cross-country driving, they will quickly foul in a short-trip, city-driving situation. On the other hand, "hot" plugs definitely are not suited to high-speed driving condition—plug life will be short and, with a two-stroke engine, generated heat must be dissipated rapidly or ignition by incandescence will result. In short, it is best to use only approved spark plug types in the SAAB.

In the SAAB 95 and 96, conventional type spark plugs are used; in the SAAB Sport (for hard driving), Bosch MGV 260 T31S surface gap plugs are used. These plugs have no side electrode and the spark gap is the space between the center electrode and the lower part of the plug. This plug remains relatively cold and is therefore especially suitable for hard driving.

MGV 260 T31S plugs have a big pre-sparking (booster) gap inside the insulator to give a better spark effect. This reduces the risk of missing and fouled plugs. The booster gap requires a special ignition system having high ignition voltage (i.e., a special ignition coil having series resistance).

Bosch MGV 260 T31S plugs should *not* be sand blasted; clean only with a wire brush. As the gap is not adjustable, the plug must be replaced when the gap reaches 0.05″. The tightening torque is 14 ft. lbs. Other plugs should be gapped to 0.022–0.024″.

the pulley coincides with the middle mark on the engine block.

4. Turn the distributor as in Step 3 of the preceding section.

5. Connect a test light between the chassis and the terminal for the primary wire on the distributor; switch on the ignition.

6. Turn the distributor housing a little to find the position in which the test light comes on. Check that the weights of the centrifugal governor are in the inner position by turning the rotor counterclockwise. Now, secure the distributor with the locking bolt.

7. Check that the ignition timing is correct by turning the crankshaft one complete turn clockwise. When the mark on the pulley again coincides with the middle mark on the engine block, the test light should come on. While in this position, check that the marks on the rotor and distributor housing coincide and that the centrifugal weights are in the inner position.

8. Switch off the ignition and remove the test light. Clean and inspect all wires, spark plugs and the distributor cap.

Maintenance

The spark gap should be checked and adjusted to 0.030″ every 3,000 miles (except UK-16 surface gap type). Plugs with large gaps require an abnormally high ignition voltage, which involves the risk of cross-firing in the distributor cap, ignition coil and plug wires. Spark plugs in two-stroke engines normally last about 6,000 miles.

Table of Approved Spark Plugs

Type of Car	Spark Plug Make and Type	Type of Driving
SAAB 95 and 96	AC M83	Easy
	AC M82	Hard
	AC 82-S-COM	Normal
	Bosch M 175T1	Easy
	Bosch M 225T1	Normal
	Bosch M 240T1	Hard
	Champion UK-10	Easy
	Champion K-9	Normal, hard
	NGK A7	Easy, normal
SAAB Sport, Sonett, and Monte Carlo	Bosch MGV 260 T31 S	Normal, hard, easy
GT-750	Bosch M 240T1	Easy
	Bosch M 270T16	Hard

SPARK PLUG WIRES

The spark plug wires are equipped with resistors to suppress the interference produced by the electrical discharge at the spark plugs, which could be picked up on television and radio sets. These resistors consist of a core of graphite-impregnated plastic wire covered with an insulating sheath.

Because of the high ignition voltage, the wires of the SAAB Sport should not be placed closer to any grounded parts than about 0.4". It is extremely important that the wires be properly connected to the plugs, distributor cap and ignition coil, to avoid bad contact and resultant radio static. Check the resistance in cables and connections if fouled spark plugs are a common occurrence. The total resistance between the ignition coil, the distributor and spark plugs should be a maximum 35,000–40,000 ohms; a minimum of 8,000 ohms.

Suppression of Interference

The SAAB 95 and 96, SAAB Sport and Monte Carlo models are equipped with suppressed ignition cables to prevent radio and television interference. When a radio is installed in the car, no separate resistors may be installed on the distributor and spark plugs, nor may suppressed spark plugs be used with suppression wiring. The total permissible resistance then would be exceeded, resulting in a reduction of the strength of the spark.

The following table shows some further methods that can be used to suppress static; make sure the front panel and grill is grounded with a multi-braid cable.

COIL

Two different ignition coils are used, both made by Bosch. One of these is of standard design and is used on the SAAB 95 and 96 up to 1965, the other is a high output unit and is used on the SAAB Sport, Monte Carlo 850 and 95 and 96 models from 1966. The high output coil requires a ballast resistor in order to prevent its being damaged when the engine is running at low speeds or when the ignition is switched on. The ignition coil is located on the right-hand wheel well.

V4 Distributor

The distributor, Bosch JFUR 4, is installed at the rear of the engine; it rotates in a clockwise direction. It is equipped with both centrifugal and vacuum advance; centrifugal advance regulating ignition timing with relation to engine speed and vacuum advance regulating ignition timing with relation to load.

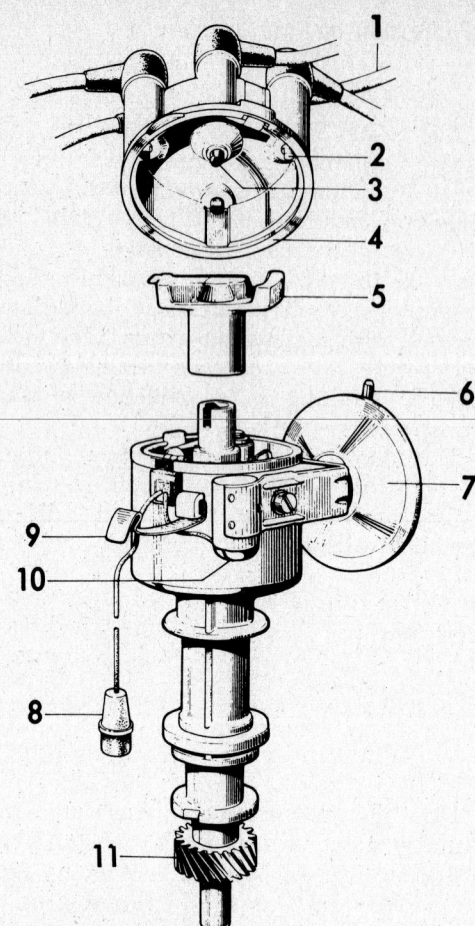

V4 distributor—typical

1. Spark plug wire
2. Contact
3. Center carbon
   button
4. Distributor cap
5. Rotor
6. Vacuum hose
   connection
7. Vacuum chamber
8. Ignition primary
   wire
9. Retaining spring
10. Condenser
11. Drive gear

REMOVAL

1. Remove wires from spark plugs.
2. Release retaining springs and remove cap.
3. Remove primary wire.
4. Remove the vacuum hose.
5. Crank engine until the mark on the rotor and the mark on the distributor housing are directly opposite each other. This is the firing position for No. 1 cylinder (6° BTDC).
6. Unscrew the retaining clamp screw and remove the clamp.
7. Remove the distributor from engine.

INSTALLATION

1. Turn the distributor until the rotor is directly opposite the assembly mark.
2. Insert the distributor into the engine.
3. See that the gears mesh properly. Rock the engine back and forth until the distributor shaft engages the oil pump driveshaft properly.
4. Check that the mark on the pulley coincides with the 6° mark on the transmission cover (firing position for No. 1 cylinder).
5. Turn the distributor housing so that the mark on the rotor is directly opposite the mark on the edge of the distributor housing.
6. Adjust the ignition timing.
7. Tighten retaining clamp slightly with the screw so that the distributor still can be turned.
8. Connect the primary wire.
9. Connect dwellmeter and adjust dwell angle at starter rpm with switch "on."
10. Install cap (correct position is indicated by rear retaining spring). Secure it with retaining springs and connect spark plug wires.

V4 distributor internal parts

1. Vacuum chamber
2. Adjustment mark
3. Adjustment rod
4. Ground lead
5. Lubricating felt
6. Assembly mark
7. Retaining spring
8. Bearing
9. Condenser
10. Primary cable
11. Fiber peg
12. Adjuster-fixed
    point
13. Breaker points
14. Locking Screw
15. Fixed breaker
    point
16. Movable breaker
    point

11. Connect a strobe light and adjust ignition timing at starter rpm, or start engine and let it run at 500 rpm. At higher engine speeds, the centrifugal governor begins to operate and invalidates the reading.

12. Tighten the distributor clamp.

13. Adjust the idle speed rpm.

BREAKER POINTS

Removal

1. Release retaining springs and remove cap.

2. Remove rotor.

3. Disconnect breaker arm lead.

4. Remove clip and washers from breaker pivot (applies to distributors 0 231 146 044 and 0 231 146 024).

5. Press leaf spring out of hole in contact support and remove breaker arm. Collect any shims (applies to distributors 0 231 146 044 and 0 231 146 024).

6. Remove retaining screw that secures the fixed breaker point.

7. Remove breaker point (breaker unit on distributor 0 231 146 033).

Installation

1. Insert the fixed breaker point or breaker unit and insert retaining screw without tightening it fully.

2. Lubricate pivot and bearing bushing on breaker arm using Bosch Ft1v 22 grease or equivalent. Do not get any oil or grease on contact surfaces, because oxidation will result.

3. Place breaker arm leaf spring in hole in contact support (applies to distributors 0 231 146 044 and 0 231 146 024). The contact surfaces of the points must be parallel to each other. Correct any misalignment with shims or by bending the fixed breaker point.

4. Install shims and clip onto the pivot (applies to distributors 0 231 146 044 and 0 231 146 024).

5. Smear the breaker arm and fiber rubbing block with Bosch Ft1v 22 grease or equivalent.

6. Connect the breaker arm lead.

7. Adjust point gap and dwell angle.

a. *Point Gap:* Crank engine until breaker arm is the greatest distance away from the fixed breaker point. Insert a screwdriver between the two adjusting lugs and slot; turn screwdriver to adjust gap. Tighten retaining screw and recheck gap.

b. *Dwell Angle:* Connect a dwellmeter between the primary coil wire and ground, then turn on ignition and crank engine with starter. Compare indicated value with specified value. Correct, if necessary, by adjusting the fixed breaker point. Tighten retaining screw and recheck gap.

8. Soak the lubricating felt in the distributor shaft with oil and install the rotor.

9. Install the distributor cap and secure with the two retaining springs.

10. Connect a strobe timing light and check the ignition timing at starter speed or with the engine running at 500 rpm, vacuum hose removed.

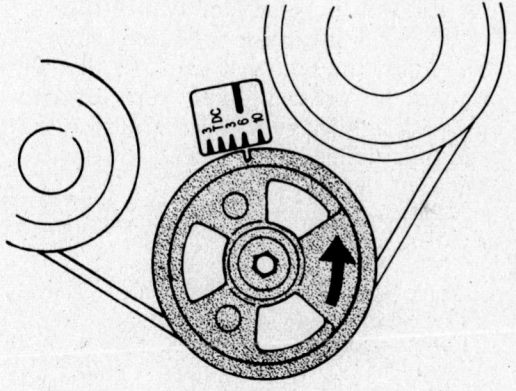

Ignition timing marks—V4 engine

Generator, Alternator

The generator on the SAAB 95 and 96 (up to and including 1966) and for the 1965 SAAB Sport is connected to a voltage and current regulator of the variode type and supplies a maximum continuous current of 300 Watts. Monte Carlo 850 models from 1966 and Saab 95 and 96 models from 1967 have an alternator. A warning lamp on the instrument panel from 1964, and an ammeter from 1960–63, shows whether or not the generator is charging the battery.

Generator Service Procedures

During driving, the generator supplies the current required by the various units and also charges the battery.

The generators used on the SAAB 95 and 96 and Sport models, up to and including 1965, have identical electrical data, but are provided with different retaining lugs for the different models. From 1966, the Monte Carlo 850 is equipped with an alternator; from 1967, all cars use an alternator.

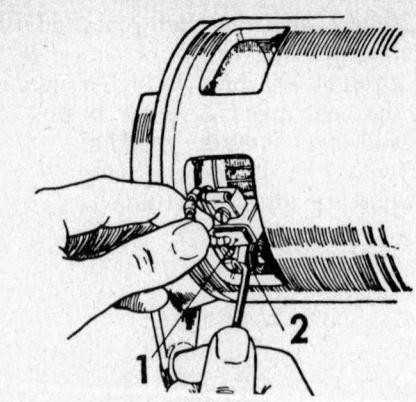

Removing carbon brushes

1. Brush   2. Spring

Removal and Installation

1. Disconnect the negative battery cable. Engines with an alternator must not be running.
2. Disconnect the generator wires, retaining and adjusting bolts, then remove fan-belt.
NOTE: *On some models, cooling system must be drained and hoses disconnected from water pump.*
3. Lift out the generator.
4. Reinstall in reverse sequence.
5. Adjust the fanbelt tension so that the belt can be pressed down approximately 0.3″ with light finger pressure halfway between the pulleys.

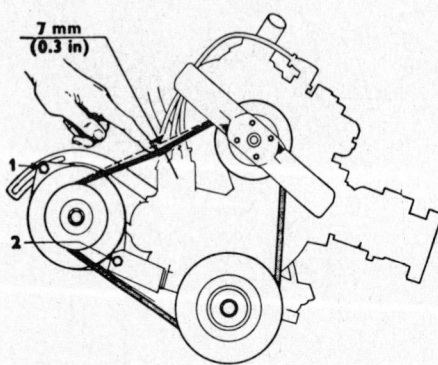

Adjusting fan belt tension

Maintenance and Inspection of Brushes

The generator brushes should be checked every 18,000 miles.
1. Disconnect the negative battery cable, then remove cables connected to DF and D+ terminals.
2. Remove the cover band over the commutator. Always disconnect the cables before removing the cover band.
3. Lift the brush springs using a wire

hook, and make sure the brushes slide freely in the holders.
4. If a brush does not slide freely in its holder, lift it out and clean both holder and brush with solvent. Do not wipe the contact surface of the brush.
5. After cleaning, install the brush in exactly the same position.
6. If a brush is damaged, or so worn so as to allow the spring to rest against the stop, a new brush must be installed. Always use genuine Bosch brushes for best results.
7. When installing, take care to prevent the spring from hitting the brush.
8. Replace the cover band, being careful not to short circuit the DF and D+ terminals.
9. Connect the DF and D+ terminal wires and the negative battery cable.

Commutator

The commutator should have a dark gray, smooth surface where the brushes contact and its surface should be free of oil and grease. If dirty, clean with a suitable solvent and dry carefully. A commutator which is scored or out-of-round must be turned down and reconditioned.

Testing the Generator

Check the voltage by connecting a voltmeter between D+ and D— terminals, after having connected DF to the chassis ground. At a maximum 2,050 rpm (1,900 rpm up to 1965), the voltmeter should read 12 volts. Check the current with an ammeter, connected in series with a rheostat

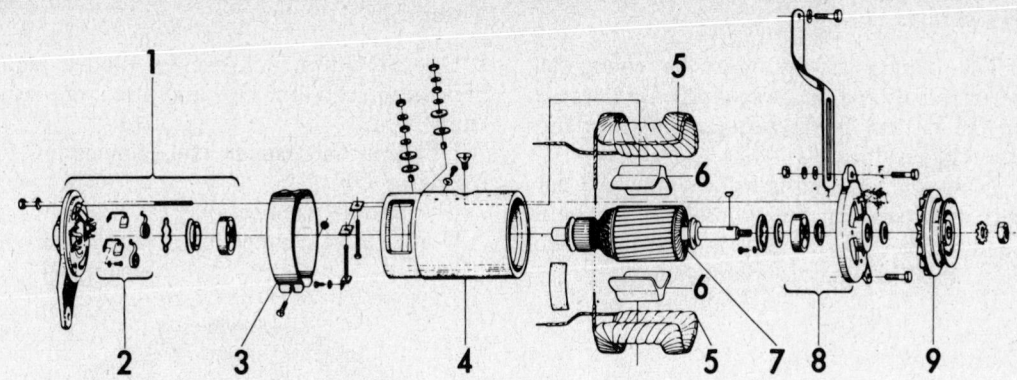

DC generator components—typical

1. Commutator frame with bearing
2. Carbon brushes with springs
3. Cover band
4. Coil housing
5. Field winding
6. Terminals
7. Armature
8. Drive end Frame
9. Belt pulley

(approximately 1 ohm) between D+ and D—. Increase the engine speed to 3,150 rpm (not more than 2,600 rpm up to 1965) and adjust the voltage to 12 volts. The current should not be less than 17 Amps (13.3 Amps up to 1965).

ALTERNATOR FOR MONTE CARLO 850 FROM 1966, SAAB 95 AND 96 FROM 1967

The SAAB Monte Carlo 850 (from 1966) and the SAAB 95 and 96 (from 1967) all are equipped with an alternator. There are some important advantages of the alternator compared to the DC generator. For example, the charging current begins earlier with an alternator and supplies the battery and electrical components at engine idle speed. Return current relays and current regulators are not used; only a voltage regulator is required. The alternator requires very little maintenance, because carbon brushes and commutators are not needed. Repair of the alternator should be done by a specialized shop.

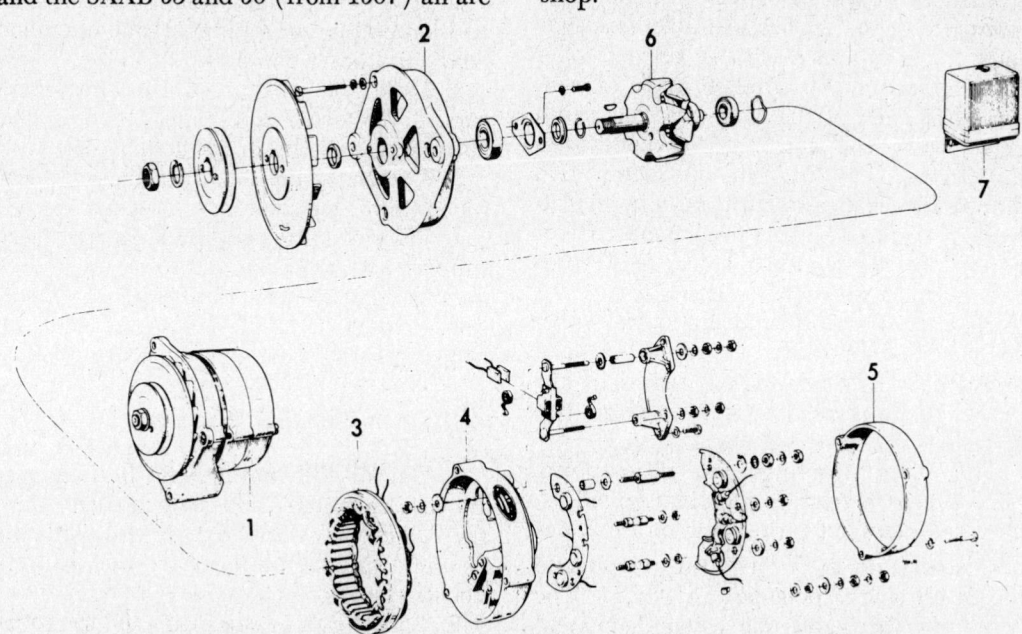

AC alternator components—typical

1. Alternator assembly
2. Bearing, gear side
3. Stator
4. Slip ring bearing
5. Protective ring
6. Rotor
7. Voltage regulator

Precautions

The battery always must be connected when the alternator is running. Do not mix up the battery leads, because serious damage will result.

If electric welding is to be done on a car with an alternator, the ground cable should be disconnected. If this is not done, the diode rectifiers may be damaged.

Designation

The Bosch designation of the alternator is
$$K1 \leftrightarrow 14U35A20$$
The interpretation of the type designation is:

20	x 100 = 2000 rpm (rpm for 2/3 of maximum current output)
35A	Maximum current
14U	Maximum voltage
←→	Direction of rotation
1	Design of alternator
K	Pole housing diameter

Description—Internal Wiring

The 12-volt alternator $K1 \leftrightarrow 14U35A20$ is internally air cooled, has a 12-pole, fork-type rotor and is equipped with six silicon diodes for rectification. An exciter diode is connected to each of the three internal windings. Their common junction constitutes the terminal D+/61. The six rectification diodes are arranged in an AC bridge network, i.e., three diodes are connected for normal polarity (anode to housing). According to polarity (positive or negative), the diode carrier is insulated from ground or connected directly to a ground contact, respectively. The insulated carrier of the exciter diode is located between these two carriers.

The stator windings are star-coupled, while the rotor carries the ring-shaped exciter coil and is of fork execution type, one fork having "north" polarity (six poles), and the other "south" polarity (six poles). The two forks then give the assembled rotor, alternately, a south and a north pole.

The exciter coil ends are connected to the slip rings, from which they receive the excitation current.

Terminals

D+/61:Output of exciter diodes, connection of regulator D+ and of charge indicator light.
DF:Input of exciter coil, connection of regulator DF.
B+:Battery connection.
D—:Ground, connection to regulator D—.

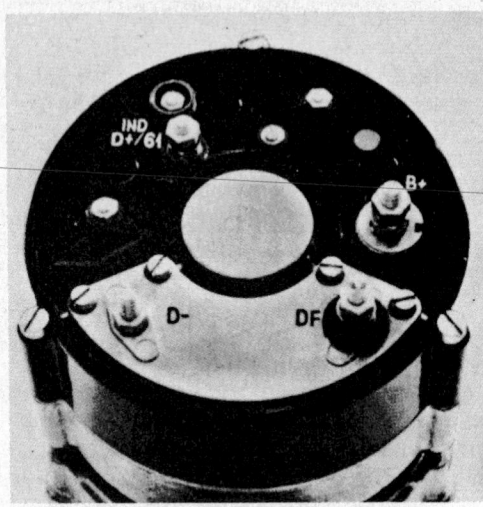

Terminal end of alternator

Alternator Bearing Replacement

1. Hold the pulley with a suitable tool and loosen the nut with a 22 mm. open end wrench. Loosen the pulley.
2. Mark the location of the attachment ear on the drive end plate. Remove the cover ring and the brush holder plate.
3. Loosen the bolts on the drive end plate, then remove the rotor and drive end plate.
4. Place the drive end plate on a suitable support and press out the rotor. It is now possible to remove the bearing.
5. Remove the ball bearing at the slip ring end, using a suitable puller.

Alternator Assembly

1. Fill the ball bearing with Bosch grease Ft 1.33 or suitable alternate grease. Press the ball bearing into the drive end plate, the enclosed side facing the drive side, using a bench vise and sockets.
2. Ease the drive end plate onto the rotor.
3. By pressing, fasten the ball bearing to the slip ring end.
4. Install the rotor and assemble the alternator. Make sure that the drive end plate

is properly positioned with relation to the slip ring end plate. Install the brush holder plate and cover ring. Torque the pulley nut to 25–29 ft. lbs.

Carbon Brush Replacement

Remove the brush holder plate, along with the carbon brushes. Remove the wire connections, using a soldering iron. When soldering the wire brush connections, take care to prevent solder flow into the cable. The minimum length of the brush is approximately 0.34″.

Testing

Diodes may be tested with DC voltages of less than 24 volts.

Glow lamps (110 volt or 220 volt) may *not* be used for insulation or short circuit tests if the diodes are in the circuit.

The 80-volt, 40 Watt test voltage for the stator winding insulation test may *not* be used unless the diodes are disconnected.

While the engine is running, battery terminals may *not* be disconnected to check the charging current.

Semiconductors (diodes) are extremely sensitive to heat. To prevent damage from heat when soldering, use a pair of longnose pliers as a heat sink on the supply wire near the diode. Use a hot iron and solder as quickly as possible. Mechanical damage to the diode wires must be avoided.

The battery must be switched off or disconnected before any work is done to the alternator, either in the car or on the bench.

Only instruments having less than an 8-volt power supply may be used to measure resistance on the assembled alternator.

On the test bench, the alternator must be driven using its own pulley. All connections must be made with the correct size cable. Do not jury rig an inadequate battery connection.

A 12-volt battery must be connected parallel to the alternator before any testing begins, except during the regulating voltage, the nominal voltage and speed tests. The battery acts as a buffer and smoothes off any peak voltages arising from switching the load on or off.

Peak voltages exceeding the maximum allowable value (50 volts) will damage the diodes.

Excitation

As opposed to DC generators, alternators can lose their self-excitation properties after long storage; therefore, a 12-volt, 2-Watt charge indicator light must be connected between terminals 61 and B+ according the wiring diagram. The pre-exciting current then will flow through the charge indicator light, D+/61 on the alternator, D+/61 on the regulator, the closed regulator contacts and DF to the exciter coil fitted to the rotor. It is most important that the charge indicator light be a minimum 2 Watts. Self-excitation begins as soon as the exciter diodes are conducting at about 1–2 volts. From there on, the voltage increases rapidly, the voltage drop across the charge indicator bulb decreases, and the bulb goes out as soon as battery voltage is achieved.

VOLTAGE REGULATOR—DC GENERATOR

The voltage regulator serves to keep the generator voltage constant within narrow limits, regardless of the generator speed and load. The regulator must prevent overcharging of the battery and limit the current take-off so that the maximum generator load is not exceeded, since this would damage the generator. To prevent the battery from being discharged through the generator when charging stops, the regulator incorporates a reverse current relay which interrupts the charging circuit when the reverse current has reached a certain point.

Function

The voltage regulator is of the variode type, meaning that it consists partly of a semiconductor regulating device called a *variode* by Bosch. This variode senses the temperature variations in the cable due to the intensity of the charging current and ambient temperature.

Regulation is achieved by varying the current through field winding (1). This is done, in three stages, at contact (4) of the regulator armature and at contacts (3) and (5).

Stage 1: Field winding grounded, armature (6) in upper position.

Stage 2: Field winding grounded through resistor (2), armature (6) in middle position.

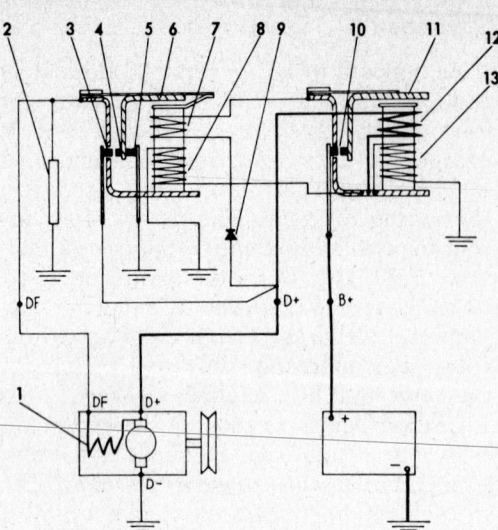

Wiring diagram—voltage regulator with variode

1. Field winding, generator
2. Resistor for field winding
3. Contact through which the field-winding can be shorted
4. Contact, armature, regulator relay
5. Contact through which the field-winding can be grounded
6. Armature, regulator relay
7. Variode pilot winding
8. Voltage winding, regulator relay
9. Variode
10. Contacts, reverse current relay
11. Armature, reverse current relay
12. Current winding, reverse current relay
13. Voltage winding, reverse current relay

Stage 3: Field winding shorted with part of the D+ cable, armature (6) in lower position.

Contact (4) will stand vibrating in one of the outer positions, depending on the voltage through the battery and connected electrical units, on the intensity of the extracted current and on the speed of the generator. All of these factors influence the force acting on the regulator armature (6), where the contact is located. The charging rate can be adjusted by changing the spring tension on armature (6)—more force gives a greater charge and vice-versa.

The variode (9) and its pilot winding (7) are connected in parallel with part of the D+ cable from the generator. The connection points are located inside the regulator casing.

The voltage over the variode and pilot winding thus will be the same as that between the connection points on the D+ cable. The resistance between the coupling points is constant for all practical purposes and the voltage is influenced only by the intensity of the generator current, which is tapped at B+.

The variode acts as a voltage-actuated and, to some extent, temperature-influenced current valve, and this feature is utilized in the voltage regulator.

When the voltage on the charging current is not high enough to open the variode, the regulator is not actuated by the pilot winding and voltage regulation is achieved with voltage winding (8) only.

If the charging current increases so much that the voltage across the variode becomes high enough to open it, part of the charging current will pass through the pilot winding, whereupon armature (6) will be attracted by the regulator coil and the field winding will be shorted through contact (3), whereupon the charging current undergoes a marked decrease. As a result, the voltage through the variode, the pilot winding and the regulator coil decreases, the armature returns and the current in the field winding increases again, thus providing a greater charging current and repeating the entire cycle. The variode thus acts as a current-limiting device in the regulator. As can be seen from the diagram, a higher voltage is required to open a cold variode. This implies that charging current will be higher when the regulator is cold (immediately after starting).

Testing

To test *closing voltage,* connect a voltmeter between ground and D+ on the regulator. Allow engine to idle and switch on the parking lights. Increase engine rpm gradually—at the instant the voltage drops slightly, then resumes its increase as rpm rises, note the voltage. The voltage immediately prior to the drop is the closing voltage—it should be 12.4–13.1 volts except for regulator RS/VA200/12/A2, which should be 12.3–13.3 volts.

To test the *no-load voltage* with a cold voltage regulator, first disconnect the battery cable, then disconnect the B+ regulator wire. This B+ wire *must not* touch ground during this test. Connect a voltmeter between ground and the B+ regulator *terminal* and increase *generator speed* to 5,000 rpm. The voltmeter should read 13.8–14.8 volts, except for regulator RS/TBA160/12/1, which should be 14.3–15.3 volts.

To test *load voltage,* switch on the headlights (high beam), windshield wipers, and heater fan. Connect a voltmeter between ground and the regulator B+ terminal (with its wire still connected). Increase *generator speed* to 5,000 rpm—voltmeter should read 13.4–14.3, except for regulator RS/TBA160/12/1, which should be 13.5–14.5.

To test the *cut-out relay* for discharge current, disconnect the B+ terminal wire and connect an ammeter between the B+ terminal and the wire just disconnected from that terminal. Increase *generator speed* to about 2,000 rpm (but less than 2,600 rpm), then slowly reduce speed to idle. During this test, the ammeter will swing from charge to discharge—the maximum ammeter minus reading should be 2.0–7.5 Amps. (except regulator RS/TBA160/12/1, which should be 3.0–9.0 Amps.).

Battery, Starter

BATTERY SERVICE PROCEDURES

The battery is a 12-volt, lead-acid type having six cells. The electrolyte is dilute sulfuric acid having a normal specific gravity of 1.28 at 68°F. with battery fully charged. The battery has a capacity of 34 Amp./hrs. up to and including the 1966 model, which means that it can supply a current of 1.7 Amps. for 20 hours at a temperature of 69°F. From 1967-1970, all cars are equipped with 44 Amp./hr. batteries. The output is 2.2 Amps. for 20 hours. 1971 models have a 60 Amp./hr. battery. The positive terminal of the battery is connected to the starter and other units, the negative terminal is grounded to the chassis.

Removal and Installation

When removing the battery, first disconnect the ground cable to prevent shorting. Engines having an alternator must be stopped before removing cables.

Loosen the wingnuts on the holder and lift out the battery.

Before installing a battery, make sure the entire battery and its terminals are clean. After battery is in place and connected, coat the terminals with Vaseline.

Electrolyte Level

Evaporation and decomposition will cause the electrolyte level to decrease. Top up, using distilled water only, until the level is approximately 0.4" above the plates. Sulfuric acid may be added *only* to compensate for leakage or to refill the battery if it has been emptied. The specific gravity must be checked whenever sulfuric acid is added.

Specific Gravity of Electrolyte

The specific gravity of the electrolyte can be checked with a syringe-type hydrometer. The result of the test indicates the charging condition of the battery; see table below.

Charging Condition	Specific Gravity
Fully charged	Approx. 1.280
Half charged	Approx. 1.210
Discharged	Approx. 1.120

Cell Voltage

A more accurate test of the state of the battery is made by using a cell tester, a voltmeter combined with a resistance, which is connected in parallel to give a load of 80–100 Amps.

Each cell is tested individually by placing the tips of the cell tester against the cell terminals. The indicated voltage should not fall below 1.6 after 10–15 seconds discharge. A bigger voltage drop indicates a defective or discharged cell.

The normal no-load cell voltage is 2.0 volts; the difference in voltage between any two cells should not exceed 0.2 volt.

Charging

The charging rate must be adapted to the capacity of the battery and should not exceed 2.5 Amps.

The battery is considered fully charged when the cell voltage is 2.5–2.7 volts, without load, and each cell has maintained the same voltage for three hours of charging.

Decomposition causes the electrolyte to boil, and release hydrogen gas, and the caps should be unscrewed while the battery is being charged.

STARTER

The starter is an electric motor, which, at the moment of starting, turns the flywheel through a pinion and ring gear. The starter pinion can slide on the armature shaft and is designed to mesh with the ring gear through operation of a solenoid. As soon as the engine has started, the pinion, driven by the flywheel ring gear, is released from the armature shaft by a freewheel mechanism, but remains in mesh with the ring gear as long as the solenoid is kept activated by the ignition key. The pinion is returned by a a spring as soon as the current for the solenoid is cut off with the key.

Removal

1. Disconnect the negative battery cable.
2. Disconnect the starter motor wires.
3. Loosen the two bolts which hold the starter to the crankcase lower half. (Use a short, open end 1/2″ wrench with two ends, one at 15° and the other at 60° with relation to the handle.)

4. Pull back the starter until it's clear, then lift it out of the engine compartment.

Installation

1. Hold the starter in place and install the two bolts.
2. Reconnect the starter wires.
3. Reconnect the negative battery cable.

Disassembly

1. Remove the cover band.
2. Lift the brush springs and remove them using a wire hook.
3. If the commutator end frame is to be removed, disconnect the brush wires and the field winding wires.
4. Separate the solenoid from the pinion housing by removing the three bolts and jumper bar from the solenoid. Lift the solenoid upwards and out.
5. Remove the solenoid lever by pulling its pivot pin.
6. Loosen and remove the two through bolts which hold the three parts of the starter assembly together.

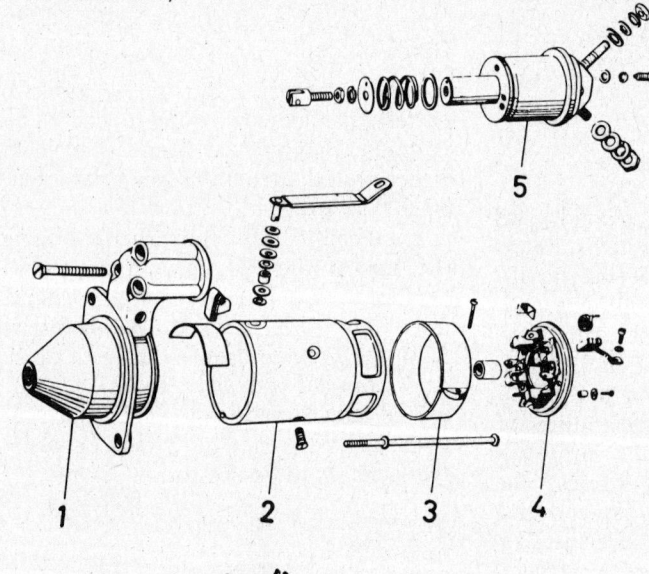

1. Pinion housing
2. Starter housing
3. Cover band
4. Commutator end frame
5. Operating solenoid
6. Starter pinion
7. Solenoid lever
8. Armature
9. Armature brake washers

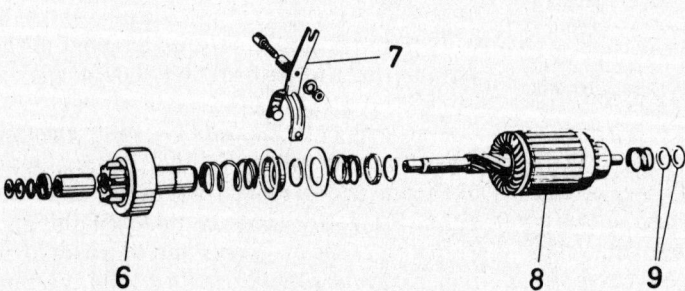

Starter motor and solenoid

7. Separate the starter assembly at the rear end frame and remove the armature and pinion. Retrieve the brake washers located on the commutator and the adjustment washers from the pinion.

8. Remove the starter pinion from the armature by pressing in the collar using a sleeve arbor, then removing the spring from inside the locating ring.

9. Clean the parts with compressed air and wash with solvent. Brushes, starter pinion and windings must *not* be washed with solvent.

Assembly

1. Relocate the starter pinion on the armature shaft and fasten using spring and locating ring. Lubricate the pinion, the shaft and the locating collar with special Bosch grease.

2. Insert the adjustment washers into the pinion housing, then install the solenoid lever and the armature.

3. Install the lever pivot pin.

4. Install the armature brake washers at the commutator. (The insulating washer goes between the two steel washers.) Lubricate using special Bosch grease.

5. If the commutator end frame was removed, attach it to the housing. Connect the wires from the carbon brushes and field windings.

6. Lubricate the bearings with oil, then assemble the armature, pinion housing and starter housing, together with the end frame, and tighten the two through bolts. The armature must have an axial clearance of 0.004–0.012″. This is adjusted with shims at the pinion housing. If new bearing bushings are to be installed, soak them in warm oil for an hour beforehand.

7. Install the solenoid and connect the jumper bar to the terminal bolt.

8. Install the brushes and cover band.

Solenoid

The solenoid has two windings, a powerful winding to attract and a weaker winding to hold. If the hold winding is defective, the solenoid will repeatedly switch on and off when starting is attempted. In such cases, a new solenoid must be installed. The distance between the pin for the lever and the operating solenoid operating flange must be adjusted according to the illustration.

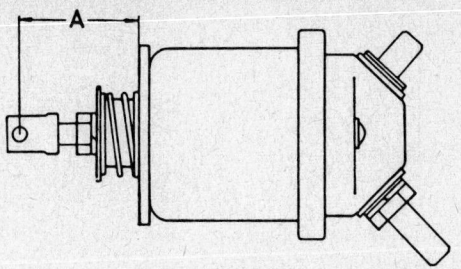

Adjusting starter solenoid yoke length, core fully extended. A=1.142 ±0.004″

Fuel System

Two-stroke models have used many carburetor types, depending on year, the more common of which are the Solex 40 AI, Solex 40 BI, and Zenith 34 VNN. SAAB Sport, Sonett two-stroke, and Monte Carlo models have always had a triple carburetor set-up, using three Solex 34 W units mounted on a common throttle body, three separate Solex 34 BIC units, or three sidedraft Solex 40 DHW units (Sonett II). A triple carburetor set-up was also available on some 95 and 96 models from 1966, although few were imported. The GT-750 was equipped with a Zenith 34 VNN carburetor originally, although a dual-downdraft Solex 44 PII carburetor was available for competition tuning.

SAAB 95, 96, and Sonett models having the V4 engine were equipped with either a Solex 28-32 PDSIT-7 or 32 PDSIT-4 carburetor up to and including 1968, a Ford C8GH-9510-H smog carburetor in 1969, and a Ford 70TW-9510-AA carburetor in 1970.

Both electric and diaphragm-type fuel pumps have been used on the various SAAB models. Of the electric pumps, the SU is the more common, although Monte Carlo models from chassis No. 168,001 are equipped with Bendix pumps, as are Sonett two-stroke models having the 40 DHW carburetors. The GT-750 model with the dual Solex 44 PII carburetor and special (2.01″) exhaust system required two SU pumps connected in tandem.

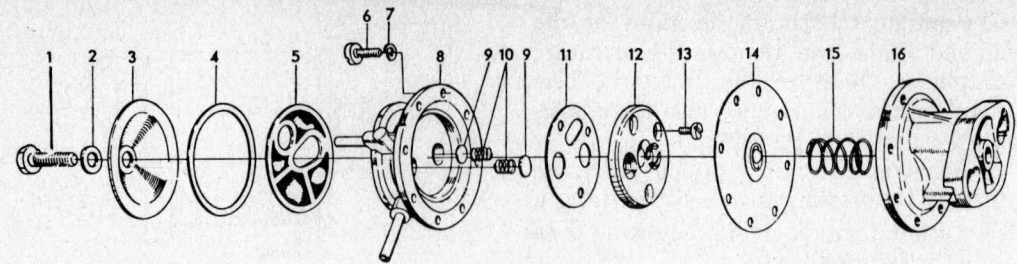

Fuel pump

1. Screw	5. Filter	9. Valve	13. Screw
2. Washer	6. Screw	10. Valve spring	14. Diaphragm
3. Cover	7. Washer	11. Gasket	15. Diaphragm spring
4. Gasket	8. Upper pump housing	12. Valve plate	16. Lower pump housing

Fuel Pump and Filter—Two-Stroke

DIAPHRAGM PUMP

The diaphragm-type fuel pump is mounted on the engine crankcase. The pressure variations in the crankcase actuate the diaphragm, causing the pump to feed fuel to the carburetor.

Cleaning the Filter

Loosen the screw on top of the pump and remove the cover with its gasket. Clean the filter. This should be done every 12,000 miles. When reassembling, make sure filter and gasket are undamaged.

Disassembly

1. Remove fuel pump from engine.
2. Mark relative positions of pump halves.
3. Loosen bolts that hold the pump halves together and separate.
4. If valves are to be changed, loosen the three bolts that hold the valve plate and remove gasket, valve discs, and valve springs.
5. Loosen the screw that holds the cover on top of the filter. Remove filter, together with gasket.
6. Check sealing surfaces of pump and correct, if necessary, using a face plate with fine valve grinding compound. Replace the diaphragm and valves.

Assembly

1. Mount the valve springs, with the small diameter turned towards the guide pin.
2. Put on the valve discs, refit the gasket and valve plate and secure the bolts by use of a centerpunch.
3. Refit the pump spring and diaphragm. Locate the diaphragm with the rivet head toward the lower part of the housing.
4. Put the pump halves together in the previously marked position and tighten the bolts.
5. Fasten the pump to engine block with a gasket on either side of thick fiber spacer that fits between block and pump.

ALTERNATE FUEL PUMP

In 1966, an alternate fuel pump was introduced with a different valve system—see illustrations for major differences.

FUEL PUMP TESTING

1. Disconnect the fuel hose at the carburetor and connect hose to a fuel pressure test gauge (0–10 psi).
2. Remove the ignition coil high-tension wire.
3. Run the starter without touching the throttle.
4. The pressure should be 2.8–3.5 psi; it must not fall appreciably when starter is turned off. If the pressure drops rapidly, there is probably leakage in gaskets, valves or diaphragm.

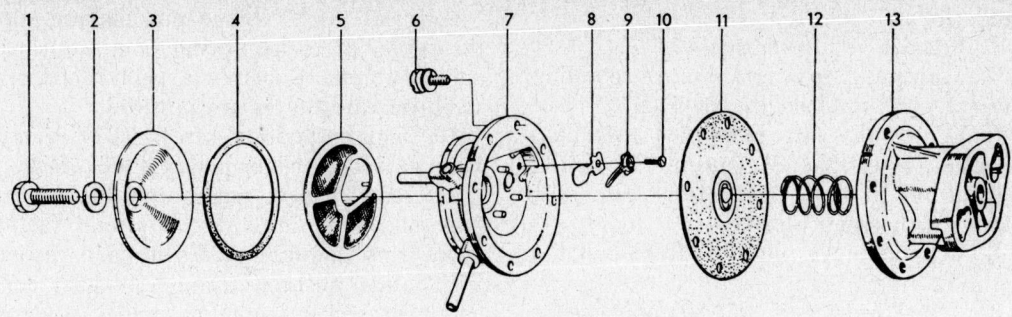

Alternate fuel pump

1. Hexagon screw
2. Gasket
3. Casing
4. Gasket

5. Filter
6. Screw
7. Upper pump
    housing

8. Inlet valve
9. Stop for inlet valve
10. Stop screw
11. Diaphragm

12. Diaphragm spring
13. Lower pump
     housing

SU ELECTRIC PUMP

The SU electric fuel pump is made up of three main parts—the pump body, containing valves and fuel filter, the magnet and diaphragm assembly and the contact breaker assembly. SU pumps can be of either 6-volt or 12-volt design. To determine the voltage designation, remove the bakelite cover and check the leads—green coil leads indicate a 6-volt unit; red, black or brown coil leads a 12-volt unit.

Disassembly

1. Remove pump from wheel housing.
2. Wash pump with kerosene or gasoline.
3. Referring to the illustration, remove the six bolts which hold the magnet housing to the pump body.
4. Separate pump into major component groups, then unscrew diaphragm assembly (3) from trunnion in contact breaker and release bronze pushrod.
5. Remove diaphragm, retrieving the 11

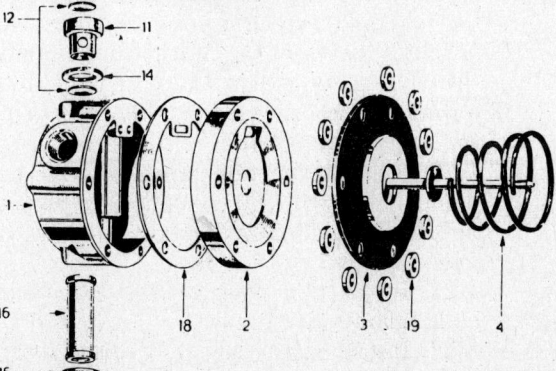

1. Pump body
2. Spacer
3. Diaphragm
4. Volute spring
5. Magnet housing
6. Throwover mechanism
7. Spring blade
8. Bakelite pedestal
9. Bakelite cover
10. Outlet union
11. Valve cage
12. Valve disc
13. Spring clip
14. Fiber washer, thin
15. Filter washer, thick
16. Filter
17. Filter plug
18. Gasket
19. Armature guide roller
20. Rocker hinge pin
21. Terminal nut
22. Cover nut
23. Pedestal screw
24. Screw for blade
25. Spring washer
26. Terminal screw
27. Lead washer
28. Nut
29. Assembly screw
30. Ground terminal

SU electric fuel pump

guide rollers (19).

6. Remove volute spring (4).

7. Turn pump over and remove retaining nut (22) and the bakelite cover (9).

8. Loosen the two bolts (23) that hold pedestal (8) to magnet housing (5). Leaving one bolt in place, completely remove the other (with ground lead).

9. Remove hinge pin (20) from bakelite molding.

10. The "throwover" unit (6) now can be removed sideways.

11. Remove bolt (24), spring blade (7) and coil terminal.

NOTE: *Unless pedestal or magnet assemblies are to be replaced, further disassembly is unnecessary.*

12. Remove nut (28).

13. Remove the other screw that holds pedestal (23).

14. Slip a thin screwdriver blade between the terminal tag and the bakelite pedestal, or use a knife to loosen lead washer (27).

15. Remove terminal, screw (26) and spring washer (25).

16. Remove outlet fitting (10) from pump body.

17. Remove fiber washer (15).

18. Remove valve cage (11). Turn pump upside down and shake out washer (14) and valve disc (12).

19. Remove filter plug (17), filter (16) and fiber washer (15).

Assembly

1. Clean all parts and blow dry with compressed air.

2. Insert square-head terminal screw into bakelite pedestal.

3. Install coil terminal tag onto screw, after installing spring washer.

4. Install lead washer.

5. Install terminal nut, concave side down, and tighten to compress lead.

6. Loosely install pedestal to magnet housing using screw (23) and spring washer.

7. Assemble "throwover" unit and insert it between pedestal and magnet housing. Adjust outer rocker to eliminate side-play, then connect ground lead.

8. Install the other screw (23)—do not tighten. Fit ground terminal tag and spring washer.

9. Install rocker hinge pin, making sure the center of rocker spring points towards contact points. Hinge pin is special hardened steel—no substitutes are possible.

10. Tighten pedestal screws (23) evenly. Do not overtighten or pedestal will crack.

11. Install volute spring onto diaphragm pushrod, with large diameter end facing away from diaphragm. Fit impact washer.

12. Slide pushrod through magnet core and turn rocker trunnion so that pushrod can be screwed in a few turns.

13. Install 11 guide rollers in position around armature, inside diaphragm.

14. Hold magnet assembly firmly in left hand in a horizontal position. Screw in diaphragm pushrod, pushing in and out on diaphragm while doing so. The breaker mechanism will at first flop over hard. Continue adjustment and stop screwing in pushrod when the mechanism flops over lightly. The pedestal contact blade should be moved out of the way during this adjustment.

15. Unscrew the diaphragm and armature 2/3 turn (four holes), then install one screw to hold the adjustment.

16. Secure the pedestal contact blade, with coil terminal tag and spring washer.

17. Check and, if necessary, adjust the spring blade so that when contacts are separated the blade rests on the ledge formed in the bakelite pedestal.

18. Check that contact points coincide when circuit is closed. If not, adjust spring blade.

19. Tension on the spring blade should be such that the outer rocker can make a full sweep to deflect blade. Contact points should close when rocker is in middle of travel. To check this, place a finger against spring blade and hold it against the ledge. There should be, in this position, a clearance of 0.030″ between the magnet housing and the white rocker roller. There should also be a 0.030″ clearance between the rocker and the bakelite pedestal.

20. Seat the suction valve disc in the pump body, with the smooth face against the seat. Install delivery valve disc in the same manner.

21. Install thin fiber washer into pump body below valve cage.

22. Install valve cage and disc; secure with spring clip (facing outwards).

23. Install thick fiber washer above valve cage.

24. Install fuel outlet fitting.

25. Install filter and fiber washer onto filter plug; install plug into pump body.

26. Place a new gasket between pump body and spacer.

27. Install spacer with concave side facing magnet housing and all holes lined up properly.

28. With pump body, spacer and magnet housing assembled, the diaphragm must be flat. This can be achieved by placing a wedge between the white rollers of the outer rocker and pressing under tips of inner rocker until pushrod trunnion is lifted as far as it will go. The six assembly bolts now can be installed. NOTE: *The drain hole must match the filter plug.*

29. Tighten six bolts.

30. Remove wedge.

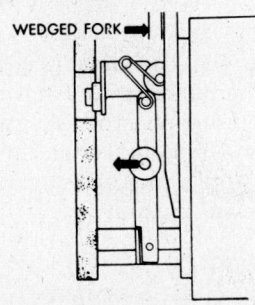

WEDGED FORK

Wedged fork being used to stretch pump diaphragm—SU electric pump

31. Lubricate rocker hinge with a few drops of light oil.

32. Test pump by hooking it up to a battery.

33. If pump operates, install bakelite cover and install pump into car.

BENDIX ELECTRIC PUMP

The Bendix fuel pump consists of a solenoid section, a breaker unit, a pump plunger, valves and a fuel filter. The Bendix gives higher pressure than the double-action SU and it always must be mounted with the bayonet cap downwards.

Cleaning Filter

1. Remove the bayonet cap from the lower end of the pump.

2. Remove filter and clean it in thinner; blow dry with compressed air.

3. Remove all particles from the magnetic plug.

4. Reassemble pump filter.

Disassembly (up to Chassis No. 201.400)

1. Remove bayonet cap, gasket and filter.

2. Loosen the three bolts which hold the valve housing. Remove the housing.

3. Remove the inlet valve, retainer and spring from valve housing.

4. Remove piston and spring from pump housing.

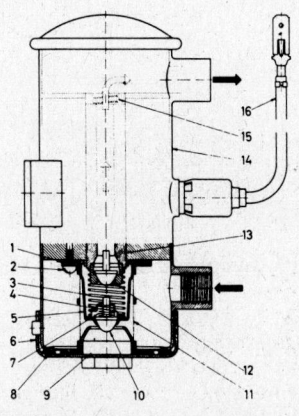

Bendix fuel pump used up to chassis No. 201,400

1. Gasket
2. Screw
3. Plunger spring
4. Spring retainer
5. Valve housing
6. Bayonet cap
7. Valve spring
8. Gasket
9. Magnetic body
10. Valve
11. Filter
12. Valve
13. Plunger
14. Pump housing
15. Damping spring
16. Electrical connection

Disassembly (from Chassis No. 201.401)

1. Remove bayonet cap, gaskets, filter and magnetic plug.

2. Unhook lock wire, remove washer, O-ring and inlet valve from the barrel.

3. Remove spring, piston and delivery valve.

Assembly (up to Chassis No. 201.400)

1. Wash all parts in thinner and blow dry with compressed air. Examine all parts for wear and replace as required.

2. Coat the plunger assembly with light oil, install the plunger spring and push plunger into the barrel.

3. Install the inlet valve, with spring and washer, into the valve housing.

4. Install the valve housing, with gasket and screws, into the pump housing; tighten the screws.

5. Install the filter and the bayonet cap, with gasket.

Assembly (from Chassis No. 201.401)

1. Wash all parts in thinner and blow dry with compressed air. Examine all parts for wear and replace as required.

2. Coat the plunger assembly with light oil, install the plunger spring and push plunger into the barrel.

3. Install inlet valve, spring and retainer into the valve housing.

4. Install O-ring, washer and lock wire.

5. Install filter into valve housing, then install bayonet cap with gasket and plug.

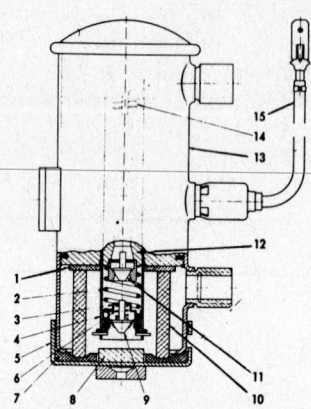

Bendix fuel pump used after chassis No. 201,401

1. Gasket
2. Plunger spring
3. Spring retainer
4. Valve housing
5. Bayonet cap
6. Valve spring
7. Gasket
8. Magnetic body
9. Valve
10. Filter
11. Valve
12. Plunger
13. Pump housing
14. Damping spring
15. Electrical connection

Fuel Pump—V4

REMOVAL

Remove the fuel line from the pump. Remove the nuts and lockwashers, then remove the pump, pushrod and the old gasket. Always use a new gasket and mark the end of the pushrod which rests against the camshaft for easy assembly.

DISASSEMBLY

1. Remove the cover, gasket and strainer.
2. Mark the upper and lower part of the pump so that they can be installed in the same relative position.

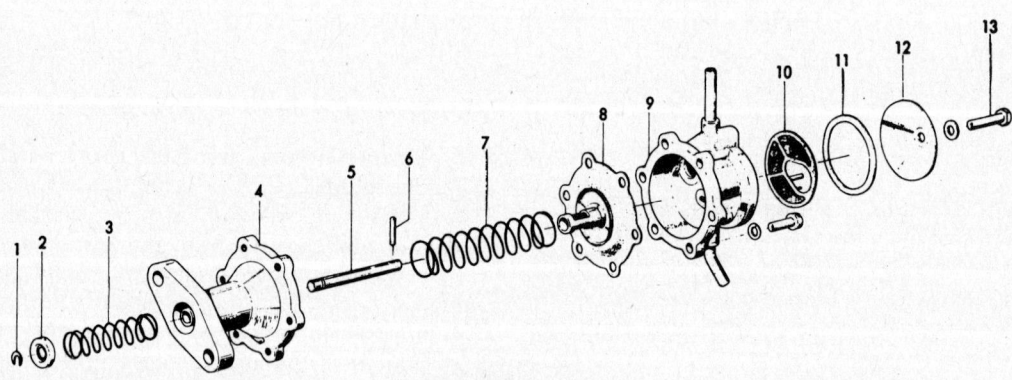

V4 engine fuel pump

1. Lockwasher
2. Sleeve
3. Spring
4. Pump body, lower part
5. Diaphragm rod
6. Retaining pin
7. Spring
8. Diaphragm
9. Pump body, upper part
10. Filter
11. Gasket
12. Cover
13. Cover screw

3. Loosen and remove the screws, then separate the upper and lower parts of the pump. The upper part containing the valves can be disassembled no further.

4. Place the lower part of the pump, with the diaphragm, on a flat surface. Press down the spiral spring lockwasher with a 10 mm. open end wrench and remove the lock-ring from its groove in the diaphragm rod. Remove the spring lockwasher and the spring; replace the lock-ring on the diaphragm rod.

5. A small seal is supplied to seal between the diaphragm rod and the lower part of the pump. This is not replaceable. Because the lips on the shaft seal face the ring groove for the lock-ring, the shaft seal would be completely ruined if the diaphragm rod was withdrawn from the lower part of the pump towards the diaphragm. Because of this, always proceed as follows:

a. Hold the lower part of the pump in the hand, press the diaphragm lightly inward and remove the lock-ring again. Release the diaphragm only far enough to allow the pins which hold the diaphragm to the diaphragm rod to be removed by pressing with a sharp pin punch.

b. Pull the diaphragm rod away from the lower part of the pump (towards the drive side). Remove the diaphragm and the compression spring.

ASSEMBLY

1. Apply a little grease to the diaphragm rod and connect it, with the pin, to the new diaphragm. Install the spring.

2. Push the lower part of the pump, against spring pressure, onto the diaphragm rod until the diaphragm makes contact.

3. Place the lower part of the pump, with the diaphragm, on a flat surface. Install the compression spring with the lockwasher. Hold the lockwasher with a 10 mm. wrench, press it down on the pushrod and insert the lock-ring.

4. Align the upper part of the pump according to the marked flanges. Press the pushrod in far enough that the diaphragm is not under tension. In this position, insert the screws and fasten the two halves together.

5. Install a new strainer and gasket; screw on the cover.

Carburetor—Two-Stroke

SOLEX 40 AI AND 40 BI CARBURETOR

These carburetors have a "cold starting device," which supplies a richer than normal fuel mixture during starting. The fuel-air ratio is determined by starting air jet (8) and fuel jet (9). The device is turned on by means of a control on the dashboard. When the cold start device is used, the throttle should be fully closed.

The high speed system includes main jet (4), emulsion jet (1), and emulsion tube (2). The correct combination of these parts gives the right carburetor compensation.

Idle speed is regulated by means of air jet (2), fuel jet (3) and the volume control screw (5). A richer mixture is obtained by unscrewing the volume control screw.

This design permits access to all the jets, except the idle air jet, without disassembly.

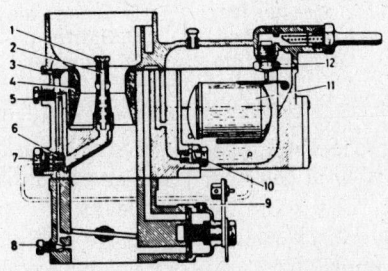

SOLEX 40 BI CARBURETOR SECTIONED

1. Emusion tube jet
2. Emulsion tube
3. Idling air jet
4. Choke tube
5. Idling fuel jet
6. Main jet
7. Jet carrier
8. Adjusting screw, idling mixture
9. Starter air jet
10. Starter fuel jet
11. Float
12. Needle valve

Disassembly and Assembly

1. Remove air cleaner.
2. Disconnect fuel line from pump.
3. Disconnect cold start control.
4. Remove rubber boot from plate on the throttle spindle.
5. Remove the carburetor.
6. Clean the carburetor externally.
7. Remove the float chamber cover.

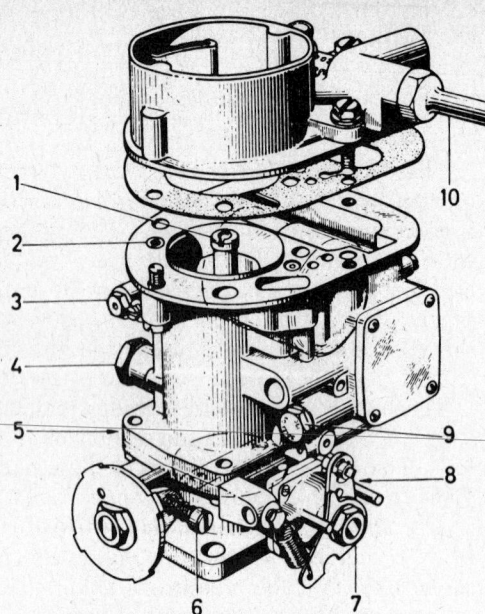

Solex 40 BI carburetor

1. Emulsion tube jet
2. Idling air jet
3. Idling fuel jet
4. Main jet carrier
5. Adjusting screw,
   idling mixture
6. Adjusting screw,
   idling speed
7. Cold-starting
   device
8. Starter air jet
9. Starter fuel jet
10. Union and filter

8. Check the needle valve and gasket.

9. Check the float lever and spindle.

10. Check the float for leaks.

11. Check the main jet, the idle jet and the emulsion jet.

12. Check the slide of the cold starting device for surface wear. Check the starting air jet and starting fuel jet, as well as the return motion.

13. Check the throttle spindle for wear.

14. Reassemble and install carburetor, after cleaning all parts.

15. Reconnect fuel line and controls and start engine.

16. Check float level, if necessary.

17. Install air cleaner; when engine is warm, adjust idle speed.

Idle Speed Adjustment

1. With engine warm, adjust idle speed to about 600–750 rpm with the slow speed adjustment screw.

2. Screw in mixture screw until bottomed, then unscrew 1½–2 turns.

3. Readjust the slow speed adjustment screw until 600–750 rpm is obtained, then recheck the volume control screws as before. Repeat until proper idle speed is obtained.

Float Level Adjustment

1. Allow engine to idle.

2. Switch off engine without touching the throttle.

3. Remove air cleaner.

4. Detach fuel line from carburetor. This must be done in order to prevent additional fuel from entering the float chamber.

5. Remove the float chamber cover.

6. Measure the float level with a caliper depth gauge. The distance from the top of float chamber to the fuel should be 0.8″ ± 0.04″. If the engine is hard to start when warm, the float level may be lowered to 0.87″.

7. Raise the float level by filing the fiber washer under the needle valve; lower it by adding an extra washer.

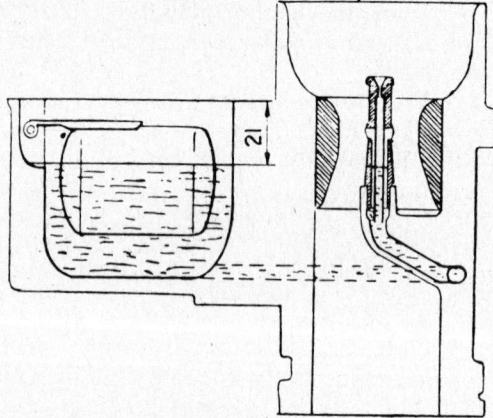

Checking float level of 40 BI carburetor

Carburetor Cleaning

1. Remove air cleaner.

2. Detach fuel line.

3. Clean filter in the banjo fitting.

4. Remove float chamber cover.

5. Clean needle valve.

6. Remove screw which acts as the float level spindle; lift out float.

7. Remove main jet (4).

8. Remove idle jet (3).

9. Remove starting jet (9).

10. Blow out the float chamber passages and jets.

11. Reassemble in reverse order, making certain the float chamber gasket is perfect.

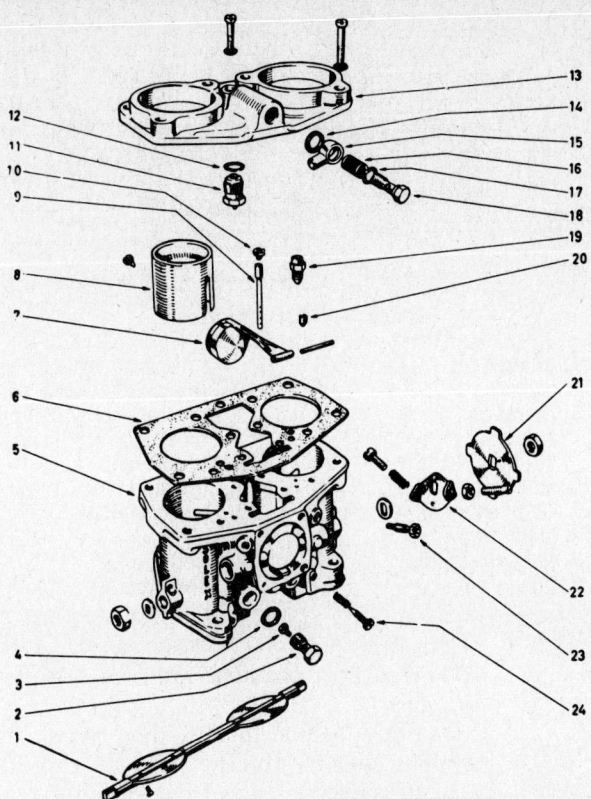

1. Throttle spindle
2. Main jet carrier
3. Main jet
4. Fiber gasket
5. Carburetor body
6. Gasket
7. Float and spindle
8. Choke tube
9. Emulsion tube
10. Emulsion jet
11. Needle valve
12. Spacer washer
13. Cover
14. Fiber gasket
15. Banjo union
16. Filter
17. Fiber gasket
18. Banjo screw
19. Emulsion tube attachment
20. Idle air jet
21. Plate for the throttle control bellows
22. Idle speed adjustment device
23. Idle fuel jet
24. Volume control screw

Solex 44 PII dual-throat carburetor used for competition tuning

Zenith 34 VNN Carburetor

The main difference between the Zenith and the Solex is the type of cold start device used—the Zenith has a butterfly valve type choke.

Pulling the choke control closes the spring-loaded butterfly valve. At the same time, linkage opens the throttle to allow the engine to idle. It is *not* necessary to depress the accelerator when starting the engine with the choke.

Disassembly and Assembly

1. Remove air cleaner.
2. Disconnect fuel line.
3. Disconnect choke control.
4. Remove rubber boot from throttle spindle plate.
5. Remove carburetor from intake manifold.
6. Clean the carburetor externally.
7. Remove the four bolts that hold the float chamber and remove chamber. Before lowering the float chamber, pull it out sideways a small distance in order to free the emulsion orifice.

8. Check the condition of the needle valve and its gasket.
9. Examine the float lever and spindle.
10. Check the float for leaks.
11. Loosen the two screws that hold the emulsion block; remove block from the float chamber.
12. Remove all jets.
13. Remove the choke and spindle.
14. Loosen stop screw (10) and remove the choke tube.
15. Check all the gaskets and blow out all passages.
16. Reassemble carburetor and adjust fast idle link.
17. Reinstall carburetor. Allow engine to warm up and adjust idle speed.

Fast Idle Link Adjustment

1. Loosen the stop screw (1) and open the throttle butterfly .043″ by inserting a No. 57 drill or a wire .043″ in diameter between the throttle butterfly and the carburetor body.

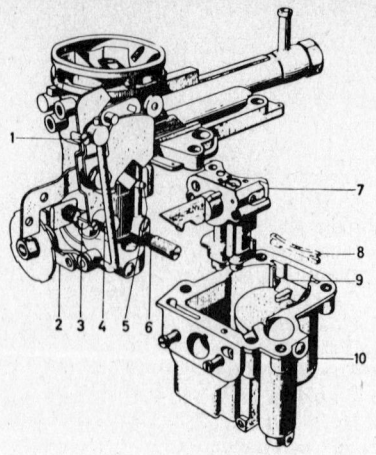

Zenith 34 VNN carburetor

1. Stop screw, throttle/choke
   link
2. Throttle-control lever
3. Adjusting screw, idling
4. Choke-control holder
5. Vacuum connection for
   distributor
6. Air-regulating screw, idling
   mixture
7. Emulsion block
8. Float carrier
9. Float
10. Float chamber

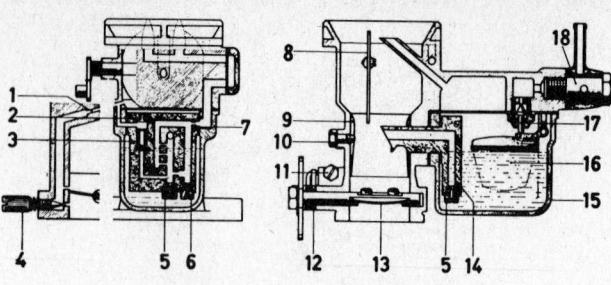

Zenith 34 VNN carburetor

1. Idling duct
2. Idling air jet
3. Idling fuel jet
4. Air-regulating screw,
   idling mixture
5. Main jet
6. Compensating jet
7. Main air jet
8. Choke butterfly
9. Choke ring

10. Stop screw, choke ring
11. Adjusting screw, idling
12. Throttle-control lever
13. Throttle flap
14. Emulsion block
15. Float chamber
16. Float
17. Needle valve
18. Fuel filter

2. Close the choke butterfly completely, then check that the lever (2) of the throttle control rests against the projection on the throttle control. Tighten stop screw (1).

Fast Idle Speed Adjustment

1. Adjust the volume control screw (6) to give the highest idle speed, after first seating it.
2. Readjust the slow speed adjustment screw (3) until the proper idle speed is obtained, 600–750 rpm, then recheck the position of the volume control screw (6) to give highest idle speed. Repeat procedure until correct idle speed is obtained.

Float Level Adjustment

The float level is determined by the thickness of the washer under the needle valve. The correct float level is obtained by using a washer with a thickness of 0.12″ (0.08″ for 1965 and earlier models). To check the

level, the float chamber must be removed as follows:

1. Allow engine to idle, then switch off without touching throttle.
2. Remove fuel line from carburetor to prevent flooding from pump.
3. Remove air cleaner.
4. Loosen the float chamber screws and lift the chamber out. Use care not to spill any of the fuel in the chamber.
5. Measure the distance from the upper edge of the float chamber to the fuel while holding the chamber in a level position. When the float is in place, the distance should be 1.0″ (0.89″ for 1965 and earlier models) (1.18″ without the float).
6. To lower the float level, install additional gasket under the float valve. To raise the level, file down the existing gasket.
7. After adjustment, recheck level.

TRIPLE CARBURETORS—
MONTE CARLO UP TO 1965

This system consists of three Solex 34 BIC carburetors mounted on a common intake manifold with separate cast-in induction passages. A thin balance channel connects the main passages. The air idle system volume screw is located on the intake manifold; this controls the amount of air fed to the individual carburetor idle systems through cast-in channels in the manifold. The carburetors have individual volume control screws that are locked and preset at the factory.

With this system, only the center carburetor contains a cold starting device. The throttle spindle between the three carburetors is equipped with an adjusting screw for synchronization purposes, while the slow idle speed is set by turning the throttle screw on each carburetor.

Carburetors and intake manifold—three carb system to 1965

1. Channel to cylinder
2. Balance channel
3. Air-idle distribution channel
4. Air volume screw
5. Air hose to volume screw
6. Mixture screw (must not be moved)

Disassembly and Assembly

1. Remove the intake manifold and carburetors from engine.

2. Remove fuel lines and carburetors from manifold.

3. Clean carburetors externally, using gasoline or thinner.

4. Remove float chamber cover from one carburetor. It is a good idea to place the other carburetors aside so that parts confusion is eliminated.

5. Inspect needle valve for scoring and gasket for cracks.

6. Inspect the float for leakage; clean float chamber.

7. Inspect main jet, pilot jet, correction jet and emulsion tube for damage.

8. Inspect cold starting device slide for excessive surface wear, then inspect fuel jet, air jet and lever free movement.

9. Check the throttle spindle for excessive wear.

10. Clean all parts in thinner and reassemble unit, then proceed to other carburetors and disassemble as above.

11. Install all reassembled carburetors onto manifold.

12. Install throttle linkage, companion screws and springs. The front carburetor gets the weakest spring, the second carburetor the next weakest and the control shaft the strongest.

13. Install carburetors and manifold, then connect fuel lines, generator bracket, throttle linkage and cold starting device linkage.

14. Install air cleaner and start engine. It may be necessary to adjust float level at this time.

Float Level Adjustment

1. Allow the engine to idle for a few minutes.

2. Turn off ignition without touching accelerator pedal.

3. Disconnect fuel line at the fuel pump (outlet).

4. Remove float chamber cover and air cleaner, if it was installed.

5. Measure the fuel level using a vernier depth gauge or steel ruler; the clearance between the float chamber top and the fuel surface should be $0.78 \pm .04''$. Because of

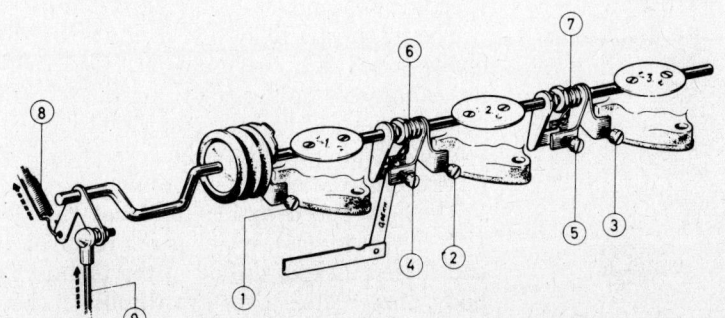

1., 2., 3. Throttle screws
for cylinders
4., 5. Companion screws
6. Stiff spring
7. Weak spring
8. Return spring
9. Throttle control

Throttle linkage—three carb system to 1965 (front cylinder is No. 3)

the installed inclination of the carburetor, take the measurement near the choke tube wall. Float level is changed by changing the thickness of the washer under the needle valve; a thicker washer lowers the float level, a thinner washer raises it.

Idle Speed Adjustment and Synchronization

1. Start the engine and allow it to warm up; turn off engine.

2. Remove the air cleaner, then unscrew the companion screws, (4) and (5), about 0.080".

3. Turn the volume control screw on the

Adjusting volume control screw—three carb system to 1965

manifold until it gently bottoms, then back it out 1½ turns.

4. Start the engine and adjust the idle speed to 600–750 rpm, using the throttle screws.

5. This step requires use of a "Synchro-Test" or "Uni-Syn" device. Place the device

Adjusting throttle screw using Uni-Syn device

on one of the carburetors and adjust the valve to bring the float to the middle of the sight tube.

6. Move the device to the next carburetor and adjust the carburetor throttle screw to bring the float to the same mark as on first carburetor. A grease pencil is handy for marking position of float on sight tube.

7. Move device to next carburetor and repeat. Continue moving device around until an idle speed of 600–750 rpm is attained with the float at the same level on all carburetors. The volume screw on the manifold can be adjusted ± 1/2 turn from its original 1 1/2 turn position to obtain smoother idle. NOTE: *If a synchronization device is not available, a short length of rubber hose can be used to determine airflow through the carburetors. Place one end of the hose at the carburetor throat and the other end near your ear. The sound level is a fair indication of flow so long as the hose is located at the same place for each carburetor.*

8. Turn in the companion screws to give 0.002" clearance, as illustrated.

9. Install the air cleaner, preheat tube and manifold hose.

TRIPLE CARBURETORS—SPORT, MONTE CARLO AND 95/96 FROM 1965

This induction system consists of three downdraft Solex 34 W units mounted on a common throttle body, each cylinder having a separate induction passage.

A balance passage is cast into the intake manifold. The carburetors have jets for four systems which include high speed, low speed, idling and cold starting systems.

The high speed system consists of the choke tube (K), the main jet (Gg), with its calibrated holder (Y) mark "A," the emulsion jet (a) and the emulsion tube (s), which combine to insure the correct fuel-air mixture for the high speed range.

The low speed system includes fuel jet (g), the air jet (u), which is not removable, and three passages drilled in the carburetor body immediately over the throttle butterfly.

The idling system consists of the fuel jet (gN) and an idling jet, which is not removable, and the air regulating screw (W) for the fuel-air mixture. Prior to 1966, the screw is located on the induction tube; since 1966, the air regulating screw is found on the float chamber.

Fuel and air first pass through separate jets, after which the two components are mixed and pass through the adjustable air regulating screw out into the induction pipe. From 1966 on, only the center carburetor has an idling system or a cold starting system. Through a special passage, this connects to the intake manifold. The cold start system consists of fuel jet (Gs), the air jet (Ga) and a slide valve for regulating the volume of the fuel-air mixture. The slide valve has two positions—one-half open and fully open. The fully open position is spring-loaded for automatic return to the one-half open position.

Disassembly and Assembly

1. Remove air cleaner.
2. Disconnect fuel line.
3. Remove rubber boot from throttle spindle plate.
4. Remove cold start control and fuel lines.

5. Remove carburetor and intake manifold as a unit.
6. Remove throttle body assembly, with carburetors, from intake manifold.
7. Clean carburetors externally and detach from throttle body.
8. Remove the cover of the float chamber and examine the retaining spring between needle valve and float arm, as well as the needle valve and its gasket.
9. Check the float lever and bearing and make sure the float does not leak.
10. Clean the bleed filter in the float chamber cover.
11. Check the main jet, low speed jet, idling jet, emulsion jet and emulsion tube.
12. Examine the cold starting device slide for wear on face. Check fuel and air jets and lever return.
13. Check the throttle spindle for wear.
14. After thorough cleaning, reassemble carburetors. Take care when assembling the lid of float chamber. The bearing pin for the float must enter both grooves in the float chamber, otherwise the pin will become bent or jammed. Also, make certain the needle valve retaining spring is connected to the float.
15. Complete assembly of carburetors and manifold to the engine. Allow engine to warm up before adjusting idle.

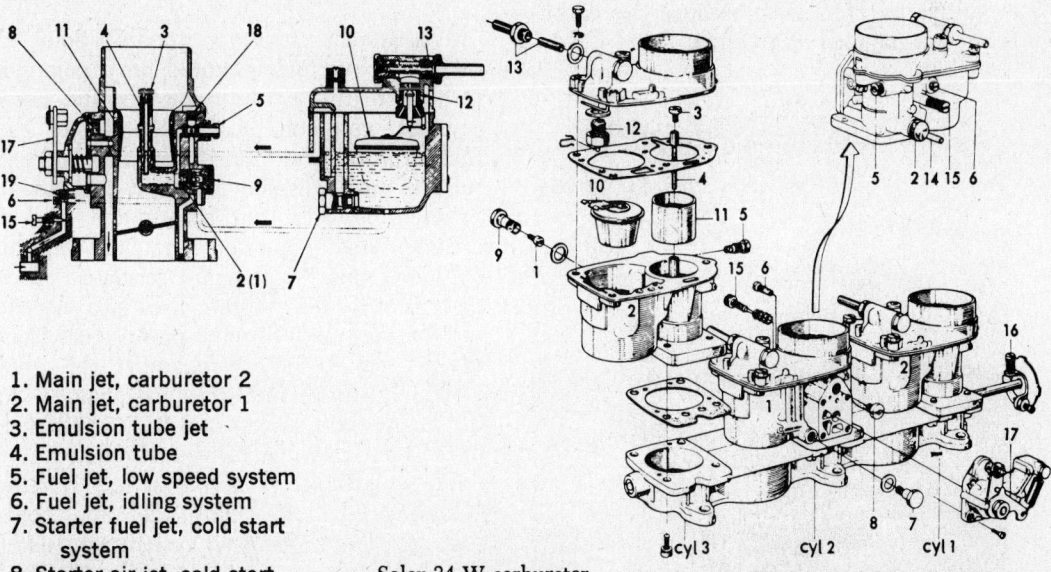

1. Main jet, carburetor 2
2. Main jet, carburetor 1
3. Emulsion tube jet
4. Emulsion tube
5. Fuel jet, low speed system
6. Fuel jet, idling system
7. Starter fuel jet, cold start system
8. Starter air jet, cold start system
9. Carrier main jet
10. Float
11. Choke tube K 28
12. Needle valve
13. Connection with filter
14. Vacuum connection
15. Air-regulating screw, idling mixture
16. Adjusting screw, idling
17. Cold start control
18. Air-jet, low speed system 80
19. Air jet, idling system 80

Solex 34 W carburetor

Float chamber cover

1. Spring for needle valve	2. Bleed filter
	3. Float bearing

Float Level Adjustment

1. Remove air cleaner.
2. Allow engine to idle about 30 seconds, then stop engine without touching throttle.
3. Disconnect the fuel line at carburetor and remove the float chamber cover and float.
4. Measure the lever with a vernier depth gauge. The distance between the dividing plane of the float chamber cover and the surface of the fuel should be $0.96 \pm 0.04''$ for the 1965 SAAB Sport, $1.04 \pm 0.04''$ for the SAAB 95 and 96 and the Monte Carlo from 1966. The measurement must be made at the carburetor neck because the carburetors are inclined at an angle.

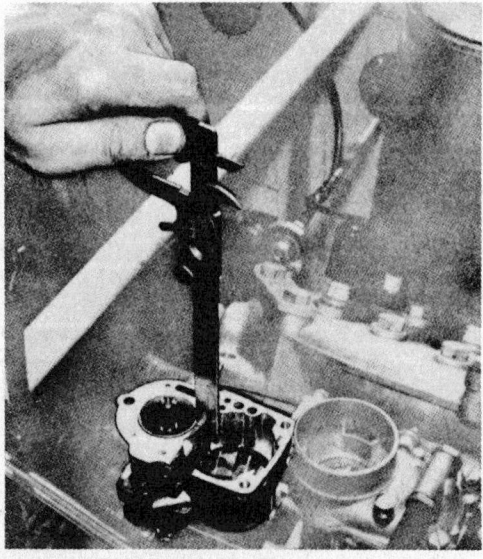

Measuring float level with a depth gauge

5. If adjustment is necessary, file down or remove the washer under the needle valve and recheck the level.

Idle Speed Adjustment

1. Allow engine to idle until warm.
2. Adjust idle speed to make engine run as slowly as possible (400–500 rpm).
3. Screw in the volume control screw 1/4 turn and wait until the engine speed stabilizes. Repeat until the engine stops.
4. Unscrew the volume screw 1/4 turn and restart engine.
5. Slowly give more fuel, and check that engine speed increases correspondingly. Should the engine speed fall momentarily, unscrew the volume control screw 1/8 turn. Recheck, and, if required, unscrew another 1/8 turn.
6. Now, if necessary, adjust the throttle screw until a suitable idle speed is obtained in the 600–750 rpm range. On cars equipped with AC alternator, switch on headlights and check idle speed.

TRIPLE CARBURETORS—SAAB SONETT

This system uses three sidedraft Solex 40 DHW carburetors mounted on a common throttle body. Through the throttle body runs a common shaft, to which the three throttle butterflies are attached. A tube is cast into the manifold to provide balance between the carburetors, and a common float chamber (mounted on the engine compartment floor) serves all three carburetors. This system uses two electric fuel pumps, one of which pumps fuel from the gas tank to the float chamber, the other of which pumps fuel from the chamber to the carburetors. Excess fuel is diverted back to the float chamber to be recirculated.

These carburetors have four fuel systems —high-speed, low-speed, idle, and cold-starting. The high-speed system consists of the choke tube, main jet, emulsion jet, and emulsion tube. The low-speed system consists of the fuel jet, air jet, and three channels drilled into the throttle body close to the butterfly of each carburetor. The idle sys-

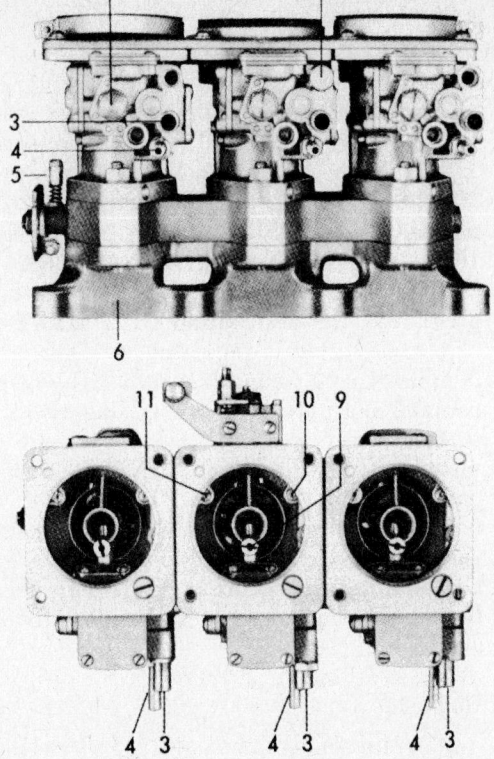

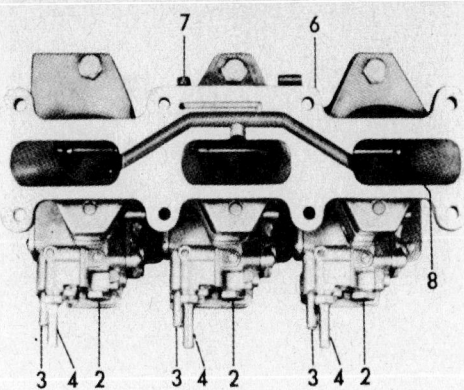

1. Idle fuel jet
2. Retainer, main jet
3. Outlet pipe, fuel
4. Inlet pipe, fuel
5. Low-speed adjustment screw
6. Suction pipe
7. Volume-control screw
8. Throttle valve
9. Emulsion jet
10. Bypass air jet
11. Idle air jet

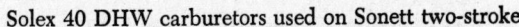

Solex 40 DHW carburetors used on Sonett two-stroke

tem consists of the fuel jet, the air jet, and the mixture regulating screw on the throttle body. Only the center carburetor has this idle system. Idle speed is adjusted by turning the air regulating screw and the setscrew on the throttle shaft. The cold-starting system consists of the fuel jet and a sliding valve to regulate the quantity of fuel-air mixture supplied to the engine. This sliding valve has two positions—one-half open and fully open. In the wide open position, a spring tends to make the valve return automatically to the one-half open position. For this reason, the accelerator must not be moved when starting the car, otherwise the cold-starting device will not operate.

Removal, Disassembly, Assembly, Installation

1. Remove the air cleaner, then disconnect the fuel line from the secondary pump at the T and plug the hose.
2. Remove the rubber cover from the throttle shaft, then remove cold-starting control cable, fuel lines, and alternator bracket.
3. Remove the intake manifold and carburetors as a unit.

4. Cover the intakes on the engine to prevent entry of dirt.
5. Remove throttle body assembly, with carburetors, from intake manifold.
6. Clean the carburetors with solvent, then remove them from the throttle body.
7. Check all jets for wear or clogging, then check the cold-starting slide for wear.
8. Check the throttle shaft for wear, then clean all parts, replace any defective parts, and reassemble carburetors.
9. Reassemble throttle body to manifold and install by reversing removal procedure. NOTE: *Always use new gaskets to prevent air leaks.*

Float Level

The float level is determined by carburetor design and cannot be adjusted. The common float chamber, while adjustable, usually does not need adjustment. The float level in this chamber can vary over a wide range without any adverse effects, and only should be disassembled if it overflows or is empty.

Adjusting the idle speed with the air regulating screw—Solex 40 DHW

Idle Speed Adjustment

1. Start the engine and allow it to warm up to operating temperature.

2. Adjust the idle speed to about 600–750 rpm, using the low-speed screw.

3. Adjust the volume screw to give the highest idle speed possible, then readjust the low-speed screw to obtain 600–750 rpm again.

4. If the car stumbles or hesitates when the accelerator is floored at about 40 mph, it may be necessary to loosen the volume screw an additional 1/4–1/2 turn, then readjust the low-speed screw to obtain 600–750 rpm.

Adjusting the idle speed with the throttle shaft setscrew

Carburetor—V4

SOLEX CARBURETOR

The carburetor is a Solex downdraft type. Up to engine No. 16,100 (chassis No. 434,-173 for the SAAB 96 and Monte Carlo, and No. 46,137 for the SAAB 95) the designation is 28–32 PDSIT-7. From engine No. 16,101 (chassis No. 434,174 for the SAAB 96 and Monte Carlo, and No. 46,138 for the SAAB 95) the designation is 32 PDSIT-4. The fuel supply is regulated by fixed jets mounted in the carburetor body. The body contains not only fuel drillings but also air drillings, and a certain amount of air is mixed with the fuel at an early stage in the emulsion tube.

The carburetor features an automatic choke device with fast idle provisions, an accelerator pump and a pressure-controlled booster system known as an Econostat.

Removal

1. Drain some of the cooling water.
2. Remove air filter.
3. Disconnect the lines from the automatic choke.
4. Disconnect the throttle control linkage and the vacuum line.
5. Disconnect the fuel line.
6. Remove the carburetor.
7. For 32 PDSIT-4, first disconnect the hose from the valve cover, then remove the intermediate flange.

Installation

On 32 PDSIT-4, first install the intermediate flange, with new gaskets.

1. Using a new gasket, install the carburetor and tighten bolts evenly.
2. Reconnect the fuel and vacuum lines.
3. Connect the throttle control.
4. Reinstall water hoses.
5. Refill the cooling system.
6. Install air filter.

Disassembly

1. Remove the retainer from the control rod between the automatic choke and the throttle butterfly, then detach the link from the throttle butterfly arm.

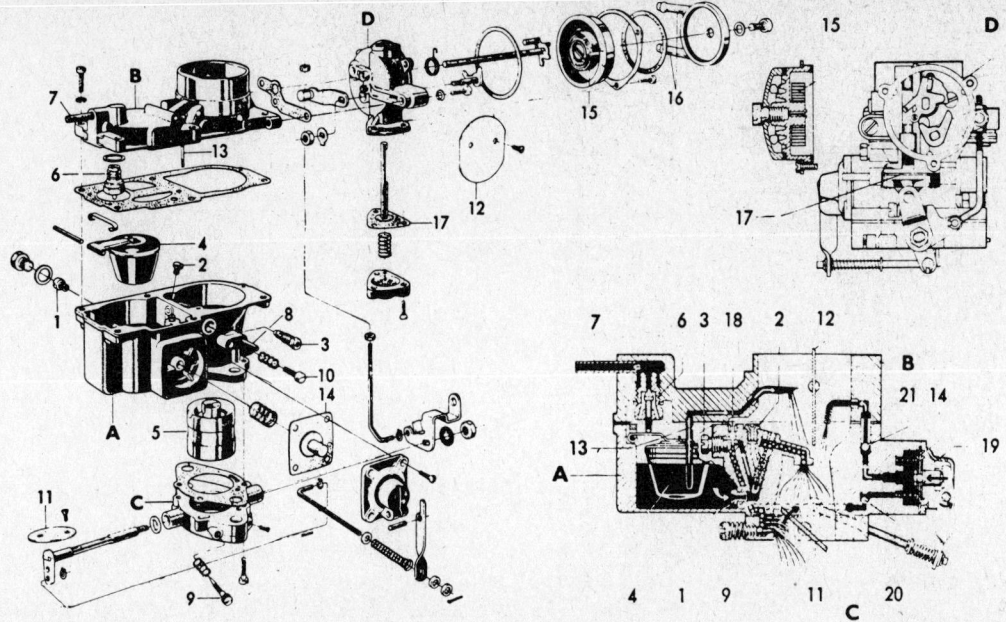

Solex 28-32 PDSIT-7 carburetor

1. Main jet	10. Adjusting screw, idling	choke
2. Emulsion jet	11. Throttle flap	18. Idling air jet (drilling)
3. Idling jet, fuel	12. Choke flap	19. Acceleration pump
4. Float	13. Ascending pipe, additional	20. Inlet valve, acceleration
5. Choke tube	system (Econostat)	pump
6. Float valve	14. Diaphragm, acceleration	21. Outlet valve, acceleration
7. Connection, fuel hose	pump	pump
8. Connection, vacuum hose,	15. Bimetal spring for	A. Float chamber
distributor	automatic choke	B. Float chamber cover
9. Air-regulating screw, idling	16. Water connections	C. Throttle body assembly
mixture	17. Diaphragm for vacuum	D. Housing, automatic choke
	control of automatic	

2. Unscrew and lift off the float chamber cover; remove the gasket.

3. Unscrew the needle valve.

4. Take out the float and float chamber.

5. Remove the plug from the float chamber and remove the main jet.

6. Pull off the accelerator pump jet (over the accelerator pump).

7. Unscrew the idle and emulsion tube jets.

8. Unscrew the accelerator pump cover and check the diaphragm.

9. Unscrew the idle mixture air regulating screw.

10. For carburetor 32 PDSIT-4, remove the intermediate flange valve.

Assembly

1. Install the spring, diaphragm and cover for the accelerator pump.

2. Insert the accelerator pump jet.

3. Screw in the idle and emulsion tube jets.

4. Advance the idling mixture air screw carefully until it bottoms, then back it off one complete turn.

5. Insert the float.

6. Screw the needle valve and gasket into the float chamber cover.

7. Install a new cover gasket.

8. Install float chamber cover.

9. Install the rod between the automatic choke and the throttle butterfly arm; fasten with the retaining ring.

10. Set the butterfly arm in the semi-open position and, at the same time, fully close the choke butterfly with the fingers. Hold the butterfly arm firmly and make sure the throttle butterfly is ajar. The clearance between the butterfly and flange must be 0.032″. This can be checked with a No. 67

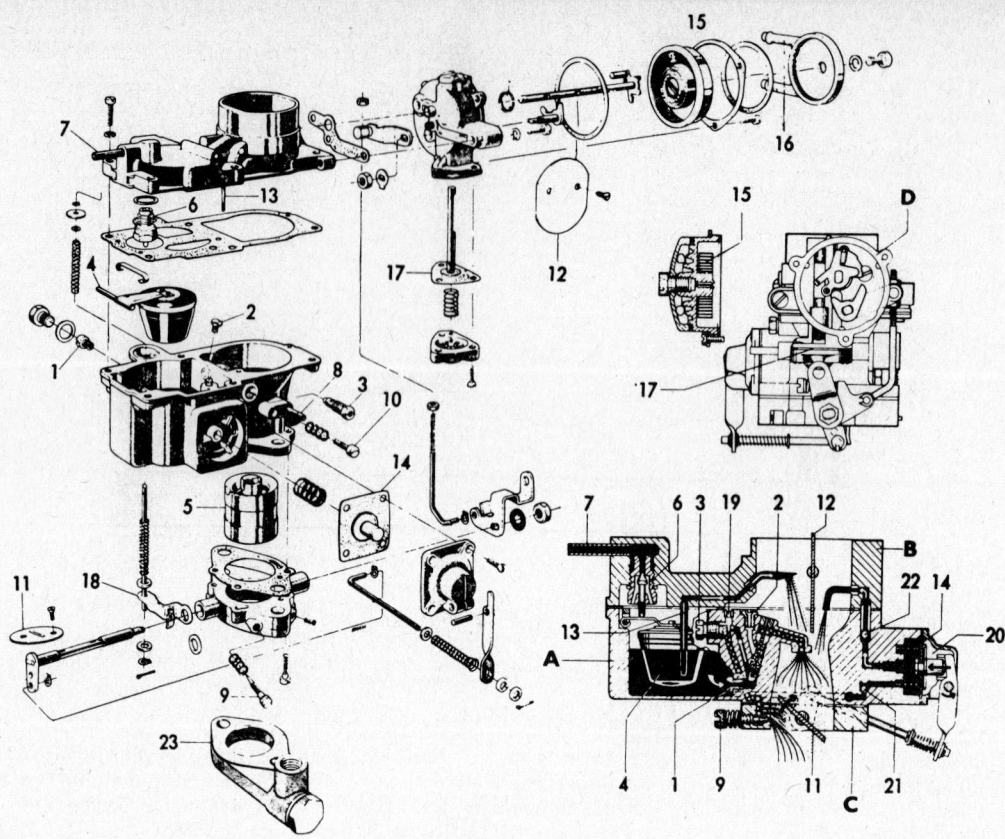

Solex 32 PDSIT-4 carburetor

1. Main jet
2. Emulsion jet
3. Idling jet, fuel
4. Float
5. Choke tube
6. Float valve
7. Connection, fuel hose
8. Connection, vacuum hose distributor
9. Air-regulating screw, idling mixture
10. Adjusting screw, idling
11. Throttle flap
12. Choke flap
13. Ascending pipe, addition system (Econostat)
14. Diaphragm, acceleration pump
15. Bimetal spring, automatic choke
16. Water connections
17. Diaphragm for vacuum control of automatic choke
18. Retaining device, float chamber ventilation
19. Idling air jet (drilling)
20. Acceleration pump
21. Inlet valve, acceleration pump
22. Outlet valve, acceleration pump
23. Intermediate flange
A. Float chamber
B. Float chamber cover
C. Throttle body assembly
D. Housing, automatic choke

drill bit or wire of the same diameter. To adjust the clearance, loosen the nuts on the linkage rod for the fast idle system, then adjust the rod so that the butterfly takes the correct position. Retighten the rod and lock in the correct position. NOTE: *For carburetor 32 PDSIT-4, install the intermediate flange valve.*

Float Level Adjustment

The level in the float chamber should be measured while the engine is idling and should be $0.59 \pm 0.04''$. The level is con-

trolled by the thickness of the float valve sealing washer. If the level is too high, a thicker washer must be fitted; a thinner washer must be fitted to raise the level. The float level is measured from the top of the float chamber cover to the fuel level. Measuring can be done with a transparent fuel standpipe connected at the location of the jet plug in the float chamber.

Idle Speed Adjustment

The idle speed must be adjusted with the engine at normal operating temperature and the headlights switched on.

1. Turn the slow speed adjustment screw slightly clockwise, so that the engine speed is slightly increased.

2. Slowly turn in the volume control screw until the engine begins to run unevenly, then slowly back off approximately 1/4 turn to achieve the best idle setting. The volume control screw never must be screwed in so hard that it bottoms.

3. Screw the volume control screw slowly in or out until the engine runs at the prescribed idling speed.

Automatic Choke Adjustment

1. Remove the air filter.

2. Connect an accurate thermometer into the water hose between the thermostat housing cover and a connector for the water hoses to the automatic choke.

3. Start the engine (cold) and note the temperature at which the choke butterfly opens wide. The correct opening temperature is 140–149°F.

4. If the choke opens at a lower or higher temperature, loosen the three clamping screws and turn the bimetal spring housing so that the proper setting is obtained.

Fast Idle Speed Adjustment

1. Remove air cleaner.

2. Warm up engine, switch on headlights.

3. Connect a tachometer to the engine (between distributor-to-coil primary wire and ground).

4. Adjust the engine to correct idle speed (800–900 rpm).

5. Close the choke a little in order to make it contact the ratchet wheel. Hold the choke in this position and keep pressing it toward the ratchet wheel.

6. Open the throttle butterfly slowly so as to allow the choke to move to the next position. Release the throttle cautiously, then the choke. The step which increases the idle speed is now in the first position of the ratchet wheel.

7. The throttle control must not be touched at this stage, as the ratchet wheel would then revert to the neutral position. For safety's sake, the control rod should be pushed up hard with the fingers.

8. With the throttle butterfly in this position, the engine speed should be 1,100–1,300 rpm. Adjust the control rod. (To increase the speed, lengthen the rod; to reduce the speed, shorten the rod.) After the adjustment, check that the control rod does not jam the throttle control lever.

9. Now check the speed of the third step (2,700–2,900 rpm).

10. Recheck idle speed.

AUTOLITE (FoMoCo) CARBURETOR (1969)

Removal

1. Remove the air cleaner.

2. Remove the water hoses from automatic choke.

3. Remove the throttle control.

4. Detach fuel and vacuum hoses.

5. Remove the carburetor.

Installation

1. Install new gaskets under the intermediate flange and carburetor. Turn the face marked "oben" up. A special gasket is required for this carburetor and must not be confused with the gasket for the Solex carburetor.

2. Reinstall the fuel and vacuum hoses, throttle control, water hoses and air cleaner.

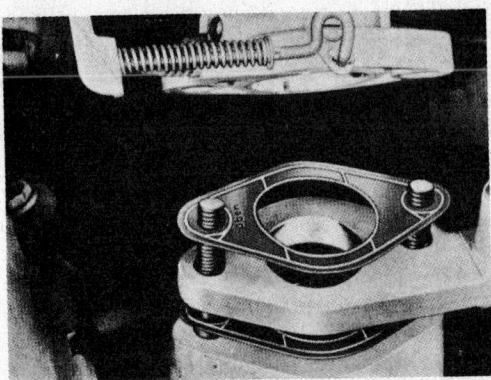

Special gasket, showing correct installation

Disassembly

1. Remove the three bolts and detach the thermostatic spring housing.

2. Unscrew the step cam from the throttle body.

3. Unscrew the bolts that hold the float

Accelerator pump fuel channel ball and weight

chamber cover and lift off the cover. Remove the spring on the float chamber cover; remove the gasket. By holding the float chamber upside down, remove the ball and weight from the accelerator fuel channel.

4. Unscrew the bolts in the accelerator pump cover, then remove cover, diaphragm and spring.

5. Remove accelerator pump rod from the lever of the throttle valve shaft; remove the lever.

6. Remove idle mixture control screw and idle speed adjusting screw; remove the springs.

7. Remove the throttle valve.

8. Remove, using a small file, any burrs from the threaded bores in the throttle valve shaft, then remove the shaft.

9. Remove the float. Unscrew the float needle valve.

10. Unscrew the main jet.

11. Unscrew the automatic choke housing from the carburetor.

12. Pull the pins of the air cleaner mounting yoke and remove.

13. Remove the choke plate.

14. Remove, using a small file, any burrs from the threaded bores in the choke plate shaft, then remove the shaft.

Assembly

Clean the carburetor. Blow out all channels, passages and jets; renew gaskets and defective parts.

1. Mount the throttle valve shaft in the throttle body. Fit the accelerator pump lever to the throttle valve shaft, turning the side marked "O" up.

2. Install the throttle valve so that the side with two punched marks faces downward when the throttle is held closed. Prior

to tightening the bolts, see that the valve centers in the closed position. Check that the throttle shaft moves freely.

3. Install the mixture control and idle adjusting screws and springs.

4. Install the accelerator pump rod between the levers of the accelerator pump and throttle valve.

5. Install the accelerator pump diaphragm and spring. The small end of the spring must face the diaphragm. Replace the cover.

6. Install the choke plate shaft and choke plate. Before tightening, make sure that the choke plate centers in the closed position. Check that the shaft moves freely.

7. Install the air cleaner mounting yoke and drive in the pins.

8. Install the automatic choke housing, with its gasket, and connect the accelerator pump rod to the choke plate shaft.

9. Screw in the main jet.

10. Screw in the needle valve and install the float.

11. Insert ball and weight into the accelerator pump channel.

12. Install the float chamber valve spring into the carburetor cover. Install, then insert the float chamber valve pushrod into the cover. Tighten the cover.

13. Screw on the step cam.

14. Install the thermostatic spring housing.

Float Level Adjustment

1. When checking the measurement "A," which must be 1.08", hold the float chamber cover vertically without pressing on the spring-loaded ball of the float valve. When adjusting, bend the stop gently at the arrow.

2. The lower end position of the float is

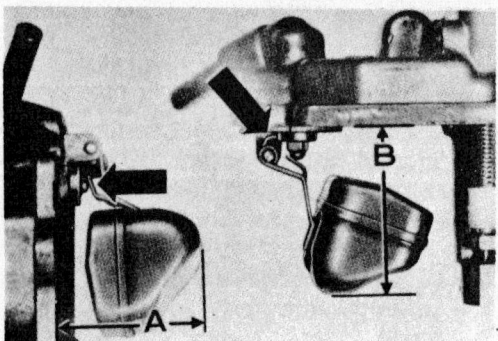

Checking float measurement (see text)

checked by measuring at "B"; (1.34").
When adjusting, bend the stop gently at the
arrow.

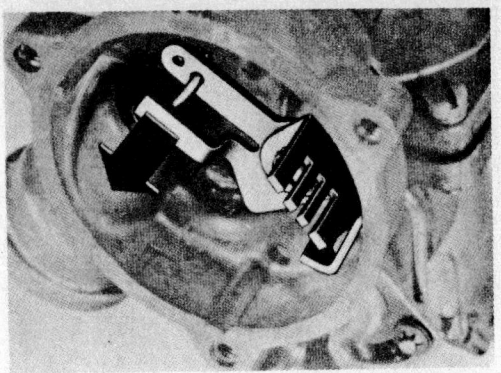

Vacuum piston and position

Accelerator Pump Adjustment

1. Loosen the idle adjusting screw until
the throttle is fully closed.
2. Using a small screwdriver, depress the
accelerating pump diaphragm until it stops.
3. The measurement "A" between the
piston and lever must be 0.09–0.10".
4. If the measurement "A" is not within
tolerance, adjust by bending or straightening the yoke of the accelerator pump rod.

Checking measurement "A"

Automatic Choke Adjustment

Normally the automatic choke setting
should not need to be altered in any way.
The setting mark on the thermostatic spring
housing is normally in line with the center
mark on the automatic choke housing, with
the free end of the thermostatic spring fitted
into the center slit of the thermostatic
spring lever.

Vacuum Operation

1. Remove the thermostatic spring housing.
2. Depress the vacuum piston fully. Move
the choke plate toward closed position until
the tongue of the thermostatic spring lever
contacts the vacuum piston lever. In this
position, the opening of the choke plate

should be 0.17–0.19"; a No. 12–17 drill may
be used as a gauge.
3. Install the thermostatic spring housing;
make sure the spring takes the proper position.
4. Check the position of the step cam by
inserting a drill gauge; see Step 2. In this
position, the mark on the third catch of the
step cam must be exactly in front of the stop
dog of the throttle valve lever; adjust by
bending the link rod.

Mechanical Operation

1. Open the throttle valve fully. This
forces the choke plate to open in such a way
that an arm (B) on the throttle spindle
contacts a stop (A) on the step cam.
2. When the throttle valve is fully open,
the choke plate should open 0.19–0.23".
This is checked using a No. 1–11 drill.

Checking choke plate opening using a drill bit for
a gauge

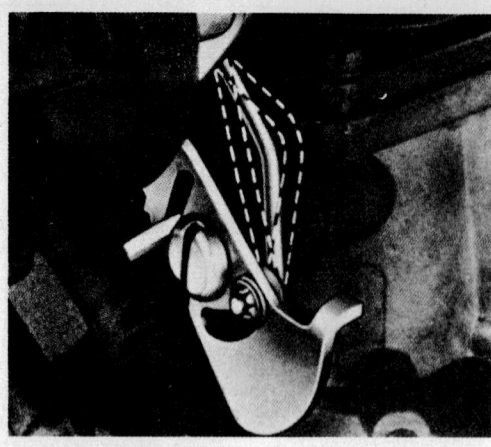

Adjusting link rod

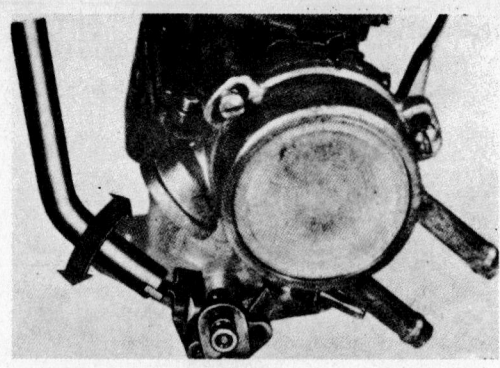

Bending throttle valve stop

Fast Idle Speed Adjustment

1. Bring engine to operating temperature; remove air cleaner.
2. Connect tachometer between distributor-to-coil primary wire and ground.
3. Hold the throttle shaft and step cam, so that the stop dog contacts the mark on the third catch of the step cam.
4. The engine speed now should be 1,800 rpm. To adjust, bend the stop of the throttle valve shaft.
5. Check the fast idle speed setting.
6. Reinstall the air cleaner.

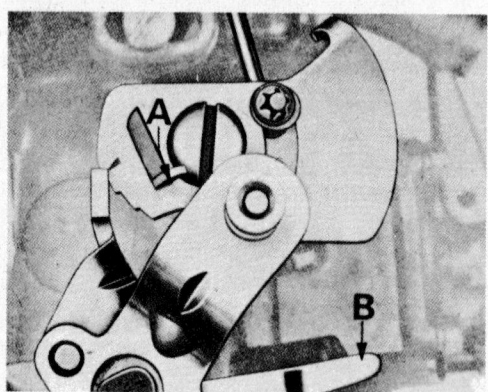

Choke plate arm (B) and step cam stop (A)

Idle Speed Adjustment

Adjust only with engine at normal operating temperature.
1. Reduce engine speed to less than 800 rpm.

2. Adjust the idle mixture control screw so that the engine runs as uniformly as possible.
3. Switch on headlights and increase engine speed, by means of the idle adjusting screw, to 800–900 rpm.

AUTOLITE (FoMoCo) CARBURETOR (1970)

This carburetor, while quite similar to the one used in 1969 USA cars, has a different choke mechanism that requires a slightly different setting procedure. When the engine is started, manifold vacuum acts on the base of the choke piston and draws the piston down into the bore. The choke bore has two narrow slots machined over part of its length, which are uncovered as the piston moves down. Atmospheric pressure then bleeds past the piston to reduce the vacuum beneath it, thus modulating piston movement considerably. This has the effect of preventing leaning out of the mixture, thus reducing the tendency to stumble and backfire.

Choke Plate Pull-Down

1. Remove the thermostatic spring and water housing.
2. Place a piece of 0.040" diameter wire in the inner slot above the piston, while holding the vacuum piston lever to keep piston and wire in position.
3. Check the choke plate—it should now be 0.080–0.100" from the carburetor body.
4. This can be checked using a drill bit, as with previous carburetors, between the

choke plate and the body. If necessary, bend the extension of the choke thermostat lever (the part that rests against the vacuum piston lever) to obtain the desired clearance.

Idle Speed

1. Start engine and allow it to warm up to normal operating temperature.
2. Connect a tachometer and CO meter.
3. Adjust idle screw to obtain 900 rpm, then adjust mixture screw to obtain 1.5–2.0% CO. The mixture screw has an internal stop, which should not be broken in an attempt to further unscrew it.

Deceleration Valve—1970 USA cars

The stricter exhaust emission standards set by the federal government required a few changes to the V4 engine. The carburetor was modified by changing the jet sizes and adding a deceleration section, the air cleaner was equipped with a thermostatically operated flap to provide better combustion when the engine is cold, the distributor advance curve was slightly modified, and a deceleration valve was added to the intake manifold.

This deceleration valve contains a spring-loaded diaphragm, which is held in position by the bottom cover. One side of the diaphragm is subject to intake manifold vacuum (top side), and the other side to atmospheric pressure. During deceleration, manifold vacuum is high enough to overcome spring tension to lift the valve from its seat. This movement operates the deceleration section in the carburetor to meter fuel-air mix to the manifold, providing better combustion. The valve must be checked every 6,000 miles and adjusted if necessary so that the car continues to comply with emission standards.

CHECKING

1. Start the engine and allow it to warm up to normal operating temperature. NOTE: *Air cleaner must be in place.*
2. Make sure the decel valve is not working at idle speed by disconnecting the hose between the carburetor and valve—if the valve is operating properly, no vacuum should be in the line. If vacuum is present, screw in the adjusting screw until valve closes.

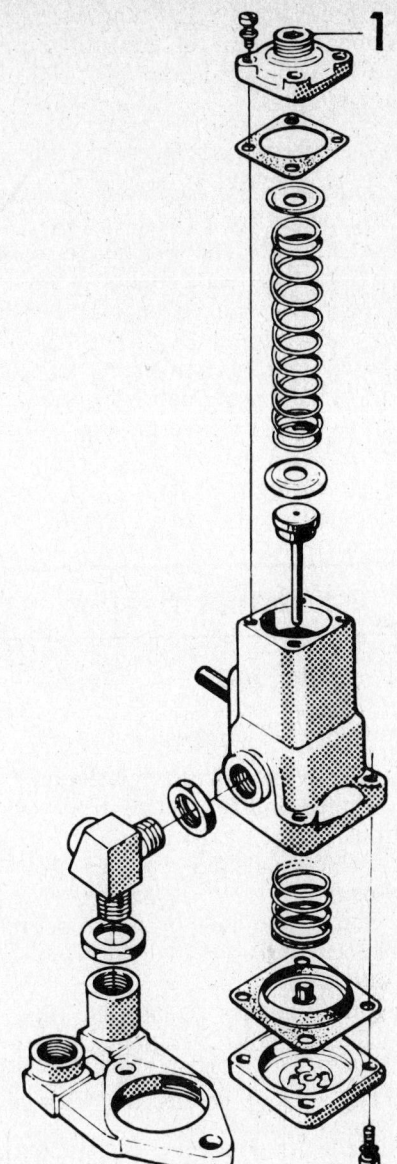

Deceleration valve—1970 USA cars. (1)=adjusting screw

3. Connect a tachometer to the engine and adjust idle speed to 850 rpm.
4. Accelerate engine to 3,000 rpm, then release the throttle and check the time it takes for the engine to drop back to idle speed.
5. If the decel valve is O.K., it should take 7–8 seconds for the speed to drop.

ADJUSTMENT

1. Remove the air cleaner.
2. If the time was greater than 8 seconds, screw in the adjusting screw until desired

time lapse is achieved; if time was less than 7 seconds, back out the adjusting screw.

3. Install the air cleaner and recheck the valve operation.

TROUBLESHOOTING THE DECELERATION VALVE

If the decel valve diaphragm is defective, air then passes from the bleed hole in the atmospheric side into the intake manifold. This massive air leak results in an overly lean mixture with attendant backfiring, stalling, and rough idle. If both carburetor adjustment and ignition timing are correct, and the above symptoms still exist, check the decel valve by covering the bleed hole with a finger. A defective diaphragm can be replaced—disassembly is obvious from the illustration.

Exhaust System

Front Muffler R&R

TWO-STROKE

1. Loosen the exhaust pipe clamp.
2. Unbolt muffler flange from exhaust manifold. Remove gasket.
3. Remove muffler support bolt and lower muffler.
4. Separate exhaust pipe from muffler and remove muffler.

To install:

1. Insert muffler connection pipe and flange through hole in engine compartment floor.
2. Slip muffler connection with clamp loosely onto exhaust pipe.
3. Install muffler support bolt loosely.
4. Install a new flange gasket and bolt on the flange.
5. Tighten the support bolt and exhaust pipe clamp.
6. Check for vibration or leaks.

V4

1. Disconnect battery ground cable.
2. Disconnect cables and remove starter.
3. Unbolt flanges from engine. Remove spacers and flange gaskets. Unbolt muffler support brackets from engine.
4. Loosen exhaust pipe clamp. Separate exhaust pipe from muffler. There are two exhaust pipes on the Sonett.

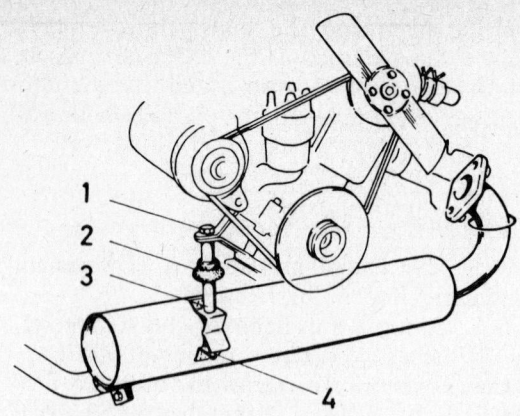

Front muffler—two-stroke
1. Bolt
2. Rubber seal
3. Spacer
4. Nut and washer

5. Lower muffler. Pull right muffler inlet pipe through engine compartment floor and turn it forward between front panel and bumper. Pull out left muffler inlet pipe.

6. Reverse procedure to install, using new flange gaskets.

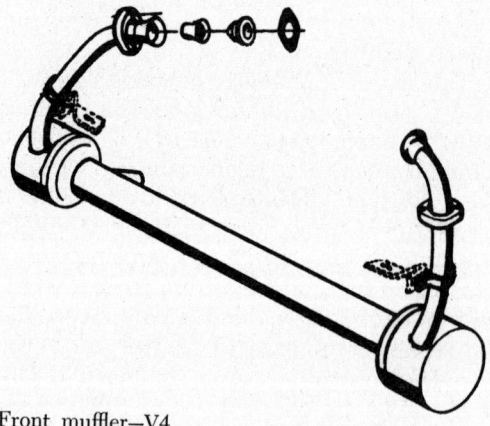

Front muffler—V4

Rear Muffler R&R

ALL MODELS

1. Remove right rear wheel.
2. Remove two muffler support bolts. On the Sonett II, there are additional muffler support bolts.
3. Loosen muffler clamp and remove muffler.
4. Reverse procedure to install.

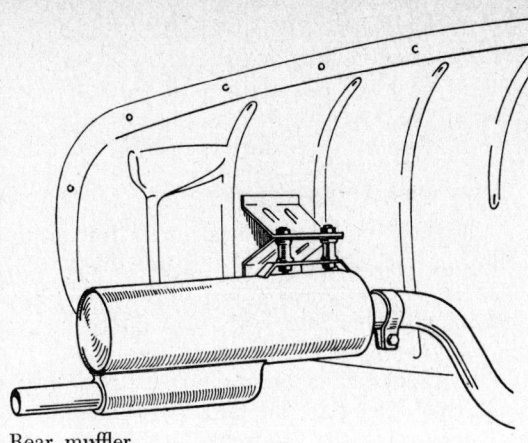

Rear muffler

Exhaust Pipe R&R

ALL MODELS

1. Remove rear muffler.
2. Loosen exhaust pipe clamp(s) and hangers.
3. Remove exhaust pipe.
4. Reverse procedure to install.

Cooling System

Radiator R&R

EARLY TWO-STROKE MODELS, RADIATOR BEHIND ENGINE

1. Drain coolant.
2. Remove radiator hoses.
3. Remove both radiator to radiator frame bolts.
4. Release radiator stay from frame. Bend frame forward carefully to permit removal of stay from hole in frame.
5. Remove two bolts holding radiator to support member.
6. Press frame forward carefully and move radiator backward until inlet connection clears frame. Lift radiator out behind frame.

To replace:

1. Replace radiator and relocate stay in frame. Bolt radiator to support member and frame.
2. Tighten nut on radiator stay.
3. Replace hoses. Refill cooling system.

LATE MODELS, RADIATOR AHEAD OF ENGINE

1. Drain coolant. Remove or open hood, as necessary.

2. Remove radiator blind cord, if installed.
3. Disconnect water hoses.
4. Back off upper and lower radiator retaining screws.
5. Lift out radiator.
6. Reverse procedure to install.

Water Pump R&R

EARLY TWO-STROKE MODELS, INTEGRAL WITH GENERATOR

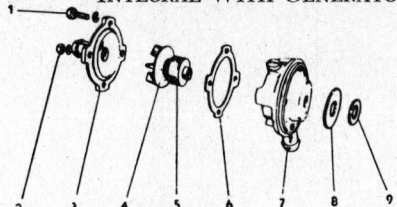

Details of water pump used with late two-stroke engines.

1. Bolt
2. Nut
3. Pump cover
4. Pump impeller
5. Shaft seal
6. Gasket
7. Pump body
8. Splash washer, brass
9. Shim

1. Drain coolant.
2. Loosen and remove belt.
3. Disconnect hoses at pump.
4. Disconnect generator cables. Remove generator and water pump together.
5. Remove bolts and pump cover.
6. Unscrew impeller from generator shaft.
7. Remove pump body.
8. Remove splash washer from generator shaft. Remove shim from behind splash washer.
9. Shaft seal is pressed onto the impeller shaft. It may be replaced if worn.

To replace:

1. Replace shim and splash washer on generator shaft.
2. Locate pump body against generator.
3. Install and tighten impeller on generator shaft.
4. Install gasket and pump cover.
5. Reinstall generator and pump.
6. Replace hoses and clamps.
7. Connect generator cables. Adjust belt. The correct belt play is .3" for all SAAB models.

LATE TWO-STROKE ENGINES

1. Drain coolant.
2. Loosen and remove belt. Remove fan and pulley.
3. Disconnect water hoses.
4. Remove pump mounting bolts.

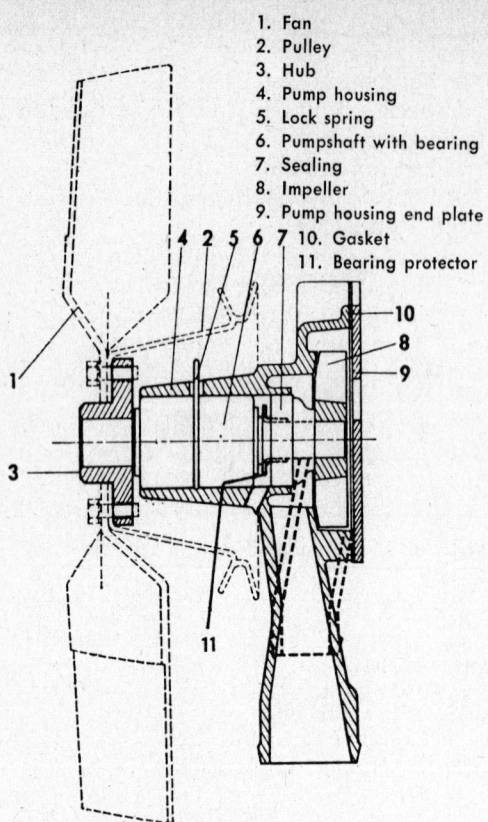

1. Fan
2. Pulley
3. Hub
4. Pump housing
5. Lock spring
6. Pumpshaft with bearing
7. Sealing
8. Impeller
9. Pump housing end plate
10. Gasket
11. Bearing protector

Integral water pump, detached from generator

5. Remove pump.

To replace:

1. Install pump.
2. Replace hoses.
3. Replace fan and pulley.
4. Adjust belt. The correct belt play is .3″ for all SAAB models.

V4 ENGINE

1. Drain coolant.
2. Remove alternator and bracket. Remove belt.
3. Unbolt and remove pump.

To replace:

1. Bolt the pump in place with a new gasket.
2. Install alternator and bracket.
3. Adjust belt. The correct belt play is .3″ for all SAAB models.

Electric Cooling Fan R&R

The two-stroke Sonett II has an electric cooling fan located in front of the radiator. The fan is controlled by a thermostatic switch in the engine water outlet. To remove the fan and motor:

1. Remove grill.

2. Detach fan motor electrical cables.
3. Remove fan motor retaining screws.
4. Remove fan and motor through the air intake.
5. Reverse procedure to install.

Thermostat

The 750 cc. engine has an aneroid type thermostat fitted in the water hose between the engine water outlet and the radiator inlet. The 850 cc. engine has a wax (flap) type thermostat mounted in the cylinder head behind the water pump. On the V4 engine, the thermostat is mounted in the front of the intake manifold casting. Standard equipment thermostats are as follow:

Engine	Average Operating Temperature
GT 750	170°F
850 cc. (1960-1964)	185°F
850 cc. (1965-1967)	189°F
Sonett (Two-stroke and V4)	180°F
95 and 96 V4	180°F

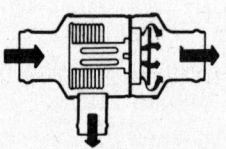

Thermostat flow diagram—750 cc. engine

THERMOSTAT R & R—V4

1. Drain coolant.
2. Remove air cleaner and carburetor.
3. Disconnect upper water hose.
4. Remove bolts, upper thermostat housing, and thermostat.

To replace:

1. Insert thermostat with retaining bracket perpendicular to the front-rear center-line of the car. If this is not done, the thermostat will be bent, rendering it useless.
2. Install a new gasket and bolt down the upper thermostat housing.
3. Replace water hose, carburetor, and air cleaner.
4. Refill cooling system.

Thermostat installation position—V4

Two-Stroke Engine

The SAAB two-stroke engine is a three-cylinder, in line, water-cooled unit employing crankcase scavenging, piston-controlled port timing and cylinder scavenging on the Schnürle principle. Lubrication is accomplished by mixing motor oil with the fuel supply, except in GT-850 models.

SAAB 95 and 96 models use an identical 850 cc. engine, while the GT-750 uses a 750 cc. unit, similar to that used in the older 93 model. The engine used in the Sonett II is basically the same as that used in the Monte Carlo 850, with the exception of a different water outlet which has a connection for a thermostatically operated switch and for a hose to an expansion tank. The oiling system of the Sonett engine has an oil tank with no glass gauge, and a capacity of 3 quarts. In addition, this engine has two fuel pumps (Bendix) and a three-carburetor system employing Solex 40 DHW carburetors.

The cylinder block and lower crankcase half are made of cast nickel alloy steel and are machined to match. Matching numbers are stamped on each side of the joint at the right rear of the engine.

The cylinder head is made of light alloy (aluminum) and the crankshaft is built up by pressing separate sections together. The crankshaft has six webs and seven crankpins, permitting the use of single ball bearings and double or single bearings as main and connecting rod bearings. A torsional vibration damper is utilized.

Seals of the piston-ring type separate the three crankcase compartments and the flywheel end of the engine. At the front of the engine, the crankcase is sealed by rubber gaskets on the covers of the distributor gear housing. With the two-stroke design, it is extremely important that the crankcase be sealed.

The connecting rods are made of drop forged and hardened steel, the wristpin being carried in a caged needle bearing and the big end designed so that its internally ground surface forms the outer race of the connecting rod bearing.

Connecting rods in later model engines (850 cc., and 750 cc. from chassis No. 118.980) are piston guided, while in earlier 850 cc. enginess and 750 cc. engines up to chassis No. 118.979 they are crank guided.

The standard 850 cc. engine uses Ringstreifin pistons, while the 750 cc. engine uses aluminum units. All engines utilize chrome-steel piston rings.

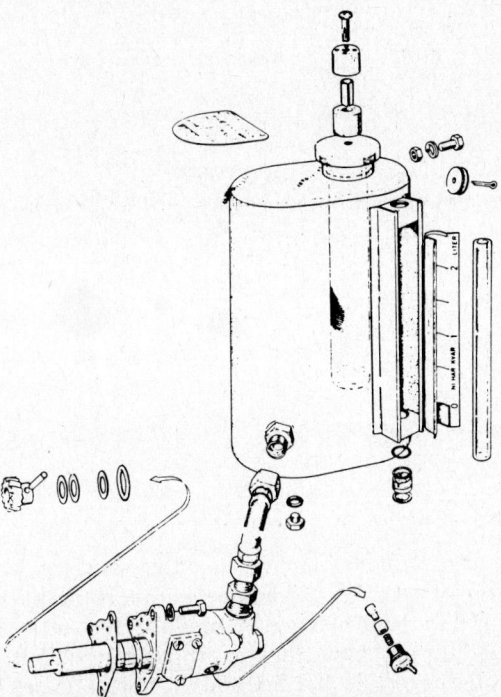

Monte Carlo oil injection tank and pump

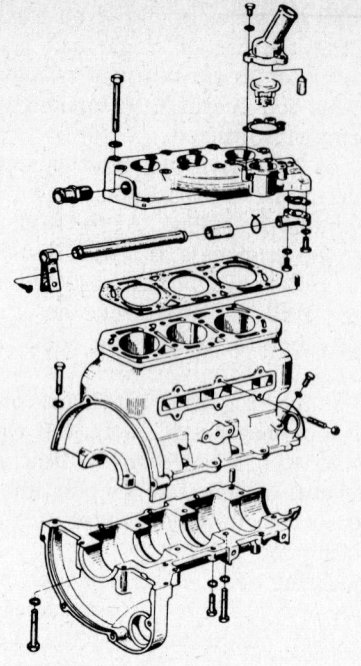

ENGINE BODY WITH CYLINDER HEAD

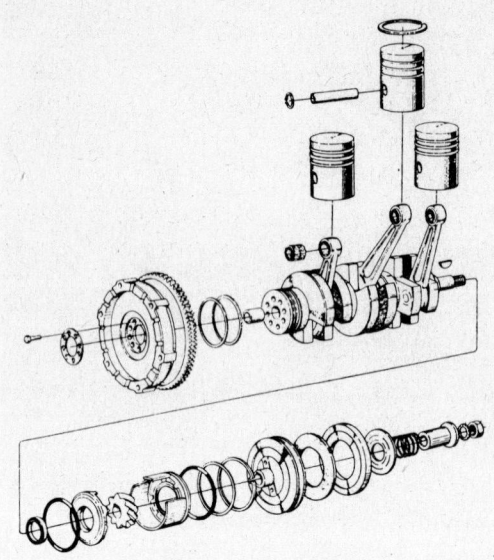

CRANKSHAFT WITH PISTONS

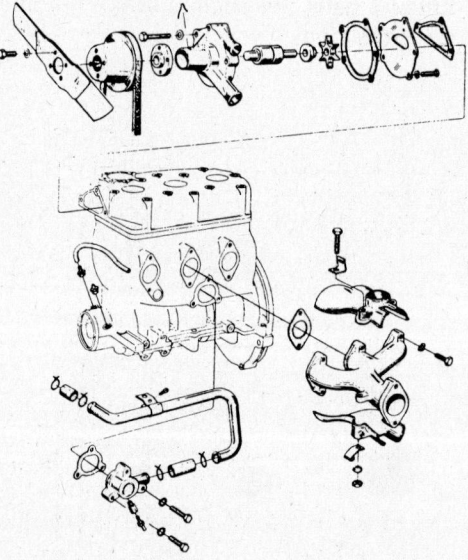

WATER PUMP AND CONNECTING PARTS, LEFT

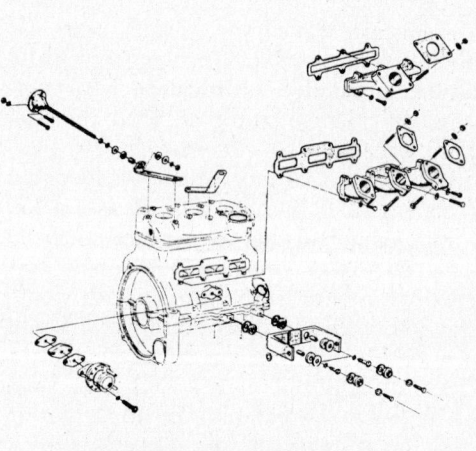

CONNECTING PARTS, RIGHT

Internal engine components—two-stroke

The GT-850 engine is lubricated in a somewhat different manner than the engines used in the 93, 95 and 96 models. Instead of adding oil to the fuel, a supply reservoir is filled every 900–1,200 miles. Steel pipes within the engine convey the oil to the three cylinders and the four main bearings under pressure from a separate oil pump. The distributor drive pinion is driven off the front of the crankshaft and is fitted with a slip clutch which operates if the oil pump jams or if the oil is too viscous.

The GT crankshaft is slightly different from the crankshaft used in other models. More material on the crank webs results in a higher crankcase compression pressure (volume is reduced) and, thus, higher power output.

IMPORTANT: The methods described here are derived from factory-recommended procedures, which require special tools. Substitutes for these tools are mentioned and other, equally suitable, procedures are possible so long as a certain amount of care is exercised. In any case, the proper tool usually can be purchased through the SAAB dealer network.

Engine Removal

1. Disconnect battery ground cable.
2. Remove the hood. Open the hood wide enough to remove the securing pins, if any, on the pivot pins. Take hold of the hinge bracket and bend it slightly inwards to release the pin on one side. The hood now may be easily lifted off. On the Sonett, simply open the hood and remove the two pivot bolts, then, with the help of an assistant, lift off the hood.
3. Drain the cooling system.
4. Disconnect the headlight and turn signal wires. On the Sonett, this must be done before removing hood.
5. Disconnect the radiator blind cord and hood lock mechanism.
6. Remove the four screws for the front panel and the two radiator supports from the body plate. Remove the clamping straps from the radiator. (*NOTE: Not necessary on Sonett.*)
7. Carefully lift off the front panel.
8. Disconnect the upper and lower radiator hoses from the engine.
9. Remove the two lower radiator bolts, then remove the radiator.
10. Disconnect the distributor primary wire, the ignition coil wire and generator wires. Remove the vent hose (if utilized) from the distributor cap.
11. Remove the air cleaner and preheat pipe.
12. Disconnect the fuel line from the pump.
13. Disconnect the cold starting (choke) control and throttle linkage from the carburetor.
14. Disconnect the two heater hoses and the temperature gauge sender from the engine.
15. Disconnect the engine side brace.
16. On the SAAB Sport and Sonett cars, disconnect the oil pressure monitor line and the hose from the oil pump. Bend the hose upward and fasten it so as to prevent losing oil from the tank. Cover all connections to keep dirt from entering the oil system.
17. Remove the two muffler flange bolts and loosen the exhaust pipe clamp.
18. Loosen the muffler retaining nut and tie the muffler out of the way to avoid damaging the pipe.
19. Remove the six front engine mount bolts from beneath the engine compartment floor.
20. Lift engine slightly and block up the transmission case with a 3½″ wood block.
21. Remove the two starter bolts and lay the starter on the floor of engine compartment with the cables still connected.
22. Loosen and remove the bolts that hold the engine to the transmission case, then pull the engine out carefully so as not to damage the clutch shaft.

Engine Installation

1. Lower engine into the car. Check the clutch shaft splines—if undamaged, coat them with grease.
2. Bolt the engine to the transmission case and reconnect the engine ground cable.
3. Install the starter.
4. Remove the wood block from under the transmission case, then lower the unit.
5. Refasten front engine mounts and the side brace.
6. Reconnect the muffler by fastening it to the exhaust manifold and muffler bracket. Don't tighten the bracket nut.
7. Tighten the flange bolts, the bracket nut and the exhaust pipe clamp—in that order.
8. On SAAB Sport and Sonett cars, reconnect the hose to the oil pump and the cable to the oil monitor on the pump. Turn the pump shaft about 100 times by hand.
9. Reconnect heater hoses and temperature gauge sender unit.
10. Reconnect throttle and cold starting device controls.
11. Install air cleaner and preheat pipe, then connect fuel hose.
12. Connect the distributor and generator wires. Replace the distributor vent hose.
13. Connect the radiator hoses.

14. Replace the front panel, along with the clamping strap and two radiator braces.

15. Install the radiator blind cord and the hood light mechanism.

16. Connect the headlight and turn signal wires.

17. Refill the radiator.

18. Replace the hood.

19. Connect the battery ground cable.

20. Check the clutch pedal free-play and adjust if necessary.

21. Adjust ignition timing and test engine.

Basic ignition timing when installing distributor is achieved by aligning mark 1 with 2, and 3 with 4.

Engine Disassembly

1. Clean the engine, using Gunk and kerosene.

2. Remove the fanbelt and generator.

3. Remove the intake manifold, complete with carburetor.

4. Remove fuel pump.

5. Remove exhaust manifold.

6. Take off radiator inlet hoses.

7. Loosen cylinder head bolts and remove head; remove head gasket.

8. If the water pump and thermostat are to be removed, take off fan and pulley, then detach water pump from the cylinder head. Disconnect the upper inlet pipe and remove the thermostat and valve.

9. Loosen the distributor clamp bolt and the distributor.

10. On SAAB Sport cars, loosen the oil pump bolts and remove the pump.

11. Turn the engine right side up, making sure the surface is clean and flat.

12. Loosen the crankshaft pulley nut and remove the vibration damper and the pulley. (Use puller 784055 if available.)

Removing front pulley using tool No. 784055

13. Insert spacers (784209 or 784065) under clutch levers and remove the retaining screws and clutch.

14. Release the lockwasher and loosen the flywheel bolts, then remove flywheel.

15. Remove the engine mounts from the lower crankcase half.

16. Remove the bolts and lift off the crankcase lower half.

17. Lift out the crankshaft, along with pistons. Take great care so as not to bend the connecting rods or damage the pistons. Removal is simplified by inserting a clutch centering tool (784064) into the flywheel end and screwing tool (784057), onto the stub at the other end of crankshaft.

18. Take off the outer cover of the distributor housing and put it aside, along with the retaining ring and shims.

19. On SAAB 95 and 96, remove the distributor pinion with a puller (784051), then

remove the inner cover together with O-ring.

On SAAB Sport, remove the distributor pinion together with the fiber washer. Remove and put aside the two slip clutch pins and springs.

20. Remove the piston retaining rings and drive out the piston pins using a brass drift or Tool 784061.

Engine Assembly

Inspect and clean all engine parts. Replace defective parts and all gaskets. A new cylinder head gasket *always* must be used regardless of the condition of the old one.

1. Install piston rings using piston ring pliers.

2. Install pistons onto connecting rods, using a dummy shaft and driver (784061) to locate needle bearing. Install piston pin with the driver and install retaining rings. Always install the pistons with the arrow pointing forward.

3. On the SAAB Sport, make certain the sealing ring is fitted at the ignition end of the crankshaft. If it has been removed, make sure the sealing rings are located with the openings 180° apart.

4. Put the Woodruff key in the end of the crankshaft. Oil the pistons and cylinder bores before assembly and use care not to damage pistons or rings. On SAAB 95 and 96 engines, make sure that the sealing rings are located vertically and that gaps are 180° apart.

5. Insert tool No. 784057 into the front end of the crankshaft and put the centering tool into the crankshaft bushing. Locate the piston ring gaps to coincide with the locking pins in the pistons and lower the crankshaft, with pistons, into the engine block. The center piston should be lowered first.

6. In SAAB Sport engines, place the two slip clutch springs and pins in the ignition end of the crankshaft, then refit the distributor pinion so that the pointed pin enters the notch on the pinion. Install the distributor pinion fiber washer. Oil all parts before continuing assembly.

7. Install the lower crankcase half, tightening the large bolts first. Begin in the middle and tighten alternately toward each end. Tighten the 5/16″ bolts to 18 ft. lbs. and the 3/8″ bolts to 29 ft. lbs. No sealing compound or gasket may be used between the lower half and the block; the surfaces must be clean and lightly oiled.

8. On SAAB 95 and 96 engines, install the inner cover of the distributor gear housing along with O-ring and shaft seals. Use tool No. 784056 (or homemade sleeve) to avoid damaging the shaft seals. Locate the cover with the cutaway opening opposite the hole for the distributor; install the distributor pinion with the chamfered side inwards.

On SAAB Sport engines, check that the ignition distributor pinion is located with the pointed pin in the groove, then insert the fiber washer.

9. Install the outer cover, with O-ring and shaft seal, (using tool No. 784057, or tool No. 784127 for the SAAB Sport engine) onto the crankshaft stub and press the cover in place by screwing in the tool.

10. Insert shims outside of the cover and install the retaining ring, making sure it is firmly seated in its groove. Loosen the tool about 1/2 turn and make sure the shims are tight against the retaining ring. If not, remove the ring and insert more shims.

11. Install the flywheel, using a new retaining ring. Tighten the bolts to 22 ft. lbs. and secure them. (Special bolts are used for the flywheel.)

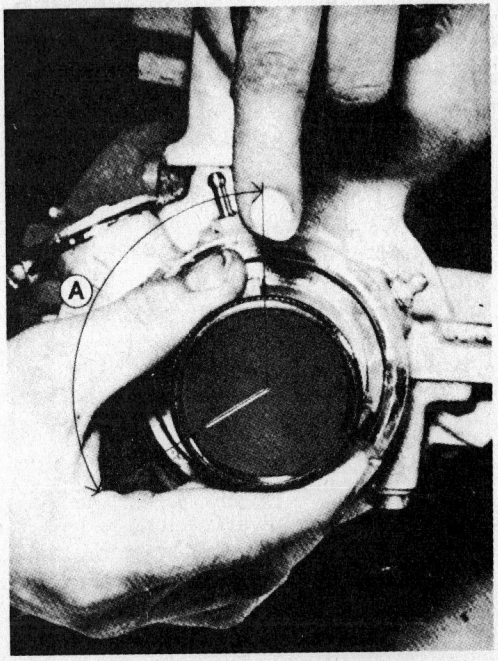

Shimming the outer cover. A=¼-⅓ turn

12. Insert the clutch plate and install the clutch, making sure the three spacers are properly positioned. Center the clutch plate with arbor No. 784069, or an old transmission main shaft while tightening the bolts, then remove arbor and spacers. Some flywheels and clutches are paint marked to indicate proper balance. These parts are to be installed with the marks 180° apart.

13. Install the pulley and vibration damper, using a new retaining ring under the nut. Torque the nut to 36 ft. lbs.

14. On SAAB Sport engines, install the oil pump and its gasket.

15. Install the engine mounts.

16. Install the lower water inlet neck and pipe; coat both sides of the gasket with Permatex.

17. With the surfaces dry and clean, place the cylinder head gasket on the block, making certain the broad part of the folded-on lining is against the cylinder head. Never use Permatex or oil on cylinder head gasket.

18. Install the cylinder head and tighten the bolts, in sequence, as described in the next part of this chapter.

19. Reconnect the water pump, pulley and fan, then hook up the hose for the engine inlet pipe.

20. Install the thermostat, the valve and the upper outlet pipe; reconnect the heater pipe.

21. Install the intake manifold and carburetor.

22. On the SAAB Sport, pour 1.7 fluid ozs. of motor oil into the distributor gear housing through the hole for the distributor.

23. Install the distributor.

24. Install the generator and fanbelt, then adjust the belt tension.

25. Install the exhaust manifold and gaskets.

26. On SAAB 95 and 96 models, fill the distributor housing with chassis grease.

Cylinder Head

The engine must be cool before the head is removed so as not to distort the casting.

Check the head surface with a straightedge and correct any irregularities with a face plate covered with valve grinding compound. Don't indiscriminately mill the head to increase compression because the piston to head clearance can be decreased to the point where contact is made. Clean the spark plug threads with a round wire brush or with a M 18 V 1.5 mm. thread chaser. Carbon deposits in the lower parts of the thread can cause damage when a new plug is installed. Such damage, if it occurs, can be repaired using Heli-Coil inserts.

The head gasket is black composition material with rolled metal O-rings around the cylinders. When installing, the head surface must be clean and dry and the gasket carefully centered with the broad side of the folded metal O-rings facing the head.

Before installing the cylinder head bolts, clean the threads with a wire brush and lightly coat the threads with oil or graphite grease. Tightening is done in steps—on 850 cc. engines, first tighten to 22 ft. lbs., then further tighten 90° (1/4 turn). This is equal to 36 ft. lbs. torque and is a better method than simply tightening to 36 ft. lbs. On 750 cc. engines, there are eight bolts instead of twelve. There are two types of bolts used as well—marked "80" and "100." The bolts marked "100" are tightened to 58 ft. lbs., the bolts marked "80" to 47 ft. lbs.

Start the engine, after assembling all other components, and allow it to warm up. Shut off the engine and allow it to cool to at least 86°F. Tighten all bolts again (without first loosening them) an additional 20° in the case of 850 cc. engines; to the prescribed torque for 750 cc. engines. After 1,200 miles, retighten an *additional* 20° or check prescribed torque (with engine cold).

Cylinder Block

The cylinder block and crankcase are machined to match and it is impossible to replace one without replacing the other. The crankcase number is stamped on both sides of the common joint at the right rear of the engine. The engine number is stamped as illustrated in Chapter 1. The bore class is stamped on the left-hand side of the block.

DISASSEMBLY AND ASSEMBLY

Follow the procedures at the beginning of this chapter, with the following hints: when crankcase is fitted to the block, the surface must be perfectly clean. No form of gasket, sealing compound or similar material may be used. The surfaces should be lightly coated with oil. There are two bolt sizes, having different tightening torques. Tighten the large bolts first, beginning in the center and tightening alternately outwards in each direction. Make sure to tighten the rear bolts on the flywheel side.

HONING CYLINDERS

When pistons are replaced due to wear or damage it is often necessary to hone the cylinder bores in order to remove ridges and scoring, as well as to match the clearance of the piston class to be used.

BORING CYLINDERS

If reboring is necessary, select an oversize that will correct any damage to the bores. The ports always must be chamfered as indicated in the illustration, otherwise broken piston rings could result. This job can be done with a scraper or a rotary grinder. Make sure that all dust and chips are removed after this operation and that the port shape is not radically changed (which could result in unbalanced gas flow).

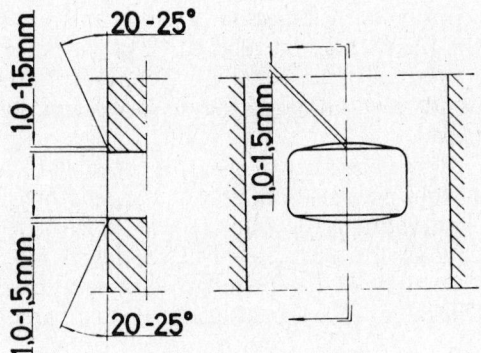

Chamfering ports after reboring cylinders

CHECKING OIL PASSAGES—SAAB SPORT AND MONTE CARLO 850

The block casting includes seven steel pipes which direct oil from the oil pump to the main bearings and the three cylinders. Check for blockage by passing a nylon thread about 0.04″ thick (fishing line) through the oil passage. If the oil passage is blocked, it can be cleaned with a piece of music wire 0.02″ thick. It is extremely important that oil passages be checked after reboring.

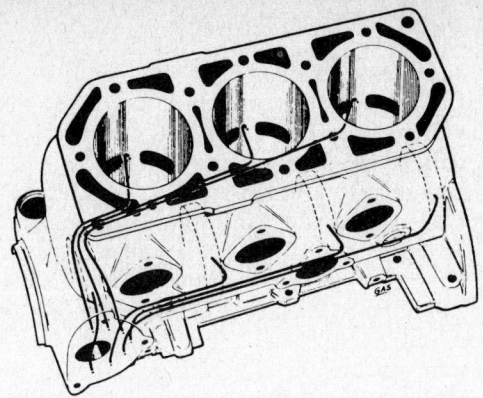

Engine block cutaway, showing oil passages—SAAB Sport and Monte Carlo 850

Pistons and Connecting Rods

PISTONS—95 AND 96

The engine in the SAAB 95 and 96 is fitted with Ringstreifen pistons. This type of piston is distinguished by a steel ring which is cast-in below the bottom piston groove. All piston rings are of hard-chrome steel and are of the same thickness.

PISTONS—SAAB SPORT, MONTE CARLO 850, AND GT-750

The pistons in the SAAB Sport and Monte Carlo are made of aluminum and have very thick skirts. The three piston rings are made of steel and are molybdenum coated all around their periphery. The bottom ring is thinner than the other two and serves as an oil scraper. (The oil scraper is beveled at the top and has a sharp bottom edge.)

CONNECTING ROD GUIDANCE

The late-model connecting rods are piston-guided, meaning that they are guided axially at the piston pin bearing and have a large clearance at the big end connecting rod bearing.

When fitting piston, pin and needle bearing to the connecting rod, it is recommended that a guide pin (No. 784061) be used. When installing the piston pin, hold the piston firmly with the hand to avoid distorting the connecting rod. Always install the piston pin retaining rings.

PISTON PIN BEARING

The piston pin bearing is a needle bearing. To ensure an accurate fit, a series of nine bearings is available.

Marking of Needle Bearings

The basic diameter of the needles is 0.07847″ and the marking indicates the deviation from this value in thousandths of a millimeter. The bearing marked —9 has the smallest needles, while the biggest needles are installed in the bearing marked +7. Bearings marked with a plus sign are a kind of oversized bearing and normally are used on replacement crankshafts. When reconditioning piston pin bearings, both piston pin and needle bearings should be replaced.

Before reassembling the piston, the piston pin must be matched with a needle bearing to give the correct fit in the connecting rod. There should be practically no play, although it should not be necessary to force the piston pin into the needle bearing when the latter is fitted in the connecting rod.

Light thumb pressure is the maximum permissible pressure when fitting needle bearings The piston pin should rotate easily between two fingers and should be free of play.

PISTONS AND CYLINDER CLASSES

The markings on the cylinder block indicate the cylinder class of each bore. This makes it possible to choose the proper piston. The choice of piston class is made from the following table.

Standard Classes	Oversize Classes
	Cyl. Bore, Piston Mark
A	O.D. 0.5 A
AB	O.D. 0.5 B
B	O.D. 1.0 A
C	O.B. 1.0 B

As shown, there are four standard classes of pistons and cylinders, and two oversizes, 0.5 and 1.0 mm. (.020″ nom. and .040″ nom.) with two classes each. Piston and cylinder class normally must agree. However, when the engine is properly broken in, or worn, pistons of a larger class can be fitted into the SAAB 95 and 96 engines. Remember that the difference between classes B and C is far greater than between other classes and that no deviations are permitted.

MEASURING CYLINDER BORES

If the cylinder bore is damaged by piston scoring, or if excessive wear is measured, the block must be rebored.

Normally, the bores are worn most at the upper part, although they also wear out-of-round.

It is necessary to measure each bore at several points—both across and lengthwise. To determine the true amount of wear, the micrometer must be set at the lower tolerance limit of the cylinder class concerned. Check taper by measuring at two points, 0.39″ and 1.97″ from the upper edge.

MEASURING PISTONS

Measure the piston diameter with a micrometer 0.8″ (0.6″ for the SAAB Sport and GT-750) from the bottom of the skirt and at right angles to the pin. Measure out-of-roundness by measuring parallel with, and at right angles to, the piston pin.

CHECKING PISTON CLEARANCE

Should the proper equipment for measuring bores and pistons be unavailable, pistons can be fittted with the aid of a feeler gauge,

Piston and block marking codes

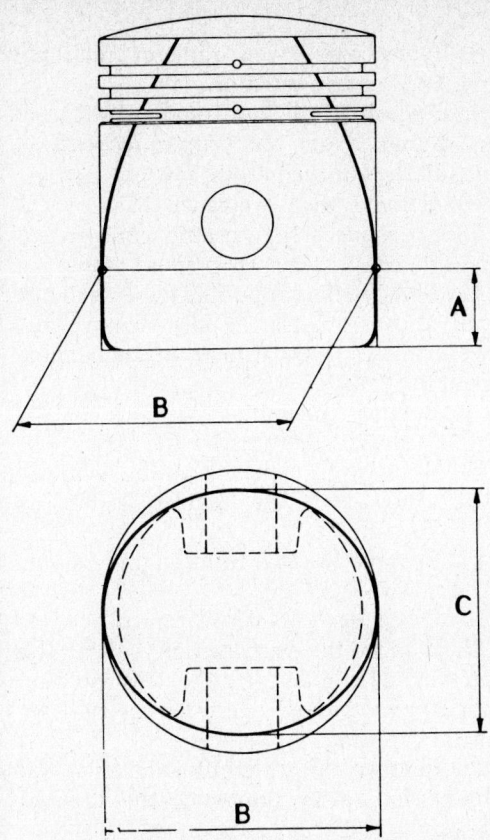

Measuring piston taper and out-of-roundness. A=distance from piston skirt bottom is 0.8″ for 95/96, 0.6″ for Sport and Monte Carlo. B= diameter at right angles to piston pin. C= diameter parallel to piston pin.

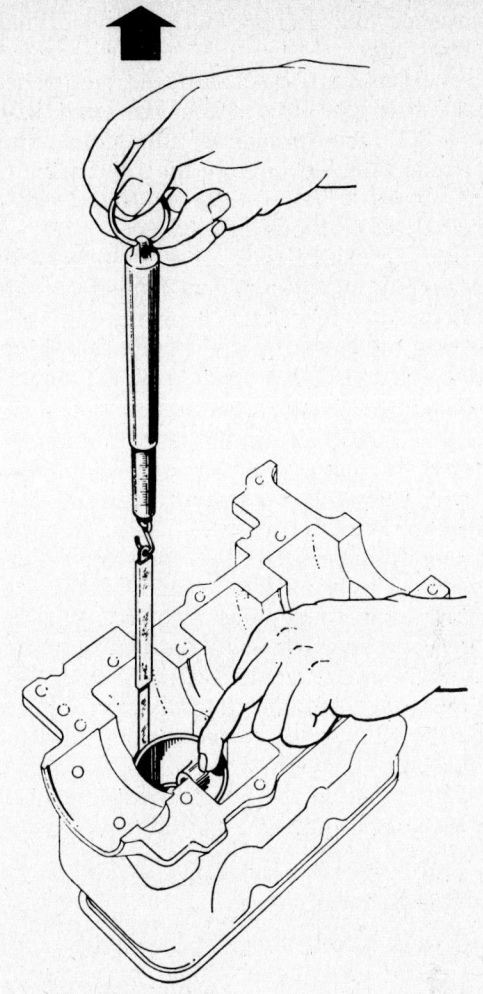

Checking piston clearance with feeler gauge and scale.

1/2″ wide and about 8″ long, and a spring scale graduated to 1,000 grams (2.2 lbs.).

Clean the bore and lightly coat with oil. Place, for example, a .002″ feeler gauge along the bore, compression side, and insert the piston into the bore (minus the rings). Measure the clearance at right angles to the pin. Now, pull the feeler gauge from the bore with the spring scale and note the amount of pull; it should be 600–1,000 grams (1 lb. 5 oz.—2 lbs. 3 oz.). If the pull is less, try pistons one class larger; if more, try pistons one class smaller. Continue until the correct fit is obtained. The amount of pull should be checked at different piston depths.

V4 Engine

This engine is a four-cylinder, four-stroke, water-cooled overhead valve unit with the cylinders arranged in a 60° vee. The carburetor is a single downdraft type having an automatic choke. The cylinder heads have separate intake ports and common exhaust ports for each bank of cylinders; the cylinder block is one-piece cast iron.

The cylinder heads are identical, with partially machined combustion chambers and 14 mm. threads for the spark plugs. The valve guides and valve seats are machined directly in the heads. The cast iron crank-shaft has three identical main bearings with hardened and ground journals and drilled oil passages.

The camshaft, case hardened and phosphated, is gear driven from the crankshaft at a 2:1 ratio through a fiber gear. The tappets, actuated directly by the camshaft, are carried in the cylinder block and move the valves, pushrods and rockers.

The connecting rods are shrunk onto the piston pins and are not detachable from the pistons; therefore, only a piston and connecting rod assembly is available as a spare part. The pistons are made of aluminum, having two compression rings and one oil control ring. The upper ring is chromeplated and plain, while the lower compression ring is of an oil scraping design. The oil control ring is tripartite. The lubrication system is force feed type, pressure being generated by a rotor-type pump driven by the camshaft. The pump is mounted inside the oil pan under the crankshaft. The pump forces the oil past a relief valve incorporated in the pump, through the full-flow oil filter and the oil passages to the various lubrication points.

The engine in the Sonett V4 is identical to those used in the 95 and 96 models with the exception of heavier valve springs.

Engine Removal

If work is to be done on the engine only, the entire power unit should be removed and the engine separated from the transmission. Removal of the engine alone is not recommended.

1. Disconnect battery ground cable.
2. To remove hood first open it wide enough to remove the locking springs for the hood hinges. Now, bend the hood brace slightly inward to release the pin on one side. On Sonett V4, remove the two pivot bolts, then, with the help of an assistant, lift off the hood.
3. Drain engine oil and cooling water.
4. Disconnect headlight and turn signal wires. (*NOTE: This must be done before removing hood on Sonett.*)
5. Loosen the four screws that hold the grill panel and remove the two radiator supports. Detach the clamping straps from the radiator, then remove the hood lock and control wire.
6. Remove the grill panel, using care so as not to damage paint.
7. Disconnect the upper and lower radiator hoses.
8. Loosen the lower radiator retaining bolts and remove radiator.
9. Disconnect all hoses and cables from the engine. Note the proper location of wires to the alternator (tag them).
10. Remove the air cleaner.
11. Disconnect the throttle control, engine side support and air preheat casing.
12. Remove the flange nuts for the exhaust pipes at the cylinder heads. Remove the lower exhaust pipe clamps at the engine mounting pads.
13. Remove the rubber cushions for the middle exhaust pipe (under the floor).
14. Remove the spacers at the cylinder heads and lower the muffler as far as possible.
15. Remove the two front engine mounts (from above).
16. Disconnect freewheel control.
17. Remove the rear retaining bolt for the clutch cylinder and wire unit out of the way. Collect any shims used between the cylinder and transmission.
18. Remove the gearshift joint from the transmission, after removing the tapered pin.
19. Disconnect the speedometer cable.
20. Lift floor mat and remove the rubber plug so the center bolt of the rear engine bracket becomes accessible. Remove the bolt, using a 9/16″ socket and extension.
21. Jack up car and place jack stands under the front edges of the sills so that the front wheels clear the floor.
22. Remove the large clamps from around the rubber boots on the universal joints.
23. Attach a lifting device (GC 6000) to the engine.
24. Connect the lifting device to a suitable lifting hook, carefully lift the engine about 2″ and pull the transmission stub out of the rear engine bracket.
25. Disconnect the inner universal joints, first on the right side, then on the left. Do this with the T-shaped pieces of the driveshafts located vertically and with the engine pushed as far as possible in the opposite direction. (Fit protective cover 731762 in the rubber boots and 783846 on the inner drivers, if available.)
26. Lift the engine-transmission unit out of the engine compartment. Make sure the distributor vacuum chamber does not hit the cross brace.

Removing engine with factory lifting brackets

Engine Installation

1. Make sure that the inner universal joints are filled with the proper grease.

2. Lower the engine-transmission unit into the engine compartment, using the lifting device.

3. Lower just far enough so that the engine brackets are about 0.2″ from the engine mounts.

4. Place the T-pieces of the inner shafts into the inner universal joints. Do this with the T-pieces located vertically and with the power unit pushed over as far as possible in the opposite direction. First assemble the left side, then the right.

5. Attach the engine side support; tighten after engine is in place.

6. Lower the engine into position and tighten the front engine mounts.

7. Lower the car onto its wheels.

8. Place new clamps on the inner universal joints.

9. Tighten the bolts for the rear engine bracket. Make sure the limit washer on the rear of the engine bracket is in position. If the washer is missing, the fan could hit the radiator.

10. Reinstall the rubber plug and replace floor mat.

11. Reconnect speedometer cable and freewheel control.

12. Install the gearshift rod joint.

13. Install the clutch cylinder, along with any shims; adjust the clutch.

14. Connect the exhaust pipes to the cylinder heads, using new gaskets.

15. Reinstall the clamps and the exhaust pipes.

16. Reconnect the throttle control.

17. Reconnect all hoses and cables to the engine. Do not confuse the leads to the alternator, as wrong wiring could ruin the unit. (Connect the black leads to D—.)

18. Install air cleaner.

19. Install radiator and hoses.

20. Install the front grill panel, radiator clamping straps, radiator braces and hood lock.

21. Reconnect the headlight and turn signal wires.

22. Fill and bleed the cooling system. The bleeding nipple is located on the front of the firewall mounted heating unit.

23. Check the oil level in the transmission.

24. Fill the engine with oil.

25. Reconnect the battery ground cable.

26. Start engine, check oil pressure and coolant temperature.

Separating Engine-Transmission Unit

DISASSEMBLY

1. Remove the flywheel housing cover plate from beneath the clutch housing.

2. Remove the bolts that connect the engine and transmission.

3. Remove the starter.

4. Separate the engine and transmission.

ASSEMBLY

1. Reinstall transmission. Make certain the guide sleeves line up correctly in the clutch housing.

2. Tighten the clutch housing bolts evenly to the proper torque.

3. Install the housing cover plate for the flywheel.

Engine Disassembly

1. Ideally, the engine should be attached to the proper SAAB engine stand (using fixture GC 6010). If one is not available, place engine upright on a sturdy wooden bench or roller stand.

2. Remove the distributor cap and wires.

3. Remove the distributor vacuum line and fuel inlet line by applying pressure with a screwdriver behind the washers at the flexible connections.

4. Remove the carburetor.

5. Remove the distributor clamping bolt, clamp and distributor.

6. Remove the fuel pump, pushrod and gasket. Mark the end of the pushrod which normally rests against the camshaft.

7. Remove the spark plugs.

8. Loosen the water supply tube clamps and slide them away from the connections. Remove the tube.

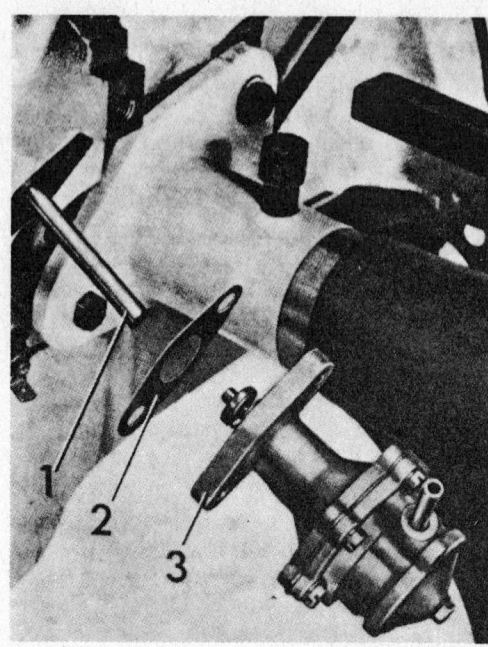

Removing fuel pump (3), gasket (2), and push-rod (1)

9. Remove the oil pressure gauge sender.

10. Remove the valve covers. Release the rocker arm assembly by loosening the two bolts alternately, then removing the oil return plates.

Removing rocker arm assembly
1. Rocker shaft and arms
2. Oil return plate

11. Remove the pushrods, keeping them in the correct order.

12. Remove the thermostat housing, thermostat and gasket.

13. Remove the intake manifold retaining bolts and nuts. It may be necessary to tap the underside of either end with a fiber mallet in order to break the seals. *Do not pry with a screwdriver or similar tool.*

14. Remove the side bracket.

15. Remove the cylinder head bolts. Lift off the heads and inspect the cylinder head gaskets for signs of leakage.

16. Remove the tappets, using a bar magnet or bent wire; keep them in the correct order.

17. Remove the oil pan and gaskets.

18. Remove the balance shaft pulley.

19. Remove the transmission cover bolts.

20. Tap the rear of the water pump with a fiber mallet to loosen the transmission cover from the intermediate plate.

21. Disconnect the water pump from the transmission cover.

Removing water pump

22. Take the oil seal for the balance shaft out of the transmission cover (using slide-hammer or tool GC 6059).

23. Remove the oil filter.

24. Remove the oil pump and its drive-shaft.

25. Remove the bolt and washer for the camshaft drive gear. Take out the camshaft gear by hand.

26. Pull off the balance shaft gear.

27. Remove the two intermediate plate retaining bolts, then remove the plate and gasket.

Engine block, as seen from the front

1. Intermediate plate   2. Retaining bolts

28. Remove the camshaft thrust plate, the key and the spacer, then carefully pull the camshaft out of the bearings (toward the front).

29. Carefully remove any ridges or carbon deposits from the upper end of the cylinder bores, using a scraper or milling cutter, without touching the piston ring travel area of the bores.

30. Mark all connecting rods and caps, so that they can be reinstalled in their original positions. Remove the bolts and caps and push the pistons, with connecting rods, out of the bores using the handle end of a hammer. When removing connecting rods and pistons, the connecting rod and cap must be marked as indicated in the illustration.

Connecting rod marking

31. Remove the bearing inserts from the connecting rods and caps, then mark the caps and rods so that they can be installed in their original positions.

32. Remove the crankshaft retaining bolt and remove the gear with tool GC 6306 or suitable gear puller.

33. Remove the flywheel. Before removing the crankshaft flange and flywheel, they must be marked with relation to one another.

34. Using a soft mallet, drive the balance shaft rearwards until the Welch plug is out. Carefully remove the balance shaft from the rear of the block.

35. Remove the bolts from the main bearing caps. Remove the main bearing caps, together with bearing inserts.

36. Lift the crankshaft carefully out of the block.

37. Remove the rear oil seal from the rear of the crank.

38. Remove the main bearing inserts from the caps and block and keep them in the proper order.

Engine Assembly

1. Place all bearings in position, after coating them lightly with oil.

2. Place the crankshaft carefully in the bearing seats.

3. Install the bearing caps and inserts. Apply a thin coat of sealing compound to the rear part of the contact surface of the rear main bearing cap. The arrows on the center and front main bearings must point to the front.

4. Tighten the front and rear bearing caps to 72 ft. lbs. Finger-tighten the bolts for the center bearing cap. Do not confuse the cylinder head bolts and the main bearing cap bolts—they are the same diameter, but the bolts for main bearing caps are 0.4" longer. After engine No. 74900, the bolts are an additional 0.4" longer and there is less danger of confusion.

5. Push the crankshaft forward and pry the center bearing cap to the rear. Tighten the cap bolts to a torque of 72 ft. lbs, while holding the crankshaft forward. This is necessary so that both halves of the bearing insert are equally capable of bearing axial loads.

6. Lubricate the inner diameter of the new crankshaft seal with engine oil and push the seal onto tool GC 6701-B (if available); in any case, drive seal into the main bearing until it bottoms. Fit piston rings, as described below, then go on to Step 7.

FITTING PISTON RINGS

New Or Rebored Cylinder

Push the piston rings one by one into the bore, using a piston turned upside down so that the ring takes the proper position. Measure the piston ring gap with a feeler gauge. The correct figures are found in the Engine Rebuilding Specifications Chart for Valves. If the gap is too small, the ring ends must be trimmed with a fine file.

Measuring piston ring end gap

Worn Cylinder

When installing piston rings into a worn bore, the ring gap must be measured with the ring in the lower piston reverse position, as the bore is the smallest at this point.

7. Install new connecting rod bolts. This should be done each time the crankshaft has been removed.

8. Coat the pistons, rings and cylinder bores with engine oil. Position the piston rings in the following manner:

The oil control ring center spring gap 180° from the mark on the top of the piston; the oil segments with the gaps staggered 1″

on either side of the center spring gap; the lower compression ring gap 150° from one side of the center spring gap, and the upper compression ring gap 150° from the other side of the center spring gap. Installation as above is essential for optimum seating and low oil consumption.

9. Install the piston, together with the connecting rod, using tool 786228 or other suitable ring compressor, by carefully driving the piston down with the handle of a hammer. Be certain the mark on the top of the piston faces forward.

10. If new bearings are installed, check the oil clearance. The procedure is described later.

11. Install the bearing inserts (dry) into the connecting rods, then coat them with oil. Put on the bearing caps and tighten the nuts to the proper torque.

12. Coat the balance shaft journals and bearings with engine oil and install the balance shaft from the rear end of the block.

13. Apply a thin coat of sealing compound to the new balance shaft Welch plug, then drive it into the block until it bottoms. Install with the flat side out.

14. Coat the two wedge-shaped seals with sealing compound and press them into the rear main bearing cap with a blunt screwdriver. The domed side of the seal must be turned to face the main bearing cap.

15. Install the flywheel, using new bolts.

Installing balance shaft cover plate

16. Locate the key in the crankshaft. Fasten the gear to the shaft using a bolt and washer; tighten to 36 ft. lbs. Do not tap the gear because this could damage the bearings.

17. Coat the camshaft bearings with engine oil and install the camshaft.

18. Install the spacer, with the countersunk side toward the camshaft; insert the key.

19. Put the thrust plate over the front of the camshaft so that it covers the main oil gallery hole. The spacer is a little thicker than the camshaft thrust plate. (The difference in measurement corresponds to the axial play in the camshaft.) To indicate the size group, the spacers have red or blue markings. When installing new parts, choose a spacer giving the correct axial play. (A red spacer gives a small clearance and a blue one a larger clearance.)

20. Apply a thin coat of sealing compound to the mounting surface of the intermediate plate on the front of the block; put the gasket on the block and install the plate loosely with the two retaining bolts. Temporarily install the two lower bolts as guide dowels, then tighten the two retaining bolts. Make sure the lower edge of the plate is in line with the level of the pan, then remove the guide bolts.

21. Turn the crankshaft until the mark on the crankshaft gear faces the camshaft.

22. Press the camshaft gear onto the camshaft so that the mark matches the mark on the crankshaft gear. Secure the camshaft gear with a retaining bolt and washer.

23. Install the balance shaft gear so that the mark matches the mark on the crankshaft gear.

24. Install a new balance shaft seal in the transmission cover (using tool GC 7600-B).

25. Apply a thin coat of sealing compound to the gasket mounting surfaces of the intermediate plate and transmission cover. Put the transmission cover gasket against the intermediate plate, then center the transmission cover (with the special pilot tool GC 6059 if possible) and fasten it with the nine bolts. To facilitate the installation of the water pump, fasten it to the transmission cover *before* installation.

26. Lubricate the inside of the balance shaft seal with engine oil. Line up the pulley keyway with the balance shaft key and install the pulley; fasten using bolt and flat washer.

27. Insert the oil pump driveshaft into the block (pointed end first). The stop plate on the shaft must be positioned 5.02" from the blunt end.

28. Install the oil pump and gasket. Tighten the pump bolts first, then the suction line bolt.

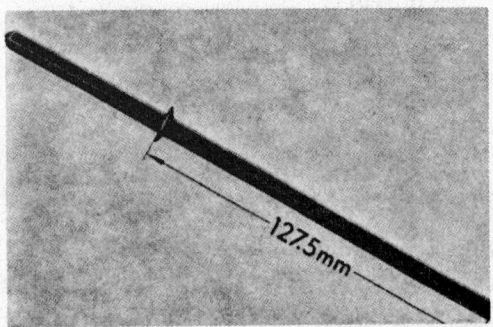

Oil pump drive shaft, with stop ring

29. Insert the rubber seal into the groove in the rear main bearing cap.

30. Apply a coat of sealing compound to the two corner joints where the transmission cover, the intermediate plate and the edges of the oil pan meet. Position the oil pan gasket on the block and insert the two tabs on the cork gasket under the recesses in the rear bearing cap rubber seal.

31. Install and secure the oil pan. Position the two bolts with the rubber washers at the rear balance shaft bearing; see arrows in illustration.

32. Lubricate the tappets and their bores with engine oil and install the tappets in their original positions.

Transmission gear timing marks properly aligned

Installing oil pan

33. Install cylinder head gaskets. The gaskets are marked "Front" and "Top."

34. Install the complete cylinder heads, insert the bolts and tighten all bolts in the sequence indicated to the correct torque, tightening in three stages: first to 40 ft. lbs., then to 50 ft. lbs. and finally to 68 ft. lbs.

35. Install the side stay bracket.

36. Dip the pushrod ends in engine oil and install the pushrods into their original tappets.

37. Lubricate the ends of the rocker arms with engine oil, then install the oil return plates and rocker arm assembly. Fasten the rocker arm assembly by alternately tightening the two bolts.

38. Apply sealing compound to the intake manifold gasket surfaces on the cylinder heads. Install the intake manifold gasket and make sure that the protruding part of the righthand cylinder head gasket enters the notch in the intake manifold gasket.

39. Install the intake manifold. Tighten the bolts and nuts in two stages, to the correct torque.

40. Install the thermostat, the gasket and thermostat housing cover.

41. Adjust the valve clearance as described later.

42. Install a new oil filter. Tighten by hand until the oiled rubber seal makes contact with the cylinder block, then tighten it another 1/2 turn.

43. Install the pump pushrod, gasket and fuel pump. Install the pushrod with the same end on the cam as before.

44. Apply sealing compound to the threads of the oil pressure gauge sender and install.

45. Install the water distribution pipe.

46. Install the clutch, after aligning the disc with tool No. 784064 or other suitable pilot shaft.

47. Install the carburetor and gasket.

48. Connect the fuel lines to the carburetor and fuel pump. Make certain the washers on connections are positioned properly.

49. Install spark plugs.

50. Install fanbelt pulley and fan.

51. Install alternator and bracket; adjust fanbelt (0.2–0.3″ deflection under thumb pressure).

52. Insert new gasket into valve cover grooves. Press the clamp ends of the gasket into the notches in the cover. Install and tighten the bolts equally to the proper torque. Cover with oil cap goes on right-hand bank. (Before replacing the covers, the lubrication of the rocker shaft should be checked with the engine running.)

53. Install the distributor.

54. Connect the vacuum line to the distributor.

55. Install the distributor cap and spark plug wires.

56. Install the dipstick.

57. Install the air filter.

SELECTING MAIN AND ROD BEARING INSERTS

Standard bearing inserts are of two thicknesses. One is marked with a red dot and one with a blue dot; they also have different part numbers. Blue inserts are slightly thicker than red ones; red inserts increase, blue inserts decrease, the clearance.

First, attempt to obtain the correct clearance by using red inserts, regardless of the color with which the engine block, the bearing caps, the crankshaft and connecting rods are marked. Should the clearance be too great with two red inserts, install a red and a blue one, or two blue ones, to obtain a lesser clearance. Should the clearance be too great with two blue insert. the crankshaft journals must be machined to the next possible undersize and inserts of the corresponding sub-class installed. *CAUTION: Never, under any circumstances, grind the bearing caps or place shims under the bearing inserts to reduce clearances.*

Measuring Bearing Oil Clearance

Clearance is measured using Plastigage. Plastigage is supplied in three thicknesses, type PG-1 (green) must be used, since this type permits measurement of 0.00098–0.00299″ clearances.

1. Support the engine with the cylinder head down to prevent crankshaft weight from affecting the measurement.

2. Make certain the parts to be measured are free of oil and dirt. Install a dry bearing insert into the bearing cap and put a strip

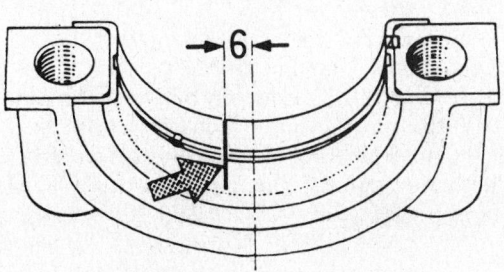

Proper location of Plastigage in bearing cap

of Plastigage into the insert, about 0.236″ off center.

3. Make sure the crankshaft is set about 30° after bottom dead center. With the crankshaft in this position, install the bearing cap with insert and Plastigage and

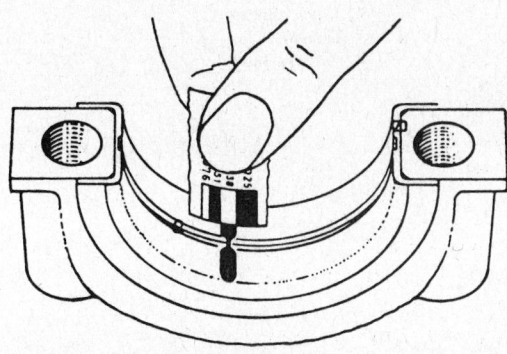

Measuring crushed Plastigage to determine oil clearance

tighten the bearing cap bolts to the prescribed torque. Do not rotate the crankshaft when measuring. When measuring connecting rod clearance, make sure the rod is not moved.

4. Remove the bearing cap. The Plastigage strip will be found pressed in the bearing cap or on crankshaft journal.

5. Using the scale printed on the Plastigage packing, measure the Plastigage at its widest point; do not touch it with the fingers.

Conicity (axial taper) of a crankshaft journal exists if one end of the flat pressed Plastigage strip is wider than the other.

After taking the above measurement, another measurement must be taken after turning the crankshaft through 90°. The difference between the two measurements indicates the ovality (egg-shape) of the journal.

Valve Train

ADJUSTING VALVE CLEARANCE

Rotate the engine by hand, while cold, until the mark on the pulley lines up with the dead center mark on the transmission cover. With both valve covers removed, rotate the engine very slightly back and forth; the rocker arms on the first (No. 1) or fourth (No. 4) cylinder will move slightly in opposite directions. If the No. 1 cylinder rockers move, rotate the engine, in the normal direction, one more full revolution and check again; No. 4 cylinder rockers should now move.

NOTE: *The balance shaft pulley, which carries the timing mark, normally rotates counterclockwise.*

With the engine in this position, check the valve clearance for No. 1 cylinder by inserting feeler gauges between the valve stems and the rocker arms. Turn locknuts to adjust clearance. Now, rotate the engine one-half turn (180°) in the normal (clockwise seen from front) direction of rotation until the No. 2 cylinder rockers move, then adjust the No. 3 cylinder valve clearance. Continue in the same manner, i.e., when the rocker arms of No. 1 cylinder move, the No. 4 cylinder valves are adjusted; when the rocker arms of No. 3 cylinder move, the No. 2 cylinder valves are adjusted. Intake valves are adjusted to 0.014″ cold; exhaust valves to 0.016″ cold.

ROCKER ARM DISASSEMBLY AND ASSEMBLY

Drive the roll pins out of the shaft, using a drift. Remove the spring washers and rocker shaft brackets. During assembly, the oil holes in the rocker arms must be turned down against the cylinder head. This position is marked by a ground area at the end of the rocker shaft; see arrow in illustration.

Drive a roll pin into the shaft, then install the various parts as indicated in the illustration. The rocker shaft bracket with the oil outlet must be positioned at the rear on the right-hand side of the engine and at the front on the left-hand side of the engine.

Engine Lubrication

Removal and replacement of the throw-away oil filter and the engine oil pan is covered under Engine Disassembly and Assembly. The oil pan cannot be removed with the engine installed in the car.

OIL PUMP CLEARANCES

To check the oil pump clearances:

1. Remove the oil pump as described under Engine Disassembly. Remove the oil pump cover.

2. Check the clearance between the sealing surface of the pump housing and the front sides of the outer and inner rotor, using a straightedge and a feeler gauge. The clearance should not exceed .004″. If necessary grind the sealing surface of the pump housing or the rotor sides with fine emery cloth on a face plate. New inner and outer rotors are available as replacement parts.

NOTE: *All grinding dust must be removed before reassembly.*

3. Check the clearance between the outer rotor and the pump housing with a feeler gauge. If the clearance exceeds .012″ with new rotors, the pump housing must be replaced.

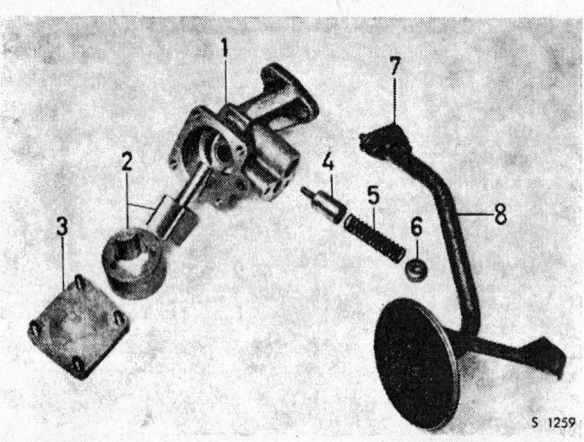

1. Housing
2. Inner and outer rotor
3. Cover
4. Relief valve

5. Spring
6. Cover plate
7. Gasket
8. Suction line

Exploded view of oil pump

Checking clearance between rotor sides and pump housing sealing surface

S 1135   Checking clearance between outer rotor and pump housing

Clutch and Transmission

Two-Stroke Clutch

The clutch in the two-stroke models is a single dry-plate type manufactured by Fichtel and Sachs or Borg and Beck.

The pressure plate assembly consists of a steel cover and cast pressure plate with six coil springs providing pressure. The unit is secured to the flywheel with six bolts.

A ball-type throwout bearing with a graphite or teflon coating is held in the clutch fork by two clip-type springs.

Clutch Removal

1. Remove engine, as previously described.

2. Loosen the six bolts that hold pressure plate to flywheel, placing spacers (tool No. 784209) as shown in the illustration.

Clutch Installation

1. Insert clutch disc and replace pressure plate assembly using spacers, as shown in illustration, to assure proper location of pressure plate in flywheel. Balanced clutch and flywheel combinations are color marked and should be assembled by locating the color marks as close to 180° apart as possible. Parts may be assembled in any position, or the same as they were before removal.

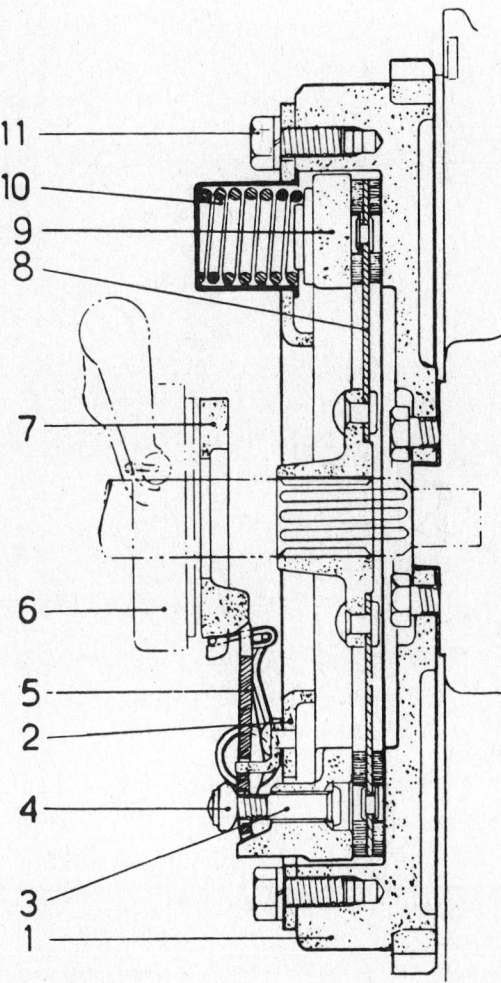

Two-stroke clutch assembly

1. Flywheel
2. Clutch cover
3. Stud
4. Adjusting nut
5. Clutch lever

6. Release bearing
7. Release plate
8. Clutch disc
9. Pressure plate
10. Spring
11. Screw

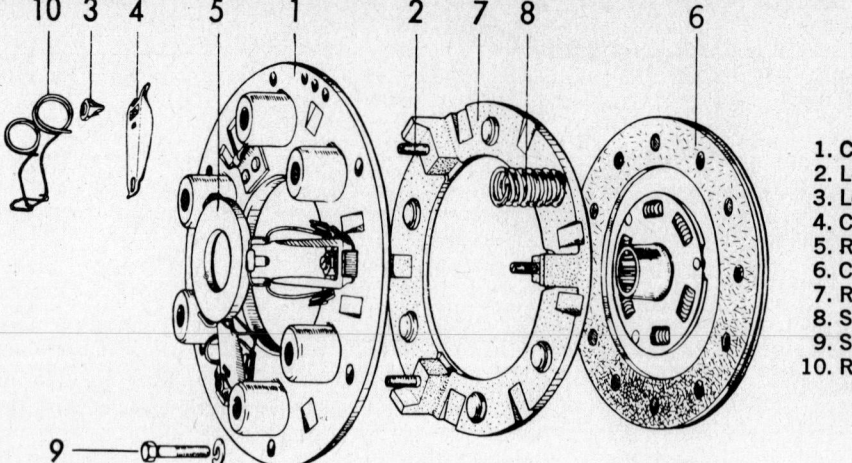

Exploded view of Fichtel and Sachs clutch assembly

1. Clutch cover
2. Lever screw
3. Locknut
4. Clutch lever
5. Release bearing
6. Clutch disc
7. Release plate
8. Spring
9. Screw
10. Retaining spring

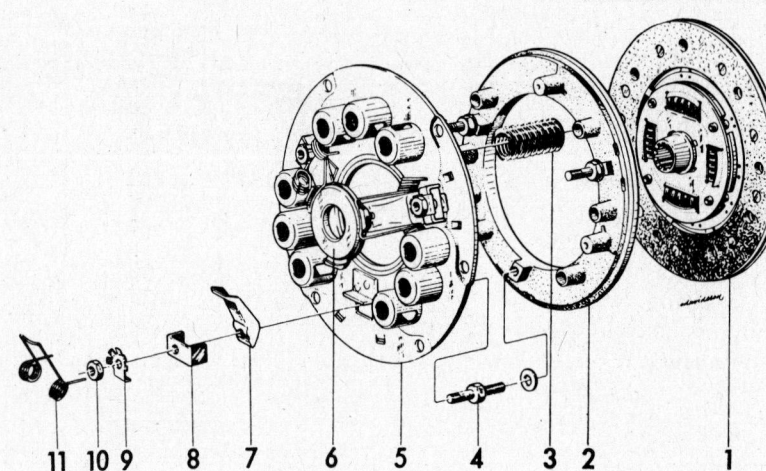

Exploded view of Borg and Beck clutch assembly

1. Disc
2. Release plate
3. Spring
4. Lever screw
5. Clutch cover
6. Release bearing
7. Clutch lever
8. Bracket
9. Washer
10. Nut
11. Spring

2. Center the clutch disc with arbor tool No. 78064 or a clutch shaft from an old transmission.

3. Tighten the six pressure plate bolts slowly and evenly and remove the spacers.

Clutch Adjustment—Hydraulic Type

The clutch pedal free-play is adjusted by means of an adjusting screw on the side of the clutch housing opposite the slave cylinder. The free-play is increased by turning the screw to the left. Check the clearance by pressing the slave cylinder connection towards the clutch arm—movement of 0.16″ (A), indicates the correct clutch clearance.

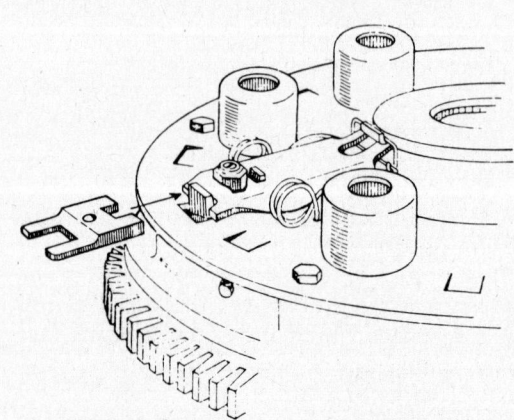

Fitting spacers when removing or installing pressure plate assembly

CLUTCH ADJUSTMENT—SONETT MECHANICAL LINKAGE

The adjustment screw on the clutch cable is accessible from the left side of the engine compartment. Screwing in increases pedal play and vice-versa. Adjust for a pedal play of 3/4–1″—clutch wear may cause the clearance to decrease to 3/8″ or so before clutch replacement is necessary.

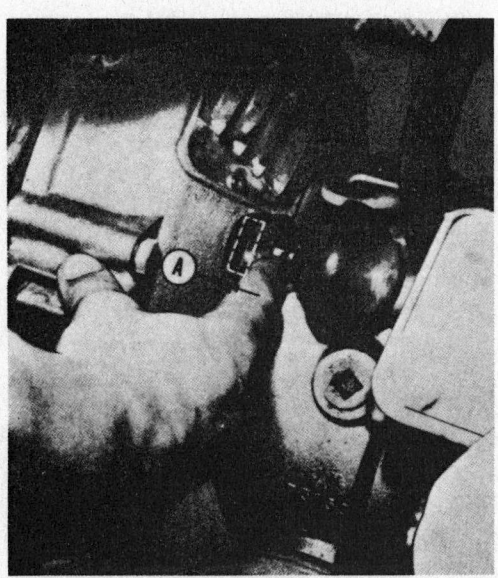

Adjusting clutch play. A=0.16″

REMOVAL AND INSTALLATION OF THROWOUT BEARING

1. Remove engine.
2. Turn clutch lever forward, along with the two spring clips that hold the bearing in the clutch fork. The graphite ring must not be worn flush with its retainer. If worn, replace ring or bearing assembly.
3. Reinstall in reverse sequence, making certain spring clips are properly located.

CLUTCH MASTER CYLINDER

Disassembly

To examine or renew parts, disconnect pushrod from pedal and remove from dash panel. Carefully move back the dust cap. Use longnose pliers to remove lock-ring. After removing pushrod, the entire piston assembly can be removed. The piston assembly can be disassembled by lifting the retainer spring leaf over the tongued end of the piston. Carefully remove the piston seal and the end seal. Push down on the piston return spring, allowing the valve spindle to slide through the key-shaped hole in the retainer so that the spring lets go. Remove the valve spacer carefully so as not to damage the elastic washer under the valve head. Remove the seal from the valve head.

If the cylinder bore is smooth, not scored or distorted, new seals may be installed safely.

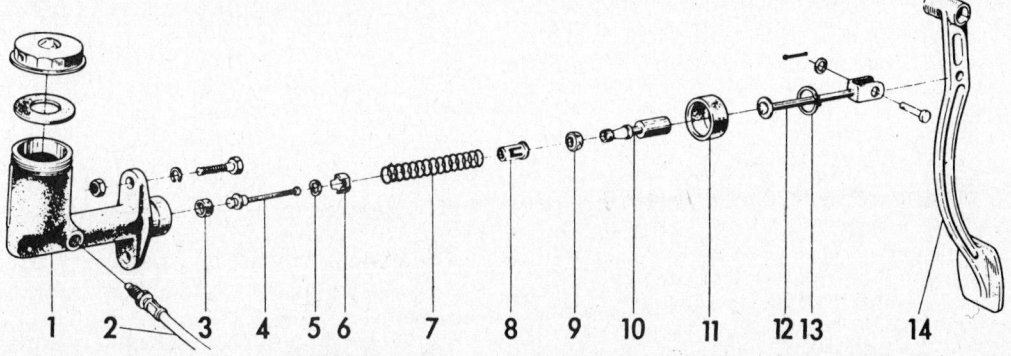

Exploded view of master cylinder, models through 1968

1. Cylinder housing
2. Hose
3. Seal
4. Rod
5. Elastic washer
6. Valve spacer
7. Spring
8. Spring retainer
9. Seal
10. Piston
11. Rubber dust cover
12. Pushrod with cupped washer
13. Lockring
14. Clutch pedal

Assembly

Place the valve seal with its flat side properly located on the valve head. Now, put on the elastic washer with the dished side facing the lower side of the valve head, holding it in position by means of the valve spacer, the legs turned toward the valve seal. Replace the piston return spring, centering it on the washer, then insert the valve spring retainer into the spring and press down until the valve spindle bottoms through the key-shaped hole. At the same time, make certain the spindle is correctly located in the middle of the retainer. Make certain the spring is still centered on spacer. Put a new piston seal onto the piston, with the flat side turned toward the front of the piston. Install a new end seal, with its lip facing the piston seal. Insert the small end of the piston into the retainer until the retainer spring engages the piston tongue; press the retainer fully home. Lubricate the piston thoroughly with Wakefield/Girling rubber grease #3 and place assembly into cylinder bore, valve end first, easing the piston seal lips slowly into the bore. Install the pushrod into the cylinder, with the dished side of the washer under the spherical head then install lock-ring and rubber cap.

SLAVE CYLINDER

Disassembly

Carefully move dust cap back and remove lock-ring with longnose pliers. Now, remove piston with seal and spring. If bore is smooth, not scored or distorted, a new seal may be installed.

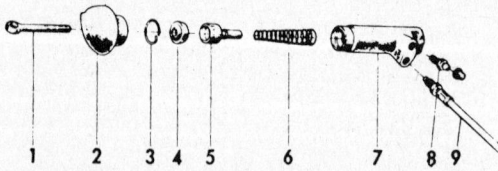

Exploded view of slave cylinder

1. Pushrod
2. Rubber dust cover
3. Lockring
4. Seal
5. Piston

6. Spring
7. Cylinder body
8. Bleedscrew
9. Hose

Assembly

Reverse the disassembly procedure, taking care to lubricate the seal and pack the rubber boot with Wakefield/Girling rubber grease #3. Always lubricate the cylinder bore with brake fluid.

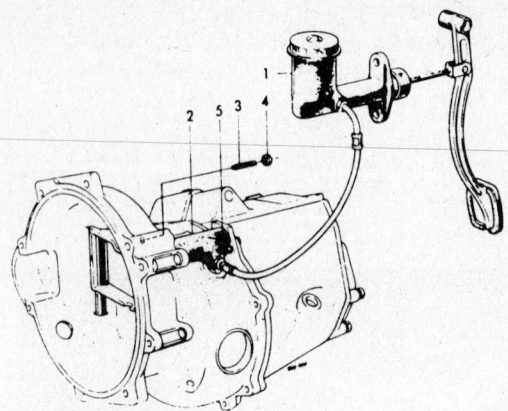

Clutch linkage

1. Master cylinder
2. Slave cylinder
3. Adjustment screw

4. Stop nut
5. Bleedscrew

BLEEDING THE MASTER AND SLAVE CYLINDER

Connect a hose to the bleed nipple on the slave cylinder and place the free end into a clean jar full of hydraulic fluid. Fill the master cylinder reservoir with brake fluid. Open the bleed nipple 1/2 turn and depress the clutch pedal. Close the bleed nipple just before the clutch pedal bottoms, then release the pedal. Repeat until no more air comes from the bleed hose. Top off the master cylinder. *NOTE: Discard the jar of fluid, because it is permeated with microscopic air bubbles.*

V4 Clutch

The clutch consists of a single dry plate disc, pressure plate assembly and release bearing.

The clutch plate consists of a resilient steel disc attached to a splined hub which slides on the clutch shaft. The clutch linings are riveted to both faces of the disc.

The pressure plate assembly, which consists of the clutch cover and a cast pressure plate kept under pressure by coil springs, is attached to the flywheel by means of bolts. The coil springs are kept in place by guides on the pressure plate and the clutch cover. Three clutch release levers are carried on struts, riveted to the clutch cover.

Clutch and flywheel assembly

1. Clutch housing and pressure plate
2. Clutch disc
3. Flywheel

The pressure plate assembly is held together by three clutch levers, which are secured by lugs on the struts. A spring-loaded steel disc, against which the release bearing is pressed during disengagement, rests on the inner ends of the clutch levers.

The release bearing consists of a ball bearing held in a bearing housing, which is retained in the clutch fork by springs. A graphite ring or teflon coating on the ball bearing presses against the release plate during disengagement. When replacing the release bearing it must be noted if the bearing has teflon coating. If so, the release plate must be surface ground and *not* teflon coated.

The clutch is hydraulically actuated, and service to this part of the system, including bleeding operations, is the same as for the similar two-stroke unit.

Clutch Removal

1. Remove the engine from the car.
2. Loosen evenly and remove the six bolts that hold the pressure plate assembly to the flywheel.
3. Remove the pressure plate assembly, then the clutch disc.

Clutch Installation

1. Place the clutch disc and pressure plate assembly against the flywheel; loosely insert the six retaining bolts.
2. Center the clutch disc with arbor tool No. 784064 or another suitable pilot shaft which fits into the pilot bearing in the crankshaft end.
3. Tighten the six retaining bolts evenly all around.
4. Install the engine.

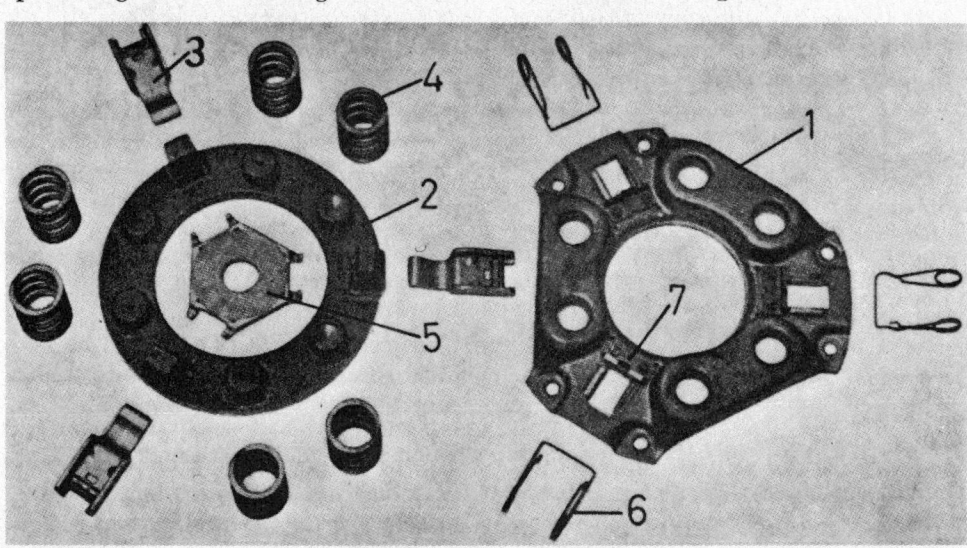

Exploded view of clutch—V4

1. Clutch cover
2. Pressure plate
3. Clutch release lever
4. Spring
5. Release plate
6. Retaining spring
7. Strut

Clutch Pedal Free-Play Adjustment

The clearance between the release bearing and release plate is gradually decreased by wear of the clutch linings.

Adjust the clutch pedal free-play by turning the screw on the clutch housing.

The free movement is increased by loosening the screw (turning to the left).

The clearance is checked by moving the slave cylinder connection to the clutch arm. A movement of 0.16″ here indicates the correct clutch clearance.

Three-Speed Transmission and Differential

Removal

NOTE: SAAB recommends that the engine and transmission be removed together, and then separated.

1. Remove engine.
2. Disconnect freewheel control.
3. Remove rear clutch cylinder bracket and wire cylinder out of way.
4. Remove gearshift shaft joint from the transmission. If both ends of the conical pin are threaded, transfer the nut and use it to remove the pin. A conical pin threaded on only one end is removed by means of tool 784083 or by backing off nut until flush with threads, then tapping gently with hammer.

5. Disconnect speedometer cable from transmission.
6. Peel back or remove front floor mat, then remove rubber plugs to provide access to rear engine mount center bolt.

On older models, a section of the pedal housing must be removed. Remove the center bolt, using a 9/16″ socket wrench.

7. If the tapered engine mount will not move, tap it off with a punch.
8. Remove the steering arm from the upper ball joint on the right steering knuckle housing, then pull the middle driveshaft from the inner joint. On the SAAB Sport, 1966 up, model 95 and 96, and the Monte Carlo 850, the steering knuckle need not be loosened.
9. As the transmission is lifted, move it slightly to the right so that the left driveshaft comes out of the joint. On the SAAB Sport, Monte Carlo 850, and SAAB 95 and 96 from 1966, use care not to remove the inner drivers (which contain needle bearings).

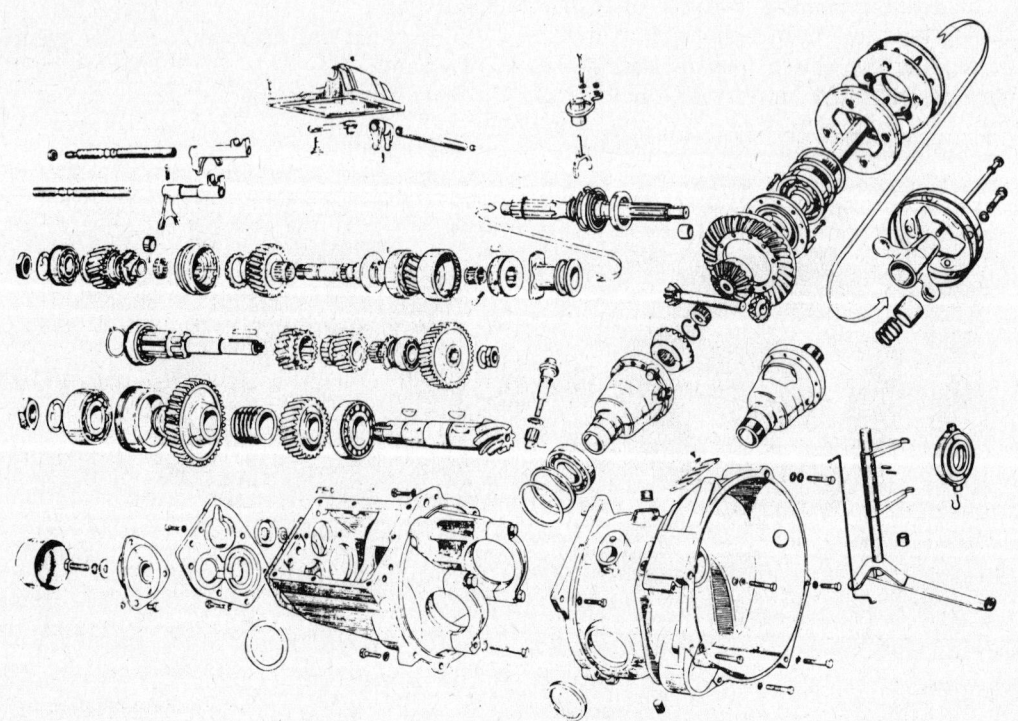

Exploded view of three-speed transmission

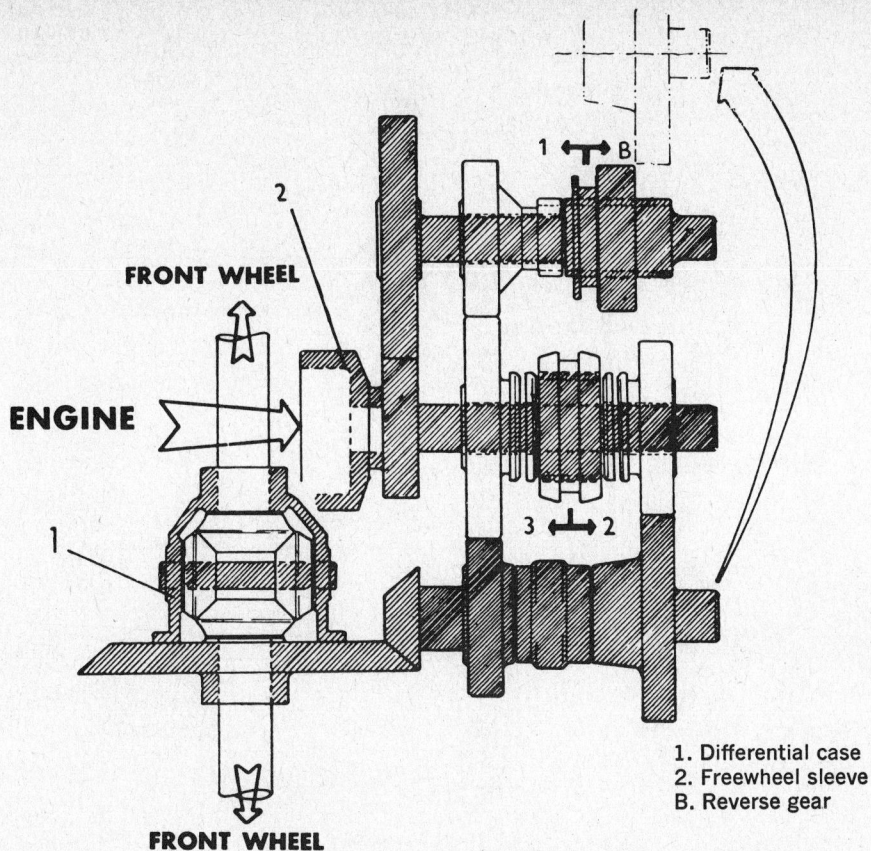

FRONT WHEEL

ENGINE

FRONT WHEEL

1. Differential case
2. Freewheel sleeve
B. Reverse gear

Power flow in three-speed transmission

DISASSEMBLY

The methods described here are derived from factory-recommended procedures, which require special tools. Substitutes for these tools will become obvious as the job progresses. For example, it would be impractical to buy the special transmission jig that the dealer uses, but a large bench vise and suitable arbors and sleeves cut from pipe or other stock can serve the same purpose.

1. Clean outside of transmission and drain all the oil.

2. Remove the inner universal joint with shafts. On the SAAB 96, the joints are connected to the side gears by means of a bolt which passes through the shaft centers.

3. Separate the transmission unit at the joint between the clutch housing and the transmission case. The clutch shaft will have to be turned to a certain position while removing the differential case.

4. Install the transmission case into the fixture, tool No. 784100, as illustrated (if available).

5. Check location of pinion and measure ring gear backlash for correct setting, as described later.

6. Remove the two bearing caps and lift out differential. Keep the spacers and shims for each of the two bearings separate and note their positions.

7. Remove freewheel hub, with the six rollers, from its sleeve, using tool No. 784068 and a strong rubber band to prevent the spring-loaded rollers from being thrown out. Next, remove the needle bearing. Make certain none of the rollers are missing.

8. If the pinion shaft or bearings are to be removed, measure the location of the pinion shaft before removing the end cover.

Gearshift Forks

9. Remove the transmission case cover.

10. Remove the end cover and attached shift fork rail for 2nd and 3rd gears. Take care to prevent the ejection of the poppet ball. Keep the shims and gasket in their respective positions.

11. If only the rear pinion shaft bearing is to be removed, it can be done now. Back

1., 3., 4. Spacers and shims
2. Differential case
5. Caps

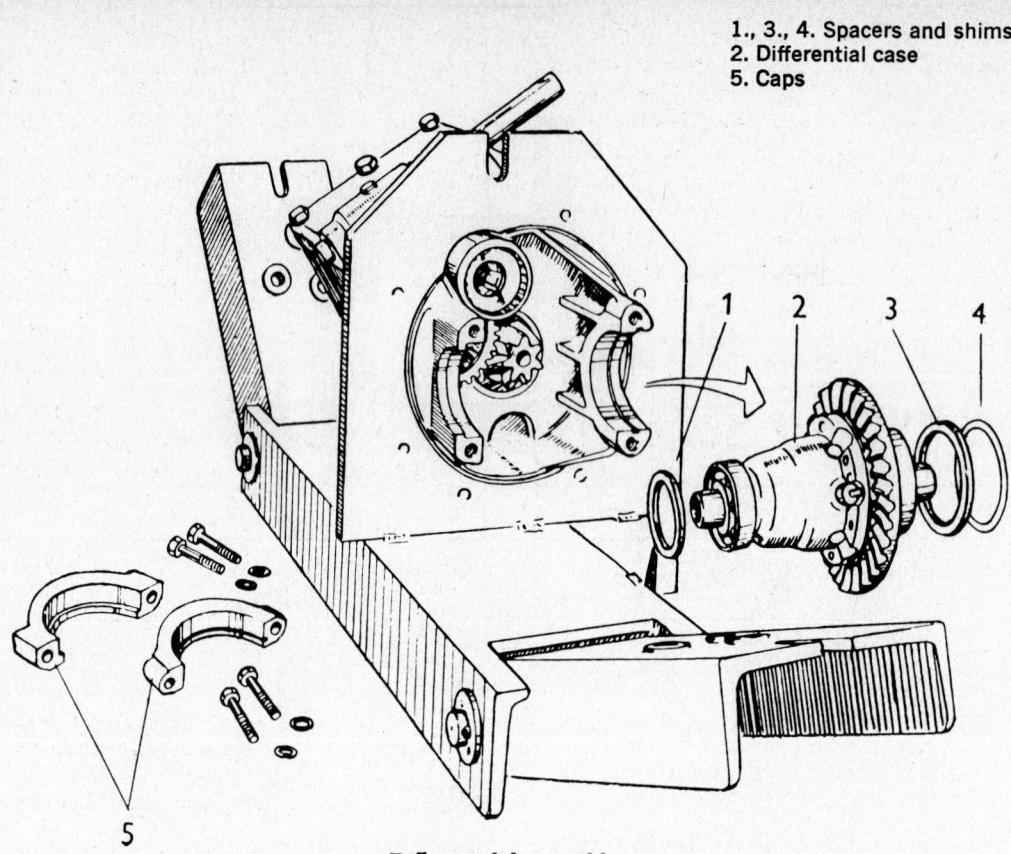

Differential disassembly

off the left-hand thread nut and extract
bearing with tool No. 784101 or other suitable puller.

12. Using a screwdriver, push 1st and
reverse shift fork rail through the end of the
transmission case. Take care to prevent
ejection of poppet ball.

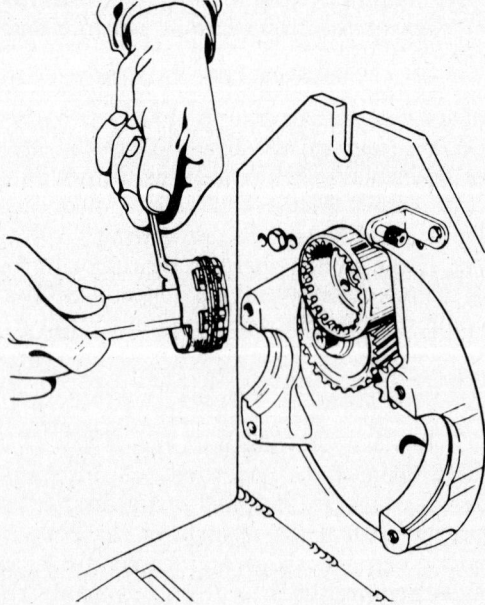

Disassembling freewheel hub using special tool
No. 784068

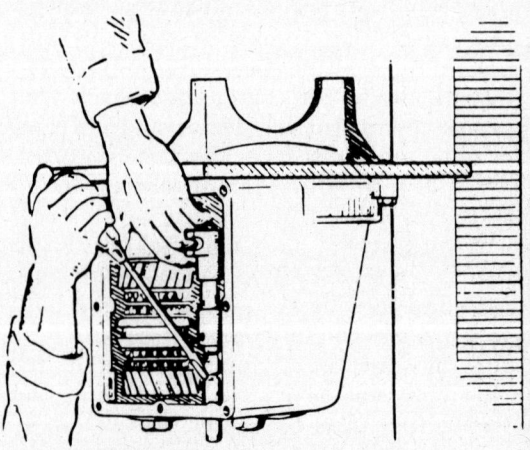

Disassembling 1st and Reverse shift fork

Countershaft with Bearings and Gears

13. Shift the synchronizer sleeves to engage two gears at the same time.

14. Back off the nut at front of countershaft. Remove friction wheel and washer. Also back off the end nuts of the primary and pinion shafts if they are to be removed. The pinion shaft nut has left-hand thread.

15. Lift the front end plate of the fixture and make it fast.

16. Locate arbor tool No. 784110, fitted with the shortest point, between the front press screw and the countershaft. Press in shaft until arbor rests hard against the gear. Change the arbor point to the next longest one and press again. Repeat procedure once more with the longest point until the bearing and countershaft are released. Remove tool and drop fixture end plate.

17. Lift the front end of the countershaft, hold the gears with one hand and pull the shaft through the rear bearing hole. Remove the gears. Note the washer between the 1st speed gear and ball bearing; take the two needle bearings from inside 1st gear.

18. Remove retaining ring and drive ball bearing off the shaft.

19. Using an arbor, carefully drive or tap the remaining bearing toward the differential side. Note the retaining ring behind the bearing.

Primary Shaft with Bearings and Gears

20. Put the rear press screw of the fixture against the primary shaft and locate the arbor tool No. 784104 between screw and shaft.

21. Press shaft out to the front until it is released from the bearings.

22. Extract shaft in forward direction.

23. Hold the synchronizer unit and gears and allow the washer to drop from between the 2nd speed gear and the ball bearing into the case. Lift out gear and synchronizer as a unit.

24. If the twin needle bearings in the 3rd speed gear hub did not come with shaft, remove shaft.

25. Remove the needle bearings from the 2nd speed hub.

26. Disassemble synchronizer.

27. Drive the rear primary shaft bearing out of the case with the press screw in the front end of the fixture, using tool No. 784109 and sleeve No. 784106.

28. Remove the thrust washer and locking pin from shaft.

29. Remove the retaining ring and press ball bearing from the shaft.

Pinion Shaft with Bearings and Gears

30. Attach puller, tool No. 784101, to pinion shaft bearing sleeve and pull sleeve out with bearing. Use the front press screw of the fixture for support against the drive pinion. Collect the spacer and shims from inside the bearing.

31. On transmissions with aluminum casings, use puller No. 784115 instead, as the construction is the same as with the four-speed unit.

32. Remove the speedometer drive gear.

33. Put the rear fixture press screw against the pinion shaft and press out forward. As soon as the unit is free, remove the shaft and lift the gears out of the transmission case.

34. If necessary, drive the roller bearings off the pinion shaft.

ASSEMBLY

1. After making certain all parts are completely clean, begin reassembly at the appropriate point.

When fitting new gears, the following are supplied in matched sets.

3rd speed gear—pinion shaft 3rd gear
2nd speed gear—pinion shaft 2nd gear
pinion shaft   —ring gear

For quiet operation, it is essential that gears be replaced in complete sets and installed with matching numbers facing the same side.

Pinion Shaft with Bearings and Gears

2. Press the roller bearing onto the pinion shaft with a sleeve or tool No. 784106 and locate the two Woodruff keys in their grooves. The keys are of different sizes, the thinner one is intended for 2nd gear.

3. Fit the 2nd and 3rd gears into the case, along with the speedometer drive gear. Locate the speedometer drive gear with the beveled side facing the differential. The matching number on the pinion shaft 3rd gear should face the same direction as the number on the 3rd speed gear.

4. Insert the pinion shaft from the front.

5. Locate the 3rd gear in relation to keyway. Make sure the speedometer drive gear is properly engaged, then locate the 2nd gear in relation to the keyway.

6. Locate the front press screw of the fixture against the pinion shaft and press carefully, a fraction of an inch, so that the pinion rides on the shaft. The pinion shaft 2nd gear will now rest against the rear of the case. Make certain that it is at right angles to the pinion shaft.

7. Back off the press screw a few turns, while supporting the gears, and locate the aligning arbor tool No. 784102 in the rear bearing seat. Be sure the shaft end passes into the arbor.

8. Press the arbor in until its flange is flush against the end of the case; leave the press screw in this position.

9. Use the opposite press screw to drive the pinion shaft in from the front until the roller bearing is hard against the 3rd gear.

10. Back off the press screws and remove arbor from the rear bearing seat.

11. Put a spacer 0.14″ thick on the end of the shaft. If the pinion shaft or any other parts have not been replaced, use the previously fitted spacer and shims.

12. Refit the twin bearing in its sleeve—the bearing marking should face inwards.

13. Drive in the bearing and sleeve assembly with the press screw and arbor tool No. 784102, using the press screw on the opposite end of fixture for support of the pinion shaft.

14. Fit a new tabbed retaining washer onto the pinion shaft and screw on the left-hand thread nut. Turn the tab of the washer outwards. Don't tighten the nut with a torque wrench until the primary shaft and countershaft have been installed.

15. Replace the speedometer drive.

Primary Shaft with Bearings and Gears

16. Drive the ball bearing onto the primary shaft and install retaining ring. Use tool No. 784107, if available.

17. Install locking pin in shaft and fit the thrust washer behind the ball bearing retainer so that the pin drops into the groove, preventing it from rotating.

18. Reassemble the 3rd speed gear, complete with twin needle bearing, synchronizer unit with rings and 2nd speed gear without its bearings. Pass this assembly into the transmission case and install aligning arbor tool No. 784114 into the end of the case so that it enters the 2nd speed gear hub.

19. Install the primary shaft from the front, turning it gently back and forth so its lands enter the synchronizer hub.

20. Fit arbor tool No. 784104 into the freewheel sleeve. The needle bearing must be removed from the freewheel sleeve to prevent damage.

21. Raise and lock both ends of the fixture and support the arbor in the 2nd speed hub with the rear press screw.

22. Drive in the primary shaft carefully, from the front towards the arbor, using the press screw. Make certain the synchronizer hub slides easily on the shaft.

23. Back off the rear press screw and remove the arbor from the 2nd speed gear hub.

24. Put the needle bearings and steel bushing in the 2nd speed gear and fit the washer onto the shaft. The beveled side of the washer should face outwards.

25. Drive in the primary shaft rear bearing with the rear press screw and tool No. 784109. The press screw and 784104 at the freewheel sleeve will help support the shaft.

26. Back off the press screws and remove the arbors.

27. Install a new tabbed washer, tab facing outwards, and the end nut. Don't tighten with torque wrench until the countershaft is installed.

Countershaft with Bearings and Gears

28. If the countershaft front ball bearing has been removed, drive it into the case from the differential side, until it is tight against the retaining ring. Raise and lock the rear plate of the fixture and drive in the bearing with the press screw and arbor tool No. 784108.

29. Put the countershaft gear on the outside of the bearing, holding it with tool No. 784108. Hold with front press screw against the bearing. The machined part of hub must face clutch housing.

30. Assemble the reverse gear and 1st speed gear, with its two needle bearings and washer. Mount these parts as a unit, inserting the countershaft through the rear bearing seat at the same time. If the rear bearing has not been removed from the shaft it can remain in position during reassembly, providing the retaining ring is taken off.

31. Drive in the shaft using the rear press screw and arbor tool No. 784104. Be certain that the shaft passes into the countershaft gear. If the shaft is driven in complete with bearing, tool No. 784109 should be used. This tool also is used to install the ball bearing after installation of the shaft. Make sure to install the ball bearing retaining ring.

32. Shift the synchronizer units to engage two gears at the same time and turn the 3rd speed gear to align the keyways in the countershaft and the countershaft gear. Using an arbor, drive in the key as far as it goes.

33. Install a new retaining ring with tab facing inwards, or mount the friction wheel, with a new friction washer and star washer. Make certain the friction wheel is not located outside the opposing gear and that there is sufficient clearance between the primary shaft ball bearing and the countershaft gear. Tighten the countershaft end nut to 60 ft. lbs. torque, and the primary shaft nut to 35 ft. lbs. Tighten the pinion shaft nut initially to a torque of 90 ft. lbs., then back off and retighten to 45 ft. lbs.

34. Return the synchronizer sleeves to the neutral position.

35. Lock the primary shaft nut. The pinion shaft nut also may be locked unless further adjustments are to be made.

36. Check the end cover shims and adjust if necessary.

Gearshift Forks

37. Insert the spring and poppet ball into the 1st and reverse gearshift fork. Put the fork in position and install shaft. To simplify this job, use tool No. 784069 to hold the poppet ball in place.

38. Put the 2nd and 3rd gearshift fork in place, with the spring and poppet ball assembled.

39. Check that the rubber washer and the plastic plug are mounted in the end cover and that the oil collector is mounted in the transmission case end.

40. Fit the 2nd and 3rd gearshift fork rail to the end cover. Coat the shims lightly with grease to hold them in place, coat both sides of the gasket with Permatex No. 3 and slide the rail and cover into place. Tighten the end cover bolts to 18 ft. lbs.

41. If necessary, back off the locknut and adjust the 2nd and 3rd gearshift fork so that it is not under axial pressure with 2nd and

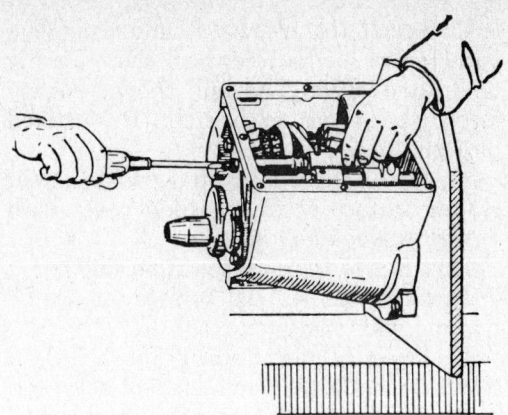

Adjusting 2nd and 3rd shift fork shaft

3rd gears engaged. There must be a definite clearance between the synchronizer sleeve and its respective gear.

Differential Freewheel

42. Check the drive pinion setting and adjust if necessary. Before measuring the drive pinion setting, be sure to tighten the pinion shaft end nut and end cover bolts to the correct torque.

43. After adjusting drive pinion, check that the shaft nut is locked.

44. Place the differential and ring gear in the bearing seats and adjust the backlash between the drive pinion and ring gear.

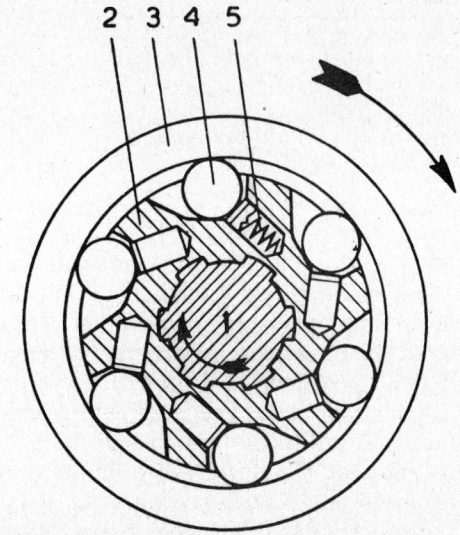

Freewheel assembly

1. Clutch shaft
2. Freewheel hub
3. Freewheel sleeve
4. Roller
5. Coil spring

45. Install the freewheel hub, complete with rollers in the freewheel sleeve, using tool No. 784068. The hub should engage firmly when turned to the right. It is marked on front face.

46. Put all gears in neutral position; coat sealing surface of transmission cover with Permatex No. 3 and install.

47. Remove transmission from fixture.

48. Coat the sealing surface of clutch housing with Permatex No. 3.

49. Place needle bearing in freewheel sleeve. Check the clutch shaft seal and

eight disassembly instructions of the three-speed unit also apply to the four-speed unit. outwards. Fill the space between the lips with grease.

50. Bolt the clutch housing to the transmission case. Turn the clutch shaft so it clears the differential; drive in the locating pin.

51. Refit the inner universal joints and shafts. Use care not to damage seals.

52. Coat the clutch shaft with graphite grease and fill the transmission with transmission oil.

Shim Selection Chart

Location of Shims or Part	4-Speed Transmission			3-Speed Transmission		
	Spare-Part No.	Thickness (in.)	Thickness (mm)	Spare-Part No.	Thickness (in.)	Thickness (mm)
On primary shaft	708093	0.004	0.10	708093	0.004	0.10
	708101	0.006	0.15	708101	0.006	0.15
	708102	0.012	0.30	708102	0.012	0.30
On countershaft	708094	0.004	0.10	708093	0.004	0.10
	708103	0.006	0.15	708101	0.006	0.15
	708104	0.012	0.30	708102	0.012	0.30
On pinion shaft	708095	0.004	0.10	708095	0.004	0.10
	708105	0.006	0.15	708105	0.006	0.15
	708106	0.012	0.30	708106	0.012	0.30
End cover	708058			710432		
Gasket	716754		(thin)	710430		(thin)

Four-Speed Transmission and Differential

DISASSEMBLY

The methods described here are derived from factory-recommended procedures, which require special tools. Substitutes for these tools will become obvious as the job progresses. For example, it would be impractical to buy the special transmission jig that the dealer uses, but a large bench vise and suitable arbors and sleeves cut from pipe or other stock can serve the same purpose.

1. The removal procedure and the first eight disassembly instructions of the three-speed unit also apply to the four-speed unit.

Gearshift Forks

2. Remove end cover bolts and drive out the 1st, 2nd and 3rd, and 4th gearshift fork shaft (from the front).

3. Remove cover rearwards, keeping the gearshift forks in position. Note the location

Mounting transmission case in factory disassembly fixture

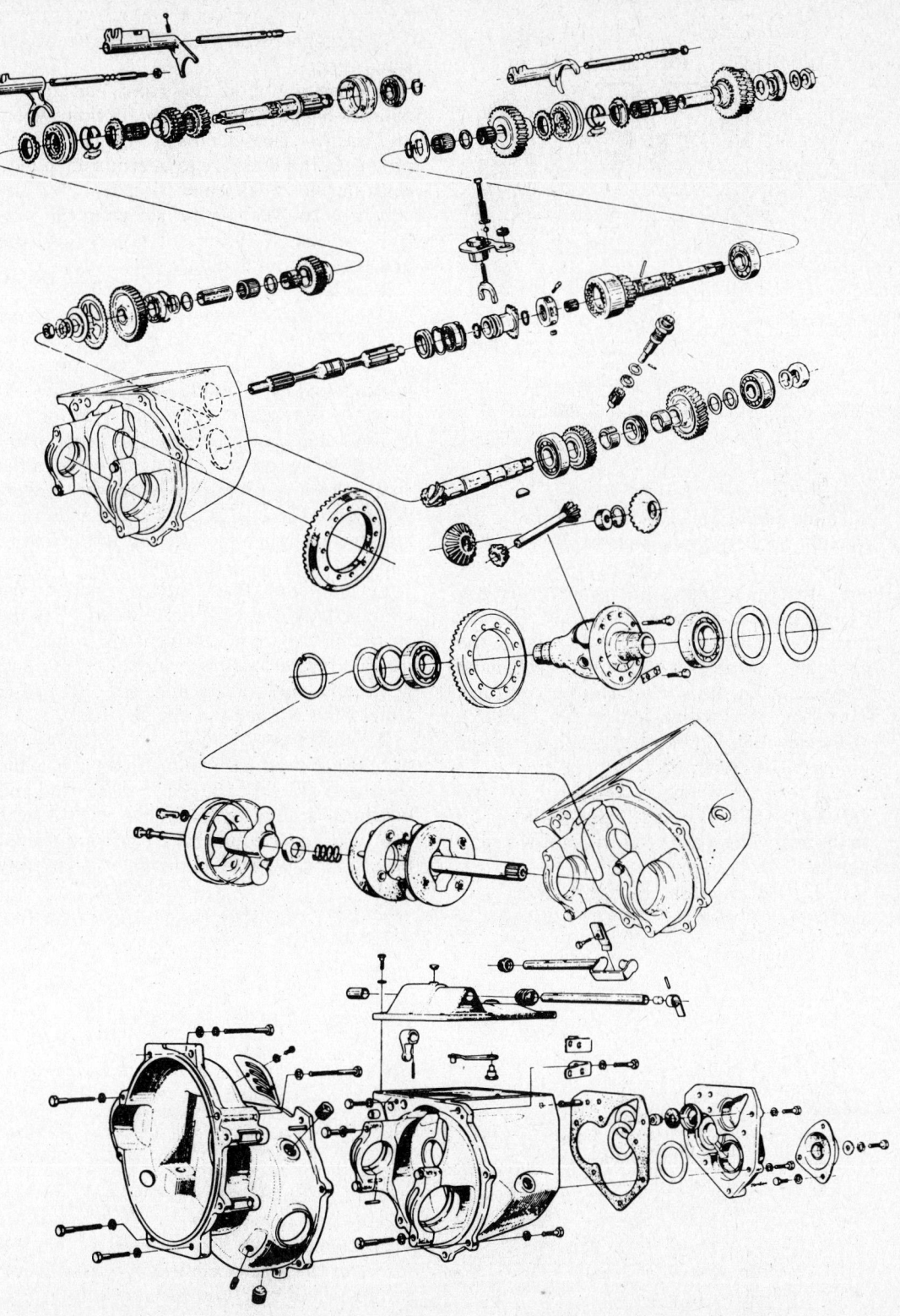

Exploded view of four-speed transmission

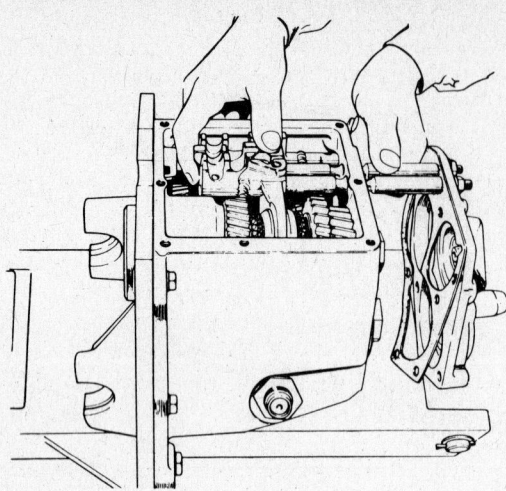

Disassembling end cover and shift fork rails

of shims and collect the shims. Prevent the ejection of the poppet balls in the gearshift forks.

4. If only the rear pinion shaft bearing is to be removed, it can be done now. Engage two gears (3rd and reverse), release the retaining washer and back off the left-hand thread nut on the shaft. The bearing now can be removed with a puller (No. 784115), and a new bearing can be installed and the pinion shaft shimmed.

5. Use a brass driver to release the reverse gearshift fork shaft and withdraw it to the rear. Prevent the ejection of the poppet ball.

6. Lift out the three gearshift forks.

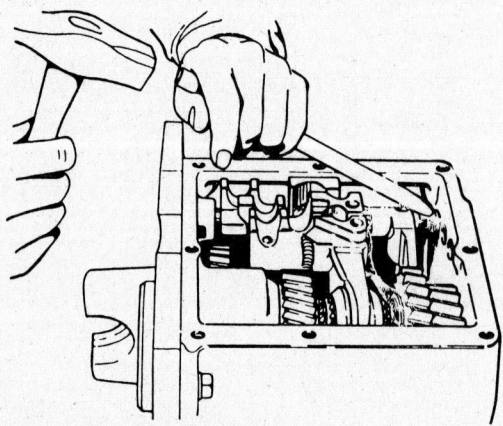

Driving out reverse shift fork rail

Countershaft with Bearings and Gears

7. Engage reverse and 3rd gears at the same time.

8. Loosen nut at the front end of the countershaft. Remove the friction wheel and washer. Loosen nuts of the primary and pinion shaft if these are to be removed; pinion shaft nut has a left-hand thread.

9. Return synchronizer sleeve to the neutral position. Lift up and fasten the front end plate of the fixture.

10. Place arbor tool No. 786058, with shortest point between the front press screw and the countershaft, and press in until the arbor is against the gear. Meanwhile, supporting tool No. 784125 should be located between 1st speed gear and rear of the transmission case. Change the arbor point to the next longer one and again press in the shaft. Repeat procedure with the longest point until the bearing and countershaft are released. Remove tools and drop the fixture end plate.

11. Pull the shaft out rearwards; the countershaft gear will be released. Let the spacer at the front bearing drop while lifting the entire assembly, including the two gears and synchronizer unit, out of the case. Collect the washer and key.

If necessary:

a. Remove the retaining ring from the shaft and drive off the rear ball bearing and bearing seat in order to remove reverse gear.

b. The front countershaft bearing cannot be changed without removing the primary shaft.

Primary Shaft with Bearings and Gears

12. Remove the end nut and retaining washer. Lift up and fasten the rear plate of the fixture.

13. Place an arbor tool (No. 784104) between the rear press screw and shaft and press in the shaft until it is released from the bearings.

14. Remove the shaft forwards; let the spacer at the rear bearing drop while lifting out gears and synchronizer as a unit.

15. After removal of primary shaft, the front bearing can be removed by tapping it gently toward the differential side.

16. Drive out the rear primary shaft bearing using the front press screw, tool No. 784109 and extension sleeve No. 784106.

If necessary:

a. Remove the thrust washer and locking pin from the shaft.

b. Remove the retaining ring and drive off the front bearing.

Pinion Shaft with Bearings and Gears

17. Remove the speedometer gear drive.

18. Remove the left-hand thread shaft nut and pull out rear pinion shaft bearing with a puller (tool No. 784115), using front press screw to support the shaft. Collect the spacer and shims from inside the bearing.

19. Locate the supporting tool (No. 784121) on the lower side of the shaft between the rear gear and the front end of the case. Make sure the tool is centered on the gear so that the gear does not tip and bind on the shaft.

20. Lift and fasten the rear end plate of fixture, then drive out the shaft forwards, using the press screw, until the roller bearing clears the front of case. Remove the tool and drop end plate of fixture. Lift out the 3rd gear while drawing shaft from case. Retrieve the Woodruff key.

If necessary:

a. Press the front roller bearing and pinion shaft 4th gear from the shaft as follows: Remove the retaining ring from the roller bearing. Place the pinion shaft and supporting tool (No. 784123) in a press and drive out shaft. Make sure the outer bearing race is flush against the gear. The bearing should not be taken apart if it is to be reused; make sure that the rollers do not fall out and install the retaining ring immediately.

b. Press oil collector gently out of the case.

When installing new gears, remember that the 3rd speed gear and pinion shaft 3rd gear are supplied in matched sets, as are the 4th speed gear and the pinion shaft 4th gear. Quiet operation is assured only if gears are replaced in sets. The pinion shaft and ring gear are also matched sets and must be replaced as sets. Install the gears so that the matching numbers face the same way.

ASSEMBLY

Pinion Shaft with Bearings and Gears

1. Locate the front roller bearing, pinion shaft 4th gear, spacers and speedometer drive gear on the pinion shaft. Using a press and tool (No. 784106), drive in the bearing and pinion shaft 4th gear until the inner bearing race is flush with the drive pinion. Check that the matching number faces the same way as on the 4th speed gear.

2. Next, put the pinion shaft into the case from the differential side and place the pinion shaft 3rd gear on the shaft inside the case. Be certain the Woodruff key for the 3rd gear is in the pinion shaft. In some older units, the pinion shaft 4th gear also is held by a key.

3. Turn the shaft to line up the Woodruff key and the keyway in the 3rd gear.

4. Place a guiding arbor tool (No. 784122) in the rear bearing seat so that the pinion shaft passes into it.

5. Secure the arbor with the rear press screw so that the flange is flush with the case.

6. Drive the pinion shaft into place using the front press screw. Be certain the key enters the groove in the 3rd gear.

7. Loosen the rear press screw and remove the arbor from the bearing seat.

8. Place a 0.14″ spacer on the end shaft. If the rear pinion bearing has a split inner ring, the spacer must be placed next to the bearing.

9. Using the press screw and arbor (No. 784122), press the rear ball bearing, with retaining ring, into the case. Use the press screw at the front end of the pinion shaft for support. In the case of a split bearing, first fit the inner ring, then the remaining part, and press in as described above.

10. Loosen the rear press screw and drop both fixture end plates.

11. Install a new tabbed washer onto the pinion shaft, with tab facing out. Install the left-hand thread nut, but don't tighten it with a torque wrench until primary shaft and countershaft are installed.

Primary Shaft with Bearings and Gears

12. Up to and including transmission No. 276503: refit the front bearing, using tool No. 784107, and place retaining ring, locking pin thrust washer and 4th speed gear needle

bearing on the primary shaft. Be certain the locking pin prevents the thrust washer from rotating.

From Transmission No. 276504: fit the oil slinger and front bearing, using tool No. 784107, and place the retaining ring, washer and 4th speed gear needle bearing on the primary shaft.

13. Before pressing in the primary shaft, the countershaft front bearing must be in position. Press in the bearing from the front, using the arbor tool No. 786134, until it is hard against the retaining ring in the bearing seat.

14. Assemble the primary shaft components, the 3rd and 4th speed gears and the synchronizer sleeve and rings, then place the entire assembly into the case while passing the aligning arbor (No. 784114) into the 3rd speed gear through the rear bearing seat. Secure the arbor with the press screw.

15. Slide in the shaft from the front until its splines enter the synchronizer hub.

16. Put arbor tool No. 784104 into the freewheel hub. The needle bearing must be removed from the freewheel sleeve while this is being done.

17. Lift and fasten the front end plate of the fixture and carefully drive in the primary shaft against the arbor in the freewheel sleeve, using the press screw if a fixture is available, until the 3rd speed gear is tight against the rear case. Check that the synchronizer hub does not tip and bind.

18. Remove the aligning arbor from the 3rd speed gear and place the needle bearing spacer sleeve and bushing for this gear onto the shaft inside the gear hub.

19. Place the spacer, with the beveled side facing outwards, and the rear bearing on the primary shaft and drive in the bearing using tool No. 784109. The front press screw and the arbor in the freewheel sleeve will support the shaft.

20. Loosen the press screws and drop the rear fixture end.

21. Place a new tabbed washer, with tab facing outward, and a nut on the shaft. Do not tighten with torque wrench until countershaft is installed.

Countershaft with Bearings and Gears

22. Raise and fasten the front plate of fixture and place countershaft gear in position, with the machined part facing the clutch bearing. Use front press screw and tool No. 786134 to hold the countershaft gear and shaft gear.

23. Reassemble the 1st and 2nd speed gears, the 2nd speed complete with needle bearing, spacer and bushing and synchronizer unit with its rings.

24. Place this assembly into the case, passing the countershaft needle bearing, complete with 1st speed gear, through the rear of the case at the same time. If the rear bearing, bearing seat and reverse gear have not been removed, they may remain on the shaft during reassembly. In this case, however, the bearing first must be pressed into the seat and the rear retaining ring removed from the shaft.

25. Put the spacer on the shaft between the 2nd speed gear and the front ball bearing, then slide the shaft through the front bearing and into the countershaft gear.

26. Drive in the countershaft with the press screw and tool No. 784109. Make certain that the shaft splines engage with the synchronizer hub and the shaft passes into the countershaft gear. Use a pin wrench, tool No. 784124, to turn the shaft. Drop both fixture end plates and fasten the rear bearing with the retaining ring (after pressing it in). If countershaft is reinstalled, complete with reverse gear and bearing, use tool No. 784109. This tool also is used if the reverse gear and the seat with the bearing are mounted separately.

27. Engage 2nd and 4th gears at the same time and turn the 3rd speed gear in order to align the keyway in the countershaft gear. Drive in the key using an arbor.

28. Refit the friction wheel, together with new friction and star washers. Tighten countershaft end nut to 60 ft. lbs. Tighten the pinion shaft nut initially to 90 ft. lbs., back off and retighten to 45 ft. lbs. The primary shaft nut must be tightened to 35 ft. lbs. Check that the friction wheel is not located outside the opposing gear and that there is enough clearance between the primary shaft ball bearing and the countershaft gear. Lock the nuts on the main and pinion shafts by bending down the tabs on the washers.

Gearshift Forks

29. Put the synchronizer sleeve and reverse gear in neutral position and insert gearshift forks. The poppet balls and springs

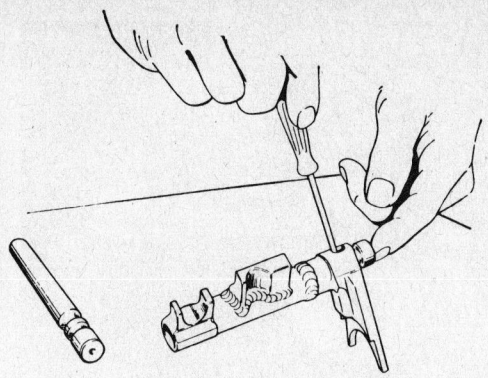

Installing poppet ball into reverse shift fork, using
tool No. 784069

must be fitted and secured with tool No.
784069 before forks are placed in case.

30. Install the reverse gearshift shaft
through the rear end and retrieve the tool
used to hold the poppet ball in position.

31. Make sure the rubber washer and
plastic plug are mounted in the end cover
and the oil collector is in place in the case
end.

32. Check the shims in the end cover.

33. Pass the 1st and 2nd and 3rd and 4th
gearshift fork shafts through the rear end,
positioning them so that the forks engage
their respective shafts.

34. Fit the poppet balls in the forks. This
is simplified if the balls are held with two
tools (No. 784069) while the cover is
pressed in.

35. Retrieve the two tools as they are
pressed out of the front ends of the forks,

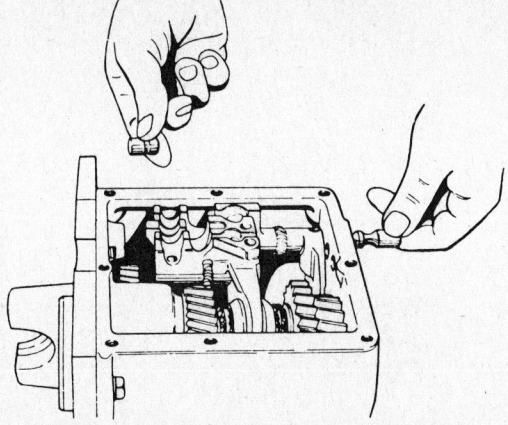

Retrieving tool No. 784069 after shift fork rail is
fully seated

then tighten the end cover bolts to 18 ft. lbs.
Check that the bolt opposite the reverse
gearshift fork is not too long (which would
impede fork movement).

36. If necessary, adjust the gearshift fork
shafts, so that the forks are not subjected to
axial pressure when a gear is engaged.
Roughly the same clearance should exist
between each synchronizer sleeve and the
gear concerned in all gear positions.

Differential

37. Reinstall differential assembly and
spacers and tighten bearing cap bolts to
28 ft. lbs. Be sure the short bolts are installed in the small bearing cap.

38. If the pinion shaft setting has been
altered, or parts in the differential were
replaced, always check the side clearance of
the bevel gear.

39. Reinstall the speedometer drive gear.

40. Coat the top cover with sealing compound and check that the three gearshift

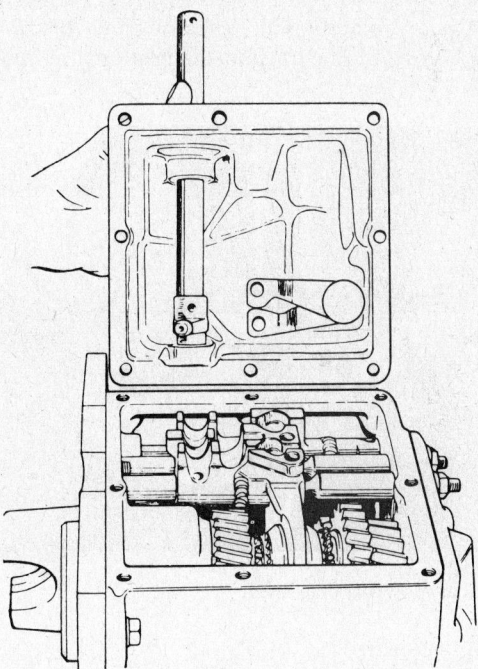

Shift mechanism and catch in transmission case
cover

forks and the dogs and catch in the cover
are in neutral, then fit the cover. Check the
function of the gearshift mechanism.

41. Insert the freewheel hub, using tool
No. 784068 in the freewheel sleeve. Be sure
an undamaged needle bearing is installed.

42. Check the clutch shaft seal and the
driveshaft seals and replace if necessary.
Install the seals so that the dust guard lips
face outwards; fill the space between the
lips with chassis grease.

1066

SAAB

43. Coat the sealing surface of the clutch housing with Permatex No. 3 and attach the clutch housing to the transmission case. Turn the clutch shaft so that it clears the differential. Be certain the clutch shaft is not subjected to lateral stress and that the freewheel hub engages the clutch shaft splines.

44. Coat the clutch shaft splines with graphite grease and fill the transmission with oil.

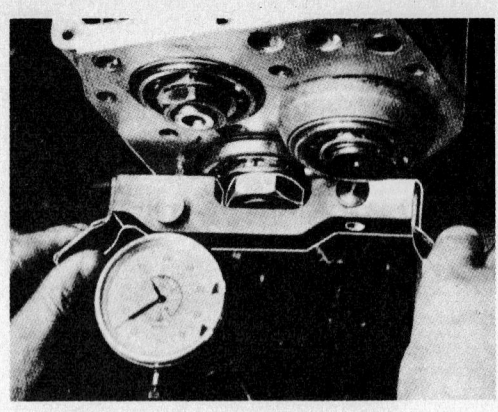

Measuring rear end

TRANSMISSION END COVER SHIMMING

1. With end cover gasket removed, sealing surfaces clean and all bearings properly installed, place a dial indicator (No. 784237) as shown in illustration; the point of the dial

Measuring rear end cover

indicator to the machined surface of the bearing to be shimmed. The measurement is to be made without shims and with a new end cover gasket.

2. Set the dial indicator to zero.

3. Place the measuring tool on the corresponding bearing in the transmission case; read the dial indicator.

4. Install, into the bearing position in the end cover, a combination of shims that correspond to the measurement, ± 0.002″.

5. Proceed in the same way for all bearings.

6. Coat both sides of gasket and reinstall end cover; torque bolts to 18 ft. lbs.

CLUTCH SHAFT SEAL REPLACEMENT

1. Remove the release bearing.

2. Pry out the seal (using tool No. 784220)

3. Install new seal—if double type, fill the space between lips with chassis grease, (use tool No. 784220).

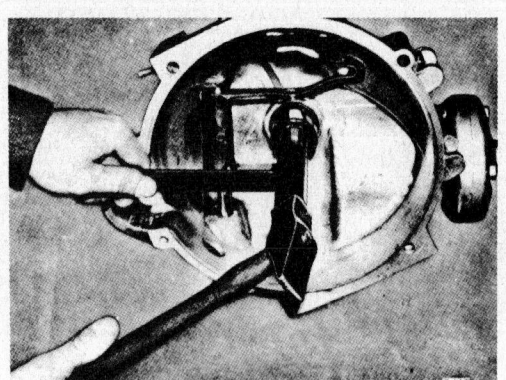

Installing clutch shaft seal

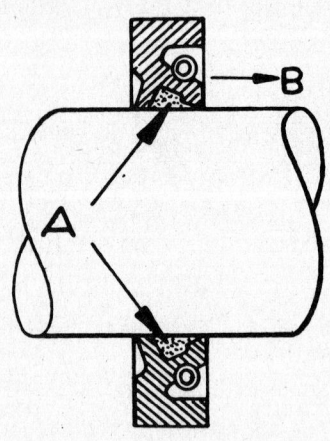

Clutch shaft seal with double seal lips

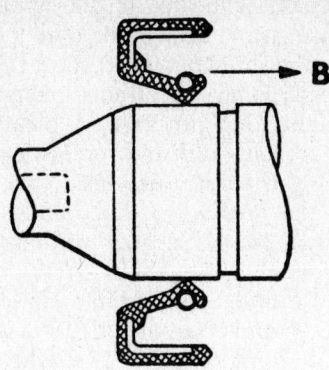

Clutch shaft seal with single seal lips

CLUTCH SHAFT OR BEARING REPLACEMENT

1. Remove inner universal joints, separate clutch housing from transmission case. Remove release bearing and clutch shaft seal.

2. Remove retainer ring from the bearing seat inside the seal. Remove the retaining ring which forms the rear stop for the locking sleeve on the shaft.

3. Pull the clutch shaft forwards and retrieve the locking sleeve and freewheel operating fork.

4. Remove the retaining rings from the shaft and drive off the bearing. This bearing's primary function is to locate the shaft in an axial direction.

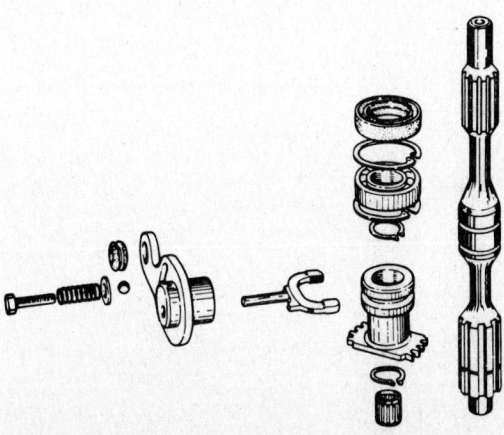

Clutch shaft, bearing, and freewheel mechanism

CLUTCH SHAFT ASSEMBLY

1. Place the rear retaining ring in the clutch housing bearing seat.

2. Press bearing onto the shaft and install the two retaining rings.

3. Place the freewheel operating fork and the locking sleeve in position in the clutch housing.

4. The clutch shaft is installed from the front so that it engages the locking sleeve. Fit the rear retaining ring onto the shaft behind the sleeve.

5. Reinstall the front retaining ring into the clutch housing bearing seat and check the function of the freewheel operating mechanism.

6. Install a new seal, then replace release bearing.

FREEWHEEL DISASSEMBLY AND ASSEMBLY

1. Remove the clutch shaft to allow removal of the locking sleeve and operating fork.

2. Back off the operating lever locking screw to provide access to the spring, operating lever and poppet ball. Reassemble in reverse order, after replacing worn parts.

Freewheel Hub

1. When the freewheel unit is disassembled for repair, it is normally necessary to replace only the hub and six rollers.

2. Remove the needle bearing from the freewheel hub.

3. Insert the prongs of tool No. 784068 between the freewheel and sleeve, then insert the other part of the tool into the hub splines. Twist the freewheel so that the rollers are firmly held against the tool prongs, then pull out the hub until the rollers are halfway out of the sleeve. Put a strong rubber band around the rollers and remove completely. If special tool is not available, any tool can be used which can grip the internal splines so that unit may be turned counterclockwise while being drawn out far enough to put on the rubber band.

4. Reassemble the freewheel hub and needle bearing in reverse order and reinstall into transmission. A spring-loaded plunger is under each roller. Always check the

plunger for wear, making certain it moves freely in its hole. Check the spring tension. Never reuse old rollers after installing a new freewheel hub. Install hub so that the unit engages firmly when the hub is turned clockwise.

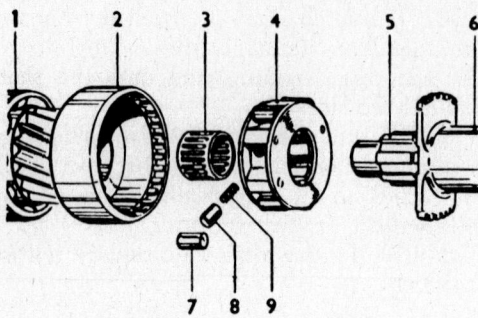

Freewheel mechanism

1. Ball bearing
2. Freewheel sleeve (primary shaft)
3. Needle bearing
4. Freewheel hub
5. Clutch shaft
6. Locking device
7. Roller
8. Plunger
9. Spring

Drive Axle, Suspension, and Steering

All four wheels have coil springs. Each front wheel is attached to a steering knuckle, which is suspended on ball joints between two conventional A-frames (transverse control arms). The inner ends of these control arms are supported by rubber-clad bearings on the body and the vertical coil spring. Wheel travel is limited by rubber bumbers.

A large, forged steering knuckle forms a frame for the front axle, its principal components being a bearing housing with two inward-inclined arms, an upper and a lower. The outer driveshaft is carried in a ball bearing enclosed in the bearing housing. The wheel hub and brake drum or disc are mounted on the outer end of the driveshaft, while the backing plate or caliper, with its front brake assembly, is bolted to the steering knuckle.

Ball joints are attached to the steering knuckle arms, where they provide flexible connections for the ends of the control arms. The steering arm, to which the tie-rod is connected, is located on the upper steering knuckle arm. The outer and inner driveshafts are interconnected through the outer universal joint, the turning center of which is on the king pin axis. A pleated rubber boot prevents dirt and foreign matter from entering the outer universal joint and contains the grease for that joint. The inner universal joint is located on the stub of the differential output shaft.

The SAAB Sport, Monte Carlo 850, and SAAB 95 and 96 from 1967 have disc brakes on the front wheels. The wheels on the latter models are different from those used on the SAAB 95 and 96 up to and including 1966. Other components, such as the control arms with their ball joints and rubber bearings, the coil springs and rubber bumpers, and the stabilizer bar, are the same as used on the 1966 model. The front wheel alignment is also identical. The Sonett suspension is identical, with the exception of the stabilizer bar, which is omitted on this model.

The SAAB Sport and Monte Carlo 850, up to and including 1966, features a special hub, to which the brake disc is bolted. The wheel is secured to the wheel hub with only four bolts. The steering knuckle, which is identical to that on the SAAB 95 and 96, carries a holder for the brake housing.

Wheel Alignment

It is of the utmost importance that the front wheels be correctly aligned, since incorrect steering geometry can cause:

1. Driver fatigue, due to impaired roadability.
2. Difficulty in keeping the car under control.

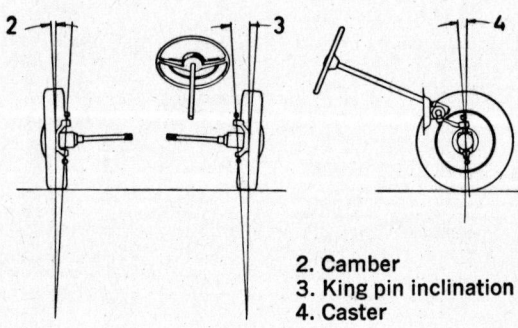

2. Camber
3. King pin inclination
4. Caster

Front wheel alignment

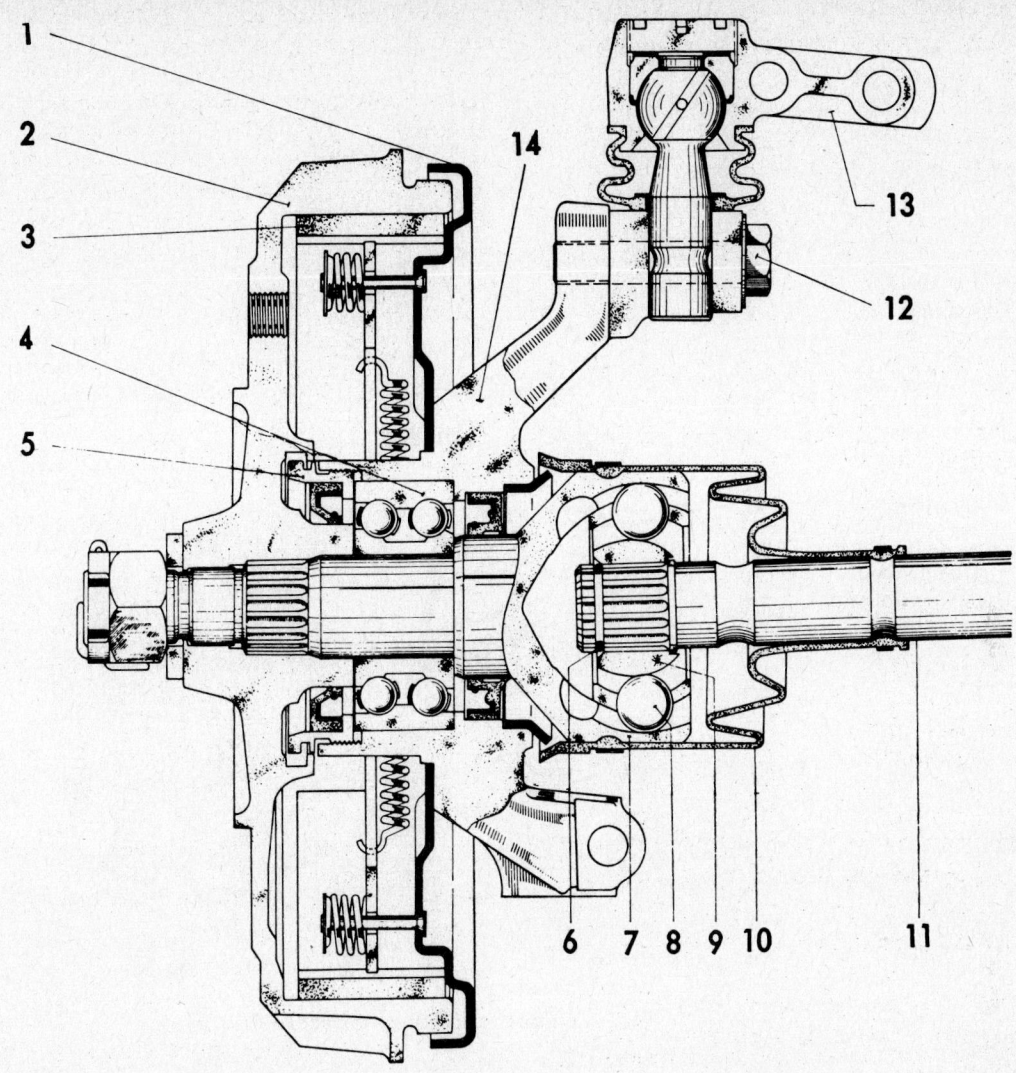

Front axle and suspension—SAAB 95 and 96 up to and including 1966

1. Backing plate	5. Nut	9. Hub	13. Ball joint
2. Brake drum	6. Lock ring	10. Rubber bellows	14. Steering knuckle
3. Brake shoe	7. Outer driveshaft	11. Inner driveshaft	housing
4. Ball bearing	8. Ball	12. Bolt	

3. Increased tire and repair costs due to abnormal wear of tires and steering components.

Checking and Adjustment

Before adjusting, the following items should be attended to:

1. Check that the tire pressure is correct on all wheels and that the tires are not too unevenly worn.

2. Check the front wheel bearings, control arm bushings, ball joints and tie-rod ends, adjusting or replacing as necessary to eliminate errors that can be caused by worn parts.

3. Check the steering gear and adjust any faults.

4. Check the function of the shock absorbers and renew any defective shock absorbers and rubber bushings.

5. If the car has been involved in an accident, driven into a ditch, etc., any dam-

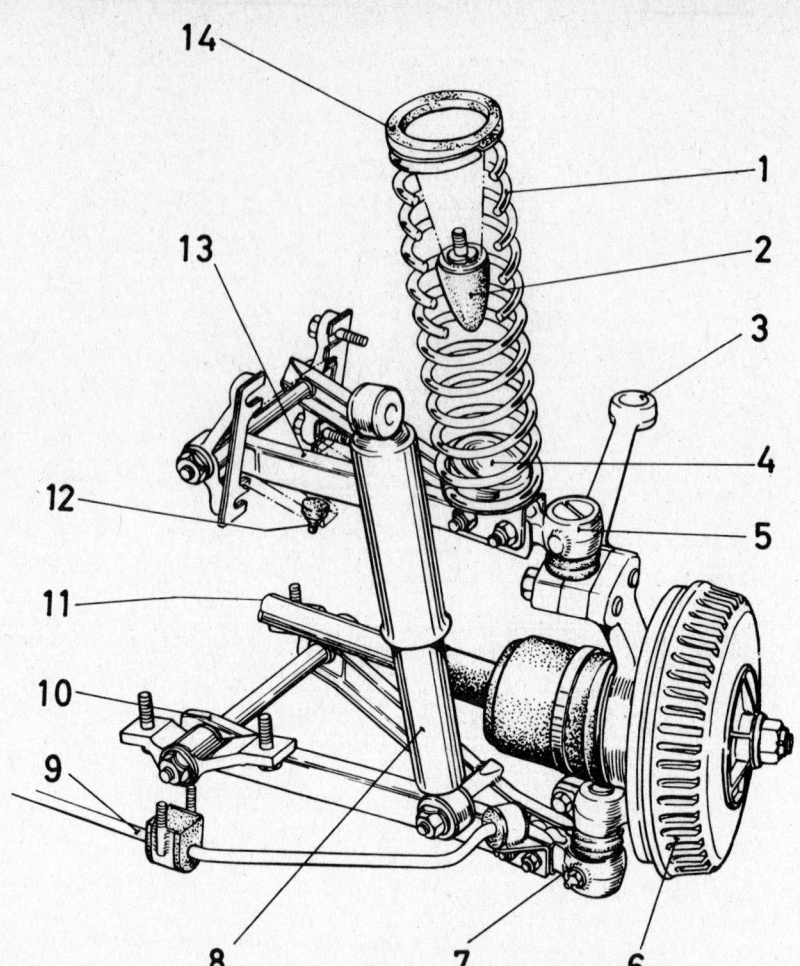

1. Coil spring
2. Rubber bumper
3. Steering arm
4. Spring seat
5. Upper ball joint
6. Brake drum
7. Lower ball joint
8. Shock absorber
9. Stabilizer bar
10. Lower control arm
11. Inner driveshaft
12. Rubber bumper
13. Upper control arm
14. Rubber spacer

Left-front suspension—typical 1960-1970

age incurred must be repaired before checking the front alignment. Bent steering arms must be replaced—straightening is not safe practice.

6. Immediately before checking, road test the car, without hard cornering, to seat the suspension components and provide a basis for evaluation of any changes made. During alignment, the car must be unloaded and on a flat surface.

Toe-In

Toe-in is the difference between measurements taken at the forward extremes of the tires and the rearward extremes of the tires. In the illustration, this is shown as the difference between X and Y.

The correct setting is 0.08″ ± 0.04″ (i.e., measurement Y should be 0.04–0.12″ less than measurement X). Toe-in is adjusted by

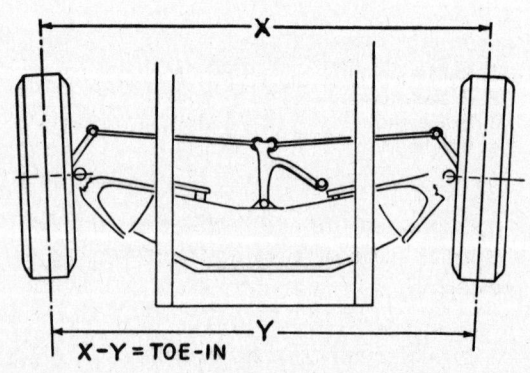

Toe-in

changing the length of the tie-rod with the wheels in the straight-ahead position. Toe-in is 0.04″ ± 0.04″ for Sonett II models.

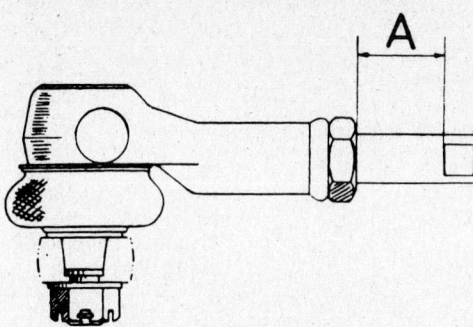

CHECKING THE LENGTH OF A TIE-ROD WITH KEY GRIP

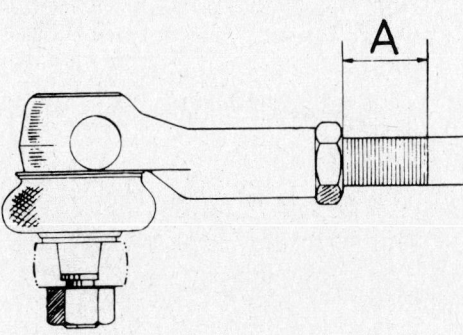

CHECKING THE LENGTH OF A TIE-ROD WITHOUT KEY GRIP

CAMBER

Camber is the amount, expressed in degrees, that the front wheels are inclined outward at the top. The purpose of camber is to take some of the load from the outboard spindle bearing. If the wheel is tilted outward at the top, the camber is positive; if inward, the camber is negative. The correct camber for SAAB models is $+3/4° \pm 1/4°$, with the exception of the Sonett II, which requires $0° \pm 1/4°$.

CASTER

Caster is the amount that the king pin is tilted toward the rear of the car, expressed in degrees. Positive caster means that the top of the king pin is tilted towards the rear; negative caster that the top is tilted towards the front. The correct caster setting for SAAB models, including the Sonett II, is $+2° \pm 1/2°$.

Brakes

The SAAB has used three separate and distinct brake systems, although some minor differences between them exist. The first type (Type I) is a four-wheel drum system having self-energizing front shoes, each shoe having a single wheel cylinder. The rear shoes are actuated by a single cylinder, but the cylinder is movable—the pushing action against one shoe resulting in an opposite reaction to move the other shoe against the drum.

The second type (Type II) is also a four-wheel drum system. It, however, has standard double-ended wheel cylinders at the rear, fixed to the backing plate.

The third type (Type III) is a four-wheel, dual-circuit system utilizing either a front drum/rear drum or a front disc/rear drum configuration. With this type system, the master cylinder controls the left front and the right rear independently of, and simultaneously with, the right front and left rear wheels. If hydraulic fluid leakage occurs, braking effort will be lost only on one diagonal pair of wheels. Leakage manifests itself by long pedal travel and by a tendency for the car to swerve toward the side where brake pressure is the greatest. A warning light system is used after 1968, consisting of a light in the speedometer housing and a switch on the pedal mechanism.

Up to and including the 1966 model, pressure regulating valves are installed in the lines to the rear brakes on the SAAB 96, SAAB Sport and Monte Carlo 850. The pressure regulating valves are to prevent premature lock-up of the rear wheels.

The mechanical handbrake acts on the rear wheels and the brake lever is located between the front seats.

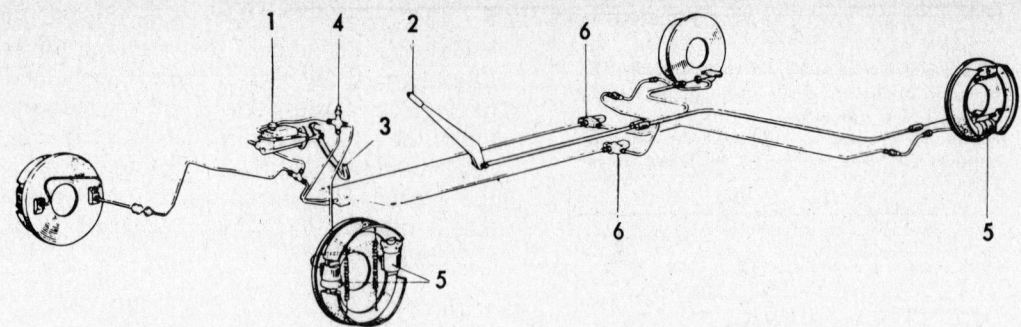

Two-circuit braking system used up to and including 1967

1. Master cylinder   4. Stop light contact   6. Pressure regulating valve
2. Handbrake lever   5. Wheel cylinders   (SAAB 96 and Monte Carlo
3. Brake pedal   850 up to and including
                                                                1966 model.)

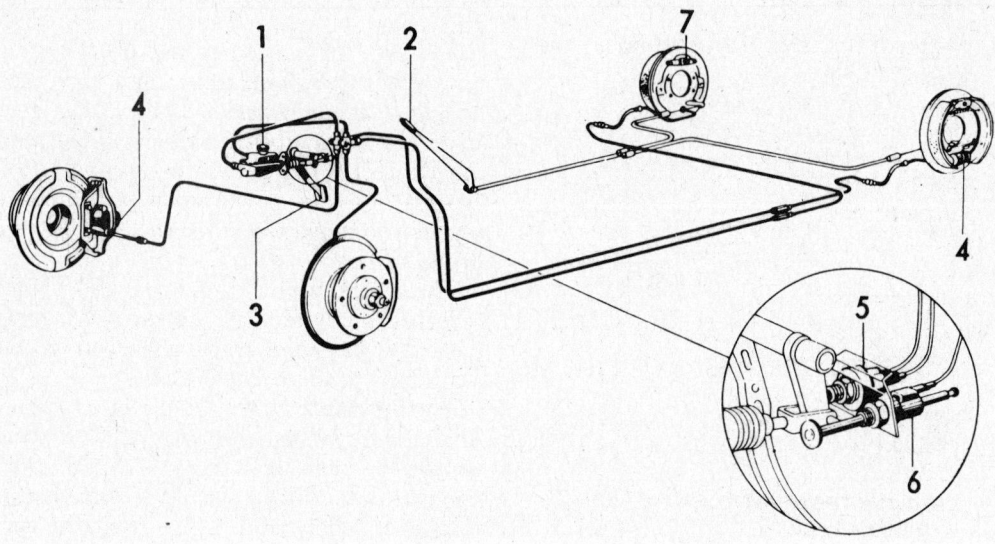

Two-circuit braking system, 1968 and later

1. Master cylinder   4. Wheel cylinder   6. Brake warning light contact
2. Handbrake lever   5. Stop light switch   7. Adjusting screw, rear brake
3. Brake pedal

Master Cylinder

The tandem master cylinder includes a body housing, a primary piston (10) and a secondary piston (14), which is actuated by a pushrod (31) from the brake pedal. The pistons are held apart by a spring (18), the distance between them being determined by a clip (17) and the retaining pin (19). The secondary piston has a primary cup (12) and a secondary cup (15). Fitted behind the primary cup is a dished piston washer (13), which prevents the cup from being extruded into the feed holes in the flange. The primary cup of the primary piston (21) also has a dished piston washer (22) and a secondary cup (26), which bears against the piston rod and prevents leakage of brake fluid. The spring (9) returns the pistons to the initial position. One-way valves are fitted in the two outlets (1 and 2).

When the brake pedal is depressed, the pushrod (31) actuates the primary piston,

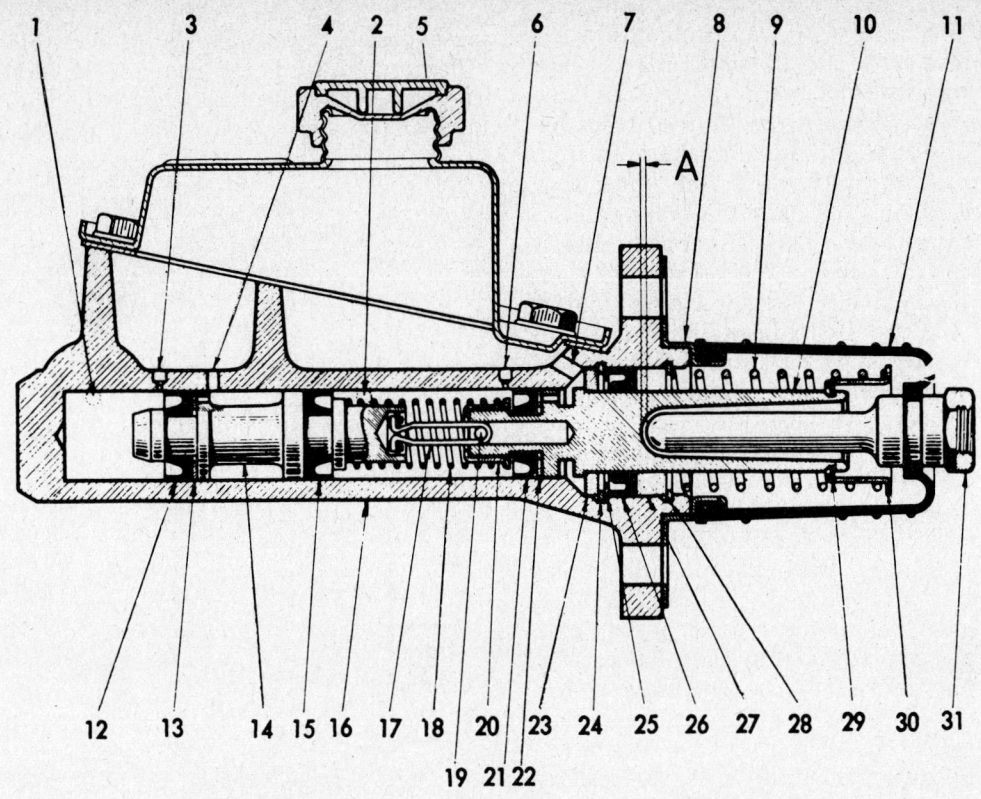

Cross-sectional view of master cylinder. A=0.024-0.047"

1. Outlet to one circuit
2. Outlet to other circuit
3. Bypass port
4. Feed hole
5. Brake fluid reservoir
6. Bypass port
7. Feed hole
8. Retaining plate
9. Spring
10. Primary piston
11. Rubber boot

12. Primary piston
13. Piston washer
14. Secondary piston
15. Secondary cup
16. Body
17. Clip
18. Spring
19. Retaining pin
20. Spring holder
21. Primary cup

22. Piston washer
23. Piston stop ring
24. Circlip
25. Washer
26. Secondary cup
27. Guide bearing
28. Circlip
29. "Spirol ox" circlip
30. Spring retainer
31. Pushrod

the thrust being transmitted by the spring (18) to the secondary piston, which forces brake fluid out through the one-way valve to one brake circuit. As the secondary chamber rises, the spring force between the pistons is overcome, and further effort on the brake pedal compresses the spring slightly, causing brake fluid to be forced to the second brake circuit. The pressure in front of the primary piston also reacts on the back of the secondary piston. Consequently, the latter forms a partition and balances the pressures until they are equal in both brake circuits.

Upon removal of the load from the brake pedal, the return spring (9) returns the pistons to the initial position faster than the

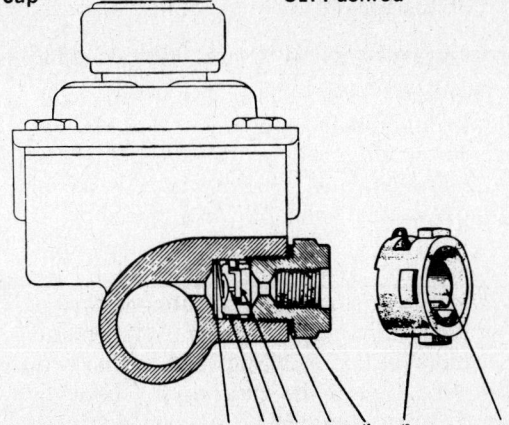

One-way valve in master cylinder

41. Spring
42. Valve body
43. Equalizing hole
44. Spring clip
45. Gasket
46. Adapter

fluid is able to flow back from the wheel cylinders. The front (or primary) cups therefore move forwards a little and the dished washers uncover the feed holes behind the cups and admit brake fluid from the reservoir. Meanwhile, the brake shoe return springs pull back the brake pistons, whereupon brake fluid flows back through the one-way valves. The brake fluid then flows back to the reservoir via the bypass ports (3) and (6), which also compensate for contraction or expansion of the brake fluid due to temperature changes. When the brake shoes have been returned, the one-way valve closes, and any residual pressure is relieved through the hole (43) in the valve. The purpose of the one-way valve is to prevent entry of brake fluid from the wheel cylinders when bleeding the brake system. This ensures that a fresh charge of brake fluid, completely free of air, will pass from the reservoir and through the systems at each stroke of the brake pedal. In the event of a leak occurring in the system operated by the primary piston, the spring (18) is compressed until the primary piston strikes the secondary piston. The latter can then function normally. If leakage occurs in the circuit operated by the secondary piston, the secondary piston will be thrust forward by the primary piston and spring until it touches the bottom of the cylinder bore, whereupon the brake fluid can be forced out into the remaining circuit. The Sonett master cylinder is similar to the ones used on other SAAB models, with the exception of the remote mounted fluid reservoir.

Front Brakes—SAAB 95 and 96 up to 1966

The front brake shoes are of the self-energizing type and each one is operated by its own single-acting wheel cylinder. The shoes are engaged in slots in the wheel cylinder piston and opposing wheel cylinder, where they are free to slide and thus to center in relation to the drum. Each shoe carries its own automatic adjustment device, consisting of an adjuster lever (4), secured to the brake shoe by a peg (13) at one end, with serrations at the other end. The lever is held to the brake shoe by two retaining washers (5), a retaining pin (10), loaded by a spring (11), and a spring retainer (12). One end of the brake shoe return spring (9) is designed as a pawl, which engages in the serrations of the adjuster lever. On the

backing plate, a peg (3) is provided, which slides in a groove in the center of the lever. The brake shoes are held against the backing plate by a spring, a washer and anchor

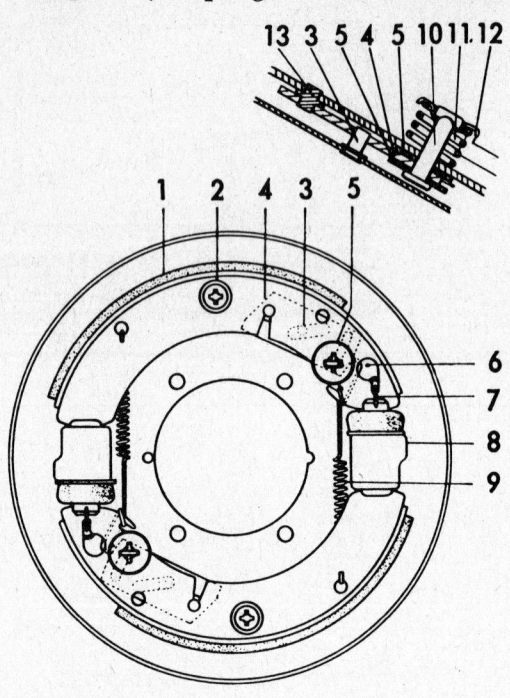

Front brake components

1. Brake shoe
2. Steady pin with spring
3. Back plate peg
4. Adjuster lever
5. Friction washers
6. Hole for locking spring
7. Piston-locking spring
8. Wheel cylinder
9. Return spring
10. Retaining pin
11. Spring
12. Spring retainer
13. Peg

pin (2). They are also held to the wheel cylinder piston by means of a piston locking spring (7).

The backing plate peg (3) always has a certain amount of clearance in the adjuster lever slot; this determines how much free-play will exist between the brake linings and the brake drums when the shoes are "off." Upon application of the brake, the shoe is forced out against the drum by the piston and is accompanied by the adjuster lever, so that the peg takes up a new position in the slot. As the brake linings wear down, the automatic adjustment device becomes effective. Further travel of the brake shoe, together with the adjuster lever, results in the detention of the lever in the middle by the peg (3). However, since the lever is carried in a bearing (2) at one end, it turns there and slides between the retaining washers (4) at the other end. The friction of these retaining washers is sufficient to hold the adjuster lever in this new position when the brake shoes return to the "off" position. When the adjuster lever has traveled far enough, the pawl on the return spring drops into the next serration and thus ensures positive retention of the adjuster lever. When the brake shoe returns to the "off" position, it will move only as much as is allowed by the free-play at the peg, which is just enough to ensure that the brake shoe clears the drum. In order to prevent any variation in the brake pedal travel due to the piston's working back into the cylinder on its own, the piston is connected to the brake shoe by a piston locking spring.

to and including 1966 are equipped with pressure regulating valves for the rear brakes in order to provide a proper distribution of braking effort. The handbrake operates through sealed Bowden cables by a lever located between the front seats.

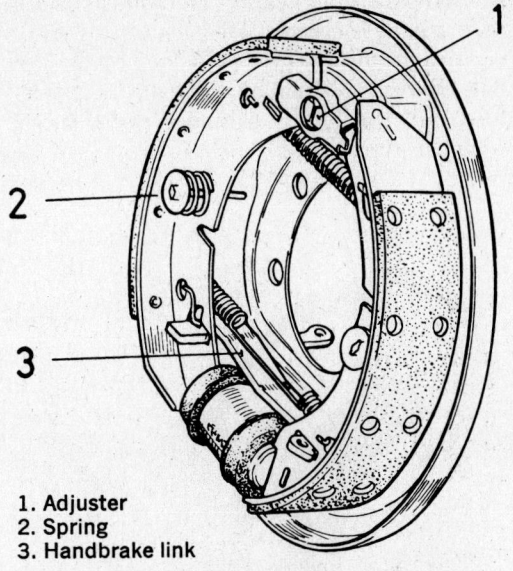

1. Adjuster
2. Spring
3. Handbrake link

REAR BRAKES

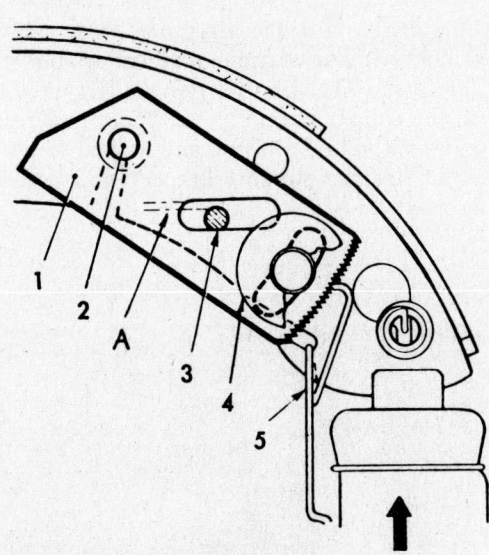

Brake shoe with worn lining, shown in applied position

A. Clearance
1. Adjuster lever
2. Bearing
3. Backing plate peg
4. Friction washers
5. Return spring with pawl catch

Rear Wheel Brakes and Handbrake

The rear wheel brakes and handbrake are, in principle, identical for all models. All have a wheel cylinder mounted in the backing plate. The cylinder is fitted with two pistons, with the exception of early 95, 96 and GT-750 models, each of which acts on one brake shoe. The shoes are adjusted manually. SAAB Sport and Monte Carlo up

Disc Brakes—SAAB Sport and Monte Carlo 850 up to and Including 1966

The front wheel disc brakes consist of a disc attached to the front hub which rotates with the wheel. On each side of the disc is a friction pad which, when the brakes are applied, is forced against the brake disc by a brake piston. The brake pistons are located in a split caliper housing which encases the brake disc. In the caliper housing, the fluid is distributed to the two brake cylinders, and a bleed screw is fitted at the highest point. The caliper housing is screwed to a holder, which is fastened to the steering knuckle. The brake pistons are 2″ in diameter. The piston seals are located in grooves in the cylinders; the pistons have a completely smooth surface. The outer seals serve to keep out dust and dirt, while the inner seals prevent leakage of brake fluid. The brake pistons act directly on the friction pads, the latter being held in position by means of two springs and cotter pins. Pads can be changed by removing the springs and pins. There are no return springs for the pads, which means that the disc brakes are self-adjusting. When the brakes are applied, brake fluid is forced from the master cylinder to the brake cylinders, and the brake pistons press the friction pads against the disc. When the pressure is removed from the brake pedal, the pistons are returned a few thousandths of an inch because of the flexibility of the piston seal. This is sufficient to prevent the friction pads from bearing on the disc. Wear on the pads is compensated for in this manner, as the piston gradually moves farther out. Excessive wear on the pads is, therefore, not revealed by excessive pedal travel with this type brake.

Disc Brakes—SAAB 95, 96 and Monte Carlo from 1967

From 1967, the front wheels are equipped with disc brakes with only one cylinder. The main parts are the support bracket, caliper assembly, cylinder body and friction pads.

The support bracket is bolted to the steering knuckle housing, which keeps the brake in place and transmits the braking force to the suspension. The caliper assembly is secured to the support bracket by means of a hinge pin and a friction unit. It is movable with relation to the support bracket, the torsional center being provided by the hinge pin. The brake cylinder is the same type as previously used with the addition of an outer wiper seal to prevent the entry of dirt, plus an inner fluid seal. The friction pads are wedge-shaped in order to compensate for the irregular wear which occurs because of the movement around the hinge pin. The outer friction pad is mounted in the caliper assembly; the inner pad rests against the brake piston and is held in position by the support bracket and caliper assembly.

Front axle assembly, showing disc brakes used up to and including 1966

1. Brake disc
2. Wheel hub
3. Caliper housing
4. Friction pads

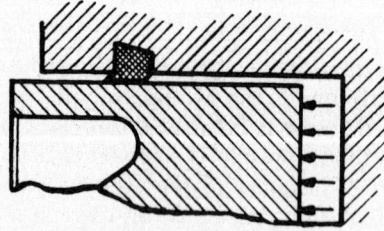

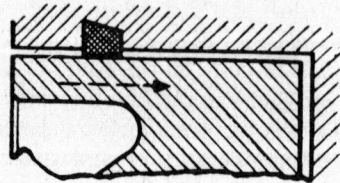

The brake piston is moved back under influence of piston seal

Front axle assembly, showing disc brakes used from 1967

1. Brake disc
2. Wheel hub
3. Caliper housing
4. Friction pads

Hydraulic pressure from the master cylinder actuates the brake piston, causing it to move outwards and press the friction pad against the disc. The movable brake unit then is influenced so that the outer friction pad is also pressed against the brake disc. The flexibility of the piston seals is sufficient to provide clearance between the friction pads and the disc when the brake pedal pressure is released.

As the friction pads wear, the brake body assembly rotates around the hinge pin, thus causing the angle of wear to be changed continuously. When the linings have become so worn as to need replacement, the angle has become so small that the lining is almost parallel to the disc.

Drum Brake Service

Because the front shoes are self-adjusting, it is not possible to detect worn linings by excessive pedal travel. It is, therefore, important to remove the wheels at regular intervals in order to check lining wear through the inspection holes in the drum. If the linings are less than 1.0 mm. (.040″) thick, replacement is necessary.

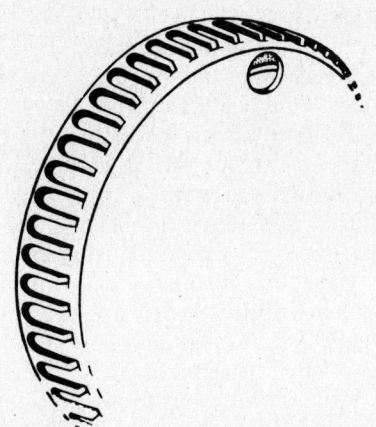

Inspection hole in brake drum

BRAKE DRUM REMOVAL

1. Remove the cotter pin and spindle nut.
2. Jack up the car.
3. Remove the wheel.
4. a. *Rear wheels:* Release the handbrake and adjust the rear shoes with the adjusting screw.

b. *Front wheels:* The front shoes must be adjusted in the following manner.

Insert a screwdriver into the extra hole in the brake drum, then into the hole (6) in the brake shoe. Then, with another screwdriver or bar bearing against the hub nut, press the brake drum and shoe against the normal direction of rotation, until a grating sound is heard, indicating that the shoe has been forced back and the pawl has released. Readjust both shoes before removing the brake drum.

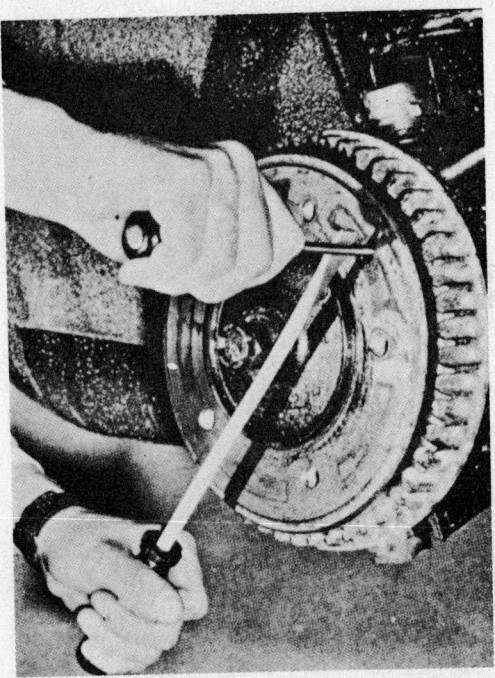

Adjusting brake shoes

5. Remove the brake drum, using puller No. 784002 for SAAB 95 and 96 and No. 784201 for SAAB Sport and Monte Carlo models. If the proper puller is not available, a standard wheel puller will do if used carefully. Never hammer on drums.

6. Examine the linings on all the shoes. If they are worn below inspection limits, cracked, burned, charred or worn unevenly, or covered with grease, new linings must be installed. Never install new linings on only one side.

7. If linings are replaced, they must be ground in a special machine to a radius of about 0.010–0.012″ less than that of the drum for perfect contact. The edges of the linings must *not* be chamfered, they should be left as sharp as possible.

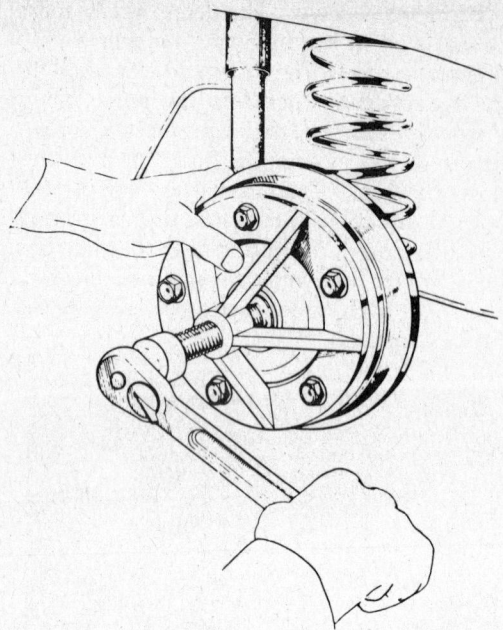

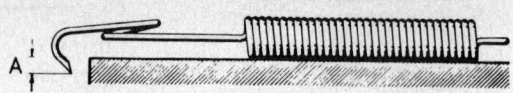

Checking return spring pawl mechanism. A=0.157″

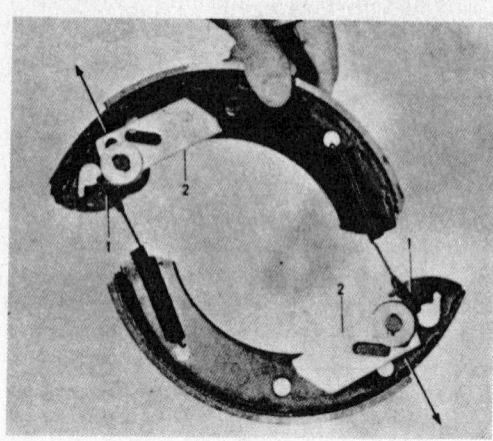

Installing return springs

Using puller No. 784002 to remove brake drum

Front Brake Shoes Disassembly

1. Remove the locking springs (7) that hold the brake piston to the brake shoe. (Unhook the spring from the piston first.)

2. Remove the anchor springs (2) for the brake shoes.

3. Ease the heel of the lower shoe out of the wheel cylinder, then move the shoe carefully outwards a little way to disengage the backing plate peg (3) from the adjuster lever groove. The toe of the shoe then can be removed from the brake piston. Use only the fingers and do not touch the return springs. Also, take care not to distort the return springs and pawl mechanism catches.

4. Remove the upper shoe in the same manner. Use a small piece of wire or some suitable device around the cylinders to prevent the pistons from falling out.

5. Remove the retaining washers, the spring and pin, then the adjuster lever from the brake shoe.

Assembly

1. If the adjuster lever and retaining washers have been removed, check them for wear, then locate the adjuster lever in its slot in the brake shoe. Install the retaining washers on either side of the adjuster lever and install the spring, retaining pin, and spring retainer. Do *not* lubricate the retaining washers.

2. Check the return springs and, if necessary, adjust the pawl mechanism catches to the correct dimension.

3. Push the adjuster levers over as far as possible towards the shoe table. Refit both return springs, making sure that their pawl mechanism catches are correctly positioned in the retaining washers.

4. Remove the wires used to retain the pistons.

5. Refit the upper shoe first, making sure that the backing plate (3) engages the oval hole in the adjuster lever.

6. Next install the lower shoe in the same manner, using the hands only, taking care not to touch the springs. It is most important that the pawl catches on the return springs are not distorted during assembly.

7. Refit the piston locking springs and the anchor springs, with retaining pins and washers.

8. Center the shoes and install the drums.

9. Adjust the front brakes by applying the brakes hard several times. Do not drive the car until this is done.

Rear Brake Shoes Disassembly

1. Use a piece of wire or clamp to keep the brake pistons in the wheel cylinder.

2. Remove the springs which hold the shoes to the backing plate.

3. Remove the shoes from the cylinder and handbrake levers; first the top, then the bottom.

ASSEMBLY

1. Hook the springs between the shoes.
2. Install the front shoe, with the handbrake lever in the oblong hole.
3. Lift the rear shoe with the handbrake lever into the large hole. Make sure the spring presses against the lever as illustrated.
4. Remove the wire or clamp used to keep the brake pistons in place.
5. Adjust the shoes approximately in the center of the backing plate. Install the springs that hold the shoes against the backing plate.
6. Install the wheel hub and wheel.
7. Adjust the brakes.

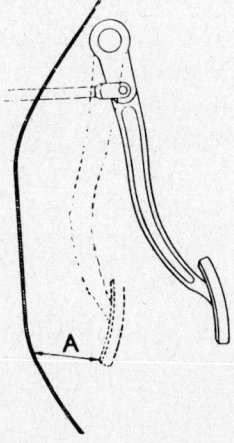

Measuring distance between brake pedal and floorboard. A=2.5″

BRAKE ADJUSTMENT

Brake wear is revealed by excessive travel of the brake pedal or handbrake lever before brakes take effect. The distance between the fully depressed pedal and the floor board should be not less than 2.5″. Since the front brakes are self-adjusting, only the rear brakes require adjustment.

1. Jack up the car so that the rear wheels clear the ground. It is possible to adjust the brakes without removing the wheels.
2. Release the handbrake and make sure that the brake levers return all the way. If the cable seems to bind, the levers must be returned by hand.
3. Press the brake pedal hard several times to center the brake shoes.
4. The adjusting screw for the rear brakes is the square peg located on the rear of the backing plate. Turn this adjuster, using the special wrench included in the tool kit of the car, until the wheel no longer rotates. Back off one or more notches until the wheel again rotates freely.

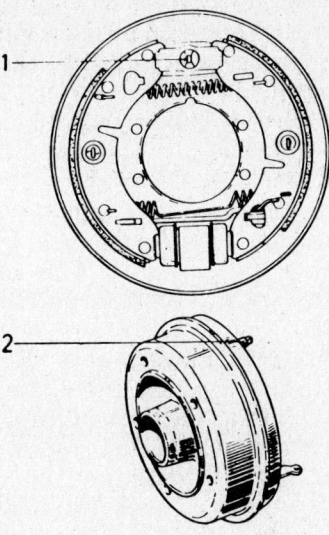

Rear brake adjusting screw (2) and adjusting device (1)

5. After adjusting, make sure that the free movement of the brake pedal is 0.12–0.24″. If the clearance is less, the brake shoes are not returning when the brake pedal is released.
6. If the adjusting screw cannot be tightened enough to lock the wheel, the brake linings are worn and must be replaced. Always change linings on both wheels at the same time. This is to be certain that braking is even. After adjusting the brakes, make sure the rear wheels turn freely.

BRAKE DRUM TURNING

If the brake drums are only moderately and equally scored, braking will not be affected to any great degree. If, on the other hand, only one drum is scored, or if both drums are severely scored, they should be replaced or machined. Replacement or machining is also necessary if the brake drum is out-of-round, a condition which manifests itself by a jerky pedal action when braking. The front drums may be machined to a maximum diameter of 9.059″ and the rear to a maximum 8.059″.

Disc Brake Service

Brake Disc Replacement up to 1966 Models

If the brake disc shows signs of heavy wear, it must be replaced. Moderate scoring, on the other hand, does not necessitate replacement. Never separate the two caliper halves except when absolutely essential. In any case, normal service can be done without dismantling the caliper.

1. Remove the hubcap and loosen the spindle nut.

2. Jack up the front of the car, take off the wheel, and remove the spindle nut.

3. Back off and remove the two bolts that hold the caliper to the steering knuckle. These bolts are accessible from inside the brake disc.

4. Lift the caliper away from the brake disc; *do not disconnect* the brake hose. Take care not to scratch the friction pads. Wire the caliper assembly to the suspension to avoid damaging the brake hose.

5. Pull off the wheel hub, with brake disc attached, using a wheel puller.

6. Remove the brake disc from the hub. Reassemble in the reverse order. Always use new tab lock plates when installing the caliper bolts.

Brake Squeal Elimination—Sport and Monte Carlo up to 1966

1. Remove the friction pads and make sure that the grooved faces of the brake pistons are pointing downwards. If they are not, rotate the pistons into the correct position using a pair of snap-ring pliers. Place the pliers inside the piston so as not to damage the outer contact surface.

2. If the noise still persists, obtain the proper shims from the dealer (anti-squeak plates), then install a shim between each brake piston and friction pad. The shim has two recesses, which should be placed downwards so as to align with the ends of the relieved faces of the pistons.

Brake Disc Replacement from 1967 Models

1. Remove hubcap and loosen the spindle nut.

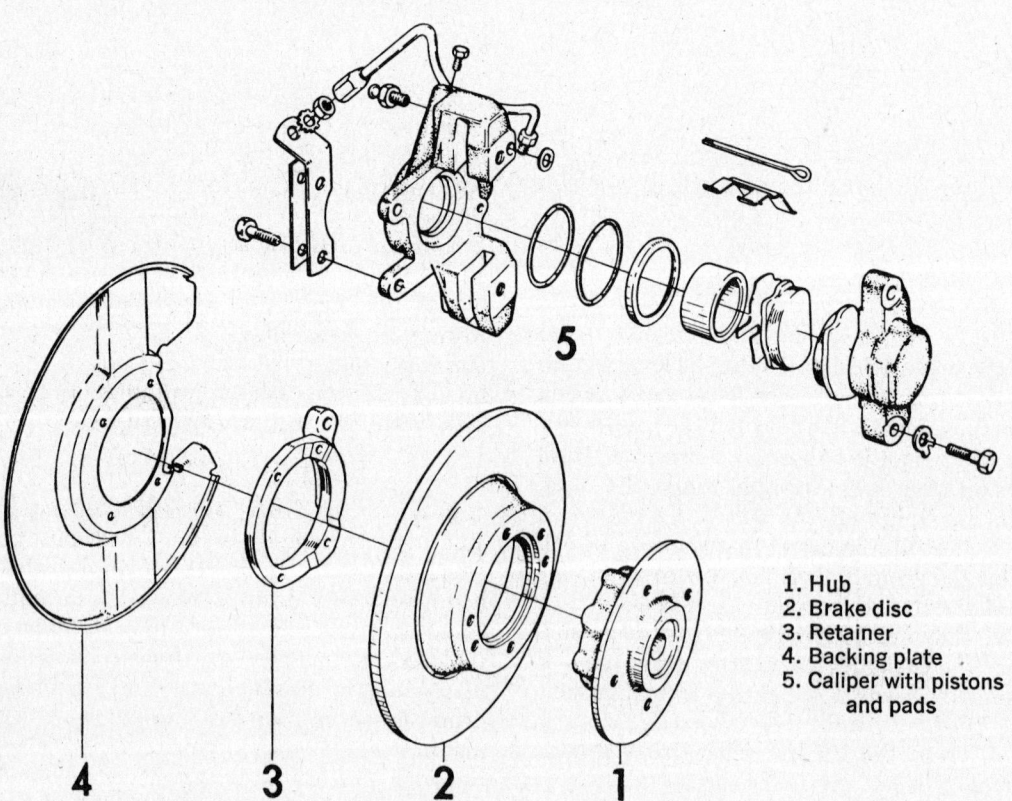

1. Hub
2. Brake disc
3. Retainer
4. Backing plate
5. Caliper with pistons and pads

Disc brake components up to and including 1966

2. Jack up the front of the car, take off the wheel and remove the spindle nut.

3. Remove the two bolts that hold the brake to the steering knuckle housing. These bolts are accessible from inside the brake disc. Lift the caliper clear of the brake disc. *Do not disconnect* the brake hose; wire the brake in such a way that the hose is not damaged.

4. Pull off the wheel hub, with disc attached, using a wheel puller.

5. Detach the brake disc from the wheel hub. Reassemble in reverse order. When installing the caliper bolts, always use a new tab lock plate. After assembly, pump the pedal a few times to seat the brake pistons.

Friction Pad Replacement—General

As the disc brakes on the SAAB Sport, Monte Carlo and SAAB 95 and 96 from 1967 are self-adjusting, it is not possible to decide by the length of the pedal stroke whether or not the linings are worn. It is, therefore,

important that the wheels be removed at regular intervals to check the thickness of the linings. The friction pads should be replaced when the thickness is less than 0.06".

Pad Replacement—Sport and Monte Carlo up to 1966

1. Jack up the car and remove the wheel.

2. Remove the cotter pins and springs that hold the friction pads. Remove one friction pad, twisting slightly to ease removal.

3. Clean the protruding part of the brake piston with brake fluid. Make sure there is no rust or dirt in the recesses for the friction pad.

4. Drive the piston back into the caliper, using tool No. 784132 or a suitable small C-clamp. When the brake pistons are forced back into the cylinders, the brake fluid in the reservoir will be displaced; therefore the surplus should be drained.

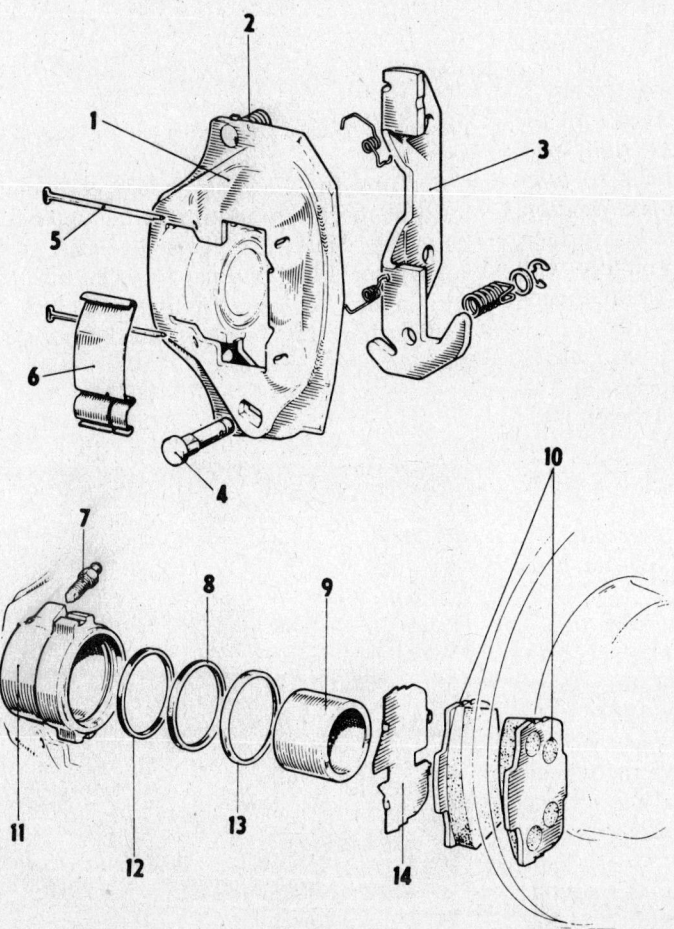

1. Brake body assembly
2. Spring-loaded steady pin
3. Support bracket
4. Hinge pin
5. Split pins
6. Spring clip
7. Bleedscrew
8. Wiper seal
9. Piston
10. Friction pad assemblies
11. Cylinder body
12. Fluid seal
13. Retainer
14. Shim

Disc brake components from 1967

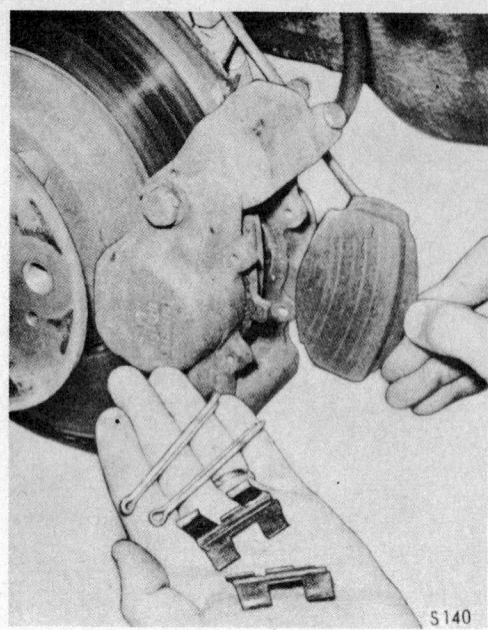

Replacing friction pads—disc brakes up to and including 1966

5. Make sure that the brake piston is correctly positioned with the recess in the contact face towards the friction pad, aligned downwards. If you have to twist the brake piston into the proper position, take care not to damage its sealing surface.

6. Clean the brake disc thoroughly with a solvent which will leave no residue, such as trichloroethylene.

7. Install the new friction pad, making sure it moves easily in its recess in the caliper. Protruding parts of the friction pads can be trimmed with a file.

8. Change the other pads in the same manner.

9. Install new springs and cotter pins.

10. Pump the brake pedal a few times to seat the pads.

11. Top up brake fluid in the reservoir.

Pad Replacement—Monte Carlo and 95 and 96 Models from 1967

1. Jack up the car and remove the wheel.

2. Remove the cotter pins and the springs that hold the friction pads. Remove the friction pads.

3. Clean the exposed part of the piston, making sure there is no rust or dirt on the friction pad surfaces which contact the

bracket and yoke. When cleaning, use only brake fluid or methylated spirits.

4. Drive the piston back into the brake housing, using tool No. 786043 or a small C-clamp. When the piston is forced back, the fluid in the reservoir will be displaced and it may be necessary to drain off the excess.

5. Clean the brake disc with a solvent which leaves no residue, such as Trichloroethylene.

Pressing back brake piston using tool No. 786043

6. Turn the movable brake component towards the wheel and install the outer friction pad. Make sure it moves easily in its yoke. Protruding pad parts can be trimmed with a file. If used friction pads are installed, they must be placed in their original positions.

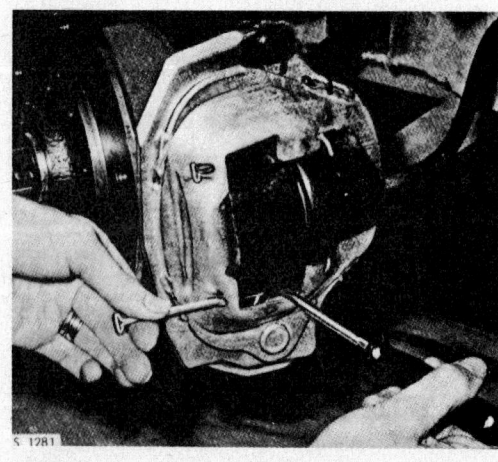

Installing friction pads

7. Turn the movable brake component backwards as far as possible.

8. Fit anti-squeak shims to the back of the friction pads, making sure they don't exceed the contours of the pressure plate.

9. Make sure the shims are installed with the two recesses directed downwards in such a way that they are centered on the ends of the piston recess. Install the inner friction pad. Make sure that the recess in the piston is directed downwards.

10. Install the spring. The recess in the spring should be as near as possible to the outer friction pad. Install new cotter pins, the upper cotter pin first. To install the lower cotter pin, press the spring upwards using a screwdriver.

11. Pump the brake pedal a few times to seat the pads.

12. Top up the brake fluid deservoir.

Hydraulic System Service

If it becomes necessary to disassemble the hydraulic system, it must be done under extremely clean conditions. Remove all dirt and grease before removing any parts. Do not use gasoline, kerosene or similar solvents, which cause damage to rubber parts. Dismantle the units on a bench covered with a sheet of clean paper. After dismantling, place all metal parts in a tray of clean brake fluid to soak. Having done this, dry off with a clean, lint-free cloth. It is recommended that all rubber parts be replaced. Parts are readily available in the form of repair kits containing all the rubber parts required for each unit. When assembling, all internal parts should be dipped in brake fluid and assembled wet. When assembling rubber parts, use the fingers only, nicks caused by sharp tools will result in brake failure.

INSPECTION

For safety reasons, it is necessary to check the brake system at regular intervals as outlined in the owner's manual.

Every 6,000 Miles

1. Check the brake fluid level. (Or once every three months.)

2. Adjust the rear brakes.

3. Check the wear on brake linings and friction pads. Brake linings should be replaced when worn to a thickness of 0.06″.

4. Road test the car to check the function of the brakes.

Every 12,000 Miles

1. Check the condition of brake hoses and lines and check the master cylinder, wheel cylinders and fittings for leakage.

2. Adjust the handbrake.

Every 36,000 Miles or Every Three Years

Replace all brake hoses, rubber cups and rubber seals throughout the system; change the brake fluid.

BRAKE FLUID

Always keep the reservoir properly filled. Check the level every 6,000 miles or every three months.

Use only brake fluid meeting the minimum requirements of specification SAE 70 R 3. For SAAB Sport and Monte Carlo 850 models, use Lockheed H D 328 brake fluid. For SAAB 95 and 96 models, use Lockheed Super Heavy Duty brake fluid.

When refilling the reservoir, always clean the cap before unscrewing it to prevent any dirt from entering the system. Be certain the air vents in the cap are not blocked.

BRAKE BLEEDING

Bleeding is not a routine procedure and is necessary only when part of the system has been disassembled or when the brake fluid has been drained. Indications that air has entered the system are excessive pedal travel, spongy pedal action or absence of braking effect until the pedal has been pumped several times.

Location of bleedscrews, front brakes—SAAB 95 and 96 up to and including 1966

A bleed screw is provided for each brake. Bleed screws for the disc brakes are located on the inner part of the caliper up to and including 1966, from 1967 the screws are located on the brake cylinder.

When bleeding the rear brakes on the SAAB Sport and 96 and Monte Carlo 850 up to chassis No. 400477, the pressure regulating valves will shut off the supply of brake fluid to the rear wheels if the brake pedal is depressed too hard before the bleed screw is opened.

To bleed the system, proceed as follows:

1. Check that the reservoir is full and that the air vents are not blocked.

2. Since the master cylinder has tandem pistons, it is necessary to bleed both rear wheels and both front wheels at the same time in order to purge the system. Begin with the rear wheels and bleed the front wheels afterwards.

3. Fit suitable hoses to the bleed screws.

4. Dip the hose ends into a glass jar full of clean brake fluid.

5. Back off both screws 1/2–1 turn.

6. Have another person quickly push the pedal down and allow to come up slowly.

Location of bleedscrews, rear brakes

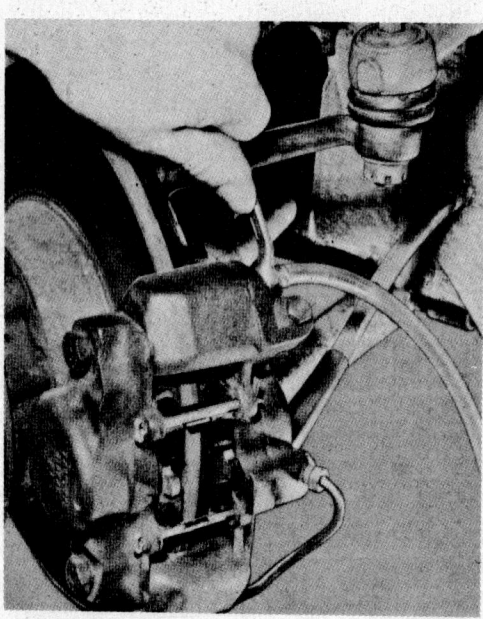

Location of bleedscrews, front brakes—SAAB Sport and Monte Carlo up to and including 1966

Continue until escaping fluid is free of air bubbles. Keep the hose ends below the fluid level in the jars during the operation.

7. Close the bleed screws, keeping the pedal depressed.

8. Be certain the fluid in the reservoir does not run out while the system is being bled; top up as you go along.

9. Top off the reservoir after bleeding both the front and rear brakes.

CAUTION: *Discard brake fluid in the jars, as it is permeated with air.*

Master Cylinder

REMOVAL

1. Disconnect the brake outlet lines from the master cylinder.

2. Remove the rubber boot from the pushrod, or back off the locking nut and unscrew the pushrod from the clevis on the brake pedal.

3. Loosen and remove the two master cylinder retaining bolts. The lower one is a stud bolt and the nut is reached from the engine compartment. The upper one is a standard bolt, accessible from inside the car.

4. Remove the master cylinder.

INSTALLATION

1. Cover all openings to prevent the entry of dirt during installation.

2. Attach the brake cylinder to the cowl plate.

3. Install the rubber boot onto the pushrod. Reassemble the pushrod if it has been disassembled.

4. Connect the brake outlet lines and refill the system with brake fluid.

5. Adjust the brake pedal free-play.

6. Bleed the hydraulic system.

DISASSEMBLY

1. Remove the rubber boot (11) from its retaining plate (8), together with the push-rod (31). Bend the four ears of the boot retaining plate away from the mounting flange and remove it from the end of the cylinder.

2. Depress the spring retainer (30) and, using a small screwdriver, unwind the "Spirolox" circlip (29) from the groove on the primary piston, taking care not to distort the coils; remove the spring retainer (30) together with the spring (9).

3. Remove the circlip (28), taking care not to damage the surface finish of the primary piston (10). Lightly tap the mounting flange of the cylinder body on the bench and remove the nylon guide bearing (27), the secondary cup (26) and the plain washer (25).

4. Using special snap-ring pliers with long narrow jaws, tool No. 784199, remove the inner snap-ring (24), taking care not to damage the surface finish of the primary piston (10).

5. Removal of the snap-ring (24) will allow both pistons to be withdrawn together with the piston stop (23).

6. Compress the intermediate spring (18), together with spring holder (20), then drive out the retaining pin (19) using a suitable pin punch. This will separate the two pistons (10 and 14), and allow the withdrawal of spring (18) and spring holder (20).

7. Remove the primary cups (12 and 21), together with the piston washers (13 and 22), from the primary and secondary pistons. Remove the secondary cup (15) from the back of the secondary piston. Do not attempt to remove the clip (17) from the secondary piston, as it is permanently peened in position.

8. Unscrew the outlet adapters (46) and remove them with the gaskets.

9. Remove the one-way valves—the spring (41), valve body (42) and spring clip (44). Take care not to distort the spring clip (44) when removing it from the valve body.

10. Remove the six bolts that hold the cover of the brake fluid reservoir (5), then take off the cover and gasket.

INSPECTION

1. Make sure the cylinder bore is not scored.

2. Check the bypass holes; probe with a thin piece of steel piano wire.

3. Check all parts; replace any defective ones. Internal rubber parts should be replaced in any event.

ASSEMBLY

Before assembling, dip all parts in brake fluid.

1. Using the fingers only, stretch the secondary cup (15) over the large end of the secondary piston, with the lip pointing toward the peened clip. Gently work around the cup with the fingers to ensure correct seating.

2. Install the piston washer onto the secondary piston, as illustrated, so that the convex edge faces the rear of the cup. Using the fingers only, ease the primary cup (12) over the nose and into the groove, with the lip of the cup pointing away from the head of the piston.

3. Use the same procedure with the primary cup (21) and piston washer (22) of the primary piston. Ease the spring holder (20) into the end of the spring (18) and fit the other end of the spring over the rear of the secondary piston (14).

4. Place the retaining pin (19) in the hole in the primary piston; do not seat fully. Compress the spring until the secondary piston clip (17) is visible. Place the clip in position in the primary piston and secure it by pushing the retaining pin fully home. Release the spring and check that the spring holder (20) is correctly positioned. ·

5. Ease the pistons gently into the cylinder bore and slide the piston stop (23) over the primary piston. Install the snap-ring (24) into the inner groove, using snap-ring pliers. Do not damage the surface finish of the primary piston because this could cause leakage past the secondary cup.

6. Install the plain washer (25) into the cylinder bore against the snap-ring, followed by the secondary cup (26).

7. Place the nylon guide bearing (27) in position and secure the outer snap-ring (28).

8. Fit the boot retaining plate (8) in

position over the mounting flange and bend the four ears over to hold it in position.

9. Mount the spring retainer (30) with the return spring (9) on the primary piston (10). Compress the spring until the piston circlip groove is visible behind the spring retainer, then install the "Spirolox" circlip. Before installing the rubber boot (11), smear the small end of the pushrod (31) and its groove with silicone grease to ensure that the rod will rotate freely when assembled.

10. Ease the pushrod into position in the rubber boot and push the boot into its groove.

11. Ease the spring clip (44) into the one-way valve body and make sure that it is correctly positioned. Install the return spring over the valve body and assemble the parts within the outlet port, inserting the spring first.

12. Screw the outlet adapter (46), together with gasket (45), into the outlet port and tighten to a torque of 28 ft. lbs. Use the same procedure for the other outlet port.

13. Place the cover of the brake fluid reservoir (5) in position, with the gasket, and secure using the six bolts, tightening them to a torque of 6 ft. lbs.

Brake Lines

The brake lines are made of 3/16″ Bundy tubing. The ends of all the lines are flanged and fitted with compression nuts, which must be pushed onto the line before the ends are flanged. All lines, rubber hoses and fittings in the brake system must be kept in good condition at all times.

New lines must fit well at both ends and at the clips. Never stretch a too short line or bend a previously installed line. Such procedures could result in stresses, which could cause leakage, line fracture or stripped threads.

Lines for connection to brake hoses are flanged as "type A"; other lines are flanged as "type B."

Brake Hoses

The brake system has two front and two rear brake hoses, providing a flexible connection between the body and the wheel cylinders. These hoses are of different lengths and must not be confused. Install the hoses with the wheels freely suspended and aligned straight ahead. When tighten-

ing the brake line, hold the brake hose (not the locknut) to prevent the hose from twisting and changing position. When installing hoses it is of extreme importance that they are correctly positioned so that they do not rub steering or suspension components or the body.

Stop Light Switch

The stop light switch is connected to the hydraulic system and is actuated by hydraulic pressure. It is found in a four-way coupling on the firewall beside the master cylinder.

From chassis No. 439334 for SAAB 96, and 46816 for SAAB 95, a mechanical stoplight switch is utilized. This switch is located on a bracket above the brake pedal.

Pressure Regulating Valve

The SAAB 96, Sport and Monte Carlo 850 up to and including the 1966 model, are equipped with two pressure regulating valves for the rear brakes.

The valves are bolted to the floor under the rear seat, and serve to limit the hydraulic pressure to the rear brakes so that the braking effect is properly distributed between the front and rear wheels. The valve is set for a given pressure and cannot be adjusted. When the pressure reaches 425–485 psi, the spring force acting on the piston is overcome, causing the piston to travel and close the passage to the rear brakes. Any additional pressure increases the effect of the front brakes, while the pressure on the rear brakes remains constant.

Wheel Cylinders

SAAB 95 and 96 up to and Including 1966—Front

The front wheel cylinders contain a single piston with a rubber sealing ring and an external rubber boot. The piston is forced toward the brake shoe by the fluid pressure.

Each of the rear wheel cylinders has two pistons which actuate separate brake shoes. Each piston is fitted with a rubber sealing ring and an external rubber boot.

Removal

1. Jack up the car and remove the wheel, brake drum, brake shoes, and backing plate.

2. Disconnect the brake hose from the wheel cylinder.

3. Disconnect the brake hose between the cylinders.

4. Remove the cylinder by unscrewing the bolts from the rear of the backing plate.

Disassembly

The illustration shows a dismantled wheel cylinder. Remove the rubber boot from the cylinder, withdraw the piston and take off the sealing ring.

Inspection

1. Clean all parts with brake fluid. Do not allow gasoline or oil to come into contact with the rubber sealing rings or boots.

2. Make sure the cylinder bore is not scored.

3. Check that the rubber sealing rings and boots are in good condition. The use of unsuitable brake fluids can cause rubber parts to swell up to 50%. Any rubber parts that are even slightly damaged or swollen must be replaced.

Assembly

Lubricate all parts with brake fluid before assembling. Install a cup onto the piston, taking care to align it as illustrated. Use the fingers only. Next, install the piston into the cylinder and put on the rubber boot.

Installation

1. Attach the cylinders to the backing plate with the bolts; don't forget the elastic washers.

2. Reinstall the brake line between the cylinders.

3. Secure the brake hose. Remember to insert the copper gasket.

4. Refit the backing plate, brake shoes, brake drum, and wheel.

SAAB 95 AND 96, SPORT AND MONTE CARLO 850—REAR

From chassis No. 400478, the SAAB 96 and Monte Carlo are equipped with smaller wheel cylinders at the rear than those of the SAAB 95. The location of their anchor pins differs from the 95 to prevent crossover. The anchor pin must not be removed.

Removal

1. Remove the wheel, brake drum and brake shoes.

2. Disconnect the handbrake cable from the levers.

3. Disconnect the brake line from the rear of the backing plate.

4. Remove the wheel cylinder retaining ring and the bleed screw from the rear of the backing plate.

5. Remove the wheel cylinder.

Disassembly

1. Remove the rubber boots from the cylinder.

2. Pull out the pistons.

3. Take the rubber seals off the pistons.

Inspection

1. Clean and dry all parts. Do not allow gasoline or grease to come in contact with the rubber seals.

2. Make sure the cylinder bore is not scored.

3. Check that all the rubber seals and cups are in perfect condition.

Assembly

Utmost cleanliness must be observed when assembling the wheel cylinder. Lubricate all parts with brake fluid when assembling. Assemble, as shown in the illustration, making certain the piston seal is facing the correct way; use no sharp tools.

Installation

1. Bolt the wheel cylinder to the backing plate and locate the retaining ring and bleed screw. The cylinder has an anchor pin which fits in a hole in the backing plate.

2. Connect the brake line.

3. Install the brake shoes, brake drum and wheel, taking care not to damage the axle seal.

4. Connect the handbrake cable. The handbrake lever must be installed with the bent part upwards. Bleed the system whenever a cylinder has been removed or a line disconnected.

Brake Pedal Free-Play Adjustment

In order to allow the piston in the master cylinder to return fully each time the pedal is released, there always must be clearance between the master cylinder piston and the brake pedal pushrod when the pedal is at

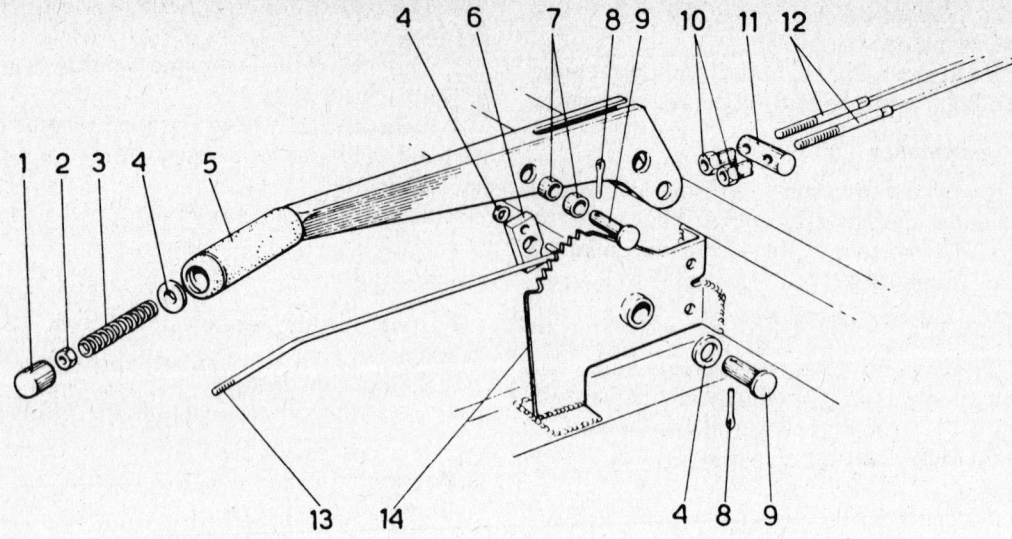

Handbrake components

1. Release button
2. Nut
3. Return spring
4. Washer
5. Handbrake lever

6. Pawl
7. Spacer sleeve
8. Cotter pin or circlip
9. Pin
10. Adjustment nut

11. Cable pin
12. Threaded wire rods
13. Pawl rod
14. Ratchet

rest. This clearance should be measured at the tip of the pedal, and should be 0.12–0.24″.

1. Loosen the locknut.

2. Turn the hexagonal section of the push-rod until the correct clearance is obtained.

3. Tighten the locknut.

Handbrake Adjustment

Adjustment of the handbrake lever travel or of the brake cables always should be preceded by adjustment of the rear brakes. If the handbrake still requires adjustment, proceed as follows:

1. Jack up the car so that both rear wheels clear the floor.

2. Remove the right front seat and move the lever to its lowest position.

3. Tighten the left-hand adjusting nut until the brake shoes contact the left brake drum.

4. Back off the nut just enough to permit the wheel to rotate, then back off one more full turn.

5. Repeat this procedure for the right-hand adjusting nut.

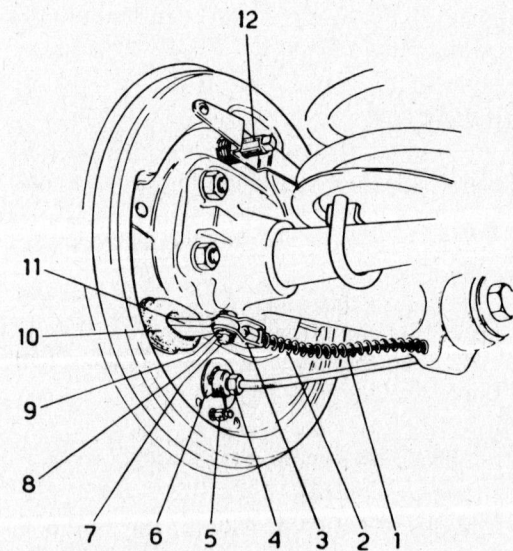

Reverse side of left-rear backing plate

1. Handbrake wire
2. Coil spring
3. Clevis
4. Brake pipe connection
5. Bleed nipple
6. Lock washer

7. Pin
8. Cotter pin
9. Washer
10. Rubber boot
11. Brake lever
12. Adjustment device

6. Test by pulling the handbrake all the way on, then releasing it. The wheels should still rotate freely with the lever pulled up two notches from off, but should be locked at the third-notch.

7. Make sure the braking effect is equal for both wheels.

Brakes—V4

The major difference between the brakes used on the 1969 and later V4 and previous models is that a power brake unit is used. It consists of a vacuum cylinder, which is actuated by the brake pedal. A hose connects the cylinder to the intake manifold of the engine. The operation of the system is described below.

INITIAL POSITION

When "off," the return spring holds the valve piston and the pushrod in the right-hand end position in the guide housing. In this position, the atmospheric air bore is kept closed and the vacuum bore open. Since the right-hand side of the diaphragm is connected with the left-hand side via the open vacuum bore in the guide housing, the pressure is equal on both sides of the diaphragm.

BRAKE POSITION

When the pedal is pressed, the vacuum bore closes and the atmospheric air bore opens, overcoming the tension of the return spring. Vacuum on the left-hand side of the diaphragm, and atmospheric pressure on the right-hand side, results in servo action being obtained. The brake effect can be increased further by greater pressure on the pedal. When the pedal pressure drops, the return spring forces the valve piston back. The vacuum bore then opens and the atmospheric air bore closes. The vacuum servo returns to its "off" position.

Should the power brake unit malfunction, the brake system in the car will still function without servo effect. CAUTION: *Individual parts are not available for the vacuum servo and the unit is not serviceable.*

Competition Modification

To prepare a car for competition, two primary areas must be improved—power and handling. A third area—safety—also must be considered when making any modifications.

Before beginning, make sure to thoroughly investigate all the pertinent rules and regulations for the particular type of competition. Another thing to remember is that each car is different and must be prepared on an individual basis. General procedures that work for one car may not work on another; some experimentation with the following procedures may be necessary to achieve the desired results.

Two-Stroke Engine

Power can be increased by altering the cylinder head to increase compression and by modifying the intake, exhaust, and transfer ports to increase breathing efficiency. Modifying the ports on a two-stroke engine is equivalent to installing a high-performance camshaft in a four-stroke engine.

The following procedures are arranged in three groups—Stage I is a mild tuning procedure for the street or gymkhanas; Stage II is for hillclimbs, sprint races, ice races, or other events where major modifications are permitted; and Stage III is for all-out competition.

850 CC. ENGINE TO 1965

Stage I

Stage I tuning consists entirely of carburetor and exhaust system modifications. Re-jet the carburetor, depending on whether a GT (2.01″ diameter) exhaust system and a modified air filter is used.

	Std. Filter and Exhaust	Modified Filter and GT Exhaust
Air throat	28 mm.	31 mm.
Main jet	135	145–150
Emulsion jet	250	250
Fuel idle jet	45	45
Air idle jet	100	100

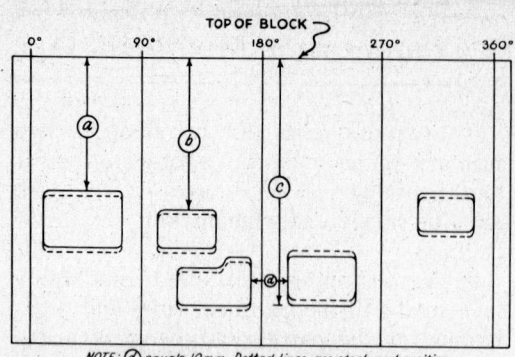

NOTE: ⓓ equals 10mm. Dotted lines are stock port positions

Engine	Exhaust ports raised ⓐ mm	Transfer ports raised ⓑ mm	Intake ports lowered ⓒ mm
850 to '65 STAGE II	47	57	96
850 to '65 STAGE III	46	56	97
750 STAGE II	46.4	57	96.2
750 STAGE III	45.7	56.8	97.8
850 1965-66	44	56	99

Port modifications—two-stroke engine

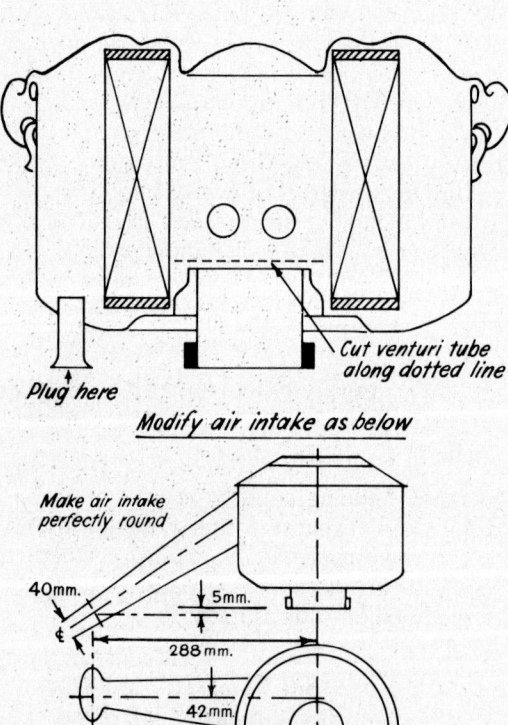

Plug here

Cut venturi tube along dotted line

Modify air intake as below

Make air intake perfectly round

40mm.
5mm.
288 mm.
42mm.

Air cleaner modifications

Stage II

Increase compression by milling the cylinder head (9.5:1). After milling, check the piston crown-to-cylinder head clearance—it must be at least 0.73 mm. (0.0285″). The combustion chambers can be flycut to correct clearance. Grind the ports to the dimensions shown in the chart, then polish and smooth the surfaces. The exhaust ports are ground upwards, as are the transfer ports, while the intake ports are extended downwards. All measurements are taken between the edge of the port and the top surface of the cylinder block.

Ignition modifications are simple—use a Bosch VJ3BR7 distributor in conjunction with copper spark plug wires and a Bosch TK12A1D ignition coil. The ignition timing can be varied, but is best set at TDC with this set-up.

Modify the air cleaner as illustrated. The 1965 air filter does not have to be modified, however. Polish the carburetor barrel, then re-jet the carburetor as follows:

Air throat   31 mm.
Main jet   150–155
Fuel idle jet   50
Fuel air jet   50

Stage III

Increase compression by milling the cylinder head 4.5 mm. (0.177″). The combustion chambers must be flycut afterwards to maintain a piston crown-to-cylinder head clearance of 0.73 mm. (0.0285″). Grind the ports to the dimensions shown in the chart, then polish and smooth the surfaces. The exhaust ports are ground upward, as are the transfer ports, while the intake ports are extended downward. All measurements are taken between the edge of the ports and the top surface of the cylinder block. The amount of material removed in this operation requires that certain care be taken to ensure adequate wall thickness. This can be checked through the coolant passages.

A great increase in power can be achieved by installing the GT crankshaft. This crankshaft has larger, full-diameter counterweights which take up more space in the crankcase than the stock unit. In a two-stroke engine, this decrease in crankcase

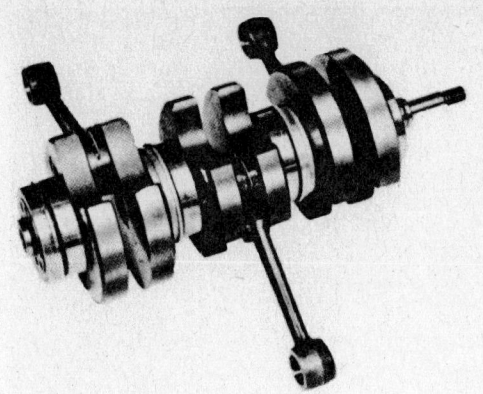

Standard crankshaft

GT crankshaft—note filled counterweights

crankshaft), a tachometer is recommended. The proper hook-up for the three-cylinder engine is illustrated.

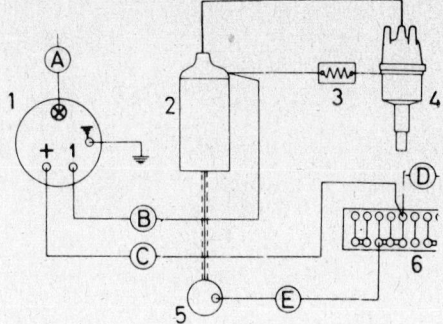

Tachometer installation schematic—two-stroke engines

1. Tachometer
2. Ignition coil
3. Resistance
4. Distributor
5. Ignition switch
6. Fuse block
A. Instrument lamp lead
B. Lead between coil and terminal 1 on Tach
C. Lead between fuse block (fuel pump) and terminal on Tach
D. Lead to fuel pump
E. Lead from ignition switch to fuse block

volume serves to increase compression.

Carburetion should be increased by replacing the stock unit with one of the three-carburetor systems or the single Solex dual-throat 44PII.

Use a Bosch VJ3BR7 distributor, a Bosch TK12A1 ignition coil, copper spark plug wires, and Bosch M310T1 spark plugs for best results. Set ignition timing to TDC.

It is advisable to install a Bendix electric fuel pump to prevent fuel starvation at high rpm. Install pistons at 0.0035–0.0040″ clearance to prevent galling, and use only SAAB two-stroke oil and high-test (at least 97 octane) gasoline.

Pay particular attention to the head torque sequence, after milling the head, to prevent gasket blowing. Initial tightening torque is 35 ft. lbs.—this should be rechecked at 300, 600, and 1,200 miles if the car is used on the street; or before every competition meet.

If 6,000 rpm is exceeded very often, the stock front vibration damper tends to become out-of-round. Since this quite often causes destruction of the front bearing (and

750 cc. Engine

The 750 cc. engine responds to the same modifications as does the 850 cc. engine up to 1965. Port timing is shown in the chart.

850 cc. Engine—1965-66

Modify the ports, as previously described, according to the illustration and chart. An especially critical area on this engine, where care must be exercised during grinding, is the water jacket directly above the exhaust ports. Smooth and polish all port areas after grinding.

Mill the head 3.0 mm. (0.1182″), then flycut the combustion chambers to maintain a piston crown-to-cylinder head clearance of 0.73 mm. (0.0285″).

When tightening the head bolts, first pre-tighten to 22 ft. lbs., then turn an additional 90°. Start the engine, allow it to warm up to operating temperature, then let it cool down and turn the head bolts an additional 20°. If the car is used on the street, tighten an additional 20° after 1,000 miles with a

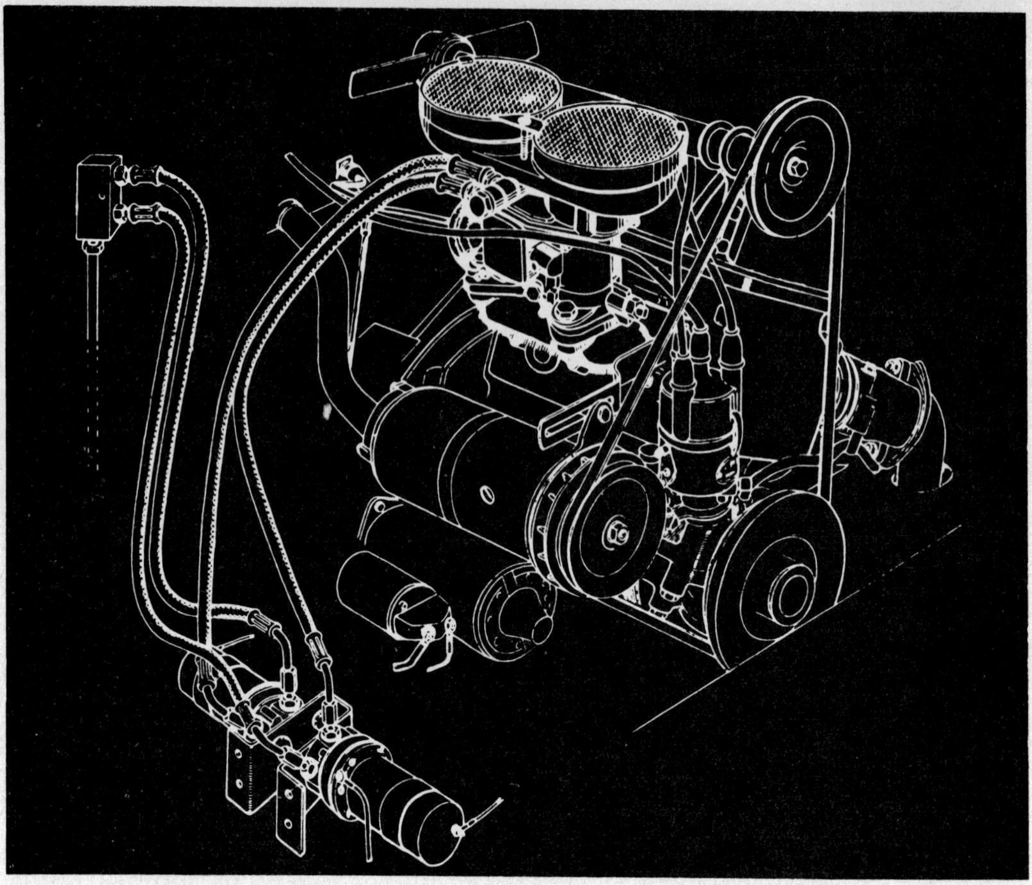

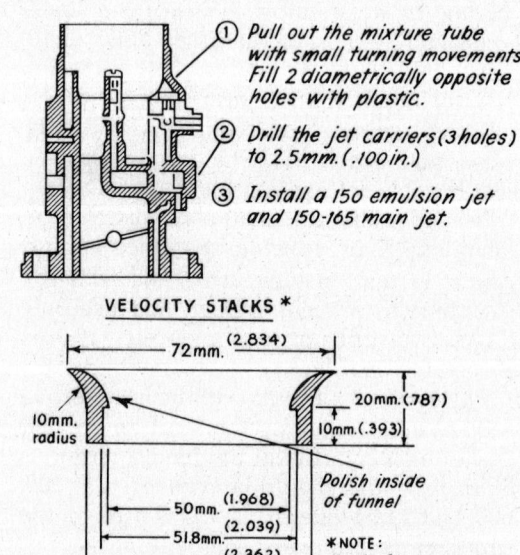

Solex dual-throat 44 PII carburetor and twin fuel pump hook-up

cold engine, or after one or two competition meets.

G.ind the intake and exhaust manifolds to match the ports and gaskets, then smooth and polish the inside runners.

Modify the carburetor according to the illustration, then re-jet as follows:

	Stage I & II	Stage III (with velocity stack)
Main jet	155	160–165
Air correction	150	150

To adjust the float level, use a different shim under the needle valve; never bend the float arm. To check the level:

1. Remove the air cleaner.

2. Start the engine and allow it to idle for 30 seconds, then turn off the ignition without touching the gas pedal.

3. Loosen the fuel lines and remove the top of the float chamber and the float.

4. Measure between the gasket surface

① Pull out the mixture tube with small turning movements. Fill 2 diametrically opposite holes with plastic.

② Drill the jet carriers (3 holes) to 2.5mm. (.100 in.)

③ Install a 150 emulsion jet and 150-165 main jet.

VELOCITY STACKS *

72 mm. (2.834)
20mm. (.787)
10mm. radius
10mm. (.393)
Polish inside of funnel
50mm. (1.968)
51.8mm. (2.039)
*NOTE: Not for Street use
60mm. (2.362)

(Fabricate from Aluminum)

Carburetor modifications

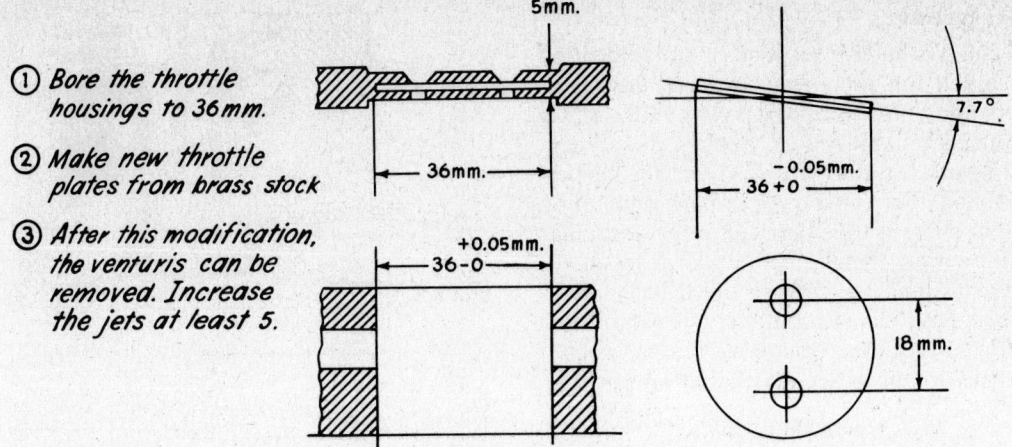

① Bore the throttle housings to 36mm.

② Make new throttle plates from brass stock

③ After this modification, the venturis can be removed. Increase the jets at least 5.

Carburetor modifications

and the fuel level, alongside the carburetor barrel, using a depth gauge—the proper level is 24.5± 1 mm. (0.9653± 0.039″).

Modify the air cleaner as illustrated. Since the preheater tube no longer operates after this modification, it may be necessary to add 2–4% isopropyl alcohol to the fuel to prevent carburetor icing under some weather conditions.

Modify the exhaust system as illustrated. For Stage I tune, the stock tailpipe can be used; for Stages II and III, a 6 1/2 foot long by 2″ diameter extension is recommended. This "straight" pipe must be so arranged to exit just behind the rear of the door.

Use copper spark plug wires, lock the ignition advance, and install a double contact breaker spring. It is also a good idea to exchange the fiber shims for steel washers (in the distributor).

When assembling the distributor, make sure there is at least 0.004″ axial shaft play, measured with a feeler gauge under the drive gear. Set the ignition timing to 20° BTDC for a start, then work from there.

For maximum vibration damper life, do not exceed 6,300 rpm. The torsional vibration damper should be inspected at regular intervals. If necessary, replace the rubber disc and the damper spring (1.125″).

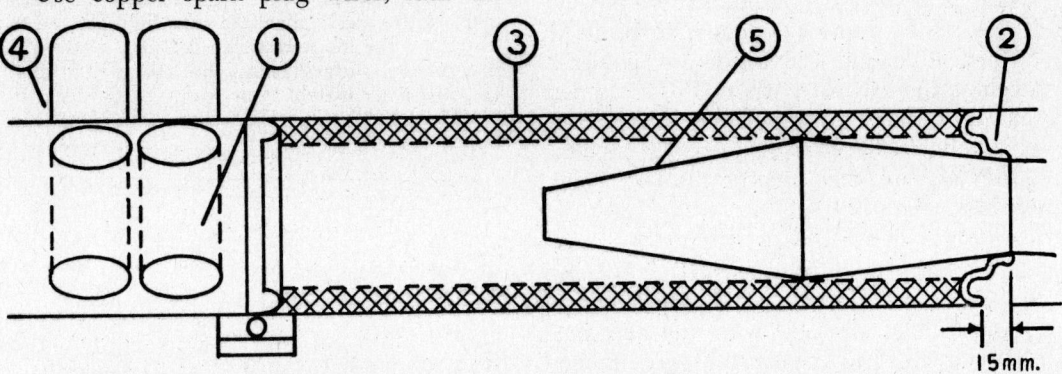

1· Remove the exhaust tubes from the inside.

2· Cut the inlet pipe at the weld and remove 110mm. (4.33 in.) of the pipe leading into the cone so the taper starts at 15mm. (.590 in.) before the inlet end of the muffer.

3· Remove the glass wool and perforated sheet tube.

4· Weld reinforcing gussets to the outlet pipes.

5· Existing cone with 80 holes moved outward 4.33 in.

Exhaust system modifications

V4 Engine

The V4 engine responds to modification in much the same way as does any four-stroke engine—increased power with slightly reduced reliability and tractability. Procedures are listed in this chapter can be performed either entirely, or in part, depending on the stage of tune desired for the particular competition. Remember, any of these modifications tend to increase the exhaust emissions above the minimum levels established for each year car; therefore the car should not be driven on the street if at all possible.

ENGINE BLOCK

It is not necessary to mill the block to increase compression, simply file or sand the decks lightly to remove any burrs, then lightly chamfer all machined surfaces. Have the block "hot tanked" before beginning assembly, because metal chips and dust often lodge in inaccessible places. These chips, if allowed to remain, will eventually circulate through the lubrication system and cause bearing and crankshaft damage.

CYLINDER HEADS

Mill the heads to increase compression ratio. Do not, however, remove more than 0.040″ from each head or the intake manifold will have to be machined to mate properly with the heads. Porting and polishing results in better gas flow, thus more power. If the 1 3/4″ exhaust system is to be used (which it should for maximum power), machine the exhaust ports to 1 3/4″ as per the illustration. Machine the flange that goes between the head and exhaust pipe to 1 3/4″ as well, then enlarge the bolt holes and use gasket No. 707712.

OVERSIZE VALVES

The ports must be modified if oversize valves are to be used. Machine the intake ports "funnel shaped" with the top port diameter, directly below the seat, opened out to 1.575″. The ports should be machined to 1.250″ in diameter about 1/4″ below the seat, then all sharp corners should be removed and the ports polished.

Machine the exhaust port "funnel shaped" with the top port diameter, directly below the seat, opened out to 1.275″. The port should be machined to 1.150″ in diameter about 1/4″ below the seat, then all sharp corners should be removed and the ports polished.

Countersink to cylinder bore

The intake ports are opened up as illustrated. The dotted lines show the original size and shape of the ports. If more than 0.040″ is milled from the heads or block, the intake manifold must be machined to match. If the block is milled 2.5 mm. (0.0985″) the seating surfaces must be milled 1.5 mm. (0.0591″) to match. Cut valve seat width to 0.0472-0.0623″ for intake valves, 0.0632-0.0787″ for exhaust valves.

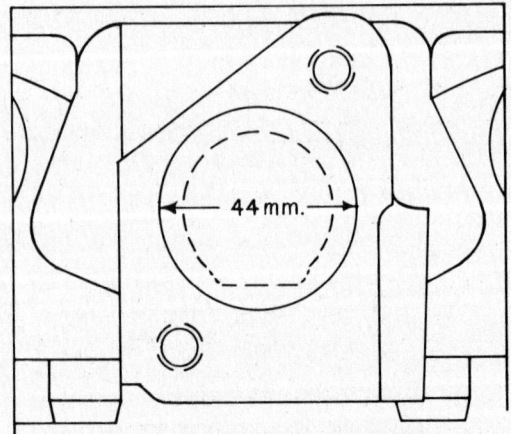

Open up the exhaust ports to 44 mm. (1.732″), as well as the manifold flange. Use gasket No. 707712, after enlarging the bolt holes.

The valve guides *must* be knurled to obtain proper stem-to-guide clearance (very light thumb press fit), then the seats must be ground. Grind the intake seats so that the width is 0.050"; the exhaust seat width must be wider to accommodate the increased temperatures in that area—0.065".

The oversize valves must be machined and polished as per the illustration, then they must be adjusted as follows (depending on camshaft used):

3/4 race cam: 0.016H (intake)
                0.018H (exhaust)
Full race cam: 0.018H (intake)
                0.020H (exhaust)
Track grind cam: 0.020H (intake)
                  0.024H (exhaust)

Use intake valve part No. 111000, exhaust valve part No. 111010.

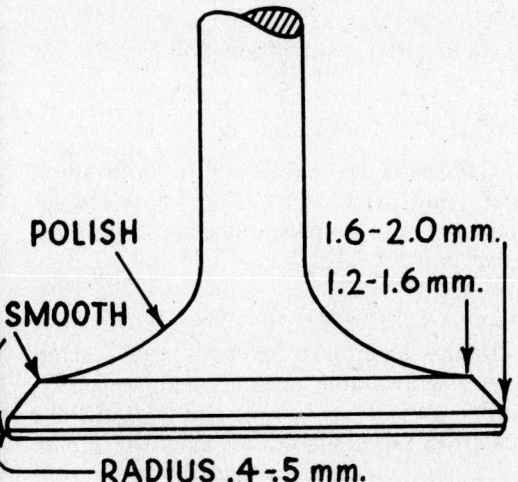

POLISH

SMOOTH

1.6-2.0 mm.

1.2-1.6 mm.

RADIUS .4-.5 mm.

Valves should be polished to remove all roughness. Radius the bottom edge to achieve a seating surface of 0.0157-0.0197" from the outer edge. Cut the seats as described in the text.

VALVE TRAIN

The pushrods need no modification, nor should any be attempted. The valve springs should be replaced with part No. 111250, and aluminum retainers, part No. 111300, used.

For best results, install full-floating Teflon valve guide seals. These seals are available from SAAB under competition part No. 111020. To install these seals, a special tool (part No. 111021) is required. The valve guide must be machined as well, to provide sufficient clearance between the spring retainer and the new seal when the valve is fully open. Cut the guide down to 0.425"

from the spring seat to obtain this clearance.

The stock valve lifters should be discarded and lighter competition lifters, part No. 112100, installed.

CARBURETOR

If the car is used in events where major modifications are not permitted, use an early Solex (part No. 786638·) single-barrel unit; this carburetor does not have exhaust emission settings. Remove the venturi from this carburetor and install 195–200 main jet for best results.

For more performance, use a Weber two-barrel 28/36 DCD carburetor (part No. 115000). A special two-barrel manifold is available from SAAB under part No. 114001. This particular carburetor and manifold is also available in a complete Stage I tuning kit, along with a chromed air filter, vented oil cap, and necessary linkage and gaskets.

For maximum performance in all-out competition events, use a Weber two-barrel 40 DFI carburetor (part No. 115001). Modify this unit by replacing the main jet with a 190–200, the air correction jet with a 160, and the idle jet with a 65. Set the float level to 6–6.5 mm. (0.2364–0.2561") between float and gasket surface with float chamber held upside down. Bore out choke tubes to 33 mm. and increase main jet size to 200–220 for all-out performance.

AIR FILTER

Modify the stock air filter as per the illustration if a single-barrel Solex is used; use chromed filter No. 115050 for the Weber 28/36 DCD.

FUEL PUMP

The stock fuel pump is sufficient and no modifications are necessary.

OIL PUMP

Replace the stock pump with a high-pressure, high-volume unit. Such a pump is available from SAAB under part No. 114200.

OIL COOLER

It is advisable to use an oil cooler, part No. 117400, for maximum engine life. The cooler increases oil capacity by 1 1/2–2 quarts.

CRANKSHAFT

The standard crankshaft can be used as is, or a 1,700 cc. stroker crankshaft can be

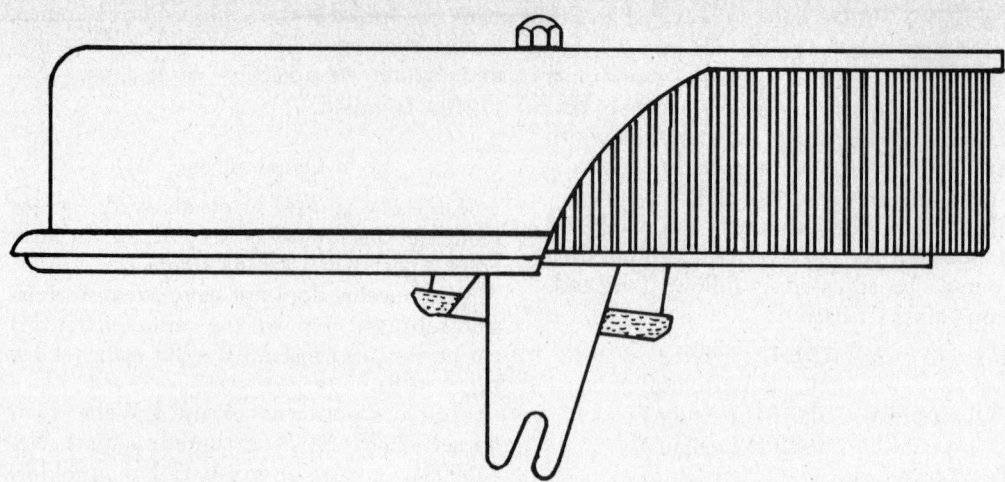

Modify the air cleaner as illustrated if a single-barrel carburetor is used.

installed (part No. 116010). If the high-pressure oil pump is used with either of these cranks, use red bearings.

FLYWHEEL

The flywheel can be lightened by some 5 lbs. as per the illustration. It is important, however, to rebalance the flywheel after any such machining operation, as well as to use new flywheel bolts during assembly.

CLUTCH

A competition pressure plate, part No. 1130300, is available. A competition clutch disc is also available, although no part number is listed yet.

PISTONS

If the 1,700 cc. crank is used, 1,700 cc. pistons and rods must be used as well. These are available under part Nos. 116011 and 116012 for early engines, No. 116020 for late-model blue engines. If the standard crank is used, use competition pistons, No. 116005. Always check that the rings are properly staggered before installation.

Compression Ratio

Part No.	Ratio
116011, 116020	10:1
116012	10.2:1
116005	11.2:1

CONNECTING ROD BOLTS

Always use competition rod bolts, part No. 113150, when assembling any modified V4 engine. The standard rod bolts, even if new, are *not* strong enough to withstand the increased loads on the lower end, and engine failure is virtually certain. When installing the competition bolts, check the

CAMSHAFT

Camshafts are available for both street and competition use. If high rpm's are anticipated, use a special steel balance shaft gear, part No. 112125.

INTAKE MANIFOLD

Intake manifolds for two-barrel carburetors are available, as mentioned previously, under parts Nos. 114000 and 114001. The manifold ports should be matched to the head ports and gaskets, and the inside runners polished for best results.

DISTRIBUTOR

Remove the vacuum advance unit and braze the breaker plate to the bottom plate that is attached to the housing. Do not change the centrifugal advance. Use a rotor without radio suppression, as well as spark plug wire (part No. 20110) without resistance. Set timing to 9°BTDC static as a starting point.

SPARK PLUGS

For the silver engine, use Autolite AE-901 plugs (part No. 120152); for the blue engine, use Autolite AG-12 plugs for the street, Autolite AG-901 plugs for racing. These are available under parts Nos. 120150 and 120151 respectively.

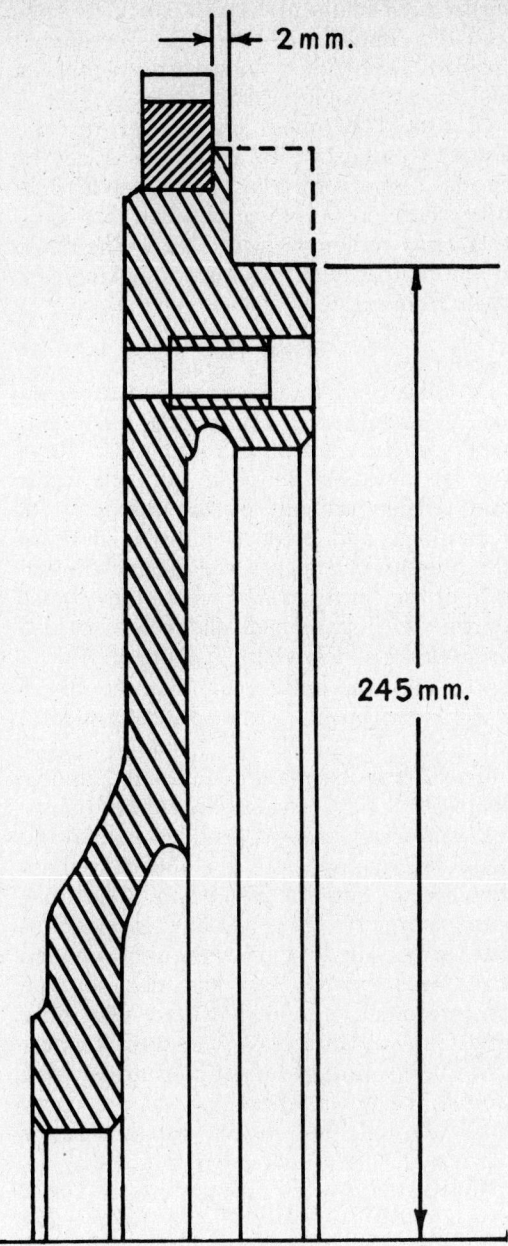

2 mm.

245 mm.

Lighten the flywheel by some 5 lbs. by turning the outside diameter down to 245 mm. (9.6456"). Leave a supporting flange 2 mm. (0.0787") wide behind the ring gear, then rebalance the entire flywheel. Maximum unbalance is 15 g. cm. (0.05280 in. oz.).

CRANKCASE VENTILATION

Intake manifold No. 114001 has an adapter plate to permit installation of full-flow crankcase ventilation. The PCV hose must be attached to the valve cover not having the oil filter tube. Change the existing oil filter cap to the vented type that comes with the Stage I tuning kit, or buy the vented cap separately.

EXHAUST SYSTEM

A simple set of headers can be made up using two lengths of 1 3/4" pipe, brought together in a Y about 51" from the block. Connect this single pipe to a muffler suitably mounted, with exhaust exiting behind one door.

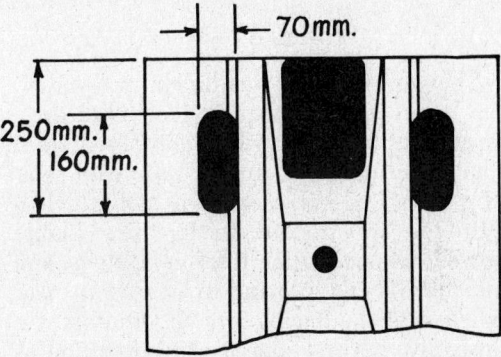

70 mm.

250 mm.
160 mm.

The exhaust pipe openings in the floor pan must be enlarged to accommodate the larger diameter exhaust pipe. All dimensions are in mm.

Chassis and Handling

Since there are so many opinions on just how to set up a SAAB suspension for each type of competition, and even for individual courses, no one procedure can be specifically prescribed. The following procedures are good general practices.

SPRINGS

The SAAB can be made to handle quite a bit better by lowering the entire car. The best way to accomplish this is to cut the coil springs 1-1/2—3 turns each. Never heat the springs in order to collapse them, as this is an unsafe practice. Coil springs are under considerable compression when installed, and can be dangerous if removed without proper precautions. Always use a good coil spring compressor, especially on the front coils. It is easier to remove the rear coils by first removing the limit straps and shocks, then lowering the rear axle far enough to release most of the compression.

SHOCK ABSORBERS

Many different shock absorbers and shock absorber combinations can be, and have been, used. The best all-around answer to the problem is to install Koni adjustable shock absorbers at all four wheels. These shock absorbers have a wide variety of adjustment combinations, which the driver can use to advantage by tailoring the handling to each specific course.

WHEELS AND TIRES

The greatest single handling improvement can be achieved by using wider tread tires, in conjunction with wider reinforced rims. The choice of racing tires is quite wide, and care should be exercised so as not to select a tire too large in diameter for the available power. Depending on track conditions, any number of tire types and tread patterns can be successful. Racing tire distributors are probably the best source of information as to the type of tire that has been proven most successful at local tracks and, of course, a look at what the competition is using also may be a help.

V4 Rally Cars

The following details show the modifications made by the SAAB factory competition department to its rally cars. Part numbers are included to aid the owner in deciding what modifications to include in his own car.

CHASSIS

The chassis is lightened as much as possible, while making sure the car retains its structural soundness. The entire chassis floor is spot welded closer than on a standard SAAB, and all undercoating is removed to save weight.

SUSPENSION

The springs are replaced with rally springs (No. 140100, 140110) and Ferodo 2430 pads (No. 140002) are used on the front discs. The rear axle (No. 140200) is more thoroughly welded at all points, espically at the center bushing, shock absorber mounts, and control arm attaching points. In addition, the axle tube is made of heavier gauge tubing. The rear control arms and the tubes that attach the control arms to the chassis are made of heavier stock as well, and the control arms are more thoroughly welded. Heavy-duty shock absorbers (No. 140150, 140151) are used.

It would be most impractical for the average enthusiast to make up a set of special rear control arms and a heavier axle tube; therefore it is recommended that these two items be bought from SAAB. Their cost is low compared to the effort of making new parts from scratch.

FRONT END

Modifications to the front end are concerned mainly with reinforcing the points where fracture is most likely to occur. Reinforcing plates are added to both the inside and outside sections of the upper shock mountings, and extra welding is done in these areas. Plates are welded on the outside of the spring towers where they attach to the floor pan, and plates are welded around the holes where the upper A-arms go through the inner fender panels. Heavy duty A-arm bushings (No. 140090, 140091) are used.

The A-arm beams are reinforced underneath (the ones that hold the rubber bumpers) and reinforcement is added behind the upper spring supports (No. 730062) where they are attached to the chassis. The front spring support (No. 730062) is made of heavier stock and is more thoroughly welded than on standard cars, and channel-type reinforcement is added where the inner fender panels attach to the outer fenders above the spring towers. Plates are welded around the holes where the steering arms come through, and heavy gauge washers are added where the rubber bumpers (No. 707601) attach to the spring brackets. Plates also are added where the upper and lower A-arms attach to the chassis.

REAR FLOOR PAN

Reinforcement plates are welded to the floor pan where the rear axle control arms attach to the chassis, and a plate is added where the center axle bushing attaches to the chassis.

NOTE: *Cars are available from SAAB built to the above specifications. These cars are built for competition only, thus do not have a warranty. Also, the drive train and engine is standard to meet the emission laws, and the engine must be modified separately. Price for the car is approximately $2,800.*

SAAB High-Performance Parts

The following list is compiled from the latest information available. Although list prices are noted, it must be kept in mind that SAAB prices are subject to change, and that this list cannot be construed to be official in any way. Any inquiries should be sent to the local SAAB dealer, or: SAAB Competition Department, 100 Waterfront Street, New Haven, Conn. 06506, phone 203-469-2331 extension 293.

111000 42 mm. oversize intake valve $6.02
Enlargement of intake port is required by machining. Modification should only be performed by a professional machine shop. Valve guides must be knurled to insure proper valve stem clearance and life.

111010 35 mm. oversize exhaust valve $9.69
Enlargement of exhaust port is required by machining. Modification should only be performed by a professional machine shop. Valve guides must be knurled to insure valve stem clearance and life.

111020 Full floating teflon $8.00
  valve guide seals (set of 8)
Machining of the valve guide is required by using cutting tool 111021. The metal housing which holds the spring loaded teflon seal is then press fitted over the guide. Oil leaking past poor valve guide seals pollutes the air fuel/mixture and gives poor combustion and carbon build up. These seals prevent oil seepage and power loss especially in higher rpm ranges.

111021 valve guide seal cutting tool $12.50
Tool required to machine valve guides before installing full floating teflon valve guide seals. Requires a 1/2" drill to perform the necessary work.

111250 valve springs (set of 8) $12.00
Heavier than stock springs. When used with retainers 11300 and lifters 12100, engine rpm redline may be increased to 7,000.

111300 aluminum spring retainers $8.00
  (set of 8)
Each retainer weighs half the weight of a standard retainer. Multiplied by eight means considerably less weight on the valve train and less chance of valve float at high rpm.

112000 3/4 race camshaft $76.00
Excellent camshaft for street use. Has excellent torque characteristics thruout entire rpm range. 111250 springs, 111300 retainers and 12100 lifters recommended.

112001 full race camshaft $82.00
May be used as a camshaft for street use. However, has rough idle and torque is in higher rpm range. Starts developing good power at 2,200 rpm. Good street camshaft for the lighter weight Sonett. 111250 springs, 111300 retainers, 112100 lifters recommended.

112002 track camshaft $85.00
Should be used for all out competition only, such as oval tracks and road racing. Power starts at 3,200 rpm. 111250 springs, 111300 retainers, 112100 lifters must be used to receive full benefit of high rpm torque.

112100 lightweight lifters (set of 8) $14.00
Standard lifter weighs 104 grams. These specially designed lifters weigh only 74 grams and have less power robbing friction in lifter bore than standard lifter. One piece cast unit.

112125 steel balance shaft gear $48.67
This gear should be installed on engines for all out competition. Replaces fibre balance shaft gear which tends to have excessive back lash after running for extended periods at high rpm.

113150 chrome moly bolts (set of 8) $14.00
Any engine being run in excess of 6,000 rpm must use these specially designed bolts if a blown engine is not desired. These bolts come complete with locknut and are very inexpensive insurance for keeping an engine together.

114000 2-barrel intake manifold $95.00
Aluminum manifold which accepts the Weber 2-barrel carburetor. Fits all SAAB 95 and 96 V4's. Because of height clearance problems this manifold cannot be used on Sonett V4's.

114001 2-barrel intake manifold $59.95
A new intake manifold designed to fit all SAAB V4 engines. Comes complete with carburetor mounting studs and spacer plate which allows the full installation of power brake hose and PCV valves on '69 and later SAAB V4's. No machining is necessary and either the 40 DFI or 28/36 DCD Weber may be used.

114200 high pressure oil pump $33.50
Recommended for all engines to be used in competition. Has constant pressure of 70 psi.

114500 Stage I tuning kit $140.00
Kit includes 114001 manifold, 28/36 DCD Weber carburetor, chrome air filter, vented oil cap, and necessary throttle linkage to complete full installation. Increases SAE horsepower rating from 73 to 90. Gas mileage of 24 to 26 mpg may be expected.

115000 28/36 DCD Weber carburetor $72.50
A progressive linkage which allows the use of one barrel at cruising speeds and the use of both barrels at full acceleration makes this a very good carburetor for increased performance while highway driving. Gas mileage figures average 24 to 26 mpg at cruising speeds.

115001 40 DFI Weber carburetor $78.00
Twin 40 mm. chokes and direct linkage. Best carburetor for competition purposes. Will clear the Sonett hood when used with intake manifold 114001. No air filters are available for this carburetor yet.

115050 chrome air filter assembly $7.50
Complete assembly with washable filter element and necessary hardware to attach filter to 28/36 DCD carburetor only,

116000　2 cycle 74 mm. pistons　　$33.00
These pistons complete with rings increase the SAAB 2-cycle displacement to 940 cc. A special copper head gasket must be made to use this type of piston.

116001　74 mm. piston rings　　$2.60 ea.
Use with piston 116000. Two per piston.

116005　1,500 cc. V4　　$62.40 ea.
　　high compression piston
Specially designed piston for the 1,500 cc. V4 engine to increase compression ratio to 11.2:1. Complete with lightweight wrist pin and rings. No machining of block or cylinder heads necessary. Used in all SAAB 1,500 cc. factory prepared rally cars.

116010　V4 stroker crankshaft　　$105.00
Increases stroke of V4 by 5/16″. Displacement increased to 1,700 cc. No machine work necessary to install. 1,700 cc. piston and rod assemblies must be used with this crankshaft as wrist pin height in piston is different.

116011　1,700 cc. piston　　$36.00
　　and rod assembly
Comes complete with rings and must be used with 116010 crankshaft in early type open block V4 engines using 1/2″ spark plugs. No machining necessary to install. Increases compression ratio to 10:1.

116012　.040″ oversize 1,700 cc. piston　$40.50
Comes complete with rings and must be used with 116010 crankshaft in early type open block V4 engines using 1/2″ reach spark plugs. Boring of the engine to .040″ oversize is necessary. Increases displacement to 1,730 cc. and compression ratio to 10.3:1.

116020　1,700 cc. piston & rod assembly　$36.00 ea.
Comes complete with rings and must be used with 116010 crankshaft in late model blue engines using 3/4″ reach spark plugs. No machining necessary to install. Increases compression ratio to 10:1.

117400　V4 engine oil cooler kit　　$59.95
Light alloy cooler with hardware and instructions included to make a complete installation. Recommended for all V4 engines to be used in competition or when considerable high speed driving is done in hot climates. Fits all SAAB 96, 95 and Sonetts.

120100　capacitive discharge　　$44.95
　　ignition system
Fits all SAAB engines 2 cycle, V4 or 99. Especially good for solving plug fouling problems on 2 cycle engines. The distributor points are used as a breaker switch only, and has no high amperage as in a standard ignition; therefore, no point burning. Test results on a V4 after 18,000 miles proved, points like new, spark plugs extremely good and two mpg better mileage experienced throughout the test. Guaranteed for one full year by the manufacturer.

120110　ignition wire　　$.96 per ft.
Wire has special silicon covering which is unaffected by gas, oil, or heat. This same wire is standard equipment on all Indy twin cam Ford engines.

120150　AG-12 Autolite spark plugs　　$1.25
Should be used for high speed highway driving on late V4 engines equipped with AG-22 spark plugs.

120151　AG-901 racing spark plugs　　$1.25
Should be used on all modified V4 engines using AG-22 spark plugs as standard equipment.

120152　AE-901 racing spark plugs　　$1.25
Should be used on all modified V4 engines using AE-22 spark plugs as standard equipment.

120200　European rectangular　　$40.00
　　headlight kit
Fits SAAB 95 and 96 from 1969 on and gives a much wider and lower frontal appearance. Kit includes all necessary parts to perform a complete change including different grille assembly. No drilling or special tools required. Now comes with brighter than standard 45/60 watt bulbs. *These are not legal in the United States* as they are not sealed beam units. Very good lighting for off road races and rallies.

130050　gearbox side support kit　　$7.00
Kit comes with all necessary hardware to perform a complete installation. A must for all SAABS in competition. When accelerating thru turns the power train tries to roll sideways, due to torque load, which is very hard on engine and gearbox mounts. The shift column u-joint is also misaligned during a power train roll which creates hard shifting. This kit substantially decreases the power train roll.

130100　close ratio gear set　　$135.00
Comparing these gears to the standard gearbox first and second are higher, third is the same and fourth is slightly lower. Gears are straighter cut for strength and will have slightly more noise than a standard gearbox. Using a 4.88:1 ring and pinion these are excellent gears for highway driving. The 5.43:1 ring and pinion and these gears are excellent for autocross and gymkhana use. However, rpm's are much higher in fourth gear while highway cruising.

130101　gearbox bearing kit　　$11.60
If close ratio gears 130100 are installed into earlier gearbox these bearings and circlips are needed to install.

130200　6.00:1 ring and pinion　　$140.00
Specially designed for rallys and off road racing. Teeth of ring and pinion are much wider than standard and much stronger. Only ring and pinion used on Swedish rally cars.

130203　4.67:1 ring and pinion　　$72.28
Highest speed ring and pinion available.

130210　nylon tie straps　　$7.50 per 50
　　　　　　　　　　　　　　　　$13.50 per 100**
U-joint boot tie straps. Takes only seconds to

install. Saves time and headaches for the mechanic. Sold only in packs of 50 and 100.

130300 competition pressure plate $25.95
Special pressure plate with heavy duty springs and fully balanced. A must for good clutch life with modified engines.

140002 competition disc brake pads $15.95
Harder racing pad which fits all V4 95, 96 and Sonetts.

140090 rally swing arm bushings $1.60 ea.
Used in front upper swing arms. Thicker rubber in bushing to give better dampening and hold the front end in alignment during rough road driving.

140091 rally swing arm bushings $2.10 ea.
(upper swing arm)
Used in front upper swing arms. Thicker rubber in bushing to give better dampening and hold the front end in alignment during rough road driving.

140100 special rally front springs $12.95
Recommended for all racing and rallying. Standard equipment on all 1970 Orange competition cars sold. Recommended for areas of U.S. where rough roads are common. Also can be used on air conditioned cars because of extra weight on front end.

140110 rally rear spring $7.50
For use on rallies or in areas of U.S. where rough roads are common. May also be used for SAABs with heavy trunk loads or pulling trailers with heavy tongue weight.

140150 rally shock absorbers (front) $32.00 ea.
Specially designed gas filled shocks for all rough terrain type driving. Used on all Swedish factory rally cars and in Baja. The only shock found to withstand the beating at Baja. Fits all V4 SAAB 95 and 96.

140151 rally shock absorbers (rear) $35.00 ea.
Specially designed gas filled shocks for all rough terrain. Used on all Swedish factory rally cars and in Baja. The only shock found to withstand the beating of Baja. Fits SAAB 96 only.

140200 heavy duty rear axle $130.00
Axle tube is made of heavier gauge tubing and more thoroughly welded at attaching points. Standard equipment on all 1970 Orange competition cars sold.

140700 4 1/2″ wide competition wheel
Discontinued. Use Sonett part number 741207.

150101 rally protection plate $160.00
Full protection aluminum skid plate with spring steel reinforcement. Use on all 95 and 96 V4's using standard exhaust system. Has special steel plate to protect front muffler and exhaust pipe as well as oil pan. Comes complete with mounting brackets.

150102 rally protection plate $126.00
Engine protection skid plate. Made from aluminum with spring steel reinforcement. Comes complete with mounting brackets.

110500 120 HP V4 engine assembly $2,095.00
Completely new, not rebuilt, 1,700 cc. high compression V4 engines. Highly tuned for top performance yet mild enough for city driving. Engine: 1,700 cc. displacement; 10:1 compression ratio; high pressure oil pump; 3/4 race camshaft; fully modified valve train; chrome moly rod bolts; modified water distribution pipe; 2-barrel manifold assembly; 28/36 DCD carburetor; chrome air filter unit. This engine does not conform to smog emission regulations. Engine is warranteed against defects in material and workmanship for 60 days. The Competition Department is not responsible for any components damaged due to improper installation. Please specify, when ordering, whether engine is to be installed in 96, 95 or Sonett. No air filter available for Sonett as hood clearance is a problem. Recommended rpm redline of 6,600. In order to insure new 1,700 cc. V4 engines SAAB does not accept the 1,500 cc. V4 engine in exchange as they do not use the 1,500 cc. V4 engine.

SAAB 99 SECTION

Index

Introduction

The SAAB 99, a new and entirely different design from earlier SAAB models, was made available to the public in 1969, after extensive development. A newly designed, aerodynamic sedan body, and an in-line, overhead cam four cylinder engine, designed by Ricardo Engineering in England are used. The Model 99 is the largest, most powerful SAAB yet produced.

In 1970, a fully automatic transmission coupled with electronic fuel injection was made available, and in 1971 a four door version and electronic fuel injection with the standard manual transmission were made optional. The electronic fuel injection, manufactured by Bosch, improves engine performance and driveability, while reducing harmful pollutant emissions.

Year and Model Identification

SAAB 99—1969-71

Vehicle and Engine Serial Number

Vehicle Serial Number

The vehicle serial number is stamped both on a plate located at the lower left-hand corner of the windshield, and on the left body sill.

Engine Number

On 1969 models, the engine number is located on a boss at the left rear of the engine, just below the valve cover. On later models, the engine number is located below the No. 1 and 2 sparkplugs.

Vehicle Serial Number Plate (1)

Engine Number—1969

Engine Number—1970-71

Vehicle Identification

Year	Serial Number
1969	99.001.001—99.014.259
1970	99.020.001–

NOTE: Body style, engine, and transmission type are also specified on the identification plate. They are coded as follows:

Code	Body Style	Engine	Transmission
2 CM	Two door	Carbureted	Manual
4 CM	Four door	Carbureted	Manual
2 FM	Two door	Fuel injected	Manual
4 FM	Four door	Fuel injected	Manual
2 FA	Two door	Fuel injected	Automatic
4 FA	Four door	Fuel injected	Automatic

General Engine Specifications

Year	Type	Cu. In. Displacement (cc's.)	Carburetor	Developed Horsepower @ rpm (SAE)	Developed Torque @ rpm (ft. lbs.)	Bore and Stroke (in.)	Comp. Ratio	Normal Oil Pressure (psi)
1969-1971	4 cylinder, inline, OHC.	104.2 (1709)	1 bbl.	87 @ 5500	97.7 @ 3000	3.29 × 3.07	9.0:1	N.A.
1970-1971	4 cylinder, inline, OHC.	104.2 (1709)	Electronic fuel injection.	95 @ 5500	97.7 @ 3000	3.29 × 3.07	9.0:1	N.A.

Tune-Up Specifications

Year	Model	Spark Plugs		Distributor		Basic Ignition Timing (deg.) @ rpm ▲	Cranking Compression Press. (psi)	Valves			Intake Opens (deg.)	Idle Speed (rpm.)
		Make (Type)	Gap	Point dwell	Point gap			Tappet (cold) Clearance (in.)				
								Intake	Exhaust		
1969-1971	99	Bosch (W175T30)	.024-.028	40° ± 2	.012-.016	9° B * 5° B **	N.A.	(1) .006-.0012 (2) .008-.010	.014-.020 .016-.018	12° B	850 ± 50 * 800 ± 50 **

B—Before top dead center
▲—Vacuum hoses disconnected
*—Carbureted engines.
**—Fuel injected engines. The idle speed of models equipped with automatic transmissions is set with the transmission in "drive".
1—Valve inspection tolerance. If clearance is outside this tolerance, adjustment should be made to within the valve adjustment tolerance (2).

Firing Order

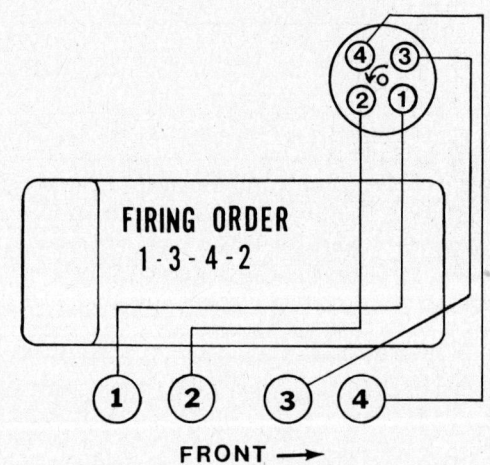

FRONT →

Distributor Specifications

Year	Model	Distributor Identification	Centrifugal Advance			Vacuum Advance	
			Start °	Intermediate °	End °	Start (in. Hg.)	End °°
1969-1971	99	Delco Remy D302 7953520	9 @ 1000	21 @ 2000	35 @ 5000	5	6-8 @ 20

*—Crankshaft degrees @ crankshaft rpm
**—Crankshaft degrees @ in. Hg.

Engine Rebuilding Specifications

Year	Model	Crankshaft								
		Main Bearing Journals (in.)					Connecting Rod Bearing Journals (in.)			
		Journal Dia.		Oil Clearance	Shaft End-Play	Thrust On No.	Journal Dia.		Oil Clearance	End-Play
		New	Min.				New	Min.		
1969-1971	99	2.1254-2.1259	N.A.	.0009-.0020	.003-.010	3	1.7499-1.7504	N.A.	.0009-.0020	N.A.

Year	Model	Pistons					Rings		
		Cylinder Bore (in.)		Piston Dia. (in.)		Wrist Pin Dia. (in.) (Fit)	Ring No.	Side Clearance (in.)	End Gap (in.)
		New	Max.	New ∘	Max. Over-size				
1969-1971	99	(F) 3.2868-3.2872 (G) 3.2873-3.2878	N.A.	(F) 3.2859-3.2864 (G) 3.2864-3.2868	N.A.	.8124-.8126 (Thumb press)	Top Middle Lower (Oil scraper)	.0015-.0035 .0015-.0035	.011-.018 .011-.018 .015-.054

∘—Measured at the lower edge of the piston skirt, perpendicular to the piston pin.

Year	Model	Valves						
		Seat Angle (deg.)	Minimum Valve Face Contact Width (in.)	Valve Lift (in.)		Spring Pressure (lb.)		
				Intake	Exhaust	Intake	Exhaust	
1969-1971	99	45	.86	N.A.	N.A.	110 ± 11	110 ± 11	

Year	Model	Spring Installed Height (in.)	Stem Diameter (in.)		Stem to Guide Clearance (in.)		Valve Guides Removable
			Intake	Exhaust	Intake	Exhaust	
1969-1971	99	1.43	.3105-.3109	.3097-.3101	N.A.	N.A.	Yes

Torque Specifications

Year	Model	Cylinder Head Bolts and Nuts (ft. lbs.)	Main Bearing Cap Bolts (ft. lbs.)	Rod Bearing Cap Bolts (ft. lbs.)	Camshaft Bearing Cap Bolts (ft. lbs.)	Crankshaft Pulley (ft. lbs.)	Flywheel to Crankshaft Bolts (ft. lbs.)	Intake Manifold (ft. lbs.)	Exhaust Manifold (ft. lbs.)
1969-1971	99	54 (∘)	58	40	17	62	44	N.A.	N.A.

∘—Cylinder head nuts and bolts are torqued in two stages. First tighten the nuts to 22 ft. lbs. and the bolts to 4 ft. lbs. in the specified sequence. Then tighten the nuts and bolts to the specified torque, in the proper sequence. Run the engine until warm, stop and allow to cool for 30 minutes, loosen and retorque the nuts and bolts to specifications.

Torque Sequences

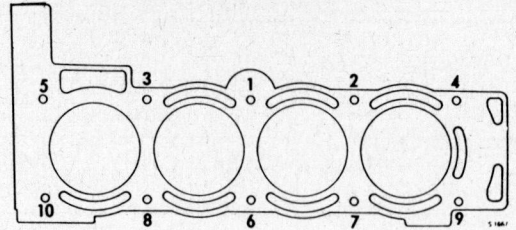

Cylinder Head

Electrical Specifications

Year	Model	Battery			Starter							Brush Spring Tension (oz.)
		Capacity (amp hrs.)	Volts	Grounded Terminal	Lock Test			No Load Test				
					Amps	Volts	Torque (ft. lbs.)	Amps	Volts	RPM		
1969-1971	99	60	12	Negative	N.A.	N.A.	N.A.	N.A.	N.A.	N.A.		42–46

Year	Model	Alternator					AC Regulator				
		Part Number °	Field Current Draw @ 12V (amps)	Output @ Alternator rpm (amps)	Brush Spring Pressure (ozs.)		Part Number	Volts to Close	Volts @ 125° F.	Air Gap (in.)	Point Gap (in.)
1969-1971	99	K1➤14V35A20	N.A.	24 @ 2000	10.5–14		AD 1 14V	13.5–14.2	N.A.	N.A.	.010–.015

°—Bosch Alternator part numbers are broken down as follows:
K—Pole housing diameter.
1—Design of alternator.
➤—Direction of rotation.

14V—Maximum voltage.
35A—Maximum current.
20—Multiplied by 100 equals rpm at ⅔ maximum current output.

Capacities and Pressures

Year	Model	Engine Crankcase Refill After Draining (qts.)		Transmission Refill After Draining (qts.)	Drive Axle (qts.)	Fuel Tank (gals.)	Cooling System With Heater (qts.)	Normal Fuel Press. (psi)	Maximum Coolant Press. (psi)
		With Filter	Without Filter						
1969-1970	99	4	3.5	3	•	12.6	9	(1) N.A. (2) 28.5	8.5
1971	99	4	3.5	3	•	11.9	9	(1) N.A. (2) 28.5	8.5

•—Differential is lubricated integrally with the transmission.
1—Carbureted engines.
2—Fuel injected engine. Pressure checked *beyond* the pressure regulator.

Brake Specifications

Year	Model	Type		Brake Cylinder Bores			Brake Disc Diameter (in.)		Maximum Disc Axial Runout (in.)
		Front	Rear	Master Cylinder (in.)	Caliper Pistons (in.)		Front	Rear	
					Front	Rear			
1969-1971	99	Disc	Disc	.687	1.890	1.063	10.614	10.614	.008

Chassis and Wheel Alignment Specifications

Year	Model	Chassis			Wheel Alignment								
		Wheel-base (in.)	Track (in.)		Caster (deg.)		Camber (deg.)			Toe-in (in.)	King-Pin Inclination (deg.)	Wheel Pivot Ratio (deg.)	
			Front	Rear	Range	Pref. Setting	Range	Pref. Setting				Inner Wheel	Outer Wheel
1969-1971	99	97.5	54.75	55.25	1.0–1.5	1.25	(1) .5–1.0 (2) –1.0 to 1.0	(1) .75 (2) 0	(1) 0 (2) 0	11.5±1	21.5±1	20

1—Front suspension
2—Rear suspension

Fuse Specifications

Year	Model	Position	Circuit	Amperage
1969-1971	99	1	Right-hand lower beam	8
		2	Left-hand lower beam	8
		3	Right rear parking lamp and license light	8
		4	Left rear parking lamp and license light	8
		5	Stop lamps	8
		6	Cooling fan	8
		7	Clock, lighter, roof lamp, and warning buzzer	8
		8	Turn signals and fuel injection pump (if so equipped)	8
		9	Windshield wiper and washers	8
		10	Heater blower fan	8
		11	Backup lamps and horn	8
		12	Extra	8

Light Bulb Specifications

Year	Model	Usage	Type	Wattage
1969-1971	99	Headlight; low and high beam	4002 •	37.5/50
		Headlight; high beam	4001 •	37.5
		Front and rear directional indicator, braking and backup lights	1073 •	21
		Front parking light, taillight, and license plate light	67 •	5
		Side marker lights	57 •	4
		Dome light	Cartridge bulb	10
		Trunk light, rear-view mirror light	Cartridge bulb	5
		Ignition switch light, hazard warning switch light	Miniature bulb	2
		Instrument and indicator lights	Glass fitting	1.2
		Heater control light	Miniature bulb	3 (24 volts)

•—SAE identification numbers.

Wiring Diagrams

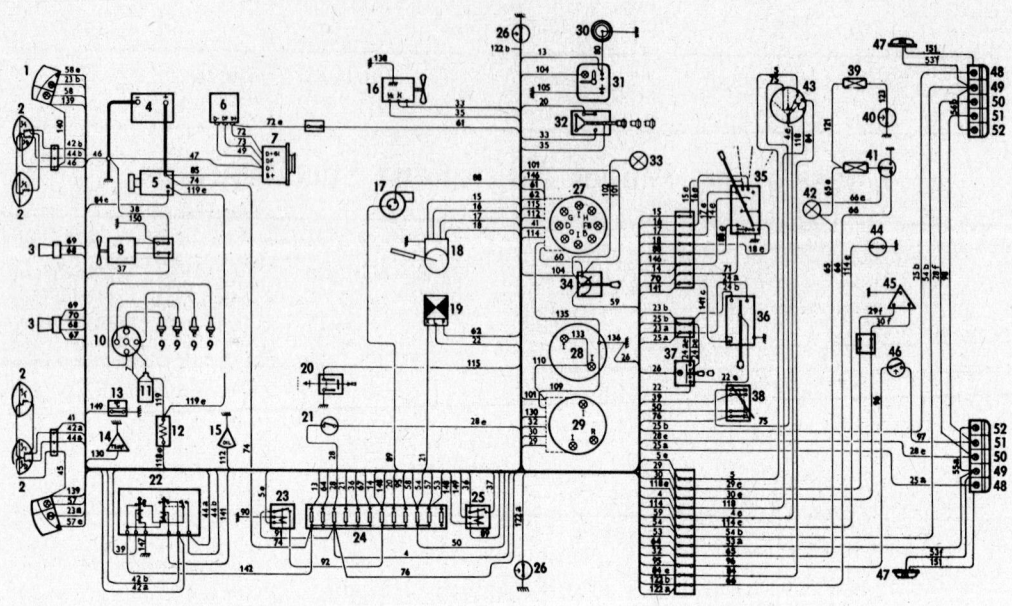

Wiring Diagram—1969

1. Parking light and direction indicator
2. Headlight
3. Horn
4. Battery
5. Starter
6. Voltage regulator
7. Alternator
8. Radiator fan motor
9. Spark plug
10. Distributor
11. Ignition coil
12. Series resistance
13. Radiator fan thermostat switch
14. Temp. transmitter
15. Oil pressure switch
16. Heater fan motor
17. Windshield washer pump
18. Windshield wiper motor

19. Flasher unit
20. Brake warning light contact
21. Brake light contact
22. Light relay
23. Ignition switch relay
24. Fuse box
25. Radiator fan relay
26. Door switch for dome light
27. Instrument light
28. Speedometer and odometer
29. Temperature and fuel gauge
30. Cigarette lighter
31. Clock
32. Heater fan motor switch
33. Heater control illumination
34. Instrument lighting rheostat
35. Windshield wiper, windshield washer and horn control switch
36. Direction indicator switch

with headlight dimmer and flasher
37. Hazard warning signal switch
38. Headlight switch
39. Trunk light
40. Contact for trunk light
41. Dome light with switch
42. Ignition switch illumination
43. Ignition and starter contact switch
44. Handbrake light contact
45. Fuel level transmitter
46. Back-up light contact
47. Side position light
48. Direction indicator
49. Tail light
50. Stop light
51. Back-up light
52. Number-plate light

No.	Color	No.	Color	No.	Color
4	gray	39	yellow	85	gray
4e	gray	41	blue/white	88	black
5	brown/white	42a	blue	88e	black
5e	brown/white	42b	white	89	yellow
7	brown/white	44a	gray	90	black
13	blue	44b	yellow	91	gray
14	brown	45	black	92	white
14e	brown	46	black	*95	white
15	red	47	black	96	red
15e	red	49	black	97	white
16	green	50	green	98	white
16e	green	53	blue	101	green
17	gray	53f	red	102	green
17e	gray	54	green	104	green
18	blue	54b	green	105	black
18e	blue	55a	blue	109	black
20	blue/white	56b	green	110	green
21	red/white	57	blue	112	blue
22	green	57e		114	white
22e	green	58	green	114e	white
23a	blue/white	58e		115	yellow
23b	red/white	59	green	118	green/white
24a	blue/white	60	green	118e	green/white
24ae	blue/white	61	red	119	black
24b	red/white	62	gray	119e	black
24be	red/white	64	yellow	121	gray
25a	blue/white	65	yellow	122a	black
25b	red/white	65e	yellow	122b	black
26	black	66	black	123	blue
28	red	66e	yellow	130	yellow
28e	red	67	red	133	green
28f	red	68	red	135	black
29	gray	69	black	136	black
29e	gray	70	black	138	black
29f	gray	71	black	139	black
30	brown	72	red	140	black
30e	brown	72e	red	141	white
30f	brown	73	yellow	141c	white
32	red	74	gray	142	gray
33	yellow	75	red	146	brown
35	gray	76	gray	147	black
36	gray	80	blue	148	red
37	green	84	yellow	149	black
38	black	84e	yellow	150	black
				151	black

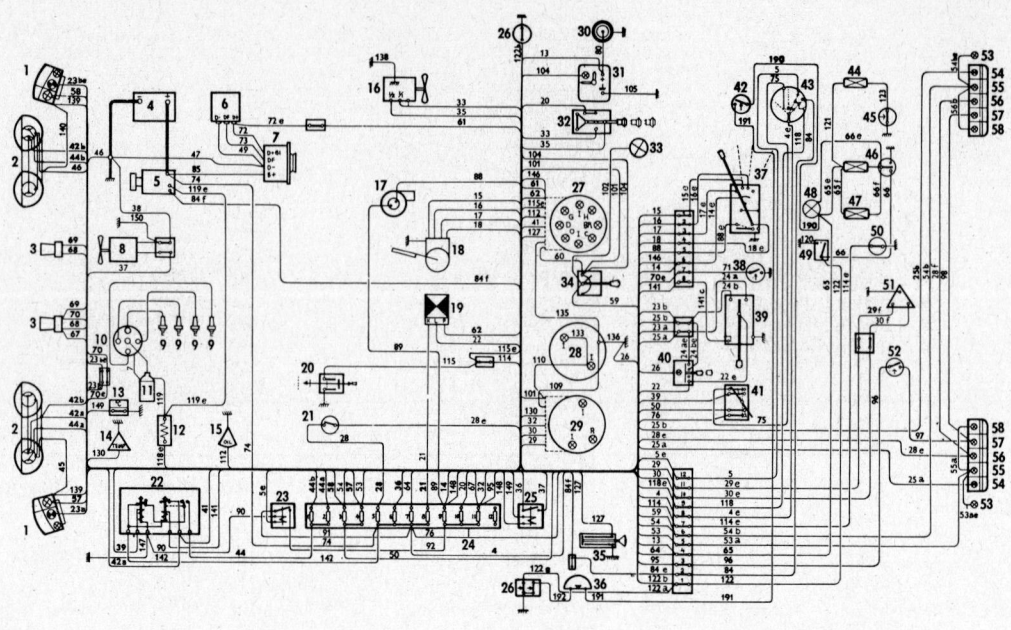

Wiring Diagram—1970-71 (carbureted engine)

1. Parking light and direction indicator
2. Headlight
3. Horn
4. Battery
5. Starter
6. Voltage regulator
7. Alternator
8. Radiator fan motor
9. Spark plug
10. Distributor
11. Ignition coil
12. Series resistance
13. Radiator fan thermostat switch
14. Temp. transmitter
15. Oil pressure switch
16. Heater fan motor
17. Windshield washer pump
18. Windshield wiper motor
19. Flasher unit

20. Brake warning light contact
21. Brake light contact
22. Light relay
23. Ignition switch relay
24. Fuse box
25. Radiator fan relay
26. Door switch for dome light
27. Instrument indicator light
28. Speedometer and odometer
29. Temperature and fuel gauges
30. Cigarette lighter
31. Clock
32. Heater fan motor switch
33. Heater control illumination
34. Instrument lighting rheostat
35. Contact for choke indicator light
36. Buzzer
37. Windshield wiper and windshield washer control switch
38. Horn contact

39. Direction indicator switch with headlight dimmer and flasher
40. Hazard warning signal switch
41. Headlight switch
42. Contact for warning buzzer
43. Ignition and starter contact
44. Trunk light
45. Contact for trunk light
46. Dome light with switch
47. Rear-view mirror light
48. Ignition switch illumination
49. Switch for interior light
50. Handbrake light contact
51. Fuel level transmitter
52. Back-up light contact
53. Side position light
54. Direction indicator
55. Tail light
56. Stop light
57. Back-up light
58. Number-plate light

No.	Color	No.	Color	No.	Color
4	gray	42b	white	88e	black
4e	gray	44	gray	89	yellow
5	brown/white	44a	gray	90	black
5e	brown/white	44b	yellow	91	gray
7	brown/white	45	black	92	white
13	blue	46	black	95	white
14	brown	47	black	96	red
14e	brown	49	black	97	white
15	red	50	green	98	white
15e	red	53	blue	101	green
16	green	53a	blue	102	green
16e	green	53ae	blue	104	green
17	gray	54	green	105	black
17e	gray	54b	green	109	black
18	blue	54be	green	110	green
18e	blue	55a	blue	112	blue
20	blue/white	56b	green	114	white
21	red/white	57	blue	114e	white
22	green	58	green	115	yellow
22e	green	59	green	115e	yellow
23a	blue/white	60	green	118	green/white
23b	red/white	61	red	118e	green/white
23be	red/white	62	gray	119	black
24a	blue/white	64	yellow	119e	black
24ae	blue/white	65	yellow	120	black
24b	red/white	65e	yellow	121	gray
24be	red/white	65f	black	122	black
25a	blue/white	66	black	122a	black
25b	red/white	66e	blue	122b	black
26	black	66f	black	123	blue
28	red	67	red	127	brown/white
28e	red	68	red	130	yellow
28f	red	69	black	133	green
29	gray	70	black	135	black
29e	gray	70e	black	136	black
29f	gray	71	black	138	black
30	brown	72	red	139	black
30e	brown	72e	red	140	black
30f	brown	73	yellow	141	white
32	red	74	gray	141c	white
33	yellow	75	red	142	gray
35	gray	76	gray	146	brown
36	gray	80	blue	147	black
37	green	84	yellow	148	red
38	black	84e	yellow	149	black
39	yellow	84f	yellow	150	black
41	blue/white	85	gray	190	yellow
42a	blue	88	black	191	gray
				192	black

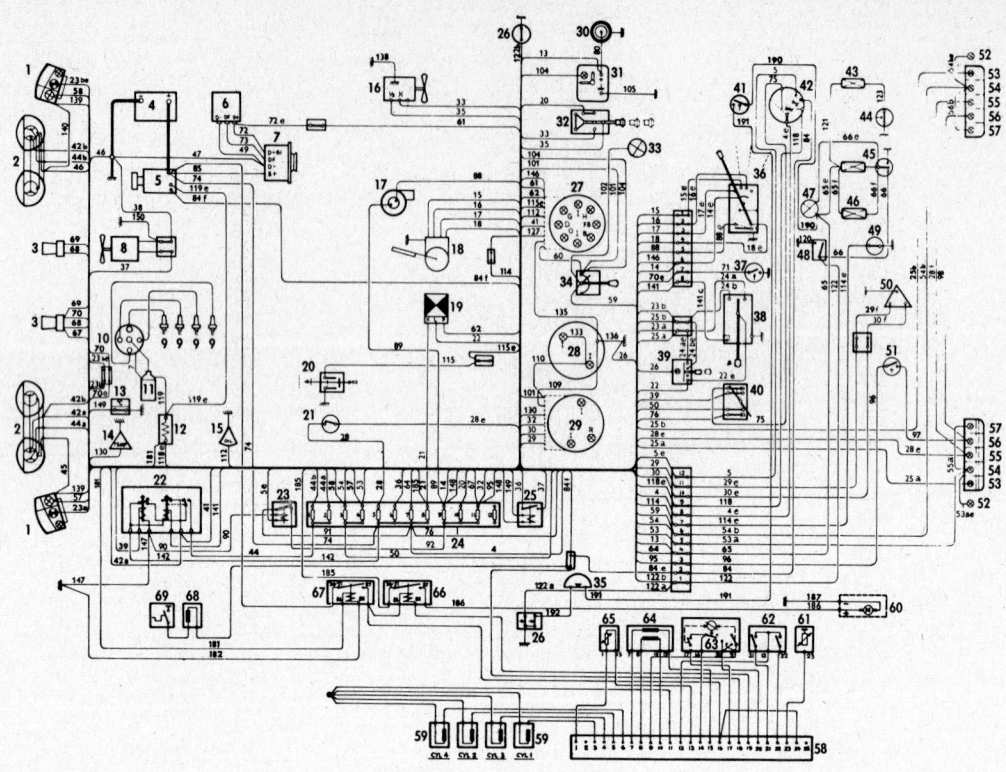

Wiring Diagram—1970-71 (fuel injected engine)

1. Parking light and direction indicator	25. Radiator fan relay	47. Ignition switch illumination
2. Headlight	26. Door switch for dome light	48. Switch for interior light
3. Horn	27. Instrument indicator lights	49. Handbrake light contact
4. Battery	28. Speedometer and odometer	50. Fuel level transmitter
5. Starter	29. Temperature and fuel gauge	51. Back-up light contact
6. Voltage regulator	30. Cigarette lighter	52. Side position light
7. Alternator	31. Clock	53. Direction indicator
8. Radiator fan motor	32. Heater fan motor switch	54. Tail light
9. Spark plug	33. Heater control illumination	55. Stop light
10. Distributor	34. Instrument lighting rheostat	56. Back-up light
11. Ignition coil	35. Buzzer	57. Number-plate light
12. Series resistance	36. Windshield wiper and windshield washer control switch	Electronic fuel injection units:
13. Radiator fan thermostat switch		58. Control unit
14. Temp. transmitter	37. Horn contact	59. Injection valves
15. Oil pressure switch	38. Direction indicator switch with headlight dimmer and flasher	60. Fuel pump
16. Heater fan motor		61. Temp. sensor II
17. Windshield washer pump	39. Hazard warning signal switch	62. Trigger contacts
18. Windshield wiper motor	40. Headlight switch	63. Throttle valve switch
19. Flasher unit	41. Contact for warning buzzer	64. Pressure sensor
20. Brake warning light contact	42. Ignition and starter contact switch	65. Temp. sensor I
21. Brake light contact		66. Pump relay
22. Light relay	43. Trunk light	67. Main relay
23. Ignition switch relay	44. Contact for trunk light	68. Start valve
24. Fuse box	45. Dome light with switch	69. Temp. switch
	46. Rear-view mirror light	

No.	Color	No.	Color	No.	Color
4	gray	44a	gray	92	white
4e	gray	44b	yellow	95	white
5	brown/white	45	black	96	red
5e	brown/white	46	black	97	white
7	brown/white	47	black	98	white
13	blue	49	black	101	green
14	brown	50	green	102	green
14e	brown	53	blue	104	green
15	red	53a	blue	105	black
15e	red	53ae	blue	109	black
16	green	54	green	110	green
16e	green	54b	green	112	blue
17	gray	54be	green	114	white
17e	gray	55a	blue	114e	white
18	blue	56b	green	115	yellow
18e	blue	57	blue	115e	yellow
20	blue/white	58	green	118	green/white
21	red/white	59	green	118e	green/white
22	green	60	green	119	black
22e	green	61	red	119e	black
23a	blue/white	62	gray	120	black
23b	red/white	64	yellow	121	gray
23be	red/white	65	yellow	122	black
24a	blue/white	65e	yellow	122a	black
24ae	blue/white	65f	black	122b	black
24b	red/white	66	black	123	blue
24be	red/white	66e	blue	127	brown/white
25a	blue/white	66f	black	130	yellow
25b	red/white	67	red	133	green
26	black	68	red	135	black
28	red	69	black	136	black
28e	red	70	black	138	black
28f	red	70e	black	139	black
29	gray	71	black	140	black
29e	gray	72	red	141	white
29f	gray	72e	red	141c	white
30	brown	73	yellow	142	gray
30e	brown	74	gray	146	brown
30f	brown	75	red	147	black
32	red	76	gray	148	red
33	yellow	80	blue	149	black
35	gray	84	yellow	150	black
36	gray	84e	yellow	181	green/white
37	green	84f	yellow	182	black
38	black	85	gray	185	red
39	yellow	88	black	186	gray
41	blue/white	88e	black	187	black
42a	blue	89	yellow	190	yellow
42b	white	90	black	191	gray
44	gray	91	gray	192	black

Engine Electrical

Distributor

The SAAB 99 uses two types of distributors, depending on engine equipment. Carbureted versions utilize a Delco distributor, while fuel injected engines use a Bosch distributor. The Bosch unit is equipped with a secondary set of contacts, mounted in the distributor lower housing, used to signal engine speed to the fuel injection computer.

REMOVAL AND INSTALLATION

Remove the distributor cap, and the primary lead from the coil. On models equipped with the Bosch distributor, separate the connector from the lower set of contacts. Rotate the engine until the mark on the flywheel indicates the basic ignition timing, with the rotor pointing toward the No. 1 tower on the distributor cap, and mark the relative position of the rotor to the distributor body, and the distributor body to the engine block. Loosen the mounting bolts and remove the distributor.

When installing, align the rotor arm approximately parallel with the crankshaft centerline and pointing toward the rear, and insert the distributor. Engage the drive gears (the shaft will rotate approximately 30° counterclockwise) and the oil pump, and check to ensure that the index marks align. Check the ignition timing using a timing light.

BREAKER POINTS

The breaker points are retained in the Delco distributor by two screws, and in the Bosch distributor by a screw and a clip. In both cases, pry slots are provided to permit adjustment of the point gap.

The lower points of the Bosch distributor are not adjustable, and must be replaced by an assembly when worn. The assembly is retained on the distributor housing with two mounting screws. Prior to installation, lightly lubricate the heels of the point arms with distributor cam lubricant.

IGNITION TIMING

The ignition timing is adjusted with the vacuum hoses disconnected and the engine running at idle speed. On carbureted engines, the timing should be adjusted with the engine cold, in order to ease lowering

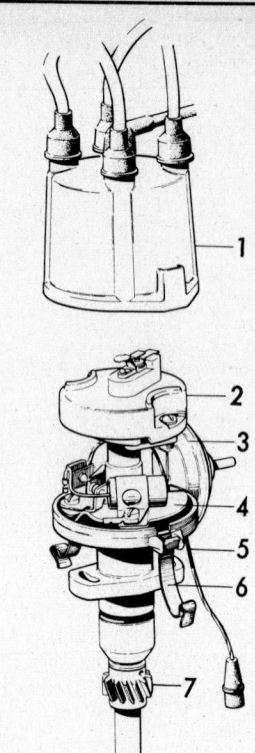

Delco distributor—exploded view

1. Distributor cap   5. Low-voltage wire
2. Rotor   6. Spring clip
3. Vacuum control unit   7. Drive gear
4. Breaker plate

the engine speed to idle speed (below 850 rpm) with the vacuum retard detached.

IGNITION TIMING MARKS

The ignition timing marks are located on the rim of the flywheel, and are visible through a port in the clutch housing, adjacent to the distributor. The marks are graduated in five degree increments, those before top dead center being numbered.

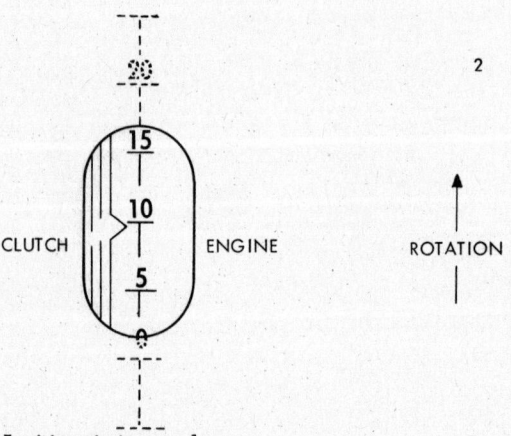

Ignition timing marks

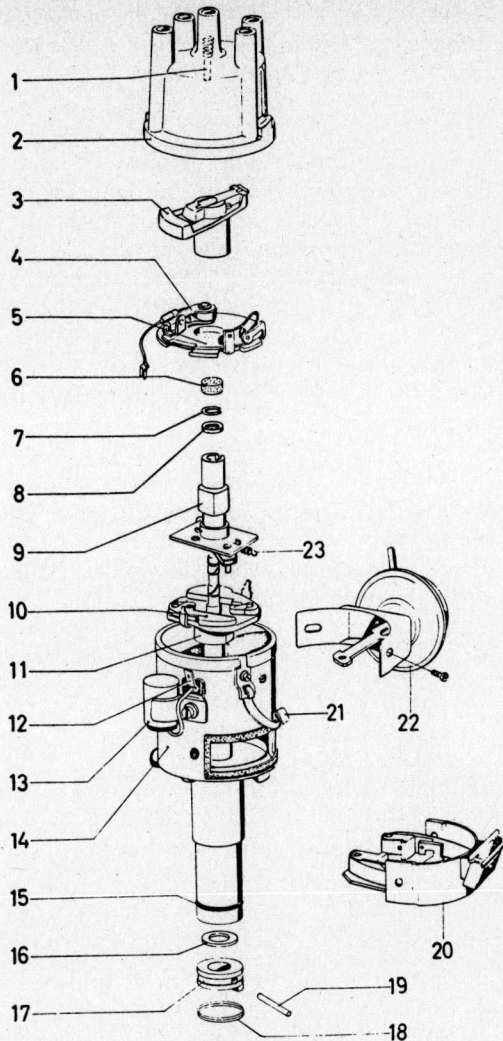

Bosch distributor—exploded view

1. Rod brush (carbon)
2. Distributor cap
3. Distributor arm
4. Contact breaker
5. Breaker plate
6. Lubricating felt
7. Circlip
8. Washer
9. Breaker cam
10. Centrifugal weight
11. Cam for triggering contacts
12. Primary terminal
13. Capacitor
14. Distributor body
15. Rubber seal
16. Washers
17. Driving collar
18. Resilient ring
19. Lock pin
20. Contact device
21. Lock clasp for dist. cap
22. Vacuum regulator
23. Centrifugal governor spring

AC Generator

When servicing the charging system of vehicles equipped with an AC generator, the following precautions should be taken to avoid damaging the system:

1. Never operate the alternator on an open circuit (battery disconnected).
2. When installing a battery, connect the gound terminal (negative) before connecting the positive terminal.
3. When arc welding *anywhere* on the vehicle always disconnect the alternator.

REMOVAL AND INSTALLATION

Disconnect the battery ground cable and all wires from the alternator. Remove the two mounting bolts and the fanbelt, and remove the alternator. Install in the reverse order of removal.

AC Regulator

A Bosch single element regulator is used. To test the regulator voltage control, connect a voltmeter between the B+ terminal of the generator and ground. Start the engine, run at 2,200 rpm and observe the voltage reading. If the voltage reading is outside specifications, remove the regula-

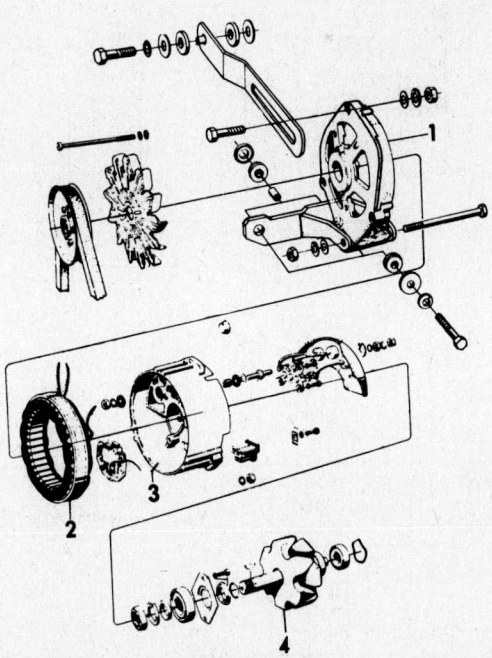

Bosch alternator—exploded view

1. Drive bearing assembly
2. Stator
3. Slip ring bearing
4. Rotor

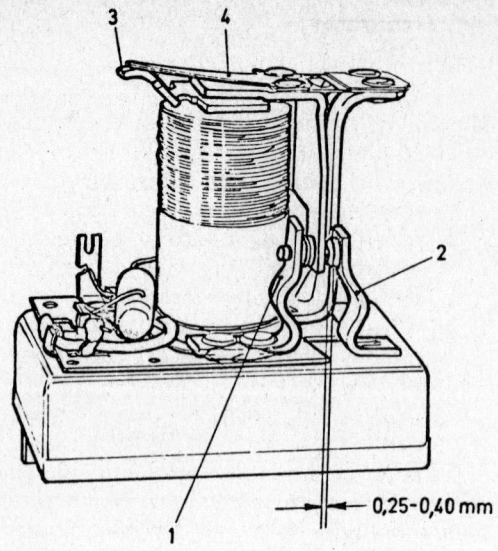

Voltage regulator

1. Lower contact
2. Upper contact
3. Adjusting arm
4. Spring

tor cover and adjust the voltage rating by bending the spring tensioner. Bending the tensioner downward will lower control voltage, and upward will increase voltage. NOTE: *After making each adjustment,*

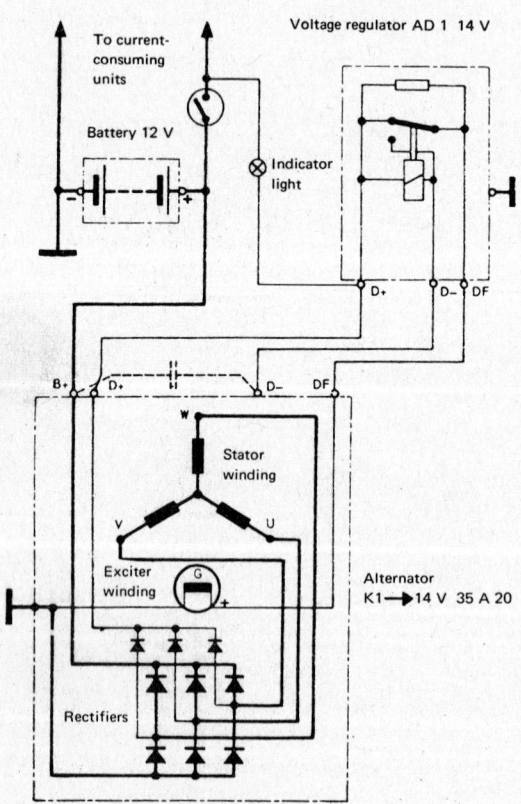

Charging Circuit Schematic

lower engine speed to idle, to avoid the influence of residual magnetism in the regulator core on voltage readings.

Battery

Battery electrolyte level must be maintained (distilled water is recommended), and the terminals kept clean, tight and free from corrosion. Should the specific gravity of the battery electrolyte fall below 1.196 at 68° F., the battery must be charged. If the battery takes the charge, and the specific gravity repeatedly falls to this level, the charging system should be investigated.

CAUTION: *When jump starting, ensure that proper polarity is observed, and that the jumper battery is disconnected as soon after starting as possible, to prevent damaging the charging system.*

Hydrometer Readings	Condition
1.260-1.310	Fully charged
1.230-1.250	¾ charged
1.200-1.220	½ charged
1.170-1.190	¼ charged
1.140-1.160	Almost discharged
1.110-1.130	Fully discharged

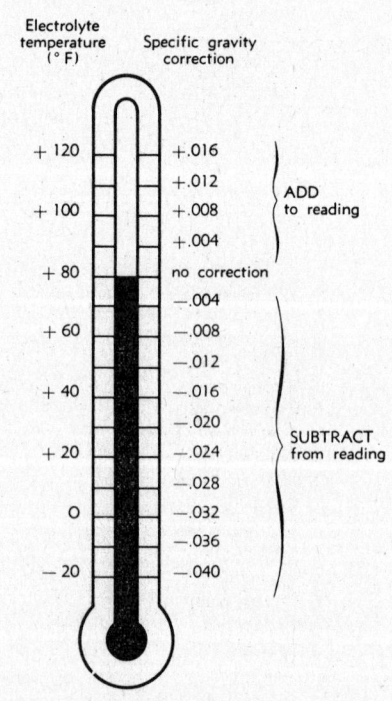

Effect of temperature on the specific gravity of battery electrolyte.

Starter

REMOVAL AND INSTALLATION

Disconnect the battery ground cable, code for identification and remove all starter wires. Unbolt and remove the flywheel cover. Remove the starter mounting bolts, slide the starter rearward until it is free, and remove.

Install in the reverse order of removal.

Fuel System

Fuel Pump (Carbureted Engines)

REMOVAL AND INSTALLATION

Remove the fuel lines from the pump and cover the ends. Unbolt the two retaining bolts, and remove the pump.

Install a new gasket on the pump and install the pump in the reverse order of removal.

SERVICE

The fuel filter and the pump diaphragm are the only serviceable parts. To replace the filter, remove the cover retaining bolt, the cover and the filter (the filter may be serviced with the pump installed in the vehicle).

To replace the diaphragm, remove the pump, and mark the relative position of the upper and lower pump halves. Separate the pump halves, press the diaphragm down and rotate it 1/4 turn clockwise, and remove the diaphragm. Install in the reverse order of removal, checking to ensure that the index marks on the pump halves align.

Electric Fuel Pump (Fuel Injected Engines)

REMOVAL AND INSTALLATION

Remove the panelling to the left of the spare tire in the trunk. Loosen the three retaining screws and pull the fuel pump panel forward. Clamp off and code the fuel hoses for identification. Unbolt the two attaching nuts, and remove the fuel pump together with the rubber pads and the fuel lines. Remove the fuel lines from the pump.

Install in the reverse order of removal. Install the fuel hoses in the following sequence: suction side, pressure side, and return side.

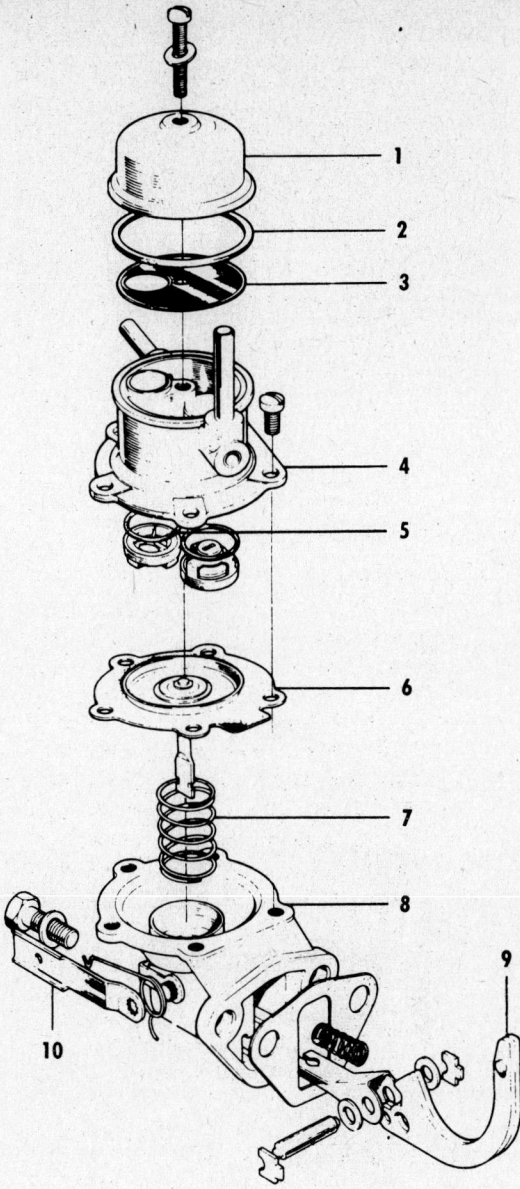

Mechanical fuel pump—exploded view

1. Cover	6. Diaphragm
2. Gasket	7. Diaphragm spring
3. Filter	8. Bottom half of pump
4. Top half of pump	9. Lever
5. Valves	10. Manual lever

SERVICE

The electric fuel pump is sealed, and therefore is serviced as a unit. A fuel filter, which must be replaced every 6,000 miles is also mounted on the fuel pump panel in the trunk. When replacing the filter, en-

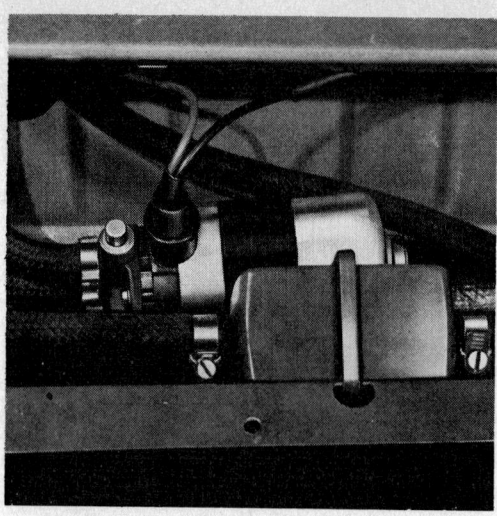

Electric fuel pump—exploded view

sure that the arrow embossed on the filter housing points in the direction of fuel flow.

Carburetor

REMOVAL AND INSTALLATION

Disconnect the preheater hose and remove the air cleaner. Detach the throttle and choke controls, and remove the fuel and vacuum lines. Unbolt the four retaining nuts, and remove the carburetor.

Install by reversing the removal procedure.

ADJUSTMENTS

Fuel mixture is factory adjusted, and a self-centering mixture needle is used, therefore no jet adjustments are necessary. Precise mixture adjustments can be made, using a CO meter, by turning the air screw

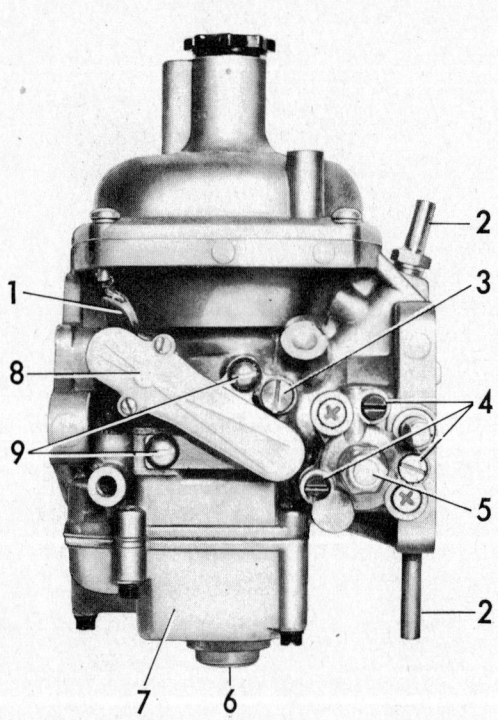

Zenith-Stromberg 175 CD-2SE—right side view

1. Sealing
2. Vacuum nipple
3. Air screw
4. Screws for removal, overflow valve
5. Overflow valve
6. Float chamber plug
7. Float chamber
8. Temperature compensator
9. Screws for removal, temperature compensator

Zenith-Stromberg 175 CD-2SE—left side view

1. Clip, choke control wire
2. Vacuum chamber cover
3. Damper cap
4. Air channel, float chamber ventilation
5. Channel, air to space under diaphragm
6. Channel, air to temperature compensator
7. Choke
8. Fast idling cam
9. Connection, choke control wire
10. Adjusting screw, fast idling
11. Idling screw

on the right side of the carburetor. The CO content of the exhaust gas should be 3.0±.5%.

NOTE: *The CO readings should be taken within 8 minutes after the opening of the coolant thermostat, on an engine that was started cold. To ensure accuracy, the float bowl must be no warmer than room temperature, the air cleaner should be in the summer position, the idle speed should be set correctly and the damper filled with oil, and there should be no backlash in the throttle linkage.*

The fast idle is adjusted after the idle has been adjusted. With the choke closed, the clearance between the fast idle cam and the adjusting screw should be .08".

If the idle speed drops off after extended idling, the temperature compensator should be adjusted. Remove the compensator cover. The valve should yield to very light pressure, and spring back when released. If the valve moves sluggishly or sticks, loosen the phillips-head screw and ensure that there is no binding. If the problem still exists, remove the compensator,

and using the adjusting nut, with the unit at room temperature, adjust the valve clearance to .004-.012". If the unit still will not operate properly, it must be replaced.

If the engine will not return to idle speed after acceleration (NOTE: *check to ensure that the choke is closed and adjusted properly, and that the fast idle cam is adjusted*), the overflow valve should be removed and cleaned. If the malfunction continues, the valve must be replaced, since no adjustment is provided.

Checking float level

The float level is checked and adjusted with the carburetor removed from the vehicle and inverted, with the float cover removed (see illustration). At the highest point, the float should be .63-.71", and at the rear end of the float .39-.47" above the float cover mounting flange. Adjust the float level by bending the tang that rests on the float needle.

OVERHAUL

Unscrew and remove the vacuum cover and the piston return spring. Remove the piston and diaphragm assembly, loosen the retaining screw, and remove the fuel needle. Separate the piston from the diaphragm, by removing the retaining screws, metal and plastic washers. Remove the temperature compensator and the overflow valve from the carburetor. Unscrew and remove the choke mechanism.

Clean all parts and check for excessive wear. Clean all holes in the carburetor and

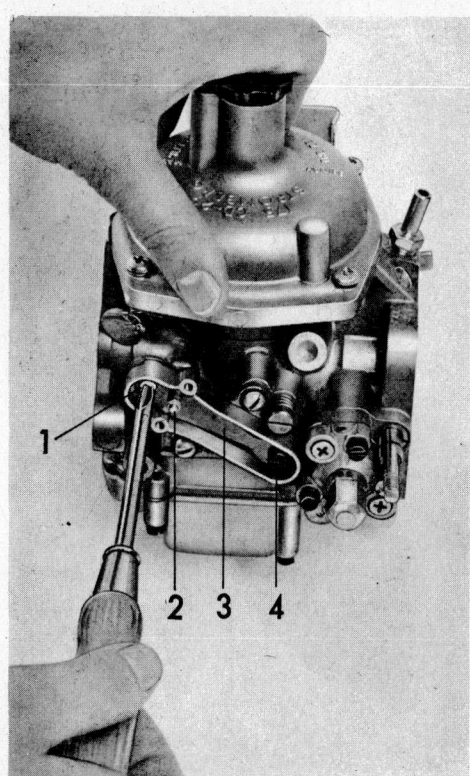
Adjusting temperature compensator

1. Screw
2. Nut
3. Bimetal spring
4. Valve

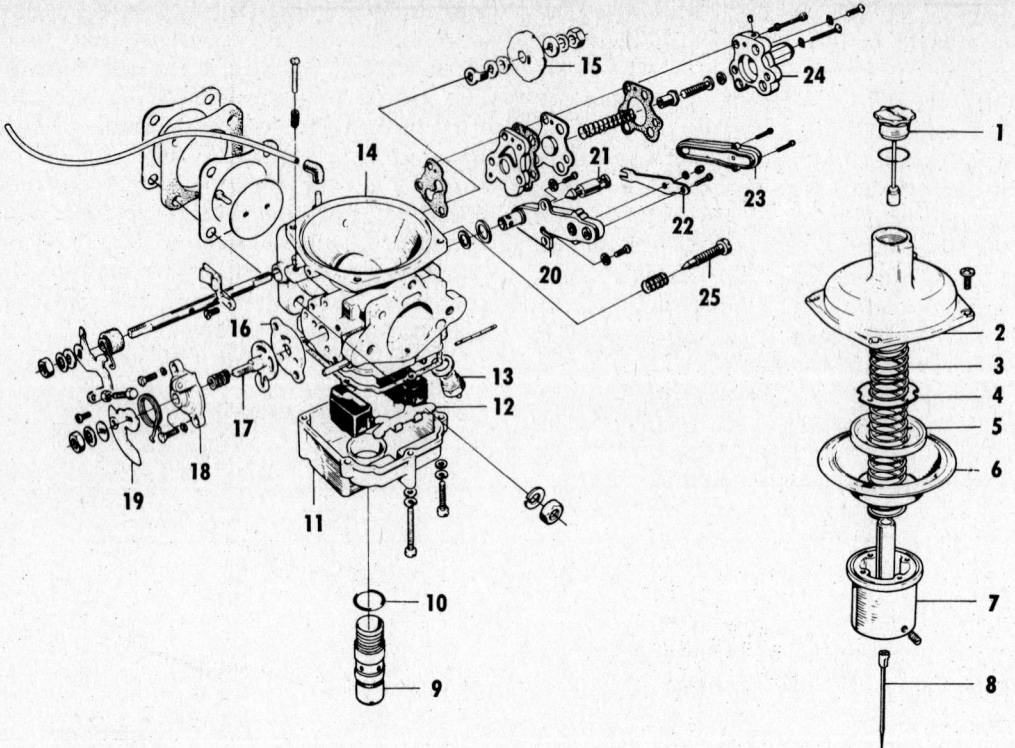

Zenith-Stromberg 175 CD-2SE—exploded view

1. Damper screw cap	10. O-ring	19. Idling cam plate
2. Vacuum chamber cover	11. Float chamber	20. Temperature compensator
3. Spring	12. Float	21. Valve
4. Metal washer	13. Float valve	22. Bimetal spring
5. Plastic washer	14. Carburetor housing	23. Cover
6. Diaphragm	15. Throttle lever	24. Overflow valve
7. Vaccum piston	16. Valve plate	25. Air screw
8. Fuel needle	17. Valve plate	
9. Float chamber plug	18. Choke mechanism housing	

choke bodies with compressed air. Ensure that the diaphragm is intact, the float valve is not overly worn, the fuel needle is straight and intact, and that the choke valve plates are not scratched.

Install the diaphragm on the piston so that the tang on the diaphragm aligns with the notch on the piston lip, insert the plastic and metal washers, and tighten the mounting screws. Insert the fuel needle into the piston so that the flat on the spring housing engages the set screw, and the plastic washer is flush with the lower surface of the piston. Install the piston assembly into the carburetor body, install the spring, mount the vacuum chamber cover according to the index marks, and tighten the retaining screws. Screw the needle valve into the carburetor body, and mount the float, flat side away from the carburetor

body. Check and adjust the float level (see above). Using a new gasket, mount the float cover. Install the retaining screws, at first loosely, then press the cover until it butts against the carburetor body, and tighten the screws. Mount the choke mechanism and the overflow valve. Check the adjustment of the temperature compensator, adjust if necessary (see above), and install on the carburetor.

Fill the damper with oil (NOTE: *same viscosity as engine oil*), install the carburetor, and adjust as shown above.

Electronic Fuel Injection

CAUTION: *Electronic fuel injection is a highly complex system, requiring specialized tools and training to service. Do not attempt other than basic adjustments described below without this equipment*

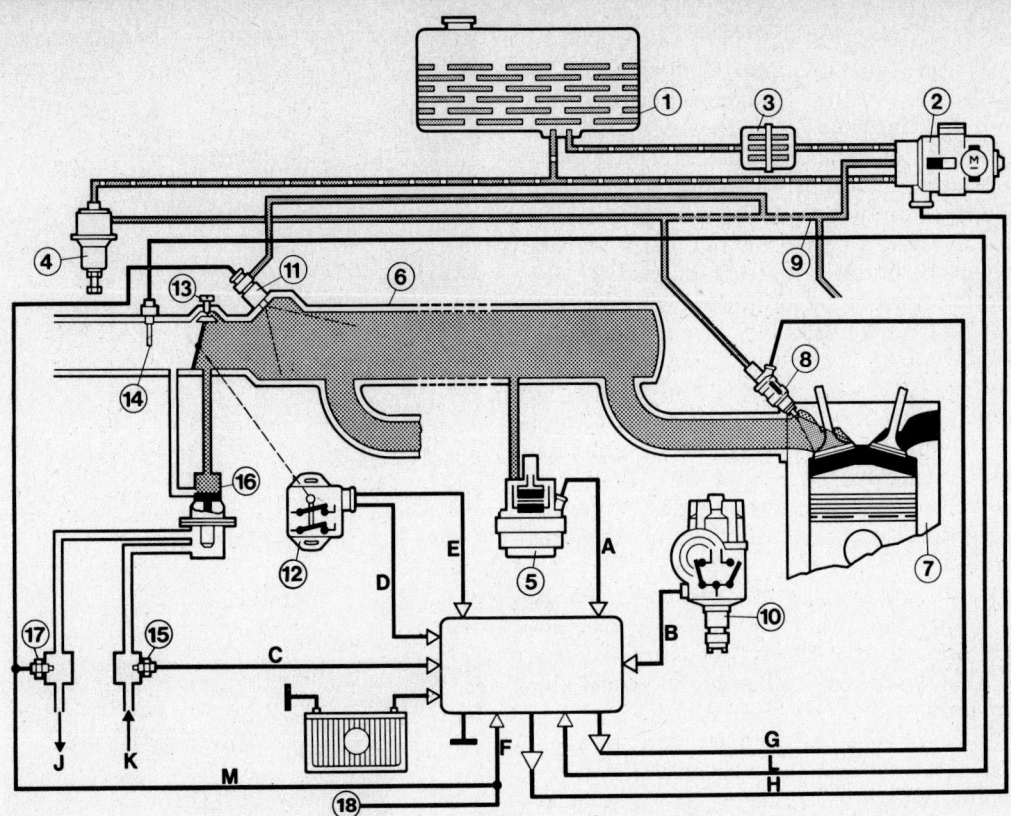

Electronic Fuel Injection Schematic

1. Fuel tank
2. Fuel pump
3. Fuel filter
4. Pressure regulator
5. Pressure sensor (manifold vacuum)
6. Common inlet duct
7. Cylinder head
8. Injection valves
9. Fuel distributor pipe

10. Ignition distributor (trigger contacts)
11. Enrichment valve
12. Throttle valve switch
13. Idling adjustment screw
14. Intake air temperature sensor
15. Coolant temperature sensor
16. Auxiliary air regulator
17. Temperature switch
18. From starter switch

and knowledge, otherwise serious damage to the system and the engine may result.

Bosch Electronic Fuel Injection is based on a computer-like device that accurately monitors engine functions. The computer monitors engine speed, engine load (manifold vacuum), throttle position, coolant and air temperature, and translates this data into injection duration for the injectors and the enrichment valve. Fuel is supplied by a constant pressure fuel loop consisting of an electronic fuel pump, fuel line, a pressure regulator, and return line. Excess fuel bypasses the injectors and is returned to the tank and pump to be recirculated, maintaining constant pressure in the fuel loop. Air is supplied, through a single throttle valve, by a four branch manifold.

Item	Signal
A — Pressure sensor (manifold vacuum)	Load condition of engine
B — Trigger contacts	Engine speed
C — Temperature sensor (coolant)	Warming up
D — Throttle valve switch	Deceleration fuel cut-off
E — Throttle valve switch	Acceleration enrichment
F — From starter terminal 50 (when temperature switch is closed)	Start enrichment
G — To injection valves	Duration
H — To fuel pump	On—Off
J — Cooling liquid to auxiliary air regulator	Auxiliary air regulator control
K — Same as J	Same as J
L — Temperature sensor (intake air)	
M — to start valve	Start enrichment

Adjustments

The pressure regulator is checked by inserting a pressure gauge, on a T-fitting, into the line leading to the regulator, and running the engine at idle speed. If pressure does not meet specifications, loosen the locknut, and turn the adjusting screw.

The throttle valve switch must actuate when the throttle plate is opened 2°. To adjust, connect an ohmmeter or powered test light to contacts No. 14 and 17 (right-hand, looking at the switch cover). Loosen the two adjusting screws, and rotate the switch until the ohmmeter reads 0 (light off). Rotate the switch clockwise until the resistance reads ∞ (light on), turn the switch counterclockwise one graduation on the switch scale, and tighten the adjusting screws.

If no fuel reaches the regulator, check to ensure that the curved fuel pump suction line (in the trunk) has not collapsed. If the line has collapsed, it must be replaced.

If the engine fails to start, and the ignition and fuel systems appear to be functioning properly, remove the connector from the coolant temperature sensor. Short across the cable plug terminals, and try to start the engine. If the engine starts, the temperature sensor must be replaced.

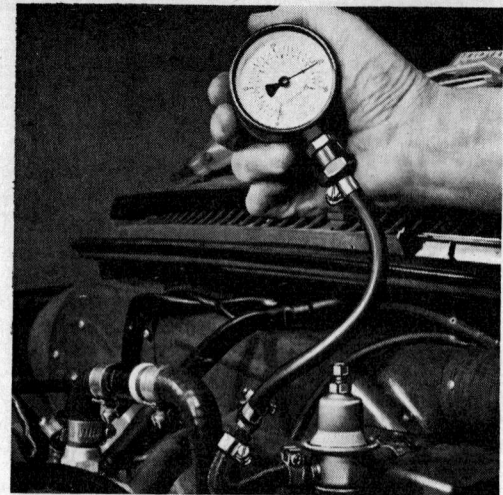

Checking pressure regulator

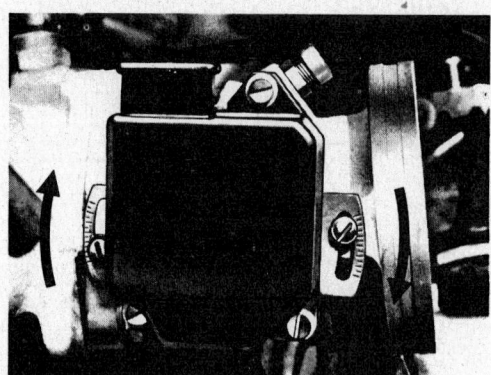

Throttle valve switch adjustment

Exhaust System

Exhaust Pipe, Muffler and Tailpipe

Removal and Installation

CAUTION: *To prevent excessive noise and vibration, ensure that no contact exists between the parts of the exhaust system and the underbody, heat shield, or fuel filler pipe.*

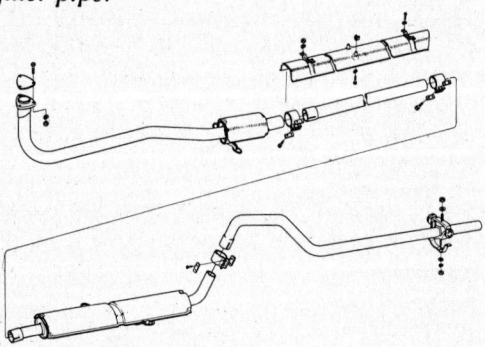

Exhaust System

Coolant temperature sensor

Front Exhaust Pipe and Muffler

Remove the preheater casing, and unbolt the exhaust pipe from the exhaust manifold. Loosen the clamp at the rear of the front muffler, unhook the rubber O-rings, and remove the muffler and pipe.

Install in the reverse order of removal, making sure that all joints are tight and leak free.

Rear Muffler and Tailpipe

Loosen the clamps at the front and rear of the rear muffler and at the rear of the tailpipe. Unhook the rubber O-rings, and slide the assembly rearward until the muffler disengages from the middle pipe. Separate the muffler from the tailpipe and remove. Remove the tailpipe by separating the tail pipe clamp, and sliding the pipe to the rear.

Install in the reverse order of removal, making sure that all joints are tight and leak free.

NOTE: *To ensure proper sealing, all clamps should be installed with the tightening plate pointing 45° downward.*

Heater bleeder nipple

Cooling System

Radiator

REMOVAL AND INSTALLATION

Drain the coolant from the radiator, loosen the upper and lower radiator hose clamps, and separate the hoses from the radiator. Disconnect the wiring terminals from the cooling fan and thermoswitch. Unbolt the four radiator retaining bolts, and lift out the radiator, the expansion tank (on 1969-70 models), and the fan assembly. Remove the sheet metal screws retaining the fan housing to the radiator, and remove the fan housing.

Installation is the reverse of removal. When filling with coolant, open the heater core bleeder, and set the heater at its maximum heat. Fill the system with coolant, start the engine, and allow it to run at moderate speed until coolant flows from the bleeder without air bubbles. Close the bleeder, stop the engine, and fill the radiator to capacity.

Water Pump

REMOVAL AND INSTALLATION

Disconnect the battery ground cable, and drain the coolant from the radiator and the engine block (below the exhaust manifold). Detach all fuel and vacuum lines and electrical connectors from the intake manifold and carburetor. On fuel injected engines, separate the fuel distributor tube from the injectors and the enrichment valve, and cap the injectors and the valve to prevent dirt from entering. Remove the preheater hose and air cleaner, and disconnect the throttle and choke control (if so equipped). Unbolt the intake manifold mounting bolts, and remove the manifold. (NOTE: *cover the inlets in the cylinder head*). Remove the water pump cover (tap lightly with a plastic hammer to unseat), and turn the impeller bolt clockwise to screw the pump shaft assembly out of the block.

With the impeller removed, slide the pump shaft into the block, engaging the drive gears. Seat the bearing housing using a large piece of tubing and a hammer, so that the housing butts against the plane of the engine block. Install the impeller and washer, tightening the bolt counterclockwise (left-hand thread).

Place an .02" spacer between the impeller bolt and the pump cover. Measure the clearance between the block and the cover (as shown), and select the appropriate spacers. Gaskets are available in three thicknesses—.01, .02, and .03". Remove the shim and tighten the cover mounting bolts.

Measuring water pump cover clearance

Install the remaining parts in the reverse of removal.

Overhaul

Holding the end of the pump shaft, remove the impeller retaining bolt (left-hand thread). Using a brass drift, tap the shaft out of the impeller. Press the pump shaft, seals, and bearings from the bearing housing. Remove the pump seal, O-ring, slinger, seal ring, and the ball bearing lock ring. Press the ball bearing from the pump shaft. Check the bearing to ensure that it ro-

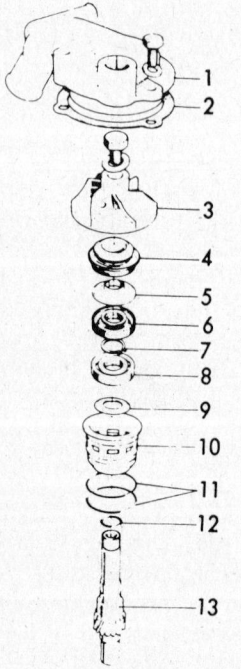

1. Pump cover
2. Gasket
3. Impeller
4. Water pump seal
5. Slinger
6. Seal ring
7. Bearing lock ring
8. Ball bearings
9. Oil slinger
10. Bearing housing
11. O-rings
12. Seal ring
13. Pump shaft

Water pump—exploded view

tates freely, replace if necessary, and renew all seals.

Place the oil slinger onto the pump shaft, press the bearing on (NOTE: *always press ball bearings on the race being installed*), and install the bearing lock ring. Press the pump shaft and bearing into the bearing housing. Install the seal ring and the slinger and tap the water pump seal into the bearing housing using a large sleeve of tubing as an installer. Mount the O-rings, and install the pump (see above).

Thermostat

When servicing the thermostat, examine the check valve in the thermostat housing. If the valve is pitted or worn, it must be replaced. NOTE: *Portions of the cooling system will not function if the check valve is not installed.*

Engine

Exhaust Emission Control

Carbureted SAAB 99's utilize distributor and carburetor modifications to control exhaust emissions. Lean carburetor jetting, and a distributor retard mechanism, drawing vacuum directly from the intake manifold, maintain low emissions at idle. Therefore, in order to meet Federal Standards, the ignition timing and the carburetor must be adjusted exactly as specified, and checked periodically to ensure accuracy.

Fuel injected models use the Bosch fuel injection computer to monitor engine functions and provide the precise fuel/air mixture necessary under varying engine conditions. For the system to function at maximum efficiency, all adjustments (ignition timing, idle speed, fuel pressure) must be made very accurately.

All models are equipped with positive crankcase ventilation. Air is drawn, from the air cleaner, through the crankcase and a valve into the intake manifold. The output hose and valve should be cleaned periodically to maintain efficiency. To clean the valve, remove the cover spring and cover, the diaphragm, the coil spring and the needle valve. Clean all parts (excluding the diaphragm) in solvent, and check the diaphragm for holes, cracks, and hardening. Replace the diaphragm if necessary, and assemble the valve.

Engine Assembly

REMOVAL AND INSTALLATION

NOTE: *The power train is removed as a unit. Removing only the engine is not recommended.*

Mark the position of the hood brackets on the hood hinges, loosen the mounting bolts, and with an assistant, lift off the hood. Detach both battery cables, unclamp and lift out the battery. Disconnect the coil and ballast resistor, temperature and oil pressure senders, radiator fan and thermostat contact. Drain the coolant from the radiator and engine block, and disconnect the upper and lower radiator hoses from the engine. Disconnect the brake assist vacuum hose from the intake manifold, and (if carbureted) the suction line from the fuel pump. If fuel injected, disconnect all injection wiring connectors, vacuum lines, and fuel input and return lines from the engine. Remove the air cleaner and preheater casing, disconnect the throttle linkage from the throttle shaft, and the choke cable from the carburetor (if so equipped).

Unbolt the slave cylinder, and hang it in an out of the way position. Move the freewheel lever into the locked position, and disconnect the cable from the transmission. Disconnect the exhaust pipe from the exhaust manifold, and remove the ground cable from the transmission.

Raise the front end of the car, put the gear lever in neutral, knock out the front taper pin from the shift rod joint, and separate the shift rod joint from the gear selector rod. Remove the speedometer cable from the transmission. Unbolt all engine mounts, and support the power train at its lifting brackets with a hoist. Remove the larger clips on the rubber bellows covering the inner U-joints.

Gear shift rod joint

On 1969 models, rotate the axle until the U-joint trunnions are horizontal, raise the power train approximately 2", move it as far right as possible and separate the left U-joint. Move the power train as far left as possible and separate the right U-joint. NOTE: *Ensure that the needle bearing caps remain on the U-joint.*

On 1970-71 models, unbolt the right-hand lower ball joint from the lower control arm. Turn the steering wheel to left lock, and separate the right U-joint. Raise the power train slightly, and separate the left U-joint.

On all models, raise the power train to gain access, and disconnect all wires from the starter and alternator. Lift the power train out of the car.

Installation of the power train is the reverse of removal. When installing, pack the inner U-joints with grease. After lowering the power train onto its mounts, ensure that the throttle control shaft is inserted into its bearing. NOTE: *When installing carbureted engines, ensure that adequate clearance (1/2") exists between the alternator belt and the fuel line.*

POWER TRAIN SEPARATION AND ASSEMBLY

Drain the engine oil (3/4" hex head plug) and remove the clutch cover. Remove the lock ring and sealing cap, and unbolt the clutch shaft center bolt, washer, and O-ring. Remove the clutch shaft using a threaded end slide hammer. Unbolt the three release bearing guide sleeve bolts, back-off the clutch adjusting screw, and disconnect the clutch lever. Remove all engine to transmission mounting bolts. CAUTION: *Do not mix the bolts. Bolts threaded into the transmission case have UNC threads, bolts threaded into the engine block have UNF threads.* While lifting the engine from the transmission, remove the release bearing guide sleeve.

Assemble in the reverse order of disassembly.

Manifolds

INTAKE MANIFOLD

Removal and Installation

Detach all fuel and vacuum lines and electrical connectors from the intake manifold and carburetor (if so equipped). On fuel injected engines, separate the fuel distributor tube from the injectors and the enrichment valve, and cap the injectors and the valve to prevent dirt from entering. Remove the preheater hose and the air cleaner, and disconnect the throttle and choke control (if so equipped). Unbolt the mounting bolts, and remove the manifold. NOTE: *Cover the inlets in the cylinder head.*

Install in the reverse order of removal.

Exhaust Manifold

Removal and Installation

Remove the air cleaner and the preheater hose and casing. Unbolt the exhaust pipe from the exhaust manifold. Unbolt the manifold mounting bolts, and remove the manifold from the cylinder head.

Install in the reverse order of removal.

Cylinder Head

Removal and Installation

CAUTION: *Remove the cylinder head only with the engine cold, to prevent warpage.*

Drain the coolant from the radiator, engine block and heater bleeder, and disconnect all coolant hoses from the cylinder head. Remove the air cleaner, the preheater hose and the preheater casing, and disconnect the brake assist vacuum line from the intake manifold. On carbureted engines, remove the fuel output line from the fuel pump, and disconnect the throttle and choke control from the carburetor. On fuel injected engines, disconnect all hoses and electrical connectors from the intake manifold, and disconnect the throttle control. Unbolt the exhaust pipe from the exhaust manifold. Remove the camshaft cover and rotate the engine until the camshaft index marks align (see illustration), screw a nut onto the threaded stud in the camshaft sprocket, and tighten securely against the mounting plate. NOTE: *The nut must prevent movement of the camshaft sprocket, otherwise the chain tensioner will adjust and the engine will have to be removed to readjust the tensioner.* Loosen and remove all cylinder head bolts and nuts in the reverse of the torque sequence. Remove two cylinder head studs using a large screwdriver and screw them into two lower bolt holes to act as guides for removal. Remove the remaining studs, and lift off the cylinder heads.

Camshaft index marks

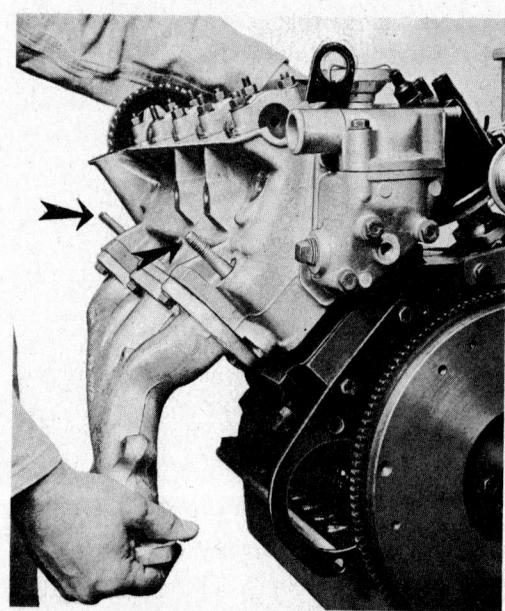

Cylinder head studs used as locating pins

Carefully scrape all old gasket material from the mating surfaces (do not use emery cloth), and check both the cylinder head and block for distortion using a straightedge. Install a new gasket (uncoated) using the studs as locating pins. Align the camshaft index marks, and install the cylinder head over the locating studs. Screw the center studs into their original position, then relocate the studs used as locating pins to their original position. Install the nuts and bolts, torque as specified, and mount the camshaft sprocket on the camshaft. NOTE: *Do not remove the nut from the camshaft sprocket center stud until the sprocket is mounted on the camshaft.* Lock the camshaft sprocket bolt, and continue in the reverse of the removal procedure.

Valve Train

Valve Adjustment

Checking

With the camshaft cover removed, the transmission in third gear, and the freewheel locked, push the car until each camshaft lobe is on the base circle. A feeler gauge of the minimum checking tolerance should insert between the valve and camshaft, while a gauge of the maximum tolerance should not. If the clearance of any valve does not meet these specifications, all valves must be adjusted.

Adjusting

Repeat the above procedure using feeler gauges to determine the exact clearance of each valve, and record the tolerances. Remove the camshaft (see below), and number the valve depressors. Pull out each valve depressor and its adjusting pallet, using a magnet or a suction cup. CAUTION: *Do not intermix valve depressors and adjusting pallets.* Using a micrometer, measure the thickness of each adjusting pallet and record. Compare the valve clearance as measured to the valve adjusting tolerances, and add or subtract the difference (depending whether the measured tolerance is larger or smaller than the required tolerance) to the thickness of the pallet. Obtain pallets of the required thickness, and install them with the valve depressors onto the valves. Install the camshaft, and check to ensure that clearances are correct.

Camshaft, Idler Shaft, and Timing Chain

Camshaft

Removal and Installation

Remove the camshaft cover, and rotate the engine until the camshaft index marks align. Install a nut on the camshaft sprocket stud, and tighten, securely clamping the sprocket to the mounting plate. NOTE:

The nut must prevent movement of the camshaft sprocket, otherwise the chain tensioner will adjust, making it impossible to install the sprocket on the camshaft. Remove the sprocket mounting bolts, gradually loosen the camshaft bearing cap nuts until valve spring pressure is released, and remove the bearing caps and camshaft.

Installation is the reverse of removal. When installing, ensure that the camshaft index marks align.

Idler Shaft

Removal and Installation

With the engine mounted in a work stand, rotate the flywheel until the camshaft index marks align. Remove the intake manifold, the water pump, and the water pump shaft. Mark the position of the distributor body on the block, and the rotor on the distributor body, and remove the distributor. Detach the fuel lines from the fuel pump (if so equipped), and remove the pump. Unbolt and remove the crankshaft pulley using a slide hammer. Remove the timing chain cover, and mark the position of the idler shaft sprocket on the block and the timing chain. Unbolt and remove the chain tensioner, loosen the curved guide rail mounting bolts, and move the rail away from the timing chain. Lift the chain away from the idler shaft sprocket, remove the idler shaft retaining plate bolts, and slide the idler shaft out of the block.

Insert the idler shaft into the block and tighten the retaining plate bolts. Align the index marks, and engage the chain and sprocket. Return the curved guide rail to its original position, and tighten the mounting bolts. Install the timing chain tensioner and adjust (see below). Check the condition of the timing cover seal and replace if necessary. Continue installation in the reverse order of removal.

Timing Chain Tensioner

Removal and Installation

With the engine on a work stand, unbolt and remove the crankshaft pulley using a slide hammer. Remove the timing chain cover, and the bolt from the back of the tensioner. Insert a hex key, and turn clockwise to slacken chain tension. Unbolt the tensioner mounting bolts and remove the tensioner.

Installing chain tensioner (early engines)

On engines up to and including Serial No. 2954, install the tensioner as follows: Loosen the curved chain guide mounting bolts, and slacken the chain. Using a hex key, rotate the tensioner sleeve clockwise to relieve spring tension, and mount the tensioner on the engine. Press the curved chain guide to remove slack from the chain, and tighten the guide mounting bolts. Turn the tensioner sleeve to release spring pressure (a click indicates release), and install the cover bolt on the back of the tensioner. Continue installation in the reverse order of removal.

On engines with Serial No. 2955 and up, install the tensioner as follows: Loosen the curved chain guide mounting bolts, and slacken the chain. Relieve spring tension by rotating the tensioner sleeve clockwise, and insert a .12" shim on the tensioner neck (shim is supplied with the tensioner). Mount the tensioner on the block with the shim installed. Press firmly on the curved

Installing chain tensioner (late engines) using shim

chain guide while removing the shim from the tensioner neck, causing the tensioner to bottom, and release slightly to actuate the tensioner. Tighten the curved chain guide mounting bolts, and continue installing in the reverse order of removal.

TIMING CHAIN

Removal and Installation

With the engine mounted on a work stand, unbolt and remove the crankshaft pulley using a slide hammer. Remove the camshaft and timing chain covers. Rotate the engine until the 0° mark on the flywheel and the mark on the side of the block align, and the camshaft index marks align (NOTE: *the marks on the idler shaft*

Crankshaft index marks

sprocket will be horizontal). Install a nut on the camshaft sprocket stud, securely tightening the sprocket to the mounting plate. Unbolt and remove the chain tensioner and the curved guide plate. Unbolt the camshaft sprocket from the camshaft, and the sprocket mounting plate from the block, and remove the timing chain from the engine.

Installation is the reverse of removal. When installing, apply light tension to the curved chain guide, rotate the crankshaft two turns, and ensure that the flywheel, camshaft, and idler index marks are properly aligned. NOTE: *When installing a used chain, install so that the sides are positioned as they were in the original installation.*

OIL SEALS

Replacement

The flywheel end oil seal may be replaced with the drive train installed in the vehicle. Remove the flywheel housing, the clutch and throwout bearing, and the flywheel. Unbolt and remove the seal cap from the engine. Pry the old seal out of the seal cap using a screwdriver and hammer.

Tap the new seal into the cap, lubricate the seal, and install the seal cap. Ensure that the seal seats properly on the crankshaft. NOTE: *When installing the flywheel, always use new bolts.*

In order to replace the timing cover oil seal, the engine must be removed from the vehicle and mounted on a work stand. Unbolt and remove the crankshaft pulley using a slide hammer. Remove the timing cover from the engine, and pry out the seal.

Tap the new seal into the timing cover, and install in the reverse order of removal.

Pistons and Connecting Rods

PISTONS

Pistons are installed with the marking "FRONT" or ➜ facing the timing chain end of the engine. Piston size class is identified by a letter stamped into the center of the piston head.

Piston Rings

The compression rings are installed with their gaps 180° apart, at each end of the piston pin. The lower compression ring should be installed with the "TOP" marking facing the top of the piston. The gaps

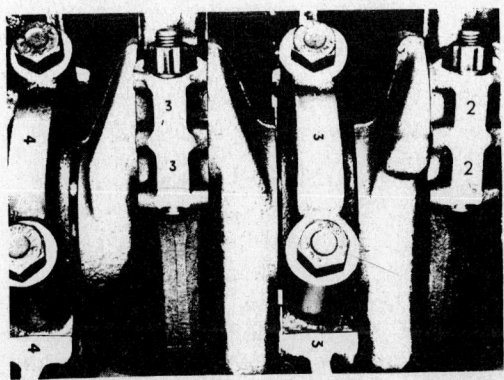

Connecting rod installation

of the top and bottom segments of the oil scraper ring should also be staggered.

CONNECTING RODS

Matching connecting rods and caps are numbered corresponding to the cylinder in which they are installed. The rods are installed so that the numbered side faces away from the idler shaft.

Clutch and Transmission

Clutch

REMOVAL AND INSTALLATION

NOTE: *A clutch-throwout bearing compression tool (SAAB No. 839207) is necessary to remove and install the clutch from the SAAB 99 drive train. Do not attempt to remove the clutch unless this tool is available.*

Mark the position of the hood brackets on the hood hinges, loosen the mounting bolts, and with an assistant, lift off the hood. Disconnect the battery ground cable, all wiring from the front sheet, the coil high tension lead from the coil, and the temperature and oil pressure switches. Drain the radiator coolant and remove all hoses from the radiator. Remove the headlight trim frames. Disconnect the hood lock

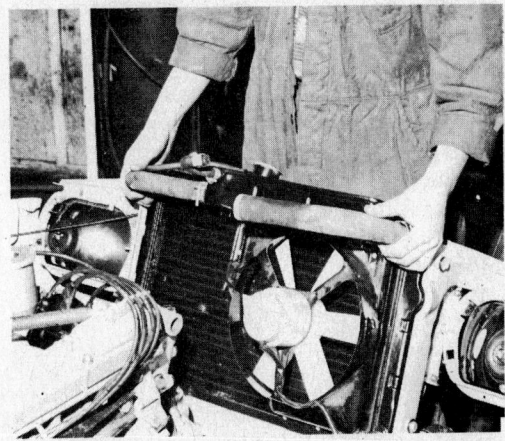

Removing the front sheet

from its connections at the firewall and the fender. Remove the eight retaining screws, and lift off the entire front sheet.

Remove the clutch cover. Unbolt the slave cylinder and support it in an out of

Clutch compression tool installed

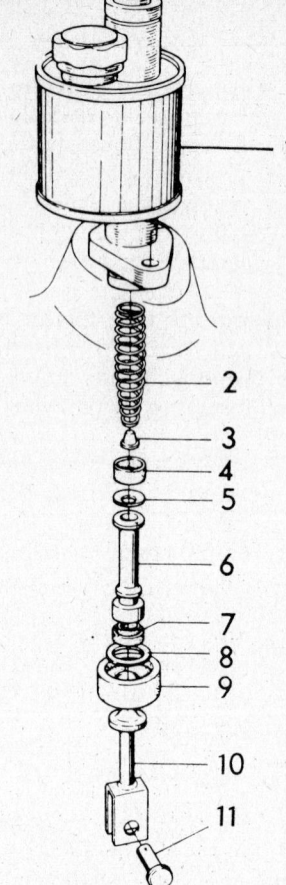

the way position, and remove the clutch lever. Remove the lock ring, the clutch shaft end cap, and the clutch shaft center bolt, washer, and O-ring. Pull the clutch shaft using a slide hammer threaded into the shaft. Back off all clutch retaining bolts, one turn at a time, until clutch pressure is released, and remove all bolts except the top two. Unbolt the throwout bearing guide sleeve. Install and tighten the clutch-throwout bearing compression tool. Remove the remaining clutch retaining bolts, and lift out the clutch disc, pressure plate, throwout bearing, and guide sleeve.

To install, assemble the pressure plate, throwout bearing and guide sleeve using the compression tool. Insert the clutch disc into the flywheel, and lower the pressure plate assembly into position. Install the clutch shaft, align the pressure plate with the locating pins, and tighten the clutch bolts finger tight. Tighten the guide sleeve retaining bolts, remove the compression tool, and tighten the clutch retaining bolts. Continue installation in the reverse order of removal.

1. Housing
2. Spring
3. Spring retainer
4. Seal
5. Washer
6. Piston
7. Seal
8. Lock ring
9. Sealing boot
10. Push rod
11. Shaft bolt

Clutch master cylinder—exploded view

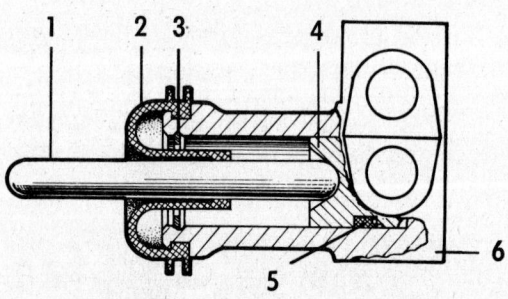

Clutch slave cylinder—exploded view

1. Push rod   4. Piston
2. Sealing cap   5. Piston seal
3. Lock ring   6. Housing

CLUTCH LINKAGE

The clutch linkage consists of a vertical master cylinder, actuated directly by the clutch pedal, and a slave cylinder, which operates the clutch lever.

Bleeding

NOTE: *The conventional method of bleeding the linkage, pumping the pedal to expel air, is not recommended on the SAAB 99, and can cause damage to the system.*

Connect a hose to the slave cylinder bleeder, and immerse the free end in a container of brake fluid. Fill the master cylinder reservoir with brake fluid, and open the slave cylinder bleeder 1/2 turn. Place a cooling system pressure tester over

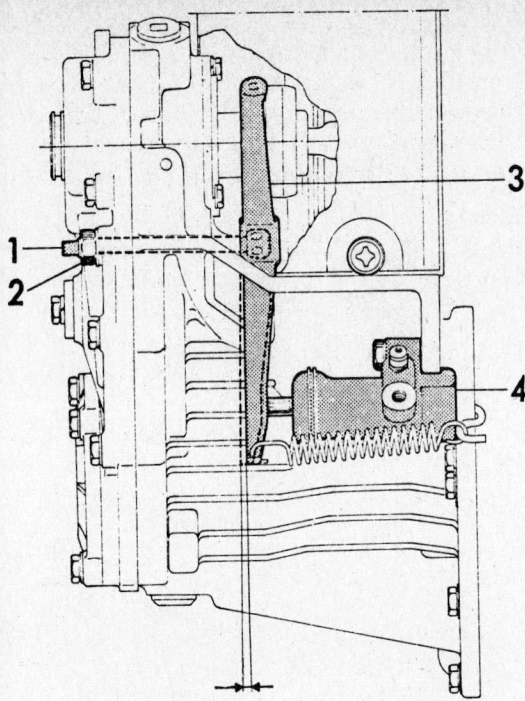

Clutch play adjustment

1. Adjusting screw
2. Lock nut
3. Clutch lever
4. Slave cylinder

the master cylinder reservoir, and pump until no air bubbles leave the bleeder hose. Close the bleeder and check the action of the clutch pedal.

Adjustments

Clutch free play is determined by the position of the clutch lever pivot in relation to the throwout bearing. To adjust, loosen the locknut, and turn the adjusting stud to obtain .12" free play at the end of the clutch lever.

Transmission

SHIFT LINKAGE

Adjustments

Engage reverse gear and turn the ignition key to the locked position. Move the shift lever back and forth, and measure the axial play of the shift rod. If the movement is not between .06 and .1", adjust by moving the shift lever housing backward or forward. Access to the shift lever housing is obtained by removing the shift knob and shift boot, the knobs from the free

wheel and heater controls, and the shift cover.

REBUILDING

With the power train removed from the car, separate the engine from the transmission, mount the transmission on a work stand, and drain the oil from the transmission. Remove the inner universal joints using a slide hammer and claw puller. Unbolt the differential bearing seats, and remove using a slide hammer and claw puller. Remove the differential assembly, the spacers, and the shims. NOTE: *Note the position of, and save all spacers and shims for use in assembly.* Remove the lock plate

Pulling out the intermediate shaft

adjacent to the pinion bearing housing, and pull out the intermediate shaft, allowing the intermediate gear set to drop free. Unbolt and separate the primary gear housing from the transmission, and lift out the intermediate gear set. Remove the transmission side cover, and the spring and ball catch for the gear selector rod. Pull out the reverse shaft, and remove the reverse gear, bearings and washers. Remove the gear shift shafts and the shift forks. Unbolt the pinion bearing housing retaining bolts, and tap the pinion shaft out of the transmission case using a drift. NOTE: *Retain the shims for use in assembly.*

Disassemble the pinion shaft by remov-

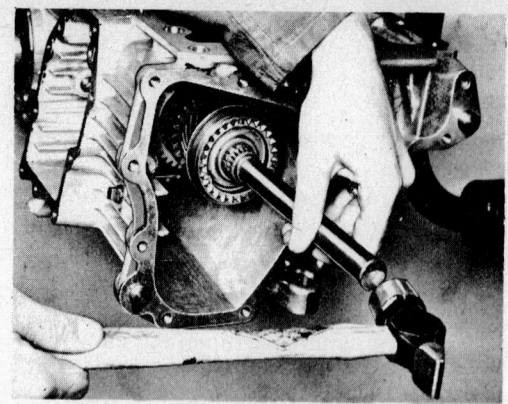

Tapping out the pinion shaft

driver gear may be pressed off the shaft, and/or the bearing removed from the case for replacement. Press the primary input gear, complete with bearing, out of the primary gear case. If necessary, remove the snap ring, press the bearing off the shaft

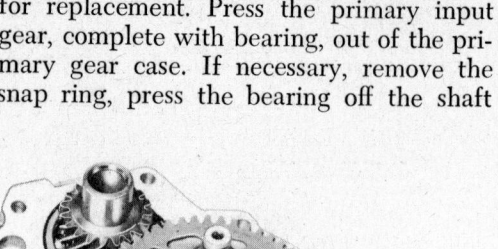

Primary gear train

Reverse gear, bearings, and washers

Disassembled pinion shaft

Center gear, shaft, and bearings

ing the lock rings and sliding off the gears and synchronizers. CAUTION: *Do not disassemble the pinion shaft beyond this point (see illustration). Doing so will require special tools for assembly of the differential.*

To disassemble the primary gear housing, unbolt and remove the primary gear case. Remove the freewheel control, and tap the freewheel shaft out of the housing. Remove the center gear and shaft from the primary gear case, and separate the shaft from the gear to replace the bearings (if necessary). Unbolt the cap from the primary gear case, free the lock ring from the shaft, and press the shaft out of the case and bearing. If necessary, the

Removing the transmission input gear bearing support

and replace. Remove the bearing support that retains the transmission input gear and bearing, and press the gear and bearing out of the primary gear housing. If necessary, remove the snap ring, press the bearing off the shaft, and replace. Check the condition of the remaining bearings installed in the primary gear housing, press out, and replace if necessary.

Disassemble the freewheel hub if necessary, by placing the freewheel assembly in a large clean rag, and pushing the hub out of the sleeve (NOTE: *the rag is necessary to prevent the loss of springs, plungers, and rollers*). If the freewheel sleeve is damaged, the entire assembly must be replaced.

When installing the freewheel hub into the sleeve, the figures on the face of the hub should face inward in the sleeve. In order to assemble and install a used hub, a special tool must be utilized (see illustration). Insert the hub into the notched end of the tool, with the figures facing the unnotched end. One by one, rotating the hub counterclockwise, install the springs, plungers, and rollers (see illustration). When the final roller is installed, push the hub into the unnotched end of the tube, so that approximately 1/2 of the hub protrudes from the tube. Insert the exposed end of the freewheel hub into the sleeve, and push and turn (clockwise) the remainder of the hub into the sleeve.

Assemble the primary gear housing in the reverse order of disassembly. When installing the transmission input gear bearing support, glue on the intermediate shaft thrust washer, and use the intermediate shaft as an alignment guide. The bearing support bolts should be secured with Loctite. Assemble the gears, synchronizers, and lock rings onto the pinion shaft in the order in which they were removed.

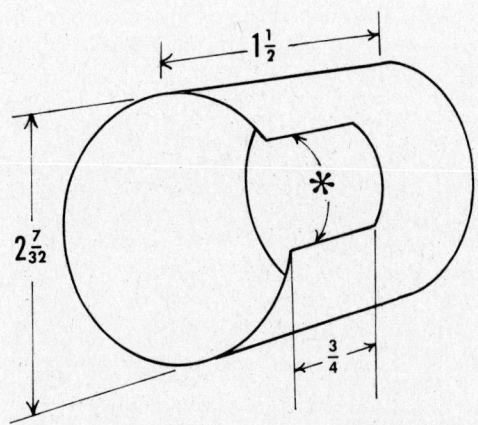

Freewheel hub assembly tool. * — Width of the notch equals the width of one roller ramp on the freewheel hub.

Pinion housing locating studs

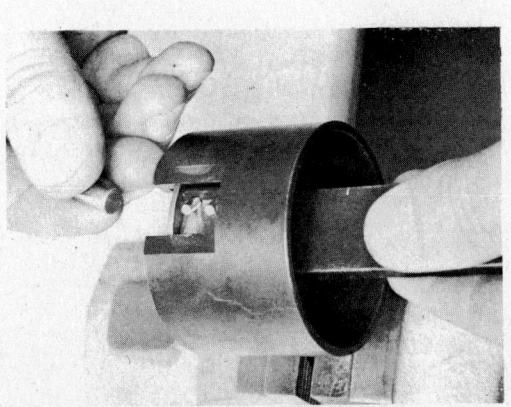

Assembling the freewheel hub

Install two aligning studs into the pinion housing mounting holes in the transmission case, and ensure that the original shims are installed on the pinion bearing housing. Insert the pinion shaft into the transmission case. Using a sleeve over the housing, tap it lightly into position, and install the four mounting bolts, securing them with Loctite. Slide the blocker rings on the pinion shaft into the neutral position, and install the shift forks and shafts.

Glue the intermediate shaft thrust washer into the transmission case, and insert the 25 loose needles into the intermediate shaft gear set, retaining them with grease. Lay the intermediate shaft in the transmission, coat the mating case flange with sealing compound, and mount the primary gear housing. NOTE: *Do not tighten mounting bolts.* Rock the transmission and/or support the intermediate gear set through the side cover opening until it is possible to insert the intermediate shaft. Tap the intermediate shaft into position, and tighten the primary gear housing mounting bolts. Install the reverse gear assembly and shaft with the thrust washer adjacent to the stationary gear. Mount the shaft lock plate adjacent to the pinion bearing housing. Install the reverse shift lever and the detent ball and spring, coat the side mating flange with sealing compound, and install the side cover.

Inspect the shaft seals in the differential bearing seats, and replace if necessary. Install the differential, the bearing seats and

shims, *exactly as they were removed.* Mount the inner driveshafts and U-joints. Coat the flange of the differential end cover with sealing compound, and mount the cover.

Fill the transmission with oil, join the power train, and install in the vehicle.

Drive Axle and U-Joints

The SAAB 99 drive axle consists of an inner U-joint, an axle shaft, an outer U-joint, a stub shaft, and a wheel hub. Due to the configuration of the U-joints, the axle shaft can slide axially as well as being jointed. 1969 models utilize an inner U-joint with two trunnions, while 1970 and later models use a joint with three trunnions.

Removal and Installation

Loosen the wheel nuts, remove the cotter pin, and loosen the castle nut. Raise the

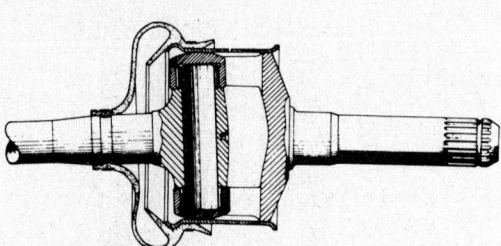
Inner U-joint, 1969 models

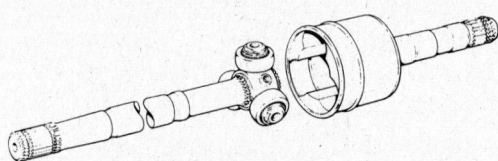
Inner U-joint, 1970 and later models

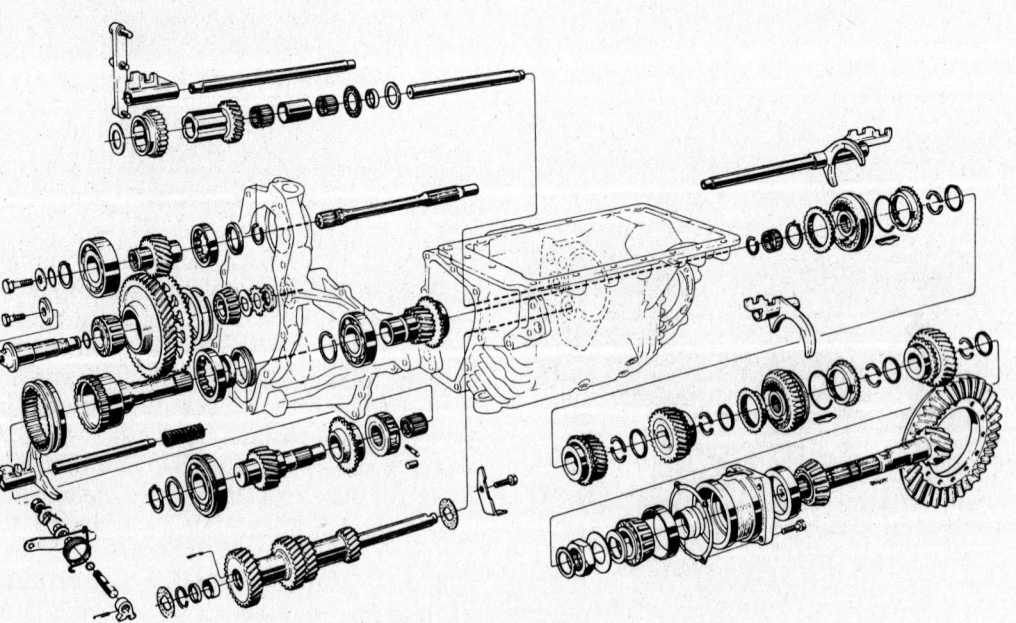
Transaxle—exploded view

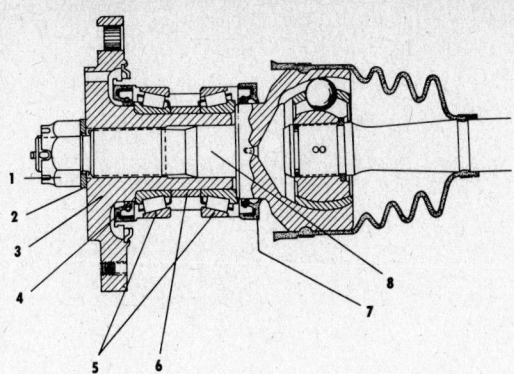

Outer U-joint

1. Castle nut
2. Washer
3. Hub
4. Outer shaft seal

5. Wheel bearings
6. Spacer sleeve
7. Inner shaft seal
8. Outer drive shaft

of the inner U-joint boot, to prevent damage to the joint.

Install in the reverse order of removal. When installing, pack the inner U-joint with grease, and tighten the castle nut to 145 ft. lbs.

Reconditioning

Using a puller attached to the wheel mounting studs, extract the stub shaft from the wheel hub. Pull the wheel hub out of the suspension upright, and pry out the

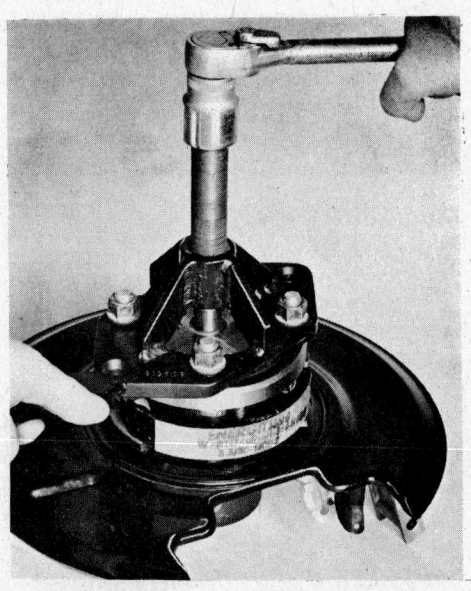

Removing the stub shaft from the hub

front of the car, and remove the wheel. Dismount the brake caliper, and support it so as not to stress the brake hose, in an out of the way position. Remove the brake disc, and disconnect the handbrake cable. Remove the large clamp from the inner U-joint boot. Free the tie rod end from the steering arm using the puller (SAAB Tool No. 819540 or equivalent; see illustration), and unbolt the upper and lower ball joints from the control arms. Pull out the entire assembly and install a cap over the end

seals with a screwdriver. NOTE: *Seals are not reusable.* Pull the bearing from the wheel hub, check the condition of all bearings, and replace if necessary.

Fill half the space between the bearing outer races, and coat the inner bearing races, with SAAB chassis lube. Mount the bearings and spacer in the suspension upright, and press in the seals. NOTE: *The seals are pressed flush with the flange. Pressing the seals further can cause bearing interference, and result in excessive bearing wear.* Mount the drive axle assembly, the suspension upright, and the wheel hub in a press, and press into their installed position. Install the castle nut, torque to 145 ft. lbs. and install cotter pin. Continue assembly in the reverse order of disassembly.

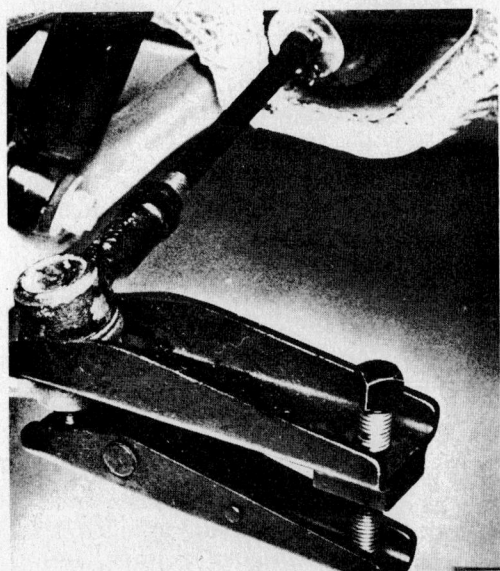

Removing the tie rod end from the steering arm using SAAB Tool No. 819568

Suspension and Steering

Suspension

FRONT

The front suspension consists of unequal length upper and lower A-arms, mounted directly to the unit body on brackets. The suspension upright, with steering arm, is mounted on ball joints bolted to the A-arms. The coil spring is mounted over the upper control arm, while the shock absorber is mounted on a stud on the lower arm. Upper and lower bump stops are utilized, the upper being progressive.

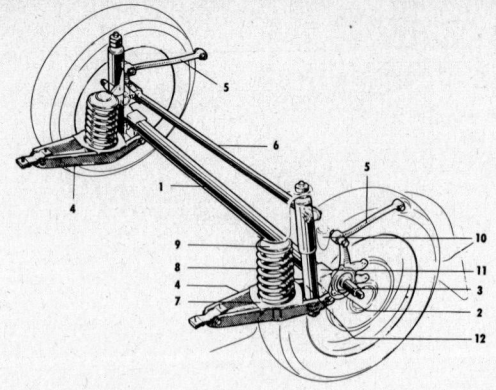

Rear suspension

1. Rear axle
2. End piece
3. Stub axle
4. Spring links
5. Rear links
6. Cross bar
7. Spring seat
8. Coil spring
9. Spring insulator
10. Bump stop
11. Stop
12. Shock absorber

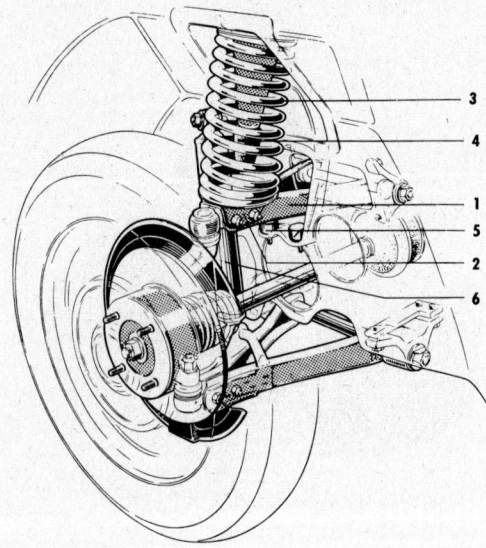

Front suspension

1. Upper control arm
2. Spring support
3. Coil spring
4. Upper bump stop
5. Lower bump stop
6. Shock absorber

Ball Joint Removal and Installation

Raise the car and remove the wheel. Unbolt the caliper, and hang it in an out of the way position, so as not to stress the brake hose. Servicing the upper ball joint is aided by compressing the coil spring. Unbolt the ball joint from the control arm, and remove the stud retaining nut. Remove the ball joint from the suspension upright with a puller (SAAB Tool No. 819540 or equivalent). Install in the reverse order of removal.

REAR

A rigid tubular rear axle is mounted by lower trailing arms and upper links. A Panhard rod is used to control lateral movement. Stub axles, pressed into the end pieces of the axle tube, support the wheel hubs on conical roller bearings. Coil springs and shock absorbers are mounted on the trailing arms. Upward suspension movement is limited by a rubber bump stop, while downward travel is limited by the shock absorbers.

CAUTION: *Never jack or support the car on its rear axle tube. To do so could distort the axle.*

Hub Bearing Replacement

Remove the wheel, unbolt the caliper, and hang it in an out of the way position so as not to stress the brake hose. Remove the brake disc, pry out the cap, and unbolt the castle nut. Pull off the hub, using a slide hammer if necessary. Pry out the seal (NOTE: *seal is not reusable*), and remove the bearing inner races.

Inspect the bearings, and if necessary, tap out the outer race using a suitable drift, and replace. Fill half the space between the bearing outer races, and coat the bearing inner races, with SAAB chassis grease. NOTE: *If used bearings are installed, they must be in their original position.* Install the inner bearing and the seal, and mount the hub. Install the outer bearing, and tight-

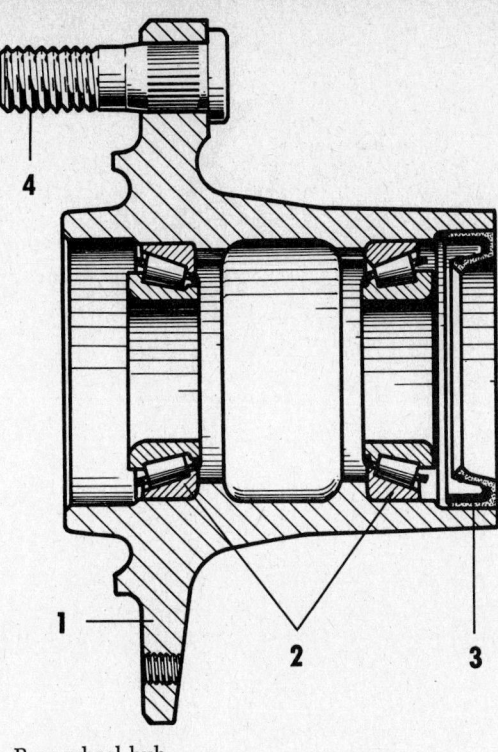

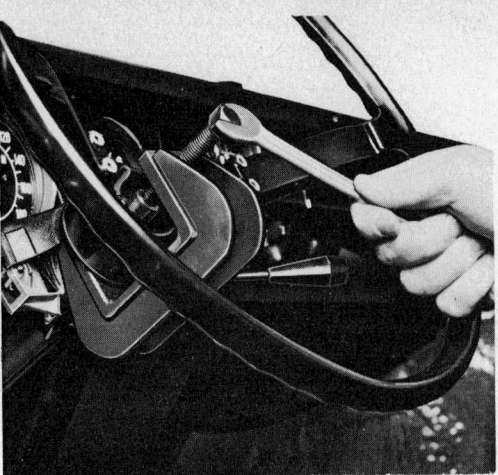

Removing the steering wheel

Rear wheel hub

1. Hub
2. Wheel bearings
3. Seal ring
4. Wheel screw

en the castle nut to zero play. Continue installation in the reverse order of removal.

Rear Axle Removal and Installation

Raise the rear of the car, and support it by the underbody. Disconnect the brake hoses in front of the rear axle and plug. Support the axle with a jack, and unbolt the shock absorbers from the trailing arms, the Panhard rod from the body, and the upper links from the axle. Lower the jack and remove the coil springs. Unbolt the axle from the trailing arms, and remove from the car.

Install in the reverse order of removal. When installing, bleed the brake system. Torque all suspension bolts with the weight of the car supported by the wheels.

Steering

STEERING WHEEL

Removal and Installation

· Remove the steering wheel padding and the steering wheel bearing lower cover. Remove the steering wheel nut, and mark

the position of the wheel and the shaft for installation. Install a puller (SAAB Tool No. 819568 or equivalent; see illustration), and remove the steering wheel.

Install the steering wheel in the reverse order of removal. CAUTION: *Extreme care must be exercised to avoid damaging the collapsible steering column. In no case should the steering wheel be forced or hammered onto the shaft.*

STEERING COLUMN

Removal and Installation

Loosen the lock bolt at the intermediate shaft. Unbolt the column at the pedal bracket and the instrument panel. Separate the electrical connector, and lift out the column.

Install in the reverse order of removal.

STEERING GEAR

A helical rack and pinion, directly actuating the steering arms by means of tie rods ball jointed at each end of the rack, is used. Early models (up to vehicle No. 99.022.278) can be lubricated and adjusted externally, later units being permanently lubricated and non adjustable.

Adjustments

Rack backlash may be adjusted, on early units, using a bolt on the underside of the pinion housing. Loosen the locknut, and tighten the adjusting bolt to zero lash. Back off the bolt 1/8-1/4 turn, tighten the locknut, and check to ensure that the unit does not bind from lock to lock.

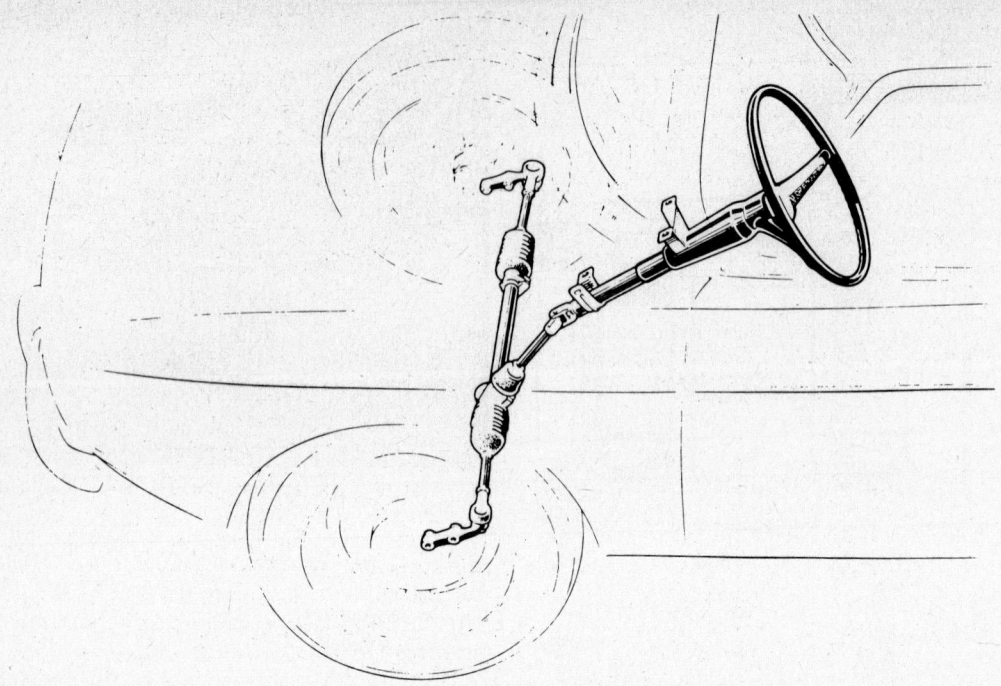

Steering mechanism

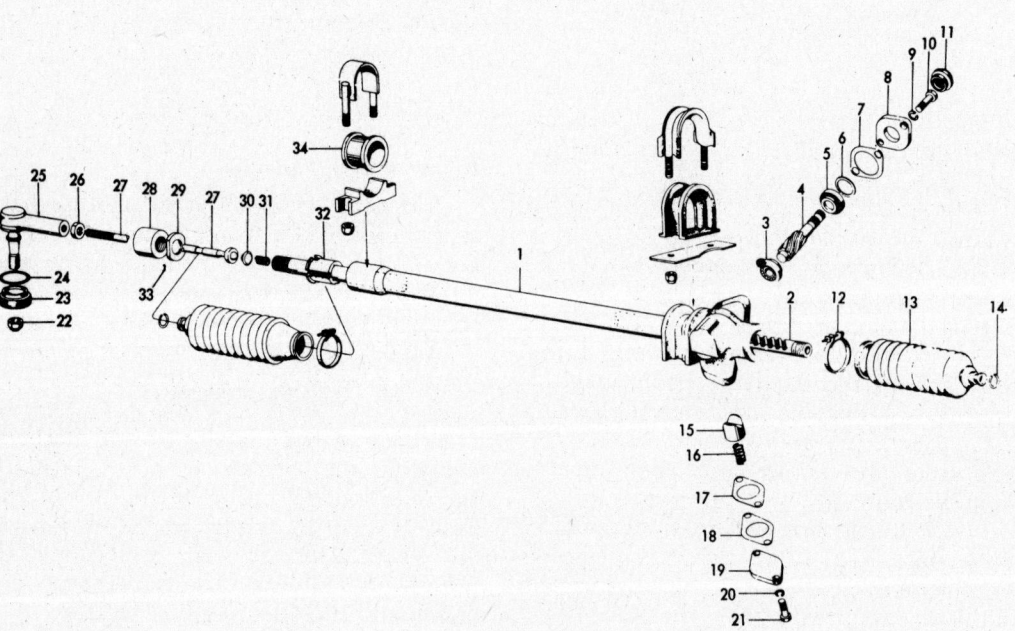

Steering gear—late

1. Steering gear housing assembly	9. Washer	18. Gasket	27. Tie rod
2. Rack	10. Screw	19. Cap	28. Outer ball joint cup
3. Ball bearing	11. Seal ring	20. Washer	29. Lock nut
4. Pinion	12. Clamp	21. Screw	30. Inner ball joint cup
5. Ball bearing	13. Boot	22. Nut	31. Spring
6. Shim	14. Clamp	23. Boot	32. Bushing
7. Gasket	15. Plunger	24. Ring	33. Cotter pin
8. Cap	16. Spring	25. Tie rod end	34. Rubber bushing
	17. Shim	26. Lock nut	

Removal and Installation

Raise the car and remove the front wheels. Unbolt, and remove the tie rod ends from the steering arms using a puller. Roll back the carpet, and loosen the lower intermediate shaft joint. Unbolt the steering column, pull back, and separate the intermediate shaft from the pinion shaft. Loosen the retaining clamp nuts, and slide the steering gear out through the left wheel well.

Install in the reverse order of removal. When installing, place the brake discs in a straight ahead position, center the rack (equal distance from each lock), and place the steering wheel in its centered position. Adjust the tie rod ends so that they insert into the steering arms as positioned above

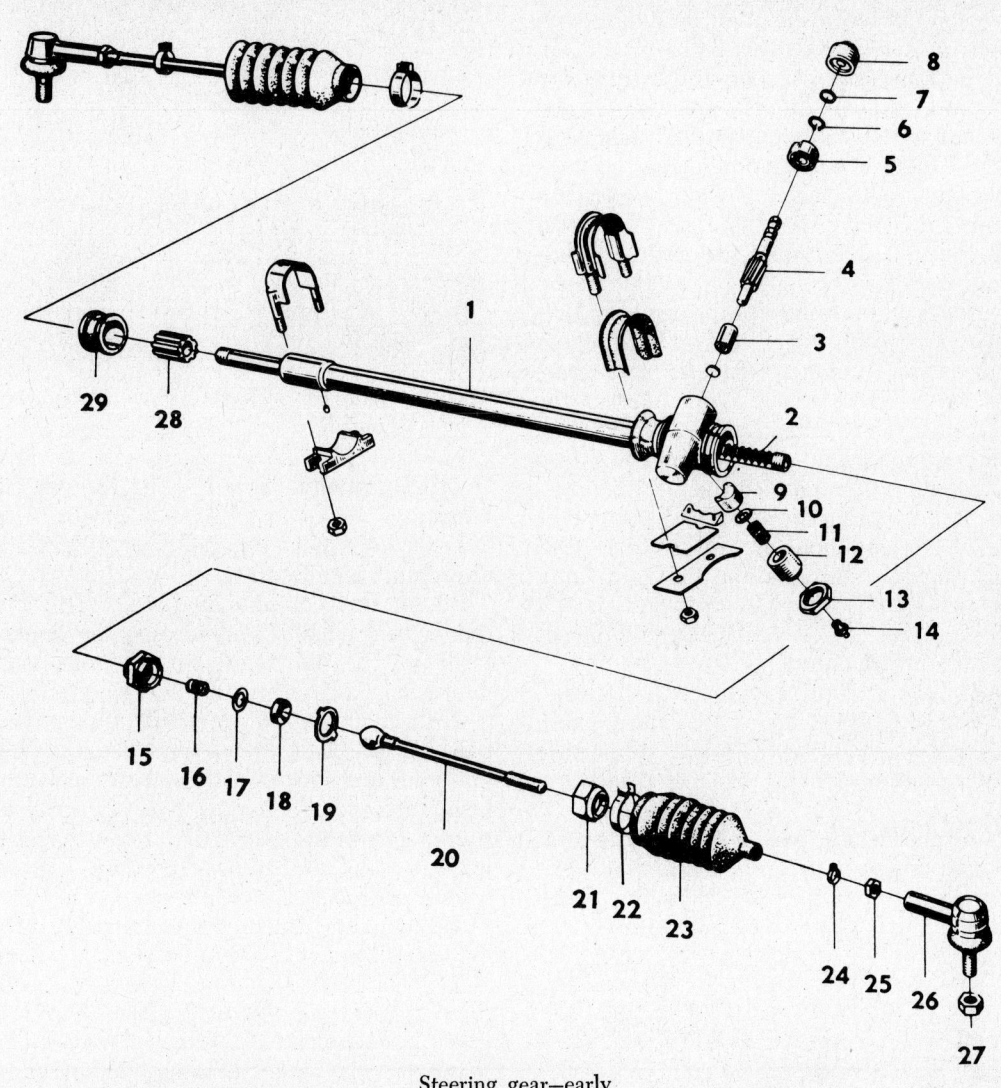

Steering gear—early

1. Steering gear housing assembly	11. Spring	22. Clamp
2. Rack	12. Fitting	23. Boot
3. Bushing	13. Lock nut	24. Clamp
4. Pinion	14. Grease fitting	25. Nut
5. Ball bearing	15. End piece	26. Tie rod end
6. Lock ring	16. Spring	27. Nut
7. Seal ring	17. Shim	28. Rubber bushing
8. Fitting	18. Inner ball joint cup	29. Bushing
9. Plunger	19. Tab lock washer	
10. Washer	20. Tie rod	
	21. Ball joint cap	

and fasten the intermediate shaft to the pinion shaft. Adjust the toe-in to specifications, and center the steering wheel.

Reconditioning

Early model steering gear (up to model No. 99.022.278) is rebuilt as follows:

Loosen the lock nuts and remove the tie rod ends from the tie rods. Unclamp and remove the rubber boots. Pry up the tab locks, and unscrew the outer ball joint cups, removing the tie rods and ball joints. Holding the rack in a vise between two blocks of wood, remove the end pieces. Loosen the lock nut on the adjusting bolt and back out the bolt, spring and plunger. Using a slide hammer attached to the pinion shaft, remove the pinion from the steering housing. Pull the rack out of the steering housing.

Inspect all bushings and bearings and replace as necessary. Lubricate all gear teeth, sliding contact surfaces, and bearings with SAAB chassis lube. Insert the rack into the steering housing. Install the pinion and bearing, and tighten the fitting against the outer race of the ball bearing. Mount the plunger spring and adjusting bolt in the steering housing. Install the large boot clamps, and holding the rack in a vise between two blocks of wood, install the rack end pieces. Stake the end pieces in position with a punch.

Assemble the tie rod inner ball joints, and adjust using shims so that the tie rod, with end installed, will be self supporting in any position without sticking. Adjust the play of the rack (see adjustments). Mount the boots, and lubricate the unit through the grease fitting. Check that lubricant (SAAB chassis lube) fills the entire

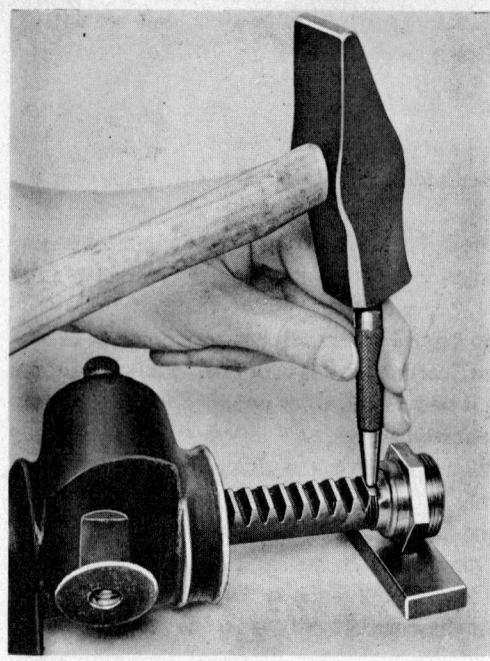

Staking end piece to rack—early steering gear

steering gear unit by squeezing the rubber boots.

Later units (from model No. 99.022.279) are rebuilt as follows:

Loosen the lock nuts, and remove the tie rod ends. Unclamp and remove the boots. Drill out the pin in the tie rod inner ball joint using a 5/32″ drill. NOTE: *The pin is 3/8″ deep. Do not overdrill.* Using two pairs of pliers, unscrew and remove the ball joint and lock nut. Unbolt the rack adjustment cap, and remove the cap, gasket, shims, spring, and plunger. Remove the pinion cap bolts, and remove the cap, gasket, shims, pinion and upper bearing. Pull the rack out of the housing, and tap the housing to remove the lower pinion bearing.

NOTE: *The steering gear should be well lubricated during assembly, as it is a sealed unit, and cannot be lubricated externally.*

Inspect the pinion bearings and replace if necessary. The rack bushings are reamed to size and are not replaceable. Install the lower pinion bearing. NOTE: *Pinion bearings are installed with the inner race extensions facing each other (see illustration).* Install the lock nut on the pinion end of the rack, fill the ball joint cup with SAAB chassis lube, and assemble the ball joint. Tighten the ball joint cup so that the tie rod, with end installed, is self supporting

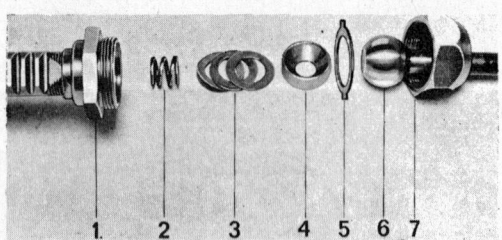

Tie rod inner ball joint—early

1. End piece   5. Lock plate
2. Spring   6. Tie rod
3. Shim   7. Outer ball joint cup
4. Inner ball joint cup

in any position without sticking. Tighten the lock nut against the ball joint cup, and recheck the adjustment. Using a 5/32″ drill, drill a new 3/8″ deep pin hole, install a lock pin, and stake the pin in position by center punching the edge of the hole. Insert the rack into the housing, and install the pinion and upper bearing. Adjust the pinion shaft so that there is no axial play using shims (.005, .0075, .010, .090″ shims are available). Insert the rack tensioner plunger and

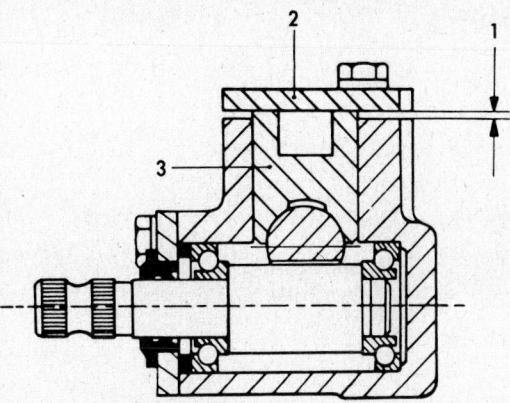

Rack plunger clearance measurement

1. Clearance (add .002-.006″)
2. Cap
3. Plunger

install the cap (without spring or gasket), tightening the bolts finger tight. Measure the clearance between the cap and the housing, add .002-.006″, and select a gasket and shims within this tolerance (.005, .0075, .010, .015, .020″ shims are available). Install the cap, spring, gasket, and shims, and ensure that the rack does not stick in any position. Assemble the remaining ball joint, adjust as above, and install the boots and tie rod ends.

Brakes

Four wheel disc brakes are utilized. Power assisted, dual brake systems operate independently on diagonally opposed pairs of wheels (left front and right rear; right front and left rear). Front to rear proportioning is provided by smaller brake cylinder bores on the rear calipers than on the front. The cable actuated parking brake consists of small brake shoes acting on drums inside the front disc rotor hats.

Master Cylinder

REMOVAL AND INSTALLATION

CAUTION: *Do not permit brake fluid to contact painted surfaces.*

Disconnect and plug all master cylinder brake lines. Unbolt the master cylinder from the power assist unit, and remove the master cylinder from the car.

Install in the reverse order of removal, and bleed the brake system.

RECONDITIONING

NOTE: *Do not rebuild the master cylinder unless there is no replacement cylinder available.*

Drain the fluid from the cylinder. Remove the lock ring that retains the primary piston, and back off the stop screw that retains the secondary piston. Pull out the pistons, springs, and seals. Remove the spring retainer screw, spring retainer, support ring and washer from the primary piston.

Ensure that no fluid passages are blocked (use a fine wire), and that the cylinder bore is not scratched. Replace all rubber seals and gaskets, and any other defective parts.

NOTE: *Dip all parts in brake fluid prior to installation.* Insert the secondary piston with spring and seals. Assemble the spring retainer, and install the primary piston and the lock ring.

Power Assist

The vacuum power assist unit cannot be disassembled, and therefore is nonserviceable.

REMOVAL AND INSTALLATION

Remove the air cleaner. Disconnect and plug the master cylinder brake lines and the power assist unit vacuum line. Unscrew the clip that holds the speedometer cable to the power assist unit. Disconnect the push rod from the brake pedal, unbolt the power assist unit from the firewall, and remove the unit. Remove the retaining nuts and separate the master cylinder from the power assist unit.

Install in the reverse order of removal, and bleed the brake system.

Disc Brakes

ATE disc brakes, with dual piston calipers and solid discs are used. A disc

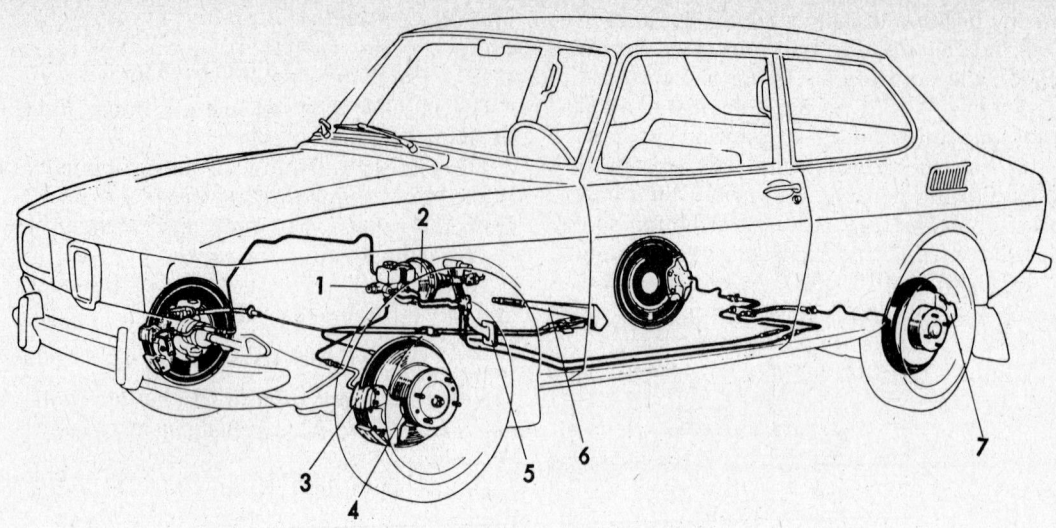

Brake system

1. Master cylinder
2. Power assist unit
3. Disc brake assembly
4. Brake shoes, handbrake

5. Brake pedal
6. Handbrake lever
7. Disc brake assembly

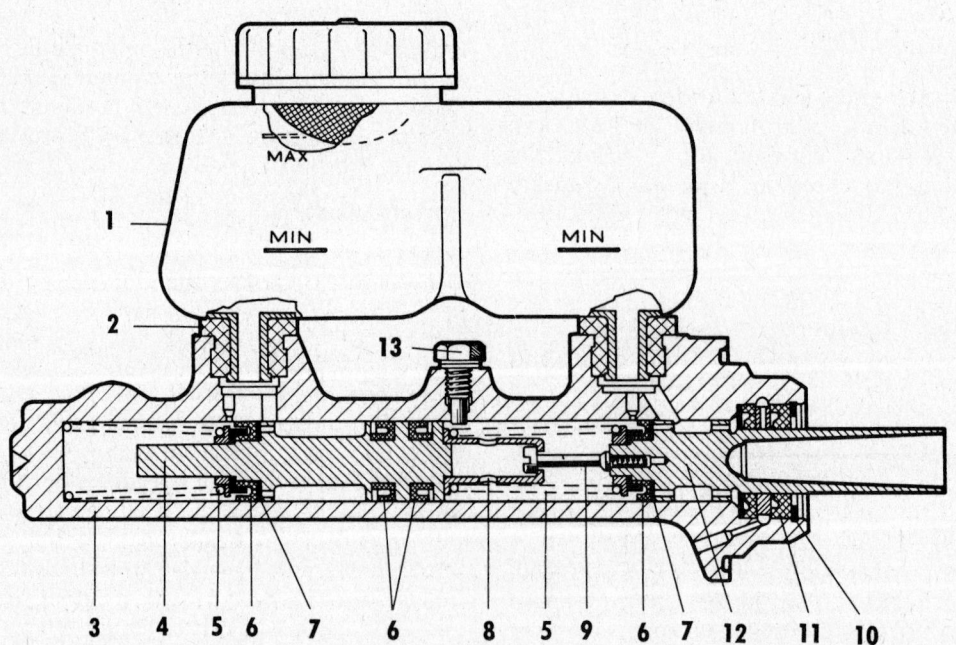

Master cylinder—cross-section

1. Container
2. Rubber seal
3. Housing
4. Secondary piston
5. Spring

6. Piston seals
7. Washer
8. Sleeve
9. Screw
10. Lock ring

11. Seal ring
12. Primary piston
13. Screw

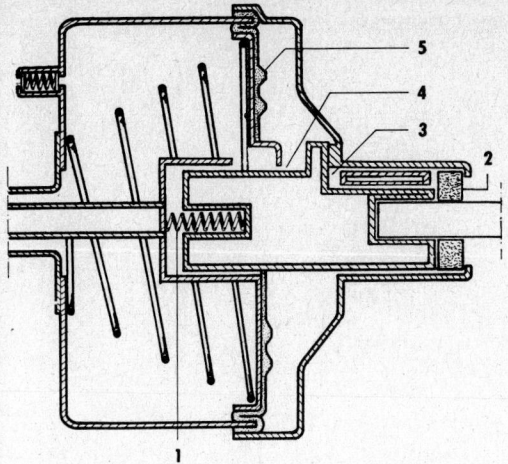

Power assist unit—cross-section

1. Return spring   4. Vacuum channel
2. Air filter   5. Diaphragm
3. Atmospheric channel

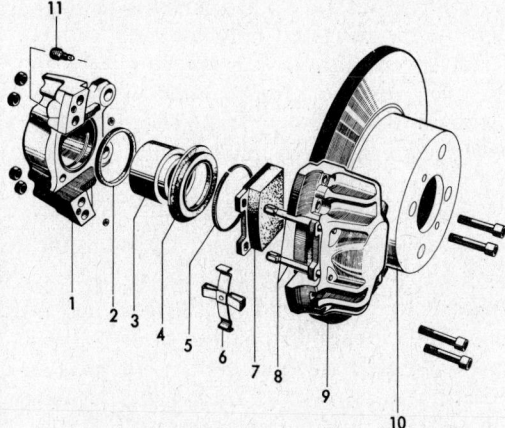

Disc brake assembly

1. Caliper half   7. Brake pad
2. Piston seal   8. Locking pins
3. Piston   9. Brake housing half
4. Gasket   10. Brake drum and disc
5. Gasket retainer   11. Bleeder screw
6. Retaining spring

throw compensator, consisting of a spring assembly behind each piston, maintains proper pad-to-disc clearance. The pad retaining spring also acts as warning device in case of excessive pad wear, causing high pedal effort when pads reach their minimum thickness.

Brake Pads

Removal and Installation

Remove the guard plate, and drive out the pad locking plates with a drift. Lift out the pads. Inspect the discs for excessive wear, scratches, or scoring, and resurface or replace if necessary. Check the caliper piston dust seals, and replace if damaged.

Press the pistons into the calipers (see illustration). NOTE: *Brake fluid level will rise when pressing pistons. Drain fluid off to prevent overflowing.* Insert the brake pads,

Pressing piston into caliper

and install the retaining spring, the pins and the guard plate. Pump the pedal to bring the pads into contact with the disc, and fill the brake reservoir if necessary.

Caliper

NOTE: *Never separate the caliper halves.*

Reconditioning

Remove the brake pads. Disconnect and plug the caliper brake line. Unbolt the caliper from the suspension upright, and remove it from the car. Press one piston into the caliper (see illustration), and force the other out of the caliper using compressed air. Pry the seal out of the caliper bore.

Coat the new seal with special disc brake lubricant, and install it into the caliper. Coat the piston with the same lubricant, and insert it into the caliper, using a template to locate the recess in the piston face (see illustration). After installation, ensure that the recess is in the proper position. If necessary, rotate the piston into position. Coat a new dust cover with the special lubricant, and press the cover and retainer onto the piston and caliper. Repeat the operation on the other piston.

Install the caliper in the reverse order of removal, and bleed the brake system.

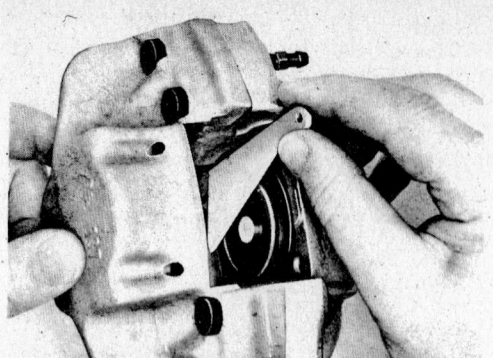

Caliper piston alignment template

Adjusting the parking brake

Parking Brake

The drum type parking brake, located inside the rotor hat of the front discs, is very similar in construction and service procedures, to a conventional service drum brake.

ADJUSTMENTS

When properly adjusted, the parking brake should begin to engage by the second ratchet notch, and fully lock the wheels by the third notch. To adjust, raise the front of the car, and support under the suspension arms. Release the parking brake,

and rotate the front wheels to ensure that no binding exists. Rotate the disc until the hole aligns with the adjuster, and using a screwdriver, tighten the adjuster until the disc can just be turned. Back off the adjuster until the shoes do not bind (1 or 2 teeth), and check the adjustment.

BRAKE SHOES

Removal and Installation

Raise the front end of the car and remove the wheels. Unbolt the brake caliper, and hang it in an out of the way position so as not to stress the brake line. Release the parking brake, and remove the disc. Using a piece of welding rod with a hook formed on the end, release the upper return spring. Rotate the hub until the hole is over the shoe hold down springs, and remove the hold down springs. Remove the shoes by pulling them down.

Loosen the cable at the lever arm end, install the shoes in the reverse order of removal, and adjust the parking brake.

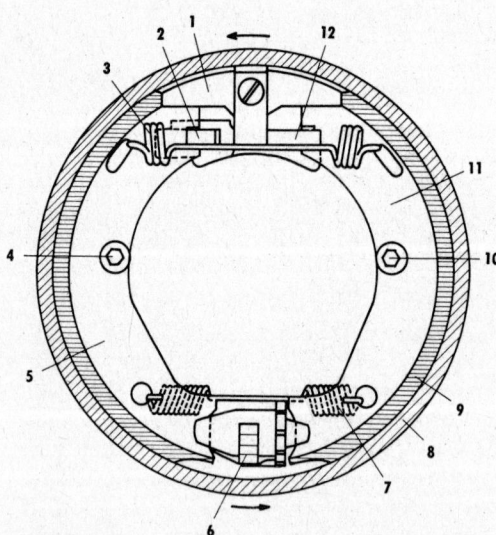

Parking brake

1. Support piece
2. Lever arm
3. Upper tension screw
4. Compression screw
5. Primary brake shoe
6. Adjustment
7. Lower tension spring
8. Brake drum
9. Brake lining
10. Retaining spring
11. Secondary brake shoe
12. Pressure rod

Heater

Blower

REMOVAL AND INSTALLATION

Code for identification and remove the three wires from the blower motor. Remove the mounting screws from the front plate, and lift out the blower motor.

Core

REMOVAL AND INSTALLATION

Open the heater bleeder, drain the coolant from the heater core, and disconnect the hoses from the heater. Disconnect and remove the throttle control shaft, and disconnect the heater water valve. Separate all air hoses from the heater casing. Unbolt and remove the left hand cover plate and the fan casing and fan (as a unit). Disconnect the engine brace from the firewall. Remove the screws under the dash panel that retain the air control valve to the heater casing. Unbolt the casing mounting bolts on the firewall, and remove the heater casing. Remove the clips that hold the halves of the casing together, and lift out the core.

Installation is the reverse of removal. Install the seal rings on the water pipes before assembling the casing. Start the engine, close the heater bleeder and open the heater water valve, and fill the cooling system. Run the engine at moderate speed, and bleed the cooling system.

Windshield Wipers

Linkage

REMOVAL AND INSTALLATION

Remove the windshield wiper blades and arms. Remove the heater hoses on the left and right of the engine compartment, unbolt and remove the heater fan housing. Unscrew the nuts from the spindles, and unbolt the motor mounting bracket. Push the spindles into the body, and slide out the linkage.

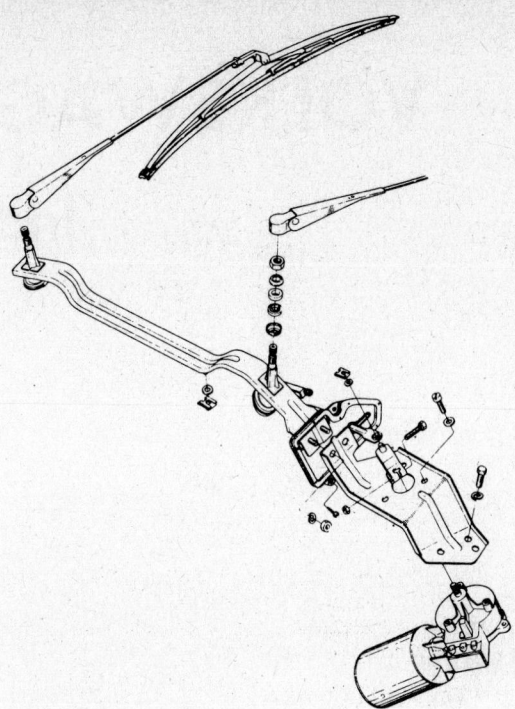

Windshield wipers

Install in the reverse order of removal. Ensure that the wiper arms are installed in the parked position with the motor in the same position.

Motor

REMOVAL AND INSTALLATION

The motor is removed with the wiper linkage (see above). After removing the linkage, unbolt the crank arm from the motor, and remove the motor from the bracket.

Install in the reverse order of removal.

VOLKSWAGEN SECTION

Index

Introduction

In 1932, Ferdinand Porsche produced prototypes for the NSU company of Germany. These led to the design of the Volkswagen. The prototypes had a rear, air-cooled engine, torsion-bar suspension, and the spare tire mounted at an angle in the front luggage compartment. In 1936, Porsche produced three Volkswagen prototypes, one of which was a 995 cc., horizontally-opposed, four-cylinder automobile. In 1945 Volkswagen production began and 1,785 beetles were built. The Volkswagen convertible was introduced in 1949, the year when only two Volkswagens were sold in the entire U.S.A. The year 1950 marked the beginning of the sunroof models and the transporter series. The Volkswagen Karmann Ghia was introduced in 1956, and is still of the same basic styling format. The "big" Volkswagen, the 1500 Squareback, was introduced in Europe in 1961, and sold in the U.S.A. in 1966 as a member of the new type 3 series (Fastback and Squareback). The type 4 was introduced to the U.S.A. with the 1971 model line.

Year and Model Identification

Basic Body Types

Karmann Ghia, Type 1

Squareback Sedan, Type 3

Micro Bus, Type 2

Sedan (Beetle), Type 1

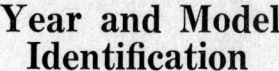

Convertible, Type 1

411 4-Door Sedan, Type 4

Fastback sedan, Type 3

411 3-Door Sedan, Type 4

Type 1 Identification

Year	Chassis Numbers	Major Body Changes	Major Mechanical Changes
1971		Super Beetle introduced; flow through ventilation; increased luggage space; towing eyes front and rear; Super Beetle 3″ longer. Normal beetle continued.	Suspension strut front axle; 1600 cc. engine with 60 hp, dual port heads, relocated oil cooler with its own cooling air supply. Front brake size increased to 9¾″.
1970	11,0,2000001–	Louvers in rear hood; modified lights and reflectors; ignition lock buzzer warning.	1600 cc. 57 hp engine; vapor emission control system (California only).
1969	119,000,001– 119,1,093,704	Electric rear window defroster; ignition lock combined with steering lock. Locking gas flap.	Double-jointed rear axle standard.
1968	118,000,000– 118,1,016,098	Raised bumpers, front and rear; vertical bumper guards eliminated. Built-in headrest in front seats; extensive padding in front compartment and dashboard. Seat belts in rear standard; external gas filler.	Exhaust emission control; collapsible steering column; optional automatic stick shift.
1967	117,000,001– 118,000,000	Back-up lights. Retractable seat belts. Armrest for driver. Locking buttons on doors. Parking light built into turn signals. Narrower chrome trim. Volkswagen nameplate on engine lid. Two-speed windshield wipers. Headlights now vertical in indented fenders.	Dual brake system. Increased horse-power, from 50 to 53. (SAE) Larger engine, from 1300 cc. to 1500 cc. 12-volt electrical system. Number of fuses increased from 8 to 10. More powerful starter motor. Equalizer spring rear axle.
1966	116,000,0001– 116,1,021,298	Number "1300" on engine lid. Flat hub caps; ventilated wheel discs. Four-way flasher system. Dimmer switch on turn signal. Defroster outlet in center of dash. Front seat backs equipped with safety locks.	Increased engine size, from 1200 cc. to 1300 cc. Increased engine output, from 40 hp. to 50 hp. (SAE)
1965	115,000,0001– 115,979,200	Larger windows, narrower window and door posts. Heater control levers now mounted on tunnel, formerly a twisting knob. Push-button handle on engine lid. Back of rear seat convertible to a flat platform.	No major changes.
1964	5,677,119– 6,502,399	Steel sliding sunroof; crank operated. Wider license plate light. Non-porous leatherette upholstery replaced by porous vinyl material.	No major changes.
1963	4,846,836– 5,677,118	Sunroof equipped with folding handle. Fresh air heating system. Nylon window guides. Introduction of leatherette headliner; formerly "mouse fuzz". Wolfsburg hood crest eliminated from front hood.	No major changes.
1962	4,010,995– 4,846,835	Spring-loaded hood. Addition of seat belt mounting points. Gasoline gauge on dashboard; formerly only a reserve fuel tap. Size of tail lights increased. Sliding covers for front floor heating outlets. Windshield washer added; compressed air type.	Worm and roller steering; formerly worm and sector. Tie rod ends permanently lubricated.

Type 1 Identification

Year	Chassis Numbers	Major Body Changes	Major Mechanical Changes
1961	3,192,507– 4,010,994	Flatter gasoline tank. Increased front luggage space. Windshield washer; pump-type. Key slot in doors now vertical; formerly horizontal. Starter switch now non-repeat.	Increased engine output, from 36 hp. to 40 hp. (SAE). Automatic choke. Push-on electrical connectors. First gear now synchromesh; all forward speeds now synchromesh.
1960	2,528,668– 3,192,506	"Dished" steering wheel. Push-button door handles; formerly lever-type. Foot rest for passenger. Padded sunvisor.	Front anti-sway bar added. Generator output increased to 180 watts, formerly 160. Steering damper added.
1959	2,007,616– 2,528,667	No major changes.	Stronger clutch springs. Fan belt improved. Frame given additional reinforcement.
1958	1,600,440– 2,007,615	Larger rear window and windshield. Front turn signal lights moved to top of fenders. Radio grill moved to far left of dashboard.	Wider brake drums and shoes.
1957	1,246,619– 1,600,439	Doors fitted with adjustable striker plates. Front heater outlets moved rearward, to within five inches of door. Tubeless tires used; formerly tube-type.	No major changes.
1956	929,746– 1,246,618	Tail light housings raised two inches. Steering wheel spoke moved lower and off-center. Heater knob moved forward. Adjustable front seat backs; formerly non-adjustable. Increased front luggage space.	Dual tail pipe; formerly single tail pipe.
1955	722,935– 929,745	Flashing turn signal lights replace "semaphore"-type flappers. Indicators mounted near outside bottom of front fenders.	No major changes.
1954	575,415– 722,934	Starter switch combined with ignition switch; formerly a separate button on dashboard. Interior courtesy light added.	Increased engine size, from 1131 cc. to 1192 cc. Addition of oil-bath air cleaner.
1953	428,157– 575,414	Oval rear window replaces two-piece split rear window. Vent window handles now provided with a lock button.	No major changes.
1952	313,830– 428,156	Vent windows added. Body vent flaps eliminated. Window crank geared down from 10½ to 3½ turns. Door added to glove compartment. Turn signal control to steering wheel; formerly on dashboard. 5.60 x 15 tires. Formerly 5.00 x16.	Top three gears synchromesh; formerly crashbox.
1951	220,472– 313,829	Vent flaps in front quarter-panel of body. Wolfsburg crest above front hood handle.	No major changes.
1950	138,555– 220,471	Ash tray added to dashboard.	Hydraulic brakes; formerly mechanical.
1949	91,922– 138,554	Pull release for front hood; formerly locking handle.	Solex carburetor now standard equipment.

Type 1 Identification

1949
(© Volkswagen)

1950
(© Volkswagen)

1951
(© Volkswagen)

1952
(© Volkswagen)

1953
(© Volkswagen)

1954
(© Volkswagen)

1955
(© Volkswagen)

1956
(© Volkswagen)

1957
(© Volkswagen)

1958
(© Volkswagen)

1959
(© Volkswagen)

1960
(© Volkswagen)

1961
(© Volkswagen)

1962
(© Volkswagen)

1963
(© Volkswagen)

1965
(© Volkswagen)

1966
(© Volkswagen)

1967
(© Volkswagen)

1968
(© Volkswagen)

1969
(© Volkswagen)

1970
(© Volkswagen)

1971 (© Volkswagen)

1971 Super Beetle (© Volkswagen)

Model Number (LHD)	Description
111	VW 1300A sedan, 1971 1600 sedan
115	VW 1300A sedan with folding sunroof
113	VW 1500 sedan, 1971 1600 Super Beetle
117	VW 1500 sedan with steel sunroof
141	VW 1500 Karmann Ghia Convertible
143	VW 1500 Karmann Ghia Coupe
151	VW 1500 Convertible (4-seater)
211–215	Delivery Van
221–225	Micro Bus
231–237	Kombi
241	Deluxe Micro Bus (9-seater)
251	Deluxe Micro Bus (7-seater)
261–267	Pick-up
271–273	Ambulance
281–285	Micro Bus (7-seater)
311	Fastback sedan (1600TL)
313	Fastback sedan with steel sunroof
315	1600A sedan
317	1600A sedan with steel sunroof
343	1600L Karmann Ghia Coupe
345	1600L Karmann Ghia Coupe with steel sunroof
361	1600L Squareback sedan
363	1600L Squareback sedan with steel sunroof
365	1600A Squareback sedan
367	1600A Squareback sedan with steel sunroof
411	411 Four door sedan
411	411 Three door sedan (wagon)

Chassis Number

The chassis number is on the frame tunnel under the back seat in the type 1 and 3. In the type 2, the chassis number is on the right engine cover plate in the engine compartment.

Beginning with the 1965 model year, a nine-digit serial number system was instituted. In this system, the first two numbers are the first two digits of the car's model number and the third digit stands for the car's model year—"5" stands for 1965, "8" stands for 1968, etc. A tenth digit was added when production passed one million.

Identification Plate

The identification plate carries the vehicle serial number and paint, body, and assembly codes. It is behind the spare tire in the luggage compartment on type 1 models, and on the right side of the overhead air duct in early type 2 vehicles. The type 3 identifica-

Vehicle and Engine Serial Number Identification

Volkswagen Types

Volkswagen models are differentiated by type. Type 1 is the beetle and Karmann Ghia. Type 2 is the transporter, or bus and truck, series. Type 3 is the Fastback and Squareback. Type 4 is the 411 sedan and wagon. The current model numbers are as follow:

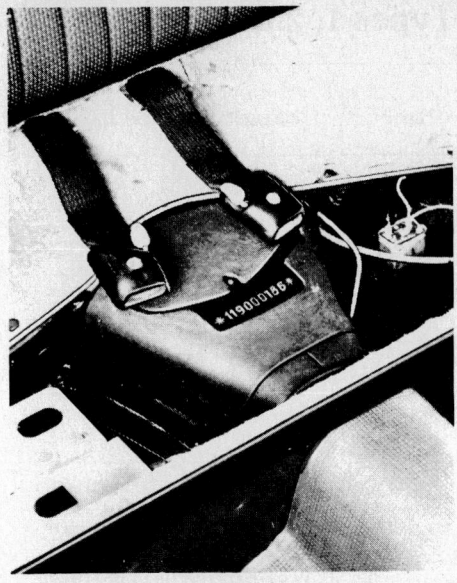

Type 1 chassis number location.

Type 1 engine number location.

Type 1 identification plate location.

tion plate is next to the hood latch, in front of the spare tire in the luggage compartment. Starting 1970, all models have an identification plate on top of the driver's side of the instrument panel. This plate may be seen through the windshield.

Engine Number

On type 1 and 2 vehicles, which have the upright engine fan housing, the engine number is on the crankcase flange for the generator support. The number can readily be seen by looking through the center of the fan belt. On type 3 and 4 engines, which have the fan on the end of the crankshaft, the number is along the crankcase joint between the oil cooler and the air cleaner. The engine can be identified by the letter preceding the serial number. Refer to the Engine Identification Chart.

Vehicle Identification—Types 1, 2 and 3

	SAE Output	from Chassis No.	Date	to Chassis No.	Date
Vehicle, Type 1					
Standard Sedan	36bhp.	1-0575 415	December 1953	6 502 399	July 1964
Standard Sedan, Sedan A	36bhp.	115 000 001	August 1964	115 979 202	July 1965
Deluxe Sedan Karmann Ghia Models VW Convertible	36bhp. 42bhp.	1-0575 415 3192 507 115 000 001	December 1953 August 1960 August 1964	3192 506 6 502 399 115 979 202	July 1960 July 1964 July 1965
1200A	42bhp.	116 000 001	August 1965	1161 021 297	July 1966
VW 1200	42bhp.	117 483 306 118 000 001 119 000 001 110 2000 001	January 1967 August 1967 August 1968 August 1969	117 844 900 1181 016 095 1191 093 701	July 1967 July 1968 July 1969
VW 1300 Sedan Karmann Ghia Models VW Convertible	50bhp.	116 000 001	August 1965	1161 021 298	July 1966
VW 1300 A	50bhp.	117 000 001	August 1966	117 403 305	Jan. 1967
VW 1300 Sedan	50bhp.	117 000 001 118 000 001 119 000 002 110 2000 002	August 1966 August 1967 August 1968 August 1969	117 844 901 1181 016 096 1191 093 702	July 1967 July 1968 July 1969
VW 1500 Sedan Karmann Ghia Models VW Convertible	53bhp.	117 000 001 118 000 001 119 000 003 110 2000 003	August 1966 August 1967 August 1968 August 1969	117 844 902 118 1016 097 119 1093 703	July 1967 July 1968 July 1969
	57bhp.	110 2000 004	August 1969		
VW 1600 Sedan Karmann Ghia Models VW Convertible	57bhp.		1970		
VW 1600 Sedan Super Beetle Karmann Ghia Models VW Convertible	60bhp.		1971		

Vehicle Identification—Types 1, 2 and 3

	SAE Output	from Chassis No.	Date	to Chassis No.	Date
Vehicle, type 2					
	36bhp.	20-069 409	December 1953	614 455	May 1960
1200		614 456	June 1960	1 328 271	July 1964
	42bhp.	215 000 001	August 1964	215 036 378	Sept. 1964
Transporter	51bhp.	1041 014	January 1963	1 328 271	July 1964
		215 000 001	August 1964	215 176 339	July 1965
1500	53bhp.	216 000 001	August 1965	216 179 668	July 1966
		217 000 001	August 1966	217 148 459	July 1967
		218 000 001	August 1967	218 202 251	July 1968
1600	57bhp.	219 000 001	August 1968	219 238 131	July 1969
		210 2000 001	August 1969		
	60bhp.		1971		
Vehicle, type 3					
		0 000 001	April 1961	0 483 592	July 1964
		315 000 001	August 1964	315 220 883	July 1965
		316 000 001	August 1965	316 316 237	July 1966
	54bhp.	317 000 001	August 1966	317 283 852	July 1967
Volkswagen 1500		318 000 001	August 1967	318 235 386	July 1968
		319 000 001	August 1968	319 264 031	July 1969
		310 2000 002	August 1969		
		0 221975	August 1963	0 483 592	July 1964
		315 000 001	August 1964	315 220 883	July 1965
		316 000 001	August 1965	316 316 238	July 1966
Volkswagen 1600	66bhp.	317 000 001	August 1966	317 233 853	July 1967
		318 000 002	August 1967	318 235 387	July 1968
		319 000 002	August 1968	319 264 032	July 1969
		310 2000 002	August 1969		

Engine Identification

Common Designation	Number Of Cylinders	C.C. Displacement (cu. in.)	Type Engine	Type Vehicle	Engine Code Letter	Year
–	4	1,131 (69.02)	Upright fan	1	–	To December, 1953
1,200	4	1,192 (72.74)	Upright fan	1,2	A	To July, 1960
1,200	4	1,192 (72.74)	Upright fan	1,2	D	From August, 1960
1,300	4	1,285 (78.4)	Upright fan	1,2	F	From August, 1965
1,500	4	1,493 (91.1)	Upright fan	1,2	H	From August, 1967 ①
1,600	4	1,584 (96.6)	Upright fan	1,2	B	From August, 1969 ②
1,500	4	1,493 (91.1)	Upright fan	2	G	To July, 1965
1,500	4	1,493 (91.1)	Suitcase engine	3	K	To July, 1965 ③ From August, 1965 ④
1,500S	4	1,493 (91.1)	Suitcase engine	3 1500S	R	To July, 1965
1,600	4	1,584 (96.6)	Suitcase engine	3	T	From August, 1965
1,600	4	1,584 (96.6)	Suitcase engine	3 injected	U	From August, 1967
1,600	4	1,584 (96.6)	Upright fan	1,2	AD	From August, 1970

① Type 2 from August, 1965
② Type 2 from August, 1967
③ High compression
④ Low compression

General Engine Specifications

Engine Code①	CC Displacement (cu. in.)	Carburetor	Developed Horsepower (SAE) @ rpm	Developed Torque (ft. lbs.) @ rpm	Bore x Stroke (in.)	Compression Ratio	Normal Oil Pressure (P.S.I.) @ 2,500 rpm
–	1,131 (69.02)	Single barrel downdraft	25@ 3,300	51@ 2,000	2.953 x 2.520	5.8:1	42 ⑤
A	1,192 (72.74)	Single barrel downdraft	36@ 3,700	60@ 2,400	3.03 x 2.52	6.6:1	42 ⑤
D	1,192 (72.74)	Single barrel downdraft	41.5@ 3,900	65@ 2,400	3.03 x 2.52	7.0:1	42 ⑤
F	1,285 (78.4)	Single barrel downdraft	50@ 4,600	69@ 2,600	3.03 x 2.72	7.3:1	42 ⑤
H	1,493 (91.1)	Single barrel downdraft	53@ 4,200	78@ 2,600	3.27 x 2.72	7.5:1	42 ⑤
B	1,584 (96.6)	Single barrel downdraft	57@ 4,400	113@ 3,000 ②	3.36 x 2.72	7.5:1 ③	42 ⑤
G	1,493 (91.1)	Single barrel downdraft	51@ 4,000	74@ 2,600	3.27 x 2.72	7.8:1	42 ⑤
K	1,493 (91.1)	Single barrel downdraft	54@ 4,200	84@ 2,800	3.27 x 2.72	7.8:1 ④	42 ⑤
R	1,493 (91.1)	Two single barrel downdraft	66@ 4,800	84@ 3,000	3.27 x 2.72	8.5:1	42 ⑤
T	1,584 (96.6)	Two single barrel downdraft	65@ 4,600	87@ 2,800	3.36 x 2.72	7.5:1	42 ⑤
U	1,584 (96.6)	Electronic fuel injection	65@ 4,600	87@ 2,800	3.36 x 2.72	7.7:1	42 ⑤
AD	1,584 (96.6)	Single barrel downdraft	60@ 4,400	81.6@ 3,000	3.36 x 2.72	7.5:1	42 ⑤

① See Engine Identification Chart in Chapter 1 for explanation of codes.
② Type 2 - 82@ 3,000
③ Type 2 - 7.7:1
④ To July 1965; 7.5:1 from August 1965.
⑤ Minimum - 28@ 2,500 rpm, 7@ idle rpm.

Tune-Up Specifications

Year	Engine Code, ⑨ SAE HP Rating Displacement	Spark Plugs Make, Type ⑧	Gap (in.)	Distributor Approx. Point Dwell (deg.)	Point Gap (in.)	Basic Ignition Timing (deg.)	Cranking Comp. Pressure (psi)	Valves Clearance (in.) Intake	Exhaust	Intake Opens (deg.) ①	Idle Speed (rpm)
To December, 1953	25 hp., 1,100	Bosch W 175 T1, Champion L-10	.026	50	.016	5 BTDC	85-107	.004	.004	2½ BTDC	550
To July 1960	A, 36 hp., 1,200	Bosch W175T1, Champion L-10	.026	50	.016	7.5 BTDC	100-114	.004	.004	2½ BTDC	550
From August, 1960	D, 42 hp., 1,200	Bosch W175T1, Champion L87Y	.026	50	.016	10 BTDC	100-128	.004 ②	.004 ②	6 BTDC	550
From August 1965	F, 50 hp., 1,300	Bosch W175T1, Champion L-87Y	.028	50	.016	7.5 BTDC	107-135	.004	.004	7½ BTDC	550
From August, 1965-Type 2, From August 1967- Type 1	H, 53 hp., 1,500	Bosch ③ W175T1, Champion L-87Y	.028	42-58	.016	7.5 ④ BTDC	114-142	.004	.004	7½ BTDC	550 ⑤
From August, 1969-Type 1, From August 1967-Type 2	B, 57 hp., 1,600	Bosch W145T1	.026	47-53	.016	0 ATDC	114-142	.004	.004	7½ BTDC	850
To July 1963	G, 51 hp., 1,500	Bosch W145T1	.028	42-58	.016	10 BTDC	121-142	.004 ②	.004 ②	7½ BTDC	550

Tune-Up Specifications

Model	Spark Plug									
K, 54 hp, 1,500 To July 1965 (6) From August 1965 (7)	Bosch W175T1	.026	.016	50	10 BTDC (6) 7.5 BTDC (7)	121-142 (6) 114-142 (7)	.004 (2)	.004 (2)	7½ BTDC	550
R, 66 hp, 1,500S To July 1965	Bosch W175T1	.026	.016	50	10 BTDC	135-164	.004 (2)	.004 (2)	7½ BTDC	750
T, 65 hp, 1,600 From August 1965	Bosch W175T1	.028	.016	50	7.5 BTDC	114-142	.004	.004	7½ BTDC	750
U, 65 hp, 1,600 From August 1967, Injected	Bosch W175T1	.028	.016	47-53	0 ATDC	114-142	.004	.004	7½ BTDC	850
AD, 60 hp, 1,600 From August 1970	Bosch W145T1	.028	.016	44-50	5 ATDC	114-142	.004	.004	7½ BTDC	850

(1) With valve clearance of .04 in. (This clearance is used for checking valve timing only.)

(2) Before 1965, some 1,200 and 1,500 cc engines used long rocker arm mounting studs which pass through the full thickness of the cylinder head. Valve clearances on engines with long studs must be set at .008 in. (intake), and .012 in. (exhaust). These engines are:

Engine Code	Up to Engine No.
D	9205699
G	0710799
K	0672748
R	0672297

(3) Type 1 - Bosch W145T1
(4) Type 1 with throttle positioner - 0° ATDC
(5) Type 1 - 850 rpm
(6) High compression
(7) Low compression
(8) The Bosch W175T1 plug can be used to replace the W145T1 for sustained high speeds
(9) See Engine Identification Chart for explanation of codes.
NOTE: If any of this tune-up information conflicts with the information on the engine sticker(s), use the sticker figures

Some of these engines have had short studs installed in one or both heads. In this case, the valves are set at .004 in. (intake and exhaust); The only sure way to determine what clearance to use on these engines is by a sticker on the engine, or by feeling the stud ends between the pushrod tubes under the engine.

Engine Rebuilding Specifications—Pistons, Cylinders and Rings

Engine	Cylinders — Cylinder Diameter (mm)									Pistons — Piston Diameter (mm)									Wrist Pin ② Diameter (in.)		Rings — Side Clearance (in.)			Rings — End Gap (in.)		
	Std			1st O/S			2nd O/S			Std			1st O/S			2nd O/S			No Mark	Green	Top	2nd	Oil Scraper	Top	2nd	Oil Scraper
	B	P	G	B	P	G	B	P	G	B	P	G	B	P	G	B	P	G								
1,131, 1,200, and 1,300 cc.	76.99	77.00	77.01	77.49	77.50	77.51	77.99	78.00	78.01	76.95	76.96	76.97	77.45	77.46	77.47	77.95	77.96	77.97	19.996-20.000①	20.001-20.004①	.002-.0027	.002-.0027	.001-.002	.012-.018	.012-.018	.010-.016
1,500 cc.	82.99	83.00	83.01	83.49	83.50	83.51	83.99	84.00	84.01	82.96	82.96	82.97	83.45	83.46	83.47	83.95	83.96	83.97	21.996-22.000	22.001-22.004	.0027-.0035	.002-.0027	.001-.002	.012-.018	.012-.018	.010-.016
1,600 cc.	85.49	85.50	85.51	85.99	86.00	86.01	86.49	86.50	86.51	85.45	85.46	85.47	85.95	85.96	85.97	86.45	86.46	86.47	21.996-22.000	22.001-22.004	.0027-.0035	.002-.0027	.001-.002	.012-.018	.012-.018	.010-.016

O/S - Oversize

Color coding of cylinders and matching pistons: B - blue
P - pink
G - green

① Pin diameter given applies to 1,131 and 1,200 cc. engines only. Pins for the 1,300 cc. engine are the same as for the 1,500 and 1,600.

② Pin should be light push fit in piston. Piston pin to connecting rod clearance: .0004-.001 in. - maximum -.002 in.

Firing Order

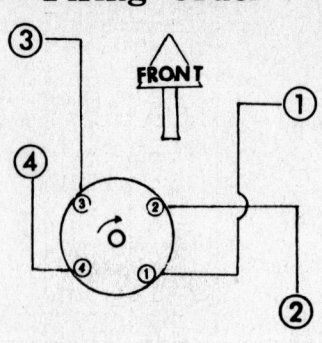

Cylinder numbering, wiring, and distributor rotation for all VW engines. The firing order is 1-4-3-2.

Engine Rebuilding Specifications—Crankshaft

Engine	Main Bearing Journals (in.)												Connecting Rod Journals (in.)						Max. Journal Out-of-Round (in.)
	Journal Diameter								Oil Clearance		Shaft End-Play	Thrust On No.	Journal Diameter				Oil Clearance	End-Play	
	Journal 1, 2, 3				Journal 4				Journal 1, 2, 3	Journal 4			Std.	1st U/S	2nd U/S	3rd U/S			
	Std.	1st U/S	2nd U/S	3rd U/S	Std.	1st U/S	2nd U/S	3rd U/S											
36 hp, A engine - type 1, and Type 2 Engine before May, 1959 ③	1.9681, 1.9675	1.9583, 1.9577	1.9484, 1.9478	1.9386, 1.9380	1.5748, 1.5742	1.5650, 1.5643	1.5551, 1.5545	1.5453, 1.5446	.002-.004	.002-.004	.0027-.005	1 (at flywheel)	1.9861, 1.9675	1.9583, 1.9577	1.9484, 1.9478	1.9386, 1.9380	.0008-.0024	.0067-.016	.001
All later engines ①	2.1648, 2.1642	2.1551, 2.1544	2.1453, 2.1445	2.1353, 2.1347	1.5748, 1.5742	1.5650, 1.5643	1.5551, 1.5545	1.5452, 1.5446	② .002-.004	.002-.004	.0027-.005	1 (at flywheel)	2.1650, 2.1645	2.1553, 2.1544	2.1455, 2.1448	2.1355, 2.1350	.0008-.003 ④	.004-.016	.001

NOTE: The crankshaft of type 1/1,200 cc, engines may be reground only twice.

U/S - undersize

① Including modified 36 hp. type 2 engine from May, 1959 (chassis 469477, engine 3400000)

② Bearings No. 1 and 3 from August, 1965: .0016 - .004 in.
Bearings No. 1, 2, 3; to engine 3520332: .0016 - .0035 in. ① to engine 3472699: .001 - .0035 in. ①
Steel backed bearing No. 2 from August, 1965 and all other steel backed bearings (used in cold countries): .001 - .0035 in.

③ Also 25 hp.

④ All 1,500 and 1,600 cc : .0008 in.

Engine Rebuilding Specifications—Valves

| Engine | Seat Angle Deg. | Valve Seat Width (in.) | | Spring Pressure (lbs. @in.) | Stem (in.) Diameter | | Stem to Guide Rock (in.) | | Valve Guide Removable |
		Intake	Exhaust		Intake	Exhaust	Intake	Exhaust	
25 hp., 36 hp., A engine - Type 1, and Type 2 engine- before May, 1959	45	.05 -.09	.05- .09	73.5+ 3.7@ 1.1	.2739- .2736	.2736- .2732	.011- .012	.011- .012	With Special Equipment
All Later Engines	45	.05- .09	.05- :09	①	.3130- .3126	.3118- .3114	.008- .009	.011- .012	With Special Equipment

Engine Code	To Engine No.	Spring Pressure
G K, R, T	0627578 0663330	96.4+ 6.6 @ 1.32 in.
D	6805938 (type 2) 6850939 (type 1)	102.0+ 5.0 @ 1.35 in.
K	0042987	
Engines with progressively wound springs		126.0+ 8.8 @ 1.22 in.

NOTE: Cylinder head combustion chamber volumes are
      are as follows:

Engine	Volume (cc.)
A	45.5 - 47.0
D	43.0 - 45.0
F	44.0 - 46.0
All 1,500 and 1,600 cc.	48.0 - 50.0

Torque Specifications—Engine

Fastener	Thread Size	Torque (ft. lbs.)
All Engines		
1-Nuts for crankcase halves	M12x1.5	25 ①
2-Screws and nuts for crankcase halves	M8	14
3-Cylinder head nuts ②	M10	23
4-Rocker shaft nuts	M8	14-18
5-Flywheel gland nut	M 28x1.5	217
6-Connecting rod bolts and nuts	M9x1	22-25 ④
7-Special nut for fan	M12x1.5	40-47
8-Generator pulley nut	M12x1.5	40-47
9-Crankshaft pulley bolt	M20x1.5	29-36
10-Spark plugs	M14x1.25	22-29
11-Oil drain plug	M14x1.5	25
12-Clutch to flywheel	M8x1.5	18
13-Self-locking nuts for engine carrier to the crankcase	M8	18 ⑤
14-Nuts for oil pump	M8	14
15-Cap nut for oil filter cover	M6	5
16-Nuts for engine mounting	M10	22
17-Screws for converter to drive plate	M8	18
25 and 36 hp. - exceptions		
1-Nuts for crankcase halves	M10	22
3-Cylinder head nuts ②	M10	26-27
11-Oil drain plug ③	M18x1.5	22-29
13-Insert for spark plug	M18x1.5	50-54
Type 3 - exceptions		
8-Generator pulley nut	M12x1.5	40-47
9-Special bolt for fan and crankshaft pulley	M20x1.5	94-108
17-Screws for converter to drive plate	M8	14
19-Self locking nuts for engine carrier to body	M8	18 ⑤

① For cap nuts: 18 ft. lbs.

② Tightening sequences are given in Chapter 4.

③ As above from August 1959.

④ Contact surfaces oiled. 1,300 cc. and earlier - 28 - 36 ft. lbs.

⑤ Renew.

Torque Specifications— Transmission and Rear Axle

Fastener	Thread Size	Torque (ft.lbs.)
Transmission and Rear Axle (Standard and Partly-synchronized) Transmission) Type 1 and 2		
Drive pinion nut (Partly-synchronized transmission) up to Chassis No. 1 454 550/238 499	M 22 x 1.5	80-87 ①
Drive pinion nut (Partly-synchronized transmission /new lock-washer) from Chassis No. 1 454 551/238 500	M 22 x 1.5	58-65 ①
Slotted nut for pinion (Standard transmission)	M 18 x 1.5	36 ②
Main drive shaft nut	M 16 x 1.5	30-36
Reverse selector fork screw	M 7 x 12	14
Ring gear screws	M 10 x 1.5	43
Selector fork clamp screw	M 8 x 1.25	18
Transmission housing nuts and bolts ③	M 8 x 1.25	14
Oil drain plug	M 18 x 1.5	22-29
Oil filter plug	M 24 x 1.5	14
Axle shaft nut	M 24 x 1.5	217
Transmission carrier to frame	M 18 x 1.5	166
Spring plate nuts/bolts	M 12 x 1.5	72
Transmission and Rear Axle (fully synchronized) all Types		
Drive pinion round nut: 1-for double ball bearing.	M 35 x 1.5	87
2-for double taper roller bearing	M 35 x 1.5	144
Pinion bearing retainer screws	M 10 x 1.5	36
Pinion nut	M 22 x 1.5	43 ④
Drive shaft nut	M 22 x 1.5	43 ④
Reverse lever guide screw	M 7 x 1	14
Selector fork screws	M 8 x 1.25	18
Nuts for gearshift housing	M 7 x 1	11
Ring gear screws	M 10 x 1.5	43
Final drive cover nuts	M 8 x 1.25	22
Axle tube retainer nuts	M 8 x 1.25	14
Rear wheel bearing retainer screws	M 10 x 1.5	43
Oil drain plug	M 24 x 1.5	14
Oil filter plug		
Rear axle shaft nut (Type 1 and 3)	M 24 x 1.5	217

Fastener	Thread Size	Torque (ft.lbs.)
Nut on driven shaft (Type 2 from August 1963)	M 30 x 1.5	108
Nut on rear axle driven shaft (Type 2) up to Chassis No. 1144302	M 24 x 1.5	217 ⑤
from Chassis No. 1144303	M 30 x 1.5	217 ⑤
Transmission carrier on frame	M 18 x 1.5	166
Spring plate/reduction gear housing screw (Type 2)	M 12 x 1.5	72-87
Additional torques for transmission and rear axle (Stickshift automatic)		
Temperature switch/ Selector switch/Starter inhibitor switch	M 14 x 1.5	18
Converter to drive plate screws	M 8 x 1.25	18
Retaining nut for taper roller bearing	M 80 x 1	159
Nut for converter housing	M 8 x 1.25	14
Screw for one-way clutch support	M 6 x 1	11 ⑥
Screw for clutch	M 6 x 1	11
Lock screw	M 8 x 1.25	7
Clamp screw for clutch lever	M 8 x 1.25	18
Screw for transmission oil pan and lock plate	M 7 x 1.25	7
Union for oil pressure line	M 12 x 1.5	25
Union for oil return line	M 14 x 1.5	25
Screw for drive shaft	M 8 x 1.25	25
Fitted screw in diagonal arm	M 14 x 1.5	87
Additional torques for transmission and rear axle (Type 3 Automatic)		
Screw for oil pump on transmission case	M 6 x 1	3
Screw for valve body on transmission case	M 6 x 1	3
Screw for transfer plate on valve body	M 5 x 0.8	2
Screw for oil strainer on valve body	M 6 x 1	2
Screw for oil pan on transmission case	M 8 x 1.25	7
Pin for operating lever on transmission case	M 10 x 1.5	4
Plug for pressure connections/transmission case	M 10 x 1	7
Vacuum unit/transmission case	M 14 x 1.5	18
Screw for bearing cap/ diff. carrier	M 10 x 1.5	40
Screw for ring gear/ differential housing	M 9 x 1	32
Screw for converter on drive plate	M 8 x 1.25	14

Torque Specifications— Transmission and Rear Axle

Fastener	Thread Size	Torque (ft.lbs.)
Screw for drive shaft on flange	M 8 x 1.25	25
Screw for front band	M 12 x 1.75	3.5 ⑦
Screw for rear band	M 12 x 1.75	3.5 ⑧
Lock nut for band adjusting screw	M 10 x 1.75	14
Nut for differential carrier on rear axle housing	M 6 x 1	6
Nut for side cover on rear axle housing	M 6 x 1	6
Nut for transmission/final drive housing	M 8 x 1.25	14
Nut and screw for spring plate	M 12 x 1.75	80
Screw for bearing cover	M 10 x 1.5	43
Fitted bolt for diagonal arm	M 10 x 1.5	87

Transmission and Rear Axle (fully synchronized) Type 2-from Chassis No. 218 000-001		
Retaining ring for double taper roller bearing/ transmission case	M 80 x 1	109
Round nut/pinion	M 35 x 1.5	144
Union nut/clamp sleeve	M 14 x 1.5	18-22
Bracket/reverse shifter shaft on gear carrier	M 8 x 1.5	18
Support/rocket lever on on gear carrier	M 8 x 1.5	18
Shift fork on shift rod	M 8 x 1.25	18
Locking screw with dog point	M 8 x 1.25	11
Clamp sleeve on gear carrier	M 14 x 1.5	32
Shift housing on gear carrier	M 7x 1	11
Nuts on gear carrier, transmission and clutch housing	M 8 x 1.25	68
Ring gear to differential housing	M 9 x 1	32
Double taper roller bearing retainer	M 9x 1.25	22 ⑨
Final drive side covers	M 8 x 1.25	14
Brake back plate to housing	M 8	18
Brake back plate to housing	M 10	25
Slotted nut on rear wheel shaft	M 30 x 1.5	230-253 ⑩
Joint to flange (socket head screw)	M 8	25
Control arm to frame	M 12 x 1.5	58
Cover/spring plate mounting	M 10	32
Control arm to bearing housing	M 14 x 1.5	94

Shock absorber to frame and bearing housing	M 12 x 1.5	43

① The nut should be tightened and not backed off.
② First tighten to 108 ft. lbs., then back off and tighten to 36 ft. lbs.
③ Note tightening sequence, illustrated in Power Train Chapter.
④ Tighten first to 86 ft. lbs. then back off and finally tighten to 43 ft. lbs.
⑤ If cotter pin holes are not in line, tighten to a maximum of 250 ft. lbs. If hole is still not in line, fit a different nut.
⑥ Use new screws
⑦ Tighten to 7 ft. lbs. first, loosen and tighten again. Turn out 1 3/4 - 2 turns from this position.
⑧ Tighten to 7 ft. lbs. first, loosen and tighten again. Turn out 3 1/4 - 3 1/2 turns from this position.
⑨ Tighten to 32 ft.lbs. first, slacken off and tighten to 22 ft. lbs.
⑩ With reinforced spacer sleeve: at least 253 ft. lbs. then turn on to cotter pin hole.

Torque Specifications— Front Axle and Steering Gear

Fastener	Thread Size	Torque (ft.lbs.)
Type 1 Front Axle		
Front axle to frame	M 12 x 1.5	36
Shock absorber screw on side plate	M 12 x 1.5	22-25
Shock absorber nut on side plate	M 10	14
Shock absorber nut on lower tension arm	M 10	22-25
Hexagon nuts for steering ball joints ⑤	M 12 x 1.5 or M 10 x 1	36-50 29-36
Inner wheel bearing nut	M 18 x 1.5	29 ①
Lock nut for wheel bearing	M 18 x 1.5	50 ①
Socket head screw in clamp nut	M 7 M 12 x 1.5	7-max. 9 ②
Slotted nut on tie-rod	M 10 x 1	22 ③
Steering damper nut on tie-rod ⑤	M 10 x 1 M 10 x 1	18 ③ 18
Steering damper screw on axle tube	M 10	29-32
Setscrew for torsion bars	M 14 x 1.5	29-36
Locknut for setscrew	M 14 x 1.5	29-36
Caliper to steering knuckle	M 10	36
Clamping screw link pin to torsion arm	M 10	32
Screw for front axle support/front axle	M 12 x 1.5	40-43
Screw for front axle/ frame	M 10	40-43

Torque Specifications— Front Axle and Steering Gear

Fastener	Thread Size	Torque (ft.lbs.)
Type 2 Front Axle		
Front axle/frame bolts (side member)	M 12 x 1.5	65-90
Shock absorber nut and bolt upper (from Chassis No. 971550)	M 12 x 1.5 M 10	36 29-32
Shock absorber securing bolt, upper (up to Chassis No. 971549)	M 12 x 1.5	25-32
Shock absorber securing nut, lower	M 10	18-22
Steering knuckle/torsion arm (link pin bolts)	M 10	29-32
Ball joints to steering knuckle ⑤	M 18x 1.5	72
Inner wheel bearing nut	M 18 x 1 or M 22 x 1.5	25 ④
Wheel bearing locknut	M 18 x 1 or M22 x 1.5	50 ④
Tie-rod and draglink nuts	M 12 x 1.5 M 10 x 1	22 ③ 18 ③
Type 1 and 3 Steering Gear		
Steering gear to axle-Type 1	M 10	18-22
Steering gear to axle-Type 3	M 10	18-22
Locknut for roller shaft adjusting screw	M 10 x 1	18
Steering gear cover screws	M 8 x 1.25	14-18
Screw securing drop arm to roller shaft	M 12 x 1.5	50
Steering wheel nut	M 18 x 1.5	36
Lock nut for steering worm adjustment screw	M 35 x 1.5	36-43
Hex. bolt for steering coupling to steering worm	M 8	14-18
Hex. nut. flange to coupling disc	M 8	11
Fillister head screw for self-cancelling ring on steering wheel	AM 3.5	3.6
Lock nut for tapered ring to tie rod	M 14 x 1.5	18
Clamping screw for tie rod retaining clip	M 8 x 1	11
Hex. bolt for steering column mounting plate to instrument panel	M 8	11
Screw for retainer eccentric bearing	M 8	11
Type 2 Steering gear		
Bracket to frame screws	M 10 x 22	29-32
Steering bos to bracket	M 10 x 40	25-36

Fastener	Thread Size	Torque (ft.lbs.)
Drop arm nut	M 20 x 1.5	58-80
Swing lever pinch bolt (from Chassis No. 20-117 901)	M 12 x 1.5	43
Upper and lower steering arm bolts (up to Chassis no.20-117 901)	M 12 x 1.5	47-54
Steering wheel nut	M 16 x 1.5	18-22
Hex. nut for flange to steering worm	M 8	14
Castellated nut for coupling disc to flange	M 8	11
Cheese head screw for steering column cap to floor plate	M 6	3.6
Steering gear case cover bolt	M 8	18
Steering gear and cover bolt	M 6	11
Steering damper/frame bolt and nut (up to Chassis No. 851 389)	M 10 x 45	32
Steering damper/axle tube screw (from Chassis No. 851 390)	M 10 x 40	29-32
Steering damper/ swing lever screw	M 10 x 72	29-32
Setscrew for torsion bars	M 14 x 1.5	29
Lock nut for setscrew	M 14 x 1.5	29
Stabilizer to torsion arm	M 10 M 8	25-36 18
Screw for brake back plate to steering knuckle	M 10	36-43
Clamping screw for link pins to torsion bar	M 10	29-36
Type 3 Front axle		
Front axle securing bolts		
a - upper and lower	M 10	22
b - center	M 10	29
Grub screw securing torsion bars	M 14 x 1.5	22
Grub screw securing stabilizer	M 14 x 1.5	32-40
Lock nut for grub screw	M 14 x 1.5	29
Torsion bar to axle beam screws	M 10	29
Clamp screw stabilizer	M 10	29
Adjusting screw for stabilizer	M 8	7 ⑥
Shock absorber to axle beam screws	M 12 x 1.5	22-25
Shock absorber nut on torsion arm	M 10	22-25
Steering arm on steering knuckle	M 10 x 1	40
Nuts for upper and lower ball joints	M 20 x 1.5 or M 18 x 1.5	80
Clamp screws for upper and lower ball joints up to Chassis No. 0273513 (October 1963)	M 10x 40 M 8 x 40	40 25
Socket head screw in split nut	M 7	7-max. 9

Torque Specifications—
Front Axle and Steering Gear

Fastener	Thread Size	Torque (ft.lbs.)
Inner wheel bearing nut up to Chassis No. 315 220 883	M 16 x 1.5	11 ②
Wheel bearing locknut	M 16 x 1.5	50 ②
Tie rod nuts	M 12 x 1.5	22 ④
	M 10 x 1	18 ④
Steering damper screw on axle	M 10	29-32
Steering damper nut on drop arm	M 10	18

① Tighten inner nut to 29 ft. lbs. first, fit new lock plate and slacken nut 72° (distance from one wheel bolt hole in drum to next). Then tighten outer nut to 50 ft. lbs.
② Tighten nut while turning wheel. Then slacken nut off until the specified axial play of .03 - .12 mm (.001 - .005 in.) is obtained. If front axle tends to be noisy, keep play to lower limit (.03 - .06 mm.) When play is correct, tighten socket head screw to the correct torque.
③ Turn on to cotter pin hole.
④ Tighten inner nut to 25 ft. lbs. first while turning wheel. Then fit new lock plate and slacken nut off until specified axial play of .03 - .12 mm. (.001 - .005 in.) is obtained. If front axle tends to be noisy, keep play to lower limit (.03 - .06 mm.) When play is correct, tighten outer locknut to 50 ft. lbs.
⑤ Always use new self-locking nuts after removal.
⑥ Tighten clamp screw to 29 ft. lbs. first, then tighten adjusting screw to 7 ft. lbs. and lock it.

Torque Specifications—
Brakes and Wheels

Fastener	Thread Size	Torque (ft.lbs.)
Brakes Type 1		
Master cylinder to frame	M 8	14-22
Screws for bearing cover/ back plate/bearing flange.	M 10	40-47
Back plate/steering knuckle screws	M 10	36
Brake hose unions	M 10 x 1	11-14
Brake pipe unions	M 10 x 1	11-14
Stop light switch	M 10 x 1	11-14
Wheel cylinder to back plate	M 8	14-22
Caliper to steering knuckle	M 10	36
Residual pressure valve in tandem master cylinder	M 12 x 1	14
Brakes Type 2		
Screws for bearing cover to rear brake back plate	M 10	40-43
Brake back plate/wheel cylinder front	M 10	40-43
Brake hose unions	M 10 x 1	11-14
Brake pipe unions	M 10 x 1	11-14
Stop light switch	M 10 x 1	11-14
Tandem master cylinder to brake servo	M 8	9
Brake servo to retaining retaining plate/front axle	M 8	9
Brakes Type 3		
Master cylinder to frame	M 8	14-22
Screws for bearing cover/ back plate rear	M 10 x 1.5	40-47
Wheel cylinders a - rear on back plate	M 8	18
b - front on back plate/steering knuckle	M 10 x 1	32
Disc brake caliper housing to steering knuckle	M 10	43
Brake hose at a - brake pipe	M 10 x 1	11-14
b - wheel cylinder	M 10 x 1	11-14
c- disc brake caliper housing	M 10 x 1	11
Stop light switch	M 10 x 1	11-14
Wheels		
Wheel bolts		
Type 1	M 12 x 1.5	72
from August 1965 (four hole wheel)	M 14 x 1.5	108
Type 2	M 14 x 1.5	94
Type 3	M 12 x 1.5	72
from August 1965 (four hole wheel)	M 14 x 1.5	108

① Only on vehicle with disc brakes. For all from Chassis No. 118 000 001.

Tightening Sequences

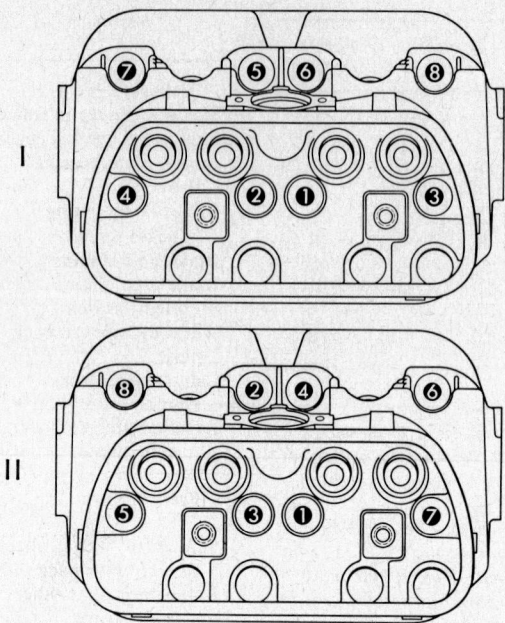

The cylinder head nuts should initially be tightened to 7 ft. lbs. in order I, then tightened to the recommended torque in order II.

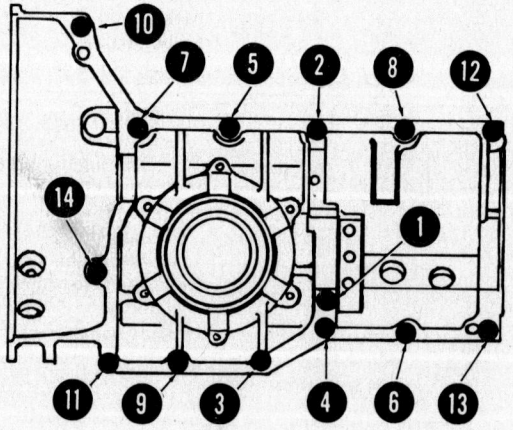

Split-type trans-axle.

Electrical Specifications—Battery and Starter

Model	Battery			Starter						
	Capacity (Amp Hours)	Volts	Grounded Terminal	Model	Lock Test			No Load Test		
					Amps	Volts	Torque (ft.lbs.)	Amps	Volts	RPM
Type 1 up to Chassis No. 929745	70	6	Neg.	25, 36 hp. Bosch EED 0.4/6L/4	500	3.5	NA	80	5.5	5,400
Type 1 from Chassis No. 929746	66	6	Neg.	40 hp. 1,200cc. Bosch EEF 0.5/ 6L/1	450-520	3.5	8	60-80	5.5	5,500-7,300
Type 1 from Chassis No. 118000001 ①	36	12	Neg.	40 hp. 1,200 and 1,300cc.- VW 113 911 021 A	450-520	3.5	8	60-80	5.5	5,500-7,300
Type 2 up to Chassis No. 117901	84	6	Neg.	40 hp. 1,200 and 1,300 cc. -Bosch 113 911 021 B	450-520	3.5	8	60-80	5.5	5,500-7,300
Type 2 from chassis No.117902	77	6	Neg.	Bosch AL/EEF 0.8/12L1 (12 Volt)	250-285	6.0	6.5 8.2	38-45	12	6,400-7,900
Type 2 from chassis No.217000001	45	12	Neg.	1,500cc.- 111 911 021 G (12 Volt) ②	250-285	NA	NA	38-45	12	7,150
Type 3 from chassis No.0000001	77	6	Neg.	–	–	–	–	–	–	–
Type 3 from chassis No. 317000001	36	12	Neg.	–	–	–	–	–	–	–

① *Excluding VW 1,200, Type 1.*

② *Test figures for 6 Volt units on 1,500 cc. engines should be the same as for previous 6 volt units.*

NA - Not Available

Electrical Specifications—Generator and Regulator

| | Generator | | | Regulator | | |
Part Number	Brush Spring Pressure (oz.)	Field Resistance (ohms.)	Max. Output	Part Number	Cut-in Voltage	Voltage Setting (No Load)
25 hp.- Bosch RED 130/ 6-2600 AL 16	16-21	1.20-1.32	NA	Bosch RS/G130/ 6/11 (on generator)	NA	7.3-8.6
36 hp. 1,200 cc. Bosch LJ/ REF 160/ -2500 L4	16-21	1.20-1.32	NA	Bosch RS/TA 160/ 6/Al (on generator)	5.5-6.3	7.3-8.6
36 hp. 1,200 cc. Bosch LJ/ REF 160/6/ 2500 L17	16-21	1.20-1.32	NA	Bosch RS/TAA 160/ 6/1 (on generator)	6.4-6.7	7.4-8.1
40 hp. 1,200 cc. Bosch 111 903 021 G	16-21	1.20-1.32	270 WATTS	Bosch RS/TAA 180 /6/A4	6.2-6.8	7.3-8.0
40 hp. 1,200 cc. -VW 113 903 021 C	16-21	1.20-1.32	270 WATTS	VW 113 903 801 C	6.4-6.7	7.4-8.1
Late 1,200 and 1,300 cc.- Bosch 113 903 021 H	16-21	1.20-1.32	NA	Bosch 113 903 801F	6.2-6.8	7.4-8.1
Late 1,200 and 1,300 cc.- VW 111 903 021 J	16-21	1.20-1.32	NA	VW 113 903 801G	6.4-6.7	7.4-8.1
Karmann Ghia 1,300 and Type 1 1,500- Bosch 131 903 021	16-21	NA	30 AMPS	Bosch 131 903 801	6.2-6.8	7.3-8.0
Bosch 450 M 12/ 3700-14 38A 32 (12 Volt)	16-21	NA	38 AMPS	Bosch UA 14 V 38A	12.5-13.2	13.5-14.5
Bosch E(L) 14V 38A 32, EG (R) 14V 38A 32 (12 Volt)	16-21	NA	38 AMPS	Bosch RS/VA 14V 38A	12.4-13.1	13.6-14.4
Bosch G(L) 14 V 30A 20	16-21	NA	30 AMPS	Bosch RS/VA 14V 30A	12.4-13.1	13.6-14.4

NA - Information not available.

Distributor Advance Characteristics

Vehicle	Engine	Distributor	Centrifugal Advance (deg. @ rpm.)				Vacuum Advance (deg. @ mm. hg.)			
			Start	Intermed-iate	Intermed-iate	End	Start	Intermed-iate	Intermed-iate	End
Type 1	25 hp.	Bosch VE 4 BRS 383	5@ O rpm	5-9 @ 600	15-20 @ 1,400	32-37 @ 2800	–	–	–	–
Type 1	36 hp. 1,200	Bosch VJU 4BR 3 mk	7.5@ O rpm	8-13 @ 1,200	13.5-16.5@ 2,000	31.5-34.5@ 3,300	0 @ 80	8.0-11.5 @200	17.5-19.5 @300	18-22 @ 370
Type 1	36 hp. 1,200	Bosch VJU 4BR 8 mk	7.5@ O rpm	10-14 @ 1,800	–	23-27 @ 3,400	0 @ 100	5-7.5 @200	11-14.5 @300	13-17 @ 350
Type 1	40 hp. 1,200	VW 113 905 205H	NA	NA	NA	NA	0 @ 140	7-13 @ 300	15-21 @ 400	19-25 @ 450
Type 1	50 hp. 1,300	Bosch 113 905 205K or VW113 905 2051	NA	NA	NA	NA	0 @ 40-110	5-11 @ 200	14-20 @ 400	23-28 @ 620-650
Type 1	53 hp. 1,500	Bosch 113905 205M	–	–	–	–	@ 40-80	17-19 @300	–	32-35 @ 800
Type 1	53 hp. 1,500, 57 hp. 1,600	Bosch 113 905 205T								
Type 1	53 hp. 1,500 Auto-matic	Bosch 113 905 205P	14-23 @ 1,500	19-23 @ 1,600	19-23 @ 2,100	30-33 @ 3,750	@ 50-100	14-20 @ 300	–	8-12 @ 230
Type 1	53 hp. 1,500 Auto-matic	Bosch 113 905 205AA	14-23 @ 1,500	19-23 @ 1,600	19-23 @ 2,100	30 -33@ 3,750	@ 50-100	3-7 @ 150	–	8-12 @ 230
Type 1	57 hp. 1,600 Auto-matic	Bosch 113 905 205AD	@ 1,050-1,200	13-15 @ 1,700	13-16 @ 2,200	25-28@ 3,900	@ 70-120 @ 60-100	– –	–	8-12@ 240 6-8(retard) @170
Type 2	57 hp. 1,600	Bosch 113 905 205M	–	–	–	–	@ 40-80	17-19 @ 300	–	32-35 @ 800
Type 2	57 hp. 1,600	Bosch 113 905 205T	–	–	–	–	@ 40-80	17-19 @ 300	–	32-35@ 800
Type 3	65 hp. 1,600	Bosch 311 905 205F	–	–	–	–	@ 10-70	–	–	23-28 @ 310-340
Type 3	65 hp. 1,600	Bosch 311 905 205G	–	–	–	–	@ 10-70	17-19 @ 300	–	23-28 @ 310-340

Vehicle	Engine	Distributor	Centrifugal Advance (deg. @ rpm.)				Vacuum Advance (deg. @ mm. hg.)			
			Start	Intermed-iate	Intermed-iate	End	Start	Intermed-iate	Intermed-iate	End
Type 3	65 hp. 1,600	Bosch 311 905 205L	@ 900 1,100	6-12 @ 1,350	10-14 @ 1,500	26-30 @ 2,600	@ 50-100	10-16 @ 300	–	8-12 @ 200
Type 3	65 hp. 1,600	Bosch 311 905 205AB	@ 900- 1,100	10-14 @ 1,500	20-23 @ 2,300	27-30 @ 2,800	@ 60-100	2-8 @ 150	–	8-12 @ 200
Type 3	65 hp. 1,600	Bosch 311 905 205M	@ 900 1,050	19-22 @ 1,600	19-22 @ 2,100	27-30 @ 2,700	@ 60- 100	17-19 @ 300	–	8-12 @ 200

NOTE: Figures given are for crankshaft degrees and rpm. To obtain distributor
       degrees and rpm, divide crankshaft figures by two.

NA - Not available.

Capacities and Pressures

Model	Crankcase Refill After Draining (pts.)	Transmission Refill After Draining (pts.)				Final Drive (pts.)	Air Cleaner (pts.) ⑧	Fuel Tank (gals.)	Normal Fuel Pressure (psi)
		Standard	Auto. Stick Shift	Fully Auto.	Reduction Gears				
Type 1	5.3	6.3	6.3 ①	N/A	N/A	②	.5 ③	10.5 ⑨	⑩
Type 2	5.3	7.4	N/A	N/A	.5 each	②	.63 ④	15.8	⑩
Type 3	5.3	6.3	N/A	6.3- 8.4 ⑥	N/A	2.1 ⑦	.85 ⑤	10.5	⑩

N/A - Not applicable to this vehicle.

① The total capacity of the Automatic Stickshift torque converter circuit is 7.6 pts. ATF. The refill capacity is somewhat less.

② in unit with transmission

③ 1,300 cc. Karmann Ghia - .63 pts., 1,500 cc. Karmann Ghia - .96 pts., 1,500 cc. sedan and convertible - .85 pts.

④ 1,200 cc. - .44 pts., Late 1,500 and 1,600 cc. -.95 pts.

⑤ Single carburetor engine; .44 pts, fuel injected engine .53 pts.

⑥ Total capacity - 12.6 pts. ATF.

⑦ Only with automatic transmission; otherwise, note ② applies.

⑧ Since so many different air cleaners have been used in production, it is best to rely on the full mark on the air cleaner body. If there is no such mark, these figures may be used.

⑨ Super Beetle - 11.1 gals.

⑩ Pump Marking

	Pressure @ RPM
Unmarked (36 hp and earlier)	1.3-1.8 @ 1,000 - 3,000
Unmarked	2.5 @ 3,000 - 3,400
VW 2	5.0 @ 3,800
VW 3	3.5 @ 3,400-3,800
VW 4	3.5 @ 3,800
VW 6	5.0 @ 3,800
VW 7	3.5 @ 3,800
VW 8	3.5 @ 3,800

Brake Specifications

Vehicle	Model	Type		Brake Cylinder Bore (in.)			Brake Drum or Disc Diameter (in.)	
		Front	Rear	Master Cylinder	Wheel Cylinder		Front	Rear
					Front	Rear		
Type 1	25 hp., 36 hp. 1,200cc.	Drum ①	Drum	.750	.750	.690	9.05 ±.008	9.05 ±.008
	40hp. 1,200 and 1,300cc.	Drum	Drum	.687	.874	.750	9.059 ±.008	9.055 ±.008
	1,500 and 1,600cc. Single Master Cylinder	Drum	Drum	.687	.875	.687	9.059 ±.008	9.055 ±.008
	1,500 and 1,600cc.– Tandem Master Cylinder	Drum	Drum	.750	.875	.687	9.059 ±.008	9.055 ±.008
	1971 Models	Drum	Drum	.750	.94	.69	9.76	9.06
	Karmann Ghia	Disc	Drum	NA	1.574	.687	10.9	NA
	Karmann Ghia, 1971	Disc	Drum	NA	NA	NA	10.9	9.06
Type 2	Tandem Master Cylinder	Drum	Drum	.875	1.00	.875	9.843 +.008	9.843 +.008
	1971 Models	Disc	Drum	.813	.874	.875	10.9	9.92
Type 3	Tandem Master Cylinder	Disc	Drum	.750	1.653	.875	10.9	9.768 +.008
	1971 Models	Disc	Drum	.813	NA	.875	10.9	9.92

① *Some early models have mechanical brakes.*

Chassis and Wheel Alignment Specifications

Vehicle	Model	Chassis (in.)			Wheel Alignment					Wheel Pivot Ratio (deg.)	
		Wheel-base	Track Front	Rear	Caster (deg.) (or in.)	Camber (deg.)	Toe-in (in.) (or deg.) ④	King-Pin Inclination (deg.)	Rear Wheel Camber (deg.)	Inner Wheel	Outer Wheel
Type 1	25 hp. and 36 hp. 1,200cc.	94.5	51	49.2	$2^{o}30'$ $\pm 30'$	$0^{o}40'$ $\pm 30'$	.04-.12	$4^{o}20'$	NA	NA	NA
	42 hp. 1,200cc.	94.5	51.4	50.7	$2^{o} \pm 15'$	$0^{o}40'$ $\pm 30'$	.08-.16	$4^{o}20'$	$3^{o} \pm 30'$	34	28
	42hp. 1,200 and 1,300 cc.- after August, 1965	94.5	51.4	51.2	$2^{o} \pm 15'$	$0^{o}30'$ $\pm 15'$	.08-.18	$4^{o}20'$	$3^{o} \pm 30'$ ①	34	28
	1,500 cc. -Swing Axles	94.5	51.4	53.5	$2^{o} \pm 15'$	$0^{o}30'$ $\pm 15'$	.08 -.18	$4^{o}20'$	① $1^{o} \pm 1^{o}$	34	28
	1,500cc. and 1,600cc - Double Jointed Rear Axles	94.5	51.57	NA	$3^{o}20'$ $\pm 1^{o}$	$30'$ $\pm 20'$	$30' \pm 15$	5°	$-1^{o}20'$ $\pm 40'$	34 ± 2	28-1
	1971 Super Beetle with suspension struts	95.3	54.3	53.2	.008 in.	$1^{o}20'$ $\pm 20'$	$20'$ ± 15	NA	$-1^{o}20'$ $\pm 40'$	40	35
Type 2	Pre-1968 -Swing Axles	94.5	54.1	53.5	$3^{o} \pm 40'$	$40' \pm 30'$	$\pm .04$ $(5' \pm 10')$	NA	$3^{o} \pm 30'$ ②	NA	NA
	After 1968- Double Jointed Rear Axles	94.5	54.5	56.2	$3^{o} \pm 40'$	$40' \pm 15'$	$10''$ $\pm 10'$	5°	$-50'$ $\pm 30'$	32	24
	1971 -Disc brakes	94.5	54.6	56.6	NA	NA	NA	NA	NA	NA	NA
Type 3	With Swing Axles	94.5	51.58	52.99	$4^{o} \pm 40'$	$1^{o}20'$ $\pm 20'$	$40'$ $\pm 5'$	NA	$2^{o}30'$ $\pm 1^{o}$ ③	NA	NA
	With Double Jointed Rear Axles	94.5	51.58	53.14	$4^{o} \pm 40'$	$1^{o}20'$ $\pm 20'$	$40'$ $\pm 15'$	$5^{o}10'$	$-1^{o}20'$ $\pm 40'$	30	27-1

NA - Information not available

① 1967 sedan: $1^{o} \pm 1^{o}$
    1967 Karmann Ghia and VW convertible: $15' \pm 1^{o}$

② After chassis No. 117 901:
    Van: $4^{o} \pm 30'$
    Kombi: $3^{o}30' \pm 30'$
    Bus: $3^{o} \pm 30'$

③ 1967 and later Notchback and Type 3 Karmann
    Ghia: $1^{o}45' \pm 1^{o}$

④ Size Wheel
    14in.
    15in.
    16in.

10' toe-in equals :
.043 in.
.047 in.
.051 in.

Carburetor Specifications—Types 1 and 2

Vehicle Engine	Carburetor	Venturi (mm dia.)	Main Jet	Air Correction Jet	Pilot Jet	Pilot Jet Air Bleed or Pilot Air Jet (mm. dia.)	Pump Fuel Jet	Pump Air Correction Jet	Power Fuel Jet (mm.dia.)	Emulsion Tube	Emulsion Tube Carrier (mm.dia.)	Float Needle Valve (mm.dia.)	Float Needle Valve Washer (mm.)	Float Weight (gms.)	Accel. Pump Cap. (cc./Stroke)	By Pass Mixture Cutoff Valve
Type 1 1,131 cc. 25 hp.	Solex 28 PCI	20	105	190	50	.8	50	2.0	–	10	–	1.5	–	12.5	–	–
Type 1 1,200 cc. 36 hp. from No. 695282	Solex 28 PCI	21.5	122.5	200	g50	.8	50	2.0	–	29	5.0	1.5	–	5.7	.4 -.6	–
Type 1 1,200 cc. 36 hp. from No. 849905	Solex 28 PCI	21.5	117.5	195	g50	.8	50	2.0	–	29	5.0	1.5	–	5.7	.4 -.6	–
Karmann Ghia- Type 1 1,200 cc. 36 hp. from No. 1118403	Solex 28 PCI	21.5	117.5	180	g50	.8	50	2.0	–	29	5.0	1.5	–	5.7	.4 -.6	–
Type 2 1,200 cc. 36 hp. from No. 991590	Solex 28 PCI															
Type 1 & 2 1,200 cc. 42 hp. from No. 5000 001	Solex 28 PICT(1)	22.5	122.5	130Y/ 140Z/ 135Z/	g55	2.0	.5	–	1.0/75	①	–	1.5	–	5.7	1.1-1.4/ .8-1.0	–
Type 2 1,500 cc. 51 hp. from No. 0143543	Solex 28 PICT-2	22.5	115	145Y/ 150Z/	g45	1.55	.5	–	.7	①	–	1.5	–	5.7	1.1-1.4/ 1.2-1.3	–
Type 1 1,300 cc. 50 hp. from No. F0 000 001	Solex 30 PICT-1	24.0	125	125Z ②	g55	150	50	–	③	①	–	1.5	–	5.7	1.3- 1.6	–

Carburetor Specifications—Types 1 and 2

Vehicle	Engine	Carburetor	Venturi (mm. dia.)	Main Jet	Air Correction Jet	Pilot Jet	Pilot Jet Air Bleed or Pilot Air Jet (mm. dia.)	Pump Fuel Jet	Pump Air Correction Jet	Power Fuel Jet (mm. dia.)	Emulsion Tube	Emulsion Tube Carrier (mm. dia.)	Float Needle Valve (mm. dia.)	Float Needle Valve Washer (mm.)	Float Weight (gms.)	Accel. Pump Cap. (cc./Stroke)	By Pass Mixture Cutoff Valve
Type 2	1,500 cc. 53 hp. from No. H0000001	Solex 30 PICT-1	24.0	115	135Z	g60	150	50	–	75	①	–	1.5	–	5.7	1.3-1.6	–
Type 1 & 2	1,600 cc. 57 hp. from No. B0000001	Solex 30 PICT-1	24.0	120	135Z	55	140	50	–	50	①	–	1.5	–	5.7	1.3-1.6	–
Type 1	1,300 cc. 50 hp. Automatic from No. F1462682	Solex 30 PICT-2	24.0	x120	170Z	55	140	50	–	50	①	–	1.5	–	8.5	1.3-1.6	–
Type 1	1,500 cc. 53 hp. Automatic from No. H0879927	Solex 30 PICT-2	24.0	x120	125Z ④	55	140	50	–	50	①	–	1.5	–	8.5	1.3-1.6/1.05-1.35	–
Type 1	1,500 cc. 53 hp. from No. H0204001	Solex 30 PICT-2	24.0	x120	125Z ④	g55	150 ⑤	50	–	50	①	–	1.5	–	5.7 ⑥	1.3-1.6/1.05-1.35	–
Type 1 & 2	1,500 cc. ⑦ 53 hp. from No. H5000001	Solex 30 PICT-2	24.0	x116	125Z	55	140/135	50	–	60	①	–	1.5	–	8.5	1.3-1.6/1.05-1.35	–
Type 1 & 2	1,600 cc. ⑦ Solex 57 hp. from No. B5000001	Solex 30 PICT-2	24.0	x116	125Z	55	140	50	–	60	①	–	1.5	–	8.5	1.3-1.6	–

Carburetor Specifications—Types 1 and 2

Vehicle	Engine	Carburetor	Venturi (mm. dia.)	Main Jet	Air Correction Jet	Pilot Jet	Pilot Jet Air Bleed or Pilot Air Jet (mm. dia.)	Pump Fuel Jet	Pump Air Correction Jet	Power Fuel Jet (mm. dia.)	Emulsion Tube	Emulsion Tube Carrier (mm. dia.)	Float Needle Valve (mm. dia.)	Float Needle Valve Washer (mm.)	Float Weight (gms.)	Accel. Pump Cap. (cc./Stroke)	By Pass Mixture Cutoff Valve
Type 1	1,600 cc. 57 hp. from No. B6000001	Solex 30 PICT-3	24.0	x122.5	125Z	65	135	–	–	100	①	–	1.5	1.5	8.5	1.2-1.35	–
Type 1	1,600 cc. 57 hp. Automatic from No. B6000002	Solex 30 PICT-3	24.0	x112.5	125Z	65	135	–'	–	100	①	–	1.5	1.5	8.5	1.2-1.35	–
Type 1	1,600 cc. 57 hp. from No. B5116437	Solex 30 PICT-3	–	–	–	–	–	–	–	–	–	–	–	–	–	–	
Type 1 & 2	1,600 cc. 60 hp. 1971 Models	Solex 34 PICT-3	–	–	–	–	–	–	–	–	–	–	–	–	–	–	

① Fixed to air correction jet. ④ Karmann Ghia - 135Z.   ⑦ With emission control.
② Karmann Ghia - 170Z.   ⑤ From engine No. H0874200 - 140.
③ Karmann Ghia - 75.   ⑥ From No. H0874200 - 8.5.

Carburetor Specifications—Type 3

Vehicle	Engine	Carburetor	Venturi (mm.dia.)	Main Jet	Air Correction Jet	Pilot Jet	Idling Air Drilling	Pump Injector Tube (mm. dia.)	Pump Air Correction Jet	Power Fuel Jet (mm. dia.)	Emulsion Tube (No.)	Emulsion Tube Carrier (mm. dia.)	Float Needle Valve (mm. dia.)	Float Needle Valve Washer (mm.)	Float Weight (gms.)	Accel. Pump Cap. (cc./Stroke)	Throttle Valve Gap (mm.)
Type 3 Single Carburetor	From No. 0 000 001	Solex 32 PHN	23.5	137.5	125	g45 g50	—	.8	—	1.05	48	—	1.5	—	12.5	.9-1.2 /1.2-1.5	.8-.9
	From No. 0 084 752	Solex 32 PHN -1	23.5	132.5	115	g45	—	.8	—	.7	48	—	1.5	—	12.5	.9-1.2	.8-.9
	From No. 0220137	Solex 32 PHN -1	23.5	127.5	115	g45	—	.8	—	.7	48	—	1.5	—	12.5	.9-1.2	.8-.9
	From No. 0319841	Solex 32 PHN	23.5	130.0	115	g50	—	.7	—	.7	48	—	1.5	—	12.5	.8-1.0	.8-.9
	From No. K0150001	Solex 32 PHN	23.5	01300	115	—	1.4	.7	—	.7	48	—	1.5	—	12.5	.8-1.0	.8
Type 3 Dual Carburetors	1,500cc. From No. 0255001	Solex ① 32 PDSIT-2(-3)	21.5	x125	180	g45	—	.5 (12 mm.)	—	.9 (9.5 mm.)	—	—	1.2	—	7.3	.35-.55	.60-.65
	1,500cc. From No. 0633331	Solex 32 PDSIT-2(-3) ①	23	x135	180	g45	—	.5 (15 mm.)	—	.8 (10.5mm.)	—	—	1.2	1.5	7.3	.35-.55	.60-.65
	1,600cc. From No. T0000001	Solex ① 32 PDSIT-2(-3)	23	x130	240	g45	—	50 (12 mm.)	—	80 (15 mm.)	—	—	1.2	1.5	7.3	.35-.55	.60-.65
	1,600cc. From No. T0244544 (Left)	Solex 32 PDSIT-2	24	x132.5	150	g50	—	.5 (9 mm.)	—	—	—	—	1.2	.5	7.3	.35-.55	.60-.65

Carburetor Specifications—Type 3

Vehicle	Engine	Carburetor	Venturi (mm.dia.)	Main Jet	Air Correction Jet	Pilot Jet	Idling Air Drilling	Pump Injector Tube (mm. dia.)	Pump Air Correction Jet	Power Fuel Jet (mm. dia.)	Emulsion Tube (No.)	Emulsion Tube Carrier (mm. dia.)	Float Needle Valve (mm. dia.)	Float Needle Valve Washer (mm.)	Float Weight (gms.)	Accel. Pump Cap. (cc./Stroke)	Throttle Valve Gap (mm.)
		Solex 32 PDSIT-3 (Right)	24	x130	120	g50	-	.5 (9 mm.)	-	-	-	-	1.2	.5	7.3	.35-.55	.60-.65
	1,600cc. From No. T0576724	Solex 32 PDSIT-2 (Left)	24	x132.5	150	50	-	.5	-	-	-	-	1.2	.5	7.0	.35-.55	.60-.65
		Solex 32 PDSIT-3 (Right)	24	x130	120	50	-	.5	-	-	-	-	1.2	.5	7.0	.35-.55	.60-.65
Type 3 Dual Carburetors —Automatic	1,600cc. From No. T0690001	Solex 32 PDSIT-2 (Left)	24	x130	155	-	135	-	-	-	-	-	1.2	.5	7.0	.3-.45	.7
		Solex 32 PDSIT-3 Right	24	x127.5	120	-	135	-	-	-	-	-	1.2	.5	7.0	.3-.45	.7
	1,600cc. From No. T0463930	Solex 32 PDSIT-2 (Left)	24	130	155	50	-	.5 (9 mm.)	-	-	-	-	1.2	.5	7.0	.25-.4	.60-.65
		Solex 32 PDSIT-3 (Right)	24	127.5	120	50	-	.5 (9 mm.)	-	-	-	-	1.2	.5	7.0	.25-.4	.60-.65
	1,600cc. From No. T069000	Solex 32 PDSIT-2 (Left)	24	130	155	-	135	-	-	-	-	-	1.2	.5	7.0	.23-.4 ②	.9
		Solex 32 PDSIT-3 (Right)	24	127.5	120	-	135	-	-	-	-	-	1.2	.5	7.0	.25-.4 ②	.9

① 2 - Left carburetor, with distributor vacuum connection
3 - Right carburetor
② Return valve for accelerator pump - .3

Fuses

Model	Circuit	Amps.
1,30 Type 1 (6 Volt)	Horn, flashers, stoplight, wipers	16
	High beam warning light, left high beam	8
	Right high beam	8
	Left low beam	8
	Right low beam	8
	Left parking light, left taillight	8
	Right parking light, right taillight license plate light	8
	Headlight dimmer, radio, interior light	16
1,500 Type 1 (12 Volt)	Turn signals, horn, Stoplights brake warning light, Automatic Stickshift and rear window defroster switch current	8
	Wipers	8
	High beam warning light, left high beam	8
	Right high beam	8
	Left low beam	8
	Right low beam	8
	Left parking light, left taillight	8
	License plate light, right parking light, right taillight	8
	Interior light, emergency blinkers	8
	Spare fuse	–
	Rear window defroster main current (under rear seat, left side)	8
	Backup lights (right side of engine fan housing)	8
	Automatic Stickshift control valve (left side of engine fan housing)	8
1,500 Type 2 (6 Volt)	Left low beam	8
	Right low beam	8
	Left high beam, high beam warning light	8
	Right high beam	8
	Left taillight	8
	Right taillight, license plate light, parking lights	8
	Stoplights, turn indicators	16
	Horn, interior lights, wipers, headlight dimmer	16
1,600 Type 3 (6 Volt)	Right parking light, left parking light left taillight, luggage compartment light	8
	Right taillight, license plate light	8
	Left low beam	8
	Right low beam	8
	Left high beam, high beam warning light	8
	Right high beam	8
	Spare fuse	–
	Emergency blinkers, interior light, horn, clock, radio	16
	Stoplights, turn signals	8
	Wipers, fuel gauge, warning lights	16

Light Bulbs

Model	Usage	U.S. Replacement Bulbs	VW Part No.	Wattage
36 hp.	Headlights	–	–	35/35
1,200	Parking lights	–	–	1.5
Type 1	Stoplights	–	–	15
(6 Volt)	Taillights	–	–	5
January,	License plate light	–	–	5
1954-August	Interior light	–	–	10
1955	All warning lights	–	–	1.2
	Instrument lighting	–	–	1.2
	Turn signals	–	–	3
36 hp.	Headlights	–	–	35/35
1,200 Type	Parking lights	–	–	2
1 (6 Volt)	Stoplights	–	–	20
from	Taillights	–	–	5
August, 1955	License plate light (tubular bulb)	–	–	5
	Interior light	–	–	10
	Semaphore-type	–	–	3
	Turn signals (tubular bulbs)	–	–	1.2
	All warning lights	–	–	1.2
	Instrument lighting	–	–	
36 hp.	Headlights	–	–	35/35
1,200 Type	Parking lights	–	–	3
1 (6 Volt)	Taillights	–	–	5
Karmann	Rear stop/turn signal	–	–	15
Ghia, from	License plate lights	–	–	5
August, 1955	Interior light	–	–	5
	Front turn signals	–	–	15
42 hp.	Headlights	–	N177051	45/40
1,200 and 1,300	Parking lights	–	N177171	4
Type 1	Stoplight/taillight	–	N177371	18/5
(6 Volt)	Turn signals	–	N177311	18
Sedan and	License plate light	–	N177191	10 ①
Convertible	Interior light	–	N177231	10
	Warning and instrument lights	–	N177221	1.2
42 hp.	Headlights	–	–	45/40
1,200 and 1,300	Parking lights	–	–	4
Type 1	Taillights	–	–	5
(6 Volt)	Stoplights	–	–	18
Karmann Ghia	Turn signals	–	–	18
	License plate lights	–	–	5
	Interior light	–	–	10
	Warning, instrument lights, clock	–	–	1.2
1,300 Type	Headlights	6012	11194126A	45/40
1 (12 Volt)	License plate light	–	–	10
	Interior light	–	–	10
	Instrument and warning lights	–	–	2
	Parking lights	–	–	4
	Turn signals	–	–	18
	Stoplight/taillight	–	–	18/5
1,500 and 1,600	Headlights	6012	111941261A	–
Type 1	Parking/turn signal, taillight/stoplight	1034	N177382	–
(12 Volt)	Rear turn signal	1073	N177322	–
Sedan and	License plate light	89	N177192	–
Convertible	Backup lights	1073	N177332	–
	Instrument and warning lights	–	N177222	–
	Sedan interior light	–	N177232	–
	Convertible interior light	–	N177252	–
	Warning lights for emergency flasher, brake, rear window defroster	–	N177512	–

Light Bulbs

Model	Usage	U.S. Replacement Bulbs	VW Part No.	Wattage
1,500 Type 2 (6 Volt)	Headlights	–	N177051	45/40
	Parking lights	–	N177171	4
	Turn signals	–	N177311	18
	Taillights/stoplights	–	N177371	5/18
	License plate light	–	N177191	10
	Warning lights, Instrument lights	–	N177221	1.2
	Dome light	–	N177251	5
	Clock	–	N177221	1.2
1,600 Type 3 (6 Volt)	Headlights	6006, Type 2	N177051	–
	Front parking/turn signal	1154	N177171	5/18
	Rear turn signal, stoplight	1129	N177311	18
	Taillight	81	N177181	5
	License plate light	81	N177191	10
	Warning, instrument lights	–	N177221	1.2
	Interior and luggage compartment lights	–	N177231	10

① *1,200 uses 5 watt bulb after August, 1965.*

Transmission Gear Ratios

Model	4th	3rd	2nd	1st	R	Final Drive	Reduction Gears or Torque Converter
1951-54 Type 1	.79	1.22	1.88	3.60	4.63	4.375 or 4.43	–
1954-60 Type 1	.82	1.23 ④	1.88 ③	3.60	4.63	4.375	–
1961-67 Type 1 and 3	.89	1.32	2.06	3.80	3.88	4.375 ①	–
1968-70 Type 1 and 3	.89	1.26	2.06	3.80	3.61	4.125	–
Automatic Stick-shift	–	.89	1.26	2.06	3.07	4.375	2.1
Fully Automatic	–	1.00	1.59	2.65	1.80	3.670	2.5
Type2 1,500 cc.	.82	1.22	2.06	3.80	3.88	4.375	1.26 ②

① *Type 3, 4.125*

② *1,200cc. Type 2, 1.4 or 1.39*

③ *1.94 also used.*

④ *1.22 also used.*

Additional final drive ratios available for special purposes: 3.875 - type 181; 5.375 - type 2 (1 ton); 5.857 - type 2 (1 ton).

Wiring Diagrams

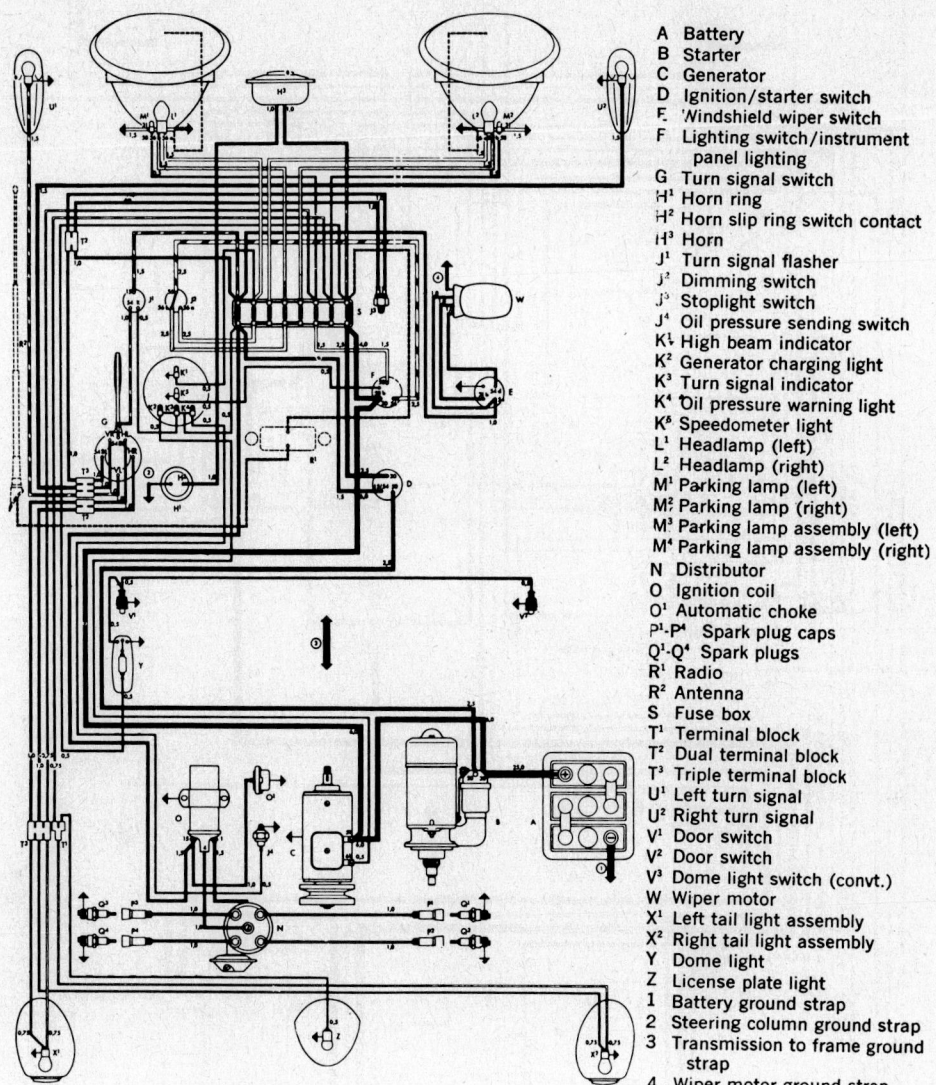

A Battery
B Starter
C Generator
D Ignition/starter switch
E Windshield wiper switch
F Lighting switch/instrument panel lighting
G Turn signal switch
H^1 Horn ring
H^2 Horn slip ring switch contact
H^3 Horn
J^1 Turn signal flasher
J^2 Dimming switch
J^3 Stoplight switch
J^4 Oil pressure sending switch
K^1 High beam indicator
K^2 Generator charging light
K^3 Turn signal indicator
K^4 Oil pressure warning light
K^5 Speedometer light
L^1 Headlamp (left)
L^2 Headlamp (right)
M^1 Parking lamp (left)
M^2 Parking lamp (right)
M^3 Parking lamp assembly (left)
M^4 Parking lamp assembly (right)
N Distributor
O Ignition coil
O^1 Automatic choke
P^1-P^4 Spark plug caps
Q^1-Q^4 Spark plugs
R^1 Radio
R^2 Antenna
S Fuse box
T^1 Terminal block
T^2 Dual terminal block
T^3 Triple terminal block
U^1 Left turn signal
U^2 Right turn signal
V^1 Door switch
V^2 Door switch
V^3 Dome light switch (convt.)
W Wiper motor
X^1 Left tail light assembly
X^2 Right tail light assembly
Y Dome light
Z License plate light
1 Battery ground strap
2 Steering column ground strap
3 Transmission to frame ground strap
4 Wiper motor ground strap

VW 1,200 type 1 (1961-62 shown).

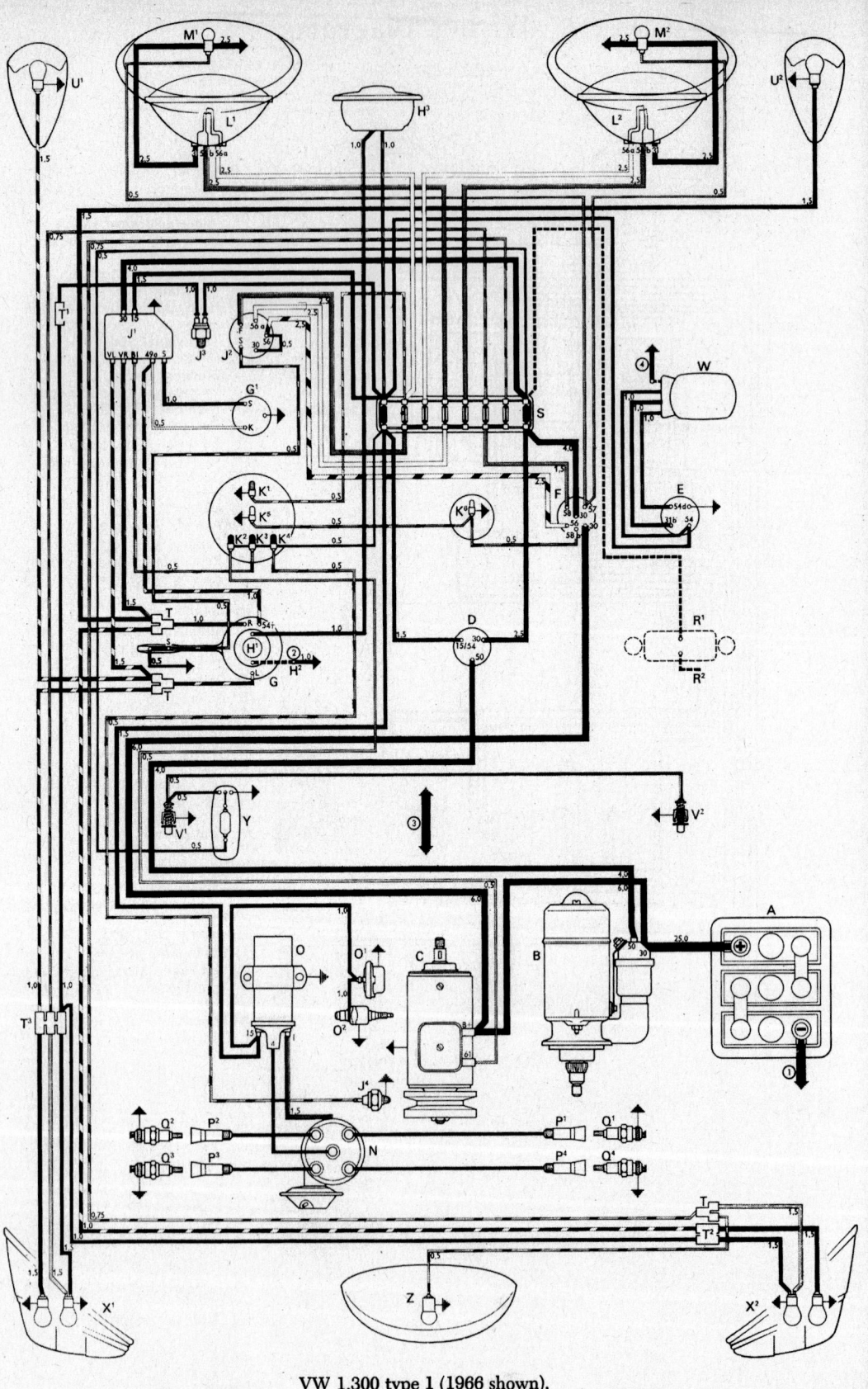

VW 1,300 type 1 (1966 shown).

A	Battery	P²	Spark plug connector, No. 2 cylinder
B	Starter		
C	Generator	P³	Spark plug connector, No. 3 cylinder
D	Ignition/starter switch		
E	Windshield wiper switch	P⁴	Spark plug connector, No. 4 cylinder
F	Lighting switch		
G	Turn signal switch with dimmer switch	Q¹	Spark plug for No. 1 cylinder
		Q²	Spark plug for No. 2 cylinder
G¹	Emergency light switch	Q³	Spark plug for No. 3 cylinder
H¹	Horn half ring	Q⁴	Spark plug for No. 4 cylinder
H²	Steering column connection	R¹	Radio
H³	Horn	R²	Aerial connection
J¹	Flasher and emergency light relay	S	Fuse box
			white fuses: 8 Ampere
J²	Dimming relay		red fuses: 16 Ampere
J³	Brake light switch	T	Cable adaptor
J⁴	Oil pressure switch	T¹	Cable connector, single
K¹	High beam warning light	T²	Cable connector, double
K²	Generator warning light	T³	Cable connector, triple
K³	Turn signal warning light	U¹	Turn signal, left
K⁴	Oil pressure warning light	U²	Turn signal, right
K⁵	Speedometer light	V¹	Door switch, left
K⁶	Fuel gauge light	V²	Door switch, right
L¹	Sealed-beam unit, left	W	Windshield wiper motor
L²	Sealed-beam unit, right	X¹	Brake, turn signal and tail lights, left
M¹	Parking light, left		
M²	Parking light, right	X²	Brake, turn signal and tail lights, right
N	Distributor		
O	Ignition coil	Y	Interior light
O¹	Automatic choke	Z	License plate light
O²	Electro-magnetic pilot jet	①	Battery to frame ground strap
P¹	Spark plug connector, No. 1 cylinder	②	Horn ring to steering coupling ground connection
		③	Transmission to frame ground strap
		④	Wiper motor to body ground strap

Black dotted line = Service installation

VW 1,300 type 1 (1966 shown).

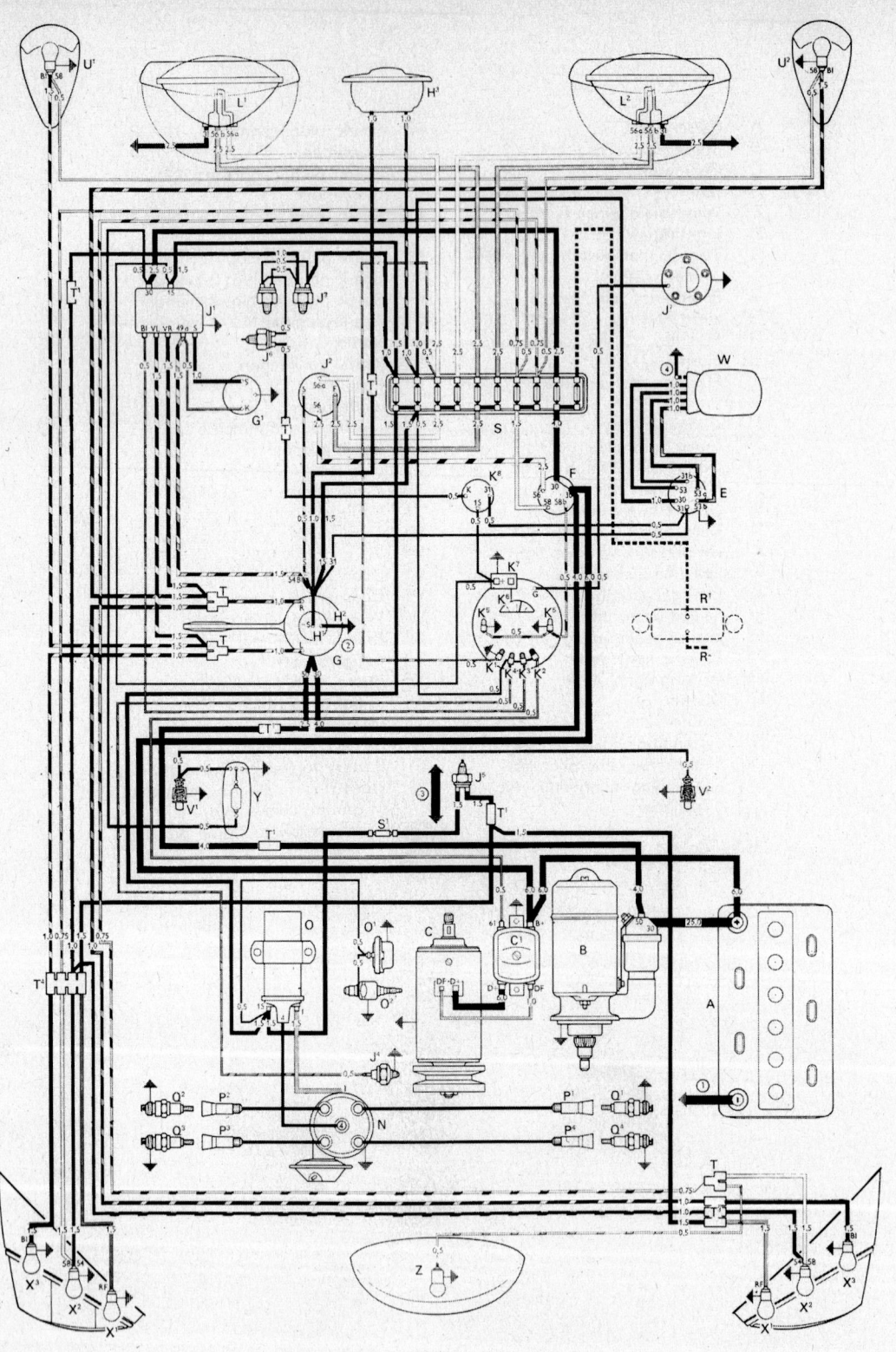

VW 1,500 type 1 (1968 shown).

A	Battery	P²	Spark plug connector, No. 2 cylinder	
B	Starter	P³	Spark plug connector, No. 4 cylinder	
C	Generator			
C¹	Regulator	P⁴	Spark plug connector, No. 3 cylinder	
E	Windshield wiper switch			
F	Lighting switch	Q¹	Spark plug for No. 1 cylinder	
G	Turn signal switch with automatic canceling, hand dimmer button and ignition/starter switch	Q²	Spark plug for No. 2 cylinder	
		Q³	Spark plug for No. 4 cylinder	
		Q⁴	Spark plug for No. 3 cylinder	
G¹	Emergency light switch	R¹	Radio	
H¹	Horn half ring	R²	Aerial connection	
H²	Steering column connection	S	Fuse box	
H³	Horn	T	Cable adapter	
J¹	Turn signal and emergency light relay	T¹	Cable connector, single	
		T²	Cable connector for horn under front luggage compartment lining	
J²	Dimmer relay			
J³	Brake light switch (2 X)			
J⁴	Oil pressure switch	T³	Cable connector, triple	
J⁵	Back-up light switch	U¹	Front turn signal and parking light, left	
J⁶	Warning switch for brake system			
		U²	Front turn signal and parking light, right	
J⁷	Fuel gauge sender unit			
K¹	High beam warning light	V¹	Door contact switch, left	
K²	Generator warning light	V²	Door contact switch, right	
K³	Turn signal warning light	W	Windshield wiper motor	
K⁴	Oil pressure warning light	X¹	Back-up lights	
K⁵	Speedometer light	X²	Brake and tail lights	
K⁶	Fuel gauge light	X³	Turn signal lights	
K⁷	Resistance for fuel gauge	Y	Interior light	
K⁸	Brake warning lamp with test button	Z	License plate light	
		①	Battery to frame ground strap	
L¹	Sealed-beam insert, left	②	Horn ring to steering coupling ground connection	
L²	Sealed-beam insert, right			
N	Distributor	③	Transmission to frame ground strap	
O	Ignition coil			
O¹	Automatic choke	④	Wiper motor to body ground strap	
O²	Electro-magnetic pilot jet			
P¹	Spark plug connector, No. 1 cylinder		Black dotted line = Optional extras or service installation	

VW 1,500 type 1 (1968 shown).

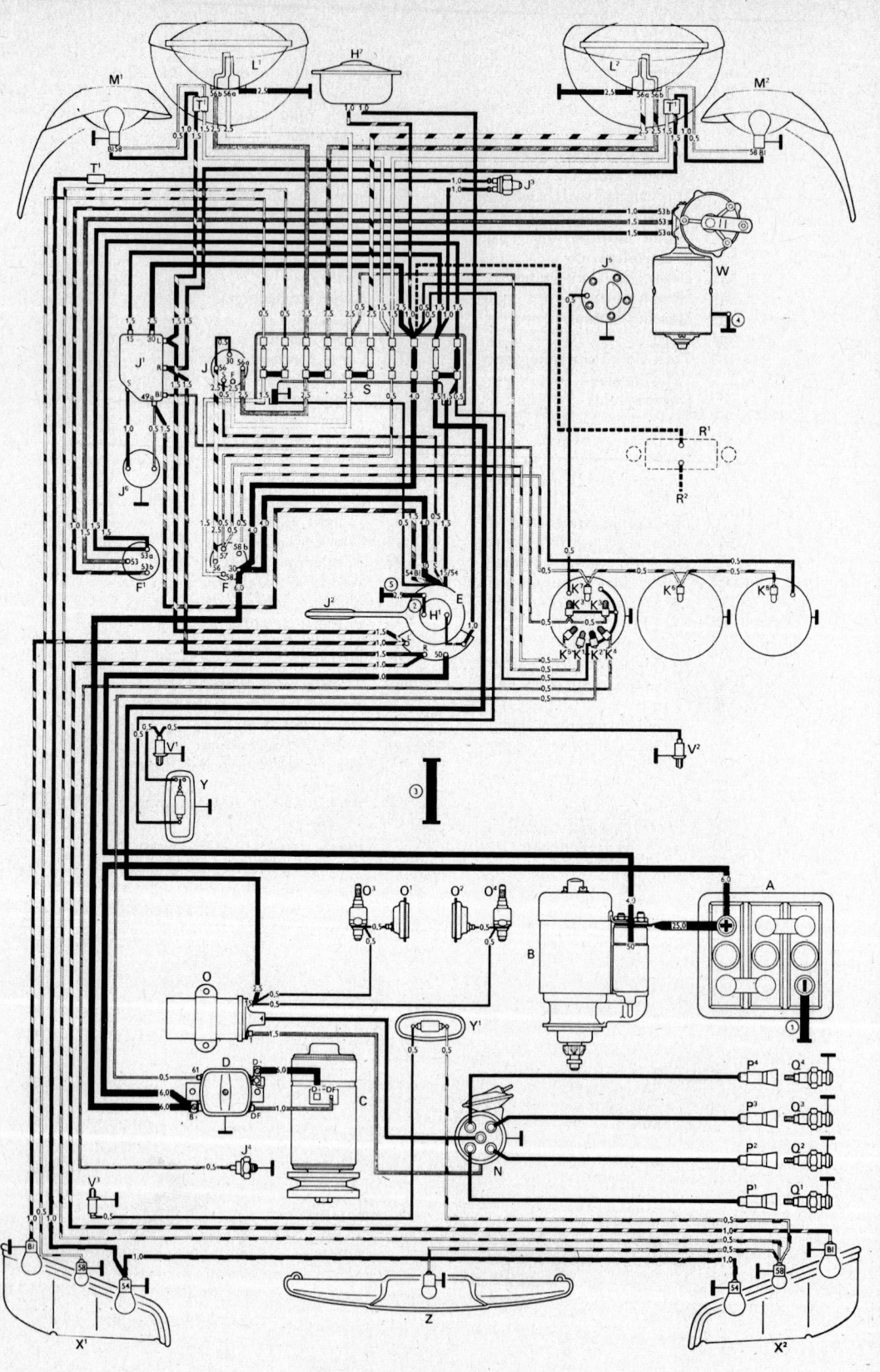

VW type 3 (1966 shown).

A	Battery	P^2	Spark plug connector, No. 2 cylinder
B	Starter		
C	Generator	P^3	Spark plug connector, No. 3 cylinder
D	Regulator		
E	Turn signal switch with ignition starter lock	P^4	Spark plug connector, No. 4 cylinder
F	Lighting switch	Q^1	Spark plug for No. 1 cylinder
F^1	Windshield wiper switch	Q^2	Spark plug for No. 2 cylinder
H^1	Horn half ring	Q^3	Spark plug for No. 3 cylinder
H^2	Horn	Q^4	Spark plug for No. 4 cylinder
J	Hand dimmer relay	R^1	Radio
J^1	Flasher and emergency light relay	R^2	Aerial connection
		S	Fuse box—10 fuses
J^2	Headlamp flasher button	T^1	Cable connector, single
J^3	Brake light switch	T^2	Cable connector, double
J^4	Oil pressure switch	V^1	Door switch, left
J^5	Fuel gauge sender unit	V^2	Door switch, right
J^6	Emergency light switch	V^3	Luggage compartment light switch
K^1	High beam warning light		
K^2	Generator warning light	W	Windshield wiper motor
K^3	Turn signal warning light	X^1	Tail light, left
K^4	Oil pressure warning light	X^2	Tail light, right
K^5	Parking light warning light	Y	Interior light
K^6	Speedometer light	Y^1	Luggage compartment light
K^7	Fuel gauge light	Z	License plate light
K^8	Clock light	①	Battery to frame ground strap
L^1	Headlamp, left	②	Horn half ring steering coupling ground connection
L^2	Headlamp, right		
M^1	Parking light and turn signal light, left	③	Transmission to frame ground connection
M^2	Parking light and turn signal light, right	④	Windshield wiper motor to body ground strap
N	Distributor	⑤	Front axle to frame ground strap
O	Ignition coil		
O^1	Automatic choke, left		
O^2	Automatic choke, right		Black dotted lines = Service installation
O^3	Electro-magnetic pilot jet, left		
O^4	Electro-magnetic pilot jet, right		1.5; 0.5 etc.: Cable cross section
P^1	Spark plug connector, No. 1 cylinder		

VW type 3 (1966 shown).

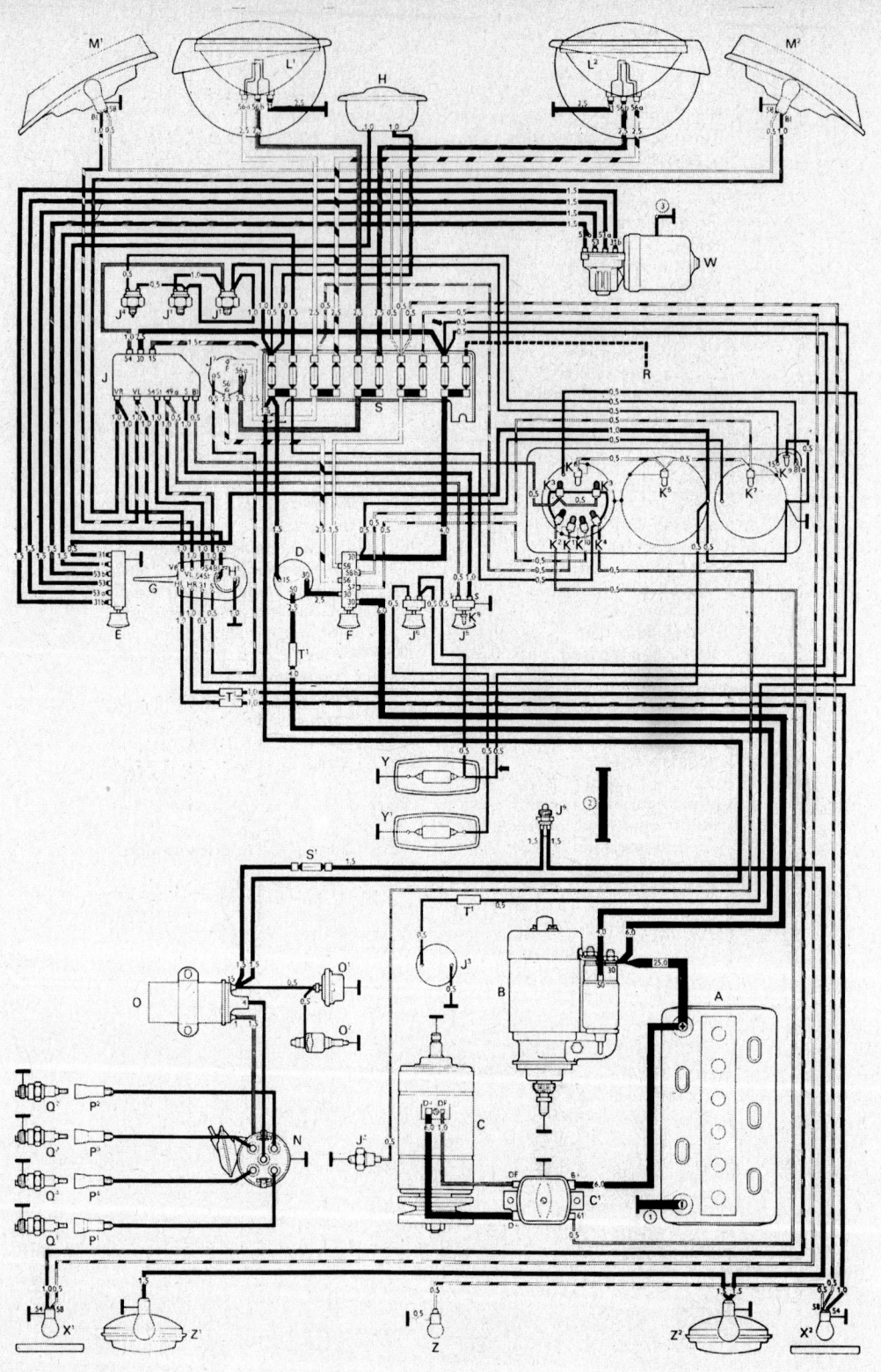

VW type 2 (1968 shown).

A	Battery	P²	Spark plug connector, No. 2 cylinder
B	Starter	P³	Spark plug connector, No. 3 cylinder
C	Generator		
C¹	Regulator	P⁴	Spark plug connector, No. 4 cylinder
D	Ignition/starter switch		
E	Windshield wiper switch	Q¹	Spark plug for No. 1 cylinder
F	Lighting switch	Q²	Spark plug for No. 2 cylinder
G	Turn signal switch and hand dimmer	Q³	Spark plug for No. 3 cylinder
		Q⁴	Spark plug for No. 4 cylinder
H	Horn	R	Radio
H¹	Horn button	R¹	Aerial connection
J	Emergency light relay	R²	Rear loudspeaker connection
J¹	Brake light switch (2 X)	S	Fuse box
J²	Oil pressure switch	S¹	Back-up light fuse
J³	Fuel gauge sender unit	T¹	Cable connector, single
J⁴	Warning switch for brakes	U¹	Turn signal, front left
J⁵	Emergency light switch	U²	Turn signal, front right
J⁶	Interior light switch	W	Windshield wiper motor
J⁷	Dimmer relay	X¹	Brake, turn signal and tail light, left
J⁹	Back-up light switch		
K¹	High beam warning lamp	X²	Brake, turn signal and tail light, right
K²	Generator and fan warning lamp		
		Y	Interior light, front
K³	Turn signal warning lamp	Y¹	Interior light, rear
K⁴	Oil pressure warning lamp	Z	License plate light
K⁵	Speedometer light bulb	Z¹	Back-up light, left
K⁶	Fuel gauge light bulb	Z²	Back-up light, right
K⁷	Clock light bulb	①	Battery to body ground strap
K⁸	Emergency light warning lamp	②	Transmission to body ground strap
K⁹	Brake system warning lamp		
L¹	Sealed beam unit, left	③	Windshield wiper motor ground connection
L²	Sealed beam unit, right		
M¹	Parking light, left		
M²	Parking light, right		
N	Distributor		
O	Ignition coil		
O¹	Automatic choke		
O²	Electro-magnetic pilot jet		Black dotted lines = Optional extras
P¹	Spark plug connector, No. 1 cylinder		All fuses: 8 amps

VW type 2 (1968 shown).

Engine Electrical

Distributor

DISTRIBUTOR R & R

Take off the vacuum hose at the distributor. Disconnect cable 1 at the ignition coil and remove the distributor cap. Mark

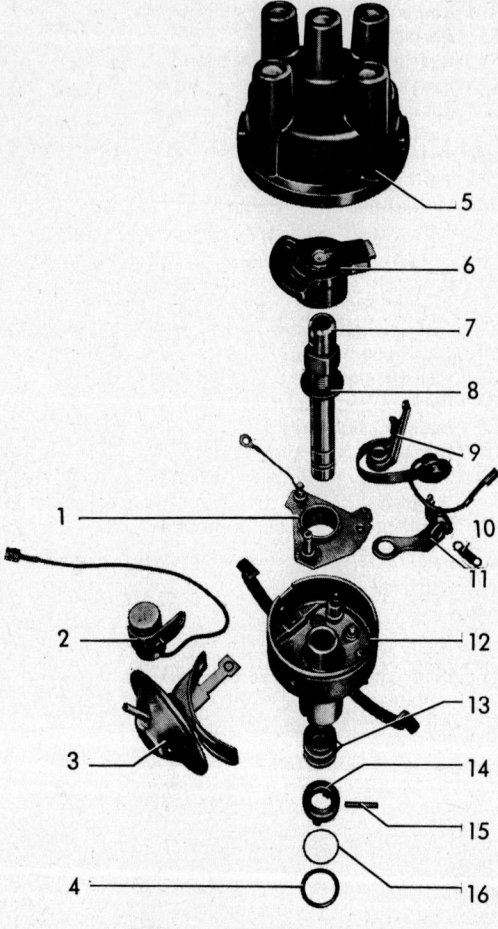

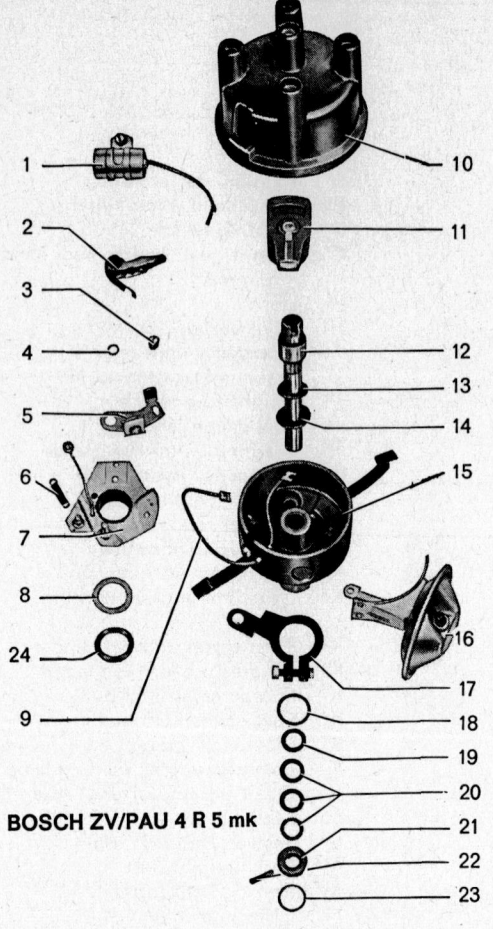

1 Condenser
2 Contact breaker arm
3 Securing screw with flat and spring washers
4 Insulating washer
5 Contact breaker point
7 Breaker plate with ground cable
8 Plastic washer
9 Low tension cable
10 Distributor cap
11 Rotor
12 Distributor shaft
13 Steel washer
14 Fiber washer
15 Distributor housing
16 Vacuum advance
17 Clip
18 Sealing ring
19 Fiber washer
20 Shim
21 Driving dog
22 Pin
23 Locking spring
24 Shim

Exploded view, typical Bosch distributor.

1 Breaker plate with ground cable
2 Condenser
3 Vacuum advance unit
4 Sealing ring
5 Distributor cap
6 Rotor
7 Distributor shaft
8 Fiber washer
9 Contact breaker arm with spring
10 Return spring
11 Contact breaker point
12 Distributor housing
13 Steel washers
14 Driving dog
15 Pin
16 Locking ring

Exploded view, typical VW distributor.

the relationship between the distributor body and the engine case. Unscrew the distributor retaining screw on the crankcase and lift out the distributor.
(NOTE: *before removing the distributor, it is best to turn the engine until the rotor points to number one cylinder lead; i.e., toward the notch in the distributor*

1. Spring for breaker arm
2. Breaker arm
3. Distributor with cam
4. Connection for contact
5. Breaker plate
6. Vacuum unit
7. Condenser
8. Insulator
9. Securing screw
10. Pins on breaker plate
11. Breaker point
12. Eccentrics for return springs
13. Return springs
14. Pull rod

Details of typical distributor.

housing. *In this way one can be sure of having the rotor pointing in the proper direction when the distributor is reinstalled.*)

Installation is in the reverse sequence. Align the marks made before removal. When the distributor is reinstalled in the engine, the timing must then be adjusted.

CONTACT POINT ADJUSTMENT

The breaker points are the heart of the Volkswagen ignition system, and must be given their share of attention. All Volkswagens ever made require a breaker point gap of .016" (COLD) and a dwell angle of 50 degrees. It is best if the engine is cold from sitting overnight or for several hours. If you are not able to rest your hand comfortably on any part of the engine, it is too warm to set the breaker point gap and the ignition timing. In adjusting the contact points, the following steps are taken:

(1) Remove distributor cap and rotor.
(2) Turn the engine by hand until the fiber block on the movable breaker point rests on a high point of the cam lobe.
(3) With a screwdriver, loosen the locking screw of the stationary breaker point.
(4) Manipulate the stationary point plate so that the clearance between the points is .016".
(5) Tighten the locking screw of the stationary point.
(6) Recheck gap, correct if it has changed from step (4) due to the tightening of the locking screw.

When replacing points, the same steps as above are followed, except that in between steps (3) and (4), the old points are taken out and the new points inserted. Points should be replaced when they have been badly burned or have been in use so long that correct adjustment is no longer possible. When checking the gap of points which have been in use for some time, it is advisable to use a round gauge rather than a flat feeler gauge. In the case of points that have a peak in one point and a valley in the other, the flat-type gauge will result in a reading which is smaller than the actual gap between the two points.

If necessary, multi-purpose grease should be applied to the breaker arm fiber block whenever the points are inspected. Use enough to do the job—but avoid excess grease that could come into contact with the breaker points and cause misfiring of the ignition system. On older Volkswagens there is a felt wick in the center of the distributor cam shaft which requires a few drops of light oil every 15,000 miles. If the indentation in the top of the cam shaft is entirely metallic, no lubrication is required. On models that have a felt ring in the contact breaker base plate, this point should receive a few drops of light oil every 3,000 miles.

IGNITION TIMING

It is only after adjusting the breaker points properly that the ignition timing should be adjusted. It is most important that the ignition timing adjustment be carried out only when the engine is dead cold, because rising engine temperature causes the setting to become different.

If, in exceptional cases, it is necessary to adjust the timing with a warm engine, not exceeding 122°F, the timing should be advanced about 2.5° beyond the normal setting. The timing must then be rechecked at the first opportunity with the engine cold.

VW engines have had several different arrangements of crankshaft pulley timing marks. On early type 1 engines, the pulley bore two timing marks, 7.5° before top dead center and 10° before top dead center, reading clockwise. Later, with the introduction of emission controls, a 0° top dead center mark was added. The 7.5° and 10° marks were subsequently removed, leaving only the 0° mark. Current engines have only a 5° after top dead center mark. Type 2 engines are generally the same as type 1 models. Early type 3 engines have marks at

7.5° and 10° before top dead center; later engines have marks at 7.5°, 10°, and 12.5° before top dead center. Fuel injected type 3 engines have marks corresponding to 0°, 7.5°, 10°, and 12.5° before top dead center.

Timing Procedure

(1) Turn the engine by hand until the appropriate mark on the crankshaft pulley is lined up with the crankcase dividing line. (On type 3 models, the mark is to be lined up with the timing setting surface, or pointer, on the fan housing. At the same time the appropriate mark is opposite the dividing line, the rotor must be pointing to the lead wire of cylinder number one (the cylinder toward the front of the car on the passenger [right] side). Number one position is indicated by a mark on the rim of the distributor. See illustration showing cylinder numbering. If the rotor is not pointed toward number one cylinder, the crankshaft must be turned one more revolution clockwise until it is. On recent models, number three cylinder is retarded about 4° compared with number one cylinder and only number one cylinder is to be used in setting the ignition timing.

(2) Loosen the clamp screw at the base of the distributor.

(3) Attach the lead of a test lamp (6 volt for 1966 and earlier models, 12 volt for 1967 and later) to terminal 1 of

Right mark is 10° BTDC, one on left is 7.5° BTDC on early type 1 and 2 engines. See text for details of markings on other engines.

A 6 or 12 volt static test lamp is used in setting the ignition timing of all pre-1968 VW engines. One lead of the test lamp is connected to terminal 1 of the coil, the other to ground.

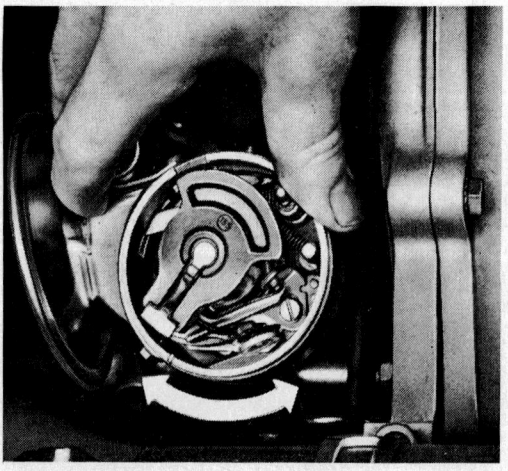

Turning the distributor body clockwise retards the ignition timing; turning counterclockwise advances the timing.

the ignition coil and ground the test lamp.

(4) With the ignition switched on, rotate the distributor body clockwise until the contact points close, and then rotate it slowly counter-clockwise until the points begin to open and the lamp lights.

(5) Without moving the distributor body, tighten the clamp screw at the base of the distributor.

(6) Recheck adjustment by turning the crankshaft pulley counter-clockwise one-half turn, and then turning clockwise until the mark is within one inch of the dividing line. At this point, proceed more slowly by tapping the right side of the fan belt with your hand. Such tapping will cause the fan belt to move in either moderate or very small jumps, depending on the strength of the tap. Slight taps toward the end of the check will ensure the finest possible check on the accuracy of the adjustment. If, upon rechecking, the lamp lights before the mark gets to the dividing line, the timing will have to be retarded slightly by loosening the clamp screw and rotating the distributor body in the clockwise direction. Rotating the distributor clockwise retards the timing, while rotation in the counter-clockwise direction advances the timing.

NOTE: *adjustment of ignition timing on 1967 and earlier engines must always be* done with a test lamp. A stroboscopic timing light should not be used, as it will alter the entire setting range. However, it is recommended that exhaust emission controlled engines (1968 and later) and type 3 fuel injected engines be timed with a stroboscopic light. These engines should be timed at idle speed, with the distributor vacuum line disconnected and the engine at normal operating temperature.

DISTRIBUTOR TRIGGER CONTACT R & R

The distributor on fuel injected engines has two breaker plates. The first is the normal breaker point plate for the ignition

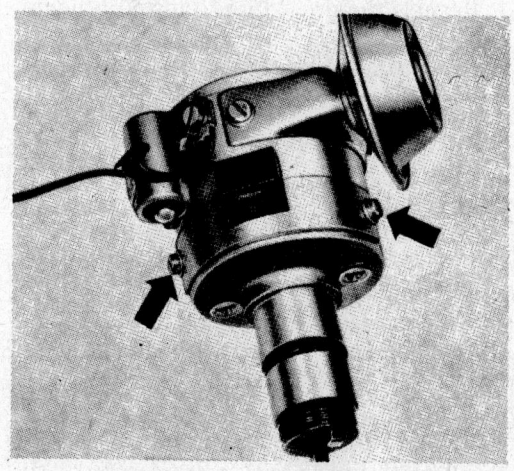

Distributor used with fuel injected engines. The two screws pointed out hold the fuel injection trigger contact plate in place.

A stroboscopic timing light must be used to set the ignition timing of all 1968 and later exhaust emission controlled VW engines.

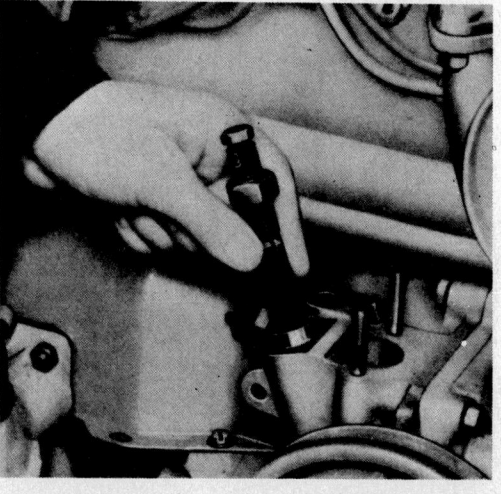

A removal tool is required to extract the distributor driveshaft.

system. The second plate, mounted in the base of the distributor head, carries two similar breaker assemblies which regulate fuel injection. There is no adjustment provided for the injection trigger contact breakers. To replace the trigger contacts:

1. Remove the distributor cap. Pull out the triple plug and disconnect the flat plug at terminal 1 of the coil. Loosen the clamp and remove the distributor after noting the rotor position and marking the relationship between the engine block and the distributor body.
2. Remove the two contact plate holding screws.
3. Pull out the plate holder.
4. Reverse the procedure to install the new plate holder. If ignition timing is correct, the injection timing will also be correct.

DISTRIBUTOR DRIVESHAFT R & R

To remove the distributor drive shaft loosen the distributor clamp bolt, turn the engine so that the rotor is pointing to number one cylinder (the notch on the distributor housing), lift out the distribu-

Engine

Type 1 and 2 (except early 1968 models with throttle positioner)

Type 3

Type 1 and 2 (early 1968 models with throttle positioner)

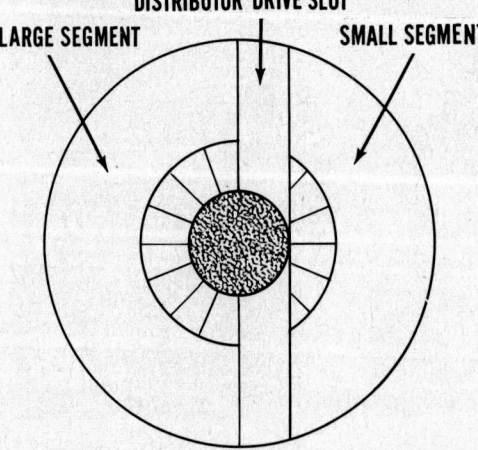

DISTRIBUTOR DRIVE SLOT

LARGE SEGMENT   SMALL SEGMENT

Detail of top of distributor driveshaft, showing off-set slot referred to in text.

tor. Remove fuel pump and intermediate flange, gaskets, and fuel pump push rod. Remove the distance spring on the distributor drive shaft. Be sure that number one cylinder is at its firing point, and withdraw the drive shaft via a removal tool by pulling with the extractor and turning the drive shaft to the left at the same time.

Remove the washer(s) under the drive shaft, being careful not to drop a washer into the crankcase. When the engine is installed, a magnet is handy for removing these washers.

When installing, the reverse of the previous procedure applies. The fuel pump push rod drive eccentric and the pinion teeth should be checked for wear. If the teeth are badly worn, the teeth on the crankshaft should also be examined. Check the washer under the drive shaft for wear and replace if necessary. Position number one cylinder at its firing point and insert the distributor drive shaft.

The slot in the top of the distributor driveshaft is offset, dividing the top of the driveshaft into two unequal segments. The driveshaft is installed as follows:

Distributor Driveshaft Installation
(No. 1 Cylinder in Firing Position)

Slot at right angles to crankcase split, small segment toward crankshaft pulley.

Slot at about 60° to crankcase split, small segment toward oil cooler.

Slot at about 60° to crankcase split, small segment toward crankshaft pulley.

Insert the distance spring, install the distributor, set the ignition timing, and install the fuel pump. (Note: When the engine has been completely disassembled, it is necessary that the oil pump, the fan housing, the fan, and the crankshaft pulley be installed before the distributor drive shaft is inserted.)

Installing the distributor driveshaft in type 1 and 2 engines.

Installing the distributor driveshaft in type 3 engines. With No. 1 cylinder at its firing point, the slot of the driveshaft must form an angle of approximately 60°, with the smaller segment toward the oil cooler. See the text for details on other engines.

Generator

Different types of generators have been used throughout the years and models. Refer to the Generator and Regulator Electrical Equipment Specifications Chart for details.

The generator warning light in the speedometer housing connects to the voltage regulator by means of terminals in the ignition switch. The warning lamp lights as soon as the ignition is turned on, and goes out when the voltage of the generator approaches that of the battery. The warning lamp simply gives a yes-no answer to the question of whether the generator is charging or not. As such, it is potentially useful in detecting broken fan belts, because when a fan belt is broken, the generator is no longer being turned and will not charge. In the type 1 or 2, a broken belt means that the entire car is out of commission, but with the type 3 the fan is mounted directly on the crankshaft and the car can be driven until the battery runs out of electricity.

The generator is equipped with ball bearings that are packed with special high melting point grease. Lubrication of the generator is not necessary under normal conditions. However, if the unit has been disassembled and/or overhauled, it is then necessary to provide new lubricant for the bearings. Under no circumstances should ordinary grease be used, for it will not hold up under operating conditions.

TESTING GENERATOR NO-LOAD VOLTAGE

In testing the no-load voltage of the generator, the cable from terminal B+(51) at the regulator must first be disconnected. The positive lead of the voltmeter to be used should be attached to terminal B+ (51) of the regulator and the negative lead of the meter grounded. With the engine running, the speed should be increased gradually until the reading of the voltmeter peaks out. If the regulator is functioning properly, the peaking point of the no-load voltage should be approximately 7.4 to 8.1 volts for the 6-volt system and 13.6 to 14.4 for the 12-volt system. When the engine is turned off, the needle of the voltmeter should drop from 6 volts (12 volts) to zero just before the engine stops.

TESTING GENERATOR WITHOUT REGULATOR

The generator can be given a very quick check without the regulator. It is most important that the duration of the test be very brief (only a few seconds) in order that the generator field windings will not be overloaded during the test.

Disconnect the two leads from the generator. Connect terminal DF of the generator to ground. Connect the positive terminal of the voltmeter to terminal D+ and the negative terminal to the generator ground. For 6 volt systems, approxi-

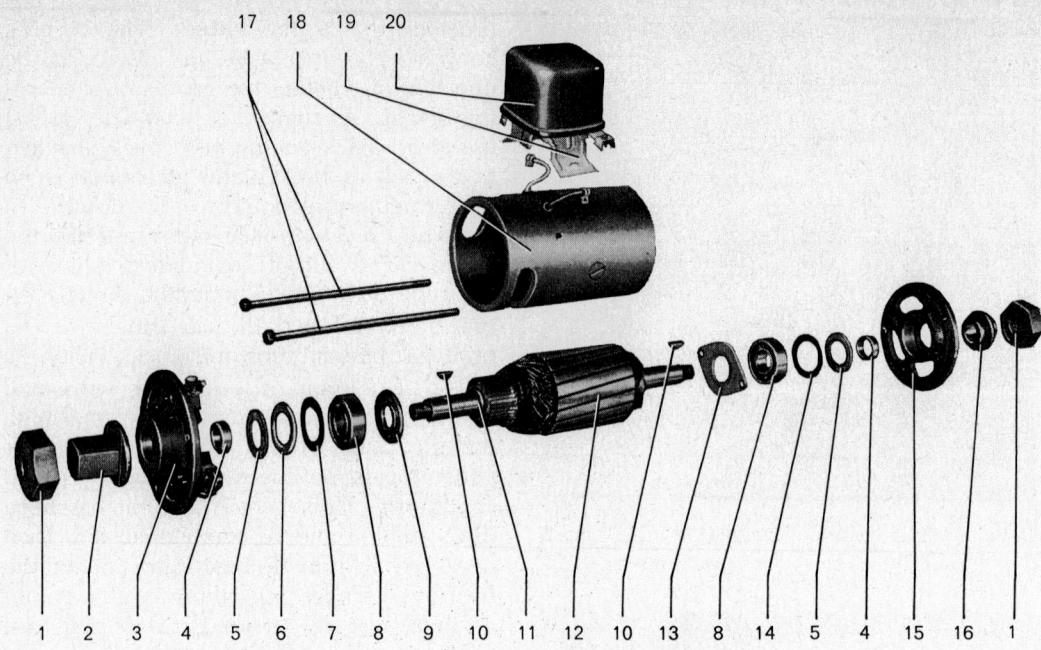

1. Nut
2. Pulley hub
3. Brush holder end plate
4. Spacer ring
5. Felt washer
6. Retainer
7. Thrust ring
8. Ball bearing
9. Washer
10. Key
11. Spacer
12. Armature
13. Bearing retainer
14. Thrust ring
15. End plate
16. Fan hub
17. Housing screws
18. Housing and field assembly
19. Slotted screw
20. Regulator

Exploded view, VW generator.

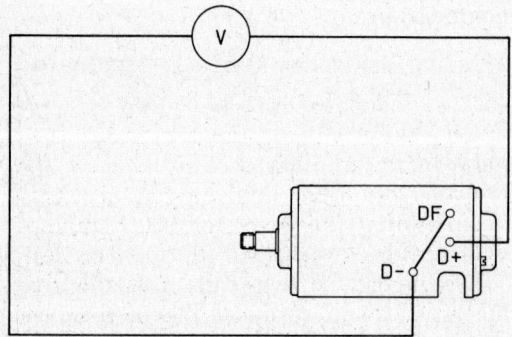

Circuit diagram for making quick check of generator without regulator. Test must not take longer
than a few seconds, or generator will be damaged.

mately 6 volts should be generated at
1500 RPM and about 15 at 3000 RPM. A
circuit diagram for this test is included
in this section.

REGULATOR R & R

On pre-1967 models, the regulator is
located on top of the generator. Take off
the connections from terminals B+ (51)
and 61 at the regulator. Remove the
screws that hold the regulator onto the
generator and remove the regulator from
its position on the generator. Disconnect the electrical cables from the bottom
of the regulator. These are marked + (D+)
and F(DF).

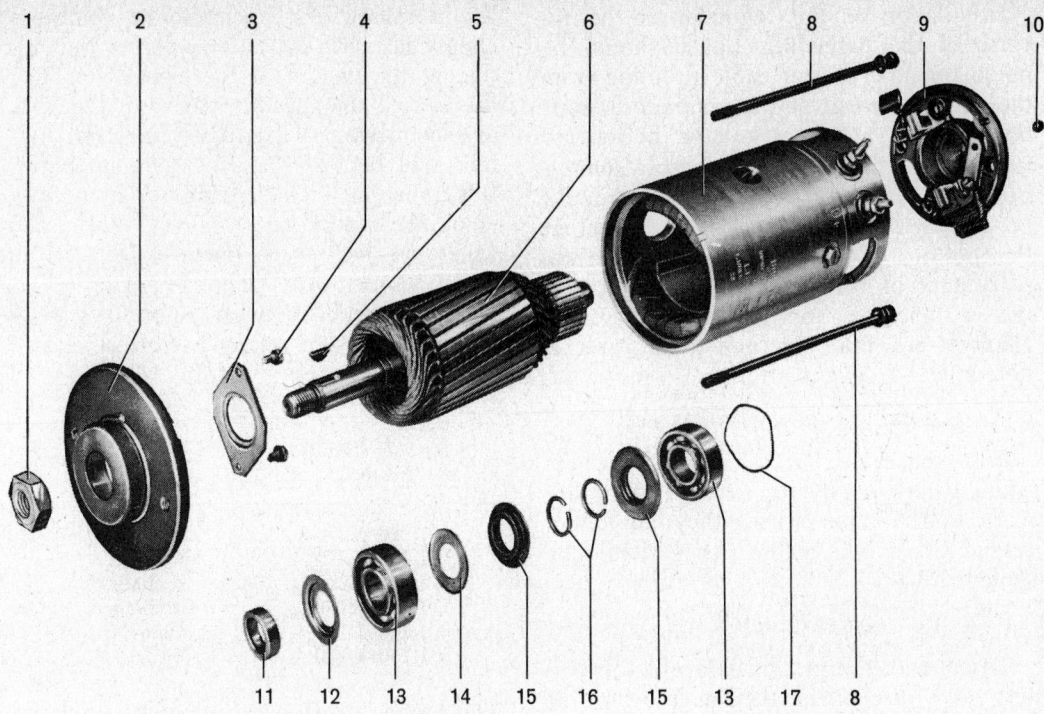

1. Nut
2. End plate
3. Retaining plate
4. Screw
5. Woodruff key
6. Armature
7. Pole housing
8. Housing screw
9. End plate with brush holders
10. Screw
11. Spacer
12. Washer
13. Bearing
14. Washer
15. Washer
16. Circlip
17. Spring ring

Exploded view, Bosch generator.

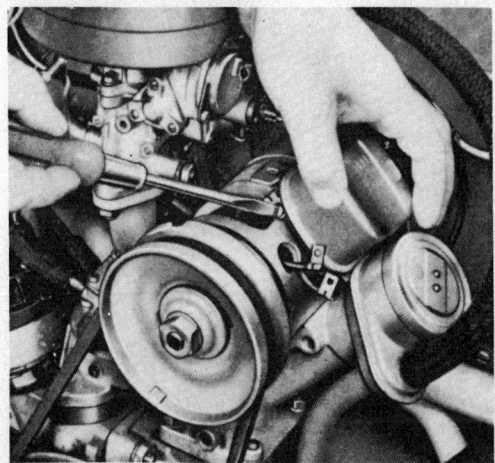

Removing voltage regulator, early type 1 vehicles.

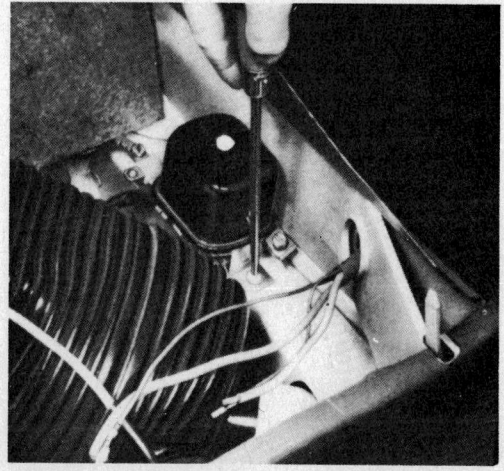

Removing voltage regulator, type 3 and late type 1 vehicles.

Installation of the regulator is the reverse of the preceding, but it should be noted that the thicker cable (coming from the positive brush of the generator) must be attached at the regulator bottom to terminal + (D+). The thin cable coming from the generator field windings should be attached to the F (DF) terminal at the bottom of the regulator. If the replacement of the regulator does not correct a deficiency in the charging system, chances are that the generator itself is defective.

CHECKING GENERATOR BRUSHES

The generator brushes should be examined periodically for wear. If they are worn to the point where they no longer extend from their holders, they should be replaced.

GENERATOR R & R

Disconnect the ground strap of the battery and disconnect the leads from the regulator. Remove the air cleaner and the carburetor and take off the fan belt. Remove the retaining strap from the generator. Remove the cooling air thermostat. Remove hot air hoses from the fan housing, take out the fan housing screws and lift off the housing. After removing the fan housing screws, the generator can be lifted off along with the fan.

Installation is the reverse of the preceding.

Battery, Starter

BATTERY

The electrical system of the Volkswagen is of the negative-ground type, the negative terminal of the battery being grounded. In most VW models, the battery is located under the right-hand side of the rear seat. In the Karmann Ghia and Transporter models it is in the engine compartment.

The six-volt electrical system was standard on all Volkswagens through the 1966 models. Beginning with the 1967 models —August 1966—the change was made to the 12-volt system.

A specific gravity test is a practical indicator of the state of charge of the battery. As a battery is discharged, a chemical change takes place within each cell.

The sulphate of the electrolyte combines chemically with the battery plates, thus reducing the weight of the electrolyte. For this reason the specific gravity of the acid, or electrolyte, of a partially charged battery will be less than that of one that is fully charged. The electrolyte in a fully charged battery is usually about 1.285 times as heavy as pure water at the same temperature. The following chart gives an indication of specific gravity value and how it relates to battery charge condition:

Specific Gravity Reading	Charge Condition
1.260–1.280	Fully charged
1.230–1.250	¾ charged
1.200–1.220	½ charged
1.170–1.190	¼ charged
1.140–1.160	Almost flat
1.110–1.130	Nil

The battery hydrometer consists simply of a glass cylinder, a moving float, and a calibrated scale. When acid is drawn into the glass cylinder, the calibrated float displaces its weight in acid, and thereby reveals the specific gravity of the battery acid and the condition of the battery. Hydrometers are available at auto supply houses at a fairly low price. It is always possible to have the specific gravity checked at a service station.

Battery Storage

If a battery is not used for a prolonged period of time, it tends to discharge itself at a slow rate. This rate varies according to the temperature—high temperatures cause stored batteries to discharge more quickly. At room temperature, the rate of battery discharge is about 1% per day. When a discharged battery is stored at room temperature, it also tends to "sulphate", or form layers of lead sulphate on the battery plates. When storing a battery for a long period of time, it should be charged before storage and the acid level and specific gravity checked and corrected if necessary. Once in storage the battery should be kept in a cool, dry location and discharged, then recharged, every 6–8 weeks. Before the stored battery is put into use, it should be charged at a low rate, not to exceed 3 amps.

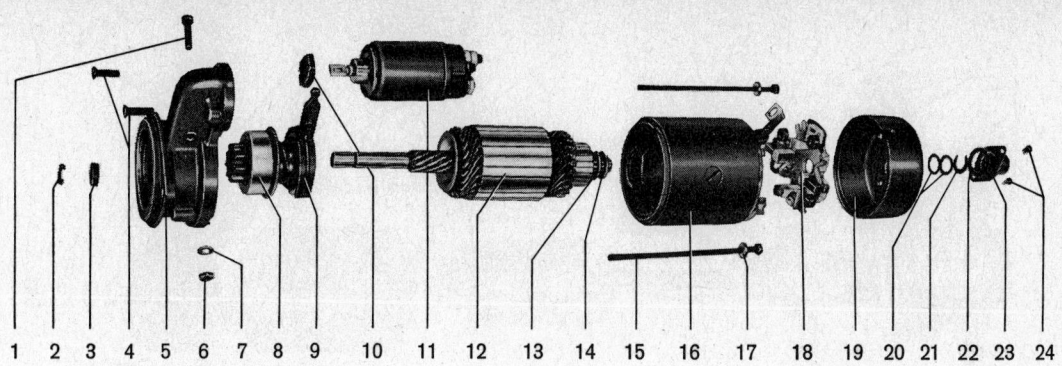

1. Lever bearing pin
2. Circlip
3. Stop ring
4. Securing screws
5. Mounting bracket
6. Nut
7. Spring washer
8. Pinion
9. Operating lever
10. Rubber seal
11. Solenoid
12. Armature
13. Steel washer
14. Synthetic washer
15. Housing screw
16. Pole housing
17. Washer
18. Brush holder
19. End plate
20. Shims
21. Lock washer
22. Sealing ring
23. End cap
24. Screws

Exploded view of typical Bosch starter.

STARTER

The starter motor of the Volkswagen is rated at about ½ horsepower. The motor used in the starter is a series wound type and draws a heavy current in order to provide the high torque needed to crank the engine during starting. The starter in current models cannot be switched on accidentally while the engine is still running—the device responsible for this safeguard is a non-repeat switch in the ignition switch. If the engine should stall for any reason, the ignition key must be turned to the "off" position before it is possible to restart the engine.

The starter is flange-mounted on the right-hand side of the transmission housing. Attached to the starter motor housing is a solenoid which engages the pinion and connects the starting motor to the battery when the ignition key is turned on. When the engine starts, and the key is released from the start position, the solenoid circuit is opened and the pinion is returned to its original position by the return spring. However, if for any reason the starter is not switched off immediately after the engine starts, a pinion free-wheeling device stops the armature from being driven so that the starter will not be damaged.

Starter R & R

Disconnect the ground strap of the battery and remove the cable from terminal 30 and the lead from terminal 50 of the solenoid. After removal of the two retaining screws, the starter can be taken out.

Prior to installation, the outboard bushing should be lubricated with special lithium grease, and sealing compound should be applied to the mating surfaces between the starter and the transmission. After putting the long screw into the hole in the flange, locate the starter on the transmission housing. Be sure that the cables are tightly connected to the terminals and that the contact points between the cables and terminals are clean.

Solenoid R & R

Unscrew the hexagon nut and remove the connector strip. Take out the two retaining screws on the mounting bracket and withdraw the solenoid after it has been unhooked from its actuating lever. When replacing a defective solenoid with a new one, care should be taken to see that the distance "a" in the accompanying diagram is 19+ or −.1 mm. when the magnet is drawn in. The actuating rod can be adjusted after loosening the lock nut.

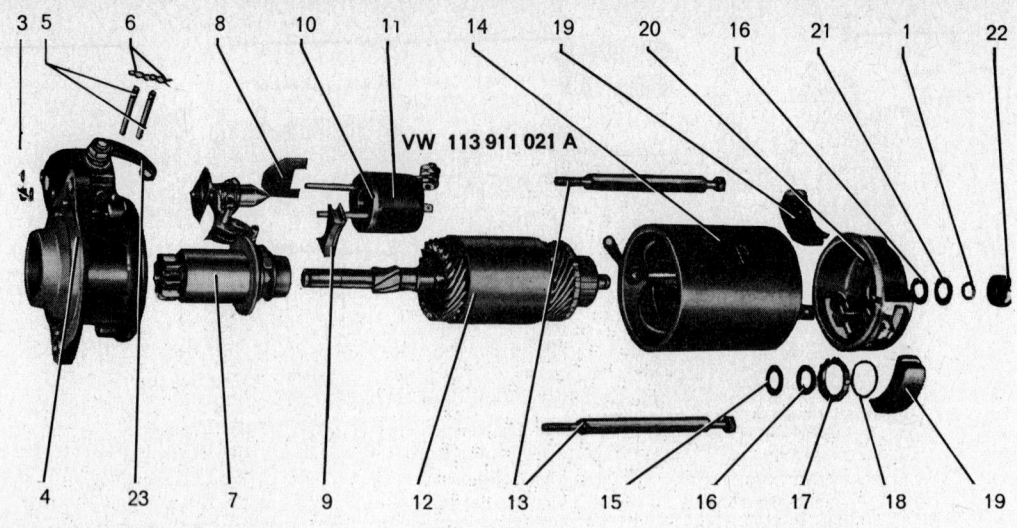

Exploded view of typical VW starter.

1 Circlip	8 Insulating plate	16 Bronze washer
2 Cup washer	9 Moulded rubber seal	17 Friction washer
3 Nuts and lockwashers	10 Insulating disc	18 Thrust ring
4 Intermediate bracket	11 Solenoid housing	19 Brush inspection cover
5 Pivot pins	12 Armature	20 Commutator end plate
6 Spring clips	13 Housing screws	21 Steel washer
7 Drive pinion with linkage	14 Housing and field assembly	22 Cap
and solenoid core	15 Steel washer	23 Connecting strip

Installation of the solenoid is the reverse of the preceding. Be certain that the rubber seal on the starter mounting bracket is properly seated. A small strip of VW Sealing Compound D 14 should be placed on the outside of the switch. In order to facilitate engagement of the actuating rod, the pinion should be pulled out as far as possible when the solenoid is inserted.

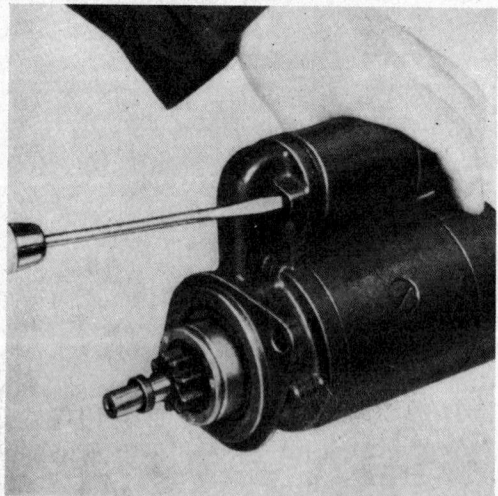

The solenoid may be withdrawn after removal of the two screws securing it to the starter motor intermediate bracket.

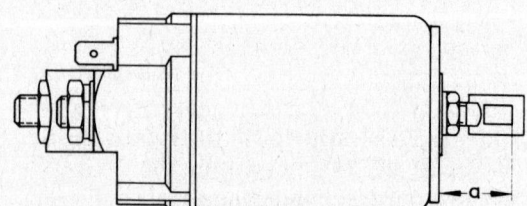

When installing a new solenoid, distance a should be 19 ± .1 mm. with the magnet drawn in.

Jump Starting

The following is the only correct, safe procedure for jump starting a car with a discharged battery. It is equally effective whether using a separate booster battery or one installed in another vehicle.

1. The basic safety principles to remember are:

    a. to avoid sparks, always connect the ground terminals last; always disconnect them first.

    b. to prevent serious electrical system damage, always connect batteries in parallel; never in series. Connect positive (+) to positive, and negative (−) to negative.

    c. batteries produce explosive hydrogen gas. Therefore, any nearby spark may cause an explosion, ruining the battery and possibly causing serious personal injury.

    d. make sure that the battery supplying the boost is of the proper voltage and amperage to handle the load. Do not use excessive voltage. Electrical system damage may result.

2. Connect the output (positive) terminals of both batteries with one jumper cable. This terminal is usually equipped with an insulated cable.

3. Connect one end of the second jumper cable to the ground (negative) terminal of the booster battery. This terminal is usually connected by a woven metal strap to the car frame or engine. To avoid sparks at the battery, connect the other end to a good ground on the car being started. The bumper or the engine is a convenient ground point.

4. Attempt to start the engine.

5. If the engine starts, disconnect the jumper cables. Always disconnect the ground (negative) cable first to avoid sparks.

6. If the engine does not start, do not leave the cables connected for any length of time, unless the engine in the car supplying the boost is running. If the batteries are left connected, without any incoming charge, the charges in both batteries will soon reach a state of equilibrium, possibly leaving both batteries too weak to start an engine.

The above procedure applies when both vehicles have negative ground electrical systems. A few vehicles, usually British, have a positive ground system. These vehicles can also be jump started or used to jump start another vehicle, provided that the safety principles in Step 1 are followed. Steps 2-6 do not apply in this case.

Fuel System

The Fuel Pump

The Volkswagen fuel pump, except on fuel injected engines, is mechanical, and of the diaphragm type, being push-rod operated from a cam on the distributor drive gear. The fuel flow is regulated automatically as the fuel is used up from the float bowl. The fuel pump consists of the top cover, containing the suction valve and the delivery valve, and the lower half, which contains the rocker mechanism.

As the distributor shaft turns, the cam on the distributor drive gear pushes the push rod against the rocker arm, which in turn pulls the diaphragm downward against the diaphragm spring. In this way a vacuum is created above the diaphragm, causing the lifting of the suction valve off its seat so that fuel can be drawn in. After the push rod moves away, the loaded diaphragm spring pushes the diaphragm upward, forcing the fuel in the pump through the delivery valve and to the carburetor. This process is repeated each time the distributor drive gear turns, which is once each two turns of the engine.

The pump pressure is determined by the amount the diaphragm spring is compressed during the suction stroke of the pump. The pressure of the spring is balanced by the upward force of the carburetor float on the needle valve. The higher the fuel level in the carburetor, the greater is the upward force on the needle valve. Under normal engine operation, the diaphragm of the fuel pump is moved only a fraction of an inch.

Other than cleaning the filter of the pump at regular intervals, no other maintenance is necessary. The push rod and pump rocker arm are lubricated by the lubricant in the lower part of the pump. The fuel pump filter on recent Volkswagen models is removed by unscrewing the hexagonal head plug from the side of the fuel pump assembly.

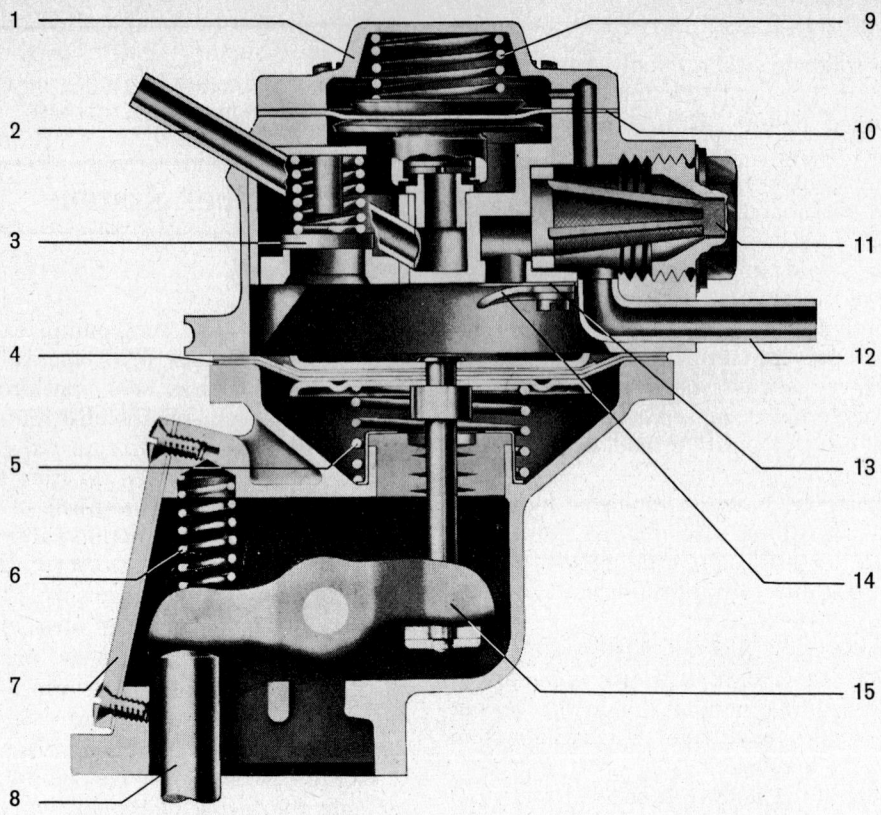

1. Cover
2. Fuel outlet
3. Pressure valve
4. Diaphragm
5. Diaphragm spring
6. Pump lever spring
7. Sealing plate
8. Push rod
9. Spring for cut-off
    diaphragm
10. Cut-off diaphragm
11. Strainer
12. Suction pipe
13. Suction valve
14. Suction valve retainer
15. Pump lever

Cross sectional view of a mechanical fuel pump.

MECHANICAL FUEL PUMP R & R

The fuel pump is removed by taking off the fuel line, disconnecting the hose from the pump, and removing the retaining nuts from the mounting studs. After the pump has been removed, the intermediate flange, push rod and gaskets can be removed. Be careful in handling the push rod, as it could be inconvenient to have to fish it out of the crankcase.

Once removed, the stroke of the fuel pump is adjusted by the insertion or removal of the proper number of flange gaskets. Adjustment is checked after installing the intermediate flange with two

gaskets and push rod, and nuts are tightened to the same tightness as if the entire pump were being installed. Normal full-stroke is approximately 4 mm. The length of the push rod stroke is measured from the pump contact surface on the intermediate flange, including gaskets.

When installing the fuel pump, care must be taken to install the intermediate flange before the push rod, otherwise the rod may fall through into the crankcase. Before installing the fuel pump, the lower chamber should be filled with universal grease. Tighten nuts to mounting studs, taking care not to overtighten. (Nuts should be retightened when the engine has

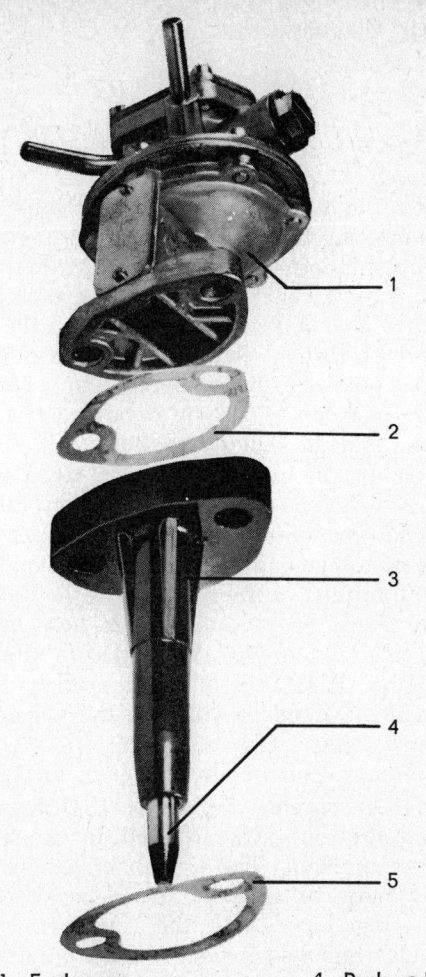

1. Fuel pump
2. Gasket
3. Plastic intermediate flange
4. Push rod
5. Gasket

Exploded view, lower portion of mechanical fuel pump.

Measuring mechanical fuel pump pushrod stroke from pump contact surface on intermediate flange.

reached operating temperature.) Connect the fuel line and hose, and check for correct seating of the fuel line rubber grommet in the panel of the engine compartment.

Fuel pump pressure can be checked by the insertion of a suitable gauge between the pump and the carburetor. Correct fuel pump pressure for various models is given in the Capacities and Pressures Chart.

Carburetor and Fuel Pump Rebuilding Kits

Carburetor and fuel pump repair and rebuilding kits are available at authorized Volkswagen dealers and various other sources. These kits contain the critical parts of the units to be rebuilt or repaired, and are well worth the money compared to the trading in of the old unit on a new one. Such kits are also handy to have on hand during long trips through low-population areas, because even the ultra-reliable Volkswagen sometimes (though rarely) becomes incapacitated due to unexpected failures in these two most important elements of the fuel system.

Electric Fuel Pump

ELECTRIC FUEL PUMP R & R

The electric fuel pump is mounted at the front of the chassis. There are three fuel lines, suction, pressure, and return.

To remove the pump:

1. Pinch clamp the fuel lines shut to prevent leakage.
2. Unplug the electrical cable plug.
3. Cut off original hose clamps. Pull off the hoses and catch the fuel which drains out.
4. Raise the pressure hose to prevent draining the fuel loop line.
5. Unbolt and remove the pump.

To replace the pump:

1. Connect the three fuel hoses. Install screw type hose clamps at all three connections.
2. Bolt the pump to the mounting supports.
3. Remove the pinch clamps from the hoses.
4. Install the cable plug. The brown negative ground wire must be to the bottom and the half circular cavity toward the right. Install the protective plug cap.

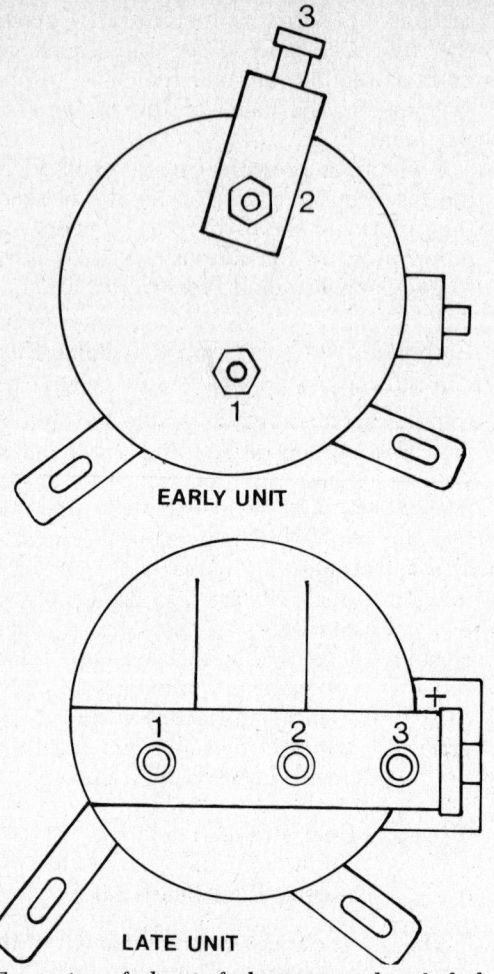

EARLY UNIT

LATE UNIT

Front view of electric fuel pumps used with fuel injection system. Suction (1), pressure (2), and return (3) connections are shown.

Air Cleaner

AIR CLEANER R & R

On type 1 models, the air cleaner is removed by taking the preheater pipe(s) from the intake tube of the air cleaner, disconnecting the thermostatic flap control wire, pulling the crankcase breather hose from the cleaner, and loosening the clamp screw that holds the cleaner onto the carburetor throat. After the air cleaner has been removed, the top part can be separated from the lower part by removing the clips that hold the halves together.

When the cleaner has been taken apart, the dirty oil should be poured out and the lower part cleaned. The upper part does not generally require cleaning. The bottom part of the air cleaner should then be filled to the mark with new engine oil of the same viscosity as that used in the engine. If there is no mark, refill with the quantity of oil specified in the Capacities and Pressures Chart.

Removal of the air cleaner in the type 3 dual carburetor engine is slightly more complex, but accomplished in much the same manner. The right-hand connecting rod must be removed from between the rotating lever and the carburetor, the cables removed from the automatic choke and electromagnetic pilot jet, the crankcase ventilation hose taken off the air

The dual carburetor type 3 engine's air cleaner is fastened down at three points. The center wingnut should always be loosened first and tightened last to avoid disturbing the linkage adjustment.

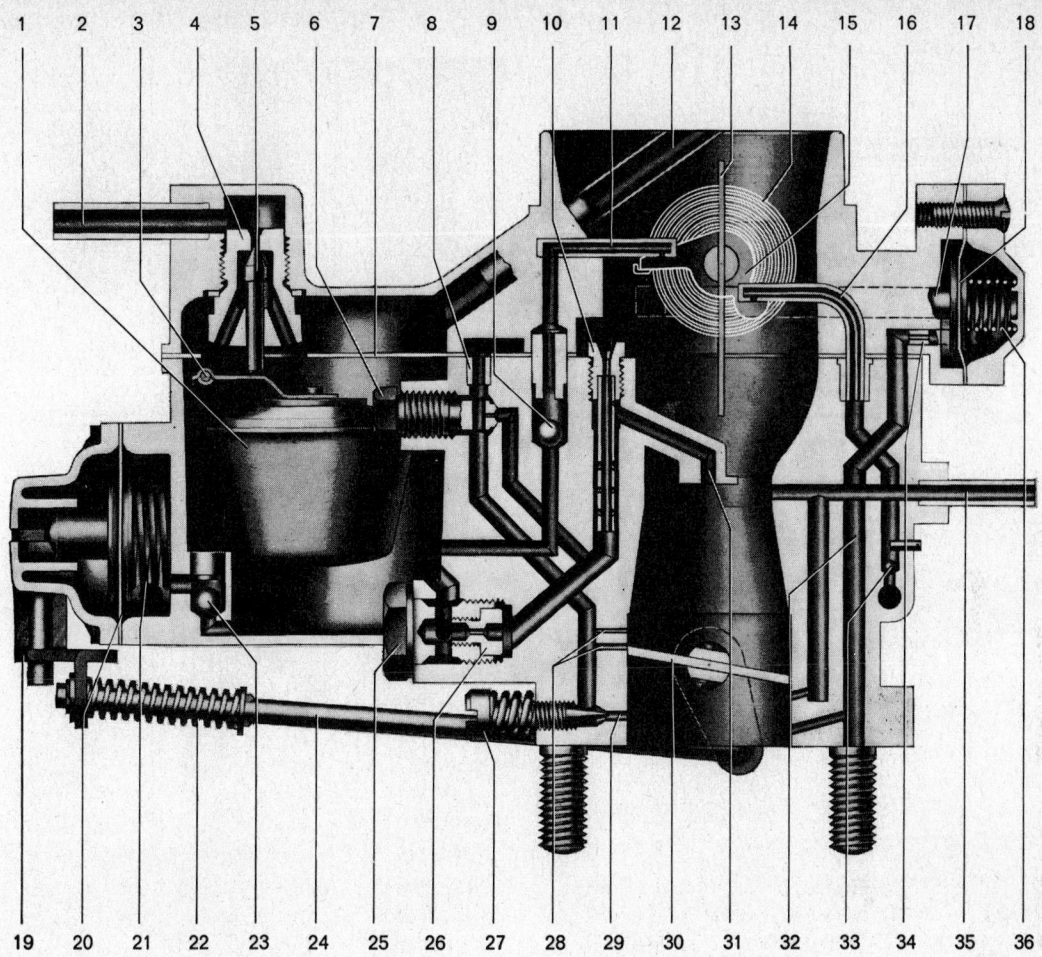

1. Float
2. Fuel line
3. Float lever
4. Float needle valve
5. Float needle
6. Pilot jet
7. Gasket
8. Pilot air drilling
9. Ball check valve in power fuel system
10. Air correction jet with emulsion tube
11. Power fuel tube
12. Float bowl vent tube
13. Choke valve
14. Bi-metal spring
15. Operating lever
16. Accelerator pump discharge tube
17. Diaphragm rod
18. Vacuum diaphragm

19. Pump lever
20. Pump diaphragm
21. Spring
22. Push rod spring
23. Ball check valve for accelerator pump
24. Pump connector rod
25. Main jet carrier
26. Main jet
27. Volume control screw
28. By-pass port
29. Idle port
30. Throttle valve
31. Discharge arm
32. Vacuum drilling
33. Ball check valve in accelerator pump drilling
34. Jet in vacuum drilling
35. Vacuum connection
36. Diaphragm spring

Solex 28 PICT-1 carburetor used on 1,200 cc. engines.

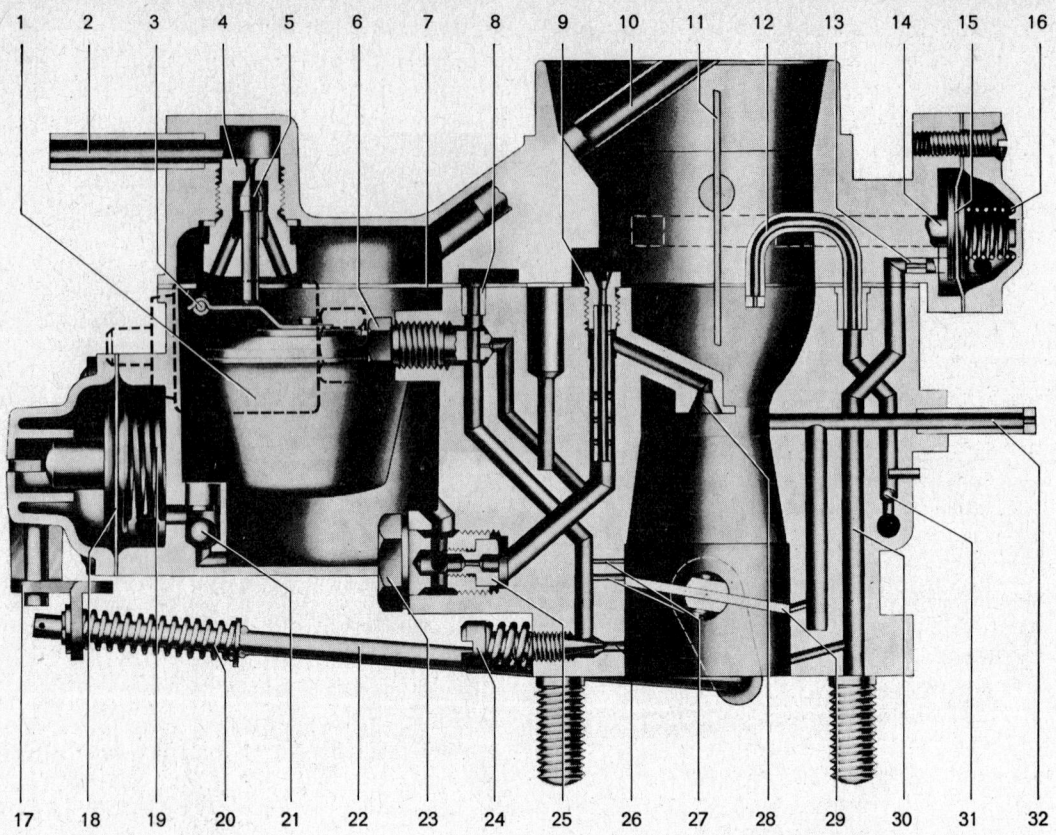

1. Float
2. Fuel line
3. Float lever
4. Float needle valve
5. Float needle
6. Electro-magnetic pilot jet
7. Gasket
8. Pilot air drilling
9. Air correction jet with emulsion tube
10. Float bowl vent tube
11. Choke valve
12. Accelerator pump discharge
    tube
13. Jet in vacuum drilling
14. Diaphragm rod
15. Vacuum diaphragm
16. Spring for vacuum diaphragm
17. Pump lever
18. Pump diaphragm

19. Pump spring
20. Spring
21. Ball check valve for accelerator
    pump
22. Pull rod for accelerator pump
23. Main jet carrier
24. Volume control screw
25. Main jet
26. Idle port
27. By-pass port
28. Discharge arm
29. Throttle valve
30. Vacuum drilling
31. Ball check valve in accelerator
    pump drilling
32. Vacuum connection

The carburetors on the Karmann
Ghia models are fitted with a power
fuel system.

Solex 30 PICT-1 carburetor used on 1,300 and 1,500 cc. engines.

cleaner, and the three wing nuts unscrewed. The center wing nut is removed before removing the air cleaner; those at each of the carburetors remain in place. After the center wing nut is removed, the air cleaner can be lifted from its position and the upper and lower parts separated.

When installing the air cleaner of the type 3 engine, care should be taken to see that the oil is up to the mark, that the rubber sealing ring on each carburetor is secure, that the water drain hole is free in the lower part of the air cleaner, and that the marks are lined up when the upper and lower halves are put back together. If the marks do not line up exactly, the intake pipe will point in the wrong direction and be either difficult or impossible to connect to the intake extension. When tightening the wing nuts of the air cleaner, it is very important that the outer wing nuts are tightened down first. There is an expansion-contraction joint between the left outer wing nut and the center wing nut which makes these not quite so critical. However, there is no such joint between the center and right-hand wing nuts. Subsequently, if the center nut is tightened first, and then the right-hand nut, the result could be a slight movement on the part of the right-hand carburetor, thus causing an alteration in a very sensitive adjustment. Tighten down the center wing nut only after the two outer wing nuts have been fully tightened.

To remove the air cleaner from fuel injected engines:
1. Detach crankcase and auxiliary air regulator hoses.
2. Loosen hose clamps at either end of air cleaner. Pull off rubber hoses.
3. Remove wingnut and air cleaner.

To clean, refill, and replace air cleaner on fuel injected engines:
1. Release three clips. Remove top section.
2. Clean filter assembly out and refill with SAE 30 oil to the red mark. SAE 10 may be used in arctic climates.
3. Be sure that red arrows on top and bottom sections are aligned when reassembling.
4. Reconnect hoses, tighten clamps and wingnut.

Carburetor

Carburetor R & R

On the type 1, remove the pre-heat hose

from the air cleaner intake pipe. Disconnect the thermostatic flap control wire. Disconnect the crankcase breather hose from the air cleaner intake. Loosen the air cleaner holding clamp and remove the air cleaner. Disconnect the fuel and vacuum hoses from the carburetor. Disconnect the wires from the automatic choke and the electromagnetic pilot jet. Disconnect the throttle cable at the carburetor and take off the spring, pin and spring retaining plate. Take off the two carburetor retaining nuts and remove the carburetor from the intake manifold. The throttle positioner may be removed in unit with the carburetor. It would, at this point, be a good idea to stuff part of a clean rag into the intake manifold hole in order to ensure that dirt and other foreign matter will not find its way into the manifold and cause damage to the engine.

Installation of the carburetor is the reverse of the previous operation. When

Main jet can be removed after unscrewing plug 1. 2 is idle mixture control screw.

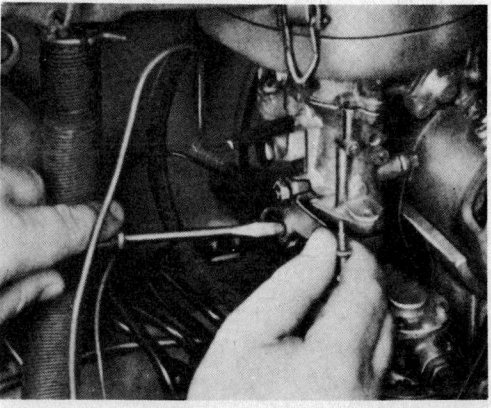

With throttle valve fully open and accelerator pedal floored, there should be a slight clearance (about 1 mm.) between the throttle lever and the stop on the carburetor body.

installing the carburetor, it is advisable that a new intake manifold gasket be used. The retaining nuts should be tightened evenly, but not too tightly. The accelerator cable should be adjusted so that there is very little play (about 1 mm.) between the throttle lever and the stop point on the carburetor body when the pedal is fully depressed. The idle speed should be checked with the engine at operating temperature.

On the type 3, remove the air cleaner as described earlier. Be sure that the electrical connections are removed from the automatic chokes and the electromagnetic pilot jets. Remove the connecting rods from between the center lever and the left- and right-hand carburetors. Disconnect the carburetor return springs and pull off the spark plug connecting caps. Remove the balance tube from between the carburetors by pulling it out of the connecting hoses on either side. Remove the nuts that hold the intake manifolds to the cylinder heads. Remove intake pipes, cylinder head gaskets, and take carburetors off of intake pipes.

Installation of the type 3 carburetors is the reverse of the preceding. New gaskets should be used on the cylinder head intake, and the carburetor gaskets should be inspected for damage and replaced if need be.

Carburetor Disassembly and Assembly

Disassembly of all Volkswagen carburetors is covered by much the same procedure. After removing the five screws that retain the top part of the carburetor, take off the upper part. Remove the float, needle valve, and needle valve gasket. Remove automatic choke housing, retaining ring, and bi-metallic spring. The choke unit is attached by three retaining screws. Remove the accelerator pump cotter pin (connects pump lever to connecting rod). Remove the four screws from pump housing, and remove the pump diaphragm and spring. The main jet and the volume control screws should be removed, along with the plug that allows access to the main jet.

After disassembly, clean all parts in a suitable solvent, except for the cover of the automatic choke unit. After cleaning through soaking and rubbing with soft cloth,

all jets, valves and drillings should be blown out with compressed air. Mouth pressure or the pressure from a simple tire pump is not enough. If necessary, pack the pieces into a box and head for the place where you usually buy gasoline. It is highly probable that the attendant will be glad to lend you the use of his compressed air hose. Especially important in the compressed air cleaning process is the cleaning of the needle valve. When cleaning the carburetor passageways and jets, do not use pins, pipe cleaners, or other pieces of wire. The drillings are finely calibrated and might be damaged or enlarged through such mistreatment.

When taking the carburetor apart for cleaning, it is not necessary that every single part be dismantled. It is sufficient for most purposes to remove only the major components, along with the needle valve, float, main jet and accelerator pump diaphragm. The most important part of the entire operation is probably the blowing out with compressed air of all passageways.

On reassembly, check the needle valve for proper operation. On the type 3, the height of the accelerator pump injector tube opening should be 12 mm. (.47″) from the upper part of the carburetor (9 mm. for engine nos. T0244544 and onward). When the carburetor is assembled, the injector tube should squirt gasoline directly into the gap between the throttle valve and the carbu-

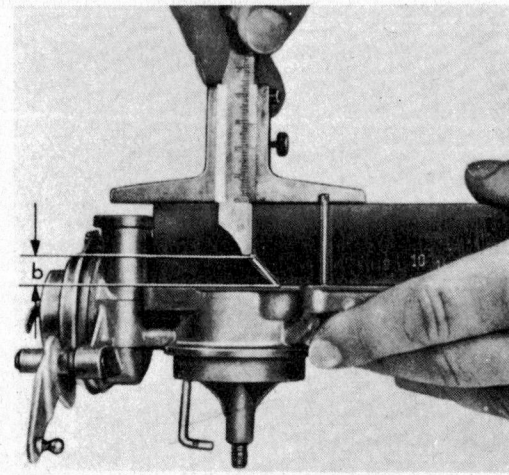

The height of the injector tube opening from the upper part of the 32 PDSIT-2/3 carburetor should be 12 mm. for engines up to number TO244544, 9 mm. thereafter.

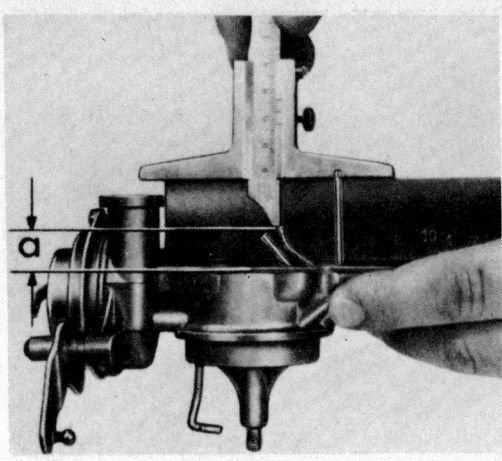

Height of power fuel tube opening from upper part of 32 PDSIT-2/3 carburetor should be 15 mm. on carburetors equipped with power fuel system.

Measuring throttle valve gap of 32 PDSIT-2/3 carburetor. Gap should be .60–.65 mm. (.024–.026″).

retor throat when the accelerator pump is displaced. The power fuel tube opening of the type 3 dual carburetor models should be 15 mm. (.59″) from the upper part of the carburetor. When the carburetor is assembled this tube should point roughly in the center of the gap between the discharge arm and the venturi. When replacing the cover of the automatic choke, be sure that the hooked end of the bi-metallic spring engages the operating lever. The mark on the cover of the choke should line up with the center lug on the upper part of the carburetor. When fastening down the automatic choke cover, care should be taken not to over-tighten the retaining screws. Be

sure to put the proper choke on the proper carburetor. They are not interchangeable.

The diaphragm of the accelerator pump should be checked for leakage, and replaced if defective. The diaphragm should be tightened down while pressed in the pressure stroke position. On the type 3, the length of the operating rod should be adjusted so that a gap of .60–.65 mm. (.024–.026″) exists at the throttle valve when the choke valve is closed. This gap should be measured with a wire feeler gauge while the throttle valve is pushed lightly in the closing direction. After tightening the two nuts on the operating rod, be sure that the parts have sufficient freedom of movement.

In the type 3, the amount of fuel injected by the accelerator pump can be adjusted by altering the position of the cotter pin on the connecting rod. Moving the cotter pin from the center to either the outer or the inner hole of the connecting rod will result in either less or more fuel injected when the throttle valve is moved from the fully closed to the fully opened position:

Hole in Rod	Quantity of Fuel
inner	larger (by .3 cc)
center	normal
outer	smaller (by .3 cc)

Checking Electromagnetic Pilot Jet

If the engine is equipped with an electromagnetic pilot jet in the carburetor, and still shows a tendency to "run-on" af-

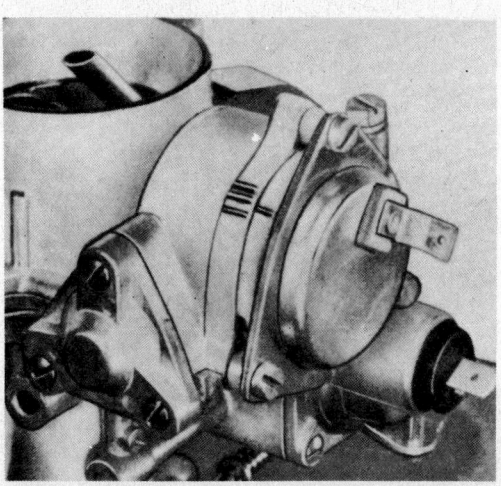

Choke housing cover alignment, type 1 single carburetor shown.

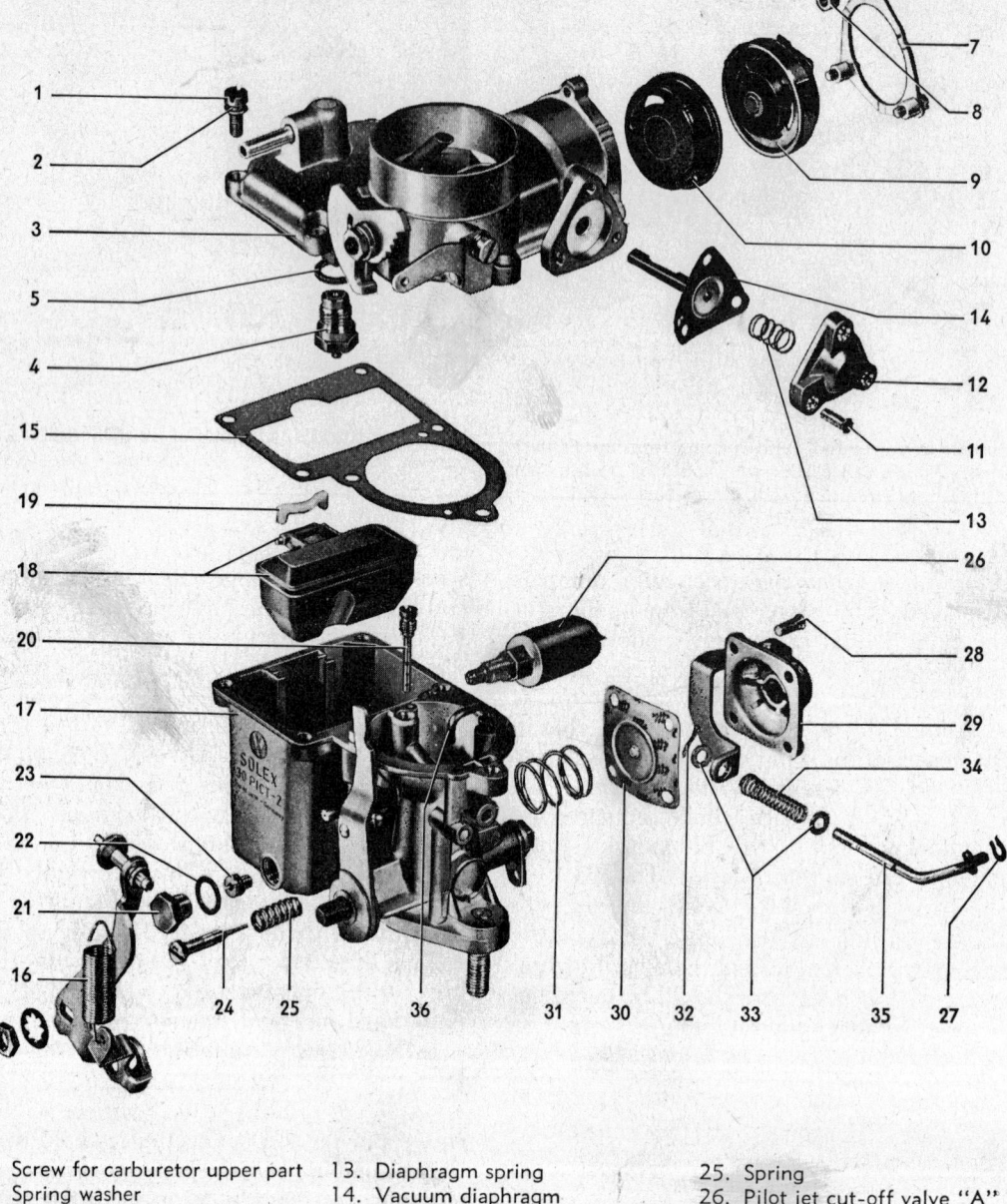

1. Screw for carburetor upper part
2. Spring washer
3. Carburetor upper part
4. Float needle valve 1.5mm diameter
5. Washer 15 x 12 x 1 mm for float needle valve
6. Screw for retaining ring
7. Retaining ring for cap
8. Spacer for retaining ring
9. Choke unit with spring and heater element
10. Plastic cap
11. Fillister head screw
12. Cover for vacuum diaphragm
13. Diaphragm spring
14. Vacuum diaphragm
15. Gasket
16. Return spring for accelerator cable
17. Carburetor lower part
18. Float and pin
19. Bracket for float pin
20. Air correction jet
21. Plug for main jet
22. Plug seal
23. Main jet
24. Volume control screw (designation 1, 2 and 3)
25. Spring
26. Pilot jet cut-off valve "A"
27. Circlip
28. Fillister head screw
29. Cover for pump
30. Pump diaphragm
31. Spring for diaphragm
32. Cotter pin 1.5 x 15 mm
33. Washer 4.2 mm
34. Spring for connecting rod
35. Connecting rod
36. Injector tube for accelerator pump

Solex 30 PICT-2 carburetor used on 1968-69 1,500 cc. engines with throttle positioner.

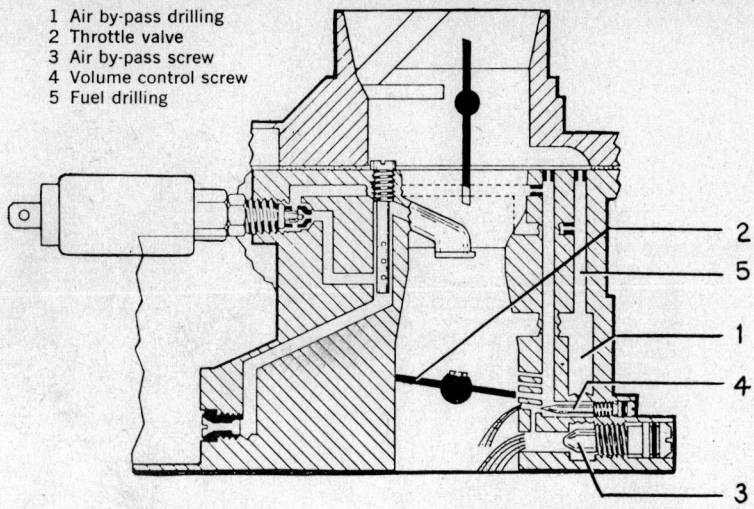

1 Air by-pass drilling
2 Throttle valve
3 Air by-pass screw
4 Volume control screw
5 Fuel drilling

Solex 30 PICT-3 carburetor used on 1970 1,600 cc. type 1 and 2 engines. Idling speed adjustments are made with the air bypass screw.

ter being shut off, chances are that the electromagnetic jet is defective. Operation can be checked by turning on the ignition and touching the slip-on connector against the terminal of the jet. If the jet is operating properly, a clicking sound will be heard each time the connector touches the terminal. When the current is off, the needle of this jet moves so as to block off the fuel supply, so when the connector is removed while the engine is running, it should stop the engine.

On 1971 type 1 and 2 engines with the Solex 34 PICT-3 carburetor, the pilot jet cutoff valve has been replaced by an idle bypass mixture cutoff valve. The new unit performs the same function.

CARBURETOR ADJUSTMENT

As a part of a routine tune-up it is necessary only to adjust the idling speed and mixture screws on the carburetors of most single carburetor Volkswagens. On 1970 and later type 1 and 2 engines, the volume control screw is factory set and the throttle valve remains closed during idling. Idling speed adjustments are made with the air bypass screw. On the 30 PICT-3 carburetor (1970), the air bypass screw is below the volume control screw. On the 34 PICT-3 carburetor (1971), the air bypass screw is above the volume control screw. Before adjustment is begun, the engine should be at normal operating temperature and the idle adjusting screw must not be resting on the

Idle speed adjustment, pre-1970 type 1 and 2.

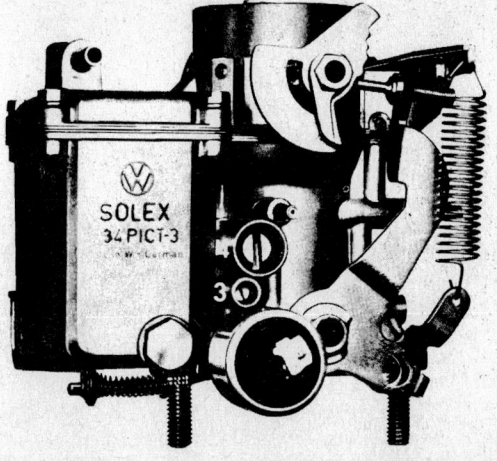

Adjustment screws on Solex 34 PICT-3 carburetor, 1971 type 1 and 2. 3 is the volume screw. 4 is the air bypass screw.

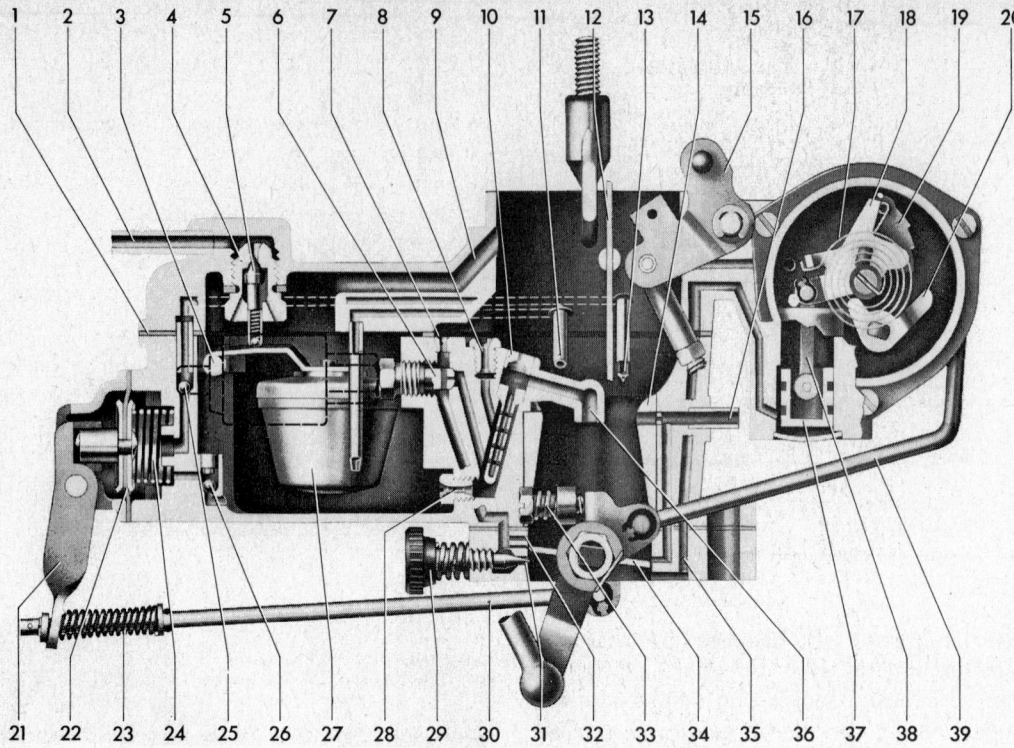

1. Gasket
2. Fuel pipe
3. Float pin
4. Float needle valve
5. Float needle
6. Pilot jet
7. Pilot air bleed drilling
8. Air correction jet
9. Vent passage for float chamber
10. Emulsion tube with ventilation jet
11. Power fuel pipe
12. Choke valve
13. Injector tube accelerator pump
14. Venturi
15. Relay lever
16. Vacuum connection
17. Bi-metal coil
18. Intermediate lever
19. Fast idle cam
20. Stop lever
21. Pump lever
22. Pump diaphragm
23. Connecting rod spring
24. Diaphragm spring
25. Ball pressure valve
26. Ball suction valve
27. Float
28. Main jet
29. Volume control screw
30. Connecting rod
31. Idling mixture port
32. By-pass port
33. Idle adjustment screw
34. Throttle valve
35. Vacuum drilling
36. Discharge arm
37. Vacuum piston
38. Piston rod
39. Operating rod

Solex 32 PDSIT-2 carburetor used on dual carburetor type 3 engine. The 32 PDSIT-2 is the left carburetor, and has a double vacuum drilling for the distributor advance mechanism.

fast idle cam of the automatic choke. The following steps should be followed in setting the idle speed and mixture adjustments on single-carburetor Volkswagen engines:

(1) With the engine warm and running, turn the idling speed adjusting screw in or out until the proper idling speed is attained. The correct speed can be found in the Tune-Up Specifications Chart and on the sticker on the engine.

(2) With the engine running at the proper idle speed, turn the idle mixture control screw slowly clockwise until the engine speed begins to drop, then turn slowly in the counterclockwise direction until the engine is running smoothly again. Now turn the mixture control screw another ¼ turn in the counterclockwise direction.

(3) If necessary, re-adjust the idle speed. With the clutch pedal depressed, the engine should continue to run after the accelerator has been quickly depressed and released. If the engine stalls, either the mixture adjustment or the idle speed adjustment is incorrect and should be remedied.

NOTE: *the setting of the slow-speed (idle) mixture will have a great influence on the performance and economy of the Volkswagen at speeds as great as fifty or sixty miles per hour. If the mixture is too rich, the result will be excess fuel consumption, stalling when the accelerator pedal is suddenly released, and possible "running on" when the ignition switch is turned off. If the mixture is too lean (too much air, not enough gasoline), the result will be better fuel consumption, but exhaust valves may suffer burning or warping. The previously-given method for adjusting the slow-speed adjustment will give the proper mixture setting. Turning the mixture screw clockwise will lean the mixture, while turning counterclockwise will enrich it.*

Carburetor Adjustment—Dual Carburetor Models

On certain type 3 models, there are two carburetors—one for each bank of two cylinders. While the current models are equipped with a fuel injection system, type 3 vehicles sold in the U.S.A. in 1966 and 1967 have dual carburetors and require slightly more sophistication in the tune-up operation. Adjusting the carburetors on the dual-carb models requires the use of a special instrument to measure air flow. A commonly-used product is that known as

1. Accelerator cable
2. Connecting rod, right
3. Connecting rod, left
4. Carburetor pull rod with return spring

Dual carburetor linkage.

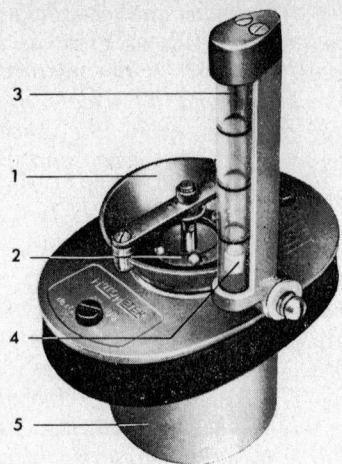

1. Funnel shaped opening
2. Adjustable throttle disc
3. Measuring glass
4. Piston in measuring glass
5. Distance piece

Device used to balance dual carburetors. The volume of air being taken in is indicated by the height of the piston in the measuring glass.

the Uni-Syn, available for under $10 from most mail-order auto accessory sources. This device measures the vacuum created by carburetor suction by means of a red piston which rides up and down inside a graded glass tube. The higher the vacuum, the higher the piston is raised.

Besides the synchronizing device mentioned above, a small frozen-juice can will also be required in order that the device will fit on the air horns of the carburetors. Because of the screws that stick straight up from the air horn for the purpose of holding the air cleaner, the small can (open on both ends) is needed. By mounting it on top of the can, the test device will clear the screws without losing vacuum. Before attempting adjustment, the engine must be at operating temperature.

Adjustment Steps

(1) Remove the right-hand connecting rod of the carburetor linkage system. This is the rod which connects the center bell crank with the right-hand carburetor throttle.

(2) Remove the air cleaner. It is held on by two wing nuts on each carburetor and one wing nut in the center. The connections to the air intake and to

the crankcase ventilation system must also be removed.

(3) With the engine running, adjust the idle speed adjusting screw of each carburetor until the correct idling speed is attained. Each carburetor should then be sucking the same amount of air. When the test device is moved from one carburetor to the other, the height of the red piston should not change more than one inch, preferably less. Because of the fine adjustment possible with the use of the idle speed adjusting screws there is no excuse for not being able to adjust the carburetor idle speeds so that the maximum variation is less than one-quarter of an inch. When checking the air flow through each carburetor, the disc on the device should be turned clockwise or counterclockwise until the piston rides approximately in the center of the range.

(4) In adjusting the volume control screw of each carburetor, slowly turn the screw clockwise until the engine speed begins to drop, then turn counterclockwise until the engine runs smoothly once again, then a further ¼ of a turn in the counterclockwise direction.

(5) Recheck the idle speed adjustment, and if necessary increase or decrease the idle speed of each carburetor so that the correct speed is maintained and the test device shows the same reading when it is moved from one carburetor to the other without moving the disc on the device.

(6) Recheck the adjustment on the mixture control screws. On the 1600 models, there is present on each screw a raised portion on the outside perimeter. This will enable one to feel the position of the screw when he cannot see it. The correct position for the mixture control screw will be approximately 1½ turns from the screwed-in position. When turning the screw fully in the closed position, care should be taken not to apply too much torque, for the seat or needle of the screw could be damaged in this way.

(7) After the mixture adjustment has been rechecked the idle speed and

balance should also be checked again and corrected if necessary.

(8) In checking the balance of the carburetors at an increased speed, it is necessary to install once again the right-hand connecting rod which was removed in step (1). By means of a suitable object (e.g. a tool box) wedged against the accelerator pedal, the engine speed should be maintained at approximately 1,200–1,500 RPM in order to check the higher-speed balance of the two carburetors.

(9) Apply the test device to the left-hand carburetor and adjust the disc until the red piston rides in the center of the range. Now move the device over to the right-hand carburetor and, without moving the disc, compare the height of the piston here with the height achieved at the left carburetor. If the height of the piston is higher on the right side, the length of the right-hand connecting rod must be increased slightly. If the height of the piston is lower on the right side, the length of the right-hand connecting rod will have to be decreased. Changing the length of the right-hand control rod is ac-

complished by loosening the nuts on both ends and twisting the rod while leaving the ends stationary. The opposite ends have threads which tighten in opposite directions. The length of the right control rod must be adjusted until there is little or no difference between the readings of the test device when it is moved from one carburetor to the other.

(Hint: for a really fine adjustment, it is possible to loosen only one of the control rod ends and turn it slightly in the desired direction. If loosening and moving this end is not sufficient to effect the adjustment needed, then the opposite end must also be loosened and moved slightly after the first end has been tightened. This is a step-by-step method which is guaranteed to be more accurate than simply loosening both ends and tightening them up again at the same time. It is quite impossible to avoid changing the setting when tightening the ends. Ordinarily the ends are offset by 90 degrees, but the step-by-step method takes into consideration that the ends may be offset slightly more or less if

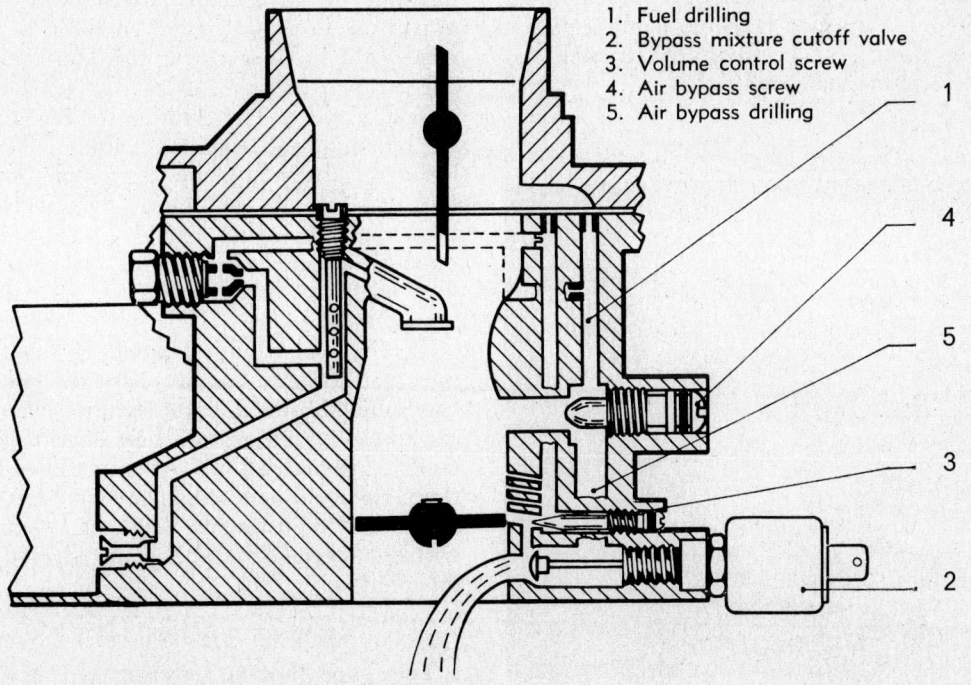

1. Fuel drilling
2. Bypass mixture cutoff valve
3. Volume control screw
4. Air bypass screw
5. Air bypass drilling

Solex 34 PICT-3 carburetor used on 1971 1,600 cc. type 1 and 2 engines. The volume control screw is factory set. Idling speed adjustments are made with the air bypass screw.

it will contribute to a more accurate balance.

(10) After low-speed and high-speed balance has been checked, the connecting rods should be lubricated at their ends with lithium grease and the carburetor's moving parts lubricated with a light oil.

(11) Reinstall the oil bath air cleaner, being careful to tighten the two outer wing nuts first, and then the center wing nut. If the center wing nut is tightened first, it is possible that the adjustment of the right-hand carburetor will be altered when the air cleaner is fastened tightly to the screw protruding from its air horn. Replace the crankcase ventilation hose and air intake connections. In order to install the air cleaner it will be necessary to remove the right-hand carburetor connecting rod temporarily. Take care not to bend this rod.

ACCELERATOR CABLE R & R, TYPE 1

The Volkswagen accelerator cable runs from the accelerator pedal to the carburetor by means of the central tunnel, the fan housing and the throttle valve lever. Guide tubes are used in both the central frame tunnel and the fan housing, while a plastic hose is present between the tunnel and the front engine cover plate.

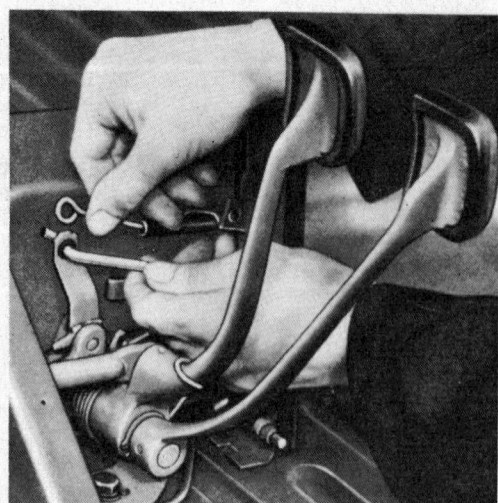

Accelerator cable is removed from the front of the car and is attached as shown.

To remove the accelerator cable, disconnect the cable from the throttle lever pin, raise the rear of the car, and pull the cable through from the front of the car after disconnecting the rod from the accelerator pedal.

Installation is the reverse of the removal. Grease the cable well before inserting from the front of the car. Be sure that the rear rubber boot and hose are properly seated, so that water will not enter the guide tubes. In order to avoid excessive strain of the throttle cable and assembly, there should be about 1 mm. (.04") clearance between the throttle stop and the carburetor body when the throttle is in the wide-open position. For this reason, it is advisable that the cable be tightened down at the carburetor end only when the accelerator pedal is at the fully-floored position.

Fuel Injection System

The Bosch electronic fuel injection system is used on all type 3 and 4 vehicles, beginning with 1968 models. Fuel pressure in the system is maintained at a constant 28 psi by an electric pump and a pressure regulator. Excess fuel bled off by the pressure regulator is routed back to the tank. Opening of the injector valves is timed by a pair of breaker trigger contacts in the base of the ignition distributor. The injector valves open in pairs; cylinders No. 1 and 4, and 2 and 3. The duration of the injector opening, and thus the volume of fuel injected, is regulated by the famous black box, or electronic computer. This unit takes into account inputs from sensors which measure engine temperature, air temperature, engine vacuum, air density, and throttle opening.

Testing and troubleshooting of the fuel injection system requires special Bosch electronic testing apparatus. For this reason, these operations are best left to qualified personnel at an authorized dealer's shop. Removal and replacement of components, and adjustments that can be made without special equipment are covered in this section.

IDLE SPEED ADJUSTMENT

The only tune-up adjustment possible on the Bosch electronic fuel injection system is that for idle speed. The adjusting

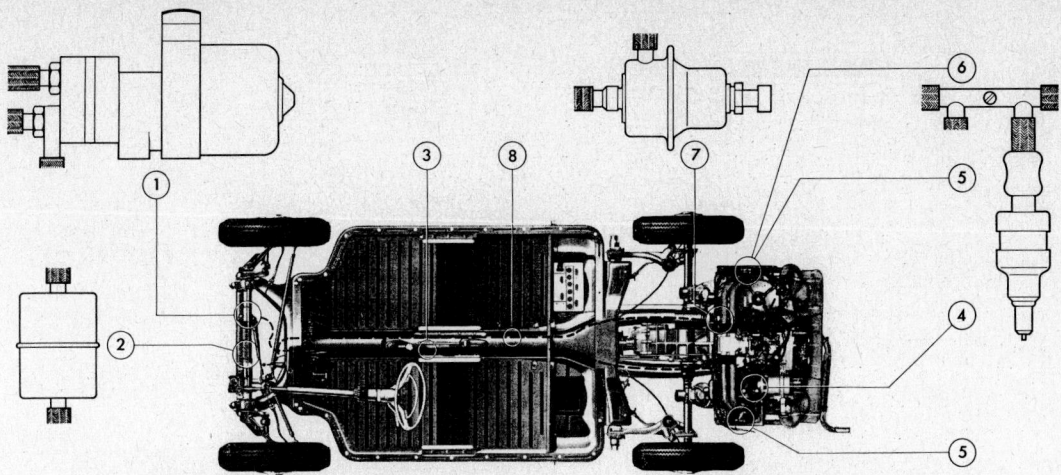

Fuel system of the fuel-injected engine: (1) electric fuel pump, (2) filter, (3) pressure line, (4) ring main, (5) electro-magnetic fuel injectors, (6) distributor pipes, (7) pressure regulator, and (8) return line.

Fuel system of the fuel injected engine.

Adjusting idle speed on fuel injected engine. Turn screw toward a to increase speed. Turn locknut toward c to tighten.

screw is located on the left side of the intake air distributor. Early models have a knurled screw with a lockspring; current models have a locknut on the adjusting screw. After adjusting idle speed to specifications, make sure that the throttle valve is completely closed at idle.

THROTTLE VALVE SWITCH ADJUSTMENT

The throttle valve switch is mounted to a base plate with graduated markings secured to the intake air distributor inlet. An align-ment mark is located on the air distributor housing. The switch is affixed by two mounting screws and an electrical plug. To adjust the switch:

1. Remove air cleaner for access.
2. Close throttle valve completely.
3. Loosen base plate mounting screws. Slowly rotate switch and plate assembly counterclockwise until a click is heard.
4. Continue rotating switch and plate assembly counterclockwise one more graduation. (Each graduation indicates 2°.)
5. Tighten base plate mounting screws.
6. Throttle valve switch should come into operation when throttle has moved 4°

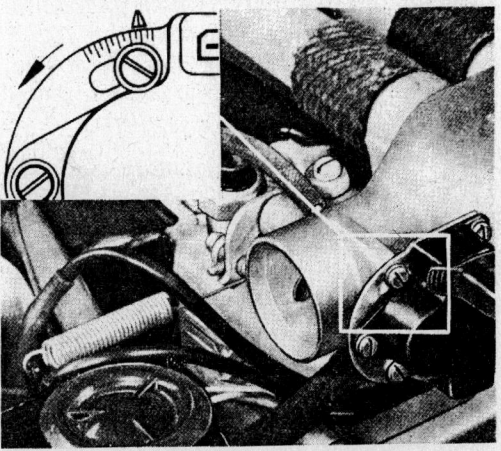

Throttle valve switch details. Each graduation indicates 2°.

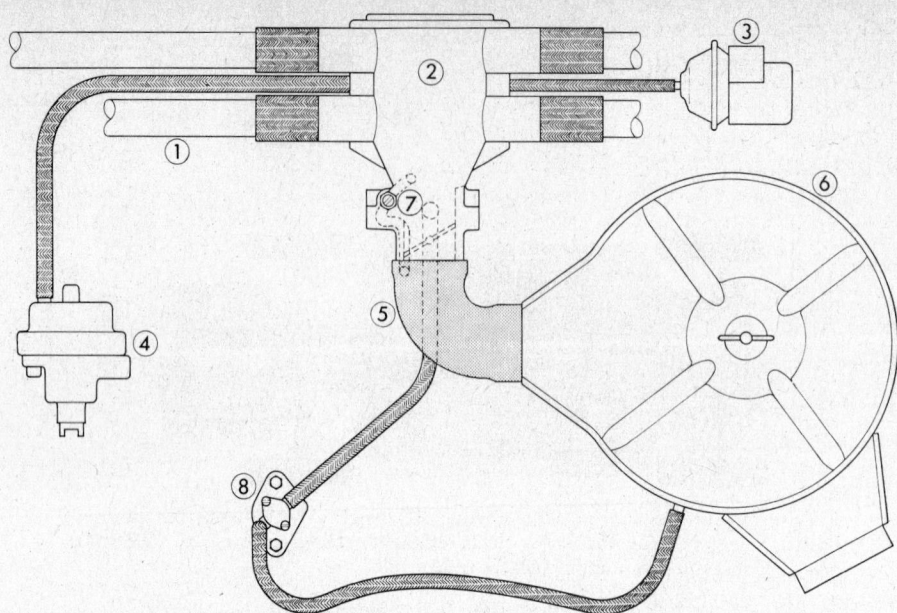

Air system of the fuel-injected engine: (1) intake pipes, (2) intake air distributor, (3) pressure switch, (4) pressure sensor, (5) idle air circuit, (6) air cleaner, (7) idling air screw, (8) auxiliary air regulator.

Air system of the fuel injected engine.

from the closed position. Unhook throttle return spring and check that throttle is not binding.

7. Replace throttle spring and air cleaner.

PRESSURE REGULATOR ADJUSTMENT

The pressure regulator is located on the front engine cover plate beneath the right side of the intake manifold. It is fitted with an adjusting nut and a locknut. There is a T-fitting for a pressure gauge in the fuel loop line between the takeoff points for the right side injector units. This fitting is normally plugged with a stop screw.

NOTE: *before making any adjustment, be absolutely certain that the pressure gauge being used is accurate.*

To adjust the pressure regulator:

1. Remove the air cleaner for access.
2. Attach the pressure gauge securely to the T-fitting.
3. Start the engine and allow it to idle. Make sure that the idle speed is correct. Adjustment of idling speed is explained in Chapter 2.
4. If the pressure reading is not 28 psi (2 atmospheres), loosen the locknut and regulate the pressure with the adjusting nut.

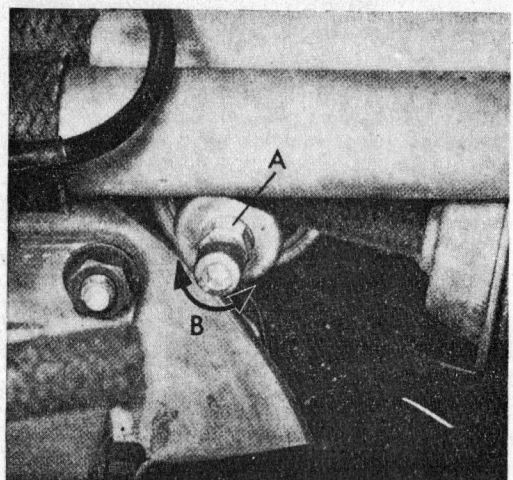

Pressure regulator, located under right side of the intake manifold. A is the locknut; B is the adjusting nut.

5. Tighten the locknut. Check that pressure is still correct.
6. Stop engine. Disconnect pressure gauge and plug T-fitting with stop screw. Replace air cleaner.

INJECTOR R & R

To remove the injectors on either side of the engine:

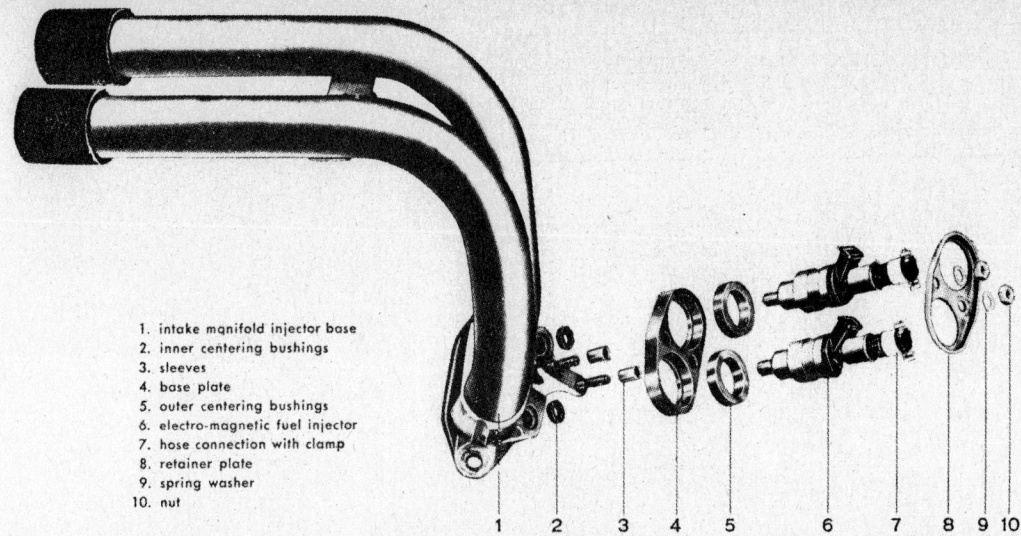

1. intake manifold injector base
2. inner centering bushings
3. sleeves
4. base plate
5. outer centering bushings
6. electro-magnetic fuel injector
7. hose connection with clamp
8. retainer plate
9. spring washer
10. nut

1   2   3   4   5   6   7   8 9 10

Details of injectors and right side of intake manifold.

1. Remove both cable plugs.
2. Unscrew both retainer plate nuts.
3. Pull out both injectors with retainer plate, centering bushings, base plate, and stud sleeves. Be sure to remove the inner bushings from the intake manifold base.
4. Loosen the hose clamps and pull out the injectors. Be careful not to damage the needles.
5. Reverse the procedure to replace the injectors. Use lockwashers under the retaining nuts. Torque them to 4.3 ft. lbs. Install cable plug with gray protective cap toward rear of car, and plug with black cap at front.

FUEL FILTER R & R

The fuel filter is in the pump suction line, either near to, or mounted on the fuel pump. It should be replaced every 6,000 miles. To replace the filter:

1. Pinch clamp the fuel lines shut on either side of the filter.
2. Remove the pin holding the filter bracket to the pump. Remove the filter.
3. Install the new filter making sure that the arrow points to the pump. Replace the bracket and pin.
4. Install screw type hose clamps on the fuel lines.

Fuel filter, which must be replaced periodically. The arrow shown must point to the pump.

Exhaust System

Exhaust Pipe, Muffler and Tail Pipe

R & R, Muffler

To remove the muffler from all Volkswagen models, first remove the clamps from the muffler and heat exchangers. (Early 1963 and earlier models do not have exchangers.) Remove clips connect-

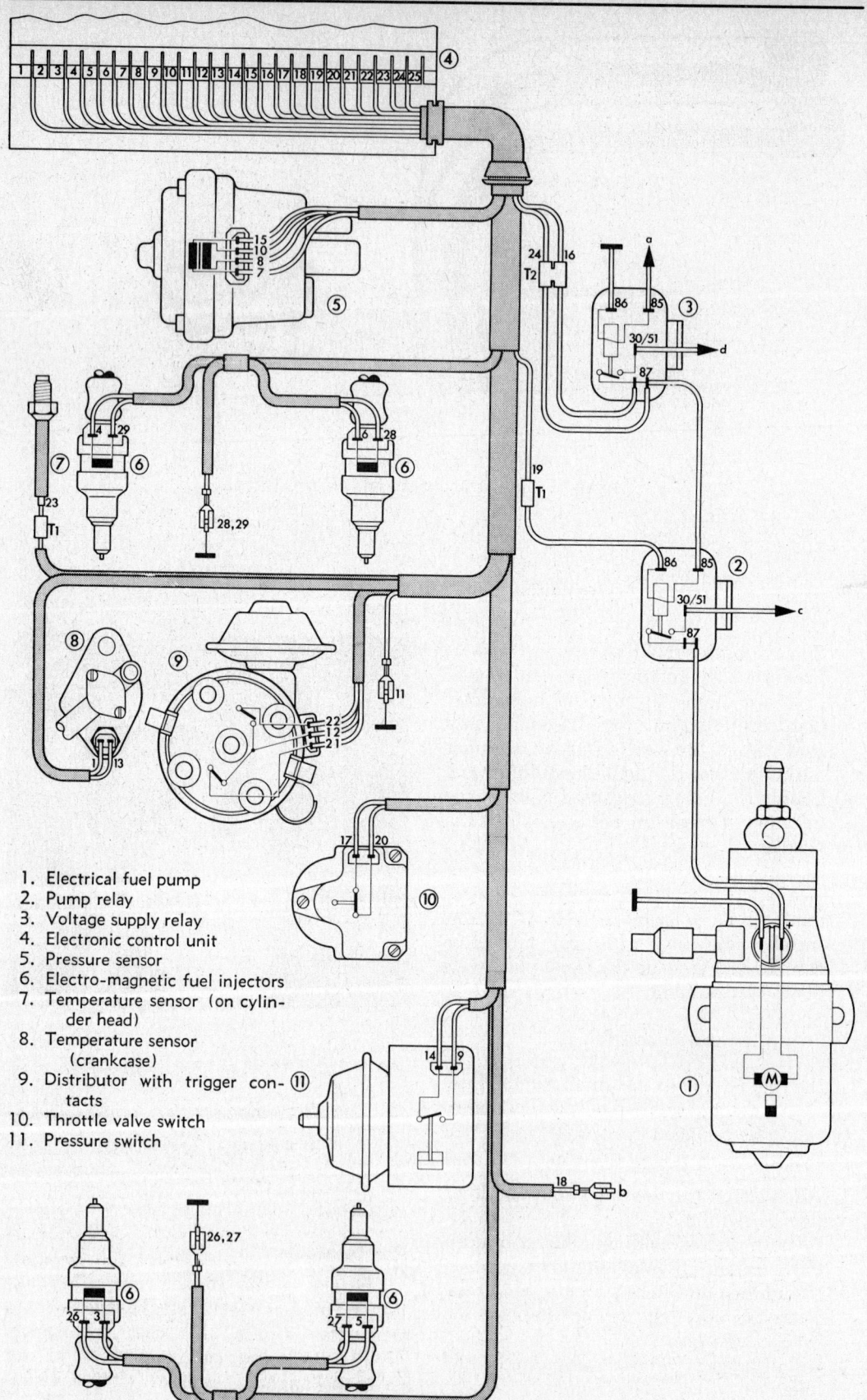

1. Electrical fuel pump
2. Pump relay
3. Voltage supply relay
4. Electronic control unit
5. Pressure sensor
6. Electro-magnetic fuel injectors
7. Temperature sensor (on cylinder head)
8. Temperature sensor (crankcase)
9. Distributor with trigger contacts
10. Throttle valve switch
11. Pressure switch

Control system and components of fuel injection system.

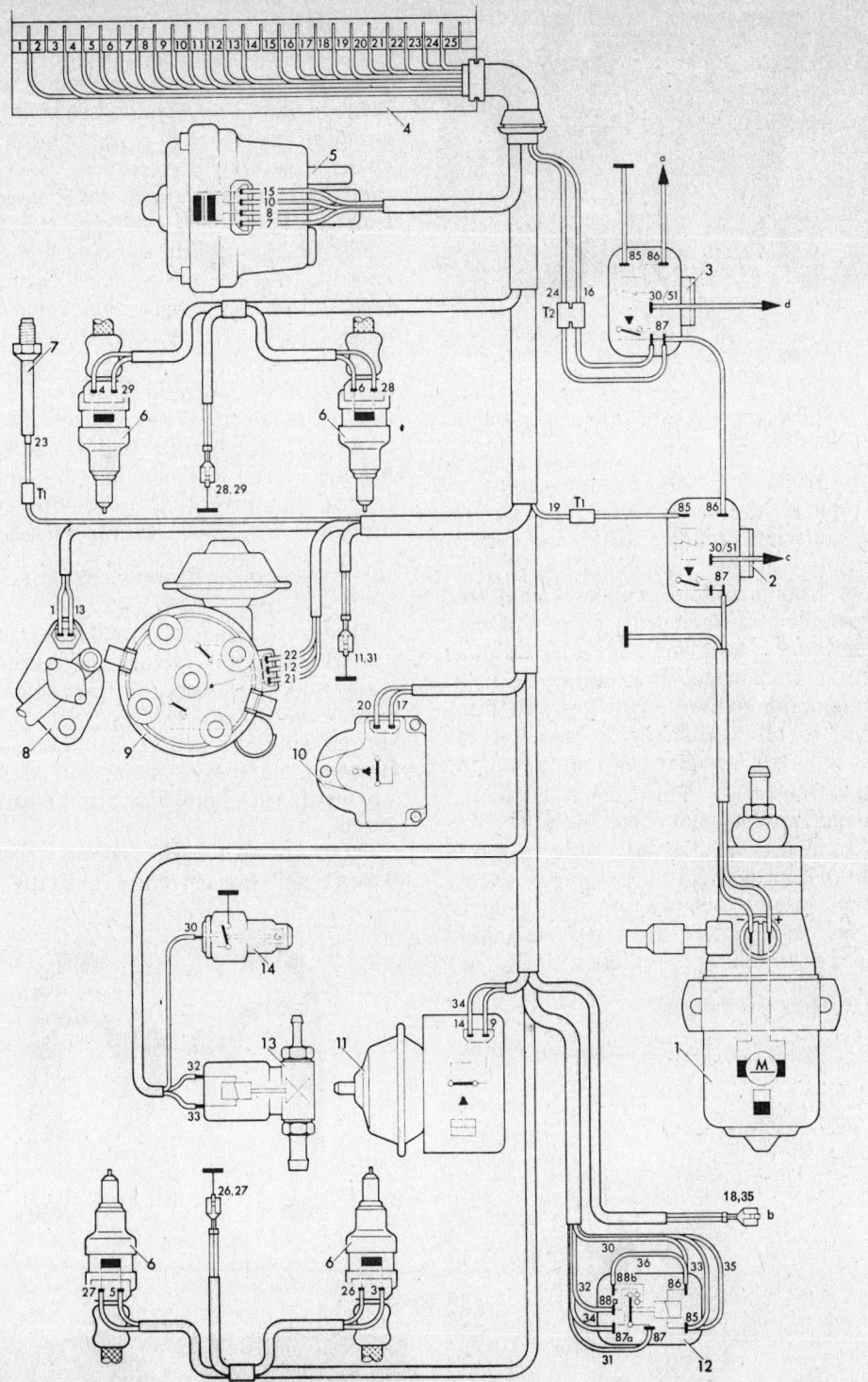

1. Electric fuel pump
2. Pump relay (relay I)
3. Voltage supply relay (relay II)
4. Electronic control unit
5. Pressure sensor
6. Elec. magnetic fuel injectors
7. Temp. sensor (cyl. head)

8. Temp. sensor (crankcase)
9. Ign. distr. with trigger contacts
10. Throttle valve switch
11. Pressure switch (no longer used)
12. Relay (cold starting jet)
13. Elec. magnetic cutoff (cold starting jet)

14. Thermo switch (cold starting)
a. Wire to ign. switch (terminal 15)
b. Wire to starter solenoid (term. 50)
c. Wire to terminal 30
d. Wire to pos. battery terminal

Control system and components of fuel injection system with cold starting device.

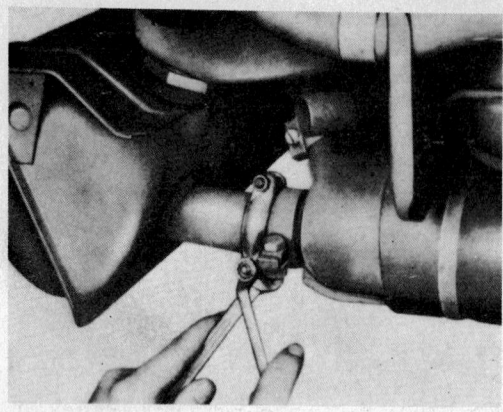

Unbolting the clamps between the muffler and the heat exchangers.

ing warm air channels. Loosen clamps on tail pipe(s) and remove tail pipe(s). Remove nuts from muffler flange and remove pre-heater adaptor pipe. Remove four screws from manifold preheater pipe and take muffler off, including gaskets. Check muffler to be installed and exhaust pipes for leaks or damage. If necessary, exhaust pipes can be re-used. However, in practice it is often difficult to remove tail pipes from old muffler without damaging them extensively. This generally occurs with old mufflers that have become rusty, and in such cases it is advisable to install new tail pipes. Type 1 tail pipes should protrude about 7.5″ on pre-1968 models; 8.3″ on later models. New gaskets should be used in installing the muffler.

R & R, Heat Exchangers

To remove the heat exchangers remove exhaust pipe clamps, the clamps between heat exchanger and exhaust pipe, and the rear engine cover plate (type 1 and 2). Remove nuts on cylinder head and warm air pipe connecting clips. The heat exchanger can now be removed. Check outer shell and exhaust pipes for damage and leakage. If the heat exchangers leak, there could be a possibility of poisonous gases entering the heating system. Sealing surfaces must be clean and smooth, and flanges that are distorted or bent through excessive tightening should be straightened or machined. Use new gaskets and ensure that all connections are gastight. Heat exchangers must be attached at the cylinder heads with self-locking 8 mm. hexagon nuts. It is not permissible for any other types of nuts to be used, even with lockwashers.

ACCESSORY EXHAUST SYSTEMS

Accessory exhaust systems are not approved by the VW factory and are not generally sold by dealers. Further, some states disapprove of any exhaust system that is not an original factory equipment type. However, accessory systems do usually give a power boost (up to 10%) and a satisfying sound.

There are two basic types of accessory exhaust systems currently available. The

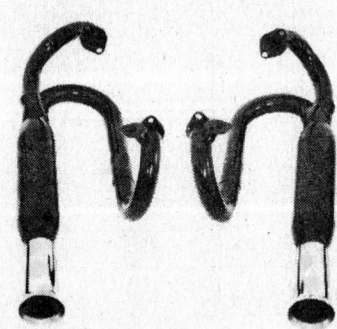

Header exhaust system, as used on VW-based dune buggies.

Removing heat exchanger attaching screws.

180° tuned, or extractor, exhaust system for VW engines.

first, the header type, has a separate muffler on each side, one for cylinders 1 and 2, and one for cylinders 3 and 4. This type of system does not allow the use of the heater and will not fit on sedans and buses, unless the rear body panels have been cut away. The header system is rather loud and rough sounding, because it is actually two completely separate two cylinder systems. It is most often seen on dune buggies, where a large ground clearance is necessary.

The second type of accessory exhaust system is known as the 180° tuned, or extractor system. In most such systems, equal length pipes are run from each cylinder, the pipes from each cylinder 180° apart in the firing order are run together, and then both these pipes are run together into a single outlet. The effect is a small horsepower boost and a smooth exhaust note. These systems are installed in much the same way as the stock muffler, and are available in models which utilize the original heater. Some extractor exhaust kits furnish canvas tubing to connect the heat exchangers to the fan housing tubing. The canvas tubing will rot out quickly, and should be replaced with stainless steel flexible tubing held with screw type hose clamps.

When fitting any low restriction exhaust system, it is advisable to rejet the carburetor to prevent an excessively lean mixture and resultant valve burning. Normally a main jet one or two sizes larger will be sufficient. It may also be necessary to replace the air correction, or air bleed, jet. The spark plugs and the inside of the tailpipe will give evidence of changes in mixture.

NOTE: *the results of rejetting, or of any other engine modifications, must be checked with suitable testing equipment to make sure that exhaust emissions remain within legal limits.*

Cooling System

R & R, Fan Housing

Removal of the type 1 and 2 fan housing is as follows: Remove two heater hoses and generator strap. Pull out the lead wire of the ignition coil. Remove distributor cap and take off spark plug connectors. Remove the retaining screws on both sides of the fan housing. Remove outer half of generator pulley and remove fan belt. Remove the thermostat securing screw and take out the thermostat. Remove lower part of carburetor preheater duct. Fan housing can now be removed with the generator. After removal, check fan housing for damage and for loose air-deflector plates. Accumulated dirt should be removed at this time.

Installation is the reverse sequence, and involves installation of fan housing flap assemblies, and the insertion of the thermostat actuating rod in the cylinder head and lower fan housing. It is necessary that the fan housing fit properly on the cylinder cover plates so that loss of cooling air will be avoided. In order to achieve proper fit, the cover plates may have to be bent slightly.

The removal of the fan housing of the type 3 is accomplished in a slightly different manner due to the different layout of the cooling system of this engine. Remove crankshaft pulley, rear fan housing half and fan. Unhook the linkage and spring at the right-hand air control flap. Remove the attaching screws of the front half of the fan housing. Prior to installation, the front half of the fan housing should be checked for damage.

In installing the fan housing, first install the front half of the fan housing, ensuring correct sealing with the cylinder cover plates. Replace and tighten two lower mounting screws slightly. Turn the two halves of the fan housing to the left until the left crankcase half is contacted by the front lug. Tighten fully the two lower mounting screws. Loosen nuts at the breather support until it can be moved. Insert and tighten the mounting screws of the upper fan housing half. Tighten fully the breather support nuts. Connect the linkage and spring to the right-hand air control flap. Install fan and rear half of fan housing.

R & R, Fan

The cooling fan of the type 1 and 2 models is removed as follows: using a T-wrench, remove the four retaining screws on the fan cover. Remove the generator and fan. While holding fan from rotating, unscrew the fan retaining nut and take off the fan, spacer washers, and hub.

Installation of the fan is as follows: place the hub on the generator shaft, making sure that the woodruff key is securely positioned. Insert the spacer washers. (Note: the distance between the fan and the fan cover should be between 1.5–1.8 mm. (.06″–.07″). Place the fan into position and tighten its retaining nut with a torque wrench and socket to 40–47 ft. lbs. Check the distance from fan to cover. Correct spacing is achieved by inserting the proper number of spacer washers between the hub and the thrust washer. When only one washer is used, the other two should be positioned between the lock washer and the fan. Insert the generator in the fan housing and tighten the retaining screws on the fan housing cover. (With 1967 and more recent models, be sure that the cooling air intake slot is at the bottom when the retaining plate is screwed onto the fan housing.)

On the type 3, fan removal begins with the removal of the crankshaft pulley, coil, and the rear half of the fan housing. The fan can then be removed.

On installation of the fan, check the condition of the oil return thread on the fan hub, and install rear half of fan housing, coil and crankshaft pulley.

Engine

The Volkswagen engine's flat four (i.e., pancake) design has proven itself in automotive, industrial and aerial applications as one of the most rugged and reliable made in the world today. The four-cycle, overhead valve engine has two pairs of cylinders horizontally opposed; it is attached to the transmission case by four bolts, and is easily removed for service.

The engine in the smaller (beetle) Volkswagens is currently capable of 60 hp. output, while that used in the larger (Fastback and Squareback) cars is rated at 65 hp. on the SAE scale. Both engines are of the same basic design as that of the original prototypes but are much more highly developed.

Because it is air-cooled, the VW engine is slightly noisier than a water-cooled powerplant of the same size due to the lack of a water jacket to provide a silencing function. In addition, air-cooled engines tend to be somewhat noisier because of clearances between parts. Higher operating temperatures of air-cooled engines require more room for expansion of parts. However, noise in the Volkswagen is damped by good insulation and the little that is present should serve to remind the Volkswagen driver that he has one of the most reliable and trouble-free engines made anywhere, anytime.

The engine in the type 3 (Fastback and Squareback) series is similar to the "beetle" engine, the main exception being the location of the cooling fan on the crankshaft rather than on the generator shaft. With the type 3 engine, there is no chance of cooling fan failure due to fan belt breakage, because there is no fan belt. If the generator belt should fail, the driver could drive some distance in daylight before running out of electricity for the ignition. In addition, the type 3 engine is slightly different in the location of the oil cooler and, of course, in the layout of the cooling ductwork. The type 4 engine is similar in design to the type 3 unit.

Fan Belt

Adjusting Fan Belt Tension

If belt tension is too great, the result will be a shortening of the life of the generator bearings due to unnecessary stress. If the belt is too loose, the result will be a loss of cooling efficiency in beetles and a loss of generating power in both the small and large Volkswagens. The following steps should be followed in adjusting the fan belt tension on all Volkswagens, regardless of year:

(1) Remove holding nut from the generator pulley shaft. In type 3 models, the pulley must be held from turning by using a suitable wrench. In the smaller Volkswagens the pulley is held by a screwdriver wedged between the notch in the generator pulley and the upper generator housing bolt.

(2) Remove the outer half of the generator pulley and adjust the fan belt tension by fitting the proper number of spacer washers between the halves of the pulley. Each washer added or removed changes the play in the belt about ¼″.

(3) If the fan belt is too loose, one or more spacer washers will have to be removed from between the pulley

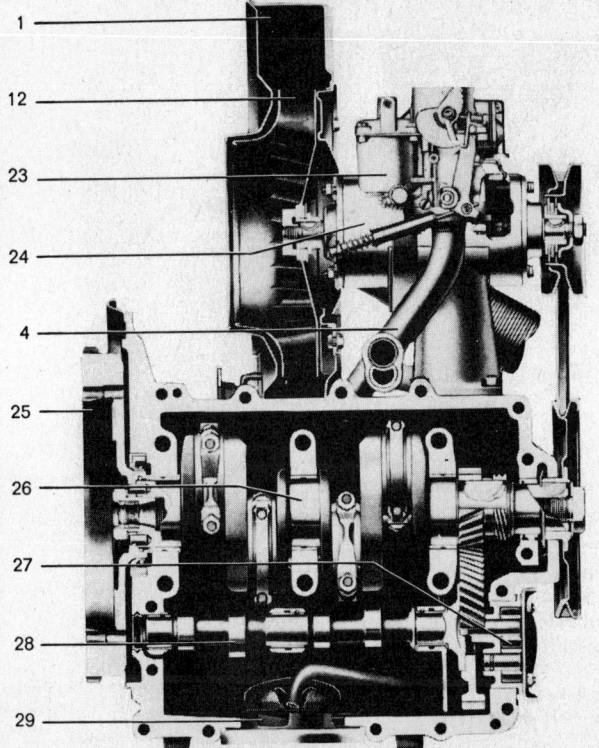

1. Fan housing
2. Ignition coil
3. Oil cooler
4. Intake manifold
5. Fuel pump
6. Ignition distributor
7. Oil pressure switch
8. Valve
9. Cylinder
10. Piston
11. Oil pressure relief valve
12. Fan
13. Oil filter and breather
14. Pre-heating pipe
15. Connecting rod
16. Spark plug
17. Cylinder head
18. Thermostat
19. Rocker arm
20. Push rod
21. Heat exchanger
22. Cam follower
23. Carburetor
24. Generator
25. Flywheel
26. Crankshaft
27. Oil pump
28. Camshaft
29. Oil strainer

Type 1 and 2 engine.

1. Intake pipe	10. Connecting rod	19. Oil pump
2. Carburetor	11. Cylinder	20. Fan
3. Valve	12. Cylinder head	21. Fan housing
4. Oil cooler	13. Spark plug	22. Crankshaft pulley
5. Piston	14. Flywheel	23. Muffler
6. Distributor	15. Camshaft	24. Coil
7. Fuel pump	16. Oil strainer	25. Cooling air intake housing
8. Air cleaner	17. Crankshaft	26. Thermostat
9. Crankcase breather	18. Camshaft drive gears	27. Heat exchanger

Dual carburetor type 3 engine.

When pressed firmly at mid-point, fan belt should yield about 15 mm. (.6″).

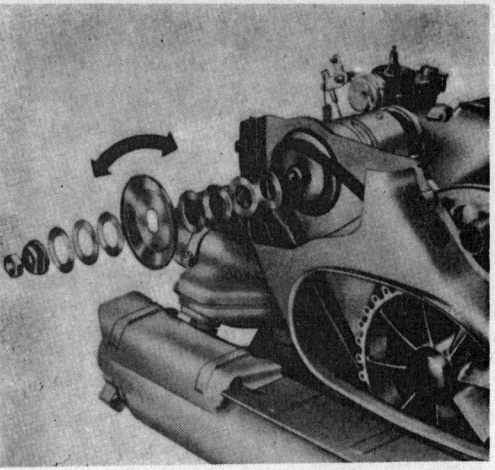

Exploded view of type 3 generator pulley and adjusting shims.

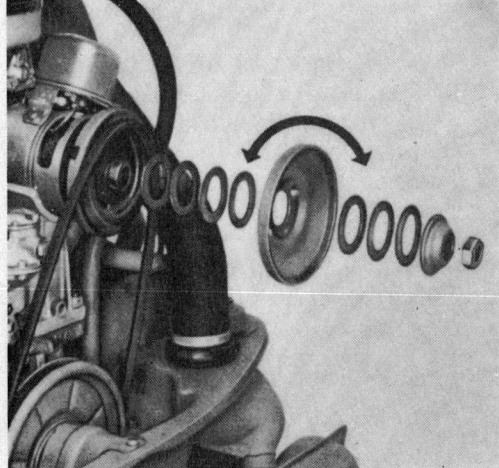

Exploded view of type 1 and 2 generator pulley and adjusting shims.

The generator pulley must be held as shown while loosening the nut.

halves. If the belt is too tight one or more washers will have to be added between the pulley halves.

(4) When correct adjustment has been achieved, the belt will deflect approximately .6 in. (15 mm.) when pressed by thumb pressure at its mid-point.

(5) When adjustment is correct, install the outer half of the generator pulley, and insert all left-over washers between the pulley nut and the outer pulley half. In this way, all spacer washers will remain on the pulley shaft and will be readily available whenever subsequent belt adjustments are required.

(6) Tighten pulley nut.

If the belt has stretched to the extent that correct adjustment can no longer be achieved by removing spacers from between the pulley halves, the belt should be replaced. Also, if a belt has frayed edges or cracks, it should be replaced. Fan belts should be kept free from grease and oil.

It is recommended that a new belt be inspected regularly during the first several hundred miles of use, since new belts have a tendency to stretch slightly.

Exhaust Emission Control

THROTTLE REGULATOR ADJUSTMENT

The exhaust emission control device used on type 1 and 2 vehicles, 1968–70, is the

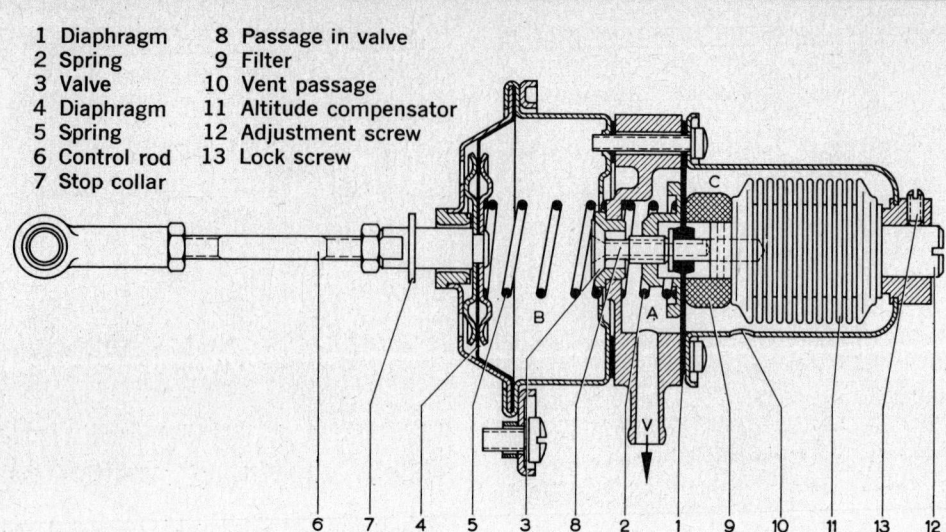

1 Diaphragm	8 Passage in valve
2 Spring	9 Filter
3 Valve	10 Vent passage
4 Diaphragm	11 Altitude compensator
5 Spring	12 Adjustment screw
6 Control rod	13 Lock screw
7 Stop collar	

Throttle regulator, 1968-1969 type 1 and 2 engines.

throttle valve regulator. This device holds the throttle open slightly on deceleration to prevent an excessively rich mixture.

On 1970 models, the throttle regulator consists of two parts, connected by a hose. The operating part is mounted at the carburetor, and the control part is located on the left sidewall of the engine compartment. The 1969 unit is one piece, mounted at the carburetor.

1. Engine must be at operating temperature, with automatic choke fully open.
2. Start engine. Turn regulator adjusting screw clockwise until control rod just starts to move throttle valve lever. The stop collar on the control rod will be against the regulator body. Engine speed should be 1,700–1,800 rpm.
3. If speed is too high, shorten control rod.
4. After adjustment, tighten lock nuts on control rod.
5. Turn regulator adjusting screw counter-clockwise until an idle speed of 850 rpm is obtained.
6. Increase engine speed to 3,000 rpm, then release throttle valve lever. Engine should take 3–4 seconds to return to idle.

Incorrect throttle regulator adjustment may cause erratic idle, excessively high idle speed, and backfiring on deceleration.

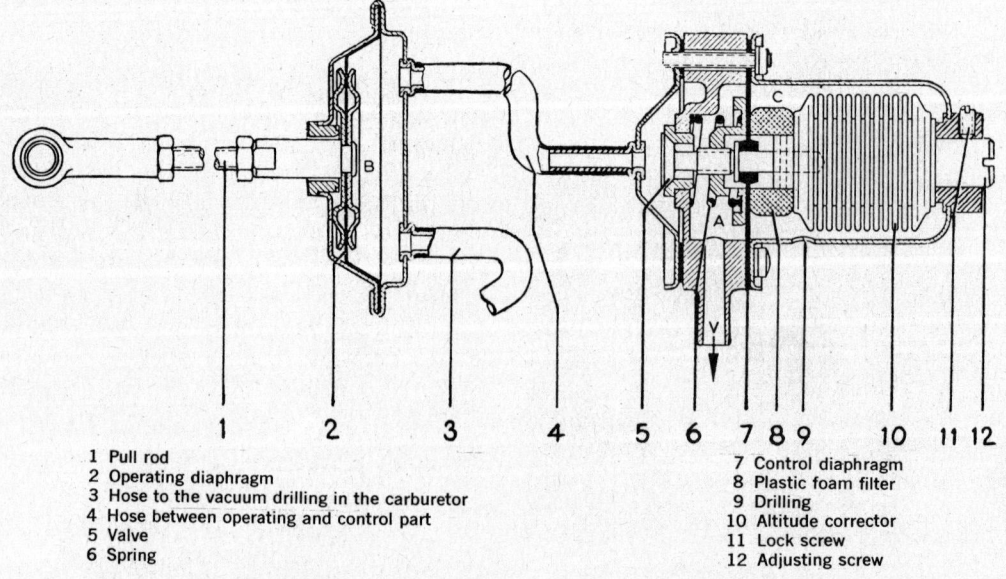

1 Pull rod	7 Control diaphragm
2 Operating diaphragm	8 Plastic foam filter
3 Hose to the vacuum drilling in the carburetor	9 Drilling
4 Hose between operating and control part	10 Altitude corrector
5 Valve	11 Lock screw
6 Spring	12 Adjusting screw

Throttle regulator, 1970 type 1 and 2 engines.

Engine Assembly

Engine Removal

The Volkswagen engine is mounted on the transmission, which in turn is attached to the frame. In the beetle models, there are four attaching points—two bolts and two studs—while on the type 3 there is an extra mounting point at the rear of the engine. Type 3 vehicles with automatic transmission have front and rear engine and transmission mounts. At the front, the gearbox is supported by the rear tubular crossmember; at the rear, a crossmember is bolted to the crankcase and mounted to the body at either end. When removing the engine from the car, it is recommended that the rear of the car be about three feet off the ground. The engine is removed by bringing it out from underneath the car. However, before raising the car, the following steps should be followed:

(1) Disconnect the ground strap from the battery, cables from generator (and, in beetle models, regulator).

(2) Remove air cleaner from engine, and the rear engine cover plate on beetle models. Remove throttle positioner.

(3) Rotate the distributor of beetle models so that this part will be able to clear the rear cover plate. (NOTE: *on 1967 and later models, the rear cover plate need not be removed, since the redesigned rear deck and compartment allow sufficient room for engine withdrawal from the car.*)

(4) Disconnect throttle cable from carburetor(s), and remove electrical connections to automatic choke, coil, electromagnetic cut-off jet, and oil pressure sending unit.

(5) Disconnect the fuel hose at the front engine cover plate and seal it to prevent leakage.

(6) On type 3 models, remove the oil dipstick and the rubber boot between the oil filler and body.

(7) Remove the cooling air intake bellows on type 3 models after loosening the clip that secures the unit.

(8) Remove the warm air hose on the type 3 models.

(9) After disconnecting the appropriate electrical and control cables, remove

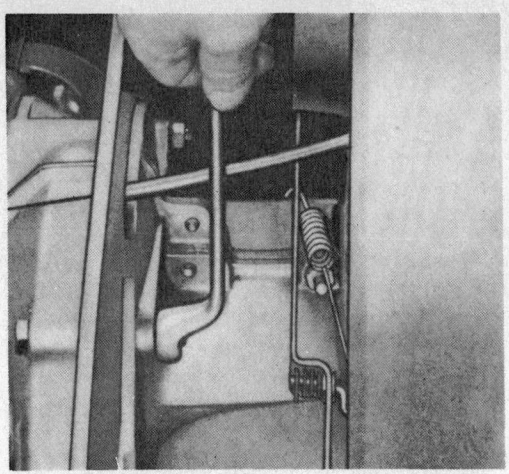

Removing upper engine mounting bolts, type 1.

Removing upper engine mounting bolts, type 3.

the rear engine support (type 3) and raise the car off the ground.

(10) After removing the flexible air hoses between the engine and heat exchangers, disconnect the heater flap cables, unscrew the two lower engine mounting nuts and slide a jack under the engine. Be sure that it is suitable for supporting the weight of the engine without placing undue strain on the components.

On type 1 Automatic Stickshift models, disconnect the control valve cable and manifold vacuum hoses. Disconnect the ATF suction line and plug it with a 16 X 1.5 mm. cap. On type 3 fully automatic models, disconnect the vacuum hose and kickdown cable. On either model, remove the four 8 mm. bolts from the converter drive plate through the holes in the transmission case. After removing the engine, hold the torque converter in place on the transmission with a strap. On fuel injected type 3 models, the fuel pressure and return lines must be clamped off and disconnected, and the injection unit wiring disconnected.

(11) Raise the jack until it just contacts the engine, and have an assistant hold the bolts of the two upper engine mounts so that you will be able to unscrew the nuts. If an assistant is not available at this stage, it is possible to wedge sockets into the proper places so that one man can do the job without having four hands.

(12) When the engine mounts are disconnected and there are no remaining cables or controls linking the engine with the car, roll the engine backwards slightly so that the release plate will be able to clear the main drive shaft.

(13) Lower the engine very slowly, and be sure that the clutch release plate does not contact the main drive shaft of the transmission.

Engine Installation

Roughly speaking, engine installation is the reverse of the preceding operation,

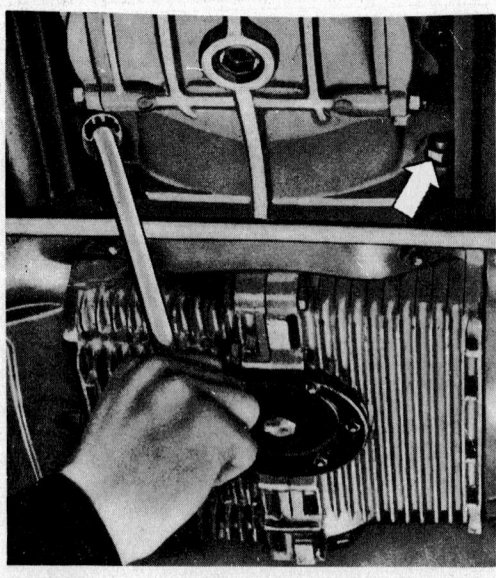

Removing lower engine mounting nuts, type 1.

although it is important that some special precautions be taken. Before replacing the engine, the clutch plate must be centered, the clutch release bearing and release plate checked for wear, and a number of components greased or cleaned. The starter shaft bush should be lubricated with lithium grease, the needle bearing in the gland nut supplied with 1 gram of universal grease, and the main drive shaft splines lubricated with molydenum-disulphide powder applied with a clean cloth or brush. Before installing the engine, care must also be taken to ensure that the mating surfaces of the engine and transmission are cleaned thoroughly.

The engine is then lifted into position and the engine rotated via the generator pulley so that the clutch plate hub will engage the transmission shaft splines. In pushing the engine home, care must be taken to see that the gland nut needle bearing, clutch release bearing, and main drive shaft are not damaged. After the engine is in position, put the lower engine mounting bolts through the holes in the flange of the transmission case and press the engine against the flange so that proper and even contact is made. Tighten the upper nuts first, then the lower ones. After this initial tightening, tighten all nuts evenly in this same sequence.

On the type 3 reinstallation, synthetic washers are used to raise the engine about 2–3 mm. when the rear engine mounting is attached and tightened. Use only enough washers in the rear mount so that the engine is lifted no more than 3 mm. when the mounting is tightened down. Care should be used when installing the rear air intake housing bellows of the type 3 engine, for this unit can be easily damaged through careless handling. Reconnect cables and controls. Attach the thick lead to terminal D+ of the generator. Adjust the accelerator cable with the engine at full throttle, and set the ignition timing.

To avoid interference with the function of the automatic stickshift clutch, take care to route the connecting hoses so that they are not kinked or jammed when installing the engine. This applies particularly to the small diameter pipe from the control valve to the carburetor venturi, which will work properly only if routed in the original production manner.

Engine Disassembly and Assembly Operations

The disassembly of the type 3 engines is different from that of the other VW engines mainly in the removal of the engine cover plates and cooling ductwork. In tearing down a Volkswagen engine, the following is the recommended sequence of operations:

(1) Drain engine oil.
(2) Remove hoses between engine and heat exchangers.
(3) Remove front engine cover plate.
(4) Remove muffler and intake manifold, including carburetor(s).
(5) Remove fan belt, cooling air intake housing, generator and crankshaft pulley.
(6) Remove rear half of fan housing, fan, and front half of fan housing.
(7) Remove distributor and fuel pump and take out distributor drive pinion.
(8) Remove cooling air ductwork from cylinder area.
(9) Remove oil cooler.
(10) Remove rocker arm shaft and cylinder heads.
(11) Remove cylinders and pistons.
(12) Remove clutch assembly and flywheel.
(13) Remove oil pump and oil strainer.
(14) Disassemble crankcase and remove camshaft, crankshaft and connecting rods.

Assembly, generally speaking, is the reverse of the foregoing procedure.

NOTE: *the torque, capacity, tune-up, and clearance figures given in the text apply, generally, to the most common engines. However, since there are so many variations in production, it is always best to consult the applicable chart for the figure in question.*

Cylinder Heads

R & R, Cylinder Head

In order to remove the cylinder head of either pair of cylinders, it is first necessary that the rocker arm assembly be removed. The cylinder head is held in place by eight studs. Since the cylinder head also holds the cylinders in place in the VW engine, if it is not desired that the cylinders be removed, they should be

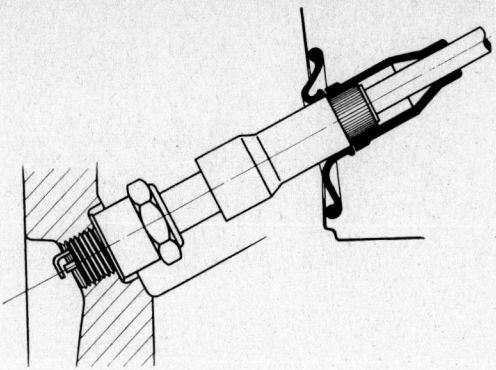

The rubber spark plug seals should fit snugly against the cooling ducts so that cooling air does not escape.

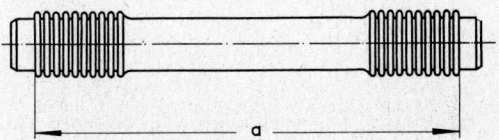

Push rod tube length (distance a) is 190–191 mm. for 1,300, 1,500, and 1,600 cc. engines, and 180.5–181.5 mm. for the 40 hp. 1,200 cc. engines. No measurement is given for earlier engines.

held in place with an appropriate holding clamp. After the rocker arm cover, the rocker arm retaining nuts and rocker arm assembly have been removed, the cylinder head nuts can be removed and the cylinder head lifted off.

When reinstalling the cylinder head, several points must be remembered. The cylinder head should be checked for cracks both in the combustion chamber and in the intake and exhaust ports. Cracked cylinder heads should be replaced. Spark plug threads should be checked at this time for tightness. If the threads are stripped, they can be corrected by means of Heli-coil threaded inserts. On 1963 and later engines, no gasket is necessary between the cylinder head and the cylinders. However, on earlier models, which do not have a fresh air heating system, a gasket should be fitted. New seals should be used on the push rod tube ends, and should be checked for proper seating.

The push rod tubes should be turned so that the seam faces upwards. In order to ensure perfect sealing, used tubes should be stretched to the correct length of 190–191 mm. before they are installed. (Note: in the 40 hp. engine, the correct length is 180.5–181.5 mm. On the 40 hp. engine,

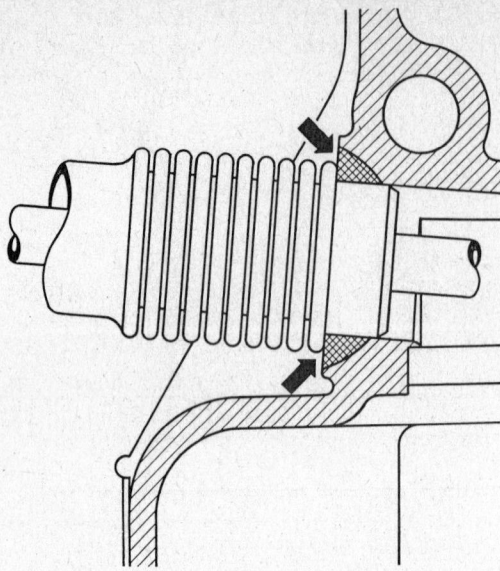

The oil seals at the ends of the pushrod tubes must be properly seated to prevent leakage.

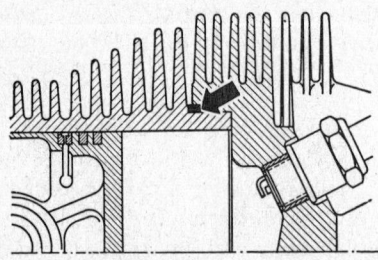

On pre-1963 engines a cylinder head gasket is used. The slotted side of the gasket must be toward the cylinder head.

the sealing ring between the outer shoulder of the cylinder and the cylinder head should be renewed, placing the slotted side of the ring toward the cylinder head. On the 50 hp. engine of 1966 and subsequent engines, no sealing ring is needed.)

After inserting the cylinder head nut washers, the cylinder head nuts should be tightened slightly, and then to a torque of 7 ft.-lbs. before fully tightening them to a torque of 23 ft.-lbs. (27 ft.-lbs. in 1959 and earlier models). The sequence of tightening shown in the tightening sequence diagram should be followed. (Note the different sequences for the initial and final tightening procedures.)

Cylinders

R & R, Cylinders

Before removing the cylinders, the cylinder head, valve push rods, push rod

tubes, and deflector plate below the cylinders must be taken out. The cylinders may then be pulled off.

Reinstall the cylinders as follows:

Cylinders should be checked for wear, and if necessary replaced with another matched cylinder and piston assembly of the same size. Also check the cylinder seating surface on the crankcase, cylinder shoulder, and gasket, for cleanliness. Foreign matter here could cause leaks due to distortion of the mating parts. When reinstalling the cylinders, a new gasket should be used between each cylinder and the crankcase.

The piston rings, and piston pin should be liberally oiled (a MoS_2 based lubri-

The deflector plates under the cylinders must be tight against the cylinder studs to prevent rattles.

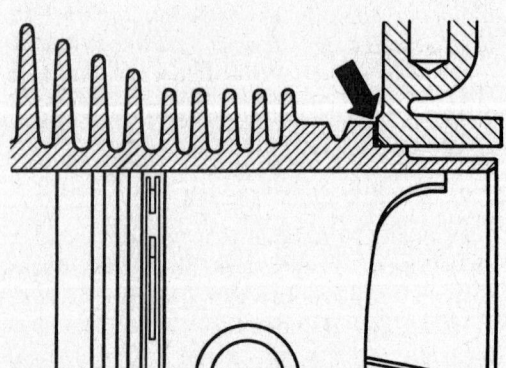

Foreign matter between the cylinder and the crankcase could cause distortion of the cylinder. The gasket indicated should not be reused.

When sliding the cylinder over the piston, the crankcase studs must not be allowed to contact the cylinder cooling fins.

cant is suitable). Compress rings with compression tool. Be sure that ring gaps are adequate and staggered on the piston with the oil ring inserted into the cylinder so that its gap is positioned UP when the pistons are in their horizontal position in the engine.

Lubricate the cylinder wall and slide cylinder over piston. Crankcase studs should not contact cylinder cooling fins. Install the deflector plates under the cylinders, bending slightly if necessary to make them seat tightly on the cylinder head studs.

Install push rod tubes and push rods, ensuring that the tubes are inserted with the seam facing upwards and are of the proper length.

Valve Train

ADJUSTING VALVE CLEARANCE

If valve clearances in the Volkswagen engine are too small, the valves can be seriously damaged by warping or burning, and compression will eventually suffer from lack of proper valve sealing. Valves are cooled by resting against the valve seat— if the valves are opened for too long, they have insufficient time to rest against their seats, and hence to transfer their heat to the cylinder head. On the other hand, if the valve clearance is too great, the result will be rough running, loss of power, and excessive wear of the valve train components. However, if error is necessary,

it is best to err in the direction of too large a clearance. A few thousandths of an inch of excess clearance will be much less harmful than the same error in the opposite direction. As long as you can hear the valves clicking, you are at least assured that they are not burning.

Before the valves can be adjusted in any Volkswagen, the engine must be stone cold, preferably after sitting overnight. Volkswagen valve clearances vary somewhat between models of different years. To determine the correct setting, refer to both the Tune-Up Specifications Chart and the engine sticker.

Preference is to be given to the valve clearance specified on the engine fan housing sticker, if one is present. On models built after late 1964, such a sticker will be on the fan housing. Such stickers will also be present on all factory rebuilt engines, regardless of horsepower output, and the clearances specified should be followed closely.

Steps in Adjustment

(1) Remove distributor cap and turn engine until rotor points to notch in distributor rim and the crankshaft pulley timing mark is aligned with the crankcase split or pointer. # 1 cylinder is now at top dead center of its compression stroke. See illustration showing cylinder numbering.

(2) Remove the rocker arm cover of cylinders #1 and #2.

(3) With the proper feeler gauge, check the clearance between the adjusting

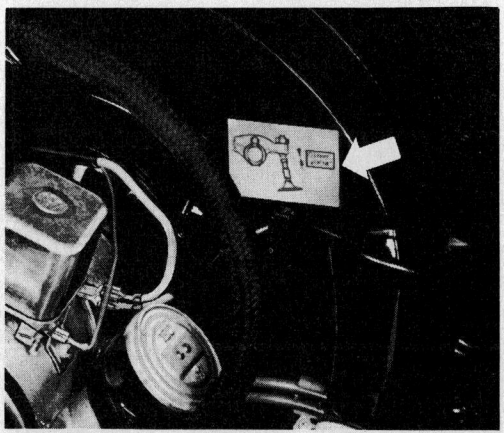

Most late model engines have the correct valve clearance indicated on a sticker on the fan housing.

When rotor points to notch in distributor rim and crankshaft pulley timing mark is aligned with crankcase split or pointer, cylinder #1 is at top dead center.

Turning adjusting screw while checking valve clearance with feeler gauge.

screw and the valve stem of both valves for #1 cylinder. If the feeler gauge slides in snugly without being forced, the clearance is correct. It would be well to use the "go—no go" gauge system in which the proper leaf slides in but one which is .002″ thicker will not.

(4) If the clearance is incorrect, the lock nut must be loosened and the adjusting screw turned until the proper clearance is attained. After tightening down the lock nut it is then advisable to recheck the clearance, because it is possible to alter the

adjustment when tightening the lock nut.

(5) Turn engine one-half revolution in the counterclockwise direction. This will turn the distributor rotor 90 degrees in the counterclockwise direction so that it will now point to the lead wire for cylinder #2. #2 cylinder is now at top dead center.

(6) Repeat adjustment process for cylinder #2.

(7) Replace valve rocker arm cover on cylinders #1 and 2, using a new gasket and cleaning off the seating surfaces to guard against leakage.

(8) Remove valve rocker arm cover on cylinders #3 and 4.

(9) Turn the engine another one-half turn in the counterclockwise direction so that the distributor rotor now points to the lead wire of cylinder #3. #3 cylinder is now at top dead center.

(10) Adjust the clearances on cylinder #3.

NOTE: *on pre-1971 type 1 and 2 engines, #3 cylinder runs hotter than the other three cylinders because its cooling air flow is partially blocked by the oil cooler. To counter a tendency for this cylinder to burn exhaust valves, some mechanics set the #3 exhaust valve clearance .001 to .002″ wider than specified.*

(11) Turn the engine a further one-half turn counterclockwise and adjust the clearances of the valves in cylinder #4.

If engine is turned backward one half revolution from the firing point for #1 cylinder, the distributor rotor will turn backward one quarter turn to the firing point for #2 cylinder. Proceeding backward in this manner, the valves can be adjusted in 1-2-3-4 order.

(12) Replace the rocker arm cover of cylinders #3 and 4, cleaning the sealing surfaces and using a new gasket.

(13) Replace distributor cap. Replace belt housing cover in type 3 models.

While correct valve clearance is important to all Volkswagen engines, it is especially important in those having a specified clearance of .008″ and .012″ (intake and exhaust). In these engines the valve clearance actually decreases as the engine warms up, so too little initial clearance, or a clearance obtained with a warm engine, can lead to trouble within a short time. On engines with .004″ clearance, the clearance increases as the engine temperature increases.

It is also possible to adjust valves in normal firing order sequence, 1-4-3-2, rotating the engine clockwise. It is helpful to mark the crankshaft pulley directly opposite the 0° mark in order to determine precisely when the engine is turned one-half revolution.

R & R, Rocker Arm Mechanism

Before the valve rocker assembly can be reached, it is necessary to undo the clip that retains the cover plate. Prior to removing the cover plate, however, it is advisable to dust off and clean the cylinder head and cover plate. This will prevent dirt from entering the assembly. Remove the cover plate after taking off the retaining clip with a screwdriver or other suitable lever. Remove the rocker arm retaining nuts, the rocker arm shaft and the rocker arms. Remove the stud seals.

Before installing the rocker arm mechanism, be sure that the parts are as clean as possible, including the inside of the cover plate. Install the stud seals and the rocker shaft, making sure that the chamfered edges of the supports are pointing outward and the slots, upward. Tighten the retaining nuts to a torque of 14–18 ft. lbs. The only type of retaining nuts which should be used are 8 mm. nuts of the 8 G grade. These nuts are distinguishable by their copper color. Ball ends of the push rods must be centered in the sockets of the rocker arms. In addition, to help valves rotate during operation, the rocker arm adjusting screws should contact the tip of the valve slightly off center. It should be neither in the center nor all the way to one side, but exactly in the middle of the two extremes. After adjusting valves to their proper clearance, reinstall the cover plate with a new gasket. Be sure that the proper cover plate gasket is used. There are two types of gaskets, early and late. The late type is straight across the top edge, while the early type has a tab in the center of the top edge. After the engine has been run for a brief period, check the cover plates for oil leakage.

Disassembly and Assembly of Rocker Arm Mechanism

Remove the spring clips from the rocker arm shaft. Remove washers, rocker arms, and bearing supports. Before installation, check the rocker arm shaft for wear, and the seats and ball sockets of the rocker arm adjusting screws. Loosen adjusting screws before installing rocker arms. Otherwise, installation is the reverse of the disassembly procedure.

R & R, Valves

In order to remove the valves, the cylinder head must first be taken off. With the cylinder head removed, compress the valve springs with a special tool and remove valve keys, valve spring caps, valve springs, and oil deflector rings. Remove valves from cylinder head after removing any burrs that

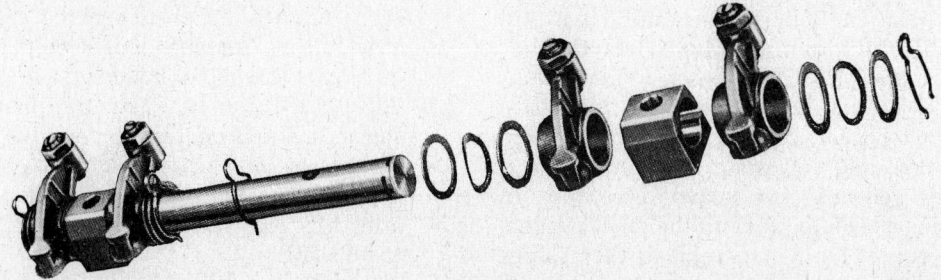

Exploded view, rocker arm mechanism.

Use of a valve spring compressor to remove valves.

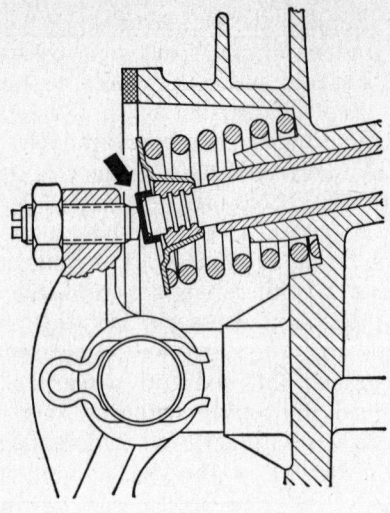

Valves with a damaged stem can be reused after fitting a cap.

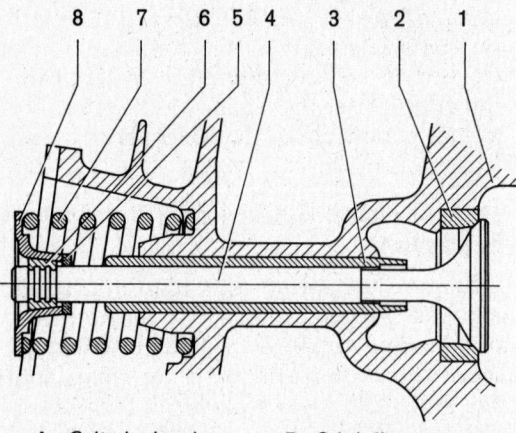

1. Cylinder head   5. Oil deflector ring
2. Valve seat insert   6. Valve cotter
3. Valve guide   7. Valve spring
4. Valve   8. Valve spring cap

Details of a typical valve.

may be present near the seating surface of the keys on the valve stem. While the valve springs are out, they should be tested. Proper valve spring pressures are given in the Engine Rebuilding Specifications Chart for Valves. Valve keys should be checked prior to installation, and new and worn keys ground at the joining faces until it is still possible to turn the valve when the key halves are pressed together. Valve stems should be checked for run-out and valve guides for wear. Valves should be checked for leaks and for wear. Because exhaust valves generally do heavy-duty work in the air-cooled engine of the Volkswagen, it is good practice to replace them since their cost is not great and the engine is already apart. If the stems of the valves are

hammered in, the valves can still be used again after valve caps have been installed. Polish rough valve stems carefully with emery cloth. After coating the valve stems with a moly paste, insert them into their guides and fit oil deflector rings. Install valve springs with the close-wound coils facing the cylinder head. Used valves must be refaced before being reinstalled. Damaged seats must also be reconditioned.

Crankcase

Disassembly and Assembly of the Crankcase

With the cylinders, pistons, and other outer parts removed, the crankcase is split as follows:

(1) Remove the oil strainer, oil pressure switch, and crankcase nuts.

(2) Keep the cam followers of the right crankcase half in position by using the retaining springs.

(3) Use a rubber hammer to break the seal between the crankcase halves. Under no circumstances insert sharp tools, wedges, etc. between the crankcase halves, for this will surely lead to serious leakage of lubricant.

(4) After the seal between the mating surfaces has been broken, remove the right-hand crankcase half, the crankshaft oil seal and camshaft end plug, and lift out the camshaft and the crankshaft.

(5) Remove cam followers, bearing shells and oil pressure relief valve.

After being loosened with a rubber mallet, the right half of the crankcase can be removed. Prying tools should never be used to separate the crankcase halves.

Assembly is generally the reverse of the foregoing procedure, but includes the following:

(1) Before reassembling crankcase, check it for damage and cracks after cleaning thoroughly. Mating and sealing surfaces should be cleaned especially well. A solvent should be used to remove traces of the old sealant from mating surfaces.

(2) Flush and blow out all ducts and oil passages.

(3) Check the oil suction pipe for leaks.

(4) Check studs for tightness. If tapped holes are worn, correction involves the installation of Helicoil inserts.

(5) Insert cam followers after checking both the followers and their bores in the crankcase.

(6) Install crankshaft bearing dowel pins and bearing shells for crankshaft and camshaft.

(7) Install crankshaft and camshaft after bearings have been well lubricated. (When installing crankshaft, note position of timing marks on timing gears.)

(8) Install camshaft end plug, using sealing compound.

(9) Install thrust washers and crankshaft oil seal. The oil seal must rest squarely on the bottom of its recess in the crankcase.

(10) Check and install oil pressure switch.

(11) Spread a thin film of sealing compound on the crankcase joining faces.

Use care so that no sealing compound enters the oil passages of the crankshaft or the camshaft bearings.

(12) Keep cam followers of right crankcase half in place by using retaining springs.

(13) Join the crankcase halves and evenly torque the fasteners to the torque specified in the Engine Torque Specifications Chart.

(NOTE: *first tighten the 8 mm. nut which is beside the 12 mm. stud of the #1 crankshaft bearing. Only then should the 12 mm. nuts be tightened fully.*)

(14) Turn the crankshaft to check for ease of movement, and check the end play of the crankshaft. The crankshaft end play is measured with the engine assembled and the flywheel installed.

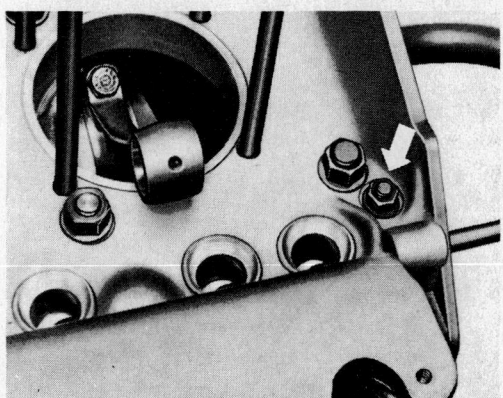

The 8 mm. nut pointed out must be tightened fully before the 12 mm. nuts.

Camshaft and Timing Gears

R & R, Camshaft

Removal of the camshaft requires that the crankcase be split. The camshaft and camshaft bearing shells are then easily removed. Before reinstalling the camshaft, it should be checked for wear of the bearing faces and bearing points. In addition, the riveted joint between the camshaft timing gear and the camshaft should be examined for security. If there is slight damage to the camshaft, it may be smoothed with a silicon carbide oilstone. A 100–120 grit stone is first used to smooth the damaged area, and then a 280–320 stone may be used for final polishing. The camshaft should be checked for run-

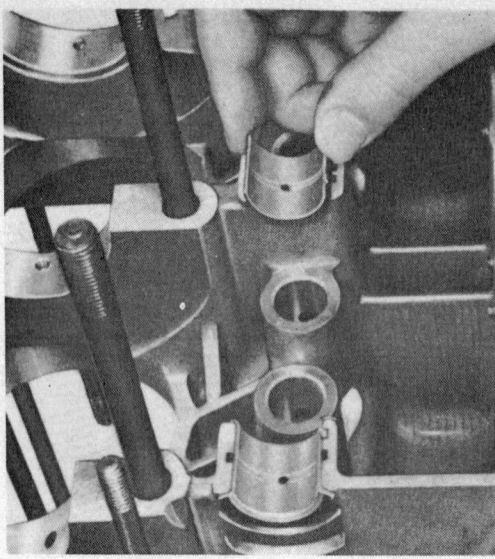

Camshaft bearings. Note the thrust flange on bearing #3, in the foreground.

out, which should not exceed .0008". The timing gear should be checked for correct tooth contact and for wear, and the edges of the camshaft bearing bores lightly chamfered to avoid seizure. If the camshaft shells removed are either worn or damaged, new shells should be fitted. The camshaft bearing shells should be installed with the tabs engaging the notches in the crankcase. Before installing camshaft, the bearing journals and cams should be generously coated with oil. When the camshaft is installed, care should be taken to ensure that the timing gear tooth marked "O" is located between the two teeth of the crankshaft timing gear marked by a

The arrow shows the proper alignment of timing marks when installing the camshaft and crankshaft.

center punch. The end play at the thrust bearing (bearing number 3) is .06–.11 mm. (.002"–.004") and the wear limit is .14 mm. (.006").

Crankshaft

R & R, Crankshaft Pulley

On the type 1 and 2, the crankshaft pulley can be removed while the engine is still in the car. However, in this instance it is necessary for the rear cover plate of the engine to be removed. Remove cover plate after taking out screws in the cover plate below the crankshaft pulley. Remove fan belt, and crankshaft pulley securing screw. Using a puller tool, remove the crankshaft pulley. The crankshaft pulley should be checked for proper seating and for proper belt contact surface. The oil return thread should be cleaned and lubricated with a molybdenum-disulphide based oil. The crankshaft pulley should be installed in the reverse sequence, and should have no run-out.

On the type 3, the crankshaft pulley can be removed only when the engine is out of the car and the muffler, generator, and cooling air intake housing are removed. After these parts have been removed, take out the plastic cap on the pulley. This can be done easily with a screwdriver. Remove the crankshaft pulley retaining bolt and remove the pulley.

Installation is the reverse of the foregoing but the following should be noted: when installing use a new paper gasket between the fan and the crankshaft pulley. If shims are used, do not forget them. No more than two shims may be used. When inserting the pulley, make sure that the pin engages the hole in the fan. The crankshaft pulley retaining bolt should be tightened to a torque of 94-108 ft.-lbs. Ensure that the clearance between the generator belt and the intake housing is at least 4 mm. and that the belt is parallel to the housing. Check the seal on the cooling air intake housing and if damaged, cement a new seal into place.

Crankshaft End Play

With engine installed, the crankshaft end play can be read with a dial indicator mounted at the pulley side of the engine. End play should be as specified with an

With the engine assembled and the flywheel installed, crankshaft end-play should be .06–.12 mm. (.003–.005″) with a wear limit of .15 mm. (.006″).

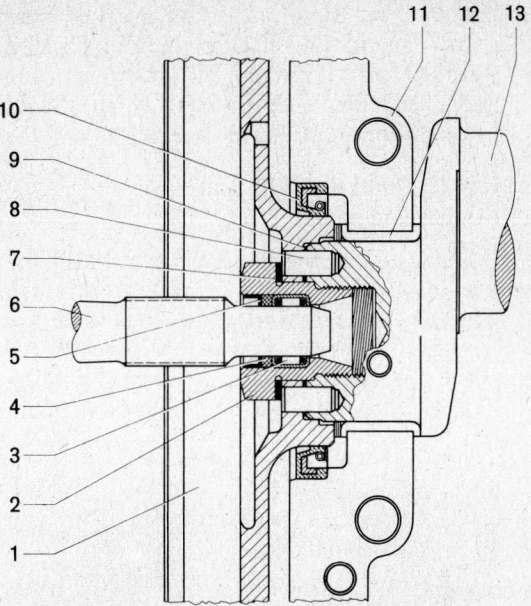

1. Flywheel
2. Gland nut
3. Needle bearing
4. Felt ring
5. Retaining ring
6. Main drive shaft
7. Lock washer
8. Dowel pin
9. Paper or metal gasket
10. Oil seal
11. Crankcase
12. Crankshaft bearing
13. Crankshaft

Cross-sectional view of flywheel and crankshaft end.

upper wear limit of .15 mm. (.006″). When the engine is not installed, crankshaft end play can be measured at the flywheel end with an indicator mounted on the flywheel. Desirable end play is obtained by adding or subtracting shims at the outer end of the main bearing. Shims for this purpose are available in various thicknesses. Never use more than one gasket.

R & R, Flywheel

The flywheel is attached to the crankshaft with a gland nut, and is located by 4 dowels. Some models have a paper gasket between the flywheel and the crankshaft; others have a metal gasket. Beginning with the 1967 model year, a metal sealing gasket is no longer present between the flywheel and crankshaft. An oil seal is recessed in the crankcase casting at #1 main bearing. A needle bearing, which supports the main drive shaft, is located in the gland nut. Prior to removing the flywheel, it is necessary to remove the clutch pressure plate and the clutch driven plate. Loosen gland nut and remove, using 36 mm. special wrench and flywheel retainer. Remove guide plate of special wrench. Remove gland nut and withdraw flywheel.

Installation is the reverse of the foregoing procedure, plus the following: check flywheel teeth for wear and damage. Check dowel holes in flywheel and crankshaft and renew dowels if necessary. Adjust crankshaft end play and check needle bearing

in gland nut for wear. Lubricate needle bearing with about 1 gram of universal grease. Insert flywheel gasket, if one is used in the engine. (Note: to minimize engine imbalance, the crankshaft, flywheel, and clutch are marked at their heaviest points. Upon assembly, be sure that the marks on these units are offset by 120°. If

The flywheel gland nut is torqued to 30 mkg (217 ft. lbs.).

but two of these parts are marked, the marks should be offset by 180°. Tighten flywheel gland nut to 217 ft.-lbs. torque and check flywheel run-out, which should be a maximum of .3 mm. (.012″).

R & R, Crankshaft Oil Seal (engine assembled)

Oil losses at the flywheel could well be the result of a leaky crankshaft oil seal. This seal is removed after removing the flywheel. After the flywheel is removed, inspect the surface on the flywheel joining flange where the oil seal makes contact.

A special tool is needed to install the crankshaft oil seal.

Remove old oil seal by prying it out of its counterbore. Before installing new crankshaft oil seal, clean the crankcase oil seal recess and coat it thinly with sealing compound. The sharp edges should be slightly chamfered so that the outer edge of the seal is not damaged. Using VW tool 204b, press in the new seal, being sure that it rests squarely on the bottom of its recess. Remove tool and reinstall flywheel after coating the oil seal contact surface with oil.

R & R, Crankshaft and Connecting Rods

Removal of the crankshaft requires the removal of the cylinder heads, cylinders, pistons, the splitting of the crankcase halves, and the withdrawal of the camshaft. When installing the crankshaft, check to see that the crankcase does not have sharp edges at points of junction. If foreign matter has become lodged in the main bearings, it will be necessary to remove it with a scraper, taking care not to remove material from the bearing shell itself. Check the dowel pins for tightness. Place one half of #2 crankshaft bearing in the crankcase. Slide on crankshaft bearing #1 so that the dowel pin hole is toward the flywheel. Install crankshaft, making sure that the dowel pins are correctly seated in the crankshaft bearings. When installing camshaft, note the marks on the timing gears.

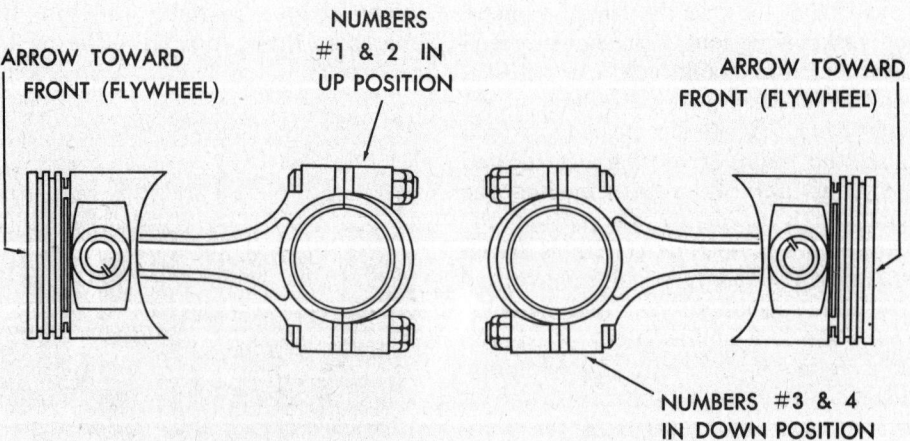

Piston and rod installation.

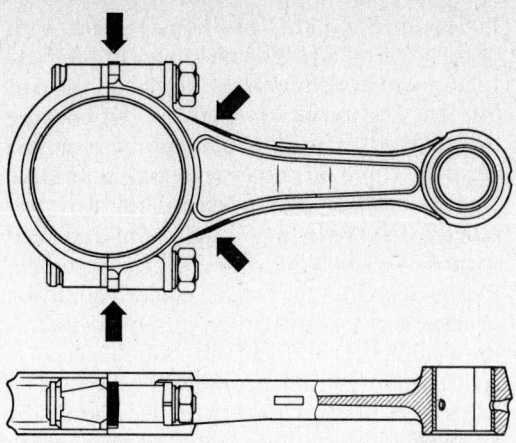

Maximum allowable weight difference between connecting rods in one engine is 10 grams. Metal may be removed from the portions of the connecting rod indicated.

After the crankshaft has been removed and clamped into position, remove the connecting rod clamping bolts and the connecting rods and caps. When installing, check the connecting rods for external damage and for weight. The difference in weight of the connecting rods in an engine must not be in excess of 10 grams in order that proper engine balance can be maintained. If necessary, metal should be removed from the heavier connecting rods at the points indicated on the accompanying drawing. Inspect the piston pin

cylinder 1   cylinder 2

cylinder 3   cylinder 4

Note that the marks on the connecting rods are pointing upward, while the rods are pointing toward their respective cylinders.

bushing. With a new bushing, the correct clearance is indicated by a light finger push fit of the pin at room temperature. Check and, if necessary, correct connecting rod alignment. Reinsert connecting rod bearing shells after all parts have been thoroughly cleaned and assemble connecting rods on crankshaft. The identification numbers stamped on connecting rods and bearing caps must both be on one side.

NOTE: *new connecting rod screws should always be used, and the wax removed from the screws before they are installed.*

Tighten connecting rod bolts to the specified torque. A slight pretension between the bearing halves, which is likely to occur when

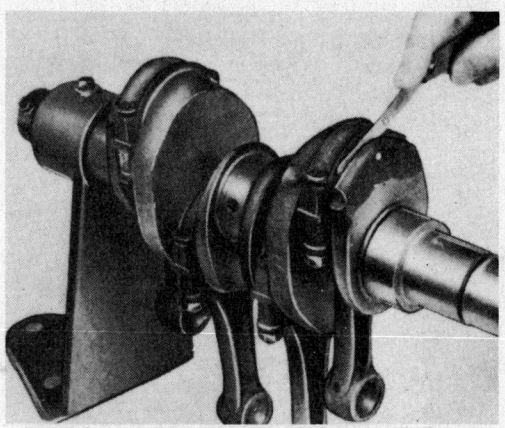

Measuring the axial (side) play of the connecting rods with a feeler gauge.

tightening connecting rod bolts, can be eliminated by light hammer taps. The connecting rods, lubricated with engine oil prior to assembly, must slide on the crank pin by their own weight. The connecting rod bushings must not be scraped, reamed or filed during assembly. Using a peening chisel, secure the connecting rod bolts in place.

Engine Lubrication

R & R, Oil Strainer

All Volkswagen models are equipped with the same type of oil strainer, a view of which is shown in the accompanying diagram. The oil strainer can be easily removed simply by removing the restraining nuts, washers, oil strainer plate, strainer and gaskets. Once taken out, the strainer

1. Gasket   4. Cover plate
2. Oil strainer   5. Cap nut with washer
3. Gasket   6. Plug with washer

Crankcase oil strainer components. The strainer must be cleaned at each oil change, and new gaskets must be used.

must be thoroughly cleaned and all traces of old gaskets removed prior to fitting new ones. The suction pipe should be checked for tightness and proper position. When the strainer is installed, be sure that the suction pipe is correctly seated in the strainer. If necessary, the strainer may be bent slightly. The measurement from the strainer flange to the tip of the suction pipe should be 10 mm., plus or minus 1 mm. The measurement from the flange to the bottom of the strainer should be 6 mm. plus or minus 1 mm. The cap nuts at the bottom of the strainer should not be overtightened, for the bottom plate may become distorted and lead to leakage of engine lubricant. If it is desired, the strainer can be equipped with a permanent magnet designed to retain metal particles that are circulating in the oil. This magnet is held in place by means of a spring clip, and should be removed and cleaned whenever the strainer is removed for the same purpose. Magnetic drain plugs are also available.

R & R, Oil Cooler

The Volkswagen oil cooler is mounted on the crankcase and is positioned in the path of the cooling air. The oil cooler in the type 1 can be removed with the engine in the car, but it is first necessary that the fan housing be removed. The oil cooler can be removed after the three oil cooler retaining nuts have been taken off. The gaskets should be removed along with the oil cooler and replaced with new ones when the cooler is installed. Before installation, the oil cooler should be checked for leaks at a pressure of 85 psi. If the cooler is found to leak, the oil pressure relief valve should also be checked. The studs and bracket on the cooler should be checked for tightness. See that the hollow ribs of the oil cooler do not touch one another. Clean the contact surfaces on the crankcase, install new gaskets, and attach oil cooler. Tighten retaining nuts. On the type 3, be sure that a spacer ring is present between the crankcase and the cooler at each securing screw. If these rings are omitted, the seals may be squeezed too tightly, resulting in a stoppage of oil flow and consequent damage to the engine. The type 3 oil cooler is similar in design to that of the type 1 and 2, except that it lies horizontally cross-wise in the path of the air, while that of the other models is in a vertical position.

Beginning 1971, the type 1 and 2 oil cooler is mounted farther forward on an intermediate flange and has its own cooling air supply through the fan housing. This prevents the oil cooler from blocking off the cooling air to No. 3 cylinder and causing that cylinder to run hot.

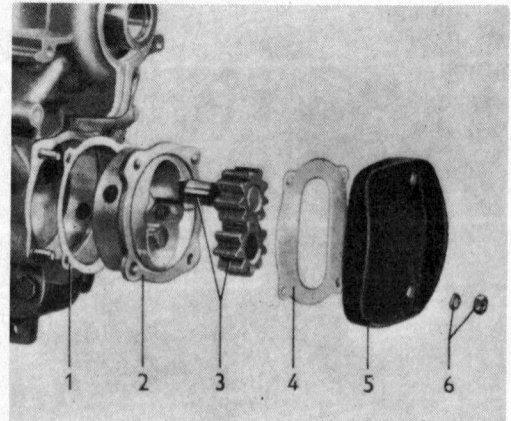

1. Gasket   5. Oil pump cover
2. Oil pump body   6. Nut and spring
3. Gears   washer
4. Gasket

Oil pump components, type 1.

R & R, Oil Pump

An exploded view of the Volkswagen oil pump is given in the accompanying illustration. In the type 3, the oil pump can be taken out only after the engine is removed from the car and the air intake housing, the belt pulley fan housing, and the fan are dismantled. On the type 1 and 2, the pump can be removed with the engine in the car, but it is first necessary to remove the cover plate, the crankshaft pulley, and the cover plate under the pulley. Removal on all model Volkswagens is similar. On Automatic Stickshift models, the torque converter oil pump is driven by the engine oil pump.

Remove the nuts from the oil pump cover and remove the cover and its gasket. Remove the gears and take out the pump body with a special extractor. Care should be taken not to damage the inside of the pump housing.

Prior to assembly, check the oil pump body for wear, especially the gear seating surface. If the pump body is worn, the result will be loss of oil pressure and possible damage to the engine. Check driven gear shaft for tightness, and if necessary peen it tightly into place or replace the pump housing. The dimension *a* in the accompanying diagram should be .5–1.0 mm. (.02–.04"). The gears should be checked for wear, backlash and end play. Backlash may be from .03–.08 mm. (.0012–.0031") and the maximum end play, without gasket, .1 mm. (.004"). The end play can be checked using a T-square and a feeler gauge. Check the mating surfaces of the pump body and crankcase for dam-

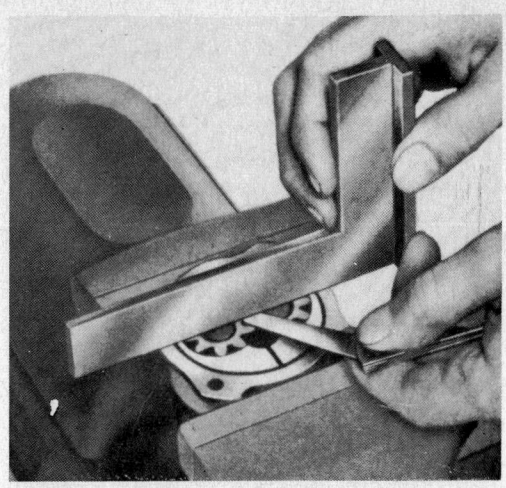

Maximum end-play of the oil pump gears, measured without a gasket, should be .1 mm.

age and clean them. Install pump body with gasket, but without sealing compound. Insert oil pump pilot instead of oil pump drive shaft into pump body. Then turn the camshaft by 360° (one complete turn of the camshaft requires two complete turns of the crankshaft.) This will ensure the centering of the pump body opposite the slot in the camshaft. Mark the pump body so that the correct fit of the oil pump can be checked after the cover has been installed. Remove the oil pump pilot and install the gears. Check the cover for wear—worn covers should be either machined or replaced. Before installing cover, new gaskets should be fitted and secured with sealing compound. Install cover and tighten nuts without disturbing the position of the pump housing.

R & R Oil Pressure Relief Valve

When the oil is cold and thick, and oil pressure is very high, the pressure relief valve plunger is in its lowest position and oil flows directly to the lubrication points and some of it back to the crankcase. When the oil warms up and thins out, the oil pressure drops, the plunger covers the by-pass port and oil flows to the lubrication points both directly and via the oil cooler. After the oil has warmed up to normal operating temperature and is thin, oil pressure is low, the plunger of the relief valve is in its highest position, and the oil goes to the lubrication points only after it has passed through the oil cooler.

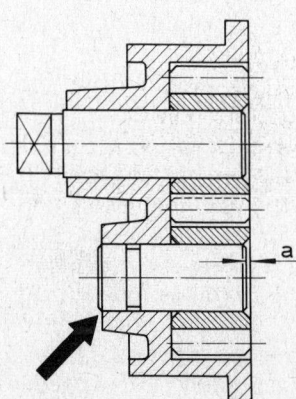

Arrow shows driven shaft of gear type oil pump. Dimension a should be .02–.04".

1. Plunger   3. Gasket
2. Spring   4. Plug

Components of oil pressure relief valve.

There are two types of oil pressure relief valve plungers available. The first is the plain type normally found in type 1 and 2 engines. The second type is longer and has an annular groove. This is used in some type 3 engines. It has been found that, if the grooved plunger is substituted for the plain plunger, the result will be more oil flow through the cooler and a drop in oil temperature of about 15°F. This, as all other engine modifications, is discouraged by the VW factory.

1970 and later type 1 and 2 engines have two oil pressure relief valves. The second valve is located at the flywheel side of the oil sump and is identical to the first.

Oil pressure relief valve plungers; the grooved type gives increased oil cooling.

The oil pressure relief valve should be checked whenever there is any disturbance in oil circulation, and especially when the oil cooler is found to be leaky. If the plunger should stick at its highest point when the oil is thick, there is danger of the oil cooler leaking from excess pressure. If, on the other hand, the plunger sticks in the bottom of its travel, the oil will tend to flow directly back to the sump and lubrication will be lacking when the engine is warm.

The oil pressure relief valve is removed by unscrewing the end plug and removing the gasket ring, spring and plunger. If the plunger is stuck, it can be removed by screwing a 10 mm. tap into it. Prior to installation, check the plunger and the bore in the crankcase for signs of seizure. If necessary, the plunger should be renewed. The spring should be checked to assure that it conforms to the following specifications:

Condition	Length	Load in lbs.
Unloaded	2.44–2.52″	0
Loaded	.93″	17.1 lbs.

When installing the relief valve, care should be taken to ensure that the upper end of the spring does not scratch the wall of the bore. The gasket should be removed and the end plug tightened securely.

Pistons and Connecting Rods

PISTONS R & R

Following the removal of the cylinder head and the cylinder, the pistons should be marked with a number (cylinder number) and an arrow (pointing to clutch side of engine) if they are to be reinstalled in the engine. The pistons are removed as follows:

Using piston circlip pliers, remove the circlips used to retain the piston wrist pin. Heat the piston to 80°C. (176°F.), remove the piston pin and take the piston off the end of the connecting rod. If it is necessary to remove the piston rings, use piston ring pliers in order to avoid damage.

Install the piston as follows: First, clean the piston and the ring grooves, taking care to see that the ring grooves are not scratched or otherwise damaged. The piston should then be checked for wear and, if necessary, replaced by one of corresponding size and weight. Weight be-

The pistons should be marked in this manner before removal.

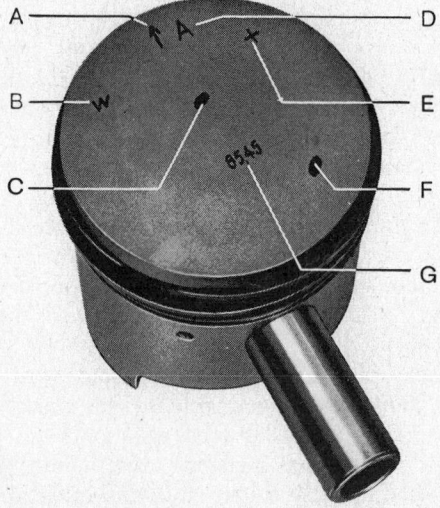

size grading. If, however, the cylinder of a worn or damaged piston shows no signs of wear, it is permissible to install a new piston of appropriate size. See accompanying diagram for piston markings.

After making a decision concerning the piston to be used, select piston rings of the correct size. After the ring has been inserted in the cylinder and pushed down about .2" by the piston, check the gap with a feeler gauge. After using a piston ring tool to install the rings, check the side clearance of the rings in their grooves with a feeler gauge.

Ring side clearance and end gap should be as specified in the Engine Rebuilding Specifications Chart for Pistons, Cylinders, and Rings.

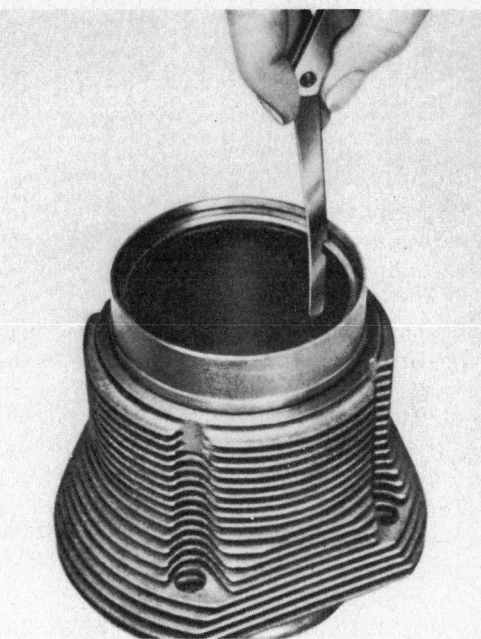

Measuring ring end gap.

A. Arrow (indented or stamped on) which must point toward the flywheel when piston is installed.
B. Details of piston pin bore size indented or stamped on (s = black, w = white).
C. Paint spot indicating matching size (blue, pink, green).
D. The letter near the arrow corresponds to the index of the part number of the piston concerned. It serves as an identification mark.
E. Details of weight grading (+ or —) indented or stamped on.
F. Paint spot indicating weight grading (brown = — weight, grey = + weight).
G. Details of piston size in mm.

An explanation of the markings on new pistons.

tween pistons must not be greater than 10 grams. If the running clearance between the piston and cylinder is .2 mm. (.008") or more, the piston and cylinder should be replaced by a set of the same

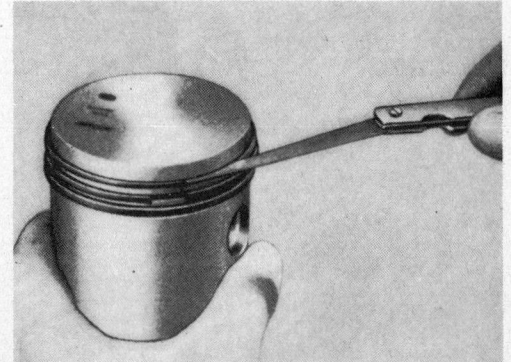

Measuring ring side clearance.

Because the compression rings are slightly tapered, they should be installed with the marking "Top" or "Oben" toward the top of the piston. Insert the piston pin circlip which faces toward the flywheel. Because piston pin holes are offset, make sure that the arrow (or word "vorn") points toward the flywheel. This offset is to help accommodate thrust loads which amplify and lead to objectionable piston slap.

Check and fit piston pin. The pin may be found to be a light finger-push fit in the piston, even when the piston is cold. However, this condition is normal, even to the extent of the pin sliding out of the piston under its own weight. Clearance between the piston pin and the connecting rod bushing should be as specified in the Engine Rebuilding Specifications Chart. If the clearance is near the wear limit, renew the piston pin and the rod bushing. It is not advisable to install an oversize pin in this case. In all cases where the pin is not a light finger push fit in the cold piston, heat the piston in oil to about 176°F. Insert the second circlip and make sure that the circlips fit perfectly in their grooves.

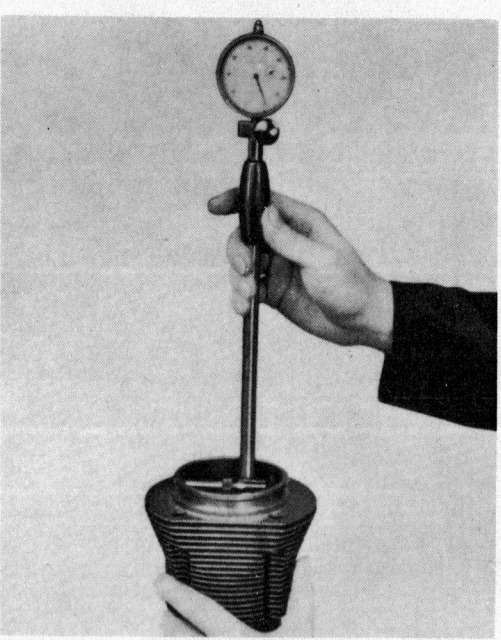

Clearance between cylinder and piston should not exceed .20 mm. (.008"). Clearance is determined by measuring both piston and cylinders. The cylinder diameter is measured 10–15 mm. below the upper edge.

A good barometer in deciding whether or not a new cylinder and piston should be installed is oil consumption. If the engine uses more than one quart of oil each 600 miles, it is quite likely that the engine is in need of reconditioning.

Clutch and Transmission

Clutch

CLUTCH R & R

Manual Transmission

To remove the clutch, first remove the engine; then remove the clutch-to-flywheel attaching bolts by gradually and alternately backing the bolts out of the flywheel; and finally take off the clutch cover and lift out the clutch driven plate.

Installation of the clutch is the reverse of the preceding. Before installing, inspect and resurface the pressure plate if it is worn in excess of .008". The friction surface should be polished. Inspect the driven plate and renew it if there is any doubt as to its reliability. Examine the release plate, release levers, and springs for damage. Check release bearing for damage and replace if necessary. If the release bearing has a plastic ring, it must be roughed up with emery cloth and lubricated sparingly with molybdenum disulphide paste. This prevents an annoying whistling sound which sometimes comes from the release bearing. Inspect the bearing points of the clutch operating shaft for wear. Lubricate the needle bearing in the flywheel gland nut with approximately 10 grams of universal grease. Then, reinstall the driven (lined) plate, using a pilot mandrel to ensure correct centering alignment. Evenly and alternately tighten the clutch-to-flywheel bolts. Check proper distance and parallelism between clutch cover contact face at flywheel and the clutch release plate with a clutch adjustment gauge. Adjust free play at the clutch pedal to .4–.8".

Automatic Stickshift

To remove the clutch, the engine and then the transmission must first be removed. Proceed as follows:

1. Pull off the torque converter. Seal off the hub opening.

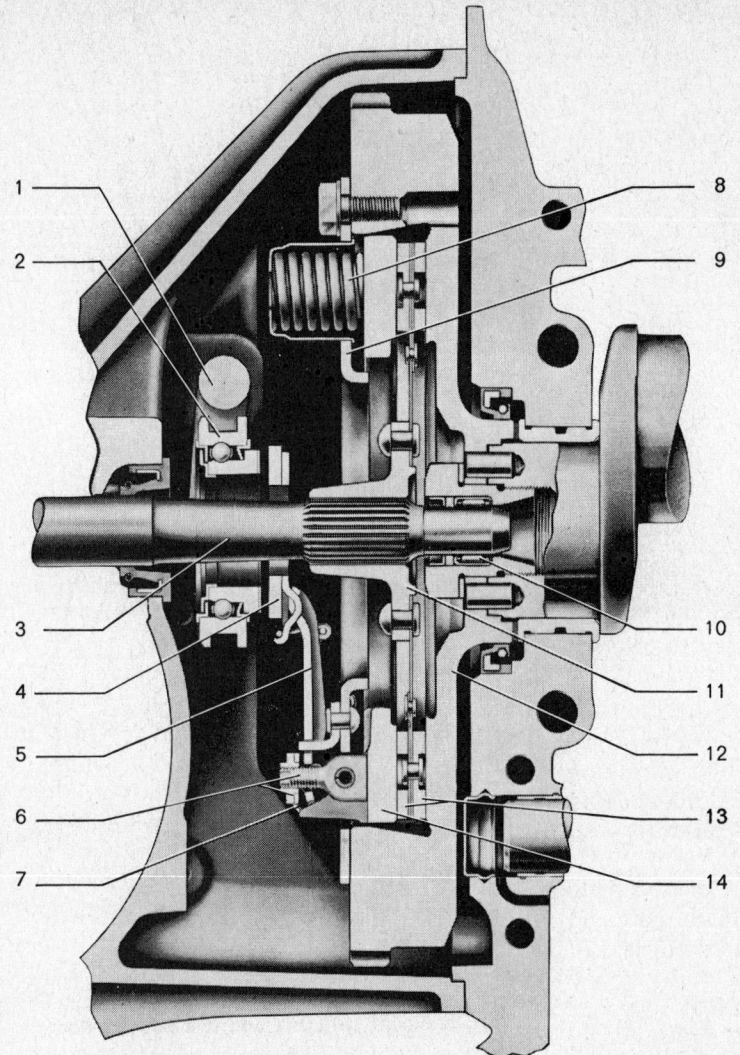

1. Operating shaft
2. Release bearing
3. Main drive shaft
4. Release plate
5. Release lever
6. Bolt and special nut
7. Release lever spring
8. Thrust spring
9. Cover
10. Needle bearing for gland put
11. Driven plate
12. Flywheel
13. Lining
14. Pressure plate

Cross-sectional view of clutch assembly.

2. Mount transmission in a repair stand or on a suitable bench.

3. Loosen clamp screw and pull off clutch operating lever. Remove transmission cover. Remove hex nuts between clutch housing and transmission case (two inside the differential housing).

4. The oil need not be drained if the clutch is removed with the cover opening up and the gearshift housing breather blocked.

5. Pull transmission off clutch housing studs.

6. Turn clutch lever shaft to disengage release bearing.

7. Remove both lower engine mounting bolts.

8. Loosen clutch retaining bolts gradually and alternately to prevent distortion. Remove bolts, diaphragm clutch, clutch plate, and release bearing.

9. Do not wash the release bearing. Wipe dry only.

To replace the clutch:

10. Check clutch plate, pressure plate, and release bearing for wear and damage. Check clutch carrier plate, needle bearing, and seat for wear. Replace all parts as necessary.

11. If clutch is wet with ATF, replace clutch carrier plate seal and clutch. If clutch is wet with transmission oil, replace transmission case seal and clutch.

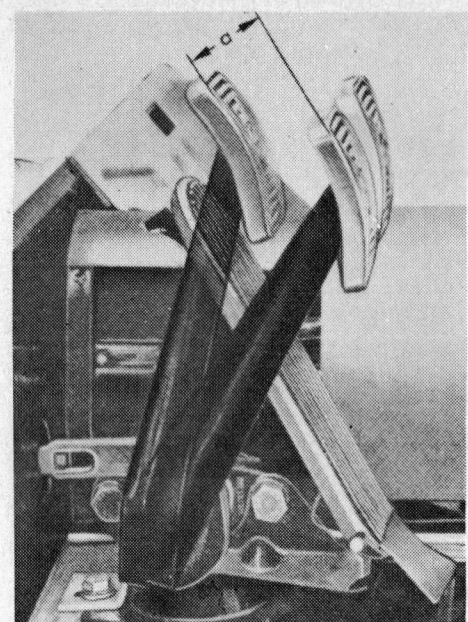

Clutch pedal free play should be 10–20 mm. (.4–.8").

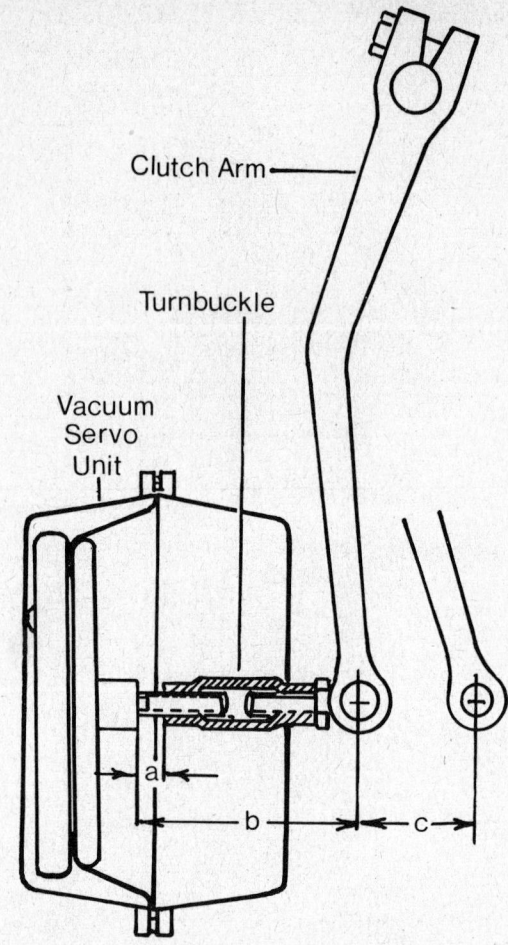

Adjustment dimensions required after installing new clutch in Automatic Stickshift unit. a should be .335", b should be 3.03", and c should be 1.6".

12. Coat release bearing guide on transmission case neck and both lugs on release bearing with lithium grease containing a molybdenum disulphide additive. Insert bearing into clutch.

13. Apply lithium grease to carrier plate needle bearing. Install clutch plate and clutch, centering the plate with an old main drive shaft or a suitable dummy shaft.

14. Tighten clutch retaining bolts evenly and alternately. Make sure that release bearing is correctly located in diaphragm spring.

15. Insert lower engine mounting bolts from front. Replace sealing rings if necessary. Some units have aluminum sealing rings and capnuts.

16. Push transmission onto converter housing studs. Insert clutch lever shaft behind release bearing lugs. Push release bearing onto transmission case neck. Tighten hex bolts holding clutch housing to transmission case.

17. Install clutch operating lever.

To adjust new clutch:

18. Clutch operating lever should contact clutch housing. Tighten lever clamp screw slightly.

19. Refer to the adjustment illustration. Adjust dimension a to .335", b to 3.03",

and c to 1.6". Tighten the clutch lever clamp screw fully.

20. Push torque converter onto support tube. Insert into turbine shaft by turning.

21. Check clutch play after installing transmission and engine.

R & R, Clutch Cable

Manual Transmission

The clutch cable runs from the pedal to the release bearing, which in turn presses against the release plate and moves it axially. To remove the cable, first remove the left rear wheel. Disconnect the cable from its operating lever on the transmission. Pull the rubber boot from the guide tube and cable. Disconnect the brake master cylinder push rod and unbolt the pedal

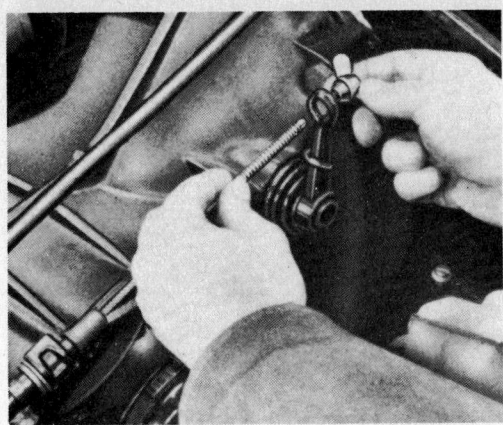

Disconnecting clutch cable from operating lever.

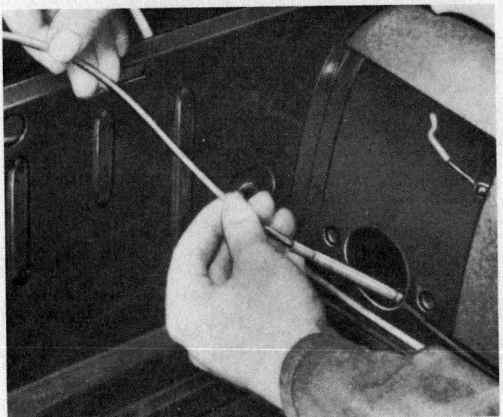

Inserting clutch cable into guide tube.

assembly. Unhook the cable from the pedal cluster and pull it forward through the hole from which the pedal cluster was removed.

Installation is the reverse of the above. The cable should be lubricated thoroughly with universal grease. While the pedal assembly is out of the frame tunnel, it is a good idea to lubricate this part well also. The cable guide should be bent slightly by inserting a suitable number of washers between the transmission case bracket and the end of the cable guide (A). (See illustration.) Adjust pedal free play.

CLUTCH ADJUSTMENT—MANUAL TRANSMISSION

The Volkswagen clutch is a dry, single-plate unit fitted to the flywheel. Earlier models had a carbon throw-out bearing, while the later models are equipped with the ball-bearing type. With the carbon type bearing, wear on the bearing was significant when the clutch pedal was depressed for any length of time, although in normal and proper use the carbon bearings generally lasted for the life of the clutch lining. Neither the carbon bearing nor the ball-type bearing requires periodic maintenance.

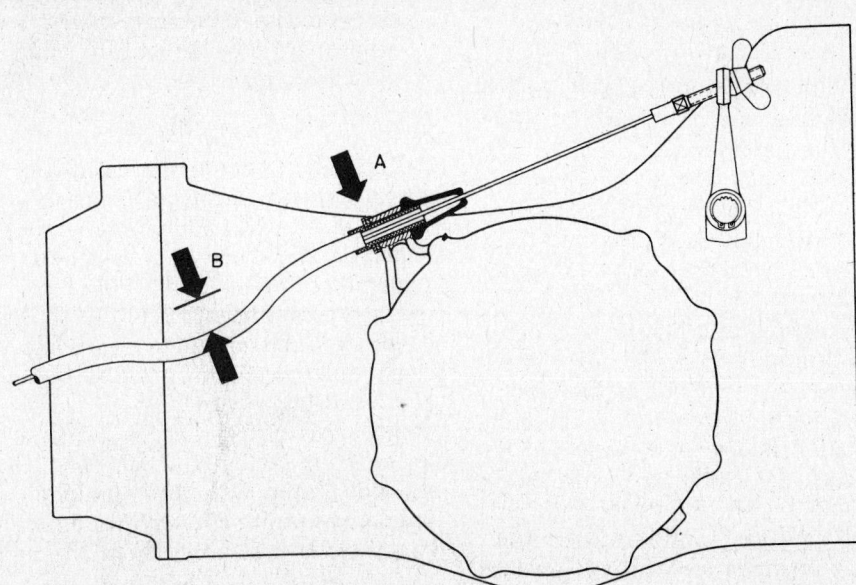

Smooth clutch action requires a slight sag in the cable. Dimension B should be 1.0–1.7″. Adjustment is made by washers at point A.

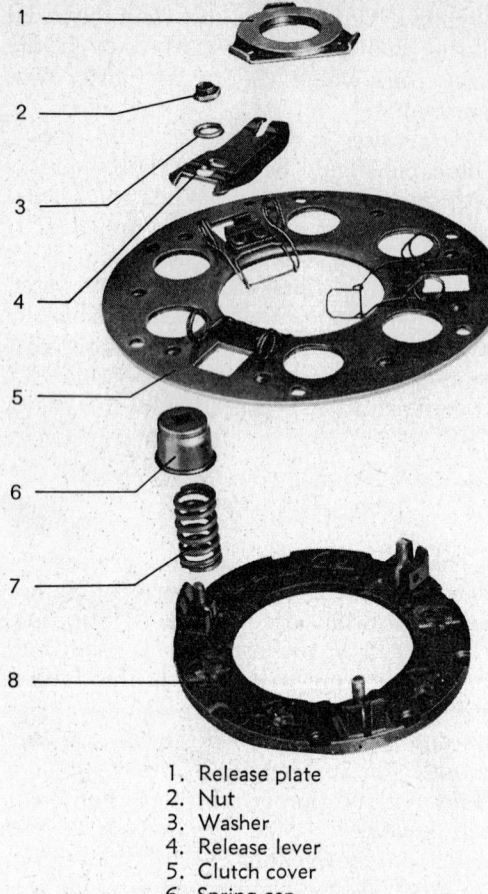

1. Release plate
2. Nut
3. Washer
4. Release lever
5. Clutch cover
6. Spring cap
7. Spring
8. Pressure plate

Exploded view, clutch assembly.

Routine clutch maintenance is limited to adjusting the free play present at the clutch pedal. As the clutch lining wears, clearance between the release bearing and release plate is reduced until these parts touch. Such a condition can lead to damage or excessive wear, as well as clutch slipping and burning of the lining. The proper clutch pedal free play is 10–20 mm. (.4–.8″) measured at the pedal.

Adjustment is carried out at the rear of the car, at the cable end of the clutch. First loosen the locking nut, and then the adjusting nut. On 1966 and subsequent models, a single wing nut serves both purposes. The adjusting nut is turned until the proper amount of free play is evident at the pedal. Then the lock nut, if present, is tightened, after which the pedal should be depressed several times and the free

play rechecked. After the clutch is adjusted, the thread on the cable end should be greased.

CLUTCH ADJUSTMENT—AUTOMATIC STICKSHIFT

Checking Clutch Play

A minimum clutch play is required to prevent slippage and excessive wear. The adjustment is made on the linkage between the clutch arm and the vacuum servo unit. To check the clutch play:

1. Pull off servo vacuum hose.
2. Measure clearance between upper edge of servo unit mounting bracket and lower edge of adjusting turnbuckle. If the clearance is .16″ or more, the clutch needs adjustment.
3. Replace vacuum hose.

Adjusting Clutch Play

To adjust the clutch:
1. Pull off servo vacuum hose. Loosen turnbuckle locknut slightly. Turn turnbuckle 5–5½ turns away from the locknut. There should now be .25″ clearance between the locknut and the turnbuckle.
2. Tighten locknut against turnbuckle.
3. Replace vacuum hose.
4. The clutch adjustment is correct when there is no slippage and reverse can be engaged silently. If the clutch arm contacts the clutch housing, there is no more adjustment possible and the clutch plate must be replaced.

Adjusting Speed of Engagement

The clutch should normally take a full second to engage after shifting down from 2 to 1, at 44 mph without accelerating. Engagement speed may be adjusted to suit personal preference, within certain limits. However, excessively fast clutch action may cause transmission damage, while excessively slow action may cause overheating and rapid lining wear. Speed of clutch engagement is adjusted at the reducing valve, to the left of the ignition coil. The adjusting screw is on top of the unit, under a cap. In the normal position, the adjusting screw has two threads protruding from the unit.

To adjust the speed of clutch engagement:

1. Remove the reducing valve cap.
2. To slow engagement, turn adjusting

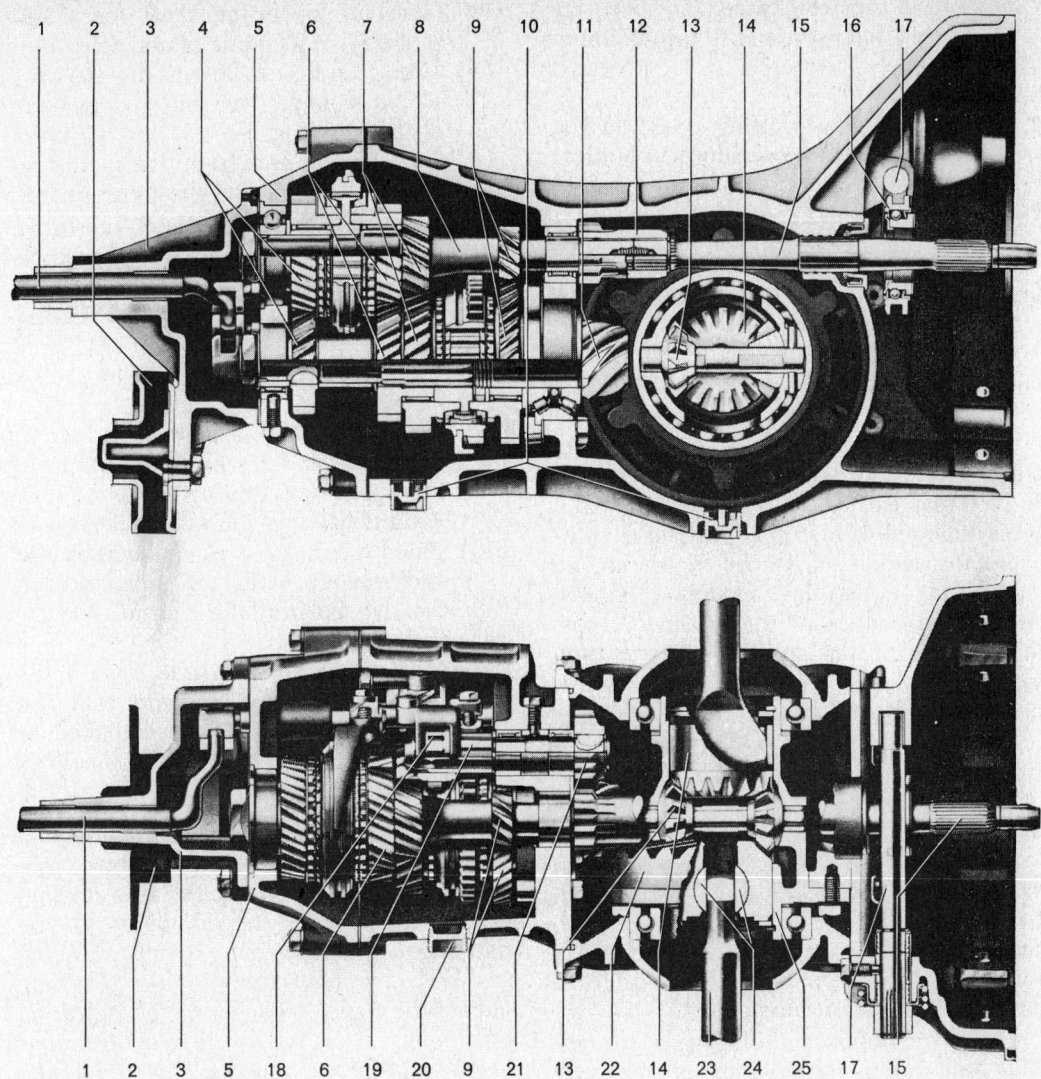

1. Transmission shift lever
2. Bonded rubber mounting
3. Gearshift housing
4. 4th speed
5. Gear carrier
6. 3rd speed
7. 2nd speed
8. Main drive shaft, front
9. 1st speed
10. Oil drain plugs
11. Drive pinion
12. Reverse gear
13. Differential pinion
14. Differential side gear
15. Main drive shaft, rear
16. Clutch release bearing
17. Clutch operating shaft
18. Reverse sliding gear
19. Reverse shaft
20. Oil filler plug
21. Reverse drive gear
22. Ring gear
23. Rear axle shaft
24. Fulcrum plate
25. Differential housing

Cross-sectional view of **one-piece transaxle** with four-speed transmission.

screw ¼–½ turn clockwise. To speed engagement, turn screw ¼–½ turn counterclockwise.

3. Replace cap.
4. Test operation by shifting from 2 to 1 at 44 mph without depressing accelerator.

Trans-Axle

The transmission, differential and engine are mounted as one unit at the rear of the car. The transmission case is rubbermounted and is supported at three points. The transmission case contains the transmission, the differential and ring gear.

Recent transmission cases are of one-piece, die-cast construction, Transmissions of 1960 and earlier models (36 hp. with a non-synchromesh first gear) are of a split-type construction. With the 40 hp. engine introduced on the 1961 models, all transmissions have been of the one-piece type. In the case of the split-type cases, both halves must be replaced at the same time, since they are cast and machined in pairs.

The transmission has four speeds forward and one reverse, with various ratios.

Selection of gears in the Volkswagen transmission is by a floor-mounted lever working through a shift rod contained in the frame tunnel. The gears are helical, and are in constant mesh. In every speed, engine power is transmitted through a pair of gears. There is no direct drive in the Volkswagen transmission.

The drive pinion and ring gear are helically-cut. These gears must be perfectly adjusted in order that long life and silent operation will be ensured.

Transmission work of any kind requires removal of the engine.

TRANS-AXLE R & R

Manual Transmission with Swing Axles

(1) With the engine removed from the car, remove the rear wheels and disconnect the brake lines at the rear wheels and plug the lines.

(2) Disconnect the parking brake cables from the push bar at the frame and withdraw the cables from their conduit tubes.

(3) Remove the bolts at the rear axle shaft bearing.

(4) Disconnect the clutch release cable from the operating shaft lever and pull it from its guide plate.

(5) From the access hole under the rear seat, disconnect the shift rod in back of the coupling.

(6) Remove the nuts from the mounting studs at the front of the transmission.

(7) Remove the lower shock absorber mounting bolts and mark the position of the rear torsion bar radius arm in relation to the rear axle bearing housing by using a chisel.

(8) Disconnect the wires from the starter motor.

(9) Disconnect the ground strap from the frame and remove the nuts from the auxiliary spring rods (1966 Squareback and 1967–68 beetles).

(10) Place a suitable jack under the unit, and remove with a 27 mm. wrench the two bolts at the transmission attachments.

(11) Withdraw the trans-axle toward the rear of the car. Be sure that the main drive shaft is not damaged or bent when the unit is placed on the ground.

Installation of the trans-axle unit is accomplished by reversing the above procedure. The two bolts at the transmission carrier should be greased before being tightened. When a new rear axle is being installed, it is advisable that the retaining nuts of the transmission cradle be tightened fully only after the front mounting has been securely tightened. This tightening sequence is necessary to prevent distortion and premature wear of the rubber mountings.

When the shift rod coupling is reinstalled, the point of the coupling screw should be correctly engaged in the recess. The screw should be secured with a piece of wire. After replacing the ground strap, install the rear axle tubes in their correct positions. The mounting bolts on the spring plate should be tightened to a torque of about 80 ft.-lbs. Tighten securely the lower mounting bolts of the shock absorbers. Install the engine and adjust the clutch pedal free play to .4–.8″ and tighten the rear axle shaft nuts to 217 ft.-lbs. If the cotter pin cannot be lined up, turn further until it can be inserted. Bleed the brakes and adjust the hand brakes. Note: when a new axle, frame, spring plate or front transmission mounting is installed, the rear wheels must be re-aligned. A special optical alignment gauge is necessary for this purpose. An accurate setting is not otherwise possible.

Manual Transmission with Double Jointed Axles

This procedure is similar to that for vehicles with swing axles; however, the rear wheels and brakes need not be removed or disconnected. The driveshafts should be unbolted at both ends and removed. If the vehicle is not to be moved, the driveshafts may be unbolted at the inner ends only and wired up to the body. It is a good idea to cover the axle joints with plastic bags to keep out dirt.

Automatic Stickshift

All Automatic Stickshift models have double jointed axles. After removing the engine:

1. Detach gearshift rod coupling.
2. Remove or disconnect and support driveshafts.
3. Disconnect ATF hoses from transmission. Seal openings. Disconnect temperature switch, neutral safety switch, and backup light switch.
4. Pull off vacuum servo hose.
5. Disconnect starter cables. (Battery ground strap was disconnected during engine removal.)
6. Remove front trans-axle mounting nuts.
7. Loosen rear trans-axle mounting bolts. Support unit and remove bolts.
8. Remove trans-axle.

To replace the trans-axle:

9. Raise trans-axle into place. Tighten nuts for front mounting. Insert rear mounting bolts loosely.
10. Replace vacuum servo hose.
11. Connect ATF hoses, using new washers.
12. Connect temperature switch and starter cables.
13. Install driveshafts, using new lockwashers. Turn the convex sides of the washers toward the screw heads.
14. Align trans-axle and tighten mounting bolts, being careful that the axle joints cannot rub on the frame fork.
15. Insert shift rod coupling, tighten screw and secure with wire.

16. After installing engine, bleed the ATF lines if return flow has not started after 2–3 minutes.

Split-Type Trans-axle, Reconditioning

While the split-type trans-axle is no longer manufactured, there are a sufficient number of units in operation to warrant the following summary of the disassembly and assembly operations:

Disassembly

(1) Remove the gear selector housing.
(2) Remove clutch release bearing assembly.
(3) Remove bolts holding the trans-axle halves together.
(4) With a rubber hammer, carefully separate the case halves, then lift off the right half.
(5) Remove the main drive shaft (the long, clutch-driven shaft).
(6) With a rubber hammer, drive the axle and differential unit from the case. (NOTE: *many shims and special purpose washers are used in this unit. It is advisable to lay out, or otherwise identify these parts to help in assembly.*)
(7) Remove lock pin at reverse sliding gear shaft and drive out the shaft.
(8) Lift out the reverse gear.

To Disassemble the Drive Pinion Shaft

(1) Straighten out the lockplate, and remove retaining nut.
(2) Remove the ball bearing, fourth gear, third-fourth synchronizer hub, and the roller bearing assembly.

To Disassemble the Main Driveshaft

(1) Straighten out the lockplate, and remove retaining nut.
(2) Remove the ball bearing and the high speed gear with a press.
(3) Spread the spacer with a screwdriver, and press off third speed gear.
(4) Remove woodruff keys, and remove the ball bearing at the first speed gear end of the shaft.

To Disassemble the Differential

(1) Cut lock wire and remove.
(2) Remove ring gear retaining bolts.
(3) Remove differential housing cover, axle shaft, differential side gears, ful-

crum plates (trunnion blocks), and the ring gear.

(4) Remove the lock pin, and pull out the differential shaft and the differential pinion gears.

To Assemble the Drive Pinion Shaft

(1) Install the roller bearing inner race by expanding it in an oil bath of 190°F., then sliding it over the shaft and into position.

(2) Install the roller bearing.

(3) Install the end play shim that was originally used. However, some modifications may be necessary, as will be described later.

(4) Slide the second speed clutch gear over the splines.

(5) Install synchronizer and second speed gear.

(6) Slide bushing into second speed gear, then install third speed gear and synchronizer ring over the bushing.

(7) Assemble synchronizer hub for third and fourth gears by sliding the operating sleeve onto the clutch gear, at the same time pulling the three plates into position and securing with the two snap rings. The ring ends must be located in one sector between two shifter plates.

(8) Slide the synchronizer unit onto the drive pinion shaft and rotate the synchronizer ring until the shifting notches engage the slots. The top of the synchronizer hub should be even with the top end of the shaft splines by plus or minus .002″.

(9) Place fourth speed synchronizer ring against the hub, then slide fourth speed gear bushing into position followed by fourth speed gear.

(10) Install thrust washer, and measure end play of the gear train. End play should be from .004″–.010″. Shims are available in various sizes for this purpose.

(11) Install the double row ball bearing.

(12) Position and hold the drive pinion assembly so that the lock nut on the end of the shaft may be torqued to 80-87 ft.-lbs. Do not lock the nut at this time.

(13) Complete assembly of first gear by installing the three coil springs and shifter plates. Be sure the plates are positioned with their ends under the snap ring.

(14) Press all shifter plates down and slide first gear over the hub.

To Assemble the Main Driveshaft

(1) Install the two woodruff keys and position third speed gear on the driveshaft.

(2) Separate the spacer tube with a screwdriver and locate it over the woodruff keys.

(3) Install fourth speed gear, then with an arbor press, push the gears into position until third gear is tightly seated against second gear.

(4) Install both bearings, the lock ring, lock plate, and the retaining nut.

(5) Torque the lock nut to 30–35 ft.-lbs., and bend the lock plate to secure the nut.

To Assemble the Differential

(1) Insert each axle shaft into its corresponding side gear and fulcrum plates. The play between axle and fulcrum plates should be from .002″–.009″. Oversize fulcrum plates are available.

(2) Install axle shaft and side gear assembly, differential gears, shaft and lock pin. Stake the pin to secure it.

(3) Install the other axle, side gear, and housing assembly. Torque bolts to 43–45 ft.-lbs. Safety wire these bolts as a security measure.

At this point special equipment is required to relate the ring gear accurately with the pinion. According to design, the face of the drive pinion is positioned 59.22 mm. from the centerline of the ring gear. This measurement must be flexible to the extent of manufacturing tolerances, and the deviation from standard is stamped on the edge of the ring gear. The ring gear and pinion gear, as on the tunnel-type trans-axle, are matched in sets. Backlash value is also etched on the edge of the ring gear.

In the absence of special differential gauges and measuring equipment, the red lead tooth patterning method has been used, however, the practice is not advisable. The following is a brief description of the recommended procedure, using special Volkswagen tools.

To establish the location of the pinion in the case, install and hold the pinion into the case as far and firmly as possible. Install the mandrel of the gauging tool in one half of the case. Install the other case half and bolt them together.

Rotate the mandrel until the spring-loaded plunger of the mandrel is at right angles to the face of the pinion. Now, release the plunger to permit contact with the face of the pinion. Lock the plunger in this position, then rotate the mandrel so that the plunger is away from contact with the pinion. Separate the two case halves so that the mandrel may be removed for measurement.

Half the diameter of the mandrel, plus the length of the extended pin, should correspond with the value etched on the edge of the ring gear. If these values do not agree, the pinion-positioning shim installed in previous Step No. 10 under To Assemble Drive Pinion Shaft must be changed.

Carrier bearings must carry a preload sufficient to spring the case .005–.007", while maintaining a good tooth pattern and a backlash value corresponding to that etched on the ring gear. This is controlled by the selection of spacers used at the differential pedestal bearings. Proper thickness of spacer rings can be determined by using the special measurement tools supplied by VW.

After installing the differential assembly into its recess in the left-hand housing, install reverse sliding gear and the shaft. Insert the lock pin through the bearing recess. Bend the lock plate over the main drive pinion shaft retaining nut, then install the assembly in the case. Before the case halves are assembled, gears should be shifted to check for free and full tooth mesh. If full mesh is not made, loosen the positioning set screw and move the shifter fork enough to centralize the gear. Reverse shaft lock screw is accessible from inside the case, the other two being reached by removing threaded plugs from outside the case.

Coat the mating surfaces of the housing halves with sealer. Assemble the two halves and torque the retaining bolts to 15 ft.-lbs. The double row rear pinion bearing must be preloaded by .001–.004". This is done by inserting shims between the bearing and the gear shift housing at the rear of the transmission. To do this, take a depth gauge reading of the bearing recess in the gear shift housing, then measure the amount that the bearing race extends beyond the surface of the case. Paper shims are available to make up this specified preload.

Repeat the above measuring and shimming procedure at the mainshaft bearing and add enough shims to produce a .001–.004" preload. Install the gearshift cover and test shift the unit.

Install the trans-axle by reversing the removal procedure.

DISASSEMBLY AND ASSEMBLY OF ONE-PIECE TRANS-AXLE

(The general repairman should not do extensive work on this unit unless he has special tools and experience.)

Disassembly

(1) Remove the gear selector housing and pry off the lock plates that secure the drive pinion and drive shaft nuts.

(2) Lock the transmission by engaging both reverse and high gears.

(3) Remove the drive pinion and main drive shaft nuts, and remove and discard the lock plates.

(4) Remove the gear carrier stud nuts, the ground strap, and the accelerator cable retainer.

(5) Position the assembly so that the left-hand final drive cover faces up.

(6) Remove the stud nuts from the left-hand final drive cover, then remove the cover.

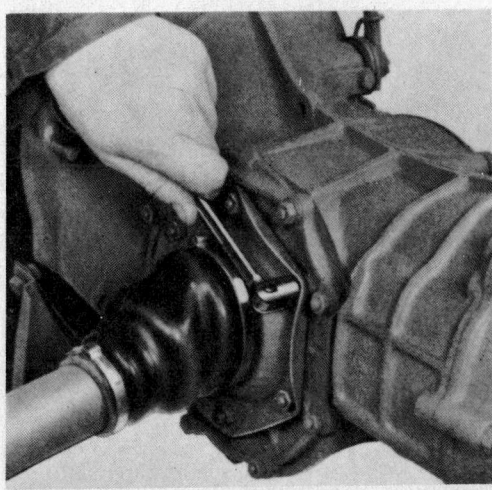

Removing nuts from rear swing axle tube retainer.

Pressing out the differential.

(7) Attach tool VW 297 to the right hand final drive cover studs, and press out the differential. Note the thicknesses and positioning of the differential shims to simplify reassembly.

(8) Loosen the retaining ring that secures reverse gear on the main drive shaft.

(9) Slide reverse gear toward the rear and screw apart the main drive shaft.

(10) Remove the reverse gear and the retaining ring and withdraw the rear main shaft toward the rear, taking care not to damage the oil seal.

(11) Remove tool VW 297 and right-hand final drive cover.

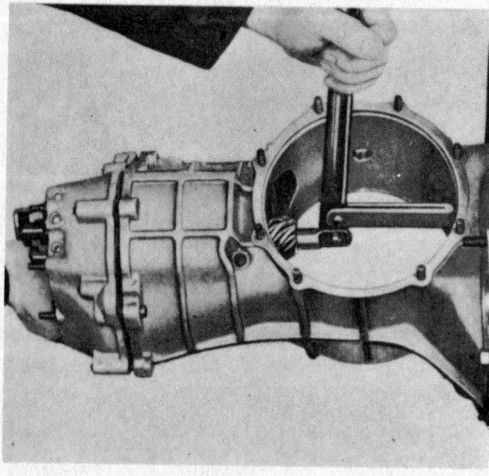

Use of special tool to remove transmission from case.

(12) Release the lock tabs and remove attaching screws, then remove drive pinion ball bearing retainer.

(13) Press the transmission out of case with tool VW 296. Note thickness of pinion shims to simplify reassembly.

(14) Spread and remove snap ring, then pull off reverse drive gear.

(15) Remove woodruff key and withdraw reverse gear shaft and thrust washer from the transmission case.

(16) Remove the security screw of the needle bearing spacer sleeve from the reverse gear shaft.

(17) With a suitable drift, drive out the reverse gear shaft needle bearings and spacer sleeve.

(18) Remove security screw from the needle bearing of the main drive shaft.

(19) With a suitable drift, drive out the main drive shaft needle bearing.

(20) Press out the ball bearings from both final drive covers, and remove the clutch release bearing and operating shaft.

Assembly

Clean and inspect the case and all components for wear, damage or any indication of malfunction, and replace as necessary. The starting motor armature, brushes and bushings should be inspected and dealt with accordingly. The clutch operating shaft and bushings should be checked and, if necessary, replaced.

(1) Press ball bearings into both final drive covers.

(2) Insert needle bearings for reverse gear shaft and spacer sleeve, then secure.

(3) Install main drive shaft needle bearing with a suitable drift, then secure.

(4) Install reverse shaft, woodruff key thrust washer and gear, then secure with a snap ring.

(5) Locate drive pinion shims over bearing, then turn two 4" guide studs into bearing retainer to assure retainer and shim alignment during transmission-to-case assembly.

(6) Push reverse selector and sliding gear onto reverse lever and engage reverse gear.

(7) With a new carrier gasket in place, carefully insert the transmission into

the case (the 4" guide screws will help at this time).

(8) Remove guide screws, then install transmission-to-case attaching screws and lock plates. Torque to 36 ft.-lbs.

(9) Lubricate lip of oil seal, and install rear half of main drive shaft.

(10) Screw both halves of the drive shaft together.

(11) Back them off until the splines of the reverse gear are in line, then install reverse gear snap ring.

(12) With new gasket in place, install right-hand final drive cover and torque to 18 ft.-lbs.

(13) With shims properly inserted, install differential in case.

(14) Install gear carrier nuts and torque to 14 ft.-lbs.

(15) Lock transmission by engaging both reverse and fourth gears at the same time.

(16) Torque the main drive shaft nut to 87 ft.-lbs.; then loosen the nut and re-tighten to a final 43 ft.-lbs. Secure with lock plate.

(17) Torque the drive pinion nut to 43 ft.-lbs. and secure with lock plate.

CAUTION: *when installing gear shift housing, make sure that the three selector shafts are in neutral.*

Gear Carrier, Disassembly and Assembly

Disassembly

(1) Remove the reverse selector fork including the reverse sliding gear from the reverse lever.

(2) Remove and note the thickness of drive pinion ball bearing shims.

(3) Clamp gear carrier in vise equipped with soft jaws.

(4) Loosen and withdraw shifting fork lock screws, and remove first-second shifting fork.

(5) Withdraw the shifting fork shaft from third-fourth shifting fork.

(6) For security, place a strong rubber band around first-second operating sleeve and main shaft, mount the assembly in a press, case end up, and press on the main shaft to remove transmission from gear carrier.

(7) Remove the screw that holds drive pinion needle bearing, and press out bearing.

(8) Press out main drive shaft bearing.

With gear carrier clamped in soft-jawed vise, locking screws of 1st-2nd and 3rd-4th selector forks are loosened prior to the removal of 1st-2nd selector fork.

(9) Clamp gear carrier in vise with soft jaws, and remove reverse lever guide screws.

(10) Withdraw reverse gear selector shaft and remove reverse lever guide.

(11) Withdraw first-second selector shaft and remove reverse lever from support.

(12) Withdraw third-fourth selector shaft.

(13) Remove plungers and detent balls, and hook out detent springs with a small screwdriver.

Assembly

All components should be checked for damage and wear, and replaced if necessary. Free length of detent springs should be 1.0". The wear, or fatigue, limit is 0.9". A force of 33–44 lbs. applied to the ends of the selector shafts should be required in order to unseat the detent balls when shifting.

(1) Insert detent springs through the selector shaft holes.

NOTE: *due to design, the springs for first-second and reverse gear detents can be more easily installed by inserting them into the top halves first.*

(2) Install reverse selector shaft, including reverse lever and reverse lever guide.

(3) Install selector shafts for first-second and for third-fourth gears. Do not forget the two interlocking plungers. This is a safety assurance against shifting two gears at the same time.

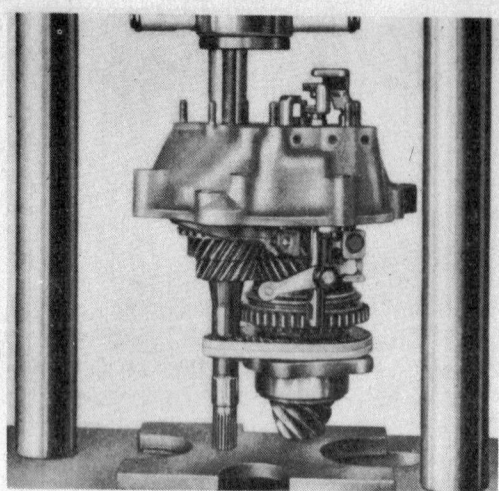

When the transmission is pressed into position, the drive pinion and main driveshaft are held together with a large rubber band.

(4) Check drive needle bearing and main drive shaft ball bearing for wear and damage, and replace if necessary.

(5) Secure drive pinion needle bearing in the gear carrier.

(6) Position gear carrier on a suitable support and press main drive shaft ball bearing into position.

(7) Check selector forks for wear. Fork-to-operating sleeve clearance should be 0.004″–0.012″. Greater clearance warrants parts replacement.

(8) Position the selector fork for third-fourth gears.

(9) Press transmission into the gear carrier. While pressing, take care that the third-fourth selector fork does not become jammed. Also, with a heavy rubber band, secure first-second gears to the main drive shaft.

(10) Install first-second selector fork.

(11) Attach reverse gear fork with reverse sliding gear onto selector lever and adjust selector forks. as described in the following section.

Selector Fork Adjustment

(In order to adjust the selector forks, special equipment is required.)

(1) Place transmission, drive pinion shims and gasket for gear carrier on test tool VW 294 and secure gear carrier with four screws.

(2) Tighten drive pinion bearing retainer with two screws located diagonally, to 36 ft.-lbs. torque.

(3) Push crank of the test tool onto splines of main drive shaft so that the main shaft is locked by the crank.

(4) Engage first and second gears.

(5) With a torque wrench, tighten the main drive shaft nut to 87 ft.-lbs.; then loosen the nut and retighten to 43 ft.-lbs. and lock it.

(6) Attach gearshift housing and shifting handle. By attaching the gearshift housing, correct seating of the main drive shaft bearing in its recess in the gear carrier is guaranteed.

(7) Position first-second and third-fourth selector forks so that they move freely in the operating sleeve while in neutral, and when various gears are engaged.

(8) Position reverse gear selector fork so that reverse sliding gear is centered between the operating sleeve and second gear of the main drive shaft with second gear engaged. The fork must also engage properly in reverse gear of the drive pinion when reverse gear is engaged.

(9) Using a T-handle torque wrench and socket, tighten the selector forks locking screws to 18 ft.-lbs. Tighten the reverse lever guide screw to 14 ft.-lbs.

(10) Remove gearshift housing and transmission from tool VW 294.

Main Driveshaft Oil Seal, Replacement

The main drive shaft oil seal can be replaced with the rear axle installed or removed. Remove the engine, clutch re-

The selector fork locking screws and the reverse lever guide screw are tightened to 18 and 14 ft. lbs., respectively.

lease bearing, and the seal from the transmission case.

Before installing the new seal, lightly coat the outer edge of the seal with sealing compound, and lubricate the main drive shaft and the lip of the seal. Then, slide the oil seal onto the main drive shaft, and drive it into position with a suitable driving sleeve or pipe. The seal should be slid onto the shaft very carefully in order to avoid mis-positioning the spring around the lip.

Drive Pinion, Reconditioning

Disassembly

(1) Press out inner race of needle bearing and fourth gear, then remove woodruff key from the shaft.
(2) Remove spacer sleeve, concave washer shims and the concave washer.
(3) Remove second and third gears with needle cage and second gear synchronizer stop ring.
(4) Remove clutch gear for first and second gears, including springs, shifting plates and operating sleeve.
(5) Disassemble parts.
(6) Inspect all components for wear and damage; replace as necessary.

If pinion and ring gear require replacement, a matched set is in order. (Note matching number on both gears.) If drive pinion or ball bearing are replaced, the drive pinion and ring gear must be adjusted. Whenever a damaged gear is re-

placed, the mating gear should also be replaced. Worn or otherwise damaged first and second speed gears require a replacement of the front main drive shaft.

Clean and check all synchronizer components for wear. Clearance between the synchronizer stop ring face and the clutch teeth of the corresponding gear should be about .043″. If the wear limit of .024″ has been reached, the stop ring should be replaced. If a gear will not engage, even though the clutch is fully released, the probable cause is wear in the slots of the stop ring. Worn parts should be replaced.

Assembly

In preparation, the inner races of the ball bearing and the needle bearing inner race for first gear should be heated in an oil bath to about 194°F.

(1) Slide the ball bearing onto the drive pinion.
(2) Slide the second inner race on so that the bearing parts numbers are exactly opposite each other.
(3) Slide first gear thrust washer and needle bearing inner race onto the drive pinion.
(4) With components mounted in a press, press all parts into correct position.
(5) Tighten the round nut to 108–144 ft.-lbs.
(6) Install shims for first gear.
(7) After the clutch gear for first and second gears has been installed,

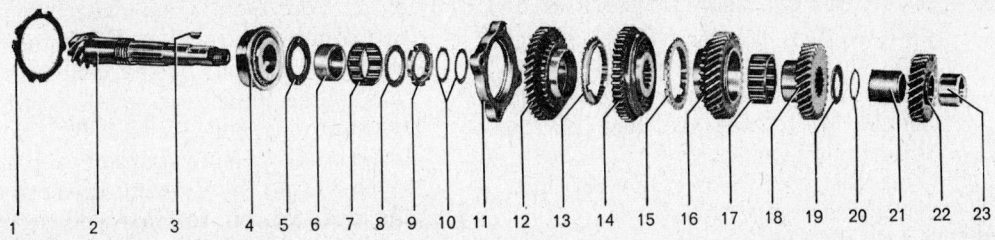

1. Shim	9. Round nut
2. Drive pinion	10. Shims, end play 1st gear
3. Woodruff key for 4th gear	11. Roller bearing retainer
4. Roller bearing	12. 1st gear
5. Thrust washer for 1st gear	13. Synchronizer stop ring (1st gear)
6. Needle bearing inner race (1st gear)	14. Clutch gear 1st and 2nd gears, and reverse gear
7. Needle cage (1st gear)	15. Synchronizer stop ring (2nd gear)
8. Thrust washer for needle bearing (1st gear)	

16. 2nd gear
17. Needle cage (2nd gear)
18. 3rd gear
19. Concave washer
20. Shims for concave washer
21. Spacer sleeve
22. 4th gear
23. Inner race, needle bearing in gear carrier

Details of drive pinion and related parts.

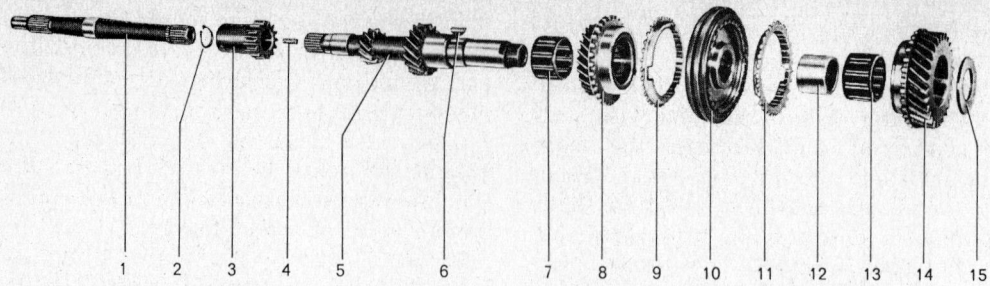

Details of main driveshaft and related parts.

1. Main drive shaft rear half
2. Circlip for reverse gear
3. Reverse gear on drive shaft
4. Stud
5. Main drive shaft front half
6. Woodruff key for clutch gear
7. Needle cage (3rd gear)
8. 3rd gear
9. Synchronizer stop ring (3rd gear)
10. Clutch gear (3rd and 4th speeds)
11. Synchronizer stop ring (4th gear)
12. Needle bearing inner race (4th gear)
13. Needle cage (4th gear)
14. 4th gear
15. Thrust washer (4th gear)

check for end play of .004″–.010″ between thrust washer and first gear. Correct if necessary; shims of various thicknesses are available for this purpose.

(8) Position first speed stop ring on the cone surface of the gear. (First and second synchronizer stop rings are not interchangeable.)

(9) Assemble the synchronizer unit for first and second gears.

(10) Slide operating sleeve on the clutch gear so that its shifting plate slots are in line with the slots in the clutch gear.

(11) With the shifting plates in position, install the two snap rings, offset to each other.

(12) Slide the synchronizer assembly onto the drive pinion. The longer hub should be toward the face of the drive pinion splines.

(13) Turn first speed stop ring until shifting plates engage with the slots.

(14) Adjust the concave washer to produce the prescribed spring travel of .007″-plus or minus .0004″.

(15) Heat the fourth speed gear and needle bearing inner race in an oil bath to 194°F. before pressing into position.

(16) Insert woodruff key for fourth gear into drive pinion.

(17) Slide fourth gear onto the drive pinion, wide shoulder facing the spacer sleeve.

(18) Press fourth speed gear and needle bearing inner race fully into position.

Main Driveshaft, Reconditioning

Disassembly

(1) Remove thrust washer, fourth gear, needle bearing cage and stop ring.

(2) Remove fourth speed needle bearing inner race, clutch gear for third and fourth speed and third gear.

(3) Remove needle bearing cage for third gear.

(4) Strip down synchronizing unit for third and fourth gears.

(5) Clean and inspect all parts for wear and damage.

(6) Place front main drive shaft between two centers and, with a dial indicator, check for run-out at the contact surface of the third gear needle bearing. Run-out must not exceed .0006″. Note: if excessive run-out warrants replacement of the front main drive shaft, the gear wheels for first and second speeds on the drive pinion must also be replaced at the same time.

(7) Check clearance between the stop ring face and the clutch teeth of the corresponding gear with a feeler gauge. Normal clearance is .043″. If a wear limit of .024″ has been reached, stop rings need replacement. If a gear resists engagement, even though the clutch is fully released, it may be due to misalignment of the teeth of the stop ring with the splines of the oper-

ating sleeve. This is caused by wear in the slots of the stop ring.

(8) Check fourth gear thrust washer for wear, and replace if necessary.

Assembly

(1) Assemble synchronizing unit for third and fourth gears. To hold lash between the clutch gear and operating sleeve to a minimum, the sleeve and clutch gear are matched and etched for identification.

(2) Position the shifting plates and install the two snap rings, offset to each other. Be sure that the ring ends engage behind the shifting plates.

(3) Insert clutch gear woodruff key into the main drive shaft.

(4) Place third gear synchronizer stop ring on the cone of the gear.

(5) Press clutch gear for third and fourth gears into position. The identifying figure 4 on the clutch gear must be toward fourth gear. Third gear is lifted slightly and turned until the stop ring engages in the shifting plates.

(6) Press fourth gear needle bearing inner race into position.

Differential, Reconditioning

Disassembly

(1) Put differential into holding fixture.

(2) Cut and remove safety lock wire and ring gear attaching screws.

(3) Lift off ring gear.

(4) After driving out the lock pin, push out the differential pinion shaft, and remove differential pinions.

Ring gear attaching bolts are torqued to 43 ft. lbs.

Assembly

(1) Check the differential pinion concave thrust surfaces in the differential housing. If scored or worn, replace differential housing.

(2) Install differential pinion gears and shaft, then install the pinion shaft lock pin and peen it into place.

(3) Examine ring gear for wear or damage. If necessary, replace. Ring and drive pinion must be replaced only in pairs, which are matched. Note: replacement of drive pinion and ring gear or differential housing requires readjustment of the transmission.

(4) Install and tighten ring gear attaching screws to a torque of 43 ft.-lbs.

(5) Insert ring gear attaching screws safety wire to effect a clockwise force on the attaching screws. Twist ends of safety wire and cut off.

Pinion and Ring Gear, Adjustment

Quiet operation with minimum wearing of the final drive is directly dependent upon pinion and ring gear relationship. For this reason, drive pinion and ring gears are produced in matched pairs and are so identified. Silent operation is obtained by adjusting the drive pinion endwise with the ring gear lifted enough out of the fully engaged position (without backlash) to ensure backlash being within the prescribed tolerance of .0067″–.0098″. Any tolerance difference from standard is measured and marked on the pinion face.

Normally, it is necessary to readjust the ring gear and drive pinion only if parts have had to be replaced which directly affect the adjustment. It is satisfactory to readjust the ring gear if the differential housing, a final drive cover or a differential bearing have been replaced. The pinion and ring gear must be readjusted if the transmission case, the gear itself, or the drive pinion ball bearing have been replaced. To be sure of silent operation, the pinion must first be adjusted by installing shims between the ball bearing and the contact surface at the transmission case. This is to reestablish the factory setting of distance from the center line of the ring gear to the drive pinion face.

Both final drive covers must be installed with a preload of .0055″. After de-

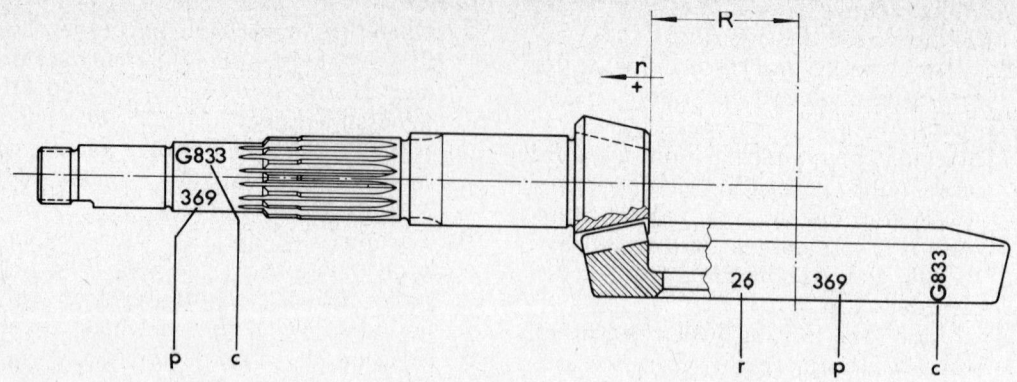

R Standard fitting dimension/ring gear center line
   to drive pinion face:
r Deviation from R (given in hundredths of a millimeter)
p Matching number of gear set
c Type of teeth (G = Gleason, K = Klingelnberg,
   and number of teeth (8:33)

Markings and dimensions of ring and pinion gear.

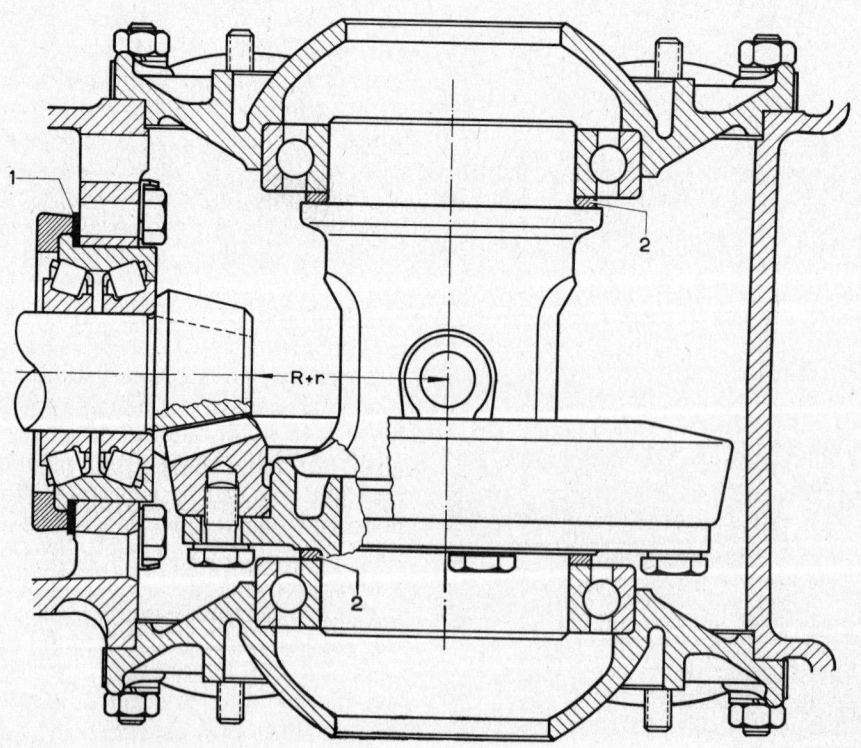

1. Pinion setting shims
2. Shims S1 (ring gear side) and S2 for the differential

Cross-section of ring and pinion gear.

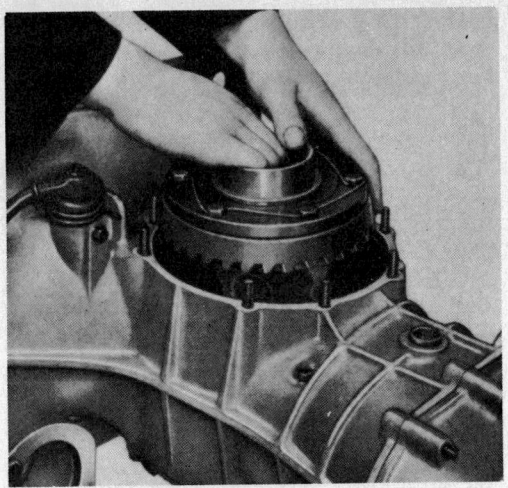

Installing differential in case.

termining the thickness of the shims, a preload of .0028" must be considered on both sides.

The Transporter, an Important Deviation

NOTE: *in the swing axle differential assembly of the VW Transporter, the ring gear is positioned on the opposite side of that in passenger cars, being on the right side of the unit instead of on the left. The reason for this difference is the presence of reduction gears on the rear of the transporter. These gears serve to make possible increased ground clearance in the Transporter and also to reduce the road speed at any given engine RPM to handle the loads allowed for in design. If the ring gear of the Transporter is accidentally installed on the wrong side of the differential unit, the result will be a Transporter with one speed forward and four in reverse.*

Automatic Stickshift Repair

Disassembly

1. Remove gearshift housing with inner transmission shift lever.
2. Remove hex nuts holding gear carrier.
3. Remove transmission cover and gasket.
4. Take out locking clip and loosen roller bearing retaining ring at pinion gear until it just contacts the ring gear. Special wrench VW 183 is normally used.

NOTE: *the transmission can also be removed with the differential in place.*

5. Press out the transmission until the retaining ring touches the case. Alternately loosen retaining ring and press out transmission until ring has been completely screwed clear of the bearing. Hinged lever VW 281 is required to press out the transmission. Press out the bearing with the transmission. Note thickness and number of drive pinion adjusting shims.
6. Support gear carrier in a vise. Remove selector fork clamping screws and remove first-reverse selector fork.
7. Remove second-third selector shaft from fork.
8. Remove circlip and dished washer from main driveshaft. The washer is under tension.
9. Press main driveshaft out of gear carrier. Be careful not to damage splines or second-third selector fork.

Assembly

1. Check all parts; replace or repair as needed.
2. Engage second-third selector fork in operating sleeve.
3. Position pinion shaft and main driveshaft in press. Press gear carrier onto main driveshaft, being careful not to damage splines or jam second-third selector fork.
4. Install dished washer and new circlip on main driveshaft. Press circlip down until it snaps into groove. Squeeze circlip all round with water pump pliers until it bottoms in the groove.

Install and adjust selector forks as follows:

5. Install the gear carrier and pinion shaft in setting appliance VW 294b. The pinion adjusting shims, but not the paper gear carrier gasket, must also be installed in the appliance.
6. Screw retaining ring on pinion roller bearing and hand tighten with C-wrench VW 183.
7. Push selector shaft into second-third fork. Install clamp screw. Install first-reverse selector fork and clamp screw.
8. Move first-reverse lower selector shaft into first gear detent groove. Slide operating sleeve and fork over synchronizer teeth until it is against first gear. Cen-

tralize fork in operating sleeve groove and tighten clamp screw. The selector forks must not rub on the sides of the groove in the sleeve when in either neutral or a gear position.

9. Select first, neutral, and reverse several times while turning the transmission. Check for clearance between fork and sleeve groove in each position. In reverse, the sleeve contacts a stop pressed into the hub. If necessary, alter the selector fork setting until there is the same clearance between sleeve and gear sleeve and stop in both end positions. Tighten clamp screw.

10. Move upper selector shaft into detent groove for third. Adjust fork as for first-reverse. Tighten clamp screw.

11. Check interlock mechanism. It must not be possible to engage two gears at once.

Resume transmission assembly:

12. Insert transmission with pinion shims and gear carrier gasket into transmission case. Drive pinion and mainshaft in with a rubber hammer. On transmission with locating screw for pinion shaft bearing, align bearing outer race hole with hole in housing.

13. If differential is still in place, the pinion bearing retaining ring must be inserted and screwed on while transmission is driven in.

14. Tighten retaining ring to 108 ft. lbs. When using torque wrench on C-wrench VW 183, the correct setting is 87 ft. lbs.

15. Tighten gear carrier nuts diagonally. Insert retaining ring locking clip and tighten screw. On transmission with pinion shaft bearing locating screw, insert and align locking clip so screw can be installed when cover is fitted.

16. Insert gearshift housing and transmission shift lever with new gasket. Tighten nuts.

17. Install transmission cover with gasket and tighten screws diagonally. Coat end of bearing locating screw with sealing compound and insert screw.

Gear Carrier Details

If difficult shifting was noted, check selector shaft detent springs. To remove the plugs holding in the springs, cut a 6 mm. thread in each. Spring free length should be 0.9–1.0″. The force required to overcome the grooves should be 33–44 lbs.

When using a replacement gear carrier from a four speed manual transmission, the holes for the reverse shift rod must be plugged. Only the old type of gear carrier with the long guide for the first-second shift rod is supplied as a replacement. When using this carrier for the Automatic Stick-shift, the hole for the first-second shift rod must be drilled about 16 mm. deep from inside with a 16 mm. dia. drill. If this is not done, the shift rod will probably jam.

Main Driveshaft Disassembly

1. Remove thrust washer, third gear, needle bearing, and synchronizer stop-ring.
2. Press off needle bearing inner race, clutch gear with operating sleeve, and second gear.
3. Take out shaft key.
4. Disassemble clutch gear.

Main Driveshaft Assembly

1. Check gears, synchronizer teeth, thrust washer, main driveshaft, and key for wear and damage.
2. Press synchronizer stop-rings onto gears and measure clearance between synchronizer ring and gear with a feeler gauge.

Gear	Installation Clearance	Wear Limit
First	.043–.070″	.023″
Second, Third	.040–.075″	.023″

3. Install second gear with needle bearing and synchronizer stop-ring.
4. Install key.
5. Fit operating sleeve and clutch gear for second and third gears together, aligning marks. Sleeve and clutch gear may be replaced in matched sets only. Install springs with ends overlapping 120°. The angled spring ends must fully engage over the shift plates.
6. Seat reassembled clutch gear. The 1 mm. deep groove on the operating sleeve must point toward third gear and the wide chamfer on one side of the clutch gear must be toward second gear.
7. Heat inner race of third gear needle bearing to about 212°F and press into position.
8. Install needle bearing, gear with synchronizer stop-ring, and thrust washer for third gear.

Drive Pinion Shaft Disassembly

1. Remove circlip, while holding third gear down with a press.
2. Press third gear and needle bearing inner race off together.
3. Take off spacer spring and remove second gear circlip. Take off second gear, first gear with synchronizer ring, first gear needle bearing, clutch gear with operating sleeve, and shim.
4. Unscrew round nut. Tool VW 293 may be used.
5. Press off bearing. Remove operating sleeve, shift plates, and spring from clutch gear.

Drive Pinion Shaft Assembly

1. Check all parts for wear and damage. Second and third gears may be replaced only in pairs. Press synchronizer ring over cone on gear and measure clearance. Clearances and wear limits are as given in Step 2 under Main Driveshaft Disassembly.
2. Heat inner races of double taper roller bearing to about 212°F and install bearing on shaft. Cool to room temperature and press on with 3 tons pressure.
3. Screw on new round nut and tighten to 159 ft. lbs. Tool VW 293 should be used. Check bearing turning torque. On used bearings, there should be no end-play. To check turning torque, install pinion shaft in transmission housing without shim, fit retaining ring and tighten to 108 ft. lbs. (87 ft. lbs. when using VW 183). Turn pinion with a torque gauge, oiling bearings lightly with hypoid oil. Turn pinion rapidly in each direction about 15–20 turns, then take reading while turning. Turning torque should be .43–1.5 ft. lbs. (6–21 cmkg) for a new bearing or .21–.51 ft. lbs. (3–7 cmkg) for a used bearing. Peen locking shoulder of round nut into pinion splines at three places 120° apart, using a blunt chisel. Be careful not to crack or burr the shoulder.
4. Find thickness of shim for round nut as follows: Measure from end of pinion gear to base of bearing race. This is dimension a. Measure from end of pinion gear to top of bearing inner race. This is b. Measure from bearing contact shoulder on pinion to upper edge of shim. This is X. X should be 44.40–44.50 mm. Shim thickness = X + b − a.
5. Assemble pinion shaft up to second gear. The clearance between second gear and its circlip should be .10–.25 mm. (.0039–.0098″). Circlips of various sizes are available.
6. Fit spacer spring and third gear.
7. Heat needle bearing inner race to about 212°F and press on with third gear.
8. Install circlip.

Differential Details

Before removing the differential, the transmission gears must be removed. Replacing and adjusting the differential requires numerous special tools and procedures. For this reason, these operations are best left to an authorized repair facility.

Differential specifications are as follow:

Backlash—.15–.25 mm (.0059–.0098″)
Side bearing turning torque (preload)— New bearings, 18–22 cmkg (1.3–1.59 ft. lbs.); used bearings, 3–7 cmkg (.21–.51 ft. lbs.)

R & R, Gear Shift Lever — Standard Transmission

The gear shift lever can be removed

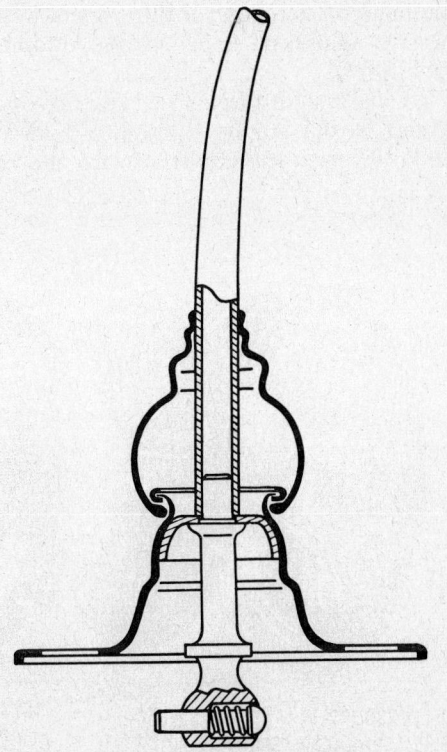

Details of gearshift lever.

after the front floor mat has been lifted and the screws removed that attach the gear shift lever ball housing to the central frame tunnel. After the two retaining screws have been removed, the gear shift lever, ball housing, rubber boot, and spring are removed as a unit. The spring will have to be turned in order to clear the pin. Remove the stop plate and clean all components and check them for wear.

Installation of the gear shift lever is the reverse of the preceding. Replace any worn parts. Be sure that the locating pin is a firm fit, but not overly tight. The spring in the steel ball should be checked for tension and replaced if necessary. When installing the stop plate, be sure that the turned-up ramp is on the right-hand side. Lubricate all parts generously with universal grease. After installation is completed, operate the various gears in order to check ease of movement.

VW Automatic Stickshift

Since 1968, Volkswagen has offered an automatic clutch control three speed transmission. This unit is called the Automatic Stickshift.

It consists of a three speed gear box connected to the engine through a hydrodynamic torque converter. Between the converter and gearbox is a vacuum-operated clutch, which automatically separates the power flow from the torque converter while in the process of changing gear ratios.

While the torque converter components are illustrated here, the picture is for familiarization purposes only. The unit cannot be serviced. It is a welded unit, and must be replaced as a complete assembly.

The power flow passes from the engine via converter, clutch and gearbox to the final drive, which, as with the conventional gearbox, is located in the center of the transmission housing.

The converter functions as a conventional clutch for starting and stopping. The shift clutch serves only for engaging and changing the speed ranges. Friction-wise, it is very lightly loaded.

There is an independent oil supply for the converter provided by an engine driven pump and a reservoir. The converter oil pump, driven off the engine oil pump, draws fluid from the reservoir and drives it around a circuit leading through the converter and back to the reservoir.

This circuit also furnishes cooling for the converter fluid.

OPERATION

The control valve is activated by a very light touch to the top of the shift selector knob which, in turn, is connected to an electro-magnet. It has two functions.

At the beginning of the selection process,

PRESSURE PLATE AND DIAPHRAGM SPRING   CLUTCH PLATE   CARRIER PLATE   TORQUE CONVERTER   IMPELLER   STATOR   TURBINE

Automatic Stickshift clutch and torque converter.

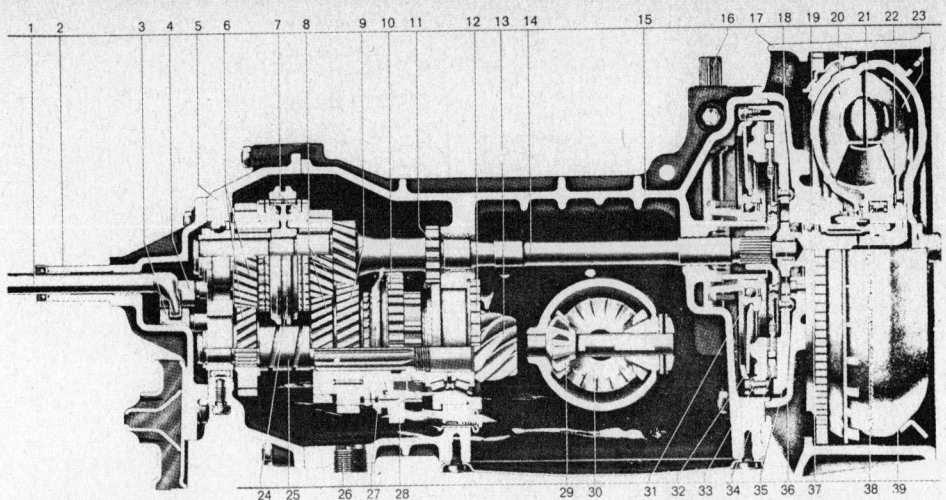

1 Inner transmission shift lever
2 Gear shift housing
3 Selector shaft for 1st and driving range
4 Selector shaft for 2nd and 3rd driving range
5 Gear carrier
6 Gear train, 3rd driving range
7 Synchronizing rings, 3rd and 4th driving range
8 Gear train, 2nd driving range
9 Gear train, 1st driving range
10 Operating sleeve, 1st and reverse driving range
11 Drive, driving range
12 Tension nut for driving pinion
13 Drive pinion
14 Drive shaft
15 Transmission housing
16 Release shaft for separator clutch
17 Converter housing
18 Support tube for converter freewheel
19 Shaft sealing ring for torque converter
20 Impeller
21 Stator
22 Freewheel
23 Turbine
24 Operating sleeve, 2nd and 3rd driving range
25 Axial spring, 2nd and 3rd driving range
26 Magnetic oil drain plug
27 Synchronizing ring, 1st driving range
28 Clutch gear, 1st and reverse driving range
29 Differential pinion
30 Differential side gear
31 Release bearing for separator clutch
32 Cup spring
33 Pressure plate
34 Drive plate
35 Clutch carrier plate
36 Shaft sealing ring for converter housing
37 Grooved ball bearing for turbine shaft
38 Turbine shaft
39 Torque converter

Cross-section of Automatic Stickshift trans-axle.

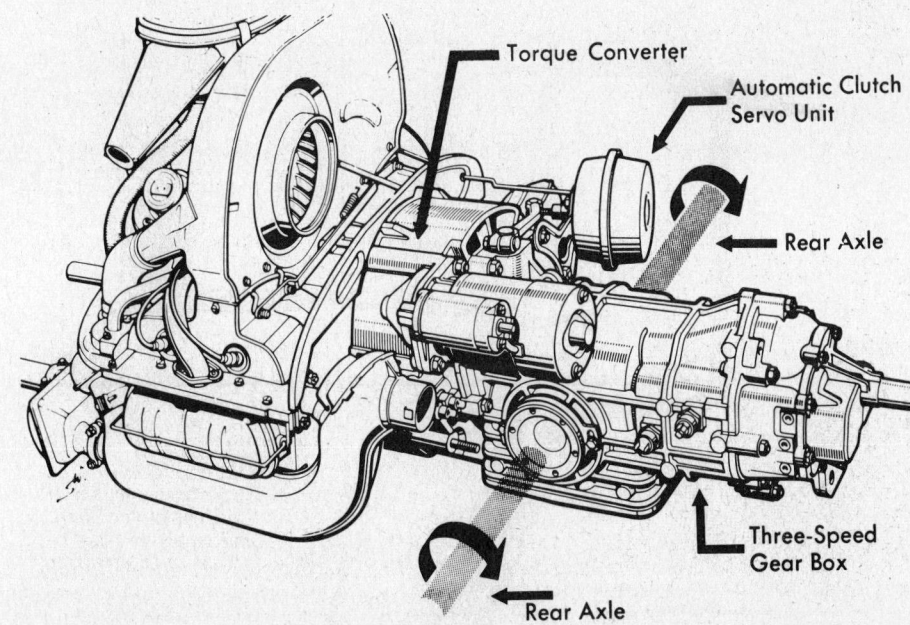

Basic components of Automatic Stickshift.

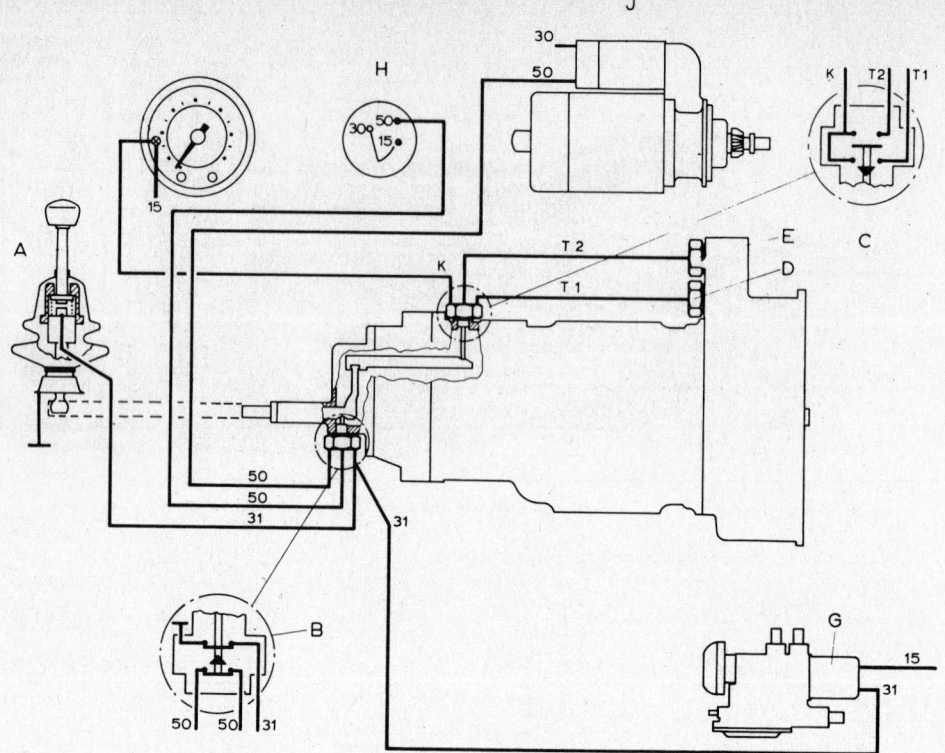

Automatic Stickshift electrical circuit.

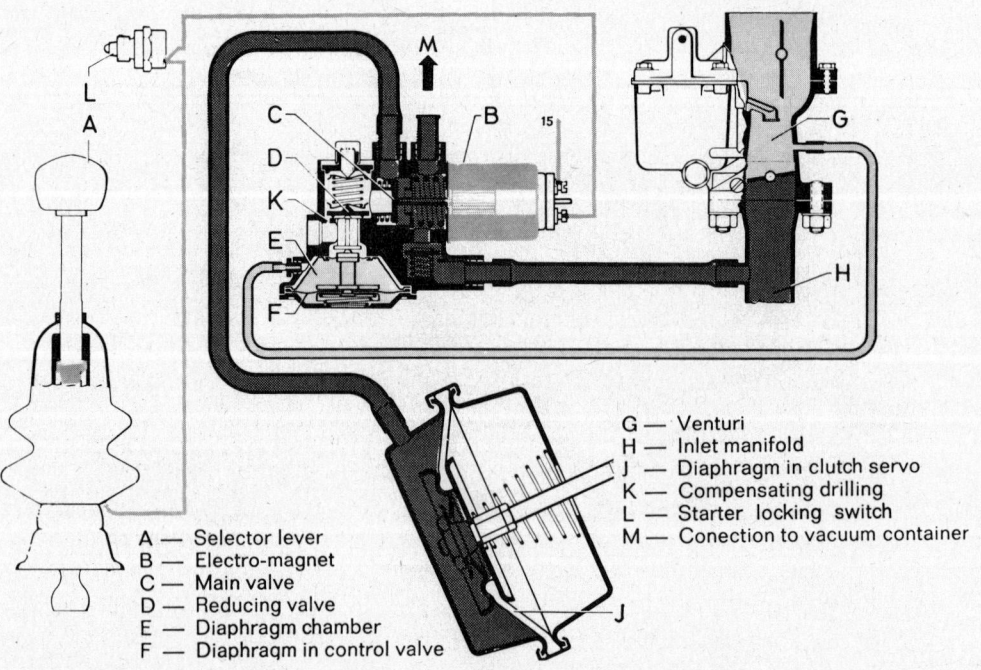

A — Selector lever
B — Electro-magnet
C — Main valve
D — Reducing valve
E — Diaphragm chamber
F — Diaphraqm in control valve

G — Venturi
H — Inlet manifold
J — Diaphragm in clutch servo
K — Compensating drilling
L — Starter locking switch
M — Conection to vacuum container

Automatic Stickshift oil circuits.

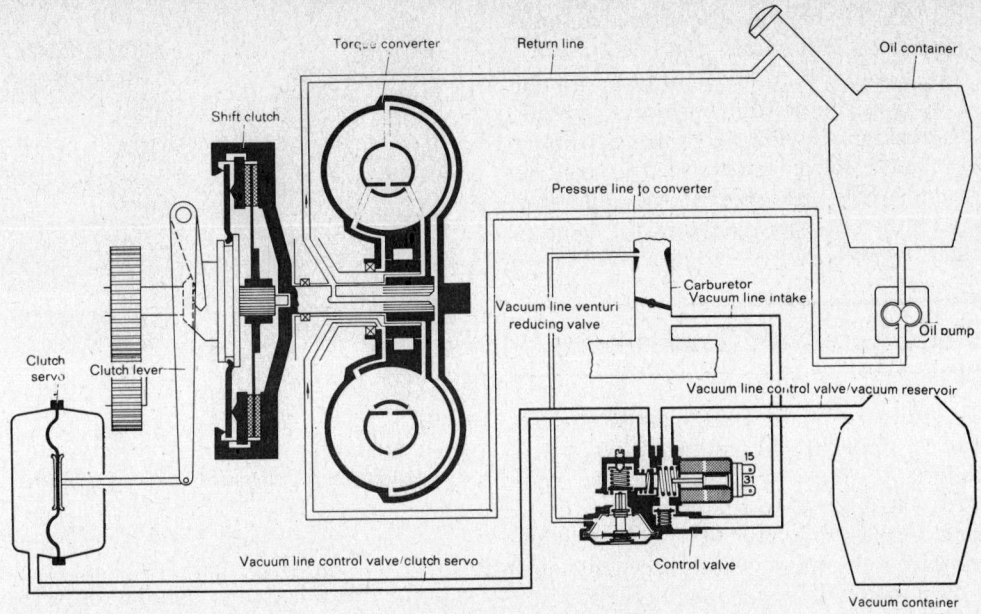

Torque converter   Return line   Oil container

Shift clutch

Pressure line to converter

Carburetor
Vacuum line venturi   Vacuum line intake
reducing valve

Oil pump

Vacuum line control valve/vacuum reservoir

Clutch
servo   Clutch lever

15

Vacuum line control valve/clutch servo   Control valve

Vacuum container

Automatic Stickshift vacuum circuits.

it has to conduct the vacuum promptly from the intake manifold to the clutch servo, so that the shift clutch disengages at once, and thus interrupts the power flow between converter and transmission. At the end of the selection process, it must, according to driving conditions, automatically ensure that the shift clutch engages at the proper speed. It may neither slip nor engage too harshly. The control valve can be adjusted for this purpose.

As soon as the selector lever is moved to the engaged position, the two contacts in the lever close the circuit. The electromagnet is then under voltage and operates the main valve. By this means the clutch servo is connected to the engine intake manifold, and at the same time the connection to the atmosphere is closed. In the vacuum space of the servo system, a vacuum is built up, the diaphragm of the clutch servo is moved by the difference with atmospheric pressure and the shift clutch is disengaged via its linkage. The power flow to the gearbox is interrupted and the required speed range can be engaged. The process of declutching, from movement of the selector lever up to full separation of the clutch, lasts about 1/10 sec. The automatic can, therefore, declutch faster than would be possible by means of a foot-operated clutch pedal.

When the selector lever is released after

changing the speed range, the switch interrupts the current flow to the electro-magnet, which then returns to its rest position and closes the main valve. The vacuum is reduced by the reducing valve and the shift clutch re-engages.

Clutch engagement takes place, quickly or slowly, according to engine loading. The clutch will engage suddenly, for example, at full throttle, and can transform the full drive moment into acceleration of the car. Or, this can be effected slowly and gently if the braking force of the engine is to be used on overrun. In the part-load range, too, the duration of clutch re-engagement depends on the throttle opening, and thus the depression in the carburetor venturi. This results in smooth, pleasant driving under all conditions.

Vanes on the outside of the converter housing aid in cooling. However, in the case of abnormal prolonged loading (lugging a trailer over mountain roads in second or third speed), converter heat may exceed maximum permissible temperature. This condition will cause a red warning light to function in the speedometer.

There is also a starter locking switch. This, combined with a bridging switch, is operated by the inner transmission shift lever. It performs two functions:

1. With a speed range engaged, the electrical connection to the starter is inter-

rupted. The engine, therefore, can only be started in neutral.

2. The contacts in the selector lever are not closed in the neutral position. Instead, the bridging switch transmits a voltage to the electromagnets of the control valve. This ensures that the separator clutch is also disengaged in the neutral shifter position.

Fully Automatic Transmission

The fully automatic transmission, consisting of an automatically shifted three speed planetary transmission and a torque converter, was introduced in 1969.

The torque converter is a conventional three element design. The three elements are an impeller (driving member), a stator (reaction member), and the turbine (driven member). Maximum torque multiplication, with the vehicle starting from rest, is two and one-half to one. Maximum converter efficiency is about 96 per cent.

The automatic transmission is a planetary unit with three forward speeds which engage automatically, depending on engine loading and road speed. The converter, planetary unit, and control system are incorporated together with the final drive in a single housing. The final drive is located between the converter and the planetary gearbox. Driving and driven shafts fit one inside the other in contrast to the manual transmission in which they are located one below the other. The planetary gear unit is controlled by two multi-plate clutches which make up the third-reverse and for-

1 Small sungear   3 Large sungear   5 Small planet gear
2 Planet carrier   4 Large sungear   6 Ring gear

Automatic transmission planetary gear unit.

ward clutch, a first gear band, a second gear band, and a roller clutch which permits the planetary ring gear to rotate only in the direction of drive.

The transmission control system includes a gear type oil pump, a centrifugal governor which regulates shift points, a throttle modulator valve which evaluates engine loading according to intake manifold pressure, and numerous other regulating components assembled in the transmission valve body.

Power flow passes through the torque converter to the turbine shaft, then to the clutch drum attached to the turbine shaft, through a clutch to a sungear. The output planet carrier then drives the rear axle shafts via the final drive.

Transmission ranges are Park, Reverse, Neutral, Drive (3), Second (2), and First (1).

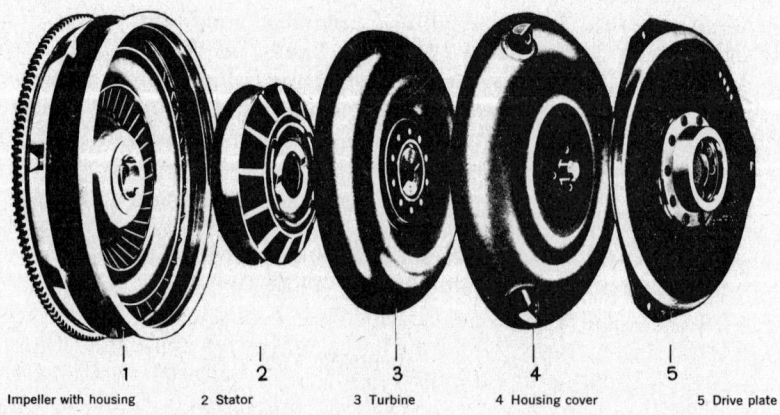

1 Impeller with housing   2 Stator   3 Turbine   4 Housing cover   5 Drive plate

Automatic transmission torque converter.

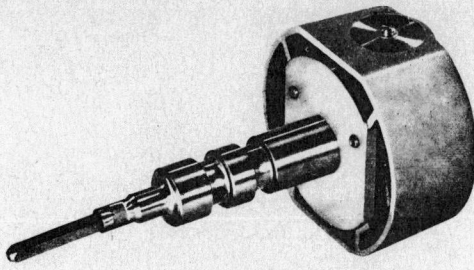

Automatic transmission centrifugal governor.

Automatic transmission oil pump.

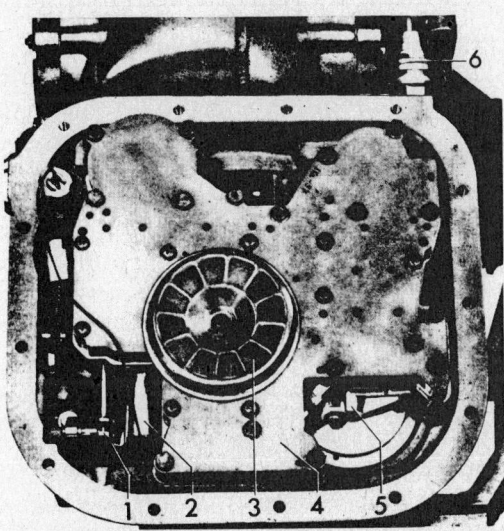

1. Manual valve
2. Solenoid for kickdown valve
3. Oil strainer
4. Transfer plate
5. Valve body
6. Vacuum unit for primary throttle modulator valve

Automatic transmission valve body.

Drive Axle

SWING AXLES

REAR AXLE TUBE AND SHAFT R & R

The rear axle tube and shaft can be removed while the transmission is still in the car.

(1) Remove the brake drum, bearing cover, back plate and rear wheel bearing.

(2) Remove the nuts of the axle tube retainer and remove the axle tube and retainer.

(3) Take off the gasket and plastic packing.

(4) Remove the differential side gear lock ring, the differential side gear thrust washer and the axle shaft.

(5) After removing the differential side gear and fulcrum plates from the differential housing, knock the dowel pin from the bearing flange.

(6) Remove the rear axle dust sleeve.

(7) Press the axle tube out of its bearing flange.

Installation is mainly the reverse of the preceding. The rear axle boot should be checked for wear and replaced if necessary. The tube retainer and its seat should be cleaned thoroughly. The clearance between the flat end of the rear axle shaft and the inner diameter of the side gear should be .03–.1 mm. (.0012–.004″). The axles and gears are coded according to color, and fall into four tolerance groups: yellow, blue, pink and green. Only parts in the same size group should be mated.

Paint Mark	Inner Diameter Side Gear	Outer Diameter Axle Shaft
Yellow	59.93–59.97 mm (2.3200–2.3610″)	59.87–59.90 mm (2.357–2.3582″)
Blue	59.98–60.00 mm (2.3610–2.3622″)	59.91–59.94 mm (2.3583–2.3598″)
Pink	60.01–60.04 mm (2.3626–2.3638″)	59.95–59.97 mm (2.3602–2.3610″)
Green	60.05–60.07 mm (2.3642–2.3650″)	59.98–60.00 mm (2.3614–2.3622″)

The maximum allowable run-out for the rear axle is .05 mm. (.002″). This measurement is taken at the seat of the ball bearing. Axles that are slightly bent can be straightened cold. A feeler gauge is used to measure the side clearance between the flat ends of the axle and the fulcrum

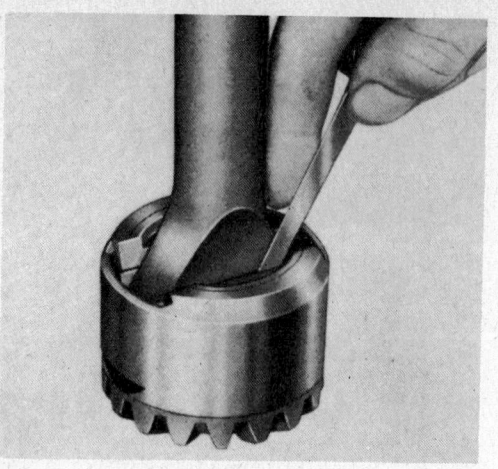

Checking clearance between rear axle shaft and fulcrum plates and between fulcrum plates and differential side gear.

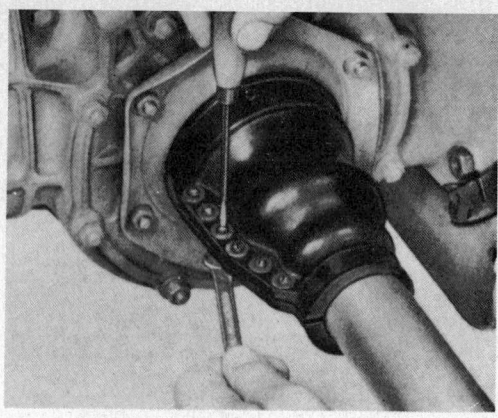

Installation of boot for rear swing axle. The seam must be horizontal, as shown.

plates. This clearance should be .035–.244 mm. (.0014–.0096″). Excessive clearance can be taken care of by installing oversize fulcrum plates, which have a groove on the face.

Install the differential side gear, axle and thrust washer in differential housing and insert lock ring. Install the retainer gasket and the axle tube with retainer. There should be no end play between the axle tube and the axle tube retainer. This is accomplished by choosing a gasket of suitable thickness. The axle tube retainer nuts should be tightened to a torque of 14 ft.-lbs. Over- or under-tightening should be avoided, for this will lead either to rapid wear or to leaks. Axle boots should not be tightened before the car is on the ground, axle intact. Otherwise, the boots may become twisted and damaged.

Rear Axle Boot R & R

The original rear axle boots (dust sleeves) are of a one-piece design and must be cut open in order to be removed for replacement. A split-type axle boot is available for replacement which can be installed and then tightened down. To remove the axle boot, take off the retaining clip at each end, and cut off the damaged boot. Clean thoroughly both the axle tube and the axle tube retainer so that the new boot will fit securely.

Upon installation, put a light coating of sealing compound on the joining faces of the boot and ensure that the smaller diameter of the boot is equal to 89 mm. When positioning the new boot, keep the joining faces in a horizontal plane and on the rear of the axle. Tighten the joining screws and the retaining clips (do not overtighten) only after the rear axle is in a loaded condition, and be sure that the boot is not twisted.

Suspension

Trailing Arm Front Suspension

The trailing arm type front suspension of the Volkswagen has taken two basically different forms over the years. Models prior to 1966 used link (king) pins to connect the front wheel spindles to the suspension trailing arms. All Volkswagens since the 1966 model year employ ball joints in the front end along with the transverse torsion bars which had always been used. The principle of torsion bars is that of springing action taking place via twisting of the bars. When a front wheel goes up or down, the torsion bars are twisted, causing a downward or upward force in the opposite direction.

The supporting part of the Volkswagen front axle is the axle beam, which is two rigidly joined tubes attached to the frame with four screws. At each end of the tubes there is a side plate designed to provide additional strength and serve as the upper mounting point for the shock absorbers. Because the front axle is all-welded, it is replaced as a unit whenever damaged.

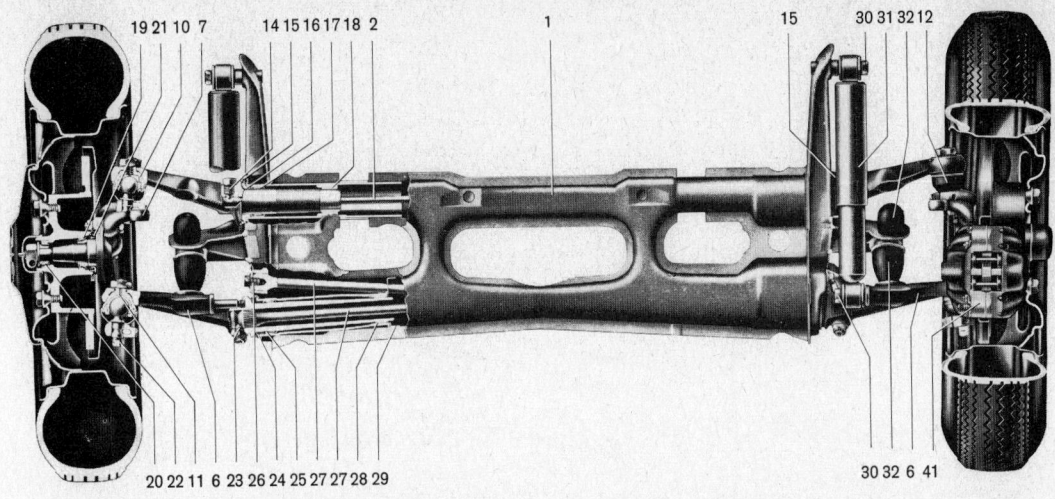

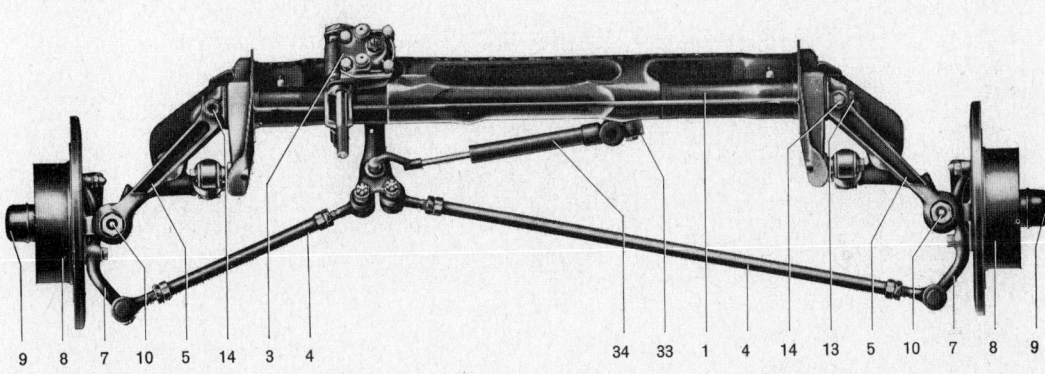

1. Front axle beam
2. Stabilizer
3. Steering gear
4. Tie rods
5. Torsion arm, upper
6. Torsion arm, lower
7. Steering arm
8. Brake disc
9. Grease cap
10. Upper ball joint
11. Lower ball joint
12. Dust seal
13. Adjust screw for upper torsion arm axial play
14. Grub screw
15. Seal, upper
16. Thrust ring
17. Needle bearing, upper
18. Plastic sleeve with metal bush
19. Front wheel bearing, inner
20. Front wheel bearing, outer
21. Seal
22. Eccentric for camber adjustment
23. Grub screw
24. Seal, lower
25. Needle bearing, lower
26. Retaining bolt
27. Torsion bars
28. Plastic sleeve with metal bush, lower
29. Reinforcement plate
30. Shock absorber mounting bolt
31. Shock absorber
32. Rubber stop
33. Steering damper mounting bolt
34. Steering damper
35. Steering gear mounting clamp
36. Steering drop arm
37. Clamping screw
38. Steering knuckle
39. Steering arm mounting bolt
40. Brake back plate
41. Caliper

Cross-sectional view of ball joint front suspension currently in use.

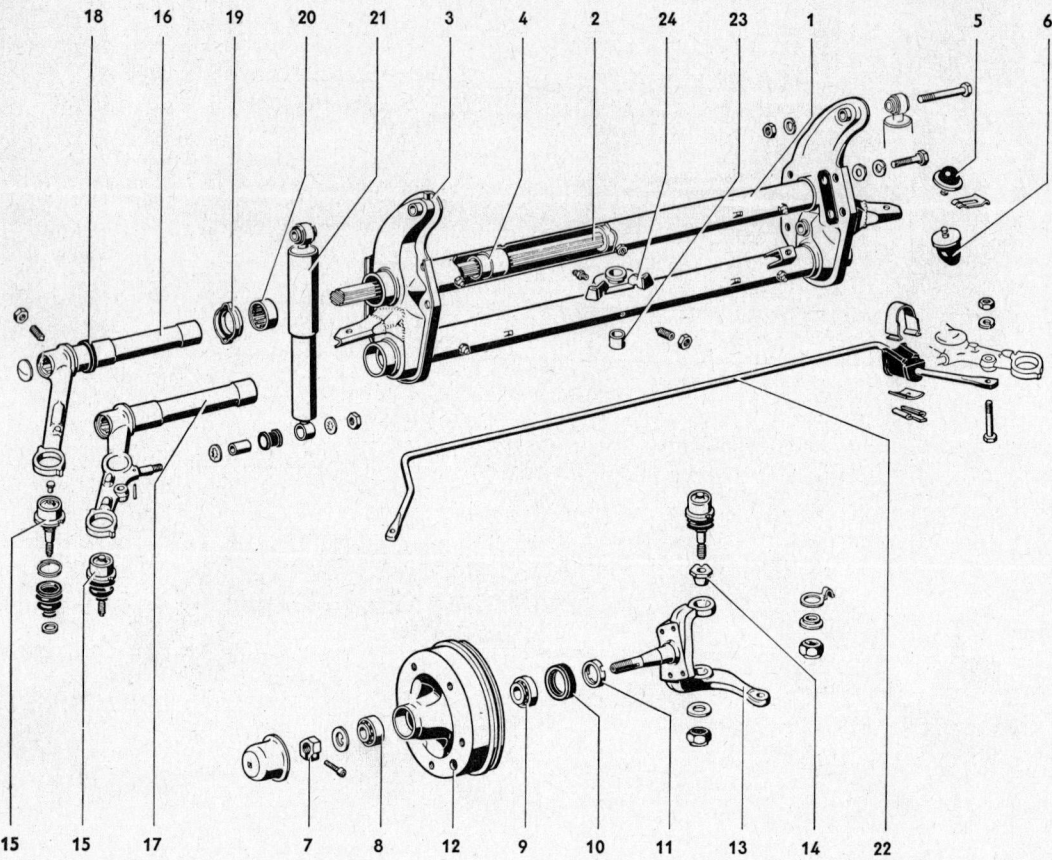

1. Front axle beam
2. Torsion bar
3. Side plate
4. Torsion arm bush
5. Upper rubber buffer
6. Lower rubber buffer
7. Clamp nut for wheel bearing adjustment
8. Outer front wheel bearing
9. Inner front wheel bearing
10. Front wheel bearing seal
11. Spacer ring
12. Brake drum
13. Steering knuckle
14. Eccentric bush for camber adjustment
15. Ball joint
16. Upper torsion arm
17. Lower torsion arm
18. Seal for torsion arm
19. Seal retainer
20. Torsion arm needle bearing
21. Shock absorber
22. Stabilizer
23. Swing lever shaft bush
24. Swing lever stop

Cross-sectional view of transporter ball joint front suspension currently in use. Note steering gear swing lever in middle of lower torsion bar housing.

1. Suspension strut
2. Track control arm
3. Stabilizer
4. Steering gear
5. Tie rods
6. Idler arm and bracket
7. Safety steering column
8. Frame head

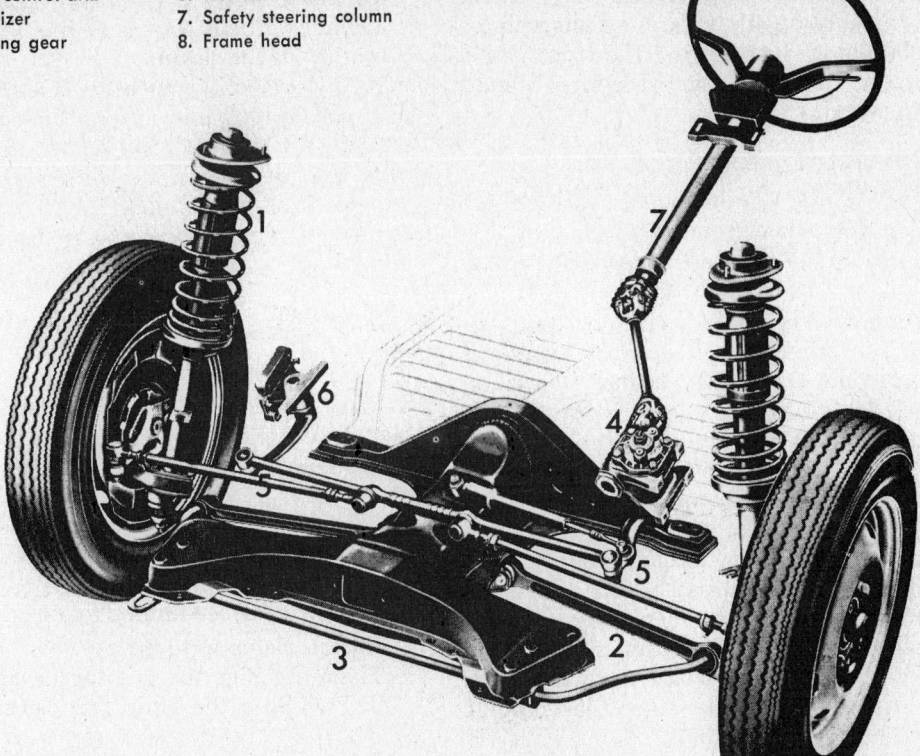

Details of the strut front suspension of the Super Beetle.

Strut Front Suspension

The type 4 and the type 1 Super Beetle use a strut front suspension. Each wheel is suspended independently on a shock absorber strut surrounded by a coil spring. The strut is located at the bottom by a track control arm and a ball joint, and at the top by a ball bearing which is rubber mounted to the body. The benefits of this type of suspension include a wider track, a very small amount of toe-in and camber change during suspension travel, and a reduced turning circle. The strut front suspension requires no lubrication. It is recommended, however, that the ball joint dust seals be checked every 6,000 miles and the ball joint play every 30,000 miles.

GREASING FRONT WHEEL BEARINGS

Beginning with the 1966 models, tapered roller bearings were used in the front wheels of all model Volkswagens. Previously, all models were equipped with

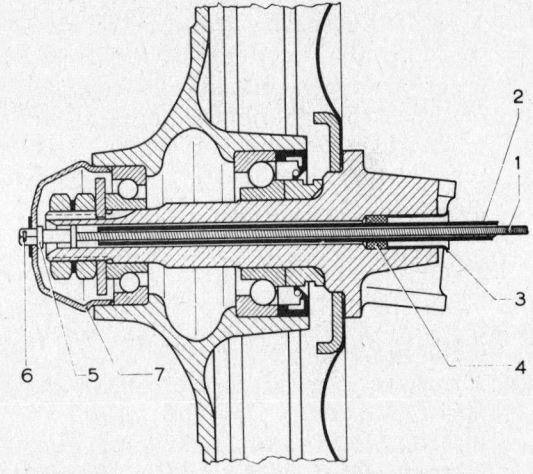

1. Cable	5. Square drive end
2. Plastic sheath	6. Cotter pin
3. Metal sleeve	7. Hub cap with square
4. Rubber sleeve	hole

Cross-sectional view of left front wheel bearing. The right side is the same, but does not have the speedometer drive assembly.

ball bearings in the front wheels. The front wheel bearings should be cleaned and repacked with grease at intervals of 30,000 miles. In servicing the front wheel bearings, the following procedures should be followed:

Ball-Bearing Equipped Models:

1. Jack up the side of the car; remove hub cap from wheel; remove wheel.
2. Remove small dust cap that covers locking nuts at tip of axle.
3. Unscrew the hexagonal lock nut, remove the locking plate, inner hexagonal nut, and the thrust washer. Nuts on left axle have left-hand thread; those on the right have right-hand thread.
4. Pull the brake drum off the axle stub, while at the same time being careful to keep the inner raceway and the cage of the outer bearing from falling in the dirt. If brake drum resists being removed, it may be necessary to back off the brake adjustment slightly and also bolt the wheel back onto the brake drum so as to have more leverage in pulling on the drum.
5. Remove plastic grease seal from hub and take out cage of inner bearing.
6. Leaving inner raceway in place on axle, and outer raceway in place in hub, clean all components in solvent and also clean the inside of the brake drum, being careful to keep any grease or oil from touching the interior surface of the drum. Caution should also be exercised in order that the brake shoes themselves will remain free of grease.
7. Repack the inner bearing cage with grease and place within the hub. Now the plastic seal can be reinstalled by tapping it in lightly until it achieves a flush position. A flat piece of wood placed atop the seal may prove helpful in this operation.
8. The inner raceway on the axle should now be greased and the wheel replaced. After repacking the outer bearing cage, this part can now be inserted in the hub. Bearing installation is completed with the installation of the inner race, thrust washer and hexagonal nut.
9. Tighten the hexagonal nut until the thrust washer can just be moved sideways with a screwdriver. Replace the locking plate (renew if unusable) and the lock nut. The locking plate tabs should be bent over, and the hexagonal nut tightened down.

NOTE: *it is always a good idea to use new plastic seals and locking plates. When working on the left front wheel, take note that this wheel drives the speedometer cable. After removing the cotter pin and the driving end of the cable, proceed normally.*

Roller-Bearing Equipped Models:

Roller-bearing equipped models include the type 3 and the type 1 Karmann Ghia and beetle models of 1966 and later.

On beetle models, equipped with drum brakes, the procedure is much the same as that listed for ball-bearing equipped models except that the final adjustment will be more exacting. Adjustment requires that the following procedure be followed:

1. Loosen clamp nut screw.
2. Tighten clamp nut to a torque of 11 ft.-lbs. while at the same time turning the wheel.
3. Loosen clamp nut until the axial play of the wheel is between .03 and .12 mm. (.001–.005″).
4. Tighten clamp nut screw to a torque of 7 ft.-lbs. and recheck axial play.
5. Install hub cap.

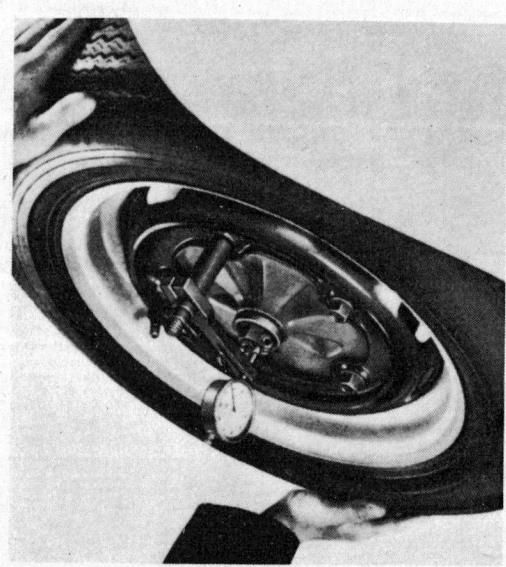

Checking axial (side) play of front wheel bearings with a dial indicator.

Loosening wheel nut pinch bolt at left front wheel. The pinch bolt should be torqued to 7 ft. lbs. on reinstallation.

The following directions apply to type 3 and 1971 and later type 2 models, and the 1500 and 1600 Karmann Ghia, supplied with disc brakes:

1. After removing front wheel and disc cap, bend up the lock plates on the caliper securing screws and remove both the screws and the caliper assembly.
2. Secure caliper to the brake hose bracket by means of a piece of wire or rope. The caliper should not be allowed to hang by the brake hose.
3. Loosen the socket head screw of the clamp nut. Unscrew clamp nut.
4. Remove the wheel bearing thrust washer.
5. Remove disc.
6. The parts removed should be cleaned thoroughly in a cleaning solvent solution. Because dirt and lining dust can act as abrasives, these particles should be kept out of the bearings for obvious reasons. Check all parts for wear, damage, and proper size.
7. Lubricate bearings with a lithium grease of the proper type, pressing grease into the cages and fill the grease cavity of the disc. Grease should not be put into the disc cap.
8. Press in outer race of inner bearing.
9. Fit the inner race and cage and insert grease seal. When fitting grease seal, drive in by tapping lightly with a rubber hammer; avoid tilting seal.
10. Press in outer race of outer bearing.

11. Install thrust washer and ensure that it is not tilted.
12. Adjust bearings so that axial play is between .03 and .12 mm. (.001 and .005″). The adjustment process is as described in the preceding section on adjusting front wheel bearings on beetle models equipped with roller bearings.

TORSION BAR R & R

1. Remove wheels and both steering knuckles complete with brake drums and backing plates. Attach assemblies to axle with wire.
2. Remove shock absorber. Remove torsion arms on one side.
3. Disconnect front gearshift rod at coupling.
4. Loosen set screw locknuts and remove screws.
5. Remove torsion bars.
  To install:
1. Coat torsion bars with lithium grease.
2. Tape end of torsion bar leaves. Insert torsion bars, noting positions of countersinks for set screws.
3. Install remaining parts and lubricate torsion arm bearings with general purpose grease.

LINK PIN R & R

1. Raise front end.
2. Remove front wheels, drums, and backing plates. Disconnect speedometer cable and outer tie rod.
3. Remove torsion arm pinch bolts.
4. Remove torsion arm link and stub axle by driving out both link pins.
5. Examine all parts carefully and replace as necessary.
  To install:
1. Measure offset of torsion arm eye faces. By using .5 mm. shims, set the offset to 7 mm.
  NOTE: *There must always be 8 shims and one retainer with dust excluder fitted to one torsion arm link pin.*
2. Install link pins and shims with universal grease.
3. Replace remaining parts.
4. Adjust torsion arm pins, front wheel bearings, front end alignment, bleed and adjust brakes.

BALL JOINT R & R

1. Remove wheel and brake drum. Dis-

connect stabilizer bar and speedometer cables.

2. Remove torsion arms.
3. Press out ball joints. Check ball joint free play (.3-2 mm. is allowable) and dust seals.

To install:

1. Ball joints and torsion arms are available in standard size and oversize. Press new joint into torsion arm, making sure that notches on ball joint align with projection on torsion arm.
2. Check camber and toe-in after reassembly.

STABILIZER BAR R & R

1. Remove clamp retaining clip.
2. Bend up clamps and remove plates.
3. Remove nut from securing bolt on lower torsion arm.
4. Remove stabilizer bar, check for damaged parts and replace as necessary.
5. Reverse procedure to install. Torque securing nut on lower torsion arm to figure specified in Torque Specifications Chart.

Swing Axle Rear Suspension

The rear wheels of the Volkswagen are independently sprung by means of torsion bars. The inside ends of the torsion bars are anchored to a body cross member via a splined tube which is welded to the frame. The torsion bar at each side of the rear suspension has a different number of splines at each end. This makes possible the adjustment of the rear suspension.

The torsion bars of different models may be slightly different in diameter, depending on the loads designed to be carried. For example, the torsion bars at the rear of the 1967 type 1 are 21 mm. in diameter compared to 23 mm. for the Squareback sedan. The length of the torsion bar also has an effect on its springing properties, and Volkswagens have, through the years and models, had torsion bars ranging in length from 21.7" (1967 type 1) to 24.7" (the first type 1 produced).

The suspension of the Squareback sedan is reinforced by a transverse torsion bar which is located above the rear axle. This bar acts progressively to soften the bumps in proportion to their size, and also to add to the handling qualities and lateral stability of the rear axle. This reinforcing spring is also present on all 1967 and 1968 models. For earlier models, there is available an accessory known as the "Camber Compensator."

This device is a transverse leaf spring which is installed below the rear axle. It reduces oversteer by resisting the tendency of the rear wheels to tuck under the body on hard cornering.

Swing axle rear suspension. This is a type 3 vehicle with a transverse reinforcing torsion bar.

Double jointed axle rear suspension. The model shown is a type 2.

The rear shock absorbers of the Volkswagen are of the double-acting type which dampen the shocks of the road as well as prevent excessive rebound when the wheel(s) are in the unloaded position.

Double Jointed Axle Rear Suspension

This rear suspension system was first introduced on the 1968 type 2 and on the Automatic Stickshift type 1. It is currently used on all Volkswagen vehicles. The axle shafts each have two constant velocity joints. The rear wheels are located by trailing arms as on swing axle models, and by diagonal control arms from the rear crossmember. The axle shafts and final drive therefore do not absorb any thrust forces. In this design, there is only a very slight change in rear wheel track and camber during suspension travel. This results in more stable handling, since rear wheel traction remains constant regardless of the suspension position.

R & R, Rear Wheel Bearing, Oil Seal

Details of the rear wheel bearing and oil seal are shown in an exploded view. To remove the oil seal and bearing, remove the rear axle nut, raise the car and take off the brake drum. The hand brake should be disengaged to make this easy. Remove the

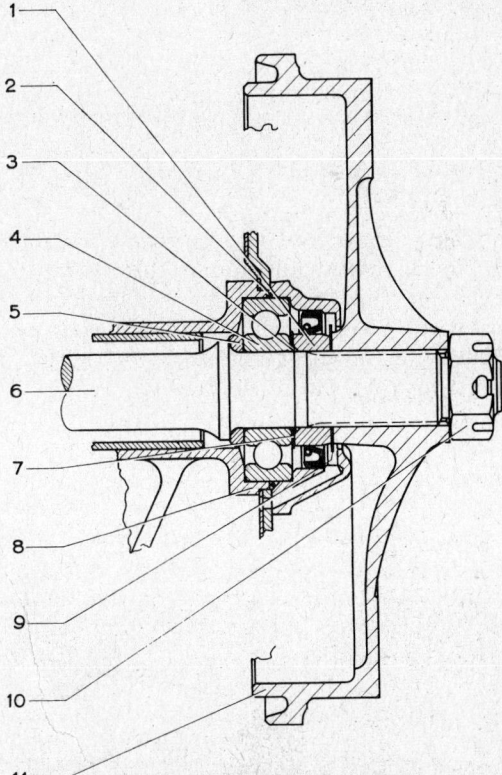

1. Outer spacer	7. Washer
2. Sealing ring	8. Bearing housing
3. Sealing ring	9. Oil seal
4. Ball bearing	10. Nut
5. Inner spacer	11. Brake drum
6. Axle shaft	

Cross-sectional view of rear wheel bearing.

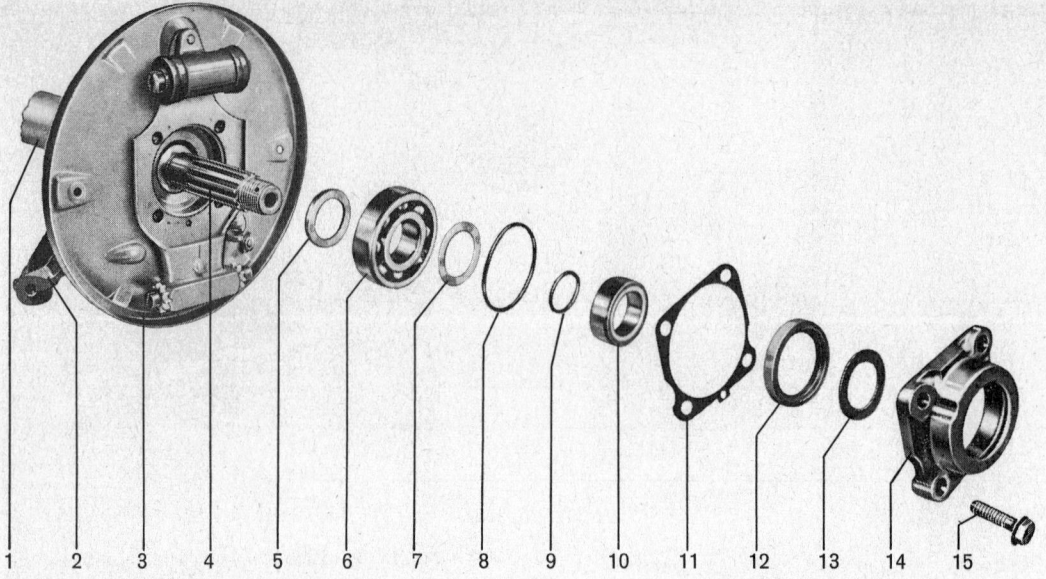

1. Rear axle tube
2. Shock absorber bracket
3. Brake back plate
4. Axle shaft
5. Inner spacer
6. Ball bearing
7. Washer
8. Sealing ring
9. Sealing ring
10. Outer spacer
11. Paper gasket
12. Oil seal
13. Oil deflector
14. Cover
15. Cover retaining screw

Exploded view of rear wheel bearing assembly.

retaining screws from the cover and take off the cover along with the oil seal. Remove brake line, and take off back plate, outer spacer, gasket between bearing and spacer, washer, and cover gasket. Remove the rear wheel bearing and inner spacer.

The correct torque for the rear wheel nut is 217 ft. lbs.

Installation is the reverse of the foregoing, but in addition, certain other steps should be taken. The condition of the bearing should be examined, and the bearing replaced if necessary. Replace the two sealing rings. If the oil seal is damaged or uneven, it should also be replaced. When installing a new oil seal, coat it with oil and press it into the bearing cover. The outer spacer should be examined for wear, replaced if scored or cracked, and lightly coated with oil when installed. Clean the oil hole in the cover and replace cover. The splines in the brake drum hub should be inspected and the brake drum replaced if the splines show signs of excessive wear. Tighten the rear axle shaft nut to a torque of 217 ft.-lbs., using a new cotter pin and turning nut slightly tighter if necessary to line up holes for cotter pin.

Check the level of lubricant in the transmission and top up if necessary. The oil should be at a level even with the lower edge of the filler hole. Bleed and adjust the brakes.

Steering

General

Type 1 and 3 steering is of the roller type. The type 2 uses worm and peg steering. All models since 1968 have collapsible or breakaway steering column arrangements for crash protection. The movements of the steering wheel are transmitted to the wheels via tie rods which are adjustable and maintenance-free. Road shocks are reduced through a hydraulic steering damper.

The worm in the steering case is adjustable, and is engaged by a roller shaft with a needle bearing mounted roller. The roller shaft is held by bronze bushings in the housing and housing cover, while the worm spindle is mounted in ball bearings. The spindle and the roller shaft are both adjustable, the former by a washer fitted under the upper bearing, and the latter by a screw in the housing cover.

Steering and Front-End Geometry

The critical geometrical angles in the front end of the Volkswagen vary significantly from model to model and even change somewhat from early models to later models. Refer to the Chassis and Wheel Alignment Chart for the correct figures for each model.

Brakes

The Hydraulic Brake System

Since 1950, all Volkswagens imported to the U.S. have been equipped with hydraulic brakes. The brakes of the Squareback and

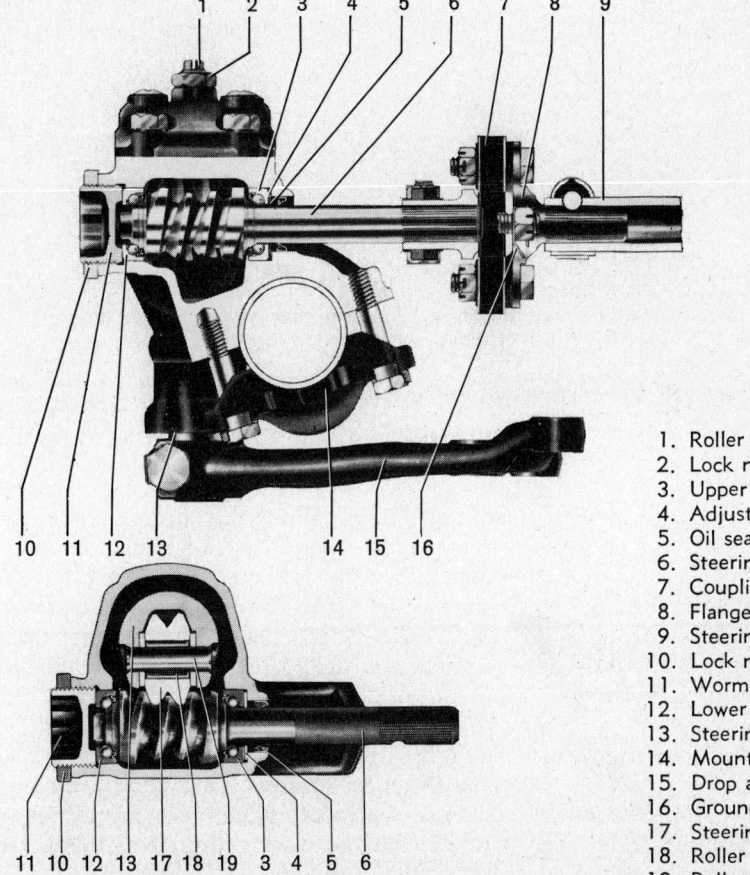

1. Roller shaft adjusting screw
2. Lock nut
3. Upper worm bearing
4. Adjusting shim for worm
5. Oil seal for worm
6. Steering worm
7. Coupling
8. Flange for coupling disc
9. Steering column
10. Lock nut
11. Worm adjusting screw
12. Lower worm bearing
13. Steering roller shaft
14. Mounting clamp
15. Drop arm
16. Ground connection terminal
17. Steering roller
18. Roller needle bearings
19. Roller support pin

Cross-sectional view of roller type steering gear.

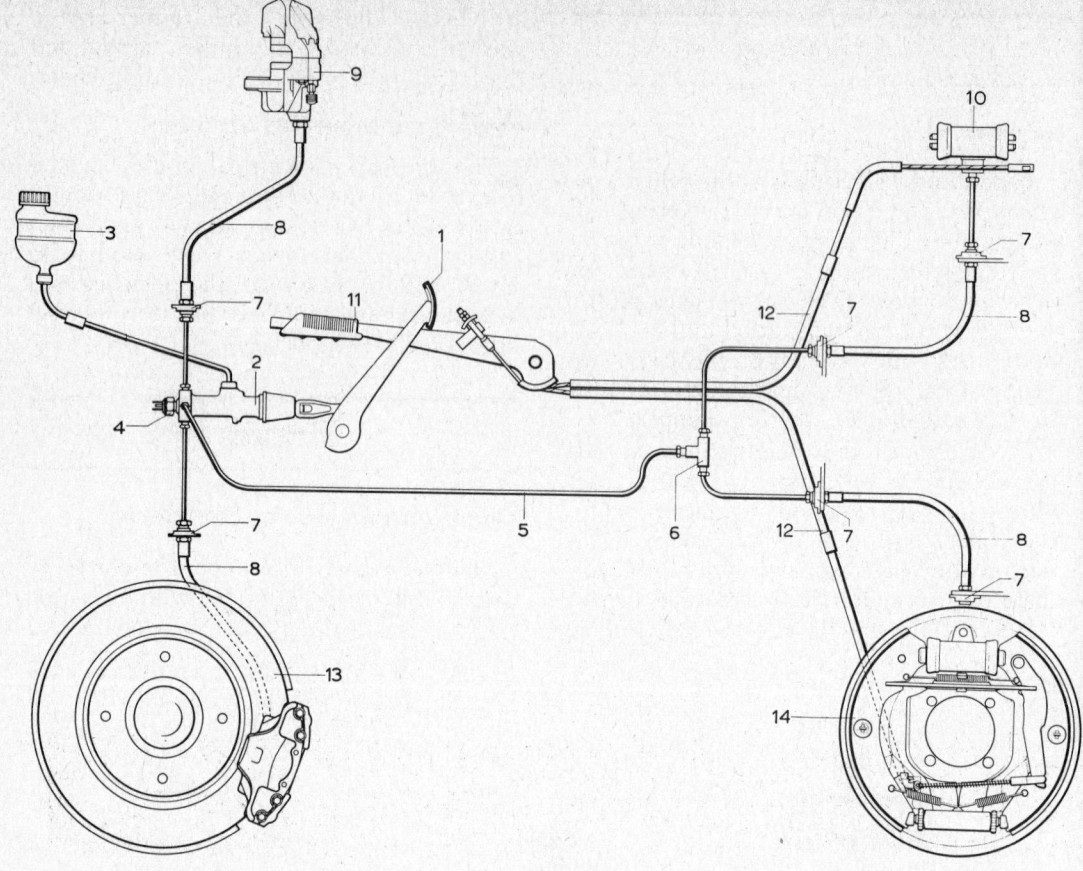

1. Brake pedal
2. Master cylinder
3. Fluid reservoir
4. Stop light switch
5. Brake line

6. Connector
7. Hose bracket
8. Hose
9. Brake caliper
10. Wheel cylinder

11. Hand brake lever
12. Cable and guide tube
13. Front wheel brakes (disk brakes)
14. Rear wheel brakes (drum brakes)

Typical single circuit disc/drum hydraulic brake system.

Fastback sedans are of the disc/drum type, with discs on the front and conventional drums at the rear. The 1500 Karmann Ghia is also provided with discs at the front, while the beetle models are, at this writing, still equipped with drums front and rear. The type 2 models were equipped with front discs starting in 1971.

The hydraulic braking system functions as follows:

When the brake pedal is depressed, force is transmitted to the master cylinder via the push rod. The pressure generated at the master cylinder then travels through the system to the wheel cylinder or caliper, depending on the type of brake at the end of the line. With the drum brake arrangement, the wheel cylinder expands and forces the brake shoes against the inside of the brake drum. In the disc brake, the caliper pinches the friction pads against the disc. Because the disc is out in the open, rather than enclosed like the drum, the heat is dissipated more rapidly, and brake fading is experienced only under the most unusual conditions. The rear brakes, which are generously proportioned relative to the work required of them, are also difficult to fade.

The VW hand brake is mechanically actuated, and operates on the rear wheels via a cable running to the rear.

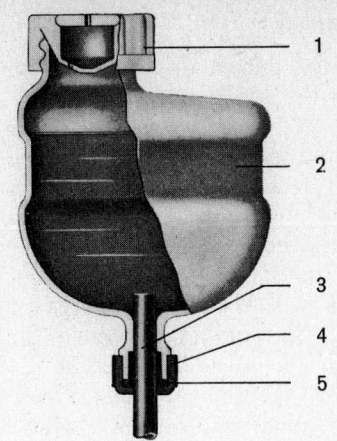

1. Screw cap
2. Fluid reservoir
3. Brake line
4. Line attaching nut
5. Seal for brake line
6. Stop light switch
7. Master cylinder body
8. Special check valve
9. Piston return spring
10. Main cup
11. By-pass port

12. Piston washer
13. Rubber plug
14. Washer for rubber plug
15. Intake port
16. Piston
17. Secondary cup
18. Piston stop plate
19. Lock ring
20. Piston push rod
21. Rubber boot

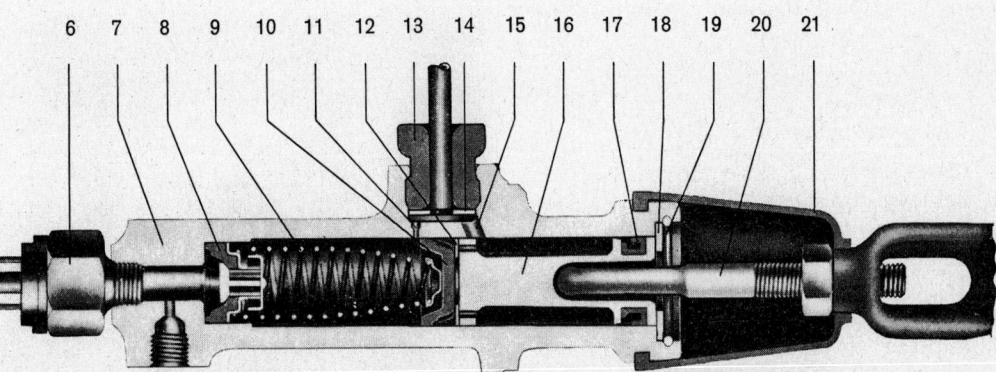

Cross-sectional view, single circuit master cylinder and reservoir.

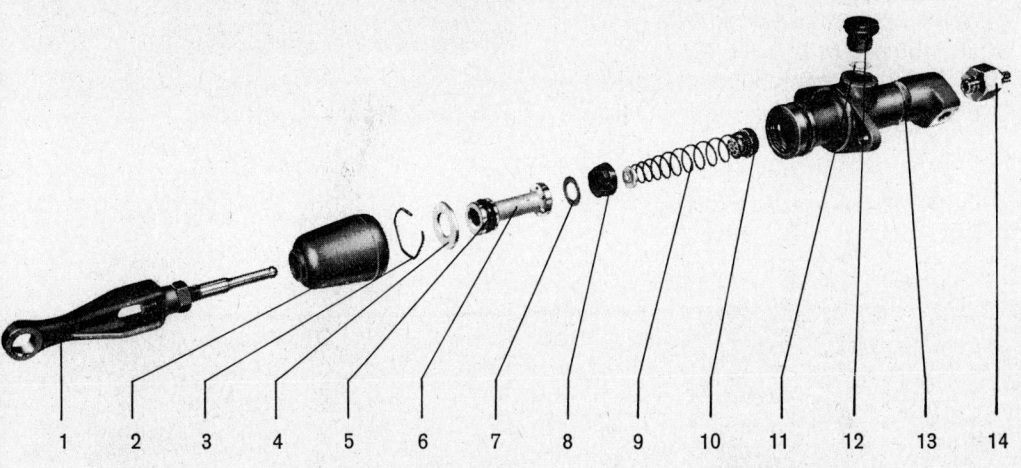

1. Push rod
2. Rubber boot
3. Lock ring
4. Stop washer
5. Secondary cup

6. Piston
7. Piston washer
8. Main cup
9. Return spring

10. Special check valve
11. Washer for sealing plug
12. Sealing plug
13. Cylinder housing
14. Stop light switch

Exploded view, single circuit master cylinder.

Master Cylinder

Steps applying to the early single cylinder-type are not covered here; only steps that apply to the dual-type are used.

Fluid Reservoir

A dual-section reservoir is used so that loss of fluid in one portion will not cause failure of the entire system.

Pushrod

To obtain proper master cylinder action, the pushrod must be set to obtain pedal free movement of 0.02-0.28″.

If a new rod is to be used, it must be an exact predetermined length. That is, from end of ball to center of pin hole— 5.433 ±.019″. Pushrod length is set at the factory.

Master Cylinder Repair

1. Remove boot.
2. Remove stop screw.
3. Remove spring stop-ring.
4. Remove internal parts.
5. Remove residual pressure valves and light switches.
6. Replace in reverse sequence of removal. All parts must be cleaned in methylated spirits or brake fluid. No burrs or corrosive conditions should be overlooked.
7. The residual pressure valves and the brake light switches should be installed and tightened to 11-14 ft. lbs.
8. Install protective cap with breather hole downward.

Bleeding the Brakes

When a brake line is disconnected for any reason or the brake pedal action becomes spongy, the hydraulic brake system must be bled and the fluid reservoir topped up. The usual cause of a spongy brake is the presence of air somewhere in the system. Only Lockheed or Genuine VW brake fluid should be used.

An assistant will make the job easier when bleeding the brakes. Remove the dust caps from the bleeder valves at the wheel cylinders. As shown, place a container of brake fluid atop the fluid reservoir to keep it full during the bleeding opera-

A fluid container of this type makes brake bleeding easier by keeping the reservoir full.

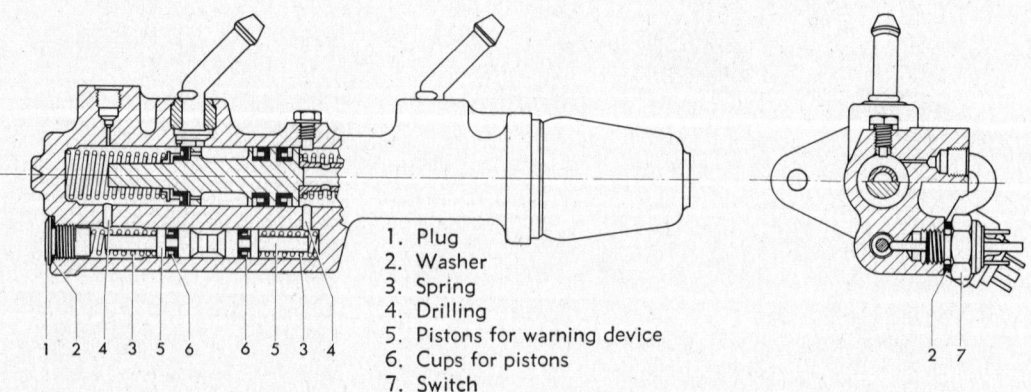

1. Plug
2. Washer
3. Spring
4. Drilling
5. Pistons for warning device
6. Cups for pistons
7. Switch

Cross-sectional view of dual circuit brake master cylinder. Each half of the system serves two brakes. A warning light tells when either half has failed.

tion. The cylinders may be bled satisfactorily in the sequence suggested by the diagram, beginning with the wheel cylinder farthest from the master cylinder. With the bleeder hose on the nipple of the wheel cylinder, loosen the bleeder valve one turn. Have an assistant press gently on the brake pedal, and allow fluid and air bubbles to escape from the valve. Close the valve and let the brake pedal back up slowly. Repeat the operation until bubbles are no longer visible in the bleeder hose. With the pedal held in the lowest part of the last downward stroke, close the bleeder valve, remove the bleeder hose and refit the dust cap to the valve. Go on to the next wheel in the sequence.

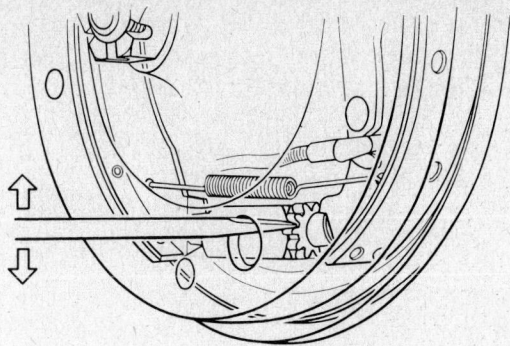

Drum brake adjustment. Later models have two adjusting holes in the backing plate.

Drum Brakes—Adjustment

The only equipment needed to adjust the drum brakes of the Volkswagen is a screwdriver. Pre-1966 Volkswagens have an adjuster hole in the outside of the brake drum for the purpose of adjustment. Models of 1966 and later have adjustment holes in the back plate.

Before adjusting the brakes press the pedal down several times to centralize the shoes in the drums. Turn the wheel so that an adjusting nut is visible through the adjustment hole. Using the screwdriver, turn the adjustment nut until a slight drag is felt when the wheel is rotated by hand. At this point, back off the adjusting nut until the wheel turns freely (about 3 or 4 teeth of the adjusting nut will pass the adjustment hole). Move on to the other adjusting nut of the wheel. The adjustment nuts on each wheel turn in opposite directions, so whichever direction of rotation was needed to tighten one shoe will loosen the adjustment of the other shoe. The handbrake is adjusted by means of adjusting nuts at the rear of the control lever inside the car. However, when the rear brakes are adjusted, the handbrake is automatically adjusted also. If this is not enough to hold the rear wheels at 4 notches, the hand brake should be adjusted by means of the adjusting nuts. When the brake lever is applied by 2 notches, both rear wheels should resist turning by an equal amount of force. If for some reason, it were necessary to use the handbrake to stop in an emergency, it could be dangerous if both rear wheels did not tend to lock equally.

Brake bleeder hose and container.

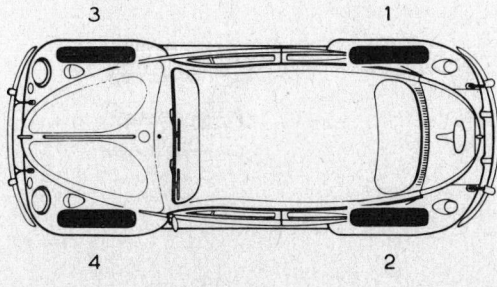

Suggested sequence of brake bleeding starts at the wheel farthest from the master cylinder.

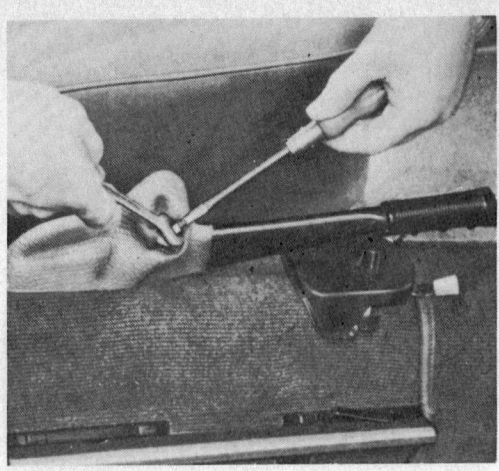

Parking brake adjustment. Each side should be adjusted equally.

PARKING BRAKE ADJUSTMENT

Unless adjustments are of major proportions, or parts replacement needed, the parking brake may be adjusted inside the vehicle.

1. Raise both rear wheels.
2. Slide off rubber ring, then fold back the parking brake lever rubber boot until cable adjusting nuts are accessible.

3. Back off locknuts, then tighten adjusting nuts to a point where the rear wheels will still turn freely when the hand-brake is in off position.
4. Pull the hand-lever up two notches, then check that both rear wheels have the same value of brake hold. Application to the fourth notch should lock the wheels to hand turning.
5. Secure the locknuts and re-position hand-lever rubber boot.

Parking Brake Repair

On parking brake levers of this type, the ratchet sometimes disengages itself, making the brake inoperative. The reason for this is that the rear wheel brakes gradually wear down, thus requiring more travel in the parking brake mechanism to tighten them. Eventually, a point is reached where the ratchet can no longer cope with the increasing travel and the unit comes apart. To repair, follow the numbered steps, but remember, a lasting repair can only be accomplished by adjusting the rear wheel brakes, thus bringing the system back to normal operating tolerance.

1. Completely remove the four nuts which secure and lock the cables to the mechanism.

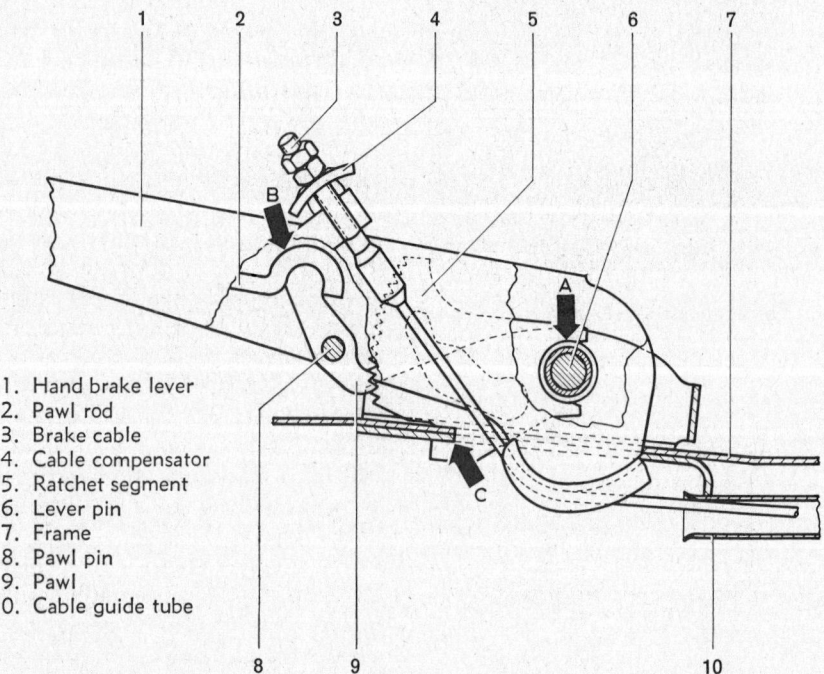

1. Hand brake lever
2. Pawl rod
3. Brake cable
4. Cable compensator
5. Ratchet segment
6. Lever pin
7. Frame
8. Pawl pin
9. Pawl
10. Cable guide tube

Details of parking brake assembly.

2. Lift the lever to its uppermost position and examine the pawl rod, checking that it is not physically broken. Slowly drop rod to about halfway position.

3. Pull the pawl rod off the pawl (see illustration) and reposition pawl so that it contacts ratchet (B). At the same time push down on the pawl rod so that it hooks over the pawl.

4. Slowly lower lever to full down position, then carefully check for proper operation by pushing button and slowly pulling up on lever a short distance. The ratchet mechanism should make a clicking sound, indicating that the pawl rod is successfully hooked over the pawl.

5. If the lever comes free, the operation must be repeated. A study of the illustration will help greatly, as it indicates the correct positioning of the components.

6. When the operation of the parking brake lever is satisfactory, place two of the nuts on the cable ends and adjust.

Drum Brakes

The drum brakes of the type 1 Volkswagen are of the conventional type, with one leading and one trailing shoe per brake drum, and should present no unusual problem to anyone familiar with this type of system. The amount of brake lining remaining can be checked by looking through the holes provided in the drums.

Shoe Replacement—Drum Brakes (Front)

Remove the front wheel and grease cap. Remove the cotter pin from the speedometer drive cable (left wheel) before removing the grease cap. Remove the brake drum, the shoe retainer spring assemblies and the front shoe return springs. Take one brake shoe out of the slot of the adjuster, and remove both shoes from the back plate. When the brake drum has been removed and the brake shoes taken out, care should be taken to ensure that the brake pedal is not depressed through accident or carelessness. If this occurs, the result will be an unchecked expansion of

1. Cylinder
2. Brake shoe with lining
3. Upper return spring
4. Spring with cup and pin
5. Lower return spring
6. Adjusting screw
7. Back plate
8. Connecting link
9. Lever
10. Brake cable
11. Adjusting nut
12. Anchor block

Rear drum brake of type 3 vehicle.

Front wheel brake

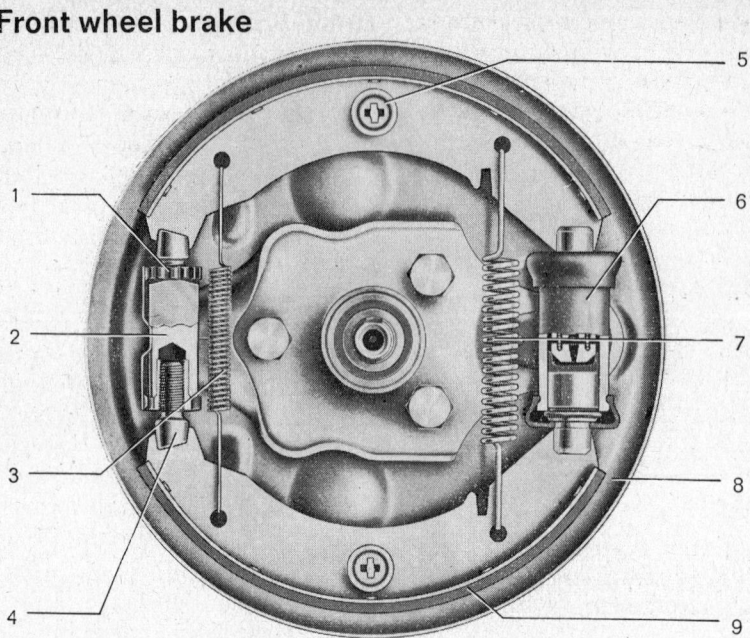

Rear wheel brake

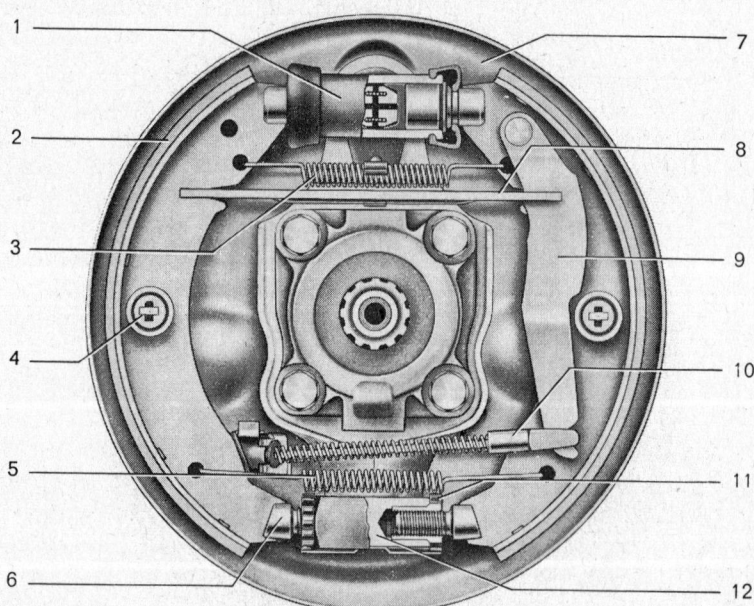

FRONT
1. Adjusting screw
2. Anchor block
3. Front return spring
4. Adjusting nut
5. Guide spring with cup and pin
6. Cylinder
7. Rear return spring

8. Back plate
9. Brake shoe with lining

REAR
1. Cylinder
2. Brake shoe with lining
3. Upper return spring
4. Spring with cup and pin

5. Lower return spring
6. Adjusting screw
7. Back plate
8. Connecting link
9. Lever
10. Brake cable
11. Adjusting nut
12. Anchor block

Front and rear drum brakes, type 1.

the wheel cylinder and its parts, and a loss of brake fluid.

Before installing new brake shoes, be sure that both front wheels are using the same type of lining. Any difference in lining type, or the use of a lining of the wrong width, can lead only to uneven braking at best, and to a dangerous accident at worst. Care should also be taken to install the shoes correctly. The stronger return spring and the slots in the brake shoes should be at the wheel cylinder side of the assembly. The adjuster slots should be positioned as shown in the accompanying illustration. The brake shoe return springs should be hooked in from the front so that there is no chance of interference with shoe operation. The two brake shoe retainers should also be replaced at this time. The slotted retainer cup should be inspected for wear and replaced if necessary. If the slot has become too large or shows evidence of possible weakness, it should be replaced. Once the brake shoes are installed and retained, they should be centered. Before replacing the brake drum inspect the oil seal. Adjust the front wheel bearings and adjust and bleed the brakes. Road test the car and check braking action.

Shoe Replacement—Drum Brakes (Rear)

Remove the wheel and brake drum. (On the type 3, the drum can be removed after the two drum retaining bolts have been taken out. This eliminates the need to re-move the axle shaft nuts in order to remove the drum.) Remove the brake shoe retainers and unhook the lower return spring. (There are two lower return springs on the rear brakes of the type 3.) Remove upper return spring, handbrake cable, and the brake shoe with lever. The lever is held onto the rear brake shoe by a circlip.

Installation of the rear brake shoes is in the opposite sequence. Be sure to install the proper linings on each of the rear wheels. Install the front brake shoe and attach its retaining assembly. The front brake shoe of the type 3 should be positioned as shown in the accompanying picture. Install the rear brake shoe with handbrake lever, connecting link, and upper return spring and clip. Fasten retainer assembly to the rear brake shoe, and attach the handbrake cable end to the lever on the rear shoe. Be sure to position the adjuster slots properly. Install lower return spring(s), adjust the brakes and bleed the brake system. If the axle nut was removed to allow removal of the brake drum, tighten it to a torque of 217 ft. lbs.

Brake Shoes—Relining

A VW parts department is the most reliable place to obtain replacement linings or shoes.

When removing linings from shoes, take care not to damage or distort the shoes. Clean the shoes and remove any burrs from the rivet holes. The linings should fit squarely on the shoe and the rivets be pressed in vertically from the center outwards.

Disconnecting parking brake cable from operating lever.

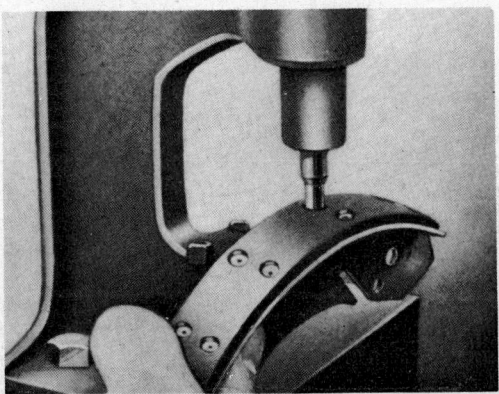

Brake lining rivets must be pressed in carefully to prevent distorting the linings.

Disc Brakes

The principal components of the disc brakes are the disc, friction pad, caliper and splash shield. The purpose of the splash shield is to protect the inside of the disc from damage due to stones or dirt. The caliper housing is in two parts, which are bolted together by four bolts. The disc brakes are self-adjusting and need no maintenance except changing the friction pads when they are worn.

When friction pads need replacing, it is best to take it easy on the new ones for the first 100 miles or so. This is because the surfaces of the pads become very hard during this period of normal usage. If the brakes are used severely during the first 100 miles after installing new friction pads, the lives of the pads will be significantly shortened. When friction pads are replaced, it is good practice to replace both pads on each of the front wheels. A special VW repair set is available for this purpose.

1. Splash shield
2. Brake disc
3. Brake caliper

Basic components of disc brake.

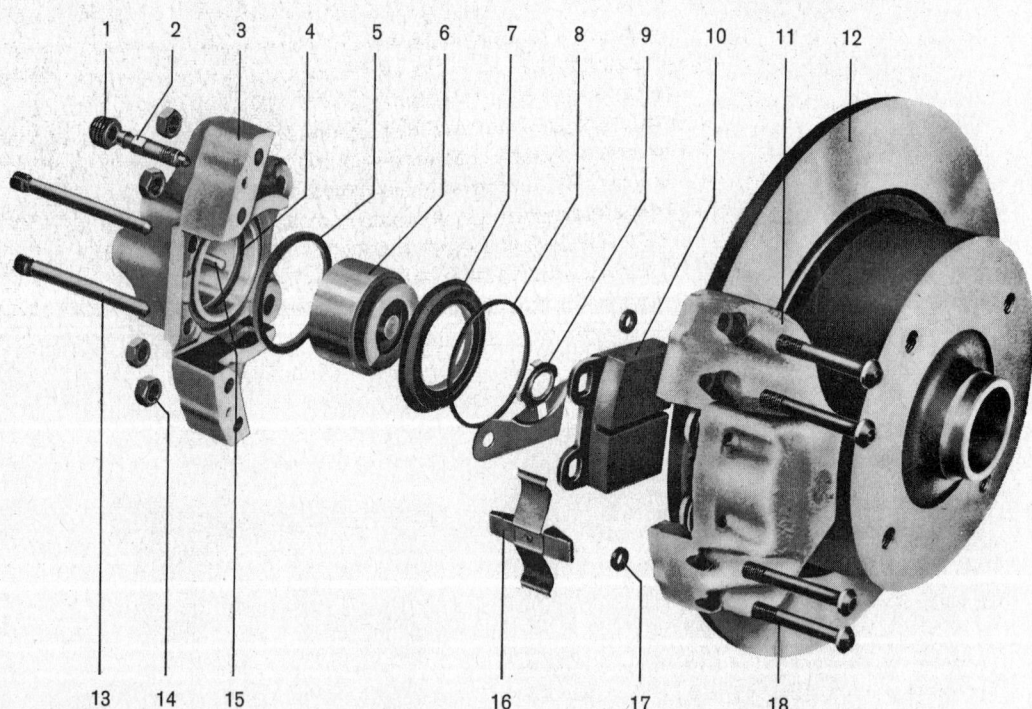

1. Bleeder valve dust cap
2. Bleeder valve
3. Brake caliper inner housing
4. Groove for rubber seal
5. Rubber seal
6. Brake caliper piston
7. Rubber boot
8. Spring ring
9. Piston retaining plate
10. Friction pad
11. Brake caliper outer housing
12. Brake disc
13. Friction pad retaining pin
14. Nut
15. Cylindrical pin (pressed in)
16. Spreader spring
17. Fluid channel "O" ring
18. Caliper housing securing bolts

Exploded view of type 3 disc brake.

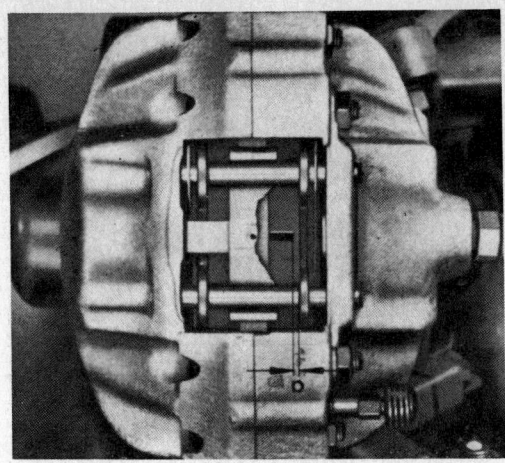

Disc brake friction pads should be checked for wear every 6,000 miles. When the pad thickness, a, is 2 mm. or less, the pads must be replaced.

These special pliers are useful in pushing the pistons back into the cylinders.

R & R Friction Pads

Replacement of the friction pads is easily done. After raising the front of the car, remove the wheel. Use a punch to drive out the upper retaining pin. Remove the friction pad expander spring, and drive out the lower retaining pin. The friction pads can now be removed via a special extractor tool.

On installation of friction pads, discard pads that are dirty or badly scored and put in four new ones. If the old pads are to be re-used, they should be carefully cleaned.

Using a special tool, push the pistons away from the disc. Before carrying out this part of the operation, however, it is a good idea to remove some fluid from the brake fluid reservoir so that it does not overflow. Clean the calipers with alcohol. Sharp edged tools and mineral based solvents should not be used. The retaining plates are removed for the purpose of cleaning, and should be replaced if damaged or corroded. When replacing the retaining plate, be sure that it is installed so that the center part is firmly pressed into the center of the piston, and is below the piston cutaway. The piston should be at an angle of 20°.

The brake pads may now be inserted. Care should be taken to ensure that they move freely in the caliper housing. Insert the lower retaining pin, using a punch of a larger diameter than the pin itself. In-

Insertion or removal of friction pads. A special hook is often needed to remove the old pads.

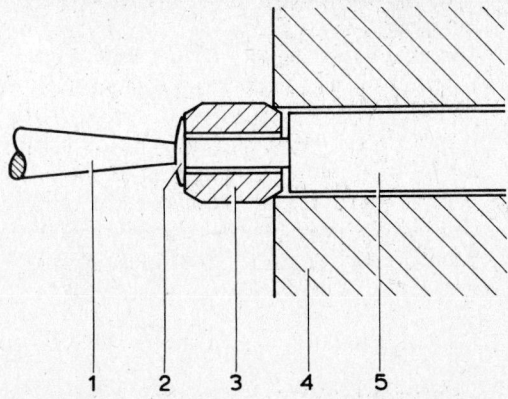

1. Punch (too small)
2. Endangered retaining pin shoulder
3. Split clamping bush
4. Housing
5. Retaining pin

The punch shown is too small to safely drive in the friction pad retaining pin. If the pin is driven in with this size punch, the pin head may shear off and allow the pin to fall out.

stall a new friction pad expanding spring. Insert the upper retaining pin while at the same time pressing down on the expander spring. While the vehicle is stationary, depress the brake pedal several times to enable the brake pads to settle into their correct positions. The level of brake fluid in the reservoir should be checked and the car taken on a test run.

Brake Caliper R & R

1. Remove front wheel.
2. Remove brake hose, cap, and bleeder valve dust cap.
3. Bend back mounting bolt lock plate.
4. Remove caliper attaching bolts.
5. Remove caliper.
6. In reinstalling, clean all mating surfaces and steering knuckle.
7. Install mounting bolts and torque to 43 ft. lbs. The bolts and locking plates should be renewed.
8. Bleed the brake system. Be sure to replace dust caps on bleeder valves.
9. Road-test.

Brake Caliper Repair

1. Remove friction pads.
2. Remove caliper.
3. Mount caliper in vise using vise clamps.
4. Remove piston retaining plates.
5. With screwdriver, pry out rubber boot spring ring. Do not damage boot.
6. With plastic rod, remove boot.
7. Remove one piston with air pressure, holding the second piston with retaining pliers.
8. Remove rubber seal with a plastic rod.
9. To reassemble, first clean with methylated spirits or brake fluid.
10. Replace any parts showing wear, corrosion or physical damage. A damaged cylinder requires the replacement of a complete caliper.
11. Install new rubber boot and spring ring.

12. Install retaining plate.
13. Now, follow above procedures for the second piston.

Brake Disc R & R

1. Remove wheel.
2. Remove caliper from knuckle and hang on the tie rod with wire hook.
3. Remove wheel bearing clamp nut and remove disc.
4. In replacing, check splash shield for damage and replace if needed.
5. Reinstall disc and adjust bearing.

Windshield Wipers

Windshield Wiper Motor R&R, Type 1

1. Disconnect battery ground cable.
2. Loosen clamp screws and remove wiper arms.
3. Remove both wiper bearing hex nuts and washers. Take off outer bearing seals.
4. Remove instrument panel back from luggage compartment.
5. Disconnect cable from wiper motor.
6. Remove glove compartment box.
7. Remove screw securing wiper frame to body.
8. Remove frame and motor, with linkage.

When replacing the motor and linkage:
1. The pressed lug on the wiper frame must engage the groove in the wiper bearing. Make sure that the wiper spindles are vertical to the windshield.
2. Check the linkage bushings for wear.
3. The hollow side of the links must face toward the frame, with the angled end of the driving link toward the right bearing.
4. The inner bearing seal should be placed so that the shoulder of the rubber moulding faces the wiper arm.

VOLVO SECTION

Index

1800 Sports Coupe

Introduction

Since Volvo built its first cars in 1927 in Gothenburg, Sweden, the company has maintained a reputation for making reliable, durable, and economical autos. The first Volvo model to become well known was the 444/544. It was introduced in 1944. In 1957 the first 121/122S was built. Other models developed during later years are: the 1800 sports coupe in 1964; the 142S (2 door) and the 144S (4 door) in 1967; the 145 station wagon in 1968; and the 164 in 1969. All Volvos currently imported into the United States are equipped to meet the latest safety and emission control standards. The following safety features are standard equipment: padded interior, disc brakes, collapsible steering wheel, shoulder and lap belts, and safety door latches. In 1970, electronic fuel injection was introduced in the 142 E and P1800E.

144S

Model Identification

544

164

122S

145

Vehicle and Engine Serial Number Identification

In all correspondence with the dealer or when ordering spare parts, the type designation, chassis number, and engine number should be quoted for proper identification.

Type designation and chassis number are stamped on the cowl under the hood (on the right door column in the 144S and 164S). The type designation is also stamped on a plate to the left of this, with

122S Wagon

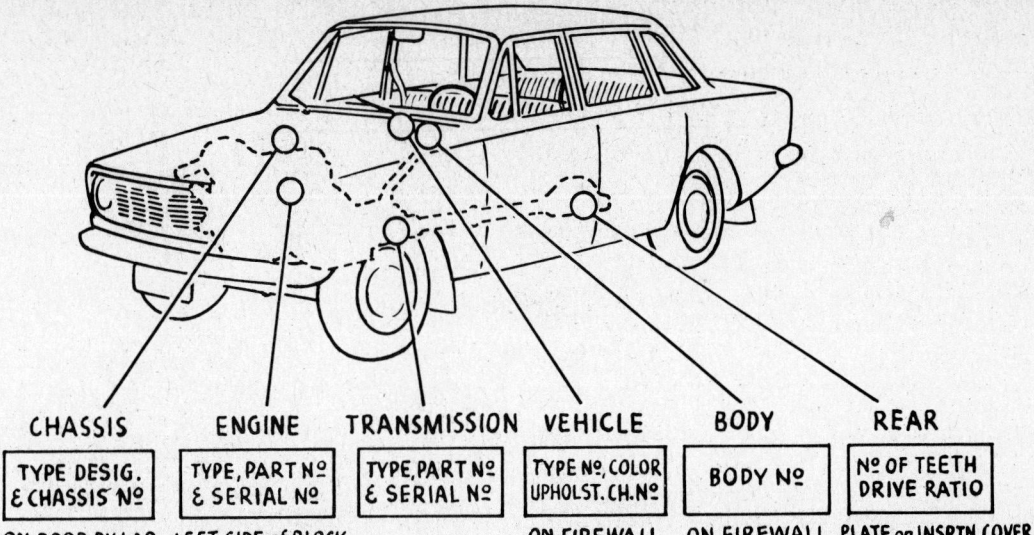

CHASSIS	ENGINE	TRANSMISSION	VEHICLE	BODY	REAR
TYPE DESIG. & CHASSIS N°	TYPE, PART N° & SERIAL N°	TYPE, PART N° & SERIAL N°	TYPE N°, COLOR UPHOLST. CH. N°	BODY N°	N° OF TEETH DRIVE RATIO
ON DOOR PILLAR	LEFT SIDE of BLOCK		ON FIREWALL	ON FIREWALL	PLATE on INSPTN. COVER

the code numbers for body color and upholstery. The engine type designation, part number and serial number are given on the left side of the cylinder block. Stamped on a tab are the last figures of the part number followed by the serial number. In identifying the engine, both the part number and serial number should be given.

Vehicle Identification

Year	Model	Starting Chassis Number
1956	PV444	–
1957	PV444	–
1958	PV444	151123
1959	PV444	18501
1959	PV544	196005
1960	PV544	240387
1961	PV544	244000
1962	PV544/C	302360/ 330100
1963	PV544	334061
1964	PV544	369000
1965	PV544	406043
1966	PV544	427078
1959	122	21000
1960	122	28167
1961	122	29000
1962	122	55741
1963	(4 door)	87743
1963	(2 door)	2461
1964	(4 door)	112000
1964	(2 door)	11600
1965	(4 door)	150532
1965	(2 door)	57555
1966	(4 door—stick)	176814
1966	(4 door—automatic)	176822
1966	(2 door—stick)	108243
1966	(2 door—automatic)	108258
1966	(Station Wagon)	22217

(1962–1966 grouped as: 122)

Vehicle Identification

Year	Model	Starting Chassis Number
1967	(4 door Sedan)	206143
1967	(4 door Sedan—automatic)	206143
1967	(2 door Sedan)	172249
1967	(2 door Sedan—automatic)	172249
1967	(4 door Wagon)	35303
1968	(2 door Sedan)	133441262715
1968	(2 door Sedan—automatic)	133441262715
1968	(4 door Wagon)	223441056880
1962	P1800	101
1963	P1800	326
1964	1800S	6001
1965	1800S	9247
1966	1800S	13679
1967	1800S	18253
1968	1800S	183451024100
1969	1800	–
1970	1800	–
1967	142	–
1968	142	1423441000001
1969	142	–
1970	142	–
1967	144	–
1968	144	1423441000001
1969	144	–
1970	144	–
1968	145	–
1969	145	–
1970	145	–
1969	164	–
1970	164	–

(1967–1968 Sedan/Wagon grouped as: 122S)

Engine Identification

Number of Cylinders	Displacement Cu. In. (cc)	Type	Model
4	86(1,410)	OHV	B14A
4	96.4(1,580)	OHV	B16A
4	96.4(1,580)	OHV	B16B
4	96.4(1,580)	OHV	B16D
4	109(1,780)	OHV	B18A
4	109(1,780)	OHV	B18B
4	109(1,780)	OHV	B18D
4	122(1,990)	OHV	B20A
4	122(1,990)	OHV	B20B
6	183(2,980)	OHV	B30A

General Engine Specifications

Type	Cu. In. Displacement (cc's)	Carburetion	SAE Horsepower @ rpm	Torque (ft. lbs.) @ rpm	Bore x Stroke (in.)	Compress. Ratio	Normal Oil Pressure (psi)
B14A	86 (1,410)	Dual Sidedraft	70 @ 5,500	75.9 @ 3,000	2.953 x 3.150	7.8:1	43–57 @ 2,000
B16A	96.4 (1,580)	Single Downdraft	66 @ 4,500	86.5 @ 2,500	3.125 x 3.150	7.4:1	36–50 @ 2,000
B16B	96.4 (1,580)	Dual Sidedraft	85 @ 5,500	87 @ 3,500	3.125 x 3.150	8.2:1	36–50 @ 2,000
B16D	96.4 (1,580)	Single Downdraft	72 @ 5,500	86.1 @ 2,600	3.125 x 3.150	8.2:1	36–50 @ 2,000
B18A	109 (1,780)	Single Downdraft	75 @ 4,500	103 @ 2,800	3.313 x 3.150	8.5:1	50–85 @ 2,000
B18B	109 (1,780)	Dual Sidedraft	100 @ 5,500	108 @ 4,000	3.313 x 3.150	9.5:1	50–85 @ 2,000
B18D	109 (1,780)	Dual Sidedraft	90 @ 5,000	105 @ 3,500	3.313 x 3.150	8.5:1	50–85 @ 2,000
B20A	122 (1,990)	Single Sidedraft	90 @ 4,800	119 @ 3,000	3.50 x 3.150	8.7:1	36–85 @ 2,000
B20B	122 (1,990)	Dual Sidedraft	118 @ 5,800	123 @ 3,500	3.50 x 3.150	9.5:1	36–85 @ 2,000
B30A	183 (2,980)	Dual Sidedraft	145 @ 5,500	163 @ 3,000	3.50 x 3.150	9.2:1	36–85 @ 2,000

Tune-Up Specifications

| Engine Model | Spark Plugs | | | Distributor | | Basic Ignition Timing (deg.) @ r.p.m. | Cranking Compress. Press. (p.s.i.) | Valves | | | Idle Speed |
	Make, Type	Gap (in.)	Point Dwell (deg.)	Point Gap (in.)			Intake ① Clear. (in.)	Exhaust ① Clear. (in.)	Intake ④ Opens (deg.)	
B14	Champion Y4A/J6	.028-.032	47	.018-.022	20 BTDC @ 1,500		.020	.020	0 @ TDC	
B16A	Bosch W175T3	.028-.032	47-53	.016-.020	19-21 BTDC @ 1,500	135-150	.016	.018	10 BTDC	
B16B	Bosch W225T3	.028-.032	47-53	.016-.020	21-23 BTDC @ 1,500	142-156	.020	.020	0 @ TDC	
B18A	Bosch W175T1	.028-.032	59-65	.016-.020	21-23 BTDC @ 1,500	156-185	.016-.018	.016-.018	10 ATDC	500-700
B18B	Bosch W225T1	.028-.032	59-65	.016-.020	17-19 BTDC @ 1,500 ③	170-200	.020-.022	.020-.022	0 @ TDC	600-800
B18D	Bosch W175T1	.028-.032	59-65	.016-.020	22-24 BTDC @ 1,500 ②	156-185	.016-.018	.016-.018	10 ATDC	
B20A	Bosch W175T35	.028-.032	59-65	.016-.020	21-23 BTDC @ 1,500	156-185	.016-.018	.016-.018	10 ATDC	700
B20B	Bosch W200T35	.028-.032	59-65	.016-.020	10 BTDC @ 600-800	156-185	.020-.022	.020-.022	0 @ TDC	700
B30A	Bosch W175T35	.028-.032	37-43	.010 min.	10 BTDC @ 600-800	156-185	.020-.022	.020-.022	0 @ TDC	750

NOTE: Emission control requires a precise approach to tune-up. Timing and idle speed are peculiar to the engine and its application, rather than to the engine alone. Data for the particular application will be found on a sticker in the engine compartment.

* With vacuum line disconnected.

① Either hot or cold.

② Some models with B18D engines are set at 17-19° BTDC @ 1,500 rpm. Check the owner's manual and engine compartment sticker.

③ B18B with emission controls — 5° BTDC @ 800 rpm.

④ When checking camshaft setting, adjust valves on cold engine to:

.045   B16B
.043   B16A, B18A, B18D, B20A
.057   B20B, B30A.

Firing Order

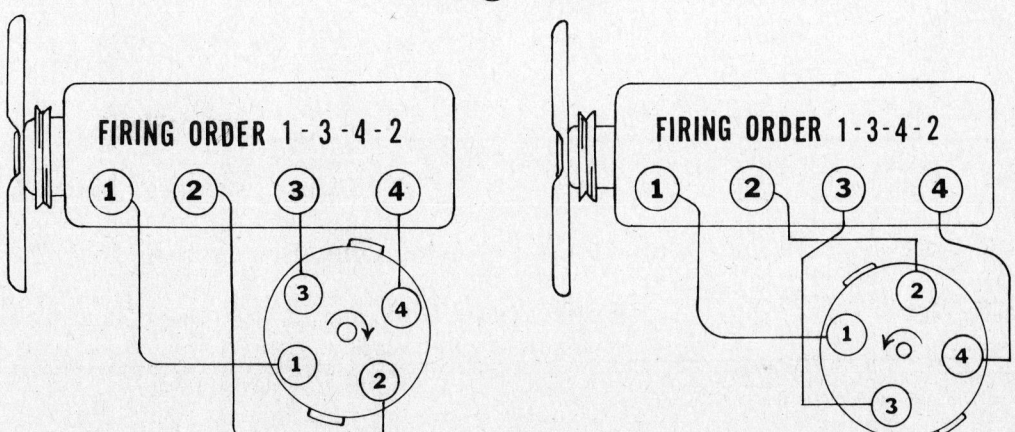

4 cylinder, 6 volt   4 cylinder, 12 volt

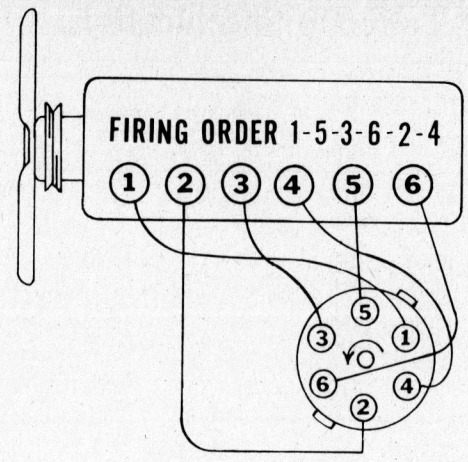

6 cylinder, 12 volt

Engine Rebuilding Specifications

Engine Model	Bore		Pistons°		Rings		
	Standard Size (in.)	Maximum Wear (in.)	Piston-to-Bore Clearance (in.)	Wrist Pin ① Diameter (in.), fit	End Gap (in.)	Oil Ring Side Clearance (in.)	Compression Ring Side Clearance (in.)
B14	2.9512-2.9516	.010	.0016-.0024		.010-.020	.0017-.0028	.0027-.0031
B16A	3.1248-3.1252	.010	.0012-.0020	.748, floating	.010-.020	.0017-.0028	.0027-.0031
B16B	3.1248-3.1252	.010	.0012-.0020	.748, floating	.010-.020	.0017-.0028	.0027-.0031
B18A	3.313	.010	.0008-.0016	.866, floating	.010-.020	.0017-.0028	.0021-.0032
B18B	3.313	.010	.0008-.0016	.866, floating	.010-.020	.0017-.0028	.0021-.0032
B18D	3.313	.010	.0008-.0016	.866, floating	.010-.020	.0017-.0028	.0021-.0032
B20A	3.500	.010	.0008-.0016	.866, floating	.016-.022	.0017-.0028	.0017-.0028
B20B	3.500	.010	.0008-.0016	.866, floating	.016-.022	.0017-.0028	.0017-.0028
B30A	3.500	.010	.0008-.0016	.866, floating	.016-.022	.0017-.0028	.0017-.0028

① Wrist pin pressed into connecting rod, slide fit in piston.
° Maximum piston weight deviation — .35 oz. (10 g.).

Engine Rebuilding Specifications

Engine Model	Crankshaft									
	Main Bearing Journals (in.)					Connecting Rod Bearing Journals (in.)				
	Journal Diameter						Journal Diameter			
	Standard Size	Max. out of Rd.	Oil Clearance	Shaft ① end-play	Thrust on No.	Standard Size	Max. out of Rd.	Oil Clearance	End-play
B16A	2.1240-2.1244	.002	.0005-.0025	.0004-.0040	rear	1.8736-1.8740	.003	.0020-.0036	.006-.014
B16B	2.1240-2.1244	.002	.0005-.0025	.0004-.0040	rear	1.8736-1.8740	.003	.0020-.0034	.006-.014
B18A	2.4977-2.4982	.002	.001-.003	.0007-.0042	rear	2.1295-2.1300	.003	.0015-.0032	.006-.014
B18B	2.4977-2.4982	.002	.0015-.0035	.0007-.0042	rear	2.1295-2.1300	.003	.0015-.0032	.006-.014
B18D	2.4977-2.4982	.002	.001-.003	.0007-.0042	rear	2.1295-2.1300	.003	.0015-.0032	.006-.014
B20A	2.4977-2.4982	.002	.001-.003	.0007-.0042	rear	2.1295-2.1300	.0028	.0015-.0032	.006-.014
B20B	2.4977-2.4982	.002	.001-.003	.0007-.0042	rear	2.1295-2.1300	.0028	.0015-.0032	.006-.014
B30A	2.4977-2.4982	.002	.0015-.0035	.0019-.0054	rear	2.1295-2.1300	.0028	.0015-.0035	.006.-014

① Maximum end-play .006 in.

Engine Rebuilding Specifications

Engine	Valves								
	Seat ① Angle (deg.)	Seat Width (in.)	Spring Press. (psi). @ Length (in.)	Spring Free Length (in.)	Stem Diameter (in.)		Stem-to-Guide Clearance (in.)		Guide Height Above Head (in.)
					Intake ③	Exhaust ③	Intake ②	Exhaust ②	
B14	45		145 @ 1.20	1.77	.3094-.3100	.3085-.3095	.0012-.0024	.0017-.0033	.83
B16A	45	.060	145 @ 1.20	1.77	.3094-.3100	.3082-.3089	.0012-.0024	.0024-.0035	.83
B16B	45	.060	145 @ 1.20	1.77	.3094-.3100	.3082-.3089	.0012-.0024	.0024-.0035	.83
B18A	45	.055	65 @ 1.57	1.77	.3413-.3438	.3403-.3409	.0010-.0021	.0025-.0037	.83
B18B	45	.055	65 @ 1.57	1.77	.3413-.3438	.3403-.3409	.0010-.0021	.0025-.0037	.83
B18D	45	.055	145 @ 1.20	1.77	.3413-.3438	.3403-.3409	.0010-.0021	.0025-.0037	.83
B20A	45	.080	65 @ 1.57	1.81	.3132-.3138	.3120-.3126	.0012-.0026	.0024-.0038	.689
B20B	45	.080	65 @ 1.57	1.81	.3132-.3138	.3120-.3126	.0012-.0026	.0024-.0038	.689
B30A	45	.080	56 @ 1.54	1.77	.3132-.3138	.3120-.3126	.0012-.0026	.0024-.0038	.689

① Valve face angle 44.5°.　　② Maximum stem to guide clearance .006 in.　　③ Maximum valve stem wear .0008 in.

Torque Specifications

Engine	Cyl. Head (Ft. Lb.)	Main Bear. Bolts (Ft. Lb.)	Rod Bear. Bolts (Ft. Lb.)	Crank-shaft Pulley Bolt (Ft. Lb.)	Flywheel to Crank-shaft Bolts (Ft. Lb.)	Camshaft Nut (Ft. Lb.)	Gen. or Alt. Bolt (Ft. Lb.)	Oil Cooler Nut (Ft. Lb.)	Oil Filter Nipple (Ft. Lb.)	Oil Pan Bolts (Ft. Lb.)
B18	61-69	87-94	38-42	51-58	33-40	94-108	25-29	22-25	33-40	6-8
B20	61-69	87-94	38-42	51-58	33-40	94-108	45-75		33-40	6-8
B30	61-69	87-94	38-42	51-58	36-40	94-108			33-40	7.3-8.7

Tightening Sequences

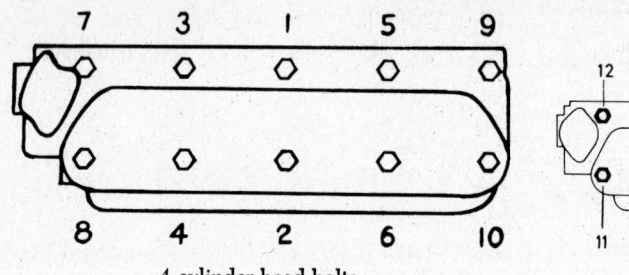

4 cylinder head bolts

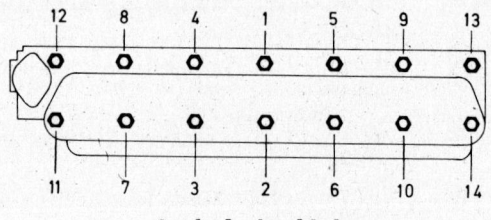

6 cylinder head bolts

Electrical Specifications

Engine	Battery Capacity (amp. hrs.)	Voltage (volts)	Grounded Terminal	Starter Lock Test Amps	Lock Test Volts	No Load Test Amps	No Load Test Volts	No Load Test RPM	Brush Spring Tension (lbs.)
B14, B16	85	6	Neg	450-500	3.5	60-80	5.5	4,000-5,000	1.75-2.00
B18, B20, B30	60	12	Neg	300-350	6	40-50	12	6,900-8,100	2.53-2.86

Engine	Generator Part Number	Brush Spring Pressure (lbs.)	Field Resistance (ohms)	Max. Output (amps)	Regulator Part Number	Cut-out Relay Cuts in at (volts)	Reverse Current at (amps)	Max. Current (amps)	Voltage Regulator Setting (volts)
B18	Bosch LJ/ GG240/12/ 2400/AR6 or 7	1.0-1.3	4.8 ± 0.5	30	Bosch RS/ VA240/12/ 12	12.4-13.1	2.0-7.5	45 cold 30 warm	14.1-14.8 idling, 13.0-14.0 loaded

Engine	Alternator Part Number	Output (amps) at rpm	Minimum Brush Length (in.)	Regulator Part Number	Voltage (volts) at alt. rpm, cold
B20	Bosch K1(R)- 14V, 35A20	35 @ 1,200	.32	Bosch AD-14V	14.0-15.0 @ 4,000
B30	S.E.V. Motorola 14V-26641	30 @ 1,500	.20	S.E.V. Motorola 14V-33525	13.1-14.4 cold, 13.85-14.25 hot

Capacities and Pressures

Engine Model	Crankcase Capacity w/o filter (with filter) Pints	Crankcase Viscosity SAE	Transmission Cap. Pints	Transmission Vis-cosity SAE	Rear Axle Cap. Pints	Rear Axle Vis-cosity SAE	Fuel Tank Cap. Gals.	Fuel Pump Press. PSI	Cooling System Cap. with Heater Qts.	Cooling System Therm. Opens °F.
B14	7 (7.75)	10W-30					9.3	2 to 3		
B16A	6 (7)	10W-30					9.3	2 to 3.5	9.5	
B16B	6 (7)	10W-30	2	90	2		9.3	2 to 3.5	9	169
B18A	7 (8)	10W-30	1.5	90	2.75	90	11.8	1.5 to 3.5	9	169
B18B	7 (8)	10W-30	1.5	90	2.75	90	11.8	1.5 to 3.5	9	169
B18D	7 (8)	10W-30	1.5	90	2.75	90		1.5 to 3.5	9	169
B20	7 (8)	10W-30	1.6	90	2.75	90		1.5 to 3.5	9	169
B30	11 (12.7)	10W-30	1.3	90	3.4	90		2.1 to 3.5	13	179

Notes: 1. Overdrive transmission requires 3.4 pints SAE 30.
2. Automatic transmissions require 13.25 pints type A oil.

Brake Specifications

Model	Type Front	Type Rear	Brake Cyl. Bore (In.) Master Cyl.	Brake Cyl. Bore (In.) Wheel Cyl. Front	Brake Cyl. Bore (In.) Wheel Cyl. Rear	Drum or Disc Diam. (In.) Front	Drum or Disc Diam. (In.) Rear
PV444	Drum	Drum					
PV544	Drum	Drum	1	1	.813	9	9
122, P1800	Disc	Drum					
142, 144	Disc	Disc	.882	1.422	1.422	10.7	11.6
145	Disc	Disc	.882	1.422	1.5	10.7	11.6
164	Disc	Disc	.95	1.422	1.422	10.7	11.6

New brake lining thickness is .394 in.

Chassis and Wheel Alignment Specifications

| | Chassis | | Wheel Alignment | | | | Wheel Pivot Ratio | |
Model	Wheelbase (In.)	Track (In.)	Caster (Deg.)	Camber (Deg.)	Toe-In (In.)	King Pin Inclin. (Deg.)	Inner	Outer
PV444, PV445, PV544	102.5	51.0(F), 51.7(R)	− ¾ to + ¼	− ¼ to + ½	0 to .118	5	22 ± 1	20
122	102.4	51.7	0 to + 1	0 to + ½	0 to .154	8		
142, 144, 145	102.4	53.1	0 to + 1	0 to + ½	0. to .16	7.5	21.5 to 23.5	20
164	106.3	53.2	0 to + 1	0 to + ½	0. to .16	7.5	21.5 to 23.5	20

Light Bulb Specifications

Model	Usage	Wattage or Candle Pr.
122	Headlights	45/40
	Parking	5
	Flashers, Front & Rear	32 CP
	Stop/Tail	32/4 CP
	Backup	15
	License Plate	5
	Interior	10
	Glove Compartment	2
	Instruments	2
	Warning:	
	Turn Signals	2
	Headlight	2
	Charging	2
	Oil Pressure	6
142, 144, 145	Headlights	45/40
	Parking	5
	Flashers, Front & Rear	4 CP
	Stop	32 CP
	Backup	32 CP
	License	32 CP
	Interior	5
	Glove	10
	Instruments	2
	Compartment	3

Light Bulb Specifications

Model	Usage	Wattage or Candle Pr.
	Lighting, Heater Controls	1.2
	Warning:	
	Charging	1.2
	Turn Signals	1.2
	Handbrake	1.2
	Headlights	1.2
	Oil Pressure	1.2
	Rear Window Heater	2
164	Headlights	45/40
	Parking	5 (4 CP)
	Flashers, Front & Rear	32 CP
	Rear Lights	5 (4 CP)
	Stop Lights	25 (32 CP)
	Backup	15 (32 CP)
	License Plate	5
	Interior	10
	Glove Compartment	2
	Engine and Luggage Compartments	18
	Instruments	3
	Lighting, Heater Controls	1.2
	Warning:	
	Instrument Panel	1.2
	Overdrive	1.2
	Rear Window Heater	1.2

Carburetor Specifications

Engine Model	Carburetor(s)	Air Intake Dia. In.	Venturi Desig.	Fuel Control Jet Dia. (in.)	Fuel Control Jet Desig.	Main Jet (Standard) Dia. (in.)	Main Jet (Standard) Desig.	Compensating Dia. (mm)	Jet Desig.	Needle Type	Idle Fuel Jet Dia. (mm)	Idle Fuel Jet Desig.	Idle Air Jet Dia. (mm)	Idle Air Jet Desig.	Accel. Dia. (mm)	Jet Desig.	Float Valve (dim.)	Float Valve Washer (thickness mm)	Fuel Level (Below Float Bowl Top)	Idling Speed RPM—Warm Engine
B14A	SU H2(2)	1.5		.09						CZ	.50		.50		.40	.40		1	18mm	400–600
B16A	Zenith 34VN		27			.97	97	.97	97			.50		.50						500–700
B16B	SU H4(2)	1.5			AUC2112					GT*										500–700
B18A	Zenith 36VN		30			117			115			70		70		40		1.75	1		500–700
B18B, D	SU H6(2)	1.75								KA										
B18D	Zenith-Stromberg 175CD-2S									4E										
B20A	Zenith-Stromberg 175CD-2SE	1.63								B2AF										700
B20B	SU HS6	1.63								KN										800
	Zenith-Stromberg 175CD-2SE																			700(1)
	SU HS6																			800
	Zenith-Stromberg 175CD-2SE	1.63								BIS										700(1)
B30A	Zenith-Stromberg 175CD-2SE	1.63																		750
	SU HS6	1.75																		750

* GW when using intake silencer air cleaner.
1. For cars equipped with automatic transmissions.

Wiring Diagrams

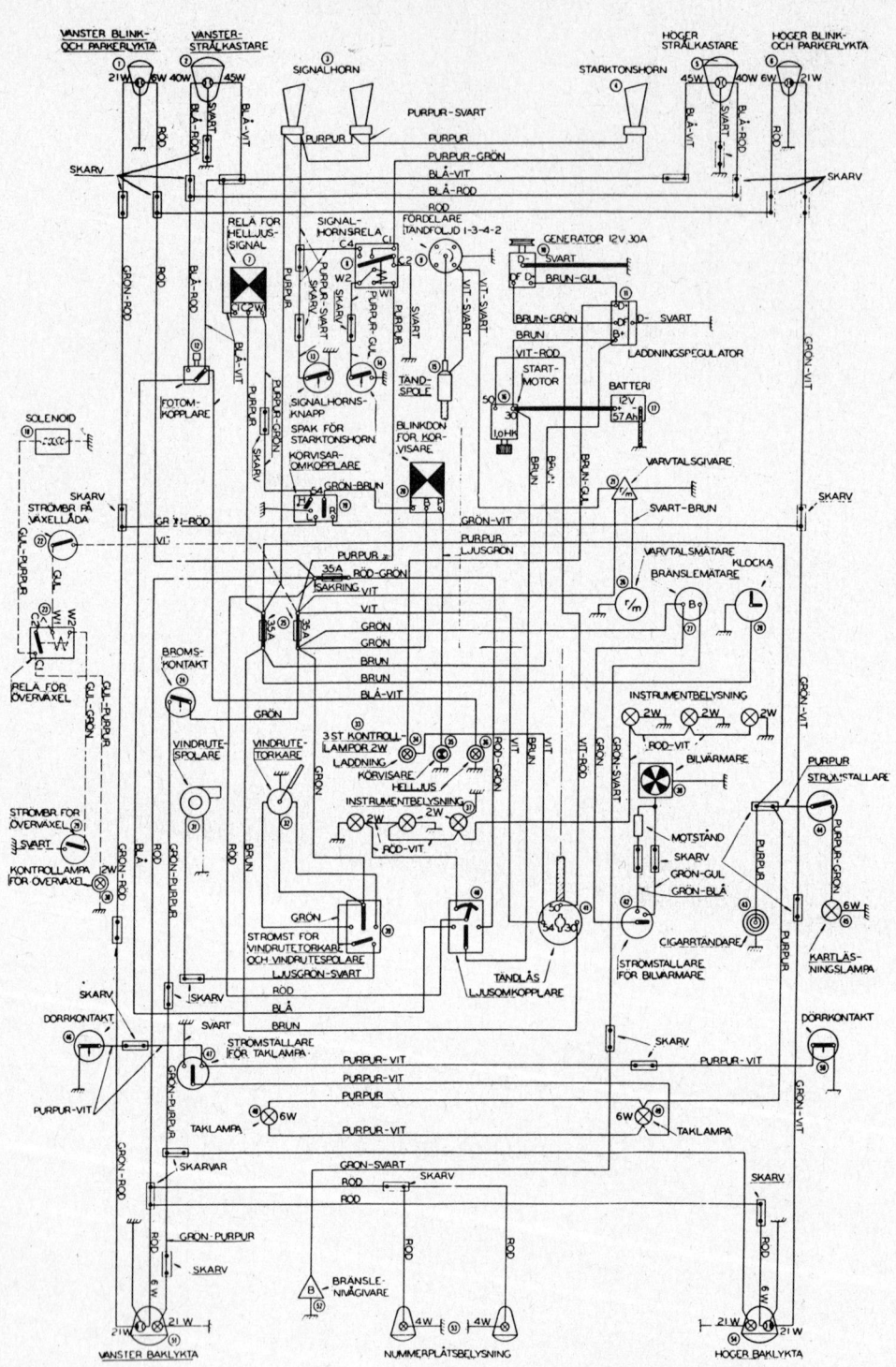

Pl800 up to chassis number 7000

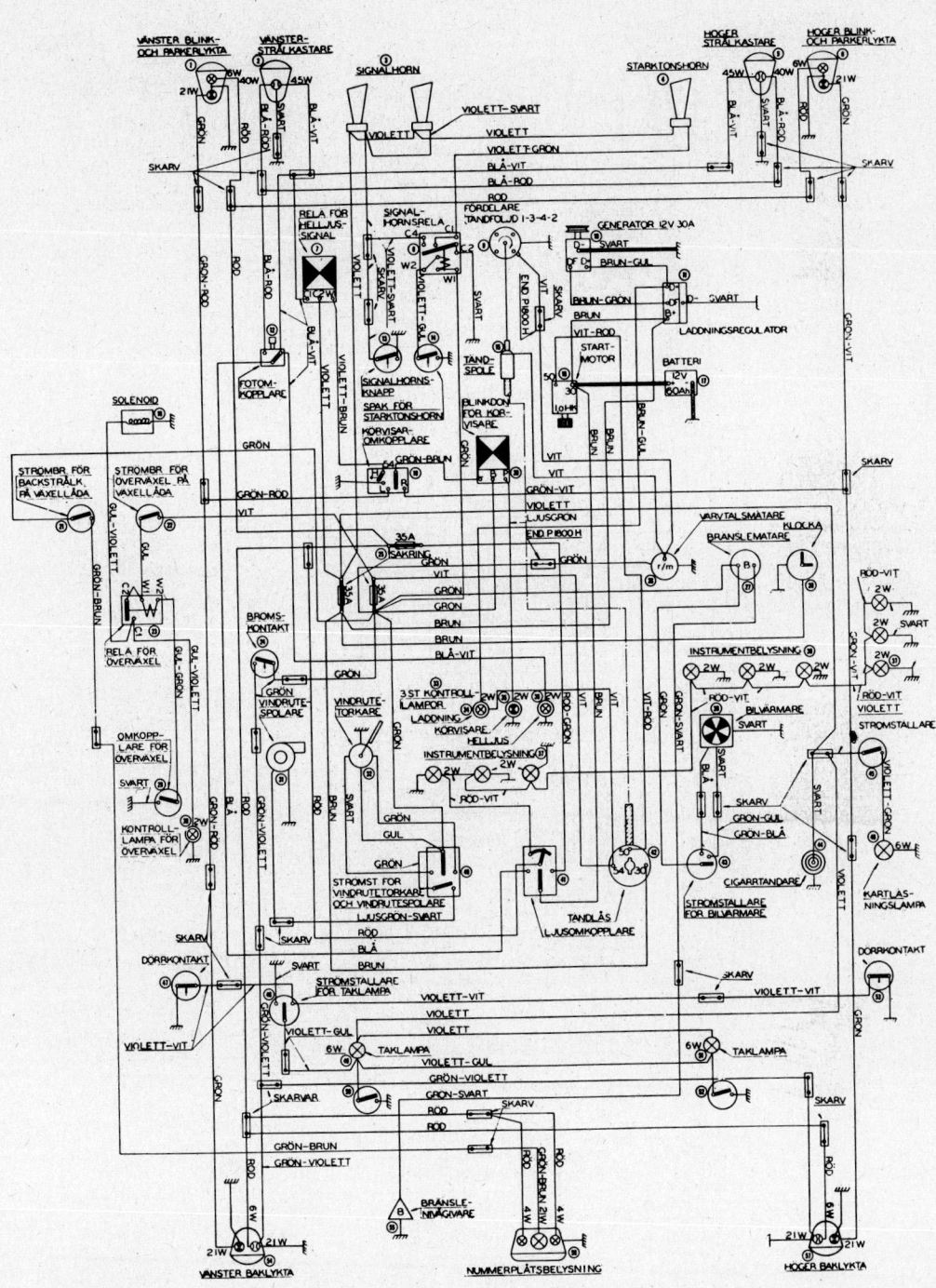

Pl800 from chassis number 10001 to 12500

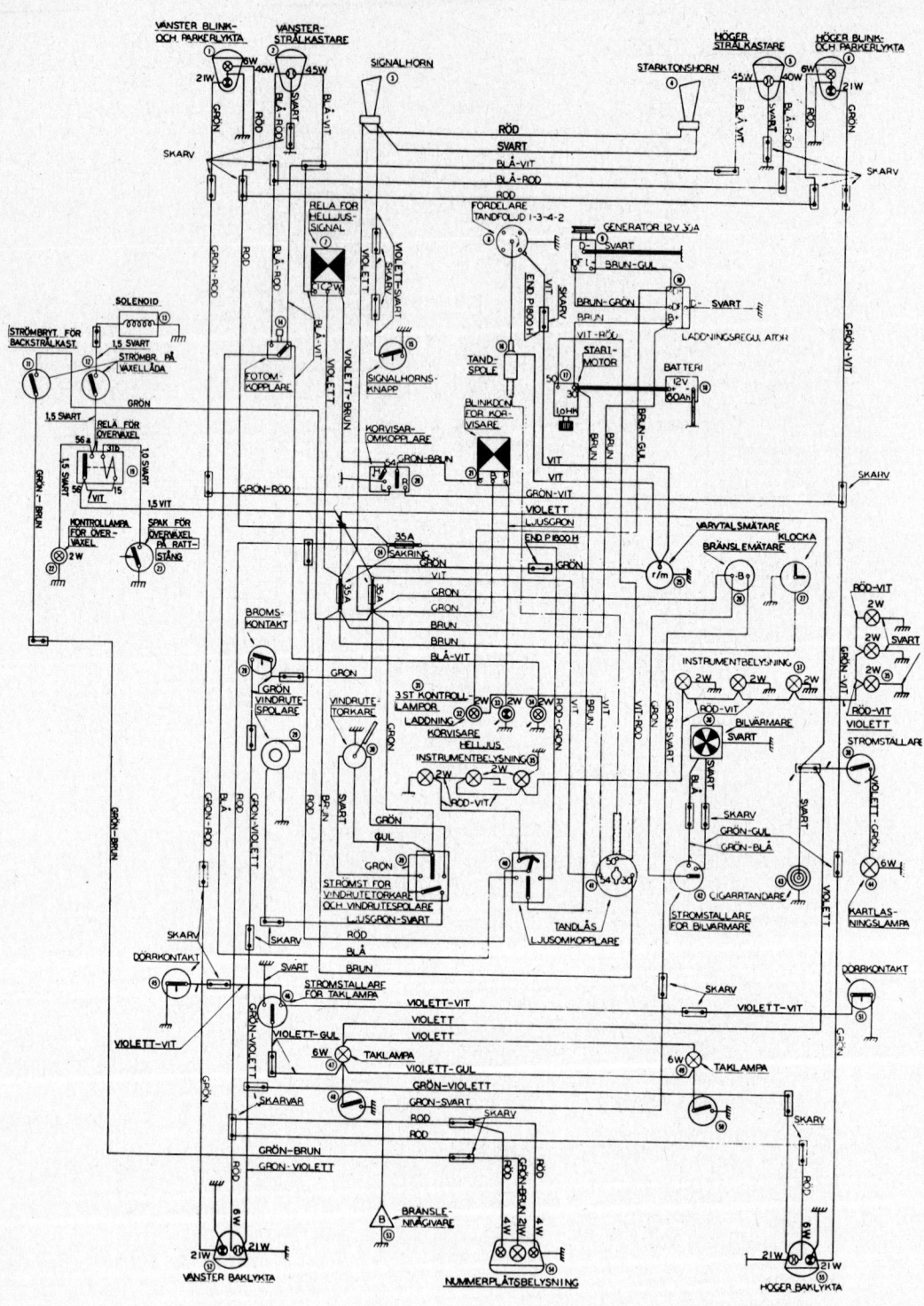

P1800 from chassis number 12501

P1800 from chassis number 10001 to 12500

1. Flasher and parking light, left
2. Headlight, left
3. Horn
4. High-tone horn
5. Headlight, right
6. Flasher and parking light, right
7. Relay for headlight signalling
8. Relay for horn
9. Distributor firing order 1, 3, 4, 2
10. Generator 12 V 30 A
11. Voltage regulator
12. Foot dimmer switch
13. Horn button
14. Lever for high-tone horn
15. Ignition coil
16. Starter motor
17. Battery
18. Solenoid
19. Turn signal switch
20. Flasher mechanism for turn signal
21. Backup light switch on transmission
22. Overdrive switch on transmission
23. Relay for overdrive
24. Brake light switch
25. Fuse
26. Tachometer
27. Fuel Gauge
28. Clock
29. Switch for overdrive
30. Warning lamp for overdrive
31. Windshield washer
32. Windshield wipers
33. 3 Warning lamps
34. Charging
35. Turn signal
36. High beam
37. Instrument lighting
38. Heater
39. Instrument lighting
40. Switch for windshield wipers and washer
41. Light switch
42. Ignition switch
43. Switch for heater
44. Cigar lighter
45. Switch
46. Map-reading lamp
47. Door switch
48. Switch for interior lamp
49. Interior lamp
50. Switch for lamp
51. Interior lamp
52. Switch for interior lamp
53. Door switch
54. Rear lamp, left
55. Fuel level pickup
56. License plate lighting
57. Rear lamp, right

P1800 from chassis number 12501

1. Flasher and parking light, left
2. Headlight, left
3. Horn
4. High-tone horn
5. Headlight, right
6. Flasher and parking light, right
7. Relay for headlight signalling
8. Distributor firing order 1, 3, 4, 2
9. Generator 12 V 30 A
10. Voltage regulator
11. Switch for backup light
12. Switch on transmission for overdrive
13. Solenoid
14. Foot dimmer switch
15. Horn button
16. Ignition coil
17. Starter motor
18. Battery
19. Relay for overdrive
20. Turn signal switch
21. Flasher mechanism for turn signal
22. Warning lamp for overdrive
23. Overdrive lever switch on steering column
24. Fuse
25. Tachometer
26. Fuel gauge
27. Clock
28. Brake light switch
29. Windshield washer
30. Windshield wipers
31. 3 Warning lamps
32. Charging
33. Turn signal
34. High beam
35. Instrument lighting
36. Heater
37. Instrument lighting
38. Switch
39. Switch for windshield wipers and washer
40. Light switch
41. Ignition switch
42. Switch for heater
43. Cigar lighter
44. Map-reading lamp
45. Door switch
46. Switch for interior lamp
47. Interior lamp
48. Switch for interior lamp
49. Interior lamp
50. Switch for interior lamp
51. Door switch
52. Rear lamp, left
53. Fuel level pickup
54. License plate lighting
55. Rear lamp, right

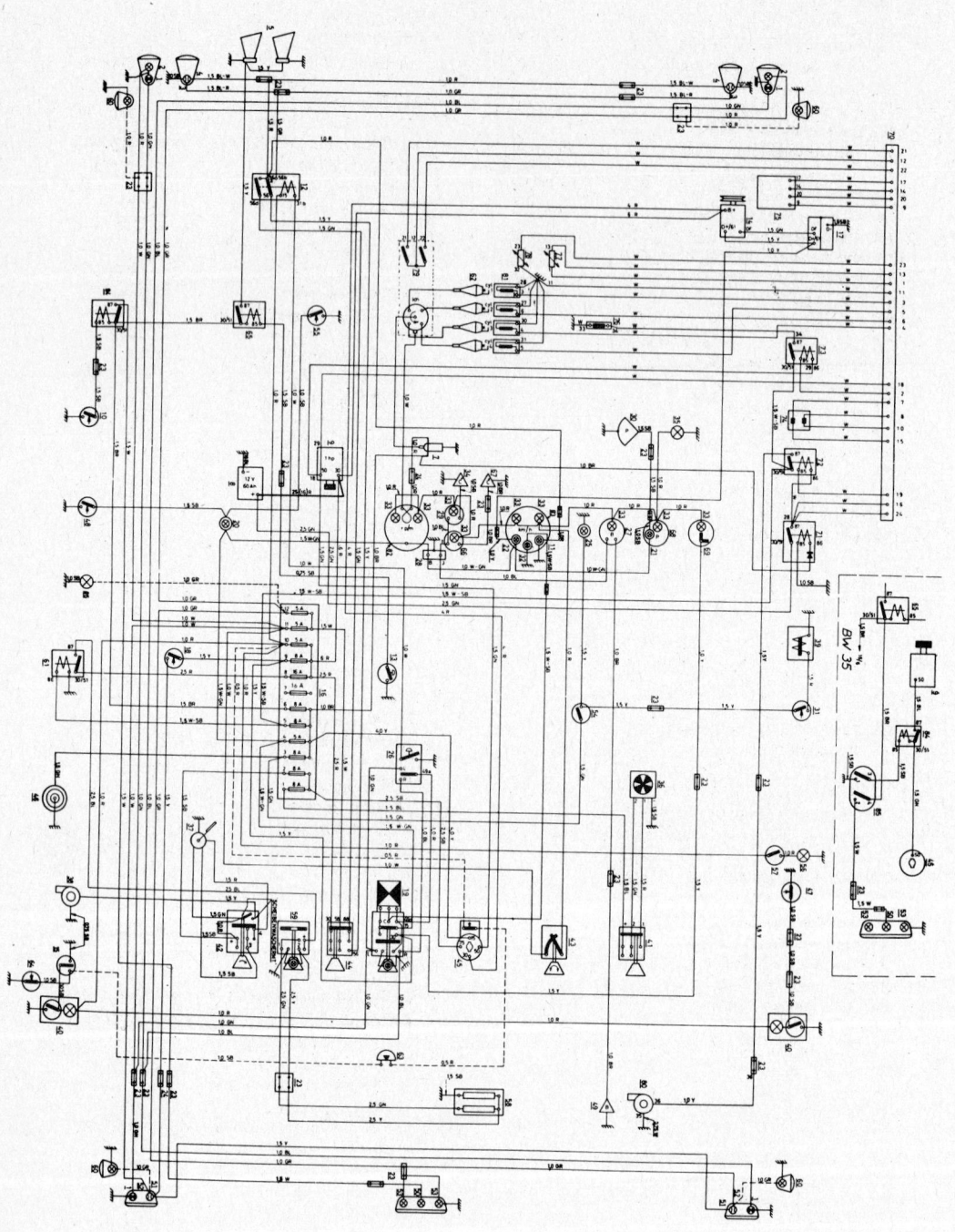

1800E, 1971

1800E, 1971

1. Directional indicators 23 CP
2. Parking lights, 4 CP
3. Low beam lights 40 W
4. High beam headlights 45 W
5. Horn
6. Distributor (firing order 1-3-4-2)
7. Ignition coil
8. Battery, 12 V, 60 Ah.
9. Starter motor, 1 hp.
10. Switch for backup light
11. Warning lamp for high beam, 3 W
12. Step relay for high beam and low beam headlights
13. Horn control
14. Alternator, 35 A
15. Switch, courtesy lighting
16. Fusebox
17. Voltage regulator
18. Brake switch
19. Emergency warning flashers
20. Warning lamp for brakes, 2 W
21. Warning lamp for oil pressure, 2 W
22. Warning lamp for battery charging, 3 W
23. Connector
24. Connector (only right-hand drive)
25. Warning lamp for overdrive, 2 W
26. Switch for directional indicators and flashers
27. Fuel gauge
28. Voltage stabilizer
29. Temperature gauge
30. Oil pressure pickup
31. Overdrive switch on transmission
32. Warning lamp for directional indicators
33. Instrument lighting
34. Temperature pickup
35. Lighting for heating controls
36. Heater
37. Windshield wipers
38. Windshield washer
39. Control solenoid for overdrive, on transmission
40. Courtesy lighting, 2x5 W
41. Switch for heater
42. Switch for windshield wipers and washer
43. Rheostat for instrument lighting

44. Lighting switch
45. Ignition
46. Cigarette lighter
47. Door switch
48. Switch for parking brake warning
49. Fuel level pickup
50. Rear lights
51. Stop lights, 32 CP
52. Backup lights, 4 CP
53. License plate lighting, 2x4 CP
54. Switch for overdrive
55. Brake warning switch
56. Map-reading lamp
57. Switch for map-reading lamp
58. Electrically heated rear window, 150/40 W
59. Switch for electrically heated rear window
60. Side marker lights (only USA), 5 W
61. Relay for electrically heated rear window
62. Spark plugs
63. Warning buzzer (only USA)
64. Door switch on driver's side
65. Horn relay
66. Oil temperature gauge
67. Oil temperature sender
68. Oil pressure gauge
69. Lock
70. Control unit for fuel injection
71. Main relay for fuel injection
72. Relay for fuel pump
73. Relay for cold start valve
74. Pressure sensor
75. Throttle switch
76. Cold start valve
77. Temperature sensor I (induction air)
78. Temperature sensor II (coolant)
79. Triggering contacts
80. Fuel pump
81. Injectors
82. Tachometer
83. Speedometer
84. Relay for rear lights
85. Switch for automatic transmission, BW35
86. Quadrant lighting (only BW35)

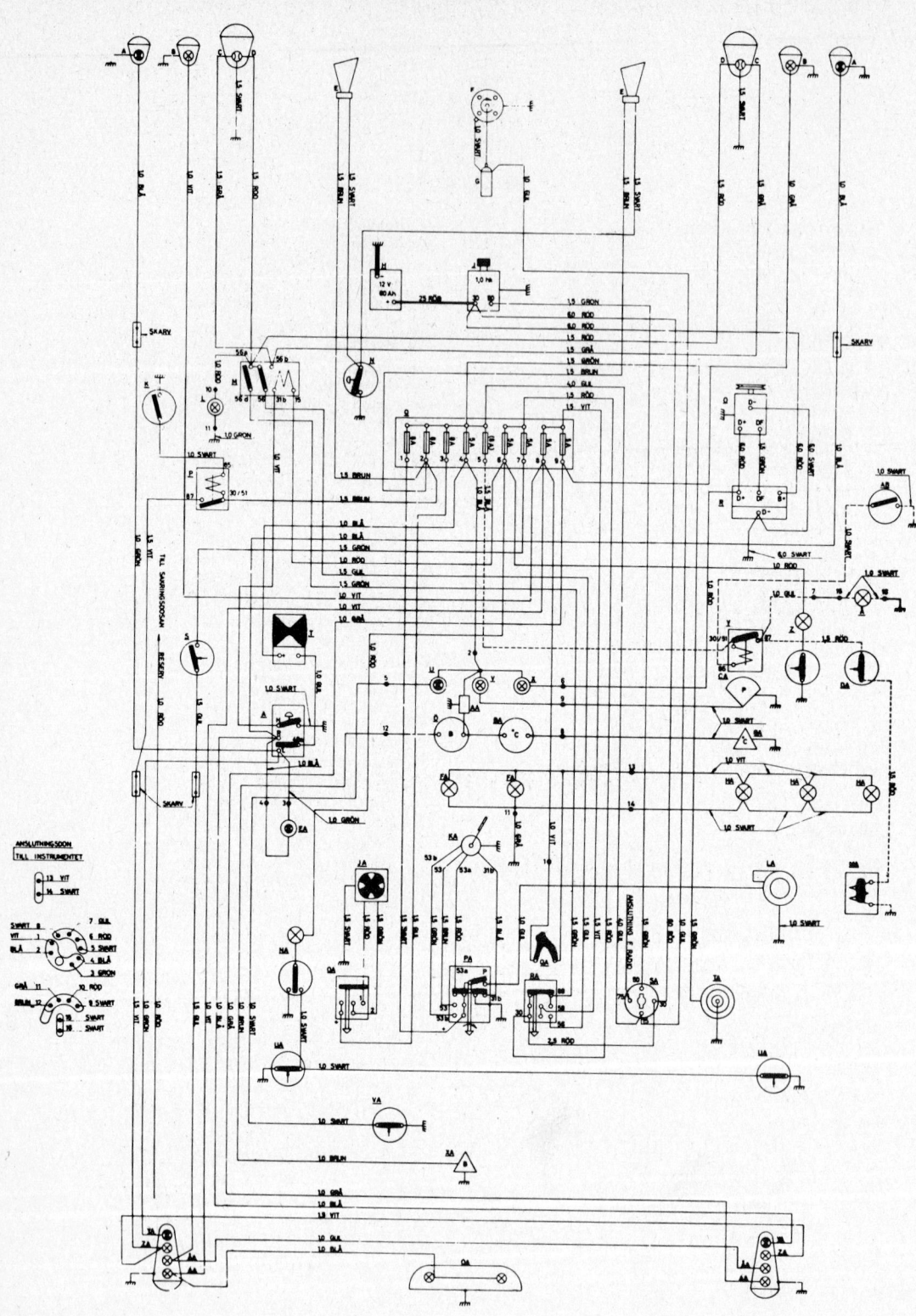

144, early model

144, early model

A — Turn signal light 32 CP
B — Parking-light 5 W
C — Low beam light 40 W
D — High beam light 45 W
E — Horn
F — Distributor, firing order 1-3-4-2
G — Ignition coil
H — Battery 12 V, 60 amp/hr
J — Starter motor 1 hp.
K — Switch for backup light on transmission
L — Control lamp for high beam light 1.2 W
M — Relay for high beam, low beam and headlight flasher
N — Horn ring
O — Alternator 12 V, 30 A
P — Relay for backup light
Q — Fuse box
R — Voltage regulator
S — Brake contact
T — Flasher unit
U — Warning light, handbrake, 1.2 W
V — Warning light, oil pressure, 1.2 W
X — Warning light, charging, 1.2 W
Y — Relay for overdrive
Z — Glove compartment light, 2 W

A — Warning lamp for overdrive 1.2 W
A — Switch for light signal and direction indicators
O — Fuel gauge
AA — Voltage regulator
BA — Temperature gauge
CA — Oil pressure warning unit
DA — Switch for overdrive on transmission
EA — Warning lamp, flashers 1.2 W
FA — Instrument lighting 2X3 W
GA — Temperature sending unit
HA — Lighting for heater controls 31.2 W
JA — Heater
KA — Windshield wipers
LA — Windshield washer
MA — Solenoid for overdrive
NA — Interior light 10 W
OA — Switch for heater
PA — Switch for windshield wipers and washer
QA — Rheostat for instrument lighting
RA — Lighting switch
SA — Ignition switch
TA — Cigarette lighter
UA — Door contact

VA — Switch for handbrake warning
XA — Fuel gauge tank sender
YA — Flasher light 32 CP
ZA — Reversing light 15 W
AA — Brake light 25 W
AA — Rear light 5 W
OA — License plate lighting 2X5 W
AB — Switch for overdrive

Connections to instruments

13	WHITE	4	BLUE
14	BLACK	3	GREEN
8	BLACK	11	GRAY
1	WHITE	12	BROWN
2	BLUE	10	RED
7	YELLOW	9	BLACK
6	RED	15	BLACK
5	BLACK	16	BLACK

Translation of diagram text

Bla = Blue
Brun = Brown
Gra = Gray
Gul = Yellow
Rod = Red
Svart = Black
Skarv = Junction
Anslutning f. radio = connection for radio

142 and 144, standard transmission, 1969-70

A — Turn signal 32 CP
B — Parking light 5 W
C — Headlight low beam 40 W
D — Headlight high beam 45 W
E — Horn
F — Distributor, firing order 1-3-4-2
G — Ignition coil
H — Battery 12 V, 60 Ah
J — Starter motor 1.0 h.p.
K — Switch for backup light on transmission
L — High beam warning lamp 1. 2 W
M — Dimmer relay for high and low beams and headlight flasher
N — Horn ring
O — Generator 12 V
P — Relay for backup light
Q — Fusebox
R — Voltage regulator
S — Brake contact

T — Warning flasher
U — Brake control lamp 1.2 W
V — Oil pressure warning lamp 1.2 W
X — Charging warning lamp 1.2 W
Y — Junction
Z — Glove compartment lighting 2 W
A — Overdrive warning lamp 1.2 W
A — Switch for headlight signalling and turn signals
O — Fuel gauge
AA — Voltage regulator
BA — Temperature gauge
CA — Oil pressure lamp
DA — Switch for overdrive on transmission
EA — Turn signal warning lamp 1.2 W
FA — Instrument lighting 2X3 W
GA — Temperature gauge sensitive head
HA — Heater control lighting 3X1.2 W

JA — Heater
KA — Windshield wipers
LA — Windshield washers
MA — Solenoid for overdrive
NA — Interior lamp 10 W
OA — Switch for heater
PA — Switch for windshield wipers and washer
QA — Instrument lighting rheostat
RA — Light switch
SA — Ignition switch
TA — Cigarette lighter
UA — Door contact
VA — Switch for handbrake warning
XA — Fuel gauge tank unit
YA — Flasher light 32 CP
ZA — Backup light 15 W
AA — Brake stoplight 25 W
AA — Tail light 5 W
OA — License plate lighting 2X5 W
AB — Switch for overdrive
BB — Warning valve

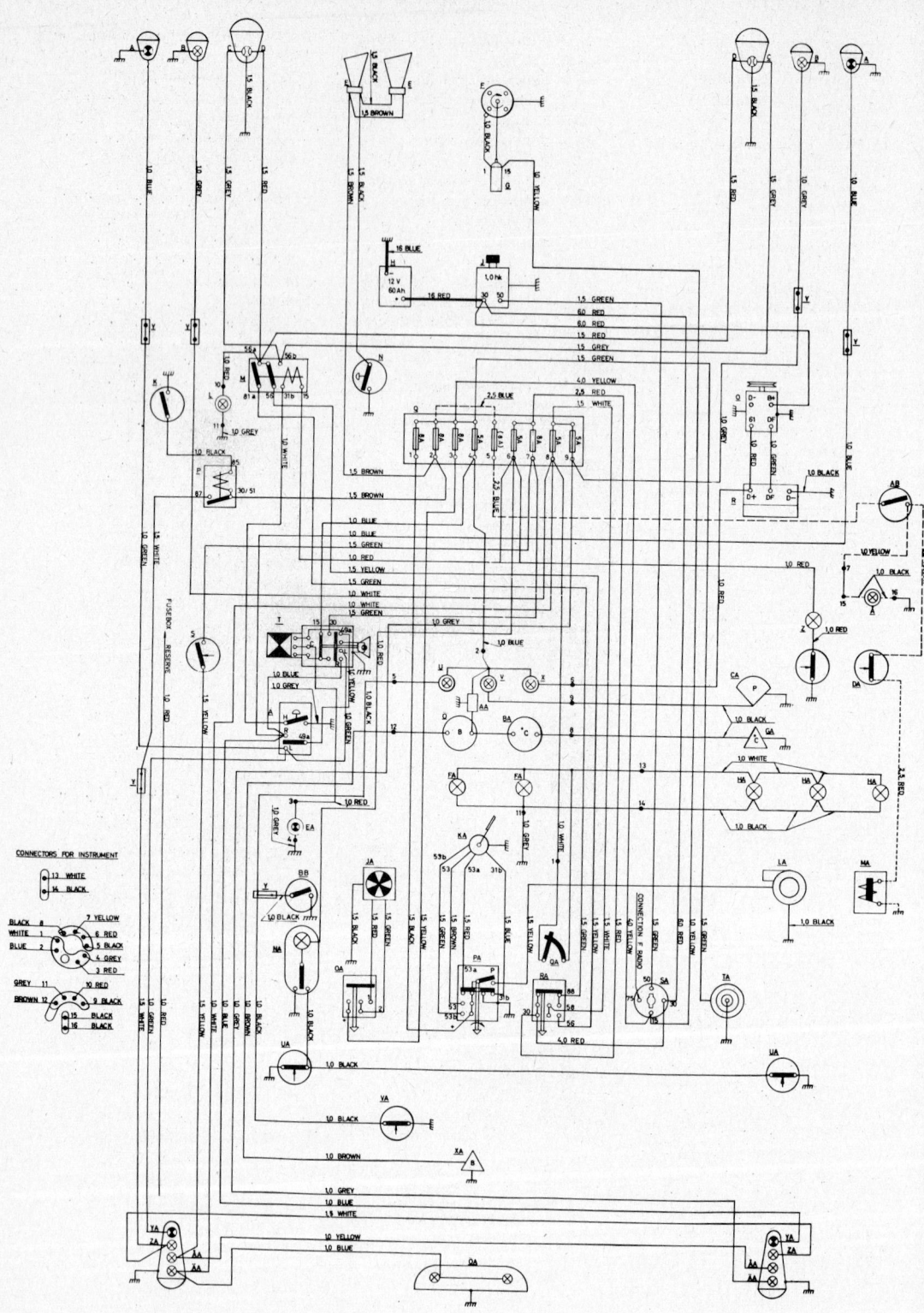

142 and 144, standard transmission, 1969-70

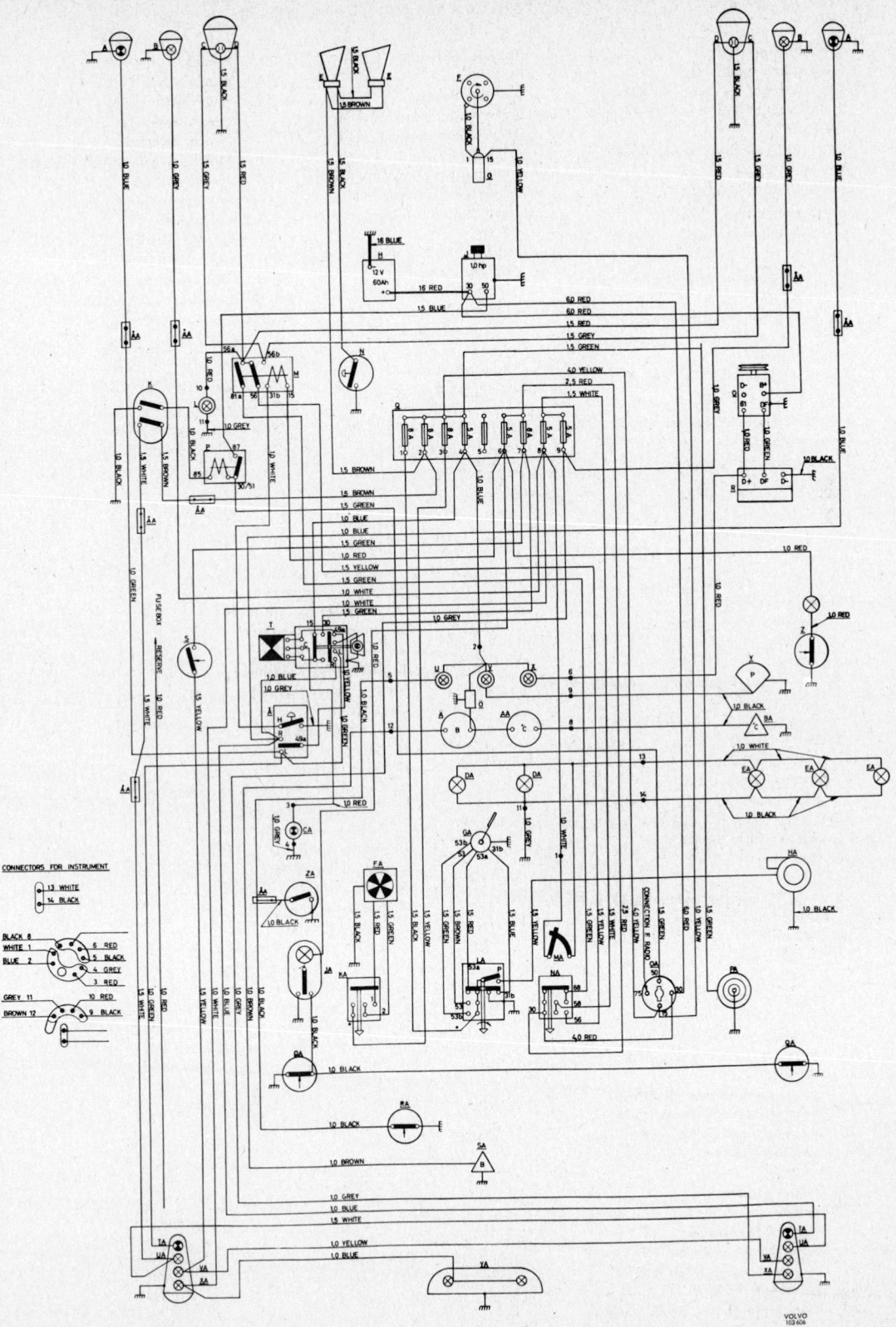

142 and 144, automatic transmission, 1969-70

142 and 144, automatic transmission, 1969-70

A — Turn signal 32 CP
B — Parking light 5 W
C — Headlight low beam 40 W
D — Headlight high beam 45 W
E — Horn
F — Distributor firing order 1-3-4-2
G — Ignition coil
H — Battery 12 V, 60 Ah
J — Starter motor 1.0 hp.
K — Switch unit for starter lockout
and backup lights
L — High beam warning lamp
1.2 W
M — Dimmer relay for high and
low beams and headlight
flasher
N — Horn ring
O — Generator 12 V
P — Relay for solenoid, on starter
motor
Q — Fusebox

R — Voltage regulator
S — Brake contact
T — Warning flasher
U — Brake warning lamp 1.2 W
V — Oil pressure warning lamp
1.2 W
X — Charging warning lamp 1.2 W
Y — Oil pressure warning
Z — Glove compartment lighting
2 W
A — Switch for headlight signalling
and turn signals
A — Fuel gauge
O — Voltage regulator
AA — Temperature gange
BA — Temperature gauge
sensitive head
CA — Turn signal warning control
lamp 1.2 W
DA — Instrument lighting 2X3 W
EA — Heater control lighting
3X1.2 W

FA — Heater
GA — Windshield wipers
HA — Windshield washers
JA — Interior lamp 10 W
KA — Switch for heater
LA — Switch for windshield wipers
and washers
MA — Instrument lighting rheostat
NA — Light switch
OA — Ignition switch
PA — Cigarette lighter
QA — Door contact
RA — Switch for handbrake warning
SA — Fuel gauge tank unit
TA — Flasher light 32 CP
UA — Backup light 15 W
VA — Brake stoplight 25 W
XA — Tail light 5 W
YA — License plate lighting 2X5 W
ZA — Warning valve
AA — Junction

142 and 144, 1971

1. Dir. ind. flashers 32 CP
2. Parking lights 5 W
3. Headlight low beam 40 W
4. Headlight high beam 45 W
5. Horn
6. Distributor firing order 1-3-4-2
7. Ignition coil
8. Battery 12 V, 60 Ah.
9. Starter motor 1.0 hp.
10. Switch for backup lights only for M40
and M41 transmission
11. High beam warning lamp 1.2 W
12. Dimmer relay for high and low beams
and headlight flasher
13. Horn ring
14. Alternator
15. Relay for backup light on M40, M41 and
starter Relay on BW35
16. Fuse box
17. Voltage regulator
18. Brake contact
19. Warning flashers
20. Brake warning lamp 1.2 W
21. Oil pressure warning lamp 1.2 W
22. Charging warning lamp 1.2 W
23. Connector
24. Glove compartment lighting 2 W
25. Overdrive warning lamp 1.2 W
26. Switch for headlight signalling and
emergency flashers
27. Fuel gauge
28. Voltage regulator
29. Temperature gauge
30. Oil pressure warning
31. Switch for overdrive on transmission
32. Flasher warning lamp 1.2 W
33. Instrument lighting 2x1.2 W
34. Temperature gauge, sending unit
35. Heater control lighting 3x1.2 W
36. Heater
37. Windshield wipers

1.0 hp.

38. Windshield washer
39. Solenoid for overdrive
40. Interior lamp 10 W
41. Switch for heater
42. Switch for windshield wipers and washer
43. Instrument lighting rheostat
44. Light switch
45. Ignition switch
46. Cigarette lighter
47. Door contact
48. Switch for parking brake warning
49. Fuel gauge tank unit
50. Backup lights 15 W
51. Brake stoplights 25 W
52. Tail lights 5 W
53. License plate lighting 2x5 W
54. Switch for overdrive
55. Brake warning contact
56. Switch on transmission, BW35
57. Switch glove comp. lighting
58. Elec. heated rear window
59. Switch elec. heater rear window
60. Side marker lamps, only for USA 5 W
61. Relay for elec. heated rear window
62. Conn. at instrument
63. Buzzer
64. Door switch on driver's side
65. Connection plate
66. Clock

Color code:
SB   Black
W   White
Y   Yellow
GN   Green
GR   Grey
BL   Blue
R   Red
BR   Brown
W-R   White-Red
BL-Y Blue-Yellow

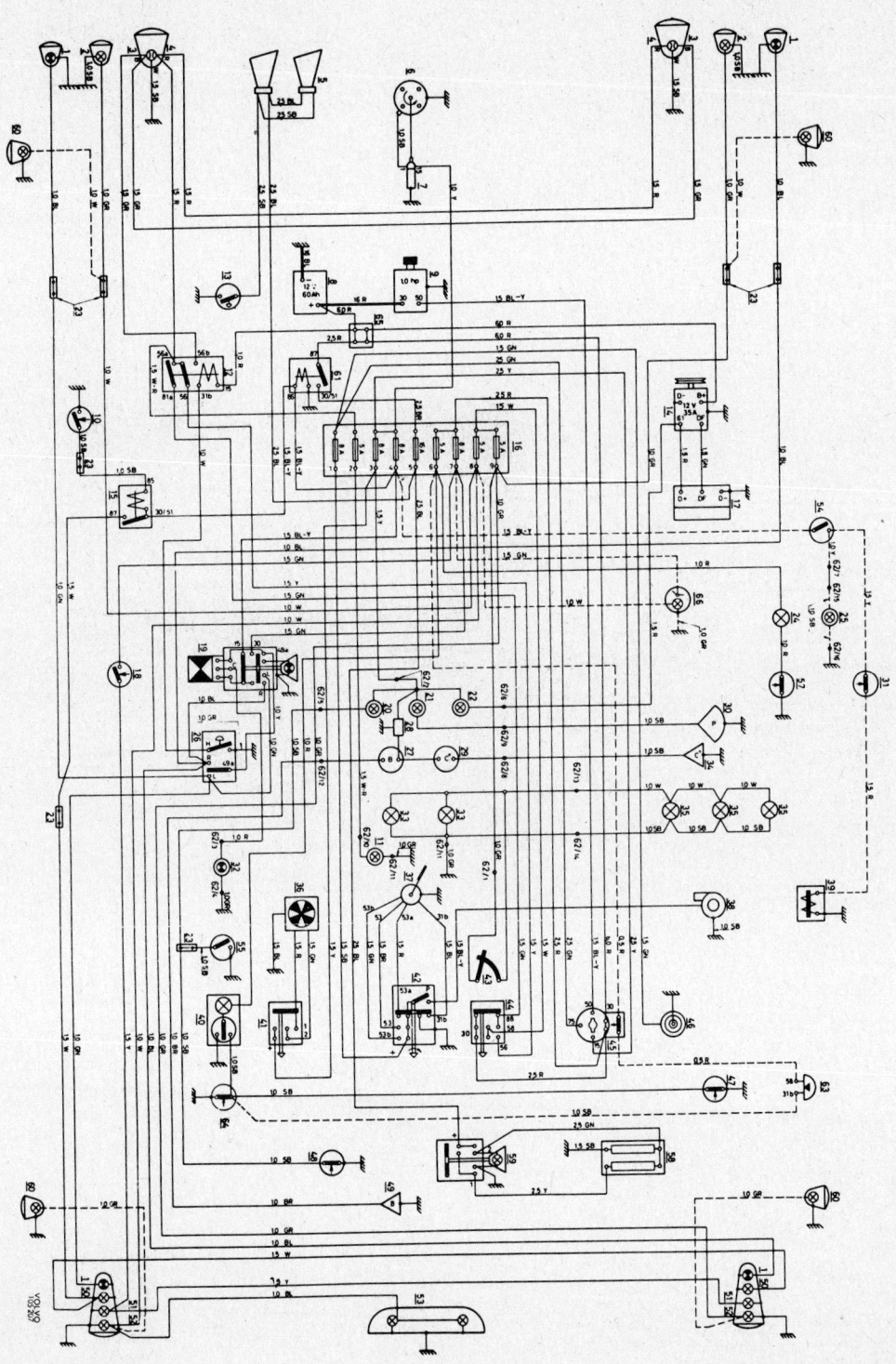

142 and 144, 1971

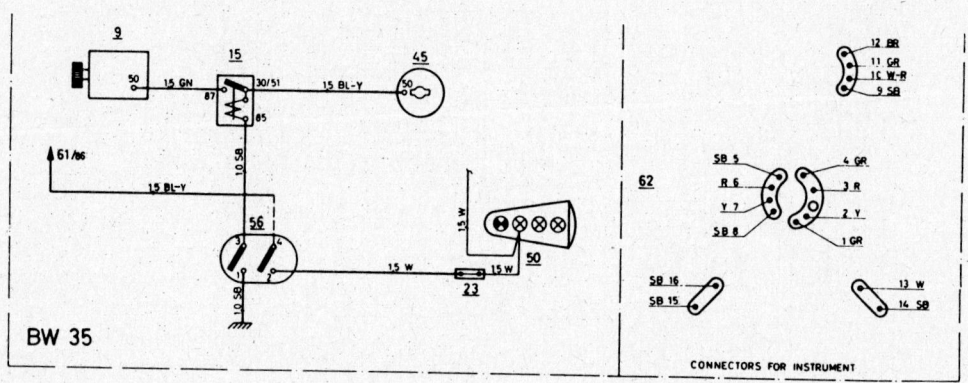

142, 144, automatic transmission, 1971

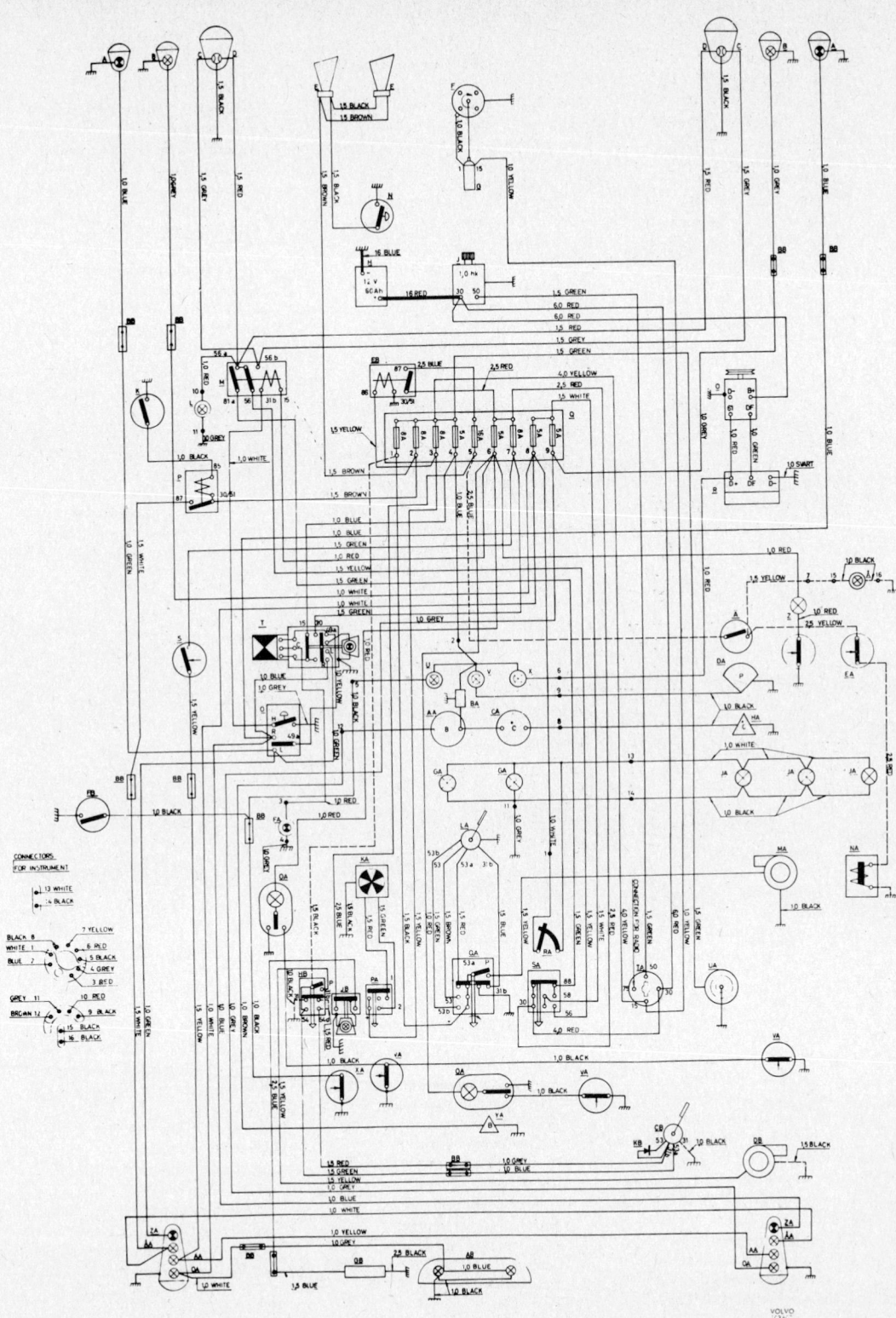

145, standard transmission, 1969-70

145, standard transmission, 1969-70

A Turn signal 32 CP
B Parking light 5 W
C Headlight low beam 40 W
D Headlight high beam 45 W
E Horn
F Distributor firing order 1-3-4-2
G Ignition coil
H Battery 12 V, 60 Ah.
J Starter motor 1.0 hp.
K Switch for backup light on
   transmission
L High beam warning lamp
   1.2 W
M Dimmer relay for high and low
   beams and headlight flasher
N Horn ring
O Generator 12 V
P Relay for backup light
Q Fuse box
R Voltage regulator
S Brake contact
T Warning flasher
U Handbrake warning lamp
   1.2 W
V Oil pressure warning lamp
   1.2 W

X Charging warning lamp 1.2 W
Y
Z Glove compartment lighting
   2 W
A Warning lamp for overdrive
   1.2 W
A Switch for overdrive
O Switch for headlight
   signalling and turn signals
AA Fuel gauge
BA Voltage regulator
CA Temperature gauge
DA Oil pressure warning
EA Switch for overdrive on
   transmission
FA Turn signal warning lamp
   1.2 W
GA Instrument lighting 2X3 W
HA Temperature gauge
   sensitive head
JA Heater control lighting
   3X1.2 W
KA Heater
LA Windshield wipers
MA Windshield washers
NA Solenoid for overdrive

OA Interior lamp 10 W
PA Switch for heater
QA Switch for windshield wipers
   and washer
RA Instrument lighting rheostat
SA Light switch
TA Ignition switch
UA Cigarette lighter
VA Door contact
XA Switch for handbrake warning
YA Fuel gauge tank unit
ZA Flasher light 32 CP
AA Backup light 15 W
AA′ Brake stoplight 25 W
OA Tail light 5 W
AB License plate lighting 2X5 W
*CB Rear window wiper
*DB Rear window washer
EB Relay for rear window heater
FB Caution contact
GB Heated rear window
*HB Switch for rear window wiper
JB Switch for rear window
   heater with warning lamp
   2 W

* Accessory

145, automatic transmission, 1969-1970

A Turn signal 32 CP
B Parking light 5 W
C Headlight low beam 40 W
D Headlight high beam 45 W
E Horn
F Distributor firing order 1-3-4-2
G Ignition coil
H Battery 12 V, 60 Ah.
J Starter motor 1.0 hp.
K Switch unit F starter lockout
   and backup lights
L High beam warning lamp
   1.2 W
M Dimmer relay for high and low
   beams and headlight flasher
N Horn ring
O Generator 12 V
P Relay F solenoid on start motor
Q Fusebox
R Voltage regulator
S Brake contact
T Warning flasher
U Handbrake warning lamp
   1.2 W

V Oil pressure warning lamp
   1.2 W
X Charging warning lamp 1.2 W
Y Caution contact
Z Glove compartment lighting
   2 W
A Junction
A Relay for rear window heater
O Switch for headlight signalling
   and turn signals
AA Fuel gauge
BA Voltage regulator
CA Temperature gauge
DA Oil pressure warning
*EA Rear window washer
FA Turn signal warning lamp
   1.2 W
GA Instrument lighting 2X3 W
HA Temperature gauge
   sensitive head
JA Heater control lighting
   3X1.2 W
KA Heater
LA Windshield wipers

MA Windshield washer
*NA Rear window wiper
OA Interior lamp 10 W
PA Switch for heater
QA Switch for windshield wipers
   and washer
RA Instrument lighting rheostat
SA Light switch
TA Ignition switch
UA Cigarette lighter
VA Door contact
XA Switch for handbrake warning
YA Fuel gauge tank unit
ZA Flasher light 32 CP
AA Backup light 15 W
AA Brake stoplight 25 W
OA Tail light 5 W
AB License plate lighting 2X5 W
BB Heated rear window
*CB Switch for rear window wiper
DB Switch for rear window heater
   with warning lamp 2 W
*EB Diode
* Accessory

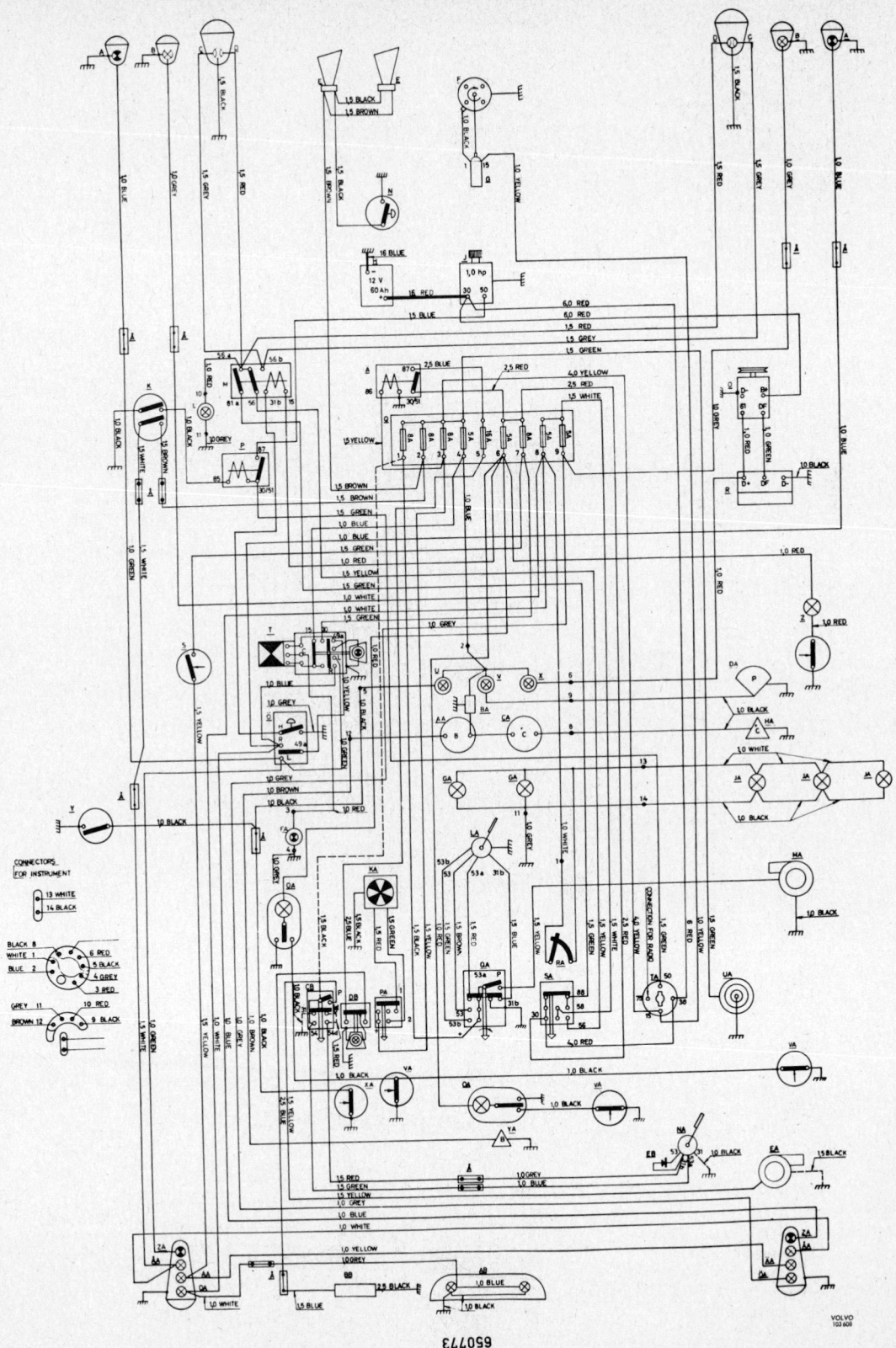

145, automatic transmission, 1969-1970

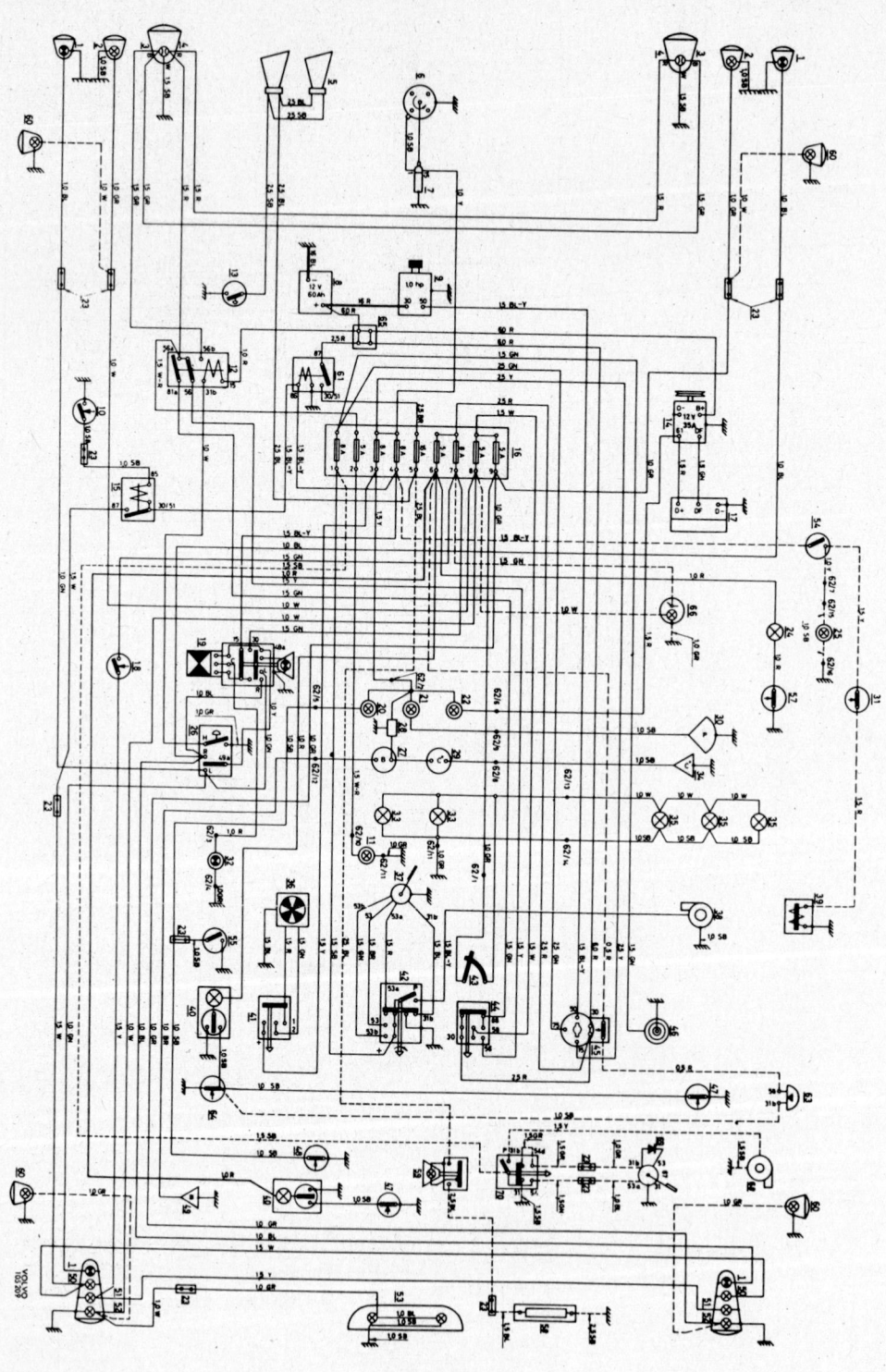

145, 1971

145, 1971

1. Dir. ind. flashers 32 CP
2. Parking light 5 W
3. Headlight low beam 40 W
4. Headlight high beam 45 W
5. Horn
6. Distributor firing order 1-3-4-2
7. Ignition coil
8. Battery 12 V 60 Ah.
9. Starter motor 1.0 hp.
10. Switch for backup lights only for M40 and M41 transmission
11. High beam warning lamp 1.2 W
12. Dimmer relay for high and low beams and headlight flasher
13. Horn ring
14. Alternator
15. Relay for backup lights on M40, M41 and starter Relay on BW35
16. Fuse box
17. Voltage regulator
18. Brake contact
19. Warning flashers
20. Brake warning lamp 1.2 W
21. Oil pressure warning lamp 1.2 W
22. Charging warning lamp 1.2 W
23. Connector
24. Glove compartment lighting 2 W
25. Overdrive warning lamp 1.2 W
26. Switch for headlight signalling and emergency flashers
27. Fuel gauge
28. Voltage regulator
29. Temperature gauge
30. Oil pressure warning
31. Switch for overdrive on transmission
32. Flasher warning lamp 1.2 W
33. Instrument lighting 2x1.2 W
34. Temperature gauge sending unit
35. Heater control lighting 3x1.2 W
36. Heater
37. Windshield wipers
38. Windshield washer
39. Solenoid for overdrive

40. Interior lamp 10 W
41. Switch for heater
42. Switch for windshield wipers and washer
43. Instrument lighting rheostat
44. Light switch
45. Ignition switch
46. Cigarette lighter
47. Door switch
48. Switch for parking brake warning
49. Fuel gauge tank unit
50. Backup lights 15 W
51. Brake stoplights 25 W
52. Tail lights 5 W
53. License plate lighting 2x5 W
54. Switch for overdrive
55. Brake warning contact
56. Switch on transmission, BW35
57. Switch glove comp. lighting
58. Elec. heated rear window
59. Switch elec. heated rear window
60. Side marker lamps, only for USA 5 W
61. Relay for elec. heated rear window
62. Conn. at instrument
63. Buzzer
64. Door switch on driver's side
65. Connection plate
66. Clock
67. Rear window wiper
68. Rear window washer
69. Diode
70. Switch for rear window wiper

Color code:
SB   Black
W   White
Y   Yellow
GN   Green
GR   Grey
BL   Blue
R   Red
BR   Brown
W-R White-Red
BL-Y Blue-Yellow

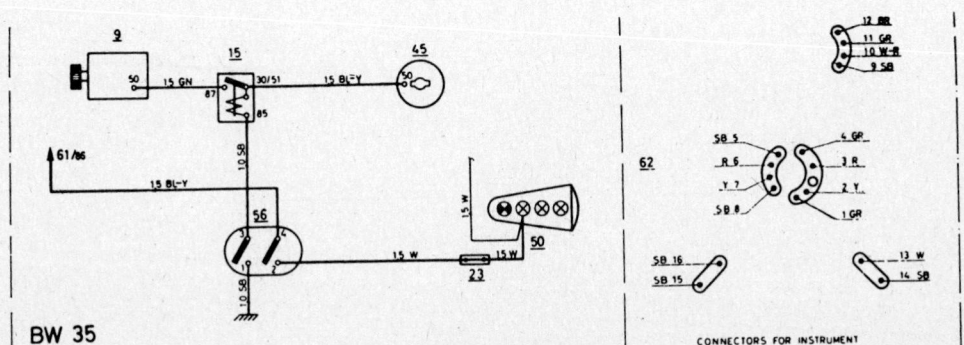

145, automatic transmission, 1971

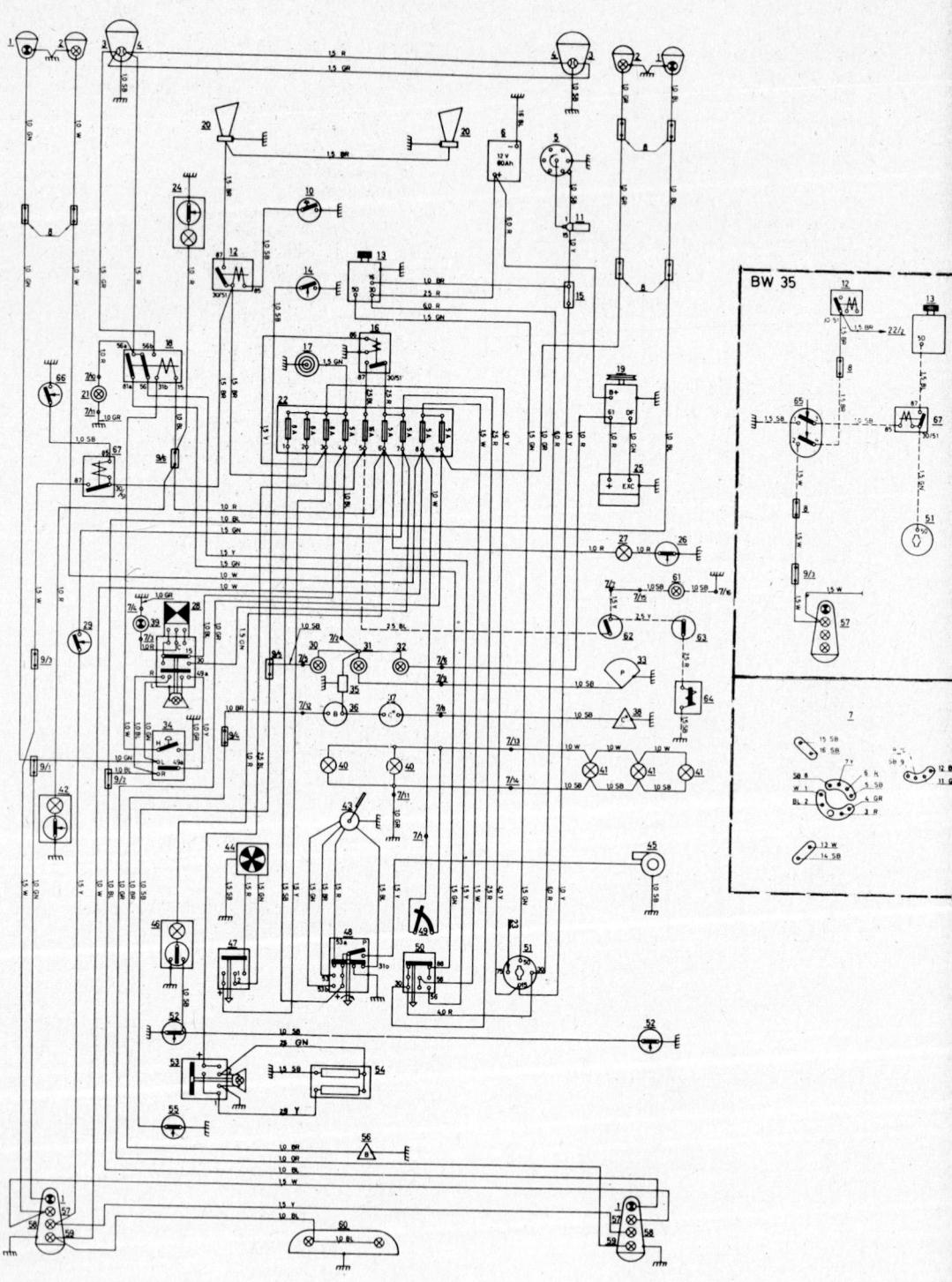

164, 1969-70

164, 1969-70

1 Turn signal flashers 32 cp
2 Parking light 5 W (4 cp)
3 Headlight low beam 40 W
4 Headlight high beam 45 W
5 Distributor firing order 1-5-3-6-2-4
6 Battery 12 V, 60 Ah.
7 Conn. at instrument
8 Junction
9 Part of 6-pole conn. unit
10 Horn ring
11 Ignition coil
12 Relay for horn
13 Starter Motor 1.0 hp.
14 Caution contact
15 Resistor
16 Relay for heated rear window
17 Cigarette lighter
18 Dimmer relay for high and low beams
   and headlight flasher
19 AC-generator 12 V, 35 A
20 Horn
21 High beam warning lamp 1.2 W
22 Fusebox
23 Radio connection
24 Engine comp. lighting 18 W
25 Voltage regulator
26 Switch glove comp. lighting
27 Glove compartment lighting 2 W
28 Warning flashers
29 Brake contact
30 Brake warning lamp 1.2 W
31 Oil pressure warning lamp 1.2 W
32 Charging warning lamp 1.2 W
33 Oil pressure warning
34 Switch for headlight-
   signalling and flashers

35 Voltage regulator
36 Fuel gauge
37 Temperature gauge
38 Temperature gauge sensitive head
39 Flasher warning lamp 1.2 W
40 Instrument lighting 2x3 W
41 Heater control lighting 3x1.2 W
42 Luggage comp. light 18 W
43 Windshield wipers
44 Heater
45 Windshield washers
46 Interior lamp 10 W
47 Switch for heater
48 Switch for Windshield wipers and washer
49 Instrument lighting rheostat
50 Light switch
51 Ignition switch
52 Door contact
53 Switch heat, rear window
54 Heated rear window
55 Switch for handbrake warning
56 Fuel gauge tank unit
57 Backup light 15 W (32 cp)
58 Brake stoplight 25 W (32 cp)
59 Tail light .5 W (4 cp)
60 License plate lighting 2x5 W
61 Overdr. control lamp 1.2 W
62 Switch for overdrive
63 Switch f. overdr. on transmission
64 Solenoid f. overdrive
65 Switch on transmission BW35
66 Switch for backup light only M400
   and M410
67 Relay for backup light on M400, M410 and
   starter relay on BW35

Engine Electrical

Models equipped with B14 and B16 engines have 6-volt electrical systems, and those with B18, B20, and B30 engines have 12-volt systems. Each consists of the battery, starter, generator or alternator, regulator, ignition, lighting, signaling and instrumentation components.

COMPONENT DESCRIPTION REMOVAL AND REPAIR

The battery for B18 and B20 engines is mounted on a shelf to the left of the radiator, with the B30 it is to the right of the radiator; it is a 12-volt, lead-acid battery with a capacity of 60 ampere hours and the negative terminal grounded. The battery for the B14 and B16 engines is mounted on a shelf on the front bulkhead. It is a 6-volt, lead-acid battery with a capacity of 85 ampere hours and the negative terminal grounded.

Battery Replacement

Loosen the bolts of the battery cable clamps. Spread the clamps with a screwdriver and then use a clamp puller if necessary, to remove the clamp. Pulling on the clamp itself may damage the battery.

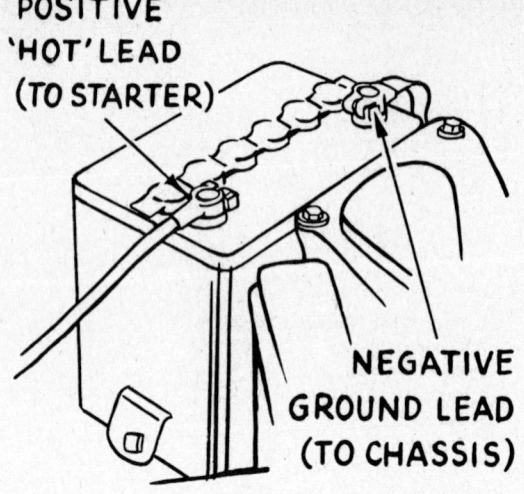

Battery connections.

Note polarity of battery connections.

Remove screws from battery clamp and remove battery from car. Clean battery with a brush and rinse with lukewarm water. Clean the battery shelf and cable clamps with a wire brush. Install new battery in proper position and install clamp and screws. Coat cable clamps and battery terminals with vaseline.

Starter

The starter is mounted on the left side

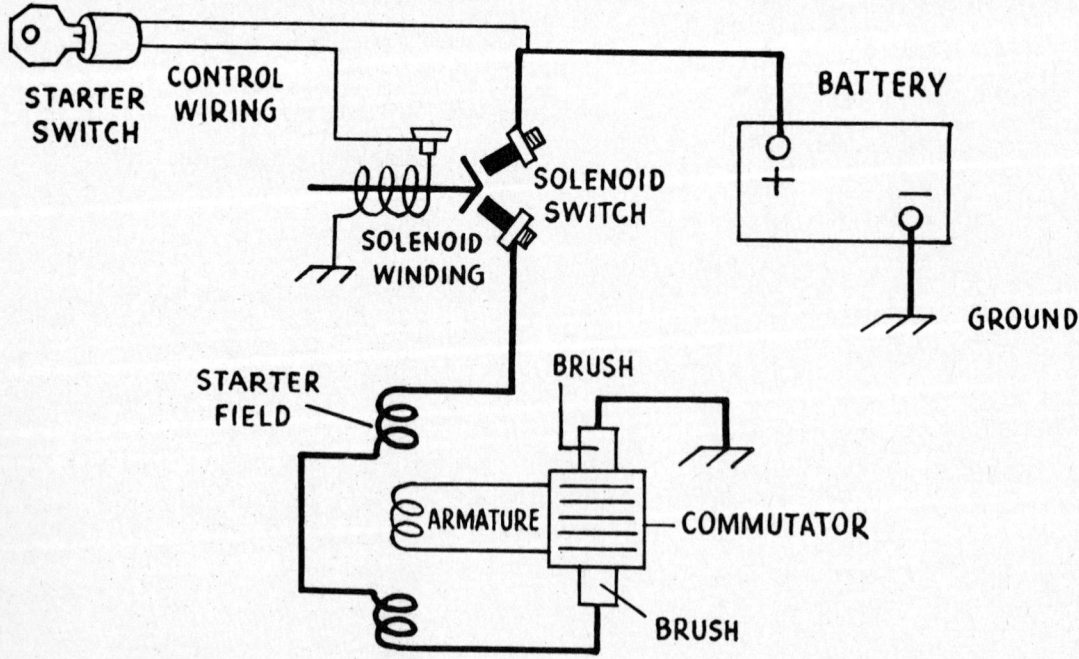

Schematic diagram of starter electrical circuit.

of the flywheel housing. It consists of a 4-pole, series-wound motor. The motor is energized by a solenoid which also engages the gear of the starter clutch assembly with the flywheel ring gear.

The field frame carries the pole shoes and the field coils. The armature has a spline which carries the overrunning clutch and gear assembly. The armature shaft is supported in two bushings which are permanently packed with lubricant.

As the starter is energized, the shift lever moves against the spring and by means of the guide ring sends the gear into mesh with the flywheel. After the gear meshes, the solenoid contact disc closes the circuit and the engine is cranked. When the engine starts, the increased speed of the flywheel causes the gear to over-run the clutch and armature. The gear continues in full mesh until the starter current is interrupted. Then the shift lever spring returns the gear to its neutral position.

STARTER REPLACEMENT

The unit can be removed from the vehicle as follows.

Remove the battery ground cable so that the cables connected to the starter are not hot. Disconnect leads from starter, noting connections. Remove bolts holding starter to flywheel housing and lift starter off. Install new starter in reverse order of above. Tighten bolts evenly, but not too tightly. Connect leads to starter terminals. Connect battery ground cable.

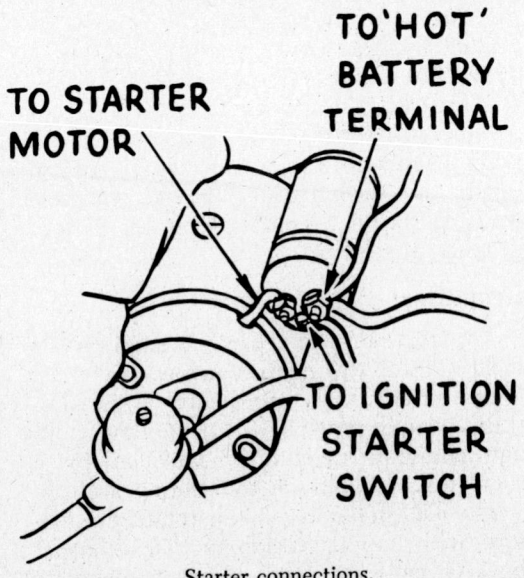

TO STARTER MOTOR

TO 'HOT' BATTERY TERMINAL

TO IGNITION STARTER SWITCH

Starter connections.

STARTER DISASSEMBLY

The starter may be disassembled for overhaul or repair as follows after removal from the vehicle:

Remove the cover protecting the brushes and commutator. Remove brush screws, lift springs and remove brushes. Mark position of front and rear end frames in relation to the housing and remove through-bolts that hold these frames to the housing. Disconnect lead between the control solenoid and housing and lift off the rear end frame with armature brake together with the housing. Remove pivot screw from solenoid engaging fork, and lift out armature and clutch assembly from housing. Remove the stop washers from the armature shaft. Three washers are removed by pulling straight off shaft. Tap the thick washer further onto the shaft about ¼" and remove the lock ring. Then remove the thick washer from the shaft.

Remove armature brake from rear end frame. Blow dirt and dust from housing, field winding and armature. Wipe clean but do not use solvents that may attack the insulation of the windings.

STARTER COMPONENT CHECKS

Examine the armature for damage such as bent or worn shaft, scored commutator or damaged windings. A defective shaft or damaged windings require armature replacement. A scored or unevenly worn armature can be turned using a special chuck.

Check the armature for electrical shorts by placing it in a growler machine and holding a thin piece of steel such as a hacksaw blade an inch or so from the armature. If the blade vibrates in any position when the armature is rotated in the growler, there is a short between frame and windings, between windings, or between commutator and frame. Locate short by checking with a low wattage lamp and test prods. A shorted armature usually must be rewound.

Examine the housing and check the field windings for damage to armature. Using test prods and the low wattage lamp, check the field winding by placing one test prod on the housing and one on the field lead. If the lamp lights, the field may be damaged, or the lead-through may be shorted at the housing. Remove lead-through and test again. If short continues,

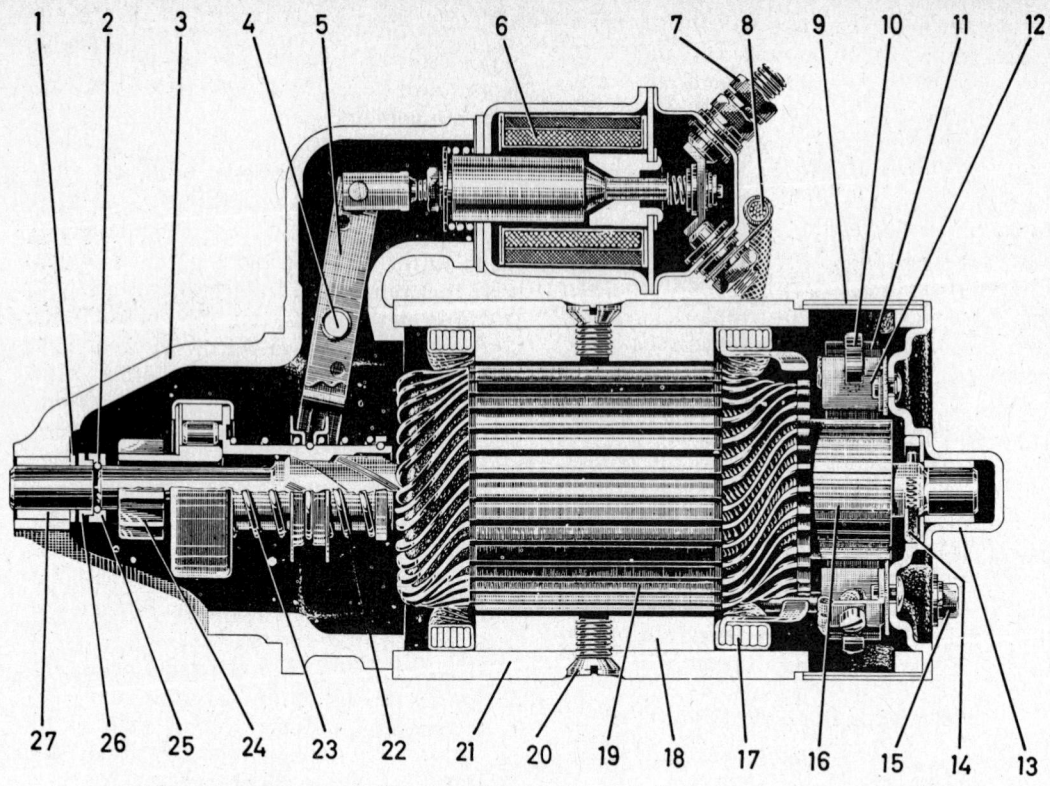

1. Adjusting washer
5. Clutch lever
6. Solenoid switch
7. Battery lead terminal
8. Starter motor terminal
11. Brush assembly

14. Armature brake
16. Commutator
17. Field winding
18. Pole shoe
19. Armature
20. Pole screw

23. Clutch spring
24. Clutch gear
25. Stop washer
26. Stop washer
27. Bushing

Starter and solenoid components.

field must be replaced. Check end head containing brush holders and test the two normally insulated holders for shorts to the end head. If brush holders are shorted replace end head assembly.

STARTER ASSEMBLY

Install armature brake in rear end frame and install electrical lead between positive brushes. Install clutch gear on armature shaft, slide on washers and secure locking ring. Lubricate armature shaft and brake with silicone grease.

Assemble armature and gear housing and place engaging arm in its position around the gear. Install solenoid on gear housing and insert pivot screw. Lubricate gear and engaging arm with silicone grease. Lubricate shaft end.

Place housing over armature, lining up with the end frame according to markings made on casing before disassembly. Place rear end frame on armature shaft in correct position and assemble end frames and housing with through bolts. Tighten bolts. Install brushes. Turn armature, and check to see that it moves freely.

Install starter on vehicle by carrying out reverse procedure from removal. Tighten bolts evenly, but not too tightly. Install brush and commutator cover. Connect leads to starter terminals. Connect battery ground lead.

Generator

The generator, which is mounted on the right side of the engine and is driven by V-belt from the crankshaft, is a DC shunt-wound type. The current and voltage charging rates are controlled by a regulator mounted on the engine firewall.

The DC generator has a rotating armature with copper windings that intersect lines of magnetic force between magnetic

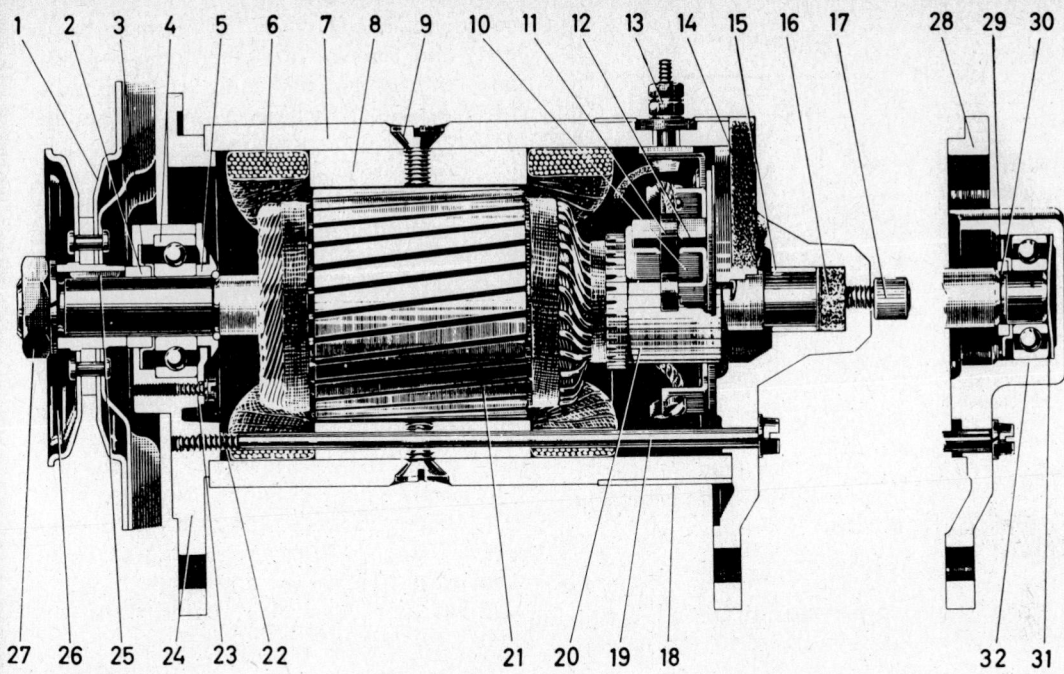

1. Belt pulley
2. Spacing ring
3. Oil seal washer
4. Ball bearing
5. Spacing ring
6. Filed winding
7. Stator
8. Pole shoe
9. Pole screw
10. Brush holder
11. Brush spring
12. Brush

13. Armature terminal
Gen. type AR6
14. End shield
15. Bushing
16. Lubricating felt
17. Lubricating cap
18. Protecting band
19. Through bolt
20. Commutator
21. Armature
22. Screw

23. Sealing washer
24. End head
25. Key
26. Spring washer
27. Nut
28. End shield
Gen. type AR7
29. Oil seal washer
30. Spacing ring
31. Spring ring
32. Ball bearing

DC generator components.

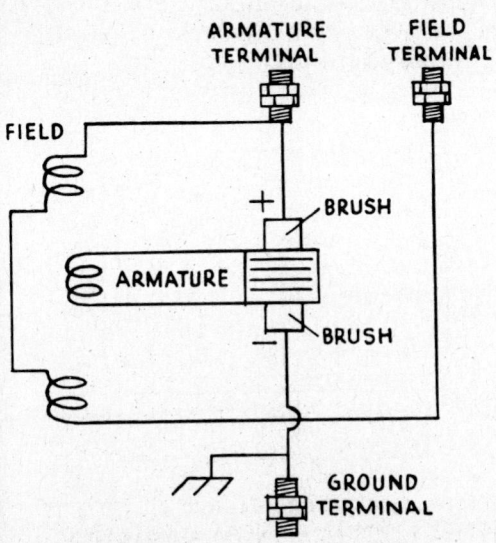

Schematic diagram of generator electrical circuit.

field poles. At the start, the magnetic field is weak because it is only residual. However, as current flows from the armature windings, part of the flow is fed into and excites the magnetic field. Increasing speed intensifies the magnetic field and thereby increases the voltage from the windings. The magnetic field becomes saturated with energy and no further increase in armature speed will add to the output.

GENERATOR REPLACEMENT

If generator is found defective, replace as follows. Remove ground cable from negative terminal of battery. Disconnect leads from generator. Loosen V-belt tensioning bracket and remove belt. Remove two bolts holding generator to engine and lift off generator. Install new generator in

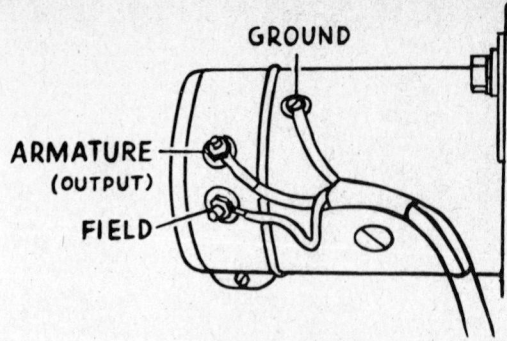

Generator connections.

reverse order of above, making sure connections are correct and that V-belt tension is adjusted for ½″ deflection.

GENERATOR BENCH TEST

Clean outside of generator with rag moistened in kerosene. Remove brush and commutator protective cover and check commutator for worn or scored surfaces. Inspect inside of generator housing around commutator for solder that may have been thrown from commutator as a result of overheating. If solder is present, generator is probably shorted and armature or field may require rewinding. If commutator and brushes are in good condition, make the following test.

Connect the generator field terminal to the generator ground terminal and to the negative terminal of a battery of the proper voltage (6V or 12V) for the generator under test. Connect the armature terminal of the generator in series with an ammeter to the positive terminal of the battery. The generator should then run as a motor at a low, even speed. If it does not run or runs very slowly, and the current is low, the trouble could be that brushes, not free in the holders, are making poor contact on the commutator, or a defective armature winding. If it does not run or runs slowly and the current is high, the trouble could be a broken or shorted field, a worn bushing, or too-high brush tension. Heavy sparking or excessive up and down movement of brushes means commutator is too far out-of-round, or brushes are damaged.

GENERATOR DISASSEMBLY

Generator may be dismantled for overhaul or repair as follows. Remove brush and commutator cover. Disconnect brush leads and remove brushes. Remove terminal connecting bar and then remove through-bolts which hold end frames together.

Pull off rear end frame with brush holders, and lift armature out of housing. Place armature in a vise having soft jaws (avoid excessive tightening) and remove pulley nut, lock washer, pulley, fan, key, and drive end frame.

NOTE: *after removing armature from vise, tap threaded end of armature shaft with a soft hammer, if necessary, to remove drive end frame.* Remove bearing parts from drive end frame. Clean and inspect the ball bearings, replace worn parts, and pack assembly with high temperature grease. Wipe generator parts with clean cloth. Grease solvents might damage insulated windings. Reassemble using reverse sequence.

DC Regulator

The regulator is mounted on the right wheel housing and automatically controls the charging voltage and current that the generator supplies to the battery.

Since voltage produced by the generator is in direct ratio to the product of armature speed and exciting current in the magnetic field, a constant voltage output can be easily maintained by making compensating adjustments to the field current. Armature speed is based on engine rpm and is therefore not independently controllable. The regulator maintains a constant voltage output by interrupting the field current.

The Bosch regulator used on the Volvo

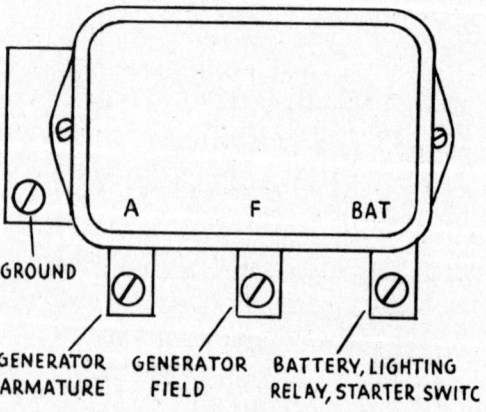

Regulator connections, 6-volt system.

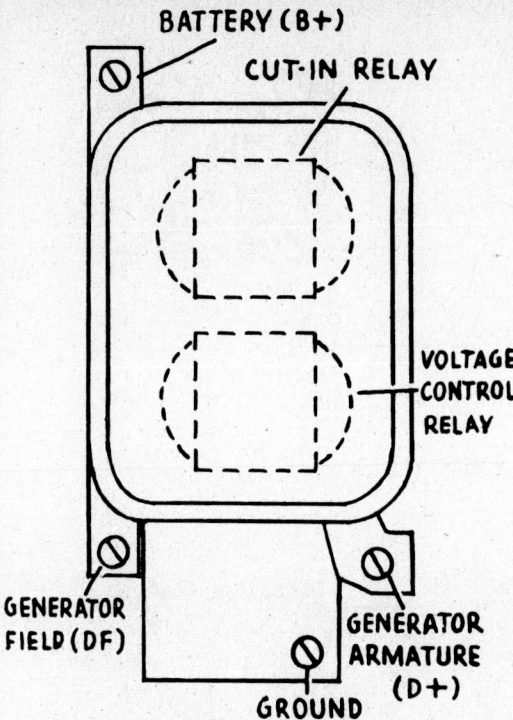

BATTERY (B+)

CUT-IN RELAY

VOLTAGE CONTROL RELAY

GENERATOR FIELD (DF)

GENERATOR ARMATURE (D+)

GROUND

Regulator connections, 12-volt system.

has a semi-conductor component, a variode, having a variable resistance under different voltage loads, ranging from high resistance at low voltages to extremely low resistance at high voltage levels. The variode lead picks up the voltage drop that resistance causes in the main current lead. The resistance of the main current lead determines the activation of the variode and should not be altered or replaced separately.

REGULATOR ADJUSTMENT–CUT-IN VOLTAGE

Connect an 0-20V DC voltmeter between the regulator terminal D+ and ground. Start engine and increase speed slowly, noting reading of voltmeter. The reading should first increase to about 6.1-6.4 (for 6V systems) and 12.1-12.8 (for 12V systems) then fall back to .1 or .2 volt when the cut-in relay is actuated, after which it should remain constant. Adjustment is carried out by decreasing the pressure of the spring on the cut-in relay. If it is too low, the adjustment is made by increasing the pressure on the spring.

REGULATOR ADJUSTMENT—CUT-OUT CURRENT

Connect an 0-50A ammeter in series

with the battery (B+) connection to the regulator. Increase engine speed to obtain a reading. Then reduce speed gradually to idle, watching the ammeter reading go down to zero and slightly into the discharge region, when it should jump up suddenly to zero. At this point, the reverse current relay has cut out. If the reverse current (into discharge region) is less than 2 amps, the reverse current is too low, and the tension of the contact spring on the cut-in relay should be lowered by bending the yoke of the cut-in contact. If the discharge reading is more than 7.5 amps, the bending of the contact spring must be increased until the cut-out current is within range.

REGULAR ADJUSTMENT—VOLTAGE CONTROL

Remove the wire from the B+ connection on the regulator. Connect a voltmeter between the B+ terminal on the regulator and ground, accelerate the engine gradually to increase the generator output. Watch the voltmeter reading increase and note the reading at which it stops increasing. This voltage for 6-volt systems should be 6.5-7.3, and for 12-volt systems, 13.9-14.9 for unloaded engines. Adjustment is made by bending the spring support to change spring pressure on the voltage control relay. Increasing spring pressure increases the voltage at which control takes place, decreasing spring pressure lowers the voltage. The engine should be thoroughly warmed before making this adjustment.

Alternator

The alternator is a three-phase, delta connected alternating unit. The rectifier, built into the slip ring end shield, consists of six silicon diodes. Also in the slip ring are the magnetizing diodes, which feed the field wiring via the voltage regulator. The alternator has a rotating field (rotor) and a stationary main wiring (stator).

Since the alternator is self limiting as far as current is concerned (35 amps), a simple mechanical voltage regulator is used with only voltage control as its function.

ALTERNATOR REPLACEMENT

If the alternator is found defective, replace as follows.

Remove the negative lead from the battery. Disconnect the leads from the alternator. Loosen the tensioning bracket and the V-belt. Remove the bolt holding the

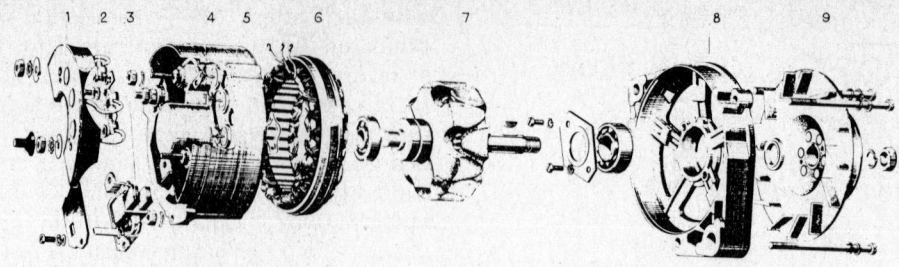

1. Rectifier (positive diode plate)
2. Magnetizing rectifier
3. Brush holder
4. Slip ring end shield
5. Rectifier (negative diode)

6. Stator
7. Rotor
8. Drive end shield
9. Pulley with fan

Bosch alternator.

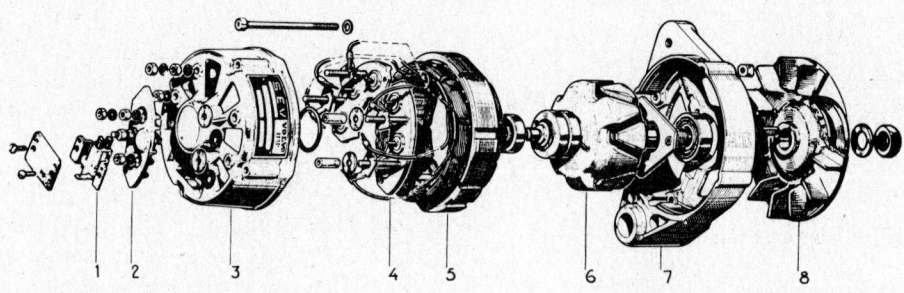

1. Brush holder
2. Insulation diode with holder
3. Slip ring end shield
4. Rectifier

5. Stator
6. Rotor
7. Drive end shield
8. Pulley with fan

Motorola alternator.

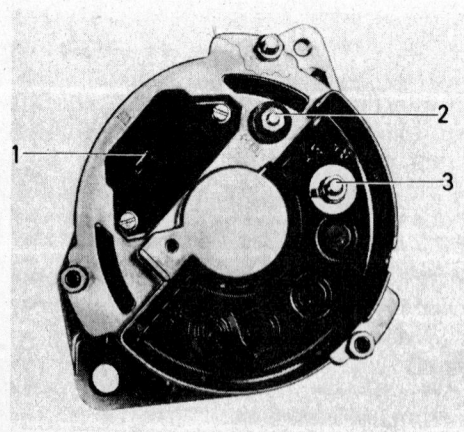

1. DF to field winding
2. 61/D+ from magnetizing rectifier
3. B+ to battery

Bosch alternator connections.

alternator to the engine block, and remove the alternator.

Install new alternator in the reverse of above, making sure connections are correct and that the V-belt tension is adjusted for ½" deflection.

ALTERNATOR DISASSEMBLY

Remove the pulley and key. Remove the bolts holding the brush holder and take off the holder. Remove the nuts, washers and screws that hold the alternator together. Take off the drive end shield and rotor from the stator and slip off the ring end shield. Press the rotor out of the drive end shield. Remove the screws for the washer which holds the drive end shield bearing and press out the bearing.

On the Bosch, remove the positive diode plate and unsolder the stator connection to remove the stator. On the Motorola, remove

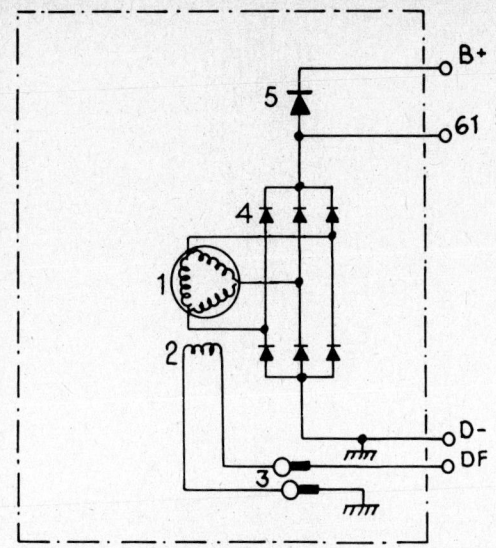

1. Stator
2. Rotor (field winding)
3. Slip rings and brush holder
4. Rectifier diode
5. Insulation diode

Motorola alternator inner circuit.

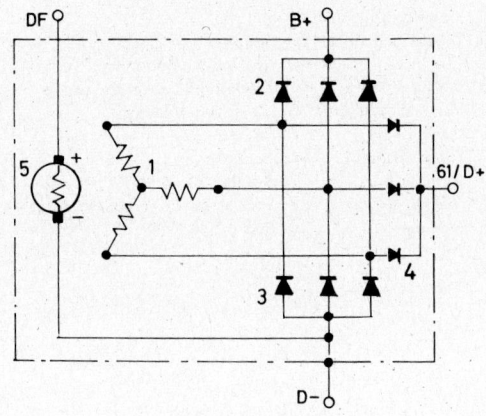

Inner wiring of Bosch alternator.

the negative diode holder and the diode holders for the slip ring end shield.

ALTERNATOR TESTING

Caution: do not use a 110 or 220 V DC or AC test lamp, or a high powered ohmmeter for any of the tests. Only a 12 V, 2-5 W test light should be used, and for testing the diodes only a battery-powered or other low powered ohmmeter should be used.

Stator

Check stator isolation by connecting a 40 V alternating current between the body and each phase lead. If arcing or a noticeable odor is present, there is a short circuit. Another test is to use a 12 V, 2-5 W test lamp between the stator plates and a terminal on the stator. If the test lamp lights, the insulation is damaged and the stator must be replaced.

Rotor

Check the rotor with a 40 V alternating current to the rotor frame and a slip ring. Arcing or a noticeable odor indicates a faulty rotor. Resistance between the slip rings should be 4 ± 0.4 ohms on the Bosch alternator, and 5 ± 0.2 ohms for the Motorola alternator. Burned or damaged slip rings may be turned on the Bosch to a minimum of 1.3 in. (31.5 mm). Maximum out-of-roundness for the slip rings is 0.0012 in. (0.03 mm.).

Diodes

Check the diodes with a diode tester or a battery-powered ohmmeter. When using an ohmmeter, resistance in one direction will be very high, and in the other direction will be very low.

To replace the diodes on the Bosch alternator, unsolder the faulty one and remove from the plate. Lubricate the replacement with silicon oil before inserting it. Paint a replaced positive diode with a chlorinated rubber enamel to prevent corrosion. If any of the magnetizing diodes are faulty, replace the entire plate with all the diodes.

To replace the diodes on the Motorola alternator, the entire diode holder must be replaced. If the isolation diode is faulty, the holder and the diode are replaced as a unit. The positive diode holder is marked with red ink and the negative diode holder is marked with black ink.

Brushes

Check the isolation of the brush holder with a 40 V alternating current as above. For the Bosch alternator minimum brush length is 0.32 in. (8 mm). For the Motorola alternator minimum brush length is 3/16 in. (5 mm). If less, replace the brushes.

ALTERNATOR ASSEMBLY

Fit the stator in the slip ring and shield, fit the diode holders and solder the stator leads to the connecting point. Grease the drive end bearing with light machine oil and fit the bearing and washer in the drive end bearing shield, then press the shield and the spacing ring onto the rotor. Lubricate the slip ring bearing and seat with a light layer of Moylkote or equivalent. Assemble alternator halves and lightly tighten the bolts. Fit the brush holder and pulley. Tighten the pulley nut to 29 ft. lbs.

AC Regulator

The regulator is mounted to the right of the radiator on the 140 series and on the right wheel well on the 164. It is a simple mechanical device since the alternator is self-limiting.

Ignition System

A battery ignition system includes the ignition coil, contact-breaker, distributor, spark plugs, ignition switch, and a source of current. Current flows from the battery through the ignition switch to the induction coil. Through primary and secondary winding arrangements in the coil, high voltage is developed to fire the spark plugs. The distributor has two functions within the circuit. It has the breaker-point assembly which times the collapse of the mag-

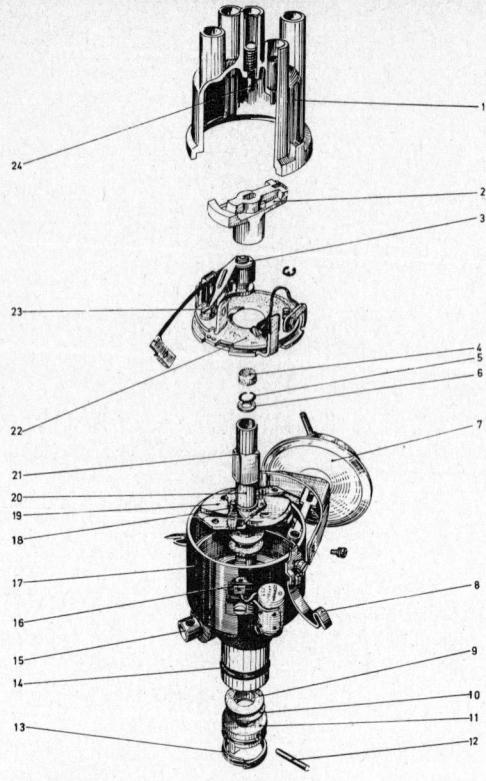

1. Distributor cap
2. Distributor arm
3. Contact breaker
4. Lubricating felt
5. Circlip
6. Washer
7. Vacuum regulator
8. Cap clasp
9. Fiber washer
10. Steel washer
11. Flange
12. Lock pin
13. Resilient ring
14. Rubber seal
15. Lubricator
16. Primary connection
17. Distributor housing
18. Centrifugal governor spring
19. Centrifugal weight
20. Breaker arm
21. Breaker cam
22. Breaker plate
23. Lock screw for breaker contacts
24. Rod brush (carbon)

Distributor, B20B

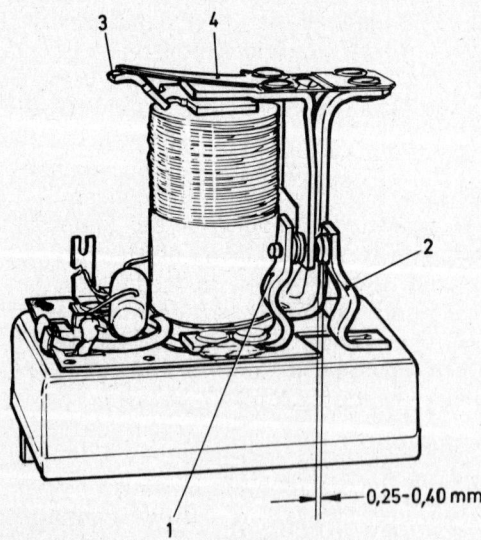

0,25-0,40 mm

1. Regulator contact for lower control range (lower contact)
2. Regulator contact for upper control range (upper contact)
3. Stop lamp
4. Spring

Bosch AC voltage regulator.

netic field in the coil so that a pulse of high voltage (secondary circuit) is sent to the spark plugs. The second function of the distributor is the distribution of spark to the correct plug. The rotor and cap provide this distribution. The condenser, arranged in parallel with the breaker-point circuit, prevents arcing between the points after they have been separated. A precise instantaneous magnetic field collapse in the coil is thus possible.

DISTRIBUTOR REPLACEMENT

To remove the distributor for overhaul or replacement, remove the distributor cap, place No. 1 cylinder in the firing position (timing marks aligned), disconnect

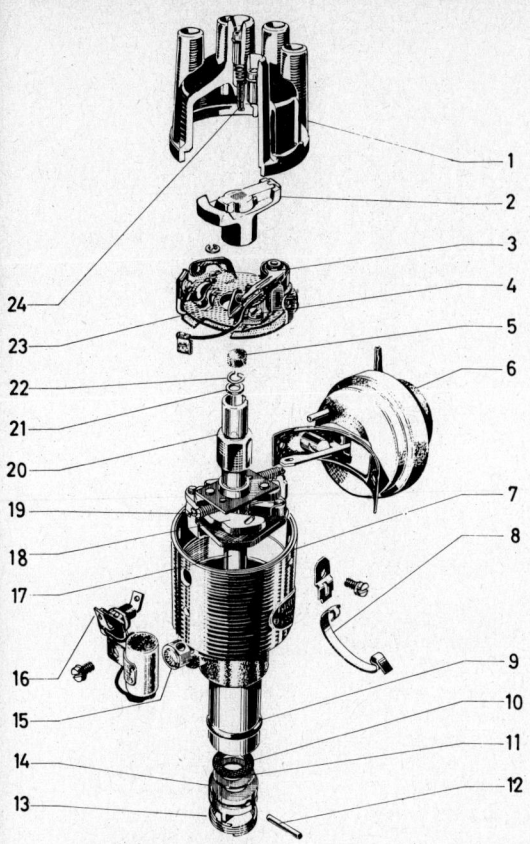

1. Distributor cap
2. Distributor arm
3. Contact breaker
4. Lock screw for breaker contacts
5. Lubricating felt
6. Vacuum regulator
7. Distributor housing
8. Cap clamp
9. Rubber seal
10. Fiber washer
11. Steel washer
12. Lock pin
13. Spring ring
14. Flange
15. Lubricator
16. Primary connection
17. Distributor shaft
18. Centrifugal weight
19. Centrifugal governor spring
20. Breaker cam
21. Washer
22. Circlip
23. Breaker plate
24. Rod brush (carbon)

Distributor, B30A

vacuum line and primary ignition wire, and remove bolt, clamp and distributor.

Replace paper gasket on distributor housing if necessary.

Install new distributor with vacuum advance unit pointing rearward and par-

allel with engine. Turn rotor to align mark on tip with breaker point hold-down screw so that the shaft seats itself. If distributor was set in wrong, rotor will be 180° out of place. Set distributor into position and hand tighten bolt. The mark on the rotor should be nearly aligned with mark on distributor housing. Align marks on rotor tip and housing, set breaker point gap or dwell angle, and adjust ignition timing.

CONTACT-POINT ASSEMBLY

When installing points, lightly lubricate distributor cam with high temperature grease. CAUTION: *excessive lubricant will throw off into contact points.* Position support on breaker plate and install lock screw loosely for later adjustment. Install breaker arm on pivot pin. Position spring insulating washer correctly in spring support. Plug-in breaker arm wire. Adjust gap to specifications. Tighten.

Point gap can be set by using a feeler gauge or a dwell meter. Accurate measurements with a feeler gauge require careful, precise usage of the feelers.

A dwell meter should be calibrated first, switched to the four- or six-cylinder position, and connected between distributor primary terminal and ground. Remove distributor cap and rotor. Loosen the breaker set screw approximately ⅛ turn. Observing the dwell meter, reset screw of stationary contact to obtain specific dwell angle. Tighten set screw and recheck

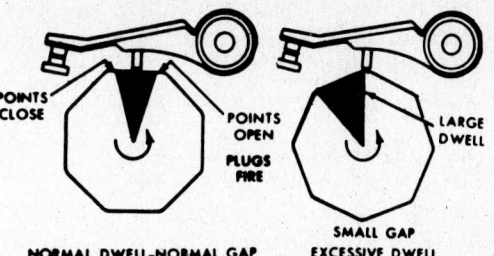

NORMAL DWELL-NORMAL GAP   SMALL GAP EXCESSIVE DWELL

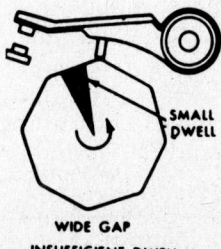

WIDE GAP
INSUFFICIENT DWELL

Distributor dwell angle.

dwell. Install rotor and cap, start engine, and make a final dwell angle check.

IGNITION TIMING

Timing marks are located on the crankshaft pulley and a raised spot is on the timing gear cover. (The B14 and B16 engines have timing marks on the flywheel and a pointer in a window on the right side of the flywheel housing.) Timing is correct when the timing marks are aligned at the moment No. 1 cylinder reaches top dead center.

Basic timing is set by rotating distributor housing counterclockwise slightly until contact points just start to open. Timing marks must line up at this point. Install distributor cap, and connect spark plugs.

Adjust ignition timing after setting point gap. A fast and easy way to adjust timing is with a stroboscope.

Connect strobe light to No. 1 spark plug. Disconnect all vacuum hoses from distributor and plug the hoses. Start engine and adjust idle to specified rpm for timing. Idle performance must be smooth. Rotate distributor as necessary to align timing marks with strobe pulses.

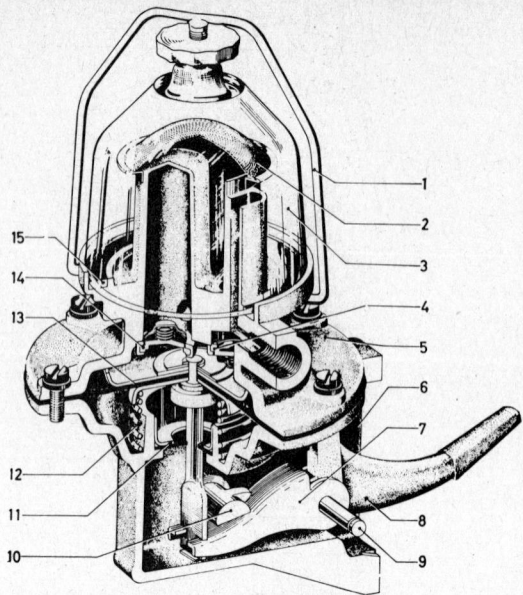

1. Retaining clamp	9. Shaft
2. Strainer	10. Stop
3. Sludge trap	11. Seal
4. Inlet valve	12. Spring
5. Upper pump housing	13. Diaphragm
6. Lower pump housing	14. Outlet valve
7. Link arm	15. Gasket
8. Rocker arm	

Type I fuel pump.

Fuel System

There are four types of fuel pumps used: Type I is an AC-UG; Type II is a Pierburg APG; Type III is an AC-YD; and Type IV is a Pierburg PV3025. Either Zenith-Stromberg or SU carburetors are used in single and dual installations.

FUEL SYSTEM PRESSURE TEST

The fuel system must supply fuel at the proper pressure (1.7-3.5 psi) for good engine operation. Fuel pump pressure is controlled by diaphragm spring pressure. A weak spring causes low fuel pressure and too strong a spring causes too much fuel pressure. To check the fuel pump pressure, connect a T-connector fuel fitting at the pump outlet to the carburetors and a pressure gauge to the fitting. Start the engine and note the reading. Then, stop the engine and see if the pressure drops gradually or immediately. An immediate pressure drop means a possible leaky pump valve or a worn carburetor float valve. Excessive fuel pump pressure may

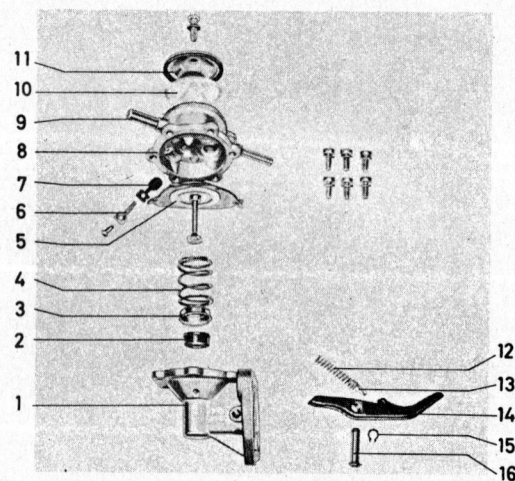

1. Lower pump housing	9. Inlet pipe
2. Rubber seal	10. Strainer
3. Guide	11. Cover and gasket
4. Spring	12. Return spring
5. Diaphragm	13. Spring retainer
6. Stop arm	14. Lever
7. Spring	15. Circlip
8. Upper pump housing	16. Lever pin

Type II fuel pump

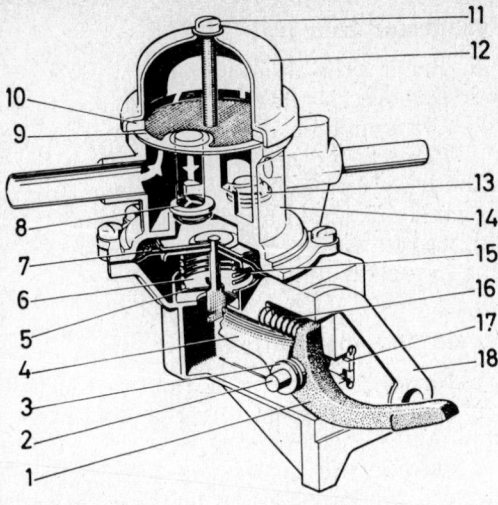

1. Rocker arm
2. Pin
3. Washer
4. Lever
5. Rubber seal
6. Washer
7. Diaphragm
8. Inlet valve
9. Strainer
10. Gasket

11. Screw with washer
12. Cover
13. Outlet valve
14. Upper pump housing
15. Diaphragm spring
16. Return spring
17. Rider
18. Lower pump housing

Type III fuel pump.

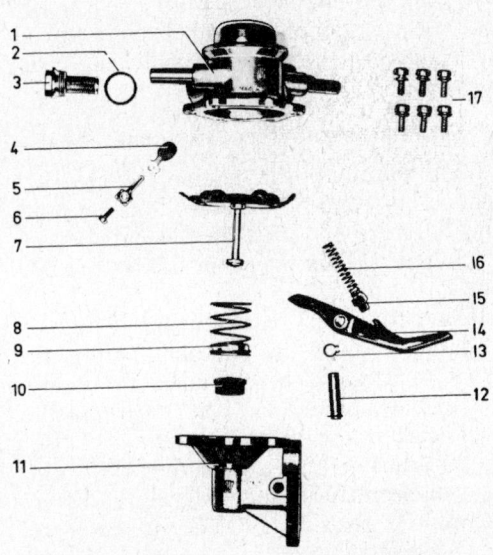

1. Upper housing
2. Sealing washer
3. Plug and strainer
4. Inlet valve
5. Stop arm
6. Screw
7. Diaphragm
8. Spring
9. Spring guide

10. Rubber seal
11. Lower pump housing
12. Lever pin
13. Snap-ring
14. Lever
15. Spring retainer
16. Return spring
17. Housing bolts

Type IV fuel pump

be caused by a dirty fuel filter strainer. Remove the plug and strainer from the fuel pump, clean it, replace it, and check the fuel pressure again.

FUEL PUMP

Fuel Pump Removal

1. Disconnect the fuel lines from the pump and plug them to exclude dirt.

2. Remove the pump mounting screws and carefully pull the pump free from the engine.

3. Remove and discard the old fuel pump gasket.

Fuel Pump Installation

1. Place new gasket on fuel pump.

2. Mount fuel pump with new gasket on engine block while inserting pump lever in engine block against camshaft.

3. Hold the pump body steady against the engine block and install the mounting screws securely.

4. Connect the fuel lines.

5. Start the engine, check for any leaks around the pump, and check the pump pressure.

Fuel Pump Overhaul

TYPE I

Separate the upper and lower parts of the pump. Remove the diaphragm by pressing it down and turning it a quarter turn. Remove rocker arm shaft lock-ring and press out shaft. Remove rocker arm, spring, link arm and washers.

Replace the valves (in an earlier design) by removing the screws for the retainer. Remove the old valves and clean recesses. Place new valves and new seats in position and install retainer.

Replace the valves (in a later design) by removing the old valves with a screwdriver and cleaning the valve recesses. Place new seals and valves in position using a sleeve. Then peen over the metal around each valve at four places with a special punch.

Assemble in reverse order, installing new diaphragm by pressing down rod in position and turning it a quarter turn. When installing make sure rocker arm lever is in correct position above its cam.

TYPES II & IV

Scratch line-up marks on the upper and

lower parts. Separate the parts. Remove rocker arm pin lockring and press out pin. Pull out rocker arm and return-spring. Remove diaphragm with spring, guide and rubber seal. The spring can be removed after the rubber seal has been pulled up over the nylon washer. Remove screw on the underside of the upper part, remove the stop arm and the spring valve. The inlet valve cannot be removed.

Reassemble by installing the leaf spring and stop arm. Tighten screw just enough for leaf spring to contact pump housing properly. Install spring and guide, and pull on rubber seal with flange inward, facing guide. Install diaphragm unit in lower part of pump. Press downward so that the rubber seal comes into correct position. Press down diaphragm, push in rocker arm and make sure that it positions correctly in relation to the diaphragm rod. Install rocker arm pin, lockring, spring retainer and return-spring.

Assemble upper and lower parts in accordance with lineup marks and bolt to housing. Make sure rocker arm is in correct position above cam.

Type III

Remove cover. Make scratch lineup marks on upper and lower parts, and separate the parts. Remove diaphragm by turning it one quarter turn. Remove diaphragm spring by turning washer so that hole coincides with wide end of diaphragm rod. With a grinding rod, remove peening for the rocker arm pin rider and remove rocker arm with pin and lever. Pull out rocker arm pin. Check parts for wear.

Assemble the pump by assembling the link arm, rocker arm with washers and the rocker arm pin. Insert linkage system with return spring into the housing. Install and lock riders in housing by peening.

ELECTRIC FUEL PUMP

An electric fuel pump is used on the 142E and the P1800E as part of the electronic fuel injection system. The pump is described and a replacement procedure given in the Fuel Injection System section. The pump is not repairable and must be replaced when defective.

CARBURETOR

Carburetor Removal

1. Remove the air cleaner.
2. Remove the link rod ball joints, fuel hoses, vacuum hose, and choke wire.
3. Remove the mounting nuts from the carburetors and pull the carburetors from the intake manifold together. Clean off the old gasket. Cover the intake holes with tape to exclude dirt.

Carburetor Installation

1. Remove tape covering from the manifold and put a new gasket in place. Install the protection plates.
2. Position the carburetors. On SU carburetors, the intermediate shaft and levers should be fitted between the carburetors before they are mounted. Install the mounting nuts and tighten evenly until the carburetors are snug against the manifold.
3. Connect the fuel hoses, vacuum hose, throttle and choke linkage. Be sure the choke dash control is pushed all the way in.
4. Adjust the carburetors.

Carburetor Adjustments

Before adjusting the carburetors, be sure that the engine has the correct valve clearance, distributor breaker point dwell angle, ignition timing, and sufficient compression.

Synchronizing Twin Carburetors

First warm up the engine, remove air cleaner, disconnect throttle linkage, and adjust for equal idling on the carburetors at a higher idling speed of 1,000 to 1,200 rpm.

If a carburetor synchronizing gauge is available, adjust it on one carburetor throat to a piston height near the middle of the scale. Switch the test gauge to the other carburetor and, if necessary, reset the air-adjustment screw of that carb until the synchronizing gauge piston returns to the middle position. NOTE: *do not reset the gauge level.*

1968 and later cars have an intake manifold which heats the intake mixture by circulating it through baffles heated by the exhaust gases in the exhaust manifold. In addition to heating the mixture, the manifold also acts as a plenum chamber, and reduces the necessity of close synchronization of the carburetors.

Idle Adjustment—Zenith-Stromberg 175CD-2S/2SE

The 175CD-2S/2SE carburetor contains a single jet with a tapered needle that is operated by an air valve and carburetor vacuum. There is no special idling system. The fuel air mixture is set at idling speed by the single adjusting screw at the bottom of the carburetor and applies to the entire speed range. There is no choke as such. Rather, a disc-like cold starting device, when actuated, depresses the jet, giving a richer mixture. Therefore, there are two adjustments, one for the proper fuel-air mixture and the fast idle stop screw for proper idling speed. To make these adjustments, remove the air cleaner and proceed as follows:

1. Press the air valve down, and screw in the fuel-air mixture adjusting screw at the bottom of the carburetor until the jet just touches the valve. Then unscrew the adjusting screw 1½ turns.
2. Run the engine until it is warm.
3. Adjust the fast idle stop screw for an idle speed of about 600 rpm.
4. Screw in the fuel mixture adjusting screw until the engine starts to run unevenly. Then slowly turn the screw in the opposite direction until the engine again starts to run unevenly. Finally turn the screw back to a point somewhere between these two positions.
5. Adjust the fast idle stop screw until it barely touches the choke cam at a point about one-half inch from the upper part of the cam when it is turned upward. (In extremely cold weather, adjust the screw so that it touches the choke cam when the choke control is pushed in fully).

Idle Adjustment—Zenith 36VN

The down-draft Zenith 36VN has a hand regulated choke, fixed main and idling jets and an acceleration pump. Fuel air mixture at idling speed is controlled by an adjustment screw.

Adjust the idle mixture with the engine at normal operating temperature. At idling speed, turn in the fuel-air mixture screw until the engine speeds up. Continue to

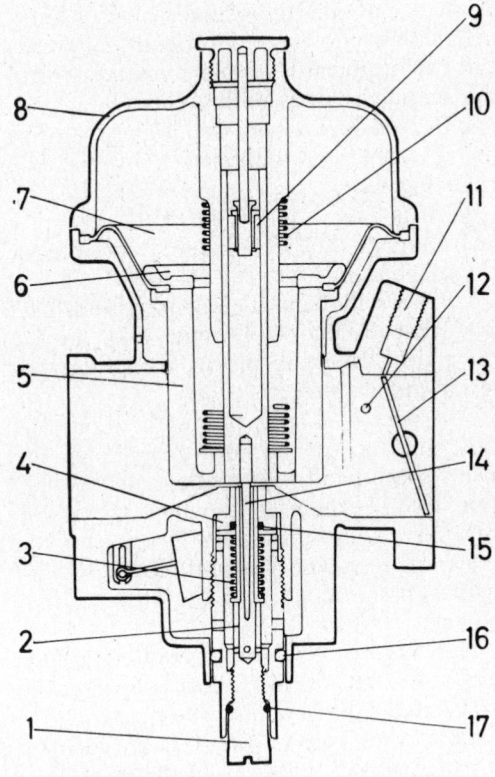

1. Orifice adjusting screw
2. Jet holder
3. Spring
4. Guide
5. Air valve
6. Washer
7. Diaphragm
8. Suction chamber
9. Damper piston
10. Spring
11. Vacuum connection
12. Cold start fuel channel
13. Throttle flap
14. Metering needle
15.-17. O-rings

Zenith-Stromberg 175CD-2S carburetor

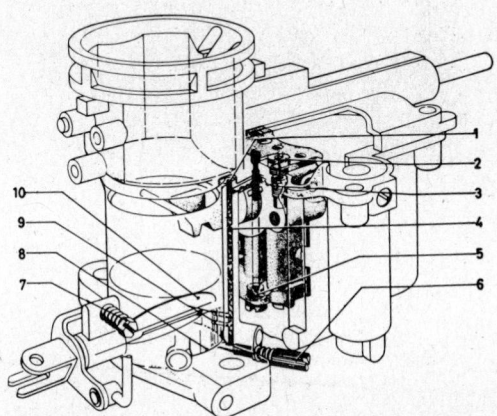

1. Air hole
2. Idling air jet
3. Idling jet
4. Idling channel
5. Main jet
6. Fuel-air mixture idling adjustment
7. Fast-idle stop screw
8. Venturi
9. Transition holes
10. Throttle flap

Zenith 36VN downdraft carburetor

turn in until the engine slows down. Back out the screw until the engine starts to run slowly and roughly, then turn it back in until the engine idles smoothly. The objective of this adjustment is to obtain the fastest possible smooth idle. Open the throttle suddenly and release it. If the engine stalls, back out the screw ¼ turn for a slightly richer mixture. If adjustment of the mixture screw seems to have no effect on idle performance, the idle passages are probably clogged.

Idle and Choke Adjustment—SU-HS6 (B18B/D Engines)

These engines are equipped with twin horizontal carburetors, Type SU-HS6. When starting with a cold engine the fuel-air mixture is enriched by a lowering of the jets through manual operation of the

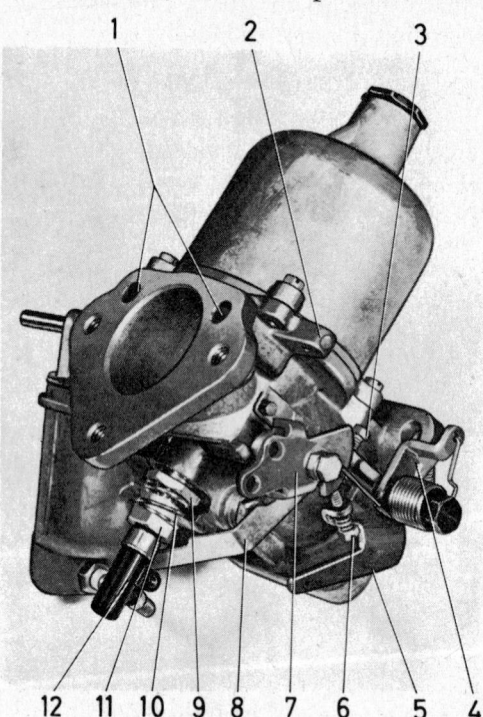

1. Ventilation holes
2. Attachment for choke control
3. Throttle stop screw
4. Throttle spindle flange
5. Cam
6. Fast idle stop screw
7. Choke control lever
8. Link (lowers jet when choking)
9. Locknut
10. Spring
11. Adjusting nut
12. Jet

SU-H6 carburetor

choke on the instrument panel. In addition, the fast idling screw is moved somewhat by a cam on the choke lever, opening the throttle plate slightly.

Obtain the proper fuel-air mixture and idling adjustment as follows after warming engine:

1. Adjust both carburetors at the same time. First, screw in the fuel-air mixture adjusting nut at the bottom of each carburetor to its upper position, and then back it off 1½ turns.

2. Adjust the idle screw on each carb equally and to obtain an engine idling speed of about 600 rpm. Turn the screws so that the intake sounds of the carbs are equal strength.

3. Without touching the idle screw, adjust the fuel-air mixture nut at the bottom of each carb one at a time, by first turning slowly downward (richer mixture) and then upward (leaner mixture) until the engine runs smoothly. The best position is reached when the highest engine speed is obtained without altering the idle adjusting screw.

4. Adjusting equally on both carburetors, adjust the idle screws for proper idling speed.

5. Check that the fuel-air mixture is correct, first in one carburetor then in the other by lifting the piston, using the pin beside the air intake.

The engine should run with about the same unevenness in both cases, and the speed should fall off to about 450 or 500 rpm. If the engine stalls when one of the carb pistons is lifted, the mixture in the other carbs is too lean. If engine speed increases, the mixture in the other carb is too rich.

The choke control and fast idling adjustments are made as follows, keeping in mind that adjustments must always be made so that both carburetors are affected to exactly the same extent by the control:

1. Pull out choke control on the instrument panel about 5/8".

2. Loosen the locking screw for the choke control cable. Lift the lever enough to let the jet start to go down.

3. Adjust the fast idle screw so that it just touches the fast idle cam on the lever when the jet starts to go down as described in Step 3. Tighten the control cable locking screw.

4. Check that both carburetors are

operated to the same extent by pulling the choke control cable and watching the jets go down. Adjust setting if jets do not go down equally.

IDLE AND CHOKE ADJUSTMENT
(B14A AND B16B ENGINES)

B14A engines employ twin horizontal Type SU-H2 carburetors, while B16B engines are equipped with twin horizontal SU-H4 types. Except for slight variations in float and choking arrangements, these carburetors are similar to the SU-HS6 twin carburetors and adjustment can be carried out as previously described for the B18B/D engines.

THROTTLE AND CHOKE LINKAGE
ADJUSTMENT

The throttle and choke linkage should be adjusted whenever the carburetor is adjusted. The choke cable should hold the choke (strangler) flap completely open when the dashboard control is fully pushed in. When the dashboard control is completely pulled out, the choke flap should be completely closed. The throttle linkage should be adjusted after the idling speed has been set. On Zenith carburetors the throttle linkage is adjusted by changing the length of the vertical push rod so there is .040″ clearance between the throttle flap lever and the full throttle stop when the accelerator pedal is fully depressed.

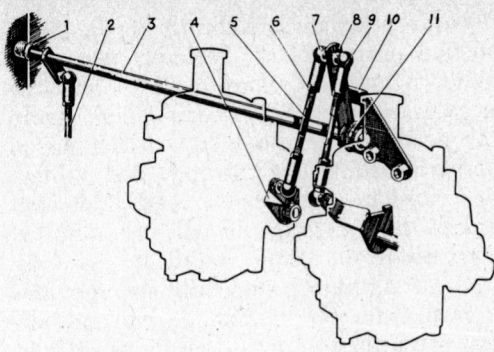

1. Bushing
2. Pedal link rod
3. Control shaft
4. Throttle lever
5. Link rod
6. Locknut
7. Ball joint
8. Control shaft lever
9. Ball joint
10. Bracket
11. Rubber mounting

Zenith-Stromberg carburetor linkage

On Zenith-Stromberg carburetors, the link rods should be adjusted so that there is .004″ clearance between each throttle lever and the throttle spindle angle on the carburetor. On SU carburetors, there should be .020″ clearance between the control shaft lever and its stop.

The throttle linkage on all carburetors should be oiled at all friction points with a light oil. Ball cups should have a light grease filling.

Carburetor Overhaul

Carburetors may be overhauled by disassembly, replacing worn parts, thorough cleaning, and reassembly. Follow the overhaul procedure applying to the particular carburetor model and then adjust as above.

SU CARBURETOR

The SU carburetor must be handled very carefully since the venturi and fuel system are made of special high precision parts.

Suction Piston and Chamber

Remove the four set screws and take off the suction chamber. Remove suction spring, nylon packing and suction piston from chamber after placing components on a flat working surface so that the inside of the chamber and the sliding part of the piston are not damaged. Use extreme care not to bend the tapered fuel jet needle on the bottom of the piston.

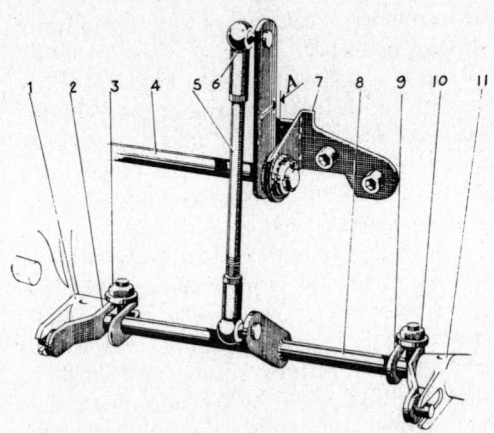

1. Throttle spindle lever
2. Intermediate shaft lever
3. Locknut
4. Control shaft
5. Link rod
6. Ball joint
7. Bracket
8. Intermediate shaft
9. Intermediate shaft lever
10. Locknut
11. Throttle spindle lever

SU carburetor linkage

Do not remove metering needle from suction piston unless absolutely necessary. When it must be removed, first loosen the needle set screw. Then with pliers, grasp the needle at its shoulder near the piston and remove by slowly turning and pulling.

Performance will be adversely affected unless the metering needle is installed correctly in the piston. To do so, carefully push needle into piston until the shoulder is flush with the bottom. Wash and air-dry parts, then apply a few drops of light oil to the piston rod and reassemble. Do not apply oil to the large end of the piston or to the inside of the suction chamber.

Fuel Jet

The fuel jet is easily removed. However, the jet itself is a precision component and should not be disassembled unless absolutely necessary because reassembly is very difficult.

To remove jet, remove small (.1575 in. dia.) screw and then the connecting plate from the jet head. This is done easier by pulling lightly on the choke lever. Next, loosen clip and remove fuel line. The fuel jet can then be removed. When the jet is removed the metering needle will stay inside. Be careful not to damage either.

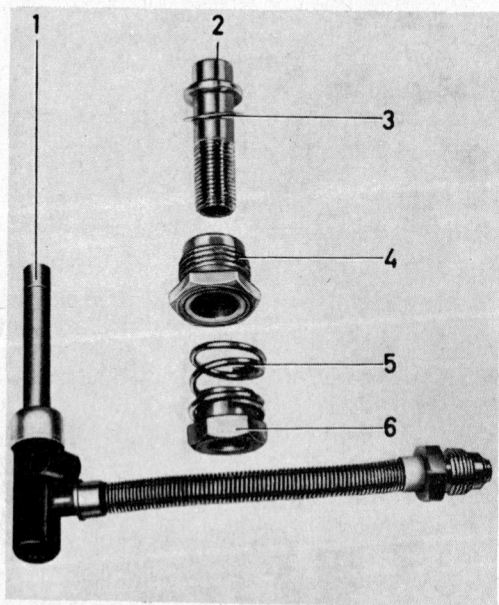

1. Jet
2. Jet sleeve
3. Washer
4. Locknut
5. Spring
6. Adjusting nut

SU carburetor jet assembly

Next, remove the idling adjusting nut and spring. The fuel sleeve is removed by removing the sleeve set screw. Clean and air-dry the jet.

Reassemble in reverse order, removing the oil cap nut to assist in centering piston in suction chamber. Set piston to its fully closed position and insert fuel jet until it contacts the jet sleeve. Then move jet sleeve slightly so that it is at right angles to the center axis, and position the jet sleeve so that the jet does not contact needle.

Raise suction piston with the finger, and lower it slowly. Piston should drop smoothly until stop-pin drops on venturi making a light striking sound. Tighten jet sleeve set screw at this position. Now remove jet and install idle adjusting spring and nut on jet sleeve and re-insert jet. Connect fuel line to jet nipple. Next, pull choke lever slightly, hold connecting plate with sleeve and .1575 in.-diameter washer and tighten it on jet head with the .1575 in.-diameter screw. In so doing, move choke lever slightly and attach sleeve firmly to connecting plate opening. Upon completion of assembly, again check that suction piston drops smoothly.

ZENITH-STROMBERG 175CD-2S/2SE CARBURETOR

Remove carburetor from vehicle after disconnecting fuel line, throttle and choke controls, vacuum line to the distributor, and removing screws holding carburetor to intake manifold.

Scratch alignment marks (for reassembly) on the suction chamber and body. Remove suction chamber and spring. Remove screws and washer, with diaphragm and piston. Loosen screw and remove metering needle.

Remove float chamber. Carefully remove float shaft from the bridge and remove the float. Unscrew and remove jet holder, adjusting screw, jet spring, guide and washers. Remove fuel inlet needle and washer. Remove choke device. Wash and air-dry components. Use kerosene only for washing diaphragm.

Check diaphragm for damage. Replace if cracked or distorted. Check metering needle for wear. If bent or worn replace needle. Check contacting and sealing surfaces for damage. Check valve disc on choke device.

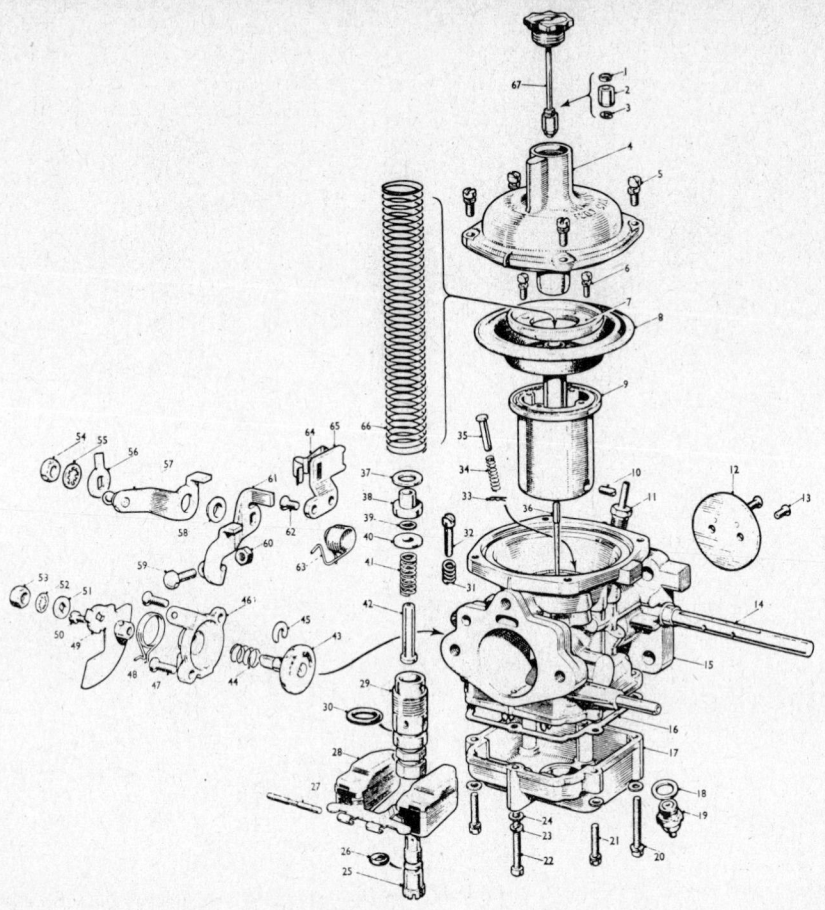

1. Washer
2. Bushing
3. Retaining ring
4. Cover
5. Screw and spring washer (4)
6. Screw and spring washer (4)
7. Retaining ring
8. Diaphragm
9. Air valve and shaft
   Air valve assy. (incl. items 6, 7, 8 and 9)
10. Locking screw
11. Vacuum adapter
12. Throttle
13. Screw (2)
14. Throttle spindle
15. Main body
16. Gasket
17. Float chamber
18. Washer
19. Needle valve
20. See item 22
21. Screw (short) (2)
22. Screw (long) (4)
23. Spring washer (6)

24. Washer (6)
25. Adjusting screw (incl. item 26)
26. O-ring for 25
27. Float pin
28. Float assembly
29. Bushing retaining screw (incl. item 30)
30. O-ring for 29
31. Spring
32. Throttle stop screw
33. Clip
34. Spring
35. Lifting pin
36. Metering needle
37. Washer for bushing
38. Bushing for jet
39. O-ring
40. Washer for O-ring
41. Spring for jet
42. Jet
43. Starter spindle assy.
44. Starter spring
45. C-washer
46. Starter cover

47. Screw for 46 (2)
    Shakeproof washer (2) (not shown)
48. Return spring
49. Cam lever assy.
50. Clamping screw
51. Spacing washer
52. Shakeproof washer
53. Nut
54. Nut for throttle spindle
55. Shakeproof washer
56. Tab washer
57. Throttle lever
58. Bushing
59. Fast idle screw
60. Locknut for 59
61. Throttle stop and fast idle lever
62. Screw for control bracket
63. Throttle return spring
64. Clip for control bracket
65. Starter control bracket
66. Air valve return spring
67. Damper assy. (incl. items 1, 2 and 3)

Zenith-Stromberg 175CD-2S carburetor

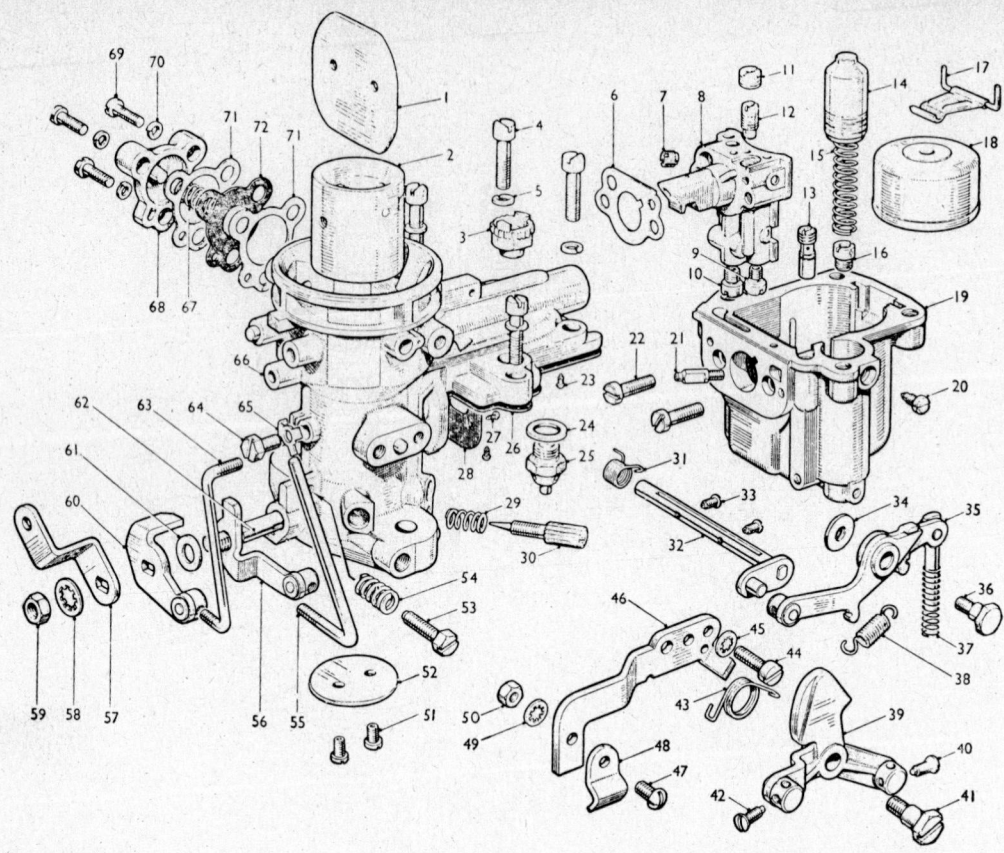

1. Choke (strangler) flap	27. Screw fixing item 28 (2) (see item 23)
2. Choke (venturi) tube	28. Gasket (bowl to barrel) (vertical face)
3. Pump stop	29. Spring for volume control screw
4. Screw and spring washer fixing bowl to barrel (4)	30. Volume control screw
5. See item 4	31. Spring
6. Gasket for emulsion block	32. Choke spindle and lever assembly
7. Not used	33. Screw fixing choke flap (2) Washer for choke spindle (not shown)
8. Emulsion block	34. Washer for pivot screw
9. Compensating jet	35. Pump lever and rod assembly (includes item 38)
10. Main jet	36. Pivot screw for pump lever
11. Plug over idle jet	37. Spring for pump rod Sealing washer for pump rod (not shown)
12. Idle jet	38. Follow-up spring
13. Pump discharge valve	39. Choke control lever
14. Pump piston	40. Screw for choke swivel
15. Spring for 14	41. Pivot screw for choke control lever
16. Pump check valve	42. Screw for interconnection swivel
17. Float arm and pivot	43. Spring for choke control lever
18. Float	44. Screw fixing choke control bracket
19. Carburetor bowl	45. Shakeproof washer
20. Stop screw for pump piston	
21. Pump jet	
22. Screw fixing emulsion block (2)	
23. Screw fixing item 26 (4)	
24. Washer for needle and seat	
25. Needle and seat	
26. Gasket (bowl to barrel) (horizontal face)	

46. Choke control bracket (includes items 47, 48, 49 and 50)
47. Screw fixing clip
48. Clip
49. Shakeproof washer
50. Nut
51. Screw fixing throttle (2)
52. Throttle
53. Throttle stop screw
54. Spring for 53
55. Interconnection rod
56. Floating lever
57. Throttle lever
58. Shakeproof washer
59. Nut
60. Throttle stop
61. Washer
62. Throttle spindle
63. Pump link
64. Screw fixing venturi tube
65. Tab washer for 64
66. Carburetor barrel assembly
67. Economizer spring
68. Economizer valve cover
69. Screw fixing 68. (3)
70. Spring washer for screw (3)
71. Gasket for economizer diaphragm(2)
72. Economizer diaphragm

Zenith 34VN carburetor

Assemble carburetor by placing diaphragm on air valve so that projection fits into recess in valve and guiding edge fits into slit. If diaphragm is too distorted to fit, replace it. Place washer over diaphragm so that screw holes line up without turning washer, and washer groove mates with guide edge of diaphragm. Tighten screws.

Fit metering needle with cylindrical section of needle against valve. Install valve and diaphragm into carb body, fitting tag into recess. Install suction chamber observing alignment marks. The slit and guiding edge should fit eaily. Insert screws.

Insert adjusting screw together with the new O-ring into jet holder, and install new O-ring on the jet holder. Install the spring, brass washer, guide, new O-ring and washer on the jet, and install the entire assembly together with the jet holder and adjusting screw into the carb body. Screw in the jet holder by hand but do not tighten it. Screw in the adjusting screw until the upper part of the jet is against the air valve when the valve is at its lowest position. Position the carburetor with the flange on the throttle plate side down and allow the air valve to fall. The needle will then enter the fuel jet orifice and automatically centralize the jet. Tighten jet assembly slowly, frequently checking to see that the needle remains free in the orifice. Raise the air valve and allow it to fall freely. The piston should then stop firmly on the bridge. After the jet is tight, if a clear striking sound is not heard when the piston is lifted and allowed to fall, repeat the centering procedure.

Install the float and shaft with the flat side of the float facing away from the carb body. Check the float level. The highest point on the float (front) should be ⅜" above the face of the body and the rear edge ¼" above. Float level can be changed by carefully bending the tab which connects to the end of the needle. Do not bend the float arm.

Install a new gasket on the float chamber and install float chamber, inserting all screws just a few turns. Then move float chamber down to the contact surface of upper section and tighten screws. Install choke device.

ZENITH 34VN/36VN CARBURETOR

To clean the carburetor, it is usually sufficient to remove the float chamber and float, remove the idling jet and the air jet located above it, remove the acceleration pump plunger and the idle fuel screw on the housing. Remove the needle valve. Wash all parts and air-dry. Blow compressed air through all channels and jets, including hole for idle fuel screw. Hold jets up to light to check for cleanliness.

To completely disassemble, remove float chamber. Remove float lever and float. Remove emulsion block and remove all jets from block. Remove acceleration pump plunger, spring inlet valve, outlet valve and acceleration jet. Remove float valve and economizer valve. Unscrew idle fuel jet. Blow all parts dry with compressed air after cleaning. Do not use wire to clean jets.

Reassemble in reverse order, making sure that all gaskets and parts are in good condition. Observe TOP markings on float and float lever. Press float chamber upward and inward against carb body and then tighten screws. Check that the emulsion block is in contact with the stay across the venturi. If not, loosen the screw, adjust the position and tighten screw.

FUEL INJECTION SYSTEM

The 142E and 1800E are equipped with an electronic fuel injection system. The system supplies fuel at constant pressure to the injectors.

The complete system contains the following units: control unit, electric fuel pump, fuel filter, pressure regulator, injectors, cold start valve, inlet duct, throttle valve switch, auxiliary air regulator, temperature sensors (induction air and coolant), pressure sensor (for pressure in inlet duct) and triggering contacts in the ignition distributor.

Briefly, the system operates as follows:

Fuel is drawn from the fuel tank by the electric fuel pump and forced through the fuel lines and filter into the fuel pressure line and to the injectors. The pressure regulator limits fuel pressure to 28 psi. If the fuel pressure is more than 28 psi, a relief valve opens and the excess fuel flows back to the fuel tank. The electromagnetic fuel injectors are mounted in the inlet ducts in the cylinder head.

The duration of fuel injection and thus fuel quantity is controlled by both engine speed and engine load. Engine speed information is supplied to the control unit

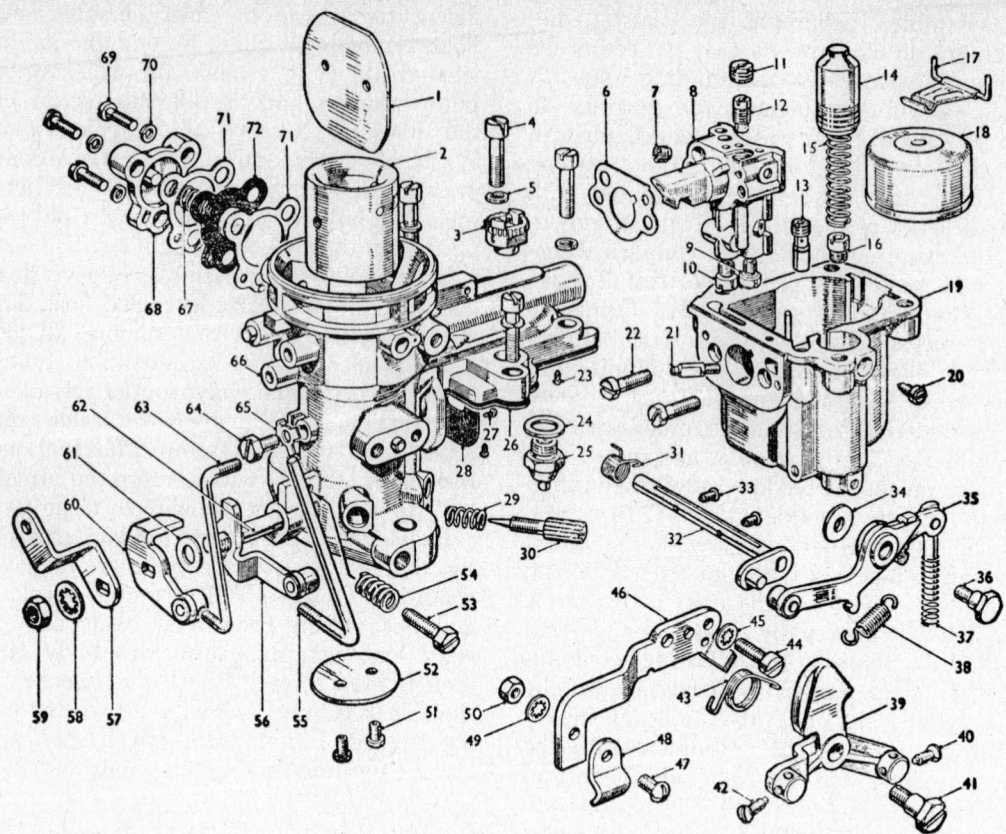

1. Choke (strangler) flap
2. Choke (venturi) tube
3. Pump stop
4. Screw and spring washer fixing bowl to barrel (4)
5. See item 4
6. Gasket for emulsion block
7. Ventilation screw
8. Emulsion block
9. Compensating jet
10. Main jet
11. Plug over idle jet
12. Idle jet
13. Pump discharge valve
14. Pump piston
15. Spring for pump piston
16. Pump check valve
17. Float arm and pivot (not used)
18. Float and arm
     Float arm pivot (not shown)
     Float arm retainer
     (not shown)
19. Carburetor bowl
20. Stop screw for pump piston
21. Pump jet
22. Screw fixing emulsion block (2)
23. Screw fixing item 26 (4)
24. Washer for needle valve
25. Needle valve
26. Gasket (bowl to barrel)
     (horizontal face)

27. Screw fixing item 28 (2)
     (see item 23)
28. Gasket (bowl to barrel)
     (vertical face)
29. Spring for volume control screw
30. Volume control screw
31. Automaticity spring
32. Choke spindle and lever assembly
     Washer for choke spindle
     (not shown)
33. Screw fixing choke flap (2)
34. Washer for pivot screw
35. Pump lever and rod assembly
     (includes item 38)
36. Pivot screw for pump lever
     Sealing washer for pump rod
     (not shown)
37. Spring for pump rod
38. Follow-up spring
39. Choke control lever
40. Screw for choke swivel
41. Pivot screw for choke control lever
42. Not used
43. Spring for choke control lever
44. Screw fixing choke control bracket
45. Shakeproof washer

46. Choke control bracket
     (assembled with items 47, 48, 49 and 50)
47. Screw fixing clip
48. Clip
49. Shakeproof washer
50. Nut
51. Screw fixing throttle (2)
52. Throttle
53. Throttle stop screw
54. Spring for throttle stop screw
55-56. Not used
57. Throttle lever
     Spring washer (not shown)
58. Shakeproof washer
59. Nut
60. Throttle stop
61. Washer
62. Throttle spindle
63. Pump link
64. Screw fixing venturi tube
65. Tab washer for screw
66. Carburetor body assembly
67. Economizer springs
68. Economizer valve cover
69. Screw fixing valve cover (3)
70. Spring washer for screw (3)
71. Gasket for economizer diaphragm (2)
72. Economizer diaphragm

Zenith 36VN carburetor

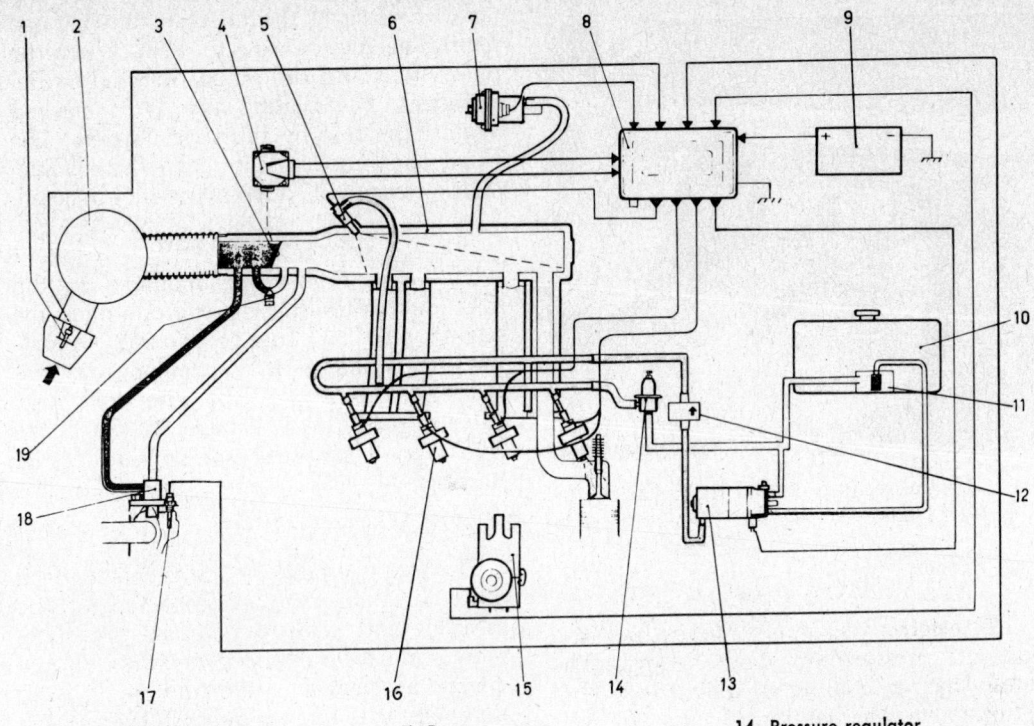

1. Temperature sensor for induction air
2. Air cleaner
3. Throttle valve
4. Throttle valve
5. Cold start valve
6. Inlet duct
7. Pressure sensor
8. Control unit
9. Battery
10. Fuel tank
11. Fuel filter, induction side
12. Fuel filter, pressure side
13. Fuel pump
14. Pressure regulator
15. Distributor with triggering contacts
16. Injectors
17. Temperature sensor for coolant
18. Auxiliary air regulator
19. Idling adjustment screw

Electronic fuel injection, B20E engine

Injection System Components

by the distributor triggering contacts. Load information is supplied by an inlet duct pressure sensor. The control unit uses this information to determine the length of time the injectors remain open. During warm-up periods, the cold start valve injects extra fuel while the starter is operated. The auxiliary air regulator supplies extra air until the engine coolant reaches normal temperature.

When the engine is accelerated, the throttle valve switch sends electrical pulses to the control unit to increase the amount of fuel injected. When decelerating, the throttle valve sends a pulse to the control unit to close off the fuel flow. When engine speed drops to about 1,000 rpm, the fuel supply is turned on again to allow a smooth changeover to idle speed.

CONTROL UNIT

The control unit receives electrical impulses from the pressure and temperature sensors. In addition, the control unit determines if and for how long the cold start valve should be open and when the fuel pump should operate. The control unit is located under the front seat on the 142E and behind the instrument panel on the 1800E. Repair of the control unit requires the use of special test equipment which is available only on the dealer level.

CONTROL RELAYS

The control relays connected to the cold start valve and the fuel pump are located on the right rear wheel arch along with the main relay.

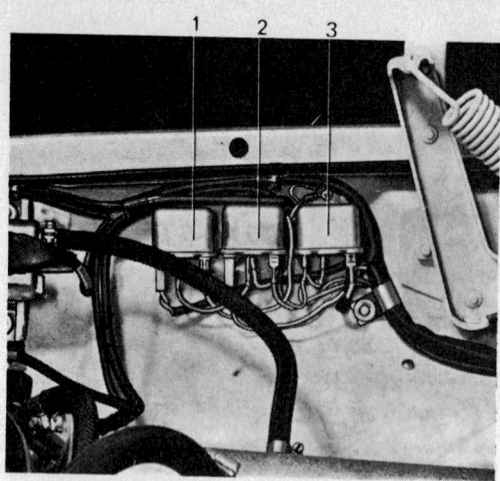

Control relays. 1 is cold start relay;
2 is pump relay; and 3 is main relay.

FUEL PUMP

The electric fuel pump pumps fuel at a constant pressure of about 28 psi. The pump has a combined relief and non-return valve. The non-return valve prevents the fuel system from losing pressure when the engine is stopped. The pump, which is located under the car on the right side of the fuel tank, is not repairable. The entire pump assembly must be replaced if defective.

FUEL FILTERS

There are two fuel filters used in the system—a suction line nylon filter in the fuel tank and a pressure line paper filter that should be replaced every 12,500 miles. The pressure line filter is located in the mounting bracket with the fuel pump.

PRESSURE REGULATOR

The pressure regulator unit is bracket mounted on the cowl and is connected between the fuel pump pressure line and the fuel tank. When the fuel line pressure is less than 28 psi, the valve is closed. When the pressure exceeds 28 psi, the valve opens and releases the excess fuel into the return line to the fuel tank.

INJECTORS

The injectors pass fuel into the intake ports in the cylinder head (one injector for each port). They operate in two groups —first injectors 1 and 3; then injectors 2 and 4. The injector operates when a pulse from the control unit energizes the mag-

netic winding of the injector, drawing the sealing needle up from the seat. When the pulse stops and the magnetic winding de-energizes, the sealing needle is pushed against the seat by the return spring. The valve opening time interval (.002-.01 seconds) controls the amount of fuel injected.

COLD START VALVE

The cold start valve, mounted in the inlet duct after the throttle, supplies the engine with extra fuel for starting. Operating time is determined by coolant temperature. At 4°F and colder, the cold start valve operates for 8 seconds. At 130°F, the cold start valve does not operate during starting.

THROTTLE VALVE SWITCH

The throttle valve switch is mounted on the inlet duct and is connected to the throttle shaft. This switch has two functions. One is to increase the fuel supply during acceleration, and the other is to shut off the fuel supply during deceleration.

INLET DUCT

The inlet duct is of aluminum, cast in one piece. It consists of a common inlet duct from which individual induction pipes lead to each induction port in the cylinder head.

A throttle valve is mounted at the mouth of the common inlet duct. During idling, the throttle valve is completely closed. Air flows in through a by-pass pipe under the throttle valve. Idling speed is adjusted by means of the idle adjusting screw forward of the throttle valve switch.

AUXILIARY AIR REGULATOR

The auxiliary air regulator is located at the front end of the cylinder head and has its expanding element projecting into the cooling system.

The regulator operating range is from -13°F, fully open, to 140°F, fully closed.

At the cold start, the auxiliary air regulator opens (how much will depend on the temperature) and admits additional air into the inlet duct. Gradually as the engine heats up, the regulator closes off the auxiliary air pipe.

TEMPERATURE SENSORS

The system is equipped with two temperature sensors, one for coolant and one for intake air.

The temperature sensor for intake air provides the control unit with information about the intake air temperature so that the control unit can increase the injection quantity somewhat at low intake air temperature. Compensation ceases when the temperature of the intake air is greater than 20°C (68°F). This sensor is located under the air intake for the air cleaner.

The temperature sensor for the coolant provides the control unit with information concerning the coolant temperature so that the control unit can adjust the injection interval and determine how long the cold start valve should remain open at cold start. This sensor is located in the cylinder head next to the auxiliary air regulator.

PRESSURE SENSOR

The pressure sensor senses the pressure in the inlet duct. It is located on the right wheel housing and is connected to the inlet duct by means of a hose.

TRIGGERING CONTACTS

Below the centrifugal governor in the distributor there is a contact device with two triggering contacts. The contacts are actuated by a cam on the distributor shaft. The function of the contacts is to supply information to the control unit about the engine speed to enable it to determine when the injection shall begin and the duration of the injection with the help of the information from the pressure sensor.

CABLE HARNESS NUMBERING

Cable No.	From	To
1	Control unit	Temperature sensor I (intake air)
2	Control unit	Cold start relay, terminal 85
3	Control unit	Injector, cyl. 1
4	Control unit	Injector, cyl. 3
5	Control unit	Injector, cyl. 4
6	Control unit	Injector, cyl. 2
7	Control unit	Pressure sensor
8	Control unit	Pressure sensor
9	Control unit	Throttle valve switch
10	Control unit	Pressure sensor
11	Control unit	Ground
12	Control unit	Distributor (triggering contacts)
13	Control unit	Temperature sensor I (intake air)
14	Control unit	Throttle valve switch
15	Control unit	Pressure sensor
16	Control unit	Main relay, terminal 87
17	Control unit	Throttle valve switch
18	Control unit	Starter motor, terminal 50
19	Control unit	Pump relay, terminal 85
20	Control unit	Throttle valve switch
21	Control unit	Ignition distributor (triggering contacts)
22	Control unit	Ignition distributor (triggering contacts)
23	Control unit	Temperature sensor I (coolant)
24	Control unit	Main relay, terminal 87
25	Not used	
26	Fuel injector, cyl. 1	Ground
27	Fuel injector, cyl. 2	Ground
28	Main relay, terminal 87	Pump relay, terminal 86
29	Cold start relay, terminal 86	Starter motor, terminal 50
30	Fuel injector, cyl. 3	Ground
31	Fuel injector, cyl. 4	Ground
32	Temperature sensor II (coolant)	Ground
33	Cold start valve	Ground
34	Cold start valve	Cold start relay, terminal 87
35	Fuel pump (−)	Ground
36	Fuel pump (+)	Connector
37	Connector	Pump relay, terminal 87
38	Main relay, terminal 86	Ignition coil, terminal 15

FUEL VAPOR CONTROL SYSTEM

US models are fitted with a gas vapor control system, which prevents gas fumes from being released into the atmosphere. The system consists of an expansion cannister and a venting filter, which is filled with active carbon. The venting filter is located in the engine compartment on the right side. The expansion container is behind the panel in the trunk.

Gas fumes are conveyed to the expansion container and from there to the venting filter where they are mixed with the active carbon.

When the engine starts, air is drawn through the venting filter and the inlet duct into the engine. Gas fumes stored in the active carbon are drawn into the engine.

The foam plastic filter at the bottom of the venting filter should be replaced every 25,000 miles.

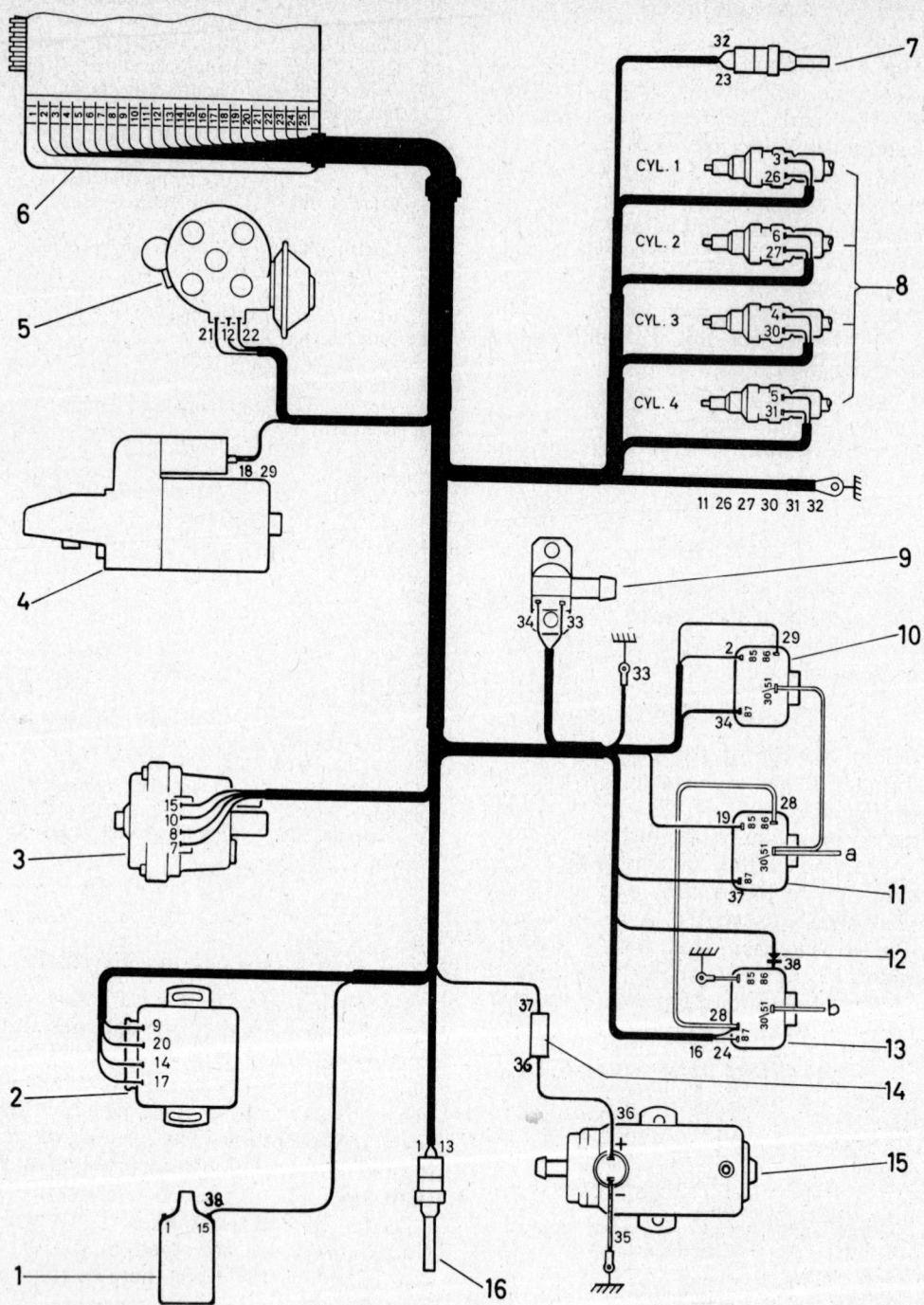

1. Ignition coil (term. 15)
2. Throttle valve switch
3. Pressure sensor
4. Starter motor (term. 50)
5. Distributor (triggering contacts)
6. Control unit
7. Coolant temperature sensor
8. Injectors
9. Cold start valve
10. Cold start relay
11. Pump relay
12. Diode (located in relay)
13. Main relay
14. Connector
15. Fuel pump
16. Intake air pressure sensor
a. To fuse 1 (small fusebox)
b. To battery, B+

Electronic injection system cable harness

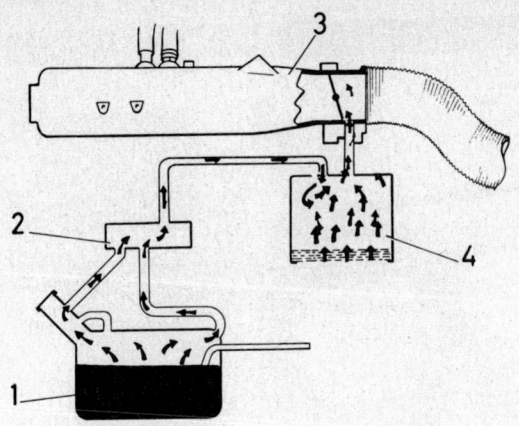

Fuel vapor control system. 1 is fuel tank; 2 is expansion container; 3 is inlet duct; and 4 is venting filter.

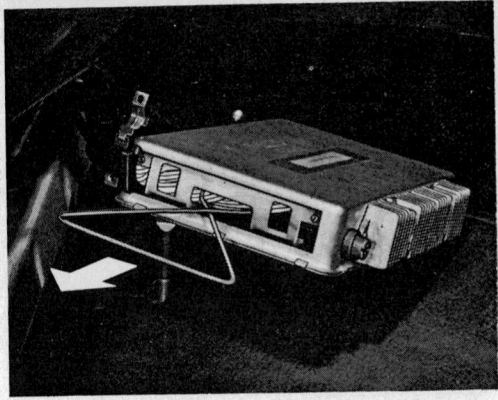

Pulling plug contact from control unit

Repairs

The fuel injection system is repaired simply by replacing the defective part. There are adjustments that can be made to the pressure regulator, throttle valve, throttle valve switch, throttle stop screw (idle speed), and the fuel mixture. To make resistance checks, an ohmmeter is necessary. If an ohmmeter is not available, a test light with a 12-volt power source may be substituted for continuity checks.

If the control unit is defective, return it to a qualified repair service and install a new unit.

CONTROL UNIT

Removal—142E

1. Move the right seat all the way back.

2. Unscrew the bolt securing the seat's front (long) adjusting screw at the tubular bend. Move the seat to the front stop position and fold it back.

3. Remove the two attaching screws and lift out the control unit.

4. Remove the screw for the cap holding the cable harness to the control unit.

5. Pull out the plastic cover strip.

6. Make a puller. Hook in the puller and pull out the plug contact carefully.

Replacement

1. Press the plug contact firmly into the control unit. Install the plastic cover strip and cap.

2. Place the control unit in position and install the screws.

3. Fold back the seat and move it to the rear stop position.

4. Bolt the seat securely at the front (long) adjusting screw.

FUEL PUMP

Replacement

1. Disconnect the cables at the pump and remove the bracket on which the pump and filter are mounted.

2. Remove the plastic clamp holding the hoses together and clean around the pump's hose connections.

3. Pinch shut the fuel hoses to the pump. Loosen the hose clamps and pull off the hoses.

4. Remove the screws holding the pump and remove the pump.

5. Place the new pump in position and secure it.

6. Connect the hoses to the pump and remove the pinch clamps.

7. Place the plastic clamp around the hoses, place the bracket in position, and secure it.

8. Connect the plug contact and check that the pump is functioning and that the hose connections do not leak.

Check

The pump should deliver 26.4 gph at a pressure of 28 psi. At this load, current consumption should be 5.0 amps.

FUEL FILTER

Replacement (every 12,500 miles)

1. Disconnect the electric cable at the

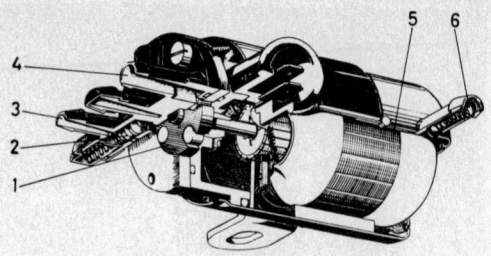

1. Pump rotor
2. Overflow valve
3. Overflow channel
4. Inlet
5. Rotor for electric motor
6. Outlet

Electric fuel pump

Pressure regulator, mounted on firewall

fuel pump. Remove the bracket on which the pump and filter are mounted.

2. Remove the plastic clamp holding the hoses together and clean around the filter's hose connections.

3. Pinch shut the fuel hoses to the filter. Loosen the hose clamps and remove the filter.

4. Place the new filter in position.

NOTE: *Make sure that the filter is fitted with the arrow pointing in the direction of fuel flow. Make sure that no dirt enters the connections for the filter.*

5. Tighten the hose clamps and remove the pinch clamps. Check for leakage.

6. Place the plastic clamp around the hoses. Mount the bracket and secure it.

7. Connect the plug contact to the fuel pump.

Pressure Regulator

Replacement

1. Place pinch clamps on the hoses next to the pressure regulator.

2. Loosen the hose clamps and remove the hoses.

3. Remove the pressure regulator from the bracket.

4. Install the new pressure regulator to the bracket.

5. Connect the hoses to the pressure regulator.

6. Remove the pinch clamps and check for leakage.

Adjustment

1. Install pinch clamps at the fuel hose between the header pipe and pressure regulator.

2. Loosen the hose clips and disconnect the hose. Connect a pressure gauge. Remove pinch clamps.

3. Run the fuel pump, either by starting the engine or by connecting a test voltage.

4. Loosen the locknut and adjust the pressure to 28 psi. (Replace regulator if pressure is not correct.)

5. Install pinch clamps on the hose between the header pipe and pressure gauge. Remove the pressure gauge. Install the hose on the pressure regulator and tighten the hose clips. Remove the pinch clamps on the hose. Check for leakage.

Injectors

Replacement

1. Pinch shut the fuel hose to the header pipe.

2. Loosen the hose clamps for all the injector fuel hoses. Lift up the header pipe.

3. Remove the plug contact from the injector and turn the lock ring counterclockwise so that it loosens from the bayonet fitting. Pull up the injector.

4. Place the new injector with washers and sealing rings in position and secure it with the lock ring.

NOTE: *The small rubber seal on the injector should be replaced each time the injector is removed.*

5. Connect the plug contact to the injector, place the header pipe in position, and tighten the hose clamps.

6. Remove the pinch clamps.

When removing all the injectors, the hose clips need not be removed since all

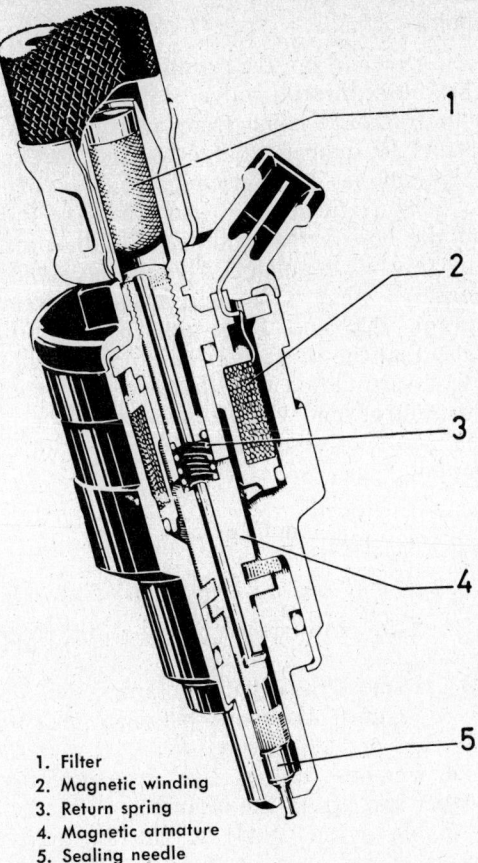

1. Filter
2. Magnetic winding
3. Return spring
4. Magnetic armature
5. Sealing needle

Injector

Cold start valve

the injectors and header pipe can be lifted up at the same time.

Check

Measure the resistance between the terminal pins. The resistance should be 2.40 ohms at 20°C (68°F).

NOTE: *Never test an injector by connecting 12 volts to the terminal. The injector will be ruined immediately.*

Maximum leakage for the injectors is two drops per minute at 28 psi.

Cold Start Valve

Replacement

1. Pinch shut the fuel hose for the cold start valve.
2. Remove the plug contact and the fuel hose from the valve.
3. Remove the screws securing the cold start valve. Remove the valve.
4. Place the new cold start valve with packing in position and screw it on.

5. Connect the fuel hose and install the plug contact to the valve.
6. Remove the pinch clamps.

Throttle Valve

Adjustment

1. Release the stop screw locknut for the throttle valve switch and back out the screw a couple of turns so that it does not lie against the stop on the throttle valve spindle. Check to make sure that the switch is fully closed.
2. Screw in the stop screw until it touches the stop on the switch spindle. Then screw it in ¼-½ turn and tighten the locknut. Check that the throttle valve switch does not jam or seize in the closed position.

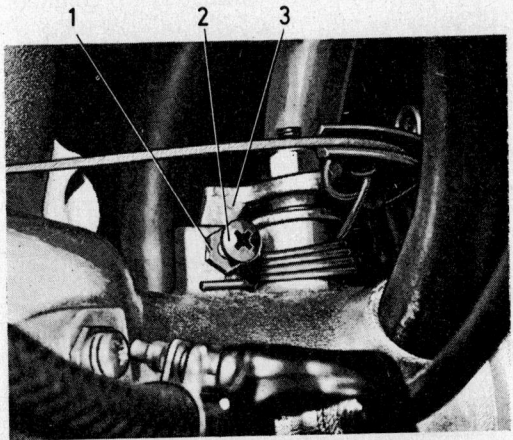

1 is locknut; 2 is stop screw for throttle valve; and 3 is stop on valve spindle.

3. Adjust the throttle valve switch.

NOTE: *The stop screw must not be used for idle adjustment.*

THROTTLE VALVE SWITCH

Replacement

1. Pull the plug contact from the throttle valve switch. Remove the two screws holding the throttle valve switch to the intake duct. Pull the throttle valve switch straight out.

2. Press on the new throttle valve switch carefully. Install the screws loosely. Connect the plug contact. Adjust the throttle valve switch as below.

Throttle valve switch

Adjustment

1. Connect an ohmmeter to contacts 14 and 17.

2. Loosen the screws in order to turn the throttle valve switch. Make a mark on the intake duct at the upper screw if there is not one there already.

3. Turn the throttle valve switch clockwise as far as possible. Then turn it slowly counterclockwise until the pointer on the instrument goes over from ∞ to 0.

Then turn further 1° (½ graduation mark on the scale upper attaching screw) and tighten down the throttle valve switch.

4. Check to make sure that the instrument pointer goes over to ∞ when the throttle valve opens about 1°. (Place a 0.02″ feeler gauge between the stop screw and stop on the throttle valve spindle.)

Check

1. Switch on the ignition. Open and close the throttle valve slowly. Clicking sounds should come from a group of injectors to indicate that extra fuel for acceleration has been injected.

2. Start the engine and warm it. Pull off the hose between the intake duct and auxiliary air regulator. The engine should now roll; that is, change speed between approx. 900 and 1,700 r.p.m. This indicates that the contacts in the throttle valve switch are closed and that the section of the control unit which regulates closing of fuel supply during engine braking is functioning.

AIR CLEANER

Replacement (every 25,000 miles)

1. Turn the steering wheel to right lock.

2. Remove the expansion tank.

3. Remove the hose between the intake duct and air cleaner.

4. Remove the screws securing the cleaner and lift off the cleaner.

5. Move the nozzle to the air intake for the new cleaner.

6. Place the new cleaner in position.

7. Connect the hose between the intake duct and cleaner.

8. Place the expansion tank in position and screw it on.

AUXILIARY AIR REGULATOR

Replacement

1. Drain coolant.

2. Remove the plug contact from the temperature sensor and disconnect the hoses from the regulator.

Remove the screws and lift off the regulator.

3. Install a new packing and screw on new regulator.

4. Connect the air hoses and plug in the contact to the temperature sensor.

5. Fill with coolant.

Check

1. Warm the engine (approx. 176°F). Note the idle speed. Then pull off the hose between the intake duct and the auxiliary air regulator. Cover the hose opening.

2. Check that the speed does not drop

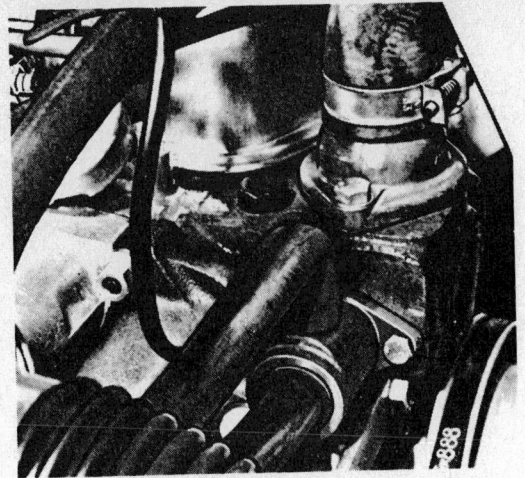

Auxiliary air regulator

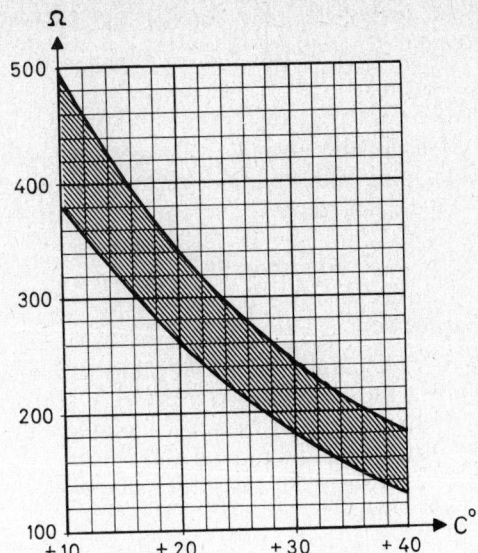

Resistance-Temperature Chart I

Temperature sensor for intake air

Check

Measure the resistance between the terminal pins and compare with the reading given in Resistance-Temperature Chart I.

TEMPERATURE SENSOR II
(COOLANT)

Replacement

1. Pull out the plug contact from the sensor.

2. Screw out the sensor.

NOTE: *Have the new sensor ready to avoid any loss of coolant.*

3. Screw in the new sensor. Do not forget the sealing ring.

noticeably in relation to the first reading. If the speed drops noticeably, there is a leak in the auxiliary air regulator, which should be replaced.

TEMPERATURE SENSOR I
(INTAKE AIR)

Replacement

1. Remove the cover plate in front of the radiator.

2. Pull out the four-way plug from the sensor.

3. Replace the sensor. Do not over tighten the new sensor.

4. Plug in the contact for the sensor.

5. Install the cover plate.

Temperature sensor for coolant

4. Install the plug contact and fill with coolant, if necessary.

Check

Measure the resistance between the terminal pins and compare with the reading given in Resistance-Temperature Chart II.

PRESSURE SENSOR

Replacement

1. Pull out the four-way plug and disconnect the hose from the pressure sensor.
2. Remove the screws holding the pressure sensor and remove the sensor.
3. Transfer the attaching bracket to the new pressure sensor.
4. Install and screw on the new sensor, connect the hose, and plug in the contact.

Check

Measure the resistance between the terminal points. The resistance should be approx. 90 ohms between 7 and 15 (primary winding). Approx. 350 ohms between 8 and 10 (secondary winding). All other combinations should give ∞ resistance.

VENTING FILTER

The foam plastic filter should be changed every 25,000 miles. This is done by loosening the bracket screws, lifting up the venting filter and removing the filter.

Pressure sensor

IDLE ADJUSTMENT

1. Run the engine until it is warm (approx. 176°F). Connect a tachometer and CO-meter.
2. Remove the hose from the air cleaner at the intake duct.
3. Check to make sure that the auxiliary air regulator is completely closed by pulling off the hose between the intake duct and the regulator and by covering the opening. The speed must not change much. (Engine is insufficiently warm or auxiliary air regulator faulty if there is much difference in the speed). Replace the hose.
4. Adjust the idling speed to 900 rpm (for automatic transmission, 800 rpm). If

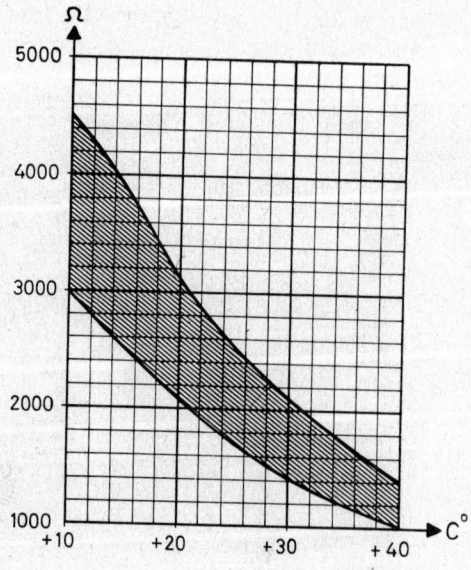

Resistance-Temperature Chart II

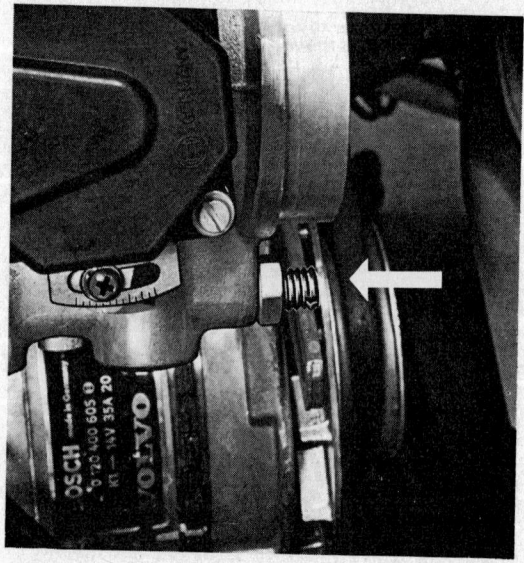

Idle adjustment screw

Screw on control unit for adjusting CO percentage

the speed cannot be lowered sufficiently, check the throttle valve setting.

5. Install the induction hose.

6. Adjust the CO-reading to 1.00-2.00% with the adjusting screw on the control unit.

IGNITION DISTRIBUTOR TRIGGERING CONTACTS

Replacement

1. Remove the ignition distributor.

2. Remove the two screws securing the the holder and pull out the holder.

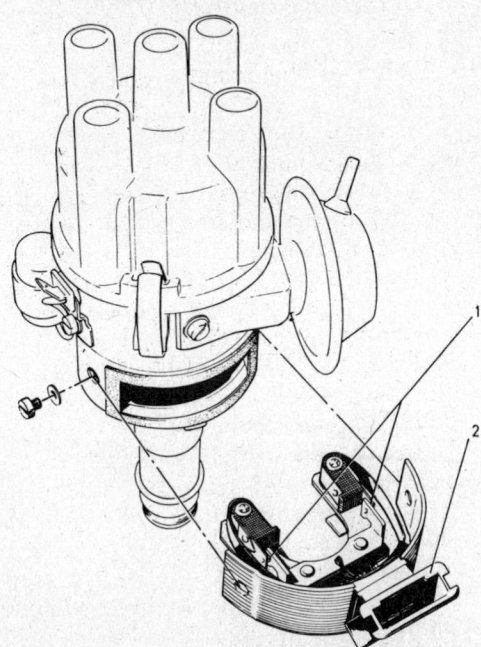

1 is distributor triggering contacts; 2 is an electrical connector on the special distributor used with fuel injection engines.

3. Apply a little grease (Bosch Ft 1V4) to the fiber pieces of the contact breaker lever on the new holder.

4. Check that the rubber ring is not damaged. Replace if necessary.

5. Install the new holder in the distributor. (It is not possible to adjust the contacts).

6. Install the distributor and adjust the ignition timing.

7. Check the contacts with an ohm-meter for resistance readings of 0 ohms and infinite resistance alternately.

Exhaust System

Safety requires that the exhaust system be kept in a sound, leak free condition. Any questionable parts should be replaced immediately.

EXHAUST PIPE REPLACEMENT

1. Unbolt the exhaust pipe from the exhaust manifold.

NOTE: *Put some penetrating oil or rust remover on the bolt threads before removing the nuts.*

2. Disconnect any hangers near the muffler.

3. Put some penetrating oil on the exhaust pipe where it joins the muffler. With a cold chisel and hammer or an air-impact chisel, cut the exhaust pipe free from the muffler after removing any clamps. In some cases, it may be possible to remove the exhaust pipe from the muffler without cutting. Remove the old exhaust pipe from under the car.

4. Install a new exhaust pipe under the car in the same position as the old pipe. Loosely attach the new exhaust pipe to the exhaust manifold until the muffler is attached and the strap hanger is connected.

5. Insert the end of the exhaust pipe into the forward end of the muffler and tighten the clamp securely.

NOTE: *The clamp should be placed on the new exhaust pipe and slid over the end of the muffler after the pipe is inserted.*

6. Attach any straphangers and then tighten the manifold bolts and nuts.

7. Start the engine and check for leaks around the exhaust manifold and the muffler.

MUFFLER AND TAIL PIPE REPLACEMENT

1. Loosen clamp attaching the muffler to the exhaust pipe. Put some penetrating oil on the joint where the pipe enters the muffler. After a few minutes, try to slide the exhaust pipe from the muffler. If the pipe is rusted to the muffler, cut it loose with a cold chisel and hammer or an air-impact chisel.

2. Attach a strap hanger to the new muffler and place it under the car.

3. Slide the clamp back on the exhaust pipe and insert the end of the pipe into the forward end of the muffler. Slide the clamp over the end of the muffler and tighten it securely.

4. Start the engine and check the muffler connection for leaks.

Cooling System

Cooling system service consists mainly of keeping the coolant solution of water and antifreeze (ethylene glycol) at the proper level and strength and flowing freely throughout the radiator and water jackets of the engine. The coolant solution should always contain enough antifreeze to protect the cooling system against freezing at temperatures down to -12°F (-24°C). The cooling system should have at least 40% antifreeze to be effective. When changing the coolant annually, drain the radiator and engine block completely. Drain cocks or plugs are located on the radiator and the right side of the engine. Flush with clean water and a cooling system cleaning solution, and drain again. Fill the radiator and engine block with clean water and enough antifreeze for a 60% water-40% antifreeze solution.

Occasionally, the radiator, water pump, and the thermostat may have to be replaced or overhauled. Procedures for these operations are given below.

THERMOSTAT REPLACEMENT

1. Drain the coolant from the radiator and the coolant hose to the thermostat housing. Be careful not to splash coolant over the engine and the alternator (generator).

2. Remove the bolts securing the thermostat housing to the cylinder head and carefully lift the housing free. Remove the old gasket and lift the thermostat from the cylinder head.

3. Test the operation of the thermostat in a container of heated water. The thermostat should open at the temperature shown in the Thermostat Chart.

Thermostat

Engine Model	Type of Thermostat	Marked	Opens at deg. F (deg. C)	Fully Open at deg. F (deg. C)
B18A, B18B, B18D, B20A	Fulton Siphon 1-1700-D3	170	167-172 (75-78)	192 (89)
B20B	Wahler	82	177-181 (81-83)	195 (90)
B30A	Wax	82	177-182 (81-83)	194 (90)

4. Install thermostat in cylinder head and install a new gasket. Set the housing in place over the thermostat and gasket and start the bolts in very carefully. Tighten the bolts evenly until snug. Do not tighten the bolts more than ¼ turn past finger-tight.

5. Refill the radiator. Start the engine and check for leaks around the thermostat housing and that the thermostat opens properly.

RADIATOR REPLACEMENT

1. Remove the caps and the plug at the bottom of the radiator and drain off the coolant.

2. Remove the expansion tank with hose and empty out the coolant.

3. Loosen the hose clamps for the lower and upper radiator hoses. Remove the upper radiator hose.

4. Remove the bolts for the radiator. Lift up the radiator and disconnect the lower radiator hose.

5. Place the new radiator in position and tighten the bolts.

6. Install the radiator hoses.

7. Install the expansion tank with hose. Install the hose from the radiator in front of the expansion tank and down to its underside so that the hose does not come into contact with the fan. Make sure that the hose has a smooth curve without any sharp bends.

8. Fill with coolant.

9. Start the engine and check for leakage.

WATER PUMP

Water Pump Replacement

1. Remove the radiator.
2. Remove the housing bolts from the water pump. Carefully remove the housing from the engine block along with all the old gasket material.
3. Pull the water pump assembly from the engine block and remove the sealing rings.

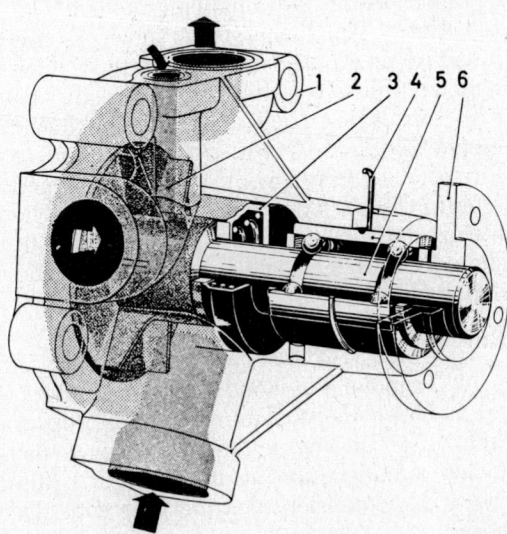

1. Housing
2. Impeller
3. Seal ring
4. Lock spring
5. Shaft with ball bearings (integral unit)
6. Hub

Water pump

4. Install a new or overhauled water pump being sure that the sealing rings on the upper side of the pump are located correctly and seated fully. Press the pump upward against the cylinder head extension to seat the rings. Be sure the sealing rings on the water pipes are not damaged while pressing the pipes in place.
5. Install the pump housing with a new gasket. Tighten the bolts evenly until snug. Do not tighten the bolts more than ½ turn further to avoid damaging or breaking the bolts or the housing.
6. Install the radiator and fan.
7. Fill with coolant. Start the engine and check for leaks around the housing and hoses.

Water Pump Overhaul

DISASSEMBLY

1. Pull out the lock spring.
2. Firmly fit a puller on the hub with the bolts for the pulley and pull off the hub.
3. Place the pump in a press. Fit a drift on the outer ring of the bearing and press out the shaft, the bearing, and the impeller.
4. Inspect the impeller and bearing. If the bearing is worn and has too much play or if it seizes, scrap the shaft and bearing. (The bearing and shaft cannot be disassembled.) If the bearing is usable, it should not be heated or washed in solvent as this would destroy its lubricant protection. If the impeller is removed, it should be replaced as its removal always results in damage. Always replace the seal ring.
5. To separate the shaft and impeller, press the seal ring down and slide in a press tool under the impeller. Then press out the shaft with a drift.

ASSEMBLY

Before assembling, check carefully that the parts are not damaged. The sealing surface of the impeller must be even and free from scratches. The bearing should run easily without seizing and may not be loose. Replace damaged parts.

1. Press down the shaft bearing into the housing with a drift, far enough that the lock wire can be inserted in its groove. Insert the lock wire.

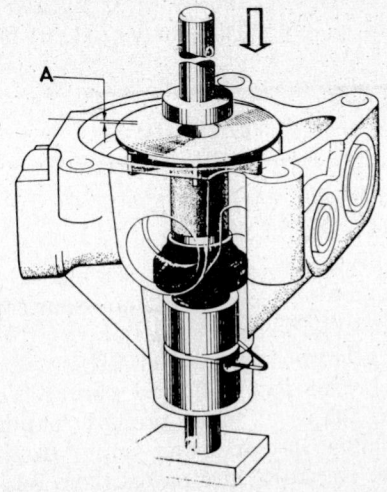

Pressing in the impeller; dimension A is .016".

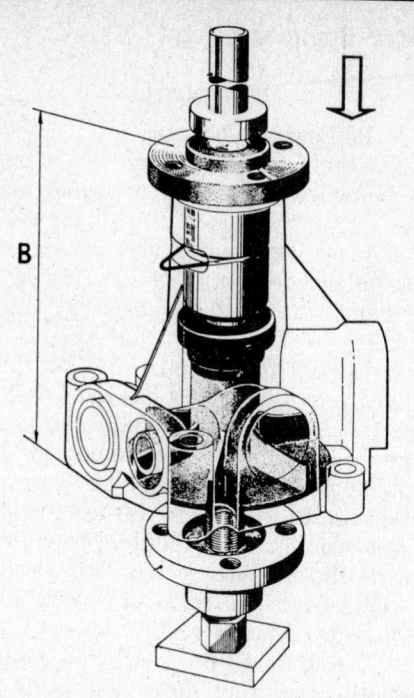

Installing the pulley; dimension B is 4.134±0.008".

2. Install the oil slinger. Install the seal ring with a drift. Coat the contact surface of the carbon washer against the impeller with molybdenum disulphide mixed in SAE 30 mineral oil. The molybdenum disulphide should be completely dry before the washer is installed.

3. Press on the impeller with a drift so that the impeller lies at a level with or 0.4 mm. (0.016") under the surface of the pump housing.

4. Turn the pump. Press on the hub with a drift. Carefully press until dimension B is 105 ±0.2 mm. (4.134 ±0.008").

Engine

EXHAUST EMISSION CONTROL SYSTEM

Volvo engines since 1968 have been equipped with an exhaust emission control system. The exhaust emission control system includes a positive crankcase ventilation system and a heated carburetor air intake manifold. The positive crankcase ventilation system draws fumes from the engine crankcase and passes them into the intake manifold to be burned in the cylinders. The heated carburetor air intake manifold warms the intake air before it passes into the cylinders. This allows the engine to be adjusted for a leaner fuel-air mixture that will burn more completely. Maintenance of the emission control system requires keeping the valves in the intake manifold free from binding and cleaning the components of the positive crankcase ventilation system periodically (every 25,000 miles).

Engine Removal and Installation

All Volvo engines may be removed and installed using the following general instructions. The lifting tools shown in the illustrations are necessary to lift the engine and transmission safely and correctly. Be sure the lifting tools are secured to the engine block as shown. Do not attempt to lift the engine with chain wrapped around the oil filter or the distributor. The lifting tools shown in the illustrations should be used if available but substitutes may be used if strong enough.

Engine Removal

1. Remove the hood from the hinges.
2. Drain the coolant. (Open the tap at right side of engine and disconnect the lower radiator hose at the radiator.) Remove the expansion tank together with the hose.
3. Remove the cover plate in front of the radiator.
4. Remove the upper radiator hose. Remove the radiator.
5. Remove the positive lead from the battery.
6. Remove the following: electric wires from the starter and ignition coil, the intake hose to the fuel pump (to be plugged), the wires from the temperature and oil pressure sending units and from the alternator (generator), the vacuum hose, the choke control, the heater hoses at the engine.
7. Remove the throttle control shaft from the pedal shaft, intermediate shaft, and bracket.
8. Remove the nuts at the branch pipe flange of the exhaust manifold.
9. Place the gears in neutral. Remove the shift lever.
10. Jack up the vehicle with four blocks or jackstands (under the front jack attachment and in front of the rear jack attachment.)

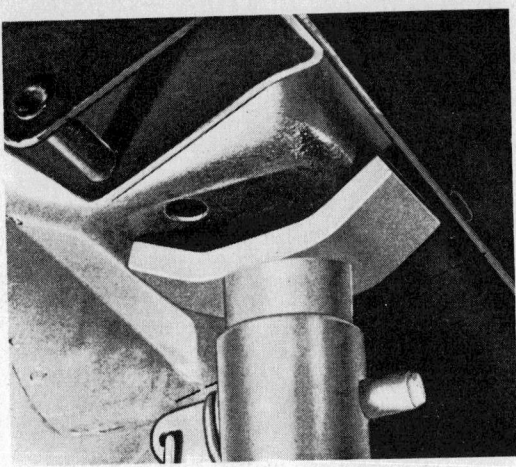

Location of the jackstand in front of rear jack attachment

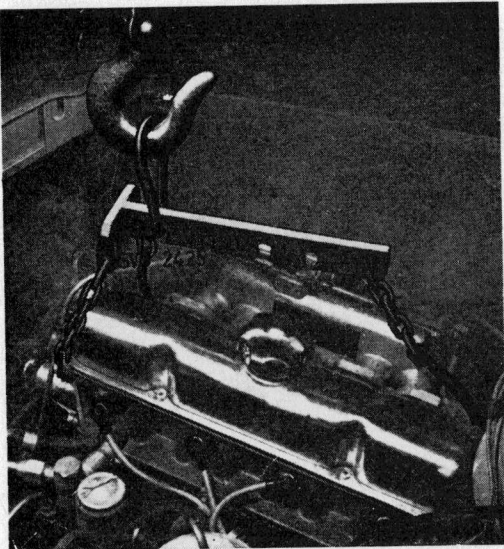

Lifting out the engine

16. Unbolt the rear crossmember.

17. Disconnect the ground cable from the engine.

18. Remove the crossmember, brackets for the exhaust manifold, and rear engine mounts.

19. Remove the lower nuts for the front engine mounts.

20. Install lifting eyes and lifting cross-bar. The lifting eyes are attached by ⅜ x 1¼ and 1" bolts. Lift out the engine and set it on an engine stand or rack.

Engine Installation

1. Install the lifting apparatus.

2. Install the engine. Place a jack under the transmission and guide the engine into position. Be careful not to damage the oil filter and oil pressure sending unit against the exhaust pipe.

3. Tighten the nuts for the front engine mounts.

4. Connect the wires for the backup lights (and overdrive).

5. Install the brackets for the exhaust manifold, rear engine mounts, the crossmember, and the nuts for the rear engine mounts.

6. Remove the jack and lifting tool.

7. Tighten the flange of the exhaust pipe against the exhaust manifold.

8. Install the clamp for the exhaust manifold, the front universal joint to the flange (make sure the contact surfaces are clean), the speedometer drive cable, the ground cable, the clutch linkage, and return spring

9. Adjust the clutch play.

10. Remove the blocks from under the vehicle.

11. Install heater hoses, wires to the temperature and oil pressure sending units, the throttle control shaft, the choke cable, the wires for the alternator (generator), starter motor, and ignition coil.

12. Install the fuel hose, vacuum hose, and battery cable.

13. Place the radiator in position and fasten it down. Install the cooling system hoses and expansion tank. Install the air cleaner.

14. Install the cover plate in front of the radiator. Fill the radiator and check the oil.

15. Install the hood. Install the shift lever.

11. Place a jack under the transmission. Remove the return spring from the throw-out fork. Disconnect the clutch cable from the throwout fork and from the flywheel housing.

12. Disconnect the wires for the backup lights and overdrive.

13. Remove the speedometer drive cable from the transmission.

14. Remove the clamp for the exhaust manifold.

15. Separate the flange of the transmission (overdrive) from the front universal joint.

ENGINE DISASSEMBLY

Manifold Removal and Installation

The intake and exhaust manifolds may be removed from the engine after removing the carburetor(s), associated linkage, and any emission control system equipment. On engines that use a carburetor air intake preheating manifold, the intake and exhaust manifolds are cast together and are removed as a unit. When installing any of these manifolds, be careful not to tighten the nuts more than is necessary to ensure a good seal. Always use a new gasket between the manifold and the engine block.

After replacing the intake/exhaust manifold, install the carburetor(s) and adjust for proper operation. Check for air leaks around the manifolds.

Cylinder Head Removal and Installation

Drain the cooling system. Disconnect the throttle and choke controls. Remove the carburetor(s). Disconnect the exhaust pipe at the exhaust manifold. Disconnect hoses to the radiator and other connections to the cylinder head. Loosen fan belt and remove rocker arm cover, rocker arm shaft, and push rods. Remove cylinder head.

When installing cylinder head, screw guide pins into the front right and left rear holes. Coat new gasket on both sides with graphite grease and lay gasket on block. Install cylinder head over the guide pins. Remove guide pins and insert bolts. Tighten bolts in the sequence illustrated, and to a torque of 61-69 ft. lb. (8.5-9.5 kgm).

Valve Train

Periodic valve train service requires adjusting the clearances for intake and exhaust valves. This should be done with the engine stationary and either warm or cold.

Adjusting valve clearance.

The valve clearances are the same for both intake and exhaust valves. Use two feeler gauges, one "Go" .40 mm. (.016") thick and the other "No-Go" .45 mm. (.018") thick. Adjust each rocker arm so the thinner feeler gauge slides in easily but the thicker feeler gauge cannot be inserted. With No. 1 piston at top dead center of the compression stroke, valves No. 1, 2, 3, and 5 (counted from the front) can be adjusted. Then, turn the crankshaft until No. 4 piston is at top dead center and adjust valves No. 4, 6, 7, and 8.

Valve adjustment for the B30A 6 cylinder engine is the same as the procedure above except for the following differences. The feeler gauges used are one "Go" .50 mm. (.020") thick and one "No-Go" .55 mm. (.022") thick. With No. 1 piston at top dead center, adjust valves No. 1, 2, 3, 6, 7, and 10 (counted from the front) so the thinner feeler gauge can be easily inserted but not the thicker feeler gauge. Then, turn the crankshaft until No. 6 piston is at top dead center and adjust valves No. 4, 5, 8, 9, 11, and 12.

Procedures for removing and reconditioning the valves and the valve train are covered in the Engine Rebuilding Section.

Camshaft and Timing Gear

Service operations for the camshaft and timing gear are detailed below. When installing timing gears, be careful that the

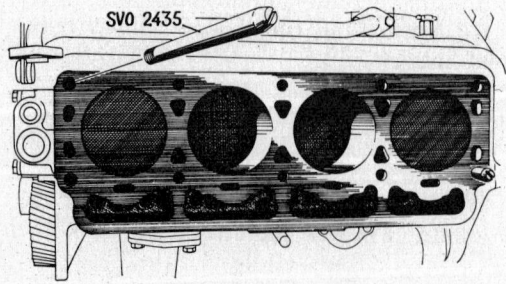

Guide pins for installing the cylinder head

alignment marks on the gears line up correctly.

TIMING GEARS, CAMSHAFT REPLACEMENT

To replace the timing gears:

1. Drain the cooling system. Remove the hood and radiator.

2. Remove the fan and pulley on the water pump. Remove the crankshaft bolt and then remove the pulley, using a puller.

3. Remove the timing gear casing. Loosen a couple of the oil pan bolts, being careful not to damage the gasket.

4. Measure tooth flank clearance. Maximum permissible gear backlash is .005". Also measure end play of camshaft. This is determined by a shim behind the camshaft gear. End play should not exceed .002".

5. Note correct relative position of gears by the markings on them. Remove the hub from the crankshaft with a puller. Remove the crankshaft gear with a puller. Pull the camshaft gear with a puller. Remove oil jet, blow air through it and replace it. Oil fed through this jet lubricates the gears.

6. If the camshaft is to be replaced, it will be necessary to remove the thrust flange and the valve lifters. The camshaft can then be pulled out the front. Valve lifters can be pushed out after removal of rocker arms, push rods, fuel pump, distributor and covers on the sides of the engine.

1. Oil jet   2. Gear markings

Observe timing gear markings.

7. Reassemble in reverse order, installing new camshaft. Install the crankshaft gear. Install the camshaft gear, making sure the gears are in the correct relative position. Do not push the camshaft backward, or the seal washer on the rear end may be forced out. Again check gear clearance and shaft end play.

8. When assembling timing gear casing, make sure drain holes in casing are open and that the casing is properly centered. Center casing using a sleeve.

TIMING GEAR CASING
OIL SEAL REPLACEMENT

B18, B20

1. Remove the fan belt. Loosen the stabilizer at the frame.

2. Screw out the bolt in the crankshaft. Remove the belt pulley.

3. Remove the circlip for the washer which retains the felt ring. Remove the washer and felt ring. Check that the casing is correctly fitted by inserting a 0.10 mm. (0.004") feeler gauge in the gap between the casing and hub on the crankshaft and moving it all around. If the feeler gauge jams at any point, the casing should be centered.

4. Install a new felt ring. Place the washer in position and install the circlip. Check that the circlip fits properly.

5. Install the remaining parts and tighten the fan belt.

B30

1. Drain coolant and remove radiator and grill.

2. Remove the fan belt. Remove the bolts for the pulley and the flywheel damper.

3. Remove the center bolt and take off the hub with a puller. (First check to see whether it is possible to pull off the hub by hand).

4. Remove the oil seal. Lubricate the sealing lip on the new seal and install the seal with a drift. First inspect the wear surface of the hub. The oil seal can be installed in three positions. With a new hub the seal will be installed in its outer position (position 1). With a wear mark on the hub, install the seal in position 2. With two wear marks on the hub, install the seal in position 3. With three wear marks, the hub should be replaced.

5. Install the hub. Before installation, the sliding surfaces of the hub should be greased. Note the marking, that is, the center punch marks on the crankshaft end and hub. Install the center bolt and tighten it to a torque of 50-57 ft.lb.

6. Install the flywheel damper and pulley.

7. Install the fan belt. This should be tightened so that the friction torque of the fan pulley is 1.2-1.7 kgm. (8.7-12.3 ft.lb.). Use a torque wrench on the alternator pulley nut. Install the radiator.

Timing Gear Case Replacement

B18, B20

1. Loosen the fan belt. Remove the fan and pulley on the water pump. Disconnect the stabilizer attachment from the frame.

2. Remove the bolt for the crankshaft belt pulley and remove the pulley.

3. Remove the timing gear casing. Loosen a couple of extra bolts for the oil pan and be careful not to damage the gasket. Remove the circlip, washer and felt ring from the casing.

4. Make sure that the gaskets are in good condition and that the drain hole is open and clean.

5. Place the casing in position and install the bolts without tightening them.

6. Center the casing with a sleeve. Turn the sleeve while tightening and ad-

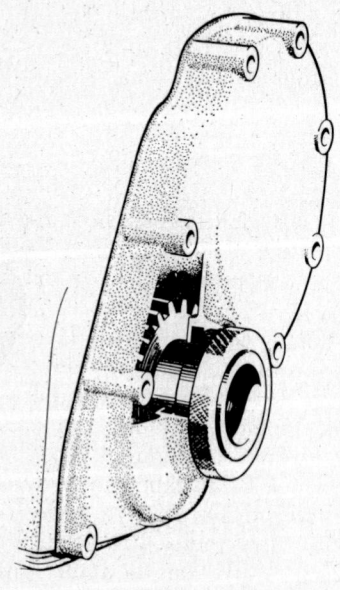

Centering the timing gear casing

just the position of the casing so that the sleeve is not jammed. Check after final tightening of the casing that the sleeve can be easily rotated without jamming.

7. Install a new felt ring, washer and circlip. Push them into their position with the centering sleeve. Check that the circlip has engaged in its groove.

8. Install the other parts and tighten the fan belt. Tighten the stabilizer attachments firmly to the frame.

ENGINE LUBRICATION

The engine employs a forced-feed lubricating system, pressure being provided by a pump driven by the camshaft and located in the oil pan under the crankshaft. The pump forces oil past a relief valve on the pump, through the oil filter and through oil passages to various lubricating points. All oil supplied to lubricating points, therefore, first passes through the oil filter.

The oil pump is a gear type. The pressure pipe from the pump to the cylinder block has no threads but is tightened in position when the pump bolts are secured. There are special rubber seals at each end of the pipe. The relief valve is mounted directly on the pump.

The oil filter is a full-flow type and on B18, B20, and B30 engines is mounted directly on the cylinder block. (On the B18B, an oil cooler is installed between the oil filter and the cylinder block.) The filter element is made of special paper and should be replaced when it becomes dirty. The oil filter contains a valve which allows oil to bypass the element if resistance to flow becomes excessive.

The oil cooler on B18B engines is installed between the oil filter and cylinder block and consists of an oil duct surrounded by a water cooling jacket. Baffles in the paths of the oil and cooling water conduct heat away from the oil.

Oil Filter Replacement

The oil filter is screwed onto a nipple in the block on B18A, B20, and B30 engines. On B18B engines, it screws onto a nipple in the air cooler.

B18, B20, B30

Remove the old filter by turning with the hands or with a chain wrench. Discard old filter. Coat the rubber gasket of the new filter with oil and make sure both

Removing oil filter.

contacting surfaces are clean. Screw on the filter by hand until it just comes to the end of its travel. Then screw in the filter a further half-turn by hand. *Do not use the chain wrench for tightening the filter.* Start engine and check for oil leaks.

B16

Loosen the center bolt on the oil filter housing, being prepared to collect the oil that runs out. Remove the oil filter. Discard the old element and clean the filter housing. Insert the new element (observing the "up" marking) and gasket in the housing, and bolt filter unit to side of engine, guiding it with the hand so that it fits into the groove correctly. Tighten bolt to 15 ft.lb. Add 1½ pints of oil to the crankcase for the new filter element. Start the engine and check for oil leaks.

B14

Drain filter by removing oil plug from the side of the filter support. Loosen center bolt on oil filter housing and remove filter. Discard old filter element and clean filter housing. Install new filter element. Install drain plug and attach oil filter assembly to support. Add 1½ pints of oil to crankcase for new filter element. Run engine and check for oil leaks.

B18B

Drain cooling system. Disconnect water connection from oil cooler. Remove oil filter. Unscrew nut on oil nipple and remove the oil cooler. The O-ring may require replacement, in which case the new O-ring should be inserted into the groove in the oil cooler after the groove is coated with gasket cement. Tighten the nut on the oil cooler to 7 ft.lb. Check that the cooler is in good contact with block, then tighten nut to 23-25 ft.lb. Install the oil filter and connect the water lines. Fill the cooling system and start the engine. Check for oil and water leaks.

Oil Cooler—B18B

The early production B18B engine is fitted with an oil cooler. The oil cooler is fitted between the oil filter and the cylinder block and consists of an inner section for the oil which is surrounded by a cooling jacket. The engine coolant is led through the cooling jacket. On its way to the oil filter, the oil passes through the cooler and some of the heat in the oil is conducted away by the coolant. The coolant cannot pass the shortest way from the inlet to the outlet, but is forced to circulate round the cooler through the channels formed by the baffles. The oil is forced between the pairs of discs in turn due to the transverse baffles on the discs and then finally passes out to the oil filter.

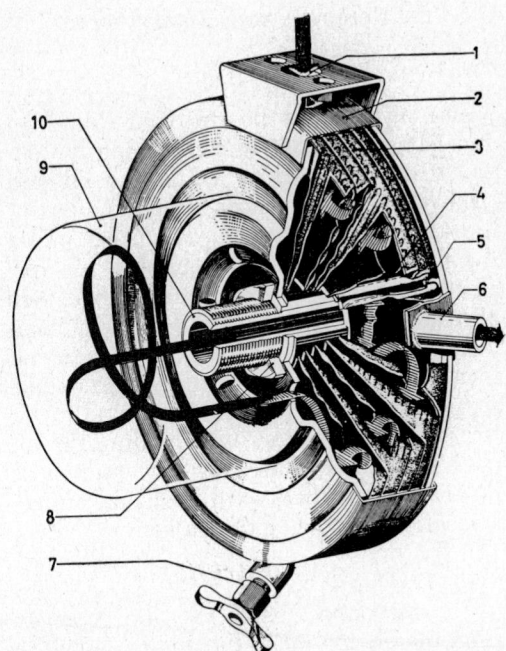

1. Coolant inlet
2. Housing
3. Discs
4. Transverse baffles
5. Baffles
6. Cooling outlet
7. Drain cock for coolant
8. Nut
9. Oil filter
10. Nipple

Oil cooler, B18B

Oil Cooler Replacement—B18B

1. Drain coolant.

2. Disconnect the coolant connections on the oil cooler. Remove the oil filter.

3. Unscrew the nut on the nipple for the oil cooler, and pull off the cooler.

4. Install the oil cooler. The O-ring against the cylinder block should be replaced if necessary, in which case it should be inserted into the groove on the oil cooler before reinstallation. Coat the groove with a thin layer of adhesive which is resistant to oil up to temperatures of 140°C (280°F), for example, Pliobond 20. With the nut tightened to a torque of 7 ft.lb., check that the cooler is in good contact with the cylinder block. The nut is finally tightened to 23-25 ft.lb.

5. Install the oil filter and connect the coolant pipes.

6. Fill up with coolant and, if necessary, also engine oil.

7. Start the engine and check for leakage.

8. If the nipple has been replaced, the new one should be tightened to 33-40 ft.lb.

Oil Pan Removal and Replacement

B14, B16

The oil pan can be removed from B14 and B16 engines without removing the engine from the vehicle. Drain the oil and remove the cover plates from the sides of the engine. Remove the cover from under the flywheel. Loosen the nuts on the forward engine supports for about one inch of travel, but do not remove them completely. Jack up the front end and slide one inch (2.5mm.) spacers between the engine supports and the motor mounts, and lower the jack. Remove the bolts holding the oil pan and remove the pan by pulling it downward and backward. Assemble in reverse order, replacing the gasket.

B18, B20, B30

The oil sump (pan) may be removed from the engine while the engine is still in the car.

Removal

1. Place supports on the frame side-members as shown. Raise the front end of the engine using lifting apparatus. Remove the dipstick.

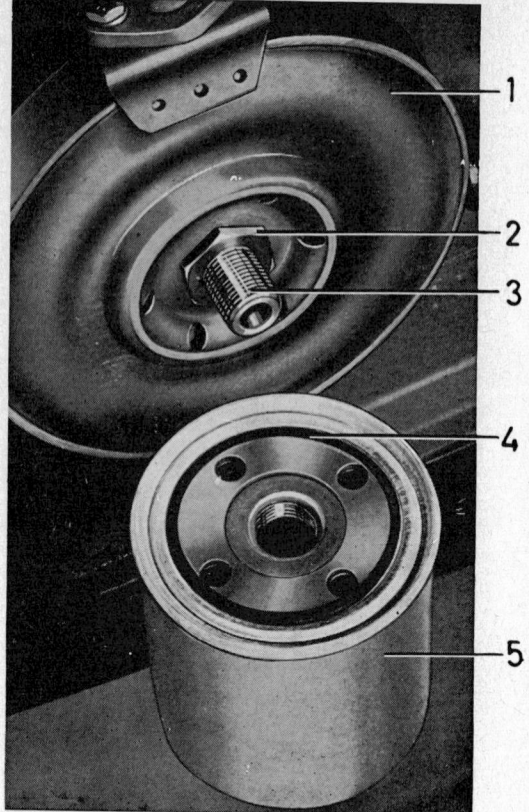

1. Cooler
2. Nut
3. Nipple
4. Gasket
5. Oil filter

Oil cooler and oil filter

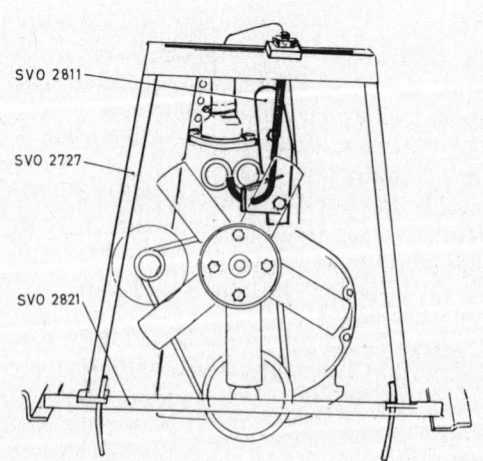

SVO 2811
SVO 2727
SVO 2821

Apparatus for lifting engine in chassis

2. Jack up the vehicle under the front jack attachments. Drain the engine oil. Remove the lower nuts for the engine mounts.

3. Place a workshop jack under the front axle member. Remove the rear bolts of the front axle member and replace with two long bolts. Remove the front bolts for the front crossmember. Lower and remove the jack so that the front axle member hangs on the two long bolts.

4. Remove the reinforcing bracket (at the flywheel casing). Unscrew the bolts and lower the pan.

5. Remove the old gasket and clean the contact surfaces of the cylinder block and oil pan.

Replacement

1. Place the oil pan and gasket in position and replace the bolts. Tighten the drain plug securely.

2. Place the reinforcing bracket in position and tighten all the bolts. Then tighten down the bolts for the flywheel casing and those for the cylinder block.

3. Raise the front crossmember and tighten down the front bolts. Remove the additional bolts, install and tighten the rear bolts.

4. Install the nuts for the engine mounts.

5. Lower the vehicle. Remove the lifting tools.

6. Fill with oil and insert the dipstick.

7. Start the engine and check for any leakage.

120 Series

Removal

1. Lift the vehicle about 12" above the floor and place blocks under it near the jacking points.

2. Apply a lifting device under the engine mounts. Do not lift on the water pump. Unscrew the nuts for the front engine mounting pads from below. Lift the engine as high as possible without pinching anything against the firewall. Allow it to hang on the hoist.

3. Place a jack under the front crossmember. Loosen but do not remove the two bolts in the front crossmember. Be careful not to lose any shims. Remove the four rear bolts and lower the front end as far as possible.

4. Remove the pan.

Replacement

1. Replace the pan.

2. Thoroughly clean the front crossmember and check that the shims are fitted correctly.

3. Lift up the front end and tighten it down.

PV544, 210

Removal

1. Lift the vehicle about 12" above the floor and place blocks under it near the jacking points.

2. Apply a lifting device under the engine mounts. Do not lift on the water pump. Unscrew the nuts for the front engine mounting pads from below. Lift the engine as high as possible without pinching anything against the firewall and allow it to hang on the hoist.

3. Place a jack under the front crossmember.

4. Clean off the brake pipe connections on the master cylinder. Disconnect the brake pipes from the master cylinder. Plug the lines in order to prevent dirt from entering the brake system.

5. Remove the four front bolts for the front crossmember. Screw in two bolts about 75 mm. (2 15/16") long in place of these, one on each side. Remove the four rear bolts for the crossmember.

6. Lower the front end so that it is supported on the two long bolts.

7. Remove the pan.

Replacement

1. Replace the pan.

2. Thoroughly clean the front crossmember and lift it up. Tighten the rear bolts. Remove the long bolts at the front and install the ordinary ones.

3. Clean around the master cylinder and brake lines. Replace the brake lines.

PISTONS AND CONNECTING RODS

Piston rings on B14 and B16 models can be replaced as follows, after the cylinder head is removed. While these instructions apply also to the B18, B20, and B30, the work is more easily accomplished on these after the engine is removed from the frame.

Lift the front end of the vehicle and support it about 8" above the floor. (Remove B18, B20, and B30 engine from frame). Drain crankcase and remove oil pan. Note connecting rod markings. Disconnect rods at the crankshaft, replacing bearing shells, caps and nuts on rods to avoid possible interchange of parts. Remove cylinder bore ridges with a ridge reamer and push out pistons and rods up through tops of cylinders. Mark cylinder numbers on pistons, connecting rods and caps, numbering 1 through 4 or 1 through 6. Remove rings.

Inspect cylinder walls for scoring, roughness, or ridges from excessive wear. With an accurate cylinder gauge or inside micrometer, check for cylinder taper and out-of-round at top, middle, and bottom of bore, both parallel with and at right angles to the center line of the engine. Wear is indicated by the difference between the highest and lowest readings. Cylinder should be rebored when wear reaches .010″ or if scoring is evident. Hone or rebore for smallest possible oversize piston and rings. Obtain piston first and then rework cylinder bore to appropriate size. Pistons should have a clearance of .0008″-0016″ between piston and cylinder wall. Piston is fitted in cylinder without the the rings.

Measure outside diameter of pistons with a micrometer at right angles to the wrist pin hole about ⅜″ from the bottom edge on B14A engines. This distance is ⅛″ on early production B18 engines and ½″ on late production B18 engines. On the B20 and B30 engines the distance is 0.098″ from the bottom.

In a new or rebored cylinder, press the rings one after another into the cylinder bore and measure the ring gap with a feeler gauge. The gap is 0.010-0.020″ for B14, B16, and B18 engines; 0.016-0.022″ for B20 and B30 engines. If the gap is too small, widen it by filing with a thin flat file. When checking the fit in a worn cylinder bore, rings must be checked at the bottom dead center position, where the diameter of the bore is smallest.

Clean piston ring grooves and check the rings in their proper grooves in the piston. Measure the clearance at a few points. Inspect ring grooves for wear, particularly the upper edge of compression ring (top) groove.

If the wrist pin hole in the piston is too worn, an oversize wrist pin is necessary. Ream out the hole to the oversize pin measurement. This is correct when the

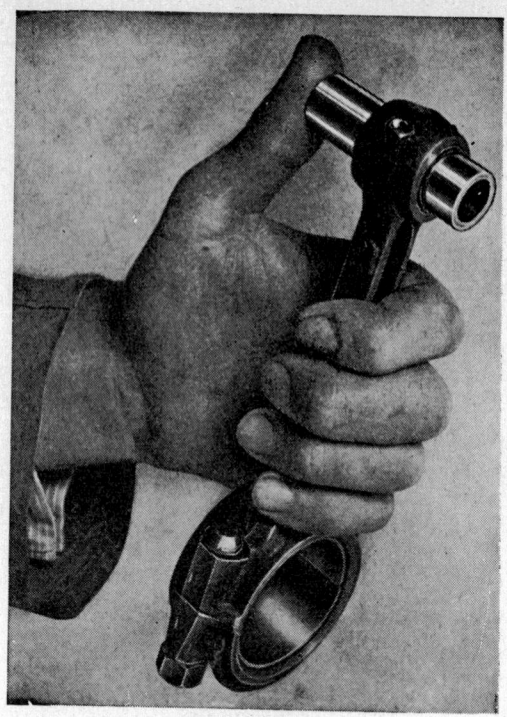

Wrist pin fit

wrist pin can be pushed through the hole by hand with light resistance.

Check to see if the connecting rods are bent or twisted and straighten them if necessary. If the bushing is worn, replace it. Make sure the oil holes line up with the holes in the connecting rod, then ream the bushing to the correct fit. The wrist pin should slide through the hole with light thumb pressure but without noticeable looseness.

When assembling, be sure that the piston is positioned in the cylinder so that the arrow (or slot) faces forward. This is important since the hole is not centered in

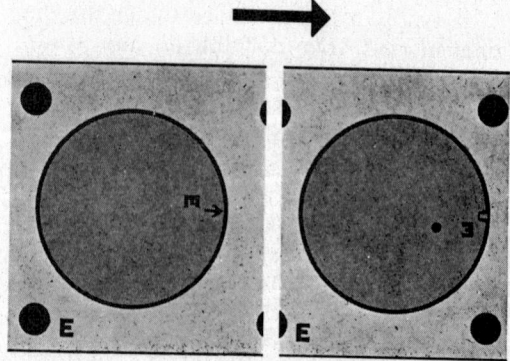

Markings on piston and engine block

the piston, and if the piston is turned the wrong way it will cause a loud noise. Also, the connecting rod should be positioned so that the number on the side faces away from the camshaft. Use a piston ring expander tool to install the rings. Position them so the gaps do not come directly under each other. The upper piston ring is chrome, and the upper side is marked TOP.

Lubricate the pistons, wrist pins and cylinder walls and install pistons in cylinders.

Install the connecting rods on the crankshaft. Tighten connecting rod bolts with a torque wrench to the proper torque.

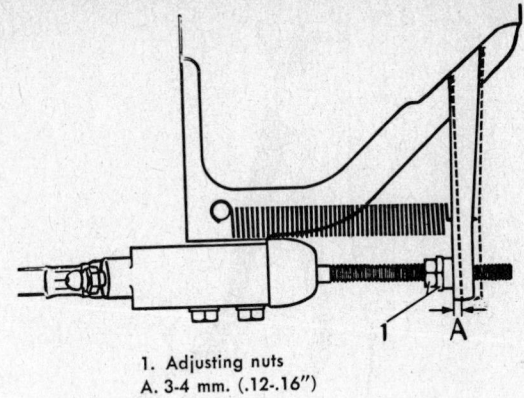

1. Adjusting nuts
A. 3-4 mm. (.12-.16")

Clutch fork free travel; 120 series, 1800 (early production)

Clutch and Transmission

CLUTCH

All manual transmission models use 8" or 8½" dry disc type clutches of Borg and Beck manufacture. Clutch control, actuated by the foot pedal, is hydraulic on 122S and 1800S and right-hand drive 164 models and mechanical on 164, 144, PV444, 445, and P210 models. Thrust on the pressure plate is provided by six strong pressure springs on all models except the 164, 145, 144, and 142 which utilize a diaphragm-type spring.

The clutch for the 142 and 144 Series cars is an 8½" diaphragm spring type. This clutch is supplied in two versions, differing mainly in the casing design. The diaphragm spring serves as a clutch lever when disengaging and as the pressure spring when engaging. Clutch action is controlled by a flexible thrust wire instead of a shaft.

Clutch Fork Free Travel Adjustment

The clutch fork travel must be checked and if necessary adjusted every 6,000 miles.

On early production 120 and 1800 models clutch fork free travel is 3-4 mm. (.12-.16").

On late production 120 and 1800 models and on the 140 series the travel is adjusted by means of nuts which secure the cable to the clutch housing.

The travel for the clutch pedal on the 120 series and 1800 should be 140 mm. (5.5"). On the 140 series (early produc-

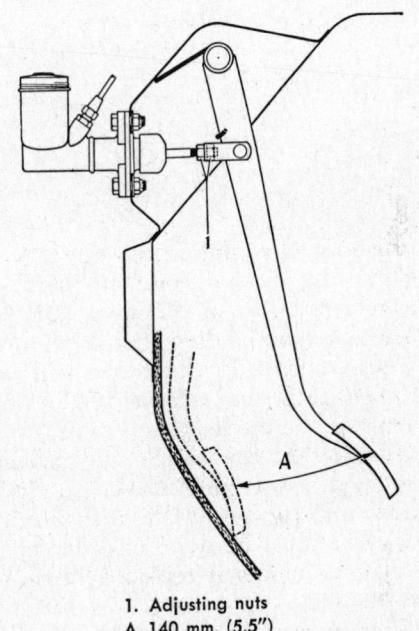

1. Adjusting nuts
A. 140 mm. (5.5")

Clutch pedal free travel; 120 series, 1800 (early production)

tion) there is an adjustable bracket with which the pedal travel can be adjusted to 125-130 mm. (4.9-5.1").

Clutch Removal

120 Series With B16 Engine

1. Remove the transmission.
2. Unhook the return spring on the clutch release fork.
3. Remove the clutch release bearing.
4. Remove the sheet metal cover under the flywheel.

1. Adjustable bracket
A. 125-130 mm. (4.9-5.1")

Clutch pedal play, 140 series (early production)

5. Remove the clutch release fork by first loosening the ball joint on the inside a few turns with a 17 mm. (21/32") wrench and then holding it still while unscrewing the bolt on which the ball joint fits. Then turn the release fork ½ turn and remove it to the rear.

6. Check that the clutch and flywheel are marked. Otherwise, mark the clutch, flywheel, and pressure plate with a center punch. This must be done in order to ensure that the clutch is replaced in the original position.

7. The six bolts securing the clutch to the flywheel should be loosened in sequence a couple of turns at a time to prevent warping. Hold up the clutch so that it does not fall. The clutch and clutch plate can now be removed downward.

120 SERIES, 1800 SERIES WITH B18 ENGINE

1. Remove the transmission.

2. Unhook the return spring on the clutch release fork. Remove the bolts for the control cylinder. Tie up the cylinder to the body. Remove the plate from the lower part of the flywheel housing. Remove the bolts for the flywheel housing and take off the housing.

3. Remove the clutch release bearing. Unscrew the bolt holding the ball joint for the release fork and remove the joint and

the fork.

4. The six bolts securing the clutch to the flywheel should be loosened in sequence a couple of turns at a time to prevent warping and then removed. Hold up the clutch to prevent it from falling to the floor. Lift off the clutch and clutch plate.

120 SERIES WITH B20 ENGINE, 140 SERIES

1. Remove the transmission.

2. Remove the upper bolt for the starter.

3. Remove the clutch release bearing. Unhook the cable from the release fork. Remove the cable sleeve from the bracket.

4. Remove the bolts and take off the flywheel housing.

5. Unscrew the bolt holding the release fork ball joint. Remove the joint and the release fork.

6. Loosen the bolts securing the clutch to the flywheel in sequence a couple of turns at a time to prevent warping. Lift off the clutch and clutch plate.

Clutch Inspection

Inspect clutch parts for wear and damage. Check friction surfaces of flywheel and pressure plate for scoring, ends of release fingers for wear, and clutch facings for wear or oil saturation. Inspect driven disc for distortion (lateral run-out should not exceed .016" at the outer diameter). Test-out disc hub on clutch gear splines for easy slip fit. Do not lubricate.

Check release bearing for wear, binding, or roughness. Do not clean disc or release bearing in solvent. Test pilot-bearing surface on clutch gear spline and check bearing in rear of crankshaft. If necessary, replace bearing.

Clutch Installation

Before installing, wash flywheel, clutch facings, and pressure plate completely free of oil with a safe solvent and wipe dry with a clean cloth. Observe markings on flywheel and clutch so that they may be aligned properly. Place clutch on flywheel so that longest projecting plate hub faces rear. Insert a clutch aligning shaft so that it centers the pilot bearing in the flywheel. Install and tighten bolts evenly in sequence. Remove aligning shaft. Install release yoke by placing in flywheel housing back to front and turning one-half turn. Install throwout bearing. Connect pedal linkage. Adjust clutch.

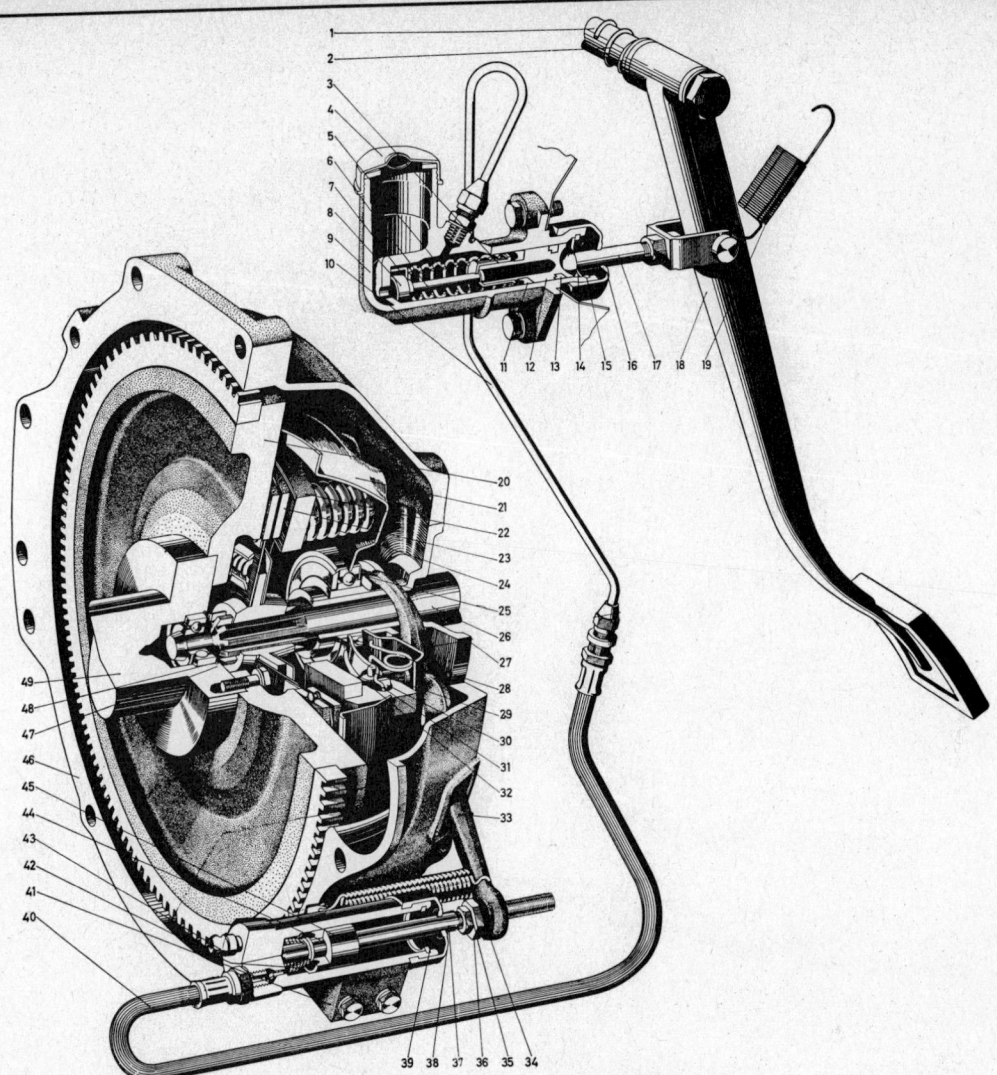

1. Pedal shaft
2. Spring
3. Retainer
4. Cap
5. Spring
6. Thrust rod
7. Retainer
8. Check valve
9. Master cylinder
10. Pipe
11. Plunger seal
12. Plunger
13. Plunger seal (early production)
14. Washer
15. Circlip
16. Rubber dust cover
17. Thrust rod
18. Clutch pedal
19. Return spring (early production)
20. Flywheel
21. Clutch cover casing
22. Pressure plate
23. Clutch plate
24. Clutch spring
25. Clutch release bearing

26. Input shaft
27. Cover
28. Spring
29. Pin
30. Lip
31. Clutch lever
32. Eyebolt
33. Clutch release fork
34. Return spring
35. Locknut
36. Adjusting nut
37. Thrust rod
38. Rubber dust cover (early production)
39. Circlip
40. Hose
41. Control cylinder
42. Spring
43. Bleeder nipple
44. Plunger seal
45. Plunger
46. Flywheel housing
47. Circlip
48. Pilot bearing in flywheel
49. Crankshaft

Clutch and clutch controls; 120 series, 1800 (early production)

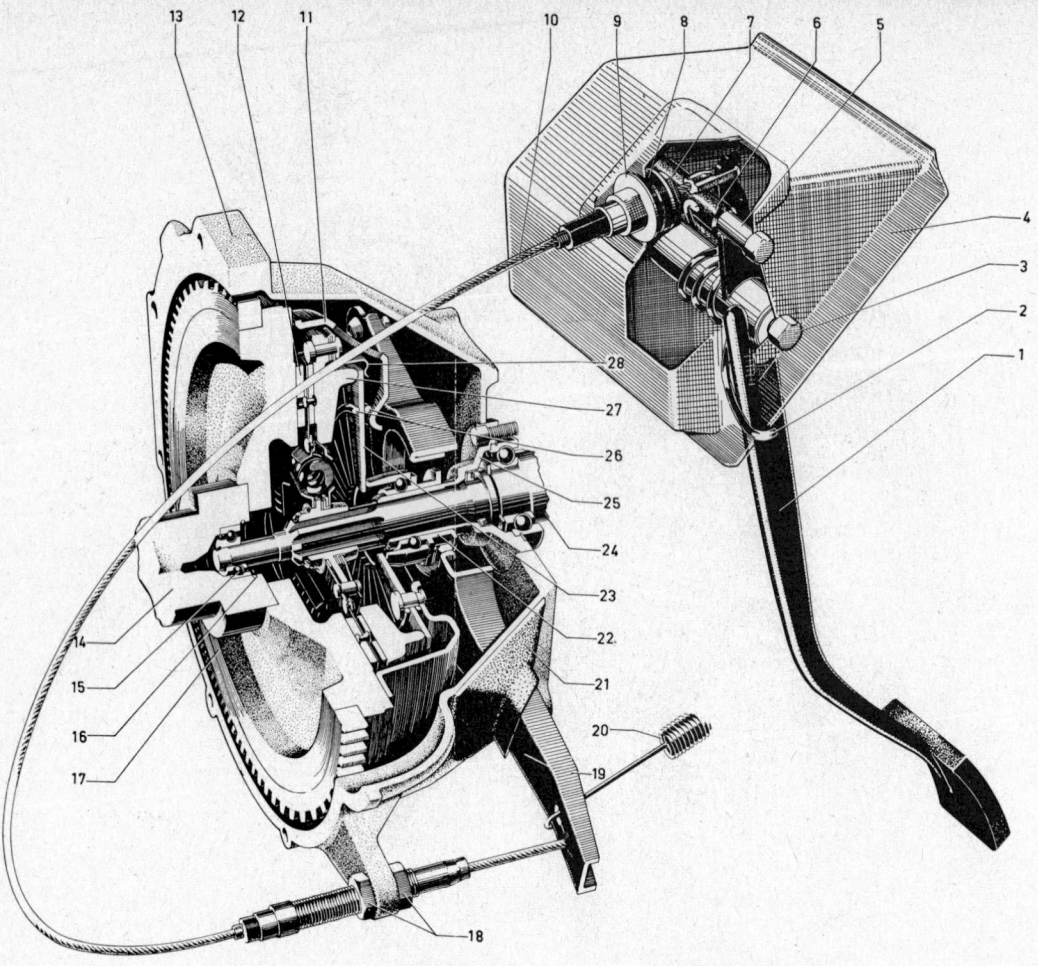

1. Clutch pedal
2. Return spring
3. Bolt
4. Pedal casing
5. Pedal stop
6. Rubber sleeve
7. Nut
8. Rubber bushing
9. Washer
10. Clutch cable
11. Clutch cover casing
12. Clutch plate
13. Flywheel housing
14. Crankshaft

15. Pilot bearing in crankshaft
16. Circlip
17. Flywheel
18. Adjusting nuts
19. Release fork
20. Return spring
21. Dust cover
22. Release bearing
23. Thrust spring
24. Plate shaft (input shaft, transmission)
25. Cover, transmission
26. Support rings
27. Thrust plate
28. Retainer

Clutch and clutch controls; 120 series, 1800 (late production)

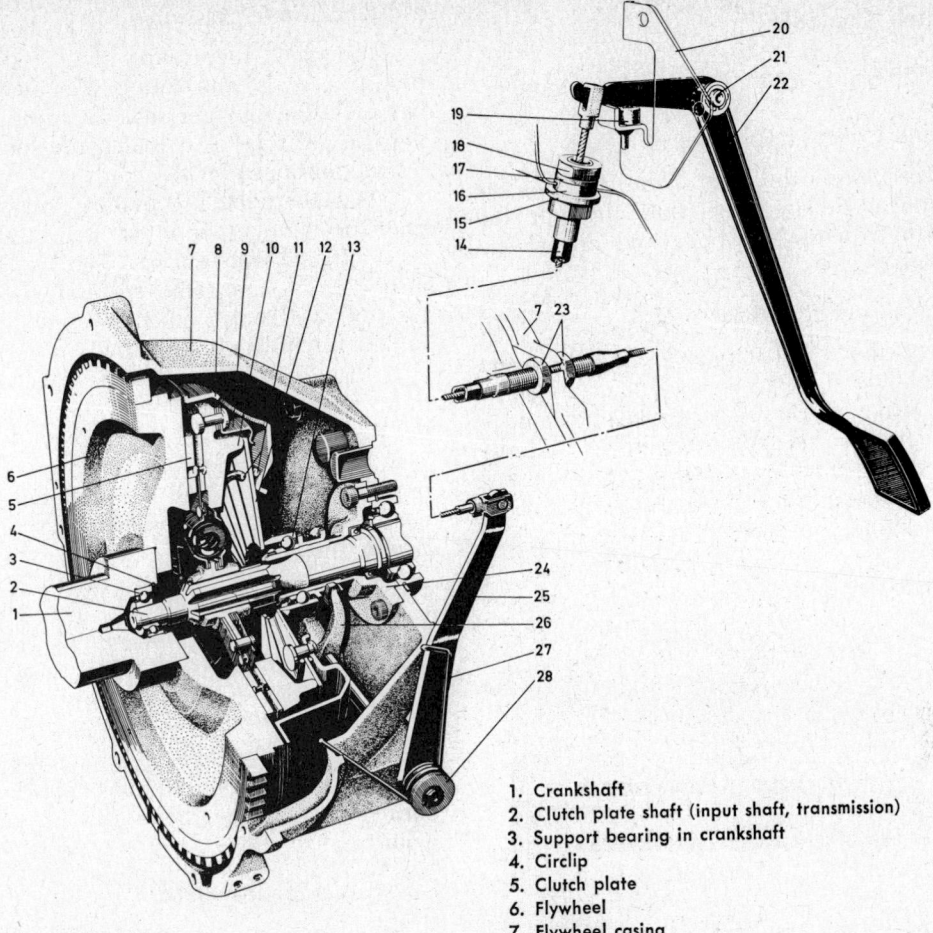

1. Crankshaft
2. Clutch plate shaft (input shaft, transmission)
3. Support bearing in crankshaft
4. Circlip
5. Clutch plate
6. Flywheel
7. Flywheel casing
8. Clutch cover
9. Retainer
10. Thrust plate
11. Support rings
12. Pressure spring
13. Release bearing
14. Clutch wire
15. Washer
16. Rubber bushing
17. Washer
18. Nut
19. Rubber stop
20. Stop bracket
21. Pedal shaft
22. Clutch pedal
23. Adjusting nuts
24. Cover, transmission
25. Lever and release shaft
26. Release fork
27. Return spring
28. Washer

Clutch and clutch controls, 164

Marking of clutch and flywheel

Clutch Controls

120 Series, 1800; Early Production

Master Cylinder Removal

Disconnect the line from the master cylinder. Remove the bolt through the pedal. Unscrew the bolts and lift off the cylinder.

Master Cylinder Disassembly

1. Remove the cap and empty out the brake fluid.
2. Take off the rubber cover and remove the circlip. Take out the plunger and the other parts from the cylinder.
3. Remove the retainer for the check valve from the plunger and separate the parts.

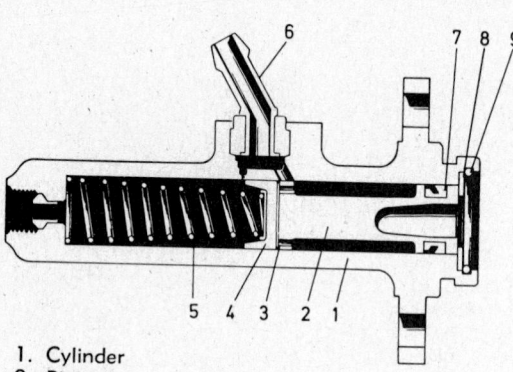

1. Cylinder
2. Piston
3. Washer
4. Piston seal
5. Spring
6. Connection pipe to
   fluid reservoir
7. Piston seal
8. Washer
9. Snap-ring

Hydraulic clutch master cylinder.

Master Cylinder Inspection

Wash all the parts in clean brake fluid and then check them for wear and other damage. The cylinder must be carefully examined internally. There must be no scoring or scratches on the polished surface. Scratches may be removed with very fine emery cloth. Examine the plunger seals for cracks or scoring on the edges. Also check that they are not swollen. The seals must be replaced if there is the slightest sign of any defect.

Master Cylinder Assembly

Note that there are two types of plungers, seals, and spring. The new type has only one plunger seal. In reconditioning the old type of cylinder, the following instructions must be observed:

When changing the plunger, make sure that the plunger is fitted with the new type of seal and spring. The outer seal must always be removed and the new type of seal spring must always be fitted. Follow the instructions below:

1. Place the seal on the plunger. Install the check valve retainers, spring, and plunger.
2. Dip the plunger and check valve in brake fluid and install them in the cylinder. Install the thrust washer, washer, and circlip. Install the rubber cover.

Master Cylinder Installation

Installation is the reverse of removal. Fill with brake fluid and bleed the system.

Slave Cylinder Removal

Disconnect the line. Remove the hose from the retainer. Unhook the return spring. Remove the bolts and lift off the cylinder.

Slave Cylinder Disassembly

Remove the rubber dust cover and the thrust rod. Remove the circlip and take out the plunger and spring.

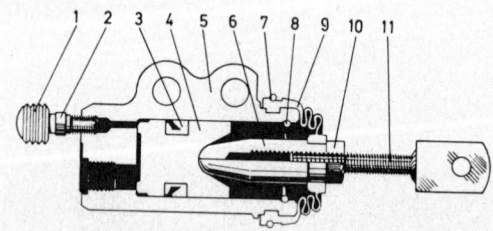

1. Rubber cover
2. Bleeding nipple
3. Piston seal
4. Piston
5. Cylinder
6. Thrust sleeve
7. Snap-ring
8. Stop ring
9. Rubber cover
10. Locknut
11. Thrust rod

Hydraulic clutch slave cylinder.

Clutch Specifications

	B16 Engine in. (mm.)	B18 Engine in. (mm.)	B20 Engine in. (mm.)	B30 Engine in. (mm.)
Clutch Pedal Free Travel	.37"—.59" (10-15)	.37"—.59" (10-15)	.37"—.59" (10-15)	.37"—.59" (10-15)
Clutch Yoke Free Travel	.12" (3)	.12" (3)	.12" (3)	.12" (3)
Type	Single plate dry disc	Single dry plate disc	Single dry plate disc	Single dry plate disc
Size	8" (203)	8.5" (215.9)	8.5" (215.9)	9"
Pedal-Actuated Control	Mechanical	Hydraulic	Mechanical [1]	Mechanical [1]
Total Friction Area	52.7 sq. in. (340)[2]	68 sq. in. (440)[2]	68,2 sq. in. (440)[2]	72.5 sq. in. (468)[2]
Installed Plate Thickness	.28"—.29" (7—7.5)	.28"—.29" (7—7.5)		
Number and Size of Rivets	16; .14" x .25" (3.5 x 6.5)	16; .14" x .21" (3.5 x 5.5)	16; .14" x .21" (3.5 x 5.5)	
Number of Springs; length, loaded under 188–199 lb. (85.5–90.5 kg)	6; 1.5" (38)	6; 1.5" (38)		
Distance between Flywheel and Contact Surface of Clutch Levers with Throw-out Bearing	1.81" (46)	1.81" (46)		
Adjustment of Clutch Levers:		Alternative 1: .29" (7.5) below adjusting jig hub (SVO2065) within ±.06" (1.5) and within .01" (.25) of each other.	Adjustment 41.5" in clutch fixture SVO2322 with packing blocks No. O.	Alternative 2: Adjustment 40.5" in clutch fixture SVO2322 with packing blocks No. O.

1 Right-hand steering and 1800S-hydraulic control.

Slave Cylinder Assembly

Dip the plunger and seal in brake fluid. Install the seal on the plunger. Install the spring and plunger in the cylinder. Install the circlip, the thrust rod, and the rubber dust cover.

Slave Cylinder Installation

Installation is the reverse of removal. Bleed the system and adjust the clutch release fork travel.

Bleeding the Hydraulic System

Check that the container is filled with brake fluid. Remove the bleeder valve rubber cap on the control cylinder. Attach a bleeder hose to the nipple and immerse the other end of the hose in a container filled with brake fluid. Open the bleeder nipple and depress the clutch pedal. Close the bleeder nipple while the pedal is fully depressed. Then release the pedal. Repeat this procedure until brake fluid free from air bubbles runs out. Fill the container with brake fluid up to the level mark (fluid level).

120 SERIES, 1800, LATE PRODUCTION; 140 SERIES

Clutch Cable Replacement

1. Unhook the return spring for the clutch release fork. Loosen the rear nut and the front nut a couple of turns. Remove the cable from the release fork.

2. Loosen the clamp holding the cable to the reinforcing member of the wheel housing.

3. Remove the panel under the instrument panel on the 140 series. Remove the bearing bolt for the pedal. Disconnect the cable from the pedal. Remove the bracket for the pedal stop (early production). Unscrew the nut for the cable sleeve. Remove the cable.

4. Install the new cable. Adjust the pedal travel and play.

TRANSMISSION

The earliest Volvo transmissions, Types H1 through H6, were three speed with synchronized second and third gears. The fully synchronized transmissions have type designations M30, M40, and M400. The M30 is a three speed unit and the M40

and M400 are four speed units. The M40 is a synchronized four speed unit with somewhat higher gear ratios in first, second and reverse. The M400 is used only on the 164. Types designated M31, M41, and M410 are M30 and M40 units equipped with overdrive. All gears, excepting reverse, are always in mesh. In neutral, gears on the main shaft rotate freely in bronze bushings.

Oil Seal Replacement

1. Carry out steps 1-4 (120 series) and 1-5 (140 series) under Removal.

2. Loosen the yoke (flange) nut. Pull off the yoke (flange).

3. Pull out the old oil seal with a seal puller. Install the new seal with the help of a sleeve.

4. Press on the yoke (flange). Install the remaining parts.

Removal—120 Series

1. Drain coolant. Disconnect the upper radiator hose and the hoses from the engine to the heater. Take off the exhaust pipe at the manifold flange. Disconnect the battery cable and the wire to the oil pressure gauge. Unscrew the thermometer body and sender of the oil pressure gauge. Disconnect the throttle control.

2. Remove the rubber boot and shift lever.

3. Jack up the vehicle and support on blocks. Drain the oil from the transmission.

4. Support the transmission with a jack. Loosen and remove the crossmember under the transmission. Disconnect the front universal joint from the transmission yoke (flange). Disconnect the speedometer cable. Place a wooden block between the engine and firewall and lower the jack. Disconnect the leads for the backup light.

5a. Vehicles with B16 engine: Loosen the bolts which hold the transmission to the clutch casing. Screw out the bolts. Pull out the transmission to the rear.

5b. Vehicles with B18 or B20 engines: Loosen the transmission retaining bolts with an 8 mm. or ⅜" socket. Pull out the transmission to the rear.

Removal—140 Series

1. Install lifting apparatus on the engine. Place the lifting hook around the exhaust pipe.

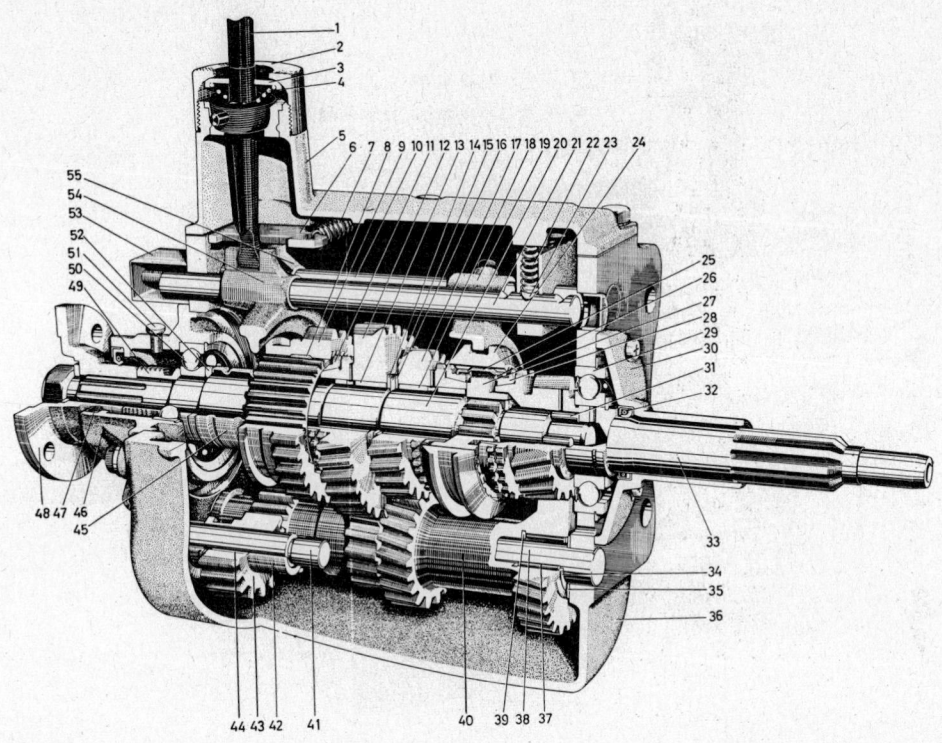

1. Shift lever
2. Cover
3. Washer
4. Spring
5. Cover
6. Sliding plate
7. Spring
8. Engaging spring
9. Engaging sleeve and reverse gear
10. Selector rail, 2nd and 3rd gears
11. Synchronizing cone
12. 1st gear
13. Bushing
14. Thrust washer
15. Circlip
16. Thrust washer
17. 2nd gear
18. Bushing
19. Selector fork for 2nd and 3rd speed

20. Mainshaft
21. Selector fork, 1st and reverse
22. Spring
23. Interlock ball
24. Engaging sleeve, 2nd and 3rd gears
25. Engaging spring
26. Snap ring
27. Synchronizing hub
28. Synchronizing cone
29. Ball bearing
30. Front cover
31. Roller bearing
32. Oil seal
33. Input shaft
34. Spacer washer
35. Thrust washer
36. Housing
37. Needle bearing

38. Countershaft
39. Spacer washer
40. Idler gear
41. Reverse shaft
42. Spacer sleeve
43. Reverse gear
44. Bushing
45. Spacer sleeve
46. Rear cover
47. Oil seal
48. Flange
49. Speedometer worm gear
50. Ball bearing
51. Air-venting nipple
52. Thrust washer
53. End casing
54. Selector fork for 1st and reverse
55. Striker

M30 transmission

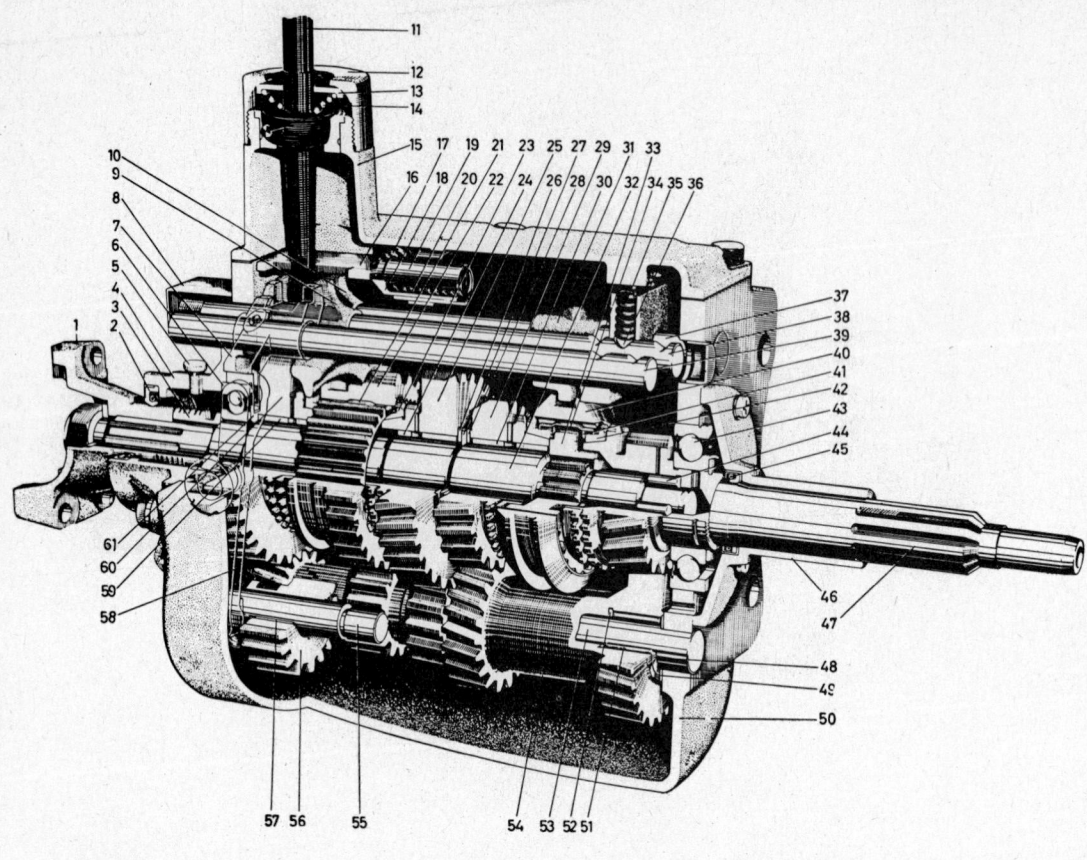

1. Flange
2. Oil seal
3. Speedometer worm gear
4. Rear cover
5. Breather nipple
6. Ball bearing
7. Striker (cutaway view)
8. End casing
9. Selector fork, 1st and 2nd gears
10. Striker
11. Gear lever
12. Cover
13. Washer
14. Spring
15. Cover
16. Sliding plate
17. Spring
18. Sleeve (reverse catch)
19. Sleeve
20. Spring
21. Engaging spring

22. Engaging sleeve and gear wheel for reverse
23. Synchronizing cone
24. Bushing
25. Gear wheel for 2nd gear
26. Thrust washer
27. Lock ring
28. Thrust washer
29. Gear wheel for 3rd gear
30. Bushing
31. Selection fork, 3rd and 4th gears
32. Mainshaft
33. Synchronizing hub
34. Engaging spring
35. Spring
36. Interlock ball
37. Selection rail for 3rd and 4th gears
38. Selection rail for 1st and 2nd gears
39. Selector rail for reverse

40. Engaging sleeve
41. Snap ring
42. Synchronizing cone
43. Ball bearing
44. Roller bearing
45. Oil seal
46. Front cover
47. Input shaft
48. Spacing washer
49. Thrust washer
50. Housing
51. Needle bearing
52. Spacing washer
53. Countershaft
54. Idle gear
55. Reverse shaft
56. Reverse gear
57. Bushing
58. Striker lever (cutaway view)
59. Bushing
60. Gear wheel for 1st gear
61. Thrust washer

M40 transmission.

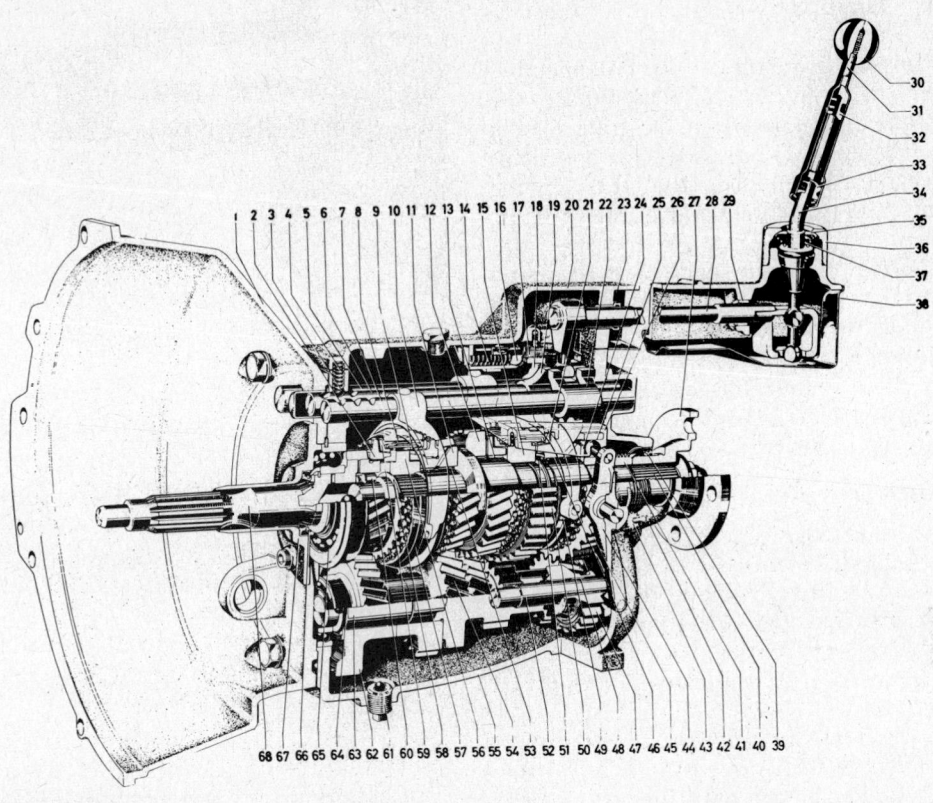

1. Clutch casing	24. Thrust washer	47. Reverse gear
2. Engaging ring	25. Ball bearing	48. Bushing
3. Interlock ball	26. Selector fork, reverse gear	49. Slide register
4. Spring	27. Flange	50. Engaging sleeve and reverse gear
5. Selector rail, reverse gear	28. Shaft	51. Circlip
6. Selector rail for 1st and 2nd gears	29. Bushing	52. Reverse gear shaft
7. Selector rail for 3rd and 4th gears	30. Shift lever knob	53. Needle bearing
8. Flange	31. Shift lever, upper section	54. Gear
9. Spring	32. Rubber bushing	55. Transmission housing
10. Selector fork	33. Rubber bushing	56. Synchronizing hub
11. 3rd gear	34. Shift lever, lower section	57. Engaging sleeve
12. 2nd gear	35. Washer	58. Circlip
13. Needle bearing	36. Cover	59. Synchronizing cone
14. Spring	37. Spring	60. Needle bearing
15. Synchronizing hub, 1st—2nd gears	38. Protective casing	61. Drain plug
16. Interlock ball	39. Oil seal	62. Gear
17. Sliding plate	40. Mainshaft	63. Countershaft
18. Flange	41. Speedometer drive	64. Ball bearing
19. Selector fork, 1st and 2nd gears	42. Rear cover	65. Ball bearing
20. Transmission cover	43. Speedometer pinion	66. Oil seal
21. Synchronizing cone	44. Shift lever	67. Cover
22. Flange	45. 1st gear	68. Input shaft
23. Bushing	46. Needle bearing	

M400 transmission

2. Remove the rubber boot and shift lever.

3. Jack up the vehicle and support on blocks. Drain the oil from the transmission.

4. Loosen and remove the crossmember under the transmission. Disconnect the front universal joint from the transmission yoke (flange). Disconnect the speedometer cable. Disconnect the rear engine mounts and the bracket for the exhaust pipe.

5. Lower the rear end of the engine about 2 cm. (0.8″). Then disconnect the backup lights and overdrive.

6. Remove the right upper and left lower transmission bolts. Install two guide pins. Remove the other two bolts. Pull the transmission backward and lower it.

Disassembly

The following description applies to units without overdrive. If the transmission has overdrive, remove the overdrive. Then carry out the operations described below as far as necessary:

1. Place the transmission in a support fixture.

2. Unscrew the bolts for the transmission cover. Lift off the cover. Remove the springs and interlock balls for the selector rails.

3. Remove the cover over the selector rails. Unscrew the selector fork bolts.

4a. M30: Slide the selector fork backward to the reverse position. Drive out the pin.

4b. M40: Slide the selector fork backward to 1st speed position. Drive out the pin slightly (it must not foul 1st gear). Then move the selector fork forward sufficiently to allow the pin to pass in front of the gear. Drive out the pin.

5. Slide out the selector rails. When doing this, hold the selector forks so that they do not jam on the rails. Remove the selector forks.

6. Unscrew the bolts for the rear cover. Turn the cover so that it does not lock the shafts for the idler and reverse gears (early production only. On late production, there is no locking tab.) Drive out the shaft for the idler gear. The shaft must be driven out backward. Let the idler gear fall into the bottom of the transmission.

7. Pull out the mainshaft.

SVO 2301
SVO 2878

Removing reverse gear shaft

8. Remove the cover over the input shaft. Pry out the oil seal from the cover with a screwdriver.

9. Drive out the input shaft. If necessary, remove the circlip and press the ball bearing off the shaft.

10. Take out the idler gear. Pull out the shaft for the reverse gear. Take out the reverse gear and other parts.

MAINSHAFT

M30 Transmission

1a. Transmission with overdrive (M31): Remove the circlip and press off the rotor for the overdrive oil pump. Remove the circlip for the mainshaft rear bearing. Slide the engaging sleeve for 1st and reverse forward. Place the shaft in a press and support under the rear cover. Press out the shaft.

1b. Transmission without overdrive: Unscrew the yoke (flange) nut. Pull off the yoke (flange). Slide the engaging sleeve for 1st and reverse forward. Place the shaft in a press and support under the rear cover. Press out the shaft with a drift.

2. Remove the thrust washer, spacer

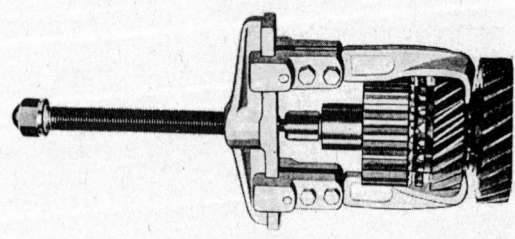

Removing front synchronizer.

sleeve, engaging sleeves, yoke (flange), and snap ring from the shaft.

3. Remove the circlip on the front end of the shaft. Pull off the synchronizing hub and 2nd gear with a suitable puller. Remove the thrust washer.

4. Remove the circlip and then the thrust washer, 1st gear, synchronizing cone and spring.

5. Remove the oil seal from the rear cover and take out the speedometer gear. If necessary, remove the circlip and press out the ball bearing.

M40 Transmission

1a. Transmission with overdrive (M41): Remove the circlip and press off the rotor for the overdrive oil pump. Remove the circlip for the mainshaft rear bearing. Slide the engaging sleeve for 1st and 2nd forward. Place the shaft in a press and support under 1st gear. Press out the shaft.

1b. Transmissions without overdrive: Unscrew the yoke (flange) nut. Slide the engaging sleeve for 1st and 2nd forward. Place the shaft in a press and support under 1st gear. Press out the shaft with a drift.

2. Remove the synchronizing cone, thrust washer, engaging sleeves, engaging springs and snap rings from the shaft.

3. Remove the circlip on the front end of the shaft. Pull off the synchronizing hub and 3rd gear with a puller. Remove the thrust washer.

4. Remove the circlip and then the thrust washer, 2nd gear, synchronizing cone and spring.

5. Remove the oil seal from the rear cover and take out the speedometer gear. If necessary, remove the circlip and press out the ball bearing.

Inspection

Check the gears, particularly for cracks or chips on the tooth surfaces. Damaged or worn gears must be replaced. Check the synchronizing cones and all the other synchronizing components. Damaged or worn parts must be replaced. Check the ball bearings, particularly for scoring or cracks on the races or balls.

Assembly

MAINSHAFT

M30 Transmission

1. Press the ball bearing into the rear

cover with a drift. Install the circlip. There are different sizes of circlips, so select one which fits snugly in the groove.

2. Transmission without overdrive: Place the speedometer gear on the bearing in the rear cover. Press in the oil seal with a drift.

3. Install the snap rings, engaging springs and engaging sleeve for the 1st gear synchronizer on the mainshaft. Install the snap rings. Install the spacer sleeve and thrust washer.

4a. Transmission without overdrive: Place the rear cover on the shaft. Ensure that the speedometer gear is positioned correctly. Install the yoke (flange). Use a sleeve which fits into the recess in the yoke (flange), press on the cover and yoke (flange). Install the washer and nut for the yoke (flange). Tighten the nut.

4b. Transmission with overdrive (M31): Place the rear cover and ball bearing on a cushioning ring or sleeve. Install the thrust washer and spacer sleeve. Press in the shaft. Select a circlip of suitable thick-

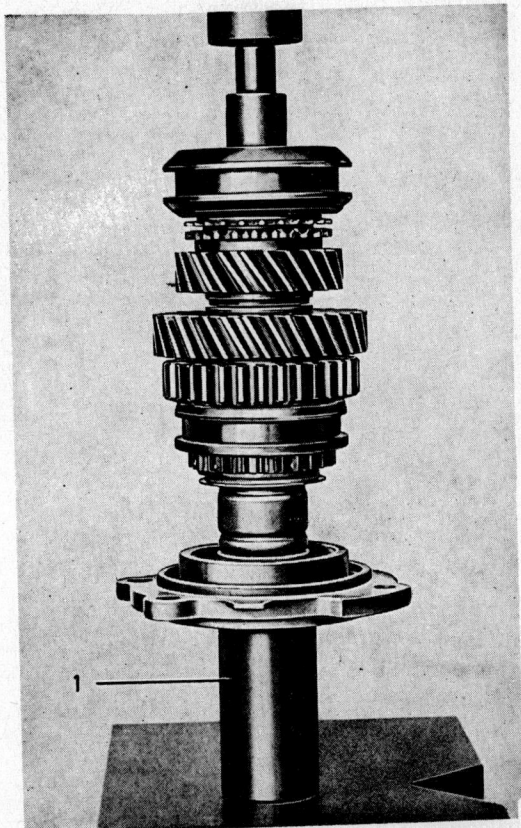

1

Installing rear cover, M31

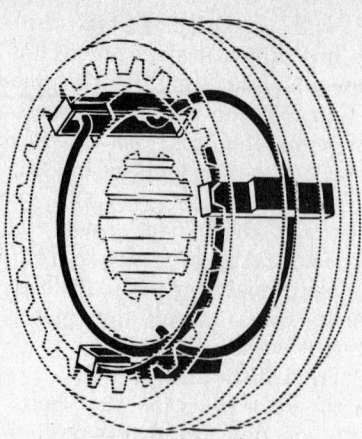

Synchronizer assembly

ness and install it. Install the key, rotor for the oil pump, and circlip.

5. Install the synchronizing cone, 1st gear, and thrust washer on the shaft. Select a circlip which fits snugly into the groove on the shaft and install the shaft.

6. Install the thrust washer, 2nd gear, and synchronizing cone on the shaft. Assemble the 2nd and 3rd gear synchronizing parts. Install the snap rings. Then install the synchronizer on the mainshaft. Be sure that the synchronizer is correctly installed. The turned groove on the engaging sleeve should face rearward. Select a circlip which fits snugly into the groove and install it.

M40 Transmission

1. Press the ball bearing into the rear cover. Install the circlip. There are different sizes of circlips, so select one which fits snugly into the groove.

2. Transmission without overdrive: Place the speedometer gear on the bearing in the rear cover. Press in the oil seal with a drift.

3. Install the parts for the 1st and 2nd gear synchronizer on the mainshaft. Install the snap rings.

4a. Transmission without overdrive: Install the synchronizing cone, 1st gear, and thrust washer. Place the rear cover on the shaft. Ensure that the speedometer gear is positioned correctly. Install the yoke (flange). Use a sleeve which fits into the recess in the yoke (flange), press on the cover and yoke (flange). Install the washer and nut for the yoke (flange). Tighten the nut.

Installing rear cover, M40

4b. Transmission with overdrive (M41): Place the rear cover and ball bearing on a cushioning ring or sleeve. Install the thrust washer, 1st gear, and synchronizing cone. Press in the shaft. Select a circlip of suitable thickness and install it. Install the key, the rotor for the oil pump, and circlip.

5. Install the synchronizing cone, 2nd gear, and thrust washer on the shaft. Select a circlip which fits snugly into the groove on the shaft and install it.

6. Install the thrust washer, 3rd gear, and synchronizing cone on the shaft. Assemble the 3rd and 4th gear synchronizing parts. Install the snap rings. Then install the synchronizer on the mainshaft. Ensure that the synchronizer is correctly fitted. The turned groove should face rearward. Select a circlip of the correct thickness and install it.

ASSEMBLING THE TRANSMISSION

1a. M30 Transmission: Install reverse gear, spacer sleeves, and reverse shaft. Ensure that the groove in the reverse shaft is turned correctly (early production). The late production reverse shaft with turned

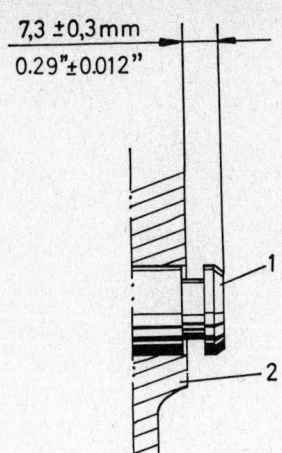

7,3 ±0,3 mm
0.29"±0.012"

Installing the reverse shaft. 1 is reverse shaft; 2 is housing.

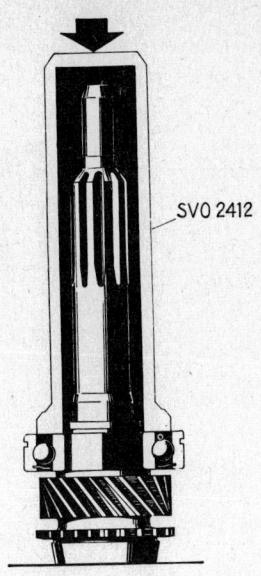

SVO 2412

Installing ball bearing on input shaft.

groove is installed so that it projects 7.0-7.6 mm. (0.276-0.300") outside the transmission housing.

1b. M40 Transmission Install the striker lever and striker. Install the reverse gear and reverse shaft. Make sure that the groove in the reverse shaft (early production) is turned correctly. The late production reverse shaft with turned groove is installed so that it projects 7.0-7.6 mm. (0.276-0.300") outside the housing.

2. Place a dummy shaft in the idler gear. Put in spacer washers and needles (24 in each bearing). Use grease to hold the needles and washers in position.

3. Attach the washers to the housing with grease and guide them into position, with the centering plugs. Lay the idler gear in the bottom of the housing.

4. Press the bearing onto the input shaft with the help of a drift. Select a circlip of suitable thickness and install it. Place the 14 bearing rollers for the mainshaft in position in the input shaft. Use grease to hold the rollers in place. Press the input shaft into position in the housing. Press the oil seal into the cover with a drift. Then install the cover over the input shaft. Do not forget the O-rings for the bolts (late production).

5. Place the mainshaft in the housing. Turn the rear cover so that the countershaft can be fitted.

6. Turn the transmission upside down. Install the countershaft from the rear. Hold against dummy shaft. Ensure that the thrust washers do not loosen and fall down.

7a. Transmissions without overdrive: Turn the rear cover correctly so that it locks the reverse shaft (early production). Install the bolts for the cover.

7b. Transmission with overdrive: Turn the rear cover correctly so that it locks the reverse shaft (early production). Make sure that the rotor for the overdrive oil pump is turned. Install the overdrive. Use new locking washers for the intermediate flange.

8. Install the selector rails and forks. Move the selector fork to the rear position when fitting the pin. Use a new pin. Fit the cover over the selector rails. If the end caps at the front end of the housing have been removed, these should be replaced so that the center end cap should project

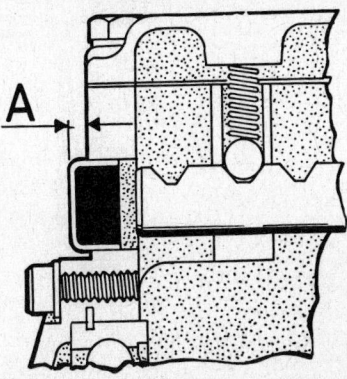

A

Installing end cap over selector rail. A should be about 0.16".

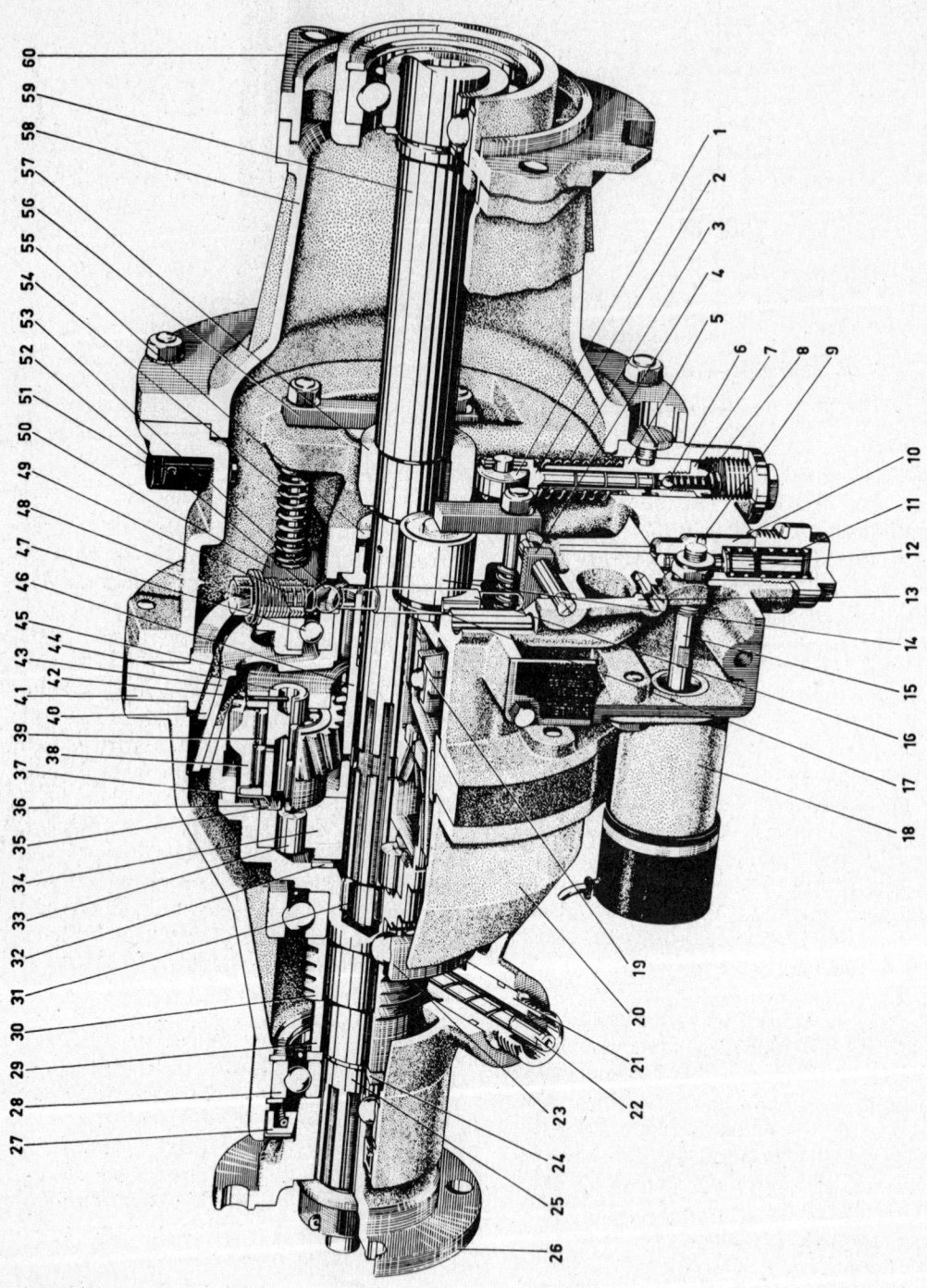

Overdrive unit.

1. Roller
2. Pump lunger
3. Spring
4. Lever
5. Pump cylinder
6. Ball
7. Valve seating
8. Spring
9. O ring
10. Valve seating, relief valve
11. Spring
12. Valve plunger
13. Lever
14. Piston
15. Armature for solenoid
16. Valve rod (cutaway view)
17. Plunger seal
18. Solenoid
19. Thrust bearing retainer
20. Housing, rear part
21. Bushing
22. Speedometer gear, small
23. Ball bearing
24. Thrust washer
25. Output shaft
26. Coupling flange
27. Sealing ring
28. Ball bearing
29. Spacing sleeve
30. Speedometer gear, large
31. Needle bearing
32. Thrust washer
33. Freewheel rollers
34. Freewheel hub
35. Oil deflector plate
36. Lock ring
37. Oil catcher
38. Planet gear
39. Needle bearing
40. Clutch facing
41. Brake drum
42. Locking pin
43. Clutch disc
44. Shaft
45. Planet gear carrier
46. Sunwheel
47. Ball bearing
48. Housing, front part
49. Plug over control valve
50. Pressure plate
51. Breather nipple
52. Tappet (cutaway)
53. Ball (cutaway)
54. Spring
55. Bushing
56. Pressure plate
57. Cam
58. Extension piece
59. Input shaft (mainshaft)
60. Rear cover, gearbox

about 4 mm. (0.16″) outside the face of the housing.

9. Place the interlock balls and springs in position. Install the transmission cover. Check that all the gears engage and disengage freely.

Installation

Make sure that the guide pins are in place. Installation is the reverse of removal. Fill up with oil.

OVERDRIVE UNIT

The overdrive unit is of the epicylic type and is attached to the rear end of the transmission. It is engaged electro-hydraulically. On the transmission cover there is

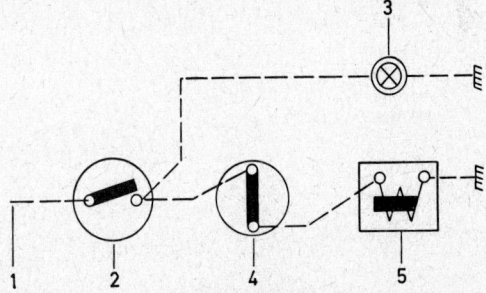

1. Lead from fusebox
2. Overdrive actuating switch
3. Warning lamp
4. Switch on transmission
5. Solenoid on overdrive unit

Overdrive electrical circuit

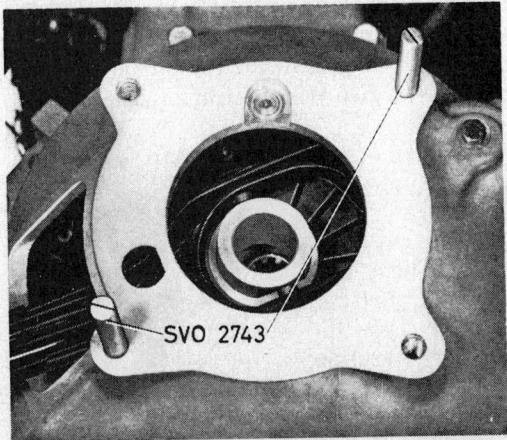

Transmission guide pins

a contact which cuts in when 2nd or 3rd gear on the M31 transmission or 4th gear on the M41 transmission is engaged. The overdrive can operate only when this contact is cut in. The overdrive is actuated by a switch underneath the steering wheel or on the instrument panel. This switch closes a circuit thru the contact on the transmission to an actuating solenoid on the overdrive.

The solenoid has two windings, a heavy operating winding and a fine holding winding. The operating winding causes the solenoid armature to move in such a way that the operating valve in the overdrive opens. After the valve has opened, the current through the operating winding is cut off

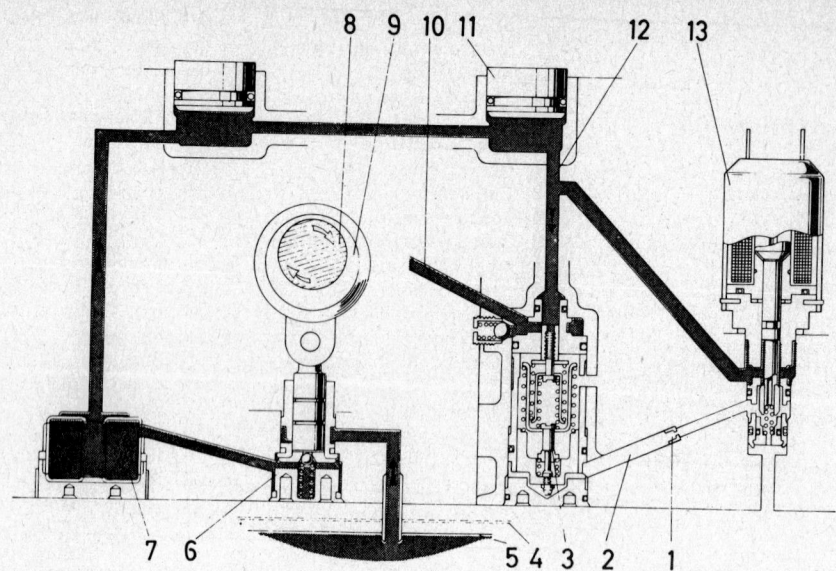

1. Nozzle (restriction)
2. Passage between control valve and relief valve
3. Relief valve
4. Pre-filter
5. Oil sump
6. Oil pump
7. Fine filter

8. Transmission mainshaft
9. Eccentric
10. Passage between relief valve and mainshaft
11. Piston
12. Channel connecting oil pump, hydraulic cylinder, and control and relief valves
13. Control valve and solenoid.

Overdrive hydraulic system (late production)

and the valve is then held in the open position by the holding winding. There is a plunger pump in the overdrive unit which is driven by a cam on the mainshaft. When the operating valve opens, oil under pressure from the pump flows through the valve to two cylinders. The pistons in these cylinders then press the clutch sliding member forward to engage with the brake ring, thus engaging the overdrive.

In-Car Service Operations

OIL PRESSURE CHECK

1. Disengage the overdrive (late production) so that any residual oil pressure is released. On the early production unit it may be necessary to engage and disengage the overdrive 10-12 times in order to do this.

2. Remove the plug over the operating valve and connect a pressure gauge. The operating valve spring, spring plunger, and ball should remain in position.

3. Start and run the vehicle. (Testing can also be done with the vehicle jacked up.) At a speed of 30-37 mph in overdrive, the pressure gauge should give a reading of 500-570 psi (early production: 470-540 psi).

OIL STRAINER CLEANING

The oil strainer should be cleaned at every transmission oil change. First drain the oil by removing the plug marked DRAIN under the oil strainer. Cleaning is as follows:

1. Remove the cover. Take out the oil strainer and magnetic element. Clean the oil strainer in a safe solvent. Blow dry with compressed air.

2. Check that the oil strainer gasket is in good condition. Turn the steel covered side to face the housing and place the gasket in position.

3. Assemble the three magnetic washers (late production) so that they adhere.

4. Fit the oil strainer, magnetic element, a new gasket, and the cover.

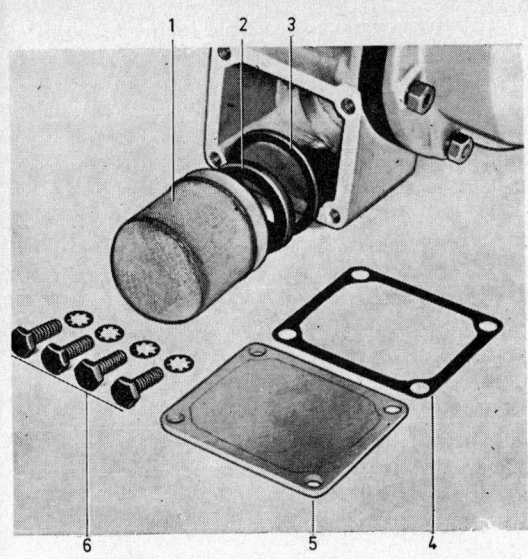

1. Strainer
2. Magnetic element (late production units only)
3. Gasket
4. Cover gasket
5. Cover
6. Bolts

Removing the oil strainer

OPERATING VALVE CHECK AND ADJUSTMENT

1. Jack up the vehicle and place blocks under the front and rear axles.

2. Remove the cover over the operating valve arm. Engage the overdrive (with engine stationary and 4th gear engaged).

Adjusting the operating valve. 1 is a .19" diameter pin.

When the operating valve is correctly adjusted it should be possible to insert a 4.75 mm. (.19") diameter pin through the hole in the arm into the body. If not, adjust the position of the arm until this can be done.

3. Check the current through the solenoid with the overdrive engaged. This should be not more than 1 amp. with a 12 volt system and not more than 2 amps. with a 6 volt system. If the current is 10-12 amps. or higher, this means that the solenoid armature does not move sufficiently to cut off the operating current. Excessive current will ruin the solenoid.

OIL PUMP CHECK

1. Disengage the overdrive (on early production units, by engaging and disengaging 10-12 times) in order to release any residual oil pressure. Jack up the vehicle and place blocks under the front and rear axles. Remove the drain plug and let the oil run out.

2. Remove the plug under the oil pump and take out the spring and ball. Remove the non-return body. Clean and check the parts.

3. Feel with a piece of wire against the pump plunger to determine that the pump operates when the output shaft is rotating. (Turn the engine a few times with the starter motor with a gear engaged and the lead from the ignition coil disconnected.) The pump plunger stroke should be 3.2 mm. (.126") early production, or 4 mm. (.157") late production. If the pump plun-

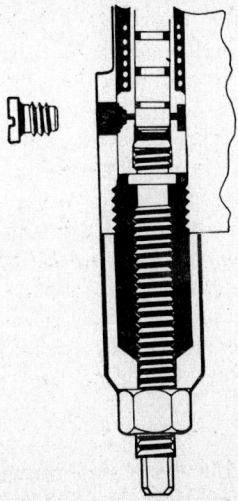

Removing the oil pump with a special puller

ger stroke is shorter than this, the pump must be removed.

4. The pump is removed as follows: Loosen the pump retaining bolt through the hole in the extension casing. Attach a puller in place of the non-return body and pull out the pump.

5. Dismantle the pump and check it carefully.

6. The pump and pump valve are replaced in the reverse order of removal. Check that the washer for the plug is in good condition. Fill with oil.

RELIEF VALVE CHECK

1. Disengage the overdrive (on early production units, by engaging and disengaging 10-12 times) in order to release any residual oil pressure. Jack up the vehicle and place blocks under the front and rear axles. Remove the drain plug and let the oil run out.

2. Remove the plug and take out the spring and valve plunger. Pull out the valve body with a small hook.

3. Clean and check oil seals carefully. Replace the parts in the reverse order of removal. When altering the oil pressure with the washer under the spring, note that a 0.1 mm. (.004″) thick washer will alter the pressure about 14 psi.

OPERATING VALVE CLEANING

1. Disengage the overdrive (on early production units, by engaging and disengaging 10-12 times) in order to release any residual oil pressure.

2. Remove the plug over the operating valve and the spring, spring plunger, ball, and valve rod. The ball can be lifted up with a small magnet or a looped piece of fine steel wire. The valve rod can be removed with a magnet or pointed piece of wood pushed into the valve rod hole.

3. Clean the parts carefully. The valve rod hole (late production units) should be cleaned out with a 3.1-3.2 mm. drill and the valve hole with a 1.1 mm. drill. For the early production valve rod use 3.1-3.2 mm. and .7 mm. drills.

4. Replace the parts in the reverse order of removal.

Removal

1. Carry out steps 1-4 under Removal Procedure for M30 and M40 Transmission. Drain the overdrive unit.

2. Disconnect the cable to the solenoid.

3. Unscrew the bolts which hold the overdrive unit to the intermediate flange and remove the unit.

Disassembly

The following procedure describes complete disassembly of the overdrive unit.

1. Remove the cover over the oil strainer and the cover over the operating lever. Take out the oil strainer. Unscrew the bolts and lift out the solenoid.

2. Bend down the locking tabs, unscrew and remove the nuts for the piston bridge pieces. Remove the bridge pieces. Pull out the pistons with the help of pliers.

3. Unscrew the nuts which hold the brake ring, front casing, and rear casing together. Loosen the bolts evenly, in sequence, in order to avoid distortion. Lift off the front casing and brake ring.

4. Lift out the clutch sliding member complete with thrust bearing and sunwheel. Remove the four return springs and thrust plate. Remove the circlips for the sunwheel and bearing. Take out the sunwheel. Pull off the bearing from the clutch sliding member. Press out the bearing from the retainer.

5. Lift off the planet gears and planet carrier. Remove the locking pins for the planet gear shafts by pressing them out with a drift and then removing them with pliers. If this cannot be done, drill out the pins. Press out the planet gear shafts and remove the planet gears. The planet gear needle bearing can be pressed out with a drift.

6. Loosen the screw and pull out the bushing and speedometer pinion. Loosen the nut for the coupling flange. Pull off the flange. Place the housing in a press. Press out the output shaft.

7. Remove the circlip (late production units) and oil thrower (retaining washer) which holds the uni-directional clutch on the output shaft. Lift out the parts of the uni-directional clutch. Remove the thrust washer. If necessary, pull out the needle bearing in the output shaft. Pull off the output shaft bearing.

8. Remove the plugs and take out the parts for the operating valve, relief valve, and outlet valve for the pump. Remove the locking screw and take out the oil pump. If the pump is difficult to remove, first re-

move the non-return body. Then pull out the pump.

Inspection

Before inspecting, wash all parts thoroughly in a safe solvent. Then carefully check all parts for wear, cracks or other damage. Check the ball and needle bearings for cracks, wear, or other damage on the balls, needles, and races.

Check the uni-directional clutch. The rollers and races must not show any signs of cracking or nicking. Check that the outer race fits securely in the output shaft. Check the planet gears. If there is any tooth damage, replace the gears. Check the linings on the clutch sliding member for burning or wear. Check that the return springs are in good condition. Check the surface on the thrust bushing for the sunwheel in the front casing. It is necessary to replace the bushing if the surface is deeply scored. Due to the close tolerances, the front casing must be replaced with the bushing. Check the oil pump for damage on the plunger and roller.

Check that the plunger slides easily in the body. Make sure that the plunger spring is not damaged. Check the non-return body and ball for burring or scoring. Check the operating valve to make sure that it moves freely in the bore in the front casing.

Check the relief valve. The relief valve plunger and seat are matched so that if either is damaged both must be replaced.

Check the cylinders for the operating pistons for scoring and wear. Make sure that the oil passages are clean.

Assembly

1. Place the front circlip for the bearing in the roller casing. Press in the bearing with a drift.

2. Press the support bearing for the transmission mainshaft in the output shaft with a drift. Press the front bearing on to output shaft.

3. Support the output shaft with a block of wood. Install the speedometer driving gear, spacer, and thrust washer. Press on the rear casing with a drift. Install the circlip for the rear bearing. Press in the oil seal with a drift. Press on the coupling flange with a suitable sleeve. Install the washer and nut. Tighten and lock the nut.

4. Assemble the uni-directional clutch,

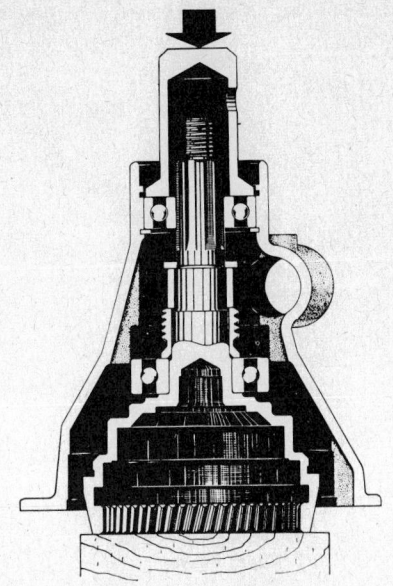

Output shaft installation

spring, and roller cage. Turn the roller cage clockwise as far as it will go and lock it in this position with a key. Put in the rollers. Tie a piece of string or rubber band around the rollers. Install the thrust washers and then the uni-directional clutch on the output shaft. Install the brass retaining washer. On early production units the washer is attached with center punch marks or chisel indentations. On late production units the washer is attached with a circlip.

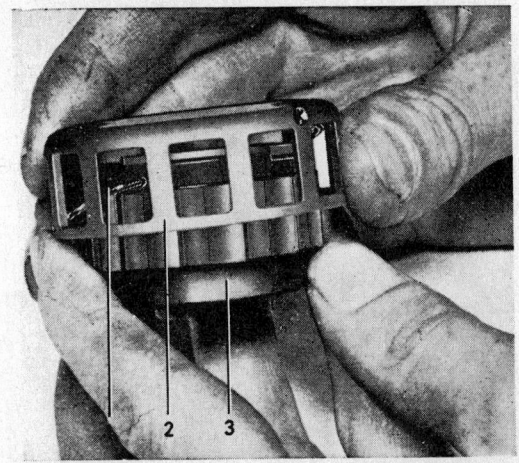

1. Spring
2. Cage
3. Uni-directional clutch

Assembling the uni-directional clutch

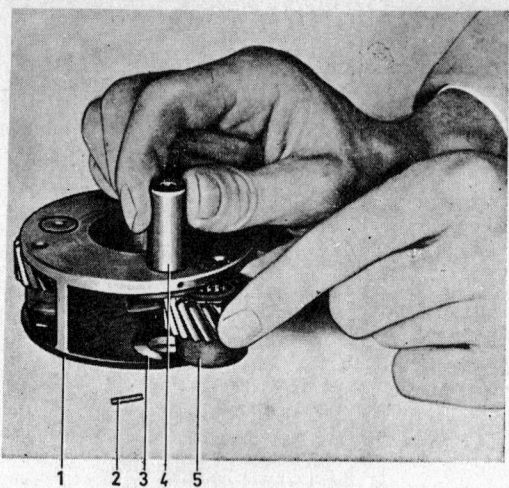

1. Planet carrier
2. Locking pin
3. Thrust washer
4. Shaft
5. Planet gear

Planet gear installation

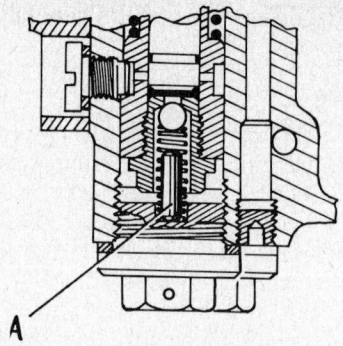

Non-return valve for oil pump. A is guide pin.

5. Press the needle bearings into the planet gears with a drift. The bearings should come slightly below the side surfaces of the gears. Assemble the planet carrier, shafts, washers and planet gears. Line up the splines in the planet carrier and uni-directional clutch with a dummy shaft.

6. Install the sunwheel in the clutch sliding member. Assemble the bolts, thrust bearing, and thrust bearing retainer. Install the thrust bearing on the clutch sliding member.

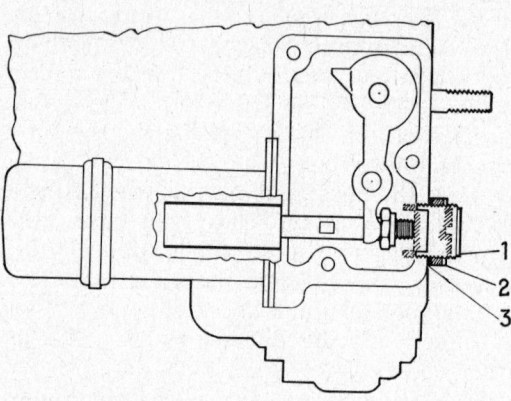

Adjusting the plug. 1 is plug, 2 is locknut, and 3 is washer.

7. Install the operating piston in the front casing. Assemble the clutch sliding member, brake ring, clutch return springs, front casing, and bridge pieces. When assembling, coat both sides of the clutch ring with sealing compound.

8. Place the assembled unit on the rear casing. Line up the splines in the planet carrier and uni-directional clutch with a dummy shaft. Install the washers and nuts. Tighten the nuts a little at a time until they are evenly tightened all around.

9. Install the other parts in the reverse order of removal. Note the following: There are two different types of plug and spring for the non-return valve of the pump. Early production plugs must not be used with late production springs or vice versa. Replacement must be in matched pairs.

Install the guide pin in the non-return valve spring.

Screw in the plug so that the solenoid armature bottoms. Then check that a 4.75 mm. (.19″) diameter pin can be inserted

Assembling the front casing

through the hole in the arm and into the body as shown. Adjust as necessary. After adjustment, screw out the plug 2½ turns, and lock with the lock nut and locking wire.

Installation

Make sure that the cam for the oil pump on the mainshaft is turned upward. Then install the overdrive unit in the reverse order of removal. Fill with oil. Overdrives number 32/3324 and later have force feed lubrication of the planet gear needle bearings and output shaft.

The part number of the transmission mainshaft is unchanged. Thus when fitting a new mainshaft in overdrive number 32/3324 and later, check that the mainshaft is drilled. If a new overdrive unit is installed on a transmission which has an early production mainshaft, the mainshaft must be replaced with an early produc-

tion type. An exception to this is the 32/3333, which does not have force feed lubrication.

AUTOMATIC TRANSMISSION

The automatic transmission is the Borg-Warner type 35. It consists of two main components:

1. A three-element torque converter coupling capable of torque multiplication at an infinitely variable rate between 2:1 and 1:1.

2. A hydraulically operated transmission having a planetary gear set with a valve system which automatically selects a suitable gear in relation to the speed of the car and position of the accelerator pedal. Selector positions are L, D, N, R, and P.

Torque Converter

The torque converter serves both as a clutch and as an extra gear between the

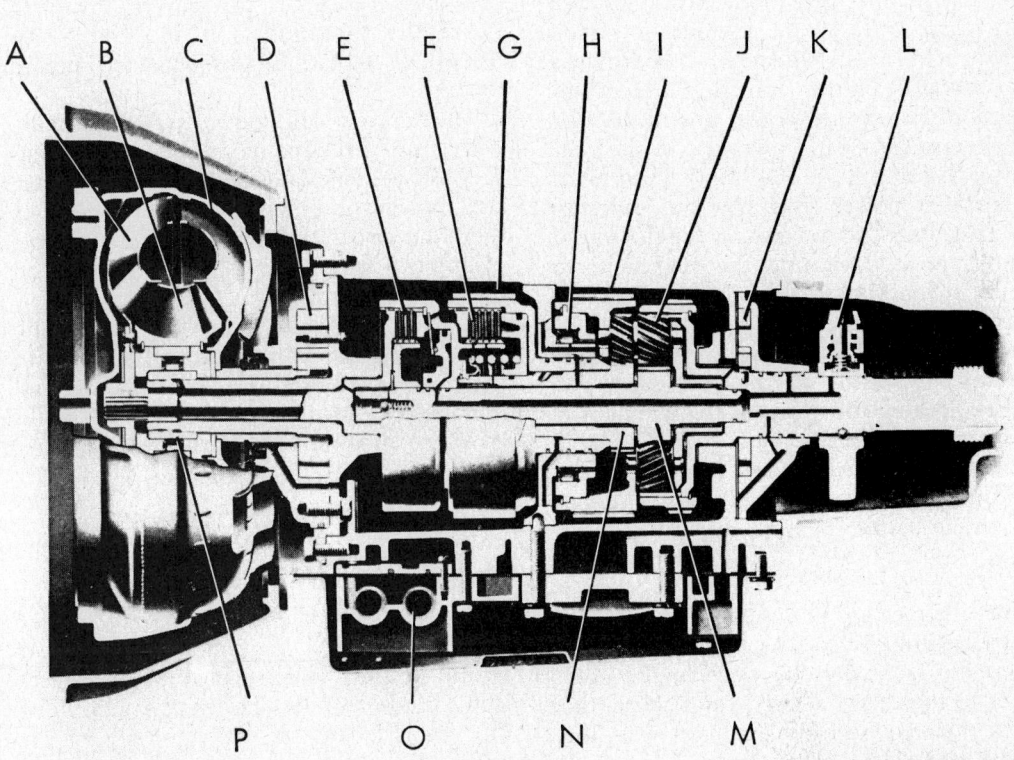

A. Turbine
B. Stator
C. Impeller and cover
D. Front pump
E. Front clutch
F. Rear clutch

G. Front brake band
H. One-way clutch
I. Rear brake band
J. Planetary gear set
K. Rear pump
L. Governor

M. Reverse sun gear
N. Forward sun gear
O. Control system
P. One-way clutch in converter

Borg-Warner type 35 automatic transmission

engine and transmission. It provides a means of obtaining smooth application of engine power to the driving wheels and additional engine torque multiplication in 1st and 2nd gears. The converter also provides low-speed flexibility in 3rd gear. The converter has three main components—an impeller connected to the engine crankshaft, a turbine connected to the input shaft of the transmission, and a stator mounted on a sprag-type one-way clutch on a fixed hub projecting from the transmission case.

Transmission

The transmission consists of a mechanical power transmission system—planetary gear, two clutches, two brake bands, and a one-way clutch—and a hydraulic system—front and rear pump, centrifugal governor, and a control valve system which regulates the fluid pressure and directs the fluid to the transmission components.

PLANETARY GEARS

The planetary gear set consists of two sun gears, two sets of pinions, a pinion carrier and a ring gear. In all forward gears, power enters through the forward sun gear; in reverse, power enters through the reverse sun gear. Power leaves the gear set by the ring gear. The pinions are used to transmit power from the sun gears to the ring gear. In reverse, a single set of pinions is used causing the ring gear to rotate in the opposite direction to the sun gear. In forward gears, a double set of pinions causes the ring gear to rotate in the same direction as the sun gear. The carrier locates the pinions relative to the two sun gears and the ring gear. The gear ratios are obtained by the engagement of hydraulically operated multi-disc clutches and brake bands.

CLUTCHES

The clutches are multi-disc units operated by hydraulic pistons. In all forward gears, the front clutch connects the converter to the forward gear; for reverse, the rear clutch connects the converter to the reverse sun gear.

BRAKE BANDS

Brake bands, operated by hydraulic servos, hold elements of the gear set stationary to effect an output speed reduction and a torque increase. In lockup, the rear band holds the pinion carrier stationary and provides the 1st gear ratio of 2.39:1, and in reverse, a ratio of 2.09:1. The front band holds the reverse sun gear stationary to provide the 2nd gear ratio of 1.45:1.

ONE-WAY CLUTCH

In the drive position, a one-way clutch is used in place of the rear band to prevent the pinion carrier from turning opposite to engine rotation, thus providing a 1st gear ratio of 2.39:1. This one-way clutch, allowing the transmission to freewheel in 1st gear, provides smooth ratio changes from 1st to 2nd and vice versa.

Oil Cooler

The automatic transmission is connected to an oil cooler in the bottom tank of the radiator.

Service

When working on the vehicle, the selector lever should be in P. If the transmission is operable, the car may be towed in N. If the transmission is inoperable the driveshaft should be disconnected before towing.

The transmission control system is made with a great degree of precision and accuracy. Fluid circulates through the converter, transmission, and control system. It is therefore necessary to observe the utmost cleanliness when carrying out any work on the transmission.

Repair instructions for the automatic transmission are limited, in this manual, to in-car service operations, and removal and replacement. More extensive repairs should be left to an authorized repair facility.

IN-CAR SERVICE OPERATIONS

Fluid Level Check

The oil level should be checked every 6,000 miles. When checking, the car should be on a level surface. Move the selector to P and let the engine idle. The dipstick is located on the right side of the engine.

NOTE: *There are different oil level marks for a warm or cold transmission.*

If necessary, fill up with oil to the Max mark. Do not overfill, or the transmission may overheat. The difference between the Min and Max mark is about 1 pint. Use an

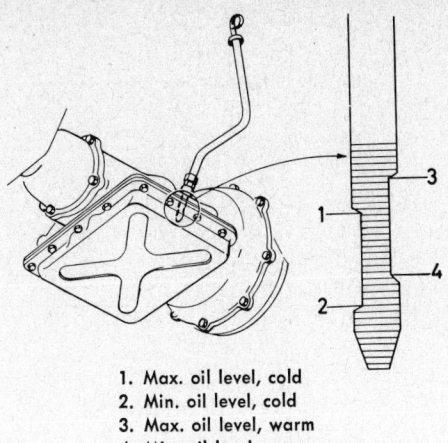

1. Max. oil level, cold
2. Min. oil level, cold
3. Max. oil level, warm
4. Min. oil level, warm

Checking oil level

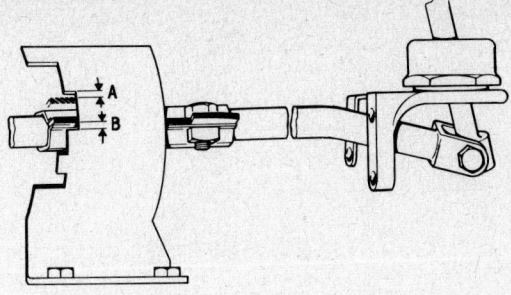

Adjusting selector controls. A should equal B.

oil which is approved as Automatic Transmission Fluid, type F.

Valve Body Assembly R & R

1. Jack up and place blocks under the vehicle. Drain the oil.

NOTE: *The oil may be very hot and cause burns if contact is made with the skin.*

2. Release the bolts for the oil pan and remove it. Carefully remove the oil tubes.

3. Release the throttle cable from the cam. Remove the three bolts securing the valve body assembly to the transmission. Remove the valve body assembly straight down so that it releases from the oil tubes at the front.

4. Make sure that the oil tubes are in position on the front pump body. Place the valve body assembly in position and secure it with the three bolts.

5. Install the throttle cable to the cam. Mount the oil tubes. Check that the magnetic element lies in the oil pan and install the pan. Use a new gasket. Coat the threads on the oil drain plug with sealant.

6. Lower the vehicle, fill with oil.

Selector Control Adjustment

1. Disconnect the pull rod from the lever on the selector shaft. Set the selector lever to N.

2. Set the lever on the transmission to the central position. Adjust the length of the pull rod so that the ball socket can easily be fastened on the ball on the lever.

3. Check the distance to the link in N and in D. The clearance should be the same for both positions.

4. Check that the selector lever pointer indicates the correct gear. If not, adjust the cable sleeve at the indicator.

5. Check that the output shaft is locked with the control lever in P.

Throttle Cable Adjustment

Correct adjustment of this cable is most important for satisfactory operation of the transmission. There are three different methods.

1. Check that engine idle speed is correct and that the inner and outer cables are correctly attached.

2. Screw up the threaded sleeve until it almost lies against the stop (for vehicles with single carburetor), and $\frac{1}{32}''$ (1 mm.) from the stop for vehicles with twin carburetors. The stop is crimped on the cable.

3. With the accelerator pedal fully depressed, check that the carburetor lever is at the full open stop and that the line pressure at converter stall speed is at least 160 psi.

If the cable stop has been damaged or moved, the cable must be adjusted as follows:

1. Connect a tachometer to the engine and a pressure gauge to the transmission.

2. Chock the wheels and apply the brakes. Start the engine and move the lever to D. Read the pressure at 500 and 1,000 rpm. At 1,000 rpm, the pressure should be 15-20 psi higher than at 500 rpm. If the pressure rise is less than 15 psi, the length of the outer cable should be increased by means of the adjuster. If the rise is more than 20 psi the length of the outer cable should be decreased. On vehicles with an exhaust emission control system, measure the pressure at 700 and 1,200 rpm. The pressure increase should be 15-20 psi.

If a new cable has to be installed, the transmission oil pan must be removed. In

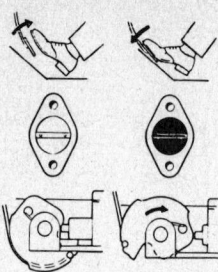

Relationship of cam to accelerator pedal

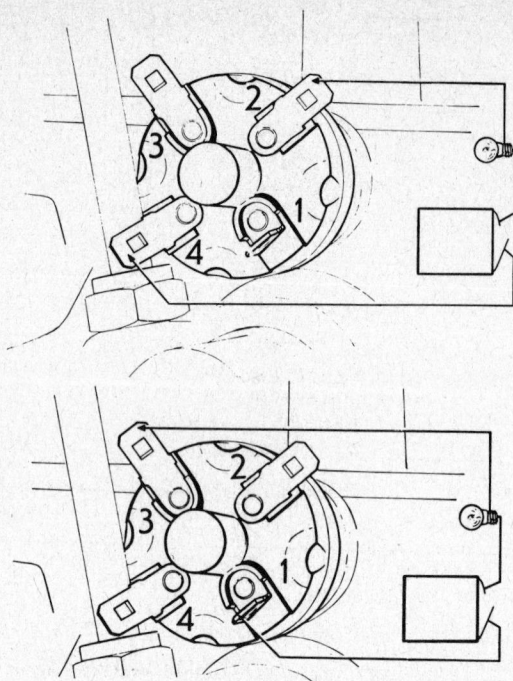

Test lamp hookup for adjusting starter inhibitor. Top figure is backup light switch test, lower figure is inhibitor switch test.

this event it is often simpler to adjust the cable by observing the movement of the cam in relation to accelerator pedal movement as follows:

1. With the accelerator pedal fully released and the carburetor lever at the idling stop, the heel of the cam should contact the full diameter of the downshift valve, with all the slack of the inner cable taken up.

2. With the accelerator pedal fully depressed and the carburetor lever at the full open stop, the constant radius area of the cam should be the point of contact with the downshift valve.

NOTE: *The cable is pre-lubricated with silicon or molybdenum disulphide lubricant and must not be oiled.*

Starter Inhibitor Switch Adjustment

The starter inhibitor switch function is to prevent the engine from being started with the selector in any position other than N or P. There are also two terminals for the backup light. It is very important that this switch be correctly adjusted.

The switch is adjusted as follows:

1. First check that the selector control is correctly adjusted. Move the selector to D.

2. Loosen the locknut for the switch. Screw out the switch until it is held only by a couple of threads.

3. Connect a test lamp to the backup light terminals. Screw in the switch until the lamp goes out. Mark this position on the housing and switch with a pencil.

4. Connect the test lamp to both the other terminals. Screw in the switch until the lamp lights again and then mark the switch again. Then screw back the switch to halfway between both the marks. Lock in place. Connect the leads.

5. Apply the brakes and chock the wheels. Check that the engine can only be

started with the selector lever in N or P. Move the selector lever to R and check that the backup light is on when the light switch is on.

Rear Brake Band Adjustment

The adjustment is made through a hole in the body tunnel under the floor mat.

1. Loosen the adjusting screw locknut.

2. Torque the adjusting screw to 10 ft.lbs. Back off the adjusting screw one turn.

3. Tighten the locknut.

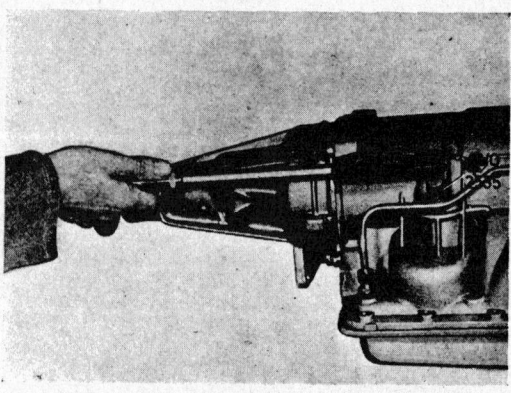

Adjusting rear brake band

REMOVAL AND REPLACEMENT

1. Pull out the dipstick and remove the clamp for the filler pipe. Remove the bracket and the throttle cable from the dashboard and throttle control. Disconnect the exhaust pipe at the flange. Jack up the car and place blocks under the front and rear axles.

2. Drain the oil.

NOTE: *The oil may be very hot and cause burns if contact is made with the skin.*

3. Place a lifting tool at the rear end of the engine. Hook the lifting hook around the exhaust pipe. Be sure that the speedometer cable or the electric wires are not damaged. Tighten the nut for the lifting hook until the sling takes the weight off the engine.

4. Disconnect the driveshaft from the transmission flange. Disconnect the controls from the selector shaft lever and the reinforcing bracket under the oil pan.

5. Remove one of the air grilles on the converter casing and unscrew the attaching bolts for the converter. With a wrench on the pulley bolt turn the crankshaft.

6. Remove the rear crossmember. Disconnect the brackets for the exhaust pipe and the rear engine mounts. Remove the speedometer cable and the oil filler pipe.

7. Lower the engine about 20 mm. (0.8″). See that the battery lead is not strained. If necessary, release the lead clamp.

8. Disconnect the wires from the starter inhibitor switch. Remove the screws for the starter inhibitor switch. Place a jack under the transmission. Unscrew the attaching bolts for the converter casing. Pull the transmission backward and release the guide pin on the converter at the same time. Lower and remove the transmission.

9. Reverse procedure to install.

Driveshaft and U-Joints, Drive Axle

DRIVESHAFT

The driveshaft is of the divided, tubular type. The rear of the front section is in the form of a splined sleeve. There is a splined shaft which also forms one of the yokes on the intermediate universal joint. The early production front and rear universal joint was carried directly in yokes on the flanges of the transmission and rear axle. The late production types have flange yokes. All three types of driveshafts can be used in the P120 and P1800 models, but only type III can be used for the 140 series.

The rear of the front section of the driveshaft is carried in a ball bearing. For types I and II the ball bearing is carried in a bearing housing suspended by two trunnions and two rubber bushes. On type III, the ball bearing is housed in a rubber cover secured to the driveshaft tunnel by a cap.

The driveshaft has three universal joints. Each joint consists of a spider with four trunnions which are carried in the yokes by needle bearings. The early production uni-

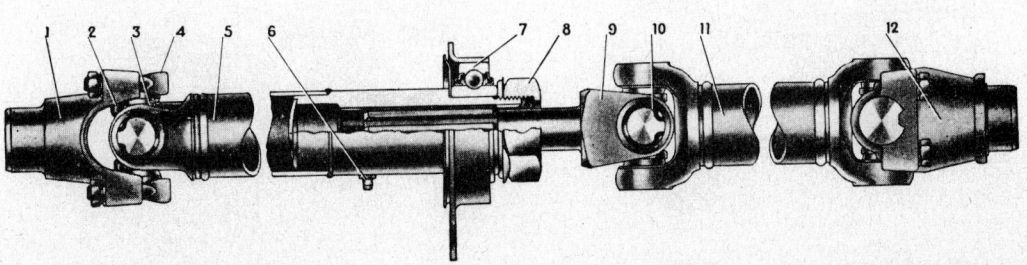

1. Yoke on transmission
2. Universal joint
3. Grease fitting
4. Clamp
5. Front section of driveshaft
6. Grease fitting
7. Support bearing
8. Nut
9. Splined shaft
10. Snap-ring
11. Rear section of driveshaft
12. Yoke on rear axle

Driveshaft, type I

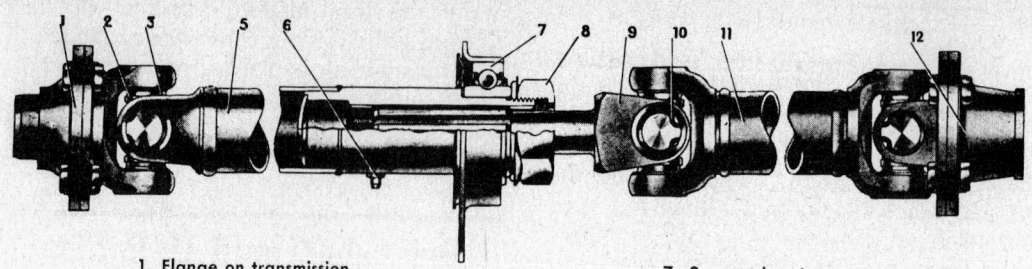

1. Flange on transmission
2. Universal joint
3. Grease fitting
4. Not used
5. Front section of driveshaft
6. Grease fitting

7. Support bearing
8. Nut
9. Splined shaft
10. Snap-ring
11. Rear section of driveshaft
12. Flange on rear axle

Driveshaft, type II

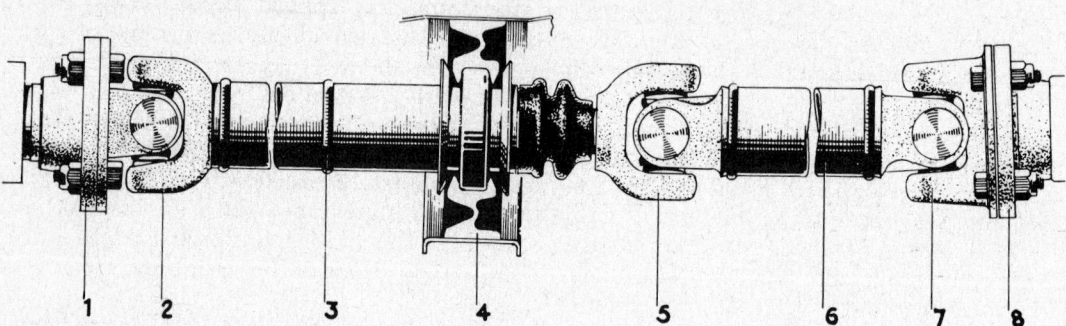

1. Transmission flange
2. Front universal
3. Front section of drive shaft

4. Support bearing
5. Intermediate universal

6. Rear section of drive shaft
7. Rear universal
8. Rear axle flange

Driveshaft, type III

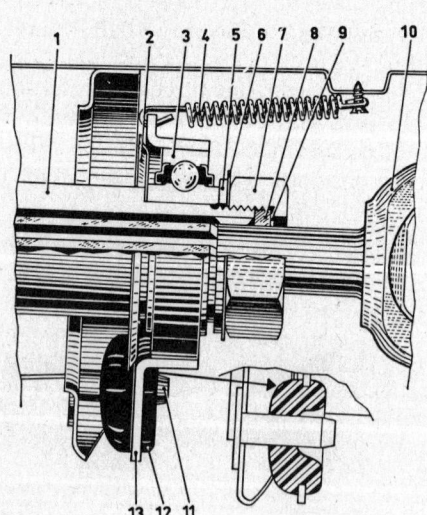

1. Front section of driveshaft
2. Dust cover
3. Ball bearing
4. Tension spring
5. Thrust washer
6. Lockwasher
7. Nut

8. Felt seal
9. Washer
10. Splined shaft
11. Pin
12. Rubber bushing
13. Retainer

Support bearing, type I

1. Front section of driveshaft
2. Dust cover
3. Ball bearing
4. Thrust washer
5. Lockwasher
6. Nut

7. Felt seal
8. Washer
9. Splined shaft
10. Tension spring
11. Retainer
12. Rubber bushing

Support bearing, type II

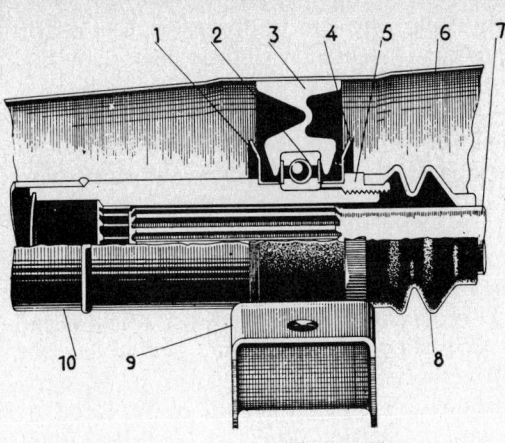

1. Dust cover
2. Ball bearing
3. Rubber housing
4. Dust cover
5. Nut
6. Floor tunnel
7. Splined shaft
8. Rubber cover
9. Cap
10. Front section of driveshaft

Support bearing, type III

versal joints and sliding joints have grease nipples for lubrication. The late types are lubricated only at assembly.

Support Bearing Replacement

TYPES I AND II

1. Jack up the vehicle and block up the front and rear axles. Loosen the clamps which retain the rear universal joint to the rear axle flange. On the type II driveshaft, the flange bolts are unscrewed after the snap rings for the bolts and nuts have been removed. Bend back the lockwasher and unscrew the nut. Pull the driveshaft rearward.

2. Disconnect the snap ring. Pull out the retainer with support bearing to the rear. Press the support bearing out of the retainer with a suitable drift. Press the new bearing into the retainer.

3. Install the retainer with the support bearing and rear section of driveshaft in

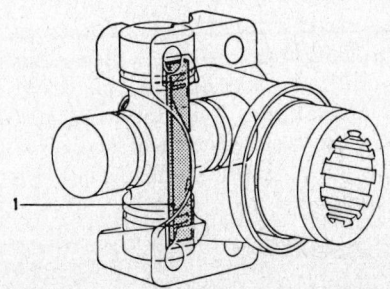

1 is sheet metal strip used on type I universal joint.

reverse order of removal. Hook on the tension spring. Lower the vehicle.

NOTE: *When fitting Type I support bearing, make sure that the sheet metal strip on the rear universal joint fits into the recesses on the flange.*

TYPE III

1. Jack up the vehicle and place blocks under the front and rear axles. Disconnect the driveshaft from the rear axle flange. Bend up the lock washer and unscrew the nut at the sliding joint. Pull the driveshaft out.

2 Remove the cap for the support bearing. Pull off the support bearing complete.

3. Pry the old bearing out of the rubber housing. Install the new bearing.

4. Install the support bearing and other parts in reverse order of removal. If the splined joint appears to be dry, lubricate it with molybdenum-disulphide grease. Lower the vehicle.

Shaft Removal

Jack up the vehicle and place blocks under the front and rear axles. Loosen the clamps and bolts holding the driveshaft to the transmission and the rear axle flange. Unhook the tension spring if fitted. For type III remove the support bearing cap and then the driveshaft. For types I and II, move the driveshaft to the rear and remove it.

Shaft Disassembly

DRIVESHAFT

1. Bend up the lock washer and unscrew the nut for the support bearing. Remove the rear section of the driveshaft. Pull off the support bearing.

2. For the late production types, remove the support bearing from the rubber housing. On the early production type, press the bearing out of the retainer with a suitable drift.

UNIVERSAL JOINT

In general, universal joints on early and late production driveshafts are disassembled in the same way. However, note that late production driveshafts have universal joints which have two flange yokes from which the spider must be disconnected.

This also applies to the intermediate universal joint on the early production driveshaft.

1. Remove the snap rings retaining the needle bearings in the yokes. Remove the grease nipple in the spider.

2. Fasten the shaft securely in a vise so that the joint is as near the vise as possible. The shaft itself is a tube which can easily be deformed.

3. With a hammer and metal drift, drive the spider in one direction as far as it can go.

4. Then drive the spider in the opposite direction as far as it will go.

5. Drive out one of the needle bearings with a light metal drift. Remove the spider. Drive out the other needle bearing.

Shaft Inspection

It is very important that the driveshaft is straight. Since even minor damage can cause vibration, very careful inspection must be made. The shaft should be set up between centers and checked along its entire length with a dial indicator while it is rotating. If it is out-of-true by more than 0.25 mm. (0.010″), the shaft must be replaced.

NOTE: *No attempt should be made to straighten a damaged driveshaft; it must be replaced.*

Check the support bearing by pressing the bearing races against each other and turning them in opposite directions. The bearing should run easily without binding at any point. If it does not do so, scrap the bearing and replace it. Check needle bearings and spiders. Worn or damaged parts should be replaced.

The flanges of type II and III driveshafts should be checked for runout and warping with a dial indicator. Runout should not exceed .003″. Warping should not exceed .004″.

Shaft Assembly

UNIVERSAL JOINTS

1. Install new washers on the spider trunnions. Install the spider in the flange yoke.

2. Fill the bearings halfway with grease. Then push the spider to one side and set the needle bearing on the trunnion. Press in the needle bearing so that

the snap ring can be installed. Use a drift having a diameter slightly less than that of the needle bearing sleeve.

3. Install the other needle bearing and snap ring in the same way. Install the spider in the other yoke in the same way.

DRIVESHAFT

1a. Types I and II: Press the support bearing into the retainer. Install the dust cover, support bearing, thrust washer, and lockwasher on the front section of the driveshaft. If the dust cover is an early production type, it should be replaced by a late production type.

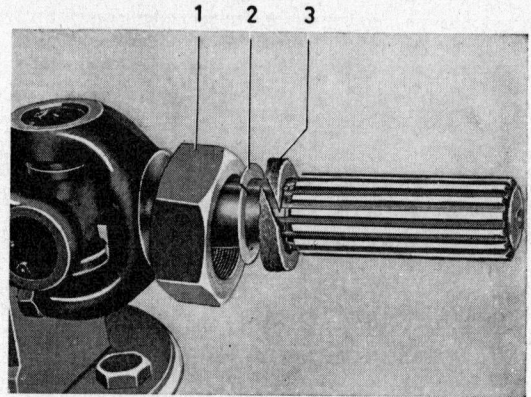

1. Nut
2. Washer
3. Felt washer

Locknut for support bearing (early production)

1b. Type III: Place the support bearing in the rubber housing. Then install the support bearing and dust covers on the front section of the driveshaft.

2. Install the nut, washer, and felt washer on the splined shaft. If the nut is the type with rubber bellows, it can be screwed directly onto the front section of the driveshaft. Do not forget the lock washer. Smear the sliding surfaces of the splined shaft with a thin layer of molybdenum-disulphide grease. Assemble the front and rear sections of the driveshaft. When assembling, it is important that the yoke on the front section of the driveshaft and the yoke on the splined shaft are correctly aligned.

Shaft Installation

Installation is the reverse of removal. Hook on the tension spring. On type I only, there is a sheet metal strip holding together two of the needle bearings on the front and rear universals. Make sure that this strip locates properly in the flange recesses, or the bearing will be pinched. Tighten the clamp nuts to 10-12 ft. lbs.

REAR AXLE AND DIFFERENTIAL

The different types of rear axles are similar in design but differ somewhat in size and certain minor details. The different types are: Salisbury, Spicer 23, Spicer 27 (Hayes, Dana), Spicer 30 (Hayes, Dana), and Volvo 1030.

The Salisbury axles are used only in the P210 and P120 Station Wagon. The Hayes axles are similar to the Spicer 27 and 30 type axles. For repair purposes, the axles can be divided into three groups: Salisbury and Spicer 23, Spicer 27, Spicer 30 and Volvo 1030.

The rear axle is of the hypoid type; that is, the drive pinion lies below the center of the ring gear. It consists of the drive pinion, ring gear and differential gears. The gear backlash and differential carrier bearing tension are adjusted by means of shims inside the differential carrier bearings. The

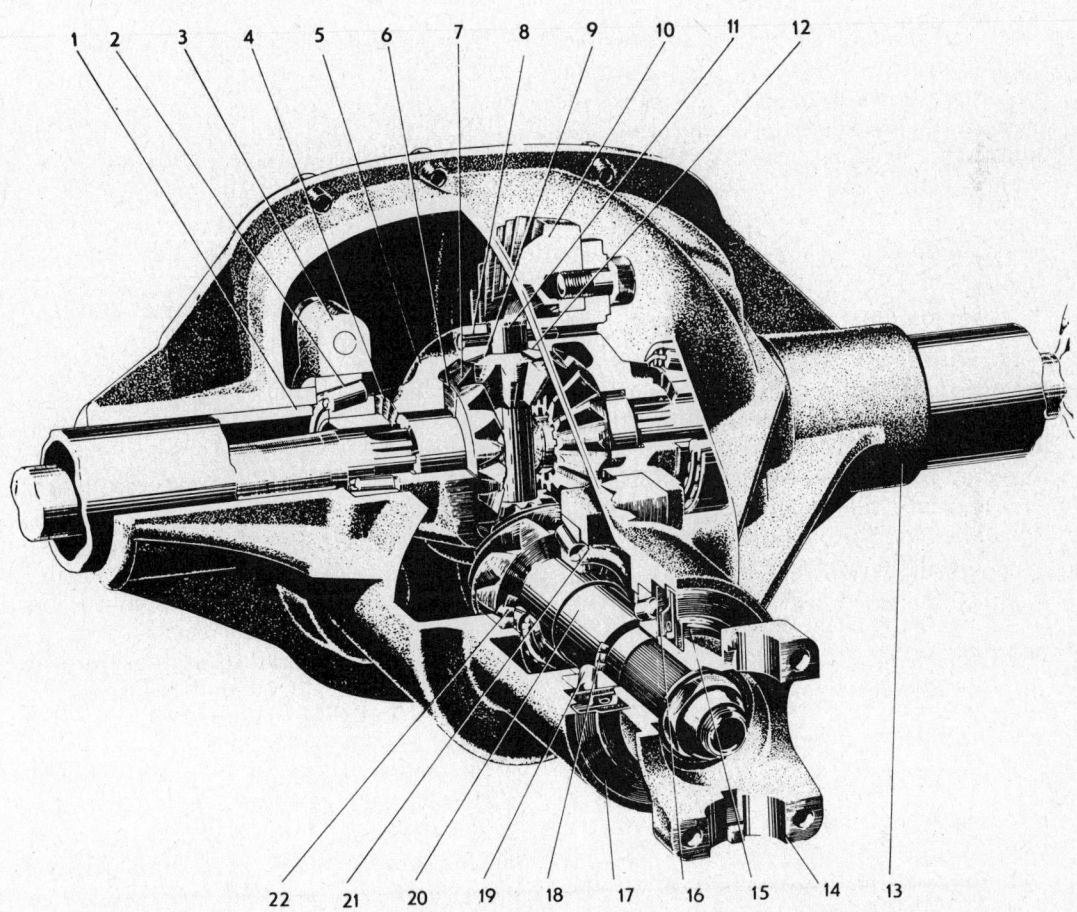

1. Tubular shaft
2. Differential shaft
3. Bearing cap
4. Shims
5. Differential carrier
6. Thrust washer
7. Differential gear
8. Lock pin
9. Differential pinion
10. Ring gear
11. Shaft
12. Thrust washer
13. Axle housing
14. Pinion flange
15. Dust cover plate
16. Oil slinger
17. Pinion oil seal
18. Shims
19. Front pinion bearing
20. Pinion
21. Rear pinion bearing
22. Shims

Rear axle and differential, 140 series

differential carrier and ring gear are jour-nalled in the final drive housing by means of two taped roller bearings. The ring gear is bolted to the differential carrier. The differential gears consist of two bevel pin-ions on trunnions and two side gears in which the driveshafts are carried by in-ternal splines. The differential gears permit the axle shafts to rotate at different speeds when the car is being driven around curves. A thrust washer is under each of the differential gears.

The drive pinion is carried in taped roller bearings. The location of the drive pinion relative to the ring gear is adjusted by shims under the front pinion bearing inner ring.

On the Volvo axles, spacer washers are used instead of shims. The spacer washer for drive pinion location is placed at the back of the rear bearing inner ring. On adjusting this type, replace the spacer washers with shims.

In-Car Service

PINION OIL SEAL REPLACEMENT

1. Disconnect the rear section of the driveshaft from the flange (yoke) on the pinion. Check for looseness of the pinion in its bearing. If it is loose, this must be corrected before a new oil seal is installed.

2. Remove the flange nut. Pull off the flange. Remove the old oil seal.

3. Install the new oil seal.

4. Press on the flange. Fit the washer and nut. Tighten the nut to 28-30 kgm. (200-220 ft.lbs.)

5. Re-connect the rear section of the driveshaft.

Axle Shaft Oil Seal Replacement

P120, P210, PV544, P1800

1. Remove the wheel and pull off the wheel hub. Remove the brake backing plate after placing a wooden block under the brake pedal and loosening the brake line on the backing plate.

2. Pull out the axle shaft.

3. Pull out the oil seal.

4. Drive in the new oil seal.

5. Clean the brake backing plate of any oil and grease. Replace brake linings if they have any oil or grease on them.

Removing the wheel hub. 1 is a puller.

6. Install the axle shaft and brake backing plate with a new felt washer.

7. Check axle shaft end play.

8. Replace the key if it has been re-moved and then replace the hub and wheel.

9. Bleed and adjust the rear brakes.

10. Check the oil level.

140 SERIES

Only Steps 1-4 and 12-15 are required to replace the inner oil seal.

1. Jack up the vehicle and place blocks under the rear axle. Remove the wheel.

2. Disconnect the brake line from the rear brake. Loosen the bolts and remove the rear brake. Unscrew the bolts for the brake disc and remove the disc.

3. Remove the return springs for the brake shoes and lift off the shoes. Discon-nect the handbrake cable from the bracket and the lever. Remove the lever and cable.

4. Unscrew the bolts for the brake backing plate and retainers. These are loosened through the hole in the axle shaft flange (yoke). Turn the brake backing plate backward so that the handbrake bracket is free of the flange. Pull out the axle shaft.

5. Fasten the driveshaft firmly in a vise so that the recess in the brake backing plate faces the rear jaw of the vise.

6. Drill a 6 mm. (¼″) hole in the lock-ring. Do not drill so deep as to damage the shaft. Split the ring with a cold chisel. Ap-ply the chisel to the outer edge of the ring in order not to damage the bearing. Re-

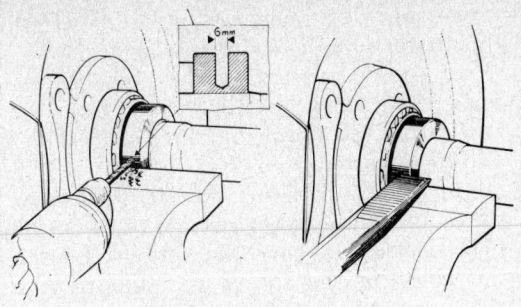

Removing lock ring

move the shaft from the vise and take off the lockring.

7. Pull loose the bearing with a puller. Then remove the brake backing plate and retainers.

8. Drive out the oil seal with a drift.

9. Clean and check all the parts. Make sure that all drill chips are removed in order to prevent damage to the bearing.

10. Drive the new oil seal into the brake retainer (adjusting nut) with a drift. Fill the space between the lips of the oil seal with grease.

11. Install the brake backing plate and retainer on the axle shaft. Press on the axle shaft until the bearing and lockring are in position.

12. Pull out the inner oil seal with a puller. Drive in the new seal with a drift. The oil seal must not be driven in so far that it bottoms.

13. Pack the bearing with multi-purpose grease and then install the axle shaft, brake backing plate, and retainer. After installing, the entire space between the oil seals should be filled with grease. Check the end play, which should be 0.05-0.13 mm. (0.0020-0.0052"), with a dial indicator. First, press out the outer rings in their bearings. If necessary, adjust. Lock the adjuster nut with a suitable tab.

14. Install the lever, handbrake shoes with spring, and the adjusting device to-

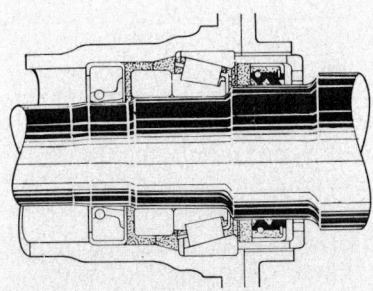

Lubricating rear axle bearing

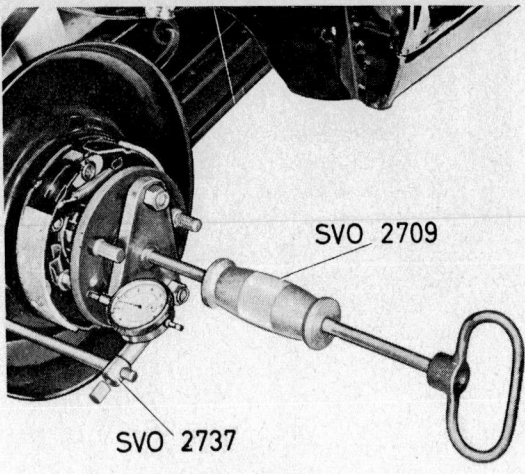

SVO 2709

SVO 2737

Measuring axle shaft end play

gether with the handbrake cable. Then install the brake disc and rear wheel brake unit. Connect the brake line. Bleed and adjust the brakes.

15. Install the wheel and wheel nuts. Lower the vehicle and tighten the wheel nuts.

Axle Shaft or Bearing Replacement

120 Series, P210, PV544, P1800

1. Remove the wheel and pull off the hub. Remove the brake backing plate after placing a wooden block under the brake pedal and loosening the brake line from the backing plate.

2. Pull out the axle shaft. Check and, if necessary, replace the oil seal.

3. Press off the bearing. Install the new bearing with the help of a sleeve.

4. Pack the bearing with multi-purpose grease. After installation, the entire space between the oil seals should be filled with grease. Install the axle shaft in the drive pinion carrier. Drive in the bearing outer ring with a sleeve.

5a. Replacement of bearing on right side: Install the brake backing plate and retainer with the felt seal. Pull the bearing outer ring out toward the brake backing plate. Install a dial indicator on the axle shaft. Set the indicator pointer facing the brake backing plate and measure the step play. Play should be .05-.15 mm. (.0019-.0059". If the play is incorrect, remove the brake drum on the left-hand side and also the brake backing plate. Then adjust the

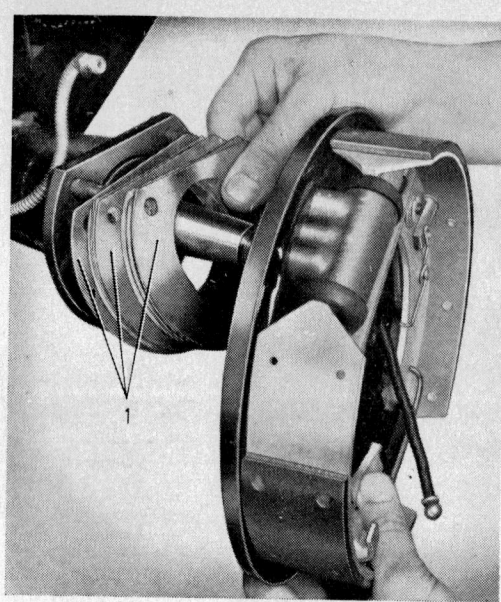

Installing the brake backing plate. 1 shows shims.

play according to steps 5b-10 below. If the play is correct proceed with steps 7-10.

5b. Replacement of bearing on left-hand side: Pull the bearing outer ring toward the plate.

6. Install a dial indicator on the axle shaft. Aim the indicator pointer at the plate, move in the shaft and zero the indicator. Pull the driveshaft outward and read the end play. To adjust the play, install suitable shims.

7. Install the brake backing plate together with the shims (left side) and the retainer with the felt seal.

8. Install the brake line, hub, brake drum, and wheel.

9. Bleed and adjust the brakes.

10. Check the oil level.

140 Series

To replace an axle shaft bearing, follow Steps 1-7, 9, and 11-15 under Axle Shaft Oil Seal Replacement.

Rear Axle Removal

120 Series, P210, PV544, P1800

1. Block the front wheels. Unscrew the rear wheel nuts and the nuts on the axle shafts. Jack up the rear. Place blocks under the body in front of the rear wheels (under the frame on P210).

2. Disconnect the rear section of the driveshaft from the flange (yoke) on the

pinion and disconnect the brake lines from the master cylinder to the rear axle.

3. Loosen the track bar, shock absorber and shock absorber straps from the rear axle. Disconnect the handbrake cables and the adjuster.

4a. P120, PV544, P1800: Unscrew the nuts for the support arms. Lower the rear axle and remove the springs. Loosen the bolts for the torque rod and remove the rear axle.

4b. P210: Slacken the spring clamps and shackles. Lower the springs and remove the rear axle.

140 Series

1. Block the front wheels. Unscrew the rear wheel nuts. Jack up the rear of the vehicle. Place blocks in front of the rear jack attachments and lower the jack slightly. Remove the rear wheels.

2. Unscrew the upper bolts for the shock absorbers. Disconnect the handbrake cables from the lever arms and brackets on the brake backing plates.

3. Disconnect the driveshaft from the flange (yoke) on the pinion. Remove the brake line union from the differential carrier.

4. Loosen the front attaching bolt for the support arms about 1 turn. Remove the rear screws for the torque rods. Disconnect the track rod from the bracket on the differential carrier. Remove the lower attaching bolts for the springs.

5. Lower the jack until the support arms release from the springs. Remove the bolts securing the differential carrier to the support arms. Lower the jack and pull the rear axle forward.

Rear Axle Disassembly

1. Place the rear axle with the pinion pointing down. Remove the brake lines.

2a. P120, P210, PV544, P1800: Remove the brake backing plates from the differential carrier. Do not lose the shims. Pull out the axle shafts with a puller.

2b. 140 Series: Unscrew the bolts for the brake backing plates and retainers. The bolts are loosened through the holes in the axle shaft flanges. Pull out the axle shafts with a puller.

3. Remove the inspection cover.

4. If the unit is being overhauled because of noise, the backlash and the gear tooth pattern should be checked before

disassembly. Clean the teeth to avoid a misleading tooth pattern.

5. Check the alignment markings on the cap and carrier. If there are no alignment marks, or if they are difficult to see, mark one side with a punch. Remove the cap.

6. Expand the pinion carrier with a special tool. Pull out the differential carrier with ring gear. A special tool is available for this purpose.

7. Turn the assembly and allow the oil to run out. Remove the nuts for the flange. Pull the flange off with a puller. Press out the pinion.

8. Drive out the front pinion bearing, the washer, and oil seal.

9. If necessary, drive out the rear bearing outer ring.

10. Clean the gasket surface. Remove all burrs with a file.

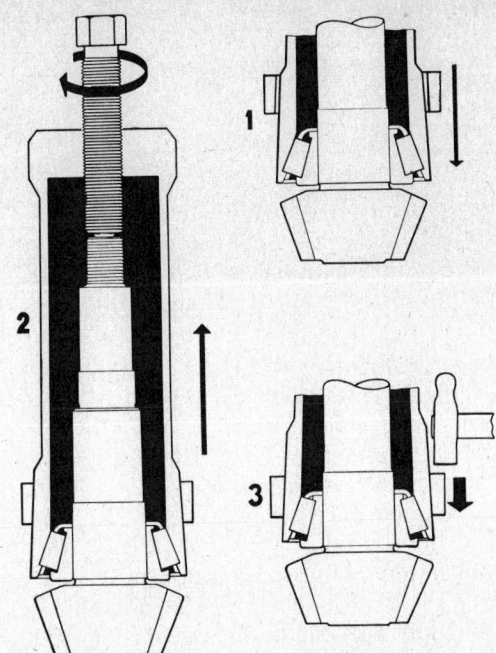

Sequence of pulling rear pinion bearing

11. If necessary, pull off the rear bearing from the pinion with a puller. Slide the puller down over the rollers and press down the lock ring. Then tighten the puller until the rollers are flush against the edge of the inner race. Tap the lock ring with a hammer.

DIFFERENTIAL DISASSEMBLY

1. Loosen the ring gear bolts and remove the ring gear.

2. Drive out the lock pin, and the shaft for the differential gears. Remove the thrust block, the differential gears, and the thrust washers.

3. Remove the differential carrier bearings with a puller. Do not lose the shims.

Inspection

Clean all the parts thoroughly. Check all the bearing races and bearings. All damaged bearings and bearing races must be replaced. Check both the pinion drive and ring gear carefully for damage to the teeth. Tooth damage is caused by incorrect break-in, wrong oil, insufficient tooth flank clearance, or faulty tooth contact.

The differential gears should also be examined for tooth damage. They should be placed in the differential carrier together with the shaft and thrust washers. Play should then be checked. If the play ex-

Alignment marks on cap and carrier

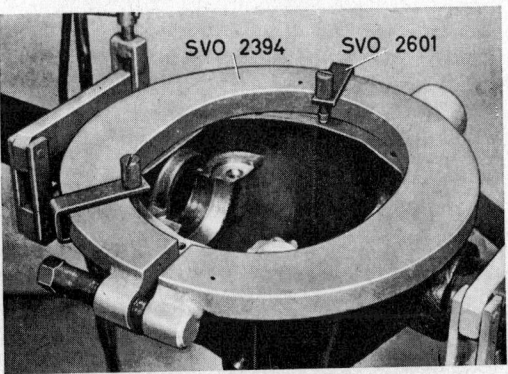

Expanding drive pinion carrier

Seized gear tooth

ceeds 0.06 mm. (0.0024″), install thicker washers. These are available in 0.78 mm., 0.86 mm., and 0.94 mm. sizes. Also check to see whether the cylindrical part of the flange which goes into the oil seal is worn or scratched. If it is, replace the flange and the oil seal.

The pinion nut has a locking slit. In time this slit loses its effectiveness. For this reason, the nut should be replaced if it has been removed more than once. The washer under the nut should also be replaced if it is deformed.

Check the oil seals and replace them if they are damaged or worn.

Check for cracks in the rear axle casing. Check that the brackets for the support arms and track rod are intact.

Rear Axle Assembly

Great cleanliness should be observed when assembling and adjusting the differential. Dirt in a tapered roller bearing can result in inaccurate measurement. When measuring the bearing clearance or pre-loading, the bearing should be oiled and rotated several turns loaded.

DIFFERENTIAL ASSEMBLY

1. Place the differential side gears and the thrust washers in the differential carrier. Then roll in the differential pinions simultaneously with the dished thrust washers.

2. Insert the thrust block and drive in the shaft.

3. Check the differential unit. If the gear play has not been measured, check it as described under inspection. If oversize washers are installed, check by turning the gears one turn. The turning torque should not exceed 1 kgm. (7.23 ft.lbs.). The tool for making this check can be easily made from a shortened axle shaft adapted to a suitable torque wrench. After checking the

replacement of the thrust washers, install the lock pin.

4. Install the ring gear. Make sure that the contact surfaces are clean and without burrs. Tighten the bolts to 45-65 ft. lbs.

NOTE: *Always use new bolts for gears in which the bolts are locked only by thread friction and the contact surface of the screw head.*

Pinion Installation

1. Polish the marking surface on the pinion with very fine emery cloth. Place the pinion in the casing so that the screw on the adjusting ring faces the larger part of the casing.

Locating pinion with adjusting tool

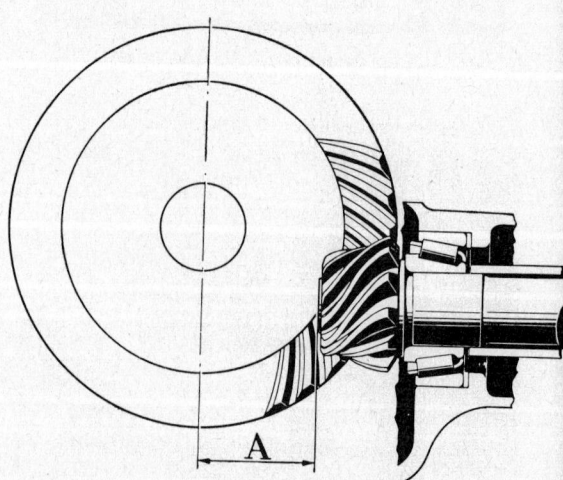

Pinion Location. A is the nominal measurement.

2. The pinion should have a certain nominal measurement to the center line of the ring gear. Due to manufacturing tolerances, there are deviations from the nominal measurement. This is indicated on the pinion.

On differentials made by Volvo, the surface is generally ground down 0.30 mm. (0.012″) so that the deviation is always indicated by plus tolerance in hundredths of a millimeter. The plus sign is not indicated. On other units, the deviation is indicated in thousandths of an inch and with a plus or minus sign. If there is a plus sign in front of the figure, the nominal measurement is to be increased and, in the case of a minus sign, the nominal measurement is to be decreased.

To check the pinion location, use a dial indicator, an indicator retainer (SVO 2284), and a measuring tool (SVO 2393), which consists of two parts: a pinion gauge and an adjuster fixture. Place the pinion

Zeroing the indicator.

Measuring pinion location

gauge on the ground end surface of the pinion and place the adjuster fixture in the differential bearing recesses. Place the indicator retainer on the drive pinion carrier and zero the indicator against the adjuster fixture. Then move the indicator retainer so that the indicator is against the pinion gauge. Read the indicator.

On a Volvo unit on which the pinion is, for example, marked 33, the pinion gauge should be 0.33 mm. (0.013″) under the adjuster fixture. On other units, if the pinion is marked 0, the adjuster fixture and pinion gauge should be at the same height; if the pinion is marked −, the pinion gauge should be higher than the adjuster fixture; and if it is marked +, the pinion gauge should be lower than the adjuster fixture. The setting is adjusted by turning the cam on the pinion until the gauge dial shows the correct figure, then locking in the adjusting ring with the lock screw. Remove the measuring tool and pinion.

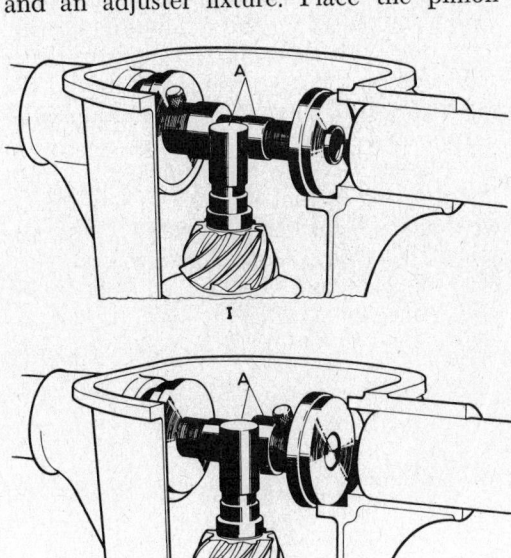

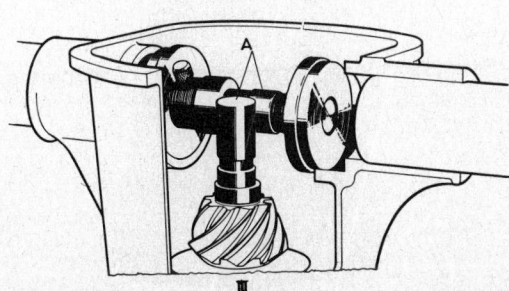

Location of measuring tool. I for Spicer 23, II for Spicer 27, III for Spicer 30 and Volvo.

3. Place the rear pinion bearing complete with the outer ring in a measuring fixture (SVO 2600). Install the plate, spring and nut. The flat side of the nut should face upward. The plate (and the bearing) should be turned forward and backward several times so that the rollers take up the correct position. Place the adjusting ring in the measuring fixture. Use an indicator retainer (SVO 2284) and a dial indicator. Place the measuring point of the gauge against the adjusting ring and set the gauge to zero. Then place the point of the gauge against the outer ring of the bearing. The gauge now shows the required size for the shims. Measure the thickness of the shims with a micrometer. It is not always possible to obtain shims with exactly the correct thickness. However, they may not be more than 0.03 mm. (0.0012″) thicker than the measured value but may be up to 0.05 mm. (0.0020″) thinner.

4. Press the rear bearing on the pinion with a sleeve. The washer under the rear bearing inner ring on a new Volvo unit should not be installed after overhaul. Install the measured shims and press in both the outer rings of the bearings.

5. Install the pinion in the carrier and mount three 0.75 mm. (0.30″) thick shims and the front pinion bearing. Tighten the pinion. If a nut remover is used when installing the pinion, the pinion must be pressed forward so that it does not strike against the bearing positions.

6. Install the pinion gauge and indicator retainer. Move the pinion down while turning it forward and backward at the same time. Set the indicator gauge to zero. Then press the pinion upward while turning it backward and forward at the same time. Read the play.

7. Remove the pinion. Remove a sufficient number of shims corresponding to the measured play plus 0.07 mm. (0.0028″). Reinstall the pinion.

8. Then check the pinion bearings with a torque gauge. The torque gauge should show a torque of 6-11 kgcm. (5-10 in.lbs.) for used bearings and 11-23 kgcm. (10-20 in.lbs.) for new bearings when the pinion rotates. On new units, turning torque may be higher due to another type of installation method.

Check the location of the pinion with a dial indicator, an indicator retainer (SVO 2284), and a measuring tool (SVO 2393).

DIFFERENTIAL INSTALLATION

1. Oil the adjusting rings internally and install them on the differential carrier. The ring with the oxidized adjusting ring is placed on the ring gear side. Also oil the bearing seal in the carrier. The differential carrier and adjusting rings are placed in the carrier. Use the dial indicator and adjust the ring so that the correct tooth flank clearance, 0.15 mm. (0.0060″) is obtained. The tooth flank clearance may vary between 0.10 mm. (0.0040″) (model 30: 0.13 mm. or 0.0052″) and 0.20 mm. (0.0080″), but should be kept as near 0.15

Determining shim thickness. 1 is adjusting ring, 2 is measuring gauge, 3 is bearing.

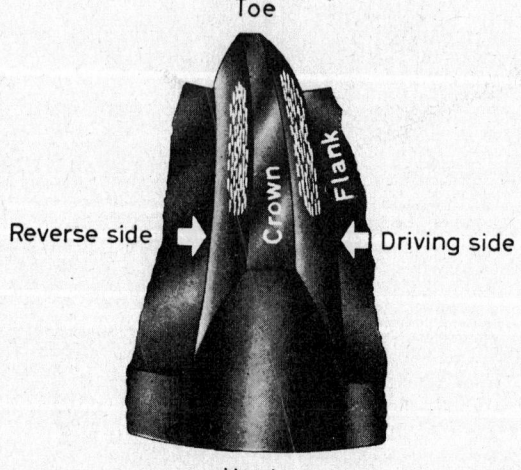

Correct tooth contact

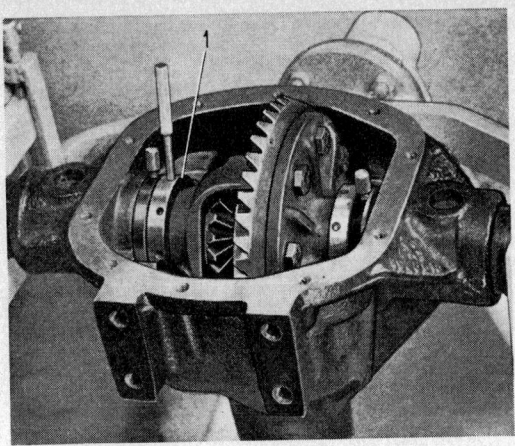

Adjusting rings for the differential

mm. (0.0060″) as possible. Tighten the lock bolts in the adjusting rings.

2. Coat several teeth with marking blue at three points on the ring gear. By this means a check can be kept on possible ring gear warping. Pull the pinion 10-12 turns in both directions and check the tooth pattern. When the tooth contact is correct, the contact pattern should be vertical in the middle of the tooth but somewhat nearer to the toe than to the heel. The contact pattern on the reverse side and driving side should lie opposite each other. If the contact pattern is incorrect, the location of the pinion must be adjusted before assembly continues. If the contact pattern lies too far toward the heel on the driving side and too far toward the toe on the reverse side, the pinion should be moved inward. If the contact pattern lies too far toward the toe on the driving side and too far toward the heel on the reverse side, the pinion should be moved outward. Note that the contact pattern will lie somewhat nearer the toe when the adjusting rings are installed than when the bearings are installed.

3. When correct tooth flank clearance and contact pattern are obtained, remove the differential and adjusting ring. Place the center washer on the measuring fixture. Place a bearing in the measuring fixture and fit the plate, spring and nut. The nut should be fitted with the flat side facing downward. Turn the plate forward and backward several times. Install the dial indicator gauge and retainer. Set the gauge to zero against the adjusting ring and then place the pointer facing the bearing. Read

the gauge. With a micrometer measure the shims. The total shim thickness should correspond to the indicator reading plus 0.07 mm. (0.0028″). Repeat with the other bearing. Keep a careful check on which side the bearing and shim are to be fitted.

4. Install the shims on the differential carrier and press on the bearings. Use a drift. When installing the second bearing, use a drift as a cushioning ring to avoid damage to the first bearing.

5. Expand the pinion carrier with a special tool. Install the differential and outer rings. Remove tool. Install the bearing caps and tighten the bolts to 35-50 ft. lbs.

6. Check the tooth flank clearance and contact pattern.

7. Install the oil slinger and the oil seal. The oil seal should be fitted with a drift. Press on the flange. Install the washer and nut. Tighten the nut to a torque of 28-30 kgm. (200-220 ft.lbs.).

8. Install the inspection cover and gasket.

AXLE SHAFT INSTALLATION

120 Series, P1800, P210, PV544

1. Pack the drive shaft bearings with multi-purpose grease and install the axle shaft. Drive in the outer bearing rings with a sleeve.

2. Install the brake backing plate and felt seal on the right side.

3. Tap several times with a hammer on both shaft ends so that the outer rings of the bearings locate in their extreme positions.

4. Install a dial indicator. Shove the axle shaft inward and set the gauge to zero. Pull the driveshaft outward and read the clearance. Adjust as described under Axle Shaft or Bearing Replacement.

5. Install the brake backing plate on the left side with the shims. Connect the brake line and brake cable at both sides. Install the hub.

140 Series

1. If the inner oil seals for the driveshafts are not installed, drive them in.

2. Pack the bearing with multi-purpose grease and then install the driveshaft, brake backing plate, and retainers. After installation, the entire space between the oil seals should be filled with grease. Check

the end play, which should be 0.05-0.13 mm. (0.0020-0.0052″), with a dial indicator. First press out the outer rings into their positions. Adjust if necessary. Lock the adjuster nut with a suitable tab.

3. Install the brake discs and the rear wheel brakes. Install the brake lines.

Rear Axle Installation

120 Series, P1800, PV544

1. Place the rear axle on a jack. Lift up the axle and install the torque rods. Slide the support arms into the retainers on the body and install the rubber blocks, washers, and nuts. The nuts should be tightened only a couple of turns to begin with.

2. Install the springs, retainers, and rubber blocks. Install bolts. Lift up the rear axle with the jack. Tighten the nuts for the support arms. Install the shock absorbers, shock absorber straps, and track rod.

3. Connect the universal joint at the flange, the brake hose, and the handbrake cables. Bleed the brake system and adjust the handbrake. Fill with oil. Use only hypoid oil.

4. Install the wheels and nuts. Lower the car and tighten the wheel nuts to 10-14 kgm. (70-100 ft.lbs.).

P210

1. Place the rear axle on a jack. Lift up the rear axle. Lift up and install the spring shackles. Install the spring clamps and shock absorbers.

2. Follow Steps 3-4 for P120, P1800, PV544.

140 Series

1. Place the rear axle on a garage jack. Move the axle in under the car and install the bolts for the support arms and torque rods.

2. Raise the jack until the track rod attachment on the shaft is at the level with the attachment on the body. Install the track rod.

3. Install the attaching bolts for the springs. Tighten the nuts for the torque rods and support arms.

4. Install the bracket, union, and brake hoses. Connect the universal joint to the flange.

5. Install the upper bolts for the shock

absorbers. Install the handbrake cable in the brackets and at the levers. Adjust the handbrake and bleed the brake system. Fill with oil.

6. Install the wheels and nuts. Lower the car. Tighten the wheel nuts to 10-14 kgm. (70-100 ft.lbs.). Fill with oil. Use only hypoid oil.

Suspension

Coil springs with hydraulic shock absorbers are used at both the front and rear. The front suspension is independent. Instructions for servicing the suspension system follow.

1. Steering knuckle
2. Upper rubber bumper
3. Rubber bushing
4. Washer
5. Upper A-arm
6. Lower A-arm
7. Shock absorber
8. Attaching plate
9. Spring
10. Lower rubber bumper
11. Stabilizer
12. Lower ball joint nut

Front suspension; 120, 1800

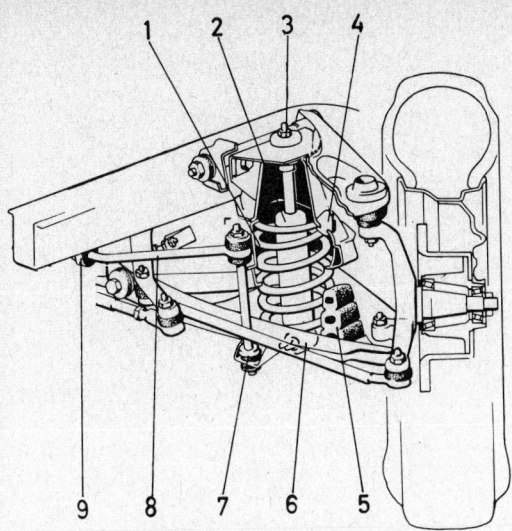

1. Spring
2. Shock absorber
3. Upper shock absorber mounting
4. Rubber bumper
5. Rubber bumper
6. Lower shock absorber mounting
7. Stabilizer attachment
8. Stabilizer bar
9. Stabilizer frame attachment

Front suspension; 140 series, 164

SPRINGS

Front Springs

REMOVAL

1. Remove the hub cap and loosen the wheel nuts a couple of turns.

2. Jack up the front end and place blocks under the front crossmember.

3. Remove the wheel nuts and the wheel.

4. Remove the shock absorber nuts and washers and take off the outer rubber bushings. Remove the bolt for the attaching plate and pull this down with the shock absorber.

5. Place a jack under the spring and jack up until the rubber bumper of the upper A-arm lifts.

6. Disconnect the stabilizer from the lower A-arm. Remove the nut for the lower ball joint.

7. Lower the jack slowly and remove the spring. If the lower ball joint does not release when the jack is lowered, use a removal tool.

INSTALLATION

Place the rubber spacer and washer in the spring housing in the front crossmember and install the spring in the reverse order of removal.

Rear Springs

REMOVAL

1. Jack up the rear of the car and place blocks under the rear jacking points.

2. Remove the wheels and release the handbrake.

3. Place a jack under the rear axle housing and jack up until the shock absorber bands loosen.

4a. 120 Series, 1800: Loosen the lower shock absorber attachment and the upper attachment for the shock absorber band on both sides. Loosen the front attachments of the support arms slightly.

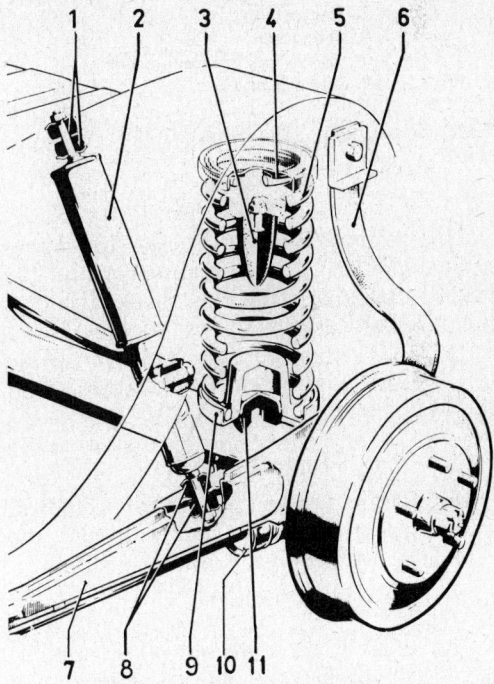

1. Upper shock absorber mounting
2. Shock absorber
3. Rubber bumper
4. Rubber spacer
5. Spring
6. Shock absorber limit band
7. Support arm
8. Lower shock absorber mounting
9. Spring seat
10. Torque rod
11. Rubber pad

Rear suspension; 120 series, 1800 (early production)

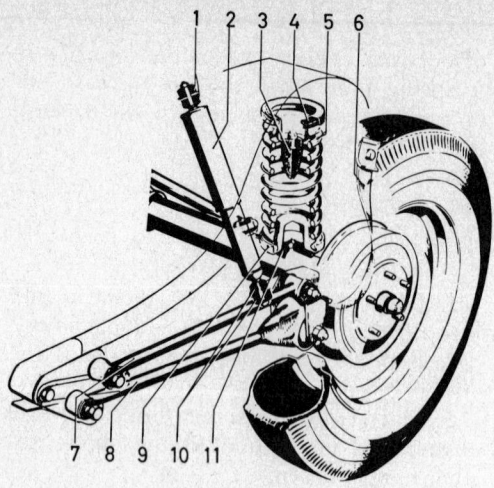

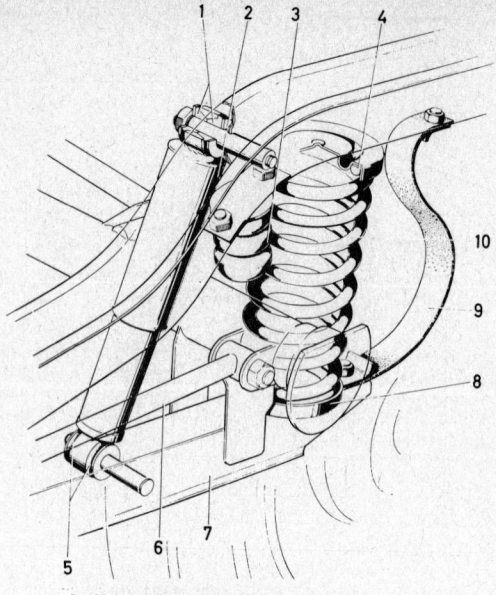

1. Upper shock absorber mounting
2. Shock absorber
3. Rubber bumper
4. Rubber spacer
5. Spring
6. Shock absorber limit band
7. Support rod
8. Torque rod
9. Spring seat
10. Lower shock absorber mounting
11. Rubber pad

Rear suspension; 120 series, 1800 (late production)

1. Upper shock absorber mounting
2. Shock absorber
3. Hollow rubber bumper
4. Rubber spacer
5. Lower shock absorber attachment
6. Support rod
7. Support stay
8. Lower spring seat
9. Shock absorber limit band
10. Spring

Rear suspension; 120 series station wagon

4b. Station Wagon: Loosen the lower attachment for the shock absorber and the lower attachment for the shock absorber band on both sides.

5. Lower the rear axle until the spring is free and then remove the spring and spacer.

INSTALLATION

Installation is the reverse of removal. Make sure that the rubber pad and the rubber spacer are in the correct position.

SHOCK ABSORBERS

The shock absorbers used on all models are of the hydraulic, double-acting, telescopic type. They need no maintenance and cannot be dismantled.

Front Shock Absorber Replacement

120 SERIES, 1800

1. Remove the upper attaching nut, washer and rubber bushing.
2. Remove the lower attaching nut, washers and rubber bushing.
3. Remove the bolt for the lower wash-

er in the lower A-arm and pull out the washer and shock absorber.

4. Installation is the reverse of removal.

140 SERIES, 164

1. Remove the upper nut, the washer, and the rubber bushing.
2. Remove the two lower attaching screws on the underside of the lower A-arm and remove the shock absorber.
3. Install the washer, the spacing sleeve, and the rubber bushing.
4. Install the shock absorber and tighten the lower screws.
5. Install the upper rubber bushing, the washer, and the nut. Tighten the nut until it makes firm contact with the spring sleeve.

Rear Shock Absorber Replacement

120 SERIES, 1800

1. Remove the upper attaching nut, washer, and rubber bushing from the

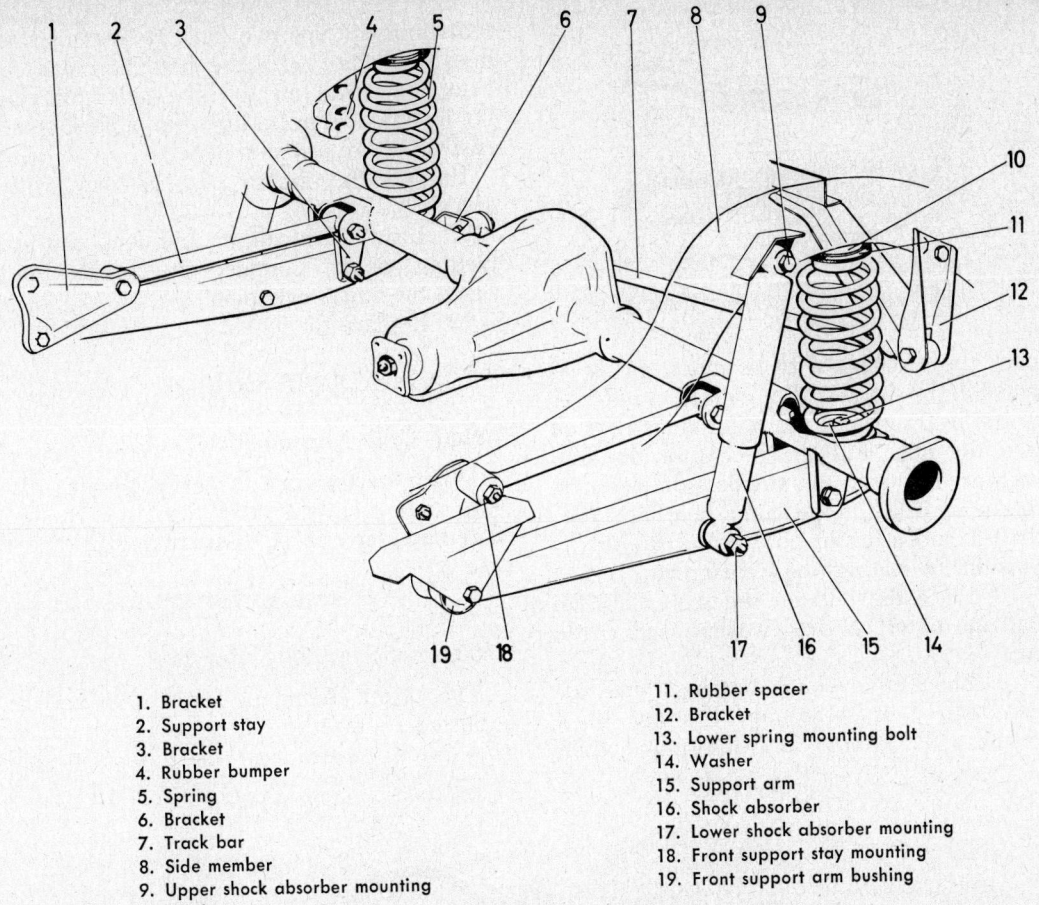

1. Bracket
2. Support stay
3. Bracket
4. Rubber bumper
5. Spring
6. Bracket
7. Track bar
8. Side member
9. Upper shock absorber mounting
10. Washer

11. Rubber spacer
12. Bracket
13. Lower spring mounting bolt
14. Washer
15. Support arm
16. Shock absorber
17. Lower shock absorber mounting
18. Front support stay mounting
19. Front support arm bushing

Rear suspension; 140 series, 164

trunk. On the 1800, remove these parts through the hole in the rear shelf.

2. Remove the lower attaching nut, washers, and rubber bushing. Remove the shock absorber.

3. Installation is the reverse order of removal. Place the washer with the larger hole on the inside of the lower rubber bushing. Tighten the nuts.

140 SERIES, 164

1. Remove the hub cap. Loosen the wheel nuts. Jack up the rear of the vehicle at the jack attachments. Remove the wheel. Unscrew and remove the shock absorber.

2. When installing, make sure that the spacing sleeve in the support arm has not been removed. Install and tighten the shock absorber. Install the wheel and wheel nuts. Lower the vehicle. Put on the hub cap.

FRONT WHEEL BEARINGS

Replacement and Adjustment

1. Jack up the front end and place blocks under lower A-arms. Remove the wheel.

2. Detach and plug the brake line. Bend up the lock washer aand screw out the attaching bolts. Lift out the caliper complete.

3. Remove the grease cap. Remove the split pin and castle nut. Pull off the hub. Pull off the inner bearing from the stub axle if the bearing remains in position.

4. Remove the bearing rings.

5. Clean the hub, brake disc, and grease cap.

6. Press in the new bearing rings.

7. Press grease into the bearings with a bearing packer. If one is not available,

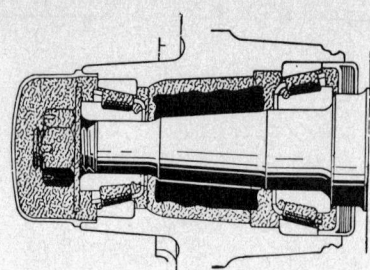

Lubricating the front wheel bearings

pack the bearings with as much grease as possible by hand. Also coat the outsides of the bearings and the outer rings pressed into the hub. Fill the recess in the hub with grease up to the smallest diameter on the outer ring for the outer bearing. Place the inner bearing in position in the hub. Press in the sealing ring with a drift.

8. Place the hub on the stub axle. Install the outer bearing, washer, and castle nut.

9. The front wheel bearings are adjusted by first tightening the nut to a torque of 7 kpm. (50 ft.lbs.), and then

loosening the nut two flats. If the nut slot does not align with the hole in the stub axle, loosen the nut until the cotter pin can be installed. Check that the wheel spins easily without any side play.

10. Fill the grease cap halfway with grease and install.

11. Install the caliper and lock the attaching bolts. Connect the brake line. Bleed the wheel cylinders.

12. Replace the wheel.

FRONT SUSPENSION

Front End Alignment

When performing wheel alignment, be sure that the front tires are properly inflated and have an equal tread depth.

CASTER ADJUSTMENT

1800, 120 Series, 140 Series, 164

The caster should be 0° to +1° and is adjusted by inserting or removing shims at the upper control arm shaft. Loosen the

1. Steering knuckle support
2. Upper control arm
3. Steering gear housing
4. Stabilizer
5. Pitman arm
6. Front axle member
7. Steering rod and tie rod
8. Lower control arm
9. Coil spring
10. Shock absorber
11. Steering knuckle
12. Steering arm

Front suspension, 544.

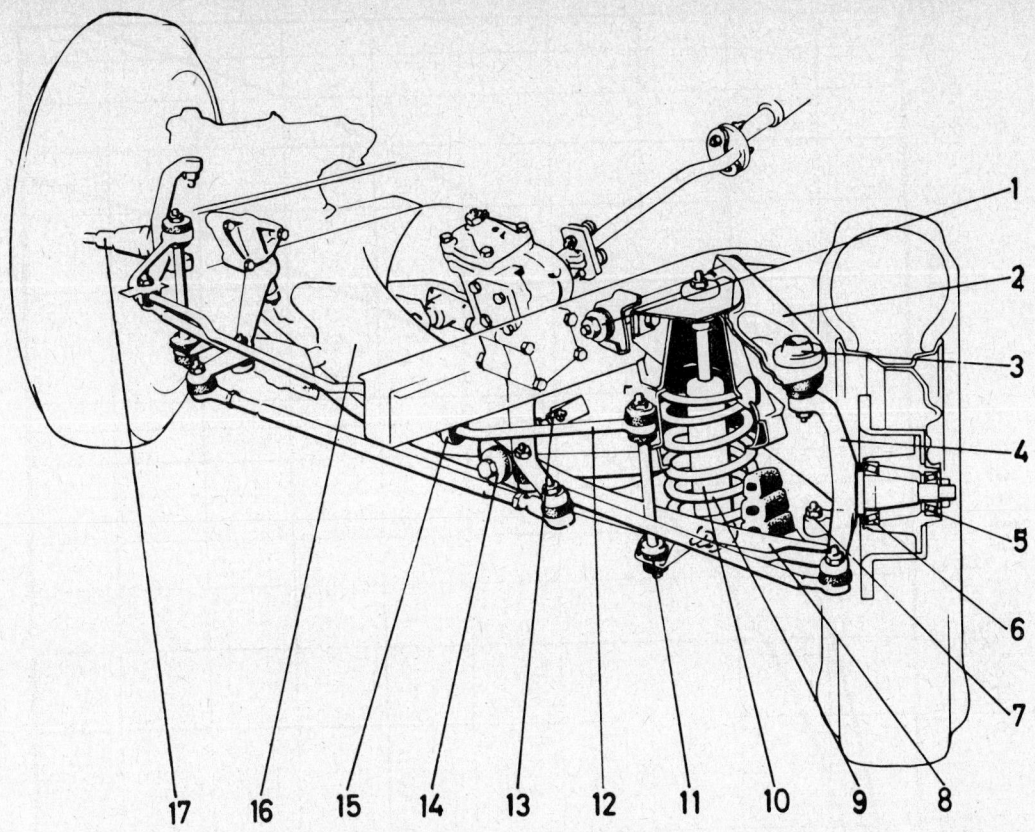

1. Upper control arm bushing
2. Upper control arm
3. Upper control arm ball joint
4. Steering knuckle
5. Outer wheel bearing
6. Inner wheel bearing

7. Lower control arm ball joint
8. Lower control arm
9. Coil spring
10. Shock absorber
11. Stabilizer attachment

12. Stabilizer
13. Stop screw max. wheel lock
14. Lower control arm bushing
15. Frame attachment for stabilizer
16. Front axle member
17. Front wheel axle

Front suspension, 140 series

Adjusting caster and camber, 140 series. A shows shims.

bolts several turns. Insert or remove shims as required.

Caster is increased toward the positive side either by inserting shims at the rear bolt, or by removing shims from the front bolt. For correct camber, the caster should be adjusted by transferring one-half the shim thickness from one bolt to the other, or simply by removing from one of the bolt positions the thickness required.

Tighten bolts before each measurement is made. (When adjustment is complete tighten bolts to 35-40 ft.lbs.).

PV444, 445, 544, P210

The caster should be −¾″ to +¼° and is adjusted by loosening the clamp bolt and

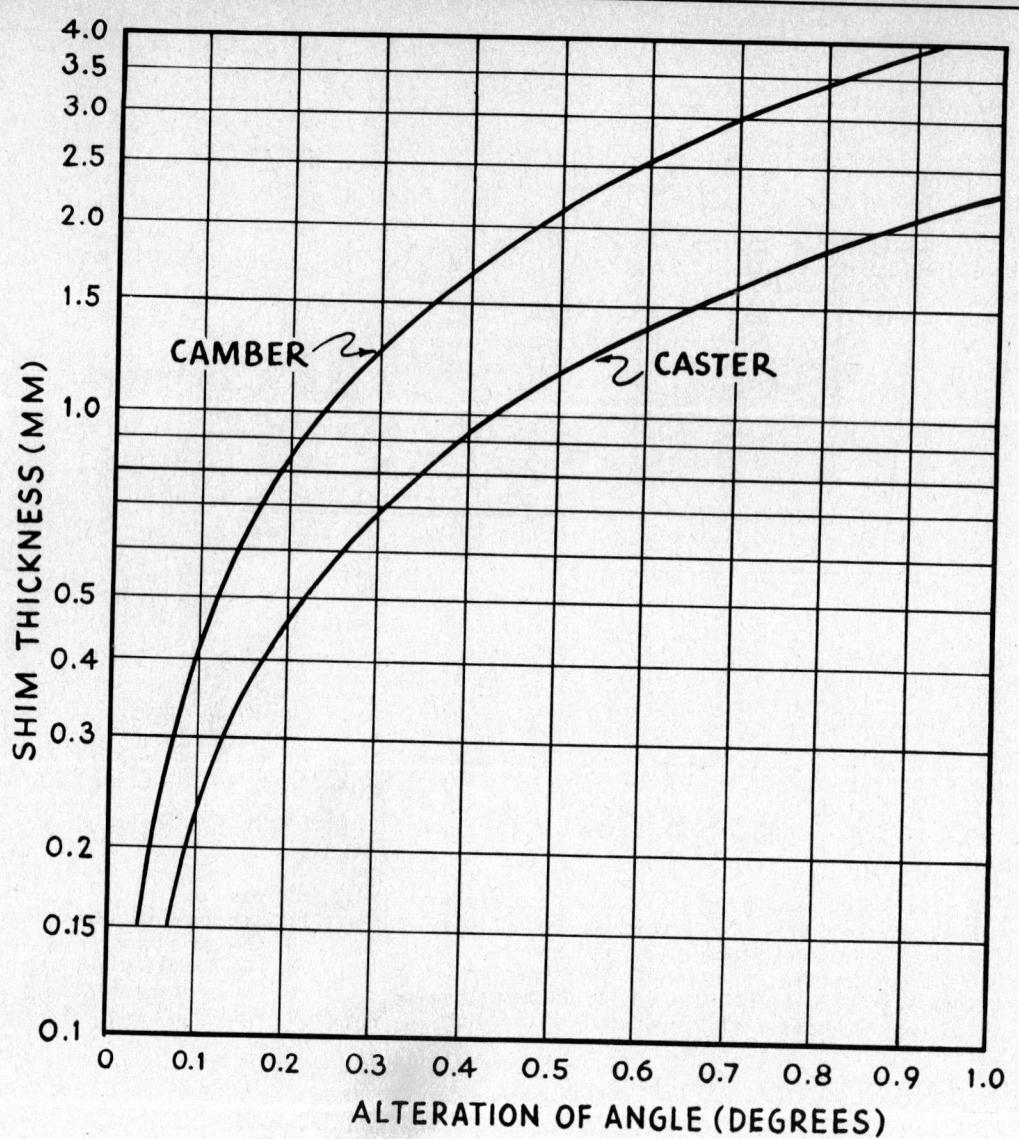

Effect of shim thickness on caster and camber angles; 140 series, 164

turning the eccentric bushing with a wrench. One complete turn alters the caster angle by ½°. NOTE: *If the wheel has the correct camber, one complete turn is necessary, otherwise the camber will be altered.* Tighten clamp bolt each time before measuring caster.

CAMBER ADJUSTMENT

1800, 120 Series, 140 Series, 164

The camber should be 0° to +½° and is adjusted by use of shims at the upper control arm shaft. Loosen bolts a few turns.

Then increase or decrease the number of shims equally at both the bolts. Camber positive angle is increased by removing shims and the negative angle increased by inserting shims. After each adjustment, tighten bolts before checking.

PV444, 445, 544, P210

After caster has been checked, camber can be adjusted to proper angle of −¼° to +½° by loosening the clamp bolt and turning the eccentric with a wrench. An alteration of camber causes a slight but negligible change in caster.

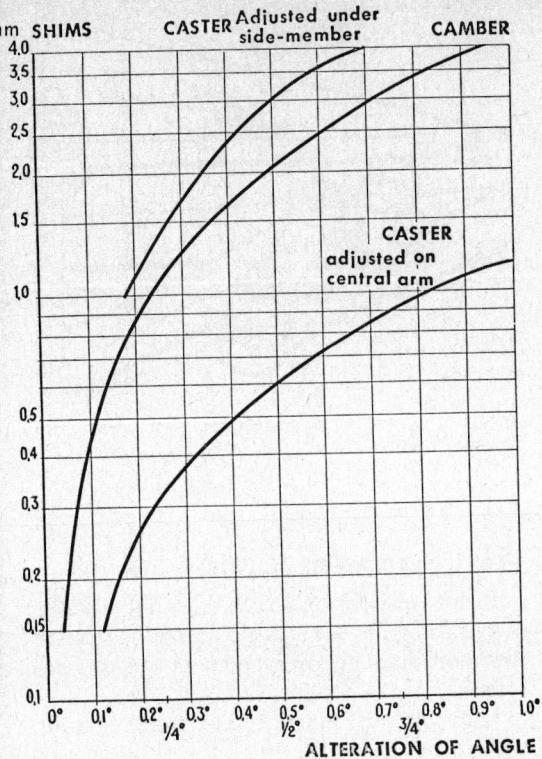

Effect of shim thickness on caster and camber angles; 120 series, 1800

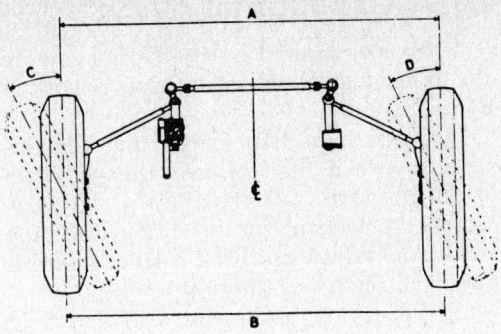

Toe-in equals B minus A.

Toe-In Adjustment

Toe-in should be ⁵⁄₃₂″ and is adjusted by loosening the clamp bolts on the tie rod, and turning the rod in the required direction. Toe-in is increased by turning the rod in the direction of forward wheel rotation. Check caster and camber before adjusting toe-in.

Steering Limit Adjustment

120 Series, P1800 (early production)

It should be possible to turn the wheels a maximum of 40° in either direction. Turning is limited by a stop screw on the pitman arm and relay arm. Adjustment is as follows:

1. Set the front wheels to point straight forward and drive them onto turntables. The turntables should be set to 0 and locked.

2. Release the turntable locking devices and turn hard left. Read the turning angle. If this is not 38-40°, loosen the locknut for the eccentric head stop screw on the pitman arm. Turn the wheel to 40°. Adjust the stop screw so that it just contacts the pitman arm and tighten the locknut.

3. Repeat this procedure with the right wheel and stop screw on the relay arm.

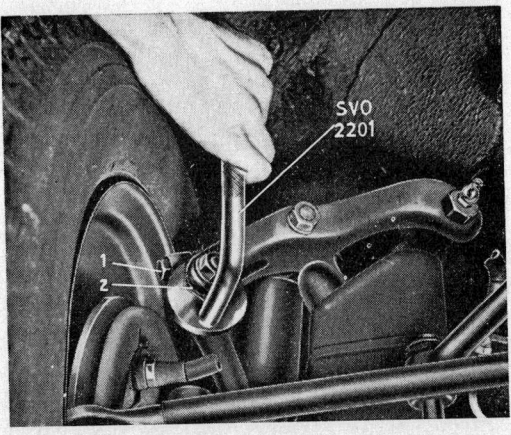

1. Clamp bolt   2. Eccentric

Adjusting caster and camber (PV544).

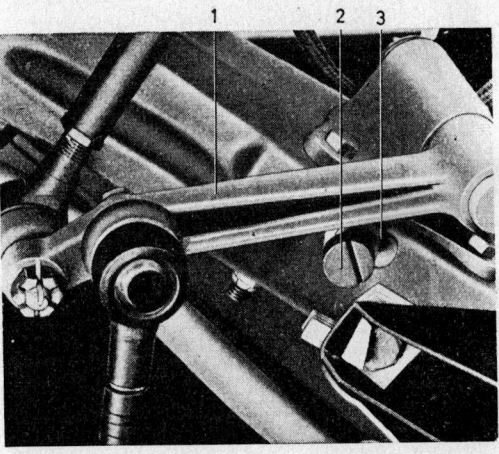

1. Relay arm
2. Eccentric screw
3. Locknut

Adjusting steering limits; 120 series, 1800

120 Series, P1800 (late production)

Turning is limited by the stop screw on the pitman arm and relay arm. Adjust as follows:

1. Turn hard left. Check that the distance between the tire and the stabilizer is 10-15 mm. (25/64-19/32″). If not, loosen the locknut for the relay arm stop screw and adjust until the correct figure is obtained. Then lock the stop screw.

2. Repeat this procedure with the right wheel and the stop screw on the pitman arm.

140 Series, 164

Wheel turning is limited by stop bolts, at the pitman arm for left turns and at the relay arm for right turns. Adjustment is as follows:

1. Turn hard left. Check that the angle of the wheels is 45°. (43-45° for 1971 140 Series.) If it is not, adjust the stop bolt at the pitman arm.

2. Repeat this procedure with the right wheel and the stop screw on the relay arm.

STEERING AXIS CANT
(KING PIN INCLINATION)

The steering axis cant or king pin inclination angle cannot be adjusted. An incorrect angle usually indicates a bent stub axle or steering part. For the 544, and P210, the correct angle is 5° at 0° camber. For the P120 and P1800, the angle is 8° at 0° camber. For the 140 series and the 164, the angle is 7.5° at 0° camber.

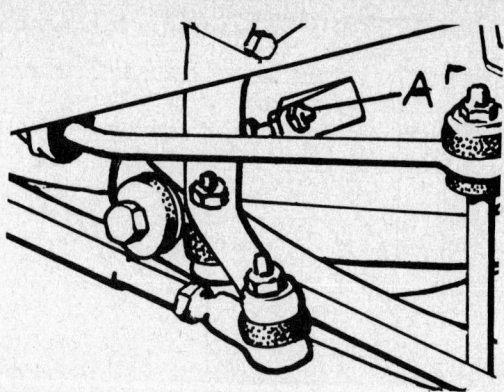

Adjusting screw for steering limits; 140 series, 164. Screw is item A.

Front Suspension Repair

Front suspension parts are not usually repairable or adjustable after excessive wear or damage. Replacement procedures follow.

Instructions for the replacement of king pins apply only to models using them—PV444, 445, 554, and P210. All other models use ball joints. Ball joints without grease fittings do not need lubrication. However, the rubber seal should be inspected at least once a year and replaced if damaged. When replacing the rubber seal on this type of ball joint, fill it with chassis grease. On ball joints with grease fittings, the rubber seal and washer must also be replaced.

COMPLETE FRONT SUSPENSION REMOVAL

120 Series, P1800

1. Remove the hub caps and loosen the wheel nuts.

2. Jack up the front end so that the wheels are clear of the ground. Place blocks under the body at the front jacking points.

3. Remove the wheels.

4. Place a support under the front of the engine.

5. Place a wooden block under the brake pedal. Disconnect the brake hoses from the body and plug the connections.

6. Remove the pitman arm with a puller.

7. Disconnect the front engine mountings. Disconnect the relay arm and stabilizer from the body.

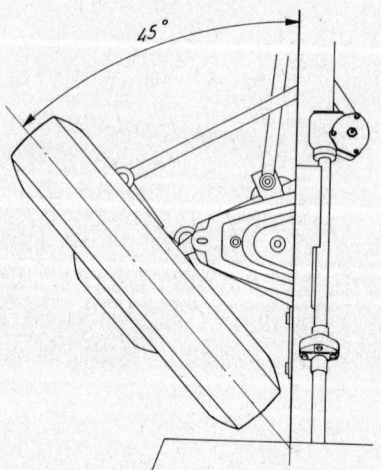

Adjusting steering limits; 140 series, 164

8. Place a jack under the front cross-member. Remove the front crossmember attaching bolts. Do not lose the shims.

9. Lower the front crossmember and pull it out.

PV444, 445, 544, P210

The procedure is very similar to that for the P120 and P1800 models except for the following: When jacking up the PV445 and P210 models, place the blocks under the frame behind the front crossmember. After removing the front engine mounting bolts, remove the front engine guard plate and put a wooden block (about 24½" x 2½" x 2½") above the frame side members but under the fan hub, inserting it from below. In addition, on the PV445 and P210, two wooden blocks (about 1½" x 2½" x 2½") should be put between the frame and above-mentioned block. On some models, a recess must be made in the wooden block.

104 Series, 164

1. Install a lifting tool. Install the plate with the upper screw (no flat washer) for the timing gear casing. Raise the engine until the weight is taken off the front engine mounts. Remove the hub caps and loosen the nuts for the front wheels.

2. Jack up the vehicle under the front jack attachments. Remove the front wheels.

3. Disconnect the steering rods from the steering arms.

4. Remove the brake hose clamps from the stabilizer screws. Remove the screws.

5. Loosen the brake hoses from the bracket at the support member.

6. Remove the lower nuts for the front engine mounts.

7. Remove the front crossmember attaching bolts, lower and remove the front end.

COMPLETE FRONT SUSPENSION INSTALLATION

120 Series, P1800

1. Place the front crossmember on a jack and move it under the vehicle.

2. Raise the crossmember into position. Install the shims and tighten the bolts.

3. Remove the support under the engine and tighten down the engine onto the front mounts.

4. Install the relay arm and stabilizer to the body.

5. Install the pitman arm; the marks on the pitman arm shaft and pitman arm should align. Install the washer and nut. Tighten the nut to 13.5-16.5 kgm. (100-200 ft.lbs.).

6. Connect the brake lines and bleed the brake system.

7. Install the wheels and lower the vehicle. Tighten the wheel nuts to 10-14 kgm. (70-100 ft. lbs.). Install the hub caps.

8. Check the wheel alignment.

PV444, 445, 544, P210

1. Lift the front suspension unit on a hydraulic jack and move it under the vehicle.

2. Place two guide pins into the body (the frame on PV445 and P210). Raise the front crossmember into position and bolt it on.

3. Remove the wooden block for supporting the engine and tighten the engine down onto the front engine mounts. Connect the brake lines.

4. Install the pitman arm.

5. Install the stabilizers.

6. Bleed the front brake system.

7. Install the wheels. Lower the vehicle and tighten the wheel nuts to a 10-14 kgm. (72-101 ft.lbs.). Install the hub caps.

8. Check the wheel alignment.

140 Series, 164

1. Install the guide pins in the front holes for the front crossmember.

2. Place a jack under the front end and raise it into position. Install the rear bolts. Remove the guide pins and install the front bolts.

3. Tighten the engine mounts.

4. Install the brake hoses. Install the bolts for the stabilizer. Firmly secure the brake hoses.

5. Install the steering rods and front wheels.

6. Bleed the brakes.

7. Lower the vehicle and remove the lifting device. Then install the timing gear casing screw with the flat washer.

KING PIN REPLACEMENT

PV444, 445, 544, P210

Loosen wheel nuts slightly, and then jack up front end and place blocks under the lower control arms. Remove wheel and wheel hub, removing inner bearing race if necessary. Remove four bolts that hold brake backing plate in place and splash guard to steering knuckle. Lift off brake backing plate and tie up to avoid straining brake line.

Remove cotter pin and nut from steering arm ball joint. Release ball joint. Loosen nut and unscrew upper control arm bolt. Remove clamping bolt and eccentric bushing. Disconnect shock absorber at bottom. Lift off steering knuckle support. Screw out lower bushing.

Drive out king pin stop key, and remove sealing washer with a pointed punch. Drive king pin downward and out. Remove grease fittings and drive out king pin bushings.

Press in new bushings. Make sure lubricating holes line up with grease fitting holes, and that the short lubricating groove faces the sealing washer. Ream bushings. Threaded bushing clearance should be .012-.023" with a wear limit of .032". King pin radial clearance should not exceed .012". Install grease fittings. Coat bushings with chassis grease.

Position the axle steering knuckle, thrust bearing, and adjusting shims, and place a centering mandrel in the upper bushing. Change shims until there is a friction torque of 4.34-56.4 in.lbs. when turning the axle. This would be a reading of 0.66-9.46 lbs. on a spring scale attached to the cotter pin hole in the axle and pulled at right angles to the axle. Drive in king pin, making sure of correct position. Insert stop key. Check to see that steering knuckle turns easily. Install sealing washers with convex

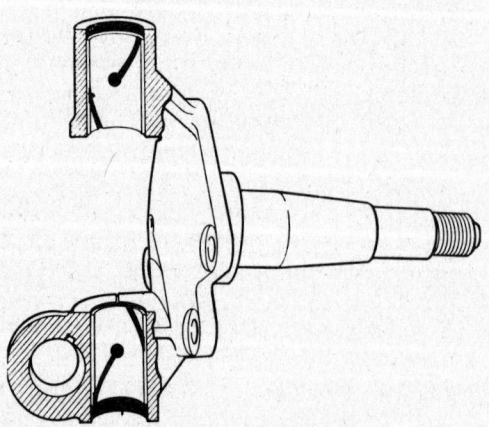

King pin bushings

side out, then knock them flat with a hammer and drift pin.

Install steering knuckle support with bushings, guard plate and bolts. Connect steering rod to steering arm. Turn ball joint so that cotter pin hole aligns longitudinally with rod. Tighten castle nut to 23-27 ft.lbs. Install brake backing plate and splash plate on steering knuckle. Install hub and wheel. Adjust wheel bearings and check front wheel alignment.

STUB AXLE REPLACEMENT— 120 SERIES, P1800, 140 SERIES, 164

1. Remove the hub cap and loosen the wheel nuts.

2. Jack up the front end and place blocks under the lower A-arms. Remove the wheel nuts and the wheel.

3. (Only applies to vehicles with disc brakes.)

Disconnect the brake line and plug. Bend back the locking plate, and unscrew the attaching bolts. Lift off the caliper complete.

4. Remove the grease cap. Remove the cotter pin and castle nut. Pull off the hub. Pull off the inner bearing from the stub axle, if the bearing remains in position.

5. Remove the ball joints.

6. Replace the stub axle and install the ball joints.

7. Place the inner bearing in position in the hub. Press in the oil seal with a drift.

8. Place the hub on the stub axle. Install the outer bearing, washer, and castle nut.

9. The front wheel bearings are adjusted by first tightening the nut to 7 kgm. (50 ft.lbs.). Then loosen the nut one third of a turn. If the slot in the nut does not align with the hole in the stub axle, loosen the nut until the cotter pin can be installed. Check that the wheel rotates easily but without any side play.

10. Fill the grease cap half full of grease and install.

11. (Only applies to vehicles with disc brakes.)

Install the caliper and lock the attaching bolts. Connect the brake line. Bleed the wheel cylinders.

12. Install the wheel. Lower the vehicle and tighten the wheel nuts to 10-14 kgm. (70-100 ft.lbs.) Install the hub cap.

BALL JOINT REPLACEMENT — 140 SERIES, 164

Upper

Jack up front of vehicle and remove wheel. Loosen nut for upper control arm ball joint. With a hammer, tap the axle around the ball joint pin until it is loosened from the axle. Remove nut completely and suspend upper end of axle to avoid straining brake lines. Loosen control arm nuts one-half turn, lift arm slightly and press out ball joint.

Before installing new ball joint, see that rubber cover is filled with grease. Bend the pin end over the slot, and be sure that the grease forces its way out. Press ball joint into control arm with sleeve and drift, making sure that slot in ball joint lines up longitudinally with shaft of control arm either externally or internally, for the pin has maximum movement in the direction of this line. Should the ball joint be incorrectly positioned, turn half a turn and then press the ball joint into the right position. Turn down the control arm and tighten the nuts on the control arm shaft. Tighten ball joint against axle. If the pin rotates, hold it with a C-clamp. Install front wheel.

Lower

Jack up front of vehicle and remove wheel. Disconnect steering rod from steering arm and disconnect brake lines from stabilizer bolt. Slightly loosen nuts on upper and lower ball joints. With a hammer, tap ball joints loose from axle. Raise lower

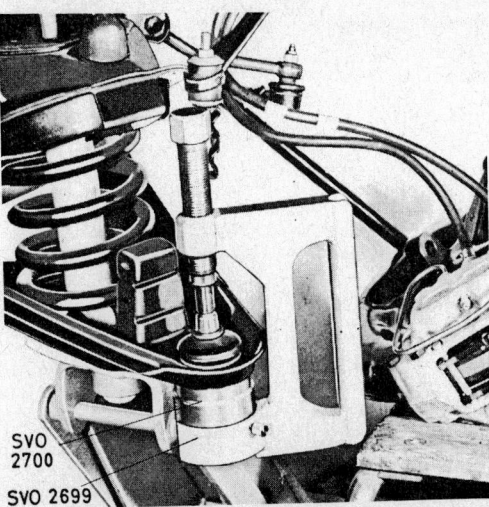

SVO 2700
SVO 2699

Removing ball joint, upper control arm.

control arm with a jack. Remove nuts. Remove steering knuckle with hub and front wheel brake unit, and support the assembly to avoid strain on brake lines. Using the same tools as for the upper arm, press ball joint out of lower arm. Before installing new joint, check to see that rubber cover is filled with grease by bending the pin to the side, forcing the grease out. Fill with grease if necessary. Press new ball joint into position in control arm. Install steering knuckle and tighten upper and lower ball joints. Install steering rod, connect brake lines to stabilizer bolt and install front wheel.

Steering

The early PV444 and PV544 models use a Ross cam and lever steering box while later PV444 and PV544 models use a Gemmer cam and roller steering box. 120 series, P1800, 140 series, and 164 use the Gemmer steering box along with other improvements in the steering linkage. Steering rod ball joints are all plastic-lined and do not need lubrication, except for the ones used in early PV444 and PV544 models with grease fittings. Ball joints with grease fittings require periodic lubrication.

The collapsible steering columns used in the 140 series and 164 are designed to absorb some of the shock of a frontal impact and to prevent the steering wheel and column from being driven back against the driver. These steering columns have a flange that breaks on impact. The 140 column is a two-piece unit that allows the lower half to move and the upper half to remain stationary. The 164 column has a collapsible sleeve between the upper and lower parts which telescope together. The 164 column has its break-away flange at the steering box.

A steering lock in unit with the ignition switch is used in the 140 series and 164.

The 164 and 1800E may be equipped with the ZF hydraulic power steering system which eases steering effort and reduces steering wheel lock-to-lock turns slightly. The hydraulic reservoir fluid level should be checked periodically to maintain it at the FULL level mark. Add only enough type A automatic transmission fluid to maintain level.

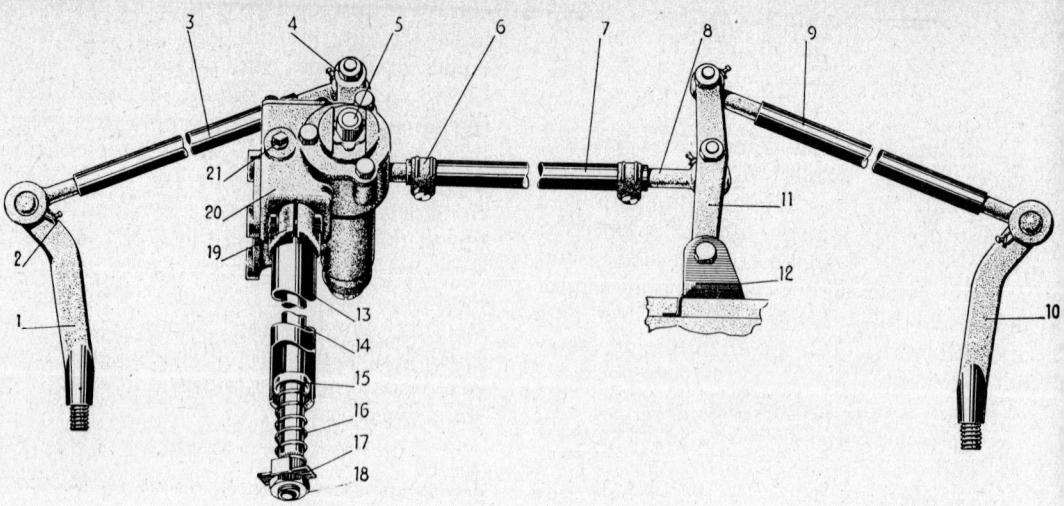

1. Left steering arm	8. Ball joint	15. Ball bearing
2. Grease nipple	9. Right steering rod	16. Spring
3. Left steering rod	10. Right steering arm	17. Locking washer
4. Pitman arm	11. Idler arm	18. Nut
5. Adjusting screw	12. Bracket for idler arm	19. Clamp for housing
6. Clamp	13. Steering column housing	20. Steering gear housing
7. Tie rod	14. Steering column	21. Grease plug

Steering gear, PV444, 445, 544, P210.

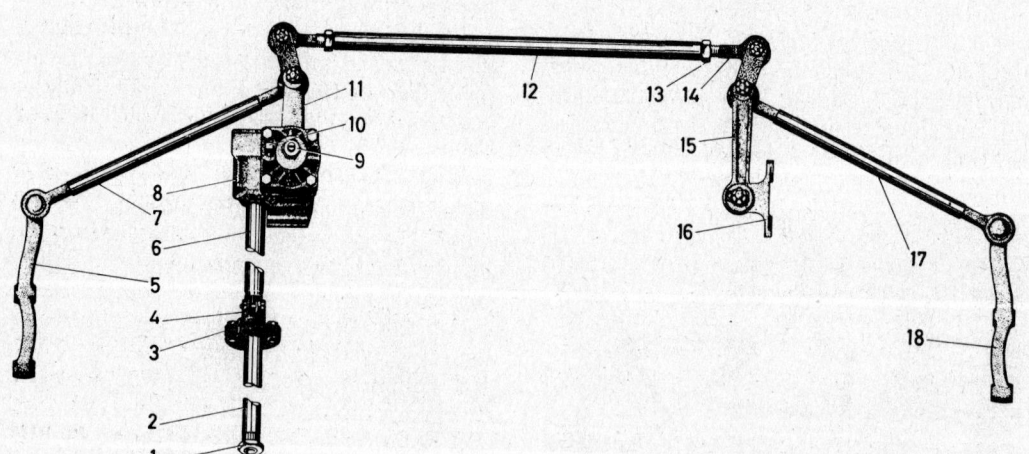

1. Steering wheel nut	7. Left steering rod	13. Locknut or clamping bolt
2. Upper steering column	8. Steering box	14. Tie rod end
3. Coupling disc	9. Adjusting screw	15. Relay arm
4. Clamp	10. Filler plug	16. Relay arm bracket
5. Left steering arm	11. Pitman arm	17. Right steering rod
6. Lower steering column	12. Tie rod	18. Right steering arm

Steering gear components, typical of P1800, 120 series, 140 series, 164, P120 (late production). Different column arrangements are used.

STEERING WHEEL R&R

PV444, 445 without Turn Signal Switch Housing

1. Remove the horn fuse.
2. Remove the horn ring by pushing it down and turning it a quarter of a turn counter-clockwise. Remove the steering wheel nut.
3. Pull off the steering wheel. A special puller is necessary.
4. Install the steering wheel so that the spokes are horizontal when the wheels are straight. Torque the nut to 3.5 kgm. (25 ft.lbs.). Place the horn ring in position, press it down and turn it a quarter of a turn clockwise. Replace the fuse.

PV444, 445 with Turn Signal Switch Housing

1. Remove the horn fuse.
2. Loosen the bolt on the left side of the steering wheel hub, turn and pull the horn ring upward. Remove the steering wheel nut. On late production models remove the lock washer first.
3. Pull off the steering wheel with a wheel puller. When doing this the turn signal switch must be in the neutral position, or it will be damaged.
4. Install the steering wheel. Check that the switch is in the neutral position and that the steering wheel spokes are horizontal when the front wheels are straight. Tighten the steering wheel nut to 3.5-5 kgm. (25-35 ft.lbs.). On late production models the nut has a lockwasher.
5. Check that the switch housing is not too near the steering wheel after installation. The distance between the upper edge of the housing and the steering wheel hub should be 1-1.5 mm. (0.04-0.06"). The distance is adjusted by loosening the clamp bolt on the side of the switch housing and moving it.
6. Install the horn ring and screw in the locking bolt. Replace the fuse.

PV544, P210

1. Remove the horn fuse.
2. Unscrew the two attaching bolts, turn the horn ring slightly, and lift it up. Bend down the lock washer and remove the steering wheel nut and washer.
3. Check that the turn signal switch is in the neutral position. Pull off the steering wheel with a puller.

4. Install the steering wheel. Check that the switch is in the neutral position and that the steering wheel spokes are horizontal when the front wheels are straight. Install the lock washer and tighten the steering wheel nut to 3.5-5 kgm. (25-35 ft.lbs.). Lock the nut.

P120

1. Remove both the attaching bolts on the underside of the steering wheel spokes and remove the horn ring.
2. Bend up the lock washer and remove the steering wheel nut. Mark the position of the steering wheel.
3. Set the turn signal switch in the neutral position. Pull off the steering wheel with a puller.
4. Install the steering wheel, noting the alignment marks. The wheel spokes should be horizontal when the wheels are straight. Tighten the steering wheel nut to 3.5-5.0 kgm. (25-35 ft.lbs.) and then lock with the lock washer.
5. Install the horn ring.

P1800

1. Pull the horn lead from the connecting block on the steering box.
2. Carefully pry out the horn button with a screwdriver or similar tool.
3. Bend back the lock washer and remove the steering wheel nut. Mark the position of the steering wheel.
4. Pull off the steering wheel. Remove the housing and hub from the steering wheel.
5. Install the steering wheel and other parts, noting the alignment marks. Tighten the steering wheel nut to 3.5-5.0 kgm. (25-35 ft.lbs.) and then lock it.

140 Series, 164

1. Remove the screws for the turn signal switch housing and lift off the housing. Remove the screws, lift up the horn ring, disconnect the ground wire, and remove the horn ring.
2. Remove the steering wheel nut.
3. Point the wheels straight. Using a steering wheel puller, remove the steering wheel.
4. Make sure that the wheels are straight. Install the steering wheel and the steering wheel nut. Tighten the nut to 3.5-5.0 kgm. (25-35 ft.lbs.).
5. Connect the ground wire and install the horn ring.

6. Install first the lower then the upper part of the direction switch housing.

STEERING BOX R&R

PV444, 445, 544, P210

1. Remove the steering wheel.
2. Disconnect the horn lead on the steering box. Pull the lead with bushing, spring, and cover up through the steering column. Remove the screw and remove the housing for the turn signal switch.
3. Remove the jacket tube support under the instrument panel. Lift the seat out of the way.
4. Remove the pitman arm nut. Pull off the pitman arm from the pitman arm shaft with a puller.
5. Disconnect the steering box from the body (on PV445 and P210, the frame) and lift out the steering box with jacket tube forward and upward.

To replace:

1. Insert the jacket tube through the hole in the firewall (do not forget to fit the rubber seal). Place the steering box in position and bolt it onto the body (on PV445 and P210, to the frame).
2. Install the support for the jacket tube but do not tighten the bolts.
3. Turn the steering column to the center position (count the number of turns) and set the wheels to point straight. Install the pitman arm onto the pitman arm shaft. On those models with a mark on the pitman arm, the mark should align with the mark on the pitman arm shaft. Install the washer nut, and pin. The nut should be tightened to 13.5-16.5 kgm. (100-120 ft.lbs.).
4. Install the turn signal switch housing.
5. Place the washer and spring, (and on Ross type steering gear, the spacing ring) on the steering column. Install the steering wheel so that the spokes are horizontal. Install the locking washer (late production) and nut, which should be tightened to 3.5-5.0 kgm. (25-35 ft. lbs.).
6. On types without turn signal switch housing, the jacket tube is now slid up under the steering wheel hub and the clamp tightened.
7. Tighten the bolts for the support under the instrument panel.
8. Adjust the turn signal switch housing so that a gap of 1-1.5 mm. (0.04-

0.06") is obtained between the upper edge of the housing and the steering wheel hub.
9. Install the horn lead and horn ring. Connect the leads on the steering box. Replace the fuse.

120 Series, P1800

1. Disconnect the horn lead from the connecting block.
2. Unscrew the two nuts and remove the bolts.
3. Remove the pitman arm with a puller.
4. Unscrew and remove the three attaching bolts.
5. Lift and turn the steering box. Pull out the horn lead from the lower section of the steering column and steering box. Lift off the steering box, being careful when moving the clamp past the brake line.

To replace:

1. Place the steering box in position. Be careful when moving the clamp past the brake line. Install the attaching bolts. On P1800 insert the horn lead through the lower section of the steering column with the help of a piece of wire. Place the steering box in position and install the attaching bolts, washers, and nuts loosely.
2. Assemble the clamp to the coupling disc. Do not forget the ground lead.
3. Adjust the position of the steering box so that the upper and lower sections of the steering column form a straight line. Tighten the attaching bolts.
4. Install the pitman arm so that the alignment mark on the pitman arm shaft aligns with the mark on the pitman arm. Tighten the nut to 13.5-16.5 kgm. (100-120 ft.lbs.).
5. Check that the steering wheel spokes are horizontal when the wheels are straight.

140 Series

1. Jack up the vehicle at the front.
2. Loosen the bolt at the lower steering column shaft flange. Remove the nuts and move the lower part of the flange as far down as possible on the steering cam.
3. Remove the lock nut for the pitman arm. Pull off the pitman arm.
4. Remove the nuts and bolts and lift out the steering box.

To install:

1. Place the steering box in position and tighten the bolts.

2. Install the pitman arm and tighten the nut to 19 kgm. (135 ft.lbs.).

3. Move the steering wheel so that the wheels point straight and tighten both halves of the steering column shaft flange.

4. Lower the vehicle.

164

1. Jack up the front end.

2. Remove the lock nut for the pitman arm. Pull the pitman arm off.

3. Loosen the clamp bolt. Remove the attaching bolts. Pull the steering box forward.

To replace:

1. Turn the steering cam to the right to the end position and then back 2½ turns. The steering gear will then be in the middle position.

2. Check that the steering wheel is straight. Place the steering box in position and install it to the flange. Install and tighten the attaching bolts. Tighten the clamp bolt.

3. Point the front wheels straight and install the pitman arm. Tighten the nut to 17.5-20 kgm, (125-145 ft.lbs.).

4. Check to make sure that the steering gear can be turned from stop bolt to stop bolt. Lower the front end of the vehicle.

POWER STEERING BOX R&R

164, 1800E

1. Jack up the front end.

2. Drain the system.

1. Nut	7. Vent screw
2. Bolt	8. Adjusting screw
3. Flange	9. Steering box
4. Clamp bolt	10. Drain plug
5. Return line	11. Mounting bolt
6. Delivery line	

Power steering box; 164, 1800E

3. Remove the lock nut for the pitman arm. Pull the pitman arm off.

4. Disconnect the lines from the steering box after the connections have been cleaned. Loosen the clamp bolt.

5. Remove the attaching bolts and pull the steering box forward.

To replace:

1. Place the steering box in the center position. A slight increase in resistance should then be felt, the position of the pitman arm shaft lands should be as marked and the alignment marks on the control spindle and housing should coincide.

2. Check to make sure that the steering wheel is straight.

3. Install the steering box spindle in the flange of the lower steering column section. Install and tighten the attaching bolts. Tighten the clamp bolt. Connect the lines. The longer delivery line should run in a curve and be clamped.

4. Point the front wheels straight and install the pitman arm. Tighten the nut to 17.5-20 kgm. (125-141 ft.lbs.).

5. Fill and bleed the system.

STEERING AND TIE ROD RECONDITIONING

Bent or otherwise damaged steering rods and tie rods must be replaced, not straightened. Ball joints cannot be disassembled or adjusted, so they must also be replaced when worn or damaged. Steering rod ball joints are made in unit with the rod, so the complete rod and ball joint assembly must be replaced. If the steering rod is to be removed, first remove the ball joint on the pitman arm and idler arm using the procedure described under King Pin Replacement. Tie rod ball joints can be replaced individually.

STEERING BOX OVERHAUL

Disassembly

Ross Unit — PV444, 445, 544, P210

1. Clean the steering box externally.

2. Loosen the clamp for the jacket tube and pull the tube out.

3. Remove the cover and drain the oil. Lift out the pitman arm shaft.

4. Unscrew the three bolts for the cover and lift it off. Do not lose the shims.

5. Pull out the steering column and steering worm. The ball bearings with outer rings will come out at the same time.

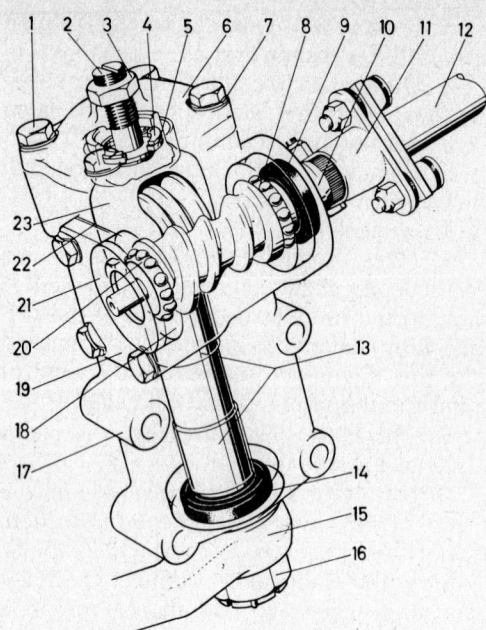

1. Bolt
2. Adjusting screw, pitman arm shaft
3. Locknut
4. Circlip
5. Adjusting washer
6. Cover
7. Tab washer
8. Upper ball bearing, steering cam
9. Oil seal, steering cam
10. Steering cam
11. Flange
12. Lower steering column section
13. Bushings, pitman arm shaft
14. Oil seal, pitman arm shaft
15. Pitman arm
16. Nut
17. Steering box
18. Lower bearing race, steering cam
19. Steering cam cover
20. Lower ball bearing, steering cam
21. Washer
22. Spacer
23. Pitman arm shaft

Steering box, 140 series

6. Remove the locking rings and ball bearings.
7. If necessary, pull out the bearing in the jacket tube with a puller.

GEMMER UNIT — P120, P1800, 140 SERIES, 164

1. Clean the steering box externally.
2. Remove the bolts for the upper cover, pull up the cover and pitman arm shaft a little and drain the oil. Pull out the cover and pitman arm shaft.

3. Remove the lower cover. Do not lose adjusting shims. On steering box part number 250051, remove the clamp and take out the jacket tube. Rap the steering column carefully and pull out the steering worm with bearings.
4. Loosen the locknut (on early production models, the cap and locking washer) and take the adjusting screw out of the cover. The adjusting screw can be removed from the pitman arm shaft after the locking ring has been removed.

Inspection

Ross Unit

Clean all parts in a safe solvent.
Check the levers on the pitman arm shaft. If these are scratched, scored, or worn the pitman arm shaft must be replaced. Examine the contact surfaces of the steering worm with the levers and the inner races of the ball bearings on the bolt. If there is any scoring or other damage, the steering worm with steering column must be replaced. Check to see whether the pitman arm shaft is loose in the bushing. If so, replace the bushings. Use a drift for removal.
Examine the outer ring and balls of the bearings.

Gemmer Unit

Clean all parts in a safe solvent.
Check the pitman arm shaft. The roller must not be scratched, scored, or worn on the contact surfaces or be loose in the pitman arm shaft. If so, the pitman arm shaft must be replaced. Examine the steering worm contact surfaces against the roller and the inner races of the ball bearings. If there are any scratches, scoring, or heavy wear, the steering worm with steering column must be replaced. Examine the outer rings and balls of the bearings. Any bearing parts which are scored or otherwise damaged must be replaced. The upper bearing outer ring is removed with a puller.
Check to see whether the pitman arm shaft is loose in the bushings. If so, replace the bushings. On steering box part number 250051 both the bushings in the housings are pressed out at the same time in the direction of the cover with a drift. The bushings in other steering boxes are removed independently in either direction

with a puller. The bushing in the cast iron cover is slotted and can be removed with a screwdriver. The bushing in the light alloy cover is cast in so that the complete cover must be replaced. If the pressed-in jacket tube must be separated from the housing it should be pressed out with a drift.

Assembly

Ross Unit

1. Press in the pitman arm shaft bushings with a drift. Ream the bushings. After reaming, clean off all metal chips.

2. Install the new sealing ring with a drift.

3. Install the ball bearings (11 balls in each bearing) onto the steering worm and install new locking rings.

4. Place the steering worm in the housing. Install the upper cover. Shim so that the steering column moves easily but without any play when the bolts are tightened. Be careful that the bearings are not damaged if too many shims are removed.

5. Place the pitman arm shaft in the housing. Check that the levers run easily in the steering worm when turned.

6. Install the adjusting screw in the cover with a new gasket.

7. Turn the steering column until the pitman arm shaft levers are about in the center of the steering worm. Tighten the adjusting screw while turning the steering column back and forth until slight binding is felt. Then loosen the adjusting screw until this binding just disappears. Lock the adjusting screw in this position.

8. Install the bearing and clamp for the jacket tube and place the felt ring on the steering column. Install the jacket tube with the slot turned up. Tighten the clamp on the type with turn signal switch housing.

9. Fill with oil. First fill as far as possible and then check the level after about 15 minutes.

Gemmer Unit

1. Press the pitman arm shaft bushings into the housing from each direction. In steering box part number 250051, the longer bushing is placed below. In late production steering boxes the upper of the original bushings has oil grooves. In this way the bushings receive slightly better lubrication when they are new. These oil grooves are not necessary. The bushings are sold without oil grooves. On cast iron upper covers, the bushing is pressed in with a drift.

2. Ream the bushings in the housing. On cast iron covers (earlier production), the bushing is first pressed in with a drift, after which it is reamed. This is first inserted through the bushings of the housing. The cover is then installed and the reaming operation carried out. After reaming, all metal chips must be removed.

3. Install the sealing ring for the pitman arm shaft with a drift.

4. If the upper bearing outer ring has been removed, this is pressed in with a drift. If the jacket tube on a steering box without a clamp has been removed, press the tube into the steering box housing so that the steering column should project 77-79 mm. (3.03-3.11″) from the jacket tube.

5. Place the steering column with bearings in the steering box housing. Install the lower cover with adjusting shims of the same thickness as were used previously. Tighten the bolts. The steering column should move easily without any play. When the bearings are correctly adjusted, a maximum torque of 1-2.5 kgcm. (0.87-2.17 in.lbs.) should be required to turn the steering column.

6. On steering box part number 250051, install the jacket tube with ball bearings and felt ring. Turn the slot of the jacket tube up and tighten the clamp.

7. Install the adjusting screw, washer, and locking ring in the pitman arm shaft. The end play of the adjusting screw should be as small as possible and should not exceed 0.05 mm. (0.002″). The play is reduced by replacing the washer with a thicker one. The adjusting screw must turn easily.

8. Install the pitman arm shaft into the steering box housing. Apply a few drops of oil to the adjusting screw in the pitman arm shaft.

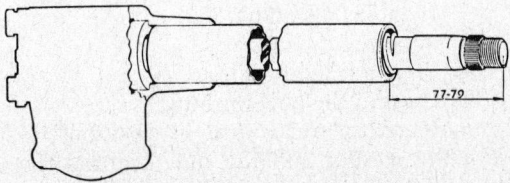

Steering column should protrude 77-79 mm.

9. Install the cover and gasket over the pitman arm shaft. Tighten the adjusting screw so that the pitman arm shaft is not pinched when the attaching bolts are tightened.

10. Install the steering wheel and attach a spring scale to the circumference of the wheel. Screw down the adjusting screw until a pull of 0.4-0.7 kg. (0.88-1.54 lb.) is required to turn the steering wheel past the center position. When the correct setting has been obtained, the locking washer and cap nut are installed (cast iron cover). There are two different types of locking washer for fine adjustment. On a light alloy cover, the adjusting screw is locked with a nut. Repeat the test after locking.

11. Fill with oil. First fill as far as possible and then check the level after about 15 minutes.

PITMAN ARM ADJUSTMENT

On steering gear with a marked pitman arm and pitman arm shaft, check that the marks align with each other. On other steering gear the pitman arm adjustment is checked as follows:

Lift up the front end of the vehicle so that the wheels are free. Turn the steering wheel to the center position (count the number of turns). Lower the vehicle. If the vehicle is correctly loaded, the wheels should now point straight forward. If the wheels do not, remove the pitman arm from the pitman shaft. Use a puller. Then set the left wheel straight forward and replace the pitman arm. The steering wheel should be in the center position. Tighten the nut to 13.5-16.5 kgm. (100-120 ft.lbs.).

RELAY ARM BUSHING REPLACEMENT

140 Series, 164

1. Jack up the vehicle at the front.
2. Disconnect the ball joints for the steering rod and tie rod from the relay arm with a puller.
3. Remove the nut and washer and remove the relay arm.
4. Press out the bushing.
5. Press in the new bushing.
6. Place the relay arm in position, install the washer and the nut. Tighten the nut to 7.0-8.5 kgm. (50-60 ft.lbs.).
7. Install the steering rod (in the inner hole on the relay arm) and the tie rod. Tighten the Nyloc nuts to 3.5-4.1 kgm. (20-30 ft.lbs.).
8. Lower the vehicle.

IDLER ARM REPAIR

PV444, 445, 544, P210

REMOVAL

Remove the cotter pin and nut for both the ball joints on the idler arm. Remove the ball joint. Remove the three attaching bolts of the bracket and lift off the bracket with idler arm.

DISASSEMBLY

Remove the locking ring and nut. Pull out the idler arm and pin and remove the washers. Press out the bushings with the help of a drift. If the pin is to be separated from the idler arm, press it out. On early production models with grease fittings, remove the fittings before pressing out the bushings.

INSPECTION

Clean and inspect all parts. Any damaged or worn parts should be replaced.

ASSEMBLY

1. Press in the new bushings 0.3-0.5 mm. (0.012-0.02″) inside the outer face with the help of a drift. Ream the bushings. Clean the bracket and check the fit of the pin in the bushings. The pin should move easily but without any noticeable play. Replace grease fittings if any were removed.

2. Press the pin into the idler arm. Coat the washer with a thin coating of chassis grease and place it on the pin. Install the pin into the bracket. Install the adjusting shims, the greased washer, and the washer. Install the nut and locking ring or locking washer. Tighten the nut to 7 kgm. (50 ft.lbs.).

3. After assembly there must be no play in the mounting. When correctly adjusted, a turning torque of 15 ±5 kgcm. (13 ±4.34 in.lbs.) is required. This means that when pulled at right-angles by means of a spring balance attached to the tie rod hole in the idler arm, a reading of 0.7-1.3 kg. (1.54-2.87 lb.) should be obtained. If this check does not give this result, the

mounting should be dismantled and adjusted by means of shims.

INSTALLATION

Install the bracket and tighten the attaching bolt. Install the ball joints and tighten their castle nuts to 3.2-3.7 kgm. (23-27 ft.lbs.) and lock them with cotter pins.

RELAY ARM AND BRACKET REPAIR

120 Series, P1800

REMOVAL

1. Jack up the front end and place blocks under the lower A-arms.
2. Remove the ball joint from the relay arm.
3. Disconnect the steering rod from the relay arm.
4. Remove the three attaching bolts for the bracket and lift off the bracket with relay arm.

DISASSEMBLY

1. Remove the cotter pin or circlip and the nut. On late production types there is no circlip. Pull out the relay arm with shaft. Do not lose the washers and shims.
2. Secure the bracket in a vise and pull out the needle bearings with a bearing puller. Remove the bushings with a drift.

ASSEMBLY

1. Press in the new needle bearings or bushings. On relay arm mounting type I, press in flush with the outer side. On type II, the needle bearings are pressed in so that the measurement A is 3.2-3.5 mm. (0.126-0.138″). The oil seals are installed with the lip turned out. On type III, the bushings are pressed in 0.3-0.5 mm. (0.012-0.020″) inside the outer face with a drift. Check the fit of the shaft in the bearings or bushings. The shaft should turn easily but without any play. On type III, ream the bushings.
2. Fill the bearings and the space between them with chassis grease. Lubricate the washers on both sides.
3. Install the other parts. The nut is tightened to 8.5 kgm. (60 ft.lbs.).
4. After assembling there must be no play in the bearings. When adjusted correctly, a turning torque of 15 ±5 kgcm. (13 ±4.3 in.lbs.) should be required. When pulling on the relay arm at the steering rod hole (the inner hole) at right angles, a spring scale should give a reading of 0.7-1.3 kg. (1.54-2.86 lb.). If this is not the case, the bearing mountings must be taken apart and adjusted with shims.

When the correct torque has been obtained the cotter pin or circlip is installed. On some late production types there is no circlip.

INSTALLATION

Place the bracket in position and tighten the attaching bolts. Install the steering rod in the inner hole of the relay arm and the tie rod in the outer hole. Tighten the castle nuts to a torque of 3.2-3.7 kgm. (23-27 ft.lbs.) and lock them with cotter pins.

JACKET TUBE AND MOUNTING REPLACEMENT

120 Series, P1800

1. Remove the steering wheel.
2. Unscrew the attaching bolts. Remove the turn signal switch and control lever. Then pull the jacket tube off the steering column.
3. If only the bushings or bearings in the jacket tube are to be replaced, the old ones are first knocked out with a drift or pulled out with a puller. After this the new parts are carefully pressed into the jacket tube.
4. Check that the rubber bushings for the jacket tube attachments are not damaged. Then install the jacket tube and other parts. The bushings on the early production type should be smeared with a thin coating of ball bearing grease. Tighten the steering wheel nut to a torque of 3.5-5.0 kgm. (25-35 ft.lbs.) and lock it.

STEERING COLUMN JACKET BEARING REPLACEMENT

140 Series, 164

To replace the upper bearing, first remove the steering wheel, spring, and seat. If the other bearings are to be replaced, the steering column must be separated from the sleeve. Release the upper steering column jacket and then the locked nut. When assembling, tighten the nut to 3-5 kgm. (20-36 ft. lbs.) and then lock nut by

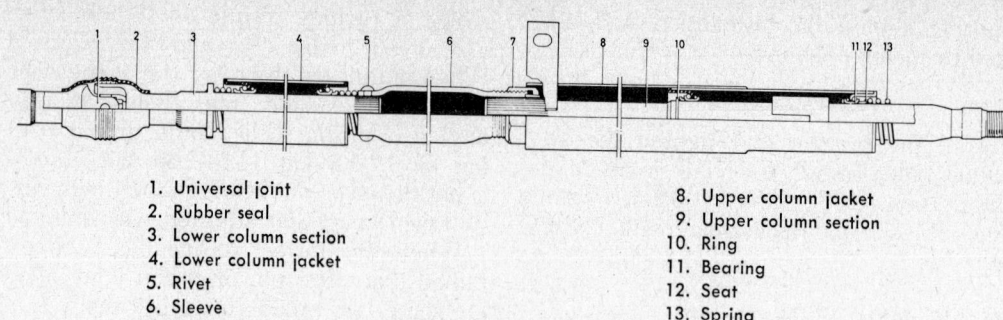

1. Universal joint
2. Rubber seal
3. Lower column section
4. Lower column jacket
5. Rivet
6. Sleeve
7. Nut

8. Upper column jacket
9. Upper column section
10. Ring
11. Bearing
12. Seat
13. Spring

Steering column components; 140 series, 164

driving the edge into one of the slits. To remove the lower steering column jacket, drill out the rivet.

STEERING LOCK

The 140 Series and 164 have a steering wheel lock. The lock mechanism is built in unit with the ignition switch and is mounted on the column with two shear-off bolts and to the dashboard with two screws.

POWER STEERING SYSTEM

The power steering system in the 164 and P1800E uses a belt-driven hydraulic pump to assist the cam and roller steering gear.

In-car Maintenance

NOTE: *Be careful that no dirt or grease gets in the hydraulic fluid. Clean all hose connections and the outside of the fluid reservoir before disconnecting or opening*

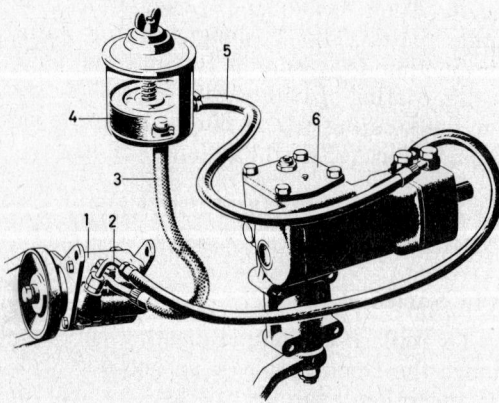

1. Hydraulic pump
2. Delivery line
3. Pump suction line

4. Reservoir with filter
5. Return line
6. Steering box

Power steering system; 164, 1800E

them. Use an approved type of automatic transmission oil when refilling the power steering system.

OIL LEVEL CHECK

Check the oil level in the reservoir every 6,000 miles. With the engine off, see that the fluid level is about ¼" above the level mark. Start the engine and see that the fluid level drops to the maximum mark. Stop the engine and see that the fluid level rises slightly.

DRAINING AND REFILLING SYSTEM

The power steering system may be drained as follows:

1. Raise the front of the car. Remove the drain plug.

2. Turn the steering wheel left to the stop position. Remove the reservoir cover.

3. Start the engine and run it for a maximum of 10 seconds until the fluid is emptied out of the pump and hoses.

4. Stop the engine and turn the steering wheel from stop to stop until all the fluid is drained out. Discard the used fluid.

To refill the system:

Two men are required for this procedure. One man adds the fluid while the other man turns the steering wheel. The total capacity of the power steering system is 2.5 US pints.

1. Fill the fluid reservoir to the edge.

2. Start the engine and add more fluid as the level drops. When the fluid level stops dropping, turn the steering wheel slowly and evenly in both directions. If necessary, add more fluid.

3. Open the bleed screw about ½-1 turn until oil starts flowing out. Then close it.

4. Continue turning the steering wheel until all the air bubbles are exhausted from the fluid.

5. Stop the engine and see that the oil level rises to about ¼″ above the maximum mark. If it rises higher than this, there is still some air in the fluid. Continue venting the system until all the air is completely exhausted. A few air bubbles may remain in the system but they will be exhausted under pressure while driving.

6. Replace the reservoir cover. Lower the car.

Brakes

The PV444, 445, 544, and P210 use drum brakes at all four wheels. The 120 series and P1800 use disc brakes on the front wheels and drum brakes on the rear. All models have an independent handbrake system that mechanically operates the rear wheel brakes. Late models have disc brakes at all wheels and, in addition, have an auxiliary brake system that operates three of the four wheel brakes in case of failure of one of the brake lines. Both front brakes and either the left or right rear brake operate. The handbrake is used to mechanically apply the rear

brakes while the car is parked. On those models that have drum rear brakes, the handbrake operates those brakes. On models with disc brakes on the rear, there is a small set of drum brakes inside each rear disc.

The handbrake systems on various models are similar in operation but different in arrangement.

MASTER CYLINDER

Master Cylinder R&R

PV444, 445, 544, P210

1. Raise the front end of the car and support it on jackstands. Remove the cylinder protector plate.

2. Disconnect the brake lines and drain the fluid into a clean container. Late production models have a separate brake fluid container which must be drained before disconnecting the lines.

3. Disconnect the wire from the stoplight switch.

4. Remove the cylinder mounting bolts. Move the cylinder forward until the thrust rod pulls free from the cylinder. Then, remove the cylinder.

To replace:

1. Mount the cylinder on the frame. Connect the link rod to the brake pedal.

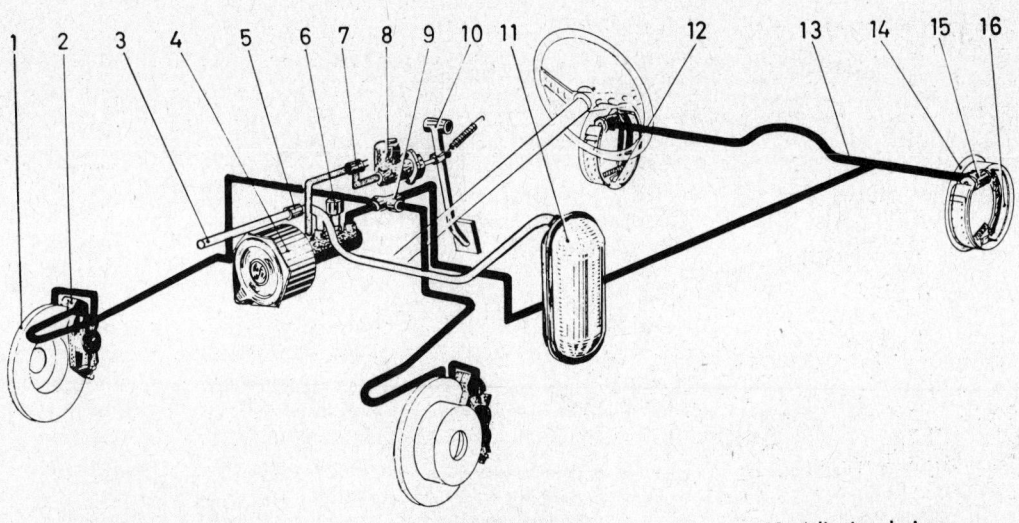

1. Brake disc
2. Front wheel brake unit
3. Vacuum line from engine
4. Vacuum booster cylinder
5. Check valve
6. Air filter
7. Brake contact
8. Master cylinder
9. Branch union
10. Brake pedal
11. Vacuum tank
12. Adjusting device
13. Brake line
14. Brake drum
15. Wheel unit cylinder
16. Brake shoe

Brake system; 120 series, 1800

1. Warning valve
2. Warning switch
3. Tandem master cylinder
4. Brake fluid reservoir
5. Vacuum line
6. Check valve
7. Brake switch
8. Electrical connection
9. Warning lamp

10. Rear brake caliper
11. Brake shoes, handbrake
12. Brake disc with drum
13. Hand brake cable
14. Brake valve, secondary circuit
15. Brake valve, primary circuit
16. Warning switch
17. Handbrake
18. Brake pedal

19. Vacuum booster cylinder
20. Front brake caliper
21. Brake disc
22. 6-branch union,
    (double 3-branch union)
23. Brake pipe
24. Brake hose
25. Cover plate

Brake system, 140 series

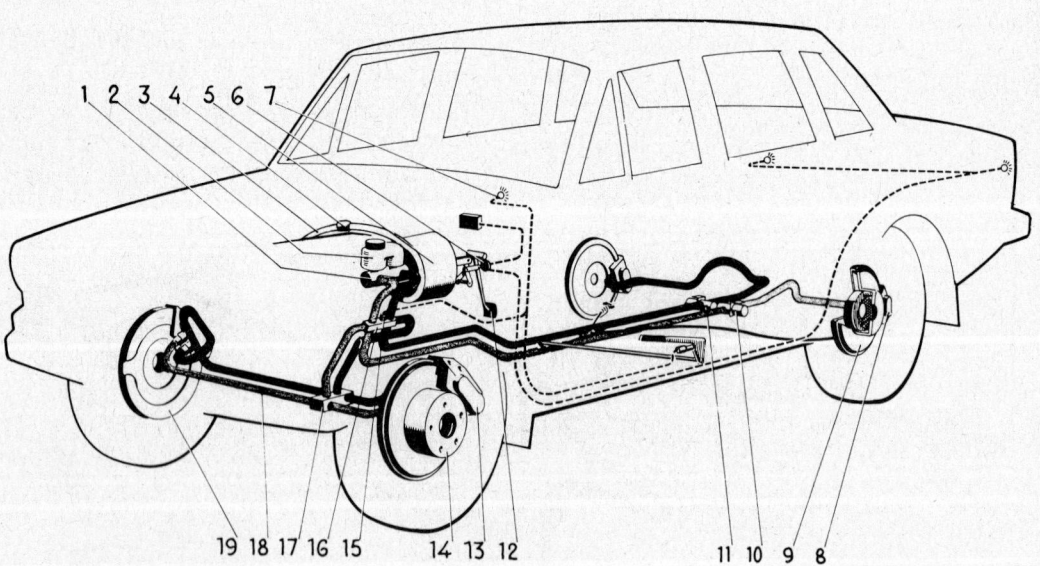

1. Tandem master cylinder
2. Brake fluid reservoir
3. Vacuum line
4. Check valve
5. Vacuum booster cylinder
6. Brake switch
7. Warning lamp
8. Rear brake caliper

9. Brake disc with drum
10. Brake valve,
    secondary circuit
11. Brake valve,
    primary circuit
12. Brake pedal
13. Front brake caliper
14. Brake disc

15. Warning switch
16. Warning valve
17. 6-branch union,
    (double 3-branch union)
18. Brake pipe
19. Cover plate

Brake system, 164

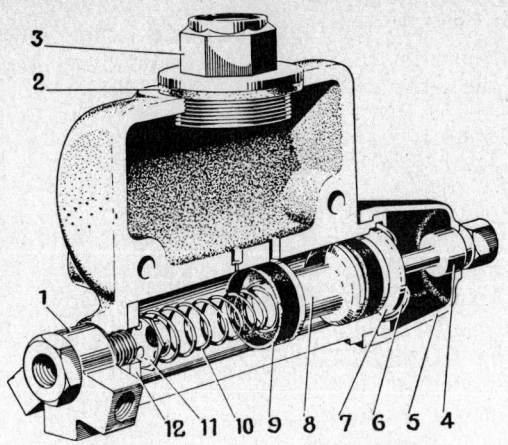

1. Branch union
2. Gasket
3. Plug
4. Thrust rod
5. Rubber cover
6. Lock ring
7. Stop washer
8. Plunger
9. Packing
10. Return spring
11. Valve
12. Packing

Master cylinder; PV444, 445, 544, P210

Connect the wire to the stoplight switch. Connect the lines to the cylinder. On cylinders that have a separate fluid container, install the container before connecting the lines. Be very careful not to let dirt or grease get into the brake cylinder or the lines.

2. Fill the master cylinder with clean brake fluid and bleed the air bubbles from the system.

3. Lower car to ground.

120 Series, P1800

1. Remove the cotter pin and attaching pin from the brake pedal linkage. Unhook the return spring. Remove the rubber cover. Disconnect the brake line and drain the fluid from the cylinder. Remove the mounting bolts from the cylinder and lift it out very carefully. Don't spill brake fluid on the painted metal.

To replace:

1. Install the master cylinder. Connect the brake line. Pull the rubber cover over the cylinder flange. Hook the return spring on the brake pedal and install the yoke on the pedal fastening it with the attaching pin and cotter pin.

2. Fill the master cylinder with brake fluid and bleed the air bubbles from the fluid.

140 Series, 164

1. Disconnect the wires and fluid lines from the cylinder.

2. Remove the mounting nuts and pull the master cylinder off the studs. Lift the cylinder from the car being careful not to spill brake fluid on the paintwork.

To replace:

1. Install the master cylinder on the studs and replace the nuts. Connect the lines. Connect the wires. Torque the nuts to 17 ft.lbs.

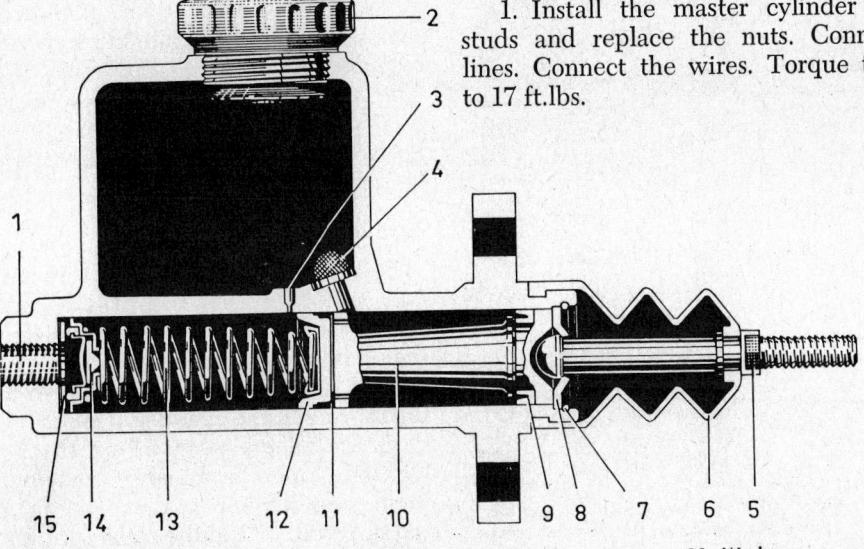

1. Connection for brake line
2. Filler cap
3. Equalizing hole
4. Strainer for overflow hole
5. Thrust rod
6. Rubber cover
7. Circlip
8. Stop washer
9. Seal
10. Plunger
11. Washer
12. Seal
13. Spring
14. Valve
15. Washer

Master cylinder; 120 series, 1800

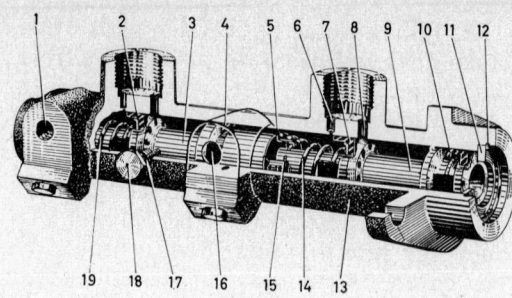

1. Connection for secondary circuit
2. Piston seal
3. Secondary piston
4. Piston seal
5. Spring guide
6. Equalizing hole
7. Piston seal
8. Overflow hole
9. Primary piston
10. Piston seal
11. Thrust washer
12. Circlip
13. Cylinder
14. Return spring for primary piston
15. Circlip
16. Connection for primary circuit
17. Sealing washer
18. Stop screw
19. Return spring for secondary piston

Master cylinder, 140 series

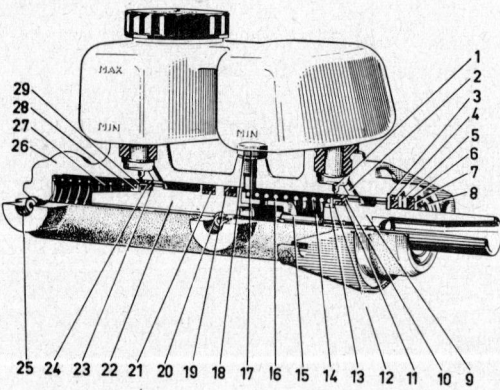

1. Equalizing hole
2. Overflow hole
3. Washer
4. Piston seal
5. Washer
6. Piston seal
7. Washer
8. Circlip
9. Primary piston
10. Washer
11. Piston seal
12. Washer
13. Thrust washer
14. Spring
15. Screw
16. Spring retainer
17. Stop screw
18. Seal
19. Piston seal
20. Connection for primary circuit
21. Piston seal
22. Secondary piston
23. Washer
24. Piston seal
25. Connection for secondary circuit
26. Cylinder
27. Spring
28. Thrust washer
29. Washer

Master cylinder, 164

2. Fill the fluid container with new brake fluid, adding fluid gradually. Then, bleed the air bubbles from the fluid.

Master Cylinder Overhaul

PV444, 445, 544, P210

Disassembly

1. Blow the master cylinder clean externally. Loosen the filler plug and empty out the brake fluid.
2. Pull off the rubber cover, and remove the snap ring and stop washer.
3. Remove the three-way union with the stoplight switch.
4. Remove the plunger, the seal, the return spring with its valve, and the seal using either a long metal punch or compressed air to force them out.

Inspection

All parts of the master cylinder assembly should be washed in clean brake fluid before inspection. Examine the cylinder internally. There must be no scars, scratches, or rust patches on the polished surface. Damage of this type can usually be removed by honing the cylinder. Clean the cylinder thoroughly after honing and check that the equalizing hole is not blocked. The clearance between the plunger and the cylinder must not exceed .25 mm. (.010″). The minimum permissible cylinder diameter is 25.25 mm. (.994″). The free length of the return spring should be 75 mm. (3″). All the seals should be replaced. Worn and damaged parts should be replaced.

Assembly

Before assembling, make sure that the two holes between the cylinder and the fluid container as well as the relief hole in the plunger are not blocked.

1. Place the seal and the valve and return spring in the cylinder.
2. Install the rear seal on the plunger. Dip the plunger and seal in brake fluid and then press them into the cylinder. Install the stop washer and the locking ring.
3. Place the push rod in the plunger and force the rubber cover over the shoulder on the master cylinder. Install the three-way union with the stoplight switch.
4. Check that the equalizing hole is not blocked by inserting a .5 mm. (.02″)

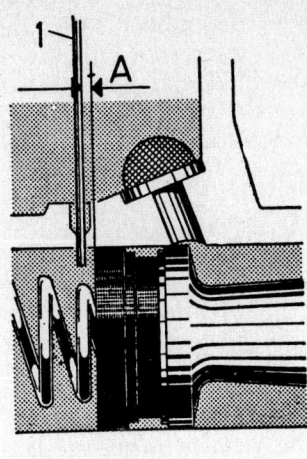

Checking the equalizing hole; 120 series, 1800, 140 series. 1 is a wire; A is .02″.

thick wire through the equalizing hole. It should then be possible to press in the plunger about .5 mm. (.02″) before the wire jams. Be careful not to damage the seal. If the equalizing hole is blocked, the master cylinder has been incorrectly assembled.

120 Series, P1800

The disassembly, inspection, and reconditioning procedures are similar to those for the PV444, 445, 544, and P210. The clearance between the plunger and cylinder must not exceed .20 mm. (.008″).

140 Series

Disassembly

1. Fasten the flange of the master cylinder firmly in a vise.
2. Place both hands under the reservoir and pull it up from the rubber seals. Remove the filler cap and strainer from the reservoir and the nuts and rubber seals from the cylinder.
3. Remove the stop screw. Remove the circlip from the primary piston with circlip pliers. Remove the pistons. If it is not possible to shake out the secondary piston, it can be removed by blowing air in the hole for the stoplight switch.
4. Remove the two seals from the secondary piston. Be careful not to damage the surfaces of the plunger. The primary piston should be replaced.

Inspection

Before inspection all the parts should be cleaned. Examine the inside of the cylinder carefully. If scored or scratched, the cylinder should be replaced. Rust formation and similar damage can be eliminated by honing the cylinder. Clean the cylinder carefully after honing and check that the holes are clear.

If wear on the cylinder or secondary piston is suspected, the diameter should be measured. The cylinder diameter may not exceed 22.40 mm. (.881″), while the diameter of the piston may not be less than 22.05 mm. (.870″). The primary piston complete should be replaced along with the secondary piston seals, the stop screw and its washer, and the circlip. The rubber seals for the container should be replaced.

Assembly

1. Install the seals on the secondary piston and make sure that they are turned correctly.
2. Coat the cylinder with brake fluid and dip the piston and seals in brake fluid before installation. Slide the spring onto the secondary piston and install the piston. Be careful when inserting the seals in the cylinder. Install the new primary piston. Press in the piston and install the washer and circlip.
3. Check that the hole for the stop screw is clear and install the screw and sealing washer. The tightening torque should be 1.3 kgm. (9.5 ft.lbs.).
4. Check the movement of the pistons and make sure that the through-flow holes are clear. The equalizing hole is checked by inserting a soft copper wire with diameter .5 mm. (25 gauge) through the hole. If the equalizing hole is not clear, then the master cylinder is improperly assembled.
5. Install the nuts with washers and rubber seals. Check that the venting hole in the cap is clear and install the strainer and filler cap. Replace the reservoir. Install the stoplight switch.

164

Disassembly

1. Fasten the flange of the master cylinder firmly in a vise.
2. Place both hands under the reservoir and pull it up from the rubber seals.

Remove the filler cap and strainer from the reservoir and the rubber seals from the cylinder.

3. Remove the stop screw. Remove the circlip from the primary piston with circlip pliers. Remove the pistons.

Inspection

Before inspection, clean all the parts. Examine the inside of the cylinder carefully. If there are any scores or scratches, the cylinder should be replaced. Rust formation and similar damage can be eliminated by honing the cylinder. Clean the cylinder carefully after honing and check that the holes are clear.

If wear on the cylinder or secondary piston is suspected, the diameter should be measured. The cylinder bore must not exceed 23.92 mm. (.942″) and the diameter of the piston may not be less than 23.66 mm. (.931″). Replace the primary piston, the secondary piston, the stop screw, washer and circlip, and the sealing ring. The rubber seals for the reservoir should be replaced.

Assembly

1. Install the secondary piston, the brass washer, and the piston seal. Check that the seal is turned correctly.

2. Coat the cylinder bore with brake fluid and dip the piston and seals in brake fluid. Install the washer, the thrust washer, and the spring on the secondary piston and install the piston. Be careful when inserting the seals in the cylinder.

3. Install the washer, the piston seal, the plastic washer, the piston seal, and the washer on the primary piston. Check that the seals are facing correctly.

4. Dip the piston and the seals in brake fluid and install the piston in the cylinder. Press in the piston and install the circlip.

5. Check that the hole for the stop screw is clear and install the screw with a new sealing washer. The tightening torque is .5-.8 kgm. (3.6-5.7 ft.lbs.).

6. Check the movement of the pistons and make sure that the through-flow holes are clear. The equalizing hole is checked by pressing the pistons in about 1.0 mm. (.04″) and by inserting a soft copper wire diameter .7 mm. (22 gauge) down through the hole. If the equalizing hole is not clear, the master cylinder is incorrectly assembled.

7. Install the rubber seals. Install the brake fluid reservoir. Fill the reservoir with brake fluid and bleed the cylinder. Check to make sure that the vent hole in the cap is open and place the strainer and cap in position.

VACUUM BOOSTER

Air Filter Element Replacement

120 SERIES, P1800

The vacuum booster air filter should be changed when replacing the rear brake linings. The element is accessible after removing the cover. When replacing, the cover should be cleaned but the element must always be replaced. Tighten the attaching bolt to 0.3-0.4 kgm. (2-3 ft.lbs.).

140 SERIES

1. Remove the master cylinder.

2. Loosen the fork from the brake pedal by removing its cotter pin and attaching pin.

3. Unscrew the 4 nuts which hold the booster to the bracket.

4. Pull the booster forward until the rubber cover is released. Do not pull it too far as this might result in the rubber cover being damaged.

5. Pry off the rubber cover, remove the plastic washer, and pull the filter forward. Remove the filter.

6. Insert the new filter. Install the plastic washer and rubber cover.

7. Put the booster on the bracket and screw on the attaching nuts.

Installing air filter for vacuum booster cylinder.

8. Install the fork on the brake pedal.

9. Install the master cylinder. Bleed the brake system.

164

1. Remove the panel under the instrument panel.

2. Remove the fuse for the brake light.

3. Remove the bracket for the brake light switch.

4. Remove the cotter pins and the attaching pins.

5. Lift up the brake pedal. Remove the rubber cover.

6. Remove the protective washer.

7. Remove the damper and the air cleaner.

To install:

1. Install the cleaner and the damper. The slots on the cleaner and damper should be 180° from each other.

2. Install the protective washer and the rubber cover. Check to make sure that the cover is pressed down properly at the inner edge of the protective washer.

3. Install the attaching pins.

4. Install the bracket and adjust the brake light switch.

5. Install the panel under the dashboard. Replace the fuse.

Check Valve Replacement

120 SERIES, P1800, 164

Remove the check valve from the vacuum hose. Install the valve so that the arrows on the valve housing point away from the booster. The vacuum hose connection should face down.

140 SERIES

Remove the vacuum hose from the check valve. Turn the valve with the help of a 28 mm. ($1/32''$) wrench and lift the valve forward. Follow this procedure in reverse when installing the check valve. Make sure that the O-ring is in the correct position. The highest point of the vacuum hose should be its attachment to the check valve.

Vacuum Booster Replacement

120 SERIES, P1800

Disconnect the hydraulic lines and vacuum line from the booster. Unscrew the three attaching bolts and lift off the cylinder. On P1800 the four attaching bolts for the bracket are first removed and the bracket lifted up so that the cylinder can be removed.

To replace, bolt the booster to the bracket. If the bracket has been removed, replace it. Connect the ingoing hydraulic line. Check that there is sufficient brake fluid in the master cylinder. Depress the brake pedal very slowly. When brake fluid just begins to run out of the booster, stop depressing the pedal. Connect the outgoing hydraulic line and vacuum line. Bleed the brake system.

140 SERIES

1. Remove the master cylinder.

2. Loosen the fork from the brake pedal by removing its attaching pin.

3. Pry off the vacuum hose from the check valve. Remove the clamp for the coupling cable and attaching screws for the support bracket.

4. Remove the attaching screws for the bracket and lift the servo cylinder forward.

5. Loosen the locknut and unscrew the fork. Remove the rubber cover and the bracket. Unscrew the thrust rod from the rear thrust rod of the cylinder.

To replace:

1. After lubricating the thrust rod, screw it into the rear thrust rod of the booster as far as possible.

2. Install the brackets on the booster. The attaching nuts should not be tightened until the brackets have been installed in the vehicle.

3. Install the rubber cover. Screw on locknut and fork. The distance between the center of the fork hole and the end of the thrust rod should be approximately 45 mm. ($1.77''$).

4. Install the booster, the upper attaching screws for the bracket, and the attaching screws for the support bracket. Then install the lower attaching screws for the bracket and tighten all the screws and nuts on the brackets.

5. Install the clamp for the coupling cable and connect the vacuum hose to the check valve. Make sure that the highest point of the vacuum hose is at the connection.

6. Connect the fork to the brake pedal and fasten with the cotter pin. Check and if necessary adjust the pedal piston.

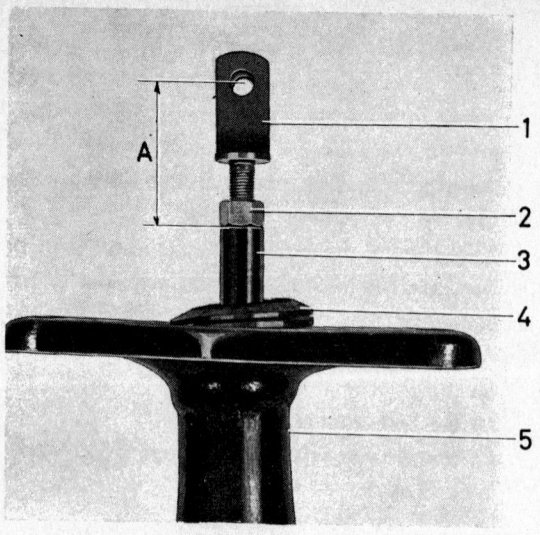

1. Fork
2. Locknut
3. Thrust rod
4. Rubber cover
5. Bracket
A. About 45 mm. (1.77")

Installing the fork, 140 series

7. Check the thrust rod clearance and install the master cylinder. Bleed the brake system.

164

1. Remove the master cylinder. Disconnect the vacuum hose from the booster.
2. Disconnect the link arm from the brake pedal. Remove the bracket with clutch pedal stop from the firewall.
3. Remove the 4 nuts securing the booster to the firewall.

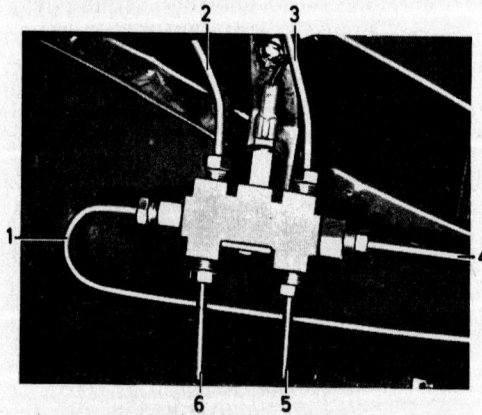

1. Primary circuit, front wheels
2. Master cylinder primary circuit
3. Master cylinder secondary circuit
4. Secondary circuit, front wheels
5. Secondary circuit, rear wheels
6. Primary circuit, rear wheels

Warning valve; 140 series, 164

4. Pull the booster forward and disconnect the fork from the link arm.

To replace:

1. Check that the rubber cover is pressed down properly at the protective washer for the cleaner. Secure the fork to the link arm. Push in the booster so that the attaching bolts are in position.
2. Place the resilient washers under the attaching nuts. Fasten the cylinder.
3. Install the bracket for the clutch pedal. Secure the link arm to the brake pedal.
4. Install the vacuum hose. The connection for the vacuum hose should face down.
5. Bleed the brake system.

BRAKE WARNING VALVE

140 Series, 164

VALVE RESETTING

1. Disconnect the wire and screw out the warning switch so that the pistons return to normal position.
2. Repair and bleed the faulty hydraulic circuit.
3. Screw in the warning switch and tighten it to 1.4-2.0 kgm. (10-14 ft.lbs.). Connect the wire.

WARNING VALVE REPLACEMENT

1. Disconnect all connections. Remove the attaching nut and then the valve.
2. Install the new valve in reverse order of removal.
3. Bleed the brake system.

BRAKE PROPORTIONING VALVE

140 Series, 164

REMOVAL

Unscrew and plug the connection to the brake line. Loosen the brake hose a maximum ¼ turn at the valve. Remove the attaching screws and unscrew the valve from the brake hose.

INSTALLATION

Screw the valve onto the brake hose. Install the attaching screws and connect the brake line. Tighten the connection. Bleed the brake system.

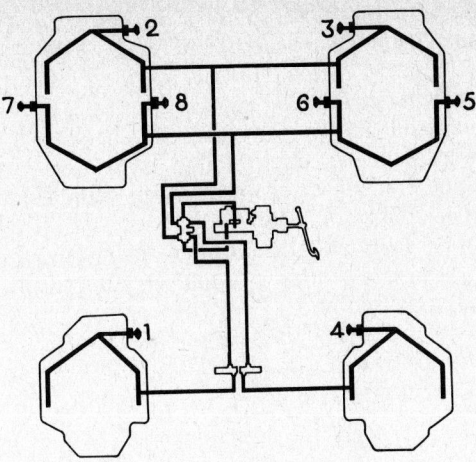

1. Adjusting screw
2. Left brake valve (secondary circuit)
3. Screw (assembling)
4. Brake hose to left rear wheel
5. Brake hose to right rear wheel
6. Bracket
7. Attaching screw
8. Right brake valve
9. From the master cylinder primary circuit
10. From the master cylinder secondary circuit

The brake valves fitted, 140 series, 164

1. Left rear wheel valve
2. Left front wheel upper inner valve
3. Right front wheel, upper inner valve
4. Right rear wheel valve
5. Right front wheel, outer valve
6. Right front wheel, lower inner valve
7. Left front wheel, outer valve
8. Left front wheel, lower inner valve

Hydraulic brake bleeding sequence, series 140 and 164.

BRAKE SYSTEM BLEEDING

To bleed the system:

1. Clean the filler plug on the master cylinder. Unscrew the plug and if necessary fill up with brake fluid. Disconnect the booster vacuum line.

2. On P1800 models up to chassis number 6999, the bleeding nipple is on the outside of the front wheel brake unit, so that the front wheels must be removed. Clean the bleeding nipple. Connect a hose onto the nipple and let the other end of the hose hang down in a container of clean brake fluid.

3. Open the nipple and have an assistant press down the brake pedal slowly. Close the nipple before releasing the pedal. Repeat the procedure as long as there are air bubbles in the fluid running out.

4. Bleed the remaining wheels in the same manner. Before each operation, check that there is sufficient brake fluid.

5. Connect the vacuum lines.

DRUM BRAKES

Wheel Cylinder Removal

1. Remove the hub.
2. Move the brake shoes to one side so far that the push rods are clear from the shoes.
3. Disconnect the brake line and remove the wheel cylinder attaching bolts.

Remove the wheel cylinder by moving it forward. Make sure that no brake fluid gets on to the brake linings.

To replace:

1. Put the wheel cylinder in place in the brake drum and install the attaching bolts. Connect the brake line. Move the brake shoes into position.

2. Fill the master cylinder with new brake fluid. Bleed the brake system until all air bubbles are exhausted from the fluid. Only the brake lines that were opened to remove the wheel cylinder need be bled.

Wheel Cylinder Rebuilding

Remove the clip, force off the rubber cover and remove the seals and the spring. Wash all the parts in clean brake fluid.

Examine the cylinder carefully internally. There must be no scars, scratches, or rust patches on the polished surface. Damage of this type can usually be repaired by honing the cylinder. Clean the cylinder thoroughly after honing. The bleeding nipple should be removed while this is done.

The clearance between the piston and the cylinder must not exceed .25 mm. (.010″). This can be determined by measuring the piston diameter with a micrometer and the cylinder with an indicator. If the clearance exceeds .25 mm. (.010"), try a new piston. If this does not help, the cylinder must be replaced.

The clearance can also be checked by using a feeler gauge. The clearance obtained by measuring in this way should not exceed .15 mm. (.006").

The seals and the rubber casing should be replaced by new units. Replace worn and damaged parts.

Assemble the parts in the reverse order of disassembly. Dip the piston and seals in brake fluid first.

Brake Drums

The friction surface and out of round of the brake drums should be checked. The out of round must not exceed .15 mm. (.006"). If the friction surface is concave, scored or cracked, the drum should be replaced. Minor rust spots can, however, be polished off or ground away.

Rear Drum Brakes

DISASSEMBLY

1. Remove the hub cap and cotter pin in the axle shaft. Loosen the castle nut and wheel nuts slightly. Jack up the car and place blocks under the rear axle. Remove the wheel.

1. Front brake shoe	7. Upper return spring
2. Lock washer	8. Rear brake shoe
3. Guide pin	9. Lever
4. Link	10. Return spring for lever
5. Spring clip	11. Adjusting device
6. Wheel cylinder	12. Lower return spring

Rear brake unit; 120 series, 1800

2. Release the handbrake. Pull off the hub.

3. Place a clamp over the wheel cylinder so that the plungers cannot be pressed out. Remove the upper return spring with brake spring pliers. Pull down the front shoe into the groove in the brake backing plate, hold against the guide pin on the other side of the backing plate, and turn and then remove the locking washer. Lift out the shoe.

4. Remove the rear shoe and disconnect it from the handbrake cable. Unhook the return spring and if necessary the handbrake link.

5. Turn in the adjusting screw slightly. Remove the adjusting plunger.

ASSEMBLY

1. Turn back the adjusting screw and install the adjusting plungers after cleaning and coating them with heat-resistant grease. Check that the plungers move easily.

2. Install the lever on the rear brake shoe. Hook on the handbrake cable and return springs. Place the shoe in position

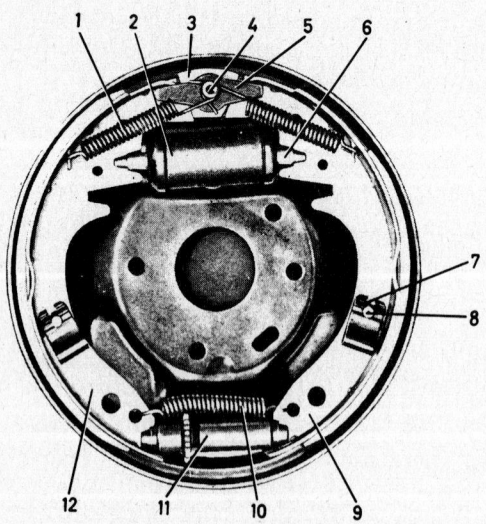

1. Return spring	7. Clip
2. Wheel cylinder	8. Guide pin
3. Centering block	9. Front shoe
4. Anchor pin	10. Locking spring
5. Guide plate	11. Adjusting device
6. Thrust rod	12. Rear shoe

Brake unit, right front; PV444, 445, 544, P210

and install the guide pin and locking clip. Make sure that the head of the guide pin enters the countersink of the clip.

3. Place the handbrake link in position, ensuring that it is turned correctly. Hook on the lower return spring and install the front brake shoe with brake spring pliers. Install the spring clip.

4. Check that the springs and locking washers are in position and that the linings are free from burrs, grease, and dirt.

5. Check that the key fits in the drive-shaft and replace the hub with brake drum. Put on the washer and tighten the castle nut. If the wheel cylinder has been removed, bleed the system. Put on the wheel after cleaning the contact surfaces between the wheel and hub.

Adjust the brakes. Lower the car and tighten the wheel nuts. Tighten alternately a little at a time until all are tightened to 10-14 kgm. (70-100 ft. lbs.). Tighten the castle nut and lock it with a cotter pin. Replace the hub cap.

Drum Brake Adjustment

Adjustment is as follows:

1. Jack up the car and place supports under the control arms and the rear axle. Release the handbrake.

2. Remove the rubber seal. Turn the wheel in its normal direction of rotation while bringing the brake shoes into contact with the drum. Use a screwdriver or adjusting tool to turn the adjuster screw. When the wheel can just be turned by using one hand, stop tightening the screw. Then back off the adjuster screw 1-2 notches. Install the rubber seal.

3. Repeat adjustment procedure on other brakes. Remove the supports and lower the car.

DISC BRAKES

Disc brakes require no adjustment. They should, however, be checked frequently for wear.

Disc Pad Replacement

The brake pads should be replaced when about 3 mm. (⅛″) of the facing thickness remains. The pads should not be allowed to wear down to below 1.5 mm. (1/16″).

1. Remove the hub cap and loosen the wheel nuts slightly.

2. Jack up the vehicle and place blocks

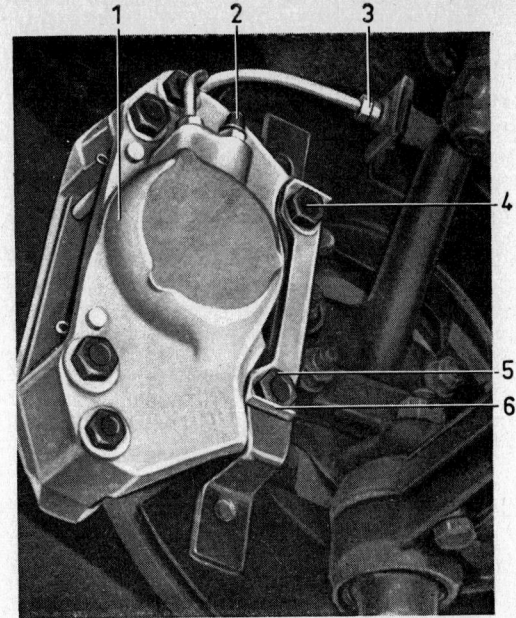

1. Caliper	4. Attaching bolt
2. Bleeding nipple	5. Attaching bolt
3. Brake line	6. Lockwasher

Front disc brake; 120 series, 1800

under the jack attachment. Remove the wheel nuts and the wheel.

3. Remove the hairpin-shaped locking clips and guide pins for the brake pads. Pull out the pads. Carefully clean out the cavity in which the pads fit. If the seal is damaged, remove the caliper unit.

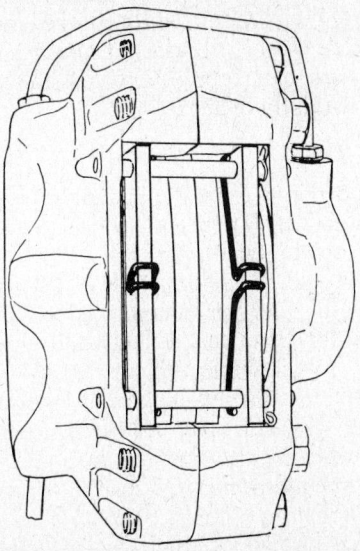

Damping springs; 120 series, 1800 (late production)

4. Carefully press the plungers into the wheel cylinders and install the new pads. The brake fluid level in the master cylinder will rise and may possibly overflow. Make sure that the guide pins and locking clips are undamaged before replacing them. Check that the pads can move and that the linings do not project outside the brake disc. Install the damping springs, if used.

5. Depress the brake pedal several times and check that the movement feels normal. Bleeding is not usually necessary after replacing the brake pads.

6. Put on the wheel after cleaning the contact surfaces of the wheel and hub. Lower the car and tighten the wheel nuts. Tighten alternately to 10-14 kgm. (70-100 ft. lbs.). Replace the hub cap.

Caliper Unit Replacement

REMOVAL

1. Remove the wheel.
2. Clean the caliper externally.
3. Disconnect the brake line and plug the connection. Make sure that no brake fluid runs onto the disc or pads. Bend back the locking plate and take out the attaching bolts. Lift off the unit complete.

INSTALLATION

Before the caliper is installed, check the brake disc. Check that the contact surfaces of the caliper and retainer are clean and undamaged. Install the caliper. Put on the locking plate, tighten the attaching bolts and lock them. Connect the brake line and bleed the wheel cylinders. Check that the brake disc can rotate between the brake pads. Install the wheel.

Brake Discs

Check the disc friction surface run-out, and thickness. There must be no rust or scoring on the friction surface. The run-out must not exceed .1 mm. (.004"). The run-out for the 140 series and 164 is .1 mm. (.004") for the front wheels and .15 mm. (.006") for the rear wheels at the outer edge of the disc. Check that the wheel bearings are correctly adjusted and that the disc fits securely on the hub. The disc can be reconditioned by turning or grinding. Machining should be done in unit with the hub. The thickness of the disc after machining must not be less than 12.2 mm. (.48"). After reconditioning, the disc

must not run out more than .10 mm. (.004") and its thickness must not vary more than .03 mm. (.0012"). If the brake disc cannot be reconditioned, or if it is cracked or damaged, it should be replaced with the hub.

BRAKE PEDAL

Free Travel Adjustment

PV444, 445, 544, P210

It is important that the brake pedal have the correct free travel. If the travel is too small the equalizing hole between the cylinder and the fluid reservoir will be blocked by the piston, with the result that the brake shoes are prevented from returning to their rest position. If the free travel is too great, the effective stroke may be insufficient.

Pedal free travel is adjusted by changing the length of the link rod. Loosen locknut and turn the thrust rod until the pedal has a free travel of 7-12 mm. (¼-½"). Tighten the locknut.

Pedal Positioning

120 SERIES, P1800

When the pedal is released, it should align with the clutch pedal. The pedal position is adjusted by loosening the locknut and turning the push rod for the master cylinder. Tighten the locknut.

140 SERIES, 164

The pedal should travel about 140 mm. (5½") before the pistons in the master cyl-

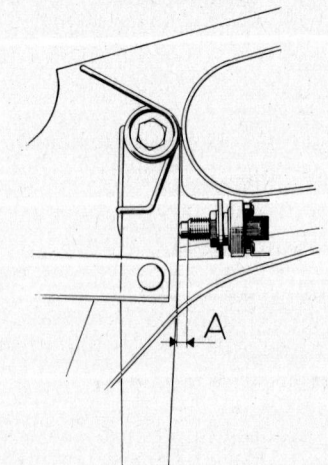

Adjusting brake light switch, 164. A is .16±.08"

inder are pressed to the bottom. Pedal travel for the 164 should be 152 mm. (6"). The travel can be measured only by bleeding both circuits simultaneously. At the bottom position, the pedal should be about 10 mm. (⅜") from the floor.

When the pedal is released, it should align with the clutch pedal provided that the clutch pedal is correctly adjusted.

The position of the pedal is adjusted by loosening the locknut, removing the attaching pin, and turning the fork. Tighten the locknut and install the cotter pin.

STOPLIGHT SWITCH

140 Series, 164

To adjust the switch, measure the distance between the brake pedal in the released position and the threaded brass hub on the switch. This distance should be 4 ±2 mm. (.16 ±.08). Move the bracket until the correct distance is obtained. Tighten the attaching screws.

HANDBRAKE

Handbrake Adjustment

PV444, 445, 544, P210

1. Adjust the rear brakes.
2. Check that the handbrake is fully on at the fourth-fifth notch on the ratchet. If not, adjust the handbrake by moving the clevis on the pull rod. On late production models with a spring on the pull rod, the rear nut is tightened so that the spring is just under tension.

120 Series, P1800

The handbrake should be fully on at the fourth-fifth notch. If not, the handbrake should be adjusted. The rear brakes should first be adjusted. The handbrake is adjusted by moving the clevis on the pull rod. Tighten the nuts after adjusting.

140 Series, 164

The handbrake should give full effect at the third-fourth notch. If it does not, adjust it.

1. Apply the handbrake, remove the hub caps of the rear wheels, and loosen the wheel nuts.
2. Jack up the rear end, place blocks under the rear axle, remove the nuts, and take off the wheels. Release the handbrake.
3. Check that the brake pads are not stuck to the brake disc. Disconnect the cable from the lever.
4. Set the drum so that its hole aligns with the adjusting screw. Insert a screwdriver and adjust the shoes by moving the screwdriver handle upward. When the drum cannot be rotated easily, stop adjusting the shoes. Turn the adjusting screw back 4-5 serrations. Check that the shoes do not drag by turning the drum in its normal direction of rotation. A very slight drag is permissible. If there is heavy drag, the adjusting screw should be released a further 2-3 serrations. Connect the cable to the lever.

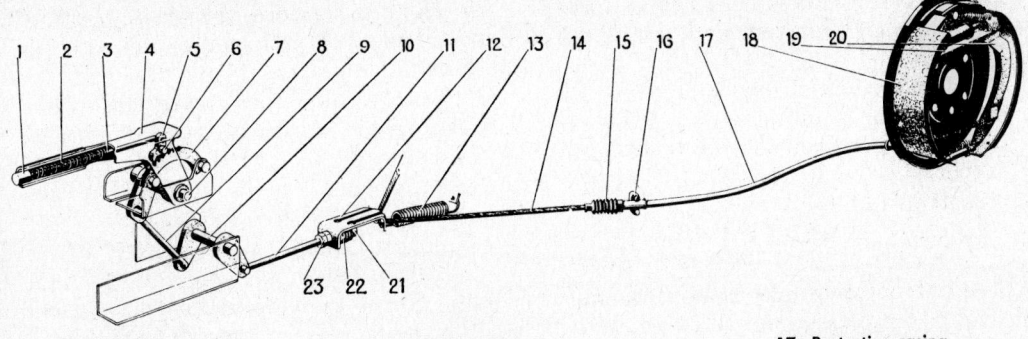

1. Release button	9. Pull rod	17. Protective casing
2. Spring	10. Countershaft	18. Brake shoe
3. Thrust rod	11. Pull rod	19. Link
4. Handbrake lever	12. Clevis	20. Lever
5. Ratchet pawl	13. Return spring	21. Nut
6. Rivet	14. Handbrake cable	22. Spring
7. Ratchet segment	15. Rubber cover	23. Nut
8. Shaft	16. Attaching clamp	

Handbrake system; PV444, 445, 544, P210

5. Repeat the adjusting procedure with the other rear wheel.

6. Apply the handbrake lever and check that the handbrake is fully on at the third-fourth notch. If it is not, tighten the cable. This is done by loosening the locknuts and screwing in the block on the pull rod. After adjusting, tighten the locknuts. Check that there is approximately the same braking effect on both rear wheels.

7. Install the wheels. Lower the vehicle and tighten the nuts. Tighten the nuts alternately to 10-14 kgm. (70-100 ft.lbs.). Install the hub caps.

Cable Replacement

PV444, 445, 544, P210

1. Apply the handbrake, remove the hub cap, loosen the wheel nuts and castle nut.

2. Lift up the rear of the car, place blocks under the rear axle and remove the wheel. Release the handbrake.

3. Remove the bolts and the cable outer casing attachment in the brake backing plate. Remove the cable outer casing front attachment and spring. Remove the cotter pin and release the pull rod. Unhook the cable from the clevis.

4. Pull off the brake drum and hub with a puller. Remove the cable from the brake shoe lever and pull the cable forward.

To replace:

1. Insert the cable in the brake shoe and hook it onto the lever.

2. Hook the cable onto the clevis and install the pull rod and cotter pin. Bolt the cable outer casing attachment to the brake backing plate and bracket, and install the spring.

3. Put on the hub, drum, and wheel.

4. Adjust the handbrake. Lower the car and tighten the wheel nuts to 10-14 kgm. (70-100 ft.lbs.). Tighten and lock the castle nut. Install the hub cap.

120 Series, P1800

1. Apply the handbrake, remove the hub cap, loosen the wheel nuts and castle nut.

2. Jack up the rear end, place blocks under the rear axle and remove the wheel. Release the handbrake.

3. Pull off the brake drum and hub with a puller. Unhook the cable from the brake shoe lever.

4. Remove the screws for the cable casing attachment on the brake backing plate.

Remove the cable casing front attachment and rubber support sleeve. Unhook the cable from the clevis and pull out the cable.

To replace:

1. Install the rubber support sleeve on the cable casing. Insert the cable into the brake backing plate and hook it onto the lever.

2. Hook the cable onto the clevis.

3. Tighten the bolts in the brake backing plate. Install the cable casing front attachment and make sure that the clamp enters the groove on the sleeve. If necessary, loosen the adjusting nuts. Install the rubber support sleeve in its bracket.

4. Install the hub with brake drum and wheel.

5. Adjust the handbrake. Lower the car and tighten the wheel nuts to 10-14 kgm. (70-100 ft.lbs.). Tighten and lock the castle nut. Install the hub cap.

140 Series, 164

1. Apply the handbrake, remove the hub caps of the rear wheels and loosen the wheel nuts.

2. Jack up the rear end, place blocks under the rear axle, remove the nuts and take off the wheels. Release the handbrake.

3. Remove the bolt and the wheel from the pulley.

4. Remove the rubber cover for the front attachment of the cable sleeve and the nut as well as the attachment for the rubber suspension ring on the frame. Remove the cable from the other side of the attachment in the same way.

5. Hold the return spring in position. Bend up the lock and remove the lock pin so that the cable releases from the lever.

6. Remove the return spring with washers. Loosen the nut for the rear attachment of the cable sleeve. Lift the cable forward after loosening both sides of the attachments.

To replace:

1. Adjust the brake shoes of the rear wheels. Check that the brake pads do not stick to the brake disc and adjust the drum so that its hole aligns with the adjusting screw. Place a screwdriver between the serrations of the adjusting screw and apply the shoes by moving the screwdriver handle upward. When the drum can no longer be turned easily, stop adjusting the shoes. Then turn the adjusting screw back 4-5 serrations.

2. Install new rubber cable guides for the cable suspension. Place the cable in position in the rear attachment and tighten the nut. Install the washers and return spring. Compress the spring. Oil the lock pin and install it together with the cable on the lever. Install the attachment and rubber cable guide on the frame.

3. Install the cable in the same way on the other side of the vehicle.

4. Place the cable sleeve in position in the front attachments and install the rubber covers.

5. Lubricate and install the pulley on the pull rod. Adjust the pulley so that the handbrake is fully on at the third-fourth notch.

6. Install the wheels.

Rear Handbrake Drums

140 SERIES, 164

Disassembly

1. Apply the handbrake, remove the hub caps of the rear wheels and loosen the wheel nuts.

2. Jack up the rear end, place blocks under the rear axle, remove the nuts and take off the wheels. Release the handbrake.

3. Screw loose the brake line from the rear brake caliper and plug the connection. Brake fluid must not spill onto the disc or brake pads. Remove the attaching bolts. Take off the caliper.

4. Remove the attaching bolts for the brake drum and take off the drum.

5. Unhook the lower return spring. Lift the shoes forward.

Inspection

First check for leakage. If there is leakage, replace the sealing ring. Clean all the parts except the brake linings. Check that the lever joint does not chafe and replace parts which are damaged or worn. If the brake linings are oily or worn down to the rivets, replace the shoes completely. The brake drum should be replaced if its friction surface is concave, or if its out-of-round exceeds .2 mm. (.008″). Rust spots can, however, be polished off. Clean the contact surfaces on the backing plate.

Assembly

1. If new linings or drums are to be

fitted, loosen the pulley to relieve cable tension.

2. Coat the 6 guide lips on the backing plate as well as the lever joint and adjusting screw with grease. Check that the lever and anchor bolt parts are correctly installed.

3. Install the brake shoes. The shorter sleeve on the adjusting device should be turned forward on the right side and backward on the left side.

4. Hook on the return spring.

5. Install the brake drum.

6. Place the brake caliper in position. Install the attaching bolts.

7. Check that the brake pads move freely and adjust the handbrake.

8. Bleed the caliper.

9. Replace the wheel.

Heating System

140 SERIES

The following heating system repair operations for the 140 series can generally be applied to other models as well.

Heater Unit Removal

Drain the coolant and disconnect the negative battery lead. Remove the hoses to the control valve. Remove the panel, below the dashboard, by loosening the two screws, one on the left side and one beside the glove compartment. Pull the upper section of the panel rearward so that it loosens from the clips in the dashboard and free the panel from the hood release control. Remove the mat on the transmission tunnel. Loosen and remove the defroster hoses and control wires, remove the switch for the fan, and disconnect the cables to the fan motor. Remove the two screws which hold the fusebox to the heater. Remove the control valve and loosen the upper hose to the heater unit. Plug the outlets on the heater so that the remaining coolant does not run into the car. Loosen the ground cables from the right bracket. Loosen and remove the four screws which hold the heater unit to the brackets and loosen the drain hose. Lift out the heater unit and control valve carefully.

Heater Unit Disassembly

Remove the four rubber bushings on the

sides of the heater unit. Mark the fan casing to ease reassembly. Remove the spring clips which hold the heater and separate the two halves.

Fan Motor Replacement

Remove the heater unit and disassemble it. Mark the mounting plate in relation to the fan casing. Loosen the mounting plate with fan motor from the fan casing by straightening the tabs. Remove the screws which hold the fan motor to the mounting plate. To reassemble, replace the fan motor and the screws which hold it to the mounting plate. Replace the mounting plate on the fan casing. Reassemble the heater unit and install it in the vehicle.

Heater Unit Assembly

Scrape off the sealant and replace it with a soft sealant. Replace the core with sensitive body and reassemble the casing halves. Replace the spring clips and the rubber bushings.

Heater Unit Installation

Place the heater unit in position and connect the drain hose. Install the four screws which hold the heater to the brackets. Connect the ground cables to the right bracket. Install the control valve and the upper hose to the heater. Install the fusebox to the heater. Connect the cables from the fan motor to the switch and mount the switch in the dashboard. Install the control wires to the shutters and control valve. Install the defroster hoses and replace the mat on the transmission tunnel. Fasten the panel in position below the instrument panel. Install the hoses to the control valve. Connect the negative battery lead and refill the coolant system.

Removal of Heater Controls

The control unit is attached to the instrument panel with three nuts. For removal, first loosen the panel below the instrument panel. Next loosen the wires on the heater unit and control valve. Remove the control lighting lamps by pulling them straight out from the holders. Remove the three nuts and take out the control unit.

Electrical

WINDSHIELD WIPERS

The windshield wipers are driven by an electric motor mounted to the wiper drive linkage under the instrument panel. The motor has two speeds which are selected by a switch on the instrument panel. The windshield washer is operated by a motor driven pump mounted at the water container under the hood.

Wiper Assembly Replacement

To replace the wiper assembly, remove wiper arms from shaft. Remove nuts, washers, and seals from wiper shafts. Label and remove leads from wiper motor assembly. Remove screw which holds wiper mechanism to the body. This is accessible from the underside of the instrument panel. Install new wiper assembly in reverse order, making sure rubber seals are in good condition. Lubricate nylon bushings on wiper linkage with grease or vaseline. Grease wiper gear housing and lubricate wiper arm shafts with light engine oil.

HORNS

Two horns are mounted between the radiator and grill. One horn gives a low note and the other a high note. Depressing the horn ring on the steering wheel closes a relay circuit which provides a ground to complete the horn circuit. If the horn does not operate, check to see that voltage is being supplied to the horn terminal from the fuse block. If the tone of the horn changes, check for loose or otherwise defective mounting.

INDICATOR LAMPS

Charging Indicator

The charging indicator lamp should light when the ignition is turned on and extinguish when the engine is running, indicating that the generator is charging the battery. If the lamp does not light when the ignition switch is turned on before the engine starts, the lamp and fuse circuit should be checked. If lamp lights while the engine is running, the generator charging circuit should be checked.

Oil Pressure Indicator

The oil pressure indicator lamp is energized through the ignition switch circuit and should light when the ignition switch is turned on. The lamp should go out when the engine starts and remain out indicating adequate oil pressure, while it is running.

If the lamp should light while the engine is running, stop the engine immediately and check oil pressure.

Turn Signal Indicators

Check for defective bulbs if the indicator lamp does not light or flashes abnormally.

High Beam Headlight Indicator

The indicator for high beam headlights is a blue lamp behind the instrument panel.

Handbrake Warning Light

The lamp is energized through the igni-tion switch. It automatically lights when the brake is applied.

FUSES

Fuses employ melt-type wires and are mounted on a fuse block on the firewall under the hood for the 444, 544, and 122, and on a fuseblock near the heater behind an opening in the protection panel under the instrument panel on the 140 series and 164. If a fuse should blow repeatedly look for trouble in the electrical circuits and components which it feeds. Do not install a higher rated fuse.

Engine Tune-Up

Engine tune-up is a procedure performed to restore engine performance, deteriorated due to normal wear and loss of adjustment. The three major areas considered in a routine tune-up are compression, ignition, and carburetion, although valve adjustment may be included.

A tune-up is performed in three steps: *analysis*, in which it is determined whether normal wear is responsible for performance loss, and which parts require replacement or service; *parts replacement or service*; and *adjustment*, in which engine adjustments are returned to original specifications. Since the advent of emission control equipment, precision adjustment has become increasingly critical, in order to maintain pollutant emission levels.

Analysis

The procedures below are used to indicate where adjustments, parts service or replacement are necessary within the realm of a normal tune-up. If, following these tests, all systems appear to be functioning properly, proceed to the Troubleshooting Section for further diagnosis.

—Remove all spark plugs, noting the cylinder in which they were installed. Remove the air cleaner, and position the throttle and choke in the full open position. Disconnect the coil high tension lead from the coil and the distributor cap. Insert a compression gauge into the spark plug port of each cylinder, in succession, and crank the engine with

Maxi. Press. Lbs. Sq. In.	Min. Press. Lbs. Sq. In.	Max. Press. Lbs. Sq. In.	Min. Press. Lbs. Sq. In.
134	101	188	141
136	102	190	142
138	104	192	144
140	105	194	145
142	107	196	147
146	110	198	148
148	111	200	150
150	113	202	151
152	114	204	153
154	115	206	154
156	117	208	156
158	118	210	157
160	120	212	158
162	121	214	160
164	123	216	162
166	124	218	163
168	126	220	165
170	127	222	166
172	129	224	168
174	131	226	169
176	132	228	171
178	133	230	172
180	135	232	174
182	136	234	175
184	138	236	177
186	140	238	178

Compression pressure limits
(C) Buick Div. G.M. Corp.)

the starter to obtain the highest possible reading. Record the readings, and compare the highest to the lowest on the compression pressure limit chart. If the difference exceeds the limits on the chart, or if all readings are excessively low, proceed to a wet compression check (see Troubleshooting Section).

—Evaluate the spark plugs according to the spark plug chart in the Troubleshooting Section, and proceed as indicated in the chart.

—Remove the distributor cap, and inspect it inside and out for cracks and/or carbon tracks, and inside for excessive wear or burning of the rotor contacts. If any of these faults are evident, the cap must be replaced.

—Check the breaker points for burning, pitting or wear, and the contact heel resting on the distributor cam for excessive wear. If defects are noted, replace the entire breaker point set.

—Remove and inspect the rotor. If the contacts are burned or worn, or if the rotor is excessively loose on the distributor shaft (where applicable), the rotor must be replaced.

—Inspect the spark plug leads and the coil high tension lead for cracks or brittleness. If any of the wires appear defective, the entire set should be replaced.

—Check the air filter to ensure that it is functioning properly.

Parts Replacement and Service

The determination of whether to replace or service parts is at the mechanic's discretion; however, it is suggested that any parts in questionable condition be replaced rather than reused.

—Clean and regap, or replace, the spark plugs as needed. Lightly coat the threads with engine oil and install the plugs. CAUTION: *Do not over-torque taper-seat spark plugs, or plugs being installed in aluminum cylinder heads.*

SPARK PLUG TORQUE

Thread size	Cast-Iron Heads	Aluminum Heads
10 mm.	14	11
14 mm.	30	27
18 mm.	34*	32
7/8 in.—18	37	35

* 17 ft. lbs. for tapered plugs using no gaskets.

—If the distributor cap is to be reused, clean the inside with a dry rag, and remove corrosion from the rotor contact points with fine emery cloth. Remove the spark plug wires one by one, and clean the wire ends and the inside of the towers. If the boots are loose, they should be replaced. If the cap is to be replaced, transfer the wires one by one, cleaning the wire ends and replacing the boots if necessary.

—If the original points are to remain in service, clean them lightly with emery cloth, lubricate the contact heel with grease specifically designed for this purpose. Rotate the crankshaft until the heel rests on a high point of the distributor cam, and adjust the point gap to specifications.

When replacing the points, remove the original points and condenser, and wipe out the inside of the distributor housing with a clean, dry rag. Lightly lubricate the contact heel and pivot point, and install the points and condenser. Rotate the crankshaft until the heel rests on a high point of the distributor cam, and adjust the point gap to specifications. NOTE: *Always replace the condenser when changing the points.*

—If the rotor is to be reused, clean the contacts with solvent. Do not alter the spring tension of the rotor center contact. Install the rotor and the distributor cap.

—Replace the coil high tension lead and/or the spark plug leads as necessary.

—Clean the carburetor using a spray solvent (e.g., Gumout Spray). Remove the varnish from the throttle bores, and clean the linkage. Disconnect and plug the fuel line, and run the engine until it runs out of fuel. Partially fill the float chamber with solvent, and reconnect the fuel line. In extreme cases, the jets can be pressure flushed by inserting a rubber plug into the float vent, running the spray nozzle through it, and spraying the solvent until it squirts out of the venturi fuel dump.

—Clean and tighten all wiring connections in the primary electrical circuit.

Additional Services

The following services *should* be performed in conjunction with a routine tune-up to ensure efficient performance.

—Inspect the battery and fill to the proper level with distilled water. Remove the cable clamps, clean clamps and posts thoroughly, coat the posts lightly with petroleum jelly, reinstall and tighten.

—Inspect all belts, replace and/or adjust as necessary.

—Test the PCV valve (if so equipped), and clean or replace as indicated. Clean all crankcase ventilation hoses, or replace if cracked or hardened.

—Adjust the valves (if necessary) to manufacturer's specifications.

Adjustments

—Connect a dwell-tachometer between the distributor primary lead and ground. Remove the distributor cap and rotor (unless equipped with Delco externally adjustable distributor). With the ignition off, crank the engine with a remote starter switch and measure the point dwell angle. Adjust the dwell angle to specifications. NOTE: *Increasing the gap decreases the dwell angle and vice-versa.* Install the rotor and distributor cap.

—Connect a timing light according to the manufacturer's specifications. Identify the proper timing marks with chalk or paint. NOTE: *Luminescent (day-glo) paint is excellent for this purpose.* Start the engine, and run it until it reaches operating temperature. Disconnect and plug any distributor vacuum lines, and adjust idle to the speed required to adjust timing, according to specifications. Loosen the distributor clamp and adjust timing to specifications by rotating the distributor in the engine. NOTE: *To advance timing, rotate distributor opposite normal direction of rotor rotation, and vice-versa.*

—Synchronize the throttles and mixture of multiple carburetors (if so equipped) according to procedures given in the individual car sections.

—Adjust the idle speed, mixture, and idle quality, as specified in the individual car sections. If adjustment of carburetors equipped with idle limiter caps is found to be impossible, the caps may be removed by inserting a sheet metal screw into the cap, and tightening until the cap slides off. Final idle adjustments should be made with the air cleaner installed. CAUTION: *Due to strict emission control requirements on 1969 and later models, special test equipment (CO meter, SUN Tester) may be necessary to properly adjust idle mixture to specifications.*

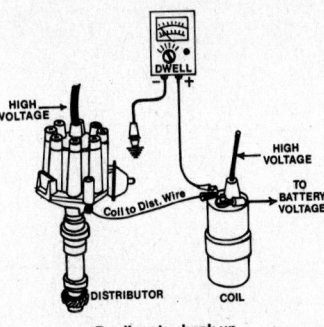

Dwell meter hook-up

Trouble-shooting

The following section is designed to aid in the rapid diagnosis of engine problems. The systematic format is used to diagnose problems ranging from engine starting difficulties to the need for engine overhaul. It is assumed that the user is equipped with basic hand tools and test equipment (tach-dwell meter, timing light, voltmeter, and ohmmeter).

Troubleshooting is divided into two sections. The first, *General Diagnosis*, is used to locate the problem area. In the second, *Specific Diagnosis*, the problem is systematically evaluated.

General Diagnosis

PROBLEM: Symptom	Begin diagnosis at Section Two, Number ——
Engine won't start:	
Starter doesn't turn	1.1, 2.1
Starter turns, engine doesn't	2.1
Starter turns engine very slowly	1.1, 2.4
Starter turns engine normally	3.1, 4.1
Starter turns engine very quickly	6.1
Engine fires intermittently	4.1
Engine fires consistently	5.1, 6.1
Engine runs poorly:	
Hard starting	3.1, 4.1, 5.1, 8.1
Rough idle	4.1, 5.1, 8.1
Stalling	3.1, 4.1, 5.1, 8.1
Engine dies at high speeds	4.1, 5.1
Hesitation (on acceleration from standing stop)	5.1, 8.1
Poor pickup	4.1, 5.1, 8.1
Lack of power	3.1, 4.1, 5.1, 8.1
Backfire through the carburetor	4.1, 8.1, 9.1
Backfire through the exhaust	4.1, 8.1, 9.1
Blue exhaust gases	6.1, 7.1
Black exhaust gases	5.1
Running on (after the ignition is shut off)	3.1, 8.1
Susceptible to moisture	4.1
Engine misfires under load	4.1, 7.1, 8.4, 9.1
Engine misfires at speed	4.1, 8.4
Engine misfires at idle	3.1, 4.1, 5.1, 7.1, 8.4

PROBLEM: Symptom	Probable Cause
Engine noises: ①	
Metallic grind while starting	Starter drive not engaging completely
Constant grind or rumble	*Starter drive not releasing, worn main bearings
Constant knock	Worn connecting rod bearings
Knock under load	Fuel octane too low, worn connecting rod bearings
Double knock	Loose piston pin
Metallic tap	*Collapsed or sticky valve lifter, excessive valve clearance, excessive end play in a rotating shaft
Scrape	*Fan belt contacting a stationary surface
Tick while starting	S.U. electric fuel pump (normal), starter brushes
Constant tick	*Generator brushes, shreaded fan belt
Squeal	*Improperly tensioned fan belt
Hiss or roar	*Steam escaping through a leak in the cooling system or the radiator overflow vent
Whistle	*Vacuum leak
Wheeze	Loose or cracked spark plug

①—It is extremely difficult to evaluate vehicle noises. While the above are general definitions of engine noises, those starred (*) should be considered as possibly originating elsewhere in the car. To aid diagnosis, the following list considers other potential sources of these sounds.

Metallic grind:
Throwout bearing; transmission gears, bearings, or synchronizers; differential bearings, gears; something metallic in contact with brake drum or disc.

Metallic tap:
U-joints; fan-to-radiator (or shroud) contact.

Scrape:
Brake shoe or pad dragging; tire to body contact; suspension contacting undercarriage or exhaust; something non-metallic contacting brake shoe or drum.

Tick:
Transmission gears; differential gears; lack of radio suppression; resonant vibration of body panels; windshield wiper motor or transmission; heater motor and blower.

Squeal:
Brake shoe or pad not fully releasing; tires (excessive wear, uneven wear, improper inflation); front or rear wheel alignment (most commonly due to improper toe-in).

Hiss or whistle:
Wind leaks (body or window); heater motor and blower fan.

Roar:
Wheel bearings; wind leaks (body and window).

Specific Diagnosis

This section is arranged so that following each test, instructions are given to proceed to another, until a problem is diagnosed.

INDEX

*—The engine need not be running.
**—The engine must be running.

SAMPLE SECTION

Test and Procedure	Results and Indications	Proceed to
4.1—Check for spark: Hold each spark plug wire approximately 1/4″ from ground with gloves or a heavy, dry rag. Crank the engine and observe the spark.	If no spark is evident: —————→	4.2
	If spark is good in some cases: —————→	4.3
	If spark is good in all cases: —————→	4.6

DIAGNOSIS

Test and Procedure	Results and Indications	Proceed to
1.1—Inspect the battery visually for case condition (corrosion, cracks) and water level.	If case is cracked, replace battery:	1.4
	If the case is intact, remove corrosion with a solution of baking soda and water (CAUTION: *do not get the solution into the battery*), and fill with water:	1.2
1.2—Check the battery cable connections: Insert a screwdriver between the battery post and the cable clamp. Turn the headlights on high beam, and observe them as the screwdriver is gently twisted to ensure good metal to metal contact. Testing battery cable connections using a screwdriver	If the lights brighten, remove and clean the clamp and post; coat the post with petroleum jelly, install and tighten the clamp:	1.4
	If no improvement is noted:	1.3

1.3—Test the state of charge of the battery using an individual cell tester or hydrometer.

Spec. Grav. Reading	Charged Condition
1.260-1.280	Fully Charged
1.230-1.250	Three Quarter Charged
1.200-1.220	One Half Charged
1.170-1.190	One Quarter Charged
1.140-1.160	Just About Flat
1.110-1.130	All The Way Down

State of battery charge

Electrolyte temperature (°F)	Specific gravity correction
+120	+.016
+100	+.012 / +.008 (ADD to reading)
+80	+.004
	no correction
+60	—.004
+40	—.008 / —.012
+20	—.016 / —.020 / —.024 (SUBTRACT from reading)
0	—.028 / —.032
—20	—.036 / —.040

The effect of temperature on the specific gravity of battery electrolyte

If indicated, charge the battery. NOTE: *If no obvious reason exists for the low state of charge (i.e., battery age, prolonged storage), the charging system should be tested:* — 1.4

Test and Procedure	Results and Indications	Proceed to
1.4—Visually inspect battery cables for cracking, bad connection to ground, or bad connection to starter.	If necessary, tighten connections or replace the cables:	2.1

Tests in Group 2 are performed with coil high tension lead disconnected to prevent accidental starting.

Test and Procedure	Results and Indications	Proceed to
2.1—Test the starter motor and sole-noid: Connect a jumper from the battery post of the solenoid (or relay) to the starter post of the solenoid (or relay).	If starter turns the engine normally:	2.2
	If the starter buzzes, or turns the engine very slowly:	2.4
	If no response, replace the solenoid (or relay).	3.1
	If the starter turns, but the engine doesn't, ensure that the flywheel ring gear is intact. If the gear is undamaged, replace the starter drive.	3.1
2.2—Determine whether ignition override switches are functioning properly (clutch start switch, neutral safety switch), by connecting a jumper across the switch(es), and turning the ignition switch to "start".	If starter operates, adjust or replace switch:	3.1
	If the starter doesn't operate:	2.3
2.3—Check the ignition switch "start" position: Connect a 12V test lamp between the starter post of the solenoid (or relay) and ground. Turn the ignition switch to the "start" position, and jiggle the key.	If the lamp doesn't light when the switch is turned, check the ignition switch for loose connections, cracked insulation, or broken wires. Repair or replace as necessary:	3.1
	If the lamp flickers when the key is jiggled, replace the ignition switch.	3.3

Checking the ignition switch "start" position

Test and Procedure	Results and Indications	Proceed to
2.4—Remove and bench test the start-er, according to specifications in the car section.	If the starter does not meet specifications, repair or replace as needed:	3.1
	If the starter is operating properly:	2.5
2.5—Determine whether the engine can turn freely: Remove the spark plugs, and check for water in the cylinders. Check for water on the dipstick, or oil in the radiator. Attempt to turn the engine using an 18" flex drive and socket on the crankshaft pulley nut or bolt.	If the engine will turn freely only with the spark plugs out, and hydrostatic lock (water in the cylinders) is ruled out, check valve timing:	9.2
	If engine will not turn freely, and it is known that the clutch and transmission are free, the engine must be disassembled for further evaluation:	Next Chapter

Tests and Procedures	Results and Indications	Proceed to
3.1—Check the ignition switch "on" position: Connect a jumper wire between the distributor side of the coil and ground, and a 12V test lamp between the switch side of the coil and ground. Remove the high tension lead from the coil. Turn the ignition switch on and jiggle the key.	If the lamp lights:	3.2
	If the lamp flickers when the key is jiggled, replace the ignition switch:	3.3
	If the lamp doesn't light, check for loose or open connections. If none are found, remove the ignition switch and check for continuity. If the switch is faulty, replace it:	3.3

Checking the ignition switch "on" position

3.2—Check the ballast resistor or resistance wire for an open circuit, using an ohmmeter.	Replace the resistor or the resistance wire if the resistance is zero.	3.3
3.3—Visually inspect the breaker points for burning, pitting, or excessive wear. Gray coloring of the point contact surfaces is normal. Rotate the crankshaft until the contact heel rests on a high point of the distributor cam, and adjust the point gap to specifications.	If the breaker points are intact, clean the contact surfaces with fine emery cloth, and adjust the point gap to specifications. If pitted or worn, replace the points and condenser, and adjust the gap to specifications: NOTE: *Always lubricate the distributor cam according to manufacturer's recommendations when servicing the breaker points.*	3.4
3.4—Connect a dwell meter between the distributor primary lead and ground. Crank the engine and observe the point dwell angle.	If necessary, adjust the point dwell angle: NOTE: *Increasing the point gap decreases the dwell angle, and vice-versa.*	3.6
	If dwell meter shows little or no reading:	3.5

Dwell meter hook-up

Dwell angle

| 3.5—Check the condenser for short: Connect an ohmmeter across the condenser body and the pigtail lead. | If any reading other than infinite resistance is noted, replace the condenser: | 3.6 |

Checking the condenser for short

Test and Procedure	Results and Indications	Proceed to
3.6—Test the coil primary resistance: Connect an ohmmeter across the coil primary terminals, and read the resistance on the low scale. Note whether an external ballast resistor or resistance wire is utilized.	Coils utilizing ballast resistors or resistance wires should have approximately 1.0Ω resistance; coils with internal resistors should have approximately 4.0Ω resistance. If values far from the above are noted, replace the coil:	4.1

Testing the coil primary resistance

Test and Procedure	Results and Indications	Proceed to
4.1—Check for spark: Hold each spark plug wire approximately $\frac{1}{4}''$ from ground with gloves or a heavy, dry rag. Crank the engine, and observe the spark.	If no spark is evident:	4.2
	If spark is good in some cylinders:	4.3
	If spark is good in all cylinders:	4.6
4.2—Check for spark at the coil high tension lead: Remove the coil high tension lead from the distributor and position it approximately $\frac{1}{4}''$ from ground. Crank the engine and observe spark. CAUTION: *This test should not be performed on cars equipped with transistorized ignition.*	If the spark is good and consistent:	4.3
	If the spark is good but intermittent, test the primary electrical system starting at 3.3:	3.3
	If the spark is weak or non-existent, replace the coil high tension lead, clean and tighten all connections and retest. If no improvement is noted:	4.4
4.3—Visually inspect the distributor cap and rotor for burned or corroded contacts, cracks, carbon tracks, or moisture. Also check the fit of the rotor on the distributor shaft (where applicable).	If moisture is present, dry thoroughly, and retest per 4.1:	4.1
	If burned or excessively corroded contacts, cracks, or carbon tracks are noted, replace the defective part(s) and retest per 4.1:	4.1
	If the rotor and cap appear intact, or are only slightly corroded, clean the contacts thoroughly (including the cap towers and spark plug wire ends) and retest per 4.1:	
	If the spark is good in all cases:	4.6
	If the spark is poor in all cases:	4.5
4.4—Check the coil secondary resistance: Connect an ohmmeter across the distributor side of the coil and the coil tower. Read the resistance on the high scale of the ohmmeter.	The resistance of a satisfactory coil should be between $4K\Omega$ and $10K\Omega$. If the resistance is considerably higher (i.e., $40K\Omega$) replace the coil, and retest per 4.1: NOTE: *This does not apply to high performance coils.*	4.1

Testing the coil secondary resistance

Test and Procedure	Results and Indications	Proceed to
4.5—Visually inspect the spark plug wires for cracking or brittleness. Ensure that no two wires are positioned so as to cause induction firing (adjacent and parallel). Remove each wire, one by one, and check resistance with an ohmmeter.	Replace any cracked or brittle wires. If any of the wires are defective, replace the entire set. Replace any wires with excessive resistance (over 8000Ω per foot for suppression wire), and separate any wires that might cause induction firing.	4.6
4.6—Remove the spark plugs, noting the cylinders from which they were removed, and evaluate according to the chart below.	See below.	See below.

	Condition	Cause	Remedy	Proceed to
	Electrodes eroded, light brown deposits.	Normal wear. Normal wear is indicated by approximately .001″ wear per 1000 miles.	Clean and regap the spark plug if wear is not excessive: Replace the spark plug if excessively worn:	4.7
	Carbon fouling (black, dry, fluffy deposits).	If present on one or two plugs:		
		Faulty high tension lead(s).	Test the high tension leads:	4.5
		Burnt or sticking valve(s).	Check the valve train: (Clean and regap the plugs in either case.)	9.1
		If present on most or all plugs: Overly rich fuel mixture, due to restricted air filter, improper carburetor adjustment, improper choke or heat riser adjustment or operation.	Check the fuel system:	5.1
	Oil fouling (wet black deposits)	Worn engine components. NOTE: *Oil fouling may occur in new or recently rebuilt engines until broken in.*	Check engine vacuum and compression:	6.1
	Lead fouling (gray, black, tan, or yellow deposits, which appear glazed or cinder-like).	Combustion by-products.	Clean and regap the plugs: (Use plugs of a different heat range if the problem recurs.)	4.7

	Condition	Cause	Remedy	Proceed to
	Gap bridging (deposits lodged between the electrodes).	Incomplete combustion, or transfer of deposits from the combustion chamber.	Replace the spark plugs:	4.7
	Overheating (burnt electrodes, and extremely white insulator with small black spots).	Ignition timing advanced too far.	Adjust timing to specifications:	8.2
		Overly lean fuel mixture.	Check the fuel system:	5.1
		Spark plugs not seated properly.	Clean spark plug seat and install a new gasket washer: (Replace the spark plugs in all cases.)	4.7
	Fused spot deposits on the insulator.	Combustion chamber blow-by.	Clean and regap the spark plugs:	4.7
	Pre-ignition (melted or severely burned electrodes, blistered or cracked insulators, or metallic deposits on the insulator).	Incorrect spark plug heat range.	Replace with plugs of the proper heat range:	4.7
		Ignition timing advanced too far.	Adjust timing to specifications:	8.2
		Spark plugs not being cooled efficiently.	Clean the spark plug seat, and check the cooling system:	11.1
		Fuel mixture too lean.	Check the fuel system:	5.1
		Poor compression.	Check compression:	6.1
		Fuel grade too low.	Use higher octane fuel:	4.7

Test and Procedure	Results and Indications	Proceed to
4.7—Determine the static ignition timing: Using the flywheel or crankshaft pulley timing marks as a guide, locate top dead center on the *compression* stroke of the No. 1 cylinder. Remove the distributor cap.	Adjust the distributor so that the rotor points toward the No. 1 tower in the distributor cap, and the points are just opening:	4.8
4.8—Check coil polarity: Connect a voltmeter negative lead to the coil high tension lead, and the positive lead to ground (NOTE: *reverse the hook-up for positive ground cars*). Crank the engine momentarily. **Checking coil polarity**	If the voltmeter reads up-scale, the polarity is correct:	5.1
	If the voltmeter reads down-scale, reverse the coil polarity (switch the primary leads):	5.1

Test and Procedure	Results and Indications	Proceed to
5.1—Determine that the air filter is functioning efficiently: Hold paper elements up to a strong light, and attempt to see light through the filter.	Clean permanent air filters in gasoline (or manufacturer's recommendation), and allow to dry. Replace paper elements through which light cannot be seen:	5.2
5.2—Determine whether a flooding condition exists: Flooding is identified by a strong gasoline odor, and excessive gasoline present in the throttle bore(s) of the carburetor.	If flooding is not evident:	5.3
	If flooding is evident, permit the gasoline to dry for a few moments and restart.	
	If flooding doesn't recur:	5.6
	If flooding is persistant:	5.5
5.3—Check that fuel is reaching the carburetor: Detach the fuel line at the carburetor inlet. Hold the end of the line in a cup (not styrofoam), and crank the engine.	If fuel flows smoothly:	5.6
	If fuel doesn't flow (NOTE: *Make sure that there is fuel in the tank*), or flows erratically:	5.4
5.4—Test the fuel pump: Disconnect all fuel lines from the fuel pump. Hold a finger over the input fitting, crank the engine (with electric pump, turn the ignition or pump on), and feel for suction.	If suction is evident, blow out the fuel line to the tank with low pressure compressed air until bubbling is heard from the fuel filler neck. Also blow out the carburetor fuel line (both ends disconnected):	5.6
	If no suction is evident, replace or repair the fuel pump:	5.6
	NOTE: *Repeated oil fouling of the spark plugs, or a no-start condition, could be the result of a ruptured vacuum booster pump diaphragm, through which oil or gasoline is being drawn into the intake manifold (where applicable).*	
5.5—Check the needle and seat: Tap the carburetor in the area of the needle and seat.	If flooding stops, a gasoline additive (e.g., Gumout) will often cure the problem:	5.6
	If flooding continues, check the fuel pump for excessive pressure at the carburetor (according to specifications). If the pressure is normal, the needle and seat must be removed and checked, and/or the float level adjusted:	5.6
5.6—Test the accelerator pump by looking into the throttle bores while operating the throttle.	If the accelerator pump appears to be operating normally:	5.7
	If the accelerator pump is not operating, the pump must be reconditioned. Where possible, service the pump with the carburetor(s) installed on the engine. If necessary, remove the carburetor. Prior to removal:	5.7
5.7—Determine whether the carburetor main fuel system is functioning: Spray a commercial starting fluid into the carburetor while attempting to start the engine.	If the engine starts, runs for a few seconds, and dies:	5.8
	If the engine doesn't start:	6.1

Test and Procedures	Results and Indications	Proceed to
5.8—Uncommon fuel system malfunctions: See below:	If the problem is solved:	6.1
	If the problem remains, remove and recondition the carburetor.	

Condition	Indication	Test	Usual Weather Conditions	Remedy
Vapor lock	Car will not re-start shortly after running.	Cool the components of the fuel system until the engine starts.	Hot to very hot	Ensure that the exhaust manifold heat control valve is operating. Check with the vehicle manufacturer for the recommended solution to vapor lock on the model in question.
Carburetor icing	Car will not idle, stalls at low speeds.	Visually inspect the throttle plate area of the throttle bores for frost.	High humidity, 32-40° F.	Ensure that the exhaust manifold heat control valve is operating, and that the intake manifold heat riser is not blocked.
Water in the fuel	Engine sputters and stalls; may not start.	Pump a small amount of fuel into a glass jar. Allow to stand, and inspect for droplets or a layer of water.	High humidity, extreme temperature changes.	For droplets, use one or two cans of commercial gas dryer (Dry Gas) For a layer of water, the tank must be drained, and the fuel lines blown out with compressed air.

Test and Procedure	Results and Indications	Proceed to
6.1—Test engine compression: Remove all spark plugs. Insert a compression gauge into a spark plug port, crank the engine to obtain the maximum reading, and record.	If compression is within limits on all cylinders:	7.1
	If gauge reading is extremely low on all cylinders:	6.2
	If gauge reading is low on one or two cylinders:	6.2
	(If gauge readings are identical and low on two or more adjacent cylinders, the head gasket must be replaced.)	

Testing compression
(© Chevrolet Div. G.M. Corp.)

Compression pressure limits
(© Buick Div. G.M. Corp.)

Maxi. Press. Lbs. Sq. In.	Min. Press. Lbs. Sq. In.	Maxi. Press. Lbs. Sq. In.	Min. Press. Lbs. Sq. In.	Max. Press. Lbs. Sq. In.	Min. Press. Lbs. Sq. In.	Max. Press. Lbs. Sq. In.	Min. Press. Lbs. Sq. In.
134	101	162	121	188	141	214	160
136	102	164	123	190	142	216	162
138	104	166	124	192	144	218	163
140	105	168	126	194	145	220	165
142	107	170	127	196	147	222	166
146	110	172	129	198	148	224	168
148	111	174	131	200	150	226	169
150	113	176	132	202	151	228	171
152	114	178	133	204	153	230	172
154	115	180	135	206	154	232	174
156	117	182	136	208	156	234	175
158	118	184	138	210	157	236	177
160	120	186	140	212	158	238	178

Test and Procedure	Results and Indications	Proceed to
6.2—Test engine compression (wet): Squirt approximately 30 cc. of engine oil into each cylinder, and retest per 6.1.	If the readings improve, worn or cracked rings or broken pistons are indicated:	Next Chapter
	If the readings do not improve, burned or excessively carboned valves or a jumped timing chain are indicated:	7.1
	NOTE: *A jumped timing chain is often indicated by difficult cranking.*	
7.1—Perform a vacuum check of the engine: Attach a vacuum gauge to the intake manifold beyond the throttle plate. Start the engine, and observe the action of the needle over the range of engine speeds.	See below.	See below

	Reading	Indications	Proceed to
	Steady, from 17-22 in. Hg.	Normal.	8.1
	Low and steady.	Late ignition or valve timing, or low compression:	6.1
	Very low	Vacuum leak:	7.2
	Needle fluctuates as engine speed increases.	Ignition miss, blown cylinder head gasket, leaking valve or weak valve spring:	6.1, 8.3
	Gradual drop in reading at idle.	Excessive back pressure in the exhaust system:	10.1
	Intermittent fluctuation at idle.	Ignition miss, sticking valve:	8.3, 9.1
	Drifting needle.	Improper idle mixture adjustment, carburetors not synchronized (where applicable), or minor intake leak. Synchronize the carburetors, adjust the idle, and retest. If the condition persists:	7.2
	High and steady.	Early ignition timing:	8.2

Test and Procedure	Results and Indications	Proceed to
7.2—Attach a vacuum gauge per 7.1, and test for an intake manifold leak. Squirt a small amount of oil around the intake manifold gaskets, carburetor gaskets, plugs and fittings. Observe the action of the vacuum gauge.	If the reading improves, replace the indicated gasket, or seal the indicated fitting or plug: If the reading remains low:	8.1 7.3
7.3—Test all vacuum hoses and accessories for leaks as described in 7.2. Also check the carburetor body (dashpots, automatic choke mechanism, throttle shafts) for leaks in the same manner.	If the reading improves, service or replace the offending part(s): If the reading remains low:	8.1 6.1
8.1—Check the point dwell angle: Connect a dwell meter between the distributor primary wire and ground. Start the engine, and observe the dwell angle from idle to 3000 rpm.	If necessary, adjust the dwell angle. NOTE: *Increasing the point gap reduces the dwell angle and vice-versa.* If the dwell angle moves outside specifications as engine speed increases, the distributor should be removed and checked for cam accuracy, shaft end-play and concentricity, bushing wear, and adequate point arm tension (NOTE: *Most of these items may be checked with the distributor installed in the engine, using an oscilloscope*):	8.2
8.2—Connect a timing light (per manufacturer's recommendation) and check the dynamic ignition timing. Disconnect and plug the vacuum hose(s) to the distributor if specified, start the engine, and observe the timing marks at the specified engine speed.	If the timing is not correct, adjust to specifications by rotating the distributor in the engine: (Advance timing by rotating distributor opposite normal direction of rotor rotation, retard timing by rotating distributor in same direction as rotor rotation.)	8.3
8.3—Check the operation of the distributor advance mechanism(s): To test the mechanical advance, disconnect all but the mechanical advance, and observe the timing marks with a timing light as the engine speed is increased from idle. If the mark moves smoothly, without hesitation, it may be assumed that the mechanical advance is functioning properly. To test vacuum advance and/or retard systems, alternately crimp and release the vacuum line, and observe the timing mark for movement. If movement is noted, the system is operating.	If the systems are functioning: If the systems are not functioning, remove the distributor, and test on a distributor tester:	8.4 8.4
8.4—Locate an ignition miss: With the engine running, remove each spark plug wire, one by one, until one is found that doesn't cause the engine to roughen and slow down.	When the missing cylinder is identified:	4.1

Test and Procedure	Results and Indications	Proceed to
9.1—Evaluate the valve train: Remove the valve cover, and ensure that the valves are adjusted to specifications. A mechanic's stethoscope may be used to aid in the diagnosis of the valve train. By pushing the probe on or near push rods or rockers, valve noise often can be isolated. A timing light also may be used to diagnose valve problems. Connect the light according to manufacturer's recommendations, and start the engine. Vary the firing moment of the light by increasing the engine speed (and therefore the ignition advance), and moving the trigger from cylinder to cylinder. Observe the movement of each valve.	See below	See below

Observation	Probable Cause	Remedy	Proceed to
Metallic tap heard through the stethoscope.	Sticking hydraulic lifter or excessive valve clearance.	Adjust valve. If tap persists, remove and replace the lifter:	10.1
Metallic tap through the stethoscope, able to push the rocker arm (lifter side) down by hand.	Collapsed valve lifter.	Remove and replace the lifter:	10.1
Erratic, irregular motion of the valve stem.*	Sticking valve, burned valve.	Recondition the valve and/or valve guide:	Next Chapter
Eccentric motion of the pushrod at the rocker arm.*	Bent pushrod.	Replace the pushrod:	10.1
Valve retainer bounces as the valve closes.*	Weak valve spring or damper.	Remove and test the spring and damper. Replace if necessary:	10.1

*—When observed with a timing light.

Test and Procedure	Results and Indications	Proceed to
9.2—Check the valve timing: Locate top dead center of the No. 1 piston, and install a degree wheel or tape on the crankshaft pulley or damper with zero corresponding to an index mark on the engine. Rotate the crankshaft in its direction of rotation, and observe the opening of the No. 1 cylinder intake valve. The opening should correspond with the correct mark on the degree wheel according to specifications.	If the timing is not correct, the timing cover must be removed for further investigation:	—

Test and Procedure	Results and Indications	Proceed to
10.1—Determine whether the exhaust manifold heat control valve is operating: Operate the valve by hand to determine whether it is free to move. If the valve is free, run the engine to operating temperature and observe the action of the valve, to ensure that it is opening.	If the valve sticks, spray it with a suitable solvent, open and close the valve to free it, and retest. If the valve functions properly: If the valve does not free, or does not operate, replace the valve:	 10.2 10.2
10.2—Ensure that there are no exhaust restrictions: Visually inspect the exhaust system for kinks, dents, or crushing. Also note that gasses are flowing freely from the tailpipe at all engine speeds, indicating no restriction in the muffler or resonator.	Replace any damaged portion of the system:	
11.1—Visually inspect the fan belt for glazing, cracks, and fraying, and replace if necessary. Tighten the belt so that the longest span has approximately ½″ play at its midpoint under thumb pressure. **Checking the fan belt tension** (© Nissan Motor Co. Ltd.)	Replace or tighten the fan belt as necessary:	11.2
11.2—Check the fluid level of the cooling system.	If full or slightly low, fill as necessary: If extremely low:	11.5 11.3
11.3—Visually inspect the external portions of the cooling system (radiator, radiator hoses, thermostat elbow, water pump seals, heater hoses, etc.) for leaks. If none are found, pressurize the cooling system to 14-15 psi.	If cooling system holds the pressure: If cooling system loses pressure rapidly, reinspect external parts of the system for leaks under pressure. If none are found, check dipstick for coolant in crankcase. If no coolant is present, but pressure loss continues: If coolant is evident in crankcase, remove cylinder head(s), and check gasket(s). If gaskets are intact, block and cylinder head(s) should be checked for cracks or holes. If the gasket(s) is blown, replace, and purge the crankcase of coolant: NOTE: *Occasionally, due to atmospheric and driving conditions, condensation of water can occur in the crankcase. This causes the oil to appear milky white. To remedy, run the engine until hot, and change the oil and oil filter.*	11.5 11.4 12.6

Test and Procedure	*Results and Indication*	*Proceed to*
11.4—Check for combustion leaks into the cooling system: Pressurize the cooling system as above. Start the engine, and observe the pressure gauge. If the needle fluctuates, remove each spark plug wire, one by one, noting which cylinder(s) reduce or eliminate the fluctuation. **Radiator pressure tester** (© American Motors Corp.)	Cylinders which reduce or eliminate the fluctuation, when the spark plug wire is removed, are leaking into the cooling system. Replace the head gasket on the affected cylinder bank(s).	11.5
11.5—Check the radiator pressure cap: Attach a radiator pressure tester to the radiator cap (wet the seal prior to installation). Quickly pump up the pressure, noting the point at which the cap releases. **Testing the radiator pressure cap** (© American Motors Corp.)	If the cap releases within ± 1 psi of the specified rating, it is operating properly: If the cap releases at more than ± 1 psi of the specified rating, it should be replaced:	11.6 11.6
11.6—Test the thermostat: Start the engine cold, remove the radiator cap, and insert a thermometer into the radiator. Allow the engine to idle. After a short while, there will be a sudden, rapid increase in coolant temperature. The temperature at which this sharp rise stops is the thermostat opening temperature.	If the thermostat opens at or about the specified temperature: If the temperature doesn't increase: (If the temperature increases slowly and gradually, replace the thermostat.)	11.7 11.7
11.7—Check the water pump: Remove the thermostat elbow and the thermostat, disconnect the coil high tension lead (to prevent starting), and crank the engine momentarily.	If coolant flows, replace the thermostat and retest per 11.6: If coolant doesn't flow, reverse flush the cooling system to alleviate any blockage that might exist. If system is not blocked, and coolant will not flow, recondition the water pump.	11.6 —
12.1—Check the oil pressure gauge or warning light: If the gauge shows low pressure, or the light is on, for no obvious reason, remove the oil pressure sender. Install an accurate oil pressure gauge and run the engine momentarily.	If oil pressure builds normally, run engine for a few moments to determine that it is functioning normally, and replace the sender. If the pressure remains low: If the pressure surges: If the oil pressure is zero:	— 12.2 12.3 12.3

Test and Procedure	Results and Indications	Proceed to
12.2—Visually inspect the oil: If the oil is watery or very thin, milky, or foamy, replace the oil and oil filter.	If the oil is normal:	12.3
	If after replacing oil the pressure remains low:	12.3
	If after replacing oil the pressure becomes normal:	—
12.3—Inspect the oil pressure relief valve and spring, to ensure that it is not sticking or stuck. Remove and thoroughly clean the valve, spring, and the valve body.	If the oil pressure improves:	—
	If no improvement is noted:	12.4

Oil pressure relief valve
(© British Leyland Motors)

Test and Procedure	Results and Indications	Proceed to
12.4—Check to ensure that the oil pump is not cavitating (sucking air instead of oil): See that the crankcase is neither over nor underfull, and that the pickup in the sump is in the proper position and free from sludge.	Fill or drain the crankcase to the proper capacity, and clean the pickup screen in solvent if necessary. If no improvement is noted:	**12.5**
12.5—Inspect the oil pump drive and the oil pump:	If the pump drive or the oil pump appear to be defective, service as necessary and retest per 12.1:	12.1
	If the pump drive and pump appear to be operating normally, the engine should be disassembled to determine where blockage exists:	Next Chapter
12.6—Purge the engine of ethylene glycol coolant: Completely drain the crankcase and the oil filter. Obtain a commercial butyl cellosolve base solvent, designated for this purpose, and follow the instructions precisely. Following this, install a new oil filter and refill the crankcase with the proper weight oil. The next oil and filter change should follow shortly thereafter (1000 miles).		

Engine Rebuilding

This chapter describes, in detail, the procedures involved in rebuilding a typical engine. The procedures specifically refer to an inline engine, however, they are basically identical to those used in rebuilding engines of nearly all design and configurations. Procedures for servicing atypical engines (i.e., horizontally opposed) are described in the individual car sections, although in most cases, cylinder head reconditioning procedures described in this chapter will apply.

The chapter is divided into two sections. The first, Cylinder Head Reconditioning, assumes that the cylinder head is removed from the engine, all manifolds are removed, and the cylinder head is on a workbench. The camshaft should be removed from overhead cam cylinder heads. The second section, Cylinder Block Reconditioning, covers the block, pistons, connecting rods and crankshaft. It is assumed that the engine is mounted on a work stand, and the cylinder head and all accessories are removed.

Procedures are identified as follows:

Unmarked—Basic procedures that must be performed in order to successfully complete the rebuilding process.

Starred (*)—Procedures that should be performed to ensure maximum performance and engine life.

Double starred (**)—Procedures that may be performed to increase engine performance and reliability. These procedures are usually reserved for extremely heavy-duty or competition usage.

In many cases, a choice of methods is also provided. Methods are identified in the same manner as procedures. The choice of method for a procedure is at the discretion of the user.

The tools required for the basic rebuilding procedure should, with minor exceptions, be those

TORQUE (ft. lbs.)*

U.S.

Bolt Diameter (inches)	Bolt Grade (SAE)				Wrench Size (inches)	
	1 and 2	5	6	8	Bolt	Nut
1/4	5	7	10	10.5	3/8	7/16
5/16	9	14	19	22	1/2	9/16
3/8	15	25	34	37	9/16	5/8
7/16	24	40	55	60	5/8	3/4
1/2	37	60	85	92	3/4	13/16
9/16	53	88	120	132	7/8	7/8
5/8	74	120	167	180	15/16	1
3/4	120	200	280	296	1-1/8	1-1/8
7/8	190	302	440	473	1-5/16	1-5/16
1	282	466	660	714	1-1/2	1-1/2

Metric

Bolt Diameter (mm)	Bolt Grade				Wrench Size (mm) Bolt and Nut
	5D	8G	10K	12K	
6	5	6	8	10	10
8	10	16	22	27	14
10	19	31	40	49	17
12	34	54	70	86	19
14	55	89	117	137	22
16	83	132	175	208	24
18	111	182	236	283	27
22	182	284	394	464	32
24	261	419	570	689	36

*—Torque values are for lightly oiled bolts. CAUTION: Bolts threaded into aluminum require much less torque.

General Torque Specifications

1471

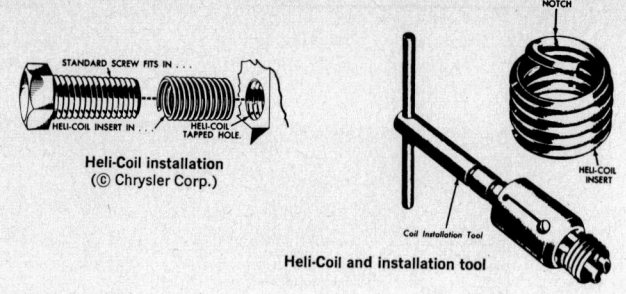

Heli-Coil installation
(© Chrysler Corp.)

Heli-Coil and installation tool

Heli-Coil Insert			Drill	Tap	Insert. Tool	Extracting Tool
Thread Size	Part No.	Insert Length (In.)	Size	Part No.	Part No.	Part No.
1/2 -20	1185-4	3/8	17/64(.266)	4 CPB	528-4N	1227-6
5/16-18	1185-5	15/32	Q(.332)	5 CPB	528-5N	1227-6
3/8 -16	1185-6	9/16	X(.397)	6 CPB	528-6N	1227-6
7/16-14	1185-7	21/32	29/64(.453)	7 CPB	528-7N	1227-16
1/2 -13	1185-8	3/4	33/64(.516)	8 CPB	528-8N	1227-16

Heli-Coil Specifications

included in a mechanic's tool kit. An accurate torque wrench, and a dial indicator (reading in thousandths) mounted on a universal base should be available. Bolts and nuts with no torque specification should be tightened according to size (see chart). Special tools, where required, all are readily available from the major tool suppliers (i.e., Craftsman, Snap-On, K-D). The services of a competent automotive machine shop must also be readily available.

When assembling the engine, any parts that will be in frictional contact must be pre-lubricated, to provide protection on initial start-up. Vortex Pre-Lube, STP, or any product specifically formulated for this purpose may be used. NOTE: *Do not use engine oil.* Where semi-permanent (locked but removable) installation of bolts or nuts is desired, threads should be cleaned and coated with Loctite. Studs may be permanently installed using Loctite Stud and Bearing Mount.

Aluminum has become increasingly popular for use in engines, due to its low weight and excellent heat transfer characteristics. The following precautions

must be observed when handling aluminum engine parts:
—Never hot-tank aluminum parts.
—Remove all aluminum parts (identification tags, etc.) from engine parts before hot-tanking (otherwise they will be removed during the process).
—Always coat threads lightly with engine oil or anti-seize compounds before installation, to prevent seizure.
—Never over-torque bolts or spark plugs in aluminum threads. Should stripping occur, threads can be restored according to the following procedure, using Heli-Coil thread inserts:

Tap drill the hole with the stripped threads to the specified size (see chart). Using the specified tap (NOTE: *Heli-Coil tap sizes refer to the size thread being replaced, rather than the actual tap size*), tap the hole for the Heli-Coil. Place the insert on the proper installation tool (see chart). Apply pressure on the insert while winding it clockwise into the hole, until the top of the insert is one turn below the surface. Remove the installation tool, and break the installation tang from the bottom of the in-

sert by moving it up and down. If the Heli-Coil must be removed, tap the removal tool firmly into the hole, so that it engages the top thread, and turn the tool counter-clockwise to extract the insert.

Snapped bolts or studs may be removed, using a stud extractor (unthreaded) or Vise-Grip pliers (threaded). Penetrating oil (e.g., Liquid Wrench) will often aid in breaking frozen threads. In cases where the stud or bolt is flush with, or below the surface, proceed as follows:

Drill a hole in the broken stud or bolt, approximately ½ its diameter. Select a screw extractor (e.g., Easy-Out) of the proper size, and tap it into the stud or bolt. Turn the extractor counter-clockwise to remove the stud or bolt.

Magnaflux and Zyglo are inspection techniques used to locate material flaws, such as stress cracks. Magnafluxing coats the part with fine magnetic particles, and subjects the part to a magnetic field. Cracks cause breaks

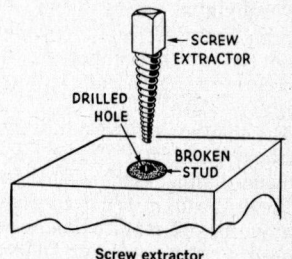

Screw extractor

in the magnetic field, which are outlined by the particles. Since Magnaflux is a magnetic process, it is applicable only to ferrous materials. The Zyglo process coats the material with a fluorescent dye penetrant, and then subjects it to blacklight inspection, under which cracks glow bright-

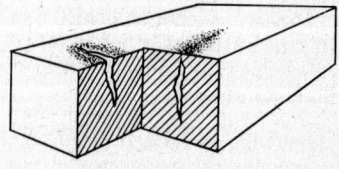

Magnaflux indication of cracks

ly. Parts made of any material may be tested using Zyglo. While Magnaflux and Zyglo are excellent for general inspection, and locating hidden defects, specific checks of suspected cracks may be made at lower cost and more readily using spot check dye. The dye is sprayed onto the suspected area, wiped off, and the area is then sprayed with a developer. Cracks then will show up bright-ly. Spot check dyes will only indicate surface cracks; therefore, structural cracks below the surface may escape detection. When questionable, the part should be tested using Magnaflux or Zyglo.

CYLINDER HEAD RECONDITIONING

Procedure	Method
Identify the valves:  **Valve identification** (© SAAB)	Invert the cylinder head, and number the valve faces front to rear, using a permanent felt-tip marker.
Remove the rocker arms:	Remove the rocker arms with shaft(s) or balls and nuts. Wire the sets of rockers, balls and nuts together, and identify according to the corresponding valve.
Remove the valves and springs:	Using an appropriate valve spring compressor (depending on the configuration of the cylinder head), compress the valve springs. Lift out the keepers with needlenose pliers, release the compressor, and remove the valve, spring, and spring retainer.
Check the valve stem-to-guide clearance:  **Checking the valve stem-to-guide clearance** (© American Motors Corp.)	Clean the valve stem with lacquer thinner or a similar solvent to remove all gum and varnish. Clean the valve guides using solvent and an expanding wire-type valve guide cleaner. Mount a dial indicator so that the stem is at 90° to the valve stem, as close to the valve guide as possible. Move the valve off its seat, and measure the valve guide-to-stem clearance by moving the stem back and forth to actuate the dial indicator. Measure the valve stems using a micrometer, and compare to specifications, to determine whether stem or guide wear is responsible for excessive clearance.
De-carbon the cylinder head and valves: 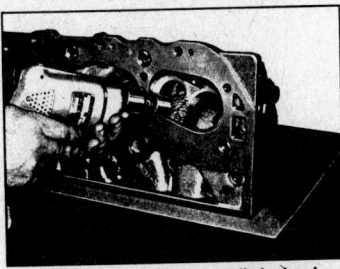 **Removing carbon from the cylinder head** (© Chevrolet Div. G.M. Corp.)	Chip carbon away from the valve heads, combustion chambers, and ports, using a chisel made of hardwood. Remove the remaining deposits with a stiff wire brush. NOTE: *Ensure that the deposits are actually removed, rather than burnished.*

Procedure	Method
Hot-tank the cylinder head:	Have the cylinder head hot-tanked to remove grease, corrosion, and scale from the water passages. NOTE: *In the case of overhead cam cylinder heads, consult the operator to determine whether the camshaft bearings will be damaged by the caustic solution.*
Degrease the remaining cylinder head parts:	Using solvent (i.e., Gunk), clean the rockers, rocker shaft(s) (where applicable), rocker balls and nuts, springs, spring retainers, and keepers. Do not remove the protective coating from the springs.
Check the cylinder head for warpage: 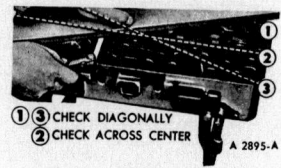 ①③ CHECK DIAGONALLY ② CHECK ACROSS CENTER A 2895-A **Checking the cylinder head for warpage** (© Ford Motor Co.)	Place a straight-edge across the gasket surface of the cylinder head. Using feeler gauges, determine the clearance at the center of the straight-edge. Measure across both diagonals, along the longitudinal centerline, and across the cylinder head at several points. If warpage exceeds .003″ in a 6″ span, or .006″ over the total length, the cylinder head must be resurfaced. NOTE: *If warpage exceeds the manufacturers maximum tolerance for material removal, the cylinder head must be replaced.* When milling the cylinder heads of V-type engines, the intake manifold mounting position is altered, and must be corrected by milling the manifold flange a proportionate amount.
** Porting and gasket matching:  **Marking the cylinder head for gasket matching** (© Petersen Publishing Co.)  **Port configuration before and after gasket matching** (© Petersen Publishing Co.)	** Coat the manifold flanges of the cylinder head with Prussian blue dye. Glue intake and exhaust gaskets to the cylinder head in their installed position using rubber cement and scribe the outline of the ports on the manifold flanges. Remove the gaskets. Using a small cutter in a hand-held power tool (i.e., Dremel Moto-Tool), gradually taper the walls of the port out to the scribed outline of the gasket. Further enlargement of the ports should include the removal of sharp edges and radiusing of sharp corners. Do not alter the valve guides. NOTE: *The most efficient port configuration is determined only by extensive testing. Therefore, it is best to consult someone experienced with the head in question to determine the optimum alterations.* 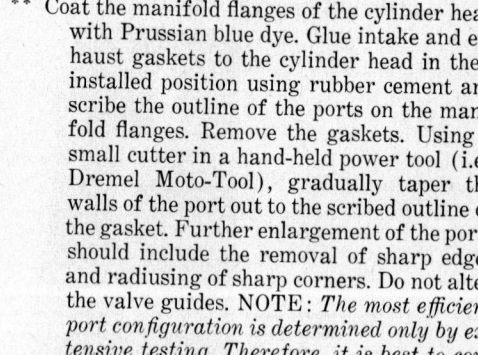

Procedure	Method
** Polish the ports:	** Using a grinding stone with the above mentioned tool, polish the walls of the intake and exhaust ports, and combustion chamber. Use progressively finer stones until all surface imperfections are removed. NOTE: *Through testing, it has been determined that a smooth surface is more effective than a mirror polished surface in intake ports, and vice-versa in exhaust ports.*

Relieved and polished ports
(© Petersen Publishing Co.)

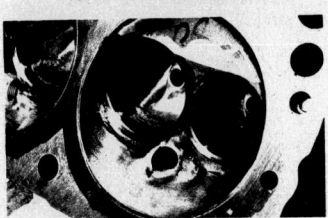

Polished combustion chamber
(© Petersen Publishing Co.)

* Knurling the valve guides:	* Valve guides which are not excessively worn or distorted may, in some cases, be knurled rather than replaced. Knurling is a process in which metal is displaced and raised, thereby reducing clearance. Knurling also provides excellent oil control. The possibility of knurling rather than replacing valve guides should be discussed with a machinist.

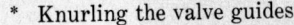

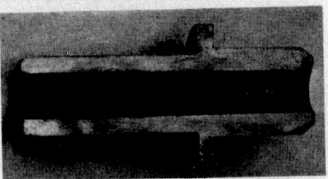

Cut-away view of a knurled valve guide
(© Petersen Publishing Co.)

Replacing the valve guides: NOTE: *Valve guides should only be replaced if damaged or if an oversize valve stem is not available.*	Depending on the type of cylinder head, valve guides may be pressed, hammered, or shrunk in. In cases where the guides are shrunk into the head, replacement should be left to an equipped machine shop. In other cases, the guides are replaced as follows: Press or tap the valve guides out of the head using a stepped drift (see illustration). Determine the height above the boss that the guide must extend, and obtain a stack of washers, their I.D. similar to the guide's O.D., of that height. Place the stack of washers on the guide, and insert the guide into the boss. NOTE: *Valve guides are often tapered or beveled for installation.* Using the stepped installation tool (see illustration), press or tap the guides into position. Ream the guides according to the size of the valve stem.

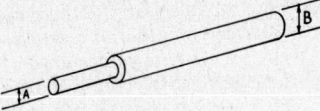

A-VALVE GUIDE I.D.
B-SLIGHTLY SMALLER THAN VALVE GUIDE O.D.

Valve guide removal tool

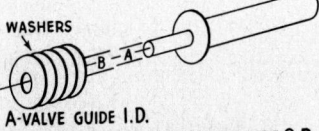

WASHERS

A-VALVE GUIDE I.D.
B-LARGER THAN THE VALVE GUIDE O.D.

Valve guide installation tool (with washers used during installation)

Procedure	Method
Replacing valve seat inserts:	Replacement of valve seat inserts which are worn beyond resurfacing or broken, if feasible, must be done by a machine shop.

Resurfacing (grinding) the valve face:

Grinding a valve
(© Subaru)

Using a valve grinder, resurface the valves according to specifications. CAUTION: *Valve face angle is not always identical to valve seat angle.* A minimum margin of 1/32″ should remain after grinding the valve. The valve stem tip should also be squared and resurfaced, by placing the stem in the V-block of the grinder, and turning it while pressing lightly against the grinding wheel.

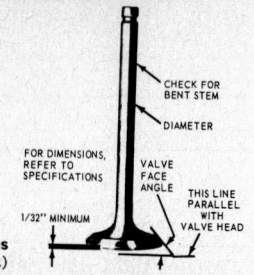

CHECK FOR
BENT STEM

DIAMETER

FOR DIMENSIONS,
REFER TO
SPECIFICATIONS

VALVE
FACE
ANGLE

THIS LINE
PARALLEL
WITH
VALVE HEAD

1/32″ MINIMUM

Critical valve dimensions
(© Ford Motor Co.)

Resurfacing the valve seats using reamers:

Reaming the valve seat
(© S.p.A. Fiat)

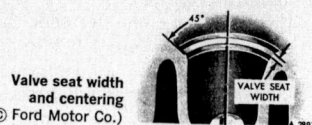

45°

VALVE SEAT
WIDTH

A 2897-A

Valve seat width and centering
(© Ford Motor Co.)

Select a reamer of the correct seat angle, slightly larger than the diameter of the valve seat, and assemble it with a pilot of the correct size. Install the pilot into the valve guide, and using steady pressure, turn the reamer clockwise. CAUTION: *Do not turn the reamer counter-clockwise.* Remove only as much material as necessary to clean the seat. Check the concentricity of the seat (see below). If the dye method is not used, coat the valve face with Prussian blue dye, install and rotate it on the valve seat. Using the dye marked area as a centering guide, center and narrow the valve seat to specifications with correction cutters. NOTE: *When no specifications are available, minimum seat width for exhaust valves should be 5/64″, intake valves 1/16″.* After making correction cuts, check the position of the valve seat on the valve face using Prussian blue dye.

* Resurfacing the valve seats using a grinder:

Valve grinder

Grinding a valve seat
(© Subaru)

Select a pilot of the correct size, and a coarse stone of the correct seat angle. Lubricate the pilot if necessary, and install the tool in the valve guide. Move the stone on and off the seat at approximately two cycles per second, until all flaws are removed from the seat. Install a fine stone, and finish the seat. Center and narrow the seat using correction stones, as described above.

Procedure	Method

Checking the valve seat concentricity :

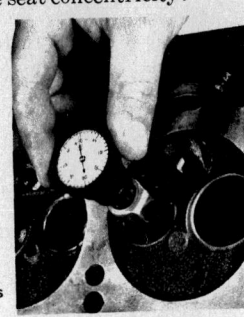

Checking the valve seat concentricity using a dial gauge (ⓒ American Motors Corp.)

Coat the valve face with Prussian blue dye, install the valve, and rotate it on the valve seat. If the entire seat becomes coated, and the valve is known to be concentric, the seat is concentric.

* Install the dial gauge pilot into the guide, and rest the arm on the valve seat. Zero the gauge, and rotate the arm around the seat. Run-out should not exceed .002″.

---

* Lapping the valves: NOTE: *Valve lapping is done to ensure efficient sealing of resurfaced valves and seats. Valve lapping alone is not recommended for use as a resurfacing procedure.*

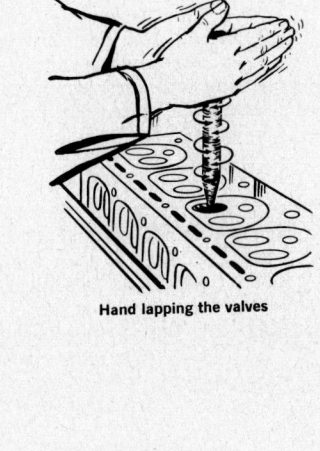

Hand lapping the valves

HAND DRILL

ROD

SUCTION CUP

Home made mechanical valve lapping tool

* Invert the cylinder head, lightly lubricate the valve stems, and install the valves in the head as numbered. Coat valve seats with fine grinding compound, and attach the lapping tool suction cup to a valve head (NOTE: *Moisten the suction cup*). Rotate the tool between the palms, changing position and lifting the tool often to prevent grooving. Lap the valve until a smooth, polished seat is evident. Remove the valve and tool, and rinse away all traces of grinding compound.

** Fasten a suction cup to a piece of drill rod, and mount the rod in a hand drill. Proceed as above, using the hand drill as a lapping tool. CAUTION: *Due to the higher speeds involved when using the hand drill, care must be exercised to avoid grooving the seat.* Lift the tool and change direction of rotation often.

Check the valve springs :

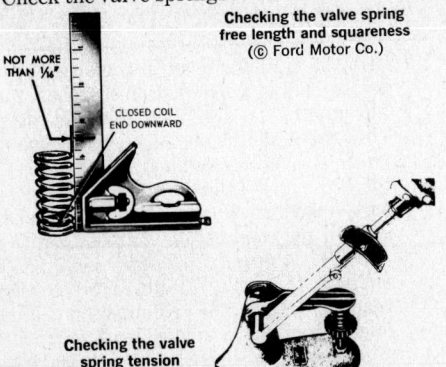

Checking the valve spring free length and squareness (ⓒ Ford Motor Co.)

NOT MORE THAN 1/16″

CLOSED COIL END DOWNWARD

Checking the valve spring tension (ⓒ Chrysler Corp.)

Place the spring on a flat surface next to a square. Measure the height of the spring, and rotate it against the edge of the square to measure distortion. If spring height varies (by comparison) by more than 1/16″ or if distortion exceeds 1/16″, replace the spring.

** In addition to evaluating the spring as above, test the spring pressure at the installed and compressed (installed height minus valve lift) height using a valve spring tester. Springs used on small displacement engines (up to 3 liters) should be ± 1 lb. of all other springs in either position. A tolerance of ± 5 lbs. is permissible on larger engines.

Procedure	Method

* Install valve stem seals :

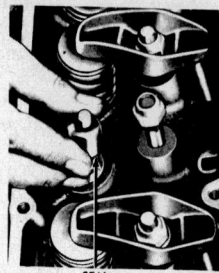

Valve stem seal installation
(© Ford Motor Co.)   SEAL

* Due to the pressure differential that exists at the ends of the intake valve guides (atmospheric pressure above, manifold vacuum below), oil is drawn through the valve guides into the intake port. This has been alleviated somewhat since the addition of positive crankcase ventilation, which lowers the pressure above the guides. Several types of valve stem seals are available to reduce blow-by. Certain seals simply slip over the stem and guide boss, while others require that the boss be machined. Recently, Teflon guide seals have become popular. Consult a parts supplier or machinist concerning availability and suggested usages. NOTE: *When installing seals, ensure that a small amount of oil is able to pass the seal to lubricate the valve guides; otherwise, excessive wear may result.*

Install the valves :

Lubricate the valve stems, and install the valves in the cylinder head as numbered. Lubricate and position the seals (if used, see above) and the valve springs. Install the spring retainers, compress the springs, and insert the keys using needlenose pliers or a tool designed for this purpose. NOTE: *Retain the keys with wheel bearing grease during installation.*

Checking valve spring installed height :

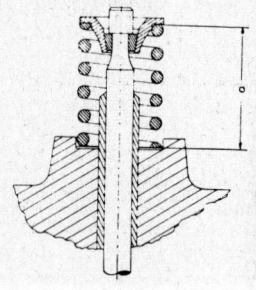

Valve spring installed height dimension
(© Porsche)

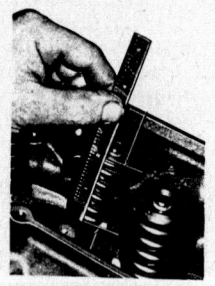

Measuring valve spring installed height
(© Petersen Publishing Co.)

Measure the distance between the spring pad and the lower edge of the spring retainer, and compare to specifications. If the installed height is incorrect, add shim washers between the spring pad and the spring. CAUTION: *Use only washers designed for this purpose.*

** CC'ing the combustion chambers :

** Invert the cylinder head and place a bead of sealer around a combustion chamber. Install an apparatus designed for this purpose (burette mounted on a clear plate; see illustration) over the combustion chamber, and fill with the specified fluid to an even mark on the burette. Record the burette reading, and fill the combustion chamber with fluid. (NOTE: *A hole drilled in the plate will permit air to escape*). Subtract the burette reading, with the combustion chamber filled, from the previous reading, to determine combustion chamber volume in cc's. Duplicate this procedure in all combustion

Procedure	Method

CC'ing the combustion chamber
(© Petersen Publishing Co.)

chambers on the cylinder head, and compare the readings. The volume of all combustion chambers should be made equal to that of the largest. Combustion chamber volume may be increased in two ways. When only a small change is required (usually), a small cutter or coarse stone may be used to remove material from the combustion chamber. NOTE: *Check volume frequently.* Remove material over a wide area, so as not to change the configuration of the combustion chamber. When a larger change is required, the valve seat may be sunk (lowered into the head). NOTE: *When altering valve seat, remember to compensate for the change in spring installed height.*

Inspect the rocker arms, balls, studs, and nuts (where applicable):

Stress cracks in rocker nuts
(© Ford Motor Co.)

Visually inspect the rocker arms, balls, studs, and nuts for cracks, galling, burning, scoring, or wear. If all parts are intact, liberally lubricate the rocker arms and balls, and install them on the cylinder head. If wear is noted on a rocker arm at the point of valve contact, grind it smooth and square, removing as little material as possible. Replace the rocker arm if excessively worn. If a rocker stud shows signs of wear, it must be replaced (see below). If a rocker nut shows stress cracks, replace it. If an exhaust ball is galled or burned, substitute the intake ball from the same cylinder (if it is intact), and install a new intake ball. NOTE: *Avoid using new rocker balls on exhaust valves.*

Replacing rocker studs:

Reaming the stud bore for oversize rocker studs
(© Buick Div. G.M. Corp.)

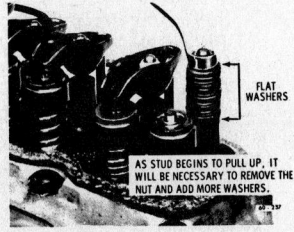

Extracting a pressed in rocker stud
(© Buick Div. G.M. Corp.)

In order to remove a threaded stud, lock two nuts on the stud, and unscrew the stud using the lower nut. Coat the lower threads of the new stud with Loctite, and install.

Two alternative methods are available for replacing pressed in studs. Remove the damaged stud using a stack of washers and a nut (see illustration). In the first, the boss is reamed .005-.006″ oversize, and an oversize stud pressed in. Control the stud extension over the boss using washers, in the same manner as valve guides. Before installing the stud, coat it with white lead and grease. To retain the stud more positively, drill a hole through the stud and boss, and install a roll pin. In the second method, the boss is tapped, and a threaded stud installed. Retain the stud using Loctite Stud and Bearing Mount.

Procedure	*Method*
Inspect the rocker shaft(s) and rocker arms (where applicable):  **Disassembled rocker shaft parts arranged for inspection** (© American Motors Corp.) 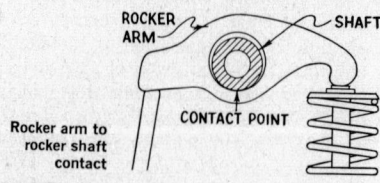 **Rocker arm to rocker shaft contact**	Remove rocker arms, springs and washers from rocker shaft. NOTE: *Lay out parts in the order they are removed.* Inspect rocker arms for pitting or wear on the valve contact point, or excessive bushing wear. Bushings need only be replaced if wear is excessive, because the rocker arm normally contacts the shaft at one point only. Grind the valve contact point of rocker arm smooth if necessary, removing as little material as possible. If excessive material must be removed to smooth and square the arm, it should be replaced. Clean out all oil holes and passages in rocker shaft. If shaft is grooved or worn, replace it. Lubricate and assemble the rocker shaft.
Inspect the camshaft bushings and the camshaft (overhead cam engines):	See next section.
Inspect the pushrods:	Remove the pushrods, and, if hollow, clean out the oil passages using fine wire. Roll each pushrod over a piece of clean glass. If a distinct clicking sound is heard as the pushrod rolls, the rod is bent, and must be replaced.
	* The length of all pushrods must be equal. Measure the length of the pushrods, compare to specifications, and replace as necessary.
Inspect the valve lifters:  Check for Concave Wear on Face of Tappet Using Tappet for Straight Edge **Checking the lifter face** (© American Motors Corp.)	Remove lifters from their bores, and remove gum and varnish, using solvent. Clean walls of lifter bores. Check lifters for concave wear as illustrated. If face is worn concave, replace lifter, and carefully inspect the camshaft. Lightly lubricate lifter and insert it into its bore. If play is excessive, an oversize lifter must be installed (where possible). Consult a machinist concerning feasibility. If play is satisfactory, remove, lubricate, and reinstall the lifter.
* Testing hydraulic lifter leak down: 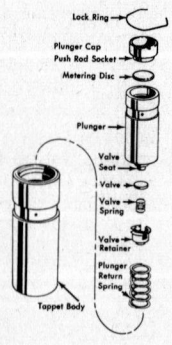 Lock Ring Plunger Cap Push Rod Socket Metering Disc Plunger Valve Seat Valve Valve Spring Valve Retainer Plunger Return Spring Tappet Body **Exploded view of a typical hydraulic lifter** (© American Motors Corp.)	Submerge lifter in a container of kerosene. Chuck a used pushrod or its equivalent into a drill press. Position container of kerosene so pushrod acts on the lifter plunger. Pump lifter with the drill press, until resistance increases. Pump several more times to bleed any air out of lifter. Apply very firm, constant pressure to the lifter, and observe rate at which fluid bleeds out of lifter. If the fluid bleeds very quickly (less than 15 seconds), lifter is defective. If the time exceeds 60 seconds, lifter is sticking. In either case, recondition or replace lifter. If lifter is operating properly (leak down time 15-60 seconds), lubricate and install it.

CYLINDER BLOCK RECONDITIONING

Procedure	*Method*

Checking the main bearing clearance:

Plastigage installed on main bearing journal
(© Chevrolet Div. G.M. Corp.)

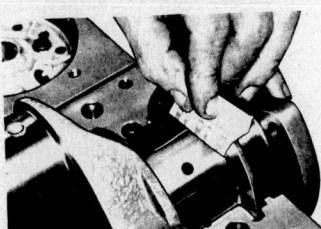

Measuring Plastigage to determine
main bearing clearance
(© Chevrolet Div. G.M. Corp.)

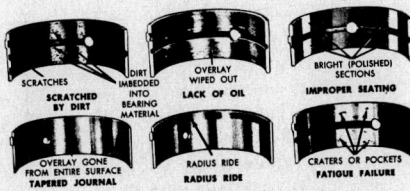

SCRATCHES — SCRATCHED BY DIRT
DIRT IMBEDDED INTO BEARING MATERIAL
OVERLAY WIPED OUT — LACK OF OIL
BRIGHT (POLISHED) SECTIONS — IMPROPER SEATING
OVERLAY GONE FROM ENTIRE SURFACE — TAPERED JOURNAL
RADIUS RIDE — RADIUS RIDE
CRATERS OR POCKETS — FATIGUE FAILURE

Causes of bearing failure
(© Ford Motor Co.)

Invert engine, and remove cap from the bearing to be checked. Using a clean, dry rag, thoroughly clean all oil from crankshaft journal and bearing insert. NOTE: *Plastigage is soluble in oil; therefore, oil on the journal or bearing could result in erroneous readings.* Place a piece of Plastigage along the full length of journal, reinstall cap, and torque to specifications. Remove bearing cap, and determine bearing clearance by comparing width of Plastigage to the scale on Plastigage envelope. Journal taper is determined by comparing width of the Plastigage strip near its ends. Rotate crankshaft 90° and retest, to determine journal eccentricity. NOTE: *Do not rotate crankshaft with Plastigage installed.* If bearing insert and journal appear intact, and are within tolerances, no further main bearing service is required. If bearing or journal appear defective, cause of failure should be determined before replacement.

* Remove crankshaft from block (see below). Measure the main bearing journals at each end twice (90° apart) using a micrometer, to determine diameter, journal taper and eccentricity. If journals are within tolerances, reinstall bearing caps at their specified torque. Using a telescope gauge and micrometer, measure bearing I.D. parallel to piston axis and at 30° on each side of piston axis. Subtract journal O.D. from bearing I.D. to determine oil clearance. If crankshaft journals appear defective, or do not meet tolerances, there is no need to measure bearings; for the crankshaft will require grinding and/or undersize bearings will be required. If bearing appears defective, cause for failure should be determined prior to replacement.

Checking the connecting rod bearing clearance:

Plastigage installed on connecting rod
bearing journal
(© Chevrolet Div. G.M. Corp.)

Connecting rod bearing clearance is checked in the same manner as main bearing clearance, using Plastigage. Before removing the crankshaft, connecting rod side clearance also should be measured and recorded.

* Checking connecting rod bearing clearance, using a micrometer, is identical to checking main bearing clearance. If no other service

Procedure	Method

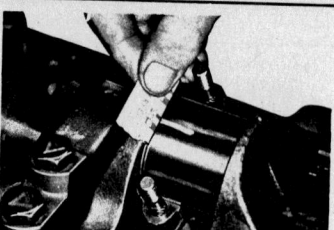

Measuring Plastigage to determine
connecting rod bearing clearance
(© Chevrolet Div. G.M. Corp.)

is required, the piston and rod assemblies need not be removed.

Removing the crankshaft:

Connecting rod matching marks
(© Ford Motor Co.)

Using a punch, mark the corresponding main bearing caps and saddles according to position (i.e., one punch on the front main cap and saddle, two on the second, three on the third, etc.). Using number stamps, identify the corresponding connecting rods and caps, according to cylinder (if no numbers are present). Remove the main and connecting rod caps, and place sleeves of plastic tubing over the connecting rod bolts, to protect the journals as the crankshaft is removed. Lift the crankshaft out of the block.

Remove the ridge from the top of the cylinder:

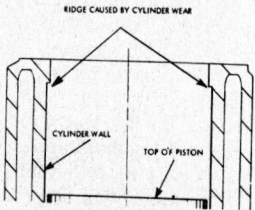

Cylinder bore ridge
(© Pontiac Div. G.M. Corp.)

In order to facilitate removal of the piston and connecting rod, the ridge at the top of the cylinder (unworn area; see illustration) must be removed. Place the piston at the bottom of the bore, and cover it with a rag. Cut the ridge away using a ridge reamer, exercising extreme care to avoid cutting too deeply. Remove the rag, and remove cuttings that remain on the piston. CAUTION: *If the ridge is not removed, and new rings are installed, damage to rings will result.*

Removing the piston and connecting rod:

Removing the piston
(© SAAB)

Invert the engine, and push the pistons and connecting rods out of the cylinders. If necessary, tap the connecting rod boss with a wooden hammer handle, to force the piston out. CAUTION: *Do not attempt to force the piston past the cylinder ridge (see above).*

Procedure	Method
Service the crankshaft:	Ensure that all oil holes and passages in the crankshaft are open and free of sludge. If necessary, have the crankshaft ground to the largest possible undersize.
	** Have the crankshaft Magnafluxed, to locate stress cracks. Consult a machinist concerning additional service procedures, such as surface hardening (e.g., nitriding, Tuftriding) to improve wear characteristics, cross drilling and chamfering the oil holes to improve lubrication, and balancing.
Removing freeze plugs:	Drill a hole in the center of the freeze plugs, and pry them out using a screwdriver or drift.
Remove the oil gallery plugs:	Threaded plugs should be removed using an appropriate (usually square) wrench. To remove soft, pressed in plugs, drill a hole in the plug, and thread in a sheet metal screw. Pull the plug out by the screw using pliers.
Hot-tank the block:	Have the block hot-tanked to remove grease, corrosion, and scale from the water jackets. NOTE: *Consult the operator to determine whether the camshaft bearings will be damaged during the hot-tank process.*
Check the block for cracks:	Visually inspect the block for cracks or chips. The most common locations are as follows: Adjacent to freeze plugs. Between the cylinders and water jackets. Adjacent to the main bearing saddles. At the extreme bottom of the cylinders. Check only suspected cracks using spot check dye (see introduction). If a crack is located, consult a machinist concerning possible repairs.
	** Magnaflux the block to locate hidden cracks. If cracks are located, consult a machinist about feasibility of repair.
Install the oil gallery plugs and freeze plugs:	Coat freeze plugs with sealer and tap into position using a piece of pipe, slightly smaller than the plug, as a driver. To ensure retention, stake the edges of the plugs. Coat threaded oil gallery plugs with sealer and install. Drive replacement soft plugs into block using a large drift as a driver.
	* Rather than reinstalling lead plugs, drill and tap the holes, and install threaded plugs.

Procedure	*Method*

Check the bore diameter and surface:

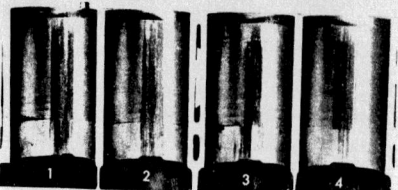

1, 2, 3 Piston skirt seizure re-
sulted in this pattern. Engine
must be rebored

4. Piston skirt and oil ring
seizure caused this damage.
Engine must be rebored

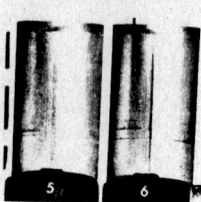

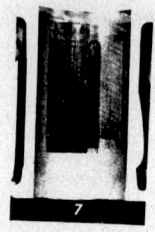

5, 6 Score marks caused by a
split piston skirt. Damage is
not serious enough to warrant
reboring

7. Ring seized longitudinally,
causing a score mark
1 3/16" wide, on the land
side of the piston groove.
The honing pattern is de-
stroyed and the cylinder
must be rebored

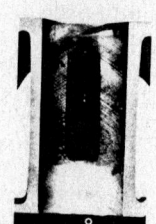

8. Result of oil ring seizure.
Engine must be rebored

9. Oil ring seizure here was not
serious enough to warrant
reboring. The honing
marks are still visible

Cylinder wall damage
(© Daimler-Benz A.G.)

Visually inspect the cylinder bores for roughness, scoring, or scuffing. If evident, the cylinder bore must be bored or honed oversize
to eliminate imperfections, and the smallest
possible oversize piston used. The new pistons should be given to the machinist with
the block, so that the cylinders can be bored
or honed exactly to the piston size (plus
clearance). If no flaws are evident, measure
the bore diameter using a telescope gauge
and micrometer, or dial gauge, parallel and
perpendicular to the engine centerline, at
the top (below the ridge) and bottom of the
bore. Subtract the bottom measurements
from the top to determine taper, and the
parallel to the centerline measurements
from the perpendicular measurements to
determine eccentricity. If the measurements
are not within specifications, the cylinder
must be bored or honed, and an oversize piston installed. If the measurements are within specifications the cylinder may be used
as is, with only finish honing (see below).
NOTE: *Prior to submitting the block for
boring, perform the following operation(s).*

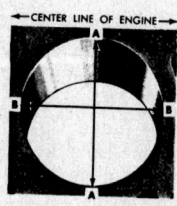

Cylinder bore measuring
positions
(© Ford Motor Co.)

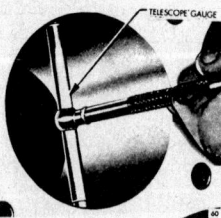

Measuring the cylinder bore
with a telescope gauge
(© Buick Div. G.M. Corp.)

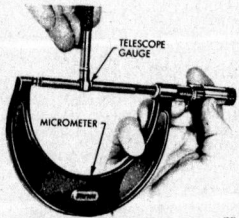

Determining the cylinder bore
by measuring the telescope
gauge with a micrometer
(© Buick Div. G.M. Corp.)

Measuring the cylinder bore
with a dial gauge
(© Chevrolet Div. G.M. Corp.)

Procedure	Method
Check the block deck for warpage:	Using a straightedge and feeler gauges, check the block deck for warpage in the same manner that the cylinder head is checked (see Cylinder Head Reconditioning). If warpage exceeds specifications, have the deck resurfaced. NOTE: *In certain cases a specification for total material removal (Cylinder head and block deck) is provided. This specification must not be exceeded.*
* Check the deck height:	The deck height is the distance from the crankshaft centerline to the block deck. To measure, invert the engine, and install the crankshaft, retaining it with the center main cap. Measure the distance from the crankshaft journal to the block deck, parallel to the cylinder centerline. Measure the diameter of the end (front and rear) main journals, parallel to the centerline of the cylinders, divide the diameter in half, and subtract it from the previous measurement. The results of the front and rear measurements should be identical. If the difference exceeds .005″, the deck height should be corrected. NOTE: *Block deck height and warpage should be corrected concurrently.*
Check the cylinder block bearing alignment:  **Checking main bearing saddle alignment** (© Petersen Publishing Co.)	Remove the upper bearing inserts. Place a straightedge in the bearing saddles along the centerline of the crankshaft. If clearance exists between the straightedge and the center saddle, the block must be align-bored.
Clean and inspect the pistons and connecting rods: 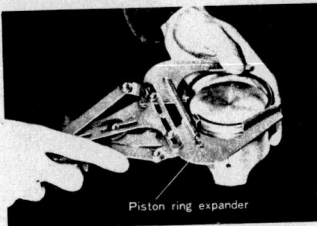 Piston ring expander **Removing the piston rings** (© Subaru)	Using a ring expander, remove the rings from the piston. Remove the retaining rings (if so equipped) and remove piston pin. NOTE: *If the piston pin must be pressed out, determine the proper method and use the proper tools; otherwise the piston will distort.* Clean the ring grooves using an appropriate tool, exercising care to avoid cutting too deeply. Thoroughly clean all carbon and varnish from the piston with solvent. CAUTION: *Do not use a wire brush or caustic solvent on pistons.* Inspect the pistons for scuffing, scoring, cracks, pitting, or excessive ring groove wear. If wear is evident, the piston must be replaced. Check the connecting rod length by measuring the rod from the inside of the large end to the inside of the small end using calipers (see

Procedure	Method

Cleaning the piston ring grooves
(© Ford Motor Co.)

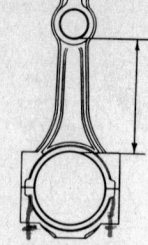

Connecting rod
length checking
dimension

illustration). All connecting rods should be equal length. Replace any rod that differs from the others in the engine.

* Have the connecting rod alignment checked in an alignment fixture by a machinist. Replace any twisted or bent rods.

* Magnaflux the connecting rods to locate stress cracks. If cracks are found, replace the connecting rod.

Fit the pistons to the cylinders:

Measuring the cylinder
with a telescope gauge
for piston fitting
(© Buick Div.
G.M. Corp.)

Measuring the piston
for fitting
(© Buick Div.
G.M. Corp.)

Using a telescope gauge and micrometer, or a dial gauge, measure the cylinder bore diameter perpendicular to the piston pin, 2½" below the deck. Measure the piston perpendicular to its pin on the skirt. The difference between the two measurements is the piston clearance. If the clearance is within specifications or slightly below (after boring or honing), finish honing is all that is required. If the clearance is excessive, try to obtain a slightly larger piston to bring clearance within specifications. Where this is not possible, obtain the first oversize piston, and hone (or if necessary, bore) the cylinder to size.

Assemble the pistons and connecting rods:

Installing piston pin lock rings
(© Nissan Motor Co., Ltd.)

Inspect piston pin, connecting rod small end bushing, and piston bore for galling, scoring, or excessive wear. If evident, replace defective part(s). Measure the I.D. of the piston boss and connecting rod small end, and the O.D. of the piston pin. If within specifications, assemble piston pin and rod. CAUTION: *If piston pin must be pressed in, determine the proper method and use the proper tools; otherwise the piston will distort.* Install the lock rings; ensure that they seat properly. If the parts are not within specifications, determine the service method for the type of engine. In some cases, piston and pin are serviced as an assembly when either is defective. Others specify reaming the piston and connecting rods for an oversize pin. If the connecting rod bushing is worn, it may in many cases be replaced. Reaming the piston and replacing the rod bushing are machine shop operations.

Procedure	*Method*

Clean and inspect the camshaft:

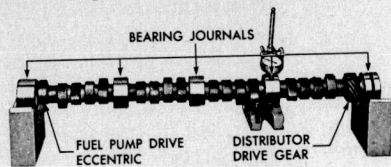

BEARING JOURNALS

FUEL PUMP DRIVE ECCENTRIC   DISTRIBUTOR DRIVE GEAR

Checking the camshaft for straightness
(© Chevrolet Motor Div. G.M. Corp.)

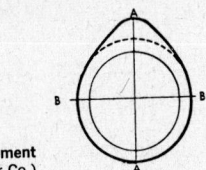

Camshaft lobe measurement
(© Ford Motor Co.)

Degrease the camshaft, using solvent, and clean out all oil holes. Visually inspect cam lobes and bearing journals for excessive wear. If a lobe is questionable, check all lobes as indicated below. If a journal or lobe is worn, the camshaft must be reground or replaced. NOTE: *If a journal is worn, there is a good chance that the bushings are worn.* If lobes and journals appear intact, place the front and rear journals in V-blocks, and rest a dial indicator on the center journal. Rotate the camshaft to check straightness. If deviation exceeds .001″, replace the camshaft.

* Check the camshaft lobes with a micrometer, by measuring the lobes from the nose to base and again at 90° (see illustration). The lift is determined by subtracting the second measurement from the first. If all exhaust lobes and all intake lobes are not identical, the camshaft must be reground or replaced.

Replace the camshaft bearings:

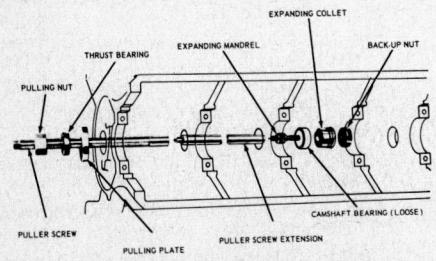

EXPANDING COLLET

THRUST BEARING   EXPANDING MANDREL   BACK-UP NUT

PULLING NUT

PULLER SCREW   CAMSHAFT BEARING (LOOSE)

PULLING PLATE   PULLER SCREW EXTENSION

Camshaft removal and installation tool (typical)
(© Ford Motor Co.)

If excessive wear is indicated, or if the engine is being completely rebuilt, camshaft bearings should be replaced as follows: Drive the camshaft rear plug from the block. Assemble the removal puller with its shoulder on the bearing to be removed. Gradually tighten the puller nut until bearing is removed. Remove remaining bearings, leaving the front and rear for last. To remove front and rear bearings, reverse position of the tool, so as to pull the bearings in toward the center of the block. Leave the tool in this position, pilot the new front and rear bearings on the installer, and pull them into position. Return the tool to its original position and pull remaining bearings into position. NOTE: *Ensure that oil holes align when installing bearings.* Replace camshaft rear plug, and stake it into position to aid retention.

Finish hone the cylinders:

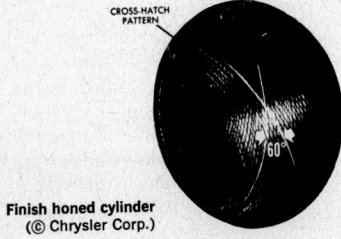

CROSS-HATCH PATTERN

60°

Finish honed cylinder
(© Chrysler Corp.)

Chuck a flexible drive hone into a power drill, and insert it into the cylinder. Start the hone, and move it up and down in the cylinder at a rate which will produce approximately a 60° cross-hatch pattern (see illustration). NOTE: *Do not extend the hone below the cylinder bore.* After developing the pattern, remove the hone and recheck piston fit. Wash the cylinders with a detergent and water solution to remove abrasive dust, dry, and wipe several times with a rag soaked in engine oil.

Procedure	*Method*

Check piston ring end-gap:

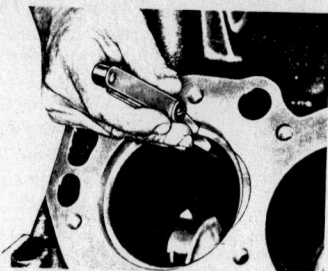

Checking ring end-gap
(© Chevrolet Motor Div. G.M. Corp.)

Compress the piston rings to be used in a cylinder, one at a time, into that cylinder, and press them approximately 1″ below the deck with an inverted piston. Using feeler gauges, measure the ring end-gap, and compare to specifications. Pull the ring out of the cylinder and file the ends with a fine file to obtain proper clearance. CAUTION: *If inadequate ring end-gap is utilized, ring breakage will result.*

Install the piston rings:

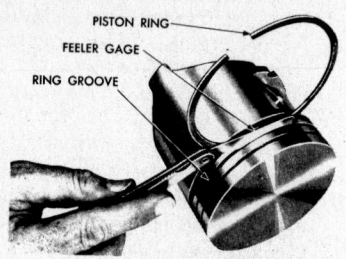

PISTON RING
FEELER GAGE
RING GROOVE

Checking ring side clearance
(© Chrysler Corp.)

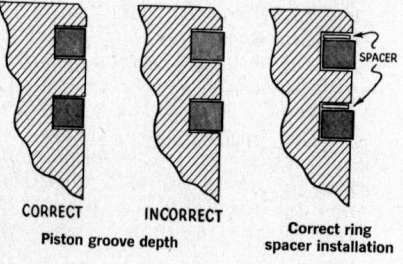

CORRECT INCORRECT
Piston groove depth

SPACER

Correct ring spacer installation

Inspect the ring grooves in the piston for excessive wear or taper. If necessary, recut the groove(s) for use with an overwidth ring or a standard ring and spacer. If the groove is worn uniformly, overwidth rings, or standard rings and spacers may be installed without recutting. Roll the outside of the ring around the groove to check for burrs or deposits. If any are found, remove with a fine file. Hold the ring in the groove, and measure side clearance. If necessary, correct as indicated above. NOTE: *Always install any additional spacers above the piston ring.* The ring groove must be deep enough to allow the ring to seat below the lands (see illustration). In many cases, a "go-no-go" depth gauge will be provided with the piston rings. Shallow grooves may be corrected by recutting, while deep grooves require some type of filler or expander behind the piston. Consult the piston ring supplier concerning the suggested method. Install the rings on the piston, lowest ring first, using a ring expander. NOTE: *Position the ring markings as specified by the manufacturer (see car section).*

Install the camshaft:

Liberally lubricate the camshaft lobes and journals, and slide the camshaft into the block. CAUTION: *Exercise extreme care to avoid damaging the bearings when inserting the camshaft.* Install and tighten the camshaft thrust plate retaining bolts.

Check camshaft end-play:

Checking camshaft end-play with a feeler gauge
(© Ford Motor Co.)

Using feeler gauges, determine whether the clearance between the camshaft boss (or gear) and backing plate is within specifications. Install shims behind the thrust plate, or reposition the camshaft gear (see car section), and retest end-play.

Procedure	Method

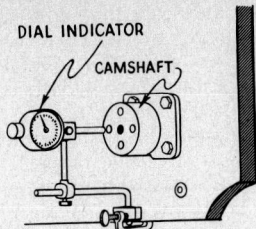

DIAL INDICATOR

CAMSHAFT

Checking camshaft end-play with a dial indicator

* Mount a dial indicator stand so that the stem of the dial indicator rests on the nose of the camshaft, parallel to the camshaft axis. Push the camshaft as far in as possible and zero the gauge. Move the camshaft outward to determine the amount of camshaft end-play. If the end-play is not within tolerance, install shims behind the thrust plate, or reposition the camshaft gear (see car section), and retest.

Install the rear main seal (where applicable):

Seating the rear main seal
(© Buick Div. G.M. Corp.)

Position the block with the bearing saddles facing upward. Lay the rear main seal in its groove and press it lightly into its seat. Place a piece of pipe the same diameter as the crankshaft journal into the saddle, and firmly seat the seal. Hold the pipe in position, and trim the ends of the seal flush if required.

Install the crankshaft:

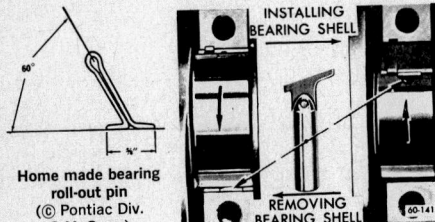

Home made bearing roll-out pin
(© Pontiac Div. G.M. Corp.)

INSTALLING BEARING SHELL

REMOVING BEARING SHELL

Removal and installation of upper bearing insert using a roll-out pin
(© Buick Div. G.M. Corp.)

Thoroughly clean the main bearing saddles and caps. Place the upper halves of the bearing inserts on the saddles and press into position. NOTE: *Ensure that the oil holes align.* Press the corresponding bearing inserts into the main bearing caps. Lubricate the upper main bearings, and lay the crankshaft in position. Place a strip of Plastigage on each of the crankshaft journals, install the main caps, and torque to specifications. Remove the main caps, and compare the Plastigage to the scale on the Plastigage envelope. If clearances are within tolerances, remove the Plastigage, turn the crankshaft 90°, wipe off all oil and retest. If all clearances are correct, remove all Plastigage, thoroughly

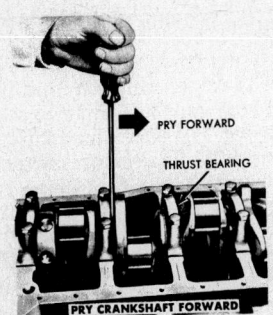
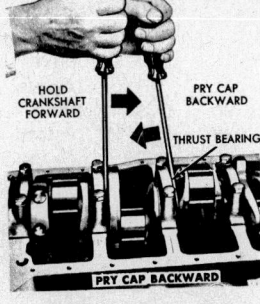
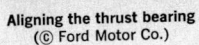
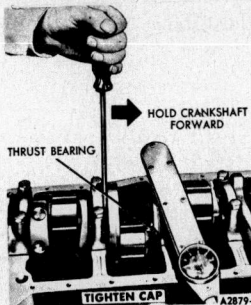

Aligning the thrust bearing
(© Ford Motor Co.)

Procedure	Method

lubricate the main caps and bearing journals, and install the main caps. If clearances are not within tolerance, the upper bearing inserts may be removed, without removing the crankshaft, using a bearing roll out pin (see illustration). Roll in a bearing that will provide proper clearance, and retest. Torque all main caps, excluding the thrust bearing cap, to specifications. Tighten the thrust bearing cap finger tight. To properly align the thrust bearing, pry the crankshaft the extent of its axial travel several times, the last movement held toward the front of the engine, and torque the thrust bearing cap to specifications. Determine the crankshaft end-play (see below), and bring within tolerance with thrust washers.

Measure crankshaft end-play:

Checking crankshaft
end-play with a
dial indicator
(© Ford Motor Co.)

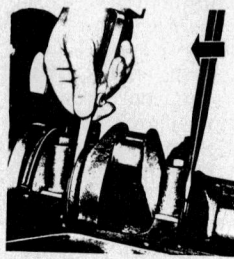

Checking crankshaft
end-play with a
feeler gauge
(© Chevrolet Div.
(G.M. Corp.)

Mount a dial indicator stand on the front of the block, with the dial indicator stem resting on the nose of the crankshaft, parallel to the crankshaft axis. Pry the crankshaft the extent of its travel rearward, and zero the indicator. Pry the crankshaft forward and record crankshaft end-play. NOTE: *Crankshaft end-play also may be measured at the thrust bearing, using feeler gauges* (see illustration).

Install the pistons:

Press the upper connecting rod bearing halves into the connecting rods, and the lower halves into the connecting rod caps. Position the piston ring gaps according to specifications (see car section), and lubricate the pistons. Install a ring compresser on a piston, and press two long (8″) pieces of plastic tubing over the rod bolts. Using the plastic tubes as a guide, press the pistons into the bores and onto the crankshaft with a wooden hammer handle. After seating the rod on the crankshaft journal, remove the tubes and install the cap finger tight. Install the remaining pistons in the same man-

Procedure	Method

Tubing used as guide when installing
a piston
(© Oldsmobile Div. G.M. Corp.)

ner. Invert the engine and check the bearing clearance at two points (90° apart) on each journal with Plastigage. NOTE: *Do not turn the crankshaft with Plastigage installed.* If clearance is within tolerances, remove *all* Plastigage, thoroughly lubricate the journals, and torque the rod caps to specifications. If clearance is not within specifications, install different thickness bearing inserts and recheck. CAUTION: *Never shim or file the connecting rods or caps.* Always install plastic tube sleeves over the rod bolts when the caps are not installed, to protect the crankshaft journals.

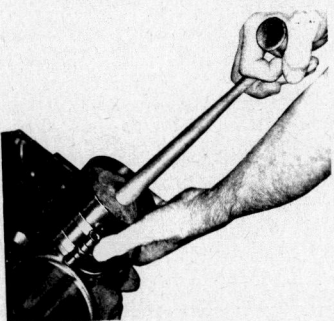

Installing a piston
(© Chevrolet Div. G.M. Corp.)

Check connecting rod side clearance:

Determine the clearance between the sides of the connecting rods and the crankshaft, using feeler gauges. If clearance is below the minimum tolerance, the rod may be machined to provide adequate clearance. If clearance is excessive, substitute an unworn rod, and recheck. If clearance is still outside specifications, the crankshaft must be welded and reground, or replaced.

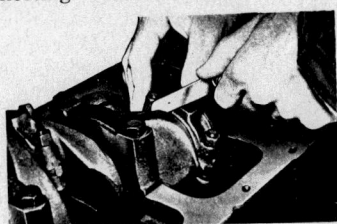

Checking connecting rod side clearance
(© Chevrolet Div. G.M. Corp.)

Inspect the timing chain:

Visually inspect the timing chain for broken or loose links, and replace the chain if any are found. If the chain will flex sideways, it must be replaced. Install the timing chain as specified in the car section. NOTE: *If the original timing chain is to be reused, install it in its original position.*

Procedure	Method

Check timing gear backlash and runout:

Checking camshaft gear backlash
(© Chevrolet Div. G.M. Corp.)

Checking camshaft gear runout
(© Chevrolet Div. G.M. Corp.)

Mount a dial indicator with its stem resting on a tooth of the camshaft gear (as illustrated). Rotate the gear until all slack is removed, and zero the indicator. Rotate the gear in the opposite direction until slack is removed, and record gear backlash. Mount the indicator with its stem resting on the edge of the camshaft gear, parallel to the axis of the camshaft. Zero the indicator, and turn the camshaft gear one full turn, recording the runout. If either backlash or runout exceed specifications, replace the worn gear(s).

Completing the Rebuilding Process

Following the above procedures, complete the rebuilding process as follows:

Fill the oil pump with oil, to prevent cavitating (sucking air) on initial engine start up. Install the oil pump and the pickup tube on the engine. Coat the oil pan gasket as necessary, and install the gasket and the oil pan. Mount the flywheel and the crankshaft vibrational damper or pulley on the crankshaft. NOTE: *Always use new bolts when installing the flywheel.* Inspect the clutch shaft pilot bushing in the crankshaft. If the bushing is excessively worn, remove it with an expanding puller and a slide hammer, and tap a new bushing into place.

Position the engine, cylinder head side up. Lubricate the lifters, and install them into their bores. Install the cylinder head, and torque it as specified in the car section. Insert the pushrods (where applicable), and install the rocker shaft(s) (if so equipped) or position the rocker arms on the pushrods. If solid lifters are utilized, adjust the valves to the "cold" specifications. If hydraulic lifters are used, torque the adjusting nut to 20 ft. lbs.

Mount the intake and exhaust manifolds, the carburetor(s), the distributor and spark plugs. Adjust the point gap and the static ignition timing. Mount all accessories and install the engine in the car. Fill the radiator with coolant, and the crankcase with high quality engine oil.

Break-in Procedure

Start the engine, and allow it to run at low speed for a few minutes, while checking for leaks. Stop the engine, check the oil level, and fill as necessary. Restart the engine, and fill the cooling system to capacity. Check the point dwell angle and adjust the ignition timing and the valves. Run the engine at low to medium speed (800-2500 rpm) for approximately ½ hour, and retorque the cylinder head bolts. Road test the car, and check again for leaks.

Follow the manufacturer's recommended engine break-in procedure and maintenance schedule for new engines.

Appendix

General Conversion Table

Multiply by	To convert	To	
2.54	Inches	Centimeters	.3937
30.48	Feet	Centimeters	.0328
.914	Yards	Meters	1.094
1.609	Miles	Kilometers	.621
.645	Square inches	Square cm.	.155
.836	Square yards	Square meters	1.196
16.39	Cubic inches	Cubic cm.	.061
28.3	Cubic feet	Liters	.0353
.4536	Pounds	Kilograms	2.2045
4.546	Gallons	Liters	.22
.068	Lbs./sq. in. (psi)	Atmospheres	14.7
.138	Foot pounds	Kg. m.	7.23
1.014	H.P. (DIN)	H.P. (SAE)	.9861
———	To obtain	From	Multiply by

Note: 1 cm. equals 10 mm.; 1 mm. equals .0394″.

Conversion—Common Fractions to Decimals and Millimeters

INCHES			INCHES			INCHES		
Common Fractions	Decimal Fractions	Millimeters (approx.)	Common Fractions	Decimal Fractions	Millimeters (approx.)	Common Fractions	Decimal Fractions	Millimeters (approx.)
1/128	.008	0.20	11/32	.344	8.73	43/64	.672	17.07
1/64	.016	0.40	23/64	.359	9.13	11/16	.688	17.46
1/32	.031	0.79	3/8	.375	9.53	45/64	.703	17.86
3/64	.047	1.19	25/64	.391	9.92	23/32	.719	18.26
1/16	.063	1.59	13/32	.406	10.32	47/64	.734	18.65
5/64	.078	1.98	27/64	.422	10.72	3/4	.750	19.05
3/32	.094	2.38	7/16	.438	11.11	49/64	.766	19.45
7/64	.109	2.78	29/64	.453	11.51	25/32	.781	19.84
1/8	.125	3.18	15/32	.469	11.91	51/64	.797	20.24
9/64	.141	3.57	31/64	.484	12.30	13/16	.813	20.64
5/32	.156	3.97	1/2	.500	12.70	53/64	.828	21.03
11/64	.172	4.37	33/64	.516	13.10	27/32	.844	21.43
3/16	.188	4.76	17/32	.531	13.49	55/64	.859	21.83
13/64	.203	5.16	35/64	.547	13.89	7/8	.875	22.23
7/32	.219	5.56	9/16	.563	14.29	57/64	.891	22.62
15/64	.234	5.95	37/64	.578	14.68	29/32	.906	23.02
1/4	.250	6.35	19/32	.594	15.08	59/64	.922	23.42
17/64	.266	6.75	39/64	.609	15.48	15/16	.938	23.81
9/32	.281	7.14	5/8	.625	15.88	61/64	.953	24.21
19/64	.297	7.54	41/64	.641	16.27	31/32	.969	24.61
5/16	.313	7.94	21/32	.656	16.67	63/64	.984	25.00
21/64	.328	8.33						

Conversion—Millimeters to Decimal Inches

mm	inches	mm	inches	mm	inches	mm	inches	mm	inches
1	.039 370	31	1.220 470	61	2.401 570	91	3.582 670	210	8.267 700
2	.078 740	32	1.259 840	62	2.440 940	92	3.622 040	220	8.661 400
3	.118 110	33	1.299 210	63	2.480 310	93	3.661 410	230	9.055 100
4	.157 480	34	1.338 580	64	2.519 680	94	3.700 780	240	9.448 800
5	.196 850	35	1.377 949	65	2.559 050	95	3.740 150	250	9.842 500
6	.236 220	36	1.417 319	66	2.598 420	96	3.779 520	260	10.236 200
7	.275 590	37	1.456 689	67	2.637 790	97	3.818 890	270	10.629 900
8	.314 960	38	1.496 050	68	2.677 160	98	3.858 260	280	11.032 600
9	.354 330	39	1.535 430	69	2.716 530	99	3.897 630	290	11.417 300
10	.393 700	40	1.574 800	70	2.755 900	100	3.937 000	300	11.811 000
11	.433 070	41	1.614 170	71	2.795 270	105	4.133 848	310	12.204 700
12	.472 440	42	1.653 540	72	2.834 640	110	4.330 700	320	12.598 400
13	.511 810	43	1.692 910	73	2.874 010	115	4.527 550	330	12.992 100
14	.551 180	44	1.732 280	74	2.913 380	120	4.724 400	340	13.385 800
15	.590 550	45	1.771 650	75	2.952 750	125	4.921 250	350	13.779 500
16	.629 920	46	1.811 020	76	2.992 120	130	5.118 100	360	14.173 200
17	.669 290	47	1.850 390	77	3.031 490	135	5.314 950	370	14.566 900
18	.708 660	48	1.889 760	78	3.070 860	140	5.511 800	380	14.960 600
19	.748 030	49	1.929 130	79	3.110 230	145	5.708 650	390	15.354 300
20	.787 400	50	1.968 500	80	3.149 600	150	5.905 500	400	15.748 000
21	.826 770	51	2.007 870	81	3.188 970	155	6.102 350	500	19.685 000
22	.866 140	52	2.047 240	82	3.228 340	160	6.299 200	600	23.622 000
23	.905 510	53	2.086 610	83	3.267 710	165	6.496 050	700	27.559 000
24	.944 880	54	2.125 980	84	3.307 080	170	6.692 900	800	31.496 000
25	.984 250	55	2.165 350	85	3.346 450	175	6.889 750	900	35.433 000
26	1.023 620	56	2.204 720	86	3.385 820	180	7.086 600	1000	39.370 000
27	1.062 990	57	2.244 090	87	3.425 190	185	7.283 450	2000	78.740 000
28	1.102 360	58	2.283 460	88	3.464 560	190	7.480 300	3000	118.110 000
29	1.141 730	59	2.322 830	89	3.503 903	195	7.677 150	4000	157.480 000
30	1.181 100	60	2.362 200	90	3.543 300	200	7.874 000	5000	196.850 000

To change decimal millimeters to decimal inches, position the decimal point where desired on either side of the millimeter measurement shown and reset the inches decimal by the same number of digits in the same direction. For example, to convert .001 mm into decimal inches, reset the decimal behind the 1 mm (shown on the chart) to .001; change the decimal inch equivalent (.039″ shown) to .00039″).

Tap Drill Sizes

National Fine or S.A.E.				National Coarse or U.S.S.		
Screw & Tap Size	Threads Per Inch	Use Drill Number		Screw & Tap Size	Threads Per Inch	Use Drill Number
No. 5	44	37		No. 5	40	39
No. 6	40	33		No. 6	32	36
No. 8	36	29		No. 8	32	29
No. 10	32	21		No. 10	24	25
No. 12	28	15		No. 12	24	17
1/4	28	3		1/4	20	8
5/16	24	1		5/16	18	F
3/8	24	Q		3/8	16	5/16
7/16	20	W		7/16	14	U
1/2	20	29/64		1/2	13	27/64
9/16	18	33/64		9/16	12	31/64
5/8	18	37/64		5/8	11	17/32
3/4	16	11/16		3/4	10	21/32
7/8	14	13/16		7/8	9	49/64
1 1/8	12	1 3/64		1	8	7/8
1 1/4	12	1 11/64		1 1/8	7	63/64
1 1/2	12	1 27/64		1 1/4	7	1 7/64
				1 1/2	6	1 11/32

Decimal Equivalent Size of the Number Drills

Drill No.	Decimal Equivalent	Drill No.	Decimal Equivalent	Drill No.	Decimal Equivalent
80	.0135	53	.0595	26	.1470
79	.0145	52	.0635	25	.1495
78	.0160	51	.0670	24	.1520
77	.0180	50	.0700	23	.1540
76	.0200	49	.0730	22	.1570
75	.0210	48	.0760	21	.1590
74	.0225	47	.0785	20	.1610
73	.0240	46	.0810	19	.1660
72	.0250	45	.0820	18	.1695
71	.0260	44	.0860	17	.1730
70	.0280	43	.0890	16	.1770
69	.0292	42	.0935	15	.1800
68	.0310	41	.0960	14	.1820
67	.0320	40	.0980	13	.1850
66	.0330	39	.0995	12	.1890
65	.0350	38	.1015	11	.1910
64	.0360	37	.1040	10	.1935
63	.0370	36	.1065	9	.1960
62	.0380	35	.1100	8	.1990
61	.0390	34	.1110	7	.2010
60	.0400	33	.1130	6	.2040
59	.0410	32	.1160	5	.2055
58	.0420	31	.1200	4	.2090
57	.0430	30	.1285	3	.2130
56	.0465	29	.1360	2	.2210
55	.0520	28	.1405	1	.2280
54	.0550	27	.1440		

Decimal Equivalent Size of the Letter Drills

Letter Drill	Decimal Equivalent	Letter Drill	Decimal Equivalent	Letter Drill	Decimal Equivalent
A	.234	J	.277	S	.348
B	.238	K	.281	T	.358
C	.242	L	.290	U	.368
D	.246	M	.295	V	.377
E	.250	N	.302	W	.386
F	.257	O	.316	X	.397
G	.261	P	.323	Y	.404
H	.266	Q	.332	Z	.413
I	.272	R	.339		

ANTI-FREEZE INFORMATION

Freezing and Boiling Points of Solutions
According to Percentage of Alcohol or Ethylene Glycol

Freezing Point of Solation	Alcohol Volume %	Alcohol Solution Boils at	Ethylene Glycol Volume %	Ethylene Glycol Solution Boils at
20°F.	12	196°F.	16	216°F.
10°F.	20	189°F.	25	218°F.
0°F.	27	184°F.	33	220°F.
−10°F.	32	181°F.	39	222°F.
−20°F.	38	178°F.	44	224°F.
−30°F.	42	176°F.	48	225°F.

Note: above boiling points are at sea level. For every 1,000 feet of altitude, boiling points are approximately 2°F. lower than those shown. For every pound of pressure exerted by the pressure cap, the boiling points are approximately 3°F. higher than those shown.

To Increase the Freezing Protection of Anti-Freeze Solutions Already Installed

Number of Quarts of **ALCOHOL** Anti-Freeze Required to Increase Protection

Cooling System Capacity Quarts	From +20°F. to					From +10°F. to					From 0°F. to			
	0°	−10°	−20°	−30°	−40°	0°	−10°	−20°	−30°	−40°	−10°	−20°	−30°	−40°
10	2	2 3/4	3 1/2	4	4 1/2	1	2	2 1/3	3 1/4	3 3/4	1	1 3/4	2 1/2	3
12	2 1/2	3 1/4	4	4 3/4	5 1/4	1 1/4	2 1/4	3	3 3/4	4 1/2	1 1/4	2	2 3/4	3 1/2
14	3	4	4 3/4	5 1/2	6	1 1/2	2 1/2	3 1/2	4 1/2	5	1 1/4	2 1/2	3 1/4	4
16	3 1/4	4 1/2	5 1/2	6 1/4	7	1 3/4	3	4	5	5 3/4	1 1/2	2 3/4	3 3/4	4 3/4
18	3 3/4	5	6	7	7 3/4	2	3 1/4	4 1/2	5 3/4	6 1/2	1 3/4	3	4 1/4	5 1/4
20	4	5 1/2	6 3/4	7 3/4	8 3/4	2	3 1/4	5	6 1/4	7 1/4	1 3/4	3 1/2	4 3/4	5 3/4
22	4 1/2	6	7 1/2	8 1/2	9 1/2	2 1/4	4	5 1/2	6 3/4	8	2	3 3/4	5 1/4	6 1/2
24	5	6 3/4	8	9 1/4	10 1/2	2 1/2	4 1/2	6	7 1/2	8 3/4	2 1/4	4	5 1/2	7
26	5 1/4	7 1/4	8 3/4	10	11 1/4	2 3/4	4 3/4	6 1/2	8	9 1/2	2 1/2	4 1/2	6	7 1/2
28	5 3/4	7 3/4	9 1/2	11	12	3	5 1/4	7	8 3/4	10 1/4	2 1/2	4 3/4	6 1/2	8
30	6	8 1/4	10	11 3/4	13	3	5 1/2	7 1/2	9 1/4	10 3/4	2 3/4	5	7	8 3/4

Test radiator solution with proper tester. Determine from the table the number of quarts of solution to be drawn off from a full cooling system and replace with concentrated anti-freeze, to give the desired increased protection. For example, to increase protection of a 22-quart cooling system containing Alcohol anti-freeze, from +10°F. to −20°F. will require the replacement of 5 1/2 quarts of solution with concentrated anti-freeze.

Number of Quarts of **ETHYLENE GLYCOL** Anti-Freeze Required to Increase Protection

Cooling System Capacity Quarts	From +20°F. to					From +10°F. to					From 0°F. to			
	0°	−10°	−20°	−30°	−40°	0°	−10°	−20°	−30°	−40°	−10°	−20°	−30°	−40°
10	1 3/4	2 1/4	3	3 1/2	3 3/4	3/4	1 1/2	2 1/4	2 3/4	3 1/4	3/4	1 1/2	2	2 1/2
12	2	2 3/4	3 1/2	4	4 1/2	1	1 3/4	2 1/2	3 1/4	3 3/4	1	1 3/4	2 1/2	3 1/4
14	2 1/4	3 1/4	4	4 3/4	5 1/2	1 1/4	2	3	3 3/4	4 1/2	1	2	3	3 1/2
16	2 1/2	3 1/2	4 1/2	5 1/4	6	1 1/4	2 1/2	3 1/2	4 1/4	5 1/4	1 1/4	2 1/4	3 1/4	4
18	3	4	5	6	7	1 1/2	2 3/4	4	5	5 3/4	1 1/2	2 1/2	3 3/4	4 3/4
20	3 1/4	4 1/2	5 3/4	6 3/4	7 1/2	1 3/4	3	4 1/4	5 1/2	6 1/2	1 1/2	2 3/4	4 1/4	5 1/4
22	3 1/2	5	6 1/4	7 1/4	8 1/4	1 3/4	3 1/4	4 3/4	6	7 1/4	1 3/4	3 1/4	4 1/2	5 1/2
24	4	5 1/2	7	8	9	2	3 1/2	5	6 1/2	7 1/2	1 3/4	3 1/2	5	6
26	4 1/4	6	7 1/2	8 3/4	10	2	4	5 1/2	7	8 1/4	2	3 3/4	5 1/2	6 3/4
28	4 1/2	6 1/4	8	9 1/2	10 1/2	2 1/4	4 1/4	6	7 1/2	9	2	4	5 3/4	7 1/4
30	5	6 3/4	8 1/2	10	11 1/2	2 1/2	4 1/2	6 1/2	8	9 1/2	2 1/4	4 1/4	6 1/4	7 3/4

Test radiator solution with proper hydrometer. Determine from the table the number of quarts of solution to be drawn off from a full cooling system and replace with undiluted anti-freeze, to give the desired increased protection. For example, to increase protection of a 22-quart cooling system containing Ethylene Glycol (permanent type) anti-freeze, from +20°F. to −20°F. will require the replacement of 6 1/4 quarts of solution with undiluted anti-freeze.

APPENDIX

ANTI-FREEZE CHART

Temperatures Shown in Degrees Fahrenheit
+32 is Freezing

Quarts of **ALCOHOL** Needed for Protection to Temperatures Shown Below

Cooling System Capacity Quarts	1	2	3	4	5	6	7	8	9	10	11	12	13
10	+23°	+11°	− 5°	−27°									
11	+25	+13	0	−18	−40°								
12		+15	+ 3	−12	−31								
13		+17	+ 7	− 7	−23								
14		+19	+ 9	− 3	−17	−34°							
15		+20	+11	+ 1	−12	−27							
16		+21	+13	+ 3	− 8	−21	−36°						
17		+22	+16	+ 6	− 4	−16	−29						
18		+23	+17	+ 8	− 1	−12	−25	−38°					
19		+24	+17	+ 9	+ 2	− 8	−21	−32					
20			+18	+11	+ 4	− 5	−16	−27	−39°				
21			+19	+12	+ 5	− 3	−12	−22	−34				
22			+20	+14	+ 7	0	− 9	−18	−29	−40°			
23			+21	+15	+ 8	+ 2	− 7	−15	−25	−36°			
24			+21	+16	+10	+ 4	− 4	−12	−21	−31			
25			+22	+17	+11	+ 6	− 2	− 9	−18	−27	−37°		
26			+22	+17	+12	+ 7	+ 1	− 7	−14	−23	−32		
27			+23	+18	+13	+ 8	+ 3	− 5	−12	−20	−28	−39°	
28			+23	+19	+14	+ 9	+ 4	− 3	− 9	−17	−25	−30	
29			+24	+19	+15	+10	+ 6	− 1	− 7	−15	−22	−30	−39°
30			+24	+20	+16	+11	+ 7	+ 1	− 5	−12	−19	−27	−35

+ Figures are above Zero, but below Freezing.

− Figures are below Zero. Also below Freezing.

Quarts of **ETHYLENE GLYCOL** Needed for Protection to Temperatures Shown Below

Cooling System Capacity Quarts	1	2	3	4	5	6	7	8	9	10	11	12	13	14
10	+24°	+16°	+ 4°	−12°	−34°	−62°								
11	+25	+18	+ 8	− 6	−23	−47								
12	+26	+19	+10	0	−15	−34	−57°							
13	+27	+21	+13	+ 3	− 9	−25	−45							
14			+15	+ 6	− 5	−18	−34							
15			+16	+ 8	0	−12	−26							
16			+17	+10	+ 2	− 8	−19	−34	−52°					
17			+18	+12	+ 5	− 4	−14	−27	−42					
18			+19	+14	+ 7	0	−10	−21	−34	−50°				
19			+20	+15	+ 9	+ 2	− 7	−16	−28	−42				
20				+16	+10	+ 4	− 3	−12	−22	−34	−48°			
21				+17	+12	+ 6	0	− 9	−17	−28	−41			
22				+18	+13	+ 8	+ 2	− 6	−14	−23	−34	−47°		
23				+19	+14	+ 9	+ 4	− 3	−10	−19	−29	−40		
24				+19	+15	+10	+ 5	0	− 8	−15	−23	−34	−46°	
25				+20	+16	+12	+ 7	+ 1	− 5	−12	−20	−29	−40	−50°
26					+17	+13	+ 8	+ 3	− 3	− 9	−16	−25	−34	−44
27					+18	+14	+ 9	+ 5	− 1	− 7	−13	−21	−29	−39
28					+18	+15	+10	+ 6	+ 1	− 5	−11	−18	−25	−34
29					+19	+16	+12	+ 7	+ 2	− 3	− 8	−15	−22	−29
30					+20	+17	+13	+ 8	+ 4	− 1	− 6	−12	−18	−25

For capacities over 30 quarts divide true capacity by 3. Find quarts Anti-Freeze for the $\frac{1}{3}$ and multiply by 3 for quarts to add.

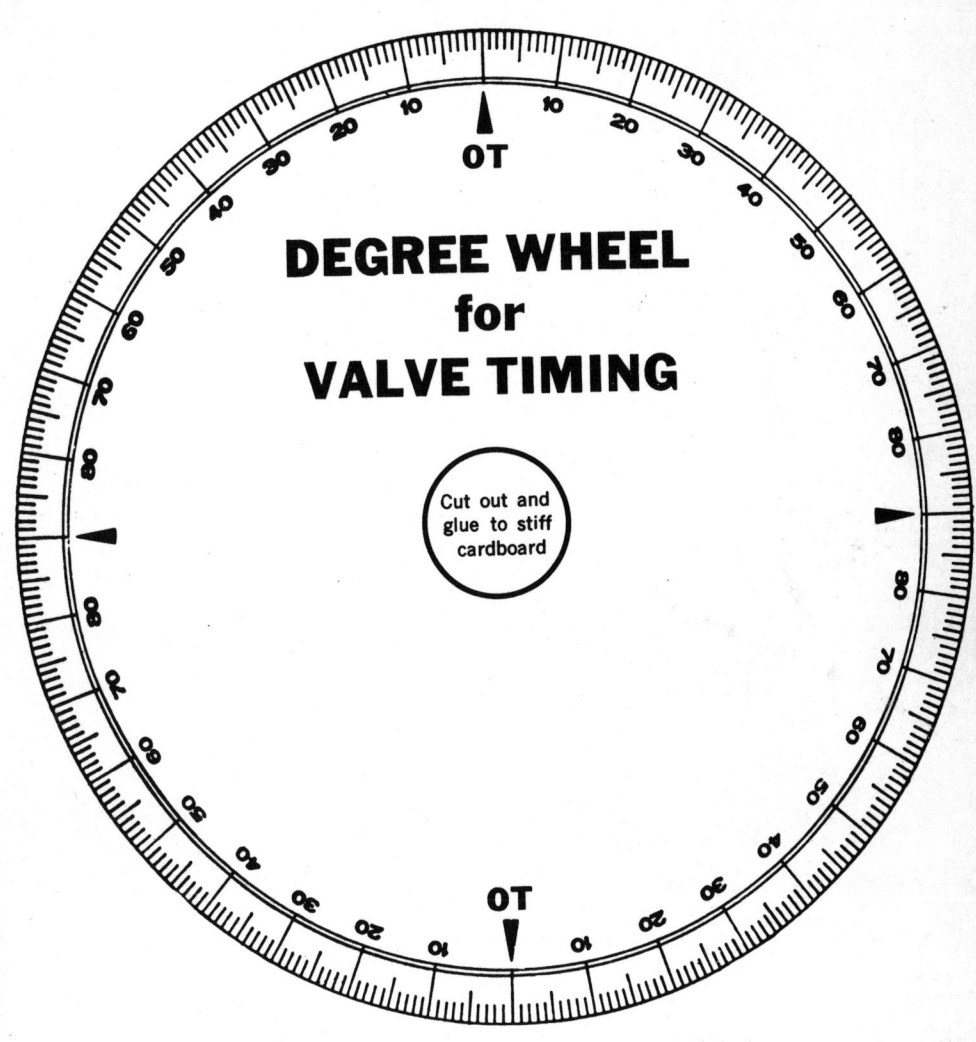